THE
PULPIT COMMENTARY

Edited by

H. D. M. Spence

and

Joseph S. Exell

Volume 9

PROVERBS, ECCLESIASTES,
SONG OF SOLOMON

Wm. B. Eerdmans Publishing Company, Grand Rapids, Michigan

THE PULPIT COMMENTARY

Edited by

H. D. M. Spence *and* Joseph S. Exell

This large-type edition republished
from new plates by

WM. B. EERDMANS PUBLISHING COMPANY
Grand Rapids, Michigan

ISBN 0-8028-8066

Reprinted 1978

PHOTOLITHOPRINTED BY EERDMANS PRINTING COMPANY
GRAND RAPIDS, MICHIGAN, UNITED STATES OF AMERICA

PROVERBS

EXPOSITION BY

W. J. DEANE

and

S. T. TAYLOR - TASWELL

HOMILETICS BY

W. F. ADENEY

HOMILIES BY VARIOUS AUTHORS

E. JOHNSON   W. CLARKSON

THE PROVERBS

INTRODUCTION

§ 1. Name of the Book.

THE book which we are about to consider takes its general title from the words with which it opens in the Hebrew original, 'The Proverbs of Solomon'—*Mishle Shelomoh*. This name, or, in an abbreviated form, *Mishle*, has always been current in the Jewish Church. Later, in rabbinical writings, it was cited under the appellation of *Sepher Chocmah*, 'Book of Wisdom,' which title also included Ecclesiastes. In the Septuagint it is headed Παροιμίαι Σαλωμῶντος in some manuscripts, though in others, and those the earliest, the name of Solomon is omitted. St. Jerome, in the Latin Vulgate, gives a longer title : 'Liber Proverbiorum quem Hebræi *Misle* appellant.'

Among the early Christian writers, in addition to the name given in the Septuagint, it was called Σοφία, 'Wisdom,' or Ἡ Πανάρετος Σοφία, 'All-virtuous Wisdom,' though this last title was also applied to Ecclesiasticus and the Book of Wisdom. Clemens Romanus, in his 'Epistle to the Corinthians' (i. 57), heads a quotation from ch. i. 23—33 thus: Οὕτως γὰρ λέγει ἡ Πανάρετος Σοφία, "Thus saith All-virtuous Wisdom." That this was commonly received as the designation of our book is clear also from Eusebius, who writes ('Hist. Eccl.,' iv. 22), "Other passages also, as if from unwritten Jewish tradition, Hegesippus cites; and not only he, but Irenæus, and the whole band of ancient writers, called the 'Proverbs of Solomon' 'Panaretos Sophia.'" It is true that in the writings which are attributed to Irenæus still extant, quotations from the Proverbs are cited simply as Scripture without further definition, but we have no reason to discredit Eusebius's testimony concerning a matter with which he must have been well acquainted. Two other titles are found, viz. Ἡ Σοφὴ Βίβλος, 'The Wise Book,' so called by Dionysius of Alexandria; and Παιδαγωγικὴ Σοφία, 'Educational Wisdom,' by Gregory of Nazianzum. Melito of Sardis (according to Eusebius, 'Hist. Eccl.,' iv. 26) states, in giving a catalogue of canonical Scriptures, that the book was known by the name of Σοφία, 'Wisdom,' as well as that of 'Proverbs of Solomon.' This title, which, better perhaps than that of Proverbs, expresses the chief subject of the work, seems not to have been invented by the primitive Christian writers, but to have been derived from still earlier times, and to have been handed down by that unwritten Jewish tradition of which Eusebius speaks.

In considering the appropriateness of the usual name of our book, we must see what is meant by the Jewish term *mishle*, "proverbs," as we translate it. The word *mashal* has a much wider significance than our word "proverb." It is derived from a root meaning "to be like," and therefore has primarily the meaning of comparison, similitude, and is applied to many discourses, sentences, and expressions which we should not class under the head of proverbs. Thus Balaam's prophecy is so called (Numb. xxii. 7, etc.); so too Job's didactic poem (Job xxvii. 1); the taunting satire in Isa. xiv. 4, etc.; the parables in Ezek. xvii. 2 and xx. 49, etc.; the song in Numb. xxi. 27, etc. It is often translated "parable" in the Authorized Version, even in the book itself (ch. xxvi. 7), and in the historical psalm (lxxviii.), the second verse of which St. Matthew (xiii. 35) tells us Christ fulfilled when he spake by parables. This would lead us to expect to find other meanings in the term and under the husk of the outward form. And, indeed, the Hebrew *mashal* is not confined to wise or pithy sayings, expressing in pointed terms the experience of men and ages; such an account would, as we see, be most inadequate to describe the various forms to which the term was applied. That there are in our book numerous apothegms and maxims, enforcing moral truths, explaining facts in men's lives and the course of society, which are proverbs in the strictest sense of the word, is obvious; but a very large proportion of the utterances therein are not covered by that designation. If the notion of comparison at first restricted the term to sayings containing a simile, it soon overstepped the bounds of such limitation, and comprehended such brief sentences as conveyed a popular truth under figures or metaphors. Of this sort is the pointed query, "Is Saul also among the prophets?" (1 Sam. x. 12); and, "The fathers have eaten sour grapes, and the children's teeth are set on edge" (Ezek. xviii. 2); and, "Physician, heal thyself" (Luke iv. 23). In many so-called proverbs the contrasted objects are placed side by side, leaving the hearer to draw his own deduction. In the longer pieces so-named a single idea is worked out at some length in rhythmical form. Further, under this general category are contained also dark sayings, riddles, intricate questions (*chidah*), which have always had great attraction for Oriental minds. The Queen of Sheba, we are told, came to try Solomon with hard questions (1 Kings x. 1); as the Septuagint renders it, "with enigmas." Probably such puzzles are found in ch. xxx., and in many of those passages which, according as they are pointed, are capable of very different interpretations. There is one other word used in this connection (ch. i. 6)—*melitsah*, which is rendered in the Authorized Version "interpretation," and in the Revised Version "a figure; " it probably means a saying containing some obscure allusion, and usually of a sarcastic nature. There are very few examples of this form in our book.

The various kinds of proverbs have been divided by Hanneberg ('Revel. Bibl.,' v. 41, quoted by Lesètre) into five classes: 1. *Historical proverbs*, wherein an event of the past, or a word used on some momentous occasion, has passed into a popular saying, expressive of some general sentiment or idea. The saying about Saul mentioned just above is of this nature. Of the historical proverb there seems to be no instance in our book. 2. *Metaphorical proverbs*. These are what we should most appropriately call proverbs. They enunciate some moral truth under a figure drawn from nature or life. Such are these: " In vain is the net spread in the eyes of any bird" (ch. i. 17); " Go to the ant, thou sluggard" (ch. vi. 6); " Let a bear robbed of her whelps meet a man, rather than a fool in his folly " (ch. xvii. 12); " The contentions of a wife are a continual dropping" (ch. xix. 13; xxvii. 15, 16). 3. *Enigmas*. These are either riddles like that of Samson (Judg. xiv. 14), or obscure questions which needed thought to elucidate them, and the kernel of which conveyed a moral truth. Such are the words of Agur, " Who hath ascended up into heaven, or descended? " etc. (ch. xxx. 4); " The horseleech hath two daughters, Give, give " (ch. xxx. 15). 4. *Parabolic proverbs*. Herein are presented things and truths in allegorical shape. Our blessed Lord has used this mode of teaching most extensively, showing himself greater than Solomon. The best example of this class is the treatment of Wisdom, *e.g.* " Wisdom hath builded her house, she hath hewn out her seven pillars" (ch. ix. 1). 5. *Didactical proverbs*, which give precise instruction on points of morals, religion, or behaviour, and of which the first nine chapters afford very perfect instances, and the rest of the book more concise and less developed examples.

§ 2. Contents.

The book is inscribed, " The Proverbs of Solomon, son of David, King of Israel." How this title is to be regarded, and to what portion or portions of the work it applies, we shall see further on. Then (ch. i. 1—6) follows a description of the writing and a recommendation of its importance and utility. Its object is partly moral and partly intellectual; it seeks to instruct in the way of wisdom, to edify those who have already made progress, and to discipline hearers to receive and assimilate the highest teaching. The wisdom (*chocmah*, and in the plural of " excellence," *chocmoth*) here first mentioned is no mere philosophical attainment, no merely secular advancement in the knowledge of things; it is this—it includes the knowledge of all that can be known; but it is much more. It is distinctly religious, and has for its object the directing man's life according to his highest interests, so that it is equivalent to " the fear of the Lord," that is, practical religion, and is often interchanged with that expression. It teaches what God requires of man, how God would have man behave in all circumstances of life; it teaches piety, duty, justice. King and peasant, the old and the young, learned and ignorant, are hereby taught what is acceptable in their several stations, ages, stages of intellectual development. Later on, Wisdom is personified as a great teacher, as dwelling with God from all eternity, assisting at the creation of the world, the original of all authority on earth. We gather from various indications in our book that wisdom is regarded in a threefold respect: first, as an essential attribute of Almighty God; secondly, as revealed in creation; thirdly, as communicated to man. It is the mind or thought of God; it is that by which he created the world; it is that which regulates and informs the moral being of man. The language used in such passages as ch. viii. 23—31 adapts itself to the idea of a representation of the Son of God, an anticipation of the incarnation of Jesus our Lord; and though we cannot suppose that Solomon had any clear notion of the Divine personality of Wisdom (for which, indeed, the stern monotheism of the age was not ripe), yet we may believe that it was not alien from the mind of the Holy Spirit that the Christian Church should see in these Solomonic utterances prophecies and adumbrations of the nature and operations of the Son of God made man, of him whom St. John calls the Word. It is of Wisdom as communicated to man that the Book of Proverbs chiefly treats, indicating the only way of obtaining and securing possession of her, and the incalculable blessings that attend her acquisition and usance.

It must further be observed, in connection with this subject, that the Hebrew, in his pursuit of Wisdom, was not like the heathen philosopher groping blindly after God, seeking to discover the great Unknown, and to form for himself a deity which should satisfy his moral instincts and solve the questions of the creation and government of the universe. The Hebrew started from the point where the heathen came to a pause. The Jew knew God already—knew him by revelation; his aim was to recognize him in all relations—in nature, in life, in morality, in religion; to see this overruling Providence in all things whatsoever; to make this great truth control private, public, social, and political circumstances and conduct. This profound conception of Divine superintendence dominates all the reflections of the thinking man, and makes him own in every occurrence, even in every natural phenomenon, an expression of the mind and will of God. Hence comes the absolute trust in the justice of the supreme Ruler, in the wise ordering of events, in the certain distribution of rewards and punishments, in the regulated dispensing of prosperity and adversity. In such ways Wisdom reveals itself, and the intelligent man recognized its presence; and idealizing and personifying it, learned to speak of it in those high terms which we read of with awe in this section, seeing therein him who is invisible.

After this introduction there follows the first part of the book (ch. i. 7— ix. 18), consisting of fifteen admonitory discourses, addressed to youth, with the view of exhibiting the excellence of wisdom, encouraging the ardent pursuit thereof, and dissuading from folly, *i.e.* vice, which is its opposite. This is especially the hortatory or wisdom section of the book. It is usually regarded as a prelude to the collection of proverbs beginning at ch. x., and is compared to the proem of Elihu in Job xxxii. 6—22, before he addresses himself more particularly to the matter in hand. An analogous preface occurs in ch. xxii. 17—21 of our book, though this is short and intercalary. The section is divided by Delitzsch as above, though the portions are not very accurately defined by internal evidence. We have adopted this arrangement in the Commentary for convenience' sake. Commonly, each fresh warning or instruction is prefaced by the address, "My son" (*e.g.* ch. i. 8, 10, 15; ii. 1, etc.), but this is not universally the case, and no subdivisions can be accurately formed by attention to this peculiarity. The unity of the section consists in the subject and the mode of treatment, rather than in a regular course of instruction proceeding on definite lines, and leading to a climacteric conclusion. The motto of the whole is the noble maxim, "The fear of the Lord is the beginning of knowledge: but the foolish despise wisdom and instruction." Taking this as the basis of his lecture, Solomon proceeds with his discourse. He warns against fellowship with those who entice to robbery and murder (ch. i. 8—19). Wisdom addresses those who despise her, showing them their folly in rejecting her offers, and the security of those who hearken to her counsels (ch. i. 20—33). The teacher points out the blessings arising from the sincere and earnest pursuit of Wisdom—it delivers from the path of evil, and leads to all moral and religious knowledge (ch. ii.). Now comes an exhortation to obedience and faithfulness, self-sacrificing devotion to God, perfect resignation to his will (ch. iii. 1—18). Wisdom is introduced as the creative energy of God, who becomes the Protector of all who hold fast to her (ch. iii. 19—26). One condition for the attainment of wisdom and happiness is the practice of benevolence and rectitude in dealing with others (ch. iii. 27—35). Having previously spoken in his own name, and having also brought forward Wisdom making her appeal, the teacher now gives some recollections of his own early home and his father's advice, especially on the subject of discipline and obedience (ch. iv.). He returns to a matter before glanced at as one of the chief temptations to which youth was exposed, and gives an emphatic warning against adultery and impurity, while he beautifully commends honourable marriage (ch. v.). Then he warns against suretyship (ch. vi. 1—5), sloth (vers. 6—11), deceit and malice (vers. 12—19), and adultery (vers. 20—35). Keeping to the theme of his last discourse, the moralist again denounces the detestable sin of adultery, and enforces his admonition by an example which he had himself witnessed (ch. vii.). Working round again to Wisdom, as the object of all his discourses, the author introduces her as inviting all to follow her, descanting on her excellence, her heavenly origin, her inestimable blessings. This is the most important section concerning Wisdom, which here appears as coeternal with God and co-operating with him in creation. Thus her supreme excellence **is an** additional reason for hearkening to her instructions (ch. viii.). Summing up in brief the warnings which have preceded, Solomon introduces Wisdom and Folly, her rival, inviting severally to their companionship (ch. ix.).

The next part of our book contains the first great collection of Solomonic proverbs, some four hundred in number; or, as others say, three hundred and seventy-five (ch. x.—xxii. 16). They are introduced with the title, " The Proverbs of Solomon," and fully correspond to their description, being a series of apothegms, gnomes, and sentences, containing ideas moral, religious, social, political, introduced apparently without order, or with only some verbal connection or common characteristics, and certainly not arranged on any systematic scheme. Of the *form* of these maxims we shall speak later; we here only mention some of the subjects with which they are concerned. This part of the work begins by drawing comparisons between the righteous and sinners, in their general conduct, and the consequences that result therefrom (ch. x.).

"Treasures of wickedness profit nothing:
But righteousness delivereth from death" (ch. x. 2).
" He that gathereth in summer is a wise son:
But he that sleepeth in harvest is a son that causeth shame" (ch. x. 5).
" The memory of the just is blessed:
But the name of the wicked shall rot" (ch. x. 7).

The same distinction is maintained in conduct to neighbours—

" A false balance is abomination to the Lord:
But a just weight is his delight" (ch. xi. 1).
" He that withholdeth corn, the people shall curse him:
But blessing shall be upon the head of him that selleth it" (ch. xi. 26).

Then we have maxims on social and domestic life—

" A virtuous woman is a crown to her husband:
But she that maketh ashamed is as rottenness in his bones " (ch. xii. 4).
" The righteous man regardeth the life of his beast:
But the tender mercies of the wicked are cruel " (ch. xii. 10).

The difference between the godly and sinners is seen in the use they respectively make of temporal goods—

"There is that maketh himself rich, yet hath nothing:
There is that maketh himself poor, yet hath great wealth" (ch. xiii. 7).
" Wealth gotten by vanity shall be diminished:
But he that gathereth by labour shall have increase" (ch. xiii. 11).

The relations between rich and poor, wise and fools, exhibit the same rule—

" He that despiseth his neighbour sinneth:
But he that hath pity on the poor, happy is he!" (ch. xiv. 21).
" The foolish make a mock at guilt:
But among the upright there is favour" (ch. xiv. 9).

The state of the heart is that to which God looks—

> "The Lord is far from the wicked:
> But he heareth the prayer of the righteous" (ch. xv. 29).

Trust in God is the only security in life—

> "Commit thy works unto the Lord,
> And thy purposes shall be established" (ch. xvi. 3).

> "He that giveth heed unto the word shall find good:
> And whoso trusteth in the Lord, happy is he!" (ch. xvi. 20).

Gentleness and long-suffering are recommended—

> "A soft answer turneth away wrath:
> But a grievous word stirreth up anger" (ch. xv. 1).

> "The beginning of strife is as when one letteth out water:
> Therefore leave off contention, before there be quarrelling" (ch. xvii. 14).

Humility is strongly enjoined—

> "Pride goeth before destruction,
> And a haughty spirit before a fall" (ch. xvi. 18).

Sloth and intemperance and other vices are severely reprobated—

> "Slothfulness casteth into a deep sleep;
> And the idle soul shall suffer hunger" (ch. xix. 15).

> "Love not sleep, lest thou come to poverty;
> Open thine eyes, and thou shalt be satisfied with bread" (ch. xx. 13).

> "He that loveth pleasure shall be a poor man:
> He that loveth wine and oil shall not be rich" (ch. xxi. 17).

A good reputation should be sought and retained—

> "A good name is rather to be chosen than great riches,
> And loving favour rather than silver and gold" (ch. xxii. 1).

The section ends with an apothegm about rich and poor which is capable of more than one interpretation—

> "Whosoever oppresseth the poor, it is for his gain;
> Whosoever giveth to the rich, it is for his loss" (ch. xxii. 16).

This is a religious statement concerning the moral government of God, affirming, on the one hand, that oppression and extortion inflicted on the poor man do in the end redound to his good; and, on the other hand, addition to the wealth of a rich man only injures him, leads him to indolence and extravagance, and sooner or later brings him to want.

There is much said in this part about the king's prerogative—

> "The king's favour is toward a servant that dealeth wisely:
> But his wrath shall be against him that causeth shame" (ch. xiv. 35).

> "He that loveth pureness of heart,
> For the grace of his lips the king shall be his friend" (ch. xxii. 11).

It is possible to take exception to the worldliness and low motives of many of the maxims in this and other parts of the book. The wisdom often seems to be that of this world rather than of heavenly aspiration. And there have not been wanting persons who say such pronouncements cannot be deemed to be inspired, and that the work containing them was not dictated or controlled by the Holy Spirit. We will quote a few of those so-called worldly maxims. Obedience to the Law is enjoined in order to gain long life and prosperity (ch. iii. 1, 2), riches and honour (ch. viii. 18); diligence is to be desired with the view of obtaining a sufficiency, and averting poverty (ch. xx. 13); the great motive for charity and bene-volence is the temporal reward and the favour of God which they secure (ch. xix. 17; xxi. 13); the same reason holds good for honouring God with our substance (ch. iii. 9, 10); humility is to be practised because it brings honour and life (ch. xxii. 4); self-control is a useful attainment because it preserves from many dangers (ch. xvi. 32; xxv. 28); a fine reputation is a worthy object of quest (ch. xxii. 1); sloth, drunkenness, and gluttony are to be avoided because they impoverish a man (ch. xxi. 17; xxiii. 20, 21; xxiv. 33, 34); we should avoid companionship with the evil because they will lead us into trouble (ch. xiii. 20; xxii. 24, etc.); it is unwise to retaliate lest we bring injury on ourselves in the end (ch. xvii. 13); we are not to exult over an enemy's fall lest we provoke Providence to punish us (ch. xxiv. 17, etc.), but rather to assist an adver-sary in order to secure a reward at the hands of the Lord (ch. xxv. 21, etc.); wisdom is to be sought for the temporal advantages which it brings (ch. xxiv. 3, etc.; xxi. 20).

Such are some of the maxims which confront us in this Scripture; and there can be no doubt that they seem at first sight to make virtue a matter of calculation; and though they are capable of being spiritualized and forced into a higher sphere, yet in their natural sense they do urge the pursuit of right on low grounds, and base their injunctions on selfish considerations. Is this what we should expect to find in a work con-fessedly appertaining to the sacred canon? Is this teaching such as tends to make a man wise unto salvation, to furnish the man of God unto good works? The whole question turns upon the due employment of secondary motives in the conduct of life. Is this method properly employed in education? Does God use it in his dealings with us? We must observe that 'Proverbs' is a book written chiefly for the edification of the young and inexperienced, the simple who were still in the early age of moral growth, those whose principles were as yet unsettled and needed direction and steadfastness. For such teaching of the highest character would be inappropriate; they could not at once appreciate more elevated doctrine; their power of assimilation was at present too feeble to admit the strong meat of heavenly lore; and they were to be led gradually to a higher stage by a slow and natural process which would make no great demand on their faith, nor conscious interruption in their daily life. It is thus that we educate children. We employ the motives of shame and emulation, reward and punishment, pleasure and pain, as incentives to goodness and activity, or as deterrents from evil; and though the actions and habits fostered by these means cannot be regarded as perfect, and have in them an element of weakness, still they are helps on the way to virtue, and facilitate the course of higher training. By such means, imperfect as they are, the moral principle is not injured, and the pupil is placed in a position where he is open to the best influences, and prepared to receive them. We have learned thus to deal with children from God's dealings with ourselves. What are gratitude to parents, faith in teachers, love of friends, loyalty to a sovereign, but secondary motives which control our lives, and yet are not distinctly religious? We build on these feelings, we expect and cherish them, because they lead to worthy action, and without them we should be selfish, loveless, animals. They keep us in the path of duty; they take us out of ourselves, make us regard others' interests, preserve us from much that is evil. Men act on such motives; they do not generally set before themselves anything higher; and he who would teach them must take them as they are, stand on their platform, sympathize with their weakness, and, by putting himself in their position, gain their confidence, and lead them to trust his guidance when he tells them of heavenly things. On such principles much of our book is framed. The moralist knew and recognized the fact that the persons for whose benefit he wrote were not wont to act from the highest motives, that in their daily life they were influenced by selfish considerations—fear of loss, censure of neighbours, public opinion, expediency, revenge, custom, example; and, instead of declaiming against these principles and in austere virtue censuring their defects, he makes the best of them, selects such as may suit his purpose, and, while using them as supports for his warnings, he intersperses so much higher teaching that every one must see that morality has another side, and that the only real and true motive for virtue is the love of God. Such teaching loses its apparently anomalous character when we consider that it is addressed to a people who were living under a temporal dispensation, who were told to expect blessings and punishments in their present life, and who saw in all that befell them providential interferences, tokens of the moral government of their Lord and King. It is consistent with the educational object of our book, and with the gradual development of doctrine observed in the Old Testament, wherein is seen that the Law was a tutor to bring men to Christ.

The first collection of proverbs is followed by two appendices enunciating "the words of the wise"—the first contained in ch. xxii. 17—xxiv. 22; the second, introduced by the words, "These things also belong to the wise," in ch. xxiv. 23—34. The former of these commences with a personal address to the pupil, recommending these sayings to his serious attention, and then proceeds to give various precepts concerning duty to the poor, anger, suretyship, cupidity, intemperance, impurity, and to urge the young to avoid evil men and those who would lead them astray. It ends with the weighty saying of moral and political importance—

> "My son, fear thou the Lord and the king:
> And meddle not with them that are given to change" (ch. xxiv. 21).

The second little appendix consists also of proverbial sayings, but is enlivened by a personal reminiscence of the writer, who in his walk passed by the field of the sluggard, noted its miserable condition, and drew a lesson therefrom (ch. xxiv. 30, etc.). This section also contains the almost evangelical precept—

> "Say not, I will do so to him as he hath done to me:
> I will render to the man according to his work."

We now arrive at the second great collection of Solomonic proverbs, "which the men of Hezekiah copied out" (ch. xxv.—xxix.). This is a series of some hundred and twenty gnomic sayings collected from previous writings, by certain scribes and historiographers, in the reign and under the superintendence of the good King Hezekiah, and intended as a supplement to the former collection, to which it bears a very marked similarity, and many sentences of which it repeats with no or very slight variations. Hezekiah, devoted to the moral and religious improvement of his people, seems to have commissioned his secretaries to examine again the works of his predecessor, and to cull from them, and from similar compilations, such maxims as would further his great purpose. Hence we do not find in this section, as in former parts, much instruction for the young, but sentences concerning government, ideas on social subjects, on behaviour, on moral restraint, and kindred topics that have to do with private and public life. There are in it some noteworthy utterances concerning the office of king—

> "The heaven for height, and the earth for depth,
> But the heart of kings is unsearchable.
> Take away dross from the silver,
> And there cometh forth a vessel for the finer;
> Take away the wicked from before the king,
> And his throne shall be established in righteousness" (ch. xxv. 3, etc.).

> "The king by judgment establisheth the land:
> But he that exacteth gifts overthroweth it" (ch. xxix. 4).

There is also a *mashal* hymn in praise of agriculture, which looks like a protest against the growing luxury of the age, and a call to the simpler, purer life of earlier days—

> "Be thou diligent to know the state of thy flocks,
> And look well to thy herds.
> For riches are not for ever:
> And doth the crown endure unto all generations?
> The hay is carried, and the tender grass showeth itself,

And the herbs of the mountains are gathered in.
The lambs are for thy clothing,
And the goats are the price of the field :
And there will be goats' milk enough for thy food,
For the food of thy household,
And maintenance for thy maidens" (ch. xxvii. 23, etc.).

There follow three appendices of various origin and authorship. The first contains "The words of Agur, the son of Jakeh, the oracle," addressed by him to two of his disciples (according to one interpretation of the words, "The man spake unto Ithiel, even unto Ithiel and Ucal"), and containing proverbial and enigmatical sayings (ch. xxx.). This unknown author begins with a confession of his faith, a humble depreciation of his own acquirements, and an acknowledgment of the fruitlessness of endeavouring to comprehend the nature of God. There is much here and in other parts of the section to remind us of the musings of Job, who felt and expressed the same perplexity. The poet then utters two prayers to God, that he may be delivered from vanity and lies, and may be supplied with daily food—

"Give me neither poverty nor riches ;
Feed me with the food that is needful for me " (ch. xxx. 8).

Then succeeds a curious collection of pictures, grouped into three or four sentences each, each stich having a certain connection in language and idea. Thus we have four wicked generations, denoting the universal prevalence of the sins therein denounced; four things insatiable; four things inscrutable; four intolerable; four exceeding wise; four of stately presence. If these utterances mean no more than what at first sight they seem to imply, they merely express the feelings of one who was a keen observer of man and nature, and took a peculiar method of enforcing his remarks: "There are three things, yea, four," etc. But if under these apparently simple statements of fact there are hidden great spiritual verities, then we have here examples of dark sayings, enigmas, difficulties, in the solution of which the opening of the Book promised assistance. That such is the case many early commentators, followed by some modern writers, have stated without hesitation; and much labour has been expended in spiritualizing the dicta of the text. Certainly in their literal shape these sentences are not of the highest type, nor distinctly religious ; and it is but natural that, feeling this, expositors should endeavour to raise these commonplace and secular allusions to a more exalted sphere.

The second appendix (ch. xxxi. 1—9) is entitled, " The words of King Lemuel, the oracle which his mother taught him." The chief interest lies in the question—Who is Lemuel? (see § 3). The section is a brief lesson addressed to kings, chiefly on the subjects of impurity and drunkenness.

The third appendix, which forms the conclusion of the book (ch. xxxi. 10—31), consists of the celebrated description of the virtuous woman, the type of the ideal wife, mother, and mistress. It is what is called an acrostic *mashal*, i.e. each verse commences with one of the twenty-two letters of the Hebrew alphabet, in the usual alphabetical order. Taking the manners and customs of his age and country as the basis of his pictures, the author delineates a woman of the highest attainments, strong-minded yet feminine, active, practical, prudent, economical. Her husband trusts her wholly; she manages the household, keeps her servants to their work, and herself sets an example of diligence; she always has funds in hand to make purchases at the right moment, and to provide for the needs of her household. She is as wise as she is beautiful, as generous and charitable as she is just; her virtue redounds to the credit of husband and children, and all connected with her.

> "Her children rise up, and call her blessed;
> Her husband also, and he praiseth her, saying,
> Many daughters have done virtuously,
> But thou excellest them all.
> Favour is deceitful, and beauty is vain:
> But a woman that feareth the Lord, she shall be praised.
> Give her of the fruit of her hands;
> And let her works praise her in the gates."

After the many passages which speak of the degradation of woman, which introduce her in the most odious light, as the temptress of youth, and the very road to death; in contrast, too, to numerous paragraphs and allusions which represent home-life as spoiled by a contentious, jealous, and extravagant wife,—it is soothing to come upon this noble description, and to close the volume with this picture of what a woman is when she is animated by love of God and duty.

We may add a slight sketch of the theology and ethics which meet us in this book. There is little distinctive Judaism. In this respect the similarity to the Book of Job is remarkable. The name of Israel is not once mentioned; there is no allusion to the Passover or the other great festivals; there is not a word about idolatry, not a warning against the worship of false gods; the observation of the sabbath is not referred to, nor the payment of tithes. At the same time, the Law is often mentioned, and the ceremonies enjoined therein are tacitly regarded as being in full use and practice (see ch. xxviii. 4, 9; xiv. 9; vii. 14, etc.). It is doubtless a providential arrangement that so little prominence is given to the external obligations of the Hebrew religion; by this reticence the book was better adapted to become a world-wide teacher; it spoke to Jew and Gentile alike; it taught a morality with which all good men could sympathize; it penetrated wherever Greek literature was understood and valued. Of its wide influence the Book of Wisdom and Ecclesiasticus are special proofs.

The dogmatic statements of "the Proverbs" are in complete accord with the religion of Israel as we know it from other sources. The special name of God in the form Jehovah occurs everywhere throughout the book, and is used more often than Elohim, thus emphasizing the great truth of which the incommunicable name was the symbol. God is incomprehensible (ch. xxx. 4), infinitely wise (ch. iii. 19, etc.; viii.), omniscient, omnipresent (ch. xv. 3). He created all things out of nothing (ch. viii. 22, etc.) ; he governs and preserves them by his providence (ch. xvi. 4) ; he teaches men by chastening and affliction (ch. iii. 11, 12); his care watches over and rewards the good, while he punishes the evil (ch. xii. 2) ; the poor and the lowly are special objects of his love (ch. xxii. 4; xvi. 19; xxiii. 11); allowing to man the exercise of free-will (ch. i. 24), God helps him by his grace to make a right choice (ch. xvi. 1, 3, 9; xx. 24), because he loves him (ch. viii. 17, 31), and wills his happiness (ch. viii. 35). Of the doctrine concerning wisdom in this book we have spoken above. Of Messianic hopes no distinct trace is found. Whether the future life is asserted has often been questioned; but it is difficult to believe that this great truth is wholly neglected in this book, as we know that long before Solomon's time it was generally admitted, and we should confidently expect traces of its influence in the treatment of man's destiny.

> " In the way of righteousness is life;
>   And in the pathway thereof there is no death " (ch. xii. 28).

> " The wicked is thrust down in his evil-doing:
>   But the righteous hath hope in his death " (ch. xiv. 32).

These are not dogmatic assertions of future rewards and punishments, but they are consistent with such a belief, and may well imply it. In the same light we may consider the many passages which speak of the recompense that awaits actions good or evil. The retribution promised is not fully satisfied by anything that befalls a man in this life as the result of his conduct; both the reward and the punishment are spoken of in terms which seem to look to something beyond the grave—something which death did not end, and which nothing here was adequate to fulfil. If it is said that impurity plunges a man into the depths of hell (ch. ii. 18; vii. 11), that sinners remain in the congregation of the dead (ch. xxi. 16), and that their expectation perishes when they die (ch. xi. 7), it is also announced that righteousness delivereth from death (ch. xi. 4), that there is a sure reward for the godly (ch. xi. 18), and that the righteous hath hope in his death (ch. xiv. 32).

The moral teaching of our book may be grouped under various heads—the result of experience, the outcome of thought, controlled by the strongest sense of religion and an overruling Providence.

1. *Duty to God.* The first of all duties, the foundation of all morality and religion, is the fear of God (ch. i. 7). This must be followed by perfect trust in him and distrust of self (ch. iii. 5, etc.). The externals of religious worship are not to be neglected (ch. xiv. 9; xx. 25), but God looks chiefly to the heart (ch. xvii. 3); it is this which makes men acceptable or abominable in his sight (ch. xi. 20; xv. 8). If we sin, we must confess

our guilt (ch. xxviii. 13), meekly submit to his chastisement (ch. iii. 11,
etc.).

2. *Duty to ourselves.* The first and chief lesson enforced is the utter
necessity of avoiding fleshly lusts and evil companionship (ch. i. 10, etc.;
xiii. 20). Among deadly sins to be avoided special mention is made of
pride, the enemy of wisdom and hateful to God (ch. xvi. 5, 18, 19); avarice
and cupidity, which lead to fraud and wrong (ch. xxviii. 20), and produce
only a transitory profit (ch. xxiii. 4, 5); envy, which is as rottenness in
the bones (ch. xiv. 30); luxury and intemperance, which, as prevalent
in the more artificial state of society, induced by wealth and contact with
other nations, are most strongly reprobated and shown to ensure most fatal
consequences (ch. ii. 18; xxiii. 1, etc., 20, etc., 29, etc.); anger, which
leads to folly, causes and embitters quarrels, makes a man detestable (ch.
xiv. 17; xv. 1; xx. 3); idleness, which ruins equally a man's character and
property (ch. xiii. 4; vi. 6, etc.). Then much is said about the necessity
of guarding the tongue, in the power of which are death and life (ch. xii.
13, etc.; xviii. 21), and avoiding self-praise (ch. xii. 9; xxvii. 2).

3. *Duty to our neighbours.* We should sympathize with the afflicted, and
try to cheer them (ch. xii. 25; xvi. 24); help the poor in their need
because they are brethren, children of the All-Father (ch. iii. 27, etc.;
xiv. 31). A neighbour should be judged honestly and truthfully (ch. xvii.
15; xxiv. 23, etc.); with him we are to live in peace (ch. iii. 29, etc.;
xvii. 13, etc.), never slandering him (ch. x. 10, etc.; xi. 12, etc.), hiding
his faults if possible (ch. x. 12), encouraging sincere friendship (ch. xviii.
24), and being strictly honest in all transactions with him (ch. xi. 1;
xx. 14; xxii. 28).

4. *Domestic duties.* Pious parents are a blessing to children (ch. xx. 7),
and should teach them holy lessons from their earliest years (ch. i. 8; iv. 1,
etc.), training them in the right way (ch. xxii. 6), correcting them when
they do wrong (ch. xxiii. 13, etc.). Children for their part should attend
to the instruction of elders, and gladden their parents' hearts by prompt
obedience and strict life (ch. x. 1; xxiii. 15, etc.). Let the mother of the
family realize her high position, and be the crown of her husband (ch.
xii. 4), and build up her house (ch. xiv. 1). If she needs a model, let her
endeavour to emulate the strong-minded virtuous woman (ch. xxxi. 10, etc.).
Be it far from her to imitate the contentious wife, whose peevish ill temper
is like the continuous dropping of a leaky roof, and renders family life
insupportable (ch. xix. 13; xxv. 24). Servants should be carefully selected
(ch. xvii. 2) and wisely treated, that they may not rise beyond their station
and prove arrogant and assuming (ch. xix. 10; xxix. 21).

5. *Maxims relating to civil life and political economy.* The king's throne
is established by righteousness, mercy, and truth (ch. xvi. 12; xx. 28);
his sentence is regarded as indefeasible (ch. xvi. 10); he pursues the
godless with righteous punishment (ch. xx. 8, 26), protects the weak (ch.
xxxi. 7, etc.), favours the pious and obedient (ch. xvi. 15; xix. 12). He

is no oppressor, nor covetous (ch. xxviii. 16) ; and he gathers round him faithful counsellors (ch. xiv. 35), whose advice he takes in all important matters (ch. xxiv. 6).   By such means he increases the stability of his throne ; he enables his subjects to advance in prosperity and virtue, and finds his honour in the multitude of his people (ch. xi. 14 ; xiv. 28).   It is the duty of men to render obedience to the powers that be ; punishment speedily overtakes the rebellious (ch. xvi. 14, etc. ; xix. 12 ; xx. 2).   God has ordained that there shall be rich and poor in the land (ch. xxii. 2) ; the rich ought to help the poor (ch. iii. 27, etc. ; xiv. 21), and not treat them roughly (ch. xviii. 23).   All commercial transactions should be conducted with the strictest honesty ; the withholding of corn is specially denounced (ch. xi. 26).   It is a foolish act to stand security for another's debt ; you are sure to smart for it, and then you can blame only yourself (ch. vi. 1, etc. ; xxii. 26, etc.).

Among miscellaneous sayings we may note the following :—

" Who can say, I have made my heart clean,
I am pure from my sin ? " (ch. xx. 9).

" It is as sport to a fool to do wickedness ;
And so is wisdom to a man of understanding " (ch. x. 23).

" A wise man is strong ;
Yea, a man of knowledge increaseth strength " (ch. xxiv. 5).

" The wicked flee when no man pursueth :
But the righteous are bold as a lion " (ch. xxviii. 1).

" Hope deferred maketh the heart sick :
But when the desire cometh, it is a tree of life " (ch. xiii. 12).

" The path of the righteous is as the shining light,
That shineth more and more unto the perfect day " (ch. iv. 18).

" The wicked earneth deceitful wages :
But he that soweth righteousness hath a sure reward " (ch. xi. 18).

" The hoary head is a crown of glory ;
It shall be found in the way of righteousness " (ch. xvi. 31).

§ 3. Authorship and Date.

Uncritical antiquity, followed in modern times by undiscriminating conservatism, had no hesitation in ascribing the whole Book of Proverbs to one author, Solomon, King of Israel.   It is true that three portions of the work are prefaced with his name (ch. i. 1 ; x. 1 ; xxv. 1) ; but two other sections are attributed respectively to Agur (ch. xxx. 1) and Lemuel (ch. xxxi. 1) ; so that apparently the volume itself professes to be composed by three authors ; and besides this, there are two appendices containing " the words of the wise " (ch. xxii. 17, etc. ; xxiv. 23, etc.), which must be distinguished from those of Solomon.   It was natural indeed for the Jews to affix their great king's name to the whole collection.   He is said to have spoken three thousand proverbs (*mashal*, 1 Kings iv. 32), a statement which implies that they had been collected into a volume, and the present work was reasonably supposed to form part of this surprisingly large storehouse of wisdom. But a more careful examination of the book necessitates the opinion of divided authorship; contents and language point to differences of date and composition; the repetition of the same proverb in identical or almost identical language, the recurrence of the same thought varied only in actual wording, the adoption of one member of an old maxim with the attachment of a different hemistich,—these blemishes could hardly have been allowed to remain in the work of a single author. There are also variations in the language, which in a marked manner differentiate the several parts, so that we are forced to allow a composite character to the work; and the difficult task is imposed of endeavouring to find some certainty on the question of its origin.

In one place alone does the book itself afford direct help towards determining the date of any portion. The section copied by Hezekiah's friends from previous records must have been put together in that monarch's reign, between two and three hundred years after the time of Solomon, who was regarded as the author of those sayings. The persons engaged in the compilation may have been those mentioned in 2 Kings xviii. 18—Shebna the secretary, and Joah, son of Asaph, the chronicler, and very possibly the Prophet Isaiah himself, as a Jewish tradition relates. Whether after so long an interval they simply reproduced his utterances, unadulterated and unaugmented, might *primâ facie* be doubted; a careful examination of the section shows that this doubt is well founded. If there are many sentences therein which in form and substance have a flavour of high antiquity, and may well have flowed from Solomon's lips and have been current in his age, there are also many which exhibit the artificiality of a later period, and presuppose a condition of things far removed from the palmy era of the Hebrew monarchy. Most critics have come to the conclusion that the earliest portion is that which is called the first great collection, contained in ch. xi.—xxii. 16. The style throughout is simple and chaste, the maxims are mostly comprised in antithetical distichs, each verse being complete in itself. This, according to Ewald, is the oldest form of the technical proverb. It is noticed that there are many phrases and expressions which are peculiar to this section, *e.g.* " fountain of life," " tree of life," " snares of death," " hand in hand," " whisperer, tale-bearer," " shall not go unpunished," " but for a moment," etc. But arguments derived from peculiarities of structure and language are generally uncertain, and strike readers in different ways. A surer criterion is found in the contents of a composition, in the references which it contains, in the circumstances which it mentions, or the environments which it implies. Now, if we compare this first collection with that of Hezekiah's " men," we shall note some very marked differences, which have been observed by many critics. There is evidently a change in the political situation. In the former section the monarchy is at its best. It is deemed "an abomination to kings to commit wickedness" (ch. xvi. 12); their "throne is established by righteousness," they "delight in righteous lips, and love him that speaketh right;" there is "life in the king's countenance, and his favour is like the latter rain" (ch. xvi. 13, etc.); mercy and truth are his safeguard, and uphold his throne (ch. xx. 28). A changed picture is presented in the Hezekiah collection. Here we have a people oppressed by a prince wanting in understanding (ch. xxviii. 19), mourning under the rule of a wicked king (ch. xxix. 2), who is likened to a roaring lion and a ranging bear (ch. xxviii. 15). There is reference to bribery and extortion in high places (ch. xxix. 4), change of dynasties (ch. xxviii. 2), unworthy favourites (ch. xxv. 5; xxix. 12)—all of which circumstances point to a political situation other than that in the former part; a period, in fact, when experience had brought knowledge of evil, and rulers had been found to be antagonistic to the interests of their subjects, liable to the worst vices, open to corrupting influences. It is impossible to suppose that many of the maxims, even in the former collection, were spoken by Solomon. What experience would make him say that the king's honour lay in the multitude of his people, and his destruction in their paucity (ch. xiv. 28)? Or, again, that a pious wife is the best of blessings (ch. xii. 4; xviii. 22), while a contentious one is a torment (ch. xix. 13, 14; xxi. 9, 19)? Such statements as these last presuppose a monogamous man, not one notorious for polygamy. Then, would Solomon have discoursed thus about himself, asserting that a Divine sentence is his word, and that his judgments are irrefragable (ch. xvi. 10), that his wrath is as messengers of death, that his favour is light and life (ch. xvi. 14, 15), that his anger is like the roaring of a lion, and he puts to the torture those who offend him, while his only claim to support at God's hands is the mercy and truth which his life exhibits (ch. xx. 2, 26, 28)? However cast in Solomonic mould, these sentences cannot have had Solomon for their author; so we must conclude that, together with his genuine sayings, a multitude of gnomes were extant, of various ages and origins, which were attributed popularly to the great king, as the founder of that kind of gnomic poetry, the great master of proverbial philosophy. That both sections contain very many sayings which had him for their author, it is reasonable to suppose, and there is nothing to discredit this notion. From what is said of his remarkable wisdom, and regarding the form which philosophy assumes in the East, we might expect such productions from his mind. If he had for his object the instruction of his people, the training of them in sound views of life and in the practice of virtue and religion, he would embody his views in terse and pithy sentences, charming the imagination and easy to be remembered; he would thus apply Divine truths to the conduct and regulation of daily life. This precedent was doubtless followed by other sages, and thus in addition to and in connection with the proverbial lore which is accumulated in every nation by the experience of ages, there grew up a gradually increasing store of maxims and apothegms, of a higher order than the vulgar sort, which was enshrined in carefully balanced sentences, and handed down as a precious heirloom to succeeding generations.

These considerations, which seem well grounded, account for the composite character of the Book of Proverbs. Many minds and many ages have been concerned in the collection; it has suffered from interpolation, transposition, addition; various editors have arranged and rearranged the materials before them; passages reflect the golden age of Israel's monarchy; passages belong to such times as those of Jeroboam II. and his successors. It has become impossible to assign assured dates to the several parts, and the attempt has led critics to ludicrous conclusions, some from the same data attributing to Solomon compositions which others affix to post-exilian times. Out of the medley of varying opinions we gather the following conclusions. When the men of Hezekiah made their collection, which is headed with the words, " These are also proverbs of Solomon," there existed already a body of maxims known as Solomon's, to which they were minded to make an addition from sources open to them. This previously existing collection we may reasonably suppose to be that which at present stands immediately before theirs, viz. ch. x. 1—xxii. 16, and which would thus be the older portion. It is expressly called " the proverbs of Solomon; " and there can be no reasonable doubt that the traditional account which assigned it to the son of David was in the main correct. Knowing the facts of Solomon's later career, no collector would have had the hardihood to attribute many of the utterances therein to him, had they not been universally recognized as his. They are doubtless the effusion of earlier days, the collected outpouring of the happy time when his heart was whole and his faith unimpaired; but who arranged it, or when it received its present shape, can only be conjectured. It is not to be supposed that Solomon sat down and deliberately composed a book of proverbs such as we now possess. It is said that he *spake* three thousand proverbs. He must have had scribes and secretaries who collected the wisdom that flowed from his lips during the various circumstances of his life and in the various stages of his career (1 Kings iv. 3). This formed the nucleus round which accretions gathered in the course of time, the acumen of Hebrew critics failing to distinguish the genuine from the spurious. From the great mass of proverbial literature thus formed Hezekiah's friends made a new selection. What became of the rest of the older collection, which is not comprised in our present volume, cannot be known. It was evidently preserved among the archives of the kingdom which contained accounts, not only of the monarch's acts, but also of his wisdom (1 Kings xi. 41). As we have said above, the repetitions of the same proverb in different places indicate a change of authors or editors, deriving their materials from the same source, oral or documentary, but writing independently.

The two appendices to this section containing the " words of the wise " (ch. xxii. 17—xxiv.) exhibit repetitions which again would indicate a variety of authors, or a lack of care in selection. Some passages found in other parts of the book occur also in these two sections. Thus ch. xxiv. 20 (as we shall notice directly) appears at ch. xiii. 9; ch. xxiv. 23, "To have respect of persons is not good," at ch. xxviii. 21; and ch. xxiv. 33, 34 at ch. vi. 10, 11. The first of the appendices is evidently later than the first collection; the structure of the verses is less terse, the parallelism is not so strongly marked, sometimes entirely wanting, and the sense is often not completed under three or even five verses. A comparison of the way in which the repetitions above indicated are introduced would lead to the impression that the former was the earlier, and that the appendix-writer derived certain sentences from that. Thus in ch. xxii. 14 we have the statement, "The mouth of strange women is a deep pit;" but in ch. xxiii. 27 this is introduced as a reason for the advice in the previous verse, and amplified thus: "For a whore is a deep ditch, and a strange woman is a narrow pit." So the verse, ch. xi. 14, is enlarged into two in ch. xxiv. 5, 6; and the unvarnished gnome (ch. xiii. 9), "The light of the righteous rejoiceth, but the lamp of the wicked shall be put out," becomes, under the manipulation of the transcriber, a warning in quite a different direction: "Fret not thyself because of evil-doers, neither be thou envious at the wicked; for there will be no reward to the evil man; the lamp of the wicked shall be put out" (ch. xxiv. 19, 20). Who can doubt that the simpler form of these sayings is the original? Hitzig claims an exilian date for this section on the strength of an Aramaic colouring which other critics deny, and a supposed borrowing of passages or phrases from Jeremiah which seems to be wholly imaginary. How could a poet, banished from his own country, make a point of not removing the ancient landmark (ch. xxii. 28; xxiii. 10), or enjoin his hearers to serve their king and avoid innovators (ch. xxiv. 21)? There is, indeed, nothing to guide us to any certainty in the question, but the style and language reflect those of the first portion of our book, and it may possibly have been written about the same period. As in ch. iii. 31, so often in this section (*e.g.* ch. xxii. 22; xxiv. 15, etc.), there are hints of oppressive rulers and iniquitous governors, which would lead us to think of Manasseh and his like. It is reasonable to conclude that this appendix was added after Hezekiah's time by an editor who had before him the first great collection. The same holds good concerning the second little appendix (ch. xxiv. 23—34), which seems to be of contemporaneous origin. Nowack, by comparing the two similar passages in ch. vi. 10, 11 and xxiv. 33, 34, concludes that the former is original, and that the appendix-writer has somewhat altered the sentence in transferring it to his own repertory.

We have in some degree indicated what may be reasonably determined about the date and authorship of the central portions of our book. It remains to investigate the beginning and the closing sections. The introduction (ch. i. 1—6), describing the character and intent of the work, applies virtually not only to the collection immediately succeeding (ch. i. 7—ix.), but to other parts of the book, whether the writer had these parts

before him or not. Who is the author of this first section, the proem, as it
has been called, is a matter of much dispute. There is some difficulty in
attributing it to Solomon himself. The opening words do not necessarily
imply that Solomon wrote all that follows. "The Proverbs of Solomon"
may be introduced as a formal heading of what may be a gathering of
fragments from many quarters, composed in Solomon's spirit and instinct
with his wisdom, but not actually received from his lips or writings. There
are passages which seem to be derived from Isaiah's prophecy; *e.g.* ch. ii.
15, "Whose ways are crooked, and they froward in their paths," is
parallel to Isa. lix. 8; ch. i. 24, 26, 27, to Isa. lxv. 12 and lxvi. 4. But the
language is not identical, and the prophet may have been indebted to the
moralist. More to the purpose is the fact that the second part (ch. x. 1—
xxii. 16) is superscribed "The Proverbs of Solomon," which would be
unnecessary and misleading if the first part was also his composition. To
this it may be answered that this title is more especially appropriate to the
section as containing proverbs rather than hortatory addresses; and if
introduced by a different editor the discrepancy is easily accounted for.
Others insist that the religious ideas and the form in which they are
expressed are quite foreign to Solomon's time and standpoint. If the
technical form of the *mashal*, consisting of distichs displaying well-
balanced and antithetical clauses, be the form which alone appertains to
Solomon's age, then it must be allowed that the introductory section
contains very few proper *mashals*, but rather is composed of odes of
varying length, in which, as it were incidentally, a few *mashals* are
inserted. The terse single proverb is remarkably absent, and descriptive
poems, lengthy exhortations, and developments of a given truth, are the
common characteristics of the piece. Here again, however, there is no
certainty that Solomon regarded himself as bound to keep to one law in
the composition of proverbs, or that he did not employ other and more
elaborate methods of expressing his sentiments. The presumption is
certainly against the two parts having the same author, but the idea is not
irrational. Delitzsch has produced another argument. He dwells upon
the different idea of Wisdom afforded by the two sections. In the former,
Wisdom appears as an independent personality, dwelling with God before
all creation, and operating in the production of the visible world, and busy-
ing itself with the affairs of men; in the latter, Wisdom is a moral quality,
which is grounded in the fear of God, teaches men to recognize the truth,
and to regulate their lives according to the rules of religion. Doubtless
the view of Wisdom in the proem is an advance on and a development of
the conception in the other section. Speculation had progressed, schools
of wise men had been formed, preceptors addressed their pupils as "son,"
and Wisdom was regarded as the chief motor of moral and religious action.
The *chokma* is no longer an idea, a code, or a subjective thought; it has
an objective existence, carried back to eternity, fellow-worker with God.
This consideration is decisive against the identity of authorship in the two

parts, and disposes one to allow more weight to the undecisive arguments mentioned above. The parænetical form adopted in the introduction, so different from the proverb proper, points to the influence of the prophetic element, hardly arrived at public utterances and documentary testimony in Solomon's time, but afterwards the great power in the state and the common support of the religious life. Many passages breathe the spirit of Deuteronomy, which in the minds of some critics would at once be a proof of very late origin, but of course have no such look for those who hold the Mosaic authorship of the Pentateuch. Others are remarkably similar to parts of the Book of Job, and are evidently more or less borrowed from that source; but as the date of that writing is still undecided, nothing can be deduced from this fact. Taking all that has been said into consideration, and carefully weighing the opinions which have been put forth on the question, we regard this section as the composition of one author, and *that* not Solomon, except in so far as it breathes his spirit and possibly embodies many of his sayings. It is no argument against this last suggestion, that Solomon would not be found discoursing against unchastity of which his own later life was a flagrant example. There is no reason why this wisest of men should not have uttered such warnings in the earlier and purer part of his career. It was probably arranged in its present shape by the editor of the first great collection of Solomonic proverbs, and placed by him as an introduction to this work. The eloquence of the piece is of the very highest order, and exhibits the inspiration of a true prophet, but the writer must remain unknown. It is only natural to consider that such magnificent passages as those contained in ch. vii. and ix. were composed by a man of no mean attainments, and one can think of no one able to write them but Solomon himself, especially inspired by God with wisdom beyond all men; but this impression does not vanquish opposing criticism, and we can only concede that the section is worthy of Solomon, and probably contains some of his lore, garnered and lovingly reproduced by a kindred spirit.

The last two chapters (xxx. and xxxi.) present some difficult questions, which have always exercised the ingenuity of critics, and which cannot even now be determined with any certainty. Ch. xxx. opens (according to the Authorized Version) thus: "The words of Agur the son of Jakeh, even the prophecy: the man spake unto Ithiel, even unto Ithiel and Ucal." Nothing whatever is known about any of the persons here supposed to be mentioned. The name Ithiel, indeed, occurs once in Nehemiah (xi. 7); but the Benjamite thus called can have nothing to do with the person in our verse. It is conjectured that Agur was some well-known sage, Hebrew or foreign, whose sayings were thought by some late editor to be worthy of a place beside the proverbs of Solomon. Jewish interpreters have explained the names symbolically of Solomon himself. Agur may mean "Gatherer," "Convener," from *agar*, "to collect," and is applied to the wise king, either as "master of assemblies" (Eccles. xii. 11), or collector of wisdom and maxims, elsewhere called *koheleth* (Eccles. i. 1), though this interpretation of the latter word is very questionable. *Jakeh* is rendered "Obedient" or "Pious," so "the Gatherer, son of the Obedient," would designate Solomon, son of David. St. Jerome countenances the allegorical interpretation by rendering, "Verba Congregantis filii Vomentis." But one sees no reason why the king, whose name has been freely used in the previous sections, should now be introduced under an allegorical appellation. Certainly, much that is contained in the chapter may be regarded as symbolical, but that is scarcely sufficient reason for making the teacher also symbolical. Why, again, should this section be separated from the rest of Solomon's words, and not incorporated with the great body of his collection? What object could there be in introducing another batch of the king's proverbs after the " words of the wise " ? If this piece had been in existence in early times, Hezekiah would surely not have omitted placing it in its proper position in his own repertory. The contents, however, leave no doubt on the subject. Solomon never could have uttered what follows :—

> " Surely I am more brutish than any man,
> And have not the understanding of a man ;
> And I have not learned wisdom" (ch. xxx. 2, 3).

Nor could he be blindly groping in darkness after the Creator (ch. xxx. 4) ; nor pray that he might have neither poverty nor riches (ch. xxx. 8). The notion, therefore, that Solomon himself is here intended must be surrendered as wholly unfounded. Some have attempted to find Agur's nationality in the word translated "the prophecy" (*hamassa*). *Massa*, "burden," is the word generally used to denote a prophet's message, either from its being borne by him to the appointed place, or expressive of its grievous nature and awful importance. The term does not seem altogether appropriate to the utterances that follow, and Hitzig has started a theory which makes the word denote the country from which Agur came. The old Venetian Version had given : Λόγοι 'Αγούρου υἱέως 'Ιακέως τοῦ Μασάου, " the words of Agur son of Jakeh the Masaite." Now, there was a son of Ishmael named Massa (Gen. xxv. 14; 1 Chron. i. 30), who may have given his name to a tribe and a district, as did his brothers Duma and Tema (Isa. xxi. 11, 14). It is mentioned in 1 Chron. iv. 38, etc., that certain Simeonites in the days of Hezekiah made a raid into the country of Edom, and established themselves in Mount Seir, driving out the Amalekites whom they found settled there. Starting from this locality and moving northwards towards Damascus, according to Hitzig, they set up the kingdom of Massa, and hence issued this piece of poetry not long after the first establishment. This, in his view, would account for the peculiarities of dialect found in the composition. Others have found a Massa in the town Mismije, on the north of the Hauran ; others place it on the north of the Persian Gulf. In fact, nothing is known with certainty about the country ; its very existence is problematical. The most likely supposition is that Agur was an Edomite, a worshipper of Jehovah, and well acquainted with

Israelitish literature, being one of the sages for whom Edom was celebrated (1 Kings iv. 30), a man whose sayings were deemed of sufficient value and inspiration to insert in the sacred canon, though he, like Job, was not one of the chosen people. The more probable rendering of the second hemistich of ver. 1 of this chapter, which is given in the margin of the Revised Version, is noted in the Exposition.

As Agur is considered a symbolical name of Solomon, so is Lemuel in the next chapter, which opens thus: "The words of King Lemuel, the burden which his mother taught him." Lemuel (or Lemoel, as ver. 4) means "Unto God," equivalent to "Dedicated to God;" and it is supposed to be applied to Solomon, who from infancy was dedicated to God, and called by him Jedidiah, "Beloved of the Lord" (2 Sam. xii. 25). But there is no good reason for supposing Solomon to be designated Lemuel. If Agur meant Solomon, why is the name now suddenly changed? And how can we suppose the following address to have been spoken by Bathsheba, the adulteress and virtual murderess? This is a difficulty not resolved by regarding "the mother" as a personification of the Hebrew Church, which is an arbitrary assumption invented to meet an objection, rather than necessitated by an observation of evidence. Those who saw in Massa the country of Agur's residence, would here likewise translate, "the words of Lemuel, King of Massa," and weave a pleasing fiction whereby Agur and Lemuel become the sons of a Queen of Massa, who is supposed to have been, like the Queen of Sheba, a diligent seeker of wisdom. This may be true, but it is a mere conjecture, which cannot be verified. If it is accepted, Lemuel would be an Ishmaelite, whose home was in North Arabia, and who belonged to the company of the wise men for whom Arabia was proverbial. At the same time, it is unlikely that the production of an alien, particularly of a jealously regarded Ishmaelite, should be admitted to the sacred canon. Of course, there is the difficulty concerning the origin of the Book of Job, but as that controversy is not settled, we cannot regard this as an objection. Laying aside the theory of Lemuel being a non-Israelite, we must regard the word as the appellation of an ideal king, whether the poet looked back to Solomon or Hezekiah, whom he represents as taught by a careful mother in the way of piety and justice. Concerning the date of these appendices there is little to guide us in our determination, except that the language points to composition at a later period than the former portions of the book. We have many dialectical variations, Aramaic and Arabic expressions, which do not occur in the earlier sections, and which were not, as far as we know, current in Southern Israel before Hezekiah's reign, nor probably for some long time after. The free, terse proverb is now wholly wanting, a strained, mechanical composition taking its place; we have enigmas instead of maxims, laboured odelets instead of neat distichs—productions in quite different style from those hitherto handled, and showing a decline of creative power and a tendency to make artificiality and mechanical skill take the place of thought and novelty. The passages which are similar to, and may have been derived from, Job cannot be used in proof of the late date of these sections, as the era of that work is undetermined; but the painful consciousness of man's ignorance in the presence of the great Creator, which meets us, as in Job, so in this appendix (ch. xxx. 2, etc.), implies a speculative activity very foreign to the earlier Hebrew mind, and indicative of contact with other elements, and acquaintance with philosophical questions far removed from the times of the primordial monarchy. Some, accordingly, have attributed the pieces to post-exilian days; but there is not a shadow of proof for this, not an expression or an allusion which confirms such a notion; and Delitzsch is probably correct when he dates their production at the end of the seventh or the beginning of the sixth century B.C.

The closing poem, the praise of the virtuous woman, is probably still later, and certainly by a different hand. The alphabetical ode is not found till the very latest period of Hebrew poetry, though it is impossible to affix any definite date for its production.

§ 4. GENERAL CHARACTER.

The whole Book of the Proverbs is rhythmical in construction, and it is rightly so printed in the Revised Version as to exhibit this characteristic. The great feature of Hebrew poetry, as every one knows, is parallelism, the balancing of thought against thought, corresponding in form and often in sound, so that one line is an echo of the other. The second member is either equivalent to the first, or contrasted with it or similar to it in construction; the whole may consist of only two lines forming a distich, which is the normal type of proverb, or of three or four or more; but all contain one thought expanded on parallel lines. The various shapes which are thus assumed by the sentences in our book are thus noted.

The simplest and earliest form is the *distich*, a sentence consisting of two lines balanced one with the other, like—

' A wise son maketh a glad father :
But a foolish son is the heaviness of his mother " (ch. x. 1).

The second part of our book (ch. x. 1—xxii. 16) consists mainly of such sentences. Sometimes the sense extends over three lines, forming a *tristich*, when the thought in the first line is repeated in the second before the conclusion is reached. Thus—

" Though thou shouldest bray a fool in a mortar
With a pestle among bruised corn,
Yet will not his foolishness depart from him " (ch. xxvii. 22).

Or the idea in the second line is developed by a contrast in the third—

" Whoso causeth the upright to go astray in an evil way,
He shall fall himself into his own pit :
But the perfect shall inherit good " (ch. xxviii. 10).

Or the additional line produces a proof in confirmation—

> "Thine own friend, and thy father's friend, forsake not;
> And go not to thy brother's house in the day of thy calamity:
> Better is a neighbour that is near than a brother that is far off" (ch. xxvii. 10).

Of *tetrastichs* we find some instances, where the last two lines make the application of the others—

> " Take away the dross from the silver,
> And there cometh forth a vessel for the finer:
> Take away the wicked from before the king,
> And his throne shall be established in righteousness" (ch. xxv. 4, 5).

In the maxims consisting of five lines, *pentastichs*, the last two or three generally supply or develop the reason of the preceding—

> " Weary not thyself to be rich:
> Cease from thine own wisdom.
> Wilt thou set thine eyes upon that which is not?
> For riches certainly make themselves wings,
> Like an eagle that flieth toward heaven" (ch. xxiii. 4, 5).

Of a proverb in six lines, *hexastich*, we have a few instances—

> "Deliver them that are carried away unto death,
> And those that are ready to be slain see that thou hold back.
> If thou sayest, Behold, we knew not this;
> Doth not he that weigheth the hearts consider it?
> And he that keepeth thy soul, doth not he know it?
> And shall not he render to every man according to his work?" (ch. xxiv. 11, 12).

Of the *heptastich* there is only one example, viz. ch. xxiii. 6—8.

The connected verses in ch. xxiii. 22—25 may be regarded as an *octastich*, but when thus extended the proverb becomes a *mashal* ode, like Ps. xxv., xxxiv., xxxvii. Of this character are the introductory part, which consists of fifteen didactic poems, the hortatory address (ch. xxii. 17—21), the warning against drunkenness (ch. xxiii. 29—35), and many other passages, especially the praise of the virtuous woman (ch. xxxi. 10, etc.), written in the form of an alphabetical acrostic.

The form of the proverb being such as we have described, it remains to distinguish the different kinds of parallelisms employed which have led to their being arranged into various classes.

1. The simplest species is the *synonymous*, where the second hemistich merely repeats the first, with some little alteration of words, in order to enforce the truth presented in the former; *e.g.*—

> "The liberal soul shall be made fat;
> And he that watereth shall be watered also himself" (ch. xi. 25).

> " He that is slow to anger is better than the mighty;
> And he that ruleth his spirit than he that taketh a city " (ch. xvi. 32).

2. The *antithetic* presents in the second member a contrast to the first, bringing forward a fact or an idea which offers the other side of the picture—

"The labour of the righteous tendeth to life:
The increase of the wicked to sin" (ch. x. 16).

"The thoughts of the righteous are judgment:
But the counsels of the wicked are deceit" (ch. xii. 5).

These are, perhaps, of more frequent occurrence than any. Sometimes the form is interrogative—

"The spirit of a man will sustain his infirmity:
But a broken spirit who can bear?" (ch. xviii. 14).

3. Synthesis in logic is an argument advancing regularly from principles conceded to a conclusion founded thereon. The term has been loosely applied to our subject, and *synthetical* proverbs are such as contain two different truths embodied in the distich, and not necessarily dependent one upon another, but connected by some feature common to both.

"The fear of the wicked, it shall come upon him;
And the desire of the righteous shall be granted" (ch. x. 24).

The idea of the future is here the connecting link. In the following distich the misery which results in both cases is the point :—

"He that is slack in his work
Is brother to him that is a destroyer" (ch. xviii. 9).

4. This last example introduces us to what Delitzsch terms the *integral* proverb, where the second line completes the thought which is only begun in the first—

"The law of the wise is a fountain of life,
To depart from the snares of death" (ch. xiii. 14).

"The eyes of the Lord are in every place,
Keeping watch upon the evil and the good" (ch. xv. 3).

This is called also *progressive*, a gradation being presented from the less to the greater, or the greater to the less, as—

"Behold, the righteous shall be recompensed in the earth :
How much more the wicked and the sinner!" (ch. xi. 31).

"Sheol and Abaddon are before the Lord :
How much more then the hearts of the children of men!" (ch. xv. 11).

5. The fifth sort of proverb is named the *parabolic*, which is, perhaps, the most striking and significant of all, and capable of manifold expression. Herein a fact in nature or in common life is stated, and an ethical lesson grounded upon it. The comparison is sometimes introduced by particles—

"As vinegar to the teeth, and as smoke to the eyes,
So is the sluggard to them that send him" (ch. x. 26).

Sometimes it is suggested by mere juxtaposition—

> " A jewel of gold in a swine's snout,
> A fair woman which is without discretion " (ch. xi. 22).

Or it is introduced by "and," the so-called *vav adæquationis*—

> " Cold water to a thirsty soul,
> And good news from a far country " (ch. xxv. 25).

> " For lack of wood the fire goeth out,
> And where there is no whisperer, contention ceaseth " (ch. xxvi. 20).

To the forms here specified must be added the *numerical* proverb (*middah*, "measure "), where a certain number is stated in the first line, which is usually increased by one in the second, and thus a kind of climax is formed which gives force and piquancy to the sentence. Familiar examples occur in Amos i., where we find a series of propositions commencing with the words, " For three, . . . yea, for four," etc. There is only one of these in our book from ch. i. to xxix., and that is the *octastich*, ch. vi. 16—19, beginning—

> "There be six things which the Lord hateth,
> Yea, seven which are an abomination unto him.'

But there are many in ch. xxx., viz. vers. 15, 18, 21, 29. These are all in the form mentioned above, the first-named number being augmented by one. Two more are of simpler form, being not climacteric, viz. vers. 7—9, 24—28. The latter, *e.g.*, says—

> " There are four things which are little upon the earth,
> But they are exceeding wise; "

and then proceeds to specify the ants, conies, locusts, and lizards.

The last two chapters possess a character of their own, quite distinct from the rest of the work; ch. xxx. being for the most part destitute of parallelism, Lemuel's words forming a continuous instruction in which the second member of each verse repeats the idea and almost the very words of the first, and the eulogium of the virtuous woman taking the shape of an acrostic ode.

Of the principles which guided the editors in their arrangement of the material before them, it is impossible to give any satisfactory account. Sometimes the proverbs are loosely connected by certain catchwords which occur in a series. Thus in ch. xii. 5—7 the link is found in the recurrence of the words " righteous " (*tsaddik*) and " wicked " (*rasha*) ; in ch. x. 8, 13, 20, 21, we have in the Hebrew continually the word *leb*, " heart; " so in ch. xii. 8, 11, 20, 23, 25, and elsewhere. Sometimes the subject supplies the connection, as in ch. xviii. 10, 11, where the fortress of faith and that of presumption are contrasted; ch. xxii. 30, 31, where the overruling of God's providence is the theme. But generally the grouping is arbitrary, and the attempt, like that of Zöckler, to give a synoptical account of the contents is far from satisfactory.

Such, then, is the *mashal* collection in this book regarded in its mechanical aspect. Viewed as poetry, it offers the greatest contrasts, ranging from the bald and commonplace to the heights of the sublime. If we meet with vulgar truisms in one place, in another we are sitting at the feet of a bard who discourses of heavenly things with pure and fervid eloquence. If in one place we find only maxims of secular tendency, to be taken as the outcome of worldly experience in matters of daily life, in another we are dealing with parables of things Divine, which need and are intended to receive spiritual handling, and cannot be thoroughly understood under any other treatment. The portrait of Wisdom is an adumbration of the eternal Son of God, who invites all to share his bounty and enrich them- selves from his boundless store. The "strange woman" is not merely a representation of vice; she is a type of the great opponent of Christ, the antichrist, the false doctrine, the harlotry of the intellect, which opposes the truth as it is in Jesus. And the virtuous woman is not merely an example of the perfect woman, wife, and mother; but also a figure of the Church of God, with all its ennobling influence, its vivifying ordinances, its super- natural graces.

The book reflects the circumstances of the times in which its various parts were composed. There are pictures of savage rapine and plunder, insecurity of life and property, and the evils that attend days of anarchy and confusion. There are pictures of peace and prosperity, quiet home-life, agriculture, grazing, farming, with its pleasures and profit. There are signs of luxury, bringing in its train excess, profligacy, fraud, covetousness. There is the ideal king, upright, discerning, pious, the enemy of all that is base, dishonourable, or vicious, the rewarder of the just and God-fearing. There is the ruler, tyrannical, oppressive, iniquitous, hated by his subjects, and caring nothing for their best interests. Here we have the judge whose verdict is as God's own judgment, pure and equitable; there the judge venal, corrupt, selling the truth, perverting the right, and making the tribunal a mart for the gain of filthy lucre. On these and such- like circumstances the Proverbs offer warnings and instructions; antidotes against evil influences; encouragements to perseverance in the right way. Much may have originally been written by Solomon for the benefit of his son Rehoboam, who in that age was exposed to peculiar temptations; but thereby the Holy Spirit has produced a manual fitted for the use of all who in active life are open to the seductions of their time and country and society. We have spoken above of the use of secondary motives in the teaching of our book; but we must not omit to observe that, under the earthly and secular element, there is present a vein of heavenly wealth. The con- sciousness of a Divine presence, of a moral Governor, of an exterior Law- giver, dominates every lesson. The heart is to be guarded whose secrets are known only to God; the tongue is to be diligently watched, though human law punishes not its transgressions. All actions are to be referred to God's will and Word, and are only right when conformed to these.

The absence of all mention of polytheism, which some have used as a reason for assigning a post-exilian date to the book, may be otherwise accounted for. If the Proverbs reflect the earlier days of Solomon's reign, before his great decline and apostasy, the days when the temple had newly been built and consecrated, and men's minds were filled with the grand ceremonies of its opening services and the marvels which attended its dedication, there would be then no tendency to idolatry, the evil propensity for unlawful worship would at any rate for a time have been checked, and the moralist would have had no reason for warning against this particular offence.

§ 5. HISTORY OF THE TEXT.

The Book of Proverbs has always been enumerated by the Jews among the twenty-two books into which they divided their canon. Thus it was found to be by Melito of Sardis, when he personally investigated the matter during his journey in the East, as mentioned by Eusebius ('Hist. Eccl.,' iv. 26). To the same effect is the testimony of Origen, adduced also by Eusebius (ibid., vi. 25). In the Christian Church the catalogues of Holy Scripture drawn up by councils and private persons never fail to include Proverbs in the canon. The frequent quotation of the work by the writers of the New Testament (e.g. Rom. xii. 16, 17; 2 Cor. ix. 7, Septuagint, etc.) placed it at once beyond the pale of doubt, and lent indisputable confirmation to its claims. The inspiration of the works attributed to Solomon was indeed denied by Theodore of Mopsuestia at the end of the fourth century, but his opinions found no support among the orthodox, and were condemned by the Fifth Œcumenical Council. Since that time no doubt has ever been thrown by Christians upon the claim of our book to its place in the sacred volume. But the settlement of the original text is quite a different matter from establishing the canonicity of the work as a whole. To compare with the existing Masoretic text we have the Targum, the Syriac, Greek, and Latin versions, all of which present variations from the original which we possess.

The Targum, which usually takes the form of a Chaldee Paraphrase, is in the present case a tolerably close version without much comment or additional matter. It is plainly dependent upon the Syriac in a great degree, though it varies from it occasionally, the translator having other sources to appeal to. In many passages the Peshito and the Targum agree in receding from the Masoretic reading, in these often coinciding with the Septuagint, which version it is most unlikely that the Targumist himself consulted, the strictest of Hebrews holding that translation in abhorrence. Nöldeke concludes that a Jew took the Syriac as the foundation of a Targum, but also consulted the Masoretic text, correcting from it certain prominent errors, but for the most part leaving the rest unaltered.

The Syriac itself offers many remarkable deviations from our text, not

only affording interpretations which denote different wording and pointing, but often introducing whole verses or clauses which have no representative in the Hebrew. It is evident that when this version was made, the Hebrew text was still unsettled, and what we now receive was not universally recognized. Very probably under these variations are concealed genuine readings which would otherwise be lost. Many of these are noticed in the Exposition. The Syriac translator has made free use of the Septuagint, and laid great weight on its renderings, often endorsing its mistakes and paraphrastic explanations.

The Latin Vulgate, the work of St. Jerome, is also greatly indebted to the LXX., though he has not always slavishly followed it against the authority of the present Hebrew; when he does do so, it is in cases where the text seemed unintelligible without the help of the Greek, or where the pointing was not determined by any traditional decision. What use he made of the old Itala cannot be determined, though it seems to be assured that many of the additions found in his version occur also in the more ancient.

Of the Septuagint Version, as the most important of all, there is more to be said. When it was made it is impossible to say, though it must have been in existence before Ecclesiasticus was written, as it seems clear that Ben-Sira had it before him when he translated his senior's work. The translator was well acquainted with Greek literature, and aimed rather at producing a respectable literary work than offering a simple representation of the original. He renders freely, paraphrasing where he thought it necessary, and even, as it seems, altering words or phrases to make his meaning clearer, or his sentence more flowing. The version shows traces of more than one hand being concerned in arranging the present text, as we find sometimes double renderings of the same passage, and sometimes two incompatible translations blended confusingly into one. Thus, ch. i. 27, after, "When affliction and siege come upon you," is added, "*or when destruction shall come upon you;*" ch. ii. 2, "Thine ear shall listen to wisdom, thou shalt also apply thine heart to understanding, *and thou shalt apply it to the instruction of thy son;*" ch. vi. 25, "Let not the desire of beauty overcome thee, *neither be thou captured with thine eyes*, neither be thou caught with her eyelids;" ch. iii. 15, "She is more valuable than precious stones, *no evil thing shall oppose her; she is well known to all who approach her*, and no precious thing is worthy of her." There is also evidence of carelessness and want of precision here as in other portions of the Greek Version. But there can be no doubt that many of the variations are owed to a different original. That the LXX. had not our Masoretic text before them is proved by more than one consideration. In the first place, the order of chapter and verse, so to speak, was not the same as in our present book. Up to ch. xxiv. 22 the two for the most part coincide, though there is some variation in ch. xv. and xvi.; and again in ch. xvii. and xx. single verses are dislocated and inserted elsewhere. But at ch. xxiv. 23 a notable change occurs. Here is

introduced ch. xxix. 27; then follow four distichs not found in the Hebrew; then ch. xxx. 1—14, succeeded by ch. xxiv. 23—34; then comes the rest of ch. xxx., viz. from ver. 15 up to ch. xxxi. 9. Thus the words of Agur are divided into two sections; and the superscriptions there and at the beginning of ch. xxx. being removed, the proverbs of Agur and Lemuel are joined without reserve to those of Solomon. The praise of the virtuous woman closes the book, as in the Hebrew. What led the translator to make these changes is a difficult question. Hitzig considers that the writer confounded the columns of the manuscript before him, two being on each page, and the proverbs of Agur and Lemuel being ranked before ch. xxv., and understood traditionally as Solomon's. That this was the translator's idea we see from the inscription which he has inserted at ch. xxiv. 23, "These things I say to you who are wise," where the speaker must necessarily be Solomon. Instead of "The words of Agur" (ch. xxx. 1), he writes, "Fear my words, my son, and receiving them repent;" and in ch. xxxi. 1, again, he finds no proper name in Lemuel, but renders, "My words have been spoken by God the King." Another circumstance which shows that the Greek translator had before him a different text from ours is that he presents us with many passages which are not found in the Hebrew, and omits many which now have a place therein.

The list of such variations would be very large. Among the additions we may notice the following: At the end of ch. iv., which seems to close somewhat abruptly, we have two verses, "For the ways which are on the right hand God knoweth, but those on the left are crooked; and he it is who will make thy tracks straight, and will guide thy goings in peace." In ch. ix. there are two great additions: after ver. 12, "He that stays himself upon lies, he shepherdeth winds, and he will pursue birds as they fly; for he has forsaken the ways of his own vineyard, and has caused the axles of his own field to go astray, and he passeth through a waterless desert, and a land established in drought, and gathers with his hands fruitlessness;" and at ver. 18, "But hasten thou away, delay not in the place, neither fix thine eye upon her, for then shalt thou go through strange water; but from strange water abstain thou, and of a strange fountain drink not, that thou mayest live long, and years of life may be added to thee." Whether these and such-like sentences are genuine or not cannot be determined. They look very commonly like explanations or amplifications of the original which have crept from the margin into the text. Thus ch. xi. 16, "A gracious woman raiseth glory for her husband, *but a seat of dishonour is a woman hating righteousness; the slothful come to lack wealth,* but the brave are supported by wealth." Here the Syriac gives, "The slothful shall be poor even with their riches; but the spirited shall sustain wisdom." The words in italics seem to be mere glosses. So ch. xviii. 22, "He who finds a good wife finds favours; and receives gladness from God. He who putteth away a good wife putteth away good things, and he that keepeth an adulteress is foolish and ungodly." Of the longer intercalations the most celebrated is that concerning the bee (ch. vi. 8), which follows the lesson on the ant: " Or go to the bee, and learn how diligent she is, and how noble a work she performeth; whose labours kings and private persons use for health, and she is desired by all and of good repute; and although she is weak in strength, yet because she regardeth wisdom she is highly honoured." There is another long interpolation respecting the king and his power which succeeds ch. xxiv. 22: "A son that keepeth the word shall be far from destruction. Receiving he receiveth it. Let no falsehood be spoken by the mouth of a king, and let no falsehood proceed from his tongue. The king's tongue is a sword, and not one of flesh; whosoever shall be delivered over to it shall be utterly crushed. For if his anger be provoked, he consumes men together with their sinews, and devoureth men's bones, and burneth them as a flame, so that they cannot be eaten by the young of eagles." The last clause seems to refer to the opinion that birds of prey will not touch carcases struck by lightning. After ch. xix. 7, which is given thus: " Every one who hates a poor brother shall also be far from friendship," we have, " Good understanding will draw near to them that know it; and a prudent man will find it. He that doth much evil perfects mischief, and he that useth provoking words shall not be saved." An additional illustration is sometimes added. Thus, in ch. xxv. 20, omitting the reference to leaving off a garment in cold weather, the LXX. give, " As vinegar is inexpedient for a sore, so suffering falling on the body afflicts the heart. As moth in a garment and worm in wood, so a man's grief injures the heart." In ch. xxvii. 20 we have, " An abomination to the Lord is he who fixeth his eye, and the uninstructed are incontinent in tongue." And in the next verse, " The heart of the lawless seeketh evils, but an upright heart seeketh knowledge." The addition in ch. xxvi. 11 occurs in Ecclus. iv. 21, " There is a shame that bringeth sin, and there is a shame that is glory and grace." The Greek origin of the translation appears plainly in some of the interpolations. Thus in ch. xvii. 4, " To the faithful belongeth the whole world of riches, but to the unfaithful not even an obole."

The minor interpolations are too numerous to specify. They are for the most part noticed as they occur in the Exposition, in which also the many deviations from the received Hebrew text in words and clauses are mentioned. The additions are not of much value morally or religiously, and cannot bear comparison with the genuine proverbs. Whether they are corruptions of the Hebrew text, or corrections and additions made by the translators themselves, cannot be decided. It must be noted, in conclusion, that the Greek Version omits many passages which are now found in our Hebrew Bibles; e.g. ch. i. 16; viii. 32, 33; xi. 3, 4; xv. 31; xvi. 1, 3; xviii. 23, 24; xix. 1, 2; xx. 14—19; xxi. 5; xxii. 6; xxiii. 23.

Of the versions of Aquila, Symmachus, and Theodotion, fragments have been transmitted in Origen's great work, which sometimes afford light in the rendering of difficult words. There is also another translation known as Veneta, very literal, and made about the ninth century of our era. It belongs to St. Mark's Library at Venice, and has been published, first in 1784, and again of late years.

§ 6. ARRANGEMENT IN SECTIONS.

The various superscriptions in the book for the most part divide it into its several parts. There is one at the very beginning, "The Proverbs of Solomon;" the same words are repeated at ch. x. 1; at ch. xxii. 17 a new section is commenced with the words, "Bow down thine ear, and hear the words of the wise;" another at ch. xxiv. 23 with the remark, "These things also belong to the wise." Then at ch. xxv. 1 we have, "These are also the Proverbs of Solomon which the men of Hezekiah copied out;" at ch. xxx. 1, "the words of Agur;" at ch. xxxi. 1, "the words of Lemuel," followed by the acrostic ode of the virtuous woman.

Thus the book may conveniently be divided into nine parts.

PART I. Title and superscription. Ch. i. 1—6.

PART II. Fifteen hortatory discourses, exhibiting the excellence of wisdom and encouraging the pursuit thereof. Ch. i. 7—ix. 18.

1. First hortatory discourse.		Ch. i. 7—19.
2. Second	„ „	Ch. i. 20—33.
3. Third	„ „	Ch. ii.
4. Fourth	„ „	Ch. iii. 1—18.
5. Fifth	„ „	Ch. iii. 19—26.
6. Sixth	„ „	Ch. iii. 27—35.
7. Seventh	„ „	Ch. iv.
8. Eighth	„ „	Ch. v.
9. Ninth	„ „	Ch. vi. 1—5.
10. Tenth	„ „	Ch vi. 6—11.
11. Eleventh	„ „	Ch. vi. 12—19.
12. Twelfth	„ „	Ch. vi. 20—35.
13. Thirteenth	„ „	Ch. vii.
14. Fourteenth	„ „	Ch. viii.
15. Fifteenth	„ „	Ch. ix.

PART III. First great collection of (375) Solomonic proverbs, mostly unconnected. Ch. x. 1—xxii. 16,—divided into four sections, viz. ch. x. 1—xii. 28; xiii. 1—xv. 19; xv. 20—xix. 25; xix. 26—xxii. 16.

PART IV. First appendix to first collection, containing "words of the wise." Ch. xxii. 17—xxiv. 22.

PART V. Second appendix to first collection, containing further "words of the wise." Ch. xxiv. 23—34.

PART VI. Second great collection of Solomonic proverbs gathered by "men of Hezekiah." Ch. xxv.—xxix.

PART VII. First appendix to second collection: "words of Agur." Ch. xxx.

PART VIII. Second appendix to second collection: "words of Lemuel." Ch. xxxi. 1—9.

PART IX. Third appendix to second collection: acrostic ode in praise of the virtuous woman. Ch. xxxi. 10—31.

§ 7. LITERATURE.

The Fathers have for the most part not formally commented on this book. Origen and Basil have commentaries hereon: 'Ex Commentariis in Proverbia,' Orig., 'Op.,' iii.; 'In Principium Prov.,' Basil., ii. Besides these there is Bede, 'Exposit. Allegor.'

Among the numerous expositions of later date the most useful are the following: Salazar, 1619; Cornelius à Lapide, 1635, etc.; Melancthon, 'Op.,' ii.; Bossuet, 'Notæ,' 1673; Hammond, 'Paraphrase,' iv.; Michaelis, 'Adnotationes,' 1720; Aben Ezra, 1620, and edit. by Horowitz, 1884; Schulteus, 1748; Umbreit, 1826; Rosenmüller, 1829; Löwenstein, 1838; Maurer, 1838; Bertheau, 1847; re-edited by Nowack, 1883; Stuart, 1852; Ewald, 'Sprüche Sal.,' 1837, 1867; Hitzig, 1858; Zöckler, in Lange's 'Bibelwerk,' 1867; Vaihinger, 1857; Delitzsch, in Clarke's 'For. Libr.;' Reuss, Paris, 1878; Plumptre, in the 'Speaker's Commentary;' Bishop Wordsworth; Nutt, in Bishop Ellicott's Commentary; Strack, in 'Kurzgef. Kommentar,' 1889. The 'Topical Arrangement' of Dr. Stock will be found useful; also the Introductions of Eichhorn, De Wette, Bertholdt, Keil, and Bleek.

THE PROVERBS

———◆———

EXPOSITION

CHAPTER I.

Vers. 1—6.—Part I. The Title and Superscription. The superscription of the Proverbs, which extends from ver. 1 to ver. 6, furnishes us with an epitome in short and concise language of the general scope and bearing of the book, and points out its specific utility, both to the inexperienced and to those already wise. Thus (1) in ver. 1 it gives the name of the author to whom the proverbs are attributed; (2) in vers. 2 and 3 it declares the aim, object, or design of the collection, which is to lead to the acquirement of wisdom generally; and (3) in vers. 4—6 it proceeds to indicate the special utility the collection will be to two main classes—to the simple and immature, on the one hand, in opening and enlarging their understanding, and so providing them with prudent rules of conduct by which they may regulate the course of life; and, on the other, to the wise and intelligent, in further increasing their knowledge or learning, and thus rendering them competent to comprehend, and also to explain to others less favourably situated than themselves, other proverbs, or enigmas, or sayings, of a like recondite nature to those now to be brought before them.

The *title* of the book embodied in the text is, 'The Proverbs of Solomon the son of David, King of Israel,' but the shorter designation by which it was and is known among the Jews is *Mishle* (מִשְׁלֵי), taken from the word with which the book begins. Analogously, in the Authorized Version it is styled 'The Proverbs,' and the heading in the LXX. is Παροιμίαι Σολομῶντος. The outside title in the Vulgate is more elaborately given as, 'Liber Proverbiorum, quem Hebræi *Misle* appellant' (' The Book of the Proverbs, which the Hebrews call *Misle*'). In the Talmud it is called the 'Book of Wisdom' (סֵפֶר חָכְמָה, *Sepher Khokhmah*); and Origen (Eusebius, 'Hist. Eccl.,' vi. 25) designates it Μισλώθ, the Greek form of the Hebrew *M'shaloth* (מְשָׁלוֹת). Among the ancient Greek Fathers, *e.g.* Clement, Hegesippus, Irenæus, the book was known by a variety of titles, all more or less descriptive of its contents as a repository of wisdom.

Ver. 1.—**The proverbs of Solomon.** The word which is here translated "proverbs" is the original *mishle* (מִשְׁלֵי), the construct case of *mashâl* (מָשָׁל), which, again, is derived from the verb *mashal* (מָשַׁל), signifying (1) "to make like," "to assimilate," and (2) "to have dominion" (Gesenius). The radical signification of *mashal* is "comparison" or "similitude," and in this sense it is applied generally to the utterances of the wise. In Numb. xxiii. 7, 8 it is used of the prophetic predictions of Balaam; certain didactic psalms, *e.g.* Ps. xlix. 5 and lxxviii. 2, are so designated, and in Job (xxvii. 1 and xxix. 1) it describes the sententious discourses of wise men. While all these come under the generic term of *m'shalim*, though few or no comparisons are found in them, we find the term *mashal* sometimes used of what are proverbs in the sense of popular sayings. Compare " Therefore it became a proverb (מָשָׁל), Is Saul also among the prophets?" (1 Sam. x. 12); and see also other instances in Ezek. xvi. 4 and xviii. 2. In this sense it is also found in the collection before us. The predominant idea of the term, however, is that of comparison or similitude, and as such it is better represented by the Greek παραβολή (from παραβάλλω, "to set or place side by side"), literally, a placing beside, or comparison, than by παροιμία, "a byword," or "a trite wayside saying," though in the Greek of the synoptic Gospels παροιμία is equivalent to παραβολή. The English word "proverb" insufficiently renders the wider scope of meaning conveyed in the Hebrew *mashâl*, and is not quite accurately rendered here, since of proverbs in our ordinary signification of that word there are comparatively few in this collection. The Hebrew word here means "maxims," "aphorisms," "wise counsels." *Of Solomon.* Most modern commentators (Delitzsch, Zöckler, Fuerst, Stuart, Plumptre, etc.), while attributing, in a greater or less degree, the authorship of the book to Solomon, regard the insertion of his name in the title as indicating rather that he is the dominant spirit among those wise men of his age, some of whose sayings are here incorporated with his own. **King of Israel**, as forming the second hemistich of the verse, goes with "Solomon," and not "David." This is indicated in the Authorized Version by the position of the comma. The Arabic Version omits allusion to David, and reads, "Proverbia, nempe documenta Salomonis sapientis, qui regnavit super filios Israel." The proverbial or parabolic form of teaching was a recognized mode of instruction among the Hebrews, and in the Christian Church is recommended by St. Clement of Alexandria ('Strom.,' lib. 11, *init.*).

Ver. 2.—**To know wisdom and instruction.** In this verse we have a statement of the first general aim or object of the Proverbs. "To know" (לָדַעַת, *ladaath*) is somewhat indefinite in the Authorized Version, and might be more accurately rendered, "from which men may know" (De Wette, Noyes); cf. *unde scias* (Munsterus). The לְ which is here prefixed to the infinitive, as in vers. 2, 3, and 6, gives the clause a final character, and thus points out the object which the teaching of the Proverbs has in view. The teaching is viewed from the standpoint of the learner, and hence what is indicated here is not the imparting of knowledge, but the reception or appropriation thereof on the part of the learner. Schultens states that the radical meaning of דַּעַת (*daath*) is the reception of knowledge into one's self. *Wisdom.* It will be necessary to go rather fully into this word here on its first appearance in the text. The Hebrew is חָכְמָה (*khokhmah*). Wisdom is mentioned first, because it is the end to which all knowledge and instruction tend. The fundamental conception of the word is variously represented as either (1) the "power of judging," derived from חָכַם, "to be wise," from

the Arabic, "to judge" (Gesenius); or (2) "the fixing of a thing for cognition," derived from the Arabic equivalent of the Hebrew חָכַם, as before, which signifies "to fasten" (Zöckler), or "compactness," from the same root as before, "to be firm, or closed." It is also variously defined (1) as "*insight* into that upright dealing which pleases God—a *knowledge* of the right way which is to be followed before God, and of the wrong one which is to be shunned" (Zöckler); (2) as "piety towards God," as in Job xxviii. 28 (Gesenius); (3) as "the knowledge of things in their being and in the reality of their existence" (Delitzsch). The word is translated in the LXX. by σοφία, and in the Vulgate by *sapientia*. The Hebrew *khokhmah* and the Greek σοφία so far agree as philosophical terms in that the end of each is the same, viz. the striving after objective wisdom, the moral fitness of things; but the character of the former differs from that of the latter in being distinctly religious. The beginning and the end of the *khokhmah*, wisdom, is God (cf. ver. 7). Wisdom, then, is not the merely scientific knowledge, or moral philosophy, but knowledge κατ' ἐξοχήν, *i.e.* religious knowledge or piety towards God; *i.e.* an appreciation of what God requires of us and what we conversely owe to God. "Sapientia est de divinis" (Lyra). Wisdom will, of course, carry with it the notions of knowledge and insight. *Instruction.* As the preceding word represents wisdom in its intellectual conception, and has rather a theoretical character, so "instruction," Hebrew, מוּסָר (*musar*), represents it on its practical side, and as such is its practical complement. The Hebrew *musar* signifies properly "chastisement," from the root *yasar* (יָסַר), "to correct," or "chastise," and hence education, moral training; and hence in the LXX. it is rendered by παιδεία, which means both the process of education (cf. Plato, 'Repub.,' 376, E.; Arist., 'Pol.,' 8. 3) and its result as learning (Plato, 'Prob.,' 327, D.). The Vulgate has *disciplina*. In relation to wisdom, it is antecedent to it; *i.e.* to know wisdom truly we must first become acquainted with instruction, and hence it is a preparatory step to the knowledge of wisdom, though here it is stated rather objectively. The words, "wisdom and instruction," are found in exactly the same collocation in ch. iv. 13 and xxiii. 23. In its strictly disciplinary sense, "instruction" occurs in ch. iii. 11, with which comp. Heb. xii. 5. Holden takes this word as "moral discipline" in the highest sense. **To perceive the words of understanding**; literally, *to discern the words of discernment;* i.e. "to comprehend the utterances which proceed from intelligence, and give expression to it" (Delitzsch). *Understanding;* Hebrew, vinah (בִּינָה), connected with the hiph. (לְהָבִין l'havin), properly "to distinguish," hence "to discern," of the same clause, signifies the capability of discerning the true from the false, good from bad, etc. With this agrees Cornelius à Lapide, who says, "Unde prudenter discernas inter bonum et malum, licitum et illicitum, utile et noxium, verum et falsum," and from which you are enabled to know what to do in any circumstances, and what not to do. The LXX. renders the word by φρόνησις, the Vulgate by *prudentia.* Φρόνησις, in Plato and Aristotle, is the virtue concerned in the government of men, management of affairs, and the like (see Plato, 'Sym.,' 209, A.; Arist., 'Eth.,' N. 6. 5 and 8), and means practical wisdom, prudence, or moral wisdom. Van Ess, Allioli, Holden, translate "prudence."

Ver. 3.—To receive the instruction of wisdom. This verse carries on the statement of the design of the Proverbs. *To receive;* Hebrew, לָקַחַת (lakakhath), not the same word as "to know" (לָדַעַת), in ver. 2, though regarded as synonymous with it by Delitzsch. Its meaning is well represented by the LXX. δέξασθαι, and the Authorized Version "to receive." The Hebrew, לָקַחַת, is infinitive, and means properly "to take, or lay hold of," hence "to receive," Greek, δέχομαι. No doubt it conveys the idea of intellectual reception (cf. ch. ii. 1). *The instruction of wisdom;* Hebrew, מוּסַר הַשְׂכֵּל (musar has'kel); i.e. the discipline or moral training which leads on to reason, intelligence, or wisdom (as Hitzig, Fuerst, Zöckler); or discipline full of insight, discernment, or thoughtfulness (as Umbreit, Ewald, Delitzsch). The phrase does not mean the wisdom which instruction imparts. The word *musar* occurs here in a slightly different sense from its use in ver. 2; there it is objective, here its meaning as a medium for the attainment of wisdom is more distinctly brought out. *Wisdom (has'kel)* is properly "thoughtfulness" (so Umbreit, Ewald, Delitzsch, Plumptre). It is strictly the infinitive absolute of שָׂכַל (sakal), "to entwine or involve," and as a substantive it stands for the thinking through of a subject, so "thoughtfulness." The LXX. renders this sentence, δέξασθαί τε στροφὰς λόγων, which St. Jerome understands as "versutias sermonum et solutiones aenigmatum" ("the cunning or craftiness of words and the explication of enigmas"). **Justice, and judgment, and equity.** These words seem to be the unfolding of the meaning contained in the expression, "the instruction of wisdom." Holden regards the last four words as objective genitives dependent on "instruc-

tion," but wrongly. Cornelius à Lapide states that "justice and judgment and equity" indicate the same thing in different aspects. *"Justice* stands for the thing itself—that which is *just; judgment* in respect of right reason, which says it is just; and *equity* in respect of its being agreeable to the Law of God." *Justice;* Hebrew, צֶדֶק (tsedek), from the root צָדַק (tsadak), "to be right, or straight;" in a moral sense it means "rectitude," "right," as in Isa. xv. 2 (Gesenius). The underlying idea is that of straightness. Heidenheim, quoted by Delitzsch, maintains that in *tsedek* the conception of the *justum* prevails; but the latter enlarges its meaning, and holds that it also has the idea of a mode of thought and action regulated, not by the letter of the Law, but by love, as in Isa. xli. 2; xlii. 6. Plumptre thinks "righteousness" would be a better translation of the word, on the ground that the Hebrew includes the ideas of truth and beneficence. Compare with this the LXX. δικαιοσύνη ἀληθής. Zöckler also renders "righteousness," i.e. "that which is in accord with the will and ordinances of God as Supreme Judge." In the Authorized Version, in ch. ii. 9, where we have the same collocation of words, *tsedek* is translated "righteousness;" cf. ch. xii. 17, "He who utters truth shows forth righteousness (tsedek)." *Judgment;* Hebrew, מִשְׁפָּט (mish'pat), from the root שָׁפַט (shapat), "to adjust, judge," corresponds with the Hebrew in meaning; it is the delivery of a correct judgment on human actions. Compare the LXX. κρίμα κατευθύνειν. *Equity;* i.e. rectitude in thought and action (Delitzsch), or integrity (Zöckler). This quality expresses upright demeanour or honourable action on one's own part individually, while "judgment" has regard both to our own and the actions of others. The Hebrew, *mesharim* (מֵשָׁרִים), used only in the plural, is from the root יָשַׁר (yashar), "to be straight or even," and is equal to "uprightness." The plural form is reproduced in the marginal reading "equities;" comp. Ps. xvii. 2, "Let thine eyes behold the things that are equal (mesharim)." The Vulgate reads *aequitas,* and the Syriac *rectitudo.* The two ideas in judgment and equity appear to be expressed in the LXX. by the phrase, κρίμα κατευθύνειν.

Ver. 4.—To give subtilty to the simple. In this verse and the following we are introduced to the classes of persons to whom the proverbs will be beneficial. The ל with the infinitive, לָתֵת (latheth), shows that in construction this proposition is co-ordinate with those in vers. 2 and 3, and not dependent as represented by ἵνα δῷ (LXX.) and *ut detur* (Vulgate). *Subtilty;* Hebrew, עָרְמָה (ar'mah), from the root עָרַם (aram), "to be crafty or wily," properly means "nakedness" or "smoothness;" hence in a metaphorical sense it expresses "the capacity for escaping from the wiles of others" (Umbreit). We have this idea expressed as follows in ch. xxii. 3, "The prudent man (עָרוּם, arum) foreseeth the evil, and hideth himself." In the Arabic Version it is rendered by calliditas, "shrewdness," in a good sense. The Hebrew ar'mah, like the Latin calliditas, also means "craftiness," as appears in the use of the cognate adjective arum in Gen. iii. 1, where we read, "The serpent was more subtle," etc. For "subtilty" the LXX. has πανουργία, a Greek word which appears to be employed altogether in a bad sense, as "trickery," "villainy," "knavery;" but that scarcely appears to be the meaning of the Hebrew here, since the aim of the Proverbs is ethical and beneficial in the highest degree. The Vulgate astutia, the quality of the astutus, beside the bad sense of craftiness, also bears the good sense of shrewdness, sagacity, and so better represents the Hebrew. "Subtilty may turn to evil, but it also takes its place among the highest moral gifts" (Plumptre). The simple; Hebrew, פְּתָאִים (ph'thaim), plural of פְּתִי (p'ti) from the root פָּתַח (pathakh), "to be open," properly means the open-hearted, i.e. those who are susceptible to external impressions (Zöckler), and so easily misled. The word occurs in ch. vii. 7; viii. 5; ix. 6; xiv. 18; and xxvii. 12. The LXX. properly renders the word ἄκακοι, "unknowing of evil." The same idea is indirectly expressed in the Vulgate parvuli, "the very young;" and the term is paraphrased in the Arabic Version, iis in quibus non est malitia ("those who are without malice"). The Hebrew here means "simple" in the sense of inexperienced. **To the young man knowledge and discretion.** The Hebrew naar (נַעַר) is here used representatively for "youth" (cf. LXX., παῖς νέος; Vulgate, adolescens) in general, which stands in need of the qualities here mentioned. It advances in idea beyond "the simple." Knowledge; Hebrew, דַּעַת (daath), i.e. experimental knowledge (Delitzsch); insight (Gesenius); knowledge of good and evil (Plumptre). The LXX. has αἴσθησις, which classically means perception by the senses and also by the mind. Discretion; Hebrew, מְזִמָּה (m'zimmah), properly "thoughtfulness," and hence "circumspection" or "caution" (Zöckler), or "discernment," that which sets a man on his guard and prevents him being duped by others (Plumptre). Ἔννοια was probably adopted by the LXX. in its primary sense as representing the act of thinking; intellectus (Vulgate), equivalent to "a discerning" (see the marginal "advisement").

Ver. 5.—**A wise man will hear, and will increase learning.** The change of construction in the original is reproduced in the Authorized Version, but has been rendered variously. Thus Umbreit and Elster, regarding the verb יִשְׁמַע (yish'ma) as conditional, translate, "if the wise man hear;" on the other hand, Delitzsch and Zöckler take it as voluntative, "let the wise man hear," etc. The principle here enunciated is again stated in ch. ix. 9, "Give instruction to a wise man, and he will be yet wiser," and finds expression under the gospel economy in the words of our Lord, "For whosoever hath, to him shall be given, and he shall have more abundance" (Matt. xiii. 12; cf. xxv. 29; Mark iv. 25; Luke viii. 18 and xiv. 26). Learning; Hebrew, לֶקַח (lekakh), in the sense of being transmitted or received (Gesenius, Delitzsch, Dunn). **And a man of understanding shall attain unto wise counsels.** A man of understanding (LXX., ὁ νοήμων; Vulgate, intelligens) is a person of intelligence who lays himself open to be instructed. Wise counsels; Hebrew, תַּחְבֻּלוֹת (takh'buloth). This word is derived from חֶבֶל (khevel), a ship-rope, a denominative of חֹבֵל (khovel), and only occurs in the plural. It signifies those maxims of prudence by which a man may direct his course aright through life (cf. regimen, Arabic). The imagery is taken from the management of a vessel, and is reproduced in the LXX. κυβέρνησις, and the Vulgate gubernatio. "Navigationi vitam comparat" (Mariana). The word is almost exclusively confined to the Proverbs, and occurs in ch. xi. 14; xii. 5; xx. 18; and xxiv. 6, usually in a good sense, though it has the meaning of "stratagem" in ch. xii. 5. In the only other passage where it is found it is used of God's power in turning about the clouds; cf. Job xxxvii. 12, "And it [i.e. the bright cloud] is turned round about by his counsels (בְּתַחְבּוּלֹתָו, b'thakh'bulothau)." It is the practical correlative of "learning," in the first part of the verse.

Ver. 6.—**To understand a proverb.** This verse carries on the idea which is stated in ver. 5. The end of the wise and intelligent man's increase in learning and prudence is that he may be thus enabled to understand other proverbs. Schultens, followed by Holden, takes the verb לְהָבִין (l'havin) as a gerund, intelligendo sententias. This rendering does not represent the end, but points to the proverbs, etc., as means by which the wise generally attain to learning and prudence. **And the interpretation;** Hebrew, מְלִיצָה (m'litsah). It is difficult to determine the exact meaning of this word. By Gesenius it is rendered "enigma, riddle;" by Bertheau and Hitzig, "discourse requiring interpretation;" by Delitzsch, "symbol;" by Havernick and Keil, "brilliant and pleasing discourse;" and by Fuerst, "figurative and involved discourse." By comparing it with the corresponding words, "dark sayings," it may be regarded as designating that which is obscure and involved in meaning; compare σκοτεινὸς λόγος (LXX.). It only occurs here and in Hab. ii. 6, where it is rendered "taunting proverb." The marginal reading is "an eloquent speech," equivalent to *facundia*, "eloquence." Vatablus says that the Hebrews understood it as "mensuram et pondus verbi." **The words of the wise;** *i.e.* the utterances of the *khakhamim* (חֲכָמִים). This expression occurs again in ch. xxii. 17, and also in Eccles. ix. 19 and xii. 11. In the latter they are described as "goads and as nails fastened by the ministers of assemblies" (*i.e.* "authors of compilations," as Mendelssohn), because they cannot fail to make an impression on everybody good or bad. The expression, as used in ch. xxii. 17, implies that other than Solomonic proverbs are included in this collection. **And their dark sayings;** Hebrew, וְחִידֹתָם (*v'khidotham*). The Hebrew *khidah* (חִידָה), as *m'litsah* (מְלִיצָה), its parallel in the preceding hemistich, designates obscure, involved utterances. It plainly has the sense of "enigma" (Fleischer, apud Delitzsch). Compare αἰνίγματα (LXX.), and *ænigmata* (Vulgate), which latter is followed by the Chaldee Paraphrase and Syriac (see also Ps. lxxviii. 2, "I will open my mouth in parables, I will utter *dark sayings* of old "). Gesenius derives it from the root חוּד (*khud*), "to tie knots," and hence arrives at its meaning as an involved or twisted sententious expression, an *enigma*.

Ver. 7—ch. ix. 18.—Part II. INTRODUCTORY SECTION. The first main section of the book begins here and ends at ch. ix. 18. It consists of a series of fifteen admonitory discourses addressed to youth by the Teacher and Wisdom personified, with the view to exhibit the excellence of wisdom, and generally to illustrate the motto, "The fear of the Lord is the beginning of knowledge," or wisdom. It urges strong encouragements to virtue, and equally strong dissuasives from vice, and shows that the attainment of wisdom in its true sense is the aim of all moral effort.

Ver. 7.—The fear of the Lord is the beginning of knowledge. This proposition is by some commentators regarded as the motto, symbol, or device of the book (Delitzsch,

Umbreit, Zöckler, Plumptre). Others, following the Masoretic arrangement of the Hebrew text, consider it as forming part of the superscription (Ewald, Bertheau, Elster, Keil). As a general proposition expressing the essence of the philosophy of the Israelites, and from its relation to the rest of the contents of this book, it seems rightly to occupy a special and individual position. The proposition occurs again in the Proverbs in ch. ix. 10, and it is met with in similar or slightly modified forms in other books which belong to the same group of sacred writings, that is, those which treat of religious philosophy—the Khokhmah; *e.g.* Job xxviii. 28; Ps. cxi. 10; Eccles. xii. 13; Ecclus. i. 16, 25. With this maxim we may compare "The fear of the Lord is the instruction of wisdom" (ch. xv. 33). *The fear of the Lord* (יִרְאַת יְהֹוָה, *yir'ath y'hovah*); literally, *the fear of Jehovah*. The expression describes that reverential attitude or holy fear which man, when his heart is set aright, observes towards God. The original word, יִרְאַת (*yir'ath*) for "fear," is properly the infinitive of יָרֵא (*yare*), "to fear or reverence," and as a substantive means "reverence or holy fear" (Gesenius). *Servile* or abject fear (as Jerome, Beda, Estius) is not to be understood, but *filial* fear (as Gejerus, Mercerus, Cornelius à Lapide, Cartwright), by which we fear to offend God—that fear of Jehovah which is elsewhere described as "to hate evil" (ch. viii. 13), and in which a predominating element is love. Wardlaw remarks that the "fear of the Lord" is in invariable union with love and in invariable proportion to it. We truly fear God just in proportion as we truly love him. The fear of the Lord also carries with it the whole worship of God. It is observable that the word *Jehovah* (יְהֹוָה) is used in the Hebrew, and not *Elohim* (אֱלֹהִים), a peculiarity which is invariably marked in the Authorized Version by small capitals. *The beginning;* Hebrew, רֵאשִׁית (*reshith*). This word has been understood in three different senses: (1) As *initium*, the beginning; *i.e.* the initial step or starting-point at which every one who wishes to follow true wisdom must begin (Gejerus, Zöckler, Plumptre). (2) As *caput*; i.e. the most excellent or principal part, the noblest or best wisdom. This sense is adopted in the marginal reading (comp. also ch. iv. 7) (Holden, Trapp). (3) As the *principium* (Vulgate); *i.e.* the origin, or basis, as in Micah i. 13, "She is the origin, or basis (*reshith*) of the sin of the daughter of Zion." Delitzsch regards the original, *reshith*, as embracing the two ideas of commencement and origin, in the same way as the Greek ἀρχή. Wisdom has its origin in God, and whoever fears him receives it if he prays in faith (cf. Jas. i. 5, *sqq.*) (Vatablus, Mercerus, Delitzsch). That the first sense, viz. that of beginning, is to be understood here appears from the parallel passage in ch. x. 10, where the corresponding word is תְּחִלָּה (*t'kil-lath*), "beginning," from the root חָלַל (*kha-lal*), "to begin;" cf. also the LXX. ἀρχὴ, in this sense, and the *initium* of the Syriac and Arabic Versions. All previous knowledge to "the fear of the Lord" is comparative folly. He who would advance in knowledge must first be imbued with a reverence or holy fear of God. But **fools despise wisdom and instruction**; or, according to the inverted order of the words in the original, *wisdom and instruction fools despise*, the association of ideas in the three words, "knowledge," "wisdom," and "instruction," thus being more continuously sustained. This arrangement links on the two latter words with "the fear of the Lord," and so helps towards the elucidation of the sense in which "fools" is to be understood. *Fools;* אֱוִילִים (*evilim*), plural of אֱוִיל (*evil*), from the root אָוַל (*aval*), "to be perverse," here properly designates the incorrigible, as in ch. xxvii. 22, and those who are unwilling to know God (Jer. iv. 22), and hence refuse and despise wisdom and salutary discipline, those "who set at nought all his counsel, and will none of his reproof." The word is opposed to the "prudent" (ch. xii. 16) and to the "wise" (ch. x. 14). Delitzsch understands it as "thick, hard, stupid," from the root *aval, coalescere, incrassari.* Schultens uses παχεῖς, equivalent to *crassi pro stupidis,* to represent the original. Dunn takes it in the same sense as "gross or dull of understanding." Fuerst, adopted by Wordsworth, regards it in the sense of having no moral stamina, from the root meaning "to be slack, weak, lax, or lazy." But none of these explanations seems, in my opinion, to coincide sufficiently with the evil and depraved activity expressed in the verb "despise," which follows, and which describes the conduct of this class. The LXX. renders the word or action by ἀσεβεῖς, equivalent to *impii,* "godless," "profane," and the Vulgate by *stulti. Despise;* בָּזוּ (*bazu*) is perfect, but is properly translated by the present, because the perfect here represents a condition long continued and still existing (Gesenius, § 126); cf. the Latin *odi, memini,* etc. The LXX. uses the future ἐξουθενήσουσιν, *i.e.* they will set at nought; the Vulgate, the present (*despiciunt*). The radical meaning is most probably contemptuous trampling under the feet (Gesenius). *Wisdom and instruction* (see ver. 2). The latter clause of this verse is antithetical to the former, but the antithesis is obscurely expressed. In the Autho-

rized Version it is marked by the adversative conjunction "but," which, however, is not in the original. The LXX. has a striking interpolation in this verse between the first and second clauses, which is partly taken from Ps. cxi. 10 (Σύνεσις δὲ ἀγαθὴ πᾶσι τοῖς ποιοῦσιν αὐτήν· εὐσέβεια δὲ εἰς Θεὸν ἀρχὴ αἰσθήσεως, "And a good understanding have all they that do it: and reverence towards God is the beginning of knowledge"). Compare the Arabic Version, which has the same interpolation: *Et intellectus bonus omnibus facientibus eam. Sana religio in Deum est initium prudentiæ.*

Vers. 8—19.—1. *First admonitory discourse. Warning against enticements to robbery and bloodshed.*

Ver. 8.—**My son, hear the instruction of thy father.** The transition in this verse from what may be regarded as filial obedience towards God to filial obedience towards parents is suggestive of the moral Law. The same admonition, in a slightly altered form, occurs again in ch. vi., "My son, keep thy father's commandment, and forsake not the law of thy mother" (cf. also ch. iv. 1). *My son;* בְּנִי (*b'ni*) from בֵּן (*ben*), "a son." The form of address here adopted was that in common use by teachers towards their pupils, and marks that superintending, loving, and fatherly care and interest which the former felt in and towards the latter. It occurs frequently in the introductory section (ch. ii. 1; iii. 1, 21; iv. 10, 20; v. 1; vi. 1; vii. 1), and reappears again towards the close (ch. xxiii. 15, 19, 26; xxiv. 13, 21; xxvii. 11) in the teacher's address. The mother of Lemuel uses it (ch. xxxi. 2) in the strictly parental sense. In other passages of the Old Testament the teacher, on the other hand, is represented as a "father" (Judg. xvii. 10; Isa. x. 12; 2 Kings ii. 21). We find the same relation assumed in the New Testament, both by St. Paul (1 Cor. iv. 15; Philem. 10; Gal. iv. 19) and by St. John (1 John ii. 1; v. 2); but under the economy of the gospel it has a deeper significance than here, as pointing to the "new birth," which, being a later revelation, lies outside the scope of the moral teaching of the Old Testament dispensation. *The instruction* (מוּסָר, *musar*); as carrying with it the sense of disciplinary education (cf. LXX., παιδεία; Vulgate, *disciplina;* see also ver. 2), and of the correction with which it may be enforced (cf. ch. xiii. 24; xxii. 15; xxiii. 13, 14), the writer attributes appropriately to the father, while the milder *torah,* "law," he uses of the mother (Delitzsch). *Father.* The nature of the exhortation conveyed in this verse requires that we should understand the terms "father" and "mother" in their natural sense as designating the parents of the persons addressed, though a symbolical meaning has been attached to them by the rabbis (see Rabbi Salomon, *in loc.*), "father" being understood as representing God, and "mother," the people. But the terms are more than merely figurative expressions (Stuart). Those who look upon the Proverbs as the address of Solomon to his son Rehoboam naturally take "father" as standing for the former. Naamah, in this case must be the mother (1 Kings xiv. 31). It is almost unnecessary to state that pious parents are presupposed, and that only that instruction and law can be meant which is not inconsistent with the higher and more perfect Law of God (Gejerus, Wardlaw). **And forsake not the law of thy mother.** *Forsake.* The radical meaning of תִּטֹּשׁ (*tittosh*) is that of "spreading," then of "scattering" (Aiken), and so the word comes to mean "forsake, reject, or neglect." The LXX. reads ἀπώσῃ, from ἀποθέω, *abjicere,* "to push away, reject." Cf. *abjicias* (Arabic). The Vulgate has *dimittas,* i.e. "abandon," and the Syriac, *obliviscaris,* i.e. "forget." *The law;* תּוֹרַת (*torath*), construct case of תּוֹרָה (*torah*), from the root יָרָה (*yarah*), "to teach," hence here equivalent to "a law" in the sense of that which teaches—a precept (*doctrina,* Jun. et Tremell., Piscat., Castal., Versions). With one exception (ch. viii. 10), it is the term which always expresses the instruction given by Wisdom (Delitzsch). The law (*torah*) of the mother is that preceptive teaching which she imparts orally to her son, but *torah* is also used in a technical sense as *lex, νόμος δέσμος,* that which is laid down and established, a *decretum* or *institutum,* and designates some distinct provision or ordinance, as the law of sacrifice (Lev. vi. 7). In Josh. i. 8 we find it employed to signify the whole body of the Mosaic Law (*sepher hatorah*). *Mother.* Not inserted here as a natural expansion of the idea of the figure required by the laws of poetic parallelism (as Zöckler), since this weakens the force of the passage. Mothers are mentioned because of their sedulousness in imparting instruction (Bayne).

Ver. 9.—**For they (shall be) an ornament of grace unto thy head.** The sentiment here expressed is put forward as an inducement to youth to observe obedience towards the instruction of the father and the law of the mother, and the meaning is that, just as in popular opinion ornaments and jewels are supposed to set off the personal form, so obedience towards parents in the ways of virtue embellishes the moral character (Bayne, Cartwright, Holden). *An ornament of grace;* Hebrew, לִוְיַת חֵן (*liv'yath khen*); literally, *a wreath or garland of grace.* We meet with the same expression in ch. iv. 9, "She [*i.e.* wisdom] shall give to thine head

an ornament of grace." The Hebrew לִוְיַה (*liv'yah*) is derived from the root לָוָה (*lavah*), "to wind a roll" (Delitzsch) or "to be joined closely with" (Gesenius), and hence signifies an ornament that is twisted, and so a wreath or garland. Gejerus and Schultens translate the phrase by *corollâ gratiosa,* i.e. "a crown full of grace," and so meaning conferring or producing grace, just as the expression, "the chastisement of our peace" (Isa. liii. 5), means the chastisement bringing or procuring our peace. So again a "precious stone," in ch. xvii. 8, margin, "a stone of grace," is one conferring gracefulness. The marginal reading, "an adding" (*additamentum,* Vatablus), conveys, though obscurely, the same idea; and this sense is again reproduced in the Vulgate, *ut addatur gratia capiti suo* ("in order that grace may be added to thy head"). The LXX. reads, στέφανος χαρίτων. **And chains about thy neck.** *Chains;* properly, *necklaces;* עֲנָקִים (*anakim*), plural of עֲנָק (*anak*), "a collar or necklace;" the κλοιὸς χρύσεος, or "golden collar," of the LXX., and *torques* (*i.e.* twisted neckchain) of the Vulgate. There is a very apposite parallel to this verse in ch. vi. 20, 21 (cf. ch. iii. 3; see also Judg. viii. 26). The gold chain round the neck was a mark of distinction, and was conferred on Joseph by Pharaoh when investing him with authority and dignity (Gen. xli. 42), and on Daniel by Belshazzar in the same way (Dan. v. 29; see Song of Solomon iv. 9). The mere adornment of the person with gold and pearls, without the further adornment of the moral character with Christian graces, is deprecated both by St. Paul and St. Peter (see 1 Tim. ii. 9, 10, and 1 Pet. iii. 3, 4). *Neck,* גַּרְגְּרֹת (*gar'g'roth*) only occurs in the plural (Gesenius). (See ch. iii. 3, 22 ; vi. 21.)

Ver. 10.—**My son, if sinners entice thee.** (As to the form of address, see ver. 8.) It is here used because the writer is passing to a warning against bad company, and hence the term is emphatic, and intended to call especial attention to what is said. It is repeated again in ver. 15, at a further stage in this address, with the same view. *Sinners;* חַטָּאִים (*khattaim*), the plural of חַטָּא (*khatta*), from the root חָטָא (*khata*), properly "to miss the mark, to err;" cf. Greek, ἁμαρτάνω, "to sin" (Gesenius), here equivalent to "habitual, abandoned sinners," and those especially who make robbery and bloodshed a profession. Not simply *peccantes,* i.e. sinners as a generic designation of the human race, for "*All* have sinned and come short of the glory of God" (Rom. iii. 23), but *peccatores* (Chaldee, Syriac, Pagin., Tigur., Versions and Vulgate), "sinners," *i.e.* those who sin habitually, knowingly, wilfully, and maliciously

(Gejerus), or those who give themselves up to iniquity, and persuade others to follow their example (Cartwright). In the New Testament they are styled ἁμαρτωλοί. They are those of whom David speaks in strikingly parallel language in Ps. xxvi. 9, "Gather not my soul with sinners (khattaim), nor my life with bloody men" (cf. Ps. i. 1). The LXX. has ἄνδρες ἀσεβεῖς (i.e. ungodly, unholy men). *Entice thee*; יְפַתּוּךָ (y'phat-tukha); the piel form, פִּתָּה (pitah), of the kal פָּתָה (patah), "to open," and hence to make accessible to persuasion, akin to the Greek πειθεῖν, "to persuade." The noun פֶּתִי (p'thi), is "one easily enticed or persuaded" (Gesenius). The LXX. reads μὴ πλανήσωσιν, "let them not lead thee astray." The idea is expressed in the Vulgate by *lactaverint*; i.e. "if sinners allure or deceive thee with fair words." The Syriac, Montan., Jun. et Tremell., Versions read *pellexerint*, from *pellicio*, "to entice." **Consent thou not.** (אַל־תֹּבֵא, al-tovē). The Masoretic text here has been emended by Kennicott and De Rossi, who, on the joint authority of fifty-eight manuscripts, maintain that תֹּבֵא (tovē) should be written תֹּאבֵא (tovē). Others read תָּבֹא (tavō), i.e. "thou shalt not go," which, though good sense, is incorrect. אַל־ (al) is the adverb of negation, i.q. μὴ, ne. The Hebrew תֹּבֵא (tovē) is derived from אָבָה (avah), "to agree to, to be willing" (Gesenius, Delitzsch), the preformative א being omitted, and is accurately rendered by the LXX., μὴ βουληθῇς, and the Vulgate, *ne acquiescas*. The warning is especially brief and striking. The only answer to all enticements of evil is a decided negative (Plumptre). Compare St. Paul's advice to the Ephesians (Eph. v. 11, "And have no fellowship with the unfruitful works of darkness, but rather reprove them").

Ver. 11.—**If they say, Come with us, let us lay wait for blood.** The teacher here puts into the mouth of the sinners, for the sake of vivid representation, the first inducement with which they seek to allure youth from the paths of rectitude, viz. privacy and concealment (Cartwright, Wardlaw). Both the verbs אָרַב (arav) and צָפַן (tzaphan) mean "to lay in wait" (Zöckler). The radical meaning of arav, from which נֶאֶרְבָה (neer'vah), "let us lay in wait" (Authorized Version) is taken, is "to knot, to weave, to intertwine." Verbs of this class are often applied to snares and craftiness (cf. the Greek δόλον ὑφαίνειν, and the Latin *insidias nectere*, "to weave plots, or lay snares"). Generally, arav is equivalent to "to watch in ambush" (Gesenius); cf. the Vulgate, *insidiemur sanguini*; i.e. "let us lay wait for blood." The LXX. paraphrases the expression, κοινώνη-

σον αἵματος, i.e. "let us share in blood." On the other hand, צָפַן (tzaphan), from which נִצְפְּנָה (nitz'p'nah), translated in the Authorized Version, "let us lurk privily," is "to hide or conceal," and intrans. "to hide one's self," or ellipt., "to hide nets, snares" (Gesenius, Holden). This sense agrees with the Vulgate *abscondamus tendiculas*; i.e. "let us conceal snares." Delitzsch, however, holds that no word is to be understood with this verb, and traces the radical meaning to that of restraining one's self, watching, lurking, in the sense of *speculari*, "to watch for," *insidiari*, "to lay wait for." The two verbs combine what may be termed the apparatus, the arrangement of the plot and their lurking in ambush, by which they will await their victims. *For blood* (לְדָם, l'dam). The context (see vers. 12 and 16), bearing as it does upon bloodshed accompanying robbery, requires that the Hebrew לְדָם (l'dam) should be understood here, as Fleischer remarks, either elliptically, for "the blood of men," as the Jewish interpreters explain, or synedochically, for the person, with especial reference to his blood being shed, as in Ps. xciv. 21. Vatablus, Cornelius à Lapide, and Gesenius support the latter view (cf. Micah vii. 2, "They all lie in wait for blood," i.e. for bloodshed, or murder. דָם (dam) may be also taken for life in the sense that "the blood is the life" (Deut. xii. 23). **Let us lurk privily for the innocent without cause.** The relation of the phrase, "without cause" (חִנָּם, khinnam), in this sentence is a matter of much dispute. It may be taken either with (1) the *verb* (as in the Authorized Version, Wordsworth, Luther, Van Ess, Noyes, Zöckler, Delitzsch, Hitzig, LXX., Syriac, Rashi, Ralbac), and then "lurk privily without cause" is equivalent to (a) without having any reason for revenge and enmity (Zöckler), i.e. though they have not provoked us, nor done us any injury, yet let us hurt them, in the sense of *absque causâ* (Munsterus, Paganini Version, Piscatoris Version, Mercerus), ἀδίκως (LXX.), *inique* (Arabic); (b) with impunity, since none will avenge them in the sense of Job ix. 12 (this is the view of Löwestein, but it is rejected by Delitzsch); or (2) it may be taken with the *adjective* "innocent," in which case it means (a) him that is innocent in vain; i.e. the man whose innocence will in vain protect (Zöckler, Holden), who gets nothing by it (Plumptre), or, innocent in vain, since God does not vindicate him (Cornelius à Lapide). On the analogy of 1 Sam. xix. 5; xxv. 31; Ps. xxxv. 19; lxix. 4; Lam. iii. 52, it seems preferable to adopt the first connection, and to take the adverb with the verb. In the whole of the passage there is an evident allusion to an evil prevalent in the age of Solomon, viz. the presence of bands of robbers, or banditti, who disturbed the security and internal peace of the country. In the New Testament the same state of things continued, and is alluded to by our Lord in the parable of the man who fell among thieves.

Ver. 12.—**Let us swallow them up alive as the grave.** A continuation of ver. 11, expanding the idea of bloodshed ending in murder, and showing the determination of the sinners to proceed to the most violent means to effect their covetous ends. The enticement here put before youth is the courage and boldness of their exploits (Wardlaw). The order of the words in the original is, " Let us swallow them up, as the grave, living," which sufficiently indicates the meaning of the passage. *Alive*; חַיִּים (khayyim), i.e. " the living," refers to the pronominal suffix in נִבְלָעֵם (niv'laem), as in the Authorized Version and Zöckler (cf. Ps. lv. 15; cxxiv. 3). Umbreit and Hitzig are grammatically incorrect in connecting כִּשְׁאוֹל (kish'ol) " as the grave," with " the living," and translating " like the pit (swallows) that which lives." The כְּ (ki) with a substantive, as here in kish'ol, is a preposition, and not a conjunction (see Gesenius, ' Lexicon'). It denotes a kind of resemblance, but does not introduce a co-ordinate sentence. The allusion is undoubtedly in the teacher's mind to the fate of Korah and his company (Numb. xvi. 30—33), and as in that case " the earth opened her mouth, and swallowed them up " in the flush of life, so here the robbers say that they will as suddenly and effectively destroy their victims. בָּלַע (dala); from which niv'laem, in a figurative sense, means " to destroy utterly " (Gesenius). The change from the singular, " the innocent " (לְנָקִי, l'naki), to the plural in " let us swallow them up," is noticeable. *Like the pit* (כִּשְׁאוֹל, kish'ol); literally, *like Sheol*, or *Hades*, the great subterranean cavity or world of the dead. The all-devouring and insatiable character of sheol is described in ch. xxvii. 20, where the Authorized Version translates " Hell (*sheol*) and destruction are never full," and again in ch. xxx. 15, where it (*sheol*, Authorized Version, " the grave ") is classed with the four things that are never satisfied. Vulgate, *infernus*; LXX., ᾅδης. **And whole, as those that go down into the pit.** The parallelism of the ideas requires that the word " whole " (תְּמִימִים, t'mimim) should be understood of those physically whole (see Mercerus, Delitzsch), and not in a moral sense, as the *upright* (Luther, Grier, Holden, Plumptre). The word is used in an ethical signification in ch. ii. 21. Gesenius gives it the meaning of " safe, secure." *Those that go down into*

the pit (יוֹרְדֵי בוֹר, yorde vor); i.e. the dead. The phrase also occurs in Ps. xxviii. 1; xxx. 4; lxxxviii. 4; cxliii. 7; Isa. xxxviii. 18). *The pit* (בוֹר, vor); or, *the sepulchre*, the receptacle of the dead, is here synonymous with *sheol*. The LXX. substitutes for the latter part of the verse, Καὶ ἄρωμεν αὐτοῦ τὴν μνήμην ἐκ γῆς, "And let us remove his memory from the earth." The robbers, by drawing a comparison between themselves and Hades and the grave, which consign to silence all who are put therein, imply their own security against detection. They will so utterly destroy their victims that none will be left to tell the tale (see Musset, *in loc.*). This, we know, is a fancied, and at the best only a temporary, security.

Ver. 13.—**We shall find all precious substance.** This verse carries on the proposal of the sinners one step further, and puts forward a third enticement, viz. that of the profit of crime, or the prospect of immediate riches, before youth to join in crime. A short cut to wealth, and to the acquirement of that which costs others long years of steady application and carefulness, is a strong inducement (Wardlaw). *We shall find*; נִמְצָא (nim'tza), from מָצָא (matza), properly " to reach to," and " to find," in the sense of " to come upon;" cf. Latin *invenio*. *Substance* (הוֹן, hon); i.e. substance in the sense of riches. The radical meaning of הוֹן (hun), from which it is derived, is the same as in the Arabic word, " to be light, easy, to be in easy circumstances, and so to be rich " (Gesenius). In its abstract sense, *hon*, " substance," means ease, comfort, and concretely riches which bring about that result (see also Fleischer, as quoted by Delitzsch); cf. the LXX. κτῆσις, i.e. collectively, possessions, property. The Piscatoris Version, for " precious substance," reads *divitias*, " riches." *Precious*; יָקָר (yakar), properly " heavy," is found with הוֹן (hon), " substance," in ch. xii. 27 and xxiv. 4. The collocation of the ideas of lightness and heaviness in these two words is striking, but we need not necessarily suppose that any oxymoron is intended, as Schultens. Such combinations occur in other languages, and reside more in the radical meanings of the words than in the mind or intention of the writer or speaker. **We shall fill our houses with spoil;** i.e. they promise not only finding, but full possession (Gejerus, Muffet). *Spoil*; שָׁלָל (shalal), from שָׁלַל (shalal), same as the Arabic verb " to draw," and hence " to strip off " (Gesenius); and equivalent to the Greek σκῦλα (LXX.), the arms stripped off a slain enemy, spoils, and the Latin *spolia* (Vulgate). *Shalal* is used generally, as here, for " prey," " booty " (Gen. xlix. 27; Exod. xv. 9). Our gains, say the robbers, will not only be valuable, but numerous and plentiful.

Ver. 14.—**Cast in thy lot among us.** The fourth and last enticement put forward, viz. *honourable union* and *frank and open-hearted generosity.* It has distinct reference to the preceding verse, and shows how the prospect of immediate wealth is to be realized (see Delitzsch, Wardlaw). *Cast in thy lot* cannot mean, as Mercerus, "cast in your inheritance with us, so that we all may use it in common," though גּוֹרָל (*goral*) does mean "inheritance" in the sense of that which comes to any one by lot (Judg. i. 3) (Gesenius), since that would be no inducement to youth to join the robbers. *Goral* properly is "a little stone or pebble," κλῆρος, especially such as were used in casting lots, and so equivalent to a "lot" here—that with which the distribution was made, as in Lev. xvi. 8; Neh. x. 34; and the custom of freebooters dividing the spoil by lot is here alluded to (Holden); comp. Ps. xxii. 18 in illustration of the practice of casting lots, "They part my garments among them, and cast lots upon my vesture." The sense is, "you shall equally with the others cast lots for your share of the spoil" (Zöckler, Delitzsch). **Let us all have one purse.** *Purse;* כִּיס (*kis*), the βαλάντιον of the LXX., the *marsupium* of the Vulgate, is the receptacle in which money is placed for security. In ch. xv. 11 it is used for the bag in which traders kept their weights, "the weights of the bag;" and in ch. xxiii. 31 it is translated "cup," the wine-cup. It here signifies the common stock, the aggregate of the gains of the robbers contributed to a common fund. The booty captured by each or any is to be thrown into one common stock, to form one purse, to be divided by lot among all the members of the band. On this community of goods among robbers, compare the Hebrew proverb, *In loculis, in poculis, in ira.* Community of goods among the wicked carries with it community in crime, just as the community of goods among the early Christians implied community in good works and in the religious sentiments of the Christian body or Church. The Rabbi Salomon Isacides offers another explanation (which leaves the choice open to youth either to share in the spoil by lot, or to live at the expense of a common fund, as he may prefer): "Si voles, nobiscum spolia partieris, si etiam magis placebit, sociali communique marsupio nobiscum vives"—"If thou wilt, thou shalt share with us the booty; ay, if it like thee more, thou shalt live with us on a confederate and common purse" (see Cornelius à Lapide).

Ver. 15.—**My son, walk not thou in the way with them.** The admonitory strain of ver. 10 is again resumed, and in vers. 16—19 the teacher states the reasons which should dissuade youth from listening to the temptations of sinners. *My son.* The recurrence of these words for the third time in this address marks the affectionate interest, the loving solicitude, in which the admonition is addressed. *Walk not thou.* Immediate and entire abandonment is counselled. The warning is practically a repetition of ver. 10, and is given again in ch. iv. 14, "Enter not into the path of the wicked, and go not in the way of evil men." *Way;* דֶּרֶךְ (*derek*) means, figuratively, the way of living and acting (Gesenius). "Mores et consuetudines" (Bayne); cf. ch. xii. 15, "the fool's way;" xxii. 25; and Ps. i. 1. The meaning is "associate not with them, have no dealings whatever with them." **Refrain thy foot from their path;** *i.e.* keep back thy foot, or make not one step in compliance, resist the very first solicitations to evil. Compare the legal maxim, *Initiis obsta.* *Refrain;* מְנַע (*m'na*) is from מָנַע (*mana*), "to keep back, restrain;" LXX., ἔκκλινον (cf. Ps. cxix. 101, "I have refrained my feet from every evil way;" Jer. xiv. 10, "Thus have they loved to wander, they have not refrained their feet"). Restraining the foot carries with it indirectly the natural inclination or propensity of the heart, even of the good, towards evil (Cartwright). *Foot* (רֶגֶל, *regel*) is, of course, used metaphorically, and means less the member of the body than the idea suggested by it; hence the use of the singular (Gejerus, Delitzsch). Bayne remarks that the Hebrews understood this passage as meaning "neither in public nor private life have any dealings with sinners." *Path* (נָתִיב, *nathiv*) is a beaten path, a pathway, a byway; from the unused root נָתַב (*nathav*), "to tread, trample;" and hence, while "way" may mean the great public high-road, "path" may stand for the bypath, less frequented or public. The same distinction probably occurs in Ps. xxv. 4, "Show me thy ways, O Lord; and teach me thy paths."

Ver. 16.—**For their feet run to evil, and make haste to shed blood.** This is the first dissuasive urged to enforce the warning against evil companionship, as showing the extremes to which entering upon the ways of the wicked lead ultimately. At once the youth who listens will be hurried along impetuously to the two crimes of robbery and murder, which God has expressly forbidden in the eighth and sixth commandments respectively of the moral code. *Evil* (רַע, *ra*) is "wickedness," τὸ κακόν, generally, but here more specifically highway robbery, latrocinism (Cornelius à Lapide), as appears from vers. 11—13, where also murder, the laying in wait for blood, is proposed. The Rabbis Salomon and Salazar understand the evil to refer to the evil or destruction which sinners bring upon themselves, and the shedding of blood to the fact that they lay themselves open to have their own blood shed by judicial process (see also Holden). The former explanation seems preferable to this, as putting a higher law than that of self-preservation before youth. The fear of judges who can condemn to death is nothing comparatively to the fear of him "who is able to destroy both body and soul in hell." This verse is wanting in the Vatican LXX., and Arabic, and hence Hitzig has concluded that it is an interpolation made from Isa. lix. 7, but upon insufficient evidence, as it is found in the Alexandrian LXX., Chaldee Paraphrase, Vulgate, and Syriac Versions, all which follow the Hebrew text. The latter part of the verse is quoted by St. Paul in Rom. iii. 15.

Ver. 17.—**Surely in vain the net is spread in the face of any bird.** The teacher here advances a *second* reason in support of his warning in ver. 15, under the form of a proverb in its strict sense. It is based on the ill-advised audacity of sinners in flying in the face of God's judgments. *In vain* (חִנָּם, *khinnam*), see ver. 11, may be taken in two senses. (1) *I.e.* to no purpose, *gratis, frustra* (Vulgate, Chaldee Paraphrase, Arabic). The meaning of the proverb here used then is, "to no purpose is the net spread before birds," *i.e.* though they see the net spread before them, they nevertheless fly into it (comp. ch. vii. 23, "As a bird hasteth to the snare, and knoweth not that it is for his life"). So sinners, when they are plotting for others, plunge into their own destruction with their eyes open. Therefore do not associate with them, do not imitate their crass folly, be warned by their example, or you will share their fate. This view is supported by the LXX. reading, Οὐ γὰρ ἀδίκως ἐκτείνεται δίκτυα πτερωτοῖς, "For not unreasonably is the net spread before birds;" *i.e.* they fall into the snare (see Luther, Patrick, Umbreit, Ewald, Hitzig, Zöckler, Plumptre). (2) Others, as Delitzsch, Ziegler, Beda, Döderlein, Bertheau, Wardlaw, take *khinnam* in a different sense, as indicating the escape of the birds—the birds see the snare and fly away, and so in vain the net is spread in their sight. This explanation is in agreement with Ovid's statement, "Quæ nimis apparent retia vitat avis." The moral motive put before youth in this case is the aggravation of his guilt if he listens to the enticements of sinners. The teacher seems to say, "Imitate the birds, flee from temptation; if you listen to sinners, you will sin with your eyes open." *Is spread;* מְזֹרָה (*m'zorah*), *expansum*, not *conspersum est*, i.e. besprinkled or strewn with corn as a bait, as Rashi. M'zorah is the participle passive of pual, זֹרָה

(*zorah*), "to be strewn," from kal זָרָה (*zarah*), "to scatter, or disperse" (Gesenius), and means *expansum*, because when a net is scattered or dispersed it is spread out (see Delitzsch). *Of any bird* (כָל־בַּעַל כָּנָף, *khal-baal khanaph*); literally, *of every possessor of a wing*, or, as margin, *of everything that hath a wing*, i.e. of every bird. Compare the same expression in Eccles. x. 20, בַּעַל הַכְּנָפַיִם (*baal hach'naphayim*); *i.e.* "that which hath wings" (Authorized Version).

Ver. 18.—**And they lay wait for their** own **blood,** etc. The *third* reason or argument why the teacher's warning should be followed, drawn from the *destruction* which overtakes the sinners themselves. "Lay wait," and "lurk privily," as in ver. 11, from which this verse is evidently borrowed. They propose, as they say, to lay wait for the blood of others; but it is, says the teacher, for their own blood. לְדָמָם (*l'dhamam*), *contra sanguinem suum;* they lurk privily, as they say, for the innocent, but in reality it is for their own lives; לְנַפְשֹׁתָם (*l'naph'shotham*); *contra animas suas* (Vulgate); or, as the LXX. puts it, Αὐτοὶ γὰρ οἱ φόνου μετέχοντες, θησαυρίζουσιν ἑαυτοῖς κακὰ, "For they who take part in murder treasure up evils for themselves;" that is, they are bringing a heavier and surer destruction upon themselves than they can ever inflict upon others (Wardlaw). The LXX. adds, at the close of the verse, Ἡ δὲ καταστροφὴ ἀνδρῶν παρανόμων κακή, "And the overthrowing or destruction of transgressors is great, or evil." The Arabic Version has a similar addition.

Ver. 19.—**So are the ways of every one that is greedy of gain.** The epiphonema or moral of the preceding address. *So are the ways*, or such is the lot (as Delitzsch), or such are the paths (as Zöckler), *i.e.* so deceitful, so ruinous, are the ways. כֵּן (*chen*) is here used as a qualitative adverb. *Ways;* אׇרְחוֹת (*ar'khoth*), the plural of אֹרַח (*orakh*), a poët. word, equivalent in the first instance to "way," *i.q.* דֶּרֶךְ (*derekh*), and metaphorically applied to any one's ways, his manner of life and its result, and hence lot, as in Job viii. 12, and hence the expression covers the three preceding verses. *That is greedy of gain* (בֹּצֵעַ בָּצַע, *botsea batsa*); literally, *concupiscentis concupiscentiam lucri;* i.e. eagerly longing after gain; he who greedily desires riches (*avari,* Vulgate). *Gain; batsa* in pause, from בֶּצַע (*betsa*), which takes its meaning from the verb בָּצַע (*batsa*), "to cut in pieces, to break," and hence means properly that which is cut or broken off and taken by any one for himself, and so *unjust gain*—anything whatever fraudulently acquired, as in ch. xxviii. 16, where it is translated "covetousness" (Authorized Version); cf. Isa. xxxiii. 15; ch. xv. 27. The idea of greed and covetousness enters largely into the word. Which taketh away the life of the owners thereof. The pronoun "which" does not occur in the original. The nominative to "taketh away" (יִקָּח, yikkath) is "gain;" the "unjust gain" (betsa) takes away the life of its owners, i.e. of those who are under its power. Owners thereof (בְּעָלָיו, b'alayo) does not necessarily imply that they are in actual possession of the unjust gain, but rather refers to the influence which the lust for gain exercises over them. The expression in this second hemistich does not mean that the rapacious take the life of their comrades who possess the gain, as Rabbi Salomon; nor, as the Vulgate, "the ways of the avaricious man take away the lives of those who possess them." For the phrase, "taketh away the life," as importing a violent taking away, cf. Ps. xxxi. 13; 1 Kings xix. 10. The sentiment of the verse is well expressed in 1 Tim. vi. 10, "For the love of money is the root of all evil; which while some coveted after, they have erred from the faith, and pierced themselves through with many sorrows."

Vers. 20—33.—2. Second admonitory discourse. Address of Wisdom personified, exhibiting the folly of those who wilfully reject, and the security of those who hearken to, her counsels. The sacred writer, in this section, as also in h. viii., uses the rhetorical figure of prosopopœia, or impersonation. Wisdom is represented as speaking and as addressing the simple, scorners, and fools. The address itself is one of the noblest specimens of sacred eloquence, expressing in rapid succession the strongest phases of feeling—pathetic solicitude with abundant promise, indignant scorn at the rejection of her appeal, the judicial severity of offended majesty upon offenders, and lastly the judicial complacency which delights in mercy towards the obedient. The imagery in part is taken from the forces of nature in their irresistible and overwhelming violence and destructive potency.

Ver. 20.—Wisdom crieth without. Wisdom. The Hebrew word (khochmoth) here used to designate Wisdom seems to be an abstract derivation from the ordinary khochmah. The form is peculiar to the Proverbs and Psalms, in the former occurring four times (ch. i. 22; ix. 1; xiv. 1; xxiv. 7), and in the latter twice only (viz. Ps.

xlix. 4; lxxviii. 15). As in ch. ix. 1 and xxiv. 7, it is a pluralis excellentiæ of the feminine gender, a variety of the pluralis extensivus, as Böttcher prefers to denominate it. The feminine form may be determined by the general law which associates purity and serenity with womanhood (Plumptre). The idea of plurality, however, is not that of extension, but of comprehension, i.e. it is not so much all kinds of wisdom which is presented to us, as all the varieties under which wisdom par excellence may be regarded and is comprehended. The plural form of the word denotes the highest character or excellence in which wisdom can be conceived; or, as the marginal reading expresses it, wisdoms, i.e. excellent wisdom. Other instances of the pluralis excellentiæ are met with in Holy Writ, e.g. Elohim, God, i.e. "God of Gods," either from the polytheistic view, or from the monotheistic view as expressive of God's might in manifestation, passim; k'doshim, "the Holy (God)," ch. ix. 10; xxx. 3; adonim, for adon, "lord" (Gesenius, 'Gram.,' § 108. 2 b). In the conception of Wisdom here presented to us in the text we have the germ of an idea which, on the principles of expansion, developed subsequently in the consciousness of the Christian Church into a definite identification of Wisdom with the Second Person of the blessed Trinity. There is a striking parallel to this passage in Luke xi. 49, where Christ speaks of himself as ἡ Σοφία τοῦ Θεοῦ, "the Wisdom of God," that shall send prophets and apostles into the world, and thereby identifies himself with Wisdom (cf. this with vers. 20, 21; ch. vii.). Again, a striking similarity is observable between the teaching of Divine Wisdom and that of the Incarnate Word, as much in their promises as in their threats and warnings. But it is difficult to determine with accuracy to what extent the Messianic import of the personification was present to the consciousness of the sacred writers, and whether Wisdom as here presented to us is simply a poetic and abstract personification or a distinct hypostatizing of the Word. Dorner ('Pers. of Christ,' Introd., p. 16), with reference to ch. viii. 22, etc., says that though Wisdom is introduced speaking as a personality distinct from God, still the passage does not lead clearly to an hypostatizing of the Khochmah. Döllinger ('Heidenthum und Judenthum,' bk. x. pt. iii. sec. 2 a, and ch. viii. 22, etc.) maintains that Wisdom is "the personified idea of the mind of God in creation," rather than the presence of "a distinct hypostasis." Lücke (see references in Liddon, 'Bampton Lects.') holds that in Proverbs Wisdom is merely a personification. It is clear that whatever is predicated

of Wisdom in ch. viii. must be also predicated of her in the passage before us, in
reference either to the hypostatic or opposite
view. On the other hand, a large number
of expositors, dating from the earliest
periods of the Christian Church down to
the present time, see in Wisdom a distinct
hypostasis, or person—the Lord Jesus Christ.
A fuller investigation of this subject will
be seen in our remarks on ch. viii. For
the present we observe that Wisdom is
essentially Divine. Her authority, her
utterances, whether of promise, threat, scorn,
or vengeance, are the authority, the utterances, of God. *Crieth;* rather, *crieth loudly,*
or *aloud.* The Hebrew verb *ranan* (רָנַן) is
"to vibrate the voice," and conveys the idea
of the clear loud ringing tones with which
proclamations were made; cf. the Vulgate
prædicare, and the Arabic *clamitate,* "to cry
with a loud voice." Fleischer remarks that
the Arabic *rannan,* which is allied to the
Hebrew verb, is used of a speaker who has
a clear piercing voice. In such a way does
Wisdom cry without when making her
address. She elevates her voice that all
may hear. The verb in the original is
tazonnah, the feminine singular of *ranan,*
and predicate to "Wisdom," according to
the rule that verbs in the singular are
construed with plural nouns having a
singular signification, especially the *pluralis
excellentiæ* (see Gesenius, 'Gram.,' § 146. 2).
Without. בַּחוּץ (*bakhuts*) is here used adverbially, as in Gen. ix. 22, and signifies
"in the open places," *i.e.* abroad, without,
as opposed to the space within the walls.
The writer here begins his enumeration of
the five places wherein Wisdom preaches,
viz. (1) without, (2) in the streets, (3) in
chief places of concourse, (4) in the opening
of the gates, (5) in the city, all of which
are public, and thus indicate the publicity
of her announcements (with these comp. ch.
viii. 1; ix. 3). **She uttereth her voice;** or,
causeth her voice to be heard; represented in
the Vulgate by *dat vocem suam,* and in the
LXX. by παῤῥησίαν ἄγει (equivalent to "she
observes free-spokenness"). The instrumentality which Wisdom uses in her public
preaching are the prophets and teachers
(Ecclus. xxiv. 33; Zöckler, Vatablus, Mercerus). **In the streets;** literally, *in the wide
spaces;* the Hebrew, רְחֹבוֹת (*r'khovoth*), being,
as in Gen. xxvi. 22, "wide spaces," and
corresponding to the πλατεία of the LXX.;
plateæ, Vulgate. The same places are indicated in Luke xiv. 21, where, in the parable
of the marriage supper, the servants are
bidden to go out into the *streets* (πλατείαι)
and lanes of the city. The word is connected with the adjective *rakhav* (רָחָב),
"broad," "wide;" and in 2 Chron. xxxii.

6 is used to designate the ample space
at the gates of Oriental cities (Gesenius),
though here it seems to refer rather to
"squares," large open spaces, not uncommon in Oriental cities—I saw one such at
Aden—or it may refer to the broad crowded
thoroughfares. The Syriac reading, *in com-
pitis,* gives a different sense, as *compitum,*
equivalent to "cross-roads."

Ver. 21.—**She crieth in the chief place of
concourse.** The *chief place* is literally the
head (רֹאשׁ, *rosh*); here used figuratively for
the place where streets or roads branch off
in different directions, as in Ezek. xvi. 25,
"the beginning of streets," or "the head of
the way;" comp. Gen. ii. 10, where it is
used of the point at which the four streams
branched off; and the corresponding expression in ch. viii. 2, "She standeth in the
top (*rosh*) of high places." *Of concourse;*
הֹמִיּוֹת (*homiyyoth*) is the plural of the adjective, הֹמִי (*homi*); literally, "those who are
making a noise," or "the tumultuous;" here,
as in Isa. xxii. 2 and 1 Kings i. 41, used
substantively for "boisterous, noisy places"
(compare the Vulgate, *in capite turbarum*).
The variation in the LXX., "on high
walls," or "on the tops of the walls" (ἐπ'
ἄκρων δὲ τειχέων, *super summos muros*),
which is adopted also in the Chaldee,
Syriac, and Arabic Versions, arises from
reading חוֹמוֹת (*khomoth*), "walls," for the
Masoretic *homiyyoth.* **In the openings of
the gates.** The *opening* (פֶּתַח, *pethakh*) is
the opening of the gate, or the entrance
by the gate (שַׁעַר, *shaar*), *i.e.* of the city,
the *introitus portæ* of the Chaldee and
Syriac Versions. The openings of the gates
would be thronged, as courts of justice were
held at the gates (Deut. xvi. 18; 2 Sam.
xv. 2); business was carried on there, as
the selling and redemption of land (Gen.
xxiii. 10—16; Ruth iv. 1); markets were
also held there (2 Kings vii. 1—18); and the
same localities were used for the councils
of the state and conferences (Gen. xxxiv.
20; 2 Sam. iii. 27; 2 Chron. xviii 9; Jer.
xvii. 19; comp. ch. xxxi. 33, "Her husband
is known in the *gates*"). In place of the
expression, "in the openings of the gates,"
the LXX. reads, Ἐπὶ δὲ πύλαις δυναστῶν
παρεδρεύει, "And at the gates of the mighty
she sits"—an interpolation which only partially represents the sense of the original, and
which is adopted in the Arabic. In the next
clause, for "in the city" is substituted ἐπὶ
δὲ πύλαις πόλεως, "at the gates of the city."
The Vulgate combines the separate clauses
of the original in one—*in foribus portarum
urbis,* "in the entrances and openings of
the gates of the city." **In the city** (בָּעִיר,
bair); *i.e.* in the city itself (so Aben Ezra,
ap. Gejerus), as opposed to the entrance by

the gates, and so used antithetically (as Umbreit, Bertheau, Hitzig). The publicity of the teaching of Wisdom, observable in the places she selects for that purpose, also marked the public ministry of our Lord and his disciples, and finds an illustration in his command, " What ye hear in the ear, that preach ye upon the housetops " (Matt. x. 27); i.e. give it all the publicity possible. The spirit of Wisdom, like that of Christianity, is aggressive (see Wardlaw, 'Lectures on Proverbs iv.,' vol. i. pp. 40, 41).

Ver. 22.—How long, ye simple ones, will ye love simplicity? etc. From this verse to the end of the chapter the sacred writer puts before us the words of Wisdom herself. The discourse begins in the same way as in Ps. iv. 2 (Zöckler), and the classification of the persons addressed—the simple, the scorners, and the sinners—closely resembles that of Ps. i. 1. In the order there is a progression from the least to the most culpable. The simple (פְּתָיִם, p'thayim), as in ver. 4, those who are indifferent through thoughtlessness and inconsiderateness, and are thereby open to evil. The scorners (לֵצִים, letsim); or, mockers, the same as the (לָצוֹן, latson) " scornful men" of ch. xxix. 8, derived from the root לוּץ (luts), " to deride, mock," probably by imitating the voice in derision. The mockers are those who hold all things in derision, both human and Divine, who contemn God's admonitions, and treat with ridicule both threatenings and promises alike. Fools; כְּסִילִים (ch'silim), a different word from the evilim of ver. 7, but signifying much the same, i.e. the obdurate, the hardened, stolidi, those who walk after the sight of their eyes and the imagination of their hearts—a class not ignorant of knowledge, but hating it because of the restraint it puts them under. The word occurs in ch. xvii. 10, in the sense of the incorrigible; in ch. xxvi. 3, 4 as a term of the greatest contempt. The enallage, or interchange of tenses in the original—the verbs " love " and " hate " being future, and " delight " being perfect—is not reproducible in English. The perfect is used interchangeably with the future where the action or state is represented as first coming to pass or in progress, and, as Zöckler remarks, may be inchoative, and so be rendered "become fond of," instead of "be fond of." But it appears to represent not so much a state or action first coming to pass as in progress (see Gesenius, 'Gram.,' § 126. 3). Böttcher (§ 948. 2) translates it by concupiverint, i.e. "How long shall ye have delighted in scorning?" The futures express "love" and "hate" as habitual sentiments (Delitzsch). It is to be noted that the language of

Wisdom, in vers. 22 and 23, is expressive of the most tender and earnest solicitude.

Ver. 23.—Turn you at my reproof. A call is here made to repentance. The meaning seems to be "return to my reproof," i.e. place yourselves under my reproof (as Gejerus, Delitzsch), the לְ being represented by ad, as in the Vulgate: convertimini ad correptionem meam. It is susceptible, however, of a different reading, i.e. "in consequence of, or because of (propter), my reproof," the prefix לְ being found in Numb. xvi. 34, " They fled at the cry," i.e. because of the cry. Reproof (תּוֹכַחַת, thochakhath); i.e. rebuke, or correction, by words. The LXX. ἔλεγχος conveys the argumentative conviction which will be present in the reproof. The word occurs again in vers. 23, 25, and 30 of this chapter, and also in ch. iii. 11; v. 12; vi. 23; xxvii. 5; xxix. 15. Behold, I will pour out my Spirit unto you. The promise consequent upon, and the encouragement to, repentance. The promise is conditioned—if those addressed will heed the reproof of Wisdom, then she will pour forth her Spirit upon them, and cause them to know her words. The verb hibbia (הִבִּיעַ), " to stream forth, or gush out," is here used figuratively. The outflow of the Spirit of Wisdom will be like the abundant and continuous gushing forth of water from the spring or fountain. The verb unites in it the figures of abundant fulness and refreshing invigoration (Umbreit, Elster); comp. ch. xv. 2, 28; Ps. lix. 7; cxix. 171; Eccles. x. 1. We have here a striking anticipation of the prophecy of Joel (ii. 28). The Spirit is that of Wisdom "and understanding, the Spirit of counsel and godly strength, the Spirit of knowledge and true godliness " (see Confirmation Office). The explanation of Beda, that it signifies her anger, is clearly inadmissible. I will make known my words unto you; i.e. as the LXX., "I will teach you my word" (διδάξω), or as the Vulgate "show" (ostendam), "expound, or make clear." My words (d'vari); i.e. precepts, or doctrine, or secrets. An intimate relation subsists between the "Spirit" of Wisdom and her "words," with which it is parallel. The former is the illuminating, invigorating principle which infuses life and power into the "words" of Wisdom, which she has already given, and which are already in our possession. Wisdom stands in the same relation to her words as the Divine Logos does to his utterances, into which he infuses himself. "It is the Spirit that quickeneth; the flesh profiteth nothing: the words that I speak unto you, they are spirit, and they are life" (John vi. 63. See Delitzsch, Wardlaw, in loc.).

Ver. 24.—Because I have called, and ye refused. A pause may be imagined, and seems to be implied, between this and the preceding verses (22 and 23), when the address passes into a new phase—from that of invitation and promise to that of judgment and stern denunciation (vers. 24—27). In the subsection the antecedent clauses are vers. 24, 25, introduced by the conjunction "because" (יַעַן, *yaan*; *quia*, Vulgate), which expresses the reason or cause for the conclusion in vers. 26 and 27, introduced by "I also," to which the "because" answers. A similar grammatical construction and judgment is to be found in Isaiah: "I also will choose their delusions, and will bring their fears upon them; because when I called, none did answer; when I spake, they did not hear" (Isa. lxvi. 4; see also Jer. vii. 13). *Refused*; i.e. refused to hearken, as signified in the LXX. ὑπακούσατε. **I have stretched out my hand.** A forensic gesture to arrest attention. The expression is equivalent to "I have spread out my hands" (Isa. lxv. 2); cf. "Then Paul stretched forth the hand (ἐκτείνας τὴν χεῖρα)" (Acts xxvi. 1). **Regarded** (מַקְשִׁיב, *mak'shiv*). The original idea of the verb קָשַׁב (*kashav*), used here, is that of erecting or pricking up the ear, like the Latin *arrigere*, sc. *aures*, in Plaut., 'Rud.,' 5. 2. 6; and cf. "arrectisque auribus adstant" (Virgil, 'Æneid,' i. 153).

Ver. 25.—**Ye have set at nought**; rather, *rejected* (Umbreit, Ewald, *et alii*). The Authorized Version rendering here is equivocal, inasmuch as it is capable of meaning "despised," whereas פָּרַע (*para*) signifies "to let loose," "to let go" (cf. the German *fahren lassen*), and hence "to overlook, or reject." Its force is fairly represented in the LXX., Ἀκύρους ἐποιεῖτε ἐμὰς βουλὰς, "Ye rendered my counsel of no effect." **Counsel** (עֵצָה, *etsah*); i.e. advice, in the sense of recommendations for doing good, as opposed to *reproofs* for the avoidance of evil (see vers. 23 and 30). **Would none.** The same verb, אָבָה (*avah*), occurs in vers. 10 and 30, hence used with the negative לֹא (*lo*) in the sense of ἀπειθεῖν (LXX.), "to refuse compliance with," as in Æschylus, 'Agam.,' 1049.

Ver. 26.—**I also will laugh at your calamity**; or, more accurately, *in the time of your calamity*; as in the Vulgate, *in interitu vestro ridebo*. The preposition prefixed to the substantive *b'eyd'chem* (בְּאֵידְכֶם) refers to the time, or state, or condition (Gesenius, 'Gram.,' 154. 3). In the time of their calamity wisdom will exult or rejoice. The LXX., Τῇ ὑμετέρᾳ ἀπωλείᾳ ἐπιγελάσομαι, however, favours the rendering of the Authorized Version. *Calamity* (אֵיד, *eyd*) is heavy overwhelming misfortune,

that which oppresses and crushes its victims. The terrific nature of the punishment of the wicked is marked by a succession of terms all of terrible import—calamity, fear, desolation, destruction, distress, and anguish (vers. 26, 27). When these come upon them, then Wisdom will laugh and have them in derision. The verbs "laugh" (שָׂחַק, *sakhak*) and "mock" (לָעַג, *laag*) are the same as in Ps. ii. 4, where they are rendered "to mock" and "have in derision." **When your fear cometh**; i.e. has actually arrived. *Fear* (פַּחַד, *pakhad*); here used metonymically for that which causes the fear or terror (*id, quod timebatis*, Vulgate). There is a similar use of φόβος in 1 Pet. iii. 14.

Ver. 27.—**When your fear cometh as desolation.** The imagery in this verse is borrowed from nature—from the tempest and whirlwind, which, in their impetuous fury, involve all in irretrievable ruin. The two leading ideas here in the writer's mind are calamity and fear. These—their fear, that which causes their fear; and their destruction, *i.e.* calamity—both representing Wisdom's, and so God's, judgment, will come on sinners as a wasting tempest and sweeping hurricane. The terror and devastation caused by these latter as they pass over the face of nature are employed to depict the alarm and ruin of sinners. **Desolation**; שׁוֹאָה (*shaavah*) is a wasting, crashing tempest (cf. ch. iii. 25; Zeph. i. 15), derived from שָׁאָה (*shaah*), "to make a crash," as of a house falling. The Vulgate reads, *repentura calamitas*; the LXX., ἄφνω θόρυβος; both bringing out the idea of suddenness, and the latter that of the uproar of the tempest. The Khetib, or traditional text of the manuscripts (כְּשׁוֹאָה), is equivalent to the Keri, or emended reading (כְּשׁוֹאָה), and both appear to have the same root-meaning. **Destruction** (אֵיד, *eyd*); the same as "calamity" in the preceding verse. **Whirlwind**; סוּפָה (*suphah*), from the root סוּף (*suph*), "to snatch, or carry away," means a whirlwind carrying everything before it—the καταιγίς of the LXX., or hurricane, as in Arist., 'Mund.,' 4. 16. **Distress and anguish** (צָרָה וְצוּקָה, *tsarah v'tzukah*). A corresponding alliteration occurs in Isa. xxx. 6 and Zeph. i. 15. The root-signification of the former is that of compression, reproduced in the LXX. θλίψις, and the Vulgate *tribulatio*; that of the latter is narrowness. LXX., πολιορκία, "a beleaguering;" Vulgate, *angustia*. The LXX. adds, at the close of this verse, ἢ ὅταν ἔρχηται ὑμῖν ὄλεθρος as explanatory.

Ver. 28.—The phase which the address now enters upon continues to the thirty-first verse. The change in this verse from the second to the third person is striking. It implies that Wisdom thinks fools no longer worthy of being addressed personally— "Quasi stultos indignos censunt ulteriori alloquio" (Gejerus and Michaelis). The declaration is the embodiment of the laughter and scorn of ver. 26. The three verbs, " they shall call," " they shall seek," " they shall find," occur in uncommon and emphatic forms in the original. They are some out of the few instances where the future terminations are inserted fully before the pronominal suffix. **I will not answer.** The distress and anguish consequent upon their calamity and fear lead them to pray, but there will be no answer nor heed given to their cry. They are not heard, because they do not cry rightly nor in the time of grace (Lapide). See the striking parallel to the tenor of this passage in Luke xiii. 24—28. **They shall seek me early** ; *i.e.* diligently. The verb שָׁחַר (*shakhar*) is the denominative from the substantive שַׁחַר (*shakar*), "the dawn, morning," and signifies to go out and seek something in the obscurity of the morning twilight (Delitzsch, Zöckler), and hence indicates diligence and earnestness in the search. Gesenius gives the same derivation, but connects it with the dawn in the sense of the light breaking forth, and thus, as it were, seeking (see also ch. ii. 27; vii. 15; viii. 17; Hos. v. 15).

Vers. 29 and 30 belong to ver. 28, and are not the antecedent clauses to ver. 31, as Zöchler remarks. They recapitulate the charges already made against the sinners in vers. 22 and 25, and now set them forth as the ground or reason why Wisdom, on her part, turns a deaf ear to their entreaties. Wisdom will disregard them because they have previously disregarded her. The connection is denoted in the LXX. by γάρ, for the Hebrew *takhath ki*, equivalent to "because," and in the Authorized Version by the punctuation. **Did not choose the fear of the Lord.** The verb "to choose" (בָּחַר, *bakhar*) combines in itself the meanings of *eligere* and *diligere* (Fleischer), and therefore signifies here not only choice of, but also the fuller sense of love for, the fear of the Lord. **They despised** ; *i.e.* rejected the reproof with scorn or derision, sneered or turned up their noses at it (μυκτηρίζειν, LXX.), disparaged it (*detrahere*, Vulgate), or, more strongly, as Gejerus says, execrated it. Their rejection of reproof is stigmatized in stronger terms than in ver. 25.

Ver. 31.—**Therefore they shall eat,** etc. A further enlargement of the declaration of Wisdom, showing that their calamity is the result of their own ways. The futures are resumed in the original from ver. 28. The word "therefore" does not occur, but it is

met with in the LXX., τοιγαροῦν ; in the Vulgate, *igitur ;* and in the Syriac, *ideo.* The truth here expressed is accordant with the tenor of the teaching of the Scripture (comp. ch. xiv. 14; xxii. 8; Job iv. 8; Isa. iii. 10 ; Gal. vi. 7, 8), and with our daily experience of God's moral government of the world (see Butler, 'Analogy,' part i. ch. ii., *ad fin.*). This sentiment of retributive punishment also found expression in Terence, " Tute hoc intristi, tibi omne est edendum " ('Phorm.,' 2. 1. 4). When we are punished, the blameworthiness lies not with God, but with us sinners (Wardlaw). **They shall be filled** ; rather, *satiated,* or *surfeited; saturabuntur* (Vulgate). The verb שָׂבַע (*shava*) means not only "to fill," but "to be satiated or cloyed" (cf. ch. xiv. 14; xxv. 16; Ps. lxxxviii. 3; cxxiii. 4). Michaelis remarks on this word, " Ad nauseam implebuntur et comedent, ita ut consiliorum suorum vehementer tandem, sed nimis sero, ipsos pœniteat" (Michaelis, ' Notæ Uberiores in Prov.'), "They shall be filled and eat *ad nauseam,* so that at length, but too late, they shall vehemently repent them of their own counsels." **Counsels** (מוֹעֵצוֹת, *moetsoth*) ; *i.e.* ungodly counsels, or evil devices. The word only occurs in the plural.

Ver. 32.—Wisdom now brings her address to a close by contrasting the destruction and ruin of the foolish, and the security of those who listen to her voice. **The turning away** ; מְשׁוּבָה (*m'shuvah*), from שׁוּב (*shuv*), "to turn about, or to return " (which is used metaphorically of conversion), here means *defection,* turning away; and hence apostasy (*aversio,* Vulgate, Chaldee Paraphrase, Syriac; *perversitio,* Cast. Version); the "backsliding" of Jer. viii. 5; Hos. xi. 7. Aben Ezra understands it to signify "case," as in the marginal reading ; but there seems no warrant for taking the word in that sense. The LXX. renders the passage quite differently, Ἀνθ' ὧν γὰρ ἠδίκουν νηπίους, φονευθήσονται, " For because they wronged the young, they shall be slain ; " so also the Arabic. The turning away is from the warnings and invitations of Wisdom, and implies rebelliousness against God. **The prosperity.** The word in the original (שַׁלְוָה, *shal'vah*) is here used in a bad sense, and means " carelessness, indolence," that carnal security which is induced by prosperity and worldly success, as in Jer. xxii. 21, " I spoke to thee in thy prosperity (security), but thou saidst, I will not hear " (cf. Ezek. xvi. 49, where it is translated "idleness." So Dathe translates, " Incuria ignavorum eos perdit." The Chaldee Paraphrase and Syriac Versions read " error." It occurs in a good sense as " tranquillity," " security," in ch. xvii. 1 and Ps. cxxii. 7. The derivation of the word is from שָׁלָה (shalah), "to be tranquil, to be safe, secure." Mariana remarks that it is more difficult to bear prosperity than adversity, because we endure adversity, we are corrupted by prosperity, and prosperity or ease makes fools mad. The false security of the prosperous is illustrated by our Lord in his parable of the rich fool (Luke xii. 16—21). The LXX. differs again from the Hebrew in the second clause of this verse, καὶ ἐξετασμὸς ἀσεβεῖς ὀλεῖ; i.e. the carefully considered judgment of God concerning them shall destroy them. The LXX. is followed by the Arabic. **Them**; i.e. the fools themselves, and not other sinners, as Ben Ezra says, though the apparent security of fools, the impunity with which they seem to go on in their wickedness, and the success of their plans, may lead others to destruction.

Ver. 33.—**Hearkeneth unto me.** Wisdom, in closing her address, draws a beautiful picture of the real security and peace of the righteous, as contrasted with the false security of the wicked. As on the one side rejection of her counsels, her warnings, and invitations, carries with it punishment and irretrievable ruin; so, on the other, the hearkening to her words, and loving obedience, are rewarded by her with the choicest blessings. **Shall dwell safely**; that is, with confidence, without danger (absque terrore, Vulgate). The phrase, שָׁכַן בֶּטַח (shachan

betakh), is used in Deut. xxxiii. 12—18 of the safety with which the covenant people should dwell in the land that God had given them; but it is capable of a further extension of meaning beyond mere temporal security, viz. to the spiritual peace of the righteous. The psalmist also employs it to describe the confidence with which he awaits the resurrection, when he says, "My flesh also shall rest in hope [or, 'dwell confidently']" (Ps. xvi. 9). So here Wisdom promises that he who hearkens to her shall dwell calmly and undisturbed amidst the distractions of the world. The promise agrees with the description of Wisdom elsewhere that "her ways are ways of pleasantness, and all her paths are peace." **And shall be quiet** (שַׁאֲנַן, shaanan, perfect pilel). Wisdom regards her assurance as already accomplished, and hence the perfect in the original is used for the future. The hearers and doers of her will shall live in tranquillity; nay, they are already doing so. It is a thing not only in prospect, but in possession. **From fear of evil**; i.e. either without any fear of evil, fear being removed (timore sublato, Vulgate), or, as the Authorized Version expresses it, connecting the phrase more intimately with the verb—"quiet from fear of evil." It is not only evil, רָעָה (raah), in its substantial form, as calamity, they are to be free from, but even the fear of it. The tranquillity will be supreme.

HOMILETICS.

Ver. 6.—*Proverbs.* It is not surprising to see that proverbs, which are found more or less in the traditional lore of almost all nations, and flourish most abundantly in the East, also enter into the circle of the inspired literature of the Jews. The general characteristics of this portion of the sacred Scriptures are well worthy of our study.

I. THE PROVERBS ARE ALL CONCISE UTTERANCES. In the present age, when time is more precious than ever, it is to be wished that public teachers would correct their prolixity by following the example of these sayings, which certainly contain "the soul of wit." 1. The conciseness of the proverbs renders them *striking.* It is not enough to state a truth; we must make it tell. Men's ears are dull to spiritual ideas. In order to penetrate, words must have point, incisiveness, force. 2. The conciseness also greatly *assists memory.* Proverbs can be handed from one to another like coins. A truth that is worth uttering is worth remembering.

II. MANY OF THE PROVERBS ARE ILLUSTRATIVE SAYINGS. They are "figures." The proverb runs into the parable; indeed, a parable is but an expanded proverb. Either by way of arbitrary illustration, or by reason of real correspondence between the material and the spiritual nature, a proverb will often afford lessons of spiritual truth which are more fresh and interesting than bare abstract statements. The popular mind naturally turns to the concrete. What strikes the senses is felt to be most forcible. How well our Lord knew this fact of human nature, and how graciously he condescended to accommodate himself to it, is seen in his own rich picture-gallery of parabolic teaching. He who can discern "sermons in stones" and "books in the running brooks" will have his eyes opened to see "good in everything."

III. SOME OF THE PROVERBS ARE SUGGESTIVE rather than direct teachings. They are "dark sayings"—possibly because the truth is so profound that it can only be approached by those who grope after it in difficult research. But more simple truth may be wrapped in enigmatic phrases for the express purpose of testing the genuineness of the desire to possess it, exciting interest, exercising the powers of thought in the learner, and becoming itself a more intelligible and more valuable thing when it is once found (see Matt. xiii. 10—17). Let no man think that the best treasures of thought are scattered prodigally on the surface of life for swine to trample underfoot. They lie deep, and must often be sought with toil and anguish of soul. Yet to the honest seeker after light, if only he follow the Light of the world, it will surely dawn, though for a season

> " The intellectual power, through words and things,
> Went sounding on, a dim and perilous way."

IV. THE PROVERBS TREAT OF HUMAN CONDUCT. 1. Next to theology, the highest knowledge is that of human life and duty. The triumphs of physical discovery seem to have thrown us into the opposite extreme from that to which Socrates tended. Surely whatever other studies we may pursue, " the *proper* study of mankind is man." No other topic is more profoundly interesting, none requires so much light, none is so replete with practical issues. 2. The wisdom of the proverbs is practical. It deals with conduct—which, as Mr. Matthew Arnold says, " is three-fourths of life." What we know is of service to us chiefly as it affects what we do. 3. This wisdom concerns itself with the moral and religious guides to practice. We find here no Machiavellian maxims of dishonest expediency, no mere worldly advice in the school of Lord Chester-field, no Jesuistic casuistry. Righteousness among men and the fear of God are the leading principles set forth. The least exalted precepts are pure and honest. The highest reach the level of Christian ethics. Though much of the Book of Proverbs falls short of the lofty requirements of the New Testament, many passages in it read like anticipations of the Sermon on the Mount. Thus are we taught that the highest wisdom is one with the purest morality and the noblest religion.

V. THE PROVERBS ORIGINATED IN WISDOM, AND NEED WISDOM FOR THEIR INTERPRE-TATION. They are words of the wise. Inspiration does not dispense with intelligence; it quickens it. Wisdom is itself a gift of the Spirit of God (Jas. i. 5). The most simple truth is often the product of the most difficult thinking which has triumphed in thus making plain what was previously obscure. Let us see, however, that the clear utterance is a word of the wise; for there is a tendency to accept a saying because of its neat and apt form, without regard to its truth or falseness. Wisdom is therefore needed in understanding proverbs and in "discerning spirits." It is not enough that the grammarian explains the words. Higher wisdom is necessary to see where the isolated truth fits into other truths, by what it is qualified, and how it is to be applied; for it is one of the disadvantages of the proverb that its very terseness gives to it an unnatural isolation, and excludes the addition of counterbalancing truths.

Ver. 7.—*The relation of religion to knowledge.* " The fear of the Lord " being the most common Old Testament name for religion, we must take it here in its large and general sense, and understand that religion in all its relations is set forth as the true basis of knowledge; though it may well be that awe and reverence for the majesty and mystery of God have a special prominence in regard to the pursuit of truth.

I. RELIGION IS AN IMPORTANT REQUISITE FOR THE ACQUISITION OF ALL KINDS OF KNOWLEDGE. Religion—not theology—claims this position. The progress of science was arrested for a thousand years by the claims of theology to dominate all regions of inquiry. Theology, or human speculations about Divine things, is the most difficult, and therefore in many respects the most uncertain, of all the sciences. When the schoolmen made the dogmatic assumptions of patristic theology, combined with elaborate deductions from Aristotelian philosophy, the touchstone of all truth, they set up an impenetrable barrier before the investigation of nature. Even when theological dicta are absolutely true, it is irrelevant to bring these to bear upon physical science. Unquestionably Bacon did a great service to the cause of truth in banishing final causes from the science of nature. But the relation of religion to science is of a totally different nature. That relation consists in the influence that religious experience, religious character, religious feelings and motives, must necessarily have upon scientific research. Religion influences all life; intellectual life is no exception. 1. Religion should *excite the thirst for truth*. It is a mistake to suppose that religion inclines to indolence and ignorance. It inspires all the noblest endeavours. It is on the side of light and truth. Rightly understood, it will impose the pursuit of science as a duty. Without religion this pursuit is too likely to be followed only from mere inclination, or possibly for ends of self-interest. 2. Religion tends *to induce the most wholesome scientific temper*. There is great resemblance between the Christian graces and the special dispositions requisite for the successful discovery of truth. The Sermon on the Mount contains the best possible precepts for the character of the model man of science. Loyalty to truth, unselfishness in sacrificing prejudices and crotchets, justice to the work of rivals, diligence in uninteresting but needful inquiries, patience in waiting for solid results, conscientiousness in refraining from mere sensationalism, humility in confessing the smallness of the area really conquered, calmness and generosity under criticism, are among the most essential requisites for the pursuit of science, and they are among the best fruits of religion. 3. Religion tends *to open the eyes to truth*. It raises us from the gross animalism which is intellectual death. Elevating the whole man, it enlarges the intellect.

II. Religion is the necessary foundation of spiritual knowledge. This fact agrees with the great modern doctrine of inductive philosophy. Experience is the basis of knowledge. To know God we must have personal relations with him. Spiritual truths in regard to human life depend on the same Source. We must do the commandment in order to know the doctrine. Indeed, there is a constant interaction between knowledge and experience—every enlargement of experience increasing our knowledge, and every increment of knowledge throwing light on our way for future experience; till, in consequence of these two processes, we rise, as one has said, by a sort of "spiritual spiral," to the coexistent perfection of knowledge and of character. Our independence upon an external and superhuman revelation for our knowledge of Divine things is no exception to this principle, as two considerations will show. 1. *Revelation was first vouchsafed through religious men*. The fear of God was the beginning of knowledge in the prophets; the love of Christ is its basis in the apostles. Nebuchadnezzar could not have written the prophecies of Isaiah, nor could Judas have written St. John's Gospel. 2. *Revelation can only be understood by religious men*. A bad man may be a good verbal commentator, but the essential truth, the spirit which quickens as distinguished from the "letter that killeth," can only be discerned by those who are in sympathy with it, because "spiritual things are spiritually discerned."

Ver. 10.—*Temptation*. I. How the temptation comes. 1. *From sinners*. (1) It comes from without. The evil of our own hearts inclines us to sin; but were we perfectly innocent we could not escape temptation. The serpent was a denizen of Eden. Christ the Sinless One was tempted. The sights and sounds of the wicked world penetrate to the most carefully guarded soul. (2) The temptation is furnished by those who have themselves succumbed to sin. It is sinners who tempt. Sin is contagious. The worst sin is that of those who, like Jeroboam, "make Israel to sin." The bad man has terrible power for harm. Example, social influence, friendship, favour his designs. 2. *By enticements*. Sin is made to be attractive; and it is most important for all of us to know that there are pleasures in sin, in order that we may not be surprised at the discovery of them. The fruit is palatable, though, like apples of Sodom, it soon turns to ashes. If it were not so, who would run the risk of tasting it? If stolen waters were not sweet, who would choose to wear the brand of a thief on his conscience? Herein is the great power of temptation. By slow degrees and soft inducements the evil is wrought. The subtle serpent succeeds where the roaring lion fails. Delilah conquers the man whom no Philistine warrior could overthrow.

"Devils soonest tempt, resembling spirits of light."

II. How the temptation is to be met. "Consent thou not." Let no man deem himself the helpless victim of temptation. "God is faithful, who will not suffer you to be tempted above that ye are able," etc. (1 Cor. x. 13). We have wills. We can say "Yes" and "No." We are not responsible for meeting with temptation, since even Christ felt the cruel force of this trial, but we are responsible for the way we behave under it.

> "'Tis one thing to be tempted,
> Another thing to fall."

Now, the resistance to temptation must be immediate and thorough. The tempter entices by gentle degrees, but the tempted must resist at once and with decision. He must not begin with the "retort courteous," but with "the lie direct." There is something brusque about the advice, "consent thou not," very different in tone from the polite *enticing* manner of the tempter. Yet this is necessary, for all that is wanted by the tempter is compliance—no active exercise of will, but a passive yielding. The resistance, however, must be active. The greatest danger is in dallying with temptation.

> "Lie in the lap of sin, and not mean harm?
> It is hypocrisy against the devil:
> They that mean virtuously, and yet do so,
> The devil their virtue tempts, and they tempt Heaven."

The difficulty is to give a decided negative. With some people the hardest word to say is "No." Remember: 1. There is a Divine grace to which we can appeal for aid in temptation, and a Saviour who can succour (Heb. ii. 18). 2. We can best keep out sin, not by bare expulsion of the spirit of evil, leaving the soul empty, swept, and garnished, and therefore ready for the advent of worse sins, but by filling our thoughts and affections with pure and worthy objects, by overcoming evil with good.

Vers. 20—23.—*The gospel call.* This cry of Wisdom is a sort of evangel of the Old Testament religion. It is an anticipation of the gracious invitation subsequently put forth by the Christian truth. That, too, is a cry of Wisdom; for is not Christ the "Wisdom of God" (1 Cor. i. 24), and "made unto us Wisdom" (1 Cor. i. 30)? We of the latter times, therefore, may hear in the preaching of Solomon the call of the glorious gospel of the blessed God.

I. THE CHARACTER OF THE CALL. It is a cry, a loud utterance, arresting attention, arousing the thoughtless. Elsewhere we read that wisdom must be sought for like hid treasures (ch. ii. 4), and her most precious gifts are always reserved for diligent inquirers. But before she is found, she calls. Though the choicest blessings of Christ may be pearls to be had only after long search, his call to us is antecedent to our desire to obtain them. God does not wait for us to return to him before he shows a willingness to welcome us. He calls at once in his revelation of truth. It is the duty of Christians to take up and repeat this call, to be heralds of a public truth, not jealous guardians of an esoteric doctrine.

II. THE SCENE OF THE CALL. 1. *Without.* Before the truth can be enjoyed in the heart it must be heard from without. It is not reserved for the initiated. It is declared in the open. 2. *In the streets.* The gospel meets men in their busy lives. The streets and lanes must be scoured to furnish guests for the King's feast. The call is too gracious to contain itself in the conventicle of the elect. Free as the air, it aims to reach all. The faithful preacher of the gospel must seek men in their haunts, not wait till they come to his snug retreat. 3. *In the chief place of concourse.* The gospel courts inquiry, it declares itself in the full light of day, it challenges comparison with all earthly voices. Let us not think that it can only live in conventual seclusion. It boldly claims a place in the busiest life of the world. If it cannot hold its own there, it is worthless. If Christians had more faith in it, they would be less afraid to bring this truth into all possible relations with science, politics, business, recreation. But alas! our ears are dull, and often when the voice of Wisdom is lifted up clear and kindly, it is drowned in the coarse din of worldly commotion.

III. THE PERSONS CALLED. Simple ones, scorners, fools. Divine wisdom is healing wisdom. It is not so much a reward to the wise as instruction for the foolish. Earthly wisdom comes most readily to those who are most advanced. The gospel of Christ seeks the ignorant, the wayward, the fallen.

IV. THE WAY TO RECEIVE THE CALL. "Turn you." It is not enough to hear, we must answer; and to answer is to obey, for the call is an invitation; and to obey is to turn and repent, for the gospel of the holy Christ must be a reproof to sinners. This gospel can be of no avail to us until we come to ourselves, turn our backs on our old life, and arise and go to our Father.

V. The BLESSING PROMISED—the outpouring of the Divine Spirit.   All Divine wisdom is an inspiration.   Christ the Wisdom of God can only be received as we are baptized with the Holy Spirit.   Thus we receive light, love, purity, peace, strength, and eternal life.

Vers. 24—30.—*Left to their doom.*   Broad and encouraging as are the promises of Divine grace, if we forget the darker facts of life we shall be deluded into a false security; for nothing could be more unreasonable than to suppose that the mercy of God takes no account of moral considerations.   Legally our sovereign is vested with an unfettered right of pardoning every criminal, but principles of justice and public order put great restraints upon the exercise of such a right.   Bald representations of prayer as a means for securing immediate deliverance from trouble, and especially as a sure door of escape from the consequences of sin, are as false as they are shallow.   It is most important that we should know under what circumstances God will reject the prayer of his troubled children and leave them to their doom.

I. An OBSTINATE REJECTION OF GOD'S INVITATIONS AND COUNSELS.   No word is here said of the great mass of the heathen world, who have never heard the full declaration of God's will.   Clearly it is implied that such men do not come under the same condemnation as that of the persons immediately referred to.   For the special accusation is based on the rejection of the overtures of grace, which must have been known to have been refused.   The guilt of this rejection may be measured in two directions.   1. *By the character of the Divine voice.*   (1) It was an invitation, not a mere declaration of truth.   " I have called."   (2) It was a persuading.   " I have stretched out my hand."   (3) It was a warning.   " Counsel " and " reproof " are referred to.   The sin was plainly demonstrated, the danger clearly revealed.   To reject such a Divine message is no slight error.   2. *By the character of the rejection itself.*   (1) It was an obstinate refusal.   There was no indecision.   But, practically, not to decide to obey the voice of God is to decide to rebel against him.   (2) It was an insulting indifference.   " No man regarded."   They refused, and went on their own ways, to their farms and merchandise and pleasure, without further thought.

II. A CRY FOR DELIVERANCE FROM TROUBLE WITHOUT REPENTANCE OF SIN.   The simple ingratitude of sin would be no barrier to the full exercise of God's pardon in Christ if it were hated and repented of, for " he is able to save to the uttermost," etc.   But without repentance the smallest sin cannot be forgiven.   And repentance is not the mere feeling of distress at the consequence of sin—every sane and sentient being would have that feeling; nor is it a mere regret that the wrong thing was done now its horrible fruits are ripening.   It must be a hearty abhorrence of the wickedness itself, and a genuine desire to do nothing of the kind in the future.   The dying sinner who is appalled at his future prospects, and shrieks for deliverance from the powers of hell, will not be heard, but will be left to his fate, and most reasonably so, if he has experienced no moral change, and feels no compunctions of conscience, but would do all his vile deeds over again if only he could ensure himself against the just penalties of them.

III. An ATTEMPT TO ESCAPE FROM THE INEVITABLE.   The earthly consequences of sin are many of them fixed immutably by laws of nature.   Prayer will not heal the shattered constitution of the drunkard, nor restore the squandered fortune of the spend-thrift, nor recover the lost reputation of the thief.   No doubt many spiritual consequences of sin are also inevitable, and, though God may pardon the sinner, he will take vengeance on his devices.   But when there is true penitence and trust in the mercy of God, the incidence of the calamity is shifted, though the calamity itself is not altered, so that it comes as wholesome chastisement, and is then not laughed at by the Divine wisdom, but graciously overruled for the discipline of the penitent.

Ver. 31.—*Punishment the natural fruit of sin.*   The punishment of sin is not an arbitrary penalty, but a natural consequence.   It follows by laws of nature.   It needs no executioner.   The sin works out its own doom.   This thought may be regarded from two points of view.   From the standpoint of nature it is a proof that Divine justice does not abrogate, but works through natural laws.   From the spiritual side it is an evidence that God has planted his moral laws in the very constitution of the world.

I. Sin bears fruit. Nothing really perishes. Deeds live on in their consequences. Evil is not simply negative; there is a terribly active and even vital power in it. Its vitality may be of a diseased, destructive order, like that of the cancer that grows and spreads to the death of the body in which it is imbedded; but it is none the less vigorous and enduring.

II. The fruit of sin has a natural affinity to the stock from which it springs. The consequences of a sin have an inherent resemblance to the sin. As the Beatitudes are specially related to the graces they crown, so the curses of evil have close relations to particular forms of evil. Each sin bears its own fruit. Hatred provokes hatred; selfishness leads to isolation; falsehood engenders distrust.

III. The fruit of sin is beyond our control. We are free to sow the seed or to refrain; we are not free to arrest the growth of the tree. A deed once done is not only irretrievable, but it passes out of our power while it lives on to work out perpetual consequences. It may become a Frankenstein, horribly tyrannizing over its creator.

IV. The fruit of sin must be eaten by the sinner. It will come back to him when it is ripe. There may be a long interval between the sowing of the seed and the gathering of the fruit, but the sower will have to devour the harvest. Herein is the peculiar horror of the doom of sin. Though a man would fain forget the past, it returns in the dreadful resemblance it bears to its consequences, now fully developed and revealed in true colours. Nauseous and poisonous, it must not only be witnessed, but eaten. He will have to receive it in his own life, in most close and intimate union with himself.

Conclusion. 1. Let us beware of the thoughtless sowing which must lead to so fearful a harvest. 2. Let us lay hold of the hope of redemption in Christ through which our sins may be buried in the depths of the sea.

Ver. 32.—*Fatal prosperity.* It is certainly not incumbent on the Christian preacher to maintain that prosperity is in itself an evil. This would involve a strange paradox, since it must be confessed that we all desire prosperity by natural instinct, and seek it in some form, and when we have met with it are exhorted to be thankful for it; all of which things would need to be deprecated if prosperity were essentially evil. So far is it from being thus represented in the Bible, that the Old Testament regards it as the reward of righteousness, and the New Testament as less important indeed and more full of danger, yet still as something to be enjoyed gratefully (see 1 Tim. iv. 4). But experience and revelation both warn us that it brings peculiar perils and temptations, and that there are some people to whom it is nothing less than fatal.

I. Consider who are the persons to whom prosperity is most fatal. It does not affect all alike. One man can stand calmly on a steep height where another reels with giddiness. The success which is fatal to one may develop magnanimous qualities in another. It is not all prosperity, but the prosperity of fools, that is destructive. The character of the men rather than the inherent evil of the thing determines its effects. Note some of the characters most injured by prosperity. 1. *The weak,* who are moulded by circumstances instead of mastering them. If a man is not strong enough to direct his course, but suffers himself to drift with the currents of external events, prosperity will lead him away into extravagance and folly. He only is safe under it who is independent of it. 2. *The short-sighted*—men whose views of life are exceptionally limited. These people will be likely to expect too much from prosperity, to forget that riches take to themselves wings and fly away. 3. *The empty-minded.* If people have other resources than external possessions they are the more free to make good use of those possessions. But if they have nothing else, if they have no "inner city of the mind," if their life is all on the outside, prosperity will become a god and the idolatry of it a fatal delusion. 4. *The vicious.* A bad man will find in prosperity only enlarged means for evil-doing, and so will increase his wickedness and bring the greater doom upon his own head. To the intemperate, the profligate, the lovers of corrupt pleasures, prosperity is nothing less than a curse.

II. Consider the way in which prosperity becomes fatal. 1. *It hides folly.* La Bruyère says, "As riches and favour forsake a man, we discover him to be a fool, but nobody could find it out in his prosperity;" and Hare remarks that "nothing hides a blemish so completely as a cloth of gold." But if folly is hidden, it is unchecked, and grows worse and ripens fatally. 2. *It encourages indolence.* Prosperity may afford ample means for generous occupation, but weak and foolish people are more likely to be satisfied with idleness and self-indulgence when they find that all their wants are supplied without any effort on their own part. Then the disuse of faculties leads to the loss of them. Hence, as the pressure of adversity quickens our powers, the relaxation of prosperity tends to a sort of atrophy of them. 3. *It affords opportunity for the exercise of bad qualities.* Many men have tendencies to particular kinds of sin that are checked for want of opportunity. Prosperity will give this with fatal results. 4. *It induces satisfaction with itself.* Thus it quenches the thirst for deeper satisfaction. Lot, prosperous in Sodom, ceases to be a " pilgrim and stranger," and forgets to seek a " better country " till he is roused by the shock that puts an end to his worldly successes.

HOMILIES BY VARIOUS AUTHORS.

Vers. 1—6.—*Design and character of proverbial wisdom.* We may regard the opening words as a general index of the contents, as a designation of the object, and a statement of the value and profit of the teaching, of the book.

I. ITS DESIGN IS TO IMPART PRACTICAL SENSE. 1. And first, this in general includes the information of the understanding and of the memory by wisdom. This Hebrew word (*chôkmâh*) denotes, strictly, all that is *fixed* for human knowledge. We may render it " insight." In other places in the Bible, the judge (1 Kings iii. 28), the artist (Exod. xxviii. 3), or the man of skill and renown in general, are thus said to be men of insight, craft, or cunning, in the original and good sense of those words. Applied to religion and conduct, it means insight into the principles of right conduct, the knowledge of how to walk before God, choosing the right and avoiding the wrong path—the knowledge of the way to peace and blessedness. 2. The training of the will. The word rendered " instruction " denotes moral education or training. Here, then, is the practical side of the matter. Not only sound intelligence is aimed at, but pure feeling, right affections, the will guided by the polar star of duty. All this is general. 3. But next, particulars, falling within this great scope, are pointed out, viz. " the attainment of justice and right and fair dealing." The first is all that pertains to God, the supreme Judge—his eternal order and will. The second refers to established custom and usage among men—to law, in the human sense. The third, an expressive word, signifying literally what is *straight*, points to straightforward, honourable, and noble conduct. 4. But the book has a *special* object in view, and a special class : " To hold out *prudence* to *simple ones*, and *knowledge* and *reflectiveness* to *boys*." Each of these words has its peculiar force. The Hebrew expression for the first class is literally the " open ones," *i.e.* those who in ignorance and inexperience are open to every impression, good or bad ; simple-minded ones (not *fools*, which is another idea), who are readily governed by the opinions and examples of stronger minds. They need that prudence, or caution, which the hints of proverbial sense may supply, to enable them to *glide out of danger* and avoid snares (for the word rendered " subtilty " denotes *smoothness*, like that of the slippery snake). Boys, or youths also, stand in peculiar need of " thoughtfulness "—a habit of reflecting with attention and forethought upon life and different modes of conduct. The Book of Proverbs, all must see, is specially adapted for these classes. But not for them alone. 5. The book is a book for all. The wise man may listen and gain instruction ; for men " grow old, learning something fresh each day." And the intelligent man may obtain guidance. For although by middle life the general principles and maxims of wisdom may have been stored up, still the applications of them, the exceptions to them, form a vast field for ever-growing acquisition. Knowledge is practically infinite ; we can think of no bounds to it. New perplexities continually arise, new cases of conscience present themselves, old temptations revive in fresh combinations ; and the records of others' experience continually flash new light from angles of observation distinct from our own.

II. THE CHARACTER AND VALUE OF THE BOOK. (Ver. 6.) 1. It is a *collection of proverbs.* Condensed wisdom. Landmarks in the field of experience. Beacons of warning from dangerous shores. Objects of interest in life's travel. Finger-posts.

The "wit of many, the wisdom of one." A portable property of the intellect. A currency honoured in every land. "Jewels five words long, that on the outstretch'd forefinger of all time sparkle for ever." They may be compared to darts, to stings, to goads. They arouse the memory, awake the conscience: they fix the floating impressions of truth in forms not easily forgotten. These Bible proverbs are in poetical form; and of them it may well be said, with George Herbert, "A verse finds him who a sermon flies." 2. The mode of speech is often *figurative*. The word rendered "dark s ying" means a profound saying, enigma, "thing hidden" (Matt. xiii. 35; Ps. lxxviii. 2), "obscure allegory" (Augustine). An example of this parabolic way of speaking is found in Agur's discourse (ch. xxx.). The power of it, like the power of pictures and of all sensuous symbols and poetical images, lies in the fact that the form "half reveals and half conceals the soul within," and thus excites the curiosity, fixes the attention, stimulates exertion of thought in the listener. The best preachers leave much for the hearers to fill up for themselves. Suggestive teaching is the richest; it makes the pupil teach himself. Such is the method of our Lord in his parables; but not the only method; to be combined, as with him and here, with the direct mode of statement. The application is: "Take heed how ye hear." "To him that hath it shall be given." All wisdom is of God; the teacher and the disciple are both listeners at the living oracle of eternal truth. Knowledge is essential to religion, and growth belongs to both (Luke xvii. 5; Eph. iv. 15, 16; Col. i. 11; ii. 19; 2 Thess. i. 3; 2 Pet. iii. 18).—J.

Ver. 7.—*Religion the true beginning.* This is the motto of the book. It is often found (ch. ix. 10; Sirach i. 16, 25, 26; Ps. cxi. 10). The Arabs have adopted it at the head of their proverbial collections.

I. THE OLD TESTAMENT DESIGNATION OF RELIGION. It is the *fear of Jehovah.* That is reverence for him who is One, who is eternal, incomparable with any of the gods of the heathen, the Deliverer of Israel in the past and ever, the All-holy, just and merciful One. Such reverence includes practical obedience, trust, gratitude, and love. With this expression we may compare *walking before Jehovah* and the *service of Jehovah*, as designations of the *practical* aspect of religion, as the former indicates the *emotional* and *intellectual*.

II. SUCH RELIGION IS THE TRUE GERM OF SOUND KNOWLEDGE. Men have divorced by a logical abstraction science, and often sense, from religion. But ideally, psychologically, historically, they are in perfect unity. Religion is "the oldest and holiest tradition of our race" (Herder). From it as the beginning the arts and sciences sprang. It is ever so. True science has a religious basis. 1. In both the Infinite is implied and is sought through the finite. 2. Both run up into mystery—science into the unknowable ground or substance behind all phenomena, religion before the inscrutable and unutterable God. 3. The true mood is alike in both, that of profound humility, sincerity, self-abnegation, impassioned love of the truth, the mood of Bacon, of Newton, etc.

III. THE REJECTION OF RELIGION FOLLY. The Hebrew word for "fool" is strong; it is *crass, stupid*, insensible. "A stock, a stone, a worse than senseless thing." Folly is always the reversal of some true attitude of the mind and temper. It is the taking a false measure of self in some relation. It is the conceit of a position purely imaginary —amusing in a child, pathetic in a lunatic, pitiful in a rational man. True wisdom lies in the sense that we have little, in the feeling of constant need of light and direction; extreme folly, in the notion that the man "knows all about it." Most pitiable are learned fools. Without religion, *i.e.* the constant habit of reference to the universal, all knowledge remains partial and shrunk, is tainted with egotism, would reverse the laws of intelligence, and make the universal give way to the particular, instead of lifting the particular to the life of the universal. Beware of the contemptuous tone in books, newspapers, and speakers. Reserve scorn for manifest evil. The way to be looked down upon is to form the habit of looking down on others. To despise any humblest commonplace of sense and wisdom is to brand one's self in the sight of Heaven, and of the wise, a *fool*.—J.

Vers. 8, 9.—*Filial piety.* The teacher speaks under the assumed form of a father, like St. Paul (1 Cor. iv. 15; Philem. 10), to give the more affectionate zest to his appeal. And the word "mother" is brought in by poetical parallelism, enhancing the parental image. We may include the parent and the teacher in one conception. The duty owed to both is analogous. And the teacher may be at the same time the parent.

I. DUTY TO PARENTS AND EARLY TEACHERS COMES NEXT TO DUTY TO GOD. It occupies that place in the Decalogue. Pythagoras and Plato, and the wise of antiquity, generally taught that parents came next to the gods, and were to be honoured even as the gods. The family is the key-stone of society. Parents are the earliest representatives to children of the principle of authority, of "other-will," and, in this sense, of God.

II. THE TRUE PARENT IS THE BEST EARLY TEACHER. 1. He has the fresh mind to deal with, the opportunity of the first word, the early and deepest impression. 2. He is the most sincere of teachers, or has the least temptation to be insincere. His one object is the child's good. 3. He is the most loving. 4. The father and the mother should combine in this work—the father to train the young mind to principle, the mother to inspire pure sentiment. The masculine influence deals with the general, with law and relation in life, with the logic or mathematics of conduct; the feminine, with the particular, with the details of behaviour, with the concrete expression of right thought and feeling. Neither can be dispensed with.

III. REVERENCE FOR PARENTS AND TEACHERS IMPARTS GRACE AND BEAUTY TO THE BEARING. The adoption of their example and instruction is compared, in Oriental illustration, to the wearing of a "pleasant chaplet" on the head (and the necklace of pearls), as at feasts and entertainments—a wreath of roses or other flowers. The former was a general custom of antiquity, both for men and women. We have no exact parallel to it, and must recur to the thought of good or graceful dress in general. What significance, as we all know, is there in dress to make or mar the personal appearance! But the spiritual, not the material "habit" is the best dress, and will set off the most ungainly form. It is natural to wish to appear graceful, and one of the first manifestations of the artistic instinct in humanity is in this attention to dress. Let the instinct, then, have a moral or religious turn, and true beauty be found above all in the moral idea, in the attire of the soul, "the ornament of a meek and quiet spirit, which in the sight of God is of great price." The complimentary deferences to one another in polite society, the slight submissions in word and deed, the trifling self-abnegations which give a transient perfume and refinement to social hours,—all these do but mimic or represent something of more permanent value, the principle of obedience, the will governed by law, the character formed by the true, which is also the good and the beautiful.—J.

Vers. 10—19.—*Warnings against the evils of the time.* An unsettled time, one of violence and insecurity of life, appears to be indicated, such as has only its occasional parallel in our society. Yet the perverted impulses which lead to open crime are those which induce every species of dishonesty and more subtle attacks upon the life or property of others. We may thus draw from a particular description some general lessons. But it seems to give more point and force to the passage if we view it as attaching to notorious and frequent forms of crime.

I. THE TEMPTER. He is always existing in every state of society, and not hard to find. There are human beings who have come to adopt evil as a trade, and, not content with practising it themselves, must have help and sympathy in their work, and turn recruiting-sergeants for the devil. The beautiful laws of our being assert themselves amidst all the perversion of depraved choice. Crime, like sorrow, is lonely, and craves partnership. Remorse would soothe itself by fixing the like sting in the bosoms of others. And the criminal, constantly on his defence against society, learns to acquire an allurement of manner which is not the least of his dangerous qualities. The warning to youth against "enticing sinners" of both sexes can never be obsolete. Beware of persons of "peculiarly fascinating manners." What is it that fascinates? Generally it will be found to be some species of flattery, overt or concealed, attacking the weak point of the tempted ones. The warning may be so far generalized into "Beware of the flatterer." Flattery is at the bottom of most temptation.

II. PICTURES OF CRIME. 1. *Its aspect of horror.* They are to be understood as drawn by the teacher's hand. He is putting the *real meaning* of the tempter's suggestions into vivid descriptions. The tempter himself will take care not to expose the bloody and hideous aspect of his trade.

> "Vice is a monster of so hideous mien,
> That to be hated needs but to be seen."

On such a principle the teacher acts. The veil is torn aside from the life of crime, and its repulsive inhumanity disclosed. It is a "lurking for blood," after the image of the hunter with nets and nooses, watching for his prey. And this too for "the vainly innocent," *i.e.* whose innocence will avail him nothing with us (comp. Ps. xxxv. 19; lxix. 5; Lam. iii. 52), or, in the other interpretation, for the innocent who has given us no cause for hatred or revenge. "Will swallow them up living like the pit [or, 'abyss']." An expression for sudden death as opposed to that by lingering sickness—the earth as it were yawning from its abysses to devour the fated lives (comp. Ps. cxxiv. 3; ch. xxx. 16). The expression *whole*, whether it denotes sound in body or in character (honest men), adds to the force of the description. 2. But there is an *attractive aspect* in crime. "Thou shalt cast thy lot into our midst," *i.e.* shalt share and share alike with us, as we say, or take an equal chance for the best of the booty, the lot in such cases being the custom of robbers and of soldiers (Ps. xxii. 19; Neh. x. 35). There is freedom, communism, good-fellowship, in the life of the banditti; no distinction of rank or class, poor or rich. In certain times the picture of such a life has proved of overwhelming fascination for young adventurous spirits. In solemn reiterated warning the teacher raises his voice against the treading of their path and way. This simple biblical figure may remind us that every mode of active life, every profession or occupation, is like a path; it *leads somewhither*. Unless we could cease from activity, we must all be advancing to some moral issue. What will it be? 3. *A summary description of the criminal.* He runs toward wickedness, hastes to shed blood. The eagerness, the swiftness, and perseverance of the criminal often arouse intellectual admiration, and shame the slothfulness of those who follow noble callings. But the devotion of ability and energy of a high order to such ends is, indeed, one of the most striking proofs we can have of the corruption of man's nature. This is crime revealed in its hatefulness, on the one hand, by its cruel and inhuman conduct and effects; on the other, in its dark source, the utter perversion of the criminal's mind itself.

III. THE RECOIL OF EVIL ON THE DOERS. Here again are powerful pictures. Like thoughtless birds, which rush with open eyes into the net, so do these miscreants, in preparing destruction for others, themselves run headlong upon their fate (comp. Job xviii. 8). While they are lurking for others' blood and laying snares for others' lives, their own are forfeited. This self-defeat of wickedness is a central thought in biblical wisdom (comp. ch. xv. 32; xvi. 27; Eccles. x. 8; Ps. vii. 16; Rom. ii. 5; Gal. vi. 8; 1 Tim. vi. 9, 10; Jas. v. 3—5). Thus wisdom and folly form an antithesis in their nature, their powers, and their result. 1. Wisdom is at one with religion and morality; folly casts off God and right. 2. Wisdom pursues good ends by good means; folly pursues evil by evil means. 3. The result of wisdom is life and blessedness, health and peace; that of folly is self-undermining, self-overthrow, or "slow suicide."

III. THE ROOT OF CRIME. It is like that of all sin, in desire, in misdirected desire, the greed of "unlawful gain," to give the fuller force of the expression. Note: 1. The *prevalence* of this passion. By far the largest proportion of men's worst actions are probably to be traced to it. Read the reports of the courts of law, listen to the gossip of the hour for illustrations. 2. Its *intoxicating, illusory* power. The victim of it deceives himself, as in other passions: it is thrift, it is due regard to what is of substantial value to one's interests, etc. And how difficult to distinguish that desire for more, which is the spring of action in commerce as in honourable ambition, the pursuit of knowledge, etc.! The question must be carried to the conscience and to God. 3. Its *unsocial* character. More than any passion, it separates man from his kind, and assimilates him to the beast of prey. 4. Its *suicidal* effect. If it does not destroy the man's body, it certainly corrodes and eats away his soul. It dehumanizes him. There is no object more shadowy in one aspect, more unreal, in another more monstrous, than the miser, as depicted by Balzac and other great writers. Covetousness is self-slaughter.—J.

Vers. 20—33.—*Warning cry of Wisdom.* In dramatic style, Wisdom is presentiated, personified, endued with visible and audible attributes. As contempt for religion has been animadverted upon, so now contempt for Wisdom calls for rebuke. The motto (ver. 7) is still in the preacher's mind.

I. THE CRY OF WISDOM IS PUBLIC AND CLEAR. In the street, "where merchants most do congregate," and in all places of general resort, the cry is heard. Hers is no esoteric doctrine; it is popularly exoteric, it is for all. She has no concealments. She is not ashamed of her message. She seeks the weal of each and of all. Like her Divine embodiment, she is the Friend of the simple and the meek, yea, of the fools and the sinners (Matt. x. 27; Luke xiv. 21). It is a voice to be heard above the mingled sounds of these thronged centres. The state of the markets and of the weather, passing events, the gossip of the hour, news of success and of failure, all have a moral meaning, run up into moral calculations, may be reduced to expressions of moral law.

II. HER TONE. 1. It is *commanding and superior.* She appeals to different classes of the frivolous, the free-thinking, the scoffers of the time. The times of Solomon, as pointed out by Delitzsch, were times of widespread worldliness and religious indifference. The *lēzim,* or "scorners," must have been a numerous class. They scoffed at sacred things, laid claim to superior sense (ch. xiv. 6), were contentious and full of debate (ch. xxii. 10). They avoided the *chakanim,* or "wise men," and hence received the name of scoffers or mockers. They were like our modern free-thinkers, and have left their clear traces on the biblical page. The "wise men" were a kind of practical philosophers, not a professional class, but belonging to different callings. Religion and worship have never been exempt from criticism, have in every age been exposed to that "ridicule which is the test of truth." In these conflicts the tone of truth is ever commanding, conscious of authority, calm; that of the scoffer irritable and wanting in weight. Wisdom is commanding, because she holds the conscience. She bandies no arguments with the scoffer, who will only find in them fuel for his contentious spirit; she aims directly at the conscience, accuses and judges the perverted heart. "Turn at my denunciation" from your evil ways! "I will cause my Spirit to stream forth upon you." 2. Her tone is *hortatory* and *promising.* The Spirit of wisdom is compared to a mighty, forth-bubbling, never-exhausted fountain. So Christ cried in the last great day of the feast in Jerusalem, "If any man thirst, let him come unto me, and drink." (1) There is a rich *fulness* in having wisdom, in contrast to which are the dry negations which are all the scoffer has to offer. (2) It is a refreshing and a strengthening supply. It is not pedantry, the wisdom of words, nor abstract science of logic and metaphysics, but vital truth, the knowledge of facts and laws of the inner and outer world, which we need for everyday consumption, for the life of the mind. (3) Its impartation is conditioned by the will of the recipient. There must be the turning and the seeking, that there may be the finding and the enjoying of it; the opening of the mouth before it can be filled. 3. Her tone is *threatening and prophetic* of retribution. The day of grace is now conceived as past, the hour gone that will not return. She has called, has stretched out the hand, in token of pleading for attention, has lavished both counsel and rebuke; but has been responded to by sullen refusal, averted looks, scornful depreciation, obstinate resistance. This relation of forbearance and good will has been strained to the last degree; in the law of things it must be succeeded by a reaction. The places will be reversed. The scoffer will be the scoffed; the mocker will afford material for mirth. And here the pictures accumulate their dread impression on the imagination; the tempest and the tempest-whirlwind answer in nature to the calamity and the horror, the anguish and constraint, of the faithless soul. All moral teaching carries in it a twofold prophetic element; a prophecy of penal *retribution* and a prophecy of *blessed recompense.* Retribution is the logical consequence of certain acts; and it involves a *correspondence.* The relation which has been wrongly denied comes in the end to be affirmed; and that which was affirmed, to be in the end denied. The manner of the sin foretells the manner of the penalty. Those who turned from pleading Wisdom, plead in the end with her in vain; seeking her now with zeal ("early"), their

search is vain. The attitude which the soul refused to assume in its pride, it is forced
into by its distress. The wheel comes full circle; the sinner is smitten in the very
place of his sin; and outraged conscience is avenged. 4. Above all, the tone of
Wisdom is *reasonable*. These are no arbitrary, cruel, capricious dealings with the
sinner. They rest upon the *law of things* (vers. 29—31). "*Because* they hated reasonable doctrine, and coveted not the fear of Jehovah, fared not on the way of my counsel,
and despised all my rebuke; *therefore* they shall eat of the fruit of their way, and be
satiated with their counsels!" It is the law of causality applied to moral things.
"The curse *causeless* shall not come!" The most obvious example of the law of cause
and effect in nature—the connection of seed and crop, sowing and reaping—best illustrates the process in the human spirit. We cannot deceive God, cannot evade law;
whatsoever we sow, we must reap, and that according to *quantity*, to *kind* or *quality*.
Again, the figure of a *surfeit* is forcible as applied to this experience of the consequences
of guilt. We find it also in Isa. iii. 10; Ps. lxxxviii. 4; cxxiii. 4. It brings out the
principle that all spurious pleasures, *i.e.* those which are rooted only in egotism, *cloy*,
and so turn the man against himself. Self-loathing, self-contempt, is the deep revelation of an inner judgment. If any one asks with the anger of the atheistic poet, "Who
made self-contempt?" let him turn to this passage for an answer. 5. Wisdom is
declarative of moral laws. The *turning away*, the resistance and recalcitrancy of the
simple, murders them (Jer. viii. 5; Hos. xi. 5), and the *security* (idle, easy, fleshly
carelessness, Jer. xxii. 21) destroys them.

> "More the treacherous calm I dread
> Than tempests sailing overhead."

(See South's powerful sermon, with his usual splendid illustrations, on "Prosperity
ever dangerous to Virtue," vol. ii. ser. vi.) 6. She is *prophetic of good* to the obedient.
In bright contrast to the spurious peace of the dulled conscience is the true peace of
the wise and God-fearing, "He who listens to me shall dwell securely, and have rest
without terror of calamity." It is like that of ordered nature—"central peace abiding
at the heart of endless agitation." In this profound union with God, the parables of
life are but superficial and transient as the waves of ocean, while the depths are calm
as eternity. The method of personified Wisdom is that of Christ, with which it may
be compared at every point. (1) Sin is clearly exposed, in its effects and its cause. (2)
Judgment is clearly announced. (3) Promises of eternal good are no less emphatically
given. (4) Refuge from evil, and the way of salvation both temporal and eternal, are
pointed out.—J.

Vers. 1—6.—*The ideal teacher.* Solomon had all possible advantages to qualify him
for the work of a teacher of men. He had (1) special endowments from the hand of
his Creator (1 Kings iii.); (2) a heritage of rich experience from the life of his father,
beside parental counsels from his lips; (3) the best instruction which the kingdom
could afford, and surely there must have been much wisdom to learn from so wise and
faithful a teacher as the Prophet Nathan (2 Sam. xii.). Who, then, should be so well
able as he was to give us the ideal of a true teacher? We are reminded by these
verses that he is the man who—
I. IS AFFECTED BY THE PRESENCE OF IGNORANCE AND ERROR. He notices the
"simple" man and the "young man" (ver. 4); he has regard to the fact that there
are those about him who need to be led into the paths of "justice and judgment and
equity" (ver. 3). His eye rests on these; his mind perceives how urgently they need
the "instruction" and "understanding" which will save them from the perils to
which they are exposed; his heart goes out to them; his sympathies embrace them;
he desires "to give subtilty to the simple, to the young man knowledge and discretion." He is, therefore, the man who—
II. CONVEYS KNOWLEDGE. 1. He seeks to impart a knowledge of *facts*; to give
"instruction" (ver. 2); to make known to the simple-minded and inexperienced the
truth that "all is not gold that glitters," that men are often very different from that
which they seem to be, that under a fair exterior there may lurk uttermost corruption,
that the sweetest morsels may be the introduction to bitterest consequences, etc. 2.
He seeks also to convey a knowledge of *principles;* to give "understanding;" to make

plain to the mind distinctions between that which is true and that which is false, that which is honourable and that which is shameful, that which elevates and that which lowers, that which is permissible and that which is desirable. He is, further, the man who—

III. IMPARTS WISDOM. He will not be content until he has instilled into the mind and introduced to the heart discretion (ver. 4) and wisdom itself (ver. 2). Wisdom is the pursuit of the highest end by the surest means. No teacher of men who recognizes his true position will ever be contented until he has led his disciples to walk in the path of wisdom—to be seeking after the noblest ends for which God gave us our being, and to be seeking them by those ways which are sure to lead thereto. 1. Our highest wisdom is to seek " the kingdom of God, and his righteousness" (Matt. vi. 33). 2. Our one " Way " is the Son of God himself (John xiv. 6). The true teacher thus becomes the man who—

IV. CONDUCTS TO MORAL EXCELLENCE. For he who is the child of wisdom will also receive the instruction of "justice and judgment and equity." He will be a man who will have continual regard to the claims of his fellow-men; who will shrink from encroaching on their rights; who will endeavour to give to them the consideration, the care, the kindness, which they may rightly look for as children of the same Father, as disciples of the same Saviour, as citizens of the same kingdom, as travellers to the same home. The ideal teacher will also be a man who—

V. FOSTERS INTELLECTUAL GROWTH. (Vers. 5, 6.) We ourselves are not truly and satisfactorily progressing except our mental capacities are being developed, and thus truth and wisdom are being seen with clearer eye and held with tighter grasp. The wise man is therefore bent on training, exercising, bracing the intellectual faculties of his disciple, so that he " will increase learning," will " attain to wise counsels," will think out and see through the proverbs and problems, the puzzles and perplexities, which come up for investigation. We know something in order that we may know much. We are wise that we may become wiser. We climb the first slope of the hill of heavenly truth that we may ascend the one which is beyond; we master the " deep things of God " that we may look into those which are deeper and darker still. Ours is ever to be the spirit of holy inquiry; not of querulous impatience, but of patient, untiring effort to understand all those truths which are within our reach, waiting for the fuller revelation of the days which are to come.—C.

Ver. 7.—*The foundation-truth.* These words invite our attention to—

I. THAT WHICH CONSTITUTES THE FEAR OF GOD. " The fear of the Lord" was the chief note of Hebrew piety. It expressed itself in that form (see Gen. xlii. 18; Exod. xviii. 21; Lev. xix. 14; Neh. v. 15; Ps. lxvi. 16; Eccles. xii. 13, etc.). What did it signify? Evidently something more and other than mere dread. The piety of the Jews was an immeasurably higher thing than the abject terror with which the heathen shrank from the capricious and malignant power of the deities they worshipped. It included: 1. Reverence for his Divine nature. 2. Sense of the Divine presence: "The Lord before whom I stand." 3. Regard for the Divine will, shown in the two ways of (1) obedience to his commands, and (2) submission to his appointments.

II. THE FACT THAT THE FEAR OF GOD CONSTITUTES THE FOUNDATION ON WHICH WE BUILD. " The fear of the Lord is *the beginning* of knowledge." The sense of God, the belief that he is, that he reigns, that he is the Source and Fountain of all life and blessing—this is the foundation on which all wisdom, all success, all excellency, rests. How truly fundamental is this fear of God is seen when we consider : 1. That it is implanted, as one of the earliest thoughts, in the human mind. The very little child can entertain it; it enters his opening mind with the first conceptions which are cherished there. As soon as we begin to think we begin to fear God. That sentiment, which never once affected the life of the most intelligent of the brute creation in any land or age, strikes deep root and bears fairest fruit in the spiritual nature of the " little child." " The fear of the Lord is the beginning of knowledge," even *in time.* 2. That the acceptance of God is the basis on which all truth must rest. There are mysteries in theism which may baffle and sometimes perplex us. But in atheism we are utterly at sea. Not to start from the acceptance of an originating, designing, fashioning, controlling, out-working Intelligence is to be " all abroad " in the region of human investigation and inquiry. Accepting that, the universe is indeed mysterious, but it is not an all-shrouding mist in which we ourselves and everything around us are hopelessly lost. The fear of the Lord, the reverent acceptance of the truth that God is, and that he reigns, lies at the foundation, is the beginning, of knowledge—of the truth which makes the world comprehensible to the understanding, and life valuable to the soul. 3. That the fear of God is the ground of all heavenly wisdom. We cannot know our own Divine Father, our own spiritual nature with all its high and ennobling capacities, the excellency of moral and spiritual worth, the supreme blessedness of self-surrender, if we do not know God, if we have not the mind of Christ revealed to us and accepted by us. The fear of the Lord is the beginning, and is the very substance of that knowledge which constitutes the "life eternal" (John xvii. 3).

III. THE FOLLY OF SPIRITUAL INDIFFERENCE. "Fools despise wisdom and instruction." The foolish man does not care even *to begin* to know; he despises the very elements of instruction; he will not take the first step in the path of wisdom. He wanders off at his own will, and he goes in the direction of the thick darkness. He is turning from him who is the Light of life, and is travelling to that dreary region where it is always night, away from God, from wisdom, from holiness, from love.—C.

Vers. 8, 9.—*The duty and the beauty of filial piety.* The wise teacher here commends to us the excellency of the filial spirit. And it is worthy of notice that he exhorts the young to be obedient to their mother as well as mindful of the counsels of their father. We think of—

I. THE DUTY OF FILIAL PIETY, based upon and arising from: 1. The relation itself. It is enough that our parents *are* our parents, and that we are their offspring. On that simple ground it behoves us to listen and to obey. 2. The fact that they have expended on us far more than any other beings. Who shall measure the thought, the anxiety, the solicitude, the prayers, the labours, the sacrifices, which they have cheerfully devoted to us? 3. The fact that it is the will of God that we should render such filial honour (Exod. xx. 12; Lev. xix. 3; Deut. v. 16; Eph. vi. 2).

II. THE BEAUTY OF FILIAL PIETY. "They shall be an ornament of grace unto thy head, and chains about thy neck" (ver. 9). Youth, especially young manhood, is apt to think that there is something unbecoming, ungraceful if not disgraceful, in rendering filial obedience; it is apt to imagine that there is something admirable in breaking away, in even early years, from parental guidance, and establishing an independence of judgment and action. In truth, there is nothing more offensive, nothing morally uglier, than such premature assertiveness. On the other hand, nothing is more comely, nothing more attractive, nothing more intrinsically beautiful, than filial devotedness. It has all the best elements of spiritual excellency: (1) humility, a lowly view of ourselves; (2) responsiveness to strong and tender love; (3) the recognition of real worth, of the claims of age and wisdom; (4) cheerful acceptance of the ordination of nature, and acquiescence in the will of God. Those who illustrate the duty of filial piety live in the admiration of the wise, and walk in the sunshine of the smile of the Supreme.—C.

Vers. 10—19.—*The peril and the wisdom of youth: a sermon to the young.* How many human lives are nothing better than failures! How many souls are there that "make shipwreck of faith and a good conscience"! Over how many of the children of men do the wise and the holy mourn, as those who might have done well and wrought good, but who have turned aside to folly, guilt, and ruin! As a rule, these have gone astray in their younger days. Temptation assailed them when they were comparatively unarmed, attacked them when least prepared to resist, and they were overcome. Our text suggests—

I. THE PECULIAR PERIL OF YOUTH. Youth is endangered by three things. 1. The invitations of the unholy. "Sinners entice it." Companionship is dear to the young, and is very powerful over it. Its heart is open, trustful, responsive. It rejoices with a keen delight in the confidences of friendship. And when one whose advances have been received, and who has been welcomed as a congenial companion, says, "Come," it is hard for friendship to refuse; this more especially when the solicitation comes from him who has a strong will or an amiable and fascinating disposition. The heart of youth is very powerfully drawn, sometimes to good, but too often to evil, by the charm of early friendship. 2. *The subtlety of sin* (ver. 17). Sin makes a very fair promise, but its word is false, its coin is counterfeit. (1) It professes disinterestedness (ver. 14), but it is utterly selfish at heart. (2) It affects to be able to hide all traces and elude all evil consequences of its acts (ver. 12), but it cannot: the blood which it sheds will cry to Heaven for retribution. (3) It offers gain and satisfaction (vers. 13, 19), but it constantly fails to secure its immediate object, and it never brings real and lasting joy to the soul. The fowler does not spread the net in sight of the bird, or he would fail. Sin keeps its snares well out of view; it proceeds with cruel cunning; it shows the present pleasure, and hides the coming shame, and so it secures its victims. 3. *The appeal of powerful instincts.* The love of daring exploits has led many a young man to consent when sinners have said, "Come, let us attack the victim, that we may seize the prey" (vers. 11, 12). Guilty violence shapes itself as manly daring. And the instinct of acquisition, the desire to obtain and to possess (vers. 13, 19), often leads astray. Greediness of gain begins in a desire to be rich, an ambition to have abundance.

II. THE EARNEST SOLICITUDE OF THE WISE. There is an air of earnestness, a tone of deep solemnity, about these words of the wise man. " My son, if sinners entice thee," etc. (ver. 10); "My son, walk not thou in the way," etc. (ver. 15). Here is the urgency of a tender solicitude; here are the pleadings of profound affection. And why? Because the wise man (the father, minister, teacher) knows; 1. That sin means ruin to others (ver. 16). The path of evil is marked with blood: it is the track which is trodden by death itself; it is red with the blood of souls. 2. That sin is the supreme mistake. It is really laying wait for itself, to compass its own miserable end (ver. 18); it is robbing itself of all the excellency of life in order to secure its gains (ver. 19). Men too often " lose their life for the sake of the means of living." They expend on the means all those resources of their manhood which should be devoted to life itself. Sin is suicidal; the young who are yielding themselves to a life of ungodliness and guilt may well be the object of the most fervent anxiety, of the most tender, tearful pity of the wise.

III. THE WAY OF VICTORY. And there is no other way than that of decisive refusal at once. As soon as the alluring voice says, " Come," let the resolute reply be heard, " I will not." Let the lips of holy resentment open at once to say, " Depart from me, ye evil-doers; I will keep the commandments of my God" (Ps. cxix. 115). To hesitate is to risk everything. Speak a strong, unwavering refusal on the spot.—C.

Vers. 20—23.—*The voice of Wisdom.* Wisdom is here personified; it is the language of poetic inspiration. Later on, " in the dispensation of the fulness of times," Wisdom was manifested in human form, and spake in the hearing of men. But its voice has never been silent altogether, from the beginning until now. We are reminded of it—

I. THAT THERE ARE MANY CHANNELS THROUGH WHICH WISDOM UTTERS ITS VOICE. The plural form of the word ("wisdoms") suggests the manifoldness of the utterance. God teaches us his truth, makes known his mind to us, through (1) the objects and laws of the physical world around us; (2) the constitution of our own frame; (3) the teachings of our own spiritual nature, the judgments of our conscience and the conclusions of our reason; (4) his providential orderings; (5) the admonitions of his Spirit; (6) the words of Jesus Christ: he is *the* " Wisdom of God" (1 Cor. i. 24).

II. THAT THE VOICE OF WISDOM IS AUDIBLE TO ALL WHO WILL LISTEN. "Wisdom crieth without; she utters her voice in the streets: she crieth in the chief place of concourse," etc. (vers. 20, 21). Wisdom, Divine truth, does not merely whisper its doctrine in secret places where there are few to hear; she does not reserve her teaching to the closed class-room to which only some favoured ones find admittance; she speaks " in the open," where the " ways meet," in " the chief places of concourse." " Upon whom doth not God's light arise?" (Job xxv. 3). The friendly voices speak in the ear of childhood; they address the mind of youth; they have a message for manhood; they find their way to the sanctuary of age. Wisdom waits upon the pure and holy, walks by the side of spiritual indifference to win its ear, and confronts sin in its most secret haunts. Nothing—or nothing but the most hardened iniquity which calls evil good and good evil—can shut its doors so fast that the monitory voice cannot enter the chambers of the soul.

III. THAT WISDOM SPEAKS WITH A HOLY AND LOVING ENERGY. Wisdom "crieth," "utters her voice in the streets." There is an energy and an urgency in her tones and in her language (vers. 22, 23). The utterance of Wisdom is none other than the voice of God. It is our Father who pleads with us; it is our Saviour who calls to us; it is our Divine Friend who implores us. It is no hard voice as of a court doomster that assaults us; it is the pleading, plaintive, pathetic voice of One who loves us with fatherly affection, and yearns over us with more than motherly solicitude, that arrests us in our course and touches the tender and sacred feelings of our heart.

IV. THAT WISDOM SPARES NOT TO TELL US EXACTLY WHAT WE ARE. She does not mince her words; she does not cut away the knots of the cord with which we are to be stirred to newness of life. She calls men simpletons, scorners, fools, and upbraids them for their stupidity and their folly (ver. 22). When we listen to the voices which are from above we must expect plain speaking. We must not start back with offence if we find ourselves condemned in strong terms. "Thou art the man!" follows the narrative which transfixes the cruel and heartless robber of his neighbour's all. "Ye fools and blind!" said the Wisdom of God, as he rebuked the hypocrisy of his day. We are not to be repelled from, but attracted to, the man who, speaking for the only wise God, puts sacred truth into the strongest and even the sternest language.

V. THAT WISDOM SEEKS TO IMPART ITS OWN SPIRIT TO ITS DISCIPLES. "Behold, I will pour out my Spirit unto you" (ver. 23). Its aim is spiritual and beneficent. God wounds only that he may heal. He sends "poverty of spirit" that he may thereby make rich for evermore. He humbles that he may exalt. His one desire is to make us like himself; to put his own Spirit within us, that we may be "the children of our Father who is in heaven."—C.

Vers. 24—33.—*The Divine ultimatum.* There is something which is fearful and appalling in these verses. We are ready to tremble as we read them. We are ready to exclaim, "How far may human perversity, and Divine retribution go!" With hushed voice, with subdued spirit, as those before whose eyes the lightnings of heaven are flashing, we consider the significance of the words. But first we see—

I. THAT GOD MAKES MANY APPEALS TO THE HUMAN SOUL. He calls, and we refuse; he stretches out his hands, and no man regards (ver. 24). He multiplies his counsel and his reproof (vers. 25 and 30). Thus his statement is sustained by his dealings with us; he gives us the repeated and manifold admonitions of our own conscience, of the home, of the sanctuary, of friendship, of his Word, of his Spirit, etc.

II. THAT HUMAN PERVERSITY GOES AS FAR AS THE DIVINE PATIENCE. Man "refuses," "regards not" (turns away his eyes, closes his ears), "sets at nought," "will not have," "hates," does not choose (deliberately rejects), all the counsel of God. Perhaps the course of human perversity may be thus traced: first temporizing, with the idea of submitting; then postponing, without any such intention; then disregarding, hearing without heeding; then positively disliking and getting away from; then actually hating, cherishing a feeling of rebellious aversion, ending in mockery and scorn. So far may human perversity go. God's wonderful patience in seeking to win is extended far, but not further than human opposition and resistance. To every "Come" from Heaven there is an answer, "I will not," in the human spirit.

III. THAT GOD FINALLY ABANDONS SIN TO ITS DOOM. We must, of course, understand the language of vers. 26, 27 as highly figurative. No proverb is to be pressed to its fullest possible meaning. The author always assumes that it will be applied with intelligence and discrimination. This is the language of hyperbole. No one could for a moment believe that the eternal Father of our spirits would, literally and actually, laugh and mock at our calamity and alarm. The significance of the passage is that, after a certain point of perverse refusal has been past, God no longer pleads and strives with his wayward children. He interposes no further between a man and the consequences of his folly. He "leaves him alone" (Hos. iv. 17). He "gives him up" (Acts vii. 42; Rom. i. 26). He permits sin to do its own sad work in the soul, and to produce its own natural results in the life; he removes his restraining hand, and suffers them "to eat of the fruit of their own way, and be filled with their own devices" (ver. 31). This *is* the end of impenitence. We see it only too often illustrated before our eyes. Men act as if they might defy their Maker, as if they might draw indefinitely on the patience of their Divine Saviour, as if they might reckon on the unlimited striving of the Holy Spirit. They are wrong; they make a fatal mistake; they commit the one unpardonable sin! They try to go beyond the Divine ultimatum. God's marvellous patience reaches far, but it has its bounds. When these are passed his voice is still, his hand is taken down, his interposing influence is withdrawn. Sin must bear its penalty. But this awful passage closes with a word of hope. Let us turn to a brighter aspect, and see—

IV. THAT SO LONG AS MAN HONESTLY DESIRES GOD'S SERVICE, HE MAY FIND PEACE AND REST. (Ver. 33.) If at any time it is in our heart to obey the voice of the All-wise, to lend an attentive ear to the Divine counsel, we may reckon on his grace and favour. Happy the heart that heeds the voice of Wisdom! Others may be rocked and tossed on the heaving billows of care and anxiety, of alarm and dread; but he, " dwelling in the secret place of the Most High," hiding in the Rock of his salvation, shall " dwell safely, and be quiet from fear of evil." God will hide him in his pavilion ; he will " rest in the Lord."—C.

Ver. 32.—" *The prosperity of fools.*" " The prosperity of fools shall destroy them." Few men fear prosperity ; but if they had enough wisdom to know their own weakness, they would see that there was nothing which they had so much reason to dread. We approach the truth of the text by seeing—

I. THAT IT IS IN OUR HUMAN NATURE TO ASPIRE TO PROSPERITY AND TO STRIVE AFTER IT. The Author of our nature has made us hunger for success as the food of the soul.

II. THAT THE PROSPERITY OF THE WISE IS AN EMINENTLY DESIRABLE THING. For it (1) will do them no harm, and (2) will multiply their influence for good.

III. THAT THE PROSPERITY OF THE FOOLISH IS A CALAMITOUS THING. 1. It results in ruin to other people—often their temporal, still more often their spiritual, ruin. 2. It ends in their own destruction. It leads down to death ; for : (1) It fosters pride, and " pride comes before a fall." (2) It ministers to passion, and passion conducts to the grave in every sense. (3) It induces worldliness, and the man who loses himself in the cares, engagements, and excitements of the world is " dead while he lives."

The conclusion of the matter is this : 1. Let those to whom God has denied prosperity cheerfully accept their lowliness. In their humble position they are comparatively safe. They live where many arrows of destruction do not fly. 2. Let those who have attained prosperity ever recognize that the post of honour and of power is the place of danger, and that they need peculiar grace from God that they may not fall. 3. Let those who are being injured by their prosperity beware lest they go down fast to utter and irretrievable ruin.—C.

EXPOSITION.

CHAPTER II.

Vers. 1—22.—3. *Third admonitory discourse, pointing out the benefits which arise from a sincere, earnest, and persevering search after Wisdom.* This discourse divides itself into three parts. (1) Vers. 1—9 : a statement of the conditions which, if fulfilled, result in the highest knowledge of Jehovah —the fear of Jehovah and the knowledge of God, who is the Source of wisdom and the Protection and Ensurer of safety to the righteous. (2) Vers. 10—19 : the negatively beneficial results of Wisdom, in delivery from the paths of evil, from destructive lusts and passions, from the temptations of wicked

men and wicked women. (3) Vers. 20—22 : the epilogue, or conclusion, combining encouragement on the one hand, and warning on the other.

Ver. 1.—The teacher here reverts to the original form of his address, as appears from the employment of the term, **my son.** It seems clear that it is no longer Wisdom personified who is the speaker, from the fact that the words, " wisdom and understanding " in ver. 2 are used without the possessive pronoun " my," which would have been undoubtedly inserted if this address had been a continuation of the discourse in the preceding chapter. Some of the ideas of that address, however, are restated, as the crying and lifting up the voice after Wisdom, and the conclusion, wherein the respective destinies of the pious and wicked are portrayed. The particle "if" (אִם) is conditional, and serves to introduce the series of clauses (vers. 1—4) which lay down the conditions upon which the promises depend, and which form the protasis to the double apodosis in vers. 5 and 9. De Wette, Meyer, and Delitzsch regard it as voluntative, as expressing a wish on the part of the teacher, and translate, "Oh that thou wouldst!" and אִם, "if," is used in this way in Ps. cxxxix. 19; but the LXX. (ἐάν) and Vulgate (si) make it conditional. It is repeated in an emphatic form in ver. 3. **Receive.** The verbs "receive" and "hide" show that the endeavour after Wisdom is to be candid and sincere. "To receive" (לָקַח) seems to be here used, like the LXX. δεχέσθαι, in the sense of "to receive graciously," "to admit the words of Wisdom." It is noticeable that there is a gradation in emphasis in the various terms here used by the teacher. Just as "commandments" is stronger than "words," so "hide" is stronger than "receive." The emphasizing is carried on in the following verses in the same way, and at length culminates in ver. 4, which sums up the ardent spirit in which the search after Wisdom is to be prosecuted in presenting it to us in its strongest form. **Hide.** The original (צָפַן, tsaphan) is here used in a different sense to that in which it occurs in ch. i. 11 and 18. It here refers, as in ch. vii. 1; x. 14; and xiii. 22, to the storing or laying up, as of treasure, in some secret repository, and means "to lay up." The Divine commands of the teacher are to be hidden in safe custody in the memory, in the understanding, in the conscience, and in the heart (cf. ch. iv. 21; vii. 1). The psalmist expresses the same idea in Ps. cxix. 11, "Thy words have I *hid* in my heart, that I might not sin against thee."

Ver. 2.—This verse is dependent on the preceding. **So that thou incline.** The literal translation is "to incline;" but the inclination of the ear and the application of the heart follow as a consequence upon the preceding ideas (cf. the Vulgate, *ut audiat sapientiam auris tua*). The root-idea of the original (קָשַׁב, kashav) is "to sharpen," viz. the ear as expressed, and so to give diligent attention to the precepts of Wisdom. In ch. i. 24 it is rendered "to regard." **To apply thine heart** is to turn the heart with the whole scope of its powers, in the spirit of humility and eagerness, to understanding. As the **ear** represents the outward vehicle of communication, so the **heart** (לֵב, lev) represents the inward, the intellectual faculty, the mind, or it may mean the affections as suggested by the LXX. καρδία and Vulgate

cor. **Understanding** (תְּבוּנָה, t'vunah) is here interchanged with "wisdom," which must determine its meaning to some extent. The LXX. interpreters take it as σύνεσις, "the faculty of comprehension." Like בִּינָה (vinah) in ch. i. 2, the word describes the faculty of distinguishing or separating; but it does not appear to be here used as representing this "as a faculty of the soul, but as a Divine *power* which communicates itself as the gift of God" (Delitzsch). A second and perhaps simpler sense may be given to the sentence. It may mean the turning or applying of the heart in an affectionate and loving way, *i.e.* with full purpose, to the discrimination of what is right and what wrong. The ideas of wisdom and understanding seem to some extent to be brought forward as personifications. They are things outside of ourselves, to which we have to give attention. Religion appeals not only to the affections, but also to the intellect, as this satisfies all the yearnings of our nature.

Ver. 3.—**Yea, if thou criest after knowledge.** The endeavour after Wisdom is not only to be sincere, it is also to be earnest, as appears from the "yea, if," and the verbs "crying" and "lifting up the voice," both of which frequently occur in Scripture as indicating earnestness. This earnestness is the counterpart of that which Wisdom herself displays (see ch. i. 20, 21). *Knowledge*; i.e. insight. In the original there is practically little difference between "knowledge" and "understanding" (בִּינָה and תְּבוּנָה). They carry on the idea expressed in "understanding" in the preceding verse, and thus throw the emphasis on the verbs. The LXX. and Vulgate, however, take "knowledge" as equivalent to σοφία, sapientia, "wisdom." The reading of the Targum, "If thou callest understanding thy mother," arises from reading אֵם for אִם, but is not to be preferred to the Masoretic text, as it destroys the parallelism.

Ver. 4.—**If thou seekest,** etc. The climax in the series of conditions is reached in this verse; and the imagery employed in both clauses indicates that the search after Wisdom is to be *persevering*, unrelaxing, and diligent, like the unremitting toil and labour with which men carry on mining operations. "To seek" (בָּקַשׁ, bakash) in the original is properly "to seek diligently" (piel), and is kindred to "to search" (קָפַשׂ, khaphas), which again is equivalent to "to dig" (חָפַר, khaphar), the Vulgate *effodere*, "to dig out." Compare the expression in Job iii. 21, "And dig for it more than for hid treasures." We trace in these verbs the idea in the mind of the teacher indicated above, which finds expression also in the object of the search, the silver, in its crude state, and the hidden treasures (מַטְמֹנִים, *mat'monim*), *i.e.* the treasures of gold, silver, and precious metal concealed in the earth. The comparison here made between the search for Wisdom and the search for the hidden treasures of the earth was not unfamiliar to the Hebrew mind, as it is found worked out with great beauty of detail in the twenty-eighth chapter of Job. Again, the comparison of Wisdom with things most precious in the estimation of man is natural and common, and occurs in Ps. cxix. 72; Job xxviii. 15—19. The same ideas and comparisons here used are presented to us in the New Testament teaching, in our Lord's parable of the man who finds the hid treasure in the field, and, in the phraseology of St. Paul, who speaks of "all the treasures of wisdom and knowledge," and of "the unsearchable riches of Christ." "Divine knowledge is an inexhaustible mine of precious ore" (Wardlaw). The language of the Proverbs would receive additional force from the circumstances of the reign of Solomon, the most splendid and prosperous era in the annals of the Jewish national history, in the means taken to secure the treasures of other and distant countries; the wealth and the riches of that reign (see 2 Chron. ix. 20—22) would help to bring out the idea of the superlative value of Wisdom. In no era of the Jewish national history was there such abundance of riches, such splendid prosperity, as in the reign of Solomon, whose ships of Tarshish brought "gold and silver" (see 2 Chron. ix. 20—22), and this state of things would give point to the comparisons which the teacher uses in our text.

Ver. 5.—**Then shalt thou understand the fear of the Lord.** *Then* (אָז), introducing the first apodosis, and answering to the conditional "if" of vers. 1, 3, 4. The earnest endeavour after Wisdom meets with its reward, and those that seek shall find (cf. Matt. vii. 7); and thus an inducement is held forth to listen to the admonition of the teacher. *Understand* implies the power of discernment, but Zöckler gives it the further meaning of taking to one's self as a spiritual possession, just as "find," meaning primarily "to arrive at," conveys the idea of getting possession of (Mercerus). The *fear of the Lord* (יִרְאַת יְהוָה, *yir'ath y'hovah*); "the fear of Jehovah," as in ch. i. 7. As it is the beginning, so it is the highest form of knowledge and the greatest good. Elsewhere it is represented as a fountain of life (ch. xv. 27). All true wisdom is summed up in "the fear of the Lord." It here means the reverence due to him, and so comprises the whole range of the religious affections and feelings, which respond to various attributes of the Divine character as they are revealed, and which find their expression in holy worship. **The knowledge of God** (דַּעַת אֱלֹהִים, *daath Elohim*); literally, *the knowledge of Elohim*. Not merely cognition, but knowledge in its wider sense. The two ideas of "the fear of the Lord" and "the knowledge of God" act reciprocally on each other. Just as without reverence of God there can be no knowledge of him in its true sense, so the knowledge of God will increase and deepen the feeling of reverence. But it is noticeable that the teacher here, as in ch. ix. 10, where, however, it is "the knowledge of the holy" (דַּעַת קְדֹשִׁים, *daath k'doshim*), gives the chief place to reverence, and thus indicates that it is the basis of knowledge, which is its fruit and result. The relation here suggested is analogous to that which subsists between faith and knowledge, and recalls the celebrated dictum of Anselm: "Neque enim quæro intelligere ut credam; sed credo, ut intelligam." *Elohim*, here interchanged with *Jehovah*, is not of frequent occurrence in the Proverbs, as it is only found therein five times, while the predominating word which is used to designate the Deity is *Jehovah*. But it is difficult to draw any distinction between them here. *Jehovah* may refer more especially to the Personality of the Divine nature, while *Elohim* may refer to Christ's glory (Plumptre). Bishop Wordsworth thinks that a distinction is made between the knowledge of Elohim and the knowledge of man which is of little worth.

Ver. 6.—**For the Lord giveth wisdom.** The Lord Jehovah is the only and true Source of wisdom. The truth stated here is also met with in Dan. ii. 21, "He giveth wisdom unto the wise, and knowledge to them that know understanding." He "giveth," or more properly, "will give" (יִתֵּן, *yitten*, future of נָתַן, *nathan*), wisdom; but the connection requires us to understand that the assurance applies only to those who seek after it earnestly and truly (cf. Jas. i. 5—7). The two coefficients to our obtaining wisdom are our efforts and God's assistance. Solomon may be adduced as a striking exemplification of this; he asked for "an understanding heart," and God graciously granted his request (see 1 Kings iii. 9, 12). **Out of his mouth** (מִפִּיו, *mippiv*); *ex ore ejus;* God is here spoken of anthropologically. He is the true Teacher. The meaning is that God communicates wisdom through the medium of his Word (Delitzsch. Pi.). The law proceeds from his mouth (Job xxii. 22). In the Book of Wisdom (vii. 25), "Wisdom is the breath of the power of God." His word is conveyed to us through men divinely inspired, and hence St. Peter (2 Pet. i. 21) says that "holy men of old spake as they were moved by the Holy Ghost."

Ver. 7.—Wisdom which is the foundation of security and safety, and hence is *sound wisdom*, is that which God treasures up for the righteous. The teacher passes to another phase of the Divine character. God is not only the Source of wisdom; he is also the Ensurer of safety, the Source of salvation to those who act uprightly. It will be noted that the use of the word is confined to the Proverbs and Job, with the exception of the two passages in Isaiah and Micah. **Buckler.** Besides storing up the treasures of sound wisdom, which the righteous may use and so obtain security in their uprightness, God is himself a *Buckler*, or *Shield* (מָגֵן, *magen*), to those who walk in innocence. This aspect of God's directly protecting power is met with in other parts of Scripture. In Gen. xv. 1 he encourages Abram with the assurance, "I am thy Shield." In Ps. xxxiii. 20; lxxxiv. 11; lxxxix. 18; cxliv. 2, Jehovah is called a Shield to his saints. He renders them security against the assaults of their enemies, and especially against the fiery darts of the wicked one. Again, in ch. xxx. 5, it is said, "God is a Shield (*magen*) unto them that walk uprightly." It is incorrect to take מָגֵן (*magen*) either as an accusative after the verb or in apposition with "sound wisdom." **To them that walk uprightly**; literally, *to the walkers in innocence* (לְהֹלְכֵי תֹם, *l'khol'key thom*). תֹם (*thōm*) is "integrity of mind," "moral faultlessness," "innocence." "To walk uprightly" is to maintain a course of life regulated by right principles, and directed to right ends. He "walks uprightly who lives with the fear of God as his principle, the Word of God as his rule, and the glory of God as his end" (Wardlaw). The *completeness* of the moral and religious character is involved in the expression which is found also in ch. x. 9 and Ps. lxxxiv. 11. The Vulgate translates the latter clause of the verse, *proteget gradientes simpliciter*, "he will protect those who walk in simplicity;" cf. 2 Cor. i. 12 in illustration of the phrase. **He layeth up;** *i.e.* he treasures up (LXX., θησαυρίζειν), or preserves and protects (*custodire*, Vulgate), as a person does "treasure or jewel, that it may not be stolen" (Zöckler). The majority of commentators read the Keri (יִצְפֹּן, "he will treasure up," future of צָפַן) in preference to the Khetib (וְצָפַן, perfect of same verb, with prefix וְ, "and he treasured up"), and this is the reading adopted in the Authorized Version. The Keri implies that God does treasure up sound wisdom, while the Khetib, as Delitzsch observes, has the force of the aorist, and so

represents the treasuring up as an accomplished fact. The same verb occurs in ch. ii. 1, where it is translated in the Authorized Version by "hide," and also in ch. vii. 1 and x. 14 by "lay up." The laying up, or treasuring, points to the preciousness of that which is treasured, "sound wisdom." **Sound wisdom.** A great variety of opinions exists as to the true meaning of the word in the original, תּוּשִׁיָּה (*tvushiyyah*), of which "sound wisdom" is an interpretation. Zöckler explains it as "wisdom, reflection;" Delitzsch, as "advancement and promotion;" Dathe, as "solid fortune;" Gesenius, as "aid." The proper meaning of the word seems to be "substance," from the root יָשָׁה, "to be, to exist, to be firm." Professor Lee remarks on the word, "From the places in which it occurs, either wealth, thought, or some such sense it manifestly requires. It occurs in Job vi. 13, in parallelism with 'help;' in ch. ii. 7, with a 'shield;' in Job xi. 6, with 'wisdom;' in Job xii. 16, with 'strength;' in ch. iii. 21, with 'discretion;' in ch. viii. 14, with 'counsel' and 'understanding;' in Isa. xxviii. 29, with 'counsel;' and so in Job xxvi. 3. In Job xxx. 22 and Micah vi. 9, 'entirely' or the like seems to suit the context; see also ch. xviii. 1, and generally 'excess,' or 'abundance,' taken either in a good or bad sense, and varied by other considerations, seems to prevail in every case in which this word is used" (see Professor Lee, on Job v. 12). The parallelism of the passage before us seems to require that it should be understood in the sense of *security*; and transferring the idea to wisdom as the means of security. This idea is reproduced in the LXX. σωτήρια, the Vulgate *salus*, and the Targum *incolumitas*.

Ver. 8.—**He keepeth the paths of judgment.** This verse is explanatory of the latter hemistich of ver. 7, and points out more fully in what way God is a Protector of his saints. Some connect the Hebrew infinitive לִנְצֹר (*lin'tsor*), "to watch or keep," with "them that walk uprightly," and translate, "them that walk uprightly by keeping the paths of judgment;" but this is to transfer the idea of protection from God to such persons. The verb signifies specially "to defend, to preserve from danger," as in ch. xxii. 12, "The eyes of the Lord preserve knowledge; *i.e.* defend or protect it from danger." It is God who "keepeth the paths of judgment," as he alone has the power to do so. He watches over all that walk therein, guides, superintends, and protects them. *The paths of judgment;* or rather, *justice,* אָרְחוֹת מִשְׁפָּט (*ar'khoth mish'pat*). The abstract is here used for the concrete, and the phrase means "the paths of the just," *i.e.* the paths in which the just walk, or "those who walk justly"

(Mercerus). This expression corresponds with " the way of his saints," just as " keep " and " preserve " are synonymous verbs, both meaning "to guard, keep safe, or protect." **He preserveth the way of his saints.** God does this (1) by his preventing grace, as in Ps. lxvi. 9, "He suffereth not our feet to slip." Cf. Hannah's song, " He will keep the feet of his saints " (1 Sam. ii. 9); (2) by angelic agency, as in Ps. xci. 11, "He shall give his angels charge over thee to keep thee in all thy ways." The saints are ever under the watchful care and mighty protection of Jehovah. *His saints* (חֲסִידָיו, *khasidav*); *i.e.* the pious towards God, the godly, those in whose hearts the principles of sanctity have been implanted, and who cherish earnest inward love to God, and "walk righteously" and "speak uprightly" (Isa. xxxiii. 15). It is remarkable that the word " saints " only occurs once (in this passage) in the Proverbs. During the period of the Maccabæan Wars, a party or sect, which aimed at ceremonial purity, claimed for themselves the title of *Chasidim* or *Asidæans* ('Ασιδαῖοι), as expressive of their piety or devotion. They are those whom Moses called " men of holiness," Exod. xxii. 31 (אַנְשֵׁי־קֹדֶשׁ, *v'an'shev-kodesh*); cf. Ps. lxxxix. 5; cxlix. 1; lxxxix. 8; Deut. xxxiii. 3; Dan. vii. 18, 21, 22, 25. Under the Christian dispensation, the saints are those who are sanctified in Christ Jesus (1 Cor. i. 2; 1 John v. 1), and who are holy in all manner of conversation (1 Pet. i. 15; 1 Macc. ii. 42; vii. 13; 2 Macc. xiv. 6); see Bishop Lightfoot, 'Colossians and Philemon,' diss. ii. p. 355.

Ver. 9.—**Then** (אָז, *az*), repeated from ver. 5, introduces the second apodosis. As the former referred to God, so this appears to refer more especially to man, and thus we have stated the whole benefit, in its twofold aspect, which Wisdom confers on those who diligently seek her. It is not to be affirmed, however, that righteousness and judgment and equity refer exclusively to man ; they must represent some aspects of our relationship to God, both from the meaning of the words themselves, and because the law which regulates our dealings and intercourse with man has its seat in the higher law of our relation to God. **Righteousness, and judgment, and equity.** These three words occur in the same collocation in ch. i. 3, which see. **Yea, every good path.** " Yea " does not occur in the original. The expression is a summarizing of the three previous conceptions, as if the teacher implied that all good paths are embraced by and included in " righteousness, and judgment, and equity; " but the term is also comprehensive in the widest degree. The literal translation is " every path of good " (כָּל־מַעְגַּל־טוֹב,

cal-ma'gal-tov), *i.e.* every course of action of which goodness is the characteristic, or, as the Authorized Version, " every good path," the sense in which it was understood by St. Jerome, *omnem orbitam bonam.* The word here used for " path " is מַעְגַּל (*ma'gal*), " the way in which the chariot rolls " (Delitzsch), and metaphorically a course of action, as in ch. ii. 15 ; iv. 26.

Vers. 10—19.—Statement of the advantages which result from the possession of Wisdom, and specially as a safeguard against evil men (vers. 12—15) and evil women (vers 16—19).

Ver. 10.—**When wisdom entereth into thine heart.** There is practically little difference as to the sense, whether we render the Hebrew כִּי by the conditional " if " or by the temporal " when " as in the Authorized Version. The conditional force is adopted by the LXX. ἐάν and the Vulgate *si.* In the previous section of this address, the teacher has shown that the search after Wisdom will result in possession; now he points out, when Wisdom is secured, certain advantageous consequences follow. The transition is easy and natural. The form of construction is very similar to that adopted previously. There is first the hypothesis, if we give this force to כִּי, though much shorter ; and secondly the climax, also shorter and branching off into the statement of two special cases. *Entereth ;* or, *shall enter* (תָּבוֹא, *thavo*) in the sense of permanent residence in the heart. Wisdom is not only to come in, but to *rest* there (cf. ch. xiv. 33). The expression is illustrated by John xiv. 23. The imagery of the verse is taken from the reception and entertainment of a guest. As we receive a welcome guest, and find pleasure in his company, so is Wisdom to be dear to the heart and soul. *Into thine heart* (בְלִבֶּךָ, *b'libecha*). The heart (לֵב) " concentrates in itself the personal life of man in all its relations, the conscious and the unconscious, the voluntary and the involuntary, the physical and the spiritual impulses, the emotions and states " (Cremer, ' Bib. Theol. Lex.,' *sub voce* καρδία). It is that in which the נֶפֶשׁ (*nephesh*)," soul," manifests itself. It is the centre of the life of will and desire, of the emotions, and of the moral life. Rudloff ('Lehre von Menscher,' p. 59, *sqq.*, apud Zöckler) remarks that everywhere in the Scriptures the heart appears to belong more to the life of desire and feeling than to the intellectual activity of the soul. But at the same time, it is to be noted that intelligent conception is attributed to the heart (לֵב); ch. xiv. 10; viii. 5; xvi. 9. The expression seems to be put here for the moral side of man's nature; and in the Hellenistic sense, καρδία, the proper equivalent of לֵב, "heart," involves all that stands for νοῦς, λόγος, συνείδησις, and θυμός; i.e. it includes, besides other things, the intellectual faculty. The word "soul" (נֶפֶשׁ, nephesh) is here found in combination with "heart." The other passages where they are mentioned together are Deut. vi. 5; Ps. xiii. 2; Jer. iv. 19; ch. xxiv. 12. The soul is primarily the vital principle, but according to the usus loquendi of Holy Scripture, it frequently denotes the entire inward nature of man; it is that part which is the object of the work of redemption. The home of the soul is the heart, as appears from ch. xiv. 10, "The heart knoweth his own bitterness [or, 'the bitterness of his soul,' Hebrew]." While the "heart" (לֵב) is rendered by καρδία and ψυχή, the only Greek equivalent to "soul" (נֶפֶשׁ) is ψυχή. The two expressions, "heart," and "soul," in the passage before us may be taken as designating both the moral and spiritual sides of man's nature. Wisdom is to be acceptable and pleasant to man in these respects. It may be remarked that an intellectual colouring is given to the word "heart" by the LXX., who render it by διανοία, as also in Deut. vi. 5 and other passages, evidently from the idea that prominence is given to the reflective faculty. Classically, διανοία is equivalent to "thought," "faculty of thought," "intellect." **Knowledge** (Hebrew, דַעַת); literally, to know, as in ch. viii. 10 and xiv. 6; here used synonymously with "wisdom." Knowledge, not merely as cognition, but perception; i.e. not merely knowing a thing with respect to its existence and being, but as to its excellence and truth. Equivalent to the LXX. αἰσθησις, "perception," and the Vulgate scientia. **Is pleasant** (Hebrew, יָנְעַם, yin'am); literally, shall be pleasant; i.e. sweet, lovely, beautiful. The same word is used impersonally in Jacob's blessing of Issachar (Gen. xlix. 15, "And he saw the land that it was pleasant"), and also in ch. xxiv. 25, "To those that punish [i.e. the judges] there shall be delight." And this usage has led Dunn to take "knowledge" as an accusative of reference, and to translate, "There is pleasure to thy soul in respect of knowledge;" but the Authorized Version may be accepted as correct. "Knowledge" is masculine, as in ch. viii. 10 and xiv. 6, and agrees with the masculine verb "is pleasant." Knowledge will be pleasant from the enjoyment and rest which it yields. The Arabic presents the idea of this enjoyment under a different aspect: "And prudence shall be in thy soul the most beautiful glory."

Ver. 11.—**Discretion shall preserve thee.** Discretion (מְזִמָּה, m'zimoth), as in ch. i. 4, is the outward manifestation of wisdom; it tests what is uncertain, and avoids danger (Hitzig). The word carries with it the idea of reflection or consideration (see ch. iii. 21; v. 2; viii. 12). The LXX. reads, βουλὴ καλή, "good counsel;" and the Vulgate, concilium. Shall preserve thee. The idea of protection and guarding, which is predicated of Jehovah in ver. 8, is here transferred to discretion and understanding, which to some extent are put forward as personifications. **Understanding** (תְבוּנָה, t'vunah), as in ch. ii. 11; the power of distinguishing and separating, and, in the case of conflicting interests, to decide on the best. **Shall keep**; i.e. keep safe, or in the sense of watching over or guarding. The two verbs "to preserve" (שָׁמַר, shamar) and "to keep" (נָצַר, natsar), LXX. τήρειν, occur together again in ch. iv. 6.

Ver. 12.—**To deliver thee from the way of the evil** man. The first special advantage resulting from the protecting guardianship of discretion and understanding. From the way of the evil man; properly, from an evil way; Hebrew, מִדֶּרֶךְ רָע (midarek ra), not necessarily, though by implication, connected with man, as in the Authorized Version. רָע (ra), "evil," "wicked," in an ethical sense, is an adjective, as in Jer. iii. 16 (לֵב רָע, lev ra), "an evil heart;" cf. the LXX., ἀπὸ ὁδοῦ κακῆς; the Vulgate, Targum, and Arabic, a viâ mala, and the Syriac, a viis pravis. "Way," is here used in the sense of "conduct," and the evil way is a line of conduct or action which is essentially wicked or evil. The teacher has already warned youth against the temptations and dangers of the way of evil men in ch. i. 10—15; he now shows that discretion, arising from wisdom being resident in the heart, will be a sufficient safeguard against its allurements. **From the man that speaketh froward things.** Perverse utterances are here brought in contradistinction to the evil way or froward conduct. Man (אִישׁ, ish) is here used generically, as the representative of the whole class of base and wicked men, since all the following verbs are in the plural. Froward things. The word תַּהְפֻּכוֹת (tah'pucoth), here translated "froward things," is derived from the root הָפַךְ (haphak), "to turn," "to pervert," and should be translated "perverseness." Perverseness is the wilful misrepresentation of that which is good and true. The utterances are of a distorted and tortuous character. The word, only found in the plural, is abstract in form, and is of frequent, though not of exclusive, occurrence in the Proverbs. It is attributed to the Israelites in Deut. xxxii. 20. It is met with again in such expressions as "the mouth of perverseness," Authorized Version "froward mouth" (ch. viii. 13); "the tongue of perverseness," "froward tongue," Authorized Version (ch. x. 31); "the man of perverseness," "froward man," Authorized Version (ch. xvi. 28). What is here said of wicked men is attributed to drunkards in ch. xxiii. 33, "Thine heart shall utter perverse things." The expression finds its explanation in ch. vi. 13, 14. The spirit which indulges in this perverseness is stubborn, scornful, self-willed, and rebellious, and it is from such a spirit that discretion is a preservative. In Job v. 13 it is said that "the counsel of the froward is carried headlong" (see also 2 Sam xxii. 27; Ps. xviii. 26; ci. 4). The LXX. rendering of this word is μηδὲν πιστόν, "nothing trustworthy," which is amplified in the Arabic, *quod nullam in se continet veritatem*, "that which contains in itself no truth."

Ver. 13.—**Who leave the paths of uprightness.** Between vers. 13 and 15 the teacher proceeds to give a more detailed description of those who speak perversely. *Who leave* (הַעֹזְבִים, *haoz'vim*); literally, *forsaking*, but the present participle has the force of the preterite, as appears from the context. The men alluded to have already forsaken or deserted the paths of uprightness (see previous note on the word "man." *The paths of uprightness* (אָרְחוֹת יֹשֶׁר, *ar'khoth yosher*); the same as the "right paths" of ch. iv. 11. The strict meaning of the Hebrew word translated "uprightness" is "straightness," and hence it stands opposed to "perverseness" in the previous verse. Uprightness is integrity, rectitude, honest dealing. The LXX. translators represent the forsaking of the paths of uprightness as a consequence resulting from walking in the ways of darkness, "O ye who have left the right ways by departing [τοῦ πορεύεσθαι, equivalent to *abeundo*] into the ways of darkness." Again, the **ways of darkness** (דַּרְכֵי חֹשֶׁךְ, *dar'chey kkoshek*) are opposed to the "paths of uprightness" which rejoice in the light. Darkness includes the two ideas of (1) ignorance and error (Isa. ix. 2; Eph. v. 8), and (2) evil deeds. To walk in the ways of darkness, then, is to persist in a course of wilful ignorance, to reject deliberately the light of knowledge, and to work wickedness, by performing "the works of darkness (τὰ ἔργα τοῦ σκότους)," which St. Paul exhorted the Church at Rome to cast away (Rom. xiii. 12), and by having fellowship with "the unfruitful works of darkness (τὰ ἔργα τὰ ἄκαρπα τοῦ σκότους)," against which the same apostle warned the Ephesians (v. 11). They are ways of darkness, because they endeavour to hide themselves from God (Isa. xxix. 15) and from man (Job xxiv. 15; xxxviii. 13, 15). In their tendency and end they lead to the blackness of darkness for ever. In Scripture darkness is associated with evil, just as

light is with uprightness (see John iii. 19, 20). The same association of ideas is discoverable in the dualism of the Persian system, as formulated by Zoroaster—Ormuzd, the good principle, presides over the kingdom of light, while Ahriman, the principle of evil, is the ruler of the kingdom of darkness.

Ver. 14.—**Who rejoice to do evil.** Another element is here brought forward, and the description increases in intensity. The wicked not only rejoice to do evil themselves, but they exult when they hear of evil in others (cf. Rom. i. 32). Such may be the interpretation, though the latter part, of the verse is capable of a different and more general rendering as signifying exultation in evil generally, whether it appears in themselves or others. The expression rendered in the Authorized Version, **in the frowardness of the wicked**, is in the original (בְּתַהְפֻּכוֹת רָע, *b'thah'pucoth ra*), *in the perverseness of evil*, or in evil perverseness, where the combination of the two nouns serves to give force to the main idea, which is that of perverseness. This rendering is adopted in the LXX., ἐπὶ διαστροφῇ κακῇ, "in evil distortion;" in the Vulgate, *in pessimis rebus;* in the Targum, Syriac, and Arabic, *in conversatione malâ*, "in a bad course of conduct;" and in the Targum, *in malitiæ perversione*, "in the perversion of wickedness." It is not perverseness in its simple and common form that these men exult in, but in its worst and most vicious form (for a similar construction, see ch. vi. 24; xv. 26; and xxviii. 5). How widely different is the conduct of charity, which "rejoiceth not in iniquity" (1 Cor. xiii. 6)!

Ver. 15.—**Whose ways are crooked;** better, perhaps, *who as to their ways are crooked.* This is the construction adopted by Fleischer, Bertheau, Zöckler, and others, though it may be remarked that the substantive אֹרַח (*orakh*), "way," is common gender, and may thus agree with the adjective עִקֵּשׁ (*ikesh*), "perverse," which is masculine. The Targum, LXX., Vulgate, Syriac, and Arabic, all make "crooked" agree with "ways," so that, grammatically, the Authorized Version may be regarded as not incorrect. *Crooked* (עִקְּשִׁים, *ik'shim*); i.e. tortuous, perverse, not straightforward (σκολιαί, LXX.). Symmachus translates the original by σκαμβαί, i.e. "bent." Theodotion, by στριβλαί, "twisted, crookt." Sinners, in their perverseness, are ever winding about, turning in every direction, and changing from purpose to purpose, as wayward caprice or shifting inclination, the alternations of evil propensity, happen to dictate (Wardlaw). (For the expression, "crooked ways," see Ps. cxxv. 5.) **And they froward in their paths;** i.e. perverse in their paths. The root-idea of the Hebrew niph. participle וְנִלוֹזִים (vun'lozim), translated "and they froward," is "to bend aside," "to turn away." They are turned aside to the right hand and to the left in their walk. The niph. participle נָלוֹז (naloz) only occurs four times in the Scriptures—here; ch. iii. 32; xiv. 2; and Isa. xxx. 12. This is the last feature in their wickedness.

Ver. 16.—**To deliver thee from the strange woman.** This is the second form of temptation against which *wisdom* (discretion) is a preservative, and the great and especial dangers arising from it to youth, owing to its seductive allurements, afford the reason why the teacher is so strong in his warnings on this subject. Two terms are employed to designate the source of this evil—"the strange woman" (אִשָּׁה זָרָה, *ishshah zara*), and "the stranger" (נָכְרִיָּה, *nok'riyah*)—and both undoubtedly, in the passage before us, mean a meretricious person, one who indulges in illicit intercourse. The former term is invariably employed in this sense in the Proverbs (ch. v. 2, 20; vii. 5; xxii. 14; xxiii. 33) of the adulteress (זָרִים, *zarim*), and Jer. ii. 25. The participle זָר (*zar*), from the verb זוּר (*zur*), of which זָרָה (*zara'*) is the feminine form, is, however, used in a wider sense, as signifying (1) one of another nation, or one of another family; or (2) some one different from one's self; (3) or strange. Thus: (1) in Isa. i. 7 we have "Strangers devour it (your land) in your presence;" but in Exod. xxx. 33 "the stranger" is one not the high priest. (2) The "stranger" is another (ch. xi. 15; xiv. 10; xx. 16; xxvii. 2, 13). (3) The "strange fire" (אֵשׁ זָרָה, *esh zarah*) is the unlawful fire as opposed to the holy fire (Lev. x. 1); the "strange god" (אֵל זָר, *el zar*) is the foreign god (Ps. lxxxi. 9). But the idea of foreign origin implied in the word is more strongly brought out in the next term, נָכְרִיָּה (*nok'riyah*), on which Delitzsch remarks that it scarcely ever divests itself of a strange, foreign origin. This word is used to designate those "strange women" whom Solomon loved in his old age, and who turned his heart aside to worship false gods (1 Kings xi. 1—8), "outlandish women," as they are termed in Neh. xiii. 26; it designates "the strange wives" of Ezra x. and Neh. xiii. 27; and is applied to Ruth the Moabitess (Ruth ii. 10). Again, it has to be further observed that the laws of the Mosaic code against prostitution were of a most stringent nature (Lev. xix. 29; xxi. 9; Deut. xxiii. 17), and no doubt served to maintain a higher standard of morality among Israelitish women than that observed among the Midianites, Syrians, and other nations. Strong prohibitions were directed against the intermarriage of

Israelites with the women of the surrounding nations; but the example set by Solomon would serve to weaken the force of these prohibitions, and would lead to a large influx of women of a different nationality. The conclusion we arrive at is that the class mentioned in the text, though not Israelitish by birth, were yet so by adoption, as the context clearly indicates (ver. 17) the fact of marriage and the acceptance of certain religious observances. Such women, after a temporary restraint, would eventually set all moral and religious obligations at defiance, and would become the source of temptation to others. The allegorical interpretation given to this passage by the LXX. is to be rejected on the ground that the previous section (vers. 12—15) speaks of perverse *men*. Which **flattereth with her words;** literally, *who has made smooth her words*, the hiph. perfect being used of חָלַק (*khalak*), "to make smooth," or "flattering." The preterite shows what her habitual practice is, and is used of an action still continuing, and so may be fitly rendered by the present, as in the Authorized Version: "She has acquired the art of enticing by flattering words, and it is her study to employ them;" cf. the Vulgate, *quæ mollit sermones suos*, "who softens her words;" and the Syriac, *quæ subvertit verba sua*, "who subverts her words," *i.e.* "uses deceit." The expression occurs again in ch. v. 3; vi. 24; vii. 5.

Ver. 17.—**The guide of her youth** (אַלּוּף נְעוּרֶיהָ, *alluph n'ureyah*); properly, *the associate* or *companion of her youth*. The Hebrew, אַלּוּף (*alluph*), being derived from the root אָלַף, (*alaph*), "to accustom one's self to," or "to be accustomed to" or "familiar with" any one. The word is rendered as "friend" in ch. xvii. 9; xvi. 28; Micah vii. 5. The idea of guidance, which is adopted in the Authorized Version, and appears also in the Vulgate *dux*, and Targum *ducatus*, is a secondary idea, and is derived probably from the relation in which the husband stands to his wife. Various interpretations have been given to the expression. It occurs again in Jer. iii. 4, where Jehovah applies it to himself, and says, through his prophet, to the religiously adulterous Judah, "Wilt thou not from this time cry unto me, My Father, thou art the Guide of my youth (אַלּוּף נְעֻרַי, *alluph n'ura*)?" It has also been understood as referring to the woman's parents, her father and mother, who were her natural guardians. But the context seems to require that it should be taken as designating her *husband*. It will then be the correlative of "the wife of thy youth" of Mal. ii. 14. **The covenant of her God;** *i.e.* the marriage covenant, called "the covenant of her God," because entered into in his presence. The forsaking of the guide of her youth is essentially bound up with a forgetfulness of the solemn covenant which she had entered into in the presence of God. No specific mention is made in the Pentateuch of any religious ceremony at marriage; yet we may infer, from Mal. ii. 14, 15, where God is spoken of as "a Witness" between the husband and "the wife of his youth," "the wife of thy covenant," that the marriage contract was solemnized with sacred rites. The Proverbs thus give a high and sacred character to marriage, and so carry on the original idea of the institution which, under the gospel dispensation, developed into the principle of the indissolubility of the marriage tie. It is no objection to this view that the monogamic principle was infringed, and polygamy countenanced. The reason of this latter departure is given in Deut. xxii. 28 and Exod. xxii. 16. The morality of the Proverbs always represents monogamy as the rule; it deprecates illicit intercourse, and discountenances divorce. It is in entire accordance with the seventh commandment. The woman who commits adultery offends, not only against her husband, but against her God.

Ver. 18.—For her house inclineth unto death; rather, *she sinks down to death together with her house* (Böttcher, Delitzsch). The objection to the Authorized Version is that it does not follow the construction of the original, the verb "sinks down" (שָׁחָה, *shakhah*) being feminine, while "house" (בַּיִת, *bayith*) is invariably masculine. Aben Ezra translates, "She sinks down to death, (which is to be) her house;" but it seems better to regard "her house" as an adjunct of the strange woman. Her house includes all who belong to her. She and they are involved in the same fate. The Authorized Version is evidently influenced by the Vulgate. *Inclinata est enim ad mortem domus ejus*, "For her house is inclined to death." The LXX. gives a different rendering, Ἔθετο γὰρ παρὰ τῷ θανάτῳ τὸν οἶκον αὐτῆς, "For she hath placed her house beside death." So the Arabic. The "for" (כִּי, *ki*) refers back to ver. 16, and indicates how great is the deliverance effected by wisdom. The meaning of the passage is aptly illustrated by ch. vii. 27, "Her house is the way to hell, going down to the chambers of death." **And her paths unto the dead.** *The dead* (רְפָאִים, *r'phaim*) are properly the quiet, or the feeble. They are the shadowy inhabitants or shades of Hades, the *inferi* of the Vulgate, and are here put for Sheol itself. Compare the εἴδωλα καμνόντων of Homer, and the *umbræ*, "shades," of Virgil. The word occurs again in ch. ix. 18; xxi. 16; and in

Ps. lxxxviii. 11; Isa. xxvi. 14, 19; Job xxvi. 5.

Ver. 19.—None that go unto her return again. The fate of the companions of the strange woman is described as irrevocable. All who visit her shall not return again. The Targum reads, "They shall not return in peace." The difficulty which they who give themselves up to the indulgence of lust and passion encounter in extricating themselves makes the statement of the teacher an almost universal truth. Hence St. Chrysostom says, "It is as difficult to bring back a libidinous person to chastity as a dead man to life." This passage led some of the Fathers to declare that the sin of adultery was unpardonable. Fornication was classed by the scholastic divines among the seven deadly sins, and it has this character given to it in the Litany: "From fornication, and all other deadly sin." St. Paul says, "No whoremonger nor unclean person . . . hath any inheritance in the kingdom of Christ and of God" (Eph. v. 5; cf. 1 Cor. vi. 9; Rev. xxii. 15). The sin which they commit who have dealings with the strange woman is deadly and leads on to death, and from death there is no return, nor laying hold of or regaining the paths of life (see Job vii. 9, 10). Compare the words with which Deiphobe, the Cumæan sibyl, addresses Æneas—

"Tros Anchysiade, facilis descensus Averno
  Sed revocare gradum superasque evadere
      ad auras,
Hoc opus, hic labor est."
          (Virgil, 'Æneid,' vi. 126—129.)

"O Trojan, son of Anchyses, easy is the path that leads to hell. But to retrace one's steps, and escape to the upper regions, this is a work, this is a task."

Vers. 20—22.—Conclusion of the discourse in which are antithetically stated the respective destinies of the good and the bad, the upright and the wicked.

Ver. 20.—That (Hebrew, לְמַעַן, *l'maan*); *in order that* (Vulgate, *ut*), carries us back properly to ver. 11. The protecting power of wisdom is developed in a positive direction. Negatively, it delivers from the evil man and from the strange woman, but it does more—"it shall keep thee in order that thou mayest walk in a good way," etc. The Hebrew לְמַעַן (*l'maan*) is co-ordinate with "to deliver thee," but it serves to bring the discourse to a conclusion. Umbreit renders it "therefore," thus making what follows an inference from the preceding discourse. So the Syriac, *ambula igitur*, "therefore walk." **In the way of good men** (בְּדֶרֶךְ טוֹבִים, *b'derek tovim*); *i.e.* in the way of the good, in an ethical sense, *i.e.* the upright, as in Isa. v. 20. The Vulgate renders, *in viâ bonâ,* "in the good way." "The way of good men" is the way of God's commandments, the way of obedience. **Keep.** The Hebrew verb שָׁמַר (*shamar*) is here used in the sense of "to observe," "to attend to," but in a different sense from Ps. xvii. 4, "I have observed the ways of the violent man," *i.e.* that I might avoid them. To keep the paths of the righteous is to carefully attend to the life of obedience which they follow. The LXX. closely connects this verse with the preceding, and renders, "For if they had walked in good ways, they would have found the paths of righteousness light."

Ver. 21.—**For the upright shall dwell in the land.** Much the same language is met with in Ps. xxxvii. 29, "The righteous shall inherit the land, and dwell therein for ever." It is the secure and peaceful dwelling in the land which is intended (cf. ch. x. 30). To dwell in the land was always put forward as the reward of obedience to God's commandments (see Exod. xx. 12; Lev. xxv. 18; xxvi. 5), and the phrase conveyed to the Hebrew mind the idea of one of the greatest, if not the greatest, of all temporal blessings. The love of country was a predominant characteristic of the race. Elster, quoted by Zöckler, remarks, "The Israelite was beyond the power of natural feeling, which makes home dear to every one, more closely bound to the ancestral soil by the whole form of the theocracy; torn from it, he was in the inmost roots of life strained and broken. Especially from psalms belonging to the period of the exile this patriotic feeling is breathed out in the fullest glow and intensity." *The land* (אֶרֶץ, *arets*) was the promised land, the land of Canaan. The word is not used here in the wider sense in which it occurs in Matt. v. 5, "Blessed are the meek: for they shall inherit the earth." **And the perfect shall remain in it;** *i.e.* they shall not, as Rabbi Levi remarks, be driven thence nor caused to migrate. The *perfect* (תְּמִימִים, *th'mimim*), the holy (LXX., ὅσιοι), the spotless (*immaculati,* Targum), those without a stain (*qui sine labe,* Syriac), the guileless (*simplices,* Vulgate). *Shall remain;* יִוָּתְרוּ (*yivvath'ru*), niph. future of יָתַר (*yathar*), properly "to be redundant," and in the niph. form, "to be left," or "to remain." LXX., ὑπολειφθή-

σονται, "shall remain;" *permanebunt,* Vulgate.

Ver. 22.—**But the wicked shall be cut off from the earth.** The punishment of the wicked is contrasted with the blessings that are promised to the upright. *Shall be cut off;* יִכָּרֵתוּ (*yikkarethu*), niph. future of כָּרַת (*karath*), "to cut off, or destroy." LXX., ὀλοῦνται; Vulgate, *perdentur.* The expression is used to convey the idea of extermination, as in Ps. xxxvii. 9 (cf. Job xviii. 17; Ps. xxxvii. 28; civ. 35). The verb is found also in Gen. xvii. 14; Exod. xii. 15. *The earth;* properly, *the land.* The same word (אֶרֶץ, *arets*) is used as in ver. 21. **The transgressors** (בּוֹגְדִים, *bog'dim*); here employed synonymously with "the wicked" (יְשָׁעִים, *y'shaim*), "the impious." The primary meaning of the verb from which it is derived (בָּגַד, *bagad*) is "to cover," "to deal treacherously," and hence the word signifies those who act treacherously or perfidiously, the faithless. They are those who perfidiously depart from God, and break away from the covenant with Jehovah. LXX., παράνομοι (cf. ch. xi. 3, 6; xiii. 2, 25; xxii. 12; Ps. xxv. 3; lix. 5; Isa. xxxiii. 1). **Shall be rooted out** (יִסְּחוּ, *yiss'khu*). This word is taken by Davidson as the future kal of נָסַח (*nasah*), "to pluck up," and hence is equivalent to "they shall pluck up," or, passively, "they shall be plucked up." Delitzsch remarks that it is as at ch. xv. 25 and Ps. lii. 7, active, "they shall pluck up," and this with the subject remaining indefinite is equivalent to the passive form, "they shall be plucked up." This indefinite "they" can be used of God, as also in Job vii. 3 (Fleischer). The expression has been understood as referring to being driven into exile (Gesenius), and this view would be amply justified by the fate which overtook the apostate nation when both the kingdoms of Israel and Judah suffered this fate (cf. LXX. ἐξωθήσονται, "they shall be driven out"). It also derives colour from the language of the preceding verse, but the imagery appears to be derived from the cutting down and rooting up of trees. The destruction of the wicked and transgressors will be complete. They shall be exterminated (cf. Targum, *eradicabuntur;* Syriac, *evellentur;* and Arabic, *exterminabuntur*).

HOMILETICS.

Vers. 1—5.—*The search for wisdom.* I. DIVINE WISDOM MUST BE SOUGHT BEFORE IT CAN BE FOUND. It is true that Wisdom cries aloud in the street and invites the ignorant and simple to partake of her stores. But the burden of her cry is to bid us seek her. It is the voice of invitation, not that of revelation. The latter is only audible to those who incline their ears purposely and thoughtfully. The thoughtless are satisfied with hasty impressions of the moment; but the only religious convictions worth considering are the outcome of thought and prayer. Still, it is to be observed that this wisdom is not reserved for the keen-sighted, the intellectual, the philosophical. It is not ability, but industry, that is required; not exceptional capacity to attain knowledge, but diligence in pursuing it. Laborious dulness can never achieve the triumphs of the brilliant scholar in secular studies. Industry alone will not make a senior wrangler. But the highest knowledge, Divine knowledge, depends so much more on moral considerations which are within the reach of all, that it can stand upon this democratic basis and offer itself to all patient inquirers.

II. THE SEARCH FOR DIVINE WISDOM MUST BEGIN IN RECEPTIVE FAITH. This wisdom is not innate; it is not attained by direct observation; it is not the result of self-sustained reasoning. It comes as revelation, in the voice of God. Thus the soul's first duty is to hear. But the right attitude towards the Divine revelation is not merely a state of receptivity. It is one of faith and careful attention, receiving the words and hiding them. All through the Bible this essential distinction between heavenly truth and philosophy, between the mere intellectual requisites of the one and the faith and obedience which lie at the root of the other, is apparent. The first steps towards receiving the wisdom of God are childlike trust and that purity and devoutness which bring the soul into communion with God.

III. THE SEARCH FOR DIVINE WISDOM MUST BE MAINTAINED WITH INCREASING EARNESTNESS. The verses before us describe a progressive intensity of spiritual effort— receiving, hiding the commandment, inclining the ear, applying the heart, crying after, lifting up the voice, seeking, searching as for hid treasure. The truth may not be found at once. But the earnest soul will not desist at the first discouragement; if his heart is in the pursuit, he will only press on the more vigorously. It is, moreover, the characteristic of Divine truth that a little knowledge of it kindles the thirst for deeper draughts. Thus we are led on to the most energetic search. Spirituality does not discourage the eager energy with which men seek worldly gain; on the contrary, it bids us transfer this to higher pursuits, and seek wisdom as men seek for silver, and sink mines after hidden treasures. Christ does not say, "Be anxious for nothing;" but, "Be not anxious for the morrow"—in order that we may transfer our anxiety to more important concerns, and "seek first the kingdom of God and his righteousness."

IV. THE SEARCH FOR DIVINE WISDOM WILL BE REWARDED WITH SUCCESS. Some question this, and, after weary pursuit, abandon the quest in despair, or settle down into indolent indifference. Perhaps they lack patience—toiling in the night and taking nothing, they cannot hold on till the dawn, when the Master will give them a rich draught; or they seek wrongly, not in spiritual faith, but in cold human reason; or they seek a mistaken goal—the explanation of mystery rather than practical wisdom as the guide of life. This wisdom is promised to those who truly seek, and it is attainable.

Ver. 6.—*Wisdom a gift of God.* I. TRUE WISDOM ORIGINATES IN DIVINE INSPIRATION. Prophets and apostles—teachers of the highest truths—claim to be delivering a message from heaven. The greater the thoughts declared to us in Scripture, the more emphatic is the ascription of them to a superhuman source. Surely this very fact—this conjunction of unique value in the thoughts with the confident assertion that they are from God—should go far in leading us to believe in the inspiration of them. But it is also urged by the men who bring these truths to us that we can only receive them when we are inspired by the Spirit of God; and experience shows that they who have most spirituality of life are able to drink most deeply of the fountains of revelation. Further, when once we admit this much, it follows that, if we recognize the constancy of God in all his methods of action, it is reasonable for us to feel that all truth must depend on a Divine illumination for its manifestation, and that all wisdom must be the outcome of some degree of inspiration. Nevertheless, it is not to be inferred that inspiration dispenses with natural channels of knowledge; on the contrary, it opens the eyes of men, who must then use their eyes to be seers of spiritual truth.

II. THE INSPIRATION OF WISDOM DEPENDS ON SPIRITUAL RELATIONS WITH GOD. If inspiration is the source, the questions arise—Who are privileged to drink of this fountain? and how do they gain access to it? Now, it is much to be assured that this is not reserved to any select class of men. Prophets have a special revelation to convey a special message, and apostles have a distinctive endowment for the accomplishment of a particular mission; but the inspiration of wisdom generally is not thus limited. On the contrary, it comes freely to all who rightly avail themselves of it. What, then, are the conditions for receiving it? 1. *Prayer.* "If any of you lack wisdom, let him ask of God, who giveth to all liberally, and upbraideth not; and it shall be given him" (Jas. i. 5). Whosoever seeks shall find. 2. *Purity.* "The pure in heart shall see God," and the highest wisdom is in the beatific vision of him who dwells in the light of eternal truth. 3. *Obedience.* As we submit our wills to God's will, we open the channel through which his Spirit enters into us, and by fellowship illumines.

III. TRUE WISDOM, BEING INSPIRED BY GOD, WILL BEAR THE STAMP OF DIVINE CHARACTERISTICS. It will differ from mere human speculation; sometimes it will be so much in conflict with that speculation as to pass for foolishness (see 1 Cor. i. 18). It will be distinctly opposed to the wisdom that is purely carnal, *i.e.* to that which takes account only of earthly facts and ignores spiritual principles, the wisdom of expediency, the cleverness of men of the world. Such wisdom is not only earthly; its low maxims and immoral devices proclaim it to be "sensual, devilish" (Jas. iii. 15). Divinely inspired wisdom, on the contrary, is spiritual—taking account of the facts and laws of the higher order; pure—not ministering to selfish greed and degraded pleasure; wholesome—strengthening and elevating the soul; "peaceable, gentle, easy to be intreated, full of mercy and good fruits, without variance, without hypocrisy" (Jas. iii. 17).

Vers. 10, 11.—*The antidote to temptation.* I. WE NEED AN ANTIDOTE TO TEMPTATION. It is not enough to trust to our own spiritual health to throw off the poison. We are already diseased with sin, and have a predisposition to yield to temptation in the corruption of our own hearts. But if we were immaculate, we should still be liable to fall; the power of temptation is so fearful that the purest, strongest soul would be in danger of succumbing. The tempter can choose the moment of his attack. When we are most off our guard, when we are faint and weary, when we are suffering from spiritual depression, the mine may be suddenly sprung, and we may be lost before we have fully realized the situation. Like the dragon in Spenser's 'Faëry Queene,' which would have stifled the Red Cross Knight with the fiery fumes it belched forth unless he had fallen into the healing fountain, the tempter would destroy our spiritual life with an atmosphere of foul thoughts after more tangible attacks have failed, were it not that we have a supply of grace outside ourselves, equal to our need. Even Christ, when tempted, did not rest on his own purity and power, but appealed for support to the sacred wisdom of Scripture.

II. THE ANTIDOTE TO TEMPTATION MUST BE SOME FORM OF POSITIVE GOOD. Fire is quenched by water, not by opposing flames. Evil must be overcome with good. The way to keep sin out of the heart is to fill the heart with pure thoughts and affections till there is no room for anything else. The citadel entered most easily by the tempter is an empty heart.

III. TRUE WISDOM IS THE SUREST ANTIDOTE TO TEMPTATION. All knowledge tends in some degree to preserve from evil. Light makes for goodness. Both are from God, and therefore they must harmonize. Secular knowledge is morally useful. A very large proportion of the criminals in our jails can neither read nor write. Ignorant of wiser courses, they are led aside to the lowest pursuits. Sound intelligence and good information introduce men at least to the social conscience. But the schoolmaster is not the saviour of the world. Higher wisdom is needed to be the successful antidote to sin— that wisdom which, in the Book of Proverbs, is almost synonymous with religion—the knowledge of God and his laws, and the practical discernment of the application of this knowledge to conduct. We must know God's will and the way of the Christian life, the beauty of holiness and how to attain it, if we are to have a good safeguard against sin. Christ, the Wisdom of God, dwelling in our hearts, is the great security against temptation.

IV. TO BE EFFECTUAL AS AN ANTIDOTE TO TEMPTATION, WISDOM MUST BE RECEIVED WITH DELIGHT. Knowledge must be "pleasant." We are most influenced by that which we love most. There is a strength in the Divine joy. So long as religious truths are accepted in cold intellectual conviction, or submitted to through hard compulsions of duty, they will have little power over us. But happily God has joined the highest truth to the purest gladness. Wisdom is a pleasure to those who welcome it to their hearts. The acquisition of all knowledge is pleasurable. The knowledge of God is joined with peculiar spiritual delights. In rejoicing in this and in love to the incarnation of this wisdom in Christ, we have the strongest safeguard against temptation.

Ver. 14.—*Rejoicing to do evil.* We often insist upon the fact that goodness is the secret of true happiness, and invite men to rejoice in the service of God; but we are here reminded of an opposite kind of joy which some find in the course of wickedness.

I. THIS IS A POSSIBLE EXPERIENCE. It is so unnatural that one who knew nothing of the world might well declare it to be impossible. But experience proves its existence, and the explanation of it is not far to seek. 1. *Naturally desirable ends lend a sense of pleasure to the evil means by which they are sought.* The miser loves his money on its own account through previous associations with the ideas of what it might purchase. So the criminal may come to delight in his crimes because the profit he gets out of them has cast a glamour over the ugly deeds themselves. 2. *Some pleasures are sinful.* Then the whole course, end as well as means, is wicked; yet, as it concerns self-indulgence, a wicked glee accompanies it. 3. *There is a sense of freedom in sin.* There is more room to range at large over the broad way than in the narrow path of righteousness. The sinner has burst the shackles of law, and he revels in the licence of self-will. 4. *Sin gives an opportunity for the exercise of power.* Much evil is done simply for the sake of effect, in order that the doer of it may find himself producing results. But it is easier to do harm than to do good. Therefore a man turns to evil for the larger realization of his power. So wicked children delight in picking flies to pieces.

II. THIS IS A SIGN OF ADVANCED WICKEDNESS. 1. *At first it is painful to sin.* The poor, weak soul gives way to temptation, but the very act of sinning is accompanied with a sense of uneasiness and humiliation. 2. *A further stage is reached when sin is committed with indifference.* This is indeed a state of moral degradation, for conscience is now practically dead, and the sinner is as willing to have his pleasure by lawless means as in an innocent manner. 3. *The lowest depth is reached when there is a positive pleasure in doing wrong.* Evil is then chosen on its own account, and not as the disagreeable or the indifferent means for reaching some ulterior end. When two courses are open, the bad one is deliberately selected as the more pleasant on its own account. A malignant joy lights up the countenance of the abandoned sinner at the mere prospect of some new villainy. This is Satanic wickedness. The abandoned sinner can now exclaim with Milton's Satan—

"Evil, be thou my good!"

III. THIS IS A DELUSIVE JOY. 1. *It is shallow.* Though it may be excited into a diabolical ecstasy, it has no heart-satisfying qualities. Beneath it there is profound unrest. The peace which accompanies the joy of holiness, and which is the sweetest ingredient in the cup of the good man, is quite wanting here. There are shooting pangs, dark misgivings, and dread sinkings of heart in the midst of this monstrous delight. 2. *It will not endure.* The pleasures of sin do but endure for a season. The sweet morsels soon turn to dust and ashes. After the wild orgie there follows deep depression or dread despair, or at best a sense of listless weariness. The appetite is soon exhausted. New and more piquant forms of wickedness must be invented to stimulate the jaded palate. At length the awful consequences must come, and anguish of soul follow the delights of sin when God's judgment takes effect.

Ver. 15.—*Crooked ways.* I. CROOKED WAYS ARE DEVIATIONS FROM THE STRAIGHT PATHS OF MORAL SIMPLICITY. The man of high character is simple in conduct. Great complexity of motive is generally a sign of moral laxity. The way of right is straight because it makes for its goal without any considerations of expediency, danger, or pleasure. To be turned aside from the steep Hill of Difficulty, or into By-path Meadow, is to forsake the right for selfish ease. When men allow considerations of momentary advantage to guide their actions, they will be perpetually swayed from side to side till their track is marked by an irregular "zigzag." "The expression of truth," says Seneca, "is simplicity."

II. CROOKED WAYS ARE SIGNS OF LACK OF PRINCIPLE. Principles are like the rails on which the train runs, keeping it in a direct course and facilitating its speed. The unprincipled man is off the rails, and the result is confusion. Like a ship without compass, rudder, or chart, the unprincipled man drifts with wind and tide, and so leaves behind him a crooked track. The security for straightforward conduct is the guidance of a deep-seated principle of righteousness.

III. CROOKED WAYS RESULT FROM SHORT-SIGHTED AIMS. The lane which is made, bit by bit, from farm to farm, is likely to wind about; but the old Roman high-road that connects two distant cities runs as directly as possible. The ploughman who looks no further than his horses' heads will make a crooked furrow; to go straight he must fix his eyes on the end of the field. He who regards only present circumstances will wander aimlessly. To go right we must look out of self to Christ; beyond present expediency to the full purpose and end of life; above all earthly pursuits to the goal of the life eternal.

IV. CROOKED WAYS ARE DECEITFUL WAYS. Bad men often fear to go straight towards their evil aims lest they shall be discovered. They beat about the bush. The assassin avoids the high-road and slinks along under a hedge, that he may come upon his victim unawares. The thief breaks into the house by the back door. Honesty is direct; dishonesty is circuitous. Crooked ways tend to become deceitful, if they are not so of set purpose. A man may wander in them till he has lost account of the points of the compass, and knows not whither he is going. The most elementary notions of right and wrong are then confused. This is the common issue of casuistic and disingenuous conduct; it results in self-deception.

V. CROOKED WAYS LEAD TO A FATAL END. The way to heaven is to "turn to the right, and keep straight on." The road that leads to destruction is broad, admitting of much irregularity of motion from one side to the other. It is the straight and narrow way that leads to life.

HOMILIES BY VARIOUS AUTHORS.

Vers. 1—9.—*The conditions of religious knowledge.* The previous chapter having shown us in a variety of representations the necessity and the worth of wisdom, the question is now dealt with—How shall it be sought and attained?

I. CONDITIONS ON MAN'S SIDE. The enumeration is climactic, proceeding from the less strong to the stronger expressions. 1. *Receptivity.* The open mind and heart, ever ready to "adopt" true sentiments and appropriate them as one's own. The point is not to ask—Who says this? By what channel does it come to me? But—Is it sound? is it true? If so, it is *for me,* and shall be made my own. Truth is common property. 2. *Attention, concentration, assimilation.* "Keeping her commands with us." The thorough student finds it necessary to exercise his memory, and to help it by the use of note-books, where he hives his knowledge. So must we hive and store, arrange and digest, our religious impressions, which otherwise "go in at one ear and out at the other." Short germ-sayings may be thus kept in the memory; they will burst into fertility some day. 3. *Active application.* In figurative language "bending the ear" and "turning the heart" in the desired direction. The mind must not be passive in religion. It is no process of "cramming," but of personal, original, spiritual activity throughout. 4. *Passionate craving and prayerfulness.* "Calling Sense to one's side, and raising one's voice to Prudence"—to give another rendering to ver. 3. We must *invoke* the spirit of Wisdom for the needs of daily conduct; thus placing ourselves in living relation with what is our true nature. Fra Angelico prayed before his easel; Cromwell, in his tent on the eve of battle. So must the thinker in his study, the preacher in his pulpit, the merchant at his desk, if he would have the true clearness of vision and the only genuine success. True prayer is always for the *universal,* not the *private,* good. 5. *Persevering and laborious exertion.* Illustrated by the miner's toil. The passage (Job xxviii.), of extraordinary picturesque power and interest, describing the miner's operations, may help us to appreciate the illustration. The pursuit of what is ideal is still more arduous than that of the material, as silver and gold. It is often said that the perseverance of the unholy worker shames the sloth of the spiritual man. But let us not ignore the other side. The toil in the spiritual region is not obvious to the eye like the other, but is not the less really practised in silence by thousands of faithful souls. We should reflect on the immense travail of soul it has cost to produce the book which stirs us like a new force, though it may appear to flow with consummate ease from the pen. Such are the conditions of "understanding the fear of Jehovah," or, in modern language, of appropriating, making religion our own; "receiving the things of the Spirit of God," in the language of St. Paul (1 Cor. ii. 14). It is the highest human possession, because permanent, inalienable, and preservative amidst life's ills.

II. CONDITIONS ON THE SIDE OF GOD. If religion be the union or identification of the soul with God, he must be related to us in such a way as makes this possible. 1. He is *wisdom's Source* and *Giver*. He not only contains in himself that knowledge which, reflected in us, becomes prudence, sense, wisdom, piety; he is an active Will and a self-communicating Spirit. The ancients had a glimpse of this when they said that the gods were not of so grudging or envious a nature as not to reveal their good to men. God is self-revealing; "freely gives of his things" to us, that we may *know*, and in knowing, *possess* them. 2. *His wisdom is saving.* "Sound wisdom" (ver. 7) may be better rendered *soundness*, or *salvation*, or *health*, or *saving health*. It seems to come from a root signifying the *essential* or *actual*. Nothing is essential but health for sensuous enjoyment; nothing but health, in the larger sense, for spiritual enjoyment. Let us think of God as himself absolute Health, and thus the Giver of all health and happiness to his creatures. 3. He is *Protector* of the faithful. The Hebrew imagination, informed by constant scenes of war, delights to represent him as the Buckler or Shield of his servants (Ps. xviii. 2; xxxiii. 20; lxxxix. 19). Those who "walk in innocence" seem to bear a charmed life. They "fear no evil," for he is with them. The vast sky is their tent-roof. They may be slain, but cannot be hurt. To be snatched from this world is to be caught to his arms. 4. He is eternal *Justice*. Being this in himself, the "way of his saints," which is synonymous with human rectitude, cannot be indifferent to him. Right is the highest idea we can associate with God. It is exempt from the possible suspicion of weakness or misdirection which may cleave to the mere idea of goodness or kindness. It essentially includes might. Thus the soul finds shelter beneath this vast and majestic conception and faith of its God. These, then, are the conditions, Divine and human, of religion. That we may realize it in ourselves, "understand right, justice, and equity"—in a word, "every good way" of life and thought, uniting piety with morality—the conditions must be faithfully fulfilled. Perfect bodily health may not be attainable; some of its conditions lie without the sphere of freedom, and within that of necessary law. Spiritual health *is* attainable, for it lies within the sphere of freedom. Then God is realized; it is the ether of the soul, and the region of love and light and blessedness.—J.

Vers. 10—22.—*The profit of religious knowledge.* It is preservative amidst the influences of evil example and of sensuous solicitation.

I. THE WAY IN WHICH IT ACTS AS A PRESERVATIVE. 1. By taking up a *central place in the consciousness.* "When wisdom enters thy heart, and knowledge is dear to thy soul." Not as a stranger or mere guest, but a beloved and confidential intimate. The heart denotes here, as elsewhere, "the centre and organic basis of the collective life of the soul, the seat of sentiment, the starting-point of personal self-determination." The soul, as used by Hebrew writers, denotes the entire assemblage of the passive and active principles of the inner life. Delitzsch terms the heart, as used in the Bible, "the birthplace of thought;" and this is true, because thought springs out of the dim chaos of feeling as the defined crystals from the chemical mixture. 2. By *counteractive force.* If the inmost thing we know and feel be a sense of right and a sense of God, a pure sentiment and a lofty idea, this must exclude the baser feelings, and displace the images of pleasure and objects of desire which are unlawful and undivine. There is watch and ward in the fortress of Man-soul against the enemy and the intruder. The "expulsive force of a new affection" operates. It is the *occupied* heart that alone is temptation-proof. "Discretion shall watch over thee, prudence guard thee." The mind, directed to what is without, and feeling for its course among uncertainties, thus appears forearmed against dangers.

II. The dangers from which it preserves. Social dangers. In society lies our field of full moral development, both in sympathy with the good and in antipathy to the evil. Two dangers are particularized. 1. *The influence of the bad man.* We know men by their talk and by their actions—their habit in both; their "style," their "form," in the expressive language of the day. (1) His *talk* is of "froward things," or "perversities"—cunning, crafty, malicious in spirit (ver. 12). Literally it is *crooked* talk, which is a relative term—the direct opposite of the "straightness" of ver. 9 being meant. Our moral intuitions appear in the mind under the analogy of relations in space, and are thus designated probably in all languages. The right line and the curve or zigzag represent what we *feel* about good and evil in conduct. The speech of *evil insinuation, covert suggestion, bad tone,* generally may be meant; or perhaps, rather, guilty topics of conversation. The East is more leisurely in its habits than are we; and the warning has peculiar adaptation to the unfilled hours of an easy life, and which bad talk so often wastes and corrupts. (2) His *habit of life.* He forsakes the "straight paths" to walk in "dark ways," such as those alluded to by St. Paul (Rom. xiii. 13; Eph. v. 11; 1 Thess. v. 5). In the like sense that darkness is antipathetic to us, is moral evil (hence its appropriateness as an emblem); we may overcome the feeling partially, but only by doing ourselves a violence. It is a step further in self-perversion to "take pleasure in the execution of evil, and to make merry over wickedness." Human nature demands sympathy; the most depraved cannot do without it or the semblance of it. We are always craving the sight of that which reflects us; hence the sight of evil gives joy to the bad man, the sight of good enrages him. For he is a deformity. His ways are crooked, twisted all his mode of mind and life; a moral deformity. The conscience, armed with the healthy perception of the true, beautiful, and good, sees all this in the bad man, recognizes him for what he is, and so is proof against him. One great lesson of Goethe's 'Faust' is that the tempted man does not see the devil in human shape, because his moral temper has been first unstrung, and so his vision vitiated. 2. *The solicitations of the bad woman.* The expressions, "strange, foreign" (ver. 16), appear to designate her as the wife of another, an adulteress (comp. ch. vi. 26; but the sense is disputed). To allegorize the passage is to weaken its force; for the actual dangers of youth are clearly indicated. She is depicted in the strongest light of reality. This is what she is in the view of the inspired conscience. (1) Her *infidelity* to her husband and her God (ver. 17). For marriage is a bond, not only between two human beings, but between each and God. Affiance is the glory of womanhood; to break her plighted troth is to wreck all her true charm and beauty. "Companion of her youth" is a beautiful designation of the husband (Jer. iii. 4; Ps. lv. 14). (2) Her *dangerous arts.* Oh, what can replace a youth defiled? or what more dangerous influence can there be than that of her whose "hatred is goaded by shame"—hatred against the virtue which confronts to reproach her? Her smooth tongue, flattering her victim with simulated admiration, and with the "hypocrisy of passion," is more deadly than the sword. (3) Her *deadly seductions.* Death, the kingdom of the shades, the ghosts who lead, according to the view of the ancient world, a faint and bloodless existence below, is the end of her and the partakers of her sins. To Sheôl, to Hades, the bourne whence no traveller returns, the steps of all her visitors tend. Her house seems ever to be tottering over the dark abyss. The truth held in this tragic picture is too obvious to need further illustration. Fatal to health of body, to peace of soul, to the very life itself, is the zymotic disease of lust. To the religious conscience thus the harlot appears; stripped of her paint and finery, her hypocrisy exposed, the poison of her being detected. It is the shadow of a life, and ends in emptiness, darkness, and ghostly gibbering.—J.

Vers. 20—22.—*The principle of moral stability.* This may be regarded as the epilogue or summary of the whole chapter. The object of all Wisdom's exhortations and warnings is the direction of youth to the good way, and that they may hold on the path of the just. For—

I. The righteous have a future before them. A "dwelling in the land "—the home-land; sound dear to an Israelitish ear. The *form* in which the happy future shall be realized may be first *material,* but only to pass into the spiritual. For ages Israel saw the promise under the image of material prosperity; afterwards, in the purification and enlightenment of her conscience by the gospel, she looked for a " better country, that is, an heavenly." Both senses may be included. The enlightened spirit knows how to idealize every material content, and will leave much undefined in the prospect. Enough to say of all the seekers of God's kingdom and righteousness, " They have a future before them." The soul itself suffices to itself for the scene of bliss, and converts the rich land of Canaan into the type of its inward joys and harvests of good.

II. THE WICKED HAVE NO FUTURE BEFORE THEM. That is, in the sense *par excellence.* Their doom is to be rooted out and cast forth from the land. What lies behind the material figure, who can say? To conceive it transcends the bounds of human thought. There is no travelling out of the analogies of experience possible. We reach at last a *negative* conception in the case both of future bliss and future woe. The Buddhists aim as their highest goal at the *Nirvana,* which is the negation of finite existence with its defects and evils. What must be the *Nirvana* of the wicked? The negation of the Infinite must mean confinement in self, and this is death indeed. They who have persistently said "No" to God and the good in their life will be confronted by an everlasting "No!" And thus again the wheel comes full circle, and they reap as they sow (comp. Matt. vii. 24—27).—J.

Vers. 1—9.—*The course, the goal, and the prize of wisdom.* These are comprehensive verses; they include the three main features of the heavenly race.

I. THE COURSE OF THE WISDOM-SEEKER. He who searches for wisdom is a wise runner in a heavenly race; he is pursuing an end which the Divine Author of his being distinctly and emphatically commends. 1. His search for life-giving truth must be characterized by *readiness to receive.* He must be wholly different in spirit from those who are disinclined to learn; still more must he be far removed from those who scornfully reject; he must be a son who "will receive the words" of wisdom—the words of the "only wise God," of him who is "the Wisdom of God" (ver. 1). 2. But there must be not only readiness; there should be *eagerness to receive.* He must "incline his ear" (ver. 2). Not only be prepared to listen when Wisdom speaks, but make a distinct and positive effort to learn the truth which affects him and which will bless him. 3. Beyond this, there must be *carefulness to retain.* The student must not let his mind be a sieve through which knowledge passes and from which it is readily lost; he must make it a reservoir which will retain; he is to "hide God's commandments" within him (ver. 1), to take them down into the deep places of the soul whence they will not escape. 4. Further, there must be *perseverance in the search.* He must "apply his heart to understanding" (ver. 2). Not by "fits and starts" is the goal to be reached, but by steady, patient, continuous search. 5. And there must also be *enthusiasm in the endeavour* (vers. 3, 4). With the impassioned earnestness with which a man who is lost in the pathless wood, or is sinking under the whelming wave, "cries" and "lifts up his voice," should the seeker after heavenly wisdom strive after the goal which is before him. With the untiring energy and inexhaustible ardour with which men toil for silver or dig for the buried treasure of which they believe themselves to have found the secret, should the soul strive and search after the high end to which God is calling it.

II. THE GOAL HE WILL SURELY REACH. He who thus seeks for heavenly truth will attain that to which he is aspiring; "for the Lord giveth wisdom," etc. (ver. 6). There is no man who desires to be led into the path of that Divine wisdom which constitutes the life and joy of the soul, and who pursues that lofty and holy end in the spirit here commended, who will fail to reach the goal toward which he runs. That earnest and patient runner shall be helped of God; Divine resources shall be supplied to him; he shall run without weariness, he shall walk without fainting, till the winning-post is clasped (see Matt. v. 6; vii. 7, 8). 1. He shall apprehend the essential elements of religion. "Thou shalt understand the fear of the Lord" (ver. 5). He will be led into a spiritual apprehension of that which constitutes the foundation and the essence of all true piety. He will be able to distinguish between the substance and the shadow, the reality and the pretence of religion. 2. He shall also—and this is a still greater thing—*attain to a vital and redeeming knowledge of God himself.* "Thou shalt find the knowledge of God" (ver. 5). To know him is eternal life (John xvii. 3).

But this knowledge must be—what in the case of the earnest disciple of heavenly wisdom it will become—a *vital* knowledge; it must be of the whole spiritual nature, and not only of the intellectual faculty. It must be a knowledge which (1) engages the whole powers of the spirit; (2) which brings joy to the soul; (3) which leads to an honest effort after God-likeness.

III. THE PRIZE HE WILL WIN. It may be truly said that the runner in the race finds a deeper satisfaction in clasping the goal while his competitors are all behind him than in wearing the chaplet of honour on his brows. And it may be truly said that the most blessed guerdon which the heavenly runner wins is in that knowledge of God which is his " goal " rather than in the after-honours which are his "prize." Yet we may well covet with intense eagerness the prize which Wisdom holds in her hand for those who are victorious. It includes much. 1. Stores of deep spiritual verities. " He layeth up sound wisdom," etc. (ver. 7)—greater and deeper insight into the most profound and precious truth. 2. Discernment of all practical wisdom. " Thou shalt understand righteousness, and judgment, and equity; yea, every good path " (ver. 9). 3. Divine guardianship along all the path of life. " He is a Buckler to them that walk uprightly. He keepeth the paths of judgment," etc. (vers. 7, 8).—C.

Vers. 10—15.—*The course of sin and the strength of righteousness.* We have here portrayed for us—

I. THE SHOCKING COURSE OF SIN. 1. It begins in departure from rectitude. Evil men first manifest their error by " leaving the paths of uprightness." They were once under the wholesome restraints of righteousness. Parental control, the influences of the sanctuary and of virtuous society, held them in check, but these are thrown off; they have become irksome, and they are rebelled against and abandoned. The old and wise principles which were received and cherished are one by one discarded, and they stand unshielded, unguided, ready to wander in forbidden paths. 2. It continues in the practice of evil. Having thrown off old restraints, they " walk in the ways of darkness " (ver. 13); they proceed to do, habitually, those things which the unenlightened do—those things which shun the light and love the darkness; deeds of error and of shame. 3. It resorts to despicable shifts. " Whose ways are crooked " (ver. 15). Sin cannot walk straight on; it would be soon overtaken by penalty, or fall over the precipice. It is like men pursued of justice, who have to turn and double that they may elude those who are behind. The course of sin is twisted and tortuous; it resorts to cunning and craftiness. All manliness is eaten out of it; it has the spirit and habit of a slave (see Rom. vi. 16). 4. It hardens into utter perversity. They " are froward in their paths " (ver. 15); they "speak froward things " (ver. 12), *i.e.* they sink down into complete hardihood and spiritual stubbornness; their hearts are turned aside from all that is devout, pure, wise, and they have gone utterly after that which is profane and base. 5. It culminates in a hateful and hurtful propagandism. They " rejoice to do evil, and delight in the frowardness of the wicked " (ver. 14). Sin can go no further in enormity, no deeper in abasement, than when, rejoicing in iniquity, it seeks to lead others into the same guilt and vileness with itself. What a pitiful zealotry is this—the anxiety and pertinacity of sin in winning from the paths of rectitude the children of innocence and truth! What a saddening thought that thousands of our fellow-men are actively occupied in this diabolical pursuit!

II. THE PERIL OF PIETY AND VIRTUE. Here, on earth, the purest virtue must walk side by side with the worst depravity. Sin sits down at the same hearth with goodness; profanity with piety. And thus brought into close contact, it is open to one to win or to seduce the other. We rejoice that godliness is seeking to gain impiety for God, but we mourn and tremble as we see sin seeking to pervert purity and goodness from " the right ways of the Lord." We are all open to human influence. The heart of man is responsive to human entreaty and example. But especially so is the heart of youth : *that* is tender, impressionable, plastic. Perhaps never a day passes but the sun looks down, in every land, on some young heart detached from truth, led into the path of evil, stained with sin, through the snares and wiles of guilty men. Who does not sigh with some feeling of solicitude as he sees the young man go forth from the shelter of the godly home into the world where the wicked wait, " rejoicing to do evil," and taking pride in the destruction they produce?

III. The strength and security of righteousness. When wisdom enters the heart and knowledge is pleasant to the soul, then discretion will preserve, and understanding will keep us (vers. 10, 11). In other words, the cordial acceptance of the truth of God is the one security against sin. Delighting to do God's will, his Law being *in the heart* as well as in the understanding (Ps. xl. 8), this will prove an effectual breakwater against the tides of evil. He that can say, "O Lord, how love I thy Law!" (Ps. cxix.) will never have to utter words of bitter remorse and black despair. Would youth know the certain path of victory, and pursue that way which leads, not down to shame, but on and up to heavenly glory? 1. Let it regard with earnest gaze him who is the Wisdom of God in fullest revelation to the sons of men. 2. Yield to him its early, unbounded love. 3. Then will it find unfading joy in the Divine truth which flowed from his lips, and which shone in his holy life. Whoso believes in him shall never be confounded.—C.

Vers. 16—19.—*The way of sin : a sermon to young men.* Reference is made here to one particular sin. While the words of the teacher are specially appropriate to it, they will also apply to all sin; they show the way it takes. Let us see —
I. That sin is the contradiction of the Divine thought. It is a "strange" thing (ver. 16). The painted harlot is "the strange woman." And while the prostitution of a human being, meant to be a helpmeet for man in all his highest and holiest pursuits to a mere ministress to his unlawful lusts, is the very saddest departure from the Divine ideal, and amply justifies the use of the word "strange woman," we may remember that *all* sin is a *strange* thing in the universe of God. How it ever entered there is the problem which can never be solved. But meeting with it here, in whatever form, we say, "This is the contrary of the thought of the Supreme," "This is the exact opposite of his design," "This is something alien, unnatural, intrusive: cannot we cast it out?"
II. That sin must stoop to falsehood if it will win its way. It "flattereth with its words" (ver. 16). Flattery is only another name for a sweet falsehood. The woman that is a sinner uses flattery to accomplish her ends. So sin cannot live without lying. That may be said of sin which was said of a great European usurper, that it "has deliberately taken falsehood into its service." But the most effective and destructive form of it is flattery. Let the young take earnest heed to their danger. When the lips of beauty speak soft and gratifying things, let purity beware; it is only too likely that temptation in its most seductive form is nigh, and that character and reputation are being insidiously assailed.
III. That sin sinks to its darkest depths through various violations. (Ver. 17.) It is uncertain whether by the "guide of her youth" is to be understood her husband (see Mal. ii. 14, 15), her parents, or her God. The second clause clearly refers to the marriage covenant, which is regarded as a sacred bond. Whichever be the correct view of the former clause, it is certain that the sinner of the text could only descend to her shameless depth by violating every promise she has made, by breaking through every fence which once stood between her and guilt. This is the inevitable course of sin. It violates first one vow, then another, until all sacred promises are broken. (1) Deliberate resolutions, (2) solemn assurances, (3) formal vows;—all are infringed.
IV. That sin leads straight to the doorway of death. (Vers. 18, 19.) It leads: 1. To physical death. Vice carries with it a penalty in the body; it robs of health and strength; it enfeebles; it sows seeds of sickness and death. The "graves of lust" are in every cemetery and churchyard in the land. 2. To spiritual death. "None that go unto her return again" as they went. Men come away from every unlawful indulgence other than they go—weaker and worse in soul. Alas for the morrow of incontinence, of whatever kind it be! The soul is injured; its self-respect is slain, its force is lessened; it is on the incline which slopes to death, and one step nearer to the foot of it. "Her house inclineth unto death." 3. To eternal death. They who resort to forbidden pleasure are fast on their way to the final condemnation; they have wandered long leagues from "the paths of life." We conclude with two admonitions: (1) Keep carefully away from the beginnings of evil. Shun not only the "strange woman's" door, but the evil glance, the doubtful company, the impure book, the mere-

tricious paper. (2) The way of escape is *immediate* and *total* abandonment of sin. Such resolution made at once, seeking God's strength and grace, will permit the wanderer to "return again."—C.

Vers. 20—22.—*Recompense and retribution.* It ought to be enough for us that wisdom is the supremely excellent thing; that the service of God is the one right thing. We should hasten to do that which commends itself to our conscience as that which is obligatory. But God knows that, in our weakness and frailty, we have need of other inducements than a sense of duty; he has, therefore, given us others. He has made wisdom and righteousness to be immeasurably remunerative; he has made folly and sin to be utterly destructive to us. We look at—

I. THE REWARD OF WISDOM. (Vers. 20, 21.) 1. The man who pursues wisdom, who seeks conformity to the will of the Wise One, will have holy companionship for the path of life. He will walk in the way in which good and righteous men walk. Instead of being "the companion of fools," he will be "the friend of the wise." Those whose hearts are pure, whose minds are stored with heavenly treasure, and whose lives are admirable, will be about him, making his whole path fragrant with the flowers of virtue, rich with the fruits of goodness. 2. He will be upheld in personal integrity. Walking in the way of the good, and keeping the paths of the righteous, he himself will be preserved in his integrity, and be set before God's face for ever (see Ps. xli. 12). His feet will not slip; he will not wander into forbidden ways; he will keep "the King's highway of holiness;" his face will be ever set toward the heavenly Jerusalem. 3. He will dwell in the land of plenty (ver. 21). To "dwell in the land," to "remain" in the land of promise, was to abide in that country where all things in rich abundance waited for the possession and enjoyment of the people of God (Exod. iii. 8). Those who are the children of wisdom now dwell in a region which is full of blessing. If outward prosperity be not always their portion, yet is there provided by God (1) everything needful for temporal well-being; (2) fulness of spiritual privilege; (3) the abiding presence and favour of the eternal Father, the unfailing Friend, the Divine Comforter.

II. THE FATE OF FOLLY. (Ver. 22.) Those who were the children of folly in the wilderness-period were shut out of the land of promise; they did not enter into rest. The threat of the Holy One to those who had inherited the land was deportation and distance from their inheritance—being "cut off" and "rooted out." The evils which foolish and stubborn souls have now to dread, as the just penalty of their folly and their frowardness, are (1) exclusion from the "kingdom of God" on earth, and (2) exile from the kingdom of God in heaven. Such impenitent and unbelieving ones, by their own folly, cut themselves off from that "eternal life" which begins in a blessed and holy union with the Lord of glory here, and which is consummated and perpetuated in the nearer fellowship and more perfect bliss of heaven.—C.

EXPOSITION.

CHAPTER III.

Vers. 1—18.—4. *Fourth admonitory discourse.* The third chapter introduces us to a group of admonitions, and the first of these (vers. 1—18) forms the fourth admonitory discourse of the teacher. To all intents and purposes this is a continuation of the discourse in the preceding chapter, for inasmuch as that described the benefits, spiritual and moral, which follow from the pursuit of Wisdom, in promoting godliness and providing safety from evil companions, so this in like manner depicts the gain flowing from Wisdom, the happiness of the man who finds Wisdom, and the favour which he meets with both with God and man. The discourse embraces exhortations to obedience (vers. 1—4), to reliance on God (vers. 5, 6) against self-sufficiency and self-dependence (vers. 7, 8), to self-sacrificing devotion to God (vers. 9, 10), to patient submission to God's afflictive dispensations (vers. 11, 12), and concludes with pointing out the happy gain of Wisdom, her incomparable value, and wherein that value consists (vers. 13—18). It is noticeable that in each case the exhortation is accompanied with a corresponding promise of reward (vers. **2, 4, 6, 8, 10**), and these promises are brought forward with the view to encourage the observance of the duties recommended or enjoined. Jehovah is the central point to which all the exhortations converge. Obedience, trust, self-sacrificing devotion, submission, are successively brought forward by the teacher as due to God, and the persons in whom they are exhibited are truly happy in finding Wisdom. The transition in thought from the former to the latter part of the discourse is easy and natural. Obedience and trust are represented as bringing favour, guidance, and health—in a word, prosperity. But God is not only to be honoured in times of prosperity, but also in adversity his loving hand is to be recognized; and in this submission to his will is true wisdom.

Ver. 1.—**My son** (*b'ni*) serves to externally connect this discourse with the preceding. **Forget not my law.** This admonition bears a strong resemblance to that in ch. i. 8, though the terms employed are somewhat different, *torah* and *mits'oth* here occupying the place respectively of *musar* and *torah* in that passage. *My law* (*torathi*), is literally, *my teaching*, or *doctrine*, from the root *yarah*, " to teach." The *torah* is the whole body of salutary doctrine, and designates " Law " from the standpoint of teaching. Forgetting here is not so much oblivion arising from defective memory, as a wilful disregard and neglect of the admonitions of the teacher. **Thine heart** (*libekha*); Vulgate, *cor*; LXX., καρδία; and so the sum total of the affections. **Keep**; *yitstsor*, from *notsar*, " to keep, or observe that which is commanded." The word is of frequent occurrence in the Proverbs, and appears about twenty-five times. **My commandments** (*mits'othay*); Vulgate, *præcepta mea*; LXX., τὰ ῥήματα μου; *i.e.* my precepts. The Hebrew verb from which it is derived means " to command, or prescribe." The law and commandments here alluded to are those which immediately follow, from ver. 3 onwards. The three main ideas combined in this verse are remembrance, affection, and obedience. Remembering the law or teaching will depend, to a large extent, on the interest felt in that law; and the admonition to "forget not" is an admonition to give "earnest heed," so that the law or teaching may be firmly fixed in the mind. In using the words, " let thy heart keep," the teacher goes to the root of the matter. There may be an historical remembrance of, or an intellectual assent to, the commandments, but these are insufficient, for the keeping of the

commandments must be based on the recognition of the fact that the affections of the heart are to be employed in the service of God, the keeping of the commandments is to be a labour of love. Again, the expression, "keep my commandments," implies, of course, external conformity to their requirements: we are " to observe to do them " (Deut. viii. 1); but it implies, further, spiritual obedience, *i.e.* an obedience with which love is combined (Deut. xxx. 20), and which arises from the inward principles of the heart being in harmony with the spirit of the commandments (see Wardlaw).

Ver. 2.—**Length of days** (*orek yamim*); Vulgate, *longitudo dierum*. The expression is literally "extension of days," and signifies the prolongation of life, its duration to the appointed limit—a meaning which is brought out in the LXX. μῆκος βίου, "length of days," the Greek word βίος being used, not of existence, but of the time and course of life. It occurs again in ver. 16, and also in Job xii. 12 and Ps. xxi. 4. "Length of days" is represented as a blessing in the Old Testament, depending, however, as in the present instance, on the fulfilment of certain conditions. Thus in the fifth commandment it is appended to the honouring of parents (Exod. xx. 12), and it was promised to Solomon, at Gibeon, on the condition that he walked in the way, statutes, and commandments of God (1 Kings iii. 14). The promise of prolongation of life is not to be pressed historically as applying to every individual case, but is to be taken as indicating the tendency of keeping the Divine precepts, which, as a rule, ensure preservation of health, and hence "length of days." **Long life** (*vush'noth khayyim*); literally, *years of life*; Targum Jonathan, Vulgate, Syriac, and Arabic, *anni vitæ*; LXX., ἔτη ζωῆς. The Authorized Version scarcely serves to bring out the sense of the original, as there is practically no difference in meaning between " length of days " and " long life." The idea conveyed in the expression, " years of life," is that of material prosperity. The thought of an extended life is carried on from the preceding expression, but it is amplified and described. The years of life will be many, but they will be years of life in its truest sense, as one of true happiness and enjoyment, free from distracting cares, sickness, and other drawbacks. The Hebrew plural, *khayyim*, " lives," is equivalent to the Greek expression, βίος βιωτός, " a life worth while living " (cf. Plat., ' Apol.,' 38, A). To the Israelitish mind, the happiness of life consisted in " dwelling in the land " (Deut. iv. 40; v. 30, etc.), and " abiding in the house of the Lord " (Ps. xv. 1; xxiii. 6; xxvii. 3) (Zöckler). The conjecture that the plural, *khayyim*, signifies the present and the future life, is unfounded. The scope of the promise before us is confined to the present stage of existence, and it is negatived also by the similar use of the plural in ch. xvi. 5, "In the light of the king's countenance is life (*khayyim*)," where *khayyim* cannot possibly refer to the future life. *Khayyim* stands for life in its fulness. "Godliness" has indeed, as St. Paul wrote to Timothy, "promise of the life that now is, and of that which is to come" (1 Tim. iv. 8). **Peace** (*shalom*). The verb *shalom*, from which the substantive *shalom* is derived, signifies "to be whole, sound, safe," and hence "peace" means internal and external contentment, and tranquillity of mind arising from the sense of safety. In ver. 17 the ways of Wisdom are designated *peace*. While, on the one hand, peace is represented by the psalmist as the possession of those who love God's Law (Ps. cxix. 165), on the other, it is denied the wicked (Isa. xlviii. 22; lvii. 21). **Shall they add to thee**; *i.e.* shall all the precepts and commands bring (Zöckler) or heap upon (Muffet) thee.

Ver. 3.—**Mercy and truth** (*khesed vermeth*); properly, *love and truth;* Vulgate, *misericordia et veritas;* LXX., ἐλεημοσύναι καὶ πίστεις. With this verse begin the commandments which are alluded to in ver. 1. The Hebrew *khesed* has to be understood in its widest sense, though the Vulgate and the LXX. confine it to one aspect of its meaning, viz. that which refers to the relation of man to man, to the pity evoked by the sight of another's misfortunes, and to almsgiving. The radical meaning of the word is "ardent desire," from the root *khasad*, "to eagerly or ardently desire." Delitzsch describes it as "well-affectedness." Predicated of God, it indicates God's love and grace towards man; predicated of man, it signifies man's love towards God, *i.e.* piety, or man's love towards his neighbour, *i.e.* humanity. Where this mercy or love is exhibited in man it finds expression in (1) mutual outward help; (2) forgiveness of offences; (3) sympathy of feeling, which leads to interchange of thought, and so to the development of the spiritual life (see Elster, *in loc.*). The word carries with it the ideas of kindliness, benignity (Targum, *benignitas*), and grace (Syriac, *gratia*). **Truth** (*emeth*); properly, *firmness*, or *stability*, and so fidelity in which one performs one's promise. Truth is that absolute integrity of character, both in word and deed, which secures the unhesitating confidence of all (Wardlaw). Umbreit and Elster designate it as inward truthfulness, the *pectus rectum*, the very essence of a true man. As *khesed* excludes all selfishness and hate, so *emeth* excludes all hypocrisy and dissimulation. These two virtues are frequently combined in the Proverbs (*e.g.* ch. xiv. 22; xvi. 16; xx. 28) and Psalms (*e.g.* Ps.

xxv. 10; xl. 11; lvii. 4—11; cviii. 5; cxxxviii. 2), and, when predicated of man, indicate the highest normal standard of moral perfection (Zöckler). The two ideas are again brought together in the New Testament phrase, ἀληθεύειν ἐν ἀγάπῃ, "to speak the truth in love" (Eph. iv. 15). There seems little ground for the remark of Salasius, that "mercy" refers to our neighbours, and "truth" to God. Each virtue, in fact, has a twofold reference—one to God, the other to man. The promise in ver. 4, that the exercise of these virtues procures favour with God and man, implies this twofold aspect. **Bind them about thy neck**; either (1) as ornaments worn about the neck (Gejerus, Zöckler); or (2) as amulets or talismans, which were worn from a superstitious notion to ward off danger (Umbreit and Vaihinger); or (3) as treasures which one wears attached to the neck by a chain to guard against their loss (Hitzig); or (4) as a signet, which was carried on a string round the neck (Delitzsch). The true reference of the passage seems to lie between (1) and (3). The latter adapts itself to the parallel expression, "Write them on the tablet of thine heart," and also agrees with ch. vi 21, "Tie them about thy neck," the idea being that of their careful preservation against loss. The former meaning, however, seems preferable. Mercy and truth are to be ornaments of the character, to be bound round the neck, *i.e.* worn at all times (comp. ch. i. 9, "For they shall be an ornament of grace unto thine head, and chains about thy neck." See also Gen. xli. 42; Song of Sol. i. 10; iv. 9; Ezek. xvi. 11). The imagery of the binding is evidently taken from Exod. xiii. 9 and Deut. vi. 8, and is suggestive of the tephillim, or phylacteries. **Write them upon the table of thine heart**; *i.e.* inscribe them, mercy and truth, deeply there, impress them thoroughly and indelibly upon thine heart, so that they may never be forgotten, and may form the mainspring of your actions. The expression implies that the heart is to be in entire union with their dictates. *The table* (*luakh*) was the tablet expressly prepared for writing by being polished, corresponding to the πινακίδιον, the writing-table of Luke i. 63, which, however, was probably covered with wax. The inscription was made with the *stylus*. The same word is used of the *tables* of stone, on which the ten commandments were written with the finger of God, and allusion is in all probability here made to that fact (Exod. xxxi. 18; xxxiv. 28). The expression, "the tables of the heart," occurs in ch. vii. 3; Jer. xvii. 1 (cf. 2 Cor. iii. 3); and is used by Æschylus, 'Pro.,' 789, δέλτοι φρενῶν, "the tablets of the heart." This clause is omitted in the LXX.

Ver. 4.—**So shalt thou find** (*vum'tsa*);

literally, *and find.* A peculiar use of the imperative, the imperative kal (*m'tsa*) with *vau* consecutive (ו) being equivalent to the future, " thou shalt find," as in the Authorized Version. This construction, where two imperatives are joined, the former containing an exhortation or admonition, the second a promise made on the condition implied in the first, and the second imperative being used as a future, occurs again in ch. iv. 4; vii. 2, " Keep my commandments, and live;" ix. 6, " Forsake the foolish, and live;" xx. 13, "Open thine eyes, and thou shalt be satisfied with bread" (cf. Gen. xlii. 18; Ps. xxxvii. 27; Job xxii. 21; Isa. xxxvi. 16; Hos. x. 12; Amos v. 4—6; Gesenius, § 130. 2). Delitzsch calls this "an admonitory imperative;" Böttcher, "the desponsive imperative." Compare the Greek construction in Menander, Οἶδ᾽ ὅτι ποίησον, for ποιήσεις, "Know that this you will do." *Find* (*matza*); here simply " to attain," " obtain," not necessarily implying previous search, as in ch. xvii. 20. **Favour** (*khen*). The same word is frequently translated " grace," and means the same thing; Vulgate, *gratia*; LXX., χάρις. For the expression, "to find favour" (*matsa khen*), see Gen. vi. 8; Exod. xxxiii. 12; Jer. xxxi. 2; comp. Luke i. 30, Εὗρες γὰρ χάριν παρὰ τῷ Θεῷ. " For thou hast found favour [or, ' grace'] with God," spoken by Gabriel to the Virgin. **Good understanding** (*sekel tov*); *i.e.* good sagacity, or prudence. So Delitzsch, Bertheau, Kamph. A true sagacity, prudence, or penetrating judgment will be adjudicated by God and man to him who possesses the internal excellence of love and truth. The Hebrew *sekel* is derived from *sakal*, " to act wisely or prudently," and has this intellectual meaning in ch. xiii. 15; Ps. cxi. 10 (see also 1 Sam. xxv. 3 and 2 Chron. xxx. 22). The Targum Jonathan reads, *intellectus et benignitas*, thus throwing the adjective into a substantival form; the Syriac, *intellectus* simply. Ewald, Hitzig, Zöckler, and others, on the other hand, understand *sekel* as referring to the judgment formed of any one, the favourable opinion or view which is entertained of him by others, and hence take it as *reputation*, or estimation. The man who has love and truth will be held in high esteem by God and man. Our objection to this rendering is that it does not seem to advance the meaning of the passage beyond that of "favour." Another, mentioned by Delitzsch, is that *sekel* is never used in any other sense than that of *intellectus* in the Mishle. The marginal reading, "good success," *i.e.* prosperity, seems inadmissible here, as the hiph. *has'kil*, "to cause to prosper," as in ch. xvii. 8; Josh. i. 7; Deut. xxix. 9, does not apply in this instance any more than in Ps. cxi. 10, margin. **In the sight**

of God and man (*b'eyney elohim v'adam*); literally, *in the eyes of Elohim and man;* i.e. according to the judgment of God and man (Zöckler); Vulgate, *coram Deo et hominibus.* A simpler form of this phrase is found in 1 Sam. ii. 26, where Samuel is said to have found favour with the Lord, and also with men. So in Luke ii. 52 Jesus found favour " with God and man (παρὰ Θεῷ καὶ ἀνθρώποις) " (comp. Gen. x. 9; Acts ii. 47; Rom. xiv. 18). The two conditions of favour and sagacity, or prudence, are not to be assigned respectively to God and man (as Ewald and Hitzig), or that finding favour has reference more to God, and being deemed prudent refers more to man. The statement is universal. Both these conditions will be adjudged to the man who has mercy and truth by God in heaven and man on earth at the same time (see Delitszch). The LXX., " after favour," instead of the text, reads, " and provide good things in the sight of the Lord and men," quoted by St. Paul (2 Cor. viii. 21).

Ver. 5.—**Trust in the Lord** (*b'takh el-y'hovah*); literally, *trust in Jehovah.* Entire reliance upon Jehovah, implied in the words, " with all thine heart," is here appropriately placed at the head of a series of admonitions which especially have God and man's relations with him in view, inasmuch as such confidence or trust, with its corresponding idea of the renunciation of reliance on self, is, as Zöckler truly remarks, a " fundamental principle of all religion." It is the first lesson to be learnt by all, and no less necessary for the Jew than for the Christian. Without this reliance on or confidence in God, it is impossible to carry out any of the precepts of religion. *Batakh* is, properly, " to cling to," and so passes to the meaning of "to confide in," "to set one's hope and confidence upon." The preposition *el* with *Jehovah* indicates the direction which the confidence is to take (cf. Ps. xxxvii. 3, 5). **Lean** (*tishshaen*); Vulgate, *innitaris;* followed by *el*, like *b'takh*, with which it is very similar in meaning. *Shaan*, not used in kal, in hiph. signifies " to lean upon, rest upon," just as man rests upon a spear for support. Its metaphorical use, *to repose confidence in*, is derived from the practice of kings who were accustomed to appear in public leaning on their friends and ministers; cf. 2 Kings v. 18; vii. 2, 17 (Gesenius). The admonition does not mean that we are not to *use* our own understanding (*binah*), *i.e.* form plans with discretion, and employ legitimate means in the pursuit of our ends; but that, when we use it, we are to depend upon God and his directing and overruling providence (Wardlaw); cf. Jer. ix. 23, 24, " Let not the wise man glory in his wisdom," etc. The teacher points out not only where we are to rely, but also where we are not to rely.

Ver. 6.—**In all thy ways.** This expression covers the whole area of life's action—all its acts and undertakings, its spiritual and secular sides, no less than its public and private. It guards against our acknowledging God in great crises and solemn acts of worship only (Plumptre). **Acknowledge** (*daehu*); Vulgate, *cogita;* LXX., γνώριζε. The Hebrew verb *yada* signifies "to know, recognize." To acknowledge God is, therefore, to recognize, in all our dealings and undertakings, God's overruling providence, which "shapes our ends, rough-hew them as we will." It is not a mere theoretical acknowledgment, but one that engages the whole energies of the soul (Delitzsch), and sees in God power, wisdom, providence, goodness, and justice. This meaning is conveyed by the Vulgate *cogitare,* which is "to consider" in all parts, "to reflect upon." David's advice to his son Solomon is, "Know thou (*ola*) the God of thy father." We may well acknowledge Jehovah ; for he "knoweth the way of the righteous" (Ps. i. 6). Acknowledging God also implies that we first ascertain whether what we are about to take in hand is in accordance with his precepts, and then look for his direction and illumination (Wardlaw). **And he shall direct thy paths** (*v'hu y'yashsher or'khotheyka*); *i.e.* he himself shall make them straight, or level, removing all obstacles out of the way ; or they shall, under God's direction, prosper and come to a successful issue ; they shall be virtuous, inasmuch as deviation into vice will be guarded against, and happy, because they are prosperous. The pronoun *v'hu* is emphatic, "he himself;" Vulgate, *et ipse.* *Yashar,* piel, is "to make a way straight," as in ch. ix. 15 ; xv. 21 ; xi. 5. Cf. the LXX. ὀρθυτομεῖν, "to cut straight" (see on ch. xi. 5). God here binds himself by a covenant (Lapide). This power is properly attributed to God, for "it is not in man to direct his steps" (Jer. x. 23).

Ver. 7.—**Be not wise in thine own eyes.** This admonition carries on the thought from the preceding verses (5, 6), approaching it from a different direction. It is a protest against self-sufficiency, self-conceit, and self-reliance. It says, in effect, "Trust in the Lord, do not trust in yourself." Wisdom, as Michaelis remarks, is to trust in God ; to trust in yourself and in your own wisdom is unwisdom. God denounces this spirit: "Woe unto them that are wise in their own eyes, and prudent in their own sight!" (Isa. v. 21), because such a spirit leads to the prohibited self-dependence, and is inconsistent with "the fear of the Lord." The precept of the text is reiterated by St. Paul,

especially in Rom. xii. 16, "Be not wise in your own conceits" (cf. 1 Cor. viii. 8 ; Gal. vi. 3). It commends humility. The diligent search for Wisdom is commanded. The great hindrance to all true wisdom is the thought that we have already attained it (Plumptre). *In thine own eyes;* i.e. in thine own estimation ; *arbitrio tuo* (Trem. et Jun.). **Fear the Lord, and depart from evil.** The connection of this with the first part of the verse becomes clear upon reflection. "The fear of the Lord" is true wisdom (Job xxviii. 28 ; ch. i. 7). Fear the Lord, therefore, because it is the best corrective of one's own wisdom, which engenders arrogance, pride, presumption of mind, which, moreover, is deceptive and apt to lead to sin. The fear of the Lord has this other advantage—that it leads to the departure from evil (ch. xvi. 6). It is the mark of the wise man that he fears the Lord, and departs from evil (ch. xiv. 16). These precepts form the two elements of practical piety (Delitzsch), an eminent example of which was Job (Job i. 1).

Ver. 8.—**It shall be health to thy navel, and marrow to thy bones.** A metaphorical expression, denoting the complete spiritual health which shall follow from fearing the Lord and departing from evil. *Health,* (*riph'uth*); properly, *healing;* LXX., ἴασις; Vulgate, *sanitas;* so Syriac and Arabic. The Targum Jonathan has *medicina,* "medicine," as the margin. The root *rapha* is properly "to sew together," and the secondary meaning, "to heal," is taken from the healing of a wound by sewing it up. Delitzsch, however, thinks *riph'uth* is not to be taken as a restoration from sickness, but as a raising up from enfeebled health, or a confirming of the strength which already exists. There shall be a continuance of health. Gesenius translates "refreshment." *To thy navel* (*l'shor'rekha*); Vulgate, *umbilico tuo;* so Targum Jonathan. *Shor* is "the navel," here used synecdochically for the whole body, just as "head" is put for the whole man (Judg. v. 30), "mouth" for the whole person speaking (ch. viii. 13), and "slow bellies" for depraved gluttons (Titus i. 12) (Gejerus, Umbreit). The idea is expressed in the LXX., Syriac, and Arabic by "to thy body" (τῷ σώματι σου; *corpori tuo*). The navel is here regarded as the centre of vital strength. For the word, see Cant. vii. 2 ; Ezek. xvi. 4. This is the only place in the Proverbs where this word is found. Gesenius, however, takes *shor,* or *l'shor'rekha,* as standing collectively for the nerves, in which, he says, is the seat of strength, and translates accordingly, "Health (*i.e.* refreshment) shall it be to thy nerves." *Marrow* (*shik'kuy*); literally, *watering* or *moistening,* as in the margin ; Vulgate, *irrigatio.* Moistening is imparted to the bones by the marrow, and thus they are strengthened: "His bones are moistened with marrow" (Job xxi. 24). Where there is an absence of marrow the drying up of the bones ensues, and hence their strength is impaired, and a general debility of the system sets in—they "wax old" (Ps. xxxii. 3). The effect of a broken spirit is thus described: "A broken spirit drieth up the bones" (ch. xvii. 22). The physiological fact here brought forward is borne witness to by Cicero, 'In Tusc.:' 'In visceribus atque medullis omne bonum condidisse naturam" (cf. Plato). The meaning of the passage is that, as health to the navel and marrow to the bones stand as representatives of physical strength, so the fear of the Lord, etc., is the spiritual strength of God's children.

Ver. 9.—**Honour the Lord with thy substance**, etc. An exhortation to self-sacrificing devotion by the appropriation and use of wealth to the service of Jehovah. *With thy substance* (*mehonekha*); Vulgate, *de tua substantia*; LXX., ἀπὸ σῶν δικαίων πόνων. *Hon*, properly "lightness," is "opulence," "wealth," as in ch. i. 13. The *min* in composition with *hon* is not partitive, as Delitzsch and Bertheau take it, but signifies "with" or "by means of," as in Ps. xxviii. 7; Isa. lviii. 12; Ezek. xxviii. 18; Obad. 9. The insertion of δικαίος by the LXX. limits the wealth to that which is justly acquired, and so guards against the erroneous idea that God is honoured by the appropriation to his use of unlawful wealth or gain (Plumptre). The Israelites "honoured Jehovah with their substance" when they contributed towards the erection of the tabernacle in the wilderness, and later when they assisted in the preparations for the building of the temple, and in the payment of tithes. The injunction may undoubtedly refer to tithes. and is in accordance with the requirement of the Mosaic Law on that and other points as to oblations, free-will offerings, etc.; but it has a wider bearing and contemplates the use of wealth for all pious and charitable purposes (see ch. xiv. 31). The word *maaser*, "tithe," does not occur in the Proverbs. **With the firstfruits** (*mereshith*); Vulgate, *de primitiis*. So Targum Jonathan, Syriac, and Arabic. The law of the firstfruits is found in Exod. xxii. 29; xxiii. 19; xxxiv. 20; Lev. xxiii. 10; Numb. xviii. 12; Deut. xviii. 4; xxvi. 1—3. The firstfruits were presented by every Israelite to the priests, in token of gratitude and humble thankfulness to Jehovah, and consisted of the produce of the land in its natural state, or prepared for human food (Maclear, 'Old Test. Hist.,' bk. iv. c. iii. a). The "firstfruits" also carried with it the idea of the best. The custom of offering the firstfruits of the field and other revenues as

a religious obligation was observed by ancient pagan nations (see Diod. Sic., i. 14; Plut., 'De Iside,' p. 377; Pliny, 'Hist. Nat.,' 18. 2 (Zöckler). Some of the ancient commentators find in this verse an argument for the support of the ministry. It is well known that the priests "lived of the sacrifice," and were "partakers of the altar," and as their support by these means tended to the maintenance of Divine worship, so those who supported them were in the highest degree "honouring God." The injunctions also show that the honouring of God does not consist simply of lip-service, of humility and confidence in him, but also of external worship, and in corporeal things. They are not peculiar to Israel, but are binding on all. They oppose all *selfish* use of God's temporal gifts, and lead to the thought that, in obeying them, we are only giving back to God what are his own. "The silver and the gold is mine, saith the Lord of hosts" (Hag. ii. 28).

"We give thee but thine own,
 Whate'er the gift may be;
All that we have is thine alone,
 A trust, O Lord, from thee."
 (Day's 'Psalter.')

Ver. 10.—**So shall thy barns be filled with plenty.** The promise held out to encourage the devotion of one's wealth to Jehovah's service, while supplying a motive which at first sight appears selfish and questionable, is in reality a trial of faith. Few persons find it easy to realize that giving away will increase their store (Wardlaw). The teacher is warranted in bringing forward this promise by the language of Moses in Deut. xxviii. 1—8, where, among other things, he promises that Jehovah will command a blessing upon the "storehouses" and industry of those who honour God. The principle is otherwise expressed in ch. xi. 25, "The liberal soul shall be made fat, and he that watereth shall be also watered himself;" and it is exemplified in Hag. i. 3—11; ii. 15, 19; Mal. iii. 10—12, and in the New Testament in Phil. iv. 14—19; 2 Cor. ix. 6—8. *Thy barns; asameykha,* the only form in which *asam,* "a storehouse," "barn," or "granary," occurs. The Hebrew *asam* is the same as the Latin *horreum* (Vulgate) and the Greek ταμιεῖον (LXX.). *With plenty* (*sava*); Vulgate, *saturitas;* i.e. fulness, abundance, plenty. The root *sava* is "to become satisfied," and that richly satisfied. This expression and the following, **and thy presses shall burst out with new wine,** depict the greatest abundance. *Thy presses* (*y'kaveykha*). The word here translated "presses" is, strictly speaking, "vats" or "reservoirs," into which the must from the wine-press flowed. The wine-press consisted of two parts, the *gath* (equivalent to the Latin *torcularium, torculum*, or *torcular;* Greek, ληνός, Matt. xxi. 33), into which the grapes were collected from the surrounding vineyard, and there trodden underfoot by several persons (Neh. xiii. 15: Isa. lxiii. 3; Lam. i. 15), whose movements were regulated by singing or shouting (Isa. xvi. 10; Jer. xlviii. 33), as among the Greeks (see 'Athen.,' v. p. 199, *a;* Anacreon, ' Od.,' xvii. 1. lii.; cf. Theocritus, vii. 25) and Egyptians (Wilkinson, 'Man. and Cust.,' vol. ii. pp. 152—157); and the *yekev*, used here, which was a trough of corresponding size, dug into the ground, or cut out of a rock, at a lower level, to receive the must. The *yekev* corresponded with the Greek ὑπολήνιον, mentioned in Mark xii. 1, and the Latin *lacus* (Ovid, ' Fasti,' v. 888; Pliny, ' Epist.,' ix. 20 ; ' Colum. de Rust.,' xii. 18): Cajeterus, indeed, reads, *lacus torcularii.* The word *yekev* is, however, used for the wine-press itself in Job xxiv. 11 and 2 Kings vi. 27. *Shall burst out (yiph'rotsu);* literally, *they shall extend themselves;* i.e. shall overflow. *Parats*, "to break," is here used metaphorically in the sense of " to be re lundant," " to overflow" (cf. 2 Sam. v. 20). It is employed intransitively of a people spreading themselves abroad, or increasing, in Gen. xxviii. 14; Exod. i. 12. *New wine (tirosh);* Vulgate, Arabic, and Syriac, *vino;* LXX., οἴνῳ; properly, as in the Authorized Version, "new wine;" Latin, *mustum* (see Deut. xxxiii. 28; Isa. xxxvi. 17; lv. 1).

Ver. 11.—**My son, despise not the chastening of the Lord.** The teacher, in vers. 11 and 12, passes to another phase of life. The thought of prosperity suggests the opposite one of adversity. Abundant prosperity shall flow from honouring Jehovah, but he sometimes and not unfrequently sends affliction, and, indeed, without this life would be incomplete. The object of the exhortation is, as Delitzsch states, to show that, as in prosperity God should not be forgotten, so one should not suffer himself to be estranged by days of adversity. Submission is counselled on the ground that, when Jehovah afflicts, he does so in the spirit of love, and for good. The " chastening " and " correction," though presenting God in an attitude of anger, are in reality not the punishment of an irate God. The verse before us is evidently copied from Job v. 17, " Behold, happy is the man whom God correcteth, therefore despise not thou the chastening of the Almighty;" and the whole passage is cited again in the Epistle to the Hebrews (Heb. xii. 5, 6). It has been said that ver. 11 expresses the problem of the Book of Job, and ver. 12 its solution (Delitzsch). *Despise not (al-timas);* Vulgate, *ne abjicias;* LXX., μὴ ὀλιγώρει. The verb *maas* is first

" to reject," and then " to despise and contemn." The Targum Jonathan puts the thought in a stronger form, *ne execreris*, " do not curse." They despise the chastening of Jehovah who, when they see his hand in it, do not humbly and submissively bow, but resist and become refractory, or, as it is expressed in ch. xix. 3, when their " heart fretteth against the Lord." Job, notwithstanding his bitter complaints, was on the whole, and in his better moments, an example of the proper state of mind under correction (see Job i. 21; ii. 10). Jonah, in treating contemptuously the procedure of God, is an exemplification of the contrary spirit, which is condemned implicitly in the text (Wardlaw). *Chastening (musar);* i.e. correction not by reproof only, as in ch. vi. 23 and viii. 30; but by punishment also, as in ch. xiii. 24; xxii. 15. The meaning here is expressed by the LXX. παιδεία, which is " instruction by punishment," discipline, or schooling (cf. Vulgate, *disciplina*). **Neither be weary** (*al-takots*); i.e. do not loathe, abhor, feel disgust nor vexation towards. The expression, " do not loathe," is a climax to the other, " despise not." It represents a more deeply seated aversion to Jehovah's plans. Gesenius takes the primary meaning of *kuts* to be that of vomiting. The word before us certainly denotes loathing or nausea, and is used in this sense by the Israelites in their complaints against God and against Moses in Numb. xxi. 5 (cf. Gen. xxvii. 46). The writer of the Epistle to the Hebrews, in quoting the passage, adopts the LXX. reading, μὴ ὀκλύου, " nor faint; " Vulgate, *ne deficias*, i.e. " do not give way to despondency." **Correction.** This word, like *musar* above, has a twofold meaning of either punishment or chastening, as in Ps. lxxiii. 14; or reproof, as in ch. i. 23 ; xxv. 30; v. 12; xxvii. 5; xxix. 15, where it also occurs. It is here used in the former sense. To loathe the correction of Jehovah is to allow it to completely estrange us from him. We faint under it when, by dwelling on or brooding over, or bemoaning the trial, the spirit sinks to faintness. To faint at correction ignores the belief in the truth that " all things work together for good to them that love God."

Ver. 12.—In this verse the motive for submissiveness to Jehovah's corrections is brought forward. They are corrections, but they are the corrections of love. One of the most touching relationships of life, and that with which we are most familiar, viz. that of father and son, is employed to reconcile us to Jehovah's afflictive dispensations. A comparison is drawn. God corrects those whom he loves after the same manner as a father corrects (" correcteth " has to be understood from the first hemistich) the son whom he loves. The idea of the passage is evidently taken from Deut. viii. 5, "Thou shalt also consider in thine heart, that as a man chasteneth his son, so the Lord thy God chasteneth thee." The idea of the paternal relationship of God to mankind is found elsewhere (Jer. xxxi. 9; Mal. ii. 10), and especially finds expression in the Lord's prayer. When the truth of this passage is learned, we shall be drawn to, rather than repelled from, God by his corrections. The gracious end of earthly trials is expressed in Heb. xii. 6, 2; cf. Rom. v. 3—5; 2 Cor. iv. 17 (Wardlaw). "These gracious words (Heb. xii.) are written in Holy Scripture for our comfort and instruction; that we should patiently and with thanksgiving bear our heavenly Father's correction, whensoever by any manner of adversity it shall please his gracious goodness to visit us" (see Visitation Office). **Even as a father the son in** whom **he delighteth** (*vuk'av eth-ben yir'tseh*); literally, *even as a father the son he delighteth in.* Various renderings have been given to this passage. (1) Delitzsch, De Wette, *et al.*, agree with the Authorized Version, and take ו *vau*, as explicative, and *yir'tseh*, "in whom he delighteth," as a relative sentence. The ו is used in this explanatory sense in 1 Sam. xxviii. 3 (see Gesenius, § 155. 1 *a*). The relative *asher*, "whom," is omitted in the original, according to the rule that the relative is omitted, especially in poetry, where it would stand as a pronoun in the nominative or accusative case (comp. Ps. vii. 16, "And he falls into the pit (which) he made;" and ch. v. 13). We have the same elision of the relative in the English colloquial expression, "the friend I met" (see Gesenius, § 123. 3, *a*). (2) Hitzig and Zöckler translate, "and holds him dear as a father his son." This, though grammatically correct, does not preserve the parallelism. It serves only to expand the idea of love, whereas the predominant idea of the verse is that of correction, to which love is an accessory idea (see Delitzsch). For similar parallels, see Deut. viii. 5 as before, and Ps. ciii. 13. In the comparison which is instituted, *yir'tseh*, "in whom he delighteth," corresponds with *eth asher ye'hav y'hovah*, "whom the Lord loveth," and not with *yokiah*, "correcteth." (3) Kamph translates, "and (dealeth) as a father (who) wisheth well to his son." This is substantially the same as the Authorized Version, except that in the relative sentence "son" is made accusative after *yir'tseh*, here translated, "wisheth well to," and the omitted relative (*asher*) is placed in the nominative instead of the accusative case. (4) The variation in the LXX., μαστιγοῖ δὲ πάντα υἱὸν ὃν παραδέχεται, "and scourgeth every son whom he receiveth," cited literally in Heb. xii. 5, evidently arises from the translators having read יְכָאֵב (*yakev*), "he scourgeth" for וּכְאָב (*vuk'av*), "even as a father." It will be seen that this alteration could be easily effected by a change in the Masoretic pointing. (5) The Vulgate renders, *et quasi pater in filio complacet sibi. He delighteth; yir'tseh* is from *ratsah*, "to be delighted" with any person or thing.

Vers. 13—18.—The teacher here enters upon the last part of this discourse. In doing so, he reverts to his main subject, which is Wisdom, or the fear of the Lord (see ver. 7 and ch. i. 7), and pronounces a panegyric upon her, comparing her, as in Job xxviii., with treasures whose value she exceeds, and showing wherein that value consists, viz. in the gifts which she confers on man.

Ver. 13.—**Happy is the man** (*ash'rey adam*); literally, *blessings of the man.* The plural of "excellence" used here, as in Job v. 17, to raise the sense. The man who has found Wisdom is supremely blessed. Beda connects this blessedness immediately with God's chastisements in the preceding verse. So Delitzsch. That **findeth** (*matsa*); properly, *hath found.* "The perfect expresses permanent possession, just as the imperfect, *yaphik*, denotes a continually renewed and repeated attaining" (Zöckler). The Vulgate also uses the perfect, *invenit*, "hath found;" LXX., ὃς εὖρε, "who found"—the aorist. **The man that getteth understanding** (*adam yaphik t'vunah*); literally, *the man that draweth out understanding*, as in the margin. *Yaphik* is the hiph. future or imperfect of *puk*, the primary meaning of which is *educere*, "to draw out," "to bring forth." This verb is used in two widely different senses. In the first place, it is equivalent to "bring forth" or "draw out" in the sense of *imparting*, as in Isa. lviii. 10, "If thou *draw out* thy soul to the hungry," *i.e.* impart benefits to them; and Ps. cxl v. 13, "That our garners may be full, *affording* all manner of store," *i.e.* yielding, giving out, presenting for our benefit. Its second sense is that of attaining, drawing out from another for one's own use. In this sense it occurs in ch. viii. 35; xii. 2; xviii. 22, where it is rendered "obtain." The latter sense is the one that suits the present passage, and best agrees with the corresponding *matsa.* The man is blessed who draws forth, *i.e.* obtains, understanding from God for himself. The Vulgate renders, *qui affluit prudentiâ*, "who overflows with understanding," or, has understanding in abundance; LXX., ὃς εἶδε, equivalent to "who saw."

Ver. 14.—**The merchandise** (*sakh'rah*);

Vulgate, *acquisitio*; LXX., ἐμπορεύεσθαι. The gain arising from trading in wisdom is better than that which arises from trading in silver. *Sakh'rah* is the gain or profit arising from merchandise, *i.e.* from trading. It denotes the act itself of gaining. The root *sakrah*, like the Greek ἐμπορεύεσθαι, signifies " to go about for the sake of traffic," *i.e.* to trade. There may be an allusion here, as in ch. ii. 4, to the new commerce (Plumptre). **The gain thereof** (*t'vuathah*); *i.e.* the gain existing in, and going along with, Wisdom herself; gain, therefore, in a different sense from that indicated in *sakh'-rah*. Gesenius takes it as "gain resulting from Wisdom," as in ch. viii. 19 and Isa. xxiii. 3. The word is used of the produce of the earth, the idea apparently embodied in the Vulgate *fructus*. In this case there may be a reference to ver. 18, where Wisdom is said to be a "tree of life." The LXX. omits the latter clause of this verse. The sense is, " The possession of Wisdom herself is better than fine gold." **Fine gold** (*karuts*); Vulgate, *aurum purum;* Syriac, *aurum puris-simum*. *Kharuts* is the poetic word for gold, so called, either (1) from its brilliancy, and then akin to the Greek χρυσός (Curtius); **or** (2) from its being dug up, from the root *kharats*, "to cut into or dig up," "to sharpen." It evidently means the finest and purest gold, and is here contrasted with silver (*keseph*). The word is translated " choice gold " in ch. viii. 10 ; " gold " simply in ch. xvi. 16; " yellow gold " in Ps. lxviii. 13; and "fine gold " in Zech. ix. 3. In the Version Junii et Tremellii it appears as *effosum aurum,* " gold dug up," *i.e.* gold in its native, unalloyed state. The Targum Jonathan understands it of "molten gold " (*aurum conflatum*).

Ver. 15.—**Rubies** (Khetib, *p'niyim*; Keri, *p'ninim*). No unanimous opinion has been arrived at as to the real signification of the word here translated "rubies." The majority of the rabbins (among them Rashi), and Bochart, Hartman, Bohlen, Lee on Job xxxviii. 18, and Zöckler, render it "pearls." Its meaning seems to lie between this and " corals," the rendering adopted by Michaelis, Gesenius, and Delitzsch (following Fleischer), who says that the Hebrew *p'ninim* corresponds with the Arabic word whose root-idea is " shooting forth," and means " a branch." The peculiar branching form in which coral is found favours this opinion, which is strengthened by the passage in Lam. iv. 7, where we get additional information as to colour, " They [the Nazarites] were more ruddy in body than rubies," a description which would apply to " coral," but is scarcely applicable to "pearls." The various versions suggest the further idea that *p'ninim* was a descriptive word used

to denote precious stones in general. The LXX. renders, " She is more precious than precious stones (λίθων πολυτελῶν)." So the Targum Jonathan, Syriac, and Arabic. The Vulgate renders, " She is more precious than all riches (*cunctis opibus*)." The word *p'ninim* only occurs here (Keri) and in ch. viii. 11; xx. 15; xxxi. 10; and in Job and Lamentations as above. This passage, as well as ch. viii. 11, which is an almost literal repetition of it, are imitations of Job xxviii. 18. The identification of *p'ninim* with "pearls" may have suggested our Lord's parable of the pearl of great price (Matt. xiii. 45, 46). **All the things thou canst desire** (*kal-khaphatseyka*); literally, *all thy desires.* Here everything in which you have pleasure, or all your precious things; LXX., πᾶν τίμιον; Vulgate, *omnia, quæ desiderantur*. The comparison, which has risen from the less to the more valuable, culminates in this comprehensive expression. There is nothing, neither silver, gold, precious stones, nor anything precious, which is an equivalent (*shavah*) to Wisdom in value. How it shows, when everything is put before us to choose from, that, like Solomon at Gibeon, we should prefer wisdom (1 Kings iii. 11—13)! In the second half of this verse the LXX. substitutes, " No evil thing competes with her ; she is well known to all that approach her."

Ver. 16.—The remaining three verses (16—18) state in what respects Wisdom is incomparable in value. **Length of days;** *orek yamim,* as in ver. 2. Wisdom is here represented as holding in her right hand that which is previously promised to obedience. Length of days is the blessing of blessings, the condition of all prosperity and enjoyment, and hence is placed in the right hand, the chief place, for among the Hebrews and other Oriental nations, as also among the Greeks the right hand was regarded as the position of highest honour (Ps. cx. 1; 1 Kings ii. 19; 1 Macc. x. 63; Matt. xxii. 24); cf. Ps. xvi. 11. in which the psalmist says of Jehovah, " In thy right hand there are pleasures for evermore." The two hands, the right and the left, signify the abundance of Wisdom's gifts. **Riches and honour** stand here for prosperity in general. The same expression occurs in ch. viii. 8, where riches are explained as "durable riches." A spiritual interpretation can, of course, be given to this passage— length of days being understood of eternal life; riches, of heavenly riches; and honour, not " the honour that cometh of men," but honour conferred by God (1 Sam. v. 44; John xii. 26); see Wardlaw, *in loc.* The thought of the verse is, of course, that Wisdom not only holds these blessings in her hands, but also confers them on those who seek her. The LXX. adds, "Out of her mouth proceedeth righteousness; justice and mercy she beareth upon her tongue;" possibly suggested by ch. viii. 3. The words of the teacher remind us of the saying of Menander, 'Ο διαφέρων λογισμῷ πάντ' ἔχει, "He who excels in prudence possesses all things."

Ver. 17.—**Ways of pleasantness** (*dar'key noam*); Vulgate, *viæ pulchræ;* LXX., ὁδοὶ καλαί. Wisdom's ways are those in which substantial delight may be found. They are beautiful and lovely to look upon, and afford happiness. **All her paths are peace** (*v'kal-n'thivo-theyah shalom*); literally, as in the Authorized Version. "Peace," *shalom,* is not genitive as "pleasantness." The character of peace is stamped upon her paths, so that in speaking of Wisdom's paths we speak of peace. She brings tranquillity and serenity and blessedness. Her paths are free from strife and alarm, and they lead to peace. (On the distinction between "ways" and "paths"—the more open and the more private walks—see ch. ii. 15.)

Ver. 18.—**A tree of life** (*ets-khayyim*); Vulgate, *lignum vitæ;* LXX., ξύλον ζωῆς. This expression obviously refers to "*the* tree of life" (*ets-hakayyim*), which was placed in the midst of the garden of Eden, and conferred immortality on those who ate of its fruit (Gen. ii. 9; iii. 22). So Wisdom becomes equally life-giving to those who lay hold on her, who taste of her fruit. She communicates life in its manifold fulness and richness (so the plural "lives" indicates) to those who seize her firmly. What is predicated of Wisdom here is predicated in other passages (ch. xi. 30; xiii. 12; xv. 4) of the fruit of the righteous, the fulfilment of desire, and a wholesome tongue. Each of these, the teacher says, is "a tree of life." Elster denies that there is any reference to "*the* tree of life," and classes the expression among those other figurative expressions—a "fountain of life," in ch. xiii. 4 and xiv. 27, and a "well of life," in ch. x. 11; but if it be once admitted that there is such a reference, and it be remembered also that Wisdom is the same as "the fear of the Lord," the point insisted on in the Proverbs and in Job, it seems difficult to deny that the teacher has in view the blessed immortality of which the tree of life in Paradise was the symbol. In this higher sense the term is used in the Revelation (ii. 7; xxii. 2, 14). Wisdom restores to her worshippers the life which was lost in Adam (Cartwright). It is remarkable that the imagery here employed is confined to these two books. After the historical record in Genesis, no other sacred writers refer to the tree of life. Old ecclesiastical writers saw in the expression a reference to Christ's re-

deeming work. "The tree of life is the cross of Christ," *lignum vitæ crux Christi* (quoted by Delitzsch). The symbol, Plumptre remarks, entered largely into the religious imagery of Assyria, Egypt, and Persia. **To them that lay hold upon** (*lammakhazikim*, hiph. participle); Vulgate, *his, qui apprehenderint;* LXX., τοῖς ἀντεχομένοις. The Hebrew verb חָזַק (*khazak*), "to tie fast," is in hiph. with בְּ (*b'*), "to take hold of," "to seize any one." **Happy is every one that retaineth her.** In the original, the participle, "they retaining her" (*tom'keyah*), is plural, and the predicate, "happy" or "blessed" (*m'ushshar*), is singular. The latter is used distributively, and the construction is common (cf. ch. xv. 22). The Authorized Version aptly renders the original. The necessity for "retaining" as well as "laying hold" of Wisdom is pointed out. The verb תָּמַךְ (*tamak*) is "to hold fast something taken." Such will be blessed who hold Wisdom tenaciously and perseveringly.

Vers. 19—26.—5. *Fifth hortatory discourse. Wisdom, the creative power of God, exhibited as the protection of those who fear God.* The teacher in this discourse presents Wisdom under a new aspect. Wisdom is the Divine power of God, by which he created the world, and by which he sustains the work of his hands and regulates the operations of nature. This eminence of Wisdom, in her intimate association with Jehovah, is made the basis of a renewed exhortation to keep Wisdom steadily in view. The elevated thought that Wisdom has her source in Jehovah might seem in itself an adequate and sufficient reason for the exhortation. But another motive is adduced intimately bound up with this view of Wisdom. Jehovah becomes the ground of confidence and the protection in all conditions of life of those who keep Wisdom.

Ver. 19.—**The Lord by wisdom hath founded the earth.** The emphatic position of the word *Jehovah*, "the Lord," at the beginning of the sentence (cf. Ps. xxvii.; xcvii.; xcix.), as well as the nature of the discourse, indicates a new paragraph. The description of the creative Wisdom of Jehovah may have been suggested to the mind of the teacher by the mention of the tree of life, in ver. 18 (Zöckler); but the connection between this and the preceding passage has to be sought for in something deeper. The scope of the teacher is to exhibit, and so to recommend, Wisdom in every respect, and after showing her excellence in man, he now brings her forward as the medium of creation, and hence in her relation to God. *By wisdom* (*b'kokhmah*); Vulgate, *sapientiâ*; LXX., τῇ σοφίᾳ. It is evident that Wisdom is here something more than an attribute of Jehovah. " By Wisdom" means " by, or through, the instrumentality of Wisdom." While the corresponding and parallel expressions, " understanding," " knowledge," militate against the idea of an hypostatizing of Wisdom, *i.e.* assigning to Wisdom a concrete and objective personality, yet the language is sufficiently strong, when we connect this passage with ch. i. and viii., to warrant our regarding Wisdom as something apart from yet intimately connected with Jehovah, as an active agency employed by him, and hence this description may be looked upon as an anticipation of that which is more fully developed in ch. viii., where the characteristics which are wanting here are there worked out at length. The rabbins evidently connected the passage before us, as well as ch. i. and viii., with Gen. i. 1, by rendering *b'reshith*, "in the beginning," by *b'kokhmah*, "by Wisdom." Our Lord identifies himself with the Divine Sophia, or Wisdom (Luke xi. 49). And the language of St. John, "All things were made by him, and without him was not anything made that was made" (John i. 3), which assigns to the Logos, or Word of God, *i.e.* Christ, the act of creation (cf. John i. 10, and especially the language of St. Paul, in Col. i. 16), argues in favour of the view of some commentators who understand Wisdom to refer to the Second Person of the Trinity. The Logos was understood by Alexandrian Judaism to express the *manifestation* of the unseen God, the Absolute Being, in the creation and government of the world; and the Christian teachers, when they adopted this term, assigned to it a concrete meaning as indicating the Incarnate Word (see Bishop Lightfoot, in Col. i. 15). For the passage, see Ps. xxxiii. 6; civ. 24; cxxxvi. 5; and especially Jer. x. 12, "He hath established the world by his wisdom," etc.; li. 55; Ecclus. xxiv. 2, *seq.* *Hath founded* (*yasad*); Vulgate, *fundavit*; LXX., ἐθεμελίωσε. The same verb is used in Job xxxviii. 4; Ps. xxiv. 2; lxxviii. 69, of the creation of the earth by God. While the primary meaning of *yasad* is " to give fixity to," " to lay fast," that of *konen*, rendered "he hath established," is "to set up," "to erect," and so "to *found*," from *kun*, or referring to the Arabic and Ethiopic cognate root, "to exist," "to give existence to." The marginal reading, "prepared," corresponds with the LXX. ἐτοίμασε. The Vulgate is *stabilivit*, "he hath established."

Ver. 20.—**By his knowledge the depths are broken up.** This is usually taken to refer to that primary act in creation, the separation of the waters from the earth, when "the waters were gathered together unto their own place," as recorded in Gen. i. 9. So Munster, Zöckler, Wardlaw. But it seems better to understand it (as Mercerus, Lapide, Delitzsch, and Authorized Version) of the fertilization of the earth by rivers, streams, etc., which burst forth from the interior of the earth. In this sense the correspondence is preserved with the second hemistich, where the atmospheric influence is referred to as conducing to the same end. The teacher passes from the creation to the wonderful means which Jehovah employs through Wisdom to sustain his work. *The depths* (*t'homoth*); Vulgate, *abyssi*; LXX., ἄβυσσοι, are here " the internal water stores of the earth" (Delitzsch), and not the depths of the ocean, as in ch. viii. 24, 27, 28, and in Gen. i. 2. *Are broken up* (*niv'kau*); properly, *were broken up*, niph. perfect of *baka*, (1) to cleave asunder, (2) to break forth, as water, in Isa. xxxv. 6. The perfect describes a past act, but one that is still continuing in effect. Cf. Vulgate *eruperunt*, "they burst forth;" LXX., ἐρράγησαν, aorist 2 passive of ῥήγνυμι, "to burst forth," Targum, *rupti sunt*; and Syriac, *ruptæ sunt*. The idea of division or separation is present, but it is not the predominant idea. There seems to be no allusion here either to the Deluge (Beda), nor to the cleaving of the waters of the Red Sea (Gejerus), though both of these historical events were undoubtedly well known to the teacher. **And the clouds drop down the dew.** *The clouds* (*sh'khakim*) are properly the *ether*, the higher and colder regions of the atmosphere, and then "the clouds," as in Ps. lxxvii. 15, which are formed by the condensation of vapours drawn by solar influence from the surface of the earth—seas, rivers, etc. The singular *shakhak* signifies " dust," and secondly " a cloud," evidently from the minute particles of moisture of which a cloud is composed. *Drop down* (*yir'aphu*, kal future of *raaph*, used as a present or imperfect); LXX., ἐρρύησαν, "let flow." The clouds discharge their contents in showers, or distil at evening in refreshing dew. Modern science agrees with the meteorological fact here alluded to, of the reciprocal action of the heavens and the earth. The moisture drawn from the earth returns again " to water the earth, that it may bring forth and bud, to give seed to the sower, and bread to the eater" (Isa. lv. 10). *Dew; tal*, here used not only of dew, but of rain in gentle and fructifying showers. The Arabic word signifies "light rain;" LXX., δρόσους, "dew." Moses, in describing the blessing of Israel, says, " His heavens shall drop down dew" in the same sense (Deut. xxxviii. 28; cf. Job xxxvi. 28). The fertilization of the earth is ordered by the Divine Wisdom.

Ver. 21.—**My son, let not them depart from thine eyes.** After the description of the power of Wisdom exhibited in creating and sustaining the earth, the exhortation to keep Wisdom steadily before the eyes, and the promises of Divine protection, appropriately follow. Since Wisdom is so powerful, then, the teacher argues, she is worthy of being retained and guarded, and able to protect. *Let them not depart* (*al-yaluzu*); *i.e.* "let them not escape or slip aside from your mind (cf. Vulgate, *ne effluant hæc ab oculis tuis*). They are to be as frontlets between your eyes, as a ring upon your finger. *Yaluzu*, from *lûz*, "to bend aside," *deflectere*, *a viâ declinare*, which see in ch. ii. 15, ought probably to be written *yellezu*, on the analogy of the corresponding passage in ch. iv. 21. The LXX. renders absolutely μὴ παραρρύῃς, "do not thou pass by," from παραρρύω, "to flow by," "to pass by, recede" (cf. Heb. ii. 1, "Therefore we ought to give the more earnest heed to these things, lest at any time we should let them slip (μή ποτε παραρρυῶμεν)," quoted probably from the LXX. of this passage). The Targum Jonathan reads, *ne vilescat*, "let it," *i.e.* wisdom, "not become worthless." *Them*, included in the verb *yaluzu*, of which it is subject in the original, is to be referred either to "sound wisdom and discretion" of ver. 21*b* —so Gejerus, Cartwright, Geïer, Umbreit, Hitzig, Zöckler, Plumptre (a similar trajection occurs in Deut. xxxii. 5, and is used, as here, to give vividness to the description); or to "wisdom, understanding, knowledge," of the preceding verses—so Delitzsch and Holden. The first view in every way seems preferable, and it is no objection to it that "sound wisdom" (*tushiyyah*) and "discretion" (*m'yimmah*) are feminine, while the verb "depart" (*yaluzu*) is masculine (see Gesenius, 'Gram.,' § 147). The Syriac reads, "Let it not become worthless (*ne vile fit*) in thine eyes to keep my doctrine and my counsels." **Keep sound wisdom and discretion.** *Keep; n'zor,* kal imperative of *nâtsar,* "to watch, guard." For "sound wisdom" (*tushiyyah*), see ch. ii. 7. Here used for "wisdom" (*kokhmah*), as "discretion" (*m'zimmah*) for "understanding" (*t'vunah*), to contrast the absolute wisdom and insight of God with the corresponding attributes in man (see Zöckler, *in loc.*). They belong to God, but are conferred on those who seek after Wisdom, and are then to be guarded as priceless treasures. The Vulgate reads, *custodi legem et consilium;* and the LXX., τήρησον δὲ ἐμὴν βουλὴν καὶ ἔννοιαν, "guard my counsel and thought."

Ver. 22.—**So shall they be life to thy soul, and grace to thy neck.** *So shall they be* (*n'yikva*); *and they shall be.* The "soul" and "neck" stand for the whole man in his twofold nature, internal and external. Life is in its highest and widest sense given to the soul (see ch. ii. 16, 18; iv. 22; viii. 35), and favour is conferred on the man, *i.e.* he becomes acceptable to his neighbours, if he has wisdom. The latter expression is very similar to ch. i. 9, where the same promise is expressed, "grace" (*hon*) being equivalent to "ornament of grace" (*liv'yath hon*). Others understand "grace to thy neck" (*hon l'garg'grotheyka*), as *gratia gutturis*, in the sense of "grace of the lips," as in Ps. xlv. 3 and ch. xxii. 11, that is, as the grace of speaking, power of eloquent and effective utterance (Gejerus, Bayne, Lapide). It is better to take it as referring to the adornment of the personal character, and so by metonymy of the favour and kindness which it procures.

Ver. 23.—**Then shalt thou walk in thy way safely.** The first of the promises of protection, which follow from vers. 23—26. He who keeps "sound wisdom and discretion" shall enjoy the greatest sense of security in all situations of life. *Safely* (*la^retakh*); either in confidence, as Vulgate *fiducialiter*, i.e. confidently, because of the sense of security (cf. LXX., πεποιθὼς ἐν εἰρήνῃ, and ver. 26); or in security: the adverb *lavetakh* is equivalent to *betakh* in ch. i. 30 and x. 9. The allusion is obvious. As he who is accompanied by an escort proceeds on his way in safety, so you protected by God will pass your life in security; or, as Trapp, "Thou shalt ever go under a double guard, 'the peace of God' within thee (Phil. iv. 7), and the 'power of God' without thee (1 Pet. i. 5).' **And thy foot shall not stumble;** literally, *and thou shalt not strike thy foot.* *Stumble* in the original is *thiggoph,* 2 singular kal future of *nagaph,* "to smite," "strike against with the foot." So in Ps. xci. 12. The Authorized Version, however, correctly gives the sense. The LXX., like the Authorized Version, makes "foot" the subject, Ὁ δὲ πούς σου οὐ μὴ προσκόψῃ, "(That) thy foot may not stumble." For a similar assurance, see ch. iv. 12. The meaning is: You will not stumble, because you will be walking in the way of wisdom, which is free from stumbling-blocks (Lapide). You will not fall into sin.

Ver. 24.—**When thou liest down thou shalt not be afraid.** This is beautifully illustrated by what David says in Ps. iv. 8, "I will both lay me down in peace and sleep: for thou, Lord, only makest me dwell in safety." No fear is to be apprehended where Jehovah is Protector (see Ps. iii. 5, 6; xlvi. 1—3; xci. 1—5; cxxi. 5—8). *When* (*im*) is rendered "if" by the Vulgate, LXX., Targum Jonathan. *Thou liest down; tish'kav,* "thou shalt lie down," kal future.

like *shakavta,* kal perfect, in the corresponding hemistich, is from *shakıv,* "to lie down," specially to lay one's self down to sleep, as in Gen. xix. 4; Ps. iii. 6. Vulgate, *si dormieris;* cf. ch. vi. 22, "when thou sleepest" בְּשָׁכְבְּךָ, *b'shok'b'ka).* The LXX. rendering, "if thou sittest" (κάθη), arises from reading תֵּשֵׁב *(teshev)* for תִּשְׁכַּב *(tish'kav).* **Yea, thou shalt lie down;** *b'shok'b'ta,* as before, with וְ prefixed, equivalent to the future, as in the Authorized Version; LXX., καθεύδης. **Shall be sweet;** *arvah,* from *arav,* "to be sweet," or "pleasant," perhaps "well mixed," as *arev,* equivalent to "to mix." Thy sleep shall be full of pleasing impressions, not restless, as in Deut. xxviii. 66 and Job vii. 4, but sweet, because of the sense of safety, and from confidence in God, as well as from a good conscience (cf. Job xi. 18, "Thou shalt take thy rest in safety," from which the idea is probably taken).

Ver. 25.—**Be not afraid;** *al-tirah,* is literally "fear thou not," the future with *al* preceding being used for the imperative in a dehortative sense, as in Gen. xlvi. 3; Job iii. 4, 6, 7 (see Gesenius, 'Gram.,' § 127. 3, c); Vulgate, *ne paveas.* Others, however, render, as the LXX., οὐ φοβηθήσῃ, "Thou shalt not be afraid," in the sense of a promise. The verb *yare,* from which *tirah,* is here followed by *min,* as in Ps. iii. 7; xxvii. 1, and properly means "to be afraid from or before" some person or thing. **Sudden;** *pithom,* an adverb used adjectively (cf. like use of adverb *khinnam* in ch. xxvi. 2). **Fear** *(pakhad);* as in ch. i. 16, the object which excites terror or fear, as any great disaster. **The desolation of the wicked** *(shôath r'shâim)* may be taken either (1) as the desolation made by the violence of the wicked, the desolation or storm which they raise against the righteous (so the LXX., Vulgate, Mariana, Michaelis, Hitzig, and others); or (2) the desolation which overtakes the wicked, the desolating vengeance executed upon them (so Doderlein, Lapide, Stuart, Muensch., Delitzsch, Wardlaw). The latter is probably the right interpretation, and agrees with the threatening language of Wisdom against her despisers, in ch. i. 27, where *shôath* also occurs. In the desolation which shall overwhelm the wicked he who has made Wisdom his guide shall be undismayed, for the Lord is his confidence. The passage was probably suggested by ch. v. 21, "Neither shalt thou be afraid of desolation when it cometh." Lee, in *loc. cit.,* says the places are almost innumerable where this sentiment occurs. Compare the fearlessness of the man of integrity and justice, in Horace—

> "Si fractus illabatur orbis,
> Impavidum ferient ruinæ."
> (Horace, 'Od.,' iii. 3. 7, 8.)

> "Let Jove's dread arm with thunders rend the spheres,
> Beneath the crush of worlds undaunted he appears."
> (Francis's Trans.)

Ver. 26.—**Thy confidence** *(v'kis'lekâ);* literally, *as thy confidence. Kesel,* primarily "loin" or "flank," as in Lev. iii. 14; x. 15; Job xv. 27, is apparently used here in its secondary meaning of "confidence," "hope," as in Job viii. 14; xxxi. 24; Ps. lxxviii. 7. The כ *(v')* prefixed is what is usually termed the כְ *essentiæ,* or כְ *pleonasticum* (equivalent to the Latin *tanquam,* "as"), and serves to emphasize the connection between the predicate "thy confidence" and the subject "Jehovah" (cf. Exod. xviii. 4; see Ewald, 'Lehrb.,' 217, *f.*; and Gesenius, 'Gram.,' § 154). Jehovah shall be in the highest sense your ground and object of confidence. Delitzsch describes *kesel* as confidence in the presence of evil: Jehovah in the presence of the "sudden fear," and of "the desolation of the wicked," the evils and calamities which overwhelm the wicked, shall be thy confidence. The sense of his all-encircling protection will render you undismayed. The meaning given to *kesel* as "foolhardiness" (Ps. xlix. 14) and "folly" (Eccles. vii. 25), and the connection of *kesel* with *k'silim* in ch. i. 22, comes from the root-idea *kâsal,* "to be fleshly, or fat," the signification of which branches out on the one side into strength and boldness, and on the other into languor and inertness, and so folly or confidence in self (Schultens, *l.c.*). The Talmudic rendering of the Rabbi Salomon approximates to this meaning, "and the things in which you seemed to be foolish *(desipere videbaris)* he will be at once present with you." Others, as Ziegler, Muentinghe, give *kesel* its primary meaning, and translate, "Jehovah shall be as thy loins," the loins being regarded as the emblem of strength. Jehovah shall be your strength. But *kesel* does not appear to have this local application here. Wherever it is used in this sense, as in Job and Leviticus cited above, there is something in the context to point it out as a part of the body. Compare, however, the Vulgate, *in latere suo,* "in thy side or flank." The LXX. renders, ἐπὶ πασῶν ὁδῶν σου, "over all thy ways." **From being taken** *(millâked);* Vulgate, *ne capiaris,* "lest thou be taken." The meaning is, Jehovah will be your protection against all the snares and traps which the impious lay for you. *Lĕkĕd,* "a being taken," is from *lâkâd,* "to take or catch animals" in a net or in snares. It only occurs here in the Proverbs. Its unusual appearance, together with other reasons, not tenable, however, has led Hitzig to reject vers. 22—26 as an interpolation.

The LXX. reads, πτόησιν, *pavorem.* Πτόησις, in Plato, Aristotle, and Plutarch, is used subjectively, and means "any vehement emotion." The word only occurs once in the New Testament in 1 Pet. iii. 6, μὴ φοβούμενη μηδεμίαν πτόησιν, where it is evidently quoted from the passage before us, in an objective sense, and designates some external cause of terror (cf. Authorized Version, "and be not afraid with any amazement;" see also Book of Common Prayer: 'Solemnization of Matrimony,' *ad fin.*).

Vers. 27—35.—6. *Sixth admonitory discourse.* In this discourse the teacher still carries on his object, which is to demonstrate the conditions upon which true wisdom and happiness are to be attained. The discourse differs from the preceding in consisting of detached proverbs, and may be divided into two main sections—the first (vers. 27—30) enjoining benevolence, that love to one's neighbour which is the fulfilling of the Law; the second warning against emulating the oppressor and associating with him, because of the fate of the wicked (vers. 31—35). It is observable that all the maxims have a negative form, and thus present a striking contrast to the form adopted by our Lord in the Sermon on the Mount (Matt. v.), and to the admonitions at the close of St. Paul's Epistles. In one instance in particular (ver. 30), the teaching does not reach the high moral standard of the gospel (see Delitzsch and Lange).

Ver. 27.—**Withhold not good from them to whom it is due.** This precept indicates the general principle of beneficence, and not merely, as the words at first sight seem to imply, restitution (as Cajet.). We are to do good to those who are in need or deserving of it, whenever we have the means and opportunity. *From them to whom it is due* (nib'âlâyv); literally, *from its owner*, from bâal, *dominus*, "lord" or owner of a thing. Cf. ch. xvi. 22, "Prudence is a fountain of life to its owner (b'âlâyv);" i. 19; xvii. 8; and also Eccles. viii. 8; vii. 12;—in all of which passages proprietorship in the thing or quality mentioned is expressed. The owners of good are those to whom good is due or belongs either by law or by morality, whether by desert or need. The latter qualification is the one emphasized in the LXX., Μὴ ἀπόσχῃ ἓν ποιεῖν ἐνδεῆ, "Abstain not from doing good to the needy." So the Arabic *pauperi.* The Targum and Syriac put the precept in more general terms, "Cease not to do good," without indicating

in particular any one who is to be the recipient of the good. But the Jewish interpreters generally (*e.g.* Ben Ezra) understand it of the poor, *egentibus.* The Vulgate puts an entirely different interpretation on the passage: *Noli prohibere benefacere eum qui potest; si vales, et ipse benefac*, "Do not prohibit him who can from doing good; if you are able, do good also yourself." It thus implies that we are to put no impediment in the way of any one who is willing to do good to others, and enjoins the duty on ourselves also. *Good (tôv); i.e.* "good" under any form, any good deed or act of beneficence. The principle brought forward in this passage is that what we possess and is seemingly our own is in reality to be regarded as belonging to others. We are only stewards of our wealth. **In the power of thine hand** (l'êl yâd'yka); literally, *in the power of thine hands.* For the dual, yâd'ykâ, the Keri substitutes the singular, yâd'kâ, to harmonize it with the similar expression, l'êl yâdi, "in the power of thy hand," which occurs in Gen. xxxi. 27; Deut. xxviii. 32; Neh. v. 5; Micah ii. 1. But there is no grammatical need for the emendation. Both the LXX. and Targum employ the singular, "thy hand." *Power* (êl); here "strength" in the abstract. Usually it means "the strong," and is so used as an appellation of Jehovah, though, as Gesenius says, those little understand the phrase who would render êl here "by God." The ? prefixed to êl indicates the condition. The meaning of the phrase is, "While it is practicable, and you have the opportunity and means of doing good, do it." Do not defer, but do good promptly. The passage receives a remarkable illustration in the language of St. Paul, "While we have opportunity, let us do good unto all men" (Gal. vi. 10).

Ver. 28.—The precept of this and that of the preceding verse are very closely related. The former precept enjoined the general principle of benevolence when we have the means; this carries on the idea, and is directed against the postponement of giving when we are in a position to give. In effect it says, "Do not defer till to-morrow what you can do to-day." This "putting off" may arise from avarice, from indolence, or from insolence and contempt. These underlying faults, which are incompatible with neighbourly good will, are condemned by implication. **Unto thy neighbour;** l'rêâykâ, "to thy friends," the word being evidently used distributively. *Rêêh* is "a companion" or "friend" (cf. Vulgate, *amico tuo*; Syriac, *sodali tuo*), and generally any other person, equivalent to the Greek ὁ πλησίον, "neighbour." The Authorized Version correctly renders "come again," as *shûv* is not merely

" to return," but to return again to something (so Delitzsch); cf. Vulgate, *revertere;* and as the words, "to-morrow I will give thee," show. The LXX. adds, "For thou knowest not what the morrow may bring forth," probably from ch. xvii. 1. If viewed in respect of the specific claims which servants have for work done, the precept is a re-echo of Lev. xxix. 13 and Deut. xxiv. 15. In illustration of the general scope of the passage, Grotius quotes, "A slow-footed favour is a favour without favour." Seneca says in the same spirit, "Ingratum est beneficium quod diu inter manus dantis hæsit," "The benefit is thankless which sticks long between the hands of the giver" (Seneca, 'Benef.,' i. 2); cf. also *Bis dat qui cito dat.*

Ver. 29.—**Devise not evil against thy neighbour.** This precept is directed against abuse of confidence. *Devise not evil (ăl tākhărôsh rââh).* The meaning of this expression lies between "fabricating evil" and "ploughing evil." The radical meaning of *khărăsh,* from which *tâkhărôsh,* is "to cut into," "to inscribe" letters on a tablet, cognate with the Greek χαράσσειν, "to cut into." But it is used in the sense of "to plough" in Job iv. 18, "They that plough iniquity *(khar'shey ăvĕn),*" and Ps. cxxix. 3, "The ploughers ploughed *(khar'shim khar'shim)* upon my back" (cf. Hos. x. 13). This also appears from the context to be the meaning in ch. vi. 14. With these we may compare such expressions as "to plough a lie" *(μὴ ἀροτρία ψεύδος,* rendered in the Authorized Version, "Devise not a lie"); see ch. vii. 12, and "to sow iniquity," ch. xxii. 8—a cognate figure. "To plough evil" is to devise evil, to prepare for it, just in the same way as a ploughman prepares the land for sowing. In this sense the verb is understood by the older commentators and by Ewald and Delitzsch. On the other hand, the verb may be used in its other signification, "to fabricate," and hence "to contrive." The noun *khârăsh* is an artificer of iron, etc. (Exod. xxxv. 35; Deut. xxvii. 15). "To fabricate evil" is, of course, as the Authorized Version "to devise evil." The LXX., *μὴ τεκτήνῃ,* from *τεκταίνομαι,* "to build," inclines to this sense. The Vulgate, *ne moliaris,* does not clear up the point, though *moliri,* usually "to contrive," is used by Virgil, 'Georg.,' i. 494, "moliri terram," of working or tilling the ground. The verb also occurs in ch. vi. 19; xii. 20; xiv. 22. **Seeing he dwelleth securely by thee;** *i.e.* as the Vulgate, *cum ille in te habet fiduciam,* "when he has confidence in thee;" so the LXX.; or, as the Targum and Syriac, "when he dwells with thee in peace." *To dwell (yâshâr)* is in Ps. i. 1 "to sit with any one." *i.e.* to associate familiarly with him

(cf. Ps. xxvi. 4, 5); but it also has the meaning "to dwell," and the participle *yôshêv,* here used; in Gen. xix. 23: Judg. vi. 21, means "an inhabitant, a dweller." *Securely (lâvĕtāh); i.e.* with full trust (see on ver. 23). Devising evil against a friend is at any time reprehensible, but to do so when he confides in and is altogether unsuspicious of you, is an act of the greatest treachery, and an outrage on all law, human and Divine. It implies dissimulation. It is the very sin by which "the devil beguiled Eve through his subtlety" (Wardlaw).

Ver. 30.—The meaning of the precept in this verse is clear. We are not to strive or quarrel with a man unless he has first given us offence. So Le Clerc, "Nisi injuriâ prior lacessiverit." The admonition is directed against those who, from spite, jealousy, or other reasons, "stir up strife all the day long" with those who are quiet and peaceable. **Strive.** The Keri here reads *ţariv* for the Khetib *taruv,* but without any change of meaning. The verb *rûv,* from which *taruv,* is "to strive or contend with the hand and with blows," as in Deut. xxxiii. 7; or with words, as in Ps. ciii. 9 (cf. the Vulgate, *ne contendas;* and the LXX., *μὴ φιλεχθήσῃς,* "Do not exercise enmity," from the unusual *φιλεχθρέω. Rûv* is here followed by * py (im),* as in Job ix. 3; xl. 2; and Gen. xxvi. 30. Its forensic sense, "to contend with in law," does not strictly apply here, though the precept may be taken as discouraging litigation (Lapide). **Without cause** *(khinnăm);* LXX., *μάτην,* equivalent to *δωρεάν* in John xv. 25; Vulgate, *frustra;* further explained in the concluding clause (see on ch. i. 17). **If he have done thee no harm.** The phrase, *gâmăl rââh,* is to bring evil upon any one (Schultens). The verb *gâmăl* signifies "to do, to give, to show to any one." Holden renders, "Surely he will return thee evil," in the sense that unprovoked attack ensures retaliation. But this is to ignore the negative force of *im-lô,* "if not." The verb sometimes means "requiting," but not in the passage before us, nor in ch. xi. 17; xxxi. 12. The Vulgate renders as the Authorized Version, *Cum ipse tibi nihil mali fecerit.* It is to be remarked that this precept falls below the moral standard of the New Testament teaching (see Matt. v. 39—41; Rom. xii. 17—21; 1 Cor. vi. 6—8), and of the example of our Lord, of whom it was predicted that "When he was reviled, he reviled not again; when he suffered, he threatened not" (see Isa. liii.).

Ver. 31.—**Envy thou not the oppressor, and choose none of his ways.** The thought of strife in the preceding verse leads to that of oppression, and the precept is directed against fellowship with those who outrage the general law of benevolence and justice.

Envy not; i.e. as Stuart, "Do not anxiously covet the booty which men of violence acquire." Success and wealth may follow from severity and extortion, but the man who acquires prosperity by these means is not to be envied even by the victim of his oppression (for the verb, see ch. xxiii. 17; xxiv. 1, 19). *The oppressor (ish khâmâs);* literally, *a man of violence* (see margin). The expression occurs in ch. xiv. 29; Ps. xviii. 41, and in its plural form, *ish khămâmîm,* "man of violences," in 2 Sam. xxii. 49; Ps. cxl. 1, 4. The man of violence is one who "grinds the faces of the poor," and whose conduct is rapacious, violent, and unjust. *And choose none of his ways;* literally, *and choose not all his ways,* i.e. with a view to acquire the same wealth, greatness, and power. The LXX. renders this verse, "Do not acquire the hatred of evil men, neither be jealous of their ways," evidently from having taken *tiv'khar,* "choose," in the second hemistich, for *tith'khar,* "be jealous."

Ver. 32.—This verse gives the reason for the previous warning. The oppressor is here included under the more general term, "the froward." **The froward;** *nâlôz,* hiph. participle from *lúz,* "to bend aside," and hence a perverted or wicked man, one who turns aside from the way of uprightness, a transgressor of the Law (cf. LXX., παράνομος); and so the opposite of "the righteous," *y'shârîm,* "the upright," those who pursue the path of justness, or the straightforward. **Abomination** *(tôêvâh);* i.e. an abhorrence, something which, being impure and unclean (cf. LXX., ἀκάθαρτος), is especially abhorrent to Jehovah. In some passages it is connected with idolatry, as in 1 Kings xiv. 24 and 2 Kings xxiii. 13, but is never used in this sense in the Proverbs, where it occurs about twenty times (see ch. xxviii. 9; xxi. 27; xi. 1, 20, etc.). The passage shows that prosperity and worldly success are not always a true measure of Divine favour. **His secret** *(sôdô);* Vulgate, *sermocinatio.* Here *sod* probably means "familiar intercourse," as in Job xxix. 4 and Ps. xxv. 14; and hence the special favour with which Jehovah regards the upright, by revealing to them what he conceals from others, or his friendship (compare what our Lord says in John xv. 14, 15). Dathe translates, "probis vero est familiaris." Gesenius says *sod* properly means "a couch," or *triclinium,* on which people recline; but Delitzsch derives it from the root *sod,* "to be firm," "compressed," and states that it therefore means properly "a being together, or sitting together." The LXX. continues the "froward man" (παράνομος) as the subject, and renders, "Every transgressor is impure before God, and does not sit together with (οὐ συνεδριάζει) the just."

Ver. 33.—**The curse of the Lord is in the house of the wicked.** From ver. 33 to the end of the discourse the contrast is continued between the condition of the wicked and the just, the scornful and the lowly, the wise and the fools. In the verse before us a further reason is given why the prosperity of the wicked is not enviable. The curse of Jehovah dwells in and rests upon his house. *The curse; m'êrâh,* from *arav,* "to curse." This word only occurs five times in the Old Testament —once in Deuteronomy, twice in Proverbs (here and in ch. xxviii. 27), and twice in Malachi. The nature of the curse may be learned from Deut. xxviii. 20, where it is the infliction of temporal misfortunes ending with the "cutting off" of the wicked (see Ps. xxxvii. 22). It is a hovering evil, the source of constant misfortune. LXX., κατάρα. Cf. "the cursing" *(âlâh)* against thieves and swearers in Zech. v. 4. **But he blesseth the habitation of the just.** The contrast to the former, as in Deut. xxviii. 2—6. *He blesseth;* i.e. both temporarily and spiritually. Blessing does not exclude affliction, but "trials" are not "curses" (Wardlaw). Both the LXX. and the Vulgate render, "But the habitations of the just shall be blessed," the LXX. having read the pual future *(y'vôrăk),* "they shall be blessed," for the piel future *(y'vâr:k),* "he shall bless," of the text. *The habitation; nâvêh,* from *nâvâh,* "to sit down," "to dwell." A poetic and nomad (Fleischer) word usually understood of a small dwelling is *tugurium,* the shepherd's hut or cottage, "the sheepcote" of 2 Sam. vii. 8. The LXX. ἔπαυλις, and the Vulgate *habitaculum,* favour the suggestion of Gejerus, that a contrast is here made between the large house or palace *(bâyith)* of the wicked and the small dwelling of the just. In ch. xxi. 20 and xxiv. 15 the word is rendered "dwelling."

Ver. 34.—**Surely he scorneth the scorners;** literally, *if with regard to the scorners he scorneth (im lăllêtsim hû yalîts); i.e.* he repays scorn with scorn; or, as Rabbi Salomon, "He renders to them so that they fall in their own derision *(reddit ipsis ut in suâ derisione corruant)."* He renders their schemes abortive. He resists them. *The scorners (lêtsim)* are those who treat with scoffing regard the precepts and truths of God; the arrogant, proud, insolent, here placed in contrast with "the lowly." Vulgate, *derisores;* LXX., ὑπερήφανοι, "the overbearing." The ל for לה *(l'ha),* prefixed to *lêtsim,* signifies "with regard to," as in Job xxxii. 4 (cf. Ps. xvi. 3, "With regard to the saints *(lik'dôshim),* in them only I delight"). **But he giveth grace unto the lowly;** or, *on the other hand,* the ל prefixed to *lăănâyim,* "to the lowly," having that antithetical force here as in Job viii. 20. *The lowly* (*anâyyîm*); Vulgate, *mansueti;* LXX., ταπεῖνοι; properly, "the afflicted," with added notion of submission and lowly demeanour, and hence the meek, gentle—the gentle towards man, and the abased and lowly before God. St. James (iv. 6) quotes the LXX. of this passage, "God resisteth the proud, but giveth grace to the humble." With the exception of substituting Κύριος for Θεός (cf. 1 Pet. v. 5), our Lord's parable of the Pharisee and publican illustrates the teaching of this verse (Luke xviii. 9—14).

Ver. 35.—**The wise shall inherit glory.** Ch. xi. 2 indicates that "the wise" here are to be identified with "the lowly" of the preceding verse. *Inherit;* succeed to it as a matter of course by hereditary right as sons. *Heirship* implies *sonship. Glory* (*kâvôd*); or, *honour;* not merely earthly distinction and splendour, the glory of man, but the "glory of God." **But shame shall be the promotion of fools;** or, as margin, *shame exalteth the fools.* The rendering of the original, *vuk'silim mêrim kâlôn,* depends upon the meaning to be given to *mêrim,* the hiph. participle of *rûm,* hiph. "to lift up, exalt;" and whether the plural, *k'silim,* in a dis-

tributive sense, as in ver. 18, or *kâlôn,* is the subject. Various interpretations have been given of the passage. (1) The Vulgate renders, *stultorum exaltatio ignominia;* i.e. as in the Authorized Version, "shame exalts fools." They "glory in their shame" (Phil. (ii. 19); or shame renders them conspicuous as warning examples (Ewald); or, as Dathe explains it, "Stulti infamiâ sunt famosi," "Fools become famous by infamy;" or as Rabbi Levi, "Shame exalts them as into the air, and makes them vanish away." (2) The LXX. renders, Αἱ ἀσεβεῖς ὕψωσαν ἀτιμίαν, i.e. "Fools exalt shame, prize what others despise" (Plumptre). (3) Umbreit, Bertheau, Zöckler, render, "Shame sweeps fools away," i.e. lifts them up in order to sweep away and destroy them (cf. Isa. lvii. 14). (4) The true rendering seems to be given by Michaelis, "Fools carry away shame" as their portion. So the Targum, Delitzsch, Hitzig, Wordsworth. They look for "promotion." They attain such as it is, but the end of their attainments is "shame and everlasting contempt." As the wise inherit glory, so fools get as their portion shame and ignominy.

HOMILETICS.

Vers. 1—4.—*Making the heart a treasury of good principles.* I. THE TREASURE. Innumerable impressions are constantly being made upon our minds, and as constantly transferring themselves into memories. Frivolous thoughts, false notions, corrupt images, once harboured, take up their abode in the soul, and ultimately modify its character to the likeness of themselves. It is most important for us to guard our memories from such things, and to fill them with more worthy stores. Consider, therefore, the best subjects for contemplation and memory. 1. *The Law of God.* Divine truth is the highest truth, the noblest theme of meditation, the supreme guide to conduct. Truth concerning our actions, the revealed will of God, is for us the most valuable Divine truth. Other forms of truth may please and help us, but this is essentially needful as a lamp to our feet. We can afford to lose sight of the stars if the harbour light shines clear on the waters over which we have to sail. This practical Divine truth—not our dreams and fancies, but utterances of God's will—we are called to remember. Hence the importance of studying the Bible, which contains it. It is well for children to store their minds with passages of Scripture. These will afford strength in temptation, guidance in perplexity, comfort in sorrow. 2. *Mercy and truth.* "The letter killeth." It is superstition that merely treasures up the words of Holy Writ, and repeats them parrot-like, as though a spell were to be wrought by the very utterance of them. The truth contained within these ancient words is what we need to recollect. And it is not the exact verbal bearing of the Law, but the wide-reaching principles underlying it, that Christians are called upon to treasure; not rules of sacrifice, but principles of mercy; not merely the prohibition, "Thou shalt not steal," but the higher precept, "Thou shalt love thy neighbour as thyself." 3. *Christ.* Christ is the Truth; he is the incarnation of mercy, our great exemplar, the visible manifestation of God's will, the perfect Ideal of our life. If we are weary of reading dry legal rescripts, and fail in contemplating bare abstract truths, we have a better way of treasuring good principles, by cherishing the vision of Christ.

II. THE TREASURY. This is the heart. It is not enough that the Law has been once for all revealed, that we come under it and under the institutions of the Church, that we treasure the Bible in our library, that we hear it read in hasty moments.

Much superstition prevails on these points. People seem to think that there is a virtue in the mere act of reading a chapter from the Bible, and some seem to go through the task as a sort of penance, imagining that they thus score some points to their credit in heaven. The Bible is valuable to us only in so far as it influences us. To influence us it must be known and remembered. The Law graven on stone, locked in the ark, and hidden behind the thick curtains of the sanctuary, could do the people of Israel little good. It needed to be written on the fleshy tables of the heart. This involves: 1. *An intelligent understanding* of Divine truth, so that it comes to us, not as a mere string of words, but as clear ideas. 2. *A good memory* of it. 3. *A love* of it, so that it is treasured thoughtfully, and becomes part of our very being, moulding our character, colouring our thoughts and affections, and directing our conduct. It is not difficult to see that such a treasury of such treasure will secure favour with God and ultimately also favour with men.

Vers. 5, 6.—*Divine guidance.* I. The need of Divine guidance. Several considerations force this upon us; *e.g.*: 1. *The complexity of life.* The longer we live, the more do we feel the profound mystery that touches us on every side. Innumerable avenues open out to us. Innumerable claims are made upon us. Conflicting duties perplex us. We feel as autumn leaves before the driving winds. We are helpless to choose and follow the right. 2. *Our ignorance of the future.* Like Columbus, we set our sails to cross unknown seas. We know not what a day will bring forth, yet we must boldly face the next day, and plan for many a day in advance. Our whole life must be arranged with respect to the future. We live in the future. Yet the future is hidden from us. How needful, then, to be guided on to that unknown land by One who sees the end from the beginning! 3. *The claims of duty.* We need a guide if we have only our own interests to consider. Much more is this the case when we are called to serve God. We are not free to choose our own path, even if we have light to do so. The servant must learn the will of his master before he can know what he is to do. Our prayer should be not so much that God should guide us safely, as that he should show us his way.

II. The condition of Divine guidance. This is trust. The lower animals are guided by God through unconscious instincts. But having endowed us with a higher nature, God has given to us the dangerous privilege of a larger liberty, and the serious responsibility of voluntarily choosing or rejecting his guidance. But then he vouchsafes this great help on the simplest of all conditions. We have not to deserve it, to attain to it by any skill or labour, but simply to trust with the most childlike faith. Consider what this involves. 1. *Self-surrender.* "Lean not to thine own understanding." We sometimes pray for God's guidance insincerely. We want him to guide us into our own way. But his guidance is useless when we should go the same way without it. It is only when human wisdom diverges from Divine wisdom that we are called expressly to follow the latter; we do so unconsciously under easier circumstances. This does not mean, however, that we are to stultify our intellect; we must rather seek God's Spirit to enlighten it—not lean to our understanding, but to God for the strengthening of that understanding. 2. *Whole-hearted faith.* "Trust in God with all thine heart." It is useless to have certain faint opinions about the wisdom of God. Every thought, affection, and desire must be given over to his direction; at least, we must honestly aim at doing this. The more completely we trust the more surely will God guide us. 3. *Active faith.* God guides, but we must follow his directions. The traveller is not carried up the mountain by his guide; he follows of his own will. It is vain for us to pray for a Divine leading unless we consent to follow the directions indicated to us.

III. The method of Divine guidance. 1. *Through our own conscience.* Conscience is our natural guide. It is not, therefore, the less Divine; for God is the Author of our nature. Conscience, clear and healthy, is the voice of God in the soul. But conscience is liable to corruption with the rest of our nature. Hence the need of prayer for the gift of the Holy Spirit to purify, enlighten, and strengthen it. 2. *Through inspired teaching.* God guides one man through his message to another. Prophets and apostles are messengers of Divine guidance. We need such direction outside our own consciences, especially in our present imperfect condition, or we may mistake the echoes of old prejudices and the promptings of self-interest for voices of God. God's word in the Bible is "a lamp to our feet." 3. *Through the disposition of events.* God guides us in his overruling providence, now closing dangerous ways, now opening up new paths.

Vers. 9, 10.—*Consecrated property.* I. WE CAN HONOUR GOD WITH OUR PROPERTY. It is not to be supposed that because religion is a wholly spiritual power it has no bearing on material things. Our religion is a mockery unless it affects the way in which we spend our money, as well as all other concerns of life. Property can be consecrated to God by being spent in conscious obedience to his will and by being used for the promotion of his glory, as in the maintenance of worship, the extension of missions, the relief of the poor, the sick, the widow and orphan.
II. GOD HAS CLAIMS UPON OUR PROPERTY. 1. It originally came from him. He created the materials and powers of nature. He gave to us our faculties. We sow the seed, but God gives the increase. 2. It is only lent to us for a season. Till recently it was not ours; soon we must leave it. While we have it, it is a talent to be used in our great Master's service, and for which we shall have to give an account. Rich men will be called to a Divine audit, where all their wealth will be reckoned and their method of spending it apprised. But so also will the poor; for we are all answerable for the use we make of our possessions, whether they be much or little. The one talent must be accounted for as well as the five talents.
III. OUR WHOLE PROPERTY SHOULD BE CONSECRATED TO GOD. It was *all* given to us by God. We shall have to give account of the use we make of *all* of it—of the substance or capital and of the increase or yearly income. We cannot compound for the abuse of the larger part of our goods by sacrificing to God a small proportion of them. If we give a tithe of our possessions to God, we do not thereby receive a dispensation to give the rest to Mammon. Is the mendicant friar, then, the typical Christian? No. An enlightened Christianity will teach us how to consecrate our possessions to God, while retaining the control of them. We are to be stewards, not beggars.
IV. THE BEST OF OUR PROPERTY SHOULD BE MORE DIRECTLY OFFERED TO THE SERVICE OF GOD. While all we have should be held sacred to God, some should be spent on objects that plainly involve self-sacrifice, and that manifestly concern the kingdom of heaven. We must not make the lofty thought of the consecration of all our property an excuse for low selfishness in spending the whole on ourselves. God expects the best. He should have the firstfruits; his claims should be recognized before all others. People often give to religious objects what they think they can spare after satisfying all other calls. They should give to these first, and see afterwards what is spared for more selfish things.
V. IT IS WELL TO DISPOSE OF OUR PROPERTY ON A CERTAIN METHOD. People who give to religious and philanthropic objects on a system of setting apart a certain portion of their income for such purposes, find that they can thus give most readily and justly. It is for each to settle in his own conscience and before God according to what proportion he should give. One may find a tithe too much, considering his duty to his family, etc. Another may find it far too little, considering his ease and affluence and the needs of the world.
VI. THIS CONSECRATION OF PROPERTY TO GOD BRINGS A BLESSING ON THE OWNER. If it is not always rewarded with temporal riches, it is repaid in better treasures— pleasures of sympathy and benevolence and the smile of God.

Vers. 11, 12.—*Chastening.* I. GOD CHASTENS HIS CHILDREN WITH SUFFERING. All suffering is not chastening. Some trouble is the pruning of branches that already bear fruit, in order that they may bring forth more fruit (John xv. 2). But when it meets us in our sins and failings, it is to be regarded as a Divine method of correction. It is not then the vengeance of a God simply concerned with his own outraged anger; before this we should tremble with alarm. It is not the chance product of the unconscious working of brute forces; such a materialistic explanation of suffering might well induce blank despair. The teaching of revelation is that suffering comes with a purpose, and that the purpose is our own good; it is a rod to chasten us for our faults, that we may be led to forsake them, and a pruning-knife to fit us for larger fruitfulness.

II. The motive with which God chastens his children is fatherly love. 1. *God must be angry with us for our sin.* His anger, however, is not the fruit of malignant hatred, but the expression of grieved love. For love can be angry, nay, sometimes must be, if it is pure and strong. The weak kindliness which is a stranger to indignation at wrong-doing is based on no deep affection. 2. *If God chastens in love, it is for our own good.* Weak love seeks the present pleasure of its objects; strong love aims at the highest welfare, even though this involve misunderstandings and temporary estrangement. 3. *God's paternal relation with us* is the ground of his chastening in love. We do not feel called upon to correct in strange children the faults for which we chastise our own family. The very love we bear to our children rouses indignation at conduct which we should scarcely heed in others. True love is not blind to the faults of those who are loved, it is rather rendered keen-sighted by sorrowful interest. Hence we may take the chastening as a proof of the love and Fatherhood of God. If we were not children, God would not thus put us to pain. Instead of regarding trouble as a proof that God has deserted us, we should see in it a sign that God is owning us and concerning himself with our welfare. The worst curse a man can receive is to be deserted by God and left unchecked in pursuit of folly and sin (Heb. xii. 8).

III. To rightly receive Divine chastening we must neither despise it nor grow weary of it. The good it will do to us depends on the reception we give it. Like other graces, the grace of correction may be received in vain, may be abused to our own hurt. We must not be satisfied, therefore, with the mere fact that we are being chastened. Two evils must be avoided. 1. *Despising* chastening. Cynical indifference and stoical hardness will render the chastening inefficacious. We must open our hearts to receive it. It blesses the broken heart. The very sorrow it induces is of the essence of its healing grace. 2. *Growing weary* of chastening. This is the opposite failing. We may despair, complain, show impatience, and rebel. Then the chastening loses its utility. The right reception is evidently to feel its grievousness, but to submit humbly and to seek to learn its bitter but wholesome lessons. The two all-essential thoughts, that suffering is for our own good, and that it is sent in love and is a proof of God's fatherly care for our welfare, should help us neither to be indifferent to it nor to rebel against it, but thus humbly to accept it.

Vers. 13—20.—"*More precious than rubies.*" We must bear in mind that the wisdom here commended to us is not mere knowledge, science, philosophy. It has two important characteristics. First, it is *religious;* it is based on the fear of God. Second, it is *practical;* it assumes the direction of human conduct. It is the knowledge of Divine truth, and the application of it to life. Why is this to be accounted most precious?

I. Wisdom is valuable on account of its own inherent qualities. (Vers. 13—15.) Paper money is worthless unless it can be exchanged for something else; but gold coins have a value of their own. If they are not used in the purchase of other things, the precious metal is valuable, and can be fashioned into objects of use and beauty. Wisdom is like solid specie. If she brings nothing else, she is a treasure in herself. While men are asking what advantages will religion give them, they should see that she is "the pearl of great price," for which all other good things may be sold, and yet the profit remain heavily on the side of him who purchases her. This is an inward treasure, a possession of the soul. It has many advantages over material treasures. 1. It is *exalted and elevating.* Its character is pure, and it raises those who possess it. There are earthly treasures that defile by contact with them, and others that materialize—make a man hard, worldly, ignoble. 2. It is *satisfying.* A man cannot live on gold, but on bread alone. There are desires of the soul that money and food do not quiet. Books, pictures, music, all works of art, all triumphs of civilization, leave a void unfilled. It is the mission of the thoughts of God in the soul to fill this void. 3. It is *never wearying.* Many things that never satisfy soon satiate. We are not full, yet we turn away with disgust, having had enough of them. The sea is beautiful, but the sailor grows tired of the endless monotony of waves. Divine wisdom never tires us. It is infinite, endlessly varied, eternally fresh. It is true that we may become wearied of religious occupations, religious books, etc. But then we have the imperfections of the human embodiment of wisdom to annoy us. 4. It is *secure*. No thief can steal it. No moth nor rust can consume it. The thief may take a man's jewels, but never his inner treasure. He may be stripped of property, home, choicest possessions, and left to bare beggary; yet if he have precious thoughts of God in his heart, no thief can touch them. They are a safe, an eternal possession.

II. WISDOM IS VALUABLE BECAUSE IT MINISTERS TO OUR EARTHLY WELFARE. (Vers. 16—18.) The temporal advantages of religion are here described with that prominence and positiveness which are characteristic of the Old Testament, and of the Book of Proverbs in particular. We have learnt to see more limitations upon these things, and, at the same time, we have had revealed to us much larger spiritual and eternal beati- tudes than those of the Jewish faith. But we may make the mistake of ignoring the truth contained in the old view. There are earthly advantages in religion. It has promises for this life as well as for that to come. 1. *Length of days*. Many good people die young; many bad men grow hoary in sin. If it were not so, we should lose the discipline that comes by our having to walk by faith. But on the whole, wisdom tends to length of days by preserving the constitution sound and healthy. A wise way of living falls in with the laws of health. Reckless folly saps the energies of life, induces disease, decrepitude, premature old age and death. 2. Ways of *pleasant- ness and peace*. The road is pleasant as well as the end. Religion may bring a cross, but she also brings grace for bearing it. All her rewards are not reserved for the future. There is a peace of God that passeth all understanding, which the world can neither give nor take away, and which will make the wilderness of the saddest life blossom like the rose. 3. A *tree of life*. Length of days is a poor blessing unless the life preserved is worth living. What boon would it be to an exile in Siberia, a convict on Dartmoor, a paralytic in an infirmary? Long existence without a source of worthy life is the curse of the Wandering Jew, not the blessing of eternal life. Wisdom— *i.e.* Divine truth, religion—supplies fruits for holy sustenance and leaves for the healing of the nations. To know God is eternal life (John xvii. 3).

III. WISDOM IS VALUABLE BECAUSE IT IS A LINK OF CONNECTION BETWEEN MAN AND GOD. (Vers. 19, 20.) Our heart is restless till it finds rest in God. All our highest life, all our deepest peace, all our truest thought, all our noblest effort, all our purest joy, depend on our union in and with God. But wisdom is an essential Divine attribute. By it God first created the earth and the heavens (ver. 13). By it he now controls all things (ver. 20). The wisdom of God is reflected in nature. All our know- ledge is just the reflection of this wisdom; it is thinking into the thoughts of God; thus it is a communion with him. Spiritual knowledge brings us nearest to God, who is Spirit. Christ as the incarnate " Word," by whom all things were made, and the Wisdom of God, is our Mediator, and unites us to God.

Vers. 27, 28.—*Dilatoriness in the payment of just debts.* I. THIS DILATORINESS IS MORALLY CULPABLE, AND MOST INJURIOUS TO SOCIETY. Through thoughtlessness in some cases, through deliberate meanness in others, many people postpone the payment of their just debts as long as possible, though they have the money by them, and are perhaps turning it to account for their own advantage. Such needless delay of justice should be regarded as a moral offence. A sad laxity prevails in this matter. It is said that preachers direct their admonitions respecting the business habits of the day too much to one side of the case. The tradesman is accused of greed, dishonesty, deceit, while little is said of the conduct of the customer. But here is an instance where the failing, nay, the sin, lies with the buyer. Most of us little know how much the trading classes suffer from delay and difficulty in calling in the money that is owing to them ; how often they pinch themselves and suffer in silence for fear of losing a customer by giving offence in too much pressing for payment, knowing that the common selfish- ness of others will readily lead them to court the patronage of the offended client. This delay is grossly unjust to more conscientious people who pay promptly, and yet are made to suffer from the high prices necessitated by the bad debts and postponed pay- ments of others. It is also a direct temptation to those shifty practices which all of us deprecate when we meet with them in trade. Feeling that he cannot recoup himself readily in the regular way, the tradesman is tempted to try some less straightforward method for making his business, thus heavily handicapped, to some extent profitable.

A new moral tone is requisite in this matter. People should see that to delay to execute justice is to commit injustice. Time is as valuable as coins. He who robs a man of time is a thief, and should wear the brand of a thief.

II. THE REMEDY FOR THIS DILATORINESS MUST BE FOUND IN A FULLER RECOGNITION OF THE CLAIMS OF HUMAN BROTHERHOOD. It is not enough to prove the abstract justice of prompt payment. The selfishness which withholds it will find some casuistic excuse for further delay. This selfishness, which is at the root of the evil, must be overcome. The spirit of Cain is dishonest as well as murderous. We are too ready to treat those with whom we have merely business dealings according to an entirely different code from that which controls our conduct with our friends. Commercial rules are so much more lax than social laws. The mere business relation is too often robbed of all human consideration, treated from a purely selfish standpoint, almost on a principle of enmity, as though it belonged to a state of war. Does a man cease to be our brother because we buy and sell with him? When he was a stranger, we felt some tie of common humanity with him. After we have entered into relations of mutual convenience, is the tie broken, and does he become as a heathen and a publican? We must remember that it is our "neighbour" who claims just payment; and are we not required to love our neighbour as ourselves? The golden rule of Christ, that we must do to others as we would that they should do to us, must be applied to business, or we have no right to profess ourselves to be Christians.

HOMILIES BY VARIOUS AUTHORS.

Vers. 1—10.—*Precepts and promises of wisdom.* I. THE CONNECTION OF PRECEPT AND PROMISE. 1. Precept needs confirmation. We cannot but ask—*Why* should we pursue this or that line of conduct in preference to another? *Why* should men be God-fearing, honest, chaste? We are rational creatures, not "dumb driven cattle," to be forced along a given road. We must have reasons; and it is to reason in us that the Divine reason ever makes appeal. 2. The confirmation is found in *experience*. This is the source of our knowledge; to it the true teacher must constantly refer for the verification of his principles, the corroboration of his precepts. The tone assumed by the teacher is indeed that of *authority*, but real authority always rests upon experience. Experience, in short, is the discovery and ascertainment of law in life. Precepts are its formulation. 3. The experience of the past enables the prediction of the future. Just as we know the science of the astronomer, *e.g.*, to be sound, because we find that he can predict with accuracy coming events, appearances of the heavenly bodies, eclipses, etc., so do we recognize the soundness of moral teaching by its power to forecast the future fates of men. Precepts are the deductions from the actual; promises the forecasts of that which, because it has been constant in the past, may be expected in the future. In science, in morality, in religion, we build on the permanence of law; in other words, on the constancy of the eternal God.

II. PARTICULAR EXAMPLES OF THIS CONNECTION. 1. *Obedience ensures earthly happiness.* (Vers. 1, 2.) The connection is first stated generally. "Extension of days," or long life, is the one aspect of this happiness; inward peace of heart, denied to the godless, the other (Isa. xlviii. 22; lvii. 21). Prolongation of days, life in the good land, dwelling in the house of the Lord, are the peculiar Old Testament blessings (Deut. iv. 40; v. 33; vi. 2; xi. 9; xxii. 7; xxx. 16; Ps. xv. 1; xxiii. 6; xxvii. 4). (1) The desire for long life is *natural*, and religion recognizes it. (2) Without *inward satisfaction*, long life is no blessing. (3) While the Old Testament promises *formally* cover the finite life only, they do not exclude the infinite. In God and faith in him the infinite is *germinally* contained. 2. *Love and good faith ensure favour with God, good will with men.* "Mercy," or "love;" the word denotes the recognition of *kinship*, fellowship in men, and the duty of *kindness* therein implied. "Truth," in the sense in which we speak of *a true man*; sincerity and rectitude, the striving to make the *seeming* and the *being* correspond to one another; the absence of hypocrisy. St. Paul gives the ideas, "dealing *truly* in *love*" (Eph. iv. 15). Let these virtues be bound about the neck, like precious objects, for the sake of security; let these commands be engraven in the only indelible way—upon the heart. Let the mind be fixed and formed, and the result will be favour in the sight of God, and a "good opinion" in the minds of men. The two relations form a *correlation*. There is no true standing with God which does not *reflect* itself in the good opinion of good men; no worthy opinion of a man which does not furnish an *index* to God's view of him. Both were united in the case of the youthful Jesus. 3. *Trust in God ensures practical direction.* (Vers. 5, 6.) (1) This trust must be *whole-hearted*. An exception to it destroys it, as one faulty link will cause the chain to break, one rotten plank the ship to leak, etc. (2) The fallacy of confidence is when we separate the particular in our intelligence from the universal. This is intellectual egoism. There is a dualism in consciousness—the private self-seeking intelligence, and the Divine mind in us. (3) Trust is *abandonment to the Divine mind*, to the universal intelligence which carries us out of self. (4) Such trust implies the "taking cognizance" of God in all we do. Of bad, unjust men, like Eli's sons, it is said that they take no cognizance of Jehovah (1 Sam. ii. 12). To ask of every action not—Is this what the generality of men would do in my position? but— Is it what God would have me to do? Not—Is it "natural"? but—Is it Divine? Such a habit ensures practical direction. All our *égarements* and stumblings arise from following the isolated intelligence, which is a true guide only for immediate sensuous relations, cannot light us for life's complex whole. Hence the way in which selfish and cunning people constantly outwit themselves, while the man who is set down by them as a fool for neglecting his own interests comes out safely in the long run. 4. *Simple piety secures health.* (Vers. 7, 8.) (1) *Conceit is opposed to piety.* This we have already seen. For what is conceit but the lifting of the merely individual into a false generality? In its extreme, the worship of self is a little god. (2) Simple piety has a positive and a negative pole: positive, reverence for God; negative, aversion from evil. The pious man affirms and denies, both with all his might. His life is emphatic, includes an everlasting "Yes" and an everlasting "No"! (3) Simple piety is the source of health. (*a*) *Physical.* It tends to promote right physical habits. It certainly reacts against the worst disorders, viz. the nervous. (*b*) *Spiritual.* It is in the mind what the sound nervous organization is in the body. The mind thus centrally right digests, enjoys, assimilates, the rich food which nature, books, and men afford. 5. *Consecration of property ensures wealth.* (Vers. 9, 10.) (1) *Ancient custom commanded this.* The consecration of the firstling of firstfruits was not confined to Israel. It was an ancient custom of the world generally. The part represents the whole, for all is God's. There seems to be no objection to the private practice of the custom by Christians still. In any case, let it be recognized that *property*, in the legal sense, is but an expression of convenience; that *really* our temporary possessions, along with ourselves, are the property of God. If this be not recognized, we merely *consume* them, or hoard them, do not use them. (2) *Plenty falls to the lot* of the giver. The exceptions to the rule are *apparent*, and perhaps language does not suffice for their statement and elucidation. The rule is *comprehensively* true, and a *comprehensive view* is necessary for its application. Rich and poor are *subjective terms*. There is a rich poverty and a miserable affluence. The promise is only truly fulfilled in the man who *feels* he has abundance, and enjoys it.—J.

Vers. 11, 12.—*Patience in affliction.* Well does this lesson contrast with the preceding picture of prosperity and opulence.

I. THE RELIGIOUS VIEW OF SUFFERING. 1. *It is not a dark doom*, a cruel fate, a blind necessity of things. Such were the ideas of the heathen. 2. *Its cause may be known.* This is ever a great solace—to be persuaded that our troubles lie in the reason of things, that nothing is chance or caprice. 3. That cause is *in the Divine mind and will.* The power of God is manifested in our suffering; we are but as the clay on the potter's wheel. Still more the love of God is manifested in our suffering. There is always some mitigation accompanying it. "It might have been worse" may be said of every pain. It serves as the foil to set off some greater good. "The ring may be lost, but the finger remains," as the Spanish proverb says. 4. *The object or final cause of suffering.* Purification from inward evil; correction of faults. The mind grows of itself; the schoolmaster can do little more than point out and correct faults. So with life's education from the religious point of view. And the most fertile minds need most the discipline of suffering. The pruning-knife is not applied to the puny plant; and languid minds are the least touched by affliction. In these adjustments, love is still revealed. 5. *Suffering must be viewed under the analogy of the parental and filial relation.* Let these words once become clear, *Father, son,* in their application to God's relation to us, and ours to him, and the theory of suffering is mastered (comp. Deut. viii. 5; Ps. cxviii. 18; Lam. iii. 31—33).

II. THE RELIGIOUS TEMPER UNDER SUFFERING. 1. *Humility.* No indignant questioning, scornful recalcitration, proud efforts of stoical fortitude. These will but *defeat* or *delay* the end. The medicine benefits not if the patient sets his mind against it as unneeded. 2. *Patient endurance.* Perseverance in a passive, receptive, attitude is far more difficult than perseverance in activity. We haste to snatch at good. But God is never in haste. His processes are slow. And to receive their benefit we must learn the wisdom of the word "wait." While we are thus waiting, things are not at a standstill; God is working, producing a spiritual shape out of the passive material.

> "Maker, remake, complete,
> I trust what thou shalt do!"
>   (R. Browning's noble poem, 'Rabbi Ben Ezra.')
>   **J.**

Vers. 13—18.—*Wisdom the best investment.* I. WISDOM COMPARABLE WITH THE MOST PRECIOUS THINGS. Silver, gold, precious stones, everything eagerly coveted and warmly prized by the senses and the fancy, may illustrate the worth of the pious intelligence. Every object in the world of sense has its analogy in the world of spirit. The worth of the ruby is due to the æsthetic light in the mind of the observer. But wisdom is the light in the mind itself.

II. WISDOM INCOMPARABLE WITH ALL PRECIOUS THINGS. For by *analogy* only can we put wisdom and precious minerals side by side, on the principle that mind is *reflected* in matter. But on the opposite principle, that mind is diverse from matter, rests the *incomparableness* of wisdom. Mere matter can breed nothing; spiritual force only is generative. When we talk of "money breeding money," we use a figure of speech. It is the mind which is the active power.

III. WISDOM MAY BE VIEWED AS THE BEST LIFE INVESTMENT. All the objects which stimulate human activity to their pursuit are derivable from this capital. Life in health and ample and various enjoyment, riches and honour, pleasure and inward peace; blessings that neither money nor jewels can purchase, are the fruit, direct or indirect, of the cultivation of the spiritual field of enterprise, the whole-hearted venture on this Divine speculation, so to say. For religion *is* a speculation; faith is a speculation in the sense that everything cannot be made certain; some elements in the calculation must ever remain undefined. (For further, see the early part of the chapter; and on ver. 17, South's 'Sermons,' vol. i. ser. 1.) The summary expression, "a tree of life," seems to symbolize all that is beautiful, all that is desirable, all that gives joy and intensity to living (comp. ch. xiii. 12; xv. 4).—J.

Vers. 19, 20.—*Wisdom the principle of the creation.* Perhaps the mention of the tree of life has reminded the writer of the early account of the creation in Gen. i., ii. He thus traces the visible world and its order to its spiritual root in the mind of God. He gives a brief sketch of the construction of the *cosmos,* according to the ancient mode of thought. Both heaven and earth are fixed and made fast; and the water-masses divided into those above and those below the "firmament;" the consequence of which is the gushing forth of the clouds in rain. The modern scientific knowledge of the world may be used to impart a rich context to these simple conceptions of the early imagination.

I. THE WORLD IS AN ORDER. The Greeks expressed this idea in the beautiful word "cosmos." It includes symmetry, beauty, variety, harmony, adaptation of means to ends. To recognize these in the visible world is an intellectual delight, and a motive to the purest reverence.

II. THIS ORDER IS REDUCIBLE TO A UNITY. Formerly we looked upon the world as a collection of independent forces. Science showed us the correlation, interdependence, interaction of these forces. Now she has risen to the grand conception of the unity of all force; and thus arrives at the same goal with religious thought.

III. THAT UNITY OF FORCE IS GOD. It is often forgotten that the generalizations of science are but logical distinctions—cause, law, force, etc. What are these without Being, Personality, as their ground? Empty names. Religion fills these forms with life, and where the scientific man speaks of law, she bows before the living God.

IV. SCIENCE AND RELIGION ARE AT ONE. When we talk of their opposition, we are using a figure of speech. What they represent, these names, is two different directions of the spiritual activity of man. What needs to be cured is narrowness and partialism on the side of both scientific and religious *men*. For there is no real cleft in the nature of our knowledge. All genuine knowledge is essentially a knowledge of God, of the Infinite revealed in and through the finite.—J.

Vers. 21—26.—*Confidence and the sense of security in the ways of God.* In rich variation the religious habit of mind is presented. What has been spoken of as worthy to be hung about the neck as precious is now referred to as to be kept continually before the eyes of the mind. The designation of wisdom or its attributes is also varied, viz. "thoughtfulness and circumspection" (ver. 21). In the next, former modes of statement recur (comp. ver. 3, *sqq.*).

I. RELIGION STRENGTHENS AND STEADIES THE PERCEPTION. (Ver. 23.) Perfect *unconsciousness of danger*, as in the child, the somnambulist, etc., is often seen to be a condition of security in walking in dangerous places. And so may the mind be unconscious of danger through the full enfolding in God. But better is the safe step which is given by the perfect knowledge both of danger and the resources against it. This is found in religion. We know what is against us, still more who is for us, and so pass on with head erect and footstep firm.

II. RELIGION CONTROLS THE IMAGINATION. (Vers. 24, 25.) The indefinable in space and time continually besets the fancy, and, especially in certain temperaments, fills it with images of gloom and terror. The timid heart forebodes some sudden "tempest of the wicked," some onrush of malice and violence out of the dark. What a chapter of "imaginary terrors" could be filled from the experience of many such a one! But faith fortifies the imagination, preoccupying it with the thought of the almighty Defender (compare the beautiful Ps. xci.).—J.

Vers. 27, 28.—*Promptitude in good actions.* I. NEGATIVE UNKINDNESS. (Ver. 27.) 1. It consists in *withholding good* which it is in our power to impart. 2. It is analogous to *the refusal to pay a just debt*. Kindness is the "due" of our fellow-men. This does not imply the giving to every beggar or borrower. No act is required which, under the *show* of kindness, involves no real benefit to another or actually involves an injustice to ourself or another. We must carry these precepts to the light of the heart and of the discriminating intelligence. Speaking generally, sullenness, unsociability, extreme taciturnity, self-absorption, are forms of the sin.

II. PROCRASTINATION CONDEMNED. (Ver. 28.) Remember: 1. That to give promptly is to give twice; that the deferred gift loses its bloom; that unnecessary delay is a fraud on the time and temper of others; that of everything we intend to do we had best make the beginning at once, which, the Roman poet says, is "half the deed." 2. To defer a duty till to-morrow may be to defer it for ever. A lost opportunity of doing good is a sad sting in the memory. These *negative* warnings infer the positive lesson of promptitude. (1) Now is the acceptable time for ourselves and our own salvation. (2) It may also be the acceptable time for others' salvation. How admirable to be one of those who, amidst whatever pressure, can find time to listen, to comfort, to help their brethren, to-day, at once!—J.

Vers. 29—31.—*Odious passions.* Let them be held up in the clear exposure of Wisdom, that their very mention may suggest their hideousness.

I. MALICE AND ITS DEVICES. (Ver. 29.) Literally, "*Forge* not ill against thy neighbour." 1. Malice, like love, is all-inventive. But as the devices of the latter are the very instruments of progress and good, so those of the former are pernicious— burglar's tools, cunning instruments of torture. 2. Directed against unsuspecting objects, malice is truly Satanic, an inspiration from hell. We have to beware of indulgence in curiosity about our neighbours; it is seldom free from some taint of malice in thought, which may pass over at any moment into action. Something in our neighbour's life may rebuke us and rouse the latent passion. How near are the angel and the devil to one another in the heart!

II. UNPROVOKED CONTENTIOUSNESS. (Ver. 30.) In other words, *quarrelsomeness.* The vicious habit and disposition to "pick quarrels," to invent occasions for fault-finding, for the exercise of pugnacity, and so on. The man of whom it is said that if left alone in the world he would fight with his own shadow. Let him contend with his own vices, of which this temper is a symptom, and expend his pugnacity upon the evils of society. There are men before whose presence all the sleeping germs of wrath start up into chaotic life. Could they but see themselves as others see them!

III. ENVY OF THE WICKED GREAT. (Ver. 31.) As emulation of the virtuous great is a noble passion, this, the *reverse side* of it, is correspondingly base. Imitation, again, is a powerful passion, the source of "fashion." The pure spirit knows nothing of fashion as such; and immoral fashion, born of mere imitation, it must avoid and denounce. 1. Every passion has its obverse and its reverse, its good and its evil side; malice may be turned to benevolence; idle quarrelsomeness to noble pugnacity; immoral envy to pure emulation. 2. Religion *intensifies, purifies, directs,* the passions to noble ends.—J.

Vers. 32—35.—*The discernment of Jehovah.* This is a leading thought of the Old Testament. In ordinary life, in civilized times, the character of individuals is concealed from us by the intermixtures of society and the complexity of its interests. Even in village life it is difficult to classify people; but God *distinguishes* in—

I. HIS VIEW OF INDIVIDUAL CHARACTER. 1. He abominates the *perverse*, the crooked, twisted, deceitful character. All in the spirit must be compared with that ideal geometrical rectitude of form, so to speak, which is the truth of his Being. 2. With the upright he "maintains good friendship" (ver. 32), or "is in secret alliance" (Job xxix. 4; Ps. xxv. 14). To enjoy the friendship of discerning minds, what greater privilege can there be? To live on such terms with God is the privilege of the true soul.

II. HIS PROVIDENTIAL ADMINISTRATION. "His curse dwells in the house of the wicked." A fatality of evil clings to him and his. But Jehovah blesses the tent of the righteous. He scoffs at the scoffer, but gives to the lowly grace (comp. Jas. iv. 6; 1 Pet. v. 5). The wise under this administration inherit glory, while ignominy carries away the fools. 1. These are, in the mode of their presentation, *generalized* or abstract truths, and as such must be understood. The study of apparent exceptions, even the admission of them, is foreign to this phase of Oriental thought. It was the presence of exceptions, insoluble to ancient thought, which excited the doubt and grief of Job and some of the psalmists. 2. While the truth must be stated, from the exigencies of language, in this sharp polar antithesis, actual human character is found, with all its merits and shades, in the intermediate region. 3. The subtle intermixtures of good and evil in human character, recognized by modern thought, defy complete analysis. We must suspend our judgment in particular cases, leaving all to him who brings to light the hidden things of darkness; conscious that there must be great "reversals of human judgment" upon the character of man (see Mozley's sermon on this subject).—J.

Vers. 1—4.—*Cherishing the truth.* We have here—
I. THE ESSENTIAL THING IMPLIED. It is implied that the Law of God has been heard and understood; also that it has been received as Divine, and taken as the true guide of life. The teacher or preacher has sometimes to assume this; but too often it is an assumption unjustified by the facts. When it *is* justified, there come—

II. TWO SPECIALLY VALUABLE VIRTUES INSISTED UPON. Mercy and truth (ver. 3) are to be exemplified. 1. *Mercy,* which includes (1) compassion, or the pity one should show to the unfortunate and the suffering; and (2) clemency, or a lenient view taken and a generous spirit shown in presence of error and wrong-doing, particularly of injury done to ourselves. 2. *Truth,* which includes (1) veracity in language; (2) sincerity of heart; (3) honesty and uprightness of action.

III. A MATTER OF GREAT MOMENT ENFORCED. This is *the* cherishing of the truth by the spirit which has received it in the love of it. "My son, forget not my law; ... let thine heart keep," etc. (ver. 1); "Bind them about thy neck; write them upon the tablet of thine heart" (ver. 3). If these precepts are to be duly carried out, and there is thus to be a *continuance* in well-doing, and even a *growth* therein, then must there be: 1. The dwelling upon them by the mind; that must be a mental habit carefully cultivated. 2. The placing ourselves where they will be urged on our attention and commended to our affection (the sanctuary, the Lord's table, the society of the holy, etc.). 3. The wise study of them as illustrated in the lives of the worthiest of our race. 4. The use of any and every means by which they will be seen by us to be the beautiful and blessed things they are. The children of Wisdom will not only receive gladly the truth of God, but they will cherish it carefully; they will water with diligent hand the plant which has been sown and which has sprung up in the soul. "Let not the workman lose what he has wrought." If we *continue* in the word of Christ, then are we his disciples indeed (see John viii. 31; xv. 9; Acts xiii. 43).

IV. A LARGE BLESSING PROMISED. (Vers. 2, 4.) Under the Law, temporal blessings were more abundantly held in view; then the wise were promised long life, comfort, and human estimation, as well as the favour of God. Under the gospel, temporal prosperity takes the second place, spiritual and heavenly well-being the first. But we may urge that conformity to the will of God as revealed in his Word: 1. Tends to bodily health and strength; if that does not secure it, assuredly disobedience will not. 2. Tends to secure a life of tranquillity. "Peace," as well as "length of days," it is likely to add; equanimity of mind and the comfort which is the consequence of right and kind behaviour. 3. Tends to win the esteem and the affection of our neighbours. "Favour in the sight of man." 4. Ensures the love and the blessing of Almighty God.—C.

Vers. 5, 6, 7 (first part).—*Self-distrust and trust in God.* If we would realize God's thought concerning us, we shall—

I. CHERISH A DEEP DISTRUST OF OURSELVES. We are not to "lean unto our own understanding," or to "be wise in our own eyes" (vers. 5, 7). 1. We shall certainly have a sense of our own insufficiency if we *weigh our own human weakness;* if we consider how little we know of (1) human nature generally; and of (2) our own hearts in particular; of (3) the real character and disposition of those connected with us; of (4) the whole circle of law by which we are surrounded on every side; of (5) the events which are in the (even) near future; of (6) the ultimate effect of our decisions on our circumstances and our character. 2. So also if we *consider the disastrous results* that have followed presumption in this matter. How often have we seen men, confident of their own capacity, staking everything on their own judgment, and miserably disappointed with the issue! Men of this spirit, who carry self-reliance (which is a virtue) to an exaggerated and false assurance of their own sagacity, not only dig a deep grave for their own happiness, but usually involve others also in their ruin. Neither in (1) the affairs of this life, nor (2) in the larger issues of the spiritual realm, should we lean all the weight of our own and of others' prosperity on our own poor finite understanding.

II. LOOK DEVOUTLY UPWARD. We are to maintain: 1. A whole-hearted trust in God (ver. 5). A profound assurance that (1) he is regarding us; (2) he is divinely interested in our welfare; (3) he will see that we have all we need, and go in the way in which it is best for us to walk. 2. A continual acknowledgment (ver. 6). We are to acknowledge God (1) by referring everything to him in our own heart; (2) by consulting and applying his will as revealed in his Word; (3) by praying for and expecting his Divine direction; so shall we acknowledge him "in all our ways." This trust and acknowledgment are *inclusive* and *not exclusive* of our own individual endeavour. We are to think well, to consult wisely, to act diligently, and then to trust wholly. Whoso does the last without the first is guiltily and daringly presumptuous; whoso does the first without the last is guiltily irreverent and unbelieving.

III. RECKON CONFIDENTLY ON DIVINE DIRECTION. "He shall direct thy paths" (ver. 6). As a very little child, left alone in the streets of a great city, can but wander aimlessly about, and will surely fail of reaching home, so we, lost in the maze of this seething, struggling, incomprehensible world—world of circumstance and world of thought—can but make vain guesses as to our true course, and are certain to wander far from the home of God. What the shrewdest and cleverest of men most urgently and sorely need is the guiding hand of a heavenly Father, who, through all the labyrinths of life, past all the by-paths of error and evil, will conduct us to truth, righteousness, wisdom, heaven. If we trust him wholly, and acknowledge him freely and fully, we may confidently expect that he will (1) lead our feet along the path of outward life; (2) guide our minds into the sanctuary of heavenly truth; (3) help our souls up the ennobling heights of holiness; (4) direct our steps to the gates of the city of God; and (5) finally welcome us within its "golden streets."—C.

Vers. 7 (second part), 8.—*A three-linked chain.* We have—
I. PIETY. "Fear the Lord." It is the faculty which distinguishes the meanest man from the noblest brute, which raises our race immeasurably above the next below it. Man can fear God. He can (1) recognize his Maker; (2) bow down in lowly but manly reverence before God; (3) render to him the gratitude of a heart mindful of his many mercies; (4) subject his will to the will Divine; (5) order his life according to the written Word.
II. MORALITY. "Depart from evil." The outcome of piety is morality. 1. The morality which rests not on the basis of piety (the fear of the Lord) is on an insecure foundation. Change of circumstance, of friends, of fashions, may blow it down. 2. The morality which depends on the "thou shalt" and "thou shalt not" of the Supreme is safe against all the winds that blow. For the dark hour of powerful temptation there is no such barrier against sin and ruin as the conviction, "How can I do this great wickedness and sin against God?" For the bright hour of obligation there is no such animating incitement as "that Christ may be magnified in me." The third link in this heaven-forged chain is—
III. HEALTH. "It shall be health to thy navel, and marrow to thy bones." Sickness of body may be the portion of the best of men or women. Some are born to suffer until they die and pass to the blessed country where the inhabitant will never say, "I am sick." But the constant tendency of piety and its invariable accompaniment morality is to give (1) health and strength of bodily frame; the pure blood, the clear eye, the strong muscle, the steady nerve, the "green old age." It regularly gives (2) an active mind; and it necessarily imparts (3) a soul that is "in health" (3 John 2). The man who fears God and departs from evil is the man who is fitted and is likely to have the largest show of vigorous, robust, healthy life in all its forms.—C.

Vers. 9, 10.—*The Divine responsiveness.* There are two ways in which God blesses us—unconditionally and conditionally. We receive very much from him in virtue of his *originating and spontaneous goodness.* We may, if we will, receive much from him also as the result of his *faithful response* to our appeal. The text suggests to us the truth, which has manifold illustrations, that if we take toward him the attitude which he desires us to assume, he will visit us with appropriate and corresponding blessings.
I. IF WE LOVE HIM, HE WILL LOVE US. True, indeed, it is that "we love him because he first loved us" (1 John iv. 19), his own Divine beneficence is the source of all human affection; but it is also true that "if a man love me (Christ), he will keep my words, and my Father will love him" (John xiv. 23). Our love of God, of Jesus Christ, will meet with a large response in the outpouring of Divine affection toward us. God will love us with the fulness of parental, rejoicing love.
II. IF WE TRUST HIM, HE WILL TRUST US. Those who believe in the Lord Jesus Christ, and thus become his sons (John i. 12), are the objects of his Divine trust. God does not prescribe to his reconciled children the hours, places, forms, methods, and means of service. He leaves these to the promptings of the filial spirit, to the decision of the understanding which has been consecrated to him. He makes known to us his will, that he should be served and his creatures blessed and saved; then he trusts us to put out our energies in all wise ways to fulfil his purpose. His treatment of us is in response to our attitude towards him.
III. IF WE HONOUR HIM, HE WILL HONOUR US. (1 Sam. ii. 30.)
IV. IF WE GIVE OF OUR SUBSTANCE TO HIM, HE WILL ENRICH US. This is the

illustration which our text supplies (see Deut. xxvi.). The children of Israel were encouraged to bring of their firstfruits and to present them unto the Lord, and to expect that, if they gave thus to God, he would give, in like way, to them, enlarging and enriching them (Mal. iii. 10—12). And not only were they taught thus to look on gifts of piety, but also of charity; these should be repaid by the observing and responsive Lord (ch. xix. 17). It may be asked how far we may go in anticipating like rewards at the hand of God now. And the answer is: 1. We are not to expect that God will enrich us in substance irrespective of other conditions (2 Thess. iii. 10). This would be a premium on idleness and imprudence. It will always be "the hand of the diligent that will make rich." 2. But labour and frugality being understood, the man who "seeks first the kingdom of God," who "acknowledges him in all his ways" (ver. 6), and who liberally gives to his cause (specially remembering his "little ones"—his poor), may look for large blessings at his hand. *At least* sufficiency now (Matt. vi. 33; Phil. iv. 19), and glorious abundance soon and for ever (John xiv. 13, 14; xvi. 9).—C.

Vers. 11, 12.—*Wrong views of affliction, and the right one.* Sorrow is a very large ingredient in the cup of human life. It begins so early and lasts so long; it lies so near the surface and it strikes so deep into our nature; it is so certain that we shall meet with it before long, and so likely that we may renew our acquaintance with it very soon, that they must be unwise indeed who do not prepare for its coming, and they must be losers indeed who do not know how to treat it when it knocks at their door. There are—

I. MANY MISTAKES WE MAY MAKE ABOUT IT. 1. We may treat it thoughtlessly; we may "despise the chastening of the Lord" (ver. 11). We may allow ourselves to have "the sorrow of the world," of which Paul speaks (2 Cor. vii. 10); *i.e.* we may decline to consider what it means; content ourselves with the sullen thought that we have something that we must endure as best we can, not attempting to discover whence it comes or what it means. 2. We may conclude that it is only accidental. This is another way of "despising the chastening of the Lord." We may take that view which is intellectually the most easy and spiritually the most barren, and refer our trouble to the "course of events;" we may recognize no guiding hand, we may decide, with off-handed readiness, that we are the unhappy victims of unkind circumstances, and go on our way "grinding our teeth" with impatient spirit. 3. We may be crushed under the weight of it. We may (to use the words in Heb. xii. 5) "faint when we are rebuked." We may suffer a spiritual collapse, may meet affliction with an unmanly spirit of prostration, and, instead of bending bravely beneath the yoke and bearing it, break down utterly and miserably. 4. We may repine under long continuance of it. We may "be weary" of God's correction. Sometimes, when affliction is long-continued, men feel that either God has nothing to do with them at all, or that he is not regarding their prayer, or that he is punishing them above that which they are able to bear, and they repine; they are weary in their spirit, querulous in their tone, perhaps positively complaining in their speech. But there is—

II. THE ONE RIGHT WAY IN WHICH TO TAKE IT. And that is to accept it as *the correction of fatherly kindness.* "For whom the Lord loveth he correcteth," etc. (ver. 12). 1. We may be God's unreconciled children, and he is seeking to win us to himself. 2. Or we may have returned to him, but need fatherly correction. He may be rebuking us for some departure from his will. He may be desirous of removing the spirit of pride or of selfishness, or of worldliness, and of leading us along paths of humility, self-surrender, spirituality. Certainly he is seeking our truest welfare, our highest good, our lasting joy. Let each afflicted heart ask—What is the lesson the Father wishes me to learn?—C.

Vers. 13—26.—*Wisdom's inestimable worth.* Here are found many strong recommendations of heavenly wisdom, and we might adopt the thirteenth verse as a refrain to each one of them: "Happy is the man that findeth wisdom, and the man that getteth understanding."

I. POSSESSORS OF IT, WE ARE SHAREHOLDERS WITH GOD HIMSELF. (Vers. 19, 20.) Only by wisdom could the Divine Founder of all visible things make them what they are. His wonder-workings in the heavens above and on the earth beneath, in sun and star, in grain and grass, in coal and iron, in rain and dew,—all are the product of Divine wisdom.

II. POSSESSORS OF IT, WE HAVE A WELL-BEING THAT ENDURES. "Length of days is in her right hand" (ver. 16). "She is a tree of life to them that lay hold upon her" (ver. 18). They who fear God are more likely than others to "be satisfied with long life" (Ps. xci. 16). For the secret of strength is with those who are obedient to law; but though they should die before old age, yet (1) so long as life lasts their well-being will continue, and (2) when their earthly life is taken, their heritage is in the everlasting life beyond, where there is "length of days" indeed.

III. IT IS THE SOURCE OF GENUINE ESTEEM. "In her left hand . . . honour" (ver. 16). It may, indeed, be that the children of wisdom are disregarded or even despised. But that is the painful exception to the rule. The rule is, everywhere and in every age, that those who consult God's will in the guidance of their life are honoured of their brethren, enjoy the esteem of the worthiest of their neighbours, live and die in the fragrance of general regard.

IV. IT IS THE ONE SECURITY AGAINST SIN. (Ver. 23.) How many are "the stumblers," those who trip and fall as they ascend or descend the hill of life! And how serious, sometimes, are these falls! Character, reputation, joy, the light of other hearts, the happiness of the home,—all gone through the one false step! We have urgent need of some security. In what shall this be found? Not in hedgings and fencings which will take away every possible danger, but in the wisdom of the wise, which will teach us where to go and how to tread the path of life, in the "wisdom which is from above."

V. IT GUARANTEES THE GUARDIANSHIP OF GOD, AND THUS ENSURES CONFIDENCE AND PEACE. (Vers. 24—26.) There are those whose life is full of slavish fear; by day they dread the evils which assail the wicked, by night the perils of the darkness. But he who keeps God's Word enjoys the guardianship of his Almighty arm. "The Lord is his confidence;" his days are spent in quietness and calmness, and "his sleep is sweet" (Ps. cxii. 7).

VI. IT IS THE PERENNIAL SPRING OF PEACE AND JOY. (Vers. 17, 18.) Other sources of gratification are to be found, but some of them do not carry the sanction of conscience, some of them are out of the reach of the lowly, others are only open to the learned or the favoured; most, if not all of them, are short-lived, and become of less worth as they are more frequently employed. The wisdom which comes from God and which leads to him, which makes the human spirit the friend and follower of the Son of God, brings a "peace which passes all understanding," the "peace of God," and "joys which through all time abide."

VII. IT IS THE REALIZATION OF HUMAN LIFE. Wisdom is a "tree of life" (ver. 18); wisdom and discretion "shall be life unto our soul" (ver. 22). Any existence which is not illumined, ennobled, sanctified, beautified (ver. 22, "grace to thy neck"), by these, is *something less than life* in the sight of God. Only with these and by these do we attain to a state of being which the Wise One who sees things as they are recognizes as the life of man.

Wherefore: 1. Count it worth while to secure this heavenly wisdom at all costs whatsoever (vers. 14, 15). Its value cannot be estimated in gold; the price of wisdom is above rubies (Job xxviii. 18). *Nothing* is to be compared with it. Part, if necessary, with the largest fortune to obtain it (Mark x. 21; ch. xxiii. 23). 2. Take care to cherish and retain it (ver. 24). Let the most precious pearl fall, but hold this with a hand that will not unclasp.—C.

Vers. 27—32.—*Four valuable virtues.* There are some graces which, though not of the first importance, are yet far from being unimportant. Many men so fashion their lives that while, upon the whole, they are rightly reckoned among the wise and good, they are much less happy, less honoured, and less useful than they might become if they heeded a few small things. If we had regard to some of the minor moralities which we are apt to neglect, there would be less friction and more beauty in our lives than is now seen of God and felt of man.

I. PUNCTUALITY IN THE PAYMENT OF THAT WHICH IS DUE. (Vers. 27, 28.) These dues may be (1) the wages of the workman; (2) the debt contracted with the trades-man; (3) the sum promised to the relative or friend. This may be denied, even when it could be easily rendered, through an "avaricious reluctance" to part with money or a culpable disregard of other men's necessities and claims. Such default is not worthy of a godly, a Christian man.

II. CONSCIENTIOUSNESS TOWARDS OUR FRIENDS. (Ver. 29.) Too many men are inclined to abuse the confidence their kindred or friends put in them, or the generosity they are prepared to show them. Such men draw unscrupulously on the trust or the bounty of others. It is a serious departure from perfect rectitude, and should be disallowed to themselves by all who fear God and would follow Christ. Those who "dwell securely by us," who have confided in us, are those whom every principle of honest self-respect demands that we should treat with scrupulous integrity.

III. PEACEABLENESS OF SPIRIT. (Ver. 30.) The lives of many are embittered by the quarrelsomeness of their neighbours. Offence, never intended, is taken, bitter words are spoken, a hostile attitude is assumed, all friendly relations are broken off, malicious insinuations are thrown out; in fact, "there is war between the house" of this man and that man, when there is positively nothing on which to found a complaint. A very small allowance of charity would cure this evil spirit, if only taken in time. Charity would hide a multitude of sins in the sense of *preventing them altogether*, if men would but attribute kind motives to their neighbours, or inquire sufficiently before they condemn, or even wait a while before they strike, to see if there is no other and better way of arranging a dispute. If it be possible—and it very often *is* possible, when men imagine it is not—we should "live peaceably with all men" (Rom. xii. 18).

IV. FREEDOM FROM FRETTING ENVY. Many good men are, upon the whole, what God would have them to be, and they have from him all that they can reasonably ask at his hand; their well-being is such as to constitute the condition of thankfulness and joy. Yet the cup of their life is made bitter and unpalatable because they are envious of the successful oppressor (ver. 31); they "fret themselves because of evil-doers," and are envious against the workers of iniquity (Ps. xxxvii. 1, 8; lxxiii. 3). They think, perhaps, that if bad men are as prosperous as they seem to be, they (the good) ought to be far more successful than they find themselves to be. Surely this is both sinful and foolish. 1. It is discontentment with God's arrangement, and a querulous chal-lenging of his administration of human affairs. 2. It is forgetfulness of the fact that God's severest anger rests on the oppressor, and that he is therefore the last man to be envied; he is "abomination to the Lord" (ver. 32). Would we change places with *him?* 3. It overlooks the fact that the righteous man is enjoying the friendship of God—surely an advantage that immeasurably outweighs the wealth or honour which the oppressor has stolen. "The secret of the Lord" is with him. He is God's trusted servant, Christ's intimate friend (see Ps. xxv. 14; John xv. 14, 15; xiv. 23).—C.

Vers. 33—35.—*The height of well-being and the depth of ill-being.* The issues of righteousness and unrighteousness are here very broadly stated. These verses indicate to us the long and large results of wisdom on the one hand and of folly on the other.

I. THOSE WHOM GOD FAVOURS AND THAT WHICH HE APPORTIONS THEM. There are three epithets by which they are here characterized; they are called "the just," "the lowly," and "the wise." In those whom God loves and means to bless there are found (1) the spirit of humility,—they are conscious of their own demerit and unworthiness; (2) the spirit of wisdom,—they are in the attitude of inquiry towards God, desirous of knowing his truth and doing his will; and (3) the spirit of conscientiousness,—they are the "just," wishful to do that which is right toward their fellows, to act honestly, fairly, considerately, in the various relations they sustain. These God loves, and on them he will bestow his Divine benediction. 1. He will give them "grace"—his own royal favour and that which draws down upon them the genial and gracious regard of men. 2. He will bless them in their home life. He "blesseth the habitation of the just." He will give them purity, love, honour, affection, peace, joy in their most intimate relations; so that their homes shall be blessed. He will be known as the "God of the families of Israel." 3. And He will give them exaltation in the end. "The wise shall inherit glory." "Unto the upright there will arise light in the darkness." Present gloom shall give place to glory, either now on this side the grave, or hereafter in " that world of light."

II. THOSE WITH WHOM GOD IS DISPLEASED AND HIS AWFUL MALEDICTIONS ON THEM. These are also thrice characterized here; they are " the wicked," " the scorners," " fools." These are they who (1) in their folly reject the counsel of God; who (2) in their guilt yield themselves up to sin in its various forms; who (3) in their arrogance scoff at all sacred things—the " scorners;" this is the last and worst development of sin, the treatment of things holy and Divine with flippant irreverence. These God regards with Divine disapproval; them he strongly condemns and visits with fearful penalty. 1. His wrath is on themselves. He " scorneth the scorners." " He that sitteth in the heavens laughs " at them, he " has them in derision " (Ps. ii. 4). His feeling toward them and his power over them are such that they have reason to apprehend overthrow and ruin at any hour (see Ps. lxxiii. 19, 20). 2. His curse is on their house (ver. 33). They may expect that in their domestic relations they will have, as in fact they do have, saddest occasions of sorrow and remorse. 3. His hand is against their hope. They may be anticipating great things for themselves in the future, their castles are high and strong in the air, their hope is great; but " lo! sudden destruction," the wind of heaven blows, and all is brought into desolation. God touches their fine structure with his finger, and it is in ruins. " Shame is the promotion of fools."—C.

EXPOSITION.

CHAPTER IV.

Vers. 1—27. — 7. *Seventh admonitory discourse.* We here enter upon the second group of admonitory discourses, as is indicated by the opening address, " my children," and which occurs again in ch. v. 7 and vii. 24. This group extends to the end of ch. vii. Its prevailing tone is that of warning rather than of positive exhortations, which have been the rule hitherto. The general aim of the discourse before us, as of those preceding, is to exalt Wisdom, to exhibit her as a subject worthy of all earnest endeavour and sacrifice, but it is noticeable that the teacher introduces a fresh feature into his teaching or mode of instruction, in order to procure attention to, and acceptance of, his precepts on the part of his hearers. He has already spoken in his own name and with his own authority; he has brought forward Wisdom personified as making her appeal; he now adduces the authority of his own father's advice to himself. But as the mode of emphasizing his admonitions varies, so Wisdom is many-sided, and the aspect under which she is now presented seems to be especially that of discipline and obedience. The key-note of the discourse seems to be struck in the word "instruction," *i.e.* discipline, in the original, *musar*, thus recalling the admonition in ch. i. 8, " My son, hear the instruction of thy father."

Bohlius, in his ' Ethica Sacra,' disp. vi. p. 65, *sqq.*, assigns " discipline" (*musar*) to this chapter; and Melancthon describes the admonitions of the chapter before us as " adhortationes ad studium obedientiæ." Discipline rising into obedience seems to be the predominant thought to which all others are made subordinate. The discourse is an enlargement or amplification of this aspect of Wisdom. In structure the discourse consists mainly of the father's advice (vers. 4—19), preceded and followed by the teacher's own admonitions in vers. 1—3 and 20—27. The chief topics touched upon are (1) the supreme importance of Wisdom as being " the principal thing " to be obtained before everything else (vers. 7—9); (2) the two ways that lie open to the choice of youth, distinguished respectively as the way of light and the way of darkness (vers. 14—19); and (3) the guarding of the heart with all diligence, as being the seat of conscience and the fountain of life in its moral sense (vers. 23—27). The first part of the discourse is characterized by exhortations accompanied by promises; the latter part takes the form of warning, and warning of an alarming nature. The harmony which exists between the allusions in the discourse and the facts recorded in the historical books of Samuel and Chronicles serves to indicate that we have before us, in substance at least, the advice which David gave to

Solomon, and that the discourse is Solomonic. Compare especially ver. 3 with 1 Chron. xxviii. 5 and xxii. 9, and ver. 18 with the last words of David in 2 Sam. xxiii. 4.

Ver. 1.—**Hear, ye children, the instruction of a father.** This exhortation is identical with that in ch. i. 8, except that the address, "ye children," indicating a new departure, is now used instead of "my son," which has been hitherto employed (see ch. i. 8; ii. 1; iii. 1, 21), and "of thy father" is altered to "of a father." The verb is the same, occurring here, of course, in the plural number. The appeal is evidently intended to rouse attention. Attention is especially necessary to secure a knowledge of Divine truth. *Ye children* (*bhânim*). This address occurs again twice in the second group of admonitory discourses—in ch. v. 7 and vii. 24, and also in the appeal of Wisdom personified in ch. viii. 32, and, with these exceptions, nowhere else in the Proverbs. It is used by David, and it is possible that when the teacher penned these words he had in mind Ps. xxxiv. 11, "Come, ye children, hearken unto me; I will teach you the fear of the Lord." The similarity in the address serves to connect the teacher of wisdom with David, and thus to identify him with Solomon, while it also leads to the conclusion that the advice which follows in vers. 4—19 is in substance that which David had given his son. On "instruction," see ch. i. 8. *Of a father* (*âv*). It is difficult, owing to the want of the pronominal suffix, to determine accurately whether the teacher is referring to himself or to his own father in the expression. The following verse (2) would indicate that he is speaking of *himself* in his capacity as a teacher or instructor of youth. But it is quite possible that he may be referring to *his own father*, whose advice he had received, and which he is now about to lay before others in vers. 4—19. Though attention to paternal advice in general, *i.e.* instruction given by any father to his children, is not intended here, still the passage may be regarded as embodying the principle that attention to parental advice is incumbent on children, and a disregard of it is the mark of ingratitude and depravity. Rabbi Levi understands the phrase as referring to our heavenly Father. **Attend** (*hakshivu*, hiph. imperative of *kâshâv*). On the force of this verb as signifying "earnest, absorbed attention," see ch. i. 24. **To know understanding** (*lâdâ᷄ath binâ*); *i.e.* in order that you may know or gain understanding. The infinitive marks the design or object of the attention (cf. the Vulgate, *ut sciatis*). The expression corresponds with *lâdâ᷄ath khokmah* in ch. i. 2, and just as this signifies "to appropriate

to yourself wisdom," so the one before us has the same force, and signifies the gaining or appropriation of understanding, *i.e.* the faculty of discernment or discrimination. Hitzig renders, "to know with the understanding;" *i.e.* to know intelligently, but this does not seem to be the meaning of the phrase.

Ver. 2.—**For I give you good doctrine.** This, while stating the reason for the exhortation in the previous verse, signifies that what the teacher has given and is giving, he has received from his father. *I give; nâthâti,* literally, "I gave," is the kal perfect of *nâthân,* "to give," but the perfect is here used for the present, as denoting not only a past action, but one that is still continuing (Gesenius, 'Heb. Gram.,' § 126. 3). *Good doctrine* (*lĕkākh tôv*). The doctrine or instruction is "good," not only intrinsically, but as to the source from which it was derived, and in its effects. *Lĕkākh* is, according to its root *lâkākh,* "something which is received or taken." From the standpoint of the teacher it is that instruction which he had received of his father. With respect to his hearers it is the instruction which is communicated to them, and which they receive (see on ch. i. 5). The LXX. renders, δῶρον ἀγαθὸν; similarly the Vulgate, *donum bonum,* "a good gift." **Forsake ye not**; *āl-tāăzôvû,* from *âzâv,* "to leave, forsake" (compare the corresponding phrase, *āl-tiltôsh,* from *nâtâsh,* "to leave, forsake," in ch. i. 8). **Law** (*tôrāh*); as in ch. i. 8.

Ver. 3.—**For I was my father's son.** This is more than the mere statement of a physical fact. It indicates that the teacher was in the highest degree an object of endearment to his father, just as he states in the second hemistich that he held a unique position in the affection of his mother. The statement agrees with the historical record. Solomon would be more than ordinarily dear to his father, as being a child of promise, as "the beloved of the Lord," and as the son whom the Divine will had pointed as the successor to his throne, and the one on whom was to devolve the building of the temple (see 2 Sam. vii. 12, 13; xii. 24; 1 Chron. xxii. 9). Bertheau explains, "I also once stood in the relation to my (actual) father in which you stand to me your paternal instructor," thus giving prominence rather to the consecution of the passage, and preparing the way for the reception of the father's advice which is to follow. But this rather loses sight of what appears an important element in the instruction, that not only was it "good," but that it was dictated by affection. The writer is fortifying and strengthening his instruction by the authority of his father, showing that what he was laying before others he had had placed before him; and as *his* father's advice was the outcome of affection, so he addresses his hearers in the same spirit. Dathe and others connect "tender" (*rāk*) with "son" (*bên*), and render, "I was a son dear to my father." So the LXX., which, however, understands "tender" in the sense of "tractable," "obedient:" "For I was an obedient son to my father"—a meaning which the word *rāk* can only bear as indicating the susceptibility of the young to receive impressions. In general, *rāk* means "tender," "soft," and has reference to the weakness and helplessness of the young; comp. Gen. xxxiii. 13, "My lord knoweth that the children are tender (*rakkîm*)." Combined with *yâkhîd*, which follows, it signifies, in the passage before us, that the teacher was an object of tender care or love. The Vulgate *tenellus*, the diminutive of *tener*, as signifying "somewhat tender or delicate," reproduces the idea of the Hebrew *rāk*. In the word the teacher recalls his early life and the instruction in wisdom which he received in it. **Only** beloved; literally, *only* (*yâkhîd*), as "beloved" does not occur in the original. The Vulgate renders, *unigenitus;* Aquila, Symmachus, and Theodotion, μονογενής, *i.e.* "only begotten;" but this was not literally the fact, as Bathsheba, the mother of Solomon, had other sons (2 Sam. v. 14; 1 Chron. iii. 5). Both the Hebrew *yâkhîd*, "only," and the Vulgate *unigenitus*, "only begotten," consequently signify what is expressed by the LXX. ἀγαπώμενος, *i.e.* "beloved." Solomon was so beloved of his mother as if he were an only child. So *yâkhîd* is used of Isaac in Gen. xxii. 2, 12 in the same way, since at the time that Isaac was so designated, Ishmael, the other son of Abraham, was still living. The word *yâkhîd* occurs in Ps. xxii. 20, where it is rendered "darling," and may possibly refer to Solomon. Jennings, in Ps. xxii. 20, understands it, however, of the life besides which the psalmist has no other—*unicam meam*, as the Vulgate, *i.e.* "his only life" (cf. Ps. xxxv. 17; and for the word *yâkhîd*, see Jer. v. 26; Amos viii. 10; Zech. xii. 10). **In the sight of my mother** (*liph'ne immi*); literally, *ad facies matris meæ*, or, *before my mother;* Vulgate, *coram matre meâ*, i.e. in her estimation (cf. Gen. xvii. 18). The mention of the mother is probably introduced here for the sake of poetic parallelism; cf. ch. i. 8 (Zöckler).

Ver. 4.—From this verse to ver. 19 inclusive, the teacher quotes the instruction which he had received of his father. His object in doing so is to show that his own teaching was in harmony with it, and therefore worthy of attention. His precepts, admonitions, and warnings are not his only, but those of his father. Other examples of David's instructions to Solomon are found in 1 Kings ii. 2; 1 Chron. xxii. 12, 13; xxviii. 9. **And he taught;** *i.e.* his father, for *vâyyorêni* is masculine. The LXX. renders, "They said and taught me (οἳ ἔλεγον καὶ ἐδίδασκόν με)," as if the precepts which follow were the combined teaching of David and Bathsheba. This variation is due to the mention of both parents in the preceding verse. **Retain;** *yith'môk*, kal future, used imperatively, of *thâmāk*, "to take hold of," and metaphorically, as here, "to hold fast" (see ch. iii. 18). The LXX. renders ἐρειδέτω, imperative of ἐρείδω, "to fix firm." Symmachus has κατεχέτω, "give heed to." **And live;** *i.e.* and thou shalt live, as the kal imperative, *kh'yêh*, from *khâyâh*, "to live," has here the force of the future (cf. Vulgate, *et vives*). The meaning is, "And thou shalt enjoy a long and happy life." Temporal life alone seems to be indicated, as in ver. 10 (cf. ch. iii. 2). The Syriac addition, "And my law as the apple of thine eye," is probably borrowed from ch. vii. 2, where we meet with the same admonition.

Ver. 5.—After the general exhortation given above, the father's instruction becomes more specific, and deals with the acquirement of wisdom. This subject seems to be continued in ver. 13, where the second and concluding branch of the instruction begins, which consists mainly of warning, as the first part does with exhortation. We are thus furnished with an example how to teach. In our teaching it is not sufficient simply to point out what is to be done, but we must show what is to be avoided. **Get wisdom, get understanding.** The father urges the acquirement of wisdom in the same way and with the same importunity as the trader or merchant presses his goods upon buyers. Wisdom and understanding are put forward as objects of merchandise; for the verb *kânâh*, from which the imperative *k'nêh*, signifies not only "to acquire for one's self," or "to possess," but especially " to buy." The verb occurs again in the same sense in ver. 7, "Get [*k'nêh*, i.e. buy] wisdom;" and in ch. xxiii. 23, "Buy (*k'nêh*) the truth, and sell it not; also wisdom, and instruction, and understanding" (cf. also ch. xv. 22; xvi. 16; xix. 9, where we also meet with the same verb). The reiteration of the word "get," as Umbreit remarks, is "an imitation of the exclamation of a merchant who is offering his wares." The importunity of the father measures the value he sets upon wisdom as an inestimable treasure, a pearl of great price (see ch. iii. 14). **Forget it not,** etc.; rather, *forget not, neither turn from the words of my mouth,*—so Zöckler, Delitzsch, Hodg., and others; Vulgate, *ne obliviscaris, neque declines à verbis oris mei.* There is no need to supply "it" after the verb *al-tish'-kakh*, "forget not," as Holden states, and as appears in the Authorized Version, since *shâkākh* is found with *min* (מן), "of" or "from," in Ps. xii. 4 (5), "I forgot to eat (*shâkākh'ti mêâkol*)," and the same construction may obtain here. The two verbs, "forget" and "decline from," are not so very wide in meaning, since the former, *shâkākh*, is to "leave" something from forgetfulness, and the latter, *nâtâh*, rendered here "decline from," is "to turn away" from something. The words of my mouth represent as it were the means by which wisdom may be purchased.

Ver. 7.—Wisdom is the principal thing; therefore get wisdom. The older versions, such as the Alexandrian LXX. (the verse is omitted by the Vatican LXX.), Targum, and Syriac, agree in rendering this verse, "The beginning of wisdom is get wisdom," which is equivalent to saying that the beginning of wisdom consists in the acquisition of wisdom, or, as Umbreit explains, "in the resolution to get wisdom." That this rendering, which is adopted by Luther, Delitzsch, and Umbreit, may be correct appears from ch. i. 7 and ix. 10, where we have the same construction, only in inverted order. Seneca's aphorism is conceived in much the same spirit: "Magna pars boni est velle fieri bonum"—"A large part of good is the wish to become good;" *i.e.* that the beginning of being good depends to a large extent upon the wish to become so. The objections to this rendering are: (1) That it is difficult to see how the beginning of wisdom can be the acquisition of it. (2) That elsewhere, as in ch. i. 7 and ix. 10, the beginning of wisdom is represented as the fear of the Lord. (3) That it does not fall in well with the context or with the aim of the father's teaching, which is to hold up wisdom as pre-eminently a blessing, as the most excellent and highest thing attainable. On the other hand, Hitzig, De Dieu, Doderlein, Zöckler, render as in the Authorized Version, "Wisdom is the principal thing, therefore get wisdom;" *i.e.* wisdom is the highest good, and therefore ought to be obtained. The word *reshith* is found with this signification in ch. xxiv. 20; 1 Sam. ii. 29; Job xl. 19; Jer. xlix. 35; Amos vi. 1—6. And with all thy getting get understanding. This does not mean, as the Authorized Version seems to imply, that while you are acquiring other things, you are to acquire wisdom, but that wisdom is to be purchased with all you have acquired or gotten. "Getting" (*kin'yon*) is the purchase money. No price is too high to be paid for her, no sacrifice too great; cf. the parables of the hidden treasure and goodly pearl (Matt. xiii. 44; Luke x. 42), in both of which the man sold "all that he had" to obtain the

prize. There is a play upon the words in the original (*kin'yân'ki k'nêh*), which is preserved in our translation.

Ver. 8.—Exalt her, and she shall promote thee. The father here proceeds to point out some of the benefits which follow from the pursuit of Wisdom. Exalt her (*sāl's'lĕâh*); Vulgate, *arripe illam*; LXX., περιχαράκωσον αὐτήν; Targum, *dilige eam*; Syriac, *blandire illi*; Arabic, *circumsepi eam*. The Hebrew, *sāl's'lĕâh*, is the pilpel imperative of *sâlāl*, "to lift up, exalt." It is equivalent to the kal form. The pilpel form only occurs here, but the kal participle is met with in ch. xv. 19, where it has the meaning of "to raise up as a causeway" (see marginal reading *in loc.*). Gesenius renders, "exalt her," *sc.* with praises. The meaning of the verb, as Delitzsch says, is to be determined by the corresponding "she shall promote thee" (*th'rôm'mēk*), and this verb *romêm* is (1) to raise or make high; (2) to exalt by bestowing honours upon one of low estate, *i.e.* raising them in general estimation; it is so used in 1 Sam. ii. 7 by Hannah, in her song of thankfulness, "He (Jehovah) bringeth low and lifteth up (*m'rômêm*);" (3) to extol by praises, as in Ps. xxx. 2. The ra lical meaning of *sâlal* seems to be "to heap up," as a road is prepared by embankments, and by the filling up of inequalities (cf. Isa. lxii. 10). In this sense the passage before us is explained by Levi ben Gersom, "Prepare the way of Wisdom, and walk assiduously in it." But the context, wherein the idea of buying is evidently used, favours Böttcher's interpretation, "Hold it or her high in price, bid high for her as a purchaser who makes offer upon offer, to secure what he wants." So Pi, *in pretio habe*. The LXX. rendering, "Circumvallate her, enclose her with a wall or hedge," which is reproduced in the Arabic, *circumsepi eam*, "hedge her around," seems out of place with the context. The Talmudists understand the verb as signifying "to examine closely," "to scrutinize, meditate, or reflect" upon Wisdom constantly, just as the Roman poet says, "Nocturna versate manu, versate diurna"— "We exalt Wisdom when we follow her precepts," *i.e.* when we esteem her—the idea which is presented to us in the Targum and Syriac cited above. The sentiment of the verse agrees with what Jehovah says in the message of the man of God to Eli, in 1 Sam. ii. 30, "Them that honour me I will honour." She shall bring thee to honour, when thou dost embrace her. The LXX. reverses the order of ideas, "Honour her in order that she may embrace thee." Embrace her; i.e. in a loving and affectionate manner, as a husband does his wife, or a son his mother. (For the verb *khâvak*, see ch. v. 20; Cant. ii. 6; viii. 3.) There are only three other instances where this verb occurs in the pilel form, *khibbêk*. Esteem and honour, the confidence of others, elevation to offices of trust and consequence, are some of the rewards with which Wisdom repays those who esteem and love her. Others follow in the next verse.

Ver. 9.—**An ornament of grace** (*liv'yath khên*). (On this, see ch. i. 9.) **A crown of glory shall she deliver to thee**; or, as margin, *she shall compass thee with a crown of glory. Deliver.* The verb *miggên*, piel, since the kal, *mâgan*, is not used. is, however, properly, "to give, or deliver," as in Gen. xiv. 20; Hos. xi. 8. That this is the meaning is clear from the corresponding "she shall give" (*tittên*, but cf. *nâthan*, "to give"). It is commonly found with an accusative and dative, but here takes two accusatives. Both the LXX. and the Vulgate render, "With a crown of glory or delights shall she protect (*ὑπερασπίσῃ, protegat*) thee; " as if it were connected with *mâgên*, "a shield," but a crown is not usually associated with protection or defence. "A crown of glory," in the New Testament, is always associated with the everlasting honours of heaven, as in Heb. ii. 9; 2 Tim. iv. 8; 1 Pet. iv. 4; Rev. ii. 20. The meaning is here, "Wisdom shall confer on thee true dignity."

Ver. 10.—Many commentators, *e.g.* Jerome, Bede, Ewald, Bertheau, and Hitzig, suppose that the father's instruction closes in the preceding verse, but it seems more appropriate to consider the father as here passing to another branch of his instruction, which is to point out the way of wisdom, and so to prepare for his warnings which follow from ver. 14 to ver. 19. **Receive**; *kakh*, from *lâkah*, "to receive" (on the force of this verb, see ch. i. 3). He who shows a delight or willingness in admitting the words of Wisdom—for such a character the father claims for his teaching, as we see from the next verse—shall receive a blessing. It is a sign of grace when any even show themselves open to listen to instruction; but it is a greater sign when this instruction is received with readiness and pleasure (Muffet). **The years of thy life** (*sh'nôth khâyyîm*); literally, *years of thy lives.* The plural "lives" expresses the idea of life in the abstract. There is no absolute statement of a *future* life here, though by the Christian this idea may be indulged in on the ground of a fuller revelation. The promise is one that not only implies the prolongation of life, but also a life of prosperity and enjoyment. **Shall be many;** literally, *shall be multiplied.*

Ver. 11.—The perfects, **I have taught** and **I have led**, in the original seem to have here the absolute signification of the past. The father recalls the instruction which he

has given in times past. So Delitzsch. But Gejerus gives them the combined force of the past and future, "I have taught and I will more fully teach," and so with the other verb. The Vulgate renders, *monstrabo*, "I will show," and *ducam*, "I will lead." In the **way of wisdom** (*b'dĕrĕk khŏk'mâh*) may mean "in the way that leads *to*, or by which you come to Wisdom; I have taught you the manner in which Wisdom may be attained;" or "the way in which Wisdom walks" (Zöckler). The ways of Wisdom are described in ch. iii. 17 as "ways of pleasantness." The next clause seems to indicate that the latter explanation is to be preferred. The ב (*b'*) indicates the subject in which instruction has been given. In **right paths** (*b'mâ'g'lê yóshĕr*); literally, *in the paths of rectitude*; i.e. of straightness, paths of which the characteristic is uprightness. (On "paths," as signifying a carriage-way, see ch. ii. 9.) *Instruction* and *direction* have formed the two elements in the father's teaching. These present us with a model of education. "To teach *duty* without *truth* is to teach *practice* without *motive*; to teach *truth* without *duty* is to teach motive without the practice to which it should lead" (Wardlaw).

Ver. 12.—In this verse the father depicts the benefits and advantages which shall follow from "receiving his words" (ver. 10), *i.e.* from attending to his counsels and imbibing the principles of wisdom. The whole course of life shall be freed from obstacles or impediments, from anxiety, perplexity, or difficulty, or from vacillation. **When thou goest** may refer to the daily walk, to the common and ordinary events or circumstances incidental to life, just as the corresponding **when thou runnest** may refer to cases of emergency when promptness and decisive action are called for. In both cases Wisdom, by inspiring unity of principle, gives freedom of movement; in ordinary cases it removes embarrassment and perplexity arising from conflicting interests drawing now in one direction, now in another, and in extraordinary cases it supplies a rule of conduct which prevents our falling into mistakes and errors. Or the verse may refer to the prosperity which shall attend all the undertakings of those who are in Wisdom's ways, whether they advance slowly or rush forward with the impetuosity of youth, whether they act with deliberation or with haste. **Shall not be straitened** (*lô-yêtsar*); i.e. shall not be narrowed or confined; Vulgate, *non arctabuntur;* LXX., οὐ συγκλεισθήσεται. The future *yêtsar* only occurs four times in the Scriptures—here, and Job xviii. 7; xx. 22; Isa. xlix. 19. It is usually derived from the root *yâtsâr*, which, however, is not found, cognate with *tsûr*, "to straiten," "to be narrow." *Yêtsâr*, however, always occurs in the passive sense. though an active signification is given it by the Rabbi Nathan ben Jechiel, quoted by Delitzsch, *in loc.*, who renders, " Thou shalt not need to bind together, or hedge up thy way." The roots *yâtsâr* and *tsûr* partake more or less of the idea of binding up, oppressing, putting into narrow and confined circumstances and limits. By the expression that "the steps are straitened" we may understand, therefore, that there is a want of freedom for their movements, and consequently that they are impeded or cramped. The Arabic expression, " to contract the feet," signifies the diminishing of good fortune. Compare the similar expression in Job xviii. 7, "The steps of his strength shall be straitened." The psalmist presents the idea of the verse under a different form, " Thou hast *enlarged* my steps under me, so that my feet did not slip" (Ps. xvii. 36). **Thou shalt not stumble;** *lô-thĭkkâshêl*, hiph. future. The niph. *nĭkshâl*, equivalent to the kal *kâshal*, signifies properly " to totter," " to sink down," used of one about to fall. The primary idea, however, usually disregarded, of *kâshâl*, is " to totter in the ankles," equivalent to the Latin *talipedare*. It occurs again in ch. iv. 16, and is a different verb from " stumble " in ch. iii. 23 (which see).

Ver. 13.—The short but urgent admonitions in this verse may be explained by the knowledge which the father has of the temptations to which youth is exposed and the liability of youth to fall into them, as well as by the fact that Instruction, or Wisdom, is the bestower of life. This latter conviction is the reason why he urges " taking fast hold " of Wisdom. The tenacious grasp with which the shipwrecked sinking sailor lays hold on any spar or plank floating near will illustrate the kind of grasp with which Wisdom is to be held. It is no less a virtue to keep and hold fast a good thing than to get it at the first beginning (Muffet). **Instruction** (*musar*), usually of a disciplinary nature (see ch. i. 3), here more particularly the instruction of the father, but in a wider sense wisdom generally, with which it is synonymous, as appears from the feminine, " let *her* not go, keep *her*," *musar* being masculine ; or the feminines may refer back to " Wisdom " in ver. 11. So Mercerus and Buxtorf. **For she is thy life** (*kî hî khăyyĕkâ*) ; i.e. she brings life to thee. Wisdom is represented as the bestower of long life, in ch. iii. 2, 16, 18. Just in proportion as Wisdom is retained and guarded, so is life secured, and so far as the hold upon her is lost, so are the hopes of life diminished. Life depends upon the observance of her precepts.

Ver. 14.—From admonition the father passes to warning. The connection with the preceding section is obvious. There are two ways diametrically opposite—the way of wisdom and the way of evil ; the one the way of life, the other fraught with death, because a way of darkness and violence. As the father has dealt with the former, so now he deals with the latter. With these warnings we may also comp. ch. i. 10—15 and ii. 10—15, where much the same warning is given, and the way of the wicked is described in almost the same terms. The warning of the father takes a threefold form : (1) enter not ; (2) go not ; (3) avoid. In effect he says this is the only course to be adopted in order to keep a firm hold of Wisdom which he has counselled in the preceding verse (13). **Enter not ;** *ăl-tâvô*, from *bô*, " to come in," " to enter," *i.e.* do not even enter. The Vulgate renders, " Delight not in," evidently from reading *tôvê*, which occurs in ch. i. 10. But our reading is to be preferred, as *ăvâh*, " to acquiesce in," from which *tôv'ê*, is not used with ־, here denoting place, but with ל. **Go not** (*ăl-t'ăshshêr*) ; *i.e.* do not walk in. The two verbs " to enter " (*bô*) and " to go " (*ĭshshêr*) stand in the relation of *entering* and *going on—ingressus* and *progressus*. So Gejerus and Delitzsch. The piel *ĭshshêr*, here used, is properly " to go straight on," like the kal *âshâr*, of which it is an intensive (cf. ch. ix. 6). It is the bold, presumptuous walk, the stepping straight out of the evil, which is here indicated, and against this the father warns his son. The sense is, " If you have entered the way of the wicked, do not continue or persevere in it." The other meanings of the verb *âshâr*, viz. " to guide straight " (ch. xxiii. 19), " to esteem happy and prosperous " (ch. xxxi. 28), are not in place here, as they destroy the parallelism of thought, and on the same ground the LXX. and Syriac renderings, " envy not " and μηδὲ ζηλώσῃς, are to be rejected. **The wicked** (*ishaim*), *i.e.* the godless (cf. Ps. i. 1), is parallel with " evil men " (*râim*), *i.e.* the habitually wicked.

Ver. 15.—**Avoid it ;** *p'râĕhu*, the kal imperative of *pârâ*, properly, " to let go," hence " to reject, or abhor." (On the verb, see ch. i. 25, where it is rendered, " set at naught.") The same verb also occurs in ch. viii. 33 ; xiii. 18 ; xv. 32. *It* ; i.e. the way. The suffix of the verb is in the original is feminine, " avoid *her* ;" *dĕrĕk*, " the way," being common. **Turn from it** (*s'tĕh mĕâlâyv*). The original is a pregnant expression equivalent to " turn aside from it, so that you do not come to stand upon it." The word *mĕâlâyv*, equivalent to the Latin *desuper ea*, has much the same force as the French *de dessus* and the Italian *di sopra* (Delitzsch). The verb *sâtâh* is, as in the Authorized Version, " to turn, or go aside." **Pass away ;** *ăvôr*, kal imperative of *âvar*, " to pass over," equivalent to Latin *transire*, here means " to pass on, or along," " to go beyond," like the German *Ger weiter gehn.* The counsel of the father is not only " turn aside from," but " put the greatest possible distance between you and it." The injunction, so absolutely stated, to have nothing to do with sin, is required, if not indeed prompted, by the knowledge of the fact that youth, confident in its own power of resistance, frequently indulges in the fatal mistake of imagining that it can dally with sin with impunity. The only course compatible with safety is to entirely avoid it.

Ver. 16.—This verse exhibits the extreme depravity and debasement into which " the wicked" (*r'shaim*) and " the evil " (*ráim*) of ver. 14 have fallen. Their sins are not sins of frailty, but arise from premeditation and from their insatiable desire to commit wickedness. Sin has become to them a kind of second nature, and, unless they indulge in it, sleep is banished from their eyes. **They sleep not;** *lo-yish'nu*, future of *yâshān*, " to fall asleep ; " the future here being used for the present, as is frequently the case in the Proverbs, and denoting a permanent condition or habit. **Unless they cause** some to fall ; *i.e.* " unless they have betrayed others into sin," taking the verb in an ethical sense (Zöckler), or, which is preferable, owing to ver. 16*a*, unless they have done them some injury (Mercerus) ; Vulgate, *nisi supplantaverint.* For the Khetib *yik'shûlû*, kal, which would mean " unless they have stumbled or fallen," the Keri substitutes the hiph. *yâk'shîhî*, " unless they have caused some to fall." The hiph. is found without any object, as here, in 2 Chron. xxv. 8). (On the verb *khâsal*, from which it is derived, see ch. iv. 12.) With the statement of the verse we may compare David's complaint of the persistent persecution of his enemies (Ps. lix. 15), " If they be not satisfied, then will they stay all night " (margin). A similar construction to the one before us occurs in Virgil : " Et si non aliqua nocuisses, mortuus esses "—" And had you not, by some means or other done him an injury, you would have died " (' Eclog.,' iii. 15) ; cf. also Juvenal : " Ergo non aliter poterit dormire; quibusdam somnum rixa facit "—" Therefore, not otherwise, would he have slept ; contention to some produces sleep." Hitzig rejects vers. 16 and 17 against all manuscript authority.

Ver. 17.—**For** (*ki*, equivalent to the Greek γὰρ) is here explanatory. It serves not so much to introduce another independent statement, as one which accounts for the statement made in the preceding verse, that the wicked sleep not unless they have done mischief, *i.e.* it states the reason why they

are so conditioned. There is no comparison expressed in the original, as the rendering adopted by Schultens and others implies, " For wickedness do they eat as bread, and violence do they drink as wine," which is evidently based on Job xv. 16, " Which drinketh up iniquity like water," and Job xxxiv. 7, " Who drinketh up scorning like water." The literal rendering is, *for they eat the bread of wickedness, and the wine of violence do they drink.* **The bread of wickedness** (*lĕkhĕm rĕshā*) is not bread which consists in wickedness, but bread which is obtained by wickedness. just as **the wine of violence** (*yiyin khâmāsim*) is not the wine which produces violence, but the wine that is procured by violent deeds. Their support, what they eat and drink, is obtained by wickedness and injustice. They live by wrong. For such expressions as " the bread of wickedness" and " the wine of violence," cf. Deut. xvi. 3, " the bread of affliction ; " Ps. cxxvii. 2, " the bread of sorrows ; " and Amos ii. 8, " the wine of the condemned." There is a change of tense in the verbs, the first being perfect, " they have eaten," and the second future, " they shall drink," which Delitzsch explains as representing the twofold act—first eating the bread, and then washing it down with wine.

Ver. 18.—A contrast is drawn in this and the following verse between the path of the just and the way of the wicked. The former is, by an extremely beautiful image, likened to the light at dawn, which goes on increasing in brightness and intensity as the day advances, until at length it reaches its meridian splendour and glory. An exactly similar figure is found in David's last words (2 Sam. xxiii. 4). **The path of the just ;** *i.e.* their moral course. **As the shining light** (*k'ôr nôgāh*) ; *i.e.* as the light of dawn. The word *nôgāh*, from *nâgāh*, " to shine," is a noun, and properly signifies " brightness," " shining," " splendour." It is used also to designate the dawn, the light of the sun when it first mounts the horizon, and sheds its beams over the landscape, as in Isa. lx. 3, " Kings (shall come) to the brightness (*nôgāh*) of thy rising;" and Isa. lxii. 1, " Until the righteousness thereof go forth as the brightness (*nôgāh*) " (cf. 2 Sam. xxiii. 4, where the same word also occurs). Michaelis and Schultens refer *nôgāh* to " the path," and render, " The path of the just is splendid as the light." So Dathe and others ; and in this sense it was understood by the LXX., " The path of the just shall shine as the light shines." The Vulgate renders, *quasi lux splendens.* **That shineth more and more** (*hôlêk vâôr*) ; literally, *going and shining*—a common Hebrew idiom denoting progression or increase. The construction of the participle *hôlêk*, from *hâlak*, " to go," with the participle of another verb, is found in 1 Sam. xvii. 41, "The Philistine came nearer and nearer (hôlêk v'kârêv);" 1 Sam. ii. 26, "The child Samuel grew on more and more (hôlêk v'hâdêl)" (cf. 2 Chron. xvii. 12; Jonah i. 11). Unto the perfect day (ăd-n'kôn hăyyôm); Vulgate, usque ad perfectam diem. The Hebrew, n'kôn hăyyôm, corresponds to the Greek, ἡ σταθερὰ μεσημβρία, equivalent to "the high noon," when the sun seems to stand still in the heavens. The figure, as Fleischer remarks, is probably derived from the balance, the tongue of the balance of day, which before or after is inclined either to the right or the left, being at midday perfectly upright, and as it were firm. So kûn, the unused kal, from which n'kôn, the niph. participle, is derived, is "to stand upright," and in hiph. "to be set," "to stand firm," "to be established," and hence the expression might be rendered, "until the steady, or established day," which, however, refers to the midday, or noon, and not to that point when day succeeds dawn, as Rosenmüller and Schultens on Hos. vi. 3 maintain. The comparison is not extended beyond the midday, because the wish of the father was to indicate the full knowledge which the just attain in God, and which can know of no decline. A similar figure of gradual development is found in our Lord's parable of the seed growing secretly (Mark iv. 28), and is visible in Ps. lxxxiv. 7, "They grow from strength to strength, every one of them in Zion appeareth before God." The verse illustrates the gradual growth and increase of the righteous in knowledge, holiness, and joy, all of which are inseparably connected in the career of such.

Ver. 19.—The way of the wicked is as darkness. In contrast with the path of the just is the way of the wicked, which is described as darkness itself; i.e. so deeply enveloped in gloom that the wicked are not able even to see the obstacles and impediments against which they stumble, and which are the cause of their ruin. It is a way dark throughout—a viâ tenebrosa (Vulgate)—terminating at length in "the blackness of darkness." As light is emblematical of knowledge, holiness, and joy, so darkness represents ignorance, unholiness, and misery (see Isa. viii. 22). Darkness (ăphêlâh); strictly, thick darkness, midnight gloom, the entire absence of light. It is the word used of the plague of "thick darkness" that settled over all the land of Egypt, even a darkness that "might be felt," when the Egyptians "saw not one another, nor any arose from his place for three days" (Exod. x. 21—23). It occurs again in ch. vii. 9, "in the black and dark night." In this darkness the wicked cannot help but stumble. Compare our Lord's

teaching, "But if a man walk in the night, he stumbleth, because there is no light in him" (John xi. 10; cf. xii. 36). The expression, they know not at what they stumble, carries with it the idea that they are so ignorant that they neither know wickedness as wickedness, nor do they apprehend the destruction which it involves. "Sins, however great and detestable they may be, are looked upon as trivial, or as not sins at all, when men get accustomed to them" (St. Augustine, 'Enchiridion,' cap. 80). On "stumble" (kâshal), see ver. 12; and on the destruction of the wicked implied in the stumbling, see ch. i. 27, seq., ii. 18—22; iii. 35.

Ver. 20.—The teacher here resumes his admonitions after thus citing the example of his father's teaching, and showing how it resembled the tenor of his own precepts, which, upon such a consideration, were most worthy of attention.

Ver. 21.—Let them not depart from thine eyes; i.e. keep them constantly in view as the guide of the whole conduct. These words are a repetition of ch. iii. 21, just as the latter part of the verse reproduces the thought of ch. ii. 1. Depart. The hiph. yăllîzû is here used instead of the kal yălûzû of ch. iii. 21, but has the same force. In the midst of thine heart; i.e. in its inmost recesses; there the words and sayings are to be guarded as a man guards a treasure stowed away in the inmost chambers of a house. The expression implies cherishing them with an internal affection. The terms of the verse may be illustrated by Deut. vi. 6, 8, "And these words, which I command thee this day, shall be in thine heart. . . . And thou shalt bind them for a sign upon thine hand, and they shall be as frontlets between thine eyes."

Ver. 22.—They are life; i.e. they bring life (khăyyîm; the plural, as usual). Unto those that find them; i.e. to those who by effort get possession of and procure them; the verb mâtsâ, "to find," embodying the idea of activity. Health; mâr'pê, derived from the root râphâ, "to heal" (like riph'ûth of ch. iii. 8, which see), and hence rather "the means of health" than "health," "healing," or, as margin, "medicine," "that which restores to health;" LXX., ἴασις; Vulgate, sanitas. The moral condition is regarded as enfeebled by sickness, from which it may be restored to health and soundness by the words of wisdom. The effect of these, however, is not only to restore to health, but to maintain in health. Their tendency is to promote "a sound mind in a sound body." To their flesh; literally, to his flesh; the singular, b'sârô, being used instead of the plural, which we should have expected, because what is said applies to each one of those who receive the precepts of wisdom. The *all* implies the completeness of the restoration ; it is not confined to one part, but pervades the whole body.

Ver. 23.—**Keep thy heart with all diligence** ; properly, *above all things that have to be guarded, keep or guard thy heart.* So Mercerus, Gesenius, Delitzsch, Zöckler. This seems to be the right meaning of the phrase, *mikkol-mish'mar*, rendered in the Authorized Version "with all diligence," *mish'mar*, from *shâmâr*, "to guard," being the object of guarding ; that which is to be guarded. It is as if the teacher said, "Guard riches, property, health, body, everything, in short, in which you have a legitimate interest, or which is advantageous ; but before and above everything else, keep a guard on your heart. The rabbins Jarchi, Ben Ezra, Rashi, however, give a different rendering, "From everything which is to be avoided (*ab omni re cavenda*) guard thy heart ; " but the objection to this is that it ignores the radical meaning of the verb *shâmâr*, from which *mish'mar* is derived, as stated above, which is not that of *avoiding*, but of *guarding*. A third rendering is, "Keep thy heart with all keeping ; " so the Vulgate, *omni custodia serva cor tuum ;* and the LXX., πάσῃ φυλακῇ τήρει σὴν καρδίαν ; on which the Authorized Version seems to be based. Another rendering, similar to the first, except that it gives *mish'mar* the active signification of guarding instead of the passive one of being kept or guarded, is, "Keep thy heart more than any other keeping (*præ omni custodia*)." Origen, 'Hex.;' Field. Again, Aquila and Theodotion render, "Keep thy heart by reason of every commandment (ἀπὸ παντὸς φυλάγματος)," thus bringing into prominence the occasion and the obligation of keeping the heart, which is that we are so commanded. *Heart* (*lev*) ; here the affections and the moral consciousness. **For out of it are the issues of life.** The conjunction "for" introduces the reason. The fact here stated is that the moral conduct of life, its actions and proceedings, are determined by the condition of the heart. If the heart is pure, the life will be pure ; if the heart is corrupt, the life will be corrupt. The heart is here compared with a fountain. The same idea which is affixed to it in its physical sense is also assigned to it in its ethical or moral sense. Physically, it is the central organ of the body ; morally, it is the seat of the affections and the centre of the moral consciousness. From this moral centre flow forth "the issues of life ; " *i.e.* the currents of the moral life take their rise in and flow forth from it, just as from the heart, physically considered, the blood is propelled and flows forth into the arterial system, by which it

is conveyed to the remotest extremities of the body. And as the bodily health depends on the healthy action of the heart, so the moral health depends on and is influenced by the state in which this spring of all action is preserved. *Issues ; tôts'âôth,* from *yâtsâr,* "to go forth," are the place from which anything goes forth, and hence a fountain. For "the issues of life," the LXX. reads, ἔξοδοι ζωῆς, the Vulgate, *exitus vitæ.* With this passage compare our Lord's teaching (Matt. xv. 19 ; Mark vii. 21—23 ; Luke vi. 43—45).

Ver. 24.—The following admonitions of this chapter bear reference to the outward conduct of life. They continue the subject of ver. 23 by showing how the guarding of the heart is to be done. There is the most intimate connection between the heart as the fountain of the moral life and of the conduct of life, which, though determined by the condition of the heart, in its turn reacts upon the heart as the moral centre, and keeps it pure. Thus the subject is treated from its two sides. On vers. 24 and 25 Hitzig remarks that they "warn against an arbitrary perverting of the moral judgment into which evil passions so easily betray, and admonish not to give misdirection to thought within the department of morality." **A froward mouth, and perverse lips ;** literally, *perverseness of mouth and waywardness of lips* (*ikk'shúth peh vulzuth s'phâthãy'm*). "Perversity of mouth" is fraudulent, deceitful speech ; that which twists, distorts, perverts, or misrepresents what is true, and hence falsehood (ch. iv. 24 ; vi. 12 ; xix. 1). The σκολιὸν στόμα of the LXX., *i.e.* the "tortuous mouth," in a metaphorical sense. The phrase is very similar in meaning with the parallel "waywardness of lips," which means speech which turns aside from what is true and right, the noun *lâzûth* being derived from *lâzâh*, or *lûz*, "to bend aside." The tongue is the unruly member (Jas. iii. 2). Speech is the index of the mind (Lapide). Vigilance over the heart is vigilance over the mouth, inasmuch as "out of the abundance of the heart the mouth speaketh" (Matt. xii. 34). The admonition may have a twofold application, and may mean either do not indulge in this kind of speech yourself, exercise an unremitting jealousy over every propensity to it ; or have no dealings with those who are guilty of it, as in Ps. ci. 5.

Ver. 25.—**Let thine eyes look right on, and let thine eyelids look straight before thee.** "To look *right on*" and "to look straight *before* one" is to fix the eyes steadily and unswervingly upon an object before them, not to allow the gaze to deflect either to the right hand or to the left. As a noun, the word *nôkākh*, rendered "right on," signifies what is straight in front of one; adverbially, it has the same meaning as that given in the Authorized Version. The corresponding "before" (*nĕgĕd*) is substantively the side of any object which is opposite one, and as a preposition is equivalent to "before," "in the presence of," like the Latin *coram*. The versions (LXX., Syriac, Targum) take *nôkākh* in the sense of "right things:" "Let thine eyes look at right things;" contemplate them, aim at justice and equity. This meaning is given to the cognate adjective *nâkôâkh* in ch. viii. 9; xxiv. 26; Isa. xxvi. 10; xxx. 10; lix. 14; but in the Proverbs the word *nôkākh* only occurs twice (here and ver. 21), either as an adverb, "right on," "straightforwardly," or as a preposition, "before." *Look straight.* Gesenius takes this verb *yâshār* in hiph., "to make straight," as used elliptically: "Let thine eyelids *direct* a way before thee;" but the meaning is the same as "Let them look straight before thee." The Syriac, Gejerus, and Holden render, "Let thine eyelids direct thy way before thee;" *i.e.* do nothing rashly, but everything with premeditation; examine thy conduct, and see that it is right. The verb *yâshār* has this meaning, "to direct," in ch. iii. 6; xi. 5, but it is here used intransitively (Mercerus). *Eyelids* (*âph'âppîm*); so called from their fluttering, rapid motion, here used by way of poetic parallelism with "eyes." What the command inculcates is simplicity of aim or principle, singleness of motive. The moral gaze is to be steadily fixed, because if it wanders indolently, lasciviously, aimlessly, it imperils the purity of the soul. This verse may be understood, as Zöckler, as containing a command levelled against dishonest practices. The man who intends to cheat his neighbour looks this way and that how he may deceive him. Such an interpretation may be maintained on the ground that the former verse is directed against falsehood in *speech;* this against falsehood in *action.* But the former view is preferable. If you wish to keep the heart, you must be guided by simplicity of aim; look not aside either to the one hand or to the other, lest you may be led astray by the seductions and temptations which imperil the onward and upward progress of

the soul. The passage reminds us of the "single eye" (ἁπλοῦς), "simple," *i.e.* intent on heaven and God, of Matt. vi. 22.

Ver. 26.—**Ponder the path of thy feet;** properly, *make straight or level the path of thy feet.* The command carries on the idea of the previous verse. Simplicity of aim in the moral life is to be accompanied by attention to the moral conduct. The sense is, remove every obstacle which may impede or render insecure the way of moral life, and thus avoid every false step. The meaning "to ponder," *i.e.* "to weigh," seems to be given to the verb *pāllēs*, piel of the unused *pā'as* here used only in Ps. lviii. 3 and possibly in ch. v. 21. Its ordinary signification is "to make level, or even," as in Isa. xxvi. 7; xl. 12; and ch. v. 6. The LXX. keeps this in view in rendering, "Make straight paths for thy feet" (cf. Heb. xii. 13). The Authorized Version would mean, "Weigh your conduct as in a balance; before acting, consider the consequences and nature of the act." The second clause, **and let all thy ways be established,** is in effect only a repetition of the preceding thought, since it signifies, "See that thy conduct is correct; let all thy ways be definite and fixed." The marginal reading, "And all thy ways shall be ordered aright," gives the literal rendering to the tense; *yikkonu* being the future hiph. of *kûn,* "to be established," "to stand firm." This would express the *result* of giving heed to one's conduct.

Ver. 27.—This verse, with which the teacher closes this discourse, is very closely connected with ver. 26, which it more fully explains. The command is the parallel of ver. 25. As in ver. 25, the gaze is to be concentrated. So here the feet are not to deflect nor turn aside to byways. Nothing is to be permitted to draw one off from the right way, neither adversity, nor prosperity, nor anything which can possess the power of temptation (Bayne and Wardlaw). **Remove thy foot from evil.** A fuller expression than "depart from evil," of ch. iii. 7. Both the LXX. and the Vulgate add, "For the Lord knows the ways which are on thy right hand; but they are perverse which are on thy left. He shall make thy paths straight, and shall advance thy ways in peace."

HOMILETICS.

Vers. 1—4.—*A family heirloom.* I. DIVINE WISDOM IS THE BEST OF FAMILY HEIRLOOMS. Solomon transmits to his son the instruction which he has received from his father. Thus he aims at making it an old household treasure. He also hands down royal power, great possessions, national fame. But wisdom is to him an inheritance more precious than all other things. The rest may go rather than that the entail shall be cut off this most prized part of the family estate. It would be well if fathers and sons had a similar opinion of the best of treasures. One labours to leave heavy legacies in his will; another aims at securing good posts for his sons; a third is proud of the unsullied family honour; but many forget that which alone secures true welfare here and eternal life hereafter. It is beautiful to see this heirloom of piety carefully guarded in the cottage of the poor; but it is more interesting to see those who might be drawn aside to lower pursuits—as, alas! Solomon was in his later days—setting the same treasure before their family as the most valuable of all possessions.

II. DIVINE WISDOM WILL NOT REMAIN AS A FAMILY HEIRLOOM WITHOUT SPECIAL CARE IN RETAINING AND TRANSMITTING IT. The estate descends from father to son by laws of inheritance or by testamentary directions. The bodily likeness, the mental characteristic, the genius, the defect, the disease, often come down through successive generations. But religion is not found in the blood; no law of inheritance will secure the succession to Divine wisdom; you cannot ensure that your son will be pious by any clause in your will. This family heirloom will pass out of the household unless it is most carefully guarded. Bad sons may follow good fathers. The religion of our parents is no guarantee of our own spiritual state, nor does our religion contain within it the promise and potency of our children's faith.

III. DIVINE WISDOM MAY BE TRANSMITTED AS A FAMILY HEIRLOOM THROUGH INSTRUCTION AND EXAMPLE. We cannot absolutely secure the inheritance because we have to deal with that most ungovernable of all elements, the free-will of souls. But failure is often to be attributed to defective instruction. Home culture has been neglected, while public ministry has been most assiduous; or there has been a harsh, unwise restraint which has provoked a rebound of licence. On the whole, we may hope that good, sound home training will not be in vain. This involves two elements. 1. *Instruction.* There must be positive, definite teaching. We must not rely on the general influence of a wholesome Christian atmosphere, on casual words and passing advice, etc. Wisdom involves knowledge; religion depends on faith; and faith follows "hearing." It is most important that the main elements of the Christian truth should be understood and remembered by children. It is not enough to tell them to love Christ. They must know him if they are to trust and follow him. 2. *Example.* Without this instruction is futile. Our deeds then give the lie to our words. Instruction is the light to show the way; example, the impulse to urge us to walk in it. Succession in genius is rare. The two Plinys, the two Pitts, the two Mills, are exceptional instances. But by right instruction and example we have much more reason to expect a succession in piety, because genius must be born in a man, but the wisdom of godliness is offered to all who will seek it.

Ver. 9.—*A coronation.* Wisdom is here represented as standing forth with garlands and crowns, rewarding her votary. The whole picture suggested to us by this brief verse may be taken as illustrative of the blessed experience of the people of God.

I. THE CROWNING AUTHORITY. It is ridiculous to offer a crown except with the right and power to make the coronation effective. It was held that no one could be an emperor in the "holy Roman empire" of the Middle Ages unless he had been crowned by the pope, as Charles the Great had been crowned. In our picture we have a greater than the highest ecclesiastic. The Wisdom of God, ideally personified, offers crowns and garlands with her own hands. It is really an act of God. God's wisdom is subsequently revealed in Christ who bestows the best blessings on his people. Coronation from such an authority must be effective.

II. THE SUBJECT CROWNED. He is the votary of Wisdom, and it is on account of his allegiance to his heavenly mistress that he receives his honour. Solomon seems to be referring directly to himself (ver. 3). If so, it is the more remarkable that the most magnificent king of Israel should set less value on his regal dignity than on his fidelity to Wisdom. Even Solomon is here crowned, not because he is David's son and sits on the throne of a great nation, but because he is a loyal servant of Wisdom. The same honour is open to all who follow the same course. Wisdom, Divine truth, the knowledge of God, the following of Christ,—these things are the true grounds for honour; not birth, rank, power, or wealth.

III. THE ACT OF CORONATION. Wisdom stands forth and crowns her votary. She does it spontaneously. The pursuit of Divine Wisdom brings honour. Here we see that there is more than bare deliverance from ruin for the people of God.   They are invited to receive honours from above.   This happens in a measure upon earth in the elevation of character, the loftiness of the whole course of life, and perhaps even the worthy reputation of a true Christian.   Yet we must remember that the coronation is not the world's admiration, but God's approval.   This will be perfected in heaven when the saints who have borne the cross on earth will receive their crowns—only to cast them at the feet of the Lord through whose grace alone they have won them (Rev. iv. 10).

IV. THE NATURE OF THE CROWNS.   There is a garland as well as a crown.   1. *A recognition of victory.*   A simple wreath has little inherent worth.   But it is a token of victory.   It is nobler to wear a true conqueror's wreath than an idle monarch's diadem. The pursuit of Divine Wisdom leads to victory over sin and the world.   2. *A possession of wealth and honour.*   After the victor's wreath comes the regal crown.   Observe how it is constructed.   (1) Gold of truth.   (2) Precious stones of heavenly experience. Precious stones are symbolical of celestial structures (Rev. xxi. 18—21).   The follower of Wisdom has the heavenly mind; he minds spiritual things.   (3) Pearls of purity. True wisdom leads to holiness.

Ver. 12.—*A free course.*   Religion is looked upon too much in the light of a restraint, and the Christian is often regarded by the world as hampered and shackled by irksome bonds.   But the very opposite is suggested by the words of our text.   We see the servant of Divine Wisdom running with freedom on his course, and at the same time carefully guarded from misadventure.

I. THE TRUTH OF GOD GIVES LIBERTY.   Christ promised that the truth should make men free (John viii. 32).   1. *The liberty of knowledge.*   Ignorance is a bondage, because the ignorant man does not know how to shape his course.   He is like a traveller lost in the African bush.   Physical knowledge gives a certain liberty of action.   Knowledge of nature helps the man of science to act where the layman would be helpless.   The engineer's knowledge of his machine enables him to work it.   When we know the way of peace and safety we can freely and fearlessly run in it.   2. *The liberty of obedience.* The wisdom of the Proverbs is practical; it is intimately connected with the fear of God.   It implies more than knowledge in its followers; it requires also submission and obedience.   Now, when we are in rebellion against the Law and will of God, we are continually arrested by his opposing action.   But when we delight to do his will, we are perfectly free.   There is no liberty so great as that which comes from harmony between our wills and the will of God.   We desire the very things that God commands; it must follow that we are free to seek them.   Then of a certainty God will give us our heart's desire.

II. THE TRUTH OF GOD SECURES SAFETY.   The follower of Divine Wisdom will not stumble.   1. *He will not run in the way of danger.*   The narrow path is the safe path. There are gins and snares in the broad road.   Though the way of life may be rugged, it is not like the flowery path of sin, in the beauty of which a deadly serpent hides.   2. *God will remove the greatest impediments out of his path.*   He is in the King's highway.   Even this road may lead over steep places and through difficult passes.   But still, as it is maintained by its Lord, it cannot be left to fall into the state of an impassable road in a neglected country.   God is with his people while they are treading the path of righteousness, and he will prepare their way for them.   3. *There will be light to see the difficulties of the way.*   It is possible to stumble even on the high-road. Christian men have fallen.   We need to be prepared to face the difficulties which will surely meet us even while we are pursuing the Christian course.   Now, God's truth is a lamp to guide us over such difficulties (Ps. cxix. 105).   With the light of heavenly wisdom we safely pass them.   4. *There will be help at hand.*   Christ is with his people on their pilgrimage.   Like Peter sinking in the waves, they may cry, "Lord, save me: I perish!" and they will be delivered.   "Hold thou me up, and I shall be safe" (Ps. cxix. 117).

Ver. 13.—*Holding fast.*   I. THE NECESSITY OF HOLDING FAST.   This is to be in regard to instruction in Divine wisdom.   There are difficulties in keeping to the truth of God.   1. *The knowledge of it is an attainment.*   It is not innate; it does not come by inevitable experience; it is not received without conscious effort. What has been won may be lost. That which is not naturally a part of our being may be detached from us. 2. *The truth is spiritual.* Therefore it belongs to a different region from that of everyday experience in the world, and it is in danger of being thrust aside by the rude demands of material facts. The rush and roar of outward life drown the whispers of the "still, small voice." 3. *It is morally exacting.* God's instruction concerns our conduct, and that in a way not always agreeable to ourselves. It urges us with lofty mandates, it seeks to regulate our lives by great principles. But weakness shrinks and self-will rebels against such a yoke. Therefore unless we hold fast to the instruction, we shall soon lose it. Mere negligence is enough to imperil the choice possession. By simple indifference we may let slip the truth of God (Heb. ii. 1).

II. How we may hold fast. 1. *Attention must be directed.* As we have a certain command of our thoughts in the power of fixing attention on certain topics in preference to others, we can turn our minds towards Divine truth by a voluntary movement. External aids are here of use. The reading of the Bible is most helpful, not merely to obtain fresh truth, but to impress and revive the truth we already know. The ordinances of public worship are also designed with this end in view. The Christian preacher has not merely to instruct the ignorant and to lead those who know some truth to higher regions of revelation. A great part of his work consists in impressing upon men what they already know, and aiding them to hold it fast. None of these means of directing attention are sufficient without the addition of personal prayer and meditation. 2. *Truth must be realized in practice.* There is no better way of holding fast to instruction than by obeying it. The greatest truths are vague ideas till we commence to put them in practice. We hold best those truths which we follow most closely in life.

III. The advantage of holding fast. It is our duty to hold the truth which God has revealed to us, and to attend to the commandments which he has sent us. But it is also for our own soul's profit. This is a matter of life and death. Divine truth is not a mere luxury for the leisured classes. It is a necessary of life. 1. *This truth is a guide from the way of ruin.* God speaks words of the utmost moment to warn us from continuing in the old course of sin, and to show us the way of salvation. 2. *It is an immediate source of life.* God gives his Spirit through his truth, and the Spirit of God is the quickening power of our souls. Thus God's truth is the soul's food. To lose it is to starve. To hold it fast is to secure eternal life. The words that Christ speaks to us are spirit and life (John vi. 63).

Vers. 14, 15.—*Bad company.* I. The duty of avoiding bad company. We are all more or less unconsciously affected by the tone of the society we frequent. Even the strongest, most independent spirit cannot wholly fortify himself against this influence. As water wears the hardest rock, the constant friction of social intercourse makes itself felt in course of time upon the most resolute character. We are naturally gregarious. Without knowing it, nay, even while protesting against it, we are carried away with the current through which our course lies. Salmon swim up against the stream; but men prefer to float with the stream. Hence the great reason for choosing society of good character. It is most essential that young men just entering business in a great city should bear this in mind. The class of companions they choose will very largely affect the whole future course of their lives. Christians are called to come out from the world; but our Lord showed his wisdom, as much as his kindliness, in instituting the Church as a fellowship of his people. Thus he sought to use the social influences of mankind in favour of purity and truth as a set-off against the strong current of a corrupt worldly society. It is always dangerous to be cut off from these good influences. Emigrants and others who go to the colonies and to foreign countries should be on their guard against the peculiar dangers of their isolated situation. Many a young man has been ruined for life by going friendless to a distant country, and there falling a prey to the corruptions of bad company.

II. Difficulties in the application of this duty. The early Church, seeing idolatrous rites associated with almost every political and social engagement, withdrew very considerably from public life. The logical outcome of her conduct was monasticism. We have not her peculiar difficulties to contend with. Yet the mere thought of avoiding bad company might lead us to a similar course unless we weighed well other considerations of duty. Thus there are Christians who eschew all connection with national affairs because they hold that politics are closely wrapped up with worldly and wicked practices. But if the worst is true, it is rather our duty to seek to mend matters. Since we must have government, we should see that this is of the best possible character. If all the good people forsake it, they hand the government of the nation over to the wicked, and thereby tacitly sanction bad government. So if they put a ban on all amusement, they indirectly degrade every kind of amusement, and increase the temptation of the great mass of people, who naturally seek some sort of recreation, and will have the bad if they do not get the good. We must remember also that our Lord was accused of keeping the worst of company, and that he did this deliberately for the good of those with whom he had intercourse. We are not to be Pharisees, proud separatists, but brothers of all men, who are our *fellow*-sinners. The important point is the motive with which men enter bad company. If this be to discharge some duty, or to benefit those who are visited, it is pure, and may be expected to ward off harm. If it be done carelessly and for selfish pleasure, there is danger in it.

Ver. 18 —*" The path of the just."* I. A shining light. 1 *It has all the great leading characteristics* suggested by light, viz. truth, purity, joy, life. Perhaps the leading idea is that of holy gladness. This is to be enjoyed here on earth in those pleasant ways and paths of peace through which Wisdom leads her votaries. The Christian may be a martyr, but he need not be a victim of melancholy. 2. *It is open to the day.* They who do evil love the darkness that hides their deeds. "The dark places of the earth are full of the habitations of cruelty." Goodness fears no exposure. Cato had no fear of his neighbours looking into his garden. Daniel could afford to let his habits be public. 3. *It is bright with reflected Divine light.* Here is the source of the brightness like that of the dawn that reflects the sun's beams. Christ shines on the soul, and it brightens under his love as the dark hills and darker valleys take on the colours of life before the rising sun. 4. *It is always giving out light around it.* It is a shining light, a glistening light; not mere colour, but radiance. The true Christian is a light of the world; it is his duty to let his light shine to the glory of God.

II. A growing light. We must not stumble at that word "just," as though it removed the whole subject to lofty regions far beyond all possible attainments of ours. The just man in the Old Testament, like the saint in the New Testament, is not necessarily a person of fully ripened perfection, but one whose course and aim and tendency are towards righteousness. Such a man will begin with many imperfections. His course, however, will be one of growing brightness. Unless there is growth there must be death. The stagnant Christian is the dead Christian, soon to become the corrupt Christian. It is for our encouragement that we may expect growth if we employ the right means. There is growth in personal piety. Every victory over sin is so much new light gained. There is growth in grace. The richest stores of God's grace are in the future. There is ever " more to follow," and the best wine is reserved for the last. There is growth in knowledge. The light of truth is a growing light. What we know not now we shall know hereafter. "Now we see as in a mirror darkly, but then face to face." There is growth in joy and peace. The best fruits of Christian blessedness take time to ripen. The young Christian is disappointed at finding them green and acid. Time must mellow them. Now, this growth is gradual like the dawn, so that the Christian is carried on from stage to stage. But the rate is not uniform. With some there is a long twilight. With others the day hastens on with tropical speed. He who has most of Christ will find his dawn spread most rapidly.

III. A light that leads to perfect day. All that we now see is but the dull, chill twilight. It may be a cheerful dawn, but it is not to be compared with the rich splendour of the noon. The Christian progress is not to cease till it reaches perfection. It is far from that as yet. With some of us but a few grey streaks have as yet broken out of the old sad night. But all Christians may have the same glad hope of the full and perfect day. Heaven will be the coincidence of ripened character with perfected blessedness. And this day has no afternoon. There are no lengthening shadows to sadden us with threats of the chill evening and the dread darkness, for " there is no night there." A greater than Joshua arrests the sun at the meridian. Or rather there will be no need of the sun, because we shall be beyond this world of successive changes in the life eternal of that new Jerusalem, where it is ever day, because " the Lord God is the Light thereof."

Ver. 19.—*The way of darkness.* The way of sin is in all respects one of darkness. It is dark in its origin, dark in its course, and dark in its end.

I. THE WAY OF SIN STARTS FROM A DARK ORIGIN. 1. *Ignorance.* Most criminals are deplorably ignorant. Vicious men are generally men whose mental cultivation has been neglected by others or by themselves. Ignorance of Divine truth leads the way to wickedness. The first preventative of evil is the religious teaching of children. 2. *Inherited tendencies to evil.* These awful consequences of a parent's sin are a dark heritage which heavily handicaps the child from the first. 3. *Satanic influences.* Temptations are all dark in their origin. Evil suggestions come up from the pit of darkness. 4. *The lower nature.* When a man gives way to sin he sacrifices his higher to his lower self. He sinks from the sunlit mountain heights of purity to gloomy depths of baser living.

II. THE WAY OF SIN PURSUES A DARK COURSE. It is a road that runs through sombre passes, like some of those Welsh paths far in the heart of the mountains, on which the sun never shines. This is worse than the Valley of the Shadow of Death, for in the fearful path of sin there is no guiding hand and no protecting staff. The darkness of this course is exhaled from the evil committed upon it. 1. *Perverted conscience.* Sin distorts a man's thoughts, blinds his eyes to the highest truth, raises a mist about the old landmarks of right and wrong, and plunges the soul into a stupor of moral indifference. From neglecting to follow the light of God, the sinner comes at last to be incapable of beholding it. 2. *Spiritual desertion.* God's Spirit will not always strive with the sons of men (Gen. vi. 3). There comes a time when God leaves the self-abandoned soul to its own devices. Then, indeed, a darkness as of winter midnight sinks upon the lost being. 3. *Corrupt conduct.* Following the way of evil, the sinner continues to blacken it with the guilt of his own misdeeds. He plunges into the spiritual darkness of wicked living—the degradation, the loss of the joy and purity of heavenly light that sin always induces.

III. THE WAY OF SIN ISSUES IN A DARK END. The sinner cannot see his way upon it, and therefore he is sure to stumble. Bruised and confused, he may still persist in his sombre career. But he has no prospect of light beyond. There are no Beulah heights for him at the further end of the gloomy valley. His night of sin will be followed by no dawn of blessed light. He presses on only to deeper and yet deeper darkness. If he will not return there is nothing before him but the darkness of death. The one way of escape is backwards—to retrace his steps in humble penitence. Then, indeed, he may see the welcome light of his Father's home, and even earlier the Light of the world, the Saviour who has come out into the darkness to lead him back to God. For the sinner who persists in his evil course there can be no better prospect than that described by Byron in his poem on " Darkness "—

" The world was void,
The populous and the powerful was a lump,
Seasonless, herbless, treeless, manless, lifeless—
A lump of death—a chaos of hard clay.
The rivers, lakes, and ocean all stood still,
And nothing stirred within their silent depths;
Ships sailorless lay rotting on the sea,
And their masts fell down piecemeal: as they dropped
They slept on the abyss without a surge—
The waves were dead; the tides were in their grave,
The moon, their mistress, had expired before;
The winds were withered in the stagnant air,
And the clouds perished; Darkness had no need
Of aid from them—she was the Universe."

Ver. 23.—*On guard.* I. WHAT IS TO BE KEPT. The heart. In the Bible the "heart" represents what we call the "head" as well as the affections and conscience to which we confine the word "heart;" *i.e.* it stands for the whole inner nature, the life of thought, feeling, and will. This is the "Town of Mansoul," and it has the various constituents of a town. 1. *Entrance gates.* The soul is always receiving thoughts and impulses from without. It is important to see that no adulterated article, no poison, no subject of infectious disease comes in. Debased, false, and immoral impressions must be warded off. 2. *Ways of exit.* The broad river bears on her bosom argosies from the busy city to many a distant port. Let us see that the cargo is of good wares, in good measure, honestly realizing professions, containing no injurious things. Some hearts export only sham products, some deadly poisons. Deeds, words, even smiles and glances carrying thought and influences out of the soul must be carefully guarded. 3. *Internal thoroughfares.* The town is a network of streets and passages. Busy thoughts run to and fro in the heart. Let the traffic be orderly, the road well preserved, lest pure thoughts should be smirched with the mire of an unwholesome mental habit. 4. *Storehouses.* Memory has her treasuries, warehouses, granaries. Let us see that they are not crowded with rubbish, left in disorder, made fever-nests by the corruption of any unhealthy contents. Nourishing truths and beautiful ideas should stock them. 5. *Factories.* In the heart we weave fine webs of fancy—see that the pattern has the beauty of holiness; there, too, we forge great engines for future work—see that they are constructed on safe and serviceable principles. 6. *Halls of amusement.* Let them be places of recreation, not of dissipation. 7. *Shrines for worship.* See that no idol takes the place of the true God, no hypocrisy does service for the incense of spiritual prayer and praise. 8. *Graveyards* of dead hopes and loves; keep them beautiful with flowers of tender memory. Are there also graves of dead sins? Plant weeping willows of penitence over them.

II. WHY IT IS TO BE KEPT. 1. For its *own sake.* The heart is the centre of the life; the soul is the true being, the self. To care for the health of the body while the soul is diseased and dying in sin is like sending for the builder to repair the house, but leaving the sick inmate to perish without attention. "What shall it profit a man if he gain the whole world and lose his own soul"—life, heart? 2. For its *fruits.* "Out of it are the issues of life." In proportion as the heart is vigorous or feeble, healthy or diseased, all the organs of the body work well or ill. Take care of the heart first, cultivate right principles, see that the affections are set on things above, and then the practice of the details of morals will follow almost as a matter of course. It is a mistake to put casuistry in the forefront of moral teaching. The result of doing so is to weaken conscience, to confuse the sense of right and wrong. Let the condition of the heart be the first concern; see that truth, justice, purity, charity, are enshrined there. Let the love of God and the love of man be well cultivated, and the spiritual directory will be greatly simplified. But it is not even enough to cultivate right principles. Deeper than these is the life. Below the particular actions come general principles; beneath these lie the character, the life, the heart of all. The fundamental requisite is not to do this or that deed, nor to cherish one or another principle, but to possess the life eternal in the heart, out of which pure blood will flow through main arteries of principles to the most remote and minute and intricate capillaries of conduct.

III. HOW IT IS TO BE KEPT. 1. *Pure.* Let us see that the heart above all things is cleansed from sin and kept holy. We cannot do this for ourselves. But we can go to the fountain that is opened for uncleanness, and there wash and be clean. The blood of Christ, which cleanses from all sin, not only removes guilt, but purges out the corruption and power of evil. By faith in Christ and the indwelling of the Divine Spirit that is a consequence of faith, the heart can be cleansed and preserved in purity. 2. *True.* The Christian is to be a servant of God. Let him be loyal—frank, too, and ingenuous and simple. 3. *Tender.* One has well said that we want "tough skins and tender hearts." There is much in the world to harden them. Let us seek to have them soft to receive Divine influences and to feel human compassions. The heart must be kept, not as a prisoner under hard restraint, nor like the jewels at the Tower, in useless seclusion; but like a garden, well weeded, but also sown with good seed and bearing fruit and flowers. Keep the heart thus by watchfulness, by self-control (the New Testament "temperance"), by prayer, above all by entrusting it to the keeping of

God. Feeling that "the heart is deceitful above all things and desperately wicked," knowing how powerful are the temptations of the world, we may well despair of keeping the heart pure and safe. God meets us in our helplessness, and offers to keep it for us if we will put our trust and love in him. " My son, give me thy heart."

Vers. 25—27.—*Spiritual drilling.* The whole man must be drilled into form and disciplined into orderly action, just as the whole armour of God is necessary for the protection of the soldier of Christ. It is not enough for safety to wear a helmet while the breast is exposed, nor to bare the head while the legs are covered; and it is not enough for service that part of our nature is trained to obedience. We must seek to have all in right order.

I. THE HEART. This must be guarded most sedulously, and before all else. We cannot have our actions right in the sight of God while the heart is perverted. The attempt to secure this only ends in hypocrisy. The first duty of the soldier is loyalty. The first duty of the Christian is fidelity. Nevertheless, though the fountain must be pure if the stream is to be pure, its purity will not secure the water against subsequent defilement. It is not enough to think of the state of the heart, we must also consider the course of our actions. A pseudo-spirituality ends in indifference to morals, and even in positive immorality. St. Paul did not think his work done when he had laid the foundation of the Christian character. He sought the "edification," the "building up," of it by detailed and earnest instruction in Christian morals.

II. THE LIPS. The first and most ready expression of the state of the heart is in our conversation. "Out of the abundance of the heart the mouth speaketh." Now, it is important to remember that we are responsible for our words. For "every idle word that men shall speak, they shall give account thereof in the day of judgment" (Matt. xii. 36). Words are deeds. They carry influence and linger in memories and are transmitted from one to another long after the speaker has forgotten them.

III. THE EYES. The eye is one of the chief gateways of knowledge. According to the objects on which we fix it, the class of our knowledge will be determined. It is the guide in our actions. Now, it is requisite that the Christian have: 1. *A straight and "single" sight* (see Matt. vi. 22), looking only at the truth, with no stray glances at the innumerable deceptions of low self-interest. 2. *A long sight,* looking at the end of the race—the Celestial City, neither allured by the fascinations of Vanity Fair nor distracted by the horrors of the Valley of the Shadow of Death. 3. *An upward gaze* fixed on God and Christ rather than on worldly loss or gain.

IV. THE FEET. All the life leads on to the outgoings of activity. The ultimate question is—In what way are we going? Here the requisite is that the feet should go straight on. There are many ways of wrong, only one of right; hence the breadth of the former and the narrowness of the latter. We must especially avoid the error of falling into extremes. While shunning the track to the left let us see that we do not go off on that to the right. The path of duty is between these extremes. Yet the way to find it is not by seeking for a mean and so only accepting a compromise, but by aiming at the true and the right and pressing straight on to them irrespective of all conflicting influences.

HOMILIES BY VARIOUS AUTHORS.

Vers. 1—13.—*The tradition of piety.* The writer, here and in ch. v. 7 and vii. 24, addresses his audience as children, thinking of himself as a son, who had been the object of fatherly counsels and warnings in his youth. He would hand on the torch of wisdom, the tradition of piety, to the next generation.

I. PIETY SHOULD BE A FAMILY TRADITION. (Vers. 1—3.) Handed down from father to son and grandson, or from mother to daughter and grandchild, from Lois to Eunice, till it dwells in Timothy also (2 Tim. i. 5). Tradition in every form is, perhaps, the strongest governing power over the minds of men in every department of life.

II. EARLY INSTRUCTION WILL BE RETAINED, RECALLED, AND REPRODUCED. As the twig is bent, so is the tree inclined; or, as Horace says so beautifully, "The cask will long preserve the odour with which when fresh it was imbued" ('Ep.,' i. 2. 69).

Every higher effort of the intellect rests on memory. Our later life is for the most part the reproduction in other forms of the deep impressions of childhood.

III. THE CONTENTS OF THIS TRADITION ARE SIMPLE, YET PROFOUND. (Vers. 4—9.) They are summed up in "the one thing needful." In opposition to the cynical maxim, "Get money, honestly if you can, but by all means get money," or the refrain of "Property, property" (Tennyson's 'Northern Farmer'), the teacher rings the exhortation out, like an old chime, "Get wisdom, get understanding."

IV. THE STYLE OR FORM OF THE TRADITION. 1. It is *iterative*. It may even seem to modern ears monotonous. But this form is peculiarly part of the habit of the stationary East. Thought is not so much expansive, travelling from a centre to a wide periphery; it swings, like a pendulum, between two extremes. Generally, for all, the best life-wisdom must be these iterations, "Line upon line, precept upon precept" or *stare super antiquas vias*—a recurrence to well-worn paths. 2. It has *variety of expression* with unbroken unity of thought. (1) In reference to the *object of pursuit*. "Wisdom" is the leading word; but this is exchanged for "training" and "insight" (ver. 1); "doctrine" and "law" (ver. 2); "words" and "commandments" (ver. 4); the same word often recurs. (2) In reference to the *active effort of the mind* itself. This is presented as "hearing" and "attending" (ver. 1); "not forsaking" (ver. 2); "holding fast in the heart," and "guarding" (ver. 4); "getting" and "not turning from" (ver. 5); "not forsaking" and "loving" (ver. 6); "holding her high" and "embracing her" (ver. 8); "receiving words" and "adhering to instruction" (vers. 10, 13). (3) In reference to the *accompanying promise*. "Thou shalt live" (ver. 4); "She shall guard thee;" "protect thee" (ver. 6); "exalt thee;" "bring thee to honour" (ver. 8); "give to thy head a chaplet of delight;" "hold out to thee a splendid crown" (ver. 9); "many years of life" (ver. 10); "Thy steps shall not be hindered" (ver. 12); "Thou shalt not stumble" (ver. 12); "She is thy life" (ver. 13).

V. THE ADVANTAGES OF THIS METHOD OF TEACHING. 1. It is simple, intelligible to all. 2. Of universal adaptation. Easily remembered by the young, impossible to forget in age. 3. It admits of infinite illustration from experience. It is a sketch or outline, given to the pupil; he fills it in and colours it as life progresses.—J.

Vers. 14—19.—*The two paths.* I. LIFE UNDER THE IMAGE OF A PATH. It is a leading biblical image. There is much suggestion in it. 1. Life, like a path, has a *starting-point, a direction*, and *an end*. 2. We have a *choice of paths* before us. The high-road may image holy tradition and custom, the bypaths the choice of caprice or personal aberration. 3. It is only safe to follow *beaten tracks*. What we call "striking out an original course" *may be* conceited folly. "Gangin' our ain gait" is a dubious expression. 4. The selection of the path must be determined by *whither we desire to arrive*. 5. We are ever drawing near to *some end*. It alone can disclose the prudence or the folly of our choice.

II. THE PATH OF THE WICKED. (Vers. 14—17, 19.) 1. Religion *passionately* warns against it. The language of *iteration* is the very language of urgency and passion. What a force there is in the mere repetition of the cry, "Fire! fire! fire!" or in the warning of the mother to the little one against some dangerous object, "Don't go near it; keep away; go further off!" Just so does Divine Wisdom deal with us children of a larger growth. Again and again she clamours, "*Enter not; go not; shun it; pass not over; turn away; pass by!*" (vers. 14, 15). This throbbing earnestness, this emotion of the Bible, gives it its hold on man; and should be shared by every teacher. 2. Religion describes it in *powerful invective* (vers. 16, 17). (1) The *sleepless malice* of the wicked. A common figure for the intense activity of the mind. As David had a sleepless ambition to build a temple for Jehovah; as the trophies of Marathon suffered not the glory-loving Themistocles to sleep; as care, or glowing study, or eager planning, breaks our nightly rest;—so the evil have no repose from their dark cupidities and pernicious schemes. (2) They are *nourished by evil* (ver. 17). To "eat bread and drink wine" is a Hebrew metaphor for living (Amos ii. 8; vii. 12). In a similar way, the "bread of misery" and the "wine of punishment" are spoken of (Deut. xvi. 3; Ps. cxxvii. 2; Amos ii. 8). They live upon villainy, as we might say. It is the root of their being. It is horrible, but true, that a man may, as it were, draw life and energy out of a perverted consciousness, as the drunkard cannot live without the alcohol which is killing him.

III. THE PATH OF THE RIGHTEOUS. (Ver. 18.) There is a change of figure; for the image of the path, the image of the advancing light of morning is substituted. 1. Light as an image of moral goodness. It is universal, suggests itself to and strikes the fancy of all. It associates with it the images of beauty, of joy, of expansion, of futurity, of infinity. 2. The *growth of light* from dawn to noon as an image of moral progress. This is true of *knowledge* and of *practice.* The good man travels out of dimmer perceptions and out of doubts, into clear convictions of reason. At first he realizes little; his will is weak and untrained. But keeping his eyes upon the ideal of the good, true, and beautiful, he embodies more and more of it in conduct. As the sun rests not (to speak and think in the dialect of poetry) till it "stands" (see the Hebrew) in high noon, so the righteous is ever advancing towards the goal of a life in perfect unity with God. 3. The safety of the light is an image of the course of the righteous. Translated into distinctively Christian thought, this is *following Christ* (John xi. 9, 10). 4. The image serves to throw into contrast the course of the wicked. "Thick darkness" represents their mind and way. It is ignorant, full of peril, yet they are unconscious of it. Instead of *growth* and progress, their doom is *sudden extinction* (comp. ch. i. 27, *sqq.*; ii. 18, 22; iii. 35).—J.

Vers. 20—22.—*Self-preservation.* The instinct of self-preservation is the very root of all our activity. "Every individual existence strives to remain what it is," and would defend its integrity from all attack.

I. THE INSTINCT IS RECOGNIZED. As it must be by all genuine teachers. It is a fact, and cannot be properly ignored; a Divine fact, and ought not to be obscured. It includes (1) the desire to live, the sense of life's sweetness; (2) the desire for health and happiness.

II. THE INSTINCT IS DIRECTED. It needs direction; for all instinct is in itself blind, and men, in seeking health and happiness, ignorantly and viciously purchase disease and death.

III. THERE IS NO SECRET OF SELF-PRESERVATION BUT (IN THE MOST COMPREHENSIVE SENSE) GODLINESS. This teaches the renunciation of the immediate for the further and lasting good. A paradox is here involved, a seeming contradiction containing a unity. To lose life is to gain it; to gain it, to lose it. For in true conduct there is ever a denial of the lower contained in the affirmation of the higher, and in evil conduct *vice versâ* (compare on this section, ch. iii. 2, 8, 13, 16; iv. 13).—J.

Vers. 23—27.—*The heart and its issues.* I. LIFE CENTRED IN THE HEART. (Ver. 23.) *Physically*, we know this is so. It is a self-acting pump, a fountain of vital force. All the physical activities are derived from it. *Spiritually*, it is so. The connection of the heart with *emotion* is recognized in all languages. It is feeling in the widest sense that makes us what we are.

II. THE HEART MUST BE, THEREFORE, THE PECULIAR OBJECT OF OUR SOLICITUDE. (Ver. 23.) The *sentiments*, to put it in another form, are the important elements in character. These lie so close to *opinion*, that we commonly say either "I feel" or "I think" in expressing our opinions. To instil right *sentiments* about the important points of behaviour, the relation of the sexes, business, honour, truth, loyalty, is the great work of moral education, and here lies its immense value as distinguished from the gymnastic of the intellect.

III. THE EXTERNAL ORGANS MUST AT THE SAME TIME BE DISCIPLINED. (Vers. 24—27.) Education must not be one-sided. The heart supplies the organs and channels of activity; but these again react upon the heart. The impulses of feeling are in themselves formless; it is the definite organs which give to them peculiar shape and determination. Hence the organs themselves must be trained to receive true impressions and to give them back. 1. *The mouth—the lips.* They are to be corrected of every "crooked," false *expression.* What wonderful variety of expression is the mouth capable of—firmness, laxity, tenderness, scorn, love, irony, hate! In controlling the mouth we do something to control the heart. Its *contents* must be purified from falsehood, coarseness, foolish jesting, malicious gossip, all of which tell upon the central consciousness, and disturb and obscure it. 2. *The eyes.* (Ver. 25.) They are to be trained to a *direct* and *straightforward* expression. The leer of lust, the oblique glance of cunning expressed on the faces of others, or the clear honest light beaming from the eyes of the pure and open-hearted, not only mirror the heart, but remind how the heart may be reached by the self-discipline of the eye. 3. *The feet.* (Ver. 26.) In like manner, they are to be trained to a straightforward walk. Even in moments of relaxation 'tis well to have an object for a walk. The mind needs self-direction and discipline even in its pleasures; otherwise it becomes dissolute, and waywardly falls into evil through sheer laxity in the spring of will. (1) Action and reaction, between the inward and the outward world, expression and impression, constitute a great law of our spiritual activity. (2) Hence self-discipline and moral education should be founded on the recognition of it. We must work from the centre to the periphery, and back again from every point of the periphery to the centre of life.—J.

Vers. 1—13.—*The solicitude of the wise father: a sermon to parents and children.* In these verses we have a peep into the royal house at Jerusalem while David was on the throne. And we have such a glimpse as we should expect to gain. We see the devout man extremely solicitous that his son should walk in the ways of Divine and heavenly wisdom. David, like the rest of human parents, and more than most of them, was under—

I. A STRONG TEMPTATION TO MAKE A FALSE ESTIMATE. So near to us is this present passing world, so powerfully do its interests appeal to us, so strong is the hold which it gains over our senses and our imagination, that we are apt to over-estimate altogether its claims and its worth. And this in proportion to the height of the dignity, the measure of the power, the extent of the fortune, to which we have attained. David, as a man subject to all human passions, would be particularly tempted to weigh the worldly advantages of his favourite son, and estimate them very carefully and very highly. He would be in danger of considering—not exclusively, but excessively—what would be the extent of his kingly rule, what the revenue he would be able to collect, what the influence he would wield over neighbouring powers, what the authority he would exercise over his own people, etc. And in the thick throng of these mundane considerations there would be no small risk of other and higher things being lost sight of. So with other if not with all parents. There is a constant danger of worldly anxieties about our children absorbing, or at any rate obscuring, the deeper and worthier solicitudes. But in the case of the devout monarch of Israel there was, as there should be with us all—

II. A WISE DISCERNMENT. David was profoundly convinced that "wisdom is the principal thing" (ver. 7), that everything is of inferior value to that. He saw clearly and felt strongly that he must induce his son Solomon to walk in the fear of the Lord, or even *his* brilliant prospects would come to nothing. For he knew: 1. That the fear of God was the living principle most likely to lead to temporal prosperity: he had proved that in the elevation of his own "house" and the rejection of that of Saul. 2. That no possible successes of an earthly kind would compensate for the loss of character: his own hour of disastrous folly had shown him that (2 Sam. xi. 27). 3. That no circumstantial misfortunes could fatally injure a man who was right at heart with God: his own experience had illustrated that truth (Ps. xli. 12). We shall be wise if we come to the same conclusions. Like David, we shall see that the outward and the visible, though they may be far more attractive and voiceful, are yet of far inferior account to the inward and the spiritual. We shall care immeasurably more for our children that they shall be wise in soul than prosperous in estate, "all glorious within" than magnificent without; we shall be far more solicitous to see them "getting wisdom" (ver. 5) than "making money," "retaining the words" of truth (ver. 4) than gaining or keeping possession of lands and houses.

III. THE WAY OF WISDOM TOWARD THE YOUNG. If we, as parents, would walk wisely, so that we may attain our heart's desire concerning the children of our love and of our charge, we shall act as David did—we shall *commend the truth* God has taught us (1) with all affectionateness of manner (ver. 3); (2) with all earnestness of spirit (vers. 4, 10, 11); (3) with all fulness of exposition. There is a strain of parental tenderness of tone and energy of manner, as well as great fulness of utterance here. The same thought is presented, is repeated, is pressed on the reason and the conscience. David evidently yearned, strove, persisted with patient and resolute zeal, that he might convince and inspire his son with the sacred truths he held so dear. He represented heavenly wisdom, the truth of God, as (1) the thing of surpassing intrinsic excellency (ver. 7); (2) a thing to be pursued in preference to other fascinations (vers. 5—7); (3) a thing to be cherished and held to the heart (ver. 6); (4) a thing to be highly honoured before men (ver. 8); (5) a thing to be retained at all costs (ver. 13); (6) a friend that would repay all attentions—that would guard and shield from evil (vers. 6, 12), that would lead to honour and esteem (vers. 8, 9), that would prolong life (ver. 10), that would lead in that way which is *the* path of life itself (ver. 13).

1. To *parents,* the lesson of the text is (1) discern the one supremely precious thing to be commended to the heart of youth; and (2) commend it graciously, earnestly, fully. 2. To *sons and daughters,* it is (1) remember all the sacred solicitude that has been expended on you; and (2) fulfil the desire of your parents' hearts. " My son, know the God of your father" (see ver. 1); this is " good doctrine " (ver. 2); it is "your life" (ver. 13).—C.

Vers. 14—17, 19.—*The prudence of piety.* We may say concerning piety or virtue —the wisdom which is from God includes both—that the *essence of it* is in right feeling, in loving him who is the Holy One and that which is the right and admirable thing, and in hating that which is evil and base ; that the *proof of it* is in right acting— in doing those things and those only which are good and honourable, which God's Word and our own conscience approve; and that the *prudence of it* is in these two things which are implied in our text.

I. Cherishing a wholesome horror of the consequences of sin. There is an insensibility and an ignorance which passes for courage, and gets a credit which is not its due. Those who do not take the trouble to know what the issues of any line of conduct are, and who go fearlessly forward, are not brave ; they are only blind. We ought to know all we can learn of the consequences of our behaviour, of the end in which the path we are treading terminates. The prudent man will see and shrink from the consequences of evil ; and if he open his eyes or consult those who can tell him, he will find that they are simply disastrous. 1. For sin is mischievous in its spirit; it gloats over the ruin which it works; it finds a horrible delight in doing harm to human souls (vers. 16, 17). 2. And it succeeds in its shameful design. It *does* " mischief ; " it makes men "to fall." It causes spiritual decline, decay, corruption— the worst of all mischief; it leads purity, sobriety, honesty, truthfulness, reverence, love, to fall down into the ruinous depths of lasciviousness, intemperance, dishonesty, false-hood, profanity, hard-heartedness. 3. It leads down to a darkness and a death of which it did not dream (ver. 19). It sinks into that awful soul-blindness in which the " eye is evil," in which the very " light is darkness " (Matt. vi. 23), in which the moral judgment, all perverted, leads astray. " The way of the wicked is as darkness : they know not at what they stumble." Their powers of moral distinction are gone ; they are " altogether gone astray." Piety, virtue, may well in godly prudence shrink with wholesome horror from this.

II. Careful avoidance of the way of the wicked, and so of the path of temptation. 1. True it is that we must be often found in perilous places at the call of daily *duty.* 2. True that at the invitation of *mercy* we shall sometimes be found there. 3. But it is also true that the wise will not needlessly expose themselves to the assaults of sin. They will refrain from so doing both because (1) we are not sure of the measure of our own strength ; there may be some very weak places in our armour, ill-fortified parts in our character ; most men are weaker than they know, *somewhere.* And also because (2) we do not know the full strength of temptation. Full often sin proves to have an unimagined force, an unsuspected skill. The full strength of the allurements and enticements of evil perhaps no man knows. The number of the slain that lie on the spiritual battle-field tells with a mournful eloquence that thousands of the children of men have over-estimated their own resisting power, or under-estimated the insidiousness, or the fascination, or the force of the foe. Therefore, if duty does not demand it, nor mercy plead for it, *shun* the dangerous path, " enter not into the way of it . . . avoid it, pass not by it, turn from it, and pass away " (vers. 14, 15).

Let it be considered that this is a Divine injunction; therefore let there be no hesitation about obeying. There is nothing unmanly or ignoble in prudence. It is not a virtue to be anywise ashamed of. There is ample scope for the utmost heroism of spirit and of life without exposing our young hearts to evils the very nature of which we may not know, the force of which we cannot measure, and from the consequences of which we might never be able to escape.—C.

Vers. 18, 19.—*Darkness and light.* We have two perfect contrasts in these two verses—the path of the just and the way of the wicked; the one is very closely connected with light and the other with darkness.

I. SIN AND DARKNESS. (Ver. 19.) We may say that: 1. Sin *is* darkness. It is (1) the ignorance of the mind; it is (2) the error of the heart—it is the soul's supreme mistake, misreading, misunderstanding every one and everything from the highest to the lowest. 2. Sin spreads darkness (1) over the soul of the sinner himself, blinding his eyes, distorting his vision, confusing his perceptions; (2) over the souls of others, leading them into the darkness of folly, superstition, wrong-doing. 3. Sin leads to the ruin which attends darkness; it ends in making the sinner blind to the true character of his own transgressions: "They know not at what they stumble;" blind, also, to the final issue of his guilt: they know not *into* what they stumble—into what a "blackness of darkness."

II. WISDOM AND LIGHT. (Ver. 18.) By "the just" in this verse we understand not particularly the man who is equitable in his dealings with his fellows, but the good and wise man—the man who, in the fear of God, seeks to act with rectitude in all his relations. This man is closely associated with the light. 1. Knowledge is light, and heavenly wisdom is the truest and best knowledge—that of God, and of the human soul, and of the path of eternal life. 2. That which reveals is light, and heavenly wisdom is the best and most beneficent revealing power. The wise, the "just" man is "making manifest" (see Eph. v. 13) the highest, the most far-reaching, deep-descending truths. He does this (1) by his direct endeavour to instruct; (2) unconsciously, by the influence of his life. "The life is the light of men" in our case as in his who was "the Life made manifest." 3. The light of the just man grows ever stronger and more illuminating: it "shineth more and more unto the perfect day." With added opportunities of inquiry and acquisition, with multiplied privileges, with more of Divine discipline, with increase of power resulting from the exercise of spiritual faculty, there is (1) growing light within, burning more steadily and lustrously; and (2) advancing influence for good which flows forth in wider, deeper, and larger streams.—C.

Vers. 20—27.—*The course of wisdom.* In these verses we may trace the course of wisdom from the beginning to its full development. We have—

I. ITS BEGINNING IN THE SOUL. (Ver. 20.) It commences in *attention.* When a man "inclines his ear unto the sayings of Wisdom," when he eagerly listens to what God says to him, when he is a disciple sitting at the feet of the great Teacher, he has taken an important step in the heavenward course. The "grace of God" is upon him (Acts xiii. 43).

II. ITS ESTABLISHMENT IN THE SOUL. (Ver. 21, latter clause.) When the counsels of the Wise One are once fairly and fully welcomed to the soul, so that they may be said to be "in the midst of thine heart," then it may be said that the decisive point is turned. When there is the "cherishing of a cordial attachment;" when we say, "How love I thy Law!" when our heart is given to the truth of God because given to him, the gracious Lord of truth;—then wisdom is established within our soul.

III. THE NEED FOR HOLY VIGILANCE CONCERNING ITS MAINTENANCE. (Ver. 23; see homily *infra.* Ver. 26, first clause.)

IV. ONE OF ITS MANIFESTATIONS. (Ver. 24.) It will show itself in clean lips; it will put far away the froward and perverse mouth. Its utterances will be pure, temperate, reverent. The child of folly is detected by his foolish, vain, culpable expressions. His "speech bewrayeth him." "By his words he is condemned." The son of wisdom is known by his blamelessness in this particular; by *his* words he is justified (Matt. xii. 36, 37; Eph. iv. 29; Jas. i. 26).

V. RESOLUTENESS IN THE RIGHT PATH. (Ver. 27.) There must be no "turning again to folly" (Ps. lxxxv. 8); no turning to the 'right or left into either main highways of vice and open sin, or any byways of error and ill-doing. Even the pleasant path that seems to skirt the King's highway so closely that at any time we may return thereto, is a danger to be avoided. The road that leads off from that highway of holiness by ever so small an angle is a road that finds its way at last to a "City of Destruction." The best preservative from the perilous wandering is here indicated; it is—

VI. STEADFAST GAZE UPON THE GOAL. (Ver. 25.) Look right on to the goal in front; be so intent on reaching that, and on attaining to the prize which awaits the winner, that there will be no temptation to depart from the straight course. We keep a straighter path by fixing our eye on the object toward which we walk than by watching the steps we take; how much more so than by looking about us on every hand! Our heavenly wisdom is to be looking "right on," "straight before us," unto Jesus, the Leader and Perfecter of the faith (Heb. xii. 2).

VII. ITS ISSUE. It issues in life and health (vers. 22, 23). Long life was promised to the wise and holy under the old dispensation; now we look confidently forward, as the issue of heavenly wisdom, to (1) a blessed life below, of spiritual wholeness, and (2) everlasting life beyond, where the inhabitants are never sick (Isa. xxxiii. 24).—C.

Ver. 23.—*Man's chief treasure.* "Keep thy heart above all keeping" (marginal reading). Evidently there is a precious treasure which, as the disciples of Wisdom, we are charged to keep. We ask—

I. WHAT ARE THE CHIEF TREASURES WE HAVE IN CHARGE? These are threefold. 1. That which belongs to us, but which is entirely without us—our money, our houses, our lands, our shares, our ships, our precious documents, our "valuables." 2. That which is more closely related to us, but is still outside ourselves—our bodily frame, the tabernacle of our spirit, and, with this, our physical health and strength; the clear eye, the healthy brain, the strong nerve. 3. Our own very selves—that spiritual nature in virtue of which we are said to be "created in the image of God" (Gen. i. 27). These are the treasures we may "keep."

II. WHICH IS THE ONE OF SUPREME VALUE, AND WHY? "Keep *thy heart* above all keeping." That which is nearest ourselves must be of more value to us than that which is further from us. To keep our temporal estate is to preserve that which is precious, but which is not ourselves. To maintain our health is most desirable, but our body is only our temporary home and organ; it is something we can lose and yet ourselves be. But our heart, that is our own very self. God made us, not *to have*, but *to be*, living souls: that in us, that of us which thinks, loves, hopes, worships, rejoices in the spiritual and the Divine, that is *ourself*, and to keep that must be the supreme duty; that is to be kept beyond all keeping. But the wise man says there is a special reason why we should keep our heart beyond all keeping; he says, "for out of it are the issues of life." In other words, a well-guarded heart is the spring and source of all that is best in human life. 1. The holy thoughts and pure feelings and kind purposes which flow therefrom are, in themselves, a large part and the very best part of human life. 2. A well-guarded heart will prove the source of a well-regulated life—of a life of honesty, virtue, peaceableness, sobriety; and these will ensure prosperity, esteem, joy. 3. A well-regulated heart will conduct to the life immortal in the heavenly land: this is the most blessed "issue" of all. With whatsoever anxiety, vigilance, diligence, we guard our temporal interests, or even our health and our mortal life, with far greater anxiety, far more eager vigilance, far more unremitting diligence, should we guard our heart—its purity, its tenderness, its devotion.

III. WHAT ARE OUR FORCES OF DEFENCE? Wherewith shall we keep these hearts of ours? What are the forces at our command? They are these. 1. The power of introspection. We can interrogate and examine our own souls, and see how we stand, what need there is for penitence and for renewal. 2. The power of self-regulation. We can acquire healthful habits, pass regulative resolutions which will (1) keep us away from temptation, and (2) take us where our souls will be nourished and strengthened in things Divine. 3. The power of the Divine Spirit. We can ask and gain the "might [which comes from] his Spirit in the inner man."—C.

EXPOSITION.

CHAPTER V.

Vers. 1—23.—8. *Eighth admonitory discourse. Warning against adultery, and commendation of marriage.* The teacher, in this discourse, recurs to a subject which he has glanced at before in ch. ii. 15—19, and which he again treats of in the latter part of the sixth and in the whole of the seventh chapters. This constant recurrence to the same subject, repulsive on account of its associations, shows, however, the importance which it had in the teacher's estimation as a ground of warning, and that he ranked it among the foremost of the temptations and sins which called the young off from the pursuit of Wisdom, and so led them astray from "the fear of the Lord." The vividness with which the ruin, bodily and moral, ensuing with absolute certainty on a life of vice, is described is a sufficient proof in itself that the subject before us is not brought forward from or for voluptuous motives, but for the purpose of conveying an impressive warning. Some commentators, *e.g.* Delitzsch, include the first six verses in the previous discourse; but the unity of the subject requires a different treatment. Zöckler's reason against this arrangement, on the ground that the previous discourse was addressed to "tender youth," and thus to youth in a state of pupilage, while the one before us refers to more advanced age —to the married man—may be true, but is not the true ground for incorporating them in the present discourse. The unity of the subject requires that they should be taken with the central and didactic part of the discourse, as being in a sense introductory to it. The discourse divides itself into three sections. (1) The earnest appeal to attention because of the counter-attraction in the blandishments of the harlot, which, however, in the end, are bitter as wormwood and sharp as a two-edged sword (vers. 1—6). (2) The main or didactic section (vers. 7—20), embracing (*a*) warnings against adulterous intercourse with "the strange woman" (vers. 7—14); (*b*) the antithetical admonition to use the means of chastity by remaining faithful to, and rejoicing with,

the wife of one's youth (vers. 15—20). And (3) the epilogue, which, in addition to the disastrous temporal consequences which follow on the violation of the sanctity of marriage, mentioned in vers. 9—14, represents the sin as one which will be examined by the universal Judge, and which brings with it its own Nemesis or retribution. All sins of impurity, all sins against *temperance, soberness,* and *chastity,* are no doubt involved in the warning, and the subject is capable of an allegorical interpretation—a mode of treatment in some instances adopted by the LXX. rendering, as that the "strange woman" stands as the representative of *impenitence* (Miller), or, according to the earlier view of Bede, as the representative of heresy and false doctrine; but the sin which is inveighed against, and which is made the subject of these repeated warnings, is not fornication simply, but *adultery*—the violation, in its most repulsive form, of the sacred obligations of marriage. The whole discourse is an impressive commentary on the seventh commandment.

Ver. 1.—The admonitory address is very similar to that in ch. iv. 20, except that here the teacher says, "Attend to *my wisdom*, bow down thine ear to *my understanding*," instead of "Attend to *my words*, and incline thine ear unto *my saying*." It is not merely "wisdom" and "understanding" in the abstract, but wisdom which he has appropriated to himself, made his own, and which he knows by experience to be true wisdom. It may therefore have the sense of experience and observation, both of which increase with years. To "bow down the ear" is to listen attentively, and so to fix the mind intently on what is being said. Compare the similar expressions in Ps. xxxi. 2 and ch. ii. 2; iv. 20; xxxiii. 12. The same idea is expressed in Marc Antony's address to his countrymen, "Lend me your ears" (Shakespeare, 'Julius Cæsar,' act iii. sc. 2).

Ver. 2.—This verse expresses the purposes or results of the preceding admonition. The first is, **that thou mayest regard discretion** (Hebrew, *lishmôr m'zimmôth*); literally, *to guard reflection;* i.e. in other words, that thou mayest maintain thoughtfulness, observe counsel, set a proper guard or control over thy thoughts, and so restrain them within proper and legitimate limits, or form such resolutions which, being well considered and prudential, may result in prudent conduct. The word *m'zimmóth*, however, does not travel beyond the sphere of what is conceived in the mind, and consequently does not mean conduct (as Holden conceives), except in a secondary sense, as that thoughts and plans are the necessary preliminaries to action and conduct. Muffet, *in loc.*, explains, " that thou mayest not conceive in mind any evil or vanity." The word *m'zimmóth* is the plural of *m'zimmáh*, which occurs in ch. i. 4. This word generally means any plan, project, device, either in a good or bad sense. In the latter sense it is applied to intrigue and deceitful conduct, as in ch. xxiv. 8. It is here used in a good sense. Indeed, Delitzsch remarks that the use of the word in a good sense is peculiar to the introductory part of the Proverbs (ch. i.—ix.). The Vulgate renders, " That thou mayest guard thy thoughts or reflection (*ut custodias cogitationes*)." So the LXX., "Ἵνα φυλάξῃς ἔννοιαν ἀγαθήν, " That thou mayest guard good reflection," the adjective ἀγαθή being introduced to note the sense in which the ἔννοια, *i.e.* act of thinking, properly, is to be understood. The prefix לְ (" to ") before *shámar*, " to guard," in *lishmór*, expresses the purpose, as in ch. i. 5; ii. 2, *et alia*. The second end in view is, that **thy lips may keep knowledge**; literally, *and thy lips shall keep knowledge*. Those lips keep or preserve knowledge which literally retain the instruction of Wisdom (Zöckler), or which allow nothing to pass them which does not proceed from the knowledge of God (Delitzsch), and which, when they speak, give utterance to sound wisdom. The meaning may be illustrated by Ps. xvii. 3, " I am purposed that my mouth shall not transgress." The same expression occurs in Mal. ii. 7, " For the priest's lips should keep knowledge," *i.e.* preserve and give utterance to it. Where " the lips keep knowledge," there they are protected against the lips of the strange woman, *i.e.* against her allurements, because they will be fortified with purity. *Thy lips; s'phâthêykâ* is the dual of the feminine noun *sáphah*, " a lip." The teacher designedly uses this word instead of " thy heart " (cf. ch. iii. 1), because of the contrast which he has in mind, and which he produces in the next verse. The LXX., Vulgate. and Arabic add, " Attend not to the deceitful woman," which Houbigant and Schleusner think is required by the context. The addition, however, is without authority (Holden).

Ver. 3.—The teacher enters upon the subject of his warning, and under two familiar figures—common alike to Oriental and Greek writers—describes the nature of the " strange woman's " allurements. **For the lips of a strange woman drop as an** honeycomb. The conjunction " for " (Hebrew *ki*) here, like the LXX. γὰρ, states the reason why the preceding exhortation is worthy of attention. Some commentators render " although," " albeit," as corresponding with the antithetical " but " in ver. 4. *The lips; siphthêy*, the construct case of *sáphâh* in ver. 2. The organ of speech is here used for the speech itself, like the parallel " mouth." *A strange woman* (*zârâh*); *i.e.* the harlot. The word occurs before in ch. ii. 16, and again in ch. v. 20; vii. 5; xxii. 14; xxiii. 33. She is *extranea*, a stranger with respect to the youth whom she would beguile, either as being of foreign extraction, or as being the wife of another man, in which capacity she is so represented in ch. vii. 19. In this sense she would be an adulteress. St. Jerome, in Ezek. vi., takes her as the representative of the allurements from sound doctrine, and of corrupt worship (Wordsworth). *Drop as an honeycomb* (*nóphêth tithóph'nâh*); rather, *distil honey*. The Hebrew *nóphêth* is properly a " dropping," *distillatio*, and so the honey flowing from the honeycombs (*tsûphim*). Kimchi explains it as the honey flowing from the cells before they are broken, and hence it is the *pure fine virgin honey*. Exactly the same phrase occurs in Cant. iv. 11, " Thy lips, O my spouse, drop as an honeycomb (*nóphêth tithóph'nâh*)." The only other places where we meet with the word *nóphêth* are Ps. xxiv. 10 (11) (there combined with *tsûphim*, which helps to determine its meaning) and ch. xxiv. 13; xxvii. 7. The meaning is the same as she " flattereth with her words " of ch. vii. 5, in which chapter the teacher gives an example of the alluring words which the strange woman uses (ch. vii. 14—20). As honey is sweet and attractive to the taste, so in a higher degree are her words pleasant to the senses. **Her mouth is smoother than oil;** *i.e.* her words are most plausible and persuasive. The Hebrew *khik* is properly " the palate," though it also included the corresponding lower part of the mouth (Gesenius). It is used as the instrument or organ of speech in ch. viii. 7, " For my mouth (*khik*) shall speak truth ; " and in Job xxxi. 30, " I have not suffered my mouth (*khik*) to sin." Under the same figure David describes the treachery of his friend in Ps. lv. 22, " His words were softer than oil, yet they were drawn swords."

Ver. 4.—The contrast is drawn with great vividness between the professions of the " strange woman " and the disastrous consequences which overtake those who listen to her enticements. She promises enjoyment, pleasure, freedom from danger, but **her end is bitter as wormwood.** " Her end," not merely with reference to herself, which may be and is undoubtedly true, but the last of her as experienced by those who have intercourse with her—her character as it stands revealed at the last. So it is said of wine, "At the last," *i.e.* its final effects, if indulged in to excess, "it biteth like a serpent, and stingeth like an adder" (ch. xxiii. 22). *Bitter as wormwood.* The Hebrew, *lăănáh,* "wormwood," Gesenius derives from the unused root *lăăn,* "to curse." It is the equivalent to the *absinthium* of the Vulgate. So Aquila, who has ἀψίνθιον. The LXX. improperly renders χολή, "gall." In other places the word *lăănáh* is used as the emblem of bitterness, with the superadded idea of its being poisonous, also according to the Hebrew notion, shared in also by the Greeks, that the plant combined these two qualities. Thus in Deut. xxix. 18 it is associated with *rosh,* "a poisonful herb" (margin), and the Targum terms it, agreeably with this notion, "deadly wormwood." The same belief is reproduced in Rev. viii. 11, "And the name of the star is called Wormwood: and many men died of the waters because they were made bitter" (cf. Jer. ix. 15; Amos v. 7; vi. 12). The apostle, no doubt, has it in mind when he speaks of any "root of bitterness," in Heb. xii. 15. The herb is thus described by Umbreit: "It is a plant toward two feet high, belonging to the genus *Artemisia* (species *Artemisia absinthium*), which produces a very firm stalk with many branches, grayish leaves, and small, almost round, pendent blossoms. It has a bitter and saline taste, and seems to have been regarded in the East as also a poison, of which the frequent combination with *rôsh* gives an intimation." Terence has a strikingly similar passage to the one before us—

" In melle sunt linguæ sitæ vestræ atque orationes
Lacteque ; corda felle sunt lita atque acerbo aceto."

" Your tongues are placed in honey and your speech is milk; your hearts are besmeared with gall and sharp vinegar" ('Trucul.,' i. 11. 75). **Sharp as a two-edged sword ;** literally, *as a sword of edges (khĕrĕv piyyóth),* which may mean a sword of extreme sharpness. Her end is as sharp as the sharpest sword. But it seems better to take the term as it is understood in the Authorized Version, which has the support both of the Vulgate, *gladius biceps,* and the LXX., μαχαίρα διστόμος, *i.e.* " a two-edged sword." Compare "a two-edged sword" *(khĕrĕv pîphiyyóth)* of Ps. cxlix. 6. The meaning is, the last of her is poignancy of remorse, anguish of heart, and death. In these she involves her victims.

Ver. 5.—Vers. 5 and 6 continue the de-

scription of the harlot. **Her feet go down to death ; her steps take hold on hell.** She leads her victims to ruin. She hastens to death and the grave, and so do all those who listen to her. In all instances where the teacher speaks of the harlot at length he gives the same description of her (cf. ch. ii. 18 ; vii. 27 ; ix. 18). An intensifying of the language is observable in the second hemistich. The descending progress to death becomes the laying hold of the grave, the underworld, as if nothing could turn her steps aside. And it is not only death, as the cessation of life, but death as a punishment, that is implied, just as the grave has in it the idea of corruption. (On " hell," *sh'ol,* see ch. i. 12.)

Ver. 6.—**Lest thou shouldest ponder the path of life, her ways are movable, that thou canst not know** them. This verse should be rather rendered, *she walks not in the path of life, her ways fluctuate, she knows not.* It consists of a series of independent propositions or statements, all of which are descriptive of the singularly fatuous conduct of " the strange woman." In the previous verse the teacher has said that her conduct leads to ruin; he here further emphasizes the idea by putting forward the same truth from the opposite, or, as we may say, from the negative point of view, and so completes the picture. "The words," as Plumptre remarks, " describe with terrible vividness the state of heart and soul which prostitution brings on its victims." Her course is one of persistent, wilful, headstrong, blind folly and wickedness. *Lest; pĕn;* here " not," equivalent to לֹא *(ló).* So the LXX., Vulgate, Targum, Syriac. The use of *pĕn* in this sense is, however, unique (Gesenius). Delitzsch and Zöckler, following Luther, Geïer, Holden, etc., assign to it an emphatic negative force, as, " She is *far removed from* entering," or, " she *never* treadeth." Others take *pĕn* as a dependent prohibitive particle, equivalent to the Latin *ne forte,* " lest," as in the Authorized Version, and employed to connect the sentence which it introduces either with the preceding verse (as Schultens) or with the second hemistich, on which it is made dependent (Holden, Wordsworth, Aben Ezra, *loc.,* Michaelis, etc.). *Thou shouldest ponder; t'phăllês,* connected by makkeph with *pĕn,* as usual (Lee), is either second person masculine or third person feminine. The latter is required here, the subject of the sentence being " the strange woman," as appears clearly from the second hemistich, " *her* ways," etc. The verb *pátãs* (cf. ch. xiv. 26) here means " to prepare," *i.e.* to walk in, or to travel over. Thus Gesenius renders, " She (the adulteress) prepareth not (for herself) the way of life: " *i.e.* she does not walk in the way of life;

cf. the LXX. εἰσέρχεται, Vulgate *ambulant* (sc. *gressus ejus*), and other ancient versions, all of which understand the verb in this sense. The meaning of the phrase, *pĕn t'phalles*, is, therefore, " she walks not " in the way of life—the way that has life for its object, and which in itself is full of life and safety. Far from doing this, the teacher goes on to say, *her ways are movable;* literally, *go to and fro, or fluctuate;* i.e. they wilfully stagger hither and thither, like the steps of a drunkard, or like the uncertain steps of the blind, for the verb *nûā* is so used in the former sense in Isa. xxiv. 20; xxix. 9 ; Ps. cvii. 27 ; and in the latter in Lam. iv. 14. Her steps are slippery (LXX., σφαλέραι), or wander (Vulgate, *vagi*) ; they are without any definite aim ; she is always straying in the vagrancy of sin (Words-worth) ; cf. ch. vii. 12. *That thou canst not know them (lô thêdâ)*; literally, *she knows not.* The elliptical form of this sentence in the original leaves it open to various inter-pretations. It seems to refer to the way of life ; she knows not the way of life, *i.e.* she does not regard or perceive the way of life. The verb *yâdā* often has this meaning. The meaning may be obtained by supplying *mah*, equivalent to *quicquam,* " anything," as in ch. ix. 13, " She knows not anything," *i.e.* she knows nothing. The objection to this is that it travels unnecessarily out of the sentence to find the object which ought rather to be supplied from the context. The object may possibly be the staggering of her feet : she staggers hither and thither with-out her perceiving it (Delitzsch) ; or it may, lastly, be indefinite : she knows not whither her steps conduct her (Wordsworth and Zöckler).

Vers. 7—14.—The ruinous consequences of indulgence in illicit pleasures.

Ver. 7.—The subject of which the teacher is treating demands the utmost attention of youth. Enough, it might be supposed, had been said to deter from intercourse with the " strange woman." She has been portrayed in her real colours, plunging recklessly into ruin herself, and carrying her victims with her ; deceitful, full of intrigues, neither walking in nor knowing the way of life. But the warning is amplified and made more impressive. There is another side of the picture, the complete bodily and temporal ruin of her victim. The *argumentum ad hominem* is applied. There is an appeal to personal interest in the details which follow, which ought not to fail in holding youth back. The form of the address which is repeated is very similar to that in ch. vii. 24. The plural form, " O ye children " (cf. ch. iv. 1 and vii. 24), immediately passes into the singular for the reason mentioned before,

that, though the address is made to all, yet each individually is to apply it to himself.

Ver. 8.—**Remove thy way far from her.** In other words, this is the same as St. Paul counsels, " Flee fornication " (1 Cor. vi. 14). *From her (mêâlĕyâh ; desuper ea).* The term conveys the impression that the youth has come within the compass of her temptations, or that in the highest degree he is liable to them. The Hebrew *mêâl,* compounded of *min* and *al,* and meaning " from upon," being used of persons or things which go away *from* the place *in* or *upon* which they had been. **And come not nigh the door of her house;** *i.e.* shun the very place where she dwells. " Be so far from coming into her chamber as not to come near the door of her house " (Patrick). She and her house are to be avoided as if they were infected with some mortal disease. The old proverb quoted by Muffet is applicable—

" He that would no evil do
  Must do nothing that 'longeth [*i.e.* be-longeth] thereto."

Ver. 9.—The reasons why the harlot is to be avoided follow in rapid succession. **Lest thou give thine honour unto others, and thy years unto the cruel.** The word rendered " honour " (Hebrew, *hôd*) is not so much reputation, as the English implies, as " the *grace* and *freshness* of youth." It is so used in Hos. xiv. 6; Dan. x. 8. The Vulgate renders " honour," and the LXX., ζώη, " life." *Hôd* is derived from the Arabic word signifying " to lift one's self up," and then " to be eminent, beautiful." *Thy years;* i.e. the best and most vigorous, and hence the most useful and valuable, years of life. *Unto the cruel* (Hebrew, *l'ăk'zârî*) ; literally, *to the cruel one;* but the adjective *âkzârî* is only found in the singular, and may be here used in a collective sense as designating the *entourage* of the harlot, her associates who prey pitilessly on the youth whom they bring within the range of her fascinations. So Delitzsch. It seems to be so understood by the LXX., which reads ἀνελεήμοσιν, *immitentibus;* but not so by the Vulgate, which adheres to the singular, *crudeli.* If we adhere to the gender of the adjective *âkzârî,* which is masculine, and to its number, it may designate the husband of the adulteress, who will deal mercilessly towards the paramour of his wife. So Zöck-ler. Again, it may refer, notwithstanding the gender, to the harlot herself (so Vatablus and Holden), who is cruel, who has no love for the youth, and would see him perish without pity. The explanation of Stuart and others, including Ewald, that the " cruel one " is the purchaser of the punished adul-terer, is without foundation or warrant, since there is no historical instance on record where the adulterer was reduced to slavery, and the punishment inflicted by the Mosaic code was not slavery, but death (Numb. xx. 10; Deut. xxii. 22), and, as it appears from Ezek. xvi. 40 and John viii. 5, death from stoning. The adjective *ākzâr*, like its equivalent *ākzâr*, is derived from the verb *kâzar*, "to break," and occurs again in ch. xi. 17; xii. 10; xvii. 11. The moral of the warning is a wasted life.

Ver. 10.—Another temporal consequence of, and deterrent against, a life of profligacy. **Lest strangers be filled with thy wealth; and thy labours be in the house of a stranger.** The margin reads, "thy strength" for "thy wealth," but the text properly renders the original *kôākh*, which means "substance," "wealth," "riches"—the youth's possessions in money and property (Delitzsch). The primary meaning of the word is "strength" or "might," as appears from the verb *kâkhākh*, "to exert one's self," from which it is derived, but the parallel *ātsâbĕykâ*, "thy toils," rendered "thy labours," determines its use in the secondary sense here. Compare the similar passage in Hos. vii. 9, "Strangers have devoured his strength [*kôākh*, i.e. 'his possessions'], and he knoweth it not" (see also Job vi. 22). *Kôākh* is the concrete product resulting from the abstract strength or ability when brought into action. *Thy labours* (*ātsâbĕykâ*); i.e. thy toils, the product of laborious toil, that which you have gotten by the labour of your hands, and earned with the sweat of your brow. Fleischer compares the Italian *i miri sudori*, and the French *mes sueurs*. The singular *ĕtsĕv* signifies "heavy toilsome labour," and the plural *ătsâvim*, "labours," things done with toil, and so the idea passes to the resultant of the labour. Compare the very similar expression in Ps. cxxvii. 2, *lĕkhĕm nâătsâvim*, equivalent to "bread obtained by toilsome labour;" Authorized Version, "the bread of sorrows." The Authorized Version properly supplies the verb "be" against those (*e.g.* Holden *et alii*) who join on "thy labours" to the previous verb "be filled," as an accusative, and render, "and with thy labours in the house of a stranger." So also the LXX. and the Vulgate, "and thy labours come" (ἔλθωσι, LXX.) or "be" (*sint*, Vulgate) "to the house of strangers" (εἰς οἴκους ἀλλοτρίων) or, "in a strange house" (*in aliena domo*). In the latter case the Vulgate is wrong, as *nôk'ri* in the phrase *bĕyth nŏk'ri* is always personal (Delitzsch), and should be rendered, as in the Authorized Version, "in the house of a stranger." The meaning of the verse is that a life of impurity transfers the profligate's substance, his wealth and possessions, to others, who will be satiated at his expense, and, being strangers, are indifferent to his ruin.

Ver. 11.—The last argument is the mental anguish which ensues when health is ruined and wealth is squandered. **And thou mourn at the last, when thy flesh and thy body are consumed.** The Hebrew *v'nâhāmtâ* is rather "and thou groan." It is not the plaintive wailing or the subdued grief of heart which is signified, but the loud wail of lamentation, the groaning indicative of intense mental suffering called forth by the remembrance of past folly, and which sees no remedy in the future. The verb *nâhām* occurs again in ch. xxviii. 15, where it is used of the roaring of the lion, and the cognate noun *nāhām* is met with in ch. xix. 12 and xx. 2 in the same sense. By Ezekiel it is used of the groaning of the people of Jerusalem when they shall see their sanctuary profaned, and their sons and their daughters fall by the sword, and their city destroyed (Ezek. xxiv. 23). Isaiah (v. 29, 30) applies it to the *roaring* of the sea. The Vulgate reproduces the idea in *gemas*, equivalent to "and thou groan." The LXX. rendering, καὶ μεταμεληθήσῃ, "and thou shalt repent," arising from the adoption of a different pointing, *nikhāmtâ*, from the niph. *nikhām*, "to repent," for *nâhāmtâ*, to some extent expresses the sense. *At the last;* literally, *at thine end;* i.e. when thou art ruined, or, as the teacher explains, *when thy flesh and thy body are consumed.* The expression, "thy flesh and thy body," here stands for the whole body, the body in its totality, not the body and the soul, which would be different. Of these two words "the flesh" (*bâsâr*) rather denotes the flesh in its strict sense as such (cf. Job xxxi. 31; xxxiii. 21), while "body" (*sh'ĕr*) is the flesh adhering to the bones. Gesenius regards them as synonymous terms, stating, however, that *sh'ĕr* is the more poetical as to use. The word *bâsâr* is used to denote the whole body in ch. xiv. 30. It is clear that, by the use of these two terms here, the teacher is following a peculiarity observable elsewhere in the Proverbs, of combining two terms to express, and so to give force to, one idea. The expression describes "the utter destruction of the libertine" (Umbreit). This destruction, as further involving the ruin of the soul, is described in ch. vi. 32, "Whoso committeth adultery with a woman lacketh understanding; he that doeth it destroyeth his own soul (*nephesh*)" (cf. ch. vii. 22, 23).

Ver. 12.—Self-reproach accompanies the unavailable groaning. **And say, How have I hated instruction, and my heart despised reproof!** *i.e.* how could it ever come to pass that I have acted in such a senseless and inexcusable manner, that I have hated instruction (*musar, disciplina,* παιδεία), the warning voice which dissuaded me from going with the harlot, and in my heart despised, *i.e.* rejected inwardly, whatever my outward demeanour may have been, the reproof which followed after I had been with her! *Despised* (*nâats*), as in ch. i. 30; comp. also ch. xv. 5, "A fool despiseth his father's instructions."

Ver. 13.—**And have not obeyed the voice of my teachers, nor inclined mine ear to them that instructed me.** The ruined profligate admits he was not without teachers and advisers, but that he gave no heed to their warnings and reproofs. *Have not obeyed the voice* (*lô-shâmá'ti b'kôl*). The same phrase occurs in Gen. xxvii. 13; Exod. xviii. 19; Deut. xxvi. 14; 2 Sam. xii. 18. The verb *shâmā* is primarily "to hear," and then "to obey," "to give heed to," like the Greek ἀκούω.

Ver. 14.—**I was almost in all evil in the midst of the congregation and assembly;** *i.e.* such was my shamelessness that there was scarcely any wickedness which I did not commit, unrestrained even by the presence of the congregation and assembly. The fact which the ruined youth laments is the extent and audacity of his sins. It is not that he accuses himself of hypocrisy in religion (Delitzsch), but he adds another element in his career of vice. He has disregarded the warnings and reproofs of his teachers and friends; but more, the presence of the congregation of God's people, a silent but not a less impressive protest, had no restraining effect upon him. The words, "the congregation and assembly" (Hebrew, *kâhâl v'êdâh*), seem to be used to heighten the conception, rather than to express two distinct and separate ideas, since we find them both used interchangeably to designate the congregation of the Israelites. The radical conception of *kâhâl* ("congregation") is the same as that of the LXX. ἐκκλησία and Vulgate *ecclesia*, viz. the congregation looked upon from the point of its being called together, *kâhâl* being derived from *kâhāl*, which in hiph. is equivalent to "to call together," while that of *êdâh* is the congregation looked at from the point of its having assembled *êdâh* being derived from *yâad*, in niph. equivalent to "to come together." The latter will therefore stand for any assembly of people specially convened or coming together for some definite object, like the LXX. συναγώγη and the Vulgate *synagoga*. The term *êdâh* is, however, used in a technical sense as signifying the *seventy elders*, or senators, who judged the people (see Numb. xxv. 7; xxxv. 12). Rabbi Salomon so explains *hâêdâh* as "the congregation," in Josh. xx. 6 and Numb. xxvii. 21. Other explanations, however, have been given of these words. Zöckler takes *kâhâl* as the convened council of elders acting as judges (Deut. xxxiii. 4, 5), and *êdâh* as the con-

course (*cœtus*) of the people executing the condemning sentence (Numb. xv. 15; cf. Ps. vii. 7), and renders, "Well nigh had I fallen into utter destruction in the midst of the assembly and the congregation." Fleischer, Vatablus, and Bayne take much the same view, looking upon *râ* ("evil," Authorized Version) as "punishment," *i.e.* the evil which follows as a consequence of sin—a usage supported by 2 Sam. xvi. 18; Exod. v. 19; 1 Chron. vii. 23; Ps. x. 6—rather than as evil *per se*, i.e. that which is morally bad, as in Exod. xxxii. 22. Aben Ezra considers that the *perfect* is used for the *future*; "In a little time I shall be involved in all evil;" *i.e.* punishment, which is looked forward to prospectively. For "almost" (*kı̄-mat*, equivalent to "within a little," "almost," "nearly"), see Gen. xxvi. 10; Ps. lxxiii. 2; cxix. 87.

Vers. 15—19.—*Commendation of tne chaste intercourse of marriage.* In this section the teacher passes from admonitory warnings against unchastity to the commendation of conjugal fidelity and pure love. The allegorical exposition of this passage, current at the period of the Revision of the Authorized Version in 1612, as referring to liberality, is not *ad rem.* Such an idea had no place certainly in the teacher's mind, nor is it appropriate to the context, the scope of which is, as we have seen, to warn youth against indulgence in illicit pleasures, by pointing out the terrible consequences which follow, and to indicate, on the other hand, in what direction the satisfaction of natural wants is to be obtained, that so, the heart and conscience being kept pure, sin and evil may be avoided.

Ver. 15.—**Drink waters out of thine own cistern,** etc.; *i.e.* in the wife of your own choice, or in the legitimate sphere of marriage, seek the satisfaction of your natural impulses. The pure, innocent, and chaste nature of such pleasures is appropriately compared with the pure and wholesome waters of the cistern and the wellspring. The "drinking" carries with it the satisfying of a natural want. Agreeably with oriental and scriptural usage, "the wife" is compared with a "cistern" and "well." Thus in the Song of Solomon the "bride" is called "a spring shut up, a fountain sealed" (Song of Sol. iv. 12). Sarah is spoken of under exactly the same figure that is used here, viz. the *bôr*, or "cistern," in Isa. li. 1. The figure was not confined to women, however, as we find Judah alluded to as "waters" in Isa. xlviii. 1,

and Jacob or Israel so appearing in the prophecy of Balaam (Numb. xxiv. 7). The
people are spoken of by David as they that
are "of the fountain of Israel" (Ps. lxviii.
26). A similar imagery is employed in the
New Testament of the wife. The apostles
St. Paul and St. Peter both speak of her as
"the vessel (τὸ σκεῦος)" (see 1 Thess. iv. 4
and 1 Pet. iii. 7). The forms of the original,
b'or and *b'er*, standing respectively for "cistern" and "well," indicate a common derivation from *bâar*, "to dig." But *bôr* is an
artificially constructed reservoir or cistern,
equivalent to the Vulgate *cisterna*, and
LXX. ἄγγειος, while *b'êr* is the natural spring
of water, equivalent to the Vulgate *putens*.
So Aben Ezra, who says, on Lev. ii. 36,
"*Bôr* is that which catches the rain, while
b'êr is that from within which the water
wells up." This explanation, however, does
not entirely cover the terms as used here.
The "waters" (Hebrew, *mâyim*) may be the
pure water conveyed into the cistern, and
not simply the water which is caught in its
descent from heaven. The parallel term,
"running waters" (Hebrew, *nôz'lim*), describes the flowing limpid stream fit, like the
other, for drinking purposes. A similar use
of the terms is made in the Song of Sol. iv.
15, "a well of living waters (*b'êr mayim
khayyim*) and streams (*v'noz'lim*) from Lebanon." It may be remarked that the allusion
to the wife, under the figures employed, enhances her value. It indicates the high
estimation in which she is to be held, since
the "cistern" or "well" was one of the
most valuable possessions and adjuncts of
an Eastern house. The teaching of the
passage, in its bearing on the subject of
marriage, coincides with that which is
subsequently put forward by St. Paul, in
1 Cor. vii. 9.

Ver. 16.—**Let thy fountains be dispersed
abroad, and rivers of waters in the streets.**
The figurative language is still continued,
and under the terms "fountains" and "rivers
of waters," are to be understood children,
the legitimate issue of lawful marriage. So
Aben Ezra and the majority of modern
commentators, Schultens, Döderlein, Holden,
Muenscher, Noyes, Wardlaw, etc. The
meaning appears to be, "Let thy marriage
be blessed with many children, who may go
forth abroad for the public good." Other
interpretations have been adopted. Thus:
(1) Delitzsch takes the words "fountains"
and "rivers of waters" as used figuratively
for the procreative power, and renders,
"Shall thy streams flow abroad, and water-
brooks in the streets?" and interprets, "Let
generative power act freely and unrestrainedly within the marriage relation." (2)
Schultens and Dathe, followed by Holden,
regard the verse as expressing a conclusion

on the preceding, "Then shall thy springs
be dispersed abroad, even rivers of waters
in the streets." The objection to this is that
it necessitates the insertion of the copulative
vau (ו) before the verb, *yâphûtzû*, "be dispersed." (3) Zöckler and Hitzig read the
verse interrogatively, "Shall thy streams
flow abroad as water-brooks in the streets?"
on the analogy of ch. vi. 30 and Ps. lvi. 7.
(4) The reading of the LXX., adopted by
Origen, Clemens Alexandrinus, places a
negative before the verb, Μὴ ὑπερεκχείσθω,
i.e. "Let not thy waters flow beyond thy
fountain;" *i.e.* "confine thyself to thy wife."
Fountains. The Hebrew *ma'yânim*, plural
of *mâyân*, derived from *âyin* ("a fountain")
with the formative *men*, is rather a stream
or rill—water flowing on the surface of the
ground. It is used, however, of a fountain
itself in Gen. vii. 11; viii. 2. *Rivers of
waters* (Hebrew, *pâl'gey-mâyim*); rather,
water-courses, or *water-brooks* (cf. Job xxxviii.
25). The *pêlĕg* represents the various streams
into which the *mâyân*, "fountain," divides
itself at its source or in its course. We
find the same expression, *pâl'gey-mâyim*,
used of tears in Ps. cxix. 136; Lam. iii. 48.
It occurs again in our book in ch. xxi. 1,
"The king's heart is in the hand of the
Lord as the rivers of waters (*pâl'gey mâyim*)."
On "abroad" (Hebrew, *khutz*), and "in the
streets" (*r'khôvôth*), see ch. i. 20.

Ver. 17.—**Let them be only thine own,
and not strangers' with thee.** By confining
yourself to chaste intercourse with your
lawful wife, be assured that your offspring
is your own. Promiscuous and unlawful
intercourse throws doubt upon the paternity
of children. Thy children may be thine,
they may belong to another. The natural
pride which is felt in a legitimate offspring
is the motive put forward to commend the
husband to confine himself exclusively to
his wife. Grotius on this verse remarks,
"Ibi sere ubi prolem metas"—"Sow there
where you may reap an offspring." *Them;*
i.e. the children referred to figuratively in
the preceding verse, from which the subject
of this verse is supplied. The repetition of
the pronoun which occurs in the original,
"let them belong to thee, to thee," is emphatic, and exclusive of others. The latter
clause of the verse, "and not strangers' with
thee," covers the whole ground. The idea
of their being strangers' is repulsive, and so
gives further point to the exhortation.

Ver. 18.—**Let thy fountain be blessed:
and rejoice with the wife of thy youth.**
The employment of the ordinary term
"wife" in the second hemistich shows in
what sense the figure which is used has to
be understood. The terms "fountain" and
"wife" denote the same person. The wife
is here called "thy fountain" (Hebrew,

m'kor'ka), just as she has been previously "thine own cistern" (*b'or*) and "thine own well" (*b'er*) in ver. 15. The Hebrew *mâkôr*, "fountain," is derived from the root *kur*, "to dig." The figure seems to determine that the blessing here spoken of consists in the wife being a fruitful mother of children; and hence the phrase means, "Let thy wife be blessed," *i.e.* rendered happy in being the mother of thy children. This is quite consistent with the Hebrew mode of thought. Every Israelitish wife regarded herself, and was regarded by others as "blessed," if she bore children, and unhappy if the reverse were the case. *Blessed;* Hebrew, *bârûk* (Vulgate, *benedicta*), is the kal participle passive of *bârak*, "to bless." Instead of this, the LXX. reads ἴδια, "Let thy fountain be thine own"—a variation which in no sense conveys the meaning of the original. *And rejoice with;* rather, *rejoice in*, the wife being regarded as the sphere within which the husband is to find his pleasure and joy. Umbreit explains, "Let thy wife be extolled." The same construction of the imperative *s'mâkh*, from *sâmakh*, "to be glad, or joyful," with *min*, occurs in Judg. ix. 19; Zeph. iii. 14, etc. The Authorized rendering is, however, favoured by the Vulgate, *lætare cum*, and the LXX., συνευφραίνω μετὰ. Compare the exhortation in Eccles. ix. 9, "Live joyfully with the wife whom thou lovest." *The wife of thy youth* (Hebrew, *îshshâh n'urĕyka*) may mean either (1) the wife to whom thou hast given the fair bloom of thy youth (Umbreit); (2) the wife chosen in thy youth (Delitzsch); or (3) thy youthful wife. The former seems the more probable meaning. Compare the expression, "companion of thy youth," in ch. ii. 17.

Ver. 19.—Let her be as **the loving hind and pleasant roe**. The words in italics do not occur in the original. The expression, "the loving hind and pleasant roe," is, therefore, to be attached to the preceding verse, as carrying on the sense and as descriptive of the grace and fascinating charms of the young wife. As combining these attributes, she is to be the object of thy love and devotion, the one in whom thine affections are to find the fulfilment of their desires. Love and grace are her possessions. *The loving hind* (Hebrew, *ayyĕlĕth âhâvim*); literally, *the hind of loves*, which may be understood, as in the Authorized Version, as pointing to the fondness of this animal for its young, or as descriptive of its beauty and the extreme gracefulness of its form. In this sense the phrase may be rendered, "the lovely hind." The *ayyĕlĕth*, or *ayyâlâh*, feminine of *ayyâl*, "stag," or "hart," was in all probability the gazelle. *Pleasant roe* (Hebrew, *yâalâth khên*); literally, *the ibex of grace*. The particular expression only occurs here in the Bible. The *yâalâth* is the feminine of *yâal*, "the ibex" or "mountain goat" according to Bochart, or the "chamois" according to Gesenius. It does not appear that it is so much "the pleasantness" or amiability of this animal which is here alluded to as its gracefulness of form. As terms of endearment, the words entered largely into the erotic poetry of the East. Thus in the Song of Sol. iv. 5 the bride likens her beloved to "a roe or young hart" (cf. also Song of Sol. iv. 17 and viii. 14), while numerous examples might be quoted from the Arabian and Persian poets. They were also employed sometimes as names for women. Compare the superscription of Ps. xxii., *Ayyeleth hash-shakar*, "Upon the hind of the dawn." **Let her breasts satisfy thee at all times.** The love of the wife is to refresh and fully satisfy the husband. The word *dadeyah*, "her breasts," only occurs here and in Ezek. xxiii. 3, 8, 21, and is equivalent to *dodeyah*, "her love." The marginal reading, "water thee," serves to bring out the literal meaning of the *y'ravvuka*, derived from *ravah*, in kal, "to drink largely," "to be satisfied with drink," but misses the emphatic force of the piel, "to be fully satisfied or satiated." This is expressed very forcibly in the Vulgate rendering, "Let her breasts inebriate thee (*inebrient te*)," which represents the strong influence which the attractions of the wife are to maintain. The LXX., on the other hand, avoiding the rather sensual colouring of the language, substitutes, "May she thine own lead thee, and be with thee always." **And be thou ravished always with her love;** *i.e.* let it intoxicate thee. The teacher, by a bold figure, describes the entire fascination which the husband is to allow the wife to exercise over him. The verb *shâgâh* is "to reel under the influence of wine," and is so used in the succeeding vers. 20 and 23, and ch. xx. 1 and Isa. xxviii. 7. The primary meaning, "to err from the way," scarcely applies here, and does not express the idea of the teacher, which is to describe "an intensity of love connected with the feeling of superabundant happiness" (Delitzsch). The Vulgate, *In amore ejus delectare jugiter*, "In her love delight thyself continually," and the LXX., "For in her love thou shalt be daily engaged," are mere paraphrases.

Vers. 20, 21.—*The adulterer to be restrained by the fact of God's omniscience and the Divine punishment.* Vers. 20 and 21 should apparently be taken together. The teaching assumes a higher tone, and rises from the lower law which regulates fidelity to the wife, based upon personal attractions, to the higher law, which brings the husband's conduct into relation with the duty he owes to Jehovah. Not merely is his conduct to be regulated by love and affection alone, but it is to be fashioned by the reflection or consciousness that the Supreme Being presides over all, and takes cognizance of human action. Without losing sight that the marriage contract has its own peculiar obligations, the fact is insisted upon that all a man's ways are open to the eyes of the Lord.

Ver. 20.—**And why**; *i.e.* what inducement is there, what reason can be given, for conjugal infidelity, except the lewd and immoral promptings of the lower nature, except sensuality in its lowest form? **Ravished.** The verb *shâgâh* recurs, but in a lower sense, as indicating "the foolish delirium of the libertine hastening after the harlot" (Zöckler). **With a strange woman** (Hebrew, *b'zarah*); *i.e.* with a harlot. On *zârâh*, see ch. ii. 16 and vii. 5. The *b'* (בְ) localizes the sources of the intoxication. **Embrace** (Hebrew, *t'khâb-bêk*). On this verb, see ch. iv. 8. **The bosom of a stranger** (Hebrew, *khêh nŏk'riyyâh*). A parallel expression having the same force as its counterpart. The more usual form of *khêk* is *khêyk*, and means "the bosom" of a person. In ch. xvi. 33 it is used of the *lap*, and in ch. xvii. 23 and xxi. 14 for the *bosom* or *folds* of a garment.

Ver. 21.—**For the ways of man are before the eyes of the Lord.** The obvious meaning here is that as "the eyes of the Lord are in every place, beholding the evil and the good" (ch. xv. 3), there is no possibility of any act of immorality escaping God's notice. The consciousness of this fact is to be the restraining motive, inasmuch as he who sees will also punish every transgression. The great truth acknowledged here is the omniscience of God, a truth which is borne witness to in almost identical language in Job: "For his eyes are upon the ways of man, and he seeth all his goings" (Job xxxiv. 21; cf. xxiv. 23 and xxxi. 4). So Hanani the seer says to Asa King of Judah, "For the eyes of the Lord run to and fro throughout the whole earth" (2 Chron. xvi. 9); and Jehovah says, in Jeremiah, "For mine eyes are upon all their ways, they are not hid from my face, neither is their iniquity hid from mine eyes" (Jer. xvi. 17; cf. xxxii. 29); and again, in Hosea, "They are before my face" (Hos. vii. 2), and the same truth is re-echoed in the Epistle to the Hebrews, in all probability gathered from our passage, "All things are naked and opened unto the eyes of him with whom we have to do" (Heb. iv. 13). *The ways of man*; i.e. the conduct of any individual man or

woman; *ish*, "man," being used generically. *Are before the eyes of the Lord*; i.e. are an object on which Jehovah fixes his gaze and scrutiny. **And he pondereth all his goings.** The word "he pondereth" is in the original *m'phâllês*, the piel participle of *phillês*, piel of the unused kal, *pâlâs*, and appears to be properly rendered in the Authorized Version. This verb, however, has various meanings: (1) to make level, or prepare, as in ch. iv. 26 and v. 6; (2) to weigh, or consider accurately, in which sense it is used here. So Gesenius, Lee, Buxtorf, and Davidson. Jehovah not only sees, but weighs all that a man does, wheresoever he be, and will apportion rewards and punishments according to a man's actions (Patrick). The German commentators, Delitzsch and Zöckler, however, look upon the word as indicating the overruling providence of God, just as the former part of the verse refers to his omniscience, and render, "he marketh out," in the sense that the Lord makes it possible for a man to walk in the way of uprightness and purity. There is nothing inherently objectionable in this view, since experience shows that the world is regulated by the Divine government, but it loses sight to some extent of the truth upon which the teacher appears to be insisting, which is that evil actions are visited with Divine retribution.

Vers. 22, 23.—*The fearful end of the adulterer.* From the universal statement of God's omniscience and the Divine judgment, the teacher passes to the fate of the profligate. His end is inevitable ruin and misery. The deep moral lesson conveyed is that sin carries with it its own Nemesis. Adultery and impurity, like all sin of which they are forms, are retributive. The career of the adulterer is a career begun, continued, and ended in folly (comp. ch. i. 31, 32; ii. 5; xviii. 7; xxix. 6; and Ps. ix. 15).

Ver. 22.—**His own iniquities shall take the wicked himself;** *i.e.* his manifold sins shall overtake and arrest him. The imagery is borrowed from the snare of the fowler. The emphatic form of the original, "His sins shall overtake him, the impious man," point conclusively to the adulterer. It is "his" sins that shall overtake *him*, not those of another, and they shall fall upon his own head; and further, his character is depicted in the condemning clause, "the impious man;" for such he is. *Shall take.* The verb *lâkâd* is literally "to take or catch animals in a snare or net," properly "to strike with a net." The wicked man becomes entangled and caught in his own sins; he is struck down and captured by them, just as the prey is struck by the snare of the fowler. The verb is, of course, used metaphorically, as in Job v. 13. *The wicked* (Hebrew, *eth-hârâsâ*); in the original introduced as explanatory of the object, "him." **And he shall be holden with the cords of his sins.** The Authorized Version follows the LXX. and Vulgate in rendering "his sins," instead of the original "his sin" (*khāttâtho*). It is not so much every sin of man which shall hold him, though this is true, as the particular sin treated of in the address, viz. adultery, which shall do this. The expression, "the cords of his sin" (Hebrew, *khāvley khāttâtho*), means the cords which his sin weaves around him. Nothing else will be requisite to bind and hold him fast for punishment (cf. "cords of vanity," in Isa. v. 18).

Ver. 23.—**He shall die without instruction.** The phrase, "without instruction," is in the original *b'eyu musar*, literally, "in there not being instruction." The obvious meaning is, because he gave no heed to instruction. So Aben Ezra and Gersom. The Authorized Version is at least ambiguous, and seems to imply that the adulterer has been without instruction, without any to reprove or counsel him. But such is not the case. He has been admonished of the evil consequences of his sin, but to these warnings he has turned a deaf ear, and the teacher says therefore he shall die. The Vulgate supports this explanation, *quia non habuit disciplinam* "because he did not entertain or use instruction." In the LXX. the idea is enlarged, "He shall die together with those who have no instruction (μετὰ ἀπαιδεύτων)." The *b'* (ב) in *b'eyn* is causal, and equivalent to *propter*, as in Gen. xviii. 28; Jer. xvii. 3. A similar statement is found in Job iv. 21, "They die even without wisdom," *i.e.* because they have disregarded the lessons of wisdom; and Job xxxvi. 12, "They shall die without knowledge." **And in the greatness of his folly he shall go astray;** better, as Delitzsch, "He shall stagger to ruin." The verb *shâgâh* is used as in vers. 19 and 20, but with a deeper and more dread significance. A climax is reached in the manner in which the end of the adulterer is portrayed. His end is without a gleam of hope or satisfaction. With an understanding darkened and rendered callous by unrestrained indulgence in lust, and by folly which has reached its utmost limits and cannot, as it were, be surpassed, in that it has persistently and wilfully set aside and scorned wisdom and true happiness, the adulterer, like the drunkard, who is oblivious of the danger before him, shall stagger to ruin.

HOMILETICS.

Ver. 15.—*Home joys.* I. THE HOME IS A DIVINE INSTITUTION OF THE FIRST IMPORTANCE FOR THE WELFARE OF MANKIND. Here and throughout the Bible the sanctity of the home is insisted on as something to be guarded inviolably. It is evident that this beautiful institution is in harmony with our nature. To live according to nature is not to indulge ill-regulated passions, to follow chance impulses, to subordinate reason and conscience to instinct and appetite. It is to live so as to secure the harmonious working of our whole nature and of the general body of mankind. Thus regarded, family life is natural; it falls in best with the requirements of the race, it ministers best to its advancement. Polygamy is always degrading. As men rise in the moral scale they cast it off. The home is the foundation of the state. Where home life is most corrupt social and political institutions are in greatest danger. The homes of England are the surest guardians of her internal order and peace. May no corrupt casuistry ever dare to lay its foul finger on these holy shrines! The worst fruits of atheism and of the confessional are seen in specious pretexts for committing that horrible sacrilege.

II. IN ORDER TO PROTECT THE HOME GOD HAS MADE IT TO BE A FOUNTAIN OF PURE AND WHOLESOME JOYS. They who break through the restraints of home life in the feverish thirst for illicit delights little know what joys they are losing. The poison-fruits of a pandemonium let a blight fall on the sweet, fresh beauty of what might have been a very garden of Eden. For the restraints which look to libertines so irksome are just the very conditions of the most lasting, most satisfying, most wholesome of human joys. The strong love of husband and wife, the parents' pleasure in their children, the innumerable little interests of the home circle, and all that is typified by the "fireside," are delights unknown to men who profess to make the pursuit of pleasure their aim in life.

> "The first sure symptom of a mind in health
> Is rest of heart and pleasure felt at home."

III. TO BE PRESERVED IN THEIR INTEGRITY, THE HOME JOYS MUST BE CAREFULLY GUARDED AND REVERENTLY CHERISHED. The serpent is in the garden; beware of its wiles. Temptations seek to break up the confidence and peace of the family circle. Not only must gross infidelity be shunned as a deadly sin, but all approaches to a breach of domestic sanctity must be dreaded. Levity, as well as immorality, may go far to spoil the waters of the purest fountain of delight. Mere indifference may wreck the home joys. These joys must be cherished. Courtship should not end with the wedding-day. Husbands and wives should beware of neglecting mutual respect and consideration under the influence of familiarity. Why should a man be more rude to his wife than to any other woman? Surely marriage is not designed to destroy courtesy. There should be an element of reverence in wedded love. Mutual sympathy —each taking interest in the occupations and cares of the other; mutual confidence— the avoidance of secrets between husband and wife on the mistaken plea of sparing pain; and mutual forbearance, are requisites for the preservation of the sweetness of the fountains of home joy.

Ver. 21.—*Under the eyes of God.* I. WE ARE ALWAYS UNDER THE WATCHFUL EYES OF GOD. God is no epicurean Divinity, retreating far above mundane affairs in celestial seclusion. He is not indifferent to what goes on in this little world. He is watchful and observant. This fact may not affect us much while we think of it in the general. But we should observe that God's watchfulness is directed to all particular, individual objects. He looks at each of us, at the smallest of our concerns. It is the property of an infinite mind thus to reach down to the infinitely small, as well as to rise to the infinitely great. Consider, then, that God searches us through and through. There is no dark cranny of the soul into which his keen penetrating light does not fall, no locked secret which does not open up freely to his magisterial warrant. We may hide the thought of God from our own minds, but we cannot hide ourselves from the sight of God. Now, what God notices chiefly in us is our conduct—our "ways," "goings." Mere profession counts for nothing with the All-seeing. Opinions, feelings, resolutions, are of secondary moment. God takes inquisition chiefly of what we do, whither our life is tending, what are the actions of the inner as well as of the outer man. But let us remember that God does all this in no mere prying curiosity, in no cruel desire to "find us out" and convict us of wrong. He does it of right, for he is our Judge; he does it with holy ends, for he is holy; he does it in love, for he is our Father.

II. THE CONSCIOUSNESS OF THE DIVINE OVERSIGHT SHOULD POWERFULLY AFFECT ALL OUR CONDUCT. 1. It should make us *true.* What is the use of paltry devices for the deception of men when the only question of consequence concerning the treatment of our conduct is—How will God regard it? What folly to wear a mask if he sees behind it! The gaze of God should shame and burn all lies out of the soul. 2. It should make us *dread to do wrong.* An Eastern legend tells how one stole a jewel called "the eye of God," but though he fled far with his treasure and hid in dark caverns, he was tortured by the piercing light that it threw out till, unable to endure the horror of it, he gave himself up to justice. We all have the eye of God on our ways. Let us beware that we never go where we should not wish him to see us. 3. It should lead to *confession of sin.* If God knows all, is it not best to make a clean breast of it, and humble ourselves before him? We cannot hide or cloke our sins from God. It is foolish to attempt to do so. But let us be thankful that we cannot. While we try to hide them they only scorch our own bosom. If we confess them, "he is faithful and just to forgive us our sins." 4. It should induce *confidence in God.* It is sometimes a relief to know that the worst is out. God knows all. Yet he endures us, yet he loves us still. He who thus watches looks upon us as a mother regards her child, grieving for what is wrong, but tenderly seeking to save and protect us from all harm. Why should we fear the gaze of God? His sleepless eye is our great security (see 2 Chron. xvi. 9). 5. It should incline us to *faithful service.* We should learn to be ashamed of the eye-service of men-pleasers, and seek to win the approval of our rightful Lord. He is no hard tyrant. When we try to please him, though ever so imperfectly, he *is* pleased, and will say, "Well done, good and faithful servant." May it be our aim to live, as Milton resolved to do when considering his life on his twenty-third birthday—

"As ever in my great Taskmaster's eye."

Ver. 22.—*Cords of sin.* I. THE SINNER IS IN BONDAGE. Such a condition is not expected when a man freely gives the reins to his passions, and weakly yields himself to temptation. On the contrary, he supposes that he is enjoying a larger liberty than they possess who are constrained to walk in the narrow path of righteousness. Moreover, even when this shocking condition is reached, he is slow to admit its existence. He will not confess his bondage; perhaps he scarcely feels it. Thus the Jews were indignant in rejecting any such notion when our Lord offered deliverance from the slavery of sin (John viii. 33). But this only proves the bondage to be the greater. The worst degradation of slavery is that it so benumbs the feelings and crushes the manliness of its victims, that some of them do not notice the yoke that would gall the shoulders of all men who truly appreciated their condition. The reality of the bondage is soon proved, however, whenever a slave tries to escape. Then the chains of sin are felt to be too strong for the sinner to break. He cries, "O wretched man that I am! who shall deliver me from the body of this death?" (Rom. vii. 24).

II. THE CORDS THAT BIND THE SINNER ARE SPUN OUT OF HIS OWN SINS. Satan does not need to build any massive prison walls, or to call upon Vulcan to forge fetters for his captives. He has but to leave them to themselves, and their own misdeeds will shut them in, as the rank new growth of a tropical forest encloses the rotting trunks of the older trees, from the seed of which it sprang. 1. This results from the *force of habit.* All conduct tends to become permanent. The way wears into ruts. Men become entangled in their own past. 2. This is confirmed by *wilful disregard of saving influences.* If the sinner repented and called for deliverance, he might be saved from the fearful bondage of his sins. But proudly choosing to continue on his own course, he has consented to the tightening of the cords that bind him.

III. CHRIST ALONE CAN LIBERATE FROM THE BONDAGE OF SIN. Left to itself, the slavery will be fatal. The sinner will never be free to live to any good purpose. He will not be able to escape in the day of doom; his own sins will tie him to his fate. In the end they will strangle him. Inasmuch as the cords are spun out of his own conduct, they are part of himself, and he cannot untie their knots or cut their strands. They are stronger than the cords with which Delilah bound Samson, while the helpless, guilty sinner is weaker than the shorn Nazarite. But it is to men in this forlorn condition that the gospel of Christ is proclaimed, with its glorious promise of liberty to the captives (Isa. lxi. 1). Christ brings liberating truth (John viii. 32), redeeming grace, and the saving power of a mighty love,—those attractive "cords of a man" (Hos. xi. 4) which are even stronger than the binding cords of sin.

HOMILIES BY VARIOUS AUTHORS.

Vers. 1—14.—*Meretricious pleasures and their results.* I. GENERAL ADMONITION. (Vers. 1—3.) Similar prefaces to warnings against unchastity are found in ch. vi. 20, etc.; vii. 1, etc. The same forms of *iteration* for the sake of *urgency* are observed. A fresh expression is, "That thy lips may keep insight." That is, let the lessons of wisdom be oft conned over; to keep them on the lips is to "get them by heart." "Consideration" (ver. 2), circumspection, forethought, are peculiarly needed in facing a temptation which wears a fascinating form, and which must be viewed in *results,* if its pernicious quality is to be understood.

II. THE FASCINATION OF THE HARLOT. (Ver. 3; comp. ch. ii. 16.) Her lips are honeyed with compliments and flattery (comp. Cant. iv. 11). Her voice is smoother than oil. A temptation has no power unless it is directed to some weakness in the subject of it, as the spark goes out in the absence of tinder. The harlot's power to seduce lies mainly in that weakest of weaknesses, vanity—at least, in many cases. It is a power in general over the senses and the imagination. And it is the part of the teacher to disabuse these of their illusions. In the word "meretricious" (from the Latin word for "harlot"), applied to spurious art, we have a witness in language to the hollowness of her attractions.

III. THE RESULTS OF VICIOUS PLEASURES. (Vers. 4—6.) They are described in images full of expression. 1. As *bitter* like *wormwood*, which has a bitter, salt taste, and is regarded in the East in the light of poison. Or "like Dead-Sea fruits, which tempt the taste, and turn to ashes on the lips." 2. As of *acute pain*, under the image of a sword, smooth on the surface, with a keen double edge to wound. 3. As *fatal*. The harlot beckons her guests as it were down the deathful way, to *sheôl*, to Hades, the kingdom of the dead. 4. They have *no* good result. Ver. 6, correctly rendered, says, "She measures not the path of life; her tracks are roving, she knows not whither." The picture of a life which *can give no account of itself*, cannot justify itself to reason, and comes to a brutish end.

IV. THE REMOTER CONSEQUENCES OF VICE. (Vers. 7—13.) A gloomy vista opens, in prospect of which the warning is urgently renewed (vers. 7, 8). 1. The *exposure of the detected adulterer*. (Ver. 9.) He exchanges honour and repute for public shame, loses his life at the hands of the outraged husband, or becomes his slave (comp. ch. vi. 34). 2. *The loss of property*. (Ver. 10.) The punishment of adultery under the Law was stoning (Lev. xx. 10; Deut. xxii. 22, *sqq.*). Possibly this might be commuted into the forfeiture of goods and enslavement to the injured husband. 3. *Remorse*. (Vers. 11—14.) Last and worst of all inflictions, from the Divine hand, immediately. In the last stage of consumption the victim of lust groans forth his unavailing sorrow. Remorse, the fearful counterpart of self-respect, is the mind turning upon itself, internal discord replacing the harmony God made. The sufferer accuses himself of *hatred to light*, *contempt of rebuke*, of *disobedience* to voices that were authoritative, of *deafness to warning*. No external condemnation is ever passed on a man which his own conscience has not previously ratified. Remorse is the last witness to Wisdom and her claims. To complete the picture, the miserable man is represented as reflecting that he all but fell into the doom of the public condemnation and the public execution (ver. 14).—J.

Vers. 15—21.—*Fidelity and bliss in marriage.* The counterpart of the foregoing warning against vice, placing connubial joys in the brightest light of poetic fancy.

I. IMAGES OF WIFEHOOD. The wife is described: 1. As a *spring*, and as a cistern. Property in a spring or well was highly, even sacredly, esteemed. Hence a peculiar force in the comparison. The wife is the husband's peculiar delight and property; the source of pleasures of every kind and degree; the fruitful origin of the family (comp. Isa. li. 1; Cant. iv. 12). 2. As "*wife of one's youth.*" (Cf. Deut. xxiv. 5; Eccles. ix. 9.) One to whom the flower of youth and manhood has been devoted. The parallel description is "companion of youth" (ch. ii. 17). Her image, in this case, is associated with the sunniest scenes of experience. 3. As a "*lovely hind, or charming gazelle.*" A favourite Oriental comparison, and embodied in the names *Tabitha* and *Dorcas*, which denote "gazelle." There are numberless uses of the figure in Arabian and Persian poets. The beautiful liquid eye, delicate head, graceful carriage of the creature, all point the *simile*. Nothing can surpass, as a husband's description of a true wife, Wordsworth's exquisite stanza beginning—

> "She was a phantom of delight,
> When first she gleam'd upon my sight;
> A creature not too bright or good
> For human nature's daily food;
> For transient sorrows, simple wiles,
> Praise, blame, love, kisses, tears, and smiles."

II. IMAGES OF THE HUSBAND'S BLISS. 1. It is like taking draughts from a fresh and ever-running stream. There is "continual comfort in a face, the lineaments of gospel books." 2. It is a *peculiar*, a *private possession*. Ver. 16 should be rendered interrogatively; it conveys the contrast of the *profaned* treasures of the unchaste woman's love, and thus fits with ver. 17. The language of lovers finds a true zest in the word, "My own!" Life becomes brutish where this feeling does not exist. 3. Yet it attracts *sympathy, admiration*, and *good will*. Ver. 18 is the blessing wished by the speaker or by any looker-on. Wedding-feasts bring out these feelings; and the happiness and prosperity of married pairs are as little exposed to the tooth of envy as any earthly good. 4. It is *satisfying*; for what repose can be more sweet and secure than that on the bosom of the faithful spouse? It is *enrapturing*, without being enfeebling, unlike those false pleasures, " violent delights with violent endings, that in their triumph die" (ver. 19).

III. CONCLUDING EXHORTATION (ver. 20), founded on the contrast just given. 1. The true rapture (the Hebrew word *shâgâh*, " reel " as in intoxication, repeated) should deter from the false and vicious. 2. To prefer the bosom of the adulteress to that of the true wife is a mark of the most vitiated taste, the most perverted understanding.—J.

Ver. 21.—*God the all-seeing Judge.* " Before Jehovah's eyes are man's paths, and all his tracks he surveys."

I. CYNICAL PROVERBS CONCERNING SECRECY ARE CONDEMNED. Such as " What the eye sees not, the heart does not grieve over; " " A slice from a cut cake is never missed ; " " Never mind so long as you are not found out."

II. NOTHING IS REALLY SECRET OR UNKNOWN. We are naked and open to the eyes of him with whom we have to do. The whisper, the inarticulate thought, will come back one day in thunder.—J.

Vers. 22, 23.—*Vice suicidal.* I. WICKEDNESS (LIKE GOODNESS) HAS UNDESIGNED RESULTS. The good comes back to nestle in the bosom of the giver and the doer. We never do right without invoking a blessing on our own heads. Evil, on the other hand, designed and executed, is like a snare set for one's self, a net in the meshes of which the crafty is entangled, self-overreached.

II. WICKEDNESS AND IGNORANCE ARE IN CLOSE CONNECTION. " He shall die for *want of* instruction "—the correct rendering of ver. 23. Socrates taught that vice was ignorance, virtue identical with knowledge. This, however, ignores the perversity of the will. The Bible ever traces wickedness to *wilful* and inexcusable ignorance.

III. WICKEDNESS IS A KIND OF MADNESS. " Through the greatness of his folly he shall reel about." The word *shâgâh* once more. The man becomes drunk and frenzied with passion, and, a certain point passed, staggers to his end unwitting, careless, or desperate.—J.

Vers. 1—20.—*Victims of vice.* One particular vice is here denounced; it is necessary to warn the young against its snares and sorrows. What is here said, however, of this sin is applicable, in most if not all respects, to any kind of unholy indulgence ; it is an earnest and faithful warning against the sin and shame of a vicious life.

I. ITS SINFULNESS. The woman who is a sinner is a " strange " woman (ver. 3). The temptress is all too common amongst us, but she is *strange* in the sight of God. She is an alien, foreign altogether to his purpose, a sad and wide departure from his thought. And all vice is strange to him ; it is a departure from his thought and from his will ; it is sin in his sight ; it is offensive to him ; he " cannot look on " such iniquity without abhorrence and condemnation. He who is tempted may well say, with the pure-minded and godly Joseph, " How can I do this great wickedness, and sin against God ? "

II. ITS SHAME. It is a shame to a man to allow himself to be deceived by a vain, shallow-minded woman (vers. 3, 4) ; it is a shame to a man to permit a mere selfish temptress to beguile him, to prevent him from entertaining the true and wise thought in his mind, to hinder him by her artifices from reflecting on what is the path of life and what the way of death (ver. 6) ; it is a shame to a man to surrender his manly virtue to one so utterly undeserving of his honour (vers. 7—9). He who yields to the solicitations of the temptress, to the impulses of a vicious nature, is forfeiting his honour, is resigning his true manhood, is a son of shame.

III. ITS FOLLY. (Vers. 15—20.) How senseless is sin ! how stupid is vice ! It embraces a guilty and short-lived pleasure only to reject a pure and lasting joy. Why should men resort to shameful lust when they can be blest with lawful and honourable love ? Why sink in debauchery when they can walk along those goodly heights of moderation and of pleasures on which God's blessing may be invoked ? Whatever the sense may be (whether of seeing, hearing, etc.), it is the pure pleasure which is not only high and manly, but is also unaccompanied by bitter and accusing thoughts, and is lasting as life itself. Why turn to devour the garbage when "angels' food" is on the table? Vice is the very depth of folly.

IV. Its penalty. This is threefold. 1. Impoverishment (ver. 10). Vice soon scatters a man's fortune. A few years, or even weeks, will suffice for dissipation to run through a good estate. Men "waste their substance in riotous living." 2. Remorse (vers. 11—14). How bitter to the soul the pangs of self-accusation! There is no poisoned dart that wounds the body as the arrow of unavailing remorse pierces the soul. 3. Death (ver. 5, "Her feet go down to death; her steps lay hold on hell"). Death physical and death spiritual are the issue of immorality. The grave is dug, the gates of the City of Sorrow are open, for the lascivious, the drunken, the immoral.—C.

Ver. 11 (first clause).—*Mourning at the last.* What multitudes of men and women have there been who, on beds of pain, or in homes of poverty, or under strong spiritual apprehension, have "mourned at the last"! After tasting and "enjoying the pleasures of sin for a season," they have found that iniquity must meet its doom, and they have "mourned at the last." Sin makes fair promises, but breaks its word. It owns that there is a debt due for guilty pleasure, but it hints that it will not send in the bill for many years;—perhaps never: but that account has to be settled, and they who persist in sinful indulgence will find, when it is too late, that they have to "mourn at the last." This is true of—

I. Slothfulness. Very pleasant to be idling when others are busy, to be following the bent of our own fancy, dallying with the passing hours, amusing ourselves the whole day long, the whole year through; but there is retribution for wasted hours, for mis-spent youth, for negligent and idle manhood, to be endured further on; there is self-reproach, condemnation of the good and wise, an ill-regulated mind, straitened means if not poverty,—mourning at the last.

II. Intemperance. Very tempting may be the jovial feast, very fascinating the sparkling cup, very inviting the hilarity of the festive circle; but there is the end of it all to be taken into account, not only to-morrow's pain or lassitude, but the forfeiture of esteem, the weakening of the soul's capacity for pure enjoyment, the depravation of the taste, the encircling round the spirit of those cruel fetters which "at the last" hold it in cruel bondage.

III. Lasciviousness. (See previous homily.)

IV. Worldliness. There is a strong temptation presented to men to throw themselves into, so as to be absorbed by, the affairs of time and sense—business, politics, literature, art, one or other of the various amusements which entertain and gratify. This inordinate, excessive, unqualified devotion to any earthly pursuit, while it is to be distinguished from abandonment to forbidden pleasure, is yet wrong and ruinous. It is *wrong*, for it leaves out of reckoning the supreme obligation—that which we owe to him in whom we live and move and have our being, and who has redeemed us with his own blood. It is *ruinous*, for it leaves us (1) without the heritage we were meant to have, and may have, in God, in Jesus Christ and his blessed service and salvation; (2) unprepared for the other and larger life which is so near to us, and to which we approach by every step we take. However pleasant be the pursuits we engage in or the prizes we win, we shall wake one day from our dream with shame and fear; we shall "mourn at the last."—C.

Ver. 21.—*Man in God's view.* This verse is added as a powerful reason why the worst sins should be avoided. A man under temptation may well address himself thus—

> "Nor let my weaker passions dare
> Consent to sin; for God is there."

I. The varied energies and actions of man. Many are "the ways of man;" "all his goings" cannot easily be told. There is (1) his innermost thought starting in his mind; (2) then his feeling or desire in some direction; (3) then his resolution, the decision of his will; (4) then his planning and arranging; (5) then his consultation and co-operation with others; (6) then his execution. Or we may consider the variety of his actions by regarding them as (1) beginning and ending with himself; (2) affecting his immediate circle, his own family; (3) reaching and influencing his neighbours; (4) acting upon those who will come after him. The forms of human activity are indefinitely numerous—so complex is his nature, so various are his relations to his kind and the world in which he lives.

II. GOD'S NOTICE OF ALL OUR DOINGS. "The ways of a man are before the eyes of the Lord." Every thought is thought, every feeling felt, every resolve made, every plan formed, every word spoken, every deed done, under his all-observing eye. "Neither is there any creature that is not manifest in his sight, but *all* things are naked and opened unto the eyes of him with whom we have to do" (Heb. iv. 13; see 2 Chron. xvi. 9; Job xxxi. 4; Ps. cxxxix. 2—12; and ch. xv. 3). The eyes of the Lord not only cover the earth and the heavens, but they look everywhere within; through the thick curtains of the night his own hand has spread, and through the thickest folds our hand can draw, and through the walls of our human frame into the inner chambers and darkest recesses of our souls.

III. GOD'S MEASURE OF OUR DOINGS. "He *pondereth* all his goings." God weighs all that he sees in the scales of his Divine wisdom and righteousness. He marks every thought, word, deed; and he estimates their worth, their excellency or their guilt. Never any way taken, any course entered upon, but *all* the motives which led to its choice and execution are before the mind of God, and are accepted or are blamed by him. And this being so, there must be—

IV. GOD'S REMEMBRANCE OF OUR PAST AS WELL AS HIS OBSERVATION OF OUR PRESENT LIFE. For the Omniscient One cannot forget; and it may be that, in some way unknown to us, but quite in accordance with some ascertained facts, all our past actions are spread out before his sight in some part of his universe. Certainly the effects of all we have done abide, either in our own character and life or in those of other men. Our ways, past and present, *are before him*; he is estimating the moral character, for good or ill, of *all* our goings.

Therefore: 1. In view of all our guilt, let us seek his mercy in Christ Jesus. For it is a truth consistent with the foregoing, that, if there be repentance and faith, all our sins shall "be cast into the depths of the sea" (Amos vii. 19). God will "hide his face from our sins, and blot out our iniquities" (Ps. li. 9). 2. In view of God's observation and judgment, let us strive to please him. If we yield our hearts to himself and our lives to his service, if we accept eternal life at his hands through Jesus Christ, and then seek to be and to do what is right in his sight, we shall do that which he will look upon with Divine approval, with fatherly delight (Gal. iv. 1; Heb. xi. 5; xiii. 16; 1 Pet. ii. 20, etc.).—C.

Vers. 22, 23.—*The end of an evil course.* There are two fearful evils in which impenitent sin is sure to end, two classes of penalty which the wrong-doer must make up his mind to pay. He has to submit to—

I. AN INWARD TYRANNY OF THE MOST CRUEL CHARACTER. (Ver. 22.) We may never have seen the wild animal captured by the hunter, making violent efforts to escape its toils, failing, desperately renewing the attempt with fierce and frantic struggles, until at length it yielded itself to its fate in sullen despair. But we have witnessed something far more romantic than that. We have watched some human soul caught in the meshes of vice (intemperance, it may be), or entangled in the bonds of sin (coveteousness, it may be), struggling to be free, failing in its endeavour, renewing the attempt with determined eagerness, and failing again, until at length it yields to the foe, vanquished, ruined, lost! "His own iniquities have taken the wicked himself, he is holden in the cords of his sins." 1. Sin hides its tyranny from view; its cords are so carried that they are not seen; nay, they are so wound around the soul that at first they are not felt, and the victim has no notion that he is being enslaved. 2. Gradually and stealthily it fastens its fetters on the soul; *e.g.* intemperance, impurity, untruthfulness, selfishness, worldliness. 3. It finally obtains a hold from which the soul cannot shake itself free; the man is "holden;" sin has him in its firm grip; he is a captive, a spiritual slave. Beside this terrible tyranny, the persistent wrong-doer has to endure—

II. AFTER-CONSEQUENCES YET MORE CALAMITOUS. (Ver. 23.) These are: 1. Death in the midst of folly. "He shall die without instruction," unenlightened by eternal truth, in the darkness of error and sin; he will die, "hoping nothing, believing nothing, and fearing nothing"—nothing which a man should die in the hope of, nothing which a man should live to believe and die in the faith of, nothing which a man should fear, living or dying. He shall die without peace to smooth his dying pillow, without hope to light up his closing eyes. 2. Exclusion from future blessedness through his folly. "In the greatness of his folly he shall go astray." While the simplest wisdom would have led him to seek and find entrance into the City of God, in the greatness of his folly he wanders off to the gates of the City of Sorrow.

1. If the path of folly has been entered upon and is now being trodden, return at once without delay. Further on, perchance a very little further on, it may be too late—the cords of sin may be too strong for the soul to snap. Arise at once, in the strength of the strong Deliverer, and regain the freedom which is being lost. 2. Enter in earliest days the path of spiritual freedom. Bear the blessed yoke of the Son of God, that every other yoke may be broken. Enrol in his ranks whose "service is perfect freedom."—C.

EXPOSITION.

CHAPTER VI.

Vers. 1—35.—The sixth chapter embraces four distinct discourses, each of which is a warning. The subjects treated of are (1) suretyship (vers. 1—5); (2) sloth (vers. 6—11); (3) malice (vers. 12—19); and (4) adultery (ver. 20 to the end). The continuity of the subject treated of in the preceding chapter appears to be somewhat abruptly interrupted to make way for the insertion of three discourses on subjects which apparently have little connection with what precedes and what follows. Their unlooked-for and unexpected appearance has led Hitzig to regard them as interpolations, but it has been conclusively pointed out by Delitzsch that there is sufficient internal evidence, in the grammatical construction, figures, word-formations, delineations, and threatenings, to establish the position that they proceeded from the same hand that composed the rest of the book and to guarantee their genuineness. But another and not less interesting question arises as to whether any connection subsists between these discourses and the subject which they apparently interrupt. Such a connection is altogether denied by Delitzsch, Zöckler, and other German commentators, who look upon them as independent discourses, and maintain that, if there is any connection, it can be only external and accidental. On the other hand, Bishops Patrick and Wordsworth discover an ethical connection which, though not clear at first sight, is not on that account less real or true. The subject treated of in the preceding chapter is the happiness of the married life, and this is imperilled by incautious undertaking of suretyship, and suretyship, it is maintained, induces sloth, while sloth leads to maliciousness. After treating of suretyship, sloth, and malice in succession, the teacher recurs to the former subject of his discourse, viz. impurity of life, against which he gives impressive warnings. That such is the true view there appears little doubt. One vice is intimately connected with another, and the verdict of experience is that a life of idleness is one of the most prolific sources of a life of impurity. Hence we find Ovid saying—

"Quæritur, Ægisthus, quâ re sit factus adulter?
In promptu causa est—desidiosus erat."

"Do you ask why Ægisthus has become an adulterer?
The reason is close at hand—he was full of idleness."

Within the sphere of these discourses themselves the internal connection is distinctly observable, vers. 16—19 being a refrain of vers. 12—15, and the phrase, "to stir up strife," closing each enumeration (see vers. 14 and 19).

Vers. 1—5.—9. *Ninth admonitory discourse. Warning against suretyship.*

Ver. 1.—The contents of this section are

not to be taken so much as an absolute unqualified prohibition of suretyship as counsel directed against the inconsiderate and rash undertaking of such an obligation. There were some occasions on which becoming surety for another was demanded by the laws of charity and prudence, and when it was not inconsistent with the humane precepts of the Mosaic Law as enunciated in Lev. xix. 19. In other passages of our book the writer of the Proverbs lays down maxims which would clearly countenance the practice (ch. xiv. 21; xvii. 17; xviii. 24; xxvii. 10), and in the apocryphal writings the practice is encouraged, if not enjoined (Ecclus. xxix. 14; viii. 13). Notwithstanding this limitation, however, it is observable that suretyship is almost invariably spoken of in terms of condemnation, and the evil consequences which it entailed on the surety may be the reason why it is so frequently alluded to. The teacher refers to the subject in the following passages: here; ch. xi. 15; xvii. 18; xxii. 26; xx. 16; xxvii. 13. **My son.** On this address, see ch. ii. 1; iii. 1, 17. **If thou be surety** (Hebrew, *ĭm-árāvtâ*); literally, *if thou hast become surety*; LXX., ἐὰν ἐγγύσῃ; Vulgate, *si spoponderis.* What the teacher counsels in the present instance is that, if by inadvertence a person has become surety, he should by the most strenuous endeavours prevail on his friend to free him from the bond. The Hebrew verb *árāv* is properly "to mix," and then signifies "to become surety" in the sense of interchanging with another and so taking his place. The frequent mention of suretyship in the Proverbs is alluded to above. The first recorded instances are those where Judah offers to become surety for Benjamin, first to Israel (Gen. xliii. 9), and secondly to Joseph (Gen. xliv. 33). It is singular that it is only once alluded to in the Book of Job, where Job says, "Lay down now, put me in surety with thee; who is he that will strike hands with me?" (Job xvii. 3); and once only, and that doubtfully, in the whole of the Mosaic writings, in the phrase *tesummat yad*, i.e. giving or striking the hand in the case of perjury (Lev. vi. 2). The psalmist refers to it in the words, "Be surety for thy servant for good" (Ps. cxix. 122). It is spoken of twice in Isaiah (xxxviii. 14; xxxvi. 8), once in Ezekiel (xxvii. 27) and in Nehemiah (v. 3), and the cognate noun, *arrabon*, "the pledge," security for payment, is met with in Gen. xxxviii. 17 and 1 Sam. xvii. 18. These scattered notices in the Old Testament show that the practice was always in existence, while the more frequent notices in the Proverbs refer to a condition of society where extended commercial transactions had apparently made it a thing of daily occurrence, and a source of constant danger. In the New Testament one instance of suretyship is found, when St. Paul offers to become surety to Philemon for Onesimus (Philem. 19). But in the language of the New Testament, the purely commercial meaning of the word is transmuted into a spiritual one. The gift of the Spirit is regarded as the *arrabon,* ῤραβών, "the pledge," the earnest of the Christian believer's acceptance with God (2 Cor. i. 22; v. 5; Eph. i. 14). **For thy friend**; Hebrew, *l'rēëka.* The Hebrew *rēëh*, more usually *rēä,* is "the companion or friend," and in this case obviously the debtor for whom one has become surety. The word reappears in ver. 3. The ל (*l'*) prefixed to *rēëh* is the *dativus commodi.* So Delitzsch and others. **If**; not in the original, but rightly inserted. **Thou hast stricken thy hand with a stranger** (Hebrew, *tākā'tâ lāzzâr kāpĕykā*); properly, *thou hast stricken thy hand for a stranger.* The analogous use of *l'* (ל) in *lāzzâr* determines this rendering. As in the corresponding *l'rēëyka*, the ל (*l'*) indicates the person *for* whose benefit the suretyship is undertaken, *i.e.* the debtor, and not the person *with* whom the symbolical act is performed, *i.e.* the creditor. Compare the following passages, though the construction with ל is wanting: "He that is surety for a stranger" (ch. xi. 15); "Take his garment that is surety for a stranger" (ch. xx. 16 and xxvii. 13). "The stranger," *zâr*, is not an alien, or one belonging to another nationality, but simply one extraneous to one's self, and so equivalent to *ākhêr*, "another." The meaning, therefore, seems to be, "If thou hast entered into a bond for one with whom thou art but slightly acquainted." Others (Wordsworth, Plumptre), however, take *zâr* as representing the foreign money-lender. The phrase, "to strike the hand," *tākā kâph*, or simply "to strike," *tākā*, describes the symbolical act which accompanied the contract. *Tākā* is properly "to drive," like the Latin *defigere,* and hence "to strike," and indicates the sharp sound with which the hands were brought into contact. The act no doubt was accomplished before witnesses, and the hand which was stricken was that of the creditor, who thereby received assurance that the responsibility of the debtor was undertaken by the surety. The "striking of the hand" as indicating the completion of a contract is illustrated by the author of the 'Kamoos' (quoted by Lee, on Job xvii. 3), who says, "He struck or clapped to him a sale . . . he struck his hand in a sale, or on his hand . . . he struck his own hand upon the hand of him, and this is among the necessary (transactions) of sale." So among

Western nations the giving of the hand has been always regarded as a pledge of *bona fides.* Thus Menelaus demands of Helena (Euripides, ' Hel.,' 838), Ἐπὶ τοῖσδε νῦν δεξιὰς ἐμῆς θίγε, "Touch my right hand now on these conditions," *i.e.* in attestation that you accept them. In purely verbal agreements it is the custom in the present day for the parties to clasp the hand. A further example may be found in the plighting of troth in the Marriage Service.

Ver. 2.—**Thou art snared with the words cf thy mouth,** etc.; *i.e.* the inevitable consequence of an inconsiderate undertaking of suretyship is that you become entangled and involved by your own promises, and hampered by self-imposed obligations. The Authorized Version rightly regards this as the conclusion. So the Vulgate. Others, however, carry on the hypothesis, and insert *īm,* "if:" "If thou art snared," etc.; but without warrant (Zöckler, Wordsworth, Plumptre). The LXX. throws the thought into the form of a proverb, as "a strong net to a man are his own words." A dist.nction is to be drawn between the verbs rendered "entangled" and "taken;" the former, *yâkôsh,* signifying to be taken unwarily, off one's guard; the latter, *lâkad,* referring, as before observed (cf. ch. v. 22), to the being stricken with the net. They are found in the same collocation in Isa. viii. 15, "Many among them shall be *snared* and *taken.*" The repetition of the phrase, "with the words of thy mouth," is not unintentional or purely rhetorical. It is made, as Delitzsch observes, to bring with greater force to the mind that the entanglements in which the surety is involved are the result of his own indiscretion.

Ver. 3.—In this verse advice is tendered as to what is to be done under the circumstances of this entanglement. The surety is to take immediate steps to be set free. The urgency of the advice is to be explained by the serious consequences which would follow in the event of the debtor not satisfying the creditor in due time. The surety became liable to the penalties inflicted by the Hebrew law of debt. His property could be distrained. His bed and his garment could be taken from him (ch. xxii. 27 and xx. 16), and he was liable as well as his family to be reduced to the condition of servitude. So we find the son of Sirach saying, "Suretyship hath undone many of good estate, and shaken them as a wave of the sea: mighty men hath it driven from their houses, so that they wandered among strange nations" (Ecclus. xxix. 18; cf. 2 Kings iv. 1; Neh. v. 3—5; and Matt. xviii. 25). Compare the dictum of Thales, the Greek philosopher, Ἐγγύα πάρα δ᾽ ἄτα, "Give surety, and ruin is near;" and that of

Chilo (Pliny, ' Nat. Hist.,' vi. 32), "Sponsioni non deest jactura"—"Loss is not wanting to a surety." The same idea is conveyed in the modern German proverb, "Bürgen soll man' würgen"—" Worry a surety." **Do this now;** or, *therefore.* The particle *éphô* is intensive, and emphasizes the command, and in this sense is of frequent occurrence (Job xvii. 15; Gen. xxvii. 32; xliii. 11; 2 Kings x. 10, etc.). It appears to be equivalent to the Latin *quod dico.* So the Vulgate, "Do therefore what I say;" similarly the LXX. renders, "Do, my son, what I bid thee (ἃ ἐγὼ σοι ἐντέλλομαι)." It carries with it the sense of instant and prompt action. **And deliver thyself, when thou art come into the hand of thy friend;** *i.e.* set thyself free when thou findest thou art actually at the mercy of thy friend for whom thou hast become surety. The *ki* (כִּי) is not hypothetical, but actual; it is not " if " you are, but " when " or because you actually are in his power. The Vulgate and LXX. render כִּי respectively by *quia* and γάρ. **Go, humble thyself;** *i e.* present thyself as a suppliant, prostrate thyself, offer thyself to be trodden upon (Michaelis), or humble thyself like to the threshold which is trampled and trode upon (Rashi), or humble thyself under the soles of his feet (Aben Ezra). The expression implies the spirit of entire submission, in which the surety is to approach his friend in order to be released from his responsibility. The Hebrew verb *hith'rappês* has, however, been rendered differently. Radically *râphâs* signifies "to tread or trample with the feet," and this has been taken to express haste, or the bestirring of one's self. So the Vulgate reads *festina,* "hasten;" and the LXX. ἴσθι μὴ ἐκλυόμενος, *i.e.* "be not remiss." But the hithp. clearly determines in favour of the reflexive rendering; comp. Ps. lxviii. 30, "Till every one submit himself with pieces of silver"—the only other passage where *râphâs* occurs. **And make sure thy friend** (Hebrew, *r'hâv rêëykâ*); rather, *importune thy friend,* be urgent with him, press upon him to fulfil his engagement. The verb *râhâv* is properly "to be fierce," "to rage," and hence with the accusative, as here, "to assail with impetuosity." In Isa. iii. 5 it is used with בּ (*b'*), and signifies to act fiercely against any one. The meaning of the passage is that if abject submission or persuasion does not avail, then sterner measures are to be resorted to to gain the desired end.

Ver. 4.—This verse carries on the thought one step further. The appeal to the friend is not to be confined to one spasmodic effort and then relinquished. He is to be followed up pertinaciously and continually, with unwearied diligence, until prevailed upon to fulfil his engagements. Of this unwearied energy in the pursuit of an object in which one is deeply interested, compare David's resolution, "I will not give sleep to mine eyes, or slumber to mine eyelids, until I find out a place for the Lord, an habitation for the mighty God of Jacob" (Ps. cxxxii. 4, 5).

Ver. 5.—The struggles of the roe and the bird to escape from the snare are employed figuratively to describe the efforts which the surety is to make to tear and free himself from his friend. From the hand of the hunter (Hebrew, *miyyâd*); literally, *from the hand*, as shown by the italics. The variation in all the ancient versions, with the exception of the Vulgate and Venetian, which read "from the snare," suggests that the original text was *mippath* instead of *miyyâd*. The Hebrew *yad*, "hand," may, however, be used by metonymy for a toil or gin; but this is improbable, as no example of this kind can be found. With regard to the addition, "of the hunter," though this does not occur in the original, the parallelism would seem to clearly require it, and Böttcher maintains, but upon insufficient evidence, and against the reading of all manuscripts, which omit it, that the word *tsâyyâd*, equivalent to "of the hunter," formed part of the original text, but has fallen out. The plain reading, "from the hand," may, however, be used absolutely, as in 1 Kings xx. 42, "Because thou hast let go out of thy hand (*miyyâd*)," in which case the hand will not be that of the hunter, but that of the person for whom the one is surety. Roe. There is a paronomasia in *ts'vi*, equivalent to "roe," and *tsippôr*, equivalent to "bird," of the original, which is lost in the Authorized Version. The *ts'vi* is the "roe" or "gazelle," so named from the beauty of its form (see also Song of Sol. ii. 7—9, 17; iii. 5; viii. 14; 1 Kings v. 3; Isa. xiii. 14). *Tsippôr* is a generic word, and represents any small bird. It is derived from the twittering or chirping noise which the bird makes, the root being *tsâphar*, "to chirp, or twitter." As to its identification with the sparrow, *Passer montanus*, or the blue thrush, *Petrocossyphus cyanens* (see 'Bible Animals,' Rev. J. G. Wood, p. 405, edit. 1876).

Vers. 6—11.—10. *Tenth admonitory discourse. Warning against sloth.* The ethical connection of this discourse with the preceding has already been pointed out. Sloth militates against prosperity; it is the prolific parent of want, and, even more surely than suretyship, leads to misfortune and ruin. The certainty with which ruin steals upon the sluggard may be the reason why the teacher closes the discourse in the way

he does. In the case of suretyship such an issue is uncertain; there is the possibility of escape, the surety may prevail upon his friend to release him from his obligation, and so he may escape ruin; but with sloth no such contingency is possible, its invariable end is disaster. So far as the grammatical structure of the two discourses is concerned, they appear to be quite independent of each other, the only points of coincidence observable being the repetition of one or two words, which is purely accidental (cf. "go" in vers. 3 and 6, and "sleep" and "slumber" in vers. 4 and 10).

Ver. 6.—Go to the ant, thou sluggard; consider her ways, and be wise. The ant (Hebrew, *n'mâlâh*) is here brought forward as supplying an example of wisdom to the sluggard. The habits of this insect, its industry and providence, have in all ages made it the symbol of these two qualities, and not only the sacred, but also profane writers have praised its foresight, and held it up for imitation. The ant is only mentioned twice in the Old Testament, and on both occasions in our book (see present passage and ch. xxx. 25). The derivation of *n'mâlâh* is either from the root *nâm*, with reference first to the silence with which it moves, and secondly to its active yet unperceived motion (Delitzsch), or from *nâmâl*, i.q. *mâlâl*, "to cut off," from its cutting off or consuming seeds (*ab incidendis seminibus*) (Buxtorf, Gesenius). The Aramaic name, *shum'sh'mânâh*, however, points to its activity and rapid running hither and thither (Fleischer). *Sluggard;* Hebrew, *âtsêl*, a verbal adjective found only in the Proverbs. The primary idea of the root *âtsâl* is that of languor and laxity. The cognate abstract nouns *âts'lâh* and *âts'luth*, equivalent to "slothfulness," occur in ch. xix. 15; xxxi. 27. *Consider her ways;* attentively regard them, and from them derive a lesson of wisdom. Her ways are the manner in which the ant displays her industry and foresight.

Ver. 7.—Which having no guide, overseer, or ruler. This statement is substantially correct, for though the most recent observations made by modern naturalists have discovered various classes of ants occupying the same ant-hill, yet there appears to be a total want of that gradation and subordination in ant-life which is noticeable among bees. The three terms used here, *kâtsâ, shôter, môshêl*, all refer to government, and correspond respectively with the modern Arabic terms, *kadi, wali*, and *emir* (Zöckler). The first refers to the judicial office, and should rather be rendered "judge," the root *kâtsâh* being "to decide" (see Isa. i. 10; iii. 6, 7; Micah iii. 9). The word, however, is used of a military commander in Josh. x. 24; Judg. ii. 6—11, and in this sense it is understood by the Vulgate, which has *dux. Shôtêr,* rendered "overseer," is literally "a scribe," and appears as the general designation for any official. In Exod. v. 6, 19 the *shôtêr* is the person employed by the Egyptian taskmasters to urge on the Israelites in their forced labour; in Numb. xi. 16 the *shôtêr* is one of the seventy elders; and in 1 Chron. xxiii. 4 he is a municipal magistrate. The meaning assigned to the word in the Authorized Version seems to be the correct one. The ant has no overseer; there is none to regulate or see that the work is done. Each ant apparently works independently of the rest, though guided by a common instinct to add to the common store. In *môshêl* we have the highest title of dignity and power, the word signifying a lord, prince, or ruler, from *mâshâl,* "to rule."

Ver. 8.—**Provideth her meat in the summer, and gathereth her food in the harvest.** It is this characteristic, combined with what has just been said, which gives point to the lesson the sluggard is to learn. The teacher, as it were, argues: If the ant, so insignificant a creature in the order of the animal kingdom, is so provident, how much more should you be—you, a man endued with superior intelligence, and with so many more resources at hand, and with greater advantages! If the ant, with none to urge, direct, or control her work, is so industrious, surely she provides an example at which you, the sluggard, should blush, since there is every external incentive to rouse you to action—your duty to the community, the urgent advice of your friends, and your dignity as a man. If she provides for the future, much more should you do so, and throw off your sloth. Objection has been taken to what is here stated of the provident habits of the ant in storing food, on the ground that it is carnivorous and passes the winter in a state of torpidity. That the ant does lay up stores for future use has, however, been the opinion of all ages. Thus Hesiod ('Days,' 14) speaks of the ant as harvesting the grain, calling it ἴδρις, "the provident." Virgil says ('Georg.,' i. 186; cf. 'Æneid,' iv. 4027)—

"Veluti ingentem formicæ farris acervum
    Quum populant hiemis memores, tectoque
    reponunt."

"So the ants, when they plunder a tall heap of corn, mindful of the winter, store it in their cave." The language of Horace ('Sat.,' i. 1. 32) might be a comment on our passage—

"Parvula (nam exemplo est) magni formica
    laboris sicut
Ore trahit quodcunque potest, atque addit
    acervo,
Quem struit, haud ignara ac non incauta
    futuri,
Quæ, simul universum contristat Aquarius
    annum
Non usquam prorepit, et illis utitur ante
Quæsitis sapiens."

"For thus the little ant (to human lore
    No mean example) forms her frugal store,
Gathered, with mighty toils, on every
    side,
Nor ignorant, nor careless to provide
For future want; yet when the stars appear
That darkly sadden the declining year,
No more she comes abroad, but wisely
    lives
On the fair store industrious summer
    gives."

(Francis' Translation.)

The same provident character is noted in Æsop's fable, 'The Ant and the Grasshopper;' see also Aristotle ('Hist. Nat.,' ix. 6). All objections on this subject appear to be based on insufficient data, and have been conclusively answered by recent observation. Apart from the remark of Buffon, that "the ants of tropical climates *lay up provisions,* and as they probably live the whole year, they submit themselves to regulations entirely unknown among the ants of Europe." The late Professor Darwin states of the agricultural ant of Texas, which in many features resembles the ant of Palestine, that it not only *stores its food,* but prepares the soil for the crops, keeps the ground free from weeds, and finally reaps the harvest (*Journal of Linnæan Society,* vol. i. No. 21, p. 29). Canon Tristram also observes, "The language of the wise man is not only in accordance with the universal belief of his own time, but with the accurately ascertained facts of natural history. Contrary to its habits in colder climates, the ant is not there dormant through the winter; and among the tamarisks of the Dead Sea it may be seen, in January, actively engaged in collecting the aphides and saccharine exudations, in long files passing and repassing up and down the trunk. Two of the most common species of the Holy Land (*Alta barbara,* the black ant, and *Alta structor,* the brown ant) are strictly seed-feeders, and in summer lay up large stores of grain for winter use. These species are spread along the whole of the Mediterranean coasts, but are unknown in more northern climates. Hence writers who were ignorant of ants beyond those of their own countries have been presumptuous enough to deny the accuracy of Solomon's statement" ('Nat. Hist. of the Bible,' p. 320). The Mishna, section 'Zeraim,' also contains a curious piece of legislation which bears testimony to the storing properties of the ant.

Ver. 9.—Vers. 9—11 contain a call to the sluggard to rouse himself from his lethargy, and the warning of the evil consequences if he remains heedless of the reproof. **How long wilt thou sleep, O sluggard?** It is the same as if it were said, " What infatuation is this which makes you lie and sleep as if you had nothing else to do?" The double question stigmatizes the sluggard's utter indolence, and suggests the picture of his prolonging his stay in bed long after every one else is abroad and about his business. *How long* (Hebrew, *ād-mâthā; * Vulgate, *usquequo*); literally, *till when?* **When;** Hebrew, *mâthā; * Vulgate, *quando.* The same words are used in the same order in introducing a question in Neh. ii. 6, " For how long will the journey be? and when wilt thou return?" **Wilt thou . . . sleep.** The Hebrew *tish'kăr* is literally " wilt thou lie," but the verb easily passes to the secondary meaning of "to sleep." The delineation of the sluggard is again drawn in ch. xxiv. 30—34 in almost identical language, but with some additions.

Ver. 10.—**Yet a little sleep, etc.** Is this the answer of the sluggard which the teacher takes up and repeats ironically, and in a tone of contempt? or is it the teacher's own language describing how the sluggard slides on insensibly to ruin? The Vulgate favours the latter view, " Thou shalt sleep a little, thou shalt slumber a little, thou shalt fold thy hands to sleep, and then," etc. Habits, as Aristotle in his 'Ethics' has shown, are the resultant of repeated acts, and habits entail consequences. So here the inspired teacher would have it learnt, from the example of the sluggard, that the self-indulgence which he craves leads on to a confirmed indolence, which in the end leaves him powerless. " Yet a little" is the phrase on the lips of every one who makes but a feeble resistance, and yields supinely to his darling vice.

Ver. 11.—**So shall thy poverty come as one that travelleth, and thy want as an armed man.** The inevitable consequences of sloth—*poverty* and *want*, two terms conveying the idea of utter destitution—are described under a twofold aspect: first, as certain; second, as irresistible. Poverty will advance upon the sluggard with the unerring precision and swiftness with which a traveller tends towards the end of his journey, or, as Michaelis puts it, "quasi viator qui impigre pergit ac proprius venit donec propositum itineris scopum contin-

gat" (Michaelis, 'Notæ Uberiores'). Muffet, *in loc.*, keeping to the figure, however, explains differently, "Poverty shall overtake thee, as a swift traveller does one who walks slowly." The Authorized Version, " as one that travelleth," correctly represents the original *kim'hǎllêk.* There is no ground whatever, from the use of the verb, for rendering the piel participle *m'hǎllêk* as " a robber." The verb *hâlăk* invariably means "to go, or walk," and the piel or intensive form of the verb means " to walk vigorously, or quickly." The participle can only mean this in the two other passages where it occurs—Ps. civ. 3 and Eccles. iv. 14. The substantive *hêlĕk* in 2 Sam. xii. 4 also signifies "a traveller." So the Vulgate here, *quasi viator.* The other view, it is stated, is required by the parallel expression in the second hemistich, " as an armed man," and receives some support from the LXX. reading, ὥσπερ κακὸς ὁδοιπόρος, " as an evil traveller," which may mean either a traveller bringing evil news, or one who wanders about with an evil intention and purpose, in the sense of the Latin *grassator*, "a highwayman." In this case the meaning would be that poverty shall come upon the sluggard as he is indulging in his sloth, and leave him destitute as if stripped by a robber. But the destitution of the sluggard will not only be certain and swift, it will be also irresistible. His want shall come upon him as *an armed man* (*k'ish mâgên*); literally, as *a man of a shield; * Vulgate, *quasi vir armatus; * i.e. like one fully equipped, and who attacks his foe with such onset and force that against him resistance is useless. As the unarmed, unprepared man succumbs to such an opponent, so shall the sluggard fall before want. The expressions, " *thy* poverty " and " *thy* want," represent the destitution of the sluggard as flowing directly from his own habit of self-indulgence. It is his in a special manner, and he, not others, is alone responsible for it. Compare, beside the parallel passage ch. xxiv. 33, the similar teaching in ch. x. 4; xiii. 4; xx. 4. The Vulgate, LXX., and Arabic Versions at the close of this verse add, " But if thou art diligent, the harvest shall come as a fountain, and want shall flee far from thee; " the LXX. making a further addition, " as a bad runner (ὥσπερ κακὸς δρομεὺς)." It is observable, in comparing this section with the preceding, that the teacher pursues the subject of the sluggard to its close, while he leaves the end of the surety undetermined. The explanation may be in the difference in character of the two. The surety may escape the consequences of his act, but there is no such relief for the sluggard. His slothfulness becomes a habit, which increases the more it is indulged in, and leads to consequences which are as irremediable as they are inevitable.

Vers. 12—19.—11. *Eleventh admonitory discourse. Warning against mischievousness as a thing hateful to God.* The connection of this with the preceding discourse is not at first sight very clear, but it may be found in the fact, attested only too unhappily by experience, that sloth leads those who indulge in it to such vices as are next enumerated. The sluggard may develop into a treacherous and deceitful man, and even if such should not happen, the characteristics of the two are nearly allied, and their end is much the same. St. Paul, in his First Epistle to Timothy, observes this same combination of character, and remarks that idlers are "tattlers also and busybodies, speaking things which they ought not" (see 1 Tim. vi. 13). The intention of the discourse is obviously to dissuade all, and especially the young, from the vices, and to preserve them from the ruin, of those men of whom "the naughty person and wicked man" is the type.

Ver. 12.—**A naughty person, a wicked man, walketh with a froward mouth.** The teacher begins by stating in general terms the nature and character of the man whom he now holds up as a warning to others, and then proceeds to point out the various features in his conduct and behaviour by which he may be known. In concise terms he is described as "a naughty person, a wicked man." This is pre-eminently his character, and the first feature in it is that his life is one of wilful and injurious misrepresentation of the truth. *A naughty person, a wicked man.* In apposition and mutually explanatory. The grammatical arrangement of the sentences which follow, each of which is introduced by a participle, and is thus co-ordinate to the others, as well as the parallel terms, "person" (*ádâm*) and "man" (*ish*), determine this apposition. So Bertheau and Delitzsch. Others (as Zöckler, Noyes, Kamph), however, connect the second expression with the series of characteristics which follow, and render, "A worthless person is a deceiver, who," etc., but wrongly. *A naughty person* (Hebrew, *ádâm b'liyyáál*); literally, *a man of Belial;* Vulgate, *homo apostata;* LXX., ἀνὴρ ἄφρων. The word "Belial" is derived from *b'li,* "without," and *yáál,* "profit" (*i.e.* "without profit"), or from *b'li* and *ól,* "yoke" (*i.e.* "without yoke"), and strictly signifies either a worthless or a lawless person. The latter derivation is, however, rejected by Gesenius and others. Its abstract signification is worthlessness, uselessness; its concrete or adjectival, worthless. The word "naughty" (Anglo-Saxon, *náht, ne aht,* "not anything," equivalent to "nothing"), in the sense of good-for-nothing, ne'er-do-well, adopted in the Authorized Version, exactly reproduces its strict etymological meaning. The word, however, always carries with it the idea of moral turpitude. In the present instance its meaning is determined by the appositional phrase, "a man of iniquity," or "a wicked man," and such iniquity as takes the form of mischief-making, deceit, and sowing discord among brethren. The "man of Belial" is not therefore simply, as its etymological derivation would imply, a worthless individual, one who is of no use either to himself or to the community at large, but a positively wicked, iniquitous, and despicable character. The meaning of the word varies in other passages. Thus in Deut. xiii. 13, where it first occurs, it is used to designate those who have fallen away into idolatry, and induce others to follow their example. In this sense it corresponds with the Vulgate, *apostata,* as signifying a defection from the worship of the true God. Again, in 1 Sam. i. 16 it is applied to the profanation of sacred places. When Hannah is accused by Eli of drunkenness in God's house at Shiloh, she replies, "Count not thine handmaid for a daughter of Belial." In the historical books (*e.g.* Judges, 1 Samuel, 1 Kings, 2 Chronicles), where it is of frequent occurrence, it has the general meaning of "wickedness," under whatever form it appears. So in the Psalms (xviii. 4; xli. 8; ci. 3) and Nahum (i. 11, 15). In the Book of Job (xxxiv. 18, once only) it is used adjectively and as a term of reproach, "Is it fit to say to a king, Thou art wicked [*b'liyyáál;* i.e. 'worthless']?" Individuals possessing the qualities of worthlessness, profanity, or wickedness are designated in Holy Scripture either as "sons," "children," "daughters," or "men of Belial." The word only occurs in two other passages in the Proverbs—ch. xvi. 27 and xix. 28. In the New Testament (2 Cor. vi. 15) the word "Belial" (Greek, βελίαρ or βελίαλ) appears as an appellative of Satan, ὁ πονηρὸς, "the evil one," as the representative of all that is bad, and as antichrist. *A wicked man* (Hebrew, *ish áven*); literally, *a man of vanity or iniquity;* Vulgate, *vir inutilis;* LXX., ἀνὴρ παράνομος. The radical idea of *áven* (from *ún,* "nothing") is that of emptiness or vanity, and has much, therefore, in common with *b'liyyáál.* Its secondary meaning, and that which it usually bears in Scripture, is iniquity. "A man of iniquity" is one who is altogether deficient in moral consciousness, and who goes about to work wickedness and do hurt and injury to others (cf. ver. 18 and Job xxii. 15). *Walketh with a froward mouth.* His first characteristic, as already observed. His whole life and conduct are marked by craftiness, deceit, perversion, and misrepresentation, and an utter want of truth. "Walking" is here, as elsewhere in Scripture, used of some particular course of conduct. So we find the LXX. paraphrase, πορεύεται ὁδοὺς οὐκ ἀγαθάς, "he enters or walks not in good ways." *With a froward mouth* (Hebrew, *ik'shûth pĕh*); literally, *with perversity of mouth*; Vulgate, *ore perverso.* Symmachus has στρεβλεύμασι στόματος, "with perversity of mouth." The mouth, or speech, is the vehicle by which this person gives outward expression to the evil thoughts which are inwardly filling his heart. The phrase occurs before in ch. iv. 24. The meaning of the passage is well illustrated in Ps. x. 7, "His mouth is full of misery, deceit, and fraud: under his tongue is mischief and vanity."

Ver. 13.—**He winketh with his eyes, he speaketh with his feet, he teacheth with his fingers.** He employs his other members for the same nefarious purpose. In the language of St. Paul, he yields his members to uncleanness, and to iniquity unto iniquity (Rom. vi. 19). "To wink with the eye (*kā-rāts āyĭn*)," as in ch. x. 10 and Ps. xxxv. 19, or "with the eyes (*kārāts b'ēynāyim*)," is properly to compress or nip them together, and so to wink, and give the signal to others not to interfere (Gesenius and Delitzsch); cf. the LXX., ἐννεύει ὀφθαλμῷ; and the Vulgate, *annuit oculis.* Aquila and Theodoret, however, read, κνίζει, "he *vexes* or *annoys.*" The observation of the teacher in ch. x. 10 is, "He that winketh with his eyes causeth sorrow." The same verb *kārūts* is also used of the compression or closing of the lips in ch. xvi. 30. *He speaketh with his feet;* i.e. he conveys signs by them to his companion; cf. the LXX., σημαίνει δὲ ποδί, and the Vulgate, *terit pede,* which conveys much the same meaning. *He teacheth with his fingers;* or, as more fully expressed in the LXX., διδάσκει δὲ ἐννεύμασι δακτύλων, "he teacheth by the signs of his fingers." Symmachus has δακτυλοδεικτῶν, which, however, in its strictly classical use (see Demosthenes, 790. 20) is pointing at with the finger. "Teaching" is only the secondary meaning of the Hebrew participle *môrĕh,* which is here used. The verb *yârâh,* to which it belongs, means properly to extend or stretch out the hand for the purpose of pointing out the way (compare the Hebrew *shâlakh yod,* and the Latin *mon-*

strare), and hence came to mean "to teach." The crafty and deceitful character which is here presented to us is strikingly reproduced in Ecclesiasticus: "He that winketh with the eyes worketh evil: and he that knoweth him will depart from him. When thou art present, he will speak sweetly, and will admire thy words: but at the last he will writhe his mouth, and slander thy sayings. I have hated many things, but nothing like him; for the Lord will hate him" (Ecclus. xxvii. 22—24). The heathen poet Nævius says of the impudent woman—

"Alium tenet, alii adnutat, alibi manus
  Est occupata: est alii percellit pedem."

Compare also Ovid's words ('Amor.,' i. iv. 16)—

    "Clam mihi tange pedem:
Me specta, mutusque meos, vultumque loquacem.

      .   .   .   .   .

Verba superciliis sine voce loquentia dicam;
  Verba leges digitis."

So Tibullus, i. 12—

"Illa viro coram nutus conferre loquaces
  Blandaque compositis abdere verba notis."

The lesson which we may learn from this verse is not to abuse the members of our bodies, by employing them for the purposes of deceit and hypocrisy, and so to promote evil, but to put them to their natural and legitimate use. Ver. 14.—From these external features the teacher passes to the heart, the seat of all this mischief and deceit. In this respect we observe a striking correspondence with the method adopted by our Saviour in his teaching, who referred everything to the heart, as the true seat of all that was good or bad in man. *Frowardness is in his heart* (Hebrew, *tāh'pŭkôth b'libbo*); *i.e.* his heart is full of perverse imaginations, it is there he nourishes his jealousy, his hatred, his malice, his ill will. It is there, too, **he deviseth mischief continually.** "Devising mischief" carries us one step further back in the history of evil. It is this feature, this deliberate premeditation to plot mischief and to devise means to carry it into execution, which makes the character of the man simply diabolical. He makes his heart as it were the workshop wherein he fabricates and prepares his villainy. The Hebrew *khârāsh* (to which the participle *khôrêsh* belongs) is equivalent to the Vulgate *machinari,* and the LXX. τεκταίνομαι, "to fabricate, devise, plot." (See ch. iii. 29 and ver. 18; and cf. Ps. xxxvi. 4, "He deviseth mischief upon his bed.") The LXX. combines the two statements in one proposition: "A perverse heart deviseth evil at all times." Similarly the Vulgate, which, how-- ever, joins "continually" (Hebrew, *b'kol-eth;* Vulgate, *omni tempore*) to the second hemistich, thus: "And at all times he sows discord (*et omni tempore jurgia seminat*)." **He soweth discord** (Hebrew, *mid'-yânim* (Keri *y'shâllêâkh*); literally, *he sends forth* (i.e. excites) *strife;* or, as the margin, *he casteth forth strife.* The Keri reading *mid'yânim,* for the Khetib *m'dânim,* is probably, as Hitzig suggests, derived from Gen. xxxvii. 36. The phrase occurs again as *shîllâkh m'dânim* in ver. 19, and as *shîllâkh mâdôn* in ch. xvi. 28 (cf. ch. x. 12). This is the culminating point in the character of the wicked man. He takes delight in breaking up friendship and in destroying concord among brethren (see ver. 19), and thus destroys one of the most essential elements for promoting individual happiness and the welfare of the community at large. This idea of the community is introduced into the LXX., which reads, "Such an one brings disturbance to the city (ὁ τοσοῦτος ταραχὰς συνίστησι πόλει)." The motive cause may be either malice or self-interest.

Ver. 15.—**Therefore shall his calamity come suddenly; suddenly shall he be broken without remedy.** Great sins, as Muffet, *in loc.,* observes, have great punishments; neither only great, but sudden. *Therefore;* Hebrew, *âl-kên.* A Nemesis or retribution awaits this man of malice and deceit. His calamity or destruction is represented as the direct result of, as flowing forth from, what he has done. *His calamity;* Hebrew, *êydô.* On *êyd,* see ch. i. 26. *Shall come suddenly;* i.e. sooner than he anticipates; when he thinks his diabolical plans are succeeding, then suddenly his victims will discover his fraud and malice, and will rise and inflict the punishment which is his due. *Suddenly;* *pêthâ,* a variation of *pithôm* just used. *Shall he be broken;* Hebrew, *yish-shâvêr;* Vulgate, *conteretur.* The verb *shâvâr,* "to break," "to break to pieces," is used of ships which are wrecked (Isa. xiv. 29; Ezek. xxvii. 34; Jonah i. 4); of an army which is defeated and dispersed (Dan. xi. 22; 2 Chron. xiv. 12); of the destruction of a kingdom, city, or people (Isa. viii. 15; Jer. xlviii. 4); and of the complete prostration of the spirit of man by affliction (Ps. xxxiv. 19); and as such, in the passage before us, conveys the idea of the complete ruin of this man. It is a destruction that shall break him up. *Without remedy* (Hebrew, *v'êyn mâr'pê;* literally, *and there is no remedy.* There shall be, as Fleischer, as it were, no means of recovery for his shattered members. His destruction shall be irremediable, or as the LXX., a συντριβή ἀνίαψτος, a *contritio insanibilis;* or as the Vulgate, *nec habebit ultra medicinam.* The idea seems to be

taken from the shattered fragments of a potter's vessel, which it is impossible to re-unite. So in the case of the man whose life has been one of fraud, deceit, and malice, there is for him no hope of any recovery. The language may seem exaggerated, but the picture is painted with this high colouring to exhibit a strong deterrent to such a line of conduct, and further, it may be remarked that, in the present day, only the most confiding would again put trust in a man who has wilfully and maliciously deceived them (cf. Isa. xxx. 14). The second hemistich of this verse occurs again *verbatim* in ch. xxix. 1.

Ver. 16.—The whole structure and arrangement of the thoughts which occur in vers. 16—19 clearly show that this is not an independent section, but one closely allied to that which has just preceded. The object is to show that those evil qualities of deceit and malice which are disastrous to man are equally odious in the sight of Jehovah, and consequently within the scope of the Divine displeasure. **These six things doth the Lord hate: yea, seven are an abomination unto him.** The use of the numerical proverb, though common to the gnomic literature of Persia and Arabia, as Umbreit shows, is by our author confined to this single instance. Other examples occur in our book in the words of Agur the son of Jakeh (see ch. xxx. 7—9, 24—28), and the midda, the name given by later Jewish writers to this form of proverb, is observable in the apocryphal Book of Ecclesiasticus (see xxiii. 16; xx. 7 and xxvi. 5—28). When, as in the present instance, two numbers are given, the larger number corresponds with the things enumerated. So in Job v. 19. In Amos i. and ii., however, there is an exception to this rule, where the numbers appear to be used indefinitely. As to the origin of the numerical proverb, the most probable explanation is that given by Hitzig and adopted by Zöckler, namely, that it is due to the exigencies of parallelism. The author first adopts one number optionally, and then a second is employed as a parallel to it. Here, however, the number determined on in the writer's mind is the larger number seven, and the smaller number six is used as a rhetorical parallel. An examination of the following verses will show that the seven exactly measures the things which are described as odious to the Lord. The Authorized Version, so far as the numbers are concerned, exactly represents the original, which, by the use of the cardinal number "seven" (*shêvā*), and not the ordinal "seventh," which would be *sh'vii,* shows that the things enumerated are equally an abomination in God's sight. The view therefore, that the seventh vice is odious to God in an especial degree above the others, is untenable, though it has found defenders in Lowenstein, Bertheau, and Von Gerlach, and is supported by the Vulgate, *Sex sunt quæ odit Dominus, et septimum detestatur anima ejus*. All the seven things are execrable, all are equally objects of the Divine abhorrence. Besides, we cannot imagine that the vice of sowing discord among brethren, of ver. 19, is more odious to God than the crime of shedding innocent blood of ver. 17. *Unto him* (Hebrew, *naph'sho*); literally, *of his soul*.

Ver. 17.—The enumeration begins with *pride*. **A proud look** (Hebrew, *êynāyim rāmôth*); literally, *haughty or lofty eyes*, as in the margin; Vulgate, *oculos sublimes;* LXX., ὀφθάλμὸς ὑβριστοῦ. It is not merely the look which is meant, but the temper of mind which the look expresses (Wardlaw). The lofty look is the indication of the swelling pride which fills the heart, the *mentis elatæ tumor*, the supreme disdain, *grande supercilium*, for everything and everybody. Pride is put first, because it is at the bottom of all disobedience and rebellion against God's laws. It is the very opposite of humility, which the apostle, in Eph. iv. 2, mentions as the basis, as it were, of all the virtues. All pride is intended, and the face of the Lord is against this pride. He "resisteth the proud;" he "knoweth them afar off;" he "hath respect unto the lowly;" he "will bring down high looks" (Ps. xviii. 27); he judgeth those that are high (Job xxi. 22). It is against this spirit that Job prays Jehovah "to behold every one that is proud, and abase him," and "to look upon every one that is proud, and bring him low" (Job xl. 11, 12). The next thing in the enumeration is **a lying tongue**. Lying is hateful to God, because he is the God of truth. In a concise form the expression, "a lying tongue," represents what has been already said in vers. 12 and 13 of "the wicked man" who "walks with a froward mouth," and whose conduct is made up of deceit. Lying is the wilful perversion of truth, not only by speech, but by any means whatever whereby a false impression is conveyed to the mind. The liar "sticks not at any lies, flatteries, or calumnies" (Patrick). Lying is elsewhere denounced as the subject which excites the Divine displeasure (see Ps. v. 6; cxx. 3, 4; Hos. iv. 1—3; Rev. xxi. 8, 27); and in the early Christian Church, in the case of Ananias and Sapphira, it was punished with death. On the subject of lying, see St. Augustine, 'Enchiridion,' c. xviii., wherein he says, "Mihi autem videtur peccatum quidem esse omne mendacium." Every lie is a sin. The third thing is

hands that shed innocent blood, *i.e.* a murderous and cruel disposition, which, rather than have its plans frustrated, will imbue the hands with innocent blood, *i.e.* the blood of those who have done it no injury. The Divine command is, "Thou shalt do no murder," and those who break it will find, even if they escape man, that the Lord is "the avenger of blood," and that he "maketh inquisition" for it (cf. ch. i. and ii., and Isa. lix. 7, which bear a close resemblance to this passage). That the shedding of innocent blood cries for vengeance, and pulls down God's heavy judgments on the murderer, appears in the case of Cain and Abel (Muffet).

Ver. 18.—The fourth thing is **an heart that deviseth wicked imaginations**. "Wicked imaginations" are literally "thoughts of iniquity;" Hebrew, *mākh'sh'vôth āvĕn;* Vulgate, *cogitationes pessimas;* LXX., λογισμοὺς κακοὺς. The same expression in Isa. lix. 7 is rendered "thoughts of iniquity." (On *deviseth*, Hebrew *khôrêsh*, see ver. 14 and ch. iii. 29.) The thought is a repetition of ver. 14*a*. There are evil thoughts in all men's hearts; but the devising, fabricating of them, and thus making the heart into a devil's workshop, is the mark of utter depravity and wickedness, and is abhorrent to God. The devices of the heart, though planned in secret, are clear to him "to whom all hearts are open, all desires known, and from whom no secrets are hid." The peculiar position which the heart occupies in the enumeration is to be accounted for on the ground that it is the fountain, not only of those vices which have been already mentioned, but of those which follow. The fifth thing is **feet that be swift in running to mischief**. Again we are reminded of Isa. lix. 7, "Their feet run to evil." "Mischief" (Hebrew, *rā*) is a re-echo of ver. 14 and ch. i. 16. "To run to mischief" is to carry out with alacrity and without delay what has already been devised in the heart. It implies more than falling or sliding into sin, which is common to all. It denotes, Cornelius à Lapide remarks, "inexplebilem sceleris aviditatem, et destinatum studium."

Ver. 19.—The sixth thing is *perjury*. **A false witness** that **speaketh lies**; literally, *he that breathes out, or utters, lies as a false witness*. So the Vulgate, *proferentem mendacia testem fallacem*. The Hebrew *pûākh* is "to breathe," "to blow," and in the hiph. form, which is used here (*yāphiākh*, hiph. future), it is "to blow out" or "utter," either in a bad sense, as in the present instance, and in ch. vi. 19; xiv. 5; xix. 5, 9 (cf. Ps. x. 5; xii. 5); or in a good sense, "to utter the truth," as in ch. xii. 17. *Lies;* Hebrew, *k'zāvim*, plural of *kāzāv*, "falsehood," "lying" (cf. ch. xxi. 28). *A false witness* (Hebrew, *êd-k'zâvim*), as in margin, "a witness of lies." The expression, "as a false witness," as it appears in the original, is explanatory, and indicates the particular aspect under which the speaking of lies is regarded. Lying in its more general sense has been already spoken of in ver. 17. The vice which is here noted as odious to God is expressly forbidden in the moral code, "Thou shalt not bear false witness against thy neighbour" (Exod. xx. 16). But this, though the chief, is only one view of the case. Perjury may be employed, not only in ruining the innocent, but also in screening the guilty. "Much hurt," says Muffet, *in loc.*, "doth the deceitful and lying witness, for he corrupteth the judge, oppresseth the innocent, suppresseth the truth, and in the courts of justice sinneth against his own soul and the Lord himself most grievously." "He that speaketh lies as a false witness," again, may be the vile instrument in the hands of unscrupulous and inexorable enemies, as those employed against our Lord and Stephen. Perjury, too, destroys the security of communities. The shipwreck of society which it occasions may be seen in the frightful misery which ensued when the system of *delatores* was not only countenanced, but encouraged under the Roman empire. Truly speaking, he that lies as a false witness must be hateful to God. **And he that soweth discord among brethren**; the seventh and last thing in the enumeration, but not, as Delitzsch holds, the *ne plus ultra* of all that is hated of God. It closes, as in ver. 14, the series, but with the addition "among brethren;" thus emphatically stigmatizing the conduct of that man as diabolical who destroys the harmony and unity of those who ought to live together in brotherly affection, and who disturbs the peace of communities.

Vers. 20—35.—**12. Twelfth admonitory discourse.** In this the teacher returns again to the subject which he has already treated in the eighth discourse. The extreme tendency of men, and especially young men, to sins of impurity is no doubt, as Delitzsch remarks, the reason why this subject is again resumed. The subject is gradually worked up to the preceding admonitions in vers. 20—23, pointing out that the way of life, the way of safety, is to be secured by obedience to the precepts of parents, whose commandment and law illumine the perilous road of life, and whose reproofs are salutary to the soul. The arguments against the sin of adultery are cogent in their dissuasiveness, and none

stronger of a purely temporal nature could be devised. It may be objected that the sin is not put forward in the higher light, as an offence before God, and that the appeal is made simply on the lines of self-interest; but who will deny that the scope of the teaching is distinctly moral, or that mankind is not influenced and dissuaded from sin by such a category of evils as includes personal beggary, dishonour, and death?

Ver. 20.—The first part of this verse is couched in almost the same terms as that of ch. i. 8, except that *mitz'rath*, "precept," *preceptum*, is here used instead of *musar*, *eruditio*, or "disciplinary instruction," while the latter part of the two verses are identical.

Ver. 21.—This verse recalls also ch. iii. 3, and reminds us of the use of the phylacteries, or *tefellim*, common among the Jews of our Lord's time, and the practice of binding which upon various parts of the person may have had its origin in this and such like passages. The "tying about" the neck may suggest the use of amulets, an Oriental custom, to ward off evil, but it is more likely that it refers to the wearing of ornaments. **Them**; *i.e.* the commandment and law of father and mother respectively, expressed in the Hebrew by the suffix *-êm*, in the verb *kosh'rem*, equivalent to *liga ea*, and again in *ŏndem*, equivalent to *vinci ea*. (For the *personal* use of this figure, see Cant. viii. 6.) **Tie them**; Hebrew, *ŏndêm*. The verb *ânâd*, "to tie," only occurs twice as a verb—here and in Job xxxi. 36. Lee prefers "to bind;" Delitzsch, however, states that it is equivalent to the Latin *circumplicare*, "to wind about." The meaning of this and similar passages (cf. ch. vii. 3; Exod. xiii. 9; Deut. vi. 8; xi. 13) is that the commandment, precept, law, or whatever is intended, should be always present to the mind. The **heart** suggests that they are to be linked to the affections, and the **neck** that they will be an ornament decking the moral character.

Ver. 22.—The going, sleeping, and awaking occur in the same order in the Pentateuch, from which the ideas of this and the preceding verse are evidently derived (see Deut. vi. 7 and xi. 19). Though only specifying three conditions, they refer to the whole conduct of life, and hence the verse promises direction, guardianship, and converse of wisdom, which will undoubtedly attend life where the precepts of parents are lovingly treasured and obediently observed. The Authorized Version conveys the impression that it is "the keeping" of the parents' precepts, etc., which is to bear such results; but it is better to understand " it " as signifying the whole teaching or doctrine of wisdom, as Delitzsch. Wisdom becomes personified in the representation, and identified with her teaching. **It shall lead thee.** The Hebrew verb *nâkhâh*, " to lead," in the sense of " to direct," like the Latin *dirigere* (Delitzsch), and as it is used in Exodus and Numbers, *passim.* In the Psalms (v. 9 ; xxvii. 11 ; xxxi. 4, etc.) it is employed of God as governing men. Hence, in the affairs of life, Wisdom will so guide and control us that we shall act uprightly. There is the further notion imported into the word of preservation from evil (cf. ch. iii. 23, " Thou shalt walk in thy way safely, and thy foot shall not stumble "). **When thou sleepest ;** or, *when thou liest down,* as in ch. iii. 24, where the same verb occurs. **It shall keep thee ;** *i.e.* watch over, keep safe, or preserve : as in the Vulgate, *custodire,* and the LXX. φυλαττεῖν. We have had the same verb, *shâmâr,* before in ch. ii. 11. Wisdom will be as it were a guardian angel in our hours of repose. When **thou awakest ;** Hebrew, *hăkitsôthâ,* the hiph. perfect of *kûtz.* This word only occurs here. The hiph. form, *hêkitz,* is intransitive, " to be aroused " (cf. the LXX., ἐγειρομένῳ). **It shall talk with thee ;** rather, *she.* Bertheau renders, " She will make thee thoughtful ; " and Dathe, " Let them be thy meditation ; " but the accusative suffix designates the person who is the object of the action of the verb, as in Ps. v. 5 ; xlii. 4 ; Zech. vii. 5 (Zöckler) and as Delitzsch remarks, the personification requires something more than a mere meditation with one's self on the precepts of Wisdom. Wisdom herself shall hold converse with thee (cf. the LXX., συλλαλῇ σοι), she shall suggest thoughts how thou art to behave thyself. The meaning of the verb, " to meditate," " to think deeply," however, need not be lost sight of.

Ver. 23.—**For the commandment is a lamp ; and the law is light.** The teacher takes up the words " commandment " (Hebrew, *mitzrah*) and " law " (Hebrew, *tôrâh*) from ver. 20, which he describes respectively as " a lamp " and " light." The " commandment " is any special or particular commandment which harmonizes with God's will, and commands what is to be done and forbids what is to be left undone. The " law " is the whole law of God in its entirety ; not here the Law of Moses technically, but the whole system of generalized instruction. They stand, therefore, in the same relation to each other as " a lamp " and " light," the one being particular, and the other general. " Light " (Hebrew, *ôr*) is light in general, as the light of the day and the sun, while " a lamp " (Hebrew, *nêr,* from *nûr,* " to shine ") is a particular light like that of a candle, which is enkindled at some other source. The " commandment " and the " law " alike enlighten the conscience and enable one to walk in his way of life. On this passage Le Clerc remarks, " Ut in tenebris lucerna, aut fax ostendit nobis, quâ eundum sit : in ignorantiæ humanæ caligine, quæ nos per hanc totam vitam cingit, revelatio divina nos docet, quid sit faciendum, quid vitandum." So the psalmist says in Ps. xix. 8, " The commandment of the Lord is pure, enlightening the eyes ; " and again in Ps. cxix. 105, " Thy Word is a lamp unto my feet, and a light unto my path ; " *i.e.* they direct and show the true way of faith and life (Gejerus). The " commandment " and the " law " may stand for the whole revelation of God without reference to any particular precept (as Scott), but they have here a specific bearing on a particular form of human conduct, as appears from the following verses. **And reproofs of instruction are the way of life.** *Reproofs of instruction ;* Hebrew, *tok'khôth mûsâr,* disciplinary reproofs, *i.e.* reproofs whose object is the discipline of the soul and the moral elevation of the character. The LXX. reads, καὶ ἔλεγχος καὶ παιδεία ; thus connecting it with education in its highest sense. Such reproofs are a way of life (Hebrew, *dĕrĕk khayyim*), *i.e.* they lead to life ; they conduce to the prolongation of life. This view of the subject, so prominent in the mind of the teacher in other passages (cf. ch. iii. 2 and 19), must not be lost sight of, though the words are susceptible of another interpretation, as indicating that the severest reproofs, inasmuch as they correct errors and require obedience, conduce to the greatest happiness (Patrick). Or again, it may mean that disciplinary reproofs are necessary to life. The soul to arrive at perfection must undergo them as part of the conditions of its existence, and, consequently, they are to be submitted to with the consciousness that, however irksome they may be, they are imposed for its eventual benefit (cf. Heb. xii. 5). But this interpretation is unlikely from what follows.

Ver. 24.—**To keep thee from the evil woman.** The specific object to which the discourse was tending. The " commandment " and the " law " illuminate the path of true life generally, but in a special degree they, if attended to, will guard the young against sins of impurity, fornication, and adultery. *The evil woman* (Hebrew, *ĕshĕth râ*) ; strictly, *a woman of evil,* or vileness, or of a wicked disposition, addicted to evil in an extraordinary degree ; *râ* being here a substantive standing in a genitive relation to *ĕsheth,* as in ch. ii. 12, " The way of evil (*dĕrĕk râ*)." Cf. also *tâh'pŭkôth râ, perverstates mali* (ch. ii. 14), and *makh'sh'voth râ, cogitationes mali* (ch. xv. 26), and *ăn'shĕy* *râ, riri mali* (ch. xxviii. 5). The Vulgate, however, gives an adjectival force to *râ*, rendering, *à muliere mala*. The LXX. ἀπὸ γυναικὸς ὑπάνδρου, *i.e.* "from the married woman," arises from reading *réâ*, "a companion," for *râ*, "evil." From the flattery of the tongue of a strange woman ; *i.e.* from her enticements; Hebrew, *mêkhĕl'kâth lâ-shôn nôk'riyyâh;* literally, "from the smoothness of a strange tongue," as in the margin. Zöckler, however, proposes an emendation of the Masoretic text, and substitutes the construct case, *l'shon*, for the absolute, *lâshôn*, rendering as in the Authorized Version, on the ground that the emphasis lies, not on the "tongue," which would be the case if we render "of a strange tongue," but on "the strange woman," who is the subject of the discourse, as in ch. ii. 16 and v. 20. But *nok'riyyah* is feminine of the adjective *nôk'ri*, and in agreement with *lâshôn*, which, though common, is more frequently feminine (Gesenius), and hence the two words may stand in agreement. The marginal reading is to be preferred (Wordsworth). Again, *mêkhĕl'kâth*, the construct case of *khĕl'kâh*, literally, "smoothness," and metaphorically flattery, with the prefix *mê*, forms one member of the phrase, while the compound expression, *lâshôn nôk'riyyah*, forms the second. Ewald and Bertheau render, "from the smooth-tongued, the strange woman," thus connecting *mêkhĕl'kâth lâshôn*, and regarding *nôk'riyyah* as a separate and distinct idea. They agree with Symmachus and Theodotion, ἀπὸ λειογλώσσου ξένης, *i.e.* "from the smooth-tongued or flattering stranger." So the Vulgate, *à blandâ linguâ extraneæ,* i.e. from the smooth tongue of the strange woman. The LXX. again favours the marginal reading, ἀπὸ διαβολῆς γλώσσης ἀλλοτρίας, "from the slander of a strange tongue." So the Chaldee Paraphrase. The Syriac reads, "from the accusation of a woman of a strange tongue," *i.e.* who uses a foreign language. If, however, the Authorized Version be retained, the Hebrew *nôk'riyyah* will, as in other passages, mean "an adulteress" (Gesenius) ; ch. v. 20; vii. 5; xxiii. 27. Under any circumstances, we have here attributed to the tongue what, in fact, belongs to the woman. It is against the enticements and blandishments of a woman of depraved moral character that the "commandment" and "law" form a safeguard to youth.

Ver. 25.—**Lust not after her beauty in thine heart.** The admonition of this verse embraces the two sides of the subject—the external allurement and the internal predisposition to vice. *Lust not after* (Hebrew, *ăl-tākh'mōd*); strictly, *desire not*, since the verb *khâmâd* is properly "to desire, or covet." The same verb is used in Exod. xx. 17, "Thou shalt not *covet* thy neighbour's wife,"

and xxxiv. 24, "Neither shall any man *desire* thy land" (cf. Micah ii. 2 and ch. xii. 12). In Ps. lxviii. 19; Isa. i. 29; liii. 2, it has the sense of *taking delight* in anything. It may be questioned whether it ever has the strong meaning given in the Vulgate (*non concupiscat*) and adopted in the Authorized Version, "to lust after" (Holden). Aquila, Theodotion, and Symmachus render μὴ ἐπιθυμήσῃς. The use of *khâmâd* here reveals the warning of the Decalogue. *In thine heart;* Hebrew, *bĭl'vâvĕkâ*, corresponding to the ἐν τῇ καρδίᾳ αὐτοῦ of Matt. v. 28. The admonition is a warning to repress the very first inclinations to unchaste desires. They may be unobserved and undetected by others, but they are known to ourselves, and the first duty of repressing them calls for an act of determination and will on our part. Our Lord teaches (Matt. v. 28, cited above), "That whosoever looketh on a woman to lust after her hath committed adultery with her already in his heart." The LXX. reading is Μή σε νικήσῃ κάλλους ἐπιθυμία, "Let not the desire of beauty conquer thee." **Neither let her take thee with her eyelids;** *i.e.* do not let her captivate thee with her amorous glances. *Take.* The Hebrew verb, *lâkâkh*, is "to captivate" with blandishments, "to allure, beguile" (cf. ch. xi. 30); LXX., μήδε ἀγρευθῇς. *With her eyelids* (Hebrew, *b'âph'ăppĕyâh*); or perhaps more literally, *with her eyelashes* (Zöckler). The eyelids; Hebrew, *âph'ăppāyim*, dual of *aph'aph*, so called from their rapid, volatile motion, are here compared with *nets*, as by Philostratus (' Epistles :' Γυναικί), who speaks of "the nets of the eyes (τὰ τῶν ὀμμάτων δίκτυα)." The eyelids are the instruments by which the amorous woman beguiles or catches her victims. She allures him by her glances. So St. Jerome says, "The eye of an harlot is the snare of her lover." The wanton glance is expressed in the Vulgate by *nutibus illius ;* cf. "The whoredom of a woman may be known in her haughty looks and eyelids" (Ecclus. xxvi. 9). Milton (' Paradise Lost,' xi. 620) speaks of the daughters of men "rolling the eye," amongst other things, in order to captivate the sons of God. Piscator and Mercerus understand the eyelids as standing metonymically for the beauty of the eye ; and Bayne, for the general adornment of the head in order to attract attention. Allusion may possibly be made to the custom of Eastern women painting the eyelids to give brilliancy and expression ; cf. 2 Kings ix. 30 (Wordsworth). A striking parallel to the verse before us occurs in Propertius, lib. i. 'Eleg.' i., "Cynthia prima suis miserum me cepit ocellis."

Ver. 26.—**For by means of a whorish**

woman a man is brought to a piece of bread. From this verse onwards to the end of the chapter the discourse consists of a series of arguments, each calculated to deter youth from the sins of fornication and adultery, by exhibiting the evil consequences of such indulgence. The first is the poverty and extreme beggary to which a man is brought. *For by means of;* Hebrew, *ki v'ād.* Lee gives the preposition *rāād* the force of "after," *i.e.* after associating with. The radical idea of the preposition is that of nearness, *by, near,* and easily passes to that of "because" (Gesenius) or "by means of," as in the Authorized Version. It is here used for *per,* "through," as in Josh. ii. 15; 2 Sam. xx. 23, and so indicates the transit through the way of fornication to extreme beggary (Gejerus). *A whorish woman;* Hebrew, *ishshâh zônâh;* Vulgate, *scortum;* LXX., πόρνη; "a harlot," here corresponding to "the adulteress" (*êshĕth îsh*), since the root *zânâh,* "to commit fornication," is attributed both to married and unmarried women (Gen. xxxviii. 24; Lev. xix. 29; Hos. iii. 3). The word *zônâh* is sometimes written alone, as in Gen. xxxviii. 15 and Deut. xxiii. 19. The fuller expression, as here, occurs in Lev. xxi. 7; Josh. ii. 1; Judg. xi. 1. *To a piece of bread;* Hebrew, *ād-kikkār lâkhĕm.* It will be noticed that there is an ellipsis in the Hebrew, which, however, may be easily supplied, as in the Authorized Version. Delitzsch supplies "one cometh down to;" so Zöckler. "A piece of bread" is properly "a circle of bread, a small round piece of bread, such as is still baked in Italy (*pagnotta*) and in the East (Arabic *kurs*), here an expression for the smallest piece" (Fleischer). The term occurs in Exod. xxix. 23; 1 Sam. ii. 36, in the latter of which passages it expresses the extreme destitution to which the members of the house of Eli were to be reduced. As illustrating the term, see also ch. xxxviii. 21 and Ezek. xiii. 19. The LXX. and Vulgate singularly render, "For the price of a harlot is scarcely that of a bit of bread," which may mean, as Castalio, that she is of so little value; but the context is opposed to this rendering, where the point brought out is not the vile character of the harlot as the ruin she inflicts or is the cause of. Besides, the Hebrew *ad* does not mean ever "scarcely," or "hardly," which the Vulgate *vix* gives to it. **And the adulteress will hunt for the precious life.** The adulteress is *ishĕth îsh,* literally, "the woman of a man," or "a man's wife," as in the margin—as, therefore, strictly an adulteress here (cf. Lev. xx. 10). *Will hunt;* Hebrew, *thâtsûd;* LXX., ἀγρεύει; Vulgate, *capit.* The Hebrew verb *tsûd,* "to lie in wait for," "to hunt," also signifies "to take, or capture," like the

Vulgate *capere.* The verb in its metaphorical use also occurs in Lam. iii. 52; Micah vii. 2; Ps. cxl. 12, and refers to those beguilements resorted to by the adulteress to seduce youth. In Ezek. xiii. 18 it carries with it the idea of death, and if understood in this sense here it may have reference to the death-penalty inflicted on adulterer and adulteress by the Mosaic Law (Lev. xx. 10), and introduces what is said more fully in vers. 32, 34, 35. *The precious life;* Hebrew, *nĕphĕsh y'kârâh.* The epithet *y'kârâh* is appropriately added to *nĕphĕsh,* as indicating the high value of the life. All is implied in the *nĕphĕsh,* "the life," moral dignity of character, the soul of man. It is the ever-existing part of the man, and therefore is precious—nothing can exceed it in value. Our Lord says (Matt. xvi. 26), "What shall a man give in exchange for his soul?" and the psalmist (Ps. xlix. 8), "For the redemption of their life is precious." But it is for this life, or soul, that the adulteress hunts, and which she destroys. Lives of fornication and adultery, therefore, carry with them the severest penalties, the loss of temporal possessions, for the enjoyment of a transient passion, and far beyond this the loss of life both temporal and eternal. We cannot imagine a more deterrent warning.

Ver. 27.—In this and the two following verses (28 and 29) the discourse proceeds from statement to illustration, and by examples of cause and effect the teacher shows "the moral necessity of the evil consequences of the sin of adultery" (Delitzsch). The meaning of the verses is plain enough, viz. that as it is in vain to suppose that a person's garment will not be burnt or his feet not be scorched if fire is brought near them, so it is equally inconceivable that a person indulging in adultery can escape its consequences or the retribution that follows. The two questions in vers. 27 and 28 imply a strong negative, and so prepare for the conclusion in ver. 30. *Take fire.* The Hebrew verb *khâthâh* signifies "*to take* burning or live coals *from the hearth*" (Piscator); and hence is used here in a pregnant sense "to take from the hearth and place in" (cf. ch. xxv. 22, "For thou wilt take coals ['and heap them:' Hebrew, *gĕkhâlim khôtheh*] on his head"). The fuller expression is met with in Isa. xxx. 14, "So that there shall not be found in the bursting of it a sherd to take fire from the hearth (*lâkh'tôth êsh miyyâkûd*)." The Vulgate renders by *abscondere,* "to hide:" *Numquid potest homo abscondere ignem;* and the LXX. by ἀποδεῖν, equivalent to the Latin *alligare,* "to tie or bind fast." Wordsworth explains "to take and heap up, as in a firepan or censer." **In his bosom;** Hebrew, *b'khêykô;* LXX., ἐν κόλπῳ; Vulgate, *in sinu suo.* The word *khêyk* is properly "an undulation" (Delitzsch), not the *lap*, but as in the Authorized Version here, "the bosom," and "the bosom of a garment," as in ch. xvi. 33; xvii. 23; xxi. 14. The answer to the question of this and the next verse is of course a decided negative, but we may note that the teacher compares adultery to a burning fire in its consequences.

Ver. 28.—**Can one go upon hot coals, etc.?** The repeated question is introduced by *im*, "if," here equivalent to the Latin *an*, used in double questions, as in Gen. xxiv. 21; Exod. xvii. 7; Judg. ix. 2, etc. *Go*; i.e. *walk upon hot coals* (Hebrew, *al-hāggĕkâlim*); literally, *upon the hot coals.* The Hebrew *gākhĕlĕth* is coals thoroughly ignited, as in Lev. xvi. 12 and ch. xxv. 22; different from *pĕkhâm* of ch. xxvi. 21, which is "a black coal," or, as Gesenius explains, charcoal unkindled. **Be burned;** Hebrew, *tĭkkâvĕynâh;* i.e. be burned or scorched so as to leave a mark by burning, as in Isa. xliii. 2; this being the force of the verb *kâvâh.* The flames of lust will certainly be visited with punishment, and with the stings of conscience. Job, speaking on this very subject, says a deviation from the paths of virtue "is a fire that consumeth to destruction." And to him who gives way to adultery it may be said, in the words of Horace, though with a different application from that in which they were used by that poet, "incedis per ignes suppositos cineri doloso." "You are walking over fire that lies hidden under deceitful ashes" (Gejerus).

Ver. 29.—**So he that goeth in to his neighbour's wife; whosoever toucheth her shall not be innocent.** It is as great a folly to suppose that an adulterer will escape punishment as to imagine that no injury will follow where fire has been applied. Delitzsch illustrates this verse by a passage from Pythagoras's maxim ('Eclog.,' c. 39), Τὸ εἰς πῦρ καὶ εἰς γυναῖκα ἐμπεσεῖν ἴσον ὑπάρχει. *Goeth in;* Hebrew, *hâbbâ el;* i.e. has intercourse with, as in Gen. vi. 4; xix. 31; xxxviii. 9; Ps. li. 2. The same in force as "toucheth." *Shall not be innocent;* Hebrew, *lô-yĭnnâkĕh;* i.e. *pœna vacuus,* "exempt from punishment," or shall be unpunished (Delitzsch, Zöckler, Gesenius); cf. ch. xi. 21, "The wicked shall not be unpunished (*lo yĭnnâkĕh*)," as here. The verb *nâkâh* signifies primarily "to be pure;" so the Vulgate renders *non erit mundus,* "he will not be pure;" but the LXX. observes the secondary meaning of the verb, οὐκ ἀθωωθήσεται, *non erit innoxius,* "he shall not be let go unpunished," from the Alexandrine verb ἀθωόω. Certain and the very heaviest punishment shall come upon him (see also ch. xvii. 5; Jer: xxv. 29; xlix. 12). With this explanation agree Gejerus and Vatablus.

Ver. 30.—**The teacher continues his argument with another illustration, still keeping in view his object, which is to show that the punishment of the adulterer is a surely impending one and severe in its character.** The argument in vers. 30—33 is one *à fortiori.* If men do not overlook but severely punish a crime which has been committed under extenuating circumstances, much less will they do so where the crime is of a much graver character and has nothing to excuse it. Theft and adultery are brought into comparison. Theft under all circumstances is a lesser crime than adultery, but here it is minimized to the lowest degree. The case of a man is taken who steals to satisfy his hunger; the extent of the theft cannot be large, but yet he is punished, and called upon to make the amplest restitution. Much more, does the teacher infer, will be the punishment, and equally certain, where adultery is in question, and the crime is of the most heinous character affecting the most precious interests, and indulged in from the lowest of motives. Men do not despise a thief, etc.; i.e. they do not condemn him under the circumstances, *non grandis est culpa* (Vulgate), "the fault is not a great one;" but they do despise an adulterer—him they hold in contempt as one "who lacketh understanding" and destroyeth his own soul (ver. 32). The verb *bûz* has, however, been otherwise rendered as "to overlook." Zöckler and Holden explain, "men do not overlook," though the former gives the literal sense as "men do not despise." Gesenius renders "despise," but explains, "*i.e.* they do not let him go unpunished." Vatablus, the Versions, Ariæ, Montani, and Munsteri, Hitzig, Delitzsch, and Gesenius, Stuart, Muenscher, and Wordsworth, all agree in regarding the proper meaning of the verb to be "to despise" or "to treat scornfully." The verb *bûz*, moreover, occurs in this sense in ch. i. 7; xi. 12; xiii. 13; xiv. 21; xxiii. 9; and Cant. viii. 1, 7. Michaelis's explanation is as follows: "although a theft is deservedly regarded as infamous in the commonwealth, nevertheless, if it be compared with adultery, it is less wicked." The rendering of the LXX., οὐ θαυμαστὸν ἐάν ἁλῷ τις κλέπτων, *i.e.* "it is not a wonder if any thief be taken," it is difficult to reconcile with the text in the original, though it may be explained as expressing the certainty of arrest which follows theft, and thus gives colour to the secondary meaning attached to the verb, *i.e.* that of overlooking. The Syriac and Arabic Versions follow the LXX., while the Chaldee Paraphrase renders, "It is not a matter of surprise if a thief steals," etc. **His soul;** Hebrew, *nâph'shô. Nĕphĕsh* is used here for desire, craving, or appetite, as in Eccles. vi. 2, 7; Ezek. vii. 19. "To satisfy his soul" is "to sustain his life." *Anima*, Vulgate; ψυχή, LXX.

Ver. 31.—**But if he be taken, he shall restore sevenfold.** Men do not despise the thief, but yet they apprehend him and insist on fullest restitution. *Be found;* i.e. seized (Delitzsch), or legally convicted (Gejerus). *He shall restore;* i.e. he must restore (Zöckler). Delitzsch, however, understands the future, *y'shālêm*, as potential, "he may restore." *Sevenfold;* Hebrew, *siv'āthâyim;* LXX., ἑπταπλάσια; Vulgate, *septulum.* On this word Geïer remarks, "Hæc vox nullibi in sacris ponitur pio numero definito;" *i.e.* "It is nowhere put in Scripture for a definite number." It is therefore to be understood indefinitely of complete restitution, or, as it is expressed in the second and parallel clauses, "all the substance of his house." The word is used in this sense in Gen. iv. 24; Lev. xxvi. 28; Job v. 19 (Lapide). Theft under the Mosaic Law was punishable by a fivefold, fourfold, and twofold restitution (Exod. xxii. 1—4, 9), and, in the event of this not forthcoming, the delinquent was to be sold into slavery (Lev. xxv. 39). In 2 Sam. xii. 6 a fourfold restitution is mentioned, and in the New Testament Zacchæus promises to restore fourfold if he could be convicted of fraud (Luke xix. 8). In the attempts to reconcile the "sevenfold" of our passage with the requirements of the Mosaic Law, Aben Ezra says that the combined penalties for two cases of theft are contemplated, and others that in the time of the writer the penalties had been increased. But proof of this is wanting. Grotius's explanation is more curious than correct, viz. that if the theft be repeated seven times, and he be "taken" seven times, the thief should only be punished by being forced to make restitution with some addition. Both the Greek and Roman law demanded a twofold restitution. Selden maintains that theft would have been subjected to the usual punishment (Selden, 'De Jure Not. et Gent.,' vi. c. 6). We may therefore come to the conclusion that "sevenfold" is used in the sense indicated above. As to any objection which may be raised on the score of inconsistency in talking of a man making restitution, and giving all his substance when he steals to satisfy his hunger, it may be remarked that he need not necessarily be without substance of some sort or other, and he could acquire subsequently sufficient to satisfy the demand. On the question whether a person is justified by extreme want in stealing, see Grotius, 'De Jure Belli et Pacis,' ii. c. 2. § 6; Puffendorf, 'De Jure Not. et Gent.,' ii. c. 6. § 5; Blackstone, 'Commentary,' iv. 2. § 4.

Ver. 32.—**But whoso committeth adultery with a woman lacketh understanding.** The adversative "but" is wanting in the original, but is clearly demanded by the contrast which is instituted. The man who steals from hunger has a motive for so doing, but the adulterer has no such excuse for *his* crime, which is an unwarrantable invasion of his neighbour's rights. Because there are honest ways for satisfying his desires, he therefore "lacketh understanding." *Committeth adultery with a woman;* Hebrew, *nôêph ishshâh;* LXX., ὁ μοιχὸς; Vulgate, *qui adulter est;* i.e. an adulterer. The Hebrew *nââph,* "to commit adultery," is here followed by an accusative, as in Lev. xx. 10 and Jer. xxix. 23. *Lacketh understanding;* Hebrew, *khăsār-lêv; deficit corde.* The verb *khâsêr* is "to be devoid of anything," "to lack." The expression, which occurs again in ch. vii. 7 and ix. 4, refers to the brutish and stupid condition to which lust has reduced him. Lust has displaced right reason. He is *expers judicii* (Syriac), devoid of judgment, without intelligence, senseless and stupid. In modern phraseology, he has taken leave of his senses. Both the LXX. and Vulgate have combined the two branches of this verse, the former rendering, "But the adulterer, on account of want of intelligence, compasses the loss of his life," and the latter, "But the adulterer, on account of want of intelligence, loses his life." **He that doeth it destroyeth his own soul;** or literally, *whoso will destroy his life he will do this,* i.e. adultery. So Ariæ Montani, Munsterus, Chaldee Targum. The man who commits adultery is a self-murderer. The phrase, *măshkith naph'sho, corrumpens animam suam,* may be resolved into the concrete "a self-destroyer," as Delitzsch. The following verses seem to indicate that it is the temporal life which is referred to in *nĕphĕsh,* but the meaning of the term may be extended to embrace not only physical loss of life, but also moral and spiritual loss. By the Levitical Law adultery was punished by death: "The man that committeth adultery with another man's wife . . . the adulterer and adulteress shall surely be put to death" (Lev. xx. 10; cf. Deut. xxii. 22; John viii. 4, 5; see also 1 Thess. iv. 6).

Ver. 33.—**A wound and dishonour shall he get; and his reproach shall not be wiped away.** Two other things more immediate await the adulterer—personal chastisement and loss of reputation. It seems clear that "a wound" (Hebrew, *nĕgāv,* "a stroke" or "blow"), used here in the singular, collectively refers to the corporal punishment, which the outraged husband will inflict upon the adulterer (Delitzsch, Zöckler, Lapide). (For the word, see Deut. xvii. 8;

xxi. 5.) It may also have reference to the punishment inflicted by the Law. In the LXX. the idea is expressed by ὀδύνας, i.e. "pains," and so gives colour to Lapide's explanation of "afflictions of every kind" The Vulgate gives a moral turn to the meaning, and co-ordinates the word with "dishonour:" *Turpitudinem et ignominiam congregat sibi*, "*Dishonour* is the ignominious treatment he will receive on all hands." The second part of the verse states that a brand of disgrace will be attached to his name which will be perpetual, not confined to this life only, but extending beyond it, so that men will never recall it but with this stigma (Patrick, Mercerus). On *shall be . . . wiped away* (Hebrew, *tĭmmâkĕh*, the niph. future of *mâkhâh*, "to wipe off, or away," and in hiph. "to be blotted out," equivalent to the Latin *delere*), see Deut. xxv. 6; Ezek. vi. 6; Judg. xxi. 17. The LXX. renders ἐξαλειφθήσεται, and adds, εἰς τὸν αἰῶνα, "for ever." The statements of the verse are illustrated by Horace, 'Satires,' lib. i. 2. 37, who describes the dangers and mishaps which befall the adulterer and fornicator.

"Hic se præcipitem tecto dedit; ille flagellis
Ad mortem cæsus: fugiens hic decidit acrem
Prædonum in turbam: dedit hic pro corpore nummos."

Ver. 34.—For jealousy is the rage of a man: therefore he will not spare in the day of vengeance. The first hemistich is adduced as a reason for what has preceded, while the concluding hemistich and the following and last verses are a deduction strengthening what has been stated before, and also showing that the punishment will be inevitable. The general *consensus* of commentators and texts is to connect the two hemistiches of this verse. Thus the LXX., Μεστὸς γὰρ ζήλου θυμὸς ἀνδρὸς αὐτῆς, οὐ φείσεται ἐν ἡμέρα κρίσεως, "For the wrath of her husband filled with jealousy shall not spare in the day of judgment;" the Vulgate, *Quia zelus et furor viri non parcet in die vindictæ*, "For the jealousy and rage of a man shall not spare in the day of vengeance;" the Syriac, *Nam quia furor mariti plenus est zelotypiâ non parcet in die retributionis*, "For because rage of a husband is full of jealousy he shall not spare in the day of retribution." So the Arabic, and the Tigurina Versio, and among the commentators Durandus. Dathe, Doderlein, Holden. But the Hebrew simply makes the statement, *hi-kĭmâh khămâth-gâver, quia zelus excandescentia viri*, i.e., as in the Authorized Version, "for jealousy is the rage of a man;" *ki*, equivalent to the Greek γὰρ, "for," and *kĭnâh* is the subject of the

sentence. The Hebrew *kĭnâh* is "jealousy" as in ch. xxvii. 4, "Who is able to stand before envy?" or, as margin, "jealousy." The ordinary copulative verb "is" is best understood as connecting the subject and the predicate; "the rage of a man," Hebrew *kămāth-gâvĕr*, as above, i.e. "the glow of a man's anger" (Delitzsch), or "a man's fierce anger" (Zöckler). Jealousy awakens and inflames the wrath and anger of a man or husband to its highest pitch. It evokes the strongest feelings for revenge. *Man;* Hebrew, *gâvĕr*, equivalent to *ish*, "a man," in opposition to "a wife"—"a *husband*," as here. The word is chiefly found in poetry. Its derivation, from *gâvār*, "to be strong," serves to bring out the idea also of the intensity or force of the jealousy—it burns or rages with all the might of the man. The latter part of the verse in the Hebrew is simply, "and he will not spare (*v'lô-yâkh'môl*) in the day of vengeance." The Authorized Version "therefore" serves to bring out the deduction, though it does not occur in the original. *He will not spare;* i.e. the injured husband will not show any clemency or mercy to the adulterer, the man who has wronged him so deeply. *In the day of vengeance;* Hebrew, *b'yôm nâkâm.* The expression may refer to the time when the adulterer is brought before the judges, but more probably to every occasion on which the husband can exercise his vengeance. So Gejerus. For the expression, cf. Isa. xxxiv. 8, "The day of the Lord's vengeance;" Job xx. 28, "The day of his wrath;" and ch. xi. 4, "The day of wrath." Jealousy is implacable (see Song of Solomon viii. 6, "Jealousy is cruel as the grave").

Ver. 35.—He will not regard any ransom; neither will he rest content, though thou givest many gifts. No recompense nor atonement, nor any gifts however great, will buy him off. These are supposed to be offered by the adulterer to the enraged husband, who, however, will never rest till he effects the utter ruin of his injurer. The literal rendering of the first hemistich is, "He will not accept the face of any ransom." The phrase *nâsâ phanim* is equivalent to the Greek πρόσωπον λαμβάνειν, and signifies "to give a favourable reception to the outward expression of any one." The figure is taken from lifting up the face of a suppliant, the radical meaning of the verb *nâsâ* being "to take up," "to lift up." The *ransom;* Hebrew, *kôphĕr* (the word usually applied to designate the price of redemption, mulct, or fine demanded for expiation of a crime; see Exod. xxi. 30; xxx. 12; Numb. xxxv. 31, 32); here the bribe offered by the adulterer to be let off will be altogether rejected, however alluring, the word *p'ney*, "face," carrying with it the idea of something recommendatory. For the expression, *nâsâ phanim*, cf. Gen. xix. 21; xxii. 21; Job xiii. 10; xlii. 8; and Mal. i. 8. The LXX. rendering is, Οὐκ ἀνταλλάξεται οὐδενὸς λύτρου τὴν ἔχθραν, "He will not commute for any redemption his enmity." *Neither will he rest content;* literally, *and he will not be willing;* Hebrew, *v'lô-yôvĕh;* LXX., οὐδὲ μὴ διαληθῇ, "nor may it, *i.e.* his enmity, be dissolved or weakened." (On the verb *âvâh*, "to consent to," or "to be willing," see ch. i. 10.) Many gifts, each increasing in value, may be offered, but he will not be willing to forego his right of revenge. *Though thou givest many gifts.* It is noticeable that the address, which has been adapted to the third person, here becomes personal, and so takes up the form originally employed in vers. 20—25. A hypothetical case has been imagined in vers. 26—35, but still with the thought underlying it that it applies to the person addressed. "Though *thou* givest many gifts," or more literally, "though thou multipliest the gift," brings the matter home to the young man. *Gifts;* Hebrew, *shôkad,* "the gift," is the word usually employed to designate the bribe offered to corrupt a judge (see Exod. xxiii. 8; Deut. x. 17; xvi. 19; xxvii. 25; 1 Sam. viii. 3). Here it refers to the money offered to free from punishment. The Vulgate gives the idea that these gifts or bribes are offered by a third party on behalf of the adulterer: *Nec acquiescet cujusquam precibus, nec suscipiet pro redemptione dona plurima.* On these two last verses Lange remarks, "Just as little as the adulterer, taken in his adultery, is left unpunished by the injured husband, so little, yea, even less, will the spiritual adulterer remain unpunished of the Lord (1 Cor. iii. 17)."

HOMILETICS.

Vers. 1—5.—*The surety.* Our Christian charity may naturally be shocked at the selfishness apparently inculcated by the frequent warnings against giving security for others that are scattered up and down the Book of Proverbs. They have done more than anything else to lead people to regard the standard of morality of the Proverbs as low and worldly. Let us consider the subject from various points of view.

I. THE STANDARD OF MORALITY OF THE BOOK OF PROVERBS IS LOWER THAN THAT OF THE NEW TESTAMENT. Let this fact be clearly recognized. Revelation is progressive. Doctrine is only revealed by degrees. The same applies to ethics. Such a method is most suited to the moral education of the race. A less-advanced people can only live up to a less-elevated principle. If the standard be raised too high, it ceases to be effective, and becomes like a counsel of perfection, which ordinary people disregard. On the other hand, Christians have no excuse for taking refuge in the lower principles of an obsolete dispensation.

II. AN EXCLUSIVE ATTENTION TO ONE DUTY WILL ALWAYS MILITATE AGAINST OTHER DUTIES. Duties cross and qualify one another. Each taken by itself and pressed to its extreme will lead to conflict with others. Now, here prudence only is commended. To enforce it the more powerfully, other duties are for the time left out of sight. When they are taken up they will qualify it considerably.

III. IT IS FOOLISH TO UNDERTAKE AN OBLIGATION WHICH WE ARE UNWILLING TO CARRY OUT. It is so easy to make chivalrous promises. But immense harm is done by overhaste in professions of generosity. Let a man count the cost enough to see whether he is morally able to bear the strain before making a very liberal offer.

IV. MUCH EVIL WAS DONE BY THE MONEY-LENDING SYSTEM OF THE JEWS. The laws of debt were most stringent, and " the goods of the sureties might be distrained, or they even sold as slaves, just as in the case of insolvent debtors." Such an outrageously cruel state of things was justly deprecated.

V. OTHER MORE PRESSING CLAIMS FORBID US TO CONTRACT SOME OF THE MOST EXACTING OBLIGATIONS. The good-natured Jew who beggared his children and lost his liberty by becoming surety to a spendthrift, robbed those who had most right to enjoy his property, and hindered himself from doing more good in the future. The duty of a man to his family is often pleaded as an excuse for some act of mean selfishness. Nevertheless, the duty is real, and must not be neglected. A man has no right to risk his children's welfare in order to oblige a friend. People who are too hasty in putting their names to bills should remember this.

VI THE SURETY IS ONLY ADVISED TO ESCAPE BY JUST MEANS. He is not told to break his promise, to hide, to leave the country. He is urged to seek a release by requesting his friend to grant it him. Such a course is humiliating. But it is not dishonest.

Ver. 6.—*The ant.* Scripture sends us to nature. Even the smallest works of nature are full of Divine lessons to him who has eyes to read them. Sometimes we are bidden to consider the heavens, but now we are invited to consider the ant. The telescope has its lessons; so also has the microscope. But when a man refuses to hear the voice of God, will he hear the voice of an insect-prophet? Possibly. It takes an eagle's eye to gaze at the sun; but any eye can look on the earth. If a man's vision is too weak to look at the burning bush, the fiery pillar, the mystic Shechinah, let him turn his eyes to the glowworm at his feet, and perhaps even that humble torch-bearer may save him from stumbling.

I. GO TO THE ANT, AND LEARN NOT TO DESPISE LITTLE THINGS. Of late the doings of the ant have been very carefully looked into, and very wonderful facts have come to light. Among ants there are *engineers*, constructing elaborate tunnels and carrying on complicated building operations; *stock-keepers*, guarding and feeding the aphis, like a cow, for the juice they extract from it; *agriculturists*, carefully clearing ground of all weeds, in order to let only certain grasses grow within the prepared area, and storing up corn underground, which by a marvellous instinct they first kill so as to prevent it from germinating; *slave-holders*, who attack tribes of black ants, carry off the young and keep these to wait on them and feed them, becoming meanwhile so helpless as to be absolutely unable to feed themselves, and dying of starvation when deprived of the help of their slaves; and some so far imitating our habits as to keep pet insects—insects which they feed and attend to but which apparently render them no service. As we look at the diminutive ant, we may well wonder

" That one little head could carry all he knew."

We must not mistake bigness for greatness. Tartary is bigger than Greece. Athens was a little city in comparison with Babylon. Despise not one of the little ones. And we too with our short lives and dwarf powers, may we not do something worth living for?

II. GO TO THE ANT, AND LEARN NATURE'S LESSON OF WORK. It is with no small labour that the agricultural ant of Syria clears its field, keeps it well weeded, gathers in the corn, and stores this in subterranean granaries. Nature is a great factory. All life involves work. Even the silent forest apparently sleeping in the hush of noon is busy, and if only we had ears to hear, we might detect the elaboration of the sap and the growth of the leaf, showing that every tree is hard at work on its appointed task. 1. Work *according to ability.* The ant cannot build a cathedral. But he can make an ant-hill. " Whatsoever thy hand findeth to do, do it with thy might." 2. Work *in face of danger.* One careless footstep may demolish a whole city of ant-life, and crush hundreds of its inhabitants. Yet the little creatures toil on without heeding a danger which they cannot avert. 3. Work *perseveringly.* Any one who has watched an ant struggling with a heavy load may well be rebuked by the patient insect. If the ant-hill is destroyed, the ants soon set to work and commence mining and building, and reducing the chaos to order again. 4. Work *harmoniously.* It is the union of great numbers that enables the ants, though a very small folk, to effect very considerable results. The Church can do what passes the power of individuals, but only when the individuals are severally doing their share of labour.

III. GO TO THE ANT, AND LEARN THE DUTY OF PROVIDING FOR THE FUTURE. The ant works from instinct, and we must admire the wisdom of the great Maker, who has taught it unconscious habits of providence. But we are endowed with powers of looking before and after, and therefore are left to our own will to be deliberately provident. It is strange that many people have no prudence in temporal things. In prosperous times they are recklessly self-indulgent. In harder times they are in destitution. These people abuse Christian charity; and unwise Christian charity is guilty of indirectly encouraging their improvidence. Thus they lose independence, self-reliance, and the wholesome discipline of present restraints for the sake of future needs. But if earthly prudence is practised, shall we stop there? Are we consistent in our providence? We have provided for the natural winter: have we provided for other, more terrible, winters? We may have a philosophy of life which suits the happy sunshine, but how are we provided against the storms and frosts of the winter of sorrow? There is a wintry blast that ultimately kills the hardiest flower. Have we made provision for the winter of death? Happy they who in bright summer, and happier they who in youth's spring-time, have found a Saviour who will be their Bread of life and their Shelter in the chills of grief, in the dread winter of death!

Ver. 14.—*Sowing discord.* I. THE SOWER. He may be of various characters. 1. *A malignant person.* Such a one delights in the mischief he makes. He flings the firebrand with fiendish glee because he loves to witness the conflagration. He is a true child of Satan, one to break the peace of Eden, one to set Cain to murder his brother. 2. *A person greedy of power.* It is easier to make trouble than to mend it. Nothing is more simple than to scatter seeds of quarrels. A single pebble flung into the middle of a mountain tarn will shatter the fair mirror of crag and sky, and spread disturbing wavelets to every shore. There is a sense of power, of producing a great effect, in mischief-making. 3. *A selfish person.* If we always claim our dues and exact our pound of flesh, we must be perpetually embroiled in quarrels. Disregard to the rights of others, which is only too common with the selfish, will lead one individual to plunge a whole society into confusion. 4. *A heedless person.* It is so easy to sow discord that we may do the mischievous thing before we are aware of our folly. It needs care and watchfulness to avoid this disastrous conduct.

II. THE SEED. 1. *A misrepresentation.* Thomas Carlyle pointed out how often national quarrels and wars spring from "misunderstandings." If we knew each other better we should be more friendly. Our acquaintances tend to become our friends. But a misrepresentation is the parent of a misunderstanding, and as such the seed of discord. 2. *A hot word.* If we approached a troublesome question calmly and patiently we might see a way of avoiding all quarrelling over it. But when the anger is roused everything appears in its worst light; there is no inclination to smooth ever a difficulty; on the contrary, opposition is magnified. 3. *An unkind word.* This may be spoken deliberately. The more cool the speaker, the more cutting his speech.

III. THE SOIL. The discord is sown "among brethren." 1. *A possible soil.* One would say that here no quarrels can grow. But, alas! they who should love most can hate with bitterest hatred, or, if no deep dislike be engendered, they may still quarrel most fiercely. The first quarrel was between brethren—Cain and Abel. Esau and Jacob, the two Hebrews whom Moses rebuked in Egypt, the nations of Israel and Judah, were all brethren in discord. 2. *A fruitful soil.* Surely it would be thought discord among brethren cannot last and spread. But experience proves the contrary. Family feuds are deep, bitter, enduring. Church quarrels are most rancorous. Civil war is sanguinary.

IV. THE HARVEST. This discord is no slight thing like the breeze that disturbs the lake for one moment and speedily leaves it to resume its normal placidity. 1. *It is painful.* Pride may conceal the wound, but the sore is not slight. No misery is greater than that of family quarrels. 2. *It is injurious.* It raises evil passions, hinders harmonious action, wastes resources in internecine strife. All men are of one blood, therefore all war is discord among brethren; and who shall measure its frightful harvest of woe? 3. *It is unchristian.* The gospel proclaims and enforces brotherhood. It helps us to realize the dream of the psalmist, "Behold how good and how pleasant it is for brethren to dwell together in unity!" (Ps. cxxxiii. 1). Christ blessed the peacemaker (Matt. v. 9).

Vers. 16—19.—*Seven hateful things.* It is certainly best for us to think most of "whatsoever things are lovely, of good report," etc. But the *couleur de rose* view of human nature that comes of a fastidious objection to look at the darker shades of character is not only false, but also dangerous, since it tempts us to ignore our own failings and to neglect the duty of rebuking sin and of labouring to better the world. The physician must study pathology. The patient must allow his disease to be examined. We must therefore sometimes set ourselves to the unwelcome task of considering hateful things. Let us look at the general features of the seven abominations.

I. THEY ARE DEFINED IN DETAIL. We are not only told that sin is odious. Particular sins are specified. A general confession of sin may be made without any admission of guilt in regard to one's own special faults. The proud man will confess himself a miserable sinner while he refuses to see the evil of his pride. Therefore we must consider our sins in the concrete. Only thus can we feel true compunction and make practical repentance. Six hateful things are mentioned; then a seventh is added as a sort of after-thought, and to suit the requirements of the poetic form of the enigma. It is thus made apparent that the seven is not a definite number intended to exclude all others. Seven is a round number, and the list might easily be lengthened. In fact, we have just seven specimen abominations. Therefore let no man flatter himself because his peculiar failing may happen to be omitted. All transgression of the Law is sin, and is hateful in the sight of God. When particular evils are denounced, remember that they are but specimens of a large and varied and wholly abominable host of sins.

II. THEY ARE DESCRIBED IN REFERENCE TO PARTICULAR ORGANS. A look, a tongue, hands, a heart, feet. All sin is the abuse of some power or faculty. The organ is innocent in itself, but it is prostituted to a base purpose. Every part of our nature is susceptible of this degradation. The more powers we have, the greater is our capacity of evil-doing as well as of well-doing.

III. THEY ARE APPARENTLY VERY UNEQUAL IN GUILT. The promiscuous collection of hateful things is surprising. It looks as though they were flung together with little consideration. Possibly this is designed, that we may not so much compare respective degrees of sin but hate and eschew all evil, the least sin being hateful to God. Pride, lying, murder, are in close juxtaposition. It is not asserted that the three are equally guilty. But no measure is given for discriminating between them. The casuistry of such measurement is demoralizing. Moreover, the difference is often not so great as we think. The crime that sends a shock of horror through the country and leads us to regard the doer of it as an inhuman monster, may come from no blacker sink of iniquity than that which sends forth a sin wearing a much less tragic hue.

IV. THEY ARE AS A WHOLE CHARACTERIZED BY FEATURES THAT ARE SPECIALLY REPROBATED IN CHRISTIAN ETHICS. The first and the last of the hateful things are the exact opposites of the first and the last of the graces named in the seven Beatitudes of the Sermon on the Mount. Pride, lying, cruelty, are the opposites of the Christian duties of humility, truthfulness, and charity. The sin of the heart and imagination is condemned as well as that of the hands.

V. THEY ARE ALL CONDEMNED ON ACCOUNT OF THEIR HATEFULNESS IN THE SIGHT OF GOD. Morality is not created by the fiat of the Divine will. It is eternal, necessary, immutable. God is holy because he lives according to it. But God's relation to morals adds a new sanction. Wickedness then becomes sin. The hatefulness of sin in God's sight should be to us its greatest condemnation, not only because God will punish it, but because it separates us from the love of God.

Vers. 20—22.—*Parental training.* I. SOUND PARENTAL TRAINING IS THE SUREST FOUNDATION FOR A GOOD AFTER-LIFE. Both parents are here named. Neither has a right to delegate to the other his or her share of the great responsibility. In early days this rests chiefly with the mother, and throughout life her moral influence is likely to be the more persuasive. Here is woman's great work. Man fills the world with the noise of his busy doings. But woman has a no less great and useful task in moulding the characters of the toilers of the future. Yet the father has his duty in parental training; and there are often special circumstances in which his knowledge of the world or his firmness of control is essential. Let parents feel that nothing can take the place of home training. The Sunday school cannot do the work of the mother's counsel. No pressure of public duty should let a man excuse himself for neglecting the religious training of his children. He deludes himself if he thinks he can do it by proxy, be the substitute ever so efficient a teacher. Nothing can take the place of the anxious watchfulness of parental love.

II. SOUND PARENTAL TRAINING IS OF LITTLE USE UNLESS IT IS RIGHTLY RECEIVED

BY THE CHILDREN. The child has his duty in regard to it as well as the parent. His will is free. The best seed may be wasted on bad soil. It is his duty to treasure up wholesome home lessons as the most valuable portion divided to him. How mad is the desire of some to escape from the control of the home to the fascinating liberty of the world, of the perils and deceits of which they are so ignorant? Why should the young man be so anxious to take a journey into a far country out of the sight of those who have his interest most at heart? Perhaps there have been unwise restraints in the home. But escape from them is no excuse for rushing to the utmost bounds of licence.

III. SOUND PARENTAL TRAINING, WELL RECEIVED AND FOLLOWED, IS A GREAT BOON FOR THE WHOLE OF LIFE. 1. It is a source of quiet restfulness. It keeps one while sleeping. After the feverish tumult of the day, to retire to rest with hallowed memories lovingly recalled, what a help it is to peace of heart! 2. It is a guide in duty and in danger. "When thou goest, it shall lead thee . . . When thou awakest, it shall talk with thee." These old memories rise up to cheer in dismal tasks or to warn from deceitful temptations. And if they have become doubly sacred because the voice that spake the words of counsel is hushed in death, shall they not also be more reverently cherished? Who knows but what those patient, gentle eyes that followed the child in his nursery griefs and joys may be looking down from the heights of heaven to watch him still as he bends to the hard toil of life?

Ver. 23.—*The object of religious teaching.* I. IT IS TO SERVE AS A LIGHT. How much so-called religious teaching "darkens counsel with words without knowledge"! We do not give right Christian instruction when we urge upon the belief of people unintelligible dogmas in phrases which are to them meaningless. Like the book Hamlet was reading, very much that is crammed into children is "words, words, words." You cannot teach that which is not understood. The first thing is to open the eyes of the scholar, to throw light on regions of the unknown. Revelation is illumination. Christianity is not a rule of dark superstition, but a religion of light.

II. THIS LIGHT GIVES A NEW INTERPRETATION TO ALL THINGS. The light does not create the objects it shines upon, it only makes manifest what was previously hidden, but not the less solidly existent. So religious revelation does not create. The doctrines of Christianity, if they are true at all, represent eternal facts. The New Testament brings these facts to light. Thus Christ has taught us to call God "Father," but he was our Father before the great Teacher came into the world. Earthly facts have new meanings as new lights fall upon them. The light of eternity transforms the whole appearance of life. Under its rays "all things become new." The pleasures, the sorrows, the duties, the gold, the food, the houses, the land, are there still, but they take on quite other hues, and range themselves in strangely altered ranks of interest. When the sun rises, the horrible monsters that loomed on us through the night resolve themselves into homely barns and familiar trees, while the distant mountain range that had been invisible before displays its silent solitudes in all their awful splendour.

III. THE MISSION OF THIS LIGHT IS TO GUIDE OUR CONDUCT. "Reproofs of instruction are the way of life." This teaching is not given merely to satisfy our curiosity, nor simply to develop our mental powers. When theology is pursued with the thirst for knowledge only, it eludes our grasp. When it is degraded to the functions of mental gymnastics, it is wrecked and ruined. The end of revelation is practical and momentous. Scripture is to serve as a "lamp to our feet." Religious teaching should not aim at merely exciting intellectual interest, nor at solving abstract problems, nor at inculcating authoritative dogmas, but at guiding men into the way of peace and life. Therefore: 1. Do not be disappointed if it adds as many mysteries as it explains; so long as it sheds light on our path we can afford to find that it makes the darkness in some other regions the more visible. 2. Do not be content with hearing, understanding, assenting to religious instruction. It fails wholly of its object if it does not lead us to obey it, to walk in its light.

Ver. 27.—*Fire in the bosom.* I. SIN IS FIRE. Fire has an activity that mocks life; it is full of noise and movement. It hisses like a demon-serpent; it sends forth its tongues of flame like living creatures. Yet it is lifeless and the deadliest enemy to all life. Though some animals are drowned in water, others are fitted to find it their natural element; but all living creatures perish in fire. The phœnix is an impossibility. So sin mocks life and beauty and healthy energy. But it is only a death-power. 1. It is *destructive*. Fire exists by consuming its victims. So sin does not simply use, it destroys the faculties it works through. 2. It tends to *spread*. Fire leaps from object to object, rushing over a wide prairie, enveloping a whole city. "Behold, how great a matter a little fire kindleth!" (Jas. iii. 5). So sin spreads through the soul, and from one man to another. 3. It *converts into fire* everything that it lays hold of. So sin turns all that comes under its power into its own nature. 4. It *rages furiously*. Nothing is so like madness as a great fire. It is infinitely more horrible than the wildest tempest of wind and water. Sin is a fury of passion. 5. It *leaves smouldering embers and dismal heaps of ashes*. When the fire of passion is burnt out, the soul is left charred, empty, dismal, as but dust and ashes.

II. The sinner carries fire in his bosom. 1. It is *in himself*. You cannot kindle the fires of your sin outside your own soul at a safe distance. You cannot even sin with your hands while your heart is untouched. When sin is indulged, it takes up its abode in a man's bosom. It enters his affections, it lies close to his heart, it coils about his very life. 2. Moreover, he who takes this fire in his bosom *cannot readily get rid of it*. It penetrates deeper and deeper and spreads further and further, till it fills the whole man. It is not possible to sin for a moment and leave the scene of guilt scatheless. He who enters the furnace of sin lets the fire of sin enter his own bosom, and when he goes forth carries it with him—himself a furnace of sins!

III. The sinner with fire in his bosom will find it burn him. Men talk of the fires of retribution as though they were kindled in some remote region by some unknown executioner, and so they are often as little moved by the thought of them as they are affected by the heat of the stars. But the fire in a man's bosom will bring its own retribution. The wicked man has a hell within him. He is becoming like Milton's Satan when he felt the impossibility of escaping from hell because of his own fearful state, and exclaimed, "Myself am Hell!" This is natural. It would require a miracle to prevent the fire in the bosom from burning. But these terrible thoughts are not intended to induce despair. Rather they should so awaken us to the horror of sin as to lead us to shun it as we would run from a house on fire, and make us so realize our danger as to seek safety in that fountain opened for all uncleanness which can quench the fires of sin and stay all their fatal consequences.

Vers. 30, 31.—*Motive and responsibility.* I. Guilt is to be measured by motive. The starving pick-pocket is not so wicked as the well-to-do house-breaker. Even in the low depths of crime moral distinctions need to be observed, lest we do grievous injustice to our most unhappy fellow-men. The principle that guilt is commensurate with motive rests on the Christian conception of it as an inward fact. This makes it always difficult to form a correct judgment of other people. The rough external standard of the law must be applied by the administrators of civil justice, because no other standard is within their power. But it still remains true that the judge who pronounces sentence may be a much worse man than the prisoner whom he sends to the hulks.

II. Primary necessaries are prior to conventional laws. It is an instinct of the most elementary character that prompts the hungry man to take food. Of course, it is still possible for moral laws to interfere with the pursuit of the object of that instinct, and we must always recognize that moral laws are higher than natural instincts. But in our complicated modern civilization we are not dealing with the direct and simple impact of those lofty and inflexible laws. We are brought into contact with very curious social arrangements, and the laws of right and justice are only allowed to work themselves out by means of an extraordinary social machinery. Under such circumstances there may be room for a protest of instinct against convention, though there can never be an excuse for the enjoyment of any personal desire when that is contradicted by absolute morality. The hero of Victor Hugo's story, 'Les Misérables,' is not regarded as a vulgar thief when he steals the loaf from the baker's shop to feed his starving family. He appears as a revolutionist protesting against what he feels to be an unjust distribution of property. A healthy Christian conscience must condemn his action; but in such a case every human heart will give great weight to "extenuating circumstances."

III. RESPONSIBILITY CANNOT BE MEASURED BY MOTIVE. Here a new element is introduced—one which cannot be lightly set aside. A man must reap the consequences of his deeds, no matter what motives prompted them. If he acts foolishly from the best of motives, he must suffer for his folly; if he offends against social law, no plea of primary necessity will exonerate him from the penalty. In a world of law and order we must look to the results of our conduct as well as to its inward urging principle. Moreover, if we injure any one without the least malice, but only through what we regard as sheer necessity, the fact of the injury does not vanish, and we are under an obligation to take the first opportunity to make ample amends. Further, it is the duty of society to see that external right is done, even though those who resist it may be acting with the best of excuses. The thief must be punished, though his starving condition rouses our pity. But surely these painful points of casuistry should never arise. It is the duty of Christians to work for a better social order, wherein no injustice can give the semblance of an excuse to crime.

HOMILIES BY VARIOUS AUTHORS.

Vers. 1—5.—*The perils of suretyship.* Here we have—
I. A FEATURE OF ANCIENT LIFE. The warnings against incurring this responsibility are very frequent in this book (ch. xi. 15; xvii. 18; xx. 16; xxii. 26). For the bail was treated like the insolvent debtor (2 Kings iv. 1; Matt. xviii. 25). He was subject to distraint or to be sold into slavery. Ben-Sira (xxix. 18, *seq.*) says, "Suretyship hath destroyed many that were doing well, and swallowed them up as a wave of the sea. It hath turned mighty men out of their homes, and they wandered among foreign peoples." The surety struck his hand into that of the debtor, as a sign that he would answer for him. This would be accompanied by a verbal declaration, and hence the man had bound and confined himself—"snared himself by the words of his mouth." The rigidity of ancient custom in this particular told with terrible severity against thoughtless incurrers of responsibility, no matter how kind the motive. Hence—
II. THE URGENT NEED OF PRUDENCE. Ver. 3: "Since thou hast come into the hand [power] of thy neighbour, stamp with thy foot, and storm thy neighbour;" *i.e.* be urgent and insistent with the careless debtor for whom thou hast pledged thyself, press upon him the fulfilment of his responsibilities before it be too late. Exercise a sleepless vigilance (ver. 4, "Tear thyself free like a gazelle from its haunt, and like a bird from the hand of the fowler").
III. MODERN REFLECTIONS AND LESSONS. 1. Let us be thankful that the severity of the ancient laws and customs concerning debt and suretyship has been mitigated. The history of the changes of law is one of the best evidences of Christianity, and proof that prior conceptions of God advance side by side with gentler conceptions of social relations and duties. 2. Prudence is a constant necessity, and its cultivation a virtue, though not the highest. We must learn to adjust the claims of prudence and of neighbourly love. 3. Independence is not only a "glorious privilege," but the firm foundation for the best life-enjoyment and life-work. These are golden words from Ben-Sira, valid for all time: "Take heed to thyself, lest thou fail. *The elements of life are water, bread, and a coat to one's back, and a dwelling to hide unseemliness.* Better the poor man's life in his hut than faring luxuriously in others' houses. . . . It is an ill life from house to house, and not to be able to open your mouth where you are sojourning." To do our own work or God's work well, we should aim at *detachment, disembarrassment, freedom of spirit.*—J.

Vers. 6—11.—*The sluggard admonished.* I. THE PICTURE OF INSECT INDUSTRY. The ant was viewed as the very picture of laboriousness in ancient as in modern times. It is interesting that the German word for "industrious" (*emsig*) seems derivable from *amessi,* "emmet, ant." The like may probably be traceable in some English dialects. 1. The industry of the ant has all the appearance of a *virtue.* For it seems unforced; there is no judge, superintendent, or onlooker, or taskmaster, to superintend its work.

Contrast with the representations on various monuments of the taskmasters with whips superintending gangs of labourers. 2. It is *provident* industry. It lays up against the rainy day. The closer study of ant-life by modern observers opens a world of marvel, and suggests other lines of thought. It is sufficient for didactic purposes to note the general principle; the external appearances of nature reveal *moral analogies*.

II. THE CONTRAST OF HUMAN SLOTH. (Vers. 9—11.) 1. The lazy man seems as if he would sleep *for ever* (ver. 9). 2. He knows not when he has reposed enough (ver. 10). An ironical imitation of his langour, his lazy attitude. The arms ever crossed, instead of being opened and ready for toil. "When I begin to turn about," said the Duke of Wellington, "I turn *out*." 3. The result of sloth (ver. 11). Poverty surprises him like a robber, and want like an armed man. A striking picture of the *seeming suddenness* with which men may sink into destitution. But it is only seeming; it has been long really preparing.

III. MORAL ANALOGY AND APPLICATION. Sloth in all its forms is ruinous to body and soul. Mental inertness and vacuity is a common form. The mind must be *aroused, interested, filled*. Here is one of the great *sources of drunkenness*, because of *depression*. If you have no occupation, *invent one*. *Goad your temper* by hopes and fears, if it will not wake up without them. In religion " be not slothful." *Work* at the practical or theoretical side of it, whichever suits your capacity best. Work out your own salvation. *Take it all for granted*, and you will presently find that all has slipped away, and naught remains but an *impoverished intellect, a stagnant will.—J.*

Vers. 12—15.—*A picture of spite.* I. THE SPITEFUL MAN DEFINED GENERALLY. (Ver. 12.) He is "naughty," the old English word being expressive; otherwise "a thing of naught," a "slight man" (Shakespeare); in German *heilloss*, "unsound," "unworthy," and so *worthless*. Gather up the sense and force of these adjectives, and we get the idea comprehensively of *badness*, the sensuous counterpart of which is *rottenness, corruption*.

II. HIS CHARACTERISTICS. (Vers. 13, 14.) 1. In *mien* and *gesture* and *language*. His mouth is twisted to a false expression, and utters false things. There is an obliquity and uncertainty in his glance (comp. ch. x. 10). He is full of shy tricks and hints— the thrust of the foot, nudges and signs with his fingers. "The shrug, the 'hum!' the 'ha!' those petty brands that calumny doth use" (Shakespeare). 2. In *spirit perverse*. It is a nature awry, inwardly deformed. Busily inventive, scheming mischief, breeding quarrels (comp. on ch. iii. 29). It is a mind naturally active and curious, which, disabled from good, swings inevitably to the other extreme.

III. HIS DESTINY. An overthrow, *sudden, utter, irremediable.* 1. This is described constantly as the common doom of all kinds of wickedness. 2. The Bible makes sharp distinctions, and opposes characters in an *absolute* manner. Fine distinctions would run into the infinite. But we must make them in every particular case. 3. The doom ever stands in the relation of *correspondence* to the guilt.—J.

Vers. 16—19.—*A catalogue of abominations.* I. WHAT IS AN ABOMINATION? The *word* (as a verb) is of Roman or pagan origin, and denoted the feeling of abhorrence for what was *ill-omened*. In the moral sphere all evil conduct is like a *bad omen*, exciting dread and aversion, because boding calamity. In the direct language of the Bible, referring all things immediately to God, abominations are defined as "things that Jehovah hates, and that are an aversion to his soul" (ver. 16).

II. AN ENUMERATION OF THESE DIVINE AVERSIONS. The particular *number* is explained by the parallelism of Oriental poetry generally. It has no direct religious significance. 1. *Proud eyes.* Literally, *lofty* eyes. The *grande supercilium*, or *haughty brow*, of the Romans. The sensuous expression contains and implies in every case the *inner mood*. This Divine aversion for pride is deeply marked in the Bible and in ancient thought generally. Pride is an *excess*—the excess of a virtue of due self-valuation. Therefore it is a disturbing element in the moral world, or God's order. It tends to disjoint the social system. 2. *A lying tongue.* The liar is thus a solvent of society. It must break up were lying to become universal, and must decay so far as the vice of individuals becomes the custom of the multitude. 3. *Hands of violence and injustice.* The tyrant is a usurper of God's authority. He "plays such tricks . . . as angels weep at." The judicial murderer sets at naught the justice both of heaven and earth, the rights of God and of men. 4. *The malicious, scheming heart.* (See on ver. 14.) That quick "forge and working-shop of thought" (Shakespeare) that we call the imagination may become a very devil's smithy, a manufactory of the newest implements of mischief, from the patterns of hell. 5. *Feet that speed to mischief.* All couriers of ill news, eager retailers of slander, all who cannot bear to be forestalled in the hurtful word, who are ambitious of the first deadly blow. 6. The "*breather of lies.*" (Ver. 19.) The false witness, the lying informer; all who trade in *falsehood*, and breathe it as their atmosphere. 7. *The mischief-maker.* The instigator of quarrels between brethren (see on ver. 14). All who partake of the leavened bread of malice, rather than of the pure, unfermented, and incorruptible bread of sincerity and truth.

1. Our aversions should be God's aversions. 2. The reasoning antipathy is the counterpart of improper sympathy. 3. Our love and our hate are liable to aberration if not governed by reason and religion. 4. *Instinctive* antipathy means only that we have found in another something that is opposed to our personal sense of well-being; conscientious antipathy, that we have found that which is opposed to the order of God's world.—J.

Vers. 20—24.—*Exhortation to chastity.* I. PREFACE. (Ver. 20; see on ch. v. 1, 2; ch. i. 8.)

II. EXHORTATION TO MINDFULNESS OF EARLY LESSONS. (Ver. 21; see on ch. ii. 3.) It is in *oblivious* moments that we sin. We may forget much that we have learned, having outgrown its need. We can never outgrow the simple, early lessons of piety. The chain that links our days each to each in moral progress is the memory of those lessons.

III. VITAL VIRTUE IN THOSE REMEMBERED LESSONS. They have a true *vis vitalis.* They *guide* in action, *protect* in passive hours (see on ch. iii. 23, 24). In wakeful hours of the night they seem to *talk* to the heart, as it "holds communion with the past." "Spirits from high hover o'er us, and comfort sure they bring." The truth becomes as a guardian angel. There is a junction of light and life in religion (ver. 23). What is seen in the intelligence as *true* translates itself into *health* in the habits.

IV. THEY ARE SPECIALLY PRESERVATIVE AGAINST THE WICKED WOMAN AND HER WILES. (Ver. 24; see on ch. ii. 16; v. 20.) Nothing is said directly of the *reflex* effect of vice upon the mind. It is always the danger externally considered that is pointed out. But this is due to the *objective* presentative form of the biblical thought and speech. We must learn to render the objective into the subjective form, to note how every outward drama has its reflex in the spirit itself; and thus we draw a double benefit from Bible lore. The pictures must be taken first in their *proper* meaning, then be converted into *figures* of the *inner life.*—J.

Vers. 25—35.—*Warning against adultery.* No candid student can ignore the fact that the view of this sin, and the motives deterrent from it, are of far lower order than those of pure Christianity. They do not rise above those of Horace, or any general morality of men of the world. In the sense that the body is the temple of the Holy Spirit, that the soul is in communion with God, we reach that loftier point of view whence the *odium* of the sin is clearly discernible, and the motives against it are the highest that can be known.

I. SIN SPRINGS FROM THE ROOT OF DESIRE. (Ver. 25.) This is the general law (Jas. i. 14, 15). Hence the last command of the Decalogue (Exod. xx. 17; Matt. v. 28). The objects of desire may be good in themselves, but not lawful for our possession, as *e.g.* anything that belongs to our neighbour. Or the object may only *seem* to be good in itself, and its possession may be both unlawful and pernicious. This is the case with the adulteress. Her beauty is a deceitful show. It is a symbol with *no* moral worth behind it. The beauty, the "twinkling eye," are only sensuous charms. We must not speak of desire abstractly as if *it* were wrong, but of the *indiscriminating* desire, which confounds the lawful with the unlawful, the real with the unreal.

II. ADULTEROUS DESIRE BOTH UNLAWFUL AND PERNICIOUS. 1. The *extravagance and avarice of the adulteress.* (Ver. 26.) This is a commonplace of observation. Excess in one passion affects the whole moral equilibrium, and she who will lavish away her honour will be reckless of other waste.   2. *She is a spendthrift of her lover's life.* The Hebrew designates the soul or life as *dear,* or *costly.* After making havoc of his possessions, she preys upon his life, more precious than all.   3. The *deadly certainty of those results of such liaisons.* (Vers. 27—29.) By two impassioned questions the teacher conveys the most emphatic denial of what they suggest.   4. The *further certainty of penal consequences on detection.* Conveyed by means of an analogy (vers. 30, 31). The act of the thief who steals to quiet his starving stomach is not overlooked. If apprehended, he is made to restore sevenfold. The Mosaic Law says four or fivefold (Exod. xxi. 36; xxii. 1, *sqq.*; cf. Luke xix. 8). The "sevenfold" merely expresses a round sum generally; the thief might have to buy off his exemption from legal prosecution with all he had. Much less, then, can the graver crime of adultery escape punishment, if detected. And hence the *senselessness* and *suicidal conduct* of the lover (ver. 32).   5. *Other risks of detection.* Castigation and ignominy at the hands of the outraged husband (ver. 33). Exposure to all the fury of excited jealousy, which is unsparing, fiercely vindictive, insatiable, unappeasable (vers. 34, 35).

1. The lower motive—fear of consequences—is the most *powerful* deterrent from crime.   2. But the higher motives, derived from the sense of what crime is in itself and in relation to the doer, are needed when the other is not acting.   3. It is not *being found out* that makes the evil evil,—that is an *accident;* the essence of the crime is in the wrong done to the soul.—J.

Vers. 1—5.—*Answering for others; danger and deliverance.* There are times when we are invited and are bound to answer for other people—it may be with our word, or it may be with our bond. We have all been indebted to the kindnesses of our friends in this direction, and that which we have received from our fellows we should be ready to give to them in return. But it is a matter in which it is very easy to go much too far; in which carelessness is wrong and even criminal; in which, therefore, wise counsel is well worth heeding.

I. THAT GOOD MEN ARE EXPOSED TO SERIOUS DANGER IN THE WAY OF SURETYSHIP. (Vers. 1—3.) Good men, as such. For it is they who are most likely to be in a position to grant the help which is desired, and who are most likely to be induced to do so. The danger is threefold. 1. The appeal is to kindness of heart. It is the young at starting, or it is the unfortunate, or it is those on whom the helpless are dependent, who supplicate our interposition; and it is difficult for the tender-hearted to turn a deaf ear to their entreaty.   2. The peril is easily incurred. It was but the taking of the hand in the presence of two or three witnesses; it is but the signing of a name at the foot of a bond, and the thing is done.   3. The result is remote and uncertain. No evil may ever happen; if it should, it will fall some day in the distance.

II. THAT GODLY PRINCIPLE REQUIRES US TO PUT A STRONG CHECK ON INCLINATION. 1. However much our sympathetic feelings may be stirred, however great the pleasure of compliance, and however deep the pain of refusal, we must forbear, when we have not wherewith to meet the demand that may be made on us. To comply, under such conditions, is simple dishonesty; it is criminal; it is an essentially false action.   2. We should imperil the comfort of our own family. Our first duty is to the wife whom we have solemnly covenanted before God to cherish and care for, and to the children whom the Father has entrusted to our charge.   3. We should be encouraging a culpable spirit of unsound speculation.   4. We should be disregarding the general good. No minister can commend to a Christian community a brother whom he believes to be unfit for the post without sinning against Christ and his Church most seriously. No man can recommend an incompetent or unworthy neighbour or friend to a position of trust and influence without doing a wrong which, if it be not condemned in the Decalogue, will be heavily scored in the Divine account.

III. THAT IF WE FIND WE HAVE ERRED, WE MUST DO EVERY POSSIBLE THING TO GAIN DELIVERANCE. (Vers. 3—7.) There should be: 1. The utmost promptitude (ver. 4). When the blow may not fall for some time to come, there is special temptation to procrastinate until it is too late. Seek safety at once; let not the sun go down before the first step is taken.   2. Energy in action (ver. 5). We should seek to extricate ourselves and those who are dear to us with the vigour with which the roe escapes from the hunter, the bird from the fowler. 3. If necessary, with self-humiliation (ver. 3). We hate to "humble ourselves," but we ought to be ready to do this rather than allow trouble and ruin to hang over our home.

IV. THAT IF THIS URGENCY BE DUE TO TEMPORAL DANGERS, HOW MUCH MORE IMPERATIVE IS OUR DUTY TO GAIN DELIVERANCE FROM SPIRITUAL PERILS! We may well give " no sleep to our eyes, nor slumber to our eyelids," until the peril is passed of being called by the Divine Creditor to meet a debt when we ' have nothing to pay."—C.

Vers. 6—11.—*Sloth and diligence.* In this land and in this age, in England in the nineteenth century, there is little room for the sluggard; there is comparatively little temptation to sluggishness; the force of a rushing stream carries all along with it at a, rapid pace. Nevertheless, it is true—

I. THAT SOME MEN FIND THEMSELVES UNDER SPECIAL TEMPTATION TO SLOTH. This may be a matter of (1) bodily infirmity, the misfortune of an exceptional physical constitution; (2) mental disposition, inherited from others, and to a large extent deserving of pity rather than censure; (3) moral character, the impress of a bad habit—a spiritual result which has to be blamed as much as to be deplored.

II. THAT IT IS TO BE REGARDED AS UNWORTHY OF CHRISTIAN MANHOOD. 1. It is rebuked by the humbler creation (vers. 6—8). That which the ant does instinctively, and without any intelligent guide or instructor, we ought to do, who are endowed with reason, and who have so many human teachers and friends to direct, admonish, and prompt us; who have, moreover, the admonitions of a Divine Teacher and Friend to enlighten and quicken us. 2. It is contemptible in the sight of man, our brother. There is something more than a tone of strong remonstrance, there is a perceptible admixture of contempt in the address, " Thou sluggard " (ver. 6), and also in the raillery of the ninth and tenth verses, " How long wilt thou sleep! . . . Yet a little sleep," etc. The industrious man cannot look at the slothfulness of the sluggard, at the supineness of the careless, at the dilatoriness of the half-hearted, without irrepressible feelings of aversion and contempt; he is compelled to scorn them in his heart.

III. THAT IT MUST BE OVERCOME IN OUR OWN TEMPORAL INTERESTS. (Ver. 11.) Sloth soon ends in ruin. Bankruptcy waits on negligence. Temporal ruin comes: 1. *Unexpectedly.* " Poverty comes as one that travelleth." It has started a long time, it has traversed many a road, crossed many a valley, surmounted many a hill; but, though travelling long, it is only in sight during the last ten minutes of its journey. So ruin begins its course as soon as a man neglects his duties; it travels far and long, its form is hidden behind the hills, it is only just toward the last that its countenance is seen and recognized; then, before he expected it, Poverty stares him in the face, and grasps his hand with cruel clutch. 2. *Irresistibly.* " Want as an armed man." At last no measures can be taken. Friends are alienated, relatives are wearied, all good habits are gone, the courage which might have risen to the occasion is broken by continued sluggishness of spirit; the man is disarmed of every weapon, and is at the mercy of well-armed Want. Indolence not only brings about ruinous circumstances, but it robs us of the spirit by which adversity might be met and mastered; it places us helpless at the feet of the strong.

" Let us, then, be up and doing; " for while sloth is rebuked on every side, and leads down to inevitable ruin, on the other hand, diligence (1) is in accordance with the will of God concerning us (Rom. xii. 11; 1 Tim. v. 8; 2 Thess. iii. 6—14); (2) commands a genuine prosperity (see ch. xxii. 29); (3) braces the character and imparts spiritual strength; (4) places us in a position to show kindness to the unfortunate (Eph. iv. 28); (5) in the sphere of religion ensures ultimate and complete salvation (2 Pet. i. 5, 10, 11; 2 Cor. v. 9).—C.

Vers. 12—15.—*The character and doom of the abandoned.* Perhaps there is no word which more aptly designates the man who is here described than the word "abandoned." The " man of Belial " (" the naughty man ") is he who is abandoned, who has abandoned himself, to the promptings of his own evil nature, to the fascinations and tyrannies of sin. Here we see the features of his character and his doom.

I. THAT IN SPEECH HE IS UTTERLY UNPRINCIPLED. "He walks with a froward mouth." He continually and remorselessly uses the language of falsehood, of profanity, of lewdness, of slander. From his mouth there constantly issues that which God hates to hear, and which is offensive and shameful in the estimation of the good and pure.

II. THAT IN PRACTICE HE HABITUALLY RESORTS TO LOW CUNNING. (Ver. 13.) He has ways of communicating with others only known to the initiated. He cannot afford to be frank and outspoken; he must have recourse to subtlety, to low tricks, to devices which will cover his thoughts from the eye of the upright. This is (1) degrading to himself, and (2) disgusting to others.

III. THAT IN HIS HEART HE IS POSITIVELY MALIGN. (Ver. 14.) He takes a demoniacal pleasure in doing evil. It is not only that he will consent to sacrifice the claims or injure the character of others if he cannot enrich himself without so doing; it is that he finds a horrible and malignant satisfaction in compassing their ruin; he "devises mischief continually; he sows discord." To the pure it is incomprehensible that men can positively delight in impurity; to the kind it seems impossible that men can enjoy cruelty, etc. But it is the last result of a sinful course that the "froward heart" scatters mischief on every hand for the sake of the evil thing itself; to him vice and misery are themselves its reward.

IV. THAT GOD WILL BRING DOWN ON HIS HEAD IRREMEDIABLE DISASTER. (Ver. 15.) The man thinks he can defy his Maker, but he is deceiving himself. God is not mocked; he that sows to the flesh *shall* reap corruption (Gal. vi. 8). He has broken away from all Divine restraints; he has thrown off him the arresting hand of a merciful Redeemer, he has silenced the voice of a pleading spirit; but God is not altogether such as we are (Ps. l. 21). He *will* rebuke, and he will set our sins before our souls again. The hour will come, quite unexpectedly, when judgment will overtake him. It may be (1) public indignation, and the stern rebuke of human society; or (2) ruin in his temporal affairs,—his schemes break down and involve him in their fall, or some one of his victims turns against him; or (3) sudden sickness and pain lay him prostrate on a bed from which he may never rise, and on which his iniquities may confront him; or (4) death and eternity present themselves, and demand that he shall look them full in the face (see ch. xxix. 1).—C.

Vers. 16, 17.—*The condemnation of pride.* The simple, strong language of the text tells us that pride is a thing which God hates. We should therefore make some inquiries concerning it, and know all we can learn about it; for who would like to have in his heart and life that which is positively odious to the Father of his spirit?

I. ITS SEAT IS IN THE SOUL. The wise man speaks of the "proud look" or the "haughty eyes," but he specifies this as it is a most common manifestation of the evil which lies within. Its seat is in the soul, in the lurking thought, in the secret sentiment, in the nursed and nourished convictions, in the false idea. It is in the habit of the heart; it is embedded in the character.

II. IT IS MANIFOLD IN ITS MANIFESTATION. It is most often shown, as intimated, in the proud look, but it may make itself felt in (1) the disdainful tone; (2) the contemptuous silence or non-observance; (3) the cutting sentence; (4) the exclusive action.

III. IT SPRINGS FROM MANY SOURCES. It may arise from: 1. A consciousness of physical superiority—elegance of figure, beauty of face, muscular strength, etc. 2. Consciousness of mental acquisitions—intellectual force, knowledge, eloquence, etc. 3. Social prominence—rank, office, distinction. 4. Recollection of great services rendered.

IV. IT IS HATEFUL IN THE SIGHT OF GOD. This thing "doth the Lord hate." He hates it, for doubtless he sees in it a heinousness and enormity we do not perceive. But he may hate it because: 1. It is an essentially *false* thing. We give ourselves credit for that which is not due. "What have we that we have not received?" The pedestal on which we stand is a false imagining. 2. It is an utterly *unbecoming* thing. Who are we, the sinful children of men, the body of whom is deserving of condemnation, that we should look down superciliously on others? In any human soul pride is unbecoming, unlovely. 3. It is a *cruel* thing. It wounds, and it wounds the most sensitive spirits worst. We place, by itself, as demanding particular reference, one evil in pride for which God condemns it, viz.—

V. IT SHUTS US OUT OF THE KINGDOM OF HIS GRACE. How can we possibly go in humility and faith to the redeeming Lord, our Saviour, while pride occupies the throne? The man in whom the proud spirit dwells stands afar from the salvation of God. "The Lord resisteth the proud, but giveth grace unto the humble." "Blessed are the poor in spirit: for *theirs* is the kingdom of heaven." "Except ye be converted, and become as little children, ye shall not enter into the kingdom of heaven."—C.

Vers. 16, 17.—*The Divine dislike of deceitfulness.* (See ch. xii. 22.) God hates "a lying tongue;" "Lying lips are abomination to the Lord." We must consider—

I. WHAT IS THE DECEITFULNESS WHICH GOD DETESTS. It is evident that the "lying tongue" and the "lying lips" are mentioned as the principal instrument of the soul in the sin which is rebuked. It is the sin itself which is the object of the Divine displeasure. That sin is deceitfulness; conveying false impressions to the mind of our neighbour, the wilful blinding of his eyes by untrue words or by false actions. This may be done by: 1. Downright falsehood—the most shameless and shocking of all ways. 2. Covert insinuation or innuendo—the most cowardly and despicable of all ways. 3. Prevarication, the utterance of a half-truth which is also half a lie—the most mischievous, because the most plausible and last detected, of all ways. 4. Acted untruth—one of the most common forms of falsehood, and perhaps as hurtful to the sinner as any, because it avoids apparent guilt, while it really is as culpable as most, if not as any, of these manifestations of deceit.

II. WHY IT IS SO ODIOUS TO THE RIGHTEOUS FATHER. What makes it "hateful," "abominable in his sight"? 1. It is inherently heinous. The soul has to make a very decided departure from rectitude to commit this sin. We may say of it, "Oh, 'tis foul! 'tis unnatural!" It is a "strange" thing in the view of the Holy One and the True. It is something which comes into direct and sharp collision with his Divine principles; which, in its own nature, is a painful, oppressive spectacle to his pure spirit. He loves and lives and desires truth—"truth in the inward parts;" and with the same intensity with which he loves truth, he must hate, with immeasurable abomination, every shape and form of falsehood. 2. It is ruinous to the soul that practises it. Nothing so surely leads down to spiritual destruction as this sin. It breaks down the walls and breaks up the very foundation of all character. For those who habitually decline from the truth, in word or deed, are constantly teaching themselves to consider that there is nothing sacred in truth at all; they are sliding down the incline at the foot of which is the sceptic's question, "What is truth?" A man who is false in language or in action is poisoning his soul by degrees; he is a spiritual suicide. 3. It is mischievous to society. "Putting away lying, speak every man truth with his neighbour; *for we are members one of another.*" Human society depends on truthfulness in its members for its prosperity, comfort, and almost for its very life. What if we constantly doubted one another's word? The men of truth and trustworthiness are the salt of society. The men of lying tongue are its pest and its peril. Our neighbours have a right to claim of us that we shall put away lying lips and shall "speak the truth in love." God, who cares for the well-being of this human world, hates to see his children weakening, wounding, endangering that world of man by falsehood and deceit.

III. WHAT GOD WILL DO WITH THOSE WHO ARE GUILTY. He will surely punish them. He does so (1) by making them bear their penalty in the shape of spiritual demoralization; (2) by bringing down upon them first the distrust and then the reprobation of their fellows; (3) by excluding them firmly and finally from his own fellowship. He that does not "speak the truth in his heart" may not abide in his tabernacle here (Ps. xv. 1); he that deserves to be denominated a liar will be banished from his presence hereafter (Rev. xxii. 15).—C.

Vers. 16—19.—*The brand of God.* God placed a brand on the first murderer's brow, and he carried the curse with him to his grave. He does not mark us thus now with such signs of guilt; nevertheless, he has made it clear as the day that there are some men who are the objects of his very high displeasure. We know from the text that among these are—

I. MEN OF A PROUD HEART. (See above.)

II. MEN OF A FALSE SPIRIT. (See above.)

III. MEN THAT ARE RESPONSIBLE FOR OTHERS' DEATH. (Ver. 17.) Those whose

" hands shed innocent blood " are strongly condemned of him. These include, not only (1) men guilty of murder and manslaughter in the literal sense, but also (2) those who are responsible for the death of the innocent through culpable carelessness (*e.g.* an indifferent and negligent judge or reckless captain), and also (3) those who, by their heartlessness in family or social life, crush the spirit and shorten the life.

IV. MEN THAT PLOT MISCHIEF. " A heart that deviseth wicked imaginations " (ver. 18). These are they who use their inventive faculties, not for the good of their race, nor for the maintenance of their families, but for the base and shameful purpose of bringing some of their fellows into distress, if not into ruin ; they contrive their overthrow only to enjoy their discomfiture.

V. CRUEL EXECUTIONERS OF WRATH. " Those whose feet are swift in running to mischief " (ver. 18) ; these are they who take a savage delight in being the instruments of punishment—the gaoler, the soldier, the executioner, who gloat over their work of severity or blood.

VI. FALSE WITNESSES. (Ver. 19.) One of the most solemn and responsible positions a man can occupy is the witness-box ; he stands there, invoking the dread Name of the Eternal himself to cause justice to be done. If then he perjures himself, and " speaketh lies " when actually under oath, he defies his Maker, perverts justice, wrongs the innocent or releases the guilty, is disloyal to his country, outrages his own conscience. Well may *he* be among those whom God especially condemns.

VII. MEN THAT DISTURB HARMONY. " He that soweth discord among brethren " (ver. 19). " Blessed are the peacemakers," said the Master. " Cursed are the mischief-makers," says the text. If we do not actively promote peace and good will, surely we need not be the abettors of strife. There are two degrees of guilt here : there is the mischief-making which is due to culpable thoughtlessness, repeating words which should have been allowed to fall to the ground, unintentional but decided misrepresentation, etc. ; and there is the darker wrong, to which a heavier penalty is due, deliberate and wanton disturbance of previous harmony. This is (1) bad in the social circle, (2) worse in the home, (3) worst in the Church of Christ.

Let it be remembered that : 1. God hates these things ; they are utterly abhorrent to him. He cannot regard them without Divine repugnance. 2. God is " much displeased " with those who do them ; his holy and awful wrath must extend to those who " do such things." 3. God will surely punish those who impenitently persist in them (Rom. ii. 2—9).—C.

Vers. 20—35.—*Sin and safety.* These verses may teach us—

I. THAT MAN LIES OPEN TO STRONG AND SAD TEMPTATIONS. The reference of the text is to the sin of sensuality ; the wise man is warning against the wiles of " the evil woman," " the strange woman " (ver. 24). This sin of sensuality may consist in irregularities, or in things decidedly forbidden, or in gross and shameful violations of law and decency ; it may be secret and hidden from every eye, or it may be unblushing and may flaunt itself before high heaven. The words of the text may, in part, apply to other sins ; *e.g.* to intemperance, and also to gambling. To all of these the strong passions of youth often urge the soul ; it finds itself drawn or driven by a powerful impulse which it is difficult to overcome. But the truth must be faced —

II. THAT VICE LEADS DOWN BY A SURE AND SHORT ROAD TO THE WORST INFLICTIONS. It leads to : 1. Self-reproach. The sinner " shall not be innocent " (ver. 29), and will carry the miserable consciousness of guilt with him into every place. 2. Corruption of character—such a one " lacketh heart " (marginal reading), " destroyeth his own soul " (ver. 32) ; losing all self-respect, his character is as a substance that is smitten, cracked through, ready to fall to pieces, worthless ; " a wound " (ver. 33), a deep wound, it has gotten. 3. Shame. Men do not despise a thief who steals to allay the gnawing pangs of hunger ; they may compel him to restore sevenfold, but they pity him as much as they despise him (vers. 30, 31). But the adulterer, or the confirmed drunkard, or the man who is impoverishing his family to gratify his lust for gambling, him men do despise in their hearts ; they dishonour him in their soul, they cry " shame " upon him (ver. 33). 4. Impoverishment. Loss of money, of occupation, beggary, the humiliation of borrowing, pledging, etc. (ver. 26). 5. Penalty from those who have been wronged (vers. 34, 35). Those who outrage the honour of their fellows may expect the bitterest revenge. To steal the love of a wife from her husband, or of a husband from his wife, is to make one enemy whose wrath nothing will appease. It is an evil thing, even if it be not a dangerous thing, to go through life bearing the malice, exposed to the intense and inextinguishable hatred of a human soul.

III. THAT THERE IS ONE PATH OF SAFETY. It is that which is suggested in vers. 27, 28, "Can one go upon hot coals, and his feet not be burned?" etc. The way to escape the evil is *not to touch it*, to steer clear of it altogether, to keep well out of harm's way—to avoid the house and company of the flippant woman, to leave the sparkling cup untasted, to refuse to stake a farthing in any kind of lottery whatever. This is the only secure ground to take. Once begin to talk with the seductive woman, or to taste the pleasure of exhilaration from intoxicants, or to enjoy the sweets of appropriating money gained by nothing but a guess, and who shall say what the end will be? Do not touch the fire, and you will not be burnt.

IV. THAT THE YOUNG SHOULD BEAR THE GUIDING LAMP OF TRUTH ABOUT THEM ALONG THE WHOLE PATH OF LIFE. (Vers. 20—23.) In order to sustain the resolution to keep away from the destroying fires, consult the Word of God. 1. Have it in continual remembrance (ver. 21). 2. Illustrate it in every way open (ver. 20). 3. Find it a steady light, accompanying the steps everywhere (vers. 22, 23).—C.

Ver. 22.—*God's Word—guide, guardian, companion.* Man is insufficient of himself; he needs help from on high. Often in the course of his life he has goings forth, and then he wants direction; often he finds himself helpless, and then he needs a guardian to preserve him; often he is alone, and then he craves a friend who will commune with him. All this he has in the Word of the living God. It is—

I. IN ACTION, OUR GUIDE. "When thou goest, it shall lead thee." We go "from home," "into business," "to sea," "abroad," etc. In all these goings forth we want that which will lead us in the right and the wise way—the way of truth, purity, righteousness, happiness. The Word of the heavenly Father will supply this.

II. IN DANGER, OUR DEFENCE. "When thou sleepest, it shall keep thee." Not only when we are "asleep" on our couch are we in danger from those who might wish to injure us, but when we are unconscious of the spiritual dangers by which we are surrounded; when in a state of "innocence," of being uninitiated into the secrets of sin; when we are not alive to duty and opportunity as we should be;—then the Word of God will be a fence, a security. Following it, coming to it to learn God's will, we shall know which way to take, what courses to avoid, how to revive and to be reanimated with holy energy and zeal.

III. IN LONELINESS, OUR COMPANION. "When we awake," when we find ourselves with our faculties all in force, and no one to hold fellowship with us, then the Word of God will "talk with us." It will speak to us of God our Father, of the supreme value of our spiritual nature, of the path of life, of the kingdom of Christ and the salvation in him, of the heavenly home. "Lamp of our feet, whereby we trace," etc. (ver. 23).—C.

EXPOSITION.

CHAPTER VII.

Vers. 1—27.—13. *Thirteenth admonitory discourse,* containing a warning against adultery, treated under a different aspect from previous exhortations, and strengthened by an example. In this chapter and the following a contrast is drawn between the adulteress and Wisdom.

Ver. 1.—**My son, keep my words.** The teacher enjoins his pupil, as in ch. ii. 1, to observe the rules which he gives. **Lay up, as a precious treasure** (see on ch. ii. 1 and 7).

The LXX. adds here a distich which is not in the Hebrew or in any other version, and is not germane to the context, however excellent in itself: "My son, honour the Lord, and thou shalt be strong, and beside him fear no other." With this we may compare Luke xii. 5 and Isa. viii. 12, 13.

Ver. 2.—**Keep my commandments, and live** (see on ch. iv. 4). As the apple of **thine eye;** literally, *the little man (ishon,* diminutive of *ish) of the eye;* so called from the miniature reflection of objects seen in the pupil, specially of the person who looks into another's eye. It is a proverbial expression for anything particularly precious and liable to be injured unless guarded with scrupulous care (comp. Ps. xvii. 8; Zech. ii. 8). Similarly the Greeks called this organ κόρη, "damsel" or "puppet," and the Latins *pupilla*.

Ver. 3.—**Bind them upon thy fingers.** Wear my precepts like a ring on thy finger, so that they may go with thee, whatever thou takest in hand. Others think that the so-called *tephillin*, or phylacteries, are meant. These were worn both on the hand and the forehead, and consisted of a leather box containing strips of parchment, on which were written four texts, viz. Exod. xiii. 1—10; 11—16; Deut. vi. 4—9; xi. 13—21. The box was attached to a leather strap wound seven times round the arm, three times round the middle finger, and the remainder passed round the hand (see (Exod. xiii. 9, 16; Jer. xxii. 24). **Write them upon the table of thine heart** (see on ch. iii. 3 and vi. 21; and comp. Deut. vi. 9).

Vers. 4 and 5 contain earnest admonitions to the pursuit of Wisdom, which is worthy of the purest love.

Ver. 4.—**Say unto Wisdom, Thou art my sister.** Wisdom is personified, and the connection with her indicated by the relationship which best expresses love, purity, confidence. In the Book of Wisdom viii. she is represented as wife. Christ calls those who do God's will his brother, and sister, and mother (Matt. xii. 50). **Call Understanding** thy **kinswoman**; *moda*, "familiar friend." Let prudence and sound sense be as dear to thee as a close friend.

Ver. 5.—**That they may keep thee from the strange woman** (see on ch. ii. 16 and vi. 24). When the heart is filled with the love of what is good, it is armed against the seductions of evil pleasure or whatever may entice the soul from God and duty. Septuagint, "That she (Wisdom) may keep thee from the strange and evil woman, if she should assail thee with gracious words."

Vers. 6—23.—To show the greatness of the danger presented by the seductions of the temptress, the writer introduces no mere abstraction, no mere personification of a quality, but an actual example of what had passed before his own eyes.

Ver. 6.—**For.** The particle introduces the example. **At the window of my house.** He gives a graphic delineation of a scene witnessed outside his house. **I looked through my casement**; *eshnâb*, "the lattice," which served the purpose of our Venetian blinds, excluding the sun, but letting the cool air pass into the room (comp. Judg. v. 28). A person within could see all that

passed in the street without being himself visible from without (Cant. ii. 9). The Septuagint reads the sentence as spoken of the woman: "For from the window glancing out of her house into the streets, at one whom she might see of the senseless children, a young man void of understanding."

Ver. 7.—**And beheld among the simple ones.** Though it was night (ver. 9), there was light enough from moon or stars or from illuminated houses to show what was passing. "The simple" are the inexperienced, who are easily led astray (see on ch. i. 4). Looking forth into the street on the throng of young and thoughtless persons passing to and fro, among them **I discerned** . . . **a young man void of understanding**; a fool, who, without any deliberate intention of sinning, put himself in the way of temptation, played on the borders of transgression. The way of escape was before him, as it is in all temptations (1 Cor. x. 13), but he would not take it. Such a one may well be said to lack understanding, or heart, as the Hebrew expresses it (ch. vi. 32, where see note).

Ver. 8.—**Near her corner.** He kept near the corner of the house of the woman for whom he waited. Another reading gives, "near a corner;" *juxta angulum.* Vulgate; παρὰ γωνίαν, Septuagint; *i.e.* he did not take to the broad, open street, but sneaked about at corners, whence he could watch the woman's house without being observed by others. **He went the way to her house.** He sauntered slowly along, as the verb signifies. Septuagint, "Passing by a corner in the passages of her house (ἐν διόδοις οἴκων αὐτῆς)."

Ver. 9.—**In the twilight, in the evening of the day.** So termed to distinguish it from the morning twilight. The moralist sees the youth pacing to and fro in the early evening hours, and still watching and waiting when the darkness was deepest (comp. Job xxiv. 15). **In the black and dark night**; literally, *in the pupil of the eye of night and in darkness.* We have the same expression in ch. xx. 20 (where see note) to denote midnight. Its appropriateness is derived from the fact that the pupil of the eye is the dark centre in the iris. Septuagint: the youth "speaking in the darkness of evening, when there is the stillness of night and gloom."

Ver. 10.—**And, behold, there met him a woman.** His long watch is rewarded; the woman comes forth from her house into the street—a proceeding which would at once show what she was, especially in the East, where females are kept secluded, and never appear at night or unattended. **With the attire of an harlot.** There is no "with" in the original, "woman" and "attire" being in apposition: "There met him a woman, a harlot's dress" (*shith*, Ps. lxxiii. 6); her attire catches the eye at once, and identifies her (comp. Gen. xxxviii. 14). In Rev. xvii. 4 the harlot is "arrayed in purple and scarlet, and decked with gold and precious stones and pearls;" and in the present case the female is dressed in some conspicuous garments, very different from the sober clothing of the pure and modest. **Subtil of heart** (נְצֻרַת לֵב); literally, *of concealed heart;* i.e. she hides her real feelings, feigning, perhaps, affection for a husband, or love for her paramour, while she seeks only to satisfy her evil passions. The versions have used a different reading. Thus the Septuagint: "Who makes the hearts of young men flutter (ἐξίπτασθαι);" Vulgate, *præparata ad capiendas animas,* "ready to catch souls."

Vers. 11 and 12 describe the character and habits of this woman, not as she appeared on this occasion, but as she is known to the writer.

Ver. 11.—She is loud; boisterous, clamorous, as ch. ix. 13. The description applies to a brute beast at certain periods. **Stubborn**; ungovernable, like an animal that will not bear the yoke (Hos. iv. 16). Vulgate, *garrula et vaga,* "talkative and unsettled;" Septuagint, ἀνεπτερωμένη καὶ ἄσωτος, "flighty and debauched." **Her feet abide not in her house.** She is the opposite of the careful, modest housewife, who stays at home and manages her family affairs (Titus ii. 5). The Vulgate inserts another trait: *quietis impatiens,* "always restless."

Ver. 12.—Now is she without, now in the streets. At one moment outside her own door, at another in the open street. Septuagint: "At one time she roams without (ἔξω ῥέμβεται)." The woman is represented not as a common prostitute, but as a licentious wife, who, in her unbridled lustfulness, acts the part of a harlot. **Lieth in wait at every corner**; seeking to entice some victim. Then the narrative proceeds; the writer returns to what he beheld on the occasion to which he refers.

Ver. 13.—So she caught him, and kissed him; being utterly lost to shame, like Potiphar's wife (Gen. xxxix. 12). **With an impudent face said**; literally, *strengthened her face and said;* put on a bold and brazen look to suit the licentious words which she spoke. Wordsworth quotes the delineation of the "strange woman" drawn by St. Ambrose ('De Cain. et Abel.,' i. 4): "Domi inquieta, in plateis vaga, osculis prodiga, pudore vilis, amictu dives, genas picta; meretricio procax motu, infracto per delicias

incessu, nutantibus oculis, et ludentibus jaculans palpebris retia, quibus pretiosas animas juvenum capit."

Ver. 14.—I have peace offerings with me. *Shelamim,* "peace or thank offerings," were divided between Jehovah, the priests, and the offerer. Part of the appointed victim was consumed by fire; the breast and right shoulder were allotted to the priests; and the rest of the animal belonged to the person who made the offering, who was to eat it with his household on the same day as a solemn ceremonial feast (Lev. iii.; vii.). The adulteress says that certain offerings were due from her, and she had duly made them. **This day have I payed my vows.** And now (the day being reckoned from one night to the next) the feast was ready, and she invites her paramour to share it. The religious nature of the feast is utterly ignored or forgotten. The shameless woman uses the opportunity simply as a convenience for her sin. If, as is probable, the "strange woman" is a foreigner, she is one who only outwardly conforms to the Mosaic Law, but in her heart cleaves to the impure worship of her heathen home. And doubtless, in lax times, these religious festivals, even in the case of worshippers who were not influenced by idolatrous proclivities, degenerated into self-indulgence and excess. The early Christian agapæ were thus misused (1 Cor. xi. 20, etc.); and in modern times religious anniversaries have too often become occasions of licence and debauchery, their solemn origin and pious uses being entirely thrust aside.

Ver. 15.—Therefore came I forth to meet thee. As though she would invite the youth to a pious rite, she speaks; she uses religion as a pretext for her proceedings, trying to blind his conscience and to gratify his vanity. **Diligently to seek thy face, and I have found thee** (see on ch. i. 28). She tries to persuade her dupe that he is the very lover for whom she was looking, whereas she was ready to take the first that offered. Spiritual writers see in this adulteress a type of the mystery of iniquity, or false doctrine, or the harlot described in Revelation (ii. 20, etc.; xvii. 1, etc.; xviii. 9, etc.).

Ver. 16.—She describes the preparation she has made for his entertainment. **Coverings of tapestry**; *marbaddim,* "cushions," "pillows." The expression occurs again in ch. xxxi. 22. It is derived from רָבַד, "to spread," and means cushions spread out ready for use. The Septuagint has κειρίαις; Vulgate, *funibus,* "cords." These versions seem to regard the word as denoting a kind of delicate sacking on which the coverlets were laid. **Carved works, with fine linen of Egypt**; literally, *striped, or variegated, coverings, Egyptian linen.* The words are in apposition, but the latter point to the material used, which is אֵטוּן, etun (ἄπαξ λεγόμενον), "linen yarn or thread," hence equivalent to "coverlets of Egyptian thread." This was of extreme fineness, costly, and much prized. By "carved works" (Hebrew, חֲטֻבוֹת, chatuboth) the Authorized Version must refer to bed-poles or bed-boards elaborately carved and polished; but the word is better taken of coverlets striped in different colours, which give the idea of richness and luxury. Vulgate, trapetibus pictis ex Ægypto, "embroidered rugs of Egyptian work;" Septuagint, ἀμφιτάποις τοῖς ἀπ' Αἰγύπτου, "shaggy cloth of Egypt." The mention of these articles denotes the foreign commerce of the Hebrews, and their appreciation of artistic work (comp. Isa. xix. 9; Ezek. xxvii. 7). The Prophet Amos (vi. 4) denounces those that "lie upon beds of ivory, and stretch themselves upon their couches."

Ver. 17.—I have perfumed my bed with myrrh, aloes, and cinnamon. The substances mentioned were dissolved in or mixed with water, and then sprinkled on the couch. The love of such things is reckoned as a sign of luxury and vice (Isa. iii. 20, etc.). The three perfumes are mentioned together in Cant. iv. 14; "myrrh, aloes, and cassia," in Ps. xlv. 8. Septuagint, "I have sprinkled my couch with saffron, and my house with cinnamon." Myrrh is nowadays imported chiefly from Bombay, but it seems to be found in Arabia and on the coasts of the Red Sea and Persian Gulf. It is a gummy substance exuding from the bark of the balsamodendron when wounded, and possessing an aromatic odour not particularly agreeable to modern tastes. It was one of the ingredients of the holy oil (Exod. xxx. 23), and was used in the purification of women (Esth. ii. 12), as well as in perfuming persons and things, and, mixed with aloes, in embalming dead bodies (John xix. 39). Aloes is the inspissated juice of the leaves of the aloe, a leguminous plant growing in India, Cochin China, Abyssinia, and Socotra. The ancients used the dried root for aromatic purposes. It is mentioned by Balaam (Numb. xxiv. 6). Cinnamon, which is the same word in Hebrew and Greek, is the fragrant bark of a tree growing in Ceylon and India and the east coast of Africa.

Ver. 18.—Let us take our fill of love; let us intoxicate ourselves (inebriemur, Vulgate); as though the reason were overthrown by sensual passion as much as by drunkenness. The bride in Cant. i. 2 says, "Thy love is better than wine" (see ch. v. 15, 19, and note there).

Ver. 19.—The temptress proceeds to encourage the youth by showing that there is no fear of interruption or detection. The goodman is not at home. "Goodman" is an old word meaning "master of the house," or husband (Matt. xx. 11, etc.); but the Hebrew is simply "the man," which is probably a contemptuous way of speaking of the husband whom she was outraging. He is gone a long journey; he has gone to a place at a great distance hence. This fact might assure her lover that he was safe from her husband's jealousy (ch. vi. 34); but she has further encouragement to offer.

Ver. 20.—He hath taken a bag of money with him; not only to defray the expenses of the journey (a fact which need not be dwelt upon), but because he has some pecuniary business to transact which will occupy his time, and prevent his return before the appointed hour. And will come home at the day appointed; better, as the Revised Version, he will come home at the full moon (in die plenæ lunæ, Vulgate). כֶּסֶא here, and כֶּסֶה Ps. lxxxi. 4, are rightly translated "the full moon," this rendering being supported by the Syriac kêso, though the etymology is doubtful. As it has before been mentioned that the night was dark (ver. 9), it is plain that there were still many days to run before the moon was full, and the husband returned.

Ver. 21.—Thus far we have had the adulteress introduced speaking; now the narrative proceeds. With her much fair speech she caused him to yield. First, she influenced his mind, and bent his will to her purpose by her evil eloquence. The Hebrew word means "doctrine, or learning"—devil's pleading (ch. i. 5; ix. 9). St. Jerome has irretivit, "she netted him;" Septuagint, "She caused him to go astray (ἀπεπλάνησε) by much converse." She talked him over, though indeed he had put himself in the way of temptation, and had now no power to resist her seductions. Then with the flattering of her lips she forced him; drew him away. His body followed the lead of his blinded mind; he acceded to her solicitations. Septuagint, "With the snares of her lips she ran him aground (ἐξώκειλε), drove him headlong to ruin."

Ver. 22.—He goeth after her straightway; suddenly, as though, casting aside all scruples, he gave himself up to the temptation, and with no further delay accompanied her to the house. Septuagint, "He followed, being cajoled (κεπφωθείς), ensnared like a silly bird" (see the article on Cepphus Larus, in Erasmus's 'Adag.,' s.v. "Garrulitas"). As an ox goeth to the slaughter. He no more realizes the serious issue of his action than an irrational beast which, without prevision of the future, walks contentedly to the slaughter-house, and is stupidly placid in the face of death. Or as a fool to the correction of the stocks. There is some difficulty in the translation of this clause. The Authorized Version, with which Delitzsch virtually agrees, is obtained by transposition of the nouns, the natural rendering of the Hebrew being " as fetters to the correction of a fool." The sense thus obtained is obvious: the youth follows the woman, as a fool or a criminal is led unresisting to confinement and degradation. Doubtless there is some error in the text, as may be seen by comparison of the versions. Septuagint (with which the Syriac agrees), " As a dog to chains, or as a hart struck to the liver with an arrow ; " Vulgate, " As a frisking lamb, and not knowing that as a fool he is being dragged to bondage." The commentators are much divided. Fleischer, " As if in fetters to the punishment of the fool," i.e. of himself; Ewald, " As when a steel trap (springs up) for the correction of a fool," i.e. when a hidden trap suddenly catches an incautious person wandering where he has no business. The direct interpretation, that the youth follows the harlot, as fetters the proper punishment of fools, is unsatisfactory, because the parallelism leads us to expect a living being instead of "fetters." We are constrained to fall back on the Authorized Version as exhibiting the best mode of reconstructing a corrupt text. The youth, with his insensate passion, is compared to the madman or idiot who is taken away, unconscious of his fate, to a shameful deprivation of liberty.

Ver. 23.—**Till a dart strike through his liver.** This clause would be better taken with the preceding verse, as in the Septuagint, or else placed in a parenthesis; then the following clause introduces a new comparison. The youth follows the harlot till his liver, the seat of the passions, is thoroughly inflamed, or till fatal consequences ensue. Theocr., ' Id.,' xi. 15—

Ἔχθιστον ἔχων ὑποκάρδιον ἕλκος
Κύπριος ἐκ μεγάλας τὸ οἱ ἥπατι πᾶξε βέλεμνον.

"Beneath his breast
A hateful wound he bore by Cypris given,
Who in his liver fixed the fatal dart."

Delitzsch would relegate the hemistich to the end of the verse, making it denote the final result of mad and illicit love. The sense thus gained is satisfactory, but the alteration is quite arbitrary, and unsupported by ancient authority. **As a bird hasteth to the snare.** This is another comparison (see ch. i. 17, the first proverb in the book, and note there). **And knoweth**

not that it is for his life ; i.e. the infatuated youth does not consider that his life is at stake, that he is bringing upon himself, by his vicious rashness, temporal and spiritual ruin (ch. v. 11).

Ver. 24.—The narrative ends here, and the author makes a practical exhortation deduced from it. **Hearken unto me now therefore, O ye children.** He began by addressing his words to one, " my son" (ver. 1); he here turns to the young generally, knowing how necessary is his warning to all strong in passion, weak in will, wanting in experience. The Septuagint has " my son," as in ver. 1.

Ver. 25.—**Let not thine heart decline to her ways.** The verb satah is used in ch. iv. 15 (where see note) of turning aside from evil; but here, as Delitzsch notes, it is especially appropriate to the case of a faithless wife whose transgression, or declension from virtue, is described by this term (Numb. v. 12). **Go not astray in her paths.** The LXX. (in most manuscripts) has only one rendering for the two clauses: " Let not thine heart incline unto her ways."

Ver. 26.—**For she hath cast down many wounded.** Delitzsch, " For many are the slain whom she hath caused to fall." The harlot marks her course with ruined souls, as a ruthless conqueror leaves a field of battle strewn with corpses. **Yea, many strong** (atsum) **men have been slain by her.** One thinks of Samson and David and Solomon, the victims of illicit love, and suffering for it. Vulgate, et fortissimi quique interfecti sunt ab ea. But the Septuagint and many moderns take atsum in the sense of "numerous," as Ps. xxxv. 18; ἀναρίθμητοι, " innumerable are her slain." The former interpretation seems preferable, and avoids tautology.

Ver. 27.—**Her house is the way to hell** (sheol). A warning found in ch. ii. 18 and ch. v. 5. Viæ inferi domus ejus. The plural דַּרְכֵי is well expressed by Hitzig: " Her house forms a multiplicity of ways to hell." Manifold are the ways of destruction to which adultery leads; but they all look to one awful end. **Going down to the chambers of death.** Once entangled in the toils of the temptress, the victim may pass through many stages, but he ends finally in the lowest depth—destruction of body and soul. Spiritual writers see here an adumbration of the seductions of false doctrine, and the fate to which it brings all who by it are led astray.

HOMILETICS.

Vers. 1—3.—*Keeping the commandments.* We are all familiar with the expression, "keeping the commandments." But do we all fully comprehend what this involves? Let us consider some of the requisites.

I. REMEMBER THE COMMANDMENTS. "Lay up my commandments with thee." The Law was treasured in the ark. It is important that great principles should be so impressed upon our minds as to perpetually haunt our memories, and recur to our vision in critical moments. The school-task of committing the ten commandments to memory will not be enough. The text does not refer to the Law of Moses, but to parental instruction. Great Christian principles are what we need to treasure up.

II. LET NOTHING TAMPER WITH THE COMMANDMENTS. "Keep my law as the apple of thine eye." We cannot bear the smallest speck of dust in the eye. The slightest wound is most painful. Let us beware of allowing the least injury to the healthy condition of the law within us. Moral scepticism is most dangerous.

III. BRING THE COMMANDMENTS TO BEAR ON DAILY LIFE. "Bind them upon thy fingers." Thus they will be always before us, and brought into contact with practical affairs. It is useless to keep the Law only in the closet. It must be carried with us to the workshop, the market-place, the senate-house. How many people's religion never reaches their fingers! Like men with feeble circulation, they have cold extremities.

IV. CHERISH THE COMMANDMENTS AFFECTIONATELY. "Write them upon the table of thine heart." This means impressing them upon the whole being—understanding, memory, affection. The secret of feeble circulation at the extremities is defective action of the heart. If we are to obey the Law we must pray that God will "incline our hearts to keep" it.

Vers. 6—27.—*Profligacy.* [It would not, perhaps, be wise for any one to discuss this subject in the presence of a general congregation. The sin is so fearfully contaminating that it is scarcely possible to touch it in any way without contracting some defilement; and the few who might benefit by a public exposure of the evils of profligacy would be greatly outnumbered by the multitude of people, especially the young, to whom the direction of attention to it would be unwholesome. But on special occasions, and before special audiences, a strong, clear denunciation of this sin may be called for. We can avoid the subject too much, and so leave the sin unrebuked. Certainly some men do not seem to realize how fearfully wicked and how fatally ruinous it is.]

I. IT IS A DESECRATION OF THE TEMPLE OF GOD. It is a sin against God as well as an offence against society. Utterly abandoned men will set little weight by such a consideration, because they have long lost all serious care for their relations with God. But it is important that they who are in danger of falling should remember the solemn words of St. Paul, and the lofty point of view from which he regards the subject (1 Cor. vi. 18, 19). The Christian is a temple of the Holy Spirit. Every man is designed to be such a temple. See that this temple is not converted into a nest of corruption.

II. IT IS RUINOUS TO ANY ONE WHO SUCCUMBS TO IT. It ruins the mind, degrading the whole tone and energy of thought. It is the most gross and disastrous *dissipation.* It ruins the physical health. It ruins wholesome interest in pure delights. It ruins business prospects. It ruins reputation. It brings other sins in its train. It ruins the soul. He who abandons himself to it is indeed a lost man.

III. IT IS HEARTLESSLY CRUEL. The heaviest guilt lies with the tempter. When a man has deluded and ruined a woman, society regards the woman with loathing and contempt, while the man often escapes with comparative impunity. This is one of the grossest instances of injustice that the future judgment will surely rectify. But in any case of profligacy great selfishness and cruelty are shown. The miserable creatures who live by sin could not continue their wretched traffic if men did not encourage it. The demand creates the supply, and is responsible for the hopeless misery that results.

IV. IT IS FATAL TO SOUND SOCIAL ORDER. It is a gangrene in society, eating out its very heart. Nothing more surely undermines the true welfare of a people. It is fatal to the sanctities of the home—sanctities on which the very life of the nation depends.

V. All this accompanies the indulgence of what is pursued solely as a selfish pleasure. The profligate man has not the thief's excuse, who may rob because he is starving (see ch. vi. 30—32); nor can he pretend that he is benefiting any one else by his wickedness.

In conclusion: 1. Let the Legislature be urged to repeal any laws that make the indulgence of this sin more easy by counteracting its natural penalties. 2. Let all men avoid the smallest temptation towards it—all amusements and scenes that lead thither. 3. Let employers endeavour to protect young people under their charge from the fearful dangers of city life. 4. Let Christians seek to save the falling and rescue the fallen in the spirit of Christ, who received penitent sinners.

HOMILIES BY VARIOUS AUTHORS.

Vers. 1—27.—*A tragedy of temptation.* This is a fine piece of dramatic moral description, and there is no reason why it should not be made use of, handled with tact and delicacy, with an audience of young men.

I. The prologue. (Vers. 1—5.) On ver. 1, see ch. i. 8; ii. 1; vi. 20. On ver. 2, see on ch. iv. 4. Here an expression not before used occurs. "Keep my doctrine as thine eye-apple;" literally, "the little man in thine eye." It is an Oriental figure for what is a treasured possession (Deut. xxxii. 10; Ps. xvii. 8). On ver. 3, see on ch. iii. 3; vi. 21. "Bind them on thy fingers," like costly rings. Let Wisdom be addressed and regarded as "sister," Prudence as "intimate friend" (ver. 4). On ver. 5, see on ch. ii. 16; vi. 24. On the prologue as a whole, remark (1) it is intense in feeling, (2) concentrated in purpose, and hence (3) exhaustive in images of that which is precious and desirable before all else. It is an overture which gives the theme of the drama with the deepest impressiveness.

II. The first act. (Vers. 6—9.) The teacher looked through a grated loophole, or *eshnâb*, and saw among the silly fools, the simple ones, who passed by or stood chatting, one simpleton in particular, who attracted his notice. He watched him turn a corner (hesitating, and looking around a moment, according to Ewald's explanation), and pass down a street. The Hebrew word finely shows the deliberacy, the measured step, with which he goes; he has made up his mind to rush into sin. It was late in the evening—"*dark, dark, dark,*" says the writer, with tragic and suggestive iteration —dark in every sense. The night is *prophetic.*

III. The second act. (Vers. 10—20.) A woman—"the attire of a harlot" (as if she were *nothing but* a piece of dress), with a heart full of wiles, meets him. She was excitable, noisy, uncontrollable, gadding—now in the streets, now in the markets, now at every corner (vers. 11, 12). Her characteristics have not changed from ancient times. And so with effrontery she seizes and kisses the fool, and solicits him with brazen impudence. Thank offerings had "weighed upon" her in consequence of a vow; but this day the sacrificial animal has been slain, and the meat which, according to the Law, must be consumed within two days, has been prepared for a feast. And she invites him to the entertainment, fires his fancy with luxurious descriptions of the variegated tapestries and the neat perfumes of her couch, and the promise of illicit pleasures. She alludes with cool shamelessness to her absent husband, who will not return till the day of the full moon (ver. 20). "This verse glides smoothly, as if we could hear the sweet fluting of the temptress's voice." But it is as the song of birds in a wood before an awful storm.

IV. The third act. (Vers. 21—23.) Her seductive speech, the "fulness of her doctrine," as the writer ironically says, and the smoothness of her lips, overcome the yielding imagination of her victim. Ver. 22 implies that he had hesitated; but "all at once," passion getting the better of reflection, he follows her like a brute under the dominion of a foreign will driven to the slaughter-house. He is passive in the power of the temptress, as the fool who has got into the stocks. "Till a dart cleave his *liver*"—the supposed seat of passion. Hastening like a bird into the net, he knows not that his life is at stake.

V. The epilogue. (Vers. 24—27.) On ver. 24, see on ch. v. 7. "Let not thy heart turn aside to her ways, and go not astray on her paths." Properly, "reel not" (*shâgâh*), as in ch. v. 20. Beware of that intoxication of the senses and fancy which leads to such an end. For she is a feller of men, a cruel murderess (ver. 26). Her house is as the vestibule of hell, the *facilis descensus Averni*—the passage to the chambers of death (see on ch. ii. 18; v. 5).

LESSONS. 1. Folly and vice are characteristically the same in every age. Hence these scenes have lost none of their dramatic power or moral suggestion. 2. Only virtue is capable of infinite diversity and charm. The pleasures of mere passion, violent at first, pass into monotony, thence into disgust. 3. The character of the utter harlot has never been made other than repulsive (even in French fiction, as Zola's 'Nana') in poetry. What exists in practical form is mere dregs and refuse. 4. The society of pure and refined women is the best antidote to vicious tastes. For to form a correct taste in any matter is to form, at the same time, a distaste for coarse and spurious quality. Perhaps reflections of this order may be more useful to young men than much declamation.—J.

Vers. 1—27.—*The two ways.* Here we have—
I. THE WAY OF SIN AND DEATH. This is: 1. The way of *thoughtlessness.* It is the "simple ones," the "young men void of understanding" (ver. 7), those who go heedlessly "near the corner," "the way to the house" of the tempter or the temptress (ver. 8). It is those who "do not consider," who do not think who they are, what they are here for, whither they go, what the end will be;—it is these who go astray and are found in the way of death. 2. The way of *darkness.* (Ver. 9.) Sin hates the light; it loves the darkness. It cannot endure the penetrating glance, the reproachful look, of the good and wise man. It prefers to be where it can better imagine that it is unseen of God. 3. The way of *shame.* (Vers. 10—20.) The result of habitual sin is to rob woman of her native purity, to make her impudent and immodest. How sad, beyond almost everything, the effect of guilt that will put shameful thoughts into a woman's mind, shameless words into a woman's lips! If sin will do this, what enormity of evil will it not work? 4. The way of *falsehood,* of pretence, of imposture. (Vers. 14, 15.) 5. The way of *weakness and defeat.* (Vers. 21, 22.) A man, under the power of sin, yields himself up; he is vanquished, he surrenders his manliness, he has to own to himself that he is miserably beaten. The strong man is slain by sin, the wounded is cast down (ver. 26). He who has gained victories on other fields, and won trophies in other ways, is utterly defeated, is taken captive, is humiliated by sin. 6. The way of *death and damnation.* (Ver. 27.)
II. THE WAY OF RIGHTEOUSNESS AND LIFE. (Vers. 1—5.) This is: 1. The way of *attention.* The will of God must first be heeded and understood. 2. The way of *holy love.* We must take Divine wisdom to our heart, and love it as that which is near and dear to us (ver. 4). 3. The way of *wise culture.* (Vers. 1—3.) We are to take the greatest pains to keep God's thought in our remembrance, before the eyes of our soul. We are to take every needful measure to keep it intact, whole, flawless in our heart. We are to find it a home in the inmost chamber, in the sacred places of our spirit. Then will this path of righteousness prove to us to be: 4. The path of *life.* Keeping his commandments, we shall "live" (ver. 2). We shall live the life of virtue, escaping the snares and wiles of the vicious (ver. 5). We shall live the life of piety and integrity, beloved of God, honoured of man, having a good conscience, cherishing a good hope through grace of eternal life.—C.

EXPOSITION.

CHAPTER VIII.

Vers. 1—36.—14. *Fourteenth admonitory discourse* concerning Wisdom—her excellence, her origin, her gifts. She is contrasted with the strange woman of ch. vii., and the exceeding greatness of the blessings which she offers exhibits in the most marked manner the nothingness of the deceiver's gifts. One is reminded of the celebrated episode of the choice of Hercules, delineated by Xenophon, 'Memorab.,' ii. 1. 21, etc. The chapter divides itself into four sections. (1) Introductory (vers. 1—3); Wisdom calls on all to listen, and gives reasons for trusting to her (vers. 4—11). (2) She displays her excellence (vers. 12—21). (3) She discourses of her origin and action (vers. 22—31). (4) She again inculcates the duty of hearkening to her instructions (vers. 32—36).

Ver. 1.—**Doth not Wisdom cry?** (see on ch. i. 20, and Introduction). The interrogative form, which expects an affirmative answer, is a mode of asserting a truth universally allowed. Wisdom is personified, though we are not so plainly confronted by an individual, as in the preceding case of the harlot. But it must be remembered that, whatever may have been the author's exact meaning, however worldly a view the original enunciation may have afforded, we, reading these chapters by the light cast upon them by later revelation, see in the description of Wisdom no mere ideal of practical prudence and good sense, no mere poetic personification of an abstract quality, but an adumbration of him who is the Wisdom of God, the coeternal Son of the Father. The open, bold, and public utterances of Wisdom are in happy contrast to the secret and stealthy enticements of Vice. So Christ, the true Wisdom, says, "I have spoken openly to the world; I ever taught in the synagogues, and in the temple, where all the Jews come together; and in secret spake I nothing" (John xviii. 20). The Septuagint changes the subject of this verse, and makes the pupil addressed: "Thou shalt proclaim (κηρύξεις) wisdom, that understanding (φρόνησις) may obey thee;" which seems to mean that, if you wish to acquire wisdom, so that it may serve you practically, you must act as a herald or preacher, and make your desire generally known. St. Gregory has some remarks about wilful ignorance of what is right. "It is one thing," he says, "to be ignorant; another to have refused to learn. For not to know is only ignorance; to refuse to learn is pride. And they are the less able to plead ignorance in excuse, the more that knowledge is set before them, even against their will. We might, perhaps, be able to pass along the way of this present life in ignorance of this Wisdom, if she herself had not stood in the corners of the way" ('Moral.,' xxv. 29).

Ver. 2.—**She standeth in the top of high places, by the way.** She takes her stand, not in thievish corners of the streets, like the harlot, but in the most open and elevated parts of the city, where she may be best seen and heard by all who pass by (see ch. i. 21, and note there). **In the places of the paths;** i.e. where many paths converge, and where people meet from different quarters.

Ver. 3.—The expressions in the text indicate the position which she takes and its capabilities. **At the hand of the gates** (1 Sam. xix. 3). She posts herself at the side of the city gates, under the archway pierced in the wall, where she is sure of an audience. **At the mouth of the city,** inside the gate, where people pass on their way to the country. **At the coming in at the doors,** by which persons enter the town. Thus she catches all comers, those who are entering, as well as those who are leaving the city. Here standing, as in the Agora or Forum, she crieth; she calls aloud, saying what follows (vers. 4—36). It is a fine picture of the comprehensiveness of the gospel, which is meant for high and low, prince and peasant; which is proclaimed everywhere, in the courts of kings, in the lanes of the country, in the hovels of the city; which sets forth the infinite love of God, who is not willing that any should perish, but would have all men come to the knowledge of the truth (2 Pet. iii. 9). Septuagint, "By the gates of the mighty she sits, in the entrances she sings aloud (ὑμνεῖται)."

Vers. 4—11.—She summons various classes of persons to attend to her, showing how trustworthy she is, and how precious her instruction.

Ver. 4.—**Unto you, O men, I call.** "Men," *ishim* (אִישִׁים); equivalent to ἄνδρες, *viri*, men in the highest sense, who have some wisdom and experience, but need further enlightenment (Isa. liii. 3; Ps. cxli. 4). **The sons of man;** בְּנֵי אָדָם, "children of Adam;" equivalent to ἄνθρωποι, *homines*, the general kind of men, who are taken up with material interests. St. Gregory notes ('Moral.,' xxvii. 6) that persons (*homines*) of perfect life are in Scripture sometimes called "men" (*viri*). And again, "Scripture is wont to call those persons 'men' who follow the ways of the Lord with firm and steady steps. Whence Wisdom says in the Proverbs, 'Unto you, O men, I call.' As if she were saying openly, 'I do not speak to women, but to men; because they who are of an unstable mind cannot at all understand my words'" ('Moral.,' xxviii. 12, Oxford transl.).

Ver. 5.—**O ye simple, understand wisdom.** "The simple," those not yet perverted, but easily influenced for good or evil. See on ch. i. 4, where also is explained the word *ormah*, used here for "wisdom;" equivalent to *calliditas* in a good sense, or πανουργία, as sometimes employed in the Septuagint; so here: νοήσατε ἄκακοι πανουργίαν, "subtlety." **Ye fools, be ye of an understanding heart.** For "fools" (*khesilim*), the intellectually heavy and dull, see on ch. i. 22. The heart is considered the seat of the mind or understanding (comp. ch. xv. 32; xvii. 16, etc.). Septuagint, "Ye that are untaught, take in heart (ἔνθεσθε καρδίαν)." The call thus addressed to various classes of persons is like the section in 1 John ii., "I write unto you, little children," etc.

Ver. 6.—I will speak of excellent things; de rebus magnis, Vulgate; σεμνὰ γὰρ ἐρῶ, Septuagint. The Hebrew nagid is elsewhere used of persons; e.g. a prince, leader (1 Sam. ix. 16; 1 Chron. xxvi. 24); so it may here be best translated "princely," "noble"—an epithet which the subject-matter of Wisdom's discourse fully confirms (comp. ch. xxii. 20, though the word there is different). Hitzig and others, following the Syriac, prefer the meaning, "plain, evident truths" (comp. ver. 9); but the former interpretation is most suitable. The opening of my lips shall be right things. That which I announce when I open my mouth is just and right (ch. xxiii. 16). Septuagint, ὀρθά.

Ver. 7.—Another co-ordinate reason for attention. My mouth; chek, "palate" (ch. v. 3, where see note); the organ of speech. Shall speak truth; emeth (see on ch. iii. 3). The verb הָגָה (hagah) properly means "to speak with one's self," "to meditate;" and so the versions translate here, meditabitur, μελετήσει; but this idea is not appropriate to the word joined with it, "the palate," and it must be taken to signify "to utter," as in Ps. xxxv. 28; xxxvii. 30, etc. Wickedness is an abomination to my lips. Resha, "wickedness," is the contrary of moral truth and right. Septuagint, "False lips are abominable in my sight."

Ver. 8.—In righteousness; i.e. joined with righteousness, equivalent to "righteous." In ch. iii. 16 the Septuagint has an addition which may perhaps be an echo of this passage: "Out of her mouth proceedeth righteousness, and she beareth upon her tongue law and mercy." But more probably it is derived partly from Isa. xlv. 23, and partly from ch. xxxi. 26. There is nothing froward or perverse in them. In the utterances of Wisdom there is nothing crooked, no distortion of the truth; all is straight-forward and direct.

Ver. 9.—They are all plain to him that understandeth. The man who listens to and imbibes the teaching of Wisdom finds these words intelligible, and "to the point." Opening his heart to receive Divine instruction, he is rewarded by having his understanding enlightened; for while "the natural man receiveth not the things of the Spirit of God" (1 Cor. ii. 14), yet "the secret of the Lord is with them that fear him" (Ps. xxv. 14), and "mysteries are revealed unto the meek" (Ecclus. iii. 19, Complutensian א²). Right to them that find knowledge (ver. 10). They form an even path without stumbling-blocks for

those who have learned to discern right from wrong, and are seeking to direct their lives in accordance with high motives. Septuagint, "They are all present (ἐνώπια) to those that understand, and right (ὀρθά) to those that find knowledge."

Ver. 10.—Receive my instruction, and not silver; i.e. acquire wisdom rather than silver, if ever the choice is yours. And knowledge rather than choice gold (comp. ver. 19; ch. iii. 14). (For "knowledge," daath, see on ch. ii. 10.) The comparison is implied rather than expressed in the first clause, while it is made clear in the second. Thus Hos. vi. 6, "I desired mercy, and not sacrifice," the second matter mentioned being, not necessarily of no importance, but always in such cases of inferior importance to the other. We may quote Horace's complaint of the worldliness of his countrymen, a marked contrast to the inspired counsel of Proverbs ('Epist.,' i. 1. 52)—

"Vilius argentum est auro, virtutibus aurum.
  O cives, cives! quærenda pecunia primum est,
  Virtus post nummos."

Ver. 11.—(See ch. iii. 14, 15, and notes.)

Vers. 12—21.—Wisdom tells of her own excellence.

Ver. 12.—I wisdom dwell with prudence; rather, as in the Revised Version, I have made subtilty (ver. 5) my dwelling. Wisdom inhabits prudence, animates and possesses that cleverness and tact which is needed for the practical purposes of life. So the Lord is said to "inhabit eternity" (Isa. lvii. 15). Septuagint, "I wisdom dwelt (κατεσκήνωσα) in counsel and knowledge," which recalls, "The Word was made flesh, and dwelt (ἐσκήνωσεν) among us" (John i. 14). In 1 Tim. vi. 16 we find the expression, "Who alone hath (μόνος ἔχων) immortality," exchanged with the phrase, "Who dwelleth (οἰκῶν) in the unapproachable light." And find out knowledge of witty inventions. This rendering refers to the production and solution of dark sayings which Wisdom effects. But the expression is better rendered, "knowledge of deeds of discretion" (ch. i. 4), or "of right counsels," and it signifies that Wisdom presides over all well-considered designs, that they are not beyond her sphere, and that she has and uses the knowledge of them. Septuagint, "I (ἐγὼ) called upon understanding," i.e. it is I who inspire all good and righteous thought.

Ver. 13.—The fear of the Lord is to hate evil. Wisdom here enunciates the proposition which is the foundation of all her teaching, only here, as it were, on the reverse side, not as the beginning of wisdom (ch. i. 7; ix. 10), but as the hatred of evil; she then proceeds to particularize the evil which the Lord hates. Taking the clause in this sense, we have no need to alter the persons and forms of the verbs to "I fear the Lord, I hate evil," as Dathe and others suggest; still less to suppress the whole paragraph as a late insertion. These violent measures are arbitrary and quite unnecessary, the present text allowing a natural and sufficient exposition. There can be no fellowship between light and darkness; he who serves the Lord must renounce the works of the devil. **Pride and arrogancy,** which are opposed to the sovereign virtue of humility, are the first sins which Wisdom names. These are among the things which the Lord is said to hate (ch. vi. 17, etc.). "Initium omnis peccati est superbia" (Ecclus. x. 15, Vet. Lat.). **The evil way;** i.e. sins of conduct, "way" being, as commonly, equivalent to "manner of life." **The froward mouth;** literally, *mouth of perverseness*, sins of speech (see on ch. ii. 12; and comp. x. 31); Vulgate, *os bilingue*.

Ver. 14.—Having said what she hates, Wisdom now says what she is, and what she can bestow on her followers. **Counsel is mine, and sound wisdom.** There is some doubt about the meaning of the word translated "sound wisdom" (*tushiyyah*). The Vulgate has *æquitas*; the Septuagint, ἀσφάλεια, "safety." The word occurs elsewhere in this book and in Job, but only in two other places of Scripture, viz. Isa. xxviii. 29 and Micah vi. 9. It means properly "elevation" or "furtherance," or, as others say, "substance;" and then that which is essentially good and useful, which may be wisdom, aid, or security (see on ch. ii. 7). Wisdom affirms that she possesses counsel and all that can help forward righteousness; see Job xii. 13, 16, passages very similar to the present (comp. Wisd. viii. 9, etc.). **I am understanding.** Wisdom does not merely possess these attributes; they are her very nature, as it is said, "God is love." St. Jerome's *mea est prudentia*, and the LXX.'s ἐμὴ φρόνησις, lose this trait. **I have strength.** Wisdom directs the energies and powers of her pupils, which without her control would be spent wrongly or uselessly (comp. Eccles. vii. 19). Wisdom, understanding, and might are named among the seven gifts of the Spirit in Isa. xi. 2; and we may see in the passage generally an adumbration of him who is called "Wonderful, Counsellor, the Mighty God" (Isa. ix. 6).

Ver. 15.—**By me kings reign.** By possession of wisdom kings are enabled to discharge their functions duly and righteously. So Solomon prayed for wisdom to enable him to rule his subjects properly (1 Kings iii. 9; Wisd. ix. 4). **Princes** (*rozenim*, ch. xxxi. 4); either those who are weighty, inflexible, or

those who weigh causes; the latter explanation seems most suitable. Vulgate, *legum conditores;* Septuagint, οἱ δυνάσται. These are said to **decree justice;** literally, *to engrave just decrees on tablets;* γράφουσι δικαιοσύνην, Septuagint. Early expositors take these words as spoken by Christ, to whom they are very plainly applicable (comp. Isa. xxxii. 1).

Ver. 16.—**Princes;** here *sarim*, "leaders." **All the judges of the earth.** These words stand without a conjunction, in apposition to what has preceded, by what is called *asyndeton summativum* (ch. i. 21), and gather in one view kings, princes, and leaders. Thus the Book of Wisdom, which speaks of the duties of rulers, commences by addressing οἱ κρίνοντες τὴν γῆν, "ye that are judges of the earth." In the East judgment of causes was an integral part of a monarch's duties. The reading of the Authorized Version is supported by the Septuagint, which gives κρατοῦσι γῆς. The Vulgate, Syriac, and Chaldee read, צדק, "justice," in place of ארץ, "earth;" but this seems to have been an alteration of the original text derived from some idea of the assertion there made being too comprehensive or universal. Nowack compares Ps. ii. 10 and cxlviii. 11, "Kings of the earth, and all people; princes, and all judges of the earth." The Fathers have taken these verses as spoken by God, and as asserting his supremacy and the providential ordering of human government, according to St. Paul's saying, "There is no power but of God; and the powers that be are ordained of God" (Rom. xiii. 1; see St. Augustine, 'De Civit. Dei,' v. 19).

Ver. 17.—**I love them that love me.** So Christ says (John xiv. 21), "He that loveth me shall be loved of my Father, and I will love him, and will manifest myself unto him." Love attracts love. "Magnes amoris est amor." They who love virtue and wisdom are regarded with favour by God, whose inspiration they have obeyed, obtaining grace for grace. So Ben Sira says, "Them that love her the Lord doth love" (Ecclus. iv. 14); so Wisd. vii. 28, "God loveth none but him that dwelleth with Wisdom." The Septuagint changes the verbs in this clause, though they are parts of the same word in the Hebrew: Ἐγὼ τοὺς ἐμὲ φιλοῦντας ἀγαπῶ. This reminds one of the passage in the last chapter of St. John (xxi. 15—17), where a similar interchange is made. **Those that seek me early shall find me** (see the contrast in ch. i. 28). "Early" may mean from tender years; but more probably it is equivalent to "earnestly," "strenuously," as people deeply interested in any pursuit rise betimes to set about the necessary work (comp. Isa. xxvi. 9; Hos. v. 15). The Septuagint, "They who seek (ζητοῦντες) me shall find."

So the Lord says (Matt. vii. 7), "Seek (ζη-τεῖτε), and ye shall find;" Ecclus. iv. 12, "He that loveth her loveth life; and they that seek to her early (οἱ ὀρθρίζοντες πρὸς αὐτὴν) shall be filled with joy" (comp. Luke xxi. 38).

Ver. 18.—**Riches and honour are with me** (see ch. iii. 16). Wisdom has these things in her possession to bestow on whom she will, as God gave them to Solomon in reward of his petition for wisdom (1 Kings iii. 13). **Durable riches and righteousness.** Things often regarded as incompatible. *Durable,* עָתֵק (*athek*), occurs only here (but see Isa. xxiii. 18), and means "old," "venerable," "long accumulated;" hence firm and lasting. Righteousness is the last reward that Wisdom bestows, without which, indeed, all material blessings would be nothing worth. Wealth obtained in a right way, and rightly used, is durable and stable. This was especially true under a temporal dispensation. We Christians, however, look not for reward in uncertain riches, but in God's favour here and happiness in another world. The Septuagint, "Possession of many things, and righteousness." What is denoted by "righteousness" is further explained in the following verses, 19—21.

Ver. 19.—**My fruit is better than gold.** We have had Wisdom called "a tree of life" (ch. iii. 18), and the gain from possessing her compared to gold and silver (ch. iii. 14). **Fine gold** (*paz*); Septuagint and Vulgate, "precious stone." The word signifies "purified gold"—gold from which all mixture or alloy has been separated. **My revenue**; Vulgate, *genimina mea;* Septuagint, γεννήματα; Hebrew, *tebuah,* "produce," "profits."

Ver. 20.—**I lead in the way** (better, *I walk in the way*) **of righteousness.** I act always according to the rules of justice. **In the midst of the paths of judgment.** I swerve not to one side or the other (ch. iv. 27). So the psalmist prays, "Teach me, O Lord, the way of thy statutes; and I shall keep it unto the end;" "Cause me to know the way wherein I should walk" (Ps. cxix. 33; cxliii. 8). And the promise is given to the faithful in Isa. xxx. 21, "Thine ears shall hear a word behind thee, saying, This is the way, walk ye in it, when ye turn to the right hand, and when ye turn to the left." Virtue, as Aristotle has taught us, is the mean between two extremes.

Ver. 21.—**That I may cause those that love me to inherit substance;** יֵשׁ (*yesh*), ὕπαρξις, "real, valuable possessions." Those who love Wisdom will walk in her path, follow her leading, and therefore, doing God's will, will be blessed with success. Such will lay up treasure in heaven, will provide bags which wax not old, will be pre-

paring for "an inheritance incorruptible, and undefiled, and that fadeth not away" (Matt. vi. 20; Luke xii. 33; 1 Pet. i. 4). The LXX. here inserts a paragraph as a kind of introduction to the important section which follows: "If I declare unto you the things which daily befall, I will remember to recount the things of eternity;" *i e.* thus far I have spoken of the advantages derived from Wisdom in daily circumstances; now I proceed to narrate her origin and her doings from all eternity. But the addition appears awkward, and is probably not now in its original position.

Vers. 22—31.—Wisdom speaks of her origin, her active operations, the part which she bore in the creation of the universe, her relation to God (see on ch. i. 20 and iii. 19, and Introduction). It is impossible to decide what was the exact view of the writer with regard to the wisdom of which he speaks so eloquently; but there can be no doubt that he was guided in his diction so as to give expression to the idea of him whom St. John calls the Word of God. The language used is not applicable to an impersonal quality, an abstract faculty of God. It describes the nature and office of a Person; and who that Person is we learn from the later Scriptures, which speak of Christ as the "Wisdom of God" (Luke xi. 49) and "the Power of God and the Wisdom of God" (1 Cor. i. 24). If we confine our inquiry to the question—What was in the mind of the author when he indited this wonderful section concerning Wisdom? we shall fail to apprehend its true significance, and shall be disowning the influence of the Holy Spirit, which inspires all Scripture, which prompted the holy men who spake to utter words of which they knew not the full spiritual significance, and which could only be understood by subsequent revelation. There is, then, nothing forced or incongruous in seeing in this episode a portraiture of the Second Person of the blessed Trinity, the essential Wisdom of God personified, the Logos of later books, and of the gospel. This interpretation obtained universally in the Church in the earliest times, and has commended itself to the most learned and reverent of modern commentators. That much which was contained in their own utterances was unknown to the prophets of old, that they did not fully perceive the mysteries which they darkly enunciated, we learn from St. Peter, who tells us that they who prophesied of the grace of Christ sought and searched diligently what the Spirit of God that was in them did point unto, and were shown that not unto themselves, but unto us, they ministered those things, secrets which angels themselves desire to look into (1 Pet. i. 10, etc.). Wisdom as a human endowment, animating all intellectual and even physical powers; Wisdom as communicating to man moral excellence and piety; Wisdom as not only an attribute of God, but itself as the eternal thought of God;—under these aspects it is regarded in our book; but under and through all it is more or less personified. *Khochmah* is contrasted in the next chapter, not with an abstraction, but with an actual woman of impure life—a real, not an imaginary, antagonist. The personality of the latter intimates that of the former (see Liddon, 'Bampt. Lects.,' ii.).

Ver. 22.—**The Lord possessed me.** Great controversy has arisen about the word rendered "possessed." The verb used is קָנָה (*kanah*), which means properly "to erect, set upright," also "to found, form" (Gen. xiv. 19, 22), then "to acquire" (ch. i. 5; iv. 5, 7, etc.) or "to possess" (ch. xv. 32; xix. 8). The Vulgate, Aquila, Theodotion, Symmachus, Venetian, give "possessed;" Septuagint, ἔκτισε, "made," and so Syriac. The Arians took the word in the sense of "created" (which, though supported by the LXX., it seems never to have had), and deduced therefrom the Son's inferiority to the Father—that he was made, not begotten from all eternity. Ben Sira more than once employs the verb κτίζω in speaking of Wisdom's origin; *e.g.* Ecclus. i. 4, 9; xxiv. 8. Opposing the heresy of the Arians, the Fathers generally adopted the rendering ἐκτήσατο, *possedit*, "possessed;" and even those who received the translation ἔκτισε, explained it not of creating, but of appointing, thus: The Father set Wisdom over all created things, or made Wisdom to be the efficient cause of his creatures (Rev. iii. 14). May we not say that the writer was guided to use a word which would express relation in a twofold sense? Wisdom is regarded either as the mind of God expressed in operation, or the Second Person of the Holy Trinity; and the verb thus signifies that God possesses in himself this essential Wisdom, and intimates likewise that Wisdom by eternal generation is a Divine Personality. St. John (John i. 1), before saying that the Word was God, affirms that "the Word was

with God (ὁ Λόγος ἦν πρὸς τὸν Θεόν)." So we may assert that Solomon has arrived at the truth that Wisdom was πρὸς τὸν Θεόν, if he has left it for later revelation to declare that ἡ Σοφία or ὁ Λόγος Θεὸς ἦν. Whichever sense we assign to the verb on which the difficulty is supposed to hang, whether we take it as "possessed," "formed," or "acquired," we may safely assume that the idea conveyed to Christian minds is this—that Wisdom, existing eternally in the Godhead, was said to be "formed" or "brought forth" when it operated in creation, and when it assumed human nature. **In the beginning of his way.** So the Vulgate, *in initio viarum suarum*. But the preposition "in" does not occur in the original; and the words may be better translated, "as the beginning of his way" (Septuagint, ἔκτισέ με ἀρχὴν ὁδῶν αὐτοῦ); *i.e.* as the earliest revelation of his working. Wisdom, eternal and uncreated, first puts forth its energy in creation, then becomes incarnate, and is now called, "the Firstborn of all creation (πρωτότοκος πάσης κτίσεως)" (Col. i. 15). Thus in Ps. ii. 7, "Thou art my Son; this day have I begotten thee" (Heb. i. 5); and, "When he bringeth in the Firstborn into the world, he saith, And let all the angels of God worship him" (Heb. i. 6). In the present clause, the ways of God are his works, as in Job xxvi. 14 and xl. 19, where behemoth is called "chief among the ways of God" (comp. Ps. cxlv. 17, where "ways" stands as a parallel to "works"). **Before his works of old.** These words are better regarded (with Delitzsch) as a second parallel object, קֶדֶם (*kedem*), translated "before," being not a preposition, but denoting previous existence. Hence we translate, "The foremost of his works of old;" *i.e.* the earliest revelation of his energy. There is a curious passage in the 'Book of Enoch,' ch. xlii., which speaks of the personality and pre-existence of Wisdom, of her desire to dwell among men, frustrated by man's wickedness: "Wisdom found no place where she could dwell; therefore was her dwelling in heaven. Wisdom came forth in order to dwell among the sons of men, and found no habitation; then she returned to her place, and took her seat among the angels." We may add Wisd. viii. 3, "In that she dwelleth with God (συμβίωσιν Θεοῦ ἔχουσα), she magnifieth her nobility."

Ver. 23.—**I was set up from everlasting.** The verb used here is remarkable. It is נָסַךְ (*nasak*), in niph.; and it is found in Ps. ii. 6, "I have set my King upon my holy hill." Both here and there it has been translated "anointed," which would make a noteworthy reference to Christ. But there seems no proof that the word has this meaning. It signifies properly "to pour forth" (as of molten metal), then "to put down," "to appoint or establish." The versions recognize this. Thus the Septuagint, "he established (ἐθεμελίωσε) me;" Vulgate, *ordinata sum;* Aquila, κατεστάθην; Symmachus, προε-χείρισμαι; Venetian, κέχυμαι (comp. Ecclus. i. 9). So what is here said is that Wisdom was from everlasting exalted as ruler and disposer of all things. To express eternal relation, three synonymous terms are used. *From everlasting;* πρὸ τοῦ αἰῶνος, Septuagint, as Delitzsch notes, points back to infinite distance. **From the beginning;** *i.e.* before the world was begun to be made; as St. John says (John i. 1), "In the beginning was the Word;" and Christ prays, "Glorify thou me with thine own self, with the glory which I had with thee before the world was" (John xvii. 5). **Or ever the earth was.** This looks to the most remote time after the actual creation, while the earth was being formed and adapted.

Ver. 24.—The pre-existence of Wisdom is still more expressly set forth. **When there were no depths** (vers. 27, 28). The waste of waters which covered the face of the earth is meant—that great deep on which primeval darkness brooded (Gen. i. 2). Before even this, man's earliest conception of the beginning of the world, uncreated Wisdom was. Septuagint, "before he made the abysses" (see on ch. iii. 20). **I was brought forth;** Vulgate, *et ego jam concepta eram;* Septuagint, at the end of ver. 25, γεννᾷ με, "he begetteth me." The verb here is חול (*chul*), which is used of the travailing of women, and is rightly translated, "brought forth by generation." It indicates in this place the energizing of Wisdom, her conception in the Divine mind, and her putting forth in operation. **When there were no fountains abounding with water;** *i.e.* springs in the interior of the earth (Gen. vii. 11; comp. Job xxii., xxvi., xxxviii.). Septuagint, "Before the springs of the waters came forward (προελθεῖν)."

Ver. 25. — **Before the mountains were settled** (Job xxxviii. 6). It is questioned *where* the mountains were supposed to be fixed, and some have thought that they are represented as fixed in the depths of the earth. But, as we learn from Gen. i. 9, they are regarded as rising from the waters, their foundations are laid in the great deep. So the psalmist, speaking of the waters, says, "They went up by the mountains, they went down by the valleys, unto the place which thou hast founded for them" (Ps. civ. 8; comp. Ps. xxiv. 2). What is here affirmed of Wisdom is said of Jehovah in Ps. xc. 2, "Before the mountains were brought forth, or ever thou hadst formed the earth and

the world, even from everlasting to everlasting thou art God."

Ver. 26.—**The earth, nor the fields.** The distinction intended is land as cultivated and occupied by buildings, etc., and waste uncultivated land outside towns. Septuagint, "The Lord made countries and uninhabited places (ἀοικήτους);" Vulgate, *Adhuc terram non fecerat, et flumina.* Hebrew, *chutsoth;* things without, abroad, hence open country. The Vulgate rendering, and that of Aquila and Symmachus, ἐξόδους, are plainly erroneous, as waters have already been mentioned (ver. 24). **The highest part of the dust of the world;** literally, *the head of the dusts of the world.* Some have interpreted this expression of "man," the chief of those creatures which are made of the dust of the ground (Gen. iii. 19; Eccles. iii. 20). But the idea comes in awkwardly here; it is not natural to introduce man amid the inanimate works of nature, or to use such an enigmatical designation for him. St. Jerome has, *cardines orbis terrarum,* "the world's hinges;" Septuagint, "the inhabited summits of the earth beneath the heavens;" according to St. Hilary ('De Trinit.,' xii.), "cacumina quæ habitantur sub cœlo." Others take the term to signify the capes or promontories of the world, the peaks and elevations; others, the clods of dry, arable land, in contrast to the untilled waste of waters; others, the chief elements, the matter of which the earth is composed. This last interpretation would lead us back to a period which has already been passed. Amid the many possible explanations, it is perhaps best (with Delitzsch, Nowack, etc.) to take *rosh,* "head" as equivalent to "sum," "mass," as in Ps. cxxxix. 17, "How great is the sum (*rosh*) of them!" Then the expression comprehensively means all the mass of earth's dust.

Ver. 27.—After asserting the pre-existence of Wisdom, the writer tells her part in the work of creation. **When he prepared the heavens, I was there.** When God made the firmament, and divided the waters above it and below (Gen. i. 7), Wisdom co-operated. **When he set a compass upon the face of the depth.** חוג (*chug*), "circle," or "circuit" (as Job xxii. 14), means the vault of heaven, conceived of as resting on the ocean which surrounds the earth, in partial accordance with the notion in Homer, who speaks of the streams of ocean flowing back into itself (ἀψόρροος), 'Iliad,' xviii. 399; 'Odyssey,' x. 508, etc. That the reference is not to the marking out a limit for the waters is plain from the consideration that this interpretation would make the verse identical with ver. 29. Thus in Isa. xl. 22 we have, "It is he that sitteth above the circle (*chug*) of the earth;" *i.e.* the vault of heaven that encircles the earth. Septuagint, "When he marked out (ἀφώριζε) his throne upon the winds." The translators have referred *tehom*, "depth," to the waters above.

Ver. 28.—**When he established the clouds above.** The reference is to the waters above the firmament (Gen. i. 7), which are suspended in the ether; and the idea is that God thus made this medium capable of sustaining them. Vulgate, *Quando æthera firmabat sursum;* Septuagint, "When he made strong the clouds above" (comp. Job xxvi. 8). **When he strengthened the fountains of the deep**; rather, as in the Revised Version, *when the fountains of the deep became strong;* i.e. when the great deep (Gen. vii. 11) burst forth with power (comp. Job xxxviii. 16). The Septuagint anticipates the following details by here rendering, "When he made secure the fountains of the earth beneath the heaven."

Ver. 29.—**When he gave to the sea his decree** (*chok.* as Job xxviii. 26; Jer. v. 22); or, *its bounds.* The meaning is much the same in either case, being what is expressed in Job xxxviii. 8, etc., "Who shut up the sea with doors . . . and prescribed for it my decree, and set bars and doors, and said, Hitherto shalt thou come, and no further, and here shall thy proud waves be stayed?" The LXX. omits this hemistich. **When he appointed the foundations of the earth.** Job xxxviii. 4, "Where wast thou when I laid the foundations of the earth? . . . Who determined the measures thereof? or who stretched the line upon it? Wherein were the foundations thereof fastened? or who laid the corner-stone thereof?"

Ver. 30.—**Then I was by him.** Wisd. ix. 9, "Wisdom was with thee; which knoweth thy works, and was present when thou madest the world." So John i. 2, "The Word was with God." **As one brought up** with him; Vulgate, *cuncta componens;* Septuagint, Ἤμην παρ' αὐτῷ ἁρμόζουσα, "I was with him arranging things in harmony." The Hebrew word is אָמוֹן (*amon*), "an artificer," "workman" (Jer. lii. 15). Thus in Wisd. vii. 22 Wisdom is called ἡ πάντων τεχνῖτις, "the worker of all things." The Authorized Version takes the word in a passive state, as equivalent to *alumnus*, "foster-child," and this interpretation is etymologically admissible, and may possibly, as Schultens suggests, be glanced at in St. John's expression (i. 18), "the only begotten Son, which is in the bosom of the Father." But as the point here is the creative energy of Wisdom, it is best to take the term as denoting "artificer." It will then accord with the expression δημιουργὸς, applied by the Fathers to the Word of God, by whom all things were made (Eph. iii. 9, Textus Receptus, and Heb. i. 2). **And I was daily his delight;** literally, *I was delights day by day*, which may mean either as in Authorized Version, or "I had delight continually," *i.e.* it may signify (1) either that God took pleasure in the wisdom which displayed his workmanship, saw that it was very good (Gen. i. 4, etc.), looked with delight on the beloved Son in whom he was well pleased (Matt. iii. 17, etc.); or (2) it may mean that Wisdom herself rejoiced in her power and her work, rejoiced in giving effect to the Creator's idea, and so "founding the earth" (ch. iii. 19). Vulgate, *delectabar per singulos dies.* The Septuagint adopts the former of these views, "I was that wherein he took delight." But the second interpretation seems most suitable, as the paragraph is stating rather what Wisdom is in herself than what she was in the eyes of Jehovah. What follows is a parallel. **Rejoicing always before him**; Vulgate, *ludens coram eo omni tempore*, as though the work of creation was a sport and pastime of a happy holiday. The expression is meant to denote the ease with which the operations were performed, and the pleasure which their execution yielded. David uses the same word, speaking of his dancing before the ark, when he says, "Therefore will I *play* before the Lord" (2 Sam. vi. 21; comp. ch. x. 23).

Ver. 31.—**Rejoicing in the habitable part of his earth.** Wisdom declares wherein she chiefly delighted, viz. in the world as the habitation of rational creatures. "And God saw everything that he had made, and, behold, it was very good" (Gen. i. 31); comp. Ps. civ. 31, and see the eloquent account of Wisdom in the book so named (vii. 22—viii. 1). **My delights were with the sons of men.** Man, made in the image of God, is the principal object of creative Wisdom's pleasure; and her joy is fulfilled only in the Incarnation. When the Word became flesh, then was the end and design of creation exhibited, and the infinite love of God towards man made, as it were, visible and palpable. Septuagint, "Because he rejoiced when he completed the world (τὴν οἰκουμένην), and rejoiced in the children of men."

Vers. 32—36.—Wisdom renews the exhortation before given (ch. v. 7; vii. 24), but now on higher, and not merely moral or social grounds. She deduces, from her Divine origin and her care for man, the lesson that she is to be sought and prized and obeyed above all things.

Ver. 32.—**Now therefore**—having regard to what I have revealed of myself—**hearken unto me, O ye children;** Septuagint, "Hear me, my son." **Blessed are they that keep my ways.** The expression is interjectional: "Blessings on the man! salvation to the man!" as in ch. iii. 13. For the *ways* of Wisdom, see ch. iii. 17.

Ver. 33.—**Be wise.** This will be the effect of attending to the injunction, **Hear instruction** (see on ch. iii. 4). The Vatican text of the Septuagint omits this verse; it is added in the Alexandrian and Sin.[2]

Ver. 34.—**Watching daily at my gates.** The idea suggested has been variously taken; *e.g.* as that of eager students waiting at the school door for their teacher's appearance; clients besieging a great man's portals; Levites guarding the doors of the temple; a lover at his mistress's gate. This last notion is supported by Wisd. viii. 2, "I loved her, and sought her out from my youth; I desired to make her my spouse, and I was a lover of her beauty." **Waiting at the posts of my doors**; keeping close to the entrance, so as to be quite sure of not missing her whom he longs to see.

Ver. 35.—**For whoso findeth me findeth life.** Here is the reason why the man is blessed who attends to the instruction of Wisdom. A similar promise is made at ch. iii. 16, 18, 22. The truth here enunciated is also spoken of the Word of God, the everlasting Son of the Father. John i. 4, "In him was life; and the life was the light of men;" John iii. 36, "He that believeth on the Son hath eternal life;" John xvii. 3, "This is life eternal, that they should know thee the only true God, and him whom thou didst send, even Jesus Christ" (comp. John viii. 51; 1 John v. 12; Ecclus. iv. 12). **Shall obtain favour of the Lord;** Vulgate, *hauriet salutem,* which happily renders the

Hebrew verb (ch. xii. 2). The grace of God bringeth salvation (Titus ii. 11). Septuagint, "For my outgoings (ἔξοδοι) are the outgoings of life, and the will is prepared by the Lord (καὶ ἑτοιμάζεται θέλησις παρὰ Κυρίου)." This latter clause was used by the Fathers, especially in the Pelagian controversy, to prove the necessity of prevenient grace (see St. Augustine, 'Enchiridion,' ii. 32; 'De Gratia,' vi. 16, 17).

Ver. 36.—**He that sinneth against me wrongeth his own soul.** So Septuagint and Vulgate. And the truth stated is obvious—he who refuses to obey Wisdom, and transgresses her wholesome rules, will smart for it. Every sin involves punishment, injures the spiritual life, and demands satisfaction. But Delitzsch and others take חֹטְאִי, "my sinning one," "my sinner," in the older sense of "missing," as Job v. 24, the derived meaning of "sinning" springing naturally from the idea of deviating from the right way or failing to hit the mark. So here the translation will be "he who misseth me," which is a good contrast to "whoso findeth me," of ver. 35. He who takes a path which does not lead to wisdom is guilty of moral suicide. **All that hate me love death** (ch. vii. 27). "He that believeth not the Son shall not see life; but the wrath of God abideth on him" (John iii. 36). They who will not hearken to Wisdom, and who scorn her counsels, do virtually love death, because they love the things and the practices which lead to death, temporal and spiritual. Job xii. 10, "They that sin are enemies to their own life" (comp. Wisd. i. 12).

HOMILETICS.

Ver. 5.—*Wisdom for the simple.* We may divide the simple into three classes. 1. There are those who think themselves wise while they are but fools: there is no hope for such. 2. There are people who make no pretence to wisdom, but who have chosen folly, and are quite indifferent to the claims and charms of wisdom. 3. There are anxious seekers after wisdom, who feel their present ignorance and incompetence with acute distress, and long to be among the wise, but despair of reaching the privileged circle. The first class will refuse to believe that the call of wisdom is for them, but to the other two it may come with effect.

I. The simple need wisdom. This reflection should concern the second class—those who as yet have despised and rejected wisdom. 1. *Wisdom is a joy.* Even pleasure is rejected in the renunciation of truth, knowledge, thought, the vision of God, and the revelation of his will. The narrow mind is a dark mind, and when the light of God breaks in it will be seen that many new delights of knowledge and joys of Divine truth, which have long been missed, can now be happily received. 2. *Wisdom is a safeguard.* Men stumble in the dark. Snares are set for the unwary. In this great, mysterious world we may easily go astray and be lost, perhaps be entrapped in fearful soul-perils. It is much to know the way, to know ourselves, to know our dangers, to know the will of God and how to have his guiding and saving help. 3. *Wisdom is life.* The foolish soul is but half alive, and it is on the road to destruction. Mere knowledge itself is a free intellectual life, and the exercise of thought in the practical application of the truth which we have assimilated, i.e. *wisdom,* is a living activity. It is most unfortunate that many young men in the present day seem to despise all intellectual pursuits, and confine the attention of their leisure moments to idle amusements or at best to athletics. They fail to see the mental death that they are courting. But infinitely worse are they who turn from the moral side of wisdom—the fear of the Lord—and pursue the folly of godlessness, for this is soul-death.

II. THE SIMPLE MAY HAVE WISDOM. Here is the encouragement for the third class of the simple. It is for children, for weak minds, and for uneducated people. 1. *Mental improvement is attainable.* Where there is a will to rise, the young man under most disadvantageous circumstances will find the means to cultivate self-education. 2. *The highest wisdom is spiritual.* This wisdom is not like Greek philosophy—only open to intellectual culture. It is the truth of God that may be revealed to "babes and sucklings" (Matt. xxi. 16), and yet it is the highest truth. To be spiritually wise we need not be mentally clever. What is wanted is a sincere love of truth, a pure heart, and a childlike teachableness. 3. *The gospel brings wisdom to the simple.* That gospel was scoffed at for its apparent simplicity. Yet it was indeed the wisdom as well as the power of God (1 Cor. i. 24). Christ comes to us as the eternal Wisdom incarnate. The simple may know him, and when such receive Christ they receive the Light of the world and a loftier wisdom than was ever reached by the sages of antiquity or can ever be attained in the cold light of science.

Ver. 9.—*Plain words.* The words of wisdom are here described as "plain words." This expression has been so often abused that it is almost as important to see what it does not mean as to consider what it does mean.

I. WHAT THE EXPRESSION DOES NOT MEAN. 1. *Lack of grace.* A mistake arising from the confusion of two meanings of the term "plain" has been pointed out by Archbishop Whately, and yet it is often repeated. "Plain" means smooth, simple, easy, intelligible; "plain" also means bare, unadorned, unbeautiful. The two meanings are quite distinct. But some have thought that a plain sermon must be a sermon wanting in all grace of style and beauty of illustration. This is an inappropriate use of the word "plain." The words of Christ were plain, *i.e.* clear and simple; yet they were very beautiful and full of living illustrations. The duty to be plain is no excuse for slovenliness of speech. 2. *Intellectual feebleness.* Some people insist on having a "simple gospel" in a way that leads one to think they would condemn all vigour of thought. They forget that the teaching of St. Paul, which they admire so much, teemed with the highest intellectuality, and that he regarded the truth of the crucified Christ as the wisdom of God, and only as falsely mistaken for foolishness by the Greeks. It is the charm of the highest thinking that it can simplify difficulties. We sometimes fail to detect the great intellectual power of a writer just because this has been so perfect as to disguise all effort and make the result of processes of thought clear; while the laboured attempts of weaker minds induce us to mistake obscurity for profundity. Any subject looks simple in the hands of a master. 3. *Rudeness and offensiveness.* Disagreeable people make a virtue of being plain-spoken when they are really harsh and inconsiderate. There is no unkindness about the plain words of the Bible. The Christian teacher should remember the admonitions, "Be pitiful, be courteous."

II. WHAT THE EXPRESSION DOES MEAN. 1. It signifies that the words of wisdom are *intelligible.* The first object of revelation, of course, is to reveal. The first object of speech is to declare thoughts. It is the neglect of this simple point that has given an excuse for the sarcasm that "words were invented to conceal thoughts." The first duty of the speaker is to be plain. Afterwards he may be ornate if he will. But when the decorations of speech encumber its free movement and prevent it from accomplishing its practical ends, they are altogether encumbrances. And when intellectual power is wasted on a mere display of its own exercise, or confined to inventing difficulties and making obscure what was originally clear and simple, this also is misdirected. The Divine wisdom of the Bible claims to be intelligible. It is true that many people find great difficulties in its pages, and all of us must confess that they are not to be fully measured and sounded. But (1) they who approach them in a right way, having a spiritual mind, so necessary for the discernment of spiritual things, will be able to understand the main, most important truths of Christianity; and (2) whatever disputes may be raised about the meaning of the more abstract doctrines, the directions of duty and the indications of the things we are to do for our soul's welfare are plain; indeed, the obscurity of religious subjects varies proportionately with their abstractness, with their separation from our life and duty. 2. It signifies that the words of wisdom indicate *a plain and simple course of action.* They are "right," or rather "straight to those that find knowledge." We are not called to any complicated course of action. The intricacies of casuistry are not to be found in the Book of Proverbs nor anywhere else in the Bible. The way of duty is simple and straightforward.

Ver. 13.—*Hatred of evil.* I. RELIGION INCLUDES MORALS. This is the broad lesson of the text. It should be accepted as a self-evident truism. Yet it has been often obscured by dangerous sophisms. Thus some have regarded religion as consisting in correctness of creed or in assiduity of devotion—things treated by God as worthless unless accompanied by righteousness of conduct (Isa. i. 10—17). There is a common impression that religious merits may be pleaded as a set-off against moral deficiencies. No assumption can be more false, nor can any be more degrading or more injurious. The reverse is true. Religiousness increases the guilt of unrighteousness of life by raising the standard up to which one is supposed to live, and also adds the sin of hypocrisy. True religion is impossible without a proportionate devotion to righteousness, because it consists in the fear of God. But God is holy; to reverence him must involve the adoration of his character—the love of goodness and the corresponding detestation of its opposite.

II. RELIGION INSPIRES MORALS WITH STRONG EMOTION. Morality is to obey the law. Religion goes further, and *hates* evil. It is not a matter of outward conduct only. It goes down to the secret springs of action. It rouses the deepest passions of the soul. We cannot accept Mr. M. Arnold's definition of religion as "morality touched with emotion," because it ignores the foundation of religion in "the fear of the Lord," in devotion to a personal God; but the phrase may serve as an apt description of an essential characteristic of religion. The difficulty we all feel is that, while we know the better way we are often so weak as to choose the worse. A cold, bare exposition of morality will be of little use with this difficulty. What we want is a powerful impulse, and that impulse it is the function of religion to supply. It makes goodness not only visible but beautiful and attractive, and it inspires a hunger and thirst after righteousness, a passion for a God-like life in the love of God, a yearning after the likeness of Christ in devotion of heart to him. It also makes evil appear hideous, detestable, by its horrible opposition to these affections.

III. AMONG RELIGIOUS EMOTIONS IS THE PASSION OF HATRED. Religion is not based upon hatred. It begins with "the fear of the Lord," with reverence for God rising up to love. No strong thing can rest on a mere negation. Neither morality nor religion starts from an attitude in regard to evil. But they lead on to this, and they are not perfect without it. The passion of hatred is natural; it has a useful, though a low, place in the array of spiritual forces. It is abused when it is spent upon persons, but it is rightly indulged against evil principles and practices. We are morally defective unless we can feel "the hate of hate, and scorn of scorn." One of the means by which we are helped to resist sin is found in this hatred of it. It is not enough that we disapprove of it. We must loathe and abhor it from the very bottom of our hearts.

IV. RELIGIOUS HATRED IS DETESTATION OF EVIL ITSELF, NOT THE MERE DISLIKE OF ITS CONSEQUENCES. When Paley, in his 'Moral Philosophy,' described the function of religion in aiding morality as the addition of the prospect of future rewards and promises, he expressed a common-sense truth, but a very low truth detached from more spiritual ideas and a very partial representation of the case. Religious morality is not simply nor chiefly the fear of God as a Judge who will punish us if we do wrong. It is reverence for a holy Father leading to hatred of all that is displeasing to him. We have no religion till we go beyond the instinctive dislike for pain that follows sin to hatred of sin itself. This is the test of true religion—that we love goodness and hate evil *for their own sakes.* It is interesting to observe that the sin selected for special abhorrence on the part of those who are inspired by "the fear of the Lord" is pride. This is spiritual wickedness of the most fatal character. In its feeling of personal merit and self-sufficiency it excludes both repentance and faith—the two fundamental conditions of spiritual religion. Therefore the spirit of the Pharisee and all pride must be hated above all things, and will be hated by those who have true reverence for the great and holy God, and true love for the lowly Christ who promised the kingdom of heaven to the " poor in spirit " (Matt. v. 3).

Ver. 17.—*The blessedness of loving and seeking Christ.* Wisdom is here personified. This is only the beginning of a process that is to grow through subsequent ages, manifesting itself in the Books of Wisdom and Ecclesiasticus, and finally developing into the doctrine of the " Logos " and the great revelation of Christ as the incarnate Word of God. We must not pretend to see the perfected thought in its earliest germ. The first personification of wisdom is little more than a figure of speech, an instance of the rich imaginative habits of Oriental thinking. Nevertheless, we know Christ to be the full, living embodiment of God's wisdom. What is true of that wisdom is true of him. And, therefore, though the writer of the words before us had no thought of Jesus Christ the Son of God and Son of man, his teaching concerning Divine wisdom may be most useful when we connect it with the one perfect revelation of wisdom in our Saviour.

I. LOVE FOR LOVE. 1. *Love to Christ must precede a deep knowledge of Christ.* We love before we seek and find. Of course, we must know something of him to arouse our love ; but when this initial knowledge is attained, Love must have her perfect work before knowledge can ripen. 2. *Love to Christ must be based on what is lovable in him.* Wisdom is beautiful and attractive, and can excite love. How much more, then, should the incarnation of Wisdom in our brother man do this ! The contemplation of the beautiful life of Christ and the study of his perfect character urge us to love him ; but surely what he has done for us, his sacrifice of himself, his death on our behalf, must be our chief grounds for loving him. 3. *This love to Christ will be met by his love in return.* It is true that his love precedes ours, nay, that it is the great source of our love. But (1) it is not felt and enjoyed till it is returned, so that then it seems to come afresh as an answer to our love ; and (2) there must be a stronger, more tender, more intimate love to those who appreciate it than can be given to others. Christ loved all men, but not as he loved St. John. Christians loving Christ enjoy his peculiar love. 4. *To be loved by Christ is the best reward of loving him.* True love is satisfied with nothing less than a return of love, but it is satisfied with this. If we have nothing else we have a pearl of great price in the love of Christ. Then we can afford to lose all earthly good things, can count them but dung, that we may win Christ.

II. FINDING FOR SEEKING. 1. *We must seek Christ if we would possess him.* He offers himself to all as a Saviour and a Master. But he must be followed and found. Our love to him will be the great attraction ever drawing us nearer to him. 2. *The search for Christ must be earnest if it is to be successful.* He will not answer a half-hearted call. Till we seek him with determination, reality, persistence, we shall meet no response. We must seek him before all things, must make Christ the chief end of life. 3. *This earnest seeking will be rewarded by the receiving of Christ.* Wisdom comes to him who seeks laboriously and patiently ; much more will Wisdom incarnate, Wisdom with a heart to sympathize. Such a response will be the best reward of seeking. Better than anything that Christ could send us will be his own coming to dwell in our hearts. This will be the satisfaction of anxious inquiry in a full response, the blessing of love with love and close communion.

Vers. 22—31.—*The primeval glory of Divine wisdom.* I. THE HIGHEST WISDOM IS CREATED BY GOD. " The Lord created me as the first of his way." This idea was suggested to the Greeks in the myth of Athene, who sprang from the head of Zeus. It is the poetic form of the great truth that God is the Creator of thoughts as well as of things ; and it suggests that he not only called individual intelligences into being, but originated the primary laws and conditions of all intelligence, just as he ordained the laws of nature and the conditions of physical existence as well as the rocks and plants and animals subsequently created.

II. DIVINE WISDOM WAS ANTECEDENT TO MATERIAL CREATION. " 'Twas wrought from everlasting, from the beginning, or ever the earth was." Thought precedes action. Design anticipates execution. The architect comes before the builder.

Archetypal ideas precede creative work. In the awful depths of primeval antiquity the great Thinker wrought out the plans of the universe which as the great Worker he has been since evolving in visible existences.

III. Wisdom accompanied and directed physical creation. " I was by him as a master-worker." Wisdom did not cease when force appeared. The two wrought together. The result of their joint operation is the energetic cosmos—force and thought triumphing over death and chaos. When we endeavour to discover the secrets of nature, we are searching out the wisdom of God. When we learn the laws and processes of nature, we are able to think the thoughts of God. The naturalist should walk reverently, for he is treading in the footsteps of the mind of God. It should be our aim in studying nature to find God in his wisdom.

IV. The Divine wisdom in creation leads on to the triumph of life and order. First there is the confusion of the elements. Gradually these elements are marshalled into order till Wisdom is able to " rejoice in his earthly world." The onward movement of all things here indicated and illustrated very fully by recent science reveals the wisdom of God with increasing clearness. Instead of thinking of that wisdom as chiefly manifested in primitive creation, we should see that it is most active and most glorious in the latest and richest development of the life of the universe.

V. This wisdom is one of the most glorious of the Divine attributes. God has glory of thought as well as glory of character. There must be all phases of perfection in the perfect Mind. God is not only to be regarded on the side of moral law and religious worship. He is the great Mathematician, Architect, Philosopher, Poet. Our thoughts of God are too " Churchy." God is not only in the church. He is much in the fields. He has his workshops as well as his temples; nay, they are his best temples. Let us try to find him in " secular " thought and work, and worship him the more for the wisdom seen in his " earthly world."

Ver. 29.—*The decree of the sea.* We live under the reign of law. This fact is taken to be the late revelation of modern science. But it is embedded in Old Testament teaching. There we see that the laws of nature, which are but the ways of God on earth, are recognized as fixed and stable. But the Bible helps us in two ways in examining those laws. First, it traces them back to their origin in a personal will. These are not merely channels of a blind force. They are decrees of an authority. Secondly, it teaches us to believe that they are good, wisely directed and tending to righteousness. They come from a wise, holy, just, and benevolent source. The decree of the sea has a special significance.

I. It has a vast domain. The sea covers three parts of the surface of the globe. Leagues upon leagues of spreading ocean roll round the earth with every tide. The sea is deep, and hides in its many waters myriads of living creatures. The fearful storms that sweep its surface tell sad tales of its more than giant strength. Here we are face to face with a frightful nature-power. Yet that power is under law. God's decree encircles it, and his hand reins it in with irresistible might. The sea is great, but God is greater; strong, but God is stronger. As we look at the fearful might and majesty of the ocean, we are called to bow before the infinitely greater Power who holds its waters in the hollow of his hand. If we tremble before its terror, we may remember that it is but the inanimate slave of our Father in heaven.

II. It is enshrined in mystery. Men have discovered some of the laws of tides, currents, storms, etc. Yet the ocean is still, in many respects, a great mystery. What caverns are hidden beneath its dark waters? What monsters of the deep may still elude the grasp of man's observation? What secret terrors may burst upon his astounded gaze? Here is indeed a mystery. Yet this is all known to God, governed by God, subject to his law, humbly obedient to his decree. God rules over all the mysteries of the universe.

III. It governs change. The sea is the symbol of fickleness and deception—to-day smooth as a mirror, " green calm below, blue quietness above" (Whittier); to-morrow a black and storm-tossed chaos. Its restless waves never cease to crawl to and fro on the quietest day; its tides are ever ebbing and flowing. Yet it obeys law. There are laws of change, as in night and day, the seasons, etc. God rules over all the vicissitudes of life. Change does not mean chance.

IV. IT OVERRULES CONFUSION. God's decree does not prevent the tempest, but the tempest itself obeys the law of God. The wild and wintry waste of waters, flecked with foam, and scoured with angry billows, is all under law and order. It is so in life. God does not prevent trouble; but he overrules it and limits its extent.

This decree of the sea is typical of the Divine government of what looks most tumultuous and lawless in life. Apply it throughout with the four points—vastness, mystery, change, and confusion—(1) to earthly circumstances; (2) to the ocean of human life; (3) to the soul, that sea of many storms.

Ver. 30.—*The pre-eminent glory of Christ.* This is affirmed of wisdom, and wisdom in the Proverbs is always an abstraction, an attribute of God, or a grace conferred upon man. Thus we have the highly imaginative picture of a certain *quality of thought* described like a personal favourite in the heavenly presence. But surely it is not necessary for us to rest with this idea. The New Testament cannot be out of our minds when we read the Old. It was not long before Jews learnt to personify wisdom, and when Christ appeared he realized in his own Person what had previously been ascribed to an abstract quality. Christ is "the Truth" (John xiv. 6) and "the Wisdom of God" (1 Cor. i. 24). His pre-existence is affirmed by himself (John viii. 58) and repeatedly asserted by his apostles (*e.g.* Col. i. 16). We may, then, think of Christ embodying this wisdom of God in the awful ages of the past, and see how truly what is here predicated of wisdom applies to him in whom that wisdom dwelt.

I. WISDOM IN CHRIST WAS WITH GOD. "I was by him." 1. *Wisdom was always with God,* always at his right hand. There was never a time when God acted blindly, imperfectly, without full consciousness. We have no ground for thinking of a lawless chaos previous to the exercise of Divine wisdom and power in creation. Even when the world was "without form and void" (Gen. i. 2), God's wise thought presided over it. God's mind did not grow like ours, from infantile simplicity. He was ever fully God. 2. *Christ was similarly eternal with God.* "The Word was with God" (John i. 1). When he came to our earth he came forth from God. His condescension was seen in this, that he left his place by the right hand of his Father and came down to dwell with men.

II. WISDOM IN CHRIST WAS CONCERNED IN CREATION. 1. *God made the universe in wisdom.* It bears the impress of thought. Deep purposes have impregnated it. Creation is a parable of infinite ideas. 2. *God created all things through Christ.* "By whom he made the worlds" (Heb. i. 2). Of course, the humanity of Jesus was not then existing. But the Divine side of our Lord was not only eternal; it was even directly active. Therefore there is a Christ-spirit in nature.

III. WISDOM IN CHRIST WAS GOD'S DAILY DELIGHT. 1. *God rejoices over his work,* as an artist over the thing of beauty that his hand has fashioned according to the dream of his heart. "God saw that it was good" (Gen. i. 10). The thought that is in God's work is his especial delight. He cares not for mere exhibitions of brute force. He loves wisdom. 2. *God rejoices over Christ.* So Christ is God's "beloved Son" (Matt. iii. 17). There are times when we grieve our Father, though at other seasons he may smile upon us. But Christ always dwelt under the smile of his Father, a daily delight—rejoiced in for his wisdom and the holy and gracious use he made of it.

IV. CHRIST, BY HIS WISDOM, WAS REJOICING ALWAYS BEFORE GOD. Wisdom is a source of joy. Wisdom devoted to God is doubly joyous. Christ had an ancient joy (John xv. 11). He left a happy home to come to us. The word for this joy is "sporting." Is there humour in nature? May there be in heaven those lighter, innocent joys which make up so much of the mirth of children on earth? Why should Christ have been always solemn?

Vers. 35, 36.—*Life and favour with God.* It is common to see this and similar passages applied directly to the soul's possession of God, or to the special Christian faith in Jesus Christ. Now, it is quite true that we have here in germ what will lead up to those experiences. But apart from the mistake of ignoring the distinction between the elementary truth and its full development, there is a practical consideration that is too often overlooked. It is thought to be good policy to "Christianize" these passages of the Old Testament; *i.e.* it is thought they are thus most profitably used. On this low ground even an answer can be given—it may be shown that the policy is bad. The more Christian idea is true in itself. But it is expressed clearly enough in the New Testament. We gain no new light, therefore, if we contrive to see it here. We simply repeat a lesson that we have learnt elsewhere. But if we take the more literal meaning of the words, then, though the thought given to us may not be so exalted nor so valuable as the perfected Christian thought, it may have a distinct worth and use of its own, and therefore may add somewhat to our knowledge of Divine things —an addition which we should not have if we read the words as a mere repetition of what we had already learnt elsewhere, however much more important that other lesson might be. The New Testament teaches us that we have life in Christ. We who have that later and fuller revelation gain little or nothing by reading the same truth in the Book of Proverbs. That life is to be found in the Divine wisdom may be a less valuable thought. But it is a distinct thought, and therefore some addition to our knowledge; and as such it should be spiritually helpful to us. For this reason, though it may be perfectly legitimate for us to show how the words of our text foreshadow the great truths of Christianity, it may be more profitable for us to keep to their simple meaning, and see how life and Divine favour are received through the finding of Divine wisdom.

I. WHAT IS MEANT BY FINDING DIVINE WISDOM. 1. It is not the mere *knowledge of religious doctrine.* Many have this, and yet miss the life eternal. We may know the Bible without knowing God. 2. It is not the results of some rare *intuition,* nor the achievements of elaborate *intellectual effort;* it is neither the vision of the mystic nor the secret of the Gnostic. For this wisdom is repeatedly offered to the simple with a most general invitation (*e.g.* vers. 4, 5). 3. To find Divine wisdom is to come to the *knowledge of God* as far as this affects our own *conduct,* to know his disposition towards us, his will regarding our conduct, the way of life to which he calls us; it is further to know so much of God's ways and thoughts as to be able to set them before us as a pattern, and thus to imbibe some of the great primeval wisdom described in the preceding verses; lastly, it is to set these thoughts in relation to practice and to make the knowledge of Divine things the rule of life.

II. HOW LIFE AND THE FAVOUR OF GOD RESULT FROM THE FINDING OF WISDOM. 1. *Life.* (1) In this wisdom we see the way to life—that life which is to Christians here on earth as well as hereafter the life eternal. (2) The only life worth living is that lived with thoughts of God and aims directed by the knowledge of God. Eternal life consists in this knowledge of God. 2. *The favour of God.* God is pleased with us in so far as we walk in his ways. Divine wisdom only can direct us aright, so that we may please God. But the very habit of mind that consists in the thinking of Divine thoughts and the desiring and attempting to accomplish the purposes of Divine wisdom must be pleasing to God.

> " Base-minded they that want intelligence;
> For God himself for wisdom most is prais'd,
> And men to God thereby are nighest rais'd."
> (Spenser.)

III. HOW SELF-INJURY AND DEATH RESULT FROM THE LOSS OF THIS WISDOM. "He that misseth me," etc. 1. The *common evils* of life will lead to our ruin unless we are saved by higher means. The traveller who rejects the guide may perish in the perils of his path; the patient who disobeys the physician may die of his disease. We shall ruin ourselves in sin "if we neglect so great salvation." 2. The *rejection of Divine wisdom* is itself a fatal sin. It is our duty to hearken to its voice. If we refuse to do this, we shall suffer as a penalty for our wilful disobedience to the message from Heaven.

HOMILIES BY VARIOUS AUTHORS.

Vers. 1—9.—*Wisdom's proclamation.* Again it is a poetical personification of truth, of God's Word, of religion, morality, sense, prudence; for all these are included in the comprehensive conception of wisdom that is placed before us.

I. THE PROCLAMATION OF TRUTH HAS NEVER FAILED IN THE WORLD. The cry is coeval with the world, with the conscience of man. The preacher has an institution second to none in antiquity and in honour.

II. THE PREACHER MUST BE CONSPICUOUS TO AND AUDIBLE BY ALL. (Vers. 2, 3.) On raised ground, in lonely paths (ver. 2), in the open air, in the field and forest; and (ver. 3) in the towns and cities, at the places of public resort and traffic, at the gates in the Orient, in the centre of Western cities, the preacher's voice has been heard. All eminent teachers in books are truly agents of Wisdom, and heralds of the kingdom of God.

III. THE SUBSTANCE OF TRUE PREACHING MUST BE THE SAME IN EVERY AGE. 1. It is *human* (ver. 3), and therefore intelligible, rational, practical. 2. It is especially addressed to *inexperience*—to the foolish and the thoughtless (see on ch. i. 4). 3. It deals with *clear* and *manifest* truth (see Hitzig's reading of ver. 6), and so commends itself to every man's conscience in the sight of God. 4. It is *disinterested*, free from sophistry and compromise (ver. 7). 5. It is *just—correct* and *accurate* in knowledge of human nature and of Divine things (ver. 8). And thus it is: 6. *Acceptable* and irresistible by the "honest and good heart" (ver. 9).—J.

Vers. 10—21.—*Wisdom's pleadings.* She has nothing novel to say concerning her nature, value, and blessings. Preaching must in the main be repetition; the iteration of the old, not with dry and sterile monotony, but with that freshness which comparison with everyday facts and illustrations gives. New combinations of facts are ever arising in which to frame the old precepts and set them forth. Besides, love gives novelty to old truth, as the old song is enjoyed from the lips of the latest sweet singer.

I. SHE APPEALS TO COMPARISON. (Vers. 10, 11.) By comparison we increase and strengthen our perceptions. In the knowledge of man, books, art, life, comparison is everything. We are to compare Wisdom with *material objects of sense*, such as gold and silver, that we may see her to be incomparable; and so each for ourselves repeat the choice of Solomon (comp. on ch. iii. 14, 15).

II. SHE APPEALS TO ASSOCIATION. (Ver. 12.) Wisdom dwells with prudence. In modern language, the general implies the particular. Wisdom is intelligence in general; prudence, the appreciation of it in particular cases. In the poetical mode of representation we should say that Piety and Prudence are sisters, and go hand-in-hand, daughters of the voice of God, as Wordsworth said of duty. So, too, Wisdom has insight into enigmas, dark sayings, and generally deep things of God (see on ch. i. 4).

III. SHE UNFOLDS THE CONTENTS OF HER MIND. (Vers. 13, 14.) One of her many *aliases* is the fear of Jehovah. And this is religion, which includes all *wholesome aversions*, viz. *wickedness* in general, and in particular *assumption, arrogance, evil habits, perverted* speech. In other words, her sympathies are all with *lowliness, purity, love,* and *truth. Insight* or sharp and deep perception is another of her attributes, and *force* (comp. on ch. ii. 7).

IV. SHE CLAIMS SUPREME AUTHORITY. (Vers. 15, 16.) Kings, rulers, princes, potentates, judges,—all received those places and fulfil those functions through her and her alone. Authority in politics rests on consent or on force, or both. And these are traceable ultimately to reason, and reason is the "inspiration of the Almighty." Exceptions form no part of this representation. In modern language, we say that government, as a principle or institute, rests on an ultimate Divine basis. The text says *no less* than this, nor does it say *more.*

V. SHE IS IN RECIPROCAL RELATION TO HER SUBJECTS. (Ver. 17.) Her love is conditioned by love; the winning of her by the wooing. The notion that we can be *passive*, whether in knowledge or goodness, is an entire illusion. Such an illusion once prevailed as the doctrine of "innate ideas" now exploded in philosophy. All that becomes the portion of head or heart *implies, necessitates* a previous spiritual activity in us. We are ignorant because we will not learn, unhappy because we will not love.

VI. SHE COMMANDS WEALTH AND HONOUR AND THE AVENUES TO THEM. (Vers. 18—21.) Riches, honour, "self-increasing goods, and righteous" (comp. on ch. iii. 16). The righteous here is elucidated by the next two verses; she shows the *right way* to all earthly good. She is a tree of life, and yields *incomparable* fruit both for value and abundance (ver. 19). She *guarantees* possessions to her votaries. The connection between *righteous* and worldly wealth is insisted on. Not that it is *always obvious*. Nor again are we to expect notice of exceptions in teaching that is from first to last absolute in form. The stringency of the connection is what we have to recognize; the knowledge of its complete application to all cases opens the relations of eternity and demands the omniscience of God.—J.

Vers. 22—36.— *Wisdom in eternity and in time.* This sublime view lifts us at once above the seeming contradictions of time, and suggests the solution of all its problems in God.

I. SHE IS OF THE DIVINE BEGINNINGS OR ELEMENTS. (Ver. 22.) An element in chemistry is the last simple substance we can reach in analysis. An element in thought is the last simple notion yielded by the dialectic of the understanding. Wisdom is thus *before* the visible creation—the earth, the sea, the mountains. The verses do but repeat and iterate this one simple and sublime thought. We may in like manner vary it in any form of thought and expression familiar to us. She is the Divine *a priori*; the logic of nature and spirit; the last and first, the ground of all existence; the eternal reason, the transcendent cause, the alpha and omega of the cosmic alphabet. We are trying to express the inexpressible, utter the unutterable, define the undefinable, find out God to perfection, if we press beyond these poor forms of speech and ignore the limit which separates the known from the unknowable, and reason from faith.

II. THE CREATION PROCEEDING FROM THE DIVINE WISDOM FULFILS ITS COURSE BY WISDOM. (Ver. 27.) What we term in science the discovery of law is for religion the revelation of the mind of God in the world and in us. The cosmos is here conceived under the forms of the poetic imagination—the heavens and their outstretched circle or vault; the clouds as massive bags or skins; the springs on earth as set in motion by direct Divine activity; the sea as bounded by a positive *fiat*; the earth as fixed on firm pillars, by one act as it were of the Divine Architect. And then was Wisdom at his side as mistress of the work (ver. 30), and was in delight day by day (ver. 30), "playing before him always; playing on the circle of the earth, and I had my delight in men" (ver. 31). One of the best illustrations of the poetical force and sense of this passage is in the Wisdom of Sirach xxiv.: "I went forth from the mouth of the Highest, and as a mist I covered the earth. I pitched my tent in the heights, and my throne was as a pillar of cloud. The gyre of heaven I encircled alone, and in the depths of abysses I walked about. In the billows of the sea, and in all the earth, and among every people and nation, I was busy" (vers. 3—6).

III. WISDOM'S APPEAL AND PROMISES. (Vers. 32—36.) 1. *The appeal.* "Listen to me, listen to instruction!" Drink out of this spring of eternity, whose currents flow through all the tracts of nature and of man. "Resist not!" for to resist is to oppose the law of things and to invite destruction. Let them be so eager to listen and to know that they shall *daily* apply, daily stand as suppliants or visitors at her door! 2. *The promises.* Happiness is repeatedly foretold (vers. 32, 34). *Life* in all senses, *intensive* and *extensive* (ver. 35). *Favour with Jehovah* (ver. 35). And it follows, as the night the day, that he who sins against Wisdom, whether by neglect or direct disobedience, is guilty of a *moral* suicide, and shows a contempt for life and happiness, a perverse preference for death (see on ch. iv. 13, 22; vii. 27; comp. Ezek. xviii. 21).—J.

Vers. 1—21.—*The excellency of Divine wisdom: No.* 1. In these verses we have portrayed to us the surpassing excellency of the wisdom of God.

I. IT IS AUDIBLE TO EVERY ONE. "Doth not Wisdom cry," etc.? (ver. 1; see homily on ch. i. 20—23).

II. IT IS URGENT AND IMPORTUNATE. (Vers. 2—4; see homily on ch. i. 20—23.)

III. IT MAKES ITS APPEAL TO UNIVERSAL MAN. (Vers. 4, 5.) "Unto you, O men,

I call," etc. There is nothing exclusive or partial in its address. Its sympathies are wide as the human soul. It draws no lines of latitude or longitude in any kingdom, beyond which it does not pass. It appeals *to man*—Jew and Gentile, male and female, bond and free, learned and ignorant, wise and foolish (simple), moral and immoral (fools).

IV. IT IS IN FULL HARMONY WITH ALL THAT IS BEST WITHIN US. Some voices that address us make their appeal to that which is lower or even lowest in our nature. Divine wisdom appeals to that which is highest and best. 1. To our sense of what is right and good (vers. 6, 7). 2. To our love of that which is true (ver. 7).

V. IT IS AN APPRECIABLE THING. (Ver. 9.) Though it takes high ground, not rooting itself in anything base, but making its appeal to that which is purest and noblest in our nature, it is still appreciable by all who can estimate anything at its true worth. To "him that understandeth," to the man who is capable of any discernment, the words of heavenly wisdom will be plain—they will "receive them gladly;" while to those who have reached any height in attainment, the teaching of wisdom will be recognized as the excellent thing it is. The students of law will find in it the illustration of all true order; the disciples of ethics will perceive in it all that is morally sound and satisfying to the conscience; those who admire "the beautiful" will recognize that which is exquisite, admirable, sublime. The teaching of Divine wisdom is "right to them that find knowledge."

VI. IT IS INTIMATELY ASSOCIATED WITH INTELLIGENT OBSERVATION. It consequently results in useful contrivances (ver. 12). So far from heavenly wisdom being confined, in its principles and its results, to the realm of the abstract and unseen, it is most closely allied with, and is constantly found in the company of, simple, homely discretion, the careful, intelligent observation of all surrounding objects and passing incidents. It issues, therefore, in "witty inventions."

VII. IT ISSUES IN, AND IS ILLUSTRATED BY, MORAL AND SPIRITUAL WORTH. (Ver. 13.) "The fear of the Lord is the beginning of wisdom," and the fear of the Lord is so intimately and essentially bound up with the hatred of evil, that they may be practically identified; we may say that "the fear of the Lord is to hate evil"—evil in all its forms, "pride, arrogancy," etc.—C.

Vers. 1—21 (continued).—*The excellency of Divine wisdom: No. 2.* We have also these features of the wisdom of God—

I. IT ENDOWS WITH THE WEALTH WHICH IS THE PRODUCT OF VIRTUE. (Vers. 20, 21.) It leads in that "way of righteousness" and those "paths of judgment" which result in "inheriting substance," and being "filled with treasures." It places in the hand of its followers all that measure of earthly good which they can regard with holy satisfaction and enjoy with a good conscience.

II. IT IS A SOURCE OF STRENGTH AND INFLUENCE IN HUMAN SOCIETY. (Vers. 14—16.) It is attended with that breadth of understanding, that knowledge of affairs, that insight into "men and things," which gives sagacity to statesmen and stability to thrones.

III. IT RECIPROCATES AN ATTACHMENT. (Ver. 17.) The more we know, the more attractive does knowledge become to our admiring spirit. The further we advance into its domain, the firmer becomes our footing and the brighter becomes the light. Moreover, the highest peaks attainable by man are only reached by those who begin to climb in the days of their youth (*vide* homily *infra*).

IV. IT IS OF INCOMPARABLE VALUE TO THE HUMAN SOUL. (Vers. 10, 11, 18, 19.) If the choice should lie between wealth and wisdom, it is better far to choose the latter; for: 1. While wealth will not buy wisdom, wisdom will lead to wealth, later if not sooner, of one kind if not of another. 2. Wisdom itself *is* wealth; it is the possession of the mind, it is the inheritance of the soul, it *is* "durable riches and righteousness."
The excellency of Divine wisdom: No. 3 (see below).—C.

Vers. 1—21.—"*Christ the Wisdom of God:*" *No.* 1. Though it is not to be supposed that Jesus Christ was in the mind of the writer of this passage, yet as he does personify wisdom, and as wisdom was incarnated in that Son of man who was the Son of God, we should expect to find that the words of the wise man in the text would apply, in large measure, to the Lord Jesus Christ. They do so, and suggest to us—

I. THE MANNER OF HIS TEACHING. (Vers. 1—3.) He "spake openly to the world,

. . . taught in the synagogue, and in the temple," etc. (John xviii. 20; see Luke iv. 15; John vii. 14, 26, 28; Mark vi. 34; Matt. v. 1, 2).

II. HIS APPEAL TO ALL CLASSES AND CONDITIONS OF MEN. (Vers. 4, 5.) He came unto the world at large, to "draw all men unto him." None were, none are, so poor or so rich, so ignorant or so learned, so simple or so subtle, so degraded or so refined, so spiritually destitute or so privileged, as to be out of range of his heavenly voice. All need his message; all are welcome to his kingdom.

III. HIS MANIFESTATION OF THE TRUTH. (Vers. 6—8.) He came "to bear witness unto the truth" (John xviii. 37). He came to *be* the living Truth himself (John xiv. 6), so that the more we know of him and grow up into him, the more of Divine truth do we receive into our souls.

IV. THE APPRECIABLENESS OF HIS MESSAGE. (Ver. 9.) When he spake with his own lips, men received his words, wondering at his wisdom and his grace (see Luke ii. 47; iv. 22, 32; Matt. vii. 28, 29). "Never man spake like this Man," said the officers to the chief priests (John vii. 46). "The common people heard him gladly" (Mark xii. 37). And now that he speaks to mankind from heaven, his message of truth and love is comprehensible to all who care to know his mind. To those who earnestly seek, the way becomes plain; to those who have "spiritual discernment," the deeper things of God are intelligible; to those who "know him," his dealings are seen to be right and true.

V. HIS RESPONSIVENESS. (Ver. 17.) (See succeeding homily.)

VI. HIS INCOMPARABLE WORTH. (Vers. 10, 11.) Jewels, *compared with him, are* empty toys; gold, compared with him, *is* sordid dust. So great is his worth to the hungering heart, to the suffering spirit, to living, dying man, that all forms of earthly good are not to be named or counted in comparison.

VII. HIS SERVICE ISSUES IN THE BEST OF ALL POSSIBLE RECOMPENSE. (Vers. 18—21.) The fruit of the service of Christ is honour, joy (including peace), righteousness (ver. 20), the "inheritance which is incorruptible, and undefiled, and that fadeth not away" (ver. 21; 1 Pet. i. 4).—C.

Vers. 10, 11.—*Wisdom and wealth.* The immeasurable preference of heavenly wisdom to earthly wealth may be seen if we consider—

I. THE FAILURE OF WEALTH. Wealth is continually found to fail; for: 1. It cannot even buy happiness. It may purchase a certain amount of excitement and jollity, but it will not secure contentment, even for one brief year. 2. Much less can it buy blessedness. That happy state of which our Lord so often spoke as blessedness—the deep and true gladness of heart which God plants within the soul, and which all may well wish to possess—this wealth is utterly unable to impart. 3. It will equally fail to buy wisdom. Indeed, it may be truly said that: 4. It often stands positively in the way of its acquisition (Mark x. 23—25).

II. THE CAPACITY OF WISDOM. 1. It tends to provide men with competency, if not with abundance. Honesty, purity, sobriety, diligence, frugality, those virtues which go with the "fear of the Lord," tend to supply a man's home with all that is needful and desirable. 2. It secures peace and joy of heart. 3. It, itself, is man's chief treasure. Better the knowledge of God, the love of Christ, a holy, manly, loving spirit, than any external advantages whatsoever (see Jer. ix. 23, 24). 4. It prepares for the enjoyment of the treasures which are in heaven (Matt. vi. 19—21).—C.

Ver. 17.—*The responsiveness of Christ.* Adapting these words to him who became, and for ever will be, the Wisdom of God, they may speak to us of—

I. CHRIST'S INITIATIVE LOVE. It is quite true that "we love him because he first loved us." We should first consider "the great love wherewith he loved us, even when we were dead in sins" (Eph. ii. 4, 5). All our love to Christ springs from, has its source in, his spontaneous love toward us, unexcited by our affection, flowing from his own exceeding grace.

II. HIS RESPONSIVE LOVE. This involves much. 1. His special interest in those who are inquiring at his feet. "Jesus beholding him, *loved him,* and said unto him, One thing thou lackest" (Mark x. 21). Zacchæus (Luke xix.). 2. His Divine favour accorded to those who have accepted him as their Lord. "I love them that love me" (see John xi. 5). These are his friends and his guests (John xiv. 23; xv. 14, 15; Rev. iii.

20). 3. Spiritual blessings which he will impart. He will dwell with us by his Spirit, and the fruits of the Spirit will abound in us. If, then, our interest in Christ, and the yielding of our hearts to him, result in his close friendship and in those highest impartations which flow therefrom, how wise must be—

III. EARLY DISCIPLESHIP TO HIM! For if we would make sure of finding him and possessing his friendship, we should seek him without delay. Delay is always dangerous. There may intervene between ourselves and him : 1. Other objects which may fascinate our souls and lead us away from him. 2. The growth of the deadly spirit of procrastination. 3. A sudden close of our present life. But early discipleship, the coming in faith to his feet, to his cross, to his kingdom, to his vineyard, means the certainty of holiness and usefulness below and the assurance of blessedness above.—C.

Vers. 22—31.—*The excellency of Divine wisdom : No. 3.* We have here additional features of the wisdom of God, viz.—

I. THAT THE WISDOM EVERYWHERE ILLUSTRATED DWELT IN THE DIVINE ONE FROM ETERNITY. (Vers. 22—26.) Before anything visible was created, in the " far backward and abysm of time," even to eternity, wisdom was an attribute of the infinite God.

II. THAT CREATION AND PROVIDENCE ARE THE DELIBERATE OUTWORKING OF THE DIVINE IDEA. " When he prepared the heavens ... then I was by him " (vers. 27—30). All things were constructed after the model in the Divine mind. Perfect intelligence, seeing through and foreseeing everything, directed everything according to absolute wisdom ; thus the kindest end was gained by the surest means ; thus beauty and serviceableness, grandeur and loveliness, are bound together in the visible world because they existed together in the mind of the great Architect (see Ps. civ. 24).

III. THAT THE WISDOM OF HIS WORK WAS A CONSTANT SOURCE OF SATISFACTION TO THE MIND OF GOD. (Ver. 30.) " I was daily his delight." We find a pure and God-given satisfaction in the execution of any work on which we have spent our utmost energy. We might have hesitated to refer this to the Supreme Intelligence, but the Word of God warrants us in doing this (Gen. i. 31 ; Ps. civ. 31). We may, therefore, believe that the glories and beauties of creation are not only the source of joy to our minds (and the deeper and fuller in proportion to our purity and piety), but that they are also a source of satisfaction to him who made them what they are.

IV. THAT MAN IS THE SPECIAL OBJECT OF THE WISE ONE'S CARE. (Ver. 31.) " My delights were with the sons of men." 1. When God made man upright he " blessed him " (Gen. i. 28), and rejoiced in him as in his noblest work on earth. 2. When man fell God was grieved ; the heavenly Father's heart was saddened at his children's disobedience and wrong-doing. 3. When man returns to righteousness God is well pleased (Luke xv. 23, 24). There is no such wisdom shown in creation or in providence as in redemption. To arrange the laws of a material universe, to direct the affairs of an illimitable kingdom,—there is wondrous wisdom in these Divine doings ; but there is deeper wisdom still in redeeming a lost world, reconciling an alienated world, cleansing a guilty world, sanctifying an unholy world and fitting it for the society of the sinless in heaven.—C.

Vers. 22—31.—" *Christ the Wisdom of God :*" *No.* 2. Again regarding the Lord Jesus Christ as the Wisdom of God incarnate, we may let these words suggest to us—

I. HIS ETERNITY. (Vers. 22—26.)

II. HIS SONSHIP. (Vers. 22, 30.)

III. HIS AGENCY IN CREATION. (Vers. 37—29 ; see also John i. 3, 10 ; Eph. iii. 9 ; Col. i. 16 ; Heb. i. 2, 3, 10 ; 1 Cor. viii. 6.)

IV. HIS PRIMAL BLESSEDNESS. (Ver. 30 ; and see John xvii. 5 ; Phil. ii. 6.)

V. HIS SUPREME INTEREST IN MAN. (Ver. 31.) " His delights were with the sons of men." The interest taken by our Lord in ourselves was that of a (1) Creator, (2) Divine Ruler, (3) Redeemer ; it is now that of a (4) sovereign Saviour.—C.

Vers. 32—36.—*The convincing argument.* Here is a very strong, " Now, therefore." The excellency of Divine wisdom has been so forcibly, so irresistibly urged that the speaker is entitled to drive his argument home and make a practical application. But the urgency of the case is summed up in the few following sentences. This is the reasoning: since—

I. INATTENTION TO THE VOICE OF WISDOM IS THE DEPTH OF FOLLY. For: 1. It is self-robbery. "He that sinneth against me wrongeth his own soul" (ver. 36). The man that shuts his ears when God speaks robs himself of all those precious things which might make his heart rich and his life noble—of spiritual peace, of sacred joy, of heavenly hope, of an elevating faith, of holy love, of Divine comfort, of the best forms of usefulness. 2. It is self-destruction. "All they that hate me love death" (ver. 36). To harden our heart against the invitations and warnings of Divine wisdom is to tread the path which leads straight to the gates of spiritual and eternal death.

II. ATTENTION TO THE VOICE OF WISDOM IS OUR HIGHEST INTEREST. 1. It leads to "blessedness" (vers. 32, 34); it ensures that state of soul which the eternal God declares to be the only enviable one, to be that which should be the object of our earnest aspiration. 2. It secures his own Divine favour (ver. 35)—the "favour of the Lord," the sunshine of his smile, the benediction of his voice; he will "lay his hand upon us" in fatherly love; he will surround us with his "everlasting arms" of powerful protection. 3. It constitutes life in its very essence and substance. "Whoso findeth me findeth life" (ver. 35). To be wise with the wisdom which is from above, to "know God and Jesus Christ whom he has sent," "to understand and know the Lord that exerciseth loving-kindness, judgment, and righteousness," to have gained "the secret of the Lord," to have learnt by blessed experience "that the Lord is gracious," "to be filled with the knowledge of his will,"—this *is* life, human life at its highest, its best, its noblest. Moreover, it is that which issues in the eternal life on the other side the river, in the land where life is enlarged and ennobled far beyond the reach of our present thought. Since these things are so, "now, therefore," we conclude that—

III. DILIGENT DISCIPLESHIP IS THE ONLY OPEN COURSE. "Hearken," "hear instruction," "refuse it not," etc. (vers. 32—34). This includes: 1. Earnest attention, hearkening, watching, waiting. Something much more than allowing ourselves by force of custom to be found where wisdom is discoursed, "putting in an appearance" at the sanctuary. It implies an earnest heedfulness of spirit; a diligent, intelligent, patient inquiry of the soul; a hungering of the heart for the saving truth of the living God. 2. Practical obedience—"keeping the ways" of wisdom (ver. 32). "If we know these things, happy are we if we do them" (John xiii. 17; see Matt. vii. 21—27). As earnest disciples of Jesus Christ, the way to "keep his ways" is (1) to accept himself as our Saviour and Lord, with our whole heart; (2) to strive daily to embody his will in all the relations we sustain. That is to say, first enter into right relation to himself, making him the Saviour of our soul, the Friend of our heart, the Lord of our life; then strive to carry out his commandments in all the transactions and relationships of our human life.—C.

EXPOSITION.

CHAPTER IX.

Vers. 1—18.—15. *Fifteenth admonitory discourse*, containing in a parabolic form an invitation of Wisdom (vers. 1—12), and that of her rival Folly (vers. 13—18). The chapter sums up in brief the warnings of the preceding part.

Ver. 1.—Wisdom was represented as having a house at whose portals persons waited eagerly for admission (ch. viii. 34); the idea is further carried on. **Wisdom hath builded her house.** (For the plural form of *khochmoth*, "wisdom," a plural of excellency, see on ch. i. 20.) As the "strange woman" in ch. vii. possessed a house to which she seduced her victim, so Wisdom is represented as having a house which she has made and adorned, and to which she invites her pupils. Spiritual writers see here two references—one to Christ's incarnation, when he built for himself a human body (John ii. 19); and another to his work in forming the Church, which is his mystical body (1 Pet. ii. 5). And the sublime language used in this section is not satisfied with the bare notion that we have here only an allegorical representation of Wisdom calling followers to her. Rather we are constrained to see a Divine intimation of the office and work of Christ, not only the Creator of the world, as in ch. viii., but its Regenerator. **She hath hewn out her seven pillars.** Architecturally, according to Hitzig and others, the pillars of the inner court are meant, which supported the gallery of the first story. Four of these were in the corners, three in the middle of three sides, while the entrance to the court was through the fourth side of the square. The number seven generally denotes perfection; it is the covenant number, expressive of harmony and unity generally, the signature of holiness and blessing, completeness and rest. So in the Apocalypse the whole Church is represented by the number of seven Churches (Rev. i. 4, etc.; see on ch. xxvi. 16). Wisdom's house is said to be thus founded because of its perfection and adaptability to all states of men. But doubtless there is a reference to the sevenfold gifts of the Holy Spirit, which rested upon the Christ (Isa. xi. 2, etc.), and which are the support and strength of the Church, being symbolized by the seven-branched candlestick in the temple.

Ver. 2.—**She hath killed her beasts.** So in the parable of the marriage of the king's son (Matt. xxii., which is parallel to the present), the king sends his servants to notify the guests that the oxen and fatlings are killed, and all things are ready. Wisdom has stores of nourishment for understanding and affection; and Christ has offered himself as a Victim in our behalf, and now makes bounteous offers of grace, and especially has ordained the sacrament of the Lord's Supper for the strengthening and refreshing of the soul. **She hath mingled her wine;** Septuagint, "She hath mingled (ἐκέρασεν) her wine in a bowl." The wine which, untempered, was too luscious or too fiery to drink, was made palatable by a certain admixture of water. It was always so mixed at the Passover; and the ancient Christian Liturgies direct the mixture in the celebration of the Holy Eucharist, doubtless from traditional use. Some, however, think that allusion is here made to the custom of adding drugs to wine in order to increase its potency. Among the Greeks, ἄκρατος οἶνος meant "wine without water," and in Rev. xiv. 10 we have ἄκρατον κεκερασμένον, "undiluted wine mixed." And probably in the text the notion is that the fluid for the guests' delectation is properly prepared, that there may be no trouble when they arrive (see on ch. xxiii. 30). **She hath also furnished her table,** by arranging the dishes, etc., thereon (Ps. xxiii. 5, "Thou preparest a table before me," where the same verb, arak, is used; comp. Isa. xxi. 5). Moralizing on this passage, St. Gregory says, "The Lord 'killed the sacrifices' by offering himself on our behalf. He 'mingled the wine,' blending together the cup of his precepts from the historical narration and the spiritual signification. And he 'set forth his table,' i.e. Holy Writ, which with the bread of the

Word refreshes us when we are wearied and come to him away from the burdens of the world, and by its effect of refreshing strengthens us against our adversaries" ('Moral.,' xvii. 43, Oxford transl.).

Ver. 3.—**She hath sent forth her maidens,** as in Matt. xxii. 3, to call them that were bidden to the feast. The Septuagint has τοὺς ἑαυτῆς δούλους, "her servants," but the Authorized Version is correct, and feminine attendants are in strict harmony with the rest of the apologue. By them are represented the apostles and preachers and ministers, who go forth to win souls for Christ. St. Gregory sees in their being called "maidens" an intimation that they are in themselves weak and abject, and are only useful and honoured as being the mouthpiece of their Lord ('Moral.,' xxxiii. 33). **She crieth upon the highest places of the city,** where her voice could best be heard, as in ch. viii. 2; Matt. x. 27. She is not satisfied with delegating her message to others; she delivers it herself. Septuagint, "calling with a loud proclamation to the cup (ἐπὶ κρατῆρα);" Vulgate, *Misit ancillas suas ut vocarent ad arcem et ad mœnia civitatis,* "She has sent her handmaids to invite to the citadel, and to the walls of the town." On which rendering St. Gregory comments, "In that while they tell of the interior life, they lift us up to the high walls of the city above, which same walls, surely, except any be humble, they do not ascend" ('Moral.,' xvii. 43).

Vers. 4—12.—Here follows the invitation of Wisdom, urging the attendance of guests at the sumptuous banquet which she has prepared (comp. Rev. xix. 9).

Ver. 4.—**Whoso is simple, let him turn in hither.** This is a direct address to the imprudent and inexperienced (see on ch. vii. 7), calling them to turn aside from the way on which they are going, and to come to her. Vulgate, *si quis est parvulus veniat ad me,* which reminds one of Christ's tender words, "It is not the will of your Father which is in heaven, that one of these little ones should perish" (Matt. xviii. 14). As for **him that wanteth understanding, she saith to him** what follows (so ver. 16). Wisdom's own speech is interrupted, and the writer himself introduces this little clause. She calls on the simple and the unwise, both as necessarily needing her teaching, and not yet inveterate in evil, nor wilfully opposed to better guidance. "The world by wisdom knew not God," and he "hath chosen the foolish things of the world to confound the wise, and the weak things of the world to confound the things that are mighty, and base things of the world, and things which are despised, hath God chosen " (1 Cor. i. 21, 26, etc. ; comp. Matt. xi. 25).

Ver. 5.—**Come, eat ye of my bread.** Wisdom now directly addresses the simple and the foolish (comp. Rev. xxii. 17). **And drink of the wine** which **I have mingled** (see on ver. 2). Bread and wine represent all needful nourishment, as flesh and wine in ver. 2. So Christ says (John vi. 51), " I am the living Bread which came down from heaven . . . and the bread that I will give is my flesh, which I will give for the life of the world." Compare the invitation in Isa. lv. 1, " Ho, every one that thirsteth!" etc. The Fathers see here a prophecy of the gospel feast, wherein Christ gave and gives bread and wine as symbols of his presence (Matt. xxvi. 26, etc.).

Ver. 6.—**Forsake the foolish, and live ;** Vulgate, *relinquite infantiam ;* Septuagint, ἀπολείπετε ἀφροσύνην, " leave folly." These versions take the plural פְּתָאיִם (*petaim*) as equivalent to an abstract noun, which gives a good sense ; but the plural is not so used in our book, so we must admit the rendering of the Authorized Version, " Quit the class, give up being of the category of fools," or else we must take the word as vocative, " Leave off, ye simple ones " (Revised Version), *i.e.* quit your simplicity, your folly. *And live* (see on ch. iv. 4). It is not a mere prosperous life on earth that is here promised, but something far higher and better (John vi. 51, " If any man eat of this bread, he shall live for ever "). The LXX. saw something of this when they paraphrased the clause, " Leave ye folly, that ye may reign for ever." **Go in the way of understanding.** Leaving folly, stay not, but make real progress in the direction of wisdom. Septuagint, " Seek ye prudence, and direct understanding by knowledge."

Vers. 7—10.—These verses form a parenthesis, showing why Wisdom addresses only the simple and foolish. She giveth not that which is holy unto dogs, nor casteth pearls before swine (Matt. vii. 6).

Ver. 7.—**He that reproveth a scorner getteth to himself shame.** He who tries to correct a scorner (see on ch. i. 22 and iii. 34), one who derides religion, loses his pains and meets with ribald mockery and insult. It is not the fault of messengers or message that this should be, but the hardness of heart and the pride of the hearer make him despise the teaching and hate the teacher (Matt. xxiv. 9). **He that rebuketh a wicked man getteth himself a blot ;** rather, *he that reproveth a sinner, it is his blot.* Such a proceeding results in disgrace to himself. This is not said to discourage the virtuous from reproving transgressors, but states the effect

which experience proves to occur in such cases. Prudence, caution, and tact are needed in dealing with these characters. Evil men regard the reprover as a personal enemy, and treat him with contumely, and hence arise unseemly bickerings and disputes, injurious words and deeds. To have wasted teaching on such unreceptive and antagonistic natures is a shameful expenditure of power. St. Gregory thus explains this matter : " It generally happens that when they cannot defend the evils that are reproved in them, they are rendered worse from a feeling of shame, and carry themselves so high in their defence of themselves, that they take out bad points to urge against the life of the reprover, and so they do not account themselves guilty, if they fasten guilty deeds upon the heads of others also. And when they are unable to find true ones, they feign them, that they may also themselves have things they may seem to rebuke with no inferior degree of justice " (' Moral.,' x. 3, Oxford transl.).

Ver. 8.—**Reprove not a scorner, lest he hate thee** (see the last note, and comp. ch. xv. 12, and note there). There are times when reproof only hardens and exasperates. " It is not proper," says St. Gregory, " for the good man to fear lest the scorner should utter abuse at him when he is chidden, but lest, being drawn into hatred, he should be made worse " ('Moral.,' viii. 67). " Bad men sometimes we spare, and not ourselves, if from the love of those we cease from the rebuking of them. Whence it is needful that we sometimes endure keeping to ourselves what they are, in order that they may learn in us by our good living what they are not " (ibid., xx. 47, Oxford transl.). **Rebuke a wise man, and he will love thee.** So Ps. cxli. 5, " Let the righteous smite me, it shall be a kindness ; and let him reprove me, it shall be as oil upon the head ; let not my head refuse it " (comp. ch. xix. 25 ; xxv. 12 ; xxvii. 6).

Ver. 9.—**Give instruction to a wise** man, **and he will be yet wiser.** The Hebrew is merely " give to the wise," with no object mentioned ; but the context suggests " instruction," even though, as in ver. 8, it takes the form of rebuke. Vulgate and Septuagint, " Give an opportunity to a wise man, and he will be wiser " (comp. Matt. xiii. 12 ; xxv. 29). To make the best use of all occasions of learning duty, whether they present themselves in a winning or a forbidden shape, is the part of one who is wise unto salvation (see ch. i. 5, and note there). **Teach a just** man, **and he will increase in learning.** Wisdom being a moral and not merely an intellectual, quality, there is a natural interchange of " wise " and " just," referring to the same individual, in the two clauses. Vulgate, *festinabit accipere*; Septuagint, " Instruct a wise man, and he shall have more given him." The wise are thus rewarded with larger measures of wisdom, because they are simple, humble, and willing to learn, having that childlike spirit which Christ commends (Matt. xviii. 3).

Ver. 10.—Wisdom returns to the first apothegm and principle of the whole book (ch. i. 7). Without the fear of God no teaching is of any avail. **The knowledge of the holy is understanding.** The word translated " the holy " is קְדֹשִׁים, a plural of excellence (see on ch. xxx. 3) like *Elohim*, and equivalent to "the Most Holy One," Jehovah, to which it answers in the first hemistich. God is called " Holy, holy, holy " (Isa. vi. 3), in his threefold nature, and as majestic beyond expression. The only knowledge worth having, and which is of avail for the practical purposes of life, is the knowledge of God (see on ch. ii. 5). Septuagint, " The counsel of the holy (ἁγίων) is understanding," with the explanatory clause; " for to know the Law is the character of good thought." This occurs again at ch. xiii. 15, though in the Hebrew in neither place.

Ver. 11.—The parenthetical explanation being concluded, in which Wisdom has intimated why it is useless to appeal to the scorner and the wilful sinner, she now resumes the direct address interrupted at ver. 7, presenting a forcible reason for the advice given in ver. 6, though there is still some connection with ver. 10, as it is from the wisdom that comes from the fear of the Lord that the blessings now mentioned spring. **For by me thy days shall be multiplied** (see ch. iii. 2, 16; iv. 10, where long life is promised as a reward for the possession and practice of wisdom). The same result is attributed to the fear of God (ch. x. 27; xiv. 27, etc.). In ver. 6 the address is in the plural; here it is singular. A similar interchange is found in ch. v. 7, 8 (where see note).

Ver. 12.—**If thou be wise, thou shalt be wise for thyself.** A transition verse. Wisdom will bring thee good; as thou hast laboured well, so will be thy reward (1 Cor. iii. 8). The LXX. (Syriac and Arabic), with the idea of perfecting the antithesis, adds, καὶ τοῖς πλησίον, " My son, if thou art wise for thyself, thou shalt be wise also for thy neighbours "—which contains the great truth that good gifts should not be selfishly enjoyed, but used and dispensed for the advantage of others (Gal. vi. 6). In support of our text we may quote Job xxii. 2, " Can a man be profitable unto God? Surely he that is wise is profitable unto himself." **But if thou scornest, thou alone shalt bear it**; *i.e.* atone for it, bear

the sin, as it is expressed in Numb. ix. 13, " For every man shall bear his own burden " (Gal. vi. 5). Thus Wisdom ends her exhortation. Septuagint, " If thou turn out evil, thou alone shalt bear (ἀντλήσεις) evils." And then is added the following paragraph, which may possibly be derived from a Hebrew original, but seems more like a congeries made up from other passages, and foisted by some means into the Greek text: " He that stayeth himself on lies shepherdeth winds, and himself pursueth flying birds; for he hath left the ways of his own vineyard, and hath gone astray with the wheels of his own husbandry; and he goeth through a waterless desert, and over a land set in thirsty places, and with his hands he gathereth unfruitfulness."

Vers. 13—18.—This section contains the invitation of Folly, the rival of Wisdom, represented under the guise of an adulteress (ch. ii. 16; v. 3, etc.; vi. 24, etc.; vii.).

Ver. 13.—**A foolish woman**; literally, *the woman of folly*, the genitive being that of apposition, so that this may well be rendered, in order to make the contrast with Wisdom more marked, " the woman Folly." She is regarded as a real person; and between her and Virtue man has to make his choice. **Is clamorous**; turbulent and animated by passion (as ch. vii. 11), quite different from her calm, dignified rival. She is **simple**; Hebrew, "simplicity," in a bad sense; she has no preservative against evil, no moral fibre to resist temptation. **And knoweth nothing** which she ought to know. Ignorance is the natural accompaniment of Folly; in this case it is wilful and persistent; she goes on her way reckless of consequences. Septuagint, " A woman foolish and bold, who knows not shame, comes to want a morsel."

Ver. 14.—**She sitteth at the door of her house.** She, like Wisdom, has a house of her own, and imitates her in inviting guests to enter. She does not send forth her maidens; she does not stand in the streets and proclaim her mission. Vice has an easier task; all she has to do is to sit and beckon and use a few seductive words. Her house is not supported by seven pillars, built on the grace of God and upheld by the gifts of the Holy Spirit, like that of Wisdom (ver. 1); it is an ordinary habitation of no stately proportions, but its meanness impedes not the uses to which she puts it, her own charms causing her victims to disregard her environments. **On a seat in the high places of the city.** Her house is in the highest and most conspicuous part of the city, and she sits before her door in reckless immodesty, plying her shameful trade (comp. Gen. xxxviii. 14; Jer. iii. 2). The mimicry of her rival again appears, for Wisdom "crieth upon the highest places of the city" (ver. 3).

Ver. 15.—**To call passengers who go right on their ways.** With shameless effrontery she cries to all that pass by, she addresses her solicitations to persons who are going straight on their way, thinking nothing of her, having no idea of deviating from their pursued object. As they walk in the path of right and duty, she tries to turn them aside. Septuagint, "Calling to herself (προσ-καλουμένη) those that pass by and are keeping straight in their ways." The Fathers find here a picture of the seductions of heretical teaching, which puts on the mask of orthodoxy and deceives the unwary. Wordsworth notes that, in the Apocalypse, the false teacher bears some emblems of the Lamb (Rev. xiii. 11). All false doctrine retains some element of truth, and it is because of this admixture that it procures adherents and thrives for a time.

Vers. 16, 17.—These verses contain the invitation which Vice, in imitation of Virtue, and assuming her voice and manner, offers to the wayfarers.

Ver. 16.—**Whoso is simple, let him turn in hither.** She uses the very same words which Wisdom utters (ver. 4). The latter had addressed the simple because they were inexperienced and undecided, and might be guided aright; the former now speaks to them because they have not yet made their final choice, can still be swayed by lower considerations, and may be led astray. Such persons find it hard to distinguish between the good and the evil, the false and the true, especially when their sensual appetite is aroused and sides with the temptress. No marvel is it that such are easily deceived; for we are told that, under certain circumstances, Satan transforms himself into an angel of light (2 Cor. xi. 14). **That wanteth understanding.** This is the other class addressed by Wisdom, and which Folly now solicits, urging them to follow her on the path of pleasure, promising sensual enjoyment and security.

Ver. 17.—This is what she says: **Stolen waters are sweet, and bread eaten in secret is pleasant.** The metaphor of "stolen waters" refers primarily to adulterous intercourse, as to "drink waters out of one's own cistern" (ch. v. 15, where see note) signifies the chaste connection of lawful wedlock. Wisdom offered flesh and wine to her guests; Folly offers bread and water. Wisdom invites openly to a well-furnished table; Folly calls to a secret meal of barest victuals. What the former offers is rich and satisfying and comforting; what Vice gives is poor and mean and insipid. Yet this latter has

the charm of being forbidden; it is attractive because it is unlawful. This is a trait of corrupt human nature, which is recognized universally. Thus Ovid, 'Amor.,' iii. 4. 17—

"Nitimur in vetitum semper, cupimusque negata;
Sic interdictis imminet æger aquis."

Things easily attained, the possession of which is gotten without effort or danger or breach of restraint, soon pall and cease to charm. To some minds the astuteness and secrecy required for success have an irresistible attraction. Thus St. Augustine relates ('Conf.,' ii. 4) how he and some companions committed a theft, not from want and poverty, nor even from the wish to enjoy what was stolen, but simply for the pleasure of thieving and the sin. They robbed a pear tree by night, carried off great loads, which they flung to the pigs, and their only satisfaction was that they were doing what they ought not ("dum tamen fieret a nobis, quod eo liberet quo non liceret"). Septuagint, "Taste ye to your pleasure secret bread, and sweet water of theft." Where water is a precious commodity, as in many parts of Palestine, doubtless thefts were often committed, and persons made free with their neighbour's tank when they could do so undetected, thus sparing their own resources and felicitating themselves on their cleverness. On the metaphorical use of "waters" in Holy Scripture, St. Gregory says, "Waters are sometimes wont to denote the Holy Spirit, sometimes sacred knowledge, sometimes calamity, sometimes drifting peoples, sometimes the minds of those following the faith." He refers to these texts respectively: John vii. 38, etc.; Ecclus. xv. 3; Ps. lxix. 1; Rev. xvii. 15 ("the waters are peoples"); Isa. xxii. 20; and he adds, "By water likewise bad knowledge is wont to be designated, as when the woman in Solomon, who bears the type of heresy, charms with crafty persuasion, saying, 'Stolen waters are sweet'" ('Moral.,' xix. 9).

Ver. 18.—The deluded youth is supposed to be persuaded by the seductions of Folly, and to enter her house. The writer, then, in a few weighty words, shows the terrible result of this evil compliance. **But he knoweth not that the dead are there** (see on ch. ii. 18 and vii. 27). There are none "there," in her house, who can be said to be living, they are *rephaim*, shadowy ghosts of living men, or else demons of the nether world. The Septuagint and Vulgate, with a reference to Gen. vi. 4, translate γηγενεῖς and *gigantes*. **Her guests are in the depths of hell** (*sheol*); Septuagint, "He knows not that giants perish at her side, and he meets with a trap of hell." The terrible warning may profitably be repeated more than once.

It is like Christ's awful saying, three times enunciated, "Where their worm dieth not, and the fire is not quenched" (Mark ix. 44, 46, 48). The LXX. has another paragraph at the end of this verse, which has no counterpart in the Hebrew: "But start away, delay not in the place, nor put thy name ['eye, *al*.] by her; for thus shalt thou pass over (διαβήσῃ) strange water; but abstain thou from strange water, and of a strange spring drink not, that thou mayest live long, and years of life may be added to thee."

HOMILETICS.

Vers. 1—5.—*The banquet of wisdom.* I. THE BANQUET-HOUSE. 1. It is *substantial.* A house, not a mere tent. The feast of wisdom is no brief repast, rarely enjoyed. It is a lasting delight, a frequent refreshment always ready. 2. It is *magnificent.* Seven pillars are hewn out for the house. It is fitting that the house of God should be more beautiful than a man's dwelling. He who enters into the habitation of God's thoughts will find it beautiful and glorious. There is nothing mean about Divine truth. It is all large, noble, magnificent. He who comes into communion with it will find himself in no poor hovel. He will be in a palace of splendour, with which the material grandeur of marble columns, delicate tracery, etc., cannot vie.

II. THE PROVISION. Rich and abundant—slaughtered beasts, spiced wine, a well-furnished table. Nothing looks more sordid than poor fare in splendid apartments. This shall not be seen in the house of Divine wisdom, but, on the contrary, enough for all, and that of the best quality. No thoughts are so full nor so rich as the thoughts of revelation. There is variety here as in the viands of the banquet. And "all things are ready." The table is spread. It waits for the guests. While we are praying for light, the light is shining about us. God has revealed his truth. Christ, the Light of the world, has appeared among us. The feast of the truths of the glorious gospel of the blessed God is ready for all who will come and share in its bounties.

III. THE INVITATION. The maidens are sent forth—not one, but many—that the message may go to all quarters. They cry in the highest places of the city, that the message may have the greatest publicity, may spread over the widest area, may reach all classes. This is the character of the call of God to us in his truth. He seeks us before we seek him. He has already sought us. The gospel is preached, proclaimed as by heralds; and this gospel contains the invitation to the rich banquet of Divine truth.

IV. THE GUESTS. "The simple;" "him that lacketh understanding." So in our Lord's parable, "the poor, and the maimed, and the halt, and the blind" are called (Luke xiv. 21). The whole need not the physician; the full need not the feast. They who are satisfied with their own knowledge will not sit humbly at the feet of a Divine revelation. It is they who feel themselves to be foolish, who acknowledge their ignorance and grope dimly after the light, who will be able to enjoy the banquet of wisdom; and these people are specially invited. The heathen, the illiterate, the weak-minded, are all called to receive the saving truth of Christ.

V. THE SATISFACTION. "Eat of my bread, and drink of the wine," etc. 1. Divine truth is *nourishing.* "By every word that proceedeth out of the mouth of the Lord doth man live" (Deut. viii. 3). Christ, the "Word," is the Bread of life. 2. Divine truth is a *source of joy.* At the banquet there is wine that maketh glad the heart of man. The gospel offers no prison fare. It kills the fatted beast. It gives wine—spiced wine, things of pleasure and luxury. Yet the pleasure is not enervating; the gospel wine is not harmfully intoxicating. How much better this banquet than the injurious and really less pleasing feast of folly (vers. 13—18)!

Ver. 8.—*Reproof.* I. HOW TO GIVE REPROOF. The duty of reproving is one of the most difficult and delicate ever attempted. The people who are most rash in adventuring upon it too often fall into the greatest blunders, while those who are really fitted to undertake it shrink from the attempt. The mere utterance of a protest is generally worse than useless. It only raises anger and provokes to greater obstinacy. Unless there is some probability of convincing a man of the wrongness of his conduct, there is little good in administering rebukes to him. It is not the duty of any man to raise up

enemies without cause. We should all seek, as far as in us lies, to live peaceably with
all men. Of course, it may be incumbent upon us sometimes so to act that we shall
provoke opposition. Jesus Christ could have avoided the enmity of the Jews, but
only by unfaithfulness to his mission. Where we are in the way of our mission, or
when any duty will be accomplished or any good done, we must not shrink from rousing
antagonism. To do so is cowardice, not peaceableness. But if no good is done, we may
only bring a nest of hornets about our heads by our indiscretion. Let us understand
that while we are never to sanction evil-doing, we are only called to rebuke it when
the rebuke will not be certainly rejected; then we must risk insult for the sake of
righteousness. The practical point, then, is that we consider the character of a man
before attempting to rebuke him, and that we be not so anxious to protest against sin
as to counsel the sinner and guide him to better ways. If he is in a hard, scornful
mood, we had better wait for a more fitting opportunity. If he is too strong for us,
we shall only injure the cause of right by attempting to grapple with him. Weak
champions of Christianity have often only hurt themselves, discredited their cause, and
afforded a triumph to powerful opponents by their rash encounters. In all cases to
reprove well requires wisdom, tact, simplicity, humanity.

II. How to receive reproof. He who hates the reprover will become himself a
scorner; the wise man will love the reprover. Our manner of accepting merited reproof
will therefore be a test of our character. Thus viewed, may not the text class many of
us with the scorners, though we had little suspected where our true place was to be
found? It is too common for a man to reject all reproof with rage. Not inquiring
whether the accusation is true, he unjustly regards it as an attack upon himself, as a
personal insult. There may be fault with the reprover—very often there is. But a
wise man will not shelter himself behind that. Granting that the method of reproof
was unwise, harsh, offensive; still, was there no ground for any reproof? To be angry
at all reproof is to be one of the worst of scorners—to scorn right and truth. For the
conscientious man will not dare to reject appeals to his conscience; he will feel bound
to listen to them, no matter how unwelcome the voice that speaks them. He will
desire to be free from faults. Should he not, therefore, thank those people who show
them to him? If he loves goodness, he ought to love those whose advice will help him
to remove the greatest hindrances to attaining it. If he hates sin as the disease of his
soul, he should accept reproof as medicine, and treat the reprover as a valuable physician.

Ver. 9.—*An open mind*. There are two classes of minds that seem to be armour-
proof against the invasion of new light. One contains those people who, to use the
phraseology of the Roman Catholic Church, are in a state of "invincible ignorance."
The other contains the much more numerous people who know just enough to feel a
pride of superiority to their fellows, and who wrap themselves up in the infallibility
of self-conceit. To these persons Pope's often misapplied maxim may be fairly
appropriated—

> " A little knowledge is a dangerous thing;
> Drink deep, or taste not the Pierian spring."

The truly wise man will be the first to see the limits of his knowledge and the infinite
night of ignorance with which the little spot of light that he has as yet gained is
surrounded. Having drunk of the wells of truth, he will have found his thirst not
slaked, but stimulated; he will be a philosopher, a lover of wisdom. Such a man will
have an open mind.

I. Consider the characteristics of an open mind. 1. It is not an empty mind.
A man may be prepared to receive fresh light without abandoning the light he already
possesses. The seeker after truth need not be a sceptic. There may be many things
clearly seen and firmly grasped in the mind of one who is ready to welcome all new
truth. 2. It is not a weak mind. If a man is not a bigot, he need not be like a
shuttle-cock, driven about by every wind of doctrine. He will sift truth. He will
consider new ideas calmly, impartially, judicially. 3. An open mind is willing to receive
truth from any quarter. It may come from a despised teacher, from a rival, from an
enemy. The open mind will not exclaim, "Can any good thing come out of Nazareth?"
4. An open mind is ready to receive unpleasant truth. The new light may threaten to

interfere with the vested interests of ancient beliefs, it may expose the folly of long-cherished crotchets, it may unsettle much of one's established convictions, it may reveal truths which are themselves unpalatable, or it may wound our pride by exposing our errors. Still, the open mind will receive it on one condition—that it *is* genuine truth. 5. Such characteristics must be based on wisdom and justice. It is the wise man and the just who is ready to receive instruction. No small amount of practical wisdom is requisite for the discernment of truth amidst the distractions of prejudice. Justice is a more important characteristic. Indeed, it is one of the fundamental conditions of truth-seeking. Science and philosophy would progress more rapidly, and theology would be less confused by the conflicts of bitter sectaries, if men could but learn to be fair to other inquirers, and to take no exaggerated views of the importance of their own notions.

II. THE ADVANTAGES OF AN OPEN MIND. 1. The open mind will attain most truth. Truth is practically infinite. But our knowledge of it varies according as we are able to attain to a large and yet a discriminating receptivity. To the nut its shell is its universe. The man who locks himself up in the dungeon of prejudice will never see anything but his own prison-walls. 2. Every attainment in knowledge prepares the way for receiving more knowledge. It intensifies the desire of possessing truth. Thus the inquirer may say—

> " The wish to know—that endless thirst,
> Which ev'n by quenching is awak'd,
> And which becomes or blest or curst
> As is the fount whereat 'tis slak'd—
> Still urged me onward, with desire
> Insatiate, to explore, inquire."

But not only is the thirst thus stimulated. Future knowledge grows upon past experience. Knowledge is not an endless level plain, to reach one district of which we must leave another. It is more like a great building, and as we rise from story to story, we gain new treasures by mounting on those previously possessed. The more we know, the easier is it to increase knowledge. This applies to religious as well as to secular things. Prophets and devout people were the first to welcome the advent of the Light of the world (see Luke ii. 25—38). The more the Christian knows, the more will he be able to see of new spiritual truths. Thus he will come to welcome instruction with thankfulness.

Ver. 12.—*True self-interest.* It is the duty of the Christian to bear his brother's burden, and the duty of every man to love his neighbour as himself; it is also the privilege of the saint to lose his life for Christ's sake, and to " spend and be spent " in the service of man. But there still remains a right and lawful, and even an obligatory, regard to self-interest. For one thing, if a man's own heart and life are wrong, his work in the world must be wrong also.

I. HE IS NOT TRULY WISE WHOSE OWN SOUL IS NOT SAFE. 1. *He may know the truth.* The wisdom that can unravel many mysteries is his. He has searched into the deep truths of revelation. A diligent reader of the Bible, he is well acquainted at least with the words that God teaches. But he has never regarded the practical bearing of all this truth. It has been to him but a shadow. Then his own soul may be wrecked, though the way to the haven is clear. 2. *He may enlighten others.* Perhaps he is a preacher of the gospel, and is able to hold up the torch to many a wayfarer. He is even urgent in pressing the truth upon his hearers. Or he is a champion for the defence of the truth, arguing vehemently with unbelievers. But all the while he never applies this truth to his own case. Saving others, he is himself a castaway (1 Cor. ix. 27). The pilot leads the imperilled mariners home, but is drowned himself. Surely this is the height of folly !

II. HE WHO IS TRULY WISE WILL PROFIT BY HIS WISDOM. 1. *He will see the necessity of applying truth to himself.* This will be a part of his wisdom. We are all sadly tempted to delude ourselves into a false sense of security, and we need light and guidance to show us our danger and our course of safety. It is a mark of God-given wisdom to choose that course. 2. *He will recognize the practical bearings of truth.* It will do little good to regard one's self only as a sort of example to which certain truths are attached. Mere self-examination of the most lucid and honest character will not save our souls. We have to go a step further, and act according to the knowledge that we gain in the light of God's truth. 3. *He will find the application of wisdom directly helpful.* When a man does not hold aloof from it as from some curiosity only to be inspected, but embraces the truth of Christ, taking it home to his own heart, he discovers that it is a saving truth. By the personal reception of this Divine wisdom he reaches the way of salvation. Above all, when we remember that Christ is "the Wisdom of God," we may see that for a man to receive that wisdom, *i.e.* to receive Christ, is to be wise for himself, because Christ brings the light of God's truth, and Christ's presence is the source of sure salvation.

Ver. 17.—"*Stolen waters.*" A fatal fascination, arising out of its very lawlessness, attaches itself to sin. Illicit pleasures are doubly attractive just because they are illicit. Let us consider the secret of these evil charms.

I. THE PROVOCATION OF RESTRAINTS. There are many things which we do not care to have so long as they are within our reach, but which are clothed with a sudden attractiveness directly they are shut out from us. If we see a notice, "Trespassers will be prosecuted," we feel an irritating restraint, although we have had no previous desire to enter the path that it blocks. Innumerable fruits grew in Eden, but the one forbidden fruit excited the greatest longing of appetite. Advertisers sometimes head their placards with the words, "Don't read this!"—judging that to be the best way to call attention to them. If you say, "Don't look!" everybody is most anxious to look. To put a book in an *index expurgatorius* is the surest means of advertising it.

II. THE VALUE GIVEN BY DIFFICULTY OF ACQUISITION. We value little what we can buy cheaply. Rarity raises prices. If we have been to great labour and have run heavy risks in obtaining anything, we are inclined to measure the worth of it by what it has cost us. Many designs of sin are only achieved with great difficulty. They involve terrible dangers. When once accomplished, they are the more valued for this. The pleasures of adventure, the Englishman's peculiar delights of the chase, are enlisted in the cause of wickedness.

"All things that are,
Are with more spirit chased than enjoyed."

III. THE SENSE OF POWER AND LIBERTY. If you have gained your end in spite of law and authority, there is a natural elation of triumph about it. When you have succeeded in breaking bounds, you taste the sweets of an illicit liberty.

IV. THE ENJOYMENT OF SECRECY. To some minds there is a peculiar charm about this. To them especially "bread eaten in secret is pleasant." Let it be all open and above-board, let it be of such a nature that one would have no objection to the world knowing it, and the pleasure loses its most pungent element. The air of mystery, the sense of superiority in doing what those about one little suspect, become elements in the pleasures of sin. But surely the highest natures must be too simple and frank to feel the force of such inducements to sin!

V. THE FASCINATION OF WICKEDNESS. Pure, naked evil will attract on its own account. There is a charm in absolute ugliness. Some men really seem to love sin for its own sake. A wild intoxication, a mad passion of conscious guilt, instils a fatal sweetness into stolen waters. But it is the sweetness of a deadly poison, the euthanasia of crime.

All these horrible charms of sin need to be guarded against. We must not trust to our own integrity; it is not proof against the fatal fascinations of temptation. To resist them we must be fortified with the love of higher joys, fed with the wholesome food of the banquet of wisdom (see vers. 1—5), attracted by the beauty of holiness, and above all, led to the pure and nourishing delights of the gospel feast by faith in the Lord Jesus Christ.

HOMILIES BY VARIOUS AUTHORS.

Vers. 1—6.— *Wisdom's banquet; or, the call to salvation.* I. THE FIGURATIVE REPRESENTATION. Wisdom was termed, in ch. viii. 30, a "workmistress," in reference to the structure of the physical world. Here she whose delight is in men and human life is represented as the builder, *i.e.* the founder of moral and social order. The *seven pillars* denote grandeur, and, at the same time, *sacredness.* Her home is a temple. Religion is "the oldest and most sacred tradition of the race" (Herder); and it contains within it art, science, polity—all that makes human life stable, rich, and beautiful. Preparation has been made for a feast. The ox has been slain, the spiced wine has been mixed (Isa. v. 22; ch. xxiii. 30), the table set forth. Her servant has been sent forth, and her invitation has been freely made known on all the heights of the city. It is an invitation to the simple, the ignorant, the unintelligent, of every degree.

II. THE SPIRITUAL CONTENTS. These receive a richer unfolding in the gospel (Matt. xxii. 1—14; Luke xiv. 16—24). Instead of the practical personification of wisdom, we have the living presence of Christ, "the Wisdom of God." Instead of the *abstract,* the concrete; for an ideal conception, a real Example and a present Object of faith. Instead of the splendid palace-temple, on the other hand, we have the thought of the kingdom of God, or the Church, resting on its foundations of apostolic truth. To the provisions of the table correspond the rich spiritual nourishment derivable from Christ, his Word and work—the true Bread sent down from heaven. To the invitation of Wisdom, the call to salvation by Christ. 1. The New Testament echoes the Old, and the gospel is essentially the same in every way. 2. The gospel of Christ is the unfolding, expansion, enrichment, of the ancient spiritual lore. 3. The relation of the Divine to the human remains constant; it is that of supply to want, knowledge to ignorance, love and light to sorrow and darkness. 4. The invitation to the kingdom of heaven is free and general, conditioned by nothing except the need of its blessings.—J.

Vers. 7—9.— *Warnings against refusal.* So, in connection with the preceding section, we may take these words.

I. EVERY REFUSAL OF WISDOM IMPLIES THE PREFERENCE OF THE OPPOSITE. It implies that the associations of folly are more congenial than those of sound sense (ver. 6), which is a preference of death to life, in its effect.

II. THE SCOFFING HABIT IS AN INDICATION OF FOLLY. (Ver. 7.) Under the general head of fools come scoffers and wicked men of every degree. The cynic may prefer to speak of evil men and actions as *fools* and *folly*—" worse than a crime, a blunder " —and he utters more truth in this than he intends.

III. THE SCOFFER IS ABUSIVE, AND THIS IS SIGNIFICANT OF HIS TEMPER. (Vers. 7, 8; comp. Exod. v. 16; Ps. cxv. 7.) 1. He neither has nor desires to have self-knowledge, and therefore hates the teacher who holds the mirror up to nature, and makes him see himself as he is. 2. He is the foil to the wise man, who is thankful for corrections, because he is set upon improvement and progress; and therefore loves the corrector, holding him creditor of his thanks, and recognizing the loyalty of the hand which wounds. 3. The great distinction of the wise man from the fool is that the former has *indefinite capacity of progress;* the latter, *quâ* fool, none. 4. As there is an indissoluble connection between folly and wickedness, so are wisdom and rectitude at one (ver. 9).—J.

Vers. 10—12.— *Recurrence to first principles.* Life is made up of circles. We are ever coming back to whence we started. As history repeats itself, so must morality and religion. The shining points of wisdom appear and reappear with the regularity of the heavenly bodies. The vault of heaven has its analogue in the star-besprinkled vault of the moral relations. Iteration and repetition of first principles are constantly necessary, ever wholesome, peculiarly characteristic of Semitic thought. Wherever life is bounded to a small circle of interests, the same truths must be insisted on " over and over again."

I. RELIGION A FIRST PRINCIPLE. 1. Religion characterized. The *fear of Jehovah.* In other words, reverence for the Eternal One. We may unfold the definition, but can we substitute a better for it? It is a relation to the eternal and unseen, to a supersensual order, as opposed to that which is visible and transient. It is deep-seated in feeling. Reverence is the ground-tone in the scale of religious feeling; we descend from it to awe and terror, or rise to joy and ecstasy. It is a relation, not to ourselves, or a projection of ourselves in fancy, but to a personal and holy Being. 2. Its connection with intelligence firmly insisted on. It is the beginning, or root-principle, of wisdom, and "acquaintance with the Holy is true insight" (ver. 10). The question, often discussed, whether religion is a matter of feeling, knowledge, or will, arises from a fallacy. We may *distinguish* these functions in thought; but in act they are one, because the consciousness is a *unity*, not a bundle of things, a collocation of organs. In feeling we know, in knowledge we feel, and from this interaction arise will, acts, conduct. Hence so far as a man is soundly religious, he is likewise soundly intelligent. In the truest conception religion and wisdom are *identical.*

II. WISDOM A FIRST PRINCIPLE. (Ver. 11.) Here we come down from the region of *speculation* to that of *practical* truth. 1. The "will to live" is the very spring of our activity. 2. Only second to it in original power is the wish to be well, *i.e.* to have *fulness, energy* of life, consciousness. The *extensive* form of this wish is naturally the earlier, the more childlike—to enjoy many years, to live to a green old age, etc. The *intensive* form is later, and belongs to the more reflective stage of the mind. "Non vivere, sed valere, est vita" (Martial). 'Tis "*more life and fuller* that we want" (Tennyson). "One hour of glorious life is worth an age without a name." This view comes more home to the modern mind than to that of the monotonous East, where the like *fulness of interest* was not possible. We say, "Better twenty years of Europe than a cycle of Cathay."

III. PERSONALITY A FIRST PRINCIPLE. (Ver. 12.) 1. We have a *distinct individual consciousness.* "I am I, and other than the things I touch." I know what *my acts* are as distinguished from my involuntary movements, *my thoughts* as distinct from the passive reflection of perceptions and phantasies unbegotten of my will. 2. Our wisdom or folly is *our own affair*, both in origin and consequences. We begot the habit, and must reap as we sow, bear the brunt of the conflict we may have provoked. 3. Neither our wisdom can enrich nor our folly impoverish God (Job xxii. 2, 3; xxxv. 6—9; Rom. xi. 35; Rev. xxii. 11, 12). (1) It is a solemn thought; the constitution of our being reveals the decree of God, and may be thus interpreted: "Let him alone!" We are not interfered with. We are suffered to develop in the air and sun. Woe to us if we pervert the kindly gifts of God, and turn his truth into a lie! (2) "Take heed to thyself." The effects of our acts may extend to others, but we cannot make others answer for them in the end.—J.

Vers. 13—18.—*The invitation of Folly.* The picture to be taken in contrast with that at the beginning of the chapter.

I. THE TEMPER OF FOLLY. 1. She is *excitable* and *passionate* (ver. 13), and may be fitly imaged as the harlot, the actress and mask of genuine feeling. 2. She is *irrational,* and knows not what is what. *True* love is *not* blind, either as to self or its objects. 3. She is like the harlot again in her *shamelessness* (ver. 14). Folly does not mind *exposure,* and rushes on publicity. 4. She is solicitous of company (ver. 15). Must have partners in guilt, and companions to keep her in countenance. Fools cannot be happy in solitude, cannot enjoy the sweet and silent charms of nature. Wisdom finds good both in the forest and the city, in the cloister or amidst the "busy hum of men." 5. Folly is gregarious. Wherever there is a crowd, there is something foolish going on (ver. 16). It may be safely said of habitual gatherings in taverns and such places, "mostly fools." The wise man goes apart to recover and strengthen his individuality; the fool plunges into the throng to forget himself. 6. Folly is sly and secretive (ver. 17). The *secret* feast is here the *illicit pleasure* (cf. ch. xxx. 20). The fact that people like what they ought not to like all the more *because they ought not,* is a complex phenomenon of the soul. The *sweetness of liberty recovered* is in it, and forms its good side. Liberty adds a perfume and spice to every pleasure, no matter what the pleasure may be. Augustine tells how he robbed an orchard as a boy, admitting that he did not want the pears, and arguing that it must therefore have been his depravity that led him to find pleasure in taking them! In the same way one might prove the depravity of the jackdaw that steals a ring. Let us repudiate the affectation of depravity, a great "folly" in its way; and rather draw the wholesome lesson that the love of liberty, of fun—in short, of any healthy exercise of energy, needs direction. The instinct for privacy and liberty gives no less zest to legitimate than to illicit pleasures.

II. THE END OF FOLLY. (Ver. 18.) 1. It is represented under images of darkness and dread. Shadows, "children of death," dead men, departed ghosts, hover about the dwelling of Folly and the persons of her guests. And these, while even they sit at her table amidst feasting and mirth, are already, in the eyes of Wisdom the spectator, in the depths of hell. Thus the shadows of coming ill "darken the ruby of the cup, and dim the splendour of the scene." 2. The indefinable is more impressive in its effect than the definable. As *e.g.* Burke has felicitously shown in his treatise on 'The Sublime and Beautiful.' The *obscure realities* of the other world, the mysterious twilight, the *chiaro-oscuro* of the imagination : in this region is found all that fascinates the mind with hope or terror. If it be asked—*What* precisely will be the doom of the wicked, the bliss of the righteous? the answer is—*Definite* knowledge has not been imparted, is impossible, and would have less effect than the vague but positive forms in which the truth is hinted. 3. The indefinable is not the less *certain*. It is the definite which is contingent, uncertain. Our life is a constant *becoming* from moment to moment. This of its nature is as indefinable as the melting of darkness into day, or the reverse.—J.

Vers. 1—6.—*The Divine invitation.* Wisdom invites the sons of men to a feast. Christ, "the Wisdom of God," is inviting us all to partake of eternal life. A feast may well be regarded as the picture and type of life at its fullest. It combines so many of the best features of human life—bounty generously offered and graciously accepted, nourishment, enjoyment, social intercourse, intellectual and spiritual as well as bodily gratification. In the gospel of Christ there is offered to us life at its very fullest—Divine, eternal. We are invited by Eternal Wisdom to partake thereof, to "lay hold" thereupon. These verses suggest to us—

I. THE COMPLETENESS OF THE DIVINE PREPARATION. (Vers. 1, 2.) The house is built, the full number of pillars hewn, the beasts killed, the wine mingled, the table set out. Everything is arranged and executed; nothing is forgotten or omitted. Every guest will find that which he needs. How complete is the preparation which God has made for us in the gospel of grace and life! The whole of the Old Testament may be said to be a part of the history of his preparation. All his dealings with his ancient people, and his control of the heathen nations, were leading up to the one great issue—the redemption of mankind by a life-giving Saviour. The New Testament continues the same account; the birth, the ministry, the life, the sorrows, the death, the resurrection and ascension of Jesus Christ, the evangelizing work and the interpretive letters of the apostles, form the last part of the Divine preparation. And now everything is complete. The house is built, the table is spread, the wine outpoured. There is nothing which a guilty, sorrowing, striving, seeking soul can hunger or thirst for which it will not find at this heavenly feast. Mercy, full reconciliation, unfailing friendship, comfort, strength, hope, joy in God, everlasting life,—everything is there.

II. THE GRACIOUSNESS OF THE INVITATION. (Vers. 3, 4.) Wisdom sends "her maidens" and "cries upon the highest places of the city." She charges those to speak who are likeliest to be listened to, and to utter her invitation where it is surest to be heard. Moreover, she does not restrict her call to those who may be said to be her own children (Matt. xi. 19); on the other hand, she addresses herself specially to those who are strange to her—to "the simple," to "him that wanteth understanding." In the gospel of the grace of God : 1. It is the gracious Lord himself who speaks to us, and in the most winning way. It is he himself who says, "Come unto me;" "If any man thirst," etc.; "I am the Bread of life," etc. 2. He has, in his providence and grace, caused the message of mercy to be sounded where all can hear it—"upon the highest places of the city." 3. He calls all men to his bountiful board, specially those who are in the greatest need (Luke xiv. 21—23; Matt. ix. 12, 13).

III. The character of the message. (Vers. 5, 6.) Wisdom calls those who hear her messengers to forsake folly, to walk in righteousness, and thus to enter into life. The Wisdom of God himself calls those who hear his voice to: 1. Turn from their iniquity, turning away from the fellowship of the unholy as well as from the practice of sin. 2. Enter into closest fellowship with him himself; thus eating of the bread and drinking of the water of life; thus walking in the way of truth, holiness, love, wisdom; thus "going in the way of understanding." 3. Partake with him the life which is Divine and eternal—life for God, life in God, life with God for ever.—C.

Vers. 7—9.—*The penalty and promise of instruction.* It is not only the function of the minister of Christ to "reprove, rebuke, and exhort" (2 Tim. iv. 2); the "man of God" is to be so furnished from Scripture as to be able to administer "reproof, correction, and instruction in righteousness" (2 Tim. iii. 16, 17). But instruction, especially when it takes the form of correction, has its penalty as well as its recompense. I. The penalty of instruction. (Vers. 7, 8.) It is in the heart of the wise to rebuke iniquity. Those who are upright and true, who hate evil even as God hates it, are stirred to a holy indignation when they behold the dark and shameful manifestations of sin, and remonstrance rises to their lips. It is as "fire in their bones" until they have "delivered their soul." 2. Rebuke is often decidedly advantageous. It not only relieves the mind of the godly speaker, but it shames those who should be made to blush for their deeds. Even when it fails to impress the principal defaulter, the arch-criminal, it may produce a wholesome influence on the minds of those who witness it. A burning flame of righteous wrath will sometimes consume much unrighteousness. 3. Nevertheless, it is true that the wise must count on the contrary being the result. It may be that remonstrance will be thrown away, that it will come to nothing but shame on the part of him that reproves—a "blot on the page," and nothing but provocation to him that is rebuked, inciting him to hatred (ver. 8). The likelihood must be reckoned, and the wise must act accordingly. If there is hope of doing good, some risk may well be run. All interposition is not here discountenanced. Good men must use their discretion. There is a time to speak, using the language of strong and even severe reproach. On the other hand—this is the truth of the text—there is a time to be silent, to leave abandoned and guilty men to be condemned of God. Reproach would be lost upon them; it would only come back with a severe rebound, and wound the speaker (see Matt. vii. 6). II. The promise of instruction. (Vers. 8, 9.) 1. There are those in whom is the spirit of docility. They are ready to learn. Of these are the young. Our Lord commended the spirit of childhood partly for this reason, viz. that it is the spirit of docility. It has openness of mind, eagerness of heart to receive instruction. Of these, also, are those in whom the spirit of wisdom dwells, but who have fallen into error. 2. Instruction in these cases will be well repaid. If we rebuke a wise man, a man who is essentially good but accidentally wrong, we shall meet with appreciation: "he will love us." If we impart instruction to those already wise, we shall add to their excellency (ver. 9). So that intelligent, well-timed instruction will do two things. (1) It will restore the erring—a most valuable and admirable action, on which the best of men may truly congratulate themselves. (2) It will multiply the power of the good. It will add knowledge and wisdom to those who are already wise; it will make good men better, happier, worthier, in themselves; it will also make them more influential for good in the sphere in which they move. This, then, is the threefold lesson of the text: 1. Know when to be silent under provocation. 2. Speak the word of reproach in season. 3. Communicate knowledge to all who will welcome it.—C.

Vers. 10, 11.—*Digging deep, rising high, lasting long.* (See homilies on ch. i. 7 and iii. 1—4.) The fact that we meet with the opening sentence of the text in no less than three other places (Job xxvii. 28; Ps. cxi. 10; ch. i. 7), gives to it a peculiar significance. It indicates that the Divine Author of the Bible would impress deeply on our minds the truth—

I. That on the fear of God, as on a solid rock, all human wisdom rests. Nothing which a man can have in his outward circumstances or in his mind will compensate for the absence of this principle from the soul. He may have every conceivable advantage in his surroundings; he may have all imaginable shrewdness, dexterity, cleverness, acuteness of intellect; but if everything be not based on the fear of the living God, his character must be fatally incomplete, and his life must be a deplorable mistake. Reverence of spirit, devotion of habit, the obedience of the life,— this is the solid ground on which all wisdom rests. Let a man be ever so learned or so astute, if this be absent Wisdom itself writes him down a fool.

II. THAT SACRED TRUTH IS THE LOFTIEST AND WORTHIEST SUBJECT OF HUMAN STUDY. It is well worth our while to give our careful and continuous thought to scientific, economical, historical, political truth. These will repay our study; they will enlarge our mind and heighten our understanding. But worthy as they are, they yield in importance to the truth which is sacred and, in an especial sense, Divine. To "understand and know God," who he is, what is his character, what are the conditions of his abiding love; to know man, who and what he is, what constitutes the real excellence and nobility of human character, what are the perils which threaten and what the habits which elevate it; to know the "path of life," the way back to God, to holiness, to heaven;—this is wisdom indeed. The knowledge of the holy is understanding. All other learning is slight in comparison with this supreme attainment.

III. THAT THE SERVICE OF GOD IS INSEPARABLY CONNECTED WITH THE LASTING WELL-BEING OF MAN. (Ver. 11.) 1. Obedience to Jehovah would have given a prolonged and enduring life to the Jewish nation in their own favoured land. Conformity to Divine Law, the practice of truth, purity, uprightness, simplicity of life and manners, —these will go far to ensure long life to any nation now. 2. Obedience to Divine Law, especially to one commandment (Exod. xx. 12), gave good hope of longevity to the children of the Law (ver. 11; ch. iii. 2, 16). Piety and virtue now have promise of life and health. The sober, the pure, the diligent, those mindful of God's will, are likely to have their days multiplied and the years of their life increased. 3. To the true servants of Christ, who are faithful unto death, there is assured a "crown of life" (Rev. ii. 10).—C.

Ver. 12.—*Wisdom and folly.* In this short verse we have some valuable thoughts suggested respecting both wisdom and folly.

I. THE DISINTERESTEDNESS OF WISDOM. If any one should urge against the claims of Wisdom that they are very high, urgent, oppressive, that God's commandment is "exceeding broad;" if it be asked by the young, "Why fling these shadows on our path? why weigh us down with these responsibilities?" it may well be replied by Wisdom, "Your services are not necessary to me. 'If I were hungry, I would not tell thee,' etc.; if I plead with you, it is for your sake. You have need of my voice and my control; apart from me you cannot be blessed, you cannot realize the end of your being. I can do well without your devotion, but you cannot do without my favour. If you are wise, you will be wise for yourself."

II. THE INALIENABLE CHARACTER OF WISDOM AS A POSSESSION. The wise man in the Book of Ecclesiastes laments that riches are things which a wise man may take much trouble to gather, but he does not know who may scatter them. A man may be laborious and frugal, but not for himself; all the good may go to others who come after him. Thus is it with various acquisitions. Men no sooner gain them than they leave them behind for others; *e.g.* the hero, his glory; the student, his learning; the conqueror or discoverer, the territory he has gained or found. But if a man is wise, he is wise *for himself* as well as for others; he has a prize of which no accident will rob him, and which death itself will not take from his hands. Once his, it is his for ever —it is an inalienable possession.

III. THE PROFOUND NATURE OF TRUE WISDOM. There is a very shallow philosophy which assumes the name of wisdom, which invites us to stake everything on securing a comfortable and prosperous career in this world, leaving out of account the supreme realities of our obligations to God, our duty to our own spiritual and immortal nature, our responsibilities to other souls. This superficial and false teaching overlooks the fundamental fact that a man is more than his means, that ourself is greater than our circumstances, that it is a poor profit to gain a world and lose a soul, that if we are wise we shall be wise *for ourselves.*

IV. The starting-point of true wisdom. Some are speaking with indignation, not insincere, against so much insistence on a man's seeking his own salvation. They say it is only a refined selfishness. It may be true that there are Christian teachers who enlarge on this aspect disproportionately; but it must ever remain a truth of great prominence that a man's first duty to God is the duty he owes to himself. First, because his own soul is his primary and chief charge; and, secondly, because he can do little or nothing for the world till his own heart is right. If a man, therefore, will be wise, he must first be wise for himself.

V. The fate of folly. "If thou scornest, thou alone shalt bear it." This does not mean that only the sinner bears the consequences of his guilt—that is deplorably untrue; sin is widespreading and far-reaching in its evil consequences—it *circulates* and it *descends*. The passage means that the foolish man will have to bear alone the condemnation of his folly; every man that lives and dies impenitent must "bear his own burden" of penalty. The remorse and self-reproach of the future none will be able to divide; it must be borne by the sinner himself. There is One that once bore our transgressions for us, and will bear them away unto the land of forgetfulness *now.*—C.

Vers. 13—18.—*The truth about sin.* Solomon, having told us of the excellency of Wisdom, and of the blessings she has to confer on her children, now bids us consider the consequences of listening to sin, when she, the foolish woman, utters her invitation. We learn—

I. That sin in its later developments is a very odious thing. What a painful and repulsive picture we have here of the foolish woman, who, though utterly ignorant and unworthy (ver. 13), assumes a conspicuous position in the city, places herself "on a seat in the high places," speaks with a "clamorous" voice, and, herself unaddressed, calls aloud to those who are going on their way! When we present the scene to our imagination, we instinctively shrink from it as repelling and odious. All sin is hateful in the sight of God; to him it is "that abominable thing" (Jer. xliv. 4). And to all the pure in heart it is also, though not equally, repulsive. In its later stages and final developments it is simply and thoroughly detestable.

II. That temptation to sin besets the unwary as well as the evil-minded. Folly addresses herself to "passengers who go right on their ways" (ver. 15). There are those who go wilfully and wantonly in the way of temptation. They seek the company of the profane, the attentions of the immoral. These walk into the net, and are ensnared. Then there are others who have no thought of evil in their heart; they are not "purposing to transgress;" but as they pass right on their way, the temptress throws her net at if not over them, that she may entangle them. The path of human life is beset with spiritual perils; it is necessary to be prepared against all forms of evil. We must not only be upright in intention, but wary and well-armed also. "Be sober, be vigilant, because your adversary," etc. (1 Pet. v. 8).

III. That to unsanctified human nature sin is sometimes a terribly seductive thing. "The foolish woman," though she is said to "know nothing," yet knows enough to say truly, "Stolen waters are sweet," etc. (ver. 17). It is useless, because it is false, to deny that vice has its pleasures. Lasciviousness, revelry, avarice, usurpation, have their delights; and there is a peculiar pleasure in snatching unlawful gratifications rather than in accepting those which are honourable. When our nature is unregenerated and unsanctified, when passion is at its height, when in the soul there is the ardour and energy of youth, vice has powerful attractions. The young may well provide themselves against the dark hour of temptation with "the whole armour of God," or they may not be able to stand victorious.

IV. That those who have abandoned themselves to sin are in the embrace of ruin. "He knoweth not that the dead are there; and that her guests are in the depths of hell" (ver. 18). Not only is it true (1) that those who yield themselves to guilty passion are on the high-road to ultimate perdition; but it is also true (2) that they are already in the depth of ruin. They are "dead while they live" (1 Tim. v. 6); they are "in the depths of hell" (text). To be sacrificing manhood or womanhood on the altar of an unholy pleasure, or an immoral gain, or an enslaving fascination; to be sinning continually against God, and to be systematically degrading our own soul;

to be falling lower and lower in the estimation of the wise until we become the object of their pity or their scorn;—this *is* ruin. No need to wait for judgment and condemnation; the guests of sin *are in* the depths of hell. If near the door, if on its step, if in its hall, "escape for thy life" (see Wardlaw, *in loc.*).—C.

EXPOSITION.

CHAPTER X.

Ver. 1—ch. xxii. 16.—Part III. FIRST GREAT COLLECTION (375) OF SOLOMONIC PROVERBS.

Ver. 1—ch. xii. 28.—First section. The sections are noted by their commencing usually with the words, "a wise son."

Ver. 1.—**The proverbs of Solomon.** This is the title of the new part of the book; it is omitted in the Septuagint. There is some kind of loose connection in the grouping of these proverbs, but it is difficult to follow. "Ordo frustra quæritur ubi nullus fuit observatus," says Mart. Geier. Wordsworth considers the present chapter to contain exemplifications of the principles and results of the two ways of life displayed in the preceding nine chapters. The antithetical character of the sentences is most marked and well-sustained. As the book is specially designed for the edification of youth, it begins with an appropriate saying. **A wise son maketh a glad father.** As wisdom comprises all moral excellence, and folly is vice and perversity, the opposite characters attributed to the son are obvious. The mother is introduced for the sake of parallelism; though some commentators suggest that, as the father would be naturally elated by his son's virtues, which would conduce to honour and high estate, so the mother would be grieved at vices which her training had not subdued, and her indulgence had fostered. If this seems somewhat far-fetched, we may consider that the father in the maxim includes the mother, and the mother the father, the two being separated for the purpose of contrast (see on ch. xxvi. 3). The word for **heaviness** occurs in ch. xiv. 13 and xvii. 21.

Ver. 2.—**Treasures of wickedness**; treasures acquired by wrong-doing (Micah vi. 10). **Profit nothing** "in the day of calamity" (Ecclus. v. 8; comp. ch. xi. 4). The LXX. renders, "Treasures will not profit the wicked;" so Aquila. "For what shall a man be profited, if he shall gain the whole world, and forfeit his soul?" (Matt. xvi. 26). **Righteousness** (ch. xiv. 34); not simply justice and moral goodness, but more especially liberality, benevolence. So in Matt. vi. 1 the Revised Version (in accordance with the best manuscripts) reads, "Take heed that ye do not your righteousness before men, to be seen of them," Christ proceeding to specify three outward acts as coming under this term, viz. almsgiving, prayer, and fasting. In some analogous passages the LXX. renders the word by ἐλεημοσύνη, *e.g.* Ps. cxi. 9; Dan. iv. 27; Tobit xii. 9 (comp. 2 Cor. ix. 10). **Delivereth from death,** shows that a man's heart is right towards God, and calls down special grace. Such a man lays up in store for himself a good foundation, that he may attain eternal life (1 Tim. vi. 19; see on ch. xvi. 6).

Ver. 3.—**The Lord will not suffer the soul of the righteous to famish** (comp. ch. xix. 23). The soul is the life (comp. ch. xiii. 25). So the psalmist says (Ps. xxxvii. 25), "I have been young, and now am old; yet have I not seen the righteous forsaken, nor his seed begging their bread." Christ speaks of the providence that watches over the lower creatures, and draws thence a lesson of trust in his care of man, concluding, "Seek ye first the kingdom of God, and his righteousness, and all these things shall be added unto you" (Matt. vi. 26, 33). **But he casteth away the substance of the wicked;** Septuagint, "He will overthrow the life of the wicked;" Vulgate, "He overturns the plots of sinners." The word rendered "substance" (*havvah*) is better understood as "desire." God frustrates the eager longing (for food or other good things) of the wicked; they are never satisfied, and get no real enjoyment out of what they crave (comp. ch. xiii. 25).

Ver. 4.—**That dealeth with a slack hand;** that is lazy and indolent (comp. ch. vi. 10, 11; see on ch. xix. 15). The Septuagint, with a different pointing, reads, "Poverty humbleth a man." **The hand of the diligent** (ch. xii. 24) **maketh rich.** The words for "hand" are different in the two clauses as Wordsworth remarks. The first word is *caph*, the open, ineffective, hand or palm; the second term is *yad*, the hand tense and braced for vigorous work. The LXX. introduces a clause here which seems to interfere with the connection: Υἱὸς πεπαιδευμένος σοφὸς ἔσται, τῷ δὲ ἄφρονι διακόνῳ χρήσεται, "A well-instructed son will be wise, and he will use a fool as his minister;" *i.e.* he is able to make even the foolish subserve his ends. The sentence is quoted by St. Augustine, 'De Civit. Dei,' xvi. 2. The Vulgate inserts another paragraph, which is also found in some manuscripts of the Septuagint at ch. ix. 12: *Qui nititur* *mendaciis, hic pascit ventos; idem autem ipse sequitur aves volantes,* "He who relieth on lies feedeth on the winds, and pursueth flying birds."

Ver. 5.—**He that gathereth the harvest** into the barn at the right season. The idea of husbandry is continued from the preceding verse. **Son** is here equivalent to "man," the maxim being addressed to the young. **That sleepeth**; literally, *that snoreth;* Vulgate, *qui stertit* (Judg. iv. 21). **A son that causeth shame.** The phrase is found in ch. xvii. 2; xix. 26; xxix. 15. The Septuagint has, "The son of understanding is saved from the heat; but the sinful son is blasted by the wind in harvest."

Ver. 6.—**Violence covereth the mouth of the wicked.** So ver. 11. This is usually explained to mean either that the consciousness of his own iniquity silences the sinner when he would speak against the righteous, or his violence and injustice, returning on his own head, are like a bandage over his mouth (Lev. xiii. 45; Micah iii. 7), reducing him to shame and silence. Others, again, consider the signification to be—in default of the good, honest words which should proceed from a man's mouth, the sinner pours forth injustice and wickedness. But it is best (as in ver. 14) to take "mouth" as the subject: "The mouth of the wicked concealeth violence," that he may wait for the opportunity of practising it. The contrast is between the manifest blessedness of the righteous and the secret sinister proceedings of the evil. The Vulgate and Septuagint give, "the blessing of the Lord." For "violence" the Septuagint has πένθος ἄωρον, "untimely grief;" the Hebrew word *chamas* bearing also the sense of "misery."

Ver. 7.—**The memory.** The lasting, fragrant perfume of a holy life is contrasted with the noisomeness and quick decay of an evil name (comp. Ps. lxxii. 17). As a commentator asks, "Who ever thinks of calling a child Judas or Nero?"

Ver. 8.—**Will receive commandments.** The wise in heart is not proud or conceited; he accepts the Divine Law with all its directions (observe the plural "commandments"), and is not above learning from others; at the same time, he makes no display of his wisdom. **The fool of lips** (ver. 10); one who is always exposing his folly. The literal antithesis is better shown by rendering "the solid in heart," and "the loose in lips." So Wordsworth. The Vulgate translates, "The fool is chastised by his lips;" *i.e.* the folly which he has uttered falls back upon him, and causes him to suffer punishment. The LXX. renders the last clause, "He who is given to prating (ἄστεγος χείλεσι), walking tortuously, shall be tripped up."

Ver. 9.—**He that walketh uprightly** (ch. ii. 7); Vulgate and Septuagint, "in simplicity," having nothing to conceal or to fear. So Christ enjoins his followers to be guileless as children, and harmless as doves (Matt. x. 16; Mark x. 15). **Surely**; equivalent to "securely;" ἀμερίμνως, Aquila, having no fear of inopportune exposure, because he has no secret sin. **He that perverteth his ways**; deals in crooked practices. **Shall be known** (ch. xii. 16). He shall be exposed and punished, and put to open shame. Having this apprehension always present, he cannot walk with confidence as the innocent does. Hence the antithesis in the text.

Ver. 10.—**He that winketh with the eye** (ch. vi. 13). This is a sign of craft, malice, and complicity with other wicked comrades. Ecclus. xxvii. 22, "He that winketh with the eyes worketh evil." **Causeth sorrow** (ch. xv. 13). He causes trouble and vexation by his cunning and secrecy. **A prating fool** (as ver. 8). The two clauses are intended to teach that the garrulous fool is even more certain to bring ruin on himself and others than the crafty plotter. The Septuagint and Syriac have changed the latter clause into a sentence supposed to be more forcibly antithetical, "He who reproveth with boldness maketh peace." But there are sentences not strictly antithetical in this chapter, *e.g.* vers. 18, 22 (comp. ch. xi. 10).

Ver. 11.—**A well of life** (ch. xiii. 14; xviii. 4). The good man utters words of wisdom, comfort, and edification. God himself is said to have "the well of life" (Ps. xxxvi. 9), and to be "the Fountain of living waters" (Jer. ii. 13); and the holy man, drawing from this supply, sheds life and health around. The second clause should be taken as in ver. 6, **but the mouth of the wicked concealeth violence**, the contrast being between the open usefulness of the good man's words and the harmful reticence of the malicious sinner. The Septuagint has, "A fountain of life is in the hand of the righteous; but destruction shall cover the mouth of the wicked." This is explained to mean that a good man's words and actions tend to spiritual health; a bad man's words bring down sorrow and punishment.

Ver. 12.—**Hatred stirreth up strife** (ch. vi. 14). **Love covereth all sins** (ch. xvii. 9). The reference is primarily to the blood-feud, the existence of which led to the establishment of the cities of refuge. Hatred keeps alive the old feeling of revenge, and seeks opportunities of satisfying it; but love puts aside, forgets and forgives all offences against itself. This sentiment comes very near the great Christian principle, "Love covereth a multitude of sins" (1 Pet. iv. 8; comp. 1 Cor. xiii. 4; Jas. v. 20). The Talmud pronounces, " To love a thing makes the eye blind, the ear deaf ; " and the Arab says, " Love is the companion of blindness." Septuagint, " Love (φιλία) covereth all those who love not strife."

Ver. 13.—**Wisdom is found** (comp. Ps. xxxvii. 30). The man of understanding is discreet in speech, and does not cause trouble by rash or foolish words. **A rod** (ch. xix. 29 ; xxvi. 3). A fool brings upon himself punishment by his insensate talk. **Void of understanding** ; Hebrew, " wanting in heart ; " Vulgate, *qui indiget corde.* The LXX. combines the two members into one proposition, " He who putteth forth wisdom with his lips is a rod to chastise the man without heart." In the Hebrew conception the " heart " is the seat, not only of the passions and affections, but also of the intellectual faculties.

Ver. 14.—**Lay up knowledge** ; like a treasure, for use on proper occasions (ch. xii. 23 ; xiv. 33 ; comp. Matt. vii. 6 ; xiii. 52). **Is near destruction.** " Near " may be an adjective, equivalent to " imminent," " ever-threatening." The versions are *proximum est* and ἐγγίζει. The foolish are always uttering carelessly what may bring trouble on themselves and others.

Ver. 15.—**His strong city** (ch. xviii. 11). Wealth is a help in many ways, securing from dangers, giving time and opportunity for acquiring wisdom, making one independent and free in action (Eccles. vii. 12 ; Ecclus. xl. 25, etc.). **The destruction of the poor is their poverty.** The poor are crushed, exposed to all kinds of evil, moral and material, by their want of means. The word for " poor " is here *dal,* which implies weakness and inability to help one's self ; the other word commonly used for " poor " is *rash,* which signifies rather " impecuniosity," opposed to " wealthy." So in the present passage the LXX. renders ἀσθενῶν, " the feeble." The poor were but lightly regarded till Christ pronounced the benediction, " Blessed be ye poor : for yours is the kingdom of God " (Luke vi. 20). The view of Theognis (' Paræn.,' 177) will speak the experience of many—

Καὶ γὰρ ἀνὴρ πενίῃ δεδμημένος οὔ τέ τι εἰπεῖν Οὔθ' ἔρξαι δύναται· γλῶσσα δὲ οἱ δέδεται.

" A man, by crushing poverty subdued, Can freely nothing either say or do— His very tongue is tied."

Ver. 16.—**Tendeth to life** (ch. xi. 19). Honest labour brings its own reward in the blessing of God and a long and peaceful life. **The fruit of the wicked.** All the profit that the wicked make they use in the service of sin, which tends only to death (Rom. vi. 21). The due reward of honourable industry is

contrasted with the gains obtained by any means, discreditable or not.

Ver. 17.—**He is in the way of life** (ch. v. 6). It is a way of life when a man keepeth instruction, taketh to heart what is taught by daily providences and the wisdom of experience. Such teachableness leads to happiness here and hereafter. **Erreth** (Jer. xlii. 20) ; not " causeth to err," as in the margin, which weakens the antithesis. Septuagint, " Instruction (παιδεία) guardeth the ways of life, but he who is unaffected by instruction goeth astray " (comp. Heb. xii. 7, etc.).

Ver. 18.—This verse ought to be translated, **He that hideth hatred is [a man] of lying lips, and he that uttereth slander is a fool.** He who cherishes hatred in the heart must be a liar and a hypocrite, speaking and acting in a way contrary to his real sentiments ; if he divulges his slander, he is a stupid fool, injuring his neighbour, and procuring ill will for himself. The LXX. reads, " Just (δίκαια) lips conceal hatred ; " but probably δίκαια is an error for ἄδικα or δόλια, though Ewald defends it, and would alter the Hebrew to suit it.

Ver. 19.—**There wanteth not sin** ; LXX., " Thou wilt not avoid sin." Loquacity leads to exaggeration and untruthfulness, slander and uncharitableness (comp. Eccles. v. 1—3 ; and Christ's and James's solemn warnings, Matt. xii. 36 ; Jas. i. 26 ; iii. 2, etc.). " Speak little," says Pinart (' Meditations,' ch. vi.), " because for one sin which we may commit by keeping silence where it would be well to speak, we commit a hundred by speaking upon all occasions " (see on ch. xvii. 27). Another rendering of the passage gives " By multitude of words sin does not vanish away ; " *i.e.* you cannot mend a fault by much talking. But this weakens the contrast, and the Authorized Version is correct. **Is wise.** St. James calls the reticent " a perfect man " (comp. ch. xiii. 3). " This sentence of Scripture," says St. Augustine, in his ' Retractations,' " I greatly fear, because my numerous treatises, I know well, contain many things, if not false, at any rate idle and unnecessary."

Ver. 20.—**Choice** (ch. viii. 10, 19) ; tested, purified by fire ; πεπυρωμένος, Septuagint. **Is little worth** ; mere dross, in contradistinction to choice silver. So the tongue is contrasted with the heart, out of whose abundance it speaketh (Ecclus. xxi. 26, " The heart of fools is in their mouth ; but the mouth of the wise is in their heart "). Septuagint, " The heart of the godless shall fail (ἐκλείψει)."

Ver. 21.—**Feed many.** The righteous by wise counsel teach, support, and guide others (Eccles. xii. 11 ; Jer. iii. 15). So the clergy are the shepherds of their flocks

(John xxi. 15; Acts xx. 28; 1 Pet. v. 2). The LXX. has a different reading, "know high things." **Fools die for want of wisdom.** Far from "feeding" others, they bring ruin on themselves (ch. v. 23). Others translate, " die through one who wanteth understanding;" but if the Hebrew will bear this rendering, it is obvious that fools need no guide to their fall; their fate is a natural result. In this case the meaning must be that the foolish man involves others in destruction. But it is best to translate as the Authorized Version.

Ver. 22.—**The blessing of the Lord.** The Septuagint adds, "upon the head of the righteous," as in ver. 6. Not chance and luck, not even industry and labour, but God giveth the increase (Eccles. v. 18, 19). **He addeth no sorrow with it;** i.e. with the blessing. In acquiring and in using wealth thus blessed, the good man is contented and happy, while unsanctified riches bring only trouble and vexation. But this seems rather feeble, and it is better to render, "And a man's own labour addeth nothing thereto." A man's own work must not be regarded as an equal cause of prosperity with the favour of God. This sentiment is in accordance with Ps. cxxvii. 1, 2, "Except the Lord build the house, their labour is but lost that build it. . . . So he giveth unto his beloved in sleep"—what others vainly labour for God giveth to the righteous without toil. The rendering of the clause, "Trouble is of no avail without it," is scarcely warranted by the wording of the text.

Ver. 23.—**As a sport.** The wicked make their pastime and amusement in doing evil. **A man of understanding hath wisdom.** As thus put, the sentence is jejune. The Revised Version expresses the meaning better: "And so is wisdom to a man of understanding;" i.e. the wise man finds his refreshment in living a wise and prudent life, which is as easy and as pleasant to him as mischief is to the vicious. The wisdom intended is practical religion, the fear of God directing and showing itself in daily action. Septuagint, "A fool doeth mischief in sport (ἐν γέλωτι), but wisdom produceth prudence for a man."

Ver. 24.—This verse is connected in thought with the preceding. The wicked, though he lightly carries on his evil practices, is troubled with the thought of the retribution which awaits him, and **that which he fears shall come upon him** (ch. i. 26; Job iii. 25; Isa. lxvi. 4); Septuagint, "The wicked is involved in destruction." **The desire of the righteous.** The righteous will desire only that which is in agreement with God's will, and this God grants, if not in this world, certainly in the life to come.

The LXX. has, "The desire of the just is acceptable."

Ver. 25.—**As the whirlwind passeth.** According to this rendering (which has the support of the Vulgate) the idea is the speed with which, under God's vengeance, the sinner is consumed, as Isa. xvii. 13; Job xxi. 18. But it is better to translate, as the LXX., "when the whirlwind is passing," i.e. when the storm of judgment falls, as Christ represents the tempest beating on the ill-founded house and destroying it, while that which was built on the rock remains uninjured (comp. ch. xii. 3; Matt. vii. 24, etc.; comp. Wisd. v. 14, etc.). **Everlasting foundation** (ver. 30; Ps. xci.; cxxv. 1); like the Cyclopean stones on which Solomon's temple was built. It is natural to see here an adumbration of that Just One, the Messiah, the chief Cornerstone. The LXX. gives, "But the righteous turning aside is saved for ever."

Ver. 26.—**Vinegar** (Ruth ii. 14; Ps. lxix. 21). As sour wine sets the teeth on edge. Septuagint, "as the unripe grape is harmful to the teeth" (Ezek. xviii. 2). **Smoke.** In a country where chimneys were unknown, and the fuel was wood or some substance more unsavoury, the eyes must have often been painfully affected by the household fire. Thus *lacrimosus,* "tear-producing," is a classical epithet of smoke (see Ovid, 'Metam.,' x. 6; Hor., 'Sat.,' i. 5. 80). To these two annoyances is compared the messenger who loiters on his errand. The last clause is rendered by the LXX., "So is iniquity to those who practise it"—it brings only pain and vexation.

Ver. 27.—**The fear of the Lord prolongeth days.** The promise of long life as the reward of a religious conversation is often found in our book, where temporal retribution is set forth (see ch. iii. 2; ix. 11; xiv. 27). **Shall be shortened,** as Ps. lv. 23; Eccles. vii. 17.

Ver. 28.—**The hope of the righteous shall be gladness.** The patient expectation of the righteous is joyful, because it has good hope of being. and is, fulfilled. So the apostle (Rom. xii. 12) speaks, "Rejoicing in hope, patient in tribulation." Septuagint, "Gladness delayeth for the just." **The expectation of the wicked;** that which the wicked eagerly hope for shall come to naught (ch. xi. 7; Job viii. 13; Ps. cxii. 10).

Ver. 29.—**The way of the Lord;** i.e. the way in which he has commanded men to walk—the way of his commandments (Ps. xxv. 12; cxix. 27), that which the Pharisees confessed that Christ taught (Matt. xxii. 16). The Septuagint renders, "the fear of the Lord," which practically gives the meaning. Or "the Lord's way" may be his moral government of the world. **Strength;** better *a fortress* (ver. 15). Doing his simple duty, a good man is safe; for, as St. Peter says, " Who is he that will harm you, if ye be zealous of that which is good?" (1 Pet. iii. 13). **But destruction shall be;** better, *but it* (the way of Jehovah) *is destruction.* The two effects of the Law of God are contrasted, according as it is obeyed or neglected. While it is protection to the righteous, it is condemnation and ruin to sinners (see on ch. xxi. 15) So Christ at one time calls himself "the Way" (John xiv. 6); at another says, "For judgment I am come into this world" (John ix. 39); and Simeon declares of him (Luke ii. 34), "This Child is set for the fall and rising again of many in Israel" (comp. 2 Cor. ii. 15, etc.).

Ver. 30.—**The righteous shall never be removed** (ch. ii. 21; xii. 3, 21; Ps. x. 6; xxxvii. 29). This is in agreement with the temporal promise made to the patriarchs and often renewed, as in the fifth commandment. St. Paul says (1 Tim. iv. 8), "Godliness is profitable for all things, having promise of the life which now is, and of that which is to come." **The wicked shall not inhabit** (or, *abide not in*) **the land.** The punishment of exile was threatened upon the Jews for their disobedience, and they are still suffering this retribution (Lev. xxvi. 33; Deut. iv. 27; Isa. xxii. 17). Christ gives the other aspect of God's moral government when he says (Matt. v. 5), "Blessed are the meek: for they shall inherit the earth."

Ver. 31.—**Bringeth forth; as a tree** produces fruit, and the fields yield their increase. The metaphor is common. Thus Isaiah (lvii. 19) speaks of "the fruit of the lips" (comp. Heb. xiii. 15 and Ps. xxxvii. 30, which latter passage occurs in the same connection as the present). The Septuagint renders, "distilleth wisdom." So Cant. v. 13, "His lips are like lilies, dropping sweet-smelling myrrh." **The froward tongue** (ch. ii. 12, 14; viii. 13, which speaks only what is perverse and evil). **Shall be cut out;** like a corrupt tree that cumbers the ground (Matt. iii. 10; Luke xiii. 7). The abuse of God's great gift of speech shall be severely punished. "For by thy words thou shalt be justified, and by thy words thou shalt be condemned" (Matt. xii. 36, 37).

Ver. 32.—**Know.** A good man's lips are conversant with what is acceptable to God and man. Such a person considers what will please God and edify his neighbour, and speaks in conformity therewith. The LXX. has, " The lips of the righteous distil graces;" ἀποστάζει χάριτας, but probably the right verb is ἐπίσταται, which is found in some manuscripts. Speaketh **frowardness**; rather, *knoweth*, or is *perverseness* (comp. Eph. iv. 29); Septuagint, ἀποστρέφεται, or, according to the Sinaitic corrector and some other scribes, καταστρέφεται, "is turned aside," or "is overthrown." Delitzsch translates, "is mere falsehood."

HOMILETICS.

Ver. 1.—*The influence of a son over his parents' happiness.* It is impossible to estimate the tremendous influence which children have on the happiness of their parents. The unfortunate thing about it is that the children are the last to realize it. It may be that a misplaced modesty inclines them to imagine that their course in life cannot be of much consequence to any one. In many cases, unhappily, gross selfishness engenders sheer indifference to the feelings of those who have most claim upon them, so that they never give a thought to the pain they are inflicting. But behind these special points there is the universal fact that no one can understand the depth and overpowering intensity of a parent's love until he becomes a parent himself. Then, in the yearning anxiety he experiences for his own children, a man may have a revelation of the love which he had received all the days of his life without ever dreaming of its wonderful power. But surely, up to their capacity for understanding it, children should realize the great trust that is given to them. They are entrusted with the happiness of their parents. After receiving from them life, food, shelter, innumerable good things and a watchful, tender love throughout, they have it in their power to make bright the evening of their father's and mother's life, or to cloud it with a deep, dark gloom of hopeless misery.

I. The SECRET OF THIS INFLUENCE IS IN THE MORAL CONDUCT OF THE SON OR DAUGHTER. "The wise son"—"The fear of the Lord is the beginning of wisdom;" "the foolish son"—the fool in the Bible is more morally than intellectually defective. In the infancy of their children fond parents often dream of the earthly prosperity they would wish for them—a brilliant career, success in business, wealth, renown, happiness. But as life opens out more fully they come to see that these are of secondary importance. The mother whose brooding fancy prophesied a young Milton in her wonderful boy is perhaps just a little disappointed as by slow degrees she undergoes disillusion, and sees him develop into an ordinary city clerk ; but she will not confess her disappointment to herself, and it is soon swallowed up in just pride and delight if he is upright and kind and good.   But if she is not mistaken about the genius of her child, but only under an error as to the moral direction that genius will take ; if her Milton becomes a Byron, then, though the world rings with his fame, she—supposing her to be a true, wise mother—will be broken-hearted with grief.   It is not the dulness, nor the failures, nor the troubles, nor the early death of children that bring a father's "grey hairs with sorrow to the grave."   It is their sins.   If these sins show direct unkind- ness, the grief reaches its saddest height.   Then the father may well say, with poor Lear—

> "How sharper than a serpent's tooth it is
> To have a thankless child!"

It is heart-rending for the mother to part with her infant if he dies an early death. But the grief she feels when she looks at the little grave, and thinks of her child quietly sleeping, safe with the God who called the children to himself—this grief is calm and endurable compared with the awful, crushing agony she would have experienced if the child had lived and had fallen into sin and brought shame upon his head. Parents are foolish as well as unsubmissive when they pray too positively for their children's lives.   Our one great Father knows what is best.   Perhaps it is safest for all that the child should be taken from the evil to come.   But, of course, if he can be spared to live a life of usefulness and honour, this is most to be desired, and the parents' prayers should chiefly go out for the safe preservation of their children's *better* life.

II. THE POSSESSION OF THIS INFLUENCE SHOULD BE A STRONG INDUCEMENT TO WORTHY LIVING.   It furnishes a new element in the obligations of right.   The son has it in his power to make his parents happy or miserable.   So great a trust involves a serious responsibility.   "No man liveth unto himself."   Besides his higher obliga- tions, the son has a life in regard to his father and mother.   He is not at liberty to run riot as he chooses, because he thinks his own future only is at stake.   By all the terrible pain he inflicts, by the deep gladness he might have conferred, the guilt of his sin is aggravated.   Should not such considerations urge strongly against yielding to temptation?   If the mad young man cares little for abstract righteousness, if he has lost the fear of God, still is it nothing that every new folly is a stab in the heart of those who have done most for him and who would even now give their lives to save him?   It is not unmanly to say to one's self, "For my mother's sake I will not do this vile thing."   It is devilish not to be capable of such a thought.   Similar considerations may help us in our highest relations.   God is our Father.   We may "grieve" his Spirit by sin.   When the prodigal returns God rejoices in the presence of his angels. Shall we not hate the sins that made Christ mourn, and seek to do better for the sake of the love of God?

Ver. 4.—*Diligence.*   Of late it has become fashionable to claim a cheap reputation for loftiness of moral aims by sneering at what are called the "smug virtues."   There is a great deal about these despised virtues in the Book of Proverbs, and consequently a very low estimate is formed of that portion of Scripture.   But is there not something hollow about this assumption of ethical elevation?   It cannot be denied that the "smug virtues" have a real obligation.   No one would venture to say that they can be dispensed with.   They are simply of a comparatively inferior value.   But till they are complied with it is often difficult to rise to more ethereal heights of goodness. Meanwhile that man is little short of a hypocrite who neglects the plain duties that lie at his door for the pursuit of some other more recondite graces.   Diligence is one of the first of these duties, and it is requisite for various reasons.   Note some of them.

I. WEALTH DEPENDS ON WORK.   This is a primary law of providence.   God might have fed us as he fed the ravens.   But instead of putting food ready for our mouths, he gives us hands with which to work for it.   Social arrangements only disguise this law.   The son inherits the fruits of his father's industry.   The idle man sucks the honey of other men's toil.   But it remains truth that work makes wealth.   Every man's wealth depends largely on the work of some one—his own or somebody else's.   It is the duty of everybody to see that he is not dependent upon other people's labours if he can help himself. The man who squanders his money in prosperous times, and throws himself on public charity directly he is ill or out of work, is guilty of gross selfishness amounting to dishonesty. It is plainly every man's duty not only to keep himself and his family, but, where it is possible, to make fit provision for the future, or he will be robbing others of their maintenance. Hence one obligation to be industrious and thrifty.

II. WORK IS FOR OUR OWN GOOD. People talk of the curse of toil, little knowing that it is one of the greatest blessings we have. Better talk of the curse of idleness. It is a happy thing that man has to earn his bread with the sweat of his brow. Work develops strength—strength of mind as well as strength of limb. The self-made man is not invariably a model of grace; but he is usually a specimen of sturdy vigour of character, as different from the limp conventionality of indolence as granite rock from drifting sea-weed.

III. WE ARE ALL STEWARDS. The servant is required to be industrious for his master's sake. His time is not his own. He is not at liberty, therefore, to lounge about in dreamy idleness. We are stewards of the things lent us by God. He has sent us to work in his vineyard. In due time he will call us to account. "To be blameless as a steward of God" a man must be faithful, honest, industrious.

IV. CHRISTIANITY INCULCATES DILIGENCE. No greater mistake can be made than to suppose that the New Testament favours indolence. The ideal of Oriental monasticism is derived from other sources. Even the monks in the West knew better. In its palmy days European monasticism was the centre of honest toil. The monks cleared forests, reclaimed bogs, built cathedrals, cultivated farms, studied, laboriously copied and preserved for us the invaluable treasures of the literature of antiquity. Amongst other fruits of grace in the Christian's heart will be increased diligence in business. Christian principle, however, is necessary to consecrate industry. Without it wealth will be a god, business an absorbing worldly influence, and success a source of low selfish pleasure. But he who is diligent on Christian principle will make his business holy by working in it as the servant of Christ, and his wealth holy by dedicating it to the use of God.

Ver. 5.—*Sleep in harvest.* I. SLEEP IN HARVEST IS FOOLISH, BECAUSE THIS IS THE TIME FOR THE HARVEST-WORK. We may afford to be slack in the winter. Through the long frosts when the ground is like iron, during heavy rains when to poach on the fields is only injurious to the crops, much work is necessarily suspended. But harvest claims all time and all energy. Every man must be at work, fresh hands taken on, and longer hours spent in the field. How preposterous to be sleeping then! There are harvest-times in life—times when we are called to awake to more than ordinary energy. Youth, though in many respects a seed-time, also has some of the characteristics of harvest. It is the summer-time when work is pleasant, and when there is little to hinder it. If a man will not work in these bright days, how can he expect to be able to labour when the cramps and agues of wintry old age seize upon him? It is also the time of a great ingathering, when knowledge must be accumulated for future use. If this harvest season is passed in idleness, it will be impossible to fill the granary of the mind with stores of knowledge in after-years. But there are other special opportunities for work. We seem to have come upon the great season of the world's harvest. "The fields are now white." India is open, China and Africa are opening up; and the call is loud for labourers to go forth and gather the precious sheaves into the garner of the Lord. If there may have been some excuse for indolence in the dark ages of tyranny and ignorance, there is none now, when communication is made easy and vast opportunities for service are afforded us.

II. SLEEP IN HARVEST IS FOOLISH, BECAUSE IT WILL RESULT IN THE LOSS OF ALL PREVIOUS LABOUR. The monotonous toil of the ploughman, the careful work of the sower, the tiresome weeding, all the labour of spring and summer, will be wasted if the harvest is to be left to rot in the fields. All this was only intended to prepare the way for the harvest. So there are times when we are called to make use of the long preparatory labours of after-years. The barrister begins to plead, the surgeon to practise, the minister to preach. If they are remiss now, their university honours will add to the discredit of failure in real life. The training is all wasted if we neglect to put it to its final use. So the Christian labourer, the missionary, the preacher, the Sunday school teacher, should feel that all their work is to tend to the gathering in of souls for Christ. If they miss that result, the rest is of little good. Care, diligence, prayer, are most called for that the previous labour may not be " in vain in the Lord." Hence the responsibility of the teachers of elder scholars in a Sunday school. The harvest-time of the school-work falls upon them. If they are unfaithful, all the previous toil of preparing the soil in the infant school and sowing the seed in the lower classes may be thrown away.

III. SLEEP IN HARVEST IS FOOLISH, BECAUSE IT WILL BRING FAMINE IN THE WINTER. The harvest is a brief, swift period. It is soon to give place to the chill autumn, and that to the dreary winter. If the fruit is not gathered then it can never be gathered in later days. Yet it will be sadly wanted. The old year's corn will run out, and a great cry for bread will go up from a famished people. Then the folly of ultimate indolence will be felt in slow agony and death. We need all to remember that there is a winter coming. Let the strong man labour in harvest for the winter of growing infirmities in old age; let the prosperous labour in seasons of plenty, that they may have by them fat kine to be devoured in years of scarcity; let the happy make use of their opportunities, that they may be ready for the sorrows of the future. Apply the lesson to national affairs. In times of peace and plenty see that debts are paid off, grievances reformed, and all things made right and strong in preparation for possible national calamities. Apply it to commercial affairs, so that times of good trade may not lead to extravagance and luxury, but to more thrift. Apply it to spiritual things—to the church generally, that in peace and liberty sound principles may be instilled and strong Christian characters built up fit to stand the shock of persecution; to the individual, and see that we gather the bread of life now which shall make us able to withstand the barrenness of the winter of death. If we sleep in this our harvest-time, what dread awaking must we look forward to?

Ver. 7.—" *The memory of the just.*" I. THE WORLD CONCERNS ITSELF WITH THE REPUTATION OF THE DEAD. The words of our text describe a fact to which all history bears witness. No study is more absorbing than history—including biography; and the most interesting part of history is that which deals with individuals and discusses character. In spite of the protests of the philosophers, we are all more attracted by Shakespeare and Scott than by Hallam and Buckle. Statistics, generalizations, great laws and principles of national growth, all have their claims on our attention; but the characters of individual men appeal to us with a quite different human interest. Even the most commonplace gossip of the street-corner has some justification in the element of sympathy with things human that it presupposes.

II. THE MOST IMPORTANT ELEMENT IN POSTHUMOUS REPUTATION IS CHARACTER. Who cares for Crœsus? But the slave Epictetus takes a high place in the world's thoughts. The reputation for wealth that brings fawning flatterers in a man's lifetime is the first to fade after death. So is that of empty titles. The present duke—say the seventh—is treated with the deference considered due to rank, but no one cares to ask in what the third duke differed from the fourth duke. Even the dazzling conqueror's renown soon tarnishes if it is not preserved by higher qualities. Few men now envy the reputation of Napoleon. Genius, perhaps, carries off amongst men the palm of fame; the first place, which is due to character, is reserved for the next world. Still, moral character counts for more in common human reputation than the cynical are ready to admit. At all events, in that inner circle where a man would most care for his reputation this takes its right place. If it is better to be loved at home than to be admired abroad, it is better to leave a fragrant memory for goodness in one's own circle than to leave sorrow in the home and to reap grand funeral honours in the outside world. It is remarkable to observe how fair is the verdict of history. A hypocrite may deceive his contemporaries. He can rarely deceive future generations.

III. IT IS OUR DUTY TO CHERISH THE MEMORY OF THE JUST. This is a duty we owe to them, to righteousness, and to succeeding ages. The honest canonization that comes from no papal authority, but from the honest conviction of admiring multitudes, is a worthy tribute to goodness. Still, let us beware of the mockery of substituting this for our duty to the living—building splendid tombs to the prophets whom we have slain. How often have great men been slighted, misunderstood, cruelly wronged, during their lifetime; and then honoured by a chorus of repentant praise as soon as death has taken them beyond the reach of it! On the other hand, beware of indiscriminate adulation of the dead. There is wholesome truth in the words, "The name of the wicked shall rot." Nothing is more false than the common style of epitaphs. A visit to a grave-yard would suggest that the world was a paradise of immaculate saints. Where you cannot justly praise, at least be decently silent. Left to itself, the name of the wicked will melt away and vanish—as all rotten things do.

IV. IT IS PROFITABLE TO CONSIDER THE LESSONS LEFT BY THE LIVES OF THE DEPARTED. We need not go the length of the early Christians, who, beginning by meeting in the catacombs where the martyrs were buried, soon came to worship the martyrs as demi-gods. But we may gain great good by contemplating the beauty of good lives. If we cherish the memory of those who have gone " to join the choir invisible," we may be helped to emulate their noble qualities.

Ver. 12.—*The cloak of charity.* One of the devices of the parallelism or rhythm of ideas, which is the general characteristic of Hebrew poetry, is the alternative treatment of the same thought from two opposite points of view—from positive and negative poles. The value of some good thing is emphasized by contrasting it with the repulsive nature of its contrary, as Venetian ladies tried to appear the more fair by having negro pages to attend them. Thus the beautiful work of love, in covering all sins, is here made most attractive by being brought out on the dark background of the ugly doings of hatred. It may be profitable, therefore, for us to glance at the more painful subject first.

I. THE DARK BACKGROUND. " Hatred stirreth up strifes." 1. *Where there is hatred strifes will be stirred up.* This hideous passion is active, powerful, and contagious. It is not content to consume itself in hidden fires; it will blaze out and spread its mis-chief abroad. (1) " Hatred stirreth up strifes" because it starts new quarrels; it is irritating, provoking. An incendiary will always find plenty of fuel. When the spark is struck the tinder is ready to receive it. It is not in human nature to submit tamely to insult. Though it takes two to make a quarrel, when one man shows himself offensively quarrelsome he will not be long in finding an antagonist. (2) Then " hatred stirreth up strifes" because it aggravates old quarrels. It pokes the fire. It freshens the smouldering embers and shakes them up so that they break out into a blaze again. It is the great mischief-maker, and where it finds a little rift it sets diligently to work to widen this into a great chasm. 2. *Where strifes are stirred up hatred is behind them.* The strifes are a sign of the presence of hatred. True, a benevolent man may be dragged into a quarrel; but he will not provoke it himself, and he will not maintain it a moment longer than righteousness requires. A quarrelsome disposition is at bottom grounded on hatred. For if we loved one another, how could we desire to be at variance? Tale-bearing, reporting words that one knows will only rouse ill feeling between two people, presenting things in their worst light so as to suggest offensive thoughts, exaggerating the unkindness of a person by imputing bad motives,—all such conduct is inconsistent with Christian charity; it is just the behaviour of the old serpent, who brought discord into Eden, and was "a murderer from the beginning."

II. THE BRIGHT PICTURE. " But love covereth all sins." This does not refer to one's own sins—to the fact that one who loves much is forgiven much (Luke vii. 47). It is the sins of others that love covers. 1. *Love covereth all sins against one's self.* " Love suffereth long, and is kind" (1 Cor. xiii. 4). The Christian must forgive his enemies because he is taught to love them. All forgiveness springs from love. God pardons us for nothing that we do, but for the sake of his love in Jesus Christ. But our Lord has told us plainly that unless we forgive men their trespasses against us neither will our heavenly Father forgive us our trespasses. This is therefore no question of counsels of perfection, but one of the first elements of the Christian life. If we cherish a vindictive spirit against any one, we are ourselves still unforgiven by God, still dead in trespasses and sins. If we do not prove our love by forgiving men, we do not possess it, and without love to our brethren we can have no love to God. Therefore so long as we obstinately refuse forgiveness to any one who has wronged us, our Christianity is nothing but hypocrisy; it is a lie. 2. *Love covereth all sins in others generally,* i.e. it leads us not to note them, not to report them, not to aggravate the guilt of them, not to make mischief by tale-bearing. Further, it is not conten t to be negatively oblivious of sin. It must be active in throwing the cloak of charity upon it. Of course, we must be just and truthful. But these obligations leave us free in most cases to labour to prevent mischief by a charitable behaviour in our social influence. The Christian is not called to be an informer. At least Christian love will make a man a peacemaker. If he cannot hide the sin without unfaithfulness to some trust, he can endeavour to prevent the rising of evil passions. This is the grand Christian method of conquering wickedness. The law chastises by punishment; the gospel reforms by forgiveness. So Christ, the incarnation of God's love, covers all our sins, and renews our hearts through the grace of forgiveness.

Ver. 19.—*Golden silence.* I. THE SINFUL CHARACTER OF MUCH ORDINARY CON-VERSATION SHOULD INDUCE GREAT CAUTION IN SPEECH. It is a grave charge to bring against the tone of general society to say that "in the multitude of words there wanteth not sin." But is it not as true now as it was in the days of Solomon? "Out of the abundance of the heart the mouth speaketh;" but "the heart is deceitful above all things, and desperately wicked," and therefore, so long as human nature is corrupt, conversation will be corrupt also. If the well is poisoned, the less water we draw from it the better. In particular two or three bad features of common conversation may be observed, viz.: 1. *Untruthfulness.* There is probably a little more conscious lying even in society that professes to follow the code of honour than its members would care to admit. But untruthfulness may appear in a more disguised form. There is the equivocation that some people practise so skilfully—blinding their own conscience while throwing dust into the eyes of other people. The tendency to exaggeration for the sake of dramatic effect is very common. The falsification by means of caricature, which is dishonest because it is not confessedly caricature, is another source of deceit. But hasty speech may fall into unconscious errors; and then, though the sin of lying is not committed, harm is done by the spread of reports that are not true. 2. *Unkindness.* How much of the gossip of the parlour is made up of the criticism of one's neighbours —at least in some circles of society! No ill feeling may be felt, but cruel injustice is done when a man's actions are discussed and his motives dissected on very insufficient evidence, in the absence of the accused, by a small coterie of persons whom he trusts as friends. But if "love covereth all sins," it is uncharitable to make even the proved offences of our neighbours the topic of idle conversation. 3. *Unholiness.* When no impure words are spoken, conversation may be more dangerously defiled by innuendo. The obscene word is disgusting in its coarseness, but the skilful *equivoque,* supposed to be more fit for ears polite, carries its poison to an unsuspecting imagination. When nothing directly immoral is suggested, how much conversation would come under the category of what our Lord calls "idle words"? Such words are very different from genuine criticisms, or even from light banter, which may not be idle, but useful as mental refreshment.

II. THE DANGEROUS INFLUENCE OF SPEECH CONFIRMS THE WISDOM OF SILENCE. 1. *Speech is remembered.* The word once out cannot be recalled. It remains to rankle in the wounded breast or to stain permanently the imagination of the hearer. What is said in the heat of passion will be remembered against us in the coolness of vindictive spite. The unseemly joke of a frivolous moment may perpetually haunt the sacred subject it tampers with. 2. *Speech is suggestive.* The utterance may be little in itself, but it starts a long train of associations. One unkindly word will suggest a whole realm of ungenerous thoughts. A single unholy phrase may bring to view a whole theatre of unclean images. The word is but a spark; yet it may kindle a great fire (Jas. iii. 5). The most hasty speech may cut deepest, like the swiftest sword-thrust.

III. IN MANY SPECIAL CIRCUMSTANCES SILENCE IS PECULIARLY DESIRABLE. 1. *In quarrelsome society.* When we know that our words will only fall like firebrands in a powder-magazine, the less said the better. If we cannot persuade a person to maintain friendly intercourse with us, we had better have no intercourse with him. 2. *In unsympathetic society.* It is foolish to cast pearls before swine. We must beware of the pharisaical use that pride will make of this maxim, leading us to preserve a silence of contempt. But in all humility and charity we may refrain from speaking where we shall only be misunderstood. If our hearer cannot receive the ideas of our speech, we only waste time in giving him the words—probably we do worse, and lead him into delusions through the wrong construction that he will put on our language. 3. *In degraded society.* When to enter into conversation will only stir up the mud that lies at the bottom of the now stagnant pool, we had better be quiet. In general a few well-weighed words have more force than many hasty, thoughtless utterances. We do not all possess the gift of laconic terseness. But we can at least set a guard on our speech, and when called to speak seek Divine grace that our words may be "seasoned with salt."

Ver. 28.—*The hope of the righteous.* I. WE ALL LIVE BY HOPE. The righteous has his "hope," the wicked his "expectation;" both live in the future. The present takes its colours chiefly from our anticipations of the future. It is dark or bright according as shadows or light fall on it from that visionary world. The man who has no hope here or hereafter is practically dead. Despair is suicide. Hence the importance of seeing to our hopes. If they are ill-grounded, all life is a mistake.

II. THE LOTS OF THE RIGHTEOUS AND THE WICKED DIFFER LESS IN THEIR PRESENT CONDITION THAN IN THE FUTURE OF THEIR HOPES. Old Testament saints were often distressed at the sufferings of the good and the prosperity of the bad. It is when we see "their end" that we discover the just allotment. The house on the sand stands as fairly as the house on the rock—till the storm comes. "When the whirlwind passeth, the wicked is no more; but the righteous is an everlasting portion" (ver. 25). Men of very different deserts may have equally bright hopes; for hope is not founded on the verdict of justice, but on a man's own ideas, or even his idle fancies. The vigour of the hope is no guarantee of the certainty of its fulfilment.

III. THE PROVIDENTIAL JUSTICE OF GOD WILL OVERRULE THE ISSUE OF ALL HOPES. Our views of the future can only be safely depended on when they are determined by what we know of God. The future is in his hands. So, of course, is the present. But it is only in the course of a long time that the modifying influence of temporary accidents is removed and great general laws exert their full force. What will then happen we cannot tell by only investigating present phenomena, because of the confusion of transient influences. We must study the character of God. Then we shall be constrained to exclaim, "Shall not the Judge of all the earth do right?" Because God is just, justice must be the ultimate outcome of all things. Through all time God is surely working on to this end. We are deceived by the tardiness of the process, yet this very tardiness is effecting the more complete final result.

"The mills of God grind slowly,
But they grind exceeding small."

IV. THE DIFFERENT NATURE OF THE HOPES OF MEN OF DIFFERENT CHARACTER LARGELY DETERMINES THE QUESTION OF THEIR FUTURE FULFILMENT. God works through means and laws. Some hopes are naturally doomed to failure, others contain seeds of immortal fruition. Now, the nature of our hopes is dependent on our character. Better than professions, words, or even deeds, as a test of character, are a man's *hopes.* Tell us what he hopes, and we can say what he is. The hope is an emanation of the very essence of the soul. Therefore bad men have bad hopes, and good men good hopes. If both seem to hope for the same thing, the hopes are still wide apart as the poles; for the same thing objectively is quite different to us according to the thoughts with which we view it. The heaven for which a wicked man hopes is very unlike the Christian's heaven. Good men hope for what is good; *i.e.* for what agrees with God's will. Thus their hope will not be disappointed. Christians have faith in "Christ in us the Hope of glory." Such an expectation presages its own satisfaction.

Ver. 31.—*Righteousness and wisdom.* These two attributes appear to belong to different spheres—the one to the moral and the other to the intellectual. Yet they are here associated as parent and child, and righteousness is seen to sprout into wisdom. Righteous men are represented as speaking wisely. Now, we know that good people have not a monopoly of intellect. Aristides the virtuous was not as clever as Themistocles. There are small-minded saints, and there are sinners of giant intellect. Where, then, is the connection between righteousness and wisdom?

1. RIGHTEOUSNESS STRENGTHENS THE WHOLE SOUL. It will not convert a peasant into a philosopher, but it will brighten the faculties of the peasant. While sin deadens the soul, dissipates its faculties, and lowers its powers, the calm and temperate life of a good man helps him to attain to such vigour of thought as is within the reach of his powers.

II. RIGHTEOUSNESS REMOVES THE HINDRANCE OF PREJUDICE. No doubt many good people have their prejudices. But that is in spite of their goodness, and the goodness is an antidote of more or less efficacy. The root of prejudice is self-will, and this is also the root of sin. Just in proportion as we learn the self-distrust of humility we shall be freed from the blindness of prejudice.

III. RIGHTEOUSNESS INSTILS THE LOVE OF TRUTH. The good man wishes to know truth; he acknowledges the duty of seeking light; he will not let indolence keep him in ignorance. Now, an earnest pursuit of truth is not likely to be rewarded with failure. They who seek Wisdom earnestly will find her (ch. viii. 17). Thus the rousing of a motive to strive after wisdom helps us to reach it, and this is the fruit of righteousness.

IV. RIGHTEOUSNESS OPENS THE EYES OF THE SOUL. It has a direct influence in purging the inward vision. There are truths which can only be revealed through channels of sympathy. The way of holiness lies hidden from the gaze of the corrupt. To be good is to see the best truth.

V. RIGHTEOUSNESS LEADS TO THE PRACTICAL USE OF TRUTH. Wisdom is not a merely intellectual attainment. While intimately connected with the thoughts of the mind, it also has vital relations with the resolves of the will. The wise man is not only one who knows the right way; he practises his knowledge by walking therein.

VI. RIGHTEOUSNESS IS TRUTHFUL. When a good man speaks he will not knowingly deceive. His earnest desire will be to utter just what he believes to be true. But such a desire will help him to put forth words of wisdom.

A practical result of this association of wisdom with righteousness is that we should look well to the character of our teachers. The merely popular preacher, or the merely clever thinker, will not be so useful a guide in the higher reaches of the spiritual life as the good man of less brilliant natural gifts and intellectual attainments. Thus true wisdom may be discovered where the world only expects foolishness (1 Cor. i. 20, 21).

HOMILIES BY VARIOUS AUTHORS.

Ver. 1.—We enter upon a mosaic-work of proverbs, which perhaps hardly admit of any one principle of arrangement except that of moral comparison and contrast. This governs the whole. Life is viewed as containing endless oppositions, to which light and darkness correspond in the world of sensuous perception.

Early appearance of moral contrast. I. THE FAMILY LIFE ELICITS CHARACTER. It is a little world, and from the first provides a sphere of *probation* and of judgment which is the miniature of the great world.

II. THE TRAINING OF THE PARENTS IS REFLECTED IN THE CHILDREN'S CONDUCT. And the conduct of the children is reflected in the parents' joy or grief. Hence the duty of wise training on the one side, loving obedience on the other; that the happy effects may be secured, the unhappy averted, in each case.

III. TO LIVE TO MAKE ONE'S PARENTS (AND OTHERS) HAPPY IS ONE OF THE BEST OF MOTIVES. To see our actions mirrored in their mirth and others' joy, what pleasure can be purer, what ambition nobler?—J.

Vers. 2—7.—*Moral contrast in earthly lot and destiny.* I. ILL-GOTTEN WEALTH AND RECTITUDE. (Ver. 2.) The former cannot avert sudden death or shame (vers. 25, 27); the latter is *vital*, and stands the man in good stead in every hour of human trial and of Divine judgment.

II. HONEST POVERTY AND PROFLIGATE GREED. (Ver. 3.) The former does not *hunger*, is contented with little, has true *satisfaction*. The latter is never satisfied, expands with every indulgence, is like the "dire dropsy." It is an unappeasable thirst. God repudiates it by fixing it in perpetual impotency, while the temperate and chastened desires are rewarded by fulfilment.

III. THE LAX AND THE INDUSTRIOUS HAND. (Ver. 4; comp. ch. xii. 24.) The one leading to poverty, the other to riches. Languor and energy have their physical conditions; but how much lies in the will? We live in a day when it is the fashion to talk of "determinism," and to extend the doctrine of "causes over which we have no control" beyond all reasonable limits. We need to fall back on the healthy common sense of mankind, and on the doctrine of these proverbs. There *is* a moral question involved. Laziness is immoral, and receives the condemnation of immorality; industry is a virtue, and brings its own reward in every sphere. The opposition is amplified in ver. 5; *active forethought* being contrasted with *supine indifference*. The hard field labour referred to belongs particularly to young men; and to young men idleness is peculiarly corrupting.

IV. ASSOCIATIONS OF BLESSING AND THOSE OF VIOLENCE. (Ver. 6.) However the verse may be rendered and interpreted, this is the opposition. *Blessing* leads the mind through such a series of associated ideas as peace, tranquillity, order, security; *violence* through a contrasted series—trouble, disquiet, disorder, and all that implies a curse.

V. BRIGHT AND DARK RECOLLECTIONS. (Ver. 7.) The good man lives in thankful memories; the bad man's name is like an *ill odour*, according to the literal meaning of the Hebrew word. When the saying is quoted, "The ill men do lives after them, the good is oft interred with their bones," we should recall by *whom* this was said, or feigned to be said, and for what purpose. In the memory of Cæsar's ambition Antony is afraid the Romans will *forget* his services. *Momentarily* good may be forgotten, but *ultimately* must come to recognition and honour. The course of time illustrates the worth of the good, and enhances the odium of evil memories.—J.

Vers. 8—10.—*Folly and wisdom in manifold contrast.* I. THE WISE MAN IS MORE READY TO RECEIVE THAN TO GIVE COUNSEL; THE FOOL, THE OPPOSITE.

II. THE WISE MAN KNOWS THE VALUE OF RESERVE; THE FOOL WILL "STILL BE TALKING."

III. THE WISE MAN IS THRIFTY, ECONOMICAL OF WORDS, A CAPITALIST OF THOUGHT; THE FOOL, A SPENDTHRIFT OF WORDS, A BANKRUPT OF THOUGHT.

IV. THE WISE MAN RISES IN REPUTATION, IN POSITION; THE FOOL COMES SOONER OR LATER TO A "FALL."

V. GUILELESSNESS IS SAFE, WHILE CRAFT AND CROOKED POLICY ARE CERTAIN, SOONER OR LATER, OF EXPOSURE. (Ver. 9.) In that widest sense in which alone the saying is noble and true, "Honesty is the best policy." Cunning overreaches itself and gets into trouble; and the *mere talker* never ends well. Speech should only be *prophetic* of deed; otherwise, "Many will *say* to me in that day," etc.—J.

Vers. 11—14.—*A fourfold opposition.* I. SPEECH THAT QUICKENS AND SPEECH THAT KILLS. (Ver. 11.) 1. The speech of the wise and good is sound, "seasoned with salt;" that of the wicked is hollow or else poisonous. 2. The former *edifies*, builds up and strengthens the good principle in the minds of those who converse with him; the latter destroys the good, and sows evil in its stead.

II. QUARRELSOMENESS AND AMIABILITY. (Ver. 12; see on ch. vi. 14.) The former *begets* evil, *increases* that already existing, *inflames* wounds, lets nothing pass that may serve as fuel to its fire. The latter *puts an end* to much evil, *prevents the rise* of more, soothes every wound, and mitigates every mischief. The former is ever dividing, the latter reconciling. They undo one another's work; but love in the end prevails (ch. xvii. 9; 1 Cor. xiii. 4; Jas. v. 20; 1 Pet. iv. 8).

III. THE GRACE OF WISDOM AND THE DISGRACE OF FOLLY. (Ver. 13.) The pure eloquence of the good man attracts admiration and wins confidence; while the fallacies of the pretender, the spurious rhetoric of the insincere, are certain to be exposed and castigated. The life of the House of Commons, or of any great assembly, furnishes constant illustrations.

IV. PRUDENT RESERVE AND PERNICIOUS LOQUACITY. (Ver. 14.) There is a time and place for silence, the wise man knows—both for the recovery of his own thoughts, and for the opportunity of watching others. By a bold figure of speech, it may often be that silence is the greatest eloquence. In many instances we think we have produced no effect, have not committed ourselves to the expression of opinion; on the contrary, our reserve has spoken. In all this lies a science and art of living. The fool does not see this; he is too self-absorbed to see anything that passes in others' minds, or too unsympathetic to feel; and hence blurts out things that had better have been left unsaid, hurts sensibilities, blackens reputations, causes false positions for himself and others.

1. The heart must be watched. There is no other source of pleasing, gentle manners, nor of sound behaviour in society. Reserve and unreserve of the right kind are simply the government of the tongue by charity. 2. The tongue must be watched. And regulated by good models of conversation. Never must it be forgotten how much we learn by *imitation.*—J.

Vers. 15—21.—*A sevenfold strain of experience.* For the most part these sayings relate to earthly goods—their value, and the means for their acquisition. Godliness has the promise of both lives. Equally incredible would a religion which ignored the future be with one which ignored the present. Equally one-sided is the expectation only of earthly good from wisdom, and the expectation *only* of heavenly good. We must beware of a false materializing and of a false spiritualizing of religion.

I. THE POWER OF WEALTH AND THE WEAKNESS OF POVERTY. The former like a strong city or fortress; the latter like a ruinous dwelling, which threatens at any moment to tumble about the dweller's head. The teacher is thinking, as the following verse shows, on the one hand, of wealth wisely and honourably won, which becomes a means to other wise ends; on the other hand, of blameworthy poverty, which leads in time to further vice and misery. To desire competent means for the sake of worthy objects, and to fear poverty because of its temptations, is a right and true attitude of mind.

II. THE TENDENCY OF WEALTH DEPENDS ON THE MIND OF THE POSSESSOR. (Ver. 16.) The " tendency of riches " is in itself an incomplete thought. Silver and gold have no tendency, except by a figure of speech. In the heart of man the directing force is found. Used *justly,* riches are a good; they are simply, like bodily strength, knowledge, skill, a *mass of available means.* Used wickedly, so that they simply feed our senses and our pride, or become corrupters of others' integrity, they simply increase the possessor's power and range of mischief. When we poetically speak of accursed gold, or base dross, we should be aware that these are figures, and that the curse can never rest on anything in God's creation except the will which perverts what is a means to good into a means to evil.

III. THE CAUSES OF DIRECTION AND MISDIRECTION IN LIFE. (Ver. 17.) Why do some men succeed, and others fail, in perpetual blundering and error? The particular cases may be complex; but as to the general rule there can be no question. In the one case there is *admission of faults* and *attention to the correction of them.* In the other, *blindness to faults, inattention to warnings, obstinate persistence in error.* Be not above taking a hint, especially from a foe. " Temper " is the bane of many. Any opportunity is sacrificed rather than the whim, the humour which seems to the man so thoroughly a part of himself that he cannot give it up. The habit of calm revision of one's progress and failures in the hour of prayer seems needful both to preserve from over self-confidence and from over-reliance on the advice of others.

IV. CONCEALED HATRED AND OPEN MALICE EQUALLY ODIOUS. (Ver. 18.) Resentment that one dares not, or thinks it polite not to, express makes the lips turn traitor; and the victim is both " contemned and flattered." God has placed a natural hatred of duplicity in our hearts. It was levelled as a reproach against Euripides that he had put into the mouth of one of his characters the sentiment, " My tongue did swear, my heart remain'd unsworn." Not so dangerous in many cases, but morally worse, is the deliberate slanderer, who goes about to despoil his neighbours of that which leaves them much poorer, makes him none the richer. He is a fool, because his arts recoil upon himself.

V. THE PERIL OF THE BABBLING TONGUE; THE PRUDENCE OF RESERVE. (Ver. 19.) The man may be confronted with his words. The " written letter remains," and " many witnesses" may serve equally well to convict of the authorship of a malicious speech. It is far more easy for men to forgive abusive things said to their faces than things reported to have been said behind their backs. And even injurious acts can be got over more readily than stinging words of sarcasm. Words have a more definite shape in thought than deeds; they reveal a certain view of you which has some truth in it. You cannot forget it, which means with most you cannot forgive it. A clean-cut sarcasm, a slander which has just that *vraisemblance* about it which gives currency to gossip, stamps a certain image of the victim in the public mind. The gentler motive to prudence is the hurt we may do others; the motive consistently here is the treatment we may experience ourselves. If a person, on grounds like these, were to take a pledge of total abstinence from "personal talk" of the critical kind, his prudence must be respected. An approach to this is found in well-bred society. And how lamentable the condition of some so-called religious circles, when there is so little culture that conversation gravitates as if by necessity to the discussion of the character and doings of popular preachers, etc. !

VI. THE TONGUE AND THE HEART ARE IN IMMEDIATE CONNECTION. (Ver. 20.) Just as Napoleon said his brain and hand were in immediate connection. The analogy will serve. The "silver tongue" (no accents are silvery but those of truth) bespeaks the fine disposition, the noble heart. And what can the produce of the "worthless" heart be but "rot" upon the tongue?

VII. GOOD BREEDS GOOD, WHILE EVIL CANNOT KEEP ITSELF ALIVE. (Ver. 21.) The lips of the just *pasture* many. Good words, good preachers, good books,—these are the food of the world, and there cannot be an over-supply. Bad books and teachers may be let alone. As Dr. Johnson said of a poem, it had not enough life in it to keep it sweet (or, "not enough vitality to preserve it from corruption").—J.

Vers. 22—25.—*Life-secrets.* Lessing says of the Old Testament, as an elementary book of childlike wisdom, that "its style is now plain and simple, now poetic, full of *tautologies*, but such as exercise the penetration of the mind, while they seem now to say something fresh, yet say the same; now seem to say the same, and at bottom signify, or may signify, something different." The Proverbs are the constant illustration of the Law.

I. THE BLESSING OF JEHOVAH INDISPENSABLE; ALL TROUBLE VAIN WITHOUT IT. (Ver. 22.) We adopt the rendering, "Trouble is of no avail without it." His blessing is all in all. The thought thus yielded is a beautiful one, identical with that in Ps. cxxvii. Jehovah gives bread to his beloved while they sleep and take no "anxious thought" about it. The thought was familiar to the ancient mind, and has been wrought up in parable and fable. The counterpart is that the blessing of God is not given to the idle; that "God loves to be helped;" that "Heaven helps those who help themselves." The opposite faults are indolence and over-anxiety.

II. THE TRUE AND THE FALSE SOURCE OF CHEERFULNESS. (Ver. 23.) The fool makes mirth out of mischief. He takes delight in seeing the image of his restless and mischievous activity everywhere. The man of principle, on the contrary, draws his serene cheerfulness from faith in the Divine law of things—the sense that he is reconciled to it, and that good must ever flow from it.

III. THE FEARFUL AND THE HOPEFUL TEMPERS TRACED TO THEIR SIGNIFICANCE. (Ver. 24.) There is a timidity bred of an evil conscience—a buoyant expectation of the future bred of a good conscience. Both are *creative* in their effect on the imagination, and thus men dwell with shapes of gloom or radiant forms of fancy. Both are *prophetic*, and tend to realize themselves. This is a profound truth. For imagination in turn influences the will, and we reap the guilty fears or the pure hopes our habits sowed.

IV. THE RESULTS OF TRIAL AND TROUBLE. (Ver. 25.) The storm sweeps by and overturns the hollow and untrue; while they who are based on the righteousness of God remain unmoved (comp. Matt. vii. 24, *seqq.*). We do not know a man's principles, nor whether he has any, until the time of suffering. Theory is one thing, fact another; it is not the statement of the engineer, but the trial of winter's floods that must prove the soundness of the bridge. We have to learn the truth of life in theory first; but we do not make it our own until it is put to the test of experience. Experience throws us back upon the truth of the theory, enriches our conception of it, and should enable us to teach it with the greater confidence to others.—J.

Ver. 26.—*The lazy man a nuisance.*   I. HE IRRITATES HIS EMPLOYERS.   The images of the teeth set on edge, the blinded, smarting eyes, give the thought with great force and great *naïveté.*
II. HE IS WORSE THAN USELESS.   The Bible shows a great aversion from idleness, sluggishness (ch. vi. 6, *seqq.*; xii. 27; xix. 24; xxii. 13). 1. Laziness is a vice and the parent of worse. 2. The swift discharge of duty is acceptable to God and man.—J.

Vers. 27—32.—*Impression by tautology.*   These verses contain mostly iterations of maxims already delivered (on ver. 27, see on ch. iii. 2; ix. 11; on ver. 28, see on ver. 24; ch. xi. 7). That religion is a protector to the man of good conscience, while over-throw awaits the ungodly, again brings out an often-expressed thought with emphasis (ver. 30; see on ver. 25; ch. iii. 21). Vers. 31, 32 again contrast the speech of the good and the wicked; the former like a sappy and fruitful tree, the latter destined to oblivion; the former appealing to the sense of beauty and grace, the latter shocking by its deformity.
I. THERE IS A SAMENESS IN GOD.   He does not and cannot change. He is invariable substance, unalterable will and law.
II. THERE IS A SAMENESS IN NATURE.   The heavens above us, with all their worlds, the great mountains and features of the landscape, the daily sights of sunrise and even-ing, form and colour. Abraham and Solomon looked upon *essentially* the same world with ourselves.
III. THERE IS A SAMENESS IN HUMAN NATURE—its passions, strength, and weakness. The same types of character appear and reappear in every age in *relatively* new forms. And it is proverbial that history repeats itself.
IV. THE ESSENTIAL RELATIONS OF MAN TO GOD MUST BE THE SAME IN EVERY AGE. Hence the teacher's deliverances must constantly recur to the same great points.
V. THAT WHICH VARIES IS THE TRIVIAL OR TRANSIENT ELEMENT; THAT WHICH DOES NOT VARY IS THE SUBLIME AND THE ETERNAL.
VI. EVERY TRUE TEACHER MAY THUS VARY THE FORM OF HIS INSTRUCTION AS MUCH AS HE WILL.   Let him see to it that he works in unison with God and nature, experience, the conscience, and leaves a few great impressions firmly fixed in the mind. "Line upon line, precept upon precept, here a little and there a little."—J.

Ver. 1.—*Our joy in our children : a sermon to parents.*   We may take it for granted, as commonly understood—
I. THAT THE FOUNDATION DUTY AND INTEREST, with us all, is to be in a right relation, personally, with God. Until we are right with God we must be wrong altogether. Then we must contend—
II. THAT THE QUESTION OF NEXT VITAL CONSIDERATION is the character of our children. It is conceivable that God might have placed the human world on an entirely different basis than that of the family. But he has rested it on the human home. This is that decision of our Creator which makes the greatest difference to us and to our life. How much it is to those who are parents that they *are such !*   How would their life have been another and a smaller thing without that pure and sacred bond !   What deep chasms of experience has it opened! what fountains of feeling has it unsealed! what secrets of life has it unlocked !   What heights of joy, what depths of sorrow, has it made possible to the heart!
III. THAT THERE IS A SONSHIP WHICH GLADDENS, as there is one that grieves, the parental heart. Who is the wise son (of the text)? Not necessarily the *learned,* or the *clever,* or the *prosperous* son. A child may be any or all of these, and yet may be a grief and not a joy, a shame and not an honour, to his parents. It is he who *has learnt wisdom of God,* who has sat diligently and effectually at the feet of that great Teacher who came to be the Wisdom of God. It is he (1) who has found his home and his heritage in a Divine Father; (2) who has secured an unfailing Friend in a Divine Redeemer; (3) who has stored his mind with eternal truth and filled his soul with everlasting principles; (4) who is building up his character by the teaching, and regu-

lating his life by the will, of Jesus Christ. This is the son of whom the father will never be ashamed, who will not use the language which it would pain him to hear, nor choose the friends he would be unwilling to acknowledge, nor be guilty of the conduct it would wound him to witness. This is the son on whose character and on whose life, in all its phases and developments, he looks with profoundest gratitude and unspeakable delight.

IV. THAT THE CHARACTER OF OUR CHILDREN depends mainly on ourselves. They will: 1. Believe what we teach them. 2. Follow the example we set them. 3. Catch the spirit we manifest in their presence.—C.

Vers. 2—6.—*Four conditions of well-being.* That we may enjoy a prosperity which is truly human, we must do well and be well in three directions—in our circumstances, in our mind (our intellectual powers), and in our character. And that which tends to build up on the one hand, or to destroy on the other hand, will be found to affect us in these three spheres. The conditions of well-being as suggested by the passage are—

I. RECTITUDE. (Vers. 2, 3.) Righteousness before God is essential to all prosperity: 1. Because, if we deliberately choose the path of iniquity, we shall have to work against the arm of Omnipotence. "He casteth away the substance of the wicked" (ver. 3). 2. Because, on the contrary, if we walk in moral and spiritual integrity, we may count on the direction and even the interposition of the Divine hand. "The Lord will not suffer," etc. (ver. 3). 3. Because righteousness means virtue and prudence; it means those qualities which work for health and for security, which "relieve from death" (ver. 2). 4. Because the gains of ungodliness are never satisfactory; they profit nothing." (1) They are unattended by the joy of gratitude, and they are (often) accompanied by the miseries of self-reproach; (2) they are spoilt by the condemnation of the good and the holy; (3) they are apt to be dispersed far more freely than they are acquired; (4) they cannot and they do not satisfy the soul, though they may continue to fill the treasury,—they leave the heart empty, aching and hungering for a good which is beyond, for a blessing which is from above.

II. DILIGENCE. (Ver. 4.) 1. The inattentive and sluggish worker is constantly descending; he is on an incline, and is going downwards. All things connected with his *vocation*, or with his own *mind*, or with his moral and *spiritual condition*, are gradually but seriously suffering; decline, decay, disease, have set in and will spread from day to day, from year to year. 2. The earnest and energetic worker is continually ascending; he is moving upwards; his hand is "making rich"—it may be in material wealth, or (what is better) in useful and elevating knowledge, or (what is best) in the acquisitions of spiritual culture, in the virtues and graces of Christian character.

III. WAKEFULNESS. (Ver. 5.) This is a very important qualification; we must be ready to avail ourselves of the hour of opportunity. To gather when the corn is ripe is necessary if the toil of the husbandman is to bear its fruit; to let the crop alone when it is ready for the sickle is to waste the labour of many weeks. Readiness to reap is of as much consequence as willingness to work. The wakeful eye must be on every field of human activity, or energy and patience will be thrown away. We must covet and must cultivate mental alertness, spiritual promptitude, readiness to strike when the hour has come, or we shall miss much of "the fruit of our labour." It is the general who knows when to give the word to "charge" that wins the battle.

IV. PEACEABLENESS. (Ver. 6.) The consequences of violence shut the mouth of the wicked. He that "seeks peace and ensues it" will "see good days" (1 Pet. iii. 10, 11).—C.

Ver. 7.—"*The memory of the just.*" It is a fact that the name of the good man is fragrant, and that long after his departure there lingers in the memories and hearts of men a sense of loss, a feeling

> "Which is but akin to pain,
> And resembles sorrow only
> As the mist resembles the rain;"

a feeling of tender regret not unmingled with sacred joy and reverent gratitude. This fact is—

I. A STRENGTH TO THE JUST MAN WHILE HE LIVES. "What has posterity done for us?" asks the cynic. "The idea of posterity has done great things for us," replies the moralist. That idea and the hope to which it gives birth have done much to fortify virtue, to establish character, to enlarge and ennoble the good man's life. That thought has been fruitful of earnest work, and has helped men to gird themselves for heroic suffering. Good men have been better, noble lives have been nobler, because we care to be tenderly remembered and kindly spoken of when we are no longer among the living.

II. A COMFORT TO THOSE WHO MOURN HIM. 1. It is true that the more admirable and loving a man is, the greater is our loss when he is taken from us. 2. But it is also true that they are blessed who lose the worthiest and the best. 3. For the sorrow we feel at such loss is a very sacred thing; it comes from God himself; it can be borne with simple and pure resignation; it is unembittered with the most painful regrets; it works for the renewal and purification of our spirit and character. 4. And it is attended with a very precious mitigation; we have a pure and holy joy in the recollection of what the departed one was, what he did, how he laboured and triumphed, how many hearts he comforted, how many lives he brightened, what he was to ourselves. And these remembrances bring sunshine over the shadowed fields; they sweeten the bitter cup; they give "the garment of praise for the spirit of heaviness."

III. AN INSPIRATION TO ALL WHO KNEW HIM. For the completion of a true and godly life *is* an inspiration. 1. It is another proof that goodness can triumph over every obstacle and persevere to the end. 2. It is an unspoken, but not inaudible summons, saying, "Follow me." 3. It is a thing of beauty as well as worth; and it attracts all who have an eye to see as well as a heart to feel. (1) Resolve that, whatever else you leave (or fail to leave) behind, you will bequeath the memory of a just man; that is the *best* legacy to leave. (2) Be drawn, as by a powerful fascination, toward the character and the destiny of the good and wise who have gone before you.—C.

Vers. 8, 10, 11, 14, 18—21, 31, 32.—*The service of speech, etc.* "Man is a talking animal," we say. But if we are distinguished from the brute creation by the mere fact of speech, how truly are we divided from one another by the use we make of that human faculty! To what height of worthiness one man may rise, and what inestimable service he may render, but to what depth of wrong another man may fall, and what mischief he may work, by the use of his tongue!

I. THE SERVICE OF SPEECH. "By our words" we may do great things, as our Master has told us, and as his apostle reminds us (see Matt. xii. 37; Jas. iii. 9). 1. We may *give deep and pure gratification* (ver. 32; and see Eccles. xii. 10). We may speak (or read) words which shall be (1) charming, soothing, comforting, encouraging, even inspiring, in the ear of man; and also (2) pleasing and satisfying to our Divine Master. 2. We may *follow in the footsteps of the Divine.* For "the mouth of the just bringeth forth wisdom" (ver. 31). We may utter in the ears, and may thus convey to the minds and hearts of men, the truths which are nothing less than the wisdom of God. Thus we may be speaking to others the very thoughts and making known the will of God. We ourselves may be, on our scale and in our sphere, like the Lord whom we serve and follow, "the Wisdom of God" (1 Cor. i. 24, 30). 3. We may *enrich the life* of our fellow-men. "The tongue of the just is as choice silver" (ver. 20). And surely fine thoughts, brilliant images, sound principles, sustaining truths, elevating conceptions of God, charitable ideas of men,—these are more enlarging and enriching than many pounds of silver or many piles of gold. 4. We may *nourish the soul.* "The lips of the righteous *feed* many" (ver. 21). Their words are spiritual bread which "strengtheneth man's heart," and makes him able to watch, to work, to battle, to endure. They are the wine which gives new life when he is ready to perish (ch. xxxi. 6), which restores him in the languor of doubt and difficulty, and fills his soul with hopefulness and energy. 5. We may thus *contribute to the true and real life* of men. Our mouth will be "a fountain of life" (ver. 11, Revised Version). Whithersoever the river of Divine wisdom, of Christian truth, runneth, there will be that spiritual upspringing which is the true life of man.

II. THE MISCHIEF OF ITS ABUSE. The abuse of the power of speech, the talking which is idle and vain, is a great and sore evil. 1. It brings the speaker into contempt;

he is thought and spoken of as "a prating fool" (vers. 8, 10), and he comes under the contempt of the wise. 2. It involves men in sin. "In the multitude of words," etc. (ver. 19). The man that is ever speaking with little forethought is sure to violate truth and righteousness before many hours have passed. 3. It works mischief of many kinds (vers. 14 and 18). It is sure to end in slander, in the robbery of reputation. The mouth of the foolish is "a present destruction" (Revised Version). The habit of bad speech, especially if it be that of falsehood, or lewdness, or profanity, is a "present destruction," (1) in that it *constitutes* a real calamity; for in the sight of God there can be few things worse than such a pitiful abuse of the powers he has entrusted to us. It is also a "present destruction," (2) in that it leads with a fatal swiftness to the deterioration and corruption of those in whose hearing it is uttered.—C.

Ver. 9.—(See homily on ch. xi. 3.)—C.

Ver. 12.—*The conquest of love.* "Love covereth all sins." It does this in that—
I. IT CARRIES THE WEIGHT OF MANY SHORTCOMINGS. 1. On the one hand, many proprieties will not atone for the absence of love. We are wholly unsatisfied if one who sustains to us a very near relationship (husband, wife, son, daughter, etc.) is scrupulously correct in behaviour if love be wanting from the heart. Nothing can compensate for that. The kindness that is not prompted by affection is of a very poor order, and it does not satisfy the soul. 2. On the other hand, the presence of pure and strong affection makes many things tolerable which in themselves are hard to bear. Not that any one has a right to excuse himself for transgressions of law, of whatever kind they may be, on the ground of his tenderness of heart. It is a complete and dangerous misreading of our Lord's word (Luke vii. 47) to suppose that he meant that sins are forgiven because of the presence of much love; it is the presence of much love that is the *proof*, not the *ground*, of forgiveness (see homily *in loc.*). But it is a patent and common fact of human life that we can not only bear with one another, but can love and honour one another when love dwells in the heart and shines in the countenance and breathes and burns in the words and actions, even though there may be much faultiness and many infirmities that have to be forgiven.
II. IT IS PREPARED WITH GENEROUS INTERPRETATIONS of much misbehaviour. Where a hard, cast-iron severity sees nothing but transgression, love sees much extenuation or even complete excuse; or it goes beyond that, and sees, or believes that it sees, a worthy and not an unworthy motive. It magnifies or invents a reason which puts conduct in another light, and makes it appear pardonable, if not creditable. It has quite a different account to give of the transaction; it is that which only generous love *could* see and could supply.
III. IT HAS A LARGE FORGIVENESS FOR EVEN GREAT OFFENCES. The Divine love "abundantly pardons." It blots out the worst misdeeds and pardons the negligence and impiety of whole periods of a sinful life. The human love that is likest to the Divine can overlook very dark misdoings, and take back to its embrace those who have gone away and astray into a very "far country" of sin.
IV. IT REDEEMS AND RESTORES. When law does not avail, love will succeed in winning the erring to wiser and better ways. It can lay its hand upon the sinner with a touch that will tell and will triumph. It has a power to break the obduracy of guilt for which violence is utterly inadequate. It alone can lead the rebellious spirit into the gate of penitence and faith, and make its future life a life of obedience and wisdom. Thus in the best way, winning the noblest of all victories, it "covers sin" by conquering it, by leading the heart to the love of righteousness and the practice of purity. Where the rough winds of penalty will fail, the soft, sweet sunshine of love will succeed most excellently.—C.

Ver. 19.—(See homily on ch. xxix. 11.)—C.

Ver. 22.—*Divine enrichment.* There is no inconsistency in the teaching of the text with that of ver. 4. For God blesses us by means of our own efforts and energy; indeed, we are more truly and fully enriched of God when his blessing comes to us as the consequence of our faith and labour.

I. THE OBJECTS AT WHICH WE AIM. Those without which we are apt to consider ourselves poor. They are these: 1. *Material substance,* or (as we commonly put it to ourselves) money. 2. *Honour.* A good measure of regard, duly and clearly paid by our fellows. 3. *Power.* The holding of a position in which we are able to decide and to direct. 4. *Learning,* or unusual sagacity; that intellectual superiority which enables us to lead or to command.

II. THE CONDITION UNDER WHICH THESE MAY BE REGARDED AS THE BLESSING OF GOD. This is when we can truly say that there is "no sorrow," *i.e.* no real cause for regret that we have come to possess and to enjoy them. But when is this? 1. When they have been acquired without any reason for self-reproach—justly, purely, honourably. 2. When we have not lost as much as we have gained by their acquisition. We may lose so much in time, or in health and energy, or in wise and elevating friendship, or in the opportunity for worship and service, that the balance in the sight of heavenly wisdom may be against us. 3. When they do not become a heavy burden which we can ill bear. This they often do become. Frequently wealth becomes more of a burden than a blessing to its possessor. He would be a much lighter-hearted and less care-encumbered man if he had not so much substance to dispose of and to preserve. And so of power and influence. 4. When they do not become a snare to us, leading us into pride, or into a selfish separateness and unneighbourliness, or into a guilty self-indulgence, or into "an unenlightened and unchristian disdain of the common people," or into an overweening and fatal miscalculation of our own power and importance, or into a deadening and suicidal worldliness. These great evils may not mean present "sorrow," as we ordinarily understand that term. But they are such evils as our Divine Father sees with Divine regret; they are such as our heavenly Friend would fain deliver us from; and when riches of any kind end in them, they cannot be said to be the result of his blessing. Moreover, they all lead on and down, sooner or later, to grievous ends; those who yield to them are on their way to "pierce themselves through with many sorrows" (1 Tim. vi. 10). Hence—

III. THE PROFOUND WISDOM OF MODERATION in all human and earthly ambitions. Who shall say how much of riches he can stand? Who can tell where that point is to be found, on the other side of which is spiritual peril and ultimate "sorrow" of the worst kind? "Give me neither poverty nor riches" is the wish and the prayer of the wise and reverent.—C.

EXPOSITION.

CHAPTER XI.

Ver. 1.—A false balance; literally, *balances of deceit* (ch. xx. 23). The repetition of the injunctions of Deut. xxv. 13, 14 and Lev. xix. 35, 36 points to fraud consequent on increased commercial dealings, and the necessity of moral and religious considerations to control practices which the civil authority could not adequately supervise. The standard weights and measures were deposited in the sanctuary (Exod. xxx. 13; Lev. xxvii. 25; 1 Chron. xxiii. 29), but cupidity was not to be restrained by law, and the prophets had continually to inveigh against this besetting sin (see Ezek. xlv. 10; Amos viii. 5; Micah vi. 11). Honesty and integrity are at the foundation of social duties, which the author is now teaching. Hence comes the reiteration of these warnings (ch. xvi. 11; xx. 10). **A just weight**; literally, *a perfect stone,* stones having been used as weights from early

times. So we read (2 Sam. xiv. 26) that Absalom weighed his hair "by the king's stone" (*eben*).

Ver. 2.—Then cometh shame (ch. xvi. 18; xviii. 12); literally, *cometh pride, cometh also shame.* Pride shall have a fall; self-assertion and self-confidence shall meet with mortification and disgrace in the end. "Whosoever exalteth himself shall be abased" (Luke xiv. 11); "Let him that thinketh he standeth take heed lest he fall" (1 Cor. x. 12). Septuagint, "Where violence (ὕβρις) entereth, there also dishonour." **But with the lowly is wisdom.** "Mysteries are revealed unto the meek" (Ecclus. iii. 19, Complutensian; Ps. xxv. 9, 14). The humble are already rewarded with wisdom, because their disposition fits them to receive grace and God's gifts (comp. ch. xv. 33). Septuagint, "The mouth of the humble meditateth wisdom."

Ver. 3.—The integrity—the simple straightforwardness—**of the upright shall**

guide them in the right way, and give them success in their undertakings with the blessing of God (comp. ver. 5). Septuagint, "the perfection of the straightforward" (ch. x. 9). **The perverseness** (*seleph*) ; ch. xv. 4, and there only. Vulgate, *supplantatio ;* Septuagint, ὑποσκελισμός, "the tripping up," making others fall, putting a stumbling-block in others' way. **Transgressors ;** treacherous and deceitful. Such persons shall be caught in their own net (Ps. xxxv. 8); they not only bring punishment on themselves when their evil designs are discovered and frustrated, but they ruin their moral nature, lose all sense of truth and right, and are rejected of God. This clause and the following verse are omitted in the Vatican and some other manuscripts of the Septuagint.

Ver. 4.—**Profit not ;** afford no refuge (ch. x. 2). **In the day of wrath** (ch. vi. 34), when God visits individuals or nations to punish them for sin (comp. Ecclus. v. 8). Such visitations are often spoken of (comp. Isa. x. 3 ; Ezek. vii. 19 ; Zeph. i. 15, 18, etc.). More especially will this be true in the great *dies iræ.* **Righteousness . . . death** (see on ch. x. 2 ; and comp. Tobit iv. 10 ; xii. 9). The Septuagint here adds a sentence which is similar to ver. 10 : "When the righteous dieth he leaveth regret, but the destruction of the wicked is easy and delightsome (πρόχειρος καὶ ἐπίχαρτος)."

Ver. 5.—**The perfect ;** the upright and honest. Vulgate, "simple ;" Septuagint, "blameless." **Shall direct**—make straight or smooth—**his way** (ch. iii. 6). The good man, not blinded by passion, follows a safe and direct path of life ; but the wicked, led by his own evil propensions, and losing the light of conscience (John xi. 10), stumbles and falls. Septuagint, "Righteousness cutteth straight (ὀρθοτομεῖ) blameless paths, but ungodliness walketh in iniquity." Ὀρθοτομέω occurs in ch. iii. 6, and nowhere else in the Septuagint. St. Paul adopts the word in 2 Tim. ii. 15.

Ver. 6.—An emphatic reiteration of the preceding sentences. **Naughtiness ;** "strong desire," as ch. x. 3, which leads to sin (ch. v. 22 ; Micah vii. 3). The indulgence of their passions destroys sinners. Septuagint, "Transgressors are taken by lack of counsel."

Ver. 7.—**His expectation ;** that which he hoped for and set his heart upon, worldly prosperity, long life, impunity,—all are cut off, and the moral government of God is confirmed, by his death (Ps. lxxiii. 17—19). (For "the hope of the ungodly," see the forcible expressions in Wisd. v. 14.) **Of unjust** men ; Vulgate, *sollicitorum ;* Septuagint, τῶν ἀσεβῶν. The word seems to mean "vanities," *i.e.* "men of vanity"—abstract

for concrete. Others translate, "godless hope," or "expectation that bringeth grief," or "strong, self-confident men ; " "men in the fulness of their vigour." But the rendering of the Authorized Version is well supported, and the two clauses are co-ordinate. The Septuagint, in order to accentuate the implied antithesis, has seemingly altered the text, and introduced a thought which favours the immortality of the soul, "When a righteous man dieth, hope perisheth not ; but the boast of the wicked perisheth " (Wisd. iii. 18).

Ver. 8.—**Out of trouble ;** *i.e.* God is at hand to help the righteous out of straits (*de angustia,* Vulgate) ; or takes him away from the evil to come (Isa. lvii. 1 ; Wisd. iv. 10—14). Septuagint, "escapeth from the chase." **In his stead** (ch. xxi. 18). The evil from which the righteous is saved falls upon the wicked. As Abraham says to Dives in the parable, "He is comforted, but thou art tormented" (Luke xvi. 25). Of this substitution many instances occur in Scripture. Thus Haman was hanged on the gallows which he had erected for Mordecai (Esth. vii. 10) ; Daniel's accusers were cast into the den of lions from which he was saved (Dan. vi. 24 ; comp. Isa. xliii. 4).

Ver. 9.—**An hypocrite** (*chaneph*) ; *simulator,* Vulgate. So translated continually in Job, *e.g.* viii. 13 ; xiii. 16, etc. Others take it to mean "profane," "godless." Such a man, by his falsehoods, insinuations, and slanders, destroys his neighbour as far as he is able (ch. xii. 6). Septuagint, "In the mouth of the wicked is a snare for fellow-citizens." **Through knowledge.** By the knowledge which the just possess, and which they display by judicious counsel, peace and safety are secured. Septuagint, "Knowledge affords an easy path (εὔοδος) for the just."

Ver. 10.—**The city ;** any city. Ewald would argue that such language could not be used of the capital of the Jews till the times of Asa or Jehoshaphat. But what is to prevent the sentence being taken generally of any city or community ? The Vatican manuscript of the Septuagint and some others give here only the first clause, "In the prosperity of the righteous the city succeeds," adding from ver. 11, "but by the mouths of the wicked it is overthrown" (see on ver. 4 ; comp. Ps. lviii. 10, etc.).

Ver. 11.—This verse gives the reason of the rejoicing on the two occasions just mentioned (comp. ch. xiv. 34 ; xxviii. 12). **By the blessing of the upright ;** *i.e.* their righteous acts, counsels, and prayers (Wisd. vi. 24). **By the mouth of the wicked.** Their impious language and evil advice bring ruin upon a city.

Ver. 12.—**He that is void of wisdom**

despiseth his neighbour; uses words of contempt about his neighbour. Septuagint, " sneers at his fellow-citizens." The following clause indicates that contemptuous language is chiefly intended. Holdeth his peace. An intelligent man is slow to condemn, makes allowance for others' difficulties, and, if he cannot approve, at least knows how to be silent. *Nam nulli tacuisse nocet, nocet esse locutum.* " Speech is silver," says the proverb, " silence is golden." Septuagint, " A man of sense keeps quiet."

Ver. 13.—A tale-bearer. The word implies one who goes about chattering, gossiping, and slandering (Lev. xix. 16); Vulgate, *qui ambulat fraudulenter;* Septuagint, " the man of double tongue." To such a man it is safe to trust nothing; he revealeth secrets (ch. xx. 19). He that is of a faithful spirit; a steadfast, trusty man, not a gadder about; he retains what is committed to him (Ecclus. xxvii. 16, " Whoso discovereth secrets loseth his credit, and shall never find friend to his mind "). Septuagint, " He that is faithful in spirit [πνοῇ, as in ch. xx. 27, where see note] concealeth matters."

Ver. 14.—Where no counsel is. The word properly means " steersmanship," " pilotage " (ch. i. 5; xii. 5; xxiv. 6). So Vulgate, *gubernator;* Septuagint, κυβέρνησις, " They who have no government fall like leaves," reading *alim* instead of *am.* In the multitude of counsellors (ch. xv. 22; xx. 18; xxiv. 6). This would go to prove the superiority of a popular government over the despotism of a single ruler. But the caution of our homely proverb is not inopportune, " Too many cooks spoil the broth."

Ver. 15.—He that is surety for a stranger; or, *for another* (see ch. vi. 1). Shall smart for it. " Evil shall fall on him evilly who is surety." He that hateth suretyship; guaranteed, as the word implies, by the striking of hands in public (ch. xvii. 18). Vulgate, " who is cautious of snares," especially of the insidious dangers that lurk in suretyship. Is sure; is at rest and has nothing to fear. There is no paronomasia in the Hebrew. The play on "suretyship" and " sure " in the Authorized Version is either accidental or was introduced with the idea of giving point to the sentence. The Septuagint translates differently, " A wicked man doeth evil when he mixes with the righteous; he hateth the sound of safety (ἦχον ἀσφαλείας)." This perhaps means that the fraudulent creditor deceives the good man who has stood security for him; and henceforward the good man cannot bear to hear immunity and safety spoken of (see note on ch. xx. 16).

Ver. 16.—A gracious woman; a woman full of grace. Septuagint, εὐχάριστος,

" agreeable," " charming." The author is thinking of personal attractions, which, he says, win favour; but we may apply his expression to moral excellences also, which obtain higher recognition. Retaineth . . . retain; better, *obtain . . . win*, as in ch. xxix. 23. The two clauses are parallel in form, not in sense, and imply that beauty is more effective than strength, and honour is better than wealth. The Septuagint takes a narrow view : " A graceful woman bringeth glory to her husband." The last clause is rendered, " The manly (ἀνδρεῖοι) are supported by wealth." Between the two clauses the LXX. and the Syriac introduce the following paragraphs: " But a seat of dishonour is a woman that hateth righteousness. The indolent come to want wealth, but the manly," etc.

Ver. 17.—The merciful man; the kind, loving man. Septuagint, ἀνὴρ ἐλεήμων. His own soul; *i.e.* himself. His good deeds return in blessings upon himself. " Blessed are the merciful : for they shall obtain mercy " (Matt. v. 7). Troubleth his own flesh; brings retribution on himself. Some commentators, comparing Ecclus. xiv. 5 (" He that is evil to himself, to whom will he be good?"), translate, " He who does good to himself is a kind man to others, and he who troubles his own body will be cruel to others." The sentiment is quite untrue. Self-indulgence does not lead to regard for others; and a severe, ascetic life, while it encourages stern views of human weaknesses, does not make a man cruel and uncharitable. The Vulgate takes "his own flesh" to mean "his neighbours," as Judah calls his brother Joseph "our flesh" (Gen. xxxvii. 27). But the parallelism confirms the Authorized Version.

Ver. 18.—A deceitful work; work that brings no reward or profit, belying hope, like " fundus mendax " of Horace, ' Od.,' iii. 1. 30. The Septuagint has, "unrighteous works," which seems a jejune rendering, and does not bring out the contrast of the sure reward in the second member (comp. ch. x. 2, 16). To him that soweth righteousness (Hos. x. 12; Gal. vi. 8, 9). To " sow righteousness " is to act righteously, to live in such a way that the result is holiness. The "reward," in a Jew's eyes, would be a long life in which to enjoy the fruits of his good conduct. We Christians have a better hope, which is, perhaps, adumbrated by this analogy : as the seed sown in the field does not produce its fruit till the time of harvest, so righteousness meets with its full recompense only in the great harvest at the end of all things. The Revised Version renders, *The wicked earneth deceitful wages : but he that soweth righteousness hath a sure reward.* This makes a good antithesis. The Septuagint renders the last clause, "but the seed of the righteous is a true reward (μισθὸς ἀληθείας)."

Ver. 19.—This verse is not to be connected with the preceding, as in the margin of the Revised Version, " so righteousness," etc., each couplet in these chapters being independent, the connection, such as it is, being maintained by the use of catchwords, such as "righteous," "wicked," "upright," etc. As righteousness tendeth to life. The various uses of the first word כֵּן (ken) have led to different renderings. The Authorized Version takes it for "as;" the Revised Version as an adjective: He that is steadfast in righteousness. It is, perhaps, better, with Nowack, to regard it as an adverb: "He who is honestly, strictly, of righteousness, is to life." The meaning is plain: real, genuine righteousness hath the promise of this life and of that which is to come (1 Tim. iv. 8). The LXX., reading כֵּן (ben), translate, "A righteous son is born for life." He that pursueth evil (ch. xiii. 21); Septuagint, "the persecution of the impious," i.e. that which an impious man inflicts. But the Authorized Version is correct, and the clause means that he who practises evil brings ruin eventually on himself—a warning trite, but unheeded (comp. ch. i. 18).

Ver. 20.—They that are of a froward heart (ch. xvii. 20); Septuagint, "perverse ways." The word means "distorted from the right," "obstinate in error." Upright in their way (ch. ii. 21; xxix. 27; Ps. cxix. 1).

Ver. 21.—Though hand join in hand (ch. xvi. 5); literally, hand to hand, which may be taken variously. The Septuagint and some other versions take the phrase in the sense of unjust violence: "He who layeth hand upon hand unjustly;" Vulgate, manus in manu, "hand in hand," which is as enigmatical as the Hebrew. Some Jewish interpreters consider it an adverbial expression, signifying simply "soon." Some moderns take it to mean "sooner or later," as the Italian da mano in mano, or, in succession of one generation after another (Gesenius, Wordsworth). Others deem it a form of adjuration, equivalent to "I hereby attest, my hand upon it!" And this seems the most probable interpretation; assuredly the Divine justice shall be satisfied by the punishment of the wicked (comp. Ps. xxxvii.). The Authorized Version gives a very good sense: "Though hands be plighted in faith, and men may associate together in evil, the wicked shall not go unpunished" (comp. Isa. xxviii. 15). St. Gregory ('Mor. in Job,' lib. xxv.) takes a very different view: "Hand in hand the wicked shall not be innocent;" for hand is wont to be joined with hand when it rests at ease, and no

laborious employment exercises it. As though he were saying, "Even when the hand rests from sinful deeds, yet the wicked, by reason of his thoughts, is not innocent" (Oxford transl.). This exposition is, of course, divorced from the context. The seed of the righteous. This is not "the posterity of the righteous," but is a periphrasis for "the righteous," as in Ps. xxiv. 6; cxii. 2, "the generation of the righteous" (comp. Isa. lxv. 23). The climax which some see here—as if the author intended to say, "Not only the good themselves, but their descendants also shall be delivered"—is non-existent and unnecessary. Septuagint, "But he that soweth righteousness shall receive a sure reward," which is another rendering of the second member of ver. 18. Shall be delivered; i.e. in the time of God's wrath (vers. 4, 23; ch. ii. 22).

Ver. 22.—This is the first instance of direct "similitude" in the book. As a jewel [a ring] of gold in a swine's snout. The greatest incongruity is thus expressed. Women in the East wore, and still sometimes wear, a ring run through the nostril, and hanging over the mouth, so that it is necessary to hold it up when taking food. Such a nezem Abraham's servant gave to Rebekah (Gen. xxiv. 22; comp. Isa. iii. 21; Ezek. xvi. 12). The Septuagint has ἐνώτιον, "an ear-ring." So is a fair woman which is without discretion; without taste, deprived of the faculty of saying and doing what is seemly and fitting. The external beauty of such a woman is as incongruous as a precious ring in the snout of a pig. Lesètre quotes an Arab proverb: "A woman without modesty is food without salt." Whether swine in Eastern countries were "ringed," as they are with us nowadays, is unknown; if they were thus treated, the proverb is still more vivid.

Ver. 23.—(Comp. ch. x. 28.) The desire of the righteous is only good. They want only what is just and honest, and therefore they obtain their wishes. The expectation of the wicked—that on which they set their hope and heart—is wrath (ch. xi. 4), is an object of God's wrath. Other commentators, ancient and modern, take the clause to imply that the wishes of evil men, animated by wrath and ill temper, are only satisfied by inflicting injuries on others. Delitzsch would translate ebrah, "excess," "presumption," as in ch. xxi. 24. But the first interpretation seems most suitable (comp. Rom. ii. 8, 9). The LXX., pointing differently, for "wrath" reads "shall perish."

Ver. 24.—There is that scattereth; that giveth liberally, as Ps. cxii. 99, "He hath dispersed, he hath given to the needy." And yet increaseth; becomes only the richer in wealth and more blessed by God (comp.

ch. xix. 17). Nutt quotes the old epitaph, "What we spent, we had; what we saved, we lost; what we gave, we have." Experience proves that no one ultimately loses who gives the tithe of his income to God (see on ch. xxviii. 27). There is that withholdeth more than is meet; *i.e.* is niggardly where he ought to be liberal. But the expression is best taken as in the margin of the Revised Version, "that withholdeth what is justly due," either as a debt or as a proper act of generosity becoming one who desires to please God and to do his duty. But it tendeth to poverty. That which is thus withheld is no real benefit to him, it only increases his want. Septuagint and Vulgate, "There are who, sowing what is their own, make the more; and there are who, gathering what is another's, suffer loss." Dionysius Cato, 'Distich. de Mor.,' liv. 4. 1—

"Despice divitias, si vis animo esse beatus, Quas qui suscipiunt mendicant semper avari."

Ver. 25.—The sentiment of the preceding verse is here carried on and confirmed. The liberal soul; literally, *the soul of blessings*, the man that blesses others by giving liberally. Shall be made fat (ch. xiii. 4; xxviii. 25). The term is used of the rich and prosperous (Ps. xxii. 29). Septuagint, "Every simple soul is blessed." He that watereth—benefits and refreshes others—shall be watered also himself; shall receive the blessing which he imparts. The Vulgate introduces another idea, *Qui inebriat, ipse quoque inebriabitur*, where the verb implies rather abundance than excess, as in ch. v. 19, etc. The Septuagint departs widely from the present text: "A passionate man is not graceful" (εὐσχήμων), *i.e.* is ugly in appearance and manner—a sentiment which may be very true, but it is not clear how it found its way into the passage. St. Chrysostom comments upon it in 'Hom.' xvii. on St. John. There are some Eastern proverbs on the stewardship of the rich. When a good man gets riches, it is like fruit falling into the midst of the village. The riches of the good are like water turned into a rice-field. The good, like clouds, receive only to give away. The rivers themselves drink not their water; nor do the trees eat their own sweet fruit, and the clouds eat not the crops. The garment in which you clothe another will last longer than that in which you clothe yourself. Who gives alms sows one and reaps a thousand.

Ver. 26.—He that withholdeth corn. The practice reprehended is not confined to any one time or place. The avaricious have always been ready to buy corn and other necessary articles of consumption when plentiful, and wait till there was dearth in the market or scarcity in the land, and then sell them at famine prices. Amos sternly reproves this iniquity (viii. 4, etc.). It is a sin against justice and charity, and it is said of him who is guilty of it, the people shall curse him (ch. xxiv. 24). Such selfishness has often given rise to tumult and bloodshed, and has been punished in a signal manner. The legend of Bishop Hatto shows the popular feeling concerning these Dardanarians, as they were called by Ulpian ('Digest. Justin.,' xlvii. 11. 6). Such a one St. Chrysostom ('Hom. in 1 Cor.,' xxxix.) calls "a common enemy of the blessings of the world, and a foe to the liberality of the Lord of the world, and a friend of mammon, or rather his slave." The Septuagint gives a curious rendering: "He who holdeth corn may he leave it for the peoples!" *i.e.* may neither he nor his heirs be benefited by his store, but may it be distributed among others far and near! That selleth it; literally, *that breaketh it*, as it is said of Joseph when he sold corn to the Egyptians (Gen. xli. 56; xlii. 6).

Ver. 27.—He that diligently seeketh good; literally, *he that seeketh in the morning*, as so often in Scripture, the phrase, "rising early," implies unimpaired powers and diligence (ch. xxvii. 14; Jer. vii. 13, etc.). Procureth favour; better, *seeketh favour;* by his very act of striving after what is good, he is striving to do what may please and benefit others, and thus to please God. Vulgate, "Well does he rise early who seeketh good." It—mischief—shall come unto him; the consequences of his evil life shall fall upon his head. Says an Indian proverb, "When men are ripe for slaughter, even straws turn into thunderbolts."

Ver. 28.—There are many expressions in this and the following verses which recall Ps. i. He that trusteth in his riches shall fall (ch. x. 2; Ps. xlix. 6, 7; lii. 7; Ecclus. v. 8). Wealth is of all things the most uncertain, and leads the heart astray from God (1 Tim. vi. 17). As a branch; "as a leaf" (Ps. i. 3; Isa. xxxiv. 4). The righteous grow in grace and spiritual beauty, and bring forth the fruit of good works. Septuagint, "He who layeth hold on what is righteous [or, 'helpeth the righteous'] shall spring up (ἀνατελεῖ)."

Ver. 29.—He that troubleth his own house; he that annoys and worries his family and household by niggardliness, bad management, and captious ill temper. So the Son of Sirach writes (Ecclus. iv. 30), "Be not as a lion in thy house, nor frantic (φαντασιοκοπῶν, 'suspicious') among thy servants." Septuagint, "he who has no friendly intercourse (ὁ μὴ συμπεριφερόμενος)" with his own house." **Shall inherit the wind**; he will be the loser in the end; no one will lend him a helping hand, and his affairs will fall to ruin. **The fool**—the man who acts thus foolishly—shall be **servant to the wise of heart**; to the man who administers his household matters in a better and more orderly manner (see on ch. xii. 24). It is implied that the troubler of his own house shall be reduced to such extremity as to have to apply for relief to the wise of heart. The other side of the question is given by the Son of Sirach: "Unto the servant that is wise shall they that are free do service" (Ecclus. x. 25). The prodigal in the parable prayed his father to make him one of his hired servants (Luke xv. 19).

Ver. 30.—**The fruit of righteousness** (*of the righteous*) **is a tree of life** (ch. iii. 18; xiii. 12); *lignum vitæ*, Vulgate. That which the righteous say and do is, as it were, a fruitful tree which delights and feeds many. A good man's example and teaching promote spiritual health and lead to immortal life. Septuagint, "From the fruit of righteousness springeth a tree of life." **And he that winneth souls is wise**; rather, *he that is wise winneth souls.* The latter member is parallel to the former. He who gives men of the tree of life attracts souls to himself, to listen to his teaching and to follow his example. With this "winning of souls" we may compare Christ's promise to the apostles that they should "catch men" (Luke v. 10; comp.

Jas. v. 20). The Septuagint introduces an antithesis not found in our Hebrew text: "But the souls of transgressors are taken untimely away." Ewald and others change the present order of clauses in vers. 29 and 30, thinking thus to improve the parallelism. They would rearrange the passage in the following way: "He that troubleth his own house shall inherit the wind; but the fruit of the righteous is a tree of life. The foolish shall be servant to the wise of heart; but he that is wise winneth souls." There is no authority whatever in the versions or older commentators for this alteration; and the existing arrangement, as we have shown, gives a very good sense.

Ver. 31.—**The righteous shall be recompensed in the earth.** There are two ways of understanding this verse. The word rendered "recompensed," שָׁלַם (*shalam*), is a *vox media*, and can be taken either in a good or bad sense. So the meaning will be, "The righteous meets with his reward upon earth, much more the sinner," the "reward" of the latter being, of course, punishment. But the versions lead to another interpretation, by which "recompensed" is rendered "chastised;" and the meaning is—if even the righteous shall be punished for their trespasses, as Moses, David, etc., how much more the wicked! The Septuagint, quoted exactly by St. Peter (1 Epist. iv. 18) has, "If the righteous scarcely be saved, where shall the ungodly and the sinner appear?"

HOMILETICS.

Ver. 1.—*Just weights.* The point of this proverb is different from that of our low-toned though often useful saying, "Honesty is the best policy." Every day we are discovering more and more how profoundly true that saying is, if not in the narrow view some take of it, yet in its broad issues and in the long run. But no man will be truly honest who puts policy before honesty, and bases his morality on selfish expediency. Therefore, if we are ever to reap the personal profit promised in the English proverb, we must mould our conduct on higher principles, such as that of the Hebrew proverb, which teaches us that dishonesty in trade is hateful to God, and that justice is his delight.

I. COMMERCE IS INCLUDED IN THE RIGHTFUL DOMAIN OF RELIGION. Few men would deny the abstract proposition that commerce has its morals, though many may be very indifferent in the application of them. But it must be further seen that commerce has its religion. There is a religious way of carrying on trade, and an irreligious way of doing it. God is in the shop as well as in the church. He is as much concerned with the manner in which we buy and sell as with the style in which we pray; nay, more so, for his chief interest is with our real, daily, practical life.

II. RELIGION REQUIRES JUST WEIGHTS IN TRADE. Religion requires them. No one would dare to admit that morality did not require them. But we have now to see that religion especially demands them. This is the place where the incidence of religion on trade is to be felt. Religion carried into business does not mean praying for prosperity and then cheating our neighbours in order to secure the answer to our prayer, nor giving to missionary collections a small dole out of the profits of swindling. It means honesty in business preserved for God's sake. He will not hear our prayers while the weights and measures are being tampered with.

III. THE RELIGIOUS REQUIREMENT OF JUST WEIGHTS IS BASED ON THE OBLIGATIONS OF TRUTH AND OF OUR DUTY TO OUR NEIGHBOURS. 1. *Truth.* God hates all lies. False balances are concrete lies. They are worse than verbal untruths; for they are deliberate and permanent. A weak man may be surprised into a hasty expression that does not accord with his convictions under the shock of a sudden temptation. But to construct and keep false balances is to deceive with full consideration of what is being done. Adulteration is a similar offence. People who construct elaborate machinery for the very purpose of adulterating articles of trade should feel that all their ingenuity aggravates their condemnation. 2. *Our duty to our neighbours.* In a Christian country surely we should have some regard for the great maxim of Christ, that we should do to others as we would that they would do unto us. The tradesman should put himself in the customer's case, the buyer in that of the seller. Brotherly kindness is the best human safeguard for integrity; but above this should be our regard for the approval of God. We please God not so much by singing hymns and offering sacrifices as by honest business. " A just weight is his delight."

Ver. 2.—*The shame of pride and the wisdom of humility.* I. THE SHAME OF PRIDE. Pride claims honour, and thinks itself secure of obtaining it. It would dread disgrace above all things, would rather starve and perish than suffer from contempt. Yet a true insight into life shows that pride is the direct precursor of shame, of the very thing it would most wish to keep off. Thus, like ambition, pride "o'erleaps itself." 1. *Pride claims too high a place.* The proud man, thinking highly of himself, thrusts himself into positions where he is unable to meet what is required of him. If he took the lower place, no one would think ill of him; he might then be respected. But he makes himself ridiculous by aiming too high. The greatest of men have found out the folly of this ambition of pride. Others besides Shakespeare's Wolsey can say—

> " I have ventured,
> Like little wanton boys that swim on bladders,
> This many summers in a sea of glory;
> But far beyond my depth : my high-blown pride
> At length broke under me; and now has left me,
> Weary, and old with service, to the mercy
> Of a rude stream, that must for ever hide me."

2. *Pride refuses to receive correction.* It will not stoop to confess itself in error. Satisfied with its own condition, it will not listen to advice, nor try for any improvement. Thus it remains stationary. The flecks and flaws of character which a humble man would allow his neighbour to point out and help him to remove become stereotyped in the proud man. Thus faults which would be forgiven and forgotten if they were only transitory in the growth of character bring disgrace by becoming permanent and characteristic. 3. *Pride provokes criticism.* No man is wise in being proud until he knows he is without reproach. For the very attitude of pride challenges attacks. It offends the pride of others, and in sheer self-defence they will set to work to discover the faults which charity or a happy indifference would otherwise leave undisturbed.

II. THE WISDOM OF HUMILITY. Humility is not only right and beautiful; it is also wise. Both the Old and the New Testaments insist upon this truth. It was the mistake of Stoicism—the highest effort of secular morality—that it failed to see this. Epictetus and Marcus Aurelius—in other respects so near to the Christian ideal—are here severed from it by an impassable chasm. They were both Pharisees. The shame which pride brings, of course, suggests the wisdom of its opposite. But this wisdom has its positive recommendations. Humility, choosing lowly places, finds refuge in safe ones; admitting imperfection, confessing sin, it is ready to repent, and therefore capable of beginning a better life and of rising to perfection. Winning the hearts of men by its unassuming character, it escapes jealous criticism, and finds that faults are covered by love. Humility need not be the confession of unworthiness. Christ the Sinless One, Christ the Son of God, was the humblest and meekest of men. The

Christian is called to walk in the steps of his Master, and to seek his joy in renouncing himself. Ultimately he will find his honour in the same course. "For every one that humbleth himself shall be exalted."

Ver. 13.—*The tale-bearer.* Tale-bearing may result from spite and malice, or it may be an incident of idle gossip; but even in its milder phases it is a most mischievous practice, and one deserving of severe reprobation. Connected with what are called the minor moralities of life, the evil of it is far too little recognized by many Christian people, people who undoubtedly endeavour on the whole to square their conduct with right principles. It is very important, therefore, that the character of this very common fault should be exposed.

I. WHEN CONFIDENCE HAS BEEN REPOSED, TALE-BEARING IS SHAMEFULLY DISHONOUR-ABLE. All of us admit in the abstract that it is mean and dastardly to betray confidence. But the practice is terribly frequent with people whose character should be proof against it. Of course, no man of principle would deliberately worm a secret out of an innocent, trusting friend for the very purpose of blazing it abroad. But there are cases in which the evil is less clearly recognized. 1. *Confidence may be implied when it is not expressed.* A man need not say in so many words that he is telling us a secret, and bind us over to keep silent by solemn promises, in order to put us under an obligation not to betray his confidence. If he evidently trusts us, calls us into his counsels as an exceptional privilege of friendship, and tells us what we know he would not wish us to make public, the duty not to repeat his words is scarcely less binding. If, through being admitted into a man's house, we have discovered the skeleton in his cupboard, by accepting his hospitality, we are pledged not to reveal it. 2. *Confidence may be betrayed through carelessness.* If any one lends a jewel to a friend, he is required not only not to sell it, but not to leave it exposed to the danger of theft. Confidence is a jewel. It must be guarded. Should we through recklessness reveal what is entrusted to us, we are culpable. Two practical considerations : (1) Do not be over-anxious to learn secrets. They bring with them painful, difficult obligations. Those people who are most careless in betraying confidence are generally most eager in their curiosity to pry into the affairs of their neighbours. Both habits imply a low moral tone. (2) Be careful how you give confidence. This is not merely a maxim of prudence; it is a rule of charity, for the trust is an obligation, possibly a very arduous one. Why should you force it upon a friend, and so increase his burdens?

II. WHEN CONFIDENCE HAS NOT BEEN REPOSED, TALE-BEARING IS UNCHARITABLE. 1. *It is unkind, even if nothing damaging to character is said.* We may know many innocent things about a man which it would be highly unbecoming to make public. The modest will respect decency of soul as well as of body. The veil of mental reserve is a requirement which should distinguish the civilized man from the savage as much as the clothing of his body. One of the penalties of royalty is the exposure of private and home life in "the fierce light that beats upon a throne." Unhappily, this evil grows upon public characters; and the tendency of "society papers" to pander to idle curiosity with personal gossip about celebrities is one of the most unwholesome habits of our day. 2. *It is often injurious when no harm is meant.* The report is misunderstood, or it is unfairly judged by going forth without the lights and shades of accompanying circumstances, like a text without its context. Thus a deed appears harsh which would be condoned if the causes which led up to it were all known. Like a rolling snowball, rumour grows as it progresses through the world. The love of dramatic effect unconsciously colours the "simple, round, unvarnished tale," till the author could no longer recognize it. 3. *It is ungenerous when it is a true tale of guilt.* We are not called to tell all the evil which we know of our neighbours. Charity would hide it. It is most inhuman to take pleasure in the vivisection of character. On the other hand, we must bear in mind that it is sometimes our duty to speak out unpleasant truths, as in bearing witness to a crime from obligations of justice, and in giving a servant's character; untruthfulness in the latter case is dishonest, unjust to employers, and directly unfair to persons of good character by the depreciation of the value of truthful testimonials in the loss of confidence in all such documents.

In conclusion, see how injurious tale-bearing is to the tale-bearer. 1. It rouses retaliation. Who among us can defy the tongue of slander thus provoked? 2. It degrades the mind. Wordsworth has described the lowering influence of narrow personal talk in contrast with conversation on topics of larger, nobler interest—

> " Sweetest melodies
> Are those that are by distance made more sweet.
> Whose mind is but the mind of his own eyes,
> He is a slave—the meanest we can meet."

Ver. 17.—*The merciful man.* It would be our duty to be merciful if we suffered thereby, and indeed we can never be truly merciful solely from motives of self-interest, since genuine mercy must spring from sympathy. Nevertheless, we sadly need all aids to righteousness—the lower as well as the higher; and therefore it may be useful for us to consider how much it makes for our own profit that we should be merciful.

I. THE MERCIFUL MAN WILL OBTAIN MERCY FROM OTHER MEN. We never know in what straits the future may find us. Proud in our independence to-day, we may be in abject need before long, or at least in circumstances which make our welfare largely dependent on others. We are so much members one of another that it is not for our own good that we should injure one another. He is in the most precarious position who has provoked enemies by his cruelty. Let him beware of the turn of the tide of fortune. The tyrant calls forth the assassin. Employers who grind down their work-people cause that very indifference to their interests of which they complain. If generosity wins friendship, surely it is a valuable grace. None love so much as they who have been forgiven much.

II. ONLY THE MERCIFUL MAN WILL OBTAIN MERCY FROM GOD. This is an absolute principle the importance of which is too little recognized. In the Old Testament God tells us that he desires "mercy, and not sacrifice" (Hos. vi. 6); *i.e.* that the practice of the former, rather than the offering of the latter, is the ground of acceptance by him. Christ signalizes mercy by giving it a place in the Beatitudes, and saying that the blessing of the merciful is that they shall obtain mercy (Matt. v. 7); calls upon us to love our enemies (Matt. v. 44); inserts in his model prayer one sole condition—that God "forgives us our debts as we have forgiven our debtors" (Matt. vi. 12); and tells us that our offerings to God must be preceded by our forgiveness of men (Matt. v. 23, 24). Therefore the cruel man troubleth his own flesh, for he excludes himself from the enjoyment of God's mercy—the one essential of his eternal welfare.

> " Consider this—
> That in the course of justice, none of us
> Should see salvation: we do pray for mercy:
> And that same prayer should teach us all to render
> The deeds of mercy."

III. THE MERCIFUL MAN IS BLESSED IN THE VERY EXERCISE OF MERCY. 1. *The exercise of mercy is pleasing.* The temptation to hatred promises a devilish pleasure; but it is a delusive promise. Once the passion is indulged, it works pain in the soul. The expression of rage is no sign of pleasure. Cruelty makes a hell within, and peoples it with demons that torture the man himself even more than its victims. By a singular law of nature the exercise of mercy begins in the pain of self-sacrifice, but it soon bears fruit in inward peace and gladness. 2. *The exercise of mercy is elevating and ennobling.* Cruelty degrades the soul. Charity refines, exalts, sanctifies. The glory of God is in his mercy.

> " Wilt thou draw near the nature of the gods?
> Draw near them then in being merciful:
> Sweet mercy is nobility's true badge."

Thus, to quote one more familiar saying of Shakespeare's, we find that mercy

> " Is twice bless'd,
> It blesses him that gives and him that takes."

Ver. 24.—*Meanness.* The Book of Proverbs is sometimes accused of taking too low and worldly a view of conduct, and of giving undue importance to prudential, self-regarding duties. Whatever truth there may be in these charges—and no doubt the New Testament does describe so pure and lofty an ideal of life as to leave the morals of Solomon and his compeers in a decidedly inferior rank—gives only the greater emphasis to those maxims of broad and noble character which are so clear and imperative as to claim attention even from moralists who observe the less exalted standards of character. Thus it is very significant that, with all its inferiority to Christianity, the ethics of the Book of Proverbs unhesitatingly and repeatedly condemns all meanness, and does honour to liberal habits. Even from a selfish and comparatively worldly point of view, meanness is shown to be a miserable mistake, and generosity a wise and profitable virtue. It is evident that high Christian principles would condemn meanness. It is interesting to see that the morals of the Proverbs are equally opposed to it.

I. MEANNESS IS UNPROFITABLE BECAUSE IT IS DISPLEASING TO GOD. Let us set this consideration first, as of highest importance. Too many leave it to the last or ignore it altogether. They calculate the consequences of their actions on narrow, earthly principles; possibly they inquire what view their neighbours may take of it. But God's judgment on it they consider to be of little or no account. Yet surely, if there is a God at all, the first question should be—How far will our conduct be approved by him? If there is a providence that "shapes our ends," schemes that ignore this leave out of account the most important factor in determining the final issue of events. If God is really overruling our life, and will mete out to us curse and blessing according to his view of it, the way in which he will regard it is no mere problem of idle speculation; it is the most pressing question of practical life, more important than all other things put together. Now, God does hate selfishness, greed, and meanness, and he loves unselfishness and generosity; he will therefore punish the one and reward the other.

II. MEANNESS IS UNPROFITABLE BECAUSE IT EXCLUDES US FROM THE SYMPATHY OF OTHERS. No vice is more anti-social. Even cruelty does not seem to sever the ties of friendship more thoroughly. Regarded only from a commercial point of view, it is short-sighted. The mean customer who strikes off the odd pence in the payment of a bill does this at the cost of checking all generosity in those who deal with him. The mean employer of labour saves a little by his grinding harshness, but he loses far more by provoking his workpeople to take no interest in their work. Meanness destroys those great pleasures and comforts of life which come from the love and friendship of our neighbours.

III. MEANNESS IS UNPROFITABLE BECAUSE IT FAILS TO SACRIFICE THE PRESENT FOR THE FUTURE. The mean farmer will not sow sufficient seed, and consequently he will reap a short harvest. In business men must launch out liberally if they are to make large returns. From the lowest up to the highest concerns of life, self-sacrifice and generosity are requisite for ultimate profit. We must be willing to give up earthly wealth for the heavenly inheritance. The miser who clutches at his gold when God claims it will fail to obtain the pearl of great price.

IV. MEANNESS IS UNPROFITABLE BECAUSE IT DEGRADES AND NARROWS THE SOUL. It is a vice that destroys all noble aspirations and all lofty aims. It dwarfs the spiritual stature. It shuts out visions of the infinite. It confines thought, affection, and desire to a miserable little world of worthless interests. In groping after the small gain that meanness idolizes, we lose all power of pursuing better things. The same meanness may be carried into religion, to our soul's undoing. The pursuit of selfish salvation to the neglect of our duty to others overreaches itself. Whosoever desires to save his life, or his soul, will lose it. But in working for the good of others while forgetting our own advantage, we find our own soul most profited. "He that watereth shall be watered also himself."

HOMILIES BY VARIOUS AUTHORS.

Vers. 1—11.—*The ways of honour and of shame.* I. JUSTICE AND INJUSTICE IN COMMON THINGS. Jehovah delights in "full weight," and abominates the tricky balance. This may be applied: 1. Literally, to commerce between man and man. 2. Figuratively, to all social relations in which we may give and receive. Work is only honest if thorough; if honest and thorough, it is religious. If principle be the basis of all our transactions, then what we do is done "unto the Lord, and not unto men." If we are indifferent to principle in the common transactions of the week, it is impossible to be really religious in anything or on any day.

II. HAUGHTINESS AND MODESTY. Extremes meet. The former topples over into shame; the latter is lifted into the heights of wisdom. 1. No feeling was more deeply stamped on the ancient mind than this. Among the Greeks *hubris,* among the Romans *insolence,* designated an offence peculiarly hateful in the eyes of Heaven. We see it reappearing in the songs and proverbs of the gospel: "He hath brought down the mighty from their seat, and exalted them of low degree;" "Every one that humbleth himself shall be exalted; but he that exalteth himself shall be abased." 2. It is stamped upon all languages. Thus, in English, to be *high, haughty, lofty, overbearing,* are terms of censure; *lowly, humble,* terms of praise. In the German the words *uebermuth, hochmuth,* point to the same notion of *excess* and *height* in the temper. 3. At the same time, let us remember that the good temper may be counterfeited. Nothing is more easy than to suppose we have humbled ourselves by putting on a *manner.* Yet nothing is more detestable than the *assumption* of this particular manner. True humility springs from seeing ourselves *as we are;* pride, from nourishing a fanciful or ideal view of ourselves. Wisdom must begin with modesty; for a distorted or exaggerated view of self necessarily distorts our view of all that comes into relation with self.

III. RECTITUDE AND FAITHLESSNESS. (Ver. 3.) The former means *guidance,* for it is a clear light within the man's own breast; the latter, self-destruction. As scriptural examples of the one side of the contrast, may be cited Joseph and Daniel; of the other, the latter, Saul, Absalom, Ahithophel, Ahab, and Ahaziah.

IV. RECTITUDE AND RICHES. (Ver. 4; see on ch. x. 2.) 1. Riches cannot purchase the grace of God, nor avert his judgments. 2. Rectitude, though not the *first cause* of salvation, is its necessary condition. To suppose that we can be saved from condemnation without being saved from sin is a gross superstition.

V. SELF-CONSERVATIVE AND SELF-DESTRUCTIVE HABITS. (Vers. 5, 6; comp. ch. iii. 6; x. 3.) Honesty and rectitude level the man's path before him; wickedness causes him to stumble and fall. Straightforwardness means deliverance out of dangers, perplexities, misconceptions; while the eager greed of the dishonest man creates distrust, embarrassment, inextricable difficulty.

> "He that hath light within his own clear breast
> May sit in the centre and enjoy bright day;
> But he that hides a dark soul and foul thoughts,
> Benighted walks under the midday sun;
> Himself is his own dungeon."
>
> (Milton.)

VI. HOPE AND DESPONDENCY IN DEATH. (Ver. 7.) The former seems implied. If the Old Testament says *expressly* so little about a future life, some of its sayings may be construed as allusions to and indications of it. It is little that *we* can know *definitely* of the future life. But the least we do know is that hope is inextinguishable in the good man's soul; it is its own witness, and "reaps not shame." But despondency and despair are the direct result of wicked living. To cease to hope is to cease to wish and to cease to fear. This must be the extinction of the soul in the most dreadful way in which we can conceive it.

VII. THE EXCHANGE OF PLACES FOLLOWS MORAL LAW. (Ver. 8.) The good man comes out of distress, and the evil becomes his substitute in sorrow. So with the Israelites and Pharaoh, a great typical example; so with Mordecai and Haman; with Daniel and his accusers. Great reversals of human judgments are to be expected; many that were last shall be first, and the first last.

VIII. THE SOCIAL PEST AND THE TRUE NEIGHBOUR. (Ver. 9.) The pernicious power of slander. The best people are most injured by it, as the best fruit is that which the birds have been pecking at; or, as the Tamil proverb says, "Stones are only thrown at the fruit-laden tree." The tongue of slander "out-venoms all the worms of Nile." It spares neither sex nor age, nor helplessness. It is the "foulest whelp of sin." It promotes nothing that is good, but destroys much. Knowledge, on the other hand—in the form of sound sense, wide experience—if readily imparted, is a boon to all. And the best of boons, for gifts and charities soon lose their benefit, while a hint of wisdom lives and germinates in the mind in which it has been deposited.

IX. OBJECTS OF SYMPATHY AND ANTIPATHY. (Ver. 10.) Gladness follows the success of the good and the downfall of the evil. The popular feeling about men's lives, as manifested at critical periods of failure or success, is a moral index, and suggests moral lessons. There is a true sense in which the voice of the people is the voice of God. Compare the scene of joy which followed Hezekiah's success in the promotion of true religion (2 Chron. xxix., xxx.), and the misery under Ahaz (2 Chron. xxviii.); also the rejoicings on the completion of Nehemiah's work (Neh. viii.); and for jubilation at evil men's deaths, Pharaoh, Sisera, Athaliah (Exod. xv.; Judg. v.; 2 Kings xi. 13—20).

X. SOUND POLITICS AND PERNICIOUS COUNSELS. (Ver. 11.) The blessing, *i.e.* the beneficial principles and administration of good and wise men exalt a city (or state). On the other hand, unprincipled counsels, even if temporarily successful, lead in the end to ruin. "It is impossible," said Demosthenes, "O men of Athens, that a man who is unjust, perverse, and false should acquire a firm and established power. His policy may answer for once, may hold out for a brief period, and flourish marvellously in expectations, if it succeed; but in course of time it is found out, and rushes into ruin of its own weight. Just as the foundation of a house or the keel of a ship should be the strongest part of the structure, so does it behove that the sources and principles of public conduct should be true and just. This is not the case at the present time with the actions of Philip." Compare the examples of Elisha (2 Kings xiii. 14, etc.), Hezekiah, and Isaiah (2 Chron. xxxii. 20—23), on the one hand; and the Babel-builders (Gen. xi. 4—9) and the Ammonites (Ezek. xxv. 3, 4) on the other; also Jer. xxiii. 10; Hos. iv. 2, 3.—J.

Vers. 12—15.—*Social sins denounced.* I. THE EFFECTS OF SOCIAL SIN. It dissolves mutual bonds of confidence, corrupts and disintegrates the social order and stability. In the mixed condition of human character and society there are elements of weakness and elements of strength. Our speech about others and behaviour to them tends either to bring out their weaknesses, so promoting discontent, suspicion, and distrust, or it tends to bring out their good qualities, so promoting genial confidence and good will.

II. SOME EXAMPLES OF SOCIAL SINS. Great stress, as usual, is laid upon the tongue. 1. There is *contemptuous talk* about our neighbour. The art of depreciation is cruel to others, and moreover is, as the text says, senseless. What good can come of it? Of Byron's poetry the great Goethe said, "His perpetual fault-finding and negation are injurious even to his excellent works. For not only does the discontent of the poet infect the reader, but the end of all opposition is negation; and negation is nothing. If I call bad *bad*, what do I gain? But if I call *good* bad, I do a great deal of mischief. He who will work aright must never rail, must not trouble himself at all about what is ill done, but only do well himself. For the great point is, not to pull down, but to build up; and in this humanity finds pure joy." 2. Still worse is *open slander* (ver. 13). Secret detraction is like an arrow shot in the dark, and does much secret mischief. Open slander is like the pestilence that rages at noonday. It sweeps all before it, levelling the good and bad without distinction. A thousand fall beside it, and ten thousand on its right hand. They fall, so rent and torn in their tender parts, as sometimes never to recover the wounds or the anguish of heart which they have occasioned (Sterne). 3. *Independent counsels* (ver. 14) are another source of social mischief. As when there was no king in Israel, and when every man did that which was right in his own eyes, and the people became the prey of their enemies (Judg. ii. 19, *seq.*; xvii. 6; xxi. 25). The spiritual forces in a nation, the intelligence and honest patriotism of its rulers, are ever of more importance than wealth, fleets, or armies. 4. *Rash undertakings.* (See on ch. vi. 1, *seq.*) To promise more than there is a reasonable prospect of performing; to enter imprudently into bargains, covenants, or treaties, not easy to abide by, yet involving disgrace and dishonour if broken. The serious penalties which follow acts of imprudence should instruct us as to their real *sinfulness.* The good intention is marred by the hasty or thoughtless execution.

III. SOME SOCIAL SAFEGUARDS. 1. *Seasonable silence.* (Ver. 12.) As we are not to believe all we hear, so neither are we to speak all we know; to be cautious in believing any ill of our neighbour, and to be cautious in repeating what we do believe, are alike duties. 2. *Kindly desire.* "The honest man's ear is the sanctuary of his absent friend's name, of his present friend's secret; neither of them can miscarry in his trust" (Bishop Hall). 3. *Fulness of counsel.* (Ver. 14.) The "multitude of counsellors" implies *association, conference,* and *co-operation.* By the exchange of ideas we enrich, define, classify, or correct our own. The same subject needs to be looked at from opposite points of view, and by minds of different habit; and the just medium is thus arrived at. 4. *Caution.* (Ver. 15.) Especially with reference to the incurring of responsibilties. To fetter or lose our freedom of action is to deprive ourselves of the very means of doing further good. One of the acts of benefaction is to contrive that neither the doer of the kindness shall be hampered by excessive responsibility nor the recipient of it by excessive obligation. 5. As the foundation of all, *intelligence* and *love*—the inner light which fills the intellect with illumination and the heart with glowing affection. These are the sources of truth in friendship, safety in counsel, general usefulness to society.—J.

Ver. 16.—*The true grace of womanhood.* Even as the mighty keep a firm hold upon their possessions, so does the virtuous woman watch over her chastity and honour, to guard it from assault.
I. THE PURITY OF WOMAN IS HER "HIDDEN STRENGTH" (Milton). "She that has that is clad in complete steel."
II. IT IS HER CHIEF ORNAMENT. It clothes her amidst dangers with "unblenched majesty" and "noble grace."
III. IT IS ROOTED IN RELIGION, FOUNDED LIKE MANLY TRUTH IN THE FEAR OF GOD.
IV. IT IS PRECIOUS IN THE SIGHT OF GOD.

> "So dear to Heaven is saintly chastity,
> That when a soul is found sincerely so,
> A thousand liveried angels lackey her,
> Driving far off each thing of sin and guilt,
> And in clear dream and solemn vision
> Tell her of things that no gross ear can hear."
>
> (Milton.)

J.

Ver. 17.—*Religion and self-interest.* The loving man does good to himself, while the cruel afflict their own souls. As examples of the former, see Joseph in prison (Gen. xl. 6), the Kenites (1 Sam. xv. 6), David and the Egyptian slave (1 Sam. xxx. 11—20), David's conduct to Jonathan (2 Sam. ix. 7; xxi. 7), Job praying for his friends (Job xlii. 10), the centurion and the Jews (Luke vii. 2—10), the people of Melita to Paul (Acts xxviii. 1—10). For examples of the latter, see Joseph's brethren (Gen. xxxvii.; xlii. 21), Adoni-bezek (Judg. i. 6, 7), Agag (1 Sam. xv. 33), Haman (Esth. ix. 25).
I. RELIGION APPEALS TO THE WHOLE RANGE OF OUR MOTIVES, FROM THE LOWEST TO THE HIGHEST. We should cultivate the higher, but not ignore the lower.
II. TO DO GOOD TO OTHERS IS TO DO CERTAIN GOOD TO OURSELVES. We thus make friends, and they are a defence.
III. TO INJURE OTHERS IS CERTAINLY TO INJURE OURSELVES. Thus we make enemies. And "he that hath a thousand friends hath not one to spare; he that hath an enemy shall meet him everywhere."—J.

Ver. 18.—*The principle of recompense.* I. EVERY ACTION IS A SECONDARY CAUSE, AND IS FOLLOWED BY ITS CORRESPONDING EFFECT.
II. THE EFFECT CORRESPONDS IN KIND AND IN DEGREE TO THE CAUSE.
III. HUMAN CONDUCT MAY THUS BE VIEWED AS A SOWING FOLLOWED BY REAPING, WORK BY WAGES, ACTION BY REACTION.
IV. THE GAIN OF THE WICKED IS DECEPTION ILLUSORY. Illustrations: Pharaoh's

attempt to decrease Israel resulted in their increase and his own destruction. Caiaphas seeking by murderous expediency to save the nation brought about its ruin. The persecution of the Church at Jerusalem led to the greater diffusion of the gospel (Acts viii.).

V. THE REWARD OF THE RIGHTEOUS IS STABLE AND SURE. Illustrations: The patient continuance in well-doing of Noah, Abraham, Joseph. Compare the sowing of St. Paul in tears, *e.g.* at Philippi (Acts xvi.), with his joyous reaping, as his Epistle to the Philippians witnesses. The reward is *eternal*—"a crown of righteousness that fadeth not away." "What we weave in time we shall wear in eternity."—J.

Ver. 19.—*The tendencies of conduct.* I. ALL ACTIONS HAVE AN IMMEDIATE AND A REMOTE RESULT.

II. IT IS THE FINAL RESULT THAT MUST BE CONSIDERED IN ESTIMATING DIFFERENT COURSES OF CONDUCT.

III. THERE ARE TWO IDEAL TERMINI TO CONDUCT—LIFE AND DEATH. An old proverb says, "We know not who live or die." But we may know towards which issue certain habits are tending.

IV. TENACIOUS RECTITUDE IS THE WAY OF LIFE; BLIND PURSUIT OF THE OBJECTS OF PASSION, THE WAY TO DEATH.—J.

Ver. 20.—*The Divine view of the oppositions in conduct.* I. GOD VIEWS PERVERSITY WITH DISPLEASURE. Moral perversity is analogous to physical deformity; the line is crooked when it should be straight.

II. HE VIEWS RECTITUDE WITH DELIGHT. The morally right is the æsthetically beautiful. The true, the beautiful, and the good are one in God, and he can only delight in that which reflects himself. Hence his delight in the well-beloved Son, and in all who are conformed to his image.—J.

Ver. 21.—*Inevitable doom and certain escape.* I. A SOLEMN ASSEVERATION OF DOOM. The first words should be rendered, "The hand upon it!" referring to the custom of striking hands in a compact, and meaning the same as "My word for it!" Experience, the laws of nature, the assurances of God's prophets, the voice of conscience, all ratify this doom; the sinner must meet his fate, and there is no ultimate deliverance.

II. AN ASSURANCE OF SAFETY. The generation of the righteous, *i.e.* all that belong to that class, will escape from affliction, distress, condemnation, all woes that belong to time; for his refuge is in the eternal arms. If exiled from earth, it is to find a home in the bosom of God.—J.

Ver. 22.—*Beauty ill set off.* The comparison of the gold ring in the swine's snout suggests the idea of *glaring incongruity.* And the like is the incongruity between beauty and impurity in woman.

I. THE SOURCE OF OUR DELIGHT IN PHYSICAL BEAUTY IS THAT IT EXPRESSES MORAL WORTH. Philosophers have always found it impossible to define the beautiful as an object. Analysis at last results in this—that in every beautiful object we detect an *analogy* to some perception in our own minds. It is a visible presentation of spiritual beauty.

II. OUR DISPLEASURE IN THE ASSOCIATION OF PHYSICAL BEAUTY WITH MORAL WORTHLESSNESS ARISES FROM THE PRESENCE OF A CONTRADICTION. And the mind is made to love harmony.

III. THUS WE HAVE A WITNESS IN OURSELVES THAT GOD DESIGNED BEAUTY AND VIRTUE TO BE INDISSOLUBLY UNITED. As the sign and the thing signified—the body and the soul. Sin ever puts asunder what God has joined, and all vice is incongruous with the beauty of his world.—J.

Ver. 23.—*Wishes and hopes.* The wishes of the righteous are only good, for God prospers and fulfils them; but the hope of the wicked is extinguished in calamity (the wrath of God).

I. WISHES AND HOPES HAVE A CERTAIN POWER TO FULFIL THEMSELVES. (See Mozley's fine sermon on this subject.)

II. The REGULATION OF THE WISHES IS AN IMPORTANT PART OF SELF-DISCIPLINE.

III. To WISH AND TO HOPE FOR NOTHING BUT THE BEST (IN ACCORD WITH THE WILL OF GOD) IS AN INSURANCE AGAINST DISAPPOINTMENT.

IV. SELFISH HOPES LEAD TO UNANSWERED PRAYERS AND TO BITTER CHAGRINS.—J.

Vers. 24—26.—*The narrow and the large heart.* I. THRIFTY SPENDING. All wise outlay of money is a form of thrift. The increase of capital depends upon the observance of certain laws and rules of prudence; and the prudence which enables to amass enables also to spend. Spending in works of benevolence is seldom known to impoverish a man, for it is seldom disjoined from calculation and economy in personal habits. But whether we can trace out the manner of the connection in every instance or not, it is real and profound. Wise distribution is the condition of steady increase. In the highest point of view benevolence is a "lending to the Lord."

II. UNTHRIFTY SAVING. Niggardliness tends to poverty, because it stints the energies. It springs from a false view of the value of money, or an exaggerated view. The true source of happiness, as of wealth, lies at last in the will, its energy, its industry. He who has so little faith in this as to put all his reliance on the mere means of living, may well become poor outwardly, as he certainly is inwardly.

III. The SATISFACTION OF DOING GOOD. Here, again, we must look to the *reflex* effect of actions. The indirect results are the wider and the more important. From every free forth-going of the heart in acts of love and kindness there is a certain return *into* the heart. It is not sufficiently considered that whatever gives *expansion* to the mind—large views, broad sympathies—is so much gain in actual power. And again, that we cannot directly do much towards the removal of our own troubles, but obliquely may quell or diminish them by aiming at removing the troubles of others. Fulness of interests in the heart will not give room for grief to gnaw.

IV. SELFISHNESS AND GENEROSITY IN COMMERCE. (Ver. 26.) In time of dearth the avaricious proprietor, keeping back his corn to secure a higher price, brings down upon himself curses; while he who thinks of humanity more than of personal profit earns the blessings of the poor. The maxim that "business is business" is true, but may be pushed too far. If a trader profits by a war or scarcity, that is an accident; but it is not an accident, it is a crime, if he votes for war or interferes with the natural action of the market with a view to personal gain. If the same conditions of trade make the man rich which impoverish the many, he will feel it to be his duty to give the more out of his abundance.—J.

Vers. 27—31.—*Temporal and eternal contrasts.* I. MEN FIND WHAT THEY SEEK. (Ver. 27.) The favour of God, which includes all the elements of happiness by well-doing, or sorrow by ill-doing. This law of antecedence and consequence in moral things, thus so reiteratedly pressed upon us, cannot be too constantly before the mind. Every moral action is a prophecy before the event; every moral result, a fulfilment of a previous prophecy.

II. The CAUSES OF DECAY AND OF PROSPERITY. (Ver. 28.) Trust in riches leads to moral downfall (comp. ch. x. 2; Ps. xlix. 6, 7). By trust in riches is meant the habit of depending on them and their accessories—luxury and ease—as the main good in life. It is in this sense that "riches slacken virtue and abate her edge." The laxity and dissoluteness of the mind may well be compared to the limp and falling leaf. He, on the other hand, whose trust is in spiritual resources—the treasures of the kingdom of God—is like a tree full of sap; his foliage is abundant; his leaf ever green (Ps. xcii. 13; Isa. lxvi. 14).

III. The RETRIBUTION OF GREED AND OPPRESSION. (Ver. 29.) The man who "troubles his house" is the close-fisted and greedy, who in his covetousness keeps his household upon scant fare or withholds from them their due pay (ch. xv. 27). Ahab is thus charged by Elijah as a "troubler of Israel" (1 Kings xviii. 17, 18). But he reaps the wind, *i.e. nothing* from his misplaced care and exertion (Isa. xxvi. 14; Hos. viii. 7). Nay, he so comes down in the scale as actually often to fall into slavery to a just and merciful lord (ver. 24). These reversals in human life—more marked or easily observable, perhaps, in ancient times than with ourselves—remind men of a

superior judgment, which constantly revises and corrects the short-sighted and superficial judgments of men.

IV. THE PRODUCTS OF RIGHTEOUSNESS. (Ver. 30.) All that the good man says and
does becomes a source of blessing and life (a "tree of life") to many. He exercises an
attractive power, and gathers many souls to his side for the service of God and the
cause of truth.

V. THE CERTAINTY OF RECOMPENSE. (Ver. 31.) This may be taken as an argument
from the greater to the less. The sins of the righteous do not escape chastisement;
how much less those of men unreconciled to God! "If the righteous scarcely be
saved, where shall the ungodly and the sinner appear?" (1 Pet. iv. 18).—J.

Ver. 1.—(See homily on ch. xvi. 11, including ch. xx. 10—23.)—C.

Ver. 2.—(See homily on ch. xvi. 18.)—C.

Vers. 3—5, 8—11, 19, 20, 28, 31.—*The pricelessness of integrity.* We have here
a view of the exceeding worth of moral integrity, or of righteousness; we see what, in
the judgment of the wise, it will do for its possessor. It will—

I. DIRECT HIS WAY. "The integrity of the upright shall guide them; ... the righteousness of the perfect [*i.e.* the upright] shall direct his way" (vers. 3—5). And we read
(ch. x. 9) that "he that walketh uprightly walketh surely." The man who honestly
and earnestly seeks guidance of God will find what he seeks; he will know what he
should do, and whither he should go, and how he should act, in the various relations of
life. Instead of moving onwards and backwards, instead of inclining this way and that,
he will walk straight on in the highway of justice, purity, devotion. And he will
walk "surely." It is not in the way of holiness that the snares of sin or the stumbling-
blocks of folly are scattered about.

II. DELIVER HIM IN DANGER OR DISTRESS. (Vers. 4, 8, 9.) "Many are the afflictions" even "of the righteous," but "the Lord delivereth him," etc.; "Unto the
upright there ariseth light in the darkness" (Ps. cxii. 4). Righteousness brings
deliverance in many ways. 1. It secures the favour, and thus the merciful interposition, of the Almighty. 2. It commands the esteem, and thus the succour, of the good
and true. 3. It confers mental and physical vigour on its subjects, and makes them
strong for the day of peril and of need. 4. It endows with those moral qualities—conscientiousness, consciousness of rectitude, courage, patience, hopefulness, perseverance—
which lead to victory.

III. MAKE HIM THE SOURCE OF ENLARGEMENT TO OTHERS. "The city is exalted"
(ver. 11). Every man is something the better for the integrity of his neighbour; and
the contribution of many righteous men to the exaltation and enlargement of the city,
or the Church, or the society, is very great. They are the salt which preserves it; they
are the fountain and the garner which supply its need and minister to its strength.

IV. PROMOTE HIS PROSPERITY. (Vers. 28, 31.) As a rule, upon the whole, the
righteous man will prosper and be recompensed "on the earth." Sobriety, purity,
justice, prudence; in fact, *integrity* conducts to well-being now and here.

V. SECURE FOR HIM THE GOOD PLEASURE OF THE HIGHEST. (Ver. 20.) What a
recompense is this—"to be a delight unto the Lord," to "have this testimony, that he
pleases God"! What a reward of the purest and most enduring kind to the Christian
man, that he is "pleasing Christ," is living every day in the sunshine of his Lord's
approval!

VI. ISSUES IN THE FULNESS OF LIFE. "He that is steadfast in righteousness shall
attain unto life." 1. Unto the fulness of spiritual life below; nearness of access to God;
a real approval by God and of delight in him; constancy of service rendered unto
him; growing likeness to his Divine spirit and character. 2. Unto the fulness of
eternal life hereafter.—C.

Vers. 7—10 (latter part).—*Two sad aspects of death.* Death is the most unwelcome
of all themes for human thought, certainly for the thought of the wicked. Yet has he
special reason for considering its approach. For it is likely to arrive sooner than if he
were righteous. As we read in this chapter, "Righteousness delivereth from death"

(ver. 4); on the other hand, "The wicked shall fall by his own wickedness" (ver. 5). "The wages of sin is death," and every departure from rectitude is a step towards the grave. But how melancholy a thing is the death of the wicked! It means—

I. A MELANCHOLY EXTINCTION. Not, indeed, of the man himself, but of his work and of his hope. When the wicked dies, everything, except, indeed, the evil influences he has created and circulated, comes to a dreary end. His expectation, his hope, perishes. He can take nothing that he has toiled for into that other world which he is entering. All his laborious exertion, his elaborate contrivances, his selfish schemes, his painful humiliations, come to nothing; they are buried in the grave. He may have a powerful and well-stored mind, but he has cherished no desire, has entertained no ambition which reaches beyond the horizon of mortal life, and with the stopping of his heart-beat, every imagination of his spirit perishes; there is an untimely and utter end of all his brightest hopes. A sad and dismal outlook for a human spirit! How great and how blessed the contrast of a good man! His largest hopes are then on the point of being realized; his purest and brightest expectations are about to be fulfilled. This earth is, more or less, the scene of disappointment; but in the country whose bourne he is about to cross, he will find himself where

> "Trembling Hope shall realize
> Her full felicity."

II. A PAINFUL RELIEF. "When the wicked perish, there is shouting." 1. It is bad enough when a man's death is only felt by a very few souls. With the many oppor-tunities we have of connecting ourselves honourably and attaching ourselves strongly to our fellows, we ought to be so much to our neighbours, that when we pass away there will be many to regret us and to speak with a kindly sorrow of our departure. Poor and fruitless must that life have been when this is not so. 2. It is seriously sad when a man's death excites no regret; when "the mourners" do not mourn; when the only thing that is real about the funereal scene is the drapery of woe. It is a pitiful thing when Christ's minister cannot pray for Divine comfort, because, though there are those who are bereaved, there is none that is afflicted. 3. It is a *most* melancholy thing when a man's death is felt to be a positive relief; when, as he is borne to the grave, those who knew him cannot help being glad that one more root of mischief is plucked up, one more source of sorrow taken away. That a *man*, created to be a light, a refuge, a blessing, a brother, a deliverer, should be put away with a feeling in every one's heart of gladness that he will be seen no more, put out of sight with the senti-ment that the sooner he is forgotten the better,—this is sad indeed. What, then, is—

III. THE CONCLUSION OF THE WISE? It is this: "Let me die the death of the righteous." But the disappointing career of the author of these words (Numb. xxiii. 10; Josh. xiii. 22) should be a solemn warning and a powerful incentive to form the firm resolution to *live the life* of the righteous, lest, as in Balaam's case, death should overtake us when we are in the ranks of the enemy.—C.

Ver. 17.—*Honourable self-love; the effect of conduct on character.* Our great temp-tation, and therefore our great peril, is to look at all things in a selfish light; to ask ourselves, concerning each event as it unfolds itself—*How will it affect me?* This is very far indeed from the spirit of Christ; his spirit is that of unselfishness, of generous regard for the welfare of others. To bear one another's burdens is to fulfil his law and to reproduce his life. Yet is there one respect in which we certainly do well to con-sider ourselves. We do well to pay very particular attention to the effect of our con-duct on our own character, to ask ourselves—How are these actions of mine telling on my manhood? Are they building up, or are they causing to crumble and decay? The consideration is twofold.

I. THE INJURY WE MAY DO OURSELVES, ESPECIALLY BY UNKINDNESS. "He that is cruel troubleth his own flesh." Habitual cruelty does even more harm to itself than to its victim. *That* indeed is bad enough; for it is not only the present suffering which is inflicted by it; it is the diseased sensitiveness and the abjectness of spirit; it is the loss of courage and of confidence and of hopefulness that is left behind, which is the deepest and the darkest mark of cruelty on the object of it. But worse than even this is the moral injury which cruelty does to itself. It not only (1) calls down the strong condemnation of man, and (2) draws forth the strong rebuke and penalty of God; (3) it *indurates the soul* of the sinner. It makes him shockingly insensitive to human suffering. It may go so far as to cause him to take a savage and a diabolical delight in inflicting and in witnessing it. Thus it drags a man down to the very lowest levels. And what is true of cruelty, or of unkindness which very soon becomes cruelty, is true in other ways of other sins. All wrong-doing, falsehood, dishonesty, lasciviousness, profanity, covetousness, intemperance, makes its mark and leaves its stain upon the soul of the evil-doer; and the further he goes and the deeper he continues in sin, the deeper is the mark and the darker and broader is the stain.

II. The blessing we may bring upon ourselves, especially by kindness. "The merciful man doeth good to his own soul." Mercy may here stand for any form of kindness or of goodness of heart. It will include kindliness of manner, generosity of disposition, practical helpfulness, pity for those who suffer or are sad, patience with the erring and the froward, magnanimity under ill treatment, considerateness toward the weak and the unprivileged. All these forms of "mercy" bring a blessing to the merciful heart. They secure the appreciation and the affection of the best among men; they gain the approval and benediction of God. And they react with most valuable benignity on the heart itself. They contribute to: 1. A tenderness of spirit, a responsiveness of heart, which allies us very closely to our Divine Lord. 2. An excellency and even nobility of action which makes us "the children of our Father in heaven" (Matt. v. 45). 3. A breadth of sympathy and largeness of view which make *us ourselves* truly wise and worthy in the sight of God.—C.

Ver. 21.—*Divine providence.* "Reckonest thou this, O man, who doest such things, that thou shalt escape the judgment of God?" (Rom. ii. 3). No doubt men do indulge the thought that they will do wrong things with impunity; that, though others suffer, yet will they succeed in eluding justice; that they will have shrewdness enough to stop at the right point and to save themselves from the penalty of indiscretion. Sin is deceitful, and it imposes on its victims with strong and fatal delusions.

I. The certainty that sin will suffer. "Though hand join in hand, the wicked shall not be unpunished." 1. How impotent must mere numbers be against the decision and the action of the Almighty! There is a certain sense of security that men have in being a part of a large multitude. But it is a false sense. What do numbers avail against the action of the elements of nature, or against the outworking of the laws which determine the well-being and ill-being of the soul? 2. Confederacies of evil men are confessedly insecure. "Hand may join in hand;" the covetous, the dishonest, the violent, may combine; but in the heart of evil there are the seeds of unfaithfulness and treachery; and the alliance will break down in time. Sin carries in its folds the germ of its own undoing. 3. Against the continued success of sin many forces are combining. (1) All honest and true men have a direct and strong interest in deposing and dishonouring it. (2) It usually inflicts on some one man, or family, or city, an injury which calls forth an intense and invincible resentment. (3) It has within it the elements of physical and moral weakness, which are sure to be developed in time. (4) It is always open to the accusation of conscience and to consequent exposure. (5) It must move and even hasten towards utter demoralization and the loss of all that is most worth keeping. (6) It has against it the decree and the overruling action of the Holy One (Ps. xxxiv. 16; and text). Sin *never is* absolutely unpunished, even when it imagines that it is; and it never *remains* unpunished, though it may seem to have excellent chances of escape. The judgment of God will overtake it in time.

II. The hope of the righteous. "The seed of the righteous shall be delivered." "The generation of the upright shall be blessed" (Ps. cxii. 2). Even if God allows a man to go on long without the proof of his Divine favour, yet will he not withhold his blessing. It will come upon the children, if not upon the upright man himself. And who is there that would not be more than willing that God should bless him through his offspring? To clothe them with honour, to satisfy them with substance, to deliver them in their time of trouble, to make them citizens of the kingdom of Christ, to employ them as ambassadors of Christ,—is not this a most ample and rich reward for all our personal fidelity? If God blesses us in our children, we are blessed indeed.—C.

Vers. 24—26.—*Expensive economy, etc.* We are accustomed to speak as if the man who spends freely is a spendthrift, and as if the man who restrains his hand is on the way to wealth. But if that is our thought, we are often and much mistaken. There is an—

I. EXPENSIVE ECONOMY. "There is that withholdeth," etc. 1. If we keep back the wage that is due to the workman, we shall miss the blessing that goes with justice, and suffer the curse which attends injustice (Jas. v. 1—4). 2. If we keep back the corn we should sow more plentifully, or the strength we should expend more liberally, or the mental power we should employ more patiently and systematically, we shall reap less bountifully, we shall make less profit, we shall do less work in the spiritual sphere. "He that soweth sparingly shall reap also sparingly" (2 Cor. ix. 6). 3. If we shut up our thought and our care to our own heart, or even our own home, we shall lose all the harvest of love and blessing we might reap if we did not withhold ourselves from those outside our door. It is a poor economy, indeed, that hides its talent in a napkin.

II. PROFITABLE EXPENDITURE. There is a bound beyond which we should not go in putting forth our resources, physical, pecuniary, mental, spiritual. What that limit is every one must decide for himself. Regard should certainly be had to the preservation of health and to the necessity for replenishment. But we may often wisely and rightly go very much further than we do; and if we did we should find that we were liberally repaid. Our scattering would mean increase, our liberality would mean nourishment, our endeavour to enrich others would result in our own growth and ripeness; watering them, we should ourselves be watered. This is true of: 1. *Human sympathy* and love. The friendly man makes many friends; and to have true friends is to be blessed indeed. 2. *The energetic pursuit* of our vocation, whatever it may be. It is the man who throws his full energies into his work who is repaid in the end. 3. *Generous helpfulness.* Give money, time, thought, counsel, whatever you have to give, unto those who need it, unto the young, the ignorant, the baffled and beaten, the unfortunate, the slain in life's battle-field; and there shall come back to you that which will be far more valuable than anything or all that you have expended. There shall come to you (1) the smile of that Divine Saviour who gave himself for us, who, though he was rich, for our sake became poor; (2) the gratitude of those whom you serve, afterwards and yonder if not now and here; (3) spiritual enlargement,—the "soul will be made fat," the heart will expand, and Christian graces of many kinds and of much beauty will make their home there.

III. THE SUPERIOR CLAIM. (Ver. 26.) A man has a right to do the best he can for himself; the best, even, for his own purse, though that is saying something very different and *much less*. But this right may soon be traversed. It *is* so crossed when a man cannot go any further without injuring his brethren; that bars his way; obligation limits claim. In other words, the claim of our fellow-men is greater far than that of our individual self. When the people are lacking bread, we may not hold back our corn. God has given us our powers and our resources, not that we may build up a fortune, but that we may be of true service in a world which is full of need. To grow rich is not at all necessary to any one, and proves to be a curse to multitudes; to feed the hungry, to minister to want and sorrow, to still the cry of pain or perishing, to make glad the heart and bright the life,—that is the real privilege and heritage of man.—C.

Ver. 30.—*Wisdom's brightest crown and hardest task.* "He that winneth souls is wise." Wisdom does many things for us; but we shall find—

I. ITS BRIGHTEST CROWN in the souls that it wins. Wisdom wins wealth, honour, friendship, knowledge; acquaintance with men and with nature; high position and commanding rule; the gratification that attends achievement. Wisdom makes great changes in the face of nature, and effects great results in the organization of men. But the crown which it wears is its beneficent work in human souls. "He that winneth souls is wise" indeed. For to do that is: 1. To arrest a stream of evil influence, the full outflow and consequence of which it is impossible to estimate. 2. To originate a stream of holy and helpful influence, the growing and widening range of which we cannot imagine. 3. To turn back a human spirit from a course which leads downward to an opposite course which leads homeward and heavenward; it is to change the direction of one in whom are boundless capacities of accomplishment and of endurance, and to change it permanently for the better. 4. It is to give joy of the purest kind to hearts of the greatest worth, and satisfaction to the Divine Saviour himself (see Jas. v. 19, 20). It is wisdom's brightest crown; but it is also—

II. ITS HARDEST TASK. He that winneth souls must be, or needs to be, wise indeed; for he has a very great thing to do. He has: 1. To oppose himself to he knows not what supernatural hostilities (Eph. vi. 12). 2. To do battle with human obduracy and the evil spirit of procrastination. 3. To contend with the spiritual blindness and insensibility which are the sad consequence of long disloyalty. 4. To baffle the arts of false friendship and overcome the blandishments of an evil world. 5. To silence the deceitful voices which whisper to the awakened soul that there is no need to render an immediate and whole-hearted decision; and thus to lead it to a full surrender to Christ and to his service. 6. To persuade to a life of earnest and habitual devotion and holy usefulness. The practical lessons of the text are: (1) That we cannot expend ourselves too lavishly in the great work of winning men to Jesus Christ. There is no room for extravagance here. (2) That we have need to put forth our whole strength to gain so great a victory. (3) That when we have done all we can do we must remember that nothing is accomplished without the influence which is from above.—C.

EXPOSITION.

CHAPTER XII.

Ver. 1.—Instruction; correction, discipline, which shows a man his faults, gives him a lowly opinion of himself, and opens his mind to receive *knowledge*, especially the knowledge of himself and of all moral obligations. Is brutish; is as insensible to higher aspirations, to regret for the past or hope of amendment, as a brute beast (comp. ch. xxx. 2). On this point St. Augustine is quoted: "Quicumque corripi non vis, ex eo sane corripiendus es quia corripi non vis. Non vis enim tua tibi vitia demonstrari; non vis ut feriantur, fiatque tibi utilis dolor, quo medicum quæras; non vis tibi tu ipse ostendi, ut cum deformem te vides, reformaturum desideres, eique supplices ne in illa remaneas fœditate" ('De Corrept. et Grat.,' v.). Such conduct is unworthy of one who is possessed of an immortal soul and infinite capacity for progress and improvement.

Ver. 2.—A good man. The word is general, the particular virtue intended being often modified by the context. In view of the contrast in the second clause, it means here "pure," "straightforward," having a heart free from evil thoughts. As the psalm says, "Surely God is good to Israel, even to such as are pure in heart" (Ps. lxxiii. 1). Obtaineth favour of the Lord (ch. viii. 35); Septuagint, "Better is he who findeth favour from the Lord." A man of wicked devices (ch. xiv. 17); one whose thoughts are perverse and artful. Will he—Jehovah—condemn; Vulgate, "He who trusts to his imaginations doeth wickedly;" Septuagint, "A man that is a sinner shall be passed over in silence (παρασιωπηθήσεται)."

Ver. 3.—A man shall not be established

by wickedness. Man is metaphorically compared to a tree, especially the olive. Wickedness gives him no firm hold for growth or life (comp. ch. x. 25). The root of the righteous shall not be moved. The righteous are planted in a good soil, are "rooted and grounded in love" (Eph. iii. 17), and the root being thus well placed, the tree is safe, and brings forth much fruit (comp. ver. 12; Job xiv. 7—9).

Vers. 4—12 contain proverbs concerning the management of a house and business.

Ver. 4.—A virtuous woman; one whose portrait is beautifully traced in ch. xxxi. The term is applied to Ruth (Ruth iii. 11). The Vulgate renders, *diligens*; Septuagint, ἀνδρεία. The expression means one of power either in mind or body, or both. The same idea is contained in ἀρετὴ and *virtus*. Such a woman is not simply loving and modest and loyal, but is a crown to her husband; is an honour to him, adorns and beautifies his life, making, as it were, a joyous festival. So St. Paul (1 Thess. ii. 19) calls his converts "a crown of glorying." The allusion is to the crown worn by the bridegroom at his marriage, or to the garlands worn at feasts (comp. Cant. iii. 11; Isa. lxi. 10; Wisd. ii. 8). The Son of Sirach has much praise for the virtuous woman: "Blessed is the man that hath a good (ἀγαθῆς) wife, for the number of his days shall be double. A virtuous (ἀνδρεία) woman rejoiceth her husband, and he shall fulfil the years of his life in peace" (Ecclus. xxvi. 1, 2). She that maketh ashamed; "that doeth shamefully" (ch. x. 5; xix. 26); one who is a terrible contrast to the woman of strong character—weak, indolent, immodest, wasteful. Is **as rottenness in his bones** (ch. xiv. 30; Hab. iii. 16). Such a wife poisons her husband's life, deprives him of strength and vigour; though she is made "bone of his bones, and flesh of his flesh" (Gen. ii. 23), far from being a helpmate for him, she saps his very existence. Septuagint, "As a worm in a tree, so an evil woman destroyeth a man." Here again Siracides has much to say, "A wicked woman abateth the courage, maketh an heavy countenance and a wounded heart: a woman that will not comfort her husband in distress maketh weak hands and feeble knees" (Ecclus. xxv. 23). Thus runs a Spanish maxim (Kelly, 'Proverbs of All Nations')—

"Him that has a good wife no evil in life that may not be borne can befall;
Him that has a bad wife no good thing in life that chance to, that good you may call."

Ver. 5.—**The thoughts of the righteous are right**; literally, *judgments;* i.e. just and fair, much more then words and actions. St. Gregory ('Mor. in Job,' lib. xxv.) takes another view, seeing in "judgments" the stings of conscience, and a rehearsal of the day of account. "The righteous," he says, "approach the secret chambers of the Judge in the recesses of their own hearts; they consider how smartly he smites at last, who long patiently bears with them. They are afraid for the sins which they remember they have committed; and they punish by their tears the faults which they know they have perpetrated. They dread the searching judgments of God, even in those sins which perchance they cannot discover in themselves. And in this secret chamber of inward judgment, constrained by the sentence of their own conduct, they chasten with penitence that which they have committed through pride" (Oxford transl.). But **the counsels of the wicked**—which they offer to others—are **deceit.** The mere "thoughts" are contrasted with the mature, expressed "counsels." Septuagint, "The wicked steer (κυβερνῶσι) deceits." (For "counsels," see notes, ch. i. 5 and xx. 18.)

Ver. 6.—**The words of the wicked are to lie in wait**—a lying in wait—**for blood** (see ch. i. 11). The wicked, by their lies, slanders, false accusations, etc., endanger men's lives, as Jezebel compassed Naboth's death by false witness (1 Kings xxi. 13). **The mouth of the upright shall deliver them**; *i.e.* the innocent whose blood the wicked seek. The good plead the cause of the oppressed, using their eloquence in their favour, as in the Apocryphal Story of

Susannah, Daniel saved the accused woman from the slanders of the elders.

Ver. 7.—**The wicked are overthrown, and are not**; or, *overthrow the wicked, and they shall be no more.* The verb is in the infinitive, and may be rendered either way; but the notion is scarcely of an overthrow. The Vulgate has, *verte impios;* i.e. change them a little from their previous state, let them suffer a blow from any cause or of any degree, and they succumb, they have no power of resistance. What the stroke is, or whence it comes, is not expressed; it may be the just judgment of God—temptation, trouble, sickness—but whatever it is, they cannot withstand it as the righteous do (see ch. xi. 7). Some commentators see in the phrase the idea of suddenness, "While they turn themselves round, they are no more" (ch. x. 25; Job xx. 5). Septuagint, "Wheresoever the wicked turn, he is destroyed." **The house of the righteous**, being founded on a secure foundation, shall stand (Matt. vii. 24, etc.).

Ver. 8.—**According to his wisdom.** A man who gives practical proof of wisdom by life and character, whose words and actions show that he is actuated by high views, is praised and acknowledged by all (see on ch. xxvii. 21). Thus we read of David, that he behaved himself wisely, "and he was acceptable in the sight of all the people" (1 Sam. xviii. 5). The Septuagint, taking *lephi* differently, renders, "The mouth of the prudent is commended by men." **He that is of a perverse heart;** Vulgate, "a vain and senseless man;" Septuagint, "one slow of heart (νωθροκάρδιος)." One who takes distorted views of things, judges unfairly, has no sympathy for others, **shall be despised.**

Ver. 9.—This verse may be translated, *Better is a man who is lightly esteemed and hath a slave, than he that boasts himself and lacketh bread;* i.e. the man who is thought little of by his fellows, and is lowly in his own eyes, if he have a slave to minister to his wants (which all Orientals of even moderate wealth possess), is better off than one who boasts of his rank and family, and is all the while on the verge of starvation. "Respectful mediocrity is better than boastful poverty." Ecclus. x. 27, "Better is he that laboureth and aboundeth in all things, than he that boasteth himself, and wanteth bread." But the words rendered, **hath a slave**, are literally, *a servant to himself.* So the Vulgate has, *sufficiens sibi,* "sufficing himself," and the Septuagint, δουλεύων ἑαυτῷ, "serving himself." And the expression implies attending to his own concerns, supplying his own wants. Hence the gnome means, "It is wiser to look after one's own business and provide for one's own necessities, even if thereby he meets with contempt and detraction, than to be in real want, and all the time assuming the airs of a rich and prosperous man." This latter explanation seems most suitable, as it is not at all clear that, at the time the book was written, the Israelites of moderate fortune kept slaves, and the proverb would lose its force if they did not do so. Says a mediæval jingle—

"Nobilitas morum plus ornat quam genitorum."

Ver. 10.—**A righteous man regardeth the life of his beast.** For "regardeth," the Hebrew word is literally "knoweth" (Exod. xxiii. 9); he knows what animals want, what they can bear, and treats them accordingly (comp. ch. xxvii. 23). The LXX. translates "pitieth." The care for the lower animals, and their kind treatment, are not the produce of modern sentiment and civilization. Mosaic legislation and various expressions in Scripture recognize the duty. God's mercies are over all his works; he saves both man and beast; he hateth nothing that he hath made (Ps. xxxvi. 6; cxlv. 9; Jonah iv. 11; Wisd. xi. 24). So he enacted that the rest of the sabbath should extend to the domestic animals (Exod. xx. 10); that a man should help the over-burdened beast, even of his enemy (Exod. xxiii. 4, 5); that the unequal strength of the ox and the ass should not be yoked together in the plough (Deut. xxii. 10); that the ox should not be muzzled when he was treading out the corn (Deut. xxv. 4); that the sitting bird should not be taken from her little brood (Deut. xxii. 6), nor a kid seethed in its mother's milk (Exod. xxiii. 19). Such humane injunctions were perhaps specially needed at a time when man's life was little regarded, and animal sacrifices had a tendency to make men cruel and unfeeling, when their symbolical meaning was obscured by long familiarity. These enactments regarding animals, and the mysterious significance affixed to the blood (Gen. ix. 4; Lev. xvii. 10—14), afforded speaking lessons of tenderness and consideration for the inferior creatures, and à fortiori taught regard for the happiness and comfort of fellow-men. Our blessed Lord has spoken of God's care of flowers and the lower creatures of his hand. But the tender mercies; literally, the bowels, regarded as the seat of feeling. The wicked cannot be supposed to have "tender mercies;" hence it is best to take the word in the sense of "feelings," "affections." What should be mercy and love are in an evil man only hard-heartedness and cruelty.

Ver. 11.—A contrast between industry and idleness, repeated at ch. xxviii. 19.

He that tilleth his land. Agriculture was the first of industries, and always highly commended among the Jews, bringing a sure return to the diligent (ch. x. 5; xx. 4; xxvii. 18, 23—27; and Ecclus. xx. 28). **He that followeth after vain** persons; rather, vain things; μάταια, Septuagint, empty, useless employments, profitless business, in contrast to active labour on the land. The Vulgate renders, qui sectatur otium, "he who studieth ease;" but the original, reikim, will not bear this meaning. **Is void of understanding;** he not only, as is implied, will be reduced to poverty, but shows moral weakness and depravity. The Septuagint and Vulgate here introduce a paragraph not found in our Hebrew text: "He who takes pleasure (ὅς ἐστιν ἡδύς) in carouses of wine will leave disgrace in his strongholds (ὀχυρώμασι)" (Isa. xxviii. 7, 8; Hab. ii. 16). Probably this verse is derived from the following, with some corruption of the text.

Ver. 12.—Modern commentators have endeavoured to amend the text of this verse by various methods, which may be seen in Nowack's note on the passage; but the existing reading gives an appropriate sense, and alteration is not absolutely needed, though it is plain that the LXX. had before them something different from the Masoretic text. **The wicked desireth the net of evil men** (Eccles. vii. 26), that he may use the means which they take to enrich themselves; or matsod may mean, not the instrument, but the prey—"such booty as evil men capture;" or yet again, the word may mean "fortress," i.e. the wicked seeks the protection of evil men. So the Vulgate, Desiderium impii munimentum est pessimorum, "What the wicked desire is the support of evil men," or, it may be, "the defence of evil men," i.e. that these may be secured from suppression and interruption. Another interpretation, which, however, seems somewhat forced, is that "the net" is a metaphor for the judgment of God, which overtakes sinners, and into which they run with such blind infatuation that they seem to "desire" it. The safest explanation is the second one given above, which signifies that the wicked man seeks by every means to obtain the prey which he sees sinners obtain, and, as is implied, gets small return for his labour, does not advance his interests. **But the root of the righteous yieldeth fruit.** The root supplies the sap and vigour needed for healthy produce. Without any evil devices or plotting, the righteous gain all that they want as the natural result of their high principles. Another rendering is, "He (the Lord) will give a root of the righteous," will enable them to stand firm in time of trial. Septuagint, "The desires of the impious are evil; but the roots of the pious are in strongholds," *i.e.* are secure.

Ver. 13.—**The wicked is snared by the transgression of his lips**; rather, *in the transgression of the lips is an evil snare* (ch. xviii. 7). A man by speaking unadvisedly or intemperately brings trouble upon himself, involves himself in difficulties which he did not foresee. Often when he has spoken in order to injure others, the slander or the censure has redounded on himself (comp. Ps. vii. 15, 16; ix. 16). **The just**; the man who does not offend with his lips, avoids these snares. The Septuagint here introduces a couplet not found in the Hebrew: "He who looketh gently (ὁ βλέπων λεῖα) shall obtain mercy; but he who frequents the gates [or, 'contends in the gates,' συναντῶν ἐν πύλαις] will harass souls." This seems to mean the man who is calm and considerate for others will himself be treated with pity and consideration (Matt. v. 7); but he who is a gossip, or a busybody, or litigious, will be always vexing his neighbours.

Ver. 14.—**A man shall be satisfied with good by the fruit of his mouth** (ch. xiii. 2; xiv. 14; xviii. 20). A man's words are like seeds, and if they are wise and pure and kindly, they will bring forth the fruit of love and favour and respect. Christian commentators see here a reference to the day of judgment, wherein great stress is laid on the words (Matt. xii. 37). **Of a man's hands.** That which a man has done, his kindly actions, shall meet with full reward (comp. Isa. iii. 10, 11; Matt. xxv. 35, etc.; Rom. ii. 6).

Ver. 15.—**The way of a fool is right in his own eyes**; *i.e.* in his own judgment (ch. iii. 7: xvi. 2). The second clause is best translated, as in the Revised Version, "But he that is wise hearkeneth unto counsel," distrusting his own unaided judgment, which might lead him astray (ch. xiii. 10; xiv. 12; xvi. 25; xxi. 2; comp. Ecclus. xxxv. 19; Tobit iv. 18). Theognis, 221, etc.—

Ὅς τις τοι δοκέει τὸν πλησίον ἴδμεναι οὐδὲν,
  Ἀλλ' αὐτὸς μοῦνος ποικίλα δήνε' ἔχειν,
Κεῖνός γ' ἄφρων ἐστὶ, νόου βεβλαμμένος ἐσθλοῦ,
  Ἴσως γὰρ πάντες ποικίλ' ἐπιστάμεθα.

"Who thinks his neighbour nothing knows,
  And he alone can see,
Is but a fool, for we perhaps
  Know even more than he."

Ver. 16.—**A fool's wrath is presently** ("in the day," αὐθημερόν) **known.** A foolish man, if he is vexed, insulted, or slighted, has no idea of controlling himself or checking the expression of his aroused feelings; he at once, in the same day on which he has been incensed, makes his vexation known. A

prudent man **covereth**—concealeth—**shame**; takes no notice of an affront at the moment, knowing that by resenting it he will only make matters worse, and that it is best to let passions cool before he tries to set the matter right (comp. ch. xx. 22; xxiv. 29). Christ's injunction goes far beyond this maxim of worldly prudence: "I say unto you that ye resist not evil;" "Unto him that smiteth thee on the one cheek, offer also the other" (Matt. v. 39; Luke vi. 29); and it is certain that these maxims might be carried into practice much more than they are, even in the present state of society. Septuagint, "A clever man (πανοῦργος; *callidus*, Vulgate) concealeth his own disgrace." Corn. à Lapide quotes a Hebrew proverb which asserts that a man's character is accurately discerned "by purse, by cup, by anger;" *i.e.* by his conduct in money transactions, under the influence of wine, and in the excitement of anger.

Ver. 17.—**He that speaketh—breatheth out fearlessly** (ch. vi. 19)—**truth showeth forth righteousness.** The truth always conduces to justice and right, not only in a matter of law, but generally and in all cases. Vulgate, "He who speaks that which he knows is a discoverer of justice;" Septuagint, "A just man announces well-proved assurance [or, 'the open truth'] (ἐπιδεικνυμένην πίστιν)." **A false witness showeth forth deceit** (ch. xiv. 5, 25); exhibits his true character, which is fraud, treachery, and wrong-doing.

Ver. 18.—**There is that speaketh.** The word implies speaking thoughtlessly, rashly; hence we may render, "a babbler," "prater." Such a one inflicts wounds with his senseless tattle. **Like the piercings of a sword.** The point of the simile is seen when we remember that the edge of the sword is called its "mouth" in the Hebrew (Gen. xxxiv. 26; Exod. xvii. 13, etc.; comp. Ps. lix. 7; lxiv. 3). The Greek gnome says—

Ξίφος τιτρώσκει σῶμα, τὸν δὲ νοῦν λόγος.

"A sword the body wounds, a word the soul."

Vulgate, *est qui promittit*, which restricts the scope of the clause to the making of vain promises (Lev. v. 4; Numb. xxx. 7—9), continuing, *et quasi gladio pungitur conscientiæ*, "And is pierced as it were by the sword of his conscience." where "conscience" is added to make the meaning plain. Such a man suffers remorse if he breaks his promise, or if, like Jephthah, he keeps it. **The tongue of the wise is health**; it does not pierce and wound like that of the chatterer, rather it soothes and heals even when it reproves (ch. iv. 22; x. 11).

Ver. 19.—**The lip of truth shall be established for ever.** Truth is consistent, invincible, enduring; and the fact belongs not only to Divine truth (Ps. cxvii. 2; Matt. xxiv. 35), but to human, in its measure. Septuagint, "True lips establish testimony," pointing the last word *ad* as *ed.* Is but for a moment; literally, *while I wink the eye* (Jer. xlix. 19; l. 44). Lying never answers in the end; it is soon found out and punished (ch. xix. 9; Ps. lii. 5). Septuagint, "But a hasty (ταχύς; *repentinus*, Vulgate) witness hath an unjust tongue." One who gives his testimony without due consideration, or influenced by evil motives, readily falls into lying and injustice. With the latter half of the verse we may compare the gnome—

’Αλλ’ οὐδὲν ἕρπει ψεῦδος εἰς γῆρας χρόνου.

"Unto old age no lie doth ever live."

"A lie has no legs," is a maxim of wide nationality; and "Truth may be blamed, but shall ne'er be shamed."

Ver. 20.—**Deceit is in the heart of them that imagine evil**; *i.e.* that give evil advice; such are treacherous counsellors, and their advice can only work mischief, not joy and comfort (see on ch. iii. 29). **But to the counsellors of peace** (health and prosperity) **is joy.** They who give wholesome advice diffuse joy around. Vulgate, "Joy attends them;" Septuagint, "They shall be glad;" but the original signifies rather to cause joy than to feel it.

Ver. 21.—**There shall no evil**—mischief—**happen to the just.** The mischief (*aven*) intended is not misfortune, calamity, but the evil consequences that follow on ill-doing (ch. xxii. 8); from these the righteous are saved. Our Lord goes further, and says (Matt. vi. 33), "Seek ye first the kingdom of God, and his righteousness; and all these (temporal) things shall be added unto you." Vulgate, "Nothing that happens can make a just man sorrowful;" for he knows it is all for the best, and he looks toward another life, where all seeming anomalies will be cleared up. Septuagint, "The just man takes pleasure in naught that is unjust." **The wicked shall be filled with mischief**; rather, *with evil,* moral and physical (Ps. xxxii. 10). The Old Testament takes a general view of God's moral government without regarding special anomalies.

Ver. 22.—(Comp. ch. vi. 17; xi. 20.) **They that deal truly**; Septuagint, ὁ δὲ ποιῶν πίστεις, "he who acts in good faith."

Ver. 23.—**A prudent man concealeth knowledge** (ver. 16; ch. x. 14). He is not wont to utter unadvisedly what he knows, but waits for fitting opportunity, either from humility or wise caution. Of course, in some cases reticence is sinful. The LXX., reading the passage differently, renders, "A prudent man is the seat of intelligence (θρόνος αἰσθήσεως)." The heart of fools

proclaimeth foolishness (ch. xiii. 16; xv. 2). A foolish man cannot help exposing the stupid ideas that arise in his mind, which he considers wisdom. Septuagint, "The heart of fools shall meet with curses."

Vers. 24—28 speak of the means of getting on in life.

Ver. 24.—**The hand of the diligent shall bear rule** (ch. x. 4). For "diligent" the Vulgate has *fortium,* "the strong and active;" Septuagint, ἐκλεκτῶν, "choice." Such men are sure to rise to the surface, and get the upper hand in a community, as the LXX. adds, "with facility," by a natural law. **But the slothful** (literally, *slothfulness*) **shall be under tribute;** or, *reduced to compulsory service,* like the Gibeonites in Joshua's time, and the Canaanites under Solomon (Josh. ix. 21, 23; 1 Kings ix. 21). So ch. xi. 29, "The fool shall be slave to the wise;" and an Israelite reduced to poverty might be made a servant (Lev. xxv. 39, 40). The LXX., taking the word in another sense, translates, "The crafty shall be for plunder;" *i.e.* they who think to succeed by fraud and trickery shall become the prey of those who are stronger than themselves.

Ver. 25.—**Heaviness**—care—**in the heart of man maketh it stoop** (ch. xv. 13; xvii. 22). Care brings dejection and despair; hence the Christian is bidden to beware of excessive anxiety, and not to perplex himself with solicitude for the future (Matt. vi. 34; 1 Pet. v. 7). **A good word maketh it glad.**

Λύπην γὰρ εὔνους οἶδεν ἰᾶσθαι λόγος.

"A word of kindness grief's keen smart can heal."

Septuagint, "A word of terror disturbs the heart of a (righteous) man, but a good message will gladden him." The "word of terror" may be an unjust censure, or evil tidings. Says a Servian proverb, "Give me a comrade who will weep with me; one who will laugh I can easily find."

Ver. 26.—**The righteous is more excellent than his neighbour.** This rendering has the authority of the Chaldee, and would signify that a good man is superior to others morally and socially, is more respected and stands higher, though his worldly position be inferior. But the clause is better translated, *The just man is a guide to his neighbour,* directs him in the right way; as the Syriac puts it, "gives good counsel to his friend." Septuagint, "The righteous wise man (ἐπιγνώμων) will be a friend to himself;" Vulgate, "He who regards not loss for a friend's sake is righteous," which is like Christ's word, "Greater love hath no man than this, that a man lay down his life for his friends" (John xv. 13). Hitzig, Delitzsch, and others, reading differently, translate, "A just man spieth out (or, looketh after) his pasture;" *i.e.* he is not like the sinner, hampered and confined by the chain of evil habits and associations, but is free to follow the lead of virtue, and to go whither duty and his own best interests call him. This gives a very good sense, and makes a forcible antithesis with the succeeding clause. **But the way of the wicked seduceth them;** "causes them, the wicked, to err." Far from guiding others aright, the wicked, reaping the moral consequences of their sin, drift hopelessly astray themselves. Before the last clause some manuscripts of the Septuagint add, "But the judgments of the wicked are harsh; evils shall pursue sinners" (ch. xiii. 21). The whole is probably a gloss.

Ver. 27.—**The slothful man (literally,** *sloth)* **roasteth not that which he took in hunting.** There is some doubt concerning the correct meaning of the word translated "roasteth" (חרך), which occurs only in the Chaldee of Dan. iii. 27, where it signifies "burned" or "singed," according to the traditional rendering. It seems to be a proverbial saying, implying either that a lazy man will not take the trouble to hunt, or, if he does hunt, will not prepare the food which he has taken in the chase, or that he does not enjoy it when he has gotten it. Others render, "will not start his prey;" or "catch his prey," Septuagint; or "secure his prey," *i.e.* will not keep in his net what he has caught, but carelessly lets it escape. The Vulgate renders, "The cheat will gain no profit." The word rendered "cheat," *fraudulentus* in the Latin, and δόλιος in the Greek, is the same as that rightly translated "slothful" (ver. 24). **But the substance of a diligent man is precious;** *i.e.* the substance which an honest, industrious man acquires by his labour is stable and of real value. This second clause, however, is variously translated. Revised Version, *But the precious substance of men is to the diligent,* or, *is to be diligent;* Delitzsch, "Diligence is a man's precious possession;" Septuagint, "A pure man is a precious possession." The Authorized Version is probably erroneous, and the rendering should be, as Delitzsch

and Nowack take it, "But a precious possession of a man is diligence."

Ver. 28.—**In the way of righteousness is life** (comp. ch. x. 2). For the promise of temporal prosperity which the Jew saw in such passages as these we substitute a better hope. **And in the pathway thereof—**of righteousness—**there is no death.** Many combine the two words thus: "no-death," *i.e.* immortality; but examples of such combination are not forthcoming, and the anomaly is not necessitated by the failure of the usual rendering to afford an adequate sense. The Greek and Latin versions are noteworthy. Septuagint, "The ways of the revengeful (μνησικάκων) are unto (אֶל, not לֹא) death." St. Chrysostom refers ('Hom. xvi. in Eph.') to this rendering: "He here speaks of vindictiveness; for on the spur of the moment he allows the sufferer to act in order to check the aggressor; but further to bear a grudge he permits not; because the act then is no longer one of passion, nor of boiling rage, but of malice premeditated. Now, God forgives those who may be carried away, perhaps upon a sense of outrage, and rush out to resent it. Hence he says, 'eye for eye;' and yet again 'The ways of the revengeful lead to death." Vulgate, "A devious path leads to death"—a path, that is, which turns aside from the right direction, a life and conversation which are alien from justice and piety. But both the Septuagint and the Vulgate have missed the right meaning of the words in question; *derek nethibah,* "pathway." Many see in this verse a plain evidence that the writer believed in the immortality of the soul. We have reason to suppose that such was his faith, but it cannot be proved from this passage, though we may consider that he was guided to speak in terms to which later knowledge would affix a deeper interpretation (see ch. xiv. 32, and note there). It is Jesus Christ "who hath brought life and immortality (ἀφθαρσίαν) to light through the gospel" (2 Tim. i. 10). Writers in Solomon's time could speak only darkly about this sublime and comforting hope, though later, as in the Book of Wisdom and throughout most of the Apocryphal books, it formed a common topic, and was used as a reason for patience and resignation.

HOMILETICS.

Ver. 3.—*The instability of wickedness.* I. WICKEDNESS MAY BRING TEMPORAL PROSPERITY. It is important to observe the limitations of our subject. The Bible is not an unreasonable book; it does not ignore the patent facts of life; it does not deny that there are pleasures of sin. The very statement that "a man shall not be *established* by wickedness" implies that he may be lifted up, and may really enjoy prosperity for a season. Though not built up, he may be puffed up. This is to be borne in mind, lest the experience come as a delusion. All the warnings about the fatality of a sinful course are given with a frank recognition of its transient advantages. Therefore the occurrence of these advantages does not contradict the warnings.

II. WICKEDNESS DOES NOT SECURE STABLE PROSPERITY. It does not *"establish."* There is no faculty for building in it. There are "tents of wickedness;" but these are frail and flimsy compared to "the house of the Lord" (Ps. lxxxiv.). When at its best and brightest, the product of evil is but a bubble that will burst with a touch of right-eous judgment. The equilibrium is unstable. There is no foundation of truth to support the poor structure; it is not built according to the laws of righteousness; it is not guarded against the shock of adverse circumstances. The bad prosperous man has many enemies. All the course of the universe is in the long run directed against him. He has not God on his side, and at any moment the suspended hand of justice may fall upon his unsheltered head.

III. WICKEDNESS WILL NOT LEAD TO PERMANENT PROSPERITY. The pleasures of sin, at the best, do but endure for a season. The sinner lives, so to speak, "from hand to mouth." If in this life only he had hope, the prospect would be poor; for most of the delights of wickedness are very brief, and the consequences of shame and trouble soon follow even upon earth. The harvest of a young man's folly may be reaped by middle age. But when we consider the eternal future, the utter inability of wickedness to establish any enduring prosperity becomes clearly visible. For no one can pretend that his wicked devices extend beyond the grave; and no one can fortify himself against the pains of a future state by any successful Macchiavellianism, however cleverly devised it may be with a view to worldly security.

IV. WICKEDNESS SECURES NO PROSPERITY TO A MAN HIMSELF. *"A man* shall not be established by wickedness." His business may be so established; his plans and devices may be made firm. But these things are not the man himself, and all the while they are prospering he may be tottering to ruin, like a consumptive millionaire or a paralytic winner of a lottery-prize. Then the whole pursuit has ended in failure; for what is the use of the huntsman's success in shooting the game if he cannot bring home and enjoy what he has acquired?

V. RIGHTEOUSNESS IS A TRUE SECURITY. It has a root in the eternal laws of God. Though the storm tear off its "peaceable fruits," this deep and hidden source remains. We cannot be satisfied with only wearing a "robe of righteousness." We must have the living thing with its deep root—a growth which Christ plants (Rom. iii. 22).

Ver. 10.—*Justice to animals.* I. ANIMALS HAVE RIGHTS WHICH MAY BE OUTRAGED BY INJUSTICE. We hear more of kindness to animals than of justice towards them. It seems to be assumed that they have no rights, and that all our consideration for them must spring from pure generosity, perhaps even from a superabundant condescension. The exercise of it is treated almost as a work of supererogation. These assumptions are based on an inordinate regard for our own supremacy. Man may consider himself as the lord of creation. If he may take this exalted view of himself, he cannot on that account shake off all obligations towards the dumb serfs on his estate. This natural feudalism requires protection, etc., from the aristocracy of creation, while it allows of the exaction of dues from the underlings. For we are all animals, though men are more than animals. All orders of creation are made by one God, and all share in many common wants and feelings. The young lions are represented as crying to God for their food, and he as giving them their meat in due season. Christ tells us that God feeds the ravens—those wild birds of the mountains, while not a homely sparrow falls to the ground without the notice of our heavenly Father. It is not for us to be above giving their due to fellow-creatures for whom God cares so tenderly. These animals not only make mute appeals to our compassion; they cannot be ill treated without injustice.

II. THE CHARACTER OF A MAN WILL BE REVEALED BY HIS TREATMENT OF ANIMALS. 1. *Character is revealed in the treatment of the helpless.* A man's cattle are his property, and they are in his power. He is more free in his treatment of them than in his behaviour towards his fellow-men. Therefore his true character will come out the more clearly when he is in his stable than when he is in his dining-room. 2. *The lower creatures claim consideration.* (1) Their very inferiority gives point to this claim. Man stands to them somewhat in the position of a God. Therefore it becomes him to show the spirit of a limited Providence in his treatment of them. (2) Moreover, when he owns any animals, he is involved in especial responsibilities. He is their guardian, and their welfare largely depends upon him. (3) Further, if they render him patient service, the least that he can do is to give them all things necessary to make their lot of bondage happy to them. (4) Lastly, their affectionateness vastly strengthens the ties of obligation. Horses and dogs learn to love their masters, and love has its sacred claims in animals as well as in men. 3. *Lack of consideration for animals is a sign of a base nature.* The very sympathy of the wicked is cruelty, but this cruelty is not possible without the evil heart, of which it is the corrupt fruit. The brutal cattle-drover, and the heartless horseman who lashes his weary, patient animal, do but make a public exhibition of their own low natures.

Ver. 17.—*Truth and righteousness.* We have here a suggestion of the close connection between truth and righteousness. This connection is based on a reciprocal relation. Truthfulness is a trait of righteousness, and righteousness is advanced by truthfulness.

I. TRUTHFULNESS IS A TRAIT OF RIGHTEOUSNESS. The truth here referred to is that which is most often mentioned in the Bible, viz. subjective truth, the agreement between our convictions and our utterances. We cannot attain to perfect objective truth, to the truth which consists in an agreement between our beliefs and the facts of the universe, because all men sometimes err even with the most innocent intention of finding the truth. We are liable to delusions from without, and to the influence of an unconscious bias from within. But we can all utter what we believe to be true. Now, this truth-speaking is one of the most solemn and absolute obligations of righteousness. 1. *The grounds of the obligation.* (1) We recognize the awful duty of truthfulness in our conscience. (2) The Teutonic conscience is supposed to respond to this duty more readily than the Oriental conscience. Yet it is clearly and firmly insisted on in the Bible. (3) It is most evident in the transparent life of Christ, who is a true Witness to the truth (John xviii. 37). (4) All social arrangements presuppose truthfulness; without it society becomes a confusion. Truth cements the social fabric; lying dissolves it. A city of universal liars would be an inferno of mutual distrust, suspicion, and necessary isolation. 2. *The bearing of the obligation.* (1) On small things. Slight inaccuracies of speech may seem to be of no importance; but they open the door for more gross forms of deceit, by generating a habit of indifference to truth. Apart from this tendency, the least untruth is treason against the royal supremacy of truth. (2) In difficult cases. When we are severely tried, it is hard to speak the truth. Yet it is just then that truthfulness becomes a positive quality. Under such circumstances only a character that is morally sound will stand the strain. Indeed, it needs the grace of Christ to keep true in word and deed under all provocations to easier paths.

II. RIGHTEOUSNESS IS ADVANCED BY TRUTHFULNESS. 1. *In the individual.* Untruthfulness is certain to issue in a lower moral tone all round. We cannot abandon one of the guardian towers of the soul without risking the whole citadel. The liar is not only a person who uses false language. His cowardly habit eats into the very heart of virtue and rots the moral fibre of his soul. On the other hand, there is no more bracing moral tonic than a loyal and reverent regard for truth. The true man is likely to be honest, just, and pure in all respects. 2. *In the world.* Truth always makes for righteousness. No greater blunder was ever made than the supposition that "pious frauds" could be used for advancing the cause of Christianity. Any temporary gain that could be produced in this way must be unsound from the first, and the ultimate issue is certain to be moral indifference and unbelief. Some truths are unpleasant, some ugly, some seemingly hurtful. Yet, in the end, truth makes for soul-health. Above all, is not he who is "the Truth" also the great Source of the world's righteousness?

Ver. 23.—*Concealing knowledge.* I. KNOWLEDGE MUST FIRST BE POSSESSED. We cannot hide what we do not hold. The idea of secreting knowledge suggests the owning of a large amount of it, or at least of knowledge of some value. The tradesman who puts all his wares in the window is not the proprietor of a large stock. It cannot be a superficial mind which conceals much knowledge. Such an action suggests a granary of truth, a storehouse of ideas, a territory rich in minerals that lie far below the surface.

II. KNOWLEDGE MUST THEN BE PRIZED. Men may hide things from various motives —from shame as much as from love, because the things are bad quite as much as on account of any value set upon them. Thus the criminal tries to hide the evidences of his crime—buries his victim in a wood, or flings the tell-tale knife into a pond. But it is not with this ugly knowledge, which a man would only too gladly banish from his own mind, that we are now concerned. There are choice secrets, rare attainments, and much-valued stores of information. Such knowledge may well be kept for its own sake.

III. KNOWLEDGE SHOULD NEVER BE DISPLAYED. The vanity which would make a show of knowledge is one of the weakest traits of humanity. It is usually a sign that but little is really known. A great pretence is made by the aid of a mere smattering of information cleverly arranged, like the scenery on a small stage adjusted to suggest a long vista. Such a parade of learning springs from more love of admiration than love of truth. The loyal seeker after truth will have little thought of "making an effect" by the exhibition of his mental properties. He will prize his possessions on their own account, though no one else may be aware of their existence.

IV. KNOWLEDGE MAY SOMETIMES BE ABUSED. We may know damaging facts about a neighbour, and then charity will urge us to hide our knowledge. The feverish passion for gossiping tears the cloak of common decency which should cover the knowledge of what is bad. It is shocking that details of crime and vice are made familiar to millions by the blare of the newspaper trumpet. But, further, the knowledge of good things may sometimes be abused. The revelation may be premature; God did not send forth his Son till "the fulness of the times." Truth may be misapprehended. The most sacred things may be degraded by irreverent handling.

V. KNOWLEDGE IS TO BE USED. We do not have it as a hidden jewel to be laid by in a secret place and forgotten. Though buried in the soul and little talked about, it is a living thing, like a seed in the soil. It is given us that it may influence our lives and become a vital part of our souls.

VI. KNOWLEDGE SHOULD BE WISELY IMPARTED. We have no right to keep to ourselves any knowledge that would be helpful to our brethren. Concealment must never go so far as to hide from others the good news of God. The gospel is for the world. All Divine truth is for all honest inquirers. "He that hath ears to hear, let him hear."

Ver. 25.—*Depression.* This proverb shows us depression of soul in its own distress and gloom, and then gives a hint of the way in which it may be remedied.

I. THE STATE OF DEPRESSION. The heart is bowed down with heaviness. This is very different from external adversity and from the natural feelings that are produced by such a condition. It may be quite independent of circumstances. The buoyant soul will face great calamities with comparative cheerfulness, while the heavy heart is depressed among signs of unbroken prosperity. 1. *Depression is caused by personal conditions.* Not being the reflection of circumstance, it must be the expression of internal experience. Frequently it is a result of a man's bodily state, a merely nervous disorder or a consequence of deranged health. We look for religious remedies when the true cure is in the hands of the physician. But it may be that melancholy thoughts have depressed the soul. Then the gloom within is projected on to the world without, and the sunniest scenes are overclouded. 2. *Depression is a deplorable state of mind.* It is a source of deep distress to the sufferer. It spreads an atmosphere of gloom among others. It checks enterprise by paralyzing hope. If the joy of the Lord is our strength, sorrow of soul must be a source of weakness. Depressed Christian people discredit the name of religion by making it appear unattractive to the world. Gratitude is scarcely compatible with depression, and the soul that has given way to this deplorable experience is not likely to sing the praises of God. Thus depression tends to check worship. On the other hand, it reveals the soul's great need of God, who in his long-suffering compassion has pity on his distressed children. "He knoweth our frame, he remembereth that we are dust."

II. The cure of depression. When it is due to physical causes, physical remedies may be needed. In many cases, change of scene and brighter circumstances may help to remove it. But there are also social and moral remedies, among which not the least valuable is a wise expression of brotherly kindness. Pure condolence may do more harm than good by aggravating the painful symptoms, and yet "a good word maketh" the heart "glad." 1. *The utterance of the word may be helpful.* Isolation and silence are depressing. "It is not good for man to be alone." The heavy heart seeks solitude, and uncongenial society cannot be helpful. But sympathetic society *is* healing, even though it be admitted with reluctance. Christ founded a Church. He sought to cheer his people amid the various scenes of their heavenward pilgrimage by means of Christian companionship. 2. *The contents of the word should be helpful.* We may not do much good by moralizing. Though advice for the depressed is easy to find, it is not often acceptable. But words of affection are wonderfully healing. Cheerful thoughts should help the depressed. 3. *It is our duty to relieve the depressed.* To blame, to shun, or to patronize are all un-Christlike methods. But the Christian should endeavour to make the world brighter by his presence. Above all, if it is possible to lead the depressed to hope in God, the surest method of cure is within our reach.

Ver. 28.—*Righteousness and life.* I. The association of righteousness and life. It is something to have two such great ideas brought into close juxtaposition. Their very proximity is a revelation. They mutually illumine one another. We know more of righteousness when we see its bearing on life, and we have a better understanding of life when we recognize its dependence on righteousness. There is thus a *relationship* of ideas to be recognized here over and above the separate forms of the ideas themselves. The limitation of the subject is also instructive. We do not see to what else righteousness may be related. It may or it may not bring happiness, wealth, and success. What it is related to is distinct from all these ends, and greater than any of them—viz. life.

II. The form of righteousness that is connected with life. This is the *path* of righteousness. It is not righteousness regarded as an abstract idea, or viewed only as a law. It is not an external garment of righteousness, nor an internal principle of righteousness. It does not consist in one or more isolated deeds of righteousness. On the contrary, what is here presented to us is a view of a continuous course of righteous action. It may not be the highest path of holiness, but it is at least a right path. The traveller may stumble upon it, loiter by the way, even forget himself at times, and sleep. Yet, on the whole, this is the course he pursues. He is trying to do the right thing in his daily experience.

III. The influence of righteousness upon life. The path *is* life. 1. It is the path of *a living soul.* No one can continuously pursue a right course unless he has the spiritual life in him. Dead souls may be galvanized into momentary spasms of goodness by an electrifying example or the shock of a great authority. But the path of righteousness can only be trodden by those who have within them the soul-energy to follow it. 2. It is the path that *quickens life.* It is not like the deadly tracts of sin, those ways of wickedness that lead down into the fatal swamps of soul-death. This path runs over bracing mountain heights. 3. It is the path that *leads to life.* There is a fuller life beyond, not yet reached; and righteousness is the way to it. Every attainment in holiness is accompanied by a deepening of the soul-life. The way of God leads to eternal life. The gospel of Christ does not set aside this Old Testament principle, but it gives the new righteousness of a new life.

IV. The fatal result of leaving righteousness. "A devious way leadeth to death." 1. *The way of evil is devious.* It is not only an alternative; it is a departure from the normal course. He who is in it is where he ought not to be. Then this way is no direct high-road; it is a wandering bypath. 2. *The deviousness of the way is fatal to the traveller upon it.* The higher way is made for the good purpose of leading to the city of life. The devious way is not purposely made; it is a lawless beaten track, which runs out into the wilderness. It must be dangerous to follow such a course. To pursue it to the end is to court soul-destruction.

HOMILIES BY VARIOUS AUTHORS.

Vers. 1—3.—*Primary truths.* I. The wisdom of submission, the folly of resistance, to reproof. As self-knowledge is the most precious and indispensable, and as it comes to us by chastisement, *i.e.* by disappointment, humiliation, pain of various kinds,—to welcome correction, to be willing and anxious to know our faults, is the mark of true wisdom. To fret at reproof, to be angry with the counsellor, to hate the revealing light, is the worst folly and stupidity.

II. The favour and the disfavour of God are discriminating. The good reap his good will; the crafty and malicious are exposed to his condemnation.

III. Moral stability and instability. Wickedness gives no firm foundation. The bad man is insecure, as a tottering wall or a leaning fence. The good man is like the oak, firmly and widely rooted, which may defy a thousand blasts and storms.—J.

Vers. 4—11.—*Blessings and miseries of domestic life.* I. Elements of happiness in the home. 1. *The virtuous wife.* (Ver. 4.) The word is literally "a woman of *power*," and the idea of force lies in the word and the idea of *virtue*. Her moral force and influence makes itself felt in all the life of the household (ch. xxxi. 10; Ruth iii. 11). She is her husband's "crown of rejoicing" (comp. 1 Thess. ii. 19), his glory and pride.

> "A thousand decencies do daily flow
> From all her thoughts and actions."

2. *Noble thoughts and words.* (Ver. 5.) This expression includes, of course, noble words and deeds, and implies all that we speak of as *high principles.* And these are the very foundations and columns of the home. But expressly also the straightforward speech of the good man is named. (Ver. 6.) There is "deliverance" in the mouth of the righteous; men may build upon his word, which is as good as his bond. 3. Hence, *stability belongs to the house of the good man.* (Ver. 7.) If we trace the rise of great families who have become famous in the annals of their country, the lesson is on the whole brought home to us that it is integrity, the true qualities of manhood, which formed the foundation of their greatness. On a smaller scale, the history of village households may bring to light the same truth. There are names in every neighbourhood known as synonyms of integrity from father to son through generations. 4. *Prudence* is an indispensable element in character and reputation. But let us give the proper extension to the idea of prudence which it has in this book. It is the wide view of life—the mind "looking before and after," the contemplation of all things in their long issues, their bearings upon God, destiny, and eternity. The prudence which often passes by that name may be no prudence in this higher sense. 5. *Self-help.* (Ver. 9.) To be "king of two hands," and bear one's part in every useful toil and art, to be a true "working man," is the only honourable and true way of living. "Trust in thyself;" every heart vibrates to that iron string. "Heaven helps those who help themselves." Proverbs unite with experience to bid us lean upon the energies God has placed in brain and hand and tongue. He is never helpless who knows the secret of that self-reliance which is one with trust in God. 6. *Mercifulness.* (Ver. 10.) The good man "knows the soul of his beast;" enters into their feelings, pains, and needs, and feeds them well. The Law of Moses is noted for its kindness to animals. And in the East generally there is a deep sense that animals are not only the slaves of man, but the creatures of God. A person's behaviour to dumb creatures is, like behaviour to women and children, a significant part of character. 7. *Industry and diligence.* (Ver. 11.) The picture of the hard-working farmer or peasant rises to the mind's eye. Enough bread, competence, is ever conditioned by industry. Times may go hard with the farmer, but the evil that is foreseen and fought against by extra diligence is no evil when it comes; and how seldom are the truly industrious known to want, even in the most unfavourable seasons! This is a bright picture of domestic soundness, happiness, and prosperity. Let us contrast it with—

II. Elements of misery in the home. 1. *The vicious wife.* Like a canker in her husband's bones. The slothful, or drunken, or extravagant, or frivolous wife is the centre of all evil in the house; she is like a stagnant pool in a weed-grown garden. One may tell in many cases by the mere aspect of the house whether there be a good wife and mother dwelling there or not. 2. *Unprincipled habits.* (Ver. 5.) Where the speech is impure, where there is mutual reserve and concealment, conspiracy and counter-conspiracy going on, neither truth nor love, how can a home be otherwise than cursed? 3. *Fierce spite.* (Ver. 6.) All spite is murderous, and if it does not issue in the last extreme of violence, at least it lacerates the heart, burns, and is self-consuming. When taunts, recriminations, answering again, fill the air of a house, the very idea of the family and its peace must vanish. 4. *Dissolution and break-up.* There are homes that go to pieces, names that sink into obscurity, families that die out; and a moral lesson may here too be often inferred. 5. *Moral perversity* is at the root of these evils (ver. 8). There is a twist in the affections, a guilty misdirection of the will. Contempt in others' minds reflects the moral basis, and prophesies its miserable end. 6. *Idle vanity and pride*, again, contrasted with that habit of honest self-help which is free from false shame, is another of the tokens that things are not going well. To be above one's situation, to shun humble employment, to stand upon one's dignity,—these are sure enough marks of want of moral power, and so of true stability. 7. *Cruelty*, again, to inferiors or to dumb creatures marks the corrupt heart. Even the comparative tenderness of the bad man is a spurious thing, for there is no real kindness from a heart without love. 8. The *frivolous pursuit of pleasure*, again, the "chase after vanity," opposed to steady industry, is one of the unfailing accompaniments of folly and conducements to failure, poverty, and misery.

LESSONS. 1. The indications of a sound state of things in the household, or the reverse, are numerous and manifold, but all connected together. Partial symptoms may point to widespread and deeply seated evil. 2. At bottom the one condition of happiness is the fear of God and the love of one's neighbour; and the cause of misery is a void of both.—J.

Vers. 12—22.—*Virtues and vices in civil life.* I. SOME VICES OF SOCIETY. 1. *Envious greed.* (Ver. 12.) The wicked desires the "takings" of the evil. It is a general description of greedy strife and competition, one man trying to forestall another in the bargain, or to profit at the expense of his loss; a mutually destructive process, a grinding of egoistic passions against one another, so that there can be no mutual confidence nor peace (Isa. xlviii. 22; lvii. 21). The hard selfishness of business life, which may be worse than war, which elicits generosity and self-denial. 2. *Tricks of speech.* (Ver. 13.) How much of this there is, in subtler forms than those of ancient life, in our day! Exaggerations of value, suppression of faults in articles of commerce, lying advertisements, coloured descriptions, etc.,—all these are snares, distinct breaches of the moral law; and were they not compensated by truth and honesty in other directions, society must crumble. 3. *Conceit of shrewdness* (ver. 14) is a common mark of dishonest men. This may seem right in their own eyes, no matter what a correct moral judgment may have to say about it. There may lurk a profound immorality beneath the constant phrase, "It pays!" Want of principle never does *pay*, in God's sense. The seeming success on which such men pride themselves is not real. They laugh at the preacher, but expose themselves to a more profound derision. 4. *Passion and impetuosity.* (Ver. 16.) The temper unfits for social intercourse and business. Flaming out at the first provocation, it shows an absence of reflection and self-control. How many unhappy wounds have been inflicted, either in word or deed; how many opportunities lost, friendships broken, through mere temper! 5. *Lying and deceit.* (Ver. 17.) The teaching of the book harps upon this string again and again. For does not all evil reduce itself to a lie in its essence? And is not deceit or treachery in some form the real canker in a decaying society, the last cause of all calamity? "We are betrayed!" was the constant exclamation of the French soldiers during the last war, upon the occurrence of a defeat. But it is self-betrayal that is the most dangerous. 6. *Foulness or violence of speech.* (Ver. 18.) The speech of the fool is compared to the thrusts of a sword. Not only all abusive and violent language, but all that is wanting in tact, imagination of others' situation, is condemned. 7. *Designing craft.* (Ver. 20.) The wicked heart is a constant forge of mischief. And yet, after this catalogue of social ills, these moral diseases that prey upon the body of society and the state, let us be comforted in the recollection (1) that all evil is transient (ver. 19); and (2) that its just and appropriate punishment is inevitable. The first and last of frauds with the wicked is that he has cheated himself and laid a train of malicious devices which will take effect upon his own soul certainly, whoever else may escape.

II. SOCIAL VIRTUES. 1. They are the *condition of security* to the practiser of them. The root of the righteous is firmly fixed (ver. 12). In time of distress he finds resources and means of escape (ver. 13). 2. They yield him a *revenue of blessing.* He reaps the good fruit of his wise counsels and pure speech. They come back to him in echoes—the words of truth he has spoken to others (ch. xiii. 2; xviii. 20). And so too with his good actions. They come back with blessing to him who sent them forth with a prayer (ver. 14). Spiritual investments bring certain if slow returns. 3. Some *characteristics* of virtue and wisdom *enumerated.* (1) It is the part of wisdom to *listen* to *all* proffered advice, from any quarter, to discriminate and select that which is good, and then *follow* it (ver. 15). In critical times we ought, indeed, to find ourselves our own best counsellors, in the privacy of prayer, in communion with the Divine Spirit. But it is ever well to consult friends. Conversation with such wonderfully helps us to clear our own perceptions, resolve our own doubts, confirm our own right decisions. (2) It is the part of prudence to *ignore affronts* (ver. 16), instead of hastily resenting them like the fool. A good illustration may be taken from Saul, as showing the contrast in the same person of wisdom and folly in this matter (1 Sam. x. 27 and xx. 30—33). In the heathen world, Socrates was a noble example of patience under injuries. He taught his disciples that the man who offered an unjust affront really more injured himself than him who received it; and that if the insulted person resented it, he did but place himself on a level with the aggressor. Either you have deserved the affront or you have not. If you have, submit to it as a chastisement; if you have not, content yourself with the testimony of your conscience. But above all, the example of our Saviour is the example for us, "who when he was reviled, reviled not again, but submitted himself to him that judgeth righteously." His whole behaviour at his trial should make a deeper impression upon us than a thousand arguments. 4. *Truthful speech* is one of the most eminent signs of virtue and godliness. How constantly is this emphasized! (1) *Truthful and right* speech can only proceed from the truthful mind. "He who breathes truth," says ver. 17, "utters right." We must make truth the atmosphere of our being, our very life itself, as in ancient thought the breath is identified with the life. (2) *Truthful and wise speech* is also known by its *effects* (ver. 18). It *heals,* it brings salvation—correction to error, comfort to the wounded heart. Compare the picture of our Lord in the synagogue at Nazareth, and the words he quotes from Isaiah as expressive of the purport of his ministry (Luke iv. 16, etc.). (3) It is *valid, abiding,* permanent in value (ver. 19). Much in our knowledge is subject to the laws of change and growth. We grow out of the old and into the new. But the simple sentiments of piety and duty common to all good men are capable of no change, no decay. Of them all the good man will ever say, "So was it when I was a boy; so is it now I am a man; so let it be when I grow old!" 5. *Joy, peace, and eternal safety* are the portion of the wise and just (vers. 20, 21). Joy in the heart, peace in the home and amongst neighbours, safety here and hereafter. Translated into the language of the gospel, "Glory, honour, immortality, and eternal life!" (Rom. ii. 7). For in one word, he enjoys the favour of his God, and this contains all things (ver. 22).—J.

Ver. 23.—*Experimental truths:* 1. *Prudent reserve and foolish babbling.* I. PRUDENCE HAS REGARD TO TIME, PLACE, AND PERSONS; FOLLY HAS NONE.

II. PRUDENCE KNOWS THAT THERE IS A TIME FOR SILENCE; THE FOOL WILL STILL BE TALKING. A quiet tongue shows a sound head.

III. ANXIETY TO MAKE KNOWN OUR OPINIONS MAY BE BUT ANXIETY TO EXALT OURSELVES. Great talkers are great nuisances. The ambitious aim to shine cannot be hidden. The fool talks as if he were ambitious to be known for a fool.

IV. SILENCE IS ALWAYS SEASONABLE IN REFERENCE TO SUBJECTS WE DO NOT UNDERSTAND. Were this rule observed, conversation would be generally more entertaining and more profitable. At the same time, a great many pulpits would be emptied, and publishers and printers would have a sorry time of it (comp. 1 Tim. i. 6, 7). Let us confess that there is a great deal of the fool in every one of us.—J.

Ver. 24.—2. *The promotion of the diligent and the subjection of the slothful.* I. THE DILIGENT RISE IN LIFE. This is too obvious to need insisting upon. But often, when wonder is expressed at the rise of ordinary men, this solution may be recurred to. As a rule, it is not the greatest wits who fill the high places of the realm, but the greatest workers.

II. HE ONLY IS FIT TO GOVERN WHO HAS BEEN WILLING TO SERVE. For in truth the spirit of the true servant and that of the true ruler are alike in principle; it is respect for law, for right beyond and above self-will and self-interest, which animates both. If this has been proved in the trials of an inferior situation, its genuineness has been discovered, and it becomes a title to promotion. Abraham's servant (Gen. xxiv. 2, 10) and Joseph (Gen. xxxix. 4, 22) are illustrations from patriarchal life.

III. THE SLOTHFUL DECAY. This too is obvious. But perhaps we often fail to fix the stigma of sloth in the right place. Many busy, energetic, fussy people miscarry because their activity is ill-placed. To neglect one's *proper vocation and work* is idleness, no matter what may be the uncalled-for activity in other directions.—J.

Ver. 25.—3. *Depression and comfort.* I. DEPRESSION IS COMMON.
II. TROUBLE AFFECTS THE HEART. When we use the word "discouragement" we point to a state that is both bodily and psychical. The action of the heart is lowered, and there is less energy to act and to endure.
III. THE IMMEDIATE EFFECT OF SYMPATHY. The kindly word, and all that it expresses of love and fellow-feeling on the part of our friend, quickens the pulse, and restores, as by magic, the tone of the mind.—J.

Ver. 26.—4. *Good guidance and misleading counsels.* The true translation seems to be, "The righteous directs his friend aright : but the way of the wicked leads them astray."
I. WE ARE ALL SUSCEPTIBLE TO THE INFLUENCES OF THOSE ABOUT US. This is true even of the strongest minds; how much more of the feebler!
II. WE ARE ALWAYS SAFE IN THE COMPANY OF MEN OF RECTITUDE. The character of the man, not his mere opinions, is the force that goes forth from him to enlighten and guide.
III. WE ARE NEVER SAFE IN THE COMPANY OF UNPRINCIPLED PERSONS; no matter how correct their conversation or unexceptionable their expressed opinions.—J.

Ver. 27.—5. *Laxity and industry.* I. LAXITY GOES EMPTY-HANDED. The proverb seems to call up the image of a hunter who is too lazy to pursue the game.
II. INDUSTRY IS ITSELF A CAPITAL. Toil is as good as treasure; such seems to be the force of the proverb. And we may be reminded of the parable of the farmer who indicated to his sons the treasure in the field; their persevering toil in digging led to their enrichment.—J.

Ver. 28.—6. *The straight road and the bypath.* I. RECTITUDE MAY BE COMPARED TO A STRAIGHT ROAD. It has a definite beginning, a clearly marked course, a happy termination.
II. ALL IMMORALITY AND IRRELIGION MAY BE COMPARED TO BYPATHS. See Bunyan's Bypath Meadow in ' Pilgrim's Progress.'
III. LIFE AND DEATH ARE THE TWO GREAT TERMINI. All the more impressive because we know not what they contain of blissful or of dread meaning : " Behold, I set before you life and death ! " is the constant cry of wisdom, of every true teacher, of the unchanging gospel.—J.

Vers. 1, 15.—*The downward and the upward paths.* Whether we are daily ascending or descending depends very much on whether we are ready or are refusing *to learn.* The man of open mind is he who moves up, but the man whose soul is shut against the light is he who is going down.

I. THE DOWNWARD PATH. We strike one point in this path when we come to: 1. *The forming of a false estimate of ourself.* When "our way is right in our own eyes" (ver. 15), and that way is the wrong one, we are certainly in the road that dips downward. The wise who love us truly are grieved when they see us imagining ourselves to be humble when we are proud of heart, generous when we are selfish, spiritual when we are worldly minded, sons of God when we are children of darkness; they know well and sorrow much that we are in a bad way, in the downward road. 2. *The consequent refusal* to receive instruction. The man who thinks himself right is one who will oppose himself to all those who, and to all things which, approach him to instruct and to correct. He takes up a constant attitude of rejection. Whenever God speaks to him by any one of his many agents and influences, he is resolutely and persistently deaf. 3. *The consequent sinking* into a lower state; he becomes "brutish." A man who never admits correcting and purifying thoughts into his mind is sure to decline morally and spiritually. If our soul is not fed with truth, and is not cleansed with the purifying streams of Divine wisdom, it is certain to recede in worth; it will partake more and more of earthly elements. The finer, the nobler, the more elevating and enlarging elements of character will be absent or will grow weaker; the man will sink; he will become brutish.

II. THE UPWARD PATH. This is, naturally and necessarily, the reverse of the other. It is that wherein: 1. We form a *true* estimate of ourselves. 2. We *open* our minds to welcome wisdom from all quarters. We hearken "unto counsel," *i.e.* to the words of those who are wiser than ourselves. And it may be that some who have much less learning, or experience, or intellectual capacity than we can claim are in a position to advise us concerning the way of life. It may be even "the little child" who will "lead" us into the circle of truth, into the kingdom of God. And not only unto "counsel" shall we hearken; we shall give heed, if we are wise, to the suggestions of nature, to the teaching of events, to the promptings of the Divine Spirit. We shall be always ready and even eager to learn and willing to apply. 3. We attain to a higher and deeper wisdom. "Whoso loveth instruction loveth knowledge." In the upward way which he of the humble heart and open mind is travelling there grow the rich fruits of heavenly wisdom. The higher we ascend, the more of these shall we see and gather. To love counsel is to love knowledge; it is to love truth; it is to become the friend and disciple and depository of wisdom. There is a knowledge which is very precious that may be had of all men; it is found on the plain where all feet can tread. There is also a knowledge which dwells upon the hills; only the traveller can reach this and partake of it; and the path which climbs this height is the path of humility and heedfulness; it is taken only by those who are conscious of their own defect, and who are eager to learn *all* the lessons which the Divine teacher is seeking to impart.—C.

Vers. 3, 12.—*Strength and fruitfulness.* Concerning the righteous man two things are here affirmed.

I. IN HIM IS STRENGTH. "The root of the righteous shall never be moved." The strong wind comes and blows down the tree which has not struck its roots far into the soil; it tears it up by the roots and stretches it prone upon the ground. It has no strength to stand because its root is easily moved. The righteous man is a tree of another kind; *his* root shall never be moved; he will stand against the storm. But he must be a man who deserves to be called and considered "righteous" because he is such in deed and in truth; for they are many who pass for such of whom no such affirmation as this can be made. The man of whom the text speaks: 1. *Is well rooted.* He is rooted (1) in *Divine truth,* and not merely in human speculation; (2) in *deep conviction,* and not merely in indolent acceptance of inherited belief, or in strong but evanescent emotion; (3) in the *fixed habit* of the soul and of the life, and not merely in occasional, spasmodic outbursts. 2. *Is immovable.* There may come against him the strong winds of bodily indulgence, or of pure affection, or of intellectual struggle and perplexity, or of worldly pressure; but they do not avail; he is immovable; his roots only strike deeper and spread further in the ground. He "stands fast in the Lord;" he is a conqueror through Christ who loves him. For: 3. He is *upheld by Divine power.* While his own spiritual condition and his moral habits have much to do with his steadfastness, he will be the first to say that God is "upholding him in his integrity, and setting him before his face."

II. IN HIM IS FRUITFULNESS. "The root of the righteous yieldeth fruit" (ver. 12). The ungodly man cannot be said to bear fruit, for the product of his soul and of his life does not deserve that fair name. 1. The *forms* of godly fruitfulness are these : (1) all excellency of spirit; (2) all beauty and worthiness of life, the presence of that which is pleasing in the sight of God and admirable in the sight of man; (3) all earnest endeavour to do good, the patient, persevering effort to instil the thoughts of Christ into the minds of men, to awaken their slumbering consciences, to lift up their lives, to ennoble their character, to enlarge their destiny. 2. The *source and the security* of such fruitfulness are : (1) Union with the living Vine. (2) Abiding in him (John xv. 1—8). (3) The wise and kind discipline of the Divine Husbandman (John xv. 2 ; Heb. xii. 10, 11).—C.

Ver. 5.—*Right (just) thoughts.* "The thoughts of the righteous are right," or are "just" (Revised Version). There is something more than a truism in these words. We may see first—

I. THE PLACE OF THOUGHT IN MAN. This is one of the greatest importance, for it is the deepest of all; it is at the very foundation. 1. *Conduct rests on character.* It is often said that conduct is the greater part of life; it is certainly that part which is most conspicuous, and therefore most influential. But it is superficial; it rests on character ; it depends on the principles which are within the soul. It is these which determine a man's position in the kingdom of God. 2. Character is determined by *our prevalent and established feeling ;* by what we have learned to love, by what we have come to hate. As a man *thinketh in his heart,* as he feels in his soul, *so is he ;* it is our final and fixed attachments and repulsions that decide our character. 3. *Feeling springs from thought.* As we think, we feel. By the thoughts admitted to our minds and entertained there are determined our loves and our hatreds. Life, therefore, is ultimately built on thought. What are we thinking?—this is the vital question. Now, the thoughts of the righteous, the upright, the good, the true man, are right, or *just.*

II. THE JUST THOUGHTS OF THE GOOD. A good man's thoughts are such as are : 1. *Just to himself.* He owes it to himself to think only those thoughts which are pure and true. If he harbours those which are impure and untrue, he is doing himself deadly injury, he is inflicting on his spirit, on himself, a fatal wound. This he has no right to do; he is bound, in justice to himself, to guard the gate of his mind against these—to admit only those which are true and pure. 2. *Just to his neighbours.* He owes it to them to think thoughts that are *honest* and *charitable.* We wrong our brethren, in truth and fact if not in appearance, when we think of them that which is not fair toward them. Every really righteous man will therefore banish thoughts which are not thoroughly honest, and also those which are uncharitable; for to be uncharitable is to be essentially and most materially unjust. 3. *Just to God.* We owe to our Divine Creator and Redeemer all thoughts which are (1) reverent, leading us to piety and devotion ; (2) grateful, leading us to thankful praise ; (3) submissive, leading us to the one decisive, all-inclusive act of self-surrender, and to daily and hourly obedience to his holy will ; (4) *trustful,* leading us to a calm assurance that all is well with us, and that the darkness or the twilight will pass into the perfect day.—C.

Ver. 9.—*Consideration or comfort ?* It is worth remarking that we might obtain a very wholesome truth from the text, if we take the exact reverse of the proverb as worded in our version ; for then we reach the wise conclusion—

I. THAT SELF-RESPECT, HOWEVER INDIGENT, is better than "being ministered unto" at the cost of reputation. It is better to lack bread, or even life itself, really *honouring ourself,* than it is to receive any amount of service from others, if we have forfeited the regard of the good, and are deservedly "despised." But taking the words as they are, and reaching the sense intended by the writer, we gather—

II. THAT DOMESTIC COMFORT AND SUFFICIENCY ARE MUCH TO BE PREFERRED TO THE GRATIFICATION OF PERSONAL VANITY. One man, in order that he may have consideration and deference from his neighbours, expends his resources on those outward appearances which will command that gratification; to do this he has to deny himself the attendance which he would like to have, and even the nourishment he needs. Another man disregards altogether the slights he may suffer from his meddlesome and intrusive neighbours, in order to supply his home with the food and the comforts which will benefit his family. It is the latter who is the wise man. For : 1. The gratification of vanity is a very paltry satisfaction; there is nothing honourable, but rather ignoble about it ; it lowers rather than raises a man in the sight of wisdom. 2. The gratification thus gained is likely to prove very ephemeral, and to diminish constantly in its value; moreover, it is personal and, in that sense, selfish. 3. Domestic comfort is a daily advantage, lasting the whole year round, the whole life long. 4. Domestic comfort not only benefits the head of the household, but all the members of it, and he who makes a happy home is contributing to the good of his country and his kind. Using now the words of the text as suggestive of truths which they do not actually hold, we learn—

III. THAT THERE IS A VALUABLE SERVICE WHICH ALL MAY SECURE. "He that hath a servant." Men are divisible into those that *are* servants and those that *have* them. Some are the slaves of their evil habits; these are to be profoundly pitied, however many menservants or maidservants they may have at their call. But we may and should belong to those who hold their habits, whether of the mind or of the life, under their control and at their command. If that be so with us, then, though we should have no dependents at all in our employ, or though we ourselves should *be* dependents, living in honourable and useful service, we shall have the most valuable servants always at hand to minister to us, building up our character, strengthening our mind, enlarging our life.

IV. THAT WE SHOULD SECURE NOURISHMENT AT ALL COSTS WHATEVER. We must never be "the man that lacketh bread." To attain to any honour, to receive any adulation, to indulge any fancy, and to "lack bread," is a great mistake. For nourishment is strength and fulness of life; it is so in (1) the physical, (2) the intellectual, (3) the moral and spiritual realm. With the regularity and earnestness with which we ask for "daily bread," we should labour and strive to secure it, for our whole nature.—C.

Ver. 16.—(See homily on ch. xxix. 11.)—C.

Ver. 24.—(See homily on ch. xxvii. 23.)—C.

Ver. 26.—*Growth and seductiveness.* The goal which a man will reach must depend on the tendency of the habits he has formed, or the way in which his life inclines, whether upward or downward. Are his habits such that we can properly speak of them as *growing* toward perfection, or such as may be more properly thought of as conducting or seducing to wrong and ruin ?

I. THE GROWTH OF GOODNESS. "The righteous is ·more *abundant* than his neighbour" (marginal reading). He is more abundant because : 1. The blessing of God rests upon him, and his reward is in fruitfulness in some direction. 2. Righteousness means or includes virtue, temperance, industry, thrift, culture; and these mean prosperity and success. 3. God's great prevailing law that "to him that hath [uses, or puts out, what powers he has] is given, and he shall have abundance," is constantly operating here and now, in all realms of human action ; consequently, the good man is reaping the beneficial result. (1) In the *physical* world, bodily, muscular exercise "is profiting," and ends in abounding health and strength and capacity of endurance. (2) In the *mental* world, study and patient observation result in abounding knowledge and intellectual grasp. (3) In the *spiritual* world, devotion and the daily learning of Christ (Matt. xi. 28) end in abounding virtue, in the "more abundant life" which the Saviour offers to confer. Thus the life of the righteous man is one of continual growth in all good directions, and he is "more abundant than his neighbour."

II. THE SEDUCTIVENESS OF SIN. "The way of the wicked seduceth them." We read (Heb. iii. 13) of "the deceitfulness of sin." And we know only too well by experience and observation how seductive and deceitful are its ways. 1. It begins with a pleasureableness which promises to continue, but which fails, which indeed turns to misery and ruin (see ch. vii. 6—27). At first it is a soft green slope, but the end is a steep and rocky precipice over which the victim falls. 2. It promises an easy escape from its hold, but it coils its cords around its subjects with quiet hand, until it holds them in a fast captivity. 3. It persuades its adherents that its ways are right when they are utterly wrong, and thus sings to sleep the conscience which should be aroused and active. 4. It pleads the crowded character of its path, and assures of safety; although the presence of a multitude is no guard or guarantee whatever against the condemnation and the retribution of the Almighty. But let youth understand that all these are "refuges of lies." For the truth is that (1) the way of transgressors is all too soon found to be "hard" indeed. (2) After a very little way is trodden, it is most difficult, and further on all but impossible to return. (3) The paths of sin are all grievously wrong in the sight of Divine purity. (4) "The wages of sin is death."—C.

Ver. 28.—*The one way of life.* "All that a man hath will he give for his life;" but of what worth is life to many men? What does it mean to them but work and sleep and indulgence? Of how many is it true that they "are dead while they live"! But "in the way of righteousness there is life, and in the pathway thereof is no death."

I. THE WAY OF RIGHTEOUSNESS THE ONE PATH OF LIFE. It is the one and only path; for the paths of sin are those of spiritual death. In them the human traveller is separated from God, from all excellency of character, from all true and lasting joy; and what is this but death in everything except the name? It is not the true, the real life of man. But righteousness in the full, broad sense in which the word is here employed, includes: 1. *Devotion;* the spirit of reverence, the act of prayer, the approach of our human spirit to God, and our habitual walking with him and worship of him. 2. *Virtue;* the practice of truthfulness, temperance, purity, integrity; the exercise of self-restraint, the discharge of the duties which we owe to our fellow-men, respecting ourselves and honouring them. 3. *Service;* the endeavour, in a spirit of loving-kindness, to raise, to succour, to guide, to bless, all whom we can reach and influence. 4. *Joy;* i.e. not mere excitement or gratification, which may expire at any moment, and may leave a sting or a stain behind, but rather that honourable and pure elation of spirit which springs from conscious rectitude, which is the consequence of our being in harmony with all that is around us, and with him who is above us, which lasts through the changes of circumstances, which "through all time abides," which "satisfies and sanctifies the soul." This *is* life; this is life *indeed;* this is worth calling *life;* and this is in the way of righteousness.

II. ITS IMMUNITY FROM DEATH. "In the pathway," etc. 1. No death during mortal life; so long as we walk in the light of Divine truth there is no fear of our stumbling into error and falling into the condition of spiritual death; our life in God and with him will be steadily maintained. 2. No real death at the end of that life; for though we must pass through "the portal we call death," yet "it is *not* death to die," when the termination of mortal existence is the starting-point of the celestial life; when the being unclothed of the earthly tenement means the "being clothed upon with our house which is from heaven," when "absence from the body" means "presence with the Lord." 3. Fulness and enlargement of life for ever; for our hope and confident expectation is that, along whatever paths our God may lead us in the heavenly spheres, the way we shall take will be one that will be ever disclosing greater grandeurs, ever opening new sources of joy, ever unfolding new secrets, and making life mean more and more to our rejoicing spirits as the years and ages pass.—C.

EXPOSITION.

CHAPTER XIII.

Ver. 1—ch. xv. 19.—Second section in this collection.

Ver. 1.—**A wise son heareth his father's instruction.** The Authorized Version introduces the verb from the second member. The Hebrew is elliptical, "A wise son, his father's discipline," *i.e.* is the object or the result of his father's education; he owes his wisdom to it. Septuagint, "A clever (πανοῦργος) son is obedient to his father." But a **scorner** (ch. i. 22) **heareth not rebuke;** one who mocks at goodness and despises filial piety will not listen to reproof. Septuagint, "A disobedient son is in destruction." Compare the case of Eli's sons, and their fate (1 Sam. ii. 25; iv. 17).

Ver. 2.—**A man shall eat good by the fruit of** his mouth (ch. xii. 14; xviii. 20). By his kindly speech and wise counsels he shall gain the good will of his neighbours and the blessing of God. Schultens observes that the word rendered "good" (*tob*) means what is pleasant to taste and smell, while that translated "violence" (*chamas*) signifies literally what is crude and unripe. **The soul of the transgressors shall eat violence** (ch. i. 31). The Authorized Version introduces the verb from the first clause unnecessarily. The meaning of this rendering is that sinners, especially the treacherous, bring on themselves retribution; the injuries which they devise against others recoil on their own heads (ch. x. 6). The Hebrew is, "The soul (*i.e.* the desire, or delight) of the perfidious (is) violence." Such men have only one thing at heart, viz. to wrong their neighbour, and to increase their own property by any, even nefarious, proceedings. Septuagint, "Of the fruits of righteousness the good man shall eat; but the lives of transgressors shall perish untimely."

Ver. 3.—**He that keepeth (guardeth) his mouth keepeth his life** (ch. xviii. 21; xxi. 23; comp. Ps. xxxix. 1; Jas. i. 26). Thus the gnome—

'Η γλῶσσα πολλοὺς εἰς ὄλεθρον ἤγαγεν.

"The tongue hath many to destruction led."

And Ecclus. xxviii. 25, "Weigh thy words in a balance, and make a door and bar for thy mouth. Beware thou slide not by it, lest thou fall before him that lieth in wait." **But he that openeth wide his lips shall have destruction** (ch. x. 14). The Vulgate paraphrases, "He who is inconsiderate in speech shall experience evils;" Septuagint, "will terrify himself"—will occasion to himself many terrible alarms and inflictions. Hence the psalmist prays, "Set a watch, O Lord, before my mouth; keep the door of my lips." So we have in the Danish, "A silent man's words are not brought into court;" and in the Spanish, "Let not the tongue say what the head shall pay for;" while the Italians tell us, "The sheep that bleats is strangled by the wolf;" and "Silence was never written down" (Kelly). (See on ch. xviii. 6; xx. 19.)

Ver. 4.—(Comp. ch. x. 4.) **The soul of the sluggard desireth, and hath nothing;** literally, *and nothing is there*—he gains nothing (ch. xiv. 6; xx. 4). He has the wish, but not the will, and the empty wish without corresponding exertion is useless (ch. xxi. 25, etc.). Vulgate, "The indolent wishes, and wishes not;" he wishes for something, but he wishes not for the labour of getting it; he would like the result, but he hates the process by which the result is to be obtained. Septuagint, "In desires every idle man is occupied;" his mind is fixed wholly on aimless wishes, not on action. **Shall be made fat** (ch. xi. 25); Septuagint, "The hands of the valiant are fully occupied (ἐν ἐπιμελείᾳ)."

Ver. 5.—**Lying;** Vulgate, *verbum mendax;* Septuagint, λόγον ἄδικον; literally, *a word of falsehood.* But *debar,* "word," is used, like ῥῆμα in Hellenistic Greek, in a general sense for "thing," *i.e.* the subject of speech. So here it is not only verbal lying that is meant, but every kind of deceit and guile. This naturally betrays itself by the speech, according to the proverb, "Show me a liar, and I will show you a thief." **A wicked man is loathsome, and cometh to shame.** The clause is variously translated. Vulgate, *confundit et confundetur,* "causes shame to others and to himself." Septuagint, "is put to shame, and shall not have licence of tongue (παρρησίαν)." The Revised Version margin, "causeth shame and bringeth reproach." Delitzsch, "brings into bad odour (Gen. xxxiv. 30) and causes shame." Hitzig, "behaveth injuriously and shamefully." The antithesis is best brought out by the rendering that marks the effect of the wicked man's "lying;" "He brings disgrace upon others (who have trusted him or have been associated with him) and causes shame."

Ver. 6.—**Righteousness keepeth (guardeth)** him that is **upright in the way;** literally, *uprightness of way,* abstract for concrete, as in the second member, "sin" for "sinner." Those who are good and innocent in the walk of life are preserved from evil, moral and material. **Wickedness overthroweth the sinner;** literally, *sin.* "Overthroweth," makes to slip. Vulgate, *supplantat.* The LXX. inverts the clause, "Sin makes the impious worthless (φαύλους)" (see ch. xi. 3, 5, 6). The verse is omitted in many Greek manuscripts.

Ver. 7.—**There is that maketh himself rich, yet hath nothing.** "Maketh" may mean "feigns." There are some who pretend to be rich while really they are poor (as ch. xii. 9), and there are some who make themselves, *i.e.* pretend to be poor (as misers) while they have much wealth. The Vulgate elucidates this meaning by rendering, *quasi dives* and *quasi pauper;* and the Hebrew verbs confirm its correctness. The proverb in both members teaches one not to trust to appearances. Septuagint, "There are who enrich themselves, having nothing; and there are who humble themselves amid much wealth." It is obvious that such a version lends itself to a Christian interpretation. The first clause reminds one of the rich fool who laid up treasure for himself, and was not rich toward God (Luke xii.

21; comp. Rev. iii. 17, 18). The second clause teaches that wealth expended in God's service makes a man rich in the treasury of heaven (Luke xii. 21, 33). One who thus uses the means entrusted to him could be spoken of like St. Paul, "as poor, yet making many rich; as having nothing, and yet possessing all things" (2 Cor. vi. 10).

Ver. 8.—**The ransom of a man's life are his riches.** A rich man can save himself from many difficulties and dangers by the sacrifice of a portion of his wealth, e.g. when his money or his life is demanded by a robber; when men in authority make extortionate demands on pain of death; or when he has incurred extreme penalty by infringement of law (Exod. xxi. 22, 30). Spiritually discerned, the passage recalls Christ's injunction, "Make to yourselves friends of the mammon of unrighteousness, that when it shall fail, they may receive you into the eternal tabernacles" (Luke xvi. 9). **The poor heareth not rebuke;** has not to listen to (Job iii. 18) threats from the covetous or abuse from the envious. He has nothing to lose, and no one can gain anything by interfering with him. So the poor man is at peace. "A hundred men cannot rob one pauper."

"Cantabit vacuus coram latrone viator."

Ver. 9.—**The light of the righteous rejoiceth;** lætificat, Vulgate. But the verb is intransitive, and means "burn joyfully," bright and clear, as the sun rejoices as a strong man to run a race (Ps. xix. 5). This light (or) is the grace and virtue which adorn the good man's life, and which beam through all his actions with a cheerful, kindly radiance (comp. ch. iv. 18, 19). This is a true light, kindled in his heart by God, different from **the lamp** (ner) **of the wicked,** which is devised and lighted by themselves, and has no element of permanence, but soon shall be put out (ch. xxiv. 20; comp. ch. xx. 20; Job xviii. 5; John i. 8; v. 35, where the distinction between "light" and "lamp" is maintained). The lamp of the wicked is the false show of wisdom or piety, which may glimmer and deceive for a time, but is ere long detected and brought to naught. There may be here an allusion to a common custom in the East. "No house, however poor," says Dr. Geikie ('Holy Land,' i. 117), "is left without a light burning in it all night; the housewife rising betimes to secure its continuance by replenishing the lamp with oil. If a lamp goes out, it is a fatal omen" (comp. 1 Kings xv. 4; Jer. xxv. 10; Rev. xviii. 23). Septuagint, "The light of the righteous is everlasting; but the light of sinners is quenched." Then is introduced a couplet not found in the Hebrew, of which

the latter part is borrowed from Ps. xxxvii. 21 or cxii. 5, "Crafty souls go astray in sins; righteous men show mercy and pity." The Vulgate inserts this paragraph after ver. 13.

Ver. 10.—**Only by pride cometh contention.** Some render "surely" (raq) for "only," as in Gen. xx. 11. Others rightly translate, "By pride cometh only, nothing but, contention." Vulgate, "Between the proud disputes are always rife." One who is haughty and overbearing, or who is too conceited to receive advice, is sure to quarrel with others. Septuagint, "An evil man with insult doeth evil." **With the well-advised is wisdom;** those who are not, like the proud, above taking advice and following it, are wise (ch. xi. 2; xii. 15). As the Vulgate puts it, "They who do all things with counsel are directed by wisdom." The LXX., reading differently, has, "They who know themselves are wise," which implies that the wise know their own weakness and imperfection, and hearken humbly to good counsel.

Ver. 11.—**Wealth gotten by vanity shall be diminished;** literally, wealth by a breath; i.e. wealth obtained without labour and exertion, or by illegitimate and dishonest means, is soon dissipated, is not blessed by God, and has no stability. Vulgate, "riches acquired hastily;" Septuagint, "substance gotten hastily with iniquity." This makes the antithesis more marked, the contrast being between wealth gotten hastily and that acquired by diligent labour. Cito nata, cito pereunt, "Quickly won, quickly gone" (see on ch. xx. 21; xxi. 5). Says the Greek maxim—

Μὴ σπεῦδε πλουτεῖν, μὴ ταχὺς πένης γένῃ.

"Haste not for wealth, lest thou be quickly poor."

He that gathereth by labour; literally, with the hand, handful after handful. Vulgate, paulatim, "little by little," by patient industry. Labor improbus omnia vincit. Septuagint, "He that gathereth for himself with piety shall be increased." Then is added, "A good man is merciful and lendeth," from Ps. xxxvii. 26. The Septuagint here uses the term εὐσέβεια, which is received in St. Paul's pastoral Epistles and St. Peter's, taking the place of the earlier phrase, φόβος Κυρίου.

Ver. 12.—**Hope deferred maketh the heart sick.** Delay in the accomplishment of some much-desired good occasions sinking of the spirits, languor, and despondence. Many refer this sentence to the impatient longing for heaven which holy men feel, such as we may read in 'De Imitatione,' iii. 48, 49, and in the hymns, "For thee, O dear, dear country," and "We've no abiding city," etc.

And St. Paul can exclaim (Rom. vii. 24), "O wretched man that I am! who shall deliver me from the body of this death?" (comp. Rom. viii. 23; Phil. i. 23). Septuagint, "Better is he who taketh in hand to aid with all his heart, than he who promises and raises hopes" (comp. Jas. ii. 15, 16). When the desire cometh—when the object of the longing is obtained—it is a tree of life (ch. xi. 30); there are then no longer languor and despondence, but strength and refreshment and vigorous action. Septuagint, "A good desire is a tree of life."

Ver. 13.—Whoso despiseth the word shall be destroyed. "The word" is either the commandment of God (Deut. xxx. 14), or warning and instruction. He who despises and neglects this word "brings on himself destruction." Many good authorities take the latter verb in another sense, "is pledged by it;" as Revised Version in margin, "maketh himself a debtor thereto," i.e. is still bound to fulfil his obligations to it; he cannot escape duty by ignoring or despising it, but is pledged to do it, and will suffer for its neglect. Hence Christ's injunction to agree with our adversary quickly while we are in the way with him (Matt, v. 25). Vulgate, "He who disparages (detrahit) anything binds himself for the future." Septuagint, "He who despises a thing (πράγματος, ? τάγματυς, 'a command') shall be despised by it." Virtus se contemnentem contemnit. He that feareth the commandment shall be rewarded (ch. xi. 31). The Vulgate rendering, "shall live in peace," and that of the Septuagint, "shall be healthful," are not so suitable. The "fearing the commandment" implies obedience to it; and reward is considered as fully pledged to obedience as punishment is to neglect. The Septuagint here adds a distich which Ewald regards as genuine, "Unto a crafty son there shall be nothing good; but to a wise servant all actions shall prosper, and his way shall be guided aright." This is also found in the Vulgate of ch. xiv. 15. The Vulgate here inserts the paragraph found in the Septuagint at ver. 9 (q.v.), Animæ dolosæ errant in peccatis; justi autem misericordes sunt et miserantur.

Ver. 14.—The law (instruction) of the wise is a fountain of life (ch. x. 11), which has and imparts life (Ecclus. xxi. 13; Ps. xxxvi. 9). The rules and teaching of wise men are a source of life to those who follow them, so that they depart from the snares of death (ch. xiv. 27). Obedience to good teaching saves from many dangers, material and spiritual, especially from the snare of the devil (2 Tim. ii. 26). With "snares of death" we may compare Ps. xviii. 5 and Horace's (' Carm.,' iii. 24. 8)

"Non mortis laqueis expedies caput."

Septuagint, "The fool shall perish by the snare."

Ver. 15.—Good understanding giveth favour (ch. iii. 4); makes one acceptable to God and man. We are told of Christ that "he increased in wisdom and in stature, and in favour with God and man" (Luke ii. 52). As a good and wise man uses his gifts and graces properly, he wins higher favour from God, and kindles the love and respect of his fellow-men. After this clause the Septuagint introduces that which occurs also in ch. ix. 10, "It belongs to a good understanding (διανοίας) to know the Law." The way of transgressors is hard; rough and rugged, leading to desolation, not to waters of comfort. Ecclus. xxi. 10, "The way of sinners is made plain with stones, but at the end thereof is the pit of hell." Vulgate, "In the way of scorners is an abyss;" Septuagint, "The ways of scorners end in destruction."

Ver. 16.—Every prudent man dealeth (worketh, acteth) with knowledge; i.e. with thought and deliberation, having previously well considered the bearings and issues of his plans. But a fool layeth open his folly; Revised Version, spreadeth out folly, as if exposing the wares of his shop (ch. xii. 23; xv. 2). One works; the other talks.

Ver. 17.—A wicked messenger falleth into mischief; misfortune, calamity (ch. xvii. 20). A messenger who is false to his employer shall be detected and punished. The LXX., reading melek for malak, renders, "A rash king shall fall into evils." Such a one adopts inconsiderate measures, makes war unadvisedly, etc. A faithful ambassador (literally, an ambassador of faithfulness, ch. xxv. 13) is health. One who faithfully performs his errand is a source of comfort and satisfaction both to his employer and to those to whom he is sent. Septuagint, "But a wise messenger shall deliver him"—the king.

Ver. 18.—Poverty and shame shall be to him that refuseth instruction; correction, discipline. Nowack takes the two nouns as predicates: "He that refuseth discipline is poverty and shame," i.e. they are his lot. Such a one indulges his own lusts and passions, is headstrong in pursuing his own plans, and thus dissipates his fortune and acquires the contempt of all good men. Septuagint, "Discipline taketh away poverty and disgrace." He that regardeth reproof shall be honoured. To listen to rebuke and to profit thereby is a proof of humility and self-knowledge, which wins respect from others. Lesètre refers to Theodosius's submission to the sentence imposed upon him by St. Ambrose as a real honour and glory to him (comp. ch. xii. 1; xv. 5, 32).

Ver. 19.—**The desire accomplished** (comp. ver. 12). This is usually taken to mean the desire of what is good and honest, when it is fulfilled and realized, is a source of highest joy and comfort to the wise. Septuagint, "The desires of the pious are sweet to the soul." **But it is abomination to fools to depart from evil.** The antithesis is not very obvious, but it may be : it is sweet to a good man to obtain his wish ; but for a wicked man to leave, to abandon evil to which he clings so fondly, is a detestable alternative. Or the latter clause may mean that the wicked will not give up the evil which makes the satisfaction of their desire impossible. But it is best to take the first clause as a general statement, viz. the satisfaction of desire is pleasant to all men ; then the latter member gives a special case and will signify, " For the sake of this pleasure bad men will not give up their evil wishes and plans ; they will pursue what they have set their heart upon because they hate the idea of foregoing their evil designs." Septuagint, The deeds of sinners are far from knowledge," i.e. from practical wisdom, prudence, and piety. The Vulgate introduces quite another thought, " Fools abhor those who flee from evil." Compare the passage in Wisd. ii. concerning the sinner's hatred of the good.

Ver. 20.—**He that walketh with wise men shall be wise** ; or, according to the Khetib, *walk with wise men, and thou shalt be wise.* Ecclus. vi. 36, " If thou seest a man of understanding, get thee betimes unto him, and let thy foot wear the steps of his door." So the Greek maxim—

Σοφοῖς ὁμιλῶν καὐτὸς ἐκβήσῃ σοφός.

" With wise conversing thou wilt wise become."

And Eurip., 'Rhesus,' 206—

Σοφοῦ παρ' ἀνδρὸς χρὴ σοφόν τι μανθάνειν.

" A man that's wise will thee true wisdom teach."

A companion of fools shall be destroyed ; literally, *shall be broken,* shall suffer moral ruin ; Revised Version margin, " shall smart for it." But the antithesis is not well brought out by this rendering ; and as the word may bear the sense of " doing ill " as well as of " suffering ill," the interpretation of the Vulgate intimates the correct idea of the clause : " The friend of fools shall turn out the same ; " " He who associates with fools shall do evil." Septuagint, " He who roams about with fools shall be known." "Tell me your companions, and I will tell you what you are."

" Talis quis esse putatur qualis ei est sodalitas."

A Dutch proverb says, " He that lives with cripples learns to limp ; " and the Spanish, " He that goes with wolves learns to howl." We have a homely English proverb, " He that lies down with dogs shall rise up with fleas ; " so the Orientals say, " He that takes the raven for his guide shall light upon carrion."

Ver. 21.—**Evil pursueth sinners.** Sinners suffer not only the natural consequences of crime in external evil, injury to body, estate, reputation, etc. (Ps. xi. 6), but also stings of conscience and remorse ; even seeming prosperity is often a chastisement, and long impunity is only augmenting the coming retribution. As the shadow attends the substance, so guilt is attached to sin, and brings with it punishment. **To the righteous good shall be repaid** ; or, *he, Jehovah, shall repay good* (comp. ch. xii. 14) ; Revised Version, "The righteous shall be recompensed with good." They shall have the answer of a good conscience, happiness here and hereafter. Septuagint, "Good shall take possession of (or, overtake) the righteous."

Ver. 22.—**A good man leaveth an inheritance to his children's children.** This would be especially notable where a system of temporal rewards and punishments was expected and generally experienced. **The wealth of the sinner is laid up for the just.** Property unjustly acquired, or wickedly used, is taken from those who have it, and ultimately finds its way into better hands. They cannot keep it, and consequently cannot leave it to their children.

" De male quæsitis non gaudet tertius hæres."

" Ill-gotten wealth no third descendant holds."

This has often been the fate of property obtained by the sacrilegious seizure of what was dedicated to God's service. For the general view of the clause, comp. ch. xxviii. 8 ; Job xxvii. 16, 17 ; Eccles. ii. 26 ; and the case of Jacob (Gen. xxxi. 9), and the Israelites (Exod. xii. 35, 36), when " the righteous spoiled the ungodly " (Wisd. x. 20).

Ver. 23.—**Much food is in the tillage** (tilled ground) **of the poor** (ch. xii. 11). The word rendered " tillage " (*nir*) means ground worked for the first time, and therefore that on which much labour is bestowed. Hence the Vulgate rightly renders, *novalibus.* It occurs in Jer. iv. 3 and Hos. x. 12, where our version has " fallow ground." The poor, but righteous man, who industriously cultivates his little plot of ground, secures a good return, and is happy in eating the labour of his hands (Ps. cxxviii. 2). Instead of " the poor," the Vulgate has, " the fathers," taking ראשים in this sense ; so that the meaning would be that children who properly cultivate their paternal or hereditary fields obtain good crops. But the Authorized Version rendering is doubtless preferable. **There is that is destroyed for want of judgment;** rather, as the Revised Version, *by reason of injustice.* Rich men are often brought to ruin by their disregard of right and justice (*mishpat*). Some (poor men) are amply supplied by honest labour; others (rich) lose all by wrong dealing. Vulgate, " For others it (food) is gathered contrary to justice ; " Septuagint, quite astray, "The righteous shall pass many years in wealth; but the unrighteous shall suddenly perish"—which seems to be an explanation or amplification of ver. 22.

Ver. 24.—**He that spareth his rod hateth his son.** Correction of children is a great point with our author (see ch. xix. 18; xxii. 15; xxiii. 13, etc.; xxix. 15, 17). So Ecclus. xxx. 1, " He that loveth his son causeth him

oft to feel the rod, that he may have joy of him in the end." Dukes, " Gold must be beaten, and a boy needs blows " ('Rabbin. Blumenlese,' 71). **Chasteneth him betimes;** literally, *early in the morning* (ch. i. 28; viii. 17), which may mean, in the morning of life, ere evil habits have time to grow, or directly after the offence. Or the expression may signify " diligently." Vulgate, *instanter;* Septuagint, ἐπιμελῶς.

Ver. 25.—**The righteous eateth to the satisfying of his soul** (comp. ch. x. 3; Ps. xxxiv. 10). The good man has always enough to satisfy his wants, because he is temperate, and his substance has the blessing of God. "The chief thing for life," says Siracides (Ecclus. xxix. 21), " is water, and bread, and clothing, and a house to cover shame." **The belly of the wicked shall want.** The wicked are punished by penury and desires never satisfied. These different results are providentially ordered.

HOMILETICS.

Ver. 1.—"*A wise son.*" The young man who considers himself to be exceptionally clever is tempted to idolize his own notions and despise parental correction. We are reminded that such conduct may be a grievous mistake and a proof of essential folly, and that true wisdom will follow a more humble course of filial duty. It is not merely obligatory on the son to submit to his father; it is for his own interest to follow paternal advice, and a mark of wisdom. Of course, this is taken as a general principle. A conscientious son may be cursed with a base-minded parent, whose directions it will be anything but wise to follow. By manly intelligence and with Christian liberty, general maxims can only be applied in view of suitable circumstances. We may take it that on the whole, when the relationship is normal, wisdom will prompt submission to paternal correction.

I. No ONE CAN TRULY ESTIMATE HIS OWN CONDUCT. We cannot stand off from ourselves and view ourselves in perspective. We make the most egregious mistakes in judging ourselves, because we cannot see ourselves as others see us. The object is also the subject, and subjective feelings colour our objective perceptions of self. It is therefore a great security for a young man to have a guide apart from himself whom he can trust, as he can trust a father.

II. A FATHER CORRECTS IN LOVE. There are brutal parents, whose chastisement implies anything but sound correction. But the true father considers the highest interests of his son. If he expresses disapproval it is because he believes some material wrong has been done. His rebuke is for wholesome improvement.

III. A FATHER HAS LARGER EXPERIENCE THAN HIS SON. His age gives him the advantage of fuller knowledge and riper judgment. It may also bring a certain stiffening of notions and aversion to innovation. But even then it may still be keen to detect real errors and right in warning against them.

IV. A FATHER HAS AUTHORITY OVER HIS SON. This was recognized longer in former times than in the present day, when many sons are over-anxious to emancipate themselves from parental control. Now, there is a certain wisdom in submitting to established authority. Rebellion can only be justified by extreme wrong. Where no plain cause for rebellion exists, it is wise as well as right to submit.

V. THE PARENTAL RELATION ON EARTH IS TYPICAL OF THE RELATION BETWEEN GOD AND HIS PEOPLE. All the arguments which point to the wisdom of a son's submitting to correction from an earthly parent apply with immensely greater force to man's position before God. God regards us with love; he knows everything; he has a right and power to direct and correct us. Whatever modern notions of domestic revolts may be entertained by any of us, it still remains clear that it is wise to bow before the correction of God, our great and good Father.

Ver. 10.—*Pride and contention.* I. THE REASONS WHY PRIDE PRODUCES CONTENTION. 1. *It is self-assertive.* The proud man claims a large and prominent place for himself. He will not endure a secondary position. He demands his rights not so much because he really wishes to enjoy them, as because they *are* his rights. He will not forego them even when he gains no advantage by the exercise of them. Now, this self-assertiveness threatens the supposed rights of others where the boundary-line is as yet uncertain. It also provokes a similar spirit in a man's neighbours. 2. It is *exacting.* Pride claims its dues. The proud lord will have every ounce of respect from his underlings. Even those who are met on equal terms are narrowly scrutinized to see if they withhold a shadow of the supposed rights from the jealousy of pride. 3. It is *overbearing.* It will not endure opposition ; it is intolerant of differences of opinion ; it would rather trespass on the rights of others than surrender any of its own claims. Thus it is perpetually challenging all who cross its path.

II. THE REGIONS IN WHICH PRIDE PRODUCES CONTENTION. 1. *Among nations.* It was thought that war sprang from the pride and jealousy of monarchs, and that when the people gained power war would cease. But republics declare war. There is a dangerous form of national pride. It is possible for a whole people to be carried away by unreasoning elation, and to make inordinate claims for itself, or to be unduly sensitive to affront. 2. *In society.* Pride is here one of the chief dangers to the order and peace of cities. The poor would endure the sight of the prosperity of the rich if they were not goaded by the more irritating spectacle of insulting pride. The least that they can do who have more than their share of the good things of life is to hold them with quiet humility. To flaunt their superiority of good fortune in the face of their miserable fellow-citizens, and to make it a ground for scorn and contempt, is to rouse the latent rage of men who are already chafing under what—whether rightly or wrongly—they regard as a grossly unjust social order. 3. *In private life.* Pride is the most direful source of family quarrels. It separates the best friends, and it sets up the most invincible barriers against a speedy reconciliation. When love would hold out the hand of forgiveness, pride hangs back in gloomy resentfulness.

III. THE WAY TO PREVENT PRIDE FROM PRODUCING CONTENTION. There is but one way ; pride must be humiliated and cast out. This monster sin is directly aimed at in the preaching of the gospel of the cross. It is found lurking in the breasts of men who are regarded as saints ; but it is no part of their saintliness. It is still a sin in the sight of God. Christ cannot endure it, and one who would follow Christ must forsake it. There is no better way of destroying it than by submission to the yoke of him who was "meek and lowly."

Ver. 11.—*Fraudulent gain.* I. THE DELUSIVE APPEARANCE OF FRAUDULENT GAIN. This looks very different from coarse, vulgar robbery. The sleek swindler owns no common brotherhood with the brutal burglar. Fraudulent gain is got in the way of business ; it is not at all like the money directly stolen from a man's pocket. The process is so very roundabout that it is difficult to trace the transition from fair dealing to cheating. The decorous thief would be horrified at hearing his true name. He knows his actions are not quite straightforward, but the crookedness of them is almost hidden from himself by neat contrivances. Now, all this makes the pursuit of fraudulent gain the more treacherous and dangerous. A man who follows such a course is lost before he owns himself to be dishonest.

II. THE TEMPTATIONS TO MAKE FRAUDULENT GAIN. They spring from various sources. 1. *Keen competition.* It is so hard to make a living in the fierce contest of business life, when every rival is treated as an enemy, that any extra advantage is eagerly sought after. 2. *Large promises.* As the margin of profits shrink while the requirements of energy and alertness grow, any expedient that promises more speedy and remunerative returns is likely to present a fascinating appearance. 3. *Compromising customs.* Business is not always conducted on perfectly honest grounds, and the dishonesty that is prevalent claims to be sanctioned by usage. Moreover, if *some* departure from absolute right is permitted, a greater degree of dishonesty is but another step in the same direction. 4. *Hopes of secrecy.* The man of business cannot afford to lose his good name, and therefore plain self-interest holds him back from open theft. But the subtle pursuit of a more refined form of dishonesty appears to be possible without any loss of character. Thus as the pressure of the opinion of society is eluded, the only conscience which some men recognize ceases to operate.

III. THE RUINOUS RESULTS OF MAKING FRAUDULENT GAIN. 1. *It is a great sin.* The delusive appearance of the pursuit blinds people to its true character. But theft cannot be made honest by becoming refined. All the laws of righteousness bristle up in front of the man who pursues dishonesty, and threaten his ruin. Even though social and civil retribution be evaded, there is a higher court of justice than any of man's jurisdiction, and before its awful bar the wealthy, respected thief must ultimately stand condemned. 2. *It is likely to lead to earthly ruin.* The man whose life is one huge lie lives in a frail shell, which may be broken at any moment to expose him to pitiless punishments. Then what has he to fall back upon? He who has laid up treasures in heaven can afford to lose his poor, earthly stores; but one who has sold his prospects of heaven for brief earthly profits loses all when the gains of this life are snatched from him. The way of peace and safety can never be any other than the way of right.

Ver. 12.—*Hope deferred.* I. THE HOPE THAT IS DEFERRED. Most men who live to any purpose live by hope. It is scarcely possible to press forward with energy to a future that is wholly dark. The prospect of some future good is a present inspiration. Thus hope takes a large place in the heart of man. Note some of its forms. 1. *The hope of youth.* It is natural for youth to believe in the future, to treat its possibilities as certainties, and to colour its grey outline with the gorgeous hues of a fresh imagination. 2. *The hope of this world.* Pursuits of business or pleasure allure those who enter them with good promises. 3. *The hope of heaven.* They who have been disappointed in all earthly anticipations may cherish this glorious dream. 4. *The hope that is unselfish.* Hope need not be centred in personal pleasure. We may hope for a great cause, and hope to see some good effected, though by the sacrifice of ourselves. 5. *The hope that is in God.* A sorrowful soul may hope in God with no distinct visions of any possible future advantage, making God himself the Hope. "Christ our Hope."

II. HOW THE HOPE IS DEFERRED. 1. *By disillusion.* From the first the hope may be too sanguine. The mirage is mistaken for the oasis. Or perhaps distance is misjudged. We think that we are near to the future that still lies in the remote distance with leagues of desert between us and it. Experience must dispel such an illusion. 2. *By direct disappointment.* The well-founded hope may be deferred by a change of circumstances, or failure of ability to accomplish it, unfaithfulness to a promise, etc. Thus in life the expected "good time coming" is continually receding as men approach it. Hope may be deferred by trying changes of circumstances, or by a man's own mistakes and failures.

III. WHY THE HEART IS MADE BITTER. To be lifted up and dropped down gives a shock which is not felt if we remain on the low ground. Disappointment is a source of keen pain in any case; but when it is repeated after vague anticipations and uncertainties, it is far more distressing. The hope deferred is not denied. We cannot banish it as a mistake. Such an act would be easier to bear; there would be first a great shock of disappointment, and then the dead hope would be buried out of sight, and the grief of the loss of it would grow lighter with time. But when the hope is deferred, it is continually present, yet as a disappointment. The mind is first on the rack of wondering expectation, and then there follows a sense of unutterable weariness—true heart-sickness. It is said that sea-sickness is produced by the sinking from beneath a person of the support on which he rests. The heart-sickness of a hope long deferred arises from a similar cause in the experience of souls.

IV. HOW THIS BITTERNESS MAY BE CURED. 1. *By the satisfaction of the hope.* Long deferred, it may yet come. When we are most despairing the tide may turn. The heart-sick mother is startled with a sudden joy in the return of her long-lost sailor-lad when she is relinquishing the weary hope of ever seeing him again. 2. *By the rising of a new hope.* If this may not be found in earthly experience, and the very mention of it sounds like treason to the faithful soul, it may indeed appear in higher regions of life. In the bitterness of earthly disappointment Christ's great hope may be received. 3. *By trusting in God.* "Oh rest in the Lord, and wait patiently for him." The earthly hope may be deferred, disappointed, shattered; yet some soul-satisfying answer will be given to the prayer of faith.

Ver. 17.—*A faithful messenger.* In early times, when no public postal arrangements existed, and when reading and writing were not generally cultivated, communications were more often sent by verbal messages and personal messengers. Great mischief would then accrue through unfaithfulness on the part of one of these agents of business or friendship. But important as would be the social effects arising out of this condition of affairs, far more momentous consequences must flow from the action of messengers between God and man. They indeed need to be faithful.

I. THE CHRISTIAN PREACHER IS A MESSENGER. 1. *He carries a message.* He has to declare the truth of God as he has received it. He is the custodian of a gospel. The prophet has to utter the word of inspiration, and the apostle to proclaim the kingdom of heaven, and Christ as its King. Something of the prophet and apostle must be found in every Christian preacher. He is to go forth with the message that God has given him. 2. *He delivers his message in person.* The message is not posted; it is carried personally, and delivered by the mouth of the messenger. It is not enough that God's truth is recorded in the Bible, and that the Bible is circulated throughout the world. The living voice of the living man is needed. The missionary is God's messenger—so also is every true preacher of the gospel.

II. THE MESSENGER IS REQUIRED TO BE FAITHFUL. 1. *He must deliver his message.* The missionary must travel; the preacher at home must work among his people. Jonah was unfaithful in fleeing to Tarshish. Mere silence is unfaithfulness when one is entrusted with a message to deliver. 2. *He must give it intact.* He may neither add to it nor detract from it. Faithfulness in a Christian preacher means not shunning to declare the whole counsel of God, and not adding "vain philosophy" or "traditions of men" thereto. Of course, there is room for thought, reasoning, imagination, adaptation of the truth to the hearer, but not so as to modify the essential message. 3. *He must disregard consequences.* It may seem to him that the message is useless. Men may reject it; they may resent his offer of it; they may turn upon him and rend him. Yet it is just his duty to give the message that is entrusted to him.

III. THE FIDELITY OF THE MESSAGE SECURES HEALTH OF SOUL. Elsewhere we read, "The tongue of the wise is health" (ch. xii. 18). 1. *It is an evidence of honesty and moral courage.* The existence of messengers who are faithful even under the most trying circumstances proves that honour and right are regarded. It is for the health of a community at large that such virile qualities should be found among the leaders of thought. 2. *It secures the presentation of truth to men.* All lies and delusions are noxious poisons. Truth is food and medicine for the soul. A community that is fed on truth, though the truth be tough or bitter, is nourished with wholesome diet. That is indeed a healthy society in which all the citizens are led by honest teachers to unsophisticated truth. 3. *It brings the most needful messages to the world.* The Christian teacher is called upon to preach Christ—to show the need of Christ in the ruin of sin, the grace of Christ to save, and the right of Christ to rule. These are health-giving truths; they constitute the direct antidote to the deadly poison of sin. He who honestly proclaims them makes for the health of his fellow-men.

Ver. 24.—*Sparing the rod.* The primitive rigour of the Book of Proverbs is repudiated by modern manners. Not only in domestic training, but even in criminal law, people reject the old harsh methods, and endeavour to substitute milder means of correction. No doubt there was much that was more than rough, even brutal, in the discipline of our forefathers. The relation between father and child was too often lacking in sympathy through the undue exercise of parental authority, and society generally was hardened rather than purged by pitiless forms of punishment. But now the question is whether we are not erring towards the opposite extreme in showing more tenderness to the criminal than to his victim, and failing to let our children feel the need of some painful discipline. We idolize comfort, and we are in danger of thinking pain to be worse than sin. It may be well, therefore, to consider some of the disadvantages of neglecting the old-fashioned methods of chastisement.

I. IT IS A MISTAKE TO SUPPOSE THE ROD TO BE CRUEL BECAUSE IT HURTS. This mistake is made quite as much by the hand that should hold the rod as by the back that should feel it. Pain may be most wholesome. The highest form of punishment is that in which the cure of the offender is aimed at. To think more of the sufferings of the offender than of his sin is to show a failure of conscience, a lack of appreciation of the really evil condition of the sinner. We should learn that it is worse to sin than to suffer.

II. THERE ARE CERTAIN SPECIAL CONDITIONS UNDER WHICH PAINFUL CHASTISEMENT IS THE MOST WHOLESOME FORM OF CORRECTION. 1. *In the offender.* Some natures are redeemed by a process of punishment which will only crush others. A low and cruel nature especially needs painful punishment. 2. *In the offence.* Sins of the morally degrading class are best punished with sharp pains. The treatment which may suit a more spiritual sin, and may well reveal the shame and evil of it, would not touch these coarser forms of wickedness.

III. IT IS A SIGN OF WEAKNESS OR SELFISHNESS TO WITHHOLD NEEDFUL CHASTISEMENT. 1. *Of weakness.* The lawful authority may not have the energy to proceed to an extremity. So serious an action requires strength of purpose. 2. *Of selfishness.* It must be simply agonizing for a kind-hearted father to have to bring pain and disgrace on his son. But to hold back from the exercise of wholesome discipline on this account is really to give way to sinful self-indulgence. The true father will hurt himself in punishing his child. No doubt a certain self-indulgent softness is to be found in the present objection of society to punish criminals with due severity.

IV. GOD'S CHASTISEMENT OF HIS CHILDREN IS FOR THEIR GOOD. He does not hate his sons; therefore, at times, he does not spare his rod (see ch. iii. 12). There is neither weakness in the Almighty nor selfishness in the All-merciful. He must and will chastise sin for the correction of the sinner. We must suffer if we sin, though it is for us to choose whether we are to endure the punishment of the impenitent or the chastisement of the penitent.

HOMILIES BY VARIOUS AUTHORS.

Ver. 1.—*General truths of health and salvation.* I. DOCILITY AS CONTRASTED WITH STUBBORNNESS. (Ver. 1.) Let us carry this into the distinctly religious sphere. To be wise is to be a good *listener.* In the expressive phrase of the Bible, to "hearken to the voice of Jehovah," to listen to the suggestions of the inward monitor, is the secret of a sober, well-balanced habit of mind, and of every safe line of conduct. All that God teaches, by the voice of inspired teachers, by our own experience, by the inner revelations of the heart, is "a father's instruction." Above all, instruction by means of suffering is God's fatherly way with souls. And we have the great example of Christ to guide us and to sweeten obedience, for he "learned" it by the things which he suffered. On the other hand, the scorner has cast aside all reverential awe in the presence of the Holy One. To refuse the faithful warnings of friends, to be no better for those lessons of experience which are written in personal suffering, is to disown one's filial relation, and to estrange one's self from God.

II. TRUE LIFE-ENJOYMENT AND ITS CONTROL. (Ver. 2.) 1. Enjoyment represented under the figure of eating. As indeed eating is a most significant act, the foundation of life, the pledge of social communism. 2. The foundation of enjoyment is in one's inward state and one's social relations. The more widely we can enter into the life of others, the richer our life-joy. The unsocial life not only dries up the springs of joy, but is positively punished—in extreme cases by law, as in crimes of violence alluded to in the text, always by the alienation of sympathy.

III. THE USE AND ABUSE OF SPEECH. (Ver. 3; see on ch. x. 19, 31; xxi. 23.) How often this lesson recurs! 1. In the lower aspect it is a lesson of prudence. Reserve and caution make the safe man; loquacity and impulsiveness of speech the unsafe man. 2. In a higher point of view, the habit of silence, implying much meditation and self-communion, is good for the soul.

> "Sacred silence! thou that art offspring of the deeper heart,
> Frost of the mouth and thaw of the mind."

How easy, on the other hand, to injure our souls by talking much about religion or subjects that lie on the circumference of religion, and falling into the delusion that talk may be substituted for life!—J.

Vers. 4, 7, 8, 11.—*The value and use of property.* I. THE WORTH OF THIS WORLD'S GOODS IS ASSUMED. It is needless to show that property is a necessary institution of life under present conditions. All the strong things said in the gospel about riches do not dispute their value; it is in the *relation of the spirit* to them that evil arises. Their value as a means to the ends of the spirit is unquestioned, and everywhere assumed.

II. THE VANITY OF RICHES WITHOUT CORRESPONDING ACTION. Wishes are a great force in our nature (compare Mozley's sermon on the 'Power of Wishes'). Still, they have no practical effect unless they are transformed into will and into exertion of means to an end. It is the very characteristic of the fool that his mind evaporates in wishes; he is always desiring, but never at the pains to get anything. He is always idly expecting something to "turn up." This is a sheer superstition, a sort of clinging to the magical belief that the course of nature can be altered for one's private benefit. The lesson is, of course, equally applicable to higher things. "He would fain go to heaven if a morning dream would carry him there." He wishes to be good, to die the death of the righteous, but, at the same time, to continue in a way of life that can lead neither to the one nor to the other. Hell is paved with good intentions.

III. THE SECRET OF PROSPERITY IS DILIGENCE. Here desire is united with exertion, and it is an almost irresistible combination, as the careers of men who have risen constantly show. To conceive a good thing with such is to desire it; to desire it is to begin at once to work for it. This course must bring "rich satisfaction"—the satisfaction, by no means the least, of the pursuit, and the satisfaction in the end of entire or partial fruition. And so in moral and spiritual progress. We cannot overcome our weaknesses and sins by direct resistance, but we may react upon them by filling the mind with profitable matter of thought. The rich satisfaction depends in every case upon the same law; the personal energies must be aroused, and an object must be aimed at. Satisfaction is the complete joy of the mind in closing with and possessing a worthy and desirable object.

IV. THE CONCEIT OF RICHES IS NOT REAL RICHES. (Ver. 7; comp. ch. xii. 9.) The saying may be directed against the foolish pride of birth and ostentation without anything real to back it up. It strikes a common vice of modern times—the aim to keep up appearances, and to pass for something greater in position than one really is. The contrasted example teaches the lesson of preferring the substance to the show, of being willing to appear much less than one is. And so in higher matters; take care to *be* what is sound and good in principle, and the *seeming* may be left for the most part to take care of itself. No appearances deceive God, and nothing that is real escapes him.

V. THE PRACTICAL SERVICE OF RICHES. (Ver. 8.) They may provide a ransom from captivity, from penal judgment, from the hand of robbers. Their power to procure deliverances from the evils of life is much wider in the present day. The poor man, on the contrary, "listens to no rebuke," *i.e.* no threats can extort from him what he has not got. He is helpless for want of means. A lesson not often taught from the pulpit, and perhaps not needed for the majority—prudent regard to the possible advantages of money, stimulating to industry in the quest for it. Still, some *do* need the lesson. And the Bible has no affectation of a false contempt for the means of living. Business men should be encouraged in their pursuit of wealth, and guided in their application of it.

VI. WEALTH ONLY PERMANENT WHEN WELL-GOTTEN. (Ver. 11.) Perhaps the translation to be preferred is, "Swindled wealth becomes small." Hastily gotten generally means hastily spent. And dishonest gain burns the fingers. How often do we see a feverish passion for spending going hand-in-hand with unlawful or unhealthy getting! A healthy acquisition of wealth is *gradual*, and the result of *steady industry*. Rapid fortune-making, or sudden "strokes of luck," are certainly not to be envied in view of the good of the soul.

LESSONS. 1. Wealth is a good in itself. When we speak of it as an evil, we are using a certain figure of speech; for the evil is in the false relation of the soul to this as to other earthly objects. 2. In the desires that relate to wealth, their proper control and direction, the moral discipline probably of the majority must ever lie. 3. Safety is to be found in the religious habit, which sees in earthly objects good only as they can be connected with that which is beyond themselves, and is Divine and eternal.—J.

Ver. 5.—*Purity and impurity of sentiment.* I. AVERSION FROM ALL UNTRUTH A LEADING CHARACTER OF PURITY. This does not imply that the good man never falls into acts or words which are untrue to his nature. But as a child of God, there is in his spiritual or ideal nature a rooted *antipathy* to lies, and a deep *sympathy* with truth in all its forms. 'Tis only truthfulness which can impart *fragrance, charm, delight,* to character.
II. THE CONTRARY DISPOSITION OF THE WICKED IS LOATHSOME AND SHAMEFUL. Antipathy to truth—and, alas! perversion may actually bring men to this—produces upon the pure moral taste an impression akin to that of nausea or deformity upon the physical sensibility. And we *blush* for it as a common odium and disgrace of human nature.—J.

Ver. 6.—*The outward correspondence with the inward.* I. UPRIGHTNESS IS THE DESIGNATION OF BOTH AN INWARD AND AN OUTWARD STATE. 1. As a sensuous image, uprightness suggests *strength, confidence, well-grounded* stability. 2. As a figure of the mind and character, it denotes *moral principle, fixed purpose,* based upon firm faith in God and his moral order. 3. Its consequence is a state of security amidst danger, freedom from evil.
II. WICKEDNESS AND RUIN ARE INTERCHANGEABLE THOUGHTS. 1. The ruin begins in the inward decay of moral principle. 2. It is consummated in outward decay—of reputation, of possessions, of health, of life.—J.

Ver. 9.—*Joy and gloom.* I. LIGHT IS THE SYMBOL OF JOY.
II. HENCE THE CHEERFUL BURNING OF A LIGHT IS THE SYMBOL OF THE GOOD MAN'S HEART. He sits in the centre and enjoys clear day.
III. GLOOM IS THE NATURAL EMBLEM OF SORROW.
IV. THE PUTTING OUT OF A LAMP IN DARKNESS IS THE EMBLEM OF THE EXTINCTION OF JOY, OF HOPE—of all that makes life worth having, and of life itself.—J.

Ver. 10.—*Pride and teachableness.* PRIDE BEGETS CONTROVERSY, WHICH CAN SELDOM BE CARRIED ON LONG WITHOUT DEGENERATING INTO EGOTISM. 1. There is contention for contention's sake, which is ever idle and baneful. 2. There is contention for truth's sake. But in the latter lie many dangers to purity of temper. Whenever we become angry in controversy, as a great man said, we cease to contend for the truth, and begin to contend for ourselves.—J.

Ver. 12.—*The sickness of disappointment and the joy of fruition.* I. HOPE DELAYED. Who has not known that sickness of the heart, that slow-consuming misery of which the text speaks? It is a sorrow of every age. Life itself is by some spent in this still lingering delay. The stern experience of the course of the world teaches us that the sentimental and romantic view of the future, so natural to youth, must give way to realities.
II. HOPE DELAYED IS THE TRIAL OF FAITH. The *duration* of the trial rather than the intensity is painful. So with Abraham in reference to Isaac (Gen. xv. 2, 3).
III. THERE IS A LOVING PROVIDENTIAL MEANING AT THE HEART OF THESE TRIALS. They are essentially *time* trials; they have an end—the " end of the Lord." So the boy named "Laughter" came to Abraham; so the Lord turned again the captivity of Zion, and the delivered were like unto them that dream! So Simeon could sing his *Nunc dimittis* on the appearance of the long-expected Saviour; and on his resurrection the disciples "believed not for joy, and wondered."
IV. A CERTAIN FRUITION IS PROMISED TO THE DESIRE OF THE RIGHTEOUS. " Yet a

little while, and he that shall come will come, and will not tarry" (comp. Rom. viii. 23; 2 Cor. v. 2—4).—J.

Vers. 13—17.—*The value of the Divine Word.* I. REVERENCE AND IRREVERENCE FOR THE DIVINE WORD. The "Word" is any revelation man receives of God, whether through nature, oracles of the prophets, or in his immediate consciousness. The last, in the deepest sense, is the condition of all other revelations. Irreverence is shown either when men are deaf and indifferent to the Divine voice, or when they suffer it to be out-clamoured by other voices—of passion, policy, etc. The *result* is that he who thus sins is "pledged" or forfeited to the Divine Law, here personified or regarded as a superhuman power. Hence appears the truth from this figure, that in disobedience our *freedom* is lost. On the contrary, reverence and obedience receive a certain reward: "Glory, honour, and peace to every man that worketh good" (Rom. ii. 10). II. THE DOCTRINE OF THE WISE. (Ver. 14.) The teaching that is founded on Divine revelation is a source of life, and a safeguard against the snares of death (comp. ch. x. 11). III. THERE MUST BE RECEPTIVITY TOWARDS THIS DOCTRINE. The Word must be "mixed with faith in those that hear." The favour of God is free in one sense, *i.e.* is no earned result of our conduct; but it is conditional in another, viz. it depends on our compliance with his will. The contrast to the life in the light of God's favour, watered by vital nourishment from the springs of truth, is the "way of the faithless," which is "barren," dry, as in "a dry and thirsty land where no water is." IV. PRUDENCE AND GOOD COUNSEL MUST BE ADDED TO REVERENCE. (Ver. 16.) *Thoughtfulness* is needed in studying the evidences, the substance, the applications of religion. And in the practical conduct of life how necessary! for more errors are committed for want of judgment and discrimination as to time, place, and circumstances, than for want of true and right purpose. The man destitute of tact pours folly abroad; temper, vanity, caprice, are exposed in all that he does and says. V. FAITHFUL AND UNFAITHFUL MINISTRY. (Ver. 17.) The wicked messenger prepares misfortune both for his master and for himself; while the faithful servant will amend even his master's mistakes. Applied to sacred things, every Christian should consider himself a messenger, an *apostle* in however humble a sphere, of God and his truth. And "it is required of stewards that they be found faithful."—J.

Vers. 18—25.—*The blessings of obedience and their counterpart.* I. THE BLESSINGS OF OBEDIENCE. 1. *Honour.* (Ver. 18.) "'Tis a good brooch to wear in a man's hat at all times," says one of our old poets. Love is common to all the creatures, as life and death; honour belongs to men alone; and dishonour must be worse than death. The praise of others is the reflection of virtue, and a good name like fragrant ointment. 2. *Satisfied desire.* (Ver. 19.) And what is sweeter than the attainment of worthy "ends and expectations"? And if we will but have faith, this satisfaction may be ours, by setting our hearts on *internal* blessings, the kingdom of God and his righteousness. 3. *Improving companionship.* (Ver. 20.) Friendship with the wise makes daylight in the understanding out of darkness and confusion of thoughts. Our wits and understanding clarify and break up in communicating and discoursing with one another. "We toss our thoughts more easily, marshal them more soberly; see how they look when turned into words; we wax wiser than ourselves, and that more by an hour's discourse than by a day's meditation" (Lord Bacon). 4. *Unfailing compensations.* All things are double, one against another. An eye for an eye, a tooth for a tooth, on the one side; measure for measure, love for love, on the other. "Give, and it shall be given you;" "He that watereth shall be watered himself." "What will you have?" saith God; "pray for it, and take it." "If you serve an ungrateful master, serve him the more. Put God in your debt. Every stroke shall be repaid. The longer the payment is withholden, the better for you; for compound interest on compound interest is the rate and usage of this exchequer." 5. *Hereditary good.* (Ver. 22.) We desire to prolong our blessings, in the view of fancy, beyond our lives; and the desire to leave behind a fortune, or a name and fame, is one of the most common and natural. The thought that all the good our life has produced will be still a germinant power with our descendants after we are gone, is one of the noblest and most inspiring. 6. *Fruitful poverty.* (Ver. 23.) The image is that of the poor man's field, which becomes rich in produce through the investment of his toil in it. The improvement of the ground is the most natural way of obtaining riches; it is our great mother's blessing, the earth. The blessing of God visibly rests upon the honest labour of the poor. 7. *Wise training of the young.* (Ver. 24.) The rod may stand as a figure for all correction, firm yet kindly discipline, and instruction. The wise father will seek to *anticipate* moral evil by subduing early the passionate temper. He will incessantly follow up his child with prayer, with discipline, with exhortations, that he may not later rue the absence of seasonable warnings. 8. *Temperate enjoyment and sufficient supplies.* (Ver. 25.) The mind governed by religion and wisdom learns to reduce its wants to a small compass; and this is a great secret of content and of true riches. He who wants only what is necessary for the life and free action of the soul may rely with confidence on the infinite bounty of Providence.

II. THE COUNTERPART. 1. *Poverty and shame.* (Ver. 18.) The one an outward misery, patent to all; the other not so patent, but more acute; for contempt, as the Indian proverb says, pierces through the shell of the tortoise. So long ago as old Homer, we find the sentiment, "Shame greatly hurts or greatly helps mankind" ('Iliad,' xxiv. 45; Hesiod, 'Op.,' 316). "Take one of the greatest and most approved courage, who makes nothing to look death and danger in the face, . . . in a base and a shameful action, and the eye of the discoverer, like that of the basilisk, shall strike him dead. So inexpressibly great sometimes are the killing horrors of this passion" (South, vol. ii. ser. vii.). The Bible designates this as a peculiar fruit of sin. 2. *The unquenchable fire of lust.* (Ver. 19.) To this the correct rendering of the second member of the verse appears to point (Jas. i. 14, 15). 'Tis hard to give up the bosom sin, which still in better moments is hated— a loathsome tyranny, yet one which cannot be cast off. 3. *Depraving companionship.* (Ver. 20.) Wicked companions invite to hell. "There are like to be short graces when the devil plays the host." 4. *Haunting troublers.* (Ver. 21.) Much romance has been woven about "haunted houses;" but what haunted house so gruesome as the bad man's heart? His sin draws God's wrath and punishments after it, even as the shadows follow his feet. 5. *Forfeited wealth.* (Ver. 22.) Riches that come from the devil go back to him. Fraud, oppression, and unjust dealing are not really retentive; or wealth obtained by flattering, complying with others' humours, and servility does not prosper. The Proverbs see the outrush of life with great clearness; they do not always explain the *inner connection* of cause and effect, which should be clear to us. 6. *Self-destruction.* (Ver. 23.) Many a man is "carried away by his unrighteousness." "In contrast with the contented, humble condition of the good man, the selfish and profligate 'lovers of themselves without a rival,' are often unfortunate; and whereas they have all their time sacrificed to themselves, they become in the end themselves sacrifices to the inconstancy of fortune, whose wings they thought by their self-wisdom to have pinioned" (Lord Bacon). 7. *Weak indulgence to children.* (Ver. 24.) A most injurious error. It tends to weaken the young minds and foster all the violent passions; just as the opposite extreme tends to debase and incite to deceit. E. Irving, in one of his works, hints that a great proportion of the inmates of lunatic asylums have been only and spoilt children. 8. *Want.* (Ver. 25.) "Great wants," it has been said, "proceed from great wealth; but they are undutiful children, for they sink wealth down to poverty."—J.

Vers. 1, 13, 18.—*The wisdom of docility, etc.: a sermon to the young.* We have the positive and negative, the happy and the sorrowful aspects of the subject brought into view.

I. THE WISDOM OF DOCILITY. The excellency of docility is seen in its results: 1. *In character.* It is a "wise son" who heareth his father's instruction. (1) *Already* he is wise. Apart from all that he will gain by his teachableness, readiness to receive instruction is in itself an admirable feature of character; it is so more particularly in the young. In them it is positively essential to spiritual beauty and worth; and it goes a long way to constitute such worth. It is an attribute of mind which is pleasing to God, and which commends itself greatly to the esteem of man. (2) It has the promise of wisdom further on. For he who is ready to learn, and more especially if he is willing to "regard reproof," is on the high-road to much attainment in knowledge, and also to heights of virtue and godliness. This habit of his will save him from many snares, and will enrich his soul with pure principles and honourable aspirations and right affections. 2. *In circumstance.* The docile son will "be rewarded," will "be honoured." The path he treads is one which leads to competence, to comfort, to health, to honour, to "a green old age." But there are three things which must be included in this readiness to learn. No one will be "wise," and no one can expect to reap these desirable results, unless he (1) is docile in the home, receiving "his father's (and his mother's) instruction (ver. 1); (2) has respect to the "commandment," the will of God as revealed in his Word (ver. 13); (3) is willing to be corrected when he has gone astray, unless he "regards reproof" (ver. 18). For all of us fall into some error, make some mistakes, go astray in some directions; and we all need the kind hand that will lead us back and replace us in the right road.

II. THE FOLLY AND THE DOOM OF THE UNTEACHABLE. What should we think of the young captain who insisted on setting sail without any chart, trusting to his native cleverness to shun the shoals and rocks, and to make his way to port? We know what to judge concerning him, and what to prophesy concerning his vessel; we are sure that the one is a fool, and that the other will be a wreck. And what shall we think of youth when it resolves to sail forth on the great sea of life, disregarding the experiences of the wise, and trusting to its own sagacity? To take this course is: 1. *To be unwise.* Apart from all consequences which are in the future, it is the indication of a foolish spirit which is in itself deplorable. It shows a very ill-balanced judgment, a very exaggerated conception of one's own ability, a lack of the modesty the presence of which is so great a recommendation, and the absence of which is so serious a drawback. It calls for and it calls forth the pity of the wise; it is well if it does not elicit their contempt. 2. *To move in the direction of disaster.* It is to be in the way which conducts (1) to the loss of much that is very valuable, to "poverty" of more kinds than one (ver. 18); (2) to shame (ver. 18), the forfeiture of good men's regard, and a descent to a condition in which self-respect also is lost; (3) to ultimate destruction (ver. 13). He that feareth not God's commandment, nor regards man's warning, is a candidate for contempt, is a swift traveller on the road to ruin.—C.

Ver. 4.—(See homily on ch. xxvii. 23.)—C.

Ver. 7.—*Wrong views of ourselves, given and received.* One proverb may have many interpretations and many applications. This is such a one. It may well suggest to us two things.

I. THE GUILT OF CONVEYING A FALSE VIEW OF OURSELVES; whether this be done by the merchant in his office, or by the charlatan on the platform, or by the quack in his surgery, or by the preacher in his pulpit, or by the "philanthropist" in the newspaper, or by the man or woman of embellishment in society, or by the artist on canvas, or by the author in his book, or whether done by the common miser or the conscienceless beggar. Here is the double iniquity of: 1. Falsehood, or, at any rate, *falseness.* The man is false to himself, and forgets what is due to himself; consequently, he does that which wrongs and injures himself. 2. Fraud; imposture. A man practises on his neighbours; he deceives them; in the worst cases he induces others to run most serious risks to their health or their fortune.

II. THE MISFORTUNE OF FORMING A WRONG ESTIMATE OF OURSELVES. 1. This is sometimes *an appropriate penalty.* For if a man "makes himself" rich or poor in the eyes of others, it is extremely likely that he will before long imagine himself to be so. It is one of the well-attested facts of human experience, that what men try to persuade their fellows to think, they come in time to believe themselves. And this holds good when the object as well as the subject is the man himself. Try to convince others that you are clever, learned, kind, pious, and before many months have been spent in the endeavour you will actually credit yourself with these qualities. And the result is an entirely mistaken view of yourself. This is a punitive consequence; for there is no moral condition from which we have such urgent need to pray and strive that we may be delivered. Is it not the last stage on the downward road? 2. It is *a grave spiritual peril.* Solemn, indeed, is the warning addressed by the risen Lord to the Church at Laodicea (Rev. iii. 14—19). But no warning can be too serious or too strong, whether addressed to the Church or the individual, when there is a false estimate of self, a supposition of wealth which is but imaginary, a false confidence which, if not awakened now, will be terribly aroused and shattered further on. 3. But a false estimate of ourselves *may* be, not a penalty, but rather *a pity*. When the heart thinks itself (makes itself) poor and destitute, while it is really "rich toward God," it suffers as it need not suffer, and it lacks the strength for doing good which it need not lack. And this is not unfrequently the case. Men have been misinstructed concerning the kingdom of Christ; and long after they have been within it they have been supposing themselves to stand outside it. Wherefore let those who teach take care how they teach, and let all disciples "take heed how they hear," that they may *not* think themselves wrong when they are right with God, rebels against the Divine Ruler when they are his accepted children.—C.

Ver. 12, with ver. 9 (first part) and ver. 19 (first part).—*Hope and disappointment.* We learn that—

I. HOPE IS PLANTED AS AN INSTINCT IN THE HUMAN HEART. "Thou didst make me hope when I was upon my mother's breasts," says the psalmist (xxii. 9). We start on our course with a precious store of hopefulness in our soul; and it takes much to kill or to exhaust it. It lasts most men through life, though the troublous experiences we pass through weaken it, if they do not wound it unto death.

II. IT IS A SOURCE OF GREAT STRENGTH AND JOY TO US. 1. It is a source of strength to us. It leads us to entertain and to enter upon new ventures. It carries us on during many toils and through many difficulties. It sustains us to the end, when we are weary, and when we are opposed and baffled. "We are saved by hope." 2. It is also a perennial source of joy. Rob life of its anticipations, and you deprive it of a very large proportion of its sweetness and satisfaction.

III. SIN HAS INTRODUCED DISAPPOINTMENT. We must regard this as one part, and one very serious part, of the penalty of sin. Not, of course, that each case of disappointment is the consequence of some particular antecedent wrong-doing; but that it forms a part of that whole burden and trial of life which is the mark and the penalty of human sin. There are *lighter* disappointments which may not count for much, though these put together would make up no small aggregate of evil. But there are *heavier* disappointments which constitute a very large and serious part of our life-sorrow. "Hope deferred" does indeed make the heart sick. The long and weary waiting for the return of the absent; for the manifestation of love ungratefully, and perhaps cruelly, withheld; for the health and strength which no treatment will restore; for the opening which would prove a great opportunity; for the signs of reformation in a beloved relative or friend; for the relenting and reconciliation of one who has been long estranged;— this does fill the soul with an aching such as no other trouble brings. It is one of life's very heaviest burdens. It is sometimes *the* burden and even the blight of a human life.

IV. IT IS THE PART OF CHRISTIAN WISDOM TO AVERT IT. Not that it *can* be wholly averted—that is quite beyond our power. Not that there is any real blessing in the absence or the littleness of expectation. But that: 1. We should discourage and renounce the perilous and injurious habit of idle day-dreams. 2. We should moderate our hopes according to our circumstances, and be contented only to look for that which, in the providence of God, we may reasonably and rightly expect to partake of.

V. IT IS THE PART OF CHRISTIAN SUBMISSION TO ACCEPT IT. We must suffer when our hopes are unfulfilled; but we may find great relief in the thought that it is the will of God that we are submitting to. The feeling that it is our Divine Friend who is letting us pass through the dark shadow of disappointment, and that it is the holy Lord seeking our highest good who is sending us through the refining fires,—this will give balm to our wounded spirit; this will lighten the heavy load we bear.

VI. GOD WILL GIVE HIS PEOPLE SOME GOOD MEASURE OF FULFILMENT. We shall prove by our experience in many ways and in many spheres—particularly in those of (1) our inner life and (2) our work for our Lord—that "the light of the righteous rejoiceth," that "when desire cometh, it is a tree of life," that "desire accomplished is sweet to the soul." If we rest in the Lord, and wait patiently for him, he will give us our heart's desires (Ps. xxxvii. 4, 7).

VII. THERE IS ONE SUPREME HOPE which may well sustain us in the darkest trials (1 Pet. i. 3, 4).—C.

Ver. 20.—*Friendship: a sermon to the young.* We have here a topic which comes very close home to us *all*, but especially to the young.

I. GOD HAS GIVEN US GREAT POWER OVER ONE ANOTHER. There are two sources of power we exercise. 1. *That of ideas.* As we speak or write to one another, we impart ideas to the mind; and as thought lies beneath feeling, and feeling beneath character and conduct (see homily on ch. xii. 5), it is clearly of the gravest consequence what ideas we do instil into the mind of another. These ideas include information or knowledge, the presentation of motive and inducement, new aspects in which things are regarded, new views and conceptions of life, etc. 2. *That of influence.* As we associate with one another, we influence one another by (1) the character which commands respect; (2) affectionateness of disposition; (3) charm of manner; (4) strength of will; (5) superiority in age or in social position; (6) facility and force of utterance. All these are elements of influence; they are sometimes united, and in combination they become a great moral force.

II. CLOSENESS OF INTIMACY SHOWS THIS POWER AT ITS HEIGHT. When two "walk together because they are agreed;" when there is a close and intimate union of heart with heart, of mind with mind,—there is an opening for the exertion of a power immeasurably great. Friendship has done more than anything else to enlarge or to warp the mind, to save or to betray the soul, to bless or to corrupt the life. The influence of a beloved friend or of a favourite author is wholly beyond calculation, and is almost beyond exaggeration. We give ourselves to one another; we impress our mind upon one another; we draw one another up or we drag one another down. Hence—

III. IT IS OF SUPREME IMPORTANCE THAT WE CHOOSE OUR FRIENDS WELL. The friendships we form will either make or mar us. We shall certainly be conformed in spirit and in character to those whom we admit to the sanctuary of our soul; our lives will move with theirs toward the same goal; and we shall share their destiny for good or evil. How needful, then, that we bring to this choice our whole intelligence, our greatest care, that we do not let the accidents of locality or family connection or business association decide the intimacies of our life! There is no action on which our future more decisively depends than on this choice we make; let youth and young manhood (womanhood) look well to it. He that walketh with wise men will himself be wise, and he will reap all the fruits of wisdom; but the companion of fools, of those who fear not God and who honour not man, of the irreligious and the immoral, will be destroyed with a terrible, because a spiritual, destruction.

IV. HOW WISE TO WALK THE PATH OF LIFE WITH A DIVINE FRIEND!—with him who himself is "the Wisdom of God;" intimacy with whom will draw our spirit up toward all that is worthiest and noblest; whose presence will ensure guardianship from all serious evil, and enrichment with every true blessing, and will gladden with all pure and lasting joy.—C.

Ver. 21.—*Penalty pursuing sin.* These are striking words, and they give us a graphic picture of penalty in pursuit of the guilt which is seeking and hoping to escape, but which is certain to be overtaken.

I. SIN AND SUFFERING ARE INSEPARABLY ASSOCIATED IN THOUGHT. In our judgment and in our feeling they go together; they belong to one another. There is no need to go beyond this point; it is ultimate. If we sin, we deserve to suffer, and must expect to suffer. It is right that we should, and the hand that brings it about is a righteous hand.

II. THEY OFTEN SEEM TO BE DIVIDED IN FACT. As we observe human life, we see that the murderer sometimes escapes the reach of law, that the swindler sometimes flourishes upon the losses of his victims, that the tyrant sometimes reigns long over the nation he has defrauded of its freedom, that sometimes the man who lives in the practice of vice continues to enjoy health for many years, that the dishonest author may reap a considerable reputation and may long remain unexposed, etc. But in this case—

III. PENALTY IS PURSUING SIN AND WILL OVERTAKE IT. "Evil pursueth sinners" Justice is on the track, and sooner or later will lay its hand upon its victim. 1. *It will most likely do so here.* Very frequently, indeed almost always, *some* penalty immediately overtakes guilt; if not in bodily loss or suffering, yet in spiritual injury. And if not at once, penalty soon follows crime, vice, wrong-doing. Or if not soon, yet after many years, the "evil" comes and lays its stern hand upon the shoulder. The man may not, probably does not, see or even believe in its approach. Its step is silent, and it may be slow, but it is constant and certain. The "evil" may be *physical*, and very often it is so; or it may be *mental*, intellectual; or it may be *circumstantial*; or it may be *in reputation*; or it may be *in character*, and this last, though least seen and often least regarded, is in truth the saddest and the most serious of all, for it affects the man himself—he "loses his own soul." Thus, "though leaden-footed," penalty is "iron-handed." 2. *It will surely do so hereafter.* (See Matt. xxv. 31, 32; 2 Cor. v. 10, etc.) Yet not inconsistent with all this—

IV. THERE IS ONE MERCIFUL INTERCEPTION. If we truly repent of our sin, we shall be freely and abundantly forgiven. 1. God will change his condemnation into acceptance and parental favour, so that we shall walk thenceforward in the light of his countenance. 2. He will avert the heavier consequences of our sin by introducing into our heart and life all the remedial and restorative influences of righteousness. And there must be considered—

V. THE CONVERSE BENEFICENT LAW AFFECTING THE RIGHTEOUS. "To the righteous good shall be repaid." 1. All right acts are immediately followed by an inner and spiritual blessing; we must be something the better in soul for every really right thing we do. 2. All right actions, done in a reverent and filial spirit, will bring God's blessing down further on. He is "not unrighteous to forget our work of faith and our labour of love." Such blessings come in many forms, and at various intervals; but they *do come*; they are following the upright, and they will overtake them and crown them. 3. The reward of integrity and faithfulness only comes in part below; God holds great things in reserve for us (Matt. xxv. 21; 1 Cor. iv. 5).—C.

Ver. 24.—*Parental correction.* Few proverbs "come home" to us like those which affect the daily government of our household. They make their appeal to the human heart, to universal experience.

I. THE PARENTAL INSTINCT. 1. This is, to let the child have his way; to give him the gratification he desires, to find a present pleasure in his momentary happiness. 2. This is, to spare him suffering. No parent can hear his child cry without suffering himself (herself). Our instinct is to save our children from every trouble, small and great, from which we can exempt them. And it "goes against the grain" to inflict punishment, to cause pain, to deprive of some known enjoyment. But we dare not be blind to—

II. THE LESSON OF EXPERIENCE. Universal experience proves that to act on mere parental instinct is nothing less than selfish cruelty. It is to act as if we positively hated our children. For it is the one sure way to spoil them for life, to ruin their character. The undisciplined child becomes the wayward boy, the dissipated young man, the wreck of manhood. He becomes self-centred, incapable of controlling his spirit, exacting in all his relations, disregardful of all law and of all claims. It is to withhold the one condition under which alone we can expect any one to attain to an admirable and honourable manhood. It is to deny to our own children the most essential element of education. Experience proves that he who spares the rod acts as if he positively *hated* his son.

III. THE PRACTICE OF WISDOM. This is the well-moderated correction of love. This correction should be: 1. Carefully proportioned to the offence; the lighter ones, such as carelessness or inaptitude, being followed by the lighter rebuke, and the graver ones, such as falsehood or cruelty, being visited with severer measures. 2. Administered, not in the heat of temper, but in the calmness of conviction, and with the manifest sorrow of true affection. 3. As free as possible from physical violence. The "rod" need not be made of wood or iron. A look of reproach (Luke xxii. 61), a just rebuke or remonstrance, a wisely chosen exclusion from some appreciated privilege, may do much more good than any blows upon the body. 4. Strictly just, with a leaning to charitable construction. For one unjust infliction will do more harm than many just ones will do good. 5. Occasional and of brief duration. Nothing defeats its own purpose more certainly than perpetual fault-finding, or constantly repeated punishment, or penalty that is unrighteously severe. It behoves us always to remember that as our heavenly Father does not " deal with us after our sins " with rigorous penalties, and is not "strict to mark iniquity" with unfailing chastisement, so it becomes us, as parents, in the treatment of our children, to let pity and charity have a very large, modifying influence on our correction. He that loveth chastens " betimes ; " he is not always chastening. He takes care to let his children know *and feel* that beneath and above and throughout his fatherly righteousness is his parental love.—C.

EXPOSITION.

CHAPTER XIV.

Ver. 1.—Every wise woman buildeth her house. Wise women order well their household matters and their families; they have an important influence, and exercise it beneficially.

Γυναικὸς ἐσθλῆς ἐστὶ σώζειν οἰκίαν.

" A good wife is the saving of a house."

The versions render as above. A different pointing of the word translated " wise " (*chakhmoth*) will give " wisdom " (*chokh-moth*), which it seems best to read here, as the parallel to the abstract term " folly " in the second member. So we have, " Wisdom hath builded her house " (ch. ix. 1 ; comp. ch. i. 20). Thus : " The wisdom of women buildeth their house " (ch. xii. 4 ; xxiv. 3). **But the foolish plucketh it down with her hands;** " but Folly plucketh it down with her own hands; " of course, the folly of women is intended.

Γυνὴ γὰρ οἴκῳ πῆμα καὶ σωτηρία.

" Bane or salvation to a house is woman."

Foolish, unprincipled women, by their bad management or their evil doings, ruin their families materially and morally. " The husband should labour," says a Servian proverb; " the wife should save."

Ver. 2.—He that walketh in his uprightness feareth the Lord. So the Septuagint. He who lives an upright life does so because he fears the Lord; and his holy conversation is an evidence that he is influenced by religious motives. The outward conduct shows the inward feeling. So he that is **perverse in his ways despiseth him**—the Lord. A man is evil in his actions because he has cast off the fear of God; and such wickedness is a proof that he has lost all reverence for God and care to please him. Delitzsch renders, " He walketh in his uprightness who feareth Jahve, and perverse in his ways is he that despiseth him; " *i.e.* the conduct of the two shows the way in which they severally regard God and religion, the former acting conscientiously and up-

rightly, the latter following his own lusts, which lead him astray. Either interpretation is admissible. Septuagint, " He that walketh in crooked ways (σκολιάζων ταῖς ὁδοῖς αὐτοῦ) shall be dishonoured." The Vulgate gives quite a different turn to the sentence, " He who walketh in the right way and feareth the Lord is despised by him who pursueth the path of shame." This intimates the hatred which sinners feel for the godly (comp. Job xii. 4 ; and especially Wisd. ii. 10—20 ; and our Lord's warning, John xv. 18—21).

Ver. 3.—In the mouth of the foolish is a rod of pride. חֹטֶר (*choter*), " rod," or " shoot," is found also in Isa. xi. 1. From the mouth of the arrogant fool proceeds a growth of vaunting and conceit, accompanied with insolence towards others, for which he is often chastised. So the tongue is compared to a sword (*e.g.* Ps. lvii. 4 ; lxiv. 3 ; Jer. xviii. 18 ; Rev. i. 16). St. Gregory ('Mor. in Job,' xxiv.) applies this sentence to haughty preachers, who are anxious to appear superior to other people, and study more to chide and reprove than to encourage; " they know how to smite sharply, but not to sympathize with humility." Septuagint, " From the mouth of fools cometh a staff of insolence." **The lips of the wise shall preserve them**—the wise (ch. xiii. 3). These do not abuse speech to insult and injure others; and their words tend to conciliate others, and promote peace and good will (comp. ch. xii. 6).

Ver. 4.—Where no oxen (*cattle*) are, the crib is clean. This does not mean, as some take it, that labour has its rough, disagreeable side, yet in the end brings profit; but rather that without bullocks to labour in the fields, or cows to supply milk—that is, without toil and industry, and necessary instruments—the crib is empty, there is nothing to put in the granary, there are no beasts to fatten. The means must be adapted to the end. **Much increase is by the strength of the ox.** This, again, is not an exhortation to kindness towards animals, which makes no antithesis to the first clause; but it is parallel with ch. xii. 11, and means that where agricultural works are diligently carried on (the "ploughing ox" being taken as the type of industry), large returns are secured. Septuagint, "Where fruits are plentiful the strength of the ox is manifest."

Ver. 5.—A repetition of ch. xii. 17 (see also ch. vi. 19). **A faithful witness** cannot be induced to swerve from the truth by threat or bribe. **Will utter;** Hebrew, *breatheth forth.* A false witness with no compulsion, as it were naturally, puts forth lies (comp. ver. 25; ch. xix. 5). Septuagint, "An unrighteous witness kindleth (ἐκκαίει) falsehood."

Ver. 6.—**A scorner seeketh wisdom, and findeth it not;** literally, *it is not—there is none* (ch. xiii. 7). A scorner may affect to be seeking wisdom, but he can never attain to it, because it is given only to him who is meek and fears the Lord (Ps. xxv. 9). Wisd. i. 4, "Into a malicious soul wisdom shall not enter; nor dwell in the body that is pledged to sin" (comp. Ps. cxi. 10). True wisdom is not to be won by those who are too conceited to receive instruction, and presume to depend upon their own judgment, and to weigh everything by their own standard. This is especially true of the knowledge of Divine things, which "scorners" never really acquire. Septuagint, "Thou shalt seek wisdom among the wicked, but thou shalt find it not." **Knowledge is easy unto him that understandeth;** "that hath understanding," *i.e.* to the man who realizes that the fear of God is a necessary condition to the acquiring of wisdom, and who seeks it as a boon at his hands. This acquisition, as it is difficult, nay, impossible for the scorner, is comparatively easy for the humble believer who seeks it with the right temper and in the right way. " Mysteries are revealed unto the meek" (Ecclus. iii. 19, in some manuscripts).

Ver. 7.—**Go from the presence of a foolish man.** There is some doubt about the rendering of this passage. The Vulgate gives, *vade contra stultum,* which is probably to be taken in the sense of the Authorized Version. The Revised Version has, "Go into the presence of a foolish man." The Hebrew מִנֶּגֶד *(minneged)* may mean "from before," "over against," "in the presence of." Hence arises an ambiguity. The Authorized Version considers the sentence to be an injunction to turn away from a stupid man when you perceive that you can do him no good. The Revised Version is equivalent to "if you go into the presence," etc. **When thou perceivest not in him the lips of knowledge;** Revised Version, *and thou shalt not perceive in him,* etc., which embodies a truism with no special point. The whole sentence is better translated, *Go forth from the presence of a foolish man, and thou hast*

not known the lips of knowledge; i.e., as Nowack explains, "Leave the presence of a fool, and you carry nothing away with you; after all your intercourse with him, you quit his presence without having gained any advance in true knowledge" (see on ch. xx. 15). The LXX. presents a very different version: "All things are adverse to a foolish man; but wise lips are the arms of knowledge (αἰσθήσεως)." A foolish man, by his inconsiderate, slanderous, or bitter words, makes every one his enemy: a wise man uses his knowledge to good purposes; his words are the instruments by which he shows what he is.

Ver. 8.—**The wisdom of the prudent is to understand his way.** The wisdom of the prudent is shown by his considering whither his actions lead, the motives from which they spring, the results that attend them. As the apostle enjoins (Eph. v. 15), "See that ye walk circumspectly, not as fools, but as wise." Or the clause may be taken as enjoining a wise choice in life, a selection of such a calling or occupation as best suits one's capabilities, station, and opportunities. **The folly of fools is deceit.** This is not self-deceit, which the word does not denote, but deceit of others. Stupid persons show their folly in trying to cheat others, though they are sure to be detected, and their fraud recoils on themselves. In the case of fools, what they would call wisdom is folly; hence the wording of the sentence.

Ver. 9.—**Fools make a mock at sin.** So the Vulgate (comp. ch. x. 23). Fools, wicked men, commit sin lightly and cheerfully, give specious names to grievous transgressions, pass over rebuke with a joke, encourage others in crime by their easy way of viewing it. But in the original the verb is in the singular number, while the noun is plural, and the clause could be translated as in the Authorized Version only with the notion that the number of the verb is altered in order to individualize the application of the maxim ('Speaker's Commentary'). But there is no necessity for such a violent anomaly. The subject is doubtless the word rendered "sin" *(asham)* which means both "sin" and "sin offering." So we may render, "Sin mocks fools," *i.e.* deceives and disappoints them of the enjoyment which they expected. Or better, as most in harmony with the following member, "The sin offering of fools mocks them" (ch. xv. 8). Thus Aquila and Theodotion, ἄφρονας χλευάζει πλημμέλεια, where πλημμέλεια may signify "sin offering" (Ecclus. vii. 31). It is vain for such to seek to win God's favour by ceremonial observances; offerings from them are useless expenditure of cost and trouble (ch. xxi. 27). The Son of Sirach has well expressed this truth: "He that sacrificeth of a thing unlawfully gotten, his offering is mockery (μεμωκημένη), and the mockeries of unjust men are not well-pleasing. The Most High is not pleased with the offerings of the godless, neither is he propitiated for sin by the multitude of sacrifices" (Ecclus. xxxi. 18, 19). It is always the disposition of the heart that conditions the acceptableness of worship. Among the righteous there is favour—the favour and good will of God, which are bestowed upon them because their heart is right. The word *ratson* might equally refer to the good will of man, which the righteous gain by their kindness to sinners and ready sympathy; but in that case the antithesis would be less marked. Septuagint, "The houses of transgressors owe purification (ὀφειλήσουσι καθαρισμόν); but the houses of the just are acceptable." This is explained to signify that sinners refuse to offer the sacrifice which they need for their legal purification; but the righteous, while they have no necessity for a sin offering, are acceptable when they present their free-will vows and thanksgivings.

Ver. 10.—The heart knoweth its own bitterness; literally, *the heart (leb) knoweth the bitterness of his soul (nephesh)*. Neither our joys nor our sorrows can be wholly shared with another; no person stands in such intimate relation to us, or can put himself so entirely in our place, as to feel that which we feel. There is many a dark spot, many a grief, of which our best friend knows nothing; the skeleton is locked in the cupboard, and no one has the key but ourselves. But *we* can turn with confidence to the God-Man, Jesus, who knows our frame, who wept human tears, and bore our sorrows, and was in all points tempted like as we are, and who has taken his human experience with him into heaven. A stranger doth not intermeddle with its joy. The contrast is between the heart's sorrow and its joy; both alike in their entirety are beyond the ken of strangers. St. Gregory remarks on this passage ('Moral.,' vi. 23), "The human mind 'knoweth its own soul's bitterness' when, inflamed with aspirations after the eternal land, it learns by weeping the sorrowfulness of its pilgrimage. But 'the stranger doth not intermeddle with his joy,' in that he, that is now a stranger to the grief of compunction, is not then a partaker in the joy of consolation." A homely proverb says, "No one knows where the shoe pinches so well as he that wears it;" and an Italian maxim runs, "Ad ognuno par più grave la croce sua"—" To every one his own cross seems heaviest." Septuagint, "The heart of man is sensitive (αἰσθητική), his soul is sorrowful; but when it rejoices, it has no intermingling of insolence;" *i.e.* when a

man's mind is sensitive it is easily depressed by grief; but when it is elated by joy, it should receive its pleasure and relief without arrogance and ribaldry.

Ver. 11.—The house . . . the tabernacle. The house of the wicked, which they build and beautify and love, and which they look upon as a lasting home, shall perish; the hope which they founded upon it shall come to a speedy end (ch. xii. 7); but the righteous rear only a tent on earth, as becomes those who are strangers and pilgrims; and yet this abode is more secure, the hopes founded upon it are more lasting, for it continues unto everlasting life. The text in its first sense probably means that sinners take great pains to increase their material prosperity, and to leave heirs to carry on their name and family, but Providence defeats their efforts; good men do their duty in their state of life, try to please God and benefit their neighbour, leaving anxious care for the future, and God prospers them beyond all that they thought or wished (comp. ch. iii. 33). Shall flourish. The word applies metaphorically to the growth, vigour, and increase of a family under the blessing of God. Septuagint, "The tents of the upright shall stand." There is a cognate proverb at ch. xii. 7.

Ver. 12.—This verse occurs again in ch. xvi. 25. There is a way which seemeth right unto a man. This may refer to the blinding effects of passion and self-will; for these make a man think his own way best and most desirable. But it seems better to take it as a warning against following a perverted or uninstructed conscience. Conscience needs to be informed by God's Word and ruled by God's will to make it a safe guide. When properly regulated, it is able to pronounce a verdict upon contemplated action, and its verdict must always be obeyed. But warped by prejudice, weakened by disuse and disobedience, judicially blinded in punishment and in consequence of sin, it loses all power of moral judgment, and becomes inoperative of good; and then, as to the way that seemed at the moment right, the end thereof are the ways of death (ch. v. 5). The man is following a false light, and is led astray, and goes headlong to destruction (comp. Rom. i. 28; 1 Tim. iv. 2; see on ver. 13). St. Gregory ('Moral.,' v. 12) has some words on this subject: "There are times when we are ignorant whether the very things which we believe we do aright, are rightly done in the strict Judge's eye. For it often happens that an action of ours, which is cause for our condemnation, passes with us for the aggrandizement of virtue. Often by the same act whereby we think to appease the Judge, he is urged to anger when favourable

Hence, while holy men are getting the mastery over their evil habits, their very good practices even become an object of dread to them, lest, when they desire to do a good action, they be decoyed by a semblance of the thing, lest the hateful canker of corruption lurk under the fair appearance of a goodly colour. For they know that they are still charged with the burden of corruption, and cannot exactly discern the things that be good" (Oxford transl.).

Ver. 13.—**Even in laughter the heart is sorrowful** (comp. ver. 10). This recalls Lucretius's lines (iv. 1129)—

"Medio de fonte leporum
Surgit amari aliquid, quod in ipsis floribus angat."

The text is scarcely to be taken as universally true, but either as specially applicable to those mentioned in the preceding verse, or as teaching that the outward mirth often cloaks hidden sorrow (comp. Virgil, 'Æneid,' i. 208, etc.). **And the end of that joy is bitterness;** it has in it no element of endurance, and when it is past, the real grief that it masked comes into prominence. In this mortal life also joy and sorrow are strangely intermingled; sorrow follows closely on the steps of joy; as some one somewhere says, "The sweetest waters at length find their way to the sea, and are embittered there." Lesêtre refers to Pascal, 'Pensées,' ii. 1: "Tous se plaignent ... de tout pays, de tout temps, de tous âges, et de toutes conditions. Une preuve si longue, si continuelle et si uniforme, devrait bien nous convaincre de l'impuissance où nous sommes d'arriver au bien par nos efforts: mais l'exemple ne nous intruit point . . . Le présent ne nous satisfaisant jamais, l'espérance nous pipe, et, de malheur en malheur, nous mène jusqu'à la mort, qui en est le comble éternel. C'est une chose étrange, qu'il n'y a rien dans la nature qui n'ait été capable de tenir la place de la fin et du bonheur de l'homme. . . . L'homme étant déchu de son état naturel, il n'y a rien à quoi il n'ait été capable de se porter. Depuis qu'il a perdu le vrai bien, tout également peut lui paraitre tel, jusqu'à sa destruction propre, toute contraire qu'elle est à la raison et à la nature tout ensemble." This illustrates also ver. 12. Proverbs like "There is no rose without a thorn" are common enough in all languages. The Latins said, "Ubi uber, ibi tuber;" and "Ubi mel, ibi fel." Greek experience produced the gnome—

Ἆρ' ἐστὶ συγγενές τι λύπη καὶ βίος.

"Sorrow and life are very near of kin."

The Christian learns another lesson, "Blessed are they that mourn: for they shall be comforted" (Matt. v. 4). The LXX. has introduced a negative, which gives a sense exactly contrary to the Hebrew and to all the other versions : "In joys there is no admixture of sorrow, but the final joy cometh unto grief." The negative has doubtless crept inadvertently into the text; if it were genuine, the sentence might be explained of the sinner's joy, which he finds for a time and exults in, but which does not last, and is felt to be a delusion as life closes.

Ver. 14.—**The backslider in heart**—he who turns away from God (Ps. xliv. 18)—**shall be filled with his own ways, shall reap** the fruits of his evil-doings (ch. i. 31; xii. 14). Matt. vi. 2, "Verily I say unto you, they have their reward." **And a good man shall be satisfied from himself.** There is no verb expressed in this clause, "shall be satisfied" being supplied by our translators. Delitzsch and others read, "and a good man from his own deeds." It is simpler to repeat the verb from the former clause: "A good man shall be filled with that which belongs to him;" *i.e.* the holy thoughts and righteous actions in which he delights. Isa. iii. 10, "Say ye of the righteous that it shall be well with him; for they shall eat the fruit of their doings." The Vulgate, neglecting the prefix, translates, "And over him shall be the good man;" Septuagint, "And a good man from his thoughts," the produce of his heart and mind.

Ver. 15.—**The simple believeth every word.** "Simple" (*pethi*), the credulous person, open to all influences (ch. i. 22). The Vulgate has *innocens*, and the Septuagint ἄκακος; but the word is best taken in an unfavourable sense. The credulous fool believes all that he hears without proof or examination : having no fixed principles of his own, he is at the mercy of any adviser, and is easily led astray. Ecclus. xix. 4, "He that is hasty to give credit is light-minded, and he that sinneth (thus) shall offend against his own soul." It is often remarked how credulous are unbelievers in supernaturalism. They who refuse to credit the most assured facts of Christ's history will pin their faith on some philosophical theory or insufficiently supported opinion, and will bluster and contend in maintenance of a notion to-day which to-morrow will prove untenable and absurd. Many who despise the miraculous teaching of the Bible accept the follies and frauds of spiritualism (comp. John v. 43). Hesiod, Ἔργ., 372—

Πίστεις δ' ἄρ τοι ὁμῶς καὶ ἀπιστίαι ὤλεσαν ἄνδρας.

"Belief and unbelief alike are fatal."

Cato, 'Dist.,' ii. 20—

" Noli tu quædam referenti credere semper; Exigua his tribuenda fides qui multa loquuntur."

The prudent man looketh well to his going (ver. 8); Vulgate, *Astutus considerat gressus suos.* The prudent man considers whither the advice given will lead him, always acts with deliberation. This maxim is attributed to Pythagoras—

" Let none persuade thee by his word or deed
To say or do what is not really good ;
And before action well deliberate,
Lest thou do foolishly."
(Χρυσ. Ἔπη, 25, *sqq.*)

Septuagint, " The clever man (πανοῦργος) cometh unto repentance [or, 'afterthought'] (μετάνοιαν) ; " *i.e.* if he, like the simpleton, is too credulous, he will smart for it. Μετάνοια, so common in the New Testament, is not found elsewhere in the Greek Version of the canonical Scriptures, though it occurs in Ecclus. xliv. 16 ; Wisd. xi. 23, etc. The Vulgate here introduces the Septuagint addition in ch. xiii. 13.

Ver. 16.—**A wise man feareth, and departeth from evil** (ch. xxii. 3). In ch. iii. 7 we had, " Fear the Lord, and depart from evil; " but here the idea is different. A wise man fears the evil that lurks in everything, and examines and ponders actions by the standard of religion, and is thus saved from many evils which arise from hastiness and inadvertence. **The fool rageth, and is confident** (ch. xxi. 24 ; xxviii. 26). The fool easily falls into a rage, and has no control over himself, and is confident in his own wisdom, in contrast to the wise man, who has trust in God, and is calm and thoughtful (Isa. xxx. 15). Revised Version, " beareth himself insolently, and is confident; " but, as Nowack remarks, the word (*mithabber*), where it occurs elsewhere, means, " to be excited," " to be in a passion " (comp. ch. xxi. 24 ; xxvi. 17 ; Ps. lxxviii. 21, 59, 62), and this usual signification gives a good meaning here. Vulgate, *transilit,* " he overleaps " all laws and restrictions. The LXX., by transposition of the letters, reads *mithareh,* and translates μίγνυται, " The fool trusting to himself mixes himself up with sinners."

Ver. 17.—**He that is soon angry dealeth foolishly.** The contrast to the irascible, passionate man is seen in the man slow to anger (ver. 29 ; ch. xv. 18). Such a one, in his haste and passion, does things which in calmer moments he must see are foolish and ridiculous. Says Euripides (' Hyp.,' Fragm.)—

Ἔξω γὰρ ὀργῆς πᾶς ἀνὴρ σοφώτερος.
" Wiser is every man from passion freed."

" Be not angry," says the Talmud, " and you will not sin." Cato, ' Dist.,' i. 37—

" Ipse tibi moderare tuis ut parcere possis."

And a man of wicked devices is hated. The contrast is not between the different ways in which the two characters are regarded, as that one is despised and ridiculed, and the other hated ; but two kinds of evil are set forth in contradistinction, viz. hasty anger and deliberate plotting against others. Septuagint, " The irascible man (ὀξύθυμος) acts without deliberation, but the prudent man endureth much." The Hebrew term, " man of devices," being ambiguous, the LXX. takes it in a favourable sense, φρόνιμος; and they have a different reading of the verb.

Ver. 18.—**The simple inherit folly.** The credulous simpleton naturally falls into possession of folly, feeds upon it, and enjoys it. The LXX. regards the simple as communicating their folly to others, and translates, " Fools will divide malice." But **the prudent are crowned with knowledge ;** put on knowledge as a crown of glory, in accordance with the Stoic saying, quoted in the ' Speaker's Commentary,' " The wise is the only king." Nowack thinks the above translation and the idea alike belong to later times, and prefers to render, " The prudent embrace knowledge," which is parallel to the sentiment of ver. 6. The word is found only in Ps. cxlii. 8, where it is translated either " shall compass me about " or "crown themselves through me." The Vulgate has *expectabunt,* i.e. " wait for it patiently," as the fruit of labour and perseverance. Septuagint, " The wise shall get possession of (κρατήσουσιν) knowledge."

Ver. 19.—**The evil bow before the good ; and the wicked stand at the gates of the righteous** (ch. viii. 34). The final victory of good over evil is here set forth. However triumphant for a time and apparently prosperous the wicked may be, their success is not lasting ; they shall in the end succumb to the righteous, even as the Canaanite kings crouched before Joshua's captains (Josh. x. 24), and, hurled from their high estate, they shall stand humbly at the good man's door, begging for bread to support their life (1 Sam. ii. 36). The contrast here indicated is seen in our Lord's parable of Dives and Lazarus, when the beggar is comforted and the rich man is tormented, and when the latter urgently sues for the help of the once despised outcast to mitigate the agony which he is suffering (comp. Wisd. v).

Ver. 20.—**The poor is hated even of his own neighbour** (ch. xix. 4, 7). This sad experience of selfishness (comp. Ecclus. vi. 8, etc.; xii. 8) is corrected by the following verse, which must be taken in connection with this; at the same time, it is a truth which has been expressed in various ways by many moralists and satirists. Says the Greek Theognis—

Πᾶς τις πλούσιον ἄνδρα τίει, ἀτίει δὲ πενιχρόν.

"The rich all honour, but the poor man slight."

Says Ovid, 'Trist.,' i. 9. 6—

"Donec eris felix, multos numerabis amicos;
Tempora si fuerint nubila, solus eris."ﻻ

"Prosperous, you many friends will own;
In cloudy days you stand alone."

In the Talmud we find (Dukes, 'Rabb. Blum.'), "At the door of the tavern there are many brethren and friends, at the poor man's gate not one." **The rich hath many friends.** Says Theognis again—

Εὖ μεν ἔχοντος ἐμοῦ πολλοὶ φίλοι· ἢν δέ τι δεινὸν
Συγκύρσῃ, παῦροι πιστὸν ἔχουσι νόον.

And again, a distich which might have been written to-day—

Πλήθει δ' ἀνθρώπων ἀρετὴ μία γίγνεται ἥδε,
Πλουτεῖν· τῶν δ' ἄλλων οὐδὲν ἄρ' ἦν ὔφελος.

"One only virtue you must needs possess
(As say the most of men), and that is wealth;
All others are of small account."

Ver. 21.—**He that despiseth his neighbour sinneth.** Taken in connection with the preceding verse, this teaches that it is a sin to despise and shun a man because he is poor or of low estate; such a one has a claim for love and pity, and it is a crime to withhold them from him for selfish considerations. The Christian view is taught by the parable of the good Samaritan. **But he that hath mercy on the poor, happy is he;** hail to him! (ch. xvi. 20). Contempt is contrasted with mercy, sin with blessing. "Blessed are the merciful," said Christ (Matt. v. 7): "for they shall obtain mercy;" and St. Paul preserves another precious word, "It is more blessed to give than to receive" (Acts xx. 35). The merciful disposition, which shows itself in works of mercy, is a proof that the soul is in union with God, whose mercy is over all his works, whose mercy endureth for ever, and therefore such a soul is blessed. "The poor," wrote James Howell, "are God's receivers, and the angels are his auditors" ('Five Hundred New Sayings'). The Vulgate here appends a line absent from the Hebrew and the other versions, "He who believeth in the Lord loveth mercy." The true believer is charitable and bountiful, knowing that he will not hereby impoverish himself, but lay up a rich store

of blessing; he acts thus not from mere philanthropy, but from higher motives; he has the grace of charity which springs from and rests upon his faith in God.

Ver. 22.—**Do they not err that devise evil?** or, *Will they not go astray?* The question is an emphatic mode of asserting the truth. They who meditate and practise evil (ch. iii. 29; vi. 14) go astray from the right way—the way of life; their views are distorted, and they no longer see their proper course. Thus the remorseful voluptuary bemoans himself, "We have erred from the way of truth, and the light of righteousness hath not shined unto us. . . . We wearied ourselves in the way of wickedness and destruction; yea, we have gone through deserts, where there lay no way; but as for the way of the Lord, we have not known it" (Wisd. v. 6, etc.). **Mercy and truth shall be to them that devise good.** God's blessing will rest upon them. The combination of "mercy and truth" is found in Ps. lxi. 7; in Wisd. iii. 9 and iv. 15, and in 1 Tim. i. 2 we have "grace and mercy" (see note on ch. iii. 3, where the two words occur in connection; and comp. ch. xvi. 6; xx. 28). The two graces in the text signify the love and mercy which God bestows on the righteous, and the truth and fidelity with which he keeps the promises which he has made. The Vulgate makes the two graces human, not Divine: "Mercy and truth procure blessings." The Septuagint renders, "The good devise mercy and truth." It adds a paraphrase not found in the Hebrew, "The devisers of evil know not mercy and faith; but alms and faith are with the devisers of good."

Ver. 23.—**In all labour there is profit.** All honest industry has a reward, and all care and pain borne for a good object bring comfort and content (comp. ch. x. 22). So the Greek distich says—

Ἅπαντα τὰ καλὰ τοῦ πονοῦντος γίγνεται.

"To him who labours all fair things belong."

In contrast to the diligent are those who talk much and do nothing. **But the talk of the lips tendeth only to penury** (ch. xxi. 5). Those who work much get profit; those who talk much and do little come to want. So in spiritual matters Christ teaches that they who think that prayer is heard for much speaking are mistaken; and he adds, "Not every one that saith unto me, Lord, Lord, shall enter into the kingdom of heaven; but he that doeth the will of my Father which is in heaven" (Matt. vi. 7; vii. 21). Septuagint, "In every one who taketh thought (μεριμνῶντι) there is abundance; he who liveth pleasantly and without pain shall be in want." Cato, 'Dist.,' i. 10—

"Contra verbosos noli contendere verbis;
Sermo datus cunctis, animi sapientia paucis."

"Against the wordy strive not thou in words;
Converse with all, but to the favoured few
Impart thy heart's deep wisdom."

Oriental proverbs: "Sweet words, empty
hands;" "To speak of honey will not make
the mouth sweet;" "We do not cook rice
by babbling" (Lane). Turkish, "The language of actions is more eloquent than the
language of words."

Ver. 24.—**The crown of the wise is their
riches.** This is taken by some ('Speaker's
Commentary') to mean the glory of the
wise man, the fame and splendour which
surround him, constitute his wealth; but
it is better to interpret it thus: Riches are
an ornament to a wise man; they enhance
and set off his wisdom in the eyes of others,
enable him to use it to advantage, and are
not the snare which they might be because
they are employed religiously and profitably
for the good of others. Eccles. vii. 11,
"Wisdom is good together with an inheritance, and profitable to them that see the
sun." The Septuagint has, "The crown of
the wise is the clever man (πανοῦργος),"
for which has been substituted by some
editors, in agreement with the present
Hebrew text, πλοῦτος αὐτῶν, "their wealth."
The Greek translators, according to their
reading, denote that one eminently clever
man is a glory to the whole body of wise
men. But **the folly of fools is only folly;**
that is, even though it were accompanied
with riches. Decorate folly as you may,
trick it out in gaud and ornament, it is still
nothing but folly, and is discerned as such,
and *that* all the more for being made conspicuous. Schultens, followed by Wordsworth, finds a play of words here. The
words rendered "fool" and "folly" imply
"fatness," like the Greek παχὺς and the
Latin *crassus*, which have also this double
meaning. So the sentence reads, "Riches
are a crown to the wise; but the abundant
fatness of fools is only fatness." The last
clause is translated by the LXX., "But the
fools' way of life (διατριβή) is evil." St.
Gregory ('Moral.,' xxii. 8) comments on this
verse thus: "It was these riches of wisdom
that Solomon having before his eyes, saith,
'The crown of the wise is their riches.'
Which same person, because it is not metals
of earth, but understanding, that he calls
by the name of riches, thereupon adds by
way of a contrary, 'But the foolishness of
fools is imprudence.' For if he called
earthly riches the crown of the wise, surely
he would own the senselessness of fools to
be poverty rather than imprudence. But
whereas he added, 'the foolishness of fools is

imprudence,' he made it plain that he called
prudence 'the riches of the wise'" (Oxford
transl.).

Ver. 25.—**A true witness delivereth souls**
(ver. 5; ch. xii. 17). A true witness saves
persons who are in danger owing to false
accusation or calumny; saves lives; "saves
from evils," says the Septuagint. But **a
deceitful witness speaketh lies,** and therewith endangers lives. Literally, *He who
breatheth out lies is deceit;* he is a personification of fraud, dominated and informed
by it; it has become his very nature.
"Falsehood is the devil's daughter, and
speaks her father's tongue." Septuagint,
"But a deceitful witness kindles (ἐκκαίει)
lies."

Ver. 26.—**In the fear of the Lord is strong
confidence.** The fear of God casts out all
fear of man, all despairing anticipations of
possible evil, and makes the believer confident and bold. St. Gregory ('Moral.,' v.
33), "As in the way of the world fear gives
rise to weakness, so in the way of God fear
produces strength. In truth, our mind so
much the more valorously sets at naught all
the terrors of temporal vicissitudes, the
more thoroughly that it submits itself in
fear to the Author of those same temporal
things. And being stablished in the fear
of the Lord, it encounters nothing without
it to fill it with alarm, in that whereas it is
united to the Creator of all things by a
righteous fear, it is by a certain powerful
influence raised high above them all." Comp.
Ps. xxvii. 1 and St. Paul's words, "If God
be for us, who can be against us?" (Rom.
viii. 31). Septuagint, "In the fear of the
Lord is hope of strength." **And his children
shall have a place of refuge** (Ps. xlvi. 1).
There is an ambiguity as to whose children
are meant. The LXX. renders, "And to
his children he will leave a support." Thus
many refer the pronoun to the Lord named
in the first clause—God's children, those
who love and trust him, and look up to
him as a Father, an expression used more
specially in the New Testament than in the
Old. But see Ps. lxxiii. 15, and passages
(*e.g.* Hos. xi. 1) where God calls Israel his
son, a type of all who are brought unto him
by adoption and grace. Others, again, refer
the pronoun to "the fear of the Lord," "its
children," which would be quite in conformity with Hebrew idiom; as we have
"sons of wisdom," "children of obedience,"
equivalent to "wise," "obedient," etc. But
most modern commentators explain it of
the children of the God-fearing man, comparing Exod. xx. 6 and Ps. ciii. 17. Such a
one shall confer lasting benefits upon his
posterity (ch. xiii. 22; xx. 7). So God
blessed the descendants of Abraham and
David; so he shows mercy unto thousands,

i.e. the thousandth generation of them that love him and keep his commandments (see Gen. xvii. 7, etc.; Exod. xxxiv. 7; 1 Kings xi. 12, etc.; Jer. xxxiii. 20, etc.).

Ver. 27.—A repetition of ch. xiii. 14, substituting **the fear of the Lord** for "the law of the wise." The fear of the Lord can be called a fountain of life, because, showing itself in obedience, it nourishes the flowers and fruits of faith, produces graces and virtues, and prepares the soul for immortality. Septuagint, "The commandment of the Lord is a fountain of life, and makes one decline from the snare of death."

Ver. 28.—**In the multitude of people is the king's honour** (glory); **but in the want of people is the destruction of the prince;** or, *of the principality.* This maxim is not in accordance with the views of Oriental conquerors and despots, who in their selfish lust of aggrandizement cared not what suffering they inflicted or what blood they shed; who made a wilderness and called it peace. The reign of Solomon, the peaceful, gave an intimation that war and conquest were not a monarch's highest glory: that a happy and numerous people, dwelling securely and increasing in numbers, was a better honour for a king and more to be desired (1 Kings iv. 20). Increase of population is not, as some political economists would teach, in itself an evil; it is rather a sign of prosperity, and is in agreement with the primeval blessing, "Increase and multiply;" and though it may be hard to maintain the exact equilibrium between production and consumers, yet wise legislation can foresee and remedy the difficulty, the abundance in one part can supply the scarcity in another, the providence of God watching over all.

Ver. 29.—He that is **slow to wrath is of great understanding.** The Hebrew expression for what the Septuagint calls μακρό-θυμος, "long-suffering," and the Vulgate, *patiens,* is "long in nostrils" (ch. xv. 18), as the contrary temper, which we had in ver. 17, is "short in nostrils." That organ, into which was breathed the breath of life (Gen. ii. 7), is taken as the seat of the inward spirit, and as showing by exterior signs the dominant feeling. The original is very terse, "long in nostrils, great in understanding." A man's prudence and wisdom are displayed by his being slow to take offence and being patient under injury. He that is **hasty of spirit exalteth folly;** *i.e.* flaunts it in the eyes of all men, makes plain exposure of it. Septuagint, "He who is short in temper is a mighty fool." "Passion," says an old saw, "makes fools of the wise, and shows the folly of the foolish" (comp. ch. xii. 23; xiii. 16). The word rendered "exalteth," מָרִים (*marim*), occurs

in ch. iii. 35, and is taken by Delitzsch and Nowack in the sense of "carries away" as the assured result. "By anger," says St. Gregory ('Moral.,' v. 78), "wisdom is parted with, so that we are left wholly in ignorance what to do, and in what order to do it. . . . Anger withdraws the light of understanding, while by agitating it troubles the mind."

Ver. 30.—**A sound heart is the life of the flesh.** The heart that is healthy, morally and physically, spreads its beneficent influence over the whole body in all its functions and relations; this is expressed by the word for "flesh" (*besarim*), being in the plural number, as the Vulgate renders, *vita carnium.* But the contrast is better developed by taking מַרְפֵּא in its other signification of "calm," "gentle," "meek," as Eccles. x. 4. Thus the Septuagint, "The man of gentle mind (πραΰθυμος) is the physician of the heart." The tranquil, well-controlled heart gives health and vigour to the whole frame (see on ch. xv. 4). **But envy is the rottenness of the bones** (ch. xii. 4). Envy, like a canker, eats away a man's life and strength; it tells on his physical as well as his moral condition. We have parallel expressions in classical authors. Thus Horace, 'Epist.,' i. 257—

"Invidus alterius macrescit rebus opimis."

Martial, 'Epigr.,' v. 28—

"Rubiginosis cuncta dentibus rodit;
    Hominem malignum forsan esse tu credas,
    Ego esse miserum credo, cui placet nemo."

Bengal proverb, "In seeing another's wealth it is not good to have the eyes smart." Arabic, "Envy is a raging fever, and has no rest" (Lane). "O invidia," cries St. Jerome ('Epist.,' 45), "primum mordax tui." "When the foul sore of envy corrupts the vanquished heart," says St. Gregory ('Moral.,' v. 85), "the very exterior itself shows how forcibly the mind is urged by madness. For paleness seizes the complexion, the eyes are weighed down, the spirit is inflamed, while the limbs are chilled, there is frenzy in the heart, there is gnashing with the teeth, and while the growing hate is buried in the depths of the heart, the pent wound works into the conscience with a blind grief." Septuagint, "A sensitive heart (καρδία αἰσθητική) is a worm (σής) in the bones." A heart that feels too acutely and is easily affected by external circumstances, prepares for itself constant vexation and grief.

Ver. 31.—**He that oppresseth the poor reproacheth his Maker,** even God, who hath placed men in their several conditions (ch. xvii. 5; xxii. 2). "The poor shall never cease out of the land" (Deut. xv. 11); "The poor ye have always with you," said Christ (Matt. xxvi. 11); therefore to harass and oppress the poor because he is in this lowly condition, is virtually to arraign the providence of God, who is the Father of all, and has made all men brothers, however differing in worldly position. Christ puts the duty of aiding the poor on the high ground of his solidarity with his people (Matt. xxv. 40, 45), how that in ministering unto the least of these his brethren men are ministering unto him. "Prosperity and adversity, life and death, poverty and riches, come of the Lord" (Ecclus. xi. 14). Even the heathen could say—

᾽Αεὶ νομίζονθ᾽ οἱ πένητες τῶν Θεῶν.

"Deem ever that the poor are God's own gift."

Septuagint, "He that calumniates (συκο-φαντῶν; calumniatur, Vulgate) the poor angers him who made him." This version refers to oppression of the poor by means of calumny or false and frivolous accusation. But he that honoureth him—the Lord—hath mercy on the poor; or, better, *he that hath mercy upon the poor honoureth him;* for he shows that he has proper regard to God's ordinance, acts on high motives, and is not led astray by worldly considerations. Christ himself has consecrated poverty by coming in low estate (2 Cor. viii. 9), and they who love and honour him are glad to minister to his brethren in their poverty and distress (comp. Jas. i. 27).

Ver. 32.—**The wicked is driven away in his wickedness.** So the Greek and Latin Versions. In his very act of sin, *flagrante delicto,* the wicked is defeated, driven from hope and life; as the Revised Version renders, "The wicked is thrust down in his evil-doing;" *i.e.* there is some element of weakness in an evil deed which occasions its discovery and punishment sooner or later. Thus "murder will out," we say. But the contrast is better emphasized by taking *ra* in its other sense of "calamity," "misfortune," thus: "In his calamity the wicked is cast down" (ch. xxiv. 16). When misfortune comes upon him, he has no defence, no hope; he collapses utterly; all his friends forsake him; there is none to comfort or uphold him (comp. Matt. vii. 26, 27). But the righteous hath hope in his death (comp. Ecclus. i. 13). Primarily, the clause means that even in the greatest danger the good man loses not his trust in God. It is like Job's word (if our reading is correct, Job xiii. 15), "Though he slay me, yet will I trust in him;" and the psalmist, "Though I walk through the valley of the shadow of death, I will fear no evil: for thou art with me; thy rod and thy staff they comfort me" (Ps. xxiii. 4).

Thus the Christian martyrs went joyfully to the stake, and gentle women and little children smiled on the sword which sent them home. It is natural to see in this clause a belief in a future life, and a state of rewards and punishments; and some commentators, holding that this doctrine was not known in pre-exilian days, have taken occasion from its plain enunciation in this paragraph to affix a very late date to our book. There are two answers to be made to this assertion. First, it is capable of proof that the belief in the immortality of the soul, with its consequences in another state, was held, however vaguely, by the Jews long before Solomon's time (see note, ch. xii. 28); secondly, the present passage is by some read differently, whence is obtained another rendering, which removes from it all trace of the doctrine in question. Thus Ewald and others would read the clause in this way: "The righteous hath hope, or taketh refuge, from his own deeds." There can be no reasonable doubt that the usual reading and translation are correct; but the above considerations show that no argument as to the date of the Proverbs can be safely founded on this verse. The LXX. has a different reading for במותו, "in his death," and translates, "But he who trusteth in his own holiness is just"—which looks like a travesty of Scripture, but probably refers to the consciousness of having a heart right with God and obedient to the requirements of the Divine Law.

Ver. 33.—**Wisdom resteth in the heart of him that hath understanding.** The wise man is not always blurting out and making a display of his wisdom; he lets it lie still and hidden till there is occasion to use it with effect (ch. x. 14; xii. 23). But that which is **in the midst of fools is made known;** literally and better, *but in the midst of fools it,* wisdom, *maketh itself known.* That is, in contrast to the folly of fools, wisdom is seen to great advantage; or, it may be, the conceited display of the fool's so-called wisdom is contrasted with the modesty and reticence of the really intelligent man. "A fool's heart is ever dancing on his lips," says a proverb. So Ecclus. xxi. 26, "The heart of fools is in their mouth; but the mouth of the wise is in their heart." Theognis, 1163—

᾽Οφθαλμοὶ καὶ γλῶσσα καὶ οὔατα καὶ νόος ἀνδρῶν
᾽Εν μέσσῳ στηθέων ἐν συνετοῖς φύεται.

"The eyes, and tongue, and ears, and mind alike
Are centred in the bosom of the wise."

Vulgate, "In the heart of the prudent resteth wisdom, and it will teach all the unlearned." Wisdom sits enshrined in the intelligent man's mind, and thence disseminates instruction and light around to all who need it. The Septuagint, with which agree the Syriac, Aquila, and Theodotion, inserts a negative in the second clause, thus: "In the good heart of a man shall rest wisdom, but in the heart of fools it is not discerned" (Wisd. i. 4).

Ver. 34.—**Righteousness exalteth a nation.** "Righteousness" (ch. x. 2) is the rendering to all their due, whether to God or man. We are taught the salutary lesson that a nation's real greatness consists not in its conquests, magnificence, military or artistic skill, but in its observance of the requirements of justice and religion. Hesiod, Ἔργ. 223—

Οἱ δὲ δίκας ξείνοισι καὶ ἐνδήμοισι διδοῦσιν
’Ιθείας καὶ μή τι παρεκβαίνουσι δικαίου,
Τοῖσι τέθηλε πόλις, λαοὶ δ’ ἀνθεῦσιν ἐν αὐτῇ.

But **sin is a reproach to any people;** *to peoples.* The words for "nation" (*goi*) and "peoples" (*leummim*) are usually applied to foreign nations rather than to the Hebrews; and Wordsworth sees here a statement *à fortiori*: if righteousness exalts and sin degrades heathen nations, how much more must this be the case with God's own people, who have clearer revelations and heavier responsibilities! חֶסֶד (*chesed*) occurs in the sense of "reproach," in Lev. xx. 17, and with a different punctuation in ch. xxv. 10 of this book. Its more usual meaning is "mercy" or "piety;" hence some have explained the clause: "The piety of the peoples, *i.e.* the worship of the heathen, is sin;" and others,

taking "sin" as put metonymically for "sin offering," render: "Piety is an atonement for the peoples." But there is no doubt that the Authorized Version is correct (comp. ch. xi. 11). Thus Symmachus renders it by ὄνειδος, "shame;" and in the same sense the Chaldee Paraphrase. The Vulgate and Septuagint, owing to the common confusion of the letters *daleth* and *resh*, have read *cheser* instead of *chesed*, and render thus: Vulgate, "Sin makes peoples miserable;" Septuagint, "Sins diminish tribes." The sin of nations contrasted with the righteousness in the first clause must be injustice, impiety, and violence. See a grand passage in the fifth book of St. Augustine's 'De Civitate Dei,' ch. xii.

Ver. 35.—**The king's favour is toward a wise servant;** *servant that dealeth wisely* (Revised Version). Thus Joseph was advanced to the highest post in Egypt, owing to the wisdom which he displayed; so, too, in the case of Daniel (comp. Matt. xxiv. 45, 47). **But his wrath is against him that causeth shame;** literally, *he that doeth shamefully shall be* (the object of) *his wrath.* The Vulgate translates, *Iracundiam ejus inutilis sustinebit;* the Septuagint makes the second clause parallel to the first, "An intelligent servant is acceptable to the king, and by his expertness (εὐστροφία) he removeth disgrace." Then is added, before the first verse of the next chapter, a paragraph which looks like an explanation of the present clause, or an introduction to ver. 1 of ch. xv.: "Anger destroyeth even the prudent."

HOMILETICS.

Ver. 10.—*Incommunicable experience.* I. THE DEEPEST EXPERIENCE IS SOLITARY. This applies both to sorrows and to joys. There are profound sorrows which must lie buried in the hearts of the sufferers, and lofty joys which cannot be breathed to another soul. Sorrow has her shrine, which no intruder can enter without desecrating it; and joy her sweet silence, to break which is to shatter the delight. 1. *Each soul lives a separate life.* We are like planets, moving in our own spheres. Though we mingle in social intercourse, we do not touch in our most vital being. The "abysmal depths of personality" are utterly solitary. 2. *No two natures are just alike.* In common we share many pleasures and pains. But when we come to what is most characteristic, we reach a line of demarcation which the most sympathetic can never cross. We cannot enter into experiences quite unlike our own. We have not the key to unlock the mystery of a lonely sorrow or a rare joy. 3. *The deepest experience is shy and reserved.* Those who feel most do not cry out the loudest. It is the silent grief that eats out a man's heart. Though yearning for sympathy, he feels that he cannot breathe a word of his awful trouble. On the other hand, there are pure and lofty joys of soul that would be sullied with a breath.

II. FORCED SYMPATHY IS HURTFUL. We ought to be able to "rejoice with them that do rejoice, and weep with them that weep" (Rom. xii. 15). When sympathy can be real, it may be most helpful. But there is no opposition between this thought and that of our text. For just as real sympathy helps, unreal sympathy hurts. Now, sympathy may be unreal without being hypocritical, and even when it is well-meant and heartfelt; if we do not understand a person's feelings, we cannot sympathize with him. We may feel kindly towards him, and may desire to show compassion. But it will be all in vain, we shall not touch the fringe of the trouble, or, if we do penetrate further, we shall jar and wound the sensitive soul by blundering incompetence. It will be like a surgeon trying to dress a wound in the dark. Thus Macduff, when robbed of all his children at one cruel stroke, is only vexed by the kindly but impotent condolence of Malcom, and cries, "He has no children." III. GOD'S SYMPATHY PENETRATES TO THE DEEPEST EXPERIENCE. 1. *He knows all.* We have not to explain our case to him, and then be misunderstood and misjudged after all, as often happens in the attempt to open out the heart to a fellow-man. For God reads our most secret thoughts, and the feelings that we will not even confess to ourselves are perfectly known to him. 2. *He feels with his children.* He is not like the scientific vivisectionist, who handles quivering nerves without a spark of compunction. God tenderly pities his children in their sorrows, and graciously smiles on their innocent joys. 3. *He can touch us with sympathy.* This sympathy of God is not a distant heavenly experience hidden in the bosom of God. It is shed abroad over his children for their consolation in sorrow and their blessedness in joy. 4. *We should confide in the sympathy of God.* It is not wholesome for the soul to be buried in the seclusion of its own feelings. There is healing in the sympathizing touch of God and a consecrating benediction in his smile. Christ is the incarnation of God's human sympathy, and Christ's sympathy can reach and save and bless us all.

Ver. 12.—*The way that seemeth right.* I. ITS ATTRACTIVE APPEARANCE. This way does not only seem pleasant; it seems to be right. This is a course of life which a man is tempted to follow because it flatters him with fair promises. 1. *It promises good.* We are greatly tempted to judge of the means by the end, and, if we think that the thing to be attained is good, to condone the questionable conduct that secures it. Thus men have justified (1) war, (2) persecution, (3) the deceit of "pious fraud," (4) business irregularities. 2. *It flatters self-will.* Men believe in their own way, just because it is the way they have chosen. The statesman makes the best of the politics of his party. In private life what accords with our desire is warped into the semblance of right. 3. *It is followed by others.* Fashion condones folly. The conduct of the multitude creates a social conscience. Men measure by the standard of the average rather than by the gauge of absolute rectitude. 4. *No evil is apparent.* At present the path is easy, pleasant, flowery, and to all appearances quite safe. Short-sighted men judge of it by so much as is in view, as though the end of a road could be known by the character of its beginning. II. ITS DELUSIVE CHARACTER. 1. It is only right *in appearance.* It "seemeth right." But "things are not what they seem." A flame seems good to a moth; thin ice, safe to a heedless child; the undermined road, sound to the hoodwinked general; the sparkling water, refreshing to one who knows not that the well from which it is drawn has been poisoned. The bad social custom appears to be innocent to the slave of fashion. The way of sin "seemeth right" to the blunt conscience. 2. It is only right *in the eye of man.* It is "to man" that this doubtful way "seemeth right." But man is not the highest surveyor of life, and the map that he draws is not the supreme authority. Man is prejudiced, confused, ignorant, self-deceiving. There is a higher Judge than man, and it may be that the way which "seemeth right to man" is seen to be wrong by God. III. ITS FATAL END. This pleasant, inviting path is a tributary to a high-road. Innocent as it looks in itself, it leads into other ways, and those the ways of death. It is like a winding lane between green hedgerows and flower-strewn banks, that brings the traveller out at length into a very different road from that he supposed he was nearing. There are questionable courses that do not seem to be evil in themselves, but they lead to evil. There are amusements that seem to be innocent enough, yet they are paths towards more dangerous things, and in the end they bring the unwary to the very gates of hell. Now, the chief question to ask about any road is—Whither does it lead? If it will bring us to a treacherous bog, a homeless waste, a dark and dangerous forest, or a perilous precipice, it matters little that its early course is harmless. Whither does the way tend? If it is the path of sin, it must lead to death (Rom. vi. 23).

IV. THE NEED OF WARNING. 1. *The preacher must warn the heedless.* There is danger of self-deception, and the end may be ruin. Then men should not be indignant if they are invited to examine their ways. 2. *Each man should consider his own ways.* We live too much by appearances. But "life is real." Let us turn from the picture that "seemeth" to the fact that is. 3. *We need Divine guidance.* He who knows all ways, and can see the end from the beginning, is the only safe Guide into the way of life.

Ver. 13.—*The sadness that lies behind laughter.* This verse reads like one of the melancholy reflections of the pessimist preacher in Ecclesiastes. Yet there is a profound truth in it, as all thoughtful minds must recognize. Physically, intense laughter produces acute pangs. Laughter "holds his sides" with pain. Shelley sang truly—

> "Our sincerest laughter
> With some pain is fraught."

A long laugh naturally fills the eyes with tears and dies away in a sigh of weariness. Further, a season of undue elation is usually followed by one of depression. The mind rebounds from glee to gloom by natural reaction. But there is a deeper experience than all this. Without taking a dark view of life, we must acknowledge the existence of a very common background of sorrow behind many of the sunniest scenes of life. We may trace the causes of this experience both to the facts and nature of sorrow, and to the quality and limitation of laughter.

I. THE FACTS AND NATURE OF SORROW. 1. *Sorrow is common.* Man is born to trouble. There may not be a skeleton in the cupboard of every house, but there are few homes in which there is no chamber of sad memories. We mistake the common nature of mankind if we suppose that the merry soul has not its griefs. The roaring clown may be acting with a broken heart. Wit that spreads a ripple of laughter in all directions may even be inspired by a very bitterness of soul. 2. *Sorrow is enduring.* We cannot divide our lives mechanically into days of pain and days of pleasure. The great sorrow that once visits us never utterly forsakes us. It makes a home in the soul. It may be toned and softened by time, and driven from the front windows to dark back chambers. Still, there it lurks, and sometimes it makes its presence sorely felt even when we would fain forget it. The very contrast of present delight may rouse its restless pains. Even when it is not thought of it lingers as a sad undertone in our songs of gladness.

II. THE QUALITY AND LIMITATIONS OF LAUGHTER. 1. *Laughter is superficial.* Even while it is rippling over the surface of life, grief may lie beneath in sullen darkness, unmoved by the feeble gaiety. This does not condemn laughter as an evil thing, for while "the laughter of fools" is contemptible, and that of scorners sinful, the mirth of the innocent is harmless and even healthful. Cæsar rightly suspected the sour visage of Cinna. The monkish notion that Christ never laughed finds no countenance in the Bible. But while sinless laughter is good and wholesome, it is never able to reach the deepest troubles. Some foolish fears and fancies may best be laughed away, but not the great soul-agonies. 2. *Laughter is temporary.* Inordinate laughter is not good; too much laughter is a sign of frivolity; and no man can laugh eternally. If a man drown care in laughter, this can be but for a season, and afterwards the dreary trouble will rise again in pitiless persistence.

The remedy for trouble must be found in the peace of God. When that is in the soul, a man is happier than if he were only hiding an unhealed sore behind the hollow mask of laughter. When Christ has cured the soul's greatest trouble, there is a possibility of the laughter of a new joy, with no tears to follow.

Ver. 15.—*Credulity.* It is the constant habit of religious teachers to encourage faith, and to regard scepticism and unbelief as evil things. Are we, then, to suppose that credulity is meritorious, and that all doubt, inquiry, suspense of mind, and rejection of bold assertions are bad? According to this view, truth would be of no importance. It would be as well to believe error as truth, and to swallow superstition wholesale would be a mark of superior piety. There are not wanting critics who scornfully ascribe habits of this character to Christians—identifying faith with credulity, and charging the believer with folly. No doubt the extravagant utterances of some Christian people have given much excuse for this libel; *e.g.* the assertion of Anselm, "Credo quia non intelligo." But such utterances are not justified by Scripture or Christian wisdom.

I. OBSERVE THE NATURE OF CREDULITY. When a person is too hasty in believing without sufficient reason, and especially when he accepts statements on slight authority in opposition to a rational view, we call him credulous. Credulity is just a disposition to believe without sufficient ground. 1. *It springs from mental weakness.* It is a mark of childishness, while faith is a sign of childlikeness. The feeble mind is credulous. Faith is virile, credulity anile. 2. *It is favoured by prejudice.* The credulous person is unduly ready to believe according to his desires. So men say, "The wish is father to the thought." 3. *It is increased by fear,* which paralyzes the reasoning faculties and inclines people to believe in the most absurd impossibility. The terrors of superstition ensnare the credulous.

II. CONSIDER THE EVIL OF CREDULITY. 1. *It dishonours truth.* When a person shows indifference to the vital question as to whether what he believes is true or false, he displays a fatal disloyalty to truth. For truth will not endure an admixture of falsehoods. Therefore those very people who vainly imagine themselves to be the loyal and humble servants of the whole round of truths are the very persons who undermine the sanctity of truth itself. 2. *It tempts to fatal acts.* Men act according to their beliefs. If they believe lies, they will have the practical side of their lives flung into confusion. Truth is a beacon-light; error sheds a false glare, like that of a wrecker's lamp on a rock-bound coast. It is dangerous to accept delusions of superstition with fatuous credulity. Life is real and earnest, and men need true lights to guide them safely.

III. NOTE THE REMEDY OF CREDULITY. 1. *This is not to be found in unlimited scepticism.* The sceptic is often the slave of foolish fancies. Escaping from Christian faith, perhaps he falls into spiritualism or some other equally wild delusion. 2. *Unbelief is not the remedy;* for unbelief is but the reverse of faith. Indeed, it is negative faith. It is believing the negative of those propositions concerning which faith believes the affirmative. 3. *Agnosticism is not the remedy;* for agnosticism is more than a confession of ignorance; it is an assertion that knowledge in certain regions is unattainable. Thus it is dogmatic and possibly credulous. 4. *The remedy lies in well-grounded faith.* We must learn lessons of patience, and be willing at first to creep along step by step. We need not wait to say, with Abelard, "Credo quia intelligo," for we may accept mysteries which we cannot explain. But we need to be satisfied that we have good ground for doing so. Fundamentally, a wise Christian faith is trust in Christ, resting on an intelligent ground of assurance—that he is trustworthy.

Ver. 30.—*A quiet spirit.* Translate the first clause of the verse thus : "The life of the body is a quiet spirit."

I. THE CHARACTERISTICS OF A QUIET SPIRIT. The habit and disposition of quietness need not be accompanied by torpor. There is, indeed, a quietness of sleep, as there is also a silence of the grave. But in the passage before us the quiet spirit is directly connected with life. The body may be busy while the spirit is quiet; nay, the mind may be nimble and alert, even full of activity, while yet the spirit is at rest. Observe, then, the marks of a quiet spirit. 1. *Peace.* There is peace within the soul, and therefore quiet. The turbulent spirit is like a mutinous crew that may make tumult on board the ship while the sea is as still as glass, and the peaceful spirit is like a well-conducted crew that works in quiet while the sea is torn with tempest. 2. *Patience.* The quiet spirit does not complain under chastisement, nor does it angrily resent unkindness. The psalmist was "dumb" under calamity. Christ was led as a lamb to the slaughter (Isa. liii. 7). 3. *Unostentatiousness.* Some give more show than service, and make more noise than profit. Eager to attract attention, they "sound a trumpet before them" (Matt. vi. 2). Not so the quiet in spirit, who labour in silence, content to be obscure so long as they know they are not living in vain.

II. THE BLESSEDNESS OF A QUIET SPIRIT. It is here set forth as a source of life. No doubt fretful restlessness wears out the life of the bad. Placidity makes for health. Moreover, the life that is dissipated in noise produces no good, and therefore does not collect the means of its own support. The quiet in spirit best make a livelihood.

Further, certain special advantages of this quietness may be noted. 1. *Depth.* "Still waters run deep." We can look far into the quiet lake, while only the surface-waves of one that is fretted with cross-winds can be seen. The calm, brooding soul knows depths of thought and secret experience that are unfathomable to the foolish, restless, noisy soul. 2. *Strength.* The silent forest grows strong. The mind is made vigorous by patient endurance. One who is calm is master of the situation, while another who is fretted and flurried feels lost and helpless. 3. *Fruitfulness.* The calm, strong, silent soul, vigorous and yet unostentatious, ripens best the fruits of experience. Such a one does most real work. 4. *Beneficence.* Noise vexes the world, and a restless, complaining spirit is a weariness to men. The quiet spirit breathes a perpetual benediction. Its very presence is soothing and healing.

III. THE ATTAINMENT OF A QUIET SPIRIT. No doubt there are great constitutional differences in this respect, and while some are naturally or by ill health restless, irritable, demonstrative, others are naturally quiet, self-possessed, even reserved. Due allowance must be made for these differences before we attempt to judge our brethren. Still, there is a measure of quietness attainable by the use of the right means, viz.: 1. *Self-mastery.* When a man has conquered himself, the tumult of civil war in his breast ceases. 2. *Faith.* To trust God, to know that he is doing all well, to seek and obtain the help of his Holy Spirit, are to find the secret of peace and quietness of soul. 3. *Love.* Selfishness makes us restless. "A heart at leisure from itself" can learn to be patient and calm.

Ver. 34.—*National righteousness.* I. RIGHTEOUSNESS IS REQUIRED IN A NATION. Morality has not yet been sufficiently applied to politics. It is forgotten that the ten commandments relate to communities as well as to individuals, because they are based on the eternal and all-embracing principles of righteousness. Men have yet to learn that that which is wrong in the individual is wrong in the society. Nations make war on one another for reasons which would never justify individual men in fighting a duel. Yet if it is wrong for a man to steal a field, it must be wrong for a nation to steal a province; and if an individual man may not cut his neighbour's throat out of revenge without being punished as a criminal, there is nothing to justify a whole community in shooting down thousands of people for no better motive. If selfishness even is sinful in one man, selfishness cannot be virtuous in thirty millions of people. The reign of righteousness must govern public and national movements if the will of God is to be respected.

II. RIGHTEOUSNESS IS A BLESSING TO A NATION. To the cynical politician such "counsels of perfection" as command conscience in government, and especially in international action, appear to be simply quixotic. He holds the application of it to be wholly impracticable; he imagines that it must involve nothing but national ruin. Hence, it is maintained, there is no right but might, because there is no international tribunal and no general authority over the nations. The two points must be kept distinct—the internal life of the nation and its foreign policy. 1. *Internal life.* There are national sins in the sense of sins committed by a great part of a nation—sins that shamefully characterize it. Thus drunkenness is to a large extent an English national sin. The oppression of one class by another, a general prevalence of business dishonesty, a frivolous pleasure-seeking fashion, all affect the nation's life when they are largely extended among any people. These things eat out the very heart of a nation. For a nation's sin the punishment is on earth, because the nation goes on while individuals die, and so there is time for the deadly fruit of sin to ripen. So was it with Israel, Babylon, Rome, etc. 2. *Foreign policy.* Wars of aggression may aggrandize the victorious people for a time. But they rouse the hatred of their victims. A high-handed policy thus multiplies a nation's enemies. It is dangerous to be an outlaw among the nations. Above all, there is a just Ruler, who will put down the tyrant and punish the guilty nation.

III. RIGHTEOUSNESS MAY BE OBTAINED IN A NATION BY FOLLOWING THE RULE OF CHRIST. It is difficult to make an unchristian nation behave in a Christian manner. The sermon on the mount was addressed to disciples of Christ (Matt. v. 1). National righteousness will follow national submission to the will of Christ. The reason why the nations snarl at one another like wild beasts is just that the inhabitants of the nations do not yet follow Christ. He came to set up the kingdom of heaven on earth, and when this kingdom is established in the hearts of the citizens, the nations, which are but the aggregates of citizens, will learn to follow righteousness.

HOMILIES BY VARIOUS AUTHORS.

Vers. 1—7.—*Traits of wisdom and folly.* I. FEMININE WISDOM. (Ver. 1.) 1. Its peculiar scope is the home. Women are *physically* and *morally* constructed with a view to the stationary life and settled pursuits of home. Its comfort, the strength of the race, the well-being of society, are rooted, more than in any other human means, in the character, the principle, the love and truth of the wife and mother. 2. The absence of it is one of the commonest causes of domestic misery. The *fact* is but too well known to all who are acquainted with the homes of the poor, and indeed of all classes. The *cause* is not far to seek. The word "home" has hardly a meaning without the presence of a virtuous woman; and a home has seldom been wrecked while a virtuous woman remained in it.

II. THE STRICT CONNECTION OF RELIGION AND MORALITY. (Ver. 2.) 1. *Fear of Jehovah* includes reverence for what is *eternal*, faith in what is *constant*, obedience to what is unchanging law. 2. *Contempt for Jehovah* means the neglect of all this; and the preference of passion to principle, immediate interest to abiding good; what is selfish and corruptible to what is pure and durable and Divine.

III. SPEECH A SCOURGE OR A SHIELD. (Ver. 3.) The word of *haste*, which is at the same time the word of *passion* and of inconsiderateness, recoils upon the speaker. As an old proverb says, "Curses come home to roost." And what can put a stronger armour about a man, or cover him more securely as a shield, than the good words he has thrown forth, or in general the *expression* of his spirit in all that is wise and loving? The successive accretions of substance from year to year in the trunk of the oak tree may typify the strength coincident with growth in the good man's life.

IV. THE CONNECTION OF MEANS AND ENDS. (Ver. 4.) Such seems to be the point of the saying. "Nothing costs nothing." If you keep no oxen, you have no manger to supply. But at the same time, nothing brings nothing in. The larger income is secured by the keeping of oxen. This is, in fact, the sense of the old saw, "Penny wise and pound foolish." In short, it is part of the science of life to know the limits of thrift and of expense. "A man often pays dear for a small frugality." "Cheapest," says the prudent, "is the dearest labour." In the more immediate interests of the soul, how true is it that only first expense of thought, time, love, upon others is the truest condition of our own blessedness!

V. TRUTH AND LIES. (Ver. 5.) Again and again we strike upon this primary stratum of character. We cannot define the truthful or untruthful man. We can *feel* them. The reason is as "simple as gravity. Truth is the summit of being; justice is the application of it to affairs. The natural force is no more to be withstood than any other force. We can drive a stone upwards for a moment into the air, but it is yet true that all stones will fall; and whatever instances may be quoted of unpunished theft, or of a lie which somebody credited, justice must prevail, and it is the privilege of truth to make itself believed."

VI. THE UNWISDOM OF THE SCOFFER. (Ver. 6.) He places himself in a false relation to truth; would measure it by his small mind, and weigh it in his imperfect scales. He has one principle only to apply to everything, and that the limited perception of his faculty or the narrow light of his experience. The description well applies to the free-thinkers, the *illuminati* so called of the last century in England, France, and Germany, and their successors in the present day. There is the *air* of superior intelligence and zeal for truth, frequently concealing some passion of a very different order. Or, again, there is the shallow assumption that absolute truth is to be found by the human intellect, which has led philosophers into many aberrations. The end is some fallacy and glaring self-contradiction. How different the spirit of him whom the teacher describes as "intelligent" in this place! It is "easy" for him to be wise. It is like opening his lungs to the bountiful and all-embracing air, or expatiating on the boundless shore, like great Newton. Wisdom springs from the sense that truth in its infinity is ever beyond us. But the reference here is more to practical wisdom, the science of living from day to day. And good sense is the main requisite for its acquirement, the very opposite of which is the supercilious temper which disdains to learn from any and all.

VII. THE EVIL OF FOOLISH COMPANY. (Ver. 7.) And of all its conversation, its atmosphere, its temper. "Cast not pearls before swine." "Avoid the mixture of an irreverent commonness of speaking of holy things indifferently in all companies" (Leighton). "Do not overrate your strength, nor be blind to the personal risks that may be incurred in imprudent efforts to do good" (Bridges). "Better retreat from cavillers" (ibid.).—J.

Vers. 8—19.—*The understanding of one's way.* I. THE GENERAL PRINCIPLE. (Ver. 8.) To note, to observe, to take heed to one's way, is the characteristic of the man who is prudent for time and wise for eternity. And, on the contrary, the very principle of folly is self-deception—to be followed in turn by a terrible awakening to sobriety and recognition of the truth (comp. Ps. vii. 15; Job iv. 8). The right way is illustrated both positively and negatively.

II. SOME PARTICULAR ILLUSTRATIONS. (Ver. 9, *sqq.*) 1. *The vanity of mere ritualism.* (Ver. 9.) According to the probably correct translation, "the guilt offering scorns the fools;" in other words, his worship is useless, missing its aim, failing of God's favour, while the righteous who has washed and made himself clean, and put away iniquity (see Isa. i.), comes with acceptance before Jehovah. 2. *Respect for others' sorrows.* (Ver. 10.) Acute distress isolates a man; he cannot communicate what he feels. And it is an unkind thing to force counsel on others at a time when they know they *cannot* be understood, when the sympathy of silence is best. To sit by our friend, to clasp his hand with loving pressure, to mingle our tears with his, will be far more delicate and soothing than to attempt to "charm ache with airs, and agony with words." 3. *Consideration of the end.* (Vers. 11—13.) The old reminder recurs, *Respice finem.* Perhaps a contrast is intended between the "house of the wicked" as seeming firmer, nevertheless doomed to overthrow, and the "tent of the righteous," seeming more frail, yet destined to "sprout," to flourish, and extend. Again, resuming the image of the way, the seeming right way is not ever the right nor the safe way. It may be broad at first and well travelled, but may narrow by-and-by, and end in the pathless forest, or the desert waste, or the fatal precipice. To be safe we must still consider the *end*; and the *beginning*, which *predicts* and virtually *contains* the end. Various are the illusions to which we are subject. One example of this is that the smiling face may hide the aching heart, and the opposite (Eccles. vii. 4) may also obtain. Boisterous and immoderate mirth is no good symptom; it foretells a sad reaction, or conceals a deep-seated gloom. Human faces and appearances are masks, which hide the real countenance of things from us. 4. *Consideration of the sources of enjoyment.* (Ver. 14.) First the vicious source. The man who has fallen away from God seeks satisfaction out of God, in something practically *atheistic*, in the fruit of godless, sinful deeds (ch. xii. 14; xiii. 2; xxviii. 19). But in the matters of the spirit that which is out of God is nothing, emptiness and vanity. He is feasting upon wind. The genuine source of enjoyment is in the spirit itself, in the consciousness, where God is known and realized and loved; in the sense of union and reconciliation of thought and affection with the Divine Object thought of and believed. The kingdom of God is within us, and is "righteousness, peace, and joy in the Holy Ghost." 5. *Credulity and caution.* (Ver. 15.) Credulity is a weakness, and certainly, like every weakness, may become a sin. It is the opposite of genuine faith: it is confidence placed where we have no right to place it. God, who has set up and kindled a light in each breast, requires us to use it, each for himself. To forsake it for any other is a desertion of our trust. Would that we might ever take heed to the light that is within us, and so steer our way! There is no true faith possible which does not begin with this. Again (ver. 16), wisdom is seen in a certain self-distrust in presence of evil. To use an expressive phrase, we should know when to "fight shy" of certain persons or associations. So powerful a passion as fear was not given us for nothing, nor should we be ashamed of a timidity which leads us to give a wide berth to danger, to keep out of the lion's path. Over-confidence springs from the want of a true estimate of our proper

strength and weakness, and the security it begets is false.   6. *Passionateness and trickiness.* (Ver. 17.)   The former precipitates men into all follies.   Seneca saith well that
" anger is like rain, which breaks itself upon that whereon it falls."   Anger is certainly
a kind of baseness; as it appears well in the weakness of those subjects in whom it
reigns—children, women, old folks, sick folks.   Bitter, unforgivable words, the revelation of secrets, the breaking off of business,—such are among the follies which anger
constantly perpetrates.   But the tricky intriguing man is both foolish and odious.
Listen to one of the greatest of Englishmen, when he bears testimony that " the ablest
men that ever were born all had an openness and frankness of dealing, and a name of
certainty and veracity."   There is a fine line between the wisdom of reserve and the
vicious cunning of concealment; nothing but the loving and true purpose of the heart
can redeem any habit of secrecy from odium.   7. *Life a progress in folly or wisdom.*
(Ver. 18.)   We are ever *gaining,* according to the image of the text.   The mind has
its accretions like those of the tree.   A man becomes a greater fool the older he grows,
or becomes of deeper sagacity, richer and wider views.   All depends on how we start.
Admit an error into thought, keep it there after it is proved an error, close the mind
in any quarter to the light and keep it closed, and ensure a bigoted and foolish age.
Let God into the mind from the first, open daily every window of the soul to the
light, and grow old " learning something fresh every day."   8. The *ascendancy of goodness.* (Ver. 19.)   The picture is presented of the envoy of a conquered people who
kneels at the palace-gate of the conqueror and waits on his commands (compare on
the thought, ch. xiii. 9, 22; Ps. xxxvii. 25).   There is a might in goodness; may we
not say the only true might is that of goodness, for it has omnipotence at its back ?   It
is victorious, irresistible, in the end.   It is content to be acknowledged in the end by
all, the evil as well as the good.   Hypocrisy is the homage paid by vice to goodness.—J.

Vers. 20—27.—*Causes and effects.* To grasp this principle—there is nothing causeless
and unaccountable in life—and to apply it is one of the main principles of wisdom.
Let us note some of its applications—
I. To SOCIAL RELATIONS.   1. *Poverty an object of dislike, and riches magnetic of
good will.* (Ver. 20.)   Widespread parallels may be found in ancient literature to
this saying.   Its truth is equally obvious to-day.   It is a truth of human nature, and
has its bad and its good side.   We are apt to be impatient of those who are always
needing help, and are disposed to serve those who need nothing.   It is a lower illustration of the law that " to him that hath it shall be given."   Independence of any kind
which implies power and self-help is attractive to all; and we should seek it by all
legitimate means.   If a man is shunned by others, it may be because they instinctively
feel there is nothing but dejection to be found in his company, while they need cheerful
confidence and helpfulness.   The good man should strive after competence that he
may secure good will, and have free scope for the cultivation of virtue and the exercise
of his powers.   Another indirect lesson is that friendship thrives best in equal conditions
of life.   2. *The sources of contempt and of compassion.* (Ver. 21.)   This seems to
correct what might appear harsh in the former saying.   Contempt for anything but
what is evil in life, or petty and trivial in thought and sentiment, springs from a bad
state of the heart.   There are things we ought all to *despise*—i.e. look down upon—but
certainly the mere poverty of our neighbour or friend is not one of them.   Compassion
upon those who are in trouble is, on the other hand, a feeling truly Divine.   It extorts
the blessing of men; it receives the approval of God, the All-compassionate One.   3.
The sources of social security. (Ver. 25.)   " Souls are saved," human life is preserved,
the bonds of intercourse are held together, by the truthful man.   Hearts are betrayed,
covenants are broken, the integrity of life is shattered, by the deceiver, the hypocrite,
and the slanderer.
II. To PERSONAL BLESSINGS AND THE REVERSE.   1. *The sources of perplexity or of
peace are in the man's own mind.* (Ver. 22.)   His errors come from the falsity and
malice of his own counsels, as the effect from the cause.   And equally the blessed
sense of the Divine presence and the Divine favour is conditioned by the seeking of it
in the mind, the heart, the life.   To imagine that we can enjoy good without being
good is a sort of superstition.   2. *Causes of gain and want.* (Ver. 23.)   One of the
most valuable of Carlyle's teachings was to this effect—the reward that we all receive

and of which we are perfectly certain, if we have deserved it, consists in *having done our work*, or at least having taken pains to do our work, for that is of itself a great blessing, and one is inclined to say that, properly speaking, there is no other reward in this world.   And men bring themselves to want by neglecting their proper work, by idle talk, and waste of time and daylight.   " Work while it is called to-day."   3. Hence, *well-gotten wealth is a testimonial to the earner of it.*   (Ver. 24.)   It is an ornament, a decoration in which he may feel a juster pride than in stars, or garters, or patents of nobility, which carry no such significance.   On the other hand, the folly of the fool is and remains folly, however he may plume himself, however by means of wealth or factitious advantages he may seek to pass for somebody before the world.   4. But deeper than these are the specifically religious blessings.   (Ver. 26.)   Security springs from religion ; and religion is the constant habit of regard for God, his will in loving obedience, his favour as the most precious possession.   God himself is a Refuge to his children, and they will not fear.   The very source of life itself is religion, and nothing but the fear of God in the heart can preserve from the deathful snares which attend our way.—J.

Vers. 28—35.—*Life-contrasts.*   I. IN PUBLIC LIFE.   1. *Fulness and scantiness of population.*   (Ver. 28.)   The Hebrew had a deep sense of the value of fruitfulness in the wedded life, and of increase in the nation.   The majesty of the monarch is the reflection of the greatness of his people, and the decay must represent itself in his feebleness for action.   It is our duty as Christian men to study with intelligence political questions, and to support all measures which tend to freedom of commerce and abundance of food.   2. *National exaltation and shame.*   (Ver. 34.)   The common ideas of national glory and shame are false.   There is no glory in victory over feeble foes, no shame in seeking peace in the interests of humanity.   Too often these popular ideas of glory represent the bully and the coward in the nation, rather than its wisdom and honour.   There is *no other* real secret of a nation's exaltation than, in the widest sense, its right dealing, and no other shame for a nation than its vices—such as drunkenness, selfishness, lust for territory.   Could Englishmen see the national character in the light in which it often appears to foreigners, it would be a humbling view.   3. *Royal favour or disfavour is an index of worth.*   (Ver. 35.)   Not, of course, the only or the truest index ; and yet how seldom it happens that a man rises to high position in the service of his sovereign and country without eminent worth of some description or other !   Here, again, moral law is exemplified.   There is nothing accidental.   If it be mere prudence which gains promotion, still prudence is of immense value to the state, and moral law is confirmed by its advancement.

II. IN PRIVATE LIFE.   1. *Patience and haste of temper.*   (Ver. 29.)   They are branded respectively with the mark of sense and of folly.   "The Scripture exhorteth us to possess our souls in patience; whosoever is out of patience is out of possession of his soul."   2. *The calm and the seething heart.*   (Ver. 30.)   The first member seems more correctly rendered, "life of the body is a gentle or tranquil mind."   Zeal, on the other hand, or envy, is a constant ferment within the soul.   Men's minds must either feed upon their own good or others' evil.   Inquisitive people are commonly envious; it is a "gadding passion," and an old proverb says that "Envy keeps no holidays."   Lord Bacon says it is the vilest passion and the most depraved.   Christian humility and love can only sweeten the heart, and dilute or wash away its natural bitterness   3. *The violent death and the peaceful end.*   (Ver. 32.)   A sudden death was viewed as a visitation from God (Ps. xxxvi. 13 ; lxii. 4).   It was thought that the wicked could hardly come to any other end.   But the righteous has confidence in his death.   Considering the great silence of the Old Testament on the future life, it can hardly be honest exegesis to force the meaning of hope of a future life into this passage.   Nor is it necessary.   It is the consciousness that all is well, the soul being in God's hands, that the future may be left with him who has revealed himself in the past, which sheds peace into the dying soul.   4. *Silent wisdom and noisy pretence.*   (Ver. 33.)   The still and quiet wisdom of the sensible man (ch. x. 14 ; xii. 16, 23) is contrasted with the eager and noisy utterances of what the fool supposes to be wisdom, but in reality is the exposure of his folly.   "There is no decaying merchant or inward beggar hath so many tricks to uphold the credit of their wealth as those empty persons have to maintain the credit of their sufficiency." Wisdom and piety are felt and fragrant, like the violet in the hedge, from humble places and silent lives. Let us aim to *be*, not to *seem*.—J.

Ver. 1.—*Woman as a builder.* Where the light of revelation has shone, woman has had a position and a power, an honour and a happiness, such as she has not enjoyed elsewhere. Under the teaching of Christian truth she has been, or is being, rapidly raised to her rightful place, and is becoming all that the Creator intended her to be. We cannot forecast the future, but we may predict that her own especial province, the sphere where she will always shine, will be, as it is now, *the home.* It is " her house " that she will either build up or pluck down " with her own hands." Whether she will do the one or the other depends on the question whether she shows—

I. GOODNESS (moral worth) or GUILT.

II. IMPARTIALITY or an unwise and unrighteous preference of one child to another.

III. DILIGENCE in the discharge of her household duties, or NEGLIGENCE.

IV. KINDNESS or ASPERITY in her bearing toward all the members of the home.

V. PATIENCE or IMPATIENCE in the government of her family and her servants.

And since the upbuilding or the down-plucking of " the house," the promotion or the ruin of domestic harmony and happiness, depends in so large a degree on the wisdom or the folly of the woman who is the wife and the mother, therefore: 1. Let every wise man think many times before he makes his choice. 2. Let every woman who is entering on this estate go forth to occupy it in (1) humility, (2) prayerfulness, (3) wise and holy resolution.—C.

Ver. 4.—*Daintiness and usefulness.* It is a very great thing to prefer the greater to the smaller, the more serious to the less serious, in the regulation of our life. It makes all the difference between success and failure, between wisdom and folly.

I. A SERIOUS MISTAKE, to prefer nicety or daintiness to fruitfulness or usefulness. This grave mistake is made by the *farmer* who would rather have a clean crib than a quantity of valuable manure; by the *housewife* who cares more for the elegance of the furniture than the comfort of the family; by the *minister* who spends more strength on the wording than on the doctrine of his discourse; by the *teacher* who lays more stress on the composition of classical verses than on the history of his country or than on the strengthening of the mind; by the *poet* who takes infinite pains with his rhymes and gives little thought to his subject or his imagery; by the *statesman* who is particular about the draughting of his bills, and has no objection to introduce retrograde and dishonouring measures; by the *doctor* who insists much on his medicine, and lets his patient go on neglecting all the laws of hygiene; etc.

II. THE WISDOM OF THE WISE. This is found in subordinating the trivial to the important; in being willing to submit to the temporarily disagreeable if we can attain to the permanently good; in being content to endure the sight and the smell of the unclean crib if there is a prospect of a fruitful field. The great thing is *increase*, fruitfulness, the reward of honest toil and patient waiting and believing prayer. This increase is to be sought and found in five fields in particular. 1. Bodily health and strength. 2. Knowledge, in all its various directions. 3. Material wealth, that ministers to the comfort and thus to the well-being of the families of man. 4. Wisdom; that noble quality of the soul which distinguishes between the true and the false, the pure and the impure, the imperishable and the ephemeral, the estimable and the unworthy, and which not only distinguishes but determinately chooses the former and rejects the latter. 5. Spiritual fruitfulness; the increase of our own piety and virtue, and also the growth of the kingdom of our Lord.—C.

Ver. 8.—*Understanding our way.* A man may be " prudent," he may be clever, learned, astute; yet he may miss his way, he may lose his life, he may prove to be a failure. *The wisdom* of the prudent, that which makes prudence or ability really valuable, that which constitutes its virtue, is the *practical understanding of life*, the knowledge which enables a man to take the right path and keep it, the discretion which chooses the line of a true success and maintains it to the end. It is to perceive and to pursue the way that is—

I. FINANCIALLY SOUND; avoiding that which leads to embarrassment and ruin; shunning those which conduct either to a sordid parsimony in one direction or to a wasteful extravagance on the other hand; choosing that which leads to competence and generosity.

II. EDUCATIONALLY WISE; forming the habits which strengthen and develop the faculties of the mind, instead of those which dwarf, or narrow, or demoralize them.

III. SOCIALLY SATISFACTORY; not going the way of an unwise and unsatisfactory ambition which ends in disappointment and chagrin; seeking the society which is suitable, elevating, honourable.

IV. IN ACCORDANCE WITH INDIVIDUAL ENDOWMENT; so that we do not expend all our time and all our powers in a way which cuts against all our individual inclinations, but in one which gives room for our particular aptitudes, and develops the special faculty with which our Creator has endowed our spirit.

V. MORALLY SAFE. It is a very great part of "the wisdom of the prudent" for a man to know what he may allow himself to do and where to go; what, on the other hand, he must not permit, and whither he must not wend his way. The path of safety to one man is the road to ruin with another. "Happy is he who condemneth not himself in that thing which he alloweth" (Rom. xiv. 22). Wise is it in those, and well is it for them, who have discerned and who have decided upon those habits of life which are establishing in their hearts all Christian virtues and making to shine in their lives all Christian graces.

VI. THE WAY OF HOLY SERVICE. The way of sacred service is so essentially *the* way of wisdom, that any "prudence" or cleverness that misses it makes the supreme mistake. On the other hand, the wisdom that leads to it and that preserves the soul in it is *the* wisdom to attain unto. This way, which is the end of our being and the crown of our life, includes (1) the service of Christ, and (2) the service of man.—C.

Ver. 9.—*The sadness of sin.* It is foolish enough to use the words "sin" and "sinner" in the light and flippant way in which they are frequently employed. But to "make a mock at sin" itself, to treat otherwise than seriously the fact and forces of sin, is folly indeed. For sin is—

I. THE SADDEST AND STERNEST FACT IN ALL THE UNIVERSE OF GOD. It is the ultimate cause of all the disorder, misery, ruin, and death that are to be found beneath any sky. There is no curse or calamity that has befallen our race that is not due to its disastrous power.

II. THE DARKEST EXPERIENCE WE HAVE IN REVIEW. We may look back on many dark passages in our life-history, but none can be so black as the experiences for which we have to reproach ourselves, as those wherein we broke some plain precept of God or left undischarged some weighty obligation.

III. A POWERFUL, HOSTILE FORCE STILL CONFRONTING US. Sin "easily besets us." 1. It is exceedingly *deceptive*, alluring, undermining, betraying. 2. It is a *very present* enemy, near at hand when least suspected, entering into all the scenes and spheres of life. 3. It *strikes deep*, going down into the innermost places of the soul. 4. It is *very extensive* in its range, covering all the particulars of life. 5. It *stretches* far into the future, crossing even the dividing-line of death, and reaching into eternity. 6. It is *fatal* in its results, leading the soul down into the dark shadows of spiritual death.

The only wise course we can take in view of such a force as this is (1) to realize its heinousness; (2) to confess its guiltiness; (3) to strive with patient strenuousness against its power; (4) to seek the aid of the Holy and Mighty Spirit that it may be uprooted from the heart and life.—C.

Vers. 10—13.—*Loneliness and laughter.* The tenth verse suggests to us the serious and solemnizing fact of—

I. THE ELEMENT OF LONELINESS IN HUMAN LIFE. "The heart knoweth its own bitterness," etc. In one aspect our life-path is thronged. It is becoming more and more difficult to be alone. Hours that were once sacred to solitude are now invaded by society. And yet it remains true that "in the central depths of our nature we are alone." There is a point at which, as he goes inward, our nearest neighbour, our most intimate friend, must stop; there *is* a sanctuary of the soul into which no foot intrudes. It is there where we make our ultimate decision for good or evil; it is there where we experience our truest joys and our profoundest griefs; it is there where we live our truest life. We may so crowd our life with duties and with pleasures that we may reduce to its smallest radius this innermost circle; but some time must we spend there, and the great decisive experiences must we there go through. There we taste our very sweetest satisfactions, and there we bear our very heaviest burdens. And no one but the Father of spirits can enter into that secret place of the soul. So true is it that

> "Not e'en the dearest heart, and nearest to our own,
> Knows half the reasons why we smile or sigh."

It is well for us to remember that there is more, both of happiness and of sorrow, than we can see; well, that we may not be overburdened with the weight of the manifold and multiplied evils we are facing; well, that we may realize how strong is the reason that, when our cup of prosperity is full, we may have "the heart at leisure from itself, to soothe and sympathize" with those who, beneath a smiling countenance, may carry a very heavy heart. For we have to consider—

II. THE SUPERFICIAL ELEMENT IN MUCH HUMAN GLADNESS. "Even in laughter," etc. A man may smile and smile, and be most melancholy. To wear a smile upon our countenance, or to conclude our sentences with laughter, is often only a mere trick of style, a mere habit of life, cultivated with little difficulty. A true smile, an honest laugh, that comes not from the lips or from the lungs, but from the heart, is a very acceptable and a very admirable thing. But a false smile and a forced laugh bespeak a double-minded soul and a doubtful character. Surely the angels of God weep almost as much over the laughter as over the tears of mankind. For beneath its sound they may hear all too much that is hollow and unreal, and not a little that is vain and guilty. But, on the other hand, to smile with the glad and to laugh with the merry is a sympathetic grace not to be despised (Rom. xii. 15, first clause).

III. THE ISSUE OF FALSE SATISFACTIONS. "The end of that mirth is heaviness." How often is heaviness the end of mirth! All enjoyment that does not carry with it the approval of the conscience, all that is disregardful of the Divine Law, all that is a violation of the laws of our physical or our spiritual nature, *must* end and *does* end, sooner or later, in heaviness—in depression of spirit, in decline of power. It is a sorry thing for a man to accustom himself to momentary mirth, to present pleasure at the expense of future joy, of well-being in later years.

LESSONS. 1. Let the necessary solitariness of life lead us to choose the *very best* friendships we can form; that we may have those who can go far and often with us into the recesses of our spirit, and accompany us, as far as man can, in the larger and deeper experiences of our life. 2. Let the superficiality of much happiness lead us to inquire of ourselves whether we have planted in our soul the deeper roots of joy; those which will survive every test and trial of life, and which will be in us when we have left time and sense altogether behind us. 3. Let the perilous nature of some gratifications impose on us the duty of a wise watchfulness; that we may banish for ever from heart and life all injurious delights which "war against the soul," and rob us of our true heritage here and in the heavenly country.—C.

Ver. 13.—(See homily on ch. xvi. 25.)—C.

Vers. 17, 29.—(See homily on ch. xvi. 32.)—C.

Ver. 21.—*The sin of contempt.* We are in danger of despising our neighbours. The rich despise the poor, the learned despise the ignorant, the strong and healthy despise the weak and ailing, the devout despise the irreverent. But we are wrong in doing this. There is, indeed, one thing which may draw down a strong and even intense reprobation—moral baseness, meanness, a cruel and heartless selfishness, or a slavish abandonment to vice. But even there we may not wholly despise our neighbour; unmitigated contempt is always wrong, always a mistake. For—

I. WE ARE ALL THE CHILDREN OF GOD. Are we not all *his* offspring, the creatures of one Creator, the children of one Father? Does it become us to despise our own brethren, our own sisters? Inasmuch as we are "members one of another," of one family, we are bound to let another feeling than that of contempt take the deepest place in our heart when we think of men and women, whoever they may be, whatever they may have been.

II. SELF-GLORIFICATION IS EXCLUDED. What makes us to differ from others? Whence came our superiority in wealth, in knowledge, in strength, in virtue? Did it not come, ultimately, from God? Trace things to their source, and we find that all "boasting is excluded." It is by the favour and the grace of God that we are who and what we are. Not a haughty contemptuousness, but a humble thankfulness, becomes us, if we stand higher than our neighbour.

III. NO MAN IS WHOLLY DESPICABLE. He may have some things about his character which we deplore and which we condemn, on account of which we do well to remonstrate with him and to make him feel that we have withdrawn our regard and confidence. But no man is wholly to be despised. 1. Much of what is bad or sad about him may be the consequence of misfortune. What did he inherit? Who were his earliest counsellors? What were his adverse influences? Against what hurtful and damaging forces has he had to contend? How few and how weak have been his privileges? how many his privations? 2. There is the germ of goodness in him. There is no man, even among the most depraved, who has not in him that on which wisdom and love may lay their merciful hold, and by which the man himself may be redeemed. Many marvellous and most cheering facts *prove* that the worst among the bad may be recovered—the most profane, besotted, impure, dishonest. The Christian thought and faith is that all men are within the reach both of the mercy and the redeeming love of God. Let Divine truth be spoken to them as it may be spoken; let Divine and human love embrace them and lay its fatherly or brotherly hand upon them; let the Divine Spirit breathe upon them, and from the lowest depths of guilt and shame they may rise to noble heights of purity and honour.—C.

Ver. 23.—*Talking and toiling.* These words contain solid and valuable truth; that truth does not, however, exclude the facts—

I. THAT MUCH LABOUR IS WORSE THAN USELESS. All that which is conceived and carried out for the purpose of destruction, or of fraud, or of vice, or of impiety. Only too often men give themselves infinite trouble which is worse than thrown away, the putting forth of which is sin, the end of which is evil—misery or even ruin and death.

II. THAT MUCH SPEAKING TENDS TO ENRICHMENT. There *is* a "talk of the lips" which is worthy of taking rank with the most profitable toil. 1. It may cost the speaker much care and effort and expenditure of vital force. 2. It may be a great power for good in the minds of men and even in the histories of peoples—

> "Like Luther's in the days of old,
> Half-battles for the free."

3. It may bring light to the darkened mind, comfort to the wounded heart, rest to the weary soul, strength and inspiration to the spirit that needs revival. But, on the other hand, the truth which the proverb is intended to impress upon us is this—

III. THAT MUCH VERBIAGE IS VERY PROFITLESS AND VAIN. There is a "talk of the lips" that does indeed tend to poverty. 1. That which does nothing more than consume time. This is pure waste; and in

> "An age (like this) when every hour
> Must sweat her sixty minutes to the death,"

this can by no means be afforded. 2. That which gives false ideas of life; which encourages men to trust to chance, or to despise honest toil, or to hope for the success which is the fruit of chicanery and dishonesty, or to find a heritage, not in the consciousness of duty and of the favour of God, but in superficial and short-lived delights.

IV. THAT CONSCIENTIOUS LABOUR IS THE ONE FRUITFUL THING. "In all labour there is profit." 1. Physical labour not only cultivates the field and builds the house and clothes the naked, but it gives strength to the muscles and health to the whole body.

2. Mental labour not only designs the painting, or the sculpture, or the oratorio, and writes the poem or the history, but it invigorates the mind and braces all the mental faculties. 3. Moral struggle not only saves from vice and crime, but makes the soul strong for noble and honourable achievement. 4. Spiritual endeavour not only refines the highest faculties of our nature, prepares us for the companionship of the holiest, and accomplishes the highest purposes of the Redeemer, but brings us into the favour and leads us into the likeness of God himself.—C.

Ver. 33.—(See homily on ch. xxix. 11.)—C.

Ver. 34.—*The strength and the reproach of nations.* I. SIN THE NATION'S SHAME. 1. *A sinful nation* in the sight of God. This is a nation of which the people have gone astray from him; do not approach him in worship; do not consult his will as revealed in his Word; have no ear to lend to those that speak in his Name; lose all sense of sacred duty in the pursuit of gain and pleasure. 2. *The flagrant guilt* to which such godlessness leads down. (1) It is *probable,* in a high degree, that impiety will lead to iniquity, that the absence of all religious restraint will end in abandonment to evil in all its forms. (2) History assures us that it does so. The denial, or the defiance, or the entire disregard of God and of his will, conducts to and ends in vice, in crime, in violence, in despotism, in the dissolution of old and honourable bonds, in the prevalence of despair and suicide, in utter demoralization. 3. This is *the reproach* to a people. A country may lose its population, or its wealth, or its pre-eminent influence, without being the object of reproach; but to fall into general impiety, and to live in the practice of wrong-doing,—this is a disgrace; it brings a nation down in the estimate of all the wise; its name is clothed with shame; its fame has become infamy.

II. RIGHTEOUSNESS A NATION'S STRENGTH. National righteousness does not consist in any public professions of piety, nor in the existence of great religious organizations, nor in the presence of a multitude of ecclesiastical edifices and officers; nations have had all these before now, and they have been destitute of real righteousness. That consists in the possession of a reverent *spirit* and an estimable *character,* and the *practice* of purity, justice, and kindness on the part of the people themselves (see Isa. lviii.; Micah vi. 6—8). In this is a nation's strength and exaltation, for it will surely issue in: 1. *Physical well-being.* Virtue is the secret of health and strength, of the multiplication and continuance of life and power. 2. *Material prosperity;* for right-eousness is the foundation of educated intelligence, of intellectual energy and vigour, of commercial and agricultural enterprise, of maritime intrepidity and success. 3. *Moral and spiritual* advancement. 4. *Estimation and influence* among surrounding nations. 5. The *abiding favour of God* (Ps. lxxxi. 13—16). We may learn from the text (1) that no measure of brilliancy in statesmanship will compensate for debauch-ing the minds of the people, for introducing ideas or sanctioning habits which are morally unsound and corrupting; (2) that the humblest citizen whose life tends to establish righteousness amongst his neighbours is a true patriot, however narrow his sphere may be.—C.

EXPOSITION.

CHAPTER XV.

Ver. 1.—**A soft answer turneth away wrath.** Two things are here to be observed: an answer should be given—the injured person should not wrap himself in sullen silence; and that answer should be gentle and conciliatory. This is tersely put in a mediæval rhyme—

"Frangitur ira gravis
    Quando est responsio suavis."

"Anger, however great,
    Is checked by answer sweet."

Septuagint, "A submissive (ὑποπίπτουσα) answer averteth wrath." Thus Abigail quelled the excessive anger of David by her judicious submission (1 Sam. xxv. 24, etc.). **But grievous words stir up anger.** A word that causes vexation makes anger rise the higher.

Ὀργῆς ματαίας εἰσὶν αἴτιοι λόγοι.

"Of empty anger words are oft the cause."

Ver. 2.—**The tongue of the wise useth knowledge aright.** This means either, brings it forth opportunely, at the right time and place, or illustrates it, makes it beautiful and pleasant, as ver. 13. The wise man not only has knowledge, but can give it appropriate expression (comp. ch. xvi. 23). Vulgate, "The tongue of the wise adorneth wisdom." The wise man, by producing his sentiments and opinions in appropriate language and on proper occasions, commends wisdom, and renders it acceptable to his hearers. Septuagint, "The tongue of the wise knoweth what is fair (καλά)." But the mouth of fools poureth out foolishness (ver. 28). A fool cannot open his mouth without exposing his folly; he speaks without due consideration or discretion; as the Vulgate terms it, ebullit, "he bubbles over," like a boiling pot, which emits its contents inopportunely and uselessly. Septuagint, "The mouth of fools proclaimeth evil."

Ver. 3.—The eyes of the Lord are in every place, beholding—keeping watch on—the evil and the good. The omnipresence and omniscience of Jehovah, the covenant God, is strongly insisted upon, and the sacred name recurs continually in this and the next chapter, and indeed throughout this Book of the Proverbs (see Wordsworth, in loc.). The LXX. renders the verb σκοπεύουσι, "are watching," as from a tower or high place. To the usual references we may add Ecclus. xv. 18, 19; xxiii. 19, 20. Corn. à Lapide quotes Prudentius's hymn, used in the Latin Church at Thursday Lauds—

> "Speculator adstat desuper,
> Qui nos diebus omnibus
> Actusque nostros prospicit
> A luce prima in vesperum."

> "For God our Maker, ever nigh,
> Surveys us with a watchful eye;
> Our every thought and act he knows,
> From early dawn to daylight's close."

Ver. 4.—A wholesome tongue is a tree of life; a tongue that brings healing, that soothes by its words. Septuagint, "the healing of the tongue." But the Vulgate rendering is better, lingua placabilis, "the gentle, mild tongue" (see on ch. xiv. 30). Speech from such a source refreshes and vivifies all who come under its influence, like the wholesome fruit of a prolific tree (comp. ch. iii. 18; xi. 30).

Ψυχῆς νοσούσης ἐστὶ φάρμακον λόγος.

"The sick soul by a healing word is cured."

But perverseness therein—in the tongue—is a breach in the spirit. The perverseness intended must be falsehood, perversion of the truth. This is ruin and vexation (Isa. lxv. 14, where the same word is used) in the spirit, both in the liar himself, whose higher nature is thus terribly marred and spoiled, and in the case of his neighbour, who is injured by his slander and falsehood to the very core. The LXX., with a different reading, translates, "But he who keepeth it [the tongue] shall be filled with the spirit."

Ver. 5.—A fool despiseth his father's instruction (ch. x. 1): but he that regardeth reproof is prudent (ch. xix. 25). The son who attends to his father's reproof dealeth prudently, or becomes wiser. Astutior fiet, Vulgate; πανουργότερος, Septuagint. The Vulgate has here a distich which is not in the Hebrew, but a similar paragraph is found in the Septuagint. Thus Vulgate, "In the abundance of righteousness virtue is greatest; but the imaginations of the wicked shall be rooted up;" Septuagint, "In the abundance of righteousness is much strength; but the impious shall be destroyed from the very root." The addition seems to have been an explanation of the following verse, which has been foisted into the text here.

Ver. 6.—In the house of the righteous is much treasure (chosen; see on ch. xxvii. 24). The good man's store is not wasted or wrongly used, and is blest by God; and therefore, whether absolutely much or little, it is safe, and it is sufficient. In a spiritual sense, the soul of the righteous is filled with graces and adorned with good works. Septuagint, "In the houses of the righteous is much strength;" plurima fortitudo, Vulgate. But in the revenues of the wicked is trouble. Great revenues acquired by wrong or expended badly bring only trouble, vexation, and ruin upon a man and his family. Septuagint, "The fruits of the wicked shall perish." Spiritually, the works of the wicked cause misery to themselves and others.

Ver. 7.—The lips of the wise disperse knowledge (ver. 2; ch. x. 31). The LXX. takes the verb יְזָרוּ in its other signification of "binding" or "embracing," and translates, "The lips of the wise are bound (δέδεται) with knowledge;" i.e. knowledge is always on them and controls their movements. The wise know when to speak, when to be silent, and what to say. But the heart of the foolish doeth not so; i.e. doth not disperse knowledge. Vulgate, cor stultorum dissimile erit, "will be unlike," which probably means the same as the Authorized Version. (Compare a similar use of the words lo-ken in Gen. xlviii. 18; Exod. x. 11.) But the contrast is stated rather weakly by this rendering, lips and heart having the same office to perform; hence it is better, with Delitzsch, Ewald, and others, to take כֵּן (ken) as an adjective in the sense of "right" or "trustworthy," and either to supply the former verb, "disperseth that which is not right," or to render, "The heart of the fool is not directed right;" the fool goes astray, and leads himself and others into error. Septuagint, "The hearts of fools are not safe (ἀσφαλεῖς)."

Ver. 8.—**The sacrifice of the wicked is an abomination unto the Lord.** The costly sacrifice of the wicked is contrasted with **the prayer**, unaccompanied with sacrifice, **of the upright.** The first clause occurs again in ch. xxi. 27, and virtually in ch. xxviii. 9. But in the latter passage the prayer of the wicked is denounced as abomination. Sacrifice, as legal and cere-monial, would be more naturally open to the charge of deadness and unreality; while prayer, as spontaneous and not legally en-joined, might be deemed less liable to for-malism; all the more hateful, therefore, it is if not offered from the heart. The worth-lessness of external worship without obedi-ence and devotion of the heart is often urged by the prophets (see 1 Sam. xv. 22; Isa. i. 11, etc.; Jer. vi. 20; Hos. v. 6; Amos v. 22; see also Ecclus. xxxi. 18, etc.). The lesson was needed that the value of sacrifice depended upon the mind and disposition of the offerer, the tendency being to rest in the *opus operatum*, as if the external action was all that was necessary to make the worshipper accepted. This text was wrested by the Donatists to support their notion of the inefficacy of heretical baptism. St. Augustine replied that the validity of the sacrament depended not on the spiritual condition of the minister, but on the appoint-ment of Christ. The text has also been applied to confirm the opinion that all the acts of unjustified man are sin. The truer view is that God's grace does act beyond the limits of his visible Church, and that the inspiration of the Holy Spirit concurs with the free-will of man before he is for-mally justified. The second clause recurs virtually in ver. 29.

Ver. 9.—This verse gives the reason for the treatment specified in the preceding verse (comp. ch. xi. 20; xii. 22). **Followeth after**; *chaseth*, implying effort and persever-ance, as in the pursuit of game (ch. xi. 19; xxi. 21).

Ver. 10.—**Correction is grievous unto him that forsaketh the way.** The verse is cli-macteric, and the first clause is better trans-lated, *There is a grievous correction for him that forsaketh the way;* then the second clause denotes what that correction is: **he that hateth reproof**—*i.e.* he that forsaketh the way—**shall die.** "The way" is the path of goodness and righteousness (ch. ii. 13). "The way of life," the Vulgate calls it; so ch. x. 17. Ecclus. xxi. 6, "He that hateth reproof is in the way of sinners." The Authorized Version is quite allowable, and is supported in some degree by the

Vulgate, *Doctrina mala deserenti viam vitæ.* The sinner is annoyed by discipline, correc-tion, or true teaching, because they curb the indulgence of his passions, make him un-easy in conscience, and force him to look to future issues. Septuagint, "The instruc-tion of the guileless (ἀκάκου) is known by passers-by; but they who hate reproofs die shamefully." The Syriac adopts the same rendering; but it is a question whether the word ought not to be κακοῦ. Menander says—

ʹΟ μὴ δαρεὶς ἄνθρωπος οὐ παιδεύεται.
"Man unchastised learns naught."

Ver. 11.—**Hell and destruction are before the Lord.** The two words rendered "hell" and "destruction" are respectively *Sheol* and *Abaddon, Infernus* and *Perditio,* Ἅιδης and ἀπώλεια (comp. ch. xxvii. 20). The former is used generally as the place to which the souls of the dead are consigned—the receptacle of all departed spirits, whether good or bad. Abaddon is the lowest depth of hell, the "abyss" of Luke viii. 31; Rev. ix. 2, etc.; xx. 1, etc. The clause means that God's eye penetrates even the most secret corners of the unseen world. As Job (xxvi. 6) says, "Sheol is naked before him, and Abad-don hath no covering" (comp. Ps. cxxxix. 7, etc.). **How much more then the hearts of the children of men?** (For the form of the expression, comp. ch. xi. 31 and xix. 7; and for the import, ch. xvi. 2; xxi. 2; Jer. xvii. 10.) If God knows the secrets of the world beyond the grave, much more does he know the secret thoughts of men on earth. The heart is the source of action (see Matt. xv. 19, etc.).

Ver. 12.—**A scorner loveth not one that reproveth him** (ch. ix. 8; Amos v. 10). For "scorner" the Vulgate has *pestilens*, and the Septuagint ἀπαίδευτος, "undisciplined." "Scorners" are spoken of elsewhere, as ch. i. 22 (where see note); they are conceited, arrogant persons, free-thinkers, indifferent to or sceptical of religion, and too self-opinionated to be open to advice or reproof. **Neither will he go unto the wise,** who would correct and teach him (ch. xiii. 20). Septuagint, "He will not converse (ὁμιλήσει) with the wise." He does not believe the maxim—

Σοφοῦ παρ᾽ ἀνδρὸς χρὴ σοφόν τι μανθάνειν.
"From a wise man you must some wisdom learn."

A Latin adage runs—

"Argue consultum, te diliget; argue stultum, Avertet vultum, nec te dimittet inultum."

Ver. 13.—**A merry heart maketh a cheerful countenance.** The face is the index of the condition of the mind.

"In the forehead and the eye
The lecture of the mind doth lie."

And, again, "A blithe heart makes a blooming visage" (comp. Ecclus. xiii. 25, etc.). Septuagint, "When the heart is glad, the face bloometh (θάλλει)." But by sorrow of heart the spirit is broken (ch. xii. 25). Happiness is shown in the outward look, but sorrow has a deeper and more abiding influence; it touches the inner life, destroys the natural elasticity, creates despondency and despair (comp. ch. xvi. 24; xvii. 22). Corn. à Lapide quotes St. Gregory Nazianzen's definition—

"Lætitia quidnam? Mentis est diffusio.
Tristitia? Cordis morsus et turbatio."

Hitzig and others translate the second clause, "But in sorrow of heart is the breath oppressed." It is doubtful if the words can be so rendered, and certainly the parallelism is not improved thereby.

Ver. 14.—The heart of him that hath understanding seeketh knowledge (ch. xviii. 15). The wise man knows that he knows nothing, and is always seeking to learn more.

Σοφία γάρ ἐστι καὶ μαθεῖν ἃ μὴ νοεῖς.

"To learn what thou hast never thought is wisdom."

The mouth of fools. Another reading, is "the face of fools;" but the former is more suitable to what follows. Feedeth on foolishness. So the Vulgate and Septuagint, "The mouth of the undisciplined knoweth evil." The fool is always gaping and devouring every silly, or slanderous, or wicked word that comes in his way, and in his turn utters and disseminates it.

Ver. 15.—All the days of the afflicted are evil. "The days of the poor are evil," says the Talmud ('Dukes,' 73); but in our verse the contrasted clause restricts the sense of "the afflicted" to mental, not material, evil. The Vulgate pauperis gives a wrong impression. The persons intended are such as take a gloomy view of things, who are always in low spirits, and cannot rise superior to present circumstances. These never have a happy moment; they are always taking anxious thought (Matt. vi. 25), and forecasting evil. The LXX., reading עיר for עני, translates, "At all times the eyes of the evil expect evil." But he that is of a merry heart hath a continual feast. The cheerful man's condition is a banquet unceasingly, a fixed state of joy and contentment. Septuagint, "But the righteous are at peace always;" Vulgate, "A secure mind is like a perpetual feast." "For," says St. Gregory ('Moral.,' xii. 44), "the mere repose of security is like the continuance of refresh-

ment. Whereas, on the other hand, the evil mind is always set in pains and labours, since it is either contriving mischiefs that it may bring down, or fearing lest these be brought down upon it by others." Our own proverb says, "A contented mind is a continual feast."

Ver. 16.—Better is little with the fear of the Lord. The good man's little store, which bears upon it the blessing of the Lord, is better than great treasure and trouble therewith, i.e. with the treasure (ch. xvi. 8; Ps. xxxvii. 16). The trouble intended is the care and labour and anxiety attending the pursuit and preservation of wealth. "Much coin, much care" (comp. Eccles. vi. 4). It was good advice of the old moralist, "Sis pauper honeste potius quam dives male; Namque hoc fert crimen, illud misericordiam." Vulgate, thesauri magni et insatiabiles, "treasures which satisfy not;" Septuagint, "Great treasures without fear (of the Lord)." Christ's maxim is, "Seek ye first the kingdom of God, and his righteousness; and all these things shall be added unto you" (Matt. vi. 33).

Ver. 17.—Better is a dinner (portion) of herbs where love is. A dish of vegetables would be the common meal, whereas flesh would be reserved for festive occasions. Where love presides, the simplest food is cheerfully received, and contentment and happiness abound (ch. xvii. 1). Lesètre quotes Horace's invitation to his friend Torquatus ('Epist.,' i. 5. 1)—

"Si potes Archiacis conviva recumbere lectis,
Nec modica cenare times olus omne patella,
Supremo te sole domi, Torquate, manebo."

"If, dear Torquatus, you can rest your head
On couches such as homely Archias made,
Nor on a dish of simple pot-herbs frown,
I shall expect you as the sun goes down."
　　　　　　　　　　　　(Howes.)

So the old jingle—

"Cum dat oluscula mensa minuscula pace quieta,
Ne pete grandia lautaque prandia lite repleta."

A stalled ox is one taken up out of the pasture and fatted for the table. Thus we read (1 Kings iv. 23) that part of Solomon's provision for one day was ten fat oxen and twenty oxen out of the pastures; and the prophets speak of "calves of the stall" (Amos vi. 4; Mal. iv. 2; comp. Luke xv. 23). The fat beef implies a sumptuous and magnificent entertainment; but such a feast is little worth if accompanied with feelings of hatred, jealousy, and ill will. This and the preceding verse emphasize and explain ver. 15.

Ver. 18.—**A wrathful man stirreth up strife** (*contention*). This clause recurs almost identically in ch. xxix. 22 (comp. also ch. xxvi. 21 and xxviii. 25). He that is **slow to anger appeaseth strife** (ch. xiv 29). In the former clause the word for "contention" is *madon*, in the latter "strife" is *rib*, which often means "law dispute." It requires two to make a quarrel, and where one keeps his temper and will not be provoked, anger must subside. Vulgate, "He who is patient soothes aroused quarrels (*suscitatas*)." Septuagint, "A long-suffering man appeases even a coming battle."

"Regina rerum omnium patientia."

The LXX. here introduces a second rendering of the verse: "A long-suffering man will quench suits; but the impious rather awaketh them."

Ver. 19.—**The way of the slothful man is as an hedge of thorns.** The indolent sluggard is always finding or imagining difficulties and hindrances in his path, which serve as excuses for his laziness. The word for "thorn" here is *chedek*. It occurs elsewhere only in Micah vii. 4, where the Authorized Version has "briar;" but the particular plant intended is not ascertained. Most writers consider it to be some spinous specimen of the *solanum*. The word refers, it is thought, to a class of plants the name of one of which, at least, the miscalled "apple of Sodom," is well known in poetry, and is a proverbial expression for anything which promises fair but utterly disappoints on trial. "This plant, which is really a kind of potato, grows everywhere in the warmer parts of Palestine, rising to a widely branching shrub from three to five feet high; the wood thickly set with spines; the flower like that of the potato, and the fruit, which is larger than the potato apple, perfectly round, and changing from yellow to bright red as it ripens. . . . The *osher* of the Arab is the true apple of Sodom. A very tropical-looking plant, its fruit is like a large smooth apple or orange, and hangs in clusters of three or four together. When ripe, it is yellow, and looks fair and attractive, and is soft to the touch, but if pressed, it bursts with a crack, and only the broken shell and a row of small seeds in a half-open pod, with a few dry filaments, remain in the hand" (Geikie, 'Holy Land and Bible,' ii. 74, 117). Cato, 'Dist.,' liv. 3. 5—

"Segnitiem fugito, quæ vitæ ignavia fertur; Nam quum animus languet, consumit inertia corpus."

To the sluggard is opposed the righteous in the second member, because indolence is a grievous sin, and the greatest contrast to the active industry of the man who fears

God and does his duty. **The way of the righteous is made plain;** "is a raised causeway;" *selulah*, as ch. xvi. 17; Isa. xl. 3; xlix. 11. The upright man, who treads the path appointed for him resolutely and trustfully, finds all difficulties vanish; before him the thorns yield a passage; and that which the sluggard regarded as dangerous and impassable becomes to him as the king's highway. Vulgate, "The path of the just is without impediment;" Septuagint, "The roads of the manly (ἀνδρείων) are well beaten." St. Gregory ('Moral.,' xxx. 51), "Whatever adversity may have fallen in their way of life, the righteous stumble not against it. Because with the bound of eternal hope, and of eternal contemplation, they leap over the obstacles of temporal adversity" (comp. Ps. xviii. 29).

Ver. 20—ch. xix. 25.—Third section of this collection.

Ver. 20.—(For this verse, see ch. x. 1.) **A foolish man despiseth his mother,** and therefore is "heaviness" to her. Or the verb may mean "shameth." "A foolish man" is literally "a fool of a man."

Ver. 21.—**Folly is joy to him that is destitute of wisdom;** literally, *void of heart;* i.e. of understanding (ch. x. 23). The perverse, self-willed fool finds pleasure in going on his evil way, and exposing the fatuity which he takes for wisdom. Septuagint, "The ways of the senseless are wanting in intelligence." **A man of understanding walketh uprightly;** goes the right way. It is implied that the fool goes the wrong way.

Ver. 22.—**Without counsel**—where no counsel is—**purposes are disappointed** (ch. xi. 14); there can be no concerted action, or the means used are not the best that could be devised. Hesiod, Ἔργ., 293—

Ἐσθλὸς δ' αὖ κἀκεῖνος ὃς εὖ εἰπόντι πίθηται·
Ὃς δὲ κε μήτ' αὐτὸς νοέῃ μήτ' ἄλλου ἀκούων
Ἐν θυμῷ βάλληται, ὁ δ' αὖτ' ἀχρήιος ἀνήρ.

(Comp. ch. xx. 18.) **In the multitude of counsellors they are established** (ch. xxiv. 6). We read of "counsellors" as almost regular officials in the Hebrew court, as in modern kingdoms (see 1 Chron. xxvii. 32; Isa. i. 26; Micah iv. 9; comp. Ezra vii. 28). There is, of course, the danger of secrets being divulged where counsellors are many; and there is Terence's maxim to fear, "Quot homines, tot sententiæ;" but, properly guarded and discreetly used, good counsel is above all price. Septuagint, "They who honour not councils (συνέδρια) lay aside (ὑπερτίθενται) conclusions (*i.e.* put off coming to any definite decision); but in the hearts of those who consult counsel abideth" (compare the parallel clause, ch. xix. 21).

Ver. 23.—**A man hath joy by the answer of his mouth.** The idea of the preceding verse concerning counsel is maintained. A counsellor gives wise and skilful advice, or makes a timely speech; and, knowing how much harm is done by rash or evil words, he naturally rejoices that he has been able to be useful, and has avoided the errors which the tongue is liable to incur. A word spoken in due season, *sermo opportunus*, is advice given at the right moment and in the most suitable manner, when the occasion and the interests at stake demand it (comp. ch. xxv. 11). The LXX. connects this verse with the preceding, and renders, "The evil man will not hearken to it (counsel), nor will he say aught in season or for the public good."

Ver. 24.—**The way of life is above to the wise;** Revised Version, *to the wise the way of life goeth upward.* The writer means primarily that the wise and good lead such a life as to preserve them from death (ch. xiv. 32). The path may be steep and painful, but at any rate it has this compensation—it leads away from destruction. It is obvious to read into the passage higher teaching. The good man's path leads heavenward, to a high life here, to happiness hereafter; his conversation is in heaven (Phil. iii. 20), his affections are set on things above (Col. iii. 2). Such an upward life tends to material and spiritual health, as it is added, that **he may depart from hell** (*Sheol*) **beneath.** Primarily, a long and happy life is promised to the man who fears the Lord, as in ch. iii. 16; secondarily, such a one avoids that downward course which ends in the darkness of hell. Vulgate, "The path of life is above the instructed man, to make him avoid the nethermost (*novissimo*) hell;" Septuagint, "The thoughts of the prudent man are the ways of life, that turning from Hades he may be safe."

Ver. 25.—**The Lord will destroy the house of the proud** (ch. xii. 7; xiv. 11; xvi. 18). The proud, self-confident man, with his family and household and wealth, shall be rooted up. The heathen saw how retribution overtook the arrogant. Thus Euripides says ('Heracl.,' 387)—

Τῶν φρονημάτων
Ὁ Ζεὺς κολαστὴς τῶν ἄγαν ὑπερφρόνων.

"Zeus, the chastiser of too - haughty thoughts."

But he will establish the border of the widow. He will take the widow under his protection, and see that her landmark is not removed, and that her little portion is secured to her. The widow is taken as the type of weakness and desolation, as often in Scripture (comp. Deut. x. 18; Ps. cxlvi. 9). In a country where property was defined by landmarks—stones or some such objects—nothing was easier than to remove these altogether, or to alter their position. That this was a common form of fraud and oppression we gather from the stringency of the enactments against the offence (see Deut. xix. 14; xxvii. 17; and comp. Job xxiv. 2; ch. xxii. 28). In the Babylonian and Assyrian inscriptions which have been preserved, there are many invoking curses, curious and multifarious, against the disturbers of boundaries. Such marks were considered sacred and inviolable by the Greeks and Romans (see Plato, 'De Leg.,' viii. 842, 843; Ovid, 'Fast.,' ii. 639, etc.).

Ver. 26.—**The thoughts of the wicked** (or, *evil devices*) **are an abomination to the Lord.** Although the Decalogue, by forbidding coveting, showed that God's Law touched the thought of the heart as well as the outward action, the idea here refers to wicked plans or designs, rather than emphatically to the secret movements of the mind. These have been noticed in ver. 11. **But the words of the pure are pleasant words;** literally, *pure are words of pleasantness;* i.e. words of soothing, comforting tone are, not an abomination to the Lord, as are the devices of the wicked, but they are pure in a ceremonial sense, as it were, a pure and acceptable offering. Revised Version, *pleasant words are pure.* Vulgate, "Speech pure and pleasant is approved by him"— which is a pharaphrase of the clause. Septuagint, "The words of the pure are honoured (σεμναί)."

Ver. 27.—**He that is greedy of gain troubleth his own house** (ch. xi. 29). The special reference is doubtless to venal judges, who wrested judgment for lucre. Such malefactors were often reproved by the prophets (see Isa. i. 23; x. 1, etc.; Micah iii. 11; vii. 3). But all ill-gotten gain brings sure retribution. The Greeks have many maxims to this effect. Thus—

Κέρδη πονηρὰ ζημίαν ἀεὶ φέρει.

And again—

Τὰ δ' αἰσχρὰ κέρδη συμφορὰς ἐργάζεται.
"Riches ill won bring ruin in their train."

An avaricious man troubles his house in another sense. He harasses his family by niggardly economies and his domestics by overwork and under-feeding, deprives his household of all comfort, and loses the blessing of God upon a righteous use of earthly wealth. The word "troubleth" (*akar*, "to trouble") reminds one of the story of Achan, who, in his greed, appropriated some of the spoil of the banned city Jericho, and brought destruction upon himself and his family, when, in punishment of the crime, he and all his were stoned in the Valley of Achor (Josh. vii. 25). So the covetousness of Gehazi caused the infliction of the penalty of leprosy upon himself and his children (2 Kings v. 27). Professor Plumptre ('Speaker's Commentary,' *in loc.*) notes that the Chaldee Targum paraphrases this clause, referring especially to lucre gained by unrighteous judgments, thus : " He who gathers the mammon of unrighteousness destroys his house ; " and he suggests that Christ's use of that phrase (Luke xvi. 9) may have had some connection with this proverb through the version then popularly used in the Palestinian synagogues. **He that hateth gifts shall live** (comp. Eccles. vii. 7). Primarily this refers to the judge or magistrate who is incorruptible, and gives just judgment, and dispenses his patronage without fear or favour; he shall "prolong his days" (ch. xxviii. 16). And in all cases a man free from covetousness, who takes no bribes to blind his eyes withal, who makes no unjust gains, shall pass a long and happy life undisturbed by care. We see here a hope of immortality, to which integrity leads. The LXX., with the view of making the two clauses more marked in antithesis, restricts the application thus : " The receiver of gifts destroyeth himself; but he who hateth the receiving of gifts liveth." The Vulgate and Septuagint, after this verse, introduce a distich which recurs in ch. xvi. 6. The Septuagint transposes many of the verses at the end of this chapter and the beginning of the next.

Ver. 28.—**The heart of the righteous studieth to answer.** The good man deliberates before he speaks, takes time to consider his answer, lest he should say anything false, or inexpedient, or injurious to his neighbour. A Latin adage runs—

" Qui bene vult fari debet bene praemeditari."

Says Theognis—

Βουλεύου δὶς καὶ τρὶς, ὅ τοί κ᾽ ἐπὶ τὸν νόον ἔλθῃ·
᾽Ατηρὸς γὰρ ἀεὶ λάβρος ἀνὴρ τελέθει.

" Whate'er comes in your mind, deliberate ;
A hasty man but rushes on his fate."

Septuagint, "The heart of the prudent will meditate πίστεις," which may mean "truth," "fidelity," or "proofs." The Vulgate has "obedience," implying attention to the inward warnings of conscience and grace, before the mouth speaks. **Poureth out** (ver. 2). The wicked man never considers ; evil is always on his lips and running over from his mouth. Septuagint, "The mouth of the ungodly answereth evil things." The LXX. here inserts ch. xvi. 7.

Ver. 29.—**The Lord is far from the wicked.** The maxim is similar to that in ver. 8 and

John ix. 31, " We know that God heareth not sinners : but if any man be a worshipper of God, and do his will, him he heareth." God is said to be "far" in the sense of not listening, not regarding with favour (comp. Ps. x. 1). His attention to the righteous is seen in Ps. cxlv. 18, 19. The LXX. introduces here ch. xvi. 8, 9.

Ver. 30.—**The light of the eyes rejoiceth the heart** (ch. xvi. 15). The beaming glance that shows a pure, happy mind and a friendly disposition, rejoices the heart of him on whom it is turned. There is something infectious in the guileless, joyful look of a happy man or child, which has a cheering effect upon those who observe it. The LXX. makes the sentiment altogether personal : "The eye that seeth what is good rejoiceth the heart." **A good report** (good tidings) **maketh the bones fat**; strengthens them and gives them health (comp. ch. iii. 8 ; xvi. 24). Sight and hearing are compared in the two clauses, "bones" in the latter taking the place of "heart" in the former. The happy look and good news alike cause joy of heart.

Ver. 31.—**The ear that heareth** (hearkeneth to) **the reproof of life abideth among the wise** (ch. vi. 23). The reproof, or instruction, of life is that which teaches the true way of pleasing God, which is indeed the only life worth living. The ear, by synecdoche, is put for the person. One who attends to and profits by such admonition may be reckoned among the wise, and rejoices to be conversant with them. Wordsworth finds a more recondite sense here : the ear of the wise dwells, lodges, passes the night (ch. xix. 23) in their heart, whereas the heart of fools is in their mouth (ch. xiv. 33). This verse is omitted in the Septuagint, though it is found in the other Greek versions and the Latin Vulgate.

Ver. 32.—This verse carries on and puts the climax to the lesson of the preceding. **He that refuseth instruction despiseth his own soul**; "hateth himself," Septuagint; commits moral suicide, because he does not follow the path of life. He is like a sick man who thrusts away (ἀπωθεῖται, Septuagint) the wholesome medicine which is his only hope of cure. **He that heareth** (listeneth to) **reproof getteth understanding**; literally, *possesseth a heart*, and therefore does not despise his soul, but "loves it" (ch. xix. 8), as the LXX. renders.

Ver. 33.—**The fear of the Lord is the instruction of wisdom**; that which leads to and gives wisdom (see ch. i. 3, 7, etc.; ix. 10). 'Pirke Aboth,' iii. 26, " No wisdom, no fear of God; no fear of God, no wisdom. No knowledge, no discernment; no discernment, no knowledge." **Before honour** is humility (ch. xviii. 12). A man who fears

God must be humble, and as the fear of God leads to wisdom, it may be said that humility leads to the honour and glory of being wise and reckoned among the wise (ver. 31). A man with a lowly opinion of himself will hearken to the teaching of the wise, and scrupulously obey the Law of God, and will be blessed in his ways. For "God resisteth the proud, but giveth grace unto the humble" (Jas. iv. 6; comp. Luke i. 52). The maxim in the second clause has a general application. "He that shall humble himself shall be exalted" (Matt. xxiii. 12; comp. Luke xiv. 11; Jas. iv. 6). It is sanctioned by the example of Christ him-self, the Spirit itself testifying beforehand his sufferings that were to precede his glory (1 Pet. i. 11; see also Phil. ii. 5, etc.). Septuagint, "The fear of the Lord is discipline and wisdom, and the beginning of glory shall answer to it." Another reading adds, "Glory goeth before the humble," which is explained to mean that the humble set before their eyes the reward that awaits their humility, and patiently endure, like Christ, "who for the joy that was set before him endured the cross, despising the shame, and is set down at the right hand of the throne of God" (Heb. xii. 2).

HOMILETICS.

Ver. 1.—*A soft answer and a bitter word.* Both of these are regarded as replies to angry words. They represent the wise and the foolish ways of treating such words. They give us a bright and a dark picture. Let us look at each.

I. THE BRIGHT PICTURE. 1. *The answer.* A soft answer need not be a weak one; nor should it imply any compromise of truth, nor any yielding of righteousness. It may be firm in substance, though soft in language and spirit. Very often the most effective reply is given in the mildest tone. It is impossible to resent it, yet it is equally impossible to answer it. But often we may go further. When no vital interest of truth or righteousness is at stake, it may be well to yield a point of our own will and pleasure in order to secure peace. 2. *Its inspiration.* Such an answer might well be prompted by wisdom, for it is suggested on the ground of prudence in "Proverbs." Yet there is a higher motive for softness in reply to wrath. Christian love will inspire the kinder method, for love is more desirous of peace and good feeling than of securing all that might be justly demanded. To stand on one's rights and resent the slightest intrusion upon them is to act from self-interest, or at best from a sense of self-regarding duty. A higher feeling enters and a larger view follows when we are considering our brother's feelings, the sorrow of a quarrel and the blessedness of peace. 3. *Its results.* It is successful—not, perhaps, in gaining one's own way, but in allaying wrath. It turns away wrath. The angry opponent is silenced. For very shame he can say no more; or his wrath dies out for want of fuel; or he is won to a better feeling by the generous treatment. At the worst he can find little pleasure in fighting an unarmed and unresisting opponent.

II. THE DARK PICTURE. The ugly contrast of this second picture is necessary in order to emphasize the beauty of the former one. But however interesting they may be in art, Rembrandtesque effects are terrible in real life; for here they represent agonies and tragedies—hatred, cruelty, and misery. Yet they need to be considered if only that they may be abolished. 1. *The bitter answer.* This is more than an angry retort. Bitterness is more pungent than wrath. While rage thunders, bitterness stabs. It contains a poisonous element of malice, and it means more ill will than the hot but perhaps hasty words that provoke it. 2. *The root of its bitterness.* No doubt this springs from a feeling of injury. The angry man has wronged his companion, or, at least, wounded him, and the retort is provoked by pain. But pain alone would not engender bitterness. A new element, a virus of ill will, is stirred when the bitter word is flung back, and it is the outflow of this ill will that gives bitterness to the answer. 3. *The anger that it rouses.* This new anger is worse than that which commenced the quarrel. Each reply is more hot, more furious, more cruel. Thus a great wrath is roused and a great fire kindled by a very little spark that has been fanned into a flame when it should have been quenched at the outset.

There is no question as to which of these two pictures best accords with Christian principle. The gospel of Christ is God's soft answer to man's rebellious wrath.

Ver. 3.—"*The eyes of the Lord.*" I. GOD HAS EYES. We must always describe the Infinite and Invisible One in figurative language. But just as we speak of the arms and hands of God when thinking of his power and activity, so we cannot better conceive of his wonderful observing faculty than by saying that he has eyes. God can see; he can watch his creatures. It would be an awful thing if the universe were governed by a blind power. Yet that is the condition imagined by those who regard force, unconscious energy, as the highest existence in the universe and the cause of all things. We could but tremble before a blind god. What awful confusion, what terrible disasters, would result from the almighty energy of such a being crashing through all the complicated and delicate machinery of the world's life!

II. GOD USES HIS EYES. He is not a sleeping deity. He never slumbers, never closes his eyes. Day and night are alike to him. There is never a moment when he ceases to observe the world and all that is in it. There are men of whom we can say, "Eyes have they, but they see not;" unobservant people, who pass by the most obvious facts without noticing them; dreamers, who live in a world of their own fancies, and fail to see the things that are really happening about them. God is not thus self-contained. He has an outer life in the universe, and he neither scorns nor fails to observe all that is happening. We have to do with an ever-watchful, keenly observant God.

III. GOD'S EYES ARE EVERYWHERE. We can only see clearly what is near to us. All but the largest objects are lost in distance, and the horizon melts into obscurity. Not so with God. 1. He sees *the distant.* Indeed, nothing is distant from him. He is everywhere, so that what we should regard as the most remote objects are under his close ken. No Siberian solitude, no far-off deserted planet, no star lost to the rest of the universe and rushing off into the awful waste of space, can be far from God's presence and observation. 2. He sees *the obscure.* No fog dims his vision; no night blots out the objects he is ever gazing upon; no hiding in secret chambers, deep cellars, black mines of the earth, can remove anything from God's sight. 3. He sees *the unattractive.* Our vision is selective. Many objects pass close before our eyes, yet we never see them, because we are not interested in them. God is interested in all things. Not a sparrow falls to the ground without his notice.

IV. GOD'S EYES SEE THE EVIL. Though he is merciful, he is too true to refuse to see the sin of his children. 1. *The sinner cannot escape by secrecy.* If God does not strike at once, this is not because he does not know. Meanwhile the deluded sinner is but "treasuring up wrath." 2. *God is long-suffering.* If he forbears to strike at once and yet knows all, it must be that he waits to give us an opportunity to repent. His gospel is offered in full view of our sin. There is nothing to be discovered later on that may turn God's mercy from us. He knows the worst when he offers grace.

V. GOD'S EYES SEE THE GOOD. 1. *He observes his children's secret devotion.* Unnoticed by men, they are not unheeded by God. Misunderstood and misjudged on earth, they are quite understood by him. Should it not be enough to know that God knows all, and will recognize faithful service? 2. *He observes his children's need.* Prayer is necessary to express our faith, etc., but not to give information to God. He knows our condition better than we do. Therefore, though he seems to neglect us, it cannot be so really. No mother ever watched over her sick infant as God watches over his poor children.

Ver. 13.—*A joyous heart or a broken spirit.* These are the two extremes. The less we have of the one the more we tend towards the other. The first is encouraged that it may save us from the disasters of the second condition.

I. THE CONDITION OF THE HEART IS OF VITAL IMPORTANCE. "Out of it are the issues of life" (ch. iv. 23). The first essential for one whose life has been wrong is the creation of "a clean heart" (Ps. li. 10). According as we think and feel in our hearts, so do we truly live. Now, it is the merit of Christianity that it works directly on the heart, and only touches the outer life through this primary inward operation. We must set little store on the external signs of prosperity if the heart is wrong. When that is right the rest is likely to follow satisfactorily.

II. THE JOY OR SORROW OF THE HEART ARE NOT MATTERS OF INDIFFERENCE. The religion of the Bible is not Stoicism. It is nowhere represented to us in this book that it matters not whether men grieve or are joyous. On the contrary, the Bible contains valuable recipes against heart-pangs. God's pity for his children would lead to his concerning himself with such matters. Christ's human sympathy, which led to his being frequently " moved with compassion," made him alleviate suffering and seek to give his joy to his disciples. The special mission of sorrow and the large healing and strengthening influence of the highest kind of joy make these experiences to be of real interest to the spiritual life.

III. THE OUTER LIFE IS BRIGHTENED BY JOY OF HEART. It is possible for the actor to assume a smiling countenance when his heart is bursting with agony, but that is just because he is an actor. It is not intended by Providence that the face should be a mask to hide the soul. In the long run the set expression of the countenance must correspond to the prevalent condition of the spirit within. The sad heart will be revealed by a clouded countenance, the heart of care by the fretted lines of a worn face, the peaceful heart by a serene expression, and the glad heart by unconscious smiles. Thus we shed gloom or sunshine by our very presence. " The joy of the Lord is your strength " (Neh. viii. 10). With the brightened countenance there comes revived energy. Moreover, the cheerful expression of a Christian is a winning invitation to others. It makes the gospel attractive.

IV. THE SPIRIT IS BROKEN BY SORROW OF HEART. It must be confessed that we have here only a partial view of sorrow. The richer revelation which the New Testament makes of the Divine gospel of sorrow gives it a new meaning and a higher blessedness. Since Christ suffered, suffering has been sanctified, and the Viâ Dolorosa has become the road to victory. Nevertheless, mere sorrow is still trying, wearing, grinding to the soul. To bear the cross for Christ's sake is to render noble service, but simply to groan under the load of pain is not to be inspired with strength. Jesus was not only "a Man of sorrows, and acquainted with grief;" he could speak of his joy just before feeling his deepest agony. A life of utter sorrow must be one of utter weariness. 1. Therefore we should seek the grace of Christ to conquer sorrow in our own hearts. There is no virtue in yielding to it with self-made martyrdom. 2. It is a good work to lessen the world's sorrow.

Vers. 16, 17.—*The better things.* Earthly good is comparative. Many things regarded by themselves appear to be eminently attractive; but if they exclude more desirable things they must be rejected. We need not make the worst of this world in order to make the best of the higher world. Taking earth at its brightest, it is still outshone by the glories of heaven. But earth is not always at its brightest; and we must make our comparison with the actual facts of life, not with ideal possibilities.

I. GODLY POVERTY IS BETTER THAN TROUBLED WEALTH. 1. *Wealth is disappointing.* It might be shown that wealth at its best cannot satisfy the soul; for (1) it is only external, and (2) it is but a means of obtaining other ends. But plain experience shows that the advantages of wealth are very commonly neutralized by trouble. (1) For wealth will not prevent trouble. Rich men suffer from disease, disappointment, discontent, the unkindness of friends, etc. The child of affluence may die. (2) Wealth may bring trouble. It has its own anxieties. Antonio, who has ships at sea, is distressed at the storms that do not trouble the poor man. Many interests lead to conflicting claims, and the cares of riches are often as great as those of poverty. (3) Wealth cannot compensate for trouble. The small vexations of life may be smoothed away by money, and of course certain specific troubles—such as hunger, cold, nakedness—may be quite prevented. But the greater troubles remain. Gold will not heal a broken heart. 2. *Godliness is satisfying.* It may be found with wealth. Then it will correct the evils and supply the defects. But it may be seen with poverty, and in this case it will prove itself the true riches which will give what money can never supply. Indeed, in presence of this real good the question as to whether even great earthly treasure is to be added need not be raised. It is lost in the infinitely greater possession. The ocean will not be concerned to know whether the trickling streamlet that flows into its abundant waters be full or failing. Further, it is to be noted that God satisfies the soul directly, while at best riches can only pretend to do so indirectly. Riches seek to buy happiness. Inward religion directly confers blessedness. To have God is to be at rest.

II. LOVE WITH PRIVATIONS IS BETTER THAN HATRED WITH SUPERFLUITY. 1. *Hatred neutralizes superfluity.* What is the use of the ox in the stall if hatred makes a hell of the home? How often is it seen that the comforts of affluence only mock the wretchedness of their master, because the more essential joys of affection have been shattered! A household of discord must be one of misery. Family feuds cannot but bring unhappiness to all concerned in them. Hatred in the house leads to wretchedness in proportion to the blessedness that love would have conferred. We are more touched by our relations with persons than by our relations with things. Therefore, if those closer relations are marred, no prosperity of external affairs can bring peace. 2. *Love can neutralize privations.* The dinner of herbs may not be hurtful in itself. Daniel and his companions throve on it (Dan. i. 15). If it is not attractive and appetizing, other considerations may withdraw our attention from it and fill the heart with joy. Love is more than meat. Nay, even bitter herbs may be not unpalatable when seasoned with affection, while an alderman's feast will be insipid to a guest who is preoccupied with vexatious thoughts.

Ver. 23.—*The word in season.* I. WHAT IT IS. The word in season is the right word spoken at the right time. It may not be the word that is sought and asked for. It may even be an unwelcome word, a startling word, a word of rebuke. What can be more seasonable than to cry, "Halt!" to one who is nearing the precipice in the dark? Yet he neither expects the word, nor for the moment accepts it with favour. The great requisite is that the word should be suitable for the occasion. This has a special bearing on the word of highest wisdom, the gospel of Jesus Christ. We should be on the look out for suitable moments—*e.g.* in sorrow, when the heart is softened; in leisure hours, when the mind is open; at new departures, when special guidance is needed; after mistakes have been made, to correct and save; when doubts have been expressed, to remove their paralyzing influence; when Christ has been dishonoured, to vindicate his holy Name. These are all times for speech, but not for uttering the same words. The occasion must determine the character of the word. II. WHY IT IS GOOD. 1. *The soil must be in a right condition,* or the seed that is flung upon it will be wasted. It is useless to cast bushels of the best wheat by the wayside, and foolish to cast pearls before swine. Men do not sow seed in the heat of August nor during a January frost. Our business is to sow beside all waters, and yet to watch for the rising of the waters and make a right use of the seasons. There is a time to speak and a time to keep silence, not because these epochs are fixed by some Divine almanack of destiny, but just because silence is golden when mind and heart need rest and privacy, and speech is precious when sympathy is craved, or when wise words can be received with thoughtful attention. There are "words that help and heal." 2. *The special condition of the hearer determines what he will best receive.* We should not preach consolation to a merry child, nor talk of the difficulties of religion before a person who has never been troubled with them. On the other hand, it is useless simply to exhort the soul perplexed with diverse thoughts to "believe and be saved." Indeed, in private conversation the peculiar characteristics of each individual will require a different mode of approach. We cannot discuss theology with an uneducated man as we may have to discuss it with a young graduate. III. HOW IT MAY BE SPOKEN. It is not easy to find the word in season, and certain conditions are absolutely essential to the production of it. 1. *Sympathy.* This is the primary condition. It may be almost affirmed that where this is strong the rest will follow. We cannot speak wisely to a fellow-man until we have learnt to put ourselves in his place. 2. *Thought.* Great considerateness is necessary that we choose the right word, and then speak it just at the right moment. If a man blurts out the first thought that comes into his mind, he may do infinite harm, though he be acting with the best intention. 3. *Courage.* Those who are most fitted by sympathy and thoughtfulness are often most backward to utter the word in season. To such it seems easier to preach to a thousand hearers than to talk directly with one soul. Yet personal conversation is most fruitful. It was Christ's method, *e.g.* with Nicodemus, the woman at the well, etc. This duty is sadly neglected from lack of moral courage.

Ver. 29.—*Character and prayer.* The character of a man has much to do with the efficacy of his prayer. The prayers of different men are not of equal value. One man's most urgent petition is but wasted breath, while the slightest sigh of another is heard in heaven, and answered with showers of blessing. Let us consider how these great diversities come to be.

I. A MAN'S NEARNESS TO GOD IS TO BE MEASURED BY HIS CHARACTER. Some men appear to have what is called a gift of prayer, but in reality they are only cursed with a fatal fluency in phrases. By long habit they have acquired a facility of pouring forth voluminous sentences with a certain unctuousness that persuades inconsiderate hearers into the notion that they are " mighty in prayer." Yet, in truth, this facility is of no account whatever with God, who does not hear our " much speaking." On the other hand, if a man's heart is wrong with God, he is cut off from access to heaven. Such a man cannot truly pray, though he may " say his prayers." It may be said that even the worst sinner can pray for pardon, and of course this is a great and glorious truth. But he can only do so effectually when he is penitent. The man whose heart and life turn towards goodness is brought into sympathy with God, so that he is spiritually near to God, and his prayers find ready access to heaven.

II. THE CHARACTER OF THE MAN WILL DETERMINE THE CHARACTER OF HIS PRAYERS. He may be known by his prayers, if only we can tell what those prayers really are. His true heartfelt desires, not his due and decorous devotions, are the best expression of his real self. Now, a bad man will desire bad things, and a good man good things. It would be most unfitting in God, indeed positively wrong, to give the bad man the desires of his heart. But he who prays in the name of Christ, *i.e.* with his authority, can only pray for the things of which Christ approves, and he will only do this when he has the spirit of Christ, and is in harmony with the mind and will of his Lord. The holy man will only pray—consciously, at least—for things that agree with holiness. It is reasonable to suppose that his prayers will be heard when the ill petitions of the bad man are rejected.

III. THE CHARACTER OF A MAN AFFECTS HIS FITNESS TO RECEIVE DIVINE ANSWERS TO HIS PRAYERS. Two men may ask for precisely similar things in the way of external blessings. Yet one is selfish, sinful, rebellious, and ungrateful. To give to this man what he asks will be hurtful to him, injurious to others, dishonouring to God. But a good man will know how to receive blessings from God with gratitude, and how to use them for the glory of his Master and the good of his brethren. Further, in regard to internal blessings, what would be good for the man whose heart and life are in the right, would be hurtful to the impenitent. Saint and sinner both pray for peace. To the saint this is a wholesome solace; to the sinner it would be a dangerous narcotic. Therefore God responds to the prayer of the one, and rejects the petition of the other.

HOMILIES BY VARIOUS AUTHORS.

Vers. 1, 2, 4, 7.—*Virtues and vices of the tongue.* I. MILDNESS AND VIOLENCE. (Ver. 1.) The soft answer is like the water which quenches, and the bitter retort, the " grievous words," like the oil which increases the conflagration of wrath. As scriptural examples of the former, may be mentioned Jacob with Esau (Gen. xxxii., xxxiii.), Aaron with Moses (Lev. x. 16—20), the Reubenites with their brethren (Josh. xxii. 15—34), Gideon with the men of Ephraim (Judg. viii. 1—3), David with Saul (1 Sam. xxiv. 9—21), Abigail with David (1 Sam. xxv. 23—32). And of the latter, Jephthah (Judg. xii. 1—6), Saul (1 Sam. xx. 30—34), Nabal (1 Sam. xxv. 10—13), Rehoboam (1 Kings xii. 12—15), Paul and Barnabas (Acts xv. 39).

II. THE ATTRACTIVENESS OF WISE SPEECH AND THE REPULSIVENESS OF FOOLISH TALK. (Ver. 2.) If this verse be more correctly rendered, it means that the tongue of the wise makes knowledge lovely, while the mouth of the fool foams with folly. The speech of the former is apt to time and place—coherent—and wins upon the listener. The latter is unseasonable, 'confused, nonsensical, repellent. Notice the *tact* of St. Paul's addresses (Acts xvii. 22, 23; xxvi. 27—29), and what he says about foolish babbling in 2 Tim. ii. 16—18; Titus i. 10.

III. MODERATION AND EXTRAVAGANCE. (Ver. 4.) A calm and measured tone should be cultivated, as well as a pure and peaceful heart; these mutually react upon one another. The extravagant, immoderate, licentious tongue is "like a blustering wind among the boughs of the trees, rushing and tearing the life and spirit of a man's self and others" (Bishop Hall). Beware of exaggeration.

IV. SPEECH A DIFFUSIVE INFLUENCE. (Ver. 7.) The lips of the wise scatter seeds of good around them; *not so* with the heart and lips of the fool. "They trade only with the trash of the world, not with the commerce of substantial knowledge." The preaching of the gospel is compared to the scattering of good seed, and evil activity is the sowing of tares in the world-field (Matt. xiii. 24, etc.).—J.

Ver. 3.—*The omnipresence of God.* I. GOD IS A SPIRIT. We cannot exhaust the sublimity, the awfulness, the comfort, the meaning, in this thought.

II. GOD SEES ALL AND KNOWS ALL. Both the good and the evil. In looking upon evil deeds which pass unchastised in appearance, we are ready to exclaim, "And yet God has never spoken a word!" But God has seen, and will requite.

III. HENCE LET US POSSESS OUR SOULS IN PATIENCE. Commit them unto him in well-doing, and wait for the "end of the Lord." He knows, among other things, the need of his children, and bethinks him of helping and delivering them.—J.

Ver. 5.—*Contempt and respect for instruction.* The fool is as a "wild ass's colt" (Job xi. 12), recalcitrant, stubborn; while he who early shows a willingness to listen to good advice has the germ of prudence, the prophecy of a safe career.

I. A MURMURING TEMPER, A RELUCTANCE TO SUBMIT TO NECESSITY AND THE COURSE OF LIFE, IS IN REALITY A CONTEMPT OF GOD.

II. SUBMISSION TO THE INEVITABLE, COMPLIANCE TO THE LAWS OF LIVING, IS DOCILITY TO GOD.—J.

Ver. 6.—*True and false gains.* I. A MAN MAY BE POOR, YET POSSESS ALL THINGS. (2 Cor. vi. 10.) *Deus meus, et omnia!*

II. A MAN MAY BE RICH, YET DESTITUTE, POOR, BLIND, AND MISERABLE. If we are not *satisfied*, we are not rich. If we are content, we are never poor.

III. GOD IS THE TRUE AND ONLY GAIN OF THE SOUL. We have a nature which will be satisfied with nothing short of the Infinite. To attempt to feed it with anything less is found to be a cheat and a self-delusion.—J.

Vers. 8, 9.—*God's hatreds and God's delights.* We all have our aversions, natural antipathies, acquired hatreds. A noted author not long ago published a book called 'Mes Haines.' What are the hatreds of him who is Love? They should be our aversions.

I. THE SACRIFICE OF THE WICKED. (Ver. 8.) It is not the man's works which make him good, but the justified man—the man made right with God—produces good works, and these, though imperfect, are well-pleasing to God. The lack of heart-sincerity must stamp every sacrifice, as that of Cain, as an abomination.

II. THE PRAYER OF THE GOOD MAN. Symbolized by fragrant incense, sweet to him are pious thoughts, wishes for the best, charitable aspirations, all that in the finite heart aims at the Infinite.

III. THE WAY OF THE WICKED. A prayerless life is a godless, and hence a corrupt life. It is a meaningless life, and God will not tolerate what is insignificant in his vast significant world.

IV. THE PURSUIT OF GOOD. He who hunts after righteousness, literally, is loved of God. We learn the necessity of patience, constancy, diligence in well-doing. In no other way can genuineness and thoroughness be shown.—J.

Ver. 10.—*The principle of judgment.* I. IT IS NEVER CAUSELESS.

II. THE CONNECTION OF CAUSE AND EFFECT IS OFTEN MYSTERIOUS. Hence we should be slow to trace the judgment of God upon sinners.

III. SOME SINS THAT FORETELL JUDGMENT. 1. Desertion of duty; forsaking of God's ways; travelling in paths we *know* to be crooked or unclean. 2. Indifference to rebuke. For even in error, if we will heed the timely warning and correct the discovered fault, judgment may be averted. If not, there is no way of avoiding the law of doom. The soul that sinneth shall and "*must* die."—J.

Ver. 11.—*The heart open to God.* I. THE HEART A PROFOUND MYSTERY. We speculate about the mysteries of the world *without* us, as if *these* were the great secrets, forgetful what an abyss of wonder is within.

II. THIS MYSTERY MAY BE COMPARED TO THAT OF HADES AND THE KINGDOM OF THE DEVIL. 1. It is equally profound. 2. It is equally fascinating. 3. It is equally hidden from our knowledge. Peruse our greatest masters of the human heart—a Shakespeare, Bacon, Montaigne—we have still not touched the bottom.

III. THE MYSTERY OF ALL WORLDS IS KNOWN TO GOD, THE INTERNAL NO LESS THAN THE EXTERNAL. 1. This is a thought of awe. 2. Still more it should be of comfort. My God, thou knowest all, *all* that fain would hide itself from others, even from myself —and yet "hast stooped to ask of me the love of this poor heart"!—J.

Vers. 12—15.—*Sullen folly and cheerful wisdom.* I. DISLIKE OF CRITICISM (Ver. 12.) Often seen in those who are most critical themselves. The jiber is easily galled by a telling retort. The satirical man least loves satire upon himself. But one of the lessons we learn from truly great minds is that of willingness to turn a jest against one's self, and to find positive pleasure in a criticism of one's own character that hits the mark, provided it be good-natured. But with ill nature no one can be pleased. Most necessary it is for the health of the soul to be often with those who know more than we do.

II. THE APPEARANCE THE MIRROR OF THE MAN. The placid, serene, smiling, winning visage reflects the soul ; and so with the downcast brow and dejected mien. It may surprise us that so commonplace an observation should be thought worth recording ; but there was a time when such flashed upon man as a new discovery. Perhaps it may be a discovery to many that they may do much by assuming a cheerful manner to regulate and calm the heart.

III. BUT APPEARANCES ARE NOTHING WITHOUT REALITY. (Ver. 14.) To be truly wise is not to know a great deal, but to be always on the track and pursuit of knowledge ; and to be utterly foolish it is only necesary to give the reins to vanity, to yield to idleness, to follow every passing pleasure. The *countenance* of the fool is expressive of what? Of the want of impressions, of vacancy and vanity.

IV. THE FOLLY OF GLOOM AND THE WISDOM OF CHEERFULNESS. (Ver. 15.) In what sense can we ever say that our days are *evil*, except that we have made them so? And how more readily can we make them so than by yielding to the dark and gloomy mood, and ever looking on the dark side of things? The side of things on which we see the reflection of our narrow selves is ever dark; that on which we see God's attributes mirrored—the beauty of his nature, the wisdom of his providence—is bright and inspiring. It is, indeed, a feast to the soul to have found God; for thought, for feeling, for every practical need, he is present, he alone "shall supply all our need." Our Lord thus speaks of his body and his blood, of which to eat is life.—J.

Vers. 16, 17.—*Alternatives.* I. POVERTY WITH PIETY, OR RICHES WITH DISCONTENT. Which shall we choose? Naturally all, or nearly all, will prefer to take riches with its risks rather than poverty with its certain privations. Our Bible is precious because it reminds us that there is *another side* in this matter. Riches are too dearly gained at the expense of peace of conscience; poverty is blessed if it brings us nearer to God.

II. SCANTY FARE WITH RICH SPIRITUAL SEASONING, OR RICH FARE WITH A POOR HEART. Which? For ourselves and our personal comfort? For others and the hospitality we should like to dispense to them? For ourselves, high thinking with low living; for others, slight fare with large welcome will make a true feast.—J.

Vers. 18—23.—*Facets of moral truth.* Again flashing upon us, mostly in the light of contrast. As, indeed, from precious stones and false paste, up to the highest truths of the spirit, we can know nothing truly except by the comparison of its opposite.

I. HASTE OF TEMPER AND LONG-SUFFERING. (Ver. 18.) Quarrelsomeness, irritable words (would that we could recall them!), a thousand stabs and wounds to the heart of our friend and to our own, the result of the former. For the latter, read the exquisite descriptions of the New Testament wherever the word "long-suffering" occurs, and see the matchless beauty, and learn to covet the possession of that character—the impress of God in human nature—and those best gifts which belong to "the more excellent way."

II. IDLENESS AND HONESTY. (Ver. 19.) The way of the former beset with difficulty. Lazy people take the most trouble, in the affairs of the soul as in everything. The honest path is the only easy path in the long run. We must remember that it *is* a *long run* we have to pass over, and must make our choice accordingly. Life is no mere picnic or excursion. For amusement of the leisure hour we may strike into a by-path, but never lose sight of the high-road of faith.

III. PARENTAL JOY AND SORROW. (Ver. 20.) On the whole, these are one of the best indices of a man's character. A truly good parent may not understand his child, as Mary misunderstood Jesus; but at the bottom of the heart, when there is filial goodness there is parental sympathy and approval.

IV. SPURIOUS JOY AND QUIET PERSISTENCE IN RIGHT. (Ver. 21.) This is a good contrast. The fool is not content with saying or doing the foolish thing; he must needs chuckle over it and make a boast of it, often gaining applause for his mere audacity. But the man of true sense is content to forego the momentary triumph, and goes on his way. Ever to forsake the way we know to be right, even in momentary hilarity, brings its after-sting.

V. FAILURE AND SUCCESS IN COUNSELS. (Ver. 22.) Wild tumultuous passion causes the former; and calm deliberation, the comparison and collision of many minds, brings about sound and stable policy. To lean upon one's own weak will, to act in haste or under impulse, how seldom can a prosperous issue come of this! See how individuals rush into lawsuits, nations into war, speculators into bankruptcy,—all for want of consultation and good advice. We need the impetus of enthusiasm, not less the direction of cool prudence; if one or the other factor be omitted, disaster must ensue.

VI. SEASONABLE WORDS. (Ver. 23.) We must consider not only the *matter*, but the *manner*, of our utterances. This requires "a mind at leisure from itself" to seize the happy opportunity, to refrain from introducing the jarring note, to turn the conversation when it threatens to strike on breakers. Oh, happy art! admirable and enviable in those that possess it, but cultivable by all who have the gentle heart. We cannot conceive that the conversations of Christ were ever other than thus seasonable.—J.

Vers. 24—33.—*Religion and common sense.* What is religion without common sense? Fanaticism, extravagance, and folly. What is common sense without religion? Dry, bald, uninspired and uninspiring worldliness. What are they united? The wisdom of both worlds, the wisdom of time and of eternity. Let us look at some of their combined teachings.

I. TEACHINGS OF COMMON SENSE. 1. *To avoid danger and death.* (Ver. 24.) This is obvious enough, but, unguided by religion, prudence may easily make mistakes. 2. *To avoid unjust gains.* (Ver. 27.) Every advantage must be *paid for*, in some coin or other. Then, "is the game worth the candle?" Will a dishonest speculation, looked at on mere commercial principles, *pay?* 3. *To be cautious in speech.* (Ver. 28.) Speech is the one thing that many think they have a right to squander. There is no more common profligacy than that of the tongue. Yet, is there anything of which experience teaches us to be more economical than the expense of the tongue? 4. *To be generous of kind looks and words.* (Ver. 30.) What can cost less, or be worth, in many cases, more? "Good words," says George Herbert, "are worth much, and cost little." 5. *To be a good listener.* (Ver. 31.) And this implies willingness to receive rebuke. All superior conversation in some way or other brings to light our ignorance and checks our narrowness. And just as he is not fit to govern who has not learned to serve, so only he who has long sat at the feet of the wise will be entitled himself to take his place among the wise. One of Socrates' disciples exclaimed that life indeed was to be found in listening to discourses like his. May we all feel the like in sitting at the feet of *our* Master, who commends those who have thus chosen the good part which shall never be taken away from them! 6. *To avoid conceit and cultivate humility.* (Ver. 32.) It is the over-estimate of self which makes us contemptuous in any sense towards others. But to look down as from a superior height on others is the most mischievous hindrance to progress in sense and knowledge. A master-mind of our times says that he hates to be praised in the newspapers, and begins to have some hope for himself when people find fault with him. 7. *To found humility upon religion.* (Ver. 33.) Its only genuine and deep foundation. What are we in relation to the God whose perfection is revealed to us in nature, in the ideals of the soul, in the fulfilment of the living Person of Christ? From this depth only can we rise; for honour springs from a lowly root; and he that exalteth himself shall be abased.

II. TEACHINGS OF RELIGION. We have already seen how they blend with those of common sense. But let us bring them into their proper distinctiveness and force. 1. *To choose the upward path and shun the downward.* (Ver. 24.) To cleave to God; to love him with mind, and heart, and soul, and strength; to be ever seeking the Divine meaning in the earthly objects, the Divine goal through the course of common events, the true, the beautiful, and the good, in their ineffable blending and unity in God;—this is the upward way. To be striving after emancipation from self, in all the coarser and grosser, in all the more refined and subtle forms of lust and greed,—this is the avoidance of hell and of the downward way. "Seeking those things which are above, where Christ sitteth on the right hand of God," implies and demands "the mortification of the members which are upon the earth." 2. *To consider the judgments of God.* (Vers. 25, 27.) There was a period in the ancient world when men thought of Divine power as blind caprice, fortune, fate, destiny, setting down and raising up whomsoever it would by no fixed moral law. It was a great revelation and a magnificent discovery when men saw that there was a law in the events of life, and this law none other than the holy will of Jehovah. One of the principles of his judgment is here set forth. Godless pride is obnoxious to his disapproval, and incurs extinction at his hands. But he is Compassion, and the poor and friendless, especially the widow, are certain of his protection. It is as if a charmed circle were drawn around her humble dwelling, and a Divine hand kept the fire glowing on her hearth. 3. *To consider the religious aspect of thoughts and words.* (Ver. 26.) Words and thoughts are one, as the body and the soul. A great thinker, indeed, defined thought as talking to one's self—as all our words to others should, indeed, be as thought overheard. Thus we are thrown back on the heart, and the elementary maxims for its guidance in purity. Keep it with all diligence! But perhaps not less important is the *reflex* influence; for if bad words be scrupulously kept from the tongue, evil images will less readily arise in the heart. 4. *To consider the conditions of access to God.* (Ver. 29.) He is a *moral* Being, and must be approached in a moral character and a moral mood. To suppose that he can be flattered with empty compliments or gifts, as if he were a barbarous Monarch and not a just God, is essentially superstitious. He is the Hearer of prayer, but only of the just man's prayer. To the aspiration of the pious soul never fails the inspiration of the holy God. But of the bad heart it must ever be true, "The words fly up, the thoughts remain below." Thus to view all life's relations in God is both "the beginning of wisdom" and "the conclusion of the whole matter."—J.

Ver. 1.—*The soft answer.* This text has been on the lips of many thousands of people since it was first penned, and has probably helped many thousands of hearts to win an honourable and acceptable victory.

I. THE FACT WHICH CONFRONTS US; viz. that in this life which we are living we must expect a large measure of misunderstanding. "It is impossible but that offences will come." With all our various and complex relationships; with all that we are expecting and requiring of one another in thought, word, and deed; with the limitations to which we are subject both in mind and in spirit;—how could it be otherwise? A certain considerable measure of mistake, and of consequent vexation, and of consequent anger, will arise, as we play our part in this world. Occasions will arise when our neighbours, when our friends, when our near relatives, will speak to us with displeasure in their hearts, and with annoyance, if not anger, in their tone. This we must lay our account with.

II. THE TEMPTATION WHICH ASSAILS US. This is to a resentment which utters itself in "grievous words." Anger provokes anger and makes it angrier still; vexation grows into positive bitterness, and bitterness ends in miserable strife. Thus the "little fire" will "kindle a great matter;" thus a spark becomes a flame, and sometimes a flame becomes a fire and even a conflagration. Many a feud may be traced back to the utterance of a few hasty words, which might have been met and quieted by a pacific answer, if they had fallen on patient and wise ears.

III. The bearing which becomes us. To return "the soft answer." It does become us, because: 1. This is the true victory over our own spirit (see homily on ch. xvi. 32). 2. It is also the worthiest victory over the man who provokes us. We "turn away wrath;" and how much nobler a thing it is to win by kindness than to crush by severity! 3. It is to render an essential service to many beside the actual spokesman. When one man starts a quarrel, a great many suffer on both sides. And when one man quenches a quarrel, he saves many from misery (and perhaps from sin) into which they would otherwise fall (see Judg. viii. 1—3). 4. It is to act in accordance with the will and the example of our Lord.—C.

Ver. 3.— *God's searching glance.* The text, with others treating of the same subject, assures us, concerning the Divine notice of us, that—

I. It is absolutely universal. The eyes of the Lord are "in every place." There is no secret place, however screened from the sight of man, which is not "naked and open unto the eyes of him with whom we have to do" (see Ps. cxxxix.; Jer. xxiii. 24; Heb. iv. 13).

II. It is constant. Absolutely unintermitted, day and night; through youth and age; in prosperity and in adversity; under all imaginable conditions.

III. It is thorough. Penetrating to the innermost sanctuary of the soul, searching its most secret places, "discerning the thoughts and intents of the heart;" discovering (1) beneath the fair exterior that which is foul within; (2) beneath the rugged surface the inward beauty which is breaking forth.

IV. It is to be feared by the rebellious and the disobedient. 1. Those who are living and are purposing to live in the commission of some flagrant sin. 2. Those who are deliberately rejecting the authority and disregarding the merciful overtures of God in Jesus Christ. 3. And also those who are continually postponing the hour of decision and of return to their allegiance. These souls may *fear* to think that the eye of the Holy One is continually upon them; or they may be *ashamed* as they think that the eye of the appealing and disappointed Saviour is regarding them.

V. It is to be courted by the true and faithful. 1. The hearts that are turning toward a Divine Redeemer may be encouraged to believe that his glance of kind encouragement is upon them (see Mark x. 21). 2. The hearts that are surrendering themselves to Christ in faith and love may fill with peace and rest as they are assured of his acceptance (Matt. xi. 28—30; John v. 24; vi. 46, 47). 3. The hearts that, in his holy service, are honestly and earnestly striving to follow and to honour him and to do his work may be glad with a pure, well-founded joy as they count on his precious regard, his loving approval. To these it will be a perpetual delight that the " eyes of the Lord are in every place," beholding every human heart and every human life.—C.

Vers. 8, 9.— *With whom God is pleased.* With whom is God well pleased? A great question, that has had many answers. The statement of the text gives us—

I. God's attitude toward the wicked. 1. *Their whole life is grievous to him.* " The way of the wicked is an abomination," etc. And this, not because they hold some erroneous opinions, nor because they make many serious mistakes, nor because they are betrayed into occasional transgressions; but because they determinately withhold themselves from his service; because they claim and exercise the right to dispose of their own life according to their own will; because they deliberately disregard the will of God. They are thus in a state of fixed rebellion against his rule, of settled disavowal of his claims upon them, of consequent neglect of his holy Law. Therefore their entire course or " way " is one of disobedience and disloyalty; it must be painful, grievous, even "abominable" in the sight of the Holy One. 2. *Their worship is wholly unacceptable to him.* If we " regard iniquity in our heart, the Lord will not hear us " (Ps. l. 16—22; lxvi. 18; Isa. i. 15). God "desireth truth in the inward parts;" he cannot and will not accept as of any value whatever the offering that comes from a heart in a state of determined disloyalty to himself and hatred of his law. 3. *Their worship is positively offensive.* It is "an abomination" unto him. And it is so, because: (1) It is an act of conscious rejection of his claim; the worshipper is taking his Name and his Law upon his lips, and at the very time he is consciously keeping back from God what he knows is his due. (2) It is an act of positive insult, inasmuch as it supposes that God will be indifferent to the wrong things the worshipper is doing, that he will take a few words or offerings instead of purity, truthfulness, integrity, submission.

II. GOD'S PLEASURE WITH THE RIGHTEOUS. 1. *Who they are.* (1) They are not the absolutely perfect in creed or conduct; for these are not to be discovered. (2) They are those who recognize in God the One whose they are and to whom they desire and intend to surrender their hearts and lives. It may be, it must be, an imperfect sacrifice; but it will be a genuine and therefore an acceptable one. 2. *With what, in them, God is well pleased.* (1) With the whole spirit and aim of their life. "They follow after righteousness;" they have set their heart on being just—to God their Creator; to their neighbours, and especially those closely related to them; to themselves. And their daily and hourly life will be an honest and devout endeavour to realize their aim (see Phil. i. 20; iii. 12—15). It is they who truly desire and steadfastly endeavour, against whatever obstacles and with whatever stumblings and haltings, to be right and to do right, with whom God is pleased. (2) With their devotion. The prayer of these "upright" souls is God's "delight." He is pleased when they reverently approach him, when they humbly confess their failures, when they gratefully bless him for his patience, when they earnestly ask him for strength and grace for coming duties and struggles.—C.

Ver. 11.—*The certainty of God's notice.* First we have—
I. THE DIFFICULTY SUGGESTED. It is not unnatural to ask—Does God in very deed take notice of such beings as we are? does he condescend to watch the workings of our mind? are the flitting thoughts that cross our brain, the fugitive feelings that pass through our weak human hearts, within the range of his observation? Is that worth his while? Are they not beyond the pale of his Divine regard?
II. THE ARGUMENT FROM SECRECY. If "Sheol" is before the Lord, if that region of darkness where "the light (itself) is as darkness," if the place of mystery and shadow is within his Divine regard, how much more are those who are living in the light of day, on whom the sunshine falls, who live their life openly beneath the heavens! The writer evidently felt that there was nothing so particularly hidden or secret about the mind of man. And we may well argue that there is nothing inscrutably hidden within our hearts; for do we not read, continually and correctly, the minds of our children? We know what they think and feel. And if their minds are open to us, how much more must our minds—the minds of the children of men—be "naked and open" to our heavenly Father! If our superior intelligence supplies us with the key to their secrets, what does not Omniscience know of us, even of those thoughts and motives we are most anxious to conceal?
III. THE ARGUMENT FROM UNATTRACTIVENESS. "Abaddon [destruction] is before the Lord." That which has no manner of interest in itself, that from which Benevolence would willingly turn its eyes, that which is repelling to the sight of love and life,—that even is before God; he never ceases to regard a scene so utterly uninviting. How much more, then, will he regard the hearts of his own offspring! There is nothing beneath the skies so interesting to him. What has the most charm to *us* in our home? Surely not any furniture or any treasures, however rare, or costly, or beautiful these may be. It is our children; it is their hearts of love for which we care. It is to them that we come home in joyful expectation. It is on them our eye rests with benignity and delight. So with our Divine Father. He does look on all the furniture of this wonderful home in which we dwell (Ps. civ. 31); he ever has before him the sphere and scene of destruction; but that which draws his eye of tender interest and kindly pity and holy love is the heart of his sons and daughters. We are poor and needy, but we are all his offspring, and "the Lord thinketh upon us." 1. With what parental grief does he look upon (1) our separation from himself in sympathy; (2) our unlikeness to himself in spirit and in character; (3) our disobedience to his will! 2. With what parental satisfaction does he view (1) our return to his side and his service; (2)

our increasing likeness to our Leader and Exemplar; (3) our filial obedience and submission to his will!—C.

Vers. 13, 15—17.—*The source of satisfaction.* We learn—

I. THAT THERE SOMETIMES RESTS A LONG AND DEEP SHADOW ON THE PATH OF HUMAN LIFE. 1. Sometimes a *long* one. "*All* the days of the afflicted are evil." They are not a few who have to make up their minds for many months or years of separation or pain, or even for a lifelong trouble. They know that they will carry their burden to the grave. 2. Sometimes a *deep* one. "By sorrow of heart the spirit is broken." The burden is greater than the spirit can bear, it breaks beneath it; the heart is simply overwhelmed; all hope has died out, all gladness is gone from the life, all light from the countenance, all elasticity from the step; the heart is fairly broken.

II. THAT FAVOURABLE CIRCUMSTANCES CANNOT COMMAND SATISFACTION TO THE SPIRIT. 1. *Wealth* will not do it. Great treasure often means great trouble (ver. 16); shares and stocks often bring as much burden as blessing with them; he who piles gold on his counter may be heaping anxiety upon his heart. 2. *Sumptuous* fare will fail (ver. 17). All the delicacies that can be spread upon the table will not give enjoyment to him that has a restless spirit, or a secret that he knows he cannot hide, or a debt he knows he cannot meet, or a bounden duty he knows he has neglected.

III. THAT HAPPINESS MUST BE HEART-DEEP, OR IT IS NOTHING. (Ver. 13.) If it is not the merry heart that produces the cheerful countenance, the smile can very well be spared, both by him who smiles and by those who are in his presence. Few things are sadder to hear than hollow laughter, or to see than a forced and weary smile.

IV. THAT A CHEERFUL SPIRIT IS A VALUABLE BESTOWMENT. (Ver. 15.) Better than the large estate or the high position, or the influential circle, is the buoyant spirit which

> "Ever with a frolic welcome takes
> The thunder and the sunshine."

V. THAT A LOVING SPIRIT IS A STILL GREATER GIFT OF GOD. "Where love is," there is peace and there is joy, however mean the home or slight the fare. He who carries with him to every table and every hearth a loving spirit is a friend of God's own sending; he is "the welcome guest;" he has a treasure in his breast which no coffers will supply.

VI. THAT PIETY IS THE ALL-COMPENSATING GOOD. 1. It makes the poor man rich —"rich in faith," "rich toward God," rich with a wealth which "no thief can steal." 2. It brings comfort to the sorrowful, and introduces that Divine Physician who can bind up the broken heart, and heal *its* wounds. 3. It speaks of a heavenly portion to those who have no hope of deliverance here; there may be "affliction all the days" of life (ver. 15), but "the righteous hath hope in his death" (ch. xiv. 32). Blessed, then, is he in whose heart is "the fear of the Lord."—C.

Ver. 29.—*God's distance from us and nearness to us.* "The Lord is far from the wicked;" and yet how near to us! "He is not far from any one of us;" "He compasses us behind and before, and layeth his hand upon us." We may, indeed, insist upon—

I. GOD'S LOCAL AND EFFECTIVE NEARNESS TO THE WICKED AN AGGRAVATION OF THEIR GUILT. The fact that "in him they do live, and move, and have their being," that by his operative presence they are momently sustained in being, that by the working of his hand around and upon them they are supplied with all their comfort, and filled with all their joys,—this great fact makes more heinous the guilt of forgetfulness of God, of indifference to his will, of rebellion against his rule. But *the* truth of the text is—

II. GOD'S DISTANCE IN SYMPATHY AND IN SPIRIT FROM THE WICKED. God is far from the wicked in that: 1. He is *utterly out of sympathy* with them in all their thought and feeling, in their tastes and inclinations, in their likings and dislikings. He hates what they love; he is infinitely repelled from that which they are drawn to. 2. He regards them with a serious *Divine displeasure.* He is "angry with the wicked every day." His "soul finds no pleasure in them." He is grieved with them; in his holy and loving heart there is the pain of strong parental disapproval. 3. He is *prac-*

tically inaccessible to them. It is only he " that has clean hands and a pure heart " who is free to draw nigh unto God. " The sacrifice of the wicked is an abomination " unto him (see homily on ver. 8). God cannot hear us if we "regard iniquity in our hearts;" we virtually withdraw ourselves from him, we place a terrible spiritual distance between our Creator and ourselves, when we take up an attitude of disloyalty toward him, or when we abandon ourselves to any evil course. Yet let it be always kept in mind, that: 4. To the penitent and believing he is always near; in whatever far country the wayward son is living, he may address himself immediately to his heavenly Father.

III. God's sympathetic nearness to his children. "He heareth the prayer of the righteous." Those who are earnestly desirous of serving God, of following Jesus Christ, may be assured : 1. Of his actual and observant nearness to them when they approach him in prayer. ·2. Of his tender and loving interest in them (Mark x. 21). 3. Of his acceptance of themselves when they offer their hearts and lives to him and his service. 4. Of his purpose to answer their various requests in such ways and times as he knows to be best for them.—C.

EXPOSITION.

CHAPTER XVI.

Vers. **1—7.**—These are specially religious maxims, and they all contain the name Jehovah.

Ver. **1.**—The Authorized Version makes one sentence of this verse without any contrast or antithesis. This is plainly wrong, there being intended a contrast between the thought of the heart and the well-ordered speech. It is better translated, *The plans of the heart are man's: but the answer of the tongue is from Jehovah.* Men make plans, arrange speeches, muster arguments, in the mind; but to put these into proper, persuasive words is a gift of God. "Our sufficiency is of God" (2 Cor. iii. 5). In the case of Balaam, God overruled the wishes and intentions of the prophet, and constrained him to give utterance to something very different from his original mental conceptions. But the present sentence attributes the outward expression of what the mind has conceived in every case unto the help of God (comp. vers. 9, 33 ; ch. xv. 23). Christ enjoined his disciples to trust to momentary inspiration in their apologies or defences before unbelievers (Matt. x. 19). This verse is omitted in the Septuagint.

Ver. **2.**—**All the ways of a man are clean in his own eyes** (ch. xxi. 2). He may deceive himself, and be blind to his own faults, or be following an ill-informed and ill-regulated conscience (ch. xii. 15; xiv. 12), yet this is no excuse in God's eyes. **The Lord weigheth the spirits.** Not the "ways," the outward life and actions only, but motives, intentions, dispositions (Heb. iv. 12). He too knows our secret faults, unsuspected by others, and perhaps by ourselves (Ps. xix. 12). The Septuagint has here, "All the works of the humble are

manifest before God, but the impious shall perish in an evil day." The next verse is omitted in the Greek; and the other clauses up to ver. 8 are dislocated.

Ver. **3.**—**Commit thy works unto the Lord.** "Commit" (*gol*) is literally "roll" (κύλισον, Theodotion), as in Ps. xxii. 8 and xxxvii. 5; and the injunction means, "Transfer thy burden to the Lord, cast upon him all that thou hast to do; do all as in his sight, and as an act of duty to him." Thus Tobit says to his son, "Bless the Lord thy God alway, and desire of him that thy ways may be directed, and that all thy paths and counsels may prosper" (Tobit iv. 19). The Vulgate, using a different punctuation (*gal*), renders, "Reveal to the Lord thy works." As a child opens its heart to a tender parent, so do thou show to God thy desires and intentions, trusting to his care and providence. **And thy thoughts shall be established.** The plans and deliberations out of which the "works" sprang shall meet with a happy fulfilment, because they are undertaken according to the will of God, and directed to the end by his guidance (comp. ch. xix. 21; Ps. xc. 17; 1 Cor. iii. 9). This verse is not in the Septuagint.

Ver. **4.**—**The Lord hath made all things for himself.** So the Vulgate, *propter semetipsum;* and Origen ('Præf. in Job'), δι' ἑαυτόν. That is, God hath made everything for his own purpose, to answer the design which he hath intended from all eternity (Rev. iv. 11). But this translation is not in accordance with the present reading, לַמַּעֲנֵהוּ, which means rather "for its own end," for its own proper use. Everything in God's design has its own end and object and reason for being where it is and such as it is ; everything exhibits his goodness and wisdom, and tends to his glory. Septuagint,

"All the works of the Lord are with righteousness." **Yea, even the wicked for the day of evil.** This clause has been perverted to support the terrible doctrine of reprobation—that God, whose will must be always efficacious, has willed the damnation of some; whereas we are taught that God's will is that "all men should be saved, and come unto the knowledge of the truth," and that "God sent his Son not to condemn the world, but that the world through him might be saved" (1 Tim. ii. 4; John iii. 17; comp. Ezek. xxxiii. 11). Man, having free-will, can reject this gracious purpose of God, and render the means of salvation nugatory; but this does not make God the cause of man's destruction, but man himself. In saying that God "made the wicked," the writer does not mean that God made him as such, but made him as he made all other things, giving him powers and capacities which he might have used to good, but which, as a fact, he uses to evil. It will be useful here to quote the wise words of St. Gregory ('Moral.,' vi. 33), "The Just and Merciful One, as he disposes the deeds of mortals, vouchsafes some things in mercy, and permits other things in anger; and the things which he permits he so bears with that he turns them to the account of his purpose. And hence it is brought to pass in a marvellous way that even that which is done without the will of God is not contrary to the will of God. For while evil deeds are converted to a good use, the very things that oppose his design render service to his design." *The day of evil* is the hour of punishment (Isa. x. 3; Job xxi. 30), which by a moral law will inevitably fall upon the sinner. God makes man's wickedness subserve his purposes and manifest his glory, as we see in the case of Pharaoh (Exod. ix. 16), and the crucifixion of our blessed Lord (Acts ii. 23; comp. Rom. ix. 22). It is a phase of God's moral government that an evil day should be appointed for transgressors, and it is from foreknowledge of their deserts that their punishment is prepared. The perplexing question, why God allows men to come into the world whom he knows will meet with perdition, is not handled here. Septuagint, "But the impious is kept for an evil day." Cato, 'Dist.,' ii. 8—

"Nolo putes pravos homines peccata lucrari;
Temporibus peccata latent, sed tempore patent."

Ver. 5.—(For the first member, see ch. vi. 17; viii. 13.) Says the maxim—

Ἀλαζονείας οὔ τις ἐκφεύγει δίκην.

"Pride hath its certain punishment."

We read in the Talmud, "Of every proud man God says, He and I cannot live in the world together." A mediæval jingle runs—

"Hoc retine verbum, frangit Deus omne superbum."

Septuagint, "Impure in the sight of God is every high-hearted man (ὑψηλοκάρδιος)." The second member is found in ch. xi. 21, and must be taken as a form of adjuration. Septuagint, "Putting hands on hand unjustly, he shall not be innocent;" *i.e.* one who acts violently and unjustly shall be held guilty—which seems a trite truism. Many commentators interpret the clause as if it meant that the co-operation and combination of sinners in evil practices will not save them from retribution. But hand clasping hand in token of completing a bargain or alliance is scarcely an early Oriental custom. There is an analogous saying in Greek which implies mutual assistance—

Χεὶρ χεῖρα νίπτει, δάκτυλός τε δάκτυλον.

"Hand washes hand, and finger finger."

The LXX. has here two distiches, the first of which occurs in the Vulgate, but the second is not found there. Neither appears in our present Hebrew text. "The beginning of the good way is to do what is just; this is more acceptable to God than to sacrifice sacrifices. He who seeketh the Lord shall find knowledge with righteousness; and they who seek him rightly shall find peace."

Ver. 6.—**By mercy and truth iniquity is purged;** *atoned for.* The combination "mercy and truth" occurs in ch. iii. 3 (where see note), and intimates love to God and man, and faithfulness in keeping promises and truth and justice in all dealings. It is by the exercise of those graces, not by mere external rites, that God is propitiated (see on ch. x. 2). A kind of expiatory value is assigned to these virtues, which, indeed, must not be pressed too closely, but should be examined by the light of such passages in the New Testament as Luke xi. 41; Acts x. 4. Of course, such graces show themselves only in one who is really devout and God-fearing; they are the fruits of a heart at peace with God and man, and react on the character and conduct. The LXX., which places this distich after ver. 27 of ch. xv., translates, "By alms and faithfulness (πίστεσιν) sins are cleansed," confining the term "mercy" to one special form, as in one reading of Matt. vi. 1, "Take heed that ye do not your righteousness [*al.* alms] before men." **By the fear of the Lord men depart from evil.** The practice of true religion, of course, involves abstinence from sin; and this seems so unnecessary a truth to be formally stated that some take the "evil" named to be physical, not moral evil; calamity, not transgression. But the two clauses are co-ordinate, and present two aspects of the same truth. The first intimates how sin is to be expiated, the second how it is to be avoided. The morally good man meets with pardon and acceptance, and he who fears God is delivered from evil. So we pray, in the Lord's Prayer, "Forgive us our trespasses, and deliver us from evil." Septuagint, "By the fear of the Lord every one declineth from evil" (comp. ch. xiv. 27).

Ver. 7.—**When a man's ways please the Lord,** which they can do only when they are religious, just, and charitable. **He maketh even his enemies to be at peace with him;** to submit themselves. Experience proves that nothing succeeds like success. Where a man is prosperous and things go well with him, even ill-wishers are content to cast away or to dissemble their dislike, and to live at peace with him. Thus Abimelech King of Gerar fawned upon Isaac because he saw that the Lord was with him (Gen. xxvi. 27, etc.). This is the worldly side of the maxim. It has a higher aspect, and intimates the far reaching influence of goodness—how it disarms opposition, arouses reverence and love, gives no occasion for disputes, and spreads around an atmosphere of peace. To the Jews the maxim was taught by external circumstances. While they were doing the will of the Lord, their land was to be preserved from hostile attack (Exod. xxxiv. 24; 2 Chron. xvii. 10). And Christians learn that it is only when they obey and fear God that they can overcome the assaults of the enemies of their soul—the devil, the world, and the flesh. Talmud, "He who is agreeable to God is equally agreeable to men."

Ver. 8.—**Better is a little with righteousness** (ch. xv. 16; Ps. xxxvii. 16). "Righteousness" may mean here a holy life or just dealing; as **without right,** or, *with injustice,* in the second clause, may refer either generally to wickedness, or specially to fraud and oppression (Jer. xxii. 13). Says Theognis—

Βούλεο δ᾿ εὐσεβέων ὀλίγοις σὺν χρήμασιν οἰκεῖν,
ʾΗ πλουτεῖν ἀδίκως χρήματα πασάμενος.

"Wish thou with scanty means pious to live,
Rather than rich with large, ill-gotten wealth."

Another maxim says to the same effect—

Λεπτῶς καλῶς ζῆν κρεῖσσον, ἢ λαμπρῶς κακῶς.

Septuagint, "Better is small getting (λῆψις) with righteousness, than great revenues with iniquity" (see on ch. xv. 29).

Ver. 9.—**A man's heart deviseth his way: but the Lord directeth his steps** (ver. 1).

"Man proposes, God disposes;" or, as the Germans say, "Der Mensch denkt, Gott lenkt" (comp. ch. xx. 24). The word rendered "deviseth" implies, by its species, intensity of thought and care. Man meditates and prepares his plans with the utmost solicitude, but it rests with God whether he shall carry them to completion or not, and whether, if they are to be accomplished, it be done with ease or with painful labour (comp. Gen. xxiv. 12, etc.). We all remember Shakespeare's words in 'Hamlet'—

"There's a divinity that shapes our ends,
Rough-hew them how we will."

Septuagint, "Let the heart of man consider what is just, that his steps may be by God directed aright" (comp. Jer. x. 23).

Ver. 10.—**A Divine sentence is in the lips of the king** . קֶסֶם (*quesem*) is "divination," "soothsaying," oracular utterance. Septuagint, μαντεῖον. The king's words have, in people's minds, the certainty and importance of a Divine oracle, putting an end to all controversy or division of opinion. It seems to be a general maxim, not especially referring to Solomon or the theocratic kingdom, but rather indicating the traditional view of the absolute monarchy. The custom of deifying kings and invoking them as gods was usual in Egypt and Eastern countries, and made its way to the West. "It is the voice of a god, and not of a man," cried the people, when Herod addressed them in the amphitheatre at Cæsarea (Acts xii. 22). The Greeks could say—

Εἰκὼν δὲ βασιλεύς ἐστιν ἔμψυχος Θεοῦ.
"God's very living image is the king."

And thus his utterances were regarded as irrefragably true and decisive. **His mouth transgresseth not in judgment.** The decisions which he gives are infallible, and, at any rate, irresistible. We may refer to Solomon's famous verdict concerning the two mothers (1 Kings iii. 16, etc.), and such sentences as ch. viii. 15, "By me (wisdom) kings reign, and princes decree justice" (see below on ver. 12; ch. xxi. 1); and David's words (2 Sam. xxiii. 3), "He that ruleth over men must be just, ruling in the fear of God" (Wisd. ix. 4, 10, 12). Delitzsch regards the second hemistich as giving a warning (consequent on the former clause), and not stating a fact, "In the judgment his mouth should not err." The present chapter contains many admonitions to kings which a wise father like Solomon may have uttered and recorded for the benefit of his son. If this is the case, it is as strange as it is true that Rehoboam made little use of the counsels, and that Solomon's latter days gave the lie to many of them.

Ver. 11.—**A just weight and balance are the Lord's** (ch. xi. 1); literally, *the balance and scales of justice (are) the Lord's.* They come under his law, are subject to the Divine ordinances which regulate all man's dealings. The great principles, of truth and justice govern all the transactions of buying and selling; religion enters into the business of trading, and weights and measures are sacred things. Vulgate, "The weights and the balance are judgments of the Lord;" being true and fair, they are regarded as God's judgment. Septuagint, "The turn of the balance is justice before God." **All the weights of the bag are his work.** Some have found a difficulty here, because the bag may contain false as well as true weights (Deut. xxv. 13), and it could not be said that the light weights were the Lord's work. This surely is captious criticism. The maxim merely states that the trader's weights take their origin and authority from God's enactment, from certain eternal principles which he has established. What man's chicanery and fraud make of them does not come into view. (For the law that regulates such matters, see Lev. xix. 35, etc.) That cheating in this respect was not uncommon we learn from the complaints of the prophets, as Micah vi. 11. The religious character of the standard weights and measures is shown by the term "shekel of the sanctuary" (Exod. xxxviii. 24, and elsewhere continually).

Ver. 12.—It is **an abomination to kings to commit wickedness.** This and the following verse give the ideal view of the monarch —that which he ought to be rather than what he is (comp. Ps. lxxii.). Certainly neither Solomon nor many of his successors exhibited this high character. The Septuagint, followed by some modern commentators, translates, " He who doeth wickedness is an abomination to kings;" but as the "righteousness" in the second clause (**the throne is established by righteousness**) undoubtedly refers to the king, so it is more natural to take the " wickedness" in the first member as being his own, not his subjects'. When a ruler acts justly and wisely, punishes the unruly, rewards the virtuous, acts as God's vicegerent, and himself sets the example of the character which becomes so high a position, he wins the affection of his people, they willingly obey him, and are ready to die for him and his family (comp. ch. xxv. 5; Isa. xvi. 5). Law-makers should not be law-breakers. Seneca, 'Thyest.,' 215—

" Ubi non est pudor,
      Nec cura juris, sanctitas, pietas, fides,
   Instabile regnum est."

Ver. 13.—**Righteous lips are the delight of kings.** The ideal king takes pleasure in the truth and justice which his subjects display in their conversation. Such a one hates flattery and dissimulation, and encourages honest speaking. **They** (kings) **love him that speaketh right;** *that which is just* (ch. viii. 6). The two clauses are co-ordinate. Septuagint, "He loveth upright words" (comp. ch. xxii. 11).

Ver. 14.—**The wrath of a king is as messengers of death.** In a despotic monarchy the death of an offender follows quickly on the offence. Anger the king, and punishment is at hand; instruments are always ready who will carry out the sentence, and that before time is given for reconsideration. The murder of Thomas à Becket will occur as an illustration (comp. Esth. vii. 8, etc.). The LXX. translates, " The king's wrath is a messenger of death," taking the plural as put by enallage for the singular; but possibly the plural may intimate the many agents who are prepared to perform the ruler's behests, and the various means which he possesses for punishing offenders. This first clause implies, without expressly saying, that, such being the case, none but a fool will excite the monarch's resentment (comp. Eccles. viii. 4); then the second clause comes in naturally. **But a wise man will pacify it.** He will take care not to provoke that anger which gluts its resentment so quickly and so fatally (ch. xix. 12; xx. 2). Septuagint, " A wise man will appease him," the king; as Jacob propitiated Esau by the present which he sent forward (Gen. xxxii. 20, 21).

Ver. 15.—**In the light of the king's countenance is life** (ch. xv. 30; Ps. iv. 6). As the king's anger and the darkening of his countenance are death (ver. 14), so, when his look is cheerful and bright, it sheds joy and life around, as the rain refreshes the parched ground. **A cloud of the latter rain.** The former rain in Palestine falls about the end of October or the beginning of November, when the seed is sown; the latter rain comes in March or April, and is absolutely necessary for the due swelling and ripening of the grain. It is accompanied, of course, with cloud, which tempers the heat, while it brings fertility and vigour. To this the king's *favour* is well compared. " He shall come down," says the psalmist, "like the rain upon the mown grass, as showers that water the earth " (Ps. lxxii. 6). The LXX., reading בנו (*beni*) for פני (*peni*), translates, "In the light of life is the son of the king; and they who are acceptable to him are as a cloud of the latter rain."

Ver. 16.—**To get wisdom than gold** (comp. ch. iii. 14; viii. 10, 11, 19); **and to get understanding rather to be chosen than silver;** Revised Version better, *yea, to get understanding is rather to be chosen than* [to get] *silver.*

If the clauses are not simply parallel, and the comparative value of silver and gold is to be considered, we may, with Wordsworth, see here an intimation of the superiority of wisdom (*chochmah*) over intelligence (*binah*), the former being the guide of life and including the practice of religion, the latter denoting discernment, the faculty of distinguishing between one thing and another (see note on ch. xxiii. 4, and the quotation from 'Pirke Aboth' on ch. xv. 33). The LXX., for *kenoh* reading *kinnot*, have given a version of which the Fathers have largely availed themselves: "The nests of wisdom are preferable to gold, and the nests of knowledge are preferable above silver." Some of the old commentators take these "nests" to be the problems and apothegms which enshrine wisdom; others consider them to mean the children or scholars who are taught by the wise man.

Ver. 17.—**The highway of the upright is to depart from evil.** To avoid the dangerous byways to which evil leads, one must walk straight in the path of duty (comp. ch. xv. 19). Septuagint, "The paths of life decline from evil;" and this version adds some paragraphs in illustration, which are not in the Hebrew: "And the ways of righteousness are length of life. He who receiveth instruction will be among the good [or, 'in prosperity,' ἐν ἀγαθοῖς], and he who observeth reproof shall become wise." **He that keepeth his way preserveth his soul.** He who continues in the right way, and looks carefully to his goings, will save himself from ruin and death (ch. xiii. 3). Septuagint, "He who watcheth his own ways keepeth his life." And then is added another maxim, "He that loveth his life will spare his mouth."

Ver. 18.—**Pride goeth before destruction.** A maxim continually enforced (see ch. xi. 2; xvii. 19; xviii. 12). Here is the contrast to the blessing on humility promised (ch. xv. 33). **A haughty spirit**—a lifting up of spirit—**goeth before a fall** (comp. Dan. iv. 29, etc.). Thus, according to Herodotus (vii. 10), Artabanus warned the arrogant Xerxes, "Seest thou how God strikes with the thunder animals which overtop others, and suffers them not to vaunt themselves, but the small irritate him not? And seest thou how he hurls his bolts always against the mightiest buildings and the loftiest trees? For God is wont to cut short whatever is too highly exalted" (comp. Horace, 'Carm.,' ii. 10. 9, etc.). Says the Latin adage, "Qui petit alta nimis, retro lapsus ponitur imis." Cæsar, 'Bell. Gall.,' i. 14, "Consuesse Deos immortales, quo gravius homines ex commutatione rerum doleant, quos pro sceiere eorum ulcisci velint, his secundiores interdum re, et diuturniorem impunitatem concedere." The Chinese say, "Who flies

not high falls not low;" and, "A great tree attracts the wind." The Basque proverb remarks, "Pride sought flight in heaven, fell to hell." And an Eastern one, "What is extended will tear; what is long will break" (Lane).

Ver. 19.—This verse is connected in thought, as well as verbally, with the preceding. Better it is to be of an humble spirit with the lowly. The Revised Version has, *with the poor;* but "meek" or "lowly" better contrasts with "proud" of the second clause. Ps. lxxxiv. 10, "I had rather be a doorkeeper in the house of my God, than to dwell in the tents of wickedness." **Than to divide the spoil with the proud.** To share in the fruits of the operations and pursuits of the proud, and to enjoy their pleasures, a man must cast in his lot with them, undergo their risks and anxieties, and participate in the crimes by which they gain their wealth. The result of such association was told in ver. 18. The Germans express the connection between abundance and folly by the terse apothegm, "Voll, toll;" "Full, fool." Septuagint, "Better is the man of gentle mind with humility, than he who divideth spoil with the violent."

Ver. 20.—**He that handleth a matter wisely.** *Dabar,* translated "matter," is better rendered "word," as in ch. xiii. 13, with which passage the present is in contrast. Thus Revised Version, *he that giveth heed unto the word.* **Shall find good;** Vulgate, *eruditus in verbo reperiet bona.* The "Word" is the Law of God; he who attends to this shall prosper. The rendering of the Authorized Version is supported by the Septuagint, "The man prudent in affairs is a finder of good things;" he attends to his business, and thinks out the best mode of accomplishing his plans, and therefore succeeds in a worldly sense (comp. ch. xvii. 20). **Whoso trusteth in the Lord, happy is he;** or, *hail to him,* as in ch. xiv. 21. To heed the Word and to trust in the Lord are correlative things; handling a matter wisely can hardly belong to the same category. The Septuagint contrasts the worldly success of one who manages business wisely and discreetly with the blessedness of him who, when he has done all, commits his cause to God and trusts wholly to him: "He who hath trusted in the Lord is blessed (μακαριστός)."

Ver. 21.—**The wise in heart shall be called prudent.** True wisdom is recognized and acknowledged as such, especially when it has the gift of expressing itself appropriately (see on ch. xxiv. 8). **The sweetness** (ch. xxvii. 9) **of the lips increaseth learning.** People listen to instruction at the mouth of one who speaks well and winningly. Such a one augments knowledge in others, and in himself too, for he learns by teaching. Knowledge ought not to be buried in one's own mind, but produced on fit occasions and in suitable words for the edification of others. Ecclus. xx. 30, "Wisdom that is hid, and treasure that is hoarded up, what profit is in them both?" (see Matt. v. 15). Septuagint, "The wise and prudent they call worthless (φαύλους); but they who are sweet in word shall hear more." Wise men are called bad and worthless by the vulgar herd, either because they do not impart all they know, or because they are envied for their learning; but those who are eloquent and gracious in speech shall receive much instruction from what they hear, every one being ready to converse with them and impart any knowledge which they possess.

Ver. 22.—**Understanding is a well-spring of life unto him that hath it** (ch. x. 11; xiii. 14). The possessor of understanding has in himself a source of comfort and a vivifying power, which is as refreshing as a cool spring to a thirsty traveller. In all troubles and difficulties he can fall back upon his own good sense and prudence, and satisfy himself therewith. This is not conceit, but the result of a well-grounded experience. **But the instruction of fools is folly;** i e. the instruction which fools give is folly and sin; such is the only teaching which they can offer. So the Vulgate, *doctrina stultorum fatuitas;* and many modern commentators. But *musar* is better taken in the sense of "discipline" or "chastisement" (as in ch. i. 7; vii. 22; xv. 5), which the bad man suffers. His own folly is the scourge which punishes him; refusing the teaching of wisdom, he makes misery for himself, deprives himself of the happiness which virtue gives, and pierces himself through with many sorrows. Septuagint, "The instruction of fools is evil."

Ver. 23.—**The heart of the wise teacheth his mouth.** Out of the abundance of his heart the wise man speaks; the spirit within him finds fit utterance. *Pectus est quod disertos facit.* The thought and mind control the outward expression and make it eloquent and persuasive (comp. ch. xv. 2). **And addeth learning to his lips;** Vulgate, "addeth grace." But *lekach,* which means properly "reception," "taking in," is best rendered "learning," as in ver. 21; ch. i. 5, etc. The intellect and knowledge of the wise display themselves in their discourse. Delitzsch, "Learning mounteth up to his lips." Ecclus. xxi. 26, "The heart of fools is in their mouth; but the mouth of the wise is in their heart." Septuagint, "The heart of the wise will consider what proceedeth from his mouth; and on his lips he will carry prudence (ἐπιγνωμοσύνην)."

Ver. 24.—**Pleasant words are as an honeycomb.** "Pleasant words" are words of comforting, soothing tendency, as in ch. xv. 26; Ps. xix. 10. The writer continues his praise of apt speech. The comparison with honey is common in all languages and at all times. Thus Homer sings of Nestor ('Iliad,' i. 248, etc.)—

"The smooth-tongued chief, from whose persuasive lips
Sweeter than honey flowed the stream of speech."
(Derby.)

So the story goes that on the lips of St. Ambrose, while still a boy, a swarm of bees settled, portending his future persuasive eloquence. **Sweet to the soul, and health to the bones** (ch. xv. 30). The verse forms one sentence. The happy results of pleasant words are felt in body and soul. Honey in Palestine is a staple article of food, and is also used as a medicinal remedy. Of its reviving effects we read in the case of Jonathan, who from a little portion hurriedly taken as he marched on had "his eyes enlightened" (1 Sam. xiv. 27). Septuagint, "Their sweetness is the healing of the soul."

Ἰατρὸς ὁ λόγος τοῦ κατά ψυχὴν πάθους.

"Speech the physician of the soul's annoy."

Ver. 25.—A repetition of ch. xiv. 12.

Ver. 26.—**He that laboureth laboureth for himself;** literally, *the soul of him that laboureth laboureth for him.* "Soul" here is equivalent to "desire," "appetite" (comp. ch. vi. 30), and the maxim signifies that hunger is a strong incentive to work—the needs of the body spur the labourer to diligence and assiduity; he eats bread in the sweat of his brow (Gen. iii. 19). Says the Latin gnome—

"Largitor artium, ingeniique magister Venter."

"The belly is the teacher of all arts, The parent of invention."

"De tout s'avise à qui pain faut," "He who wants bread thinks of everything." There is our own homely saw, "Need makes the old wife trot;" as the Italians say, "Hunger sets the dog a-hunting" (Kelly). **For his mouth craveth it of him;** his mouth must have food to put in it. The verb אָכַף (akaph) does not occur elsewhere; it means properly "to bend," and then to put a load on, to constrain, to press. So here, "His mouth bends over him, i.e. urgeth him thereto" (Revised Version). Eccles. vi. 7, "All labour of man is for his mouth;" we should say stomach. Hunger in some sense is the great stimulus of all work. "We commanded you," says St. Paul (2 Thess. iii. 10), "that

if any would not work, neither should he eat."
There is a spiritual hunger without which
grace cannot be sought or obtained—that
hungering and thirsting after righteousness
of which Christ speaks, and which he who
is the Bread of life is ready to satisfy (Matt.
v. 6; John vi. 58). The Septuagint expands
the maxim: " A man in labours labours for
himself, and drives away (ἐκβιάζεται) his
own destruction; but the perverse man upon
his own mouth carrieth destruction."

Ver. 27.—This and the three following
verses are concerned with the case of the
evil man. **An ungodly man**—a man of
Belial—**diggeth up evil.** A man of Belial
(ch. vi. 12) is a worthless, wicked person,
what the French call a *vaurien.* Such
a one digs a pit for others (ch. xxvi. 27;
Ps. vii. 15), devises mischief against his
neighbour, plots against him by lying and
slandering and overreaching. Wordsworth
confines the evil to the man himself; he
digs it as treasure in a mine, loves wickedness for its own sake. But analogy is
against this interpretation. Septuagint,
" A foolish man diggeth evils for himself."
So Ecclus. xxvii. 26, " Whoso diggeth a pit
shall fall therein; and he that setteth a trap
shall be taken therein." As the gnome says—

Ἡ δὲ κακὴ βουλὴ τῷ βουλεύσαντι κακίστη.

And in his lips there is **as a burning fire**
(ch. xxvi. 23) His words scorch and injure
like a devouring flame. Jas. iii. 6, " The
tongue is a fire; the world of iniquity
among our members is the tongue, which
defileth the whole body, and setteth on fire
the wheel of nature, and is set on fire by
hell." Septuagint, " And upon his lips he
treasureth up fire."

Ver. 28.—**A froward man soweth strife**
(ch. vi. 14, 19). The verb means, literally,
" sends forth," which may signify " scatters
as seed" or "hurls as a missile weapon."
The character intended is the perverse man,
who distorts the truth, gives a wrong impression, attributes evil motives; such a one
occasions quarrels and heartburnings. **And a
whisperer separateth chief friends** (ch. xvii.
9). *Nirgan* is either " a chatterer," or " a
whisperer," " calumniator." In ch. xviii. 8
and xxvi. 20, 22 it is translated " tale-bearer."
" Be not called a whisperer (ψίθυρος)," says
the Son of Sirach (Ecclus. v. 14), speaking
of secret slander. " Slanderers," says an old
apothegm, " are Satan's bellows to blow up
contention." Septuagint, " A perverse man
sendeth abroad evils, and kindleth a torch
of deceit for the wicked, and separateth
friends." The alternative rendering of the
second clause, "estrangeth a leader," *i.e.*
a icnates one leader from another, or from
his army, is not confirmed by the authority
of the versions or the best commentators.

Ver. 29.—**A violent man enticeth his
neighbour.** The man of violence (ch. iii. 31)
is one who wrongs others by injurious conduct, by fraud or oppression. How such a
one " enticeth," talks a man over, we see in
ch. i. 10, etc. Septuagint, " The lawless
man tempts (ἀποπειρᾶται) friends." And
leadeth him into the way that is not good
(Ps. xxxvi. 4; Isa. lxv. 2); a position where
he will suffer some calamity, or be induced
to commit some wickedness.

Ver. 30.—This verse is better taken as
one sentence (so the Septuagint), and translated, as Nowack, " He that shutteth his
eyes in order to contrive froward things,
he that compresseth his lips, hath already
brought evil to pass;" he has virtually
effected it. From such a crafty, malignant
man you need not expect any more open
tokens of his intentions. **He shutteth his
eyes** (comp. Isa. xxxiii. 15); either that he
may better think out his evil plans, or else
he cannot look his neighbour in the face
while he is plotting against him. The
Vulgate has, *attonitis oculis;* Septuagint,
" fixing (στηρίζων) his eyes." **Moving his
lips;** rather, *he who compresseth his lips,* to
hide the malignant smile with which he
might greet his neighbour's calamity (comp.
ch. vi. 13, etc.; x. 10), or that neither by
word nor expression he may betray his
thoughts. Others take the two outward expressions mentioned as signals to confede-
rates; but this is not so suitable, as they are
the man's own feelings and sentiments that
are meant. One who gives these tokens
bringeth evil to pass; he has perfected his
designs, and deems them as good as accomplished, and you will do well to note what
his bearing signifies. Some take the meaning to be, brings punishment on himself;
but the warning is not given for the sinner's
sake. Septuagint, " He defines (ὁρίζει) all
evils with his lips; he is a furnace of evil."

Ver. 31.—**The hoary head is a crown of
glory** (ch. xx. 29). (For " crown," see on
ch. xvii. 6.) Old age is the reward of
a good life, and therefore is an honour to
a man (comp. ch. iii. 2, 16; iv. 10; ix. 11; x.
27). If **it be found**—rather, *it shall be found*
—**in the way of righteousness;** the guerdon
of obedience and holiness; whereas "bloody
and deceitful men shall not live out half
their days" (Ps. lv. 23). It is well said in
the Book of Wisdom (iv. 8, etc.), " Honourable age is not that which standeth in
length of time, nor that is measured by
number of years. But wisdom is the grey
hair unto men, and an unspotted life is old
age."

Ver. 32.—He that is **slow to anger** (ch.
xiv. 29) **is better than the mighty.** The
long-suffering, non-irascible man is more of
a hero than the valiant commander of a

great army. One overcomes external foes or obstacles; the other conquers himself; as it is said, **And he that ruleth his spirit than he that taketh a city** (ch. xxv. 28). 'Pirke Aboth,' iv. 1, "Who is the hero? The man that restrains his thoughts." Maxims about self-mastery are common enough. Says an unknown poet, " Fortior est qui se quam qui fortissima vincit Mœnia, nec virtus altius ire potest." So Publ. Syr., 'Sent.,' 795, " Fortior est qui cupiditates suas, quam qui hostes subjicit." And the mediæval jingle—

"Linguam frænare
Plus est quam castra domare."

At the end of this verse the Alexandrian Manuscript of the Septuagint, followed by later hands in some other uncials, adds, "and a man having prudence [is better] than a great farm."

Ver. 33.—**The lot is cast into the lap.** The bosom or fold of the garment (ch. vi. 27; xvii. 23; xxi. 14). It is not quite clear what articles the Jews used in their divinations by lot. Probably they employed stones, differing in shape or colour, or having some distinguishing mark. These were placed in a vessel **or** in the fold of a garment, and drawn or shaken thence. Such a practice has been common in all ages and countries; and though only cursorily mentioned in the Mosaic legislation (Numb. xxvi. 55), it was used by the Jews from the time of Joshua, and in the earliest days of the Christian Church (see Josh. xviii. 10; Judg xx. 9; 1 Sam. x. 20, 21; Acts i. 24,

etc.). As by this means man's agency was minimized, and all partiality and chicanery were excluded, the decision was regarded as directed by Providence. There is one case only of ordeal in the Law, and that under suspicion of adultery (Numb. v. 12, etc.). In the Epistle to the Hebrews, in place of the lot we read (vi. 16), " An oath for confirmation is to them an end of all strife." **The whole disposing thereof is of the Lord.** In these cases the Jew learned to see, in what we call chance, the overruling of Divine power. But this was not blind superstition. He did not feel justified in resorting to this practice on every trivial occasion, as persons used the *Sortes Virgilianæ* or even the verses of the Bible for the same purpose. The lot was employed religiously in cases where other means of decision were not suitable or available; it was not to supersede common prudence or careful investigation; but, for example, in trials where the evidence was conflicting and the judges could not determine the case, the merits were ascertained by lot (comp. ch. xviii. 18). After the effusion of the Holy Spirit, the apostles never resorted to divination, and the Christian Church has wisely repudiated the practice of all such modes of discovering the Divine will. Septuagint, " For the unrighteous all things fall into their bosom, but from the Lord are all just things," which may mean either that, though the wicked seem to prosper, God still works out his righteous ends; or the evil suffer retribution, and thus God's justice is displayed.

HOMILETICS.

Ver. 1.—*Man's thought and God's work.* Theology and philosophy have ever been confronted with the problem of the inter-relation of the Divine and the human in life. If God is supreme, what room is there for man's will, thought, and individual personality? If man has freedom and power, how can God be the infinite Ruler and Disposer of all things? It may not be possible to reconcile the two positions. But it must be unwise to ignore either of them. If we cannot mark their confines, we can at least observe the contents of the domain of each.

I. MAN HAS FREEDOM OF THOUGHT. "Man's are the counsels of the heart." Though externally constrained by circumstances, he is free to roam at large in the ample fields of imagination. The mind has a certain originative power. It is well-nigh a creator of thoughts—at least it can select the ideas that occur to it, arrange them, draw deductions from them; or it can let its fancies grow into new shapes; or, again, it can organize schemes, project plans, formulate purposes. Now, this liberty and the power it implies carry with them certain momentous consequences. 1. *We are responsible for our thoughts.* They are all known to God, and they will all be judged by him. Let us therefore take heed what follies and fancies we harbour in our most secret " chambers of imagery." 2. *We may exercise power with our thoughts.* These thoughts are seeds of actions. Inasmuch as we can direct them, we can turn the first springs of events. Here it is, in this inner workshop of the mind, that a man must forge his own future, and strike out works of public good. 3. *We cannot be coerced in our thoughts.* The tyrant may fling a man into a dungeon, but he cannot destroy the convictions that are enthroned in the bosom of his victim; he may tear out his tongue, but he can never tear out his thoughts. Here the powers of despotism fail; here the inalienable "rights of man" are ever in exercise.

II. God works through man's life. "The answer of the tongue is from the Lord." Though a man thinks out his ideas with originative power, when he comes into the world of action other influences lay hold of him, and his utterances are not wholly his own. This is conspicuously true of the prophet, who is not a mere mouthpiece of Divine words, but a living, thinking man; and yet whose utterances are inspired by God. The remarkable fact now is that it is true also of every man, of the godless man as well as the devout man. God controls the outcome of every man's life. 1. *He controls through internal impulses.* Conscience is the voice of God, and every man has a conscience. When conscience is disobeyed, the willing service of God is rejected, but still an unconscious doing of God's will may be brought about. In the days of the Exodus God was guiding even the stubborn Pharaoh to consent at last to the Divine purpose in the liberation of the Hebrews. 2. *He controls through external circumstances.* These modify a man's words and deeds. Even after he has spoken, they give point and direction to what he has said and done.

Ver. 4.—*The purpose of creation.* It is commonly asserted that God made the world in love, that he created it from the goodness of his heart, because he desired to have creatures to bless. From this point of view, creation represents grace, giving, surrender, sacrifice, on the part of God. But another and apparently a contrary view is suggested by the words before us. Here it would seem that God created all things from self-regarding motives, as a man makes a machine for his own use. The contradiction, however, is only superficial. For if we take the second view, we must still bear in mind what the character of God is. Now, God is revealed to us as essentially love. Therefore only those things will please him that agree with love. A cruel Being might make for himself creatures that would amuse him by exhibiting contortions of agony, but a fatherly Being will be best pleased by seeing his family truly good and happy. If the universe is made to please Divine love, it must be made for blessedness. Yet it cannot be made for selfish happiness. It must be created so as to find its own good in God, and thus to give itself up to him as the End of its being. Apply this principle—

I. In regard to the universe at large. The law of gravitation is universal. All things tend to rush to their centres of attraction. In a large way the universe is drawn to God, its Centre. 1. *It is ever more and more realizing the purpose of God.* This is seen in all growth—the seed becomes the flowering plant, etc. It is strikingly exemplified in the doctrine of evolution. The great thought of God concerning the universe is slowly emerging into fact. 2. *It is continually approaching the thought of God.* The higher orders of creatures are nearer to the nature and thought of the Infinite Spirit than the lower. The upward movement is a Godward movement. 3. *It is growingly fulfilling the purpose of God.* From the formless and void past the universe moves on to "one far-off Divine event," when God's will shall be completely accomplished.

II. In regard to evil. Evil in itself, moral evil, cannot have been made by God, who is only holy. But in two respects evil may come within God's purposes. 1. *Physical evil directly works out God's purposes.* It is only evil to our eyes, as shadows look gloomy and winter feels painful. Really it is good, because it is part of the whole good plan of the universe. God sends pain in love, that the issue of it may be the higher blessedness of his children. 2. *Moral evil will be overruled for Divine purposes.* The bad man has his uses. Nebuchadnezzar was essential to the chastisement of Israel. Judas Iscariot was an agent in the chain of events that issued in Christ's great work of redemption.

III. In regard to individual souls. We are all made for God. He is the End of our being, not only as the home and rest we need, but as the goal after which we should aim. The great aim of Christ's work is to bring all things in subjection to God, that he "may be All in all" (1 Cor. xv. 28). The mistake of men is in seeking their own good first, even though this be the higher good of "other-worldliness." For our great end is to forget self in God.

Ver. 24.—*Pleasant words.* I. PLEASANT WORDS ARE GOOD IN SOCIAL INTERCOURSE. They are said to cost little, while they are worth much. But often they are not to be had without trouble. 1. *Sympathy.* We must put ourselves to the trouble of entering into our brother's feelings if we would speak with real kindness to him. 2. *Self-suppression.* Angry words may be the first to rise to our lips; bitter words of scorn or melancholy words springing from the gloom of our own minds may come more readily than the pleasant words that are due to our neighbours. 3. *Thought.* Words of honey soon cloy if no satisfying thoughts lie behind them. Pleasant words should be more than words—they should be messengers of healing, suggestions of helpfulness. Now, as some trouble is required for the production of this kind of speech in daily intercourse, it is well to consider how valuable it is. It draws hearts together. It lightens the load of life and oils its wheels. There are enough of clouds about the souls of most men to make it desirable that we should shed all the sunshine that we possibly can. It would be like a migration from Northern gloom to Southern sunshine for all speech to be seasoned with truly pleasant words.

II. PLEASANT WORDS ARE NEEDED IN CHRISTIAN TEACHING. The preacher is not to be a false prophet of smooth sayings, whispering, " Peace, peace," when there is no peace. There are times when hard words must be spoken, and most unpleasant truths do need to be driven home to unwilling hearers. But it will be only the pressing necessity of the subject that will force men of tender hearts to utter painful words. When the topic is not of this character, the most winning words should be chosen. 1. *In teaching the young.* The gloom of some good people has repelled the young. Children ought to see the sunny side of religion. All who are themselves bright and happy should know that there is a greater gladness for them in Christ. The preacher of the gospel belies his message when he proclaims it like a funeral dirge. 2. *In interesting the careless.* We cannot frown men into the Church. If we show the attractiveness of the gospel by cheerful manners, we help to commend it to the world. 3. *In comforting the sorrowful.* It is not necessary to speak sad words to the sad in order to prove our sympathy. It should be our aim to lighten the load of their sorrow.

III. PLEASANT WORDS ARE FOUND IN THE GOSPEL OF CHRIST. Christ preached so that " the common people heard him gladly." Men wondered at the " gracious words " that fell from his lips. Christianity is a religion of Divine grace. Surely there must be found many pleasant words in the description of it. The words of the gospel are pleasant, in particular, on several accounts. 1. *They tell of God's love.* 2. *They portray Christ.* 3. *They invite men to salvation.* 4. *They reveal the blessedness of the kingdom of heaven.*

Ver. 25.—*The treacherous path.* What way have we here referred to? If the path be so deceptive, surely the guide should indicate it. Yet the way to destruction is not named, nor is its place pointed out on the chart of life. No doubt the reason of this indefiniteness of expression is just that the dangerous way is a broad road, very easy to discover, yet there are many tracks along it, and each person may take his own course. It is so broad that any description of it may possibly leave out some of its devious paths. Therefore it is better only to indicate its character and leave it for each to consider the warning, that an attractive appearance in the path is no proof of a safe end.

I. THE APPARENT RIGHTNESS OF THE WAY. 1. *The fact.* It is not only said that the way of death is attractive, like a smooth garden-path winding among flower-beds, while the way of life is a steep and rugged mountain-track; but this way even seems to be right. There is an apparent justification for following it. Conscience is in danger of being deluded into giving it a quasi-sanction. 2. *The cause.* We are always tempted to condone the agreeable. If no danger is apparent, sanguine minds refuse to believe that they are approaching one. Convention simulates conscience. The multitude who tread the broad way tempt us into trusting the sanction of their example. It is difficult to believe that that is wrong which fashion encourages. 3. *The limitations.* (1) The way only " seemeth " right. We need to be guarded against succumbing to the bondage of appearances. The question is not as to what a thing seems, but what it is. (2) It is right in the eyes of the man who is tempted to follow it. But it is not right in the eyes of God. We have to look to the higher standard of

God's approval. It is of no use that our course seems right to ourselves if it is wrong before God. On the other hand, it may be objected that these considerations destroy the validity of conscience; for if we are not to follow our own conscience, what higher guide can we have? The answer may be threefold. (1) Seeming right may not be the verdict of our true consciences, but only the too readily accepted conclusion of more worldly considerations. (2) Conscience may be perverted. (3) At all events, while we have the light of revelation in Scripture and especially in Christ, we have a guide for conscience, to neglect which is to be left without excuse.

II. THE FATAL END OF THE WAY. 1. *The importance of the end.* The great question is—Whither are we going? The purpose of a road is not to serve as a platform for stationary waiting, but to lead to some destination. It is foolish for the traveller to neglect the sign-post, and only follow the attractiveness of the road, if he wishes to reach his home. In life the value of the course chosen is determined by its issues. 2. *The character of the end.* The end is "the way of death." This is true of every course of sin. Dark and dreadful, without qualification of any kind, this goal ever stands at the end of the way of wickedness. Disappointment may come first, and sorrow, and weariness; it will be well for us if they warn us before we take the final plunge into soul-destruction. 3. *The manner of reaching the end.* The pleasant way does not lead directly into the pit of destruction. It is only a preliminary stage in the downward journey. It brings the traveller to "the ways" of death. It may be regarded as a by-path running into the broad road. There are questionable amusements and dangerous friendships that are not themselves fatal, but they incline the careless to ways of evil. They are perilous as subtle tempters fashioned like angels of light.

Ver. 31.—*The glory of old age.* I. OLD AGE MAY BE CROWNED WITH GLORY IN THE COMPLETION OF LIFE. It is not natural to die in youth. We talk of the bud gathered before it has opened on earth, that it may bloom with perfection in heaven, etc.; but we must confess that there is a great mystery in the death of children. If God so wills it, it is better to live through the whole three score years and ten into full old age. The broken column is the symbol of the unfinished life. "Such a one as Paul the aged" could say, "I have finished my course." 1. *Life is good.* It may be sorrow-stricken and it may be wrecked on the rocks of sin. Then, indeed, it is evil. There was one of whom it was said, "It had been good for that man if he had not been born" (Matt. xxvi. 24). But in itself life is good. Men in mental sanity prize it. The Old Testament idea of the value of a full long life is more healthy than the sickly sentimentalism that fancies an early death to be a Heaven-sent boon. 2. *Time is for service.* Therefore the longer the time allotted to one, the more opportunity is there for doing good. This, again, may be abused and misspent in sin. But the old age of a good man means the completion of a long day's work. Surely it is an honour to be called into the field in the early morning of life, and to be permitted to toil on till the shadows descend on a long summer evening.

II. OLD AGE MAY BE CROWNED WITH GLORY IN ITS OWN ATTAINMENTS. A bad old age presents a hideous picture. A hoary-headed sinner is, indeed, a spectacle of horror. Mere old age is not venerable in itself. Reverence for years implies a belief that the years have gathered in a harvest of venerable qualities. Old age has its defects, not only in bodily frailty, but in a certain mental stiffening. Thus Lord Bacon says, "Men of age object too much, consult too long, adventure too little, repent too soon, and seldom drive business home to the full period, but content themselves with a mediocrity of success;" and Madame de Staël says, "To resist with success the frigidity of old age, one must combine the body, the mind, and the heart; to keep these in parallel vigour one must exercise, study, and love." But, on the other hand, there are inward attainments of a ripe and righteous old age that give to the late autumn of life a mellow flavour which is quite unknown in its raw summer. "Age is not all decay," says a modern novelist; "it is the ripening, the swelling, of the fresh life within, that withers and bursts the husk." It has been remarked that women are most beautiful in youth and in old age. The wisdom, the judiciousness, the large patience with varieties of opinion which should come with experience, are not always found in old people, who sometimes stiffen into bigotry and freeze into dreary customs. But when these graces are found in a large and healthy soul, no stage of life can approach the glory of old age.

Even when there is not capacity for such attainments, there is a beautiful serenity of soul that simpler people can reach, and that makes their very presence to be a benediction.

III. OLD AGE MAY BE CROWNED WITH GLORY IN ITS PREPARATION FOR THE FUTURE. In unmasking the horrible aspect of death and revealing the angel-face beneath, Christianity has shed a new glory over old age. It is the vestibule to the temple of a higher life. The servant of God has been tried and disciplined by blessing, suffering, and service. At length he is "meet for the inheritance of the saints in light." He can learn to resist the natural melancholy of declining powers with the vision of renewed energy in the heavenly future. Or, if he cares for rest, he may know that it will be a rest with Christ, and he can say, with the typical aged saint Simeon, "Lord, now lettest thou thy servant depart in peace, for mine eyes have seen thy salvation."

Ver. 32.—*Self-control.* The world has always made too much of military glory. From the days of the Pharaohs, when brutal monarchs boasted of the number of cities they had sacked, to our own time, when successful generals receive thanks in Parliament, and grants of money far beyond the highest honours and emoluments ever bestowed upon the greatest and most useful civilians, it has been the habit of men to flatter and pamper soldiers out of all proportion to their deserts. But we are here reminded of a simple and private victory which is really greater than one of those great military exploits that send a shock of amazement round the world. It is a more noble feat to be able to rule one's own spirit than to capture a city. Consider some of the ways in which this supreme excellence of self-control is apparent.

I. IT IS GREATER IN EFFORT. In ancient days, before the invention of heavy ordnance, a siege taxed all the energies of the most skilful and powerful general. This provincial city of Jerusalem was long able to hold out against the legions of Rome. But self-control is even more difficult. 1. *The enemy is within.* The war of the soul is a civil war. We may be successful in external life, and yet unable to cope with the inner foes of our own hearts. 2. *The enemy is turbulent.* Some races are harder to rule than others; but no half-savage, wholly fanatical dervishes, could be more fierce than the wild passions that rage within a man's own breast. 3. *The enemy has acquired great power.* The uprising of passion is not a veiled sedition; it is out-and-out rebellion. Long habit has given it a sort of vested interest in the privileges of its lawlessness. 4. *The enemy is subtle.* "The heart is deceitful above all things." It is plotting treason when all looks safe. The careless soul slumbers over a mine of dynamite in the region of its own passions. It needs a supreme effort to quell and curb and rule such a foe.

II. IT IS GREATER IN RESULTS. At first sight this proposition must appear absurd. The man who curbs his own spirit does something inward, private, secret. The man who takes a city makes his mark on history. How can the self-control be the more fruitful thing? 1. *It means more to the individual man.* The successful general has won a name of glory. Yet at its best it is but superficial and empty. He may be despising himself while the world is shouting his praises. But the strong soul that has learnt to control itself has the inward satisfaction of its self-mastery. 2. *It means more to the world.* Weak men may win a temporary success, but in the long run their inner feebleness is certain to expose itself. Such men may take a city, but they cannot rule it. They may do startling things, but not really great things, and the mischief of their follies will be more disastrous than the gain of their successes.

III. IT IS GREATER IN CHARACTER. True greatness is not to be measured by achievements, which depend largely upon external circumstances. One man has an opportunity of doing something striking, and another is denied every chance. Yet the obscure person may be really far greater than the fortunate instrument of victory. True greatness is in the soul. He is great who lives a great soul-life, while a Napoleon may be mean in spite of his brilliant powers and achievements. In the sight of Heaven he stands highest who best fights the enemies in his own breast, because he exercises the highest soul-powers. It is the province of Christian grace to substitute the glory of self-victory for the vulgar glare of military success.

Ver. 33.—*The lottery of life.* I. LIFE APPEARS TO BE A LOTTERY. "The lot is cast into the lap." We seem to depend largely on chance. 1. *We are ignorant of important facts.* We are obliged to grope our way through many dark places. Life comes to us veiled in mystery. It may be that certain material considerations would greatly modify our action if only we knew them, yet we must act without regard to them, from sheer ignorance. 2. *We cannot predict the future.* Even when we do grasp the essential points of our situation in the present, we cannot tell what new possibilities may emerge. A sudden turn of the kaleidoscope may give an entirely novel complexion to life. 3. *We are unable to master our circumstances.* We find ourselves surrounded by innumerable influences which we may understand, more or less, but which we cannot alter. Sometimes it appears as though we were no more free agents than the driftwood that is cast up on the beach by the angry surf. Circumstances are too strong for us, and we must let circumstances take their course. 4. *We cannot control the course of events.* Many things happen quite outside the range of our lives, yet their results will strike across the path of our own actions. Other people are busy planning and working, and we do not all consult together and work in harmony. When many hands throw the shuttle it is impossible to bring out any sure design.

II. God disposes of the lottery of life. Voltaire says, "Chance is a word void of sense; nothing can exist without a cause." It is but a name for our ignorance of the course of events. Nevertheless, if there were no mind behind the apparent confusion of life, universal causation would but give us a blind and purposeless fate—no better, surely, than a wild and chaotic chance. But to one who believes in God the terrible uncertainty of the lottery of life is a great reason for prayer and trust. 1. *God knows all.* He knows every fact, and he foresees the whole future. Herein we have a grand reason for faith. One who knows so much more than we do must needs often act in a way that we do not understand. But his infinite knowledge is a reason for our unlimited trust in him. 2. *God controls all.* Events seem to be tossed about in the lap of chance. Yet just as surely as laws of motion govern the slightest movement of all the leaves that are blown by an autumn wind, Divine purposes control all human events, in the midst of their seeming confusion. This must be so if God is God.

> "He maketh kings to sit in sovereignty;
> He maketh subjects to their power obey;
>   He pulleth down, he setteth up on high;
>   He gives to this, from that he takes away;
>   For all we have is his; what he will do, he may."

(Spenser.)

HOMILIES BY VARIOUS AUTHORS.

Vers. 1—3.—*The rule and guidance of Jehovah.* I. God the Object and fulfilment of human desire. We are wishful, craving creatures, "with no language but a sigh." The answer of the praying tongue and heart is God himself—in the fulness of his wisdom and love, the generosity of his gifts, the accessibility of his presence. A philosopher of this century actually taught that God was the Creator of human wishes and imagination. Let us rather say, it is God who creates and calls forth the longings of the finite heart, which (as Augustine says) is restless till it rests in him.

II. God the Corrector of our false judgments. (Ver. 2.) We are prone to judge of actions and choices by their *æsthetic* value, *i.e.* by reference to our feeling of pleasure and pain; God pronounces on their *ethical* value, their relation to his Law and to the ideal of our own being.

III. God the Support of our weakness. (Ver. 3.) What is the source of all care and over-anxiety, but that we are unequal to the conflict with laws mightier than our frail energies and endeavours? Without God, we stand trembling in the presence of a giant fate which can crush us. But there is no such fate to the believer in God, only a holy power and immovable will. "We are a care to the gods," said Socrates. Much more can the Christian say this, and learn to get rid of his troubles by making them in childlike faith God's troubles, his cares God's cares. Our plans become fixed, our purposes firm, when we are conscious that they are God's plans and purposes being wrought out through us.—J.

Vers. 4—9.—*The administration of rewards and punishments.* I. THE MORAL DESIGNS OF GOD. (Ver. 4.) The creation is *teleological*; it has a beginning, a process, and an end in view, all determined by the will and wisdom of God. If this is true of every plant, of every mollusc, it is true of every man. We are formed to illustrate his praise. Disobedience, with its consequences, ratifies his just and holy laws.

II. THE MORAL FEELINGS OF GOD. (Ver. 5.) Only that which stands in a true relation to him can be true. Haughtiness and arrogance are, so to speak, in the *worst taste*. In the eyes of God they are not beautiful, and cannot escape his criticism and correction.

III. HIS PROVISION FOR THE OBLIVION OF GUILT AND THE CURE OF MORAL EVIL. (Ver. 6.) In social relations he has opened a fountain, sweet and healing, for mutual faults and sins. Love hides a multitude of sins. " I say unto thee, Her sins, which are many, are forgiven; for she loved much" (comp. Isa. lviii. 7; Dan. iv. 27). But prevention is better than healing, and in religion is the prophylactic against evil.

IV. GOD'S RECONCILING LOVE. (Ver. 7.) What sweeter pleasure does life yield than reconciliation? 'Tis a deeper blessing than peace which has never been broken. Life is full of the principle of opposition; and God is manifested, first in the drawing of us to himself, and then in the union of estranged human hearts to one another.

V. THE LAW OF COMPENSATION. (Ver. 8.) He hath set the one over against the other, that we should seek nothing after him. Poverty has great advantages, if we will see it so—is more favourable, on the whole, to moral health than the reverse condition. And the hard crust of honest poverty, how sweet! the luxurious living of the dishonest rich, how insipid! or how bitter!

VI. DIVINE RECTIFICATIONS. (Ver. 9.) We must take heed to our own way; yet with all our care, we cannot ensure right direction or security. We need God's rectification and criticism at every point, and hence should ever say to ourselves, " If the Lord will, we will do this or that" (Jas. iv. 15). The blending of human with Divine counsel, human endeavour with God's guidance, may defy analysis, but is known in experience to be *real.*—J.

Vers. 10—15.—*Divine and human authority.* I. THE DERIVATION OF AUTHORITY AND LAW FROM GOD. (Ver. 10.) The true ruler is the representative of God. Royal decrees and legal statutes profess to rest, and must rest ultimately, if they are to be binding, upon the moral Law itself. Hence the reverence in old days for " the Lord's anointed," though in the person of a Charles Stuart, was the popular witness to a deep truth, which lies at the foundation of society.

II. PRINCIPLES OF STABLE RULE. (Ver. 11.) The pair of scales have ever been viewed as the emblems of justice, and so the expressions, symbolically, of the nature of God. The second allusion is to the stone weights which the Oriental merchant carries in his bag, serving the purpose the more exactly, as not liable to rust. The exact balance and the just weight, then, if symbols of Jehovah, must be the symbols of every righteous human government.

III. THE PRINCIPLES OF ROYAL FAVOUR AND DISFAVOUR. (Vers. 12—15.) 1. The ruler must be of *pure sentiment, abhorring all kinds of immorality*, keeping his court pure, "rearing the white flower of a blameless life in the fine light that beats upon the throne." How much we owe in these respects to the example of our sovereign and her husband is written on the thankful heart of every religious Englishman. 2. *Strong moral convictions.* That the throne securely rests, not upon might, but right; not upon bayonets, but upon the Word of God. The influence proceeding from such a mind will be constantly felt as antipathetic to falsehood and corruption, and the other eating mildews of high places. 3. *Sympathy with honest policies.* How common is it to assume that politics have little or nothing to do with morality! No one who believes in the teaching of his Bible can accept such a dogma. He who acts upon it is already a traitor to his country and his God. As Greece had its Demosthenes, who has been called a "saint in politics," so we have had, thank God, in our time men of eloquent tongue and true heart in the national councils. May their line and tradition never become extinct! 4. *Their dread judicial power.* (Ver. 14.) The authorities who represent the penal powers of law are a terror to evil-doers. There must be the power to punish. And a measured and well-tempered severity does in a sense "reconcile" numbers, not to be affected otherwise, to a course of law-abiding and just conduct. 5. *The attractions of their smile.* (Ver. 15.) Ever, while human nature continues what it is, the smile of the sovereign, the tokens of his favour—the star, the medal, the garter, the uniform—will be sought after with eagerness and worn with pride. There may be a side of idle vanity in this, yet equally a side of good. It is good to seek association with greatness, though the ideal of greatness may often be mistaken. Only let us see that there is no real greatness which does not in some way reflect the majesty of God.—J.

Vers. 16—26.—*The Divine justice in respect to the wise and fools.* We see the moral order of God revealed in the character and life of men in various ways. Their conduct has a good or evil effect on themselves, on their fellows, and is exposed to Divine judgment. Let us take these in their order.

I. THE REFLEXIVE EFFECT OF MAN'S CONDUCT. 1. Wisdom is *enriching* (ver. 16). To acquire it is better than ordinary wealth (ch. iii. 14; viii. 10, 11, 19). 2. Rectitude is *safety* (ver. 17). It is a levelled and an even way, the way of the honest and good man; not, indeed, always to his own feeling, but in the highest view, "He that treads it, trusting surely to the right, shall find before his journey closes he is close upon the shining table-lands to which our God himself is Sun and Noon." The only true way of self-preservation is the way of right. 3. The *truth of contrast* (ver. 18). Pride foretells ruin; the haughty spirit, overthrow and destruction (ch. xv. 25, 33). The thunderbolts strike the lofty summits, and leave unharmed the kneeling vale; shiver the oak, and pass harmless over the drooping flower. We are ever safe upon our knees, or in the attitude of prayer. A second contrast appears in ver. 19. The holy life with scant fare better than a proud fortune erected on unjust gains.

> "He that is down need fear no fall;
> He that is low, no pride."

4. The *effect of religious principle* (ver. 20). We need constantly to carry all conduct into this highest light, or trace it to this deepest root. Piety here includes two things: (1) obedience to positive command; (2) living trust in the personal God. Happiness and salvation are the fruit. "I have had many things in my hands, and have lost them all. Whatever I have been able to place in God's hands, I still possess" (Luther).

II. EFFECTS IN RELATION TO OTHERS. 1. The good man is *pleasing* to others (vers. 21, 24). There is a grace on his lips, a charm in his conversation, in a "speech alway with grace, seasoned with salt." How gladly men listened to our great Exemplar, both in public and in private! Thus, too, the good man sweetens instruction, and furthers its willing reception in the mind of his listeners. 2. He earns a good reputation for *sense, discretion, prudence* (vers. 21, 22). And this not only adds to his own happiness (for we cannot be happy without the good will of our fellows), but it gives weight to his teaching (ver. 23). The teacher can produce little effect whose words stand not out in relief from the background of character. The true emphasis is supplied by the life. 3. The *contrast* (ver. 22). The folly of fools is self-chastising. The fool makes himself disagreeable to others; even if he chances upon a sound word or right action, it is devoid of the value and weight which only character can give. He incurs prejudice and opposition on every hand, sows thorns in his own path, and invites his own destruction.

III. THE PRINCIPLE OF DIVINE JUDGMENT IN ALL. Every one of these effects marks in its way the expression of the Divine will, the laws of a Divine order. But, above all, the *end* determines the value of choice and the quality of life. The great distinction between the *seeming* and the *real* is the distinction between facts as they appear in the light of our passions, our wishes, our lusts, our various illusions and self-deceptions, and facts as they are in the clear daylight of eternal truth and a judgment which cannot err (ver. 25). To guard against the fatal illusions that beset us, we should ask: 1. Is this course of conduct according to the definite rules of conduct as they are laid down in God's Word? 2. Is it according to the best examples of piety? Above all, is it Christ-like, God-like?—J.

Ver. 26.—*The blessing of hunger.* I. AT BOTTOM, HUNGER, THE NEED OF BREAD, IS THE GREAT STING AND GOAD TO ALL EXERTION, TO USEFUL ACTIVITY IN GENERAL.

II. HENCE HUNGER IS THE HELPER OF OUR TOIL. And we may thank God for every stimulus to do our best. Have not the best things been done for the world in every department by poor men?

III. AS APPLIED TO RELIGION, IT IS THE HUNGER OF THE SOUL WHICH PROMPTS US TO SEEK FOR RIGHTEOUSNESS; the emptiness of other joys which sends us to the feast of the gospel. Through toil and trouble, the worst unrest and distress can alone be overcome.—J.

Vers. 27—30.—*Penal judgments on guilt.* GODLESS STRIVINGS. Life is full of success and failure. There are successes which cost the soul, and failures in which is contained the reaping of life eternal. The activity of the worthless man (ver. 27). 1. It is *mischievous in spirit and in end.* He is depicted as one who digs a grave for others (ch. xxvi. 27; Jer. xviii. 20, *sqq.*). And his words are like fire that scorches, blasting reputation, withering the buds of opening good in the sentiment of the young, scoffing down the right and true. 2. It is *contentious;* breeding quarrels, creative of strife, introducing breaches between friends, disuniting households. "Envy and every evil work" is wherever he goes. 3. It is the activity of the *tempter,* the *seducer.* Not content with error himself, he would have partners in sorrow and in guilt. It is thus truly *diabolical.* 4. It is *meditated* and *determined* (ver. 30). Very striking is the picture of this verse—the eyes half closed, the bit lips, the firm line about the mouth of one resolved on dark designs and their determined execution. What a power is thought for good or evil! Oh for its right direction by the loving and creative Spirit of all wisdom and goodness, that it may be ever inventive of kind and healing deeds, that may "seal up the avenues of ill," rather than open them more widely to the processions of darkness and hate!—J.

Vers. 31, 32.—*The gentle life.* Portrayed with exquisite sweetness and beauty.

I. AN HONOURED AGE. The biblical pictures of the aged pious are very charming, and Polycarp, with his eighty-six years upon him, passing to another crown, that of martyrdom, is sublime; also "Paul the aged and the prisoner." The text points out what we must all recognize for an æsthetic truth, that it is the association of age with goodness which makes it truly respectable, venerable, beautiful.

II. MORAL HEROISM. The heathen type of heroism was strength of arm—bodily strength, manly courage against an outward foe. The spiritual and the Christian type is in strength of will against evil, self-mastery, self-conquest, sublime patience. Better than to be members of any knightly order, "Companions" of the Bath, or any similar society speaking of the lower and carnal virtues, to be "companions in tribulation, and in the kingdom and patience of Jesus Christ."—J.

Ver. 33.—*Chance and providence.* I. CHANCE IS BUT AN EXPRESSION OF HUMAN IGNORANCE. When we speak of that which is contingent, we mean something the law of which is not yet known.

II. MAN'S CONTROL OVER EVENTS IS LIMITED. We can give the external occasion to a decision; the decision itself rests with a higher power.

III. GOD OVERRULES ALL THINGS, AND OVERRULES THEM FOR THE BEST. To pretend that we are not free is to deny our nature, and so to deny him; and it is also a denial of him to think that we can be absolute masters of our fate. Between night and day—truths that are obscure and convictions that are clear—our life is balanced. Life rests on two pillars—the providence of God and the responsibility of man.—J

Vers. 1, 3, 9.—*Thought, action, prayer.* It may be said that the three main elements of human experience are those of thinking, of acting, and of praying. We have not done our best until we have done all of these.

I. Thought. "The preparations of the heart belong to man" (Revised Version). "Thy thoughts" ("thy purposes," Revised Version). We are told of Peter, after the denial, that "when he *thought* thereon, he wept" (Mark xiv. 72). But if he had thought beforehand what grief he would cause his Master by such unworthiness, he would not have had occasion to weep at all. "When Judas saw that he was condemned, he repented." But if he had thought, he would have seen that this was the plain and inevitable issue of his action. The pity is that we do not think as we should before we act. The preparation of the heart belongs to us; it is our most bounden duty to think, and to think well, before we act. And we must remember that *speech is action*, and often most important and decisive action too. We should include in our thought, when we are forming our "purposes" (Revised Version), the consideration of the effects of our prepared action upon (1) our whole nature—bodily, mental, spiritual; (2) our family and our friends; (3) our neighbours and associates; (4) our fellow-worshippers and fellow-workers; (5) the cause of Jesus Christ; (6) not only the immediate, but the further future. We should, so far as we can, think the whole subject through, look at it from all those points of view that we command; above all, we should take a decreasingly selfish and an increasingly generous and devout view of the subjects that come before us.

II. Action. "Thy works." Thought must be followed by vigorous effort, or it will "lose the name of action." Our works include not only those industries in which we are professionally engaged,—these are of great importance to us, as those which occupy the greater part of our time and most of our strength; but they include also our contributions, larger or smaller, worthy or unworthy, to the condition of our homes, to the character and the destiny of our children, to the comfort and well-being of our dependents or our employers, to the improvement of our locality, to the stability and freedom and success of the institutions (social, literary, ecclesiastical, municipal, national) upon which we can bring any influence to bear. We may move in a humble sphere, and yet, when all is told that the chronicles of heaven can tell, we may include in a busy and conscientious life many "works" that will not want the Divine approval or the blessing of mankind.

III. Prayer. "The answer of the tongue is from the Lord . . . and thy thoughts shall be established." The two clauses imply, respectively, (1) that God sometimes makes other issues to result than those which we expect; (2) that God continually brings to pass that which we strive to accomplish, especially when we commend our cause to his Divine favour. The practical conclusions are these, respectively: 1. That we must be quite willing for the hand of God to give a different direction to our activities; quite prepared to accept another issue from that which we had set before our own minds. For God "seeth not as we see," and he works out his gracious purposes in other ways than those of our choosing. 2. That we should always realize our dependence on God for a favourable issue, and earnestly ask his blessing on our labour. It is the touch of his Divine hand that must quicken into life, that must crown with true success.—C.

Ver. 2.—(See homily on ver. 25.)—C.

Ver. 6.—*The penitent's review and prospect.* Placing ourselves in the position of the man who has sinned and suffered, and has been led to repentance and submission, of the man who is earnestly desirous of escaping from the sinful past and of becoming a new man and of living a new life, let us ask—What is his hope? what are his possibilities?

I. In view of the past and of his relations with God. What is his hope there? What are the possibilities of his sins being forgiven, his iniquity purged away? What he must rely upon, in this great domain of thought, is this—*truth in himself* and *mercy in God*. 1. He himself must be a true penitent, one that '

> ". . . feels the sins he owns,
> And hates what he deplores;"

that intends with full purpose of heart to turn from all iniquity and to cleave to righteousness and purity. 2. He must cast himself on the boundless mercy of God gained for him and promised to him in Jesus Christ his Saviour.

II. IN VIEW OF THE PAST AND OF HIS RELATIONS WITH MEN. God accepts true penitence of spirit and right purpose of heart, for he can read our hearts, and knows what we really are. But *man* wants more. Before he receives the sinner to his confidence and restores him to the position from which he fell, he wants clear proofs of penitence, manifestations of a new and a clean heart. The man who has put away his sin can only "purge" the guilty past by the practice of "mercy and truth," of kindness and integrity, of grace and purity. He has done that which is wrong, false, hurtful. Let him now do that which is just, true, right; that which is kind, helpful, pitiful, generous; then we shall see that he means all that he says, that his professions are sincere; then he may be taken back—his iniquity purged—to the place which he has lost.

III. IN VIEW OF THE FUTURE, HAVING REGARD TO HIMSELF. How shall the penitent make good the promises he has made to his friends? How shall he ensure his future probity and purity? how shall he engage to walk in love and in the path of holy service, as he is bound to do, taking on him the name of Christ? The answer is, by walking on *in reverence* of spirit, by proceeding in "the fear of the Lord;" thus will he "depart from evil," and do good. It is the man who cultivates a reverent spirit, who realizes the near presence of God, who walks with God in prayer and holy fellowship, who treasures in his mind the thoughts of God, and reminds himself frequently of the will of God concerning him—it is he who will "never be moved from his integrity;" he will redeem his word of promise, he will live the new and better life of faith and holiness and love.—C.

Ver. 11 (and see ch. xi. 1; xx. 10, 23).—*Honesty in business.* The repetition of this maxim (see above) is an indication of the importance that should be attached to the subject. It is one that affects a very large proportion of mankind, and that affects men nearly every day of their life. The text reminds us—

I. THAT BUSINESS IS WITHIN THE PROVINCE OF RELIGION. The man who says, "Business is business, and religion is religion," is a man whose moral and spiritual perceptions are sadly confused. "God's commandment is exceeding broad," and its breadth is such as will cover all the transactions of the market. Commerce and trade, as much as agriculture, are "the Lord's;" it is an order of human activity which is in full accord with his design concerning us; and it is a sphere into which he expects us to introduce our highest principles and convictions, in which we may be always serving him.

II. THAT DISHONESTY IS OFFENSIVE IN HIS SIGHT. "A false balance is his abomination" (ch. xi. 1; xx. 10). Dishonesty is evil in his sight, inasmuch as: 1. It is a flagrant violation of one of his chief commandments. The second of all the commandments is this, "Thou shalt love thy neighbour as thyself" (see Matt. xxii. 29). But to cheat our neighbour in the market is to do to him what we should strenuously protest against his doing to us. 2. It is a distinct breach of what is due to our brother. It is a most unbrotherly action; it is an act done in conscious disregard of all the claims our fellow-men have on our consideration. Moreover, it is an injury to the society of which we are members; for it is one of those wrongs which are *crimes* as well as sins; it is an act which strikes at the root of all fellowship, all commerce between man and man. 3. It is an injury done by a man to himself. No man can rob his brother without wronging his own soul. He is something the worse for every act of dishonesty he perpetrates. And he who is systematically defrauding his neighbours is daily cutting into his own character, is continually staining his own spirit, is destroying himself.

III. THAT HONESTY IS ACCEPTABLE TO GOD. "A just weight is his delight." Not that all honest dealing is equally acceptable to him. Much here, as everywhere, depends upon the motive. A man may be honest only because it is the best policy, because he fears the exposure and penalty of fraud: there is small virtue in that. On the other hand, he may be strictly fair and just in all his dealings, whether his work be known or unknown, because he has a conviction of what is due to his neighbour, or because he has an abiding sense of what God would have him be and do. In this case his honesty is as truly an act of piety, of holy service, as was a sacrifice at the temple of Jehovah, as is a prayer in the sanctuary of Christ. It is an act rendered " unto the Lord," and it is well-pleasing in the sight of God his Saviour; he "serves the Lord Christ" (Col. iii. 23, 24). It is a great thing that we need not leave the shop or the ship, the office or the field, in order to render acceptable sacrifice unto the Lord our God. By simple conscientiousness, by sterling and immovable integrity, whatever the post we occupy, maintained by us with a view to the observant eye of our ever-present Master, we may honour and please him as much as if we were bowing in prayer or lifting up our voice in praise in the worship of his house. —C.

Ver. **16.**—(See homily on ch. viii. 10, 11.)—C.

Vers. 18, 19 (ch. xi. 2; xviii. 12).—*Pride and humility.* Great insistance is laid in Scripture on the evil of pride and the value of humility. The subject has a large place in those "thoughts of God," which are communicated to us in his Word.

I. The evil of pride. 1. *It is based on falsity.* For what has the richest or the strongest or the cleverest man, what has the most beautiful or the most honoured woman, that he or she has not received (1 Cor. iv. 7)? Ultimately, we owe *everything* to our Creator and Divine Benefactor; and the thought that our distinction is due to ourselves is an essentially false thought. Hence: 2. *It is irreverent and ungrateful;* for it is constantly forgetful of the heavenly source of all our blessings. 3. *It is ugly and offensive* in the sight of man. That self-respect which makes a man superior to all meanness and all unworthiness of himself is honourable and excellent in our eyes; but pride, which is an overweening estimate of our own importance or virtue, is wholly unbeautiful; it marks a man's character as a scar marks his countenance; it makes the subject of it a man whom we look upon with aversion rather than delight—our soul finds no pleasure in regarding him. It is positively offensive to our spirit. 4. *It is repeatedly and severely condemned by God* as a serious sin (ch. viii. 13; Ps. xii. 3; xxxi. 23; ci. 5; cxxxviii. 6; Isa. ii. 12; Mark vii. 22; 1 Tim. iii. 6; 2 Tim. iii. 2; Jas. iv. 6, etc.). 5. It is spiritually perilous in a very high degree. No truth is more constantly illustrated than that of the text, "Pride goeth before destruction," etc. Pride begets a false confidence; this begets unwariness, and leads into the place of danger; and then comes the fall. Sometimes it is in *health;* at other times, in *business;* or it may be in *office* and in *power;* or, alas! it may be in *morals* and in *piety.* There is no field of human thought and action in which pride is not a most dangerous guide. It leads up to and (only too often) over the precipice.

II. The excellence of humility. "Better to be of a humble spirit with the lowly," etc. And it is better because, while pride is open to all these condemnations (as above), humility is to be commended and to be desired for the opposite virtues. 1. It is founded on a true view of our own hearts. The lowlier the view we take of ourselves, the truer the estimate we form. There *is* a lowliness of word and demeanour that is feigned and that is false. A man may be "proud of his humility," and may declaim his own sins with a haughty heart. But real humility is based on a thorough knowledge of our own nature, of its weakness and its openness to evil; on a full acquaintance with our own character, with its imperfection and liability to fail us in the trying hour. 2. It is admirable in itself. We do not, indeed, admire servility; we detest it heartily. But we do admire genuine humility. It is a very valuable adornment of a Christian character; it graces an upright life with a beauty no other quality can supply. There is no one whom it does not become, whom it does not make much more attractive than he (or she) would otherwise be. 3. It is the very gateway into the kingdom of God. It is the humble heart, conscious of error and of sin, that seeks the Teacher and the Saviour. It is the guide which conducts our spirit straight to the feet and to the cross of our Redeemer. 4. It is an attribute of Christian character which commends us to the love and to the favour of our Lord. 5. It is the only ground on which we are safe. Pride is a slippery place, where we are sure to slip and fall; humility is the ground where devotion finds its home, which a reverent trustfulness frequents, where God is ready with the shield of his guardianship, from which temptation shrinks away, where human souls live in peace and purity and attain to their maturity in Jesus Christ their Lord.—C.

Ver. 25 (see ch. xiv. 12).—*The supreme mistake.* We may well be startled, and we may well be solemnized, as we witness—

I. THE MARVELLOUS RANGE OF HUMAN COMPLACENCY. It is simply wonderful how men will allow themselves to be deceived respecting themselves. That which they ought to know best and most thoroughly, they seem to be least acquainted with—their own standing, their own spirit, their own character. They believe themselves to be all right when, in fact, they are all wrong. They suppose themselves to be travelling in one way when they are moving in the very opposite direction. This strange and sad fact in our experience applies to: 1. *Our direct relation to God.* We may be imagining ourselves reconciled to him, in favour with him, enjoying his Divine friendship, engaged on his side, promoting his kingdom, while, all the time, we are far from him, are condemned by him, are doing the work of his enemies, are injuring his cause and his kingdom. Witness the hypocrites of our Lord's time, and the formalists and ceremonialists of all times; witness also the persecutors of every age; witness those of every land and age who have failed to understand that it is he, and only he, who "doeth righteousness that is righteous" in the sight of God. 2. *Our relation to our fellow-men.* How often men have thought themselves just when they have been miserably unjust, kind when they have been heartlessly cruel, faithful when they have been guiltily disloyal! 3. *What we owe to ourselves.* Only too often men think that conduct pure which is impure, consistent with sobriety which is a distinct step toward insobriety, agreeable which is objectionable, safe which is seductive and full of peril.

II. THE DISASTROUS END OF A SERIOUS MISTAKE. The way seems right to a man, and he goes comfortably and even cheerily along it, but the end of it is—*death.* 1. In some cases this end is premature physical decline and dissolution. 2. In all cases it is spiritual decay and the threatened death of the soul, the departure and ultimate loss of all that makes human life honourable, all that makes a human spirit fair in the sight of God. 3. The death which is eternal.

III. OUR CLEAR WISDOM IN VIEW OF THIS POSSIBILITY. It is: 1. *To ask ourselves how we stand in God's sight.* Man may be accepting us on our own showing, but God does not do that. "The Lord weigheth the spirits" (ver. 2). He "looketh upon the heart;" he considers the aim that is before us and the spirit that is within us; what is the goal we are really seeking; what is the motive by which we are really animated; what is the deep desire and the honest and earnest endeavour of our heart. 2. *To be or to become right with him.* If we find ourselves wrong in his view, to humble our hearts before him; to seek his Divine forgiveness for all our wandering; to ask his guidance and inspiration to set forth upon a new course and to maintain it to the end. He alone can "show us the path of life."—C.

Ver. 28.—(See homily on ch. xvii. 9.)—C.

Ver. 31.—*The crown of old age.* Many are the crowns which, in imagination, we see upon the head. Many are eagerly desired and diligently sought; such are those of fame, of rank, of wealth, of power, of beauty. These are well enough in their way; but (1) that which is spent in winning them is often far more valuable than the good for which the sacrifice is made; and (2) the crown, when it is worn, usually weighs heavier and gives less satisfaction than was imagined in the ardour of pursuit. Old age is a crown. It is natural that men should desire it, for two reasons. 1. It means a *prolongation of life;* and life, under ordinary conditions, is greatly desired, so that men cling to it even tenaciously. 2. It means *the completion of the course of life.* Age is one of its natural stages. It has its privations, but it has also its own honours and enjoyments; those who have passed through life's other experiences may rightly wish to complete their course by wearing the hoary head of old age. But in connection with age, there is—

I. THE CROWN OF SHAME. For it is *not* always found in the way of righteousness. An old man who is still ignorant of those truths which he might have learned, but has neglected to gather; or who is addicted to dishonourable indulgences which he has had time to conquer, but has not subdued; or who yields to unbeautiful habits of the spirit which he should long ago have expelled from his nature and his life; or who has not yet returned unto that Divine Father who has been seeking and calling him all his days;—such an old man, with his grey hairs, wears a crown of dishonour rather than of glory. But while we may feel that he is to be condemned, we feel far more inclined to pity than to blame. For what is age not found in the way of righteousness —age without excellency, age without virtue, age uncrowned with faith and hope? Surely one of the most pitiable spectacles the world presents to our eyes. It is pleasant, indeed, to be able to regard—

II. THE CROWN OF HONOUR. When old age *is* found in the way of righteousness, it is a crown of honour, in that: 1. It has upon it the *reflection of an honourable past.* It speaks of past *virtues* that have helped to make it the " green old age " it is; of past *successes* that have been gained in the battle of life; of past *services* that have been diligently and faithfully rendered; of past *sorrows* that have been meekly borne; of past *struggles* that have been bravely met and passed; for it was in the rendering and in the bearing and in the meeting of these that the hair has been growing grey from year to year. 2. It has *the special excellency of the present.* " A crown of beauty " (marginal reading). In the " hoary head " and in the benignant countenance of old age there is a beauty which is all its own; it is a beauty which may not be observable to every eye, but which is there nevertheless; it is the beauty of spiritual worth, of trustfulness and repose, of calmness and quietness; it is *a* beauty if not *the* beauty of holiness. He who does not recognize in the aged that have grown old in the service of God and in the practice of righteousness something more than the marks of time, fails to see a crown of beauty that is visible to a more discerning eye. 3. It has *the blessed anticipation of the future.* It looks homeward and heavenward. A selfish and a worldly old age is grovelling enough; it " hugs its gold to the very verge of the churchyard mould; " but the age that is found in the ways of righteousness has the light of a glorious hope in its eyes; it wears upon its brows the crown of a peaceful and blessed anticipation of a *rest* that remains for it, of a *reunion* with the beloved that have gone on before, of a *beatific vision* of the Saviour in his glory, of a *larger life* in a nobler sphere, only a few paces further on.—C.

Ver. 32 (with ch. xiv. 17, 29).—*The command of ourselves.* Our attention is called to the two sides of the subject.

I. THE EVIL OF IMPATIENCE. How bad a thing it is to lose command of ourselves and to speak or act with a ruffled and disquieted spirit appears when we consider that : 1. It is *wrong.* God gave us our understanding, our various spiritual faculties, on purpose that we might have ourselves under control; and when we permit ourselves to be irritated and vexed, to be provoked to anger, we do that which crosses his Divine purpose concerning us and his expectation of us; we do that which disappoints and grieves our Father. 2. It is *a defeat.* We have failed to do that which was set us to do. The hour when our will is crossed is the hour of trial; then it is seen whether we succeed or fail; and when we lose control of our spirit we are defeated. 3. It is an *exhibition of folly.* He that is hasty of spirit " exalteth folly " (ch. xiv. 29). He gives another painful illustration of folly; he shows that he is not the wise man we could wish that he were. He shows once more how soon and how easily a good man may be overcome, and may be led from the path of wisdom. 4. It *conducts to evil.* " He that is soon angry will deal foolishly " (ch. xiv. 17). A man who loses the balance of a good temper will certainly " deal foolishly." We are never at our best when we are angry. Our judgment is disturbed; our mental faculties are disordered; they lose their true proportion. We do not speak as wisely, we do not act as judiciously, as we otherwise should. In all probability, we speak and act with positive folly, in a way which brings regret on our own part and reproach from our neighbour. Very possibly we say and do that which cannot easily, if ever, be undone. We take the bloom off a fair friendship; we plant a root of bitterness which we are not able to pluck up; we start a train of consequences which will run we know not whither.

II. THE TRUE CONQUEST. To be master of ourselves is to be " of great understanding," to be " better than the mighty," or than " he that taketh a city." It is so, inasmuch as : 1. It is an *essentially spiritual* victory. To take a city is, in part, to triumph over physical obstacles, over walls and moats and bullets; but he that ruleth his spirit is doing battle with evil tempers and unholy inclinations and unworthy impulses. He is striving " not against flesh and blood," but against the mightier enemies that couch and spring on the human soul; he is fighting with far nobler weapons than sword or bayonet or cannon—with thought, with spiritual energy, with deep resolve, with strenuous will, with conscience, with prayer. The victory is fought and won on the highest ground, the arena of a human spirit. 2. It is a *victory over ourself.* And this is worthier and better than one gained over another. (1) There is no humiliation in it; on the contrary, there is self-respect and a sense of true manfulness. (2) Our first duty is that we owe to ourselves. God has committed to each human spirit the solemn charge of his own character. We have other high and sacred functions to discharge, but the first and greatest of them all is to honour, to train, to rule, to cultivate, to ennoble, our own spirit. We are therefore carrying out the express will of God when we victoriously command ourselves. 3. It is *bloodless and beneficent.* The warrior may well forget the honours he has received when he is obliged to remember the cries of the wounded on the battle-field, and the tears of the widows and the orphans who are the victims of war. But he who rules his own spirit has no sad memories to recall, no heart-rending scenes to picture to his mind. His victories are unstained with blood; by the conquest of himself he has saved many a heart from being wounded by a hasty word, and he has preserved or restored that atmosphere in which alone happiness can live and prosperity abound.—C.

EXPOSITION.

CHAPTER XVII.

Ver. 1.—(Comp. ch. xv. 16, 17; xvi. 8.) **Better** (sweeter) **is a dry morsel, and quietness therewith.** Dry bread was soaked in wine or water before it was eaten. Thus Boaz bid Ruth "dip her morsel in the vinegar" (Ruth ii. 14); thus Jesus gave the sop to Judas when he had dipped it (John xiii. 26). The Septuagint is pleonastic, "Better is a morsel with joy in peace." Aben Ezra connects this verse with the last two of ch. xvi., confining the application to the patient man; but the sentence seems rather to be independent and general. **Than an house full of sacrifices with strife.** Of the thank or peace offerings part only was burnt upon the altar, the rest was eaten by the offerer and his family; and as the victims were always the choicest animals, "a house full of sacrifices" would contain the materials for sumptuous feasting (see on ch. vii. 14). The joyous family festival often degenerated into excess, which naturally led to quarrels and strife (see 1 Sam. i. 5, 6, 13; ii. 13, etc.). So the agapæ of the early Church were desecrated by licence and selfishness (1 Cor. xi. 20, etc.). Septuagint, "than a house full of many good things and unrighteous victims with contention." With this verse compare the Spanish proverb, "Mas vale un pedazo de pan con amor, que gallinas con dolor."

Ver. 2.—**A wise servant shall have rule over a son that causeth shame.** Here is intimated the supremacy of wisdom over folly and vice. The contrast is better emphasized by translating, *A servant that dealeth wisely shall have rule over a son that*

doeth shamefully; i.e. a son of his master. (For similar contrast between "wise" and "shameful," comp. ch. x. 5; xiv. 35.) Slaves were often raised to high honour, and might inherit their master's possessions. Thus Abraham's servant, Eliezer of Damascus, was at one time considered the patriarch's heir (Gen. xv. 2, 3); Ziba, Saul's servant, obtained the inheritance of his lord Mephibosheth ("the Shameful," 2 Sam. xvi. 4); Joseph was advanced to the highest post in Egypt. Ecclus. x. 25, "Unto the servant that is wise shall they that are free do service; and he that is wise will not grudge when he is reformed." Septuagint, "A wise household servant shall rule over foolish masters." "I have seen," says Ecclesiastes (x. 7), "servants upon horses, and princes walking as servants upon the earth." **Shall have part of the inheritance among the brethren;** shall share on equal terms with the sons of the house. This innovation on the usual disposition of property could happen only in the case of an abnormally intelligent and trusted slave. In 1 Chron. ii. 34, etc., mention is made of a case where a master, having no son, gave his daughter in marriage to a slave, and adopted him into the family. Delitzsch understands the clause to mean that the slave shall have the office of dividing his master's inheritance among the heirs, shall be the executor of his deceased master's will; but this explanation hardly seems to do justice to the merits of the "wise servant," and takes no account of the idea involved in "shameful son." But the Septuagint appears to countenance this view, rendering, "and among the brethren he shall divide the portions."

Ver. 3.—**The fining-pot is for silver, and the furnace for gold.** The word *matsreph*, "fining-pot," occurs also in ch. xxvii. 21. It is not certain what is meant by it. There is no evidence that the Israelites were acquainted with the use of acids in the manipulation of impure or mixed metals; otherwise the "pot" and the "furnace" would represent the two usual modes of reduction; but it is most probable that both allude to the same method of smelting the ore in crucibles, for the purpose of separating the pure metal from the dross. That silver and gold were plentiful in Solomon's time is abundantly evident; indeed, the amount of the precious metals collected by David and his son is almost incredible (see 1 Chron. xxii. 14; xxix. 2, etc., from which and similar passages it is inferred that the sums enumerated equalled more than nine hundred millions of pounds sterling). **But the Lord trieth the hearts** (ch. xv. 11; xxiv. 12). That which fire does for the metals, the Lord does for men's hearts; he purifies them from dross, brings forth the good that is in them, purged from earthly infirmities. God's process is the application of sorrow, sickness, temptation, that, duly meeting these, the soul may emerge from the trial as pure gold, fit for the Master's use (comp. Jer. xii. 3; Mal. iii. 2; 1 Pet. i. 7; Rev. iii. 18).

Ver. 4.—**A wicked doer giveth heed to false (evil) lips.** A bad man delights in and hearkens to evil words; he takes pleasure in those who counsel wickedness, because they are after his own heart. Like mates with like. **And a liar giveth ear to a naughty (*mischievous*) tongue.** One who is himself mendacious listens with avidity to any tale that may injure a neighbour, however monstrous and improbable it may be. Septuagint, "A wicked man listens to the tongue of transgressors; but a just man heedeth not false lips." The Greek adds here, or in some manuscripts, after ver. 6, a paragraph which is not found in the Hebrew, Syriac, or Latin: "To him who is faithful the whole world-wealth belongs; but the unfaithful is not worth an obole." On this the Fathers have frequently commented (see Corn. à Lapide, *in loc.*).

Ver. 5.—**Whoso mocketh the poor** (see ch. xiv. 31, which is nearly identical). He that is glad at calamities shall not be unpunished (ch. xi. 21; xxiv. 17, 18). The particular calamity primarily intended seems to be that which reduces a person to poverty. Delight in others' misfortunes, even those of enemies, is a most detestable form of selfishness and malice. Job, testifying to his own integrity, was thankful to think that he was free from this vice (Job xxxi. 29). The Greeks had a name for it, and called it

ἐπιχαιρεκακία, which is used by Aristotle (' Eth. Nic.,' ii. 6. 18). The pious author looks for retributive punishment on such spitefulness. The LXX. tries to improve the contrast by inserting a gloss, "He who rejoices at one who perishes shall not go unpunished; but he who hath compassion shall obtain mercy," which is remarkably like Christ's sentence, "Blessed are the merciful: for they shall obtain mercy."

Ver. 6.—**Children's children are the crown of old men** (comp. Ps. cxxvii.; cxxviii.). (For the term "crown," comp. ch. xvi. 31.) Thus St. Paul calls his converts his "joy and crown" (Phil. iv. 1; 1 Thess. ii. 19). In the East a large number of children is considered a great blessing, being a guarantee of the stability of the family. Thus writes Euripides (' Iph. Taur.,' 57)—

Στύλοι γὰρ οἴκων παῖδες εἰσιν ἄρσενες.

"Male children are the pillars of the house."

The glory of children are their fathers. A long line of good or celebrated ancestors is the glory of their descendants, and brings a blessing on them (see 1 Kings xi. 13; xv. 4). Hereditary nobility, based on descent from some eminent progenitor, may be a source of not unseemly pride, and a spur to a life worthy of such excellent ancestry.

Ver. 7.—**Excellent speech becometh not a fool.** שְׂפַת יָתֶר; *verba composita*, Vulgate, *i.e.* studied, complicated, expressions; χείλη πιστά, "faithful lips," Septuagint. Others translate, "arrogant," "pretentious." It is literally, *a lip of excess* or *superabundance*, and is best taken in the above sense, as arrogant or assuming. A *nabal*, a "vicious fool," ought not to flaunt his unwisdom and his iniquities before the eyes of men, but to keep them hidden as much as possible. As such presumptuous behaviour is incongruous in the case of a fool, much less do lying lips [become] a prince; a noble person, such a one as is called in Isaiah (xxxii. 8) "liberal," where the same word, *nadib*, is used. This is an illustration of the saying, "Noblesse oblige." Thus the Greek gnome—

Ἐλευθέρου γὰρ ἀνδρὸς ἀλήθειαν λέγειν.

"A free man's part it is the truth to speak."

To John the Good, King of France, is attributed the noble maxim which well became his chivalrous character, "Si la bonne foi était bannie du reste du monde, il faudrait qu'on la retrouvât dans le cœur des rois" (Bonnechose, 'Hist. de France,' i. 310). "My son," says the rabbi in the Talmud, "avoid lying first of all; for a lie will tarnish the brightness of thy honour." For "prince," the Septuagint has, "a just man," which makes the maxim a mere truism.

Ver. 8.—There is a breath of satire in this verse. A gift is as a precious stone in the eyes of him that hath it. "A precious stone" is literally "a stone of grace" (ch. i. 9). The gnome expresses the idea that a bribe is like a bright jewel that dazzles the sight and affects the mind of him who receives it (see on ch. xv. 27; comp. Deut. xvi. 19; 1 Sam. xii. 3). Ovid, 'Art. Amat.,' iii. 653—

"Munera, crede mihi, capiunt hominesque deosque;
Placatur donis Jupiter ipse datis."

It is possible that the gnome may have a more general application, and apply to gifts given to appease anger or to prove friendship (ch. xix. 6; xxi. 14). Septuagint, "A reward of graces is discipline to those who use it;" *i.e.* moral discipline brings an ample reward of graces to those who practise it. Whithersoever it turneth, it prospereth. The Authorized Version refers these words to the gift. Delitzsch points out that the words are more properly taken of the person who receives the gift, so that they should be rendered, "Wheresoever he turneth himself he dealeth wisely." Inflamed by sordid hopes and the love of gain, he acts with all possible skill and prudence in order to work out his wages and show that he was rightly selected to receive the present. The verse merely states a common trait among unscrupulous men, and pronounces no judgment upon it.

Ver. 9.—He that covereth a transgression seeketh love; *i.e.* strives to exercise, put in practice, love (comp. Zeph. ii. 3; 1 Cor. xiv. 4). Thus Nowack. One who bears patiently and silently, extenuates and conceals, something done or said against him, that man follows after charity, obeys the great law of love (comp. ch. x. 12). Some explain the clause to mean, "procures love for himself;" but the second member certainly is not personal, therefore it is more natural to take the first in a general sense. He that repeateth (harpeth on) a matter separateth very friends (ch. xvi. 28). He who is always dwelling on a grievance, returning to it and bringing it forward on every occasion, alienates the greatest friends, only embitters the injury and makes it chronic. Ecclus. xix. 7, etc., "Rehearse not unto another that which is told unto thee, and thou shalt fare never the worse. Whether it be to friend or foe, talk not of other men's lives; and if thou canst without offence, reveal them not. For he heard and observed thee, and when time cometh he will hate thee. If thou hast heard a word, let it die with thee; and be bold, it will not burst thee." So the rabbis said: "Abstain from quarrels with thy neighbour; and if thou hast seen something bad of thy friend, let it not pass thy tongue as a slander" (Dukes, § 61). The Mosaic Law had led the way to this duty of forbearance: "Thou shalt not avenge, nor bear any grudge against the children of thy people, but thou shalt love thy neighbour as thyself" (Lev. xix. 18). Septuagint, "He who concealeth injuries seeketh friendship; but he who hateth to conceal them separateth friends and households."

Ver. 10.—A reproof entereth more (deeper) into a wise man than an hundred stripes into a fool. A deserved rebuke makes a deeper impression upon a man of understanding than the severest chastisement upon a fool. Hitzig quotes Sallust, 'Jug.,' xi., "Verbum in pectus Jugurthæ altius, quam quisquam ratus est, descendit." Quint. Curt., liv. 7, "Nobilis equus umbra quoque virgæ regitur, ignavus ne calcari quidem concitari potest." The antithesis is put more forcibly in the Septuagint, "A threat breaks the heart of a prudent man; a fool even scourged feels it not."

Ver. 11.—An evil man seeketh only rebellion. So the Greek and Latin Versions; but, as Nowack intimates, a bad man seeks many other things which do not come directly in the category of rebellion; and it is better to take *meri*, "rebellion," as the subject, regarding it as put for the concrete, thus: "A rebellious man striveth only for what is evil." From the point of view of an Eastern potentate, this is true enough. Absolute government looks upon any rising against constituted authority, any movement in the masses, as necessarily evil, and to be repressed with a high hand. Hence the succeeding clause, Therefore a cruel messenger shall be sent against him. The "cruel messenger" (ch. xvi. 14) is the executioner of the king's wrath (comp. 1 Kings ii. 29, etc.). He is called "cruel" because his errand is deadly, and he is pitiless in its performance. This seems to be the sense intended. The LXX. gives a different notion, derived from the ambiguous term *malak*, like the Greek ἄγγελος: "The Lord will send forth a pitiless angel against him." The verse then becomes a statement concerning the retribution inflicted by God on obstinate sinners, such as Pharaoh and the Egyptians. These are delivered over to "the tormentors" (Matt. xviii. 34), the angels that execute the wrath of God, as in Ps. lxxviii. 49 and Rev. viii. 6, etc. As all sin is rebellion against God, it is natural to read into the passage a religious meaning, and for homiletical purposes it is legitimate to do so. But the writer's intention is doubtless as explained above, though his language may be divinely directed to afford a further application.

Ver. 12.—Let a bear robbed of her whelps meet a man. The Syrian bear was once common throughout Palestine; it is now found in but few localities, such as the hills of Hermon and Lebanon, and in the wilds east of the Jordan, the destruction of wood and forest having deprived these animals of the shelter necessary to their existence. The ferocity of the bear when deprived of its young had become proverbial (see 2 Sam. xvii. 8; Hos. xiii. 8; Hart, 'Animals of the Bible,' 28, etc.). **Rather than a fool in his folly**; *i.e.* in the paroxysm of his passion. Compare Saul's ungoverned language to Jonathan (1 Sam. xx. 30), and Herod's murder of the children (Matt. ii. 16). So we read of the people being filled with ἄνοια against Jesus (Luke vi. 11). Oort supposes that this proverb arose from the riddle, "What is worse to meet than a bear?" Septuagint, "Care will fall upon a man of understanding; but fools imagine evils." The Greek translators take "bear" as used metaphorically for terror and anxiety, but go far astray from the Hebrew text.

Ver. 13.—Whoso rewardeth evil for good. This was David's complaint of the churlish Nabal (1 Sam. xxv. 21). Ingratitude shall surely be punished. **Evil shall not depart from his house.** Terribly has the ingratitude of the Jews been visited. They cried in their madness, "His blood be on us and on our children!" and their punishment is still going on. Injunctions on this subject are frequent in the New Testament (see Matt. v. 39; Rom. xii. 17; 1 Thess. v. 15; 1 Pet. iii. 9). The Talmud says, "Do not throw a stone into the well whose waters you have drunk." The Greeks felt the sting of ingratitude. Thus Leiodes complains to Ulysses ('Od.,' xxii. 319)—

Ὡς οὐκ ἔστι χάρις μετόπισθ' εὐεργέων.

Two sayings of Publius Syrus are quoted ('Sent.,' vv. 219, 274): "Ingratus unus omnibus miseris nocet;" "Malignos fieri maxime ingrati docent."

Ver. 14.—The beginning of strife is as when one letteth out water. The small rift in the bank of a reservoir of water, if not immediately secured, is soon enlarged and gets beyond control, occasioning widespread ruin and destruction; so from small and insignificant causes, which might at first have been easily checked, arise feuds and quarrels which extend in a wide circle, and cannot be appeased. Palestine was largely dependent upon its reservoirs for the storage of water, perennial springs being of rare occurrence. The three pools of Solomon in the neighbourhood of Bethlehem, which were connected by channels with Jerusalem, are still to be seen in all their massive grandeur; and, indeed, every town had its reservoir, or tank, as we find in India at the present time. These receptacles had to be kept in good repair, or disastrous consequences might ensue. On the tendency of a quarrel to grow to a dangerous extent, a Bengal proverb speaks of " going in a needle and coming out a ploughshare." Vulgate, *Qui dimittit aquam, caput est jurgiorum*, which seems to mean that the man who needlessly lets the water of a cistern run to waste gives occasion to quarrels. But St. Gregory ('Moral.,' v. 13), commenting on the passage, interprets differently: " It is well said by Solomon, ' He that letteth out water is a head of strife.' For the water is let out when the flowing of the tongue is let loose. And he that letteth out water is made the beginning of strife, in that, by the incontinency of the lips, the commencement of discord is afforded " (Oxford transl.). Probably, however, in the Latin, as in the Hebrew, the particle of comparison is suppressed, so that the clause means, " As he who lets out water, so is he who gives occasion to strife." **Therefore leave off contention, before it be meddled with.** The last word הִתְגַּלָּע is of doubtful interpretation. It occurs in ch. xviii. 1 and xx. 3, and is variously translated, "before it rushes forward," "before it grows warm," "before a man becomes wrathful." But Hitzig, Nowack, and others take it to signify, "before men show their teeth," like angry dogs snarling at one another. The moralist advises men to subdue angry passions at once before they become exacerbated. The Vulgate seems to have quite mistaken the clause, translating, *Antequam patiatur contumeliam, judicium deserit*, which seems to mean that a patient, peace-loving man (in contrast with the irascible) avoids lawsuits before he is involved in a lasting quarrel. Septuagint, "The beginning (ἀρχή) of justice gives power to words; but discord and contention lead the way to want." The Greek commentators see here an allusion to the clepsydra, the water-clock which regulated the length of the speeches in a court of law; but the reference is by no means clear.

Ver. 15.—He that justifieth—in a forensic sense, declares righteous, acquits—the wicked, etc. Two forms of the perversion of justice are censured, viz. the acquittal of a guilty person and the condemnation of an innocent one (comp. ch. xxiv. 24 ; Isa. v. 23).

Ver. 16.—Wherefore is there a price in the hand of a fool to get wisdom? A fool thinks that there is a royal road to wisdom, and that it, like other things, is to be purchased with money. Vulgate, *Quid prodest stulto habere divitias, cum sapientiam emere non possit?* The rabbis in later time were not allowed to take fees for teaching; but it was customary to make offerings to seers and wise men, when their services were engaged or their advice was asked (see the case of Saul and Samuel, 1 Sam. ix. 7. 8). The last clause gives the reason why it is useless for a fool to try to learn wisdom even at a large expenditure on teachers. Seeing he hath no heart to it; *i.e.* no capability for receiving it; his mental digestion cannot assimilate it. The heart, as we have already noticed, is regarded as the seat of the understanding. Thus the LXX., "Why doth a fool have wealth? for a man without heart cannot acquire wisdom." In the Gospel Christ calls his disciples "fools and slow of heart to believe what the prophets had written, and himself opened their mind (τὸν νοῦν), that they might understand the Scriptures" (Luke xxiv. 25, 45). The Septuagint and Vulgate here introduce a distich derived from portions of vers. 19, 20, "He who raises his house high seeketh destruction; and he who perversely declineth from learning (ὁ δὲ σκολιάζων τοῦ μαθεῖν) shall fall into evils."

Ver. 17.—**A friend loveth at all times, and a brother is born for adversity.** Some find a climax in the two clauses, and translate the last as Revised Version margin, "And is born as a brother for adversity," the same person being meant in both members of the sentence. A real friend loves his friend in prosperity and adversity; yea, he is more than a friend in time of need—he is a brother, as affectionate and as trusty as one connected by the closest ties of relationship (comp. ch. xviii. 24). Siracides gives a very cruel version of this proverb, " A friend cannot be known in prosperity; and an enemy cannot be hidden in adversity. In the prosperity of a man enemies will be grieved; but in his adversity even a friend will depart" (Ecclus. xii. 8, etc.). Cicero had a truer notion of the stability of friendship when he quoted Ennius's dictum, "Amicus certus in re incerta cernitur" (' De Amicit.,' xvii.). Misfortune, says our maxim, is the touchstone of friendship; and one Greek gnome enjoins—

Ἰδίας νόμιζε τῶν φίλων τὰς συμφοράς.

" Thy friend's misfortunes deem to be thine own ; "

while another runs—

Κρίνει φίλους ὁ καιρὸς, ὡς χρυσὸν τὸ πῦρ.

" The crisis tests a friend, as fire the gold."

Septuagint, " Have thou a friend for every crisis, and let brethren be useful in adversities; for for this they are made." Commenting on the expression, "is born," Wordsworth fancifully remarks, "Adversity brings him forth. He comes, as it were, out

of the womb of calamity, and seems to be born for it."

Ver. 18.—**A man void of understanding** (Hebrew, *heart*) **striketh hands**; clinches the bargain which makes him responsible (see on suretyship, ch. vi. 1, etc. ; and note, xx. 16). **Becometh surety in the presence of his friend**; to his friend for some third party. What is here censured is the weakness which, for the sake of perhaps worthless companions, lets itself be hampered and endangered by others' obligations. For, as our adage runs, he that is surety for another is never sure himself. The Septuagint takes the "striking of hands" to be a sign of joy (Vulgate, *plaudet manibus*), "The foolish man claps (ἐπικροτεῖ) and rejoices in himself, so also he who pledges himself for his friend."

Ver. 19.—**He loveth transgression that loveth strife**, because strife leads to many breaches of the commandments (comp. ch. xxix. 22; Jas. i. 20). Septuagint, "He who loveth sin rejoices in battles." And **he that exalteth his gate seeketh destruction.** He who builds a sumptuous house and lives in the way that his magnificent surroundings demand draws ruin on himself, either because he affects a state which he is unable to support, or acts so as to provoke reprisals and injurious consequences. The entrance to a Palestinian house would usually be of humble dimensions and sparse ornamentation; any doorway of great architectural pretensions would be uncommon, and would be regarded as a token of extraordinary wealth or reprehensible pride. Aben Ezra, taking " gate " as a metaphor for " mouth," explains the hemistich of the danger of random or excessive speech. This makes a good parallel with the first clause; but it is doubtful whether the words will bear this interpretation (see Hitzig); and the two clauses may present two forms of selfishness, captiousness and ostentation, both of which lead to quarrels and ruin (comp. ch. xvi. 18).

Ver. 20.—**He that hath a froward heart findeth no good.** (For " froward," see on ch. xi. 20; for " find good," on ch. xvi. 20.) The perverse, wilful man shall not prosper, shall win no blessing in his worldly matters, much less in spiritual things. Septuagint, " He who is hard of heart meeteth not with good things." **He that hath a perverse tongue falleth into mischief**; literally, *he who turns himself about with his tongue*, saying one thing at one time and something quite contrary at another. Vulgate, *qui vertit linguam*; Septuagint, ἀνὴρ εὐμετάβολος γλώσσῃ, " easily changed in tongue " (comp. ch. viii. 13; x. 31, where the word is different). "Mischief" (*ra*) " is trouble," "calamity," as in ch. xiii. 17. Speaking of the various aspects which words may assume, Cato (' Dist.,' iv. 20) says—

"Sermo hominum mores et celat et indicat idem."

> "Man's words his character reveal,
> But often they his mind conceal."

Ver. 21.—**He that begetteth a fool** doeth it **to his sorrow** (comp. ver. 25). The words for "fool" in the two clauses are different. Here it is *kesil*, which implies bold, self-confident folly, the worst form of the vice; in the second hemistich it is *nabal*, which rather denotes dulness and stupidity, a want of mental power. A conceited, offensive fool causes infinite trouble to his father, both from his need of constant correction, and the watchfulness required to repair the consequences of his foolish actions. There is also the grief at seeing instruction and warning thrown away on a worthless object. Septuagint, "The heart of a fool is a pain to him who possesseth it." **The father of a fool hath no joy.** The contrast in the case of a good son is seen in ch. xv. 20 and xxiii. 24. The LXX. adds a clause from ch. x. 1, with the view of improving the parallelism, "But a prudent son rejoiceth his mother."

Ver. 22.—**A merry heart doeth good** like **a medicine.** So Aben Ezra, understanding the particle of comparison, which is not in the Hebrew. The word translated "medicine" (*gehah*) occurs nowhere else, and probably means "healing," "relief." The clause is better rendered, *a cheerful heart maketh a good healing* (comp. ch. xv. 13; xvi. 24). Vulgate, *ætatem floridam facit*; Septuagint, εὐεκτεῖν ποιεῖ, "makes one to be in good case." A cheerful, contented disposition enables a man to resist the attacks of disease, the mind, as every one knows, having most powerful influence over the body. Ecclus. xxx. 22, "The gladness of the heart is the life of man, and the joyfulness of a man prolongeth his days." **A broken spirit drieth the bones;** destroys all life and vigour (comp. ch. iii. 8; Ps. xxii. 15; xxxii. 4). We all remember the distich—

> "A merry heart goes all the day,
> Your sad tires in a mile-a."

So the rabbis enjoin, "Give care no room in thine heart, for care hath killed many" (Dukes, p. 68). Religious gladness is a positive duty, and "low spirits," as Isaac Williams says, "are a sin." Asks the Greek moralist—

Ἀρ' ἐστὶ συγγενές τι λύπη καὶ βίος;

And Lucretius (iii. 473) affirms—

"Nam dolor ac morbus leti fabricator uterque est."

"Workers of death are sorrow and disease."

Ver. 23.—**A gift out of the bosom;** *i.e.* secretly from the fold of the garment, and not from the purse or bag wherein money was ostensibly carried. A corrupt judge "taketh," *i.e.* receives a bribe conveyed to him secretly (ch. xxi. 14). **To pervert the ways of judgment.** The judges had no appointed salaries; hence the unprincipled among them were open to bribery. The strict injunctions of the Law, and the stern denunciations of the prophets, were alike ineffectual in checking corruption (see Exod. xxiii. 8; Deut. xvi. 19; Isa. i. 23; Jer. xxii. 17; Ezek. xiii. 19; Hos. iv. 18, etc.). Septuagint, "The man that receiveth gifts in his bosom unjustly, his ways shall not prosper." For, as Job avows (xv. 34), "Fire shall consume the tabernacles of bribery." The LXX. adds, "The impious turns aside from the ways of righteousness."

Ver. 24.—**Wisdom is before [the face of] him that hath understanding.** The idea is that the intelligent man directs his look towards Wisdom, and therefore she beams upon him with all her light; as the Vulgate puts it, "In the face of the prudent wisdom shines." He has one object to which he directs all his attention (ch. xv. 14). The Septuagint rendering is not so satisfactory: "The countenance of a prudent man is wise;" he shows in his look and bearing the wisdom that guides him. Thus Eccles. viii. 1, "A man's wisdom maketh his face to shine, and the hardness of his face is changed." **The eyes of a fool are in the ends of the earth.** A fool has no one definite object in view; he pursues a hundred different things, as they happen to come in his way, but misses the most important quest of all, and fritters away the powers which might have aided him to obtain wisdom.

Ver. 25.—This verse is more or less a repetition of ver. 21; ch. x. 1; xv. 20; and comp. xix. 13. **A grief** (*kaas*). The Vulgate and Septuagint translate, "anger." A foolish son provokes the wrath of his father, and is **bitterness to her that bare him.** "Bitterness" (*memer*) occurs nowhere else; *mar* and *marar* are common enough.

Ver. 26.—**Also** (*gam*). This may be intended to connect this verse with what was said above (ver. 23) about the perversion of justice; or, as is more probable, it is used to emphasize what is coming. **To punish the just is not good.** *Damnum inferre justo,* Vulgate; ζημιοῦν, Septuagint; and the word has a special reference to punishment by fire. **Nor to strike princes for equity;** the expression, "is not good," being understood from the former clause. "Princes" are the noble in character rather than in position only. Two forms of evil are named, viz. to punish the innocent, and to visit with contumely and injury the man of high character who cannot be induced to pervert justice. Revised Version, *nor to smite the noble for their uprightness.* So virtually the Vulgate, Septuagint, and Syriac. Another rendering is, "to strike the noble is against right," which seems feeble and less suitable to the parallelism.

Ver. 27.—**He that hath knowledge spareth his words**; Revised Version, *he that spareth his words hath knowledge;* he shows his common sense, not by rash talk or saying all he knows, but by restraining his tongue (comp. ch. x. 19; Jas. i. 19). 'Pirke Aboth' (i. 18), "All my days I have grown up amongst the wise, and have not found aught good for a man but silence; not learning but doing is the groundwork, and whoso multiplies words occasions sin." Say the Greek gnomes—

Ἐνίοις τὸ σιγᾶν ἐστὶ κρεῖττον τοῦ λέγειν.
Κρεῖττον σιωπᾶν ἢ λαλεῖν ἃ μὴ πρέπει.

And Theognis (v. 815) writes—

Βοῦς μοι ἐπὶ γλώσσης κρατερῷ ποδὶ λὰξ ἐπιβαίνων
Ἴσχει κωτίλλειν καίπερ ἐπιστάμενον.

"Speech for a shekel, silence for two; it is like a precious stone" ('Qoheleth Rabbah,' v. 5). Septuagint, "He who spareth to utter a harsh speech is prudent" (ἐπιγνώμων). **A man of understanding is of an excellent spirit**; Revised Version, *he that is of a cool spirit is a man of understanding;* i.e. he who considers before he speaks, and never answers in hot haste, proves that he is wise and intelligent. Septuagint, "The long-suffering man is prudent." The above is the reading of the Khetib, followed by

most interpreters. The Keri gives, "of a precious spirit" (*pretiosi spiritus,* Vulgate), that is, one whose words are weighty and valuable, not lavishly thrown about, but reserved as costly jewels.

Ver. 28.—**Even a fool, when he holdeth his peace, is counted wise.** Not betraying his ignorance and incapacity by words, a foolish man is credited with possessing sense (comp. Job xiii. 5). Proverbs to this effect are found in all languages. Thus the Greek—

Πᾶς τις ἀπαίδευτος φρονιμώτατός ἐστι σιωπῶν.

Cato, 'Dist.,' i. 3—

"Virtutem primam esse puta compescere linguam;
Proximus ille Deo qui scit ratione tacere."

Talmud, "Silence becomes the wise, much more fools." The Dutch have appropriated this maxim, "Zweigen de dwazen zij waren wijs," "Were fools silent, they would pass for wise." "Si tacuisses, philosophus mansisses." "Silence," says the Sanskrit gnome, "is the ornament of the ignorant." "Talking comes by nature," say the Germans, "silence of understanding." The LXX. gives a different turn to the first clause: "A foolish man inquiring of wisdom will have wisdom imputed to him;" the expressed desire of knowledge will be taken as a proof of intelligence. The second clause is co-ordinate with the former. **He that shutteth his lips** is esteemed **a man of understanding**; Revised Version, *when he shutteth his lips, he is esteemed as prudent;* Septuagint, "A man making himself dumb will seem to be prudent." Theophrastus is said to have thus addressed a guest who was very silent at table: "If you are a fool, you act wisely; if you are wise, you act foolishly." "Let every man," says St. James (i. 19), "be swift to hear, slow to speak."

HOMILETICS.

Ver. 5.—*Mocking the poor.* The terrible inequality of human lots was never more apparent than it is in the present day. England is renowned for her wealth; yet England is a haunt of hungry misery. It is nothing but selfish hypocrisy to justify this condition of affairs by quoting the words of our Lord, "The poor always ye have with you" (John xii. 8). If they are always with us in abject need and distress, so much the worse for the condition of society. The statement of a distressing fact is no justification for it. Meanwhile, if the huge evil of pauperism cannot be abolished at once, it is our duty to lessen, not to aggravate it.

I. CONSIDER IN WHAT WAYS THE POOR ARE MOCKED. 1. *When their condition is disregarded.* There are thousands of people living in affluence who simply ignore the fact that they have needy brethren. Dives at his feast does not give a thought to Lazarus pining at his gate. Surely it is a mockery to the awful misery of the East End that the West End feasts and *fêtes* itself with undisturbed complacency. 2. *When their rights are neglected.* This happens in many ways, even in an age and a country that boasts of its administration of justice. (1) The so-called "sweating system" is nothing better than robbery, by means of which the strong take advantage of the necessities of the weak. (2) It is hard for poor people to avail themselves of the law-courts; so that the cry is raised that "there is one law for the rich and another for the poor." (3) Poor men have the natural rights of their manhood treated with contempt. The courtesy which is offered to the well-to-do is denied to them. Rough treatment is meted out to them. Common politeness is refused to a man with a threadbare coat. 3. *When their deficiencies are ridiculed.* The poor man is generally illiterate, his "speech bewrayeth him." He has never learnt the manners of good society. So the classes above him put up their eye-glasses to inspect him, as though he were some strange, repulsive animal. 4. *When their merits are ignored.* There is honest poverty. There are brave men fighting against adverse circumstances with the courage of heroes. Are these people to be mocked at simply because they cannot put money in their purses? The kindness of the poor to the poor is a rebuke to the cynicism of the rich. Yet how difficult it is for poor men to be duly recognized! Dr. Johnson spoke from experience when he said—

> " This mournful truth is everywhere confess'd,
> Slow rises worth by poverty depressed."

The world mocks the poor when it judges people by the fashion of their clothes and the size of their houses, instead of looking to their character and lives.

II. CONSIDER THE GREAT SIN OF MOCKING THE POOR. He who does this "reproacheth his Maker." For the God who made the rich man also made the poor man. The reproach of the child is a reproach of his Father. We do more than wrong our brethren when we treat the unfortunate with contempt; we insult our God. He is the God of the poor, and he takes their wrongs as injuries to himself. This is no slight, shadowy offence. It is an awful sin in the sight of Heaven. The only reason that is suggested why Dives should be writhing in torments of fire is that he was a rich man who gave no heed to the misery of his neighbour. Here is an awful prospect for the careless comfortable classes of England! The evil is aggravated with us, because we profess that religion which preaches a gospel to the poor. In the Church of Christ rich and poor meet together. For the rich man to despise his fellow-Christian, then, is for him to deny his Master, " who had not where to lay his head." Let it be remembered that Christ, who was rich, "for our sakes became poor." He is the Friend and Brother of the poor.

Ver. 10.—*The wisdom of accepting a reproof.* I. IT IS DIFFICULT TO ACCEPT A REPROOF. Only the wise man will take it. Many difficulties stand in the way. 1. *It is hard to believe that the reproving counsellor is a true friend.* He appears to be censorious. We think he takes a pleasure in finding fault with us. We accuse him of a Pharisaic self-satisfaction in comparing his own virtue with our fault. 2. *It is difficult to admit the application of the accusation to ourselves.* David is indignant at Nathan's recital of the parable of the ewe lamb. Yet he fails to see that the moral of it comes home to himself till the prophet exclaims, "Thou art the man!" 3. *It is not easy to confess our own humiliation.* When we see that we are accused, pride rises up to defend us. It is possible for a large amount of pride to lodge with a great quantity of folly. Indeed, the more a person is emptied of real worth the more room is there in him for self-inflation. 4. *It is troublesome to yield to a reproof.* To do so we must not merely admit our fault, but consent to mend our ways. We must allow the reproof to work actively in us as if it is to be of any use. The drunkard is often ready to confess his sin, but he is not so eager to renounce the cause of it. 5. *It is distressing to bear the reproof of God.* In reading the Bible people are tempted to appropriate the promises to themselves and to leave the threatenings for their brethren. It needs a divinely inspired wisdom to help us to profit by the warnings of Scripture.

II. IT IS WISE TO ACCEPT A REPROOF. Many as are the obstructions that stand in the way of our receiving and acting upon it, we should do well to conquer them. He is but a foolish person who despises correction. The wise man may shrink from it, but he will not reject it. 1. *A true reproof is justly due.* We have earned it by our own fault. It is foolish to kick against the consequences of our own conduct. 2. *A reproof is a wholesome corrective.* It is not a judge's sentence, but a friend's counsel.

Its object is not condemnation, but salvation. 3. *A reproof is a mild substitute for harder treatment.* While we foolishly rail at its harshness, we should be thankful for the lenity of the most stern well-deserved reproof. It might have been dispensed with, and we might have received condign punishment. The reproof is not so hard to bear as the "hundred stripes" that may follow if it is disregarded. It is wise to close with the earlier counsel. 4. *A reproof is an element of Divine grace.* Christ sends the Comforter to convict the world of sin as well as of righteousness and judgment (John xvi. 8). It is to our own cost that we receive this gracious Guest with resentful discourtesy. But, on the other hand, we plainly need Divine grace to accept a reproof in a meek and humble spirit. The wisdom to receive a reproof well is so difficult to attain that we need to seek it as an inspiration from God.

Ver. 14.—"*The beginning of strife.*" I. STRIFE MAY HAVE A SMALL BEGINNING. It is not necessary to intend great mischief if a quarrel is to be started. One word of an unfriendly character may be enough to mar the peace of brethren. A single act of unkindness may be the beginning of discord, provoking retaliation, and so originating a long-continued state of war. A quarrel may arise among very insignificant persons. It may be concerned with very unimportant questions. It may appear as a very slight affair—"a tempest in a tea-cup."
II. STRIFE GROWS WIDER. The small hole in the dyke through which a little water oozes is worn by the escaping stream so that it becomes larger, and the larger it is the more water pours through it; and this, in turn, will tear still greater pieces from the banks. A little rift within the lute is the commencement of the mischief that will silence all the music. A dispute between two frontier officers may lead to a war between two nations. Thus the strife between a few grows into a quarrel between many persons.
III. STRIFE GROWS MORE INTENSE. It not only involves more persons; it also becomes aggravated in its violence. Increasing in volume, it also grows in vehemence. The flood rushes with alarming velocity. The misunderstanding becomes a war. The coldness between friends turns into the bitterness of enmity. Anger degenerates into hatred.
IV. STRIFE BECOMES UNCONTROLLABLE. It might be arrested in its early stage. A boy pressing his knee against the small hole in the dyke could hold back the trickling stream. But if the mischief is not checked in an early stage, "all the king's horses" cannot arrest the mad career of the escaping river. An insignificant person may start a quarrel, which many wise and strong men will fail to allay. It is easier to be a war-maker than a peace-maker. Events grow too strong for the most powerful energies of man.
V. STRIFE ISSUES IN INCALCULABLE RESULTS. The flood pours down through the valley and over the plain, uprooting trees, devastating fields, deluging homesteads, drowning men and cattle. The mischief is enormous, and the course and extent of it cannot be measured beforehand. No one can tell what harm may grow out of his meddlesome mischief-making. A foolish person may mean to do no real harm, only to show a little passing spite. But he has let out the waters; the flood-gates are open; the huge army of destruction is scouring the country. Amazed and aghast at the unexpected consequences of his folly, he would fain undo the reckless deed or stay its fatal consequences. But it is too late. Those consequences have passed beyond his reach. He can never tell how far the evil effects of what he has done may extend.
VI. STRIFE SHOULD BE CHECKED IN ITS EARLIEST STAGE. It is best to avoid the very beginning of it. But if, unhappily, it has been started, it should be stayed at once. To nurse a quarrel is worse than to cherish a viper in one's bosom. Fling it away and crush it, before it spawns a deadly brood of evil. The great human quarrel with heaven, begun in Eden, was like the letting out of waters. So is the soul's quarrel with God. It is best to make peace at once, through repentance and contrition.

Ver. 17.—*The true friend.* I. THE PORTRAIT OF THE TRUE FRIEND. We must study its lineaments that we may know the original. The word "friend" is used so loosely, often as a term of mere politeness, that some such inquiry is necessary if we would disentangle it from frivolous associations and affix it to its worthy object.

1. *The essential note of true friendship is invariability of affection.* The friend "loveth at all times." This does not mean that he is always displaying his affection. Effusiveness is no proof of sincerity. "Still waters run deep." Neither are we to suppose that the affection must be always shown in the same way. The manifestation of it must vary according to the moods and feelings of the friend, and also according to the circumstances and behaviour of the object of affection. There are times when friendship must be angry, when love must frown. Still the love must remain. (1) True friendship is independent of time. It does not wear out with years. The true friend of youth is the friend of manhood. (2) It is independent of circumstances. It survives the loss of social delights. It holds on through poverty (3) It is not shaken by slander. (4) It even outlives unworthy treatment. 2. *The great test of true friendship is adversity.* (1) Then the friendship is most valuable. If it will not serve then it is of little use. We want friends to whom we can go in the hour of need. (2) Then its quality is proved. The shallow, selfish man cuts his acquaintances in their trouble. Poverty severs the cords of pretended friendship. But real friendship is proved and comes out at its best under adverse circumstances. Then its brotherly character is revealed. The friend of prosperous days becomes the brother in days of trouble. 3. *The secret of true friendship is love.* Love is stronger than death, and love can survive the loss of all things. It endures through time and change, and in spite of violent strains upon its strength.

II. THE DISCOVERY OF THE TRUE FRIEND. The portrait is ideal. Do we ever see the ideal realized? In a measure, yes, and that repeatedly. The cynical pessimism that disbelieves in any generous, unselfish friendship is false to the nature of man, and false to the noble tale of good lives. Generosity is not dead. Friendship is possible. But every human friend is imperfect. Surely the portrait of the true friend must suggest to us One who alone perfectly answers to its noble features. We discover the true Friend in Christ. 1. He gives us the note of true friendship in *invariability of affection.* His love to the race endures through the ages. His love to each individual of his people is ever-abiding and constant. It outlasts many provocations, frequent unfaithfulness, great unworthiness on their part. Christ did not cease to love St. Peter when the apostle denied his Master. 2. *He is a Brother in affliction.* The Companion of our joys, he is especially our Helper in trouble; he came expressly to save from the terrible evil of sin. He is the sympathizing Friend for all sorrow. 3. *The secret of his friendship is love.* It is not our claim or attractiveness, but the love of Christ, that makes him our abiding, faithful Friend. If we would measure the durability of his friendship, we must gauge the greatness of his undying love.

Ver. 22.—*The healing effects of cheerfulness.* I. CHEERFULNESS IS COMMENDED IN SCRIPTURE. The Bible does not put a premium on sombreness. It never suggests that there is a merit in gloom. It urges the need of repentance, calls upon men to grieve for their sins, threatens the wrath of God against impenitence, and so brings up occasions for distress of soul; it also rebukes "the laughter of fools," the empty merriment of frivolity and the riot and revelry of dissipation (Eccles. vii. 6). But it does not commend sorrow on its own account. On the contrary, it brings joy and encourages gladness. Christ gave his joy to his people (John xv. 11). St. Paul emphatically reiterated his advice to his readers to rejoice (Phil. iv. 4). God loves his children and delights in their happiness. God is blessed, therefore happy ; and he desires for his children a share in his blessedness, which must involve a participation in his gladness.

II. CHEERFULNESS EXERTS A HEALING INFLUENCE OVER THE INDIVIDUAL SOUL. Too much indulgence in sorrow induces a morbid condition. It is not healthy in itself, for man is not meant to be a perpetual incarnation of pain. The natural merriment of children is not only innocent; it is positively helpful to the sane growth of their minds. Cheerful Christians are strong Christians; for "the joy of the Lord is your strength" (Neh. viii. 10). It is easier to bear disappointment when the spirit is free and buoyant. Temptation is less powerful against a contented soul than against one that is enfeebled by fretful dissatisfaction. We can do our work best when we do it gladly. In a cheerful mood we take the widest, wisest, healthiest views of truth. Sour feelings lead to false estimates of the world. Even after sin and repentance, when the sinner is pardoned, a sober, humble cheerfulness is healthier than perpetual lamentation. Therefore the fatted calf is killed, etc.

III. CHEERFULNESS IS A SOURCE OF HEALTHY INFLUENCE FOR OTHERS. The gloomy saint cultivates his own sombre sanctity at the expense of his neighbours. He should be helping them and attracting them into the way of life. But he is repelling and hindering them. Children are best won by a cheerful presentation of religion. The indifferent are made to see that the cross of Christ does not mean perpetual distress and trouble to the Christian. The lost and fallen have hopes inspired within them when they are approached with hopes of better things. The gospel is goodness; it should be preached with a cheerful spirit; its "glad tidings of great joy" speak healing to the nations.

IV. CHEERFULNESS IS TO BE BEST ATTAINED IN THE CHRISTIAN LIFE. The merry soul may be only superficially glad, or even sinfully delighted, when it should be humbled in repentance. But after repentance and pardon God gives his own deep, sure joy. This joy rests on the love of God and fellowship with him. It is confirmed by service. When one can say, "I delight to do thy will, O my God" (Ps. xl. 8), he has reached the true fountain of a cheerful spirit. Such a joy can master adversity and rejoice in tribulation (2 Cor. vi. 10). It was when engaged in an apostolic mission that Paul and Silas were able to sing in prison (Acts xvi. 25).

HOMILIES BY VARIOUS AUTHORS.

Vers. 1—9.—*Traits of outward and inward happiness. Happiness depends more on the inward state than on the outward condition.* Hence—

I. CONTENTMENT AS AN ELEMENT OF HAPPINESS. (Ver. 1.) The dry morsel, with rest and quiet in the spirit, is better, says the preacher, than the most luxurious meal; the allusion being to slaughtered sacrificial animals as the chief constituents of a rich repast (ch. ix. 2; Gen. xliii. 16). It suggests the picture of "holy love, found in a cottage" (Matthew Henry). The secret of happiness lies rather in limiting our desires than in increasing our substance.

II. PRUDENCE AND THRIFT. (Ver. 2.) The prudent servant may rise, and probably not seldom did rise in ancient times, to superiority over the idle and dissipated son of the house. In this light Abraham looked upon Eliezer—that he might probably step into the place of a son in his house. How much more depends, in reference to power and influence in this world, upon sense and prudence than upon birth and every external advantage!

III. THE TRUE HEART. (Ver. 3.) The heart which has been tried in the scales of Jehovah, assayed by the tests of an infallible truth. We need to remind ourselves how little we know of the depths of human character. Our inquiries and our teachings are inadequate and deceptive. The search of the human heart is a royal privilege of God. Without the true, the divinely approved heart, there is no real root of good or bliss.

IV. A SINCERE TEMPER. (Ver. 4.) This is suggested, as often, by the hideous contrast of the wicked, inwardly corrupt heart, which willingly takes note of and inclines to lying words, to the tempter and his wishes. It takes pleasure in the "naughty words" it dares not, perhaps, utter itself; is glad to borrow words from another to fit its own evil thoughts. In contrast to this, the spirit of the candid and sincerely good man is that expressed by Bishop Hall, "If I cannot stop other men's mouths from speaking ill, I will either open my mouth to reprove it, or else I will stop my ears from hearing it, and let him see in my face that he hath no room in my heart."

V. COMPASSION, PITY, AND SYMPATHY. (Ver. 5.) Contempt of the poor is contempt of the majesty of God. The greater part of poverty is not wilful; it is in the course of the providence of God. "To pour contempt on the current coin with the king's image on it is treason against the sovereign." There is something worse than even this, viz. to rejoice in the calamities of others. It is a peculiarly inhuman view, and is certain to be punished in the remorse of the conscience, in the closing up of the way to God's heart in the time of one's own need.

VI. FAMILY JOYS. (Ver. 6.) To leave out these would be to leave out that which gives to life its chief fragrance and charm. As children are the pride and ornament of the parents, so the sons, on the other hand, so long as they themselves are not fathers, can only fall back upon the father. The family tree, the higher it rises and the more widely it extends, increases the honour of the race.

VII. NOBLENESS OF SPEECH. (Ver. 7.) The first element of this is, as so often insisted upon, truthfulness in the inward parts. The second is appropriateness, regard to what is becoming. Thus a high assuming tone ill befits the fool; much less falsity, affectation, hypocrisy, a noble mind. To recollect what is *becoming* in us is a great safeguard to morality and guide to conduct. In the common affairs of life we should not seek to rise above our station, nor should we fall below it. In religion there is also a just mean—the recollection of what it is to be a Christian; and the effort not to rise above the humility of that position, as not to fall below its grandeur and nobility. "If truth be banished from all the rest of the world," said Louis IX. of France, "it ought to be found in the breast of princes." Let us substitute the word "Christians."

VIII. THE VALUE OF GIFTS. (Ver. 8.) There seems to be no reason for taking this only in the bad sense with reference to bribery. Lawful gifts and presents have their charm as well as unlawful. The power of gold to corrupt; the saying of Philip of Macedon, that there was no fortress so strong but that it might be stormed if an ass laden with gold were driven to the gate;—all this is well known. But equally true is it that honest gifts of kindness, having no impure purpose in view, are like jewels. They sparkle with the lustre of human love when turned in any light, and win friends and good will for the giver wherever he goes. It is the generous freedom to give, not necessarily of silver and gold, but of "such things as we have," which is here commended and noted as one of the secrets of happiness. The deepest joy is, in all true gifts, to be expressing the one great gift of the heart to God.

IX. CONCEALING AND FORGIVING LOVE. (Ver. 9.) Let us remind ourselves that in the Law the word for forgiving or atoning is "cover." And frequently we read of God covering the sins of the penitent. This relation is for the imitation of Christians, " followers of God as dear children." "Love covers a multitude of sins." Like the healing hand of Nature, which we see everywhere busy concealing unsightliness, veiling the old ruin with the beautiful ivy and other creeping plants. On the contrary, the talebearer has an eye for every crack and seam in the structure of society; tears open and causes to bleed the wounds that might have been healed. Be true, be gentle, be generous, be God-like and Christ-like,—such are the main lessons of this section.—J.

Vers. 10—15.—*Dark phases of human character.* We may take ver. 10 as an introduction to what follows. Exhortations are to be given, and the preacher would prepare us to receive them. On the sensitive mind the censure of the good makes a deeper impression than a hundred blows on the back of the fool. Sincerity, love of truth and tender sympathy, become the exhorter, and humble docility the object of his warnings or rebukes. "Let the righteous smite me, and it shall be a kindness " (Ps. cxli. 5).

I. THE CONTENTIOUS SPIRIT. (Ver. 11.) 1. *His temper.* He seeks rebellion. In private life he may be the man who revolts from the established usages of society, delights in singularity for its own sake, in defying opinion, showing disrespect to names of authority. In public life he may become the heartless demagogue and pest of the commonwealth. 2. *His doom.* A cruel angel shall be sent against him by God; that is, generally, his offence will be visited upon him severely. The curse upon the contentious spirit is the counterpart of the great evangelical blessing on the peacemakers, who shall be called " the children of God." 3. *His dangerous qualities.* (Ver. 12.) Rage is the principle of his action, the motive of his life. To irritate him, to thwart him, is like bringing on one's self the fierce attack of the bear robbed of her whelps. Rage united with intelligence is the most fearful combination of deadly force known in the world. From so dread a picture we turn with the prayer, "From hatred and malice, good Lord, deliver us!" "Oh, may we live the peaceful life!"

II. THE UNGRATEFUL MAN. (Ver. 13.) 1. *His conduct.* He requites good with evil. As there is no virtue so natural, so spontaneous, so pleasurable, as gratitude, so there is no mere *negative* vice so odious as ingratitude. But the positive reversal of gratitude in returning evil for good—for this there is no one word in our (nor probably in any) language. It is a wickedness indeed *unutterable*. 2. *His doom* is punishment from God. And the severity of the punishment teaches by contrast how dear is gratitude to God. As evil shall ever haunt the house of the dark rebel against light and love, so shall joy and peace attend the steps of the peaceful child of God.

III. THE CONSEQUENCES OF MISCHIEF INCALCULABLE. (Ver. 14.) A homely figure impresses the truth in a way not to be forgotten. Similarly, James compares the progress of mischief to the sparks which may be easily fanned into a great conflagration (iii. 5). How great the service that may be rendered by those who, in the interests of peace, at once trample out the sparks or seal up the avenues of the flood. These rules are good for the avoidance of strife. Consider: 1. Whether the dispute is not about words rather than things. 2. Whether we really understand the subject. 3. Whether it is worth disputing about.

IV. MORAL INDIFFERENCE. (Ver. 15.) To speak the bad man fair, to justify or excuse his evil, and to censure or criticize or condemn the good, from prudence or other motive,—this shows a blindness to moral distinctions, a wilful insensibility which is incompatible with religion, and incurs the deep disapproval and judgment of Jehovah. We have examples in Ezra iv. 1—16; Acts xxiv. 1—9. Religion teaches us to distinguish between things that differ; if we have not learnt that lesson, we have learned nothing. If, having learned it, we disregard it, our profession of religion becomes converted into an hypocrisy and an abomination.—J.

Vers. 16—20.—*Light in the head, love in the heart.* I. MONEY USELESS WITHOUT SENSE. (Ver. 16.) The true view of money is that of means to ends. But if the ends are not seen, or, being seen, are not earnestly desired, of what avail the means? If our heart be set upon the right objects of life, opportunities will always present themselves. If blind to life's meaning, no advantages will seem to be advantages.

II. THE BEAUTY OF FRIENDSHIP. (Ver. 17.) 1. *In general.* It is constant; it is unvarying; it is adapted to all the various states and vicissitudes of life. 2. *In particular.* It takes new life out of sorrow. In distress, the friend is developed into the " brother," and is taken close to the heart. True friendship gladdens at the opportunity of self-devotion for the beloved one's good. It is the distress of our sin which makes us acquainted with him " that sticketh closer than a brother." But thank God for all those who are new-born to us in the freshly revealed grace and goodness of their hearts amidst the scenes of suffering.

III. THE STRICT DUTY OF CAUTION IN REFERENCE TO RESPONSIBILITY. (Ver. 18.) The consequences of becoming bail for a defaulter were in ancient life very terrible. Nowadays there are prudent men who will never set their hand to an acceptance. Although all moral duties are not equally amiable in their aspect, it must be remembered that the ability to do good to others rests upon strict prudence with reference to one s self. We may be maimed or destroyed by imprudence.

IV. RESISTANCE TO THE BEGINNINGS OF EVIL. (Ver. 19.) Contention or temper and passion in general leads on to graver sin. Open the way to one sin, and others will immediately troop forward in its rear. Again, contentiousness and pride are in close connection; the latter is generally the spring of the former. And both are ruinous in their tendency. High towers invite the lightning; but he that does not soar too loftily will suffer the less by a fall. A modest way of life, within our means, is the only truly Christian life.

V. THE TRUE HEART AND THE GUILELESS TONGUE. (Ver. 20.) There is no health, no salvation for self or others, in the false heart and the tongue that flickers and wavers between opposing impulses. Old Homer has the sentiment that he who speaks one thing and thinks another in his heart is hateful as the gates of hell. 1. There is no true light in the head without love in the heart. 2. There is no dualism in our moral character. 3. There is a correspondence between our outward lot and our inward choice.—J.

Vers. 21—28.—*Varied experiences of good and evil in life.* We may divide them into the sorrowful, the joyous, and the mixed experiences.

I. SAD EXPERIENCES. *The sorrow of thankless children.* (Vers. 21, 25.) To name it is enough for those who have known it. It has its analogue in Divine places. How pathetically does the Bible speak of the grief of God over the rebellious children he has nourished and brought up! and of Christ's lamentation as of a mother over Jerusalem! Let us remember that our innocent earthly sorrows are reflected in the bosom of our God.

II. JOYOUS EXPERIENCES. (Ver. 22.) The blessing of a cheerful heart, who can overprize it in relation to personal health, to social charm and helpfulness? Contrasted with the troubled spirit, like a parching fever in the bones, it is the perpetual sap of life and source of all its greenness and its fruit. A simple faith is the best known source of cheerfulness. It was a fine remark of a good friend of Dr. Johnson's, that "he had tried to be a philosopher, but somehow always found cheerfulness creeping in."

III. MIXED EXPERIENCES OF HUMAN CHARACTER. 1. *The briber.* (Ver. 23.) How strongly marked is this sin in the denunciations of the Bible! and yet how little the practice seems affected in a land which boasts above others of its love for the Bible! The *stealth* and so the *shame*, the evil *motive*, the perverse result, all are branded here. "He that shaketh his hands from holding of bribes, he shall dwell on high" (Isa. xxxiii. 15). 2. *The quick perception of wisdom and the warning glance of folly.* The one sees before him what is to be known or done at once; the other is lost in cloudy musings. The more a man gapes after vanity, the more foolish the heart becomes. In religion we see this temper in the restless roving to and fro, the constant query, "Who will show us any good?" "He is full of business at church; a stranger at home; a sceptic abroad; an observer in the street; everywhere a *fool*." 3. *Harshness in judges.* (Ver. 26.) Fining and flogging are mentioned. The writer had observed some such scene with the horror of a just man. Iniquity or inhumanity in the judge seems an insult against the eternal throne of Jehovah. 4. *The wisdom of a calm temper and economy of words.* (Vers. 27, 28.) An anxiety to talk is the mark of a shallow mind. The knowledge of the season of silence and reserve may be compared to the wisdom of the general who knows when to keep his forces back and when to launch them at the foe. The composed spirit comes from the knowledge that truth will prevail in one way or another, and the time for our utterance will arrive. Lastly, the wisdom of *silence,* so often preached by great men. Even the fool may gain some credit for wisdom which he does not possess by holding his tongue; and this is an index of the reality. Our great example here is the silence of Jesus, continued for thirty years; out of that silence a voice at length proceeded that will ever vibrate through the world.—J.

Ver. 3.—*Divine proving and purifying.* Heat, like water, is a very bad master but a very excellent servant. It *proves* whether our acquisition has or has not any value, whether it should be carefully preserved or be "trodden underfoot;" and it *refines* that which has any worth at all, separating the dross and securing for us the pure metal which we want for use or ornament. What we do with our materials God does with ourselves; but the fires through which he sends us are of a very different kind from those we kindle.

I. THE FIRES THROUGH WHICH GOD PASSES US. These are the disciplinary experiences through which, in his holy providence and in his fatherly love, he causes us to pass. And of them we may say that their name is legion, for "they are many." They vary as do the histories of human life. It may be (1) a change for the worse, sudden or gradual, permanent or transient, in our temporal conditions, affluence sinking into competence, or competence into pecuniary embarrassment, or into hard toil and scant enjoyment; or (2) bereavement and consequent loneliness of spirit, the loss of some near companion whose fellowship was sweet beyond expression, or whose guidance was incalculably helpful; or (3) disappointment, the going out of some bright hope in the light of which our path had been trodden and the extinction of which throws the future into thick darkness; or (4) the loss of health and strength, when we are taken away from activities which were congenial or apparently necessary to us, and are shut in to an enforced idleness, from which we long to be delivered; or (5) the endurance of pain; or (6) our failure to accomplish some good work on which we had set our heart and put our hand.

II. HIS TRIAL OF OUR SPIRIT. God thus *proves* us. These troubles are trials; they show to our Creator and to ourselves what manner of men we are, what is "the spirit we are of." They prove to him and to us whether we care more about our circumstances than we do about ourselves and our character; they prove whether we have a deep spirit of submission and of trustfulness, or whether our subjection to the will of God is very shallow and departs as soon as it is tested; they prove whether in the hour of need we look above us for strength and succour, or whether we have recourse only to those persons and things which are around us, or whether we descend to props and stays that are positively beneath us. They prove the quality of our Christian character; they sometimes demonstrate its actual unreality.

III. GOD'S REFINING GOODNESS AND WISDOM. God tries our hearts, not merely that he or we may see what is in them, but that they may be purified (see Isa. xlviii. 10). Many purifying, practical lessons we learn in affliction which we are very slow to receive, and which, but for its discipline, we might never gain at all. They are these, among others. 1. The unsatisfying character of all that is earthly and human. 2. The transitoriness of the present, and the wisdom of laying up treasures in heaven. 3. The secondariness of all claims to those that are Divine, and our consequent obligation to give the first place to the will and the cause of our Redeemer. 4. Our deep need of Christ as the Lord whom we are to be faithfully serving and the Friend in whose fellowship we are to spend our days. With these great spiritual truths burnt into our souls by the refining fires, we shall have our worldliness and our selfishness expelled, and be vessels of pure gold, meet for the Master's use.—C.

Vers. 6, 21, 25.—*Fatherhood and sonship.* Certainly, some of our very greatest mercies are those that come to us in our domestic relationships.

I. THE JOY AND CROWN OF FATHERHOOD AND OF GRANDFATHERHOOD. Our Lord speaks of the mother forgetting her anguish " for joy that a man is born into the world " (John xvi. 21). The joy of parentage is *keen,* and it is common; it may, indeed, be said to be *universal.* And it is *pure* and good; it elevates and enlarges the soul, taking thought and care away from self to another, and by so doing it distinctly benefits and blesses the nature. And, like all pure joys, it is *lasting;* it does not evaporate with time; on the other hand, it grows and *deepens* as the child of its affection develops and matures. Moreover, in the kind providence of God, it is *renewable* in another generation; for the grandfather has almost as much delight in his grandson as the father in his child (text; Gen. l. 23; Ps. cxxviii. 6). Fatherhood (motherhood) is: 1. A *natural desire* of the human heart. 2. Often the reward which God gives to patient industry and virtue in earlier days; for the setting up of a home is, in many if not in most cases, the attainment of a hope for which the young have striven and waited. 3. Sometimes a source of grievous disappointment and saddest sorrow (vers. 21, 25). There is no one in the world who can pierce our souls with such bitter anguish as can our own child when he or she goes astray from wisdom and righteousness. 4. Always an entail of the most serious responsibility; for what we are in spirit and in character it is most likely that our children will become. 5. Therefore a noble opportunity; for it is in our power, by wisdom and virtue, by kindness and piety, to lead our sons into the gates of privilege and up to the gates of the kingdom of Christ. 6. And therefore usually a source of profoundest gratitude and gladness, and the means by which we can hand down our principles and our influence, through our own direct endeavours, to the second and the third generation.

II. THE GLORY OF CHILDHOOD. "The glory of children are their fathers." 1. It is the greatest of all earthly heritages to have parents that can be esteemed and loved. Happy is the son who, as his judgment matures, can honour his father with an undiminishing or even a growing regard and deepening joy. 2. It is a very real delight to be able to look back, through all the later years of life, and recall the memories of the beloved and revered parents who have "passed into the skies." 3. It is the duty of childhood to make the very best response it can make for the love, care, pains, patience, prayerful solicitude, its parents have expended upon it. 4. It will remain a lasting source of thankfulness and joy that every possible filial attention was paid that could be paid; lighting and smoothing the path of the parents to the very door of heaven.—C.

Ver. 9 (with ch. xvi. 28).—*Friendship; the silence that saves and the speech that separates it.* We may learn—

I. THE GOODLINESS OF FRIENDSHIP. " Very friends," or " chief friends," points to intimate friendship. This is one of the very fairest and worthiest things under the sun. The man to whom God gives a lifelong faithful friendship is rich in a treasure which wealth cannot buy and the excellency of which it does not equal. It should be : 1. Founded on *common attachment* to the same great principles, and on mutual esteem. 2. Independent of the changes that occur in circumstances and conditions. 3. Strengthened by adversity. 4. Elevated by piety. 5. Lasting as life. Then it is something which, for intrinsic beauty and substantial worth, cannot be surpassed.

II. THE SILENCE THAT MAY SAVE IT. There *is a speech* that saves it. Often the interposition of a few words of *explanation*, removing an offence which would have grown into seriousness, will save a rupture. Sometimes a kindly word of *counsel* or *remonstrance* to the imprudent or to the mistaken may have the same happy effect. But, at other times, *silence* will save it. We are often tempted, even strongly tempted, to say that which would come between two human hearts. To say what we know would only be to speak the truth; it would gratify the curiosity of those present; it would be a pleasant exercise of power or the use of an advantage we happen to possess. The words rise to our very lips. But no ; it is not always our duty to say all that we know ; it is often our duty to be silent. There are times when to "cover transgression" is an act of wisdom, of kindness, of generosity, of Christ-likeness (see John viii. 1—11). Let the fact remain untold ; let the hearts that have been united remain bound together ; seek and secure the permanence of " love."

III. THE SPEECH THAT WILL SEPARATE IT. A whisperer, one that repeats a matter, does separate friends. 1. There is always some occasion for silence in every man's life. No man is so correct in thought and speech that he could afford to have every utterance repeated to any one and every one. We all want the kindly curtain of silence to be drawn over some sentences that pass our lips. 2. There are always some thought-less speakers—men and women who will carry injurious reports from house to house, from heart to heart ; there are some who are *cruelly careless* what things they promul-gate ; there are some who consciously and guiltily enlarge and misrepresent, who form the dangerous and deadly habit of exaggeration, of false colouring, and who end in systematic falsehood. Those who idly and foolishly report what is true are, indeed, less guilty than they who enlarge and pervert. But they are far from guiltless. We are bound to speak with sufficient caution to save ourselves from the charge of circu-lating evil and spreading sorrow. We are responsible to God not only for the carefully prepared speech, but also for the casual interjection ; that is the meaning of our Lord in his familiar words (Matt. xii. 36). It behoves us to remember that our brother's reputa-tion, usefulness, happiness, is in our charge, and *one slight whisper* may destroy it all. One breath of unkindness may start a long train of sad consequences which we have no power at all to stop. A very few unconsidered and unhappily uttered words may sever hearts that have been beating long in loving unison, may disunite lives that have been linked long in the bonds of happy love.—C.

Ver. 14.—*The growth of strife.* Experience shows us that—

I. STRIFE IS A GROWTH. It is as when one letteth out water ; first it is the trickling of a few drops, then a tiny rill, then a stream, etc. So with strife ; first it is a disturb-ing thought ; then it becomes a warm or a hot feeling ; then it utters itself in a strong, provoking word which leads to an energetic resentment and response ; then it swells into a decided, antagonistic action ; then it grows into a course of opposition, and becomes a feud, a contention, a war.

II. THE GROWTH OF STRIFE IS A CALAMITY. 1. It is the source of untold and incalculable misery to many hearts. 2. It betrays several souls into feelings and into actions which are distinctly wrong and sinful. 3. It presents a moral spectacle which is grievous in the sight of Christ, the Lord of love. 4. It rends in twain that which should be united in one strong and happy circle—the home, the family connection, the Church, the society, the nation. 5. It arrests the progress which would otherwise be made in wisdom and in worth ; for it causes numbers of men to expend on bitter controversy and contention the energy and ingenuity they would otherwise expend on rendering service and doing good.

III. OUR DUTY, OUR WISDOM, IS TO ARREST IT AT ITS BEGINNING. You cannot extinguish the conflagration, but you can stamp out the spark; you cannot stop the flow of the river, but you can dam the rill with the palm of your hand. You cannot heal a great schism, but you can appease a personal dispute; or, what is better, you can recall the offensive word you have yourself spoken; or, what is better still, you can repress the rising thought, you can call in to your aid other thoughts which calm and soothe the soul; you can remember him who "bore such contradiction of sinners against himself," who "as a sheep before her shearers is dumb, so he opened not his mouth," and you can maintain a magnanimous silence. When this is no longer possible, because the first inciting word has been uttered and resented, then let there be an earnest and determined effort to quell all heat in your own heart, and to pacify the one whose anger has been aroused. "Blessed are the peacemakers," etc. (see also Matt. v. 25; Rom. xii. 18).—C.

Vers. 16, 24.—*Use and neglect.* "There is everything in use," we say. And certainly a man's position at any time depends far less upon his bestowments and advantages than upon the use he has made of them. The wise man, in these verses, laments the fact that the price of wisdom should so often be in the hand of a man who fails to turn it to account (ver. 16), and that the foolish man wastes his capacities by directing them to things at a distance instead of giving his attention to that which is within his reach. The facts of human life abundantly justify the lament.

I. THE PRESENCE OF OPPORTUNITY. The price of wisdom, and also of worth and of usefulness, is "in our hand." It is not afar off, that we should ask—Who will ascend to the height or travel across the sea to find and fetch it? Opportunity is amongst and even "within us." We find it in: 1. *Our natural capacities;* here represented by the eyes of a man (ver. 24). We have the power of vision, not only bodily, but mental and spiritual. God has given us the faculty of perception, of observation, of intuition; we can see what is before us—our interest, our duty, our possibilities. 2. *Our various advantages;* the education we receive, the friends and kindred who surround us, the literature which is at our command, the resources we inherit, the openings and facilities that are offered us as we move on into life. These are "the price" wherewith we may "buy wisdom" and happiness, usefulness and power. "The gift of God" is a valuable opportunity (see John iv. 10).

II. OUR FOOLISH AND GUILTY NEGLECT OF IT. Those who have the very fairest chance of attaining to wisdom and usefulness sometimes wantonly throw it away. The foolish boy, at the best school in the land, will refuse to learn, and comes out a dunce. The foolish apprentice, with the best sources of technical or professional knowledge at his command, wastes his hours in frivolity, and when his time is up is utterly unfit for the occupation of his life. Information of what is happening all over the world may now be had for a penny a day, and, what is far more precious, the knowledge of the will of God as revealed in the life and by the lips of Jesus Christ may be had for twopence; but, with "the price of wisdom" at these figures, there are those who know nothing of the hopes or struggles of mankind, and nothing of the way to eternal life. Duty, secular and sacred, is immediately before the eyes of the foolish, but their gaze is fixed upon anything and everything else; they are dreaming, by day and by night, of impossible or of hopelessly improbable fortune, and while they might be patiently and successfully building up a good estate, the chances of life are slipping through their hands. Such neglect of God-given opportunity is: 1. A most serious sin. It is the act of hiding our talent in the earth which calls forth the strong condemnation, "Thou wicked and slothful servant" (Matt. xxv. 24—26). 2. The greatest possible folly. It is a practical renunciation of the fair heritage of life which our heavenly Father offers us; it is the act of flinging the price of wisdom "into the waste."

III. OUR WISE USE OF IT. The wise man is he who makes the most and the best he can make of that which is within his reach, that which is "before his face." He does not spend time in looking and longing for that which is "at the ends of the earth;" he sets himself to cultivate the patch of ground, however small and poor, that is just outside his door. He puts out his talents, however mean they may be. He works his capital, however small it may be. He reads well his books, however limited his library may be. He tries to serve others, however narrow his sphere may be. So doing, he is in the way of constant growth and of a large reward (Matt. xxv. 20—24).—C.

Ver. 17.—*The friend in need.* However we read this passage (see **Exposition**), we have before us the subject of true and lasting friendship. As is stated in a previous homily (see on ver. 9), this is founded on a common attachment to the same great principles, moral and religious; and also on a mutual esteem, each heart holding the other in a real regard. When such intelligent esteem ripens into strong affection, we have a result that deserves to bear the beautiful and honourable name of friendship. The true friend is one that "loves at *all* times," and he is a "brother born for adversity." A false or a weak friendship will not bear the strain which the changeful and hard experiences of life will put upon it; it will break and perish. But a true friendship, well founded and well nourished upon Christian truth, will bear all strains, even those of—

I. Distance.

II. Change of view and of occupation. Friendship usually begins in youth or in the earlier years of manhood; then will come, with maturity of mind and enlargement of knowledge and change of occupation, difference of view on things personal, political, literary, social. But true friendship will endure that strain.

III. Reduction. The loss of health; of property or income, and the consequent reduction in style and in resources; mental vigour with the lapse of time or from the burden of oppressive care and overwork. But faithfulness will triumph over this.

IV. Prosperity. One may ascend in circumstances, in social position; may be attended and even courted by the wealthy and the powerful; may have his time much occupied by pressing duties; and the friendship begun years ago, in a much lower position, may be threatened; but it should not be sacrificed.

V. Dishonour. It does occasionally happen to men that they fall into undeserved reproach. They are misunderstood or they are falsely accused; and the good name is tainted with some serious charge. Neighbours, casual acquaintances, those associated by the slighter social bonds, fall away; they "pass by on the other side." Then is the time for the true friend to make his faithfulness felt; then he is to show himself the man who "loves at all times," the "brother born for adversity." Then he will not only remember where his friend is living, but he will identify himself with him in every open way, will stand by him and walk with him, and honour him, not reluctantly and feebly, but eagerly and energetically.

VI. Declension. It *may* happen that one to whom we have given our heart in tender and loyal affection, between whom and ourselves there has existed a long and intimate friendship, will yield to temptation in one or other of its seductive and powerful forms. It may be that he will gradually decline; it may be that he will fall with some sad suddenness into serious wrong-doing. Then will come to him compunction, humiliation, desertion, loneliness. All his ordinary companions will fall from him. It will be the extreme of adversity, the lowest deep of misery. Then let true friendship show its hand, offer its strong arm, open its door of refuge and of hope; then let the friend prove himself a "brother born for adversity." 1. Be worthy to love the best, that you may form a true friendship. 2. Ennoble your life and yourself by unwavering fidelity in the testing hour, when your friend is most in need of your loyalty. 3. Secure the abiding love of that Friend who is "the same yesterday, and to-day, and for ever."—C.

Vers. 21, 25.—(See homily on ch. x. 1.)—C.

EXPOSITION.

CHAPTER XVIII.

Ver. 1.—This is a difficult verse, and has obtained various interpretations. The Authorized Version gives, Through desire a man, having separated himself, seeketh and intermeddleth with all wisdom; *i.e.* a man who has an earnest desire for self-improvement will hold himself aloof from worldly entanglements, and, occupying himself wholly in this pursuit, will become conversant with all wisdom. This gives good sense, and offers a contrast to the fool in ver. 2, who "hath no delight in understanding." But the Hebrew does not rightly bear this interpretation. Its conciseness occasions ambiguity. Literally, *For his desire a man who separates himself seeks; in* (or *against*) *all wisdom he mingles himself.* There is a doubt whether the life of isolation is praised or censured in this verse. Aben Ezra and others of Pharisaic tendencies adopt the former alternative, and explain pretty much as the Authorized Version, thus : " He who out of love of wisdom divorces himself from home, country, or secular pursuits, such a man will mix with the wise and prudent, and be conversant with such." But the maxim seems rather to blame this separation, though here, again, there is a variety of interpretation. Delitzsch, Ewald, and others translate, " He that dwelleth apart seeketh pleasure, against all sound wisdom he showeth his teeth " (comp. ch. xvii. 14). Nowack, after Bertheau, renders, " He who separates himself goes after his own desire; with all that is useful he falls into a rage." Thus the maxim is directed against the conceited, self-willed man, who sets himself against public opinion, delights in differing from received customs, takes no counsel from others, thinks nothing of public interests, but in his mean isolation attends only to his own private ends and fancies (comp. Heb. x. 25). The Septuagint and Vulgate (followed by Hitzig) read in the first clause, for *taavah,* " desire," *taanah,* " occasion ; " thus : " He who wishes to separate from a friend seeks occasions ; but at all time he will be worthy of censure." The word translated " wisdom " (*tushiyah*) also means " substance," " existence ; " hence the rendering, " at all time," *omni existentia,* equivalent to *omni tempore.*

Ver. 2.—**A fool hath no delight in understanding.** This may mean that he takes no pleasure in the wisdom of others, is self-opinionated ; or, it may be, does not care for understanding in itself, apart from the use which he can make of it. Vulgate, " The fool receives not the words of wisdom ; " Septuagint, " A man of no sense has no need of wisdom." To try to teach a fool is to cast pearls before swine, and to give that which is holy unto dogs. **But that his heart may discover itself;** *i.e.* his only delight is in revealing his heart, displaying his un-wisdom and his foolish thoughts, as in ch. xii. 23 ; xiii. 16 ; xv. 2. He thinks that thus he is showing himself superior to others, and benefiting the world at large. The LXX. gives the reason, " For rather by folly he is led."

Ver. 3.—**When the wicked cometh, then cometh also contempt.** The contempt here spoken of is not that with which the sinner is regarded, but that which he himself learns to feel for all that is pure and good and lovely (Ps. xxxi. 18). As the LXX. interprets, " When the wicked cometh into the depth of evil, he despiseth," he turns a despiser. So the Vulgate. Going

forward in evil, adding sin to sin, he ends by casting all shame aside, deriding the Law Divine and human, and saying in his heart, " There is no God." St. Gregory, " As he who is plunged into a well is confined to the bottom of it ; so would the mind fall in, and remain, as it were, at the bottom, if, after having once fallen, it were to confine itself within any measure of sin. But when it cannot be contented with the sin into which it has fallen, while it is daily plunging into worse offences, it finds, as it were, no bottom to the well into which it has fallen, on which to rest. For there would be a bottom to the well, if there were any bounds to his sin. Whence it is well said, ' When a sinner hath come into the lowest depth of sins, he contemneth.' For he puts by returning, because he has no hope that he can be forgiven. But when he sins still more through despair, he withdraws, as it were, the bottom from the well, so as to find therein no resting-place " (' Moral.,' xxvi. 69, Oxford transl.). Even the heathen could see this terrible consequence. Thus Juvenal is quoted (' Sat.,' xiii. 240, etc.)—

" Nam quis
Peccandi finem posuit sibi ? quando recepit
Ejectum semel attrita de fronte ruborem ?
Quisnam hominum est, quem tu contentum
    videris uno
Flagitio ? "

And with ignominy cometh reproach. Here again it is not the reproach suffered by the sinner that is meant (as in ch. xi. 2), but the abuse which he heaps on others who strive to impede him in his evil courses. All that he says or does brings disgrace, and he is always ready to revile any who are better than himself. Both the Septuagint and the Vulgate make the wicked man the victim instead of the actor, thus : " but upon him there cometh disgrace and reproach." The Hebrew does not well admit this interpretation.

Ver. 4.—**The words of a man's mouth are as deep waters.** " Man " (*ish*) here means the ideal man in all his wisdom and integrity, just as in ch. xviii. 22 the ideal wife is intended under the general term " wife." Such a man's words are as deep waters which cannot be fathomed or exhausted. The metaphor is common (see ch. xx. 5 ; Eccles. vii. 24 ; Ecclus. xxi. 13). For "mouth," the Septuagint reads "heart:" " Deep water is a word in a man's heart." The second hemistich explains the first : **The well-spring of wisdom as a flowing** (*gushing*) **brook.** A man's words are now called a wellspring of wisdom, gushing forth from its source, the wise and understanding heart, pure, fresh, and inexhaustible. Septuagint, "And it leapeth forth (ἀναπηδύει) a river and a fountain of life." Or we may, with Delitzsch, take the whole as one idea, and consider that a man's words are deep waters, a bubbling brook, and a fountain of wisdom.

Ver. 5.—It is **not good to accept the person of the wicked.** To "accept the person" is to show partiality, to be guided in judgment, not by the facts of a case, or the abstract principles of right or wrong, but by extraneous considerations, as a man's appearance, manners, fortune, family. (For the expression, comp. Lev. xix. 15; Deut. i. 17; and in our book, ch. xxiv. 23; xxviii. 21.) The Septuagint phrase is θαυμάσαι πρόσωπον, which St. Jude adopts (ver. 16). Other writers in the New Testament use λαμβάνειν πρόσωπον in the same sense; e.g. Luke xx. 21; Gal. ii. 6). **To overthrow (turn aside) the righteous in judgment** is not good (comp. Isa. x. 2). The construction is the same as in ch. xvii. 26. The LXX. adds in the second clause, οὐδὲ ὅσιον, which makes the sentence clear; not seeing this, the Vulgate renders, *ut declines a veritate judicii.* The offence censured is the perversion of justice in giving sentence against a righteous man whose cause the judge has reason to know is just.

Ver. 6.—**A fool's lips enter into contention**; literally, *come with quarrel* (comp. Ps. lxvi. 13); *i.e.* they lead him into strife and quarrels; *miscent se rixis*, Vulgate; "lead him into evils," Septuagint. The foolish man meddles with disputes in which he is not concerned, and by his silly interference not only exposes himself to reprisals, but also exacerbates the original difficulty. **His mouth calleth for strokes.** His words provoke severe punishment, "stripes for his back," as it is said in ch. xix. 29. Septuagint, "His mouth which is audacious calls for death."

Ver. 7.—The results of the fool's disposition and actions are further noted. **A fool's mouth is his destruction** (comp. ch. x. 14; xiii. 3; Eccles. x. 12). A mediæval adage pronounces, "Ex lingua stulta veniunt incommoda multa." **His lips are the snare of his soul;** bring his life into danger (see on ch. xii. 13; comp. ch. xiii. 14; xiv. 27; xvii. 28). So St. Luke (xxi. 35) speaks of the last day coming upon men like "a snare (παγίς)," the word used by the Septuagint in this passage.

Ver. 8.—The **words of a tale-bearer are as wounds.** *Nèrgan*, "tale-bearer," is better rendered "whisperer" (see on ch. xvi. 28). The Authorized Version reminds one of the mediæval jingle—

"Lingua susurronis
Est pejor felle draconis."

The verse recurs in ch. xxvi. 22; but the word rendered "wounds" (*mitlahamim*) is to be differently explained. It is probably the hithp. participle of *laham*, "to swallow," and seems to mean "dainty morsels," such as one eagerly swallows. Thus Gesenius. Schultens, Delitzsch, Nowack, and others. So the clause means, "A whisperer's words are received with avidity; calumny, slander, and evil stories find eager listeners." The same metaphor is found in ch. xix. 28; Job xxxiv. 7. There may, at the same time, be involved the idea that these dainty morsels are of poisonous character. Vulgate, *Verba bilinguis, quasi simplicia,* "The words of a man of double tongue seem to be simple," which contains another truth. **They go down into the innermost parts of the belly** (ch. xx. 27, 30). The hearers take in the slanders and treasure them up in memory, to be used as occasion shall offer. The LXX. omits this verse, and in its place introduces a paragraph founded partly on the next verse and partly on ch. xix. 15. The Vulgate also inserts the interpolation, "Fear overthrows the sluggish; and the souls of the effeminate (ἀνδρογύνων) shall hunger."

Ver. 9.—**He also that is slothful (*slack*) in his work.** A man that does his work in some sort, but not heartily and diligently, as one who knows that labour is not only a duty and necessity, but a means of sanctification, a training for a higher life. **Is brother to him that is a great waster; a destroyer.** "Brother" is used as "companion" in ch. xxviii. 24 (comp. Job xxx. 29), for one of like attributes and tendencies; as we say, "next door to;" and the destroyer is, as Nowack says, not merely one who wastes his property by reckless expenditure, but one who delights in such destruction, finds a morbid pleasure in havoc and ruin. So the maxim asserts that remissness in duty is as mischievous as actual destructiveness. "An idle brain," say the Italians, "is the devil's workshop." The word rendered "great" is *baal* (ch. i. 19), "owner," *patrono* (Montanus), *domino* (Vatablus); and, taking this sense, according to Wordsworth and others, the sentence implies that the servant who is slothful is brother to a master who is a prodigal. But the interpretation given above is best founded. The LXX., reading מחרפא instead of מתרפה, renders, "He who healeth not (ὁ μὴ ἰώμενος) himself in his works is brother to him who destroyeth himself." Maxims concerning laziness are found in other places; e.g. ch. x. 4; xii. 11, 24; xxiii. 21.

Ver. 10.—The **Name of the Lord is a strong tower.** The Name of the Lord signifies all that God is in himself—his attributes, his love, mercy, power, knowledge; which allow man to regard him as a sure Refuge. "Thou hast been a Shelter for me," says the psalmist (Ps. lxi. 3), "and a strong Tower from the enemy." The words bring before us a picture of a capitol, or central fortress, in which, at times of danger, the surrounding population could take refuge. Into this Name we Christians are baptized; and trusting in it, and doing the duties to which our profession calls, with faith and prayer, we are safe in the storms of life and the attacks of spiritual enemies. The righteous runneth into it (the tower), and is safe; literally, *is set on high; exaltabitur*, Vulgate; he reaches a position where he is set above the trouble or the danger that besets him. Thus St. Peter, speaking of Christ, exclaims (Acts iv. 12), "Neither is there salvation in any other; for there is none other Name under heaven given among men, whereby we must be saved." "Prayer," says Tertullian ('De Orat.,' 29), "is the wall of faith, our arms and weapons against man who is always watching us. Therefore let us never go unarmed, night or day. Under the arms of prayer let us guard the standard of our Leader; let us wait for the angel's trumpet, praying." Septuagint, "From the greatness of his might is the Name of the Lord; and running unto it the righteous are exalted."

Ver. 11.—In contrast with the Divine tower of safety in the preceding verse is here brought forward the earthly refuge of the worldly man. The rich man's wealth is his strong city. The clause is repeated from ch. x. 15, but with quite a different conclusion. And as an high wall in his own conceit. The rich man imagines his wealth to be, as it were, an unassailable defence, to preserve him safe amid all the storms of life. בְּמַשְׂכִּתוֹ (*bemaskitho*), rendered "in his own conceit," is, as Venetian has, ἐν φαντασίᾳ αὐτοῦ, "in his imagination," *maskith* being "an image or picture," as in Lev. xxvi. 1; Ezek. viii. 12; but see on ch. xxv. 11. Aben Ezra brings out the opposition between the secure and stable trust of the righteous in the Lord's protection, and the confidence of the rich worldling in his possessions, which is only imaginary and delusive. Vulgate, *Et quasi murus validus circumdans eum*, "Like a strong wall surrounding him;" Septuagint, "And its glory (δόξα) greatly overshadows him;" *i.e.* the pomp and splendour of his wealth are his protection, or merely paint him like a picture, having no real substance. The commentators explain the word ἐπισκιάζει in both senses.

Ver. 12.—(Comp. ch. xvi. 18; xv. 33; where the maxims are found in almost the same words.)

Ver. 13.—He that answereth a matter, etc. Thus Ecclus. xi. 8, "Answer not before thou hast heard the cause; neither interrupt men in the midst of their talk." A remi-

niscence of the passage occurs in the Talmud ('Aboth,' 5. 10), "I weighed all things in the balance, and found nothing lighter than meal; lighter than meal is the betrothed man who dwells in the house of his intended father-in-law; lighter than he is a guest who introduces a friend; and lighter than he is the man who answers before he has heard the other's speech" (Dukes, p. 72, § 21). So Menander—

Ὁ προκαταγιγνώσκων δὲ, πρὶν ἀκοῦσαι σαφῶς
Αὐτὸς πονηρός ἐστι, πιστεύσας κακῶς.

Seneca, 'Medea,' 199—

"Qui statuit aliquid, parte inaudita altera,
Æquum licet statuerit, haud æquus erit."

Ver. 14.—The spirit of a man will sustain his infirmity. That high property or faculty of man called "spirit" enables the body to bear up against trouble and sickness (comp. ch. xvii. 22). The influence of the mind over the body, in a general sense, is here expressed. But taking "spirit" in the highest sense, in the trichotomy of human nature, we see an intimation that the grace of God, the supernatural infusion of his presence, is that which strengthens the man and makes him able to endure with patience. But a wounded (*broken*) spirit who can bear? The body can, as it were, fall back upon the support of the spirit, when it is distressed and weakened; but when the spirit itself is broken, grieved, wearied, debilitated, it has no resource, no higher faculty to which it can appeal, and it must succumb beneath the pressure. Here is a lesson, too, concerning the treatment of others. We should be more careful not to wound a brother's spirit than we are to refrain from doing a bodily injury; the latter may be healed by medical applications; the former is more severe in its effects, and is often irremediable. In the first clause, רוּחַ, "spirit," is masculine, in the second it is feminine, intimating by the change of gender that in the former case it is a manly property, a virile moral quality, in the latter it has become weakened and depressed through affliction. Septuagint, "A prudent servant soothes a man's wrath; but a man of faint heart (ὀλιγόψυχον) who will endure?" The LXX. take "spirit" in the sense of anger, and "infirmity" as standing for a servant, though where they find "prudent" is difficult to say. Vulgate, *Spiritum vero ad irascendum facilem, quis poterit sustinere?* The Latin interpreter takes one form of weakness of spirit, viz. irascibility, as his interpretation of נכאה, "wounded." St. Gregory ('Moral.,' v. 78) has yet another version, "Who can dwell with a man whose spirit is ready to wrath?" adding, "For he that does not regulate his feelings by the reason that is proper to man, must needs live alone like a beast."

Ver. 15.—The first clause is similar to ch. xv. 14; the second gives a kind of explanation of the former—the understanding of the wise man is always expanding and increasing its stores, because his ear is open to instruction, and his ability grows by wholesome exercise (comp. ch. i. 5). *Daath*, " knowledge," which is used in both clauses, the LXX. translates by two words, αἴσθησιν and ἔννοιαν.

Ver. 16.—**A man's gift maketh room for him** (comp. ch. xix. 6). *Mattam*, "gift," has been taken in different senses. Some consider it to mean a bribe offered for underhand or fraudulent purposes; but the context does not lead to this conclusion, and the parallel passage mentioned above makes against it. Hitzig sees in it a spiritual gift, equivalent to χάρισμα; but such a meaning is not elsewhere attached to the word. The term here signifies the present which duty or friendship offers to one whom one wishes to please. This paves a man's way to a great person's presence. **Bringeth him before great men.** The Oriental custom of offering suitable gifts to one in authority, when a favour or an audience is desired, is here alluded to (comp. 1 Sam. x. 27; 1 Kings iv. 21; x. 25). So the Magi brought gifts to the new-born King at Bethlehem (Matt. ii. 11). In a spiritual sense, the right use of riches opens the way to eternal life, evincing a man's practical love of God and man; as Christ says (Luke xvi. 9), "Make to yourselves friends by means of the mammon of unrighteousness; that, when it shall fail, they may receive you into the eternal tabernacles" (Revised Version).

Ver. 17.—**He that is first in his own cause seemeth just;** Revised Version, *he that pleadeth his cause first seemeth just.* A man who tells his own story, and is the first to open his case before the judge or a third party, seems for the moment to have justice on his side. **But his neighbour cometh and searcheth him out** (ch. xxviii. 11). The "neighbour" is the opposing party—ὁ ἀντίδικος, Septuagint, which recalls Matt. v. 25—he sifts and scrutinizes the statements already given, shows them to be erroneous, or weakens the evidence which appeared to support them. Thus the maxims, "One story is good till the other is told," and "Audi alteram partem," receive confirmation. Vulgate, *Justus prior est accusator sui.* So Septuagint, "The righteous is his own accuser in opening the suit (ἐν πρωτολογίᾳ)." He cuts the ground from under the adversary's feet by at once owning his fault. St. Gregory more than once, in his ' Moralia,' adduces this rendering. Thus on Job vii. 11, "To put the mouth to labour is to employ it in

the confession of sin done, but the righteous man doth not refrain his mouth, in that, forestalling the wrath of the searching Judge, he falls wroth upon himself in words of self-confession. Hence it is written, 'The just man is first the accuser of himself'" (so lib. xxii. 33).

Ver. 18.—**The lot causeth contentions to cease** (comp. ch. xvi. 33). If this verse is taken in connection with the preceding, it refers to the decision in doubtful cases, where the evidence is conflicting and ordinary investigation fails to elicit the truth satisfactorily. The lot, being considered to show the judgment of God, settled the question. **And parteth between the mighty.** If it were not for the decision by lot, persons of eminence and power would settle their differences by violent means. This peaceful solution obviates all such contentions. The Septuagint, in place of " lot" (κλῆρος), reads now σιγηρός, "silent;" but it is evidently originally a clerical error, perpetuated by copyists. The error is noted by a second hand in the margin of the Sinaitic Manuscript.

Ver. 19.—**A brother offended** is harder to be won **than a strong city.** Something must be supplied on which the comparative notion *min*, "than," depends. So we may understand "resists more," or something similar. A brother or a once close friend, when injured or deceived, becomes a potent and irreconcilable enemy. The idea of the preceding verses is carried on, and the primary thought is still concerning lawsuits and matters brought before a judge. This is shown in the second clause by the use of the word "contentions" (*midyanim*). **And their contentions are like the bars of a castle.** They close the door against reconciliation, shut the heart against all feeling of tenderness. True it is, Χαλεποὶ πόλεμοι ἀδελφῶν (Eurip., ' Fragm.'). And again, ' Iph. Aul.,' 376—

Δεινὸν, κασιγνήτοισι γίγνεσθαι λόγους
Μάχας θ', ὅταν ποτ' ἐμπέσωσιν εἰς ἔριν.

Aristotle also writes thus (' De Republ.,' vii. 7): "If men receive no return from those to whom they have shown kindness, they deem themselves, not only defrauded of due gratitude, but actually injured. Whence it is said, ' Bitter are the quarrels of friends;' and, 'Those who love beyond measure also hate beyond measure.'" An English maxim gloomily decides, "Friendship once injured is for ever lost." Pliny (' Hist. Nat.,' xxxvii. 4), " Ut adamas, si frangi contingat malleis, in minutissimas dissidit crustas, adeo ut vix oculis cerni queant; ita arctissima necessitudo, si quando contingat dirimi, in summam vertitur simultatem, et ex arctissimis fœderibus, si semel rumpantur, maxima nascuntur dissidia." Ecclus. vi. 9, " There is a friend, who being turned to enmity will also discover thy disgraceful strife," *i.e.* will disclose the quarrel which according to his representation will redound to thy discredit. The Vulgate and Septuagint have followed a different reading from that of the present Hebrew text: "Brother aided by brother is like a strong and high city, and he is powerful as a well-founded palace," Septuagint. The last clause is rendered in the Vulgate, *Et judicia quasi vectes urbium;* where *judicia* means "lawsuits," legal disputes; these bar out friendship. The first member of the sentence in the Greek and Latin recalls Eccles. iv. 9, etc., "Two are better than one; because they have a good reward for their labour," etc. St. Chrysostom, commenting on Eph. iv. 3 ('Hom.,' ix.), writes, "A glorious bond is this; with this bond let us bind ourselves together alike to one another and to God. This is a bond that bruises not, nor cramps the hands it binds, but it leaves them free, and gives them ample play and greater energy than those which are at liberty. The strong, if he be bound to the weak, will support him, and not suffer him to perish; and if again he be tied to the indolent, he will rather rouse and animate. 'Brother helped by brother,' it is said, 'is as a strong city.' This chain no distance of place can interrupt, neither heaven, nor earth, nor death, nor anything else, but it is more powerful and stronger than all things."

Ver. 20.—With the first clause, comp. ch. xii. 14, and with the second, ch. xiii. 2. **A man's belly**; *i.e.* himself, his mind and body, equivalent to **shall he be filled**, or *satisfied*, in the second clause. A man must accept the consequences of his words, good or evil. The next verse explains this.

Ver. 21.—**Death and life are in the power of the tongue;** literally, *in the hand of the tongue.* The tongue, according as it is used, deals forth life or death; for speech is the picture of the mind (comp. ch. xii. 18; xxvi. 28). The vast importance of our words may be learned from Jas. iii.; and our blessed Lord says expressly (Matt. xii. 36, etc.), "Every idle word that men shall speak, they shall give account thereof in the day of judgment. For by thy words thou shalt be justified, and by thy words thou shalt be condemned." Hence the gnome—

Γλῶσσα τύχη, γλῶσσα δαίμων,

intimating that the tongue is the real controller of man's destiny; and another—

Λόγῳ διοικεῖται βροτῶν βίος μόνῳ.

"By words alone is life of mortals swayed."

And they that love it (the tongue) **shall eat the fruit thereof.** They who use it much must abide the consequences of their words,

whether by kind and pure and edifying conversation they contribute health and life to themselves and others, or whether by foul, calumnious, corrupting language they involve themselves and others in mortal sin. For "they that love it," the Septuagint has, οἱ κρατοῦντες αὐτῆς, "they who get the mastery over it."

Ver. 22.—**Whoso findeth a wife findeth a good** thing. A good wife is meant (as the Septuagint has it, γυναῖκα ἀγαθήν; *mulierem bonam*, Vulgate), a virtuous, prudent helpmate, as in ch. xii. 4; xix. 14; and xxxi. The epithet is omitted, because the moralist is thinking of the ideal wife, the one whose union is blessed, who alone deserves the holy name of wife. Thus in ver. 4 we had the ideal man spoken of. Septuagint, εὖρε χάριτας, "findeth graces," viz. peace, union, plenty, order (see a different view, Eccles. vii. 26—28). **And obtaineth favour of the Lord** (ch. viii. 35; xii. 2); or, *hath obtained* (ch. iii. 13), as shown by the consort whom God has given him. *Ratson*, "good will," "favour," is rendered by the Septuagint ἱλαρότητα, and by the Vulgate, *jucunditatem*, "cheerfulness," "joyousness" (see on ch. xix. 12). Ecclus. xxvi. 1, etc., "Blessed is the man that hath a good wife, for the number of his days shall be double. A virtuous (ἀνδρεία) woman rejoiceth her husband, and he shall fulfil the years of his life in peace. A good wife is a good portion which shall be given in the portion of them that fear the Lord." "A good wife," says the Talmud, "is a good gift; she shall be given to a man that feareth God." And again, "God did not make woman from man's head, that she should not rule over him; nor from his feet, that she should not be his slave; but from his side, that she should be near his heart" (Dukes, p. 69). A Greek gnome runs—

Γυνή δικαία τοῦ βίου σωτηρία.

The Septuagint and Vulgate here introduce a paragraph which is not in the Hebrew, and only partly in the Syriac. It seems to be a further explanation of the statement in the text, founded on the practice prevalent at the time when the Septuagint Version was composed, which appears to have made divorce a recognized necessity in the case of adultery: "He who casteth away a good wife casteth away good things; but he who retaineth an adulteress is a fool and impious." The advice of Siracides concerning a wicked wife is austere: "If she go not as thou wouldest have her, cut her off from thy flesh" (Ecclus. xxv. 26). Nothing is here said about the marriage of divorced persons; but the absolute indissolubility of the marriage bond was never held among the Jews, a certain laxity being allowed because of the hardness of their heart (Matt

v. 32; xix. 8, etc.). The original integrity of the marriage contract was re-established by Christ.

Ver. 23.—This and the following verse, and the first two verses of the next chapter, are not found in the chief manuscripts of the Septuagint, though in later codices they have been supplied from the version of Theodotion. The Codex Venetus Marcianus (23, Holmes and Parsons) is the only uncial that contains them. **The poor useth intreaties; but the rich answereth roughly.** The irony of the passage is more strongly expressed by Siracides : "The rich man hath done wrong, and yet he threateneth withal : the poor is wronged, and he must intreat also" (Ecclus. xiii. 3). The rich man not only does wrong, but accompanies the injury with passionate language and abuse, as if he were the sufferer; while the poor man has humbly to ask pardon, as if he were in the wrong. Thus the Roman satirist writes—

" Libertas pauperis hæc est :
Pulsatus rogat et pugnis concisus adorat,
Ut liceat paucis cum dentibus inde reverti."
(Juv., 'Sat.,' iii. 299.)

Aben Ezra explains the verse as denoting that a poor man making a submissive request from a rich man is answered cruelly and roughly. The hardening effect of wealth is seen in our Lord's parables of Dives and Lazarus (Luke xvi.), and the Pharisee and the publican (Luke xviii.).

Ver. 24.—**A man that hath friends must show himself friendly.** The Authorized Version is certainly not correct. The Hebrew is literally, *a man of friends will come to destruction.* The word הִתְרֹעֵעַ (*hithroea*) is the hithp. infinitive of רעע, "to break or destroy" (comp. Isa. xxiv. 19); and the maxim means that the man of many friends, who lays himself out to make friends of bad and good alike, does so to his own ruin. They will feed upon him, and exhaust his resources, but will not stand by him in the day of calamity, nay, rather will give a helping hand to his downfall. It is not the number of so-called friends that is really useful and precious. **But there is a friend that sticketh closer than a brother** (ch. xvii. 17; xxvii. 10).

Νόμιζ' ἀδελφοὺς τοὺς ἀληθινοὺς φίλους.

" Thy true friends hold as very brethren."

The Vulgate has, *Vir amabilis ad societatem magis amicus erit quam frater,* "A man amiable in intercourse will be more of a friend than even a brother."

HOMILETICS.

Ver. 10.—"*A strong tower.*" These words suggest to us an image of a disturbed country with a massive fortified tower standing in its midst, ready to serve as a refuge for the peasants, who till the fields when all is peaceful, but who flee to the tower for shelter when they see the enemy scouring over the plain. The baronial castles of England served the same purpose when our own country was suffering from the ravages of war. In the dangers of life the Name of the Lord is a similar refuge for his people.

I. NOTE THE NATURE OF THE TOWER. "The Name of the Lord." 1. *God himself.* " God is our Refuge and Strength" (Ps. xlvi. 1). He does not send an angel to protect us. The Church is not a citadel for those who have not first found their shelter in God. But God is with his people for their protection. Even when we have sinned we must "flee from God to God"—from his wrath to his mercy. 2. *The God of Israel.* The Lord, Jehovah. He is known in revelation, and he has been proved in history. This is no new tower that has not been tried and may be found faulty in the hour of need, like a fortress that has never been besieged. The story of God's people in all ages is one long confirmation of its venerable strength. 3. *God as he is revealed*—in his Name. This implies two things. (1) Our knowledge of God. The name is significant of the attributes. God is what his Name signifies. (2) God's own glory and faithfulness. He is sometimes appealed to for his Name's sake. For the sake of his glory, and also his fidelity to his promises, his protecting grace is expected.

II. OBSERVE THE CHARACTER OF THE REFUGE. A tower. 1. *Strong.* God is a Fortress. We do not confide in a weak goodness. Our security is in God's strength. 2. *Lofty.* The tower stands high up above the plain. It is the opposite to a mine. We must look up for shelter. We must climb to God. Our safety is in aspiration. 3. *In our midst.* Though the top of the tower soars above our heads, its foundation is at our feet, and we can enter it from where we stand. God is near at hand for shelter and safety. 4. *Conspicuous.* A cave may not be easily discovered among the rocks of the hillside, but a tower is visible to all. Though the presence of God is not visible to the eye of sense, the revelation of the gospel is open and conspicuous.

III. CONSIDER HOW THE REFUGE MAY BE USED. 1. *For the righteous.* The tower is a shelter from undeserved suffering, as in the case of Job. Here wronged innocence is safe. It is also for all the redeemed who stand before God in the new righteousness of Christ. We cannot be sheltered by God till we are reconciled to God. 2. *By entering it.* There is no safety in looking at it. It is necessary to flee to God in order to be protected by him. The fugitive may even need to run to reach the tower before the foe overtakes him. 3. *With safety.* It is not a palace with a banqueting-hall and couches of ease. It is a fortress, and therefore it may not always be comfortable; but it is safe. We are safe with God.

Ver. 13.—*The folly of hasty judgment.* We may observe some of the cases in which this folly of answering a matter before it is heard is commonly practised.

I. THE SOCIAL RELATIONS. Men are often too quick in forming their opinions of other people. A superficial glance is considered enough for an irrevocable verdict. The sentence is pronounced and the neighbour is characterized before he has had a fair chance of revealing his true nature. 1. This is *ungenerous.* We ought to give a man every opportunity of showing the good that is in him, and to be ready to believe that there may be an unseen goodness that is slow to come to the surface. 2. It is *untruthful.* The verdict should never go beyond the evidence. 3. It is *hurtful.* Much harm has been done by the hasty circulation of raw tales of idle calumny. It would be well to take warning, pause, and inquire before encouraging such mischievous gossip. 4. It is *foolish.* Surely we ought to know that a human character is not to be thus rapidly read off. If we are wise we shall be slow in forming a judgment on our neighbours.

II. IN RELIGIOUS BELIEF. Men are only too hasty in forming their opinions in religion. A minimum of evidence and a maximum of prejudice contribute to form the faith of many people. The same is equally true in regard to unbelief. It does not require much knowledge to show that prejudice is rife in the camp of those who venture to call themselves "free-thinkers." Bigotry is always blind. No men are so perverse as the dogmatic. Just in proportion to their assurance is the weakness of the grounds on which they base their assertions. On the other hand, the fear of forming a false judgment should not drive us into a perpetual suspension of inquiry. We can *hear* the matter of Divine revelation. Our duty is neither to rush to a hasty conclusion nor to retreat into paralyzing doubt, but to "search the Scriptures," "try the prophets," and "hear" the teaching on which we can found our convictions. To fail of this is foolishness that must end in shame, because in the end truth must conquer, and then all the votaries of prejudice will be confounded.

III. IN OUR CONDUCT TOWARDS GOD. This is more personal and practical than the question of religious belief, although the two things are very closely connected. We are tempted to misjudge providence, rebel against the action of God, and try to answer him who is unanswerable. Yet we have not the materials for judging God if the very thought of so doing were not presumptuous. We cannot understand his ways, which are other than ours—higher, wider, wiser, better. Perhaps we shall hear the matter at some future time. It may be that when we have reached the other side of the grave we may be able to look back upon the course of life with the light of heaven upon it, and so to solve some of the enigmas of earth. Meanwhile we have no alternative but to walk by faith. Any attempt at a higher flight will but reveal our folly and issue in our shame.

Ver. 14.—*Strong in spirit.* This thought is near akin to that of ch. xvii. 22, where the medicinal properties of a merry heart are commended. But there is some difference between the two. Both ascribe vital energy to the inner life, and commend such a cultivation of it as shall conquer weakness and suffering ; but the verse now before us treats of vigour of spirit, while the earlier passage commends cheerfulness.

I. A MAN'S TRUE STRENGTH RESIDES IN HIS INNER LIFE. Samson was a weak man, although he had bodily strength, because he had not strength within. St. Paul was regarded as contemptible in bodily appearance (2 Cor. x. 10), yet he was a hero of fiery energy and rock-like steadfastness. He could say, "When I am weak, then am I strong" (2 Cor. xii. 10). The true self is within. All real weakness or power, failure or success, must ultimately spring from this true self. Therefore the first question is as to the condition of the inner life. Those people who live only in the outer experiences do not yet know the deeper meaning of life. We have all to learn how to cultivate the powers of the spirit.

II. STRENGTH IN THE INNER LIFE CAN SUPPORT EXTERNAL INFIRMITY. 1. *Weakness of body.* No doubt the normal condition of health would be one of *mens sana in corpore sano.* But when that is not attained, mental health will do much to counteract the evil effects of bodily disease. The mind has so great power over the body that some forms of functional disease are actually cured through mental influences, as in what is called "faith-healing." The will to live is a great help to recovery from an illness. A crushed and broken spirit too often brings the body into a condition which is the despair of the physician. Higher considerations tell in the same direction, and spiritual health—though, perhaps, not what is meant in our text—will sustain, under disease, if it will not lead to bodily cure. 2. *Temporal trouble.* Misfortune can be borne by a brave, strong spirit; while a crushed, feeble spirit succumbs under it. 3. *Spiritual infirmity.* It is difficult to resist the frailty of our own souls. But when we cultivate our better selves we are best able to overcome infirmities of temper, selfishness, etc.

III. STRENGTH OF SPIRIT IS A DIVINE GRACE. 1. *A gift of God.* He can make the weak strong. "He giveth power to the faint, and to them that have no might he increaseth strength" (Isa. xl. 29). 2. *An acquisition of faith.* "They that wait upon the Lord shall renew their strength" (Isa. xl. 31). It is possible for the weak to become strong, because all can "wait upon the Lord." No grace is more needed, and no grace proves itself to be more fruitful.

Ver. 17.—*Private judgment.* The Protestant claim to the right of private judgment is not without its limitations. Applied to general truths it is unanswerable; but carried out in personal affairs it is often very dangerous. Every man may say that he is the best judge of what concerns himself. But two considerations modify that contention. 1. No one truly knows himself. 2. A man's doings are not confined to himself. They cross the boundaries of other lives and interests. Therefore, while a man is seemingly making an innocent demand concerning his own business, he is really claiming to be the judge of what affects his neighbours. Hence the need of caution.

I. PRIVATE JUDGMENT IS APPARENTLY JUST, EVEN WHEN IT IS ERRONEOUS. It is rarely that a man will own himself to be in the wrong when he is engaged in any contention with his neighbour. 1. Judgment is prejudiced by previous opinions. We all approach a subject with a stock of prepossessions. Even while honestly intending to make a fair estimate, we cannot but apply the standards of our old set notions. Hence the need of working out "the personal equation." 2. It is biassed by *self-interest.* This may be quite unintentional and unconscious. We may not be aware that we are showing any favour to ourselves. Yet so long as the selfishness of human nature remains as it is, there must be a secret weight in the scale inclining it to our own side. 3. It is distorted by *self-deception.* Not knowing ourselves, we misread our own position. We give ourselves credit for aims that do not exist, and we disregard the real motives that actuate our conduct. 4. It is perverted by *ignorance of the position of other people.* We think we are acting justly when we do not know all the circumstances of the case. If we could see all the rights and claims of our neighbours we might be ready to admit our own error.

II. PRIVATE JUDGMENT MAY BE CORRECTED BY GENERAL TESTIMONY. We recognize in the law-courts that it is only right for both parties to a suit to be heard. The same concession is necessary for obtaining a just estimate of all matters in regard to which differences of opinion are expressed. In private life, in public affairs, in theological controversies, we want to learn how to hear the other side. The very difficulties of private judgment call for the correction that may be thus afforded. But other considerations also demand it. 1. *Truth is many-sided.* Even if we be right, it is possible that our neighbours may not be wrong. Our narrowness prevents us from seeing the solid form of truth and its various facets. 2. *Other people have rights.* Until these have been considered we cannot be sure that what looks like a most just contention on our own part may not be a trespass upon them. 3. *Justice may require*

investigation. We see the way in which a skilful counsel will break down the most
plausible evidence by probing into its weak places; how he will worm secrets out of
the most reticent witness. Truth is often revealed through antagonism. The man
who prides himself on hoodwinking his fellows is foolish and short-sighted. If his
insincerity is not discovered on earth, it will be revealed at the great judgment.

Ver. 22.—*The blessedness of true marriage.* The Bible does not regard marriage as
" a failure," nor does it treat celibacy as a more saintly condition. Even St. Paul, who
does not seem to have been a married man, and who is thought by some to undervalue
marriage, gives to it a eulogium in describing the union of husband and wife as a copy
of the mystical union of Christ and his Church (Eph. v. 22—32).
   I. The blessedness of marriage. 1. *The companionship of love.* The creation
of woman is ascribed to the need of this. " And the Lord God said, It is not good that
the man should be alone " (Gen. ii. 18). In a true marriage a man's wife is his best
friend. Fellowship of soul makes the union more than a mere contract of external
relationship. Now, this fellowship is greatly needed for solace amid the cares of life,
and strength to face its difficulties. The wife is able to give it to her husband, and
the husband to the wife, as no persons in the outer circle of social relationship can hope
to offer it. 2. *Mutual helpfulness.* In the narrative of the creation, God says, concerning Adam, " I will make him a help meet for him " (Gen. ii. 18). Woman is
degraded when she is treated as a toy of idle hours, to amuse in the drawing-room, but
not to take her share in the serious concerns of life. No true woman would desire so
idle a position. The wife who understands the Christian calling will aim at ministering
to her husband in all ways of helpfulness that are within her power, but chiefly in
helping his higher life; and the duty of the husband towards the wife will be similar.
3. *Variety of ministration.* The wife is not the counterpart of the husband, but the
complement. Human nature is completed in the union of the two. Therefore it is
not the part of women to imitate men, nor is inferiority to be assigned to women
because they differ from men. The rich, full, perfect human life is attained by the
blending of differences.
   II. The secret of this blessedness. No ideal of human life can be more beautiful
than that of the happy home. The serious question is how it shall be realized. 1. *By
adaptation.* Every woman is not suitable for every man. Hasty courtships may lead to
miserable marriages. So serious a matter as the choice of a companion for life is not
to be lightly undertaken if there is to be any hope of its issuing in happiness. 2. *By
sympathy.* There must be mutual confidence between husband and wife if the marriage
is to be one of true and lasting blessedness. The Oriental cruelty of imprisonment in
the harem, and the Western cruelty of degradation in domestic drudgery, are both fatal
to the idea of marriage. Whatever be their position in the social scale, it is possible for
husbands and wives to share one another's interests and enlarge one another's lives by
conceding the fullest mutual confidence. 3. *By self-sacrifice.* Selfishness is fatal to
marriage. Love must learn to give, to suffer, to endure. The happiness is most
complete when each seeks it chiefly for the other. 4. *By religion.* The true marriage
must be ratified in heaven. Its happiness may be wrecked on so many hidden rocks
that it is not safe to venture on to the unknown sea without the assurance that God
is guiding the voyage.

Ver. 24.—" *The Friend that sticketh closer than a brother.*" Without determining
for certain which of the various renderings of the first clause of this verse should be
adopted, there can be little doubt that it points to the difficulty of maintaining a wide
circle of friends in true affection, contrasted with the blessedness of enjoying one deep
and real friendship. The second cause which describes that friendship claims our
attention on its own account.
   I. The nature of brotherly affection. If the true friend is even more than
a brother, he will have the marks of brotherhood in an exceptional degree. Now,
we have to ask—What are those peculiarities of the relation of brotherhood that determine the brother's affection? 1. *Blood-relationship.* We must all feel the peculiar
oneness that belongs to membership in the same family. 2. *Close companionship*
Brothers are usually brought up together. They share the same hardships, and they

enjoy the same family favours. They are knit together by similarity of experience. 3. *Community of interests.* Brothers share certain family interests in common. Thus families learn to hold together for the general well-being of the members. 4. *Similarity of constitution.* Brothers resemble one another, more or less. To some extent they have common traits of mind, feelings, sympathies, desires. Hence they are drawn together. How great and wonderful must be the friendship that exceeds even this close brotherly affection! Without the natural cause, it yet surpasses the love of brotherhood!

II. THE SIGN OF BROTHERLY AFFECTION. It is seen in cleaving to one's friend. With the highest type of friendship this will be observed under the most trying circumstances. 1. *In spite of the lapse of time.* Some friendships are but temporary. But brotherhood is lifelong. So also is the truest friendship. 2. *In sore need.* Then shallow friendship proves to be false. But at such a time brother should stand by brother. 3. *When faithfulness is costly.* Possibly one is under a cloud and cruelly misjudged; the brotherly soul will claim this as the most suitable time for showing true affection. Or it may be that some great sacrifice must be made to render needed assistance; this requirement will discover the nature of a friendship, and show whether it be truly that of a brother. 4. *When love is tried by indifference or enmity.* Though a man be unworthy of his brother, still true brotherly love will not cast him off. This is also the case with the highest friendship.

No doubt the object of Solomon was simply to give us a type and picture of true friendship. But as in a previous case (ch. xvii. 17), it is impossible for Christians not to recognize the application of the picture to Jesus Christ. His friendship is in all senses truly brotherly. He became a brother Man in order that he might enter into closest relations of love and sympathy with us, and he proves his friendship by doing more than any man ever did for his brother.

HOMILIES BY VARIOUS AUTHORS.

Vers. 1—9.—*Unsocial vices.* There is an inner connection between them all.

I. MISANTHROPY. (Ver. 1.) If this verse be more correctly rendered, this is the meaning yielded. From a diseased feeling the man turns aside to sullen solitude, and thus rejects wisdom. This affords a fine meaning. It is one thing to feel the need of occasional solitude, another to indulge the passion for singularity.

II. OBTRUSIVENESS. (Ver. 2.) Contrast ver. 4. The talkative fool is the very opposite of the misanthrope in his habits; yet the two have this in common—they both unfit themselves for society. We may go out of solitude to indulge our spleen, or into society to indulge our vanity. Talking for talking's sake, and all idle conversation, are here marked, if as *minor* vices, still vices.

III. BASENESS. (Ver. 3.) The word rendered "contempt" points rather to deeds of shame. And the meaning then will be that the evil of the heart must necessarily discover itself in the baseness of the life. As the impure state of the blood is revealed in eruptions and blotches on the skin, so is it with moral evil.

IV. CONSPIRACY AND PLOTTING. (Ver. 5.) The figure employed, literally, to *lift up a person's face,* signifies to take his part. All party-spirit is wrong, because it implies that truth has not the first place in our affections. But party-spirit on behalf of the wicked is an utter abomination, for it implies a positive contempt for, or unbelief in, right and truth.

V. QUARRELSOMENESS. (Vers. 6, 7.) "The apostle, when giving the anatomy of man's depravity, dwells chiefly on the little member with all its accompaniments—the throat, the tongue, the lips, the mouth. It is 'a world of iniquity, defiling the whole body.'" It leads to *violence.* The deadly blow is prepared for and produced by the irritating taunting word. But there is a *recoil* upon the quarrelsome man. The tongue to which he has given so evil licence finally ensnares him and takes him prisoner. And the stones he has cast at others fall back upon himself. Thus does Divine judgment reveal itself in the common course of life.

VI. SLANDEROUSNESS. (Ver. 8.) The word "tale-bearer" is represented more expressively in the Hebrew. It is the man that "blows in the ear." And the picture comes up before the mind of the calumnious word, whispered or jestingly uttered, which goes deep into the most sensitive places of feeling, and wounds, perhaps even unto death.

VII. IDLENESS. (Ver. 9.) Here we strike upon the root of all these hideous vices. It is the neglect of the man's proper work which suffers these vile weeds to grow. What emphasis there needs to be laid on the great precept, " Do thine own work " ! The idler is brother to the corrupter, or vicious man, and his kinship is certain sooner or later to betray itself. The parable of the talents may be compared here. Then, again, how close are the ideas of *wickedness* and *sloth !*—J.

Vers. 10—16.—*Some conditions of weal and woe.* I. CONSTITUTIONS OF LIFE-WEAL. 1. *First and foremost, religion* (ver. 10) and *humility* (ver. 12). The Name of Jehovah stands for all that God *is* (the "I am"). Trust in the Eternal is the real ground of confidence for a creature so *transient* and frail as man. To put the same truth in another way, it is religious principle which can alone sustain the soul calm and erect amidst distress. And with true religion is ever connected humility. The knowledge of one's *just position* in the world is, on the whole, humbling. It is the conceit that one is greater than one really is which is so pernicious *inwardly*, and will prove so outwardly. 2. *Competence of worldly means.* (Ver. 11.) It is the worst hypocrisy and affectation to deny the good of money, even with reference to the culture of the soul. Here we have the common view of riches ; they are a *source of strength.* Truly ; but one easily exaggerated. 3. *A cheerful temper.* (Ver. 14.) Health is the grand elementary and all-inclusive blessing. Well ! one of the main conditions of health is a merry heart, or a disposition to look on the best side of things. " I thank it, poor fool ; it keeps on the windy side of care." 4. *An open mind.* (Ver. 15.) The intelligent heart and the ever-listening ear,—these are the great instruments or means of knowledge and wisdom. It is good to have many and large windows in the house ; and to keep the soul open on all sides to the light of God. 5. *Judicious liberality.* (Ver. 16.) We found this lesson insisted on in ch. xvii. 8. The heathen poet said, " Gifts persuade the gods, gifts persuade dread kings." Often as the principle is made bad use of, let us recollect it has an opposite aspect, and make friends to ourselves of the " mammon of unrighteousness."

II. SOURCES OF TROUBLE. 1. *Pride.* (Ver. 12.) How emphatic by repetition is the warning against this *inward* vice (ch. xvi. 18) ! Like the clouds going *up the hill,* portending rain, so does self-conceit prophesy sorrow. 2. *Excessive eagerness.* (Ver. 13.) " Condemn no one," says the Book of Jesus Sirach (Ecclus. xi. 7), " before thou knowest the matter in question : know first, and then rebuke. Thou shalt not judge before thou hearest the matter; and let others speak first." Ignorance and self-conceit are ever forward ; wisdom holds its strength in reserve. 3. *Indulgence in depression.* (Ver. 14.) " A cast-down spirit who can bear ? " We must remember that the ailments of the mind are strictly analogous to those of the body ; and if the latter are to an indefinite degree under the control of the will, so too are the former. We must believe in the God-given power of the will, or no medicine can avail us.—J.

Vers. 17—21.—*Evils of the tongue and of contention.* I. THE FOLLY OF HASTE IN DEBATE. (Ver. 17.) " One tale is good till another be told." This saw holds good of private life, of lawsuits, of controversies in philosophy and theology. *Audi alteram partem,* " Listen to both sides." This is the duty of the judge, or of him who for the time being plays the judicial part. If we are parties in a debate or a suit, then nothing will hold good except to have the " conscience void of offence."

II. THE ADVANTAGE OF ARBITRATION. (Ver. 18.) The lot was the ancient mode of arbitration and settlement of disputes in a peaceful manner. Something corresponding to it in modern times may be adopted as a wise resource where other means of reconciliation have failed. Still better, the general lesson may be drawn—commit the decision to the wisdom of God.

III. THE MISERY OF DISSENSION. (Ver. 19.) The alienated brother or friend is compared to an impregnable fortress. " Oh how hard to reconcile the foes that once were friends !" The sweeter the wine, the sharper the vinegar ; and the greater the natural love, the more violent the hate where that love has been injured.

IV. The satisfaction of wise counsels. (Ver. 20; comp. ch. xii. 14; xiii. 2.) The mode of expression is strange to a modern ear, but the thought is familiar and welcome. Words here stand for thoughts; the fruit of the lips comes from the root of the heart. When an intensely modern writer says, "Nothing can bring you peace but the triumph of your principles," he puts the old truth in a new light.

V. Life and death in the tongue. (Ver. 21.) Here is another great principle, vast in its sweep. "Life and death are in the power of witnesses according to the testimony they bear, of judges according to the sentence they pass, of teachers according to the doctrine they preach, of all men who by their well or evil speaking bring death or life to themselves or to others" (Gill). Perhaps it is true that the tongue has slain its ten thousands where the sword has slain only its thousands. The employment of the tongue, whether for good or for evil, in blessing or in cursing (Jas. iii. 9; 1 Cor. xii. 3), brings its own fruit and reward to the speaker. "By thy words thou shalt be justified, and by thy words thou shalt be condemned."—J.

Vers. 22—24.—*Love in different relations.* I. Conjugal love. (Ver. 22.) The blessing of a good wife. "Young men's mistresses; companions for middle age; and old men's nurses" (Lord Bacon). On the choice of a wife none but a recluse or a pedant would pretend to lay down infallible precepts or counsels. But every man who has been happy in the married relation will recognize his happiness as among the chiefest of blessings from above. It is indeed a good that is *found*, cannot be inherited nor deserved.

II. Compassion. (Ver. 23.) Here, as so often, the duty is suggested by means of a dark picture of the opposite, of its neglect. The rich man who "against the houseless stranger shuts the door," or who, like Dives, fares luxuriously while Lazarus lies in sores at his gate,—these revolt the heart and may more move the conscience than declamations on the positive duty. When chilled by the coldness and severity of selfish man, let the poor and afflicted turn to the "God of all compassion," and to the revelation of him in the "good Samaritan," in Jesus Christ.

III. Friendship. (Ver. 24.) 1. The *spurious friendship.* The more correct rendering of the first half of the verse seems to be, "a man of many companions will prove himself to be worthless." Mere agreeableness may be a surface quality, may spring more from variety than anything else, will soon wear out, cannot be counted on. Number counts for little in friendship. 2. The *genuine friendship.* More tenacious than the mere natural love of kindred, because founded on the affinity of soul with soul. All the purest types of earthly affection and friendship are but hints of the eternal love of him who calls the soul into espousal, friendship, and eternal communion with himself.—J.

Ver. 2.—(See homily on ch. xvii. 16, 24.)—C.

Ver. 4.—*The utterances of wisdom.* Taking the sense of this passage to be continuous and not antithetical, and understanding it to refer to the utterances of the wisdom which is from above, we notice their constant characteristics, viz.—

I. Their depth. The words which come from the mouth of wisdom are "as deep waters." How shallow is much, if not most, that is spoken in our hearing! It strikes no deeper than "the hour's event," than the mere gilding of our life; it only extends to the circumstances or to the conventionalities of life; it deals with tastes and customs, with regulation and proprieties; it goes no further than pecuniary or social expectations; it lies upon the surface and does not touch "the deep heart and reality of things." But the wisdom of the wise strikes deep; it goes down into the character; it touches first principles; it has to do with the sources and springs of human action; it concerns itself with the intrinsically true, the really beautiful, the solidly and permanently good.

II. Their spontaneity. The utterances of men who are not truly wise are lacking in this. They can only repeat what they have learned; they have to consult their "authorities" in order to know what they should say; they have to labour and strive in order to express themselves. Not so the truly wise. Their words come from them as water from a well-spring; their speech is the simple, natural, unconstrained outflow of their soul; they speak from the heart, not from the book. Their spirit is full of Divine wisdom; they "have understanding" (ch. xvii. 24); they have knowledge, insight, love of the truth; they "cannot but speak" the truth they have learned of God, the things they have heard and seen. And the spontaneity of their utterance is one real element in their eloquence and their influence.

III. Their communicativeness. They are "as a flowing brook." As water that is not pent up like a reservoir, but flows on through the thirsty land, communicating moisture, and thus ministering to life and growth, so the words of the wise are continually flowing; they spread from heart to heart, from land to land, from age to age. And as they flow they minister to the life and the growth of men; they communicate those living truths which enlighten the mind, which soften and change the heart, which transform and ennoble the life. Their career is never closed, for from soul to soul, from lip to lip, from life to life, wisdom passes on in its blessed, unbroken course. 1. Be ever learning of God. He himself, in the book which he has "written for our learning," is the Divine Source of such wisdom as this. Only as we receive from him who is "the Wisdom of God" shall we be partakers and possessors of this heavenly wisdom. And therefore: 2. Come into the closest communion and connection with Jesus Christ himself. 3. Open your mind to all sources of truth whatsoever.—C.

Ver. 8.—(See homily on ch. xvii. 9.)—C.

Ver. 9.—*Needless destitution.* This strong utterance suggests—

I. The prevalence of destitution. How much of human life is needlessly low! how many men live low down in the scale who might just as well be living high up it! how sadly do men bereave themselves of good! This applies to: 1. *Their circumstances:* their daily surroundings; the homes in which they live, their food and raiment, the occupations in which they are engaged; their companionships, etc. 2. *Their intelligence:* their intellectual activity, their knowledge, their acquaintance with their own complex nature and with the world in which they live, their familiarity with (or their ignorance of) men and things. 3. *Their moral and spiritual condition:* their capacity or incapacity to control their temper, to govern their spirit, to regulate their life, to form honourable and elevating habits, to worship God, to set their lives in accordance with the will and after the example of Christ.

II. The two main sources of it. These are those which are indicated in the text. 1. *The absence of energy* in action; being "slothful [or, 'slack,' Revised Version] in work." Men who fail in their department, of whatever kind it may be, are usually those who do not throw any heart, any earnestness, any continuous vigour, into their work. They do what is before them perfunctorily, carelessly, or spasmodically. Hence they make no profits, they earn low wages, they have poor crops, they gain few customers or patients, they win no success; hence they read few instructive books, they make no elevating and informing friendships, they acquire no new ideas, they store up no new facts, they make no mental progress; hence they do not cultivate their moral and spiritual nature, they do not "build themselves up" on the foundation of truth; they are adding no stones to the living temple; they do not grow in wisdom, or in worth, or in grace. The other source is: 2. *The presence of prodigality.* He that is slothful in work is "brother to him that is a great waster." What sad wastefulness is on every hand! what dissipation of gathered treasure! what expenditure of means and of strength on that which does not profit! For these are the two forms of waste. (1) Allowing to depart that which it would be wise to hold in hand—money, goods, friends, supporters, resources. (2) Expending power on that which does not profit; letting our time, our strength, our mental forces, our moral energies, be employed upon those things which yield no return, or no adequate and proportionate return. Were men to spend their money on profitable and fruit-bearing labour, their brains on enlightening and enlarging study, their spiritual energies on intelligent worship or redeeming work, instead of wasting them as now they do, how would the desert become a fruitful field, in every sphere! But we must not overlook the fact that there is—

III. A solid remainder, not thus accounted for. Although sloth and waste together explain a very large part indeed of the destitution on the earth, they leave much still to be accounted for. And of this remainder part is due to simple and pure misfortune or incapacity, and part to the guilt of others who are not the sufferers. All this destitution is the proper field for Christian effort. It is the proper object of our genuine compassion, and of our strenuous endeavour toward removal. But to those who are culpably destitute we have to go and say—Your way upward is before you; you must exert yourselves if you would rise. No one can really enrich a human soul but himself. 1. Bring a sustained energy to bear on the work in which you are engaged. 2. Guard with a wise watchfulness what you have won. 3. Put out your powers upon that which is worthy of them and that which will repay them.—C.

Ver. 10.—*God our Refuge.* By "the Name of the Lord" we understand the Lord as he has revealed himself to us, the Lord as he has taught us to think and to speak of him. He is our strong Tower in the time of trouble.

I. OUR NEED OF A REFUGE IN THE BATTLE OF LIFE. There may be much in our life that may lead us to speak of it as a song or a tale, or as a march or pilgrimage; but there is much that compels us to consider it a battle or a struggle. Many are the occasions when we have to look about us for a refuge to which we may flee; for we have, at different times and under different circumstances, to confront: 1. *Oppression.* Ill treatment, severity; the injustice, or the inconsiderateness, or the assumption of those who can afflict us. 2. *Disaster.* The loss of that which is valuable or of those who are precious to us. 3. *Difficulty.* The uprising of great obstacles which seem to be insurmountable. 4. *Temptation.* Which may act upon us quietly but continuously, and therefore effectively, or which may come down upon us with almost overwhelming suddenness and force. Then we ask ourselves—What is the refuge, the high tower, to which we shall resort?

II. TWO RESOURCES WHICH ARE GOOD, BUT INSUFFICIENT. 1. *Our own fortitude.* This is that to which Stoicism, the noblest form of ancient philosophy, had recourse— our courage and determination as brave men, who are

"Strong in will
To strive, to seek, to find, and *not to yield.*"

2. *The sympathy and succour of our friends.* The kind heart and the helping hand of those who love us, with whom we have walked along the path of life, and who have linked their heart and hand with ours. Both of these are good; but, as all history and observation teach us, they do not suffice. We want another heart that comes nearer to us, another power that can do more for us than these. So we thankfully turn to—

III. THE REFUGE WE HAVE IN GOD. We know that with him is: 1. *Perfect sympathy.* He is "afflicted in all our affliction;" he is "touched with a feeling of our infirmity;" he "knows what is in" us—what pain of body, what desolateness of spirit, what wrestlings and agonies of the soul. 2. *Boundless wisdom.* He knows what to save us from, and what to let us suffer; how far and in what way he may relieve and restore us; how he can help us so as to bless us truly and permanently. 3. *Almighty power.* Our eyes may well be lifted up unto him, for he can "pluck our feet out of the net." "Our God is a Rock;" all the billows of human rebellion will break in vain upon his power. Into the "strong tower" of his Divine protection we may well "run and be safe." "Who is he that can harm us" there?—C.

Ver. 12.—(See homily on ch. xvi. 18.)—C.

Ver. 14.—*The wounded spirit.* How much is a man better than a sheep? By the whole range of his spiritual nature. The joys and sorrows of a man are those of his spirit; yet no inconsiderable proportion of his experiences come to him through the flesh. The text tells us—

I. THAT THE CONQUERING SPIRIT WITHIN US TRIUMPHS OVER THE BODILY INFIRMITY. There have been times when, and people by whom, the very worst bodily afflictions have been borne with lofty indifference or with still loftier and nobler resignation. Such was the Roman whose right hand was consumed in the fire without a groan; such were the Christian martyrs; such have been and such are they who are condemned to long years of privation or of suffering, and who wear the face of a holy contentment, of even a beautiful cheerfulness of spirit. Beneath the infirmity of the flesh is the sustaining spirit: *but what of the wounded spirit itself?*

II. That it is the wounded spirit for which help is needed. There are many ways in which our spirit may be wounded. 1. There is the *merciful wound from the hand of God.* For God does wound; he wounds in part in order that he may heal altogether; for the moment, that he may make whole for ever. The weapon (or one weapon) with which he smites the soul is the human conscience. We have all felt the smart from its righteous blow. We have before us the alternative of either *blunting* the edge of the instrument or learning the lesson and turning away from the sin. To do the former is to take the path which leads to wrong and ruin; to do the latter is to walk in the way of life. 2. *The faithful wound from the hand of man.* There are circumstances under which, and there are relations in which, we are simply *bound* to wound one another's spirit. As Christ wounded the spirit of Peter with a reproachful glance (Luke xxii. 61, 62); as Paul wounded the Corinthian Christians (2 Cor. ii. 1—10); so will the faithful minister of Christ, the conscientious parent or teacher, the true and loyal friend, now administer rebuke, offer remonstrance, address an appeal which will fill the heart with compunction and regret. 3. *The cruel wound from the hand of man.* This includes (1) the wound of neglect,—often a very deep and sore wound is this, coming from the hand that should sustain and heal; (2) of hastiness and rashness; (3) of malice. 4. *Spare to wound another's spirit.* It is worse to hurt the feelings than to filch the purse; to cause a bad heart-ache than any suffering of the nerve. "The spirit of a man can sustain his infirmity; but a wounded spirit *who can bear?*" 5. *When your heart is wounded repair to the One who can heal it.* There is only One who can " heal the broken heart, and bind up its wounds."—C.

Ver. 17.—*Hear the other side.* There is no truer, as there is no homelier maxim, than that we should " hear the other side," or—what is virtually the same thing— " there are two sides to everything." This is the idea in the text; the lessons are—

I. We should not expect absolute accuracy when a man tells his own case. 1. He may intentionally misrepresent it. 2. He may unconsciously misstate it. How things shape themselves to our mind depends on our individual standpoint; and when two men regard a subject from different and even opposite points of view, they necessarily see it, and as necessarily state it, with considerable variation. Such are the limitations of our mental faculties, and such is our tendency to be biassed in our own favour, that no wise man will expect his neighbour to give him the whole case, without either addition, colouring, or omission, when he pleads his own cause.

II. We should remember the inequality in men's capacity of presentment. Some men can make a very lame cause look like a sound one; but others cannot give to a good cause the appearance of justice to which it is entitled. Truth often yields to advocacy.

III. We should insist on hearing the other side. This is due to both sides. 1. *It is in the true interest of the complainant,* or he will persuade us to give him credence to which he is not morally entitled; he will then wrong his brother; he will be an oppressor or a defamer; from this evil end we should save him by our good sense. 2. *It is due to the defendant;* for otherwise he will have judgment passed when things have been left unspoken which certainly ought to be taken into the account. Justice imperatively demands that we should never condemn our neighbour un il we have heard what he has to say for himself. 3. *It is due to ourselves;* otherwise we shall not be just, and it is our Saviour's express desire that we should "judge righteous judgment" (John vii. 24), and we shall not be like unto "him who judgeth righteously." Our Christian character will be incomplete and our life will be blemished. Moreover: 4. *It is due to the cause of Christ;* for if we condemn or acquit without full and impartial inquiry, we shall do injustice to many, and we shall certainly do injury in many ways to the cause and kingdom of our Lord.—C.

Ver. 19.—*Brethren at strife.* The reference in the text is to—

I. A difficulty everywhere acknowledged. It seems to have been universally felt that a " brother offended " is very hard indeed " to be won." It is more easy to effect a reconciliation between strangers than between those united by ties of blood.

Hence a family feud is usually a very long as well as a very sad one. This does not seem to be a local or a national peculiarity. What Solomon wrote in his land and age might be written by any English or continental moralist to-day. It is human.

II. ITS EXPLANATION. 1. It is an aggravated difficulty, inasmuch as the bitterness aroused is more intense. For always in proportion to the fulness of our love is the greatness of our wrath. Anger is love reversed. Whom we love the most we are in danger of disliking the most; it is against his own wife that the madman first turns his hand. And how should we love another with all the affection we feel for the companion of our childhood and our youth, the sharer of our joys and sufferings from the very cradle and under the parental roof? 2. We shrink with greatest sensitiveness from humbling ourselves before our kindred. Reconciliation usually means apology, and apology means a measure of humiliation. And we do not like to humble our hearts before one with whom we have had and may have so much to do. 3. We are inclined to "stand upon the order of our going;" each thinks the other should make the first move; the younger thinks the elder should because he *is* the elder, and the elder the younger because he *is* the younger. 4. We are apt to resent interposition as interference; to any peacemaker who would intervene we are inclined to say, "Do not intrude into our family secrets."

III. OUR DUTY IN VIEW OF THIS FACT. It is clearly this: 1. To avoid all serious differences with our near kindred; (1) to heal at once the first small breach that may occur, for while a rupture may be beyond remedy, a small difference is easily healed; (2) to consider that almost any sacrifice of money, or of position, or of goods is worth making to retain the love of the children of our own parents, the playmates of our childhood and our youth. 2. To make a determined effort, after earnest thought and prayer, to master the difficulty we find in our heart, and make the first overture to the offended brother. So shall we win a really noble victory over ourselves; so shall we gain the warm approval of the Prince of peace.—C.

Ver. 24.—*The unfailing Friend.* If these words had occurred in a book written any time A.D., we should unhesitatingly have referred them to our Lord; they are beautifully and perfectly applicable to him. For closer than any brother is he who is "not ashamed to call us brethren."

I. HE COMES NEARER TO US THAN ANY BROTHER CAN. A human brother can draw very near to us in his knowledge of us and his brotherly sympathy with us; but not as Christ, our Divine Friend, can and does. His *knowledge* of us is perfect—of our hopes and fears, of our struggles and our sorrows, of our aspirations and endeavours, of all that passes within us. And his *sympathy* with us and his *succour* of us are such as man cannot render. He can pity us with a perfect tenderness of spirit, and he can touch our hearts with a sustaining and healing hand as the kindest and wisest of men cannot.

II. HE IS ALWAYS THE SAME TO US; OUR BROTHER IS NOT. We can never be quite sure that our kindest brother will be in a mood or in a position to lend us his ear or his hand. But we have not to make this qualification or enter into this consideration when we think of Christ. We know we shall not find him too occupied to hear us, or indisposed to sympathize with us, or unable to aid us. He is always the same, and ever ready to receive and bless us (Heb. xiii. 8).

III. HIS PATIENCE IS INEXHAUSTIBLE; OUR BROTHER'S IS NOT. By our importunity, or by our infirmity, or by our unworthiness, we may weary the most patient human friend or brother; but we do not weary the Divine Friend; and even though we do that or be that which is evil and hurtful, which is painful and grievous in his sight, still he bears with us, and at our first moment of spiritual return he is prepared to welcome and restore us.

IV. HE EVER LIVETH; OUR BROTHER MAY BE TAKEN FROM US. 1. Seek the lasting favour and friendship of Jesus Christ. 2. Realize the honour of that friendship, and walk worthily of it. 3. Gain from it all the comfort, strength, and sanctity which a close and living friendship with him will surely yield. 4. Introduce all whom you can to him, that they may share this invaluable blessing.—C.

EXPOSITION.

CHAPTER XIX.

Ver. 1.—Better is the poor that walketh in his integrity. The word for " poor " is, here and in vers. 7, 22, *rash*, which signifies " poor " in opposition to " rich." In the present reading of the second clause, **than he that is perverse in his lips, and is a fool,** there seems to be a failure in antithesis, unless we can understand the fool as a rich fool. This, the repetition of the maxim in ch. xxviii. 6 (" Than he that is perverse in his ways, though he be rich "), would lead one to admit. The Vulgate accordingly has, *Quam dives torquem labia sua, et insipiens*, " Than a rich man who is of perverse lips and a fool." With this the Syriac partly agrees. So that, if we take this reading, the moralist says that the poor man who lives a guileless, innocent life, content with his lot, and using no wrong means to improve his fortunes, is happier and better than the rich man who is hypocritical in his words and deceives others, and has won his wealth by such means, thus proving himself to be a fool, a morally bad man. But if we content ourselves with the Hebrew text, we must find the antithesis in the simple, pious, poor man, contrasted with the arrogant rich man, who sneers at his poor neighbour as an inferior creature. The writer would seem to insinuate that there is a natural connection between poverty and integrity of life on the one hand, and wealth and folly on the other. He would assent to the sweeping assertion, *Omnis dives aut iniquus aut iniqui heres*, " Every rich man is either a rascal or a rascal's heir."

Ver. 2.—Also, that the soul be without knowledge, it is not good. " Also " (*gam*), Wordsworth would render " even," " even the soul, *i.e.* life itself, without knowledge is not a blessing; " it is βίος οὐ βιωτός. At first sight it looks as if some verse, to which this one was appended, had fallen out; but there is no trace in the versions of any such loss. We have had a verse beginning in the same manner (ch. xvii. 26), and here it seems to emphasize what follows—folly is bad, so is ignorance, when the soul lacks knowledge, *i.e.* when a man does not know what to do, how to act in the circumstances of his life, has in fact no practical wisdom. Other things " not good " are named in ch. xviii. 5; xx. 23; xxiv. 23. **And he that hasteth with his feet sinneth;** misseth his way. Delitzsch confines the meaning of this hemistich to the undisciplined pursuit of knowledge : " He who hasteneth with the legs after it goeth astray," because he is

neither intellectually nor morally clear as to his path or object. But the gnome is better taken in a more general sense. The ignorant man, who acts hastily without due deliberation, is sure to make grave mistakes, and to come to misfortune. Haste is opposed to knowledge, because the latter involves prudence and circumspection, while the former blunders on hurriedly, not seeing whither actions lead. We all have occasion to note the proverbs, *Festina lente;* " More haste, less speed." The history of Fabius, who, as Ennius said,

" Unus homo nobis cunctando restituit rem,"

shows the value of deliberation and caution. The Greeks recognized this—

Προπέτεια πολλοῖς ἐστιν αἰτία κακῶν.

" Rash haste is cause of evil unto many."

Erasmus, in his 'Adagia,' has a long article commenting on *Festinatio præpropera*. The Arabs say, " Patience is the key of joy, but haste is the key of sorrow." God is patient because he is eternal.

Ver. 3.—The foolishness of man perverteth his way; rather, *overturns*, turns from the right direction and causes a man to fall (ch. xiii. 6). It is his own folly that leads him to his ruin; but he will not see this, and blames the providence of God. **And his heart fretteth against the Lord.** Septuagint, " He accuseth God in his heart " (comp. Ezek. xviii. 25, 29; xxxiii. 17, 20). Ecclus xv. 11, etc., " Say not thou, It is through the Lord that I fell away; for thou oughtest not to do the things that he hateth. Say not thou, He has caused me to err; for he hath no need of the sinful man," etc. The latter part of this important passage St. Augustine quotes thus : " Item apud Salomonem : Deus ab initio constituit hominem et reliquit eum in manu consilii sui : adjecit ei mandata et præcepta ; si voles præcepta servare, servabunt te, et in posterum fidem placitam facere. Apposuit tibi aquam et ignem, ad quod vis porrige manum tuam. Ante hominem bonum et malum, vita et mors, paupertas et honestas a Domino Deo sunt " (' De Perf. Just. Hom.,' cap. xix. § 41). And again, " Manifestum est, quod si ad ignem manum mittit, et malum ac mors ei placet, id voluntas hominis operatur : si autem bonum et vitam diligit, non solum voluntas id agit, sed divinitus adjuvatur " (' De Gest. Pelag.,' cap. iii. § 7). Homer, ' Od.,' i. 32, etc.—

" Perverse mankind! whose wills, created free,

Charge all their woes on absolute decree;

All to the dooming gods their guilt translate,
And follies are miscalled the crimes of
fate."

(Pope.)

Ver. 4.—**Wealth maketh many friends**
(vers. 6, 7; ch. xiv. 20). A Greek gnome
expresses the same truth—

'Εὰν δ' ἔχωμεν χρήμαθ' ἕξομεν φίλους.

The poor is separated from his neighbour.
But it is better to make the act of separation emanate from the friend (as the Hebrew
allows), and to render, with the Revised
Version, *The friend of the poor separateth
himself from him.* The word for " poor " is
here *dal,* which means " feeble," " languid ; "
so ver. 17; and the same word (*rea*), " friend "
or " neighbour," is used in both clauses.
The idea of man's selfishness is carried on in
vers. 6 and 7. The Law of Moses had tried
to counteract it (Deut. xv. 7, etc.), but it
was Christianity that introduced the practical realization of the law of love, and the
honouring of the poor as members of Christ.
Septuagint, " But the poor is deserted even
by his whilom friend."

Ver. 5.—This verse **is** repeated below
(ver. 9). It comes in awkwardly here, interrupting the connection which subsists
between vers. 4 and 6. Its right place is
doubtless where it occurs below. The Law
not only strictly forbade false witness (Exod.
xx. 16; xxiii. 1), but it enacted severe
penalties against offenders in this particular
(Deut. xix. 16, etc.); the *lex talionis* was to
be enforced against them, they were to
receive no pity : " Life shall be for life, eye
for eye, tooth for tooth, hand for hand, foot
for foot." He that **speaketh lies shall not
escape.** The Septuagint confines the notion
of this clause to false accusers, Ὁ δὲ ἐγκαλῶν
ἀδίκως, " He who maketh an unjust charge
shall not escape," which renders the two
clauses almost synonymous. We make a
distinction between the members by seeing
in the former a denunciation against a false
witness in a suit, and in the second a more
sweeping menace against any one, whether
accuser, slanderer, sycophant, who by lying
injures a neighbour. The History of Susanna
is brought forward in confirmation of the
well-deserved fate of false accusers.

Ψευδὴς διαβολὴ τὸν βίον λυμαίνεται.

" A slander is an outrage on man's life."

Ver. 6.—**Many will intreat the favour of
the prince**; literally, *will stroke the face of
the prince,* of the liberal and powerful man,
in expectation of receiving some benefit from
him (ch xxix. 26; Job xi. 19). **Every man
is a friend to him that giveth gifts** (see on
ch. xvii. 8). The LXX., reading כָּל־הָרָע for

כָּל־הָרָע, renders, " Every bad man is a reproach to a man," which may mean that a
sordid, evil man brings only disgrace on himself; or that, while many truckle to and try
to win the interest of a prince, bad courtiers
bring on him not glory, but infamy and
shame.

Ver. 7.—This is one of the few tristichs
in the book, and probably contains the
mutilated remains of two distichs. The
third line, corrected by the Septuagint,
which has an addition here, runs into two
clauses (Cheyne). **All the brethren of the
poor do hate him.** Even his own brothers,
children of the same parents, hate and shun
a poor man (ch. xiv. 20). **Much more do his
friends go far from him.** There should be
no interrogation. We have the expression
(*aph-ki*) in ch. xi. 31; xv. 11, etc. Euripides,
' Medea,' 561—

Πένητα φεύγει πᾶς τις ἐκποδὼν φίλος.

" Each single friend far from the poor man
flies."

Septuagint, " Every one who hateth a poor
brother will be also far from friendship."
Then follows an addition not found in the
Hebrew, " Good thought draweth nigh to
those who know it, and a prudent man will
find it. He who doeth much evil brings
malice to perfection (τελεσιουργεῖ κακίαν);
and he who rouses words to anger shall not
be safe." **He pursueth** them with words,
yet they **are wanting** to him; or, *they are
gone.* He makes a pathetic appeal to his
quondam friends, but they hearken not to
him. But the sense is rather, " He pursueth
after, craves for, words of kindness or
promises of help, and there is naught, or
he gets words only and no material aid."
Wordsworth quotes Catullus, ' Carm.,'
xxxviii. 5—

" Quem tu, quod minimum facillimumque
est,
Qua solatus es adloculione?
Irascor tibi. Sic meos amores?"

Vulgate, *Qui tantum verba sectatur, nihil
habebit,* " He who pursues words only shall
have naught." The Hebrew is literally,
" Seeking words, they are not." This is
according to the Khetib; the Keri, instead
of the negation לֹא, reads לֹו, which makes
the clause signify, " He who pursues words,
they are to him ; " *i.e.* he gets words and
nothing else. Delitzsch and others, supplying the lost member from the Septuagint,
read the third line thus : " He that hath
many friends, or the friend of every one, is
requited with evil; and he that seeketh
(fair) speeches shall not be delivered."
Cheyne also makes a distich of this line,
taking the Septuagint as representing the

original reading, "He that does much evil perfects mischief: He that provokes with words shall not escape." That something has fallen out of the Hebrew text is evident; it seems that there are no examples of tristichs in this part of our book, though they are not unknown in the first and third divisions. The Vulgate surmounts the difficulty by connecting this third line with the following verse, which thus is made to form the antithesis, *Qui tantum verba sectatur, nihil habebit; Qui autem possessor est mentis, diligit animam suam, et custos prudentiæ inveniet bona.*"

Ver. 8.—**He that getteth wisdom loveth his own soul.** "Wisdom" is, in the Hebrew, *leb*, "heart;" it is a matter, not of intellect only, but of will and affections (see on ch. xv. 32). Septuagint, ἀγαπᾷ ἑαυτόν, "loveth himself." The contrary, "hateth his own soul," occurs in ch. xxix. 24. By striving to obtain wisdom a man shows that he has regard for the welfare of his soul and body. Hence St. Thomas Aquinas ('Sum. Theol.,' i. 2, qu. 25, art. 7, quoted by Corn. à Lapide) takes occasion to demonstrate that only good men are really lovers of themselves, while evil men are practically self-haters, proving his position by a reference to Aristotle's enumeration of the characteristics of friendship, which the former exhibit, and none of which the latter can possess ('Eth. Nic.,' ix. 4). **He that keepeth understanding shall find good** (ch. xvi. 20). A man must not only strive hard and use all available means to get wisdom and prudence, he must guard them like a precious treasure, not lose them for want of care or let them lie useless; and then he will find that they bring with themselves innumerable benefits.

Ver. 9.—A repetition of ver. 5, except that **shall perish** is substituted for "shall not escape." Septuagint, "And whosoever shall kindle mischief shall perish by it." The Greek translators have rendered the special reference in the original to slanderers and liars by a general term, and introduced the notion of Divine retribution, which is not definitely expressed in the Hebrew.

Ver. 10.—**Delight is not seemly for a fool** (comp. ch. xvii. 7; xxvi. 1). *Taanug*, rendered "delight," implies rather delicate living, luxury; τρυφή, Septuagint. Such a life is ruin to a fool, who knows not how to use it properly; it confirms him in his foolish, sinful ways. A man needs religion and reason to enable him to bear prosperity advantageously, and these the fool lacks. "Secundæ res," remarks Sallust ('Catil.,' xi.), "sapientium animos fatigant," "Even wise men are wearied and harassed by prosperity," much more must such good fortune try those who have no practical

wisdom to guide and control their enjoyment. Vatablus explains the clause to mean that it is impossible for a fool, a sinner, to enjoy peace of conscience, which alone is true delight. But looking to the next clause, we see that the moralist is thinking primarily of the elevation of a slave to a high position, and his arrogance in consequence thereof. **Much less for a servant to have rule over princes.** By the unwise favouritism of a potentate, a slave of lowly birth might be raised to eminence and set above the nobles and princes of the land. The writer of Ecclesiastes gives his experience in this matter: "I have seen servants upon horses, and princes walking as servants upon the earth" (Eccles. x. 7). The same anomaly is mentioned with censure (ch. xxx. 22 and Ecclus. xi. 5). What is the behaviour of unworthy persons thus suddenly raised to high position has formed the subject of many a satire. It is the old story of the "beggar on horseback." A German proverb declares, "Kein Scheermesser schärfer schiest, als wenn der Bauer zu Herrn wird." Claud., 'In Eutrop.,' i. 181, etc.—

"Asperius nihil est humili, quum surgit in
　　altum;
Cuncta ferit, dum cuncta timet; desævit
　　in omnes,
Ut se posse putent; nec bellua tetrior ulla
Quam servi rabies in libera colla fu-
　　rentis."

As an example of a different disposition, Cornelius à Lapide refers to the history of Agathocles, Tyrant of Syracuse, who rose from the humble occupation of a potter to a position of vast power, and, to remind himself of his lowly origin, used to dine off mean earthenware. Ausonius thus alludes to this humility ('Epigr.,' viii.)—

"Fama est fictilibus cœnasse Agathoclea
　　regem,
Atque abacum Samio sæpe onerasse luto;
Fercula gemmatis cum poneret horrida
　　vasis,
Et misceret opes pauperiemque simul.
Quærenti causam, respondit: Rex ego qui
　　sum
Sicaniæ, figulo sum genitore satus.
Fortunam reverenter habe, quicunque re-
　　pente
Dives ab exili progrediere loco."

Ver. 11.—**The discretion of a man deferreth his anger;** *maketh him slow to anger.* "A merciful man is long-suffering," Septuagint; "The teaching of a man is known by patience," Vulgate. (See ch. xiv. 17, 29.) The Greek moralist gives the advice—

Νίκησον ὀργὴν τῷ λογίζεσθαι καλῶς.

"Thine anger quell by reason's timely aid."

The contrary disposition betokens folly (ch. xiv. 17). **It is his glory to pass over a transgression.** It is a real triumph and glory for a man to forgive and to take no notice of injuries offered him. Thus in his poor way he imitates Almighty God (Micah vii. 18, "Who is a God like unto thee, that pardoneth iniquity, and passeth by the transgression of the remnant of his heritage? he retaineth not his anger for ever, because he delighteth in mercy"). Here it is discretion or prudence that makes a man patient and forgiving; elsewhere the same effect is attributed to love (ch. x. 12; xvii. 9). The Septuagint Version is hard to understand: Τὸ δὲ καύχημα αὐτοῦ ἐπέρχεται παρανόμοις, "And his glorying cometh on the transgressors;" but, taken in connection with the former hemistich, it seems to mean that the patient man's endurance of the contradictions of sinners is no reproach or disgrace to him, but redounds to his credit and virtue. "Vincit qui patitur," "He conquers who endures."

Ver. 12.—**The king's wrath is as the roaring of a lion,** which inspires terror, as preluding danger and death. The same idea occurs in ch. xx. 2 (comp. Amos iii. 4, 8). The Assyrian monuments have made us familiar with the lion as a type of royalty; and the famous throne of Solomon was ornamented with figures of lions on each of its six steps (1 Kings x. 19, etc.). Thus St. Paul, alluding to the Roman emperor, says (2 Tim. iv. 17), "I was delivered out of the mouth of the lion." "The lion is dead," announced Marsyas to Agrippa, on the decease of Tiberius (Josephus, 'Ant.,' xviii. 6. 10). The moralist here gives a monition to kings to repress their wrath and not to let it rage uncontrolled, and a warning to subjects not to offend their ruler, lest he tear them to pieces like a savage beast, which an Eastern despot had full power to do. **But his favour is as dew upon the grass.** In ch. xvi. 15 the king's favour was compared to a cloud of the latter rain; here it is likened to the dew (comp. Ps. lxxii. 6). We hardly understand in England the real bearing of this comparison. "The secret of the luxuriant fertility of many parts of Palestine," says Dr. Geikie ('Holy Land and Bible,' i. 72, etc.), "lies in the rich supply of moisture afforded by the sea-winds which blow inland each night, and water the face of the whole land. There is no dew, properly so called in Palestine, for there is no moisture in the hot summer air to be chilled into dewdrops by the coolness of the night, as in a climate like ours. From May till October rain is unknown, the sun shining with unclouded brightness day after day. The heat becomes intense, the ground hard; and vegetation would perish but for

the moist west winds that come each night from the sea. The bright skies cause the heat of the day to radiate very quickly into space, so that the nights are as cold as the day is the reverse. . . . To this coldness of the night air the indispensable watering of all plant-life is due. The winds, loaded with moisture, are robbed of it as they pass over the land, the cold air condensing it into drops of water, which fall in a gracious rain of mist on every thirsty blade. In the morning the fog thus created rests like a sea over the plains, and far up the sides of the hills, which raise their heads above it like so many islands. . . . The amount of moisture thus poured on the thirsty vegetation during the night is very great. Dew seemed to the Israelites a mysterious gift of Heaven, as indeed it is. That the skies should be stayed from yielding it was a special sign of Divine wrath, and there could be no more gracious conception of a loving farewell address to his people than where Moses tells them that his speech should distil as the dew. The favour of an Oriental monarch could not be more beneficially conceived than by saying that, while his wrath is like the roaring of a lion, his favour is as the dew upon the grass." רָצוֹן (ratson), "favour," is translated by the Septuagint, τὸ ἱλαρόν, and by the Vulgate, hilaritas, "cheerfulness" (as in ch. xviii. 22), which gives the notion of a smiling, serene, benevolent countenance, as contrasted with the angry, lowering look of a displeased monarch.

Ver. 13.—With the first clause we may compare ch. x. 1; xv. 20; xvii. 21, 25. **Calamity** in the Hebrew is in the plural number (contritiones, Pagn.), as if to mark the many and continued sorrows which a bad son brings upon his father, how he causes evil after evil to harass and distress him. **The contentions of a wife are a continual dropping** (comp. ch. xxvii. 15). The flat roofs of Eastern houses, formed of planks loosely joined and covered with a coating of clay or plaster, were always subject to leakage in heavy rains. The irritating altercations and bickering of a cross-grained wife are compared to the continuous drip of water through an imperfectly constructed roof. Tecta jugiter perstillantia, as the Vulgate has it. The Scotch say, "A leaky house and a scolding wife are two bad companions." The two clauses of the verse are co-ordinate, expressing two facts that render home life miserable and unendurable, viz. the misbehaviour of a son and the ill temper of a wife. The Septuagint, following a different reading, has, "Nor are offerings from a harlot's hire pure," which is an allusion to Deut. xxiii. 18.

Ver. 14.—**House and riches are an inheri-**

tance of (*from*) **fathers.** Any man, worthy or not, may inherit property from progenitors; any man may bargain for a wife, or give a dowry to his son to further his matrimonial prospects. **But a prudent wife is from the Lord.** She is a special gift of God, a proof of his gracious care for his servants (see on ch. xviii. 22). Septuagint, Παρὰ δὲ Κυρίου ἁρμόζεται γυνὴ ἀνδρί, "It is by the Lord that a man is matched with a woman." There is a special providence that watches over wedlock; as we say, "Marriages are made in heaven." But marriages of convenience, marriages made in consideration of worldly means, are a mere earthly arrangement, and claim no particular grace.

Ver. 15.—**Slothfulness casteth into a deep sleep;** "causes deep sleep to fall upon a man" (comp. ch. vi. 9; xiii. 4). The word for "sleep" (תַּרְדֵּמָה, *tardemah*) is that used for the supernatural sleep of Adam when Eve was formed (Gen. ii. 21), and implies profound insensibility. Aquila and Symmachus render it, ἔκστασιν, "trance." Slothfulness enervates a man, renders him as useless for labour as if he were actually asleep in his bed; it also enfeebles the mind, corrupts the higher faculties, converts a rational being into a witless animal. *Otium est vivi hominis sepultura*, "Idleness is a living man's tomb." **An idle soul shall suffer hunger.** We have many gnomes to this effect (see ch. x. 4; xii. 24; xx. 13; xxiii. 21). The LXX. has introduced something of this verse at ch. xviii. 8, and here render, Δειλία κατέχει ἀνδρόγυνον, "Cowardice holdeth fast the effeminate, and the soul of the idle shall hunger." "Sloth," as the proverb says, "is the mother of poverty."

Ver. 16.—**Keepeth his own soul.** Obedience to God's commandments preserves a man's natural and spiritual life (comp. ch. xiii. 13; xvi. 17). So we read in Eccles. viii. 5, "Whoso keepeth the commandment (*mitsvah*, as here) shall feel no evil thing." **He that despiseth his ways shall die.** He that cares nothing what he does, whether his life pleases God or not, shall perish. Ἀπολεῖται, Septuagint; *mortificabitur*, Vulgate. The result is understood differently. The Khetib reads, יָמַת (*iumath*), "shall be punished with death" according to the penalties enacted in the Mosaic Law. The Keri reads, יָמוּת (*iamuth*), "shall die," as in ch. xv. 10; and this seems more in agreement with what we find elsewhere in the book, as in ch. x. 21; xxiii. 13. This insensate carelessness leads to ruin, whether its punishment be undertaken by outraged law, or whether it be left to the Divine retribution.

Ver. 17.—**He that hath pity upon the poor lendeth unto the Lord.** English

Church-people are familiar with this distich, as being one of the sentences of Scripture read at the Offertory. The word for "poor" is here *dal*, "feeble" (see on vers. 1 and 4). It is a beautiful thought that by showing mercy and pity we are, as it were, making God our debtor; and the truth is wonderfully advanced by Christ, who pronounces (Matt. xxv. 40), "Inasmuch as ye have done it unto one of the least of these my brethren, ye have done it unto me" (see on ch. xi. 24; xxviii. 27). St. Chrysostom ('Hom.,' xv., on 1 Cor. v.), "To the more imperfect this is what we may say, Give of what you have unto the needy. Increase your substance. For, saith he, 'He that giveth unto the poor lendeth unto God.' But if you are in a hurry, and wait not for the time of retribution, think of those who lend money to men; for not even these desire to get their interest immediately; but they are anxious that the principal should remain a good long while in the hands of the borrower, provided only the repayment be secure, and they have no mistrust of the borrower. Let this be done, then, in the present case also. Leave them with God, that he may pay thee thy wages manifold. Seek not to have the whole here; for if you recover it all here, how will you receive it back there? And it is on this account that God stores them up there, inasmuch as this present life is full of decay. But he gives even here also; for, 'Seek ye,' saith he, 'the kingdom of heaven, and all these things shall be added unto you.' Well, then, let us look towards that kingdom, and not be in a hurry for the repayment of the whole, lest we diminish our recompense. But let us wait for the fit season. For the interest in these cases is not of that kind, but is such as is meet to be given by God. This, then, having collected together in great abundance, so let us depart hence, that we may obtain both the present and the future blessings" (Oxford transl.). **That which he hath given will he pay him again;** *Vicissitudinem suam reddet ei*, Vulgate, "According to his gift will he recompense him." גְּמֻל (*gemul*), "good deed" (ch. xii. 14, where it is rendered "recompense"). Ecclus. xxxii. (xxxv.) 10, etc., "Give unto the Most High according as he hath enriched thee; and as thou hast gotten give with a cheerful eye. For the Lord recompenseth, and will give thee seven times as much." There are proverbs rife in other lands to the same effect. The Turk says, "What you give in charity in this world you take with you after death. Do good, and throw it into the sea· if the fish does not know it, God does." And the Russian, "Throw bread and salt behind you, you get them before you" (Lane).

Ver. 18.—**Chasten thy son while there is hope**; or, *seeing that there is hope.* Being still young and impressionable, and not confirmed in bad habits, he may be reformed by judicious chastisement. The same expression occurs in Job xi. 18; Jer. xxxi. 16. " For so he shall be well hoped of " (εὔελπις), Septuagint (comp. ch. xxiii. 13). **And let not thy soul spare for his crying.** "It is better," says a German apothegm, "that the child weep than the father." But the rendering of the Authorized Version is not well established, and this second clause is intended to inculcate moderation in punishment. Vulgate, *Ad interfectionem autem ejus ne ponas animam tuam;* Revised Version, *Set not thine heart on his destruction.* Chastise him duly and sufficiently, but not so heavily as to occasion his death, which a father had no right to do. The Law enjoined the parents who had an incorrigibly bad son to bring him before the judge or the elders, who alone had the power of life and death, and might in certain cases order the offender to be stoned (Deut. xxi. 18, etc.). Christianity recommended moderation in punishment (see Eph. vi. 4; Col. iii. 21). Septuagint, "Be not excited in the mind to despiteful treatment (εἰς ὕβριν); " *i.e.* be not led away by passion to unseemly acts or words, but reprove with gentleness, while you are firm and uncompromising in denouncing evil. This is much the same advice as that given by the apostle in the passages just cited.

Ver. 19.—Some connect this verse with the preceding, as though it signified, "If you are too severe in chastising your son, you will suffer for it." But there is no connecting particle in the Hebrew, and the statement seems to be of a general nature. **A man of great wrath**; literally, *rough in anger;* Vulgate, *impatiens;* Septuagint, κακόφρων ἀνήρ. Such a one **shall suffer punishment**; shall bear the penalty which his want of self-control brings upon him. **For if thou deliver** him, **yet must thou do it again.** You cannot save him from the consequences of his intemperance; you may do so once and again, but while his disposition is unchanged, all your efforts will be useless, and the help which you have given him will only make him think that he may continue to indulge his anger with impunity, or, it may be, he will vent his impatience on his deliverer.

Βλάπτει τὸν ἄνδρα θυμὸς εἰς ὀργὴν πεσών.

"Anger," says an adage, "is like a ruin, which breaks itself upon what it falls." Septuagint, "If he destroy (ἐὰν δὲ λοιμεύηται), he shall add even his life; " if by his anger he inflict loss or damage on his neighbour, he shall pay for it in his own person; Vulgate, *Et cum rapuerit, aliud apponet.*

Another interpretation of the passage, but not so suitable, is this : " If thou seek to save the sufferer (*e.g.* by soothing the angry man), thou wilt only the more excite him (the wrathful) : therefore do not intermeddle in quarrels of other persons."

Ver. 20.—(Comp. ch. viii. 10; xii. 15.) The Septuagint directs the maxim to children, "Hear, O son, the instruction of thy father." **That thou mayest be wise in thy latter end.** Wisdom gathered and digested in youth is seen in the prudence and intelligence of manhood and old age. Job viii. 7, "Though thy beginning was small, yet thy latter end should greatly increase." Ecclus. xxv. 6, "O how comely is the wisdom of old men, and understanding and counsel to men of honour! Much experience is the crown of old men, and the fear of God is their glory." " Wer nicht hören will," say the Germans, "muss fühlen," " He that will not hear must feel." Among Pythagoras's golden words we read—

Βουλεύου δὲ πρὸ ἔργου ὅπως μὴ μῶρα πέληται.

" Before thou doest aught, deliberate,
  Lest folly thee befall."

Ver. 21.—The immutability of the counsel of God is contrasted with the shifting, fluctuating purposes of man (comp. ch. xvi. 1, 9; Numb. xxiii. 19; Mal. iii. 6). Aben Ezra connects this verse with the preceding, as though it gave the reason for the advice contained therein. But it is most natural to take the maxim in a general sense, as above Wisd. ix. 14, " The thoughts of mortal men are miserable, and our devices are but uncertain." **The counsel of the Lord, that shall stand**; *permanebit,* Vulgate; εἰς τὸν αἰῶνα μενεῖ, "shall abide for ever," Septuagint (Ps. xxxiii. 11).

Ver. 22.—**The desire of a man is his kindness.** The Revised Version rather paraphrases the clause, *The desire of a man is the measure of his kindness;* i.e. the wish and intention to do good is that which gives its real value to an act. The word for " kindness " is *chesed,* "mercy ; " and, looking to the context, we see the meaning of the maxim to be that a poor man's desire of aiding a distressed neighbour, even if he is unable to carry out his intention, is taken for the act of mercy. "The desire of a man " may signify a man's desirableness, that which makes him to be desired or loved; this is found in his liberality. But the former explanation is most suitable. Septuagint, "Mercifulness is a gain unto a man," which is like ver. 17; Vulgate, *Homo indigens misericors est,* taking a man's desire as evidencing his need and poverty, and introducing the idea that the experience of misery conduces to pity, as says Dido (Virgil, ' Æn.,' i. 630)—

" Non ignara mali miseris succurrere disco."

A poor man is better than a liar. A poor man who gives to one in distress his sympathy and good wishes, even if he can afford no substantial aid, is better than a rich man who promises much and does nothing, or who falsely professes that he is unable to help (comp. ch. iii. 27, 28). Septuagint, " A poor righteous man is better than a rich liar." A Buddhist maxim says, " Like a beautiful flower, full of colours, but without scent, are the fine but fruitless words of him who does not act accordingly" (Max Müller).

Ver. 23.—**The fear of the Lord** tendeth to **life** (ch. xiv. 27). True religion, obedience to God's commandments, was, under a temporal dispensation, rewarded by a long and happy life in this world, an adumbration of the blessedness that awaits the righteous in the world to come. **And he that hath it shall abide satisfied.** The subject passes from " the fear " to its possessor. Perhaps better, *and satisfied he shall pass the night*, which is the usual sense of לִין (*lun*), the verb here translated " abide " (so ch. xv. 31). God will satisfy the good man's hunger, so that he lays him down in peace and takes his rest (comp. ch. x. 3). Vulgate, *In plenitudine commorabitur*, " He shall dwell in abundance." **He shall not be visited with evil,** according to the promises (Lev. xxvi. 6: Deut. xi. 15, etc.). Under our present dispensation Christians expect not immunity from care and trouble, but have hope of protection and grace sufficient for the occasion, and conducive to edification and advance in holiness. The LXX. translates thus: " The fear of the Lord is unto life for a man; but he that is without fear (ὁ δὲ ἄφοβος) shall sojourn in places where knowledge is not seen; " *i.e.* shall go from bad to worse, till he ends in society where Divine knowledge is wholly absent, and lives without God in the world. The Greek interpreters read יְד (*dea*), " knowledge," instead of יְר (*ra*), " evil."

Ver. 24.—**A slothful** man **hideth his hand in** his **bosom**; Revised Version, *the sluggard burieth his hand in the dish.* The word *tsallachath*, translated " bosom" here and in the parallel passage, ch. xxvi. 15 (where see note), is rightly rendered " dish " (2 Kings xxi. 13). At an Oriental meal the guests sit round a table, on which is placed a dish containing the food, from which every one helps himself with his fingers, knives, spoons, and forks being never used (comp. Ruth ii. 14; Matt. xxvi. 23). Sometimes the host himself helps a guest whom he wishes to honour (comp. John xiii. 26). **And will not so much as bring it to his mouth again.** He finds it too great an exertion to feed himself, an hyperbolical way of denoting the gross laziness which recoils from the

slightest labour, and will not take the least trouble to win its livelihood. An Arabic proverb says, " He dies of hunger under the date tree." Septuagint, " He who unjustly hideth his hands in his bosom will not even apply them to his mouth; " *i.e.* he who will not work will never feed himself.

Ver. 25.—**Smite a scorner, and the simple will beware;** *will learn prudence*, Revised Version (comp. ch. xxi. 11 ; and see note on ch. i. 22). The scorner is hardened to all reproof, and is beyond all hope of being reformed by punishment; in his case it is retribution for outraged virtue that is sought in the penalty which he is made to pay. Τιμωρία, not κόλασις—retributive, not corrective punishment. Seeing this, the simple, who is not yet confirmed in evil, and is still open to better influences, may be led to take warning and amend his life. So St. Paul enjoins Timothy, " Them that sin rebuke before all, that others also may fear " (1 Tim. v. 20). There is the trite adage—

" Felix quem faciunt aliena pericula cautum."

" Happy they
Who from their neighbours' perils caution learn."

Septuagint, " When a pestilent fellow is chastised, a fool will be cleverer (πανουργότερος)." So Vulgate, *Pestilente flagellato stultus sapientior erit.* **Reprove one that hath understanding, and he will understand knowledge.** The scorner does not profit by severe punishment, but the intelligent man is improved by censure and admonition (comp. ch. xiii. 1; xv. 12). Says the adage, " Sapientem nutu, stultum fuste (corripe)," " A nod for the wise, a stick for the fool."

Ver. 26—ch. xxii. 16.—Fourth section of this collection.

Ver. 26.—**He that wasteth his father.** The verb *shadad*, used here and in ch. xxiv. 15, may be taken in the sense of " to spoil," " to deprive of property; " but it is better to adopt a more general application, and to assign to it the meaning of " to maltreat," whether in person or property. **Chaseth away his mother;** by his shameless and evil life makes it impossible for her to continue under the same roof with him; or, it may be, so dissipates his parents' means that they are driven from their home. **A son that causeth shame, and bringeth reproach** (comp. ch. x. 5; xiii. 5; xvii. 2).

Ver. 27.—**Cease, my son, to hear the instruction that causeth to err from the words of knowledge.** This version fairly represents the terse original, if *musar*, " instruction," be taken in a bad sense, like the " profane and vain babblings and oppositions of the knowledge which is falsely so called," censured by St. Paul (1 Tim. vi. 20).

But as *musar* is used in a good sense throughout this book, it is better to regard the injunction as warning against listening to wise teaching with no intention of profiting by it: "Cease to hear instruction in order to err," etc.; *i.e.* if you are only going to continue your evil-doings. You will only increase your guilt by knowing the way of righteousness perfectly, while you refuse to walk therein. The Vulgate inserts a negation, "Cease not to hear doctrine, and be not ignorant of the words of knowledge;" Septuagint, "A son who fails to keep the instruction of his father will meditate evil sayings." Solomon's son Rehoboam greatly needed the admonition contained in this verse.

Ver. 28.—**An ungodly** (*worthless*) **witness scorneth judgment**; derides the Law which denounces perjury and compels a witness to speak truth (Exod. xx. 16; Lev. v. 1), and, as is implied he bears false testimony, thus proving himself "a witness of Belial," according to the Hebrew term. Septuagint, "He who becometh security for a foolish child outrages judgment." **The mouth of the wicked devoureth iniquity**; swallows it eagerly as a toothsome morsel (ch. xviii. 8).

So we have in Job xv. 16, "A man that drinketh iniquity like water" (see on ch. xxvi. 6). Such a man will lie and slander with the utmost pleasure, living and battening on wickedness. Septuagint, "The mouth of the impious drinketh judgments (κρίσεις)," *i.e.* boldly transgresses the Law.

Ver. 29.—**Judgments are prepared for scorners** (see on ver. 25). The judgments here are those inflicted by the providence of God, as in ch. iii. 34. Scorners may deride and affect to scorn the judgments of God and man, but they are warned that retribution awaits them. **And stripes for the back of fools**; Vulgate, *Et mallei percutientes stultorum corporibus* (comp. ch. x. 13; xxvi. 3). We had the word here rendered "stripes" (מַהֲלֻמוֹת, *mahalumoth*) in ch. xviii. 6. The certainty of punishment in the case of transgressors is a truth often insisted on even by heathens. Examples will occur to all readers, from the old Greek oracle, Οὐδεὶς ἀνθρώπων ἀδικῶν τίσιν οὐκ ἀποτίσει, to Horace's "Raro antecedentem scelestum," etc. (See on ch. xx. 30, where, however, the punishment is of human infliction.)

HOMILETICS.

Ver. 1.—*Poverty and integrity.* I. IT IS POSSIBLE FOR POVERTY TO BE FOUND WITH INTEGRITY. We do not always see integrity leading to wealth. Circumstances may not open up an opportunity for attaining worldly prosperity. Illicit "short cuts" to riches may be within the reach of a person who refuses to use them on grounds of principle. A man may be honest and yet incapable, or he may refuse to pursue his own advantage, preferring to devote his energies to some higher end. No one has a right to suppose that God will interfere to heap up riches for him on account of his integrity. He may be upright, and yet it may please God that he shall also be poor.

II. IT IS POSSIBLE FOR INTEGRITY TO BE FOUND WITH POVERTY. We now approach the subject from the opposite side. Here we first see the poverty, and we then find that there is no reason why the character should be low because the outside circumstances are reduced. There is no more vulgar or false snobbishness than that which treats poverty as a vice, and assumes that a shady character must be expected with shabby clothes. We sometimes hear the expression, "Poor *but* honest," as though there were any natural antithesis between the two adjectives! It would be quite as just to think of an antithesis between wealth and uprightness. But experience shows that no one section of society holds a monopoly of virtue.

III. WHEN INTEGRITY AND POVERTY ARE FOUND TOGETHER, THE ONE IS A CONSOLATION FOR THE OTHER. It may be said that a hungry man cannot feed upon his honesty. But when pressing wants are supplied, it is possible to endure a considerable amount of hardship if a person is conscious of being upright and true. The sturdy independence of the honest man will lift him out of the shame of penury. If he feels that he is walking in the path of duty, he will have a source of strength and inward peace that no wealth can bestow. The gold of goodness is better than the guineas of hoarded wealth.

IV. INTEGRITY WITH ANY EXTERNAL DISADVANTAGES IS BETTER THAN CORRUPTION OF CHARACTER WITH ALL POSSIBLE WORLDLY PROFIT. Here is the point of the subject. It is not affirmed that poverty is good in itself—the natural instincts of man lead him to endeavour to escape from it as an evil. It is not even asserted that it is right for upright men to be poor, for surely one would desire that the power of wealth should be in the hands of those people who would use it most justly. But when we have to compare integrity joined to the disadvantages of poverty with an unworthy character in no matter what circumstances, the infinite superiority of moral to material worth should lead us to prefer the former. In higher regions, the Christian character is itself a source of blessedness, whatever be the condition of the outer life. Character and conduct are the essentials of life; all other things are but the accidents.

Ver. 3.—*Fretting against the-Lord.* This is a condition of inward rebellion, or at best of grieving over the will of God instead of submitting to it in silence if it is not yet within our power to embrace it with affection. Consider this condition in its various relations.

I. IT IS POSSIBLE. It might be supposed that, however one fretted against his circumstances, he would not carry his complainings back to God. But Moses told the Israelites that when they murmured against him they were really murmuring against God (Exod. xvi. 8). If we resist God's ordinances we resist God himself. He who fires on the meanest sentry is really making war on that sentry's sovereign. We may not intend to act the proud part of Milton's Satan, and wage war against Heaven. Overt blasphemy and rank rebellion may be far from our thoughts. Yet complaints of our lot and resistance to Providence have the same essential character. We may even try to confine our rebellious thoughts to our own breasts, and simply fret inwardly. But to God, who reads hearts and dwells within, this is real opposition.

II. IT SPRINGS FROM VARIOUS SOURCES. 1. *Trouble.* It is easy for Dives to talk of submission to Providence; the difficulty is with Lazarus. Job in prosperity offers glad sacrifices without constraint: will Job in adversity "curse God and die"? 2. *Self-will.* We naturally desire to follow the way of our own choice, and when that is crossed by God's will we are tempted to fret, as the stream frets itself against an obstruction, though it may have been flowing silently and placidly so long as it had a free course. It is just this crossing of wills that is the test of obedience, which is easy so long as we are required only to follow the path of our own inclinations. But that cannot be always allowed. 3. *Sin.* Direct sinfulness resists God's will of set purpose, just because it is his will. The evil heart will fret against God in all things.

III. IT IS FOOLISH. "The foolishness of man" is at the root of this mistake. 1. *We do not know what is best.* It is but foolish for the fractious child to fret against his father's commands, for he is not yet able to judge as his father judges. All rebellion against God implies that the soul is in a position to determine questions that lie in the dark, and which only he who is resisted can answer. 2. *We cannot succeed in rebellion.* The poor heart that frets itself against God can but wear itself out, like the wave that breaks on the rock it can never shake. How foolish to raise our will in opposition to the Almighty!

IV. IT IS CULPABLE. We must never forget that "foolishness" in the Bible stands for a defect that is more moral than intellectual. It is next door to perversity. This fretting of the heart against the Lord is foolish in the biblical sense; it is sinful. 1. *He is our Master.* It is our duty·to obey him, whether we like it or not. When we resist ordinances of man we may be fighting for rights of liberty. But we have no liberty to claim against the Lord of all. 2. *He is our Father.* This murmuring against him is a sign of domestic ingratitude. Impatience under the rod is even sinful, for we know that it can only smite in love.

V. IT IS DANGEROUS. 1. *It means present unrest.* There is peace of soul in submission; to rebel is to be plunged into turmoil and distress. 2. *It leads to future ruin.* The foolishness of man not only " perverteth his way," but, as the phrase may be better rendered, "hurls his way headlong to destruction." It is like the avalanche that sweeps the mountain-path, and carries all on it to an awful death.

Ver. 11.—*Deferred anger.* I. DEFERRED ANGER IS SAVED FROM FATAL ERROR. "Anger," says the familiar Latin proverb, "is a short madness." While it lasts a man loses full control of himself. Then he utters strong, hot words without weighing the meaning of them or considering how they may strike their object. He is tempted to hit out wildly, and to do far more mischief than he would ever approve of in calmer moments. The words and deeds of anger are but momentary ; yet their fatal effects are irrevocable. These effects endure and work harm long after the fierce flame of passion out of which they sprang has died down into grey ashes of remorse. Inasmuch as it is not possible to reason calmly when under a fit of anger, the only safe expedient is to hold back and wait for a more suitable occasion of speaking and acting.

II. DEFERRED ANGER WILL MOST PROBABLY BURN ITSELF OUT. Anger is like

> "A full-hot horse, who, being allow'd his way,
> Self-mettle tires him."
>
> (Shakespeare.)

It is of the nature of anger to be more fierce than the occasion demands. Therefore it is to be expected that time for reflection will moderate it. Now, if it is modified by time, its earlier excess is demonstrated, and it is made evident that delay saved us from disaster. For it is not simply the case that we tire of anger, that we have not energy enough to be perpetually angry, that well-earned wrath expires of its own feebleness. The fact is we are all tempted to show needless anger against those who in any way injure us. Time may reveal unexpected excuses for their conduct, or lead us to see the better way of forgiveness. We do but need an opportunity to go into our chamber, and shut to the door, and pray to our Father in secret, to discover how wrong and foolish and dangerous our hasty wrath was, and to learn the wisdom of meekness and patience.

III. DEFERRED ANGER MAY YET BE EXERCISED. There are circumstances under which we should do well to be angry ; for, as Thomas Fuller says, " Anger is one of the sinews of the soul." Christ was " moved with indignation " when his disciples forbad the mothers of Israel to bring their children to him (Mark x. 14), and he showed great anger against the hypocrisy of the Pharisees. It is not right that we should witness cruel injustice and oppression with equanimity. It may reveal a culpable weakness, cowardice, or selfishness in us for sights of wrong-doing not to move us to anger. But such anger as is earned and needed by justice can bear to be reflected on. Even with this justifiable wrath haste may lead to disaster. Thus the violent explosion of popular indignation that follows the discovery of some foul crime or some grievous wrong is in great danger of falling into fatal blunders; sometimes it makes a victim of an innocent person, simply for want of consideration. There is no excuse for " lynch law." " The courts are open," and calm investigation and orderly methods will not lessen the equity of the punishment they deliberately bring on an offender. Justice is not to behave like a ravenous beast raging for its prey. There is room for calmness and reflection in connection with those great waves of popular indignation that periodically sweep over the surface of society. When the anger has been wisely deferred, and yet has been ultimately justified, its outburst is the more terrible ; it is the flowing out of wrath " treasured up against the day of wrath." Dryden says—

> " Beware the fury of a patient man."

Ver. 16.—*Soul-keeping.* The " Power that makes for righteousness," though not impersonal, as Mr. Matthew Arnold assumed, is nevertheless active as by a constant law. It is so ordered in nature and providence that goodness preserves life, and badness tends to ruin and death. Let us endeavour to see how the process is worked out.

I. THE GREAT RESULT OF RIGHTEOUSNESS IS SOUL-KEEPING. 1. *It may not be wealth.* We cannot assume that goodness tends to riches. Keeping the commandments does not always result in a man's making his fortune. Christ was a poor man. 2. *It may not be earthly happiness.* Other things being equal, a clear conscience should bring peace and inward joy. But there are troubles that fall upon us independently of our conduct. There are distresses that come directly from doing right. Christ was a " Man of sorrows." 3. *It may not be long life on earth.* No doubt this was expected in Old Testament times, for then but dim notions of any existence beyond the grave ever entered the minds of men. On the whole, no doubt, goodness tends to health of body and mind. Still, very good people may die young. Christ died at thirty-three years of age. 4. *It will be the real preservation of the soul.* The true life will be safe. The self will abide. Now, all our being really resides in our personal self. If this continues in safety, we have the highest personal security. But if not, all other gain is but a mockery; for "what is a man profited if he should gain the whole world, and lose his own soul—his life, himself?" (Matt. xvi. 26).

II. RIGHTEOUSNESS LEADS TO SOUL-KEEPING BY NATURAL LAWS. It is a matter of Divine ordering that obedience should be followed by life, disobedience by death. This was seen in the trial of Adam (Gen. iii. 3). It lies at the root of the great sanctions of the Mosaic Law (Ezek. iii. 18). He who gave the commandments also gives life. Our life is in the hand of our Lawgiver. It is in his power to withhold the life if we break the law. But we may look more closely into this process. God's commandments are not arbitrary. They follow the natural lines of spiritual health. His prohibitions are really the warnings against the course that leads naturally and inevitably to death. Goodness is itself vitality, and badness has a deadening effect on the soul. The faculties are quickened by use in the service of what is right, and they are dwarfed, perverted, paralyzed, and finally killed by reckless, lawless conduct. The profligate is a suicide.

III. CHRISTIANITY HELPS US TO TRUE SOUL-KEEPING BY LEADING US TO RIGHTEOUS-NESS. We find ourselves in the unhappy condition of those who have not kept the commandments. Therefore we are in danger of death. We have "despised our ways." The law and the promise are not addressed to us as to new beings; but they meet us in our sin and on our road to ruin. Therefore, if there were no gospel, there would be no hope. Hence the need of a Saviour. But when we enter the realm of Christian truth we cannot turn our backs on the principles of the older economy. We cannot regard them as the laws of another planet, out of the reach of which we have escaped. They are eternal truths, and we are still within their range. Christ helps us, not by teaching us to despise moral considerations as though they were irrelevant to those who had entered into the covenant of grace, but by giving us his own righteousness to be *in* us as well as *on* us. He puts us in the way of obedience, while he cancels the consequences of the old disobedience. Thus he saves our souls by helping us to preserve them in a new fidelity to the ancient, eternal right.

Ver. 17.—*Lending unto the Lord.* I. IN WHAT LENDING TO THE LORD CONSISTS. It is having pity upon the poor. This is more than almsgiving. Doles of charity may be given to the needy from very mixed motives. Inasmuch as "the Lord looketh at the heart," the thoughts and feelings that prompt our charity are of primary importance with him. In the same way, also, sympathy is prized by our suffering brethren on its own account, and the gifts that are flung from an unfeeling hand bring little comfort to the miserable. Therefore, both for God's sake and for the sake of our suffering brethren, the first requirement is to cultivate a spirit of sympathy with the helpless. When this spirit is attained, the application of practical remedies will require thought. It is easy to toss a sixpence to a beggar, but the inconsiderate act may work more harm than good. True sympathy will lead us to inquire into the unfortunate man's circumstances, and to see whether there may not be some wiser way of helping him. This is one of the most pressing problems of our complicated condition of society. It is not so easy to be wisely helpful to the poor as it was in the simpler circumstances of ancient times. A true Christian sympathy must lead us to study the deep, dark problem of poverty. How can the lowest classes be permanently raised? How can they be really saved? How can we help people to help themselves?

II. HOW THIS COMES TO BE LENDING TO THE LORD. In the olden times people thought to offer to God in material, visible sacrifices by slaying animals on the altar. Now money and service given to a Christian Church and to directly missionary agencies for spreading the kingdom of heaven, and so glorifying God, are regarded as devoted to God. Thus we are to see that we can serve him by ministering directly to the well-being of our fellow-men. 1. *Men are God's children.* He who helps the child pleases the father. 2. *God has pity on the suffering.* Therefore for us to have pity is to be like God, and so to please him; it is to do his will, to do the thing he would have us do, and so to render him service. 3. *This is within our reach.* The difficulty is to see how we can do anything to help the Almighty, or give anything to enrich the Owner of all things. The cattle upon a thousand hills are his. But the poor we have always with us. Inasmuch as we do a kindness to one of the least of these, Christ's brethren, we do it unto him (Matt. xxv. 40). All real love to man is also love to God. The noblest liturgy is the ministry of human charity. " Pure religion and undefiled before God and the Father is this, to visit the fatherless and widows in their affliction, and to keep himself unspotted from the world " (Jas. i. 27).

III. Why this is only lending to the Lord. It is returned to the giver. Such a thought seems to lower the tone of the subject. To give, hoping for no return, is Christ's method, and this lifts us to a higher level. Love asks for no payment. The pity that calculates its recompense is a false and selfish sentiment. Assuredly we must learn to love for love's sake, and to pity because we are moved with compassion, irrespective of returns. 1. *Yet the fact that there is a return remains.* It may be well for selfish men who refrain from showing sympathy for the needy to reflect on this. Their selfishness is short-sighted. 2. *The return is spiritual.* We are not to look for our money back again. That would involve no real giving. The return is different in kind. It is of a higher character, and comes in peace of soul, in enlargement of affection, in the satisfaction of seeing good results flowing from our sympathy.

Ver. 18.—*Timely chastisement.* I. Chastisement should be timely. " Prevention is better than cure." If we wait till the weeds run to seed it is in vain for us to pull them up—they will have sown another and larger crop. The lion's cub may be caught and caged; the full-grown beast is dangerous to approach, and out of our power. Consider some practical applications of these truths. 1. *They show us the importance of early home-training.* The first seeds are sown at home. If an evil disposition reveals itself there, it should be checked before it develops into a fatal habit. Foolishly fond parents laugh at exhibitions of bad temper and other faults in very young children, amused at the quaintness and pitying the helplessness of these miniature sins. But surely a wiser course would be to nip the evil in the bud. 2. *They enhance the value of Sunday school work.* Five million children were under Sunday school teaching in England during the year 1888. The great mass of the population passes through this instruction. Surely more should be made of the golden opportunity thus afforded of giving a right course to the lives of the people. Most working men will not go to church. But they will permit their children to attend Sunday school. We have the working classes with us in their childhood. 3. *They point to an enlargement of the agency of industrial schools.* Already juvenile crime has been reduced by one-half—this is one of the most cheering signs of the times. But still there are multitudes of children who breathe an atmosphere of crime from their cradles. There is no more Christian work than the effort to save these victims of the vices of their parents. The juvenile offender should be an object of peculiar solicitude to one who has the well-being of society at heart.

II. Chastisement should be hopeful. There is hope for all in their youth. We may not be able to recover the degraded, besotted wrecks of humanity in their more advanced years. But the children are amenable to saving influences, and the treatment of them should be inspired with a belief that they may be trained. Directly any parent or teacher despairs of a child he proves himself no longer competent to have the charge of him. Reading the second clause of the verse in the language of the Revisers, we are warned against vindictive chastisement: " And set not thy heart on his destruction." The old notion of punishment was purely retributive; the newer notion of it is more disciplinary. We want fewer prisons and more reformatories. But for encouragement in such efforts we must have grounds of hope. Observe some of these. 1. *The elasticity of youth.* The young are capable of great changes and of large development. 2. *The Divine direction.* The providence of God overruling our attempts at correction is needed to bring them to a successful issue. But we have a right to look for this end, for God desires the salvation and recovery of his children. 3. *The power of love.* We can never correct to good purpose unless we do so from motives of love. When these motives are felt they cannot but make themselves effective in the end. Then, though the chastisement may have been resented at first, the good purpose that instigated it will be ultimately recognized, and may rouse the better nature of the wrong-doer.

HOMILIES BY VARIOUS AUTHORS.

Vers. 1—7.— *The lowly and gentle life.* He who is truly humble before his God will be sweet, kind, and peaceable in his relations to men.

I. THE ATTRIBUTES OF THIS LIFE. (Vers. 1—3.) 1. It is the life of *innocence*, in the seeking to have a conscience " void of offence toward God and toward men." This makes poverty rich and privation blessed, for the kingdom of heaven is for such. The consciousness of being dear to God is the true wealth of the soul; the sense of being alienated from him darkens and distresses even amidst wealth and luxury. In addition to this, let us recollect the paradox of the apostle, " Poor, yet making many rich." It is such lives that have indeed enriched the world. 2. It is the life of *thoughtfulness.* 3. It is the life of *content.*

II. ITS TRIALS AND CONSOLATIONS. 1. It often incurs the *coldness of the world* (ver. 4). A man who goes down in the scale of wealth finds, in the same degree, the circle of ordinary acquaintances shrink. 2. But there is *consolation*—a sweetness even in the heart of this bitter experience, for the soul is thrown the more entirely upon God. When friends, when even father and mother forsake, the Lord takes up. *Deus meus et omnia!* We are naturally prone to rely more upon man than upon God ; and have to rewrite upon our memories the old biblical maxim, " Put not your trust in man." Poverty may separate us from so-called friends, but " who shall separate us from the love of Christ ? "

III. THE REPULSIVE CONTRAST TO THIS LIFE. A victim of vice and moral poverty amidst outward wealth. 1. *Folly and untruth.* (Ver. 1.) The words and the thoughts are interchangeable. The godless, selfish rich man's life is a *living lie.* The outward parts of Dives and Lazarus are in the sight of Heaven reversed. 2. *Thoughtless rashness.* (Ver. 2.) The " making haste to be rich," so strong a passion of our day, may be chiefly thought of. But any excessive eagerness of ambitious desire, or sensual pleasure which blinds the soul to thought, and indisposes for serious reflection, comes under this head. But the unreflective life is neither *safe* nor *happy.* It is to such thoughtless ones the solemn warning comes, " Thou fool! thy *soul* shall be required of thee." 3. *Murmuring discontent.* (Ver. 3.) The source of the vicious kind of discontent is a conscience at war with itself, and perversely mistaking the true nature of the satisfaction it needs. The " Divine discontent" which springs from the sense of our inward poverty carries in it the seed of its own satisfaction. It is the blessed hunger and thirst which shall be fed. 4. *False social relations.* (Ver. 4.) Of the friends made by riches it is true that " riches harm them, not the man " (Bishop Hall). And the great man lives amidst illusions; and, in moments of insight, doubts whether among the obsequious crowd there be a heart he can claim as his own. In such an atmosphere, false witness and lies, in all their forms of scandal, slander, destruction, spring up (ver. 5). It is a *hollow* life, and the fires of judgment murmur beneath it. Yet the *fulsome flattery* which rises like a cloud of incense before the rich man, and the throng of easily bought "friends," still hide from him the true state of the case. Well may Divine Wisdom warn of the difficulty which attends the rich man's entrance into the kingdom. Here there are great lessons on compensation. God hath set the one thing over against the other, to the end that we should seek nothing after him (Eccles. vii. 14). The gentle and humble poor may convert their poverty into the fine gold of the spirit; while the rich man too dearly buys " position " at the expense of the soul.—J.

Vers. 8—17.—*Maxims of intelligence.* I. THE WORTH OF INTELLIGENCE. 1. It is *self-conservative* (ver. 8). We all love our own soul or life in any healthy state of body and mind. We all want to live as long as possible. It is natural to desire to live again beyond the grave. Then let us understand that there is no way to these ends except that of intelligence, in the highest and in every sense. 2. *It is the source of happiness.* (Ver. 8.) The truth is very general and abstract, like the truth of the whole of these proverbs. It does not amount to this—that good sense will in every case *procure* happiness, but that there is no true happiness without it.

II. SOME MAXIMS OF INTELLIGENCE. 1. *The sorrow that falsehood brings.* (Ver. 9.) It is *certain.* Many a lie is not immediately *found out* in the ordinary sense of these words; but it is always *found in* the man's mind. It vitiates the intelligence, undermines the moral strength. The rest must follow in its time—*somewhere, somehow.* 2. *Vanity stands in its own light.* (Ver. 10.) Those who have given way to overweening self-esteem and arrogance of temper—like Rehoboam, or like Alexander the Great, or Napoleon—become only the more conceited and presumptuous in success. The opposite of vanity is not grovelling self-disparagement, but the sense which teaches us to *know our place.* 3. *The prudence of toleration and of conciliation.* (Vers. 11, 12.) Socrates was a noble example of these virtues in the heathen world. We who have "learned Christ" should not at least fall behind him. To bear our wrongs with patience is the lower degree of this virtue. Positively to "overcome evil with good" stands higher. Highest of all is the Divine art to turn persecutors into friends (1 Pet. ii. 19; Matt. v. 44, *sqq.*). 4. *The arcana of domestic life.* (Vers. 13, 14.) (1) *The foolish son.* "Many are the miseries of a man's life, but none like that which cometh from him who should be the stay of his life." "Write this man childless" would have been a boon in comparison. (2) *The tiresome spouse.* Wearing the heart that is firm as stone by her continual contentions. (3) *The kind and good wife.* No gift so clearly shows the tender providence of God. 5. *The inevitable fate of idleness.* (Ver. 15.) (1) *It produces a lethargy in the soul.* (Ch. vi. 9, 10.) The faculties that are not used become benumbed and effete. (2) Thus *it leads to want.* Although these are general maxims of a highly abstract character, still how true on the whole—if not without exception—they are to life! "He that will not work, neither let him eat." 6. *The wisdom of attention to God's commands.* (Ver. 16.) (1) To every man his soul is dear; *i.e.* his life is sweet. (2) The great secret, in the lower sense of self-preservation, in the higher of salvation, is *obedience to law.* (3) Inattention is the chief source of calamity. In the lower relation it is so. The careless crossing of the road, the unsteady foot on the mountain-side seems to be *punished* instantly and terribly. And this is the type of the truth in higher aspects. 7. *The reward of pity and benevolence.* (Ver. 17.) Sir Thomas More used to say there was more rhetoric in this sentence than in a whole library. God looks upon the poor as his own, and satisfies the debts they cannot pay. In spending upon the poor the good man serves God in his designs with reference to men.—J.

Vers. 18—21.—*The true prudence.* I. IN THE PARENTAL RELATION. (Ver. 18.) 1. *The necessity of discipline.* The exuberance of youth needs the hand of the pruner; the wildness of the colt must be early tamed, or never. Weak indulgence is the worst unkindness to children. 2. *The unwisdom of excessive severity.* Cruelty is not discipline; too great sharpness is as bad as the other extreme. Children are thus made base, induced to take up with bad company, and to surfeit and run to excess when they become their own masters.
II. IN THE RELATION OF SELF-GOVERNMENT. 1. *The folly and injuriousness of passion.* (Ver. 19.) Not only in the harmful deeds and words it may produce towards others, but in the havoc it produces in one's own bosom. How fine the saying of Plato to his slave, "I would beat thee, but that I am angry"! "Learn of him who is meek and lowly of heart." 2. *The wisdom of a teachable spirit.* (Ver. 20.) Never to be above listening to proffered advice from others, and to find in every humiliation and every failure an admonition from the Father of spirits,—this is life-wisdom. And thus a store is being laid up against the time to come, that we may lay hold on eternal life.
III. PRUDENCE BUT A FINITE WISDOM. (Ver. 21.) God is our best Counsellor; without him our prudence avails not, and along with all prudence there must be the recognition of his overruling, all-controlling wisdom. To begin with God is the true secret of success in every enterprise. May he *prevent*, or go before, us in all our doings!—J.

Vers. 22—29.—*Mixed maxims of life-wisdom.* I. HUMAN KINDNESS. (Ver. 22.) There is no purer delight than in the feelings of love and the practical exercise of universal kindness. If the mere *pleasure* of the selfish and the benevolent life be the criterion, without question the latter has the advantage.
II. TRUTHFULNESS. (Vers. 22, 28.) So the honest poor outweighs the rich or successful liar in intrinsic happiness as well as in repute. The worthless witness is a pest to society, an abomination to God.

III. PIETY. (Ver. 23.) It is a *living* principle in every sense of the word—hath the promise of life in both worlds. It provides for the soul satisfaction, rest, the consciousness of present and eternal security.

IV. IDLENESS. (Ver. 24.) Exposed by a vivid picture of the idle man's attitude. It reminds one of the saying concerning a certain distinguished writer's idleness, that were he walking through an orchard where the fruit brushed against his mouth, he would be too idle to open it to bite a morsel. No moral good can be ours without seeking.

V. SCOFFING FOLLY CONTRASTED WITH SIMPLICITY AND SENSE. (Vers. 25, 29.) He that places himself above instruction ends by bringing himself beneath contempt. Scorn for good has, like every sin, its own determined punishment. And "God strikes some that he may warn all."

VI. FILIAL IMPIETY. (Vers. 26, 27.) The shame and sorrow that it brings to parents is constantly insisted on as a lesson and a warning to the latter. If these bitter experiences are to be avoided, let children be timely trained to obedience, respect, and reverence for God. God's Word is the true rule and guide of life, and he who departs from it is a corrupt and seductive teacher.—J.

Ver. 2.—*The evil of ignorance.* Manifold are the evils of ignorance. All evil of all kinds has been resolved into error; but, if we do not go so far as this, we may truly say—

I. THAT IGNORANCE OF GOD IS FATAL. "This is life eternal, to *know God*;" and if the knowledge of God is life, what must the ignorance of him be? History and observation only too fully assure us what it is: it is spiritual and moral death; the departure of the soul from all that enlightens and elevates, and its sinking down into grovelling and debasing superstitions. To be without the knowledge of God is simply fatal to the soul of man.

II. THAT IGNORANCE OF OUR HUMAN NATURE IS PERILOUS. 1. Not to know its nobler possibilities is to be without the needful incentive to lofty aspiration and strenuous endeavour. 2. Not to know its weaknesses and its possibilities of evil is to go forward into the midst of bristling dangers, unarmed and undefended.

III. THAT IGNORANCE OF THE WORLD (OF MEN AND THINGS) IS HIGHLY UNDESIRABLE. 1. To study, and thus to be acquainted with nature as God has fashioned it, to be familiar with the ways and with the arts and sciences of man,—is to be braced and strengthened in mind, is to be far better able to understand and to apply the truth of God as revealed in his Word. 2. To be ignorant of all this is to be correspondingly weak and incapable. Knowledge is power, and ignorance is weakness, in every direction. To go on our way through the world, failing to acquire the grasp of fact and truth which intelligent observation and patient study would secure,—this is to leave untouched one large part of the heritage which our heavenly Father is offering to us. There is one particular consequence of ignorance which the wise man specifies; for he reminds us—

IV. THAT PRECIPITANCY IN WORD AND DEED IS POSITIVELY GUILTY. "He that hasteth with his feet sinneth." An unwise and hurtful precipitancy is the natural accompaniment of ignorance. The man who knows only a very little, does not know when he has heard only one-half of all that can be learnt; hence he decides and speaks and acts off-hand, without waiting for additional, complementary, or qualifying particulars. And hence he judges falsely and unjustly; hence he acts unrighteously and foolishly, and often cruelly; he takes steps which he has laboriously and ignominiously to retrace; he does harm to the very cause which he is most anxious to help. It is the man of wide knowledge and expanded view, it is the large-minded and well-informed soul, that bears the best testimony, that does the worthiest and most enduring work, that lives the largest and most enviable life.—C.

Ver. 3.—*Disquietude and complaint.* We have—

I. GOD'S RIGHTEOUS WAY. The way in which God intended man to walk was that way of wisdom, all of whose paths are peace. This divinely appointed way is that of holy service. Man, like every other being above him, and every other creature below him in the universe, was created to serve. We were created to serve our God and our kind; and in this double service we should find our rest and our heritage. This, which is God's way, should have been our way also.

II. MAN'S PERVERTED WAY. Man, in his sin and his folly, has "perverted his way; " he has attempted another path, a short cut to happiness and success. He has turned out of the h gh-road of holy service into the by-path of selfishness; he has sought his satisfaction and his portion in following his own will, in giving himself up to worldly ambitions, in indulging in unholy pleasure, in living for mere enjoyment, in making himself the master, and his own good the end and aim of his life.

III. HIS CONSEQUENT DISQUIETUDE. When anything is in its wrong place, there is certain to be unrest. If in the mechanism of the human body, or in the machinery of an engine, or in the working of some organization, anything (or any one) is misplaced, disorder and disquietude invariably ensue. And when man puts his will above or against that of his Divine Creator, that of his heavenly Father, there is a displacement and reversal such as may well bring about disturbance. And it does. It is hardly saying too much to say that all the violence, disease, strife, misery, poverty, death, we see around us arise from this disastrous perversion—from man trying to turn God's way of blessedness into his own way. Man's method has been utterly wrong and mistaken, and the penalty of his folly is heart-ache, wretchedness, ruin.

IV. HIS VAIN AND GUILTY COMPLAINT. He "fretteth against the Lord." Instead of smiting himself, he complains of God. He fails to see that the source of his unrest is in his own heart; he ascribes it to his circumstances, and he imputes these to his Creator. So, either secretly or openly, he complains of God; he thinks, and perhaps says, that God has dealt hardly with him, has denied to him what he has given to others; in the dark depths of his soul is a guilty rebelliousness.

V. THE ONE WAY OF REST. This is to return unto the Lord in free and full submission. 1. To recognize God's righteous claim upon us, as our Creator, Preserver, Redeemer. 2. To acknowledge to ourselves and to confess to him that we have guiltily withheld ourselves from him, and sinfully complained of his holy will. 3. To ask his mercy in Jesus Christ our Saviour, and offer our hearts to himself and our lives to his service. This is the one way of rest and joy; it is " the path of life."—C.

Vers. 8, 16.—*Making the most of ourself and our life.* How shall we most truly "love our own soul " but by making all we can make of the nature and the life God has entrusted to our care! And how shall we do this? Surely by "getting wisdom " and " keeping understanding." To look at the subject negatively and, beginning at the bottom, to take an upward path, we remark—

I. THAT CONTEMPTUOUS CARELESSNESS MEANS CERTAIN RUIN. "He that despiseth his ways shall die." The man who never pauses to consider what he can accomplish, how he shall spend his days and his powers, but who goes aimlessly onward, letting youth and manhood pass without any serious thought at all, and content to snatch the enjoyment of the passing hour,—is a man of folly, and he can expect nothing, as he certainly will find nothing, but the most meagre portion and a very speedy end of everything. He sows to the flesh, and of the flesh he reaps corruption. To "despise our way " in this fashion is to forfeit our inheritance and come to utter destitution. Moving higher up, but still failing to reach the right standard, we remark—

II. THAT ANY COUNSEL WHICH IS NOT OF GOD WILL PROVE DISAPPOINTING. There is much cleverness and keenness that is not wisdom; there is much concern about ourself and our future which is not a true " love for our own soul." There are many counsellors who will advise us to seek certain pleasures, or to aim at certain honours, or to climb to a certain position, or to seek entrance into some particular society, or to secure a certain treasure,—and it will be well with us. But any counsel which falls short of telling us the will of God, which leaves untold the wisdom which is from above, will certainly prove to be unsound. A point will come in our experience where it will break down. It will not meet the deeper necessities of our nature nor the darker passages of our life. We must take higher ground—that on which we see—

III. THAT DIVINE WISDOM WILL LEAD US TO TRUE AND LASTING BLESSEDNESS. "The fear of the Lord, *that* is wisdom; and to depart from evil is understanding " (Job xxviii. 28; see ch. i. 7; ix. 10). And surely : 1. To know God is, in itself, a real and a great blessing (Jer. ix. 24). To know God as he is revealed in Jesus Christ is to be enriched in the most precious and valuable knowledge; it is "to be wiser than the ancients;" it is to have that in our mind which is of more intrinsic worth than all that men can put into their pockets. 2. To know God in Jesus Christ is to have rest of heart (Matt. xi. 28, 29). Those who love themselves will surely care for spiritual rest—for a peace which no favouring circumstances can confer. 3. To learn of Christ and keep his commandments is to be preserved in moral and spiritual integrity; he that "keepeth the commandments" by consulting the will of Christ will certainly "keep his own soul" from all that stains and slays a human spirit and a human life —from impurity, insobriety, untruthfulness, dishonesty, profanity, selfishness; he will "keep his soul" in the love of God, in the light of his countenance, under his guardian care. To remain loyal to the wisdom of God (to·"keep understanding") is to find every good that is open to us. It is to move along that path which is evermore ascending; which conducts to the loftier heights of moral excellency, of exalted spiritual joy, of holy and noble service; which leads to the very gates of heaven and the near presence of God.—C.

Ver. 17 (see also ch. x. 14, 31; xvii. 5).—*Valuable kindness.* We gather—
I. THAT HAUGHTY UNKINDNESS IS A HEINOUS SIN. To mock the poor or to oppress the poor is to reproach our Maker. For he that made us made them; and, in many instances, made them to be as they are. The Son of man himself was poor, having nowhere to lay his head; and although it is true that poverty is very often the consequence and penalty of sin, yet, on the other hand, it is often (1) the accompaniment of virtue and piety; and (2) frequently it has been the penalty of faithfulness to conviction, and therefore the sign of peculiar worth. To treat with disdain a condition which God himself has associated with piety and even with nobility of character is to mock our Maker. And to oppress such is to be guilty of a flagrant sin; it is to take advantage of weakness in order to do a neighbour wrong; this is to add meanness to cruelty and injustice. It is, moreover, to do that which our Lord has told us he will consider to be directed against himself (Matt. xxv. 42, 43).
II. THAT PRACTICAL PITIFULNESS IS A MUCH-REWARDED VIRTUE. 1. It is accepted by our Divine Lord as a service rendered to himself (text; Matt. xxv. 35, 36). How gladly would we minister to Jesus Christ were we to recognize in some weary and troubled neighbour none other than the Redeemer himself clothed in human form again! But we need not long for such an opportunity; nor need we wait for it. It is ours. We have but to show practical kindness to "one of the least" of his brethren, and we show it unto him, the Lord himself (Matt. xxv. 40). And what we do shall be rendered unto us again; *i.e.* we shall receive in return from our Father that which will fully compensate us. Our reward will include not only this gracious acceptance, but: 2. We shall earn the gratitude of thankful hearts; and if (as is likely enough) we go sometimes unblessed of man, yet at other times we shall not want the cordial, loving, prayerful gratitude of a human heart; and what better treasure could we hold than that? 3. God will bless us in our own hearts for every kindness we render. He has so made our spirits that they are affected for good or evil by everything we do. Each thought, each deed, leaves us other than we were; stronger, wiser, worthier, or else weaker, less wise, less excellent, than before. Our character is the final result of everything that we have ever done, both in mind and in the flesh. So that each gracious word we speak, each kindly service we render to any one in need, is one more stroke of the chisel which is carving a beautiful character, fair in the sight of God himself. 4. We gain the present favour of our Divine Lord, and may look for his strong succour in our own time of need. 5. We shall receive his word of honour in the day "when every man shall have praise of God" (1 Cor. iv. 5).—C.

Ver. 18.—(See homily on ch. xiii. 24.)—C.

Ver. 20.—*Ready at the end.* The wise man always shows his wisdom by looking well before him. It is the sure mark of a fool to content himself with the immediate present. We do not wonder that proverbs should deal much with the future. "Passion and Patience" is the picture which is always being exhibited before the eyes of men.

I. THE NEED OF READINESS AT THE END. "How shall we enjoy the present time?" asks one; "How shall we make ready for the end?" asks another and a wiser soul. The question presents itself to the *youth*, as he looks forward to the end of the term and the coming of the examination or the writing of the report; to the *young man*—the apprentice, the articled clerk, the student—as he considers how he shall go through his trial-hour and be prepared for his business or profession; to the *man in middle life*, as he foresees the time coming when he can no longer do as he is doing now, and must have something to fall back upon in his declining days; to the *man in later life*, as he is compelled to feel that his powers are fast failing, and that the hour is not distant when he will stand on the very verge of life and confront the long and solemn future. It should also be present in the mind of those who are *soon to go forth* into the sterner conflict of life, to meet alone, away from home-influences, the serious and strong temptations of an evil world. Whatever the stage through which we are now passing, it moves towards its close—an end which is sure to open out into something beyond, and, most likely, something more important, weighted with graver responsibilities and leading to larger issues. Are we so living, the wise will ask, that we shall be ready for that end when it comes?

II. THE CONSEQUENT NEED TO LEARN OF GOD. "Hear counsel," etc. 1. There is much need to *learn of men*—from our parents, from our teachers, from every form of instructive literature, from all that the experiences of men, as we watch their life, are saying to us. Whoso would be wise at the end of his career should have an open mind that every one and everything may teach him. Lessons are to be learnt from every event, however simple and humble it may be. The wide world is the school which the wise will never "leave." 2. There is much more need *to learn of God, to learn of Christ*. For: (1) He can speak *authoritatively*, as man cannot. (2) He gives us *wisdom unmingled with error*, as man does not. (3) He can tell us how to find his Divine favour and how to reach his nearer presence, as no man can. Let us learn of Christ and be wise.—C.

Ver. 21.—*The mind of man and the mind of God.* Here is a contrast which we do well to consider. Between our human spiritual nature and that of the Divine Spirit it is possible to find resemblances and contrasts. Both are interesting and instructive.

I. THE THOUGHTS OF MAN'S MIND. We know how fugitive these are; how they come and go like the flash of the lightning; and even those which linger are but short-lived, they soon give place to others. Even those thoughts which become "fixed," which settle down into plans and purposes, have but a brief tenure in our brain; they, too, pass away and make room for others in their turn. Our thoughts are: 1. *Fluctuating and therefore many.* We care for one pleasure, we pursue one object now; but in a few weeks, or even days, we may weary of the one, we may be compelled to turn our attention from the other. 2. *Feeble and therefore many.* We propose and adopt one method, but it fails; and then we try another, and that fails; then we resort to a third, which also fails. We pass from thought to thought, from plan to plan; our very feebleness accounting for the manifoldness of our devices. 3. *False and therefore many.* We hold certain theories to-day; to-morrow they will be exploded, and we shall entertain another; before long that will yield to a third. 4. *Sinful and therefore many.* Nothing that is wrong can last; it must be dethroned, because it is evil, immoral, guilty. 5. *Selfish and therefore many.* We are concerning ourselves supremely about our own affairs or those of our family; but these are passing interests, changing with the flitting hours.

II. THE THOUGHTS WHICH ARE IN THE MIND OF GOD. His counsel stands (text). "The counsel of the Lord standeth for ever, the thoughts of his heart to all generations" (Ps. xxxiii. 11). God's purpose holds from age to age. For: 1. He rules in righteousness. He is governing the world by Divine and unchanging principles. "With him is no variableness," because he ever loves what is righteous and hates what is unholy and impure and unkind. He cannot change his course, because he cannot change his character. 2. He is working out one great beneficent conclusion. He is redeeming a lost world, reconciling it unto himself, uprooting the multiform sources of wrong and wretchedness, establishing the blessed kingdom of Christ, the kingdom of heaven on the earth. 3. He has ample time and power at his command; he has no need to change his plan, to resort to " devices."

> " His eternal thought moves on
>   His undisturbed affairs ; '

and is working out a glorious consummation which nothing shall avail to avert. 4. His perfect wisdom makes quite unnecessary the adoption of any other course than that which he is employing. (1) Steadfastness is one sign of wisdom. If we see a man or a Church perpetually changing its methods, we may be sure that it is weak. (2) Let us make God's great and holy purpose ours; (a) for it is that with which our eternal interest is bound up; (b) it is certain to be victorious. 3. Let us work on for our Lord and with him, in the calmness that becomes those who are confident of ultimate success.—C.

Ver. 23.—*The praise of piety.* What could be said more than is said here in praise of piety? What more or better could anything do for us than—

I. ENSURE OUR SAFETY. So that we shall not be visited with evil. But is not the good man visited with evil? Do not his crops fail, his vessels sink, his shares fall, his difficulties gather, his children die? Does not his health decline, his hope depart, his life lessen? Yes; but: 1. From the *worst* evils his piety secures him. The " fear of the Lord," that Holy One before whom he stands and with whom he walks, keeps him from folly, from fraud, from vice, from moral contamination, from that " death in life " which is *the* thing to be dreaded and avoided. 2. And the troubles and sorrows which do assail him lose all their bitterness as they wear the aspect of a heavenly Father's discipline, who, in all that he sends or suffers, is seeking the truest and the lasting well-being of his children. The man who is living in the fear of God, and in the love of Jesus Christ, may go on his homeward way with no anxiety in his heart, for he has the promise of his Saviour that all things shall work together for good—those things that are the least pleasant as well as those that are the most inviting.

II. SATISFY OUR SOUL. " Shall abide satisfied." Certainly it is only the man of real piety of whom this word can be used. Discontent is the mark which " the world and the things which are in the world " leave on the countenance and write on the heart of man. Nothing that is less than the Divine gives rest to the human spirit. Mirth, enjoyment, temporary happiness, may be commanded, but not abiding satisfaction. That, however, is found in the devoted service of a Divine Redeemer. Let a man yield himself, his whole powers and all his life, to the Saviour who loved him unto death, and in following and serving him he will " find rest unto his soul." Not half-hearted but whole-hearted service brings the joy which no accident can remove and which time does not efface or even lessen. The secret of lifelong blessedness is found, not in the assertion of an impossible freedom from obligation, but in an open, practicable, elevating service of the living God, our Divine Saviour.

III. CONSTITUTE OUR LIFE AND CONDUCT TO A STILL HIGHER FORM OF IT. " The fear of the Lord tendeth to life." It is not merely that a regard for God's will conduces to health and leads to long life (Ps. xci. 16); it is not only that it tends to secure to its possessor an honourable and estimable life among men. It is much more than this; it is that it *constitutes* human life. " This *is* life eternal, to know thee, the only true God." For man to live in ignorance or in forgetfulness of his Divine Father is to miss or to lose his life while he has it (or seems to have it). On the other hand, to live a life of reverence, of trustfulness in God, of love to him, of filial obedience and submission, of cheerful and devoted co-operation with him in the great redemptive work he is outworking, to be attaining more and more to his own spiritual likeness,— this *is* life itself, life in its excellency, its fulness, its beauty. Moreover, it itself, with all its worth, is but the prelude of that which is to come. It is the " fair beginning " of that which shall realize a glorious consummation a little further on. With all that hinders and hampers taken away, and with all that facilitates and enlarges bestowed upon us, we enter upon the nobler life beyond, which we have no language to describe because we have no faculty that can conceive its blessedness or its glory. 1. Let the perils of human life point to a Divine Refuge. 2. Let the weariness of earthly good

lead to the Divine Source of rest and joy.
lay hold on eternal life.—C.

3. In the midst of the deathfulness of sin,

EXPOSITION.

CHAPTER XX.

Ver. 1.—**Wine is a mocker**; or, *scorner*, the word (*luts*) being taken up from the last chapter. The liquor is, as it were, personified, as doing what men do under its influence. Thus inebriated persons scoff at what is holy, reject reproof, ridicule all that is serious. Septuagint, 'Ακόλαστον οἶνος, " Wine is an undisciplined thing;" Vulgate, *Luxuriosa res, vinum*. **Strong drink is raging**; *a brawler*, Revised Version. *Shekar*, σίκερα (Luke i. 15), is most frequently employed of any intoxicating drink not made from grapes, *e.g.* palm-wine, mead, etc. The inordinate use of this renders men noisy and boisterous, no longer masters of themselves or restrained by the laws of morality or decency. Septuagint, 'Υβριστικὸν μέθη, " Drunkenness is insolent." Theognis has some sensible lines on this matter (' Paræn.,' 479)—

Ὅς δ' ἂν ὑπερβάλλῃ πόσιος μέτρον, οὐκέτι κεῖνος
Τῆς αὑτοῦ γλώσσης καρτερὸς, οὐδὲ νόου·
Μυθεῖται δ' ἀπάλαμνα, τὰ νήφοσι γίγνεται αἰσχρά·
Αἰδεῖται δ' ἔρδων οὐδὲν, ὅταν μεθύῃ,
Τὸ πρὶν ἐὼν σώφρων τότε νήπιος.

Whosoever is deceived thereby is not wise. No one who reels under the influence of, is overpowered by, wine is wise (Isa. xxviii. 7). Septuagint, " Every fool is involved in such." Says a Latin adage—

" Ense cadunt multi, perimit sed crapula plures."

" More are drowned in the wine-cup than in the ocean,' say the Germans (comp. ch. xxiii. 29, etc.; Eph. v. 18).

Ver. 2.—**The fear of a king is as the roaring of a lion** (see ch. xix. 12). The terror which a king causes when his anger is rising is like the roar of a lion, which betokens danger. Septuagint, " The threat of a king differeth not from the wrath of a lion." **Whoso provoketh him to anger sinneth against his own soul**; imperils his life, which he has no right wilfully to jeopard. Septuagint, " He who enrageth him (ὁ παροξύνων αὐτόν)." The Complutensian and some Greek versions introduce the words, καὶ ἐπιμιγνύμενος, " and has intercourse with him;" *i.e.* he who having aroused a king's resentment does not avoid his presence, exposes himself to certain death.

Ver. 3.—**It is an honour to a man to cease**

from strife; or better, as Delitzsch and others, *to remain far from strife*. A prudent man will not only abstain from causing quarrel, but will hold himself aloof from all contention, and thus will have due care for his own honour and dignity. How different is this from the modern code, which makes a man's honour consist in his readiness to avenge fancied injury at the risk of his own or his neighbour's life! Septuagint, " It is a glory to a man to hold himself aloof from revilings." **Every fool will be meddling** (see on ch. xvii. 14 ; xviii. 1). Delitzsch, " Whoever is a fool showeth his teeth," finds pleasure in strife. Septuagint, " Every fool involves himself in such," as in ver. 1.

Ver. 4.—**The sluggard will not plough by reason of the cold**; *propter frigus*, Vulgate. But חֹרֶף (*choreph*) denotes the time of gathering—the autumn ; so we would translate, " At the time of harvest the sluggard ploughs not"—just when the ground is most easily and profitably worked. " The weakness of the coulter and other parts of the plough requires that advantage be taken, in all but the most friable soils, of the softening of the surface by the winter or spring rains; so that the peasant, if industrious, has to plough in the winter, though sluggards still shrink from its cold, and have to beg in the harvest " (Geikie, ' Holy Land and Bible,' ii. 491). **Therefore shall he beg in harvest, and have nothing.** So the Vulgate, *Mendicabit ergo æstate, et non dabitur illi*. But this does not accurately represent the meaning of the clause. If ever the prosperous are disposed to relieve the needy, it would be at the time when they have safely garnered their produce ; an appeal to their charity at such a moment would not be made in vain. Rather the sentence signifies that the lazy man, having neglected to have his land ploughed at the proper time, " when he asks (for his fruits) at harvest-time, there is nothing." He puts off tilling his fields day after day, or never looks to see if his labourers do their duty, and so his land is not cultivated, and he has no crop to reap when autumn comes. " By the street of By-and-by one arrives at the house of Never " (Spanish proverb). Taking a different interpretation of the word *choreph*, the LXX. renders, " Being reproached, the sluggard is not ashamed, no more than he who borrows corn in harvest."

Ver. 5.—**Counsel in the heart of man is like deep water.** The thoughts and purposes of a man are hidden in his breast like deep water (ch. xviii. 4) in the bosom of the earth, hard to fathom, hard to get. But a man of understanding will draw it out. One who is intelligent and understands human nature penetrates the secret, and, by judicious questions and remarks, draws out (ἐξαντλήσει, Septuagint) the hidden thought.

Ver. 6.—Most men will proclaim every one his own goodness; *chesed*, "kindness," "mercy," "liberality," as in ch. xix. 22. So Ewald and others. Hitzig and Kamphausen translate, "Many a man one names his dear friend;" Delitzsch and Nowack prefer, "Most men meet a man who is gracious to them;" *i.e.* it is common enough to meet a man who seems benevolent and well disposed. Vulgate, "Many men are called merciful;" Septuagint, "Man is a great thing, and a merciful man is a precious thing." The renderings of most modern commentators imply the statement that love and mercy are common enough, at least in outward expression. The Authorized Version pronounces that men are ready enough to parade and boast of their liberality, like the hypocrites who were said proverbially to sound a trumpet when they performed their almsdeeds (Matt. vi. 2). Commenting on the Greek rendering of the clause given above, St. Chrysostom observes, "This is the true character of man to be merciful; yea, rather the character of God to show mercy. . . . Those who answer not to this description, though they partake of mind, and are never so capable of knowledge, the Scripture refuses to acknowledge them as men, but calls them dogs, and horses, and serpents, and foxes, and wolves, and if there be any animals more contemptible" ('Hom. iv. in Phil.' and 'Hom. xiii. in 1 Tim.,' Oxford transl.). The contrast between show, or promise, and performance is developed in the second clause. But a faithful man who can find? The faithfulness intended is fidelity to promises, the practical execution of the vaunted benevolence; this is rare indeed, so that a psalmist could cry, "I said in my haste, All men are liars" (Ps. cxvi. 11; comp. Rom. iii. 4). Lesètre refers to Massillon's sermon, 'Sur la Gloire Humaine,' where we read (the preacher, of course, rests on the Latin Version), "Ces hommes vertueux dont le monde se fait tant d'honneur, n'ont au fond souvent pour eux que l'erreur publique. Amis fidèles, je le veux; mais c'est le goût, la vanité ou l'intérêt, qui les lie; et dans leur amis, ils n'amient qu' eux-mêmes. . . . En un mot, dit l'Ecriture, on les appelle miséricordieux, ils ont toutes les vertus pour le public; mais n'étant pas fidèles à Dieu, ils n'en ont pas une seule pour eux-mêmes."

Ver. 7.—The just man walketh in his integrity. It is better to connect the two clauses together, and not to take the first as a separate sentence, thus: "He who as a just man walketh in his integrity"—Blessed are his children after him (comp. ch. xiv. 26). So the Septuagint and Vulgate. The man of pure life, who religiously performs his duty towards God and man, shall bring a blessing on his children who follow his good example, both during his life and after his death. The temporal promise is seen in Exod. xx. 6; Deut. iv. 40; Ps. cxii. 2, etc. Some see here an instance of utilitarianism; but it cannot be supposed that the writer inculcates virtue for the sake of the worldly advantages connected with it; rather he speaks from experience, and from a faithful dependence on Providence, of the happy results of a holy life.

Ver. 8.—A royal and right noble maxim. A king that sitteth in the throne of judgment scattereth away all evil with his eyes. The king, sitting on the tribunal and executing his judiciary office, sees through all devices and pretences which cloak evil, and scatters them to the winds, as the chaff flies before the winnowing-fan. Nothing unrighteous can abide in his presence (comp. ver. 26; ch. xvi. 10, etc.). See here an adumbration of the characteristic of the Messiah, the great King whose "eyes behold, whose eyelids try, the children of men" (Ps. xi. 4): who is "of purer eyes than to behold evil" (Hab. i. 13); who "with righteousness shall judge the poor, and reprove with equity for the meek of the earth: and shall smite the earth with the rod of his mouth; and with the breath of his lips shall slay the wicked" (Isa. xi. 4; comp. Matt. iii. 12). Septuagint, "When the righteous king shall sit upon his throne, nothing that is evil shall offer itself before his eyes."

Ver. 9.—Who can say, I have made my heart clean, I am pure from my sin? The question implies the answer, "No one." This is expressed in Job xiv. 4, "Who can bring a clean thing out of an unclean? not one." At the dedication of the temple, Solomon enunciates this fact of man's corruption, "There is no man that sinneth not" (1 Kings viii. 46). The prophet testifies, "The heart is deceitful above all things, and it is desperately sick: who can know it?" (Jer. xvii. 9). And St. John warns, "If we say that we have no sin, we deceive ourselves, and the truth is not in us" (1 John i. 8). The heart is cleansed by self-examination and repentance; but it is so easy to deceive one's self in this matter, sins may lurk undetected, motives may be overlooked, so that no one can rightly be self-righteous, or conceited, or proud of his spiritual state. The "my sin" at the end of the clause is rather possible than actual sin; and the expression means that no one can pride himself on being secure from yielding to temptation, however clean for a time his conscience may be. The verse, therefore, offers a stern corrective of two grievous spiritual errors—presumption and apathy.

Ver. 10.—**Divers weights, and divers measures**; literally, *stone and stone, ephah and ephah*. The stones were used for weighing; dishonest traders kept them of different weights, and also measures of different capacities, substituting one for the other in order to defraud unwary customers. The Septuagint makes this plain by rendering, "A weight great and small, and measures double" (see on ch. xi. 1 and xvi. 11; and comp. ver. 23). The ephah was a dry measure, being one-tenth of the homer, and occupying the same position in solids as the bath did in liquids. It equalled about three pecks of our measure. **Both of them are alike abomination to the Lord** (ch. xvii. 15; comp. Lev. xix. 36; Deut. xxv. 13, etc.); Septuagint, "Are impure before the Lord, even both of them, and he who doeth them." Pseudo-Bernard ('De Pass. Dom.,' xvii.), applying the passage mystically, teaches that a man may be said to keep a double measure, who, being conscious of his own evil character, endeavours to appear righteous to others; who, as he puts it, "Suo judicio terræ proximus est, et aliis cupit elevatus videri." Others, connecting this verse in thought with the preceding, see in it a warning against judging a neighbour by a standard which we do not apply to ourselves. The Septuagint Version arranges the matter from ver. 10 onwards differently from the Hebrew, omitting vers. 14—19, and placing vers. 10—13 after ver. 22.

Ver. 11.—**Even a child is known** (*maketh himself known*) **by his doings.** (For " even " (*gam*), see on ch. xvii. 26.) A child is open, simple, and straightforward in his actions; he has not the reserves and concealments which men practise, so you see by his conduct what his real character and disposition are. Ewald takes מַעֲלָלָיו in the sense of "play," "games;" but it seems never to have this meaning, and there is no need to change the usual signification. The habits of a life are learned in early age. The boy is father of the man. Delitzsch quotes the German proverbs, "What means to become a hook bends itself early," and "What means to become a thorn sharpens itself early;" and the Aramæan, "That which will become a gourd shows itself in the bud." **Whether his work be pure** ("clean," as ver. 9 and ch. xvi. 2), **and whether it be right.** His conduct will show thus much, and will help one to prognosticate the future. Septuagint (according to the Vatican), "In his pursuits (ἐπιτηδεύ-

μασιν) a young man will be fettered in company with a holy man, and his way will be straight," which seems to mean that a good man will restrain the reckless doings of a giddy youth, and will lead him into better courses.

Ver. 12.—**The hearing ear, and the seeing eye, the Lord hath made even both of them.** This apothegm, which seems to be nothing but a trite truism, brings to notice many important consequences. First, there is the result noted in Ps. xciv. 9, "He that planted the ear, shall he not hear? He that formed the eye, shall he not see?" Hence we learn the sleepless providence of God. So 'Pirke Aboth,' "Know that which is above thee, an eye that seeth all, an ear that heareth all." We learn also that all things are directed and overruled by God (comp. ch. xv. 3; xvi. 4). Then there is the thought that these powers of ours, being the gift of God, should be used piously and in God's service. "Mine ears hast thou opened . . . Lo, I come . . . I delight to do thy will, O my God" (Ps. xl. 6, etc.). The eye should be blind, the ear deaf, to all that might defile or excite to evil (see Isa. xxxiii. 15). But it is the Lord alone that enables the spiritual organs to receive the wondrous things of God's Law; they must be educated by grace to enable them to perform their proper functions. "God hath given us eyes," says St. Chrysostom ('Hom. xxii. in 1 Cor.'), "not that we may look wantonly, but that, admiring his handiwork, we may worship the Creator. And that this is the use of our eyes is evident from the things which are seen. For the lustre of the sun and of the sky we see from an immeasurable distance, but a woman's beauty one cannot discern so far off. Seest thou that for this end our eye was chiefly given? Again, he made the ear, that we should entertain not blasphemous words, but saving doctrines. Wherefore you see, when it receives anything dissonant, both our soul shudders and our very body also. And if we hear anything cruel or merciless, again our flesh creeps; but if anything decorous and kind, we even exult and rejoice." "He that hath ears to hear, let him hear." Septuagint, "The ear heareth and the eye seeth, and both are the works of the Lord."

Ver. 13.—**Love not sleep lest thou come to poverty** (see ch. vi. 9, etc.). The fate of the sluggard is handled again in ch. xxiii. 21, as often before; e.g. ch. xii. 11; xix. 15. The LXX., taking שֵׁנָה (*shenah*), "sleep," as perhaps connected with the verb שָׁנָה (*shanah*), translate, "Love not to rail, that thou be not exalted (ἵνα μὴ ἐξαρθῇς)," i.e. probably, "Do not calumniate others in order to raise yourself;" others translate, "lest thou be cut off." **Open thine eyes,**

and **thou shalt be satisfied with bread.**
These words seem to connect this clause with
ver. 12. God gives the faculty, but man
must make due use thereof. The gnomist
urges, "Do not slumber at your post, or sit
down idly waiting; but be up and doing, be
wakeful and diligent, and then you shall
prosper."

Ver. 14.—It is **naught, it is naught, saith
the buyer.** The purchaser depreciates the
goods which he wants, in order to lower the
price demanded—a practice as common now
as in old time. "I don't want it, I don't
want it," says the Spanish friar; "but drop
it into my hood." The Scotch say, "He
that lacks (disparages) my mare would buy
my mare" (Kelly). **But when he is gone
his way, then he boasteth.** When he has
completed his purchase and obtained the
goods at his own price, he boasts how he has
tricked the seller. The LXX. omits vers.
14—19.

Ver. 15.—**There is gold, and a multitude
of rubies.** For *peninim*, which is rendered
"rubies," "pearls," or "coral," see on ch.
iii. 15. There is gold which is precious,
and there is abundance of pearls which are
still more valuable. **But the lips of knowledge are a precious jewel,** and worth more
than all. We had the expression, "lips of
knowledge," in ch. xiv. 7; it means lips that
utter wisdom. *Keli*, often translated "jewel"
in the Authorized Version, also bears the
meaning of "vessel," "utensil." So here
the Vulgate, *vas pretiosum;* and the wise
man's lips are called a vessel because they
contain and distribute the wisdom that is
within. (On the excellence and value of
wisdom, see ch. iii. 14, etc.; viii. 11, etc.)
Connecting this with the preceding verse,
we are led to the thought of buying, and
the Lord's parable of the merchant seeking
goodly pearls, and bartering all his wealth
to gain possession of a worthy jewel (Matt.
xiii. 45, etc.).

Ver. 16.—**Take his garment that is surety**
for a stranger. The maxim is repeated in
ch. xxvii. 13; and warnings against suretyship are found in ch. vi. 1, etc.; xi. 15; xvii.
18; xxii. 26, etc. The second portion of
the clause is translated also, "For he is
surety for another." If a man is so weak
and foolish as to become security for any
one, and is unable to make good his engaged
payment, let him lose his garment which
the creditor would seize; his imprudence
must bring its own punishment. **And take
a pledge of him for a strange woman.** The
Authorized Version probably adopts this
rendering in conformity with ch. xxvii. 13,
where it occurs in the text, as here in the
margin (the Keri). But the Khetib has, "for
strangers," which seems to be the original
reading; and the first words ought to be

translated, "hold him in pledge;" *i.e.* seize
his person for the sake of the strangers for
whom he has stood security, so as not to
suffer loss from them. The Law endeavoured
to secure lending to needy brethren without
interest (see Ps. xv. 5; Ezek. xviii. 8, 13,
etc.; xxii. 12); but it allowed the creditor to
secure himself by taking pledges of his
debtor, while it regulated this system so as
to obviate most of its severity and oppressiveness (see the restrictions in Exod. xxii.
26, etc.; Deut. xxiv. 6, 12, etc.). "Where the
debtor possessed nothing which he could
pledge, he gave the personal security of
a friend. This was a very formal proceeding. The surety gave his hand both to the
debtor and to the creditor before an assembly
legally convened, he deposited a pledge, and,
in accordance with this twofold promise, was
regarded by the creditor in just the same
light as the debtor himself, and treated
accordingly. If the debtor, or in his place
the surety, was unable to pay the debt when
it fell due, he was entirely at the mercy of
the creditor. The authorities troubled
themselves but little about these relations,
and the law, so far as it is preserved to us,
gave no directions in the matter. We see,
however, from many allusions and narratives,
what harsh forms these relations actually
took, especially in later times, when the
ancient national brotherly love which the
Law presupposed was more and more dying
out. The creditor could not only forcibly
appropriate all the movable, but also the
fixed property, including the hereditary
estate (this at least till its redemption in
the year of jubilee), nay, he could even (if
he could find nothing else of value) carry
off as a prisoner the body of his debtor, or
of his wife and child, to employ them in his
service, though this could only be done for
a definite period" (Ewald, 'Antiquities,' p.
184, etc., transl.).

Ver. 17.—**Bread of deceit is sweet to a
man**; Revised Version, *bread of falsehood;*
i.e. bread gained without labour, or by
unrighteous means (comp. ch. x. 2). This is
agreeable because it is easily won, and has the
relish of forbidden fruit. "Wickedness is
sweet in his mouth" (Job xx. 12). **But
afterwards his mouth shall be filled with
gravel.** He will find in his "bread" no
nourishment, but rather discomfort and positive injury (comp. Job xx. 14). The expression, "to eat gravel," is intimated in Lam.
iii. 16, "He hath broken my teeth with
gravel-stones;" it implies grievous disappointment and unprofitableness. See here
a warning against evil pleasures—

Φεῦγ' ἡδονὴν φέρουσαν ὕστερον βλάβην.

"Sperne voluptates: nocet empta dolore
    voluptas."

Oort supposes that the gnome in the text is derived from a riddle, which asked, "What is sweet at first, but afterwards like sand in the mouth?"

Ver. 18.—**Every purpose is established by counsel** (comp. ch. xv. 22, where see note). The Talmud says, "Even the most prudent of men needs friends' counsels;" and none but the most conceited would deem himself superior to advice, or would fail to allow that, as the Vulgate puts it, *cogitationes consiliis roborantur.* This is true in all relations of life, in great and small matters alike, in peace, and, as our moralist adds, in war. **With good advice make war;** Vulgate, *Gubernaculis tractanda sunt bella;* Revised Version, *By wise guidance make thou war.* The word here used is *takebuloth,* for which see note, ch. i. 5. It is a maritime metaphor, rightly retained by the Vulgate, and might be rendered "pilotings," "steerings." War is a necessary evil, but it must be undertaken prudently and with a due consideration of circumstances, means, etc. Our Lord illustrates the necessity of due circumspection in following him by the case of a threatened conflict between two contending kings (Luke xiv. 31, etc.). Grotius quotes the gnome—

Γνῶμαι πλέον κρατοῦσιν ἢ σθένος χερῶν.

"Than strength of hands availeth counsel more."

To which we may add—

Βουλῆς γὰρ ὀρθῆς οὐδὲν ἀσφαλέστερον.

"Good counsel is the safest thing of all."

(Comp. ch. xxiv. 6, where the hemistich is re-echoed.)

Ver. 19.—**He that goeth about as a talebearer revealeth secrets.** Almost the same proverb occurs in ch. xi. 13. The gadding gossiper is sure to let out any secret entrusted to him; therefore, it is implied, be careful in what you say to him. **Meddle not with him that flattereth with his lips;** rather, *that openeth wide his lips*—that cannot keep his mouth shut, a babbler, as ch. xiii. 3 (where see note). The Vulgate erroneously makes one sentence of the verse, "With him who reveals secrets, and walketh deceitfully, and openeth wide his lips, have no dealings." Talmud, "When I utter a word, it hath dominion over me; but when I utter it not, I have dominion over it." Says the Persian poet, "The silent man hath his shoulders covered with the garment of security." Xenocrates used to say that he sometimes was "sorry for having spoken, never for having kept silence" (Cahen).

Ver. 20.—This is an enforcement of the fifth commandment, by denouncing the punishment which the moral government

of God shall exact from the unnatural child. The legal penalty may be seen (Exod. xxi. 17; Lev. xx. 9); but this was probably seldom or never carried into execution (comp. Matt. xv. 4; Mark vii. 10). **His lamp shall be put out in obscure** (*the blackest*) **darkness** (comp. ch. xiii. 9). The expression is peculiar; it is literally, according to the Khetib, *In the apple of the eye of darkness,* as in ch. vii. 9; *i.e.* in the very centre of darkness; he will find himself surrounded on all sides by midnight darkness, without escape, with no hope of Divine protection. "Lamp" is a metaphor applied to the bodily and the spiritual life, to happiness and prosperity, to a man's fame and reputation, to a man's posterity; and all these senses may be involved in the denunciation of the disobedient and stubborn child. He shall suffer in body and soul, in character, in fortune, in his children. His fate is the exact counterpart of the blessing promised in the Law. Septuagint, "The lamp of him that revileth father and mother shall be extinguished, and the pupils of his eyes shall behold darkness." Talmud, "Whosoever abandons his parents means his body to become the prey of scorpions." Cato, 'Dist.,' iii. 23—

"Dilige non ægra caros pietate parentes;
Nec matrem offendas, dum vis bonus esse parenti."

One of the evil generations denounced by Agur (ch. xxx. 11) is that which curseth parents.

Ver. 21.—**An inheritance may be gotten hastily at the beginning**—or, *which in the beginning is obtained in haste*—but the end thereof **shall not be blessed**; or, *its end shall not be blessed.* The Khetib gives מְבֹהֶלֶת, which (comp. Zech. xi. 8) may mean "detested," but this gives no sense; it is better, with the Keri, to replace *kheth* with *he,* and read מְבֹהֶלֶת (*meboheleth*), "hastened," "hastily acquired" (see ch. xiii. 11, Septuagint). The maxim, taken in connection with the preceding verse, may apply to a bad son who thinks his parents live too long, and by violence robs them of their possessions; or to one who, like the prodigal in the parable, demands prematurely his portion of the paternal goods. But it may also be taken generally as denouncing the fate of those who make haste to be rich, being unscrupulous as to the means by which they gain wealth (see on ch. xxiii. 11; xxviii. 20, 22). A Greek gnome says roundly—

Οὐδεὶς ἐπλούτησεν ταχέως δίκαιος ὤν.

'No righteous man e'er grew rich suddenly."

Ver. 22.—**Say not thou, I will recompense**

evil (ch. xxiv. 29). The *jus talionis* is the natural feeling of man, to do to others as they have done unto you, to requite evil with evil. But the moralist teaches a better lesson, urging men not to study revenge, and approaching nearer to Christ's injunction, which gives the law of charity, "Whatsoever *ye would* (ὅσα ἂν θέλητε) that men should do to you, do ye even so to them" (Matt. vii. 12). The Christian rule is expounded fully by St. Paul (Rom. xii. 14, 17, etc.). It was not unknown to the Jews; for we read in Tobit iv. 15, "Do that to no man which thou hatest;" and Hillel enjoins, "Do not thou that to thy neighbour which thou hatest when it is done to thee." Even the heathens had excogitated this great principle. There is a saying of Aristotle, preserved by Diogenes Laertius, "Act towards your friends as you would wish them to act towards you." The Chinese have a proverb, "Water does not remain on the mountain, or vengeance in a great mind." **Wait on the Lord, and he shall save thee.** The pious writer urges the injured person to commit his cause to the Lord, not in the hope of seeing vengeance taken on his enemy, but in the certainty that God will help him to bear the wrong and deliver him in his own good time and way. The Christian takes St. Peter's view, "Who is he that will harm you if ye be followers of that which is good?" (1 Pet. iii. 13), knowing that "all things work together for good to them that love God" (Rom. viii. 28; comp. Ecclus. ii. 2, 6). Septuagint, "Say not, I will avenge myself on my enemy, but wait on the Lord, that (ἵνα) he may help thee." The last clause may be grammatically rendered thus, but it is more in accordance with the spirit of the proverb, as Delitzsch observes, to regard it as a promise. Vulgate, *et liberabit te.*

Ver. 23.—This is a repetition, with a slight variation, of ver. 10 and ch. xi. 1 (where see notes). **Is not good.** A *litotes*, equivalent to "is very evil," answering to "abomination" in the first member. Septuagint, "is not good before him" (comp. ch. xxiv. 23).

Ver. 24.—**Man's goings are of the Lord.** In the first clause the word for "man" is *geber*, which implies "a mighty man;" in the second clause the word is *adam*, "a human creature." So the Septuagint has ἀνήρ in one clause and θνητὸς in the other. The proverb says that the steps of a great and powerful man depend, as their final cause, upon the Lord; he conditions and controls results. Man has free-will, and is responsible for his actions, but God foreknows them, and holds the thread that connects them together; he gives prevent-

ing grace; he gives efficient grace; and man blindly works out the designs of Omnipotence according as he obeys or resists. A similar maxim is found in Ps. xxxvii. 23, "A man's goings are established of the Lord," but the meaning there is that it is God's aid which enables a man to do certain actions. Here we have very much the same intimation that is found in ch. ii. 6 and xix. 21; and see note on ch. xvi. 9. Hence arises the old prayer used formerly at prime, and inserted now (with some omissions) at the end of the Anglican Communion Service: "O almighty Lord, and everlasting God, vouchsafe, we beseech thee, to direct, sanctify, and govern, both our hearts and bodies, our thoughts, words, and actions, in the ways of thy laws, and in the works of thy commandments; that through thy most mighty protection we may be preserved both here and for ever." If man cannot see all sides, as God does, cannot comprehend the beginning, middle, and end in one view, **how then can a man (a weak mortal) understand his own way?** How can he find out of himself whither he should go, or what will be the issue of his doings (comp. ch. xvi. 25; Jer. x. 23)? St. Gregory, "It is well said by Solomon [Eccles. ix. 1], 'There are righteous and wise men, and their works are in the hand of God; and yet no man knoweth whether he is deserving of love or of hatred; but all things are kept uncertain for the time to come.' Hence it is said again by the same Solomon, 'What man will be able to understand his own way?' And any one doing good or evil is doubtless known by the testimony of his own conscience. But it is said that their own way is not known to men, for this reason, because, even if a man understands that he is acting rightly, yet he knows not, under the strict inquiry, whither he is going" ('Moral.,' xxix. 34).

Ver. 25.—**It is a snare to the man who devoureth that which is holy.** This verse, which is plainly a warning against rash vows, has received more than one interpretation. The Vulgate has, *Ruina est homini devorare sanctos*, which is explained to mean that it is destruction for a man to persecute the saints of God. But the word *devorare* is not certain, as the manuscripts vary between this and four other readings, viz. *devotare, denotare, devovere*, and *devocare.* The Authorized Version signifies that it is a sin to take for one's own consumption things dedicated to God, as firstfruits, the priests' portions, etc.; or a man's snare, *i.e.* his covetousness (1 Tim. vi. 9), leads him to commit sacrilege. So Wordsworth. But it is best, with Delitzsch, to take יָלַע (*yala*) as the abbreviated future of לוּעַ or לָעַע, "to speak rashly;" and then *kodesh*, "holiness," will be an exclamation, like *korban* (Mark/ vii. 11). The clause will then run, "It is a snare to a man rashly to cry, Holiness!" equivalent to "It is holy!" *i.e.* to use the formula for consecrating something to holy purposes. Septuagint, "It is a snare to a man hastily to consecrate something of his own" (comp. Eccles. v. 2, 4, etc.). **And after vows to make inquiry;** *i.e.* after he has made his vow, to begin to consider whether he can fulfil it or not. This is a snare to a man, strangles his conscience, and leads him into the grievous sins of perjury and sacrilege. Septuagint, "For after vowing ensueth repentance."

Ver. 26.—**A wise king scattereth the wicked** (ver. 8). The verb is *zarah*, which means "to winnow, or sift." The king separates the wicked and the good, as the winnowing fan or shovel divides the chaff from the wheat. The same metaphor is used of Christ (Matt. iii. 12), "Whose fan is in his hand, and he will throughly purge his floor, and gather his wheat into the garner; but he will burn up the chaff with unquenchable fire" (comp. Jer. xv. 7). Septuagint, "A winnower (λικμήτωρ) of the ungodly is a wise king." **And bringeth the wheel over them.** The threshing-wheel is meant (see Isa. xxviii. 27; Amos i. 3). This was a wooden frame with three or four rollers under it armed with iron teeth. It was drawn by two oxen, and, aided by the weight of the driver, who had his seat upon it, it crushed out the grain, and cut up the straw into fodder. Another machine much used in Palestine was made of two thick planks fastened together side by side, and having sharp stones fixed in rows on the lower surface. It is not implied that the king employed the corn-drag as an instrument of punishment, which was sometimes so used in war, as possibly may be inferred from 2 Sam. xii. 31; 1 Chron. xx. 3; and Amos i. 3. The idea of threshing is carried on, and the notion is rather of separation than of punishment, though the latter is not wholly excluded. The wise ruler will not only distinguish between the godless and the good, but will show his discrimination by visiting the evil with condign punishment. Septuagint, "He will bring the wheel upon them;" the Vulgate has curiously, *Incurvat super eos fornicem*, "He bends an arch over them," which Latin commentators explain as a triumphal arch, meaning that the king conquers and subdues the wicked, and celebrates his victory over them. A patent anachronism which needs no comment!

Ver. 27.—**The spirit of man is the candle** (*lamp*) **of the Lord.** *Neshamah*, "spirit," or "breath," is the principle of life breathed into man by God himself (Gen. ii. 7), distinguishing man from brutes—the conscious human soul. We may consider it as equivalent to what we Christians call conscience, with its twofold character of receiving light and illumination from God, and sitting as judge and arbiter of actions. It is named "the Lord's lamp," because this moral sense is a direct gift of God, and enables a man to see his real condition. Our Lord (Matt. vi. 23) speaks of the light that is in man, and gives a solemn warning against the danger of letting it be darkened by neglect and sin; and St. Paul (1 Cor. ii. 11) argues, "Who among men knoweth the things of a man save the spirit of the man, which is in him?" As Elihu says (Job xxxii. 8), "There is a spirit in man, and the breath of the Almighty giveth them understanding." And Aristotle speaks of practical wisdom (φρόνησις) combined with virtue as "the eye of the soul (ὄμμα τῆς ψυχῆς)." **Searching all the inward parts of the belly;** *i.e.* the very depths of the soul, probing thoughts, desires, affections, will, and approving or reproving, according as they are in conformity with or opposition to God's Law. We must remember that Eastern houses, before the introduction of glass, had very scanty openings to admit light, and lamps were necessary if for any purpose the interior had to be thoroughly illuminated. Hence the metaphor used above would strike an Oriental more forcibly than it strikes us. Septuagint, "The breath (πνοή, as ch. xi. 13) of man is a light of the Lord, who searches the chambers of the belly." St. Gregory ('Moral.,' xii. 64), "We ought to bear in mind that in holy Writ by the title of the 'belly,' or the 'womb,' the mind is used to be understood. For the light of grace, which comes from above, affords a 'breathway' to man unto life, which same light is said to 'search all the inward parts of the belly,' in that it penetrates all the secrets of the heart, that the things which were hidden in the soul touching itself it may bring back before the eyes thereof" (Oxford transl.).

Ver. 28.—**Mercy and truth preserve the king.** (For "mercy and truth," see note on ch. iii. 3.) The love and faithfulness which the king displays in dealing with his subjects elicits the like virtues in them, and these are the safeguard of his throne. **His throne is upholden by mercy;** or, *love.* So the king is well called the father of his people, and in modern times the epithet "gracious" is applied to the sovereign as being the fountain of mercy and condescension. Sallust, 'Jugurtha,' x., "Non exercitus neque thesauri præsidia regni sunt, verum amici, quos, neque armis cogere neque auro parare queas; officio et fide pariuntur." Septuagint,

"Mercy (ἐλεημοσύνη) and truth are a guard to a king, and will surround his throne with righteousness." "The subject's love," says our English maxim, "is the king's life-guard."

Ver. 29.—**The glory of young men is their strength.** That which makes the ornament (*tiphereth*) of youth is unimpaired strength and vigour, which can only be attained by due exercise combined with self-control. The moralist (Eccles. xi. 9) bids the young man rejoice in his youth, and let his heart cheer him in those happy days, but at the same time remember that he is responsible for the use which he makes of his powers and faculties, for for all these things God will bring him to judgment. The Greek gives a needful warning—

Μέμνησο νέος ὢν ὡς γέρων ἔσῃ ποτέ.

"In youth remember thou wilt soon be old."

Septuagint, "Wisdom is an ornament to young men." But *koach* is bodily, not mental, power. **The beauty of old men is the grey head** (ch. xvi. 31). That which gives an honourable look to old age is the hoary head, which suggests wisdom and experience (comp. Ecclus. xxv. 3—6). On the other hand, the Greek gnomist warns—

Πολιὰ χρόνου μήνυσις οὐ φρονήσεως.

"Grey hairs not wisdom indicate, but age."

Ver. 30.—**The blueness of a wound cleanseth away evil.** So the Vulgate, *Livor vulneris absterget mala. Chaburoth* means "stripes," and the proverb says that deep-cutting stripes are the only effectual cure of evil; *i.e.* severe punishment is the best healing process in cases of moral delinquency (ch. xix. 29). Painful remedies, incisions, cauteries, amputations, are often necessary in the successful treatment of bodily ailments; spiritual sickness needs sterner,

more piercing, remedies. **So do stripes the inward parts of the belly;** or better, *and strokes that reach*, etc. The stings of conscience, warnings and reproofs which penetrate to the inmost recesses of the heart, chastisement which affects the whole spiritual being,—these are needful to the correction and purification of inveterate evil. Aben Ezra connects this verse with the preceding thus: as strength gives a glory to young men, and hoar hairs adorn an old man; so wounds and bruises, so to speak, ornament the sinner, mark him out, and at the same time heal and amend him. It may also be connected with ver. 27. If a man will not use the lamp which God has given him for illumination and correction, he must expect severe chastisement and sternest discipline. Septuagint, "Bruises (ὑπώπια) and contusions befall bad men, and plagues that reach to the chambers of the belly." St. Gregory, 'Moral.,' xxiii. 40, "By the blueness of a wound he implies the discipline of blows on the body. But blows in the secret parts of the belly are the wounds of the mind within, which are inflicted by compunction. For as the belly is distended when filled with food, so is the mind puffed up when swollen with wicked thoughts. The blueness, then, of a wound, and blows in the secret parts of the belly, cleanse away evil, because both outward discipline does away with faults, and compunction pierces the distended mind with the punishment of penance. But they differ from each other in this respect, that the wounds of blows give us pain, the sorrows of compunction have good savour. The one afflict and torture, the others restore when they afflict us. Through the one there is sorrow in affliction, through the other there is joy in grief" (Oxford transl.).

HOMILETICS.

Ver. 1.—*Wine the mocker.* Intemperance was not so common a vice in biblical times as it has become more recently, nor did the light wines of the East exercise so deleterious an effect as the strong drink that is manufactured in Europe is seen to produce. Therefore all that is said in the Bible against the evil of drunkenness applies with much-increased force to the aggravated intemperance of England to-day.

I. WINE IS A MOCKER BECAUSE IT ALLURES THE WEAK. It makes great promises. Strong drink is pleasant to the palate. The effect of it on the nervous system is at first agreeably stimulating. In weakness and weariness it seems to give comfortable relief. The associations connected with it are made to be most attractive. It goes with genial companionship, and it appears to favour the flow of good fellowship. In sickness it promises renewed strength; it offers consolation in sorrow; at festive seasons it pretends to heighten the joy and to take its place as a cheering friend of man. Moreover, all these attractive traits are aggravated with the weak. The need of the stimulus is more keenly felt by such persons; the early effects of it are more readily and pleasantly recognized; there is less power of will and judgment to resist its alluring influence.

II. WINE IS A MOCKER BECAUSE IT DECEIVES THE UNWARY. The danger that lurks in the cup is not seen at first, and the sparkling wine looks as innocent as a divine nectar. The evil that it produces comes on by slow and insidious stages. No one thinks of becoming a drunkard on the first day of tasting intoxicating drink. Every victim of the terrible evil of intemperance was once an innocent child, and, whether he began in youth or in later years, every one who has gone to excess commenced with moderate and apparently harmless quantities. Happily, the majority of those who take a little are wise or strong enough not to abandon themselves to the tyranny of drinking habits. But the difficulty is to determine beforehand who will be able to stand and who will not have sufficient strength. Under these circumstances, it is a daring piece of presumption for any one to be quite sure that he will always be so wary as to keep out of the snare that has been fatal to many of his brethren who once stood in exactly the same free and healthy position in which he is at present. It is far safer not to tempt our own natures, and to guard ourselves against the mockery of wine, by keeping from all use of the strong drink itself.

III. WINE IS A MOCKER BECAUSE IT BRINGS RUIN ON ITS VICTIMS. It has no pity. It hounds its dupes on to destruction, and then it laughs at their fate. When once it holds a miserable wretch it will never willingly release him. Too late, he discovers that he is a slave, deceived by what promised to be his best friend, and flung into a dungeon from which, by his unaided powers, he can never effect an escape. There is a peculiar mockery in this fate. The victim is disgraced and degraded. His very human nature is wretched, insulted, almost destroyed. His social position is lost; his business scattered to the winds; his family life broken up and made unutterably wretched; his soul destroyed. This is the work of the wine that sparkles in the cup. We should allow no quarter to so vile a deceiver.

Ver. 3.—*The honour of peace.* The old world looked for glory in war; the Christian ideal—anticipated in Old Testament teaching—is to recognize honour in peace. It is better to keep peace than to be victorious in war, better to make peace than to win battles. Consider the grounds of this higher view of conflict and its issues.

I. THE HONOUR OF PEACE MAY BE SEEN IN SELF-SUPPRESSION. It is much more easy to give the reins to ill will and hasty passion. Men find it harder to fight their own temper than to do battle with alien foes. It is the same with nations when the spirit of war has maddened them. Heedless of consequences to themselves, and blind to the rights of their neighbours, they hurl themselves headlong into the horrors of battle. But if men could learn to curb their own strong feelings, they would really show more strength than by raging in unrestrained fury.

II. THE HONOUR OF PEACE MAY BE RECOGNIZED IN MAGNANIMITY. It may be that we are in the right, and our foes unquestionably in the wrong. Still, it is not essential that we should fight to the bitter end. We may forego our right. It may be a generous and noble thing to suffer wrong without resisting it. We cannot but see how much more harm is done in asserting just claims by force than would result from silent submission after a dignified protest. Often the more magnanimous conduct will result in the very end that would have been sought through violent measures. For it is possible to appeal to the generous instincts of opponents.

III. THE HONOUR OF PEACE MAY BE OBSERVED IN CHARITY. We should ever remember that even those who behave to us as enemies are still our brethren. We have their welfare to consider even while they may be plotting evil against us. Christ prayed for his persecutors (Luke xxiii. 34). So did St. Stephen (Acts vii. 60). Indeed, our Lord died for his enemies. He came to make an end of the fearful strife between man and God. But while he did so, he suffered from the fray. The Peacemaker was the victim of the passions of the rebellious. By suffering in meek dignity he made peace. If the mind that was in Christ is found in us, we shall be the earnest advocates of peace for the good of the very people who delight in war.

IV. THE HONOUR OF PEACE MAY BE RECOGNIZED IN HUMILITY. The special form in which the recommendation of peace is thrown is that of a *cessation of strife.* This implies a case in which there has been warfare; but one of the parties refrains from prosecuting the quarrel any further, although he has neither been worsted nor won the victory. This means a change of policy. Now, it is particularly difficult to effect such a change in the midst of a conflict. One's motives are likely to be suspected, and what is done from love of peace is likely to be set down to cowardice. It needs humility thus to withdraw and sacrifice one's pretensions. Having taken a certain position we are tempted to hold it at all hazards from sheer pride. This is especially true in the soul's conflict with God. Here we are called upon to humble ourselves enough to confess ourselves entirely in the wrong. When the "fearful striving" has ceased there is honour in repentance and the new life of peace with God.

Ver. 9.—*Universal sinfulness.* We must distinguish between the idea of universal sinfulness and that of total depravity. We may hold that there is some gleam of goodness in a human heart without maintaining its immaculate purity. It is possible to believe that there are great varieties of character, many different degrees of sin, and yet to see that the highest saint has his faults.

I. NO ONE CAN CLEAR HIMSELF FROM THE CHARGE OF SINFULNESS. Who can say, "I have made my heart clean from all imputations of guilt'? 1. *The best confess that they are sinful.* Canonized by their admiring brethren, they cast themselves down in humility and shame before the holiness of God. No men have so deep a sense of the sinfulness of their own hearts as those who live most near to God. 2. *The most skilful cannot excuse themselves.* It is possible to formulate specious pleas that will deceive unwary men; but we have to do with the great Searcher of hearts, before whose piercing gaze all sophistries and pretences melt as the mists before the sun. 3. *The deceitfulness of the heart blinds many to their own guilt.* Men naturally desire to defend themselves; they are excellent advocates of themselves to themselves. The familiar sin is softened by habit. The conventional sin is condoned by custom. 4. *False standards of holiness confuse men's estimate of their own sinfulness.* Some people seem to take a feeling of placidity as an assurance of inward perfection, as though not to be conscious of strife were to be assured of peace with God. But it is possible to slumber under the influence of spiritual narcotics. A keener conscience might rouse a new, unlooked-for sense of sin and shame. It is thought that there is no shortcoming simply because the surrounding mists hide the far-off goal. Or it may be that negative correctness is mistaken for a satisfactory condition, while many positive active duties are left undone. Perhaps the soul that thinks its aspiration after purity satisfied is wanting in charity, or in the very act of claiming sinlessness it may be puffed up with pride. The most dangerous delusion is that which denies the ownership of guilt because sin is supposed to be relegated to bodily infirmity, while the true self is spotless. This is a most deadly snare of the devil.

II. NO ONE CAN CLEAR HIMSELF FROM THE SINS WHICH HE HAS COMMITTED. Who can say, "I have purged my own conscience, cleansed my own heart, cleared off my record of guilt?" 1. *It is impossible to undo sins.* Deeds are irrevocable. What has been committed is stereotyped in the awful book of the changeless past. What I have written, spoken, done—I have written, spoken, done. 2. *It is impossible to compensate for past sins by future service.* The future service is all owing; at our best we are "unprofitable servants"—there is no margin of profit—for "we have only done that which it was our duty to do." 3. *It is impossible to atone for our sins by any sacrifice.* The hardest penance can be of no value with God. Its only use could be in self-discipline. For God is not pleased with the sufferings of his children. We can offer him nothing; for "the cattle on a thousand hills" are his. 4. *It is impossible to change our own inner sinfulness by ourselves.* We cannot create clean hearts in our own breasts. We cannot kill our own love of sin. 5. *It is only possible for sin to be cleansed in the blood of Christ.* "There is a fountain opened for all uncleanness." The admission of guilt, the repentance that turns from the old sin and seeks forgiveness, the renunciation of all claims but that of the grace of God in Christ,—these things open the door to the true way of making the heart clean, both in pardon and in purification.

Ver. 11.—*A child and his doings.* I. A PICTURE OF CHILDHOOD. First, let this picture be regarded on its own account. Childhood is worthy of study. 1. *A child has his character.* Very early in life varieties of disposition may be seen in the several members of a young family. One is hot-tempered, another patient; one demonstrative, another reserved; one energetic, another inactive. Moral distinctions are painfully and glaringly apparent. As childhood advances these varieties of disposition merge in deeper differences of character. Though the character is supple and mobile, it is nevertheless real. There are good and bad children—children who are pure, true, honest, kind; and children who are marked with the reverse of these qualities. 2. *A child is responsible for his deeds.* Unless he is crushed by tyranny, within the scope of a reasonable child-liberty he has room in which to play his small part on the stage of life. He must not be brought up with the notion that he is an irresponsible agent because he is young and weak. Conscience needs to be enlightened, trained, and strengthened in early days. 3. *A child's character is revealed in his deeds.* The character may be slight and feeble; and the deeds may be simple and insignificant. Yet even in the nursery cause and effect are at work; fruits reveal the nature even of saplings. Even children cannot be judged by outward appearance. With them innocent looks may cover sinful thoughts. Children also may deceive themselves, or make false pretences, though we do not see the hardened hypocrisy of the world in the simpler deception of the nursery. Still, it is to the conduct of children that we must look for indications of their true characters.

II. A LESSON FOR ALL AGES. If even a child is to be known by his doings, the inference is that much more may a man be known in a similar way. 1. *Character ripens with years.* If it begins to appear in childhood, it will be much more vigorous in manhood. There is something dolefully prophetic in the vices of infancy. Though often laughed at by foolish observers, these vices are the early sprouts of terrible evils that will increase with growing strength and enlarging opportunities. The more clearly we are able to detect differences of character even in childhood, the more certain is it that similar differences are aggravated in manhood. 2. *Responsibility grows with opportunity.* The deeds of children are to be regarded as characteristic—as either culpable or praiseworthy according to their moral tone. How much more must this be the case with grown men and women, who know more, have larger powers, and suffer from fewer restrictions! If the child who has continual restraint upon him, and who lives under perpetual tutelage, yet manifests characteristic conduct, the free man cannot escape from the responsibility of his doings. 3. *Conduct is always a sure sign of character.* It is so even with children who know little, and who are constantly hampered by superior authority. It must be so with double certainty in the case of adults. It is vain, indeed, for men and women to pretend that the index hand does not point truly. In the freedom of adult age there is no excuse to be urged against the inference that our deeds are the fruits of our character. Therefore, if the conduct is evil, the heart needs to be renewed.

Ver. 14.—*The buyer.* I. THE CONDUCT OF THE BUYER CALLS FOR CONSIDERATION. It is usual to discuss questions of trade morality chiefly in regard to the conduct of the man who sells. Deception, adulteration, dishonest work, the grinding of *employés*, etc., are denounced by indignant onlookers. But the conduct of the customer is less severely handled. Yet there are many reasons why it should not be overlooked. All are not sellers, but everybody buys. Therefore when commercial morality is discussed in regard to buying, the subject does not only apply to traders, it concerns all people. Moreover, if men cheat and do wrong in their business when selling, though there is no fair excuse for their conduct, it may be urged that they are driven to extremes by the pressure of competition and by the difficulty of earning a livelihood. But when many people are making ordinary purchases they are not in the same position and under the same temptation. Traders, of course, are buyers in the way of business. But people of affluent circumstances are also buyers without any consideration of business exigencies, but solely for their own convenience. If such people do not behave honourably they are doubly guilty.

II. THE BUYER IS SUBJECT TO MORAL OBLIGATIONS. 1. *He owes justice to the seller.* He has no right to squeeze the unfortunate trader's profit by the pressure of undue influence, threatening to withdraw his custom or to injure the connection among his friends, taking advantage of the fact that the seller is in want of money, etc. It is his duty to pay a fair price, even though by the stress of circumstances he might force a sale at a lower rate. 2. *He owes truth to the seller.* He may misrepresent the absolute value of his purchase, perhaps knowing more of its true worth than the seller, but trying to deceive him. Thus the skilled connoisseur may take an unfair advantage of the ignorance of the trader from whom he buys some rare article of *vertu*. Or a person may pretend not to want what he secretly covets most eagerly. Such a device is false and unworthy of a Christian profession. 3. *He owes humanity to the seller.* It is a gross abuse of trade to make it a condition of warfare. A man is not necessarily one's enemy because one does business with him. The unfortunate person who must needs sell at a great loss rather than not sell at all, is not the legitimate prey of the first greedy customer who is able to pounce upon him. The curse of trade is hard, cruel, brutal selfishness. Christianity teaches us to regard the man with whom one does business as a brother. The buyer should learn to treat the seller as he desires to be treated in turn, and so to fulfil the law of Christ. The same principle requires kindliness of manner.

III. The obligations of the buyer are commonly neglected. The causes of this negligence are manifold; *e.g.*: 1. *Inconsiderateness.* Often there is no intention of doing an injustice. The buyer simply forgets the rights of the seller. This inconsiderateness does harm in various ways. Careless customers give needless trouble to shop-people. Some order for view more goods than they need to effect a purchase; some persist in shopping late in the evening, etc. 2. *Selfishness.* The chief cause of the evil is a sole regard for self. People who are reasonable and kind in their own homes will manifest the most tyrannical spirit, the most cynical selfishness, in their shopping. When the veneer of social habits is broken this ugly vice is more visible in the most polished society than among rougher people. 3. *Sinfulness.* The evil heart is seen here as elsewhere. For the buyer to force injustice and to cheat the seller is for him to reveal himself as a slave of sin as truly as if he broke out in wanton violence and open robbery.

Ver. 22.—*Revenge and its antidote.* I. The sin and folly of revenge. This passion appears to spring from a natural instinct; it pretends to justify itself as the fair return for some wrong, and it offers a compensation for the wrong suffered in the triumph which it gains over the wrong-doer. But it is both culpable and foolish. 1. *It is culpable.* Even if revenge were desirable, we have no right to wreak it on the head of the offender. We are not his judge and executioner. God says, "Vengeance is mine, I will repay." We have no excuse for antedating the Divine vengeance in our impatience by taking the law of retribution into our own hands. If another has hurt us, that fact is no excuse whatever for our hurting him. Two wrongs do not make one right. The spirit of vengeance in man is a spirit of hatred, and therefore one for which there is no excuse. Much as an enemy may have injured us, he is still our fellow-man to whom we owe charity and forgiveness. 2. *It is foolish.* At best it can offer but a gloomy compensation. Unless our nature delights in malignity, there can be no real satisfaction in seeing an enemy suffer. Though a natural passion may seem to be satisfied with a gleam of fierce joy in the moment of triumph, this must be succeeded by a dismal sense of the vanity of any such feelings. The after-thought of revenge must be bitter. Moreover, the exercise of vengeance will not cure enmity, but only intensify it. Therefore it may just provoke a second and greater wrong than that which it is avenging. There is no prospect before it but increasing rancour, hatred, strife, misery.

II. The antidote to revenge. We are not to be left to suffer wrong without compensation or hope. We may find a prospect of something better than the bitter harvest of vengeance if we turn from sinful man to God. Then we shall see the true antidote. 1. *It springs from faith.* We have to be assured that God can and will help us. We can thus afford to ignore the wrong that has been done us, or, if that be impossible, we can learn to look above it and feel confident that, if God undertakes our cause, all will be well in the end. This faith will not desire the ruin of our enemy. It is not an entrusting of vengeance to God, though he must see justice done to the wrong-doer. But it is a quiet confidence in God's saving grace. It is better to be delivered from the trouble brought on us by the misconduct of others than to remain in that trouble and see the guilty persons punished. We can afford to be magnanimous and forget the unkindness of man when we are enjoying the kindness of God. 2. *It is realized through prayer, patience, and hope.* (1) *Prayer.* We must wait on the Lord. Vengeance is lost in prayer. We shall cease to feel the boiling of rage against our foe when on our knees before God. There we cannot but remember how utterly we depend upon mercy. (2) *Patience.* Waiting on God generally implies some delay. We must *wait* for the answer. Deliverance does not come at once. Hasty revenge must be restrained by patience in prayer. (3) *Hope.* God will save at last, if not immediately. The prospect of this deliverance is a pleasing substitute for the hideous vision of revenge on an enemy.

Ver. 29.— *Young men and old.* I. EVERY TIME OF LIFE HAS ITS OWN PECULIAR EXCELLENCE. 1. *Every age of man has some excellence.* Youth appears vain in the grave vision of age, and age looks gloomy to the bright eyes of youth. Yet both youth and age have their mead of praise. It is possible for a man to miss all excellence in life and to live in dishonour from youth to age. But that depends upon his own conduct, and he only will be to blame for spoiling every age of his life if he does thus live in dishonour. There are honourable and desirable conditions for life throughout its whole length. 2. *The excellences of the various ages of man are different.* The glory of a young man is not identical with the beauty of an old man. The common mistake is that in the narrowness of our personal experience we judge of other periods of life by the standards that only apply to those in which we are severally living. Hence either undue admiration or unreasonable disgust. It is cheering to know that a very different condition from that which floats before us as our ideal may be equally happy and honourable.

II. THE PECULIAR EXCELLENCE OF YOUTH IS FOUND IN ITS ENERGY AND THE USE IT MAKES OF IT. 1. *Energy is a characteristic of youth.* Then the fresh unfaded powers are just opening out to their full activity. This is the time for service. The young men go to the wars. "It is well for a man to bear the yoke in his youth." All kinds of fresh activities spring out of the fertile soil of youth. An indolence in youth is simply disgraceful. 2. *Youthful energy is admirable.* (1) *Physical strength.* This is a gift of God. It is a natural perfection of bodily life. It carries with it possibilities of manly work. "Muscular Christianity" may be as holy as feeble asceticism. (2) *Mental strength.* The intellectual feats of brain-athletics indicate noble energies and arduous industry. The mind is from God, and its ripened powers render him glory. (3) *Moral strength.* Daniel was stronger than Samson. The chief glory of youthful strength is here—the power to resist temptation, to live a true life, to fight all lies and shameful thoughts and deeds, and stand up firmly for the right. 3. *Youthful energy should be used in the service of Christ.* Then its glory is radiant. A lower use of it dims its lustre. Degradation to purposes of sin turns its splendour into shame.

III. THE SPECIAL EXCELLENCE OF AGE IS TO BE SEEN IN ITS RIPENED EXPERIENCE. 1. *Experience ripens with years.* The suggestion of that fact may be seen in the picture of the grey head, the beauty of which chiefly resides in the thought of the harvest of years that it represents. Strength may be lost, but experience is gained. There is an exchange, and it is not for any to say on which side the real advantage lies. 2. *The experience of years has a beauty of its own.* We usually associate youth and beauty, and we think of beauty declining with advancing years. Painful signs of life's stern battle break the fair charms of youth. But old age brings a new beauty. This is often seen even in the countenance, finely chiselled with delicate lines of thought and feeling into a rare grace and dignity. But the higher beauty is that of soul, the beauty of Simeon when he held the infant Saviour in his arms. The crowning beauty of age is in a perfected saintliness. To attain to this is to go beyond the glory of youth. Yet there must accompany it a certain melancholy at the thought of the lost energy of earlier years, until the old man can look forward to the renewed youth, the eternal energy of the life beyond.

HOMILIES BY VARIOUS AUTHORS.

Vers. 1—5.— *Evils to be avoided.* I. SOME SPECIAL EVILS AND DANGERS. 1. *Drunkenness.* (Ver. 1.) The spirit or demon of wine is spoken of as a personal agent. It leads to frivolity, scoffing, profane and senseless mirth. To be drunk with wine, as St. Paul points out (Eph. v. 18), is the opposite of being "filled with the Spirit" (see F. W. Robertson's sermon on this subject). 2. *The wrath of kings.* (Ver. 2.) In those times of absolute rule, the king represented the uncontrollable arbitration of life and death. As in the case of Adonijah, he who provoked the king's wrath sinned against his own soul. What, then, must the wrath of the eternal Sovereign be (Ps. xc. 11)? To invoke the Divine judgment is a *suicidal* act. 3. *Contentiousness.* (Ver. 3.) Quick-flaming anger is the mark of the shallow and foolish heart. The conquest of anger by Christian meekness is one of the chiefest of Christian graces. "Let it pass for a kind of sheepishness to be meek," says Archbishop Leighton; "it is a likeness to him that was as a sheep before his shearers." 4. *Idleness.* (Ver. 4.) The idle man is unseasonable in his repose, and equally unseasonable in his expectation. To know our time, our opportunity in worldly matters, our day of grace in the affairs of the soul, all depends on this (Rom. xii. 11; Eph. v. 15—17).

II. THE SAFEGUARD OF PRUDENCE. (Ver. 5.) The idea is that, though the project which a man has formed may be difficult to fathom, the prudent man will bring the secret to light. "There is nothing hidden that shall not be made known." 1. Every department of life has its principles and laws. 2. These may be ascertained by observation and inquiry. 3. In some sense or other, all knowledge is power; and that is the best sort of knowledge which arms the mind with force against moral dangers, and places it in constant relation to good.—J.

Vers. 6—11.—*The frailty of mankind.* I. THE RARITY OF TRUE FRIENDSHIP. (Ver. 6.) Many are ready to promise, few willing to perform. Many eager to say, "Lord, Lord!" comparatively few to do the will of the Father in heaven. There is no want of good notions in the world; but, according to the Italian proverb, many are so good that they are good for nothing. The spirit may be willing, the flesh is weak. Inclination to good needs to be fortified by faith in God.

II. THE JUST AND GOOD MAN. (Ver. 7.) We cannot but feel that he is an ideal character. Poets and preachers have delighted to describe him, have surrounded him with a halo, depicted the safety and blessedness of his life. But how seldom does he appear on the actual scene! Our being is a struggle and a series of failures. The one thing needful is to have a lofty ideal before us, and never to despair of approaching a little nearer to it with every right effort.

III. THE IMPARTIAL JUDGE. (Ver. 8.) The earthly judge upon his seat reminds us of the mixed state of human nature—of the need of a process of sifting, trial, purification, ever going on. Judgment is an ever-present fact, a constant process. We are being tried, in a sense, every day, and "must all stand before the judgment-seat of Christ." Let us "labour that we may be accepted of him."

IV. THE CLEAN CONSCIENCE. (Ver. 9.) This pointed question silences our boasting, and checks the disposition to excuse ourselves. By unwise comparison with others we may seem to stand well; but in the light of his own mere standard of right and duty, who is not self-condemned? "If we say that we have no sin, we deceive ourselves, and the truth is not in us" (1 John i. 8, 9).

V. EQUITABLE CONDUCT. (Ver. 10.) How common are the tricks and evasions of trade! And there is something more in this than mere desire for gain. The general experience of the world is so strong against dishonesty, as seen in common proverbs, as "bad policy," that we must look to a deeper cause of its existence, viz. the perversity of man's heart.

VI. EARLY SYMPTOMS OF CHARACTER. (Ver. 11.) Tendencies of evil and (never let us omit to acknowledge) tendencies of good are seen very early in children. The Germans have a quaint proverb, "What a thorn will become may easily be guessed." How much depends on Christian culture; for "as the twig is bent, so is the tree inclined."—J.

Vers. 12—19.—*Religion, industry, prudence, and honesty.* I. GOD THE SOURCE OF ALL GOOD. 1. Of all bodily good. The eye, the ear, with all their wondrous mechanism, with all their rich instrumentality of enjoyment, are from him. 2. Of all spiritual faculty and endowment, the analogues of the former, and "every good and perfect gift" (Jas. i. 16). The new heart, the right mind, should, above all, be recognized as his gifts. 3. In domestic and in public life. Good counsels of Divine wisdom, and willing obedience of subjects to them, are the conditions of the weal of the state; and it may be that these are designed by the preacher under the figures of the eye and the ear.

II. VIRTUES INDISPENSABLE TO HAPPINESS. 1. *Laboriousness.* (Ver. 13.) This is a command of God: "If any man will not work, neither let him eat;" for which the seeing eye and hearing ear are needed. Viewed in one light, of imagination, labour may appear as a curse; for it thwarts our natural indolence, our love of ease, and our sentimental views in general. But viewed in the light of actual experience, the law of labour is one of the divinest blessings of our life-constitution. 2. *Honesty.* (1) *Craft and trickiness exposed.* (Vers. 14, 17.) Here the cunning tricks of trade are struck; in particular the arts of disparagement, by which the buyer unjustly cheapens the goods he desires to invest in. The peculiar manner in which trade is still conducted in the East, the absence of fixed prices, readily admits of this species of unfairness. But the rebuke is general. (2) *The deceptiveness of sinful pleasures.* (Ver. 17.) There *is*, no doubt, a certain pleasure in dishonesty, otherwise it would not be so commonly practised in the very teeth of self-interest. There is a peculiar delight in the exercise of skill which outwits others. But this is only while the conscience sleeps. When it awakes, unrest and trouble begin. The stolen gold burns in the pocket; the Dead Sea fruits turn to ashes on the lips. 3. *Sense and prudence.* (Vers. 15, 16, 18.) (1) *Sense is compared to the most precious things.* What in the affairs of life is comparable to judgment? Yet compared only to be contrasted. As the common saying runs, "There is nothing so uncommon as common sense." The taste for material objects of price may be termed universal and vulgar; that for spiritual qualities is select and refined. (2) *Good sense is shown by caution and avoidance of undue responsibility.* This has been before emphasized (ch. vi. 1—5; xi. 15; xvii. 18). We have enough to do to answer for ourselves. (3) *Prudence in war.* There are justifiable wars; but even these may be carried on with folly, reckless disregard of human life, etc. "The beginning, middle, and end, O Lord, turn to the best account!" was the prayer of a prudent and pious general. 4. *Reserve with the tongue, or caution against flatterers.* (Ver. 19.) The verse may be taken in both these senses. In all thoughtless gossip about others there is something of the malicious and slanderous spirit; there is danger in it. As to the listener, rather let him listen to those who point out his faults than to those who flatter.—J.

Vers. 20—23.—*Smitten sins.* I. HATRED TO PARENTS. (Ver. 20.) 1. It is unnatural beyond most vices, like hating the hand that lifts food to the mouth. 2. It is disobedience to a primary Divine command. 3. It incurs the Divine curse and the darkest doom.

II. THE VICE OF GRASPING. (Ver. 21.) It springs from excessive, irregular, disordered desire, and generally from an ill-led life. We must wait upon God's order; must distinguish the necessary from the superfluous and the luxurious, and seek no enterprises that lie out of our proper vocation, if we would arm ourselves against this unholy temptation, and avoid the curse which attends compliance with it. For illgotten wealth can never prosper.

III. THE REVENGEFUL SPIRIT. (Ver. 22.) It costs more to avenge injuries than to endure them. "He that studieth revenge keepeth his wounds open." Let us recall the lessons of the sermon on the mount, and if there is any one who has aroused our dislike, pray for him (not in public, but in the privacy of the heart).

IV. IN EQUITY, WHETHER IN COMMERCE OR IN GENERAL RELATIONS. (Ver. 23; see ver. 10.) What is shameful when detected is no less hideous in the sight of God, though concealed from men.—J.

Vers. 24—30.—*The truth of life in diverse aspects.* We may divide the matter as follows.

I. DIVINE PROVIDENCE. (Ver. 24.) It is needful, for human wisdom is shortsighted, and human direction inadequate. It is a gracious fact, and, if acknowledged, brings blessing to the trustful mind and heart. Each man has a life-vocation. God appoints it, and will reveal the means for the attainment of it. We cannot enter the kingdom except through the guidance of Christ.

II. HUMAN RESPONSIBILITY. (Ver. 27.) There is a light within us, or conscience in the most comprehensive sense. By the help of reason we may judge other men; by that of conscience, ourselves. It is in another statement the power of reflection, the inner mirror of the soul.

III. GENERAL RELATED TRUTHS. 1. *The necessity of pondering well our wishes.* (Ver. 25.) We should think thrice before we act once. To act first and reflect afterwards is foolish and helpless; thus we reap the good of neither thought nor action. 2. *The necessity of discrimination in rulers.* (Ver. 26.) The figure is borrowed from agriculture, from the process of sifting and threshing—the latter in a *penal* sense (2 Sam. xii. 31; 1 Chron. xx. 3; Amos i. 3). It is carried into the gospel. The Divine Judge's "fan is in his hand, and he will throughly purge his floor." We must submit to law or be crushed by its penal action. 3. *The necessity of love and faithfulness in government.* (Ver. 28.) For human government, to be sound, stable, and respected, must be a reflection of the Divine government. And the eternal features of the latter are love and faithfulness. Clemency and severity are but two sides of the one living and eternal love which rules men only for their salvation. 4. *The beauty of piety in youth and age.* (Ver. 29.) Let the young man in Christ approve his strength by manful self-conquest, and the old man by riper wisdom and blameless conversation (1 John ii. 13, 14). 5. *The necessity of inward purification.* (Ver. 30.) And to this end the necessity of chastisement. In bodily disease we recognize the struggle of life against that which is inimical to it; and in the afflictions of the soul the struggle of the God-awakened soul against its evils. Luther says, "Evil is cured, not by words, but by blows; suffering is as necessary as eating and drinking."—J.

Ver. 1.—*Strong drink: four delusions.* That may be said to mock us which first professes to benefit us, and then proceeds to injure and even to destroy us. This is what is done by strong drink. First it cheers and brightens, puts a song into our mouth, makes life seem enviable; then it weakens, obfuscates, deadens, ruins. How many of the children of men has it deceived and betrayed! how many has it robbed of their virtue, their beauty, their strength, their resources, their peace, their reputation, their life, their hope! There are—

I. FOUR DELUSIONS IN WHICH MEN INDULGE REGARDING IT. 1. That it is necessary to health. In ordinary conditions it has been proved to be wholly needless, if not positively injurious. 2. That it is reliable as a source of pleasure. It is a fact that the craving for intoxicants and anodynes continually increases, while the pleasure derived therefrom continually declines. 3. That it renders service in the time of heavy trial. Woe be unto him who tries to drown his sorrow in the intoxicating cup! He is giving up the true for the false, the elevating for the degrading, the life-bestowing for the death-dealing consolation. 4. That it is a feeble enemy that may be safely disregarded. Very many men and women come into the world with a constitution which makes any intoxicant a source of extreme peril to them; and many more find it to be a foe whose subtlety and strength require all their wisdom and power to master. An underestimate of the force of this temptation accounts for many a buried reputation, for many a lost spirit.

II. THE CONCLUSION OF THE WISE. 1. To avoid the use of it altogether, if possible; and thus to be quite safe from its sting. 2. To use it, when necessary, with the most rigorous carefulness (ch. xxxi. 6; 1 Tim. v. 23). 3. To discourage those social usages in which much danger lies. 4. To act on the principle of Christian generosity (Rom. xiv. 21).—C.

Ver. 3.—(See homily on ch. xxix. 11.)—C.

Vers. 6, 7.—*The blessings of goodness.* Here are brought out again, in proverbial brevity, the blessings which belong to moral worth.

I. THE DOUBTFUL VALUE OF SELF-PRAISE. "Most men will proclaim," etc. 1. On the one hand, nothing is better than the approval of a man's own conscience. "Populus me sibilat, at mihi plaudo," says the Roman writer. Let a man have the commendation of his own conscience, and he can hear the hisses of the people with very little concern. It has been in this spirit that the very noblest things have been done by honourable and even heroic men. 2. On the other hand, there is a vast amount of self-congratulation amongst men which is nothing more or better than mere complacency. It is self-flattery, and that is not beautiful, but ugly; it is not true, but false. And such is the tendency in man to assure himself that he is right, even when he is thoroughly and lamentably wrong, that we have to wait and to inquire before we take men's word about themselves. Between the heroic spirit of a Luther, or a Columbus, or a Galileo, and the miserable self-satisfaction of some petty tyrant gloating over his tyranny, there is the entire breadth of the moral world. It is well for us all to be able to do without the honour that cometh from man only; it is well for us also to recognize the truth that our own commendation, so far from being the voice of God within us, may be nothing but the very unsightly crust of a dangerous and even deadly complacency.

II. THE EXCELLENCY OF FAITHFULNESS. Solomon seemed to find fidelity a rare thing. "Who can find it?" he asked. With Christian truth sown in so many hearts, we do not feel the lack of it as he did. We thank God that in the home and the school, in the shop and the factory, in the pulpit and the press, in all spheres of honourable activity, we find instances of a solid and sound fidelity—men and women occupying their post and doing their work with a loyalty to those whom they serve, which is fair indeed in the sight both of heaven and of earth. There is abundance of unfaithfulness also, it has to be owned and lamented; and this is sometimes found where it is simply disgraceful—among those who wear the name of that Master and Exemplar who was "faithful in all his house." It is required of us, who are all stewards, that we be found faithful (1 Cor. iv. 2); and we must not only expect to give account to our brother here, but to the Divine Judge hereafter.

III. THE WORTH OF GUIDING PRINCIPLES. "A just man walketh in his integrity." What fairer sight is there beneath the sun? A just or upright man, a man who is (1) yielding to God that which is due to his Creator and his Redeemer, viz. his heart and his life; who is (2) giving to his neighbours what is due to them; and who is (3) honouring himself as is his due;—this man is "walking" along the path of life in his integrity, every step directed by righteous principles and prompted by honourable impulses; his way is never crooked, but lies straight on; it is continuously upward, and moves to noble heights of virtue and wisdom and piety. Who would not be such as he is—a man God owns as his son, and the angels of God as their brother, and all his fellow-men as their helper and their friend?

IV. THE CROWN OF HUMAN BLESSEDNESS. "His children are blessed after him." Then is a good man crowned with an honour and a joy which no diadem, nor rank, nor office, nor emolument, can confer, when his children are found "walking in the truth" of God, their affections centred in that Divine Friend who will lead them in the path of heavenly wisdom, their life governed by holy principles, themselves enriched and encircled by a holy and beautiful character, their influence felt on every hand for good—"a seed which the Lord hath blessed."—C.

Ver. 9.—*Purity of heart.* A subject that stretches back and looks onward as far as the limits of human history. But Jesus Christ has introduced into the world a power for purity which is peculiar to his gospel.

I. THE UTTER UGLINESS OF IMPURITY. To the eye of holy men there is an unspeakable offensiveness in any form of impurity—selfishness, worldliness, covetousness, sensuality, whatever it may be. And how much more hideous and intolerable must it be in the eyes of the Holy One himself (Hab. i. 13; Ps. v. 5)! This is one explanation of choosing leprosy as a type and picture of sin, viz. its fearful loathsomeness in the sight of God.

II. ITS EXCLUSION FROM THE PRESENCE AND KINGDOM OF GOD. (See Ps. l. 16; lxvi. 18; ch. xv. 29; xxviii. 9; Isa. i. 10—17; Matt. v. 8; Heb. xii. 14.)

III. THE ONE WAY OF RETURN. When the heart sees, and is ashamed of, its corruption, and returns in simple penitence to God, then there is mercy and admission. But sincere repentance is the only gateway by which impurity can find its way to the favour and the kingdom of God.

IV. THE ESTABLISHMENT OF INWARD PURITY. When the heart, conscious of guilt, has sought and found mercy of God in Jesus Christ, and is "cleansed of its iniquity," so that there is "a clean heart and a right spirit" before God, all is not yet done that has to be accomplished. What Christian man can say, "I have made my heart clean; I am pure from my sin"? "If *we* [who are in Christ Jesus] say that we have no sin, we deceive ourselves, and the truth is not in us" (1 John i. 8). "In many things we offend all" (Jas. iii. 2). We are washed, but we "need to wash our feet" (John xiii. 10). There yet lingers within the heart of the humble and the pure that which needs purification before they will be "holy as he [the Lord] is holy." What are these cleansing forces which will best do this much-needed and most desirable work? Are they not: 1. The avoidance of that which defiles; the deliberate turning away of the eyes of the soul (so far as duty to others will allow) from all that stains and soils? 2. Much fellowship with Jesus Christ the Holy One, and much intercourse with his true friends and followers? 3. The earnest, determined pursuit of that which is noblest in man, especially by the study of the worthiest lives? 4. Prayer for the cleansing influences which come direct from the Holy Spirit of God (Ps. li. 10; cxxxix. 23, 24; 2 Thess. ii. 17; Heb. xiii. 20, 21)?—C.

Ver. 10.—(See homily on ch. xvi. 11.)—C.

Ver. 11.—*Childhood: a transparency, a prophecy, a study.* It is not apparent why Solomon says, "*Even* a child is known." It is a familiar fact, at which we may glance, and which seems to be the main thought of the text.

I. THE TRANSPARENCY OF CHILDHOOD. Some men are full of guile and of hypocrisy; they have acquired the power of concealing their real thought and feeling beneath their exterior, and you are never quite sure what they mean. You dare not trust them; for their words, or their demeanour, or their present action may entirely belie them. Not so the child. He means what he says. If he does not love you, he will not affect any liking for you. You will soon find from his behaviour what he thinks about men and things, about the studies in which he is occupied, about the service in which you want him to engage. And whether he is living a pure and faithful life, whether he is obedient and studious, or whether he is obstinate and idle, you will very soon discover if you try. It requires but very little penetration to read a child's spirit, to know a child's character. But the truth which is not so much on the surface respecting the knowledge we have of or from the child relates to—

II. THE PROPHECY OF CHILDHOOD. "Even a child" will give some idea of the man into whom he will one day grow. "The child is father to the man." In him are the germs of the nobility or the meanness, the courage or the cowardice, the generosity or the selfishness, the studiousness or the carelessness, the power or the weakness, that is to be witnessed later on. He that has eyes to see *may* read in the child before him the future—physical, mental, moral—that will be silently but certainly developed. Hence we may regard—

III. CHILDHOOD AS A STUDY. If men have found an insect, or a flower, or a seed, or a stone well worth their study, how much more is the little child! For, on the one hand, *ignorant assumption* may spoil a life. To conclude hastily, and therefore falsely, respecting the temper, the tastes, the capacities, the inclinations, the responsibilities, the culpability or praiseworthiness of the child, and to act accordingly, may lead down into error and unbelief and despair the spirit that might, by other means, have been led into the light of truth and the love of God. And, on the other hand, *a conscientious and just conclusion* on these most important characteristics of childhood may make a life, may save unimaginable misery, may result in an early, instead of a late, unfolding of power and beauty, may make all the difference in the history of a human soul. And only the Father of spirits can tell *what that difference is.*—C.

Ver. 12.—*God our Maker.* Truly we are "wonderfully made;" and "the hand that made *us* is Divine." The human ear and eye are—

I. INSTANCES OF DIVINE SKILL AND POWER. That we should be able, by means of this small apparatus included in "the ear," to detect such a variety of notes, to distinguish sounds from one another so readily, through so many years, to perceive the faintest whisper in the trees, and to enjoy the roll of the reverberating thunder; that we should be able, by means of two small globes in our face, to see things as minute as a bud or a dewdrop and as mighty as a mountain or as the "great wide sea," to detect that which is dangerous and to gaze with delight and even rapture on the beauties and glories of the world;—this is a very striking instance of the wonderful skill and power of our Creator.

II. EVIDENCES OF DIVINE GOODNESS. For what sources of knowledge, of power, of pure gladness of heart, of mental and moral cultivation and growth, has not God given to us in sculpturing for us " the hearing ear," in fashioning for us " the seeing eye"?

III. SUGGESTIVE OF THE DIVINE KNOWLEDGE. "He that planted the ear, shall he not hear? he that formed the eye, shall he not see?" (Ps. xciv. 9). The wonderful Worker who has supplied us, his finite and feeble creatures, with such power of hearing and of vision, with such sources of knowledge,—how great, how perfect, how boundless, must be his own Divine perception! How certainly must he hear the whisper we would fain make inaudible to him! how inevitably must he see the action we would gladly hide from his searching sight! How absolute must God's knowledge be, both of our outward life and of the inner workings of our soul!

IV. OPPORTUNITY FOR DIVINE SERVICE. For here are the means we want of learning of God, of knowing, that we may do, his holy will. Our eye not only conveys to us the sight of the beautiful, the richly stored, the glorious world that God has made for us, but it enables us to read "the book he has written for our learning," wherein we can find all that we need to know of his nature, his character, and his will. And our ear not only conveys to us the melodies of the outer world, but it places within the reach of our spirit the Divine truths which are uttered in our presence. These, as they come from the lips of parent, or teacher, or pastor, can "make us wise unto salvation," can fill our hearts with holy purpose, with true and pure emotion, with abiding peace. And we may add that the speaking lips are also that which "the Lord hath made;" and what an opportunity these give us of uttering his truth, of helping his children, of furthering his cause and kingdom! Such excellent service can our bodily organs render to our immortal spirit; and so may they be impressed into the holier service of their Divine Author.—C.

Ver. 17.—(See homily on ch. xxi. 6—8.)—C.

Ver. 22 (ch. xxiv. 29).—*Resentment and forgiveness.* The Christian doctrine of forgiveness finds here a distinct anticipation; but that doctrine was not found in the highway, but rather in the byway of pre-Christian morals. It made no mark. It did not find its way into the thought and the feeling of the people.

I. WE MUST EXPECT TO BE WRONGED, OR TO BELIEVE OURSELVES WRONGED, AS WE GO ON OUR WAY. So conflicting are our interests, so various our views, so many are the occasions when an event or a remark will wear an entirely different aspect according to the point of view from which it is regarded, that it is utterly unlikely, morally impossible, that we should not be often placed in a position in which we seem to be wronged. It may be some sentence spoken, or some action taken, or some purpose settled upon, slight or serious, incidental or malevolent, but we may take it that it is one part of the portion and burden of our life.

II. BITTER RESENTMENT IS DISTINCTLY DISALLOWED. It is natural, it is human enough. As man has become under the reign of sin, it finds a place in his heart if not in his creed, everywhere. *It seems to be right.* It has one element that *is* right—the element of indignation. But this is only one part of the feeling, and by no means the chief part. A bitter animosity, engendered by the thought that something has been done *against us*, is the main ingredient. And this is positively disallowed. "Say not, I will recompense evil;" "It hath been said, . . . hate thine enemy; but I say unto you, Love your enemies . . . do good to them that hate you;" "Avenge not yourselves, but rather give place unto wrath;" "Let all bitterness and wrath and anger . . . be put away from you, with all malice" (Matt. v. 43, 44; Rom. xii. 19; Eph. iv 31).

III. WE HAVE AN ADMIRABLE ALTERNATIVE. We can "wait on the Lord," and he will "save us." We can: 1. Go to God in prayer; take our wounded spirit to him; cast our burden upon him; seek and find a holy calm in communion with him. 2. Commit our cause unto him; be like unto our Leader, "who, when he was reviled, reviled not again; when he suffered, he threatened not; but committed himself to him that judgeth righteously" (1 Pet. ii. 23). We shall thus ask God to save us *from our-selves*, from indulging thoughts and feelings toward our neighbour which shame rather than honour us, which separate us in spirit from our great Exemplar (1 Pet. ii. 21); and to save us *from those who would injure us*, working out' or us, in his own way and time, our deliverance and recovery.

IV. WE WIN THE TRUE VICTORY. To be avenged on our enemy is a victory of a certain kind; the moment of success is a moment of triumph, of exultation. But: 1. *That is a victory which is greatly and sadly qualified.* When we regard the matter disinterestedly and dispassionately, can we really envy such triumph? Should we like to have in our heart the feelings which are surging and swelling in the breast of the victor—feelings of bitter hatred, and of positive delight in a brother's humiliation, or suffering, or loss? 2. *The victory of forgiveness is pre-eminently Christian.* It places us by the side of our gracious Lord himself (Luke xxiii. 34), and of the best and worthiest of his disciples (Acts vii. 60; 2 Tim. iv. 16). 3. *It gives to us a distinct spiritual resemblance to our heavenly Father himself.* (Matt. v. 45.)—C.

Ver. 23.—(See homily on ch. xvi. 11.)—C.

Ver. 27.—*The inward light.* Man may be said to be governed from above, from without, and also from within; by the power which is from heaven, by human society, and also by the forces which are resident in his own spiritual nature.

I. OUR SPIRITUAL NATURE. God created man in his own image; *i.e.* he created him a spirit. God is a spirit; so also is man, his offspring, his human child. Our spiritual nature is endowed with the faculties of perception, of memory, of imagination, of reason. These include—some would say that to these there has to be added—the power which is usually called conscience, the exercise of our spiritual faculties directed to all ques-tions of morality. This moral judgment, or conscience, of ours: 1. *Distinguishes between right and wrong.* Decides what is good and what evil, what is just and what unjust, what is pure and what impure, what is true and what false, what is kind and what cruel. It is an inward light; it is "the candle of the Lord," etc. 2. *Approves of the one and disapproves of the other.* 3. *Acts with such force* that, on the one hand, there is a distinct satisfaction, and even joy; that, on the other hand, there is distinct dissatisfaction, and even pain, sometimes amounting to an intolerable agony. There is hardly any delight we can experience which is so worthy of ourselves as the children of God, as is that which fills our heart when we know that, regardless of our own interests and prospects, we have *done the right thing;* there is no wretchedness so unbearable as remorse, the stinging and smarting of soul when our conscience rebukes us for some sad transgression. 4. *Is a profoundly penetrating power.* It "searches all the inward parts" of the soul; it considers not only what is on the surface, but what is far beneath. It deals with thoughts, with feelings, with purposes and desires, with the motives which move us, and with the spirit that animates us.

II. THE INJURY OUR NATURE SUFFERS FROM OUR SIN. He that sinneth against Divine wisdom, and therefore against the Divine One, does indeed "wrong his own soul." Every wrong action tends to weaken the authority of conscience, and, after a while, it disturbs its judgment, so that its decision is not as true and straight as it was. This is the saddest aspect of the consequence of sin. When the inward light, the candle of the Lord, begins to grow dim, and ultimately becomes darkened, then the soul is con-fused and the path of life is lost. If our eye is evil, our whole body is full of dark-ness; if the light that is in us be darkness, how great must the darkness be (Matt. vi. 23)! When that which should be directing us into the truth and wisdom of heaven is misleading us, and is positively directing us to folly and wrong, we are far on the road to spiritual ruin. We have to mourn the fact that this is no rare occurrence; that sin does so confuse and blind our souls that men do very frequently fall into the moral condition in which they "call evil good, and good evil." The light that is in them is darkness.

III. OUR RESTORATION THROUGH CHRIST OUR LORD. Jesus Christ offers himself to us as the Divine Physician; he says to us, "Wilt thou be made whole?" And he who so graciously and mightily healed the bodies heals also the souls of men. He does so by recalling our affection to God our Father, by *setting our heart right.* Then loving him, we love his Word, his truth; we study and we copy the life of our Lord. And as the *heart* is renewed and the *life* is changed, the *judgment* also is restored; we see all things in another light; we "see light in God's light." The candle of the Lord is rekindled, the lamp is trimmed; it gives a new light to all that are in the house—to all the faculties that are in the house of our nature. Let us yield ourselves to Christ our Lord, let us study his truth and his life, and our conscience will become more and more true in its decisions, and in its peaceful light we shall walk "all the day long," truly happy in heart, enjoying the constant favour of "the Father of lights."—C.

Ver. 28.—(See homily on ch. xvi. 12.)—C.

Ver. 29.—*The glory of young manhood.* A weak young man is not a sight that we like to see. Between young manhood and weakness there is no natural agreement; the two things do not accord with one another. In young men we look for strength, and delight to see it there. Moreover, youth itself is proud of the strength of which it is conscious, and "glories" in it. We look at—

I. THAT WHEREON WE CONGRATULATE IT. We look with satisfaction, and perhaps with pride, upon the young man who possesses: 1. *Physical strength.* Well-developed muscular power and skill, the attainment of the largest possible share of bodily vigour and capacity, this is one element of manliness, and, although it is not the highest, it is good in itself, and so far as it goes. 2. *Intellectual power.* The possession of knowledge, of mental vigour and grasp, of reasoning faculty, of business shrewdness and capacity, of imaginative power, of strength of will; but especially: 3. *Moral and spiritual strength.* Power to resist the evil forces which are around us; to put aside, without hesitation, the solicitations to unholy pleasure or unlawful gain; to decline the fellowship and friendship which might be pecuniarily or socially advantageous, but which would be morally and spiritually injurious; to move onward in the way of duty, unscathed by the darts and arrows of evil which are in the air; to undertake and to execute beneficent work; to range one's self with the honourable and holy few against the unworthy multitude; to bear a brave witness on behalf of truth, purity, sobriety, righteousness, whatever the forces that are in league against it;—this is the noblest element of strength, and this is pre-eminently the glory of young manhood.

II. ITS PECULIAR TEMPTATION. The temptation of the strong is to disregard and even to despise the weak, to look down with a proud sense of superiority on those who are less capable than themselves. This is both foolish and sinful. For comparative weakness is that from which the strong have themselves come up, and into which they will themselves go down. It is a question of time, or, if not of time, of privilege and bestowment (see *infra*), and a proud contempt is quite misplaced. The young should clearly understand that strength, when it is modest, is a beautiful thing, but when haughty and disdainful, is offensive in the sight both of God and man.

III. ITS CLEAR OBLIGATION. The first thing that human strength should do is to recognize the source whence it came, and to let its recognition find expression in devout and reverent action. "Thy God hath commanded thy strength." As, ultimately, all strength of every kind proceeds from God; and as he constantly sustains in power, and the strong as much as the weak are dependent on his fatherly kindness; and as the strong owe more to his goodness than the weak (inasmuch as they have received more at his hand);—the first thing they should ask themselves is—*What can we render unto the Lord?* And they will find that to devote their strength to the service of their Saviour and of their kind is to find a source of blessedness immeasurably higher, as well as far more lasting, than that which comes from the sense of power. It is not *what we have*, but *what we give*, that fills the soul with pure and abiding joy.—C.

Ver. 29 (latter clause).—(See homily on ch xvi. 31.)—C.

EXPOSITION.

CHAPTER XXI.

Ver. 1.—**The king's heart is in the hand of the Lord, as the rivers of water.** We are to think of the little channels used for irrigation. As these are altogether under the gardener's control, so the heart of the king, who might seem to have no superior, is directed by God. **He turneth it whithersoever he will.** By hidden influences and providential arrangements God disposes the monarch to order his government so as to carry out his designs, to spread around joy and plenty. The system of irrigation signified in this passage is still to be seen in Eastern lands. "Flower-beds and gardens of herbs are always made at a little lower level than the surrounding ground, and are divided into small squares, a slight edging of earth banking the whole round on each side. Water is then let in, and floods the entire surface till the soil is thoroughly saturated; after which the moisture is turned off to another bed, by simply closing the opening in the one under water, by a turn of the bare foot of the gardener, and making another in the same way with the foot, in the next bed, and thus the whole garden is in due course watered. . . . Only, in this case, the hand is supposed to make the gap in the clay bank of the streamlet, and divert the current" (Geikie, 'Holy Land and Bible,' i. 9). So in Virgil we find ('Ecl.,' iii. 111)—

"Claudite jam rivos, pueri; sat prata bibe-
    runt."

"Now close the cuts; enough the meads
    have drunk."

Ver. 2.—This is similar to ch. xvi. 2 (where see note. Comp. also ch. xiv. 12; xvi. 25; xx. 24). See here a warning against self-deception and that silly self-complacency which thinks its own ways the best. Septuagint, "Every man appears to himself righteous, but the Lord directs the hearts."

Ver. 3.—**To do justice and judgment is more acceptable to the Lord than sacrifice.** The superiority of moral obedience to ceremonial worship is often inculcated (see note on ch. xv. 8, and below, ver. 27; and comp. Micah vi. 6—8 and Matt. xii. 7). "Justice" and "judgment" (*tsedakah* and *mishpat*) are combined in Gen. xviii. 19; 2 Sam. viii. 15; Job xxxvii. 23; Isa. lvi. 1, etc. They imply equity and justice proceeding, not from bare regard to law, but from the principle of love. Septuagint, "To do justly and to speak the truth are more pleasing to God than the blood of sacrifices."

Ver. 4.—**An high look and a proud heart;** Vulgate, *exaltatio oculorum est dilatatio cordis*, "The lifting up of the eyes is a swelling of the heart." But it is best to make the whole verse one idea, as in the Authorized Version. The lifting of the eyes is a term implying pride, as shown in supercilious looks, as if other people were of inferior clay and not worthy of notice. So we have "haughty eyes" in ch. vi. 17 (where see note); and in ch. xxx. 13 we read, "There is a generation, oh how lofty are their eyes! and their eyelids are lifted up." "The enlargement of the heart" is the cause of the proud look, for it signifies the evil affections and concupiscence of the will, wholly filled up with self, and controlling the actions and expression of the body. Septuagint, "A high-minded man (μεγαλόφρων) is stout-hearted in his pride." And the ploughing of the wicked is sin. The Authorized Version takes the reading נִר (*nir*), which means "tillage" (ch. xiii. 23), or, as Delitzsch supposes, "land ploughed for the first time" (*novale*). The proverb, taken thus, will mean, "high look, proud heart, even all the field which the godless cultivate, all that they do, is sin." "Pride," says the Talmud, "is worse than sin." But another pointing gives a different and very appropriate (comp. ch. xiii. 9; xxiv. 20) meaning. נֵר (*ner*) signifies "a lamp." Thus the Vulgate, *Lucerna impiorum peccatum*, "The lamp of the wicked is sin;" and the Septuagint, Λαμπτὴρ δὲ ἀσεβῶν ἁμαρτία. "Lamp" is, as often, a metaphor for prosperity and happiness (comp. 2 Sam. xxii. 29; 1 Kings xi. 36); and it is here said that the sinner's outward prosperity and joyousness, springing from no good source, being founded in self, and not resting on virtue and godliness, are in themselves sinful and displeasing to God.

Ver. 5.—**The thoughts of the diligent tend only to plenteousness.** Patient industry is rewarded by a certain increase (comp. ch. xii. 11; xiii. 11; xiv. 23). Says an English maxim, "Diligence is a fair fortune, and industry a good estate." The Greek gnomists have said tersely—

Απαντα τὰ καλὰ τοῦ πονοῦντος γίγνεται.
Τῷ γὰρ πονοῦντι καὶ Θεὸς συλλαμβάνει.

"To him who labours all good things accrue.
The man who labours God himself assists."

But of every one that is hasty only to want. Diligence is contrasted with hastiness. The hasting to be rich by any, even nefarious, means (ch. xx. 21; xxviii. 20) will bring a man to poverty. There are numerous proverbs warning against precipitancy, which will occur to every one: *Festina lente;* "More haste, less speed;" "Eile mit Weile."

Προπέτεια πολλοῖς ἐστὶν αἰτία κακῶν.

(See a long dissertation on *Festinatio præpropera* in Erasmus's ' Adagia.') This verse is omitted in the chief manuscripts of the Septuagint.

Ver. 6.—**The getting of treasures by a lying tongue**—the acquisition of wealth by fraud and falsehood—is a vanity tossed to and fro of them that seek death. The latter clause is variously rendered and interpreted. The Hebrew is literally, *a fleeting breath, those seeking death.* The Revised Version makes the last words a separate proposition, "They that seek them seek death." But this seems unnecessary, and somewhat opposed to the gnomic style, which often combines two predicates in one construction; and there is no reason why we should not render the words, as in the Authorized Version, "of seekers of death." Such a mode of obtaining wealth is as evanescent and unstable as the very breath, and ends in death, which is practically the result of their quest. Thus Wisd. v. 14, "The hope of the ungodly is like dust that is blown away with the wind; like a thin froth that is driven away with the storm; like as the smoke which is dispersed here and there with the tempest, and passeth away, as the remembrance of a guest that tarrieth but a day." Some think that the comparison regards the mirage of the desert, which deceives travellers with the phantasms of cool waters and refreshing shade. Such an allusion is found in Isa. xxxv. 7. The Talmud enjoins, "Speak no word that accords not with the truth, that thy honour may not vanish as the waters of a brook." The Septuagint and Vulgate have followed a different reading (מוק שי־מות), and render thus: Vulgate, *Vanus et excors est, et impingetur ad laqueos mortis,* "He is vain and foolish, and will be taken in the snares of death;" Septuagint, "pursues vain things unto the snares of death (ἐπὶ παγίδας θανάτου)" (ch. xiii. 14; xiv. 27). So St. Paul says (1 Tim. vi. 9), "They that desire to be rich fall into a temptation and a snare (παγίδα), and many foolish and hurtful lusts, such as drown men in destruction and perdition."

Ver. 7.—**The robbery of the wicked shall destroy them;** Vulgate, *rapinæ impiorum detrahent eos;* Revised Version, "The violence of the wicked shall sweep them away," like ch ff before the wind. The violence with which they treat others shall rebound on themselves, shall bring its own punishment; they shall sink in the pit that they made, and their foot shall be taken in the net which they hid (Ps. ix. 15; comp. ch. i. 18, 19).

Septuagint, "Destruction shall sojourn as a guest (ἐπιξενωθήσεται) with the ungodly." The reason of this fate is given in the concluding hemistich: Because they refuse to do judgment. This is a judicial retribution on them for wilfully declining (ver. 25) to do what is right.

Ver. 8.—**The way of man is froward and strange;** Vulgate, *Perversa via viri, aliena est.* Both this and the Authorized Version miss the antithesis between the guilty and the pure man, which is intended. In חַיְ, translated "and strange" (which seems to mean "alien from what is right"), the *vav* is not the copulative, but part of the word, which is an adjective signifying "laden with guilt;" so that the clause ought to be rendered, "Crooked is the way of a guilty man" (see note on ch. ii. 15, where, however, the word is different, though the idea is analogous). An evil man's way of life is not open and straightforward, simple and uniform, but stealthy, crooked, perverse, whither his evil inclinations lead him. Septuagint, "To the crooked (σκολιοὺς) God sendeth crooked ways;" which recalls Ps. xviii. 26, "With the pure thou wilt show thyself pure; and with the perverse thou wilt show thyself froward." God allows the wicked to punish themselves by falling into mischief. As for the pure, his work is right; or, *straight* (ch. xx. 11). The pure in heart will be right in action; he follows his conscience and God's law, and goes direct on his course without turning or hesitation. The LXX. refers the clause to God: "for pure and right are his ways."

Ver. 9.—**It is better to dwell in a corner of the housetop.** One is to think of the flat roof of an Eastern house, which was used as an apartment for many purposes; *e.g.* for sleeping and conference (1 Sam. ix. 25, 26), for exercise (2 Sam. xi. 2), for domestic matters (Josh. ii. 6), for retirement and prayer (Ps. cii. 7; Acts x. 9). This, though exposed to the inclemency of the weather, would be not an uncomfortable situation during a great part of the year. But the proverb implies a position abnormally inconvenient as an alternative preferable to a residence inside. Hence, perhaps, it is advisable to render, with Delitzsch, "Better to sit on the pinnacle of a house-roof." Septuagint, "It is better to dwell in a corner of a place open to the sky (ὑπαίθρου)." Than with a brawling (*contentious*) woman in a wide house; literally, *a house of society;* i.e. a house in common (comp. ver. 19 and ch. xxv. 24). A solitary corner, replete with inconveniences, is to be preferred to a house shared with a woman, wife or other female relation, of a quarrelsome and vexatious temper. The LXX. puts the matter forcibly, "than in cieled rooms with unrighteousness and in a common house." So the Latin proverb, "Non quam late, sed quam læte habites, refert." The Scotch have a proverb to the same effect: "A house wi' a reek and a wife wi' a reerd (scold) will sune mak' a man run to the door." "I had rather dwell," says the Son of Sirach (Ecclus. xxv. 16), "with a lion and a dragon, than to keep house with a wicked woman."

Ver. 10.—**The soul of the wicked desireth veil.** A wicked man cannot rest without planning and wishing for some new evil thing. Nothing is safe from his malignant activity (comp. ch. iv. 16; x. 23). **His neighbour findeth no favour in his eyes** (Isa. xiii. 18; xxvi. 10). He does not look with pity on friend or neighbour, if they stand in the way of the gratification of his desires; he will sacrifice any one, however closely connected, so that he may work his will. Nothing makes a man more atrociously selfish and hard-hearted than vice (see ch. xii. 10, and the note there). The LXX. takes the sentence in a passive sense, "The soul of the ungodly shall not be pitied by any one." They who have no pity for others shall meet with no pity themselves; while, on the other hand, the Lord says, "Blessed are the merciful: for they shall obtain mercy" (Matt. v. 7).

Ver. 11.—**When the scorner is punished, the simple is made wise.** We had the same thought at ch. xix. 25 (where see note). The simple (*parvulus*, Vulgate) profit by the punishment of the incorrigibly evil. But the wise need not chastisement for their improvement. **When the wise is instructed** (Ps. xxxii. 6), **he** (the wise) **receiveth knowledge.** The wise man uses every opportunity, takes advantage of every circumstance and event, to increase his knowledge and experience. The Vulgate carries on the subject, "And if he (the simple) follow the wise man, he shall attain knowledge." Septuagint, "When the intemperate man is punished, the simple is made cleverer; and a wise man understanding will receive knowledge." "For it often happens," says St. Gregory ('Moral.,' xviii. 38), "that the mind of the weak is the more unsteadied from the hearing of the truth, as it sees the despisers of the truth flourishing; but when just vengeance takes away the unjust, it keeps others away from wickedness."

Ver. 12.—**The righteous man wisely considereth the house of the wicked: but God overthroweth the wicked for their wickedness.** The Authorized Version introduces the words "but God" in order to eke out the sense desired; the Revised Version, for the same reason, has, "how the wicked are overthrown;" and both versions signify that the good man contemplates the fortunes and

seeming prosperity of the wicked, and, looking to the end of these men, sees how hollow is their success and what a fatal issue awaits them. The Vulgate refers the passage to the zeal of the righteous for the salvation of sinners—a thought quite foreign to the present subject—thus: *Excogitat justus de domo impii, ut detrahat impios a malo,* "The righteous man reflects concerning the house of the wicked how he may deliver them from evil." The Hebrew is literally, *A righteous one looketh on the house of the wicked: he precipitates the wicked to destruction.* There is no change of subject in the two clauses, and "a righteous One" (*tsaddik*) is God, put indeterminately to excite the greater awe (comp. Job xxxiv. 17). The Lord keeps the sinners under his eye, that he may punish them at the fit moment (comp. ch. xxii. 12; Job xii. 19). The notion of God's moral government of the universe prevails most strongly in every pronouncement of the writer. The LXX. interprets "the house" as heart and conscience, and renders, "A righteous man understands the hearts of the godless, and despises the impious in their wickednesses;" he sees through their outward felicity, knows well its unreality, and despises them for the low aims and pursuits which satisfy them.

Ver. 13.—**Whoso stoppeth his ears at the cry of the poor.** A twofold retribution is threatened on the unmerciful man. **He also shall cry himself, but shall not be heard.** He himself shall fall into distress, and shall appeal to his neighbours for help in vain. "With the same measure that ye mete withal, it shall be measured to you again" (Luke vi. 38). This is true also in spiritual matters and in the final judgment (see on ch. xiv. 21 and xix. 17; and comp. Matt. xviii. 23, etc.; xxv. 41, etc.; Jas. ii. 13).

Ver. 14.—**A gift in secret pacifieth anger.** We have had above various maxims about bribes and presents; *e.g.* ch. xvii. 8, 23; xviii. 16. The word translated "pacifieth" is from the ἅπαξ λεγόμενον verb כָּפָה, "to turn away," "avert." Septuagint, ἀνατρέπει; Vulgate, *extinguit;* Venetian, κάμψει. A gift offered secretly to one incensed, whether personal enemy, judge, or prince, averts the consequences of the offence. The next hemistich is parallel in meaning. **And a reward** (*present*) **in the bosom strong wrath.** A present kept handy in the bosom of the petitioner's garment, ready to be transferred at a fitting moment, as experience proves, calms the most violent wrath. Septuagint, "He that is sparing of gifts arouses strong wrath."

Ver. 15.—**It is joy to the just to do judgment.** The righteous feel real pleasure in doing what is right; they have the answer of a good conscience, and the feeling that they are, as far as they can, making God's will their will, and this brings deep comfort and stable joy (see some contrary experiences, ver. 10 and ch. x. 23; xv. 21). But destruction shall be to the workers of iniquity. The Authorized Version, by inserting " shall be," and making this clause a separate assertion, obscures the force of the original, which, as in ch. x. 29 (where see note), contrasts the effect of right-doing on the good and the evil. It is a joy to the former, " but destruction [or, ' terror '] to them that work iniquity." Et pavor operantibus iniquitatem, Vulgate. They cannot trust themselves to do rightly without fear; they cannot commit the result to God, as the righteous do; if ever they do act uprightly, it is against their inclination, and such action will, as they fear, bring them to ruin. Septuagint, " It is the joy of the righteous to do judgment; but a holy man is abominable (ἀκάθαρτος) among evil-doers." So Wisd. ii. 15, " He [the righteous] is grievous unto us even to behold: for his life is not like other men's, his ways are of another fashion . . . he abstaineth from our ways as from filthiness (ἀκαθαρσιῶν)."

Ver. 16.—The man that wandereth out of the way of understanding. (For הַשְׂכֵּל, " understanding," see note on ch. i. 3.) He who forsakes the way of wisdom, the path of virtue, the religious life, and thus becomes in proverbial language "a fool," he shall remain (rest, dwell) in the congregation of the dead; in coetu gigantum commorabitur. "The dead" is, in the Hebrew, rephaim, for which see note on ch. ii. 18. The denunciation means primarily that the sinner shall soon be with the shades of the dead, shall meet with a speedy death. Wordsworth considers that the writer is saying in bitter irony that the evil man shall rest as a guest at a banquet, shall lie down and be regaled, but it will be in the company of the dead. The contrast seems to lie between the wandering and the rest, and this rest is regarded as penal; so that one must needs see here an intimation of retribution after death; and comp. ch. xxiv. 14, 20. The Fathers regarded the Rephaim, " the giants," as the descendants of the rebel angels, in accordance with their interpretation of Gen. vi. 1—4. Thus St. Gregory writes ('Moral.,' xvii. 30), quoting our passage, " For whosoever forsakes the way of righteousness, to whose number does he join himself, saving to the number of the proud spirits?"

Ver. 17.—He that loveth pleasure shall be a poor man; qui diligit epulas, Vulgate; for feasts are chiefly, though not exclusively, intended. He shall become "a man of want" (machsor) as ch. xi. 24. He that loveth wine and oil shall not be rich. " Wine and oil " were the usual adjuncts of banquets (Ps.

xxiii. 5; civ. 15). Some unguents used for anointing honoured guests were very costly. The pound of spikenard expended by Mary of Bethany was worth more than three hundred pence—the wages of a labourer for nearly a whole year (see John xii. 3; Matt. xx. 2). Indulgence in such luxuries would be a token of prodigality and extravagance, which are the sure precursors of ruin; while, on the other hand, according to the trite proverb, Magnum vectigal est parsimonia. That fulness of meat and luxurious habits tend to spiritual poverty and the loss of grace, need not be insisted on. Septuagint, " A man in want (ἐνδεὴς) loveth mirth, loving wine and oil unto wealth (εἰς πλοῦτον)." Some translate the last words, "in abundance," as if the meaning was that the poor endeavours to mitigate the severity of his lot by getting all the pleasure he can from creature comforts however procured. Others think that a negative has fallen out of the Greek, which should be, "not unto wealth," i.e. he shall not be enriched thereby.

Ver. 18.—The wicked shall be a ransom for the righteous. The same thought occurs in ch. xi. 8 (where see note). כֹּפֶר (kopher), " price of atonement," means of reconciliation. Delitzsch instances that the great movement which gathered the nations together for the destruction of Babylon, put an end to Israel's exile; and that Cyrus, the scourge of so many heathen peoples, was the liberator of the Jews (comp. Isa. xliv. 28). And the transgressor for the upright. The faithless takes the place of the upright; the stroke passes over the latter, to fall on the former, as in Egypt the destroying angel spared the houses of the Israelites, and poured his wrath on the Egyptians. Septuagint, " A transgressor is the offscouring (περικάθαρμα, perhaps equivalent to 'ransom') of a righteous man."

Ver. 19.—A variant of ver. 9. Here, instead of the " corner of the roof," we have a wilderness, a desert land, as the refuge to which the persecuted man must flee. Than with a contentious and an angry (fretful) woman. So the Vulgate. But it seems better, with many modern commentators, to take וָכָעַם, not as another epithet, but as equivalent to " and vexation," i.e. a quarrelsome wife, and the vexation that accompanies such an infliction. The LXX. adds a word to the text, as being at the root of the matter, " Than with a quarrelsome, talkative, and passionate woman."

Ver. 20.—There is treasure to be desired and oil in the dwelling of the wise. Precious treasure and store of provision and rich unguents (ver. 17) are collected in the house of the wise man, by which he may fare sumptuously, exercise hospitality, and lay up for the future (comp. ch. xxiv. 4). But a foolish man spendeth it up. "A fool of a man" (ch. xv. 20) soon swallows, runs through and exhausts, all that has been accumulated (ver. 17). Septuagint, "A desirable (ἐπιθυμητὸς) treasure will rest on the mouth of the wise, but foolish men will swallow it up." It is obvious to apply the maxim to spiritual things, seeing in it the truth that the really wise man stores up treasures of Divine love and the oil of God's grace, while the foolish man wastes his opportunities, squanders his powers, and drives the Holy Spirit from him.

Ver. 21.—He that followeth after righteousness and mercy. "Righteousness" (tsedakah), in the first hemistich, signifies the virtue which renders to all, God and man, their due, which is the characteristic of the righteous man (see on ch. xv. 9). "Mercy" (chesed) is the conduct towards others, animated by love and sympathy (see note on ch. iii. 3). Findeth life, righteousness, and honour. "Righteousness" here is the gift of God to his faithful servants, grace to live a holy life. This becomes habit, and forms the righteous character (Job xxix. 14; xxxiii. 26). "Life" is a long and prosperous life in the world (ch. iii. 16); "honour" is respect and reverence among fellow-men, and glory in another world. "Whom he justified, them he also glorified" (Rom. viii. 30). "Life and honour" stand together in ch. xxii. 4. "The fear of the Lord," says Siracides, "is honour, and glory, and gladness, and a crown of rejoicing . . . maketh a merry heart . . . and giveth long life" (Ecclus. i. 11, etc.). The LXX. omits the second "righteousness" by mistake: "The way of righteousness and mercy will find life and glory" (Matt. vi. 33).

Ver. 22.—A wise man scaleth the city of the mighty. The courage and strength of valiant men cannot defend a city against the skilful counsel of a wise strategist. And he casteth down the strength of the confidence thereof. He lays low the strength in which the defenders trusted; he not only takes the fortress, but also demolishes it. Wisdom is stronger than bodily might (ch. xx. 18. See the apologue, Eccles. ix. 14, etc.). Septuagint, "A wise man cometh upon strong cities, and casteth down the stronghold (καθεῖλε τὸ ὀχύρωμα) in which the ungodly trusted." Thus St. Paul, speaking of the weapons which God gives us to fight withal in the spiritual battle, says (2 Cor. x. 4) that they are "mighty before him to the casting down of strongholds (πρὸς καθαίρεσιν ὀχυρωμάτων)."

Ver. 23.—We have had similar maxims before (ch. xiii. 3 and xviii. 21, where see notes). He keepeth his mouth, who knows when to speak and when to be silent; and he keepeth his tongue, who says only what

is to the purpose. We have all heard the proverb, "Speech is silver, silence is gold." One who thus takes heed of his words, keepeth his soul from troubles. The troubles (angores, Vulgate) are such as these—remorse for the evil occasioned, distress of conscience, vexation and strife with offended neighbours, danger of liberty and life, and, above all, the anger of God, and retribution in the judgment.

Ver. 24.—Proud and haughty scorner is his name, who dealeth in proud wrath. (For "scorner" (לֵץ), the esprit fort, the free-thinking sceptic of Solomon's day, see notes on ch. i. 22 and xiv. 6.) The verse is better translated, A proud, arrogant man, scoffer is his name, who worketh in superfluity of pride. עֶבְרָה (ebrah), translated "wrath," denotes also want of moderation, excess, presumption (see note on ch. xi. 23). The proverb explains the meaning of the name, letz, given to these rationalists; their contempt of revealed religion proceeds from pride of intellect, which refuses instruction, and blinds the eyes to the truth. The warning comes home to us in these times, when the "higher criticism" too often runs into gross scepticism and infidelity. Septuagint, "A bold and self-willed and insolent man is called a pest (λοιμὸς), and he that remembers injuries is a transgressor."

Ver. 25.—The desire of the slothful killeth him. The craving for ease and rest, and the consequent disinclination for labour, prove fatal to the slothful man. Or, it may be, the mere wish, combined with no active exertion to secure its accomplishment, is fatal to soul, body, and fortune (comp. ch. xiii. 4; xix. 24). Lesètre quotes Bossuet, "Le paresseux spirituel s'expose aussi à la mort éternelle; car les bons désirs ne suffisient pas pour le salut; il faut encore les œuvres" (see Matt. vii. 21; Rom. ii. 13).

Ver. 26.—St. Jerome and many commentators connect this verse with the preceding, considering the two to form a tetrastich, thus: The desire of the slothful . . . he coveteth greedily all the day long, but the righteous giveth and spareth not. But in this division of our book there are only pure distichs; and, as Delitzsch observes, to make the contrast, one requires in the first hemistich an expression like, "and hath nothing" (ch. xiii. 4; comp. ch. xx. 4). So it is correct to consider this distich independent, and to translate, There is that (or one) desireth greedily always, but the righteous giveth and withholdeth not. There are claims made on all sides, demands for help, importunate prayers, such as one would think no man could satisfy; but the righteous has means enough and to spare, he is generous and charitable, he is industrious, and uses his stewardship well (Luke xvi. 9), and so arranges his expenditure that he has to give to him that needeth (Eph. iv. 28). Septuagint, "An ungodly man devises evil devices all the day long, but the righteous pitieth and showeth compassion unsparingly."

Ver. 27.—The first hemistich occurs in ch. xv. 8 (where see note). **How much more, when he bringeth it with a wicked mind!** rather, *for evil,* equivalent to "in order to atone for wickedness." The sacrifice of the sinner is abominable, as offered formally without repentance and faith; much more abominable, when he brings his offering to win, as it were, God's connivance in the sin which he commits and has no intention of renouncing,—brings it as a kind of bribe and recompense to compensate for his transgression. Such an outrage on God's purity and justice may well be called an abomination. Septuagint, "The sacrifices of the ungodly are abomination unto the Lord, for they offer them wickedly (παρανόμως)." The notion of propitiating the Deity by sharing with him the proceeds of sin is expressed in proverbial language. We have the homely saw, "Steal the goose, and give the giblets in alms;" and the Spaniards say, "Huerto el puerco, y dar los pies por Dios," "Steal the pig, and give away the pettitoes for God's sake" (Kelly). (See Ecclus. xxxi. 18, etc.)

Ver. 28.—(For the first hemistich, see ch. vi. 19; xix. 5, 9.) **Shall perish.** His testimony is worthless, and both he and it come to nothing. **The man that heareth speaketh constantly;** Vulgate, *vir obediens;* Septuagint, Ἀνὴρ ὑπήκοος φυλασσόμενος λαλήσει, "An obedient man will speak guardedly." "The man that heareth" is one who is attentive, who listens before he speaks, and reports only what he has heard. Such a one will speak "for continuance," so that what he says is never falsified, or silenced, or refuted. Vulgate, *loquetur victoriam.* And so Aquila, Theodotion, and Symmachus, εἰς νῖκος. Revised Version, *unchallenged.* The expression thus rendered is *lanetsach,* which means, in Hebrew at any rate, *in perpetuum,* "for continuance." But St. Jerome's rendering has been much used by the Fathers, who have drawn therefrom lessons of obedience. Thus St. Augustine, 'In Psalm.,' lxx., "Sola obedientia tenet palmam, sola inobedientia invenit pœnam." St. Gregory, 'Moral.,' xxxv. 28, "An obedient man in truth speaketh of victories, because, when we humbly submit ourselves to the voice of another, we overcome ourselves in our heart" (Oxford transl.). See a long dissertation on obedience in the note of Corn. à Lapide on this passage of Proverbs.

Ver. 29.—**A wicked man hardeneth his face; is shameless (as ch. vii. 13), and is insensible to rebuke or any soft feeling.** This obduracy he shows with his countenance. Septuagint, "An ungodly man shamelessly withstands with his face." **But as for the upright, he directeth his way.** He gives it the right direction (2 Chron. xxvii. 6). This is the reading of the Khetib, יָכִין but, though generally adopted by the versions (except the Septuagint), it does not make a suitable antithesis to the rash stubbornness of the wicked. Hence modern commentators prefer the reading of the Keri, יָבִין, "he considereth, proveth," his way; he acts only after due thought, giving proper weight to all circumstances. Septuagint, "But the upright man himself understands (συνιεῖ) his ways." The contrast lies in the audacious self-confidence of the unprincipled man, and the calm circumspection and prudence of the saint.

Ver. 30.—**There is no wisdom, nor understanding, nor counsel against the Lord;** *i.e.* in opposition to him, which can be compared with his, or which can avail against him (comp. Job v. 13; Ps. xxxiii. 10, 11; Isa. xxix. 14; 1 Cor. i. 20; iii. 19). Septuagint, "There is no wisdom, there is no courage (ἀνδρεία), there is no counsel, in respect of the ungodly;" πρὸς τὸν ἀσεβῆ, *neged Jahve,* being taken as "that which is against Jahve," equivalent to "impious." Wordsworth quotes Horace, 'Carm.,' iii. 6. 5, etc.—

"Dis te minorem quod geris, imperas:
Hinc omne principium, huc refer exitum."

The following verse carries on and applies the import of this one: As men's wisdom is nothing worth, equally vain is all trust in external means and appliances.

Ver. 31.—**The horse is prepared against the day of battle.** The horse is an emblem of military power and activity. To the earlier Jews, who were unaccustomed to its use, and indeed forbidden to employ it (Deut. xvii. 16), the horse and horse-drawn chariots were objects of extreme terror (Josh. xvii. 16; Judg. iv. 3), and though Solomon had largely imported them from Egypt (1 Kings iv. 26; x. 26, etc.), these animals were used exclusively for war, and, at this time, their services were never applied to agricultural purposes. The proverb asserts that, though all preparations are made for the battle, and material forces are of the best and strongest description, but **safety** (*victory*) **is of the Lord** (see Ps. xx. 7; xxxiii. 16, etc.). Septuagint, "But from the Lord is the help (ἡ βοήθεια)." The great truth here taught may be applied to spiritual matters. The only safety against spiritual enemies is the grace of God; we can cry, with St. Paul (1 Cor. xv. 57), "Thanks be to God, which giveth us the victory through our Lord Jesus Christ." "By the name 'horse,'" says St. Gregory ('Moral.,' xxxi. 43), " is understood the preparation of right intention, as it is written, 'The horse is pre- | pared,' etc. ; because the mind prepares itself indeed against temptation, but contends not healthfully unless it be assisted from above."

HOMILETICS.

Ver. 5.—*Patient industry.* The contrast between diligence and haste suggests the idea that there must be an element of patience and perseverance in the former if it is to be crowned with success. This may be very different from the Herculean efforts of genius, which astonish the world with spasms of effort and then sink into indifference. It is a quiet, constant, persistent activity. We are to see how much this is superior to the more flashy performances which are not seconded by diligence.

I. PATIENT INDUSTRY IN COMMERCE. This is the direct opposite of the gambler's method. The terrible evil of gambling has not been sufficiently weighed. Its awful temptations, its widespread influence, the frightful moral havoc it is making in all classes of society, are not yet appreciated ; for if those evils were duly considered, all who are concerned about the welfare of England would start up in horror at the sight of a stupendous cause of ruin that is rampant in our midst. One of our leading judges has pronounced gambling to be the greatest national evil of England. Now, the spirit of gambling is seen in trade, and the Stock Exchange is with many no better than a huge betting-saloon. The greedy race for wealth makes men reckless. But experience shows that it is highly dangerous. The solid success of business men is not attained in this way. The lives of such men as George Moore and Samuel Morley show that honourable industry is a better road to wealth. Even when riches are not acquired— and but a few can ever win the prizes—it is the road of safety and peace. This means self-denial, hard work, patient waiting, courage under adverse circumstances. In these respects the difference between success and failure depends on our character and effort. When a man is in calm earnest his very thoughts are fertile.

II. PATIENT INDUSTRY IN LEARNING. There is a temptation for beginners to seek some royal road to knowledge; but it has never yet been found. The true student must "scorn delights, and live laborious days." Genius may be more than an unlimited capacity for hard work ; but assuredly the highest genius will fail of its best fruits if it be swathed in indolence. The lives of great men are nearly always lives of hard-working men. Old-fashioned scholarship may appear less tempting than a short cut to popularity over the flowery fields of literary smartness. But the notoriety that is won so easily is an empty bubble that vanishes at a touch. Study, thought, intellectual industry, will always secure more solid and enduring rewards.

III. PATIENT INDUSTRY IN CHRISTIAN WORK. The modern temptation is to snatch at superficial success. An empty popular style and light attractive methods seem to secure results that are denied to more serious conscientious labours. But such a success is a rotten fruit, worthless, and soon ending in shame and bitterness. It is the duty of all who undertake Christian work to adapt it to the people. It is useless to preach if none will come to hear. The preacher ought to try to interest and win his congregation. There is no merit in dulness. The diligent must have his "thoughts." St. Paul was too wise to waste his efforts in "beating the air" (1 Cor. ix. 26). But the main efforts must be serious, persistent, persevering. If the seed is sown deeply, it will be slow to show itself; but it will be safely buried in the soil. In the mission field patient industry succeeds, while more exciting and hasty efforts only end in an ultimate collapse.

Ver. 10.—*Desiring evil.* I. MEN'S DESIRES ARE DETERMINED BY THEIR NATURES. Good men have good desires, and bad men bad desires. No doubt natural desires may spring up in an innocent heart under circumstances which forbid the satisfaction of them without sin. Only so can one be tempted as Christ was tempted, *i.e.* without sin. Some indeed have maintained that even Christ, in becoming a partaker of "sinful flesh" (Rom. viii. 3), actually took upon him a sinful nature, which he purged and redeemed. But we have no scriptural or historical evidence of any such transactions in the Person of Christ. 1. *We must distinguish, therefore, between desires suggested and desires encouraged.* The first may be brought by the tempter to the innocent. It is in the case of the second that the desires become signs of sin. 2. *Many desires are in themselves sinful.* Such desires find no place in a pure heart. The very fact that they exist is an evidence of indwelling sin.

II. THE WORST NATURES ARE THOSE THAT DESIRE EVIL FOR ITS OWN SAKE. 1. *It is possible to be surprised into sin* without having previously cherished any desire for it. It is a darker thing to sin deliberately, after nursing the vile project and waiting long for an opportunity to carry it out. 2. Or it may be that the desire is for *some definite object which is thought to be attractive on its own account.* Then there is no wish to sin; on the contrary, the fact that there is no reaching the goal without transgressing the law of righteousness may be regarded with regret. The desire is gratified in spite of its sinfulness, not because of its sinfulness. 3. The worst state is that of *desiring the sin,* loving evil, finding a fascination in it—of two paths choosing the downward just because it descends. This is diabolic wickedness.

III. EVIL DESIRES ARE SINFUL. This is the clear teaching of Christ (Matt. v. 28). 1. They are sinful as *indicating a wicked heart.* The bad fruit condemns the bad tree. The world may not detect the hidden fires of suppressed desire; but they are known to the All-seeing. 2. They are sinful as *showing the exercise of sin;* i.e. if they are entertained. When we resist and seek to crush evil desires, this second stage of sinfulness is not reached. But brooding over them and giving them good room to live and grow in the heart add to their guilt. 3. They are sinful as *leading to wicked deeds.* Evil desires are seeds buried in the soul. Left to themselves and unchecked, they are sure to grow up and reveal their badness in wicked conduct.

IV. EVIL DESIRES SHOULD BE CHECKED AT ONCE. The above considerations should show us that it would be wrong to wait until the desires had reached the outer door of action in the world. They should be checked for various reasons. 1. Because they are *already evil.* Even if we were sure that we could always keep them secret and inoperative, their natural and present wickedness makes it incumbent on us to destroy them. The snake should be destroyed, though it lurks hidden in the thicket. 2. Because they can be *most readily destroyed in an early stage.* It is easier to kill the young brood in the nest than to slay the monsters when they have grown to full size. 3. Because they will be *beyond our control* when they have issued in actions. Deeds are irrevocable; but desires can be suppressed. Therefore men need the grace of Christ before they have fallen into actual sin. The best form of redemption is for the heart to be cleansed from its evil desires.

Ver. 13.—*Ignoring the cry of the poor.* I. THE SIN. 1. *The cry of the poor is exceedingly bitter.* It may not be clamorous, but it is grievous. There is no more pressing problem for society in the present day than the question how to deal with the wretched, overcrowded, poverty-stricken quarters of our great cities. (1) The evil is *widespread.* It concerns the misery of tens of thousands of people. (2) It is *intense.* No one who has not inquired into the subject can conceive of the depth of misery that it represents—pale children crying for bread, weary women heart-sick with despair, strong men enfeebled with hunger and embittered with the sight of wealth that seems to mock their misery. The wonder is that the poor bear their hard lot so patiently that the world of wealth scarcely heeds it. (3) It is *moral.* Overcrowding, ignorance, and despair, lead to gross moral degradation, drunkenness, reckless animalism, brutality, hatred, and outrage. 2. *It is our duty to hear this bitter cry.* The very poor are our fellow-men—our brothers and sisters. Only the Cains among us can dare to ask, "Am I my brother's keeper?" Christ has bidden us to love our neighbour as ourselves, and in the parable of the good Samaritan he has shown who is our neighbour. We cannot pass by on the other side without guilt in the sight of God. 3. *The neglect of this bitter cry is wilful.* The sin is that of a man who "stoppeth his ears." It is true he does not now hear the cry. But he is not the less guilty, for he refuses to hear it. There is a culpable ignorance. Well-to-do people may say that they do not know of the miserable condition of their brethren. It is the more shameful that they are thus ignorant. It is their duty to inquire into it. If the West End luxuriates in pleasures while the East End toils and starves in misery, the more fortunate section of society has ample means of ascertaining the condition of the unhappy portion. Heedless indifference is cruel selfishness.

II. THE PUNISHMENT. "He also shall cry himself, but shall not be heard." 1. *His own circumstances may bring him into distress.* We see strange reverses of fortune. Some of the most wretched denizens of the lowest quarters were once in affluent circumstances. The breaking of a bank, the failure of a mine, the losses of speculation, the ruin of gambling, may bring a wealthy man down to destitution. Then if he has encouraged the neglect of the poor by his conduct in more fortunate days, he will suffer from the bad social custom that he has helped to foster. 2. *A social revolution may bring fearful punishment on the scornful who now neglect the cry of their brethren.* So it was in France a hundred years ago. There are not wanting signs that the whole civilization of Europe may be endangered by a huge social upheaval. The scandalous inequality of lots is glaringly apparent to all, and the privileges of the few may be ruthlessly torn from them in the interest of the many. If the volcano overflows there will be little respect for vested interests, abstract rights, or personal claims. But if we dread a violent revolution which might shatter the whole fabric of civilization, we must attend to the cry of poverty. To disregard this is to sit on the safety-valve while we wait for the coming explosion. 3. *In the future world the cry of the cruel and negligent will be unheeded.* Dives in torment cries in vain for Lazarus to cool his burning tongue. He is the very type of those who stop their ears against the cry of the poor. His punishment is to suffer from a similar neglect.

Ver. 17.—*The love of pleasure.* The love of pleasure is here described as a cause of poverty. No doubt this was meant to refer to physical destitution. But we cannot fail to see many other forms of poverty resulting from the same foolish infatuation.

I. IT IMPOVERISHES A MAN'S PURSE. This direct meaning of the text is not without its value. No man desires to come down in the social scale and to lose the comforts of life. But least of all will the pleasure-lover welcome such a prospect. High-minded, unselfish, unworldly men submit to the loss of all things, and "count them but dung" for the sake of some noble end. The pleasure-lover is not of this category. To him earthly loss must be a terrible infliction. Therefore, while the text may be of use for all, it is a direct *argumentum ad hominem* for such a person. Now, experience proves the truth of it. 1. For pleasure a man *neglects his business.* In the present day of hard competition such folly is fatal. 2. Many pleasures are *costly.* They cannot be had without great expenditure, and the passion for them leads to reckless extravagance. 3. Some pleasures *destroy the business powers of a man.* They are literally dissipations. Brain and nerves are weakened, and the degraded slave of self-indulgence becomes a wreck, unable to fight the stern battle of life. The drunkard is incompetent. The dissolute man is lacking in business promptness and energy. Other men will not trust the pleasure-seeker, and so business forsakes him. 4. There are pleasures that *directly impoverish.* Gambling—now so fearfully prevalent—is a direct road to poverty.

II. IT IMPOVERISHES A MAN'S INTELLECT. Even though the pleasure-seeker be prudent enough to preserve his fortune from shipwreck, or so exceedingly wealthy that he cannot easily squander all his possessions, he may and he will impoverish himself. Though he may always have money in his purse, his own mind will be emptied of all worthy possessions. The love of pleasure directly weakens the intellect. The physical effect of dissipation impoverishes the brain. The exciting distractions of a life of gaiety destroy the powers of deep, continuous thinking. The mind is thus wasted away in frivolity. The pleasure-seeker will not have patience to study solid literature, to think out great truths, to discuss with serious men grave questions of life and death. Exciting novels and plays will be his staple intellectual food, and the result will be mental ruin.

III. IT IMPOVERISHES A MAN'S HEART. The pleasure-seeker is often supposed to be a good-natured man because he is a genial companion. No doubt many loose-living, self-indulgent men have shown great generosity to their friends. But that is because they are not given up to pure pleasure-seeking. In itself pleasure-seeking is selfish, hard, cruel. The Romans of the old empire made a fine art of the cultivation of pleasure, and they became monsters of cruelty. The tortures of the amphitheatre furnished them with the most exquisite delights. Pleasure-loving Roman ladies treated their poor slave-girls with heartless cruelty. It is a gross mistake to suppose that kindliness goes with pleasure-seeking, and that its opposite is a sour, ill-natured Puritanism.

IV. IT IMPOVERISHES A MAN'S SOUL. The greatest loss is not that of money, nor even that of thought or heart. The chief treasure which the pleasure-lover loses is the pearl of great price—the kingdom of heaven. He may gain the whole world, but he loses his own soul. Pleasure-seeking destroys the spiritual faculties. It is not required that the Christian should be an ascetic, denying himself innocent delights, nor is it to be supposed that all pleasures are evil. The evil is the *love* of pleasure. Even the love of pleasures that are innocent in themselves may be the rock on which a soul is ruined, if this be the supreme passion of that soul, eclipsing the love of God.

Ver. 31.—*National defence.* The Jews were repeatedly warned against keeping cavalry. Cavalry were for pitched battles, and could only be used on the plains. But the old successful Jewish warfare was among the hills. As a question of military tactics, the advice meant that it was better for the Jews to act on the defensive in their impregnable strongholds than to descend into the field for open warfare. A deeper thought was that, while defensive warfare might sometimes be required, the Jews were not to embroil themselves in the affairs of their neighbours. This was especially desirable for a little state wedged in between the two great empires of Egypt and Assyria, like Afghanistan between Russia and India. A still deeper and more momentous thought has yet to be reached. The Jews were to learn that their true defence was not in armies, not in military prowess, not in naturally strong fortresses. God was their Rock and Tower of strength. Now, we have no reason to consider that the idea which was brought out in the history of Israel with magnificent emphasis applies to that little ancient race alone. It is true of every nation that will recognize God, that "safety is of the Lord." We undergo periodical panics concerning our national dangers. It would be well if we could rise to the position urged upon Israel by the teachers of Old Testament days.

I. OBSERVE HOW SAFETY COMES FROM GOD. 1. *By a providential control of events.* God delivered Israel from Egypt by opening a path through the Red Sea. He saved Jerusalem from Sennacherib by the sword of the destroying angel. He protected England from the Spanish Armada by the tempest that strewed the coast of Norway with the wrecks of Spanish galleons. When no such marked events occur, God can save his people by the quiet, unseen control of the course of history. 2. *By a Divine influence exerted over the minds of men.* God is in the secret counsels of the most astute statesmen. He can suggest and direct their thoughts and plans. He can awaken conscience in the reckless invader, and allay the passions of the enraged enemy. Thus God saved Jacob from Esau. 3. *By help given to the attacked in the hour of danger.* God's interference may be so as to guide and strengthen those who trust in him, and so to lead them on to safety. There is much to be done through wise counsels, righteous decisions, and brave, true actions. These God can inspire. 4. *By final deliverance from all trouble.* (1) After death. God's people may be killed; yet he will save them and take them home to himself. (2) On earth. National deliverance may come after national calamity. It may be just and right and necessary that a fearful defeat should come. Yet God may bring ultimate salvation—a rising up of the fallen from their shame and distress.

II. CONSIDER HOW SAFETY MAY BE OBTAINED FROM GOD. We have no right to believe ourselves to be privileged people whom God will favour in preference to Russia, or France, or Germany. All the nations are cared for by God, and no nation can be assured of his protection without pursuing the right means to find it. We have no right to pray that God will scatter our enemies, if they are in the right, and our's are the "knavish tricks." How, then, is safety to be found in God? 1. *By acting justly towards our neighbours.* God will never protect us when we are wronging another nation. 2. *By living at peace with God.* If our conduct at home is inimical to God, we cannot expect him to defend us in the field. Godlessness in peace will bring God-desertion in war. National sin will alienate the protection of God. The first step must be national repentance. 3. *By trusting God.* If we are reconciled to God, and seeking to do the right, we can pray for his help, and believe we shall have it, with our armies if they must be called out; but, better far, without them, in maintaining peace.

HOMILIES BY VARIOUS AUTHORS.

Vers. 1—3.—*The providence and government of God.* I. THE DIVINE CONTROL OF HUMAN PURPOSES. (Ver. 1.) As the streams of water are led by canals and trenches through the land, that it may be refreshed and fructified, so are the thoughts and counsels of the ruler, if wise and true, a means of strength and blessing to the people. And all such wise counsels are of God. He forms and turns the purposes of the heart, as the potter with the clay. To Cyrus he says, "I have called thee by name, have surnamed thee, though thou hast not known me" (Isa. xlv. 4. See Dr. Bushnell's fine sermon on this text in 'The New Life'). II. ALL HUMAN ACTIONS ARE WEIGHED IN THE SCALES OF DIVINE JUDGMENT. (Ver. 2.) We can say little about *motives*; we may be blind to our own, but God is not. Hence the duty of *pondering* (notice the original meaning of the word) our own doings and plans, *weighing* them, that is, in the scales of a judgment enlightened by his holy Word. III. THE TRUE DIVINE SERVICE. (Ver. 3.) There is an *outward* and an *inward* side of the religious life. The outward, viz. ritual and moral conduct, is only of value as it is an expression of true desires in the heart. The inward worship of God in spirit and in truth (John iv. 24) must precede and accompany the outward worship, or the latter is nothing worth (ch. xv. 8; Ps. l. 7, *sqq.*; 1 Sam. xv. 22; Micah vi. 6—8).—J.

Vers. 4—9.—*A family of vices.* There is a kinship between all vices as between all virtues. All sins spring from a disturbance of our true relations to God, as all virtues rest upon the deep consciousness of that relation. I. THE SIN OF PRIDE. (Ver. 4.) Its *aspect*—the lofty eyes, the haughty glance—and its principle in the heart are struck by the Divine rebuke. The meaning of the second clause is not quite clear; probably it is, "The light of the wicked is only sin," *i.e.* his haughty and overweening temper is compared to a flaming or a lurid light, contrasted with the mild serene ray that seems to stream from a good man's life. II. THE VICE OF COVETOUSNESS. (Ver. 5.) Shown by an eager and selfish haste to obtain the wealth which Providence has apportioned only as the reward of pains-taking toil. Religion teaches us moderation, *measure* in all things. "Unhasting, unresting," expresses the measure of diligence in all our life-business. III. THE USE OF DISHONEST MEANS. (Ver. 6.) This can never lead to aught but a *seeming* success (see the exegesis of this passage). "Man is a shadow's dream," said Pindar. "What shadows we are! and what shadows we pursue!" said a great Englishman. But of none is the word more true than of him who seeks gain at the expense of inner truth, profit by the loss of the soul! IV. VIOLENT DEEDS. (Ver. 7.) All violence recoils upon the perpetrator. The desolation which godless men bring upon others finally carries away themselves. No one who persistently sets himself against right can stand, can abide, for right is the very foundation and constitution of things in the order of God. And so of *criminality* or *impurity* in general (ver. 8). It is a crooked way, a twisted web. Perplexities, miserable intricacies of doubt, are generally to be traced to the fault of the will; and the straightforward man is he who walks by the light of a pure heart. V. THE CONTENTIOUS TEMPER. (Ver. 9.) It unfits for society. It makes the home intolerable. The vexing, captious, irritable temper makes a solitude around it, and calls it peace. The very idea of the Christian household is peace. Wherever struggle may be necessary, it is certainly out of place there. Let us seek the "things that make for peace"—these first and foremost. Every wife, mother, daughter, should be in reality, if not in name, a "Salome!" ("a peaceful one").—J.

Vers. 10—13.—*Lessons and warnings from life-experience.* I. THE MERCILESSNESS OF EVIL DESIRE. (Ver. 10.) There is nothing more cruel than unbridled appetite of any kind. All bad desires are perversions of self-love, and men thus became " hateful and hating one another." It is the grace of God which converts the selfish imagina-tion, ever fixed on one narrow object, to the all-embracing imagination which is neces-sary to the fulfilment of the "golden rule" (Matt. vii. 12)

II. The lessons of punishment and of reward. (Vers. 11, 12.) Daily life is full of this contrast, will we but heed its warnings. When the evil meet their just doom, let us say with the psalmist, "Thou puttest away the wicked of the earth like dross; therefore I love thy testimonies" (Ps. cxix. 119). And not less when the wise and good are made happy (this is the sense of the next clause) let us own the hand of him who pronounces concerning every good deed, "It shall in no wise lose its reward."

III. Retribution on the hard heart. (Ver. 13.) The pitiless man closes the door of pity against himself in the time of need. If the cries of the poor are not heard *by us*, they will be heard *against us* (Exod. xxii. 23; Matt. xviii. 30—34). The parable of the unmerciful servant is the best commentary on this text.—J.

Vers. 14—17.—*Lights and shades of the earthly scene.* I. The power of gifts. (Ver. 14.) They are neither good nor evil in themselves, but may be employed for good or evil ends. Let us make a *good* use of this text. We learn that gifts should be *quiet, unobtrusive, unobserved*; and the same is true of all acts of kindness, which are real gifts from the heart. They should neither irritate pride nor depress independence. By such little attentions and marks of love, how much evil may be warded off, how many asperities of temper or circumstance may be soothed!

II. Delight in or disgust for right conduct. (Ver. 15.) There is no joy in the world to be compared for depth and purity to that of the good conscience; no exercise that brings so much health and pleasure as acting rightly and doing good. But the corrupt mind of evil men can take no delight in looking at goodness, in contemplating pure and noble conduct. For the consequences can only be the judgment and punishment of their own iniquity.

III. The end of all moral observations. (Ver. 16.) One of the most solemn passages of the Bible. Taken literally or figuratively, of the present or of the future, they contain a *statement*, a *prophecy*, a *fact*. The wicked and unrepentant pass into a night without the hope of a sunrise to follow.

IV. The end of idle and frivolous mirth. (Ver. 17.) He that will squander more than his plough can earn must utterly waste (Sirach viii. 32). *Magnum vectigal est parsimonia*, or "Economy is income;" "Waste not, want not." "Better than merry Nineveh" is recorded as an old proverb (see Zeph. ii. 15).—J.

Vers. 18—20.—*Alternatives presented to choice.* I. The just and upright, the faithless and wicked life. (Ver. 18.) It occurs in many cases that the Divine wrath in judgment turns aside from the just man to roll upon the head of the sinner. See this in a *natural* light in Isa. xliii. 3, and in the great Christian light of redemption (2 Cor. v. 21; 1 Pet. iii. 18). Christ became *as* sin, or in the place of the sinner, for us. We must not, however, confuse the evident meaning of the text, which is that in critical moments of calamity the faithful minority appear to escape unscathed; and the lesson that righteousness alone is safe.

II. Solitude or unpleasant society. (Ver. 19; see on ver. 9.)

III. Wise storing or foolish squandering. (Ver. 20.) Thrift and economy give meetness to every home enjoyment they purchase. Waste is without zest, and brings positive dishonour.—J.

Vers. 21—23.—*The wise and the loving life.* I. It is an ardent enthusiastic life. (Ver. 21.) Literally, he who *hunts after* justice and love *will find life, righteousness, and honour*. So in other figures—of hungering and thirsting, of digging eagerly for hid treasures, etc.—the earnest enthusiasm of the true life is depicted.

II. It is a life of present possession and enjoyment. So in the New Testament (Rom. iii. 26; Gal. iii. 21).

III. The resistless power of wisdom. (Ver. 22.) The like penetrative power to that which we ascribe to the subtlest forces of nature—heat, magnetism, etc.—is possessed, but in a higher degree, by the intelligence and the will of man. The barriers of time and space seem to fall before him who *knows* and him who *loves*. Let none rely on walls and fastnesses. What man's hands have raised man's hands can break to pieces. We are truly strong only by means of the arts and works of intelligence and love.

IV. THE SAFETY OF THE PRUDENT TONGUE. (Ver. 23.) As one quaintly says, "God, as the Creator, has placed a double wall before the mouth—the teeth and lips, to show that we ought to use and guard the tongue with all care." "He that hath a satirical vein, as he maketh others afraid of his wit, so he had need to be afraid of others' memory." "Discretion of speech is more than eloquence; and to speak agreeably with him with whom we deal is more than to speak in good words or in good order" (Bacon).—J.

Vers. 24—26.—*The process of vice.* I. VICES HANG TOGETHER LIKE THE LINKS OF A CHAIN. (Ver. 24.) Contempt is born of pride, wrath of contempt, and from wrath scoffing and manifold injuries.

II. IDLENESS LIES IN CLOSE AFFINITY TO MANY VICES. (Vers. 25, 26.) We have here a brief anatomy of idleness. It is wishing without corresponding exertion. The idle man would rather sit still and starve than set his hand or head to painful toil. He would live by wishing. The effort to rise from the easy-chair, to take the hand from the bosom, is too great for him; hence he is consumed with vain desires. The hope of enjoyment is out of reach, though not out of sight, for want of exertion. In religion *mere* wishes, idle prayers, will not bring us good. The knocking and seeking must go with the asking. And again (ver. 26), in this analysis we are reminded of the selfishness which is at the root of this indolence. In contrast to a habit of coveting for self, we have the hand of the righteous man, who "gives and spares not." Willing labour, surrender of time and thought for others' good,—this, indeed, enriches the soul, and the man who waters others waters himself, and is a "blessing in the land."—J.

Vers. 27—31.—*The just judgments of the Eternal.* I. ON RELIGIOUS ACTS. (Ver. 27; ch. xv. 8.) The hypocrisy of devotion, the play-acting of religion, is as hideous a sight as true worship is beautiful. All the conditions of genuine worship are wanting in the bad man; there is no *heart*, no *way of access*, no faith (Bridges). We have scriptural examples in Balaam (Numb. xxiii.), Saul (1 Sam. xiii.), Absalom (2 Sam. xv.), Jezebel, the Pharisees. Compare the terrible invective of Isaiah (i.) against those who come with hands full of blood to worship and offer vain oblations.

II. ON FALSEHOOD. (Ver. 28.) Compare the ninth commandment. "The essence of a lie is the intention to deceive." But *exaggeration*, the vice of those who perpetually talk for talking's sake, seems also pointed at. The second clause describes the quality of the trustworthy witness. To hear before we speak; and witness to nothing but what we have heard and seen and known to be true. It is more from carelessness about truth than unintentional falsehood, that there is so much untruth in the world (Dr. Johnson).

III. ON INSOLENCE AND PRESUMPTION. (Ver. 29.) *Effrontery*, which assumes the brazen brow upon guilt. There was nothing among the heathen which was thought more to expose a man to the wrath of Heaven than presumption. The picture of the opposite temper is given as a willing docility to rebuke, anxiety for improvement, which brings honour in the sight of God and of man. Insolent presumption would force its will and way in spite of God; true humility would seek direction in its way by the will of God. Ver. 30 reminds us of the folly and presumption of vain human creatures to lift themselves up in rivalry to heaven. Earthly greatness, state policy, pride, stoical firmness, avail nothing against the Divine wisdom and the eternal will. Entire obedience and resignation are our duty and our safety. May all our doings be begun, continued, and ended in God! There is no success without God (ver. 31). The horse may be ready for the battle, the "powder may be dry," but all is vain unless his blessing has been sought and gained; and this cannot be unless our enterprise is just. Never act without dependence on God, nor without attention to the appropriate means of success.—J.

Ver. 1.—*Human power and Divine direction.* The course of human affairs impresses, we might perhaps say *oppresses*, us with the thought—

I. HOW MUCH POWER IS IN ONE MAN'S HAND. We shall always have kings amongst us—of one kind or another. They may not bear that name; they may not occupy the precise social position indicated by the word; but there will always be men who will exercise such distinguished power and hold such eminent position that they will be "as kings," if they are not so called by their fellows. God endows us very differently, and he puts it in the power of a few to wield commanding influence, to rise to high rank, to sway a wide and powerful control over their countrymen. And it has often been a matter for serious concern that, to a very large extent indeed, the prosperity and well-being of an entire people has rested with the decision of, has been held in the balance by, a single hand. Then we naturally think that—

II. How HIS HAND WILL MOVE DEPENDS UPON· HIS HEART. As the heart feels the hand directs. Behaviour is the outcome of character. Given a stern, insensitive heart, and we count on a hard and cruel policy ; but given a kind and considerate heart, and we reckon on a just and humane career. A country has therefore the deepest interest in the character of its rulers, as it has in the moral and spiritual condition of its leaders in any and every sphere of thought and action. We therefore gladly remember that—

III. THE HEART OF THE POWERFUL IS IN THE HAND OF GOD. "As rivers of water he turneth it," etc. In the formation of this globe, in the arrangement of land and water, in the upbuilding of the great mountains, in the cutting of the fruitful plains, in the tracing of the fertilizing streams, we recognize the hand of God. He has used a great variety of agencies to bring about all these and all such results ; but everything on the surface of the globe bears the impress of his wise hand. The rivers do not run where they list—they flow along the water-courses which his wisdom has arranged. And so with the hearts of the great and the strong, of the king and the counsellor, of the warrior and the minister. God has access to them ; he can as easily touch and affect them in their thoughts and judgments as he can determine the channels in which the springs shall run. He can arrest them in their purpose; he can change or even reverse their course. Our human minds, as well as all material objects, are subject to his sway, and own the touch of his controlling hand. Therefore we conclude that—

IV. WE NEVER NEED DESPAIR, BUT SHOULD ALWAYS HOPE. For in the darkest hour we know that we have one resource. When we can touch no other human or earthly springs, we can make our appeal to God. We can seek to "move the hand which moves the universe," and which "turneth the hearts of kings whithersoever he will." We are sure that : 1. God is never regardless of, or indifferent to, the course which his strong sons are taking. 2. He is ruling the world in the interest of righteousness. 3. He is willing, and indeed wishful, to be sought by those who love and trust him. Let the people of God, therefore, cherish hope in the midst of dire trouble and impending evil ; and let the enemies of God beware. One touch of the Divine finger, and their fine fabric of oppression falls instantly to the ground.—C.

Ver. 2.—(See homily on ch. xvi. 2.)—C.

Ver. 3.—*Devotion and duty.* It is certainly noticeable that this truth should be expressed by Solomon. For the one great work of his life was the erection of the temple wherein sacrifice should be offered to the Lord. He might have been excused if his leaning had been toward the ceremonial rather than the moral. But he was not the first Hebrew thinker to give utterance to the idea. It is interesting to trace—

I. ITS HISTORY IN HEBREW THOUGHT. We find : 1. Samuel holding this view, and declaring it in firm and powerful language (1 Sam. xv. 22). 2. David filled with a deep sense of it as he humbled his soul before God (Ps. li. 10, 15—19). 3. Asaph powerfully affected by it as he wrote his sacred song (Ps. l. 8—15). 4. Isaiah, Jeremiah, and Micah insisting upon this truth in strong and fervent words (Isa. i. 11—17; Jer. vii. 22, 23 ; Micah vi. 6—8). 5. John the Baptist making nothing of ceremonial religion, and making everything of a true and genuine repentance. 6. Our Lord himself, by his teaching and his attitude, preferring the penitent publican and harlot to the much-sacrificing but hard-hearted Pharisee ; while by his own sacrificial death he removed for ever the need of any further offering on any altar whatsoever. 7. His inspired apostles declaring the needlessness of any sacrifice except those which are of a spiritual order (Rom. xii. 1 ; Heb. ix. 28 ; x. 12 ; xiii. 15, 16).

II. ITS SIGNIFICANCE TO OURSELVES. We naturally ask—What is the relation of devotion to duty or righteousness? and we answer : 1. No measure of devotion can make up for moral laxity. We might be worshipping in the house of the Lord day and night; but if we were false, or cruel, or dishonest, or impure in our daily practice, we should certainly incur his righteous anger. 2. Moral probity by itself will not take the place of the direct approach of our hearts to God. It is much that a man should be just in all his dealings, kind in his various relationships, blameless in his bearing and behaviour—*very much*. But it is not everything; it leaves out one essential thing. God desires and demands of us that we ourselves come into close and living union and communion with himself, that we look to him and address him, and trust and love him as our Divine Father and Redeemer. And no propriety of behaviour, no excellency of life, will take the place of this. 3. Devotion and duty must coexist, and will sustain one another. (1) We should so worship God that we shall be stronger to obey his commandments in the home and in the school and in the shop—everywhere. We may safely conclude that our sacrifice on the sabbath is altogether imperfect and unsatisfactory if it does not lead to a worthier life in the week. (2) And we should so act in all the various paths of life that " with clean hands and a pure heart" we can go up to the house of the Lord, and render acceptable service of prayer and praise as we bow before him in the sanctuary. They are complementary one to the other; and no wise man will disregard or disparage either.—C.

Ver. 5.—(See homily on ch. xxvii. 23.)—C.

Vers. 6—8.—*Marks of sin.* Here we have four marks of that many-sided evil which God condemns as sin.

I. ITS MANIFOLDNESS OF FORM. Of its varied developments we have four forms here specified. 1. *Falsehood*, with a view to temporal enrichment, or the sin of cheating—a crime which has dishonoured the markets and counting-houses of every land. 2. *Violence*, with the same end in view—the breaking into the neighbour's treasury, or the assault committed on his person. 3. *Injustice*, or the sin of withholding from our neighbour that which we know is his due; whether it be a weekly wage (Jas. v. 4), or whether it be the appointment to which he is entitled by his merit, or the honour he has gained by his services. 4. *Perversity*, or frowardness—the attitude of wanton and determined rebelliousness against God's rule, or insubmission to his claim, or disobedience of his particular commandment.

II. THE UNSUBSTANTIAL NATURE OF ITS SUCCESS. Enrichment by falsehood is " a vanity [or, ' a vapour '] tossed to and fro." It is proverbial that wealth that is ill-gotten is quickly lost; this is to be accounted for by the action of God's righteous punitive laws apart from the doctrine that sin commands his condemnation. Independently of this, it is certain that the satisfaction which comes from sin is short-lived and continually declines. Sin allures its victims with fine promises, but it breaks every one of them; its bread may be sweet for a moment, but " afterwards the mouth is filled with gravel" (ch. xx. 17). The hope of the sinner is very fair, but soon comes the strong wind of penal law, and its castle is on the ground; it is " swept away " (ver. 7, Revised Version).

III. ITS SUICIDAL CHARACTER. These guilty ones are " of them that seek death." " Death is the wages of sin," and those who consciously live in sin and those (more especially) who know that this is so may be fitly spoken of as " seeking death." Suicide is not confined to those who deliberately take away their life with the pistol-shot, or the cup of poison, or the fatal plunge. It is a folly and a crime that is being committed day by day at the hearth and at the table, in the office and in the study. Men are transgressing those known laws of God on the observance of which life as well as health depends. They who live in conscious wrong-doing are determinately travelling toward death, and are guiltily " seeking " it.

IV. ITS DEEP AND WIDE DEPARTURE FROM THE HOLY PURPOSE OF GOD. The way of (the) man (of whom we are speaking) is " strange " (ver. 8). It is quite foreign to the thought and contrary to the will of God. He is saying, " Go not along this path; turn from it, and pass away." It is sin which has cut this path for the feet of the human traveller, and it is one which lies quite outside the King's highway. So strange is it to him, so alien to his purpose, so far from his present desire, that he is ever saying to his erring children, " Return, return ! " And he has made, in the gospel of his Son, a way of return and restoration. Indeed, it is his Son Jesus Christ who *is* " the Way." To know him and to love and serve him is to have our feet planted in " the path of life."—C.

Ver. 13.—*Sowing and reaping.* It is true, indeed, that as we sow we reap. It is not only true that God will in some way or other cause iniquity to suffer and righteousness to be recompensed, but we find that sin meets with its *appropriate* penalty, and worth with its *appropriate* reward. " *Whatsoever* a man soweth, *that* shall he also reap." We have an illustration of this in the text, as we find many others elsewhere.

I. INHUMANITY AND PITY. "Whoso stoppeth his ears," etc. Men will have no mercy on the merciless. Let a man be known to be hard-hearted, selfishly and cruelly indifferent to the distress of his neighbours, and when the time of his calamity comes he will discover that there is no eye to pity and no hand to help him. On the contrary, his misfortune will give a secret if not an open satisfaction. But let a man be pitiful and generous in the day of his prosperity, then when adversity overtakes him the hearts and the hands of many will open to sympathize and succour. The same principle is applicable to an evil which is similar though not quite so serious, and to its corresponding virtue, viz.—

II. SEVERITY AND LENIENCY. Our fellow-men will be sure to treat us with the same severity we impose on them. Austerity constantly begets austerity; it is not long before it hears the echo of its own harshness. Be down with rigid particularity on every offence you detect in your child, or your servant, or your neighbour, and you may reckon confidently on having the same unbending rigorousness of judgment applied to any deviation that can be discovered in yourself. But leniency brings forth leniency; charity is the beautiful mother of charity. Make every kind and just allowance as you judge your brother, and you shall have every extenuation granted you when your infirmity leads you into error. We have the same thing showing itself, the appropriateness and correspondence of the penalty or the reward to the offence or the virtue in—

III. GROSSNESS AND PURITY. "He that soweth to the flesh, *of the flesh* reaps corruption; and he that soweth to the Spirit, *of the Spirit* reaps life everlasting" (Gal. vi. 8). Bodily indulgence means bodily degeneration; spiritual culture means spiritual enlargement.

IV. GODLESSNESS AND GODLINESS. The man who lives without God has to do without God in life and at the end of life as well as he can. He has to dispense with all the comfort and support of the consciousness of God's favour and that Divine indwelling which only comes with faith and love. But he who walks with God and lives unto him enjoys all the unspeakable and inestimable advantages of the near presence, the gracious power, the continual comfort and succour of the Divine Spirit. As he sows, he reaps.—C.

Ver. 21.—*The successful search.* What a lamentable history might be written of human lives that would be correctly described as unsuccessful searches! Who, save the Omniscient One, can tell how many have lived and toiled, have struggled and suffered, in search of a goal which they never reached?—it may have been in business, or in the domain of the affections, or in the pursuit of art or of science, or in politics, or in exploration on land or sea. It is a thought of relief and comfort that no human life need be a failure—none, at least, on which the light of Divine truth has shone. It is also pleasant to think that the higher we aim the likelier we are to reach our mark. He who seeks satisfaction on the lower and grosser levels is most likely to fail; but he whose aspiration is toward wisdom and worth, toward goodness and God, is a seeker that will find—

I. THE TRUE QUEST OF A HUMAN HEART. Solomon speaks of "following after righteousness and mercy." These two words may be taken as covering the entire field of rectitude and love, being just in all our relations, and being animated by the spirit of kindness toward all with whom we have to do. Thus understood, they point to the endeavour of the human soul to find : 1. *Acceptance with the living God;* for there is no happy sense of rightness or rectitude until his favour has been secured, and we feel that we stand before him as those that are true and loyal, his faithful subjects, his reconciled children. 2. *Purity of heart and life*—deliverance from the power and bondage of sin, of the evil forces which stir within and which play around the soul. 3. *A course of honesty and equity* in the sight of man; such a regulation of conduct as will result in doing to others as we would that they should do to us, walking along the path which brings no regrets and no reproaches. 4. *A heart of kindness*; nourishing within ourselves the prevailing feeling of considerateness for others; the blessed faculty of forgetting our own personal tastes and preferences and passing interests in order to remember the wants and well-being of our friends and our fellow-men; the mental and spiritual habit of sympathizing with sorrow and succouring need with an open and a willing hand.

II. THE WAY TO THE GOAL. We who have learnt of Christ need not miss our way; we may, and (if we are in earnest) we shall, find all that we seek. We shall attain to: 1. *Righteousness.* (1) Acceptance with God, being right with him by faith in Jesus Christ (Rom. v. 1, 2; viii. 1). (2) The growth within us of those virtues and graces which come with the service of the holy Lord, with the study and the love of the sinless Friend, with prayer for the sanctifying influences of the indwelling Spirit. 2. *Life*; for he that lives thus unto God, who is becoming daily like God, who is rejoicing in the friendship of God, does *live* indeed. *This is life*—life spiritual, Divine, eternal. 3. *Honour.* No small share of the honour which comes from those whose esteem is worth possessing; and in the end the honour which will come from the appraising and approving Lord, when he says, "Well done!" to his faithful servants.—C.

Ver. 22.—(See homily on vers. 29—31.)—C.

Ver. 27.—(See homily on ch. xv. 8.)—C.

Vers. 29—31 (with ver. 22).—*The achievements and limitations of wisdom.* There is great virtue in wisdom; Solomon never wearies of praising it. Here he adds another commendation, but he calls attention to a boundary beyond which it may not pass.

I. THE ACHIEVEMENTS OF WISDOM. "A wise man scaleth the city of the mighty," etc. (ver. 22). How often have men stood behind their strong ramparts—not of stone or rock only—and looked down with complacent contempt upon the despised adversaries outside and below them; but when the shock of the battle came they found, to their dismay, that wisdom is stronger than all defences that could be raised, and that it can cast down the confidence of the proud! It is not only the city which is built of brick or stone which is at the command of the truly wise; it is also the city of falsehood and of error; it is the city of oppression and of wrong; it is also the city of knowledge and of truth. However hard to win may be its walls, the wise man—who is the man of rectitude, of unselfishness, of purity, of diligence, of earnestness, of patience, of devotion—will strive and toil until he stands within the citadel.

II. ONE OF ITS CHIEF CHARACTERISTICS. On the one hand, a wicked (who is an unwise) man "hardeneth his face." He may be proved to be in the wrong; he may be suffering seriously for his folly; but he will not change his course. He is obstinate, perverse, proud; he will go on his way, come what will. But, on the other hand, the upright (who is the wise) man directeth (or rather, *considereth*) his way. Even when he is right, and things are profitable and promising with him, he is often pondering his path, looking to his chart, carefully considering whether he is moving on in the right direction. But when he has been induced to wander into some byway, and when he is admonished either by God's providence or by man's fidelity, then he seriously considers his way, and, if he finds that he has erred, he immediately retraces his steps, until he is found again in the King's highway. The habit of considering is one of the clearest marks of wisdom.

III. TWO OF ITS LIMITATIONS. 1. It cannot succeed *against* God (ver. 30). Good men and true, who are within the kingdom of Christ, may put forth all their mental powers and moral energies to bring about that which God has condemned; they have watched and thought and striven for the cause which has *not* been, as they imagined, the cause of Christ, and they have hopelessly failed. History will supply abundant illustrations. 2. It cannot succeed *without* God (ver. 31). Equip your cavalry, arm your infantry, and collect your artillery for the day of battle; bring forth your most experienced general, who will be ready with his most brilliant tactics; still the issue will not be determined thus. There may arise a sudden unaccountable panic; there may be a movement made by the enemy's captain wholly unexpected and practically irresistible; there are forces at work on the great battle-field of the world against which no military skill can provide. God is present there. He can act upon the mind of one man or of many men in such wise that the battle will *not* be to the strong, the victory *not* be to the seasoned troops and the confident commander. Without God's consent, without his blessing, any battle on any field whatever, military or moral, must be lost.—C.

EXPOSITION.

CHAPTER XXII.

Ver. 1.—**A good name is rather to be chosen than great riches.** It will be observed that "good" in the Authorized Version is in italics, showing that the epithet is not expressed in the Hebrew, which is simply שֵׁם (*shem*), "name." But this word carried with it the notion of good repute, as in Eccles. vii. 1; for being well known implied honour and reputation, while being nameless (Job xxx. 8) signified not only obscurity, but ignominy and discredit. Hence the versions have ὄνομα καλόν, *nomen bonum*, and Ecclus. xli. 12, "Have regard to thy name (περὶ ὀνόματος), for that shall continue with thee above a thousand great treasures of gold. A good life," the moralist continues, "hath but few days; but a good name endureth for ever" (contrast ch. x. 7). And **loving favour rather than silver and gold**; or, more accurately, *and before gold and silver grace is good;* i.e. grace is far better than gold. Grace (*chen*) is the manner and demeanour which win love, as well as the favour and affection gained thereby; taken as parallel to "name," in the former hemistich, it means here "favour," the regard conceived by others for a worthy object. Publ. Syr., "Bona opinio hominum tutior pecunia est." The French have a proverb, "Bonne renommée vaut mieux que ceinture dorée." The latter hemistich gives the reason for the assertion in the former—a good name is so valuable because it wins affection and friendship, which are far preferable to material riches.

Ver. 2.—**The rich and poor meet together** (ch. xxix. 13): **the Lord is the Maker of them all** (Job xxxiv. 19). God has ordained that there shall be rich and poor in the world, and that they should meet in the intercourse of life. These social inequalities are ordered for wise purposes; the one helps the other. The labour of the poor makes the wealth of the rich; the wealth of the rich enables him to employ and aid the poor. Their common humanity, their fatherhood in God, should make them regard one another as brethren, without distinction of rank or position; the rich should not despise the poor (ch. xiv. 31; xvii. 5; Job xxxi. 15), the poor should not envy the rich (ch. iii. 31), but all should live in love and harmony as one great family of God.

Ver. 3.—**A prudent man foreseeth the evil, and hideth himself.** The whole verse is repeated in ch. xxvii. 12. St. Jerome has *callidus*, and the LXX. has πανοῦργος, as the translation of עָרוּם (*arum*); but it must be taken in a good sense, as cautious, far-seeing, prudent (see note on ch. i. 4). Such a man looks around, takes warning from little circumstances which might escape the observation of careless persons, and provides for his safety in good time. Thus the Christians at the siege of Jerusalem, believing Christ's warnings, retired to Pella, and were saved. A Spanish proverb runs, "That which the fool does in the end, the wise man does at the beginning." **The simple pass on, and are punished.** The subject of the former hemistich is in the singular number, for a really prudent man is a comparatively rare being; the second clause is plural, teaching us, as Hitzig observes, that many simple ones are found for one prudent. These silly persons, blundering blindly on their way, without circumspection or forethought, meet with immediate punishment, incur dangers, suffer loss. A Cornish proverb runs, "He who will not be ruled by the rudder must be ruled by the rock." Septuagint, "An intelligent man (πανοῦργος) seeing a wicked man punished is himself forcibly instructed; but fools pass by, and are punished" (comp. ch. xxi. 11).

Ver. 4.—**By humility** and the fear of the **Lord**, etc. This does not seem to be the best rendering of the original. The word rendered "by" (עֵקֶב *ekeb*), "in reward of," is also taken as the subject of the sentence: "The reward of humility ['and,' or, 'which is'] the fear of God, is riches," etc. There is no copulative in the clause, and a similar asyndeton occurs in ver. 5; so there is no reason why we should not regard the clause in this way. Thus Revised Version, Nowack,

and others. But Delitzsch makes the first
hemistich a concluded sentence, which the
second member carries on thus: "The reward of humility is the fear of the Lord; it
[the reward of humility] is at the same time
riches," etc. Vulgate, *Finis modestiæ timor
Domini, divitiæ et gloria et vita;* Septuagint, "The generation (γενεὰ) of wisdom
is the fear of the Lord, and wealth," etc.
It is preferable to translate as above, taking
the two expressed virtues as appositional,
thus: "The reward of humility, the fear of
the Lord." Humility brings with it true
religion, which is expressed by "the fear
of the Lord." The feeling of dependence,
the lowly opinion of self, the surrender of
the will, the conviction of sin, all effects
which are connected with humility, may
well be represented by this term, "the fear
of God," which, in another aspect, is itself
the source of every virtue and every blessing; it is **riches, and honour, and life.** These
are God's gifts, the guerdon of faithful service (see notes on ch. iii. 16 and xxi. 21;
and comp. ch. viii. 18). The Easterns have
a pretty maxim, "The bending of the humble
is the graceful droop of the branches laden
with fruit." And again, "Fruitful trees
bend down; the wise stoop; a dry stick and
a fool can be broken, not bent" (Lane).

Ver. 5.—**Thorns and snares are in the
way of the froward.** The words are in the
Hebrew without the conjunction (see note,
ver. 4), though the versions generally add it.
Thus the Septuagint, τρίβολοι καὶ παγίδες;
Vulgate, *arma et gladii;* but the Venetian,
ἄκανθαι παγίδες. It is a question whether
the thorns are what the perverse prepare for
others, or what they themselves suffer. In
ch. xv. 19 the hedge of thorns represented
the difficulties in the sluggard's path; but
here, viewed in connection with the following hemistich, the thorns and snares refer
to the hindrances proceeding from the
froward, which injuriously affect others;
"thorns" being a figure of the pains and
troubles, "snares" of the unexpected dangers
and impediments which evil men cause as
they go on their crooked way. The word
for "thorns" is צִנִּים, which occurs in Job
v. 5. The plant is supposed to be the
Rhamnus paliurus, but it has not been
accurately identified. **He that doth keep
his soul shall be far from them** (comp. ch.
xiii. 3; xvi. 17). The man who has regard
to his life and morals will go far, will keep
wholly aloof, from those perils and traps
into which the perverse try to entice them.

Ver. 6.—**Train up a child in the way he
should go.** The verb translated "train"
(*chanak*) means, first, "to put something
into the mouth," "to give to be tasted," as
nurses give to infants food which they have
masticated in order to prepare it for their

nurslings; thence it comes to signify "to
give elementary instruction," "to imbue,"
"to train." The Hebrew literally is,
Initiate a child in accordance with his way.
The Authorized Version, with which Ewald
agrees, takes the maxim to mean that the
child should be trained from the first in the
right path—the path of obedience and religion. This is a very true and valuable
rule, but it is not what the author intends.
"His way" must mean one of two things—
either his future calling and station, or his
character and natural inclination and
capacity. Delitzsch and Plumptre take the
latter interpretation; Nowack and Bertheau
the former, on the ground that *derek* is not
used in the other sense suggested. But, as far
as use is concerned, both explanations stand
on much the same ground; and it seems more
in conformity with the moralist's age and
nation to see in the maxim an injunction to
consider the child's nature, faculties, and
temperament, in the education which is
given to him. If, from his early years, a
child is thus trained, **when he is old, he
will not depart from it.** This way, this
education in accordance with his idiosyncrasy, will bear fruit all his life long; it
will become a second nature, and will never
be obliterated. The Vulgate commences
the verse with *Proverbium est,* taking the
first word substantively, as if the author
here cited a trite saying; but the rendering
is a mistake. There are similar maxims,
common at all times and in all countries.
Virg., 'Georg.,' ii. 272—

"Adeo in teneris consuescere multum est."

Horace, 'Epist.,' i. 2. 67—

"Nunc adbibe puro
Pectore verba, puer."

For, as he proceeds—

"Quo semel est imbuta recens, servabit
odorem
Testa diu."

Thus we have two mediæval jingles—

"Cui puer assuescit, major dimittere nescit."

"Quod nova testa capit, inveterata sapit."

Then there is the German saw, "Jung
gewohnt, alt gethan." "What youth
learns, age does not forget," says the Danish
proverb. In another and a sad sense the
French exclaim, "Si jeunesse savait! si
vieillesse pouvait!" All the early manuscripts of the Septuagint omit this verse;
in some of the later it has been supplied
from Theodotion.

Ver. 7.—**The rich ruleth over the poor.**
"The rich man (singular) will rule over
the poor" (plural); for there are many poor
for one rich (see on ver. 3). This is the way

of the world (ch. xviii. 23). Aben Ezra explains the gnome as showing the advantage of wealth and the inconvenience of poverty; the former bringing power and pre-eminence, the latter trouble and servitude; and hence the moralist implies that every one should strive and labour to obtain a competency, and thus avoid the evils of impecuniosity. **The borrower is servant to the lender.** (For the relation between borrower and lender, or debtor and creditor, see on ch. xx 16; and comp. Matt. xviii. 25, 34.) Delitzsch cites the German saying, "Borghart (borrower) is Lehnhart's (lender's) servant." We have the proverb, "He that goes a-borrowing goes a-sorrowing." The Septuagint departs from the other versions and our Hebrew text, translating, "The rich will rule over the poor, and household servants will lend to their own masters"— a reading on which some of the Fathers have commented.

Ver. 8.—**He that soweth iniquity shall reap vanity;** shall gain nothing substantial, shall have nothing to show for his pains. But *aven* also means "calamity," "trouble," as ch. xii. 21; so the gnome expresses the truth that they who do evil shall meet with punishment in their very sins—the exact contrast to the promise to the righteous (ch. xi. 18). "To him that soweth righteousness shall be a sure reward." Thus we have in Job iv. 8, "They that plough iniquity, and sow wickedness, reap the same;" and the apostle asserts (Gal. vi. 7, etc), "Whatsoever a man soweth, that shall he also reap. For he that soweth to his flesh shall of the flesh reap corruption; but he that soweth to the Spirit shall of the Spirit reap life everlasting." Eastern proverbs run, "As the sin, so the atonement;" "Those who sow thorns can only reap prickles" (comp. ch. xii. 14). **And the rod of his anger shall fail.** The writer is thinking especially of cruelty and injustice practised on a neighbour, as Delitzsch has pointed out, and he means that the rod which he has raised, the **violence intended against** the innocent victim, shall vanish away or fall harmlessly. Ewald and others think that the rod is the Divine anger, and translate the verb (*kalah*) "is prepared," a sense which here it will not well bear, though the LXX. has lent some countenance to it by rendering, "And shall fully accomplish the plague (πληγὴν. ? 'punishment') of his deeds." The rendering, "shall fail," "shall be consumed, or annihilated," is confirmed by Gen. xxi 15; Isa. i. 28; xvi. 4, etc. The Septuagint adds a distich here, of which the first member is a variant of ver. 9a, and the second another rendering of the latter hemistich of the present verse: "A cheerful man and a giver God blesseth

(ἄνδρα ἱλαρὸν καὶ δότην εὐλογεῖ ὁ Θεός); but he shall bring to an end (συντελεσεῖ) the vanity of his works." The first hemistich is remarkable for being quoted by St. Paul (2 Cor. ix. 7), with a slight variation, Ἱλαρὸν γὰρ δότην ἀγαπᾷ ὁ Θεός. So Ecclus. xxxii. (xxxv.) 9, "In all thy gifts show a cheerful countenance (ἱλάρωσον τὸ πρόσωπόν σου)."

Ver. 9.—**He that hath a bountiful eye shall be blessed.** The "good of eye" is the kindly looking, the benevolent man, in contrast to him of the evil eye, the envious, the unfriendly and niggardly man (ch. xxiii. 6; xxviii. 22). St. Jerome renders, *Qui pronus est ad misericordiam.* Such a one is blessed by God in this world and the next, in time and in eternity, according to the sentiment of ch. xi. 25. Thus in the temporal sense (Ecclus. xxxiv. (xxxi.) 23), "Him that is liberal in food lips shall bless, and the testimony of his liberality will be believed." Septuagint, "He that hath pity upon the poor shall himself be continually sustained (διατραφήσεται)." The reason is added, **For he giveth of his bread to the poor.** The blessing is the consequence of his charity and liberality. 2 Cor. ix. 6, "He that soweth bountifully shall reap also bountifully (ἐπ᾽ εὐλογίαις)." The Vulgate and Septuagint add a distich not in the Hebrew, *Victoriam et honorem acquiret qui dat munera; animam autem aufert accipientium;* Νίκην καὶ τιμὴν περι ποιεῖται ὁ δῶρα δούς, τὴν μέντοι ψυχὴν ἀφαι ρεῖται τῶν κεκτημένων, "Victory and honour he obtaineth who giveth gifts; but he takes away the life of the possessors." The first hemistich appears to be a variant of ch. xix. 6b, the second to be derived from ch. i. 19b. The second portion of the Latin addition may mean that the liberal man wins and carries away with him the souls of the recipients of his bounty. But this, though Ewald would fain have it so, cannot be the signification of the corresponding Greek, which seems to mean that the man who is so liberal in distributing gifts obtains the power to do so by oppressing and wronging others.

Ver. 10.—**Cast out the scorner, and contention shall go out;** Septuagint, ἔκβαλε ἐκ συνεδρίου λοιμόν, "Cast out of the company a pestilent fellow" Chase away the scorner (ch. i. 22), the man who has no respect for things human or Divine, and the disputes and ill feeling which he caused will be ended; for "where no wood is, the fire goeth out" (ch. xxvi. 20). **Yea, strife and reproach shall cease.** The reproach and ignominy (קָלוֹן, *kalon*) are those which the presence and words of the scorner bring with them; to have such a one in the company is a disgrace to all good men. Thus Ishmael and his mother were driven from Abraham's dwelling (Gen. xxi. 9, etc.), and the apostle quotes (Gal. iv. 30), "Cast out (ἔκβαλε) the bondwoman and her son." Septuagint, "For when he sits in the company he dishonours all." The next verse gives a happy contrast.

Ver. 11.—**He that loveth pureness of heart;** he who strives to be pure in heart (Matt. v. 8), free from guile, lust, cupidity, vice of every kind. The next clause carries on the description of the perfect character, and is best translated, **And hath grace of lips, the king is his friend.** He who is not only virtuous and upright, but has the gift of graciousness of speech, winning manner in conversation, such a man will attach the king to him by the closest bonds of friendship. We have had something very similar at ch. xvi. 13. Some of the versions consider that by the king God is meant. Thus the Septuagint, "The Lord loveth holy hearts, and all blameless persons are acceptable with him." The rest of the clause is connected by the LXX. with the following verse, "A king guides his flock (ποιμαίνει) with his lips; but the eyes of the Lord," etc.

Ver. 12.—**The eyes of the Lord preserve knowledge.** The expression, "preserve knowledge," is found at ch. v. 2 (where see note) in the sense of "keep," "retain," and, taken by itself, it might here signify that the Lord alone possesses knowledge, and alone imparts it to his servants (1 Sam. ii. 3); but as in the following clause a person, the transgressor, is spoken of, it is natural to expect a similar expression in the former. The Revised Version is correct in rendering the abstract "knowledge" by the concrete "him that hath knowledge;" so that the clause says that God watches over and protects the man who knows him and walks in his ways, and uses his means and abilities for the good of others (see ch. xi. 9). **But he (the Lord) overthroweth the words of the transgressor.** The transgressor here is the false, treacherous, perfidious man; and the gnome asserts that God frustrates by turning in another direction the outspoken intentions of this man, which he had planned against the righteous (comp. ch. xiii. 6; xxi. 12). Septuagint, "But the eyes of the Lord preserve knowledge, but the transgressor despiseth words," i.e. commands, or words of wisdom and warning.

Ver. 13.—**The slothful man saith, There is a lion without** (ch. xxvi. 13). The absurd nature of the sluggard's excuse is hardly understood by the casual reader. The supposed lion is without, in the open country, and yet he professes to be in

danger in the midst of the town. **I shall be slain in the streets.** Others consider that the sluggard makes two excuses for his inactivity. If work calls him abroad, he may meet the lion which report says is prowling in the neighbourhood; if he has to go into the streets, he may be attacked and murdered by ruffians for motives of plunder or revenge. "Sluggards are prophets," says the Hebrew proverb. Septuagint, "The sluggard maketh excuses, and saith, A lion is in the ways, there are murderers in the streets." Lions, though now extinct in Palestine, seem to have lingered till the time of the Crusades, and such of them as became man-eaters, the old or feeble, were a real danger in the vicinity of villages (comp. Jer. xlix. 19; l. 44).

Ver. 14.—**The mouth of strange women is a deep pit.** The hemistich reappears in a slightly altered form at ch. xxiii. 27. (For "strange woman" as equivalent to "a harlot" or "adulteress," see note on ch. ii. 16.) By her "mouth" is meant her wanton, seductive words, which entice a man to destruction of body and soul. It may be that theology rather than morals is signified here—rather false doctrines than evil practice. In this case the mention of the strange or foreign woman is very appropriate, seeing that perversions of belief and worship were always introduced into Israel from external sources. **He that is abhorred of the Lord shall fall therein.** He who has incurred the wrath of God by previous unfaithfulness and sin is left to himself to fall a prey to the allurements of the wicked woman (comp. Eccles. vii. 26). Septuagint, "The mouth of a transgressor (παρανόμου) is a deep ditch; and he that is hated of the Lord shall fall therein." Then are added three lines not in the Hebrew, which, however, seem to be reminiscences of other passages: "There are evil ways before a man, and he loveth not to turn away from them; but it is needful to turn away from a perverse and evil way."

Ver. 15.—**Foolishness is bound in the heart of a child.** Foolishness (ivveleth) here implies the love of mischief, the waywardness and self-will, belonging to children, bound up in their very nature. Septuagint, "Folly is attached (ἐξῆπται) to the heart of the young," in which version Cornelius à Lapide sees an allusion to the ornament hung by fond parents round the neck of a child whom they were inclined to spoil rather than to train in self-denying ways. To such a child folly adheres as closely as the bulla with which he is decorated. But **the rod of correction shall drive it far from him.** Judicious education overcomes this natural tendency, by punishing it when exhibited, and imparting wisdom and piety (see on ch. xiii. 24 and xix. 18; and comp. ch. xxiii. 13; xxix. 15; Ecclus. xxx. 1, etc.). The LXX. pursue their notion of the tco-indulgent parents letting the child have his own way, for they render the last clause, "But the rod and discipline are far from him."

Ver. 16.—He that oppresseth the poor to increase his riches (so the Vulgate), and he that giveth to the rich, shall surely come to want. There are various renderings and explanations of this verse. The Authorized Version says that he who oppresseth the poor to enrich himself, and he who wastes his means by giving to those who do not need it, will come to poverty. But the antithesis of this distich is thus lost. The Hebrew literally rendered brings out the contrast, *Whosoever oppresseth the poor, it is for his gain; whosoever giveth to the rich, it is for his loss.* Delitzsch explains the sentence thus: "He who enriches himself by extortion from the poor, at any rate gains what he desires; but he who gives to the rich impoverishes himself in vain, has no thanks, reaps only disappointment." One cannot but feel that the maxim thus interpreted is poor and unsatisfactory. The interpretation in the 'Speaker's Commentary' is more plausible: The oppressor of the poor will himself suffer in a similar mode, and will have to surrender his ill-gotten gains to some equally unscrupulous rich man. But the terse antithesis of the original is wholly obscured by this view of the distich. It is far better, with Hitzig, Ewald, and others, to take the gain in the first hemistich as that of the poor man, equivalent to "doth but bring him gain;" though the sentence is not necessarily to be explained as suggesting that the injustice which the poor man suffers at the hand of his wealthy neighbour is a stimulus to him to exert himself in order to better his position, and thus indirectly tends to his enrichment. The maxim is really conceived in the religious style of so many of these apparently worldly pronouncements, and states a truth in the moral government of God intimated elsewhere, *e.g.* ch. xiii. 22; xxviii. 8; and that truth is that the riches extorted from the poor man will in the end redound to his benefit, that by God's providential control the oppression and injustice from which he has suffered shall work to his good. In the second hemistich the loss is that of the rich man. By adding to the wealth of the rich the donor increases his indolence, encourages his luxury, vice, and extravagance, and thus leads to his ruin—"bringeth only to want." Septuagint, "He that calumniates (συκοφαντῶν) the poor increaseth his own substance, but giveth to the rich at a loss (ἐπ᾽ ἐλάσσονι)," *i.e.* so as to lessen his substance.

Ver. 17—ch. xxiv. 22.—Part IV. FIRST APPENDIX TO THE FIRST GREAT COLLECTION, containing "words of the wise."

Vers. 17—21.—The introduction to this first appendix, containing an exhortation to attend to the words of the wise, an outline of the instruction herein imparted, with a reference to teaching already given.

Ver. 17.—Incline thine ear (comp. ch. iv. 20; v. 1). The words of the wise; *verba sapientium,* Vulgate. "Wise" is in the plural number, showing that this is not a portion of the collection called, 'The Proverbs of Solomon' (ch. x. 1), but a distinct work. (For the term, see note on ch. i. 6.) My knowledge. The knowledge which I impart by bringing to notice these sayings of wise men. Septuagint, "Incline (παράβαλλε) thine ear to the words of wise men, and hear my word, and apply thine heart, that thou mayest know that they are good."

Ver. 18.—This verse gives the reason for the previous exhortation. It is a pleasant thing if thou keep them within thee; in thy mind and memory (comp. ch. xviii. 8; xx. 27). Thus Ps. cxlvii. 1, "It is good to sing praises unto our God; for it is pleasant, and praise is comely." They shall withal be fitted in thy lips. This rendering hardly suits the hortatory nature of the introduction. It is better to take the clause in the optative, as Delitzsch, Ewald, Nowack, and others: "Let them abide altogether upon thy lips;" *i.e.* be not ashamed to profess them openly, let them regulate thy words, teach thee wisdom and discretion. Septuagint, "And if thou admit them to thy heart, they shall likewise gladden thee on thy lips."

Ver. 19.—That thy trust may be in the Lord. The Greek and Latin versions make this clause depend on the preceding verse. It is better to consider it as dependent on the second hemistich, the fact of instruction being placed after the statement of its object. All the instruction herein afforded is meant to teach that entire confidence in the Lord which, as soon as his will is known and understood, leads a man to do it at any cost or pains, leaving the result in God's hands. I have made them known to thee this day, even to thee. The repetition of the personal pronoun brings home the teaching to the disciple, and shows that it is addressed, not merely to the mass of men, but to each individual among them, who thus becomes responsible for the use which he makes of it (comp. ch. xxiii. 15). The expression, "this day," further emphasizes the exhortation. The learner is not to remember vaguely that some time or other he received this instruction, but that on this particular day the warning was given. So in Heb. iii. 7, 13 we read, "As the Holy Ghost saith, To-day if ye will hear his voice, harden not your hearts. . . . Exhort one another daily, so long as it is called To-day, lest any of you be hardened by the deceitfulness of sin." Septuagint, "That thy hope may be in the Lord, and he may make thy way known unto thee." Cheyne ('Job and Solomon') quotes Bickell's correction of this verse, "That thy confidence may be in Jehovah, to make known unto thee thy ways;" but the alteration seems arbitrary and unnecessary.

Ver. 20.—**Have not I written to thee excellent things in counsels and knowledge?** There is a difficulty about the word rendered "excellent things." The Khetib has שׁלשׁום, "the day before yesterday, formerly;" but the word occurs nowhere alone, and, as Nowack says, can hardly have been the original reading. However, Ewald, Bertheau, and others, adopting it, suppose that the author refers to some earlier work. Cheyne cites Bickell's rendering, "Now, years before now, have I written unto thee long before with counsels and knowledge," and considers the words to mean either that the compiler took a long time over his work, or that this was not the first occasion of his writing. One does not see why stress should be here laid on former instruction, unless, perhaps, as Plumptre suggests, in contrast to "this day" of the previous verse. The LXX. renders the word τρισσῶς thus, "And do thou record them for thyself triply for counsel and knowledge upon the table of thine heart." St. Jerome has, *Ecce descripsi eam tibi tripliciter, in cogitationibus et scientiis.* Other versions have also given a numerical explanation to the term. In it is seen an allusion to the three supposed works of Solomon—Proverbs, Ecclesiastes, Canticles —which is absurd; others refer it to the threefold division of the Testament—Law, Prophets, and Hagiographa; others, to three classes of youths for whom the admonitions were intended; others, again, think it equivalent to "oftentimes," or "in many forms." But the reading is as doubtful as the explanations of it are unsatisfactory. The genuine word is doubtless preserved in the Keri, which gives שָׁלִישִׁים (*shalishim*), properly a military term, applied to chariotfighters and men of rank in the army. The LXX. translates the word by τριστάτης *e.g.* Exod. xiv. 7; xv. 4), which is equivalent to "chieftain." Hence the Hebrew term, understood in the neuter gender, is transferred to the chief among proverbs—"choice proverbs," as Delitzsch calls them. The Venetian, by a happy turn, gives τρισμέγιστα. Thus we come back to the rendering of the Authorized Version as most correct and intelligible.

Ver. 21.—**That I might make thee know the certainty of the words of truth. The** object intended is to teach the disciple the fixed rule (*firmitatem*, Vulgate) by which truthful words are guided (see Luke i. 4). Septuagint, "I therefore teach thee a true word and knowledge good to learn." **That thou mightest answer the words of truth to them that send unto thee.** This implies that the pupil will be enabled to teach others who apply to him for instruction; "will be ready," as St. Peter says, "always to give an answer to every man that asketh you a reason of the hope that is in you" (1 Pet. iii. 15). But the last expression is better translated, "them that send thee;" *illis qui miserunt te,* Vulgate (see ch. xxv. 13); and we must conceive of these as being parents or tutors who send a youth to a school or wise man to be educated. The moralist expresses his desire that the disciple will carry home such wholesome, truthful doctrines as will prove that the pains expended upon him have not been useless. Septuagint, "That thou mayest answer words of truth to those who put questions to thee (τοῖς προβαλλομένοις σοι)." The Syriac adds, "That I may make known unto thee counsel and wisdom." Bickell's version (quoted by Cheyne) is, "That thou mayest know the rightness of these words, that thou mayest answer in true words to them that ask thee."

Ver. 22—ch. xxiv. 22.—Here commence the "words of the wise."

Ver. 22.—This and the following verse form a tetrastich, which connects itself in thought with ver. 16. **Rob not the poor, because he is poor.** The word for "poor" is here *dal*, which means "feeble," "powerless" (see on ch. xix. 4), and the writer enjoins the disciple not to be induced by his weakness to injure and despoil a poor man. **Neither oppress the afflicted in the gate.** The gate is the place of judgment, the court of justice (comp. Job xxxi. 21). The warning points to the particular form of wrong inflicted on the lowly by unjust judges, who could give sentences from which, however iniquitous, there was practically no appeal.

Ver. 23.—**For,** though they are powerless to defend themselves, and have no earthly patrons, the Lord will plead their cause (ch. xxiii. 11). Jehovah will be their Advocate and Protector. **And spoil the soul of those that spoiled them;** rather, *despoil of life those that despoil them.* So the Revised Version. God, exercising his moral government on human concerns, will bring ruin and death on the unjust judge or the rich oppressor of the poor. Jerome has, *Configet eos qui confixerunt animam ejus.* The verb used is קבע (*kabah*), which is found only here and Mal. iii. 8, where it means "to defraud" or "despoil." In the Chaldee and Syriac it may signify "to fix," "to pierce." Septuagint, "The Lord will judge his cause, and thou shalt deliver thy soul unharmed (ἄσυλον):" i.e. if you refrain from injustice and oppression, you will be saved from evil and dwell securely.

Vers. 24, 25.—Another tetrastich. **Make no friendship with an angry** (irascible) **man. Have no close intercourse with a man given to fits of passion. And with a furious man thou shalt not go.** Avoid the society of such a one. The reason follows: **Lest thou learn his ways;** his mann r of life and conduct, as ch. i. 15 (where s e note). Anger breeds anger; impatience, impatience. St. Basil ('De Ira'), quoted by Corn. à Lapide, enjoins, "Take not your adversary as your teacher, and be not a mirror to reflect the angry man, showing his figure in thyself." **And get a snare to thy soul;** bring destruction on thyself. Anger unsubdued not only mars the kindliness of social life, but leads to all sorts of dangerous complications which may bring ruin and death in their train (comp. ch. xv. 18).

Vers. 26, 27.—A warning against suretyship, often repeated. **Be not thou one of them that strike hands;** i.e. that become guarantees for others (see on ch. xvii. 18; xx. 16; and comp. ch. vi. 1; xi. 15). **Sureties for debts.** The writer explains what kind of guarantee he means. **Why should he** (the creditor) **take away thy bed from under thee?** Why should you ("from respect of person." Septuagint) act so weakly as to give a creditor power to seize your very bed as a pledge? The Law endeavoured to mitigate this penalty (Exod. xxii. 26, 27; Deut. xxiv. 12, 13). But doubtless its merciful provisions were evaded by the moneylenders (see Neh. v. 11; Ezek. xviii. 12, "hath not restored the pledge").

Ver. 28.—The first line is repeated at ch. xxiii. 10. (On the sanctity of landmarks, see note on ch. xv. 25.) Some of the stones, exhibiting a bilingual inscription, which marked the boundaries of the Levitical city of Gezer, were discovered by Ganneau in 1874 ('Quart. Statement Pal. Explor. Fund,' 1874). The Septuagint calls the landmarks ὅρια αἰώνια.

Ver. 29.—A tristich follows. **Seest thou a man diligent in his business?** Mere diligence would not commend a man to high notice unless accompanied by dexterity and skill; and though מָהִיר (mahir) means "quick," it also has the notion of "skilful," and is better here taken in that sense. **He shall stand before kings.** This phrase means to serve or minister to another (Gen. xli. 46; 1 Sam. xvi. 21, 22; 1 Kings x. 8; Job i. 6). A man thus expert is fitted for any, even the highest situation, may well be employed in affairs of state, and enjoy the confidence of kings. **He shall not stand before mean men.** "Mean" (חֲשֻׁכִּים) are the men of no importance, ignobiles, obscure. An intellectual, clever, adroit man would never be satisfied with serving such masters; his ambition is higher; he knows that he is capable of better things. Septuagint, "It must needs be that an observant (ὁρατικὸν) man, and one who is keen in his business, should attend on kings, and not attend on slothful men."

HOMILETICS.

Ver. 1.—A good name and loving favour. Both of these blessings—which, indeed, are closely allied—are here preferred to great riches. It is better to be poor with either than rich with neither. Let us examine the excellence of each of them.

I. THE EXCELLENCE OF A GOOD NAME. Why is this rather to be chosen than riches? 1. Because it is a higher order of good. Wealth is a material thing. The best of it is empty and vain by the side of what is intellectual, moral, or spiritual. It is possible to have great riches and yet to be miserable and degraded, if the higher reaches of life are impoverished. 2. Because it is personal. A man's good name is nearer to him than all his property. The most personal property is distant and alien compared with the name he carries; the reputation that attaches to him is his closest garment—it is wrapped round his very self. If a person wears sackcloth next his skin, he can have little comfort in being clothed outside this with purple and fine linen. 3. Because it is social. The good name is known among a man's fellows. It is this that gives him his true status. Now, we cannot afford to neglect social considerations. It is a terrible thing to live under the stigma of the rebuke of mankind. He is either more or less than a man who can look with indifference on the good or the ill opinion of his brethren. Mere fame may be of little value. A good name is far more desirable than a great name. It is not necessary that people should have a high opinion of us. But it is important that our name should be free from disgrace, should be honoured for purity and integrity of character. 4. Because it is a sign of other excellences. It may be given by mistake to a worthless deceiver, or it may be withdrawn from a worthy person through some cruel misapprehension. We cannot always take a man's reputation as a true measure of his character. But when it is justly earned, the good name is the sacrament of a good character, and therefore an outward and visible sign of what is most excellent, for it is better to be good than to own riches.

II. THE EXCELLENCE OF LOVING FAVOUR. Why is this better than silver and gold? 1. *Because it is human.* Silver and gold are but dead metals. They may be bright, beautiful, and precious; but they can have no sympathy with their possessors. Riches are heartless things, that take themselves wings and fly away without a qualm of compunction. But human interests and affections touch our hearts and rouse our sympathies in return. It is better to be poor among friends than to be rich but loveless and friendless. 2. *Because it brings direct blessings.* Riches are at best indirect sources of good. But love is a good itself, and it breathes a benediction on all to whom it is extended. Reputation is good, but affection is better. The best love cannot be enjoyed if the good name has been lost by wrong-doing. But there may be no fame, no great name in the world, and yet much love. It is better to be loved by one than admired by a thousand. 3. *Because it is the type of higher blessings.* The loving favour of man is an earthly emblem of the grace of God. This is better than silver and gold, first, as a human source of peace and power, and then as a promise of eternal life and wealth in the heavenly inheritance, after death has robbed a man of all his silver and gold.

Ver. 2.—*Social distinctions.* I. THE SAD CONDITION OF SOCIAL DISTINCTIONS. 1. *These distinctions are very marked.* There is an enormous separation between the condition of the rich and that of the poor. The one class is overwhelmed with luxury, the other pinched with penury. There seems to be a tendency to an aggravation of this separation. As wealth grows, poverty does not perceptibly recede. Three millions are on the borders of starvation among the riches of England. 2. *These distinctions are not determined by desert.* No doubt honest industry tends to prosperity, while idleness and dissipation lead to poverty. But there are bad rich men and good poor men. 3. *These distinctions are grossly unjust.* It is impossible to maintain that there is equity in the present distribution of property throughout the community, though it may be urged that most attempts at remedying the injustice that have been proposed hitherto would be worse than the disease. 4. *These distinctions generate greater evils.* They destroy the sense of human brotherhood, fostering a spirit of pride on the part of the rich, and rousing passions of hatred among those who feel themselves to be robbed of their share of the world's wealth. One man is not to be thought of as necessarily superior to his neighbour simply because he is in possession of more property; nor, on the other hand, should the owner of wealth be regarded as a wholesale brigand.

II. THE MEANS OF RECONCILING SOCIAL DISTINCTIONS. "The rich and poor meet together." 1. *It is desirable that there should be more intercourse between the various classes of society.* Very much of the antagonism of the classes arises from ignorance. The simple, honest, poor man, seeking his rights in the rough style natural to his circumstances, is regarded as a red-handed revolutionist by the fastidious upper-class person, who, in turn, is treated by his indigent neighbour as a monster of cruelty and selfishness, a very ogre. The first step towards a better understanding is more freedom of intercourse. It is the same with the quarrel between capital and labour. Mutual conferences might bring about a common understanding. 2. *In the Church of God rich and poor meet on common ground.* Here pride of class is utterly inexcusable. Happily, the old distinction between the curtained, carpeted, and cushioned squire's pew, and the bare benches of the villagers, is being swept away. But the spirit that this distinction suggested is not so easily exorcised. Christian brotherhood should bring all together in a common family spirit. It was so in early ages, when the slave might be a privileged communicant, while the master was a humble catechumen on the threshold of the Church. 3. *Death levels all class distinctions.* Rich and poor meet together in the grave. After death new distinctions emerge. Dives cannot scorn Lazarus in Hades.

III. THE MOTIVE FOR OVERCOMING SOCIAL DISTINCTIONS. This is to be discovered in a consideration of the common relation of men to their Maker. Nothing short of religion will heal the fearful wounds of society. Forcible methods will not succeed;

e.g. in the French Revolution. A universal redistribution of property would soon be followed by the old distinctions. Socialism would destroy virtues of independence and energy. But faith in God will work inwardly towards a reconciliation. 1. *All classes are equally low before God.* The highest earthly mountains vanish in astronomy. 2. *Our common relation to God is the ground of our mutual relations with one another.* All men have one Father; therefore all men must be brethren. The recognition of the Fatherhood of God will lead to the admission of family duties and claims among men. Christ, who teaches the Fatherhood of God, inspires the " enthusiasm of humanity."

Ver. 4.—*Two graces, and their reward.* I. Two GRACES. 1. *The social grace.* " Humility." This is becoming in all men, but it is especially seemly where its attainment is most difficult; *e.g.* among the high in station, the wealthy, the famous, the gifted, the popular. It is as difficult for the demagogue to be humble as for the lord— perhaps more difficult, for the former is more conscious of his own powers, and more recently lifted above his fellows. Humility is difficult to acquire, because it is so essentially different from mere weakness and self-effacement. It is seen best in the strongest and most pronounced natures. There is no virtue in falling back from one's highest aims in order to escape notice. The grace of humility is discovered in an earnest effort to press forward energetically, without a thought of self or a care for the admiration of the world. 2. *The religious grace.* " The fear of the Lord." Pride excludes true religion. In the childlike spirit of humble dependence we are open to the influence of Heaven. Thus the one grace is linked to the other. Now, the whole of the Old Testament conception of religion is summed up in " the fear of the Lord "—not because there was no room in it for any emotion but terror, but because the root of the ancient faith was reverence. This is the root of all religion. It may be so richly mingled with love as we come to discern the Fatherhood of God, that its more dread features are utterly lost. Yet love without reverence would not be a religious emotion, or, at all events, not one suited for God as he is revealed to us in the Bible. The Greeks seemed to dispense with the fear of God in their light, gay religion; but they also dispensed with conscience. A feeling of sin and a perception of the holiness of God must lay a deep foundation of awe beneath the most happy and trustful religious experience.

II. A THREEFOLD REWARD. 1. *Riches.* This is the lowest aspect of the reward. It is in the spirit of the Proverbs, which calls especial attention to the secular consequences of good and ill. We know that the humble and good are often poor and oppressed. But there is a tendency for quiet self-renunciation to be recognized and rewarded. The meek are to be blessed with the inheritance of the earth (Matt. v. 5). When full justice is done, the best men will receive the best things in this world as well as the life of that to come. At present we wait for the accomplishment of this social rectification. 2. *Honour.* The humble who do not seek honour shall have it, while the proud are cast down in shame. The first shall be last, and the last shall be first. Men delight to honour self-forgetful merit. But the highest honour comes from God, who discerns the heart, puts down the proud, and exalts them of low degree. 3. *Life.* Whether this is given in the Hebrew manner—in old age—or not, Christ has taught us to see his true eternal life as the greatest blessing for his people. The humility in which a man loses his life is the very means of finding the true life; the reverence of religion leads us from the shallow frivolity of earth to the deep life of God.

Ver. 6.—*The training of a child.* I. THE NEED OF THE TRAINING. This arises from various causes. 1. *An undeveloped condition.* Each child begins a new life. If all that were desirable could be found wrapped up in his soul, this would need to be developed by education. 2. *Ignorance.* The child does not come into the world with a ready-made stock of knowledge. He must learn truth and be made to see the right path, which is at first unknown to him. 3. *Weakness.* The child needs not only to be taught, but to be trained. He must be helped to do what is at first too much for his strength. His better nature must be drawn out, nourished, and confirmed. 4. *Evil.* A child's mind is not a *tabula rasa.* We need not go back to Adam for evidences of hereditary evil. The child inherits the vices of his ancestors. Thus " foolishness is bound up in the heart of a child." Before he is guilty of conscious sin the tendency to wickedness begins to work within him.

II. THE AGE OF THE TRAINING. This is to be in childhood, for various reasons. 1. *Its susceptibility.* (1) Susceptibility to training. The young mind is plastic; habit is not yet confirmed. It is easier to form a character than to reform it. (2) Susceptibility to religion. "Of such is the kingdom of heaven." Young children are peculiarly open to religious impressions.

> " Heaven lies about us in our infancy!
> Shades of the prison-house begin to close
> Upon the growing boy,
> But he beholds the light, and whence it flows,
> He sees it in his joy."
>
> (Wordsworth.)

Faith is natural to children. They cannot become theologians, but they may be citizens of the kingdom of heaven. Thoughts of God and Christ, and the call to the better life, can be well received by them. 2. *Its dangers.* Children are open to temptation. If not trained in goodness, they will be trained in evil. Some have thought that children should not be biassed in their religious ideas, but left in freedom to choose for themselves. We do not do this in secular matters, trusting them to choose their own methods of spelling and to manufacture their own multiplication-table. If we believe our religion to be true and good and profitable, it is only a cruel pedantry that will keep it from children for fear of prejudicing their minds. 3. *Its duties.* Early years should be given to Christ. He seeks the opening bud, not the withered leaf.

III. THE LAW OF THE TRAINING. 1. *In action.* There is a practical end in education. We are not merely to teach doctrine, but chiefly to train conduct. 2. *According to right.* This is not a question of taste. There is a way in which a child ought to go. It is his duty to tread it, and ours to lead him in it. 3. *According to future requirements.* While the main principles of education must be the same for all children, the special application of them will vary in different cases. We have to apply them to the specific career expected for each child. The prince should be trained for the throne, the soldier for the field, etc. 4. *According to personal qualities.* Each child's nature needs separate consideration and distinctive treatment. The training that would ruin one child might save another. We have not to drill all children into one uniform fashion of behaviour; we have rather to call out the individual gifts and capacities, and guard against the individual faults and weaknesses. Thus the training of a child will be the directing of his own specific nature.

IV. THE CONSEQUENCES OF THE TRAINING. " When he is old, he will not depart from it." Age stiffens. It is well that it should grow firm in the right. Here is the reward of teaching the young. The work is slow and discouraging, and at first we see few results; perhaps we imagine that all our efforts are wasted upon thoughtless minds. But if the work is hard to begin, there is this compensation in it—when it has fairly laid hold of a child, it is not likely to be ever effaced. The teachings of the Sunday school are remembered after many a long year.

Vers. 20, 21.—*Certainty.* I. THE TRUTH-SEEKER DESIRES CERTAINTY. With him " the certainty of the words of truth" is the great object sought after. 1. *Certainty must be distinguished from positiveness.* Doubt is often violent in assertion, as though to silence the opposition that cannot be answered. We may be very positive without being at all certain. 2. *Certainty must be distinguished from certitude.* Certitude is the feeling of certainty. Now, we may feel no doubt on a subject, and yet we may be in error. Real certainty is a well-grounded assurance. 3. *Certainty is desired because truth is precious.* If a person is indifferent to truth, he may be satisfied with doubt, or acquiescent in error. This is the contemptuous condition of the cheerful Sadducee. His scepticism is no pain to him, because he does not feel the loss of truth. Not valuing truth, it is a light matter to him that he misses it. Such a condition of mind is an insult to truth itself. A man who recognizes the royal glory of truth will be in the greatest distress if he thinks it has eluded his grasp. To him the feeling of doubt will be an agony. 4. *Certainty is sought because it is not always present.* It may be very difficult to find. We grope in ignorance, error, and confusion of mind. Then the great want is some solid assurance of truth. Without this the world is dark, our voyage may end in shipwreck, and we cannot know God, ourselves, or our destiny.

II. THE TRUTH-SEEKER MAY SECURE CERTAINTY. The Bible denies agnosticism. It offers revelation. 1. *Truth is revealed.* The written Word contains the record of revelation. God has spoken to us through his prophets, but chiefly in his Son (Heb. i. 1, 2). Everything that lifts the Bible above common books and impresses its message upon our hearts as from God, urges us to believe in the truth of what it teaches, for God is the Source of all truth. If the Bible does not teach truth, the Bible must be an earthly book, uninspired by God. 2. *Truth must be practised and studied.* " Excellent things in counsels and knowledge " are written in the Bible. But to find their truth we must do the commandment, follow the counsel, enter thoughtfully into the knowledge. 3. *Truth should be taught.* " That thou mightest answer the words of truth to them that send unto thee." (1) Inquirers need counsel and guidance. (2) Truth is no private possession, but a public trust. (3) They who teach others especially need to know the truth themselves.

Ver. 28.—*Ancient landmarks.* I. ANCIENT LANDMARKS OF PROPERTY. The stone that divided one man's vineyard from his neighbour's was regarded as a sacred thing, on no account to be touched. This arrangement helped to perpetuate family holdings. It prevented the accumulation of large estates by the wealthy, and the alienation of the land from the poor. It guarded the weak from the oppression of the strong. It was a protection against deceit, error, and confusion. Ahab transgressed the Law in seeking to acquire Naboth's vineyard. It would be well if we could appreciate the spirit of the old Hebrew sanctity of the landmark. It would be well, too, if there were more people who had a personal interest in the soil of the country. The " sacred rights of property " cannot confer on the owner any power to oppress the tiller of the soil ; but, on the other hand, they should protect the owner from the violence of social revolution.

II. ANCIENT LANDMARKS OF HISTORY. The field-stones of Palestine were historic. Their very presence served as a record of the lives and doings of a past ancestry. As such they gathered a certain sanctity of association. It is no small thing that we in England belong to a historic nation. The forward movement that is so characteristic of our day should not blind us to the lessons of the past. Noble lives and great events are landmarks on the vast field of history. They help us to map out the past, and they also assist us to gain wisdom for the present. We cannot dispense with the landmarks of Scripture history. Christianity, without the facts of the life of Christ, would be boneless and shapeless. It is strong as a historical religion. Directly it is treated merely as an idea, a sentiment, or a " spirit," it will languish by the loss of the old landmarks of concrete facts in the Birth, Life, Passion, Death, and Resurrection of Christ.

III. ANCIENT LANDMARKS OF DOCTRINE. We live in an age when many of these have been uprooted and flung on one side. No doubt some of them had been converted into obstructions standing up in the middle of the road of truth. We need to ascertain whether we are really dealing with the truly ancient landmarks, and are not deceived by fraudulent inventions of later ages. The primary landmarks of Christianity are in the teachings of Christ and his apostles. We may have to clear away a great deal of the rubbish of the ages in order to get back to these original truths of Christianity. It is not right to accuse those who are loyal to Christ with removing the *ancient* landmarks, when they are only taking away these later accretions. But we cannot dispense with the truly ancient landmarks. If we forsake the New Testament, we forsake Christianity.

IV. ANCIENT LANDMARKS OF MORALS. Many practices of antiquity may be abandoned. Some may be superseded by better ways, others left behind as unsuited to the circumstances of the new times. But behind and beneath all these changing fashions there are the solid rocks of truth and righteousness. Whatever else may be shaken, we cannot afford to shift these landmarks. We may improve upon old customs ; but we cannot cast away the ten commandments.

HOMILIES BY VARIOUS AUTHORS.

Vers. **1—16.**—The theme of the earlier part of the chapter may be said to be the good name: the blessings in the possession of it, and the conditions for the acquirement of it—partly negatively, partly positively, described.

Vers. **1—5.**—*The general conditions of a good name.* I. WHAT DOES NOT CONSTITUTE ITS FOUNDATION. 1. *Riches.* (Ver. 1.) Riches have their worth; reputation has its worth; but the latter is of an order altogether different from the former. The former gives a *physical*, the latter a *moral*, power. It is right that we should have regard to the opinion of good men. "An evil name shall inherit disgrace and reproach," says Sirach **vi. 1.** And we have, as Christians, clearly to think of the effect a good or evil name must have upon "them that are without" (1 Cor. v. 12; x. 31, *sqq.*; Phil. iv. 8). 2. Again, poverty with a good name is infinitely preferable to riches associated with an evil character (ver. 2). It is according to general laws of providence that one is rich, the other poor. The great point is to recognize that we cannot all possess the lower good, but that the higher good is offered to all, made the duty of all to seek. Let the poor man not exaggerate the worth of riches, nor murmur against God, but humble himself under his hand, and trust the promises of his Word (Matt. v. 3). And let the rich man not put his confidence in riches (1 Tim. vi. 17), but lay up an inward store against the time to come. It is religion alone which solves the contradiction between riches and poverty by reducing both under the true standard of value.

II. THE POSITIVE CONDITIONS OF THE GOOD NAME. 1. *Prudence.* (Ver. 3.) To *foresee* evil at a distance—to have a cultivated spiritual sense, analogous to the keen scent of the lower animals, that may enable us to detect the danger not apprehensible by the duller sense—is necessary to our safety. And what is necessary to safety is necessary ultimately with a view to the good name. To go too near the fire may lead to the *scorching* of the reputation, if not to the loss of the life. To conceal ourselves beneath the wings of the Almighty and to abide in communion with God (Ps. xci. 1) is the best refuge from all danger. 2. *Humility.* (Ver. 4.) He that would attain to the glory must first " know how to be abased." Clearly to recognize our position and part in life always implies humility. For it is always less and lower than that which imagination dreams. Another important lesson from this verse is that reputation and the good attached to it come through seeking something else and something better. To do our *own work* is really to do something that has never been attempted before. For each of us is an original, and success in that which is peculiar to us brings more honour than success in a matter of greater difficulty in which we are but imitators of others. 3. *The fear of God.* (Ver. 4.) Religion gives *reality* to character. And reputation must at last rest on the presence of a reality; and those who have it not are perpetually being found out. 4. *Rectitude of conduct.* (Ver. 5.) What pains, anxieties, what dangers, rebuffs, and disappointments, and what loss of all that makes life sweet and good, do not the dishonest in every degree incur! The path of rectitude and truth seems rugged, but roses spring up around it, so soon as we begin fairly to tread it; the way of the transgressors seems inviting, but is indeed " hard."—J.

Vers. **6—12.**—*Means to the preservation of the good name.* I. EARLY TRAINING. (Ver. 6.) The young twig must be early bent. Experience teaches us that nothing in the world is so mighty for good or evil as custom; and therefore, says Lord Bacon, " since custom is the principal magistrate of man's life, let man by all means endeavour to obtain good customs. Custom is most perfect when it beginneth in young years; this we call education, which is in effect but an early custom. The tongue is more pliant to all expressions and sounds, the joints more supple to all feats of activity and motions, in youth than afterwards. Those minds are rare which do not show to their latest days the ply and impress they have received as children."

II. INDEPENDENCE. (Ver. 7.) How strongly was the worth of this felt in those ancient times! Poverty and responsibility to others are to be avoided. Many are forced into distress of conscience and to the loss of a good name by being tempted, for the sake of the rich man's gold or the great man's smile, to vote contrary to their convictions. Others will sell their liberty to gratify their luxury. It is an honest ambition to enjoy a competence that shall enable one to afford to be honest, and have the luxury of the freest expression of opinion. Hence frugality becomes so clear a moral duty.

III. INTEGRITY. (Ver. 8.) Ill-gotten gains cannot prosper. "The evil which issues from thy mouth falls into thy bosom," says the Spanish proverb. The rod wherewith the violent and unjust man struck others is broken to pieces.

IV. NEIGHBOURLY LOVE. (Ver. 9.) "Charity gives itself rich, covetousness hoards itself poor," says the German proverb. "Give alms, that thy children may not ask them," says a Danish proverb. "Drawn wells are never dry." So give to-day, that thou mayest have to give to-morrow; and to one, that thou mayest have to give to another. Let us remember, with the Italian proverb, that "our last robe is made without pockets." Above all, if our case is that "silver and gold we have none, let us freely substitute the kindly looks and the healing words, which are worth much and cost little."

V. A PEACEFUL TEMPER. (Ver. 10.) Let the scoffing, envious, contentious temper be cast out of our breast first. As for others, let us strike, if possible, at the cause and root of strife. Let there be solid argument for the doubter, and practical relief for actual grievances. Let us learn from the old fable, and follow the part of Epimetheus, who, when evils flew abroad from the box of Pandora, shut the lid and kept hope at the bottom of the vessel.

VI. A FAITHFUL AND CONSTANT HEART. (Ver. 11.) The greatest treasure to an earthly monarch, and dear above all to the King of kings. "He who serves God serves a good Master." Grace and truth are upon the lips of God's Anointed for evermore. And to clench these proverbs, let us recollect that nothing but truth in the inward parts can abide before the eye of Jehovah. "A lie has no legs." It carries along with itself the germs of its own dissolution. It is sure to destroy itself at last. Its priests may prop it up, after it has once fallen in the presence of the truth; but it will fall again, like Dagon, more shamefully and irretrievably than before. Truth is the daughter of God (Trench).—J.

Vers. 13—16.—*Hindrances to the attainment of a good name.* I. SLOTH. (Ver. 13.) It is full of ridiculous excuses here satirized. While a noble energy refuses to own the word "impossible," it is ever on the lips of the indolent. As in the Arabic fable of the ostrich, or "camel-bird," they said to it, "Carry!" It answered, "I cannot, for I am a bird." They said, "Fly!" It answered, "I cannot, for I am a camel." Always, "I *cannot!*" He who in false regard to his own soul refuses to go out into the world and do God's work, will end by corrupting and losing his soul itself (John xii. 25).

II. PROFLIGACY. (Ver. 14.) Lust digs its own grave. Health goes, reputation follows, and presently the life, self-consumed by the deadly fire, sinks into ruin and ashes. If men saw how plainly the curse of God is written on vice, it would surely become as odious to them as to him.

III. UNGOVERNED FOLLY. (Ver. 15.) Nothing more pitiable than an old fool, whose folly seems to stand in clear relief against the background of years. Hence, again, the urgent need of firm discipline for the young. And what occasion for thankfulness to him who, in his wise chastisements, will not "let us alone," but prunes and tills the soul by affliction, and plucks up our follies by the root!

IV. OPPRESSIVENESS. (Ver. 16.) To become rich at the expense of other's loss is no real gain. The attempt cuts at the root of sound trade and true sociality. Hastily gotten will hardly be honestly gotten. The Spaniards say, "He who will be rich in a year, at the half-year they hang him." Mammon, which more than anything else men are tempted to think God does not concern himself about, is given and taken away by him according to his righteousness—given sometimes to his enemies and for their greater punishment, that under its fatal influence they may grow worse and worse (Trench).—J.

Vers. 17—21.—*The words of the wise to be taken to heart.* I. THEY YIELD DIVINE PLEASURE (Ver. 18.) And all the pleasure of the world is not to be weighed against it. Let those who have " tasted of the good Word of God" bear their witness. The human soul is made for truth, and delights in it. There is pleasure in grasping a mathematical demonstration or a scientific law; and the successful inquirer may shout his " Eureka!" with joy over every fresh discovery. But above all, " how charming is Divine philosophy!"—that which traces the clear path of virtue, warns against vice, shows the eternal reward of the former and the doom of the latter. Received with the appetite of faith, Divine truth is food most sweet.

II. THEY LEAD US ON TO CONFIDENCE IN GOD. (Ver. 19.) And this is our true foundation. He is Jehovah, the Eternal One. He is the Constant One. His Name is the expression of mercy, of truth, and of justice. To love and to trust him is to be in living intercourse with all that is true and beautiful and good.

III. THEY ARE RICH IN MANIFOLD INSTRUCTION. (Ver. 20.) They are " princely words," *i.e.* of the highest and noblest dignity. Prone to sink into the commonplace, the mean, the impure, they lift us to high views of our calling, our duty, and our destiny.

IV. THEY PRODUCE JUSTICE OF THOUGHT AND SOUNDNESS OF SPEECH. (Ver. 21.) Thought and speech together form the garment of the soul. It is only the living sap of God's truth within us which can impart greenness and beauty, blossom and fruit, to the life. As water rises to the level from which it descended, so does all truth received into the soul go back in some form to the imparter, in thanks and in blessing.—J.

Vers. 22—29.—*Right in social relations.* I. RELATIONS TO THE POOR. (Vers. 22, 23.) 1. Robbery and oppression are a breach of the positive external law (Exod. xx. 15), much more of the inward and eternal law written in the heart, "Thou shalt love thy neighbour as thyself." 2. The perversion of law and magisterial authority to this end is an aggravation of the offence. It makes the refuge of the poor the market for bribery. 3. Above all, such oppression shows contempt for the authority of God. Among his titles to the throne of the world are these—that he is Protector of the helpless, Father of the fatherless, Judge of widows. The judgment on Ahab and the Captivity in Babylon (1 Kings xxi. 18—24; Isa. xxxiii. 1) may be referred to as examples of retributive judgment on the spoilers of the poor.

II. AGAINST ASSOCIATION WITH PASSIONATE AND PRECIPITATE MEN. (Vers. 24, 28.) It is a *contagious* temper. How soon is the habit of hot and violent language caught up from another! It is a *dangerous* temper. "Never anger made good guard for itself." It becomes more hurtful than the injury which provoked it. It is often an affected temper, compounded of pride and folly, and an intention to do commonly more mischief than it can bring to pass.

III. AGAINST THE RASH INCURRING OF LIABILITIES. (Vers. 26, 27; see on ch. vi. 1—4; xi. 15; xvii. 18; xx. 16.)

IV. AGAINST THE REMOVAL OF THE OLD LANDMARKS. (Ver. 28. See the express commands of the Law, Deut. xix. 14; xxvii. 17; Job xxiv. 2; Hos. v. 10.) A strict respect for the *rights* of others is the foundation of all social order. And connected with this is the duty of respect for the *feelings* for what is ancient and time-honoured. There should be no violent change in old customs of life and thought. Necessity may compel them; caprice should never dictate them. A spirit ever restless and bent on innovation is a nuisance in society. The existence of a custom is a proof of its meaning and relative worth; until it is discerned that the significance is now a false one, it should not be swept away.

V. ON THE PRINCIPLES OF SUCCESS. (Ver. 29.) 1. A man *must know his business* in the world. This is determined partly by his talents, partly by providential circumstances. "Know thy work" is as important a precept as "Know thyself." 2. He *must be diligent in his business,* doing " with his might" what his hand finds to do, labouring " with both hands earnestly " in every good cause. 3. The result will be *advancement and honour.* We have shining examples in Joseph, Nehemiah, Daniel. Ability and capacity are no less *acquired* than natural; use alone fully brings to light the talent, and to it Providence opens the suitable sphere of activity. Men may seem to be failures in this world who are not really so. He alone can judge of the fidelity of the heart who is to utter at the end of the sentence, " Well done, good and faithful servant!" "Many that are first will be last, and the last first."—J.

Ver. 1.—*Riches or reputation?* Both of these things are good in their way and in their measure. They may be held together, for many wealthy men have enjoyed a good name and much "loving favour." But it is not given to all men to command both of these. A large proportion of rich men have lost their reputation for equity and humanity by the way in which they have gained their wealth. And they must necessarily be many who are compelled to take and keep their place among the poor. But if only one of these two desirable things is open to us, we may be very well satisfied that this is not the wealth, but the worthiness, not the full treasury, but the good name and the kind regard. For—

I. WEALTH IS VERY LIMITED IN ITS CAPACITIES. It is true that it commands considerable material advantages, and that it puts it in the power of its possessor to enlarge his own mind, to extend his social circle, and to multiply his usefulness. This, however, it only does *as an instrument.* It does not ensure any of these things. Men may possess it, and they may, as very many of them do, altogether neglect to avail themselves of the opportunity. It does not even *dispose* men to do these wise things; it is as likely as not to allure them in other and even contrary directions. The power of mere wealth, apart from the character of its owner, is very much slighter than it seems. It only really secures bodily comforts and the *means* of advancement. 1. It does not confer even happiness, for mere jollity or transient excitement is not happiness. 2. It does not supply knowledge, much less capacity, and still less wisdom. 3. It does not provide the friendship which is worthy of the name, for no man who respects himself will be the friend of the rich simply because he *is* rich. We do not *love* a man because he has a large account at his bank. 4. It does not include the possession of any estimable moral qualities, nor, therefore, the favour of God. Moreover—

II. WEALTH HAS ITS SERIOUS DRAWBACKS. 1. It involves heavy burdens, great anxieties lest it should be lost. 2. It entails the most serious responsibility, lest its misuse or its non-use should bring down the weighty condemnation of God (Matt. xxv. 26). 3. It tempts to a dishonourable and degrading self-indulgence; also to a cynical and guilty contempt of the poor and lowly.

III. A GOOD REPUTATION INCLUDES OR IMPLIES THE BEST THINGS. Of course, men *may* acquire a fair name and even loving favour by very superficial qualities; but if they do, it is usually but short-lived. It breaks down under the weight of hard fact and accumulated experience. The good name which Solomon is thinking of, and which is the only thing of the kind worth pursuing, is that which is built upon or which springs from *a sound character.* It therefore implies the possession of uprightness, of purity, of truthfulness, of kindness, of reverence; and it therefore implies the possession of *piety* and the *favour of God.*

IV. A GOOD REPUTATION IS A SOURCE OF TRUE AND PURE SATISFACTION. 1. *It satisfies our self-respect;* for we rightly wish to enjoy the intelligent esteem of our neighbours. We are rightly troubled when we lose it; we are justified in our satisfaction that we possess it. It is a pure and lasting gratification. 2. *It satisfies our affections.* To have the "loving favour" of men is to have much true gladness of heart.

V. A GOOD REPUTATION IS A SOURCE OF MUCH POWER. While the bad rich man is steadily declining in his command, his humbler neighbour, who is esteemed for his wisdom and his worth, is gaining an influence for good with every passing year.—C.

Ver. 2.—"*Rich and poor.*" The great problem of excessive wealth and pitiable poverty confronts us still, and seems likely to task our united wisdom for many years, if not for several generations. We may regard—

I. THE BROAD AND NAKED FACT VISIBLE TO EVERY EYE. The fact that, while this world is stored with wealth beneath the ground, and is capable of bringing forth upon its surface ample supplies for all the need of the race, there is found amongst us a vast mass of miserable indigence. Children are born into the world in homes where parents do not know how to feed and clothe them, where an early death would seem to be the happiest fate; and other children are born into and brought up in homes where parents have a great deal more than they need to provide for their necessities, and where life offers every opportunity for enjoyment with no necessity for labour.

II. How FAR THIS DISTINCTION IS OF GOD. 1. Such deep and wide distinctions as now exist must be contrary to his purpose. We cannot possibly suppose that it is in accordance with his mind that thousands of his children should be starving, unclad or ill clad, homeless, exposed to the saddest sufferings and the darkest evils, while other thousands of his children have more than they need or know how to make good use of. 2. These distinctions are the ultimate result of the laws which he ordained. Poverty has its origin in sin; it is one of the penalties of wrong-doing. All the evil we see and sigh over, of every kind, we must trace to sin and to the consequences which sin entails. It is a Divine law that sin and suffering go together. 3. Some inequalities amongst us are directly due to his Divine ordering. He creates us with very different faculties. Some are fitted and enabled to do great things, which raise them in position and in circumstance above their brethren; others are not thus qualified Much, though **very** far indeed from everything, depends upon our natural endowments.

III. THE UNDESIRABLE SEPARATION WHICH EXISTS BETWEEN THE RICH AND THE POOR. We do not know our neighbours as we should. We pass one another with cold indifference. Too often men turn away from their inferiors (in circumstance) with a contemptuous disregard which signifies that the poor man is beneath their notice; too often men fail to appeal to their fellows because they think themselves unworthy to address them. Between man and man, between brother and brother, there is a gulf of isolation which must be painful and pitiful in the sight of the common Father, the Maker of them both.

IV. THE OCCASIONS WHEN THEY MEET. 1. Those on which they *must* feel the distinction between them—in business and in society. 2. Those on which they *should not* do so—when they meet in public worship or for Christian work, then all differences of a material and social kind should be forgotten and ignored. (1) What are these in presence of that which separates both rich and poor from the Infinite and Almighty One? (2) What are these in comparison with the question of moral and spiritual worth? In the sight of God, the poor but holy man is far more acceptable than the rich but unholy man. With him all questions of income or of title are utterly insignificant, positively invisible in presence of the questions of moral rectitude and spiritual worth. 3. One on which *they will not* do so (Rev. xx. 12).

1. Do your best to bridge the gulf, or, still better, to fill up the chasm which separates one class from another. 2. Take care to have that distinction which will survive the shocks of time and change.—C.

Ver. 3.—*Thoughtfulness and thoughtlessness.* All men might be divided into the thoughtful and the thoughtless. They belong either to those who look before them and prepare for the struggle or the danger that is coming, and avoid it; or else to those who go blindly on and stumble over the first impediment in their way. The " prudent man " of the text is not only the cautious man; he is the man of sagacity and foresight, who takes large and extended views of things. There are many illustrations of the thought, of which we may select.

I. THE EVIL OF PECUNIARY ENTANGLEMENT. The prudent man forbears to enter into that alliance, or into those relationships, or on to that course of action which will demand more resources than he can supply. But the simple "pass on "—become involved, and pay the penalty of prolonged anxiety, of great distraction, of painful humiliation, of grave dishonour, of financial ruin.

II. THE STRAIN OF UNWISE COMPANIONSHIP. A prudent man will consider well what company he can wisely keep, whose society will be beneficial and whose injurious to him, whether or not he can bear the pressure that will be put upon him to indulge in this or that direction, and he will shun the social circle that would be perilous to his integrity. But the simple take no heed, accept the first invitation that comes to them, become associated with those whose influence is deteriorating, succumb to their solicitation, and pay the penalty of serious spiritual declension.

III. THE FORCE OF SOME PARTICULAR TEMPTATION. The wise perceive the danger of the intoxicating cup, of the saloon, of the racecourse, of the gambling-table, and they keep steadfastly away. The simple pass on—self-confident, presumptuous, doomed, and they *are* punished indeed.

IV. THE PASSAGE OF YOUTH. The prudent recognize the fact that, unless youth yields its own particular fruit of knowledge, of acquisition, of capacity for work in one field or other, the prizes of life must be foregone; and, recognizing this, they do not waste the golden hours of study in idleness or dissipation. But the simple take no heed, trust to the chapter of accidents, wait upon fortune, fling away their precious chances, and are "punished" by having to take the lower path all the rest of their days.

V. THE RISK OF LOSING HEALTH. The prudent man sees that, if he urges his powers beyond the mark which kind and wise nature draws for him, he will gain a present advantage at the cost of future good, and he holds himself in check. The simple pass on—over-work, over-study, strain their faculties, and break down long before their time.

VI. THE LOSS OF LIFE. The wise man will count on this; he will reckon that any day he may be called to pass *from* his business and his family and his pleasure *to* the great account and the long future; and he lives accordingly, ready for life or for death, prepared to encounter the hour when he will look his last on time and confront eternity. The simple leave this stern fact out of their account; they pass on their way without making preparation either for those whom they must leave behind or for themselves when they enter the world where material treasures are of no account whatever; they pass on, and they "are punished," for they, too, reach the hour of departure, but they awake to the sad fact that that has been left undone for which a long life is not too long a preparation.—C.

Ver. 5.—*The path of the perverse.* By "the froward" we understand the spiritually perverse—those that will go on their own way, deaf to the commandments and the entreaties of their heavenly Father.

I. THE PATH OF THE PERVERSE. This is: 1. *One of guilt.* These froward souls who choose their own way, declining that to which God calls them, are most seriously guilty. Whether their disobedience be due to *careless inattention* or whether to *deliberate recusancy*, it is disloyal, ungrateful, presumptuous, offensive in a high degree. It is no wonder that it proves to be: 2. *One of suffering.* No wonder that "thorns" are in that way, thorns that pierce and pain—grievous troubles, poverty, sickness, loneliness, fear, remorse, forsakenness of God. Departure from God leads down to tangled places, causes men to be lost in thorny wildernesses where suffering abounds. It is also: 3. *One of danger.* It is a place of "snares." Without the "lamp unto the feet and the light unto the path," how should the traveller in "this dark world of sin" do otherwise than fall? Outside the service of Christ, and apart from his guidance, when the heart is uncontrolled from above, there is the greatest danger of the spirit giving way to one evil after another, of yielding to that multitude of strong temptations which attend the traveller's steps.

II. THE WAY OF THE WISE. There is no necessity for man finding the path of his life a path full of thorns and snares. It is true that no prudence or wisdom will prove an absolute guard therefrom; but if a man will "keep his soul" as he may keep it, he will be preserved in his integrity, he will even "be far" from the worst evils which overtake the froward and perverse. To "keep our soul" is to: 1. Understand its inestimable worth; to understand that it far transcends in value any property we may hold, or any position we may reach, or any prizes or pleasures we may snatch. 2. Realize that God claims it as his own; that to the Father of spirits, to the Saviour of souls, our hearts and lives belong; that to him they should be willingly and heartily surrendered, that they may be placed in his strong and holy keeping. 3. Guard it by the help of Divine wisdom; apply those precious truths which are in the pages of God's Word to its necessity; study the life and form the friendship of that One who himself *is* the Wisdom of God, walking with whom along the path of life we shall be safe from the wiles of the wicked one.—C.

Ver. 6.—*Parental training.* Very many parental hearts have leaned their weight of hope on these cheering words—many to be sustained and gladdened, some to be disappointed. We look at—

I. THE BROAD SPHERE OF PARENTAL TRAINING. What is the way in which a child should be trained to go? It is one that comprehends much. It includes: 1. *Manners.* These are not of the first importance, but they have their value. And if politeness, demeanour, bearing, be not engraven in the young, it will not be perfectly attained afterwards. 2. *Mind.* The habit of observing, of thinking, of reasoning, of sound reading, of calm consideration and discussion. 3. *Morals.* The all-important habits of truthfulness, of temperance, of industry, of self-command, of courage, of pure and stainless honesty, of unselfish considerateness, of generous forgiveness. 4. *Religion.* The habit of reverence in the use of the Divine Name, of public worship, of private prayer, of readiness to learn all that in any way God is willing to teach us.

II. The strength of the parental hope. Let the child be trained in these right ways, "and when he is old," etc. 1. *The assurance of habit.* When we have firmly planted a good habit in the mind and in the life, we have done a very great and a very good thing—we have gone far toward the goal we seek. For habit, early formed, is not easily broken. We sometimes allude to habit as if it were an enemy. But, in truth, it is our best friend. It is a gracious bond that binds us to wisdom and virtue. Without it we should have no security against temptation; with it we have every reason to hope that youth will pass into prime, and prime into old age, clothed with all the wisdom and adorned with all the grace that it received in its early years. What makes the assurance the more strong is that habit becomes more powerful with each effort and each action. Every day the good habits we have formed and are exercising become more deeply rooted in the soil of the soul. 2. *The assurance of the common experience of mankind.*

III. The necessary limit. Not the very best training of the very wisest parents in the world can positively *secure* goodness and wisdom in their children. For when they have done everything in their power, there must remain that element of individuality which will choose its own course and form its own character. Our children *may* choose to reject the truth we teach them, and to slight the example we set them, and to despise the counsel we give them. In the will of every child there is a power which cannot be forced, which can only be won. Therefore: 1. Let all parents seek, beside training their children in good habits, to *win* their hearts to that Divine Wisdom in whose friendship and service alone will they be safe. Where sagacity may fail, affection will triumph. Command and persuasion are the two weapons which parental wisdom will do its best to wield. 2. Let all children understand that for their character and their destiny they must themselves be responsible. All the very worthiest and wisest influences of home will lead to no good result if they oppose to them a rebellious spirit, if they do not receive them in the spirit of docility. There is but one gate of entrance into life, and that is the *personal, individual* acceptance of Jesus Christ as the Lord and Saviour of the spirit. The parent may lead his child up to it, but that child must pass through it of his own accord.—C.

Ver. 13.—*Excuses.* Few things are oftener on human lips than excuses. Men are continually excusing themselves from doing what they know in their hearts they ought to do. There is no sphere from which they are excluded, and there is hardly any evil to which they do not lead.

I. The spheres in which they are found. The child excuses himself from the obedience which he should be rendering to his parents; the scholar, from the application he should be giving to his studies; the apprentice, from the attention he should be devoting to his business; the agriculturist, from the labour he should be putting forth in the fields; the captain, from setting sail on the troubled waters; the unsuccessful tradesman or merchant, from investigating his books and seeing how he really stands; the failing manufacturer, from closing his mill; the statesman from bringing forward his perilous measure; the minister, from seeking his delicate and difficult interview; the soul not yet reconciled to God, from a searching inquiry into its own spiritual condition and present obligation.

II. Their moral character. 1. There is a decided ingredient of *falsehood* about them. Those who fashion them know in their hearts that there is something, if not much, that is imaginary about them. The lion is *not* without; the slothful man will *not* be slain in the streets. The evil which is anticipated in all cases of excuse is exaggerated, if it is not invented. We do not, at such times, tell ourselves the whole truth; we "deceive our own selves." 2. There is something of *meanness* or unmanliness about them; we "let 'I dare not' wait upon 'I would.'" We allow a craven feeling of apprehension to enter in, to take possession, to prevail over our better self. 3. There is an element of *disobedience* and unfaithfulness. We shrink from doing the thing which is our duty to do; we relegate to the rear that which we should keep in the front; we prefer that which is agreeable to that which is obligatory; we obey the lower voice; we leave unfulfilled the will of God.

III. THE FATE OF THOSE WHO INDULGE THEM. 1. To have a very pitiable retrospect; to have to look back, self-condemned, on work left undone, on a life not well lived. 2. To lose all that might have been gained by energy and decision, and which has been lost by sloth and weakness. And who shall say what this amounts to in the years of a long life? 3. To miss the "Well done" of the Master, if not, indeed, to receive his final and sorrowful condemnation.—C.

Ver. 15.—(See homily on ch. xiii. 24.)—C.

Vers. 16, 22.—(See homily on ver. 28.)—C.

Vers. 24, 25.—(See homily on ch. xvi. 32.)—C.

Vers. 26, 27.—(See homily on ch. vi. 1—5.)—C.

Ver. 28.—*The ancient landmark.* The text clearly refers to the ancient division of property by which the land was carefully marked out, and each family had its own proper share. The man who removed these boundaries in his own material interest was simply appropriating what did not belong to him. Perhaps "the removal of the ancient landmark" became a proverbial phrase to signify any serious departure from rectitude. It will be worth while to consider—

I. WHAT IS NOT FORBIDDEN IN THIS PRECEPT. 1. A change in social customs. It is found by experience that we are all the better for leaving certain usages behind us. We outgrow them, and they become hindrances rather than aids to us. 2. The remodelling of old institutions. The time comes when the old order changes, giving place to new, by common consent and to the general advantage. With new methods, new organizations, there may come new life and renewed power. 3. The change of religious vocabulary. There is nothing wrong in putting the old doctrine in new forms; indeed, it becomes more living and more telling when uttered in the language of the time. Ancient phraseology is to be respected, but it is not sacred; it may and must give place to new. 4. The modification of Christian doctrine; not, indeed, a change of "the faith once delivered to the saints"—a departure from "the truth as it is in Jesus," but such a varying account and statement of it as comes with increased light from the study of nature or of man, and with further reverent research of the Word of God. But what is—

II. THE WRONG WHICH IS HERE FORBIDDEN. It is *all criminal selfishness*, more especially such as that referred to—the appropriation of land by immoral means, or the securing of any kind of property by tampering with a deed or other document. It may include the act of obtaining any advantage in any direction whatever by means that are dishonourable and unworthy. In all such cases we need the ear to hear a Divine, "Thou shalt not." To act thus is a sin and a mistake. It is: 1. To disobey the voice of the Lord, who emphatically denounces it. Especially does God rebuke and threaten the wronging of the poor and feeble because they *are* such; to do this is to add meanness and cowardice to selfishness and crime (see vers. 16, 22). 2. To injure ourselves far more seriously and irremediably than we hurt our neighbour. It is to lose the favour of God, the approval of our own conscience, and the esteem of the just.—C.

Ver. 29.—(See homily on ch. vi. 6—11; xxvii. 23.)—C.

EXPOSITION.

CHAPTER XXIII.

Vers. 1—3.—A hexastich closely connected with the last verse of the preceding chapter, as if the warning was addressed to the man of skill whom his talents had made the guest of kings.

Ver. 1.—When thou sittest to eat with a ruler. This, of course, would be a great honour to a man of lowly birth, or to one of the middle class, to whom the manners of courts and palaces were practically unknown. Consider diligently what is before thee. So the Vulgate, Quæ apposita sunt ante faciem tuam ; and the Septuagint, Τὰ παρατιθέμενά σοι. Take heed lest the unusual dainties on the table tempt thee to excess, which may lead not only to unseemly behaviour, but also to unruly speech, revealing of secrets, etc. But the latter words may also be rendered, "him that is," or, "who is before thee." And this gives a very appropriate sense. The guest is enjoined to fix his attention, not on the delicate food, but on the host, who is his superior, and able to exalt and to destroy him (compare the cautious maxims in Ecclus. xiii. 2, 6, 7, 11, etc.).

Ver. 2.—And put a knife to thy throat, if thou be a man given to appetite. "Stab thy gluttony," Wordsworth. Restrain thyself by the strongest measures, convince thyself that thou art in the utmost peril, if thou art a glutton or wine-bibber (Ecclus. xxxiv. [xxxi.] 12). The LXX. gives a different turn to the injunction, "And apply (ἐπίβαλλε) thy hand, knowing that it behoves thee to prepare such things." This is like the warning of Siracides, in the chapter quoted above, where the disciple is admonished not to attend the banquets of rich men, lest he should be tempted to vie with them, and thus ruin himself by attempting to return their civilities in the same lavish manner. The earlier commentators have used the above verses as a lesson concerning the due and reverent partaking of the Holy Communion, thus: "When you approach the table of Christ, consider diligently what is represented by the elements before you, and have discernment and faith, lest you eat and drink unworthily ; and after communicating walk warily, mortify all evil desires, live as in the presence of the Lord Jesus, the Giver of the feast."

Ver. 3.—Be not desirous of his dainties. (For "dainties," see on ver. 6.) Be not too greedy of the bounties of the royal table, so as to forget discretion, and be led to say and do things which are inexpedient or unseemly. For they are deceitful meat. Oftentimes

such entertainment is not offered for friendship's sake, but for some sinister purpose—to make a man expose himself, to get at a man's real character or secrets. Far from being a sign of favour and good will, the seeming honour is deceptive and dangerous. We all know Horace's lines, 'Ars Poet.,' 434, etc.—

" Reges dicuntur multis urgere culullis
Et torquere mero, quem perspexisse laborant,
An sit amicitia dignus."

Hitzig quotes the Eastern proverb, "He who eats of the sultan's soup burns his lips, even though it be after a length of time." We have too the Indian saying, "An epicure digs his grave with his teeth," which is true in more senses than one. "Keep thee far from the man that hath power to kill," says Siracides (Ecclus. ix. 13) ; "so shalt thou not be troubled with fear of death : and if thou come unto him, commit no fault, lest he presently take away thy life ; remember that thou goest in the midst of snares, and that thou walkest upon the battlements of the city." Then for the reasons which induce a ruler to ply a guest with wine, we have, "In vino veritas. Quod est in corde sobrii, est in ore ebrii." Theognis writes—

'Εν πυρὶ μὲν χρυσόν τε καὶ ἄργυρον ἴδριες ἄνδρες
Γιγνώσκουσ', ἀνδρὸς δ' οἶνος ἔδειξε νόον,
Καὶ μάλα περ πινυτοῦ, τὸν ὑπέρ μέτρον ἤρατο πίνων,
῾Ωστε καταισχῦναι καὶ πρὶν ἐόντα σοφόν.

The Septuagint combines the ending of ver. 2, "But if thou art more insatiable, desire not his victuals, for these appertain to (ἔχεται) a false life."

Vers. 4, 5.—These form a pentastich.

Ver. 4.—Labour not—weary not thyself —to be rich. John vi. 27, "Labour not for the meat that perisheth," where the warning is against that absorbing eagerness for wealth which leads to evil-doing and neglect of all higher interests. Cease from thine own wisdom. The wisdom (binah, ch. iii. 5) is that which is necessary for making and keeping wealth. Vulgate, Prudentiæ tuæ pone modum. This is not the highest form of wisdom (chochmah), but rather the faculty of distinguishing one thing from another, mere discernment, which may exist without any religious or keen moral sense (see note on ch. xvi. 16, where possibly the contrast is expressed). Talmud, "He who augments his riches augments his cares." Erasmus, 'Adag.,' quotes or writes—

"Jupiter ementitur opes mortalibus ipse,
Sic visum ut fuerit, cuicunque, bonove,
  malove."

Septuagint, "If thou art poor, measure not thyself (μὴ παρεκτείνου) with a rich man, but in thy wisdom refrain thyself."

Ver. 5.—**Wilt thou set thine eyes upon that which is not?** more literally, *wilt thou let thine eyes fly upon it, and it is gone?* Why cast longing looks towards this wealth, and so prepare for yourself loss and disappointment? The pursuit is vain, and the result is never secure; what you gained by long toil and prudent care may be lost in an hour. Do you wish to incur this danger? Wordsworth quotes Persius, ' Sat.,' iii. 61—

" An passim sequeris corvos testaque lutoque?"

For riches certainly make themselves wings. The subject, unexpressed, is riches, and the Hebrew phrase implies absolute certainty: *Making they will make for themselves.* **They fly away as an eagle toward heaven;** or, *like an eagle that flieth toward heaven,* where not even sight can follow. Publ. Syr., 255, " Longinquum est omne quod cupiditas flagitat." The Telugu compares worldly prosperity to writing upon water. Says the Greek moralist—

Βέβαιον οὐδέν ἐν βίῳ δοκεῖ πέλειν.

" There's naught in life that one can deem secure."

Septuagint, " If thou fix thine eye upon him (the rich patron), he will nowhere be seen, for wings like an eagle's are ready prepared for him, and he will return to the house of his master (τοῦ προεστηκότος αὐτοῦ), and leave you to shift for yourself."

Vers. 6—8.—Another maxim, here a heptastich, concerning temperance.

Ver. 6.—**Eat thou not the bread of him that hath an evil eye;** the envious and jealous man, in contrast to the "good of eye" (ch. xxii. 9). Vulgate, *Ne comedas cum homine invido.* Septuagint, ἀνδρὶ βασκάνῳ, the man who has the evil eye that fascinates, which, however, is a later idea; here the notion is rather of a grudging, sordid temper, that cannot bear the sight of others' happiness or prosperity (comp. Deut. xv. 9; Matt. xx. 15). Ecclus. xvi. 8, Πονηρὸς ὁ βασκαίνων ὀφθαλμῷ, "The envious man hath an evil eye; he turneth away his face, and he is one who despiseth men." **Dainty meats;** as in ver. 3. The word (*matammoth*) occurs also throughout Gen. xxvii., where it is rendered, "savoury meat." Talmud, " To ask a favour from a miser is as if you asked wisdom from a woman, modesty from a harlot, fish on the dry land."

Ver. 7.—**For as he thinketh in his heart,**

so is he. The verb here used is שָׁעַר (*shaar*), " to estimate," " to calculate," and the clause is best rendered, *For as one that calculates with himself, so is he.* The meaning is that this niggardly host watches every morsel which his guest eats, and grudges what he appears to offer so liberally. In the Authorized Version the word " heart " occurs twice in this verse, but the Hebrew words are different. The first is *nephesh,* " breath," equivalent to " mind; " the second is *leb,* " heart." The Vulgate paraphrases the clause, *Quoniam in similitudinem arioli et conjectoris, æstimat quod ignorat,* " For like a soothsayer or diviner he conjectures that of which he is ignorant." **Eat and drink, saith he to thee.** He professes to make you welcome, and with seeming cordiality invites you to partake of the food upon his table. **But his heart is not with thee.** He is not glad to see you enjoy yourself, and his pressing invitation is empty verbiage with no heart in it. The Septuagint, pointing differently, translates, " For as if one should swallow a hair, so he eats and drinks." The Greek translators take the gnome to apply to one who invites an envious man to his table, and finds him eating his food as if it disgusted him. They go on, " Bring him not in to thee, nor eat thy morsel with him; for (ver. 8) he will vomit it up, and outrage thy fair words." In agreement with the gnome above, we find in the Talmud, " My son, eat not the bread of the covetous, nor sit thou at his table. The bread of the covetous is only pain and anguish; the bread of the generous man is a source of health and joy."

Ver. 8.—**The morsel which thou hast eaten shalt thou vomit up.** Food thus grudgingly bestowed will only create disgust, and do thee no good; thou wilt feel annoyed to have eaten it, and wilt long to get rid of it. **And lose thy sweet words.** You will have expended in vain your civil speeches and thanks for the entertainment provided for you; you really owe no gratitude for fare so grudgingly bestowed. Some think that by the " sweet words " are meant the conversation at table with which you have endeavoured to amuse your host—the witty sayings, enigmas, and apothegms, which entered so largely into the programme of a good talker. All such efforts are thrown away on the jealous, morose host. But the former explanation is more agreeable to the context.

Ver. 9.—Here is another case in which " sweet words " are lost. **Speak not in the ears of a fool.** This does not mean, as it would in our English phrase—whisper not to a fool; but do not take the trouble to try to make him understand, impart nothing to him. The " fool " here (*kesil*) is the dull, stolid, stupid man, who cannot be moved from his own narrow groove (see on ch. i. 22). It is a mere casting of pearls before swine (Matt. vii. 6) to speak to such a man of high aims, righteous motives, self-sacrifice (comp. ch. ix. 8). **He will despise the wisdom of thy words.** He cannot enter into the meaning of words of wisdom; he has no appetite for them, he cannot assimilate them; and in his self-satisfied dulness he feels for them nothing but contempt (Ecclus. xxii. 7, etc., "Whoso teacheth a fool is as one that glueth a potsherd together, and as he that waketh one from a sound sleep. He that telleth a tale to a fool speaketh to one in a slumber: when he hath told his tale, he will say, What is the matter?")

Vers. 10, 11.—An enlargement of ch. xxii. 28 combined with ch. xxii. 22, 23.

Ver. 10.—**Enter not into the fields of the fatherless.** Do not think to appropriate the fields of orphans, as if there were no one to defend their rights (comp. ch. xv. 25).

Ver. 11.—**For their Redeemer is mighty.** The redeemer (*goel*) is the near kinsman, who had to avenge bloodshed, carry on the blood-feud, or vindicate the cause of a relation otherwise unsupported (see Numb. xxv. 12, 19, 21; Lev. xxv. 25; Ruth iii. 2, 9, 12). God himself will be the orphans' Goel. This term is often applied to God; *e.g.* Job xix. 25; Ps. xix. 14; Jer. l. 34. **He shall plead their cause with thee.** He will, as it were, conduct their cause, try thee, convict thee of injustice, and pronounce thy condemnation (ch. xxii. 23).

Ver. 12 commences a new series of proverbs of wisdom. This general admonition is addressed to all, tutor and disciple, educator and educated. **Apply thine heart unto instruction.** (For *musar*, "instruction," see note on ch. i. 2.)

Ver. 13.—An injunction to the tutor or parent (comp. ch. xiii. 24; xix. 18; xxii. 15; xxix. 17). **For if thou beatest him with the rod, he shall not die.** This has been understood in various senses; *e.g.* "Though thou scourge him, that correction will not kill him;" "If thou chastise him, thou wilt save him from the doom of the rebellious son" (Deut. xxi. 18—21); or, "He shall not die eternally," which rather anticipates the conclusion in the next verse. The expression merely means—Do not be weak, thinking that you will injure your child by judicious correction, and in this fear withholding your hand; but punish him firmly when necessary, and, far from harming him, you will be doing him the greatest good.

Ver. 14.—**Shalt deliver his soul from hell** (*sheol*); *de inferno*, Vulgate; ἐκ θανάτου, Septuagint. Premature death was regarded as a punishment of sin, as long life was the

reward of righteousness. Proper discipline preserves a youth not only from many material dangers incident to unbridled passions, but saves him from spiritual death, the decay and destruction of grace here, and the retribution that awaits the sinner in another world (comp. Ecclus. xxx. 1—12).

Ver. 15.—The moralist now addresses the disciple, and so to the end of the chapter. **If thine heart be wise;** become wise by profiting by discipline, and having its natural folly (ch. xxii. 15) eradicated. **My heart shall rejoice, even mine.** The pronoun is repeated for the sake of emphasis (as in ch. xxii. 19), the speaker thus declaring his supreme interest in the moral progress of his pupil.

Ver. 16.—**My reins shall rejoice.** The "reins" (*kelayoth*), kidneys, are regarded as the seat of feeling and sensation (Job xix. 27), or of the inner nature generally (Ps. xvi. 7; Rev. ii. 22). **I shall rejoice in my very soul when thy lips speak right things;** *i.e.* when thy heart is so replete with wisdom, thy mind so well instructed as to utter naught but what is true and sensible (ch. viii. 6). The composition of these two verses is noteworthy, 15*a* being parallel to 16*b*, and 15*b* to 16*a*. Septuagint, "And thy lips shall linger in words (ἐνδιατρίψει λόγοις) with my lips, if they be right," which seems to mean, "If thy lips utter what is right, they will gather wisdom from my words and impart it to others."

Ver. 17.—**Let not thine heart envy sinners,** when thou seest them apparently happy and prosperous (comp. ch. iii. 31; xxiv. 1, 19; Ps. xxxvii. 1; lxxiii. 3). The Authorized Version, in agreement with the Septuagint, Vulgate, Arabic, and other versions, takes the second clause of this verse as an independent one; but it seems evidently to be constructionally connected with the preceding, and to be governed by the same verb, so that there is no occasion to insert "be thou." **But be thou in the fear of the Lord all the day long.** Jerome, corrected, would read, *Non æmuletur cor tuum peccatores, sed timorem Domini tota die.* As Delitzsch and Hitzig, followed by Nowack, have pointed out, the Hebrew verb, קנא (*kana*), is here used in two senses. In the first clause it signifies to be envious of a person; in the second, to be zealous for a thing, both senses combining in the thought of being moved with eager desire. Ζηλοτυπέω is used in this double sense, and *æmulor* in Latin. So the gnome comes to this—Show your heart's desire, not by envy of the sinner's fortune, but by zeal for true religion, that fear of the Lord which leads to strict obedience and earnest desire to please him.

Ver. 18.—**For surely there is an end.**

Some take the hemistich conditionally, rendering אם "when," or "if the end comes;" but one sees no object in the thought being expressed conditionally; and it is best, with the Authorized Version, Nowack, and others, to take כי אם equivalent to "assuredly," as in Judg. xv. 7; 2 Sam. xv. 21. "End" (*acharith*) is the glorious future that awaits the pious (ch. xxiv. 14; Jer. xxix. 11). The prosperity of sinners is not to be envied, for it is transitory and deceptive; but for the righteous, however depressed at times, there is a happy end in prospect. **And thine expectation** (*hope*) **shall not be cut off.** The hope of comfort here and reward hereafter shall be abundantly realized. The writer has a firm belief in the moral government of God, and in a future life which shall rectify all anomalies (comp. ch. xiv. 32; Wisd. v. 15, etc.; Ecclus. i. 13). Septuagint, "For if thou keep them, thou shalt have posterity, and thy hope shall not be removed" (Ps. xxxvii. 9; Job xiii. 12).

Vers. 19—21.—An exhortation to temperance, as one of the results of the fear of God, prefaced by an exhortation to wisdom.

Ver. 19.—Hear thou. The pronoun gives force and personality to the injunction (Job xxxiii. 33). **Guide thine heart in the way.** (For אשר, "to guide straight," see on ch. iv. 14.) "The way" is the right way, in distinction to the many wrong paths of life— the way of understanding, as it is called (ch. ix. 6). Septuagint, "Direct aright the thoughts of thy heart," for right thoughts lead to right actions.

Ver. 20.—Wine-bibbers; persons who meet together for the express purpose of drinking intoxicating liquors. **Among riotous eaters of flesh.** The Hebrew is "of flesh for themselves," whence some take the meaning to be "of their own flesh," *i.e.* who by their gluttony and luxury ruin their own bodies. But the parallelism with the wine-drinker shows plainly that the flesh which they eat is meant, and the idea is that they eat for the gratification of their own appetites, caring nothing for anything else. The combination of glutton and wine-bibber was used as a reproach against our blessed Lord (Matt. xi. 19). The versions of Jerome and the LXX. point to the contributed entertainments, where each guest brought some article to the meal, like our picnics. Thus Vulgate, "Be not among parties of drinkers, nor at the banquets of those who contribute flesh to eat;" Septuagint, "Be not a wine-bibber, and strain not after contributed feasts (συμβολαῖς) and purchases of meats."

Ver. 21.—Intemperance leads to prodigality, carelessness, and ruin. **And drowsiness shall clothe a man with rags.** The luxury and excess spoken of above lead to

drowsiness and inability to work, and poverty follows as the natural result (comp. ch. xix. 15; xxiv. 33, etc.). The Vulgate still harps on the same string as in the previous verse, "Those who waste time in drinking, and who give picnics (*dantes symbola*), shall be ruined, and somnolence shall clothe with rags." The LXX. introduces a new idea, which the Hebrew does not warrant, "For every drunkard and whoremonger shall be poor, and every sluggard shall clothe himself with tatters and rags."

Vers. 22—25.—An octastich, containing an earnest exhortation to the disciple.

Ver. 22.—That begat thee. This is a claim on the attention and obedience of the son. **When she is old.** When old age with its consequent infirmities comes upon thy mother, despise her not, but rather thank God for giving her long life, and profit by her love and long experience (comp. Ecclus. iii. 1, etc., where the exhortation to honour parents is very full and touching).

Ver. 23.—Buy the truth, and sell it not (comp. ch. iv. 5, 7; xvi. 16). Consider truth as a thing of the highest value, and spare no pains, cost, or sacrifice to obtain it, and, when gotten, keep it safe; do not barter it for earthly profit or the pleasures of sense; do not be reasoned out of it, or laughed out of it; "sell it not," do not part with it for any consideration. The second clause gives the sphere in which truth moves, or the three properties which appertain to it. These are: **wisdom** (*chochmah*), practical knowledge; **instruction** (*musar*), moral culture and discipline; and **understanding** (*binah*), the faculty of discernment (see notes on ch. i. 2). This verse is omitted in the chief manuscripts of the Septuagint.

Ver. 24.—The father of the righteous shall greatly rejoice. The father of a righteous son who has won truth and profited by the possession has good cause to be glad (ch. x. 1). Septuagint erroneously, "A righteous father brings up children well." The second clause repeats the first in different words, with the further idea that the wise son affords his father practical proof of the excellence of his moral training. The contrast is seen in ch. xvii. 21.

Ver. 25.—Shall be glad; or, *let them be glad; gaudeat*, Vulgate; εὐφραινέσθω, Septuagint. **She that bare thee.** As in ver. 24 the father's joy was expressly mentioned, so here prominence is given to that of the mother. In the former case it is "he that begetteth;" here, "she that beareth."

Vers. 26—28.—A hexastich, in which Wisdom herself is the speaker, and warns against unchastity.

Ver. 26.—Give me thine heart. Do not waste thy powers and affections on evil objects, but set thy soul with all its best faculties on me, Wisdom, who alone can satisfy its desires and aspirations. There is an eloquent passage in a tract that has gone by St. Bernard's name, though not written by him ('Epist. de Reg. Vitæ Spirit.,' ii. 1604, Mab.), which is worth quoting: "Cor nostrum nihil dignius perficere potest, quam ut ei se restituat a quo factum est: et hoc a nobis Dominus expetit dicens, ' Fili, da mihi cor tuum.' Tunc siquidem cor hominum Deo datur, quando omnis cogitatio terminatur in eum, gyrat et circumflectitur super eum, et nihil vult possidere præter eum. Sicque colligato sibi animo, eum diligit, ut sine ipso amarus sit omnis amor. Nec aliud dixerim cor Domino dare, quam ipsum captivare in omne obsequium ejus, et ita voluntati ejus ex toto supponere, ut nihil aliud velit, quam quod noverit eum velle." Let thine eyes observe my ways; keep closely to the paths of virtue which I teach thee, especially the path of purity, as the next verse shows. Vulgate, Vias meas custodiant; Septuagint, 'Εμὰς ὁδοὺς τηρείτωσαν. This is the reading of the Keri, תִּצֹּרְנָה; the Khetib, which Delitzsch and others prefer, reads תִּרְצֶנָה, "delight in" my ways.

Ver. 27.—The need of the emphatic injunction in ver. 26 is exemplified by the dangers of impurity. A deep ditch; as ch. xxii. 14. A strange woman is a narrow pit. (For "strange woman," equivalent to "harlot," see on ch. ii. 16.) A narrow pit is one with a narrow mouth, from which, if one falls into it, it is difficult to extricate one's self. The verse indicates the seductive nature of the vice of unchastity: how easy it is to be led into it! how difficult to rise from it! Thus St. Chrysostom ('Hom. xi. in 1 Cor.'), "When by unclean desire the soul is made captive, even as a cloud and mist darken the eyes of the body, so that desire intercepts the foresight of the mind, and suffers no one to see any distance before him, either precipice, or hell, or fear; but thenceforth, having that deceit as a tyrant over him, he comes to be easily vanquished by sin; and there is raised up before his eyes as it were a partition wall, and no windows in it, which suffers not the ray of righteousness to shine in upon the mind, the absurd conceits of lust enclosing it as with a rampart on all sides. And then, and from that time forward, the unchaste woman is everywhere meeting him—before his eyes, before his mind, before his thoughts, in station and presence. And as the blind, although they stand at high noon beneath the very central point of the heaven, receive not the light, their eyes being fast closed up; just so these also, though ten thousand doctrines of salvation sound in their ears from all quarters, having their soul preoccupied with this passion, stop their ears against all discourses of that kind. And they know it well who have made the trial. But God forbid that you should know it from actual experience!" The LXX. has changed the allusion: "For a strange house is a pierced wine-jar (πίθος τετρημένος), and a strange well is narrow," where the idea seems to be that the private well, which is dug for the convenience of one family only, is not to be relied upon, and will yield not enough to supply others' wants. Hence would arise a warning against coveting a neighbour's wife. There is a Greek proverb about drawing wine into pierced jars (Xen., 'Œcon.,' vii. 40).

Ver. 28.—She also lieth in wait as for a prey. "Yea, she [ch. xxii. 19] lieth in wait," as is graphically described in ch. vii. (comp. Jer. iii. 2). Chetheph is better taken, not as "prey," but in a concrete sense as the person who snatches it, the robber. Vulgate, Insidiatur in via quasi latro (comp. Ps. x. 9). And increaseth the transgressors among men. The Greek and Latin versions have taken רֹסִף as meaning "kills," "destroys." But the verb yasaph always means "to add," here "to multiply." The special transgression indicated is treachery or faithlessness. The harlot leads her victim to be faithless to his God, his wife, his parents, his tutor, his master. Septuagint, "For he shall perish suddenly, and every transgressor shall be destroyed."

Vers. 29—35.—Here follows a mashal ode or song on the subject of drunkenness, which is closely connected with the sin mentioned in the previous lines.

Ver. 29.—Who hath woe? who hath sorrow? Hebrew, lemi oï, lemi aboï, where oï and aboï are interjections of pain or grief. So Venetian, τίνι αἶ, τίνι φεῦ; Revised Version margin, Who hath Oh? who hath Alas? The Vulgate has stumbled at the second expression, which is an ἅπαξ λεγόμενον, and resolving it into two words, translates, Cujus patri væ? Contentions; the brawling and strife to which drunkenness leads (ch. xx. 1). Babbling; שִׂיחַ (siach) is rather "meditation," "sorrowful thought" showing itself in complaining, regret for lost fortune, ruined health, alienated friends. Others render "misery," "penury." St. Jerome's foveæ is derived from a different reading. The LXX. has κρίσεις, "lawsuits," ἀηδίαι καὶ λέσχαι, "disgust and gossipings." Wounds without cause; wounds which might have been avoided, the result of quarrels in which a sober man would never have engaged.

Redness of eyes. The Hebrew word *chakli-luth* is commonly taken to mean the flashing of eyes occasioned by vinous excitement. The Authorized Version refers it to the bloodshot appearance of a drunkard's eyes, as in Gen. xlix. 12, according to the same version. But Delitzsch, Nowack, and many modern commentators consider that the word indicates "dimness of sight," that change in the power of vision when the stimulant reaches the brain. Septuagint, "Whose eyes are livid (πελιδνοί)?" The effects of intemperance are described in a well-known passage of Lucretius, ' De Rer. Nat.,' iii. 475, etc.—

"Denique, cor hominum quom vini vis penetravit
Acris, et in venas discessit diditus ardor,
Consequitur gravitas membrorum, præpediuntur
Crura vacillanti, tardescit lingua, madet mens,
Nant oculei; clamor, singultus, jurgia gliscunt."

We may refer to the article in Jeremy Taylor's 'Holy Living' on "Evil Consequents to Drunkenness," and to Ecclus. xxxiv. (xxxi.) 25, etc.

Ver. 30.—The answer to the above searching questions is here given. They that tarry long at the wine (Isa. v. 11), who sit till late hours drinking. They that go to seek mixed wine; *i.e.* go to the wine-house, place of revelry, where they may taste and give their opinion upon "mixed wine," *mimsak*, wine mingled with certain spices or aromatic substances, or else simply with water, as it was too luscious to be drunk undiluted (see on ch. ix. 2). Septuagint, "those who hunt out where carousals are taking place."

Ver. 31.—Look not thou upon the wine when it is red. Be not attracted by its beautiful appearance. The wine of Palestine was chiefly "red," though what we call white wine was not unknown. The Vulgate *flavescit* points to the latter. When it giveth his colour in the cup. For "colour" the Hebrew has "eye," which refers to the sparkling and gleaming which show themselves in wine poured into the cup. It is as though the cup had an eye which glanced at the drinker with a fascination which he did not resist. When it moveth itself aright. Having warned against the attraction of sight, the moralist now passes to the; seduction of taste. Hebrew, *when it goeth by the right road.* This may refer to its transference from the jar or skin to the drinking-cup; but it more probably alludes to the drinker's throat, and is best translated, " when it glideth down smoothly." Vulgate, *ingreditur blande.* The wine pleases

the palate, and passes over it without roughness or harshness (comp. Cant. vii. 9). The LXX. has enlarged on the original thus: "Be ye not drunk with wine, but converse with just men, and converse in public places (ἐν περιπάτοις). For if thou set thine eyes on goblets and cups, afterwards thou shalt walk more bare than a pestle (γυμνότερος ὑπέρου)." This last expression, *pistillo nudior*, is a proverb. Regarding the danger of looking on seductive objects, the Arab, in his sententious language, says, "The contemplation of vice is vice."

Ver. 32.—At the last it biteth like a serpent. Wine is like the subtle poison of a serpent, which affects the whole body, and produces the most fatal consequences (comp. Ecclus. xxi. 2). *Nachash* is the generic name for any of the larger tribe of snakes (Gen. iii. 1, etc.); the poisonous nature of its bite was, of course, well known (Numb. xxi. 9). Stingeth like an adder. The Hebrew word is *tsiphoni*, which is usually rendered "cockatrice" in the Authorized Version, but the particular species intended has not been accurately identified. There was some confusion in men's minds as to the organ which inflicted the poisonous wound. Thus a psalmist says, "They have sharpened their tongue like a serpent" (Ps. cxl. 3). But the verb "sting" is to be taken in the sense of puncturing, making a wound. Vulgate, *Sicut regulus venena diffundet*, "It will diffuse its poison like a basilisk:" Septuagint, "But at the last he stretches himself like one stricken by a serpent, and the venom is diffused through him as by a horned snake (κεράστου)."

Ver. 33.—The excitement occasioned by wine is now described. Thine eyes shall behold strange women. Ewald, Delitzsch, and others take זָרוֹת to mean "strange things," as affording a better parallel to the "perverse things" of the next clause. In this case the writer intends to denote the fantastic, often dreadful, images produced on the brain by the feverish condition of the inebriated. But the often denounced connection between drunkenness and incontinence, the constant reference to "strange women" in this book, and the general consensus of the versions, lead one to uphold the rendering of the Authorized Version. It seems, too, somewhat meagre to note these illusions as one of the terrible effects of intemperance, omitting all mention of the unbridling of lust, when the eyes look out for and rove after unchaste women. Thine heart shall utter perverse things (comp ch. xv. 28; Matt. xv. 19). The drunkard's notions are distorted, and his words partake of the same character; he confuses right and wrong; he says things which he would never speak if he were in full possession of his senses. Septuagint, "When thine eyes shall see a strange woman, then thy mouth shall speak perverse things."

Ver. 34.—**As he that lieth down in the midst of the sea.** The dazed and unconscious condition of a drunkard is described by one familiar with sea life, as in Ps. civ. 25, etc.; cvii. 23, etc. The Hebrew has "in the heart of the sea" (Jonah ii. 4), i.e. the depth. Many understand the idea to be that the drunkard is compared to a man asleep in a frail boat, or to one slumbering on board a ship sunk in the trough of the sea. But the "lying" here does not imply sleep, but rather immersion. The inebriated person is assimilated to one who is drowned or drowning, who is cut off from all his former pursuits and interests in life, and has become unconscious of surrounding circumstances. This much more exactly represents the case than any notion of sleeping amid danger. Septuagint, " Thou shalt lie as in the heart of the sea." Or as **he that lieth upon the top of a mast;** the extreme point of the sailyard, where no one could lie without the greatest peril of falling off. The drunkard is exposed to dangers of all kinds from being unable to take care of himself, and yet is all the time unconscious of his critical situation. Corn. à Lapide, followed by Plumptre, considers that the cradle, or look-out, on the top of the mast is meant, where, if the watchman slept, he would be certain to endanger his life. Vulgate, " like a pilot fallen asleep, who has dropped the tiller," and is therefore on the way to shipwreck. Septuagint, "as a pilot in a great storm."

Ver. 35.—The drunkard is represented as speaking to himself. The LXX. inserts, "and thou shalt say," as the Authorized Version does : **They have stricken me, shalt thou say, and I was not sick;** or, *I was not hurt.* The drunken man has been beaten (perhaps there is a reference to the "contentions," ver. 29), but the blows did not pain him ; his condition has rendered him insensible to pain. He has some vague idea tha he has suffered certain rough treatment at the hands of his companions, but it has made no impression on him. **They have beaten me,** and I felt it not; did not even know it. Far from recognizing his degradation and profiting by the merited chastisement which he has incurred, he is represented as looking forward with pleasure to a renewal of his debauch, when his drunken sleep shall be over. **When shall I awake? I will seek it** (wine) **yet again.** Some take מתי (*mathai*) as the relative conjunctive : "When I awake I will seek it again;" but it is always used interrogatively, and the expression thus becomes more animated, as Delitzsch observes. It is as though the drunkard has to yield to the effects of his excess and sleep off his intoxication, but he is, as it were, all the time longing to be able to rouse himself and recommence his orgies. We have had words put into the mouth of the sluggard (ch. vi. 10). The whole verse is rendered by the LXX. thus : " Thou shalt say, They smote me, and I was not pained, and they mocked me, and I knew it not. When will it be morning, that I may go and seek those with whom I may consort ? " The author of the ' Tractatus de Conscientia ' appended to St. Bernard's works, applies this paragraph to the case of an evil conscience indurated by wicked habits and insensible to correction.

HOMILETICS.

Vers. 1—3.—*Sycophancy and independence.* The reader is here warned against the danger of depending too much on the favour of great people. Possibly that favour is only offered as a bribe, and the unwary recipient of it may be no better than a dupe, who has unconsciously sold himself. At the best it tends to destroy the spirit of independence.

I. HE WHO DEPENDS ON THE FAVOUR OF A GREAT MAN PUTS HIMSELF IN HIS POWER. In proportion to the power to help is the power to hurt. It is a dangerous thing to trust one's interests to man at all ; but it is doubly dangerous where there is no equality of relationship.

II. DEPENDENCE ON THE FAVOUR OF THE GREAT TEMPTS TO DISHONOURABLE CONDUCT. The sycophant is in danger of stooping to unworthy actions in order to please his patron. He is tempted to deceive and flatter in the hope of winning favour. The will of the great man supersedes the conscience of his dependant. Thus sycophancy wrecks the moral nature.

III. THIS DEPENDENCE DESTROYS TRUE MANLINESS. The poor creature who lives on the favour of the great loses all self-reliance. The honest industry that earns a night's repose is exchanged for miserable tricks of cringing slavery. Such conduct may earn the dainties of luxury, but only at the cost of all that life is worth living for. It is infinitely better to be independent, though compelled to live on the coarsest fare.

IV. SUCH A DEPENDENCE ON THE GREAT IS SURE TO BE DISAPPOINTING. The sycophant succeeds in obtaining a place at the banquet. But he cannot enjoy the feast like those guests who meet the host on terms of equality. He sits in constant dread or offending the great man. Though hungry, he shrinks from eating too much. He must almost put a knife to his throat to check his appetite; *i.e.* he must be always nervously on his guard against trespassing too far on the good will of his host. Surely such a condition must be miserable at the best!

V. THE ONLY SAFE DEPENDENCE IS THAT OF MAN ON GOD. This is not degrading, but ennobling; for God is worthy of all trust, honour, and adoration. He never deceives those who put their confidence in him. There is no painful fear for those who accept his gracious invitation to the "wedding-feast," for he is kind and merciful.

VI. AMONG MEN THE SAFEST CONDITION IS ONE OF MANLY INDEPENDENCE. This does not mean churlish indifference and selfish isolation from all social intercourse. The text supposes a person's presence at the great man's table, while it warns against the danger of the situation. We want to learn to be friendly with all men, and, at the same time, self-reliant through inward dependence on God alone.

Ver. 4.—*Labouring to be rich.* Never was the advice of the wise man more appropriate than it is in the present day; but never were people more slow to accept it. Let us consider the grounds on which is based the warning, "Labour not to be rich."

I. IT IS IMPOSSIBLE FOR MOST PEOPLE TO BECOME RICH. In the lottery of life the prizes are few and the blanks many. If the race for wealth is accelerated, the stakes are not multiplied. Or, if it be by production rather than by commerce that the riches are to be got, so that greater industry may actually create more wealth, still each of the multitude of the toilers can share but a fraction of the total produce. Riches only fall into the hands of a very small number of persons. Consequently, labouring to be rich often becomes just a species of gambling. It frequently partakes of the selfish, cruel character of gambling, the few fortunate persons enriching themselves at the expense of the large number of unfortunate persons. If a man can be content to work with his fellows and share with them, he will be saved from a multitude of anxieties that must besiege him the moment he enters the exciting race for riches.

II. THE COST OF LABOURING TO BE RICH IS EXORBITANT. 1. *In energy.* The fierce battle of life tries a man who only strives to keep his ground. They who would force their way on to marked success must toil with double effort. Rising early, sitting up late, taking no holidays, working at high pressure, they must put out every effort if they would pass equally eager competitors. 2. *In time.* The riches are not usually reached soon. As a rule, it takes many years to pile up a great fortune, and when the coveted end is attained, the tired toiler is too old and weary to enjoy it. 3. *In higher riches.* The wealth-seeker sinks into a low materialism. He becomes a mere machine for coining guineas, and his soul is ground to dust in the money-making mill.

III. WHEN THE PURSUIT OF RICHES IS SUCCESSFUL, THE ATTAINMENT IS DISAPPOINTING. Riches bring new cares. There is an anxiety to retain what has been won at so great a cost. They may make themselves wings, and "fly away as an eagle toward heaven" (ver. 5). If no fear is felt on this account, wealth itself is found to be unsatisfactory. The mere money-seeker has not cultivated any taste for the finer enjoyments which his wealth could buy him. He cannot satisfy his soul with money; he has no soul to enjoy the best things in art, etc., which money can purchase. But even if he could enjoy those things, they would not satisfy; for man has deep wants which neither money nor its purchases can ever meet. Riches are a poor salve for a breaking heart.

IV. LABOURING TO BE RICH LEADS TO THE NEGLECT OF THE NOBLER PURSUITS OF LIFE. 1. *Mind-culture.* It might be better to be more poor and to have time for reading, music, meditation. 2. *Social intercourse.* Buried in business, the fierce toiler after money has no leisure or heart for cultivating the friendship of his neighbours. 3. *The service of God.* "Life is more than meat;" "Seek first the kingdom of God and his righteousness." Labouring to be rich too often means working for self and toiling for earth. Men sometimes make family claims an excuse for doing nothing directly in the service of Christ; when, if they were honest, they would confess that they are simply labouring to be rich. The family, which in this case is a larger self, becomes a shield for selfishness.

Ver. 11.—*The mighty Redeemer.* I. THE HELPLESS NEED A MIGHTY REDEEMER. In simple, rough times some provision had to be made to protect the weak from the overbearing insolence and tyranny of the strong. When the arm of the law was not capable of maintaining justice, private friends were required and authorized to take up the cause of the wronged. The *goel*, or avenger, was then needed to stand up for his helpless kinsfolk. But there were extreme cases in which no such assistance could bring deliverance, either because no relative was living who could undertake the task, or because the distress was so desperate that no human hand could relieve it. This might happen with heart-broken widows robbed of husband, children, and land, and left penniless and friendless. But even such cases of the utmost distress are not so desperate as that of the soul in its sin and wretchedness, utterly and hopelessly undone unless some mighty hand of redemption is stretched out to save it. II. GOD IS A MIGHTY REDEEMER. Two essential conditions were required in the redeemer. He must have a right to interfere, and he must have power to succeed. God has both. 1. *The right.* The right of the old Hebrew redeemer was blood-relationship. The nearest kinsman was called to act as *goel*. God is nearly related to man. He is the Father of all. The friendless poor have One left who regards them as of his family. Christ came as a brother-man to be the Redeemer of the human race. 2. *The power.* (1) God has power as the Almighty. He can overthrow the greatest. If the poor man has God on his side, he need not fear the most imperious tyranny ; it is as child's play before the majesty of heaven. (2) *Christ has power as the crucified Saviour.* The great redemption from man's worst enemy, sin, is won by the cross of Christ. Now he is " *able* to save unto the uttermost." III. GOD'S MIGHTY REDEMPTION IS AVAILABLE. He is not only a mighty Redeemer ; he is willing to help, and he does afford succour. 1. *He acts in justice.* " Shall not the Judge of all the earth do right ? " (Gen. xviii. 25). At present we witness cruel injustice. The poor are oppressed by the strong. Hard-toiling men, women, and children in manufacturing centres are ground into penury by the fierce mill of competition, while ruthless " middle-men " fatten on their ill-paid labour. The few in prosperity revel in luxury that they wring out of the many in penury. God will not permit such cruel wrongs to last for ever. The Redeemer is an Avenger. The blood of the victims of those who make haste to be rich at the expense of their starving brethren cries out to heaven for vengeance. It will not always cry in vain. (1) Meanwhile, seeing that the Redeemer of the poor is mighty, it would be well for the reckless oppressors to repent before the sword of judgment is unsheathed. (2) They who are working at the apparently hopeless task of helping the poor and oppressed have a great encouragement. God, the mighty Avenger, is on their side. 2. *He acts in mercy.* He pities the suffering poor. They are his children, and he will not forget their needs. Love is the inspiration of Divine redemption. This is the secret of Christ's great redemption of sinners. Justice is ultimately satisfied here ; but the first motive is mercy, for the helpless are also the ill-deserving. Yet even their Redeemer is mighty.

Vers. 17, 18.—*Envying sinners.* I. THERE IS A GREAT TEMPTATION TO ENVY SINNERS. The wise man would waste words in giving a warning if he saw no danger. This temptation is fascinating on various accounts. 1. *Sinners prosper.* This was the old ground of the psalmist's perplexity. The righteous were suffering while the wicked were fattening in ill-earned luxury (Ps. lxxiii. 3—9). 2. *Sinners take forbidden paths with impunity.* They trespass and are not arrested. Thus they attain their ends by easy ways from which conscientious people are restrained. They are not troubled with scruples. 3. *Sinners escape onerous duties.* There are great and weighty obligations that rest like a heavy yoke on the shoulders of an earnest man who tries to do his duty to God and his fellows, all of which are simply ignored by the man of lower morals. Hence the apparently easier course of the latter. He can refuse the subscription list, decline to work in the benevolent society, and shirk all the burdens that come from sympathy with the suffering. 4. *Sinners enjoy wicked pleasures.* They are pleasure-seekers, and they seem to obtain pleasure. Thus at a superficial glance they appear to have sources of happiness from which those who are more rigorous in regarding the law of righteousness are excluded. The child of the Puritan home envies the gay cavalier his merry revelry.

II. IT IS WRONG TO ENVY SINNERS. 1. *This is to doubt God's justice.* Though we cannot yet see the issue of events, we must believe that God will not allow injustice to flourish for ever, unless he cares not for the course of the world or is unable to set it right. To suppose any such condition is to distrust God. 2. *This is to form a low estimate of the purpose of life.* We are not sent into the world simply to enjoy ourselves, but primarily to do our duty. If we are fulfilling that great purpose, it is a degradation to envy those who seem to be more fortunate than ourselves in the mere enjoyment of worldly pleasures. 3. *This is to yield to the attraction of unworthy delights.* The pleasures of sinners are sinful. To lust after such forbidden fruit is to have a depraved appetite. The soul that is truly pure will loathe the delights of sin. It will not be hard on a good man that his conscience forbids him to frequent the haunts of vicious revelry. He could find no true pleasure for himself amid such scenes.

III. IN THE END THE MISTAKE OF ENVYING SINNERS WILL BE DEMONSTRATED. " For surely there is an end." The pleasure-seeker is short-sighted. To judge of the wisdom of following his course, we must see what it leads to. 1. *The pleasure must end.* The delights of evil are brief, and they are followed by wretchedness. The wild devotee of pleasure soon becomes a debauched and *blasé* wreck of humanity. If one is prudent enough to avoid extreme folly, still death will soon come and put an end to all worldly pleasure. 2. *Sinful pleasure produces suffering.* It corrupts body and soul; it sows seeds of disease and misery. They who sow to the flesh will reap corruption. 3. *There will be retribution in the next world.* There is a future. Does the sinner consider this? Does the foolish man who envies him remember it?

Ver. 26.—*Our Father's claim.* I. GOD CLAIMS NOTHING LESS THAN THE HEART. 1. Some offer *belief of the intellect.* It is well to understand truth and to believe in that which is revealed about God. We may give many thoughts to God; but these, without the heart, will not satisfy him. 2. Some offer *external service.* This is claimed by God, but only as the fruit of a loving heart. Given in hard, mechanical work, without love or devotion, it is worthless in the sight of God. 3. Some offer *money, sacrifices, worship.* All such things are acceptable only as growing out of the heart. In heartless worshippers these are but mockery, and are rejected by God. 4. God's true children must give their *hearts.* They must give themselves, their inmost being, their very lives, thoughts, affections, desires.

II. THE HEART IS CLAIMED BY GOD ABOVE ALL. 1. *The world* tries to claim it. Some men are enchained in its fascinations, and so withdrawn from God. 2. *Sin* endeavours to ensnare it. If it is not a divine possession, it will be held by sin. It cannot be detached. It will be given to evil if not to God. 3. *Self* hopes to hold it. In selfishness men would retain their hearts, their love and devotion, for their own interests. Yet in doing so their hearts harden, shrink, and perish. 4. *God* has the supreme claim on the heart. We must not be satisfied with devotion to the Church or with good will towards men. The first duty is to love the Lord our God with all our heart. He must be first.

III. THE HEART MUST BE WHOLLY GIVEN TO GOD. We must not be content to love God half-heartedly. We must *give* our heart to God, and give it wholly, if we would satisfy his claim. 1. Give it in *affection.* This means a supreme surrender of our heart's love to God. 2. Give it in *devotion.* God expects loyal service, not merely the adoration of the lips or the work of the hands, but the consecration of the very soul and life and being to him. 3. Give it in *trust.* If one truly gives his heart to God, it is put in a safe place, to be guarded from harm and sin. God is the safest treasury for man's most precious treasure. When the heart is entrusted to God, he will not betray it; its affection and devotion will lead it not to desire evil; it will be in a sanctuary amid the storms and battles of life.

IV. GOD CLAIMS THE HEART OF HIS SON BECAUSE HE IS A FATHER. This is a family claim. The call, " My son," justifies the claim, " Give me thine heart." 1. The claim *rests on the obligations of the filial tie.* A young man may freely choose or refuse a particular person to be his friend. But he is not thus free in regard to his father. He owes duty and love to a father. God is represented by Malachi as saying, "A son honoureth his father . . . if then I be a Father, where is mine honour?" (Mal. i. 6). 2. The claim is *strengthened by the love of God.* He is a good Father; he does not ask his son to do what he has not done himself. God first gives his heart to his child, and then seeks the child's heart in return.

V. THE HEART MUST BE GIVEN VOLUNTARILY TO GOD. God is Lord of all, and he has a right to enforce universal obedience. But he cares not for loveless, compulsory service. Therefore he condescends to wait for willing devotion, and to ask for the heart of his son. 1 *Perhaps the heart is not yet given to God.* God seeks what he has not received. 2. *The heart can only be given by decision of will.* We shall remain away from God unless we decide to respond to the call of our Father, and freely offer him our hearts.

Vers. 31, 32.—*The danger of strong drink.* I. IT IS TERRIBLY FASCINATING. 1. *It is beautiful to the eye.* The wine sparkles in the cup. 2. *It is palatable.* Though children at first shudder at it, as at some unnatural product, the early dislike is easily surmounted, and then nothing can be more attractive. 3. *It is exhilarating.* It gives pleasurable excitement, stimulates jaded energies, enlivens conversation, drowns sorrow, and promises still larger enjoyments. 4. *It is recommended by social influences.* Good-fellowship seems to go with the use of strong drink. In some circles to decline it appears unsociable.

II. IT IS FEARFULLY DANGEROUS. The mischief is not seen at first. It is "at last" that "it biteth like a serpent." Hence its snake-like deception, as well as the deadliness of its venom. But this venom is so deadly that all need to be warned against its fatal consequences. It bites in many places; *e.g.*: 1. *The purse.* Money runs out like water, business fails, the home is wrecked and broken up as the effect of this serpent-bite of strong drink. 2. *The health.* The firm hand becomes palsied, the bright eye dimmed, and the strong body diseased when this venom of intoxication is in the blood. 3. *The mental powers.* The brain is weakened with the body. Thought is paralyzed or reduced to inanity. The lawyer, the doctor, the scholar, lose the faculties necessary for their avocations. 4. *The moral nature.* The one sin of intemperance too often debauches the conscience and prepares the way for other sins (see ver. 33). 5. *Reputation.* The drunkard loses his character. His good name vanishes in smoke when this deadly serpent lays hold of him. 6. *Soul-life.* This, too, is poisoned and slain. Religion is wrecked. The drunkard cannot enter the kingdom of heaven.

III. IT SHOULD BE UTTERLY SHUNNED. It is urged that all these indisputably evil things only come from drinking to excess. They are the results of the abuse, not of the use of strong drink. Men should be wise enough to take warning, and not to go to excess with what, used in moderation, is perfectly harmless. This was not the opinion of the wisest man. He not only urged his reader to refrain from excess; he would have him not even *look* at the fascinating cup, lest he should be ensnared by its snake-like charms. Many things concur to demand this extra caution. 1. *The terrible extent and evil of intemperance.* This is no small failing, but a national vice, and a source of wide and awful wretchedness. As no ordinary enemy has to be faced, so no ordinary means will secure us against it. 2. *The insidious nature of the temptation.* It works by slow degrees. At first it appears to be harmless. The fatal steps lead down slowly and without a shock of surprise, till it is too late to return. It is best to hold back at first. 3. *The needlessness of the strong drink.* Except in particular conditions of weakness and illness, it is not required. To renounce it is not to sacrifice any really good thing.

HOMILIES BY VARIOUS AUTHORS.

Vers. 1—8.—*Hints and warnings on conduct.* I. PERILS OF COURTLY LIFE. (Vers. 1—3.) The Arab proverb says, "He who sups with the sultan burns his lips," and, "With kings one sits at the table for honour's sake, not for that of appetite." Horace says that kings are said to press dainties and wine upon those whom they desire to scrutinize and test, as to whether they be worthy of friendship. The caution is therefore one dictated by prudence. And in general it may be thus understood: Beware of going to places and frequenting society where watchfulness and prudence are likely to be overborne; and take care that the body, by being pampered, becomes not the master of the soul.

II. PERILS AND VANITY OF RICHES. (Vers. 4, 5.) This precept does not forbid industry and diligent toil for worldly gain; but only excessive carefulness in regard to it, over-valuation of its worth, and the burning lust of avarice, which implies want of confidence in God and of the sense of our true position in the world. The antidote is the exhortation of the Saviour to lay up treasures in heaven—to make certain of the incorruptible riches (Matt. vi. 19, 20). "It is a wise course to be jealous of our gain, and more to fear than to desire abundance. It is no easy thing to carry a full cup with an even hand" (Leighton).

III. CORRUPTION FROM EVIL ASSOCIATIONS. (Vers. 6—8.) The man of the evil eye is the jealous or envious temper; his heart is dyed in its dark colour. There is no genuine hospitality here; it is like that of the Pharisees who invited our Lord. This bitter sauce of envious hatred will presently be found giving a disgusting flavour to his delicacies. Discontent will poison the best food and wine. "Men's minds will either feed on their own good or others' evil, and whoso wanteth the one will prey upon the other." Envy takes no holidays. The devil is represented as the envious man who sows tares among the wheat at night. Always it works subtly, in the dark, and to the prejudice of good things, such as is the wheat (Bacon). Instead of seeking the pleasures which bring disgust, let us secure a humble fare with Christian content (Phil. iv. 11).—J.

Vers. 9—11.—*Holding aloof from evil.* I. THE FOOL. (Ver. 9.) There is "a time to keep silence." Truth may be desecrated in certain company by speech and honoured by silence. Pearls are not to be cast before swine. The silence of Christ was equally eloquent with his words. How much does the sentence convey, "He answered him never a word"! Beyond a certain point explanations are worse than useless; the caviller only takes them as food for his folly and encouragement to his perversity.

II. THE OPPRESSOR. (Ver. 10.) The property of the widow and the fatherless is in the protection of the Almighty. He is the Eternal Vindicator of down-trodden right. In the bright evangelical picture of conduct it is the very opposite of violence and oppression to the weak that is held up for our emulation: "To visit the fatherless and the widow in their affliction." And the negative side is, in one word, "to keep one's self unspotted from the world."—J.

Vers. 12—18.—*Discipline in Divine wisdom.* I. THE TEMPER OF DOCILITY. (Ver. 12.) It is *submission of the affections* to a higher law. It is the *resignation of the will* to a higher leading. It is the *opening of the understanding* to Divine counsels. It is the realization, on the one hand, of dependence and need; on the other, of the light, the wisdom, and the goodness which ever meet that need.

II. THE NECESSITY OF DISCIPLINE FOR THE YOUNG. (Vers. 13, 14; see on ch. iii. 27; xix. 18; xxii. 15.) Luther says, in his blunt way, "Beat your son, and the hangman will not beat him. There must be a beating once for all; if the father does it not, Master Hans will; there is no help for it. None ever escaped it; for it is God's judgment." Another sternly says, "Many parents deserve hell on their children's account, because they neglect to train them in piety."

III. JOY IN DUTIFUL CHILDREN. (Vers. 15, 16.) It is next to the joy in the personal sense of God's grace. None but a parent knows the heart of a parent—the "travailing in birth" over their souls, the joy of discovering symptoms of the new life. "May all my sons be Benaiahs, the Lord's building; then will they all be Abners, the father's light: all my daughters Bithiahs, the Lord's daughters; and then they will be all Abigails, their father's joy" (Swinnock). What must be the joy in heaven and in the bosom of God over his returning and dutiful children!

IV. ENVY OF THE WICKED REBUKED. (Vers. 17, 18.) When Socrates was asked what was most troublesome to good men, he replied, "The prosperity of the wicked." Here, then, is a great temptation. It needs an antidote in reason. There is *no* reason for this envy. They are not truly happy. We look at them from the outside; the dark discontent of the heart is concealed from us. To live in the communion of God, on the other hand, is a secret, a certain, a profound and all-compensating joy. The enjoyment of the wicked, such as it is, must have its end; while the child of God ends only to begin anew—sinks below the horizon to rise in the power of an endless life.

We have thus three resources against sin: the avoidance of evil example; reverence before God; and constant recollection of the blessings of piety and virtue.—J.

Vers. 19—25.—*The perils of dissipation and the antidote.* "Who hath ears to hear, let him hear."

I. PERILS OF DISSIPATION. (Vers. 20, 21.) Gluttony and wine-bibbing. As the stomach is the centre of health, so it is also of disease. A wise man (Dr. Johnson) said that if one did not care for one's stomach, one was not likely to care for anything. It is equally true that he who cares only or chiefly for the flesh will make a wreck of everything else. Gluttony has been pointed to as "the source of all our infirmities, the fountain of all our diseases. As a lamp is choked by superabundance of oil, a fire extinguished by excess of fuel, so is the natural heat of the body destroyed by intemperate diet." By slow degrees, and more and more, the habits of self-indulgence undermine the strength of body, still more certainly the vigour of mind, until poverty comes like an armed man.

II. THE ANTIDOTE. 1. *Early instruction to be constantly recalled.* (Ver. 22.) Along with the affectionate association of the parents who gave it. That "men shall be disobedient to their own parents" (2 Tim. iii. 2) is one of the marks of the great apostasy in Scripture. But "comely and pleasant to see, and worthy of honour from the beholder," is a child understanding the eye of his parent (Bishop Hall). 2. *The truth of life to be held in supreme value.* (Ver. 23.) Wisdom, discipline, insight,—these are various names of the one thing, different aspects of the pearl of great price. There are required in the truth-seeker—attention, willingness for toil, judgment, the constant preference of reason to prejudice, teachableness, humility, self-control. Translated into Christian terms, this pearl of great price is "the excellency of the knowledge of Christ Jesus our Lord." Bunyan beautifully describes the pilgrims answering the sneering reproach, "What will you buy?" They lifted their eyes above: "We will buy the truth!" And no sacrifice is too costly with this end in view, as the example of holy men and martyrs teaches—Moses, Paul, the Hebrews (Heb. xi. 24—26). To sell one's birthright for a mess of pottage (as Esau, Judas, and Demas) is indeed to "gain a loss." 3. *Consideration of the joy we give to others by well-doing.* (Vers. 24, 25.) That heart must be unnatural or utterly depraved which feels not the force of this motive—to repay a father's anxious love, and the yearning tenderness of her that bare him. A selfishness may supply the motive even here, since parental gladness is the child's own joy as he walks in the ways of pleasantness and peace.—J.

Vers. 26—28.—*The harlot's true character.* I. IT IS DANGEROUS AND PERNICIOUS. (Vers. 27, 28.) It may be compared to a deep pit or to a narrow and deep well, out of which, if one falls therein, there is no easy escape. Or to a fell robber lying in wait for the unwary and the weak.

II. THE TRUE RESOURCE OF SAFETY. This is in the heart given up to God (ver. 26). If that heart be already polluted, he can wash it and make it clean. But he who yields his heart to the prince of this world becomes the enemy of God and of his eternal wisdom.—J.

Vers. 29—35.—*The perils of drunkenness.* I. THE IMMEDIATE EXTERNAL EFFECTS. (Vers. 29, 30.) Trouble, quarrels, violence, deformity. "No translation or paraphrase can do justice to the concise, abrupt, and energetic manner of the original." "Oh that men should put an enemy in their mouths to steal away their brains! that we should with joy, revel, pleasure, and applause, transform ourselves into beasts!"

II. THE ULTIMATE CONSEQUENCES. (Ver. 32.) It "bites like a serpent, and spits poison like a basilisk." This is the course of all sin; like Dead Sea fruits that tempt the taste, and turn to ashes on the lips. It is the "dangerous edge of things," against which men have to be on their guard. The line between use and abuse is so easily passed over. *Corruptio optimi pessima.*

III. THE EFFECT ESPECIALLY ON THE INTELLIGENCE. (Vers. 33—35.) The mind falls into bewilderment, and sees double or awry. The victim of intoxication is indeed "at sea," and like one sleeping on the very verge of danger and sudden death. In a spiritual sense he is drunk who does not perceive the great danger of his soul, but becomes more secure and stubborn under every chastisement (Jer. v. 3). It is the dreadful *insensibility*—depicted by ver. 35 which imitates the thought and speech of the drunkard—which is among the worst consequences of the vice. "The sight of a drunkard is a better sermon against that vice than the best that was ever preached upon the subject." "He who hath this sin, hath not himself; whosoever doth commit it, doth not commit sin, but he himself is wholly sin" (Augustine).—J.

Vers. 1—3.—*The temptation of the table.* It is probable that Solomon had in view those who did not often sit down to a "good dinner," and who, when they were invited to a feast by some one who was able to spread his table with delicacies, found themselves subjected to a strong temptation to unusual indulgence. Dr. Kitto tells us that, in the East, men would (and now will) eat an almost incredible amount of food when a rare opportunity offered itself. From the moral and the religious standpoint this matter of appetite demands our attention to—

I. A SPECIAL SPHERE OF OBEDIENCE AND SELF-CONTROL. Appetite is undoubtedly of God; and for few things, on the lower level, have we more occasion to thank our Creator than for the fact that he has made our food to be palatable, and caused us so to crave it that the partaking of it is a pleasure. Otherwise, the act of eating in order to keep ourselves alive and strong would be a daily weariness and penalty to us. But as it is, the necessary act of eating is a constant source of pleasure. But with the pleasure there enters inevitably a temptation. Appetite in man, strengthened as it is by man's imaginative faculty, and fostered as it is by the inventiveness which provides all kinds of inviting dainties, becomes one of those things which allure to excess, and thus to sin. To maintain the golden mean between asceticism on the one hand and epicurism or gluttony on the other hand is not found to be an easy task. Medical science inclines now to the view that a very large proportion of people take more to eat than is really for their good—especially in later life. Frequently, perhaps generally, this is rather a mistake than an offence. But the wise man will carefully consider how far he should go, and where he should draw the line. In doing this he will more especially consider two things. 1. How he should act at the table, so as not in any way to weaken his intelligence by what he eats or drinks. 2. How he should act so as to keep himself in health and strength for all useful activity in the days to come. By resolving to act with a firm self-command, with the higher and indeed the highest end in view, he may, in eating and drinking, do what he does "to the glory of God" (see 1 Cor. x. 31).

II. THOSE TO WHOM THIS FORMS A SPECIALLY STRONG TEMPTATION. "If thou be a man given to appetite." Some men are so constituted that to have the greatest delicacies in the world before them would be no temptation to them; others have an appetency which they have the greatest difficulty in controlling,—this may arise either from heredity, or from their individual bodily organization, or (as is oftenest the case) from the habit of indulgence. There are also—

III. OCCASIONS WHEN THIS TEMPTATION IS SPECIALLY SEVERE. Such as that indicated in the text (see also 1 Cor. x. 27). There are times when it would be churlish, and even unchristian, to refuse an invitation; but the presence of food or of stimulants upon the table may be a serious inducement to transgression. Then "put a knife to thy throat;" determinately stop at the point of strict moderation; resolutely and fearlessly refuse that of which you know well that you have no right to partake; distinctly and definitely decline the dish or the cup which you cannot take with a good conscience. For consider—

IV. THE FOLLY AND THE SIN OF INDULGENCE. "They are deceitful meat." Excess may bring some momentary enjoyment, but: 1. It is quickly followed by pain, disorder, feebleness, incapacity; even if not of a serious order, yet humiliating enough to a man who respects himself. 2. The habit of it leads with no uncertain step to physical and also to mental and moral degeneracy. 3. The pleasure afforded, like all the grosser gratifications, declines with indulgence. 4. All excess is sin. It is a misuse and profanation of that body which is given us as the organ of our own spirit, and should be regarded and treated as "the temple of the Holy Ghost" (1 Cor. vi. 19).—C.

Vers. 4, 5.—*The worthlessness of wealth.* Wealth is not, indeed, absolutely worthless; it has a distinct value of its own; but relatively to man's deeper necessities, and to his other, spiritual resources, it is to be held in slight esteem.

I. THE UNSUBSTANTIAL AS DISTINGUISHED FROM THE REAL. "Wilt thou set thine eyes upon that which is not?" Money regarded as that which purchases food, clothing, shelter, books, etc., has a certain value not easily overstated. But mere wealth, as wealth, has but a fictitious and unreal virtue. A man may have it and have it not at the same time. A rich man may be, to all intents and purposes, a very poor one. He may own land the scenery upon which he is wholly unable to appreciate; soil which he has not the spirit or the wisdom to cultivate; houses which he neither inhabits nor causes to be inhabited; gardens whose paths no feet are treading, and whose beauty no eyes are admiring; books which he has not the taste or even the power to read, etc. In fact, his wealth is only a possibility and not a reality to him. Practically, he "sets his eyes upon that which is not." And it is quite a common thing for men to be wealthy far beyond their capacity of enjoyment; their riches do not serve them any real purpose; they remain unused, and are as if they were not at all (see Matt. xxv. 29; Luke viii. 18). On the other hand, knowledge, wisdom, pure and holy love, a generous interest in the welfare of others, joy in God and in the friendship of the good,—these are real blessings. A man who has these must be and *is* enriched thereby.

II. THE TRANSIENT AS DISTINGUISHED FROM THE ABIDING. "Riches certainly make themselves wings," etc. 1. *They are insecure.* It is impossible to mention any "investment" that is absolutely secure. Even "real property" has been found to become depreciated and even positively worthless in the market. And of the more ordinary sources of wealth, it is proverbial that they have all a limited, and many of them but a slight, security. A revolution in government, in trade, even in fashion or in taste, and the ample means are reduced to nothing, the millionaire is brought down to bankruptcy. A poor foundation, indeed, on which to build the structure of human happiness and well-being is the possession of riches. 2. *They must soon be laid down.*

III. THE HUMAN AS DISTINGUISHED FROM THE DIVINE. To "labour to be rich" is of man. To work for wealth, and even to live for it is to be borne along on the current of human energy, is to breathe the atmosphere which human society is throwing round him. It is "our own wisdom." But it is not the wisdom of God. That says to us, "Labour *not* for the meat which perisheth;" "Lay *not* up for yourselves treasures on earth;" "A man's life does *not* consist in the abundance of the things which he possesseth." The wisdom which is from above speaks to us of "forsaking all to follow Christ;" of parting with everything for one inestimable pearl; of agonizing to enter in at the strait gate. It tells us that the service of God, the friendship of Jesus Christ, the life of holy usefulness, the life-testimony to a Divine Redeemer, the rest of soul which comes with spiritual rectitude, the inheritance which is incorruptible and undefiled and which fadeth not away,—that all this is not only more precious than gold, it is absolutely priceless; it is the one thing for which it is worth our while to labour with all our strength, to sacrifice all that we have.—C.

Vers. 6—8.—*The graces of giving, receiving, and refusing.* The text treats of a hospitality which does not deserve the name, and of our duty when we are invited to accept a gift that is grudged. It thus opens the whole subject of giving and receiving. There are three graces here.

I. THE GRACE OF GIVING. This is one which is readily recognized as heaven-born. 1. God commends it to us. He says, "Give, and it shall be given unto you" (Luke vi. 38); "Give to him that asketh thee" (Matt. v. 42); "He that giveth let him do it with liberality" (Revised Version); "given to hospitality" (Rom. xii. 8, 13). 2. It is the best reward of labour (Eph. iv. 28). 3. It is the most God-like of all graces. For God lives to give; he is ever giving forth to all his creation; he is feeding the multitudes and millions of his creatures beneath every sky. 4. It is the source of the purest and most elevating joy. "It is more blessed to give than to receive."

II. THE GRACE OF RECEIVING. If it is right and good for some men to give of their abundance, then the correlative act of receiving must also be right and good. There is, indeed, a virtue, a grace, in receiving cheerfully and cordially as well as gratefully, which may be almost, if not quite, as acceptable to God as that of generosity itself. There is truth in Miss Proctor's lines—

"I hold him great who for love's sake
Can give with generous. earnest will;
Yet *he who takes* for love's sweet sake,
I think I hold more generous still."

III. The grace of refusing. 1. We may rightly refuse a gift, whether it be in the way of hospitality or not, which we are sure the giver *cannot honestly afford*; we do not wish to be enriched or entertained at the expense of his creditors. 2. We may properly decline a gift if we feel that it is offered us under a misconception; when we are imagined to be, or to believe, or to be working toward, that which is contrary to our spirit, our creed, our aim 3. We do well to decline the hospitality which does not come from the heart. The host is "as he thinketh in his heart." His fair or "sweet words" are no real part of himself; they only come from his lips; and if he is grudging us what he gives us, we may well wish ourselves far away from his table. No man who has any self-respect whatever will wish to take a crust from the man who counts what he gives his friends. Such food as that, however dainty, would choke us as we ate it. Nor is it begrudged hospitality alone that we should have the independence to refuse, but all else that is in the shape of gift; all money, all position, all friendship. Better to go entirely without than to have abundance at the cost of our own self-respect. Better to toil hard and wait long than to accept such offers as those. Better to turn to him "who giveth liberally and upbraideth not," and ask of him.—C.

Ver. 10.—(See homily on ch. xxii. 28.)—C.

Vers. 13, 14.—(See homily on ch. xiii. 24.)—C.

Vers. 17, 18.—*God's righteous judgment.* Nothing is more foolish than to endeavour to found a proof of the righteousness of God's rule upon a single case of human experience. Yet is that often done. A good man seizes upon a piece of good fortune in a godly man's life, and exaggerates its importance; a bad man pounces upon a piece of bad fortune and draws unwarrantable conclusions therefrom. But are there not indications, if not proofs, to be had for the seeking, that all things are under the direction of a just and righteous Ruler? Yes; if we look far and wide enough. For as we look, we see that *all* men, good and bad, are rewarded according to their works.

I. All the laws which regulate the recompense of labour exist for the unrighteous as well as for the righteous. Take, *e.g.*: 1. *The covetous man.* Consider all that he foregoes in order to reap his harvest—all the physical, social, domestic, literary, philanthropic, religious advantages and delights that he sacrifices; consider all the immense and ceaseless pains and toils he goes through, and the risks he runs, to achieve his object. And he gets his prize; he has earned it. He will find it weighted with more burdens and freighted with fewer and smaller blessings than he thought, and it will not last him long. Do not envy him or begrudge him what he receives; he has paid a very heavy price for it, and is surely welcome to it. 2. *The hypocrite.* He is a very painstaking, hardworking man; he spares himself no trouble, no sacrifice; he makes long prayers, for which he has no heart; he abstains from food he would fain be eating; he parts with money which he longs to keep; he goes through the most wearisome experiences in order that he may win a little passing honour. He has his reward; he is very welcome to it. He has earned it; we will not envy him; there is nothing more for him to receive (Matt. vi. 5). 3. *The man of pleasure.* He also pays a very high price for his momentary gratifications—the degradation of his powers, the disregard of his friends, the loss of his self-respect, the decline of his health, etc.; and all this for mere enjoyment which becomes less keen and vivid every day. We will not envy him. Unholy pleasure is the costliest thing in the whole world.

II. All the laws which regulate the recompense of labour exist for the righteous man as well as for the unrighteous. 1. By returning unto God in penitential self-surrender we seek reconciliation, peace, joy, the full re-establishment of our filial relations with God; and we find what we seek. "Surely there is a reward" (Revised Version) for us, and "*our* expectation is not cut off." 2. By "walking in the fear of the Lord all the day long," consulting his will and endeavouring to follow him, we seek his Divine favour and a growing measure of likeness to our Lord. And we find what we seek. 3. By kind Christian helpfulness, by sympathy and succour freely and gladly given to those in need, we seek the blessedness of him that gives (Acts xx. 35), the gratitude of true and loving hearts, the present smile and final benediction of the Son of man (Matt. xxv. 34—40). And we find and shall find it. Surely there *is* a reward for us; our hope shall not be cut off. No; let us "envy not the sinner;" let us make him welcome to all he has; let us try to elevate and enlarge his hope and his reward by changing the spirit of his mind. As for ourselves, let it be in our hearts to say, "God is faithful who hath called us to the fellowship of his Son;" let us anticipate the anthem of the angels,-and sing already, "Great and marvellous are thy works, Lord God Almighty, *just and true* are thy ways, O thou King of saints!"—C.

Vers. 20, 21.—(See below.)—C.

Ver. 23.—*The freedom and the price of truth.* We have often to insist upon—

I. THE FREEDOM OF THE TRUTH. In one sense, truth is essentially free. If firm and strong as the granite rock, it is also fluent as the water, elastic as the air. It belongs to no man, and cannot be patented or monopolized; it is the inheritance of mankind. We are all of us bound to communicate it freely, to "pass it on like bread at sacrament." This is emphatically the case with the truth of the gospel. "Ho! every one that thirsteth, come ye to the waters, and he that hath no money; come ye, buy, and eat . . . without money and without price;" "Whosoever will, let him take the water of life *freely.*" But the lesson of the text is—

II. THE PRICE OF TRUTH. Truth has sometimes to be paid for; it has its own price, and we must be willing to buy it. 1. *That truth for which we involuntarily pay some price.* We go forth into the world with crude, immature notions, which we find, by painful experience, have to be corrected and perhaps changed. Sometimes this necessary lesson is very costly to us. In this way we have to buy the truth as to: (1) The checkered character of our human life. We have to learn, painfully enough, that it does not answer to our early dreams, but is sadly dashed with disappointment, with failure, with loss, with trouble; that it is many-coloured, with a large admixture of the dull or even the dark. (2) The imperfections of the good. That there is a large amount of profession without any reality at all; that *some* really good men allow themselves to be overtaken in serious fault; that all good men have some defects which tarnish the perfect brightness of their character; that human excellency is not so much an attainment as an earnest and admirable endeavour. (3) The strength and weakness of our own character. We have to find, at the cost of much humiliation, where our strength ends and our weakness begins. Such truths as these we buy without bargain; we do not agree to the price that we pay. There is not the freedom of contract we usually have in any purchase we make. But we may part willingly, and even cheerfully, as we are called upon to do, with that which we lose, thankfully accepting the truth we acquire; and so doing we practically and wisely " buy the truth." 2. *The truth for which we voluntarily pay the price.* (1) A completer knowledge of God's Word. Our knowledge of the book of God is very varied; it may be very slight or it may be very deep and full. How deep or how full depends on whether or not we will pay the price of this excellent wisdom; the price is that of *patient, reverent study.* (2) The surpassing blessedness of true consecration; the peace and the joy to be had in Christ and in his holy and happy service. We do not know as much as we might, and as we should, of this; but we do not pay the price of knowledge. That price is whole-hearted surrender of ourselves to our Saviour and to his service. So long as we "keep back part of the price" we cannot know this experience; but if we will "yield ourselves unto God" unreservedly, we shall know the truth in its fulness. We may make a special point of (3) the beauty and excellency of Christian work; and the price of knowing this is the act of hearty and faithful labour, sustained by much earnest prayer for the inspiration and the blessing of God. We complete the thought of the text by considering—

III. THE ABSOLUTE PRICELESSNESS OF THE TRUTH. "Sell it not." Heavenly wisdom, once gained, is not to be parted with for any consideration whatever. Nothing on earth represents its value. To lose it is to sign away our inheritance. It is to be held at all costs whatever.—C.

Vers. 24—26.—(See homily on ch. x. 1.)—C.

Vers. 29—35 (with vers. 20, 21).—*Drunkenness.* A most striking picture is given as here of the manifold evils of this great curse. In a few strokes Solomon brings before us most, if not all, of its painful and pitiable consequences. Their name is legion, for they are indeed many.

I. THE CONTEMPT OF THE SOBER. (Ver. 20.) The very word "drunkard," or " wine-bibber," is indicative of the deep disregard in which the victim of this vice is held by sober men.

II. POVERTY. (Ver. 21.) It is striking and surprising how soon men of large means are brought down to straitness of circumstance, and even poverty itself. It is what they *spend* on this craving, and what they *lose* by its ill effects upon them, that drag them down.

III. PHYSICAL DETERIORATION. (Ver. 29.) Dissipation soon tells on a man's personal appearance; he shows by his garments, and still more by his countenance, that he is mastered by that which he puts into his mouth. Vice means ugliness.

IV. CONTENTIOUSNESS. (Ver. 29.) We need all our powers in good balance to control ourselves so that we are not provoked to the hasty word and to the lasting quarrel. But the man who is excited by wine is in the worst possible condition for ruling his spirit and commanding his tongue. He is likely enough to speak the sentence which is followed by the blow, or, what is worse, the long-continued feud.

V. IMPURITY. (Ver. 33.) The excitement of the intoxicating cup has had much to do with the saddest departures from the path of purity and honour; with the entrance upon the road of utter ruin.

VI. INFATUATION. (Vers. 34, 35.) The drunkard is seen by his friends to be sinking and falling; in his circumstances, his reputation, his health, his character, he is palpably perishing. Those who really love and pity him warn him with earnest remonstrance, with affectionate entreaty, but it is of no avail. He acts with as much infatuation as would a man who made a bed of the waves or the top of a mast. After he has been stricken and has suffered, he goes back to his cups, and is stricken and suffers again.

VII. THE AGONY OF REMORSE. "At the last it biteth like a serpent," etc. The sting of remorse which a man suffers when he awakes to a full sense of his folly is something pitiful to witness, and must be far more terrible to endure. The man suffers a penalty which is worse than bodily torture; it is the just punishment in his own soul for his folly and his sin. In one sense it is self-administered, for it is the stern rebuke of conscience; in another sense it is the solemn and strong condemnation of the Supreme.

VIII. BITTER BONDAGE. Worse, if possible, than the sting of remorse is the sense of helpless bondage in which he finds that he is held. "At the last" is a tyranny which the evil habit, the strong craving, exercises over the man's spirit. He knows and feels his humiliation and loss; he essays to escape; he strives, he writhes to become freed; but he tries in vain; he is "holden with the cords of his sins" (ch. v. 22); he is a poor, miserable captive, the slave of vice.

Such are the consequences of departure from sobriety. It is the first step which is the most foolish and the most avoidable. When a certain stage is reached, restoration, though not impossible or impracticable, is very difficult. Let all men, as they love their soul, keep well within that boundary-line that divides sobriety from intemperance. Moderation is good; abstinence is better, for it is safer, and it is kinder to others. "Look not " on the tempting cup; turn the eyes to purer and nobler pleasure.—C.

EXPOSITION.

CHAPTER XXIV.

Ver. 1.—We return here to the more usual form, the tetrastich. Be not thou envious against evil men (see on ch. xxiii. 17, where a similar warning is given, and comp. ver. 19 below). "Men of wickedness," wholly given over to evil. Neither desire to be with them. Their company is pollution, and association with them makes you a partner in their sinful doings. The Septuagint prefaces the paragraph with the personal address, *vié.* "son."

Ver. 2.—For their heart studieth destruction. The grounds of the warning are here given, as in ch. i. 15. "Destruction" (*shod*); Vulgate, *rapinas*, "violence" of all kinds, *e.g.* robbery, murder. Their lips talk of mischief; utter lies and slanders which may injure other people or bring themselves profit. Admiration of such men and intercourse with them must be repugnant to every religious soul. The LXX. refers the verse to evil imaginations issuing in evil talk; "For their heart meditates falsehoods, and their lips speak mischiefs (πόνους)."

Vers. 3, 4.—In contrast with the conversation of the evil, wisdom is commended.

Ver. 3.—**Through wisdom is an house builded** (see on ch. xiv. 1). By prudence, probity, and the fear of God a family is supported and blessed, maintained and prospered. **Established** (see on ch. iii. 19); Septuagint, ἀνορθοῦται.

Ver. 4.—(Comp. ch. i. 13 and note ch. iii. 10.) **With all precious and pleasant** (ch. xxii. 18) **riches.** Material prosperity, copious store of necessaries, and wealth, follow on wisdom; how much more do spiritual blessings attend the fear of God!

Vers. 5, 6.—Wisdom is beneficial in peace and war.

Ver. 5.—**A wise man is strong.** בעוֹז, "in strength," full of strength, because, however feeble in body, he is wise in counsel, firm in purpose, brave in conduct, thoroughly to be depended upon, and supported by his perfect trust in God (comp. ch. xxi. 22). The Septuagint, with which agree the Syriac and Chaldee, reading differently, renders, "A wise man is better than a strong man"—a sentiment which Lesêtre compares to Cicero's "cedant arma togæ." **A man of knowledge increaseth strength**; literally, *strengtheneth power;* shows greater, superior power, as Amos ii. 14. The Septuagint, from some corruption of the text, renders, "And a man having prudence (is better) than a large estate (γεωργίου μεγάλου);" *i.e.* wisdom will bring a man more worldly advantages than the possession of extensive farms. The gnome is proved by what follows.

Ver. 6.—**Thy war**; war for thyself, for thy profit, equivalent to "successful war" (comp. Exod. xiv. 14). The clause is an echo of ch. xx. 18 (where see note). The last line is a repetition of ch. xi. 14 (comp. also ch. xv. 22). Septuagint, "War is made with generalship (κυβερνήσεως), and help with a heart that counsels."

Vers. 7—10.—Some distichs now follow, concerned with wisdom and its opposite.

Ver. 7.—**Wisdom is too high for a fool.** It is beyond his reach, he cannot follow its lead, and has nothing to say when his counsel

is asked, and no ability to judge of any question presented to him. "Wisdom" (*chochmoth*) is in the plural number, intimating the various attributes connoted by it, or the different aspects in which it may be regarded (see note on ch. i. 20). "Too high" (רָאמוֹת, *ramoth*) is also plural; and Delitzsch and Nowack take it to mean, not so much "high things" as "precious things," such as pearls or precious stones, in accordance with Job xxviii. 18, "No mention shall be made of coral or of crystal; yea, the price of wisdom is above rubies." In this sense Delitzsch translates, "Wisdom seems to the fool to be an ornamental commodity," a costly and unnecessary appendage, which is not worth the sacrifices entailed by its pursuit. Whichever way we take it, the point is the rarity and inaccessibility of wisdom, and the repugnance of fools to make any exertion in order to obtain it. St. Augustine thus sums up the steps by which wisdom is reached: fear of God, piety, knowledge, fortitude, mercifulness, sincerity ('De Doctr. Christ.,' ii. 7). **He openeth not his mouth in the gate.** When men gather in the usual place of assembly (ch. viii. 3; xxii. 2), to take counsel on public matters, he has nothing to say; he listens fatuously, and is silent. Septuagint, "Wisdom and good thought are in the gates of the wise; the wise turn not aside from the mouth of the Lord, but reason in assemblies."

Ver. 8.—**He that deviseth to do evil.** He who shows a certain kind of misapplied cleverness (in contrast to the true wisdom) in planning and pursuing evil schemes. **Shall be called.** Defined and explained, as ch. xvi. 21 (comp. ch. xxi. 24). **A mischievous person;** literally, *lord of mischief;* i.e. owner, possessor of mischief. One must not be led by such a man's apparent astuteness to attribute to him wisdom; he is an impostor, a mere intriguer, who is sure to be exposed ere long. Septuagint, "Death befalls the undisciplined."

Ver. 9.—**The thought of foolishness is sin.** "Sin" is the subject in this clause as "the scorner" is in the next; and what it says is that sin is the excogitation, the contriving of folly. The sinner is the real fool, in that he does not pursue his proper end, prepares misery for himself, is blind to his best interests. The connection between sin and folly, as between wisdom and righteousness, is continually enforced throughout the book. **The scorner is an abomination to men.** The man who scoffs at religion and every high aim is an object of abomination to the pious, and is also a cause of evil to others, leading them to thoughts and acts which are hateful in the eyes of God. Septuagint, "The fool dieth in sins (John viii. 24), and uncleanness belongeth to a pestilent man." The text here followed, as in other passages of this chapter, is quite different from the received one.

Ver. 10.—**If thou faint in the day of adversity, thy strength is small.** The gnome seems to be unconnected with the preceding. There is a paronomasia between צָרָה (*tsarah*), "adversity," and צַר (*tsar*), "small," narrow, which is retained by Fleischer: "Si segnis fueris die angustiæ, angustæ sunt vires tuæ." So we may say in English, "If thou faint in time of straitness, straitened is thy strength." If you fail, and succumb to anxiety or danger, instead of rising to meet the emergency, then you are but a weakling or a coward, and the strength which you seemed to possess, and of which you boasted, perhaps, is nothing worth. Such a man hearkens not to the Sibyl's counsel (Virgil, 'Æneid,' vi. 95)—

"Tu ne cede malis, sed contra audentior ito,
Quam tua te fortuna sinet."

The LXX. again varies from the received text, "He shall be polluted in an evil day, and in a day of affliction, until he fail," or "die" (ἐκλίπῃ).

Vers. 11, 12.—A hexastich, inculcating humanity on the ground of God's omniscience.

Ver. 11.—**If thou forbear to deliver them that are drawn unto death.** The sentence is not conditional, אִם in the second line being equivalent to לוּ, *utinam*, "oh that!" "would that!" So the first hemistich should be rendered, "Deliver them that are haled to death," and the second, "And those that are tottering to slaughter, oh, hold them back!" The sentence is somewhat obscure, but Cheyne well explains it thus: "Some victims of a miscarriage of justice are about to be dragged away to execution, and the disciple of wisdom is exhorted to use his endeavours to deliver them" ('Job and Solomon'). In the case supposed a moral obligation lies on the pious and well-informed to save a human life unjustly imperilled. At the same time, there is nothing in the passage which absolutely shows that the punishment of the guiltless is here deprecated; it looks rather as if Wisdom had no pleasure in the death of men, innocent or not, and that the victims of an extreme sentence claimed pity at her hands, whatever might be the circumstances of the verdict. Septuagint, "Deliver those that are being led away to death, and redeem (ἐκπρίου) those that are appointed to be slain; spare not (to help them)" (comp. Ps. lxxxii. 3, 4).

Ver. 12.—**If thou sayest, Behold, we knew it not.** The disciple of Wisdom may excuse himself from making any effort for the prisoners' release, by saying he had not heard of the case. St. Jerome makes the excuse to be inability, *vires non suppetunt*. The LXX. makes it a personal matter, ignoring the plural form of the previous paragraph. "I know him not, he is no friend of mine; why should I trouble myself about him?" Such a selfish person, like the priest and Levite in the parable, would "pass by on the other side." **Doth not he that pondereth the heart consider it?** God knows the truth—knows that the excuse is vain; for he is the Weigher and Searcher of hearts (ch. xvi. 2; xxi. 2). Cain's plea, "Am I my brother's keeper?" is unavailable; the law of love is limited by no circumstances. **He that keepeth thy soul, doth not he know it?** The expression, "keeping the soul," may be equivalent to "preserving the life;" but it more probably means watching, observing, the inmost secrets of the nature (Job vii. 20). The verb used is נָצַר (*natsar*), which has both significations. The sense of "forming," which some give it, seems not allowable. (For "heart" (*leb*) and "soul" (*nephesh*), see note on ch. ii. 10.) **Shall not he render to every man according to his works?** Knowing the heart and the motive, God deals out retributive justice (ch. xii. 14; Ps. lxii. 12; Rom. ii. 6). Septuagint, "But if thou say, I know not this man, know that the Lord knoweth the hearts of all; and he who formed (πλάσας) breath for all, himself knoweth all things, who rendereth to every man according to his works."

Vers. 13, 14.—An exhortation to the study of wisdom, with an analogy.

Ver. 13.—**Eat thou honey, because it is good.** Honey entered largely into the diet of the Oriental, and was regarded not only as pleasant to the taste and nutritious, but also as possessed of healing powers. It was especially used for children's food (Isa. vii. 15), and thus becomes an emblem of the purest wisdom. "I have eaten my honeycomb with my honey," says the lover in Cant. v. 1; and the psalmist says that the ordinances of the Lord are "sweeter than honey and the honeycomb" (Ps. xix. 10; see on ch. xxv. 16). Palestine was a land flowing with milk and honey (Exod. iii. 8); hence is derived the continual reference to this article of diet in the Bible.

Ver. 14.—**So shall the knowledge of wisdom be unto thy soul;** better, *know, apprehend wisdom to be such for thy soul*— to be as pleasant and nourishing and profitable to thy soul, as honey is to thy taste and thy body. The moralist would have his disciple feel the same relish for wisdom that he has for sweet food, recognize it not simply as useful, but as delightful and enjoyable. When thou hast found it. To find wisdom is to get possession of it and use it (comp. ch. iii. 13, and note there). **Then** there shall be a reward. The apodosis begins here. We have had the same assurance in ch. xxiii. 18 (where see note). The word is literally *future*. One who has obtained wisdom has a glorious hope before him; *habebis in novissimis spem*, Vulgate; but his hope is better than that— it goes with him, not in his last hour only, but all his life long. Septuagint, "Then shalt thou perceive wisdom in thy soul; for if thou find it, fair shall be thine end, and hope shall not fail thee."

Vers. 15, 16.—A warning against plotting for the ruin of a good man's house, with a view doubtless of profiting by the disaster.

Ver. 15.—Lay not wait, O wicked man, against the dwelling of the righteous. רָשָׁע (*rasha*) is vocative (comp. Ezek. xxxiii. 8); taken appositionally, as in Revised Version margin, "as a wicked man," it is senseless; for how could he lay wait in any other character? Spoil not his resting-place. "Spoil," as ch. xix. 26 (where see note). Drive him not from his house by violence and chicanery. Vulgate, "Seek not impiety in the house of the righteous;" do not attempt to cloak your insidious designs by detecting some evil in the good man, and making yourself the instrument of retribution, as if you were doing God service in afflicting him (John xvi. 2). Septuagint, "Bring not an ungodly man into the pasture (νομῇ) of the righteous, neither be thou deceived by the feasting of the belly."

Ver. 16.—A just man falleth seven times, and riseth up again. The fall may be taken of sin or of calamity. Preachers, ancient and modern, have made much use of this text in the first sense, expatiating how a good man may fall into venial or more serious sins, but he never loses his love of God, and rises from his fall by repentance on every occasion. We also often find the words *in die*, "a day," added, which indeed occur in some manuscripts, but are not in the original. But the verb *naphal* seems not to be used in the sense of "falling" morally; and the meaning here is that the just man frequently falls into trouble,—he is not secure against worldly cares and losses, or the insidious attacks of the man mentioned in ver. 15; but he never loses his trust in God or offends by fretfulness and impatience, and always God's providence watches over him and delivers him out of all his afflictions. "Seven times" means merely often, that number being used to express plurality or completeness (see on ch. vi. 31; xxvi. 16; and comp. Gen. iv. 24; Job v. 19 (which is like our passage); and Matt. xviii. 22). The expectation which the sinner conceived when he saw the good man distressed, that he might seize the opportunity and use it

to his own benefit, is woefully disappointed. In contrast with the recovery and reestablishment of the righteous, when the wicked suffer calamity there is no recuperation for them. The wicked shall fall into mischief; Revised Version better, *are overthrown by calamity* (comp. ch. xiv. 32, and note there). Septuagint, " But the ungodly shall be weak in evils."

Vers. 17, 18.—A warning against vindictiveness, nearly approaching the great Christian maxim, "Love your enemies" (Matt. v. 44).

Ver. 17.—Rejoice not when thine enemy falleth. "Thou shalt love thy neighbour" was a Mosaic precept (Lev. xix. 18); the addition, "and hate thine enemy," was a Pharisaic gloss, arising from a misconception concerning the extermination of the Canaanites, which, indeed, had a special cause and purpose, and was not a precedent for the treatment of all aliens (see ch. xxv. 21, 22). When he stumbleth; rather, *when he is overthrown*. The maxim refers to private enemies. The overthrow of public enemies was often celebrated with festal rejoicing. Thus we have the triumph of Moses at the defeat of the Amalekites, and over Pharaoh's host at the Red Sea; of Deborah and Barak over Sisera (Exod. xv.; xvii. 15; Judg. v.); and the psalmist, exulting over the destruction of his country's foes, could say, "The righteous shall rejoice when he seeth the vengeance; he shall wash his feet in the blood of the wicked" (Ps. lviii. 10). But private revenge and vindictiveness are warmly censured and repudiated. So Cato, 'Distich.' iv. 46—

"Morte repentina noli gaudere malorum;
Felicesobeunt quorum sine crimine vita est."

Of very different tone is the Italian proverb, " Revenge is a morsel for God;" and "Wait time and place to act thy revenge, for it is never well done in a hurry" (Trench).

Ver. 18.—Lest the Lord see it, and it displease him. This malignant pleasure at others' misfortunes (which Aristotle, 'Eth. Nic.,' ii. 7. 15, calls ἐπιχαιρεκακία) is a sin in the eyes of God, and calls for punishment. And he turn away his wrath from him; and, as is implied, direct it upon thee. But it seems a mean motive to adduce, if the maxim is taken baldly to mean, "Do not rejoice at your enemy's calamity, lest God relieve him from the evil;" for true charity would wish for such a result. Bede considers "his wrath" to be the enemy's ill will against thee, which God by his grace changes to love, and thou art thus covered with confusion and shame for thy former vindictiveness. But the point is not so much the removal of God's displeasure from the enemy as the punishment of the malignant man, either mentally or materially. To a malignant mind no severer blow could be given than to see a foe recover God's favour and rise from his fall. The moralist then warns the disciple against giving way to this ἐπιχαιρεκακία, lest he prepare for himself bitter mortification by having to witness the restoration of the hated one, or by being himself made to suffer that evil which he had rejoiced to see his neighbour experience (comp. ch. xvii. 5, and note there).

Vers. 19, 20.—A warning against envying the prosperity of the wicked.

Ver. 19.—Fret not thyself because of evil men (comp. ver. 1 and Ps. xxxvii. 1). The verb (charah) means "to burn," "to be angry;" so here we may render, "Be not enraged on account of evil-doers." The anger would arise on account of the apparent inequitable distribution of blessings. St. Jerome has, Ne contendas cum pessimis; Septuagint, "Rejoice not over (ἐπί) evil-doers." Neither be thou envious at the wicked; i.e. do not fancy that their prosperity is to be desired, nor be led to imitate their doings in order to secure like success. The next verse shows the solemn reason for this warning.

Ver. 20.—For there shall be no reward to the evil man. He has no happy "future" to expect, as ver. 14; ch. xxiii. 18 (where see note). The candle, etc. (see ch. xiii. 9, where the clause appears). Septuagint, "For the evil man shall have no posterity, and the torch of the wicked shall be quenched."

Vers. 21, 22.—An injunction urging loyalty to God and the king.

Ver. 21.—Fear thou the Lord and the king. The king is God's vicegerent and representative, and therefore to be honoured and obeyed (see Eccles. viii. 2; x. 20; 1 Pet. ii. 17). Meddle not with them that are given to change. There is some doubt about the interpretation of the last word שׁוֹנִים (shonim), which may mean those who change, innovators (in which transitive sense the verb does not elsewhere occur), or those who think differently, dissidents, who respect neither God nor the king. The verb שָׁנָה signifies transitively "to repeat," and intransitively "to be changed;" so it may be most accurately translated here, with Delitzsch, "those who are otherwise disposed," who have not the proper sentiments of fear and honour for God and the king. St. Jerome has, Et cum detractoribus non commisscearis, by which word he probably means what we call revolutionists, persons who disparage and despise all authority. Septuagint, "Fear God and the

king, and disobey neither of them." The verse has been largely used as a text by preachers who desired to recommend loyalty and to censure disaffection and rebellion. It has been a favourite motto for discourses on the Gunpowder Treason and the execution of Charles I.

Ver. 22.—For their calamity shall rise suddenly. Though these dissidents seem to succeed for a time, yet retribution shall fall suddenly upon them. And who knoweth the ruin of them both? This seems to mean the two classes, those who dishonour God and those who dishonour the king; but no such distinction is made in the previous verse; the rebels are classed under one category. Wordsworth renders, "the stroke of vengeance from them both," i.e. from God and the king. Otherwise, we must give another signification to שְׁנֵיהֶם, and, with the Syriac and many modern commentators, take it in the sense of "years," which שְׁנֵיהֶם will bear, as Job xxxvi. 11, and translate, "The destruction [equivalent to 'end'] of their years, who knoweth?" No one can tell when the crisis of their fate shall come; but it will arrive some day, and then the time of their prosperity will be at an end. Septuagint, "For they (God and the king) will suddenly punish the ungodly; and who shall know the vengeance of both (τὰς τιμωρίας ἀμφοτέρων)?" After this the LXX. inserts three proverbs not found now in the Hebrew, which, however, Ewald ('Jahrb. der Bibl. Wissensch.,' xi. 17, etc.) considers to have been translated from a Hebrew original: "A son that keepeth the commandment shall be safe from destruction (ch. xxix. 27, Vulgate), and he hath fully received it (the word). Let no lie be spoken by the tongue of the king; and no lie shall proceed from his tongue. The king's tongue is a sword, and not of flesh; and whosoever shall be delivered unto it shall be destroyed; for if his anger be inflamed, he consumes men with their nerves, and devours men's bones, and burns them up as a flame, so that they are not food for the young eagles." The allusion at the end is to animals killed by lightning. Here follows the series of proverbs (ch. xxx. 1—14) called in the Hebrew, "The words of Agur." The second part of "the words of Agur," and "the words of Lemuel" (ch. xxx. 15—xxxi. 9) follow in the Greek after ch. xxiv. 34 of the Hebrew. Delitzsch explains the matter thus: In the copy from which the Alexandrines translated, the appendix (ch. xxx.—xxxi. 9) was divided into two parts, half of it standing after "the words of the wise" (ch. xxii. 17—xxiv. 22), and half after the supplement containing further sayings of wise men (ch. xxiv. 23—34).

Vers. 23—34.—Part V. A SECOND COL-
LECTION, forming a second supplement to
the first Solomonic book, and containing
further "words of the wise."

Vers. 23—25.—Partiality and impartiality
a hexastich.

Ver. 23.—These things also belong to the
wise; are the sayings of wise men. The
following proverbs, as well as the preceding,
are derived from wise men. Mistaking this
superscription, the LXX. makes it a personal
address: "This I say to you who are wise,
so that ye may learn." The first line is not
a proverb, but the introduction to the ensuing
collection. It is not good to have respect
of persons in judgment (see ch. xviii. 5,
and note there; and xxviii. 21, where the
expression is the same as here). To regard
one person before another is to be partial
and unjust. To say this error is "not good"
is a meiosis, the meaning being that it is
very evil and sinful (comp. ch. xx. 23).
The statement is developed and confirmed
in the next two verses, which show the
results of partiality and its opposite.

Ver. 24.—He that saith unto the wicked,
Thou art righteous. The judge is supposed
to be acquitting a guilty person. Him shall
the people curse. The Hebrew is "peoples,"
as Septuagint and Vulgate, maledicent eis
populi. Nations shall abhor him. Not
individuals, nor families only, but the whole
community, wherever such an iniquitous
ruler is found, shall execrate and hate him.
The voice of the people is universally against
him; no one is so blind and degraded as
openly to applaud his acts. The verb nakab,
"to curse," means primarily "to bore or
pierce;" hence some have translated it here,
"him shall the peoples stab." But the
word is used in the sense of distinguishing
by a mark or brand, and thence passes into
the sense of cursing, as at ch. xi. 26; Lev.
xxiv. 11; Job iii. 8. In ch. xvii. 15 the
unjust judge is called an abomination to the
Lord. In this case the vox populi is vox Dei.

Ver. 25.—But to them that rebuke him
shall be delight (see on ch. ii. 10). They
who punish the wicked, with them it is
well; they are approved by God and
applauded by the people. Vulgate, Qui ar-
guunt eum, laudabuntur, "They who convict
him shall be praised." And a good blessing
shall come upon them; literally, a blessing
of good—one that has in it all good things,
the happy contrast to the curses which meet
the unjust judge. Septuagint, "But they
that convict them (the guilty) shall appear
more excellent, and upon them shall come
blessing."

Ver. 26.—A distich connected with the
subject of the preceding paragraph. Every
man shall kiss his lips that giveth a right

answer; or better, he kisseth the lips who
giveth a right answer. An answer that is
fair and suitable to the circumstances is as
pleasant and assuring to the hearers as a
kiss on the lips. Such a salutation would
be a natural sign of sympathy and affection.
Thus Absalom won the hearts of the people
by kissing those who came to court with
their suits (2 Sam. xv. 5). In Gen. xli. 40,
where the Authorized Version has, "According to thy word shall all my people be
ruled," the Hebrew runs, "Thy mouth shall
all my people kiss," i.e. they shall do homage
to thee, which is another signification of
this action. This, however, would not be
suitable here, as the kiss is supposed to be
given by the speaker, though the LXX.
mistakenly translates, "But men will kiss
lips that answer good words."

Ver. 27.—Prepare thy work without. The
proverb enjoins a man to look well to his
resources before he undertakes to build a
house or to establish a family. "Without"
(chuts) (ch. vii. 12; viii. 26); in the fields.
Put in due order all immediate work in thy
farm. And make it fit for thyself in the
field; and get ready for what has to come
next. That is, in short, steadily and with
due foresight cultivate your land; provide
abundant means of subsistence before you
attempt to build up your house. A suitor
had, as it were, to purchase his bride from her
relations by making considerable presents;
it was therefore necessary to provide a certain amount of wealth before contemplating
matrimony. And afterwards build thy house.
This is, indeed, the meaning of the passage;
but the Hebrew makes a difficulty, as it is
literally, "afterwards and thou shalt build."
Some have supposed that some words have
dropped out of the text (Cheyne, 'Job and
Solomon'). But vav in וּבָנִיתָ, coming after
a date or notification of time, as here after
אַחַר (comp. Gen. iii. 5), "has the future signification of a perfect consecutive" (Delitzsch),
equivalent to "after that, then, thou mayest
build." Septuagint, "Prepare thy works for
thy going forth (εἰς τὴν ἔξοδον), and get
ready for the field, and come after me, and
thou shalt build up thine house." In a
spiritual sense, the heart must be first cleared
of thorns, and opened to genial influences,
before the man can build up the fabric of
virtuous habits, and thus arrive at the
virtuous character.

Ver. 28.—Be not a witness against thy
neighbour without cause (chinnam); gratuitously (ch. iii. 30; xxiii. 29; xxvi. 2), when
you are not obliged in the performance of
a plain duty. Persons are not to put
themselves forward to give testimony to a
neighbour's discredit, either officiously as
busybodies, or maliciously as slanderers.
The maxim is expressed in general terms

and is not to be confined to one category, as the Syriac and Septuagint render, "Be not a false witness against thy fellow-citizen." **And deceive not with thy lips.** The Hebrew is really interrogative, "And wouldest thou deceive with thy lips?" (Ps. lxxviii. 36). The deceit is not so much intentional falsehood as misrepresentation arising from haste and inconsiderateness consequent on this unnecessary eagerness to push forward testimony unsought. Septuagint, " Neither exaggerate (πλατύνου) with thy lips."

Ver. 29.—The subject is still continued, as if the moralist would say, " Though a man has done you an injury by gratuitously testifying against you, do not you retaliate in the same way." **Say not, I will do so to him as he hath done to me** (see ch. xx. 22, and note there). The *lex talionis* should not be applied to private wrongs. The high morality of the Christian code is here anticipated, the Holy Spirit guiding both.

Vers. 30—34.—A *mashal* ode concerning the sluggard (for similar odes, comp. ch. vii. 6—23; Job v. 3—5; Ps. xxxvii. 35, etc.; Isa. v. 1—6).

Ver. 30.—**The field . . . the vineyard;** the two chief objects of the farmer's care, which need constant labour if they are to prove productive. Moralizing on this passage, St. Gregory ('Moral.,' xx. 54) says, " To pass by the field of the slothful, and by the vineyard of the man void of understanding, is to look into the life of any careless liver, and to take a view of his deeds."

Ver. 31.—**Thorns.** *Kimmashon* is the word here used. but the plant has not been certainly identified (comp. Isa. xxxiv. 13). **Nettles** (*charul*). The stinging-nettle is quite common in Palestine, but the plant here meant is probably the prickly acanthus, which quickly covers any spot left uncultivated (Job xxx. 7). Revised Version margin suggests wild vetches. Ovid, ' Trist.,' v. 12. 21—

"Adde, quod ingenium longa rubigine læsum
　Torpet, et est multo, quam fuit ante, minus.
Fertilis, assiduo si non renovetur aratro,
　Nil, nisi cum spinis gramen, habebit ager."

So spiritual writers have used this apologue as teaching a lesson concerning the soul and the life of man, how that spiritual sloth allows the growth of evil habits, and the carelessness which maintains not the defence of law and prayer, but admits the enemy, and the result is the loss of the true riches and the perishing of the heavenly life. The two verses are thus rendered, or morally applied, in the Septuagint: " A foolish man is as a farm, and a man wanting in sense is as a vineyard; if you leave him, he will be barren, and will be altogether covered with weeds, and he will become deserted, and his fences of stone are broken down."

Ver. 32.—**Then I saw, and considered it well** (ch. xxii. 17). I looked on this sight, and let it sink into my mind. **I looked upon it, and received instruction** (ch. viii. 10). I learned a lesson from what I saw.

Vers. 33, 34.—These verses are a repetition, with very slight variations, of ch. vi. 10, 11 (where see notes), and possibly have been introduced here by a later editor. Ver. 33 seems to be the sluggard's own words; ver. 34 shows the result of his sloth. There are numberless proverbs dedicated to this subject in all languages; *e.g.* "No sweat, no sweet;" " No pains, no gains;" " He that wad eat the kernel maun crack the nut;" "A puñadas entran las buenas hadas," " Good luck enters by dint of cuffs" (Spanish); " Nihil agendo male agere discimus;" " The dog in the kennel," say the Chinese, " barks at his fleas; the dog that hunts does not feel them" (Kelly). " Sloth and much sleep," say the Arabs, "remove from God and bring on poverty." The LXX. is somewhat dramatic in its rendering: " Afterwards I repented (μετενόησα), I looked that I might receive instruction. 'I slumber a little, I sleep a little, for a little I clasp (ἐναγκαλίζομαι) my hands across my breast.' But if thou do this, thy poverty will come advancing, and thy want like a good runner (ἀγαθὸς δρομεύς)." The word ἐναγκαλίζομαι occurs in ch. vi. 10, but nowhere else in the Septuagint. It is used by St. Mark (ix 36; x. 16). It has been thought that the original *mashal* ended with ver. 32, the following passage being added by a scribe as illustrative in a marginal note, which afterwards crept into the text.

HOMILETICS.

Ver. 9.—*Sin and folly.* However these words are read, they point to an association of sin and folly. This may be regarded from two points of view, according as we start with the thought of the sin or with that of the folly.
I. SIN IMPLIES FOLLY. 1. *It chooses the worse of two courses.* Thus it blunders into self-injury. Evil is not only culpable in the sight of God; it is hurtful to the evil-doer. Its path is dark, degraded, disappointing. It is foolish to turn from the way of light and honour and satisfaction to such a course. 2. *It is short-sighted.* In

choosing a way one should look to the end of it. It is madness for the belated traveller to turn aside to the grassy path when the rough, stony road would take him home, and he knows not whither the pleasanter way will lead him. "The wages of sin is death;" it is, then, nothing but folly to work for the master without considering his direful payment. 3. *It perverts the thoughts.* Sin involves folly, and it also leads to greater folly. Many sins directly poison and paralyze the intellectual faculties. All sins confuse the lines of right and truth. Thus the man who lives in sin is blinding his eyes to the greatest facts. To know of the doctrine we must do the commandment (John vii. 17). The wilful sinner obscures the doctrine by breaking the commandment.

II. FOLLY ISSUES IN SIN. We now look at the conjunction from the opposite point of view. We start with the folly. This is to be regarded as a seed of sin. It is true that sin is primarily concerned with the moral nature. A man cannot really sin altogether in ignorance, because if he does not know that he is doing a wrong thing, to him the thing is not wrong. But, on the other hand, there is a culpable ignorance, arising from carelessness, disregard for truth, moral obliquity. Now, as sin is at the root of that ignorance, so the ignorance may, in such a case, serve as a link in the miserable chain of consequences that drags new sins into existence. These facts should lead us to certain practical conclusions. 1. *It is our duty to seek the light that we may avoid sin.* Truth is not merely given as a luxury. It is, first of all, a beacon-light. It is to guide us over the wilderness in the right way. 2. *The teaching of children is a moral and religious duty.* The advantages of education are usually discussed from a utilitarian standpoint. But the chief advantage is that it should open the eyes of children to the wisdom of doing right and to the folly of wickedness. Many poor children grow up among scenes of vice and crime without having an opportunity of knowing of a better way. The Christian Church is called to be a light in the world, leading from sin, not forcibly, but by showing the clear wisdom of goodness, as well as its moral obligation.

Ver. 10.—*Fainting in the day of adversity.* I. STRENGTH IS TESTED BY THE DAY OF ADVERSITY. 1. *The day of adversity will come.* All have not an equally painful lot. It is only the pessimist who refuses to admit that God sends a happy life to some; and if the lines have fallen in pleasant places, nothing but ingratitude or sentimentality will deny the fact. Nevertheless, the dark day of adversity will rise on every soul of man. It cannot be eluded, though in youth and health the spirit refuses to anticipate it. It is well to be prepared to meet it. 2. *Strength is wanted for the day of adversity.* This will be a time of assault, strain, pressure. The soul will then be besieged, buffeted, and in danger of being crushed. Therefore there is need of sufficient strength, not only for prosperous times, but for this harder occasion. The lighthouse must not only be strong enough to stand in calm weather; it should be able to resist the battering-rams of the tempest. The ship must be built for the storm. The army that can look smart in a review is useless if it goes to pieces on the field of battle. The model navy is an extravagant ornament if it will not serve us in action. The lamp is useless if it goes out in the hour of darkness. Religion is for the time of trial and temptation. The spiritual life needs to be strong enough to hold on through terror, temptation, and trouble; or it is a delusion. 3. *Faulty strength will fail in the day of adversity.* Trouble is trial. The season of affliction will assuredly be severe enough to prove our strength. It is vain for any one to live on empty boasts and idle pretences. The hollowness of such folly will be exposed at the fatal moment. The soft-metal sword will certainly double up in the battle and bring disaster on its unhappy owner.

II. FAITH AND COURAGE WILL GIVE STRENGTH IN THE DAY OF ADVERSITY. 1. *To faint in the day of adversity is to make one's strength small.* Such a collapse will undermine one's energy. The coward is always weak. To fear is to fail. But courage inspires strength, and he who is able to keep up a brave heart in the day of adversity is most likely to conquer. Few men have been called upon to endure such hardships and to face such perils as Livingstone, alone in the heart of Africa. Now, Livingstone was characterized by a wonderful buoyancy of temperament, by high spirits and unfailing cheerfulness. Nelson is said not to have known fear. Gordon was as ready to face death as to go to his daily duty. No doubt such heroic courage is largely due to the natural greatness of the men who possessed it But it is not independent of moral qualities. For: **2.** *The secret of the highest courage is faith.* He who trusts God is armed with the might of God. This is higher than natural strength, because "even the youths shall faint and be weary, and the young men shall utterly fall: but they that wait upon the Lord shall renew their strength; they shall mount up with wings as eagles; they shall run, and not be weary; and they shall walk, and not faint" (Isa. xl. 30, 31). Thus there is a strength that is perfected in weakness (2 Cor. xii. 9). **3.** *Therefore we have no excuse to faint in the day of adversity.* With such stores of strength for the weakest, failure is culpable. Note: We are not to blame for meeting with adversity—we cannot escape it; nor for suffering under it—this is natural; but only for fainting, *i.e.* for collapse and despair. Yet even this may not mean utter failure. We may still have some strength, though it be sickly and fast ebbing away. Like Gideon's heroes, we may be "faint, yet pursuing" (Judg. viii. 4).

Vers. 11, 12.—*Culpable negligence.* Following the Revised Version and the now generally accepted rendering of these verses, we will read the first as an exhortation to deliver men from death, and the second as a warning against neglecting this duty.

I. THE EXHORTATION. "Deliver them that are carried away unto death, and those that are ready to be slain see that thou hold back." Note first the grounds, and then the application, of this exhortation. **1.** *The grounds of it.* (1) It springs from human need. Men are in danger in war, famine, poverty, disease, sin. The world cannot go on without mutual assistance. The selfish policy of *sauve qui peut* would be fatal to society. (2) It is based on human brotherhood. God has made all men of one blood (Acts xvii. 26). Our fellow-creatures of the animal world have claims upon us; for, like us, they are sensitive, and God made both us and them. Much more are our fellow-men in our care. (3) It is urged by Divine commands. The Bible teaches duty to man as well as to God, on Divine authority. The mainly negative requirements of the ten commandments do not cover all our duty. We are called upon to love our neighbours as ourselves. (4) It is confirmed by the example of God. He has given us our lives, spared them when forfeited by sin, and saved them from many dangers. He has given his Son in death to save us from ruin. Such redeeming mercy makes churlish negligence on our part doubly culpable. **2.** *The application of it.* (1) There should be mercy in war. It is heathenish to refuse quarter. The Christian soldier will dress the wounds of his enemy. (2) We should render assistance in cases of accident and danger. It is horrible to read in the newspapers of men who would watch a child drown because they were not officers of the Royal Humane Society, because it was not their business to save life, and even because they had good clothes which they did not wish to soil. Selfish people will see a man half murdered in a street-quarrel without interfering. (3) We should help the poor. This applies to our own poor first, then to those of our neighbourhood, but the obligation extends as far as a China famine. (4) Hospitals deserve support, for ministrations to the sick directly tend to preserve life. (5) Social reforms demand Christian assistance. (6) It is our supreme duty to spread the gospel throughout the world. This is a " Word of life " (Phil. ii. 16). To let men perish for lack of the bread of life is culpable negligence. The lepers of Samaria rebuke such conduct (2 Kings vii. 9).

II. THE WARNING. **1.** *Ignorance is no excuse.* "Behold, we knew it " (or "him ") "not." Of course, this does not apply to unavoidable ignorance. But the rich should know the condition of the poor. It is the duty of the West End to investigate the condition of the East End. While this duty is neglected the comfortable complacency of ignorance is unpardonable. Further, if the attempted excuse be that the sufferer is personally unknown to us, this must not be admitted. He is still our brother. The parable of the good Samaritan shows that the perfect stranger has claims upon us. **2.** *God observes this negligence.* He "pondereth the heart." He reads our secret thoughts and weighs our motives. Thus he knows whether we are kept back by unavoidable ignorance or inability to help, or whether the negligence is wilful. With this awful fact before us, that there is One who " pondereth the heart," all flimsy excuses must shrivel up and leave the negligence of the needy in its naked guilt. **3.** *God will treat us according to our treatment of our fellow-men.* " With what measure ye mete it shall be measured to you again " (Matt. vii. 2). Moreover, in regard to the duty now before us, it is to be observed that God takes note of omissions as well as of transgressions. The "eternal fire" is not spoken of by our Lord for thieves, murderers, etc., but for those who failed to help the hungry, the thirsty, the needy (Matt. xxv. 41—46).

Ver. 16.—*The fall of a good man.* I. IT IS POSSIBLE FOR A GOOD MAN TO FALL. 1. *Here is a warning against presumption.* "Let him that thinketh he standeth take heed lest he fall" (1 Cor. x. 12). No one is so perfect as to be impeccable. Peter, who little expected it, failed in the moment of trial. 2. *He is a warning against wrong judgments.* If a good man stumbles it is commonly thought that he proves himself to have been a hypocrite from the first. No notion could be more unwarrantable. It is possible that the former life was honest and true and up to its profession, but that a sudden change for the worse has occurred through yielding to overpowering temptation. The citadel was honestly guarded; but in an unwary moment, when the custodian was sleeping, or careless, or weak, it fell before the assaults of the ever-watchful foe. This may even be repeated many times. We can scarcely think of a really good man lapsing utterly from the right way as many as seven times and as often returning to it. But some measure of sin is committed many times. There is not a Christian who does not fall into numerous sins.

II. IF A GOOD MAN FALLS HE IS LIKELY TO RISE UP AGAIN. We need not now discuss the thorny doctrine of "final perseverance." Without retreating into the tangled thicket of *à priori* dogmatics, we may discover certain plain and practical considerations which will encourage us to believe in the recovery of the lapsed. 1. *The bent of a good man's life is towards goodness.* He is a just man. Righteousness is characteristic of him. It is his habit. His fall is an event, his righteousness is his life. He is not the less guilty in his sin. He cannot shake it off and disown it, fortifying himself against the charge of it under the guise of his habitual righteousness. A long career of goodness is no excuse for a single wrong deed. Nevertheless, beneath and behind the sin into which the man has been surprised are the general tone and temper of his life. This will make his fall an agony. One look from Christ, and the shame-faced disciple goes out to weep bitterly (Matt. xxvi. 75). The Christian who has been surprised in an hour of weakness will be in the greatest distress afterwards. He can have no rest till he is forgiven and restored. Hence there is a hope for him which we cannot cherish on behalf of the bad man who has had no experience of the better way and who has no inclination to follow it. 2. *A good man may return.* There is danger in despair. The miserable penitent fears that he may have committed the unpardonable sin, forgetting that his very grief is a proof that that dark eternity of guilt has not yet been reached. God is long-suffering and merciful. Seven times the poor man falls; seven times he is forgiven and restored by his compassionate Lord. 3. *The grace of God assists recovery.* Indeed, without this it were impossible. But with it who shall despair? On the other hand, after a wicked man has indulged in sin he refuses to open his heart to Divine grace. The one means by which he might climb up out of his deep ruin is rejected by him.

In conclusion, we may gather from a consideration of this subject that the first essential is the character of a man's life, rather than that of isolated and perhaps exceptional deeds. God notes every deed, and not one can go unavenged. But the fundamental question is—How does a man live in the main? is the set of his life towards goodness? does he habitually face the light or the darkness? Though with many stumbles and shameful bruises, is he, on the whole, going up, not down? If so, he is one of God's sons.

Ver. 19.—*A needless trouble.* I. THERE IS A TEMPTATION TO BE DISTRESSED AT THE PROSPERITY OF BAD MEN. 1. *It is unjust.* This was an ancient source of perplexity and trouble of mind. While good men often suffer, bad men are often exceptionally free from the world's ills. This pains us as a frightful discord in the psalm of life. It raises doubts as to the presence, or the power, or the justice of God. If the just Lord is in our midst and is almighty to rule, why does he permit such a condition of society? 2. *It is hurtful.* Prosperity confers power. Thus great resources are at the disposal of bad men, who are able to expend them in extensive schemes of wickedness. A successful Napoleon can deluge a continent with blood, and bring misery into thousands of households. The triumph of bad men not only enables them to inflict suffering to a frightful extent; it gives them exceptional opportunities for spreading the infectious malaria of their sin. When a bad man prospers he contaminates his trade, lowers the character of business generally, and tempts his *employés* to do wrong on a scale that is proportionate to his enterprises. 3. *It seems to be envi*.*ble.* Sin looks like a short cut to success. It is hard for a good man who resists temptations to be rewarded with distresses which he would have escaped if he had yielded.

II. IT IS FOOLISH TO BE DISTRESSED AT THE PROSPERITY OF BAD MEN. 1. *Prosperity is infinitely inferio*. *to character.* The great question is not as to what a man has, but as to what he is. It is far more important to be upright and holy in life than to be rich, successful, and happy in one's circumstances. Surely he who values true goodness will feel that it is a pearl of great price—the cost of which would not be compensated for by all the wealth of the Indies. Therefore to envy the prosperi y of the wicked is to turn aside from the higher possession which may be enjoyed in poverty and adversity. 2. *The prosperity of the wicked is delusive and unsatisfactory.* It professes to give pleasure, but it cannot afford real happiness, for it has nothing in it to respond to the deeper cravings of the soul. He who feasts upon it is like a man who would fill himself with chaff and saw-dust. In his very satiety he is miserably hungry. Full, he yet starves. Or worse, he is like one who drinks madly of salt water, and is plunged into an agony of thirst in consequence. If, as may happen, however, he feels a measure of satisfaction, this can only be by deadening his higher nature. Such a state is delusive and more terrible than open complaining. 3. *This prosperity is short-lived.* " The candle of the wicked shall be put out " (ver. 20). The psalmist who was alarmed at the prosperity of the wicked saw another picture when he came to consider their end. He who would share the purple and fine linen of Dives on earth must also share his bed of fire after death. It is only the short-sighted, earthly minded man who will much envy the prosperity of the wicked. A deeper-thinking man will dread it, and be well satisfied if he has the true blessedness of life eternal.

Ver. 29.—*Rendering evil for evil.* It is interesting to note that this conduct is not only rebuked by Jesus Christ, but also forbidden in the Old Testament, and even in the Book of Proverbs, which is thought to deal too much in temporal and self-regarding motives. So utterly is it foreign to right-mindedness. Yet it is most common, and apparently most natural.

I. LET US CONSIDER HOW IT SEEMS NATURAL TO RENDER EVIL FOR EVIL. 1. *It appears to be just.* There is a natural fitness in things, and this seems to be satisfied by the *lex talionis,* " An eye for an eye, and a tooth for a tooth." 2. *It offers to check evil.* It appears to be a natural form of punishment. Indeed, it was sanctioned in rough, primitive times, though subject to judicial inquiry (Exod. xxi. 24). 3. *It satisfies the craving for revenge.* This is the reason which encourages it far more than considerations of abstract justice or anxiety about the public weal. " Revenge is sweet," and to restrain the impulse to strike an offender in return for his blow is hard and painful. 4. *It agrees with prevalent customs.* It is " after the manner of man " to avenge a wrong, and apparently the habit springs from innate instincts. At all events, it works without reflection. Therefore it appears to be a part of the economy of nature. To refuse it is like denying a natural appetite.

II. LET US LEARN WHY IT IS WRONG TO RENDER EVIL FOR EVIL. 1. *The sense of revenge lies in our lower nature.* It is shared by the brute creation, like hunger and lust. But it is aggravated by the sin of hatred and by selfishness. There is nothing noble or elevating in it. On the contrary, it drags us down. Long-suffering braces the moral fibres of the soul; revenge relaxes them. 2. *We are not called upon to execute sentence on our fellow-men.* If there is to be a requital, this must come from God, to whom belongs just vengeance (Rom. xii. 19). We are usurping the rights of God when we impatiently take it into our own hands. Moreover, we are the worst possible judges of our own rights. When deeply wounded, or irritated by insults, or blinded by passion, we are not in a fit condition to exercise judicial functions. Yet it is just on such occasions that we are most tempted to wreak vengeance on the head of an offender. 3. *It is our duty to forgive and save our fellow-man.* Even if punishment

be due to him, vengeance from us is not owing. Our business is to seek to reclaim by
"heaping coals of fire" on our wrong-doer. Instead of doing to him as he has done to
us, our Christian motto is to do to him as we would that he should do to us. 4.
Revenge is un-Christlike. Christians are called to follow in the footsteps of the patient
and brave Jesus, who was patient under provocation, even praying for his enemies. 5.
Revenge is unseemly in those who need forgiveness. We are dependent on the mercy of
God. He has not taken vengeance on us. But if we forgive not men their trespasses,
neither will our heavenly Father forgive us our trespasses. Thus Portia rightly says
to Shylock—

> " Consider this—
> That in the course of justice, none of us
> Should see salvation : we do pray for mercy ;
> And that same prayer doth teach us all to render
> The deeds of mercy."

Vers. 30—34.—*The field of the slothful.* Nothing is more characteristic of the Book
of Proverbs than its scorn of slothfulness and its strenuous inculcation of industry.
No doubt these subjects were especially important in view of the perennial indolence
of Orientals. But slothfulness is not unknown in the West, and in the fierce competition of modern life a smaller indulgence in idleness will bring sure disasters. Men
often blame their circumstances, the injustice of fate, etc., when they should accuse their
own lack of energy. The difference between the successful and those who fail to
attain anything in life is more often than not just that between hard work and self-
indulgent, easy living. Moreover, many men who are diligent in business are most
slothful in spiritual matters. Hence applications of the parable in the present day.

I. THE STATE OF THE FIELD. 1. *This is visible to the casual wayfarer.* The writer
simply "went by" it; yet he took in enough at a glance to understand its condition.
A man's character is impressed upon his work. A slovenly man will have a slovenly
hand. The neglected field and the ill-kept vineyard reveal the idle and foolish nature
of their owner. 2. *The field is seen to be in a miserable condition.* (1) It is overgrown with thorns and nettles. It is not left empty if it is untilled. Weeds grow on
the neglected land. If we fail to do our duty, positive mischief will follow. If we
neglect the field of the world, briars of ignorance, folly, and sin will spring up; if we
fail to train the vineyard of our own family, nettles of evil will appear in the minds of
our children, to sting us for our indolence. Thus was it with Eli, who failed to
rebuke his sons. If we do not cultivate the gardens of our own souls, rank weeds of sin
will certainly grow up there and bear their poisonous fruits. (2) Its defences are
broken down. The indolent man lets his walls fall into dilapidation. Thus his
property lies open to the robber and the destroyer. The wild boar from the wood will
root up his vine. If we are not watchful and careful, evil will come in from without
and spoil our work, our home, our souls. It needs care to guard against aggression.

II. THE CONDUCT OF THE OWNER. 1. *It is slothful.* (1) His evil is negative. He
commits no offence. Yet he is ruined. We may be undone by simple omission
without any transgression. (2) His evil is in delaying to do his duty. He does not
mean to forego it. He only postpones fulfilment. Yet he is ruined and disgraced. We
owe duties to time. We do wrong by not accomplishing our work promptly, though
we intend to accomplish it ultimately. We have not unlimited time before us. To-
day's neglected task cannot be performed to-morrow without hindering to-morrow's
work. The foolish virgins failed by being too late. 2. *It is self-indulgent.* The
sluggard enjoys his sleep. Selfishness is the root of idleness. But this, in turn, is
stupefying. One does not note how the fresh morning glides away while he lies with his
eyes closed in sinful sleep. So also the slumber of the soul that neglects the call to its
highest duty is a selfish sleep. 3. *It is foolish.* The sleep is a poor compensation for
poverty and shame.

III. THE CERTAIN CONSEQUENCES. 1. *Ruin follows.* Poverty comes on the slothful
man of business as a natural punishment. Poverty of soul, emptiness, fruitlessness,
and finally death follow spiritual sloth. 2. *This may be unsuspected.* "Like a
highwayman." 3. *It will be irresistible.* The want will come "as an armed man."

CONCLUSION. Sloth is peculiarly liable to creep into one's habits without being
noticed. Therefore the need of ver. 32.

HOMILIES BY VARIOUS AUTHORS.

Vers. 1, 2.—*Warning against evil company.* I. THE LOVE OF SOCIETY IS A NATURAL INSTINCT.

II. EVIL COMPANY IS OFTEN MOST FASCINATING.

III. THE ASSOCIATIONS THAT ARE FOUNDED UPON MERE FELLOWSHIP IN PLEASURE ARE SELDOM SATISFACTORY, OFTEN CORRUPTING.

IV. THE BAD MAN'S COMPANY IS MORE TO BE SHUNNED THAN THAT OF ONE SUFFERING FROM A CONTAGIOUS DISEASE. "Wicked companions," said a man of the world, the novelist Fielding, "invite us to hell." "They are like to be short graces when the devil plays the host," said another.—J.

Vers. 3—6.—*Wisdom edifies and invigorates.* How fine a word is "edification," *building up,* in its moral and Christian uses! Here the image of the house is directly introduced, and may be variously applied.

I. WISDOM THE FOUNDATION OF DOMESTIC STABILITY AND HAPPINESS. (Vers. 3, 4.) The same great principles apply in the least as well as the most important things. Every day brings humble occasions for the practice of the grandest laws, no less in the house, the farm, or the shop, than in the council-chamber or on the battle-field. "Method is as efficient in the packing of firewood in a shed, or the harvesting of fruits in a cellar, as in Peninsular campaigns or the files of a department of state." Let a man keep the Law, and his way will be strewn with satisfactions. There is more difference in the quality of our pleasures than in the amount. Comfort and abundance in the home are the certain signs of prudence and sense and action constantly applied.

II. WISDOM THE SOURCE OF MANLY STRENGTH. (Vers. 5, 6.) It was a great man who said, "Knowledge is power." It is not the force of brute strength, but that of spiritual energy, which in the long run rules the world. The illustration of the text is aptly selected from war, where, if anywhere, brute force might be supposed to prevail. Experience shows that it is not so. The complete failures of men like Hannibal and Napoleon show it in one way. Recent wars have illustrated the truth that it is the deliberate and matured designs of the strategist and far-seeing statesman which command success, rather than the "great battalions" on the side of which Providence was said to be. And in another application, sheer force of intellect is often surpassed and outdone by the steady and constant employment of humbler powers. Strength in any form without prudence is like a giant without eyes. Violence and craft may seem the readiest way to wealth; yet experience shows that prudence and piety lead most surely to desirable prosperity.—J.

Vers. 7—10.—*Some traits of folly and sin.* I. THE GROVELLING MIND. (Ver. 7.) Wisdom is too high for the indolent to climb to, for the sensual and earthly to admire and love. They are like Muck-rake, in Bunyan's parable. From such no good counsel ever comes. They are dumb "in the gate," on every important occasion, when help, light, sympathy, are needed. The base prudence which inspires many popular proverbs—the prudence "which adores the rule of three, which never subscribes, never gives, seldom lends, and asks but one question of any project, 'Will it bake bread?'"—is indeed folly. "Self's the man," says a Dutch proverb. But those who would gain all for self end by losing self and all.

II. THE MALICIOUS TEMPER. (Ver. 8.) There are degrees in vice as in virtue. It is a short step from grovelling egotism to active malice. Extract the root of self-seeking out of any dispute, private or public, in Church or state, and the other differences may soon be adjusted. To make mischief is a diabolic instinct, and it certainly springs up in the mind void of healthy occupation and of interest for the true, beautiful, and good; for the mind's principle is motion, and it cannot cease to act.

III. SIN IN THE THOUGHT AND THE MOOD. (Ver. 9.) When busy invention and meditation are at work in the mind of the wicked and the fool, nothing good is produced. Still more is it the case with the scoffer. In him the ripened and practised powers of the mind are brought into alliance with evil desire. Such a habit of mind, once detected, excites the utmost odium and abhorrence. The man who can sneer at goodness, or hold what is by common consent good and beautiful in contempt, is already an outcast from his kind, and need not complain if he is treated as such.

IV. COWARDLY FAINT-HEARTEDNESS. (Ver. 10.) The pressure of circumstances should rouse in us the God-given strength. The man who makes duty his polar star, and trusts in God, can actually do more when things seem to be against him than when all is in his favour. Moral cowardice is closely connected with the root-sin of unbelief. Indulgence in it impoverishes and weakens the soul, so that the man ends by being actually unable to do what once he only fancied himself unable to do. Here is an illustration of Christ's saying, "To him that hath shall be given, and from him that hath not shall be taken that which he hath."—J.

Vers. 11, 12.—*Compassion for the wronged.* I. THE HEART AND HAND SHOULD EVER BE READY AT THE CALL OF DISTRESS. (Ver. 11.) The picture seems to be placed before us of one arriving at the place of judgment, seeing an innocent sufferer yet, like the priest and the Levite in the parable, passing by "on the other side."

> "To see sad sights moves more than hear them told;
> For then the eye interprets to the ear
> The heavy motion that it doth behold."

To respond to these mute appeals from any of God's creatures is to obey a law immediately known within our breast; to resist them is to sin against him and against our own souls.

II. NEGLECT OF DUTY CANNOT ESCAPE PUNISHMENT. (Ver. 12.) 1. *Human nature is fertile in excuses.* For the burden of blame and of conscious guilt is the heaviest we can bear. But searching is the truth of the proverb, "Whoso excuses, accuses himself." Ignorance of duty needs no excuses; but excuses for neglect can never be valid. 2. *Excuses may avail with man, but not with God.* With fallible men they may and often do pass for truth. At all events, they must often be accepted by those who need in turn to make them. But God knows the truth of every heart, and in every case; and to him excuses are either needless or worse. 3. *Judgment will be executed in spite of our excuses.* For God is the Vindicator of the wronged, and the Recompenser of all according to their deeds. Scripture is very impressive on the sin of *neglect* of kindly duties to others, in regard to which the conscience is so often dull (Luke xiv. 18, etc.). Men content themselves with the reflection that they have not done others positive harm—a negative position. But the other negative position, that we have not done the good we had a call to do, on this the teaching of Christ fixes a deeper guilt. Noble as it is to save a life from bodily death, still more glorious in its consequences is it to save a *soul* from death, and hide a multitude of sins.—J.

Vers. 13, 14.—*Zeal in the pursuit of wisdom.* I. THE SWEETNESS OF WISDOM. (Ver. 13.) Not without deep meaning is the sense of knowing the truth compared to the sensuous relish of the palate for sweet food. Here is, indeed, a

> "Perpetual feast of nectared sweets,
> Where no crude surfeit reigns."

(Cf. Ps. xix. 11.)

II. ENCOURAGEMENT IN ITS PURSUIT. (Ver. 14.) It brings a true satisfaction both during the pursuit and at its end, which can be said of few other objects of eager ambition in this world. The seeker for truth may be compared to the maiden of the parable, who timely fills her lamp with oil, and "hope that reaps not shame." The pursuit of wisdom, or of truth as understood and taught in this book, is no chase of dreams or abstractions; it is the affair of all. Truth is all that touches and convinces man, whether as an individual, or as a member of society, or the citizen of a nation. It is that which tells him that he is not isolated in the midst of unknown beings; but that beyond his individual life he partakes in a life that is universal. All that in the past, whether facts, thoughts, or sentiments, are in question, that makes us contemporary with the facts, fellow-heirs with humanity in great thoughts, sympathetic with great sentiments, is truth.—J.

Vers. 15—18.—*Violence and shameful joy defeated.* I. THE ATTITUDE OF THE MAN OF FRAUD AND VIOLENCE DEPICTED. (Ver. 15.) He is like the prowling wild beast, seeking whom he may devour. God the Creator has not armed us with tooth or tusk or other means of defence, like the wild beasts which are formed for making war on others. We are strongly furnished for defence, not for attack. Ferocity is distinctly an unnatural vice in us.

II. HIS ACTIVITY IS DEVASTATING. Here, again, he resembles the wild beast in his blind fury, the boar that uproots and overturns in the cultivated garden.

III. THE SELF-RECOVERY OF THE RIGHTEOUS. (Ver. 16.) To fall into sin and to fall into trouble are two different things. Avoid the former, and God will not forsake thee in the latter. Seven falls stand for many—an indefinite number of falls. There is an elasticity in rectitude like that of the young sapling; bent to the earth, it rebounds with strong upspring. "It may calm the apprehension of calamity to see how quiet a bound nature has set to the utmost infliction of malice. We rapidly approach a brink over which no enemy can follow us." But evil, being purely negative, a zero, the absence of internal power and virtue, has but an illusory existence, and quickly passes away.

IV. BASE JOY TURNED INTO SHAME. (Vers. 17, 18.) He who rejoices in the trouble of another, his own trouble stands behind the door. Why should he fear who takes his post with Omnipotence at his back?

> "Souls that of God's own good life partake
> He loves as his own self; dear as his eye
> They are to him; he'll never them forsake.
> When they shall die, then God himself shall die;
> They live—they live in blest eternity."

The tyrant and his victim are made to change sides. The "wrath" which seems expressed in the calamities of the latter is transformed into the revelation of an "everlasting kindness," while terror strikes the heart of him who sought to infuse it into his foe (compare R. Browning's striking poem, 'Instans Tyrannus').—J.

Vers. 19—22.—*Religion fortifies the heart against envy.* I. THE TEMPTATION TO ENVY THE PROSPERITY OF THE WICKED. It is very marked in the Old Testament. It is a common temptation. For we look at the outside of man's condition, and are deceived by illusions. A pirate's vessel in the distance, a mansion built and inhabited by infamy, are beautiful objects of æsthetic contemplation. So it is that the show and bravery of success master our senses.

II. THE ANTIDOTE TO THESE FEELINGS. (Ver. 20.) "Consider the end"—darkness and the blackness of darkness. The wicked have *no* future. When this is once clearly seen, the charm on the surface fades away, and the edifice of proud but godless prosperity sinks almost into a smoking ruin.

III. RELIGION AND MORALITY THE ONLY FOUNDATION OF SECURITY AND BLESSED-NESS. (Vers. 21, 22.) The one comprehensive word for religion is the "fear of Jehovah, reverence for God, and for all that, being true, is of the very nature of God. And obedience to the king includes all those civil and social duties which we incur as members of an ordered commonwealth. Religion and loyalty go together; and the best way to make good subjects to the queen is to make men good servants of God. They will not make conscience of civil duties who make none of Divine.—J.

Vers. 23—25.—*Partiality and equality in judgment.* I. RESPECT OF PERSONS. The literal translation is, "To distinguish persons in judgment is not good." The judge should be impartial as the pair of scales, the emblem of his office, and blind to the persons who appear before him, that is, to their rank and position, as the symbolical figure of Justice is represented to be. "One foul sentence doth more hurt than many foul examples; these do but corrupt the stream, the other corrupteth the fountain."

II. THE WILFUL PERVERSION OF RIGHT. (Ver. 24.) When the just man is suffered to fail in his cause before his adversary, the very nerve of public right is unstrung. It strikes a direct blow at the common weal, and hence brings down the curses of peoples and the enmity of states.

III. EQUAL AND JUST JUDGMENT. (Ver. 25.) "A judge ought to prepare his way to a just sentence, as God useth to prepare his way, by raising valleys and taking down hills ; so when there appeareth on either side a high hand, violent persecution, cunning advantages taken, combination, power, great counsel, then is the virtue of a judge seen to make inequality equal; that he may plant his judgment as upon an even ground" (Bacon). In the present text the glance is towards a proper and due severity, which will not allow the wicked to escape. " Odium may equally be incurred by him who winks at crime and by him who has no regard to mercy. For in causes of life and death, judges ought, as far as the law permits, in justice to remember mercy, and to cast a severe eye upon the example, but a merciful eye upon the person" (Bacon). The purity of the judicial bench is one of the greatest of public blessings. Let us be thankful that we enjoy it in our country, and-pray that it may ever continue.—J.

Vers. 26—29.—*Just conduct to our neighbour.* I. TRUE WITNESS. (Ver. 26.) He who gives true and faithful answers—especially in courts of justice—delights, even as the sweetest kiss upon the mouth delights. The poet alludes to the effect upon the *ear.* The understanding can no more be delighted with a lie than the will can choose an apparent evil. " Strange as it may seem," says one playfully, " the human mind loses truth." We may add, " when passion does not blind the intellect to its beauty." In the court of justice, all but the guilty and those interested in his fate see the beauty of truth, and prize it above all things. Hence to speak the truth, the whole truth, and nothing but the truth, is the solemn oath of witnesses.
II. FALSE AND UNCALLED-FOR WITNESS. (Ver. 28.) To bear false witness strikes at the very root of conscience and moral obligation. But criminal, though in a less degree, is the volunteering of evidence without cause against another ; *i.e.* when no object but private hatred and revenge is to be served. Compare the case of Doeg (1 Sam. xxii. 9, 10); the Pharisees with the wretched sinner in John viii. ; the words of the Lord in John xv. 25. Speak evil of no man, not only that evil which is altogether false and groundless, but that which is true, when speaking of it will do more harm than good (Matthew Henry).
III. DELIBERATE DECEPTION. About a court of justice, which represents truth, there gathers a dark shade of roguery and falsehood ; " persons that are full of sinister tricks and shifts, whereby they pervert the plain and direct courses of courts, and bring justice into oblique lines and labyrinths."
IV. BLIND INDULGENCE OF VINDICTIVE TEMPER. (Ver. 29 ; comp. ch. xx. 22.) Nothing is more deeply impressed in the Bible than the truth of compensation or retribution. But men must not take the law into their own hands. " Vengeance is mine, I will repay, saith Jehovah." " Revenge is a kind of wild justice, which the more man's nature runs to, the more ought law to weed it out. In taking revenge a man is but even with his enemy; but in passing it over he is superior. It is the glory of a man to pass by an offence. The man who studies revenge keeps his own wounds green, which otherwise would heal and do well " (Bacon).—J.

Ver. 27.—*The prudence and policy of industry.* I. ALL LABOUR IS ROOTED IN THE TILLAGE OF THE EARTH. 'Tis thus that bread was first wrung from her—by universal field-labour. Our ancestors were all agricultural labourers. All other industry must be fruitless and stop without the action of this spring. It is therefore the part of all prudent and good men to encourage cultivation, to improve the condition of the labourer and the farmer. All honour to the great statesmen of our time who have wrought in this cause. It is edifying to recollect that God has made Mother Earth the eternal mediator and minister to us of material blessings which lie at the foundation of all our life.
II. DOMESTIC COMFORT AND INDEPENDENCE REST UPON LABOUR. It is the " prudence of a higher strain " than that which begins and ends with mere sensual comfort that is taught in this book. It is attention to law, it is unbelief in luck, which constitutes its principle. Self-command, unslothful habits, constant exertion, put the bread a man eats at his own disposal, so that he stands not in bitter and false relations to other men.—J.

Vers. 30—34.—*The sluggard's vineyard : a parable of sloth.* I. A PICTURE OF

INDOLENCE. (Vers. 30, 31.) The vineyard in the East corresponds to the garden, orchard, or small farm in the West. In the parable it is overgrown with nettles and thorns. The stone fence is crumbling for want of repair. We may contrast the picture in Isa. v. 1, *sqq.*, of what a vineyard ought to be. The way in which God tilled the chosen people is the way in which he would have each of us attend to the garden of the soul.

II. THE SIGHT CARRIES A LESSON AND A WARNING. (Vers. 32—34.) Let us attend to the parables of Nature. The eye is the great critical organ, and we never want lessons if we use it. The *lesson* here is—the effect has a cause—the wildness of Nature betrays the sin of man. Neglect marks itself on her truthful face. The sluggard's soul is revealed in her aspect not less than in the unkempt hair and squalid face of the human being. Here is the " vile sin of self-neglect," which involves all other neglect, clearly mirrored. In such spectacles and in the gloomier ones of malarious swamps, once smiling fields, God writes his judgment on the broad earth's face against the crime of sloth. The *warning* is against poverty and want, which stride on with noiseless footsteps, rushing in at last with sudden surprise upon dreaming self-indulgence, like an armed robber. Sudden-seeming woes are long preparing, and no curse " causeless comes."

III. THE MORAL APPLICATION. 1. The analogy of Nature and the human spirit. Both are of God. Both contain principles of life, beauty, and use. Both need cultivation in order to their perfection. In both sloth and neglect are punished by loss and ruin. 2. The personal moral duty. To " awake from sleep," to " stir up the gift within us," to " work out our salvation," to be good husbandmen, good and faithful servants in this garden of the Lord—the soul. If not faithful here, how can it be expected that we shall be faithful in spheres more remote ?—J.

Ver. 1.—(See homily on ch. xxiii. 17, 18.)—C.

Vers. 3—6.—*Building with wisdom.* God is the Divine Builder. " He that built all things is God " (Heb. iii. 4). Man, also, is a great builder. The whole scenery of the earth is not a little changed by the houses and temples, by the bridges and factories, by the manifold structures of every size and shape, that he has built. But these are not the most serious and important of his works. We look at—

I. THE HOUSES WE ARE BUILDING. Of these, three are the most deserving of attention. 1. *Our estate.* The position and provision we secure for ourselves and our family ; an honourable place we take among men, as neighbours and fellow-citizens. Every man has to set this before him as a thing to be patiently pursued and ultimately attained. Some men think of little else or nothing else, therein making a fatal mistake ; but it is the manifest duty as well as the clear interest of us all, to build up a house of this kind. 2. *Our character.* This is " a house " of the first importance. We are here for this express purpose—that we may be daily and hourly building up a noble and estimable character ; such a character as God will himself approve ; such as man will admire, and will do well to copy ; such as will command the commendation of our own conscience ; such as will stand firm and strong against all the perils by which it is beset ; such as will contain many virtues and graces in its various " chambers " (ver. 4). " Precious and pleasant rubies," indeed, are these. 3. *Some cause of Christian usefulness.* We should all be diligently occupied in raising or sustaining some " work " of holy usefulness, by which the seeds of truth may be scattered, hearts may be comforted, lives may be brightened, souls may be won to righteousness and wisdom, Christ may be honoured, and his kingdom advanced.

II. THE INDISPENSABLE MATERIALS. The wisdom which is from above. " Through wisdom is a house built, and by understanding it is established " (ver. 3). For wisdom includes or secures : 1. *The fear and therefore the favour of God.* (See ch. i. 7; ix. 10.) (1) To walk and to work in the fear of God is to do all things uprightly and honourably, truly and faithfully, heartily and thoroughly ; and this is the way to build up any one of these three " houses." (2) To enjoy the favour of God is to have behind us that energizing and sustaining power without which all labour is vain (Ps. cxxvii. 1); it is to possess the protecting care which will shield us from the storms that might otherwise overthrow us (Ps. cxxi.). 2. *The various orders of strength* which we need for good building (ver. 5). (1) It tends to physical health and strength. (2) It conduces to mental strength and the increase of knowledge; it supplies us with good judgment, with tact, with prudence, with patience, with the very implements of successful labour. (3) It ministers to moral and spiritual strength; for it brings us into communion with God and to the study of his Word. 3. *The power of resistance and attack.* By "wise counsel we make war" (ver. 6). It is a very great matter, in all spheres of activity, to know when to make peace and when to show a fearless front of opposition. And when the latter course has to be taken, there is much true wisdom needed in order that our house, our stronghold, may not be carried and dismantled. We need courage, decision, watchfulness, energy, self-command, readiness to make terms at the right moment. To attain to the wisdom which will thus build up our house, we need to (1) yield our hearts fully to the only wise God and Saviour; (2) open our minds daily to receive his heavenly wisdom; (3) ask of him who "giveth to all men liberally, upbraiding not."—C.

Ver. 9.—"*The thought of foolishness.*" It will be well to be on our guard against a possible mistake here; for next in importance to our knowledge of what things are wrong and hurtful, is our freedom from imaginary fears and morbid anxieties respecting those things which are perfectly innocent and pure. We look, then, at—

I. THOUGHTS WHICH MAY SEEM TO BE, BUT ARE NOT, CONDEMNED BY THESE WORDS. 1. The serious but mistaken thoughts of childhood or of uneducated manhood. It is not every thought which cannot be characterized as wisdom that must be condemned as "foolishness." The honest attempts of artless simplicity to solve problems or to execute commands may be honourable and even commendable failures; they are the conditions of growth. 2. The lighter thoughts of the cultured and mature, thoughts of merriment and frolicsomeness, moving to honest laughter, are far from being sinful. They are clearly in accordance with the will of the Divine Father of our spirits, who is the Author of our nature, with its faculties and tendencies; they are often found to be a necessary relief under the otherwise intolerable strain of oppressive care and burdensome toil. One of the most serious and one of the most kind-hearted and successful servants of our race (Abraham Lincoln) was only saved from complete mental derangement during the terrible time of the civil war by finding occasional refuge in humour. But what are—

II. THE THOUGHTS WHICH ARE HERE CONDEMNED? The thoughts of foolishness. 1. *Our responsibility for our thoughts.* Impalpable and fugitive as they are, our thoughts are a very real part of ourselves, and they constitute a serious part of our responsibility to God. That they do so is clear, for: (1) On them everything in human life and action ultimately depends. Action depends on will, will on feeling, and feeling on thought. It is *what* we think and *how* we think that determines what we do and what we are. "As a man thinketh in his heart, so is he." Thought is the very foundation of character. (2) Thought is free. We may be compelled to speak or to act in certain prescribed ways; but we are masters of our own minds, and we can think as we like. How we think depends on our own volition. (3) We either choose deliberately the subject of our thoughts (by selecting our friends, our books and papers, our topics of conversation), or we are led to think as we do by the mental and moral character which we have been deliberately forming; we are responsible for the stream because we are responsible for the spring. 2. *The sinful character of foolish thoughts.* Foolish thoughts may be (1) *irreverent*, and all irreverence is sin; or they may be (2) *selfish*, and all selfishness is sin; or (3) *impure*, and all impurity is sin; or (4) *unkind* and inconsiderate, unloving or vindictive, and all unkindness is sin; or (5) *short-sighted and worldly*, and all worldliness is sin (1 John ii. 15—17). The conclusion of the whole matter is that if we would be right with God, "harmless and blameless," we must be right in our "inward thought" (see Heb. iv. 12); and that if we would be right there, in those central depths of our nature, we must (*a*) place our whole nature under the direct rule of the Holy One himself; (*b*) seek daily for the cleansing influences of his Holy Spirit, the continual renewal of our mind by his inspiration; (*c*) "keep our hearts beyond all keeping" (ch. ii. 23), especially by welcoming, with eagerness and delight, all the wisdom of God that we can gather from his Word.—C.

Vers. 10, 15.—*The test of adversity.* We have all of us to expect—

I. The testing-time that comes to all men. It is true that prosperity has its own perils, and makes its own demands on the human spirit. But when the sky is clear above us, when loving friends stand round us with protecting care, when privileges abound on every side, it is comparatively easy to maintain an equable and obedient mind. We can all row with the stream and sail with the favouring wind. But the hour must come to us that comes to all in time, when we have to face difficulty, or to bear obloquy, or to sustain heavy loss, or to go on our way with a lonely heart, or to suffer some keen and all but crushing disappointment. When we are moved to say with Jacob, "All these things are against me;" with Elijah, "Lord, take away my life;" we faint and fall in the day of adversity.

II. The resources that should be at our command. When that hour comes to us, as it certainly will, we should be prepared to bear ourselves bravely and well; for there are many sources of strength with which we should be supplied. There is: 1. *Ordinary human fortitude.* Such manliness and strength of will as have enabled many thousands of souls—even without any aid from religion—to confront danger or death, or to show an undisturbed equanimity of mind in the midst of severe sorrows. But beyond this there is for us: 2. *Christian resignation.* The willingness to leave the whole disposal of our lives to the wisdom and the love of God; readiness to endure the holy will of a Divine Father, of our best Friend. 3. *Christian faith.* The assurance that God is dealing with us in perfect wisdom and parental love at those times when we can least understand his way. 4. *Christian hope.* The confidence that " unto the upright there will arise light in the darkness;" that God will grant a happy issue out of all our afflictions; that though the just man fall seven times, he will rise again (see ver. 15); that though weeping may endure even for a long and stormy night, joy will come in the morning (Ps. xxx. 5). 5. *Communion with God.* To the distressed human spirit there remains that most precious refuge, the leaning of the heart on God, the appeal of the soul to him in earnest, believing prayer.

III. The inference we are obliged to draw. If, with all these resources at our command, we "faint;" (1) if we indulge a rebellious spirit, repining at our lot and thinking ourselves hardly used; or (2) if we yield ourselves to misery and melancholy, showing ourselves unequal to the duties that devolve upon us, resigning the useful activities in which we have been engaged;—then we must conclude that " our strength is small;" we have failed to enrich our souls with that spiritual power of which we might and should have become possessed. But that we may not have to deplore our weakness in the day of adversity, and that we may not give a sorry illustration of Christian life as it ought not to be seen, let us learn what is—

IV. Our wisdom at the present time. And that is to be gaining strength, to be continually becoming " strong in the Lord, and in the power of his might." This is an *imperative duty* (Eph. vi. 10; 2 Tim. ii. 1; 2 Pet. iii. 18). And we are not without the necessary means. If, in the days of sunshine and prosperity, we are daily nourishing our faith, our love, our hope, our prayerfulness, by *constant exercise* in devotion and in sacred duty, by *using* the privileges so amply supplied to us, by cultivating and cherishing our union with Jesus Christ our Lord, we shall be strong, and we shall not faint.—C.

Vers. 11, 12.—*Inexcusable indifference.* The principles contained in this passage are these—

I. That all human need is a claim for help. God has so " fashioned our hearts alike," and has so bound together our lives and our interests, that we are under serious obligation to one another. No man is at liberty to live an isolated life; he owes too much to those that have gone before him, and is too closely related to those who are around him, to allow of such a course. To wish it is unnatural, to attempt it is immoral. " We are members one of another;" we are brethren and sisters one of another. And whenever any one about us—whoever or whatever he or she may be— is in any kind of difficulty or distress, is in need of sympathy and succour, there is an imperative demand, as clear as if it came from an angel's trumpet or straight out of the heavens above us, that we should stop, should inquire, should help as best we can (see 1 John iii. 17, 18).

II. That the extremity of human need is a most powerful plea. If *any* sufferer on life's highway is a man to be pitied and relieved, how much more are they who are " drawn unto death," who are " ready to be slain " ! To see our brother or our sister—made like ourselves, and capable as we are of intense suffering, holding life as precious as we ourselves regard it—in circumstances of keen distress or of utmost danger, and to withhold our pity and our aid,—this is condemned of God. Whether we " pass by *on the other side* " (Luke x. 31), so as to hide our cruel indifference as well as we can from our own sight; or whether we pass close by, clearly recognizing our duty, but cynically and heartlessly declining to do it ; or whether we stand awhile and pity, but conclude that help will be too costly, and so pass on without helping ; —we are guilty, we are unbrotherly, inhuman, altogether unlike our Lord.

III. That excuses will not avail us. If we want to escape from our plain duty we seldom refuse it *point-blank*. We do not say to our Lord or to ourselves, " We will not ; " we say, " We would if——," or " We will when—— " When our brother is in difficulty or in sorrow, and urgently needs the extricating hand, the sympathizing word, we may plead, to ourselves or to our neighbours, our ignorance of the sufferer, our imperfect acquaintance with the circumstances, our want of time, our incapacity for assisting in that kind of trouble, our multitudinous and pressing duties and claims, etc. These may succeed with men, but they will not avail with God. God knows the hollowness of these poor pleas ; to his eye they are only thin veils that do not hide our cruel selfishness ; he judges that nothing justifies us in abandoning the perishing to their fate, and he condemns us.

IV. That God is grieved with us for our own sake. He " that keepeth our soul" knows it. And because God does " keep our soul," he is grieved to see us take up an attitude towards our brother which (1) proves us to be unbrotherly, and (2) helps to fix us in our cold-heartedness. For every act and instance of selfishness hardens our heart and makes it more capable of cruel indifference than before.

V. That cruelty and kindness move to their reward. " Shall he not render," etc.? Cruelty and kindness must be cursed or blessed by the immediate effects they leave in the soul of the agent. But they also move toward a day of award. Then will a selfish indifference hear its strong, Divine condemnation (Matt. xxv. 41—45). Then, also, will a generous kindness listen to its warm, Divine commendation (Matt. xxv. 34—40).—C.

Vers. 17, 18, 29.—*The ignobler and the nobler spirit.* (See homily on ch. xx. 22.) There can be no question at all, for the testimony of human history is everywhere and at all times the same, as to—

I. Our disposition under sin, in view of our enemies. These two passages indicate it. It is both passive and active. 1. A disposition to rejoice at their discomfiture ; to exult in the secret places of the soul when we hear of their failure, of their defeat, or even of their suffering. 2. A disposition to inflict some injury on them by our own effort. The impulse of the man who is struck is to strike again ; that of the man who is cheated is to take the next opportunity of overreaching the treacherous neighbour ; the prevalent feeling, under the long reign and malignant influence of sin, is to compass, in some way or other, the humiliation, or the loss, or the anger of the man who has injured us. We rejoice when our enemy falls ; we do more and worse than that—we do our best, we use our ingenuity and put forth even our patient labour, to bring about his overthrow. So common, so universal, is this sentiment of revenge and retaliation, that no one is in a position to speak severely of his neighbour or to condemn him harshly. Yet we understand now—

II. Its unworthiness of our nature. It was not to cherish such thoughts as these, nor was it to act in such a way as this, that our Divine Father called us into being, and gave to us our powers. 1. We were made to love and to pity ; and for us to harbour in our souls a feeling of positive delight when we witness the misery or misfortune of a brother or a sister is *really* inhuman ; it is a perversion, under the malign power of sin, of the end and purpose of our being. 2. We were made to help and bless ; and for us to expend the powers with which we are endowed to injure, to inflict suffering and loss, to send as far as we can on the downward road a human heart or human life,—this is wholly unworthy of ourselves, it is a sad departure from the intention of our Creator. We see clearly—

III. ITS OFFENSIVENESS TO GOD. "Lest the Lord see it, and it displease him." 1. God has told us fully what is his mind respecting it (Matt. v. 43—48; Rom. xii. 14, 20). 2. It is altogether unlike his own action; for he is daily and momently blessing with life and health and innumerable bounties those who have forgotten or disregarded or even denied him. 3. There are two aspects in which it must be obnoxious to him. (1) He is the Father of our spirits, and how can he look with anything but sorrow on antagonism and hatred between his children? (2) He is the Holy and the Loving One, and how can he see with anything but displeasure the hearts of men filled with the feelings of malevolence, the hands of men occupied in dealing bitter blows against one another? What, however, is the way by which this deep-rooted disposition can be expelled, and another and nobler spirit be planted in our souls? What is the way to—

IV. THE WORTHIER AND NOBLER SPIRIT. The one way to rise above vindictiveness and retaliation and to enter into the loftier and purer air of forgiveness and magnanimity is to connect ourselves most closely with our Lord Jesus Christ. 1. To surrender ourselves wholly to him, and thus to receive his Divine Spirit into our hearts (John vii. 38, 39; xv. 4; xvii. 23). 2. To have our hearts filled with that transforming love to our Father and our Saviour which will make us to become, unconsciously and gradually, like him in spirit and behaviour. 3. To let our minds be filled with the knowledge of his will, by patient and prayerful study of his Word and of his life.—C.

Vers. 30—34.—*The neglected garden.* The whole scene is before us. The sluggard is asleep while everything is going wrong; instead of the flower is the thorn; the ground is coloured with the green weeds; the wall is breaking down; where should be beauty is unsightliness; where should be fruitfulness is barrenness or wilderness; ruin is written, on everything, everywhere. So is it with the farmer, with the tradesman, with the merchant or manufacturer, of the sluggard order. Consider it well. Negligence, dilatoriness, half-heartedness, in any department means decay, break-down, ruin. *Poverty* is on its way, and will certainly be knocking at the door; *want* will present itself with a force that cannot be resisted. 1. We have all of us a garden, an estate of our own, which God has given us to cultivate—that which is of more value than many thousands of acres of fertile soil, that which no riches can buy—*our own true self,* our own human spirit. God has solemnly charged us to cultivate that, to *weed* it of error and prejudice, of folly and of passion; to *plant truth* there, his own living, abiding truth; to *plant righteousness* there, purity of heart, integrity of soul; to *plant love* there, such as fills his own gracious Spirit; to *build* there walls of wise, strong, protecting *habits,* which will fence and guard the soul from intruding enemies. 2. There are all too many who treat this garden, this estate, with careless negligence; they throw their energy and force into everything else—business, love, politics, art, pleasure, society; but *themselves,* their own spirit, their own character, they leave to fare as best it may without care and without culture. 3. Very sad indeed are the results of this foolish and guilty negligence. This picture of the sluggard's garden will tell us what they are.

I. UNSIGHTLINESS. What a dreary picture—weeds, thistles, thorns, a broken wall! The eye turns from it with repugnance. And the neglected garden of the soul? Instead of the beautiful flowers of Christian reverence and love, and the fair fruits of holiness and zeal, and the strong walls of a noble character, there are seen by God and man the unsightly weeds of transgression, of selfishness, of untruthfulness—perhaps the thorns of intemperance and impurity and profanity.

II. WASTE. African travellers tell us that passing over uncultivated regions they have to make their way through all kinds of rank growth, grass, or shrub which is high, strong, or thorny, covering many miles at a stretch. What waste is there! What corn, what fruit, would not that land produce? Alas! for the pitiful waste of an uncultured human soul! What beauties might not be seen there, what fruits might not be grown there, what graces and virtues might not be produced there, if only the truth of Christ were received into the mind and welcomed to the heart!

III. MISCHIEF. These weeds will not be confined to the sluggard's garden; their seeds will be carried by the winds into his neighbour's, and do mischief enough there.

A neglected soul is a mischief-working soul. It cannot confine its influence to itself or its own life. Those influences cross the wall and get into the neighbour's ground. And the seeds of sin are hurtful, poisonous things, spreading error, falsehood, delusion, into the minds of men. If we are not blessing our neighbours by the lives we live, we are an injury and an evil to them.

IV. RUIN. The man who neglects his estate is really, steadily, ruining himself. He may not see it until it is too late. Poverty has been travelling toward him, but only at the last bend of the road does it come in sight. Want suddenly appears " as an armed man," strong, irresistible; there is no way of escape; bankruptcy is before him. The soul that is neglected is being ruined; day by day it is being enfeebled, enslaved, deteriorated; the good that was there is lessening and disappearing; the hard crust of selfishness and worldliness is thickening. The soul is being lost; it is perishing. "I considered it well"—"set my heart up on it" (marginal reading). This is, indeed, a thing to be well considered, to " set the heart upon," for the issues of it are those of life or death. There is time to restore it; but a little more negligence, and the hour of " ruin " will have struck.—C.

EXPOSITION.

CHAPTER XXV.

Ver. 1—ch. xxix.—Part VI. SECOND GREAT COLLECTION OF SOLOMONIC PROVERBS, gathered by "the men of Hezekiah," in which wisdom is set forth as the greatest blessing to the king and his subjects.

Ver. 1.—The *superscription:* These are also proverbs of Solomon, which the men of Hezekiah King of Judah copied out. The word "also" implies that a previous collection was known to the compiler of the present book—probably the one which we have in ch. x.—xxii. 16, of which nine proverbs are inserted here. But there was still a large number of proverbial sayings attributed to Solomon, and preserved partly by oral tradition and partly in writing, which it was advisable to collect and secure before they were lost. The zeal of Hezekiah took this in hand. He was not, as far as we know, an author himself, but he evidently felt a warm interest in literature, and " the men of Hezekiah," not mentioned elsewhere, must have been his counsellors and scholars, to whom was entrusted the duty of gathering together into a volume the scattered sayings of the wise king. Among these contemporaries, doubtless, Isaiah was eminent, and it is not improbable that Shebna the scribe and Joah the chronicler were members of the learned fraternity (2 Kings xviii. 18). The verb rightly translated " copied out " (*athak*) means, properly, " to remove," " to transfer " from one place to another (*transtulerunt*, Vulgate); hence it signifies here to copy into a book words taken from other writings or people's mouths. The sayings thus collected, whether truly Solomon's or not, were extant under his name, and were regarded as worthy of

his reputation for wisdom. The title is given in the Septuagint, thus: Αὗται αἱ παιδεῖαι Σαλωμῶντος αἱ ἀδιάκριτοι, ἃς ἐξεγράψαντο οἱ φίλοι Ἐζεκίου τοῦ βασιλέως τῆς Ἰουδαίας. What is meant by ἀδιάκριτοι is uncertain. It has been translated " impossible to distinguish," equivalent to " miscellaneous; " " beyond doubt," equivalent to " genuine," " hard to interpret," as in Polyb., xv. 12. 9. St. James (iii. 17) applies the term to wisdom, but the interpreters there are not agreed as to the meaning, it being rendered " without partiality," " without variance," " without doubtfulness," etc. It seems best to take the word as used by the LXX. to signify " mixed," or " miscellaneous."

Vers. 2—7.—Proverbs concerning kings.

Ver. 2.—It is the glory of God to conceal a thing. That which is the chief glory of God is his mysteriousness, the unfathomable character of his nature and attributes and doings. The more we search into these matters, the more complete we find our ignorance to be; finite faculties are utterly unable to comprehend the infinite; they can embrace merely what God chooses to reveal. "Secret things belong unto the Lord our God" (Deut. xxix. 29), and the great prophet, favoured with Divine revelations, can only confess, " Verily, thou art a God that hidest thyself" (Isa. xlv. 15; comp. Eccles. viii. 17; Rom. xi. 33, etc.). But the honour of kings is to search out a matter. The same word is used for " glory " and " honour " in both clauses, and ought to have been rendered similarly. It is the king's glory to execute justice and to defend the rights and safety of his people. To do this effectually he must investigate matters brought before him, look keenly into political difficulties, get to the bottom of all complications, and watch against possible dangers. The contrast between the glory of God and that of the king lies in this—that whereas both God and the king desire man's welfare, the former promotes this by making him feel his ignorance and littleness and entire dependence upon this mysterious Being whose nature and designs mortals cannot understand; the latter advances the good of his subjects by giving them confidence in his zeal and power to discover truth, and using his knowledge for their benefit. Septuagint, "The glory of God concealeth a word (λόγον): but the glory of a king honoureth matters (πράγματα)."

Ver. 3.—This proverb is connected with the preceding by the idea of "searching" (chakar) common to both. Such emblematic proverbs are common in this second collection (see ver. 11). Three subjects are stated, of which is predicated the term unsearchable, viz. The heaven for height, and the earth for depth, and the heart of kings. As you can never rise to the illimitable height of the heavens, as you can never penetrate to the immeasurable depth of the earth, so you can never fathom the heart of a king, can never find out what he really thinks and intends (comp. Job xi. 8). It may be that tacitly a warning is intended against flattering one's self that one knows and can reckon on the favour of a king; his good disposition towards you may be only seeming, or may any moment become changed. The Septuagint has for "unsearchable" (אֵין חֵקֶר) ἀνεξέλεγκτος, "unquestionable." The commentators refer to a passage in Tacitus ('Ann.,' vi. 8), where M. Terentius defends himself for being a friend of Sejanus by the fact of the impossibility of investigating a great man's real sentiments. "To us," he says to Tiberius, "it appertains not to judge whom you exalt above all others and for what reason you do so. Facts which are obvious we all notice. We see who is the man upon whom you heap wealth and honours, who it is that has the chief power of dispensing rewards and punishments; that these were possessed by Sejanus no one can deny. But to pry into the hidden thoughts of a prince, and the designs which he meditates in secret, is unlawful and hazardous; nor would the attempt succeed."

Vers. 4, 5.—A tetrastich in an emblematical form.

Ver. 4.—Take away the dross from the silver. Silver was most extensively used by the Hebrews (see 'Dictionary of the Bible,' sub voc.), whether obtained from native mines or imported from foreign countries ; and the process of separating the ore from the extraneous matters mixed with it was well known (Ps. xii. 6 ; Ezek. xxii. 20, etc.; see on ch. xvii. 3). And there shall come forth a vessel for the finer (tsaraph); the goldsmith. The pure silver is ready for the artist's work, who from this material can make a beautiful vessel. Septuagint, "Beat untested silver, and all shall be made entirely pure," where the allusion is to the process of reducing minerals by lamination.

Ver. 5.—Take away the wicked from before the king. Let the wicked be removed from the presence of the king, as dross is separated from the pure silver (see the same metaphor, Isa. i. 25 ; Jer. vi. 29, etc.). And his throne shall be established in righteousness (ch. xvi. 12 ; xxix. 14). The king detects the evil and punishes them ; and this confirms his rule and secures the continuance of his dynasty. Thus righteousness triumphs, and wickedness is properly dealt with. Septuagint, "Slay the ungodly from the face of the king, and his throne shall prosper in righteousness."

Vers. 6, 7.—Another proverb (a pentastich) connected with kings and great men.

Ver. 6.—Put not forth thyself in the presence of the king. Do not make display of yourself as though vying with the king in outward circumstances. Septuagint, "Boast not thyself (μὴ ἀλαζονεύου) in the presence of a king." Stand not in the place of great men. Do not pretend to be the equal of those who occupy high places in the kingdom (ch. xviii. 16). Septuagint, "And take not your stand (ὑφίστασο) in the places of chieftains." Says a Latin gnome, "Qui cum fortuna convenit, dives est;" and Ovid wrote well ('Trist.,' iii. 4. 25, etc.)—

"Crede mihi ; bene qui latuit, bene vixit ;
et intra
Fortunam debet quisque manere suam…
Tu quoque formida nimium sublimia semper ;
Propositique memor contrahe vela tui."

Ver. 7.—For better it is that it be said unto thee, Come up hither. It is better for the prince to select you for elevation to a high post; to call you up near his throne. The reference is not necessarily to position at a royal banquet, though the maxim lends itself readily to such application. This warning against arrogance and presumption was used by our blessed Lord in enforcing a lesson of humility and self-discipline (Luke xiv. 7, etc.). Septuagint, "For it is better for thee that it should be said, Come up unto me (ἀνάβαινε πρὸς μέ)" (προσανάβηθι ἀνώτερον, Luke xiv. 7). Than that thou shouldest be put lower in the presence of the prince whom thine eyes have seen. The last words have been variously interpreted :

"to whom thou hast come with a request for preferment;" "into whose august presence thou hast been admitted, so as to see his face" (2 Sam. xiv. 24); "who knows all about thee, and will thus make thee feel thy humiliation all the more." But *nadib*, rendered "prince," is not the king, but any noble or great man; and what the maxim means is this—that it is wise to save yourself from the mortification of being turned out of a place which you have knowingly usurped. Your own eyes see that he is in the company; you are aware of what is his proper position; you have occupied a post which belongs to another; justly you are removed, and all present witness your humiliation. The moralist knew that the bad spirit of pride was fostered and encouraged by every act of self-assertion; hence the importance of his warning. The Septuagint makes a separate sentence of these last words, "Speak thou of what thine eyes saw," or, perhaps, like St. Jerome, the Syriac, and Symmachus, attach them to the next verse.

Ver. 8.—A tristich with no parallelism. **Go not forth hastily to strive.** The idea is either of one entering into litigation with undue haste, or of one hurrying to meet an adversary. St. Jerome, taking in the final words of the previous verse, renders, *Quæ viderunt oculi tui, ne proferas in jurgio cito*, "What thine eyes have seen reveal not hastily in a quarrel." This is like ver. 9 below, and Christ's injunction, "If thy brother shall trespass against thee, go and tell him his fault between thee and him alone" (Matt. xviii. 15). **Lest thou know not what to do in the end thereof.** The Hebrew is elliptical, "Lest by chance (פֶּן) thou do something (bad, humiliating) in the end thereof." But Delitzsch, Nowack, and others consider the sentence as interrogative (as 1 Sam. xx. 10), and translate, "That it may not be said in the end thereof, What wilt thou do?" Either way, the warning comes to this—Do not enter hastily upon strife of any kind, lest thou be utterly at a loss what to do. **When thy neighbour hath put thee to shame,** by putting thee in the wrong, gaining his cause, or getting the victory over thee in some way. Septuagint, "Fall not quickly into a contest, lest thou repent at the last." There is an English proverb, "Anger begins with folly and ends with repentance;" and "Haste is the beginning of wrath, its end is repentance."

Vers. 9, 10.—A tetrastich without parallelism, connected with the preceding maxim.

Ver. 9.—**Debate thy cause with thy neighbour** himself (Matt. xviii. 15; see on ver. 8). If you have any quarrel with a neighbour, or are drawn into a controversy with him,

deal with him privately in a friendly manner. **And discover not a secret to another;** rather, *the secret of another*. Do not bring in a third party, or make use of anything entrusted to you by another person, or of which you have become privately informed, in order to support your cause.

Ver. 10.—**Lest he that heareth it put thee to shame;** *i.e.* lest any one, not the offended neighbour only, who hears how treacherous you have been, makes your proceeding known and cries shame upon you. **And thine infamy turn not away.** The stigma attached to you be never obliterated. Thus Siracides: "Whoso discovereth secrets loseth his credit; and shall never find friend to his mind. Love thy friend, and be faithful unto him: but if thou bewrayest his secrets, follow no more after him. For as a man hath destroyed his enemy; so hast thou lost the love of thy neighbour" (Ecclus. xxvii. 16, etc.; comp. also xxii. 22). The motive presented in our text is not the highest, being grounded on the fear of shame and disgrace in men's eyes; but it is a very potent incentive to right action, and the moralist has good reason for employing it. That it does not reach to the height of Christian morality is obvious. The gnome is thus given in the Greek: "When thy friend shall reproach thee, retreat backward, despise him not, lest thy friend reproach thee still; and so thy quarrel and enmity shall not pass away, but shall be to thee like death." Then the LXX. adds a paragraph, reproduced partly by St. Jerome, "Kindness and friendship set a man free (ἐλευθεροῖ); preserve thou these, that thou become not liable to reproach (ἐπονεί-διστος, *exprobabilis*); but guard thy ways in a conciliating spirit (εὐσυναλλάκτως)."

Ver. 11.—One of the emblematical distiches in which this collection is rich. **A word fitly spoken.** עַל־אָפְנָיו may be translated "in due season," or "upon its wheels" (Venetian, ἐπὶ τῶν τροχῶν αὐτῆς). In the latter case the phrase may mean a word quickly formed, or moving easily, spoken *ore rotundo*, or a speedy answer. But the metaphor is unusual and inappropriate; and it is best to understand a word spoken under due consideration of time and place. Vulgate, *Qui loquitur verbum in tempore suo;* Aquila and Theodotion, ἐπὶ ἁρμόζουσιν αὐτῷ, "in circumstances that suit it;" the Septuagint has simply οὕτως. Is like **apples of gold in pictures of silver.** In these emblematical distichs the words, "is like," in the Authorized Version, are an insertion. The Hebrew places the two ideas merely in sequence; the object with which something is compared usually coming before that which is compared with it, as here, "Apples of gold—a word fitly spoken" (so in vers. 14, 18, 19, 26, 28). There is a doubt about the meaning of the word rendered "pictures," *maskith* (see on ch. xviii. 11). It seems to be used generally in the sense of "image," "sculpture," being derived from the verb שָׂכָה, "to see; " from this it comes to signify "ornament," and here most appropriately is "basket," and, as some understand, of filagree work. St. Jerome mistakes the word, rendering, *in lectis argenteis*. The Septuagint has, ἐν ὁρμίσκῳ σαρδίου, "on a necklace of sardius." "Apples of gold" are apples or other fruits of a golden colour, not made of gold, which would be very costly and heavy; nor would the comparison with artificial fruits be as suitable as that with natural. The "word" is the fruit set off by its circumstances, as the latter's beauty is enhanced by the grace of the vessel which contains it. The "apple" has been supposed to be the orange (called in late Latin *pomum aurantium*) or the citron. We may cite here the opinion of a competent traveller: "For my own part," says Canon Tristram ('Land of Israel,' p. 605), "I have no hesitation in expressing my conviction that the *apricot* alone is the 'apple' of Scripture. . . . Everywhere the apricot is common; perhaps it is, with the single exception of the fig, the most abundant fruit of the country. In highlands and lowlands alike, by the shores of the Mediterranean and on the banks of the Jordan, in the nooks of Judæa, under the heights of Lebanon, in the recesses of Galilee, and in the glades of Gilead, the apricot flourishes, and yields a crop of prodigious abundance. Its characteristics meet every condition of the 'tappuach' of Scripture. 'I sat down under his shadow with great delight, and his fruit was sweet to my taste' (Cant. ii. 3). Near Damascus, and on the banks of the Barada, we have pitched our tents under its shade, and spread our carpets secure from the rays of the sun. 'The smell of thy nose (shall be) like tappuach' (Cant. vii. 8). There can scarcely be a more deliciously perfumed fruit than the apricot; and what fruit can better fit the epithet of Solomon, 'apples of *gold* in pictures of silver,' than this golden fruit, as its branches bend under the weight in their setting of bright yet pale foliage?" Imagery similar to that found in this verse occurs in ch. x. 31; xii. 14; xiii. 2; xviii. 20. There is a famous article on the analogies between flowers and men's characters in the *Spectator*, No. 455.

Ver. 12.—Another distich concerning the seasonable word, of the same character as the last. **As an earring of gold, and an ornament of fine gold.** In this, as in many of the proverbs, the comparison is not expressed, but is merely implied by juxtaposi-

tion. *Nezem*, in ch. xi. 22, was a nose-ring, here probably an earring is meant; *chali*, "ornament," is a trinket or jewel worn suspended on neck or breast. The two, whether worn by one person or more, form a lovely combination, and set off the wearer's grace and beauty. Vulgate, *Inauris aurea et margaritum fulgens*, "A golden earring and a brilliant pearl." Septuagint, "A golden earring a precious sardius also is set." So is a wise reprover upon an obedient ear. The obedient ear receives the precepts of the wise reprover, and wears them as a valued ornament. In ch. i. 9 the instruction of parents is compared to a chaplet on the head and a fair chain on the neck. Septuagint, "A wise word on an obedient ear."

Ver. 13.—A comparative tristich concerning words. **As the cold of snow in the time of harvest.** This, of course, does not mean a snowstorm or hailstorm in the time of harvest, which would be anything but a blessing (ch. xxvi. 1; 1 Sam. xii. 17, 18), but either the distant view of the snow on Hermon or Lebanon, which gave an idea of refreshment in the heat of autumn, or more probably snow used to cool drink in warm weather. This luxury was not unknown in the time of Solomon, who had a summer palace on Lebanon (1 Kings ix. 19), though it could have been enjoyed by very few, and would not speak to the personal experience of the burgher class, to whom the proverbs seem to have been addressed. Xenophon writes of the use of snow to cool wine ('Memorab.,' ii. 1. 30). Hitzig quotes a passage from the old history of the Crusades, called 'Gesta Dei per Francos,' which runs thus: "Nix frigidissima a monte Libano defertur, ut vino commixta, tanquam glaciem ipsum frigidum reddat." So in the present day snow is sold in Damascus bazaars. The LXX., not realizing what harm such an untimely storm might effect, translates, "As a fall (ἔξοδος) of snow in harvest is of use against heat, so a faithful messenger benefits those who sent him." So is a faithful messenger to them that send him. (For "faithful messenger," see on ch. xiii. 17; and for "them that send," see on ch. xxii. 21.) The comparison is explained. For he refresheth the soul of his masters. He brings as great refreshment to his masters' mind as would a drink of snow-cooled water *in* the burning harvest-field.

Ver. 14.—The Hebrew is, Clouds and wind without rain—he that boasteth himself in a gift of falsehood (see on ver. 11). The proverb is concerned with promises disappointed. Clouds and wind are generally in the East the precursors of heavy rain, as we read in 1 Kings xviii. 45, "In a little while the heaven was black with clouds and wind, and there was a great rain." After such phenomena, which, according to current meteorological observation, gave every hope of a refreshing shower in the time of summer drought, to see the clouds pass away without affording a single drop of rain is a grievous disappointment. The metaphor is found in the New Testament. St. Jude (ver. 12) calls false teachers " clouds without water, carried along by winds." "A gift of falsehood," equivalent to "a false gift," one that deceives, because it is only promised and never given. A man makes a great parade of going to bestow a handsome present, and then sneaks out of it, and gives nothing. Such a one is, as St. Jerome renders, *Vir gloriosus, et promissa non complens.* The old commentators quote Ovid, 'Heroid.,' vi. 109—

"Mobilis Æsonide, vernaque incertior aura,
 Cur tua pollicito pondere verba carent?"

"Deeds are fruits," says the proverb, "words are but leaves;" and "Vain-glory blossoms, but never bears fruit." Concerning the folly of making stupid boasts, the Bengalee proverb speaks of a pedlar in ginger getting tidings of his ship. The Septuagint is incorrect, "As winds, and clouds, and rains are most evident (ἐπιφανέστατα), so is he who boasts of a false gift."

Ver. 15.—By long forbearing; *i e.* by patience, calmness that does not break out into passion whatever be the provocation, even, it is implied, in the face of a false and malicious accusation (comp. ch. xiv. 29). Is a prince persuaded. *Katson* is rather "an arbiter," or judge, than "a prince," and the proverb says that such an officer is led to take a favourable view of an accused person's case when he sees him calm and composed, ready to explain the matter without any undue heat or irritation, keeping steadily to the point, and not seduced by calumny or misrepresentation to forget himself and lose his temper. Such a bearing presupposes innocence and weighs favourably with the judge. The LXX. makes the gnome apply to monarchs alone, "In longsuffering is prosperity unto kings." A soft tongue breaketh the bone. A soft answer (ch. xv. 1), gentle, conciliating words, overcome opposition, and disarm the most determined enemy, and make tender in him that which was hardest and most uncompromising. "Gutta cavat lapidem, non vi, sed sæpe cadendo." Similar proverbs are found elsewhere, though probably in a different sense. Thus in modern Greek, "The tongue has no bones, yet it breaks bones;" in Turkish, "The tongue has no bone, yet it crushes;" again, "One drop of honey," says the Turk, "catches more bees than a ton of vinegar."

Ver. 16.—Hast thou found honey? Honey would be found in crevices of rocks, in hollow trees (1 Sam. xiv. 27), or in more unlikely situations (Judg. xiv. 8), and was extensively used as an article of food. All travellers in Palestine note the great abundance of bees therein, and how well it answers to its description as "a land flowing with milk and honey." Eat so much as is sufficient for thee. The agreeable sweetness of honey might lead the finder to eat too much of it. Against such excess the moralist warns: Lest thou be filled therewith, and vomit it. Thus wrote Pindar, 'Nem.,' vii. 51—

Ἀλλὰ γὰρ ἀνάπαυσις ἐν παντὶ γλυκεῖα ἔργῳ.
κόρον δ᾽ἔχει
Καὶ μέλι καὶ τὰ τέρπν᾽ ἄνθε᾽ Ἀφροδίσια.

Μηδὲν ἄγαν, *Ne quid nimis,* is a maxim continually urged by those who wished to teach moderation. Says Homer, 'Iliad,' xiii. 636—

"Men are with all things sated—sleep, and love,
 Sweet sounds of music, and the joyous dance."

(Lord Derby.)

Says Horace, 'Sat.,' i. 1. 106—

"Est modus in rebus, sunt certi denique fines,
 Quos ultra citraque nequit consistere rectum."

The honey is a figure of all that pleases the senses; but the maxim is to be extended beyond physical matters, though referring primarily to such pleasures. The mind may be overloaded as well as the body; only such instruction as can be digested and assimilated is serviceable to the spiritual nature; injudicious cramming produces satiety and disgust. Again, "To 'find honey,'" says St. Gregory ('Moral.,' xvi. 8), "is to taste the sweetness of holy intelligence, which is eaten enough of then when our perception, according to the measure of our faculty, is held tight under control. For he is 'filled with honey, and vomits it' who, in seeking to dive deeper than he has capacity for, loses that too from whence he might have derived nourishment." And in another place (ibid., xx. 18), "The sweetness of spiritual meaning he who seeks to eat beyond what he contains, even what he had eaten he 'vomiteth;' because, whilst he seeks to make out things above, beyond his powers, even the things that he had made out aright, he forfeits" (Oxford transl.).

Ver. 17.—Withdraw thy foot from thy neighbour's house; literally, *make thy foot precious, rare;* Septuagint, "Bring thy foot sparingly (σπάνιον) into thy friend's house." The proverb seems to be loosely connected with the preceding, as urging moderation. Do not pay too frequent visits to your neighbours' house, or make yourself too much at home there. The Son of Sirach Las an utterance on a somewhat similar subject, "Give place, thou stranger, to an honourable man; my brother cometh to be lodged, and I have need of mine house. These things are grievous to a man of understanding; the upbraiding of houseroom, and reproaching of the lender" (Ecclus. xxix. 27, etc.). Lest he be weary of thee, and so hate thee. Such a result might easily arise from too constant intercourse. Cornelius à Lapide quotes from Seneca ('De Benefic.,' i. 15), "Rarum esse oportet quod diu carum velis," "That should be rare which you would enduringly bear." And Martial's cynical advice—

"Nulli te facias nimis sodalem ;
Gaudebis minus, et minus dolebis."

The same poet ('Epigr.,' iv. 29. 3) writes—

"Rara juvant; primis sic major gratia pomis,
Hibernæ pretium sic meruere rosæ."

Ver. 18.—Hebrew, A maul, and a sword, and a sharp arrow—a man that beareth false witness against his neighbour (see on ver. 11). One who bears false witness against his neighbour prepares for him the instruments of death, such as those mentioned here. "A maul" (mephits), usually a heavy wooden hammer (compare malleus and "mallet"); here a club, or mace, used in battle, ῥόπαλον (Septuagint; comp. Jer. li. 20). There is a kind of climax in the three offensive weapons named—the club bruises, the sword inflicts wounds, the arrow pierces to the heart; and the three may represent the various baneful effects of false testimony, how it bruises reputation, spoils possessions, deprives of life. The second clause is from the Decalogue (Exod. xx. 16).

Ver. 19.—Hebrew (see on ver. 11), A broken tooth, and a foot out of joint—confidence in an unfaithful man in time of trouble. A faithless man is as little to be relied on in a time of need as a loose or broken tooth, and a foot unsteady or actually dislocated. You cannot bite on the one, you cannot walk on the other; so the perfidous man fails you when most wanted. Septuagint, "The way [ὁδὸς, Vatican, is probably a clerical error for ὁδοὺς, al.] of the wicked, and the foot of the transgressor, shall perish in an evil day." A Bengal maxim runs, "A loose tooth and a feeble friend are equally bad" (Lane).

Ver. 20.—As he that taketh away a garment in cold weather. The proverb gives three instances of what is wrong, incongruous, or unwise, the first two leading up to the third, which is the pith of the maxim. But there is some doubt about the rendering of the first clause. The Authorized Version has the authority of the Syriac, Aquila, and others, and gives an appropriate sense, the unreasonable proceeding being the laying aside of some of one's own clothes in cold weather. But the verb here used, עָדָה (adah), may also mean "to adorn," e.g. with fine garments; hence some expositors understand the incongruity to be the dressing one's self in gay apparel in winter. But, as Delitzsch remarks, there is no reason why fine clothes should not be warm; and if they are so, there is nothing unreasonable in wearing them. The rendering of our version is probably correct. St. Jerome annexes this line to the preceding verse, as if it confirmed the previous instances of misplaced confidence, Et amittit pallium in die frigoris. "Such a one loses his cloak in a day of frost." Vinegar upon nitre. Our nitre, or saltpetre, is nitrate of potash, which is not the substance intended by נֶתֶר (nether). The substance signified by this term is a natural alkali, known to the ancients as natron, and composed of carbonate of soda with some other admixture. It was used extensively for washing purposes, and in cookery and bread-making. It effervesces with an acid, such as vinegar, and changes its character, becoming a salt, and being rendered useless for all the purposes to which it was applied in its alkaline condition. So he who pours vinegar on natron does a foolish thing, for he spoils a highly useful article, and produces one which is of no service to him. Septuagint, "As vinegar is inexpedient for a wound (ἕλκει), so suffering falling on the body pains the heart." Schultens, Ewald, and others, by referring nether to an Arabic source, obtain the meaning "wound," or "sore," thus: "As vinegar on a sore." This gives a most appropriate sense, and might well be adopted if it had sufficient authority. But this is doubtful. Cornelius à Lapide translates the Septuagint rendering, Ὥσπερ ὄξος ἕλκει ἀσύμφορον, "Sicut acetum trahit inutile;" and explains that vinegar draws from the soil the nitre which is prejudicial to vegetation, and thus renders ground fertile—a fact in agricultural chemistry not generally known, though Columella vouches for it. A somewhat similar fact, however, is of common experience. Land occasionally becomes what farmers term "sour," and is thus sterile; if it is then dressed with salt, its fertility is restored. So is he that singeth songs to an heavy heart. The inconsistency lies in thinking to cheer a sorrowful heart by singing merry songs. "A tale out of season," says Siracides, "is as music in mourning" (Ecclus. xxii. 6). The Greeks denoted cruel incongruity by the proverb, Ἐν πενθοῦσι παίζειν; "Ludere inter mærentes." As the old hymn says—

" Strains of gladness
Suit not souls with anguish torn."

The true Christian sympathy teaches to
" rejoice with them that rejoice, to weep
with them that weep" (Rom. xii. 15).
Plumptre, in the 'Speaker's Commentary,'
suggests that the effervescence caused by
the mixture of acid and alkali is taken as a
type of the irritation produced by the inopportune songs.　But this is importing a
modern view into a paragraph, such as
would never have occurred to the writer.
The Septuagint, followed partially by
Jerome, the Syriac, and the Targum, introduces another proverb not found in the
Hebrew, " As a moth in a garment, and a
worm in wood, so the sorrow of a man hurts
his heart."

Vers. 21, 22.—This famous tetrastrich is
reproduced (with the exception of the fourth
line) from the Septuagint by St. Paul (Rom.
xii. 20).

Ver. 21.—The traditional hatred of
enemies is here strongly repudiated (see ch.
xxiv. 17, 18, and notes there).　Thus Elisha
treated the Syrians, introduced blindly into
the midst of Samaria, ordering the King of
Israel to set bread and water before them,
and to send them away unharmed (2 Kings
vi. 22).　" Punish your enemy by benefiting
him," say the Arabs, though they are far
from practising the injunction;　" Sweet
words break the bones;"　" Bread and salt
humble even a robber," say the Russians.

Ver. 22.—For thou shalt heap coals of fire
upon his head.　This expression has been
taken in various senses.　It has been thought
to mean that the forgiveness of the injured
person brings to the cheek of the offender the
burning blush of shame.　But heaping coals
on the head cannot naturally be taken to
express such an idea.　St. Chrysostom and
other Fathers consider that Divine vengeance is implied, as in Ps. xi. 6, " Upon the
wicked he shall rain snares; fire and brim-
stone and burning wind shall be their portion; " and Ps. cxl. 10, " Let burning coals
fall upon them."　Of course, in one view,
kindness to an evil man only gives him
occasion for fresh ingratitude and hatred,
and therefore increases God's wrath against
him.　But it would be a wicked motive to
act this beneficent part only to have the
satisfaction of seeing your injurer humbled
or punished.　And the gnome implies that
the sinner is benefited by the clemency
shown to him, that the requital of evil by
good brings the offender to a better mind,
and aids his spiritual life.　" Coals of fire "
are a metaphor for the penetrating pain of
remorse and repentance.　The unmerited
kindness which he receives forces upon him

the consciousness of his ill doing, which is
accompanied by the sharp pain of regret.
St. Augustine, " Ne dubitaveris figurate
dictum . . . ut intelligas carbones ignis
esse urentes pœnitentiæ gemitus, quibus
superbia sanatur ejus, qui dolet se inimicum
fuisse hominis, a quo ejus miseriæ subveni-
tur" (' De Doctr. Christ.,' iii. 16).　Lesètre
quotes St. Francis de Sales, who gives again
a different view, " You are not obliged to
seek reconciliation with one who has
offended you; it may be rather his part to
seek you; yet nevertheless go and follow
the Saviour's counsel, prevent him with
good, render him good for evil; heap coals
of fire on his head and on his heart, which
may burn up all ill will and constrain him
to love you" (' De l'Am. de Dieu,' viii. 9).
And the Lord shall reward thee.　This consideration can scarcely be regarded as the
chief motive for the liberality enjoined,
though it would be present to the kind person's mind, and be a support and comfort to
him in a course of conduct repugnant to the
natural man.　He would remember the
glorious reward promised to godliness by
the prophet (Isa. lviii. 8, etc.), and how Saul
had expressed his consciousness of David's
magnanimity in sparing his life.　" Thou art
more righteous than I; for thou hast rewarded me good, whereas I have rewarded
thee evil . . . wherefore the Lord reward
thee good for that thou hast done unto me
this day" (1 Sam. xxiv. 17, 19 and xxvi. 21).

Ver. 23.—The north wind driveth away rain.
So St. Jerome (Ventus Aquilo dissipat plu-
vias), Symmachus, Aben Ezra, and others.
The north wind is called by the natives of
Palestine " the heavenly," from the bright
effect which it produces in the sky.　" By
means of the north wind cometh he (the sun)
forth as gold " (Job xxxvii. 22).　But the
verb here used (חול) means " to bring forth,
produce " (Ps. xc. 2); hence the Revised
Version rightly renders, " The north wind
bringeth forth rain."　This is quite true if
" north wind " be taken as equivalent to
" wind from the dark quarter " (Umbreit),
like ζόφος in Greek; and, in fact, the north-
west wind in Palestine does bring rain. Septuagint, " The north wind arouseth (ἐξεγεί-
ρει) clouds."　So doth an angry countenance a
backbiting tongue.　Carrying on the interpretation intended by the Authorized Version, this clause means that an angry look
will check a slanderer and incline him to
hold his peace from prudential motives.
But with the rendering given above,
" bringeth forth," another explanation is
involved, viz. " So does a secret, slandering
tongue cause a troubled countenance."
When a man discovers that a secret slanderer
is working against him, he shows it by his
gloomy and angry look, as the sky is dark

with clouds when a storm is threatened. "Countenance" is plural in the Hebrew, denoting, as Hitzig points out, that the calumniator does not affect one person only, but occasions trouble far and wide, destroys friendly relations between many, excites suspicion and enmity in various quarters. Septuagint, "An impudent countenance provokes the tongue."

Ver. 24.—A repetition of ch. xxi. 9, taken therefore from the Solomonic collection.

Ver. 25.—As cold waters to a thirsty soul. The particle of comparison is not in this first clause in the Hebrew. (For "cold waters," comp. Jer. xviii. 14.) So is good news from a far country. The *nostalgia* of an exile, and the craving for tidings of him felt by his friends at home, are like a parching thirst. The relief to the latter, when they receive good news of the wanderer, is as refreshing as a draught of cool water to a fainting, weary man. We do not know that the Hebrews were great travellers in those days; but any communication from a distant country would be very uncertain in arriving at its destination, and would at any rate take a long time in transmission. In most cases there would be nothing to rest upon but vague report, or a message carried by some travelling merchant. There is a somewhat similar proverb found at ver. 13 and ch. xv. 30. The ancient commentators have seen in this news from a distant country the announcement of Christ's birth by the angels at Bethlehem, or the preaching of the gospel that tells of the joys of heaven, the land that is very far off (Isa. xxxiii. 17).

Ver. 26.—Hebrew (see on ver. 11), A troubled fountain, and a corrupted spring—a righteous man giving way to the wicked. A good man neglecting to assert himself and to hold his own in the face of sinners, is as useless to society and as harmful to the good cause as a spring that has been defiled by mud stirred up or extraneous matter introduced is unserviceable for drinking and prejudicial to those who use it. The mouth of the righteous should be "a well of life" (ch. x. 11), wholesome, refreshing, helpful; his conduct should be consistent and straightforward, fearless in upholding the right (Isa. li. 12, etc.), uncompromising in opposing sin. When such a man, for fear, or favour, or weakness, or weariness, yields to the wicked, compromises principle, no longer makes a stand for truth and purity and virtue, he loses his high character, brings a scandal on religion, and lowers his own spiritual nature. It is this moral cowardice which Christ so sternly rebukes (Matt. x. 33), "Whosoever shall deny me before men, him will I also deny before my Father which is in heaven." Some have assumed that the gnome is concerned with a

good man's fall into misfortune owing to the machinations of sinners; but in this case the comparison loses its force; such persecution would not disturb the purity or lower the character of the righteous man; it would rather enhance his good qualities, give occasion for their exercise and development, and therefore could not be described as fouling a pure spring.

Ver. 27.—It is not good to eat much honey. The ill effects of a surfeit of honey have been already mentioned (ver. 16); but here the application is different, and occasions some difficulty. The Authorized Version, in order to clear up the obscurity of the text, inserts a negative, so for men to search their own glory is not glory, which seems to be a warning against conceit and self-adulation. This is hardly warranted by the present Hebrew text, which is literally, as Venetian renders, Ἐρευνά τε δόξας αὐτῶν δόξα, "The search of their glory [is] glory." But who are meant by "their"? No persons are mentioned in the verse to whom the suffix in כְּבוֹדָם can be referred, and it is not improbable that some words have dropped out of the text. At the same time, we might naturally in thought supply "for men" after "it is not good," such omissions being not uncommon in proverbial sayings; the suffix then would refer to them. Commentators have endeavoured to amend the text by alterations which do not commend themselves. Schultens supposes that the suffix had reference to the Divine law and revelations, and, as כבד may mean both "glory" and "weight," translates, "Vestigatio gravitatis eorum, gravitas." Bertheau takes *kabod* in two different senses, "The searching out of their glory is a burden." So Delitzsch, by a little manipulation of the pointing (כְּבֹדָם) obtains the rendering, "But to search out hard things is an honour." Taken thus, the maxim says that bodily pleasures sicken and cloy, but diligent study brings honour. This, however, is not satisfactory; it gives a word two different senses in the same clause, and it affords a very feeble contrast. One would naturally expect the proverb to say that the excess, which was deprecated in the first hemistich as regards one department, must be equally rejected in another sphere. This is somewhat the idea given by Jerome, *Sic qui scrutator est majestatis opprimetur a gloria.* The truth here stated will be explained by translating our text, "The investigation of weighty matters is a weight." Thus the clauses are shown to be well poised. Honey is good, study is good; but both may be used so as to be prejudicial. Eating may be carried to excess; study may attempt to investigate things too hard or too high. That this is a real danger we know well from the controversies about predestination and election in time past, and those concerning spiritualism and theurgy in our own day (see Jeremy Taylor, 'Certainty of Salvation,' iii. 176, edit. Heb. ; and 'Holy Living,' ch. iii. § 5). This is the view taken of the passage by St. Gregory ('Moral.,' xiv. 32), 'If the sweetness of honey be taken in greater measure than there is occasion for, from the same source whence the palate is gratified, the life of the eater is destroyed. The "searching into majesty" is also sweet; but he that seeks to dive into it deeper than the cognizance of human nature admits, finds the mere gloriousness thereof by itself oppresses him, in that, like honey taken in excess, it bursts the sense of the searcher which is not capable of holding it." And again (ibid., xx. 18), "For the glory of the invisible Creator, which when searched into with moderation lifts us up, being dived into beyond our powers bears us down" (Oxford transl.). (Comp. Deut. xxix. 29; Ecclus. iii. 21, etc.) Septuagint, "To eat much honey is not good, but it behoves us to honour glorious sayings."

Ver. 28.—A proverb like the last, concerned with self-control. In the Hebrew it runs thus (see on ver. 11): **A city that is broken down without wall—a man on whose spirit is no restraint.** "A city broken down" is explained by the next words, "without wall," and therefore undefended and open to the first invader

(comp. 2 Chron. xxxii. 5; Neh. ii. 13). To such a city is compared the man who puts no restraint on his passions, desires, and affections; he is always in danger of being carried away by them and involved in sin and destruction; he has no defence when temptation assaults him, having lost self-control (comp. ch. xvi. 32). The old gnomes hold always true—

Θυμοῦ κρατῆσαι κἀπιθυμίας καλόν.

"Desire and passion it is good to rule."

Ταμιεῖον ἀρετῆς ἐστι σωφροσύνη μόνη.

"Virtue's true storehouse is wise self-control."

A Chinese maxim says, "Who can govern himself is fit to govern the world." Septuagint, "As a city whose walls are broken down and which is unwalled, so is a man who does aught without counsel." St. Jerome, by the addition of the words, *in loquendo*, applies the proverb to intemperance in language, "So is he who is not able to restrain his spirit in speaking." Commenting on this, St. Gregory ('Moral,' vii. 59) says, "Because it is without the wall of silence, the city of the mind lies open to the darts of the enemy, and when it casts itself forth in words, it exhibits itself exposed to the adversary, and he gets the mastery of it without trouble, in proportion as the soul that he has to overcome combats against its own self by much talking" (Oxford transl.).

HOMILETICS.

Ver. 1.—*Ancient lore.* This superscription gives us a hint of a very interesting historical event of which we have no account elsewhere. It suggests a picture of the days of Hezekiah; we see his scribes busily engaged in ransacking the ancient libraries, and bringing together the long-forgotten sayings of his famous predecessor.

I. A REVIVAL OF RELIGION SHOULD LEAD TO A REVIVAL OF LEARNING. The Renaissance preceded the Reformation, and, because it had no deep spiritual basis, it threatened to degenerate into dilletantism and pedantry. But after the second movement had taken hold of Europe, real, solid learning received a powerful impulse, because men were then in earnest in the search for truth. It would seem that a similar result was produced in the days of Hezekiah. Then there was a religious reformation, and that was followed by a newly awakened interest in the national literature. Of course, this was the more natural among the Jews, because their national genius was religious, and their literature was the vehicle of their religious ideas. The danger of a time of religious excitement is that it shall be accompanied by attenuated knowledge. But the more the religious feelings are roused, the more reason is there that they should be directed by truth. Revival preachers should be studious men if they wish their work not to be perverted into wrong and false courses through ignorance.

II. IT IS WISE TO PROFIT BY THE THOUGHTS OF OTHER MEN. The men of Hezekiah were not above learning from Solomon, who had left a reputation for unparalleled wisdom. But lesser lights have also their claims. It is a mistake to live on one's own thoughts without guidance or nourishment derived from the thoughts of other men. Private thinking tends to narrowness unless it is enlarged by the reception of a variety of ideas from external sources. The mind will ultimately starve if it is left to feed upon its own juices. We must judge for ourselves, and only accept what we honestly believe to be true—seek truth, and think out our own convictions. But we shall do those things the better if we also allow that others may have light to give us. Above all, the Christian thinker needs to found his meditations on the Bible. Of the New Testament it may be said, "A Greater than Solomon is here." If the men of Hezekiah did well to collect the proverbs of Solomon, much more is it desirable to treasure up the sayings of him who spake as never man spake.

III. WE MAY LEARN LESSONS FROM ANTIQUITY. Nearly three hundred years had passed between the days of Solomon and the time of Hezekiah—a period equal to that which separates us from the great Elizabethan writers; so that Solomon was as far anterior to Hezekiah as the poet Spenser is to our own generation. He belonged to the antique age. Yet the glamour of the great Hezekiah did not blind men to the glory of the greater Solomon. In the splendid achievements of the present day we are threatened with an extinction of antiquity. The nineteenth century is the new image of gold that has been set up on our Plain of Dura for all men to worship. We shall suffer an irreparable loss, and our mental and spiritual life will be sadly stunted, if we fail to hearken to the teachings of our forefathers. We are not to be the slaves of the past. The new age may have its new truths, as well as its new needs and duties. But what was true in the past cannot cease to be so by simply going out of fashion; for truth is eternal. The very diversity of the ages may instruct us by widening our notions and correcting the follies of prevalent customs. The age of Solomon was very different from that of Hezekiah; yet the wisdom of the royal sage could profit the newer generation.

Ver. 11.—*Apples of gold in a framework of silver.* This is a picture of Oriental decoration. A gorgeous chamber is richly and elaborately ornamented with the precious metals, by fruit carved in gold being set in dainty work of silver—as brilliant a piece of decoration as can well be imagined. This finely turned metaphor is chosen by the writer in order to give the highest possible praise to " the word fitly spoken."

I. THE NATURE AND CHARACTER OF THE WORD FITLY SPOKEN. 1. *It is a word.* Here we see an immense value set upon a word. Words have weight to crush, force to drive, sharpness to pierce, brightness to illumine, beauty to delight, consolation to cheer. He is a foolish man who despises words. 2. *It may be but one word.* We cannot value words by the length of them, nor weigh them by their bulk. Many words may be worthless, while one word is beyond all price—if only it be the right word. 3. *It must be a real word.* It must not be a mere sound of the lips. A word is an uttered thought. The soul of it is its idea. When that has gone out of it, the empty sound is a dead thing, though it be voluminous and thunderous as the noise of many waters. 4. *It needs to be an apt word;* i.e. (1) true; (2) fit to be uttered by the speaker; (3) suitable for the hearer; (4) adapted to the occasion; (5) shaped with point and individual character—a word that will go home and stick. 5. *It should be a spoken word.* There is a world of difference between living speech and written or printed sentences. The press can never supersede the human voice. We see that the newspaper has not suspended the functions of the political orator; it has only given breadth and additional enthusiasm to his utterances. The publication of the daily paper has not prevented St. James's Hall from being crowded nor Hyde Park from being thronged by thousands of eager listeners when some great question is agitating the public mind. It is the same with the pulpit. The vocation of the preacher can never cease while the sympathy of personal presence is a power. In private life a short word goes further than a long letter. 6. *It ought to be wisely spoken.* Here, too, aptness is needed, to find the right moment and speak in the best manner. Formalism, pomposity, hardness or coldness of manner, may spoil the effect of the most suitable word.

II. THE SUPREME EXCELLENCE OF THE WORD FITLY SPOKEN. 1. *It is rare.* Such decoration as is described in the text could not have been often witnessed even amid the " barbaric splendour" of Solomon's days. It is not often that the best words are spoken. We live in a din of speech; it rains words. But most of the words we hear are neither gold nor silver. 2. *It is costly.* The ornamentation of gold and silver would be very expensive, first in material, then in artistic skill. It cannot always be truly said that " kind words cost little." The best words cost time, care, consideration, self-suppression, sympathy. What costs the speaker nothing is likely to be valued by the hearer at the same price. 3. *It is beautiful.* The metaphor describes what would be regarded as exceedingly lovely in Oriental art. But good words are more beautiful still. Poetry is more lovely than sculpture, for it has more soul and life and thought in it. Words of wisdom and love have the beauty of the graces that inspire them. 4. *It is precious.* Some costly things are of little value, for one may squander wealth for what is worthless. But words of truth and goodness are beyond price. How supremely is this true of the words of Christ! How well also does it apply to the wise proclamation of the gospel!

Vers. 21, 22.—" *Coals of fire.*" I. THE CHRIST-LIKE DUTY. 1. *It is positive.* It is more than turning the other cheek to the smiter, or letting the thief of the cloak carry off the coat also. Passive non-resistance is to be surpassed by active kindness. The command is not merely to refrain from acts of vengeance; it is to bestir one's self in active benevolence for the good of an enemy—to return good for evil. 2. *It is difficult.* Perhaps this is not so exceedingly difficult as silence under provocation; for nothing seems so hard as to be still when one is wronged. Now, a new channel for the energy of vengeance is provided—to do good to the offender. Still this is very difficult. 3. *It is Christ-like.* We have—what Solomon had not—the great example of Christ; not merely led as a lamb to the slaughter, but also freely giving himself in suffering and death for the salvation of those who persecuted him. If we would be Christians, we must walk in the footsteps of our Master. Here, indeed, is a case in which the disciple is called upon to deny himself—to deny the natural impulse of revenge—and to take up his cross and follow Christ. 4. *It is only possible with Divine grace.* We ask for grace to bear our troubles. We should seek further grace to inspire us with more than a forgiving spirit—with active benevolence towards a foe.

II. ITS MIRACULOUS CONSEQUENCES. 1. *Enmity is conquered.* This is the last result that worldly men would expect. They would rather suppose that, if they gave their enemy an inch, he would take an ell. But there are two ways of conquering a foe— by coercing him and by destroying his enmity. When one makes a friend out of an old enemy he does most effectually vanquish and utterly destroy his enmity. 2. *This results from the rousing of generous sentiments.* It goes on the presumption that there are noble sentiments present, if latent, in the breast of an antagonist. The tendency of enmity is to paint our foe with the blackest colours. But he may be no worse than we are. Or, if he be an exceptionally bad man, still he is not a perfect demon. Though a man does wrong, we dare not assume that there is no capacity for better things in him. Now, the heathen method is to address him only on his evil side; but the Christian method—already anticipated in the Old Testament—is to appeal to his higher self. This is God's way in saving sinners. We deserve wrath and vengeance. But instead of our deserts, God has given us grace and a gospel of salvation. He heaps coals of fire on our heads, and conquers enmity with love. The enemy who is thus treated loses the satisfaction of having provoked his victim. He is chagrined at discovering his own impotence. It is useless to spit malice at a man who is strong and grand enough to give back kindness. Such action reflects on the degradation of the conduct of the enemy. If he has a sense of self-respect, it comes to him as burning coals of shame. 3. *This method may be successful in various regions.* (1) In private quarrels. (2) In religious differences. If the sects laboured to help one another, instead of biting and devouring each other, sectarianism would be consumed in the burning coals of Christian love. (3) In national quarrels. We have tried the old heathen method of war long enough, and with no good results. It is time we turned to the Christian method of magnanimity. 4. *This method receives the approval of God.* Besides conquering the foe, it secures God's favour, which the method of revenge loses.

Ver. 25.—" *Good news from a far country.*" I. THE LITERAL APPLICATION OF THE PROVERB. 1. It may be that a rumour has come that a distant ally is marching to succour a nation in its distress, when it had thought itself forgotten, isolated, and help-less. 2. Or perhaps, when there is famine in the land, the news arrives that " there is corn in Egypt." 3. Or, again, the nation, like Tyre in antiquity, like Venice and Holland later, like England in the present day, may do business on the great waters. She has possessions in distant lands, and her wealth is entrusted to the sea. As she learns that her enterprises are prospering, she rejoices at the good news from a far country. 4. Another way of applying the proverb is in relation to our kinsfolk across the sea. It would be well if England took more interest in her colonies. Coldness, inconsiderateness, and officialism may do much to alienate our children in the new worlds. If we would be drawn together in closer ties of mutual assistance, we must give more attention to colonial affairs. 5. Those who have relations in distant lands anxiously watch for the post. How refreshing to his widowed mother is the soldier's cheering letter from a distant land, telling of his safety! how much more so if it breathes words of love and gratitude, and reveals a heart kept true among sore temptations! 6. Lastly, good news from the mission-field is most refreshing for the Churches at home. We should all be the better for taking a wider view of the world, and rejoicing in everything good and hopeful among our fellow-men.

II. THE SYMBOLICAL SUGGESTION OF THIS PROVERB. Such a proverb as that before us cannot but suggest a reference to the good news of which the angels sang at the birth of Christ, and, although we cannot assert that any such idea was in the mind of Solomon, the principle being true in itself, may be applied by us to the Christian gospel. 1. *This comes from a far country.* (1) It comes from heaven. Christ came down from heaven, sent to us by his Father. The highest truth is a revelation. Christianity is a God-given religion. If we had to deal with "cunningly devised fables," it would not be worth while to pay much attention to the Christian legend. Its great importance rests on its truth as a message from God. (2) Heaven is a far country, while we are in our sin. Though God is locally near, spiritually he is far away. The prodigal has strayed into a far country. Yet even there he is not forgotten. God has sent from his distant heavens a message to his wandering children. 2. *It is good news.* (1) It tells of God's love and mercy. (2) It declares Christ's mission to save—his incarnation, ministry, death, and resurrection. (3) It brings to us the offer of free deliverance from all evil and of a heavenly inheritance. The Siberian exile learns from the capital that he is pardoned. The pauper is told that he is heir to untold wealth in a distant land. (4) It is of universal application. The good news is for all. 3. *It is most refreshing.* It is "as cold waters to a thirsty soul." (1) It is much needed. The soul of man naturally thirsts for knowledge of the unseen. A deeper need is that of blessedness in union with God. (2) It refreshes. We have not enough truth to clear up all mysteries, but we have enough to invigorate us and cheer us on our way. Not yet the full feast, but refreshing waters on the journey.

Ver. 28.—"*A city that is broken down.*" Elsewhere the wise man has told us that it is greater for a man to get the victory over his own passions than to take a city (ch. xvi. 32). Now we learn the reverse truth—the shame, misery, and ruin of lack of self-control.

I. THE LACK OF SELF-CONTROL. We need to see what this condition really is. Every man is permitted, in a large measure, to be his own sovereign. No tyrant can invade the secret sanctuary of his thoughts. His ideas, passions, and will are his own. Moreover, God has given to us freedom of will, so that we can give the rein to our passions or restrain them. The inner man is like a city full of life. We are each called upon to keep order in our own cities, and, if we do not respond to the call, the result will be riotous confusion. There are wild beasts within that must be chained and caged, or they will break loose and ravage the streets—murderous propensities that must be shut in a deep dungeon; ugly and vile tendencies to sin that need to be crushed lest they usurp the control of the life. When the will is not fortified and exercised against these evil things, we suffer from lack of self-control.

II. THE CONSEQUENCES OF LACK OF SELF-CONTROL. The "city is broken down, and without walls." 1. *Dilapidation.* The city falls into ruins; its palaces and temples are wrecked; rain penetrates its broken roofs; the wind blows through the crevices of its ill-kept tenements. There is such a thing as a dilapidated soul. Remains of its former glory may yet be detected, but they only add to the shame of its present condition. By failing to control himself, the foolish man has let his passions tear his very soul to pieces. His character is a wreck. 2. *An unprotected condition.* The walls have vanished. The city lies open to the invader. Self-control serves as a wall to protect the soul from temptation; when this disappears, the soul's shelter is lost. Then worse evils follow. Wolves from the forest join with the unclean creatures of the city in wasting the miserable place. It is given over to the enemy. Such is the final condition of one without self-control. He is subject to all sorts of bad foreign influences. In the end he becomes like a city sacked by devils.

III. THE CAUSE AND THE REMEDY OF THE LACK OF SELF-CONTROL. 1. *The cause*— weak self-indulgence. At first the man might have held himself under; but he commenced to indulge his passions, and now they have the mastery over him. He did not begin by choosing evil; indeed, he has never decidedly chosen it. All he has done has been to permit " sin to reign " in his " mortal body." This was not the choice of sin, but it was culpable weakness. 2. *The remedy*—Divine strength. We are all too weak to stand alone; but when we have lost control over ourselves, there is no remedy but in the mighty salvation of Christ. This gives strength for the future, by means of which we may crucify the flesh. If we cannot rule our spirits, we may seek that Christ shall take possession of them and reign within. He will build up the broken walls and restore the ruined dwellings.

HOMILIES BY VARIOUS AUTHORS.

Vers. 2—5.—*Kings: their attributes and duties.* I. CONTRAST BETWEEN DIVINE AND HUMAN GOVERNMENT. Divine government is a mystery in its principles and its ends. Partial revelation only is given of its method in the Scriptures and in the actual course of the world. Actual relations are one thing, their secret spring another. The former may be known, the latter is veiled from our scrutiny. On the contrary, human government should be founded on principles intelligible to all and commendable to the conscience and reason of all. In the kingdom of God, says Luther, we must not seek to be wise, and wish to know the why and wherefore, but have faith in everything. In the kingdom of the world a governor should know and ask the why and wherefore, and trust in nothing.

II. THE RESERVE OF RULERS. (Ver. 3.) If the heart in general is unsearchable, much more must theirs be who have not their own merely, but the secrets of nations in their keeping. The lesson is taught of abstaining from hasty censure of the actions and policy of those in power; the grounds of that policy may be far deeper than anything that meets the eye.

III. THE DUTY OF DISCERNMENT IN RULERS. (Vers. 4, 5.) As the refiner separates the dross from the silver, which mars its beauty and purity, so should the king exclude from his presence and counsels the profligate and the base. A pure or vicious court has immense influence on the manners and morals of the community. Christ speaks in like manner of gathering out of his kingdom at the day of judgment all offenders and workers of iniquity.

IV. THE TRUE FOUNDATION OF AUTHORITY. (Ver. 5.) Not force, but moral power; not might, but right. How often in our time have thrones tottered or the occupant fallen when physical force alone was recognized as the basis of security! Justice is imprinted upon the nature of man. And let rulers who would maintain their power ever appeal to reason and to right. He who takes the motto, " Be just and fear not," for the maxim of his policy lays the only stable foundation of law and government.—J.

Vers. 6, 7.—*A lesson in courtly manners.* Nothing in conduct is unimportant. Fitting and graceful manners are those which become our station in life. Here the relations to our superiors are touched upon.

I. WE SHOULD KNOW OUR PLACE, AND NOT STEP OUT OF IT. (Ver. 6.) As the Arabic proverb finely says, " Sit in thy place, and no man can make thee rise." " All that good manners demand," says a great writer, " is composure and self-content." We may add to this " an equal willingness to allow the social claims of others as to rely upon our own." Self-respect is complemented by deference. We need a ready perception of worth and beauty in our companions. If it is folly to refuse respect to admitted external rank, much more to the native rank of the soul.

II. WE SHOULD ASSUME THE LOWEST RATHER THAN THE HIGHEST PLACE. (Ver. 7.) The lesson runs all through life, from the outward to the inward and the spiritual (see Luke xiv. 8—11). " *Comme il faut*—'as we must be '—is the Frenchman's description of good society." The lesson is mainly against *presumption* in any and all of its forms, an offence hateful to man and God. To take the lowly place in religion here becomes us, and it leads to exaltation; to grasp at more than our due is to lose all and earn our condemnation. Christianity has a deep relation to manners. There is nothing so beautiful as the code of manners given in the New Testament.

> "How near to good is what is fair!
> Which we no sooner see,
> But with the lines and outward air,
> Our senses taken be." J.

Vers. 8—10.—*Some social pests.* I. THE CONTENTIOUS PERSON. (Ver. 8.) He is irritable, easily takes offence, is readily p ovoked, barbs even the playful darts of jest with poison. When the consequences of this ill temper have broken out in full force, its mischief is seen and exposed too late. Beware, then, of "entrance to a quarrel." The contentious man may make real in the end the enmity of which he only dreams.

II. MANFUL CONDUCT IN DISPUTES. (Ver. 9.) If an unavoidable dispute has begun, bear thyself in it with energy, but with honour. It is unmanly and base to employ against one's opponent the secrets that have been learned from him in some earlier confidential moment. Go first to your adversary, and seek a cordial explanation of the difference, and a fair and honourable settlement. And do not be tempted to mix up foreign matters with it. "Agree with thine adversary quickly."

III. THE EVIL OF NOURISHING QUARRELS. (Ver. 10.) Lawsuits consume time, money, rest, and friends. Worst of all consequences, however, is that in the man's own mind. He lights a fire in his own bosom, and keeps it ever supplied with the fuel of passion, and may turn his heart, and perhaps his home, into a hell.—J.

Vers. 11—15.—*Similitudes of moral beauty and goodness.* I. THE APT WORD. Compared to "golden apples in silver frames." Carved work adorning the ceilings of rooms is perhaps alluded to. The beauty of the ground sets off the worth of the object. Just so the good word is set off by the seasonableness of the moment of its utterance (1 Pet. iv. 11). The apt word is "a word upon wheels, not forced or dragged, but rolling smoothly along like chariot-wheels." Our Lord's discourses (*e.g.* on the bread and water of life) sprang naturally out of the course of passing conversation (John iv.; Luke xiv.). So with Paul's famous discourse on Mars' Hill (Acts xvii.).

II. WISE CENSURE IN THE WILLING EAR IS COMPARED TO A GOLDEN EARRING. (Ver. 12.) For if all wisdom is precious as pure gold, and beautiful as ornaments in that material, to receive and wear with meekness in the memory and heart such counsels is better than any other decoration. "The wisest princes need not think it any diminution to their greatness or derogation to their sufficiency to rely upon counsel. God himself is not without, but hath made it one of the great names of his blessed Son, 'The Counsellor'" (Bacon). He who willingly gives heed to wise chastisement does a better service to his ears than if he adorned them with the finest gold and with genuine pearls.

III. A FAITHFUL MESSENGER IS COMPARED TO COOLING SNOW. (Ver. 13.) In the heat of harvest-labour a draught of melted snow from Lebanon is like a "winter in summer" (Xen., 'Mem.,' ii. 1. 30). A traveller says, "Snow so cold is brought down from Mount Lebanon that, mixed with wine, it renders ice itself cold." So refreshing is faithfulness in service. The true servant is not to be paid with gold.

IV. IDLE PRETENSIONS COMPARED TO CLOUDS AND WIND WITHOUT RAIN. (Ver. 14.) Promise without performance. Let men be what they would seem to be. "What has he done? is the Divine question which searches men and transpierces every false reputation. . . . Pretension may sit still, but cannot act. Pretension never feigned an act of real greatness. Pretension never wrote an 'Iliad,' nor drove back Xerxes, nor Christianized the world, nor abolished slavery."

V. THE POWER OF PATIENCE. (Ver. 15.) Time and patience are persuasive; a proverb compares them to an inaudible file. Here patience is viewed as a noiseless hammer, silently crushing resistance. "He who would break through a wall with his hand," says an old commentator, " will hardly succeed!" But how do gentleness and mild-ness win their way! "I Paul beseech you by the meekness and gentleness of Christ" (2 Cor. x. 1).—J.

Vers. 16—20.—*Excesses and errors.* I. WARNING AGAINST SATIETY. (Vers. 16, 17.) The stories of Samson and of Jonathan may be read in illustration of the saying (Judg. xiv. 8, 9; 1 Sam. xiv. 26). Ver. 27 points the warning against incurring the pain of satiety. "Honey, too, hath satiety," says Pindar—

> "A surfeit of the sweetest things,
> The deepest loathing to the stomach brings."

1. We should beware of a too frequent repetition of even innocent pleasures. "If a man will not allow himself leisure to be thirsty, he can never know the true pleasure of drinking." Self-indulgence far more than suffering unnerves the soul. It may well be asked—How can men bear the ills of life, if its very pleasures fatigue them? 2. A special application of the warning. Do not weary your friends. There should be a sacred reserve of a delicate mutual respect even in the most intimate relations of friendship. To invade a busy privacy, with a view to enjoy a snatch of gossip or secure some paltry convenience, is an offence against the minor morals. Defect in manners is usually owing to want of delicacy of perception. Kindly utterance must rest on the conscientious observance of great Christian principles; let daily life be evan-gelized by their all-pervading power. Let us make our "foot precious" to our neigh-bour by not intruding it too often in his home. Better that our visits should be like angels', few and far between, than frequent and wearisome as those of a beggar or a dun.

II. THE TONGUE OF THE FALSE WITNESS. (Ver. 18.) Compared to destructive weapons (comp. Ps. lii. 4; lvii. 4; lxiv. 4; cxx. 4). "The slanderer wounds three at once—himself, him he speaks of, and him that hears" (Leighton). Not only falsehood, but the perverse and distorted way of telling the truth, comes under this ban. "In the case of the witness against our Lord, the words were true, the evidence false; while they reported the words, they misrepresented the sense; and thus swore a true false-hood, and were truly foresworn (Matt. xxvi. 60)" (Bishop Hall).

III. MISPLACED CONFIDENCE. (Ver. 19.) Compared to a broken tooth and a disjointed foot. It is a too common experience, and suggests the counsel to select as confidants only good men. "Be continually with a godly man, whom thou knowest to keep the commandments of the Lord, whose mind is according to thy mind, and will sorrow with thee, if thou shalt miscarry; ... and above all, pray to the Most High, that he will direct thy way in truth" (Ecclus. xxxvii. 12—15). Above all, "let God be true, and every man a liar."

IV. INAPT AND UNREASONABLE MIRTH. (Ver. 20.) It is like the mixture of acid with soda, by which the latter is destroyed; while the combination with oil, etc., pro-duces a useful compound. It is like laying aside a garment in cold weather. Dis-cordant behaviour, the words or the manner out of tune with the occasion, is the fault pointed at. It springs from thoughtlessness and want of sympathy. The Spirit of Christ teaches us to cultivate imagination and sympathy with others. "Rejoice with them that do rejoice, and weep with them that weep."—J.

Vers. 21, 22.—*Love to our enemy.* I. LOVE DELIGHTS IN ITS OPPORTUNITY. (Ver. 21.) And to true Christian love there is no opportunity sweeter than the distress of a foe.

II. LOVE DELIGHTS IN SUPPLYING NEED. It is the opposite of egotism, which clamours for personal satisfaction, and closes the avenues of pity to the distressed.

III. LOVE IS VICTORIOUS OVER EVIL. (Ver. 22.) A wholesome pain is excited in the mind of the enemy. He begins to feel regret and remorse. The torch of a love divinely kindled dissolves the barrier of ice between soul and soul. Evil is overcome by good.

IV. LOVE IS SURE OF ITS REWARD. Both present, in conscience; and eternal in the fruits and in the award of God. Not a cup of cold water shall be forgotten.—J.

Vers. 23—28.—*Moral invectives.* I. AGAINST SLANDER. (Ver. 23.)   Here is a striking picture.   Cunning and slanderous habits beget a dark and gloomy expression on the brow ; as a homely German proverb says, " He makes a face like three days' rainy weather."   The countenance, rightly read, is the mirror of the soul.   Without the candid soul the brow cannot be clear and open.   If we look into the mirror, we may see the condemnation which nature (that is, God) stamps upon our evil and unholy moods.

II. AGAINST CONTENTIOUSNESS. (Ver. 24.)   Better solitude than the presence of the quarrelsome in the home.   A wife is either the husband's most satisfying delight or the cruellest thorn in his side.

III. UNHOLY COWARDICE. (Ver. 26.)   Faint-heartedness springs from need of genuine faith.   To see the chief struck down in battle dismays the band.

> " He is gone from the mountain, he is lost to the forest,
> Like a summer-dried fountain, when our need was the sorest ! "

And if the good man is a fountain of help and encouragement by his example, how does the drying up of such a spring—the failure to assert the truth and confront the gainsayer—dismay and paralyze those who look on !

IV. EXCESS IN SPECULATIVE THOUGHT. (Ver. 27.)   There may be *too much* of any good thing, even of the pursuit of knowledge.   It is too much when it disturbs the health ; as a common proverb of the Germans says, " To know everything gives the headache."   It is too much when it disturbs the moral balance and unfits for society. We must know when to leave the heights of speculation and nestle in the lowly vale of faith.

V. WANT OF SELF-CONTROL. (Ver. 28.)   It is like an undefended city or one in ruins. How weak is it to be able to endure nothing, to deem it a mark of strength to resist every provocation and injury !   Let us learn, after Christ's example, to be abused without being angry ; to give soft words and hard arguments ; and to cultivate self-control in matters of small moment, in preparation for those of greater.   For " if we have run with the footmen, and they have wearied us, how shall we contend with horses ? "—J.

Ver. 25.—*Good news from abroad.* I. IT IS REFRESHING AND EVER WELCOME.   This needs no illustration.   Absence and distance raise a thousand fears in the fancy. Division and space from loved ones chill the heart.   The arrival of good tidings bridges over great gulfs in thought.

II. IT IS A PARABLE OF THE SPIRITUAL SPHERE.   God has sent us good news from what, in our sins and ignorance, seems a far country.   We have friends there.   There is a real link between us.   We are really near.   There is the prospect of a final reunion.—J.

Ver. 2.—*God's glory in concealing.*   A contrast is here drawn between the glory of God and the honour of man, especially of one class of men—the order of kings.

I. THE HONOUR OF MAN IN INVESTIGATING.   1. *The honour of royalty.*   This is " to search out a matter."   The king is acting in a way that honours him when (1) he searches human nature and knows all that he can learn about mankind, all, therefore, that he can know about his subjects ; (2) he acquaints himself with the character, the disposition, the career, of those immediately about him, in whom he trusts, on whom he leans ; (3) he investigates different affairs as they arise, probing and sifting most carefully, not satisfied until he has searched the whole thing through.   It becomes a king to make the most complete and patient investigation into all national affairs. 2. *The honour of mankind generally.*   This is to " search out " and become practically familiar with (1) all the resources this earth will yield us for our use and our enlargement ; (2) the physical, mental, moral, and spiritual necessities of those around us ; (3) what is the true way to supply their need.   This is that which most honours the disciples of that Son of man who came to minister and to redeem.

II. THE GLORY OF GOD IN CONCEALING.   The thought of the writer is obscure. We shall certainly get into the track of it if we consider the three truths : 1. *That God has no need to investigate.*   " All things are naked and open to the eyes of him with whom we have to do ; " all the dark places of the earth, the hearts of men, the most abstruse problems which are so perplexing in our sight. 2. *That he himself is the Inscrutable One.* "His thoughts are very deep," his "ways past finding out." 3. *That it is necessary for him to conceal* in order that he may *truly bless*; that he knows more than he can wisely reveal at once. Parents readily understand this, for they have frequently, constantly, to keep some truths out of sight, ready for a later day and fuller powers; also to decline to reveal, and to leave their children to find out by their own patience and ingenuity. This is very frequently the case with our heavenly Father. For our own sake he half reveals to us and half conceals from us (1) the way to become materially enriched, leaving us to find out what we need to know about agriculture and the stores of wealth that are far below the surface; (2) the way to be mentally enlarged and established; (3) the way to moral and spiritual good. God has designedly and for our ultimate benefit and blessing left much to be searched for and brought out of the *Bible*—his *providential* dealings with us, *our future*, both here and hereafter. It is the glory of man that he can discover and reveal what his fellow-men are unable to make out. It is the glory of God that he cannot make known to us all that is present to his eye, or such revelation of present good and future blessedness would injure us; that he must hide from us a part of his infinite wisdom, some of his inexhaustible stores, and leave us to search and ascertain, that by our searching we may be "lifted up and strengthened."—C.

Vers. 6, 7.—*Modesty and self-assertion.* Some amount of self-assertion is no doubt necessary for honourable success and fruitful achievement. But nothing is more common than for this quality to go beyond its true limit and become distasteful and even offensive both to God and man. What Solomon here deprecates, our Lord also condemns; what he honours, the Divine Teacher also prefers (see Luke xiv. 9).

I. THE DANGER OF SELF-ASSERTION. Its temptation is to assume such proportions that (1) it becomes immodesty, and this is a positive evil, a blemish in character, and a blot upon the life; and (2) it defeats its own ends, for it provokes antagonism and is discomfited and dishonoured. Every one is pleased when the presumptuous man is humiliated.

II. THE PREFERENCE OF MODESTY. 1. It is *frequently successful.* Modesty commends us to the good; we secure their good will; they are inclined to help us and to further our desires; they promote our prosperity. Every one is gratified when the man who "does not think more highly of himself than he ought to think" is the object of esteem, and takes the place of honour. 2. It is *always beautiful.* It is quite possible that, as a matter of worldly policy, modesty may not "answer." It may be, it will often happen, that a strong complacency and vigorous self-assertion will pass it in the race of life. Yet it is the fitting, the becoming, the beautiful thing. It is an adornment of the soul (see 1 Pet. iii. 3). It makes the other virtues and graces which are possessed to shine with peculiar lustre. It gives attractiveness to Christian character and lends a sweetness and influence which nothing else could confer. *To be lowly minded* is a far better portion than to *have the gains and honours* which an ugly assertiveness may command (see homily on Luke xiv. 7—11).—C.

Vers. 8, 9.—*The wise way of settlement.* We look at—

I. THE INEVITABLENESS OF DISPUTES. It is quite impossible that, with our present complication of interests—individual, domestic, social, civic, national—differences and difficulties should not arise amongst us. There must be a conflict of opinion, a clash of wishes and purposes, the divergence which may issue in dissension. What reason would teach us to anticipate experience shows us to exist.

II. THE TEMPTATION OF THE HASTY. This is to enter at once upon *strife*; to "carry it to the court," to "enter an action," to make a serious charge; or (in the case of a community) to take such hostile action as threatens, if it does not end in, war. The folly of this procedure is seen in the considerations: 1. That it interposes an insurmountable barrier between ourselves and our neighbours; we shall never again live in perfect amity with the man with whom we have thus striven; we are sowing seeds of bitterness and discord which will bear fruit all our days. 2. That we are likely enough to be discomfited and ashamed. (1) Those who judge "hastily" are usually in the wrong. (2) No man is a wise and good judge in his own cause; to every man that which makes for himself seems stronger, and that which makes for his opponent seems weaker, than it appears to a disinterested observer. (3) Whether a case will prosper or not at law depends on several uncertainties; and even if we have a righteous cause we may be entirely defeated—a brilliant advocate against us will easily "make the worse appear the better cause." (4) The issue may be such that we shall be impoverished and ashamed. And that which will aggravate our misery will be that we have so foolishly neglected—

III. THE WAY OF THE WISE. To go at once to the offender and to state our complaint to him. This is in every way right and wise. 1. It is the way of manliness and honour. To talk to a third person about it is more easy and pleasant "to the flesh," but it is not the straightforward and manly course. 2. It is the way that is becoming. It is not the fitting thing to disclose our secrets to another; personal and domestic and ecclesiastical contentions are hidden by the wise and the worthy rather than made known to the world. 3. It is the way of peace; for, in the majority of cases, a very little explanation or a very simple apology *at the beginning* will set everything right. 4. It is the distinctly Christian way (Matt. v. 25, 26; xviii. 15).—C.

Ver. 11.—*Welcome words.* But what are—
I. THE WORDS THAT ARE WELCOME. They are: 1. Words that *travel;* "words upon wheels" (literally). They are words that do not "fall to the ground like water which cannot be gathered up again;" but words which are *not* allowed "to fall to the ground," which pass from lip to lip, from soul to soul, from land to land, from age to age. 2. Words that are *level with our human understanding;* which do not require special learning, or profundity, or experience to be appreciated, but which make their appeal to the common intelligence of mankind. 3. Words that *meet our spiritual necessities;* that direct us in doubt, that comfort us in sorrow, that strengthen us in weakness, that nerve us in duty, that calm us in excitement, that sustain us in disappointment, that give us hope in death.

II. THEIR COMMENDATION. They are like golden apples in silver caskets; *i.e.* they are things that *excite our admiration and bring us refreshment.* We do well to *admire* the true and wise word; the saying or the proverb, the terse, sagacious utterance which holds a little world of wisdom in its sentences, is a thing to be admired by us all. The man who first launches it is a benefactor of his people. And we do still better to *appropriate and employ it;* to find refreshment and even nourishment in it. Many a wise word has given needed strength to a human soul in the very crisis of its destiny.

III. THEIR CULTIVATION. How shall we learn to speak these "words upon wheels" —these fitting, wholesome, strengthening words? They come: 1. From a *true* heart; a heart that is true and loyal to its God and Saviour. First of all we must be right with him; only from a pure fountain will come the healing stream. 2. From a *kind* heart. It is love, pity, sympathy, that will prompt the right utterance. Where the learned deliverance or the brilliant *bon-mot* would entirely fail, the simple utterance of affection will do the truest work, will hit the mark in the very centre. Love is the best interpreter and the ablest spokesman as we make the pilgrimage and bear the burdens of our life. 3. From a *thoughtful spirit.* It is not the superficial talker, that discourses upon every possible topic, but rather the man who thinks, who ponders and weighs what he knows and sees, who tries to look *into* things, and who takes the trouble to look back and to look onward,—it is he who has something to say which it will be worth our while to listen to. 4. From *practised lips.* We do not acquire this sacred art of wise and helpful speech in a day or in a year; it is the happy and exquisite product of patient effort, it is a growth, it is a holy and beneficent habit, it is a thing to be cultivated; we may begin poorly enough, but by earnest endeavour we shall succeed if we will only "continue in well-doing."—C.

Vers. 16, 27.—*The wisdom of moderation.* We can only eat a small quantity of honey; if we go beyond the limit we find out our mistake. Of this, as of all very sweet things, the words of the great dramatist are true, that "a little more than enough is by much too much." This is particularly applicable to that to which it is here referred.

I. SELF-PRAISE. We may go a little way in that direction, but not far. If we transgress the narrow bounds allowed, we shall soon find that we have done ourselves harm in the estimation of our neighbour. And even to talk, without praise, of ourselves is a habit to be held well in check, or it will run into an offensive and injurious egotism (see homily on ch. xvii. 2).

II. SELF-EXAMINATION. To "search out our own glory" is not glorious, but rather inglorious. It is allowable enough for a man sometimes to recall what he has been to others, and what he has done for others; but he may not practise this beyond a very circumscribed limit. To hold up his own achievements before his own eyes is to beget a very perilous complacency; to find them out for other people's edification is quite as dangerous. And, on the other hand, for men to be searching their hearts or their lives to discover what is evil in them, to be instituting a constant examination of their souls to ascertain whereabouts they stand,—this is open to grave mistake, and may soon become unwise and hurtful. Self-examination is very good up to a certain point; beyond that point it becomes morbid and is a serious mistake.

III. BODILY EXERCISE AND INDULGENCE. This is very pleasant and (the latter) very "sweet," like the eating of honey. And to go some way in both of these is good and wise. But let the athlete beware lest his very love of bodily exercise betrays him into excesses which undermine his strength and bring on premature decline and death. And as to bodily indulgence, let us be often reminding ourselves that only in the cup of strict moderation—whatever that cup may be—is real pleasure or lasting health to be found. All excess here is as foolish as it is sinful.

IV. SPIRITUAL NOURISHMENT. Can we have too much of this? Undoubtedly we can. Those who are perpetually partaking of one particular kind of religious nourishment, however good that may be in its way and measure, are over-eating of one kind of food, and they will suffer for so doing. They will not grow as God meant them to grow, proportionately and symmetrically; there will be a lopsidedness about their mind or character which is very noticeable and very ugly. Whether it be the contemplative, or the poetical, or the speculative, or the evangelistic, or the didactic, or any other side of truth in which men surfeit their souls, they make a mistake in so doing. They should understand that Divine truth has many sides and aspects, that there is not any one of them that constitutes wisdom or is sufficient to fill the mind and build up the character of a man. Our wisdom is to partake of the various dishes which are on the table our bountiful Host has provided for us; for as the body is the better for eating of many "meats," so is the soul all the stronger and all the fairer for partaking in moderation of all the various sources of spiritual nutrition that are within its reach.—C.

Vers. 20, 25.—*The inopportune and the acceptable.* "A man that hath friends must show himself friendly" (ch. xviii. 24). And if we would do this we must be careful to choose our time for speaking the truth to our friends, and must study to do not only the right but the appropriate thing. We must—

I. ABSTAIN FROM THE INOPPORTUNE. (Ver. 20.) It should require but a very humble share of delicacy to understand that what is very valuable at one time is altogether misplaced and unpalatable at another. We should carefully abstain from: 1. All merriment in the presence of great sorrow. By indulgence in it then we only add fuel to the fire of grief. 2. The discussion of business or the proposals of pleasure in the presence of earnest spiritual solicitude. When men are profoundly anxious about their relations with God, they do not want us to harass and burden them with talk about temporal affairs or about social entertainments; these are good in their time, but not at such a time as that. 3. Entering into the affairs of life in the presence of the dying. Those who stand very near indeed to the future world do not want to be vexed with matters which they are leaving behind for ever. Similarly, it is a mistake to be always or even often discussing death and the future with those who, while not unready for either, are charged with the duties and responsibilities of active life. 4. An urgent insistance upon spiritual obligations in presence of acute bodily suffering or severe destitution. The Christian course, in such a case, is to call in the doctor or the baker.

II. CULTIVATE THE ACCEPTABLE. (Ver. 25.) How acceptable to the human heart is: 1. Good news from our friends and kindred when afar off from us. It is worth while to take much trouble, to "put ourselves quite out of our way," in order to convey this; it is one of the friendliest of friendly acts.　2. Society in loneliness; the kindly visit paid to the solitary, a conversation (however brief and simple) with those whose hearth is uncheered by companionship.　3. Encouragement in depression.　The heart often aches and hungers for a word of cheer, and one very short sentence may lift it up from depths of disappointment and depression into the bracing air of hopefulness and determination.　4. Sympathy in sorrow.　Grief does not crave many or fine words; it asks for genuine *sympathy*—the "feeling with" it; if it has this, it will gratefully accept any simplest utterance in word or deed, and will be comforted and strengthened by it.　Real sympathy is *always* the acceptable thing.　5. Guidance in perplexity. When we do not know which way to turn, then the brief word of direction from one who has "gone that way before us" is valuable indeed.　There is no kinder friend than the true and faithful guide.　If we would take our part well and be to our brethren all that it is in our power to become, we must study to do the congenial and acceptable thing.　The man who has acquired this art is worthy of our admiration and our love; we are sure that he will not go without our Master's commendation; for is it not he who is feeding the hungry, and giving the thirsty to drink? is it not he who is clothing the naked and healing the sick?　While we do these two things, should we not also—

III. BE PREPARED FOR EVERY POSSIBLE CONDITION?　We may be sure that uncongenial and congenial things will be said to us, timely and untimely attitudes will be taken toward us; some men will aggravate and others will heal our spirits.　The wise man will see to it that he is (1) rooted in those principles which never change but always sustain; (2) has his strength in the One " with whom is no variableness nor shadow of turning."—C.

Ver. 21.—*The true triumph.*　(See homily on ch. xxiv. 17, 18, 29.)　To the truth on this subject there affirmed, may be added the consideration that to return good for evil is the true triumph; for—

I. TO BE AVENGED IS REALLY UNSATISFACTORY.　It is, indeed, to have a *momentary gratification.*　But of what character is this satisfaction?　Is it not one that we share with the wild beast, with the savage, nay, even with the fiend?　Is it one that we can approve in our calmer hour, that we can look back upon with any thankfulness or pure delight?　In fact, it is to be really and *inwardly defeated;* for we then give way to a malevolent passion—we are "overcome of evil" instead of overcoming it.　We allow thoughts to enter our mind and feelings to harbour in our heart of which, in worthier moments, we are utterly ashamed.

II. TO ACT MAGNANIMOUSLY IS THE VICTORIOUS THING.　1. It is to gain a very real victory over our self, over our lower passions.　2. It is to win our enemy.　To make him suffer, to wound him, to damage his reputation, to cause him serious loss and injury,—that is a very poor thing indeed to do.　Any one is, in a moral sense, equal to that; mere malevolence can do that and can be at home in the act of doing it. But to *win* an enemy, to turn his hatred into love, his contempt into esteem, his cruelty into kindness, his hostility into friendship,—that is to triumph over him indeed, it is to "heap coals of fire upon his head."

III. TO ACT MAGNANIMOUSLY IS TO ACT DIVINELY.　For it is: 1. To carry out a Divine commandment (text; Matt. v. 43—48; Rom. xii. 14, 19, 21).　2. To act as the Divine Father does, and as Jesus Christ did when he was with us (Matt. v. 45; Luke xxiii. 24).　3. To receive a Divine reward (text).　God will bestow a bountiful, spiritual blessing on those who thus resolutely keep his word, gain dominion over themselves, bless their neighbour, and follow in the footsteps of their Lord.—C.

Ver. 26.—(See homily on ch. xxvi. 1.)—C.

Ver. 28.—(See homily on ch. xvi. 32.)—C.

EXPOSITION.

CHAPTER XXVI.

Vers. 1—12.—Certain proverbs concerning the fool (*kesil*), with the exception, perhaps, of ver. 2 (see on ch. i. 22).

Ver. 1.—**As snow in summer, and as rain in harvest.** Snow in summer would be quite unnatural and unheard of (see on ch. xxv. 13). Rain falls in the usual course of things only at stated times; whence arose the phrase of "the early and of latter rains" (see on ch. xvi. 15). From spring to October or November was the dry season, and a storm at harvest-time was regarded, not merely as destructive or inconvenient, but as portentous and even supernatural (see 1 Sam. xii. 17, etc.). The two cases are types of all that is incongruous and unsuitable. The LXX., apparently regarding their experience in Egypt rather than the actual text, translate, "As dew in harvest, and as rain in summer." **So honour is not seemly for a fool** (ver. 8; ch. xix. 10). It is quite out of place to show respect to a stupid and ungodly man, or to raise him to a post of dignity; such conduct will only confirm him in his folly, give others a wrong impression concerning him, and afford him increased power of mischief. The Greeks had a proverb about giving honour to unsuitable objects: they called it washing an ass's head with nitre.

Ver. 2.—**As the bird by wandering, as the swallow by flying.** "Bird" (*tsippor*) is the sparrow, which is found throughout Palestine; "swallow" (*deror*), the free flier. The Authorized Version hardly gives the sense. The line should be rendered, *as the sparrow in* (in respect of) *its wandering, as the swallow in its flying.* The point of comparison is the vagueness and aimlessness of the birds' flight, or the uselessness of trying to catch them in their course. **So the curse causeless shall not come.** It shall, as it were, spend its force in the air, and fall not on the head on which it was invoked. A causeless curse is that which is uttered against one who has done nothing to deserve such denunciation. Septuagint, "As birds and sparrows fly, so a causeless (ματαία) curse shall come upon no one" (comp. 1 Sam. xvii. 43; Neh. xiii. 2.) Bailey, 'Festus'—

"Blessings star forth for ever; but a curse
Is like a cloud—it passes."

Closely connected with the superstition that dreads a curse is that which is alarmed by omens. Against this irrational fear we find some Eastern proverbs directed; *e.g.* "The jackal howls: will my old buffalo die?" "The dog barks—still the caravan passes: will the barking of the dog reach the skies?" (Lane). Instead of אל, "not," the Keri reads לו, "to him." This makes the proverb say that the unprovoked curse shall return upon him who uttered it. But this reading is not to be accepted, as it does not suit the terms of comparison, though it seems to have been used by St. Jerome, who translates, *Sic maledictum frustra prolatum in quempiam superveniet.* This retributive justice is often alluded to elsewhere; *e.g.* ver. 27 (where see note). So we find in various languages proverbs to the same effect. Thus in English, "Harm watch, harm catch;" Spanish, "Who sows thorns, let him not walk barefoot;" Turkish, "Curses, like chickens, always come home to roost;" Yoruba, "Ashes always fly back in the face of him that throws them" (Trench).

Ver. 3.—**A whip for the horse, a bridle for the ass.** We should be inclined to invert the words, and say a bridle for the horse, and a whip for the ass; but it must be remembered that in early times the horse was not ridden, but only driven. The animals used in riding were the ass and mule, and sometimes the camel. The Eastern ass is really a fine animal, larger, more spirited, and more active than the poor creature which we are wont to see. Or the whip and bridle may be intended to apply to both animals, though divided between the two for rhythmical or antithetical reasons (see on ch. x. 1). **A rod for the fool's back.** Sharp correction is both useful and necessary for the fool (so ch. x. 13; xix. 29). Similar treatment Siracides advises to be employed in the case of an idle servant (Ecclus. xxx. 24—28). Septuagint, "As a whip for a horse and a goad for an ass, so is a rod for a lawless nation."

Ver. 4.—**Answer not a fool according to his folly.** Do not lower yourself to the fool's level by answering his silly questions or arguing with him as if he were a sensible man. **Lest thou also be like unto him;** lest you be led to utter folly yourself or to side with him in his opinions and practices. Our blessed Saviour never responded to foolish and captious questions in the way that the questioner hoped and desired. He put them by or gave an unexpected turn to them which silenced the adversary. Instances may be seen in Matt. xxi. 23, etc.; xxii. 21, 22; Luke xiii. 23, etc.; John xxi. 21, etc.

Ver. 5.—**Answer a fool according to his folly.** This maxim at first sight seems absolutely antagonistic to the purport of the preceding verse; but it is not so really. The words, "according to his folly," in this verse mean, as his folly deserves, in so plain a way as to expose it, and shame him, and bring him to a better mind. **Lest he be wise in his own conceit**; thinking, it may be, that he has said something worth hearing, or put you to silence by his superior intelligence.

Ver. 6.—**He that sendeth a message by the hand of a fool.** This clause comes in the Hebrew after the next. **Cutteth off the feet, and drinketh damage.** To entrust an important commission to a fool is to deprive one's self of the means of having it properly executed, and to bring upon one's self shame and injury. A man who is so silly as to employ such an unfit messenger, as it were, cuts off the feet which should bear him on his errand, and, instead of enjoying the satisfaction of seeing the business well performed, he will be mortified and damaged by the blunder and stupidity of his emissary. Septuagint, "He maketh for himself reproach from his own ways (ὁδῶν, ? ποδῶν) who sendeth a word by a foolish messenger." The Vulgate reads the first participle in a passive sense, *claudus pedibus;* but this is unnecessary. We have similar phrases to "drinketh damage" elsewhere; *e.g.* Job xv. 16, "drinketh in iniquity;" xxxiv. 7, "drinketh up scorn;" and with a different word, ch. xix. 28, "devoureth iniquity."

Ver. 7.—**The legs of a lame man are not equal.** The first word of this verse, דליו, has occasioned some difficulty. It is considered as an imperative from דלה, "draw off," "take away." Thus the Septuagint, ἀφελοῦ; Venetian, ἐπάρατε. But the verb seems never to have this meaning; nor, if it had, would the sense be very satisfactory, for, as Delitzsch points out, lame legs are better than none, and there is a great difference between the perfectly crippled or paralytic who has to be carried, and the lame man (פסח) who can limp or get along on crutches. And when we explain the proverb in this sense (as Plumptre), "Take away the legs of the lame man and the parable from the mouth of fools," for both alike are useless to their possessors, and their loss would not be felt—we must recognize that the conclusion is not true. No one would think of amputating a man's legs simply because he was lame, and such a one's legs cannot be considered absolutely useless. Others regard the word as third plural kal, "the legs hang loose;" though the form is not sufficiently accounted for. All explanations of the word as a verbal form have such difficulties, that some take it as a noun, meaning "dancing," which is

Luther's interpretation, "As dancing to a cripple, so it becometh a fool to talk of wisdom." But the word could never signify anything but "limping," and could not express the elegant motion of dancing. The Authorized Version considers the Hebrew to mean, "are lifted up," *i.e.* are unequal, one being longer or stronger than the other; but this loses the force of the comparison. There seems to be no better interpretation than that mentioned above, "The legs of the lame hang loose," *i.e.* are unserviceable, however sound in appearance. St. Jerome has expressed this, though in a strange fashion, "As it is vain for a lame man to have seemly legs." **So is a parable in the mouth of a fool.** "Parable" (*mashal*), sententious saying, the enunciation of which, as well as the recital of stories, was always a great feature in Eastern companies, and afforded a test of a man's ability. A fool fails in the exhibition; he misses the point of the wise saying which he produces; it falls lame from his mouth, affords no instruction to others, and makes no way with its hearers. Siracides gives another reason for the incongruity, "A parable shall be rejected when it cometh out of a fool's mouth; for he will not speak it in its season" (Ecclus. xx. 20). Septuagint, "Take away the motion of legs, and transgression (παρανομίαν,? παροιμίαν, Lag.) from the mouth of fools."

Ver. 8.—**As he that bindeth a stone in a sling.** So Septuagint, Ὃς ἀποδεσμεύει λίθον ἐν σφενδόνῃ. This gives a very good sense, the point being either that the stone, after being firmly fitted in its place, quickly passes away from the sling, or, if more stress is laid on the word "bindeth," that the stone is so firmly fixed that it cannot be slung, and therefore never reaches the mark. The alternative rendering adopted by the Revised Version is this, "As a bag of gems in a heap of stones;" where the incongruity would consist either in exposing jewels on a cairn, or sepulchral monument, whence they could easily be filched, or in attracting undesirable attention. But there are grammatical and etymological reasons against this interpretation; and the Authorized Version is to be considered correct. The Vulgate is curious: *Sicut qui mittit lapidem in acervum Mercurii.* This rendering points to the custom, with which Jerome must have been familiar, of erecting statues of Mercury on the highways, which were thus placed under his protection. Round these statues were ranged heaps of stones, to which every wayfarer contributed by throwing a pebble as he passed. The absence of the critical faculty which discerned no absurdity in this anachronism is sufficiently remarkable. The Latin saying seems intended to denote useless labour, as we speak of "carrying coals to Newcastle." So is he that giveth honour to a fool. You pay respect to a fool, or place him in an honourable position, but your labour is wasted; he cannot act up to his dignity, he cannot maintain the honour; it passes away like the stone from the sling, or, if it remains, it is useless to him.

Ver. 9.—As a thorn goeth up into the hand of a drunkard. There is here no idea of the drunkard's hand being pierced with a thorn while he is insensible to the pain, but rather of his being armed with it, and ripe for mischief. So it is best to render, "A thornbush cometh into the hand of a drunkard;" he somehow gets possession of it, and in his stupid excitement is liable to become dangerous. Some understand עָלָה of the growth of the thorn; thus the Septuagint, "Thorns grow in the hand of a drunkard;" Vulgate, "As if a thorn grew in the hand of a drunkard." But one does not see the bearing of such an expression; and the translation given above is more appropriate. So is a parable, etc. (as ver. 7). In that passage the wise saying in a fool's mouth was compared with something useless, here it is compared with something injurious. He employs it purposely to wound others; or by the ignorant use of some sharp-edged word he does much mischief. In this hemistich the LXX. has read מָשָׁל with a different vocalization, and renders, "servitude (δουλεία) in the hand of fools." This seems to mean that it comes natural to fools to be manacled and restrained by force.

Ver. 10.—Few passages have given greater difficulty than this verse; almost every word has been differently explained. The Authorized Version is, The great God that formed all things both rewardeth the fool, and rewardeth transgressors; Revised Version, As an archer (Job xvi. 13) that woundeth all, so is he that hireth the fool and he that hireth them that pass by. At first sight one would hardly suppose that these could be versions of the same passage. To show the diversity that obtained in early times we quote the Greek and Latin versions. Septuagint, "All the flesh of fools is much distressed (πολλὰ χειμάζεται), for their distraction (ἔκστασις) is brought to nought;" Vulgate, "Judgment decides causes, and he who imposes silence on a fool appeases wrath." From the various interpretations of which this proverb is capable, it may be surmised that it was originally one of those hard sayings which were intended to exercise the ingenuity of auditors. It has certainly had that effect in modern times. We may at once eliminate the rendering of the Authorized Version, though the sense is good and scrip-

tural, denoting that the great Creator recompenses the good and punishes sinners. So the mediæval jingle—

"Ante Dei vultum nihil unquam restat inultum."

"God" is not in the Hebrew, and rab, "great," is never used absolutely as equivalent to "God." Nor is the word used elsewhere to mean "head-workman;" so the Revised Version margin, "a master-worker formeth all things," is suspicious. Some translate, "A great man woundeth [equivalent to ' punisheth'] all; he renders their due to fools and to transgressors." One does not see why this should be attributed to the great man; it certainly is not generally true. Rosenmüller, "The mighty man causes terror; so does he who hires the fool and the transgressor;" but it is not clear why the hiring of a fool should occasion terror. The rendering in the Revised Version, or something very similar, has found favour with many modern commentators, though quite unknown to the more ancient versions. According to this interpretation, the proverb says that a careless, random way of doing business, taking into one's service fools, or entrusting matters of importance to any chance loiterer, is as dangerous as shooting arrows about recklessly without caring whither they flew or whom they wounded. To this view Nowack objects that it is unparalleled to present an archer as a picture of what is unusual and profitless; that it does not explain why "hireth" is twice repeated; that the connection between shooter and the hire of fool and loiterer is not obvious; and that עֹבְרִים does not mean "vagabonds" or "passers-by." None of these objections are of much importance; and this interpretation still holds its ground. There is also much to be said for the rendering of the Revised Version margin, which is virtually that of Gesenius, Fleischer, Wordsworth, Nutt, and others: A skilful man, a master-workman, produces, makes, everything by his own care and superintendence; but he that hires a fool to do his work hires, as it were, any casual vagabond who may know nothing of the business. One objection to this interpretation is that the verb חוּל, does not elsewhere have the meaning here attributed to it. Considering all the above interpretations unsatisfactory, Hitzig, after Umbreit, followed herein by Delitzsch and Nowack, translates, "Much bringeth forth all," which means that he who possesses much can do anything, or, as St. Matt. xiii. 12, "Whosoever hath, to him shall be given" (comp. ch. i. 5). But the second hemistich comes in rather lamely, "But he who hires a fool is as one who hires a vagabond." Hence Delitzsch reads

וְשֵׂכָר for the first וְשֵׂכָר, and renders, "But the hire and the hirer of the fool pass away," *i.e.* what the fool gets as wages is soon squandered, and the person who took him into his service is ruined by his incapacity. In this case the connection of the two clauses would be this: A rich man, in the nature of things, grows richer; but there are exceptions to this rule; for he who employs stupid and incapable people to do his business suffers for it in property, reputation, and probably in person also; and the incompetent person derives no benefit from the connection. It is impossible to give a decided preference to any of these expositions; and the passage must be left as a crux. It is most probable that the Hebrew text is defective. This would account for the great variations in the versions.

Ver. 11.—**As the dog returneth to his vomit** (see 2 Pet. ii. 22, which, however, is not quoted from the Septuagint), **so a fool returneth to his folly**; or, *repeateth his folly*. The fool never frees himself from the trammels of his foolishness; his deeds and words always bear the same character to the end. The same truth holds good of the sinner, especially the drunkard and the sensualist. If they feel temporary compunction, and reject their sin by partial repentance, they do not really shake it off wholly; it has become a second nature to them, and they soon relapse into it. Septuagint, "As when a dog goes to his own vomit and becomes hateful, so is a fool who returns in his wickedness to his own sin." The LXX. adds a distich which is found in Ecclus. iv. 21, "There is a shame that bringeth sin, and there is a shame that is glory and grace."

Ver. 12.—**Seest thou a man wise in his own conceit?** (ch. iii. 7). Nothing so shuts the door against improvement as self-conceit. "Woe unto them," says Isaiah (v. 21), "that are wise in their own eyes, and prudent in their own sight." Such persons, professing themselves wise, become fools (Rom. i. 22; xii. 16; Rev. iii. 17, 18). Touching conceit, *Qui sibi sapit, summe desipit.* The Oriental speaks of the fox finding his shadow very large, and of the wolf when alone thinking himself a lion. There is more hope of a fool than of him (ch. xxix. 20). A fool who is conscious of unwisdom may be set right; but one who fancies himself perfect, and needing no improvement, is beyond cure; his case is hopeless. So the sinner who feels and acknowledges his iniquity may be converted; but the self-righteous Pharisee, who considers himself to have no need of repentance, will never be reformed (see Matt. ix. 12; Luke xv. 7; xviii. 14). St. Chrysostom ('Hom. in Phil.,' vii.), "Haughtiness is a great evil; it is better to be a fool than haughty; for in the one case the folly

is only a perversion of intellect, but in the other case it is still worse; for it is folly joined with madness. The fool is an evil to himself; but the haughty man is a plague to others too. One cannot be haughtyminded without being a fool. . . . The soul which is puffed up has a worse disease than dropsy, while that which is under restraint is freed from all evil" (Oxford transl.).

Vers. 13—16.—Proverbs concerning the sluggard.

Ver. 13.—This is virtually the same as ch. xxii. 13. The words for "lion" are different in two parts of the verse, *shakhal* being the lion of advanced age, *ari* the fullgrown animal; the latter may possibly be assumed to be the more dangerous of the two, and so a climax would be denoted. There is a proverb current in Bechuana, which says, "The month of seed-time is the season of headaches."

Ver. 14.—**As the door turneth upon its hinges.** The door moves on its hinges and makes no progress beyond its own confined sphere of motion; so the slothful man turns himself on his bed from side to side, but never leaves it to do his work. Other analogies have been found in this proverb. Thus: The door opens to let the diligent go forth to his daily business, while the sluggard is rolling upon his bed; the door creaks when it is moved, so the lazy man groans when he is aroused; the door now is opened, now is shut, so the sluggard at one time intends to rise, and then falls back in his bed, and returns to his sleep (comp. ch. vi. 9, 10; xxiv. 33).

Ver. 15.—Very nearly identical with ch. xix. 24. It forms a climax to the two preceding verses. Wordsworth takes "the dish" as a type of sensual pleasure, which the slothful loves, while he has no liking for active work.

Ver. 16.—**The sluggard is wiser in his own conceit.** The sluggard is here one who is too idle to think a matter out, and considers his own cursory view as sure to be right. He is one who deems study to be an unnecessary weariness of the flesh (Eccles. xii. 12), and flatters himself that he is quite able without it to give a satisfactory account of any question presented to him. **Than seven men that can render a reason.** "Seven" is the number of completeness (comp. ch. vi. 31; ix. 1; xxiv. 16). The idle fool sets more value by his own judgment than by the sense of any number of wise men. Revised Version margin, "that can answer discreetly," is perhaps nearer the Hebrew, which implies the being able to return a wise and proper answer to anything asked of them. The LXX. reading a little differently, renders, "Wiser seems a sluggard to himself than one who in satiety (ἐν πλησμονῇ) brings back a message." This is explained to mean that a sluggard thinks himself wise in not helping a neighbour with an errand or a message, though he would have probably been repaid with a good dinner for his kindness.

Vers. 17—28.—A series of proverbs connected more or less with peacefulness and its opposite.

Ver. 17.—He that passeth by, and meddleth with strife belonging not to him. "Meddleth with strife" should be "vexes, excites himself, with a quarrel." Is like one that taketh a dog by the ears, and thus needlessly provokes him to bark and bite. Regarding the position of the two participles in this verse, without any connecting link, Delitzsch takes "passing by" as attributed to the dog, thus: "He seizes by the ears a dog passing by, who is excited by a strife that concerns him not." The stray dog corresponds to the quarrel with which one has nothing to do. The present accentuation does not support this view; otherwise it is suitable and probable. Septuagint, "As he who lays hold of a dog's tail, so is he who sets himself forth as champion in another's cause." Ecclus. xi. 9, "Strive not in a matter that concerns thee not." Says a Greek gnome—

Πολυπραγμονεῖν τἀλλότρια μὴ βούλου κακά.

Our English proverb says, "He that intermeddles with all things may go shoe the goslings." The Telugu compares such interference to a monkey holding a snake in his paw; it is hard to hold, dangerous to let go (Lane).

Vers. 18, 19.—A tetrastich, but without parallelisms. As a mad man who casteth firebrands, arrows, and death. The word rendered "madman" is an ἅπαξ λεγόμενον, and has been variously explained; but the Authorized Version is probably correct. "Firebrands" are darts with some blazing material attached to them. "Death" forms a climax with the other dangers mentioned, which the madman deals forth recklessly and indiscriminately. So is the man that deceiveth his neighbour, and saith, Am not I in sport? When a man has injured his neighbour by lies or malice, the plea that he was only in joke is not allowed; the injury is not less real because he excuses it by alleging it was done not seriously, but playfully; no more than the fatal effects of the use of murderous weapons are lessened by their being employed by the hands of a maniac. Practical joking is often a most serious matter. A mediæval adage says wisely—

"Cum jocus est verus, jocus est malus atque severus."

Septuagint, "Even as those who are under medical treatment (ἰώμενοι) throw words at men, and he who first meets the word will be overthrown; so are all they that lay wait for their own friends, and when they are seen, say, I did it in jest." As insane persons who abuse and ill treat their physicians are excused by reason of their infirmity, so those who injure friends in secret try to excuse themselves when found out by alleging that they were only joking.

Ver. 20.—Some proverbs follow concerning the slanderer. Where no wood is, there the fire goeth out. Where the wood fails, and that was the only fuel then used, the fire must go out. So where there is no talebearer, the strife ceaseth; comes to silence (ch. xxii. 10). (For nirgan, "whisper," see on ch. xvi. 28.) Septuagint, "With much wood fire groweth, but where there is not one discordant (δίθυμος), strife is at rest."

Ver. 21.—As coals are to burning coals. As black, cold charcoal feeds glowing charcoal, as wood feeds a lighted fire, so a quarrelsome man (ch. xxi. 9; xxvii. 15) supports and nourishes strife. The verse is the counterpart of the preceding. Septuagint, "A hearth for coal and logs for fire, and a reviling man for tumult of strife."

Ver. 22.—(See ch. xviii. 8, where the gnome occurs.) Septuagint, "The words of knaves (κερκώπων) are soft, but they strike to the secret chambers of the bowels."

Ver. 23.—The next proverbs are concerned with hypocrisy. The Hebrew denotes the comparison simply by position (see on ch. xxv. 11), thus: An earthen vessel (or, potsherd) overlaid with silver dross—glowing lips and a wicked heart. So-called "silver dross" is litharge, an oxide of lead used to this day to put a glaze on pottery (comp. Ecclus. xxxviii. 30). The comparatively worthless article is thus made to assume a fine appearance. Thus lips that seem to burn with affection, and give the kiss of glowing love, may mask a heart filled with envy and hatred. Judas kisses and words of friendship hide the bad feelings that lurk within. Septuagint, "Silver given with guile is to be considered as a potsherd; smooth (λεῖα) lips hide a grievous heart" (comp. Matt. xxiii. 27).

Ver. 24.—He that hateth dissembleth with his lips. This and the next verse form a tetrastich. St. Jerome, Labiis suis intelligitur inimicus. But the verb here used, נכר, bears the meaning "to make one's self unknown," as well as "to make one's self known," and hence "to make one's self unrecognizable" by dress or change of countenance (1 Kings xiv. 5). This is much more appropriate in the present connection than the other explanation. The man cloaks his hatred with honeyed words. And layeth up deceit within him; meditating all the time treachery in his heart (Jer. ix. 8). Septuagint, "An enemy weeping promises all things with his lips, but in his heart he contriveth deceits." The tears in this case are hypocritical signs of sorrow, intended to deceive the dupe.

Ver. 25.—**When he speaketh fair, believe him not.** When he lowers his voice to a winning, agreeable tone, put no trust in him. Septuagint, "If thine enemy entreat thee with a loud voice, be not persuaded." **For there are seven abominations in his heart.** His heart is filled with a host of evil thoughts (see on ver. 16), as if seven devils had entered in and dwelt there (Matt. xii. 45; Mark xvi. 9). Ecclus. xii. 10, etc., "Never trust thine enemy; for like as iron rusteth, so is his wickedness. Though he humble himself, and go crouching, yet take good heed and beware of him." Plato's verdict concerning hypocrisy is often quoted, Ἐσχάτη ἀδικία δοκεῖν δίκαιον εἶναι μὴ ὄντα, "It is the very worst form of injustice to appear to be just without being so in reality" ('De Rep.,' ii. p. 361, A). With this Cicero agrees ('De Offic.,' i. 13), "Totius injustitiæ nulla capitalior est quam eorum, qui tum cum maxime fallunt id agunt ut viri boni esse videantur."

Ver. 26.—**Whose hatred is covered by deceit;** or, *hatred may be concealed by deceit,* as was said above (ver. 24). (But) **his wickedness shall be showed before the whole congregation.** The hater's real wickedness, at some time or other, in spite of all his efforts to hide it, will be openly displayed. He will show it before some third party and thus it will be divulged. At any rate, this will be the case at the judgment-day, when he who hateth his brother shall be shown to be not only a murderer, but a hater of God also (1 John iii. 15; iv. 20). Septuagint, "He that hideth enmity prepareth deceit, but he revealeth his own sins, being well known in assemblies."

Ver. 27.—**Whoso diggeth a pit shall fall therein.** This thought is found often elsewhere; *e.g.* Ps. vii. 16; ix. 16; Eccles. x. 8; Ecclus. xxvii. 25, 26. The pit is such a one as was made to catch wild animals; the maker is supposed to approach incautiously one of these traps, and to fall into it. **And he that rolleth a stone, it will return upon him.** This does not refer to throwing stones into the air, which fall upon the head of the thrower, but to rolling stones up a height in order to hurl them down upon the enemy (comp. Judg. ix. 53; 2 Sam. xi. 21). Of such retributive justice we have numerous examples; *e.g.* Haman hung on the gallows which he had prepared for Mordecai (Esth. vii. 9, etc.). So the old story tells how Perillus, the inventor of the brazen bull in which prisoners were to be burned alive, was himself made to prove the efficacy of his own invention by the tyrant Phalaris; as Ovid says—

" Et Phalaris tauro violenti membra Perilli
      Torruit; infelix imbuit auctor opus."
                              ('Art. Amat.,' i. 653.)

So we have, "Damnosus aliis, damnosus est sibi;" Ἡ δὲ βουλὴ τῷ βουλεύσαντι κακίστη. St. Chrysostom speaks of the blindness of malice: "Let us not plot against others, lest we injure ourselves. When we supplant the reputation of others, let us consider that we injure ourselves, it is against ourselves that we plot. For perchance with men we do him harm, if we have power, but ourselves in the sight of God, by provoking him against us. Let us not, then, injure ourselves. For as we injure ourselves when we injure our neighbours, so by benefiting them we benefit ourselves" ('Hom. xiv. in Phil.,' Oxford transl.).

Ver. 28.—**A lying tongue hateth those that are afflicted by it;** or, *those whom it crusheth* (ch. xxv. 15). There is a consensus of the Vulgate, Septuagint, Syriac, and Targum to translate דכיו "truth," thinking apparently of the Aramæan דְכְיָא, "that which is pure." But the hemistich would thus state the baldest truism, and modern commentators unite in assigning to the word some such sense as that given above in the Authorized Version. A liar shows his want of charity by slandering his neighbour; and that men dislike those whom they have injured is a common experience. "It is a characteristic of human nature," says Tacitus ('Agric.,' 42), "to hate those whom one has injured." Seneca, 'De Ira,' ii. 33, "Hoc habent pessimum animi magna fortuna insolentes, quos læserunt, et oderunt." **A flattering mouth worketh ruin;** brings destruction on those who succumb to its seductive words. Vulgate, *Os lubricum operatur ruinas;* Septuagint, "A mouth uncovered (ἄστεγον) causeth tumults." (For "the smooth mouth," comp. ch. v. 3; Ps. xii. 3; lv. 21; Isa. xxx. 10.) The word for "tumults" is ἀκαταστασίας, which does not occur elsewhere in the Septuagint, but is common in the New Testament; *e.g.* Luke xxi. 9; 1 Cor. xiv. 33.

HOMILETICS.

Ver. 2.—*The curse causeless.* I. GOD WILL NOT HEAR A SINFUL PRAYER. A curse is a prayer. No one has the power of inflicting direct harm upon his victim by sheer force of malignant words. Only the superstition of magic could suppose any such thing to be possible. A curse is just a prayer for evil to come on the head of the devoted person. But God will not heed such a petition if he disapproves of it. Prayer is not a force that compels God ; it is but a petition that seeks his aid, and the response to it is entirely dependent on his will.

II. THERE IS A PROVIDENCE OVER LIFE. Curses cannot fly about like black-plumed birds of evil, roosting wherever their authors choose. Above the most potent and direful curse of man is the calm, fair, equable government of God. Though the whole human race combined to curse one on whom God smiled, not a shadow of real evil could light on his head. Balaam saw the uselessness of trying to curse a people whom God had blessed (Numb. xxiii. 8).

III. IT IS MORE IMPORTANT TO WIN THE FAVOUR OF GOD THAN TO ESCAPE FROM THE CURSES OF MAN. This conclusion must necessarily result from the previous considerations. Man cannot really curse or bless. Our whole future depends, not on man's opinions, but on God's treatment of us. Yet many men are in an agony of distress when they are visited with the disapproval of society, while they take no steps to secure the favour of God. This "fear of man bringeth a snare." It is a cowardly thing, and reveals great weakness. We need a more tough moral fibre. How grand was the courage of John Bright, when, after standing on the pinnacle of popular fame in his triumph over the corn laws, he suddenly stepped down into a position of isolation and unpopularity by denouncing the Crimean War!

IV. IT IS WORSE TO DESERVE THE CURSE THAT IS NOT GIVEN THAN TO RECEIVE THE CURSE THAT IS NOT DESERVED. It may be that vile conduct is concealed or condoned by a low tone of social morality; while right conduct is misinterpreted or condemned by a false standard. Men shudder at crimes when they are guilty of more sinful vices. Nevertheless, what is evil deserves execration, and for the quick conscience ill desert is more dreadful than public disapproval.

V. NO MALIGNITY CAN ULTIMATELY FRUSTRATE THE CAUSE OF TRUTH AND RIGHTEOUSNESS. The curse causeless was flung at Christ. It appeared to alight on his head and he died in gloom a shameful death. Then he rose and triumphed, and shook off the harmless curse in his joyous victory. The enemies of Christ have cursed his gospel. But they have failed to destroy it. On the contrary, it flourishes under the curses of bad men. Though Satan and all his hosts combined against it they could not stay its glorious progress.

VI. NO SATANIC CURSES CAN HURT THE TRUE DISCIPLE OF CHRIST. All the curses of hell cannot touch a hair of the head of him who is sheltered by the grace of Christ. Even the deserved curses of his sin are not to hurt the Christian, pardoned and renewed.

Vers. 4, 5.—*The wise treatment of folly.* These two verses need not be taken as mutually contradictory. They balance one another.

I. IT IS DIFFICULT TO ANSWER FOLLY. Whichever way we take it, we are in danger of blundering. If we meet it on its own ground we may share its shame. If we treat it soberly we may only incur ridicule. Both courses are beset with difficulties. This is especially true of folly in the biblical sense of the word, according to which it is not so much stupidity as wilful perverseness, light-hearted but depraved. It is not easy to find any point of attachment through which to influence this condition of soul. We need great grace in endeavouring to recover the thoughtless, foolish evil-livers. The sad may be approached through their troubles, but the frivolous elude our grasp.

II. IT IS A FATAL MISTAKE TO IMITATE THE FOLLY OF THE FOOLISH. St. Paul would become all things to all men in the hope that he might by any means save some. But he would never descend to frivolity; that would have been lowering to his true dignity as a servant of Christ. It is not necessary to be always grave. We may arouse and interest thoughtless people by using methods that would not be desirable or acceptable in the case of earnest men and women. Assuredly there is no virtue in pretence, pomposity, pride, a stilted style, etc. But it can never be right nor wise to say or do anything that would lower the majesty of truth and righteousness or degrade the ideal of Christian conduct. It may be possible to "draw" crowds by such more than questionable methods, but it is certainly impossible to "raise" them by such means, and what is the use of massing people together under pretence of religious work when our course of action is not likely to inspire the reverence which is the root of religion? It would be a far more successful method, as well as a more worthy one, to have much humbler aims in regard to numbers, but much higher ones in regard to the spiritual character of our work.

III. It is necessary to treat the foolish in regard to their folly. We are not to give back foolish answers to foolish questions, nor to attempt to attract the frivolous by frivolous methods. But, on the other hand, it is not wise, nor is it right, to treat foolish people as though they were serious and thoughtful. Thus, if questions are raised in mockery, it is our duty to treat them accordingly, and therefore to refuse to answer them. If it is evident that an inquirer is not in earnest it is not for his good nor for the honour of truth to meet him with the language which would be suitable for an honest truth-seeker. To do so would be to cast pearls before swine. It may be well to meet folly with gravity and to rebuke frivolity. This is answering a fool according to his folly, in the right way; for it is taking note of his folly and directing attention to it. Mockery should not go unchastised. Insincerity ought to be exposed. Pompous folly is sometimes best met by ridicule. Thus Erasmus castigated hypocritical pretences to piety with the keen rapier of his wit. It is wise to prick a wind-bag.

Ver. 12.—*Self-conceit.* I. Its character. Self-conceit is just the cherishing of an undue opinion of one's own worth, powers, character, or attainments. This is not pride, because pride need not make special pretences, so long as it asserts itself with dignity, while self-conceit is concerned with the actual contents of the mental life. This is not vanity, for it is not merely a desire to be admired; it may, and probably will, stimulate this desire; but possibly it will be too proud to cherish it. Self-conceit is absorbed with an inordinate conception of its possessor's own inner wealth. It makes a weak man believe that he can carry the gates of Gaza like a second Samson, and a foolish man think that he can solve the riddle of the Sphinx. It is profoundly honest in this. No Don Quixote could be more grave in the service of an illusion than the self-conceited man in pursuit of his hopeless aims.

II. Its mischief. 1. *It blinds to self-knowledge.* It stands between a man and a true vision of his condition and character. It substitutes its own inventions for the facts of his inner life. Instead of seeing himself as he is, the conceited man only sees himself as he is painted by his besetting weakness. He mistakes the flattering picture for a photographic likeness. 2. *It shuts the door on true knowledge.* The conceited man will not learn, for he will not believe in his own ignorance. He starts with a consciousness of omniscience. 3. *It refuses to follow guidance.* In his exalted opinion of himself the poor deluded self-worshipper declines to be guided by those who are far more capable than he is. The captain dispenses with the pilot, the patient doctors himself, the suitor conducts his own case; in religious matters the self-conceited man prefers his own notions to the teachings of prophets and apostles. His "views" out-weigh Bible truths.

III. Its causes. 1. *It springs from self-love.* Dwelling much on one's own excellences generates an inordinate conception of them. Love is a flatterer, and self-love flatters self. 2. *It is nourished in ignorance.* It is usually through a lack of perception of the narrowness of the horizon that the self-conceited man believes so much in himself. His village is the world. In looking at a panorama the picture seems to retreat into a great distance, whereas it is but a few feet from the observer. 3. *It is sheltered by indolence.* The conceited man will not rouse himself to inquire.

IV. Its remedies. These must follow the diagnosis of the disease and its causes. 1. *Enlarged knowledge.* As knowledge grows, the consciousness of ignorance increases. 2. *Failure.* Give it time, and self-conceit will work its own cure, through humiliating disasters. 3. *Grace.* A vision of the truth and righteousness of God and an endowment of the grace of Divine wisdom and goodness will humble a man into shame at his own previous self-conceit.   So Nicodemus was humbled when Christ sent him back to his cradle.

Ver. 13.—" *A lion in the way.*"   I. INDOLENCE CREATES DIFFICULTIES.   The hindrance is not real; it is purely imaginary.   The lion is not *in the way,* but in the fancy of the slothful man.   If a man is not in earnest in undertaking any work, he is certain to picture to himself insuperable obstacles.   Thus missionary enterprises are discouraged by those who have no missionary zeal.   The call of Christ to service and sacrifice is shirked by men whose inventive ingenuity has manufactured unsound excuses.   The course of the Christian life is forsaken by some who see it beset with dangers that only spring out of their own reluctance to deny themselves, take up their cross and follow Christ.   Often when the slothful man cries, "There is a lion in the way," it is a lie; there is no lion.

II. INDOLENCE IS COWARDLY.   It is possible that the indolent person really believes that the beast of the forest has actually invaded the city, is indeed prowling about its streets.   He shrinks from a danger that he truly fears.   Perhaps there is real danger. We do meet with difficulties and dangers in life.   Threatening lions roar on the devoted servant of Christ.   But then the true-hearted man will be brave to face difficulty, and only the coward will shrink and fail.

III. DANGER IS NO EXCUSE FOR INDOLENCE.   If there be a lion in the street it may be all the more incumbent on a true man to go out of his house.   For the lion has no right to be in the city.   He should be slain forthwith.   To leave him there at large is to yield to him.   Are the streets to be given up to the daring intruder because no one is bold enough to face him?   Meanwhile he may work fearful havoc.   There may be children in the street.   While the idle coward bolts and bars his doors and sits shivering in his house, the helpless little ones are left unprotected, a sure prey for the fierce brute.   To shrink from the task of expelling the lion is to be guilty of shameful negligence.   Because of the hindrances and difficulties of Christ's work cowardly and idle people permit the souls of their fellow-men and the poor ignorant children of miserable degraded families to be destroyed.

IV. DANGER IS OVERCOME BY BEING FACED.   Perhaps the lion's roar is worse than his bite.   Who can tell but that he is a coward and will turn tail directly he is faced? Possibly, like Bunyan's lions, he is chained.   But we shall never know till we go boldly up to him.   Many apparent dangers are but empty threats.   There are difficulties that need only to be confronted to vanish.   The valiant Christian soldier will find that his enemies will give way before the "sword of the Spirit."

V. FOR THE INDOLENT MAN THERE IS A LION IN THE HOUSE.   While he shrinks with terror from venturing forth there is greater danger at home.   The hypochondriacal patient who dreads meeting the chill of fresh air for fear of catching cold becomes a martyr to dyspepsia at home.   The idle man is slain by his own indolence.   Satan, who goes about as a roaring lion seeking whom he may devour, is kept out by no locks and finds his victims in their most private retreats.

Ver. 20.—*The fuel of strife.*   I. STRIFE WILL DIE OUT IF IT BE NOT SUPPLIED WITH FRESH FUEL.   The fire will not burn after the stock of wood is all exhausted.   The quarrel will not continue if the angry feelings that rage in it are not fed by fresh provocations.   The unhappy experience of most quarrels is that these provocations are too readily supplied.   But if one party to a quarrel really wishes for peace, he can often obtain it by simply abstaining from maintaining his contention.   His opponent will tire of a one-sided war.   Patience, meekness, and quiet endurance will thus make peace in the end.   This was Christ's method.   He brought peace by peaceably submitting to wrong.

II. STRIFE IS TOO OFTEN MAINTAINED WITH THE FRESH FUEL ADDED BY STRANGERS. If the two principals in a quarrel were left to themselves, they might tire of perpetual disputes.   But a third party interferes, not as a peacemaker, but to take one side; or to meddle in pure mischief-making, delighting to stir up the embers of strife; or to show his own power and importance.   This conduct is the opposite of that of one who serves the Prince of Peace.

III. TALE-BEARING ADDS FUEL TO STRIFE.   1. *It may be true.*   We may hear something of one party in a quarrel which we know to be correct, and report it to the other, though it was never intended to be repeated. This rouses angry passions and renews the old battle. Immense harm is done by merely inconsiderate gossip. When an element of spite is added and there is a deliberate attempt to aggravate a quarrel, the conduct of the tale-bearer is simply diabolical. 2. *It is likely to be exaggerated.* Most tales, like snowballs, grow as they proceed. Passing from one to another, they are unintentionally exaggerated. Surmise and inference are mixed up with the original narrative as part of the story. Rhetorical point is gained at the expense of accuracy.

IV. It is the duty of the Christian to allay strife. His should be the blessedness of the peacemaker (Matt. v. 9). If we have Christian love we shall desire to do this, for charity covers a multitude of sins (1 Pet. iv. 8). Immense harm would be prevented by the merely negative course of refraining from repeating all words that have the slightest tendency to provoke ill will between other people. There is virtue in reticence. Silence here is indeed golden. But sometimes we should go further, and endeavour to make the best of people to one another, and so to heal quarrels.

V. No tale-bearer can revive the strife between the soul and God. If there be no more fuel, this will vanish. God desires to be reconciled with his children. If they will but lay down their arms, the old quarrel will cease at once. 1. *God knows the worst of us.* He knows all. Therefore he never makes discoveries that will rouse his wrath against our pardoned past. 2. *He cannot be misled by deceivers.* Tale-bearers may malign our character before men, never before God. 3. *The only thing to continue our strife with God is to continue our rebellious lives.* While we seek peace, peace is secure.

Ver. 27.—*Caught in one's own snare.* One man may be supposed to have dug a pit in some dark place in the road, or to have concealed it by covering it with boughs and earth—like an Indian tiger-trap—so that he may catch some wild animal, or perhaps make a prisoner or a victim of his enemy. Then, not heeding its whereabouts, he falls into his own snare. Another may be rolling a stone against his enemy, when it falls back and crushes the author of the mischief. Consider first some cases in which these things might happen, and then the principle that underlies them.

I. Instances. 1. *The deceiver.* The pit is a snare. It is meant to deceive. Those who deceive others are likely to be deceived. They brand and blind the faculty of truth. They acclimatize themselves in a zone of falsehood. In the very belief that they think this well for them, they prove themselves deluded. 2. *The swindler.* This man may entrap unwary folk who trust his offers, and at first he may thrive and fatten on his ill-gotten gains; but his success is almost sure to be short-lived. Swindlers rarely prosper till old age. 3. *The tempter.* One who imitates the work of the devil may have the devil's wicked triumph over weakness and ignorance. He may succeed in luring his victims to shame and ruin, and he may find a hellish glee in the awful ease with which he overcomes their virtue. But he is a short-sighted self-deceiver. There is a pit prepared for the devil and his angels, and the tempter is one of the latter. Satan makes hell, and every tempter prepares his own pit of destruction. 4. *The opponent of Christ.* The Jews rejected their Lord and laid snares for catching him. He was keen to reply, and turned the shame on the head of each party in succession —Pharisee, Sadducee, Herodian. In the end they accomplished his death. But they were punished in the frightful overthrow of their city. The world's rejection of Christ would mean the world's ruin. Every soul that plots against the kingdom of heaven unwarily plots for its own undoing.

II. The underlying principle. This principle is that sin brings its own retribution. There is no need for the conception of a *Deus ex machinâ*. No heralds of justice are wanted to proclaim the guilt of the offender; no heavenly executioners with flaming swords are required to bring swift vengeance on the guilty. If only the foolish sinner is left to himself, he will certainly reap the fatal consequences of his wickedness. Sin is naturally fatal. "Whatsoever a man soweth, that shall he also reap. For he that soweth to the flesh shall of the flesh reap corruption." The vile harvest of death grows in the soil of the man's own life. He is his own executioner. No doubt this terrible fact is based on a Divine decree that lies deeply embedded in the very constitution of the universe. Therefore, as the forest traveller unconsciously makes a circuit and returns to his old camp-fire, so the sinner comes back to his own evil deeds, but to find them now as snares to entrap him and stones to crush him.

HOMILIES BY VARIOUS AUTHORS.

Vers. 1—3.—*Sayings against folly.* I. THE INAPTNESS OF HONOURS TO THE FOOLISH MAN. (Ver. 1.) According to Jerome, it is something unheard of or impossible to ex erience, rain in the harvest-time (see 1 Sam. xii. 17, *sqq.*). The advancement of the fool appears to all men unseasonable, even shocking. High place reveals the more clearly the smallness of small souls. Honour is the just reward of virtue and ability. Let men be virtuous and wise, that they may be honoured, and that external distinctions may not rather invite the contempt of observers.
II. THE HARMLESSNESS OF UNMERITED CURSES. (Ver. 2.) Aimless as the wayward flight of sparrow or swallow, they fail to strike their object (see that in 2 Sam. xvi. 5, *sqq.*; 1 Kings ii. 8). "I would not hesitate to say," observes Trench, "that the great glory of proverbs in their highest aspect, and that which makes them so full of blessing to those who cordially accept them, is the conviction, of which they are full, that, despite all appearances to the contrary, this world is God's world, and not the world of the devil or of those wicked men who may be prospering for the hour. *A lie has no legs.*" Truth may be temporarily depressed, but cannot fall to the ground (Ps. xciv. 15; 2 Cor. iv. 9). But as for the lie; its priests may set it on its feet again after it has once fallen before the presence of the truth, yet this will all be labour in vain; it will only be, like Dagon, again to fall.
III. FOLLY INVITES ITS OWN CHASTISEMENT. (Ver. 3.) The instincts of flesh and blood show like untamed and unbroken-in animals, especially in idleness, and demand the like severe treatment. "Our flesh and sense must be subdued," not flattered and fed. If we do not practise self-control, God will administer his chastisements.—J.

Vers. 4—12.—*Discussion of folly and its treatment.* I. HOW TO ANSWER THE FOOL. (Vers. 4, 5.) 1. *Not according* to his folly; *i.e.* so chiming in with his nonsense that you become as he is. Do not descend into the arena with a fool. Preserve self-respect, and observe the conduct of the Saviour when to folly he "answered not again." 2. *According* to his folly; that is, with the sharp and cutting reply his folly invites and deserves. We have also examples of this in the conduct of our Lord; *e.g.* in reference to the inquiry of the Jews concerning the purging of the temple, which he answered by a reference to John's baptism (Matt. xxi. 25, etc.). The twofold treatment of the fool reminds that the spirit and motive must determine the act, and that opposite methods may be equally good at different times.
II. THE FOOL IS NOT TO BE TRUSTED. (Vers. 6, 7.) 1. *With messages and commissions.* (Ver. 6.) He who does so is like one who amputates his own limbs, deprives himself of the means of gaining his object, or who voluntarily drinks of an evil brewage. 2. *His words are not to be trusted.* (Ver. 7.) Sayings in the mouth of the fool are purposeless and pointless, when they even do no harm. Fools will not be prudent, says Luther, and yet would ever play the part of wise men. "A wise saying doth as ill become a fool as dancing does a cripple." The wise and weighty saying becomes in his mouth a jest. He who would instruct others in Divine wisdom must first have embraced it himself. Solemnity may be a cover for a sot; and the greatest folly is to impose on one's self.
III. THE FOOL IS NOT TO BE HONOURED. (Ver. 8.) To lift him out of his place by compliments or honours is as inapt as to lay a jewel upon a common heap of stones. The sling makes the stone bound in it an implement of death; and to flatter the undeserving brings disgrace upon one's self. It is like putting sword or pistol into a madman's hand. But the other interpretation is better. Ver. 9 shows how mischievous are even good things in the lips and hands of those who only abuse them. Luther quaintly says, "If a drunkard sports with a briar, he scratches more with it than he allows to smell the roses on it; so does a fool often work more mischief with the Scripture than good." (The meaning of ver. 10 is so obscure, it must be left to exegetes; it appears to coincide with the foregoing—the fool is not to be trusted.)

IV. The fool is incorrigible. (Vers. 11, 12; see 2 Pet. ii. 22.) He returns to his exploded nonsense, his often-repeated fallacies; and to his exposed errors of conduct (Matt. xii. 45; John v. 14; Heb. vi. 4—8). Relapses into sin, as into sickness, are dangerous and deadly. "A raw sin is like a blow to a broken leg, a burden to a crushed arm." The cause of these relapses and this incorrigibility is pointed out— deep-rooted self-conceit. This is the fruitful mother of follies. Let none deem himself perfect, but let every one cultivate humility as his dearest possession. God giveth grace to the lowly, but resisteth the proud and them that are wise in their own conceits.—J.

Vers. 13—16.—*The vice of idleness.* I. It is full of excuses. (Ver. 13.) There is always some pretext for evading duty, however frivolous and absurd, with the idle man. Idleness is the parent of almost every sin; here of cowardice. He who excuses, accuses himself. Every manly act of exertion is imagined to be full of danger by the lazy mind. The sluggard does not see what danger of another and deadlier kind there is in stagnation. Danger is the brave man's opportunity, difficulty the lion in the way, by victory over which he may earn the laurel of victory and gain the joy of new conscious power.

II. It loves repose and self-indulgence. (Ver. 14.) As the door swings perpetually upon its hinges, without moving a step from its fixed position, so with the sluggard. He "turns round and round, with dull stupidity, like the dyer's horse in the ring" (ch. xix. 24). How often the *cannot* of the slave of vice or evil habit only disguises the *will not* of the sloth-eaten heart! To make mere rest our life-object is to contend against the order of God.

III. It hates exertion. (Ver. 15.) Even the most necessary exertion may become by habit distasteful. To take his hand from his bosom, even merely to reach after the bread of life, is too much labour for him. And thus his life, instead of being a continual feast, sinks into spiritual indigence and starvation. "The idle soul shall suffer hunger."

IV. It breeds conceit and folly. (Ver. 16.) This is the strange irony of the vice, that the empty hand shall fancy itself full of wisdom. But such fancies are the very growth of the soil of indolence. It is impossible to make such a one understand his ignorance, for it requires knowledge to perceive it; and he who can perceive it has it not (Jeremy Taylor). The evil may creep into the Church. One may fall into an idle and passive piety, content with sitting still, hearing, praying, singing, from one end of the year to the other, without advancing one step in the practical Christian life (1 Thess. v. 6).—J.

Vers. 17—19.—*Wanton petulance.* I. Meddling in others' quarrels. (Ver. 17.) By a very homely image the folly of this is marked. To interfere in disputes which do not concern one is to get hurt one's self. No doubt the proverb admits of a very selfish application. We may excuse indifference to right on such a plea. But a true instinct of Christian justice and love will find a middle course. We should be sure of our *call to act* before we meddle in others' affairs. It is rare that it can be our duty to volunteer the office of judge. Benevolent neutrality is generally our most helpful attitude.

II. Making sport of mischief. (Vers. 18, 19.) There is an ape-like line of mischief in human nature that needs to be watched. Amusing in trifling matters, it may, if encouraged, fly at high game. He that purposely deceives his neighbour under colour of a jest is no less prejudicial to him than a lunatic that doth wrong out of frenzy and distraction (Bishop Hall). The habit of teasing should be corrected in children. What seems comparatively harmless in itself at first may readily become a habit and harden into a vice. It is in the little delicacies of daily life, no less than in the greatest matters, that we are called to practise the golden rule. We must consider the *effect*, as well as the *intention*, of our actions; for, as in the old fable, what is sport to us may be grievous hurt to another.—J.

Vers. 20—28.—*Spite, cunning, and deceit.* I. The tale-bearer and mischief-maker. (Vers. 20—22.) 1. *His inflammatory character.* (Vers. 20, 21.) He keeps alive quarrels which, but for his vice, would die down for want of fuel. It is easy to fire the imagination with tales of evil, not so easy to quench the flames thus kindled. If the character is odious, let us beware of countenancing it by opening our ears to scandal. Personal gossip has in our day become an offence in the public press. But were there no receivers, there would be no thieves. If we cannot stop the scandal-monger's mouth, we can stop our own ears; and "let him see in our face that he has no room in our heart." 2. *The pain he causes.* (Ver. 22.) Slander is deadly—it "outvenoms all the worms of Nile." "A whispered word may stab a gentle heart." "What weapon can be nearer to nothing than the sting of a wasp? yet what a painful wound may it give! The scarce-visible point how it envenoms and rankles and swells up the flesh! The tenderness of the part adds much to the grief." If God has given us a sting, or turn for satire, may we use it for its proper work—to cover evil with contempt, and folly with ridicule, and not at the devilish instigation of envy and spite. Let us dread and discourage the character of the amusing social slanderer.

II. THE BAD HEART. (Vers. 23—25.) 1. *It may be varnished over, but is still the bad heart.* It is like the common sherd covered with impure silver, the common wood with veneer. The *burning lips* seem here to mean glowing professions of friend-ship, like the kiss of Judas. 2. *Duplicity is the sign of the bad heart.* The dissembler smiles, and murders while he smiles. The fair face hides what the false heart doth know.

> "Neither man nor angel can discern
> Hypocrisy, the only evil that walks
> Invisible, except to God alone.
>   Oft, though wisdom wakes, suspicion sleeps
> At wisdom's gate, and to simplicity
> Resigns her charge, while goodness thinks no ill
> Where no ill seems."

3. *The need of prudence and reserve.* "Trust not him that seems to be a saint." Indeed, it is an error to place perfect trust in anything human or finite. But the special warning here is against suffering flattery to blind us to the real character of one who has once been revealed in his true colours.

III. THE EXPOSURE OF WICKEDNESS. (Vers. 26, 27.) Vain is the attempt of men to conceal for any length of time their real character. What they say and what they do not say, do and do not do, reveals them sooner or later. And the revelation brings its retribution. The intriguer falls into his own pit, is crushed beneath the stone he set in motion. Curses come home to roost; the biter is bitten; and the villain suffers from the recoil of his own weapon. This appears also to be the sense of ver. 28. Though a lie has no legs, it has wings, and may fly far and wide, but it "hates its own master" (according to one rendering), and flies back to perch on his shoulder and betray him to his ruin.—J.

Vers. 1, 6, 9.—*Honouring the unworthy.* There are different ways in which we may honour men, whether the wise or the unwise. We may (1) put them in positions of rank and dignity, in which men bow (or fall) before them (ch. xxv. 26); or (2) entrust to them offices of importance and responsibility (ver. 6); or (3) allow them to under-take the work of public instruction (vers. 7, 9). It is only the wise and good that we should honour in these ways. Unfortunately, in the confusion and perversity which sin has wrought in the world, it often happens that it is not the wise man but the fool who is chosen for the post or the task. How foolish it is to honour the unworthy is seen if we consider—

I. ITS PAINFUL INCONGRUITY. "As snow in summer, and as rain in harvest, so honour is not seemly for a fool." To hear a fool attempting lamely to discourse wisdom is suggestive of the motion of a man whose "legs are not equal." For the post of honour to be occupied by one who has disgraced himself by guilty foolishness, or who has neglected his opportunities, and is empty-minded and incapable, this is something which is manifestly unfitting; it offends our sense of the appropriate and the becoming. Shamelessness and honour, stupidity and responsibility, have no sort of agreement; they are miserably and painfully ill-mated.

II. ITS POSITIVE REVERSAL OF THE TRUE ORDER OF THINGS. The fool ought to be *positively dishonoured.* He need not be actually despised. There is too much of capacity, of indefinitely great possibility in every human spirit to make it right for us to despise our brethren. We are to "honour all men" because they *are* men, because they are, with us, the offspring of God, and may be his children in the highest and deepest sense (1 Pet. ii. 17). Yet is it our clear duty to see that folly is dishonoured, that it is made to take the lowest place, that the man who does shameful things is put to shame before his fellows. Let those who dishonour God, disregard their fellows, and disgrace themselves, feel the edge of holy indignation; they should be smitten in faithfulness that they may be healed in mercy.

III. ITS INJURIOUSNESS. To honour the fool by giving him rank, or responsibility, or the opportunity of speech, is: 1. *To injure him.* For it is to make him "think himself to be something [or, 'somebody'] when he is nothing [or, 'nobody']." It is to fasten him in his present position of unworthiness, and thus to do him the most serious harm we can inflict upon him. The flatterer of the fool is his deadliest enemy. 2. *To injure the community.* It is "to drink damage," to bind a stone in a sling that is most likely to hit and hurt our neighbour, to smart with a wound from some sharp thorn. The foolish, the guilty, the wrong in heart and mind, do serious harm when they hold the reins of office or sit in the seat of honour. Their very elevation is itself an encouragement to folly and vice, and a discouragement to wisdom and virtue. They administer injustice instead of justice. They let all things down instead of raising them up. They advance those who are like-minded with themselves, and neglect those who deserve honour and promotion. Speaking from "the chair," they make falsity and foolishness to appear to be truth and wisdom, and so they mislead the minds and darken the lives and betray the souls of men.—C.

Vers. 2, 3.—*What to fear.* Fear enters largely into human experience. It is an emotion which is sometimes stamped upon the countenance so that it is legible to all who look upon it. Under its baleful shadow some men have spent a large part of their life. We may well ask what to fear and how to be delivered from its evil. There are some—

I. THINGS THAT HAVE BEEN, BUT NEED NOT HAVE BEEN, FEARED. 1. Men and women have dreaded "the evil eye" of their fellow-men. They have been alarmed by evil omens, by signs and portents that have boded misfortune or calamity, by presentiments of approaching death, etc. All these things have been purely imaginary, and they have added largely and lamentably to the burdens and sorrows of existence. It is painful to think how many thousands, how many millions of mankind have had their hearts troubled and their lives darkened, or even blighted, by fears that have been wholly needless—fears of some evil which has never been more or nearer to them in fact than the shadow of the bird's wing as it circles in the air or flies away into the forest. 2. Of these imaginary evils that which is conspicuous among others is *the curse of the wicked*—"the curse that is causeless." The bitter imprecation of the heart that is full of unholy hatred may make the spirit quiver at the moment, but its effect should be momentary. Let reason do its rightful work and the anxiety will disappear. What possible harm can come of the bad man's curse? He has no power to bring about its fulfilment. Not in his hand are the laws of nature, the issues of events, the future of the holy. Let the feeling of apprehension pass away with a reflection that all these things are in the hand of the Supreme. Let it be as the wing of the flitting bird, out of sight in a moment. Let it be "as the idle wind which we regard not."

II. THINGS THAT MUST SOMETIMES BE BRAVED. Although we may entirely disregard the malediction of the guilty and the godless, we are obliged to attach some importance to their active opposition. When imprecation passes into determined hostility, we have then to lay our account with it. We have then to consider what we must do to meet it. But if we are obviously and consciously in the right, we can afford to brave and breast it. We are not alone. God is with us. Almighty power, irresistible wisdom, Divine sympathy, are with us; we may go on our way, doing our duty and bearing our testimony, fearless of our foes and of all their machinations. There is, however—

III. ONE THING FROM WHICH IT IS NATURAL TO SHRINK; the enmity of a human heart. We may make light of the weapons of our adversaries; we may be fearless of their designs and their doings; but from the feeling of hatred in their hearts we do well to shrink. It is far from being nothing that human hearts are actually hating us, malevolently wishing us evil, prepared to rejoice in our sorrow, in our downfall. We should not surely be entirely unaffected by the thought. It is a consideration that should move us to *pity* and to *prayer*. We should have a sorrowful feeling that ends in prayer that God would turn their heart, that leads also to the first available opportunity of winning them to a better mind. And there are those who should cherish—

IV. ONE SALUTARY FEAR. (Ver. 3.) Those who are wrong in heart and life may dread the coming down upon them of that rod of correction which is found to be the only weapon that will avail.—C.

Vers. 4, 5.—*The two ways of meeting folly.* They are these—

I. THE CAREFUL AVOIDANCE OF REPEATING IT. (Ver. 4.) Only too often men allow the foolish to draw them into a repetition of their folly, so that one fool makes another. Folly is contagious, and we are all in some danger of catching it. This is the case with us when: 1. We let the word of anger provoke us to a responsive bitterness; then we are " overcome of evil " instead of " overcoming evil with good " (Rom. xii. 21). 2. We allow one exaggeration to lead us into another. When two men are in conversation, one is often tempted to lead the other into statements that exceed the truth; and exaggeration is only another name for falsehood. 3. We accept a foolish challenge. The young, more particularly, are fond of exciting one another to deeds of folly, and it often requires courage, steadfastness, even nobility of spirit, to refuse to follow the leading of unwisdom. 4. We indulge in idle gossip; letting the first statement about our neighbour, which is unfounded and slanderous, conduct us to idle and mischievous talk in the same foolish strain. 5. We permit ourselves to follow the lead of the man whose thoughts and words are in the direction of a doubtful, or a dishonourable, or a defiling region. In all these cases it behoves us "not to answer a fool according to his folly," to be silent altogether; or else to break away into another and worthier strain; or even to " take up our parable" against that which has been said in our hearing. But here we reach the other method, viz.—

II. THE WISE CONDEMNATION OF IT. Folly is sometimes to be rebuked (ver. 5). Silence on our part would be mistaken and abused; it would be regarded as acquiescence or as incapacity to meet what has been said, and folly would go on its way, its empty head held higher than before. We must use discretion here; must understand " when only silence suiteth best," and also when silence would be a mistake and even a sin. The times to answer a fool according to his folly, *i.e.* in the way which is demanded by his folly, are surely these: 1. When ignorance needs to be exposed. 2. When pretentiousness and presumptuousness want to be put down. 3. When irreverence or actual profanity requires to be rebuked and silenced. 4. When vice or cruelty deserves to be smitten and abashed. Then let the true and brave man speak; let the name and the honour of his holy Saviour, let the cause of truth and righteousness, let the interests of the young and the poor and the weak unloose his tongue, and let him pour forth his indignation. In so doing he will be following in the footsteps of the Lord of truth and love, and of the noblest and worthiest of his followers.—C.

Ver. 13.—(See homily on ch. xxii. 13.)—C.

Vers. 18, 19.—*The condemnation of sin.* We have here, in a few strong sentences, a most forcible presentation of the evil and the guiltiness of wrong-doing. We see—

I. ITS UGLIEST FEATURE—DECEPTION. " The man that deceiveth his neighbour " is not here simply the man who overreaches his customer or who introduces a low cunning into his business; he is rather the man who deliberately misleads his acquaintance, his " friend," and induces him to do that which is unwise and unworthy. He is the man who knows better himself, but who indoctrinates the inexperienced and the unwary with the principles, or rather the vain imaginations, of folly. He stoops so low that he does not hesitate: 1. To recommend forbidden pleasure as an object worthy of pursuit, though he knows well (or ought to know, if he can learn from experience) that guilty gratification is the very costliest thing that any man can buy. 2. To persuade men that an unprincipled life is a profitable life, as if " a man's life consisted in the abundance of the things which he possessed; " as if a life without integrity were not the most utter and miserable failure. 3. To recommend selfishness and indulgence as a condition of liberty, when in fact it *is* the beginning and is sure to end in the most humiliating bondage.   4. To represent the service of God and of man as a drudgery and a dreariness, when in truth it is the height of human nobility and the very essence of enjoyment.   5. To prevail upon the young to snatch at honour and success instead of honestly labouring and patiently waiting for it.   There is no more painful and repulsive thing under heaven than the sight of experience and maturity breathing its fallacies, its sophisms, its delusions, into the ear of inexperience and innocency.

II. ITS BITTER FRUIT.   What do these delusions bring forth?   The deceiver is a man who "scatters firebrands, arrows, and death."   The ultimate consequences of the "deceitfulness of sin" are sad indeed; they are: 1. Impoverishment in circumstance. 2. The loss of the love and the honour of the wise and good.   3. Remorse of soul and, frequently, if not usually, the departure of self-respect.   4. Hopelessness and death.   5. The extension of the evil which has been imbibed to those around; becoming a source of poisonous error, a fountain of evil and wrong and misery.

III. ITS PRACTICAL INSANITY.   The fool who does wantonly scatter the seeds of deadly delusions in the minds of men is "as a madman."   There is no small measure of insanity in sin.   Sin is a spiritual disease; it is our spiritual nature in a state of complete derangement, our mind filled with false ideas, our heart affected with delusive hopes and fears.   There is no soundness, no wholeness or health about us, so far as we are under the dominion of sin.   We do things which we could not possibly have done if only reason and rectitude held sway within us.

IV. ITS POOR AND PITIFUL APOLOGY.   "He saith, Am not I in sport?"   When a man deludes and betrays, when he wrongs and ruins a human soul, and then makes a joke of it, he only adds meanness to his transgression.   Who, outside the bottomless pit, can see any fun in a blighted life, in a wounded and bleeding spirit, in a soiled and stained soul, in the ruin of reputation, in the blasting of a noble hope, in the shadow of spiritual death?   Human life and character and destiny are infinitely serious things; they are not to be the butt of fools.—C.

Ver. 22.—(See homily on ch. xvii. 9.)—C.

Vers. 23—28.—*On guard.*   Unfortunately, we have to treat men as we find them, not as we wish that they were and as their Creator meant them to be.   We are compelled to learn caution as we pass on our way.

I. OUR FIRST DUTY AND ITS NATURAL REWARD.   Our first duty, natural to the young and the unsophisticated, is to be frank, open-minded, sincere, trustful; to say all that is in our heart, and to expect others to do the same; to believe that men mean what they say and say what they mean.   And the reward of this simplicity and truthfulness on our part is an ingenuous, an unsuspicious spirit, a spirit as far removed as possible from that of cunning, of artifice, of worldliness.

II. THE CORRECTION OF EXPERIENCE.   All too soon we discover that we cannot act on this theory without being wounded and hurt.   We find that what looks like pure silver may be nothing better than "earthenware of the coarsest kind lacquered over with silver dross."   Behind the lips that burn and breathe affection for us and interest in us is a wicked heart in which are "seven abominations," in which dwells every evil imagination.   We find that those who affect to be our friends when they stand in our presence are in fact our bitterest and most active enemies.   We discover that our words, spoken in good faith and purity of heart, are misrepresented, and are made a sword to smite us.   Experience compels caution, reticence, sometimes absolute silence.

III. THE TWO MAIN EVILS AGAINST WHICH TO GUARD.   These are: 1. *Fair speaking which is false.*   The false words that are ostensibly spoken in our interest, by one that means us harm; words which would lead to trust and expectation when we should be alive with solicitude and alert to avoid the danger which impends.   By these our treasure, our position, our friendship, our reputation, our happiness, may be seriously endangered.   2. *Flattery.*   The invention and utterance of that which is not felt at all, or the careless and perhaps well-meant exaggeration of a feeling which *is* entertained in the heart.   Few things are more potent for harm than flattery.   (1) It is readily received.   (2) It is carefully treasured; men's self-love prompts them to accept and to retain that which, if it were of an opposite character, they would reject.   (3) It is harmful in three different directions: (*a*) It gives a wrong impression of our estate, and may lead to financial "ruin" (ver. 28). (*b*) It encourages an over-estimate of our capacity, and may lead to our undertaking that for which we are incompetent, and thus to an humiliating and distressing failure. (*c*) It engenders a false idea of our personal worth, and may lead to spiritual infatuation, and thus to the *ruin of ourselves*.

IV. THE DUTY AND THE WISDOM OF WARINESS. As these things are so, as human society does hold a large number of dissemblers (ver. 24), as it is possible that the next acquaintance we make may be an illustration of this sad fact, it follows that absolute trustfulness is a serious mistake. We must be on our guard. We must not open our hearts too freely. We must know men before we trust them. We must cultivate the art of penetration, of reading character. To be able to distinguish between the true and the false in this great sphere is a very large part of wisdom. Next to knowing God, and to acquainting ourselves with our own hearts, is the duty of studying men and discerning between the lacquered potsherd and the pure silver.

V. THE DOOM OF DECEIT. To be rigorously exposed, to be unsparingly denounced, to be utterly ashamed (vers. 26, 27).—C.

EXPOSITION.

CHAPTER XXVII.

Vers. 1—6.—These verses are grouped in pairs, each two being connected in subject.

Ver. 1.—**Boast not thyself of to-morrow.** He boasts himself (ch. xxv. 14) of to-morrow who counts upon it presumptuously, settles that he will do this or that, as if his life was in his own power, and he could make sure of time. This is blindness and arrogance. **For thou knowest not what a day may bring** forth. Our Lord gave a lesson on this matter in the parable of the rich fool (Luke xii.); and an analogous warning, based on our verse, is given by St. James (iv. 13, etc.). On this topic moralists and poets are always dilating. Very familiar are the words of Horace (' Carm.,' iv. 7. 17)—

"Quis scit, an adjiciant hodiernæ crastina
    summæ
Tempora di superi?"

Euripides, ' Alc.,' 783—

Οὐκ ἔστι θνητῶν ὅστις ἐξεπίσταται
Τὴν αὔριον μέλλουσαν εἰ βιώσεται.
Τὸ τῆς τύχης γὰρ ἀφανὲς οἷ προβήσεται,
Κἄστ' οὐ διδακτόν, οὐδ' ἁλίσκεται τέχνῃ.

"Every day in thy life," says the Arab, "is a leaf in thy history." Seneca wrote (' Thyest.,' 621)—

"Nemo tam divos habuit faventes,
    Crastinum ut possit sibi polliceri,
Res deus nostras celeri citatas
    Turbine versat."

There is the adage, "Nescis quid serus vesper vehat." The LXX. has, as at ch. iii. 28, "Thou knowest not what the next day (ἡ ἐπιοῦσα) shall bring forth." (For the expression, ἡ ἐπιοῦσα, comp. Acts vii. 26; xvi. 11.)

Ver. 2.—**Let another man praise thee, and**

not thine own mouth; Septuagint, "Let thy neighbour (ὁ πέλας) laud thee." **A stranger;** נָכְרִי, properly, "an unknown person from an unknown country;" but, like זר in the former hemistich, used indifferently for "another" (see on ch. ii. 16). "If I honour myself," said our Lord (John viii. 54), "my honour is nothing" And as St. Paul testifies (2 Cor. x. 18), "Not he that commendeth himself is approved, but whom the Lord commendeth."

Ὑπὲρ σεαυτοῦ μὴ φράσῃς ἐγκώμια,

said the Greek gnomist; and

Φίλων ἔπαινον μᾶλλον ἢ σαυτοῦ λέγε.

And a trite maxim runs, "In ore proprio laus sordet;" and an English one decides, "He who praises himself is a debtor to others." Delitzsch quotes a German proverb (which loses the jingle in translation), "Eigen-lob stinkt, Freundes Lob hinkt, fremdes Lob klingt," "Self-praise stinks, friends' praise limps, strangers' praise sounds."

Ver. 3.—**A stone is heavy, and the sand weighty;** literally, *heaviness of a stone, weight of the sand.* The substantives are more forcible than the corresponding adjectives would be; the versions rather weaken the form of the expression by rendering, *Grave est saxum,* etc. The quality in the things mentioned is weight, heaviness, ponderosity; that is what we are bidden regard. **A fool's wrath is heavier than them both.** The ill temper and anger of a headstrong fool, which he vents on those about him, are harder to endure than any material weight is to carry. Ecclus. xxii. 15, "Sand and salt and a mass of iron are easier to bear than a man without understanding." The previous verse asks, "What is heavier than lead? and what is the name thereof [*i.e.* of the heavier thing], but a fool?" Job speaks of his grief being heavier than the sand of the sea (Job vi. 3).

Ver. 4.—**Wrath is cruel, and anger is outrageous.** Again substantives are used, as in ver. 3, "Cruelty of wrath, and overflowing of anger." Figure to yourself the fierceness and cruelty of a sudden excitement of anger, or the bursting forth of passion which, like a flood, carries all before it; these may be violent for a time, yet they will subside when they have spent themselves. **But who is able to stand before envy?** or rather, *jealousy*. The reference is not so much to the general feeling of envy as to the outrag d love in the relation of husband and wife (see ch. vi. 34, and note there). Cant. viii. 6, " Love is strong as death; jealousy is cruel as the grave: the flashes thereof are flashes of fire, a very vehement flame." Such jealousy does not blaze forth in some sudden outbreak, and then die away; it lives and broods and feeds itself hourly with fresh aliment, and is ready to act at any moment, hesitating at no means to gratify itself, and sacrificing without mercy its victim. Septuagint, " Pitiless is wrath, and sharp is anger; but jealousy (ζῆλος) submits to nothing."

Ver. 5.—**Open rebuke is better than secret love.** Love that is hidden and never discloses itself in acts of self-denial or generosity, especially that which from fear of offending does not rebuke a friend, nor speak the truth in love (Eph. iv. 15), when there is good reason for such openness—such disguised love is worse, more objectionable, less beneficial, than the plain speaking which bravely censures a fault, and dares to correct what is wrong by well-timed blame. To hold back blame, it has been said, is to hold back love. "I love not my friend," wrote Seneca ('Ep.,' 25), " if I do not offend him." Plautus, 'Trinum.,' i. 2. 57—

"Sed tu ex amicis certis mi es certissimus.
Si quid scis me fecisse inscite aut improbe,
Si id non me accusas, tu ipse objurgandus."

Publ. Syr., 'Sent.,' 16, " Amici vitia si feras, facis tua," which Erasmus expounds by adding, " If you take no notice of your friend's faults, they will be imputed to you." Cicero ('De Amicit.,' xxiv., xxv.) has some sensible remarks on this subject: " When a man's ears are shut against the truth, so that he cannot hear the truth from a friend, the welfare of such a one is hopeless. Shrewd is the observation of Cato, that some are better served by bitter enemies than by friends who seem to be agreeable; for the former often speak the truth, the latter never. . . . As therefore both to give

and receive advice is the characteristic of true friendship, and that the one should act with freedom, but not harshly, and that the other should accept remonstrance patiently and without resistance, so it should be considered that there is no deadlier bane to friendship than adulation, fawning, and flattery."

Ver. 6.—**Faithful are the wounds of a friend.** This and the next verse afford examples of the antithetic form of proverb, where the second line gives, as it were, the reverse side of the picture presented by the first. The wounds which a real friend inflicts by his just rebukes are directed by truth and discriminating affection (see Ps. cxli. 5). **But the kisses of an enemy are deceitful.** So St. Jerome, *Fraudulenta oscula odientis.* But the verb here used (עתר) has the meaning, among others, " to be abundant or frequent;" hence it is better to take it in this sense here, as "plentiful, profuse." An enemy is lavish with his Judas kisses to hide his perfidy and hatred. Septuagint, " More to be trusted are the wounds of a friend than the spontaneous (ἑκούσια) kisses of an enemy." " Non omnis qui parcit," wrote St. Augustine (' Ep.,' 48, 'ad Vincent.'), "amicus est, neque omnis qui verberat, inimicus."

Ver. 7.—**The full soul loatheth an honeycomb.** For " loathes" the Hebrew is literally " treads upon," " tramples underfoot," which is the expression of the greatest disgust and contempt; or it may mean that the well-fed man will not stoop to pick up the comb which may have dropped in his path from some tree or rock. But whichever way we take it, the same truth is told— Self-restraint increases enjoyment; over-indulgence produces satiety, fatigue, and indolence. Horace, 'Sat.,' ii. 2. 38—

" Jejunus raro stomachus vulgaria temnit."

But to the hungry soul every bitter thing is sweet. So the prodigal in the parable would fain fill himself with the husks which the swine did eat. So we say, " Hunger is the best sauce;" the Germans, " Hunger makes raw beans sweet;" and the Portuguese, " Brackish water is sweet in a dry land."

Ver. 8.—**As a bird that wandereth from her nest.** Jerome's *avis transmigrans* conveys to us a notion of a migratory bird taking its annual journey. But the idea here is of a bird which leaves its own nest either wantonly or from some external reason, and thereby exposes itself to discomfort and danger (comp. Isa. xvi. 2). **So is a man that wandereth from his place;** *i.e.* his own home (comp. Ecclus. xxix. 21, etc., and xxxvi. 28 in Vet. Lat., " Quis credit ei qui non habet nidum, et deflectens ubicumque obscuraverit, quasi succinctus latro exsil ns de civitate in civitatem?"). The proverb indirectly inculcates love of one's home and one's native land. To be "a fugitive and a vagabond" (Gen. iv. 12) was a terrible punishment, as the Jews have learned by the experience of many centuries. Language and religion placed a barrier against residence in any country but their own (see Ps. lxxxiv.); and though at the time when this book was probably written they knew little of foreign travel, yet they regarded sojourn in a strange land as an evil, and centred all their ideas of happiness and comfort in a home life surrounded by friends and countrymen. The word "wander" may have the notion of going into exile. Septuagint, "As when a bird flies down from its own nest, so is a man brought into bondage when he is banished (ἀποξενωθῇ) from his own place." Some have reasoned from this expression that the idea of exile had become familiar to the writer, and hence that this portion of the Proverbs is of very late origin (Cheyne) —surely a very uncertain foundation for such a conclusion. The love of Orientals for their native soil is a passion which no sordid and miserable surroundings can extinguish, and a man would consider even a change of home an unmixed evil, though such change was not the result of exile. Our view of the fortunes of one who is always shifting his abode is expressed in the adage, "A rolling stone gathers no moss."

Ver. 9.—**Ointment and perfume rejoice the heart.** (For the use of unguents in the honourable treatment of guests, see ch. vii. 16, etc.; xxi. 17.) Similarly, perfumes prepared from spices, roses, and aromatic plants were employed; rooms were fumigated, persons were sprinkled with rose-water, and incense was applied to the face and beard, as we read (Dan. ii. 46) that Nebuchadnezzar ordered that to Daniel, in recognition of his wisdom, should be offered an oblation and sweet odours (see 'Dict. of Bible,' and Kitto, 'Cyclop.,' voc. "Perfumes"). The heat of the climate, the insalubrious character of the houses, the profuse perspiration of the assembled guests, rendered this attention peculiarly acceptable (comp. Cant. iii. 6). The LXX., probably with a tacit reference to Ps. civ. 15, renders, "The heart delighteth in ointments, and wines, and perfumes." So doth **the sweetness of a man's friend by hearty counsel.** This is rather clumsy; the Revised Version improves it by paraphrasing, *that cometh from hearty counsel.* The meaning is that as ointment, etc., gladden the heart, so do the sweet and loving words of one who speaks from the depths of his soul. The idea is primarily of a friend who

gives wise counsel, speaking the truth in love, or shows his approval by discreet commendation. The LXX. has pointed differently, and translates, "But the soul is broken by calamities (καταρρήγνυται ὑπὸ συμπτωμάτων);" Vulgate, "The soul is sweetened by the good counsels of a friend."

Ver. 10.—Another proverb, a tristich, in praise of friendship. It seems to be a combination of two maxims. **Thine own friend, and thy father's friend, forsake not.** A father's friend is one who is connected with a family by hereditary and ancestral bonds; φίλον πατρῷον, Septuagint. Such a one is to be cherished and regarded with the utmost affection. **Neither go into thy brother's house in the day of thy calamity.** The tried friend is more likely to help and sympathize with you than even your own brother, for a friend is born for adversity, and there is a friend that sticketh closer than a brother (ch. xvii. 17; xviii. 24, where see notes). The mere blood-relationship, which is the result of circumstances over which one has had no control, is inferior to the affectionate connection which arises from moral considerations and is the effect of deliberate choice. We must remember, too, that the practice of polygamy, with the separate establishments of the various wives, greatly weakened the tie of brotherhood. There was little love between David's sons; and Jonathan was far dearer to David himself than any of his numerous brothers when. **Better is a neighbour that is near than a brother far off.** "Near" and "far off" may be taken as referring to feeling or to local position. In the former case the maxim says that a neighbour who is really attached to one by the bonds of affection is better than the closest relation who has no love or sympathy. In the latter view, the proverb enunciates the truth that a friend on the spot in time of calamity is more useful than a brother living at a distance (μακρὰν οἰκῶν, Septuagint); one is sure of help at once from the former, while application to the latter must occasion delay, and may not be successful. Commentators quote Hesiod, Ἔργ. καὶ Ἡμ., 341—

Τὸν δὲ μάλιστα καλεῖν ὅστις σέθεν ἐγγύθι ναίει.
Εἰ γάρ τοι καὶ χρῆμ' ἐγκώμιον ἄλλο γένηται,
Γείτονες ἄζωστοι ἔκιον, ζώσαντο δὲ πηοί.

Ver. 11.—**My son, be wise, and make my heart glad.** The exhortation of a father to his son, or of a teacher to his pupil. Such address is not found elsewhere in this latter portion of the book, though common in previous parts. Delitzsch translates, "become wise." Σοφὸς γίνου, Septuagint. Such development of wisdom delights a father's heart, as ch. x. 1; xxiii. 15, 24. **That I may** answer him that reproacheth me (Ps. cxix. 42; comp. Ps. cxxvii. 5; Ecclus. xxx. 2). If the pupil did not show wisdom and morality in his conduct, the teacher would incur blame for the apparent failure of his education; whereas the high tone of the disciple might be appealed to as a proof of the merit and efficacy of the tutor's discipline. On the other hand, the evil doings of Hebrews often made the Name of God to be blasphemed among the Gentiles; just as nowadays the inconsistent lives of Christians are the greatest impediment to the success of missionary efforts in heathen countries. St. Jerome has, *Ut possis exprobanti respondere sermonem.* So Septuagint, "And remove from thyself reproachful words." But the first person is in accordance with the Hebrew.

Ver. 12.—A repetition of ch. xxii. 3. The sentence is asyndeton.

Ver. 13.—A repetition of ch. xx. 16. The LXX., which omits this passage in its proper place, here translates, "Take away his garment, for a scorner passed by, whoever lays waste another's goods."

Ver. 14.—**He that blesseth his friend with a loud voice, rising early in the morning.** What is meant is ostentatious salutation, which puts itself forward in order to stand well with a patron, and to be beforehand with other servile competitors for favour. Juvenal satirized such parasitical effusion ('Sat.,' v. 19)—

"Habet Trebius, propter quod rumpere somnum
Debeat et ligulas dimittere, sollicitus, ne
Tota salutaris jam turba peregerit orbem,
Sideribus dubiis, aut illo tempore, quo se
Frigida circumagunt pigri surraca Bootæ."

The "loud voice" intimates the importunate nature of such public trumpeting of gratitude, as the "rising early" denotes its inopportune and tactless insistency, which cannot wait for a convenient opportunity for its due expression. **It shall be counted a curse to him.** The receiver of this sordid adulation, and indeed all the bystanders, would just as soon be cursed by the parasite as blessed in this offensive manner. This clamorous outpouring of gratitude is not accepted as a return by the benefactor; he sees the mean motives by which it is dictated—self-interest, hope of future benefits—and he holds it as cheap as he would the curses of such a person. The nuisance of such flattery is mentioned by Euripides, 'Orest.,' 1161—

Παύσομαί σ' αἰνῶν, ἐπεὶ
Βάρος τι κἂν τῷδ' ἐστίν, αἰνεῖσθαι λίαν.

"Duo sunt genera prosecutorum," says St. Augustine ('In Psalm.,' lxix.), "scilicet vituperantium et adulantium; sed plus prosequitur lingua adulatoris, quam manus prosecutoris." "Woe unto you," said Christ (Luke vi. 26), "when all men shall speak well of you." "Do I seek to please men?" asked St. Paul (Gal. i. 10); "for if I yet pleased men, I should not be the servant of Christ."

Vers. 15 and 16 form a tetrastich on the subject of the termagant wife.

Ver. 15.—The single line of the second clause of ch. xix. 13 is here formed into a distich. **A continual dropping in a very rainy day.** "A day of violent rain," סַגְרִיר (*sagrir*), which word occurs nowhere else in the Old Testament. **And a contentious woman are alike.** The word rendered "are alike" (נִשְׁתָּוָה) is usually taken to be the third perf. nithp. from שׁיה; but the best-established reading, according to Hitzig, Delitzsch, and Nowack, is נִשְׁתָּוָה, which is regarded as a niph. with a transposition of consonants for נִשְׁוָתָה. Septuagint, "Drops of rain drive a man out of his house on a stormy day." The ill-constructed roofs of Eastern houses were very subject to leakage, being flat and formed of porous material.

Ver. 16.—**Whosoever hideth her hideth the wind.** Whoever tries to restrain a shrewish woman, or to conceal her faults, might as well attempt to confine the wind or to check its violence. **And the ointment of his right hand, which bewrayeth itself.** He might as well try to hide the ointment which signifies its presence by its odour. But there is no "which" in the original, which runs literally, "his right hand calls oil," or, "oil meets his right hand." The former is supposed to mean that he is hurt in the struggle to coerce the vixen, and needs ointment to heal his wound; but the latter seems the correct rendering, and the meaning then is that, if he tries to hold or stop his wife, she escapes him like the oil which you try in vain to keep in your hand. An old adage says that there are three things which cannot be hidden, but always betray themselves, viz. a woman, the wind, and ointment. The LXX. has read the Hebrew differently, translating, "The north-wind is harsh, but by name it is called lucky (ἐπιδέξιος):" *i.e.* because it clears the sky and introduces fine weather. The Syriac, Aquila, and Symmachus have adopted the same reading.

Ver. 17.—**Iron sharpeneth iron.** The proverb deals with the influence which men have upon one another. **So a man sharpeneth the countenance of his friend.** So the Vulgate, *Homo exacuit faciem amici sui.* The action of the file is probably meant (1 Sam. xiii. 21); and the writer names iron as the sharpener rather than the whetstone, because he wishes to denote that one man is of the same nature as another, and that this identity is that which makes mutual action possible and advantageous. Some have taken the proverb in a bad sense, as if it meant that one angry word leads to another, one man's passion excites another's rage. Thus Aben Ezra. The Septuagint perhaps supports this notion by rendering, Ἀνὴρ δὲ παροξύνει πρόσωπον ἑταίρου. But the best commentators understand the maxim to say that intercourse with other men influences the manner, appearance, deportment, and character of a man, sharpens his wits, controls his conduct, and brightens his very face. Horace uses the same figure of speech, 'Ars Poet.,' 304—

"Fungar vice cotis, acutum
Reddere quæ ferrum valet, exsors ipsa secandi."

On the subject of mutual intercourse Euripides says, 'Androm.,' 683—

'Ἡ δ' ὁμιλία
Πάντων βροτοῖσι γίγνεται διδάσκαλος.

"Companionship
Is that which teaches mortals everything."

Ver. 18.—**Whoso keepeth the fig tree shall eat the fruit thereof.** He who watches, tends, and cultivates the fig tree will in due time have the reward of his labour in eating its fruit. The abundance of the produce of this tree makes it a good figure of the reward of faithful service. Septuagint, "He that planteth a fig tree shall eat the fruits thereof" (2 Tim. ii. 6). **So he that waiteth on his master shall be honoured.** He who pays attention, has loving regard to his master, shall meet with honour as his reward at his master's hands, and also from all who become acquainted with his merits. The gnome may well be applied to the case of those who do true and laudable service to their heavenly Master, and who shall one day hear from his lips the gracious word, "Well done, thou good and faithful servant: thou hast been faithful over a few things, I will make thee ruler over many things: enter thou into the joy of thy Lord" (Matt. xxv. 21).

Ver. 19.—**As in water face** answereth **to face, so the heart of man to man;** Vulgate, *Quomodo in aquis resplendent vultus prospicientium, sic corda hominum manifesta sunt prudentibus.* As in clear water the face of the gazer is reflected, so man finds in his fellow-man the same feelings, sentiments, passions, which he has himself. He sees in others the likeness of himself; whatever he knows himself to be, he will see others presenting the same character. Self-knowledge, too, leads to insight into

others' minds; "for what man knoweth the things of a man, save the spirit of man which is in him?" (1 Cor. ii. 11). There is a solidarity in human nature which enables us to judge of others by ourselves. The difficulties in the construction and wording of the sentence do not affect the interpretation. They are, however, best met by rendering, with Delitzsch, "As it is with water, face corresponds to face, so also the heart of man to man." Septuagint, "As faces are not like faces, so neither are the thoughts of men;" which is like the saying of Persius, 'Sat.,' v. 52—

"Mille hominum species, et rerum discolor usus;
Velle suum cuique est, nec voto vivitur uno."

Ver. 20.—**Hell and destruction are never full.** "Hell" is *sheol,* the under-world, Hades, the place of the departed; "destruction" is the great depth, the second death, personified (see on ch. xv. 11, where the terms also occur). These "are never satisfied," they are insatiable, all-devouring (comp. ch. xxx. 16; Isa. v. 14; Hab. ii. 5). **So the eyes of man are never satisfied.** The verb is the same in both clauses, and ought to have been so translated. The eye is taken as the representative of concupiscence in general. What is true of "the lust of the eyes" (1 John ii. 16) is true of all the senses; the craving for their gratification grows as it is fed. Therefore the senses should be carefully guarded, lest they lead to excess and transgression. "Turn away mine eyes from beholding vanity," said the psalmist, "and quicken me in thy way" (Ps. cxix. 37). The LXX. here introduces a paragraph not in the Hebrew or the Latin Versions: "He that fixes (στηρίζων) his eye [*i.e.* staring impudently] is an abomination to the Lord, and the uninstructed restrain not their tongue."

Ver. 21.—**Fining-pot,** etc. (see on ch. xvii. 3; comp. also ch. xxv. 4). **So is a man to his praise.** The Hebrew is literally, *The crucible for silver, and the furnace for gold, and a man according to his praise;* i.e. as the processes of metallurgy test the precious metals, so a man's public reputation shows what he is really worth, as is stated in ch. xii. 8. As the crucible brings all impurities to the surface, so public opinion drags forth all that is bad in a man, and he who stands this test is generally esteemed. Certainly praise is a stimulus to exertion, an incentive to try to make one's self worthy of the estimation in which one is held, especially if he purifies it from the dross and earthliness mixed with it, and takes to himself only what is genuine and just. But public opinion is very commonly false, and is always a very unsafe criterion of moral excellence. Hence other interpretations have been proposed. Ewald renders, "and a man according to his boasting," that is, according to that which he most praises in himself and others. So virtually Hitzig, Böttcher, Zöckler, and others. In this view the gnome denotes that a man's real character is best examined by the light cast upon it by his usual line of thought, what he most prides himself upon, what he admires most in other men. Plumptre, after Gesenius and Fleischer, has, "So let a man be to his praise," i.e. to the mouth which praises him; let him test this commendation, to see what it is worth, before he accepts it as his due. The explanation first given seems on the whole most suitable, when we reflect that the highest morality is not always enunciated, and that secondary motives are widely recognized as factors in action and judgment. There are not wanting men in modern days who uphold the maxim, Vox populi, vox Dei. Septuagint, "The action of fire is a test for silver and gold, so a man is tested by the mouth of them that praise him." No surer test of a man's true character can be found than his behaviour under praise; many men are spoiled by it. If a man comes forth from it without injury, not rendered vain, or blind to his defects, or disdainful of others, his disposition is good, and the commendation lavished upon him may be morally and spiritually beneficial. Vulgate, Sic probatur homo ore laudantis, "So is a man proved by the mouth of him that praises him." The following passage from St. Gregory, commenting on this, is worth quoting, "Praise of one's self tortures the just, but elates the wicked. But while it tortures, it purifies the just; and while it pleases the wicked, it proves them to be reprobate. For these revel in their own praise, because they seek not the glory of their Maker. But they who seek the glory of their Maker are tortured with their own praise, lest that which is spoken of without should not exist within them; lest, if that which is said really exists, it should be made void in the sight of God by these very honours; lest the praise of men should soften the firmness of their heart, and should lay it low in self-satisfaction; and lest that which ought to aid them to increase their exertions, should be even now the recompense of their labour. But when they see that their own praises tend to the glory of God, they even long for and welcome them. For it is written, "That they may see your good works, and glorify your Father which is in heaven" ('Moral.,' xxvi. 62, Oxford transl.). The LXX. adds a verse which is not found in the Hebrew, but occurs in some manuscripts of the Latin Version. "The heart of the transgressor

seeketh out evils, but an upright heart seeketh knowledge."

Ver. 22.—Though thou shouldest bray a fool in a mortar among wheat with a pestle. "To bray" is to pound or beat small. "Wheat," רִיפוֹת, riphoth (only in 2 Sam. xvii. 19), "bruised corn." Vulgate, In pila quasi ptisanas (barley-groats) feriente; Aquila and Theodotion, Ἐν μέσῳ ἐμπτισσομένων, "In the midst of grains of corn being pounded." The LXX., reading differently, has, "Though thou scourge a fool, disgracing him (ἐν μέσῳ συνεδρίου) in the midst of the congregation." Of course, the process of separating the husks from the corn by the use of pestle and mortar is much more delicate and careful than threshing in the usual clumsy way; hence is expressed the idea that the most elaborate pains are wasted on the incorrigible fool (see on ch. i. 20). His foolishness will not depart from him. An obstinate, self-willed, unprincipled man cannot be reformed by any means; his folly has become a second nature, and is not to be eliminated by any teaching, discipline, or severity. There is, too, a judicial blindness, when, after repeated warnings wilfully rejected and scorned, the sinner is left to himself, given over to a reprobate mind "Whoso teacheth a fool," Siracides pronounces, "is as one that glueth a potsherd together, and as he that waketh one from a sound sleep" (Ecclus. xxii. 7). Again, "The inner parts of a fool are like a broken vessel, and he will hold no knowledge as long as he liveth" (Ecclus. xxi. 14). In Turkey, we are told, great criminals were beaten to pieces in huge mortars of iron, in which they usually pounded rice. "You cannot straighten a dog's tail, try as you may," says a Telugu maxim (Lane). There is a saying of Schiller's which is quite proverbial, "Heaven and earth fight in vain against a dunce." Horace, 'Epist.,' i. 10. 24—

"Naturam expellas furca, tamen usque recurret."

Juvenal, 'Sat.,' xiii. 239—

"Tamen ad mores natura recurrit Damnatos, fixa et mutari nescia."

Vers. 23—27.—A mashal ode in praise of a pastoral and agricultural life. The moralist evidently desires to recall his countrymen from the luxury of cities and the temptations of money-making to the simple ways of the patriarchs and the pleasures of country pursuits—which are the best foundation of enduring prosperity.

Ver. 23.—Be thou diligent to know the state of thy flocks. "State;" פָּנִים (panim);

vultum, Vulgate; the face, look, appearance. The LXX. has ψυχάς, which may perhaps mean "the number"—a necessary precaution when the sheep wandered on the downs and mountains, and had to be collected in the evening and folded. These precepts are naturally applied to all rulers, and especially to Christian pastors who have the oversight of the flock of Christ (1 Pet. v. 2—4). Ecclus. vii. 22, "Hast thou cattle? have an eye to them; and if they be for thy profit, keep them with thee."

Ver. 24.—**For riches are not for ever;** as ch. xxiii. 5. Money and other kinds of wealth may be lost or wasted; it is therefore expedient to have the resources of agriculture, land and herds, to depend upon. *Chosen* (ch. xv. 6), translated "riches," is "strength," "abundance," "treasure laid up." Delitzsch renders, "prosperity;" Septuagint, "A man has not strength and power for ever;" Vulgate, *Non habebis jugiter potestatem*, i.e. "you will not always be able to tend your flocks; infirmity and old age will prevent you." **And doth the crown endure to every generation?** The crown or diadem, נֵזֶר (*nezer*), is the symbol of royal authority, or of the highest dignity of the priesthood (Exod. xxix. 6; xxxix. 30). These positions are not secure from generation to generation; much less stable, in fact, than the possession of farms and cattle. St. Jerome, *Sed corona tribuetur in generationem et generationem*, where *corona* is the headship of the family. Septuagint, "Neither doth he transmit it (his strength) from generation to generation."

Ver. 25.—As ver. 23 commended the rearing of cattle, and ver. 24 supported the injunction by showing its comparative permanence, so this and the following verses discuss the material advantages of such occupation. **The hay appeareth;** rather, *the grass passeth away*, is cut and carried. This is the first stage in the agricultural operations described. **And the tender grass showeth** itself; the aftermath appears. **And the herbs of the mountain are gathered;** the fodder from off the hills is cut and stored. All these verbs are best taken hypothetically, the following verses forming the apodosis. When all these operations are complete, then come the results in plenty and comfort. Septuagint, "Have a care of the herbage (χλωρῶν) in the plain, and thou shalt cut grass, and gather thou the mountain hay."

Ver. 26.—**The lambs are for thy clothing.** Thy sheep will provide thee with clothing by their skin and wool, and by the money which thou wilt obtain by the sale of them. **The goats are the price of the field;** the sale of thy goats and their produce will pay for thy field if thou wish to buy it (see on ch. xxx. 31). Septuagint, "That thou mayest have sheep for clothing; honour thy land that thou mayest have lambs."

Ver. 27.—**Goats' milk.** Dr. Geikie ('Holy Land and Bible,' i. 311) notes that in most parts of Palestine goats' milk in every form —sour, sweet, thick, thin, warm, or cold— makes, with eggs and bread, the main food of the people. **And maintenance for thy maidens;** who milk the goats, etc., and tend the cattle, and do the household work. There is no mention of the use of animal flesh as food. It was only on great occasions, as high festivals, or the presence of an honoured guest, that kids, lambs, and calves were killed and eaten. This picture of rural peace and plenty points to a time of security and prosperity, free alike from internal commotion and external danger. The famous passage in Cicero, 'De Senect.,' xv., on the pleasures and advantages of the agricultural life. will occur to all classical readers. So also Horace ('Epod.,' 2), "Beatus ille qui procul negotiis," etc. The LXX. makes short work of this verse, "My son, thou hast from me sayings mighty for thy life and for the life of thy servants."

HOMILETICS.

Ver. 1.—*Boasting of the morrow.* I. ITS FOLLY. No man is a prophet. At the best we can but calculate probabilities. The man who has never had a day's illness may be suddenly laid low, struck down with paralysis, arrested by unsuspected heart-disease, blood-poisoned by a whiff of bad air from a drain, at death's door from pneumonia caught in an unheeded draught. The business which looks fair and prosperous may suddenly collapse. The trusted bank may break. Our life is dependent upon so many unseen sources, and is affected by so many complicated circumstances, that no man can unravel the tendencies or predict the results. Astronomy is a simple science compared with sociology. The movements of the solar system are altogether more intelligible than those of the homeliest soul. We cannot predict our own conduct. Moreover, there are other minds to be considered. Above all, there is the inscrutable providence of God.

II. ITS DANGER. "Boasting of the morrow" leads to carelessness. The man who is confident without warrant is likely to be off his guard. Believing that all is safe, he does not fortify himself against a possible surprise of mischief. He is just in the condition most favourable for attack. The wily tempter is aware of this. Therefore the danger is all the greater because it is ignored. Thus Peter, weakened through over-confidence, fell into sin, even though he had been warned against it.

III. ITS SIN. This is not merely a question of prudence and personal welfare. It touches our relations with God. He who boasts himself of the morrow acts either *atheistically*, denying the Divine control of life, or *presumptuously*, assuming without reason that God will aid his plans. Such conduct reveals a guilty pride. It is opposed to the humility of one who would bow low before the inscrutable providence of the Almighty.

IV. ITS PUNISHMENT. Such boasting is certain to be punished by failure. It would not be well to let it proceed to success, for such a result would only confirm and aggravate the evil habit. Partial and temporary victory may be attained, but ultimate triumph cannot be won in this way. God casts down and humbles the boaster, and in his shame he has an opportunity of learning wisdom.

V. ITS ANTIDOTE. This is not to be found in a cowardly shrinking from the future, nor is it to be had in a habit of despair, ever painting the days to come in the blackest hues, with the melancholy motto, "Blessed is he that expecteth little; for he shall not be disappointed." The true antidote is to be discovered in a spirit of trust. God has indeed hung an impenetrable curtain between our vision and the land of the future. Even the very morrow dwells as yet in a land of darkness, and we vainly try to discern its features. But it is perfectly familiar to God, before whom all eternity is as a clear picture ever present. And God, who knows the future, controls it. Therefore we are safe when we trust; and, eschewing boastfulness, we can learn not to be anxious about the morrow, because we can trust our Father who holds the secrets of all the morrows in his hand.

Ver. 2.—*Self-praise.* I. SELF-PRAISE IS ILL-FOUNDED. It may be true to fact, but we cannot be sure that it is. 1. *Possibly it is insincere.* So many motives of vanity and self-interest urge a person to pretend to be better than he is, that a certificate of merit given by himself on behalf of himself cannot be taken at a high value. 2. *Probably it is delusive.* Even when it is perfectly sincere it is likely to be perverted by unconscious misconceptions. It is very easy to be honestly mistaken as to one's own worth. We are the worst conceivable judges of our own characters and deserts. Even when we can calmly and fairly estimate our powers we are likely to be very wrong in valuing our use of them.

II. SELF-PRAISE SPRINGS FROM SELFISHNESS. 1. *It reveals a self-regarding habit.* If a man is given to expatiate on his own merits, he must be accustomed to turn his thoughts inwards; he must be familiar with the contemplation of himself. Now, this is not wholesome. The less a man thinks about himself the better for his own soul's health. 2. *It implies a desire of self-aggrandizement.* There is usually a motive behind the habit of self-praise, and, though this may be nothing worse than childish vanity, it carries with it a desire for exciting the admiration of others; it aims at reaping a harvest of laudation. But possibly the end sought is more far-reaching, and the pretentious person indicts his own testimonials with a deliberate intention of securing some tangible advantage thereby. The self-praise is then just an ugly, glaring blossom of selfishness.

III. SELF-PRAISE PROVOKES JEALOUSY. It rarely secures the admiration that it seeks. On the contrary, it is generally received with suspicion; and even when it is honest and true, a large discount is taken off its claims. 1. *Its defective authority is perceived.* This is a point to which vanity is singularly blind. Yet all the weakness of the situation is apparent to every beholder; for it is universally recognized that a man is strongly tempted to make out a good case for himself, and that he is likely to be deceived into an inordinate estimate of his own value. Therefore self-praise is usually wasted. 2. *It irritates the vanity of others.* The tendency is for the hearer to imagine that the vain speaker desires to exalt himself at the expense of others. A comparison of merit seems to be challenged, and this at once rouses the jealousy of the audience. Thus self-praise does not win friends. What it may perhaps succeed in extracting in the form of admiration is paid for dearly by the dislike that it also creates.

IV. SELF-PRAISE IS CONTRARY TO CHRISTIAN HUMILITY. It represents a wholly alien spirit. Doubtless it is a common weakness of men who are truly Christian and kind-hearted, for no man is perfect; but still it is a weakness, and it is foreign to the genius of the religion under which it finds a shelter. The often-repeated rule of Christ is that "Whosoever exalteth himself shall be abased;" "The first shall be last." The true disciple is not to choose the upper seat in the synagogue. Humility, self-forgetfulness, the preference of others, are the Christian graces. Self-praise is useless before God.

V. SELF-PRAISE ONLY AIMS AT WHAT CAN BE BETTER ATTAINED WITHOUT IT. "Let another man praise thee." Self-praise silences the lips of admiration from others. The truly humble man will not crave such admiration. But all men of right feeling must desire to stand well with their fellows. It is happy to feel that we have the respect and confidence of those whose opinion we value. Now, these encouragements are better secured by unpretentious merit, and humility in earnest, simple attempts to do right.

Ver. 6.—*The wounds of a friend.*" The principle implied in this verse is apparent at a glance. It is better that one who loves and truly considers the interests of another should wound him for his good than that a superficial flatterer should refrain from doing so for the sake of pleasing and winning continuous favour. The only difficulties lie in the practical application of the principle.

I. TRUE FRIENDSHIP WILL DARE TO WOUND. It is painful and difficult to do that which we know will grieve one who is greatly loved. Therefore if it is really necessary it will put the love to the test. 1. *True friendship considers the welfare of another.* The chief thought is not on behalf of agreeable companionship, but as to what will really benefit one's friend. 2. *The welfare of another may require a painful treatment.* There are so-called "candid friends," who secretly delight in saying unpleasant things. With such people there is no merit in giving pain, nor is it likely that much advantage will result from their rough conduct. But it may be possible to point out a friend's mistakes, to warn him against temptation, to gravely deprecate his wrongful conduct, to make him feel his deterioration of character. Then, though the process must be keenly painful on both sides, love will attempt it.

II. THE WOUNDS OF TRUE FRIENDSHIP SHOULD BE PATIENTLY RECEIVED. 1. *The cost of them should be considered.* If they do indeed come from a friend they show his genuine regard, his unselfish devotion. They also indicate how thorough is his confidence; for they show that he expects to be rightly understood, and that his painful action will not be resented. He risks a breach of the friendship for the sake of benefiting his friend. This is a generous action, and it should be generously accepted. But it needs magnanimity both to give and to take the wounds of friendship. 2. *The value of them should be appreciated.* The first impulse is to feel aggrieved, to resent the intrusion, to treat the well-meant rebuke as an insult, to justify one's self, perhaps even to overwhelm the friend who wounds with rage and revenge. This is as foolish as it is ungrateful. If we only knew it, we should confess that we have no better friends than those who dare to wound us. It is just from such friends that we can learn wisdom. Flattery kisses and slays; friendship wounds and saves.

III. THE DIVINE FRIENDSHIP WOUNDS TO SAVE. The world flatters and promises only pleasant things to its slaves when it first enthralls them. God treats us in the opposite way, warning us of danger, rebuking our sins, even chastising us with heavy blows. But "whom the Lord loveth he chasteneth." 1. *God proves himself to be our Friend by wounding us.* He might have left us alone to rot in our own wretched ruin. But in his great love he has interfered to save, though his advances are met with insult and anger. God loves enough to give pain. 2. *It would be wise to receive God's wounding as that of a Friend.* It is for our good; then the best course is to take it accordingly, to endeavour to profit by it. Christ lays a cross on his disciples, and saves them by leading them to follow in his *Via Dolorosa*, and to be crucified with him (Gal. ii. 20).

Ver. 8.—*A bird wandering from her nest.* Let us consider first in what respects a man may be said to be wandering from his place, and then how the evil of this condition may be illustrated by the metaphor of a bird wandering from its nest.

I. HOW A MAN MAY WANDER FROM HIS PLACE. 1. *He may leave the work he is suited for.* There is no reason why a man should not endeavour to rise in the social scale. Christianity does not consecrate any system of caste. But there are works for which certain men have natural aptitude, or for which they have been trained, and other works for which they are not thus suited. Unhappily, our inclination does not always coincide with our capacity. To follow one's likings outside the range of one's powers is to wander from one's place. 2. *He may forsake his duty.* Every man's rightful place is at the post of duty. No danger, no difficulty, no disagreeableness, can justify any one in forsaking that place. 3. *He may depart from God.* Then indeed will he have wandered from his true place. For the home of the soul is with God. Absence from God is to be out of one's place, (1) though in a very paradise of delights, (2) though among the most congenial companions, (3) though with an eminently attractive occupation. 4. *He may renounce his human status.* (1) In descending to that of an animal. Bestial lust and brutal cruelty are inhuman. He who plunges into such vile things necessarily wanders from himself as a man. He gives up the rank of a human being. (2) In degrading himself to diabolical living. This happens to one who chooses evil for its own sake, loving wickedness and pursuing it.

II. HOW SUCH A MAN MUST SUFFER AS A BIRD THAT WANDERS FROM HER NEST. 1. *He loses peace.* The nest is typical of quiet and restfulness. To forsake it is to be at large in the noisy, tumultuous world. So one who is out of his place is cast adrift on a homeless waste. He sacrifices peace in pursuit of novelty. 2. *He is removed from congenial companionship.* The poor young bird leaves her fellows and flies into unknown regions, where she finds herself alone among strange creatures. A man who is out of his element will be equally alone and friendless. The very fact that he is in the wrong place implies that he cannot find true sympathy in his new sphere. Perhaps he has been foolishly aiming at entering some higher circle of life than one that he is fitted for. If so, he will only be supremely uncomfortable, perpetually regarded as an intruder or ridiculed as a blunderer. It is better to cultivate the affections of one's own home circle and true old friends. 3. *He is not able to fulfil his mission.* It may be that a mother-bird is here thought of. In wandering from her nest she forsakes her young. So he who leaves his rightful place neglects his obligations. He fails to do his duty to those naturally dependent on him. Charity begins at home. 4. *He is exposed to danger.* The poor wandering bird may be lost in the forest; she may starve for want of food; birds of prey may pounce upon her in the darkness. There is no safety off the path of duty. Even unsuitable spheres are dangerous, because a man does not know how to behave himself in them. Away from God there is danger of ruin without hope of escape.

Ver. 12.—*Foresight of evil.* I. IT IS NOT POSSIBLE TO FORESEE ALL FUTURE EVIL. God, in his great mercy, has drawn a thick veil over the face of futurity. We can reason of probabilities; in some cases we can almost predict certainties; but taking the whole round of life, and the full reach of futurity, we have to recognize the fact that the evil to come as well as the good are largely hidden from our view. It would not be possible for us to bear the sight if all dark experiences were crowded into one horrible picture and presented before our imagination at once. We can take one by one the evils that would crush us if we beheld them all together in a mighty, terrible phalanx. When the trouble comes the strength may be given to bear it, but not before.

II. IT IS FOOLISH TO FRET OURSELVES WITH ANXIETIES ABOUT THE MORROW. This is the distinct teaching of Christ, based on various grounds. 1. *We have enough to bear in the present.* "Sufficient unto the day is the evil thereof." 2. *We cannot command the future.* No man by being anxious can add one cubit to his stature or change the natural colour of his hair. 3. *God is our Father.* He feeds the wild birds and clothes the fields. Much more will he feed and clothe his own children. 4. *We have higher considerations to absorb our attention.* "Seek first the kingdom of God, and his righteousness."

III. WE NEED TO MAKE A REASONABLE PROVISION FOR THE FUTURE. It may appear that the prudence of the Book of Proverbs is rebuked by teachings of Christ. No doubt our Lord does lift us into a higher atmosphere. But there is no contradiction between the two positions. Indeed, we are best able to banish needless care when we have made proper provision for the future. Thrift does not create anxiety. The man who has insured his house against fire does not dread the incendiary more than the man who has not provided himself against the contingency of a conflagration. He who is prepared for death need not fear death.

IV. IT IS A MARK OF TRUE WISDOM TO GUARD AGAINST THE EVIL THAT MAY BE AVOIDED. 1. *This obtains in secular pursuits.* Ignorance is no excuse for not providing against a disaster when reasonable thoughtfulness would have foreseen it. The reckless general who burns the bridges behind him is guilty of the blood of his soldiers who are slaughtered after a great defeat. 2. *This is most true in the spiritual world.* (1) Here we may foresee danger. For God has revealed the fatal consequences of sin. No one who reflects can say that he has no reason to expect that his sin will be punished. The very nature of sin foreshadows its own dreadful doom. (2) Here we may provide against it. It is not an inevitable destiny. "God has opened up a way of escape." It is wise to consider the danger of sin, in order to flee from it to safety in Christ (1 John ii. 1).

Ver. 17.—*The advantages of society.* I. OBSERVE IN WHAT THE ADVANTAGES OF SOCIETY CONSIST. We have ancient authority for the idea that it is not good for man to be alone (Gen. ii. 18). Man is naturally a gregarious being. Though some people are more sociable than others, no one can be healthy in perpetual solitude. The isolation of the hermit engendered the wildest hallucinations of fanaticism together with the narrowest conception of the world. Prisoners of the Bastille, in solitary confinement, were reduced to a condition of semi-idiocy. Robinson Crusoe made the best of his situation, yet he could not live without the companionship of animal pets, and he was glad of the humble friendship of a poor savage. 1. *Society quickens a man's intelligence.* Even Wordsworth was thought by some to have deteriorated mentally in his comparative seclusion at Rydal Mount, and yet there were other men of high mental power in his neighbourhood. Men's thoughts are stimulated and sharpened by conversation. 2. *Society rouses a man's energy.* Empty society of mere pleasure-seekers only dissipates a man's powers in frivolity. But the society of earnest men stimulates by sympathy, emulation, and encouragement. 3. *Society broadens a man's views.* He is able to see how other men think and feel. They may not all have greater advantages than he possesses; but at least they are differently constituted and situated from himself. Thus he is lifted out of the narrowness of his own single vision. Such breadth gives strength when it is accompanied by an earnest love of truth and right.

II. CONSIDER HOW THE ADVANTAGES OF SOCIETY MAY BE REALIZED. 1. *They are dependent on a man's residence.* Horace's old dispute between the town and the country mouse has never been settled. Cowper wrote, "God made the country, man made the town;" and no doubt there is to be seen a certain restfulness, a purity, and a quiet power in nature that those men miss who reside in the heart of a wilderness of houses. Nevertheless, there are compensations for the disagreeable pressure of population in great cities. The mind is quickened. Still, as evils also result from this manner of living, it is certainly important that those who are able to select their own residences should consider wholesome society to be as important as a pure water supply. 2. *They can be found in sympathetic friendship.* One good, true friend is more helpful than a score of mere acquaintances. It is in the close intercourse of genuine friendship that the best results of the mutual play of thought and feeling can be obtained. Hence the supreme importance of cultivating friendship with the wise and good. 3. *They should be obtained in the Christian Church.* Christ not only called disciples to himself, one by one; he founded the Church, and his apostles established local Churches wherever they could gather together a few converts. Christian companionship should be a help to Christian life and thought. There was a time when they who feared the Lord spake often one to another (Mal. iii. 16). Above this earthly friendship the Christian finds a mental and spiritual quickening in the friendship of Christ (Luke xxiv. 32).

HOMILIES BY VARIOUS AUTHORS.

Vers. 1—6.—*Boastfulness, jealousy, and hypocrisy.* I. OVER-CONFIDENCE REBUKED. (Ver. 1.) 1. On the ground of our limited knowledge. The homely proverb says, " Do not count your chickens before they are hatched." The future exists for us only in imagination. "Who knows," asks Horace, "whether the gods above will add to-morrow's time to the sum of to-day?" ('Od.,' iv. 7. 17); and Seneca, "None hath gods so favourable as that he may promise himself to-morrow's good." 2. On the ground of the Divine reserve of the secrets of destiny. To boast is to lift ourselves in effect out of that finite sphere of thought and feeling in which we have been placed by the Divine ordination. So says Horace again (and a distinctly Christian turn may be given to his exhortation), "Shun to inquire into the future and the morrow; and whatever day fortune shall afford thee, count it as gain" ('Od.,' i. 9. 13). Common sense and religious humility unite to teach us to "live for the day."

II. SELF-PRAISE CENSURED. (Ver. 2.) "Let another praise thee, and not thine own mouth." "Self-praise stinks," and "Not as thy mother says, but as the neighbours say," are Arabic proverbs. Every individual has a certain value; the sense of this is the foundation of all self-respect and virtue. But to show an over-consciousness of this worth by self-praise is a social offence, because it is an *exaction* of that which ought to be a free tribute, and betrays a desire of self-exaltation above others not easily forgiven.

III. THE PASSION OF THE FOOL INTOLERABLE. (Ver. 3.) Whether it be envy, furious resentment of rebuke, or jealousy, it is a burden intolerable to the person himself and to those with whom he has to do. The pious may readily sin in their anger, how much more the ungodly!

> "Ira furor brevis est; animum rege; qui, nisi paret,
> Imperat; hunc frœnis, hunc tu compesce catena."
> (Horace, 'Ep.,' i. 2. 62.)

It is like a weight of stone or sand, being without cause, measure, or end (Poole).

IV. THE TERRIBLE FORCE OF JEALOUSY AND ENVY. (Ver. 4.) It exceeds all ordinary outbursts of wrath in violence and destructiveness. Envy is the daughter of pride, the author of revenge and murder, the beginner of sedition, and the perpetual tormentor of nature (Socrates). It never loves to honour another but when it may be an honour to itself. "From envy . . . good Lord, deliver us!"

V. FALSE LOVE AND FAITHFUL FRIENDSHIP CONTRASTED. (Vers. 5, 6.) False love refuses to tell a friend of his faults, from some egotistic and unworthy motive. "If you know that I have done anything foolishly or wickedly, and do not blame me for it, you yourself ought to be reproved" (Plaut., 'Trinum.,' i. 2. 57). "It is no good office," says Jeremy Taylor, "to make my friend more vicious or more a fool; I will restrain his folly, but not nurse it." "I think that man is my friend through whose advice I am enabled to wipe off the blemishes of my soul before the appearance of the awful Judge" (Gregory I.). Christians should "speak the truth in love" (Eph. iv. 15). If the erring one does not learn it from the lips of love, he will have to learn it from a harsher source and in ruder tones (comp. Job v. 17, 18; Ps. cxli. 5; Rev. iii. 19; ch. xxviii. 23). There cannot be a more worthy improvement of friendship than in a fervent opposition to the sins of those we love (Bishop Hall).—J.

Vers. 7, 8.—*The blessing of contentment.* I. THE CONTENTED MIND. (Ver. 7.) "Enough is as good as a feast;" "Hunger is the best sauce." To know when we are well off is the cure for the canker of envy and discontent. Deprivation for a time teaches us the need of common blessings. The good of affliction is that it brings us nearer to God; and of poverty of spirit, that it is never without food.

II. THE EVIL OF RESTLESSNESS. (Ver. 8.) "The rolling stone gathers no moss." Rarely does the wanderer better his condition. Unstable as water, he doth not excel. Those who seek satisfaction for the soul out of God are like those who wander into a far country, like the prodigal. "O my wandering ways! Woe to the soul which presumed, if it departed from thee, that it should find anything better! I turned on every side, and all things were hard, and thou alone wast my Rest. Thou hast made us for thyself, O God, and our heart is restless till it finds rest in thee."—J.

Vers. 9, 10.—*The praises of friendship.* I. ITS SWEETNESS. (Ver. 9.) It is compared to fragrant unguent and incense (Ps. civ. 15; cxxxiii. 2). It is more delightful to listen to the counsel of a dear friend than sternly to rely on self. It is in human nature to love to see itself reflected in other objects; and the thoughts we approve, the opinions we form, we recognize gladly on another's lips. Talking with a friend is better than thinking aloud.

II. TIME-HONOURED FRIENDSHIP SHOULD ABOVE ALL BE HELD DEAR. (Ver. 10.) The presumption is that your own and your father's friend is one tried and approved, and may be depended upon.

> " The friends thou hast and their adoption tried,
>   Grapple them to thy soul with hooks of steel."

III. FRIENDSHIP IS FOUNDED UPON SPIRITUAL SYMPATHY. And this ranks before the ties of blood. The thought meets us in the proverbs of the ancient world in general. In the touching story of the friendship of Orestes and Pylades, *e.g.*, it has its application. " This is what people say, ' Acquire friends, not relations alone;' since a man, when he is united by disposition, though not of kin, is better than a host of blood-relations for another man to possess as his friend " (cf. Euripides, ' Or.,' 804). And Hesiod says, " If aid is wanted, neighbours come ungirt, but relations stay to tuck up their robes." Divine friendship is the highest illustration of this love. Christ is above all the " Friend that sticketh closer than a brother."—J.

Vers. 11—13.—*The need of prudence.* I. PRUDENT CONDUCT REFLECTS CREDIT UPON ONE'S PARENTS. (Ver. 11.) The graceless children of gracious parents are a special reproach, bringing dishonour even upon the Name of God (Gen. xxxiv. 30; 1 Sam. ii. 17). The world will generally lay the blame at the parents' door. The Mosaic Law severely punished the sins of the priest's daughter for the disgrace brought upon the holy office (Lev. xxi. 9).

II. THE NEED AND ADVANTAGE OF FORETHOUGHT. (Ver. 12.) Prudence has been described as " the virtue of the senses." It is the science of appearances. It is the outward action of the inward life. It is content to seek health of body by complying with physical conditions, and health of mind by complying with the laws of intellect. It is possible to give a base and cowardly interpretation of the duty of prudence; that " which makes the senses final is the divinity of sots and cowards, and is the subject of all comedy. The true prudence admits the knowledge of an outward and real world." Thus true prudence is only that which foresees, detects, and guards against the ills which menace the life of the *soul;* for there is no profit in the prudence which seeks the world and risks the soul. Those are "simple" who, often with the utmost regard for their material interests, go on heedless of the moral perils which their habits incur.

III. THE FOLLY OF THOUGHTLESS SURETYSHIP. (Ver. 13.) This, as we have seen, is often dwelt on in this book. It refers to a different condition of society from our own. We may generalize the warning. Prudence includes a proper self-regard, a virtuous egotism, so to speak. When good-natured people complain that they have been deceived, taken in, and turn sourly against human nature, do they not reproach themselves for having lacked this primary virtue of prudence? The highest virtues can grow only out of the root of independence (see ch. xx. 16).—J.

Ver. 14.—*Insincerity in friendship.* The picture is that of one who indulges in the noisy ostentation of friendship, without having the reality of it at his heart.

I. EXCESS IN PRAISE OR BLAME IS TO BE GUARDED AGAINST. Luther shrewdly observes, " He who loudly scolds, praises; and he who excessively praises, scolds. They are not believed because they exaggerate." Too great praise is half-blame. Language should be used with sobriety and temperance.

II. INSINCERITY IS SUBJECT TO A CURSE. It is odious to God and to man. One of the constant moral trials of life is in the observance of the golden mean of conduct in social relations—to be agreeable without flattery, and sincere without rudeness. Here, as ever, we must walk in the bright light of our Saviour's example, the All-loving, yet the All-faithful.—J.

Vers. 15, 16.—*The quarrelsome wife.* She is compared to the continual dropping of a shower; and the attempt to restrain her is like seeking to fetter the wind or to grasp at oil.

I. THE MONOTONY OF ILL TEMPER. It persists in one mood, and dyes all it touches with one colour, and that a dismal one.

II. THE CORRODING EFFECT UPON OTHERS' MINDS. Fine tempers cannot resist this perpetual wear and tear; the most buoyant spirits may be in time depressed by this dead weight.

III. THE INFLEXIBILITY OF ILL TEMPER. Alas! it is one of those things we are temp'ed to say cannot be mended. Nothing indeed but that Divine grace which can turn the winter of the soul into summer is able to remedy this ill. In reliance upon this, the exhortation may be given, " Purge out the old leaven ! "—J.

Vers. 17—22.—*Wisdom for self and for others.* I. THE BENEFIT OF INTELLIGENT SOCIETY. (Vers. 17, 19.) 1. *The collision of mind with mind elicits truth, strikes out flashes of new perception.* A man may grow wiser by an hour's discourse than by a day's meditation. " Speech is like embroidered cloth opened and put abroad," said Themistocles to the King of Persia. In the collision of minds the man brings his own thoughts to light, and whets his wits against a stone that cuts not (Bacon). 2. *The reflection of mind in mind.* (Ver. 19.) For we are all " like in difference," and never see so clearly what is in our own spirit as through the manifestation of another's. As we have not eyes in the back of our head, so is introspection difficult—perhaps, strictly speaking, impossible. Self-knowledge is the reflection of the features of other minds in our own.

II. SPIRITUAL LAWS. 1. *Diligent husbandry is rewarded.* (Ver. 18.) Whether we cultivate the tree, the master, the friend, our own soul, this law must ever hold good. Everything in this world of God's goes by law, not by luck; and what we sow we reap. Trust men, and they will be true to you; treat them justly, and they will show themselves just, though they make an exception in your favour to all their rules of conduct. 2. *The quenchless thirst of the spirit.* (Ver. 20.) Who can set a limit to the human desire to know, to do, to be? The real does not satisfy us; we are ever in quest of the ideal or perfect. Evil excesses and extravagances of vicious passion are the reverse of this undying impulse of an infinite nature. God is our true Good; our insatiable curiosities are only to be satisfied by the knowledge of himself. 3. *The criterion of character.* (Ver. 21.) According to the scale of that which a man boasts of, is he judged. If he boasts of praise, worthy things, he is recognized as a virtuous and honest man; if he boasts of vain or evil things, he is abhorred. " Show me what a man likes, and I will show you what he is " (this according to what seems the true rendering of this proverb). 4. *Folly in grain.* (Ver. 22.) In the East the husk is beaten from the corn by braying in a mortar. But from the fool the husk of folly will not depart. It is possible to despise the lessons of affliction, to harden one's back against the rod. Mere punishment cannot of itself correct or convert the soul. The will, the conscious spiritual activity, must co-operate with God. A great man speaks of "that worst of afflictions—an affliction lost."—J.

Vers. 23—27.—*The man diligent in his business.* I. ECONOMY AND FORESIGHT. (Vers. 23—25.) He looks after the outgoings of his farm, well aware that there is in all things constant waste, that even the royal crown is a perishable thing. All knowledge is useful, and prudence applies through the whole scale of our being. Let the man, " if he have hands, handle; if eyes, measure and discriminate; let him accept and hive every fact of chemistry, natural history, and economy ; the more he has, the less he is willing to spare any one. Time is always bringing the occasions that disclose their value. Some wisdom comes out of every natural and innocent action." To preserve and hold together are as necessary as to gain in every kind of riches.

II. THE FRUITS OF INDUSTRY. (Vers. 26, 27.) Joyous is the sight when man's toil,

united with the forces of nature, has been blessed with the abundant harvests and the
rich flocks. Let a man keep the laws of God, and his way will be strewn with satisfactions. To find out the secret of "working together with God" in all the departments
of our life is one of the deepest secrets of satisfaction and blessedness.—J.

Ver. 1.—*Man in presence of the future: our greatness and our littleness.* It is well
to glance at—

I. OUR GREATNESS IN REGARD TO THE FUTURE. 1. There need be *no bound at all* to
our hope and aspiration in respect of the future. We are warranted in looking forward
to an endless life beyond, to an actual and absolute eternity of blessedness and glory.
Whosoever believeth in Jesus Christ has everlasting life. 2. We can and we should
prepare for a *very long time to come.* The legislator should devise his measures, the
religious leader or organizer should lay his plans, the architect should make his designs,
and the builder provide his materials with a view to the next century as well as to the
next decade. 3. We should have regard to the *coming years* as well as to the passing
days; teaching our pupils so that they will not only pass the approaching examination, but be ready for the battle of life; offering and enforcing truths and principles
which will not only tide men over to-morrow, but carry them victoriously through all
the vicissitudes of their course, and solace and strengthen them in their declining days.
But *the* lesson of the text is—

II. OUR LITTLENESS IN REGARD TO THE FUTURE. We do not know what a day
may bring forth. 1. How our purposes may be deranged, and all that we are pro-
posing to do may have to be abandoned in favour of some more imperative duty (see
Jas. iv. 13—15). 2. How our prospects may be affected; we may possibly rise from
indigence to affluence, but we are much more likely to be suddenly and seriously
reduced. Financial calamities are many, but "windfalls" are few. 3. How our circle
of friendship may be narrowed, or how soon we may be called on to leave home and
kindred. 4. How our hope of health or life may be extinguished. "Between the
morning and the evening" (see Job iv. 19—21, Revised Version) we may discover
that we are afflicted with a disease which will complete its work in a few months at
most, or we may be stricken down with a blow which will bring us face to face with
death and eternity. With this uncertainty there are three lessons we should learn.
(1) All unqualified and unreserved declarations are unbecoming. If there be no verbal
qualification, there should be a mental reservation, a feeling below the surface that all
our plans and movements are subject to the will of God. (2) We should do to-day's
work before its hours are over. Since we may not be able to do a stroke to-morrow,
let us see that every day's work is well and thoroughly done. We are not responsible
for the future, but we are for the present. And not only is it *of no use* for us to be
anxious to do much in the coming years, but it is *foolish and unfaithful* of us to be
concerned about it. Our Master sets us our work, and he gives us our time. All that
we should be solicitous about is the diligent and devoted discharge of our duty in his
appointed time and way. If he takes the weapon out of our hand here, it will be
because he has a better one to give us in a brighter and broader sphere. (3) We ought
to be prepared for any and every event. We should have within us principles that
will sustain or preserve us in any trouble or in any elevation that may be awaiting us.
We should have our house in such order that, if death should come suddenly to our
door, those whom we leave behind us will suffer the least possible affliction, and we
ourselves shall pass to the great inheritance beyond.—C.

Vers. 2, 21.—*The praise of man.* How far we should go in praising others, and in
what spirit we should accept their praise, is a matter of no small importance in the
conduct of life.

I. THE DUTY OF PRAISING OTHERS. "Let another man praise thee" can hardly be
said to be imperative so far as he is concerned. But it suggests the propriety of
another man speaking in words of commendation. And the duty of praising those
who have done well is a much-forgotten and neglected virtue. 1. It is the correlative
of blame, and if we blame freely (as we do), why should we not freely praise the
scholar, the servant, the son or daughter, the workman, etc.? 2. With many hearts,
perhaps with most, a little praise would prove a far more powerful incentive than a

large quantity of blame. 3. To praise for doing well is to follow in the footsteps of Jesus Christ and of his apostles; it is to act as the most gracious and the most useful men and women have always acted. 4. It is to do to others as we would they should do to us. We thirst for a measure of approval when we have done our best, and what we crave from others we should give to others.

II. THE WISDOM OF ABSTAINING FROM SELF-PRAISE. The injunction of Solomon appeals to our common sense. Yet is it by no means unrequired. Many men are guilty of the unseemliness and the folly of praising themselves—their ingenuity, their shrewdness, their persuasiveness, their generosity, etc. Probably if they knew how very little they commend themselves by so doing, how very soon they weary their audience, how often their language becomes positively nauseous, they would abstain. Self-vindication under a false charge is a duty and even a virtue; a very minute modicum of self-commendation may be occasionally allowable; anything beyond this is, at least, a mistake.

III. THE NECESSITY OF TESTING PRAISE. "The ordinary interpretation makes *the praise try the man*, but the words . . . in the original make *the man try the praise*" (Wardlaw). What the fining-pot is to silver, that a man should be to his praise—he should carefully and thoroughly test it. For praise is often offered some part of which should be rejected as dross. The simple-minded and the unscrupulous will praise us beyond the bounds of our desert, and to drink too much of this intoxicating cup is dangerous and demoralizing to us.

IV. THE PRACTICAL PROOF OF PRAISE. The duties and the difficulties that are before us will be the best possible proof of the sincerity and of the truthfulness of the praise we receive. We shall either be approved as the wise men we are said to be, or we shall be convicted of being less worthy than we are represented to be. Therefore let us be (1) judicious as well as generous in our praise of others, remembering that they will be thus tested; and let us (2) be contented with a modest measure of honour, realizing that we have to live up to the esteem in which we are held. But we may learn a valuable lesson from the common (if not the correct) interpretation, and consider—

V. THE TEST WHICH PRAISE AFFORDS. We stand blame better than praise; though it is right to recollect that we cannot stand more than a certain measure of blame, and few people are more objectionable or more mischievous than the scold. But much praise is a great peril. It elates and exalts; it "puffs up." It too often undermines that humility of spirit and dependence on God which are the very root of a strong and beautiful Christian character. 1. Discourage all excess in this direction; it is dangerous. 2. Care more for the approval of an instructed and well-trained conscience. 3. Care most for the commendation of Christ.—C.

Vers. 5, 6, 9, 10, 17, 19.—*Four services of friendship.* (And see homily on "Friendship," ch. xiii. 20.) We have suggested in the nineteenth verse two conditions of friendship: (1) likeness of character; and (2) reciprocity in action. There can be no true friendship where one heart does not *answer to another* as the face reflected from a mirror answers to that which is before it. Men must be like-minded in their principles and sympathies; and they must be sensitive enough to feel with one another and to give back the thoughts which are expressed by one or the other, if their intimacy is to be worthy of the sacred name of friendship. There are four services which this most precious gift of God secures for us.

I. CORRECTION. (Vers. 5, 6.) "Open rebuke is better than hidden love"—better than the love which hides from a friend its disappointment or its dissatisfaction with him. The wounds of friendship are faithful. Many are they whose character is seriously defective, and whose usefulness suffers considerable abatement from want of discipline; they are not told of their faults, they are allowed to go on deepening their roots and multiplying their fruits, because no wise and faithful friend is near to say, "Pluck out and prune." What no authority may dare to speak, love can say without fear and with excellent result.

II. REFRESHMENT. (Ver. 9.) We who are weary travellers along the path of life often need that which refreshes our spirit and turns languor into energy, gloom into gladness of heart. For that we look to friendship; it is as "ointment and perfume" to the senses. We may be jaded and worn, but the look, the grasp, the words, of our friend reanimate and renew us.

III. CONSOLATION. (Ver. 10.) We may do well to avoid the house of our kindred in the day of our calamity, especially if we have passed it by in the time of our prosperity; if our "brother" has been kept or has kept himself at a distance. But the "neighbour that is near," the friend that has been "sticking closer than a brother" will not shut the door of his heart against us. *He* is the "brother who is born for adversity;" he will claim the right of friendship to open his heart, to pour forth his sympathy, to offer his succour, to *befriend us* in every way in which affection can solace and strength can sustain us.

IV. INCITEMENT. (Ver. 17.) It is the opportunity and the high privilege of friendship to urge to honourable achievement, to rekindle the lamp of holy aspiration when the light burns low; to sustain Christian devotedness when it is putting forth its strength, by every possible encouragement; to hold up the hands of that consecrated activity which is fearlessly speaking the truth and diligently building up the kingdom of Jesus Christ.—C.

Ver. 7.—*Superabundance and scarcity.* We have here—

I. A FAMILIAR FACT OF OUR PHYSICAL NATURE. Those who are well fed become very choice and dainty, while those who "lack bread" are thankful for the coarsest food. There are thousands of the sons and daughters of luxury whose appetite can hardly be tempted; for them cookery has to be developed into one of the fine arts, and nothing is palatable to their exquisite taste but delicacies. Living within five minutes' walk of their residence, and sometimes smelling the odours that come from their kitchens, are poor, pinched, struggling men and women, who will devour with great delight the first soiled crust that is offered them. There are thousands in our great cities that weigh long and seriously the question what nice beverage they shall drink at their table; and there *are* to be found those who would gladly quench their thirst in the first foul water they can find. Indulgence makes all things tasteless, while want makes all things sweet to us.

II. A CORRESPONDING TRUTH IN OUR MORAL NATURE. 1. Superabundance tends to selfishness and ingratitude. We are apt to imagine that we have a prescriptive right to that which is continued to us for any time; and as soon as it is withdrawn we murmur and rebel. There are no more thankless, no more querulous hearts to be found anywhere than in the homes of the affluent, than among those who can command all that their hearts desire. They find no pleasure in what they have, and they give God no thanks for it. 2. On the other hand, scarcity is very frequently associated with contentment and piety. When our resources are not so large and full that we do not stop to ask ourselves whence they come, when some solicitude or even anxiety leads us to look prayerfully to the great "Giver of all," then we recognize the truth that everything we are and everything we have, the cup itself and all that it holds, all our powers and all our possessions, are of God, and our hearts fill with gratitude to our heavenly Father. And thus it is not exceptionally but representatively and commonly true that—

> "Some murmur when their sky is clear
>   And wholly bright to view,
> If one small speck of dark appear
>   In their great heaven of blue.
> And some with thankful love are filled
>   If but one streak of light,
> One ray of God's good mercy, gild
>   The darkness of their night.
>
> "In palaces are hearts that ask,
>   In discontent and pride,
> Why life is such a dreary task,
>   And all good things denied.
> And hearts, in poorest huts, admire
>   How love has, in their aid—
> Love that not ever seems to tire—
>   Such rich provision made."

(Trench.)

III. ITS APPLICATION TO CHRISTIAN PRIVILEGE. Here we have: 1. *The peril of abundance.* We are tempted to become indifferent to that which we can employ and enjoy at any time, and consequently to neglect it. 2. *The compensation of scarcity.* That which is often out of reach, of which we can only occasionally avail ourselves, we appreciate at its true worth. Hence, while persecuted Christians have been willing to walk many miles to take part in the worship of God, or to give large sums of money for a few pages of Scripture, those who live in the full light of privilege are negligent of the sanctuary and the Word of God. This will apply to prayer, to praise, to Christian work, to Christian fellowship.—C.

Ver. 8.—(See homily on vers. 23—27.)—C.

Ver. 14.—(See homily on ch. xxv. 20.)—C.

Ver. 18.—*The reward of faithful service.* This is a question which very intimately and importantly concerns us; for—

I. SERVICE CONSTITUTES THE GREATER PART OF HUMAN LIFE. We have to consider how large a proportion of our race is formally and regularly engaged in service *as the occupation of their life.* When we have counted domestic servants, agricultural labourers, and all orders of "workmen;" and when we have included all those who, in the press, or the pulpit, or the legislature, are the avowed and actual servants of the public, we have referred to a very large portion indeed of the whole population. So that "he that waiteth on his master," though he may (in the literal sense of the phrase) be confined to a small section, yet actually stands for the majority of mankind. Indeed, we must be occupying a very strange position if we are not of those who are engaged in serving in some form or other.

II. MANY THINGS DEMAND THAT SERVICE SHALL BE FAITHFUL. 1. *God is requiring it of us.* It is required by him that we who are stewards be found faithful (1 Cor. iv. 2; Col. iii. 22—25). 2. *The best and noblest men,* whose character and course we admire, were men "faithful in all their house" (see Heb. iii. 5). 3. *We can only retain our self-respect* by faithfulness. To do our work slowly or slovenly, in such wise that we should be ashamed to have it inspected by "the master" (whoever he may be), in such a manner that it will not stand the test of time, is to undermine all respect for ourselves, is to sink sadly and pitifully, if not fatally, in our own esteem. 4. *Faithfulness has a large and a sure reward.* Careful culture of the fig tree is sure to be rewarded with the eating of its fruit in due time. Faithful service is sure to bring its due recompense. (1) It brings *honour.* We respect the true and conscientious labourer in our own hearts, and we do not fail to honour him in the estimation of others. Loyal and valuable service commands no small esteem when it has had time to make an impression on the mind. (2) It brings *personal attachment* and even affection. Often between those who serve and those who are served there arises a true and deep affection which is very honourable to both, very beautiful in its character, and lasting as long as life. (3) Due *material recompense.* This may be delayed, but it comes in time. (4) *Enlargement of capacity.* Perhaps the best reward of faithful service is found here—in the enlargement of the faculty of service. Do, and you will do better; serve to-day, and you will serve more skilfully and efficiently to-morrow; put out your one talent in the lowly sphere, and you will soon have two talents (of faculty and aptitude) to put out in a higher one.

> "I will ask for no reward,
> Except to serve thee still"

—and to serve thee *better.* But if it be said that, after all, human service *is* sometimes unappreciated and unacknowledged, that the labourer's hire is withheld and *not* paid, that the "master" does *not* render the honour that is due to him who has "waited on" him long and served him well—as it may sometimes be truly said—then let us retire to the truth that—

III. THERE IS ONE SERVICE IN WHICH THERE IS NO DISAPPOINTMENT. We are the servants of Christ. We delight to call him Master (John xiii. 13). We owe him everything, and we offer him the subjection of our will, the trust of our hearts, the service of our lives. He will not disappoint us. He will not forget our work of faith and our labour of love. The slightest service shall "in no wise lose its reward." He will generously regard what we do for his humble disciples as something rendered to himself. Here we shall possess his loving favour, and there his bountiful recompense.—C.

Vers. 23—27 (and ver. 8).—*A commendation of diligence.* It is likely enough that Solomon, oppressed with the burdens and vexations, with the difficulties and dangers, of the throne, looked longingly toward those pastoral scenes which he here describes. But, keen and shrewd man that he was, he must have known that contentment does not always find a home in the homestead, and that there may be as much disquietude of heart in the fields of the beautiful country as there is in the streets of the crowded city. We look for something more than an ordinary "pastoral" in these verses. We recognize in them a royal commendation of diligence.

I. THERE IS NEED OF DILIGENCE IN EVERY SPHERE. "Be diligent to know the state of thy flocks, and look well to thy herds." Pastoral prosperity demands the care and the labour of the shepherd or the herdsman, as well as do the transactions of princes and the affairs of state. It will be a poor season and a bad harvest if the farmer is dreaming all day long. It is true that kids and calves and lambs grow up "of themselves," and that "the earth bringeth forth fruit of itself" (Mark iv. 28); but it is also true that without watchful care on the shepherd's part the flock will be sickly and small, and that without toil and skill on the part of the farmer the hay crop and the wheat crop will be quite disappointing. And so in everything. Whatever the sphere may be, diligence is the invariable condition of success. The man who will not take pains, who does not work and strive, who does not throw his strength and energy into his occupation, will soon find how great is his mistake.

II. DILIGENCE MUST BE CONCENTRATED IF IT IS TO BE REMUNERATIVE. (Ver. 8.) A man that is everywhere but at home, who is interested in everybody's business but his own, who can tell his neighbours how to improve their estate while his own is neglected, who has a hand in a hundred activities, may be exceedingly busy and (in his way) diligent; but he is not a "man of business," and he does not show the diligence which yields a good result. Let a man know "his place" and keep it; and, while selfishness and narrowness of spirit are bad and blameful enough, it is needful for him to give his strength to his own sphere, his forces to his own fields.

III. A WISE DILIGENCE WILL BE WELL REWARDED. 1. It will procure domestic comfort (vers. 25—27). 2. It will lead to honour and reputation (ch. xxii. 29). 3. It will invest with power (ch. xii. 24). 4. It will enrich with various kinds of human wealth (ch. x. 4; xiii. 4; xxi. 5). Patient industry is the source of all the good which beautifies and brightens, which adorns and enlarges, human life.

IV. THERE IS A SERIOUS UNCERTAINTY AGAINST WHICH TO PROVIDE. (Ver. 24.) You may be the son of a king, but the crown sometimes changes hands; dynasties are not immortal. You may have a large treasure at command, but the thief, who wears many guises and comes to us in many forms, may steal it away. Better depend on self-reliance than on such props as these; have the diligent hand at your side, and you will be able to defy the chances and the losses that come in the hour and in the way when we look not for them.

V. THERE IS ONE SPHERE IN WHICH DILIGENCE IS OF INESTIMABLE VALUE—THE KEEPING OF OUR OWN HEART. With the most devout and the most sedulous care should we "keep" our spiritual nature, for from it flow the streams of life or death (see homily on ch. iv. 23).—C.

EXPOSITION.

CHAPTER XXVIII.

This chapter is still part of the Hezekiah collection, and not a new series by another author. It may be regarded as describing the various destinies of the powerful and the weak, the sinner and the righteous.

Ver. 1.—The wicked flee when no man pursueth. The unreasoning terror of the sinner arises partly from his uneasy conscience, which will not permit him to transgress without warning of consequences, and partly from the judgment of God, according to the threats denounced in Lev. xxvi. 36, 37. A terrible picture of this instinctive fear is drawn in Job xv. 20, etc., and Wisd. xvii. 9, etc. There are numerous proverbs about unreasonable timidity, such as being afraid of one's own shadow (see Erasmus, 'Adag.,' s.v. "Timiditas"). As the Eastern puts it, "The leaf cracked, and your servant fled;" and "Among ten men nine are women" (Lane). On the cowardice of sinners St. Chrysostom says well, "Such is the nature of sin, that it betrays while no one finds fault; it condemns whilst no one accuses; it makes the sinner a timid being, one that trembles at a sound; even as righteousness has the contrary effect. . . . How doth the wicked flee when no man pursueth? He hath that within which drives him on, an accuser in his own conscience, and this he carries about everywhere; and just as it would be impossible to flee from himself, so neither can he escape the persecutor within, but wherever he goeth he is scourged, and hath an incurable wound" ('Hom. in Stat.,' viii. 3, Oxford transl.). **But the righteous are bold as a lion.** They are undismayed in the presence of danger, because their conscience is at rest, they know that God is on their side, and, whatever happens, they are safe in the everlasting arms (see Ps. xci.). Thus David the shepherd-boy quailed not before the giant (1 Sam. xvii. 32, etc.), remembering the promise in Lev. xxvi. 7, 8. The heathen poet Horace could say of the upright man ('Carm.,' iii. 3. 7)—

"Si fractus illabatur orbis,
　　Impavidum ferient ruinæ."

"Whoso feareth the Lord shall not fear nor be afraid; for he is his Hope" (Ecclus. xxxi. (xxxiv.) 14, etc.). St. Gregory ('Moral.,' xxxi. 55, "The lion is not afraid in the onset of beasts, because he knows well that he is stronger than them all. Whence the fearlessness of a righteous man is rightly compared to a lion, because, when he beholds any rising against him, he returns to the confidence of his mind, and knows that he overcomes all his adversaries because he loves him alone whom he cannot in any way lose against his will. For whoever seeks after outward things, which are taken from him even against his will, subjects himself of his own accord to outward fear. But unbroken virtue is the contempt of earthly desire, because the mind is both placed on high when it is raised above the meanest objects by the judgment of its hopes, and is the less affected by all adversities, the more safely it is fortified by being placed on things above" (Oxford transl.).

Ver. 2.—For the transgression of a land many are the princes thereof. This implies that the wickedness of a nation is punished by frequent changes of rulers, who impose new laws, taxes, and other burdens, which greatly oppress the people; but regarding the antithesis in the second hemistich, we take the meaning to be that when iniquity, injustice, apostasy, and other evils abound, a country becomes the prey of pretenders and partisans striving for the supremacy. The history of the northern kingdom of Israel, especially in the disastrous period succeeding the death of Jeroboam II., affords proof of the truth of the statement (comp. Hos. viii. 4). Septuagint, "Owing to the sins of ungodly men, quarrels (κρίσεις, lawsuits) arise." **But by a man of understanding and knowledge the state thereof shall be prolonged.** "The state" is the stability, the settled condition of the country. The word is כֵּן (ken), here a substantive, equivalent to "station," "base." Umbreit, Nowack, and others translate it, "justice," "authority," "order." When a wise and religious man is at the helm of state, justice continues, lives, and works; such a man introduces an element of enduring good into a land (comp. ch. xxi. 22; Eccles. ix. 15). The good kings Asa, Jehoshaphat, Uzziah, and Hezekiah had long and prosperous reigns. Septuagint, "But a clever man (πανοῦργος) will quench them (quarrels)."

Ver. 3.—A poor man that oppresseth the poor. The words rendered "poor" are different. The former is *rash*, "needy," the latter *dal*, "feeble" (see on ch. x. 15). Delitzsch notes that, in accordance with the accents in the Masoretic text, we should translate, "A poor man and an oppressor of the lowly—a sweeping rain without bringing bread," which would mean that a tyrant who oppresses the lowly bears the same relation to the poor that a devastating rain does to those whom it deprives of their food. But it is pretty certain that "the poor" and "the oppressor" designate the same person (though the vocalization is against it); hence the gnome refers to a usurper who, rising to power from poor estate, makes the very worst and most tyrannical ruler. Such a one has learned nothing from his former condition but callous indifference, and now seeks to exercise on others that power which once galled him. Thus among schoolboys it is found that the greatest bully is one who has himself been bullied; and needy revolutionists make the most rapacious and iniquitous demagogues. Of such tyrants the prophets complain (see Isa. v. 8, etc.; Micah ii. 2). Wordsworth refers, as an illustration, to Catiline and his fellow-conspirators, who were moved by selfish interests to overthrow the commonwealth.

Many modern commentators (*e.g.* Hitzig, Delitzsch, Nowack), in view of the present text, regarding the combination גבר רש, and noting that elsewhere the oppressor and the poor are always introduced in opposition (comp. ch. xxix. 13), read רָאשׁ, or consider רש as equivalent to it—*rosh*, "the head," in the signification of "master," "ruler." The gnome thus becomes concinnous, the ruler who ought to benefit his dependents, but injures them, corresponding to the rain which, instead of fertilizing, devastates the crops. The LXX. had a different reading, as it renders, "A bold man in his impieties (ἀνδρεῖος ἐν ἀσεβείαις) calumniates the poor." *Is like a sweeping rain which leaveth no food;* literally, *and not bread.* A violent storm coming at seed-time and washing away soil and seed, or happening at harvest-time and destroying the ripe corn. Vulgate, *Similis est imbri vehementi, in quo paratur fames.* Ewald supposes that such proverbs as these and the following belong to the time of Jeroboam II., when the prosperity of the people induced luxury and arrogance, and was accompanied with much moral evil, oppression, and perversion of justice ('Hist. of Israel,' iii. 126, Eng. transl.). The Bengalee compares the relation of the rich oppressor to the poor, not with the rainstorm, but with that of the carving-knife to the pumpkin.

Ver. 4.—**They that forsake the Law praise the wicked.** This they do because they love iniquity, and like to see it extend its influence, and arm itself against the good, who are a standing reproach to them. St. Paul notes it as a mark of extreme wickedness that gross sinners "not only do the same iniquities, but have pleasure in them that do them" (Rom. i. 32). **Such as keep the Law contend with them;** are angry with them. They are filled with righteous indignation; they cannot hold their peace when they see God's Law outraged, and must have the offenders punished (comp. 1 Kings xix. 14; Ps. lxxiv. 11, etc.; cxix. 136, 139; cxxxix. 21). The LXX. connects this verse with the latter part of the preceding, thus: "As an impetuous and profitless rain, thus those who forsake the Law praise ungodliness; but they who love the Law raise a wall around themselves."

Ver. 5.—**Evil men understand not judgment;** or, *what is right.* An evil man's moral conception is perverted, he cannot distinguish between right and wrong; the light that was in him has become darkness (comp. ch. xxix. 7). Many men, by giving themselves over to wickedness, are judicially blinded, according to John xii. 39, 40. **They who seek the Lord understand all things.** Those who do God's will, seeking him in prayer, know what is morally right in every circumstance, have

a right judgment in all things (comp. Eccles. viii. 5; 1 Cor. ii. 15). So 1 John ii. 20, "Ye have an unction from the Holy One, and ye know all things;" and our Lord has declared, "If any man willeth to do his will, he shall know of the doctrine" (John vii. 17).

Ver. 6.—This is almost the same as ch. xix. 1, but varies a little in the second hemistich : **than he that is perverse in his ways, though he be rich.** The Hebrew literally is, *perverse of two ways;* i.e. who, going one way, pretends to go another; the "two ways" being the evil which he really pursues, and the good which he feigns to follow. Delitzsch calls him "a double-going deceiver." So Siracides imprecates, "Woe to the sinner that goeth two ways" (Ecclus. ii. 12). "A double-minded man," says St. James (i. 8), "is unstable in all his ways." It is not the endeavouring to serve God and mammon at the same time that is meant, but putting on the appearance of religion to mask wicked designs—in the present case in order to gain wealth. Septuagint, "A poor man walking in truth is better than a rich liar."

Ver. 7.—**Whoso keepeth the Law is a wise son.** "Law" is *torah,* as ver. 4; but it seems here to include not only the Decalogue, but also the father's instruction and commands. Such an obedient and prudent son brings honour and joy to a parent's heart (see ch. x. 1; xxix. 3). **He that is a companion of riotous men shameth his father;** literally, *he that feedeth, hath fellowship with, gluttons* (ch. xxiii. 20). The son who herds with debauchers, and wastes his substance in riotous living, brings shame on, wounds, and insults, all connected with him. Such a one transgresses the Law and his father's commands, and brings them into contempt (comp. ch. xxvii. 11). Hence the antithesis of the two clauses. Septuagint, "He that cherishes debauchery (ποιμαίνει ἀσωτίαν) dishonours his father." Ἀσωτία occurs only in 2 Macc. vi. 4, but is common in the New Testament; *e.g.* Eph. v. 18; Titus i. 6.

Ver. 8.—**He that by usury and unjust gain increaseth his substance.** "Usury" (*neshek*) is interest on money lent taken in money; "unjust gain" (*tarbith*) is interest taken in kind, as if a man, having lent a bushel of corn, exacted two bushels in return. All such transactions were forbidden by the Law of Moses, at any rate between Israelites (see Lev. xxv. 36, 37, "Thou shalt not give thy brother thy money upon usury (*neshek*), nor lend him thy victuals for increase [*marbith*, equivalent to *tarbith*, which is used in ver. 36]"). Septuagint, Μετὰ τόκων καὶ πλεονασμῶν, "With interest and usury." (For censure of usury, see Ps. cix. 11; Ezek. xviii. 13; and contrast Ps. xv. 5; Ezek. xviii. 8.) **He shall gather it for him that will pity the poor.** He shall never enjoy it himself, and shall fall into the hanls of one who will make a better use of it (see on ch. xxii. 16; and comp ch. xiii. 22; Job xxvii. 16, etc.). In our Lord's parable the pound is taken from one who made no good use of it and is given to a more profitable servant (Luke xix. 24).

Ver. 9.—**He that turneth away his ear from hearing the Law.** He who refuses to hearken to and to practise the dictates of the Divine Law (comp ch. i. 24). **Even his prayer** shall be abomination (comp. ch. xv. 8, and note there). "God heareth not sinners" (John ix. 31). Such a man's prayer, if he does pray, is not hearty and sincere, and therefore lacks the element which alone can make it acceptable. He will not resolve to forsake his favourite sin, even while paying outward worship to the God whose Law he breaks: what wonder that the prophet so sternly denounces such offenders (Isa. i. 11, etc.), and the psalmist cries with terrible rigour, "When he shall be judged, let him be condemned; and let his prayer become sin" (Ps. cix. 7)? St. Gregory ('Moral.,' x. 27), "Our heart blames us in offering up our prayers, when it calls to mind that it is set in opposition to the precepts of him whom it implores, and the prayer becomes abomination, when there is a 'turning away' from the control of the Law; in that verily it is meet that a man should be a stranger to the favours of him to whose bidding he will not be subject." And again (ibid., xviii. 9, 10), "If that which he bids we do, that which we ask we shall obtain. For with God both these two do of necessity match with one another exactly, that practice should be sustained by prayer, and prayer by practice" (Oxford transl.).

Ver. 10.—A tristich. **Whoso causeth the righteous to go astray in an evil way.** It is doubtful whether physical danger or moral seduction is meant. The gnome is true in either case; he who misleads one who trusted him, and who, being simple and good, ought to have been respected and to have received better treatment, shall fall into the destruction which he prepared for the other (ch. xxvi. 27). Taking the proverb in a moral sense, we find this truth: If the good man does ever yield to the temptations of the sinner, the latter does not reap the enjoyment which he expected from the other's lapse, rather he is made twofold more the child of hell, he himself sinks the deeper and more hopelessly for playing the devil's part, while the just rises from his temporary fall more humble, watchful, and guarded for the future. **But the upright shall have good things in possession;** or, *shall inherit good* (ch. iii. 35). He shall be abundantly rewarded by God's grace and protection, by the comfort of a conscience at rest, and by prosperity in his worldly concerns—an adumbration of the eternal recompense awaiting him in the life to come. St. Jerome has changed the incidence of the gnome by inserting *ejus,* thus: *Et simplices possidebunt bona ejus,* which makes the meaning to be that the righteous shall be the instruments of retribution on the deceiver, whose riches shall pass over into their possession. But the Hebrew gives no countenance to this interpretation. Septuagint, "The transgressors shall pass by good things, and shall not enter into them," where the translator has misunderstood the original.

Ver. 11.—**The rich man is wise in his own conceit** (comp. ch. xviii. 11). A rich man thinks so highly of his position, is so flattered by parasites, and deems himself placed so immeasurably above social inferiors, that he learns to consider himself possessed of other qualifications, even mental and intellectual gifts, with which wealth has no concern. This purse-proud arrogance which looks upon financial skill and sharpness in bargaining as true wisdom, is confined to no age or country. **But the poor man that hath understanding searcheth him out** (ch. xviii. 17). Wisdom is not to be bought with money. A poor man may be wise, his poverty probably making him a keener critic; and if he is brought into communication with this self-deluding plutocrat, he soon sees through him and recognizes his real value. Septuagint, "An intelligent poor man will condemn him."

Ver. 12.—**When righteous** men **do rejoice, there is great glory** (comp. ch. xxix. 2; xi. 10). "Rejoice," rather *triumph,* as conquerors, right prevailing and wickedness being overcome. Then there is great show of joy, and, as the expression implies, men put on their festal garments to do honour to the occasion. See the description of Solomon's time (1 Kings iv. 20, 25). If we take this verse in connection with ver. 2, we may see in it the triumph of order after a period of confusion and anarchy. Septuagint, "Through the help of righteous men great glory arises." **But when the wicked rise, a man is hidden** (comp. ver. 28, where, however, the verb is different). The Authorized Version means that when the wicked rise to power, people have to hide themselves in order to escape danger to life and property. The verb is more literally rendered, "are searched for," *i.e.* they have betaken themselves to hiding-places, and have to be looked for; they fear oppression and injury, and venture no longer into the streets and open places. Vulgate, *Regnantibus impiis ruinæ hominum*, "When evil men are in power, there is general ruin;" Septuagint, "In the places of the ungodly men are caught." Other interpretations of the proverb have been suggested, though none is so satisfactory as that given above. Thus some take the searching out to mean testing, in the sense that evil times try men's characters, and bring out their true nature (1 Cor. xi. 19). Others explain that, under the reign of the impious, men do not come forward to take part in public affairs, but retire sullenly into private life.

Ver. 13.—**He that covereth his sins shall not prosper.** To cover one's sins is either absolutely to disown them or to make excuses; a man who does this is never free from a burden of guilt, as the psalmist says, "When I kept silence, my bones waxed old through my roaring all the day long. For day and night thy hand was heavy upon me" (Ps. xxxii. 3, etc.). **Whoso confesseth and forsaketh** them shall have mercy. Confession alone without amendment, or what is called theologically satisfaction, does not win pardon and mercy. It is when the sinner acknowledges his transgression, and turns from it to newness of life, that God heals his backsliding, and turns away his anger and renews the tokens of his love (Hos. xiv. 4). Confession is made to God, against whom all sin is committed (Josh. vii. 19; Job xxxi. 33; 1 John i. 8, etc.); and to man, if one has transgressed against him, or if he be in a position to give spiritual counsel. Thus the people confessed their sins before John the Baptist (Matt. iii. 6) and the apostles (Acts xix. 18; comp. Jas. v. 16). Among the Jews, the high priest, acting as the mouthpiece of the people on the great Day of Atonement, confessed their iniquities, laying them on the scapegoat; and particular confession was also enjoined, and was part of the ritual accompanying a sacrifice for sin, by which legal purification was obtained (Numb. v. 6, 7, "When a man or woman shall commit any sin . . . then they shall confess their sin which they have done;" so Lev. v. 5). And the very offering of a trespass offering was a public recognition of guilt, which was exhibited by the offerer laying his hand on the head of the victim (Lev. i. 4). Such confession is spoken of strongly by Siracides, "Be not ashamed to confess thy sins, and force not the course of the river" (Ecclus. iv. 26); *i.e.* do not attempt the impossible task of trying to hide them. The LXX. has, "He who sets forth accounts (ἐξηγούμενος ἐλέγχους, *i.e.* blames himself) shall be loved." Lesètre quotes Sedulius, 'Carm. Pasch.,' iv. 76—

"Magna est medicina fateri
Quod nocet abscondi; quoniam sua vulnera nutrit
Qui tegit, et plagam trepidat nudare medenti."

"Mighty relief
T' expose what rankles while 'tis hidden still.
He feeds who hides his wounds and shuns to show
His heart's plague to the good physician."

Ver. 14.—**Happy is the man that feareth alway.** Some have taken the fear mentioned to be the fear with which God is to be regarded. Thus Aben Ezra. But it is rather the fear of sin which is meant—that tender conscience and watchful heart which lead a man to be prepared for temptation and able to resist it when it arises. Such a one distrusts himself, takes heed lest he fall (1 Cor. x. 12), and works out his salvation with fear and trembling (Phil. ii. 12; comp. ch. xiv. 16). "Grow not thoughtless of retribution" ('Pirke Aboth,' i. 8). A horror of sin cannot be instilled too early into the young. Septuagint, "Happy is the man who piously (δι' εὐλάβειαν) fears all things." St. Bernard ('In Cant. Serm.,' liv. 9), "In veritate didici, nil æque efficax esse ad gratiam promerendam, retinendam, recuperandam, quam si omni tempore coram Deo inveniaris non altum sapere, sed timere. Time ergo cum arriserit gratia, time cum abierit, time cum denuo revertetur; et hoc est semper pavidum esse." **He that hardeneth his heart shall fall into mischief;** or, *calamity* (ch. xvii. 20). A man hardens his heart who attends not to the voice of conscience, the restraints of religion, the counsel of friends, the warnings of experience (comp. ver. 26; ch. xxix. 1; Exod. viii. 15; Ps. xcv. 8). This man scorns the grace of God, loses his protection, and must come to misery.

Ver. 15.—**A wicked ruler over the poor people;** a people weak and resourceless. To such a powerful tyrant is as fatal as a roaring lion or a hungry bear prowling in quest of food. The prophets compare evil rulers to ravenous lions (see Jer. iv. 7; Ezek. xix. 6). They are like lions in strength and cruelty, like bears in craft and ferocity. Septuagint, "A hungry lion and a thirsty wolf is he, who, being poor, rules over an indigent nation." The poverty of the subjects embitters the conduct of the ruler.

Ver. 16.—**The prince that wanteth understanding is also a great oppressor;** literally, *and rich in oppression.* Ewald, Delitzsch, Nowack, and others take the verse, not as a statement, but as a warning addressed to the ruler, as we have so many addressed to a son, and as the author of the Book of Wisdom calls upon the judges of the earth to listen to his admonitions. They therefore render thus: " O prince, void of understanding, but rich in oppression! " The wording and accentuation of the passage confirm this view. Caher renders, "A prince that wants understanding increases his exactions." The want of intelligence makes a prince cruel and tyrannical and callous to suffering; not possessing the wisdom and prudence necessary for right government, he defrauds his subjects, treats them unjustly, and causes great misery. See the prophet's denunciation of Shallum and Jehoiakim for these very crimes (Jer. xxii. 13—19). Septuagint, " A king wanting revenues is a great oppressor (συκοφάντης)." He that hateth covetousness shall prolong his days (ch. xv. 27). The prince addressed is thus warned that his oppressive acts will be visited upon him judicially; that only a ruler who deals with his subjects liberally and equitably can attain to old age, and that his conduct will shorten his life. An early death is reckoned as a token of God's indignation. The second hemistich Caher translates, " But he who hates lucre shall reign long." Septuagint, " He who hateth iniquity shall live a long time." (For " covetousness " (betsa), see on ch. i. 19.)

Ver. 17.—A man that doeth violence to the blood of any person shall flee to the pit. This should be, a man oppressed (Isa. xxxviii. 14), burdened, with the blood of any one. The wilful murderer, with his guilt upon his soul, flies in vain from remorse; his crime pursues him even to the grave. For inadvertent manslaughter the cities of refuge offered an asylum, but for deliberate murder there was no safe refuge, either from the stings of conscience or from the avenger of blood, but death. The homicide, like Cain (Gen. iv. 14), must be a fugitive and a vagabond in the earth. " Pit " (bor), some take to mean any hiding-place, " a cave, or well; " but it is very commonly found in the sense of " sepulchre " (Ps. xxviii. 1; Isa. xiv. 19, etc.), and is so explained here by most commentators. Let no man stay him. We had in ch. xxiv. 11, etc., an injunction to save human life; but the case was quite different from this of wilful murder. Here it is directed that no one attempt to save him from the punishment which he has incurred, or to comfort him under the remorse which he suffers. Let him be left alone to meet the fate which he has merited. The LXX. gives a different idea to the gnome, " He who becomes bail for a man charged with murder shall be banished and shall not be in safety." They add a verse which we shall meet again, almost in the same words (ch. xxix. 17, 18), " Chasten thy son, and he will love thee, and will give honour to thy soul; he shall not obey a sinful nation."

Ver. 18.—Whoso walketh uprightly shall be saved. "Uprightly" (tamim); innocently, blamelessly (Ps. xv. 2). Vulgate, simpliciter; Septuagint, δικαίως; Aquila, Symmachus, τέλειος. "He is helped (βεβοήθηται)," Septuagint. Things shall prosper with him; God will work with him, and save him in dangers temporal and spiritual. But he that is perverse in his ways shall fall at once. " He that is perverse of two ways," or " in a double way," as ver. 6. The man who is not straightforward, but vacillates between right and wrong, or pretends to be pursuing one path while he is really taking another, shall fall suddenly and without warning. בְּאֶחָת means " all at once," or " once for all," and so that nothing else is possible, equivalent to penitus. Schultens quotes Virgil, ' Æneid,' xi. 418—

" Procubuit moriens et humum semel ore momordit."

Septuagint, " He that walketh in crooked ways will be entangled."

Ver. 19.—A variation of ch. xii. 11. Shall have poverty enough. The new clause marks the antithesis more clearly than that above.

Ver. 20.—A faithful man shall abound with blessings. "Faithful," as in ch. xx. 6, one on whom one can depend, honest and upright. Septuagint, ἀξιόπιστος. The blessings signified are such as come from God and man. Men will utter his name with praise and benediction (comp. Job xxix. 8, etc.), and God will show his approval by sending material prosperity. He that maketh haste to be rich shall not be innocent (comp. ver. 22, and note there; ch. xiii. 11; xx. 21; xxi. 5). One who is only anxious to become quickly rich, and is unscrupulous as to means, cannot be " a faithful man," and therefore cannot be blessed. Instead of " innocent," many expositors render " unpunished " (as ch. xvii. 5), which better contrasts with the blessings mentioned in the first hemistich, though the two ideas are co-ordinate. On this haste of covetousness, Juvenal writes (' Sat.,' xiv. 173)—

" Inde fere scelerum causæ; nec plura venena
Miscuit aut ferro grassatur sæpius ullum
Humanæ mentis vitium, quam sæva cupido
Immodici census; nam dives qui fieri vult,
Et cito vult fieri. Sed quæ reverentia legum,
Quis metus aut pudor est unquam properantis avari? "

The Septuagint waters down the gnome, " But the wicked shall not be unpunished."

Ver. 21.—The first hemistich occurs a little fuller in ch. xxiv. 23, referring there, as here, to the administration of justice.

For for a piece of bread that man will transgress. Thus translated, this clause confirms the former, and says that a judge given to favouritism will swerve from right under the smallest temptation. But to bribe a judge with a morsel of bread seems an unlikely idea; and the gnome is of general application, "And for a morsel of bread a man [not 'that man'] will transgress." As some men in responsible positions are often swayed by low and unworthy considerations, so in social life a very insignificant cause is sufficient to warp the judgment of some per ons, or draw 'hem aside from the line of rectitude. (For "a piece of bread," as denoting abject poverty or a thing of no value, see on ch. vi. 26) The commentators cite Aul. Gell., 'Noct. Att.,' i. 15, "Frusto panis conduci potest vel uti taceat vel uti loquatur." Septuagint, "He that regards not the persons of the just is not good; such a one will sell a man for a morsel of bread."

Ver. 22.—He that hasteth to be rich hath an evil eye (see ver. 20); better, *the man of evil eye hasteth after riches.* The man of evil eye (ch. xxiii. 6) is the envious and covetous man; such a one tries to improve his position and raise himself speedily to the height of him whom he envies, and is quite unscrupulous as to the means which he uses to effect his purpose, and keeps all that he gains selfishly to himself. And yet he is really blind to his own best interests (comp ch. xx. 21). And considereth not that poverty shall come upon him (comp. ch. xxiii. 4, 5). His grasping greed brings no blessing with it (ch. xi. 25), excites others to defraud him, and in the end consigns him to merited poveity. The LXX. here reads somewhat differently, and translates, "An envious man hasteth to be rich, and knows not that the merciful man (*chasid* instead of *cheser*) will have the mastery over him," *i.e.* will take his wealth, as ver. 8. Proverbs concerning hastily gotten wealth have already been given. Here are a few more: Spanish, "Who would be rich in a year gets hanged in half a year;" Italian, "The river does not become swollen with clear water;" says a Scotch proverb, "Better a wee fire to warm us than a meikle fire to burn us."

Ver. 23.—He that rebuketh a man afterwards shall find more favour. The word rendered "afterwards" (*postea*, Vulgate), אַחֲרַי (*acharai*), creates a difficulty. The suffix cannot be that of the first person singular, which would give no sense; hence most interpreters see in it a peculiar adverb attached to the following verb, "shall afterwards find." Delitzsch, Löwenstein, and Nowack take it for a noun with the termination -*ai*, and translate, "a man that goeth backward," "a backslider" (as Jer. vii. 24).

Hence the translation will run, "He who reproveth a backsliding man," *i e.* one whom he sees to be turning away from God and duty. He shall find more lavour than he that flattereth with the tongue (comp. ch. xxvii. 6; xxix. 5). A faithful counsellor, who tells a man his faults, brings them home to his conscience, and checks him in his downward course, will be seen to be a true friend, and will be loved and respected both by the one whom he has warned and advised and by all who are well disposed. Jas. v. 19, "If any of you do err from the truth, and one convert him, let him know that he which converteth the sinner from the error of his way shall save a soul from death, and shall hide a multitude of sins." "Laudat adulator, sed non est verus amator." The flatterer says only what is agreeable to the man whom he flatters, and thus makes him conceited and selfish and unable to see himself as he really is; the true friend says harsh things, but they are wholesome and tend to spiritual profit, and show more real affection than all the soft words of the fawning parasite. Septuagint, "He that reproveth a man's ways shall have more thanks than he who flattereth with the tongue."

Ver. 24.—Whoso robbeth his father or his mother (comp. ch. xix. 26); taking from them what belongs to them. Septuagint, "He who casts off (ἀποβάλλεται) father or mother." And saith, It is no transgression. He salves his conscience by thinking all would be his ere long in the course of nature; or he uses the plea of *Corban* denounced by our Lord (Mark vii. 11, etc.). The same is the companion of a destroyer (ch. xviii. 9); is no better than, stands in the position of, one who practises openly against his neighbour's life and property. He is a thief, and fails in the simplest duty. Vulgate, *particeps homicidæ est.* There may be an allusion to the guilt incurred by a witness in concealing his knowledge of a crime, which is denounced in Lev. v. 1 (comp. Judg. xvii. 2).

Ver. 25.—He that is of a proud heart stirreth up strife (ch. xv. 18; xxix. 22); literally, *he that is of a wide soul.* This may certainly denote pride (*qui se jactat et dilatat,* Vulgate), in which case the gnome says that one who thinks much of himself and despises others is the cause of quarrels and dissensions, occasioned by his struggles for pre-eminence and the ill feeling arising from his overbearing and supercilious conduct. Others, and rightly, take the wide soul to denote covetousness (comp. ch. xxiii. 2; Isa. v. 14; Hab. ii. 5). It is the man of insatiable desire, the grasping avaricious man, who excites quarrels and mars all peace, and in the end destroys himself. "Whence come wars," asks St. James (iv. 1), "and whence come fightings among you? come they not hence, even of your pleasures that war in your members? Ye lust, and have not; ye kill, and covet, and cannot obtain: ye fight and war." Septuagint, "An unbelieving [ἄπιστος, Alexand. ἄπληστος, insatiate] man judgeth rashly." **But he that putteth his trust in the Lord shall be made fat** (ch. xi. 25; xvi. 20; xxix. 25). The character here opposed to the covetous is that of the patient, God-fearing man, who is contented to do his duty, and leave the result in the Lord's hands. This man shall be made fat, shall be comforted and largely blessed, while he who puts his hope in material things shall fall into calamity. Septuagint, "He who trusts in the Lord will be in his care (ἐν ἐπιμελείᾳ ἔσται)."

Ver. 26.—**He that trusteth in his own heart is a fool** (see Gen. vi. 5; viii. 21). What is here censured is that presumptuous confidence in one's own thoughts, plans, and imaginations which leads a man to neglect both God's inspirations and the counsel of others (comp. ver. 14; ch. xiv. 16). "Let him that thinketh he standeth take heed lest he fall" (1 Cor. x. 12). Septuagint, "Whoso trusteth to a bold heart, such a one is a fool." **Whoso walketh wisely, he shall be delivered.** This man looks outside himself for direction; he trusts in the wisdom which is from above; he walks in the fear of the Lord, and is saved from the dangers to which self-confidence exposes the fool. The best commentary on the gnome is Jer. ix. 23, 24, "Let not the wise man glory in his wisdom, neither let the mighty man glory in his might, let not the rich man glory in his riches: but let him that glorieth glory in this, that he understandeth and knoweth me, that I am the Lord which exercise loving-kindness, judgment, and righteousness, in the earth: for in these things I delight, saith the Lord."

Ver. 27.—**He that giveth unto the poor shall not lack** (see ch. xi. 24, etc.; xix. 17). God in some way compensates what is spent in almsdeeds by shedding his blessing on the benevolent. "Der Geiz," runs the German maxim, "sammlet sich arm, die Milde giebt sich reich," "Charity gives itself rich; covetousness hoards itself poor" (Trench). "Alms," said the rabbis, "are the salt of riches." **But he that hideth his eyes shall have many a curse** (ch. xi. 26). The uncharitable man either turns away his eyes that he may not see the misery around him, or pretends not to notice it, lest his compassion should be claimed. The expression, "hiding the eyes," occurs in Isa. i. 15, "When ye spread forth your hands, I will hide mine eyes from you." The unmerciful man meets with the curses of those whom he has neglected to relieve when he had the power, and such curses are ratified and fulfilled because they are deserved, and Divine retribution attends them (see the opposite view, ver. 20). "Turn not away thine eye from the needy," says the Son of Sirach, "and give him none occasion to curse thee; for if he curse thee in the bitterness of his soul, his prayer shall be heard of him that made him" (Ecclus iv. 4, etc.; comp. Tobit iv. 7). So in the 'Didache,' ch. iv., we have, Οὐκ ἀποστραφήσῃ τὸν ἐνδεόμενον, "Thou shalt not turn thyself from one in need." Septuagint, "He that turneth away his eye shall be in great distress;" Vulgate, *Qui despicit deprecantem sustinebit penuriam.*

Ver. 28.—**When the wicked rise, men hide themselves** (see ver. 12); Septuagint, "In the places of the ungodly the righteous groan." **But when they perish, the righteous increase** (ch. xi. 10; xxix. 2, 16). The overthrow of the ungodly adds to the prosperity of the righteous, removes an opposing element, and promotes their advancement in influence and numbers.

HOMILETICS.

Ver. 1.—*The cowardice of guilt and the courage of righteousness.* I. THE COWARDICE OF GUILT. "The wicked flee when no man pursueth." 1. *This cowardice springs from a natural feeling of ill desert.* "Conscience doth make cowards of us all." Apart from all authoritative revelation, when no prophet of God is charging a man with his sin, an awful voice within clamours against his guilt and shakes the very foundations of his confidence. Though he has never breathed a word of his misdeed in the ear of a fellow-man, though all the world is deceived into believing him to be innocent, he cannot silence that dread inner voice. In many cases it utterly unnerves a man, though outwardly he dwells in perfect security. 2. *This cowardice is nourished by a perception of Divine justice.* A person who knows the revealed will of God, and his wrath against sin, must be prepared to expect judgments of condemnation on guilt. Though the avenging hand is stayed, it may fall at any moment. The miserable guilty man is like one in the condemned cell under sentence of death, who does not know the day or hour of execution, but who trembles at every footfall lest it should be that of the messenger who summons him to his doom. 3. *This cowardice gives rise to needless alarms.* The murderer starts at the fall of a leaf—so utterly unstrung is he under the tremendous consciousness of guilt. Can any condition be more dreadful? Rather than endure this agony of apprehension, men, who were in no danger of being arrested, have confessed their crimes and given themselves up to justice. When we consider the relation of sin to God and to his judgments, it is foolish indeed to live in the cowardly shame of guilt. For there are peace and pardon for the penitent.

II. THE COURAGE OF RIGHTEOUSNESS. 1. *This courage is based on a clean conscience.* (1) The feeling of innocence. Una can brave the lion and subdue its savage nature to her service because the panoply of her innocence is her perfect protection. The martyr can face the fury of the persecutor, strong in the consciousness of right and truth. It is painful to be wrongly accused, but a sensible man should learn to bear calumny when he knows that he is not guilty in the sight of God. (2) The new experience of regeneration. One who has been redeemed by Christ and renewed by the Holy Spirit need not live in the perpetual fear of guilt and shame. He is forgiven and restored. He is like the prisoner who can walk boldly out of the jail with a royal pardon. Yet his confidence can never be the same as that of original innocence. It must always have a certain humility. 2. *This courage is justified by experience.* The true man does not find his boldness fail him. He is as safe as he feels himself. The first guarantee of success in any cause is a clear consciousness that we are in the right. In the end, right and truth must triumph. But if they meet with temporary defeat, their champion need fear no real evil. He now gives his life, as he has before given his strength, to the good cause. Whether he serves it by life or by death, he does nobly, and he need not fear that he will be deserted by God.

Ver. 9.—*The prayer that is an abomination.* God does not hear all prayer. There are even prayers that he rejects with wrath. The broken words of the penitent, the simple cry of the little child, and the ungrammatical sentences of the ignorant person may be all acceptable to God, while prayers faultless in form and impressive in utterance are flung back as insults to the Divine majesty. The first consideration is not as to the nature of the prayer, but as to the character of the supposed worshipper. The prayer that is an abomination is one which, however perfect it may appear to be in itself, comes from contaminated lips. We need to examine ourselves rather than to weigh our phrases.

I. THE CONDUCT THAT MAKES THE PRAYER AN ABOMINATION. This is the conduct of one "that turneth away his ear from hearing the Law." Such conduct carries with it two evil things. 1. *Wilful error.* The heathen who do not know the Law may well be dealt with leniently when they blunder into superstition, and even confuse their consciences with degraded forms of religion, for their error is involuntary. But when a man has an opportunity of coming to a knowledge of the truth, but rejects it in indolence or aversion, he is to blame for the wrong notions which would have been corrected but for his voluntary acceptance of darkness rather than light. Devotion ought to be enlightened by instruction. The Bible should be read in public worship. Scripture truth is needed as a guide to prayer. 2. *Deliberate disobedience.* The turning aside from hearing the Law is not likely to spring from a mere reluctance to learn its doctrines. Behind this there lies a dislike to obeying its precepts, which reveals a stubborn self-will in opposition to the will of God. Now, such an evil state of the heart precludes all favour from Heaven.

II. THE REASON WHY THE PRAYER IS AN ABOMINATION. This may be looked for in two directions. It may lie in the prayer itself, or it may be found in the man who utters it. 1. *A bad prayer is offered.* If the worshipper is wilfully ignorant, he is to blame for asking for things which he would refrain from seeking when in a more enlightened condition. If he is self-willed and disobedient, he is guilty of asking amiss for what he may spend on his own lusts (Jas. iv. 3), instead of seeking what is in accordance with the will of God. 2. *A prayer proceeds from sinful lips.* There are moments of distress when the most undevout man would be glad of heavenly aid, if only it would come like the help given by Homer's gods and goddesses to his heroes in their times of danger. There is no spiritual religion in the cry for help under such circumstances. If the soul is alienated from God, and there is no sign of penitence, the prayer for deliverance, though genuine and heartfelt, may well be rejected. But worse than this is the mock-worship of one who would have the honour of being religious together with the profit of being sinful. There can be no true religion without right conduct. God looks to the behaviour of the life more than to the language of the prayer. He cares nothing for reverence in the temple if he sees wickedness in the market-place.

Ver. 10.—*The tempter.* I. THE GREATEST SIN IS TEMPTING ANOTHER TO SIN. This is Satanic wickedness, following the example of the devil. 1. It is most guilty because it *tends to increase wickedness.* It is sowing evil seeds. It is bad enough to cultivate the deadly fruit in one's own life, but to propagate it elsewhere is to be a source of trouble and manifold wickedness. 2. It is particularly guilty because it *ruins souls.* It is an attack upon other men. The tempter is a murderer. At least, he is an enemy who sows tares in his neighbours' fields, and so brings trouble wantonly on others.

II. THIS SIN IS COMMITTED BY MEANS OF EVIL EXAMPLE. The tempter need not whisper enticing words, much less need he approach his victim in the attitude of "a roaring lion, seeking whom he may devour." It is enough that his conduct sets a pattern of wickedness. We are responsible for the examples we exhibit before the world. Most important in the presence of children, who are naturally imitative, and who take their patterns from the manners of the elder people among whom they live, the example of heads of families is peculiarly impressive. Therefore the guilt of such persons is grave indeed when their reckless wickedness drags poor children down to sin.

III. THIS SIN MAY BE SUCCESSFUL. It is possible to cause the righteous to go astray in an evil way. 1. This may happen with *innocent children.* They are naturally righteous; for "of such is the kingdom of heaven." But they are not unassailable in their simplicity and early purity. The most awful fact in life is the corruption of childhood by the wickedness of older and stronger life. 2. It is possible with *good men and women.* To be good is not to be above temptation. Even Christ was tempted, though he resisted successfully. Therefore (1) when a good man is led astray we have no proof that his goodness was a hypocritical pretence; and (2) no one can be so secure in his consciousness of integrity as to afford to play with temptation and to boast of his own strength. There are joints in the thickest armour, and keen darts that find out the smallest weak places.

IV. THE SIN OF TEMPTING ANOTHER TO SIN WILL BRING RUIN ON THE TEMPTER. Of all sins this one cannot be let go unchecked and unpunished. For the sake of the victims who are threatened by it God will assuredly visit it with wrath. The tempter is a deadly serpent, whose horrible enticements only make its venom the more dangerous; and all the resources of righteousness must be put forth to crush and destroy such a pest. But no miraculous interference is needed to punish the sin of tempting. We have not to summon the Archangel Michael to fight the dangerous reptile. In the end it will turn its sting on itself. The tempter will fall into his own pit. He will alienate his victims, and he will make an enemy of all that is good. Friendless and helpless, he must perish in the hour of his need.

Vers. 13, 14.—*Confession.* I. IT IS DANGEROUS FOR A MAN TO DENY HIS SIN. 1. *It is false.* If a man pretends to be virtuous when he knows that he is guilty, that man's life is a lie. He lives in a continuous falsehood. Such a condition is rotten, turning his whole course into a delusion, and leading to a confused estimate of right and wrong. The very landmarks of righteousness are lost sight of in a fog of bewildering pretences. 2. *It precludes forgiveness.* God will only pardon the penitent, and penitence is impossible without an admission of guilt. Therefore the Divine covering of sin which will utterly bury it and allow of no ugly resurrection in a revival of old accusations, is hindered by the sinner's foolish, cowardly attempt to cover it in his own way by a paltry concealment. The wretched rags that he draws over the foul thing will not really hide it, but they will prevent the massive shield of Divine forgiveness from being cast over it. 3. *It confirms the sin.* Sin is not destroyed by being covered. It is no more killed than the seed of a poison plant is killed when it is sown in the soil, and so temporarily buried out of sight. Driven back to the secret chambers of the soul, the evil thing grows there and spreads its deadly influence. Confession would clear out the noxious malaria of guilt; concealment only shuts it up to breed in the stifling atmosphere of its own corruption. Such a condition hardens the heart in wickedness.

II. IT IS HAPPY FOR A MAN TO CONFESS HIS SIN. 1. *This confession must mean an earnest desire to be free from it.* The man who conceals his sin keeps it while he covers it, and holds it tight even when he is denying it. But one who confesses his sin aright hates it though he admits it. Three things are here implied. (1) He owns his guilt. Confession includes an admission both of the fact and of its evil character. He who confesses a sin must own that he did the deed, and that it is bad. (2) He forsakes the sin. A right confession is accompanied by repentance. It is the very opposite of the brazen-faced guilt that glories in its shame, because it loathes what still it cannot but own. (3) He first fears to sin again. He has learnt a wholesome lesson. He looks back in owning his guilt, and then forward in fear of repeating it. 2. *Such confession will be followed by God's forgiveness and a new joy to the penitent.* (1) God will forgive the penitent. He "shall have mercy." Pride claims high deserts, but the humility of confession only seeks for mercy. It inspires the publican's prayer, "God be merciful to me a sinner!" Now, as God is waiting to be gracious and loves mercy, as soon as the obstruction of impenitence is removed, his grace is free to flow in and heal the humbled soul. (2) The penitent will experience a new joy. He will be happy even in his fear. He will "rejoice with trembling." No longer living in the miserable fear of being "found out," the new fear that makes him trust his soul to God will be associated with the blessedness of forgiveness and the peace of a Divine protection.

Ver. 20.—"*A faithful man.*" I. HIS CHARACTER. Nothing can be more grand than fidelity. When found in a man it is an image of the eternal constancy of God; it is like that Divine righteousness which the psalmist compared to the "everlasting hills" —so firm, so enduring, so changeless. It would be well if this grand Old Testament grace were more prized and cultivated in the Christian Church. Let us consider it in some of its manifold aspects. What is the character of the faithful man? 1. *He is true to himself.* This fidelity must lie at the root of his fidelity to others. The faithful man must act out honestly what he feels to be demanded by his own inner convictions. 2. *He is true to his God.* The man of God is faithful as well as trustful. Thus his faith has the two sides of passive submission and active loyalty. The primary duty to God must be observed before the secondary duty to man can be kept. 3. *He is true to his friend.* This does not merely mean that he keeps his pledges. It also involves his regarding the welfare of his friend and coming to his aid in the hour of need, danger, and helpful service. 4. *He is true to his word*—one who "sweareth to his own hurt and changeth not." It is nothing that we keep our promises when they run along the lines of our own inclinations. The test is that they are equally honoured when they involve self-sacrifice. 5. *He is true when unobserved.* Faithful service is the opposite of eye-service. The faithful man will do well, though he never expects to be called to account. Faithful work is that which never meets the eye, and yet is as well wrought as the most conspicuous work. 6. *He is true in face of danger.* Here is the test of fidelity. The faithful servant of Christ is one who will not forsake his Lord when persecution threatens him. The martyr is "faithful unto death" (Rev. ii. 10). II. HIS FRUITFULNESS. He "abounds with blessings." He is like Abraham, "the father of the faithful," who was both blessed himself and a blessing to others (Gen. xii. 2). 1. *He is a recipient of abundant blessings.* It is a happy thing to be faithful even though fidelity be met with misunderstanding or persecution. (1) Fidelity is itself a blessing. This grace is its own reward. To have grace to live a strong, true, noble life is to be one of God's blessed sons, though no further reward be anticipated. (2) Fidelity brings many earthly blessings. It may not secure worldly wealth, though generally integrity is a safer road to success in life than the crooked paths of dishonour. But it will secure peace, and in the long run it is likely to be recognized and rewarded with well-merited honour. To be accounted a faithful servant is to be crowned with better than Olympian garlands. (3) Fidelity will be rewarded with heavenly favour. This is just the chief of Divine approvals singled out by Christ for his servants, "Well done, good and faithful servant" (Matt. xxv. 21). 2. *He is a source of abundant blessings.* One true, faithful soul—what a tower of strength! what a treasury of help! what a haven of refuge!. He is rich indeed who has a faithful friend. The faithful man can be relied on to help in time of need, when the faithless man, who perhaps is much stronger, deserts his trusting friend. Christ is faithful (2 Thess. iii. 3), and as such is a source of abundant blessings to his people. His fidelity is the ground of our faith.

Ver. 26.—*The folly of trusting one's own heart.* I. WHAT IT IS TO TRUST IN ONE'S OWN HEART. 1. *It is to trust in one's own wisdom.* The heart here, as throughout the Bible, stands for the intellectual as well as the emotional nature. Therefore we may be said to trust in it when we lean to our own understanding (ch. iii. 5) rather than seek counsel from God in prayer and the use of the Scriptures. 2. *It is to trust in our own character.* We may think highly of our own goodness and moral strength, and so venture into temptation needlessly or rush into difficult enterprises without counting the cost. 3. *It is to trust in our own affections.* Thus we are led to believe, like Peter, that our love to Christ will not fail (Matt. xxvi. 35). 4. *It is to trust in our own energy.* Thinking we can do more than we are capable of accomplishing, through over-estimating our mental or spiritual powers we unduly rely on our own resources.
II. HOW ONE IS TEMPTED TO TRUST IN ONE'S OWN HEART. 1. *Pride tempts.* It is humiliating to own weakness. A high opinion of one's own merits inevitably leads to a dangerous self-confidence. 2. *Unbelief tempts.* If men had more faith in God they would not be so content to rely on their own poor resources. It is the worldly spirit that leads to the limitation of view to human powers. 3. *Self-will tempts.* Men naturally desire to have their own will fulfilled. The less they look away from themselves, the more does it appear that they can do as they like. A selfish life tends to be a self-contained life.
III. WHY IT IS FOOLISH TO TRUST IN ONE'S OWN HEART. 1. *The heart is deceitful.* "Deceitful above all things" (Jer. xvii. 9). We do not know our own hearts. There are hidden weaknesses, unsuspected snares, unlooked-for limits. Ignorance of our own inner selves makes the self-trust a confidence without foundation. 2. *The heart is sinful.* "Desperately wicked" (Jer. xvii. 9). Too often he who trusts in his own heart trusts in an evil heart. Therefore he is likely to be led astray by his thoughts and desires. Until the heart is cleansed and renewed, the worst possible course is to trust it. On the contrary, it must be distrusted, resisted, restrained. 3. *The heart is frail.* Even when it has been freed from the dominion of sin, the heart of man is liable to fall, open to temptation, and in danger of yielding in the moment of trial.
IV. IN WHAT WAY ONE CAN AVOID TRUSTING IN HIS OWN HEART. It is not enough to see the danger and folly of this trust, for a man must have something to rest upon, and if the best foundation is unstable he will still build upon it rather than abandon himself to despair. Now, the cure for the tendency to trust in a wrong security is to be found in the possession of a better faith, a faith that is wise and safe. One great mischief of a man's trusting in his own heart is that he is thus led to forsake God. The remedy is found in returning to the true ground of the soul's confidence in God. He who thus trusts is wise. 1. *God is true.* Unlike the fickle heart, he is faithful and can always be trusted. 2. *God is good.* Therefore we should turn from the sinful heart to the holy and gracious God. 3. *God is strong.* The frail heart fails; the mighty God is a steadfast Rock.

HOMILIES BY VARIOUS AUTHORS.

Vers. 1—5.—*Canons of moral truth.* I. WICKEDNESS IS FEARFUL, GOODNESS IS COURAGEOUS. (Ver. 1.) A good conscience is better than a thousand witnesses; an evil conscience unmans (Job xv. 21). What passes by the name of courage is often the effect of fear of men; and that which is discountenanced as want of spirit may proceed from the profoundest reverence for God. We shall never find anything in the world more to be feared than the warring presence within our own breast. True courage is the knowledge that we are for the time at one with God. The light of his countenance is life, dispersing the darkest cloud, and calming the most turbulent tempest. An evil conscience is " the worm that dies not."

II. POLITICS AND MORALS. (Ver. 2.) Rebellion arising from the collision of party and personal interests must be very injurious to the well-being of a small state. Rebellion can only be justified when there is not only the greatest wrong existing, but also the clearest possible prospect of success. If peoples in time of distress, instead of cursing and rising against their rulers, would patiently search into the causes of their grievances, a shorter way would often be found to redress. A certain unity of feeling is essential to the well-being of a state. " When any of the four pillars of government are mainly shaken or weakened (which are religion, justice, counsel, and treasure), men had need to pray for fair weather " (Bacon).

III. THE ODIUM OF PETTY TYRANNY. (Ver. 3.) There is nothing more detestable than the oppressive rule of an upstart. A base mind becomes more corrupt from hasty elevation, a narrow heart more cruel, as in the case of Robespierre and other historical examples. As with learning, so with power; the smatterers are the most ostentatious of their knowledge; those " dressed in a little brief authority " love to

> " Play such fantastic tricks before high heaven,
> As make the angels weep."

The Divine rule is strong in gentleness.

IV. THE SECRET OF MORAL SYMPATHY AND ANTIPATHY. (Ver. 4.) Those that secretly love sin have pleasure in them that do it. " The world loveth its own." It is fearful to sin; more fearful to delight in it; yet more to defend it (Bishop Hall). The pure heart has no " fellowship with the unfruitful works of darkness." We reveal or betray ourselves by our sympathies. The homely proverb says, " Like lips, like lettuce." And the important lesson arises here—that we should dwell on the best and brightest examples, for the sake of their effect on our character; the eye becomes sunny as it gazes at the sun.

V. THE EFFECT OF VICE ON THE INTELLIGENCE. (Ver. 5.) It is a most important principle that insight into intellectual relations of truth is affected by the mood of the heart. The clearest knowledge of the letter is here of no avail. " If any man shall do God's will, he shall know of the doctrine." The pure conscience conditions the bright intelligence. The understanding is darkene l " because of the blindness of men's heart ; " and these call darkness light, and light darkness. Many things dark to reason are simplified to knowledge. The Divine mysteries are mysteries of love, and through love only may be known.—J.

Vers. 6—12.—*The moral quality of life.* Nothing we can touch, no relation we can enter into or observe, but has its moral bearing. This, indeed, is the great lesson, in hundredfold iteration, of this book.

I. POVERTY WITH INNOCENCE, WEALTH WITH PERVERSITY. (Ver. 6.) Whatever be the compensations of poverty in a lower point of view, most men would vote for riches if they had the opportunity at the price of all its inconveniences, and we need to be reminded that he who would sell his peace of conscience for wealth does but " gain a loss." Better go to heaven in rags than to hell in embroidery. Better God than gold; better be poor and live, than rich and perish.

II. A MAN IS KNOWN BY THE COMPANY HE KEEPS. (Ver. 7.) The first example is that of the man whose delight is in the Law, who is in fellowship with the truth, and who is therefore a companion " of all them that fear God and keep his precepts." The second is that of one who keeps company with the dissipated, stains his name, and brings dishonour on his family. In society lie the greatest perils and the greatest safeguards. The Christian Church is the Divine society which aims at the true and holy ideal of living. As with books, so with men; the rule is—keep company only with the best.

III. ILL-GOTTEN WEALTH DWINDLES. (Ver. 8.) Wealth is not his who gets it, but his who enjoys it. And if gotten by ill means, it cannot be enjoyed; and " Ill got, ill spent, " says the proverb. Wealth, diverted by force or fraud from its natural channels, flows back by a law of economic gravitation. A man labours for himself with selfishness and wickedness, and the harvest falls into better hands; "not intending it of himself; but it is so done through God's secret providence."

IV. PRAYERS ARE VITIATED BY INJUSTICE. (Ver. 9.) They are tainted by a horrible lie. In prayer the goodness, the moral perfection, of God is assumed; and prayer implies that the holy will ought to be done. Yet how great the contradiction between such prayers on the lips and the heart bent upon defeating that will! "Just reason that God shall refuse to hear him who refuses to hear God." Without the "ceasing to do evil, and the learning to do well," sacrifices are vain oblations, and incense is an abomination to God (Isa. i. 11—15).

V. THE SEDUCER IS SELF-SEDUCED. (Ver. 10.) So the snare of Balaam, laid for Israel, became the cause of his own ruin. If the retribution is not visible, it is a fact in the soul. Among the ingredients of remorse, none is more bitter than the recollection of having led youth and innocence astray. It is a sin most difficult of self-forgiveness. But the righteous inherit salvation. There is a real sense in which men should seek to realize the character of "just men that need no repentance." There is no salvation in selfishness—none which does not imply a regeneration of the social consciousness.

VI. POVERTY AND RICHES HAVE THEIR COMPENSATION. (Ver. 11.) Confidence in riches begins in illusory self-confidence; and there is much to abet and foster it in the opinion of the multitude; for, as the old saying runs, "Rich men have no faults." But the poor man, endued with sense and with religion, sees through these false estimates; knows that the rich feel misfortunes which pass over his own head; that they pay a tax of constant care and anxiety; and that it is ever better to fare hard with good men than to feast with bad.

VII. "THE VOICE OF THE PEOPLE THE VOICE OF GOD." (Ver. 12.) Whatever be the love of greatness and splendour, of rank and position, in the common mind, the people cannot but rejoice in good rulers, and be depressed under evil. A generous acclamation breaks from the popular heart when good men are raised to honour. "When Mordecai went out from the presence of the king in the king's royal apparel, . . . the city of Shushan rejoiced and was glad. The Jews had light, and gladness, and joy, and honour; in every province . . . a feast and a good day" (Esth. viii. 15—17).—J.

Vers. 13, 14.—*The inner conditions of peace and of misery.* I. THE CONCEALMENT OF SIN. (Ver. 13.) It is like a worm in the bud, preying upon the cheek and upon the heart. The deepest way of such concealment is when the sinner persuades himself that "he has no sin," apologizing to himself, giving a false colour to his wrong. The sense of a dualism in our being unreconciled will not admit of peace and rest.

II. THE CONFESSION AND RENUNCIATION OF SIN. To admit the truth about ourselves, neither extenuating nor exaggerating our sin and fault; to allow the detecting and discriminating light of God's judgment to fall clear and full on the conscience;—this is what confession requires. But it must be completed by renunciation; otherwise it is a mockery. To say—

> " We're sorry and repent,
> And then go on from day to day,
> Just as we always went "

—in the words of the child's hymn—is mere sentimentality and weakness. But never are these conditions fulfilled without a sense of the Divine pity striking into the heart. God is faithful and just to forgive our sins; and the conscience is assured that he is too just to permit the sinner who has become a sufferer from godly sorrow to be tormented by remorse one moment longer than is necessary for his healing.

III. THE TENDER CONSCIENCE. (Ver. 14.) It is well with him whose heart is in the constant habit of reverential dependence upon God. His law for human conduct envelops all life from the greatest to the minutest matters. It is the atmosphere of the soul that we need to keep pure; it is the fellowship with the Spirit who is holiness that we need most jealously to guard.

IV. THE HARDENING OF THE HEART. (Ver. 14.) Making light of sin leads to its repetition; repetition indurates the conscience. Disregard of the delicacies of the soul leads surely to a benumbed, and presently to a lost, sensibility. It is better to feel too keenly than not to feel at all; better the weak conscience than no conscience at all. He who presumes upon the mercy of God will have to reckon with his justice.—J.

Vers. 15, 16.—*The wicked ruler.* I. THE SIMILE. (Ver. 15.) He is like a fierce and devouring beast. No pity softens his bosom; no justice regulates his conduct. Complaint provokes further exactions; resistance kindles him into fury. He looks upon his people, not as a flock to be tended, but to be preyed upon. He roars around them like the nightly bear about the fold. Such monsters have often appeared in history.

II. THE SOURCE OF OPPRESSION. It lies in the *ignorance* of the oppressor's heart—ignorance of *policy*, of *humanity*, of Divine and eternal *right*. The great generalization, "They know not what they do," covers, indeed, all kinds of sin, but does not exempt from guilt. Men might know better; but, without the practice of what we know, our light itself becomes darkness.

III. THE GOOD RULER. (Ver. 16.) The trait that "he hates covetousness" may be made general; for false or perverted desire is the real motive of all such wickedness. "Lust and desire to have" gold, territory, power, etc., is selfish and cruel, and turns every man governed by it into a being more or less resembling the non-moral brute. Politics can never be excluded from Christianity; and the immense effect for good or evil of the acts of those in power is a reason why all good Christians should take a close interest in politics, and not permit any rank or station to be exempt from criticism.—J.

Vers. 17—22.—*Judgments on transgressors.* I. THE VIOLENT MAN. (Ver. 17.) His doom, here as elsewhere, is viewed as sudden; he hastes to Hades—lives not out half his days. The truth is general, reflecting the intuition of the moral order. And in accordance with that order it is that pity will be turned away from him that shows no pity. This is no argument for capital punishment, but it is an argument for such a treatment of criminals as will best deter from crime.

II. THE INSECURITY OF EVIL WAYS. (Ver. 18.) Integrity is alone safe; and in one or other of his crooked ways (such may be one meaning of the text) the sinner will ultimately fall. The dangerous feat is tried once too often. Our interest is attracted to "the dangerous edge of things," and we are astonished that men can stand upon it so often without falling. We do not see the result of the last and fatal attempt; or, seeing it, v e do not surmise the previous successful attempts to defy the law of things. Scripture is right; but we do not know enough of events absolutely to verify its truths.

III. POVERTY AS A JUDGMENT. (Ver. 19.) Here, again, we have a general truth—an abstract from the great broad field of life's facts. On the whole, there is no secret of abundance but industry; nor of poverty but idleness and indulgence in pleasure and amusement as a pursuit. Repose and pleasure are the illu-ions from which the stern voice of God, speaking through daily experience, is ever rousing us. Hardly any disease of body or of mind, any social evil, is there which may not be traced to self-indulgence and inertia.

IV. HASTE TO BE RICH. (Ver. 20.) This temper is contrasted with that of the faithful man. There is a different scale of value in the two cases. The good man values things by the moral standard, the covetous man only by the standard of gold. The true way of looking at wealth is as an available means to all *ends* of health, wisdom, benevolence. These alone are rational ends; but they may be lost sight of in the passionate pursuit of the means. It was a thought deeply impressed on the ancient world that over-eagerness for riches must involve dishonesty. "No one quickly grows rich, being at the same time a just man," says Menander. "For he who desires to become rich desires to become rich quickly. But what reverence for the laws? what fear or shame is there ever in the covetous man who hastes to be rich?" says Juvenal. To lessen our desires rather than to increase our means is the true wisdom of life—to study to give account of our little rather than to make our little more.

V. RESPECT OF PERSONS IN JUDGMENT. (Vers. 21, 22.) The vice springs from some mean source—from fear, covetousness, or obsequiousness. Cato used to say of Cælius the tribune, that he might be hired for a piece of bread to speak or hold his peace. To prefer interest to the truth, this is the fiery temptation in one form or other of us all. And the keeping back of a part of the truth may be as injurious to others as the utterance of direct falsehood. Any meanness harboured in the soul exposes to constant danger. Timidity may fall into worse sins than those it seeks to avoid. And in other ways extremes meet. While the haster to be rich casts an evil, envious eye on the property of others, he is blind to the menace of poverty from behind. In any case, poverty of soul follows from the constant drain of thought and energy towards things that "perish in the using." How much need have all to beware of those passions which are the "thorns" that spring up and choke the good word of God in the heart!—J.

Ver. 23.—*Faithful counsel.* I. To GIVE IT MAY REQUIRE THE HIGHEST MORAL COURAGE. It may be in the teeth of the interest of the adviser; it may turn a friend into an enemy; it may inflict a keen smart. Nothing but the highest regard to truth on the one hand, to love on the other, may be sufficient to nerve for the task.

II. THE TEMPORARY DISPLEASURE OF A FRIEND IS TO BE FACED RATHER THAN THAT HE SHOULD SUFFER LASTING EVIL. To save a soul from death, this is the great duty imposed by Christian love. And to that principle we must be true, whether we gain or lose a brother to our heart.

III. FLATTERY TURNS OUT TO BE BITTER, GOOD COUNSEL HUMBLY RECEIVED EVER SWEET IN THE END. The former, swelling our self-conceit, blinds us to both our advantage and our duty; lures us to folly and, perhaps, to ruin. The latter opens our eyes to ourselves and to our circumstances, and turns our foot from the precipice. We have reason to be thankful for the warning word that has saved us, and to bless the faithful heart which dictated it; reason ourselves to pray that we may miss no such opportunity of another's salvation.—J.

Vers. 24, 25.—*Sins of greed.* I. THEY MAY LEAD TO UNNATURAL VICES—EVEN THE ROBBERY OF PARENTS. (Ver. 24.) The heart must be profoundly corrupted that can sacrifice filial affection on the shrine of the base lust for gain. Theft is not less but more a crime if committed against one's own blood.

II. THEY LEAD TO STRIFE. (Ver. 25.) They overcome the instinct for justice and social right, and the man becomes an oppressor and a murderer—if not in act, in spirit and purpose—of his kind. Wars and fightings come of the "lusts in our members." It is confidence in the eternal God—his gracious providence and goodness, which calms excessive desire, and fills the heart with peace and content. And the riches the soul thus gains are surer and more permanent than any treasures laid up on earth.—J.

Ver. 26.—*Folly and wisdom in the personal relation.* I. THE PRINCIPLE OF FOLLY IS LIFE IN AND FOR SELF ALONE. The thought that is superior to counsel and comparison with other minds; the feeling which shuts out consideration and sympathy; the will which would act as if it knew no law but its own;—these are manifestations of that folly which is at once immoral and irreligious.

II. PRACTICAL WISDOM WELL COMPARED TO A WALK. This is the rising in thought towards universal truth. It is governed by the pulse of charity in the soul; it moves towards all worthy Divine and human ends. In folly we advance to perdition, in aiming at our weal, in wisdom, renouncing self, we enter blessedness.—J.

Vers. 27, 28.—*The life that "breeds perpetual benediction."* I. THE KINDLY AND GENEROUS HEART. (Ver. 27.) This prompts the generous hand; gathers more than it sows; is not suffered to want any good thing. It stands out in bright colours and winning aspect against the dark background of the selfish, self-concentrated, hardhearted life. Let us cultivate the open eye which drinks in the knowledge of all that concerns our fellows, and the open hand in harmony with it.

II. ITS WORTH IS HEIGHTENED BY CONTRAST. (Ver. 28.) Men cower, their brows contract, their mien becomes depressed, their soul enslaved, their manhood unmanned, beneath the proud man's oppression and the wicked's scorn. Persecution drives the moral sunshine out of the world, and tends to depopulate its moral life. As the increase of goodness depends largely on sound social and political conditions, it must be an object of prayer and of endeavour with all good men to overthrow tyranny and abolish fraud, that "the fruits of righteousness may abound and increase on every hand."—J.

Vers. 1, 13, 25 (latter part).—*The source of disturbance and the secret of security.* We hardly need the pen of the wise man to assure us that—

I. SIN MEANS DISTURBANCE TO OUR SOUL. 1. *It is bad enough to be unfortunate;* to suffer from privation or loss. 2. *It is far worse to be guilty.* We soon accommodate ourselves to our misfortunes; we readily adjust ourselves to our circumstances, even though these may be very narrow. But sin strikes deep, and its wound lasts long. Among other painful consequences it fills the soul with a tormenting fear. (1) *It dreads the pursuing penalty of God's ordaining.* And it has reason to do so, for "evil pursueth sinners" (see homily on ch. xiii. 21). In accordance with Divine Law, suffering, sorrow, shame, death, are following in the track of iniquity, and, except there be merciful interposition, will lay their hand upon it. (2) *It dreads the pursuing penalty of man.* More often than not sin is pursued by man, either by public law or by private resentment; and he who has wronged his neighbour, either by fraud or force, has reason to expect arrest and punishment. It is well that it should be so. We have come lately to understand that it is our wisdom to abandon the heavy sentence which was seldom inflicted for the lighter one which is far more freely dispensed. The great thing in administering justice is to *connect penalty with sin* as closely as possible in the mind of those who are tempted to violate the law. (3) *It dreads penalty when there is no punishment at all.* "The wicked flee when no man pursueth." The murderer cannot, dare not, stay in the presence of the body he has slain. The thief turns aside from the officer who has no intention of apprehending him. He who has inflicted the greatest wrong that one man can do another shrinks from his neighbour's eye long before his sin has been suspected. Sin fills the soul with a harassing, a tormenting, fear. The guilty heart imagines a hundred dangers before the hand of judgment is outstretched to seize, or even its pursuing feet are on the path of apprehension. We reckon badly indeed if we only count the actual and palpable inflictions of justice which evil pays; in that penalty must be included all the anxieties, the alarms, the quakings and shiverings of the soul, the abject and haunting terrors which agitate the soul before the chains are on the wrist or the prisoner is at the bar. 3. *There are two alternatives open to guilt.* (Ver. 13.) (1) It may try concealment; but this is a mistaken as well as a wrong course. It will "not prosper;" the time of concealment will be one of constant disquietude, and it will end in exposure and humiliation, for again and again it is seen that there is "nothing hidden which is not revealed." (2) It should adopt the course of confession and amendment; whoso does this "shall have mercy" of God, and will very likely indeed have mercy of man also. But even if not, the way of confession and of penalty is less hard and thorny than the path of sin and secrecy, of cowardice and terror. It is often true that while to bear punishment is tolerable, the miserable effort to escape it is absolutely intolerable.

II. RIGHTEOUSNESS MEANS SECURITY AND SERENITY. "The righteous are bold as a lion." To the upright there are two sources of rest and strength. 1. *The consciousness of integrity.* He that knows and feels his purity, his innocency, has a fearless heart, and shows a brave front to the enemy. He does not fear that the shafts of falsehood will pierce his strong armour of truth and equity. 2. *The favour of God.* (Ver. 25.) He "puts his trust in the Lord;" he commits his cause to the Righteous One; he is assured that God is on his side, and he "does not fear what man can do unto him." "The Lord is his salvation; whom should he fear?" (see Ps. xxvii. 1—3; lxxxiv. 11, 12).—C.

Vers. 4, 5.—*The practice and effect of sin and righteousness.* We have a double contrast here between the practice of the sinner and of the righteous man, and between the consequence of sin and of goodness upon the mind of the guilty and of the good.

I. THE PRACTICE OF SINFUL MEN. They "praise the wicked;" they "bless the covetous" (Ps. x. 3). 1. It is *a fact that they do so.* We hear the voice of ungodliness lifted up in favour of what is utterly wrong in the sight of God; it is expressed in the language of the lips and in every form of literature. There is hardly an evil thing perpetrated by men which does not find its advocate in some quarter. 2. It is *comprehensible that they would* do so. And this for two reasons. The wicked, as such, have an interest in lowering the standard of public morals; the more they can reduce this, the less will be their own condemnation, and the higher they may hope to move in the society they affect. But perhaps the main account of it is found in—

II. The blinding influence of sin. Those who break God's Law praise those who are wicked and that which is unworthy, because they "understand not judgment" (ver. 5). It is the fearful and fatal effect of sin upon the soul to pervert the moral judgment, to deprave the conscience, to make men regard with a diminishing disapproval the wrongness of evil deeds, until they become absolutely indifferent to it, until they positively approve the actions which they once hated and denounced. Then the light that is in them is darkness, and how great and how sad that darkness is (see Matt. v. 23)! Everything is seen in a false light; truth appears as falsehood, good as evil, wisdom as folly; and, on the other hand, all those miserable delusions which a sinful heart holds, and which are leading it down to death, appear as truth, and wrong and guilty actions appear as right, and lives which are dismal failures seem to be successes.

III. The function of the righteous. Their duty, or one of their duties, is to "contend with the wicked." This was the office, the service, of righteous Noah, of Lot, of Elijah, of Daniel, of Nehemiah, of John the Baptist, of Paul; it has been the function of every true and loyal-hearted man placed in the midst of those who are opposing the will of God. Contention is not the highest, as it certainly is not the most inviting, duty we have to take in hand. But it is often very necessary, and is sometimes quite noble service. 1. We may have to contend with the flagrantly bad, to denounce violence, oppression, injustice, vice, profanity, etc.; or with the mere hypocrite, who is right in form but wrong in heart; or with those who are half-hearted, and who are practically opposing the truth and the kingdom of God. 2. We should be very sure of our ground before we take up the attitude and use the weapons of hostility. 3. We should oppose ourselves to those who are wrong in no spirit of animosity against men, but of hatred of all evil.

IV. The effect and reward of righteousness. "They that seek the Lord understand all things." It is the most blessed effect of obedience that it elevates the doer; it purifies his heart, it clarifies his vision, it unlocks the door within which are rare treasures of immortal truth, it makes the soul to see and to rejoice in that to which it had been wholly blind. It unveils the living truth of God. It enables us: 1. To know ourselves as God knows us. 2. To understand our life as God intended us to regard it. 3. To appreciate the words and to recognize the will of the Divine Teacher. 4. To know *him* himself, " whom to know is life eternal."—C.

Ver. 8.—(See homily on vers. 20, 22.)—C.

Ver. 9.—(See homily on ch. xv. 8.)—C.

Vers. 12, 28.—*Hidden manhood.* The two main truths here taught have been anticipated by a foregoing proverb, viz. the advantage to society of promoting the good ; and the injury done by the advancement of the wicked (see ch. xi. 10). But there is a truth suggested by the wise man's language which does not elsewhere appear; he says that when the wicked rise "a man is hidden," that "men hide themselves." The fact here alluded to is clear enough; we have often read, or have frequently observed, that the best men retire to seclusion and inactivity when iniquity is on the throne, when unprincipled cleverness holds the reins; they will not serve under a sovereign whom they despise, or in circumstances which make office-holding a disgrace, if not a danger. But beyond and beneath this fact the language is fitted to suggest to us that there is much of hidden manhood amongst us. We find it in—

I. Premature retirement. Not only under the conditions stated in the text, when the withdrawal of honourable men is necessary to the upright and the high-minded, but also under very different conditions. When men are allured by a desire for quietude and ease, or when they are disheartened by disappointment, or are disgusted by the slowness of their ascent to place and power, or when they underestimate their capacity and their opportunity, and they therefore lay down the weapon and leave the field. This is a serious loss. Then "a man is hidden;" a man is burying the wisdom of maturity, the large result of manifold experience, the gathered fruit of many years. He is hiding in his own home the cultured capacity he should be expending on the city, on the country of his birth.

II. UNDEVELOPED FACULTY. We do not know how often it happens that men are born with great capacities in their nature, and who live and die without manifesting them to the world. They fail to receive the education which would bring them forth, or they are confined within a range so narrow that they have no chance of showing what they could be and do. They "die with all their music in them;" they pass away, unknown, unproved, unfelt. That is expended upon unimportant trifles which might have directed the affairs of some great company, or guided the activities of some influential Church, or decided the course of some powerful nation. A "man is hidden," and a community is left unenriched.

III. UNDISCIPLINED FORCE. When God gives to a human spirit a strong power of will, there is an imperative necessity that it should be wisely and rightly guided and controlled in youth. Faithfully disciplined, such a one becomes a most useful man, who will contribute largely to the advancement and happiness of the world. But if that discipline be withheld, and the clever, wilful boy be allowed to grow up into untrained and uncultured manhood, there will be a sad waste of power. He will be more likely than not to do harm rather than good to his generation; he may be a blight instead of a blessing. There is "a man hidden;" one who has it in him to be one of the highest and worthiest, but who, as it is, is lost or even worse than lost, to his contemporaries and his country.

IV. UNRESCUED WRONG. Even when we see humanity at its very worst, in its very foulness and baseness, we do well to feel that beneath the humiliating and pitiful exterior is a hidden manhood. It is the noble work of Christian beneficence to get down to this, to lay its kind and holy hand upon it, to raise and to restore it, to bring it into the sunshine of truth and love, to make it visible and even beautiful in the sight of God and in the estimate of man.—C.

Ver. 18.—(See homily on ch. xi. 3.)—C.

Ver. 19.—(See homily on ch. xxvii. 23.)—C.

Vers. 20, 22 (and ver. 8).—*Wealth or faithfulness? a sermon to young men.* What shall the young man set before him as his goal when he stands face to face with active life? Shall he make up his mind to be rich, or shall he resolve that, whatever his circumstances may be, he will be counted among those who are faithful to their trust? Shall he fix his mind upon and find his heritage in a large estate or in an honourable and a useful life? Let such an inquirer consider—

I. THE GRAVE DOUBT ABOUT WEALTH. To have sufficiency of money for a comfortable home, for education, for the furtherance of the cause of God, and for the relief of human want,—this is certainly a very desirable thing. He who is facing the future may honestly desire to attain it, and he who has won it may well give God hearty thanks for the goodness which has placed this blessing in his power. But the mere acquisition of wealth, on which so many set their hearts, to which they devote their lives, and for which they sacrifice the best and highest things of all, *ensures nothing at all* of that which is valuable to a man who uses his reason and cares for his character. For who can be sure: 1. *How it will be gained.* There are temptations on every hand to gain money dishonestly or, if not fraudulently, by questionable means; by taking advantage of the weak and struggling in a way which, if it be not positively unjust, is inconsiderate and unkind. Of those who "make haste to be rich," how very large a proportion fail to "be innocent" (ver. 20)! They either deviate from the straight line of perfect equity, or they wander into ways of rank injustice and shameful wrong. Who shall say whether the next aspirant will not be counted in their number? And what does it profit a man to gain a fortune and to lose his integrity? 2. *How long it will stay.* He "considereth not that poverty shall come upon him." Few things are less certain than the duration of wealth. Who that has reached middle life has not frequently known of those that were supposed to be beyond the reach of misfortune being suddenly reduced or positively beggared (see ch. xxiii. 5)? 3. *How much it will do for its possessor.* "He that hasteth . . . hath an evil eye;" so far is he from being satisfied with his fortune, and from looking graciously and generously upon all his neighbours, rich and poor, that he looks *enviously* upon those that are wealthier than himself, *proudly* upon those that are less successful, and *grudgingly* upon those that are poor, lest they should want his aid and diminish his store. 4. *Whither it will go.* If dishonestly obtained, it is likely enough that wealth will soon meet with the penalty it deserves, and pass to another holder. It may go to him that will " pity the poor," or it may get into the hands of " the fool," who will squander it in some kind of folly (Eccles. ii. 18, 19, 21). There is, then, an utter uncertainty about riches. It may be that God has not intended a man to be rich, but to be happy in a very humble station (ch: xxx. 9); and a pertinacious endeavour to secure what God has not placed within reach *must* end in a wretched failure and a badly bruised spirit. To such as these the strong words of Paul are applicable (1 Tim. vi. 9, 10).

II. THE CERTAINTY ABOUT FAITHFULNESS. "A faithful man shall abound with blessings." And there is no room for questioning it. Let a man be faithful to his convictions; let him be to God, his Father and his Saviour, what he knows in his heart he should be; let him be true and upright in all his relations with his fellow-men, and he will be regulating his life by a sovereign principle which will " abound with blessings." It will: 1. Build up a strong and noble character. 2. Establish an honourable reputation and win the confidence of men. 3. Secure as large a measure of peace and of happiness as is the lot of disciplined humanity. 4. Dispense much good of many kinds to those around, both in public and in domestic life. 5. Lead *down* to a peaceful end, and *on* to a glorious future. What wise man would endanger the loss of these priceless blessings for the uncertain and transient good of worldly wealth ?—C.

Ver. 23.—(See homily on ch. xxvii. 5, 6.)—C.

Ver. 24.—*Filial duty.* These words may be taken not only as condemnatory of filial wrong, but as suggestive of filial obligation. We look first at—

I. THREE FORMS OF FILIAL WRONG. 1. *Culpable carelessness.* Doing things or leaving them undone, so that the money of parents (which, perhaps, can ill be spared) is wasted. 2. *Unconscientious appropriation.* Which may ascend from picking out of the pot or taking from the cupboard up to a serious appropriation of property. 3. *Unprincipled involvement.* Either in the form of (1) contracting debts which (it may be well known) will have to be paid out of the father's purse; or, what is still worse (2) following an evil course of conduct which will discredit the family name and rob it of its honoured and prized reputation.

II. ITS GUILTINESS BEFORE GOD. They who do such things may justify them to their own minds; they may say to themselves, "It is no transgression; what is our parents' is our own;" but this is *not* the light in which it shows to Heaven. It is not only the wise man, but the Son of God, who has affixed his solemn condemnation to filial shortcoming (Matt. xv. 5). Undutiful conduct toward parents is a very heinous sin. 1. It is in most distinct violation of the Divine command (Exod. xx. 12; Deut. xxvii. 16; Matt. xix. 19; Eph. vi. 1, 2; Col. iii. 20). 2. It is a wrong done to those who, in virtue of their relationship, have the strongest claim upon us. 3. It is a sin against those who have spent on us the most patient, sacrificial love. To rob them to whom we owe more than we can owe any other human being is an aggravated offence indeed. It is well to consider—

III. THE TRUE FILIAL FEELING. A true son, who realizes what is due to his parents, will not only shrink from taking the advantage which his father's trustfulness places in his power, but he will consider how he may make some return for all that he has received at his parents' hands. And he will understand that this is to be rendered by : 1. Responsive affection. 2. Prompt and cheerful obedience. 3. Ready acquiescence in those things which are beyond his reach; docility and submissiveness of spirit. 4. Practical willingness to share the burdens of the home. Thus he will lighten the labour and brighten the lives of those who were the first, and will perhaps be the longest, if not the last, to love him.—C.

Vers. 25 (latter part) and 26 (former part).—*In whom to trust.* They who look *forward* to human life from the sanguine standpoint of youth may see in it little to be afraid about; but they who have reached the latter end of it, and look *back* upon it, know how much there is in it to give ground for serious apprehension. It is they who are concerned for the young, and who are so devoutly solicitous that these should put their trust in that which will sustain them. There are three principles which are applicable.

I. SELF-RELIANCE IS BETTER THAN LEANING UPON OTHERS. To be kept from "the evil which is in the world" by the authority, or the counsel, or the entreaty of others is quite unsatisfactory in any but the very young. These human props will be taken away, and where, then, is our virtue?

II. MORAL PRINCIPLE IS BETTER THAN RIGHT DISPOSITION. It is well enough to inherit or to imbibe right inclinations, pure impulses, honourable feeling. But these may go down before the force of some one very strong temptation, or be (as indeed they often are) worn down and worn out by the droppings of hostile influences. Moral principle, well rooted in the soul, will stand the rough wind and still lift up its head to heaven.

III. TO TRUST IN GOD IS INCOMPARABLY WISER THAN RESTING IN OURSELVES. 1. *To "trust in our own heart" is great folly.* For, on the one hand, we *do not* know what we may have to encounter. Possibly our life may be comparatively free from evil, material and moral; but perhaps it may not be so. There may be before us *trials* of the utmost severity, for which the very greatest endurance will be required; or there may be *temptations* of the severest kind, which will assail us with tremendous and overwhelming force; or there may be demanded of us *high duties*, large services of even heroic order, only to be rendered by a noble self-abnegation; or there may await us *splendid opportunities*, to be unequal to which would be a lifelong regret, to avail ourselves of which would crown us with joy and honour. And, on the other hand, we *do* know that, associated even with moral principle, there is some measure of human weakness. Every man has his vulnerable point; and to every man's strength of mind and character there is a limit which is only too easily reached. Who of us would dare to say that he, of himself, however fortified he may be even by sound convictions as well as excellent inclinations, is strong enough to withstand *any* storm that may beat against him, to swim *any* current into which he may be cast, to rise to *any* height that he may be called upon to climb? 2. *To trust in God is the true wisdom.* For (1) God is *able* to make us stand (Rom. xiv. 4). He can make us to know "the exceeding greatness of his power to usward who believe." We can "do all things in Christ who strengtheneth us." (2) He has promised to sustain and to enable us, if we do put our trust in him (Ps. xxxii. 10; cxxv. 11; Isa. xxvi. 3; xl. 30, 31; 2 Tim. i. 12). God has given us abundant reason to believe that, if we practically and devoutly trust in him, he will see us safely through every evil we may have to meet and master, and will guide us to his own home and glory.—C.

EXPOSITION.

CHAPTER XXIX.

This chapter reinforces many precept given previously.

Ver. 1.—**He that being often reproved hardeneth his neck;** literally, *a man of reproofs*—one who has had a long experience of rebukes and warnings. Compare "a man of sorrows" (Isa. liii. 3). The hardening of the neck is a metaphor derived from obstinate draught animals who will not submit to the yoke (Deut. x. 16; Jer. ii. 20; xxvii. 8). Christ calls his yoke easy, and bids his followers to bear it bravely (Matt. xi. 29, etc.). The reproofs may arise from the Holy Spirit and the conscience, from the teaching of the past, or from the counsel of friends. The LXX. (as some other Jewish interpreters) takes the expression in the text actively, "A man who reproves (ἐλέγχων) is better than one of stiff neck." **Shall suddenly be destroyed, and that without remedy** (ch. vi. 15; xv. 10). The incorrigible and self-deluding sinners shall come to a fearful and sudden end, though retribution be delayed (comp. Job xxxiv. 20; Ps. ii. 9; Jer. xix. 11). And there is no hope in their end; despising all correction, they can have no possibility of restoration. We may refer, as an illustration, to that terrible passage in the Epistle to the Hebrews (vi. 4, etc.), and to the fate of the Jews unto the present day. Septuagint, "For when he is burning suddenly, there is no remedy."

Ver. 2.—**When the righteous are in authority;** rather, as in ch. xxviii. 28, *when the righteous are increased;* Vulgate, *in multiplicatione justorum.* When sinners are put away, and the righteous are in the majority. Septuagint, "when the just are commended." When good men give the tone to society and conduct all affairs according to their own high standard, **the people rejoice;** there is general happiness, prosperity abounds, and voices ring cheerfully (ch. xi. 10; xxviii. 12). **When the wicked beareth rule, the people mourn;** they suffer violence and injustice, and have bitter cause for complaint and lamentation. This proverb is not applicable to the age of Solomon.

Ver. 3.—The first hemistich is a variation of ch. x. 1 (where see note). **Keepeth company with;** literally, *feedeth,* as ch. xxviii. 7. **Harlots** (see on ch. vi. 26). Such vice leads to the wasting of substance (Luke xv. 13), and the great sorrow of the parent. Septuagint, "But he that pastureth (ποιμαίνει) harlots shall waste wealth."

Ver. 4.—Many of the proverbs in this chapter seem to suit the time of Jeroboam II. (see on ch. xxviii. 3). **The king by judgment establisheth the land.** The king, the fountain of justice, by his equitable government brings his country into a healthy and settled condition (1 Kings xv. 4; comp. ver. 14; ch. xvi. 12; xxv. 5). In the security of the throne the land and people participate. **He that receiveth gifts overthroweth it.** The expression, אִישׁ תְּרוּמוֹת (*ish terumoth*), "man of offerings," "man of gifts," is ambiguous: it may mean "the taker of bribes," the unrighteous ruler who sells justice (ch. xv. 27), or it may signify "the imposer of taxes" (Ezek. xlv. 13, etc.) or forced benevolences. Aquila and Theodotion have ἀνὴρ ἀφαιρεμάτων, "man of heave offerings," and Wordsworth regards him as a man who claims and receives gifts, as if he were a deity on earth. Whichever sense we give to the phrase, the contrast lies between the inflexibly upright ruler and the iniquitous or extortionate prince. The Septuagint gives παράνομος, "a transgressor;" Vulgate, *vir avarus.*

Ver. 5.—**A man that flattereth his neighbour;** says only what is agreeable, applauds his words and actions indiscriminately, and makes him think too well of himself, he is no true friend (see ch. xxviii. 23). **Spreadeth a net for his feet; his steps** (ch. xxvi. 28; Job xviii. 8, etc.). If a man listens to such flattering words, and is influenced by them, he works his own ruin; self-deceived, he knows not his real condition, and accordingly makes grievous disaster of his life. The LXX. gives a different turn

to the sentence, "He that prepareth a net before his friend entangles his own feet therein" (comp. ch. xxvi. 27; xxviii. 10).

Ver. 6.—**In the transgression of an evil man there is a snare** (ch. xii. 13). The snare is that the sinner is caught and held fast by his sin, and cannot escape, as he knows nothing of repentance, and has no will to cast off evil habits (ch. xxiv. 16). (For "snare," comp. ch. xviii. 7; xx. 25; xxii. 25.) Septuagint, "For a man sinning there lies a great snare." **But the righteous doth sing and rejoice.** The antithesis is not very obvious. It may mean that the good man has a conscience at peace, is free from the snare of sin, and therefore is glad; or that, in spite of a momentary fall, though he has transgressed, he knows that God forgives him on his repentance, and this makes him happy; or, generally that he rejoices in the happy life which his virtue procures for him here and hereafter (Matt. v. 12). In the original "sing" represents the sudden outburst of joy, "rejoice" the continued state of happiness. "The righteous shall be in joy and gladness (ἐν χαρᾷ καὶ ἐν εὐφροσύνῃ)," Septuagint.

Ver. 7.—**Considereth the cause;** recognizes the claims, and, as the word *din* implies, supports them at the seat of judgment (comp. Job xxix. 12, 16; Ps. lxxxii. 3, etc.). Septuagint, "A righteous man knows how to judge for the poor." **The wicked regardeth not to know it.** This is a clumsy translation; it means, pays no attention so as to become fully acquainted with its details and bearings. But the words signify rather, as in the Revised Version margin, "understandeth not knowledge" (ch. xix. 25; xxviii. 5), has no knowledge which would lead him to enter into the poor man's case, and to sympathize with him in his distress: the claims of the feeble to recognition and relief at his hands are utterly unknown and disregarded. He can daily look on Lazarus at his gate, and find no call for his pity and charity; he can see the wounded traveller in the road, and pass by on the other side. The LXX. offers two translations of the latter clause, reading the second time רָשׁ instead of רָשָׁע, and thereby not improving the sense: "But the ungodly understandeth not knowledge, and the poor man hath not an understanding mind."

Ver. 8.—**Scornful men bring a city into a snare.** "Men of derision" (Isa. xxviii. 14) are those who despise and scoff at all things great and high, whether sacred or profane (see on ch. i. 22). These are the persons who raise rebellion in a country and excite opposition to constituted authority. The rendering of יָפִיחוּ, "bring into a snare," as in the Authorized Version, is supported by some of the Jewish versions and commentaries; but the more correct rendering is "blow into a blaze, inflame," as the Revised Version (comp. Job xx. 26; Ezek. xxii. 20, 21). These scorners excite the populace to acts of fury, when all respect for piety and virtue is lost; they fan the passions of the fickle people, and lead them to civil discord and dangerous excesses (comp. ch. xxii. 10). Septuagint, "Lawless men burn up a city." But wise men turn away wrath; by their prudent counsels allay the angry passions roused by those evil men (see ver. 11 and ch. xv. 1, 18).

Ver. 9.—If a wise man contendeth with a foolish man—if a wise man has a controversy, either legal or social, with a wicked fool—whether he rage (is angry) or laugh, there is no rest. It is a question whether the wise man or the fool is the subject of this clause. St. Jerome makes the former the subject, Vir sapiens, si cum stulto contenderit, sive irascatur, sive rideat, non inveniet requiem. It matters not how the wise man treats the fool; he may be stern and angry, he may be gentle and good-tempered, yet the fool will be none the better, will not be reformed, will not cease from his folly, will carry on his cavilling contention. Hitzig, Delitzsch, and others, deeming that the rage and the laughter are not becoming to the character of the wise man, take the fool as the subject; so that the sense is, that after all has been said, the fool only falls into a passion or laughs at the matter, argument is wasted upon him, and the controversy is never settled. This seems to be the best interpretation, and is somewhat supported by the Septuagint, "A wise man shall judge the nations, but a worthless man, being angry, laughs and fears not [καταγελᾶται καὶ οὐ καταπτήσσει, which may also mean, 'is derided and terrifies no one']." Wordsworth notes that the irreligious fool is won neither by the austere preaching of John the Baptist nor by the mild teaching of Christ, but rejects both (Matt. xi. 16—19).

Ver. 10.—The bloodthirsty hate the upright; him that is perfect, Revised Version; ὅσιον, Septuagint. His life is a tacit reproach to men of blood, robbers, murderers, and such-like sinners, as is finely expressed in the Book of Wisdom ii. 12, etc. (comp. 2 Cor. vi. 14). But the just seek his soul. The explanation of this hemistich is doubtful. The following interpretations have been offered: (1) The just seek the soul of the upright to deliver him from death temporal and spiritual (comp. ch. xii. 6; Ps. cxlii. 4). (2) The just seek the murderer's life, take vengeance on him (comp. Ps. lxiii. 9, 10). (3) "As for the just, they (the murderers) attempt his life," where the change of subject, though by no means unparalleled,

is awkward (comp. Ps. xxxvii. 14). The second explanation makes the righteous the executioners of vengeance on the delinquents, which does not seem to be the idea intended, and there is no confirmation of it in our book. The interpretation first given has against it the fact that the phrase, "to seek the soul," is used of attempts against the life, not of preserving it. But this is not fatal; and the above seems to be the most likely explanation offered, and gives a good antithesis. Men of blood hate a virtuous man, and try to destroy him; the righteous love him, and do their utmost to defend and keep him safe. If this interpretation is rejected, the third explanation is allowable, the casus pendens—"the just, they seek his life"—may be compared with Gen. xxvi. 15; Deut. ii. 23. Septuagint, "But the upright will seek (ἐκζητήσουσι) his life."

Ver. 11.—A fool uttereth all his mind; his spirit; רוּחוֹ, i.e. "his anger;" θυμόν, Septuagint (comp. ch. xvi. 32). The wording of the second hemistich confirms this rendering. A fool pours out his wrath, restrained by no consideration. It is a wise maxim that says, "Command your temper, lest it command you;" and again, "When passion enters in at the foregate, wisdom goes out at the postern." So we have the word attributed to Evenus Parius—

Πολλάκις ἀνθρώπων ὀργὴ νόον ἐξεκάλυψε
Κρυπτόμενον, μανίας πουλὺ χερειότερον.

"Wrath often hath revealed man's hidden mind,
Than madness more pernicious."

A wise man keepeth it in till afterwards. This clause is capable of more than one explanation. The Authorized Version says that the wise man restrains his own anger till he can give it proper vent. The term בְּאָחוֹר occurs nowhere else, and is rendered "at last," "finally," and by Delitzsch, "within," i.e. in his heart. The verb rendered "keepeth in" (shabach) is rather "to calm," "to hush," as in Ps. lxv. 7; lxxxix. 10, "Which stilleth the noise of the seas." So we have the meaning: The wise man calms the anger within him; according to the proverb, Iræ dilatio, mentis pacatio. Or the anger calmed may be that of the fool: The wise man appeases it after it has been exhibited; he knows how to apply soothing remedies to the angry man, and in the end renders him calm and amenable to reason. This seems the most suitable explanation. Septuagint, "A wise man husbands it (ταμιεύεται) in part."

Ver. 12.—All his servants are wicked. The ruler is willing to be deceived, and does not care to hear the truth, so his servants flatter and lie to him, and the whole atmosphere is charged with unreality and deceit. *Qualis rex, talis grex.* Ecclus. x. 2, "As the judge of the people is himself, so are his officers; and what manner of man the ruler of the city is, such are all that dwell therein."· Claudian, 'IV. Cons. Hon.,' 299—

" Componitur orbis
Regis ad exemplum: nec sic inflectere sensus
Humanos edicta valent, ut vita regentis.'
Mobile mutatur semper cum principe vulgus."

" By the king's precedent
The world is ordered; and men's minds are moved
Less by stern edicts than their ruler's life.
The fickle crowd aye by the prince is swayed."

Cicero, 'De Leg.,' iii. 13, "Ut enim cupiditatibus principum et vitiis infici solet tota civitas, sic emendari et corrigi continentia." And ibid., 14, "Quo perniciosius de republica merentur vitiosi principes, quod non solum vitia concipiunt ipsi, sed ea infundunt in civitatem; neque solum obsunt, ipsi quod corrumpuntur, sed etiam quod corrumpunt, plusque exemplo, quam peccato, nocent."

Ver. 13.—**A variation of ch. xxii. 2. The deceitful man.** This makes no contrast with the poor. "The man of oppressions" (*tekakim*) is the usurer, from whom the poor suffer most wrong and cruelty. The needy man and the rich lender are thrown together in social life. St. Jerome calls them *pauper et creditor.* Septuagint, "When the creditor and debtor meet together, the Lord maketh inspection (ἐπισκοπὴν) of both." **The Lord lighteneth both their eyes.** Both rich and poor, the oppressor and the oppressed, owe their light and life to God; he makes the sun to rise on the evil and on the good; he sends rain on the just and the unjust; he is the Father, Ruler, and Judge of all. Here is comfort for the poor, that he has a tender Father who watches over him; here is a warning for the rich, that he will have to give an account of his stewardship. The former proverb spoke only generally of God being the Maker of both (comp. Ps. xiii. 3; Eccles. xi. 7).

Ver. 14.—**The king that faithfully judgeth the poor** (comp. ch. xvi. 12; xx. 28; xxv. 5). Inflexible fidelity to duty is intended—that perfect impartiality, which dispenses justice alike to rich and poor, uninfluenced by personal or social considerations. **His throne shall be established for ever.** Being founded on righteousness, it shall pass on to his descendants for many generations

(comp. Jer. xxii. 3, etc.). The LXX., pointing differently, have, "His throne shall be established for a testimony" (*lahed*, instead of *lahad*).

Ver. 15.—**The rod and reproof give wisdom** to the young. The former denotes bodily correction, what we call corporal punishment; the latter, discipline in words, rebuke administered when any moral fault is noticed. The idea here enunciated is very common in this book (see ch. x. 1, 13; xiii. 24; xxiii. 13). **But a child left to himself bringeth his mother to shame.** The verb translated "left" (שָׁלַח, *shalach*) is used in Job xxxix. 5 of the wild ass left to wander free where it wills. A child allowed to do as he likes, undisciplined—spoiled, as we call it—is a shame to his mother, whose weakness has led to this want of restraint, fond love degenerating into over-indulgence (comp. ch. xvii. 21; xxviii. 7). Septuagint, "A son that goeth astray shameth his parents."

Ver. 16.—**When the wicked are multiplied, transgression increaseth.** The verb *rabah* is used in both parts of the sentence, and should have been so translated, *When the wicked increase, transgression increaseth.* Septuagint, "When the godless are many, sins become many." Where the wicked get the upper hand in a community, their evil example is copied, and a lowering of moral tone and a general laxity in conduct prevail (see on ver. 12; comp. also ver. 2; ch. xxviii. 12, 28). **But the righteous shall see their fall.** Retribution shall overtake them, and God's justice shall be vindicated. This the righteous shall witness, and shall rejoice in the vengeance, when his eye shall see its desire upon his enemies (Ps. liv. 7; see also Ps. xxxvii. 34; lxxiii. 17, etc.). Septuagint (punctuating differently), "But when they (the godless) fall, the righteous become fearful (κατάφοβοι);" they are awestruck at the sudden and grievous fall of sinners.

Ver. 17.—**Correct thy son, and he shall give thee rest** (ch. xix. 18); Septuagint, ἀναπαύσει σε. He will be no longer a source of care and disquiet to you. **Delight** (*maadanim*); properly, *dainty dishes,* and then any great and special pleasure (comp. Ecclus. xxx. 1—12). Septuagint, "He shall give ornament (κόσμον) to thy soul." This verse and the following are presented by the Greek version in a mutilated form after ch. xxviii. 17 (where see note).

Ver. 18.—**Where there is no vision, the people perish;** rather, *cast off restraint,* become ungovernable, cannot be reined in (Exod. xxxii. 22, 25). " Vision " (*chazon*), prophecy in its widest sense, denotes the revelation of God's will made through agents, which directed the course of events, and was intended to be co-ordinate with the supreme secular authority. The prophets were the instructors of the people in Divine things, standing witnesses of the truth and power of religion, teaching a higher than mere human morality. The fatal effect of the absence of such revelation of God's will is stated to be confusion, disorder, and rebellion; the people, uncontrolled, fall into grievous excesses, which nothing but high principles can restrain. We note the licence of Eli's time, when there was no open vision (1 Sam. iii.); in Asa's days, when Israel had long been without a teaching priest (2 Chron. xv. 3); and when the impious Ahaz "made Judah naked" (2 Chron. xxviii. 19); or when the people were destroyed by reason of lack of knowledge of Divine things (Hos. iv. 6). Thus the importance of prophecy in regulating the life and religion of the people is fully acknowledged by the writer, in whose time, doubtless, the prophetical office was in full exercise: but this seems to be the only passage in the book where such teaching is directly mentioned; the instructors and preceptors elsewhere introduced as disseminating the principles of the *chochmah* being parents, or tutors, or professors, not inspired prophets. **But he that keepeth the Law, happy is he!** "The Law" (*torah*) is not merely the written Mosaic Law, but the announcement of God's will by the mouth of his representatives; and the thought is, not the blessedness of those who in a time of anarchy and irreligion keep to the authorized enactments of the Sinaitic legislation, but a contrast between the lawlessness and ruin of a people uninfluenced by religious guidance, and the happy state of those who obey alike the voice of God, whether conveyed in written statutes or by the teaching of living prophets. (For "happy is he," comp. ch. xiv. 21; xvi. 20.) Septuagint, "There shall be no interpreter (ἐξηγητής) to a sinful nation, but he that keepeth the Law is most blessed."

Ver. 19.—A servant will not be corrected by words. Mere words will not suffice to teach a slave, any more than a child, true, practical wisdom. He needs severer measures, even the correction of personal discipline. Septuagint, "By words a stubborn (σκληρὸς) slave will not be instructed." The next clause gives an explanation of this necessity. **For though he understand he will not answer.** The answer is not merely the verbal response to a command, as, "I go, sir;" but it implies obedience in action. The reluctant slave thoroughly understands the order given, but he pays no heed to it, will not trouble himself to execute it, and therefore must meet with stern treatment (comp. ver. 15; ch. xxiii. 13, etc.; xxvi. 3). "That servant which knew his

Lord's will, and made not ready, nor did according to his will, shall be beaten with many stripes" (Luke xii. 47). Septuagint, "For even if he understand, he will not obey."

Ver. 20.—Seest thou a man that is hasty in his words? (comp. ch. xxvi. 12); Vulgate, *velocem ad loquendum;* Septuagint, ταχὺν ἐν λόγοις. Jas. i. 19, "Let every man be swift to hear, slow to speak." "A talkative (γλωσσώδης) man is dangerous in his city; and he that is rash (προπετής) in his words shall be hated" (Ecclus. ix. 18). We might also translate, "hasty in his matters," "hasty in business," and the gnome would be equally true (see note on ch. xix. 2). There is **more hope of a fool than of him.** The dull, stupid man (*kesil*) may be instructed and guided and made to listen to reason; the hasty and ill-advised speaker consults no one, takes no thought before he speaks, nor reflects on the effect of his words; such a man it is almost impossible to reform (see Jas. iii. 5, etc.). "Every one that speaks," says St. Gregory, "while he waits for his hearer's sentence upon his words, is as it were subjected to the judgment of him by whom he is heard. Accordingly, he that fears to be condemned in respect of his words ought first to put to the test that which he delivers—that there may be a kind of impartial and sober umpire sitting between the hear and tongue, weighing with exactness whether the heart presents right words, which the tongue taking up with advantage may bring forward for the hearer's judgment" ('Moral.,' viii. 5, Oxford transl.).

Ver. 21.—He that delicately bringeth up his servant from a child. The verb *panak*, which is not found elsewhere in the Old Testament, is rightly here translated as in the Vulgate, *qui delicate nutrit.* It refers to the spoiling a person by over-refinement, luxury, and pampering—a treatment peculiarly unsuitable in the case of a bond-servant, and one which makes such forgetful of his dependent position. Septuagint, "He that liveth wantonly (κατασπαταλᾷ) from childhood shall be a servant." **Shall have him become his son at the length;** *i.e.* at length, like "at the last," equivalent to "at last" (ch. v. 11). The word rendered "son" (מָנוֹן, *manon*) is of doubtful meaning, and has been variously understood or misunderstood by interpreters. Septuagint, "And in the end shall have pain (ὀδυνηθήσεται) over himself;" Symmachus, "shall have murmuring (ἔσται, γογγυσμός);" Vulgate, *l'ostea sentiet eum contumacem.* Ewald translates "ungrateful;" Delitzsch, "place of increase," *i.e.* a household of pampered scapegraces; but one does not see how the disaster can be called a place or a house. It seems safest in this uncertainty to adopt the Jewish interpretation of "progeny:" "he will be as a son." The pampered servant will end by claiming the privileges of a son, and perhaps ousting the legitimate children from their inheritance (comp. ch. xvii. 2; and the case of Ziba and Mephibosheth, 2 Sam. xvi. 4). "Fodder, a stick, and burdens are for the ass; and bread, correction, and work for a servant. If thou set thy servant to labour, thou shalt find rest; but if thou let him go idle, he will seek liberty" (Ecclus. xxxiii. 24, etc.). Spiritual writers have applied this proverb to the pampering of the flesh, which ought to be under the control of its master, the spirit, but which, if gratified and unrestrained, gets the upper hand, and, like a spoiled servant, dictates to its lord.

Ver. 22.—**An angry man stirreth up strife.** This is a variation of ch. xv. 18 and ch. xxviii. 25 (which see). **A furious man aboundeth in transgression.** "A furious man" is a passionate person, who gives way to violent fits of anger (ch. xxii. 24). Such a man both makes enemies by his conduct and falls into manifold excesses of word and action while under the influence of his wrath. "The wrath of man worketh not the righteousness of God" (Jas. i. 20). The Greek gnome says—

'Οργὴ δὲ πολλὰ δρᾶν ἀναγκάζει κακά.

And again—

Πόλλ' ἔστιν ὀργῆς ἐξ ἀπαιδεύτου κακά.

"Unchastened anger leads to many ills."

Septuagint, "A passionate man diggeth up sin"—a forcible expression, which is not unusual in reference to quarrels.

Ver. 23.—**A man's pride shall bring him low.** The same thought is found in ch. xv. 33; xvi. 18; xxv. 6, etc.; Luke xiv. 11. **Honour shall uphold the humble in spirit;** better, as the Revised Version, *he that is of a lowly spirit shall obtain honour* (comp. ch. xi. 16; Isa. lvii. 15). The humble man does not seek honour, but by his life and action unconsciously attains it (comp. Job xxii. 29). Septuagint, "Haughtiness brings a man low, but the lowly-minded the Lord upholdeth with glory."

Ver. 24.—**Whoso is partner with a thief hateth his own soul.** The accomplice of a thief puts his own safety in danger. This is explained by what follows: **He heareth cursing, and bewrayeth it not**; better, *he heareth the adjuration, and telleth not.* This refers to the course of proceeding defined by Lev. v. 1, and intimated in Judg. xvii. 2. When a theft was committed, the person wronged or the judge pronounced an imprecation on the thief and on any one who was privy to the crime, and refrained from giving information; a witness who saw and knew of

it, **and was silent** under this formal adjuration, has to bear his iniquity; he is not only an accomplice of a criminal, he is also a perjurer; one sin leads to another. Some commentators explain the first hemistich as referring only to the crime of receiving or using stolen goods, by which a man commits a crime and exposes himself to punishment; but it is best taken, as above, in connection with the second clause, and as elucidated thereby.

Ver. 25.—**The fear of man bringeth a snare.** He who, through fear of what man may do to him, think or say of him, does what he knows to be wrong, lets his moral cowardice lead him into sin, leaves duty undone,—such a man gets no real good from his weakness, outrages conscience, displeases God. See our Lord's words (Matt. x. 28; Mark viii. 38; and comp. Isa. li. 12, etc.). **Whoso putteth his trust in the Lord shall be safe** (ch. xviii. 10). Such trust carries a man safe through all dangers; fearing to offend God, living as always under his eye, he feels Divine protection, and knows that whatever happens is for the best. The LXX. joins this to the preceding verse, thus: "He who shareth with a thief hateth his own soul; and if, when an oath is offered, they who hear it give no information, they fearing and reverencing men, are overthrown, but he that trusteth in the Lord shall rejoice." They add another rendering of the last verse, " Ungodliness causeth a man to stumble, but he who trusts in the Lord (ἐπὶ τῷ δεσπότῃ 2 Pet. ii. 1) shall be saved." Δεσπότης is used for *Jehovah* in the New Testament, e.g. Luke ii. 29; Acts iv. 24.

Ver. 26.—**Many seek the ruler's favour;** literally, *the countenance of the ruler.* A variation of ch. xix. 6. There are numbers who are always trying, by means fair or surreptitious, to curry favour with a great man who has anything to bestow (comp. 1 Kings x. 24; Ps. xlv. 12). **But every man's judgment cometh from the Lord.** The real and only reliable judgment comes, not from an earthly prince (who may be prejudiced and is certainly fallible), but from the Lord, whose approval or disapproval is final and indisputable. Therefore one should seek to please him rather than any man, however great and powerful (comp. 1 Sam. xvi. 7; Isa. xlix. 4; 1 Cor. iv. 5).

Ver. 27.—**An unjust man is an abomination to the just.** This great moral contrast, marked and universal, is a fitting close of the book. The word "abomination" (*toebah*) occurs more than twenty times in the Proverbs; it is appropriate here because the good man looks upon the sinner as the enemy of God, as the psalmist says, "Do not I hate them, O Lord, that hate thee? and am not I grieved with those that rise up against thee? I hate them with perfect hatred: I count them thine enemies" (Ps. cxxxix. 21, etc.). He that is upright in the way is abomination to the wicked; because he is a standing reproach to him, and by every tone and look and action seems to express his condemnation (see on ch. xxi. 15, and the Septuagint Version there; and comp. 1 Kings xxi. 20; Isa. liii. 3; Matt. viii. 34; John xv. 19). Septuagint, "A direct way is an abomination to the lawless." The Vulgate ends the chapter with a paragraph which is found in some manuscripts of the Septuagint after ch. xxiv. 22 (where see note), *Verbum custodiens filius extra perditionem erit.*

HOMILETICS.

Ver. 1.—*Hardened under reproof.* I. REPROOF MAY BE REJECTED. It is not violent and compulsory correction. We have free wills, and God does not destroy our wills in order to reform our conduct, for he only delights in voluntary obedience; but he sends warnings and chastises us as his children. This treatment should lead to repentance. Still, it is addressed to our reason, our conscience, our affections. Pharaoh repeatedly rejected Divine reproofs, when he refused to let the Hebrews go after each successive plague was removed. The Israelites in the wilderness murmured and rebelled again and again, in spite of continuous mercies and numerous sharp rebukes. God is often warning his children now. The faithful preaching of his truth is a rebuke to the thoughtless and the sinful. The interior voice of conscience utters its own solemn Divine reproof. If we sin heedlessly, we do not sin unwarned. The rejection of the reproof is no sign of its weakness or insufficiency. Even the warning words of Christ failed to arrest the wilful people of Jerusalem in their headlong race to destruction (Matt. xxiii. 37). II. REPROOF IS REJECTED BY STUBBORN SELF-WILL. The neck is hardened. The obstinate man is like a horse that will not obey the reins; like one that has taken the bit into its teeth and will rush on in its own wild course. 1. *This implies determination.* One who was unreproved might plead ignorance or forgetfulness. Such an excuse cannot be put forward by the man who has been often reproved. His disregarded warnings will rise up in the judgment to condemn him. Meanwhile his continuous refusal to give heed to them is a sure sign of deliberate sinfulness. 2. *This also implies hardness of heart.* It is the hard heart that makes the neck hard. The stiff-necked generation is a stony-hearted generation. The repeated rejection of reproof tends to harden the heart more and more. The ear grows deaf to the often-neglected alarum. III. REPROOF, WHEN REJECTED, IS FOLLOWED BY RUIN. The reproof is a warning. Its very sternness is inspired by love, because it is intended to guard the foolish soul against impending danger. But after this has been heard unheeded there can be no escape. 1. *There is no excuse.* The warning has been uttered. Everything possible has been done to arrest the downward career of the stubborn reprobate. 2. *There is double guilt.* The rejection of the reproof is an additional sin—an insult to the Divine righteousness and love. 3. *There can be no hope of escape.* The destruction may be sudden, after its long delay, and "that without remedy." IV. REPROOF, WHEN HEEDED, LEADS TO RESTORATION. 1. *It contains hope.* For if there were no way of escape open the language of reproof would be wasted. In that case it would come too late, and might as well be spared. The sternest reproof is a call to repentance, and this call points to a restoration. 2. *It prepares for the gospel.* John the Baptist makes straight the way for Christ. After we have humbly submitted to reproof, we shall hear the joyous message of the gospel.

Ver. 2.—*The religion of politics.* I. RELIGION IS CONCERNED WITH POLITICS. Too often the two spheres are kept disastrously distinct. On the one hand, it is pretended that the sacred character of religion would be desecrated by its being dragged into the political arena; and on the other hand, the claim of religion to have a voice in public affairs is set down to the ambition and tyranny of priestcraft. Now, it is not to be supposed that purely religious subjects should be obtruded on the uncongenial platform of a public meeting. Very possibly they would be resented; we are not to cast pearls before swine. Moreover, there is a time for everything. But religion claims to influence politics, to be a leading factor in public movements, to hold the standard by which all political actions are to be judged. It must do this if it is to carry out its mission of leavening the whole lump. It should leave no region of life untouched; commerce, literature, art, science, recreation, society, and politics must all come under its influence. For religion to withdraw from politics is to hand that important region of life over to the devil. We find that the Bible has much to say on the conduct of public affairs.

II. THE WELFARE OF A PEOPLE IS LARGELY DETERMINED BY THE MORAL CHARACTER OF THE GOVERNMENT. 1. *The principal influence of religion on politics must be moral.* In public life nice distinctions of creed, fine varieties of abstract dogma, and academic discussions of theoretical divinity are brushed aside as mere cobwebs compared to the serious, practical, present-day questions that are at stake. But the moral influence of religion does not belong to any of these categories. That influence is direct, practical, and real. The religion of politics is the morality of public life viewed in the light of God. 2. *The moral character of public affairs is of vital interest to the people.* States are ruined by immoral government. Bad passions stir up needless strife. Wicked greed, jealousy, or revenge are at the root of most wars. A government of a high moral character would have found a means of keeping the peace, where one of lower tone has plunged the nation into all the horrors of war. The right and peaceable relation of class to class within the community can only be preserved when justice and humanity are observed in the conduct of public affairs.

III. IT IS THE DUTY OF CHRISTIAN MEN TO SEE THAT THE RIGHTEOUS ARE IN AUTHORITY. 1. *In a system of popular government all who have a voice should make that voice heard.* It is a distinct dereliction of duty for any Christian man to withdraw from all influence in public life. It may be urged that the tone of that life is worldly. If so there is the more reason why unworldly men should enter it in order to give it a higher character. The Christian is not a recluse. He is called to be the salt of the earth, to season all society with wholesome thought and action. It is unfair to leave the burden of public affairs to others, and then to profit by their labours; and yet this is what is done by those people who are too devout to assist in the making of good laws, but by no means too devout to avail themselves of those laws when they are made. 2. *Religion will best influence politics by good men being at the head of affairs.* Good men will make good measures. It is therefore necessary to select men of high character for parliament and also for municipal offices.

Ver. 8.—*Scornful men.* The evil of a contemptuous treatment of life and duty is to be seen in many relations. Let us consider some of them.

I. SCORN FOR THE PEOPLE. This was the temper of the old monarchical and aristocratic systems. The mischief of it was seen in the explosion of the French Revolution. The "dim multitude" cannot be treated as so much chaff of the threshing-floor. The nation is the people. The first interest of the nation is the welfare of the great bulk of the population, not the luxury of what is regarded as "the cream of society."

II. SCORN FOR THE POOR. This was the attitude of the wealthy Jews in ancient Israel, which called forth stern rebukes from the prophets of God (*e.g.* Amos vi. 3—6); and the same fault was detected in the Christian Church by St. James (Jas. ii. 1—3). The indifference which too many of the prosperous feel for their hard-pressed, suffering brethren is one of the most dangerous symptoms of society. It lies at the root of socialism.

III. SCORN FOR INJUSTICE. In some cases there is worse than poverty; there is positive wrong-doing. The powerful oppress the weak. Strong masters hold down miserable slaves. This evil condition was a perpetual cause of danger to Rome in its most prosperous age. It is seen in the "sweating system" in England to-day.

IV. SCORN FOR DANGER. Misery and injustice are sources of danger. But other and direct dangers may menace a country. The scorn of pride will be no security against those dangers. We shall not be protected by singing, "Rule, Britannia," or by shouting, "Britons never shall be slaves."

V. SCORN FOR WICKEDNESS. The greatest danger of the state is not in poverty at home; nor is it in war from abroad. It lies in the moral corruption of the people. Wholesale debauchery, widespread drunkenness, a perfect epidemic of gambling, profligacy, dishonesty,—these are the cankers that eat out the vital strength of a nation. Indifference to such evils is contempt for moral law.

VI. SCORN FOR RELIGION. In the race for wealth, in the dance of pleasure, in the mad orgy of worldly engagement, multitudes treat the claims of religion with scorn. Others, in their misery and despair, refuse to believe that any help or hope can come to them from heaven. This scornful attitude towards the first duties and the highest interests of life must be fraught with fatal consequences. Meanwhile the scornful attitude entirely excludes the beginnings of better things. Humility and repentance are impossible so long as this defiant mood is cherished.

Ver. 18.—*No vision!* The revelation of ancient prophecy was not continuous and uninterrupted, but it came in flashes, between which there were intervals of darkness. Sometimes those intervals were long and most distressing to a people that had learnt to draw its chief lessons from Divine oracles. Such a time was experienced in the days of Eli, for "the word of the Lord was rare in those days; there was no open vision" (1 Sam. iii. 1); and another and longer period was that of the "four centuries of silence" between the closing of the Old Testament and the opening of the New Testament.

I. MEN NEED A HEAVENLY VISION. This requirement was recognized in Israel on especial grounds, because the people felt themselves to be a divinely directed nation, with God for their King and Leader. The fading away of the prophet's vision would be like the vanishing of the pillar of cloud and fire in the wilderness; a necessary guidance would be lost. But heavenly visions are not less needed by all men. 1. *Men need to know heavenly truth.* (1) In order to do the will of God. The servant must know his master's will if he is to do his duty. Earthly knowledge is not enough. Heavenly messages are wanted, or the duty to God will be neglected. (2) For the saving of a man's own soul. We are not merely earthly animals. We are naturally related to heaven. To be starved of heavenly truth is to be left to perish in earthly-mindedness. 2. *Men cannot discover heavenly truth.* It must be revealed. Without a vision from God the world is in spiritual darkness.

II. MEN CAN HAVE A HEAVENLY VISION. God has not left his people to grope in a gross Cimmerian darkness. Light has fallen from heaven on earth. 1. *This is given in the Bible.* That record of old revelation enshrines a perpetual vision of God for all who have eyes to behold it. Therefore it is the duty of Christian people (1) to study the Scriptures, (2) to circulate them throughout the world, and (3) to teach and expound them to children and the ignorant. 2. *This is enjoyed in personal experience.* Every man can have his own vision, nay, must have it if he would really see truth. It is not to be supposed that everybody can be a Daniel or an Ezekiel, can behold Isaiah's wonderful vision of God (Isa. vi.) or St. John's glorious apocalypse of the heavenly Jerusalem (Rev. xxi.). Much less is each man to look for his own separate gospel, and to feel called upon to write his own *newer* Testament. But in the understanding and appreciation of truth we must each see it for ourselves by the aid of a Divine inspiration. This was predicted by Joel of the new dispensation (Joel ii. 28), and claimed by St. Peter (Acts ii. 16—21).

III. MEN MAY LOSE THEIR HEAVENLY VISION. God is not capricious. If the Divine voice is silent, this must be because there are no obedient ears to receive it. The vision is only withdrawn when the eyes of men are so blinded by sin and worldliness that they cannot behold it. Then God may send a famine of the Word of truth (Amos viii. 11). It is a fearful thing to be incapable of seeing the truth of God or hearing his voice. But this condition is dependent on our own conduct. We blind our eyes against the light of heaven when we plunge into the mire of sin. We need to pray, "Open thou mine eyes, that I may behold wondrous things out of thy Law" (Ps. cxix. 18). Christ came to open blind eyes (Luke iv. 18), and to give new visions of God's truth (John xviii. 37).

Ver. 25.—*The fear of man.* I. THE FEAR. 1. *In what it consists.* This fear is a dread of the disfavour of man, and its hurtful results. It may take various forms. (1)

Fear of human authority. Thus, in days of persecution, the weak shrink from martyrdom. Wrongs are often permitted for fear of the consequences of agitating against them. (2) Fear of the great. Some men have an awe of mere rank and station. They bow obsequiously before riches; they dread to oppose important personages. (3) Fear of society. "Mrs. Grundy" is regarded with awe. It is thought to be a dreadful thing to be out of the fashion. Social impropriety, in the eyes of the fastidious, is regarded as worse than moral delinquency. (4) Fear of the multitude. This is the new fear of man peculiarly mischievous in our democratic age. There is a danger lest men should concede to popular clamour what they do not believe to be good or right. (5) Fear of those we love. Perhaps this is the most difficult fear to resist (but see Mat. x. 37). 2. *How it originates.* (1) In cowardice. This is an unworthy fear. It is selfish and immoral. It springs from too much regard for our own feelings, and too little reverence for duty. (2) In godlessness. Man takes the place of God. The mob is deified. Human action is treated as supreme.

II. ITS SNARE. 1. *The deception of it.* (1) In regard to duty. Fear takes the place of conscience. It blinds us to the sense of right and wrong, blurring the great outlines of morality. Instead of asking, "What is right?" a person who is haunted by this shameful fear only inquires, "What is safe?" Now, there is no more self-deluded mortal than the man who is only sure of being "safe." When he folds his arms in smug complacency, he is really "in the gall of bitterness and the bonds of iniquity." (2) In regard to danger. Subservience to the opinion of other people can never afford real security. It is but a shallow and tricky device. We can never please all men, and in attempting to escape the wrath of one party we rouse that of another. If, however, the sleek time-server were clever enough to propitiate all human enmity, he would have left himself exposed to the far more terrible wrath of Heaven. 2. *The fatality of it.* This fear brings a snare. It entraps its unwary victim. When once the craven-hearted man is caught in the meshes of worldly fears, he finds it vain to struggle for liberty. This fear creates a miserable bondage. No serf under the old feudal system was more bound to his lord than the poor slave of public opinion is to his hydra-headed master. This wretched fear of man is fatal to all true manliness. It will make shipwreck of the most honourable career. The only needful fear is fear of doing wrong, fear of the devil (Matt. x. 28).

III. ITS ANTIDOTE. We are to find a refuge from the ensnaring fear of man by putting our trust in the Lord. God is mightier than the whole world. A howling mob hounding its victims to death cannot shake the confidence of one who has made the Lord his Refuge. Trust in God saved Shadrach, Meshach, and Abednego from cowardice when threatened by cruel Nebuchadnezzar and cast into the burning fiery furnace. Christ was calm and fearless before all his foes, fortified by the prayers of Gethsemane. We need to rise into a higher atmosphere above all the mists of popular opinion. Men may frown and rage, or laugh and ridicule; but he who dwells in the secret place of the Most High shall abide under the shadow of the Almighty (Ps. xci. 1).

"Earth may be darkness; Heaven will give thee light."

Ver. 26.—*The supreme Arbiter.* I. IT IS A COMMON MISTAKE TO ASCRIBE TO MAN THE INFLUENCE WHICH BELONGS ONLY TO GOD. In the previous verse we have been warned against falling into the snare of the fear of man, and encouraged to find our safety in trust in God. A similar contrast is again presented to us, but from the opposite side. We are tempted to flatter the great in order to win their favour; but we are now reminded that our destiny does not lie in their hands, but in the hands of One who is supreme in judgment, though his rule is too often ignored by us. Helena, in 'All's Well that ends Well,' says—

> "It is not so with him that all things knows,
> As 'tis with us that square our guess by shows;
> But most it is presumption in us when
> The help of Heaven we count the act of men."

1. This common mistake arises partly from the fact that the human influence is visible, while that of God is *unseen.* The molehill at our feet thus seems to be more important

than the mountain that bounds our horizon but is wrapped in mist. 2. It is also caused by the further fact that much of God's judgment is *postponed.* We do not yet experience the full effect of the Divine arbitrament.

II. GOD'S JUDGMENT WILL BE EXPERIENCED BY EVERY MAN. He is not only the Arbiter of the fate of those who call in his aid; he is the "Judge of all the earth" (Gen. xviii. 25). Abraham recognized the fact that God was the Judge of Sodom and Gomorrah, though no doubt the wicked cities of the plain utterly repudiated his authority. The godless will be judged by God. Those men who do not choose to put their case in the hands of God will nevertheless receive their sentence from him.

III. IT IS GOOD NEWS FOR THE WORLD THAT GOD IS THE SUPREME ARBITER. This is not set before us as a truth of terror. On the contrary, it is declared as a great consolation among the ills of life. 1. God is *just.* He is perfectly fair, utterly impartial, no Respecter of persons. Rich and poor stand on equal grounds before his judgment-seat. 2. God is *wise.* The most acute human judge may be deceived. But he that searcheth the heart knows all facts about all men. His judgment must be based on truth. 3. God is *strong.* He is able to execute his sentence. When he declares what is right, he will also establish his judgment.

IV. IT IS WELL FOR MEN TO ACKNOWLEDGE GOD AS THEIR ARBITER. We shall all have to submit to his judgment in the end. It would be wise for us to acknowledge his rule throughout life. Surely it is most fatally foolish to labour for the favour even of the most influential men, if this involves disregarding the thoughts and will of God. The verdict of the lower court will be overridden by the judgment of the higher court. Therefore what is most incumbent on all men is to see that they are right and straight in the eyes of the One supreme Judge. By sin, as we must acknowledge, we are all wrong in his eyes. Therefore no human favour can save us till we have been put right and justified through the grace of Christ.

HOMILIES BY VARIOUS AUTHORS.

Vers. 1—7.—*Private morality and the public weal.* 1. TRUTHS OF PERSONAL CONDUCT. 1. *The obstinate offender and his doom.* (Ver. 1.) The repeated complaint against Israel was that they were a "stiff-necked people." Self-willed, haughty, persistent, defying rebuke and chastisement, is the habit described. It invites judgment. "When lesser warnings will not serve, God looks into his quiver for deadly arrows." They who will not bend before the gentle persuasions of God's Holy Spirit must feel the rod. Men may make themselves outlaws from the kingdom of God. 2. *Wisdom and virtue inseparable in conduct.* (Ver. 3.) So much so that the same word may occasionally do duty for either notion. Thus the French mean by one who is "sage" one who is chaste and virtuous. The effects are alike. Joy is given to parents by the sage conduct of children; and vice is seen to be folly by the waste and want it brings in its train (comp. ch. vi. 26; x. 1; xxviii. 7). 3. *The dishonesty of flattery.* (Ver. 5.) It may be designed to deceive, and is then coloured with the darkest hue of treachery. Or it may be undesigned in its effects. But in either case, the web of flattering lies becomes a snare in which the neighbour stumbles to his fall (comp. ch. xxvi. 24, 25, 28). The kiss of the flatterer is more deadly than the hate of a foe. "When we are most praised for our discernment, we are apt to act most foolishly; for praise tends to cloud the understanding and pervert the judgment." 4. *Delusive and genuine joy.* (Ver. 6.) The serpent is concealed amidst the roses of illicit pleasures; a canker is at the core of the forbidden fruit. A "shadow darkens the ruby of the cup, and dims the splendour of the scene." But ever there is a song in the ways of God. See the example of Paul and Silas even in prison (Acts xvi. 25). "Always there are evil days in the world; always good days in the Lord" (Augustine, on Ps. xxxiii.).

II. THE INFLUENCE OF PERSONAL GOODNESS ON SOCIAL AND PUBLIC WEAL. 1. *The general happiness is dependent on the conduct of individuals.* (Ver. 2; comp. ch. xxviii. 12, 28.) For society is a collection of individuals. "It is no peculiar conceit, but a matter of sound consequence, that all duties are by so much the better performed, by how much the men are more religious from whose abilities the same proceed.

For if the course of political affairs cannot in any good sort go forward without fit instruments, and that which fitteth them be their virtues, let polity acknowledge itself indebted to religion, godliness being the chiefest, top, and well-spring of all true virtue, even as God is of all good things." "Religion, unfeignedly lived, perfecteth man's abilities unto all kinds of virtuous services in the commonwealth" (Hooker, 'Eccl. Pol.,' v. 1). 2. *The effect of just administration and of bribery.* (Ver. 4.) The best laws are of no avail if badly administered. God's throne is founded on justice (Ps. lxxxix. 14). And this only can be the foundation of national stable polity and of the common weal. "We will sell justice to none," says the Magna Charta. The theocracy was overthrown in the time of Samuel by the corruption of his sons. The just administration of David "bore up the pillars" of the land (2 Sam. viii. 15). The greed of Jehoiakim again shook the kingdom to its foundations (Jer. xxii. 13—19). Righteousness alone exalteth a nation. 3. *Justice to the poor.* (Ver. 7.) The good man enters into the feelings of others, and makes the lot of the oppressed, in sympathy and imagination, his own. The evil and hard-hearted man, looking at life only from the outside, treats the poor as dumb driven cattle, and easily becomes the tyrant and the oppressor. Peculiarly, sympathy, consideration, compassion for the lowly and the poor, have been infused into the conscience of the world, and made " current coin " by the example and spirit of the Redeemer.—J.

Vers. 8—11.—*Dishonourable passions.* Such is the designation given by St. Paul (see Revised Version of the New Testament, Rom. i. 26, etc.) to the various workings of the evil leaven in the soul. Here is a description of some of these " lusts."

I. SCOFFING. (Ver. 8.) Set on fire of hell, it inflames others, disturbs the peace of communities, produces failures and tumults in public life. But wisdom calms, and turns all things to the best. The scoffer, the malevolent critic of existing institutions, is a public pest; the judicious man, a public blessing. The one raises tumults, the other quells them.

II. CONTENTIOUSNESS. (Ver. 9.) It delights in dispute for dispute's sake. The man of this vice does not want to elicit truth, but to find fuel for his passion. Alternating between rage and ridicule, he uses words merely as weapons of offence and defence. Egotism is at the root of all his activity.

III. THE SANGUINARY TEMPER. (Ver. 10.) All hatred to the truth involves hatred to the truth-speaker and the truth-doer. Here lies the secret of all persecution and of all judicial murders. But in ourselves, whenever we detect the rising of resentment against him who exposes our faults or fallacies, we may find something of the dark temper of him " who was of the wicked one, and slew his brother " (1 John iii. 12).

IV. WANT OF SELF-CONTROL. (Ver. 11.) The impetuous, unbridled temper, which explodes with wrath at the smallest provocation, or with ill-considered opinions. He is wise who knows when to hold his peace. We are not always to speak all we feel or think, but when we do speak should ever think what we say. We must remember that " there is a time to speak, and a time to keep silence."—J.

Vers. 12—17.—*Government in truth and equity.* I. THERE MUST BE THE FORCE OF EXAMPLE. (Ver. 12.) Especially in regard to truthfulness. Nothing is more easily caught than an example of untruthfulness, evasion, hypocrisy. Servants' manners reflect their masters' characters. The more conspicuous the station, the further the influence of the example extends.

II. THERE MUST BE RESPECT TO THE RULER AND JUDGE OF ALL. (Ver. 13.) He is no Respecter of persons; but he is the Protector of all, and the Judge between man and man. The distinctions of ruler and subject, of rank and rank, of class and class, are temporary; the common relation of all to God is spiritual and eternal.

III. THERE MUST BE REGARD TO THE LOWLY. (Ver. 14.) Must not the test of every government be at last this—What did it accomplish for the poor, for the burdened, for the slave and the oppressed? "Glorious" wars and additions of territory can never compensate for injustice at home; the renown of arms for a people's misery. The throne that is not propped by bayonets, but built upon a people's gratitude and loyalty, may defy the storms of revolution.

IV. DOMESTIC GOVERNMENT TEACHES THE SAME TRUTHS ON A SMALLER SCALE.

(Vers. 15—17.) 1. There is the same need of firmness and discipline. Absolute liberty is licence. All our freedom is bounded by necessity. The good of the whole demands fixed law; and this must be observed in the household as in the body politic. A weakness in the administration of acknowledged law is fatal to the purity of the home, to the welfare of nations. Evil-doers must be kept down; if their character cannot be changed, their power to work mischief must be taken from them by the unflinching administration of law. And lastly, firmness, so far from alienating, really wins the good will, the respect, and obedience of subjects in the petty commonwealth of home and in the larger sphere of the state.—J.

Vers. 18—23.—*Fatal defects in the social state.* I. THE WANT OF COMMANDING RELIGIOUS TEACHING. The great prophets of Israel were the great instructors of the people. They declared Jehovah's living oracles; they made clear the eternal principles of the moral law; they forecast what *must* be the future under moral conditions. The Christian preacher has succeeded to the office of the Jewish prophet. Woe to the nation if the supply of preachers ceases! if, sunk in material interests, they are allowed to forget that the "Word of the Lord" lives and endures, and obedience to it must be the foundation of all private blessing, all public prosperity!

II. THE WANT OF FIRM POLICY AND CONDUCT. (Ver. 19.) There always will be a class more or less of "slaves," who must be governed, not by mere rhetoric or the appeal to feeling, but by the knowledge that words will be backed by deeds. God means what he says. The laws of nature are no mere abstract statements of truth; they are stern and solemn *facts*, which cannot be defied with impunity. And the lawless must understand that what *ought* to be *shall* be.

III. THE WANT OF CALM DELIBERATION. (Ver. 20.) Whether in private or in public life, this too may be a ruinous defect. Thus rash enterprises are begun, hostilities break out without warning, a lifelong alienation or the misery of a generation may spring from the passion or the pique of the moment.

IV. WANT OF DUE SEVERITY IN DISCIPLINE. (Ver. 21.) The exegesis of the verse certainly points to this meaning. Men are stung by the ingratitude or contumacy of those whom they had weakly petted, and whose faults they had nourished by their smiles. But human nature will only respond to just and true treatment; and injurious kindness will reap a thorny crop of ingratitude.

V. WANT OF SELF-CONTROL AND OF SELF-KNOWLEDGE. (Vers. 22, 23.) (For the first, see ch. xv. 18; xxviii. 25.) Wrath is the very hot-bed of transgression and every "evil work." And self-esteem is a neighbour vice. So near are extremes in life: the moment we are highest in our own imagination we are really lowest in power, in position, in prospect. "He that would build lastingly must lay his foundation low. As man falls by pride, he recovers by humility." And the more God honours men, the more they should humble themselves.—J.

Vers. 24—27.—*Prudence in alliance with religion.* I. PRUDENCE AND RELIGION ARE EVER IN HARMONY. There can be no divorce between them. We are not placed between cross-lights here. What intelligent regard to self prescribes, God's Law commands. Approach the facts of life from these two opposite sides, travel by either of these two paths, they meet at last in duty, in safety, in peace, and salvation.

II. SOME EXAMPLES OF THIS HARMONY. 1. *All dishonesty or complicity with it is self-destructive.* (Ver. 24.) Enlightened experience says so, and stamps itself in the clear dictum, "Honesty is the best policy." God's Word says so, and here and in a thousand similar declarations and warnings pronounces a curse upon the sin. 2. *Fear of man is perilous; confidence in the Eternal is safety.* (Ver. 25.) Experience again ratifies this. The coward dies a thousand deaths; the brave, but once. The feeble-hearted daily miss opportunities; the brave create them. Moral cowardice springs from want of inner conviction of the might of truth; moral strength, from the inner certainty that nothing but truth is victorious. Positive revelation here again fortifies the hints of common knowledge. 3. *The vanity of honour from others; the true honour that comes from God.* (Ver. 26.) What bitter things have been written down in the experience of men of the world concerning the favour of the great, and the folly of courting it and depending upon it! and how does the same lesson echo back from the page of Holy

Writ! Act well your part in Jehovah's sight; seek the honour that cometh from him only;—how common and Divine wisdom effect a juncture once more! 4. *Eternal antipathies.* (Ver. 27.) What experience teaches us in one form, that fellowship must be founded on sympathy, that tastes must be respected, that deep, undefinable feelings attract us to or repel us from others, God's Word again confirms: " Have no fellowship with the unfruitful works of darkness." Acquaintance is mere collocation of persons; friendship and Christian communism are the eternal affinity of souls in God.—J.

Ver. 1.—*The doom of obduracy.* There are four stages which conduct to spiritual ruin.
I. HUMAN DISLOYALTY. Man is found (or finds himself) at enmity with God; he does not reverence, love, honour, serve, him. He owes everything to his Maker and Preserver and generous Benefactor; but he has not paid his great debt, and now he is estranged in spirit, and his life is one of disloyalty and rebellion.
II. DIVINE SUMMONS TO RETURN. God is saying, "Return unto me, and I will return unto you;" "Let the wicked forsake his way . . . and let him return unto the Lord." By many messengers, in many voices, God calls us to repentance and reconciliation.
III. HUMAN RECUSANCY. God calls, but men will not hearken or they will not heed. They either (1) deliberately decline to listen; or they (2) do listen without being seriously impressed; or they (3) are impressed without coming to any right and wise decision; they linger and delay; they continually postpone; and every new procrastination makes indecision easier and delay more dangerous.
IV. DIVINE PATIENCE. God "bears long" with men. We see his merciful and wonderful patience when we look at: 1. *The time* during which he continues to them preservation and privilege. Through childhood and youth, through manhood and the days of decline, up to extreme old age, God continues to men his sustaining and preserving *power*, and all the fulness of Christian *privilege* ; though all the while they are abusing his gift of life by retaining it for their own personal enjoyment, and his gift of opportunity by slighting, or despairing, or misusing it. 2. The *various means* he employs in order to reach and restore us. (1) God *invites* men, through his Word, and through the Christian ministry, and by the voices of the home and of human friendship. (2) He *commands*; he requires that all men should repent and believe. (3) He *warns*. (4) He *reproves*; he *often* reproves. "He that is often reproved;" and very commonly a disloyal heart *is* often rebuked of God. Time after time he receives the admonition of his fellows, or he suffers the penalty of his guilt. God makes him to understand that "the way of transgressors is hard;" the merciful hand of the Divine Father interposes many obstacles in the way of his children's ruin, that they may be stopped and may be led to return on their way. But sin does its fatal work of indurating the heart, of paralyzing the conscience, of blinding the eyes of the children of men; and the man who is "often rebuked" only "hardens his neck," and then comes the end—
V. SUDDEN AND IRREMEDIABLE RUIN. 1. Sometimes (perhaps *frequently*, in the case of those who are guilty of flagrant sin) the day of probation ends with startling suddenness: "They are brought into desolation in a moment." Death comes down upon them without any warning. In the full flow of iniquity their soul is that very night required of them, and they pass from guilt to judgment. 2. Commonly, the end comes without expectation, and so without preparation. Men are going on with the engagements and the indulgences of life; and they are *expecting to go on* indefinitely. Then comes the serious illness, the sick-chamber, the medical attendant, the anxious inquiry, the unfavourable response, the solemn communication, and the distressed and agitated soul has to say, " My hour is come, and I am not ready for its coming."—C.

Ver. 2.—(See homily on ch. xi. 10.)—C.

Ver. 5.—(See homily on ch. xxvii. 5, 6.)—C.

Ver. 7.—(See homily on ch. xix. 17.)—C.

Vers. 8—10.—*The senselessness of scorn, etc.* Here is a triplet of truths we may gather from these three texts.

I. THE SENSELESSNESS OF SCORN. (Ver. 8.) To be of a scornful spirit, to bestow scornful looks, to use scornful language,—this is gross folly. 1. *It is utterly unbecoming.* Not one of us is so removed above his fellows as to be entitled to treat with entire disregard what they may have to say or what they propose to do. 2. *The wisest men,* and even the Wise One himself, think well to listen to what the humblest can suggest. 3. It leads to a *blind opposition* to true wisdom; for often wisdom is found with those in whom no one expects to discover it; even as the scornful Greek and the proud Roman found it in the despised teachers from Judæa. 4. *It ends disastrously.* It "brings a city into a snare," "sets a city in a flame." It refuses to consider the serious danger that is threatened, or it provokes to uncontrollable anger by its disdainfulness; and the end is discord, confusion, strife. 5. *It deliberately neglects* the one way of peace. A wise man who does *not* refuse to listen and to learn, who prefers to treat neighbours and even enemies with the respect that is their due, "turns away wrath," and saves the city from the flame. Scorn is thus a senseless thing in every light.

II. THE USELESSNESS OF CONTENTION. (Ver. 9.) We are not to understand that it is a vain or foolish thing to endeavour (1) to enlighten the ignorant, or (2) to convince the mistaken. Where there is an honest and loyal spirit, it may be of great service to do this. What *is* useless is (3) to *debate with the contentious.* Nothing comes of it but the clatter of the tongue and the triumph of the complacent "fool." He may "rage" or he may "laugh;" he may passionately declaim or he may indulge in banter and in badinage, but he does not seek, and he will not find, the truth. He is no nearer to wisdom at the end than he was at the beginning. Time is wasted; the heart of the wise is disappointed; the wayward man is confirmed in his folly;—let him alone.

III. THE AIM OF THE UPRIGHT. This is twofold. 1. *Peace.* The wise man, who is the upright man, "turns away wrath;" and he objects to a contest with the contentious, because "there is no rest." Those in whom is the Spirit of Christ are always setting this before them as a goal to be reached; they speak and act as those that "make for peace." They feel that everything which can be should be avoided that makes for dissension and strife; they are the "peacemakers," and theirs is the blessing of the children of God (Matt. v. 9). 2. *Life.* They (the upright) "seek the soul," or the life, of the man whom the bloodthirsty hate (ver. 10). To "seek the soul" or the life of men is the characteristic of the good. (1) They care, in thought and deed, for the preservation and the protection of human life; they seek the removal of all that threatens it. (2) They care much for all that enlarges and ennobles human life—education, morality, sound discipline. (3) They care most of all for that one thing which crowns human life, and may be said to constitute it—the return of the soul to God and its life in him. In this deepest and truest sense they "seek his soul;" for they are regarding and pursuing its spiritual and eternal welfare.—C.

Ver. 11 (and see ch. xii. 16; xiv. 33).—*The time to be silent.* There is a time to keep silence as well as a time to speak (see Eccles. iii. 7). According to our individual temperament we need the one injunction or the other. There are few, however, of either sex or of any disposition who do not need to be urged to guard the door of the lip. This is one of those things in which we all offend in our time and in our way. *Impatience* most frequently leads to transgression; but there are other provocations—there are other occasions when the warning word is wanted. We should carefully command our tongue when there is in our mind—

I. THE IDEA OF ACHIEVEMENT. It is unwise to talk of what we are going to do as soon as it occurs to us to act. We may think ourselves capable or our circumstances favourable when, on further consideration or inquiry, we find that we are not equal to the task or that our position makes it impossible to us. We should *think* before we *undertake.*

II. THE THOUGHT OF IGNORANCE. Nothing but harm can come of counsel given in ignorance of any case before us. Either we persuade our friends and colleagues to take action which is unwise and will prove to be injurious and possibly disastrous; or we are at once corrected by those who know better, and we are ashamed. Do not go to the council without learning the facts and understanding the matter, or else wait well and learn patiently before you speak at all.

III. THE FEELING OF RESENTMENT. " A fool uttereth all his anger, but a wise man keepeth it back and stilleth it " (Revised Version ; ch. xii. 16). Nothing more distinctly marks the presence of wisdom or folly than the habit of speaking quickly or restraining speech under provocation. It is an unfailing criterion. The reasons for silence at such a time are obvious enough, and they should be strong enough. 1. Hasty speech is (1) very likely indeed to be incorrect, imperfect, if not wholly wrong, for our judgment is sure to be disturbed and unhinged when our spirit is wounded ; (2) most likely to provoke our opponent to feel strongly and to strike severely, and thus the flood-gates of strife are opened ; (3) unworthy of the wise and strong, lowering in the eyes of our best friends and in our own regard ; (4) condemned of God (Jas. i. 19, 20). 2. Conscientious silence under provocation is (1) an admirable victory over our lower nature (ch. xvi. 32); (2) the way of peace in the council, in the home, in the Church ; (3) the path in which we follow Christ our Lord, and gain his Divine approval (Matt. xxvii. 12; vi. 9).—C.

Ver. 13.—(See homily on ch. xxii. 2.)—C.

Vers. 15—17.—(See homily on ch. xiii. 24.)—C.

Ver. 18.—*Spiritual ignorance and obedience.* (See also homily on ch. xix. 2.) Two things are clear : 1. That God has provided us with many sources of knowledge. We have, for materials to work *with*, a very complex and richly endowed nature ; and we have, for materials to work *upon*, (1) that same nature of ours with all its instincts, impulses, desires, hopes ; (2) the great visible system around us into which we can constantly be looking, and of which we might be expected to learn much ; (3) human life, and the providence of God as manifested therein. 2. That these sources of wisdom, which are constant and common to our race, prove to be lamentably insufficient. Man, under the dominion and depression of sin, cannot read aright the lessons which his own nature, the visible universe, and the providence of God are fitted and intended to teach him. He shows himself utterly incapable ; he is completely false in his ideas, and pitiably wrong in his course of action. Hence we come to the conclusion of the text—

I. THE LAMENTABLE RESULT OF SPIRITUAL IGNORANCE. " Where there is no vision, the people perish." Where there is no special Divine revelation, supplementing the knowledge and correcting the ignorance of the unenlightened, there is a " perishing " or a " nakedness " in the land. The sad and miserable result, as all lands and all ages testify, is : 1. *Literal, physical death.* Without the knowledge of God, and in the absence of the control which the knowledge of his will can supply, (1) there is *strife,* violence, war, and of this death is the continual fruit ; (2) there is *vice,* and this, when it is finished, bringeth forth death. 2. *Loss of character.* Not only of that which is sometimes understood by character, viz. *reputation,* but also of character itself. Where God's Word and will are unknown, there is such a deplorable descent into the erroneous and the immoral, that both of these go down and perish. 3. *Absence of spiritual life.* The life of our life is in God, and not only in his kindness to us, but in our knowledge of him. To be in utter ignorance of him, to have lost all belief in him, to be spending our days in spiritual separation from him,—is not this to be so destitute of all that beautifies and brightens, of all that enlarges and ennobles, human life, as to be " dead while we live " ? So thought and taught the great Teacher and his great apostle (Luke ix. 60 ; John v. 24 ; 1 Tim. v. 6). It is not merely that there is a sad exclusion, at the end, from the heavenly kingdom; it is that spiritual ignorance of God *constitutes death,* and they who are living without God, and becoming more and more alienated from and unlike to him, are perishing " day by day."

II. THE BLESSEDNESS OF OBEDIENCE. " He that keepeth the Law," etc. Happy is the man who walks in the fear of God, in the love and the service of Jesus Christ ; for : 1. He is walking in the path where all the worst evils cannot harm him ; he is defended from " the evil which is in the world ; " he is upheld in his purity and his integrity. 2. He is living a life which will command the esteem and win the love of the wise and the worthy. 3. He abides under the wing of a heavenly Father's favour; he is enjoying the friendship of a Divine Saviour. 4. He is expending his powers in the conscious, the happy service of him "whose he is," and in whose service is true and lasting freedom. 5. He is exerting a benignant influence in every circle in which he moves. 6. He is travelling homewards.—C.

Vers. 20, 22.—(See homily on ver. 11.)—C.

Ver. 23.—(See homily on ch. xvi. 18.)—C.

Vers. 25, 26.— *Two temptations and two resources.* As responsible human souls, we find ourselves exposed to two dangers, and we have two sources of refuge and strength of a very similar character.

I. TWO TEMPTATIONS. 1. To be unduly affected by the fear of man's displeasure. "The fear of man," etc. Now, the fear of man: (1) May be *dutiful.* It is the duty of children to have a reverential regard for their parents, and to shun most carefully their disapproval. There is a "fear" appropriate to servants (Eph. vi. 5). We should fear to dissatisfy those who have a right to our faithful service. (2) May be *desirable.* We should, as wise co-workers with God, fear to do that which, instead of conciliating, will disaffect those whom we want to win to righteousness and wisdom. But the fear of which Solomon writes (3) *is dishonourable and dangerous.* It is a fear which is born of cowardice, a slavish disinclination to encounter the anger or the opposition of those who are in the wrong. It is an undue concern about the action of those who may claim a right, but who cannot sustain it, to keep us back from duty or to compel us to some unworthiness. By this unmanly and unholy fear we may be (1) prevented from entering the kingdom or the Church of Christ; (2) deterred from speaking his truth with fulness and faithfulness; (3) hindered from bearing the testimony we should otherwise offer against some evil course; (4) led into actual and even active fellowship with wrong. Then, indeed, our fear is "a snare," and it betrays us into sin. 2. To be unduly impelled by a desire for man's favour. "Many seek the ruler's favour." There is, of course, nothing wrong in seeking the interest of the powerful. It is simple wisdom, on the part of those who are struggling and rising, to do that. But it may easily be and often is overdone. Our Lord used very decisive language on this subject (John v. 44). When (1) the desire is excessive; (2) language is used or action is taken which is untruthful or dishonest, or which makes a man fall in his own regard; (3) there is so much solicitude that a man loses self-reliance as well as self-respect, and forgets the help which is to be had from above;—then "seeking the ruler's favour" is a mistake, and even more and worse than that.

II. TWO SOURCES OF STRENGTH. 1. *A sense of Divine approval.* "Every man's judgment cometh from the Lord." Why be troubled about man's condemnation so long as we have his acquittal? Let Judas complain, if Jesus excuses and commends (John xii. 1—8). Let the critics pass their sentence; it is a small thing to a man who is living under an abiding sense that "he that judgeth him is the Lord" (1 Cor. iv. 3, 4; Rom. ii. 29).

> "Men heed thee, love thee, praise thee not;
> The Master praises;—what are men?"

And it is not only the *present* judgment and acceptance of God to which we have recourse, but his *future* judgment also, and the commendation he will pass upon our fidelity (see Rom. xiv. 10—13; 1 Cor. iv. 5). 2. *A hope of Divine succour.* "Whoso putteth his trust in the Lord shall be safe." Again and again, in the Old and New Testaments, by psalmists and prophets and apostles, as well as by our Lord himself, we are invited and exhorted to "put our trust in the Lord;" and we are assured that, so doing, we shall not be ashamed. If God does not deliver us *from* our enemies, and from the trouble they occasion us, he will certainly deliver us *in* our adversity; he will give us strength to endure, grace to submit, courage to bear and brave the worst, sanctity of spirit as the result; he will turn the well of our affliction into a fountain of spiritual blessing.—C.

Ver. 27.—*How to hate the wicked.* There is a hatred we have to endure, and there is also a hatred which we have to cherish. The question of any difficulty is—What is the feeling we should cultivate in our hearts towards the guilty? We may glance at—

I. THE HATRED OF US BY THE WICKED. "He that is upright in the way is abomination to the wicked." 1. This is a well-verified *fact*, attested by Scripture, by history, by observation, probably by experience. 2. Its explanation is at hand. (1) Wicked men are utterly out of sympathy with the righteous. Their tastes, inclinations, habits, are all at variance with those of the good and pure. (2) The upright are obliged to condemn them, either in private or in public. (3) The life of the one is a standing reflection upon the conduct of the other. 3. There is one right way to meet it; viz. (1) to *endure* it as Jesus Christ endured it (Heb. xii. 3; 1 Pet. ii. 23), and as seeing the invisible but present and approving Lord (Heb. xi. 27); (2) to make an honest effort to remove it by winning those who indulge it. But the more difficult question is how we are to bear ourselves toward those whose conduct we reprobate, whose character we detest, whose persons we are not willing to admit into our homes. How shall we order—

II. OUR HATRED OF THE WICKED? That there is a very strong feeling *against* the wrong-doer in the minds of the holy is obvious enough. It is a fact that "an unjust man *is* an abomination to the just." "Do not I hate them that hate thee? . . . I hate them with perfect hatred: I count them mine enemies," said David (Ps. cxxxix. 21, 22). Jesus Christ "looked round about on them with anger" (Mark iii. 5). God is "angry with the wicked every day" (Ps. vii. 11). He "hateth all the workers of iniquity" (Ps. v. 5). Our feeling, therefore, is the reflection of that which is in the heart of the Holy One himself. Of what elements should it be composed? 1. *One element that should be absent.* There should be no trace of personal ill will, of a desire for the suffering of the man himself; for the soul of the sinful we should wish well, and we fall into a mistake, if not into a sin, when we allow ourselves to find a pleasure in witnessing or in dwelling upon the humiliation or the sorrow of the wicked. We ought only to wish for that as a means of their purification and recovery. 2. *The elements that should be present.* (1) Pure resentment, such as God feels, such as our Lord felt when he lived amongst us (see Matt. xxiii.),—a feeling of strong reprobation, which we are obliged to direct against them *as the doers* of unrighteousness. (2) Faithful but measured condemnation. There is, in this view, a time to speak as well as a time to keep silence; and both publicly and privately it behoves us to blame the blameworthy, and even to denounce the shamefully unjust or cruel. But here we are bound to take care that we are well acquainted with the matter on which we speak, and that our judgment is an impartial one. (3) Fearless and unflinching opposition. We must actively and steadfastly oppose ourselves to the iniquitous, and do our best to bring their purposes to the ground. (4) Sincere and practical compassion. With all this that is adverse, we may and should conjoin such pity as our Divine Saviour has felt for ourselves, and such honest and earnest endeavour to win them to the truth and to the practice of righteousness as he put forth when he came to redeem us from sin and to raise us to the likeness and restore us to the kingdom of God.—C.

EXPOSITION.

CHAPTER XXX.

Vers. 1—33.— Part VII. FIRST APPENDIX TO THE SECOND COLLECTION, containing "the words of Agur." A short introduction, teaching that the Word of God is the source of wisdom (vers. 1—6), is followed by apothegms on different subjects (vers. 7—33). Cornelius à Lapide offers the following opinion concerning this appendix, which no one can hesitate to say is well founded, if he attempts to give it a spiritual interpretation, and to discern mysteries under the literal meaning: "Quarta hæc pars elegantissima est et pulcherrima. æque ac difficillima et obscurissima: priores enim tres partes continent Proverbia et Paræmias claras, ac antithesibus et similitudinibus perspicuas et illustres; hæc vero continet ænigmata et gryphos insignes, sed arcanos et perdifficiles, tum ex phrasi quæ involuta est et ænigmatica, tum ex sensu et materia, quæ sublimis est et profunda."

Ver. 1.—**The words of Agur the son of Jakeh, even the prophecy.** This seems to be the correct rendering of the passage, though it has been made to bear very different interpretations. It is plainly the title of the treatise which follows. Who Agur and Jakeh were is utterly unknown. The Jewish interpreters considered that "Agur son of Jakeh" was an allegorical designation of Solomon — *Agur* meaning "Gatherer," or "Convener" (see Eccles. i. 1; xii. 11); *Jakeh*, "Obedient," or "Pious," which thus would indicate David. St. Jerome somewhat countenances the allegorical interpretation by translating, *Verba Congregantis, filii Vomentis*, "The words of the Collector, son of the Utterer." But what follows could not apply to Solomon; he could not say, "I have not learned wisdom" (ver. 3), or ask blindly after the Creator (ver. 4). Many have endeavoured to find Agur's nationality in the word that follows, translated "the prophecy" (הַמַּשָּׂא, *hamassa*). *Massa*, "burden," is usually applied to a solemn prophetical speech or oracle, a Divine utterance (Isa. xiii. 1; xv. 1, etc.), and as this designation was deemed inappropriate to the character of this appendix, it has been thought that allusion is here made to a land of Massa, so called after a son of Ishmael (Gen. xxv. 14), who dwelt in the country of Edom or Seir, and whose inhabitants were among those children of the East whose wisdom had become proverbial (1 Kings iv. 30). Others find Massa in the Hauran, or on the north of the Persian Gulf. The Venetian Version gives, Λόγοι Ἀγούρου υἱέως Ἰακέως τοῦ Μασάου. But we have no satisfactory account of a country thus called, and its existence is quite problematical; therefore the ingenious explanations founded on the reality of this *terra ignota* need not be specified (see Introduction, pp. xxi., etc.). Grätz has suggested that in place of *hamassa* should be read *hammoshel*, "the proverb-writer;" but this is a mere conjecture, unsupported by any ancient authority. If, as seems necessary, we are compelled to resign the rendering, "of Massa," or "the Massan," we must fall back on the Authorized Version, and consider the term "oracle" as applied loosely and abnormally to these utterances of wisdom which follow. That they are not of the nature of Divine communications can be seen at once by consideration of their contents, which are mainly of human, and not of the highest type, and, though capable of spiritual interpretation, do not possess that uniqueness of purpose, that religious

character and elevation of subject, which one expects in the enunciations of an inspired prophet. This view does not militate against their claim to be regarded as Holy Scripture; their place in the canon is secured by other considerations, and is not affected by our suspicion of the inappropriateness of the term applied to them; and, indeed, it may be that the very human element in these utterances is meant to be unsatisfying, and to lead one to look for the deep spiritual truths which underlie the secular surroundings. Agur is some poet or moralist, well known in Solomon's time, probably one of the wise men referred to in ch. xxiv. 23 (see below). The rest of the paragraph is of greater obscurity than the former portion. **The man spake unto Ithiel, even unto Ithiel and Ucal.** According to this rendering, the man is Agur, who is introduced as uttering what follows in ver. 2, etc., to Ithiel and Ucal, two of his sons, pupils, or companions. The name Ucal occurs nowhere else in the Old Testament; Ithiel is found once, in Neh. xi. 7, as the name of a Benjamite. Wordsworth regards the names as symbolical of the moral character of those whom the author designs to address, explaining the former as equivalent to "God with me," and the latter as denoting "consumed" with zeal, or "strong," "perfect." It is as if the writer said, "You must have God with you; yea, you must have God with you, if you are to be strong. You must be Ithiels, if you are to be Ucals." He refers to 1 Cor. xv. 10; 2 Cor. iii. 5; Phil. iv. 13. That the Masorites regarded these words as proper names is evident; אֻכָל, indeed, can have no other application. The Syriac takes this view of the words; to the same opinion lean, more or less, the Jewish translators Aquila and Theodotion, Aben Ezra, Vatablus, Pagninus, and others, and it is the simplest and easiest solution of the difficulties which have been seen in the clause. But many modern commentators have declared against it; *e.g.* Hitzig, Zöckler, Delitzsch, Böttcher, Nowack. The repetition of *Ithiel* seems unmeaning; one sees no reason why it should be repeated more than *Ucal.* The second verse begins with כִּי, which, as Hebraists agree, cannot stand abruptly at the commencement of a discourse, but rather establishes something that has preceded. But if we take the words in dispute as proper names, no statement to be confirmed has been made. We are, then, constrained to take them in another sense. St. Jerome translates them, writing, *Visio quam locutus est vir, cum quo est Deus, et qui Deo secum morante confortatus.* The LXX. (which introduces vers. 1—14 of this chapter after ch. xxiv. 23) gives, "These things saith the man to those who believe God, and I cease; " τοῖς πιστεύουσι Θεῷ being the translation of the doubled *Ithiel*, equivalent to " God with me," and וָאֻכָל (παύομαι) being considered to be a formation from the root כלה. Ewald takes the two words to be the name of one man, equivalent to " God with me, so I am strong; " in his own language, *Mitmirgott —sobinich stark*; but his idea of a dialogue between the rich mocker (vers. 2—4) and the humble believer (vers. 5—14) is not well founded, though a late editor, Strack, agreeing, considers that the only possible interpretation of these verses (2—4) is to make the speaker utter them as the outcome of his unbelief and scoffing, to which Agur answers in ver. 5. Under all circumstances, it has seemed to many scholars best to surrender the notion of proper names, and, altering the vocalization, to interpret, " The oracle of the man, 'I have wearied myself, O God, I have wearied myself, O God,'" or, as others say, "about God." The utterance commences here, and not at ver. 2. The repetition forcibly expresses the laborious and painful investigation of the seeker after truth. The final word, vocalized וָאֵכֶל, is rendered, "And I have withdrawn; " or, as Bickell, quoted by Cheyne, gives, *v'lo ukal*, "I have not prevailed." We arrive thus at this interpretation: first comes the superscription, "The words of Agur," etc., "the oracle of the man; " then begins the utterance, which opens with the melancholy avowal that, though he had longed and striven to know God, his nature, his attributes, his working, he had failed in this object, and expended his labour in vain. Both Agur and Lemuel who is named in ch. xxxi. 1, seem to have been persons not of Israelitish nationality, but dwelling in the neighbourhood of Palestine, and acquainted with the religion and sacred literature of the chosen people (see ver. 5). It is by no means unlikely that they were of the race of Ishmael, from which stock many wise men had risen, and where wisdom was so cultivated as to have become proverbial (see Jer. xlix. 7; Obad. 8). In what follows Agur shows himself as a philosopher and a critic, but at the same time a firm believer.

Vers. 2 and 3 confirm what is said in ver. 1 concerning the fruitlessness of the investigation there mentioned; the more he sought and studied, the more conscious he became of his own ignorance and of God's incomprehensibility.

Ver. 2.—**Surely I am more brutish than any man** "Surely " (*ki*) should be "for " (see note on ver. 1). Cheyne, " I am too stupid

for a man; " **I am a mere irrational beast** (comp. ch. xii. 1; Ps. lxxiii. 22). **And have not the understanding of a man.** I am not worthy to be called a man, as I possess not the intellectual faculty which a man ought to have. This is not ironical, as if he did not desire the statement to be taken in its full sense, and meant to say, " Of course it is my own stupidity that is in fault; " but it is a genuine confession of incompetence to investigate the subject-matter, which is too mysterious for his mental powers to penetrate. Thus Solomon acknowledges that he is but a little child, and prays for an understanding heart (1 Kings iii. 7, 9; comp. Wisd. ix. 5; Matt. xi. 25).

Ver. 3.—**I neither learned wisdom.** With all my eager longing and striving I did not attain to such wisdom, that I should have **the knowledge of the Holy One** (Revised Version margin); *k'doshim*, plural of "excellence," like *elohim* (ch. ix. 10; Hos. xii. 1 (Hebrew); see note on ch. i. 20; and comp. Eccles. v. 8; xii. 1). The knowledge of the all-holy God was beyond his grasp (Job xi. 7, etc.). Theology is a higher science than metaphysics, and cannot be reached by that ladder. The LXX. gives an affirmative sense to this verse, " God hath taught me wisdom, and I know the knowledge of the holy (ἁγίων)."

Ver. 4.—The questions contained in this verse are such as compelled Agur to acknowledge his ignorance and nothingness before the thought of the glory and power of the great Creator. We may compare Job xxxviii., etc. **Who hath ascended up into heaven, or descended?** Who is he that hath his seat in heaven, and doeth works on earth? Who is he whose universal providence is felt and experienced? Where is this mysterious Being who hides himself from human ken? Christ has said something like this, " No man hath ascended up to heaven, but he that came down from heaven, even the Son of man which is in heaven " (John iii. 13); and St. Paul (Eph. iv. 9). In biblical language God is said to come down from heaven in order to punish, to aid, to reveal his will, etc. (Gen. xi. 7; Ps. xviii. 9, etc.); and he returns to heaven when this intervention is finished (Gen. xvii. 22; xxxv. 13). **Who hath gathered the wind in his fists?** Who hath the control of the viewless wind, so as to restrain it or release it at his pleasure? (Ps. cxxxv. 7; Amos iv. 13). Septuagint, " Who hath gathered the winds in his bosom (κόλπῳ)?" **Who hath bound the waters in a garment?** The waters are the clouds which cover the vault of heaven, and are held, as it were, in a garment, so that, in spite of the weight which they contain, they fall not upon the earth. As Job says (xxvi. 8), "He bindeth

20

up the waters in his thick clouds; and the cloud is not rent under them." And again (xxxviii. 37), "Who can number the clouds by wisdom? or who can pour out the bottles of heaven?" So the psalmist, "Thou coveredst it [the earth] with the deep as with a vesture" (Ps. civ. 6). (See above, ch. viii. 27, etc.) Who hath established all the ends of the earth? Who hath consolidated the foundations, and defined the limits, of the remotest regions of the earth? (comp. Job xxxviii. 4, etc.). The answer to these four questions is "Almighty God." He alone can order and control the forces of nature. What is his name, and what is his son's name, if thou canst tell? or, *if thou knowest*. It is not enough to acknowledge the power and operation and providence of this mysterious Being; Agur longs to know more of his nature, his essence. He must have personality; he is not an abstraction, a force, a quality; he is a Person. What, then, is his name, the name which expresses what he is in himself? Men have different appellations for this Supreme Being, according as they regard one or other of his attributes: is there one name that comprehends all, which gives an adequate account of the incomprehensible Creator? The question cannot be answered affirmatively in this life. "We know that if he shall be manifested, we shall be like him; for we shall see him even as he is" (1 John iii. 2). The further question, "What is his son's name?" has given some difficulty. The LXX. has, "What is the name of his children (τοῖς τέκνοις αὐτοῦ)?" as if there was reference to Israel, the special children of God. But the original does not bear out this interpretation, which is also opposed to the idea of the enigma proposed. The inquiry might mean—Are we to apply to the Supreme Being the same notion of natural relationship with which we are familiar in the human family? But this seems a low and unworthy conception. Or the "son" might be primeval man (Job xv. 7) or the sage; but the answer would not be satisfactory, and would not tend to solve the great question. There are two replies which can be made to Agur's interrogation. Looking to the marvellous description of Wisdom in ch. viii. 22, etc., we may consider Wisdom to be a denotation of the Son of God, and the inquirer desires to know the name and nature of this personage, of whose existence he was certified. Or he may have arrived at a knowledge of the only begotten Son of God, as the idea of the Logos is more or less developed in the Book of Wisdom, in Philo's treatises, and in the Alexandrian school; and longs for more perfect knowledge. This, indeed, is hidden: "He hath a

name written, which no one knoweth but he himself" (Rev. xix. 12). It is useless to put such question to a fellow-man; no human mind can fathom the nature of the Godhead, or trace out its operations (Ecclus. xviii. 4, etc.).

Vers. 5, 6.—The following tetrastich is connected with what has preceded in this way: As the light of nature and metaphysical speculation are of no avail in obtaining the perfect knowledge of God which the seeker craves, he must be all the more thankful for the revealed Word of God, which teaches him as much as he is capable of learning.

Ver. 5.—**Every word of God is pure.** "Word" is here *imrah*, which does not occur elsewhere in our book, which is the case also with *Eloah*, the term used for "God." Every declaration of God in the inspired record, the Torah, is pure, as if refined in the fire (Ps. xviii. 30). Vulgate, *Omnis sermo Dei est ignitus;* Septuagint, "All the words of God are tried in the fire (πεπυρωμένοι)." God's words are true, sincere, with no mixture of error, certain of accomplishment (comp. Ps. xii. 6; cxix. 140). **He is a shield.** He is perfect protection to all those who, relying on the word of revelation, fly to him for refuge (see on ch. ii. 7). The knowledge of God is obtained in two ways—by his revelation in his Word, and by the experience of those who trust in him.

Ver. 6.—**Add thou not unto his words.** God's will, as announced in revelation, is to be simply accepted and acted upon, not watered down, not overstrained. This injunction had already been given in the old Law (Deut. iv. 2; xii. 32); it is repeated in the New Testament with awful emphasis (Rev. xxii. 18, 19). No human speculations or traditions may be mingled with God's words; the glosses and explanations and definitions, affixed by rabbinical ingenuity to plain enactments, and proved to be false in morality and fatal to vital religion, are a commentary on the succeeding sentence, **Lest he reprove thee, and thou be found a liar.** The reproof is found in the consequences of such additions; the results to which they lead are such as show that he who asserts that these things are contained in the Word of God is a liar.

Vers. 7—9.—A mashal ode, containing two requests, and a *rationale* of the latter. The matter of the two prayers connects it with ver. 6, whether we consider that the limitation of man's desire follows naturally the limitation of his knowledge (Plumptre) or that the warning against being reproved as a liar is corroborated by the prayer against vanity and lies (but see below, on ver. 9). It is the first of Agur's numerical proverbs.

Ver. 7.—**Two things have I required of thee.** The personal pronoun applies to God, who, according to our interpretation, has been invoked in ver. 1; otherwise it stands without reference to anything preceding. **Deny me not before I die;** *i.e.* grant me these two things for the rest of my life. Septuagint, "Take not grace (χάριν) from me before I die."

Ver. 8.—Here is the first request: **Remove far from me vanity and lies.** *Shav*, "vanity," is inward hollowness and worthlessness, and "lies" are the expression cf this in words. The prayer might indeed be taken as an entreaty against being polluted with the companionship of the evil, like "Lead us not into temptation, but deliver us from evil;" but it is best taken subjectively, as a supplication for personal truthfulness and sincerity in all relations both towards God and man. **Give me neither poverty nor riches.** Both extremes are deprecated: the mean is the safest and the happiest. Horace, 'Carm.,' iii. 16. 42—

"Multa petentibus
Desunt multa; bene est, cui deus obtulit
Parca, quod satis est, manu."

"The 'ever craving' is Want's slave and thrall;
The gods most wisely thus their gifts accord,
Giving 'enough,' they amply give to all."
(Stanley.)

Theognis, 'Parœn.,' 1155—

Οὐκ ἔραμαι πλουτεῖν οὐδ' εὔχομαι, ἀλλά μοι εἴη
Ζῆν ἀπὸ τῶν ὀλίγων, μηδὲν ἔχοντι κακόν.

"I want not wealth; I only ask to live
On frugal means without corroding care."

Feed me with food convenient for me; literally, *give me to eat the bread of my portion;* that which by God's providence is determined for me (comp. Gen. xlvii. 22, which speaks of the portion assigned for the support of the priests; Job xxiii. 14; and below, ch. xxxi. 15). It is natural to refer to τὸν ἄρτον ἡμῶν τὸν ἐπιούσιον of the Lord's Prayer (Matt. vi. 11); but the idea is not the same. In the latter, bread for the needs of the coming day is meant; in our passage it is more indefinite, a casting one's self on the Divine love, in readiness to take what that love assigns. "Having food and covering," says St. Paul (1 Tim. vi. 8), "we shall be therewith content." Septuagint, "Appoint for me what is necessary

and what is sufficient (τὰ δέοντα καὶ τὰ αὐτάρκη)."

Ver. 9.—The reason for the latter prayer follows, unless, as some consider, the prayer is one, as if Agur asked, "Take from me riches which lead to vanity, and poverty which leads to lying and deceit." In this case the ground of the request would embrace both parts of the petition. **Lest I be full, and deny thee, and say, Who is the Lord** (*Jehovah*)? Great wealth and temporal prosperity tempt to forgetfulness of God, to self-confidence and practical unbelief in Divine providence. Like Pharaoh, the haughty rich man asks with scorn, "Who is the Lord, that I should obey his voice?" (Exod. v. 2; comp. Deut. viii. 12, etc.; Job xxi. 14, etc.; Ps. xiv. 1). Septuagint, "Lest being filled I become false, and say, Who seeth me?" **Or lest I be poor, and steal;** lest my necessities lead to dishonesty. **And take the name of my God in vain.** The verb *taphas* means "to grasp at, seize violently, handle roughly," and the sin intended may be either false swearing in denial of his theft and to escape punishment, or the arraignment of God's providence which has allowed him to fall into such distress. Thus Isa. viii. 21, "They shall pass through it, hardly bestead and hungry; and it shall come to pass that, when they shall be hungry, they shall fret themselves, and curse their king and their God." In view of the proverbs that follow, the clause seems to be best taken of the blasphemy attending on impatience and want of resignation to God's will (comp. ch. xix. 3).

Ver. 10.—**Accuse not a servant unto his master.** Calumniate, slander not; μὴ καταλαλήσῃς, Theodotion; μὴ διαβάλῃς, Symmachus. Do not secretly bring a charge against a man's slave, and make his master suspicious of him; have a kind feeling for those in lowly condition, and do not render their lot more unbearable by insinuating false or frivolous accusations against them. Ewald and others would render, "Entice not a servant to slander his master;" but there is no need so to take the expression, as the hiph. of the verb is used in post-biblical Hebrew in the sense of "to calumniate." The Septuagint has, "Deliver not a servant into the hands of his master," which seems to refer to the treatment of runaway slaves (Deut. xxiii. 15). **Lest he curse thee, and thou be found guilty,** and have to atone for it. The slandered slave imprecates a curse on his slanderer, and, as the latter has incurred vengeance by his word or action, the curse will not fall harmless (ch. xxvi. 2); God's righteous retribution will overtake him, and he shall suffer for it.

Vers. 11—31 contain six groups of four

sentences each, each quaternion having a certain connection in language and concinnity of idea. First (vers. 11—14) come four generations that are evil—four being taken as the symbol of universality. The sins herein specified had become so general that they affected the whole generation.

Ver. 11.—There is a generation that curseth their father. The words, "there is," are not found in the Hebrew, and the four subjects are without a predicate. Delitzsch calls the group "a mutilated priamel," which is explained to be a kind of gnomic poetry containing a series of antecedents or subjects followed by an epigrammatic conclusion applicable to all the antecedents. In the present case the conclusion is wanting, so that we are left in doubt whether the author meant merely to describe classes of men in his own time or to affirm that such are abominable. Septuagint, "A wicked generation curseth its father (ἔκγονον κακόν)," which expression is repeated at each of the four verses. The first sin is that which offends against the commandment to honour and obey parents. This was judged worthy of death under the old Law (Exod. xxi. 17; see ch. xx. 20, and note there). And doth not bless their mother. This is a litotes, "not to bless" being equivalent to "to curse."

Ver. 12.—A generation that are pure in their own eyes (ch. xx. 9). The second characteristic is hypocrisy and Pharisaical self-righteousness (see Luke xviii. 11). And yet are not washed from their filthiness; have not cleansed their heart by complete repentance, either because they have not examined themselves and know nothing of the real state of their conscience, or because they care nothing about it and will not regard it in its true light. There is a similar expression in Isa. iv. 4. Septuagint, "A wicked generation judgeth themselves to be just, but have not washed themselves clean (τὴν ἔξοδον αὐτοῦ οὐκ ἀπένιψεν)."

Ver. 13.—A generation, oh, how lofty are their eyes! The third sin is pride and arrogance (see on ch. vi. 17; xxi. 4). "Lord," said the psalmist, "my heart is not haughty, nor mine eyes lofty" (Ps. cxxxi. 1). The prophet rebukes "the stout heart of the King of Assyria and the glory of his high looks" (Isa. x. 12). Their eyelids are lifted up; in supercilious disdain. "Inde Proverbio dicimus," says Erasmus ('Adag.'), "attolli supercilium, fastidium indicantes" (s.v. "Arrogantia").

Ver. 14.—A generation, whose teeth are as swords, and their jaw teeth as knives. The fourth evil is insatiable cupidity, which leads to oppression and injurious treatment of the helpless and poor, which makes men

as cruel and remorseless in destroying others and despoiling them of their substance, as the very steel which they use in their operations. Similarly, the psalmist speaks of his enemies as men "whose teeth are spears and arrows, and their tongue a sharp sword" (Ps. lvii. 4; comp. Isa. ix. 12; Jer. v. 17). To devour the poor from off the earth; i.e. so as to be no more seen in the world. Amos viii. 4, "Hear this, O ye that would swallow up the needy, and cause the poor of the land to fail" (comp. Ps. xiv. 4).

Vers. 15, 16.—Having spoken of insatiate cupidity, the writer now introduces four things which are insatiable. The form of the apothegm is climacteric, mounting from two to three, and thence to four, like the famous passage in Amos i. 3, etc. (comp. ch. vi. 16, though there is no special stress there laid on the last member of the climax; Job v. 19; xxxiii. 29; Eccles. xi. 2).

Ver. 15.—The horseleach hath two daughters, crying, Give, give. The word "crying" is not in the Hebrew, which says, "The alukah hath two daughters : Give! Give!" The insatiable appetite of this creature is represented by two words, which are personified as daughters, whom the mother has produced and dearly loves. This word alukah is not found again in the Old Testament; but in later Hebrew and in Aramaic it means "leech" or "bloodsucker;" and so it is translated by the Septuagint, βδέλλα, and by St. Jerome sanguisuga. The word is derived from a root which in Arabic means "to adhere." There are several kinds of leeches common in Palestine, and their bloodthirsty nature is well known; as Horace says, 'Ars Poet.,' 476—

"Non missura cutem, nisi plena cruoris, hirudo."

It seems simple and quite satisfactory to accept the word thus, and to see in the voracity of the leech an example of the greed further developed in the following clauses; but commentators have not been contented with this explanation, and have offered various suggestions which are either unnecessary or inadmissible. Thus the Talmud considers alukah to be an appellation of hell, and the two daughters to be the Power of the world, and Heresy. Some of the Fathers regard it as a symbol of the devil and his dominion; others, as a personification of cupidity with its two offshoots, avarice and ambition. Some moderns deem it to mean a vampire or bloodthirsty demon, a ghoul, in accordance with Eastern myth. But, as we have said, such interpretations are unnecessary and unsupported by sufficient authority. The allusion to the tastes of the leech is found elsewhere. Thus Theocritus, 'Idyll.,' ii. 55—

Αἲ, αἲ, ἔρως ἀνιαρέ, τί μευ μέλαν ἐκ χροὸς αἷμα

Ἐμφὺς ὡς λιμνᾶτις ἅπαν ἐκ βδέλλα πέπωκας;

And Plautus, 'Epidic.,' ii. 2. 5—

"Jam ego me convortam in hirudinem atque
    Eorum exsugebo sanguinem,
    Senati qui columen cluent."

Ewald and others find traces of mutilation in this proverb, and endeavour to supply what is lost in various ways; but the text as it stands is intelligible, and needs no addition. The rest of the verse is an application of the truth first stated. The type of cupidity there enunciated is instanced and exemplified in four special cases. **There are three things that are never satisfied.** And then a corrective climax is addressed. **Yea, four things say not, It is enough.** The four in the following verse are divided into two plus two. Septuagint, "The leech had three daughters dearly beloved, and these three did not satisfy her, and the fourth was not contented to say, Enough."

Ver. 16.—The four insatiable things are now named: first, **the grave,** sheol (ch. xxvii. 20), which can never be filled with its victims. Horace talks of a man as—

" Victima nil miserantis Orci."
                    (' Carm.,' ii. 3. 24.)

And Hesiod (' Theog.,' 456) of Hades as—

Νηλεὲς ἦτορ ἔχων.

" A heart possessing that no pity knows."

The second thing is **the barren womb**; " the closing of the womb," as Gen. xx. 18; .Isa. lxvi. 9. The burning desire for children, characteristic of an Israelitish wife, is here denoted, like the passionate cry of Rachel to Jacob, " Give me children, or else 1 die " (Gen. xxx. 1). The barren woman, says Corn. à Lapide, " concubitus magis est avida quam ceteræ, tum propter desiderium habendæ prolis, tum quod fœcundæ et gravidæ naturaliter non appetant concubitum." The third insatiable thing is **the earth** that is not filled (satisfied) with water; the parched and thirsty soil which no amount of water can satisfy, which drinks in all that is poured upon it and is not benefited, what Virgil (' Georg.,' i. 114) calls "bibula arena." The fourth is **the fire** that saith not, It is enough; the " devouring element," as the newspapers term it. The more you heap on fire, the more material you supply, the fiercer it rages. Septuagint, " Hades, and the love of woman, and earth not satisfied with water, and water, and fire, will not say, It sufficeth." Cheyne and others quote from the Sanscrit 'Hitopadesa,'

" Fire is never satisfied with fuel; nor the ocean with rivers; nor death with all creatures; nor bright-eyed women with men."

Ver. 17.—This is an independent proverb, only connected with the preceding by being founded on an allusion to an animal. **The eye** that **mocketh at his father.** The eye is named as the mind's instrument for expressing scorn and insubordination; it is the index to the inner feeling; and look may be as sinful as action. **And despiseth to obey his mother**; i.e. holds obedience to his mother to be a thing of no importance whatever. The word translated " to obey " (ליקּהת) is rendered by St. Jerome partum; by others, " weakness," or " wrinkles," or "old age," as Septuagint, γῆρας. But etymology has led most modern commentators to give the sense of " obedience " (see Gen. xlix. 10). **The ravens of the valley shall pick it out.** Such an undutiful son shall die a violent death; his corpse shall lie unburied, and the birds of prey shall feed upon him. It is well known that ravens, vultures, and other birds that live on carrion first attack the eyes of their prey; and in our own islands we are told crows and birds of this sort will fix on the eyes of young or sickly animals. Corn. à Lapide quotes Catullus, ' Carm.,' cviii. 5—

" Effossos oculos voret atro gutture corvus,
    Intestina canes, cetera membra lupi."

"His eyes, plucked out, let croaking ravens gorge,
    His bowels dogs, his limbs the greedy wolves."

" The valley," or brook, reminds one of Elijah's miraculous support (1 Kings xvii. 4). **Young eagles.** The nesher must here mean one of the vulture tribe, as eagles do not feed on carrion (but see Job xxxix. 30). St. Gregory (' Moral.,' xviii. 49) applies the proverb thus : " 'The eye that sneereth at his father, and despiseth the travail of his mother, lo! the ravens from the torrents shall pick it out.' For bad men, while they find fault with the judgments of God, do ' sneer at their Father;' and heretics of all sorts, whilst in mocking they contemn the preaching of holy Church and her fruitfulness, what else is this but that they ' despise the travail of their mother'? whom we not unjustly call the mother of them as well, because from the same they come forth, who speak against the same."

Vers. 18—20.—A proverb concerning four inscrutable things, connected with the last by mention of the eagle.

Ver. 18.—**There be three things which are too wonderful for me, yea, four which I know not.** The great point is the fourth, to which the three previous things lead up, all of them being alike in this, that they leave no trace. The facts are marvellous; Agur feels like Job, " I have uttered that which I understood not, things too wonderful for me, which I knew not " (Job xlii. 3).

Ver. 19.—**The way of an eagle in the air.** You cannot by any outward sign know that an eagle has passed this or that way. Wisd. v. 11, " As when a bird hath flown through the air, there is no token of her way to be found," etc. **The way of a serpent upon a rock.** The snake's mode of progression by the lever-like motion of its ribs might well awake surprise, but the point is still the tracklessness of its course. On sand or soft ground its movements might be traced by the impression made, but this could not be done on hard rock; it could push itself along on such a surface without leaving any track. **The way of a ship in the midst** (*heart*) **of the sea;** *i.e.* in the open sea. You can trace a ship's course while she is near land or within sight, but when she reaches the open sea, you can follow her furrow no longer. Wisd. v. 10, " As a ship that passeth over the waves of the water, which when it is gone by, the trace thereof cannot be found, neither the pathway of the keel in the waves." **The way of a man** (*geber*) **with a maid** (בְּעַלְמָה); Septuagint, " The ways of a man in youth (ἐν νεότητι)." So Vulgate, *Viam viri in adolescentia.* But this is feeble, and *almah* is without doubt rightly rendered " maid," " virgin." The proverb says that the sinful act to which it alludes leaves no outward sign by which it can generally be recognized; it escapes man's knowledge. This is exemplified and confirmed in the following verse. It is not sufficient to refer the saying to the insidious arts of the seducer, by which he saps the principles and inflames the passions of his victim. The sin of unchastity is signified, which demands secrecy and affords no token of its commission. Two of the above parallels, says Cheyne, are given in a quatrain of a Vedic hymn to Varuna—

" The path of ships across the sea,
    The soaring eagle's flight he knows."

Some of the Fathers and earlier commentators, and among moderns, Bishop Wordsworth, have not been content with the literal sense of this gnomic, but have found in it, as in the others, deep spiritual mysteries. Christ is the great Eagle (Rev. xii. 14), who ascended beyond human ken; the serpent is the devil, who works his wily way in secret, and who tried to pass into the mind of Christ, who is the Rock; the ship is the Church, which preserves its course amid the waves of this troublesome world, though we cannot mark its strength or whither it

is guided; and the fourth mystery is the incarnation of Jesus Christ our Lord, when " the virgin (*almah*) conceived and bare a son " (Isa. vii. 14), when " a woman encompassed a man (*geber*) " (Jer. xxxi. 22). We can see the greater or less appropriateness of such accommodation, but the proverb must have been received by contemporaries only in its literal sense, whatever were the inner mysteries which the Holy Spirit wished to communicate thereby.

Ver. 20.—This verse is **a** kind of gloss or illustration of the last thought of the preceding verse, and seems not to have formed an original part of the numerical proverb. It might well be placed in a parenthesis. Many commentators consider it to be an interpolation. Such is **the way of an adulterous woman.** What Agur had said of a man above, he now applies to the practised adulteress, whose sin cannot be traced. **She eateth.** This is a euphemism for the sin which she commits. " Stolen waters are sweet, and bread eaten in secret is pleasant " (ch. ix. 17; comp. ch. v. 15). **And wipeth her mouth,** as if to leave no trace of her illicit repast. **And saith, I have done no wickedness.** As she has sinned in secret, and there is no outward proof of her guilt, she boldly denies it. Septuagint, " Such is the way of an adulterous woman, who, when she has committed the act, having washed herself, says she has done nothing amiss." She forgets him who seeth in secret, and is quite content to escape detection at man's eyes, and to assume the character of a virtuous wife, which popular report assigns to her.

Vers. 21—23.—Then follows a proverb concerning four things which are intolerable, examples of incongruous associations or positions—two in the case of men, two in the case of women.

Ver. 21.—**For three things the earth is disquieted;** better, *under three things the earth doth tremble,* as if oppressed by an overwhelming burden. The form of expression does not allow us to think of an earthquake. " The earth " is equivalent to " the inhabitants thereof." **And for four which it cannot bear;** or, *under four it cannot stand* (comp. Amos vii. 10). These four evils destroy the comfort of social life, uproot the bonds of society, and endanger the safety of a nation.

Ver. 22.—**For a servant when he reigneth;** or, *under a slave when he becometh king.* This startling vicissitude was not uncommon in Eastern states; and even if the slave was not preferred to regal power, he was often advanced by unwise favouritism to high position, for which he was wholly unfitted, and which he used only to aggrandize himself at the expense and to the injury of others.

This incongruity has been already noticed at ch. xix. 10 (where see note). And a fool when he is filled with meat. "Fool" is here *nabal*, a low, profligate fellow, who is rich and without care. When such a one rises to high position, or has power over others, he becomes arrogant, selfish, unbearable (comp. ver. 9; ch. xxviii. 12; xxix. 2).

Ver. 23.—For an odious woman when she is married; or, *under an unloved woman when she is married.* The sentence does not refer to an unbeloved wife, a Leah, becoming the favourite, a Rachel; the expression, "when she is married," can hardly have this sense; but the gnome speaks of a woman who has passed much of her life without love, having nothing about her attractive either in looks, attainments, or manner, and is consequently soured and ill-tempered. If such a one does at last win a husband, she uses her new position to vex those who formerly depreciated her, and to make them as miserable as she can. And a handmaid that is heir to her mistress. The maidservant that obtains her mistress's property, either by supplanting her or by right of inheritance, is supposed to make a bad use of it, to become conceited, arrogant, and odious to all around her. The LXX. transposes the last two members of the comparison, placing the unloved woman in the fourth place as the most intolerable of all: "And if a maidservant should cast out (ἐκβάλη, Gen. xxi. 10) her own mistress, and a hateful woman should obtain a good husband."

Vers. 24—28.—Four things small and weak, and yet wise.

Ver. 24.—There be four things which are little upon the earth, in contrast with the intolerable pretensions of the last group. The Vulgate has *minima;* but the original is not superlative, which would not be true of some of the creatures named. But they are exceeding wise; "quick of wit, wise," the participle מְחֻכָּמִים meaning "rendered wise, cunning" (Delitzsch). The Septuagint and Vulgate translate in the comparative, "These are wiser than the wise," the instincts of these animals being more marvellous than human wisdom.

Ver. 25.—The ants are a people not strong. The ant is proposed as an example to the sluggard (ch. vi. 6, etc.). He calls the ants a people, *am*, because they live in a community, and have authorities which they obey, and their actions are regulated by certain definite laws. So Joel (i. 6) calls the locusts a nation, and Homer ('Iliad,' ii. 87) speaks of ἔθνεα μελισσάων ἀδινάων, "the tribes of thronging bees." Yet they prepare their meat in the summer. In countries where ants hybernate the

object of this commended foresight is mistaken; but the statement, as that in ch. vi 6—8, is in accordance with the popular belief of the day, and serves well to point the moral intended. We know certainly that in Europe these insects fill their nests with heterogeneous articles—grain, seeds, husks, etc., not as stores to be consumed in the winter, but for warmth and comfort's sake. Scripture is not intended to teach science; it speaks of such matters phenomenally, with no attempt at a precision which would not have been understood or appreciated by contemporaries. But in the present case more careful observation has confirmed the correctness of the assertions in our proverbs. In countries where ants do not hybernate, they do make granaries for themselves in the summer, and use these supplies as food in the winter months (see note on ch. vi. 8).

Ver 26.—The conies are but a feeble folk. The term "coney" (*cuniculus*) is applied to the rabbit, but this is not the animal here intended; and indeed rabbits are not found in Palestine. The word *shaphan* designates the *Hyrax Syriacus*, called by some the rock-badger (see Hart, 'Animals of the Bible,' pp. 64, etc.). The coney, says Dr. Geikie ('Holy Land and Bible,' ii. 90), "abounds in the gorge of the Kedron, and along the foot of the mountains west of the Dead Sea. It is of the size of the rabbit, but belongs to a very different order of animals, being placed by naturalists between the hippopotamus and rhinoceros. Its soft fur is brownish-grey over the back, with long black hairs rising through this lighter coat, and is almost white on the stomach; the tail is very short. The Jews, who were not scientific, deceived by the motion of its jaws in eating, which is exactly like that of ruminant animals, fancied it chewed the cud, though it did not divide the hoof, and so they put its flesh amidst that which was forbidden. It lives in companies, and chooses a ready-made cleft in the rocks for its home, so that, though the conies are but a 'feeble folk,' their refuge in the rocks gives them a security beyond that of stronger creatures. They are, moreover, 'exceeding wise,' so that it is very hard to capture one. Indeed, they are said, on high authority, to have sentries regularly placed on the look out while the rest are feeding; a squeak from the watchman sufficing to send the flock scudding to their holes like rabbits. The coney is found in many parts of Palestine, from Lebanon to the Dead Sea." In the rocks. This fact is noticed in Ps. 'civ. 18. The Septuagint calls them χοιρογρύλλιοι here and Ps. civ. 18, also in Lev. xi. 6 and Deut. xiv. 7. This notion of the animal as a kind of little pig is not more accurate than that of St. Jerome, who renders the term by *lepusculus*.

Ver. 27.—**The locusts have no king** (ch. vi. 7), yet they show discipline, guidance, and order. **They go forth all of them by bands**; so that Joel (ii. 7, 8) speaks of them as a well-ordered army, as it were men of war, marching every one on his ways, not entangling their ranks, walking every one in his path. Septuagint, "The locusts are without a king, yet march at one command in good order."

Ver. 28.—**The spider taketh hold with her hands.** *Semamith* or *shemamith* is some sort of lizard, probably the gecko. Καλαβώτης, Septuagint; *stellio*, Vulgate. The Authorized Version alludes either to its fanlike foot, which enables it to run up walls and to cling to ceilings, or to its power of exuding from its feet a certain poisonous humour by which it catches flies and other insects. But the above translation, as well as that of the Septuagint and the Vulgate *manibus nititur*, is incorrect. The first line, in accordance with the method pursued in the three cases previously, ought to give some expression denoting weakness or littleness, whereas by the above rendering it is rather strength and activity that are signified. The translation therefore should run, as in the Revised Version margin, "The lizard thou canst seize with thy hand," and yet **it is in king's palaces.** Small as it is, and easy to catch and crush, it is agile and clever enough to make its way into the very palace of the king, and to dwell there. Septuagint, "And the lizard, supporting itself by its hands, and being easy to catch (εὐάλωτος), dwelleth in kings' strongholds." This combines the two interpretations given above. St. Gregory takes the lizard as the type of the simple, earnest man, who often succeeds better than the clever. "Many that are quick-witted, while they grow slack from carelessness, continue in bad practices, and the simple folk, which have no wing of ability to stand them in stead, the excellency of their practice bears up to attain to the walls of the eternal kingdom. Whereas, then, 'the lizard climbeth with his hands,' he 'is in kings' palaces;' in that the plain man, by earnestness of right practice, reaches that point whereunto the man of ability never mounts" ('Moral.,' vi. 12, Oxford transl.). The ancient expositors see in these verses a presentation of the Church of God, weak on its human side and despised by men, yet exceeding wise (1 Cor. i. 27)—like the ant, laying up treasure in heaven, providing for death and eternity; like the coney, making the Rock her refuge; like the locusts, moving forward a mighty army in battle array; like the lizard, active in movement, holding the truth tenaciously,

and dwelling in the palace of the great King.

Vers. 29—31.—**Four things of stately presence.**

Ver. 29.—**There be three things which go well** (*tob*); are of stately and majestic carriage. **Comely in going;** "stately in going."

Ver. 30.—**A lion which is strongest among beasts.** The word here used for "lion," *laish*, occurs elsewhere only in Job iv. 11 and Isa. xxx. 6. The LXX. renders it, "a lion's whelp." "Strongest" is *gibbor*, a mighty one, a hero. **Turneth not away for any;** Septuagint, "turneth not away, nor feareth any beast." So Job describes the war-horse, "He mocketh at fear, and is not dismayed, neither turneth he back from the sword" (Job xxxix. 22).

Ver. 31.—**A greyhound;** זַרְזִיר מָתְנַיִם (*zarzir mothnayim*), "girt in the loins" (περιεσφιγμένος τὴν ὀσφύν, Symmachus), an expression very vague, and, as the name of an animal, occurring nowhere else in the Old Testament. In post-biblical Hebrew *zarzir* is found as the name of some pugnacious bird, and the Septuagint, Vulgate, and Syriac call it here the cock. So also Aquila and Theodotion. But if the word is onomatopoetic, it would seem to apply with more propriety to one of the raven tribe; and then what is to be made of the allusion to the loins? And how comes it that amid the quadrupeds in the gnome a bird should suddenly be introduced, as one stately in going? It seems certain that some quadruped is here meant, but what? What animal has as characteristic tight-girded loins or slender or active loins? There are, indeed, many that might be so designated, but none that, as far as we know, appropriated this unique appellation. Hence various opinions are held by commentators concerning the identification. The zebra, say some, with its stripes, which may be thus denoted; the war-horse, say others, comparing Job xxxix. 19, 25, and considering the trappings with which, as we see in ancient sculptures, he was adorned; others, again, fix upon the leopard as the beast intended. But that of the Authorized Version seems, on the whole, to be the most likely rendering, the slender, agile make of the greyhound having given cause for the appropriation of the term used in the text. Delitzsch compares the German word *windspiel*, which designates the greyhound without the necessity of using the full term, *windspielhund*. The only points which may be considered adverse to this view are these two, viz. the ill repute in which dogs were held by the Hebrews, Scripture consistently disparaging and despising them; and the fact that, as far as we have information, the Jews did not use dogs for hunting purposes, though nowadays the Arabs keep a kind of Persian greyhound for sporting, and Assyrian monuments have familiarized us with the appearance of hounds employed in the chase of the lion and the wild ox. Agur may be referring to what he has seen elsewhere, but what was well known to those for whom he wrote. Gesenius suggests (253), "a warrior girt in the loins," which is adopted by Wordsworth, and gives a suitable idea. This would correspond with the king in the last line; but the interpretation is quite arbitrary, and supported by no ancient authority, resting on the fact that girding the loins is always spoken of human beings. The cock strutting among his hens is, as we have hinted, the idea which approves itself to many ancient translators. Thus the Septuagint, ἀλέκτωρ ἐμπεριπατῶν θηλείαις εὔψυχος. We are not disposed to adopt this identification, more especially as common poultry were unknown in Palestine till long after Solomon's time. Certainly what we call cocks and hens, or barn-door fowls, are never mentioned in the Old Testament, and seem to have been introduced from Persia after the rise of the Persian empire. The latest editors decide for the war-horse; but the conflicting claims cannot be reconciled, and the matter must be left undetermined. An he-goat also. This is a very natural comparison, as the stately manner in which the he-goat (tayish, "the butter") heads the flock has been always observed. The LXX. expresses this, paraphrasing, "and the he-goat leading the herd." "Flocks of goats are very numerous in Palestine at this day, as they were in former ages. We see them everywhere on the mountains, in smaller or larger numbers; at times also along with sheep, as one flock, in which case it is usually a he-goat that is the special leader of the whole, walking before it as gravely as a sexton before the white flock of a church choir" (Geikie, 'Holy Land,' i. 232). A king, against whom there is no rising up; Vulgate, nec est rex qui resistat ei, which ought to mean "and a king whom nothing resists," but can scarcely be compelled to produce this meaning without violence. The difficulty in the sentence arises from the word אלקום, which in the above rendering is regarded as composed of the negative al, and kum, the infinitive, "to rise against, oppose." But this is contrary to grammatical usage, and would be a solecism. To some it has seemed that a proper name was intended, and they have invented a King Alkum or Alkimos, whom they suppose to have been celebrated in or after Solomon's time. Many modern commentators take the word to be an Arabic expression, consisting of al, the definite

article, and kum, "people," and consider the meaning to be "a king with whom is the people," i.e. surrounded by his people or army. This is certainly a stately sight, and may well stand parallel to the hero-lion among beasts, and the bold he-goat at the head of the flock. Other Arabic expressions may probably be found elsewhere in this chapter; e.g. vers. 15, 16, 17, aluka, etc. Septuagint, "a king haranguing before a nation (δημηγορῶν ἐν ἔθνει)." This passage, again, has been taken in a spiritual sense as referring to Christ, the Lion of the tribe of Judah, the Warrior girt with the sword, the Leader of the flock, the King of kings.

Vers. 32, 33.—Agur's last proverb, exhorting to discreet demeanour.

Ver. 32.—If thou hast done foolishly in lifting up thyself (Numb. xvi. 3). If thou hast had the folly to be arrogant, proud, and overbearing in conduct. Or if thou hast thought evil, lay thine hand upon thy mouth. The verb zamam, though possibly used in a bad sense, "to devise evil," is more suitably rendered "to meditate," "purpose;" so here it is the thought of lifting up one's self that is censured, the act and the thought being contrasted. Hast thou acted arrogantly, or even only meditated doing so, restrain yourself, keep silence (Job xxi. 5; xl. 4). St. Jerome gives a different rendering, enforcing another lesson, "There is one who shows himself a fool after he is raised to high position; if he had had understanding, he would have laid his hand on his mouth." Septuagint, "If thou give thyself up to mirth, and stretch forth thy hand in a quarrel, thou wilt be dishonoured." Insensate mirth and a quarrelsome disposition alike lead to disgrace. St. Gregory ('Moral.,' xxx. 10) applies the Vulgate rendering to antichrist, "For he in truth will be lifted up on high, when he will feign that he is God. But he will appear a fool when lifted up on high, because he will fail in his very loftiness through the coming of the true Judge. But if he had understood this, he would have laid his hand on his mouth; that is, if he had foreseen his punishment, when he began to be proud, having been once fashioned aright, he would not have been raised up to the boastfulness of such great pride" (Oxford transl.).

Ver. 33.—Surely the churning of milk bringeth forth butter. The same word, mits, is used for "churning," "wringing," and "forcing;" it means "pressure" in all the cases, though with a different application. At the present day milk is churned in the East by enclosing it in a leathern bottle, which is then suspended in the air and jerked to and fro till the butter is produced. This process could scarcely be called "pressure," though, possibly, the squeezing of the udder is meant, as the Septuagint and Vulgate take it. But most probably the reference is to cheese, the term used, *chemah*, being applied indifferently to curdled milk and cheese. To produce this substance, the curdled milk is put into little baskets of rush or palm leaves, tied closely, and then pressed under heavy stones. What the proverb says is that, as the pressure applied to milk produces cheese, and as pressure applied to the nose brings blood, so the pressure of wrath bringeth forth strife; the irritation and provocation of anger occasion quarrels and contentions. They say in Malabar, remarks Lane, "Anger is a stone cast into a wasp's nest." Septuagint, "Press out milk, and there shall be butter; and if thou violently squeeze the nostrils, blood will come forth; and if thou draw forth words, there will come forth quarrels and strifes." It is the third clause which is important, and to which the others lead up; and the verse must be taken in connection with the preceding, as enforcing the duty of self-restraint and silence under certain circumstances. Some of the Fathers, commenting on the Vulgate rendering (*Qui fortiter premit ubera ad eliciendum lac, exprimit butyrum; et qui vehementer emungit, elicit sanguinem*), apply the passage to the handling of the Word of God. Thus St. Gregory ('Moral.,' xxi. 3), "Divine sentences require sometimes to be viewed externally, sometimes to be explored internally. For we 'press the udder strongly' when we weigh with minute understanding the word of sacred revelation, by which way of pressing whilst we seek milk, we find butter, because, whilst we seek to be fed with but a little insight, we are anointed with the abundance of interior richness. Which, nevertheless, we ought neither to do too much, nor at all times, lest, while milk is sought for from the udder, there should follow blood. For very often, persons, whilst they sift the words of sacred revelation more than they ought, fall into a carnal apprehension. For 'he draws forth blood who wringeth violently.' Since that is rendered carnal which is perceived by an overgreat sifting of the spirit" (Oxford transl.).

HOMILETICS.

Vers. 1—4.—*The weary search for God.* If we read ver. 1 thus: "Words of Agur the son of the Princess of Massa. The man's saying, I have wearied myself about God, wearied myself about God—then did I withdraw!" we are led to the contemplation of one who has grown tired and despairing in a hopeless search for God.

I. IT IS NATURAL FOR MAN TO SEEK GOD. Agur appears to have lived far away from the borders of the favoured land of Israel. If he was a Jew, he was one in exile, separated from the home of his people. If he was an Ishmaelite, he was even outside the covenant of Israel, and in that case we have the striking picture of an Arab of antiquity anticipating Mahomet in breaking from the idolatry of his fathers. Like Balaam, like Job, this resident in a heathen land looks up to the true God. St. Paul spoke to the Athenians of those who could "seek God, if haply they might feel after him, and find him" (Acts xvii. 27); and St. Peter could acknowledge God's acceptance of all who look to him truly, no matter what race they might belong to (Acts x. 35). The natural search of the soul for God springs from certain great fundamental facts, viz.: 1. God is the Father of all men. 2. All men need God. 3. All men are separated from God by sin, and therefore must feel naturally at a distance. The world needs God. But the world has lost God. Hence the natural search for God.

II. THE NATURAL SEARCH FOR GOD RESULTS IN WEARINESS. This is not the weariness of protracted thinking, the reaction from high mental tension. It is worse than that; it is the weariness of a long and apparently fruitless search. Man cannot by searching find out God. God does not appear to respond to the inquiry of the seeking mind. Even to the wisest of the Greeks he was "an Unknown God" (Acts xvii. 23). For God is not visible to the natural reason, nor is he ever seen excepting when he reveals himself. Now, there is no weariness like that of a long and hopeless search. The sickness of despair then begins to tire the soul. Such weariness drives men at last to abandon the vain pursuit. Agur said, "Then did I withdraw!" He gave up the inquiry. This is the refuge of agnosticism.

III. THE GREATNESS OF GOD'S WORKS MAKES THE SEARCH FOR HIM A WEARINESS. How vast is his created universe! No man can reach up to the starry altitudes of heaven, or dive into the deep mysteries of antiquity, to find the scope and range of the Divine activity. The tremendous energy of nature overwhelms us. Science can investigate its laws, and in a measure make use of its forces; but they come out of a terrible darkness, and they transcend the control of so feeble a creature as man. Agur did not simply distress himself with his own fruitless thinking. He knew something of the history of philosophy, and yet he had not been able to find one inquirer who had solved the terrible enigma over which his own heart was breaking.

IV. THE SEARCH FOR GOD IS SATISFIED IN THE REVELATION OF CHRIST. St. Paul said to the Athenians, " Whom therefore ye ignorantly worship, him declare I unto you " (Acts xvii. 23). This is not an authoritative declaration of a dogma of D vinity. 1, The revelation of Christ is such that we can see it and understand it for ourselves. We can see that God is in Christ by observing the stamp of the Divine on his countenance—the signs of God in his life and work. Then in knowing Christ we know God (John xiv. 9). 2. Moreover, this revelation of God in Christ flashes a light on the huge mystery of the universe, and helps us to find God in nature. 3. The reconciliation between man and God, effected by the cross of Christ, removes the dark barrier of sin, which is the greatest hindrance to the soul in its search for God, and brings us into the presence of God, where we can behold " the beatific vision."

Vers. 5, 6.— *The purity of God's words.* I. THE REFUGE FROM VAIN SPECULATION IS PRACTICAL REVELATION. The search for God in thought and nature has ended in weariness. But Agur does not subside into agnosticism, much less does he renounce all higher thinking as " vanity of vanities," and plunge into Sadducean worldliness and Epicurean materialism. On the contrary, though he gives up his ambitious quest with a sigh of disappointment, he learns to take a humbler path, on which he finds that God has shed light. The mysteries of pure theology are wrapped in clouds, but the path of man's duty and the way of practical religion are illumined by the light of God's revealed truth. This truth consists in more than those " regulative ideas," which are all that Mansel would have us expect to know, for it corresponds to the actual; it is fact and law of God's real spiritual world. The Word of God is with us in the Bible and in Christ. In this Word the weary seeker after light may not find a star-spangled heaven, but he will see " a lamp to his feet" (Ps. cxix. 105).

II. THE REVELATION OF GOD IS PURE. 1. *It is free from error.* This is not a matter of the language of the Bible, which is but the case that enshrines the holy revelation. The frame is not the picture. When we crack the nut we find that the kernel is sound and flawless. The spiritual contents of revelation are infallible. 2. *It is free from moral corruption.* Prurient minds have affected to be shocked at immoral stories in the Bible. But what is most wonderful about the Scripture writers in respect to such matters is that, though they are bold enough to touch the most repulsive subjects, they never soil their fingers, nor do *they* ever soil the minds of their readers. Only impure minds draw impure suggestions from the Bible, and such minds may find them anywhere. The Bible reveals man to himself, and declares God's estimate of sin. It cannot cover over the foulest evil with a cloak of social propriety. The horrible things must be exposed in the interest of purity, that they may be denounced, and the doers of them put to shame.

III. THE PURITY OF GOD'S WORD SHOULD INSPIRE TRUST AND REVERENCE. 1. It should inspire *trust*. For " he is a Shield to them that put their trust in him." We cannot understand all mysteries; the deep counsels of God must ever lie beneath our most searching inquiry; but we have light in God's words for our help and guidance. The purity of this light is a security against danger. It will not allure us into error, and it will not permit us to live in sin unrebuked and unwarned. Therefore the light is guiding, healing, saving. With such a revelation we can afford to endure the insoluble character of great mysteries of theology. When vexed, perplexed, and wearied out, we can turn to the God who has thus made himself known to us, and quietly rest in his sheltering care. 2. It should also inspire *reverence*. "Add not thou unto his words." The truth of God is too sacred for man to be permitted to tamper with it. This is a great warning that men have rarely heeded. We may think and utter our thoughts. But the fatal mistake is when we put forth our speculations as though they were a part of God's revelation. This is a common sin of authoritative theology. Men's opinions—harmless enough in themselves, perhaps—

have been added to the Scripture truths, and set before the world as unquestionable and Divine. The interpretation of Scripture has been made as sacred as the text. Church dogma has claimed Divine authority. This is adding to God's words, and the danger of it is (1) Divine disapproval—"lest he reprove thee;" and (2) human disloyalty to truth—"and thou be found a liar."

Vers. 8, 9.—"*Neither poverty nor riches.*" A wise man here points out the danger of the two extremes of poverty and riches, and seeks for himself the happier middle position. In the present day the enormous wealth of one class and the penury of another suggest serious social questions, and raise alarms as to great possible dangers unless the terrible anomaly of this artificial condition is not remedied.

I. THE EVIL OF POVERTY. The thought is of extreme poverty, of absolute destitution, or, at least, of that precarious livelihood that is always on the verge of want, and is therefore oppressed with an ever-haunting fear of the distress which can never be quite out of sight. Now, what is to be remarked here is that the great evil of excessive poverty pointed out in the passage before us is *moral* in character. The sufferings of penury are sad to contemplate. Those of us who have never known what it is to be really hungry cannot understand the pangs of the starving. More fearful must be the trouble of parents who see their children crying for bread and cannot satisfy them. Yet the worst evil is not this suffering; it is the moral degradation that follows it. Wolf-like hunger assimilates its victims to the nature of the wolf. It is hard to be honest when in want of food. The temptations of the poor are frightful to contemplate. It is wonderful that there is so little crime, seeing that there is so much poverty. The grinding cares of poverty tend to wear the soul out, and blind its vision to spiritual truth. The patience and good behaviour of the dumb, suffering multitudes of the distressed is indeed a sight to move our sympathy and excite our admiration.

II. THE EVIL OF WEALTH. The temptation of riches is not very unlike that of poverty in its character, but more deadly. Both extremes tempt to worldliness—poverty to worldly care, riches to worldly satisfaction. The "care of this world" and "the deceitfulness of riches" stand together as the thorns that choke the good seed (Matt. xiii. 22). But riches goes further. It tempts a man to dispense with God. Poverty tempts to theft, often, indeed, with extenuating circumstances. But riches tempts to scornful atheism. Christ saw this danger when he said, "How hardly shall they that have riches enter into the kingdom of God!" (Mark x. 23). On the other hand, when we see rich men who have conquered the exceptional temptations of their position, and who live a humble and useful Christian life, devoting their talents to the service of Christ, we should acknowledge that such victors over the world are deserving of especial honour.

III. THE CHOICE OF A MIDDLE COURSE. We are here reminded of Aristotle's doctrine of "the mean." There are circumstances in which the true mean is not just the middle way between two diverse policies. The lowering of the standard of right and wrong that comes from the peace-loving tendency to accept a compromise is disastrous to all conscientious conduct. But now we have to do with a middle course between two external states, both of which are dangerous. If Christian people understood their mission in the world aright, in its breadth and humanity, they would know that the call to preach the gospel of the kingdom includes the inculcation of those social principles which tend to blot out the present ugly picture of extreme poverty set off by extreme wealth. A life that is neither crushed by care nor intoxicated by riches is the life in which it is least difficult to serve God and do right. Therefore we should labour to help on a state of society in which more of such lives will be possible.

Vers. 12, 13.—*Self-deception.* Self-deception in regard to the guilt of sin is the most common delusion of minds that have not been spiritually enlightened. However much men may know and acknowledge about themselves in other respects, on this vital point they are most tempted to go astray.

I. LET US CONSIDER THE TEMPTATION TO SELF-DECEPTION. People have strong motives to think well of themselves. 1. *Conscience* is so powerful and urgent that few men are able to brave a confession of sin before its awful bar, and yet continue in the practice of sin with equanimity. For the sake of the peace of his mind, everybody naturally desires to stand well with his own conscience. Therefore there is a strong motive to lie to it, hoodwink it, cajole it ; or, if these measures fail, to gag it, drown it, brand, or crush, or stamp it out—if possible to murder it. 2. *Pride* also makes a man desire his own self-approval. The "lofty eyes" are disinclined to see any evil within. It is inwardly humbling to hear, amidst the plaudits of a bamboozled world, a keen inner voice exclaiming, "Thou art a hypocrite, a liar, a knave!" 3. *Fear of coming judgment* drives a man into a refuge of lies rather than to remain out in the open, exposed to the pitiless storm. It is absurd, ostrich-like to hide one's head in the sand ; but men are not always logical in their conduct. The feeling of danger disappears when a man persuades himself that he is innocent.

II. LET US INQUIRE INTO THE CAUSES OF THIS SELF-DECEPTION. 1. It springs from *inclination*. The temptation to flatter one's self helps to produce the delusion. Thus "the wish is father to the thought." 2. It is aided by *a low standard of morals*. Only when such a standard is prevalent and accepted will any sinful generation be capable of appearing pure in its own eyes. The higher the standard, the greater the feeling of guilt. Therefore the most holy men, being also the most spiritually enlightened, have the deepest consciousness of sin. 3. It is further encouraged by *the example of others*. There is a whole "generation" of these self-deluded people. Each man finds his neighbour as bad as himself. A single black sheep in the fold is marked by contrast with its fellows, and cannot but acknowledge its abnormal colour, but a whole flock of black sheep may readily forget that it is not white.

III. LET US OBSERVE THE EVIL OF THIS SELF-DECEPTION. The generation is pure in its own eyes, but it is not washed from its filthiness. 1. Self-deception *does not cleanse*. It only asserts what is false; it goes no way to make its assertion true. It rather tends the other way, because there can be no effectual cleansing of the soul without confession and repentance. 2. It does *not hide sin*. It is not even a cloak thrown over what remains as foul as ever, though no longer visible. The generation may walk with lofty eyes, but its pride only deludes itself. Others can see the shame in spite of all the guilty people's loud protestations. Self-deception does not lead to a deluding of God. 3. Self-deception must be *exposed and punished*. It is itself sinful. For the sinner to walk with a lofty gait is for him to court his doom. The safer course is to follow the example of the publican, who would not so much as lift up his eyes to heaven while he smote his breast and cried, "God be merciful to me a sinner!" (Luke xviii. 13).

Vers. 18, 19.—*The mystery of love.* Agur sees four things that cannot be traced out. 1. "The way of an eagle in the air." No track is followed by the king of birds as it cleaves the invisible fluid and takes its own wild course from crag to crag. 2. "The way of a serpent upon a rock." Creeping out of a dark cranny, the reptile lies and basks on the hot stone, and then at the approach of an intruder darts into another cranny—its course unknown. 3. "The way of a ship in the midst of the sea." We talk of the ocean highway, but there is no beaten track, no worn course. The ship cuts the surface for a moment, and then the waves roll over its path, and in a short time every trace of its passage is lost in the wash of the waters. So it is with the fourth mystery. The course of human love cannot be predicted or explained. It cannot be made to follow rule and precedent or to correspond to fond parental wishes. Love will go its own way free as the eagle in the air, unsuspected as the serpent on the rock, untracked as the ship in the sea. The three earlier wonders lead on to the fourth, and help to give colour and weight to it. The whole sentence thus gathers up its force into a climax. Nothing is so wonderful in the natural world as the great mystery of love. This may take three forms—

I. THE WILD FREEDOM OF THE EAGLE'S FLIGHT. Love can never be coerced. A forced marriage cannot be a love-match. It is natural that man and maid should learn to love one another of their own accord, by the drawing of mutual sympathy. Friends may guide, warn, encourage, or hinder. But a matter which concerns the lifelong happiness of two souls cannot be well arranged by worldly contrivances. Nevertheless, love that is untamed and utterly uncontrolled may lead to frightful mistakes, to folly and sin and shame. The eagle is a wild and dangerous bird—a terror to the helpless lamb. Love becomes a cursed thing, near to hatred, when it is no better than a wild, unfettered passion.

II. THE SUBTLE SECRET OF THE SERPENT'S TRAIL. This is a very ugly picture, from which we start back shuddering and in horror. There is a snake-like cunning in selfish lust that wickedly usurps the sacred name of love, when it is really the very incarnation of hellish venom, seeking to allure its prey to destruction. All low, carnal lust is of the type of the serpent. The wild passion that follows the eagle's flight may be dangerous, but the cold, loveless course of deliberate vice is deadly as that of a viper.

III. THE UNCERTAIN VOYAGE OF THE SHIP. The ship is a home on the waters. She carries freight and passengers—wealth and life. She sails from one port and she seeks another in a far-off land. But she cannot see her distant haven; she knows not what fierce tempests she may have to encounter; her way is uncertain and dangerous. Married life is a voyage over unknown waters. But where there is true love the vessel is well ballasted; she carries a cargo richer than untold ingots of gold; her crew work peacefully without fear of mutiny. Under such circumstances, though there is mystery, hearts that trust in God need fear no shipwreck of love and happiness.

Vers. 24—28.—*Four weak things, and the greatness of them.* The four little creatures that are here mentioned all illustrate the wonderful way in which the disadvantages of weakness may be overcome by some countervailing quality. In the spiritual world Christianity teaches us to look for the triumph of weakness—the weak things of the world confounding the things which are mighty (1 Cor. i. 27). Now, we have illustrations from nature for the same principle. Each of the four creatures teaches us its own special lesson, as each conquers its weakness by some separate and distinctive quality. The ant succeeds by foresight, the coney by finding shelter, the locust by organization, and the lizard by quiet persistency.

I. THE ACHIEVEMENTS OF FORESIGHT. 1. This is a triumph of *mind*. The ant is in some respects the most wonderful creature in the world; for it seems to be about equal in intelligence to the elephant, which is not only the greatest, but also the most intelligent of the larger animals. A bull, so immensely greater than an ant in body, is far smaller in mind. Similarly, man's lordship over the animal world is a triumph of mental power. The driver is weaker in body than the horse he drives, but he has a stronger mind. We shall triumph in the world just in proportion as we develop our inner life. 2. This is a triumph of *industry*. The ant rebukes the sluggard (ch. vi. 6). 3. It is a triumph of *patience*. The ant toils for the future. Herein is its true strength. Men who care only for the passing moment are shallow and weak. We are strong in proportion as we live in the future.

II. THE SAFETY OF A SOUND SHELTER. "The conies are but a feeble folk," and they have not the compensating intelligence of the ants. But their instinct leads them to live among the rocks, and hide themselves in dark caves and inaccessible crevices. Thus the strength of the hills is theirs. When there is no hope of holding our ground in the open field, we may find shelter in the Rock of Ages. If souls have their instincts in a healthy condition, these will drive them to the true shelter, and there weakness will be safe.

III. THE TRIUMPH OF ORGANIZATION. Though the locusts have no king, they are able to make successful marches over miles of country, and to completely devastate the lands they visit. They do not waste their time by flying hither and thither, and by opposing one another. They all move on in solid phalanx. This instinctive order secures success. It teaches us that the welfare of the individual must be subordinate to that of the community. If a small stream has to be crossed, the myriads of locusts who are so unfortunate as to be in the van of the mighty army fall in and fill up the bed till they make a causeway that can be used by their fellows. The victory of man is got through the suffering and death of many self-sacrificing heroes. In the Church the cause of Christ will best triumph when all Christians move together in harmony, all seeking to win the world for the kingdom of heaven.

IV. THE SUCCESS OF PERSISTENCY. The little lizard is found in king's palaces because he can stick to the walls, and so run into unlooked-for places out of the way of men. It is a great thing to be able to hold on. Quiet perseverance wins many a victory. Patient endurance is crowned in the end with glorious success. In the highest things, "he that endureth unto the end, the same shall be saved" (Mark xiii. 13).

Vers. 29—31.—*Fourfold triumph.* Each of the four here brought before us excites admiration for a successful course. As in former illustrations, the images rise up to a climax, and what is exhibited separately in the earlier ones is united and completed in the final image.

I. A TRIUMPHANT COURSE EXCITES EMULATION. 1. *True success is good.* There are various forms of success. Some are more disgraceful than failure. A low end easily won, or a desirable goal reached by foul means, gives a worthless and even a detestable victory. But when both means and end are good, there is something admirable in success. 2. *This success is continuous.* The most worthy triumph is not that of a sudden victory snatched at the end of a long, doubtful contest, but the carrying out of a course that is good throughout—a constant series of small daily victories over danger. Thus the lion is admired, not merely because he can bring down his prey by means of a long chase, or after patiently waiting for it in ambush, but because "he turneth not away for any," and of all four the excellence is that they "go well." With every man the true note of triumph is that he "goes well" day by day along the path of duty. 3. *This success is measured by the difficulties overcome.* We gauge strength by what it can do, and the best standard may not give visible results in acquisition. The proof may be seen more in triumph over obstacles. He who persists through all hardship and danger enduring to the end, and faithful unto death, is the true soldier of Christ.

II. A TRIUMPHANT COURSE MAY BE VARIOUSLY RUN. The good and admirable may be of different forms. Success of the highest kind will be got by each using his own talents, not by any vainly imitating those of another. The lion cannot copy the goat's agility, nor the greyhound the lion's strength. Four methods of success are here suggested. 1. Success may be won by *indomitable energy.* This is the characteristic of the lion. He is strong, and he "turneth not away for any." 2. It may be got by *swiftness.* The greyhound is a feeble creature compared to the lion. Its glory is in its speed. There is a victory for nimbleness of mind as well as of body. 3. It may be reached by *agility.* The hound can fly like the wind over the plain; and the he-goat can pick its way among the crags of the precipice and climb to dizzy heights. They are not like the eagle that soars on its wings, for the quadruped must always have some foothold, but with this it can stand without fear in the most precarious positions. Skilful agility will enable one to triumph over difficulties, escape snares and pitfalls, and rise to daring heights. 4. It may be attained by *human qualities.* Man is feeble as a coney compared to the lion, slow as a tortoise in the presence of the greyhound, lame and timorous beside that audacious mountaineer the goat. But he can master and outdo all these creatures by the use of mental and spiritual powers.

III. A TRIUMPHANT COURSE WILL DEVELOP UNIQUE CHARACTERISTICS. Each of the four is known by its success, as none would be known if the animals were caged in a menagerie, and the king left to enjoy empty pageantry. The kingly faculty is not only recognized on a throne. As the power to govern, it is witnessed in business, in society, and in intellectual regions. There are born kings. We see how stirring times bring such men to the front as the Civil Wars revealed Cromwell. The noblest earthly career is to be a true leader of men. He who stands at the head of the great human family was and is a Divine King, and his triumph is in his ruling even through shame and death.

Ver. 32.—*Self-suppression.* I. WHEN SELF-SUPPRESSION IS NEEDED. It is not always equally demanded of us. There are times for expression, times when we should break reserve and give forth freely the thoughts and purposes of our souls. But other times demand peculiar self-suppression. 1. *In rebuke of foolish vanity.* "If thou hast done foolishly in lifting up thyself." A magnified image of self needs to be reduced. Too much pretension must be humbled. Selfish ambition must be cast down. 2. *In restraint of evil thinking.* "Or if thou hast thought evil." Jesus Christ has taught us that evil thinking is sin (Matt. v. 28). But the sooner the sin is checked the better, and it can be best checked before it has emerged in word or deed. Expression emphasizes an evil thought. A publication of it makes it hurtful to others. The viper-brood should be scotched in the nest.

II. WHAT SELF-SUPPRESSION WILL EFFECT. 1. It will prevent *future evil*. We cannot undo the past; we cannot deny our inner self. But at least we may seek for grace that the sin may proceed no further. 2. It will *prepare for better conduct*. In itself it is but negative. It has the merit of silence. It is a "masterly inactivity." We must stop before we can turn back. There is therefore a moment of silence, cessation, even death, in the act of conversion. We cannot proceed at once from evil living to good service. St. Paul had his period of silence in Arabia. It would be an immense gain in this noisy age if we could practise more of the golden virtue.

III. HOW SELF-SUPPRESSION MAY BE ATTAINED. "Lay thine hand upon thy mouth." To the noisy and expressive this is no more easy than it is for the glutton to "put a knife to" his "throat" when he is eating "with a ruler" (ch. xxiii. 1, 2). Frank and open natures are not able readily to recognize the merits of reticence, while, on the other hand, reserved and secretive natures shrink from a requisite confession. 1. There must be a *perception of the evil of giving unrestrained vent to one's thoughts and desires*. Many people do not perceive the dangers of speech. They blurt out the most unseemly things where the sensitive shrink into silence. But a horror of the harm that may be done by heedless words will assist in the cultivation of a habit of self-restraint. 2. There must be *energy of will*. The unrestrained nature that is a victim to every rousing impression is no better than an unwalled city open to the invasion of the first chance foe (ch. xxv. 28). Now, it is a work of Divine grace to strengthen the will so that the weak may acquire more control over themselves. At the first blush of it there seems to be more energy in noisy, bustling restlessness, while quiet self-restraint appears inert. But this results from a very superficial view of life. Nothing less than Heaven-sent grace can make us strong enough to keep silent under great provocation or to be still when the heart is boiling over with passion.

HOMILIES BY VARIOUS AUTHORS.

Vers. 1—6.—*Agur's sayings: God's Word the fountain of all wisdom*. These are the words, probably, of a believer in Jehovah who was a stranger in a foreign land. Among the sworn foes of Israel and her faith, we have in him an example of Puritan rectitude, of unflinching fidelity to conscience, that is highly instructive. The purity of God's eternal truth, and the safety of all believers in him (ver. 5),—this is his simple and sublime leading theme.

I. THE BEING OF GOD AN UNUTTERABLE MYSTERY. (Ver. 1.) In vain had he sought to explore the unfathomable secret of his essence, by searching to find out the Almighty unto perfection. It was higher than heaven—what could he do? deeper than Hades—what could he know? This was substantially the confession, expressed in different forms, of all the great prophets. Compare the accounts of Isaiah's consecration, Jeremiah's and Ezekiel's. True religion is rooted in this sense of the Divine mystery. All piety is shallow without it. In every conscious feeling, thought, aspiration, we are but travelling on the edge of a great abyss, moving towards an horizon which still recedes. In our deeper moments we are all mystics, and there are times when all talk about God seems babble, and we would fain take refuge in the "sacred silence of the mind."

II. THE INTELLIGENCE OF MAN DULL AND INADEQUATE IN RELATION TO DIVINE THINGS. (Vers. 2, 3.) No words are too self-contemptuous to express the sense of the immense gulf which separates our thought from God. Applied to definable objects, our intelligence seems bright and piercing; applied to the Infinite Might and Wisdom and Purity, no better than the vacant gaze of the ox in the pasture. Look into those beautiful brown eyes; there is a depth of pathos in them, but no "speculation," no power to grasp the unity and law of things that print themselves in pictures on the retina. And what are we, though raised above the "creatures that lead a blind life within the brain," but helpless gazers into infinity? Well did Sir Isaac Newton and all the great seers of science realize this feeling. Their consummate knowledge was, viewed on another side, consummate ignorance. They had not thereby attained absolute wisdom, nor " won the knowledge of the Holy." There have been, indeed, modern philosophers who have proposed an " absolute philosophy ; " but time has discovered the idleness of their " o'er-vaulting ambition," and made a fable of their folly.

III. THE INACCESSIBLE IN NATURE RECOGNIZED. (Ver. 4.) One of the first principles laid down by the great Goethe was—Learn to distinguish between the accessible and the inaccessible in nature to your thought. For want of this, theologians on the one hand, scientists on the other, have rushed into presumption in seeking to wrest the inscrutable secrets of nature from the hand of God. The unknowableness of the first beginnings of things was recognized by the ancient thinker. The height of heaven, the movements of winds and waves, the changes of the earth's surface,—all may be brought under law; but the word "law" conceals the greater mystery—the nature of the Lawgiver himself. God is not identical with law, any more than we are identical with speech. Law is but the partially understood speech of God to our intelligence. Examine all the sublime names which have been given to God in the course of revelation, in the process of religious thought; behind them all lies the unutterable and unthinkable Somewhat.

IV. THE SELF-REVELATION OF GOD RECOGNIZED. (Ver. 5.) 1. To say that God is *utterly unknowable* is as great an error as to say that he is perfectly knowable by the human understanding: Such an admission must cut at the root of religion. On the contrary, religion implies revelation. Because God has spoken to us, we may speak to him; because he has stooped to us, we may rise towards him. In manifold ways—through nature, through inspired men, through the Son, through the conscience—God " has spoken to the world." If this be denied, religion is an entire illusion. 2. *The quality of his oral revelation.* The writer is thinking of the oral and written Law. Because definite, articulate, it may be spoken of as *the* Word of God *par excellence ;* but by no means are the indefinable and inarticulate revelations through nature to our spirit excluded. From every sight of beauty and every sound of music in the world we may derive unspoken messages of him " whose nature and whose name is Love." And God's Word is pure. The refined silver of the furnace is a favourite image of this, its quality. From the alloy of duplicity, flattery, hypocrisy, it is free. God deals sincerely with us. And, therefore, it is purifying. We behold the true life of the soul in its mirror. 3. *The practical blessing of trust in him.* He who speaks to us is to be trusted. And in this trust in One who is eternal and infallible, pure and true, we have security. The Law or Word which declares his will is like a broad hand stretched above us to command, and, in commanding, to protect, reward, and bless. 4. *The duty of strict reverence and loyalty towards his words.* (Ver. 6.) Much they leave unsaid, which it is not for us to supply. The general lesson seems to be respect for that element of reserve and mystery which lies behind all that is or may be known. We may " lie " against God by saying more than he has actually said to us by any channel of knowledge. To exceed or exaggerate seems ever a readier temptation than to keep within the modest bounds of positive declaration. And certain penalties await all distortions of the truth of every kind; they work themselves out in the conscience and the course of history.—J.

Vers. 7—9.—*The golden mean.* I. THE WAY OF LIFE: TRUTH IS THE MEAN BETWEEN TWO EXTREMES. (Ver. 8.) Extremes exist in logic ; life shows that extremes meet, and that the path of sense in opinion and of safety in conduct lies intermediate between them.

II. GREAT RICHES ARE NOT IN THEMSELVES DESIRABLE. Not by the wise and religious man. They bring perils to the soul. Full of his gifts, it is tempted to deny the Giver. The deepest atheism springs from self-sufficiency. Prospering in the flesh, men are often impoverished in the spirit. " How deep a knowledge of the heart is implied in the petition of the Litany, 'In all *time of our wealth,* good Lord deliver us' ! " (Bridges).

III. EXTREME POVERTY MAY BE EQUALLY INJURIOUS TO THE SPIRITUAL LIFE. It tempts to dishonesty, even to perjury. "Too poor to be honest " is a cynical saying which points out a real danger. The old proverb, " It is hard for an empty sack to stand on end," points the same way. More stinging still is the word, " Poor men have no souls."

IV. THE GOLDEN MEAN IS THEREFORE TO BE DESIRED AND SOUGHT. (Comp. Phil. iv. 11, 12; 1 Tim. vi. 6—10.) Horace says, " Whoever loves the golden mediocrity is safe, free from the sordid misery of the tumble-down dwelling, free from the envied hall in his sobriety " ('Carm.,' ii. 10). But let us be careful to note that the true state is to be found in the spirit itself—the inward, not the outward sufficiency. " I have learned in whatsoever state I am, therewith to be content." Rich in estate, yet poor in spirit; poor in estate, yet rich in grace;—this is the true solution of the problem, the true object of pious prayers.—J.

Ver. 10.—*Caution in the use of the tongue.* I. THE THOUGHTS ONE FEARS TO EXPRESS HIMSELF ONE MAY BE TEMPTED TO ELICIT FROM ANOTHER.

II. IT IS BASE TO TEMPT AN HONEST HEART TO THOUGHTS AND WORDS OF DISCONTENT. One of the most active forms of evil consists in the " putting into the head " of others feelings towards their employers or superiors which would not otherwise have arisen.

III. THE BITER MAY THUS BE BIT; THE TEMPTER THUS BRING A RECOIL UPON HIMSELF. (Comp. ch. xxvi. 2.)—J.

Vers. 11—14.—*Detestable phases of human character.* I. THOSE UNGRATEFUL TO PARENTS. (Ver. 11.) " Without natural affection." Solon, asked why he had made no law against parricides, said that he could not conceive of any one so impious and cruel. In the Law of Moses the cursing of a parent was visited with the same punishment as the blaspheming of God (Lev. xx. 9; xxiv. 11—16; comp. Isa. xlv. 9, 10; 2 Tim. iii. 2).

II. CRASS SELF-CONCEIT AND PRIDE. (Vers. 12, 13.) The Pharisees in the gospel (Matt. xxiii. 25—27), the Laodicean Church (Rev. iii. 17, 18), are examples. But the character is a constant one, and reappears in every age as a foil to genuine Christianity. Compare Mozley's powerful sermon on the Pharisees. But it was a noble Pharisee who learned, in the humility of Christ, to " have no confidence in the flesh " (Phil. iii. 3).

III. PITILESS CRUELTY AND OPPRESSION. (Ver. 14.) Wolves in human guise or in sheep's clothing. Similar pictures are to be found in Ps. lvii. 5; lviii. 7; Isa. ix. 12; Jer. v. 17; xxx. 16, 17. These pictures of the heart, its exceeding deceitfulness and desperate wickedness, should lead us to examine our own. The germs of all the world's evil are to be found in these *microcosmi*—these " little worlds." When we know ourselves truly, the prayer will the more sincerely arise to him to whom all hearts are open, that he will cleanse the thoughts of our hearts by the inspiration of his Holy Spirit.—J.

Vers. 15, 16.—*Reflections on the insatiable.* I. THE EXTERNAL LIFE IS THE MIRROR OF THE INTERNAL. Our spirit finds analogies to itself in the objects of nature, of history, and in the general course of human life. And all that we observe *there*, in the great world, may serve as a light to reveal to us what passes *here*, in the world of each man's heart.

II. IMAGES OF INSATIABLE APPETITE. Hades; the barren womb; the thirsty earth; the all-devouring fire. The vampire, or bloodsucker, seems to be intended in the first example; it is supposed to suck the blood of the sleeping by night.

III. THE SPIRIT OF MAN IS INSATIABLE. And whether this appetite is rightly or wrongly directed, upon this depends his weal or woe. It may be directed to what is perishable or pernicious—to gold, power, pleasure, etc. Drunkenness is the commonest illustration of the insatiety of man's nature. Or it may be directed to righteousness, to the knowledge of the truth, to the enjoyment of the good; and then it carries the power and promise of the " endless life."—J.

Ver. 17.—*The punishment of unfilial conduct.* I. THE DENUNCIATION IS IN FIGURATIVE FORM.

II. ITS FULFILMENT LITERALLY HAD BEEN A MATTER OF ACTUAL OBSERVATION.

III. THE GENERAL TRUTH MUST BE CARRIED INTO THE LIGHT OF CONSCIENCE. On the whole, as Bishop Butler soundly taught, the constitution of things tends to punish evil and reward good conduct.—J.

Vers. 18—20.—*The mystery of actions.* I. THERE ARE ACTIONS WHICH, LIKE THE FLIGHT OF THE EAGLE, OR THE PASSAGE OF THE SHIP, LEAVE NO VISIBLE TRACE BEHIND. What seems to strike the mind of the simple-hearted Agur is the fact that criminal deeds may be committed and, seemingly, leave as little trace behind. II. BUT THE MYSTERY AND SECRECY OF ALL ACTIONS ARE KNOWN TO GOD. We are naked and open to the eyes of him with whom we have to do. And God shall bring every secret work into judgment. Every act leaves its trace in the world of spirit.—J.

Vers. 21—23.—*Intolerable things.* I. THE EXAMPLES. 1. *The slave in authority.* (Ver. 22.) The inversion of objects is intolerable to the trained eye; things standing upside down, etc. So in social relations and in political. Government belongs to the wise and the strong; the feeble in mind and the narrow in heart are emphatically the wrong men in the wrong place, in seats of power. 2. *The self-satisfied fool.* His fatuous smile is a satire upon himself and upon the condition of things which permits him to bask in so fantastic a paradise. Those are sights to make the " angels weep." 3. *The ill-tempered wife.* (Ver. 23.) She, again, is emphatically " out of place." For *home*, in any sweet sense, is the place which woman's presence makes a delight. 4. *The ambitious maidservant.* The effort to supplant, to grasp a place beyond one's rights and deserts, hurts our intuitive perceptions of what is right. An Oriental proverb says, " Sit in your place, and none shall make you rise," on which we have a pointed commentary from Christ in Luke xiv. 11, " He that humbleth himself shall be exalted." II. THE GENERAL LESSONS. Order and rank are Divine institutions. To overturn this is no work of the true reformer or friend of the social weal. Rule rests ultimately upon ability to rule; government, upon power; authority, upon wisdom. When these relations are *actually* reversed, society is disturbed, matters are unhappy. When they only *seem* to be reversed, there will be distress and discomfort in right minds, until the just order and the nominal state of things shall be restored.—J.

Vers. 24—28.—*The significance of little things.* I. EXAMPLES. 1. *The ant* (ver. 25); tiny in frame, yet full of providence, making wise provision against the rainy day. 2. *The hedgehog* (" coney," ver. 26); though feeble, finds compensation in the strength of the dwelling it selects. 3. *The locust* (ver. 27); a creature, as an individual, easily crushed, yet gaining immense force by union with others. Joel (ii.) gives a splendid description of the raid of locusts under the figure of an invading army, with which the accounts of travellers in tropical lands may be closely compared. 4. *The lizard* (ver. 28); another tender and feeble creature, nevertheless penetrates human dwellings, and makes itself at home in the palaces of kings. II. LESSONS. The lower creatures show unconscious mind. What they do, apparently with blind mechanical impulse, is exemplary in many respects to us who have reason and will. The profoundest lessons may be derived from the lowliest things. Mr. Darwin's work on 'Worms' shows how the most despised of creatures, by the very law of its being, labours for others and blesses a world. It is folly to seek to explore the heights of wisdom until we are familiar with what it teaches us in the little and the low. The " little flower in the crannied wall " contains in its life the secret and mystery of all existence.—J.

Vers. 29—31.—*Grandeur in natural objects.* Our æsthetic as well as our teleological perceptions are appealed to in the objects of nature. Certain creatures express grandeur, sublimity, or beauty in their form and carriage. I. EXAMPLES. 1. The *lion.* (Ver. 30.) He is in nature and for art the very symbol of strength and prowess. Literally, he is the " hero among beasts," and turns his magnificent front from the face of no foe. 2. The *greyhound* (ver. 31), with its slender form, is the very type of swiftness, which is another idea lying close to the sublime. His name (in German, *Windspiel*, or *Windhund*) compares him with the wind. 3. The *goat ;* in its active capability, its nimble movement, and secure footing in dangerous places, gives another variety of the same idea. II. A PARALLEL IN HUMAN LIFE. The king in his majesty should combine in his person and bearing the fearless brow of the lion, the swiftness of decision and action of the other animals. The ideal majesty of man includes in itself all lower perfections in the thought of the Creator. And every man should be taught to realize the royal dignity of his being in Christ. He is made a "little lower than the angels;" and God's purpose cannot be fulfilled until we men rise to claim the glorious heritage of the ideal manhood.—J.

Vers. 32, 33.—*Moral prudence.* I. IT TEACHES THE CONTROL OF THE TONGUE. The folly and pride of the heart may be choked, if expression is denied them on the tongue. No evil or foolish thought is full-born till it is clothed in words. Give no formula to the momentary impulse of wrath or other passion, and the soul of evil will perish if it find no body to inhabit.

II. IT POINTS TO CONSEQUENCES. The quaint illustrations of Agur exhibit the certainty of evil consequences to evil thoughts and desires. As certain as any of the *physical* sequences mentioned, is the *metaphysical* sequence, the moral or immoral consequences of passion. Therefore, *obsta principiis*, resist the beginnings, "seal up the avenues of ill."—J.

Vers. 1—6.—*Reverence and docility.* Whoever Agur may have been, it is certain that he was a sage who could express his thoughts in strong and trenchant language. If, as seems probable, these opening words had reference to the compliments or the questions of his disciples, we may glean, before we proceed further, three lessons by the way. 1. That rightful acknowledgment too easily passes into adulation. 2. That it is a very easy thing for the uninstructed to ask questions which the most enlightened cannot answer. 3. That true genius is modest, and knows well the bounds of its capacity. The main lessons are—

I. OUR DUTY TO DISCLAIM WHAT IS NOT TRUE CONCERNING US. Agur, using the language of hyperbole, energetically disclaims any such elevation as he was imagined to have attained (vers. 2, 3). Men will sometimes deny us the virtue or the wisdom which we may claim; but they will often offer us an honour which is not our due. We may be taken to be wealthier, or wiser, or stronger, or more generous, or more devout than we know ourselves to be. We should then distinctly and determinately decline to receive what does not belong to us. To accept it (1) is dishonest, and any kind of dishonesty is sinful; (2) is likely to inflate our minds with fond and vain conceptions, hurtful if not fatal to our humility; (3) will sooner or later end in exposure and humiliation.

II. THE GREAT OBLIGATION TO REVERENCE. (Ver. 4.) We may know many things, but, when it is all told, what an infinitesimal fraction is this when compared with all that is unknown! What vast, what inexhaustible treasures of truth and wisdom are hidden, and must remain hidden, in the air, in the earth, in the sea! How little, then, can we understand of him, the Eternal and Infinite One, who reigns in the heavens! How unfathomable the depth of the riches, both of the wisdom and knowledge of God" (Rom. xi. 33)! 1. How foolish to expect to understand his purpose, whilst he is outworking it, either concerning our individual life or the destiny of our race! 2. How prepared we should be to accept what God has taught us respecting our nature, or our duty, or our prospects, or respecting his own nature and his will! 3. How unwise to attempt to add to his teaching by any inventions of our own! Not, indeed, that we are not to make new applications, and find out truer interpretations of his Word; but that we are not to think and speak as if we had sources of wisdom apart from his Divine communication.

III. THE REWARD OF DOCILITY. (Ver. 5.) To learn of God is: 1. *To repair to the fountain of purity.* Everything God has said to us tends to purity, to freedom from a degrading selfishness, from a corrupting worldliness, and from an enslaving and a shameful sensuality. To fill our minds and hearts with his holy truth lifts us up into an atmosphere where our whole nature is elevated and refined, where we are capacitated for the vision and fitted for the presence and the home of God (Matt. v. 8; Heb. xii. 14). 2. To learn of God and to connect ourselves with him by faith in Jesus Christ is to be well shielded in the battle of our life. For it is to have (1) strong, sustaining principles within us, and (2) the active and efficient guardianship of God around us as we pass through the *sorrows* of our life, and mingle in its many *conflicts*, and discharge its varied and weighty *duties.*—C.

Vers. 7—9.—*A new year's prayer.* We have in these most instructive words a wise and good man—

I. CALMLY CONFRONTING THE FUTURE. Whether we read "before I die" or "until I die" (Wardlaw), we have a good man deliberately facing the future of his life. He realizes that before him stretches out a tract of time which he has to cross; he knows that he must keep steadily, incessantly, moving forward; that he will meet with difficulties and dangers on his way; that he will want all and more than all the power and the wisdom he has at his command; and he is sobered and solemnized by the thought. In view of this serious aspect of things, we find him—

II. EARNESTLY ADDRESSING HIMSELF TO GOD. "Two things have I required *of thee.*" To whom, thus situated, should we go? Surely unto him who is: 1. The Lord of the future, who holds all time in his sovereign hand, who alone "can set new time upon our score." 2. The Father of our spirits, who is deeply interested in our highest welfare, and cares more about our well-being than does any human relative or friend. 3. The Lord of our life, who traces the path our feet will tread, who can and will hedge that path with his protecting care, who can and will lead us along the road we travel. And what better "requirement" or request could he prefer than that of—

III. ASKING FOR DELIVERANCE FROM DELUSION? From "vanity and lies." Whatever may have been the form which this evil took in the land and time of Agur, we know what withering and wasting delusions we need to be preserved from now. 1. *From under-estimating the value of our life.* There are many—are there not many more than there once were?—that say, "Who will show us any good?" Their name is legion who are discussing and even denying the worth of human life. Indifference, *ennui*, weariness and dreariness of spirit, disgust—leading down to a pessimistic philosophy in theory, and to suicide in action—this is the strain and spirit, and this is the current of our time. It is a delusion, both sorrowful and sinful. For it is a virtual abandonment of a noble heritage, and it is a rejection of a good and a great gift from the hand of God. A life of holy service, of unselfish devotion, of spiritual growth, of filial gratitude and joy, of Christian hopefulness, is a blessing of simply inestimable value. 2. *From over-estimating the value of the sensuous and the material.* Always and everywhere men have been in the gravest danger of supposing that "a man's life *does* consist in the abundance of the things which he possesses," or the number and sweetness of his bodily gratifications. This also is vanity; it is a falsehood which sin sows freely and which quickly takes root in the minds of men. What we need to know, what we may well ask God to teach us so that we shall not only accept but realize it, is that all the rivers of earthly good and of sensuous satisfaction may run into the sea of an immortal spirit, made for God and for goodness, and they will not fill it.

IV. PRAYING TO BE EXEMPT FROM THE EXTREMES OF CIRCUMSTANTIAL TRIAL. "Give me neither poverty nor riches." 1. *The trial of poverty.* This we can all understand, and it takes but little wisdom or sanctity to pray for exemption from its evil. 2. *The trial of wealth.* We think we could endure this without suffering. Nearly all those who have not experienced it are inclined to slight the danger of being rich. Those who have never walked on the ice imagine that *they* could do so without slipping; those who have never gambled indulge the idea that *they* could stop at the moment of prudential retirement. We do not know ourselves. He who "knew what was in man" knew how great is the peril of worldly wealth (see Mark x. 23). We do well to strive and to toil for an honourable maintenance; but we do *not* well to sacrifice health or usefulness—how much less our self-respect and the love of Christ!—in order to be rich. We do wisely to ask God to save us from the temptation—the real, the strong, the frequently whelming temptation—of great worldly success.

V. ASKING FOR THE GOOD WHICH WILL PROVE TO BE A BLESSING. "Feed me with food convenient for me;" *i.e.* which thou knowest to be suited to my need. God only knows what we want—what *we* want; what will be really and abidingly food for us, *considered in all our relations.* God knows what will nourish our spiritual nature, what will supply us as citizens of this life, what is our bodily need for those few years which he is about to give us here before he translates us to a heavenly sphere. Let us ask him to grant us what he knows is best, surely believing that what he gives in answer to our prayer is the best for us to receive—that, whatever the measure be, and not something sweeter, or finer, or more enduring. But let us, understanding what it is we ask—as they who first used the words did not—say continually, "Lord, evermore give us this bread."—C.

Ver. 14.—*From cruelty to kindness.* To those who are even ordinarily humane, the accounts which are sometimes given of horrible cruelty seem to be barely credible; it is difficult to understand how a heart that is anywise human *can* hold such fearful feelings as are thus expressed. On the other hand, to those who have been brutalized by the long practice of cruelty, it is often found almost incredible that men and women can be capable of great generosity either of heart or hand. From the lowest depth of cruelty to the noblest height of kindness there is a very large ascent.

I. THE MORAL SCALE. At the very bottom of this scale is: 1. An absolute and even a keen delight in inflicting and in witnessing pain: this is nothing short of fiendish. Then comes, perhaps: 2. A hard indifference; an utter unconcern when suffering is beheld; a perfect readiness that it should be inflicted and endured. Less iniquitous, perhaps, than this is: 3. The steeling of the heart against the appeal which is made by suffering, and which is not altogether unfelt; the presence of some sensibility, but the endeavour, for some reason, to suppress the emotion that is excited. 4. The inward acknowledgment that interposition is due and should be rendered, but the careful and ingenious avoidance of the duty; the passing by *on the other side.* 5. The compounding of a felt obligation to help by tendering some almost worthless contribution. Then, moving upward, we arrive at: 6. The act of practical kindness to the sorrowful or the needy. 7. The act of *generous* succour, wherein that which is given is really felt. 8. The summit of self-sacrificing love, on which we "lay down our lives for the brethren," even as our Lord laid down his life for us all.

II. OUR PLACE IN THIS SCALE. The question for us to answer is—Where do we stand? How far from the height? how near to the depth? Must we stand condemned? or may we hope that it is well with us in this most serious feature of human character?

III. THE WAY UPWARD. We shall probably conclude that, although our spirit is far from that of the "generation whose teeth are as swords," etc., it is not as truly and as thoroughly the spirit of Christ, the pitiful, the merciful, the magnanimous One, as we would that it were. And we want to know what we can do to leave all cruelty, all unkindness, and even all inconsiderateness, far below us, and to rise to the exalted altitude of pure and noble beneficence. Our best plan will be to make an earnest endeavour: 1. To realize the essential brotherhood of man as being based upon that great fact of the Fatherhood of God. 2. To dwell upon the great and almost boundless capacities of mankind, on the extent to which we can suffer both in body and in spirit, and the degree of joy and excellency to which we may be raised. 3. To study with devout diligence the life and the language, the spirit and the will, of Jesus Christ. 4. To move freely and frequently, both in actual life and in the paths of literature, amongst the gracious and the generous, the kind-hearted and the noble-minded. 5. To address ourselves seriously to the work of showing kindness in every open way to those whom we can reach. Whom we help we pity, whom we serve we love.—C.

Vers. 15, 16.—*The unsatisfied human heart.* There are many things in nature which are not satisfied; but there is one thing in that which is above nature which is much less easily satisfied—an intelligent, responsible, immortal spirit.

I. THE INSATIABLE IN NATURE. Agur specifies four things; in these we find three features which supply a contrast to the craving of the human soul. The insatiable: 1. *Limited by consciousness.* The grave never says, "It is enough;" though millions have descended into its dark void, and though many ages have witnessed its consumption, it is as recipient as ever; it is, and it will remain, unfilled. But it is unconscious of its reception; it is only in imagination that it can be said to crave or to cry, "Give! give!" 2. *Limited by time.* Childless womanhood is *not* unconscious; its craving is real and keen enough; but it is not lasting; it only extends over a few years of life; there is a large proportion of life, before and after, when no such longing is cherished. 3. *Limited by quantity.* The parched earth drinks in the rain hour after hour, and even day after day, as if it would not be satisfied with any quantity; but there is a measure of moisture which saturates and suffices; beyond that, anything that falls or flows is redundant.

II. THE UNSATISFIED HUMAN HEART. Here there are practically no limitations. The human heart: 1. *Is painfully conscious of its deep craving.* Unlike the grave, unlike the fire, which seems animated indeed, but is actually unconscious, the human soul is profoundly moved as it yearns for something more and better than anything it holds; down to its depths it is disturbed, troubled, agitated. Its voice, crying, "Give! give!" is not merely poetical, it is pathetic and even passionate. 2. *Is unlimited by time.* Unlike childless womanhood, its yearning for what it has not is not confined to a few years of its existence; it extends through life; it reaches on to old age, to the very hour of departure. It does not grow, thrive, fade, and die; *it lasts;* it is often found to be as keen and vigorous at the end as at the beginning, in the near neighbourhood of death as in the prime of life. 3. *Is unlimited by quantity.* Nothing that is human or earthly does satisfy the human heart. All affection, all honour, all power, all occupation, all pleasures, run into it, but they do not fill it (see Eccles. i. 7; ii. 1—11). The heart of man, created for that which is highest and best, is not satisfied with anything that falls short of that. It is profoundly conscious that something is wanting of which it is not possessed. It says, blindly perhaps, but earnestly and sometimes passionately, "*Give! give!* I have not enough. I eat, but am still an hungered; I drink, but am still athirst."

III. THE SATISFIED HUMAN SOUL. There is one source of satisfaction; it is found in God himself. "O Lord, thou hast made us for thyself, and our heart findeth no rest until it resteth in thee;" but in him, "who is our home," we do find rest and peace. To us to whom the Son of God and Saviour of mankind has spoken, the voice of cheer and hope is ever calling, "Come unto me . . . I will give you rest." In (1) the friendship, (2) the service, (3) the likeness, of Jesus Christ, and in (4) the good hope through his grace of eternal life, we find the supreme and the lasting satisfaction of the soul. He is the Bread of life, and eating of him we do not hunger more.—C.

Vers. 24—28.—*Success within success.* Many things go to make a man successful, in a true and large sense of that word. A man may have many elements of success, and yet, for want of one more, he may fail. The best part of our succeeding is this— that if we are labouring for some present and visible reward, we are, whilst so doing and in the very act, securing a deeper and a larger good, as the schoolboy seeking the prize is really storing up knowledge and power. We may learn from some of the least and humblest of God's creatures what are the elements of success in the ordering of our life and, at the same time, in the construction of our character.

I. THE ORDERING OF OUR LIFE. If we would live such a life before men as is most honourable and gratifying, we must show the qualities which are manifested by those little creatures of our text. 1. *Forethought.* (Ver. 25.) The man who does not look forward and prepare for the day and the hour when some special demand will be made upon him, must go down. A wise provision made in the time of leisure or abundance is essential to outward and visible success. We must "buy up the opportunity ['redeem the time']" (Col. iv. 5); otherwise, " when the occasion comes, we shall not be equal to the occasion; " *e.g.* the apprentice, the student, etc. 2. *Securing a retreat,* or having a reserve (ver. 26). To be able to run to the rocks or fastnesses is necessary for the feeble. And in the ordering of our life it is necessary to count on our being sometimes defeated. He is but a poor captain who conducts his campaign without " securing his base; " and he does not know the practical wisdom of life who does not provide for himself a retreat, a reserve, when fortune goes against him, as it sometimes will, in "the battle of life." 3. *Co-operation.* (Ver. 27.) It is an essential part of personal equipment that a man be able to co-operate with others. And in the great majority of cases this means readiness to take an inferior place, to obey instructions, to fall in with the suggestions of other people, to forego our own preference and adopt another man's method. It means listening and learning, conciliation and concession, punctuality and politeness. 4. *Aspiration and patience.* (Ver. 28.) For the little and unwelcome spider (or lizard) to establish itself in king's palaces there is demanded this twofold virtue. And for our success we need this also—ambition to attempt and assiduity to win our way, in spite of all the obstacles that may intervene. He that has no heart for enterprise will certainly achieve nothing; and he who lacks patience to wait his time, perseverance to renew his efforts as often as he is foiled, or as often as one success opens the way to another, will reach no king's palace, no place of honour or of influence.

II. THE CONSTRUCTION OF OUR CHARACTER. God has so ordered all things with us and for us that, as we are striving for one thing, we do gain another. As we seek an honourable position in life, we are building up our character. All these elements of success are features of human character, so that while we are "making our way," we are making *ourselves* also. Much that is most valuable in our moral and spiritual constitution is constructed by us in ways and at times when we think not of it; it is like the seed that grows secretly, night and day, the farmer "knoweth not how" (Mark iv. 27). Hence the very great importance that we should be always and everywhere acting on sound, Christian principles; for it is not so much by the direct endeavours we put forth for the purpose, as it is by the constantly and silently operating influence of our daily and hourly actions, that we become what we do become in the sight of God. Beyond and within the success of which men take notice, and on which they congratulate us, is a success which is deeper and truer, for which we may well give to God our heartier thanksgiving.—C.

Vers. 29—31.—*Spiritual comeliness.* Agur mentions four things which are "comely" (Authorized Version) or are "stately" (Revised Version) in their going; their movement is regarded with pleasure, with admiration, by those who observe it. Such demeanour on their part is suggestive of moral and spiritual attractiveness on ours.

I. WE MUST SECURE THAT WHICH IS NECESSARY. We cannot truly live without the favour of God, without entering his service, without possessing something of his likeness, without cherishing a hope of future blessedness. To miss all this is to forfeit *the* heritage of our manhood. We can by no means do without it. This we *must* gain or be undone. But we should go beyond that.

II. WE SHOULD AIM AT THE ADMIRABLE. We ought not to be at all satisfied with ourselves unless our "walk" (1 Thess. iv. 1; 1 John ii. 6), the manner of "our going," is such as to please God, and is such also as to *win men*. Our daily lives should not only be consistent enough to save us from self-reproach and from condemnation; they should be excellent enough, admirable enough, to attract, to call favourable attention to the Divine source of all that we are and have. We should not only worship, but live and work in "the beauty of holiness;" we should aim to add the things that are "lovely" to those which are true, honest, just, and pure; we should endeavour to "adorn the doctrine of Christ our Saviour *in all things*" (see Phil. iv. 8; Titus ii. 10).

III. THESE ELEMENTS OF THE SPIRITUALLY ADMIRABLE. Beginning with that illustration with which Agur ends, which may come first as the most honourable, we have: 1. *The power of command.* "A king against whom is no rising up" (Authorized Version); "a king when his army is with him" (Revised Version, marginal reading); or, a king "at the head of his army." Either way, the idea is that of a man in command. There is something very attractive and even fascinating in this exercise of authority; it elicits not only notice, but admiration. There is one sphere in which it is open to all of us to exercise and to exhibit command—*over our own spirit*. There is nothing more worth our admiring regard than the sight of a man maintaining a perfect control of his spirit under circumstances of great trial or provocation (ch. xvi. 32). To exercise a sovereign control over our fear, or our anger, or our affection, or our curiosity, or our sorrow; of our impulses, or our emotions;—this is excellent and admirable indeed: then are we "comely [or, 'stately'] in our going." 2. *The possession of strength.* "A lion which is strongest among beasts." It is the conscious possession of power which gives such dignity to the "king of beasts." To this also we should attain: (1) intrinsic power, by the devout and diligent cultivation of all our God-given faculties, (2) communicated power, by the indwelling of the Spirit of God, being of those who are "strong in the Lord, and in the power of his might." Self-sufficiency and conceit are indeed ugly enough; but conscious power, associated, as it may be and should be, with humility and kindness, is admirable and attractive. It is well to walk on our way as those who know that they have no need to fear, because God is for us and will be with us and in us. 3. *Moral symmetry.* The greyhound and the he-goat are pleasing because they are well proportioned throughout their frame. To be spiritually beautiful, our character must be symmetrical. Each quality must be balanced by its opposite virtue—firmness by gentleness, thoughtfulness by readiness for action, courage by caution, generosity by conscientiousness, etc. Thus will our character and (consequently) our demeanour be comely in the view of man as well as acceptable in the sight of God.—C.

EXPOSITION.

CHAPTER XXXI.

Vers. 1—9.—Part VIII. SECOND APPENDIX TO THE SECOND COLLECTION, containing "the words of Lemuel" on the subjects of impurity and intemperance.

Ver. 1.—*The superscription.* **The words of King Lemuel, the prophecy which his mother taught him.** Who is intended by "Lemuel king" is much disputed. Those who connect the following word *massa* ("oracle") with the preceding *melek* ("king"), translate "King of Massa," as ch. xxx. 1 (where see note). Of the country, or the king, or his mother, we have absolutely no information. The name Lemuel, or Lemoel (ver. 4), means "unto God," *i.e.* dedicated to God, like Lael (Numb. iii. 24); hence it is regarded by many authorities, ancient and modern, as an appellation of Solomon, one from infancy dedicated to God and called by him Jedidiah, "beloved of the Lord" (2 Sam. xii. 25). But there is nothing in the contents of this section to confirm this idea; indeed, there are expressions which militate against it. Possibly Hezekiah may be meant, and his remarkable piety somewhat confirms the opinion; yet we see no reason why he should be here addressed under a pseudonym, especially if we consider that he himself was concerned in making this collection. On the whole, it seems best to take Lemuel as a symbolical name, designating an ideal king, to whom an ideal mother addressed the exhortation which follows. Solomon's own proverbs contain many warnings against the very sins of which this mother speaks, so that the section is conceived in the spirit of the earlier portion of the book, though it is assigned to a different author and another age. *The prophecy* (*massa*); the inspired utterance (see on ch. xxx. 1). This maternal counsel forms one compact exhortation, which might with more propriety be so termed than the words of Agur. *His mother.* The mother of a reigning king was always regarded with the utmost respect, taking precedence of the king's wife. Hence we so often find the names of kings' mothers in the sacred record; *e.g.* 1 Kings ii. 19; xiv. 21; xv. 2; 2 Kings xii. 1. It is difficult to

say what reading was seen by the LXX., who render, " My words have been spoken by God, the oracle of a king whom his mother instructed." There are many wise women mentioned in Scripture; *e.g.* Miriam, Deborah, the Queen of Sheba, Huldah, etc., so there is nothing incongruous in Lemuel being instructed by his mother in wisdom.

Vers. 2—9.—Here follows *the exhortation*, which seems to come from the same source as the "burden" of Agur above. In this section the connection and parallelism of the parts are exhibited by repetition of thought and often of words in the several clauses.

Ver. 2.—**What, my son?** *Mah,* "what," is repeated thrice, both to enforce the attention of the son, and to show the mother's anxious care for his good. She feels the vast importance of the occasion, and asks as in perplexity, "What shall I say? What advice shall I give thee?" "Son" is here not *ben,* but *bar,* one of the Aramaic forms which are found in these two last chapters. The word occurs also in Ps. ii. 12. **Son of my vows.** This might mean, "son who wast asked in prayer," like Samuel (1 Sam. i. 11), and dedicated to God, as the name Lemuel implies; or it may signify, " thou who art the object of my daily vows and prayers." Septuagint, "What, my son, wilt thou observe ($\tau\eta\rho\eta\sigma\epsilon\iota\varsigma$)? What? the sayings of God. My firstborn son, to thee I speak. What, son of my womb? What, son of my vows?"

Ver. 3.—*Exhortation to chastity.* **Give not thy strength unto women** (comp. ch. v. 9). *Chayil* is "vigour," the bodily powers, which are sapped and enervated by sensuality. The Septuagint has $\sigma\grave{o}\nu\ \pi\lambda o\hat{v}\tau o\nu$; the Vulgate, *substantiam tuam;* but the prayerful, anxious mother would consider rather her son's personal well-being than his worldly circumstances, which, indeed, an Eastern monarch's licentiousness would not necessarily impair. **Nor thy ways to that which destroyeth kings;** or, with a slight alteration in the punctuation (and an improved parallelism), *to them that destroy kings;* "expugnatricibus regum," as Schultens terms them. Women are meant; and the prince is enjoined not to surrender his life, conduct, and actions to the influence of women, who, both by the dissipation and sensuality which they occasion, and the quarrels which they provoke, and the evil counsels which they give, often ruin kings and states (see the injunction, Deut. xvii. 11). The Vulgate rendering, *ad delendos reges*, looks as if the warning was against making wars of conquest against neighbouring kings; but this is not a satisfactory parallel to the former clause. Septuagint, " Give not thy wealth unto women, nor thy mind, nor thy life unto remorse (ὑστεροβουλίαν). Do all things with counsel; drink wine with counsel." This seems to belong to the next verse.

Vers. 4—7.—*The second admonition.* A warning against inebriety, and concerning a proper use of strong drink.

Ver. 4.—It is **not for kings; or,** as others read, *far be it from kings.* The injunction is repeated to indicate its vast importance. **Nor for princes strong drink;** literally, *nor for princes* (the word), *Where is strong drink?* (see on ch. xx. 1; and comp. Job xv. 23). The evils of intemperance, flagrant enough in the case of a private person, are greatly enhanced in the case of a king, whose misdeeds may affect a whole community, as the next verse intimates. St. Jerome reads differently, translating, " Because there is no secret where drunkenness reigns." This is in accordance with the proverb, " When wine goes in the secret comes out;" and, " Where drink enters, wisdom departs;" and again, " Quod latet in mente sobrii, hoc natat in ore ebrii." Septuagint, " The powerful are irascible, but let them not drink wine." " Drunkenness," says Jeremy Taylor ('Holy Living,' ch. iii. § 2), " opens all the sanctuaries of nature, and discovers the nakedness of the soul, all its weaknesses and follies; it multiplies sins and discovers them; it makes a man incapable of being a private friend or a public counsellor. It taketh a man's soul into slavery and imprisonment more than any vice whatsoever, because it disarms a man of all his reason and his wisdom, whereby he might be cured, and, therefore, commonly it grows upon him with age; a drunkard being still more a fool and less a man."

Ver. 5.—This gives a reason for the warning. **Lest they drink, and forget the Law.** That which has been decreed, and is right and lawful, the appointed ordinance, particularly as regards the administration of justice. Septuagint, " Lest drinking, they forget wisdom." **And pervert the judgment of any of the afflicted;** literally, *of all the sons of affliction;* i.e. the whole class of poorer people. Intemperance leads to selfish dis-

regard of others' claims, an inability to examine questions impartially, and consequent perversion of justice. Isaiah (v. 23) speaks of intoxication as inducing men to " justify the wicked for reward, and take away the righteousness of the righteous from him."

Ver. 6.—There are cases where strong drink may be properly administered. **Give strong drink unto him that is ready to perish** (Job xxix. 13; xxxi. 19). As a restorative, a cordial, or a medicine, wine may be advantageously used; it has a place in the providential economy of God. " Use a little wine for thy stomach's sake and thine often infirmities," was St. Paul's advice to Timothy (1 Tim. v. 23). It is supposed to have been in consideration of the injunction in the text that the ladies of Jerusalem provided for criminals on their way to the place of execution a drink of medicated wine, which might deaden the pain of suffering. This was the draught rejected by Christ, who willed to taste the full bitterness of death (Matt. xxvii. 34; Mark xv. 23). The Septuagint has, " to those that are in sorrow;" so the Vulgate, *mærentibus*, but this makes the two clauses tautological. **Wine unto those that be of heavy hearts** (Job iii. 20). " Wine," says the psalmist, " maketh glad the heart of man" (Ps. civ. 15). Says Homer, 'Iliad,' vi. 261—

" Great is the strength
Which generous wine imparts to wearied men."

" Wine," says St. Chrysostom ('Hom. in Ephes.,' xix.), " has been given us for cheerfulness, not for drunkenness. Wouldest thou know where wine is good? Hear what the Scripture saith, 'Give wine to them, etc. And justly, because it can mitigate asperity and gloominess, and drive away clouds from the brow" (comp. Ecclus. xxxiv. [xxxi.] 25, etc.).

Ver. 7.—**Let him drink, and forget his poverty.** Ovid, 'Art. Amat.,' i. 237—

" Vina parant animos, faciuntque caloribus aptos :
Cura fugit multo diluiturque mero.
Tunc veniunt risus; tunc pauper cornua sumit :
Tunc dolor, et curæ, rugaque frontis abit."

Thus is shown a way in which the rich can comfort and encourage their poorer brethren, which is a better method of using God's good gifts than by expending them on their own selfish enjoyment.

Vers. 8, 9.—The third exhortation, admonishing the king to judge righteously.

Ver. 8.—**Open thy mouth for the dumb.** The " dumb" is any one who for any reason whatever is unable to plead his own cause; he may be of tender age, or of lowly station, or ignorant, timid, and boorish; and the prince is enjoined to plead for him and defend him (comp. **Job xxix. 15**). **In the cause of all such as are appointed to destruction**; literally, *the sons of passing away* (Isa. ii. 18); i.e. not orphans, children whose parents have vanished from the earth, nor strangers from a foreign country, nor, generally, mortals, subjects of frail human nature (all of which explanations have been given), but persons who are in imminent danger of perishing, certain, if left unaided, to come to ruin (comp. Job xxix. 12). Septuagint, "Open thy mouth for the Word of God, and judge all men soundly (ὑγιῶς)."

Ver. 9.—**Plead the cause**; rather, *minister judgment*, or *do right*; act in your official capacity so that the effect shall be substantial justice (comp. Zech. viii. 16).

Vers. 10—31.—Part IX. THIRD APPENDIX TO THE SECOND COLLECTION. This section contains an ode in praise of the virtuous woman, derived from a different source from that of the words of Agur, and belonging to a different age (see Introduction). It is an acrostic; that is, each verse begins with one of the twenty-two letters of the Hebrew alphabet, arranged in the usual order. We may compare this *mashal* with the alphabetical psalms, "Psalmi abcedarii," which are, more or less, of similar structure, but of which one only, the hundred and nineteenth, is so marked in the English versions. Other examples are Ps. ix., x., xxv., xxxiv., xxxvii., cxi., cxii., cxlv.; also Lam. i., ii., and iii. One object of this artificial construction was to render the matter easier to commit to memory. The spiritual expositors see in this description of the virtuous woman a prophetic representation of the Church of Christ in her truth and purity and influence. Thus Bede: "Hic sapientissimus regum Salomon laudes sanctæ Ecclesiæ versibus paucis sed plenissima veritate depingit. . . . Cujus (carminis) ordine perfectissimo alphabeti typice innuitur, quam plenissime hic vel animæ cujusque fidelis, vel totius sanctæ Ecclesiæ, quæ ex omnibus electis animabus una perficitur Catholica, virtutes ac præmia describantur."

Ver. 10.—ALEPH. **Who can find a virtuous woman?** The expression, *ishshah chayil*, "woman of force," has occurred in

ch. xii. 4 (where see note). *Mulierem fortem*, St. Jerome terms her; γυναῖκα ἀνδρείαν is the rendering of the LXX., which places this section as the end of the whole Book of Proverbs. The expression combines the ideas of moral goodness and bodily vigour and activity. It is useless to try to fix the character upon any particular person. The representation is that of an ideal woman—the perfect housewife, the chaste helpmate of her husband, upright, God-fearing, economical, wise. See an anticipation of this character (ch. xviii. 22; xix. 14); and a very different view (Eccles. vii. 26). It is very remarkable to meet with such a delineation of woman in the East, where the female generally occupies a most degraded position, and is cut off from all sphere of activity and administration. To paint such a portrait needed inspiration of some sort. Such a one is hard to find. **Her price is far above rubies**; or, *pearls* (see on ch. xx. 15 and iii. 15). Septuagint, "Such a one is more valuable than precious stones." There **may** be allusion to the custom of giving treasure in exchange for a wife, purchasing her, as it were, from her friends (comp. Hos. iii. 2). At any rate, few only are privileged to meet with this excellent wife, and her worth cannot be estimated by any material object, however costly. St. Jerome, with a slight difference in the reading, has, *Procul, et de ultimis finibus pretium ejus.* You may go to the ends of the earth to find her equal in value.

Ver. 11.—BETH. **The heart of her husband doth safely trust in her.** The husband of such a wife goes forth to his daily occupations, having full confidence in her whom he leaves at home, that she will act discreetly, and promote his interests while he is absent (see the contrast in ch. vii. 20). So that he shall have no need of spoil; rather, *he shall not lack gain (shalal)*. The wife manages domestic concerns so well that her husband finds his honest gains increase, and sees his confidence profitably rewarded. Septuagint, "Such a woman shall want not fair spoils." It is obvious to see in this an adumbration of the Church winning souls from the power of the enemy, especially as *shalal* is used for an enemy's spoils (Ps. lxviii. 12; Isa. liii. 12; and elsewhere).

Ver. 12.—GIMEL. **She will do him good and not evil** (comp. Ecclus. xxvi. 1—3). She is consistent in her conduct towards her husband, always pursuing his best interests. **All the days of her life**; in good times or bad, in the early spring-time of young affection, and in the waning years of declining age. Her love, based on high principles, knows no change or diminution. The old commentator refers to the conduct of St. Monica to her unbelieving and unfaithful husband, narrated by St. Augustine in his 'Confessions,' ix. 9 : "Having been given over to a husband, she served him as her lord; and busied herself to win him to thee, revealing thee to him by her virtues, in which thou madest her beautiful, and reverently amiable, and admirable to her husband."

Ver. 13.—DALETH. **She seeketh wool, and flax.** She pays attention to these things, as materials for clothing and domestic uses. Wool has been used for clothing from the earliest times (see Lev. xiii. 47; Job xxxi. 20, etc.), and flax was largely cultivated for the manufacture of linen, the processes of drying, peeling, hackling, and spinning being well understood (see Josh. ii. 6; Isa. xix. 9; Jer. xiii 1, etc.). The prohibition about mixing wool and flax in a garment (Deut. xxii. 11) was probably based on the idea that all mixtures made by the art of man are polluted, and that what is pure and simple, such as it is in its natural state, is alone proper for the use of the people of God. **And worketh willingly with her hands;** or, *she worketh with her hands' pleasure;* i.e. with willing hands. The rendering of the Revised Version margin, after Hitzig, "She worketh at the business of her hands," is feeble, and does not say much. What is meant is that she not only labours diligently herself, but finds pleasure in doing so, and this, not because she has none to help her, and is forced to do her own work (on the contrary, she is represented as rich, and at the head of a large household), but because she considers that labour is a duty for all, and that idleness is a transgression of a universal law. Septuagint, "Weaving (μηρυομένη) wool and flax; she makes it useful with her hands."

Ver. 14.—HE. **She is like the merchants'** ships. She is like them in that she extends her operations beyond her own immediate neighbourhood, and **bringeth her food from afar,** buying in the best markets and on advantageous terms, without regard to distance, and being always on the look out to make honest profit. Septuagint, "She is like a ship trading from a distance, and she herself gathereth her livelihood." The expressions in the text point to active commercial operations by sea as well as land, such as we know to have been undertaken by Solomon, Jehoshaphat, and others (1 Kings ix. 26; xxii. 48), and such as the Hebrews must have noticed in the Phœnician cities, Sidon and Tyre.

Ver. 15.—VAV. **She riseth also while it is yet night.** Before dawn she is up and stirring, to be ready for her daily occupation. A lamp is always kept burning at night in Eastern houses, and as it is of very small dimensions, the careful housewife has

to rise at midnight to replenish the oil, and she often then begins her household work by grinding the corn or preparing something for next day's meals (comp. ver. 18). Early rising before any great undertaking is continually mentioned in Scripture (see Gen. xix. 2; xxii. 3; Ps. lvii. 8; Jer. vii. 13; xxv. 4, etc.; Mark xvi. 2; John xx. 1). **And giveth meat to her household;** *dedit quæ prædam domesticis suis,* Vulgate. The word for "meat" is *tereph,* which means "food torn in pieces" with the teeth (Ps. cxi. 5), and hence food to be eaten. The wife thus early prepares or distributes the food which will be wanted for the day. **And a portion to her maidens.** *Chok,* "final portion," may apply either to work or food. The Vulgate has *cibaria,* "meat;" Septuagint, ἔργα, "tasks." The former, which is in accordance with ch. xxx. 8, would be merely a repetition of the second clause, the meat mentioned there being here called the allotted portion, and would be simply tautological. If we take it in the sense of "appointed labour," we get a new idea, very congruous with the housewife's activity (comp. Exod. v. 14, where the same word is used in the case of the enforced labour of the Israelites).

Ver. 16.—ZAYIN. **She considereth a field, and buyeth it.** She turns her attention to a certain field, the possession of which is for some cause desirable; and, after due examination and consideration, she buys it. One is reminded of Christ's parable of the treasure hidden in a field, which the finder sold all that he had to purchase (Matt. xiii. 44). **With the fruit of her hands she planteth a vineyard.** Her prudent management and economy give her means to buy vines and plant a vineyard, and thus to increase her produce. Possibly it is meant that she sees the field she has gotten is more fitted for grapes than corn, and she cultivates it accordingly. Virgil, 'Georg.,' ii. 229—

"Altera frumentis quoniam favet, altera Baccho,
Densa magis Cereri, rarissima quæque Lyæo."

Ver. 17.—KHETH. **She girdeth her loins with strength** (ver. 25). This seems at first sight a strange assertion to make concerning one of the weaker sex; but the phrase is metaphorically expressive of the energy and force with which she prepares herself for her work. Strength and vigour are, as it were, the girdle which she binds round her waist to enable her to conduct her operations with ease and freedom. So we have a similar metaphor boldly applied to God (Ps. xciii. 1): "The Lord reigneth, he is apparelled with majesty; the Lord is apparelled, he hath girded himself with strength " (cf. Job xxxviii. 3). **Strengtheneth her arms.** By daily exercise she makes her arms firm and strong, and capable of great and continued exertion.

Ver. 18.—TETH. **She perceiveth that her merchandise is good;** Vulgate, *Gustavit et vidit quia bona est negotiatio ejus,* where the paraphrase, "she tastes and sees," expresses the meaning of the verb *taam* here used. Her prudence and economy leave her a large surplus profit, which she contemplates with satisfaction. There is no suspicion of arrogance or conceit. The pleasure that is derived from duty done and successfully conducted business is legitimate and healthy, a providential reward of good works. Septuagint, "She tastes that it is good to work." This comfort and success spur her on to further and more continued exertion. **Her candle** (*lamp*) **goeth not out by night.** She is not idle even when night falls, and outdoor occupations are cut short; she finds work for the hours of darkness, such as is mentioned in the next verse. One recalls Virgil's picture of the thrifty housewife ('Æneid,' viii. 407)—

" Inde ubí prima quies medio jam noctis abactæ
Curriculo expulerat somnum, cum femina primum,
Cui tolerare colo vitam tenuique Minerva
Impositum, cinerem et sopitos suscitat ignis,
Noctem addens operi, famulasque ad lumina longo
Exercet penso."

Some take the lamp here in an allegorical sense, as signifying life, happiness, and prosperity, as ch. xiii. 9 and xx. 20 ; others, as denoting a bright example of diligence and piety (Matt. v. 16). But the simple meaning seems to be the one intended. Wordsworth notes that the passage in Rev. xviii., which speaks of the "merchandise" of the false Church, also affirms that "the light of a candle" shall shine in her no more, the two metaphors in our passage applied to the true Church being there applied to Babylon.

Ver. 19.—YODH. **She layeth her hands to the spindle.** כִּישׁוֹר (*kishor,* a word not occurring elsewhere) is probably not the spindle, but the distaff, *i.e.* the staff to which is tied the bunch of flax from which the spinning-wheel draws the thread. To this she applies her hand ; she deftly performs the work of spinning her flax into thread. **Her hands hold the distaff.** פֶּלֶךְ (*pelek*) is the spindle, the cylindrical wood (afterwards the wheel) on which the thread

winds itself as it is spun. The hands could not be spared to hold the distaff as well as the spindle, so the first clause should run, " She stretches her hand towards the distaff." In the former clause *kishor* occasioned some difficulty to the early translators, who did not view the word as connected with the process of spinning. The Septuagint translates, " She stretches out her arms to useful works (ἐπὶ τὰ συμφέροντα);" Vulgate, *Manum suam misit ad fortia.* So Aquila and Symmachus, ἀνδρεῖα. This rather impedes the parallelism of the two clauses. There was nothing derogatory in women of high rank spinning among their maidens, just as in the Middle Ages noble ladies worked at tapestry with their attendants. We remember how Lucretia, the wife of Collatinus, was found sitting in the midst of her handmaids, carding wool and spinning (Livy, i. 57). Catullus, in his ' Epithal. Pel. et Thet.,' 312, describes the process of spinning—

" Læva colum molli lana retinebat amictum ;
Dextera tum leviter deducens fila supinis
Formabat digitis ; tum prono in pollice torquens
Libratum tereti versabat turbine fusum."
(' Carm.,' lxiv.)

Ver. 20.—CAPH. She is not impelled by selfish greed to improve her means and enlarge her revenues. She is sympathizing and charitable, and loves to extend to others the blessings which have rewarded her efforts. **She stretcheth out her hand to the poor.** "Hand" is here *caph,* "the palm," evidently containing alms. She knows the maxim (ch. xix. 17), "He that hath pity upon the poor lendeth unto the Lord," etc. ; and she has no fear of poverty. **Yea, she reacheth forth her hands to the needy.** "Hand," is here *yad,* with its nerves and sinews ready for exertion (see on ch. x. 4) ; and the idea is that she puts forth her hand to raise and soothe the poor man, not being satisfied with dealing alms to him, but exercising the gentle ministries of a tender love. Septuagint, "She opens her hands to the needy, and reaches forth her wrist (καρπὸν) to the poor." Like Dorcas, she is full of good works and almsdeeds (Acts ix. 36). It is doubtless implied that the prosperity which she experiences is the reward of this benevolence (ch. xxii. 9).

Ver. 21.—LAMED.. **She is not afraid of the snow for her household.** " Snow," says Dr. Geikie (' Holy Land,' ii. 58), " covers the streets of Jerusalem two winters in three, but it generally comes in small quantities, and soon disappears. Yet there are sometimes very snowy winters. That of 1879, for example, left behind it seventeen inches of snow, even where there was no drift, and the strange spectacle of snow lying unmelted for two or three weeks was seen in the hollows on the hillsides. Thousands of years have wrought no change in this aspect of the winter months, for Benaiah, one of David's mighty men, 'slew a lion in the midst of a pit in the time of snow' (2 Sam. xxiii. 20)." She has no fears concerning the comfort and health of her family even in the severest winter. **For all her household are clothed with scarlet**; with warm garments. The word used is עָשָׁן (*shanim*), derived from a verb meaning "to shine," and denoting a crimson or deep scarlet colour. This colour was supposed, and rightly, to absorb and retain heat, as white to repel it; being made of wool, the garments would be warm as well as stately in appearance. St. Jerome has *duplicibus* (*shenaim*), "with double garments," *i.e.* with one over the other. Warm garments were the more necessary as the only means of heating rooms was the introduction of portable chafing-dishes containing burning charcoal (see Jer. xxxvi. 22, etc.). The Septuagint has taken liberties with the text, " Her husband is not anxious concerning domestic matters when he tarries anywhere [χρονίζη, for which Delitzsch suggests χιονίζη], for all her household are well clothed." Spiritually, the Church fears not the severity of temptation or the chill of unbelief, when her children take refuge in the blood of Christ.

Ver. 22.—MEM. **She maketh herself coverings of tapestry** (*marbaddim*); as ch. vii. 16 (where see note). Pillows for beds or cushions are meant, though the translators are not of one mind on the meaning. St. Jerome has, *stragulatam vestem;* Aquila and Theodotion, περιστρώματα; Symmachus, ἀμφιτάπους, "shaggy on both sides;" Septuagint, "She makes for her husband double garments (δισσὰς χλαίνας)." **Her clothing is silk and purple.** שֵׁשׁ (*shesh*) is not "silk," but "white linen" (βύσσος, *byssus*) of very fine texture, and costly. Purple garments were brought from the Phœnician cities, and were highly esteemed (see Cant. iii. 10; Jer. x. 9). The wife dresses herself in a way becoming her station, avoiding the extremes of sordid simplicity and ostentatious luxury. "For my own part," says St. François de Sales, quoted by Lesètre, "I should wish any devout man or woman always to be the best-dressed person in the company, but at the same time, the least fine and affected, and adorned, as it is said, with the ornament of a meek and quiet spirit. St. Louis said that every one ought to dress according to his position, so that good and sensible people should not be able to say you are over-dressed, nor the younger under-dressed "

('Vie Devot.,' iii. 25). So the Church is clothed in fine linen, clean and white, even the righteousness which Christ bestows (Rev. xix. 8), and invested in her Lord's royal robe, who hath made her children kings and priests unto God (Rev. i. 6; v. 10).

Ver. 23.—NUN. **Her husband is known in the gates.** Such a woman advances her husband's interests, increases his influence, and, by attending to his domestic concerns, enables him to take his share in public matters, so that his name is in great repute in the popular assemblies at the city gates (ver. 31; ch. viii. 3). She is indeed " a crown to her husband " (ch. xii. 4). **When he sitteth among the elders of the land.** Homer introduces Nausikaa speaking to her father of her duty to see that he is honourably clad when he goes to the council—

Καὶ δὲ σοὶ αὐτῷ ἔοικε μετὰ πρώτοισιν ἐόντα
Βουλὰς βουλεύειν καθαρὰ χροῒ εἵματ᾽ ἔχοντα.
('Odyssey,' vi. 60.)

"For our costly robes,
All sullied now, the cleansing stream require;
And thine especially, when thou appear'st
In council with the princes of the land,
Had need be pure."

(Cowper.)

St. Gregory sees here an adumbration of the day of judgment: " For the Redeemer of mankind is the 'Husband' of holy Church, who shows himself 'renowned' (*nobilis*, Vulgate) in the gates. Who first came in sight in degradation and in mockings, but shall appear on high at the entering in of his kingdom ; and 'he sitteth among the elders of the land,' for that he shall decree sentence of condemnation together with the holy preachers of that same Church, as himself declares in the gospel (Matt. xix. 28)" (' Moral.,' vi. 9).

Ver. 24.—SAMECH. **She maketh fine linen, and selleth it.** The word for "fine linen" is *sadin*, not the same as in ver. 22, but equivalent to σινδών, and denoting linen garments; Delitzsch calls it "body-linen" (comp. Judg. xiv. 12, 13; Isa. iii. 23). **Delivereth girdles unto the merchant;** literally, *unto the Canaanite;* i.e. the Phœnician merchant, a generic name for all traders (see Isa. xxiii. 8; Zech. xiv. 21). Girdles were necessary articles of attire with the flowing robes of Eastern dress. The common kind were made of leather, as is the use at the present day; but a more costly article was of linen curiously worked in gold and silver thread, and studded with jewels and gold (see 2 Sam. xviii. 11; Dan. x. 5). So Virgil (' Æneid,' ix. 359) speaks of "aurea bullis cingula." We read of Queen Parysatis having certain villages assigned her for girdle-money, εἰς ζώνην δεδομέναι (Xen., 'Anab.,' i. 4. 9). Cicero alludes to the same custom in his Verrine oration (ch. iii. 33): "Solere aiunt barbaros reges Persarum ac Syrorum plures uxores habere, his autem uxoribus civitates attribuere hoc modo: hæc civitas mulieri in redimiculum prœbeat, hæc in collum, hæc in crines" (comp. Plato, 'Alcib. I.,' p. 123, B). Such rich and elaborately worked girdles the mistress could readily barter with Phœnician merchants, who would give in exchange purple (ver. 22) and other articles of use or luxury. On this passage St. Gregory thus moralizes: "What is signified by a garment of fine linen, but the subtle texture of holy preaching? In which men rest softly, because the mind of the faithful is refreshed therein by heavenly hope. Whence also the animals are shown to Peter in a linen sheet, because the souls of sinners mercifully gathered together are enclosed in the gentle quiet of faith. The Church therefore made and sold this fine garment, because she imparted in words that faith which she had woven by belief; and received from unbelievers a life of upright conversation. And she delivered a girdle to the Canaanite, because by the might of the righteousness she displayed, she constrained the lax doings of the Gentile world, in order that that might be maintained in their doings which is commanded, 'Let your loins be girded about'" ('Moral.,' xxxiii. 33).

Ver. 25.—AYIN. **Strength and honour are her clothing** (ver. 17); ἰσχὺν καὶ εὐπρέπειαν, Septuagint. She is invested with a moral force and dignity which arm her against care and worry; the power of a righteous purpose and strong will reveals itself in her carriage and demeanour. And thus equipped, **she shall rejoice in time to come**; or, *she laugheth* (Job v. 22; xxxix. 7) *at the future* (Isa. xxx 8). She is not disquieted by any fear of what may happen, knowing in whom she trusts, and having done her duty to the utmost of her ability. The Greek and Latin versions seem to take the expression as referring to the day of death; thus the Vulgate, *Ridebit in die novissimo;* Septuagint, "She rejoices in the last days (ἐν ἡμέραις ἐσχάταις)." But it is best interpreted as above. The true servant of God is not afraid of any evil tidings, his heart being fixed, trusting in the Lord (Ps. cxii. 7).

Ver. 26.—PE. **She openeth her mouth with wisdom.** She is not merely a good housewife, attending diligently to material interests; she guides her family with words of wisdom. When she speaks, it is not gossip, or slander, or idle talk, that she utters, but sentences of prudence and sound sense, such as may minister grace to the

hearers. The Septuagint has this verse before ver. 25, and the first hemistich again after ver. 27. So in Lam. ii., iii., iv., the *pe* and *ayin* verses change places. This is also the case in Ps. xxxvii. In the former passage the LXX. renders, "She openeth her mouth heedfully and lawfully (προσεχόντως καὶ ἐννόμως);" and in the other, "wisely and in accordance with law (σοφῶς καὶ νομοθέσμως)." **In her tongue is the law of kindness** (*thorath chesed*); i.e. her language to those around her is animated and regulated by love. As mistress of a family, she has to teach and direct her dependents, and she performs this duty with gracious kindness and ready sympathy. Septuagint, "She places order on her tongue."

Ver. 27.—TSADE. **She looketh well to the ways of her house;** the actions and habits of the household. She exercises careful surveillance over all that goes on in the family. **Eateth not the bread of idleness;** but rather bread won by active labour and conscientious diligence. She is of the opinion of the apostle who said "that if any would not work, neither should he eat" (2 Thess. iii. 10). Septuagint, "The ways of her house are confined (στεγναὶ διατριβαὶ οἴκων αὐτῆς), and she eats not idle bread." The first of these clauses may mean that the proceedings of her household, being confined to a narrow circle, are readily supervised. But the meaning is very doubtful; and Schleusner renders, "continuæ conversationes in ædibus ejus." St. Gregory applies our verse to the conscience, thus: "She considers the ways of her house, because she accurately examines all the thoughts of her conscience. She eateth not her bread in idleness, because that which she learned out of Holy Scripture by her understanding, she places before the eyes of the Judge by exhibiting it in her works" ('Moral.,' xxxv. 47).

Ver. 28.—KUPH. **Her children arise up, and call her blessed.** She is a fruitful mother of children, who, seeing her sedulity and prudence, and experiencing her affectionate care, celebrate and praise her, and own that she has rightly won the blessing of the Lord. **Her husband also, and he praiseth her;** in the words given in the next verse. Having the approbation of her husband and children, who know her best, and have the best opportunities of judging her conduct, she is contented and happy. Septuagint, "Her mercy (ἐλεημοσύνη) raises up her children, and they grow rich, and her husband praises her."

Ver. 29.—RESH. **Many daughters have done virtuously, but thou excellest them all.** The versions and some commentators take the encomium in the mean and restricted sense of praise for the acquisition of riches.

Thus the Vulgate, *Multæ filiæ congregaverunt divitias;* Septuagint, "Many daughters have obtained wealth." But it adds another rendering, "Many have wrought power (ἐποίησαν δύναμιν)," which is nearer the meaning in this place. *Chayil* (as we have seen, ver. 10) means "force," *virtus*, "strength of character" shown in various ways (comp. Numb. xxiv. 18; Ps. lx. 12). "Daughters," equivalent to "women," as Gen. xxx. 13; Cant. vi. 9. Roman Catholic commentators have, with much ingenuity, applied the whole description of the virtuous woman, and especially the present verse, to the Virgin Mary. We may regard it as a representation of the truly Christian matron, who loves husband and children, guides the house, is discreet, chaste, good, a teacher of good things (1 Tim. v. 14; Titus ii. 3, etc.).

Ver. 30.—SHIN. The writer confirms the husband's praise by assigning to it its just grounds. **Favour is deceitful, and beauty is vain.** *Chen,* "favour," may signify either the good will with which one is regarded, or gracefulness, beauty. As being in close parallelism with the next words, it is best taken as referring to loveliness of form. Mere gracefulness, if considered as a token of a wife's work and usefulness, is misleading; and beauty is transitory and often dangerous. Neither of them is of any real value unless accompanied by religion. As the gnomic poet says—

Μὴ κρῖν', ὁρῶν τὸ κάλλος, ἀλλὰ τὸν τρόπον.

"Judge not at sight of beauty, but of life."

But a woman that **feareth the Lord, she shall be praised.** So we come back to the maxim with which the whole book began, that the foundation of all **excellence is the** fear of the Lord (ch. i. 7). Such, too, is the conclusion of Ecclesiastes (xii. 13), "Fear God, and keep his commandments: for this is the whole duty of man." Septuagint, "False are charms (ἀρέσκεται), and vain is the beauty of woman; for a prudent woman is blessed, and let her praise the fear of the Lord."

Ver. 31.—TAV. **Give her of the fruit of her hands.** So may she enjoy the various blessings which her zeal, prudence, and economy have obtained. Ps. cxxviii. 2, "Thou shalt eat the labour of thine hands; happy shalt thou be, and it shall be well with thee." Septuagint, "Give her of the fruit of her lips." **And let her own works praise her in the gates.** She needs no far-fetched laudation; her lifelong actions speak for themselves. Where men most congregate, where the heads of the people meet in solemn assembly, there her praise is sung, and a unanimous verdict assigns to her the highest honour. Septuagint, "Let her husband be praised in the gates." This frequent introduction of the husband is curious. St. Gregory thus spiritualizes the passage: "As the entrance of a city is called the gate, so is the day of judgment the gate of the kingdom, since all the elect go in thereby to the glory of their heavenly country.... Of these gates Solomon says, 'Give her of the fruit of her hands, and her own works shall praise her in the gates.' For holy Church then receives of 'the fruit of her hands,' when the recompensing of her labour raises her up to the possession of heavenly blessings; for her 'works then praise her in the gates,' when in the very entrance to his kingdom the words are spoken to his members, 'I was an hungred, and ye gave me meat,' etc." ('Moral.,' vi. 9).

HOMILETICS.

Ver. 1.—*A mother's counsel.* The last chapter of the Book of Proverbs gives us the picture of a mother's counsel to her son—wise and good and eloquent with love and yearning anxiety. Here is a picture to suggest the inestimable advantage to a young man of a mother's guidance. In thoughtless, high-spirited youth this too often passes unheeded, and precious advice is then wasted on ungrateful ears. It would be more seemly to consider its unique merits.

I. IT SPRINGS FROM A WOMAN'S NATURE. We have many beautiful pictures of women in the Bible. Inspired women have conveyed to us some parts of the biblical teaching. Deborah (Judg. v. 7), the mother of Samuel, and now the mother of Lemuel, all help us with great Divine truths or holy thoughts and influences. It is the gift of women to see into truth with a flash of sympathy. The wonder is that we have so small a part of the Bible from the tongue and pen of women.

II. IT IS INSPIRED BY A MOTHER'S HEART. The biblical gallery of holy women does not introduce us to the cloisters. The Hebrew heroines were "mothers in Israel," not nuns. Maternity completes woman. "The perfect woman, nobly planned," is one who can think, love, and act with the large heart of a mother.

III. IT IS CHARACTERIZED BY UNSELFISH DEVOTION. There is nowhere in all creation such an image of utterly unselfish, of completely self-sacrificing love as that of a woman for her child. She almost gives her life for his infant existence. All through his helpless years she watches over him with untiring care. When he goes forth into the world, she follows him with never-flagging interest. He may forget her; she will never forget him. If he does well, her joy is unbounded; if he does ill, her heart is broken. Without a thought of self, she spends herself on her child, and finds her life or her death in his conduct.

IV. IT IS GUIDED BY DEEP KNOWLEDGE. The mother may not know much of the outer world; she may be quite ignorant of the most recent dicta of science; some of her notions may seem old-fashioned to her modern-minded son. But foolish indeed will he be if he dares to despise her counsels on such grounds. She knows *him*—his strength and his weakness, his childish faults and his early promises. Here lies the secret of her wisdom.

V. IT CANNOT BE NEGLECTED WITHOUT CRUEL INGRATITUDE. The son may think himself wiser than his mother, but at least he should give reverent attention to her advice. So much love and care and thoughtfulness do not deserve to be tossed aside in a moment of impatience. The wise son will acknowledge that his mother's wishes deserve his most earnest consideration. It may be, then, that he will be held back in the hour of temptation by the thought of the poignant grief that his shameful fall would give to his mother. It is much for a life to be worthy of a good Christian mother's counsel.

Vers. 10—31.—*The typical woman.* I. HER SPHERE. This is domestic. 1. *In marriage.* The typical woman is a wife and mother, not a St. Agnes, the mystical bride of Christ, nor even a Virgin Mary. We see her in Sarah, in Naomi, in Hannah, in Eunice. There is invaluable service for the world which only women who are free from the ties of home can accomplish; there is a noble mission for single women. But there is nothing in Scripture, reason, or conscience to suggest that virginity is more holy than marriage, that the maiden is more saintly than the matron. 2. *In the work of the home.* Moreover, for unmarried women household cares and quiet home duties usually have the first call. Some women may be called to more public positions. A queen may adorn a throne. A Florence Nightingale may live as an angel of mercy to the suffering. But these are exceptional persons. Every Jewess was not a Deborah, and even the martial prophetess, unlike her French counterpart, Joan of Arc, was "a mother in Israel." 3. *Therefore with domestic responsibility.* The typical woman will be judged primarily in regard to domestic duties. The true wife is the helpmeet of her husband. Her first aim will be to "do him good" (ver. 12). If she fails here, her public service is of little account.

II. HER CHARACTER. This is described in a graphic picture of her life—a picture which is in striking contrast to the ignorance, the indolence, the inanity of an Oriental harem. Observe its chief features. 1. *Trustworthiness.* The true wife is her husband's confidant. She must be worthy of confidence by being (1) faithful, (2) sympathetic, (3) intelligent. 2. *Industry.* Nothing can be more foolish than the notion that a "lady" should have no occupation. The ideal woman rises early and busies herself with many affairs. In old days, when the spinning was done at home and most of the family garments were made by the women of the house, the clothing of husband and children bore testimony to the industry of the wife. Machinery has destroyed this antique picture. Yet the spirit of it remains. The true wife still finds an abundance of domestic occupations. 3. *Thrift.* The wife of the Proverbs is quite a business woman, selling the superfluous work of her hands to merchants, and buying land with the proceeds. Yet by her foresight she provides warm clothing for the winter, and therefore she can afford to laugh when the snow cometh. 4. *Strength.* "She girdeth her loins with strength." The physical education of women is just now receiving especial attention, and rightly so. It is a woman's duty to be strong, if by means of wholesome food and exercise she can conquer weakness. No doubt the ailments of many women spring from lassitude, indolence, and self-surrender. But even when bodily frailty cannot be conquered, strength of soul may be attained. 5. *Charity.* The strong and thrifty wife might be hard, cold, and selfish. But the true woman "stretcheth out her hand to the poor" (ver. 20). 6. *Gracious speech.*

So energetic a woman might still be thought somewhat unlovable if we had not this final trait: "in her tongue is the law of kindness" (ver. 26). How much may the tone of a woman's conversation do to keep peace in a household, and shed over it a spirit of love and gentleness! 7. *True religion.* This is the root of the matter. The typical woman "feareth the Lord" (ver. 30).

III. HER REWARD. 1. *In her influence.* "Her husband is known in the gates." She helps him to honour. Herself too busy in the private sphere to take her part directly in public life, yet indirectly she is a great force in the large world through her influence over her husband. 2. *In the success of her energies.* We have here a picture of a wife in affluence—not of a poor domestic drudge in the squalor of abject poverty. Nevertheless, the prosperity of the home largely depends upon her. Her thoughtfulness, energy, careful oversight of others and kindness of heart and words, are the chief causes of the welfare of her happy, comfortable home. 3. *In the honour of her family.* "Her children arise up, and call her blessed; her husband also, and he praiseth her" (ver. 28). Surely this is a better reward than public fame. 4. *Continued influence.* This true woman deserves to have "the fruit of her hands." If she is to be spoken of "in the gates," it should be in praise of her domestic duties, which cannot but be known to her neighbours, however modest and retiring her manners may be.

Ver. 30.—*Rival attractions.* Lemuel's mother warns her son against the fascinations of superficial charms in his choice of a wife, and points to the attractiveness of a God-fearing woman.

I. THE VANITY OF BEAUTY. 1. *It is but temporary.* The bloom of beauty fades with youth; but a wife is to be a man's helpmeet throughout life, and, if both are spared, his companion in age. In making a choice for life a man should consider enduring traits. 2. *It is superficial.* Beauty of face and grace of form are only bodily attributes. They may have no corresponding mental, moral, and spiritual merits. 3. *It is deceptive.* The fascination of a pretty face may delude a man into neglecting more important considerations in the woman of his choice. Ill temper may be taken for strength of character, frivolity for liveliness, mere softness of disposition for love. But the great disillusion of lifelong companionship will dispel all these mistakes, when the discovery is too late to be of any use. On the other hand, there is no need to take refuge in a monkish contempt of beauty. All beauty is a work of God. It is the duty of a woman to make herself pleasing to others. The finest beauty is a product of health, good temper, and the expression of worthy sentiments—all of them desirable things. Note: The vanity of beauty shows the mistake of pursuing "art for art's sake," to the neglect of morality, duty, truth, and charity.

II. THE GRACE OF RELIGION. The "woman that feareth the Lord" is to be praised. Though, perhaps, less beautiful in form and countenance, she has the higher beauty of holiness. The Madonna stands infinitely above the Venus. The grace of the God-fearing woman has its own true attraction for those who can appreciate it. 1. It is *enduring.* Beauty fades; goodness endures. This should ripen with years into a more rich and mellow grace. 2. It is *deep.* The prolonged acquaintanceship that reveals the utter hollowness and unreality of those attractions which consist only in bodily form and skin-complexion only makes more apparent the treasures of a true and worthy character. Trouble that ploughs fatal furrows in the cheek of the mere "beauty" unveils the tender grace of the truly godly woman. Those scenes wherein earthly beauty fails open up wondrous treasures of heavenly grace. 3. It is *satisfying.* A feverish excitement accompanies the adoration of earthly beauty; but the beauty of a sweet, true, generous soul is restful and comforting. 4. It is *worthy of honour.* Poets give us their dreams of fair women. A higher subject would be the praises of God-fearing women. How much of the world's blessedness springs from the devotion of unselfish women—the self-sacrifices of true wives, the toils and prayers of good mothers!

Ver. 31.—*Woman's rights.* The strenuous advocacy of the rights of women by shrill oratory has injured the true cause of women by covering a serious subject with ridicule, and suggesting the unreality of the grievances urged. When extravagant demands are made, people assume that every just right has been conceded; and when the self-elected advocates of women put forth a programme which the great body of wives and daughters repudiate, it is supposed that there is no ground for considering any complaint as to the legal and social treatment of women. But this is unreasonable and unjust. There are women's rights, and these rights are by no means universally conceded.

I. WOMEN HAVE A RIGHT TO WORK. The Oriental notion, that women are but idle ornaments of the harem, finds no place in the Bible. Here they appear freely in the world, and, though their first duties are in the home, they are not idle, nor are they wanting in enterprise. The ideal woman in the Book of Proverbs is a manufacturer, a merchant, and a landowner. Woman's work cannot be wholly the same as man's, because nature has placed limitations upon her physical energies. But she has spheres for work, and it is cruel, unjust, and selfish to keep her out of any region of activity where she can do good service, by law or by social displeasure. Two wrongs in particular need to be swept away. 1. *The notion that work is degrading to a woman.* Surely idleness is more degrading. It is rightly said that woman's sphere is the home. But it is not every woman who has a home. Surely it is a degrading and insulting idea that the main business of a young woman is to secure a husband, and so obtain a home. There are women who are manifestly cut out for other positions; many women never have an opportunity of obtaining a home of their own except by sacrificing themselves to men whom they do not love. In early life young girls are not the better for being kept in idleness, waiting for the chance that may turn up. Half the ailments of women of the comfortable classes come from want of occupation. It needs to be known and recognized that it is a right and honourable thing for a woman to be engaged in any ordinary occupation that is suitable to her powers. 2. *The fear of rivalry with men.* There have been professions the members of which have bitterly resented the invasion of their ranks by women. Such trade-unionism is most ungenerous. It is an humiliation to have to confess that men could not hold their own unless under a system of protection against the competition of women. Certainly no Christian principle can justify such selfishness.

II. WOMEN HAVE A RIGHT TO THE RESULTS OF THEIR WORK. 1. *In payment.* The wife who earns wages has a right to her purse as much as the husband to his. Where there is a true marriage, no thought of separate interests will rouse any jealousy as to the several possessions of the two. But true marriage is not always realized. We see brutal husbands living idly on the earnings of their wives. It is not enough that the poor women are supposed to be protected by a Married Woman's Property Act, for the husband is still too often the tyrant of the home. We shall only see a more just arrangement when Christian principles are applied to domestic practices. 2. *In honour.* " Let her own works praise her in the gates." Women who contribute to the service of society are deserving of double honour, because they have had to work under exceptional disadvantages. Women who have proved themselves wise, industrious, and generous in the home-life do not receive their meed of praise. Too much is taken for granted, and accepted without thanks, because the service is constant and the sacrifice habitual. In after-years, when it is too late to give the due acknowledgment, many a man has had to feel sharp pangs of regret at his heedless treatment of a wife's patient toil or a mother's yearning love. 3. *In position.* Opportunity should be proportionate to capacity. If women can work, they should have scope for work. It is the duty of Christian society to give to woman her true position. If she be " the weaker vessel," she needs more consideration, not less justice. Christ gave high honours to women, accepted their devoted service, and laid the foundation of Christian justice in regard to them.

HOMILIES BY VARIOUS AUTHORS.

Vers. 1—31.—*The words of Lemuel.* The fear of God is the leading thought in these meditations; and this in a twofold relation—to the king in his rule in the state, and the woman in her rule in the house.

Vers. 2—9.—*A mother's maxims.* The mother's heart, deep in emotions of affection and urgent solicitude, is expressed in the passionate form of the address.

I. On WOMEN, OR THE DUTY OF CHASTITY. (Ver. 3.) The weakness of this passion was one of the things, Alexander the Great was wont to say, which reminded him that he was mortal. David and Solomon were both warnings and beacon-lights against yielding to it (2 Sam. xii. 9, 10; comp. ch. ii., v., vii.).

II. On WINE, OR THE DUTY OF TEMPERANCE. (Ver. 4. *sqq.*) Here is a sin in close affinity to the former (Hos. iv. 11). 1. *A vice degrading in all, drunkenness is most especially unbefitting those in high station.* Elah (1 Kings xvi. 8, 9), Benhadad (1 Kings xx. 16), and Belshazzar (Dan. v. 2—4), were all dark examples of the danger (comp. Hos. vii. 5). 2. *It may lead to moral perversion.* (Ver. 5.) The woman wrongly condemned by Philip of Macedon exclaimed, "I appeal from Philip drunk to Philip sober." Ahasuerus (Esth. i. 10, 11) and Herod (Mark vi. 21—28) appear to have been guilty of arbitrary conduct under the same besotting influence. Men "err through strong drink" (Isa. xxviii. 7). 3. *The true use of wine.* (Ver. 6.) It is a medicine for the fainting. It is a restorative under extreme depression. The Bible tolerates and admits the blessing of wine in moderation as promotive of social cheerfulness. It "maketh glad the heart of man," and is even said to "cheer God" (Judg. ix. 13). Hence libations were a part of the sacrificial feast offered to the Majesty on high. As an *anodyne* it is admitted here (ver. 7). But all this does not exempt from close circumspection as to time, place, persons, and circumstances in its use. The priests, when performing their sacred functions in the tabernacle and temple, were to abstain from wine. But here, as in other matters, there is large latitude given to the exercise of the private judgment, the personal Christian conscience. Any attempt to overrule the right of personal freedom creates a new class of evils. Let those who see their duty in that light adopt total abstinence; and others labour according to their ability to strike at the indirect and deeper causes of what many regard as a national vice. Wherever there is a widespread vice, it is rooted in some profound misery. The surest, though longest, cure is by the eradication of the pain of the mind which drives so many towards the nepenthes, or draught of oblivion.

III. On THE FREE AND FULL ADMINISTRATION OF JUSTICE. (Vers. 8, 9.) The royal heart and hand are to be at the service of those who cannot help themselves—the widow, the orphan, the poor, and "all that are desolate and oppressed" (Job xxix. 15, 16). He is to be both advocate and judge. He is to be an earthly type of God. "Let his representatives on earth study the character of their King in heaven, and be conformed more fully to his image of forgiveness and love."—J.

Vers. 10—31.—*The virtuous housewife.* I. HER INFLUENCE IN THE SPHERE OF HOME. (Vers. 10—22.) 1. *Her exceeding worth.* (Vers. 10—12.) A costly treasure not everywhere to be found; no commonplace blessing: an ornament and a joy above all that earth affords of rare and beautiful. A treasure on which the heart of the possessor ever dwells with delight.

> "Continual comfort in a face,
> The lineaments of gospel books."

She is the rich source of revenue to her husband in all good things.

> "All other goods by fortune's hand are given;
> A wife is the peculiar gift of Heaven."
>
> (Pope.)

"If women be good," said Aristotle, "the half of the commonwealth may be happy where they are." "The greatest gift of God is a pious, amiable spouse, who fears God, loves his house, and with whom one can live in perfect confidence" (Luther). 2. *The picture of her domestic industry.* (Vers. 13—22.) It is an antique picture, the form and colouring derived from ancient custom; but the general moral effect is true for all times. The traits of the housewifely character are: (1) *The personal example of diligence.* She is seen from day to day spinning at her loom, the chief occupation of women in ancient times. She is an early riser (ver. 15). (2) *Her unrelaxing energy.* (Ver. 17.) She has no idle hour; her rest is in change of occupation. (3) *Her personal attention to business.* (Vers. 16, 18.) Whether examining land with a view to invest her savings in purchase and cultivation, or inspecting goods, her mind is in all she does.

She is not slothful in business, but glowing in spirit, and all that she does is done with heart. (4) *Her benevolence.* Her thrift is not of the odious form which begins and ends with home, and breeds a sordid miserliness out of hard-won gains. Her open hand outstretched to the poor (ver. 20) is one of the most winning traits in the picture. She has no lack of good herself, and always something over for the needy. (5) *Her care both for comfort and for ornament.* (Vers. 21, 22.) Both the very spheres of woman's activity. But she observes their true order. Her first thought is for the health of her household; she provides the warm "double garments" against the winter's snow. Her leisure is occupied with those fine works of artistic needlework by which elegance and beauty are contributed to the scene of home. Refinement adorning comfort,—this is the true relation. In finery without solid use and comfort there is no beauty nor worth.

II. FURTHER TRAITS AND DETAILS OF THE PICTURE. (Vers. 23—31.) 1. *She reflects consideration on her husband.* Her thrift makes him rich; her noble character gives him additional title to respect. His personality derives weight from the possession of such a treasure, the devotion of such a heart. Her business capacity, her energy, and the quiet dignity of her life and bearing; the mingled sense and shrewdness, charm and grace of her conversation (vers. 24—27);—are all a source of fame, of noble self-complacency, of just confidence to the man who is blessed to call her "mine." 2. *Her life and work earn for her perpetual thanks and benedictions.* (Vers. 28, 29.) Her children, as they grow up, bless her for the inestimable boon of a mother's care and love. She has revealed to them God; and never can they cease to believe in goodness so long as they recollect her. She basks in the sunshine of a husband's constant approval. "Best of wives!" "Noblest of women!" is the thought ever in his heart, often on his lips. 3. *It is religion which gives enduring worth and immortality to character.* (Vers. 30, 31.) Beauty is a failing charm or a deception of the senses. But religious principle gives a spiritual beauty to the plainest exterior. Being and doing from religious motives, to religious ends,—this is a sowing for eternal fruits. And the works of love for God's sake and man's fill the air with fragrance to the latest end of time, and are found unto praise, honour, and glory at the appearing of Jesus Christ.—J.

Vers. 1—3.—*Motherhood.* We have not many words from women's lips in the inspired record, and we may therefore esteem the more highly those we possess. The verses bring out—

I. THE STRONG CLAIMS OF MOTHERHOOD. "The son of my womb;" "the son of my vows." These claims are based upon: 1. *Motherhood as such.* Upon all that motherhood means to us; upon the fact that the mother has borne her child, has cherished him at her own breast, has watched over his infancy and childhood with sedulous care, has shielded and succoured him, has fed and clothed him; as we say in one word—has "mothered" him. 2. *Motherly training and dedication.* The early experiences of the mother include much beyond the physical realm; they include the education of the intellect, the training of the will, the first imparting of religious instruction, the solemn dedication of her child to the service of God, repeated and earnest prayer on his behalf. Her child is not only her offspring; he is "the son of her vows," the one on whom she has expended her most fervent piety. 3. *Maternal affection and anxiety.* The words of Lemuel's mother are charged with deep affection and profound solicitude. And it is those who truly love us, and who are unselfishly devoted to our interest, that have the strongest claim upon us. A claim which is only that of natural relationship, and is not crowned and completed by affection, falls very short indeed of that which is strengthened and sanctified by sacrificial love.

II. THE HOPE OF MOTHERHOOD. The mother hopes for good and even great things for and from her child; he is to stand among the strong, the wise, the honoured, the useful.

III. ITS BITTER AND CRUEL DISAPPOINTMENT. When the son of much sorrow and prayer, of much patient training and earnest entreaty, who had a noble opportunity before him—when he virtually signs away his inheritance, "gives his strength" to the destroyer, takes the path which leads to entire dethronement and ruin, then is there such a bitter and such a cruel disappointment as only a mother's heart can feel and know. Then perishes a fond and proud and precious hope; then enters and takes possession a saddening, a crushing sorrow.

IV. Its right to remonstrate. " What, my son ? This of thee ?—of thee whom I have loved and taught and trained ? of thee for whom I have yearned and prayed ? of thee from whom I have had a right to hope for such better things ? Oh, lose not thy fair heritage ! take the portion, live the life, wear the crown, still within thy reach ! " A true and faithful mother has a right which is wholly indisputable, and strong with surpassing strength, to speak thus in affectionate expostulation to one who owes so much to her, and has returned her nothing. And what is—

V. The filial duty ? Surely it is to receive such remonstrance with deep respect ; to give to it a patient and dutiful attention ; to take it into long and earnest consideration ; to resolve that, cost what it may, the path of penitence and renewal shall be trodden ; that anything shall be endured rather than a mother's heart be pierced by the hand of her own child !—C.

Ver. 6.—*The allowable as the exceptional.* It is often the case that that which is wrong as a rule is right as an exception ; what it would be unwise, if not unlawful, to do under ordinary circumstances, it may be most wise and even obligatory to do in emergencies. This applies particularly, but not exclusively, to the subject of the text—

I. The use of stimulants. In a state of health and during the discharge of daily duties, shun the use of stimulants ; depend upon that which nourishes and builds up. " Give strong drink unto him that is ready to perish ; " to the man who, by exposure or by some suddenly inflicted wound, or by starvation, is brought down to the brink of death, administer the reviving cordial. What we should not depend upon for daily strength we do well to fall back upon in the time of extremity, or in the case of special need.

II. The employment of strong language or very vivid illustration. It is a great mistake to be always speaking in superlatives, or to be habitually indulging in expletives, or to be regularly resorting to highly coloured illustrations. It is a sign and also a source of weakness. These very soon lose their power by repetition, and then there is nothing in reserve. And the man who has no power in reserve is he who will find himself beaten in the battle. Temperate language, moderation in the use of imagery and the expression of disapproval, is the true and wise course. Strong language is for quite exceptional cases ; it has its opportunity, but should be content to wait for it.

III. Resort to violence. There are occasions when physical force should be and must be employed. The magistrate is compelled to resort to it ; so also is the schoolmaster, and even the parent. But the less the better. Bodily chastisement is always regrettable, and only to be resorted to when all other means have failed. Its constant exercise only hardens the object of it, and it is not unlikely to harden the hand that administers it. The wise teacher and the wise parent will do his best to reduce it to its very lowest point.

IV. Affectionate demonstrativeness. This has its time and place, but it is an exceptional rather than a constant one in the conduct of our life. When any one has lacked the tenderness and the affection which our heart craves, and is hungry for human love, when the free and full manifestation of heartfelt kindness will be like water to the parched lips, let it be freely and fully given. But the perpetual exhibition of endearment, whether in word or deed, is a mistake.

V. The appeal to self-interest on the part of the moralist and religious teacher. We should, as a rule, place moral obligations and religious duty on the ground of conviction ; we should continually endeavour to impress men with the feeling that they are sacredly bound to respect themselves, to regard the rights of their brethren, to respond to the claims of God, their Father and their Saviour. Religion is the response of the human soul to the boundless claim of Infinite Goodness and Love. But Christ has himself taught us that it is right and well sometimes to make our appeal to the sense of self-interest—to say to men, " If not for God's sake, who has a sovereign and supreme claim on your attention ; if not for the sake of those who are related to you and dependent on you ; yet for your own sake, because you love life and hate death, hearken and obey " (see Mark viii. 36, 37).—C.

Vers. 8, 9.—*The function and the privilege of power.* God gives to some men place and power; they may inherit it, or they may win their way to it by the force of their talent or their merit. When they have reached it, what should be the use they make of it? We may look first at—

I. WHAT HAS BEEN ITS HABIT. Only too often the actual use that has been made of high station and of civil or military power is that of (1) indulgence; or (2) appropriation; or (3) oppression. Men have used their elevation only to drink the sweet cup of pleasure; or to secure to themselves the spoils of high office, the treasures which lay within their grasp; or to find a mean and despicable gratification in the enforcement of their own dignity and the humiliation of those beneath them. This is "human," if by human we understand that which is natural to man as sin has dwarfed and spoilt his nature, perverting his powers and degrading his delights. But of man as God meant him to be, and as a Divine Redeemer is renewing him, all this is utterly unworthy. Let us see—

II. WHAT IS ITS TRUE FUNCTION. It is that of *righteousness*. A man is placed on high in order that he may "judge righteously." Whether he be the king, as in David's and Solomon's time; or whether he be the magistrate, as in our own time; or whether he be the teacher, or the manufacturer, or the farmer, or the master or father in the home; whatever be the kind or measure of authority enjoyed, the function of power is to judge righteously; it is to do justice; it is to see that innocency is acquitted and guilt condemned; it is to take pains and exercise patience in order that worth may be rewarded and that sin may be shamed; it is to be a tower of refuge to those who are conscious of rectitude, and to be a source of fear to those who know that they have been "doing evil;" it is to be a strength to the righteous and a terror to the guilty.

III. WHAT IT SHOULD COUNT ITS PECULIAR PRIVILEGE; IT IS TO BEFRIEND THE FRIENDLESS. There are those who are too weak to be of much service to their neighbours; there are those who are too selfish to cherish the ambition; but the strong man who is the good man, the man in power who has in him the spirit of his Master, will rejoice in his power mainly because it enables him to help those who would otherwise go on and go down without a helper; (1) those suffering from physical privation —the blind, the deaf, the dumb; (2) those lacking mental qualifications—the weak-minded, the timid, the reserved; (3) those too poor to purchase the aid that is sometimes essential to justice and right; (4) those over whom some great disaster, which is at the same time a cruel wrong, impends—"appointed to destruction." To lift up those who have been wrongfully laid low, to befriend the unfortunate and the desolate, to stand by the side of those who cannot assert their own claims, to be eyes to the blind and a voice to the dumb, to "make the widow's heart to sing for joy," to place the destitute in the path which leads up to competency and honour,—to act in the spirit and to promote the cause of beneficence is the true privilege, as it is the brightest crown and the deepest joy, of power.—C.

Vers. 10—31.—*Christian womanhood.* If Solomon did write these words, we need not be surprised that he speaks of the rarity of the ideal woman; for she is hardly to be found in a crowded harem. It is the Christian home that contains her. We look at—

I. HER CHARACTERISTICS. And these are: 1. *Piety.* "She feareth the Lord" (ver. 30). She has within her the spirit of reverence, and the life she lives is one in which worship and the study of the will of God have no small share. She has a seat and is at home in the sanctuary; she is also constant and earnest in the quiet chamber of devotion; she knows well that the happiness of her home and the well-being of her household depend upon the favour of the heavenly Father. 2. *Purity.* She is a "virtuous woman" (ver. 10). She gives her whole heart to her husband, and enjoys his full confidence (ver. 11). 3. *Industry.* The writer dwells upon the labours she puts forth for the sake of her husband and her household. 4. *Wisdom.* (Ver. 26.) Her conversation is far removed from mere idle gossip or the vanities of an empty curiosity. She is familiar with "the Law of the Lord;" she knows what is the secret of lasting happiness. She can guide her sons and daughters in the way of life; and she instils her heaven-born wisdom into minds that welcome it and will never lose it. 5. *Kindness.* "The law of kindness is on her lips." She is one that does not rule by the "constant droppings" of censure, but by the never-failing stream of gentleness and encouragement. Love, not fear, is the sceptre which she holds, and is the source of her strength. 6. *Beneficence.* (Ver. 20.)

II. HER REWARD. 1. *Affection and honour* on the part of those who are nearest to her. Her husband trusts and praises her (ver. 28), and her children " rise up and call her blessed." 2. *Strength and dignity* in her home. She is "clothed upon with " the tributes woven by love and esteem. Her influence is felt much oftener than it is recognized, and long after her face and her voice are no longer seen and heard. 3. *Security* against future want. She "laugheth at the time to come," while those who lack her prudence and her skill have reason to shrink from the thought of it. 4. *The prosperity* of her relatives. Her husband, relieved of care and worry at home, is able to do his proper work, and succeeds in his sphere (ver. 23).

III. HER COMMONNESS IN THE KINGDOM OF CHRIST. It might be difficult to find " the virtuous woman" in the land and the time when Lemuel dwelt (ver. 10); but she may be found to-day in any number of Christian homes. Holding the faith of Jesus Christ, governed by his principles, living his life, animated by his Spirit, fulfilling his law of love, the wife and mother is to be seen taking an honoured place, filling her home with the sweet fragrance of purity and affection, exerting her benign and gracious influence on her husband and her children. You have not to take a long journey to reach her, nor to take much pains to find her; she is at home in "the castle of the noble, in the mansion of the wealthy, and in the cottage of the poor and the lowly."

1. Let us freely acknowledge our great indebtedness to her. Those who have had the priceless advantage of a mother possessed of the Christian virtues and graces have more to thank God for than if they had inherited a titled name or an ample fortune. 2. If it be open to us, let us join her ranks. To be a woman living under the commanding influence of Christian principle, breathing a Christian spirit, and shedding a Christian influence in the home in which we live,—what is there, this side the gate of heaven, that any human spirit could more wisely wish to be? To be such is to be doing a most excellent work of God; it is to be filling a most honourable and useful sphere.—C.

HOMILETICAL INDEX

TO

THE PROVERBS

618

INDEX.

[*The Exposition of the first six chapters of this book is by the Rev. S. T. Taylor-Taswell; and that on the remaining chapters by the Rev. W. J. Deane*]

ECCLESIASTES

EXPOSITION BY

W. J. DEANE

HOMILETICS BY

T. WHITELAW

HOMILIES BY VARIOUS AUTHORS

J. R. THOMSON   W. CLARKSON

J. WILLCOCK

ECCLESIASTES ; OR, THE PREACHER

INTRODUCTION

§ 1. TITLE OF THE BOOK

THE book is called in the Hebrew *Koheleth*, a title taken from its opening sentence, " The words of Koheleth, the son of David, King in Jerusalem." In the Greek and Latin Versions it is entitled 'Ecclesiastes,' which Jerome elucidates by remarking that in Greek a person is so called who gathers the congregation, or *ecclesia*. Aquila transliterates the word, Κωλέθ ; what Symmachus gave is uncertain, but probably Παροιμιαστής, ' Proverb-monger.' The Venetian Greek has Ἡ Ἐκκλησιάστρια and Ἡ Ἐκκλησιάζουσα. In modern versions the name is usually 'Ecclesiastes; or, The Preacher.' Luther boldly gives 'The Preacher Solomon.' This is not a satisfactory rendering to modern ears; and, indeed, it is difficult to find a term which will adequately represent the Hebrew word. *Koheleth* is a participle feminine from a root *kahal* (whence the Greek καλέω, Latin *calo*, and English " call "), which means, " to call, to assemble," especially for religious or solemn purposes. The word and its derivatives are always applied to people, and not to things. So the term, which gives its name to our book, signifies a female assembler or collector of persons for Divine worship, or in order to address them. It can, therefore, not mean " Gatherer of wisdom," " Collector of maxims," but " Gatherer of God's people " (1 Kings viii. 1) ; others make it equivalent to " Debater," which term affords a clue to the variation of opinions in the work. It is generally constructed as a masculine and without the article, but once as feminine (ch. vii. 27, if the reading is correct), and once with the article (ch. xii. 8). The feminine form is by some accounted for, not by supposing Koheleth to represent an office, and therefore as used abstractedly, but as being the personification of Wisdom, whose business it is to gather people unto the Lord and make them a holy congregation. In Proverbs sometimes Wisdom herself speaks (*e.g.* Prov. i. 20), sometimes the author speaks of her (*e.g.* Prov. viii. 1, etc.). So

Koheleth appears now as the organ of Wisdom, now as Wisdom herself, supporting, as it were, two characters without losing altogether his identity. At the same time, it is to be noted, with Wright, that Solomon, as personified Wisdom, could not speak of himself as having gotten more wisdom than all that were before him in Jerusalem (ch. i. 16), or how his heart had great experience of wisdom, or how he had applied his heart to discover things by means of wisdom (ch. vii. 23, 25). These things could not be said in this character, and unless we suppose that the writer occasionally lost himself, or did not strictly maintain his assumed personation, we must fall back upon the ascertained fact that the feminine form of such words as Koheleth has no special significance (unless, perhaps, it denotes power and activity), and that such forms were used in the later stage of the language to express proper names of men. Thus we find *Sophereth*, "scribe" (Neh. vii. 57), and *Pochereth*, "hunter" (Ezra ii. 57), where certainly males are intended. Parallels are found in the Mishna. If, as is supposed, Solomon is designated Koheleth in allusion to his great prayer at the dedication of the temple (1 Kings viii. 23—53, 56—61), it is strange that no mention is anywhere made of this celebrated work, and the part he took therein. He appears rather as addressing general readers than teaching his own people from an elevated position; and the title assigned to him is meant to designate him, not only as one who by word of mouth instructed others, but one whose life and experience preached an emphatic lesson on the vanity of mundane things.

§ 2. Author and Date.

The universal consent of antiquity attributed the authorship of Ecclesiastes to Solomon. The title assumed by the writer, " Son of David, King in Jerusalem," was considered sufficient warrant for the assertion, and no suspicion of its uncertainty ever crossed the minds of commentators and readers from primitive to mediæval times. Whenever the book is referred to, it is always noted as a work of Solomon. The Greek and Latin Fathers alike agree in this matter. The four Gregories, Athanasius, Ambrose, Jerome, Theodoret, Olympiodorus, Augustine, and others, are here of one consent. The Jews, too, although they had some doubts concerning the orthodoxy of the contents, never disputed the authorship. The first to throw discredit upon the received opinion was Luther, who, in his 'Table Talk,' while ridiculing the traditional view, boldly asserts that the work was composed by Sirach, in the time of the Maccabees. Grotius followed in the same strain. In his 'Commentary on the Old Testament' he unhesitatingly denies it to be a production of Solomon, and in another place assigns to it a post-exilian date. These opinions attracted but little notice at the time; but towards the close of the last century, three German scholars, Döderlein, Jahn, and Schmidt, revived the objections urged by Luther and Grotius, and henceforward a continuous stream of criticism, opposed to the earlier tenet, has flowed forth both in England, America, and Germany. The array of writers on both sides is enormous. The discussion has evoked the energies of innumerable controversialists, though the opponents of Solomon have in late years far outnumbered his supporters. If the more ancient opinion is upheld by Dr. Pusey, Bishop Wordsworth, Mr. Johnston, Mr. Bullock, Motais, Gietmann, etc., the later view is strongly supported by Keil, Delitzsch, Hengstenberg, Vaihinger, Hitzig, Nowack, Renan, Ginsburg, Ewald, Davidson, Noyes, Stuart, Wright, etc. The question cannot be settled by the authority of writers on either side, but must be calmly examined, and the arguments adduced by both parties must be duly weighed.

Let us see what are the usual arguments for the Solomonic authorship. We will endeavour to set them forth very briefly, but fairly and intelligibly.

1. The first and most potent is the unanimous verdict of all writers who have mentioned the book from primitive times to the days of Luther, whether Christian or Jewish. The common opinion was that the three works, Canticles, Proverbs, and Ecclesiastes, were composed by Solomon; the first, as some said, being the production of his earlier days, the second written in his maturity, and the third dictated at the close of life, when he had learned the vanity of all that he had once valued, and had repented of his evil ways and turned once more to the fear of the Lord as the only stable comfort and hope. St. Jerome, in his 'Commentary,' gives the opinion which was prevalent in his day: "Itaque juxta numerum vocabulorum tria volumina edidit: Proverbia, Ecclesiasten, et Cantica Canticorum. In Proverbiis parvulum docens et quasi de officiis per sententias erudiens; in Ecclesiaste vero maturæ virum ætatis instituens, ne quicquam in mundi rebus putet esse perpetuum, sed caduca et brevia universa quæ cernimus; ad extremum jam consummatum virum et calcato sæculo præparatum, in Cantico Canticorum sponsi jungit amplexibus."

2. The book purports to be written by Solomon; the writer speaks continually in the first person; and as the work is confessedly inspired and canonical, any doubt as to the literal accuracy of the inscription throws discredit on the truth and authority of Scripture. In a treatise of this nature it is altogether unlikely that the author should attribute his own sentiments to another.

3. There is nothing in the contents which militates against the Solomonic authorship.

4. There is nothing in the language which is not compatible with the time of Solomon.

5. It is a composition of such consummate skill and excellence that it could have proceeded from no one but this wisest of men.

6. There are such a multitude and variety of coincidences in expression and phraseology with Proverbs and Canticles, which are confessedly more or less the work of Solomon, that Ecclesiastes must proceed from the same author.

Such are the grounds upon which Ecclesiastes is attributed to Solomon. The opinion has a certain attraction for all simple believers, who are content to take things on trust, and, provided a theory makes no very violent demands on credulity, to accept it with unquestioning confidence. But in the present case the arguments adduced have not withstood the attacks of modern criticism, as will be seen if we take them *seriatim*, as we proceed to do.

1. The universal consensus of uncritical antiquity concerning authorship is of little value. What was not questioned was not specially examined; the conventional opinion was regarded as certain; what one writer after another, and Council after Council, actually or virtually stated, was accepted generally and without any controversy. So the authorship, being taken for granted, was never criticized or investigated. Of how small importance in such a matter are the opinions of the Fathers, we may learn from their view of the Book of Wisdom. Unhesitatingly many of them attribute this work to Solomon. Clemens Alexandrinus, Cyprian, Origen, Didymus, and others express no doubt whatever on the subject; and yet no one nowadays hesitates to say that they were absurdly wrong in holding such an opinion. Similarly, many Councils decreed the canonicity of Wisdom, from the third of Carthage, A.D. 397, to that of Trent; but we do not give our adhesion to their decision. So we may reject tradition in discussing the question of authorship, and pursue our investigation independently, untrammelled by the utterances of earlier writers. As to the assertion that Solomon penned this treatise in sorrowful repentance for his idolatry and licentiousness and arrogant selfishness, it must be said that there is no trace of any such change of heart in the historical books; as far as we are told, he goes to his grave after he had turned away from the Lord, in that hard, unbelieving temper which his foreign alliances had produced in him. Not a hint of better things is anywhere afforded; and though, from the commendation generally accorded to him, and the typical character which he possessed, one would be inclined to think that he could not have died in his sins, but must have made his peace with God before he departed, yet Scripture supplies no ground for such an opinion, and we must travel beyond the letter to arrive at such a conclusion. He records his experience of evil pleasure, relates how he revelled in vice for a time, took his fill of luxury and sensuality, with the view, as he says, of testing the faculty of such excesses to give happiness; but he never hints at any sorrow for this degradation; not a word of repentance falls from his lips. " I turned, and tried this and that," he says; but we find no confession of sin, no remorse for wasted talents. He learns, indeed, that all is vanity and vexation of spirit; but this is not the cry of a broken and contrite heart; and to ground his repentance upon this declaration is to raise a structure upon a foundation that will not bear its weight.

2. There can be no doubt that the writer intends to assume the name and characteristics of Solomon. He calls himself in the opening verse " son of David " and " King in Jerusalem." Such a description applies

only to Solomon. David, indeed, had many other sons, but none except Solomon could be designated " King in Jerusalem." It is true also that the first person is continually used in narrating experiences which are especially appropriate to this monarch; e.g. "I am come to great estate, and have gotten more wisdom than all that were before me" (ch. i. 16) ; "I made me great works; I builded me houses " (ch. ii. 4) ; "All this have I proved by wisdom : I said, I will be wise " (ch. vii. 23). But not thus is Solomon demonstrated to be the actual author ; cleverly personated authorship would use the same expressions. And this is what we conceive to be the fact. The writer assumes the *rôle* of Solomon in order to emphasize and add weight to the lessons which he desired to teach. The idea that such personation is fraudulent and unworthy of a sacred writer springs from ignorance of precedents or a misunderstanding of the object of such substitution. Who thinks of accusing Plato or Cicero of an intention to deceive because they present their sentiments in the form of dialogues between imaginary interlocutors ? Who regards the author of the Book of Wisdom as an impostor because he identifies himself with the wise king ? So common was this system of personation, so widely spread and practised, that a name was invented for it, and *Pseudepigraphal* was the title given to all such works as assumed to be written by some well-known or celebrated personage, the real author concealing his own identity. Thus we have the ' Book of Enoch,' the ' Ascension of Isaiah,' the ' Assumption of Moses,' the ' Apocalypse of Baruch,' the ' Psalter of Solomon,' and many more, none of them being the production of the person whose name they bear, which was assumed only for literary purposes. A moralist who felt that he had something to impart that might serve his generation, a patriot who desired to encourage his countrymen amid defeat and oppression, a pious thinker whose heart glowed with love for his fellow-men,—any of these, humbly shrinking from obtruding upon notice his own obscure personality, thought himself justified in publishing his reflections under the mantle of some great name which might gain for them credit and acceptance. The *ruse* was so well understood that it deceived nobody ; but it gave point and definiteness to the writer's lucubration, and it also had the effect of making readers more ready to accept it, and to look in its contents for something worthy of the personage to whom it was attributed. There is nothing in this derogatory to a sacred writer, and no argument against the personation can be maintained on the ground of its incongruity or inappropriateness. And when we more carefully examine the language of the book itself, we see that it contains virtual, if not actual, acknowledgment that it is not written by Solomon. His name is not once mentioned. Other of his reputed writings are inscribed with his name. The Canticles begin with the words, " The song of songs, which is Solomon's ; " the Proverbs are, " The proverbs of Solomon, son of David, King of Israel." Ps. lxxii. is entitled, " A Psalm of Solomon." But our author gives himself an enigmatical appellation, which by its very form might show that it was ideal and representative, and not that of an existing personality. To suppose that Solomon uses this name (which may be interpreted " Gatherer ") for himself, with the abstruse idea that he who had *scattered* the people by his sins now desired to *gather* them together by this exhibition of wisdom, is to task the imagination beyond limit, and to read into Scripture notions which have no existence in fact. There can, indeed, be no adequate reason given why Solomon should have desired thus to conceal his identity; the plea of humility and shame is a mere invention of commentators anxious to account for what is, in their view, really inexplicable. He calls himself " King in Jerusalem "—an expression occurring nowhere else, and never applied to any Hebrew monarch. We read of " King of Israel," " King over all Israel," how that Solomon "reigned in Jerusalem over all Israel; " but the title " King in Jerusalem " is unique, and seems to point to a time when Jerusalem was not the only royal city, after the disruption of the kingdom, that is, subsequent to the epoch of the historical Solomon.

The same conclusion is reached by the occasional wording of the text itself, which speaks of Solomon as belonging to the past age. " I *was* king," the monarch is made to say (ch. i. 12), speaking, not as a reigning monarch himself would speak, but rather as one who, from the other world, or by the mouth of another, was relating his past earthly experiences. Solomon was king to the day of his death, and could never have used the past tense in reference to himself. Delitzsch and Ginsburg have called attention to a Talmudic legend based on this expression. According to this story, Solomon, driven from his throne on account of his idolatries and other sins, roamed through the country lamenting his follies, and reduced to the extremity of want, ever crying, with miserable iteration, " I, Koheleth, was King over Israel in Jerusalem!" The legend is noticeable only as conveying the significance of the preterite tense found in the text. This tense cannot, in view of the immediate context, be translated, " I have been and still am king; " nor is he saying that he was king when he applied his mind to wisdom. He is simply introducing himself in his assumed character, not comparing his present with his past life, but from his standpoint, as once an earthly and powerful king, giving the weight of his experiences. In another passage (ch. i. 16) he talks of having gotten more wisdom than all that were before him in Jerusalem. Now, this city did not fall into the possession of the Hebrews till some years after the accession of David: how could Solomon refer to previous kings in these terms, when really only one had preceded him? And that his reference is to rulers, and not to mere inhabitants, is denoted by the use of the preposition *al*, which ought to be translated " over," not " in " Jerusalem. Commentators have endeavoured to answer this objection by asserting that Solomon hereby indicates the ancient Canaanitish kings, such as Melchizedek, Adonizedek, Araunah; but is it likely that he would thus introduce the thought of these worthies of past generations as though he and his father were their natural successors? Would he condescend to compare himself with such? and would his readers be impressed by a superiority to these princelets, mostly heathens, all of them beyond the pale of Israel, and, with one exception, in no respect celebrated? It is surely much more probable that the author for the moment forgets, or throws aside, his assumed character, and alludes to the long succession of Jewish monarchs who had reigned in Jerusalem up to his own time. A further intimation that a fictitious use is made of the name of the great king is given in the epilogue, supposing it, as we do, to be an original portion of the work. Here (ch. xii. 9—14) the real author speaks of himself and the composition of his book; he is no longer "*the* Koheleth," the Solomon, who hitherto has been the speaker (as in ver. 8), but *a* koheleth, a wise man, who, founding his style on his great predecessor, sought to please and edify the people of his generation by means of proverbial sayings. This is the way in which he describes his undertaking, and in which it is impossible that the historical Solomon should have written: "Moreover, because Koheleth was wise, he still taught the people knowledge; yea, he pondered, and sought out, and put in order many proverbs," and, as the next verse implies, he adopted a form and style which might make the truth "acceptable" to his hearers.

3. Besides the notice mentioned above, there are many statements in the book wholly irreconcilable with the circumstances of Solomon's reign and epoch. In ch. iii. 16; v. 8, etc., we read of oppression of the poor and high-handed perversion of judgment, and are bidden not to wonder thereat. That such a condition of things obtained in the time of Solomon is not conceivable; if it did exist, one would have expected that this powerful monarch would immediately have set about a reformation, and not contented himself with urging patience and acquiescence. But the writer appears to have no power to redress these crying wrongs, which, if he is king, must have been owing to his neglect or misgovernment. He tells what he has seen, sympathizes with the sufferers, offers advice how to make the best of such trouble, but gives no hint that he considers himself answerable for this miserable state of things, or could in any way alleviate or remove it. If, as alleged, this book is the result of Solomon's repentance, the outcome of the revulsion of feeling caused by the warnings of the Prophet Ahijah and the grace of God working in his softened heart, here, surely, was an opportunity of expressing his changed sentiments, acknowledging the wrongdoing which occasioned the disorders in the administration of government, and avowing a determination of redress. But there is nothing of the kind. He writes as an uninterested observer, one who had no hand in producing, and possesses no influence in checking, oppression. So, too, Solomon could not have written of his own class and country in such terms as we read in ch. x. 16, "Woe to thee, O land, when thy king is a child, and thy princes eat in the morning!" It is doing violence to language, if not to common sense, to argue that Solomon is alluding to his son Rehoboam, who must have been more than forty years old at this time; and it does not speak well for the king's repentance if, knowing that his son would turn out so

badly, he made no effort for his reformation, nor, following the precedent observed in his own case, attempted to nominate a more worthy successor. Here and in other remarks about kings (*e.g.* ch. x. 20) the writer speaks, not as though he himself were a monarch, but merely as a philosopher or student of human nature. If he introduces the great king as uttering the sentiments, they arc his own experiences which he records (ch. x. 4—7): the spirit of the ruler rising against a subject, a fool set in high dignity and the rich debased to low places, servants upon horses, and princes walking as servants upon the earth;—such circumstances one can ill imagine the historical Solomon to have known and recorded, though they might readily enough have been witnessed by one who made him the vehicle of his life-history.

Again, can one suppose that Solomon would call the heir to his throne "the man that should be after" him (ch. ii. 18), and hate his labour because its fruits would fall into such unworthy hands? Or that, being well aware who his successor would be, he should speak as if it were quite uncertain— one of those future contingencies which no one could determine (ch. ii. 19)? To minimize the force of the objection here made, some critics assert that Solomon utters this sentiment after Jeroboam's attempted rebellion, and with the fear of this restless and unscrupulous leader's success lying heavy on his mind; but there is no historical ground for this notion. As far as we know, no dread of a revolution troubled his last days. Jeroboam had been driven into exile; and it is quite a gratuitous assumption that the fear of his return and forcible seizure of the throne dictated the words in the text.

There are other incongruities in connection with the relation of monarch and subject. The passage ch. viii. 2—5, 9 contains advice, not from a ruler to his dependents, but from a subject to his fellow-subjects: "I counsel thee to keep the king's commandment," etc. It is a prudent exhortation, showing how to behave under a tyrannical government, when "one man ruleth over another to the other's hurt," and could never have emanated from great David's greater son.

Again, is it compatible with the modesty of a refined disposition that Solomon should boast unrestrainedly of his intellectual acquirements (ch. i. 16), his possessions, his greatness (ch. ii. 7—9)? Such exultation might proceed naturally enough from a fictitious person, but would be most unseemly in the mouth of the real character. Is he satirizing himself when he denounces the royal spendthrift, glutton, and debauchee, and describes the misery which he brings on the land (ch. x. 16—19)? Is it not much more likely that Koheleth is drawing from his own experience of licentious rulers, which concerns not Solomon at all? Then, again, the course of philosophical investigation into the *summum bonum* depicted in the book is wholly incompatible with the historical Solomon. There is no evidence whatever that he entered into any such inquiry and pursued it with the view herein intimated. The writer gives a fair account of many of the king's great undertakings—his palaces, gardens, reservoirs, his feasts, sensuality, and carnal enjoyments; but there is no hint in the history that these things were only parts of a great experiment, steps on the path that might lead to the knowledge of happiness. Rather they are represented in the annals as the outcome of wealth, luxury, pleasure-seeking, selfishness. It is impossible, too, that, in recounting his performances, Solomon should have omitted all mention of that which was the chief glory of his reign—the erection of the temple at Jerusalem. Yet his connection with it is not noticed by the remotest allusion, though there is possibly some mention of the worship there (ch. v. 1, 2) : "Keep thy foot when thou goest to the house of God."

Further, if, as we have seen, the references to Solomon himself are often inconsistent with what we know of his history, the state of society presented by intimations scattered here and there is certainly not that which obtained in his reign. We read of violent oppression and wrong, when tears of agony were wrung from the persecuted, whose misery was so great that they preferred death to life under such intolerable circumstances (ch. iv. 1—3); whereas, in these palmy days of the kingdom, all was peace and plenty : "Judah and Israel were many, as the sand which is by the sea in multitude, eating and drinking, and making merry " (1 Kings iv. 20). Two more antagonistic scenes could scarcely have been depicted, and we cannot suppose them to refer to the same period. It is true that after Solomon's death the people complained that his yoke had been grievous (1 Kings xii. 4); it is also true that he dealt sternly with the strangers and the remnant of the idolatrous nations left in the land (2 Chron. ii. 17, 18; viii. 7, 8); but the former allegation was doubtless exaggerated, and referred chiefly to the taxes and imposts laid upon the people in order to supply the means for carrying out magnificent designs ; there was no complaint of oppression or injustice; it was relief from excessive taxation, and perhaps from enforced labour, that was demanded. The typical character of Solomon's reign would not have afforded a theme of prophetical representation of Messiah's kingdom, had it been the scene of violence, turbulence, and unhappiness which stands before our minds in Koheleth's page. With regard to the possible sufferings of the aboriginals, from whom was exacted bond-service (1 Kings ix. 21), we have no record that they were treated with undue severity; and it is certain that, in any case, Koheleth would not be thinking of them in recounting the misery which he had witnessed. No Hebrew, indeed, would take them into consideration at all. Hewers of wood and drawers of water they became in the nature of things, and of them nothing more was to be said.

Another aspect of affairs, incongruous with Solomon's time, is seen in an allusion to the system of espionage practised under despotic governments (ch. x. 20), where the writer warns his readers to beware how they utter a word, or even cherish a thought, in disparagement of the ruling power; walls have ears ; a bird shall carry the word ; and punishment is sure to follow. Can we believe that Solomon used such a system ? And is it credible that, if he did encourage this odious practice, he would explain and dilate upon it in a popular work ? Once more, it must have been at a much later period that the admonition against unsanctified and diffuse study was needed (ch. xii. 12). The national literature in Solomon's time must have been of the scantiest nature; the warning could have been applicable only when the theories and speculations of Greece and Alexandria had found their way into Palestine (Ginsburg).

Further, it must be noticed that, though God is spoken of continually, it is always by the name of Elohim, never by his covenant appellation, Jehovah. Is it conceivable that the historical Solomon, who had experienced such remarkable mercies and special endowments at the hands of Jehovah, should ignore this Divine relation, and speak of God merely as the Maker of the world, the Governor of the universe ? In Proverbs the name Jehovah occurs nearly a hundred times, Elohim hardly at all; it is preposterous to account for this difference by asserting that Solomon wrote one work while in a state of grace, and hence used the covenant name, and the other after he had fallen, and felt himself unworthy of God's favour. As we said before, there is no trace of repentance in his life; and the picture of "the aged, penitent king, stung with poignant anguish of mind for his sins, and unable to utter the adorable name," if true to nature (Wordsworth), is not true to history. Rather, one would have expected one who had been betrayed into idolatry to be careful to use the name of the true God in contradistinction to that which was common to the false and the true.

Other discrepancies might be pointed out, such, for instance, as the absence of all allusion to idolatry, which the king, if repentant, could not have refrained from mentioning; but enough has been said to show there are many statements which are unsuitable to the character, epoch, and circumstances of the historical Solomon.

4. The allegation that the language of the book is wholly compatible with the time of Solomon would require too great space to be examined in detail. We should have to enter into technicalities which could be appreciated by none but Hebrew scholars, and only by those few who were fully acquainted, not merely with the writings of the Old Testament, but also with the language of Targums, etc., the rabbinic literature which came into existence by slow degrees after the Babylonish captivity. Suffice it to say generally that the language and style of the book have marked peculiarities, and that many words and many forms of expression either occur nowhere else in the Bible, or are found solely in the very latest books of the sacred canon. Delitzsch and Knobel and Wright have given lists of these *hapax legomena* and words and forms which belong to the later period of Hebrew. The catalogue, which extends to nearly a hundred items, has been closely examined by various scholars, and careful criticism has eliminated a very large number of the incriminated expressions. Many of these are abstract words, formed from roots naturally enough, though not occurring elsewhere; many have derivatives in the earlier books; many

cannot be proved to belong exclusively to the Chaldee, and may have been common to other Semitic dialects. But after making all due allowances, there remain enough instances of late and rabbinical words and phrases to prove that the work belongs to a period posterior to Solomon. Certainly it is quite possible to press the grammatical and etymological argument too far, and to lay too much stress on details often most difficult to dissect, and frequently more questions of taste and delicate judgment than of stern and indubitable fact; but the present case does not rest on isolated examples, some of which may be found faulty and weak, but on a large induction of particulars, the cumulative importance of which cannot be set aside.

How is this argument attempted to be met? The linguistic peculiarities cannot be wholly denied, but it is argued that the Aramaisms and foreign expressions are owing to Solomon's wide intercourse with external nations, and the bent of his mind, which inclined to comprehensiveness, and led him to prefer what was rare and removed from the intercourse of common life. Some suppose that this was done with the view of making the work more acceptable to non-Israelites. Others deem that the subject-matter necessitated the peculiar phraseology employed. Such allegations, however, will not account for grammatical peculiarities and verbal inflections, which are found rarely or never in earlier books, or for the absence of forms which are most common elsewhere. Foreign words might be introduced here and there in a work of any age; but it is different with changes in syntax and inflection; these denote another epoch or stage in language, and cannot be adequately explained by any of the above arguments. The assertion that the writer desired to commend his treatise to external nations is entirely unsupported by evidence, and is negatived by the fact that idolatry, the crying sin of other peoples, is never alluded to. Compare the bold denunciations of the Book of Wisdom, and it will at once be seen how a true believer deals with those who are enemies to his religion and worship. There is another consideration which supports the view for which we contend. The whole style of the work is indicative of a later development. Critics point to the very frequent employment of conjunctions to express the most diverse logical relations, which were not needed in the simpler lucubrations of early times. Then there is the pleonastic use of the personal pronoun after the verbal form; the mode of expressing the present by the participle, often in connection with a personal pronoun; the almost entire absence of the imperfect with *vav* conversive; and many other peculiarities of a similar nature, all of which indicate neo-Hebraism.

5. That no one but Solomon could have written a book of such consummate excellence is, of course, a mere assumption. We know so little of the literary history of those days, and our information concerning writers and educationists is so scanty, that it is impossible to say who could or who could not have composed such a work. Because we can fix the authorship definitely upon no other person, we are not compelled to subscribe to the traditional view. One of equal mental capacities and attainments with the

writer of Job might, under inspiration, have produced Koheleth; and, like the other, have remained unknown. The apocryphal compositions of post-exilian days show a large amount of literary talents, and the age which gave them birth might have been fruitful in other authors.

6. The coincidences between Ecclesiastes, Proverbs, and Canticles may be explained without resorting to the supposition that the three works are the production of one author, and that author Solomon. Not to discuss the genuineness of the Song of Songs, the Book of Proverbs is confessedly derived from many sources, and quotation from its pages would not serve to establish the Solomonic origin of the passage cited. All that can be decided from the parallelism with the other books attributed to Solomon is that the author had evidently read those works, as he certainly had perused Job, and perhaps Jeremiah, and, consciously or unconsciously, borrowed sentiments and expressions from them. And, on the other hand, there are confessedly such marked variations of style between those writings and Ecclesiastes, that it is difficult to allow that they came from the same pen, though wielded, as is said, at different ages of life.

From these premisses it must be concluded that the Solomonic authorship cannot be maintained, and that the book belongs to a much later epoch than that of Solomon. Surrendering the traditional opinion, we are, however, at once cast upon an ocean of surmises, which are wholly derived from internal evidence as this strikes different readers. In assigning the date of the book, critics are hopelessly divided, some giving B.C. 975, others B.C. 40, and between these dates others have, on various grounds, taken their respective stand. But eliminating theories which the work itself contravenes, we find that most reliable authorities are divided between the times of Ezra and Nehemiah, the Persian, and the Greek epochs. The theory of its composition in the time of Herod the Great, enunciated by Grätz, needs no refutation, and is only noticeable as showing, by the legend on which it is based, that at that day Koheleth was generally regarded as an integral portion of Holy Scripture. The first period mentioned would take us to the time of the Prophet Malachi, B.C. 450—400. But that seer writes much purer Hebrew than Koheleth, and the two could hardly have been contemporaneous. At any rate, we cannot be wrong in taking the genera-tion after Malachi as the *terminus a quo* of our inquiry. The *terminus ad quem* seems to be defined by the use made of Ecclesiastes by the author of the Book of Wisdom. That the latter is the later of the two is evident from its Hellenistic form and environment, of which Koheleth shows no trace, and from its exhibiting a development of the doctrines of wisdom and eschatology far beyond what is found in our book. Koheleth complains that increase of wisdom brings increase of trouble (ch. i. 18); the later pseudo-Solomon asserts that to live with Wisdom hath no bitterness, but is stable joy and gladness (Wisd. viii. 16). On the one hand, we read that there is no remembrance of the wise man more than of the fool for ever (ch. ii. 16); on the other hand, it is maintained that wisdom makes the memory of its possessor ever fresh, and confers upon him immortality (Wisd. viii. 13 ; vi. 20). If one argues sadly that the good and the evil have the same fate (ch. ix. 2), the other often comforts himself by thinking that their destinies are very different, and that the righteous are at peace, and live for evermore, and their reward is with the Most High (Wisd. iii. 2, etc.; v. 15, etc.). And generally the future judgment which Koheleth inti- mates vaguely and indefinitely, has, in the later book, become a settled belief, and a recognized motive of action and endurance. Both writings virtually assume the authorship of Solomon ; and many passages of the later work, especially ch. ii., seem to be designed to correct erroneous impressions gathered by some minds from Koheleth's unexplained statements. There is good reason to suppose that certain free-thinkers and sensualists in Alex- andria had ventured to support their immoral opinions by citing the authority of the wise king, who in his book urged men to enjoy life, accord- ing to the maxim, "Let us eat and drink; for to-morrow we die." This misapprehension of inspired teaching the author of Wisdom unhesitatingly condemns and confutes. The passages referred to are noted as they occur in the Exposition. But a comparison of the reasoning of the materialists in Wisdom with the statements in ch. ii. 18—26 ; iii. 18—22 ; v. 13, 20, will show whence was derived the perverted view of life which needed correction.

Now, the Book of Wisdom was composed not later than B.C. 150; so the limits between which lies the production of Ecclesiastes are B.C. 400 and B.C. 150. The nearer definition must be determined by other considerations. Mr. Tyler and Dean Plumptre have traced a connection between Ecclesiastes and Ecclesiasticus, and, by a series of contrasted citations, have endeavoured to prove that Ben-Sira was well acquainted with our book, and used it largely in the composition of his own. Plumptre also considers that the name Ecclesiasticus was given to Ben-Sira's work from its connection with Ecclesiastes, following the track there set. But be this idea well founded, it will not help us much, as the date of Ecclesiasticus is still a disputed question, though most modern critics assign it to the reign of Euergetes II., commonly called Physcon, B.C. 170—117. This, if it is accepted, gives the same result as the previous supposition. But a surer criterion is found in the social and political circumstances revealed incidentally in our book.

We read of the arbitrary exercise of power, the corruption, the dissolute- ness and luxury of rulers (ch. iv. 1, etc.; vii. 7; x. 16) ; perversion of justice and extortion in provinces (ch. v. 8) ; the promotion of base and unworthy persons to high positions (ch. x. 5—7) ; tyranny, despotism, revelry. These doings are graphically depicted by one who knew from experience that of which he wrote. And this condition of affairs points with much cer- tainty to the time when Palestine lay under Persian rule, and irresponsible satraps oppressed their subjects with iron hands. For the same con- clusion makes also the comparison of the inexorable law of death to the cruel obligation of military service which obtained among the Persians, and which allowed of no evasion (ch. viii. 8); so, too, the allusion to spies

and the trade of the secret informer (ch. x. 20) suits the government of
the Achæmenidæ. The oppressive rule under which the Palestinians
groaned led to a widespread disaffection and discontent, to a readiness
to seize any occasion to revolt, and rendered suitable the caution against
hasty action and the exhortation to patience (ch. viii. 3, 4). The social
and political condition induced two evils—first, a reckless disregard to
moral and religious restraint, as though God took no care of men and
paid no heed to their welfare; secondly, a scrupulous attention to the
externals of religion, as though by this one could constrain Heaven to
favour him—the offering of perfunctory sacrifices, the making of vows
as a barren duty. This state of things we know to have been existent
from the age of Nehemiah and before the Maccabæan period; and many
observations of Koheleth are directed against these abuses (ch. v. 1—7).
The remark about the multiplication of books (ch. xii. 12) could not have
applied to any period previous to the Persian. The absence of any trace
of Greek influence (which we shall endeavour to prove further on)
removes the writing from Macedonian times; nor could it be reasonably
attributed to the Maccabæan epoch. There is no trace of the patriotic
feeling which animated the Hebrews under the tyranny of the Syrians.
The persecutions then experienced had made future retribution no longer
a vague speculation or a dim hope, but an anchor of patience—a practical
motive for constancy and courage. This was a great advance upon the
misty conception of Koheleth. The conclusion at which we arrive is that
Ecclesiastes was written about B.C. 300.

In deciding thus we are not precluded from considering that many
of the proverbs and sayings contained herein come from an earlier age,
and may have been popularly attributed to Solomon himself. Such time-
honoured sentences would be readily inserted in a work of this nature and
would favour its reception and currency. The author must be deemed
wholly unknown; he has so completely veiled his identity that any attempt
to draw him from his purposed obscurity is hopeless. That he wrote in
Palestine seems most probable. Some have fancied that the expression
(ch. xi. 1), "Cast thy bread upon the waters," etc., refers to the sowing
of seed on the inundated banks of the Nile, and that, therefore, we are
justified in considering Alexandria as the scene of our author's labours.
But this interpretation of the passage is inadmissible; the words have
nothing to do with Egyptian cultivation, and give no clue to the writer's
domicile. Indeed, there are allusions to rainy seasons and the dependence
of the land for fertility, not on the river, but on the clouds of heaven
(ch. xi. 3; xii. 2), which pointedly debar any notion of Egypt being
intended, and plainly indicate another country subject to very different
climatic influences. The peculiarities of the Palestinian weather are
characterized in ch. xi. 4, "He that observeth the wind shall not sow; and
he that regardeth the clouds shall not reap." Such warnings would have
no significance in a land where rain rarely ever fell, and no one ever con-

sidered whether or not the wind was in what we call a rainy quarter.
Again, no one but a Jew living in his own country would talk familiarly
of frequenting the temple-worship (ch. v. 1) ; of seeing evil men honoured
in the holy place, Jerusalem (ch. viii. 10) ; of a fool not knowing the way
to " the city " *par excellence* (ch. x. 15). Such expressions indicate a dweller
in or near Jerusalem, and such we consider the author to have been—
one who addresses his countrymen in their own language, as it was spoken
in his time and locality. Had he lived in Egypt, he would doubtless
have used Greek as the vehicle of his instructions, as did the writer of
the Book of Wisdom ; but dwelling in Palestine, he, like the composer
of Ecclesiasticus, published his lucubrations in the native Hebrew. At
the same time, his travels had probably extended beyond the limits of his
own country, and made him in some sort familiar with foreign courts.

Dean Plumptre has arranged his idea of the author, plan, and purpose of
the book in the form of an ideal biography, which indeed seems to solve
many of the vexed questions that meet the student, but is evolved entirely
from internal considerations, and is invented to support the writer's foregone conclusions. It is very ingenious and captivating, and worthy of
study, whether one agrees with the view taken or dissents from it. Conceiving Ecclesiastes to be the production of an unknown author writing about
B.C. 200, and, in spite of the personation of King Solomon, really uttering
his autobiographical confessions, the dean proceeds to delineate Koheleth's
life and character from the hints contained, or thought to be contained, in
his pages. According to his biographer, Koheleth, an only son, was born
somewhere in Judæa (not Jerusalem), about B.C. 230. Well taught in the
usual lore, he early learned to reverence Solomon as the pattern of wisdom
and wise experience—in this respect being superior to the mass of his countrymen, who, neglecting their own history and their own sacred books, were
inclined rather to follow the modes of thought of the Greeks and Syrians,
with whom they were brought in contact, and if they conformed to the
national religion, it was rather from conventionality and a regard to routine
than from heartfelt conviction and devout feeling. Koheleth saw and
marked this vain ceremonialism and lip-worship, and learned to contrast
such pretenders with those who really feared the Lord. As he grew up, his
father, though wealthy, made him take his share in the labours of the vineyard and corn-field, and taught him the happiness of a life of activity. But
he was not long content with this quiet existence; he panted for a wider
sphere, larger experience ; and, with his parents' consent, and with ample
means at his disposal, he set out on foreign travel. Alexandria was the
place to which he directed his steps. Here, having good introductions, he
was admitted to the highest society, saw the life of courts, joined in the
revelry prevailing there, indulged in all the enervating luxury and immorality which made the life of the pleasure-seeking inhabitants of this corrupt
city. Satiety produced disgust. While staining his soul with degrading
passions, he had preserved the memory of better things, and the struggle

between the opposing elements is faithfully retraced in his book. On the one side, we have the weariness and pessimism of the *blasé* profligate; on the other, the revolt of the higher nature leading to a truer view of life. The course of his experience conducted him to a friend who was pure and sincere, and to a mistress who was beyond measure abandoned and false; and while he could thank God for the gift of the former, who had proved to be a wise and loving counsellor, he was no less thankful for being enabled to tear himself from the snares of the latter, whom he had found " more bitter than death." Deceived and disappointed, and dissatisfied with the scanty literature of his own nation, he turned for solace to the literature and philosophy of Greece; her poets supplied him with language in which to clothe the sentiments which arose from his new experiences; philosophers, Epicureans and Stoics, for a time charmed him with their teaching concerning nature, morality, life, and death. Such doctrines confirmed the notion of the vanity of most of the objects that men eagerly pursue, and encouraged the opinion that it was one's duty and interest to enjoy moderately all the pleasures that are available. Koheleth now discovered that there was something better than sensuality; that charity, benevolence, reputation, afforded joys more comforting and lasting. Admitted a member of the *Museum*, he joined in the philosophical discussions which were there carried on; heard and talked much about the *summum bonum*, happiness, immortality, free-will, destiny; but here was little to satisfy his cravings, though for the time he was interested and cheered by this intellectual activity. And now his excesses and his close study told upon his constitution, sapped his strength, and condemned him to premature old age. Partly paralyzed, weakened in body, but with the brain still active, he sat waiting the inevitable stroke, musing upon the past, and learning from the reflection that the soul could be satisfied by nothing but religion. Childhood's teaching came back with new force and meaning; God's love, justice, and power were living and energizing truths; the Creator was also the Judge. These verities, which he at length was compelled to acknowledge, were such as ought not to be kept unrevealed. Others, like himself, might have passed the same ordeal, and might need the instruction which he could give. How better could his enforced leisure be employed than in presenting to his countrymen his experiences, the course of thought which carried him through the pessimism of the sated sensualist, the wisdom of the Epicurean thinker, to the faith in a personal God? So he writes this record of a soul's conflicts, under the pseudonym of Koheleth, " the Debater," " the Preacher," shielding himself under the ægis of the great ideal of wisdom, Solomon King of Israel, whose life of enjoyment and late repentance, as tradition affirmed, bore a close analogy to his own.

It will be seen that there are many utterances in Ecclesiastes which spring naturally from the mouth of one situated as Koheleth is supposed to be, and which are readily explained by the above theory. It is also easy so to analyze the work, and so to interpret the allusions, as to give strong ground for its acceptance. And Dean Plumptre deserves great credit for the invention of the story, and its presentation in a most fascinating form. But regarded by sober criticism, does it satisfy the requirements of the case ? Is it necessitated by the language of the book ? Is there no other theory, less novel and violent, which will equally or better meet the circumstances ?   The objections to the "ideal biography " may here be very briefly stated, as we shall have occasion to discuss many of them more fully in our account of the plan and object of our book.   The whole romance is based on the assumption that the work is replete with Grecisms, traces of Alexandrian thought, echoes of Greek philosophy and literature. Remove this foundation, and the beautiful edifice crumbles into dust.   Our study of the book has led to a very opposite conclusion from that enter-tained in this very ideal biography.   The alleged Hellenisms, the Stoicism and Epicureanism, do not stand the test of unprejudiced criticism, and are capable of being explained without going so far afield.   The particular examination of these items we defer to another section, but thus much may be here said—the adduced expressions and views are the natural outcome of Hebrew thought, have nothing extraneous in their origin, and are analogous to post-Aristotelian sentiments, not because they are consciously derived from this fount, but because they are the produce of the same human mind, reflecting upon problems which have perplexed thinkers in every age and country.   Restless speculation, combined with a certain infidelity, was rife among men; Koheleth reflects this mental activity, this endeavour to grapple with difficult questions, and to offer solutions from varying points of view : what wonder that, in the course of his disquisition, he should present parallels to the opinions of the Stoic or Epicurean, who had gone over the same ground as himself ?   There is no plagiarism, no borrowing of ideas here ; the evolution is, as it were, inspired by the subject.

> " We do not make our thoughts ; they grow in us
>   Like grain in wood : the growth is of the skies ;
>   The skies, of nature ; nature, of God. The world
>   Is full of glorious likenesses ; and these
>   'Tis the bard's task, beside his general scope
>   Of story, fancy framed, to assort, and make
>   From the common chords man's heart is strung withal,
>   Music ; from dumb earth heavenly harmony."
>   (Bailey, ' Festus.')

In short, the book is a product of the *chokma* literature, practically religious, and more concerned with the life and circumstances of man generally than with man as a member of the commonwealth of Israel. The Hebrew, in this and similar works, divests himself in some degree of his peculiar nationality, and speaks as man to man, as one of the great human family, and not as an item in a narrow fraternity. Not that revelation is ignored, or the writer forgets his theocratical position ; he simply places it in the background, takes it for granted, and, virtually grounding his lucubrations thereon, does not bring it forward prominently and distinctly. So Koheleth, in all his warnings of the vanity of earthly things, shows that beneath this sad experience and melancholy view lies a firm faith in the justice of God, and belief in the future judgment, which could be derived only from the inspired history of his people.

§ 3. Contents, Plan, and Object.

The following is an analysis of our book as it lies before us :—

After announcing his name and position, "Koheleth, son of David and King in Jerusalem," the author puts forth the thesis which forms the subject of his treatise: "Vanity of vanities; all is vanity." Man's labour is profitless; nature and human life repeat themselves in monotonous succession, and all must fall ere long into oblivion. Nothing is new, nothing is lasting (ch. i. 1—11). This is the prologue; the rest of the book is taken up with the writer's various experiences and deductions therefrom.

He had been king, and had tried to find some satisfaction in many pursuits and under various circumstances, but in vain. The striving for wisdom is a feeding on wind; there is always something that eludes the grasp. There are anomalies in nature and in human affairs that men are powerless to comprehend and to rectify; and sorrow grows with increasing knowledge (ch. i. 12—18). He takes a new quest; he tries pleasure, he tests his heart with folly: in vain. He turns to art, to architecture, horticulture, kingly state and magnificence, luxury, and the amassing of wealth; there was no profit in any of them (ch. ii. 1—11). He studied human nature in its manifold phases of wisdom and folly, and he learned thus much, that the former excels the latter as light excels darkness; yet with this came the thought that death levelled all distinctions, placed wise man and fool in the same category. Besides this, be one never so rich, he must leave the results of his labours to another, who may be unworthy to succeed him. All this bitter experience forces the conclusion that temperate enjoyment of the goods of this life is the only proper aim, and that this is entirely the gift of God, who dispenses this pleasure or withholds it according to man's actions and disposition. At the same time, this limitation impresses on man's labour and enjoyment a character of vanity and unreality (ch. ii. 12—26). Now, man's happiness depends upon God's will, and he has arranged all things according to immutable laws, so that even the minutest matters have each their proper time and season. General experience proves this; it is useless to struggle against it, however inexplicable it may seem to be; man's duty and comfort is to recognize this providential government and practically to acquiesce therein (ch. iii. 1—15). There are injustices, disorders, anomalies in the world, which man cannot remedy by any exertion of his own, and which impede his peaceful enjoyment; but, doubtless, there shall be a day of retribution, when all such iniquities shall be punished and corrected, and God allows them for a time to continue, with the view of proving men, and to teach them humility, that in one sense they are not superior to brutes. (For man and brute succumb to the universal law of death; and that there is a distinction in the destination of their spirits, though it may well be believed, is incapable of proof.) Hence man's happiness and duty consist in making the best of the present life, and improving the opportunities which God offers, without anxious care for the future (ch. iii. 16—22). He gives further illustrations of man's inability to secure his own happiness. See how man is oppressed or wronged by his fellow-man. Who can remedy this? And in face of such things, what pleasure is there in life? Success only leads to envy. Yet labour is necessary, and none but the fool sinks into apathy and indolence. Turn to avarice for consolation, and you are isolated from your fellows, and haunted with a sense of insecurity. High place itself has no assurance of permanence. Foolish kings are supplanted by young and clever aspirants; yet the people do not long remember their benefactors or profit by their meritorious services (ch. iv. 1—16). Turn to popular religion: is there any satisfaction or comfort to be found there? Nay, all is hollow and unreal. The house of God is entered thoughtlessly and irreverently; verbose prayers are uttered with no feeling of the heart; vows are made only to be broken or evaded; dreams take the place of piety, and superstition stands for religion (ch. v. 1—7). In the political life, too, there is much that is disheartening, only to be supported by the thought of an overruling Providence (ch. v. 8, 9). The pursuit and possession of wealth give no more satisfaction than other mundane things. The rich are always wanting more; their expenses increase with their wealth; they are not happy in life, and may lose their property at a stroke, and leave nothing to the children for whom they laboured (ch. v. 10—17). All this leads again to the old conclusion that we should make the best of life such as it is, seeking neither riches nor poverty, but being content to enjoy with sobriety the good that God gives, remembering that the power to use and enjoy is a boon that comes solely from him (ch. v. 18—20). We may see men possessed of all the gifts of fortune, yet unable to enjoy them, and soon obliged to leave them by the inexorable stroke of death (ch. vi. 1—6). If desires were always accomplished, we might have a different tale to tell; but they never are fully satisfied; high and low, wise and foolish, are equally victims of unsatisfied cravings (ch. vi. 7—9). These desires are profitless, because circumstances are not under man's control; and, not being able to forecast the future, he must make the best of the present (ch. vi. 10—12).

Koheleth now proceeds to apply to practice the truths which he has been establishing. As man knows not what is best for him, he must accept what is sent, be it joy or sorrow; and let him learn hence some salutary lessons. Life should be solemn and earnest; the house of mourning teaches better than the house of feasting; and the rebuke of a wise man is more wholesome than the mirth of fools (ch. vii. 1—7). We must learn patience and resignation; it is no wisdom to quarrel with things as they are or to praise the past in contrast with the present. We cannot change what God has ordered; and he sends good and evil that we may feel our entire dependence, and not disquiet ourselves about the future, which must be wholly unknown to us (ch. vii. 8—14). Anomalies occur; all excesses must be avoided, both on the side of over-righteousness and of laxity; true wisdom is found in the observance of the mean, and this is the only preservative from errors in the conduct of life (ch. vi. 15—22). Having thus far been aided by Wisdom, he desires, by her assistance, to solve deeper and more mysterious questions, but is wholly baffled. But he learned some further practical truths, viz. that wickedness was folly and madness, that of all created things woman was the most evil, and that man was made originally upright, but had perverted his nature (ch. vii. 23—29). His experience now leads him to consider man as a citizen. Here he shows that it is useless to rebel; true wisdom counsels obedience even under the worst oppression, and submission to Providence. Subjects may well be patient, for sure retribution awaits the tyrant (ch. viii. 1—9). But he is troubled by seeming anomalies in God's moral government, noting the contradiction to expected retribution in the case of the good and evil. God's abstention and the impunity of sinners make men incredulous of Providence; but in spite of all this, he knows in his heart that God is just in reward and punishment, as the end will prove. Meantime, unable to solve the mystery of God's ways, man's right course is, as before said, to make the best of existing circumstances (ch. viii. 10—15). This conclusion is confirmed by the fact that one fate awaits all men, and that the dead are cut off from all the feelings and pursuits and interests of life in the upper world (ch. ix. 1—6). Hence the lesson is repeated that man's wisest course is to use his earthly life to the best advantage, without being greatly disturbed by the inscrutability of the moral government of the world (ch. ix. 7—12). Wisdom, indeed, is not always rewarded, and the wise man who has done good service is often forgotten; but there is a real power in wisdom which can effect more than physical strength (ch. ix. 13—18). On the other hand, a little folly mars the effect of wisdom, and is quite sure to manifest itself in word or conduct (ch. x. 1—3). Koheleth then gives his experience of what he has seen in the case of capricious rulers, who often advanced to high stations the most incompetent men; and he offers some advice for conduct under such circumstances (ch. x. 4—7). Wisdom teaches caution in all undertakings, whether in private or political life; a man should count the cost and make due preparation before attempting reformation in government or any other important matter (ch. x. 8—11). See the strong contrast between the gracious words and acts of the wise man, and the objectless prating and useless labours of the fool (ch. x. 12—15). The lesson of caution under the government of dissolute and unprincipled rulers is strongly enforced (ch. x. 16—20). Drawing towards the conclusion of his work, Koheleth gives some direct practical advice under three heads. We should leave unanswerable questions, and endeavour to do our duty with diligence and activity; especially we ought to be largely beneficent, as we know not how soon we ourselves may meet with adversity and need help (ch. xi. 1—6). This is the first remedy for impatience and discontent; the second is found in a spirit of cheerfulness, which enjoys the present discreetly and moderately, with a due regard to the future account to be rendered (ch. xi. 7—9). The third remedy is piety, which ought to be practised from early years; life should be so guided as not to offend the laws of the Creator and Judge, and virtue should not be postponed till the failure of faculties makes pleasure unattainable and death closes the scene. The last days of old age are described under various images and analogies, which contain some of the most beautiful traits in the book (ch. xi. 10—xii. 7). The conclusion of the whole is the echo of the beginning, " Vanity of vanities; all is vanity " (ch. xii. 8).

The book ends with an epilogue (ch. xii. 2—14), commendatory of the writer, explaining his standpoint and the object of his work. The real Koheleth here speaks, tells of the care with which he has prepared himself for his task, and assumes the gift of inspiration. It is better to know a little well than to weary one's self with reading many things; and the whole course of the discussion in the present case tends to give one lesson, viz. that man's true wisdom lies in fearing God and looking forward to the judgment.

Such are the contents of this work as presented by the writer. But never was there a book whose plan, design, and arrangement were more widely disputed. While some enthusiastic admirers have found herein an elaborate artistical structure, a formal division into sections rhythmically distributed, others have deemed it a mass of loose thoughts heaped together without any attempt at coherence or logical system. Others, again, give the work a colloquial character, hearing in it the language of two voices —that of the wearied and exhausted seeker, and that of the warning and correcting teacher. Tennyson's poem, ' The Two Voices,' has been used in illustration of this view of Koheleth. By others the unity of the book is wholly denied, and it is considered to be derived from many authors, being, in fact, a collection of philosophical and didactic poems, interspersed with gnomes and proverbs, hard questions, and some solutions of the same. Few will now be found to uphold this theory, the identity of thought throughout, and the orderly progress of the one underlying reflection, being conspicuous to any unprejudiced reader, and (if we regard the closing verses as an integral portion of the treatise) leading to a grand and satisfying conclusion.

Among the various theories concerning the design of the author in presenting this work, we may mention a few very briefly. Rosenmüller divides it into two parts—a theoretical (ch. i.—iv.) and a practical (ch. v.—xii. 7); the former showing the vanity of human pursuits and generally of mundane things, and the latter directing men's life to worthy objects, and giving rules for obtaining pleasure and contentment. Tyler

and Plumptre see in it a struggle between revealed religion and the theories
of Greek philosophies, in the form of an autobiographical confession without any regular plan.   Renan looks upon the author as a sceptic; Heine
calls the book 'The Canticle of Scepticism;' these critics consider that
the leading thought of the vanity of human affairs, and the call to enjoy
life, point to a disbelief in a present Providence and a future retribution.
Schopenhauer and his school read pessimism in every utterance concerning
the shortness of man's life, the vanity of his pursuits, the disorders which
prevail in nature and in society.   One critic deems that the treatise points
out the vanity of everything of earth ; another, that its object is to indicate
the *summum bonum;* another, that the point proved is the immortality of
the soul ; and yet another, that the author labours to show the limits of
philosophy, and the excellence of religion in comparison therewith.

One school of interpreters sees in our book a discussion between a pious
Israelite and a Sadducee, or a youth vexed by his daily experiences and a
senior who tries to allay his misgivings and calm his excitement.   Others
find a Hebrew, under the guise of Solomon, employing Greek sophisms,
and a Jewish believer refuting him by citing maxims and proverbs ; or a
Solomon objecting to the common theory of Divine providence and placing
man's happiness in sensual pleasure, and a prophet arguing for the moral
government of the world and assigning its right position to human
enjoyment.   In this view all apparent contradictions are explained away ;
all unorthodox sentiments appertain to the caviller, while the correction is
that which the Holy Spirit would enforce.   We may say at once that it is
impossible to support this idea by reference to the text.   There is no trace
of different interlocutors; objections have no immediate answer, and what
are regarded as replies present no connection with preceding statements.
The idea of dialogue must be considered as wholly chimerical.   Equally
without foundation is the theory of the "two voices."   What are regarded
as the utterances of fatalist, materialist, Epicurean, are not refuted or
retracted ; the voice that should have taken the opposite side in the controversy is obstinately silent, and the poison—if poison it be—is left to
work its dire effect.

Of course, those who maintain the traditional view of the authorship
hold a totally distinct opinion concerning its scope and object.   With them
it is the result of a late repentance, seeking to atone for past follies, and to
enforce the warnings of a bitter experience, and thus to *gather together* the
people whom Solomon foresaw would be scattered by his sins.   Having
prescience of the fate that awaited Israel after his death, he thus endeavours
to comfort his countrymen in the evil days that were coming.   He teaches
the vanity of earthly things—things " under the sun "—that the blessedness
of eternity may be realized ; union with God implies detachment from the
world.   He surveys nature, he recalls his own varied experience, he looks
abroad : there is nothing satisfying in this view.   He thinks of his successor,
Rehoboam, a youth of weak intellect, but strong passions, and finds no

comfort there; he owns his infatuation, he calls himself " an old and foolish king " (ch. iv. 13), and already he sees the throne occupied by Jeroboam, " the poor and wise child " who should usurp his seat.   He remembers his countless wives and concubines, who had led him astray, and exclaims that women are the pest of the world, and that not one in a thousand is good. He anticipates times of confusion and misrule, and counsels obedience and submission.   Then, at the close of the book, he pictures himself aged, enfeebled, laid on his death-bed, and in solemn tones he urges early piety, the emptiness of everything apart from God, and utters the moral of his wasted life, and sums up man's duty in the weighty climax of the book.   If the treatise were Solomon's, such, indeed, might have been the course of thought.

Before we offer our own opinion concerning the purpose of the book, let us look at the views which others have formed respecting Koheleth's standpoint and sentiments.

First of all, is our author a pessimist, as many suppose ?   Does he take the worst view of things, find no benevolence in the Creator, see no hope of happiness for man ?   Certainly, his ever-recurring cry is, " Vanity of vanities; all is vanity; " certainly, he affirms that death is better than life, that the lot of those is most to be envied who never have been born, that men's labours and aims and ambitions end in disappointment, that the pursuit of wisdom, or art, or wealth, or pleasure is alike unsatisfying ; but these and such-like mournful utterances must not be considered apart from their context and the place which they occupy in the treatise.   They do not represent the object or teaching of the book ; they occur as passing obser- vations which met the thinker in the course of his investigation, and which he notes in order to trace the line taken by his inquiry.   His pessimism, such as it is, is only a cloud seeming to obscure for a time the heaven of his faith, and dissipated by the clear shining behind it.   When he speaks in desponding tones of mundane objects, he desires to call attention to the weak point in all such things, the fault that underlies them all.   Men's mistake is to think that they can secure happiness by their own efforts, whereas they are conditioned by a higher power, and can neither achieve success nor enjoy it when won except by the gift of God.   If he affirms that the day of death is preferable to the day of birth, he is virtually repeat- ing Solon's celebrated gnome that no man can be accounted happy till he has closed his life happily—that the new-born infant has a time before him full of trial and trouble, the course and end of which no one can foresee, while with the dead all is over, and we can calmly judge of his career. His faith in God's justice and benevolence is the exact contradictory of Schopenhauer's school.   His word is, " God hath made everything beautiful in its time " (ch. iii. 11) ; he believes in the moral government of the universe ; he acknowledges the reality of sin ; he looks to a life beyond the grave.   He would not paralyze exertion, and hold back from work ; he recommends diligence in one's own duties, beneficence towards others ; he leads men to expect happiness in the path on which God's providence leads them. There is no real hopelessness, no cynical despair, in his utterances taken as a whole. If he lacks the bright faith of the Christian, he in his measure feels that all works together for good for them that love God, if not in this world, yet assuredly in another. So the charge of pessimism falls to the ground when the treatise is considered in its totality, and not estimated by isolated passages.

A strong plea for the prevalence of traces of Gentile teaching has been put forward by modern critics. Let us, then, examine the grounds on which rests the idea of the potent influence of Greece (for the external influence means Hellenism) in the foundation and expression of Koheleth's sentiments. First, as to language, we have certain phrases cited which are alleged to be derived *Græco fonte*. In ch. iii. 11 *ha-olam*, translated "the world" in our version, is supposed to be the Greek αἰών, whereas it is truly Hebraic in form and signification, and is probably not used in the sense of "world" in the Old Testament. In the next verse the phrase, "to do good," is taken as equivalent to εὖ πράττειν, "to fare well, to prosper;" but this is not its use in the Bible, and it is best taken in the ethical sense of being beneficent, etc. The phrase, καλὸς κἀγαθός, is found in the "good and comely" of ch. v. 18, *tob asher-yapheh*, where, however, the correct rendering is, "Behold, what I have seen as good, which is also beautiful," and the Hellenistic source is wholly unrecognizable. *Pithgam*, "sentence," is not φθέγμα, but a Persian word Hebraized. "I gave my heart to seek and search out," "I considered in my heart," etc. (ch. i. 13; ix. 1),—such-like expressions do not imply a formal course of philosophizing, but simply the mental process of an acute observer and thinker. "That which is" (ch. vii. 24) is not τὸ τί ἐστιν, the real nature of things, but that which is in existence. Dean Plumptre deems the book to be "throughout absolutely saturated with Greek thought and language." His chief proofs are such as these: the phrase, "under the sun," to express all human things (ch. i. 9, 14; iv. 15, etc.); "seeing the sun," for living (ch. vi. 5). But what more natural term could be found than "under the sun"? And why should it be borrowed? And the periphrasis for life, or its equivalent, is found in Job and the Psalms. "Be not over-righteous or over-wise" (ch. vii. 16) is a maxim, regarded contextually, by no means identical with the gnome μηδὲν ἀγάν, *ne quid nimis*. The proverbial warning respecting the bird of the air reporting a secret (ch. x. 20) surely need not have been derived from the story of Ibycus and the cranes; as stimulating the mind under teaching it was more natural for a Hebrew to speak of "goads" than a Greek (ch. xii. 11). We need not go to Euripides or the social life of Hellas to account for Koheleth's disparagement of women; his own country and age, cursed with the evils of polygamy and the degraded condition of the female sex, gave him reason enough for his remarks. Some other instances are adduced by critics who see what they desire to see; but they are all capable of easy explanation without recourse to a foreign origin being necessary. So we may safely conclude that the language of our book exhibits no trace of Greek parentage.

An apparently strong case has been produced by those who see evidences of Greek philosophy in Ecclesiastes. Echoes of Stoical teaching are heard in the language that speaks of the endless recurrence of the same phenomena in the life of man (ch. i. 5—7, 11, etc.), which is paralleled by the theory of the cycles of events presented by history, as M. Aurelius says (xi. 1), "There will be nothing new for posterity to gaze at, and our ancestors stood upon the same level of observation. All ages are uniform and of a colour, insomuch that in forty years' time a tolerable genius for sense and inquiry may acquaint himself with all that is past and all that is to come." There is similarity, doubtless, in the ideas of these authors, but no greater than might be expected in two thinkers writing of a consideration of facts which struck them in reviewing the past. The thought of the vanity of man's life and labour, his aims and pleasures, is deemed to be derived from the apathy of the Stoic and his contempt for the world; whereas it springs from the teaching of bitter experience which needed no foreign stimulus to animate its expression. The fatalism characteristic of Stoic doctrine, which to a superficial reader seems to obtrude itself constantly, is really not found in our book. The writer is too religious to fall into any such error. The sad refrain, "Vanity of vanities; all is vanity. What profit hath a man of all his labour?" seems to some to savour of that philosophic fatalism which regards man as the prey of blind destiny. Now, the things of which Koheleth predicates vanity are wisdom, wealth, pleasure, power, speculation; and why? Not because they are the working of irresponsible and uncontrollable destiny, but because they fail in themselves to bestow that for the sake of which they are pursued, or accrue only to those persons whom Providence thus blesses. He recounts his own experience and his attempts to find satisfaction in various pursuits, and he concludes that all such strivings are vain, in so far as all are conditioned by the dispensation of God, who permits enjoyment and possession according to his good pleasure. The things themselves cannot secure and are not the cause of any happiness which accompanies them; this is solely the gift of God. Man, too, does not know what is best for him, and often seeks eagerly for what is pernicious; Providence overrules his efforts and controls the final result. Providence governs the most minute as well as the most important events of man's life (ch. iii. 1—8); everything is thus regulated according to mysterious rules which are beyond our ken. But this profound conviction does not lead Koheleth to regard man as a mere machine, possessed of no free-will, whose liberty of action is entirely controlled by higher power, who is as completely under the rule of necessity as the external physical world. He does allow that, as there are laws that direct the forces of material nature, so there are laws that control man's intellectual and moral nature; and it is from his obedience or disobedience that happiness or pain ensues. The infringement of these laws does not always bring punishment in this world, nor their observance reward, but retribution is certain in the life beyond the grave (ch. xi. 9) ; and the Preacher counsels men to fear God and to practise piety and virtue, not as though they were the victims of cruel destiny, but as responsible beings who in many respects had their life in their own hands. The second division of the book (ch. vii.—ix.) contains a collection of practical suggestions how to make the best of the present in remembrance of the omnipotent control of Providence. If the fatalist pronounces that all is left to chance, and that God hides his face and cares nought for human concerns, Koheleth warns against the error of supposing that, because retribution is delayed or falls in some unexpected way, Heaven takes no interest in mundane matters. Moral government does certainly exist, and seeming exceptions only show that we cannot understand its course, while we must submit to its decrees. If, again, unbelief asserts that human efforts are vain and sterile, the Preacher, on the contrary, urges men to do their part with energy, to use with profit the time granted to them, to make the best of their position; not that they can always command success, but generally wisdom is more powerful than physical force, and at any rate diligence and action are man's duty, and results may be left in higher hands. The vexed question of free-will and omniscience is not handled ; man's liberty and God's decree are both main-tained, but their compatibility is not explained. They are set side by side, and both are taken into account, but there is no formal attempt at recon-ciliation ; it is enough to hold, on the one hand, that Providence rules supreme, and, on the other, that piety and wisdom are better worth than folly or greatest natural power. The bitter and reiterated cry of " Vanity " does not argue disbelief in man's free-will or in God's providential care ; it issues from a soul that has learned its own weakness and its dependence upon God ; that has learned that happiness is his gift and is dispensed according to his good pleasure.

Another loan from Stoic teaching is supposed to be found in the frequent combination of "madness and folly" (ch. i. 17 ; ii. 12, etc.), which is com-pared with the view that regarded all weaknesses and delinquencies as forms of insanity. But Koheleth is offering no definition of human frailty ; his intention is to show how he pursued his investigation. As *contrariis contraria intelliguntur*, he learned wisdom by watching the results of unwisdom, confusion of thought and purpose ("madness"); that he thus designates moral error is natural to one taking a philosophical view of human nature. Why he should have borrowed the expression from the Stoics is hard, indeed, to see.

The alleged Epicureanism is equally unfounded. That parallels are met with can surely be explained without supposing that the Preacher "drank from a common source" with Lucretius and Horace. With regard to physical science, had Koheleth to go to Epicurus that he might learn the mystery of the daily rising and setting of the sun, or that rivers flow into the sea, or that the waters somehow find their way back again? These are matters of observation which must strike any thinker. Is the doctrine concerning the dissolution of man's compound being at death derived from Lucretius? Ecclesiastes says that men and beasts have one destiny; they have a living principle, and, when this is withdrawn, their bodies crumble into dust. He learned this great fact from his own sacred books; if Greek philosophers taught it, they evolved the idea from their own minds and observation, or it was a traditionary knowledge handed down from antiquity. But Koheleth sees a difference between the spirit of man and that of the lower animals, in that the former goeth, as he holds, upward (ch. iii. 21), returns to God (ch. xii. 7), the latter goeth downward to the earth. He is here not thinking of the absorption of man's spirit in the *anima mundi;* he has been taught that God breathed into Adam the breath of life, and that at death that "breath," the living soul, goes back to its source, not losing its identity, but coming more immediately in connection with its Creator, retaining its personality, and, as the Targum paraphrases, "returning to stand in judgment before him who gave it." Concerning the ignorance of what comes after death, our author is quite in accord with the reticence of the Old Testament, and has not learned from a Greek school to speak in this cautious manner. But it is in regard to the enjoyment of life that Ecclesiastes is said to have chiefly borrowed from Epicurean teaching. That, as some have supposed, he recommends a coarse sensuality needs no refutation; but even the "modified Epicureanism" which some read in his pages has no place there; the misconception arises from a false interpretation of certain phrases, especially as taken in connection with their context. There is one which often occurs, *e.g.* "It is good and comely for one to eat and to drink, and to enjoy the good of all his labour that he taketh under the sun all the days of his life" (ch. v. 18; comp. ch. ii. 24; iii. 22; viii. 15). This expression, "to eat and drink," had not, to the ears of a Hebrew, simply the lower meaning which it carries now, as if it implied only the enjoyment of the pleasures of the table. Reproaching Shallum for his declension from righteous ways, Jeremiah (xxii. 15) asks, "Did not thy father eat and drink, and do judgment and justice, and then it was well with him?" Does the prophet signify that Josiah pleased God by his Epicurean life? Is it not evident that the phrase is a metaphor for prosperity, ease, and comfort? When Koheleth inquires (ch. ii. 25), "Who can eat, or who can have enjoyment, more than I?" he means that no one has had better opportunities than he for enjoying life generally. One would have thought it scarcely necessary to insist on the extended signification of this metaphor. The bountifulness of Jehovah is thus expressed: "The Lord is the Portion of mine inheritance and of my cup;" "Thou preparest a table before me" (Ps. xvi. 5; xxiii. 5); and the joys of heaven are adumbrated by terms appropriate to a glorious banquet: "I appoint unto you a kingdom," said Christ (Luke xxii. 29), "that ye may eat and drink at my table in my kingdom;" "Blessed is he that shall eat bread in the kingdom of God," cried one, in reference to the life of glory beyond the grave (Luke xiv. 15 ; comp. Rev. xix. 9). In this and similar phrases used by the Preacher, such as "to rejoice," "to see good," etc., the idea intended is not to encourage the selfish sensuality of the voluptuary, but a well-regulated contentment with and enjoyment of the good which God gives. Nothing more than this is in man's power, and to this he ought to confine his aim ; that is, he ought to make the best of the present, knowing that he is not the architect of his own happiness, but that this is the gift of God, to be thankfully accepted as a boon from heaven, whenever and in whatever fashion it may come. It is true that the good and the evil often seem to be and are treated in the same manner (ch. ix. 1, 2) ; but this is no reason for despair and inaction ; nay, as the present life is the only time for work, it behoves us to use it in the best way : "Whatsoever thy hand findeth to do, do it with thy might." Here is no counsel of Epicurean ἀταραξία, a passionless tranquillity which disturbs itself about nothing, but rather a call to an active performance of duties as the best guarantee of happiness. The only other passage which seems to favour licence and immorality is one towards the end (ch. xi. 9) : "Rejoice, O young man, in thy youth ; and let thy heart cheer thee in the days of thy youth, and walk in the ways of thine heart, and in the sight of thine eyes." These words at first sight, and taken by themselves, do seem to encourage youth to give free scope to its passions ; but they must not be separated from their solemn conclusion : "But know thou, that for all these things God will bring thee into judgment." And the advice really comes to this : youth is the time for enjoyment, while the senses are keen, and the taste is unimpaired, and you do well to make the best of this time ; this is your portion and lot given by God ; but in all that you do, remember the end, remember the account which you will have to give ; take your pleasure with this thought always before you.

That Ecclesiastes cannot be justly accused of scepticism has been already shown incidentally. This and such-like errors are imputed by readers who regard isolated expressions divorced from the context, and neglect the general tone prevalent in the treatise. The idea is supported by such passages as ch. i. 8, 12—18 ; iii. 9 ; and viii. 16, 17, in which Koheleth professes man's inability to understand God's doings, and the uselessness of wisdom in satisfying human aspirations. He does not affirm that man can know nothing, apprehend nothing ; he is not a disciple of agnosticism— that mean excuse for declining to assent to revealed truth—he asserts that human reason cannot fathom the depth of God's designs. Reason can receive facts, and compare and arrange and argue from them ; but it cannot explain everything ; it has limits which it cannot pass ; perfect intellectual satisfaction is beyond mortals' attainment. Is this equivalent to denying to man the power of gaining any certitude or mastering any verity ? Again, when he intimates the vanity of wisdom and knowledge, he is stating the truth that the course of events is beyond man's control, that no human wisdom can secure happiness, which is absolutely the gift of God. A profound belief in a governing Providence underlies all his utterances; it is the mysteriousness, the secret working, of this government that arrests his attention and leads him to contrast with it man's ignorance and impotence, and to lay skill, prudence, science, under the feet of the great Disposer of hearts and circumstances. In all this he is not speculative; there is no theorizing or philosophizing; it is wholly practical, tending to rules of daily life, not to questions of metaphysics or minute theology.

There is another point on which the Preacher is said to exhibit the taint of scepticism, and that is on the question of the immortality of the soul. Some would make him a predecessor of the Sadducees; some cannot find a trace of the orthodox doctrine in his pages, and indeed consider it to have been unknown at his epoch; others venture to say that he had not even the Greek's idea of the soul and immortality, and held that man, in the matter of life, differed nothing from the beast, had nothing to expect after death. Without entering upon the general question how far the Old Testament countenances the dogma of the immortality of the soul, we will see what Koheleth says upon this absorbing topic. The first passage which bears upon the subject is found in the last five verses of the third chapter, where the destiny and being of men are compared with those of beasts. Properly translated and explained, the words enunciate certain unimpeachable facts. First they say that man, regarded as a mere animal, irrespectively of the relation in which he stands to God, has no more power than the lower creatures; is, no more than they, master of his own fate. Then it is added that the lot of men and beasts is the same; both have the breath of life; when this is withdrawn, both die; so in this respect man has no advantage over the beast—both come from dust and both return to dust. There is no question here of the soul's continued existence; the animal life alone is spoken of, the physical breath or power which gives life to all animals of whatever nature they may be; and all are placed in the same category by having to succumb to the law of death. There is no scepticism thus far; but round the twenty-first verse controversy has gathered. This is rendered in the Revised Version, "Who knoweth the spirit of man whether it goeth upward, and the spirit of the beast whether it goeth downward to the earth?" If we surrender the Authorized translation, "The spirit of man that goeth upward," etc., which states a truth not before enunciated, we must see whether the charge of scepticism is sustained by the Revised Version, which has the authority of the Septuagint, Vulgate, Syriac, and Targum. Now, it may be that Koheleth merely affirms that there are but few who arrive at any knowledge on the subject, or he may say that no one knows for certain anything about the respective destinies of the life of man and brute; but he does not deny, if he refrains here from expressly affirming, the continued existence of the personal soul. If we conceive that he is referring only to the animal life, he intimates that in the manner of death no one can tell what difference there is between the withdrawal of

life from man and from brute.   If he refers to the spirit, the *ego* of man,
his question implies belief in a continued existence after death; if it was
annihilated, if it perished with its earthly tabernacle, there could be no
inquiry as to what became of it.   To assert that no one can track its
course is to certify that it has a course before it, though this be not
capable of demonstration.   Plainly, too, he differentiates the fate of man
and beast.   The vital principle of the latter may go with the body to the
dust; the spirit of the former may, as he says later (ch. xii. 7), return to
the God who gave it; to hold the impossibility of attaining to certainty in
this mysterious subject by human reason or senses, does not make a man a
sceptic.   The stage of the argument required this unsatisfying statement
of the case; it is not till the close of the book that doubt is cleared away,
and faith shines forth undimmed.   There is a further difficulty in the final
clause of this paragraph : " For who shall bring him [back] to see what
shall be after him ? " Some have explained this clause, " What shall become
of him after his death ? " by which may be signified a doubt whether he has
any future or not.   But what is intended is either the thought that we
cannot tell whether after death we shall have any knowledge of what passes
on earth, or else that we cannot foresee what will happen to us or to any
one in the future in this world.   In either case there is no denial of the
great verity of the immortality of the soul.   But what is Koheleth's view
of the judgment to come ? In ch. ix. he speaks of the dead thus : " To him
that is joined with all the living there is hope: for a living dog is better
than a dead lion.   For the living know that they shall die : but the dead
know not anything, neither have they any more a reward; for the memory
of them is forgotten.   As well their love as their hatred . . . is now perished;
neither have they any more a portion for ever in anything that is done under
the sun . . . Whatsoever thy hand findeth to do, do it with thy might; for
there is no work, nor device, nor knowledge, nor wisdom, in Sheol whither
thou goest."   The existence of the soul after death is here presupposed ; its
condition in the other world is the point elaborated.   This is considered· in
accordance with the view that obtains in Job, the Psalms, and other writings
of the Old Testament.   Sheol is a place beneath the earth, gloomy, awful,
whither go, the souls of the dead.   In the utterances of the poets it has
its ʼgates, bars, valleys; its inhabitants are called *rephaim*, " the weak."
Their mode of existence differs from that of their brethren in the upper
world.   They know nothing ; they are cut off from action; they have no
scope for the exercise of passion or affection ; they are joyless, deprived of all
that made life worth living ; but they retain their individuality and have
to undergo a particular judgment.   That Koheleth believed in this last
event has been questioned, and passages which seem to warrant the idea
have been distorted and explained away, or boldly dismissed as interpolations.   But taking for granted the integrity of the book as it has come
down to us, we cannot fairly escape from such inference.   Thus, in view of
the partiality and iniquity of men in high position, our author comforts

himself with the reflection that in good time God will judge the righteous and the wicked (ch. iii. 16, 17). The vague but emphatic "there"— "there is a time *there*"—implies the world beyond the grave, the adverb referring probably to God, who is named in the preceding clause. This same thought enables the wise man to endure affliction patiently, "for to everything there is a time and judgment" (ch. viii. 6)—the oppressor shall meet with his reward. It is plain that retribution in the present life is not meant; for Koheleth's complaint is that moral government is not invariably enforced in this world; he must therefore refer to another state of existence, wherein full justice shall be done. This is made quite clear by the warning to the young in ch. xi. 9, "Know thou, that for all these things God will bring thee into judgment;" and the solemn close of the whole treatise, "God shall bring every work into judgment, with every hidden thing, whether it be good, or whether it be evil." This judgment is supposed to take place when the soul returns to God. Of its course and details nothing more is said; neither Koheleth nor any Old Testament scribe throws any light upon this mysterious subject, in this respect differing materially from the heathen who have treated of the same. Had he borrowed from the works of Egyptians, Greeks, or Romans, he would have been at no loss for descriptions of Hades and its denizens; the mythologies of those peoples would have supplied prolix details. But a sacred reticence restrains our author; he speaks as he is moved, and gives no rein to his imagination. Human thought could not pierce the darkness which enveloped the abode of the dead, and could deal only in vague conjecture or unsubstantial dreams, contrasted with earthly, sensible realities. So at this stage of revelation seers could describe the future only on its negative side, as the privation of the joys, emotions, and pursuits of this present life. To elucidate the positive side of this state, further revelation was needed. Only of the great fact the writer is absolutely certain, and he employs the truth as a consolation in trouble, as an explanation of God's long-suffering, as a motive for restraint and self-denial, as an event which shall solve the difficulties and remove the anomalies which are found in the course and constitution of this world.

Having thus endeavoured to relieve Ecclesiastes from the misapprehensions to which it has been subjected; having, as we hope, shown the unfounded nature of the accusations of Stoicism, Epicureanism, fatalism, scepticism, Hellenism,—we are in a position to state briefly our own view of the plan and scope of the book. What do we gather to have been the circumstances under which it was composed? The case seems to have been the following: The period was a trying one. Oppression and injustice reigned; fools and proletarians were promoted to high positions; wise and pious men were wronged and crushed. Where was that moral government which the Law of Moses enunciated, and which had been the guide and support of the Hebrew people in all their early history? Did injustice meet with the punishment which they had been taught to expect? Did the good and obedient prosper and live long in the land ?   Did not daily experience give the lie to the promise of temporal retribution set forth in Scripture ?   And if revelation was false in this respect, why not in others also ?   By this doubt the very foundation of religion was sapped; the hopes that the exiles had brought with them, on their return to their native land, were cruelly crushed, and the bitter cry arose, "Is there a God that judgeth the earth ?"   Malachi had been gathered to his rest; no prophet was there to lead the way to better things or to console the desponding people for the falsification of their expectations.   What was the result ?   Some took refuge in simple unbelief, saying in their hearts, "There is no God;" some, laying aside all consideration of the future, revelled in the present, lived in debauchery and sensuality, with the thought, "Let us eat and drink; for to-morrow we die;" others, as if to constrain God to fulfil old prophecies, and to grant their temporal desires, practised a scrupulous observance of the outward duties of religion, a formal rigorism which anticipated that later Pharisaism which meets us in the gospel history.   These tendencies are reflected in Ecclesiastes, and are more or less corrected herein.   This rectification is not effected in a formal, logical method.   The work is by no means a regular treatise, moral or religious.   Some have likened it to St. Augustine's 'Confessions,' or to Pascal's 'Pensées.'   It is, perhaps, not quite analogous to either of these, especially as it is written under an assumed name; but it does unveil the author's hidden self, and teaches by recounting personal experiences, and may thus be termed 'Confessions,' or 'Thoughts,' rather than a dissertation or poem.   Its subject is the vanity of all that is human and earthly, and by contrast and implication the steadfastness and importance of the unseen.   The writer desires, in the first place (virtually, though not expressly), to comfort his countrymen under their present depressed circumstances, to teach them not to set their hopes on earthly success, or to fancy that their own efforts could secure happiness, but to make the best of the present, and to receive with thankfulness the good that God sends or permits.   He also urges the avoidance of externalism in religion, and shows wherein true devotion consists.   And, in the second place, he warns against despair or reckless licence, as though it mattered not what one did, as if there were no higher Power that regarded; he solemnly asserts his faith in an overruling providence, though we cannot trace the reason or course of its working; his conviction that all is ordered for the best; his unswerving faith in the life everlasting and in a future judgment, which shall remedy the seeming anomalies of this present existence.   In all the problems of life, in all the disappointments and difficulties that meet our best and noblest efforts, there is nothing to cling to, no anchor on which to rest, but the fear of God and obedience to his commands.   Whatever happens, or however things may seem to go contrary to one's wishes and aspirations, amid the outward prosperity of the wicked and the humiliation of the good, he triumphs in the assurance that he knows certainly that it shall be well with them that fear God (ch. viii. 12).   To convey this instruction the author does not compose a carefully ordered and well-arranged dissertation, nor does he propound a moral discourse; he takes another method; he puts forth his views under the mask of Solomon, the king whose name had become proverbial for wisdom. He makes this celebrated personage recount his wide experiences, and, under this veil, hiding his own personality, he presents his peace offering to his contemporaries. No one had such varied knowledge of man's powers and circumstances as Solomon; no one like him could command attention and respect at the hand of the Hebrew people; the impersonation secured an audience, and enabled the writer to say much to them that would have come with less grace and weight from another. Though the work has a certain unity, and its great subject is continually recurring, the writer does not confine himself within narrow limits; he takes occasion to give rules of life; he mingles practice with theory. It is as though he commenced his work with some idea of writing formally and methodically, and then, carried away by the influence of his subject, overwhelmed by the thought of the nothingness of human endeavour, he cannot get beyond this reflection, and while uttering maxims of wisdom and parables of common sense, he connects them with his predominant view, mingling aphorisms and confessions with some incongruity. It seemed good to him to record the opinions which crossed his mind at various times, and the modifications which he felt constrained to admit; thus he shows the progress of his thought towards the great conclusion which closes the treatise. This conclusion is the clue to the interpretation of the whole. Resting on this rock, Koheleth could relate his doubts, perplexities, disquietudes, without fear of being misunderstood or leading others astray.

The work has its natural place in the teaching of revelation and the progress of true religion. If the literal tendency of Mosaic legislation was in the direction of the strong belief in temporal rewards and punishments, and if this notion cramped all higher aspirations and set the heart on gross earthly hopes, it was Koheleth's business to introduce a spiritual element in these expectations, to supplement the earlier reticence concerning the life beyond the grave by giving expression to the belief in immortality. By showing the inapplicability of the ancient idea to all the circumstances of the present life, he led men to look to another life, and to see another meaning in those antique utterances which spake of temporal rewards and punishments, earthly success, earthly calamity. It was ordered by Providence that religious knowledge should be communicated gradually, that it should be revealed as men were able to bear it, here a little, there a little. Each book adds something to the store of dogma, just as each saint in old story reflects some feature of perfect manhood, and helps the conception of the character of Jesus Christ. The doctrine of future retribution, which is taken for granted in the New Testament, forms a very slight portion of the teaching of the earlier Scriptures; and the Holy Spirit has allowed the writers of Job, Psalms, and Ecclesiastes to express the sense of perplexity which the apparent anomalies in moral government presented to the thoughtful observer. Our author, indeed, finds a solution; but it is only by an exercise of faith in God's justice and goodness that he rises superior to the depressing effect of experience; and beyond this conviction of the ultimate victory of goodness he has nothing definite to offer. The way to the fuller revelation of the gospel is thus laid open. The mental struggles of this ancient Hebrew seer are a lesson for all time, and point to a need of further explication, which was duly to be given. And as the same questions have always been a source of solicitude and disquieted men's minds in every age, it has seemed good to Divine Providence to set these trials of faith in the pages of Scripture, that others, reading them, may see that they stand not alone, that their doubts have been the experience of many minds, and that as such as Koheleth, with imperfect knowledge and a partial revelation, rose superior to difficulties and let faith conquer mistrust, so Christians, who are better instructed, who stand in the full light of completer knowledge, should never for a moment feel misgiving concerning the dealings of God's providence; but in unswerving trust "commit the keeping of their souls to him in well-doing, as unto a faithful Creator," casting all their care upon him, knowing that he careth for them.

§ 4. Canonicity, Unity, and Integrity

Ecclesiastes has been received without controversy in the Christian Church as a book of the Bible. In all the extant catalogues, conciliar and private, it occurs undisputed. The Jewish Church, however, has not been quite so unanimous in its full acceptance; for although it is found in all the lists of sacred books, and had its place among the five rolls (*Megilloth*), there was, towards the end of the first Christian century, some hesitation in rabbinical schools to recognize its complete inspiration, and to commend its public recitation. Objections were made on the ground of apparent contradictions contained in different parts, of its want of harmony with other portions of Holy Scripture, and of certain heretical statements. Of these objections it is to be observed that they regard rather the retention of the book in the canon than its admission therein; and that, appearing first in the first Christian century, they show that up to that time, at any rate, Ecclesiastes had been included in the sacred catalogue. The seeming contradictions and discrepancies arise from a partial view of the contents, from taking isolated passages uncorrected and unexplained by other statements and the general tendency. For instance, Koheleth is said, in ch. ii. 2 and viii. 15, to commend mirth; and in ch. vii. 3 to prefer sorrow to laughter; in one place to praise the dead (ch. iv. 2); in another to prefer a live dog to a dead lion (ch. ix. 4). So again we read, "Rejoice, O young man, in thy youth, and walk in the ways of thine heart" (ch. xi. 9), whereas Moses warns against seeking after one's own heart and one's own eyes (Numb. xv. 39). These misapprehensions were soon set at rest, the orthodoxy of the final verses could not be questioned, the inspiration of the work was acknowledged, and it has ever since been received alike by the Jewish and Christian Churches. That it is not quoted in the New Testament, and is thus far deprived of the authorization afforded by such reference, detracts in no respect from its Divine character, nor is this affected by the transference of its authorship from Solomon to an unknown writer. The grounds on which it has been admitted into the sacred canon are independent of any such external confirmation, and the Holy Spirit compels recognition at the hands of the Church by evidence that is self-revealing and indubitable. It is clear also that, in our Lord's time, Ecclesiastes formed one of the twenty-two books of the Hebrew Scripture, most of which were endorsed by citation, and a virtual sanction was thus given to the rest of the collection.

The unity and integrity of our book have been called in question, chiefly by those who have noted the apparent contradictions which it contains, and have failed to apprehend the author's standpoint, and his reason for the introduction of these anomalies. Thus exception is taken by some against the seeming want of connection between ch. iv. 13, 14 and verses 15, 16; others have discovered dislocations in various passages, and wished to arrange the work in different fashion, according to their view of the writer's intention. Others, again, have detected interpolations and later additions. Thus Cheyne, having made up his mind that Koheleth did not believe in future retribution, strikes out as spurious all passages that favour the idea of a coming judgment; in a similar spirit Geiger and Nöldeke affect to see late insertions in ch. xi. 9 and xii. 7. But all this is surely uncritical. There is no pretence of proving that the incriminated passages differ *toto cœlo* in language and treatment from the rest of the work, or that they could not have been written by the author. An opinion concerning Koheleth's dogma is adopted and boldly asserted, and any expression which opposes this idea is at once attributed to a later editor, who foisted his own sentiments into the text. If this free handling of ancient documents is allowed when they seem to be in advance of what a perhaps shallow criticism deems to be the spirit of the age, how are we to maintain the genuineness of any unfettered thinker's work? Concerning the epilogue, however, there is a little more difficulty made by those who do not look upon it as the crown and conclusion of the whole, without which the work would be unsatisfactory and lack completion. The objections to this paragraph are twofold—linguistic and dogmatic. It is said that it contains expressions deviating from those that occur in the former parts. The discussion seems to end at ver. 8 of the last chapter; and the final passage differs in style and other particulars from the rest. But an examination of the language shows that it can be paralleled in every particular from the earlier pages, and the difference in style is necessitated by the subject. In this appendix, or postscript, the writer reveals himself, *in propria persona*, no longer under the veil of

Solomon, but taking the reader, as it were, into his confidence, showing what he really is, and his claim to attention. Far from being superfluous, the addition puts the seal to the whole production. Speaking of Koheleth in the third person, he virtually acknowledges the fictitious use of Solomon's authority. At the same time, he maintains that the work has not lost its value because it cannot vindicate its authorship at the hands of the great king. He himself has been inspired to write it; the same " Shepherd " who guided the pens of Solomon and other wise men directed him likewise. As to the momentous conclusion, every one who thinks with us concerning the religious views of the writer, and the design of his work, will agree that it is most apposite, and is the only conceivable summing-up that satisfies the requirements of the treatise. It is also in full accord with what has preceded. The solution of the anomalies in life, offered by the fact of a future judgment, has been intimated more than once in other parts of the book; it is here only presented again with more emphasis and in a more striking position. We may add that no doubt concerning the genuineness of the epilogue was ever raised by the Jewish schools which hesitated to allow full inspiration to Ecclesiastes. Indeed, it was the undoubted orthodoxy of the closing verses which finally overcame all opposition.

§ 5. LITERATURE

The literature connected with Ecclesiastes is of enormous extent. We can here only enumerate a few of the most useful commentaries and kindred works.

Among the Fathers we have these: Origen, 'Scholia;' Gregory Thaumaturgus, 'Metaphrasis;' Gregory Nyssen., 'Conciones;' Jerome, Version and 'Commentary;' Olympiodorus, 'Enarratio.' The mediæval and later expositions are innumerable: Hugo A. S. Victore, 'Homiliæ;' the Jews, Rashi, Rashbam, and Ibn Ezra; Luther, 'Annotationes;' Pineda, 'Commentarii;' Cornelius à Lapide; Grotius, 'Annotationes;' Reynolds, 'Annotations;' Smith, 'Explicatio;' Schmidt, 'Commentarius;' Mendelssohn, 'D. Buch Koheleth;' Umbreit, 'Uebers. und Darstell.,' and 'Koheleth Scepticus;' Knobel, 'Comment.;' Herzfeld, 'Uebers. und Erläut.;' Hitzig, 'Erklärung;' Stuart, 'Commentary;' Vaihinger, 'Uebers. und Erklär.;' Hengstenberg, 'Auslegung;' Ginsburg, 'Koheleth;' Plumptre, 'Ecclesiastes;' Wright, 'Book of Koheleth;' Tyler, 'Ecclesiastes;' Renan, 'L'Ecclésiaste Traduit;' Zöckler, in Lange's 'Bibelwerk,' and edited by Tayler Lewis; Delitzsch, in Clarke's 'For. Library;' Grätz, 'Kohélet;' Gietmann, in 'Cursus Script. Sacr.' (1890); Motais, 'Solomon et l'Ecclésiaste,' and in 'La Sainte Bible avec Commentaires;' Nowack, in 'Kurzgef. Exeg. Handbuch;' Volck, in 'Kurzgef. Kommentar' (1889); Bishop Wordsworth, 'Bible with Notes;' Bullock, in 'Speaker's Commentary;' Salmon, in Bishop Ellicott's 'Commentary for English Readers;' Cox, 'Expository Lectures,' and 'Book of Ecclesiastes' (1891).

§ 6. DIVISION INTO SECTIONS

The attempts to dissect the book and to arrange its contents methodically have been as numerous as the editors themselves. Every exegete has tried his hand at this work, and the difference of the results arrived at is at once a proof of the difficulty of the subject. Between the idea, on the one hand, that the book is a rough mass of materials, without form, argument, or method, and that which regards it as a well-balanced poem, with strophes and antistrophes, etc., there is wide scope for disagreement and dispute. Rejecting as arbitrary and unwarranted the transposition of verses, to which some critics have had recourse, we note a few of the most feasible arrangements offered by those who recognize the unity of the work, and the existence of a central idea which throughout is kept more or less prominently in view.

Many divide the book into four parts. Thus Zöckler, Keil, and Vaihinger: I. ch. i., ii.; II. ch. iii.—v.; III. ch. vi. 1—viii. 15; IV. ch. viii. 16—xii. 7; epilogue, ch. xii. 8—14. So Ewald, except that his second division comprises ch. iii. 1—vi. 9. M'Clintock and Strong: I. ch. i., ii.; II. ch. iii. 1—vi. 9; III. ch. vi. 10—viii. 15; IV. ch. viii. 16—xii. 8. According to Tyler, the work separates into two chief parts—the first, ch. i. 2—vi. 12, being the negative side, exhibiting the author's disappointments; the second, ch. vii. 1—xii. 8, the positive side, giving the philosophy of the matter, with some practical rules of life. Kleinert, in Herzog and Plitt's 'Real-Encyclop.,' analyzes thus: I. ch. i. 12—ii. 23, inductive proof of vanity from experience; II. ch. ii. 24—iii. 22, God's ordering; III. ch. iv.—vi., a collection of shorter sentences, expressing partly the result of I. and II.; IV. ch. vii. 1—ix. 10; V. ch. ix. 11—xii. 8. Ginsburg gives, prologue, four sections, and epilogue, viz.: prologue, ch. i. 2—11; I. ch. i. 12—ii. 26; II. ch. iii. 1—v. 19; III. ch. vi. 1—viii. 15; IV. ch. viii. 16—xii. 7; epilogue, ch. xii. 8—14.

From the above given details it will be seen that it is no easy matter to systematize the treatise, and to force it into logical periods. It was plainly never intended to be so taken, and cannot, without violence, be made to assume precise regularity. There is, indeed, no designed plan; it has a theme which gives it consistency and adherence; but, satisfied with this central idea, the author allows himself a certain liberty of treatment, and often branches off into collateral subjects. We think, however, that it contains two main divisions, the first of which conveys the extended proof of the vanity of earthly things, obtained by personal experience and observation; while the second deduces certain practical conclusions from the previous considerations, presenting warnings, counsels, and rules of life. Taking this view, we divide the book in the following manner :—

TITLE of the book. Ch. i. 1.

PROLOGUE. Vanity of earthly things, and their oppressive monotony. Ch. i. 2—11.

DIVISION I. Proof of the vanity of earthly things from personal experience and general observation. Ch. i. 12—vi. 12.
  Section 1. Vanity of striving after wisdom and knowledge. Ch. i. 12—18.
  Section 2. Vanity of striving after pleasure and wealth. Ch. ii. 1—11.
  Section 3. Vanity of wisdom, in view of the fate that awaits the wise and the fool, and the uncertainty of the future. Ch. ii. 12—26.

Section 4. The impotence of man before the providence of God, and the consequent duty to make the best of the present. Ch. iii. 1—22.

Section 5. Things which interrupt or destroy men's happiness, such as oppression, envy, useless toil, isolation, fickle popularity. Ch. iv. 1—16.

Section 6. Vanity in popular religion, worship, and vows. Ch. v. 1—7.

Section 7. Dangers in a despotic state, and the unprofitableness of wealth. Ch. v. 8—17.

Section 8. Man should enjoy all the good which God gives him. Ch. v. 18—20.

Section 9. Vanity of wealth without power of enjoying it. Ch. vi. 1—6.

Section 10. The insatiability of desire. Ch. vi. 7—9.

Section 11. Man's short-sightedness and powerlessness against Providence. Ch. vi. 10—12.

DIVISION II. Deductions from the above-named experiences, with warnings and rules of life. Ch. vii. 1—xii. 8.

Section 1. Practical rules of life set forth in proverbial form, recommending earnestness in preference to frivolity. Ch. vii. 1—7.

Section 2. True wisdom is shown in resignation to the ordering of God's providence. Ch. vii. 8—14.

Section 3. Warnings against excesses, and praise of the golden mean. Ch. vii. 15—22.

Section 4. Wickedness is folly; woman is the most evil thing in the world; man has perverted an originally good nature. Ch. vii. 23—29.

Section 5. True wisdom counsels obedience to the ruling powers, however oppressive, and submission to the decrees of Providence. Ch. viii. 1—9.

Section 6. The difficulty concerning the prosperity of the evil and the misery of the righteous in this world: how to be solved and met. Ch. viii. 10—15.

Section 7. The course of God's moral government is inexplicable. The uncertainty of life and the certainty of death ought to lead man to make the best of the present. Ch. viii. 16—ix. 10.

Section 8. The issues and duration of life cannot be calculated upon. Ch. ix. 11, 12.

Section 9. Wisdom is not always rewarded when it does good service. Ch. ix. 13—16.

Section 10. Some proverbs concerning wisdom and folly. Ch. ix. 17, 18.

Section 11. Wisdom is marred by the intrusion of a little folly. Ch. x. 1—3.

Section 12. Illustration of wise conduct under capricious rulers. Ch. x. 4—7.

Section 13. Proverbs intimating the benefit of prudence and caution. Ch. x. 8—11.

Section 14. Contrast between words and acts of the wise man and of the fool. Ch. x. 12—15.

Section 15. The misery of a state under a foolish ruler, and advice to subjects thus cursed. Ch. x. 16—20.

Section 16. The first remedy for the perplexities of life: the duty of benevolence; one should do one's duty diligently, leaving results to God. Ch. xi. 1—6.

Section 17. The second is a cheerful and contented spirit. Ch. xi. 7—9.

Section 18. The third is piety practised in early life, and before the faculties are numbed by the approach of age. The last days of the old man are graphically described under certain images and analogies. Ch. xi. 10—xii. 7. The book ends with the refrain, "All is vanity." Ch. xii. 8.

EPILOGUE. Observations commendatory of the author, explaining his standpoint, the object of the book, and the grand conclusion to which it leads. Ch. xii. 9—14.

ECCLESIASTES; OR, THE PREACHER

EXPOSITION

CHAPTER I.

Ver. 1.—THE TITLE.

Ver. 1.—**The words of the Preacher, the son of David, King in Jerusalem;** Septuagint, " King of Israel in Jerusalem" (comp. ver. 12). The word rendered "Preacher" is *Koheleth*, a feminine noun formed from a verb *kalal*, "to call" (see Introduction, § 1), and perhaps better rendered "Convener" or "Debater." It is found nowhere else but in this book, where it occurs three times in this chapter (vers. 1, 2, 12), three times in ch. xii. 8, 9, 10, and once in ch. vii. 27. In all but one instance (viz. ch. xii. 8) it is used without the article, as a proper name. Jerome, in his commentary, translates it, 'Concionator,' in his version 'Ecclesiastes.' It would seem to denote one who gathered around him a congregation in order to instruct them in Divine lore. The feminine form is explained in various ways. Either it is used abstractedly, as the designation of an office, which it seems not to be; or it is formed as some other words which are found with a feminine termination, though denoting the names of men, indicating, as Gesenius notes (§ 107, 3 *c*), a high degree of activity in the possessor of the particular quality signified by the stem; *e.g.* Alemeth, Azmaveth (1 Chron. viii. 36; ix. 42), Pochereth (Ezra ii. 57), Sophereth (Neh. vii. 57); or, as is most probable, the writer desired to identify Koheleth with Wisdom, though it must be observed that the personality of the author often appears, as in ch. i. 16—18; vii. 23, etc.; the *rôle* of Wisdom being for the nonce forgotten. The word "king" in the title is shown by the accentuation to be in apposition to "Koheleth" not to "David;" and there can be no doubt that the description is intended to denote Solomon, though his name is nowhere actually given, as it is in the two other works ascribed to him (Prov. i. 1; Cant. i. 1). Other intimations of the assumption of Solomon's personality are found in ch. i. 12, "I Koheleth was king," etc.; so in describing his consummate wisdom (ch. i. 13, 16; ii. 15; comp. 1 Kings iii. 12; v. 12), and in his being the author of many proverbs (ch. xii. 9; comp. 1 Kings iv. 32)—accomplishments which are not noted in the case of any other of David's descendants. Also the picture of luxury and magnificence presented in ch. ii. suits no Jewish monarch but Solomon. The origin of the name applied to him may probably be traced to the historical fact mentioned in 1 Kings viii. 55, etc., where Solomon gathers all Israel together to the dedication of the temple, and utters the remarkable prayer which contained blessing and teaching and exhortation. As we have shown in the Introduction (§ 2), the assumption of the name is a mere literary device to give weight and importance to the treatise to which it appertains. The term, "King in Jerusalem," or, as in ver. 12, "King over Israel in Jerusalem," is unique, and occurs nowhere else in Scripture. David is said to have reigned in Jerusalem, when this seat of government is spoken of in contrast with that at Hebron (2 Sam. v. 5), and the same expression is used of Solomon, Rehoboam, and others (1 Kings xi. 42; xiv. 21; xv. 2, 10); and the phrase probably denotes a time when the government had become divided, and Israel had a different capital from Judah.

Vers. 2—11.—PROLOGUE. The vanity of all human and mundane things, and the oppressive monotony of their continued recurrence.

Ver. 2,—**Vanity of vanities, saith the**

Preacher, vanity of vanities; all is vanity (comp. ch. xii. 8). "Vanity" is *hebel*, which means "breath," and is used metaphorically of anything transitory, frail, unsatisfying. We have it in the proper name Abel, an appropriate designation of the youth whose life was cut short by a brother's murderous hand. "Vanity of vanities," like "heaven of heavens" (1 Kings viii. 27), "song of songs" (Cant. i. 1), etc., is equivalent to a superlative, "most utterly vain." It is here an exclamation, and is to be regarded as the key-note of the whole subsequent treatise, which is merely the development of this text. Septuagint, ματαιότης ματαιοτήτων; other Greek translators, ἀτμὶς ἀτμίδων, "vapour of vapours." For "saith" the Vulgate gives *dixit;* the Septuagint, εἶπεν; but as there is no reference to any previous utterance of the Preacher, the present is more suitable here. In affirming that "all is vanity," the writer is referring to human and mundane things, and directs not his view beyond such phenomena. Such a reflection is common in sacred and profane writings alike; such experience is universal (comp. Gen. xlvii. 9; Ps. xxxix. 5—7; xc. 3—10; Jas. iii. 14). "Pulvis et umbra sumus," says Horace ('Carm.,' iv. 7. 16. "O curas hominum! O quantum est in rebus inane!" (Persius, 'Sat.,' i. 1). If Dean Plumptre is correct in contending that the Book of Wisdom was written to rectify the deductions which might be drawn from Koheleth, we may contrast the caution of the apocryphal writer, who predicates vanity, not of all things, but only of the hope of the ungodly, which he likens to dust, froth, and smoke (see Wisd. ii. 1, etc.; v. 14). St. Paul (Rom. viii. 20) seems to have had Ecclesiastes in mind when he spoke of the creation being subjected to vanity (τῇ ματαιότητι), as a consequence of the fall of man, not to be remedied till the final restitution of all things. "But a man will say, If all things are vain and vanity, wherefore were they made? If they are God's works, how are they vain? But it is not the works of God which he calls vain. God forbid! The heaven is not vain; the earth is not vain: God forbid! Nor the sun, nor the moon, nor the stars, nor our own body. No; all these are very good. But what is vain? Man's works, pomp, and vain-glory. These came not from the hand of God, but are of our own creating. And they are vain because they have no useful end. . . . That is called vain which is expected indeed to possess value, yet possesses it not; that which men call empty, as when they speak of 'empty hopes,' and that which is fruitless. And generally that is called vain which is of no use. Let us see, then, whether all human things are not of this sort" (St. Chrysostom, 'Hom. xii. in Ephes.').

Ver. 3.—**What profit hath a man of all his labour which he taketh under the sun?** Here begins the elucidation of the fruitlessness of man's ceaseless activity. The word rendered "profit" (*yithron*) is found only in this book, where it occurs frequently. It means "that which remains over, advantage," περισσεία, as the LXX. translates it. As the verb and the substantive are cognate in the following words, they are better rendered, *in all his labour wherein he laboureth.* So Euripides ('Androm.,' 134) has, Τί μόχθον μοχθεῖς, and ('And. Fragm.,' vii. 4), Τοῖς μοχθοῦσι μόχθους εὐτυχῶς συνεκπόνει. Man is *Adam*, the natural man, unenlightened by the grace of God. *Under the sun* is an expression peculiar to this book (comp. vers. 9, 14; ch. ii. 11, 17, etc.), but is not intended to contrast this present with a future life; it merely refers to what we call sublunary matters. The phrase is often met with in the Greek poets. Eurip., 'Alcest.,' 151—

Γυνή τ᾽ ἀρίστη τῶν ὑφ᾽ ἡλίῳ μακρῷ.

"By far the best of all beneath the sun."

Homer, 'Iliad,' iv. 44—

Αἳ γὰρ ὑπ᾽ ἠελίῳ τε καὶ οὐρανῷ ἀστερόεντι
Ναιετάουσι πόληες ἐπιχθονίων ἀνθρώπων.

"Of all the cities occupied by man
Beneath the sun and starry cope of heaven."
(Cowper.)

Theognis, 'Parœm.,' 167—

Ὄλβιος οὐδεὶς
Ἀνθρώπων, ὁπόσους ἥλιος καθορᾷ.

"No mortal man
On whom the sun looks down is wholly blest."

In an analogous sense we find in other passages of Scripture the terms "under heaven" (ver. 13; ch. ii. 3; Exod. xvii. 14; Luke xvii. 24) and "upon the earth" (ch. viii. 14, 16; Gen. viii. 17). The interrogative form of the verse conveys a strong negative (comp. ch. vi. 8), like the Lord's word in Matt. xvi. 26, "What shall a man be profited, if he shall gain the whole world, and forfeit his soul?" The epilogue (ch. xii. 13) furnishes a reply to the desponding inquiry.

Ver. 4.—**One generation passeth away, and** another **generation cometh.** The translation rather weakens the force of the original, which is, *a generation goeth, and a generation cometh.* Man is only a pilgrim on earth; he soon passes away, and his place is occupied by others. Parallelisms of this sentiment will occur to every reader. Thus Ben-Sira, "All flesh waxeth old as a garment: for the covenant from the beginning is, Thou shalt die the death. As of the green leaves on a thick tree, some fall and some grow; so is the generation of flesh and blood, one cometh to an end, and another is born. Every work rotteth and consumeth away, and the worker thereof shall go withal" (Ecclus. xiv. 17, etc.; comp. Job x. 21; Ps. xxxix. 13). The famous passage in Homer, 'Iliad,' vi. 146, etc., is thus rendered by Lord Derby—

"The race of man is as the race of leaves :
Of leaves, one generation by the wind
Is scattered on the earth; another soon
In spring's luxuriant verdure bursts to light.
So with our race : these flourish, those decay."

(Comp. ibid., xxi. 464, etc.; Horace, 'Ars Poet.,' 60.) **But** (and) **the earth abideth for ever.** While the constant succession of generations of men goes on, the earth remains unchanged and immovable. If men were as permanent as is their dwelling-place, their labours might profit; but as things are, the painful contrast between the two makes itself felt. The term, "for ever," like the Greek εἰς τὸν αἰῶνα, does not necessarily imply eternity, but often denotes limited or conditioned duration, as when the slave is engaged to serve his master "for ever" (Exod. xxi. 6), or the hills are called "everlasting" (Gen xlix. 26). This verse gives one instance of growth and decay in contrast with insensate continuance. The following verses give further examples.

Ver. 5.—**The sun also ariseth, and the sun goeth down.** The sun is another instance of ever-recurring change in the face of an enduring sameness, rising and setting day by day, and resting never. The legendary 'Life of Abram' relates how, having been hidden for some years in a cave in order to escape the search of Nimrod, when he emerged from his concealment, and for the first time beheld heaven and earth, he began to inquire who was the Creator of the wonders around him. When the sun arose and flooded the scene with its glorious light, he at once concluded that that bright orb must be the creative Deity, and offered his prayers to it all day long. But when it sank in darkness, he repented of his illusion, being persuaded that the sun could not have made the world and be itself subject to extinction (see 'Abraham: his Life and Times,' p. 12). **And hasteth to his place where he arose**; literally, and panteth (equivalent to hasteth, longeth to go) to its place arising there; i.e. the sun, sinking in the west, eagerly during the night returns to the east, duly to rise there in the morning. The "place" is the region of reappearance. The Septuagint gives, "The sun arises, and the sun sets, and draws (ἕλκει) unto its

place;" and then carries the idea into the following verse: "Arising there, it proceedeth southward," etc. The Vulgate supports the rendering; but there is no doubt that the Authorized Version gives substantially the sense of the Hebrew text as accentuated. The verb שָׁאַף (shaaph), as Delitzsch shows, implies "panting," not from fatigue, but in eager pursuit of something; and all notions of panting steeds or morning exhalations are quite foreign from the conception of the passage. The notion which Koheleth desires to convey is that the sun makes no real progress; its eager panting merely brings it to the old place, there to recommence its monotonous routine. Rosenmüller quotes Catullus, 'Carm.,' v. 4—6, on which Doering cites Lotich., 'Eleg.,' iii. 7. 23—

"Ergo ubi permensus coelum sol occidit,
　　idem
Purpureo vestit lumine rursus humum;
Nos, ubi decidimus, defuncti munere vitæ,
Urget perpetua lumina nocte sopor."

But our passage does not contrast the revival of the sun every morning with man's eternal sleep in death.

Ver. 6.—**The wind goeth toward the south, and turneth about unto the north**; literally, going towards the south, and circling towards the north. These words, as we have seen above, are referred to the sun by the Septuagint, Vulgate, and Syriac; but it is best to make this verse refer only to the wind—a fresh example of motion continually repeated with no real progress to an end. Thus each verse comprises one subject and idea, ver. 4 being concerned with the earth, ver. 5 with the sun, ver. 6 with the wind, and ver. 7 with the waters. There seems to be no particular force in the naming of north and south, unless it be in contrast to the sun's motion from east to west, mentioned in the preceding verse. The words following show that these two directions are not alone intended. Thus the four quarters are virtually included. **It whirleth about continually.** The original is more forcible, giving by its very form the idea of weary monotony. The subject is delayed till the last, thus: Going towards the south . . . circling, circling, goeth the wind; i.e. it blows from all quarters at its own caprice. **And the wind returneth again according to his circuits.** And on its circlings returneth the wind; it comes back to the point whence it started. The wind, seemingly the freest of all created things, is bound by the same law of immutable changeableness, insensate repetition.

Ver. 7.—**All the rivers run into the sea; yet the sea is not full.** Here is another instance of unvarying operation producing no tangible result. The phenomenon mentioned is often the subject of remark and speculation in classical authors. Commentators cite Aristophanes, 'Clouds,' 1293—

Αὕτη μὲν (sc. ἡ θάλαττα) οὐδὲν γίγνεται
'Επιρρεόντων τῶν ποταμῶν πλείων.

" The sea, though all the rivers flow therein,
Waxeth no greater."

Lucretius attempts to account for the fact,
' De Rer. Nat.,' vi. 608—

"Nunc ratio reddunda, augmen quin nesciat
æquor.
Principio mare mirantur non reddere majus
Naturam, quo sit tantus decursus aquarum,
Omnia quo veniant ex omni flumina parte."

This Dr. Busby thus versifies—

"Now in due order, Muse, proceed to show
Why the deep seas no augmentation know,
In ocean that such numerous streams discharge
Their waters, yet that ocean ne'er enlarge,"
etc.

No particular sea is intended, though some have fancied that the peculiarities of the Dead Sea gave occasion to the thought in the text. Doubtless the idea is general, and such as would strike every observer, however little he might trouble himself with the reason of the circumstance (comp. Ecclus. xl. 11). **Unto the place from whence the rivers come, thither they return again**; rather, *unto the place whither the rivers go, thither they go again.* As Wright and Delitzsch observe, שָׁם after verbs of motion has often the signification of שָׁמָּה; and the idea is that the streams continue to make their way into the sea with ceaseless iteration. The other rendering, which is supported by the Vulgate *unde*, seems rather to favour the Epicurean poet's solution of the phenomenon. Lucretius, in the passage cited above, explains that the amount of water contributed by rivers is a mere drop in the ocean; that a vast quantity rises in exhalations and is spread far and wide over the earth; and that another large portion finds its way back through the pores of the ground to the bed of the sea. Plumptre considers that this theory was known to Koheleth, and was introduced by him here. The rendering which we have given above would make this opinion untenable; it likewise excludes the idea (though that, indeed, may have been entertained by the Hebrews, Ps. civ. 10 and Prov. viii. 28) of the clouds being produced by the sea and feeding the springs. Thus Ecclus. xl. 11, "All things that are of the earth do turn to the earth again; and that which is of the waters doth return into the sea."

Ver. 8.—**All things are full of labour.** Taking the word *dabar* in the sense of " word " (compare the Greek ῥῆμα), the

LXX. translates, "All words are wearisome;" *i.e.* to go through the whole catalogue of such things as those mentioned in the preceding verses would be a laborious and unprofitable task. The Targum and many modern expositors approve this rendering. But besides that, the word *yaged* implies suffering, not causing, weariness (Deut. xxv. 18; Job iii. 17); the run of the sentence is unnecessarily interrupted by such an assertion, when one is expecting a conclusion from the instances given above. The Vulgate has, *cunctæ res difficiles.* The idea, as Motais has seen, is this—Man's life is constrained by the same law as his surroundings; he goes on his course subject to influences which he cannot control; in spite of his efforts, he can never be independent. This conclusion is developed in succeeding verses. In the present verse the proposition with which it starts is explained by what follows. All things have been the object of much labour; men have elaborately examined everything; yet the result is most unsatisfactory, the end is not reached; words cannot express it, neither eye nor ear can apprehend it. This is the view of St. Jerome, who writes, "Non solum de physicis, sed de ethicis quoque scire difficile est. Nec sermo valet explicare causas naturasque rerum, nec oculus, ut rei poscit dignitas, intueri, nec auris, instituente doctore, ad summam scientiam pervenire. Si enim nunc ' per speculum videmus in ænigmate; et ex parte cognoscimus, et ex parte prophetamus,' consequenter nec sermo potest explicare quod nescit; nec oculus in quo cæcutit, aspicere; nec auris, de quo dubitat, impleri." Delitzsch, Nowack, Wright, and others render, "All things are in restless activity;" *i.e.* constant movement pervades the whole world, and yet no visible conclusion is attained. This, however true, does not seem to be the point insisted on by the author, whose intention is, as we have said, to show that man, like nature, is confined to a circle from which he cannot free himself; and though he uses all the powers with which he is endowed to penetrate the enigma of life and to rise superior to his environments, he is wholly unable to effect anything in these matters. **Man cannot utter it.** He cannot explain all things. Koheleth does not affirm that man can know nothing, that he can attain to no certitude, that reason will not teach him to apprehend any truth; his contention is that the inner cause and meaning elude his faculties, that his knowledge is concerned only with accidents and externals, and that there is still some depth which his powers cannot fathom. **The eye is not satisfied with seeing, nor the ear filled with hearing.** Use his sight as he may, listen to the sounds around him, attend to the instructions of professed teachers, man makes no real advance in knowledge of the mysteries in which he is involved; the paradox is inexplicable. We have, in Prov. xxvii. 20, "Sheol and Abaddon are never satisfied; and the eyes of man are never satisfied." Plumptre quotes Lucretius's expression (ii. 1038), "Fessus satiate videndi." "Remember," says Thomas à Kempis ('De Imitat.,' i. 1. 5), "the proverb, that the eye is not satisfied with seeing, nor the ear with hearing. Endeavour, therefore, to withdraw thy heart from the love of visible things, and to transfer thyself to the invisible. For they that follow their sensuality do stain their conscience and lose the grace of God."

Ver. 9.—**The thing that hath been, it** is that **which shall be.** The LXX. and the Vulgate render the first clauses of the two parts of the verse in both cases interrogatively, thus: "What is that which hath been? The very thing which shall be. And what is that which hath been done? The very thing which shall be done." What has been affirmed of phenomena in the material world is now affirmed of the events of man's life. They move in an analogous circle, whether they are concerned with actions or morals. Plumptre sees here an anticipation or a reproduction of the Stoic doctrine of a recurring cycle of events, such as Virgil mentions in his fourth 'Eclogue'—

"Magnus ab integro sæclorum nascitur ordo," etc.

But Koheleth is speaking merely from experience, and is indulging in no philosophical speculations. There is **no new** thing **under the sun.** The Vulgate transfers this clause to the next verse, which, indeed, supports the assertion. From classical authors commentators have culled examples of the same thought. Thus Tacitus, 'Annal.,' iii. 55, "Nisi forte rebus cunctis inest quidam velut orbis, ut quem ad modum temporum vices, ita morum vertantur." Seneca, 'Epist.,' xxiv., "Nullius rei finis est, sed in orbem nexa sunt omnia; fugiunt ac sequuntur. . . . Omnia transeunt ut revertantur, nihil novi video, nihil novi facio. Fit aliquando et hujus rei nausea." M. Aurelius, 'Medit.,' vi. 37, "He that sees the present has seen all things, both that which has been from everlasting and that which shall be in the future. All things are of one birth and one form." Again, vii. 1, "There is nothing new; all things are common and quickly over;" xii. 26, "Everything that comes to pass was always so coming to pass, and will take place again." Justin Martyr, 'Apol.,' i. 57, has, perhaps, a reminiscence of this passage when he writes, Οὐ γὰρ δεδοίκαμεν θάνατον· τοῦ πάντως ἀποθανεῖν

ὁμολογουμένου, καὶ μηδενὸς ἄλλου καινοῦ ἀλλ' ἢ τῶν αὐτῶν ἐν τῇδε τῇ διοικήσει ὄντων.

Ver. 10.—**Is there** any **thing whereof it may be said, See, this is new?** The writer conceives that objection may be taken to his statement at the end of the preceding verse, so he proceeds to reiterate it in stronger terms. "Thing" is *dabar* (see on ver. 8). Septuagint, "He who shall speak and say, Behold, this is new," *scil.* Where is he? Vulgate, "Nothing is new under the sun, nor is any one able to say, Lo! this is fresh." The apparent exceptions to the rule are mistaken inferences. **It hath been already of old time, which was before us.** In the vast æons of the past, recorded or unrecorded, the seeming novelty has already been known. The discoveries of earlier time are forgotten, and seem quite new when revived; but closer investigation proves their previous existence.

Ver. 11.—**There is no remembrance of former** things; rather, *of former men*—persons who lived in former times. As things are considered novel only because they had been forgotten, so we men ourselves shall pass away, and be no more remembered. Bailey, 'Festus'—

"Adversity, prosperity, the grave,
 Play a round game with friends. **On some** the world
 Hath shot its evil eye, and they are passed
 From honour and remembrance; **and a** stare
 Is all the mention of their names receives;
 And people know no more of them than they know
 The shapes of clouds at midnight a year hence."

Neither shall there be any **remembrance of** things **that are to come with** those **that shall come after;** rather, *and even of later generations that shall be there will be no remembrance of them with those that shall be in the after-time.* Wright quotes Marcus Aurelius, who has much to say on this subject. Thus: cap. ii. 17, "Posthumous fame is oblivion;" cap. iii. 10, "Every man's life lies all within the present; for the past is spent and done with, and the future is uncertain;" cap. iv. 33, "Those words which were formerly current and proper are now become obsolete and barbarous. Alas! this is not all: fame tarnishes in time, too, and men grow out of fashion as well as language. Those celebrated names of ancient story are antiquated; those of later date have the same fortune; and those of present celebrity must follow. I speak this of those who have been the wonder of their age, and shined with unusual lustre; but as for the rest, they are no sooner dead than forgotten" (comp. Wisd. ii. 4). (On the keen desire to live in the memory of posterity, see Ecclus. xxxvii. 26; xliv. 7, etc.)

Ver. 12—ch. vi. 12.—Division I. PROOF OF THE VANITY OF EARTHLY THINGS FROM PERSONAL EXPERIENCE AND GENERAL OBSERVATION.

Vers. 12—18.—Section 1. *Vanity of striving for wisdom and knowledge.*

Ver. 12.—**I the Preacher was king over Israel in Jerusalem.** Koheleth relates his own experience as king, in accordance with his assumption of the person of Solomon. The use of the past tense in this verse is regarded by many as strong evidence against the Solomonic authorship of the book. " I have been king" (not "I have become king," as Grätz would translate) is a statement introducing the supposed speaker, not as a reigning monarch, but as one who, in time past, exercised sovereignty. Solomon is represented as speaking from the grave, and recalling the past for the instruction of his auditors. In a similar manner, the author of the Book of Wisdom (viii. 1—13) speaks in his impersonation of Solomon. That king himself, who reigned without interruption to his death, could not have spoken of himself in the terms used here. He lost neither his throne nor his power; and, therefore, the expression cannot be paralleled (as Mr. Bullock suggests) by the complaint of Louis XIV., unsuccessful in war and weary of rule, "When I was king." Solomon *redivivus* is introduced to give weight to the succeeding experiences. Here is one who had every and the most favourable opportunity of seeing the best side of things; and yet his testimony is that all is vanity. In the acquisition of wisdom, the contrast between the advantage of learned leisure and the interruptions of a laborious life is set forth in Ecclus xxxviii. 24, etc. *King over Israel.* The expression indicates a time before the division of the kingdom. We have it in 1 Sam. xv. 26, and occasionally elsewhere. The usual phrase is "King of Israel." (For *in Jerusalem,* see on ver. 1.)

Ver. 13.—**I gave my heart** (ver. 17; ch. vii. 25; Dan. x. 12). The heart, in the Hebrew conception, was the seat, not of the affections only, but of the understanding and intellectual faculties generally. So the expression here is equivalent to "I applied my mind." **To seek and search out.** The two words are not synonymous. The former verb (שׁוּר, *darash*) implies penetrating into the depth of an object before one; the other word (תּוּר, *tur*) taking a comprehensive survey of matters further away; so that two methods and scopes of investigation are signified. **By wisdom**; ἐν τῇ σοφίᾳ (Septuagint). Wisdom was the means or instru-

ment by which he carried on his researches, which were directed, not merely to the collecting of facts, but to investigating the causes and conditions of things. **Concerning all things that are done under heaven**; *i.e.* men's actions and conduct, political, social, and private life. We have "under the sun" in ver. 9, and again in ver. 14. Here there is no question of physical matters, the phenomena of the material world, but only of human circumstances and interests. **This sore travail** (rather, *this is a sore travail that*) **God hath given to the sons of man to be exercised therewith.** The word rendered "travail" (עִנְיָן, *inyan*) occurs often in this book (*e.g.* ch. ii. 23, 26, etc.), and nowhere else in the Old Testament. The same root is found in the word translated "exercised;" hence Wright has, "It is a woeful exercise which God has given to the sons of men wherewith to exercise themselves." If we keep to the word "travail," we may render, "to travail therein." It implies distracting business, engrossing occupation. Septuagint, περισπασμόν; Vulgate, *occupationem.* Man feels himself constrained to make this laborious investigation, yet the result is most unsatisfactory, as the next verse shows. "God" is here *Elohim,* and so throughout the book, the name *Jehovah* (the God of the covenant, the God of Israel) never once occurring. Those who regard Solomon as the author of the book account for this on the plea that the king, in his latest years, reflecting sadly on his backsliding and fall, shrank from uttering with his polluted lips the adorable Name once so often used with filial reverence and beloved. But the true reason is found in the design of Koheleth, which was to set forth, not so much Israel's position under the covenant, as the condition of man in the face of the God of nature. The idiosyncrasies and peculiar features of the chosen people are not the subject of his essay; he deals with a wider sphere; his theme is man in his relation to Divine providence; and for this power he uses that name, common alike to the true and false religions, *Elohim,* applied to the Supreme Being by believers and idolaters.

Ver. 14.—Here is the result of this examination of human actions. **I have seen all the works that are done under the sun.** In his varied experience nothing had escaped his notice. **And behold, all is vanity and vexation of spirit**; *reuth ruach; afflictio spiritus* (Vulgate); προαίρεσις πνεύματος, "choice of spirit," or, "wind" (Septuagint); νομὴ ἀνέμου (Aquila and Theodotion); βόσκησις ἀνέμου, "feeding on wind" (Symmachus). This last translation, or "striving after wind," seems to be most agreeable to the etymology of the word רְעוּת, which, except in this book (ch. ii. 11, 17, 26, etc.), occurs elsewhere only in the Chaldee portion of Ezra (v. 17; vii. 18). Whichever sense is taken, the import is much the same. What is implied is the unsubstantial and unsatisfying nature of human labours and endeavours. Many compare Hos. xii. 2, "Ephraim feedeth on wind," and Isa. xliv. 20, "He feedeth on ashes." In contrast, perhaps, to this constantly recurring complaint, the author of the Book of Wisdom teaches that murmuring is unprofitable and blasphemous (Wisd. i. 11). Bailey, in 'Festus,' sings—

" Of all life's aims, what's worth the thought
    we waste on't?
How mean, how miserable, seems every
    care!
How doubtful, too, the system of the mind!
And then the ceaseless, changeless, hope-
    less round
Of weariness, and heartlessness, and woe,
And vice, and vanity! Yet these make
    life—
The life, at least, I witness, if not feel.
No matter, we are immortal."

Ver. 15.—That which is **crooked cannot be made straight.** This is intended as a confirmation of ver. 14. By the utmost exercise of his powers and faculties man cannot change the course of events; he is constantly met by anomalies which he can neither explain nor rectify (comp. ch. vii. 13). The above is probably a proverbial saying. Knobel quotes Suidas: Ξύλον ἀγκύλον οὐδέποτ' ὀρθόν. The Vulgate takes the whole maxim as applying only to morals: " Perverse men are hardly corrected, and the number of fools is infinite." So too the Syriac and Targum. The Septuagint rightly as the Authorized Version. The writer is not referring merely to man's sins and delinquencies, but to the perplexities in which he finds himself involved, and extrication from which is impracticable. **That which is wanting cannot be numbered.** The word חֶסְרוֹן, " loss, defect," is ἅπαξ λεγόμενον in the Old Testament. We cannot reckon where there is nothing to count; no skill in arithmetic will avail to make up for a substantial deficit. So nothing man can do is able to remedy the anomalies by which he is surrounded, or to supply the defects which are pressed upon his notice.

Ver. 16.—Koheleth now arrives at his first conclusion, that wisdom is vanity. **I communed with mine own heart.** The expression suggests, as it were, an internal dialogue, as the Greek Venetian puts it, Διείλεγμαι ἐγὼ ξὺν τῇ καρδίᾳ μου (comp. ch. ii. 1, 15). **Lo, I am come to great estate.** If this be taken by itself, it makes Koheleth speak of his power and majesty first, and of his progress in wisdom afterwards; but it is best

to connect it with what follows, and to confine the clause to one idea; thus: " I have obtained great and ever greater wisdom"— I have continually added to my stores of knowledge and experience. **Than all they** (*above all*) **that have been before me in** (*over*) **Jerusalem.** Who are the rulers alluded to? Solomon himself was only the second of the Israelite kings who reigned there; of the Canaanite princes who may have made that their capital, we have no knowledge, nor is it likely that Solomon would compare himself with them. The Targum has altered the approved reading, and gives, " Above all the wise men that were in Jerusalem before me." The reading, " in [instead of ' over '] Jerusalem," has indeed some manuscript authority, and is confirmed by the Septuagint, Vulgate, and Syriac, but it is evidently a correction of the text by critics who saw the difficulty of the authorized wording. Motais and others assert that the preposition in the Masoretic text, עַל (*al*), often means " in," as well as " over," when the reference is to an elevated spot; *e.g.* Isa. xxxviii. 20; Hos. xi. 11. But even granting this, we are still uncertain who are the persons meant. Commentators point to Melchizedek, Adonizedek, and Araunah among rulers, and to Ethan, Heman, Chalcol, and Darda (1 Kings iv. 31) among sages. But we know nothing of the wisdom of the former, and there is no tangible reason why the latter should be designated " before me in Jerusalem." Doubtless the words point to a succession of kings who had reigned in Jerusalem, and the writer, involuntarily, perhaps, betrays his assumed character, involving an excusable anachronism, while giving to the personated monarch a position which could not belong to the historical Solomon. **Yea, my heart had great experience of** (*hath seen abundantly*, κατὰ πολύ Venetian) **wisdom and knowledge.** הַרְבֵּה used adverbially qualifies the word before it, "hath seen." The heart, as we have observed (ver. 13), is considered the seat of the intellectual life. In saying that the heart hath seen wisdom, the writer means that his mind has taken it in, apprehended and appropriated it (comp. ch. viii. 16; Job iv. 8). *Wisdom and knowledge; chokmah* and *daath*; σοφίαν καὶ γνῶσιν (Septuagint), the former regarding the ethical and practical side, the latter the speculative, which leads to the other (comp. Isa. xxxiii. 6; Rom. xi. 33).

Ver. 17.—**And I gave my heart.** He reiterates the expression in order to emphasize his earnestness and energy in the pursuit of wisdom. And knowing, as St. Jerome says, that " contrariis contraria intelliguntur," he studies the opposite of wisdom, and learns the truth by contrasting it with error. And to know madness and folly (ch. ii. 12). The former word, *holeloth* (intensive plural), by its etymology points to a confusion of thought, *i.e.* an unwisdom which deranges all ideas of order and propriety; and folly (here *sikluth*), throughout the sapiential books, is identified with vice and wickedness, the contradictory of practical godliness. The LXX. has παραβολὰς καὶ ἐπιστήμην, "parables and knowledge," and some editors have altered the Hebrew text in accordance with this version, which they consider more suitable to the context. But Koheleth's standpoint is quite consistent. To use the words of St. Jerome in his 'Commentary,' "Æqualis studii fuit Salomoni, scire sapientiam et scientiam, et e regione errores et stultitiam, ut in aliis appetendis et aliis declinandis vera ejus sapientia probaretur." On the other hand, Ben-Sira gives a much-needed warning against touching pitch (Ecclus. xiii. 1), and argues expressly that "the knowledge of wickedness is not wisdom" (Ecclus. xix. 22). Plumptre unnecessarily sees in the use of the term "madness" an echo of the teaching of the Stoics, who regarded men's weaknesses as forms of insanity. The moralist had no need to travel beyond his own experience in order to learn that sin was the acme of unwisdom, a declension from reason which might well be called madness. The subject is handled by Cicero, 'Tusc. Disput.,' iii. 4, 5. We are reminded of Horace's expression ('Carm.,' ii. 7. 27)—

"Recepto
Dulce mihi furere est amico."

And Anacreon's (xxxi.), Θέλω, θέλω μανῆναι. Thus far we have had Koheleth's secret thoughts—what he communed with his own heart (ver. 16). The result of his studies was most unsatisfying. **I perceived that this also is vexation of spirit**; or, *a striving after wind*, as ver. 14, though the word is somewhat different. All such labour is wasted, for man cannot control issues.

Ver. 18.—**For in much wisdom is much grief.** The more one knows of men's lives, the deeper insight one obtains of their actions and circumstances, the greater is the cause of grief at the incomplete and unsatisfactory nature of all human affairs. **He that increaseth knowledge increaseth sorrow;** not in others, but in himself. With added experience and more minute examination, the wise man becomes more conscious of his own ignorance and impotence, of the unsympathizing and uncontrollable course of nature, of the gigantic evils which he is powerless to remedy; this causes his sorrowful confession (ver. 17*b*). St. Gregory, taking the religious view of the passage, comments, "The more a man begins to know what he has lost, the more he begins to bewail the sentence of his corruption, which he has met with" ('Moral.,' xviii. 65); and, "He that already knows the high state which he does not as yet enjoy is the more grieved for the low condition in which he is yet held" (ibid., i. 34). The statement in our text is paralleled in Ecclus. xxi. 12, "There is a wisdom which multiplieth bitterness," and contrasted in Wisd. viii. 16 with the comfort and pleasure which true wisdom brings.

HOMILETICS.

Vers. 1, 12.—*Koheleth, the Preacher.* I. THE PREACHER'S NAME. Koheleth, signifying: 1. *The Assembler,* or Collector (Delitzsch, Bleek, Keil), not of sentences (Grotius), but of people. Hence: 2. *The Preacher* (Delitzsch, Wright), since the object for which he calls or convenes the assembly is to address it with words of wisdom (ch. xii. 9). 3. *The Debater* (Plumptre), since "the *Ecclesiastes* was not one who called the ecclesia or assembly together, or addressed it in a tone of didactic authority; but rather an ordinary member of such assembly (the political unit of every Greek state) who took part in its discussions" (ibid.).

II. THE PREACHER'S PERSON. 1. *Solomon.* In support of this, the traditional view, may be urged: (1) That the work is, or seems to be, ascribed to him by the writer (ver. 1). (2) That the experiences assigned to the Preacher (ch. ii. 1—3), the works declared to have been wrought by him (ch. ii. 4, 5), and the wisdom represented as possessed by him (ver. 17), are in perfect accord with what is known of the historical Solomon. (3) That the composition of this book cannot be proved to have been beyond the ability of Solomon (1 Kings iii. 12; x. 3, 4; xi. 41; 2 Chron. i. 12; ix. 22, 23). (4) That the writer obviously wished his words to be accepted as proceeding from Solomon. (5) That if Solomon was not the author, then the author is unknown—which is, to say the least, unfortunate. 2. *A late writer,* belonging to the Persian period (Delitzsch, Bleek, Keil, Plumptre, Hengstenberg, Wright, Cox). Arguments in support of this view are: (1) The author expressly distinguishes himself from

Solomon (ch. xii. 9—14), which, however, assumes that the Preacher could not have spoken about himself in the third person. (2) The Preacher writes of himself in the past tense (ver. 12), which Solomon would not have done, it is thought, though a late writer might have done so, putting his words into Solomon's mouth. This argument loses part of its validity if "was" is taken as equivalent to "was and still am" (Professors Douglas and Given), or if Solomon wrote towards the end of his reign (Fausset). (3) The Preacher talks of kings as having been before him in Jerusalem (ver. 16; ch. ii. 9), whereas anterior to Solomon only David reigned in Jerusalem. But a late writer could just as little as Solomon have used the expression cited, since it was Solomon whom the late writer intended to represent as speaking. Besides, as Jerusalem had been a royal city from the days of Melchizedek, it was open quite as much to Solomon to take into his mouth as to a post-exilic author to put into his mouth the words alluded to. (4) The real Solomon could not have written as the Preacher represents (ch. iv. 1; v. 8; x. 4, 7, 16, 20); which once more assumes that Solomon could only write of what he beheld in his own dominions, and not of what he may have learnt concerning other peoples with whom he had come into contact. (5) The language bears the stamp of the post-exilic period, being full of Aramaisms or Chaldaisms (see Exposition). If this be undeniable, it is partly counterbalanced by the fact that Ecclesiastes contains Solomonic words occurring in Proverbs—which may certainly have been derived by a late writer from a study of pre-existing Solomonic writings, but which may also be explained by common authorship—and partly accounted for by supposing that Solomon adopted them from pre-existing Aramaic writings, "owing to the Aramaic influences which surrounded and pressed upon him, and owing to the influence which he desired to exert throughout his widely extended dominions, which embraced the whole of the Aramaic communities as far as the Euphrates" (Professor Douglas, in Keil). (6) "The gloomy view of the world, and the philosophy of life which meet us in it, point us at once to the times after the exile" (Keil); but similar views and philosophies have more or less characterized all periods. (7) The complaint about much book-making must have issued from a late age (Bleek). Probably the preponderance of argument will be held as lying on the side of the non-Solomonic authorship of the book; though from the considerations just advanced two things will appear—*first*, that the Solomonic authorship is not destitute of foundation; and *second*, that the non-Solomonic authorship is not absolutely unassailable.

III. THE PREACHER'S CHARACTER. 1. *Not an atheist.* Since besides making frequent (thirty-seven times) mention of the name of God, he expressly recognizes God as the true God, exalted above the world (ch. v. 8), the Object of man's fear (ch. v. 7; xii. 13) and worship (ch. v. 1, 2), and the Disposer and Governor of all (ch. vii. 13); acknowledges the existence in man of a spirit (ch. xii. 7), and of such things as truth and error, right and wrong, holiness and sin (ch. v. 4—6; vii. 15, 16; ix. 2, 3); places the sum of duty as well as the secret of happiness in fearing God and keeping his commandments (ch. xii. 13); and hints his belief in the coming of a day when God will bring the secrets of all into judgment (ch. xi. 9). 2. *Not a pantheist.* The God he believes in is a personal Divinity, distinguished from the works he has made (ch. iii. 11) and the man he has created (ch. xii. 1); who issues commandments (ch. xii. 13), and can be worshipped by prayer, sacrifice, and vows (ch. v. 1—7); who should be feared (ch. v. 7), and who can accept the service of his intelligent creatures (ch. ix. 7). 3. *Not a pessimist.* Though at times seeming to indulge in gloomy views of life, to imagine that all things on earth are going to the bad, that the sum of human happiness is more than counterbalanced by that of human misery, that life is not worth living, and that the best a wise man can do is to escape from it in the easiest and most comfortable way he can; yet that these were not his deliberate opinions may be gathered from the frequency with which he exhorts men to cultivate a cheerful mind, and to enjoy the good of all their labour which God giveth them under the sun (ch. ii. 24—26; iii. 12; ix. 7; xi. 9), and from the emphatic manner in which he repudiates morose conclusions concerning the degeneracy of the times (ch. vii. 10). 4. *Not a libertine.* This notion (Plumptre) may appear to derive countenance from what the preacher says of himself (ch. ii. 1—3); but his language hardly warrants the conclusion that the author of this book had in his lifetime been a person of dissolute morals and profligate manners. If he was, before he penned this work he must have seen the error of his way. 5. *But a deeply thinking and religious man.* When he looked upon the mystery of life he felt perplexed. He saw that, apart from God and religion, life was an emptiness and vanity. Yet was he not thereby driven to despair, or impelled to renounce life as an unmixed evil; but rather offered it as his opinion that man's highest duty was to fear God and keep his commandments, to accept whatever good Providence might pour into his cup, bear with equanimity and submission whatever trials might be mingled in his lot, and prepare himself for the moment when he should pass into the unseen to render an account for the things done in the body (2 Cor. v. 10).

IV. THE PREACHER'S AIM. Neither: 1. *To expound the doctrines of pessimism*—to show " that the past has been like the present," and "the present like that which is to come," that "the present is bad," that "the past has not been better," and "that the future will not be preferable " (Renan). Nor: 2. *To furnish an autobiographical confession* (ideal, but based on personal experiences) of the progress of a Jewish youth from scepticism through sensuality to faith (Plumptre). But possibly: 3. *To comfort God's people*, the Hebrew Church, *under oppression*—that of Persian rule, *e.g.*, supposing the book to be a late composition, by showing them the vanity of earthly things, and exhorting them " to seek elsewhere their happiness; to draw it from those inexhaustible eternal fountains, which even at that time were open to all who chose to come " (Hengstenberg). And certainly: 4. *To exhibit the true secret of felicity in the midst of life's vanities*, which consisted, as above explained, in fearing God and keeping his commandments.

LESSONS. 1. The inspiration of a Scripture not dependent on a knowledge of its date or author. 2. The value of the Bible as a key to the problem of the universe. 3. The succession of Heaven-sent preachers that have appeared all down the centuries.

Vers. 2—11.—*" Vanity of vanities."* I. THE UNPROFITABLE CHARACTER OF ALL HUMAN LABOUR. (Ver. 3.) Passing over the pathetic picture these words instinctively call up of human life as a ceaseless round of toil—a picture which modern civilization, with all its appliances and refinements, has not obliterated, but rather, in the experience of many, painted in still more lurid colours; a picture which has always possessed for poetic minds, sacred (Job vii. 1, 2) no less than profane (Thomas Hood, 'Song of the Shirt '), a peculiar fascination—readers may note the melancholy truth to which the Preacher here adverts, viz. that the solid outcome of human labour, in the shape of permanent advantage to either society at large or the individual, is comparatively small. 1. *This cannot mean that labour is wholly useless* (ch. v. 19), since without labour man cannot find that bread which is needful for his bodily sustenance (Gen. iii. 19). It would be misconceiving the Preacher to suppose he disapproved of all that has been effected by human industry and genius to enrich, enlighten, and civilize the race, or desired to teach that men had better times of it on earth when they lived like savages upon the spontaneous fruits of the earth. 2. *Nor is it likely that he designed to glance at what has been a sore evil under the sun ever since men began to divide themselves into labourers and capitalists*, viz. *the small portion of labour's fruits which usually fall to the former*, without whom there would be little or no fruits at all. 3. *It is rather probable that the writer was thinking, not of labourers so called, to the exclusion of other workers, but of all toilers without distinction*, when he said that the outcome of man's activity, so far at least as attaining to felicity was concerned, was practically nothing.

II. THE UNCEASING CHANGE TO WHICH ALL MUNDANE THINGS ARE SUBJECT. (Vers. 4—7.) 1. *Illustrated in four particulars.* (1) The passing by of human generations, in comparison with which the globe seems stable (ver. 4); (2) the daily revolution of the sun (ver. 5); (3) the circling of the winds (ver. 6); and (4) the returning of the rivers to the seas (ver. 7). The writer means not to assert that these different cycles have no uses in the economy of nature—which uses may be here illustrated; merely he pitches upon what belongs to them in common, the element of changefulness, to him a picture of man's condition on the earth generally. 2. *Explained by four clauses.* It is as if he said, " Look around and behold ! All things on earth are perpetually on the move—the sun in the sky, the winds in the firmament, the clouds in the air, the waters in the ocean, the rivers on the meadow, man himself upon the surface of the globe. Nothing bears the stamp of finality. Everything is shifting. Nothing remains long in one stay. 'All things are full of labour and weariness; man cannot utter it: the eye is not satisfied with seeing, nor is the ear filled with hearing'" (ver. 8)—by which he means that the changeful condition is never done; there never comes a time when the eye says, "Enough!" or the ear repeats, "Behold! I am full." This view of life had occurred to many before the Preacher's day (Gen. xlvii. 9; 1 Chron. xxix. 15; Job iv. 19, 20; vii. 6; viii. 9), as it has occurred to some since—to the Greek philosophers who described nature as in a state of perpetual flux, to modern poets such as Shakespeare, and to sacred writers like John (1 John ii. 17) and Paul (1 Cor. vii. 31.)

III. THE WEARISOME MONOTONY OF LIFE. (Vers. 9, 10.) 1. *What the Preacher could not have meant.* That no new occurrence ever happens on the earth, that no new contrivance ever is devised, that no new experience ever emerges. Because since the Preacher's day multitudes of new discoveries and inventions have been made in all departments of science; while in the sphere of religion at least one new thing has taken place, viz. the Incarnation (Jer. xxxi. 22), and another will take place (Isa. lxv. 17). 2. *What the Preacher did mean.* That the general impression made by life upon beholders is that of sameness. Going back to the above illustrations, he would have said, "See how it is in nature. No doubt one new day succeeds another, one gale of wind follows another, and one body of waters hastens after another. But every day and always it is the same thing over again; the same old sun which reappears in the east; and the same gusts of wind to which we are accustomed that blow from the north to the south, and whirl about continually to all points of the compass; and the same stream that keeps on filling up its fountains and sending forth its waters to the sea. And if you will look at the world of humanity it is the same. A new generation appears on the globe every thirty years, and every hour of every day new individuals are being born; but they are substantially the same old men and women that were here before. 'Fed by the same food, hurt by the same weapons, warmed and cooled by the same summer and winter' as those who preceded them, they go through the same experiences their fathers and mothers went through before them." This feeling of monotony is even more emphasized when attention is fixed on the individual. Try to think of how monotonous and wearisome an ordinary human life is! An attempt to realize this will awaken surprise.

IV. THE UNIVERSAL OBLIVION INTO WHICH MEN AND THINGS MUST EVENTUALLY SINK. (Ver. 11.) So obvious is this that it scarcely needs illustration. Consider what a small portion of the earth's incidents during the past six thousand years have survived in history, and how few of the world's great ones have left behind them more than their names. The memory has been preserved of a Flood, but what about the ordinary words and actions that make up everyday life during the years between the Creation and the Deluge? A few particulars have been preserved of the histories of an Abraham and a David, a Sennacherib and a Nebuchadnezzar, an Alexander and a Cæsar; but what about the myriads that formed their contemporaries? How much has been transmitted to posterity of the history of these islands? How few of the events of last year have been recorded? How many of those who then died are still remembered? This is, no doubt, all as it should be; but still it is a proof of the vanity of things below, if these be regarded simply in themselves.

CONCLUSION. This view of life should not be possible to a Christian who enjoys the fuller and clearer light of the New Testament revelation, and views all things in their relations to God, duty, and immortality.

Ver. 15.—*Concerning crooked things and things wanting.* I. IRREGULARITIES AND DEFECTS EXIST IN THE WORLD'S PROGRAMME. This the teaching of the two proverbs, that crooked things cannot be straightened, *i.e.* by man, or wanting things numbered. To the seeker after wisdom, who surveys all the works that are done under the sun, and gives his heart to search into and to seek out by wisdom with regard to these what is their end and issue, there appear in the physical, mental, and moral worlds anomalies, irregularities, excrescences, deviations from the straight line of natural order, as well as defects, wants, imperfections, gaps, cleavages, interruptions, failures to reach completeness, which arrest attention and excite astonishment. 1. *Of irregularities or crooked things,* such phenomena as these may be cited: (1) In the physical world, storms, tempests, accidents, diseases, sudden and unexpected calamities. (2) In the mental world, perverted judgments, erroneous beliefs, false conclusions. (3) In the moral world, wicked principles and depraved actions, sins of every kind, transgressions of human and Divine law. 2. *Of things wanting or defects*, may be reckoned these: (1) In the material realm, scenes where some element is wanting to complete their beauty or utility, as *e.g.* a Sahara without a green leaf to refresh the eye, or a well at which to quench the thirst; or forms of life that never attain to maturity, as *e.g.* buds that drop before ripening into flowers or fruit. (2) In the intellectual sphere, ignorance, limited knowledge, defective education, one-sided apprehension of truth, narrow and imperfect views. (3) In the moral domain, actions that, without being wholly wrong, yet fall short of being fully right, as *e.g.* where one tells a half-truth, or does less in particular circumstances than duty demands of him.

II. SUCH IRREGULARITIES AND DEFECTS ARE BEYOND THE POWER OF MAN TO REMOVE OR REMEDY. This, at least, is the doctrine of the above two proverbial sayings. 1. *The doctrine, however, is not absolutely and universally true.* In the physical, mental, and moral worlds, man can do something to straighten what is crooked and supply what is lacking. For instance, by skill and foresight he can guard himself to some extent against the virulence of disease, the violence of storms and tempests, the destructiveness of unexpected calamities; by education he can protect himself and others against the perils arising from defective knowledge and erroneous judgments; by personal cultivation of virtue he can at least diminish the quantity of its opposite, vice, in the world. If he cannot straighten out all the crooks, he can even some; if he cannot remedy every defect, he can remove a few. 2. *Yet the doctrine is true in the sense intended by the Preacher.* This is, that after man has done his utmost there will remain anomalies that baffle him to explain, a sense of incompleteness which nothing he can attempt will remove. Let him prosecute his investigations ever so widely and vigorously, there always will be " more things in heaven and earth than are dreamt of in his philosophy"—enigmas he cannot solve, antinomies he cannot reconcile, defects he cannot fill up.

III. THE EXISTENCE OF SUCH IRREGULARITIES AND DEFECTS SUGGESTS SOME IMPORTANT LESSONS. As: 1. *That the present system of things is not final.* Nothing that is imperfect can be final. The crooked things that want straightening and the lacking things that need supplying contain a dim prophecy of a future and better order, in which the crooked things will be straightened and the defective things supplied. 2. *That man's power of apprehending things is incomplete.* From this probably arises not a little of that sense of disorder and incompleteness in the outer world of which he complains. 3. *That things impossible to man may be possible to God.* Though man's faculties are limited, it does not follow that God's power is. The crooked things that man cannot straighten, God can straighten if it seem good to his wisdom. 4. *That man's duty meanwhile is to submit and wait.* Instead of fretting at what he cannot rectify, he should aim at extracting from it that moral discipline which, doubtless, it is intended to impart; and instead of rushing to hasty conclusions from what he only imperfectly apprehends, he ought in a spirit of hopefulness to wait for further light.

Ver. 18.—*Increase of knowledge, increase of sorrow.* I. BECAUSE NOT WITHOUT LABOUR AND PAIN, OFTENTIMES PROTRACTED AND ACUTE, CAN KNOWLEDGE OF ANY KIND BE INCREASED. No royal road to wisdom any more than to wealth. He who would acquire knowledge must dig for it as for hidden treasures (Prov. ii. 4). Those who have attained to greatest distinction, as philosophers, poets, astronomers, etc., have all been hard workers. The information that renders them so wise and their society so agreeable has been slowly and painfully collected by diligent and unremitting effort, sustained through years, often amid hardships, and by means of self-denials which would have caused them to abandon their enterprises had they been common men, sometimes at the expense of restless days and sleepless nights, and in the midst of bodily infirmities not soothed but aggravated by close and severe study. No doubt, to one inspired with a love of knowledge, such labours and anxieties are more than compensated by the knowledge so acquired; but the proposition of the Preacher is that the largest amount of wisdom one may gather is an insufficient requital for all this toil and anxiety, if the knowledge be only earthly and secular—*i.e.* has no connection with God, duty, or immortality—and one cannot help asking if the Preacher is not right.

II. BECAUSE, AS THE CIRCLE OF KNOWLEDGE WIDENS, THE SPHERE OF IGNORANCE APPEARS TO ENLARGE. One is prone to imagine that, as the circle of information widens, that of ignorance contracts—which it does in the sense that, the more one knows, the sum of what remains to be known diminishes; but in another and important sense the amount of what remains to be known increases. As in mountain-climbing, the higher one ascends he sometimes discovers heights beyond of which previously he had no suspicion, so in footing it up the steep and difficult slopes of Parnassus, one actually comes to see that the more extensive the boundaries of this knowledge become, the vaster grow the regions beyond into which he has not yet penetrated. A child, for instance, looking up for the first time into the evening sky, imagines he has understood it all at a glance; but afterwards, when he has learnt the elementary truths of astronomy, there rushes on him the conviction that what he knows is but a small part of a very large whole; and as he prosecutes his search into the wonders of star-land, he realizes that the more he knows of it the more there remains to be known, till he feels that with respect to this, at least, " he that increases knowledge increases sorrow." Nor is this experience confined to one department of knowledge, but in every department it is the same; the larger and clearer one's acquaintance becomes with it, it only seems to open up untrodden realms beyond, the bare contemplation of which exercises on the mind a strangely depressing influence.

III. BECAUSE AS ONE EXTENDS HIS KNOWLEDGE HIS DIFFICULTIES SEEM TO MULTIPLY. Especially in dealing with the problem of existence. Contrast the states of childhood and manhood, of ignorance and learning, of savage peoples and of civilized nations. The child is unconscious of anxieties that oppress the parental bosom. The peasant, innocent of geology, biology, astronomy, and history, is not troubled with mental, moral, and religious difficulties such as perplex those acquainted with these themes. The heathen, with crude and ill-defined ideas of God, duty, and immortality, are incapable of appreciating those questionings concerning the future life that proceed in Christian minds. Not that it is not better to increase in knowledge, even should such increase awaken and foster doubts; only to increase in knowledge does not necessarily bring peace to the heart or happiness to the soul. It enables one to discern dark problems where none were discerned before; it pushes one on to inquire after solutions for those problems which, nevertheless, constantly elude the grasp. In the region of morals and religion especially it burdens one with a sense of weariness and pain, because of the endless questionings it raises and cannot answer. One who has never been launched upon this sea of doubt can hardly appreciate the wretchedness of those who have been tossed by its raging billows. Those who can hold on by ideas of God, duty, and immortality for the most part escape these perplexities; the man who tries to solve the problem of the universe without these fundamental and regulative conceptions does not, but becomes entangled in a labyrinth of difficulties, and commonly ends by finding himself " in wandering mazes lost."

IV. BECAUSE AS ONE EXTENDS HIS KNOWLEDGE, HE EXTENDS AT THE SAME TIME HIS ACQUAINTANCE WITH THE WORLD'S SORROW. Often said, " One half of the world knows not how the other half lives." How much, *e.g.*, does the civilized Briton know of the degradation of " darkest Africa; " or the religiously educated youth or maiden of the sin that runs rampant in modern society; or the well-fed, well-clothed, and well-housed citizen of the aching hearts and miserable lives of the houseless and breadless poor who herd in great cities? Because these things are not known, the Christians of Great Britain are comparatively indifferent to the sad and sorrowful condition of the poor and criminal classes at home, and of the heathen abroad. Did they properly consider these things, they would be filled with sorrow. Should this be adduced as a reason why one should not trouble himself with such disagreeable subjects, the answer is that if God, duty, and immortality are fictions, it is perhaps better to let the world stew in its own wretchedness and profligacy, and to guard one's felicity from being invaded by such disquieting influences; but if God, duty, and immortality are realities, it may be perilous to exhibit such indifference towards the world's wretchedness and sin.

V. BECAUSE INCREASE OF KNOWLEDGE AUGMENTS MAN'S POWER BOTH OF CAUSING AND OF FEELING SORROW. Knowledge is power. Insight into nature's laws enables one to apply these to mechanical uses which, in the absence of such insight, would be impossible. A person of large intelligence and mature experience can do things transcending the capacity of youth. Yet this increased efficiency, which springs from increased knowledge, does not always augment the sum of happiness. If it helps man to multiply instruments for good, it also enlarges his ability to perpetrate evil. It was once believed that crime and misery would disappear from society with the general diffusion of education. No one believes that now. Mere knowledge has no tendency to make men good. (Milton's Satan was not a fool.) It will help such as are good to means and opportunities for doing good; but just as certainly it will aid the wicked in their wickedness, and add to their power of causing misery. Then, in so far as knowledge or education has a tendency to refine the nature, intensify the feelings, quicken the susceptibilities, to that extent it augments the sum of human sorrow.

Learn: 1. Not to glorify ignorance or despise knowledge, but to seek first that "wisdom which cometh from above" (Jas. i. 5; iii. 17). 2. To seek other knowledges, not so much for their own sakes, as for the purpose of using them in God's service and for his glory.

HOMILIES BY VARIOUS AUTHORS

Ver. 2.—"*All is vanity.*" If we regard this book as Solomon's own record and statement of his remarkable experience of human life, it must be deemed by us a most valuable lesson as to the hollowness and emptiness of worldly greatness and renown. If, on the other hand, we regard the book as the production of a later writer, who lived during the troubled and depressed period of Jewish history which followed the Captivity, it must be recognized as casting light upon the providentially appointed consequences of national sin, apostasy, and rebellion. In the former case the moral and religious significance of Ecclesiastes is more personal, in the latter case more political. In either case, the treatise, as inspired by Divine wisdom, demands to be received and studied with reverential attention. Whether its lessons be congenial or unwelcome, they deserve the consideration of those of every age, and of every station in society. Some readers will resent the opening words of the treatise as gloomy and morbid; others will hail them as the expression of reason and wisdom. But the truth they contain is independent of human moods and temperaments, and is only to be fully appreciated by those whose observation is extensive and whose reflection is profound. The wise man makes a broad and unqualified statement, that all things earthly and human are but vanity.

I. THIS MAY BE A STATEMENT OF A MERE MOOD OF FEELING OWING TO INDIVIDUAL EXPERIENCE. There are times when every man who lives is distressed and disappointed, when his plans come to nought, when his hopes are blasted, when his friends fail him, when his prospects are clouded, when his heart sinks within him. It is the common lot, from which none can expect to be exempt. In some instances the stormy sky clears and brightens, whilst in other instances the gloom thickens and settles. But it may be confidently asserted that, at some period and in some circumstances, every human being, whose experience of life is large and varied, has felt as though he has been living in a scene of illusion, the vanity of which has been perhaps suddenly made apparent to him, and then the language of the writer of Ecclesiastes has risen to his lips, and he has exclaimed in bitterness of soul, "Vanity of vanities; all is vanity!"

II. THIS MAY BE A STATEMENT OF PAINFUL EXPERIENCE, DEPENDENT UPON THE SPECIAL TIMES—POLITICAL AND ECCLESIASTICAL—IN WHICH THE LOT IS CAST. Such is the mutability of human affairs, that every nation, every Church, passes through epochs of prosperity, confidence, energy, and hope; and again through epochs of adversity, discouragement, depression, and paralysis. The Israelites had their times of conquest and of progress, and they had also their times of defeat, of captivity, of subjection, of humiliation. So has it been with every people, every state. Nor have the Churches into which Christian communities have been formed, escaped the operation of the same law. So far as they have been human organizations, they have been affected by the laws to which all things human are subject. In times when a nation is feeble at home and despised abroad, when faction and ambition have reduced its power and crippled its enterprise, there is proneness, on the part of the reflecting and sensitive among the citizens and subjects, to lament over the unprofitableness and vanity of civil life. Similarly, when a Church experiences declension from the Divine standard of faith, purity, and consecration, how natural is it that the enlightened and spiritual members of that Church should, in their grief over the general deadness of the religious community, give way to feelings of discouragement and foreboding, which find a fitting expression in the cry, " Vanity of vanities; all is vanity! "

III. THIS MAY BE A STATEMENT OF PHILOSOPHICAL REFLECTION UPON THE FACTS OF NATURE AND OF HUMAN LIFE. It would be a mistake to suppose that the cry of " Vanity! " is always the evidence of a merely transitory though powerful mood of morbid feeling. On the contrary, there have been nations, ages, states of society, with which it has been a settled conviction that hollowness and emptiness characterize all human and earthly affairs. Pessimism may be a philosophical creed, as with the ancient Buddhists and some of the modern Germans; it may be a conclusion reached by reflection upon the facts of life. To some minds unreason is at the heart of the universe, and in this case there is no ground for hope. To other minds, not speculative, the survey of human affairs is suggestive of aimlessness in the world, and occasions despondency in the observant and reflective mind. Thus even some who enjoy health and prosperity, and in whose constitution and circumstances there is nothing to justify discouragement and hopelessness, are nevertheless found, without any serious satisfaction in existence, ready to sum up their conclusions, derived from a perhaps prolonged and extensive survey of human life, in the words of the writer of Ecclesiastes, "All is vanity! "

IV. THIS MAY BE A STATEMENT OF RELIGIOUS CONVICTION, BOTH SPRINGING FROM AND LEADING TO THE KNOWLEDGE OF THE ETERNAL AND GLORIOUS GOD. The student of physical science looks at facts; it is his duty to observe and to classify facts; their arrangement under certain relations, as of likeness and of sequence, is his business, in the discharge of which he renders a great service to mankind. But thought is as necessary as observation. A higher explanation than physical science can give is imperatively required by human nature. We are constrained, not only to observe *that* a thing is, but also to ask *why* it is. Here metaphysics and theology come in to complete the work which science has begun. Human life is composed not only of movements, which can be scientifically accounted for, but of actions, of which the explanation is hyperphysical, is spiritual. Similarly with the world at large, and with human life and history. The facts are open to observation; knowledge accumulates from age to age; as experience widens, grander classifications are made. Still there is a craving for explanation. Why, we ask, are things as they are? It is the answer to this question which distinguishes the pessimist from the theist. The wise, the enlightened, the religious, seek a spiritual and moral significance in the universe—material and psychical. In their view, if things, as they are and have been, be regarded by themselves, apart from a Divine reason working in and through them, they are emptiness and vanity. On the other hand, if they be regarded in the light of that Divine reason, which is order, righteousness, and love, they are suggestive of what is very different indeed from vanity. To the thoughtful and reverent mind, apart from God, all is vanity; seen in the light of God, nothing is vanity. Both these seeming contradictions are true, and they are reconciled in a higher affirmation and unity. Look at the world in the light of sentience and the logical understanding, and it is vanity. Look at it in the light of reason, and it is the expression of Divine wisdom and Divine goodness.

APPLICATION. It is well to see and feel that all is vanity, if we are thus led to turn from the phenomenal to the real, the abiding, the Divine. But it will be to our hurt if we dwell upon the vanity of all things, so that pessimism be fostered, so that we fail to recognize Infinite Reason at the heart of all things, so that we regard this as the worst of all worlds, so that for us the future has no brightness.—T.

Vers. 3, 4.—*The vanity of man's life.* At the very outset of his treatise, the wise man gives his readers to understand that the vanity which is ascribed to all things that are, is distinctive in an especial and obvious manner of human life. This is the most interesting of all things to observe and study, as it is the most precious to possess. And there is some danger lest, if the study of it lead to despondency, the possession of it should cease to be valued.

I. THE FACTS UPON WHICH THE CONVICTION OF THE VANITY OF LIFE IS FOUNDED. 1. The unsatisfying character of human toil. Labour is the destiny of man, and is in most cases the indispensable condition of not only life itself, but of those things for the sake of which many men value life—wealth, comfort, pleasure, and fame. Yet in how many cases does toil fail to secure the objects for the sake of which it is undertaken! Men labour, but reap no harvest of their painful, wearying efforts. And when the result is obtained, how commonly does it yield little or nothing of the satisfaction desired! Men toil for years, and when they attain that upon which their hearts were set, disappointment and dissatisfaction take possession of their nature. 2. The brevity of human life, and the rapid succession of the generations. The reflection of the wise man is a reflection which must have been current among men from the earliest ages. No sooner has a laborious and successful man reached the summit of his ambition, grasped the object of his desire, than he is taken away from the enjoyment of that for the sake of which he was content to " scorn delights, and live laborious days." The next generation renews the quest, only to repeat the experience of disappointment. Changes and improvements take place in many details of our life; but life itself remains throughout the ages, subject to the same limitations and the same calamities, to the same uncertainties and the same close. 3. The contrast between the transitoriness of human life and the stability of the unconscious earth. It appears strange and inexplicable that man, with the great possibilities of his nature, should be so short-lived, and that the earth should outlast generation after generation of mankind. The writer of Ecclesiastes felt, as every reflecting observer must feel, the sadness of this contrast between the perpetuity of the dwelling-place and the brief sojourn of its successive inhabitants. 4. The impossibility of any generation reaping the harvest for which it has sown. The toil, the genius, the enterprise of a generation may indeed bear fruit, but it is the generation which follows that enjoys that fruit. All men labour more for posterity than for themselves. " This also is vanity."

II. THE CHARACTER OF THE INFERENCE FROM THESE FACTS, VIZ. THAT LIFE IS PROFITLESS AND VAIN. 1. It is attributable to the reflecting and aspiring nature of man. A being less endowed with susceptibilities and imagination, with moral capacities and far-reaching aims and hopes, would be incapable of such emotions and such conclusions as this book expresses. The brute is content to eat and drink, to sleep, and to follow its several instincts and impulses. But of man we may say that nothing that he can be and do can give him perfect rest and satisfaction. It is owing to an innate and noble dissatisfaction that he is ever aiming at something better and higher, and that the narrow range and brief scope of human life cannot content him, cannot furnish him with all the opportunity he desires in order to acquire and to achieve. 2. It is attributable to the very nature of earthly things, which, because they are finite, are incapable of satisfying such a nature as that described. They may and do answer a high purpose when their true import is discerned—when they are recognized as symbolical and significant of what is greater than themselves. But no material good, no terrestrial distinctions, can serve as " profit" of labour. If so regarded, their vanity must sooner or later be apparent. There is a divinely ordained disproportion between the spirit of man and the scenes and occupations and emoluments of earth.

APPLICATION. 1. There is in human life a continuity only discerned by the reflecting and the pious. The obvious and striking fact is the disconnection of the generations. But as evolution reveals a physical continuity, philosophy finds an intellectual and moral continuity in our race. 2. The purpose of God is unfolded to successive generations of men. The modern study of the philosophy of history has brought this fact prominently and effectively before the attention of the scholarly and thoughtful. We see this continuity and progress in the order of revelation; but all history is, in a sacred sense, a revelation of the Eternal and Unchanging. 3. It is well that what we do we should do deliberately and seriously, not for our own good merely, but for mankind, and in the truest sense for God. This will lend " profit " to the unprofitable. 4. This state is not all. Life explains school; summer explains spring; and so eternity shall explain the disappointments, perplexities, and anomalies of time.—T.

Vers. 5—7.—The cycles of nature. This is not to be taken as the language of one who makes complaints of nature, wishing that the great forces of the world were ordered otherwise than they actually are. It is the language of one who observes nature, and is baffled by its mysteries; who asks what all means, and why everything is as it is. Even at that distant time it was recognized that the processes of nature are cyclic. The stars accomplish their revolutions, and the seasons return in their appointed order. There is unity in diversity, and changes succeed one another with remarkable regularity. These observations seem to have suggested to the writer of Ecclesiastes the inquiry—Is man's life and destiny in this respect similar to the order of nature? Is our human experience as cyclic as are the processes of the material universe? Is there no real advance for man? and is he destined to pass through changes which in the end will only leave him where he was?

I. NATURE PRESENTS A SPECTACLE OF CONSTANT CHANGE AND RESTLESSNESS. The three examples given in these passages are such as must strike every attentive observer of this earth and the phenomena accessible to the view of its inhabitants. The sun runs his daily course through the heavens, to return on the next morning to fulfil the same circuit. The wind veers about from one quarter to another, and quits one direction only in a few hours, or a few days, or at most a few weeks, to resume it. The rivers flow on in an unceasing current, and find their way into the sea, which (as is now known) yields in evaporation its tribute to the clouds, whence the water-springs are in due time replenished. Modern science has vastly enlarged our view of similar processes throughout all of the universe which is accessible to our observation. "Nothing continueth in one stay." There is in the world nothing immovable and unchangeable. It is believed that not an atom is at rest.

II. NATURE SEEMS TO EFFECT NO PROGRESS BY ALL THE CHANGES EXHIBITED. Not only is there a want, an absence, of stability, of rest; there is no apparent advance and improvement. Things move from their places only to return to them; their motion is rather in a circle than in a straight line. It was this cyclic tendency in natural processes which arrested the attention and perplexed the inquiring mind of the wise man. And modern science does not in this matter effect a radical change in our beliefs. Evolutionists teach us that *rhythm* is the ultimate law of the universe. Evolution is followed by involution, or dissipation. A planet or a system evolves until it reaches its climax, and thenceforward its course is reversed, until it is resolved into the elements of which it was primevally composed. In the presence of such speculations the intellect reels, dizzy and powerless.

III. REFLECTION MAY, HOWEVER, SUGGEST TO US THAT THERE IS UNITY IN DIVERSITY, STABILITY IN CHANGE; THAT THERE IS A DIVINE PURPOSE IN NATURE. If there be evidence of reason in the universe, if nature is the expression of mind, the vehicle by which the Creator-Spirit communicates with the created spirits he has fashioned in his own likeness, then there is at least the suggestion of what is deeper and more significant than the cycles of phenomena. There is rest for the intelligence in such a conviction as that of the theist, who rises above the utterances to the Being who utters forth his mind and will in the world which he has made, and which he rules by laws that are the expression of his own reason. He looks behind and above the mechanical cycles of nature, and discovers the Divine mind, into whose purposes he can only very partially penetrate, but in whose presence and control he finds repose.

IV. ANALOGY POINTS OUT THAT IN AND BENEATH THE MUTABILITY OF THE HUMAN LOT AND LIFE THERE IS DIVINE PURPOSE OF INSTRUCTION AND BLESSING. If, as it seems, it occurred to the mind of the wise man that, as in nature, so in human existence, all things are cyclic and unprogressive, such an inference was not unnatural. Yet it is not a conclusion in which the reasonable mind can rest. The fuller revelation with which we have been favoured enlightens us with respect to the intentions of Eternal Wisdom and Love. Our Saviour has founded upon earth a kingdom which cannot be moved. And the figures which he himself has employed to set forth its progress are an assurance that it is not bounded by time or space; that it shall grow until its dimensions and beneficence exceed all human expectations, and satisfy the heart of the Divine Redeemer himself. Each faithful Christian, however feeble and however lowly, may work in his Master's cause with the assurance that his service shall be not only acceptable, but effective. Better shall be the end than the beginning. The seed shall give rise to a tree of whose fruit all nations shall taste, and beneath whose shadow humanity itself shall find both shelter and repose.—T.

Ver. 8.—*The insatiability of sense.* Man is on one side akin to the brutes, whilst he is on the other side akin to God. Sense he shares with the inferior animals; but the intellect and conscience by which he may use his senses in the acquisition of knowledge, and his physical powers in the fulfilment of a moral ideal, these are peculiar to himself. On this account it is impossible for man to be satisfied with mere sensibility; if he makes the attempt, he fails. To say this is not to disparage sense—a great and wonderful gift of God. It is simply to put the senses in their proper place, as the auxiliaries and ministers of reason. Through the exercise of sense man may, by Divine aid, rise to great spiritual possessions, achievements, and enjoyments.

I. AN INFINITE VARIETY OF OBJECTS APPEAL TO THE SENSES OF SIGHT AND HEARING. These are chosen as the two noblest of the senses—those by whose means we learn most of nature, and most of the thoughts and purposes of our fellow-men and of our God. Around, beneath, and above us are objects to be seen, sounds and voices to be heard. The variety is as marvellous as the multiplicity.

II. WONDERFUL IS THE ADAPTATION OF THE SENSES TO RECEIVE THE VARIED IMPRESSIONS PRODUCED BY NATURE. The susceptibility of the nerves of the eye to the undulations of ether, of the ear to atmospheric vibrations, has only been fully explained in recent times. There is no more marvellous instance of design than the mutual adaptations of the voice, the atmosphere, and the auditory nerve; of the molecular structure of coloured body, the ether, and the retinal structure of the optic nerve. And these are only some of the arrangements between nature and sense which meet us at every turn and at every moment of our conscious existence.

III. IT IS IMPOSSIBLE THAT THE MERE EXERCISE OF SENSE SHOULD AFFORD A FULL SATISFACTION TO THE NATURE OF MAN. It is not to be supposed that any reasonable being should seek his gratification merely in the enjoyment of the impressions upon the senses. But even curiosity fails to find satisfaction, and those who crave such satisfaction make it manifest that their craving is in vain. The restlessness of the sight-seer is proverbial. When the impressions of sense are used as the material for high intellectual and spiritual ends, the case is otherwise. But it remains true as in the days of Koheleth, "The eye is not satisfied with seeing, nor the ear filled with hearing."

IV. IT WOULD BE AN ERROR TO REGARD THIS FACT AS A PROOF OF THE INHERENT BADNESS OF THE SENSES. Such an inference has sometimes been drawn by enthusiastic minds; and mystics have inculcated abstinence from the exercise of the senses as essential in order to intellectual and spiritual illumination. The error here lies in overlooking the distinction between making ourselves the slaves of our senses, and using the senses as our helpers and servants.

V. BUT IT IS JUST TO REGARD THIS FACT AS AN INDICATION THAT MEN SHOULD SEEK THEIR SATISFACTION IN WHAT IS HIGHER THAN SENSE. When the eyes are opened to the works of God, when we look upon the form of the Son of God, when we hear the Divine Word speaking in conscience and speaking in Christ, our senses then become, directly or indirectly, the instrumentality by means of which our higher nature is called into exercise and finds abundant scope. Our reason may thus find rest in truth; our sympathies may thus respond to the revealed love of the Eternal Father known by his blessed Son; our whole heart may rise into fellowship with him from whom all our faculties and capacities are derived, and in whom alone his spiritual children can find a perfect satisfaction and an unshaken repose.—T.

Vers. 9, 10.—*Novelty.* If, in the ancient days in which this book was written, men were already experiencing the weariness which comes from their familiarity with the scenes of earth and the incidents of life, how much more must this be the case at the present time! It is, indeed, ever characteristic of the favourites of fortune, that they "run through" the possibilities of excitement and of pleasure before their capacity for enjoyment is exhausted, and cry for new forms of amusement and distraction. It is remarkable how soon such persons are reduced to the painful conviction that there is nothing new under the sun.

I. THE LOVE AND QUEST OF NOVELTY ARE NATURAL TO MAN. When we examine human nature, we find there a deep-seated interest in change. What is called "relativity," the passage from one experience to another, is indeed an essential condition of mental life. And transition from one mode of excitement to another is a constituent of a pleasurable life. Thus, in the case of the intellectual man, the aim is to know and to study ever new things; whilst in the case of the man of energy and activity, the impulse is to view new scenes, to undertake new enterprises. It is this principle in our nature which accounts for the efforts men put forth, and for the sacrifices to which men willingly submit.

II. THE IMPOSSIBILITY OF REAL NOVELTY IN THE NATURAL WORLD AND IN HUMAN AFFAIRS. A little reflection will convince us that continuous novelty is unattainable. The laws of nature remain the same, and their sameness produces effects which with familiarity produce the effect of monotony. The conditions of human life do not materially vary from year to year, from age to age. And human nature possesses certain constant factors, in virtue of which men's employments and pleasures, hopes, sufferings, and fears remain substantially as they were in former times. The chief exception to this rule arises from the fact that what is old to one generation is for a while new to its successor. But it must not be forgotten that the individual, if favourably circumstanced, soon exhausts the variety of human experience. The voluptuary offers a reward to him who can invent a new pleasure. The hero weeps for want of a new world to conquer. The child of fortune experiences in the satisfaction of his wants, and even his caprices, the *ennui* which is a proof that he has followed the round of occupations and pleasures until all have been exhausted. Thus the most favoured are in some cases the least happy, and the most ready to join in the complaint, " Vanity of vanities; all is vanity ! "

III. IT IS THE SPIRITUAL REALM WHICH IS ESPECIALLY CHARACTERIZED BY NEWNESS. If it is impossible that the Book of Ecclesiastes should be written over again in the Christian ages, the reason is that the fuller and sublime revelations made by the Son of God incarnate have enriched human thought and life beyond all calculation. There is no comparison between the comparative poverty of knowledge and of life, even under the Mosaic economy in ancient times, and " the unsearchable riches of Christ." None can exhaust the treasures of knowledge and wisdom, the possibilities of consecrated service and spiritual progress, distinctive of the Christian dispensation. Christianity is emphatically a religion of newness. It is itself the new covenant; its choicest gift to man is the new heart; it summons the disciples of the Redeemer to newness of life; it puts in their mouth a new song; whilst it opens up in the future the glorious prospect of new heavens and a new earth. God comes in the Person of his Son to this sin-stricken humanity, and his assurance and promise is this: " Behold, I make all things new." And in fulfilment of this assurance, the Church of Christ rejoices in the experience expressed in the declaration, "Old things have passed away; behold, all things are become new."—T.

Vers. 12—18.—*The vanity of human wisdom.* Solomon was one of the great, magnificent, and famous kings of the East, and was eminent both for possessions and abilities. The splendour of his court and capital may have impressed the popular mind more profoundly than anything else attaching to him. But his wisdom was his most distinctive and honourable peculiarity. At the beginning of his reign he had sought this from God as his supreme gift, and the gift had been bestowed upon him and continued to him. Its evidences were striking and universally acknowledged. As a king, a judge, an administrator, a writer, a religious teacher, Solomon was pre-eminently wise. It must be admitted that he did not always make the best use of the marvellous talents entrusted to him. But he was well able to speak from his own experience of the gift of wisdom; and none was ever better able to speak of its vanity.

I. THE POSSESSION AND EXERCISE OF WISDOM. 1. This implies natural ability, as a foundation; and, if this be absent, eminence is impossible. 2. It implies also good opportunities. There are doubtless many endowed with native powers, to whom are denied the means of calling forth and training those powers, which accordingly lie dormant throughout the whole of life. 3. It implies the diligent cultivation of natural powers, and the diligent use of precious opportunities. 4. It implies prolonged experience—"years that bring the philosophic mind."

II. THE LIMITATION OF HUMAN WISDOM. To the view of the uncultivated and inexperienced, the knowledge of the accomplished student seems boundless, and the wisdom of the sage almost Divine. But the wise man knows himself too well to be thus deluded. The wisest man is aware that there are (1) problems he cannot solve; (2) errors he cannot correct; (3) evils he cannot remedy. On every side he is reminded how limited are his speculative and his practical powers. He is often all but helpless in the presence of questions that baffle his ingenuity, of difficulties that defy his endeavours and his patience.

III. THE DISAPPOINTMENT AND DISTRESS OF WISDOM. 1. One erroneous inference from the considerations adduced must be carefully guarded against, viz. the inference that folly is better than wisdom. The wise man may not always come to a just conclusion as to belief and practice, but the fool will usually be misled by his folly. 2. The wise man is gradually disillusioned regarding himself. He may start in life with the persuasion of his power and commanding superiority; but his confidence is perhaps by slow degrees undermined, and he may end by forming a habit of self-distrust. 3. At the same time, the wise man becomes painfully conscious that he does not deserve the reputation which he enjoys among his fellow-men. 4. But, above all, he feels that his wisdom is folly in the presence of the all-wise God, to whose omniscience all things are clear, and from whose judgment there is no appeal. 5. Hence the wise man acquires the most valuable lesson of modesty and humility— qualities which give a crowning grace to true wisdom. The wise man assuredly would not exchange with the fool, but he would fain be wiser than he is; and he cherishes the conviction that whatever light illumines him is but a ray from the central and eternal Sun.—T.

Vers. 2, 3.—*Human life and human labour.* What is the worth of our human life? This is an old and ever-recurring question; the answer to it depends far less on what surrounds us than on what is within us, far less upon our circumstances than upon our spirit. But it must be acknowledged—

I. THAT THE WORTH OF OUR LIFE DEPENDS LARGELY UPON ITS ACTIVITIES. We have to ask—How are we related to our fellows? What is the number and what the nature of the objects that minister to our comforts? What opportunities are there for leisure, for repose, for recreation? But the largest of all questions is this: *What is the character of our activities?* Are these congenial or uninviting, burdensome or moderate, tedious or interesting, fruitful or barren, passing or permanent in their effects?

II. THAT HUMAN ACTIVITY HAS ITS DEPRESSING ASPECTS. So depressing were they to " the Preacher," that he pours forth his dejection of spirit in the strong exclamation of the text. The valuelessness of all human labour made life itself seem to him to be vain. Three things there are that dwarf it. 1. *Its slightness.* A few men accomplish that which is observable, remarkable, worthy of being chronicled and remembered, making its mark on the page of history or of poetry; but how few they are! The great majority of mankind spend all their strength in doing that which is of small account, which produces no calculable effect upon their times, of which no man thinks it worth while to speak or sing. 2. *Its dependence on others.* There are but very few indeed whose labour can be said to be original, independent, or creative. Almost every man is so working that if any of those who are co-operating with him were to withdraw *their* labour, his would be of no avail; his work would be quite unprofitable but for their countenance and support. 3. *Its insecurity.* This is the main thought of the text. What is the use of a man building up that which his neighbour may come and pull down; of gathering laboriously together that which the thief may take away; of expending toilful days and exhausting energies on something which may be taken from our grasp in the compass of an hour, at the bidding of one strong human will; of making long and weary preparation for later life, when the tie that binds us to the present sphere may be snapped in a moment? Insecurity, arising from one of a number of sources—the elemental forces of nature, the malice and treachery of men, despotism in government, the chances and changes of trade and commerce, failure of health and strength, sudden death, etc.—marks all the products of human activity with its own stamp, and brings down their value, who shall estimate how much? The Preacher says *to nothing.* But let it be remembered—

III. THAT HUMAN ACTIVITY HAS ITS REDEEMING QUALITIES. This is only one view of it. Another and a healthier view may be taken of the subject. 1. All honest and faithful labour is worthy in the sight of the wise man and of the Wise One (Prov. xiv. 23). 2. All conscientious labour provides a sphere for the active service of God; by its honourable and faithful discharge, as in his sight, we can serve and please our Lord. 3. All such labour has a happy reflex influence on ourselves, strengthening us in body, in mind, in character. 4. All earnest work is really constructive of the kingdom of Christ. Although we see not its issues and cannot estimate its worth, we may be sure that " the day will declare it," and that it will be found at last that every true stroke we struck did tell and count for truth and righteousness, for the cause of humanity and of Christ.—C.

Vers. 4—7.—*The stability of nature.* The Preacher was struck with the strong contrast between the permanence of nature and the transiency of human life; and the thought oppressed and pained him. We may take his view of the subject—and our own. We look at the stability of nature—

I. As IT APPEARS TO OUR SENSES. To the outward eye things do continue as they were—

> " Changeless march the stars above,
>   Changeless morn succeeds to even,
> And the everlasting hills,
>   Changeless, watch the changeless heaven."

The hills, " rock-ribbed and ancient as the sun; " the " unchanging, everlasting sea; " the rivers that flow down the centuries as well as through the lands; the plains that stretch for long ages beneath the skies;—these aspects of nature are impressive enough to the simplest imagination; they make this earth which is our home to be charged with deepest interest and clothed with truest grandeur. No man, who has an eye to see and a heart to feel, can fail to be affected by them.

II. As IT APPEALS TO OUR REASON. The stability of all things about and above us: 1. Gives us time to study the nature and the causes of things, and enables one generation to hand down the results of its researches to another, so that we are constantly accumulating knowledge. 2. Gives us proof of the unity of God. 3. Assures us of the mighty power of the great Author of nature, who is seen to be strong to sustain and preserve and renew.

III. As IT AFFECTS OUR LIFE. For what would happen if everything were inconstant and uncertain? What would be the effect on human labour and on human life if there were no dependence to be placed on the continuance, as they are, of land and sea, of earth and sky, of hill and plain? How does the security of all the great objects and systems of the world add incentive to our industry! how does it multiply our achievements! how does it enlarge and enrich our life! That we shall be able to complete what we have begun, and that we have a good hope of handing down our work to our successors,—is not this a large factor, a powerful inspiration, among us?

IV. As IT DWARFS OUR INDIVIDUAL CAREER. The Preacher seemed to feel this acutely. What a small, slight, evanescent thing is a human life when compared with the long ranges of time that the ancient earth and the more ancient heavens have known! A generation comes and goes, while a river hardly changes its course by a single curve; many generations pass, while the face of the rocks is not visibly affected by all the waves that beat upon its surface night and day; all the generations of men, from the time that a human face was first turned up to heaven, have been looked down upon by those silent stars! Why make so much of so transient a thing as a human life? Ay, but look at it—

V. IN THE LIGHT OF THE SPIRITUAL AND THE ETERNAL. 1. The worth of spiritual life is not determined by its duration. The life of a human spirit—if that be the life of purity, holiness, reverence, love, generosity, aspiration—is of more account in the estimate of Divine wisdom, even though it be extended over a mere decade of years, than the existence which knows nothing of these nobilities, even though *it* should be extended over many thousands of years. 2. Moreover, holy human life on earth leads on and up to the life which is eternal. So that we, whose course upon the earth is so short, who are but of yesterday and with whom to-morrow may not be, do yet begin upon the earth a life which will abound in all that is beautiful and blessed, in all that is great and noble, when the "everlasting hills" have crumbled into dust.—C.

Vers. 7, 8.—*Weariness and rest.* We have here—

I. THE COMPLAINT OF THE UNSATISFIED. "All things are full of weariness" (Revised Version). 1. There are many obvious sources of satisfaction. Life has many pleasures, and many happy activities, and much coveted treasure. Human affection, congenial employment, the pursuit of knowledge, "the joys of contest," the excitements of the field of sport, the attainment of ambition, etc. 2. All of them together fail to satisfy the heart. The eye is *not* satisfied with seeing, nor the ear with hearing, nor the tongue with tasting, nor the hand with handling, nor the mind with investigating and discovering. All the streams of temporal and worldly pleasure run into the sea of the human soul, but they do not fill it. The heart, on whatsoever it feeds, is still a-hungred, is still athirst. It may seem surprising that when so much that was craved has been possessed and enjoyed, that when so many things have ministered to the mind, there should still be heart-ache, unrest, spiritual disquietude, the painful question —Who will show us any good? Is life worth having? The profundity, the common- ness and constancy of this complaint, is a very baffling and perplexing problem. We surely ought to be satisfied, but we are not. The unillumined mind cannot explain it, the uninspired tongue "cannot utter it." What is the solution?

II. ITS EXPLANATION. Its solution is not far to seek; it is found in the truth so finely uttered by Augustine, "O God, thou hast made us for thyself, and our heart findeth no rest until it resteth in thee." The human spirit, created in God's image, constituted to possess his own spiritual likeness, formed for truth and righteousness, intended to spend its noble and ever-unfolding powers in the high service of the Divine,—is it likely that such a one as this, that can *be* so much, that can *know* so much, that can *love* the best and highest, that can *aspire* to the loftiest and purest well-being, can be *satisfied* with the love that is human, with the knowledge that is earthly, with the treasure that is material and transient? The marvel is, and the pity is, that man, with such powers within him and with such a destiny before him, *can* sometimes sink so low as to be filled and satisfied with the husks of earth, unfilled with the bread of heaven.

III. ITS REMEDY. To us, to whom Jesus Christ has spoken, there is a plain and open way of escape from this profound disquietude. We hear the Master say, "Come unto me, all ye that labour and are heavy laden, and I will give you rest. Take my yoke upon you . . . and ye shall find rest unto your souls." (1) In the reconciliation to God, our Divine Father, which we have in Jesus Christ; (2) in the happy love of our souls to that Divine Friend and Saviour; (3) in the blessed service of our rightful, faithful, considerate Lord; (4) in the not unavailing service we render to those whom he loved and for whom he died; (5) in the glorious hope of immortal life beyond the grave, we do "find rest unto our souls."—C.

Vers. 9, 10.—*The changing and the abiding.* We are not to take the Preacher's words in too absolute a sense. There is that which has been but which is not now. We are sometimes powerfully affected by—

I. THE CHANGING. Of those things which bear the marks of time, we may mention : 1. The face of nature. 2. The handiwork of man. We look on prostrate palaces, fallen temples, buried cities, disused and decaying harbours, etc. 3. Historical characters. We have been familiar with the faces and forms of men that have played a great part in their country's history or created an epoch in philosophy, or poetry, or science; but where are they now? 4. Human science. Whether medical or surgical, whether geographical, geological, philosophical, theological, or of any other order, human science is changing continually. The top-stone of yesterday is the stepping-stone of to-day. 5. The character of philanthropic work. This was once represented by almsgiving, but to-day we feel that almsgiving is as much of an evil as a good, and that we want to do that for men which will remove for ever all "charity" on the one side and all dependence on the other. But look at—

II. THE ABIDING. Many things remain and will remain; among these are: 1. *The main features of human life.* Labour, sorrow, care, struggle, death; love, pleasure, success, honour. 2. *Typical human characters.* We still have with us the false, the licentious, the cruel, the servile, the ambitious, etc.; and we still have the meek, the grateful, the generous, the pure-hearted, the devout, etc. 3. *The spiritual element.* Men have not done, and they never will have done, with the mysterious, the supernatural, the Divine. They still ask—Whence came we? By whose power are we sustained? To whom are we responsible? Whither do we go? How can we know and serve and please God? 4. *The truth of Jesus Christ.* Heaven and earth may pass away, but his words "will not pass away." They are with us still, and they will remain, amid all wreckage, to enlighten our ignorance, to cheer our sorrow, to accompany our loneliness, to conquer our sin, to light up our departure, to bless and to enrich us, ourselves, with the blessings and the treasures that are not of earth but of heaven.—C.

Ver. 11.—*Oblivion and its consolations.* We have here—

I. A NATURAL HUMAN ASPIRATION. We do not like to think that the time is coming when we shall be wholly forgotten; we should like to live on in the memory of men, especially in the memory of the wise and good. We shrink from the idea of being entirely forgotten; we do not care to think that the hour will come when the mention of our name will not awaken the slightest interest in any human circle. There is something exceedingly attractive in the thought of fame, and repelling in that of oblivion. There is that within us which responds to the fine line of Horace, in which he tells us that he has built for himself a monument more enduring than brass; and to the aspiration of our own Milton, that he might prove to have written something which "the world would not willingly let die."

II. ITS INEVITABLE DISAPPOINTMENT. 1. It is indeed true that "the memory of the just is blessed," and that they who have lived well, loved faithfully, wrought nobly, suffered meekly, striven bravely, will be remembered and honoured after death; they may be long, even very long, remembered and revered. 2. There are just a few men whose names and histories will go down the long stream of time, of whom the very last generation will speak and learn. 3. But the vast majority of men will soon be forgotten. Their names may be inscribed on memorial-stones, but in a very few years none will care to read them; the eye that lights upon them will glance from them with indifference; there will be "no remembrance" of them. The world will take its way, will do its work and find its pleasure, regardless altogether of the fact that these men once trod its surface and now lie beneath it.

III. OUR TRUE CONSOLATION. This is certainly not found in the commonness of our lot. It is no consolation to me that my neighbour is as ill off as myself; that ought to be an aggravation of my trouble. It is, in fact, twofold. 1. We may be always living in the deathless *influence* our faithful lives exerted and handed down. For good influences do never die; they are scattered and lost sight of, but they are not extinguished; they live on in human hearts and lives from generation to generation. 2. We shall be loved and honoured otherwhere. What if we be forgotten here upon the earth? Are there not other parts of the kingdom of God? And is there not one where God will have found for us a sphere, and in the minds and hearts of those who will be our friends and fellow-labourers there we shall hold our place, honouring and honoured, loving and beloved?—C.

Ver. 18.—*Knowledge and sorrow.* This is one of those utterances which contain much truth and leave much to be supplied. "In much wisdom *is* much grief," but there is much beside grief to be found in it. So we look at—

I. THE TRUTH WHICH IT CONTAINS. Of the wisdom or the knowledge which brings sadness to the heart we have to reckon the following. 1. Our deeper insight into ourselves. As we go on we find ourselves capable of worse things than we once supposed we were—selfish aims, evil thoughts, unhallowed passions, etc. Neither David nor Peter supposed himself capable of doing the deed to which he fell. 2. Childhood's corrected estimate of the good. We begin by thinking all good men and women perfect; then, as experience enlarges, we have reluctantly and sorrowfully to acknowledge to ourselves that there are flaws even in the life and character of the best. And

disillusion is a very painful process. 3. Maturity's acquaintance with evil. We may
go some way into life before we know one-half of " the evil which is in the world."
Indeed, it is the wisdom and the duty of many—of even a large proportion of the race
—*not* to know much that might be revealed. But as a widening knowledge unveils
the magnitude and heinousness of moral evil, there is sorrow indeed to the pure and
sympathetic soul. The more we know of the sins and the sorrows of our race—of its
cruelties on the one hand and its sufferings on the other, of its enormities and its
privations, of its toils and troubles, of its degradation and its death in life—the more
we are distressed in spirit ; "in much wisdom is much grief."

II. ITS LARGE QUALIFICATIONS. There is much truth belonging to the subject
which lies outside this statement, qualifying though not contradicting it. 1. There is
much pleasure in the act of acquisition. The study of one of the sciences, the reading
of history, the careful observation of nature and mastery of its secrets, the investigation
of the nature of man, etc.,—there is a pure and invigorating delight in all this.
2. Knowledge is power ; and it is power to acquire that which will surround us with
comfort, with freedom, with friendship, with intellectual enlargement. 3. The knowledge which is heavenly wisdom is, in itself, a source of elevation and of deep spiritual
thankfulness and happiness. 4. The knowledge of God, as he is known to us in Jesus
Christ, is the one unfailing source of unfading joy.—C.

Vers. 1—11.—*The summary of a life's experience.* " Solomon and Job," says Pascal,
" had most perfect knowledge of human wretchedness, and have given us the most
complete description of it : the one was the most prosperous, the other the most
unfortunate, of men ; the one knew by experience the vanity of pleasure, the other the
reality of sorrow." In such diverse ways does God lead men to the same conclusion—
that in human life, apart from him, there is no true satisfaction or lasting happiness,
that the immortal spirit cannot find rest in things seen and temporal. The words,
" Vanity of vanities, all is vanity : what profit hath man of all his labour wherein he
laboureth under the sun ? " (Revised Version), are the key-note of the whole book—the
theme which the author maintains by arguments and illustrations drawn from a most
varied experience. If Solomon be not the speaker, if we have in Ecclesiastes the composition of a later writer, no more appropriate personage could have been found than the
ancient Jewish king to set forth the teaching which the book contains. For he had
tasted all the good things human life has to give. On him God had bestowed wisdom
and knowledge, riches, wealth, honour, and length of days. All these he had enjoyed
to the full, and therefore speaks, or is made to speak, as one from whom nothing had
been kept that his soul desired, and who found that nothing results from the mere
satisfaction of appetites and desires but satiety and loathing and disappointment.
We may contrast with this retrospect of life that given us by One whose aim it was to
fulfil the Law of God and secure the well-being of his fellow-men ; and we may thus
discover the secret of Solomon's failure to win happiness or to reach any lasting result.
At the close of his life the Redeemer of mankind summed up the history of his career
in the words addressed to God, " I glorified thee on the earth, having accomplished the
work which thou hast given me to do " (John xvii. 4). It may seem to some a dreary
task to follow the course of Solomon's morbid thoughts, but it cannot fail to be profitable,
if we undertake the task in the earnest desire to discover the causes of his melancholy
and disappointment, and learn from the study how to guide our own lives more successfully, and to enter into the peace and contentment of spirit which, after all his efforts,
he failed to make his own. In the first eleven verses of this chapter we have revealed
to us the despair and weariness which fell upon the soul of him whose splendour and
wisdom raised him above all the men of his time, and made him the wonder of all
succeeding ages. Life seemed to him the emptiest and poorest thing possible—" a
vapour that appeareth for a little time, and then vanisheth away." He might have used
the words of the modern philosopher Amiel, " To appear and to vanish,—there is the
biography of all individuals, whatever may be the length of the cycle of existence
which they describe ; and the drama of the universe is nothing more. All life is the
shadow of a smoke-wreath, a gesture in the empty air, a hieroglyphic traced for an
instant in the sand and effaced a moment afterwards by a breath of wind, an air-bubble
expanding and vanishing on the surface of the great river of being—an appearance, a

vanity, a nothing. But this nothing is, however, the symbol of universal being, and this passing bubble is the epitome of the history of the world." It seemed to him that life *yielded no permanent results*, that it was *insufferably monotonous*, and that it was *destined to end in utter oblivion*. The futility of effort, the monotony of life, and the oblivion that engulfs it at last are the topics of this opening passage of the book. Let us take them up one after the other.

I. THAT LIFE YIELDS NO PERMANENT RESULTS. (Vers. 1—3.) We have before us, then, the deliberate judgment of one who had full experience of all that men busy themselves with—"the labour wherein they labour under the sun"—the pursuit of riches, the enjoyment of power, the satisfaction of appetites and desires, and so on, and his conclusion is that there is no profit in it all. And his sentence is confirmed by the words of Christ, "What shall it profit a man, if he shall gain the whole world, and lose his own soul?" In the case of Solomon, therefore, we have a record of permanent significance and value. We cannot deprive his sombre utterances of their weight by saying that he spoke simply as a sated voluptuary, and that others might with more skill or discretion extract from life what he failed to find in it. For, as we shall see, he did not confine himself to mere pursuit of pleasure, but sought satisfaction in intellectual employments and in the accomplishment of great tasks, for which the power and wealth at his disposal were drawn upon to the utmost. His melancholy is not a form of mental disease, but the result of the exhaustion of his energies and powers in the attempt to find satisfaction for the soul's cravings. And in melancholy of this kind philosophers have found a proof of the dignity of human nature. "Man's unhappiness," says one of them, "comes of his greatness: it is because there is an infinite in him, which, with all his cunning, he cannot quite bury under the finite. . . . He requires, if you consider it, for his permanent satisfaction and saturation, simply this allotment, no more and no less: God's infinite universe altogether to himself, therein to enjoy infinitely, and fill every wish as fast as it rises. . . . Try him with half of a universe, of an omnipotence, he sets to quarrelling with the proprietor of the other half, and declares himself the most maltreated of men. Always there is a black spot in our sunshine; it is even the shadow of ourselves" (Carlyle). The very consciousness of the unprofitableness of life, of failure to attain to perfect satisfaction in the possession of earthly benefits, painful as it is, should convince us of the value of the higher and better inheritance, which may be ours, and in which alone we can find rest; and we should take it as a Divine warning to seek after those things that are eternal and unchangeable. Our dissatisfaction and our sorrows are like those of the exile who pines for the pleasant land from which by a hard fate he is for a time dissevered; like the grief of a king who has been deposed. And it is to those whose hunger and thirst cannot be satisfied by things of earth, who find, like Solomon, that there is " no profit in a man's labour wherein he laboureth under the sun," that God issues the gracious invitation, " Ho, every one that thirsteth, come ye to the waters, and he that hath no money; come ye, buy, and eat; yea, come, buy wine and milk without money and without price. Wherefore do ye spend money for that which is not bread? and your labour for that which satisfieth not? hearken diligently unto me, and eat ye that which is good, and let your soul delight itself in fatness." The idea of the unprofitableness of human labour expressed by Solomon is calculated, if carried too far, to put an end to all healthy and strenuous effort to use the powers and gifts God has bestowed upon us, and to lead to indifference and despair. If no adequate result can be secured, if all that remains after prolonged exertion is only a sense of weariness and disappointment, why should we labour at all? But such thoughts are dishonouring to God and degrading to ourselves. He has not sent us into the world to spend our labour in vain, to be overcome with the consciousness of our poverty and weakness. There *are* ways in which we can glorify him and serve our generation; and he has promised to bless our endeavours, and supply that wherein we come short. Every sincere and unselfish effort we make to help the weak, to relieve the suffering, to teach the ignorant, to diminish the misery that meets us on every hand, and to advance the happiness of our fellows, is made fruitful by his blessing. Something positive and of enduring value may be secured in this way, even " treasure laid up in heaven, where neither moth nor rust doth corrupt, and where thieves do not break through nor steal." We may so use the goods, the talents, now committed to our charge, as to create for ourselves friends, who will receive us into everlasting habitations when the days of our stewardship are over, and this visible, tangible world fades away from us.

II. The second reflection of the royal Preacher is that HUMAN LIFE IS INSUFFERABLY MONOTONOUS; that under all outward appearances of variety and change there is a dreary sameness (vers. 4—10). Generation succeeds generation, but the stage is the same on which they play their parts, and one performance is very like another. The incessant motion of the sun, travelling from east to west; the shifting of the wind from one point to another, and then back again; the speedy current of the rivers to join the ocean, which yet is not filled by them, but returns them in various ways to water the earth, and to feed the springs, " whence the rivers come; " the commonplace events of human life, are all referred to as examples of endless and monotonous variation. The law of mutability, without progress, seems to the speaker to prevail in heaven and in earth— to rule in the material world, in human society, and in the life of the individual. The lordship over creation, bestowed upon man, appeared to him a vain fancy. Man himself was but a stranger, sojourning here for but a very short time, coming like a wandering bird from the outer darkness into the light and warmth of a festive hall, and soon flitting out back again into the darkness. And, to one in this sombre mood, it is not wonderful that all natural phenomena should wear the aspect of instability and change. To the pious mind of the psalmist the sun suggested thoughts of God's glory and power; the majesty of the creature gave him a more exalted idea of the greatness of the Creator, and he expatiated upon the splendour of that light that rules the day. "The heavens were his tabernacle; " morning by morning he was as " a bridegroom coming forth from his chamber, and rejoicing as a strong man to run a race." Our Saviour saw in the same phenomenon a proof of God's impartial and bountiful love to the children of men : " He maketh his sun to rise upon the evil and the good." But to the melancholy and brooding mind of our author nothing more was suggested by it than monotonous reiteration, a dreary routine of rising and setting. "The sun also ariseth, and the sun goeth down, and hasteth to his place where he arose." " He issues forth, day after day, from the east, mounts up the vault of heaven until he has reached the meridian, and then he descends at once towards the western horizon. He never stops in his course at midday, as though he had attained the end for which he issued forth with the dawn; he never sinks beneath the horizon to enjoy repose. Even throughout the night he is still hastening onward, that, at the appointed hour, he may again reach his eastern starting-place. The wind, great though its changes may be, seems never to have accomplished the purpose for which it puts forth its power. It never subsides into a state of lasting quiescence; it never even finds a station which it can permanently occupy. It ' veereth about continually,' yet it ever ' bloweth again according to its circuits.' The streams flow onward to the ocean; but the time never comes when the sea, filled to overflowing, refuses to receive their waters. The thirst of the sea is never quenched; the waters of the rivers are lost; and yet, with unavailing constancy, they still pour their contributions into its bosom " (Tyler). And so with regard to all the other things on which the eye rests, or of which the ear hears—weariness clothes everything; an unutterable monotony amid their changes and variations. Human life, too, all through, is characterized by the same unrest and ceaseless, fruitless labour. Sometimes a new discovery seems to be made; the monotony seems to be broken, and fresh and great results are anticipated by those who are ignorant of the world's past history. But the initiated, those whose experience has made them wise, or whose knowledge has made them learned, recognize the new thing as something that was known in times long ago; they can tell how barren it was of results then, how little, therefore, can be expected from it now. There is scarcely anything more discouraging, especially to the young, than this kind of moralizing. We feel, perhaps, that we can carry out some scheme that will be of benefit to the society about us, and are met with lamentable accounts of how similar schemes were once tried and failed disastrously. We feel moved to attack the evils that we meet in the world, and are assured that they are too great and our own strength too puny for us to accomplish anything worth while. And in the mean time our fervour grows cold, our courage oozes away, and we really lose the power for good we might have had. Now, this teaching of Solomon is not meant for the young and hopeful. Indeed, those who collected together the books of the Old Testament were rather doubtful about including Ecclesiastes among the others, and it ran a narrow chance of being omitted from the sacred canon. But it has its place in the Word of God; and those who have known anything of the doubts and speculations contained in it will find it profitable to trace the course of thought that runs through it, until they find the solid and positive teaching which the Preacher at lasts gives. The distressing fact remains, and must be encountered, that to those who have had long experience of the world, and whose horizon is bounded by it, who see only the things that are done "under the sun," in the midst of ever-recurring changes, there seems to be little or no progress, and that which appears to be new is but a repetition of the old. But they should remember that this world is meant as a place of probation for us—a school in which we are to learn great lessons; and that all the changing circumstances of life serve, and are meant to serve, to develop our nature and character. If it were to be our abiding-place, many improvements in it might be suggested. It is not by any means the best of possible worlds; but for purposes of education, discipline, and testing, it is perfectly adapted. "Rest yet remaineth for the people of God;" it is not here, but in a world to come. This truth is admirably stated by the poet Spenser, who perhaps unconsciously reproduces the melancholy thoughts of Solomon, and answers them. He speaks of Mutability seeking to be honoured above all the heavenly powers, as being the chief ruler in the universe, and as indeed governing all things. In a synod of the gods, she is silenced by Nature, who combats her claims, and speaks of a time to come when her present apparent power will come to an end—

> " But time shall come that all shall changed bee,
>   And from thenceforth none no more change shall see."

And then the poet adds—

> " When I bethinke me on that speech whyleare [former]
>   Of Mutability, and well it way,
>   Me seemes, that though she all unworthy were
>   Of the Heav'ns Rule; yet, very sooth to say,
>   In all things else she bears the greatest sway:
>   Which makes me loath this state of life so tickle [unsure],
>   And love of things so vain to cast away;
>   Whose flow'ring pride, so fading and so fickle,
> Short Time shall soon cut down with his consuming sickle.

> " Then gin I thinke on that which Nature sayd,
>   Of that same time when no more Change shall be,
>   But stedfast rest of all things, firmely stayd
>   Upon the pillours of Eternity,
>   That is contrayr to Mutability;
>   For all that moveth doth in Change delight:
>   But thence-forth all shall rest eternally
>   With him that is the God of Sabbaoth hight:
> O! that great Sabbaoth God, grant me that Sabbaoth's sight!"

III. LIFE DESTINED TO END IN UTTER OBLIVION. To all these considerations of the resultlessness of life, of changefulness and monotony, is added that of *the oblivion* that sooner or later overtakes man and all his works (ver. 11). "There is no remembrance of the former generations; neither shall there be any remembrance of the latter generations that are to come, among those that shall come after" (Revised Version). One generation supersedes another; the new come up with fresh interests and schemes of their own, and hustle the old off the stage, and are themselves in their turn forced to give place to those who come up after them. Nations disappear from the earth's surface and are forgotten. The memorials of former civilizations lie buried in the sand, or are defaced and destroyed to make room for something else. On every page of creation we find the sentence written, that there is nothing here that lasts. Almost no means can be devised to carry down to succeeding generations even the names of the greatest conquerors, of men who in their time seemed to have the strength of gods, and to have changed the history of the world. The earth has many secrets in her keeping, and is sometimes forced to yield up a few of them. " The ploughshare strikes against the foundations of buildings which once echoed to human mirth; skeletons of men to whom life once was dear; urns and coins that

remind the antiquary of a magnificent empire now long passed away." And so the
process goes on. Everything passes. A few years ago and *we* were not; a hundred
years hence, and there may be none who ever heard our names. And a day will come
when

> 'The cloud-capp'd towers, the gorgeous palaces,
> The solemn temples, the great globe itself,
> Yea, all which it inherit, shall dissolve;
> And . . . leave not a rack behind. We are such stuff
> As dreams are made on, and our little life
> Is rounded with a sleep."

Abundant material, then, had the Preacher, the son of David, for sombre meditation;
abundant material for contemplation does he suggest to us. And if we cannot get
much further on in speculation than he did, if since his time very little new light has
been cast upon the problems which he discusses, we may still refuse to be depressed by
melancholy like his. Granted that all is vanity, that restlessness and monotony mark
everything in the world, and that its glories soon pass away and are forgotten; still it
is not our home. It may dissolve and leave us no poorer. The tie that binds together
soul and body may be loosened, and the place that knows us now may soon know us no
more. Our confidence is in him, who has promised to take us to himself, that where
he is we may be also. "God is our Refuge and Strength, . . . therefore will not we fear,
though the earth be removed." In contrast with the Preacher's desponding, despairing
words about the fruitlessness of life, its monotony and its brevity, we may set the
hopeful, triumphant utterance of Christ's apostle: "The time of my departure is at
hand. I have fought a good fight, I have finished my course, I have kept the faith:
henceforth there is laid up for me a crown of righteousness, which the Lord, the
righteous Judge, shall give me at that day: and not to me only, but unto all them also
that love his appearing."—J. W.

Vers. 12—18.—*Speculative study of the world.* Solomon has made serious allegations
concerning human life, and he now proceeds to substantiate them. He has declared
that it yields no permanent results, that it is tedious beyond expression, and that it is
soon overtaken by oblivion. "Vanity of vanities; all is vanity!" The monotony of
things in the natural world—the permanence of the earth in contrast with the changes
in human life, the mechanical routine of sunrise and sunset, the ceaseless agitation of
the atmosphere, the constant course of rivers to the sea, and so on—had not been the
sole ground for his conclusions. He had considered also "all the works that are done
under the sun," the whole range of human action, and found in them evidence justifying
his allegations. Both in natural phenomena and in human efforts and attainments he
found that all was vanity and vexation of spirit. He had, he tells us (ver. 12), all the
resources of a great monarch at his command—riches, authority, capacity, and leisure;
and he applied himself,—he gave his heart to discover, by the aid of wisdom, the nature
of earthly pursuits, and found that they were fruitless. He concentrated all his mental
energy upon the course of investigation, and continued in it until the conclusion was
forced upon him that "in much wisdom is much grief, and he that increaseth knowledge increaseth sorrow." So different is the estimate of wisdom and knowledge formed
by the Jewish king from that held by other great philosophers and sages, that it is
worth while to inquire into the cause of the difference. The explanation is to be found
in ver. 15, "That which is crooked cannot be made straight: and that which is wanting
cannot be numbered." It was a practical end that Solomon had in view—to remedy
evils and to supply deficiencies. He did not engage in the pursuit of wisdom and knowledge for the sake of the pleasure yielded by intellectual activity. In the case of
ordinary philosophers and scientists the aim is a different one. "A truth, once known,
falls into comparative insignificance. It is now prized, less on its own account than
as opening up new ways to new activity, new suspense, new hopes, new discoveries,
new self-gratulation. It is not knowledge, it is not truth, that the votary of science
principally seeks; he seeks the exercise of his faculties and feelings. Absolute certainty
and absolute completion would be the paralysis of any study; and the last worst
calamity that could befall man, as he is at present constituted, would be that full and

final possession of speculative truth which he now vainly anticipates as the consummation of his intellectual happiness. And what is true of science is true, indeed, of all human activity. It is ever the contest that pleases us, and not the victory. Thus it is in play; thus it is in hunting; thus it is in the search of truth; thus it is in life. The past does not interest, the present does not satisfy; the future alone is the object which engages us. ' It is not the goal, but the course, that makes us happy,' says Richter " (Hamilton, ' Metaphysics '). But in the case before us we find that the pleasure afforded by intellectual activity is not regarded by the Preacher as an end sufficient in itself to engage his energies. It is a practical end he has in view; and when he finds that earthly pursuits cannot alter destinies, cannot change the conditions under which we live, cannot set right that which is wrong, or supply that which is wanting for human happiness, he loathes them altogether. The very wisdom and knowledge which he had acquired in his investigations seem to him useless lumber. He wanted to find in life an adequate aim and end, something in which man could find repose. He found it not. " The light which the wisdom he had learned cast on human destiny only exhibited to him the illusions of life, but did not show him one perfect object on which he might rest as a final aim of existence. And therefore he says that ' he that increaseth knowledge increaseth sorrow,' since he only thus perceives more and more illusions, whilst nothing is the result, and nihilism is only sorrow of heart " (*vide* Martensen, ' Christian Ethics'). The Preacher then says about the pursuit of wisdom, that though it is implanted by God in the heart of man (ver. 13), it is (1) *a severe and laborious task*, and (2) *the results it yields are grief and sorrow.*

I. In the first place, then, HE DESCRIBES THE PURSUIT OF WISDOM AS A SEVERE AND LABORIOUS TASK. He looks back upon the course of inquiry he had followed, and declares that it has been a rugged, thorny road. " This sore travail hath God given to the sons of man to be exercised therewith." And it is quite in harmony with the spirit of the book that the name of God, which occurs here for the first time, should be coupled with the thought of his laying heavy burdens upon men, since it was by him that this profitless search had been appointed. He remembers all the labours of the way by which he had come—the weariness of brain, the laborious days, the sleepless nights, the frustrated hopes, the disappointments he had experienced; and he counts the pursuit of wisdom but another of the vanities of life. The common run of men, who have no high aims, no desires after a wisdom more than that needed for procuring a livelihood, who are undisturbed by the great problems of life, are spared this painful discipline. It is those who rise above their fellows, that are called to spend their strength and resources, to deny themselves pleasures, and to separate themselves from much of that in which mankind delight and find solace, only to find keener sorrows than those known to their fellows. They do indeed hear and obey the voice of God, but it calls them to suffering and to self-sacrifice. In these days, when the sciences open up before men vast fields for research, there must be many who can verify from their own experience what Solomon says about the laboriousness of the methods used. The infinite patience needed, the observation and cataloguing of multitudinous facts, the inventing of fresh mechanical appliances for facilitating research, the varied experiments, the careful examination of evidence, and the construction and testing of new theories and hypotheses, are the " sore travail " here spoken of.

II. In the second place, THE WISDOM AND KNOWLEDGE SO LABORIOUSLY GAINED ONLY MEAN INCREASE OF GRIEF AND SORROW. (Ver. 18.) There is abundant evidence of the truth of this statement in the experience of those who have made great attainments in intellectual wisdom. For progress in knowledge only convinces man of the little he knows, as compared with the vast universe of being that lies undiscovered. He is convinced of the weakness of his powers, the shortness of the time at his disposal, and the infinite extent of the field, which he desires, but can never hope to take possession of. This thought is expressed in the well-known words of Sir Isaac Newton : " I seem to have been only like a boy playing on the seashore, and diverting myself now and then with a smoother pebble or a prettier shell than ordinary, while the ocean of truth lay undiscovered before me." With increase of intellectual knowledge, with enlarged acquaintance with the thoughts of men, and the various theories of the universe that have been held, and the various solutions of difficulties that have been given, there often comes, too, unwillingness or inability to rest content with any theory or any solution. Doubts, which frequently settle down into definite agnosticism, beset the man who is given to great intellectual activity. And then, too, the fact remains that we cannot by sheer reasoning come to any definite conclusions as to any of the great questions which most concern our happiness. No one can by searching find out God—reach definite knowledge concerning him, his existence, nature, and character; or be assured of the fact of there being an overruling Providence, of the efficacy of prayer, of a life beyond the grave, or of the immortality of the soul. Probable or plausible opinions may be formed, but certainty comes only by revelation and faith. Hence it is that Milton describes some of the fallen angels as wandering hopelessly through these labyrinths of thought and conjecture, and finding in so doing intellectual occupation, but neither solace nor rest.

> " Others apart sat on a hill retired,
>   In thoughts more elevate, and reason'd high
>   Of providence, foreknowledge, will, and fate;
>   Fix'd fate, free-will, foreknowledge absolute,
>   And found no end, in wandering mazes lost.
>   Of good and evil much they argued then,
>   Of happiness and final misery,
>   Passion and apathy, and glory and shame,
>   Vain wisdom all, and false philosophy."

And it has been said that one of the attractions which this Book of Ecclesiastes has for the present age is in its sceptical questioning, and restless, fluctuating uncertainty. The age can adopt as its own its sombre declarations.   " Science boasts vaingloriously of her progress, yet mocks us with her grand discovery of progress through pain, telling of small advantages for the few purchased by enormous waste of life, by internecine conflict and competition, and by a deadly struggle with Nature herself, ' red in tooth and claw with ravin,' greedy to feed on the offspring of her own redundant fertility. The revelations of geology and astronomy deepen our depression. The littleness of our lives and the insignificance of our concerns become more conspicuous in comparison with the long and slow procession of the æons which have gone before, and with the vast ocean of being around us, driven and tossed by enormous, complicated, and unresting forces. A new significance is thus given to the words, ' In much wisdom is much grief : and he that increaseth knowledge increaseth sorrow ' " (Tyler). In his celebrated engraving of ' Melancolia,' Albert Dürer has with wonderful skill depicted this mood of intellectual depression. He represents a winged figure, that of a woman seated by the seashore and looking intently into the distance, with bent brows and proud, pensive demeanour. Her thoughts are absorbed in sombre meditation, and her wings are folded. A closed book is in her lap. Near her stands a dial-plate, and above it a bell, that strikes the hours as they pass. The sun is rapidly nearing the horizon-line, and darkness will soon enshroud the earth.   In her right hand she holds a compass and a circle, emblematic of that infinity of time and space upon which she is meditating. Around her are scattered the various implements of art, and the numerous appliances of science. They have served her purpose, and she now casts them aside, and listlessly ponders on the vanity of all human calculations. Above her is an hour-glass, in which the sands are running low, emblematic of the shortness of the time yet left for fresh schemes and efforts. In like manner the Preacher found that on the *moral* side increase of knowledge meant increase of sorrow. Knowledge of the true ideal only made him the more conscious of the distance we are from it, and of the hopelessness of our efforts to reach it. The further the research is carried, the more abundant is the evidence discoverable of our moral nature being in a condition of disorder. We find that conscience too often reigns without governing, that natural appetites and desires refuse to submit to her rule, that often motives and feelings which she distinctly condemns, such as pride, envy, selfishness, and cruelty, direct and animate our conduct. All schools of philosophy have recognized the fact of moral disorder in our nature. It is, indeed, unfortunately too evident to be denied or explained away. Aristotle says, " We are more naturally disposed towards those things which are wrong, and more easily carried away to excess than to propriety of conduct."   And Hume, " We naturally desire what is forbidden, and often take a pleasure in performing actions merely because they are unlawful.

The notion of duty when opposite to the passions is not always able to overcome them; and when it fails of that effect, is apt rather to increase and irritate them, by producing an opposition in our motives and principles." But it is not necessary to mulitply testimony to a fact so generally acknowledged. How this moral disorder originated in human nature is a problem which philosophy is unable to solve, just as it is lacking in ability to correct it. It can discern the symptoms and character of the disease, and describe the course it takes, but cannot cure it. And so the existence of disturbing and lawless forces in our moral nature, the power of evil habit, the social inequalities and disorders which result from the perversity of the individuals of whom society is made up, and the varying codes of morals which exist in the world, are all calculated to distress and perplex him who seeks to make that straight which is crooked, and to supplement that which is defective. Increase of knowledge brings increase of sorrow. —J. W.

EXPOSITION.

CHAPTER II.

Vers. 1—11.—Section 2. *Vanity of striving after pleasure and wealth.*

Ver. 1.—Dissatisfied with the result of the pursuit of wisdom, Koheleth embarks on a course of sensual pleasure, if so be this may yield some effect more substantial and permanent. **I said in mine heart, Go to now, I will prove thee with mirth.** The heart is addressed as the seat of the emotions and affections. The Vulgate misses the direct address to the heart, which the words, rightly interpreted, imply, translating, *Vadam et affluam deliciis.* The Septuagint correctly gives, Δεῦρο δὴ πειράσω σε ἐν εὐφροσύνῃ. It is like the rich fool's language in Christ's parable, "I will say to my soul, Soul, thou hast much goods laid up for many years; take thine ease, eat, drink, be merry" (Luke xii. 10). **Therefore enjoy pleasure;** literally, *see good* (ch. vi. 6). "To see" is often used figuratively in the sense of "to experience, or enjoy." Wright compares the expressions, "see death" (Luke ii. 26), "see life" (John iii. 36). We may find the like in Ps. xxxiv. 13; Jer. xxix. 32; Obad. 13 (comp. ch. ix. 9). The king now tries to find the *summum bonum* in pleasure, in selfish enjoyment without thought of others. Commentators, as they saw Stoicism in the first chapter, so read Epicureanism into this. We shall have occasion to refer to this idea further on (see on ch. iii. 22). Of this new experiment the result was the same as before. **Behold, this also is vanity.** This experience is confirmed in the next verse.

Ver. 2.—**I said of laughter, It is mad.** Laughter and mirth are personified, hence treated as masculine. He uses the term "mad" in reference to the statement in ch. i. 17, "I gave my heart to know madness and folly." Septuagint, "I said to laughter, Error (περιφοράν);" Vulgate, *Risum reputavi errorem.* Neither of these is as accurate as the Authorized Version. **Of mirth, What doeth it?** What does it effect towards real happiness and contentment? How does it help to fill the void, to give lasting satisfaction? So we have in Prov. xiv. 13, "Even in laughter the heart is sorrowful; and the end of mirth is heaviness;" though the context is different. The Vulgate renders loosely, *Quid frustra deciperis?*

Ver. 3.—**I sought in mine heart;** literally, *I spied out* (as ch. i. 13) *in my heart.* Having proved the fruitlessness of some sort of sensual pleasure, he made another experiment in a philosophical spirit. **To give myself unto wine;** literally, *to draw (mashak) my flesh with wine;* i.e. to use the attraction of the pleasures of the table. **Yet acquainting my heart with wisdom.** This is a parenthetical clause, which Wright translates, "While my heart was acting [guiding] with wisdom." That is, while, as it were, experimenting with pleasure, he still retained sufficient control over his passions as not to be wholly given over to vice; he was in the position of one who is being carried down an impetuous stream, yet has the power of stopping his headlong course before it becomes fatal to him. Such control was given by wisdom. Deliberately to enter upon a course of self-indulgence, even with a possibly good intention, must be a most perilous trial, and one which would leave indelible marks upon the soul; and not one person in a hundred would be able to stop short of ruin. The historical Solomon, by his experiment, suffered infinite loss, which nothing could compensate. The Septuagint renders not very successfully, "I examined whether my heart would draw (ἑλκύσει) my flesh as wine; and my heart guided me in wisdom." The Vulgate gives a sense entirely contrary to the writer's intention; "I thought in my heart to withdraw my flesh from wine, that I might transfer my mind to wisdom." **And to lay hold on folly.** These words are dependent upon "I sought in my heart," and refer to the sensual pleasures in which he indulged for a certain object.

"Dulce est desipere in loco," says Horace ('Carm.,' iv. 12. 28); Ἐν μὲν μαινομένοις μάλα μαίνομαι (Theognis, 313). **Till I might see.** His purpose was to discover if there was in these things any real good which might satisfy men's cravings, and be a worthy object for them to pursue **all the days of their life.**

Ver. 4.—This commences a new experience in the pursuit of his object. Leaving this life of self-indulgence, he takes to art and culture, the details being drawn from the accounts of the historical Solomon. **I made me great works;** literally, *I made great my works*; Septuagint, Ἐμεγάλυνα ποίημά μου; Vulgate, *Magnificavi opera mea.* Among these works the temple, with all its wonderful structural preparations, is not specially mentioned, perhaps because no one could think of Solomon without connecting his name with this magnificent building, and it was superfluous to call attention to it; or else because the religious aspect of his operations is not here in question, but only his taste and pursuit of beauty. But the omission tells strongly against the Solomonic authorship of the book. **I builded me houses.** Solomon had a passion for erecting magnificent buildings. We have various accounts of his works of this nature in 1 Kings vii. and ix.; 2 Chron. viii. There was the huge palace for himself, which occupied thirteen years in building; there was the "house of the forest of Lebanon," a splendid hall constructed with pillars of cedar; the porch of pillars; the hall of judgment; the harem for the daughter of Pharaoh. Then there were fortresses, store-cities, chariot-towns, national works of great importance; cities in distant lands which he founded, such as Tadmor in the wilderness. **I planted me vineyards.** David had vineyards and oliveyards (1 Chron. xxvii. 27, 28), which passed into the possession of his son; and we read in Cant. viii. 11 of a vineyard that Solomon had in Baal-hamon, which some identify with Belamon (Judith viii. 3), a place near Shunem, in the Plain of Esdraelon.

Ver. 5.—**I made me gardens and orchards.** Solomon's love of gardens appears throughout the Canticles (vi. 2, etc.). He had a king's garden on the slope of the hills south of the city (2 Kings xxv. 4); and Beth-haccherem, "the House of the Vine," at Ain Karim, about six miles east of Jerusalem (Jer. vi. 1); and at Baal-hamon another extensive vineyard (Cant. viii. 11). The word rendered "orchard" (*parder*) occurs also in Cant. iv. 13 and Neh. ii. 8. It is a Persian word, and passed into the Greek form παράδεισος (Xenophon, 'Anab.,' i. 2. 7), meaning "a park" planted with forest and fruit trees, and containing herds of animals.

It is probably derived from the Zend *pairidaeza*, "an enclosure." (For the trees in such parks, see Cant. iv. 13, 14; and for an estimate of Solomon's works, Josephus, 'Ant.,' viii. 7. 3.)

Ver. 6.—**Pools of water.** Great care was exercised by Solomon to provide his capital with water, and vast operations were undertaken for this purpose. "The king's pool," mentioned in Neh. ii. 14, may have been constructed by him (Josephus, 'Bell. Jud.,' v. 4. 2); but the most celebrated work ascribed to him is the water-supply at Etham, south-west of Bethlehem, and the aqueduct leading from thence to Jerusalem. Most modern travellers have described these pools. They are three in number, and, according to Robinson's measurement, are of immense size. The first, to the east, is 582 feet long, 207 wide, and 50 deep; the second, 432 by 250, and 39 feet deep; the third, 380 by 236, and 25 feet deep. They are all, however, narrower at the upper end, and widen out gradually, flowing one into the other. There is a copious spring led into the uppermost pool from the north-east, but this supply is augmented by other sources now choked and ruined. The water from the pools was conveyed round the ridge on which Bethlehem stands in earthen pipes to Jerusalem. Dr. Thomson ('The Land and the Book,' p. 326) says, "Near that city it was carried along the west side of the Valley of Gihon to the north-western end of the lower Pool of Gihon, where it crossed to the east side, and, winding round the southern declivity of Zion below *Neby Dâûd*, finally entered the south-eastern corner of the temple area, where the water was employed in the various services of the sanctuary." Etham is, with good reason, identified with the beautiful valley of Urtas, which lies south-west of Bethlehem, in the immediate neighbourhood of the pools of Solomon. The fountain near the present village watered the gardens and orchards which were planted here, the terraced hills around were covered with vines, figs, and olives, and the prospect must have been delightful and refreshing in that thirsty land. **To water therewith the wood that bringeth forth trees;** Revised Version, *to water therefrom the forest where trees were reared;* literally, *in order to irrigate a wood sprouting forth trees;* i.e. a nursery of saplings. So we read how the Garden of Eden was watered (Gen. ii. 10; xiii. 10)—a most necessary feature in Eastern countries, where streams and pools are not constructed for picturesque reasons, but for material uses.

Ver. 7.—**I got me**—I bought, procured—**servants and maidens.** These are distinct from those mentioned immediately afterwards, **servants born in my house** ; Septuagint, οἰκογενεῖς ; called in the Hebrew, " sons of the house" (Ger. xv. 3). They were much more esteemed by their masters, and showed a much closer attachment to the family than the bought slaves or the conquered aboriginals, who were often reduced to this state (1 Kings ix. 20, 21). The number of Solomon's attendants excited the wonder of the Queen of Sheba (1 Kings iv. 26, etc. ; x. 5), and with good reason, if Josephus's account is to be believed. This writer asserts that the king had some thousand or more chariots, and twenty thousand horses. The drivers and riders were young men of comely aspect, tall and well-made; they had long flowing hair, and wore tunics of Tyrian purple, and powdered their hair with gold dust, which glittered in the rays of the sun (' Ant.,' viii. 7. 3). Attended by a cavalcade thus arrayed, Solomon used to betake himself to his " paradise " at Etham, to enjoy the refreshing coolness of its trees and pools. **Great and small cattle** ; *oxen and sheep.* The enormous amount of Solomon's herds and flocks is proved by the extraordinary multitude of the sacrifices at the consecration of the temple (1 Kings viii. 63), and the lavish provision made daily for the wants of his table (1 Kings iv. 22, 23). The cattle of David were very numerous, and required special overlookers (1 Chron. xxvii. 29—31). Job (i. 3) had, before his troubles, seven thousand sheep, three thousand camels, five hundred yoke of oxen, and five hundred she-asses, and these items were all doubled at the return of his prosperity. Among Solomon's possessions, horses are not here mentioned, though they formed no inconsiderable portion of his live stock, and added greatly to his magnificence. Koheleth, perhaps, avoided boasting of this extravagance in consideration of the religious sentiment which was strongly opposed to such a feature. **That were in Jerusalem before me** (so ver. 9; see ch. i. 16). But the reference here may not necessarily be to kings, but to chieftains and rich men, who were celebrated for the extent of their possessions.

Ver. 8.—**I gathered me also silver and gold.** Much is said of the wealth of the historical Solomon, who had all his vessels of gold, armed his body-guard with golden shields, sat on an ivory throne overlaid with gold, received tribute and presents of gold from all quarters, sent his navies to distant lands to import precious metals, and made silver as common in Jerusalem as stones (see 1 Kings ix. 28; x. 14—27 ; 2 Chron. i. 15 ; ix. 20—27). **The peculiar treasure of kings and of the provinces.** The word rendered " the provinces" (*hammedinoth*), in spite of the article, seems to mean, not the twelve districts into

which Solomon divided his kingdom for fiscal and economical purposes (1 Kings iv. 7, etc.), but countries generally exterior to Palestine, with which he had commercial or political relations, and which sent to him the productions for which they were each most celebrated. So the districts of the Persian empire were required to furnish the monarch with a certain portion of their chief commodities. His friendship with Hiram of Tyre brought him into connection with the Phœnicians, the greatest commercial nation of antiquity, and through them he accumulated riches and stores from distant and various lands beyond the limits of the Mediterranean Sea. The word מְדִינָה (*medinah*) occurs again in ch. v. 7 and in 1 Kings xx. 14, etc. ; but is found elsewhere only in exilian or post-exilian books (*e.g.* Lam. i. 1 ; Esth. i. 1, etc. ; Dan. ii. 48, etc.). The "kings" may be the tributary monarchs, such as those of Arabia (1 Kings iv. 21, 24 ; x. 15); or the expression in the text may imply simply such treasure as only kings, and not private persons, could possess. **Men-singers and women-singers.** These, of course, are not the choir of the temple, of which women formed no part, but musicians introduced at banquets and social festivals, to enhance the pleasures of the scene. They are mentioned in David's days (2 Sam. xix. 35) and later (see Isa. v. 12 ; Amos vi. 5 ; Ecclus. xxxv. 5 ; xlix. 1). The females who took part in these performances were generally of an abandoned class; hence the warning of Ben-Sira, " Use not much the company of a woman that is a singer, lest thou be taken with her attempts " (Ecclus. ix. 4). Such exhibitions were usually accompanied with dancing, the character of which in Eastern countries is well known. The Jews, as time went on, learned to tolerate many customs and practices, imported often from other lands, which tended to lower morality and self-respect. **And the delights of the sons of men** ; the sensual pleasures that men enjoy. The expression is euphemistic (comp. Cant. vii. 6). **Musical instruments, and that of all sorts** (*shiddah veshiddoth*). The word (given here first in the singular number and then in the plural emphatically to express multitude) occurs nowhere else, and has, therefore, been subjected to various interpretations. The Septuagint gives, οἰνοχόον καὶ οἰνοχόας, " a male cupbearer and female cupbearers ; " and so the Syriac and Vulgate, *Scyphos et urceos in ministerio ad vina fundenda*—which introduces rather a bathos into the description. After the clause immediately preceding, one might expect mention of Solomon's numerous harem (1 Kings xi. 3; Cant. vi. 8), and most modern commentators consider the word to mean "concubine," the whole expression denoting multiplicity, " wife and wives." The

Authorized Version is not very probable, though somewhat supported by Kimchi, Luther, etc., and the Greek Venetian, which has, σύστημα καὶ συστήματα, a musical term signifying "combination of tones," or harmony. Other interpretations are "captives," "litters," "coaches," "baths," "treasures," "chests," "demons." Ewald, followed by Motais and others, suggests that the word implies a strong or high degree of a quality, so that, connecting the two clauses together, we should render, "And in a word, all the delights of the sons of men in abundance." This seems a more appropriate termination to the catalogue than any specification of further sources of pleasure; but there is no very strong etymological reason to recommend it ; and we can hardly suppose that, in the enumeration of Solomon's prodigalities, his multitudinous seraglio would be omitted. Rather it comes in here naturally as the climax and completion of his pursuit of earthly delight.

Ver. 9.—**So I was great** (see on ch. i. 16). This refers to the magnificence and extent of his possessions and luxury, as the former passage to the surpassing excellence of his wisdom. We may compare the mention of Abraham (Gen. xxvi. 13), "The man waxed great, and grew more and more until he became very great" (so Job i. 3). **Also my wisdom remained with me ;** *perseveravit mecum* (Vulgate); ἐστάθη μοι (Septuagint). In accordance with the purpose mentioned in ver. 3, he retained command of himself, studying philosophically the effects and nature of the pleasures of which he partook, and keeping ever in view the object of his pursuit. Voluptuousness was not the end which he sought, but one of the means to obtain the end ; and what he calls his wisdom is not pure Divine wisdom that comes from above, but an earthly prudence and self-restraint.

Ver. 10.—**Whatsoever mine eyes desired.** The lust of the eyes (1 John ii. 16), all that he saw and desired, he took measures to obtain. He denied himself no gratification, however foolish (ver. 3). **For my heart rejoiced in all my labour ;** *i.e.* found joy in what my labour procured for it (comp. Prov. v. 18). This was the reason why he **withheld not his heart from any joy;** kept it, as it were, ready to taste any pleasure which his exertions might obtain. **This was my portion of all my labour.** Such joy was that which he won from his labour. He had his reward, such as it was (Matt. vi. 2; Luke xvi. 25). This term "portion" (*cheleq*) recurs often (*e.g.* ver. 21 ; ch. iii. 22; v. 18, etc. ; so Wisd. ii. 9) in the sense of the result obtained by labour or conduct. And what a meagre and unsatisfying result it was which he gained! Contrast the apostle's teaching, "All that is in the world,

the lust of the flesh, and the lust of the eyes, and the vain-glory of life, is not of the Father, but is of the world. And the world passeth away, and the lust thereof : but he that doeth the will of God abideth for ever" (1 John ii. 16, 17).

Ver. 11.—**Then I looked on—I turned to contemplate—all the works which my hands had wrought.** He examined carefully the effects of the conduct and proceedings mentioned in vers. 1—10, and he now gives his matured judgment concerning them. They had contributed nothing to his anxious inquiry for man's real good. His sorrowful conclusion again is that all was vanity, a hunting of wind ; in all the pursuits and labours that men undertake there is no real profit (ch. i. 3), no lasting happiness, nothing to satisfy the cravings of the spirit.

Vers. 12 — 26. — Section 3. *Vanity of wisdom, in view of the fate that awaits the wise man equally with the fool, and the uncertainty of the future of his labours, especially as man is not master of his own fate.*

Ver. 12.—**And I turned myself to behold wisdom, and madness, and folly** (ch. i. 17). He studied the three in their mutual connection and relation, comparing them in their results and effects on man's nature and life, and deducing thence their real value. On one side he set wisdom, on the other the action, and habits which he rightly terms "madness and folly," and examined them calmly and critically. **For what can the man do that cometh after the king ? even that which hath been already done.** Both the Authorized Version and Revised Version render the passage thus, though the latter, in the margin, gives two alternative renderings of the second clause, viz. *even him whom they made king long ago*, and, as in the Authorized Version margin, *in those things which have been already done.* The LXX., following a different reading, gives, "For what man is there who will follow after counsel in whatsoever things he employed it ?" Vulgate, "What is man, said I, that he should be able to follow the King, his Maker?" Wright, Delitzsch, Nowack, etc., "For what is the man that is to come after the king whom they made so long ago ?" *i.e.* who can have greater experience than Solomon made king in old time amid universal acclamation (1 Chron. xxix. 22) ? or, who can hope to equal his fame ?—which does not seem quite suitable, as it is the abnormal opportunities of investigation given by his unique position which would be the point of the query. The Authorized Version gives a fairly satisfactory (and grammatically unobjectionable) meaning—What can any one effect who tries the same experiment as the king did? He could not do so under more favourable conditions, and will only repeat the same process and reach the same result. But the passage is obscure, and every interpretation has its own difficulty. If the *ki* with which the second portion of the passage begins ("for what," etc.) assigns the reason or motive of the first portion, shows what was the design of Koheleth in contrasting wisdom and folly, the rendering of the Authorized Version is not inappropriate. Many critics consider that Solomon is here speaking of his successor, asking what kind of man he will be who comes after him—the man whom some have already chosen? And certainly there is some ground for this interpretation in vers. 18, 19, where the complaint is that all the king's greatness and glory will be left to an unworthy successor. But this view requires the Solomonic authorship of the book, and makes him to refer to Rehoboam or some illegitimate usurper. The wording of the text is too general to admit of this explanation; nor does it exactly suit the immediate context, or duly connect the two clauses of the verse. It seems best to take the successor, not as one who comes to the kingdom, but as one who pursues similar investigations, repeats Koheleth's experiments.

Ver. 13.—**Then** (*and*) **I saw that wisdom excelleth folly, as far as light excelleth darkness;** or, *there is profit, advantage* (περίσσεια, Septuagint, ch. i. 3) *to wisdom over folly, as the advantage of light over darkness.* This result, at any rate, was obtained—he learned that wisdom had a certain value, that it was as much superior to folly, in its effects on men, as light is more beneficial than darkness. It is a natural metaphor to represent spiritual and intellectual development as light, and mental and moral depravity as darkness (comp. Eph. v. 8; 1 Thess. v. 5).

Ver. 14.—**The wise man's eyes are in his head; but the fool walketh in darkness.** This clause is closely connected with the preceding verse, showing how wisdom excelleth folly. The wise man has the eyes of his heart or understanding enlightened (Eph. i. 18); he looks into the nature of things, fixes his regard on what is most important, sees where to go; while the fool's eyes are in the ends of the earth (Prov. xvii. 24); he walks on still in darkness, stumbling as he goes, knowing not whither his road shall take him. **And I myself also** (*I even I*) **perceived that one event happeneth to them all.** "Event" (*mikreh*); συνάντημα (Septuagint); *interitus* (Vulgate); not chance, but death, the final event. The word is translated "hap" in Ruth ii. 3, and "chance" in 1 Sam. vi. 9; but the connection here points to a definite termination; nor would it be

consistent with Koheleth's religion to refer this termination to fate or accident. With all his experience, he could only conclude that in one important aspect the observed superiority of wisdom to folly was illusory and vain. He saw with his own eyes, and needed no instructor to teach, that both wise and fool must succumb to death, the universal leveller. Horace, in many passages, sings of this: thus 'Carm.,' ii. 3. 21—

"Divesne prisco natus ab Inacho,
Nil interest, an pauper et infima
De gente sub divo moreris,
Victima nil miserantis Orci."

(Comp. ibid., i. 28. 15, etc.; ii. 14. 9, etc.) Plato ('Phædo,' lvii. p. 108, A) refers to a passage in 'Telephus,' a lost play of Æschylus, which is restored thus—

Ἁπλῆ γὰρ οἶμος πάντας εἰς "Αιδου φέρει.

"A single path leads all unto the grave."

Ver. 15.—**Then** (*and*) **said I in my heart** (ch. i. 16), **As it happeneth to the fool, so it happeneth even to me.** He applies the general statement of ver. 14 to his own case. The end that overtakes the fool will ere long overtake him; and he proceeds, **Why was I then more wise?** "Then" (אז), may be understood either logically, *i.e.* in this case, since such is the fate of wise and foolish; or temporally, at the hour of death regarded as past. He puts the question—To what end, with what design, has he been so excessively wise, or, as it may be, wise overmuch (ch. vii. 16)? His wisdom has, as it were, recoiled upon himself—it taught him much, but not content; it made him keen-sighted in seeing the emptiness of human things, but it satisfied not his cravings. **Then I said in my heart, that this also is vanity.** This similarity of fate for philosopher and fool makes life vain and worthless; or rather, the meaning may be, if the superiority of wisdom over folly conduces to no other end than this, that superiority is a vanity. The LXX. has glossed the passage, followed herein by the Syriac, "Moreover, I spake in my heart that indeed this is also vanity, because the fool speaks out of his abundance"—ver. 16 giving the substance of the fool's thoughts. Vulgate, *Locutusque cum mente mea, animadverti quod hoc quoque esset vanitas.* Our Hebrew text does not confirm this interpretation or addition.

Ver. 16.—**For there is no remembrance of the wise man than of the fool for ever;** Revised Version, more emphatically, *for of the wise man, even as of the fool, there is no remembrance for ever.* This, of course, is not absolutely true. There are men whose names are history, and will endure as long as the world lasts; but speaking generally, oblivion is the portion of all; posterity soon forgets the wisdom of one and the folly of another. Where the belief in the future life was not a strong and animating motive, posthumous fame exercised a potent attraction for many minds. To be the founder of a long line of descendants, or to leave a record which should be fresh in the minds of future generations, these were objects of intense ambition, and valued as worthy of highest aspirations and best efforts. The words of classical poets will occur to our memory; *e.g.* Horace, ' Carm.,' iii. 30.

" Exegi monumentum ære perennius . . .
Non omnis moriar, multaque pars mei
      Vitabit Libitinam."

Ovid, ' Amor.,' i. 15. 4—

" Ergo etiam, cum me supremus adederit
      ignis,
Vivam, parsque mei multa superstes
      erit."

But Koheleth shows the vanity of all such hopes; they are based on grounds which experience proves to be unsubstantial. Though Solomon's own fame gives the lie to the statement received without limitation (comp. Wisd. viii. 13), yet his reflections might well have taken this turn, and the writer is quite justified in putting the thought into his mouth, as the king could not know how subsequent ages would regard his wisdom and attainments. **Seeing that which now is in the days to come shall all be forgotten.** The clause has been variously translated. Septuagint, "Forasmuch as the coming days, even all the things, are forgotten;" Vulgate, "And future times shall cover all things equally with oblivion." Modern editors give, " Since in the days that are to come they are all forgotten ; " " As in time past, so in days to come, all will be forgotten ; " " In the days which are coming [it will be said by-and-by], ' The whole of them are long ago forgotten.' " This is a specimen of the uncertainty of exact interpretation, where the intended meaning is well ascertained. "All" (הכל) may refer either to wise and foolish, or to the circumstances of their lives. **And how dieth the wise** man ? **as the fool.** Better taken as one sentence, with an exclamation, *How doth the wise man die with (even as) the fool!* (For " with " (*im*), equivalent to "as," comp. ch. vii. 11; Job ix. 26; Ps. cvi. 6.) " How " (אֵיךְ) is sarcastic, as Isa. xiv. 4, or sorrowful, as 2 Sam. i. 19. The same complaint falls from a psalmist's lips, " He seeth that wise men die; the fool and the brutish together

perish" (Ps. xlix. 10). So David laments the death of the murdered leader, "Should Abner die as a fool dieth?" (2 Sam. iii. 33). Plumptre considers that the author of the Book of Wisdom expands this view with the design of exposing its fallacy, and introducing a better hope (ch. ii. 1—9). But that writer would not have designated Solomon's sentiments as those of "the ungodly" (ἀσεβεῖς), nor foisted these utterances of sensualists and materialists upon so honoured a source. At the same time, it is only as being victims, *nil miserantis Orci*, the prey of the pitiless and indiscriminating grave, that the wise and foolish are placed in the same category. There is the widest difference between the death-beds of the two, as the experience of any one who has watched them will testify, the one happy with the consciousness of duty done honestly, however imperfectly, and bright with the hope of immortality; the other darkened by vain regrets and shrinking despair, or listless in brutish insensibility.

Ver. 17.—**Therefore I hated life ;** *et idcirco tæduit me vitæ meæ.* Be a man wise or foolish, his life leads only to one end and is soon forgotten; hence life itself is burdensome and hateful. The bitter complaint of Job (iii. 20, etc.; vi. 8, 9) is here echoed, though the words do not point to suicide as the solution of the riddle. It is the *ennui* and unprofitableness of all life and action in view of the inevitable conclusion, which is here lamented. **Because the work that is wrought under the sun is grievous unto me;** literally, *for evil unto me* (Esth. iii. 9) *is the work which is done under the sun.* The toil and exertions of men pressed upon him like a burden too heavy for him to bear. Symmachus, Κακόν μοι ἐφάνη τὸ ἔργον; Septuagint, Πονηρὸν ἐπ' ἐμὲ τὸ ποίημα, κ.τ.λ. He repeats the expression, " under the sun," as if to show that he was regarding human labour only in its earthly aspect, undertaken and executed for temporal and selfish considerations alone. The apostle teaches a better lesson, and the worker who adopts his rule is saved from this crushing disappointment: " Whatsoever ye do, do it heartily, as to the Lord, and not unto men; knowing that of the Lord ye shall receive the recompense of the inheritance : ye serve the Lord Christ" (Col. iii. 23, 24). **For all is vanity.** He comes back to the same miserable refrain ; it is all emptiness, striving after wind.

Ver. 18.—Such had been his general view of men's actions; he now brings the thought home to his own case, which makes his distress more poignant. **Yea** (*and*), **I hated all my labour which I had taken under the sun.** He is disgusted to reflect upon all the trouble he has taken in life, when he thinks of what will become of the productions of his genius and the treasures which he has amassed. Because I should leave it (my labour, *i.e.* its results) unto the man that shall be after me. It is impossible that Solomon could thus have spoken of Rehoboam; and to suppose that he wrote thus after Jeroboam's attempt (1 Kings ii. 26, etc.), and in contemplation of a possible usurper, is not warranted by any historical statement, the absolute security of the succession being all along expected, and the growing discontent being perfectly unknown to, or contemptuously disregarded by, the king. The sentiment is general, and recurs more than once; *e.g.* ch. iv. 8; v. 14; vi. 2. Thus Horace, 'Epist.,' ii. 2. 175—

"Sic quia perpetuus nulli datur usus, et heres
Heredem alterius velut unda supervenit undam,
Quid vici prosunt aut horrea?"

Ver. 19.—Who knoweth whether he shall be a wise man **or a fool?** The bitter feeling that he has to leave the fruits of his lifelong labour to another is aggravated by the thought that he knows not the character of this successor, whether he will be worthy or not. As the psalmist says, "He heapeth up riches, and knoweth not who shall gather them" (Ps. xxxix. 6). Again in the parable, "The things which thou hast prepared, whose shall they be?" (Luke xii. 20; comp. Ecclus. xi. 18, 19). **Yet shall he have rule,** etc. Whatever may be his character, he will have free use and control of all that I have gathered by my labour directed by prudence and wisdom. Vulgate, *Dominabitur in laboribus meis quibus desudavi et sollicitus fui.*

Ver. 20.—Therefore I went about to cause my heart to despair; Ἐπέστρεψα ἐγὼ (Septuagint). "I turned" in order to examine more closely. So in ver. 12 we had, "I turned myself," though the verbs are not the same in the two passages, and in the former the LXX. has ἐπέβλεψα. I turned from my late course of action to give myself up to despair. I lost all hope in labour; it had no longer any charm or future for me. Septuagint, Τοῦ ἀποτάξασθαι τὴν καρδίαν μου ἐν παντὶ μόχθῳ μου, κ.τ.λ.

Ver. 21.—For there is a man whose labour is in wisdom. "In," בְּ, "with," directed and performed with wisdom. The author speaks of himself objectively, as St. Paul (2 Cor. xii. 2) says, "I know a man in Christ," etc. His complaint now is, not that his successor may misuse his inheritance (ver. 19), but that this person shall have that on which he has bestowed no skill or toil, shall enjoy what modern phraseology terms "unearned increment." This, which was set forth as one of the blessings of the promised land

(Deut. vi. 10, 11), Koheleth cannot bear to contemplate where it touches himself—not from envy or grudging, but from the feeling of dissatisfaction and want of energy which it generates. **In** (*with*) **knowledge and in** (*with*) **equity.** *Kishron,* translated " equity" in the Authorized Version; ἀνδρεία, "manliness," in the Septuagint: and *sollicitudine* in the Vulgate, seems rather here to signify " skill" or "success." It occurs also in ch. iv. 4 and v. 10, and there only in the Old Testament.

Ver. 22.—What hath man of all his labour? *i.e.* what is to be the result to man? Γίνεται ἐν τῷ ἀνθρώπῳ; (Septuagint); *Quid enim proderit homini?* (Vulgate). There is, indeed, the pleasure that accompanies the pursuit of objects, and the successful accomplishment of enterprise; but this is poor and unsubstantial and embittered. **And of the vexation of his heart;** the striving, the effort of his mind to direct his labour to great ends. What does all this produce? The answer intended is, "Nothing." This striving, with all its wisdom and knowledge and skill (ver. 21), is for the labourer fruitless.

Ver. 23.—All his days are sorrow, and his travail grief (comp. ch. v. 16, 17). These are the real results of his lifelong efforts. All his days are pains and sorrows, bring trouble with them, and all his labour ends in grief. "Sorrows" and " grief" are predicated respectively of "days" and "travail." Abstract nouns are often so used. Thus ch. x. 12, "The words of a wise man's mouth are grace." The free-thinkers in Wisd. ii. 1 complain that life is short and tedious (λυπηρός). **Yea, his heart taketh not rest in the night.** He cannot sleep for thinking over his plans and hopes and disappointments. Not for him is the sweet sleep of the labouring man, who does his day's work, earns his repose, and frets not about the future. On the one hand care, on the other satiety, murder sleep, and make the night a torment.

Vers. 24—26.—From what has been said, Koheleth concludes that man may indeed enjoy the good things which he has provided, and find a certain happiness therein, but only according to God's will and permission; and to expect to win pleasure at one's own caprice is vain.

Ver. 24.—There is nothing better for a man, than that he should eat and drink. The Vulgate makes the sentence interrogative, which the Hebrew does not sanction, *Nonne melius est comedere et bibere?* Septuagint, Οὐκ ἔστιν ἀγαθὸν ἀνθρώπῳ ὃ φάγεται καὶ ὃ πίεται, "There is naught good to a man to eat or drink;" St. Jerome and others insert *nisi,* "except for a man to eat," etc.

This and the Authorized Version, which are more or less approved by most critics, make the writer enunciate a kind of modified Epicureanism, quotations in confirmation of which will be found set forth by Plumptre. It is not pretended that the present Hebrew text admits this exposition, and critics have agreed to modify the original in order to express the sense which they give to the passage. As it stands, the sentence runs, "It is not good in (בְּ) man that he should eat," etc. This is supposed to clash with later statements; e.g. ch. iii. 12, 13; viii. 15; and to condemn all bodily pleasure even in its simplest form. Hence commentators insert מ ("than") before שֶׁיֹּאכַל, supposing that the initial *mem* has dropped out after the terminal of the preceding word, *adam* (comp. ch. iii. 22). This solution of a difficulty might be allowed were the Hebrew otherwise incapable of explanation without doing violence to the sentiments elsewhere expressed. But this is not the case. As Motais has seen, the great point lies in the preposition בְּ, and what is stated is that it does not depend on man, it is not in his power, he is not at liberty to eat and drink and enjoy himself simply at his own will; his power and ability proceed wholly from God. A higher authority than his decides the matter. The phrase, "to eat and drink," is merely a periphrasis for living in comfort, peace, and affluence. St. Gregory, who holds that here and in other places Koheleth seems to contradict himself, makes a remark which is of general application, "He who looks to the text, and does not acquaint himself with the sense of the Holy Word, is not so much furnishing himself with instruction as bewildering himself in uncertainty, in that the literal words sometimes contradict themselves; but whilst by their oppositeness they stand at variance with themselves, they direct the reader to a truth that is to be understood" ('Moral.,' iv. 1). They who read Epicureanism into the text fall into the error here denounced. They take the expression, "eat and drink," in the narrowest sense of bodily pleasure, whereas it was by no means so confined in the mind of a Hebrew. To eat bread in the kingdom of God, to take a place at the heavenly banquet, represents the highest bliss of glorified man (Luke xiv. 15; Rev. xix. 9, etc.). In a lower degree it signifies earthly prosperity, as in Jer. xxii. 15, "Did not thy father eat and drink, and do judgment and justice? then it was well with him." So in our passage we find only the humiliating truth that man in himself is powerless to make his life happy or his labours successful. There is no Epicureanism, even in a modified form, in the Hebrew text as it has come down to us. With other supposed traces of this philosophy we shall

have to deal subsequently (see on ch. iii. 12; vi. 2). **And that he should make his soul enjoy good in his labour;** *i.e.* taste the enjoyment of his labour, get pleasure as the reward of all his exertions, or find it in the actual pursuit. **This also I saw, that it was from the hand of God.** This is the point—the power of enjoyment depends on the will of God. The next verse substantiates this assertion.

Ver. 25.—**For who can eat, or who else can hasten hereunto, more than I?** This is the translation of the received text. "Eat" means enjoy one's self, as in the preceding verse; "hasten hereunto" implies eager pursuit of pleasure; and Koheleth asks— Who had better opportunity than he for verifying the principle that all depends upon the gift of God? Vulgate, *Quis ita devorabit, et deliciis affluet ut ego?* The Septuagint had a different reading, which obtains also in the Syriac and Arabic versions, and has been adopted by many modern critics. Instead of מִמֶּנִּי, they read מִמֶּנּוּ, "without him," *i.e.* except from God. "For who shall eat or who shall drink without him (πάρεξ αὐτοῦ)?" This merely repeats the thought of the last verse, in agreement with the saying of St. James (i. 17), "Every good gift and every perfect boon is from above, coming down from the Father of lights." But the received reading, if it admits the rendering of the Authorized Version (which is somewhat doubtful), stands in close connection with the personal remark just preceding, "This also I saw," etc., and is a more sensible confirmation thereof than a tautological observation can be. The next verse carries on the thought that substantial enjoyment is entirely the gift of God, and granted by him as the moral Governor of the world.

Ver. 26.—**For God giveth to a man that is good in his sight.** The subject "God" is not, in the Hebrew, an omission which is supposed to justify its virtual insertion in ver. 25. The Vulgate boldly supplies it here, *Homini bono in conspectu suo dedit Deus.* To the man that finds favour in God's sight (1 Sam. xxix. 6; Neh. ii. 5), *i.e.* who pleases him, he gives blessings, while he withholds them or takes them away from the man who displeases him. The blessings specified are **wisdom, and knowledge, and joy.** The only true wisdom which is not grief, the only true knowledge which is not sorrow (ch. i. 18), and the only joy in life, are the gifts of God to those whom he regards as good. **But to the sinner he giveth travail, to gather and to heap up.** The sinner takes great pains, expends continuous labour, that he may amass wealth, but it passes into other (more worthy) hands. Horace, 'Carm.,' ii. 14. 25—

"Absumet heres Cæcuba dignior
    Servata centum clavibus."

The moral government of God is here recognized, as below, ch. iii. 15, 17, etc., and a further thought is added on the subject of retribution: That he may give to him that is good before God. This idea is found in Prov. xxviii. 8, "He that augmenteth his substance by usury and increase, gathereth it for him that hath pity upon the poor;" and ch. xiii. 22, "The wealth of the sinner is laid up for the righteous" (comp. Job xxvii. 16, 17). So in the parable of the talents, the talent of the unprofitable servant is given unto him who had made best use of his money (Matt. xxv. 28). This also is vanity. It is a question what is the reference here. Delitzsch considers it to be the striving after pleasure in and from labour (ver. 24); Knobel, the arbitrary distribution of the good things of this life; but, put thus baldly, this could hardly be termed a "feeding on wind;" nor could that expression be applied to the "gifts of God" to which Bullock confines the reference. Wright, Hengstenberg, Grätz, and others deem that what is meant is the collecting and heaping up of riches by the sinner, which has already been decided to be vanity (vers. 11, 17, 18); and this would limit the general conclusion to a particular instance. Taking the view contained in ver. 24 as the central idea of the passage, we see that Koheleth feels that the restriction upon man's enjoyment of labour imposed by God's moral government makes that toil vain because its issue is not in men's hands, and it is a striving for or a feeding on wind because the result is unsatisfying and vanishes in the grasp.

HOMILETICS.

Vers. 1—11.—*The vanity of pleasure—an experiment in three stages.* I. THE WAY OF SENSUOUS ENJOYMENT. (Vers. 1, 2.) In this first stage Solomon, whether the real or the personated king, may be viewed as the representative of mankind in general, who, when they cast aside the teachings and restraints of religion, exclude from their minds the thought of a Divine Being, erase from their bosoms all convictions of duty, and refuse to look into the future, commonly addict themselves to pleasure, saying, "Enjoyment, be thou my god;" prescribing to themselves as the foremost task of their lives to minister to their own gratification, and adopting as their creed the well-known maxim, "Let us eat and drink; for to-morrow we die" (1 Cor. xv. 32). 1. *The investigation was vigorously conducted.* The Preacher was in earnest, not merely thinking in his heart, but addressing it, rather like the rich farmer in the parable (Luke xii. 19) than like the singer in the psalm (xvi. 2), and stirring it up as the brickmakers of Babel did one another: "Go to now!" (Gen. xi. 3, 4). That the investigation was so conducted by the real Solomon may be inferred from the preserved details of his history (1 Kings x. 5; xi. 1, 3); that it has often been so conducted since, not merely in fiction, as by Goethe's 'Faust,' but in actual life, as by 'Abelard and Heloïse' in the eleventh century, admits of demonstration; that it is being at present so conducted by many whose principal aim in life is not to obey the soul's noblest impulses, but to hamper the body's lower appetite, is palpable without demonstration. 2. *The result has been clearly recorded.* The Preacher found the way of pleasure as little fitted to conduct to felicity as that of wisdom; discovered, in fact, that laughter occasioned by indulgence in sensual delights was only a species of insanity, a kind of delirious intoxication which stupefied the reason and overthrew the judgment, if it did not lead to self-destruction, and that no solid happiness ever came out of it, but only vanity and striving after wind. So has every one who has sought his chief good in such enjoyment found. They who live in pleasure are dead while they live (1 Tim. v. 6)—dead to all the soul's higher aspirations; are self-deceived (Titus iii. 3); and will in the end have a rude awakening, when they find that their short-lived pleasures (Heb. xi. 25) have only been nourishing them for slaughter (Jas. v. 5).

II. THE WAY OF BANQUETING AND REVELRY. (Ver. 3.) In this second stage of the experiment, neither Solomon nor the Preacher (if he was different) stood alone. The path on which the ancient investigator now depicts himself as entering had been and still is: 1. *Much travelled.* The number of those who abandon themselves to wine and wassail, drunkenness and dissipation, chambering and wantonness, may not be so great as that of those who join in the pursuit of pleasure, many of whom would disdain to partake of the intoxicating cup; but still it is sufficiently large to justify the epithet employed. 2. *Appallingly fatal.* Apart altogether from the rightness or the wrongness of total abstinence, which the Preacher is not commending or even thinking of, this much is evident, that no one need hope to secure true happiness by surrendering himself without restraint to the appetite of intemperance. Nor is the issue different when the experiment is conducted with moderation, *i.e.* without losing one's self-control, or abandoning the search for wisdom. Solomon and the Preacher found that the result was, as before vanity, and a striving after wind. 3. *Perfectly avoidable.* One requires not to tread in this way in order to perceive whither it leads. One has only to observe the experiment, as others are unfortunately conducting it, to discern that its goal is not felicity.

III. THE WAY OF CULTURE AND REFINEMENT. (Vers. 4—11.) In the third stage of this experiment the picture is drawn from the experiences of Solomon—whether by Solomon himself or by the Preacher is immaterial, so far as didactic purposes are concerned. Solomon is introduced as telling his own story. 1. *His magnificence had been most resplendent.* (1) His works were great. He had prepared for himself buildings of architectural beauty, such as " the house of the forest of Lebanon, the pillared hall [porch], the hall of judgment, the palace intended for himself and the daughter of Pharaoh " (1 Kings vii. 1—12); he had strengthened his kingdom by the erection of such towns as Tadmor in the wilderness, the store-cities of Hamath and Baalath, with the two fortresses of Beth-horon the Upper and Beth-horon the Nether (2 Chron. viii. 3—6); he had planted vineyards, of which Baal-hamon, with its choicest wine, was one (Cant. viii. 11), and perhaps those of Engedi (Cant. i. 14) others; he had caused to be constructed, no doubt in connection with his palaces, gardens and orchards, with all kinds of fruit trees, and " pools of water to water therefrom the forest where trees were reared " (Cant. iv. 13; vi. 2). (2) His possessions were varied. In addition to those above mentioned, he had slaves, male and female, purchased with money (Gen. xxxvii. 28), and born in his house (Gen. xv. 3; xvii. 12), with great possessions of flocks and herds. The number of the former was so large as to excite the Queen of Sheba's astonishment (1 Kings x. 5), while the abundance of the latter was proved both by the daily provision for Solomon's household (1 Kings iv. 22, 23), and by the hecatombs sacrificed at the consecration of the temple (1 Kings viii. 63). (3) His wealth was enormous. Of silver and gold, and the peculiar treasure of the kings and of the provinces, he had amassed a heap. The ships of Hiram had fetched him from Ophir four hundred and twenty talents of gold (1 Kings ix. 28); the Queen of Sheba presented him with one hundred and twenty talents of gold (1 Kings x. 10); the weight of gold which came to him in one year was six hundred and sixty-six talents (1 Kings x. 14); while as for silver " the king made it to be in Jerusalem as stones " (1 Kings x. 27). " The peculiar treasure of kings and of the provinces " may either signify such rare and precious jewels as were prized by foreign sovereigns and states and presented to him as tribute; or describe Solomon's wealth as royal and public, in contradistinction from that of private citizens. (4) His pleasures were delicious. He had singing-men and singing-women to regale his jaded senses with music at court banquets, after the manner of Oriental sovereigns; while over and above he had " the delights of the sons of men," or " concubines very many "—" a love and loves " (Wright), " mistress and mistresses " (Delitzsch). Clearly Solomon had conducted the experiment of extracting happiness from worldly glory under the most favourable circumstances; hence special interest attaches to the result he obtained. What was it? 2. *His misery was most pronounced.* Although he had had every gratification that eye could desire, heart wish, or hand procure, he had found to his chagrin that true happiness eluded him like a phantom; that all was vanity and a striving after wind; that, in fact, there was no profit of a lasting kind to be derived from pleasure in its highest any more than in its lowest forms.

Learn: 1. The way of pleasure, however inviting, is not the way of safety or the way of peace. 2. While it cannot impart happiness to any, it may lead to everlasting misery and shame. 3. The pursuit of pleasure is not only incompatible with religion, but even at the best its sweets are not to be compared with religion's joys.

Vers. 12—16.—*Wisdom and folly.* I. FOLLY AS GOOD AS WISDOM. Three things seemed to proclaim this. 1. *The chances of life.* These appeared to be as favourable to the fool as to the wise man. The experiences of both were much alike; the lot of each little different. "I perceived," said he, "that one event happeneth to them all" (ver. 14). "As it happeneth to the fool, so will it happen even to me; and why was I then more wise?" (ver. 15). This observation apparently had struck him with much force, as he refers to it more than once (ch. viii. 14; ix. 2). It was not an original observation, as long before Job had remarked upon the seeming indifference with which providential allotments were made to the righteous and the wicked (Job ix. 22; xxi. 7). Nevertheless, it was and is a true observation that, so far as purely external circumstances are concerned, it may be doubtful if the wise man fares better than the fool. 2. *The onrush of oblivion.* With pitiless maw this devours the wise and the fool alike (ver. 16). If the human heart craves after one thing more than another, it is an assurance that name and memory shall not quite perish from the earth when one himself is gone. Such as are indifferent to a personal immortality beyond the grave in a realm of heavenly felicity, are often found to be supremely desirous of this lesser immortality which men call posthumous fame. For this the Egyptian Pharaohs erected pyramids, temples, mausoleums; for this men strive to set themselves on pinnacles of power, fame, wealth, or wisdom before they die; yet the number of those who are remembered many weeks beyond the circle of their immediate friends is small. Even of the so-called great who have flourished upon the earth, how few are rescued from oblivion!

> "Their memory and their name are gone,
> Alike unknowing and unknown."

Who beyond a few scholars knows anything of the Pharaohs who built the pyramids, or of Assurbanipal, the patron of learning in Assyria, of Homer, of Socrates, or of Plato? If one thinks of it, the amount of remembrance accorded to almost all the leaders of mankind consists in this—that their names will be found in dictionaries. 3. *The descent of death.* The wise man might have derived consolation from the fact—had it been a fact—that though after death his fate would be hardly distinguishable from that of the fool, nevertheless before and at death, or in the manner of dying, there would be a wide distinction. But even this poor scrap of comfort is denied him, according to the Preacher. "How doth the wise man die? as the fool!" (ver. 16). To appearance, at least, it is so, because in reality a difference wide asunder as the poles separates the dying of "him who is driven away in his wickedness," and "him who has hope in his death" (Prov. xiv. 32). But contemplating death from the outside, as a purely natural phenomenon, it is the same exactly in the experience of the wise man as in that of the fool. In both the process culminates in the loosening of the silver cord and the breaking of the golden bowl (ch. xii. 6).

II. WISDOM SUPERIOR TO FOLLY. As light excelleth darkness, so wisdom excels folly. Three grounds of superiority. 1. *The path of wisdom a way of light; that of folly a way of darkness.* That the latter is essentially a way of darkness, and therefore of uncertainty, difficulty, and danger, had been declared by Solomon (Prov. ii. 13; iv. 19). The Preacher adds an explanation by likening the foolish man to a person walking backwards, or "with his eyes behind;" so that he knows neither whither he is going, nor at what he is stumbling, nor the peril into which he is advancing. Had the Preacher said nothing more than this, he would have been entitled to special thanks. Thousands live in the delusion that the way of pleasure, frivolity, dissipation, extravagance, prodigality, is the way of light, wisdom, safety, felicity—which it is not. The traveller who would journey in comfort and security must walk with his eyes to the front, considering the direction in which he moves, pondering the paths of his feet, and turning neither to the right hand nor to the left (Prov. iv. 25—27). In other words, the wise man's eyes must be in his head, exercising at once forethought, circumspection, and attention. 2. *The source of wisdom from above; that of folly from beneath.* As the light descends from the pure regions of the upper air, so this wisdom of which the Preacher speaks, like that to which Job (xxviii. 23), David (Ps. li. 6), Solomon (Prov. ii. 6), Daniel (ii. 23), Paul (1 Cor. i. 30), and James (i. 5; iii. 15) allude, comes from God (ver. 26). As the darkness may be said to spring from the earth, so folly has its birthplace in the heart. The individual that turns away from the light of wisdom presented to him in the moral intuitions of the heart, the revelations of Scripture, or the teachings of nature, by that act condemns his spirit to dwell in darkness. 3. *The end of wisdom, safety ; that of folly, destruction.* The light of wisdom illuminates the path of duty for the individual; the darkness of folly covers it with gloom. Specially true of heavenly wisdom as contrasted with wickedness and sin. Even with regard to ordinary wisdom, its superiority over folly is not to be denied. The wise man has at least the satisfaction of knowing whither he is going, and of realizing the unsatisfactory character of the course he is pursuing. It may not be a great advantage which the wise man has over the fool, that whereas the fool is a madman and knows it not, the wise man cannot follow after wisdom (in itself and for itself) without discovering that it is vanity; but still it is an advantage—an advantage like that which a man has who walks straight before him, with his eyes in his head and directed to the front, over him who either puts out his eyes, or blindfolds himself, or turns his eyes backward before he begins to travel.

LESSONS. 1. Get wisdom, especially the best. 2. Eschew folly, more particularly that which is irreligious. 3. Learn to discriminate between the two; much evil will thereby be avoided.

Vers. 17—26.—*The vanity of toil.* I. THE SECRET OF HAPPINESS LIES NOT IN BUSI-NESS. Granting that one applies himself to business, and succeeds through ability, perseverance, and skill in building up a fortune, if he looks for felicity either in his labour or in his riches, he will find himself mistaken. Three things are fatal to a man's chances of finding happiness in the riches that come from business success. 1. *Sorrow in the getting of them.* Toiling and moiling, labouring and striving, drudging and slaving, planning and plotting, scheming and contriving, rising up early and lying down late, hurrying and worrying—by these means for the most part are fortunes built up. How expressive is the Preacher's language concerning the successful man of business, that "all his days are sorrows, and his travail is grief," or "all his days are pains, and trouble is his occupation," "yea, even in the night his heart taketh no rest" (ver. 23)! 2. *Sorrow in the keeping of them.* A constant anxiety besets the rich man, night and day, lest the riches he has amassed should suddenly take wings and flee away; by day looking out for safe investments, and by night wondering if his ventures will prove good, if the money he has painfully collected may not some day disappear and leave him in the lurch. And even should this not happen, how often is it seen that when a man has made his fortune, he finds there is nothing in it; that success has been too long in coming, and that now, when he has wealth, he wants the power to enjoy it (ver. 22 ; cf. ch. vi. 2); as the duke says to Claudio in the prison—

> "And when thou art old and rich,
> Thou hast neither heat, affection, limb, nor beauty,
> To make thy riches pleasant."
>
> ('Measure for Measure,' act iii. sc. 1.)

3. *Sorrow in the parting with them.* The results of all his labour he must leave to the man who shall be after him, without knowing whether that successor shall be a wise man or a fool (vers. 18, 19; cf. ch. v. 15); and though this does not greatly trouble the Christian, who knows there is laid up for him a better and more enduring substance in heaven, yet for the worldly or insincerely religious man it is an agitating thought. Mazarin, the cardinal, and first minister of Louis XIV., was accustomed, as he walked through the galleries of his palace, to whisper to himself, "I must quit all this;" and Frederick William IV. of Prussia on one occasion, as he stood upon the Potsdam terrace, turned to Chevalier Bunsen beside him, and remarked, as they looked out together on the garden, "This too I must leave behind me" (see Plumptre, *in loco*).

II. BUSINESS MAY MINISTER TO MAN'S ENJOYMENT. The Preacher does not wish to teach that happiness lies beyond man's reach, but rather that it is attainable, if sought in the right way. He recognizes: 1. *That there is nothing wrong in seeking after happiness, or even earthly enjoyment.* He admits there is nothing better, more per-missible or desirable, among men than that one "should eat and drink, and make his soul enjoy good in his labour" (ver. 24). He even allows that this is from the hand of God, which makes it plain that he is not now alluding to sinful indulgence of the bodily appetite, but speaking of that moderate enjoyment of the good things of life God has so richly provided for man's support and entertainment. It is not God's wish, he says, that man should be debarred or should debar himself from all enjoyment. Rather it is his earnest desire that man should eat and drink and enjoy what has been furnished for his entertainment, should not make of himself an ascetic, under pretence of religion denying himself of lawful pleasures and gratifications, but should so use them as to contribute to his highest welfare. 2. *That no man can make a good use of life's provisions unless in connection with the thought of God.* "Who can eat or have enjoyment, apart from him [*i.e.* God]?" (Revised Version, margin). This corrective thought the Preacher lays before his readers, that while the world's good things cannot impart happiness by themselves and apart from God, they can if enjoyed in conjunction with him, *i.e.* if recognized as coming from him (1 Chron. xxix. 14; 1 Tim. vi. 17; Jas. i. 17), and used for his glory (1 Cor. x. 31). The last passages show that this was the New Testament ideal of life (1 Tim. iv. 4). 3. *That he who seeks happiness in this way will succeed.* "For God giveth to a man that is good in his sight [or, 'that pleaseth him'] wisdom, and knowledge, and joy" (ver. 26). So far from pronouncing felicity a dream, an unattainable good, a shadow without a substance, the Preacher believes that if a man will take God and religion with him into the world, and, remembering both the shortness of time and the certainty of a future life, will enjoy the world's good things in moderation and with thankfulness, he will derive therefrom, if not absolute and unmixed happiness, as near an approximation to it as man can expect to reach on earth. God will graciously assist such a man to gather the best fruits of wisdom and knowledge, both human and Divine, and will inspire him with a joy the world can neither give nor take away (Job xxii. 21; Ps. xvi. 8, 9; cxii. 1, 7, 8; John xvi. 22). This, if not happiness, is at least a lot immensely superior to that God assigns to the sinner, *i.e.* to the man who excludes God, religion, and immortality from his life. The lot of such a man is often as the Preacher describes, to toil away in making money, to heap it up till it becomes a pile, and then to die and leave it to be scattered to the winds, enjoyed by he knows not whom, and not unfrequently by the good men he has despised (Job xxvii. 16, 17; Prov. xiii. 22; xxviii. 8).

LESSONS. 1. Be diligent in business (Rom. xii. 11). "Whatsoever thy hand findeth to do," etc. (ch. ix. 10). 2. But be "fervent in spirit, serving the Lord" (Rom. xii. 11). 3. Seek happiness in God himself rather than in his gifts (Ps. iv. 7; ix. 2; xl. 16; Luke i. 47; Phil. iii. 1).

HOMILIES BY VARIOUS AUTHORS.

Vers. 1—11.—*The vanity of wealth, pleasure, and greatness.* There is certainly a strange reversal here of the order of experience which is usual and expected. Men, disappointed with earthly possessions and satiated with sensual pleasures, sometimes turn to the pursuit of some engrossing study, to the cultivation of intellectual tastes. But the case described in the text is different. Here we have a man, convinced by experience of the futility and disappointing character of scientific and literary pursuits, applying himself to the world, and seeking satisfaction in its pleasures and distractions. Such experience as is here described is possible only to one in a station of eminence; and if Solomon is depicted as disappointed with the result of his experiment, there is no great encouragement for others, less favourably situated, to hope for better results from similar endeavours.

I. THE WORLDLY MAN'S AIM. This is to learn what the human heart and life can derive from the gifts and enjoyments of this world. Man's nature is impulsive, acquisitive, yearning, aspiring. He is ever seeking satisfaction for his wants and desires. He turns now hither and now thither, seeking in every direction that which he never finds in anything earthly, in anything termed "real."

II. THE WORLDLY MAN'S MEANS TO THIS END. How shall satisfaction be found? The world presents itself in answer to this question, and invites its votary to acquisition and appropriation of its gifts. This passage in Ecclesiastes offers a remarkable and exhaustive catalogue of the emoluments and pleasures, the interests and occupations, with which the world pretends to satisfy the yearning spirit of man. There are enumerated: 1. Bodily pleasure, especially the pleasure of abundance of choice wine. 2. Feminine society. 3. Riches, consisting of silver and gold, of flocks and herds.

4. Great works, as palaces, parks, etc. 5. Household magnificence. 6. Treasures of art, and especially musical entertainments. 7. Study and wisdom, associated with all diversions and distractions of every kind. It seems scarcely credible that one man could be the possessor of so many means of enjoyment, and it is not to be wondered at that "Solomon in all his glory" should be mentioned as the most amazing example of this world's greatness and delights. It needed a many-sided nature to appreciate so vast a variety of possessions and occupations; the largeness of heart which is ascribed to the Hebrew monarch must have found abundant scope in the palaces of Jerusalem. It is instructive that Holy Writ, which presents so just a view of human nature, should record a position so exalted and opulent and a career so splendid as those of Solomon.

III. THE WORLDLY MAN'S FAILURE TO SECURE THE END BY THE USE OF THE MEANS DESCRIBED. 1. All such gratifications as are here enumerated are in themselves insufficient to satisfy man's spiritual nature. There is a disproportion between the soul of man and the pleasures of sense and the gifts of fortune. Even could the wealth and luxury, the delights and splendour, of an Oriental monarch be enjoyed, the result would not be the satisfaction expected. There would still be "the aching void the world can never fill." 2. It must also be remembered that, by a law of our constitution, even pleasure is not best obtained when consciously and deliberately sought. To seek pleasure is to miss it, whilst it often comes unsought in the path of ordinary duty. 3. When regarded as the supreme good, worldly possessions and enjoyments may hide God from the soul. They obscure the shining of the Divine countenance, as the clouds conceal the sun that shines behind them. The works of God's hand sometimes absorb the interest and attention which are due to their Creator; the bounty and beneficence of the Giver are sometimes lost sight of by those who partake of his gifts. 4. The good things of earth may legitimately be accepted and enjoyed when received as God's gifts, and held submissively and gratefully "with a light hand." 5. Earth's enjoyments may be a true blessing if, failing to satisfy the soul, they induce the soul to turn from them to God, in whose favour is life.—T.

Vers. 12—17.—*The comparison between wisdom and folly.* To the ordinary observer the contrast between men's condition and circumstances is more expressive than that between their character. The senses are attracted, the imagination is excited, by the spectacle of wealth side by side with squalid poverty, of grandeur and power side by side with obscurity and helplessness. But to the reflecting and reasonable there is far more interest and instruction in the distinction between the nature and life of the fool, impelled by his passions or by the influence of his associations, and the nature and life of the man who considers, deliberates, and judges, and, as becomes a rational being, acts in accordance with nature and well-weighed convictions. Very noble are the words which the poet puts into the lips of Philip van Artevelde—

> "All my life long
> Have I beheld with most respect the man
> Who knew himself, and knew the ways before him;
> And from amongst them chose deliberately,
> And with clear foresight, not with blindfold courage;
> And having chosen, with a steadfast mind
> Pursued his purposes."

I. THE NATURAL CONTRAST BETWEEN WISDOM AND FOLLY. 1. The distinction is one founded in the very nature of things, and is similar to that which, in the physical world, exists between light and darkness. This is as much as to say that God himself is the All-wise, and that reasonable beings, in so far as they participate in his nature and character, are distinguished by true wisdom; whilst, on the other hand, departure from God is the same thing as abandonment to folly. 2. The distinction is brought out by the just exercise or the culpable misuse of human faculty. "The wise man's eyes are in his head," which is a proverbial and figurative way of saying that the wise man uses the powers of observation and judgment with which he is endowed. The position and the endowments of the organs of vision is a plain indication that they were intended to guide the steps; the man who looks before him will not miss his way or fall into danger. Similarly, the faculties of the understanding and reason which are bestowed upon man are intended for the purpose of directing the voluntary actions, which, becoming habitual, constitute man's moral life. The wise man is he who not only possesses such powers, but makes a right use of them, and orders his way aright. The fool, on the contrary, "walketh in darkness;" *i.e.* he is as one who, having eyes, makes no use of them—shuts his eyes, or walks blindfold. The natural consequence is that he wanders from the path, and probably falls into perils and into destruction.

II. THE APPARENT EQUALITY OF THE LOT OF THE WISE MAN AND THAT OF THE FOOL. The writer of this Book of Ecclesiastes was impressed with the fact that in this world men do not meet with their deserts; that, if there is retribution, it is of a very incomplete character; that the fortune of men is not determined by their moral character. This is a mystery which has oppressed the minds of observant and reflecting men in every age, and has been to some the occasion of falling into scepticism and even atheism. 1. The wise man and the fool in many cases meet with the same fortune here upon earth : "One event happeneth to them all." Wisdom does not always meet with its reward in earthly prosperity, nor does folly always bring down upon the fool the penalty of poverty, suffering, and shame. A man may be ignorant, unthinking, and wicked; yet by the exercise of shrewdness and cunning he may advance himself. A wise man may be indifferent to worldly ends, and may neglect the means by which prosperity may be secured. Moral means secure moral ends; but there may be spiritual prosperity which is not crowned by worldly greatness and wealth. 2. The wise man and the fool are alike forgotten after death. "All shall be forgotten;" "There is no remembrance of the wise more than of the fool for ever." All men have some sensitiveness to the reputation which shall survive them; the writer of this book seems to have been particularly sensitive upon this point. He was impressed by the fact that no sooner has a wise and good man departed this life than straightway men proceed to forget him. A few years past, and the memory of the dead itself dies, and good and bad alike are forgotten by a generation interested only in its own affairs. A common oblivion overtakes us all. Such considerations led the author of this book into distress and disheartenment. He was tempted to hate life; it was grievous unto him, and all was vanity and vexation of spirit. A voice within, plausible and seductive, urges—Why trouble as to the moral principles by which you are guided? Whether you are wise or foolish, will it not soon be all the same? Nay, is it not all the same even now?

III. THE REAL SUPERIORITY OF WISDOM OVER FOLLY. If we were to look at some verses of this book only, we might infer that the author's mind was quite unhinged by the spectacle of human life; that he really doubted the superintendence of Divine providence; that he did not care to make a fight for truth, righteousness, and goodness. But although he had doubts and difficulties, though he passed through moods of a pessimistic character, it appears plain that when he came to state his deliberate and reasoned convictions, he showed himself to be a believer in God, and not in fate; in resolute and self-denying virtue, and not in self-indulgence and cynicism. In this passage are brought together facts which occasion most men perplexity, which bring some men into scepticism. Yet the deliberate conclusion to which the author comes is this : "I saw that wisdom excelleth folly." He had, as we all should have, a better and higher standard of judgment, and a better and higher law of conduct, than the phenomena of this world can supply. It is not by temporal and earthly results that we are to form our judgments upon morality and religion; we have a nobler and a truer standard, even our own reason and conscience, the voice of Heaven to which to listen, the candle of the Lord by which to guide our steps. Judged as God judges, judged by the Law and the Word of God, "wisdom excelleth folly." Let the wise and good man be afflicted in his body, let him be plunged into adversity, let him be deserted by his friends, let him be calumniated or forgotten; still he has chosen the better part, and need not envy the good fortune of the fool. Even the ancient Stoics maintained this. How much more the followers of Christ, who himself incurred the malice and derision of men; who was despised and rejected and crucified, but who, nevertheless, was approved and accepted of God the All-wise, and was exalted to everlasting dominion! "Wisdom is justified of her children." The wise man is not to be shaken either by the storms of adversity or by the taunts of the foolish. His is the right path, and he will persevere in it; and he is not only sustained by the approbation of his conscience, he is satisfied with the fellowship of his Master, Christ.—T.

Vers. 18—23.—*Concern for posterity.* It is distinctive of man that he is a being that looks before and after; he cannot be satisfied to regard only the present; he investigates the former days, and the ancestry from which he has derived life and circumstances; he speculates as to the days to come, and "all the wonder yet to be." It appeared to the "Preacher" of Jerusalem that too great solicitude regarding our posterity is an element in the "vanity" which is characteristic of this life.

I. IT IS NATURAL THAT MEN SHOULD ANTICIPATE THEIR POSTERITY WITH INTEREST AND SOLICITUDE. Family life is so natural to man that there is nothing strange in the anxiety which most men feel with regard to their children, and even their children's children. Men do not like the prospect of their posterity sinking in the social scale. Prosperous men find a pleasure and satisfaction in "founding a family," in perpetuating their name, preserving their estates and possessions to their descendants, and in the prospect of being remembered with gratitude and pride by generations yet unborn. In the case of kings and nobles such sentiments and anticipations are especially powerful.

II. IT IS A MATTER OF FACT THAT IN MANY INSTANCES MEN'S ANTICIPATIONS REGARDING POSTERITY ARE DISAPPOINTED. The wide and accurate observations of the author of Ecclesiastes convinced him that such is the case. 1. The rich man's descendants scatter the wealth which he has accumulated by means of labour and self-denial. It need not be proved, for the fact is patent to all, that it is the same in this respect in our own days as it was in the Hebrew state. In fact, we have an English proverb, "One generation makes money; the second keeps it; the third spends it." 2. The wise man's descendant proves to be a fool. Notwithstanding what has been maintained to be a law of "hereditary genius," the fact is unquestionable that there are many instances in which the learned, the accomplished, the intellectually great, are succeeded by those bearing their name, but by no means inheriting their ability. And the contrast is one painful to witness, and humiliating to those to whose disadvantage it is drawn. 3. The descendants of the great in many instances fall into obscurity and contempt. History affords us many examples of such descent; tells of the posterity of the noble, titled, and powerful working with their hands for daily bread, etc.

III. THE PROSPECT OF AN UNFORTUNATE POSTERITY OFTEN DISTRESSES AND TROUBLES MEN, ESPECIALLY THE GREAT. The "wise man" knew what it was to brood over such a prospect as opened up to his foreseeing mind. He came to hate his labour, and to cause his heart to despair; all his days were sorrow, and his travail grief; his heart took not rest in the night; and life seemed only vanity to him. Why should I toil, and take heed, and care, and deny myself? is the question which many a man puts to himself in the sessions of silent thought. My children or my children's children may squander my riches, alienate my estates, sully my reputation; my work may be undone, and my fond hopes ,may be mocked. What is human life but hollowness, vanity, wind?

IV. THE TRUE CONSOLATION BENEATH THE PRESSURE OF SUCH FOREBODINGS. It is vain to attempt to comfort ourselves by denying facts or by cherishing unfounded and unreasonable hopes. What we have to do is to place all our confidence in a wise and gracious God, and to leave the future to his providential care; and at the same time to do our own duty, not concerning ourselves overmuch as to the conduct of others, of those who shall come after us. It is for us to "rest in the Lord," who has not promised to order and overrule all things for our glory or happiness, but who will surely order and overrule them for the advancement of his kingdom and the honour of his Name.—T.

Ver. 24.—*All good is from God.* Revelation ever presents to man a standard of conduct equally removed from selfish gratification and from proud asceticism. It condemns the habit, too common with the prosperous and fortunate, of seeking all satisfaction in the pleasures and luxuries of the world, in the enjoyments of sense; and it at the same time condemns the tendency to despise the body and the things of time and sense, as if such independence of earth were of necessity the means to spiritual enrichment and blessing. On the one hand, we are invited to partake freely and gladly of the gifts of Divine providence; on the other hand, we are admonished to receive all things as "from the hand of God."

I. GOD'S BOUNTY PROVIDES THE FAVOURS BY WHICH MAN'S EARTHLY LIFE IS ENRICHED. Food and drink are mentioned here as examples of the good gifts of the Eternal Father, who "openeth his hand, and supplieth the wants of every living thing." Manifold is the provision of the Divine beneficence. The whole material world is an apparatus by which the bounty of the Creator ministers to the wants of his creatures. And all God's gifts have a meaning and value beyond themselves; they reveal the Divine character, they symbolize the Divine goodness. To despise them is to despise the Giver.

II. GOD'S KINDNESS BESTOWS FACULTIES ADAPTED TO THE ENJOYMENT OF HIS GIFTS. The adaptation is obvious and instructive between the bounties of God's providence, and the bodily constitution in virtue of which man is able to appropriate and enjoy what God bestows. Food and drink presuppose the power to partake of them, and to use them for the continued life, health, and vigour of the body. The correspondence may be traced throughout the whole of our physical nature; between the eye and light, between hearing and sound, between the lungs and the atmosphere—in fact, between the organism and the environment.

III. GOD EXPECTS THAT WE SHOULD USE HIS GIFTS AS HE COMMANDS, AND FOR HIS GLORY. All Divine bestowments are a kind of test and trial for man, who does not of necessity follow appetite, but who can exercise his reason and his will in dealing with the circumstances of his being, with the provisions of God's bounty. All are susceptible of use and of abuse. The Preacher gives us the key to a right use of providential bounties, when he reminds us that all is "from the hand of God." The man who sees the Giver in the gift, who partakes with gratitude of that which is bestowed, recognizing its spiritual significance, and using it as the means to spiritual improvement,—such a man fulfils his probation aright, and does not live the earthly life in vain.

IV. UPON COMPLIANCE WITH OR NEGLECT OF THE DIVINE REQUIREMENT DEPENDS THE EFFECT OF GOD'S GIFTS UPON US, WHETHER THEY SHALL BE A BLESSING OR A CURSE. It would be very easy to read amiss the teaching of this Book of Ecclesiastes. Let a man read it when under the influence of a hedonistic and optimistic temper of mind, and he may be encouraged to abandon himself to the pleasures of life, to the joys of sense, to seek his welfare and satisfaction in what this world can give. Let a man read the book when passing through bitter experience of the ills and woes and disappointments of life, in a pessimistic mood, and he may be encouraged to dejection, despondency, and cynicism. But the true lesson of the book is this: Life is a Divine discipline, and its purpose should never be lost sight of; the gifts of Providence are intended for our enjoyment, our grateful appropriation, but not for the satisfaction of the spiritual nature; Divine wisdom summons us to the reverential service of the Eternal himself; we should then receive with joy what God bestows, and give up without undue mourning what God takes away, for all of life is "from the hand of God."—T.

Ver. 26.—*Retribution.* Here at length the Preacher propounds the doctrine of God's moral government, which in the earlier part of the book has been kept in abeyance. It is one thing to treat of human life, and another thing to treat of theology. The first may, and does to the thoughtful mind, suggest the second; but there are many who never take the step from the one to the other. The author of this book has recorded his experience, with such generalizations and obvious lessons as such experience naturally suggests; he has drawn such conclusions as an observant and reflecting student could scarcely avoid. But hitherto he has refrained from the province of faith, of insight, of revelation. Now, however, he boldly affirms the fact that the world is the scene of Divine retribution; that behind all natural law there is a law which is supernatural; that the Judge of all the earth doeth right.

I. GOD IS INTERESTED IN HUMAN CHARACTER AND LIFE. The ancient Epicurean notions that the gods were above all care for the concerns of men is not extinct; for many even now deem it derogatory to the Deity that he should be considered to interest himself either in the experiences or in the character of men. This passage in Ecclesiastes justly assumes that what men are and what they pass through are matters of real concern to the Creator and Lord of all.

II. GOD ALLOWS IN HUMAN LIFE SCOPE FOR THE DEVELOPMENT OF MEN'S MORAL

CHARACTER. He endows man with a constitution properly supernatural, with capacities and faculties higher than those which are amenable to physical law. Interesting as is the necessary development of the universe under the control of natural forces, far more interesting is the unfolding of the moral character of men. This, indeed, is for us the most significant and momentous of all things that exist. Man is made not merely to enjoy or to suffer, but to form character, to acquire habits of virtue and piety; to become assimilated, in moral disposition and purpose, to the Divine Author of his being. To this end all circumstances may conduce; for experience shows us that there is no condition of human life, no range of human experience, which may not minister to spiritual improvement and welfare.

III. GOD IS THE RIGHTFUL RULER AND JUDGE OF MEN. All human relationships fail adequately to set forth the character and offices of the Eternal; yet many such relationships serve to afford us some glimpse into the excellences of him who is judicially and morally the Supreme. There is no incompatibility between the representation that God is a Father, and that which attributes to him the functions of a Judge. The human relationships are based upon the Divine, and it is unjust to regard the human as simply figures of the Divine. Having all power, God is able to apportion the lot of the creature; being infinitely righteous, such apportionment on his part must be beyond all criticism and censure. The life of man should be lived under a constant sense of the Divine observation and judgment; for thus the probationer of earth will secure the advantage of the loftiest standard of righteousness, and the motive to rectitude and to progress which the Divine government is fitted to supply. Distributive justice—to use the expression familiar in moral philosophy—is the function of the Supreme.

IV. GOD HIMSELF DETERMINES THE MEASURE IN WHICH RETRIBUTION SHALL BE CARRIED OUT IN THIS EARTHLY LIFE. The passage now under consideration lays stress upon the earthly reward and penalty, though it does not represent these as exhaustive and complete. "God giveth to a man that is good in his sight wisdom, and knowledge, and joy." This is something very different from what is termed "poetical justice;" these are gifts which are consistent with adversity and affliction. In fact, the lesson seems to be conveyed that moral goodness meets with moral recompense, as distinct from the doctrine of children's story-books, which teach that "virtue will be rewarded with a coach-and-six"! And the sinner is warned that he will receive the reward of his sin in travail, disappointment, and dissatisfaction. "Whatsoever a man soweth, that shall he also reap." A man must be blind who does not see in the constitution of human nature and human society the traces of a righteous Lawgiver and Administrator; and at the same time, the man must be short-sighted who does not detect indications of incompleteness in these judicial arrangements.

V. GOD GIVES US IN THE PARTIAL RETRIBUTION OF THE PRESENT A SUGGESTION OF A LIFE TO COME, IN WHICH HIS GOVERNMENT SHALL BE COMPLETED AND VINDICATED. That the convictions and expectations of the ancient Hebrews with regard to a future existence were as developed and decisive as those of Christians, none would contend. But this and other books afford indications that the enlightened Jews had an anticipation of judgment to come. If this world were all, vanity and vexation of spirit would have been the only impression produced by the experience and contemplation of human life. But it was seen, even if dimly, that this earthly state requires, in order to its completeness, an immortality which is the scene of Divine judgment and of human retribution.—T.

Vers. 1—11.—*The trial of pleasure.* We have to consider—

I. THE CONSTANT QUESTION OF THE HUMAN HEART. In what shall we find the good which will make our life precious to us? What is there that will meet the cravings of the human heart, and cover our whole life with the sunshine of success and of contentment?

II. A VERY NATURAL RESORT. We have recourse to some kind of excitement. It may be that which acts upon *the senses* (vers. 3, 8). Or it may be that which gratifies *the mind;* the sense of possession and of power (vers. 7—9). Or it may be found in agreeable and inviting *activities* (vers. 4—6).

III. ITS TEMPORARY SUCCESS. "My heart rejoiced" (ver. 10). It would be simply false to contend that there is *no* delight, no satisfaction, in these sources of good. There is, for a while. There is a space during which they fill the heart as the wine fills the cup into which it is poured. The heart rejoices; it utters its joy in song; it declares itself to be completely happy. It " sits in the sun ; " it rolls the sweet morsel between its teeth. It flatters itself that it has found its fortune, while the angels of God weep over its present folly and its coming doom.

IV. ITS ACTUAL AND UTTER INSUFFICIENCY. (Ver. 11.) Pleasure may be coarse and condemnable; it may go down to fleshly gratifications (vers. 3, 8); it may be refined and chaste, may expend itself in designs and executions; it may be moderated and regulated with the finest calculation, so as to have the largest measure spread over the longest possible period; it may "guide itself with wisdom " (ver. 3). But it will be a failure; it will break down; it will end in a dreary exclamation of " Vanity ! " Three things condemn it as a solution of the great quest after human good. 1. *Experience.* This proves, always and everywhere, that the deliberate and systematic pursuit of pleasure fails to secure its end. Pleasure is not a harvest, to be sedulously sown and reaped; it is a plant that grows, unsought and uncultivated, all along the path of duty and of service. To seek it and to labour for it is to miss it. All human experience shows that it soon palls upon the taste, that it fades fast in the hands of its devotee; that there is no company of men so utterly weary and so wretched as the tired hunters after pleasurable excitement. 2. *Philosophy.* This teaches us that a being made for something so much higher than pleasure can never be satisfied with anything so low ; surely we cannot expect that the heart which is capable of worship, of service, of holy love, of heroic consecration, of spiritual nobility, will be filled and satisfied with " the delights of the sons of men." 3. *Religion.* For this introduces the sovereign claims of the Supreme One; it places man in the presence of God; it shows a life of frivolity to be a life of culpable selfishness, of sin, of shame. It summons to a purer and a wiser search, to a worthier and a nobler course; it promises the *peace* which waits on rectitude; it offers the *joy* which only God can give, and which no man can take away.—C.

Vers. 12—14.—*Sagacity and stupidity.* The " wisdom " and the " folly " of the text are perhaps best represented by the words " sagacity " and " stupidity." The distinction is one of the head rather than of the heart; of the understanding rather than of the entire spirit. We are invited, therefore, to consider—

I. THE WORTH OF SAGACITY. 1. It stands much lower down than heavenly wisdom ; *that* is the direct product of the Spirit of God, and makes men blessed with a good which cannot be taken away. It places them above the reach of adversity, and makes them invulnerable to the darts of death itself (see ver. 14). 2. It has its own distinct advantages. "The wise man's eyes are in his head; " he sees whither he is going ; he does not delude himself with the idea that he can violate all the laws of his nature with impunity. He knows that the wages of sin is death, that if he sows to the flesh he will reap corruption; he understands that, if he would enjoy the esteem of men and the favour of God, he must subdue his spirit, control his passions, regulate his life according to the standards of truth and virtue. This sagacity of the wise will therefore (1) save him from some of the most egregious and fatal blunders; (2) keep him sufficiently near to the path of virtue to be saved from the darker excesses and more crushing sorrows of life; (3) secure for himself and his family some measure of comfort and respect, and place some of the purer pleasures within his reach; (4) keep him within hearing of the truth of God, where he is more likely to find his way into the kingdom of God.

II. THE PITIFULNESS OF STUPIDITY. "The fool walketh blindly." 1. He has no eye to see the fair and the beautiful around him, no heart to appreciate the nobility that might be within him or the glories that are above him. 2. He fails to discern the real wretchedness of his present condition—his destitution, his condemnation, his exile. 3. He does not shrink from the evil which impends. He is walking toward the precipice, below which is utter ruin, eternal death. Truly " the fear of the Lord is the beginning of wisdom, and to depart from evil, *that* is understanding."—C.

Vers. 18—24.—*The complaint of the successful.* The man who labours and who fails to acquire may be pitied, and if he finds his life to have a large measure of vanity he may be excused for complaining; but here is—

I. THE COMPLAINT OF THE SUCCESSFUL. The speaker (of the text) is made (or makes himself) miserable because he has gained much by the expenditure of time and strength, and he has to leave it behind him when he dies; he has to leave it to one who "has not laboured" (ver. 21), and possibly to a man who is not as wise as himself, but is "a fool" (ver. 19), and he may scatter or misuse it. And the thought of the insecurity of life, together with the certainty of leaving all behind to the man who comes after, whoever or whatever he may be, makes day and night wretched (ver. 23).

II. WHEREIN IT IS SOUND. It is quite right that a man should ask himself what will become of his acquisition. To be satisfied with present pleasure is ignoble; to be careless of what is coming after us—" Après moi le deluge "—is shamefully selfish. It becomes every man to consider what the *long* results of his labour will be, whether satisfactory or unfruitful.

III. WHEREIN IT IS UNSOUND. 1. There is nothing painful in the thought of parting with our treasure. We inherited much from those who went before us, and we may be well content to hand down all we have to those who come after us. *We* spent no labour on that which we inherited: why should we be aggrieved because our heirs will have spent none on what they take from us? 2. If we did not hoard our treasures, but distributed them while we lived, putting them into the hands of the wise; or if (again) we chose our heirs according to their spiritual rather than their fleshly affinities, we should be spared the misery of accumulating the substance which a fool will scatter. But let us look at a still better aspect of the subject.

IV. THE LEGACY AND THE HOPE OF THE WISE. 1. His best legacy. We may and we should so spend our time and our strength that what we leave behind us is not wealth that *can* be dissipated or stolen, but worth that cannot fail to bless—Divine truth lodged in many minds, good principles planted in many hearts, a pure and noble character built up in many souls. This is what no fool can divert or destroy; this is that which will live on, and multiply and bless, when we are far from all mortal scenes. Immeasurably better is the legacy of holy influence than that of "uncertain riches;" the former must be a lasting blessing, the latter may be an incalculable curse. 2. His best and purest hope. What if the dying man feels that his grasp on earthly gain is about to be finally relaxed? is he not about to open his hand in a heavenly sphere, where the Divine Father will enrich him with a heavenly heritage, which will make all material treasures seem poor indeed?—C.

Ver. 24.—(See homily on ch. iii. 12, 13, 22.)—C.

Ver. 26.—*Piety and impiety; recompense and penalty.* We ask and answer the twofold question, viz. what is—

I. OUR EXPECTATION. We should certainly expect two things, judging antecedently. 1. That piety would be richly rewarded; for who would not expect that the bountiful, just, and resourceful Father would give liberally, in many ways, to those who sought his favour, and were "good in his sight"? 2. That impiety would bear plain marks of Divine disapproval; for who would suppose that men would defy their Maker, break his laws, injure his children, spoil his holy and benignant purpose, and *not* suffer marked and manifold evils as the just penalty of their presumption and their guilt? We naturally look for much happiness and prosperity for the former, much misery and defeat for the latter.

II. OUR EXPERIENCE. What do we find? 1. *That God does reward his servants.* The Preacher mentions three good gifts of his hand; they are not exhaustive, though they include or suggest much of the righteous man's heritage. (1) *Knowledge.* Most of all and best of all, the knowledge *of God* himself; and to know God is the very essence and substance of true human life. Beside this, the knowledge of man. It is, in truth, only the good man who understands human nature. Vice, iniquity, flatters itself that it has this knowledge. But it is mistaken; its conception of mankind is distorted, erroneous, fatally mistaken. It does not know what it is in man to be and to do and to become. "Only the good discern the good," and only they have a knowledge of our race which is profoundly true. (2) *Wisdom.* An enlightened conception of human life, so that its beauty and its blessedness are appreciated and pursued, so that, on the other hand, its ugliness and its evil are recognized and shunned. The wisdom of the wise includes also that practical good sense which keeps its disciples from the mistakes and entanglements that lead to destitution, which also leads its possessors to heights of honour and well-being. (3) *Joy.* In the worship of Christ, in the service of man, in the culture of our own character, in walking along the path of sacred duty and holy usefulness, is abounding and abiding joy. 2. *That sin is visited with penalty.* Do we find that God giveth " to the sinner travail, to gather and to heap up"? We do. (1) Sin necessitates the worst of all bad labours—that of deliberately and persistently breaking down the walls of conscience, of breaking through the fences which the God of righteousness and love has put up to guard his children from moral evil. (2) Sin includes much hurtful and damaging struggle against the will and against the laws of the wise and good. Bad men have to encounter and to contest the opposition of the upright. (3) Sin frequently means low and degrading toil. The " sinner " is brought down so low that he is fain to " go into the fields to feed swine ; " to do that from which he would once have indignantly recoiled. (4) Sin constantly condemns the toiler to labour on in utter discontent, if not positive wretchedness of soul. Life without the light of heavenly truth and the song of sacred service proves an intolerable burden.—C.

Vers. 1—3.—*An experiment : riotous mirth.* Solomon had found that wisdom and knowledge are not the means by which the search after happiness is brought to a successful issue. He then resolved to try if indulgence in sensual delights would yield any lasting satisfaction. This, as he saw, was a course on which many entered, who like him desired happiness, and he would discover for himself whether or not they were any nearer the goal than he was. And so he resolved to enjoy pleasure—"to give his heart to wine," and " to lay hold of folly." Like the rich man in the parable, who said to his soul, " Soul, thou hast much goods laid up for many years ; take thine ease, eat, drink and be merry," so did he address his heart, " Come, I will prove thee with mirth." He had tried wisdom, and found it fruitless for his purpose, and now would try folly. He lays aside the character and pursuits of a student, and enters the company of fools, to join in their revelry and mirth. The conviction that his learning was useless, either to satisfy his own cravings or to remedy the evils that exist in the world, made it easy for him to cast away, for a time at any rate, the intellectual employments in which he had engaged, and to live as others do who give themselves up to sensual pleasures. Wearied of the toil of thought, sickened of its illusions and of its fruitlessness, he would find tranquillity and health of mind in frivolous gaiety and mirth. This was not an attempt to stifle his cravings after the highest good, for he deliberately determined to analyze his experience at every point, in order to discover whether any permanent gain resulted from his search in this new quarter. " I sought," he says, " in mine heart to give myself unto wine, yet acquainting mine heart with wisdom ; and to lay hold on folly, till I might see what was that good for the sons of men, which they should do under the heaven all the days of their life." For the sake of others as well as for himself, he would try this pathway and see whither it would lead. But the experiment failed. In a very short time he discovered that vanity was here too. The laughter of fools was, as he says elsewhere (ch. vii. 6), like the crackling of burning thorns ; the blaze lasted but for a moment, and the gloom that followed was but the deeper and more enduring. Where the fire of jovial revelry and boisterous mirth had been, there remained but cold, grey ashes. The mood of reckless enjoyment was followed by that of cynical satiety and bitter disappointment. He said of laughter, " It is mad," and of mirth, " What doeth it ? " In his moments of calm reflection, when he communed with his own heart, he recognized the utter folly of his experiment, and felt that from his own dear-bought experience he could emphatically warn all in time to come against seeking satisfaction for the soul in sensual pleasures. Not in this way can the hunger and thirst with which the spirit of man is consumed be allayed. At most, a short period of oblivion can be secured, from which the awakening is all the more terrible. The sense of personal responsibility, the feeling that we are called to seek the highest good and are doomed to unrest and misery until we find it, the conviction that our failures only make ultimate success the more doubtful, is not to be quenched by any such coarse anodyne. Various reasons may be found to explain why this kind of experiment failed and must fail.

I. In the *first* place, it consisted in AN ABUSE OF NATURAL FACULTIES AND APPETITES. Some measure of joy and pleasure is needed for health of mind and body. Innocent gaiety, enjoyment of the gifts God has bestowed upon us, reasonable satisfaction of the appetites implanted in us, have all a rightful place in our life. But over-indulgence in any one of them violates the harmony of our nature. They were never intended to rule us, but to be under our control and to minister to our happiness, and we cannot allow them to govern us without throwing our whole life into disorder.

II. In the *second* place, THE PLEASURE EXCITED IS ONLY TRANSITORY. From the very nature of things it cannot be kept up for any long time by mere effort of will; the brain grows weary and the bodily powers become exhausted. A jest-book is proverbially very tiresome reading. At first it may amuse, but the attention soon begins to flag, and after a little the most brilliant specimen of wit can scarcely evoke a smile. The drunkard and the glutton find that they can only carry the pleasures of the table up to a certain point; after that has been reached the bodily organism refuses to be still further stimulated.

III. In the *third* place, SUCH PLEASURE CAN ONLY BE GRATIFIED BY SELF-DEGRADATION. It is inconsistent with the full exercise of the intellectual faculties which distinguish man from the brute, and destructive of those higher and more spiritual faculties by which God is apprehended, served, and enjoyed. Self-indulgence in the gross pleasures of which we are speaking actually reduces man below the level of the beasts that perish, for they are preserved from such folly by the natural instincts with which they are endowed.

IV. In the *fourth* place, THE INEVITABLE RESULT OF SUCH AN EXPERIMENT IS A DEEPER AND MORE ENDURING GLOOM. Self-reproach, enfeeblement of mind and body, satiety and disgust, come on when the mad fit is past, and, what is still worse, the apprehension of evils yet to come—the knowledge that the passions excited and indulged will refuse to die down; that they have a life and power of their own, and will stimulate and almost compel their slave to enter again on the evil courses which he first tried of his own free will and with a light heart. The prospect before him is that of bondage to habits which he knows will yield him no lasting pleasure, and very little of the fleeting kind, and must involve the enfeeblement and destruction of all his powers. Mirth and laughter and wine did not banish Solomon's melancholy; but after the feverish excitement they produced had passed away, they left him in a deeper gloom than ever. "Like phosphorus on a dead man's face, he felt that it was all a trick, a lie; and like the laugh of a hyena among the tombs, he found that the worldling's frolic can never reanimate the joys which guilt has slain and buried." "I said of laughter, It is mad: and of mirth, What doeth it?" The well-known story of the melancholy patient being advised by a doctor to go and see Grimaldi, and answering, "I am Grimaldi," and that of George Fox being recommended by a minister whom he consulted to dispel the anxieties which his spiritual fears and doubts and aspirations had excited within him, by "drinking beer and dancing with the girls" (Carlyle, 'Sartor Resartus,' iii. 1), may be used to illustrate the teaching of our text. Some stanzas, too, of Byron's last poem give a pathetic expression to the feelings of satiety and disappointment which are the retribution of sensuality—

> "My days are in the yellow leaf;
>   The flowers and fruits of love are gone;
> The worm, the canker, and the grief
>   Are mine alone!

> "The fire that on my bosom preys
>   Is lone as some volcanic isle;
> No torch is kindled at its blaze—
>   A funeral pile.

> "The hope, the fear, the jealous care,
>   The exalted portion of the pain
> And power of love I cannot share,
>   But wear the chain."

                                                                    J. W.

Vers. 4—11.—*Another experiment: refined voluptuousness.* Riotous mirth having failed miserably to give him the settled happiness after which he sought, our author records another and more promising experiment which he made, the search for happiness in a life of culture—" the pursuit of beauty and magnificence in art." More promising it was, because it brought into play higher and purer emotions than those to which ordinary sensuality appeals; it cultivated the side of the nature which adjoins, and almost merges into, the spiritual. The Law of Moses, forbidding as it did the making of images or representations of natural objects or of living creatures for purposes of worship, had prevented much advance being made in sculpture and painting; but there were still extensive fields of artistic development left for cultivation. Architecture and gardening afforded abundant scope for the exhibition and gratification of a refined taste. And so Solomon built splendid palaces, and planted vineyards, and laid out parks and gardens, and filled them with the choicest fruit trees, and dug pools for the irrigation of his plantations in the time of summer drought. Nothing was omitted that could minister to his sense of the beautiful, or that could enhance his splendour and dignity. A large household, great flocks of cattle, heaps of silver and gold, precious treasures from distant lands, the pleasures of music and of the harem are all enumerated as being procured by his wealth and power, and employed for his gratification. All that the eye could rest on with delight, all that the heart could desire, was brought within his reach. And all the time wisdom was with him, guiding him in the pursuit of pleasure, and not abandoning him in the enjoyment of it. Nothing occurred to prevent the experiment being carried through to the very end. The delights he enumerates were in themselves lawful, and therefore were indulged in without any uneasy sensation of transgressing against the Law of God or the dictates of conscience. Nay, the very fact that he had a moral end in view when he began the experiment seemed to give a high sanction to it. He was not interrupted by the intrusion of other thoughts and cares. No foreign enemy disturbed his peace; sickness did not incapacitate him; his wealth was not exhausted by the large demands made upon it for the support of his magnificence and luxury. And so he went to the utmost bounds of refined enjoyment, and found much that for a time amply rewarded him for the efforts he put forth. "My heart," he says, "rejoiced in all my labour" (ver. 10). His busy mind was kept occupied; his senses were charmed by the beauty and richness of the treasures he had gathered together, and of the great works which gave such abundant evidence of his taste and wealth. His experiment was not quite fruitless, therefore. Present gratification he found in the course of his labours; but when they were completed, the pleasure they had yielded passed away. The charm of novelty was gone. Possession did not yield the joy and delight which acquisition had done. When the palaces were finished, the gardens planted, the gems and rarities accumulated, the luxurious household established, and nothing left to do but to rest in the happiness that these things had been expected to secure, the sense of defeat and disappointment again fell upon the king. "Then I looked on all the works that my hands had wrought, and on the labour that I had laboured to do: and, behold, all was vanity and vexation of spirit, and there was no profit under the sun." He does not try to explain the cause of his failure, but simply records the fact that he did fail. "He does not moralize, still less preach; he just paints the picture of his soul's sad wanderings, of the baffled effort of a human heart, and passes on." But we may find it highly profitable to inquire what were the causes why the life of culture—which, without harshness, may be called a refined voluptuousness—fails to give satisfaction to the human soul.

I. In the *first* place, IT IS A LIFE OF ISOLATION FROM GOD. As Solomon represents the course he followed, we see that the thought of God was excluded from his mind. The Divine gifts were enjoyed, the love of the beautiful which is implanted in the soul of man was gratified, every exquisite sensation of which we are capable was indulged, but the one thing needed to sanctify the happiness obtained and render it perfect was omitted. "God," says St. Augustine, "has made us for himself, and we cannot rest until we rest in him." Emotions of gratitude, adoration, humility, and self-consecration to His service cannot be suppressed without great loss—the loss even of that security and tranquillity of spirit which are essential to true happiness. All the resources upon which Solomon drew may furnish helps to happiness, but none of them, nor all of them together, could, apart from God, secure it. Compare with the failure of Solomon the success of those who have often, in circumstances of extreme discomfort and suffering, enjoyed the peace of God that passeth all understanding. The sixty-third psalm, written by David in the time of exile and hardship, illustrates the truth that in communion with God the soul enjoys a happiness which cannot be found elsewhere. "A man's life does not consist in the abundance of the things which he possesseth." Apart from the favour of God and the service of God, the richest possessions and the most skilful employment of them can secure no lasting satisfaction. For we are so constituted as creatures that our life is not complete if we are dissevered from our Creator.

II. In the *second* place, IT IS A SELFISH LIFE. All that Solomon describes are his efforts to secure certain durable results for himself; to indulge his love for the beautiful in nature and art, and to surround himself with luxury and splendour. He would have been more successful in his search for happiness if he had endeavoured to relieve the wants of others—to clothe the naked, to feed the hungry, to comfort the afflicted, and to instruct the ignorant. Self-denial and self-sacrifice for the sake of others would have brought him nearer the goal of his desire. The penalty of his selfish pursuit fell heavily upon him. He could not live at a height above mankind, in the enjoyment of his own felicity, for long; "the riddle of the painful earth" filled him with thoughts of self-loathing and despair, which shattered all his happiness. Do what he might, old age, disease, and death were foes he could not conquer, and all about him in human society he could discern moral evils and inequalities which he could not set right nor even explain. Such selfish isolation as that into which for a time he had withdrawn himself failed to secure the object he had in view, for he could not really dissever his lot from that of his fellows, or escape the evils which afflicted them. The idea of a life of luxurious ease, undisturbed by the sight or thought of the miseries and hardships of life, was a vain dream, from which he soon awoke. In his poem, 'The Palace of Art,' Tennyson has given a most luminous and suggestive commentary upon this portion of the Book of Ecclesiastes. In it he represents the soul as seeking forgiveness for the sin of selfish isolation by penitence, prayer, and self-renunciation, and as anticipating a resumption of all the joys of culture and art in companionship with others. In communion with God, in fellowship with others, all things that are noble and pure and lovely are taken into holy keeping, and form a lasting source of joy and happiness.—J. W.

Vers. 12—17.—*The value and the futility of wisdom.* Solomon had now made many experiments to try and discover something that was good in itself, that was an end for which one might labour, a goal for which one might make, a resting-place for the soul. The acquisition of knowledge had first of all attracted him, but after a long course of study, in which he traversed the whole field of learning and reached the limits of human thought, the futility of his labours dawned upon him. Then he turned to sensual enjoyments, and gave himself up to them for a time, with the deliberate purpose of seeking to discover if there were in this quarter any permanent gain; if it were possible so to prolong the pleasures of life as to silence, if not to satisfy, the cravings of the soul. The experiment was but a short one; he soon found out that pleasure is short-lived, and that mirth and laughter are followed by weariness and melancholy. His resources were not, however, yet exhausted. A new course was open to him, and one which his richly endowed nature qualified him for trying, and his kingly power and wealth laid open to him. This was the cultivation of those arts by which human life is beautified; the gratification of those tastes that distinguish man from the lower creatures, and that have something in them that is noble and pure. He built stately palaces, planted gardens and forests; he surrounded himself with all the luxury and pageantry of an Oriental court; he accumulated treasures such as kings only could afford to procure; music and song, and whatever could delight a refined taste, and a love of the beautiful were sedulously cultivated. But all in vain; æstheticism proved as fruitless as the pursuit of knowledge, or the indulgence of the coarser appetites, to give rest to the soul. And now in sober meditation he reviewed all his experience; having come to the end of his resources, he inquires into actual results attained, and pronounces upon them. First of all, he is convinced that he has given a fair trial to all the various means by which men seek for the highest good.   He had failed to find that satisfaction, but it was not because he had been ill equipped for carrying on the search.   No one that came after him (ver. 12) could surpass him by a more complete and thorough investigation.   God had given him "a wise and understanding heart," and had endowed him with wealth and power; and in both particulars he excelled all his fellows.   Accordingly, he has no hesitation in laying down great general principles drawn from careful observation of the phenomena of human life.

I. THE GREAT ADVANTAGE WHICH WISDOM HAS OVER FOLLY.   The wise man walks in light, and has the use of his eyes; the fool is blind, and walks in darkness.   The wisdom here praised is not that holy, spiritual faculty which springs from the fear of God and obedience to his will (Job xxviii. 28; Deut iv. 6; Ps. cxi. 10), and which is so strikingly personified, almost deified, in the Book of Proverbs and in that of Job (Prov. viii., ix.; Job xxviii. 12—28); but is ordinary science, knowledge of the laws of nature, and of the powers and limitations of human life.   This wisdom can only be acquired by long and painful labour, and though by it we cannot discover God or find out the way of winning and retaining his favour, or provide for the wants of the soul, it has, in its sphere, high value.   It gives some pleasure; it affords some guidance and direction to its possessor.   It enables him to acquire some good; it teaches him to avoid some evils.   Progress in civilization is only possible by the cultivation of this wisdom.   Wider acquaintance with the laws of health, for example, has enabled men to stamp out certain forms of disease, or, at any rate, to prevent their frequent recurrence, and to alleviate the sufferings caused by others.   Consider the immense benefit to the race the progress of medical science has secured.   The inventions that we owe to the cultivation of natural knowledge are beyond number, and by them incalculable benefits have been brought within our reach—better cultivation of the soil, less exhausting labour, discovery of the uses of the metals stored up in the bowels of the earth, more rapid distribution of the productions of nature and of human industry, swifter means of communication between one part of the world and another.   "The improvement of natural knowledge," says a great authority, "whatever direction it has taken, and however low the aims of those who may have commenced it, has not only conferred practical benefits on men, but in so doing has effected a revolution in their conceptions of the universe and of themselves, and has profoundly altered their modes of thinking and their views of right and wrong" (Huxley, 'Lay Sermons').   Does not this amply justify Solomon's assertion that "wisdom excels folly, as light darkness; that the wise man hath the use of his eyes, the fool is blind"?

II. THE FUTILITY OF WISDOM.   All the delight in the charms of wisdom is quenched by the thought of the levelling power of death, which overwhelms both the wise and the foolish indiscriminately (vers. 14b—17).   For a brief space there is a distinction between them—the one endowed with priceless gifts, the other ignorant and poor.   But what, after all, was the use of the short-lived superiority?   Like an extinguished torch, the wisdom of the sage is blown out by death, and the very memory of his attainments and triumphs is buried in oblivion.   For a time, perhaps, he is missed, but the gap is soon filled up, the busy world goes on its way, and in a very short time it forgets all about him.   Thus even the posthumous fame, after which the purest and noblest minds have longed, to secure which they have been content to endure poverty, hardship, and neglect in their lifetime, is denied to the vast majority, even of those who have richly deserved it.   There were wise men before Solomon (1 Kings iv. 31), but no memorial survives of them but their names; no illustrations of their wisdom are given to explain their reputation.   And how faint is the impression which the wisdom of Solomon himself makes upon the actual life of the present world!   Enshrined though it is in the sacred volume, it seems foreign to our modes of thought; its voice is not heard in our schools of philosophy.   The fact of death is a certainty both to the wise and to the fool; the manner of it may be similar; the doubts and fears and anxieties concerning the life to come may perplex both.   What can we suggest to relieve the sad picture, or to counteract the paralyzing effect which the spectacle of the futility of wisdom and effort is calculated to produce?   The conviction that this life is not all, that there is a life beyond the grave, is the great corrective to the gloom in which otherwise every thinking mind would be enwrapped.   This present life is a state of infancy, of probation, in which we receive education for eternity.   And to ask in melancholy tones what is the use of acquiring wisdom if death is so soon to cut short our career here, is as foolish as to ask what is the use of a sapling growing vigorously in a nursery garden if it is to be afterwards transplanted. The place from which it was taken may soon know it no more. But the loss is slight; the tree itself lives and flourishes still under the eye and care of the almighty Husbandman. No fruitless regrets over the brevity and uncertainty of human fame need interfere with present effort. We may soon be forgotten on earth, but no attainments in wisdom or holiness we have made will have been in vain; they will have qualified us for a higher service and a truer enjoyment of God than we could otherwise have known.—J. W.

Vers. 18—23.—*Riches, though obtained by much toil, are vanity.* The thought of death, which sweeps away the wise man as well as the fool, and of the eternal oblivion which swallows up the memory of them both, was very depressing; but a new cause for deeper dejection of spirit is found in the reflection that the man who has toiled in the accumulation of wealth must leave it all to another, of whom he knows nothing, and who will perhaps dissipate it in a very brief time.

I. The *first* mortifying thought is—HE BUT GATHERS FOR A SUCCESSOR. (Ver. 18.) He himself, when the moment of death comes, must leave his possessions and depart into the world of shadows as naked as he was when he entered upon life. The fact that such a reflection should be bitter proves how deeply the soul is corroded by covetous and selfish aggrandizement. The heart is absorbed in the things of the present, and the anticipation of heavenly and spiritual joys grows faint and dies away. To be torn from the wealth and possessions acquired upon earth is regarded as losing everything; to be forced to leave them to another, even to a son, is almost as bad as being plundered of them by a thief. This feeling of bitter regret at having to give up all they possess at the call of death, has often been experienced by those who have found their chief occupation and happiness in life in the acquisition of earthly treasures. "Mazarin walks through the galleries of his palace and says to himself, 'Il faut quitter tout cela.' Frederick William IV. of Prussia turns to his friend Bunsen, as they stand on the terrace at Potsdam, and says as they look out on the garden, 'Das auch, das soll ich lassen' ('This too I must leave behind me')" (Plumptre).

II. The *second* mortifying thought is—THAT IT IS QUITE UNCERTAIN WHAT CHARACTER THE SUCCESSOR WILL BE OF, AND WHAT USE HE WILL MAKE OF HIS INHERITANCE. (Ver. 19.) He may be a wise man, or he may be a fool; he may make a prudent use of his inheritance, or he may in a very short time scatter it to the winds. The very change in his circumstances, the novelty of his new situation, may turn his head and lead him into courses of folly which otherwise he might have avoided. Some have thought that the character of the youthful Rehoboam was already so far developed as to suggest this mortifying reflection to Solomon. But this is quite conjectural. The early career of the headstrong, arrogant sovereign whose folly broke up the kingdom of Israel is an illustration of the truth of this general statement, and may have been in the thoughts of the writer, if he were not Solomon but some later sage. The special reference to this one historical example of an inheritance dissipated by an unworthy son need not be pressed. For, unfortunately, in every generation there are only too many instances of a like kind. So frequent are they, indeed, as to suggest very humiliating reflections to every one who has spent his life in acquiring riches or collecting treasures of art. As he sees fortunes squandered and collections of rarities broken up, the thought must recur to his mind whose are to be the things which he has treasured up so carefully (Ps. xxxix. 6; Luke xii. 20).

III. The *third* mortifying thought is—THAT THE CHARACTER OF THE SUCCESSOR MAY NOT BE A MATTER OF DOUBT; he may be a man of a positively foolish and vicious disposition (ver. 21). The case presents itself of a man who has laboured in wisdom and knowledge and equity having to leave to another who is devoid of these virtues, who has never sought to acquire them, all that his prudence and diligence have enabled him to acquire. There is thus a climax in the thoughts of the writer. First of all, there is some matter for irritation, especially to a selfish mind, in the idea of giving up to another what one has spent years of laborious toil in gathering together. Then there is the torturing doubt as to the possible character of the new owner, and the use he will make of what is left to him. But worst of all is the conviction that he is both foolish and vicious. This is enough to poison all present enjoyment, and to paralyze all further effort. Why should a man spend laborious days and sleepless nights, if this is to be the end of it all? What has he left to show for all his exertions? What but weariness and exhaustion, and the bitter reflection that all has been in vain? Yet a little time after he has been forced by death to part with his possessions, and they will be made to minister to the frivolity and vice of one who has never laboured for them, and ultimately will be scattered like chaff before the wind. Thus a final discovery of the vanity of all earthly employments is made. The acquisition of wisdom and knowledge, the gratification of the pleasures of sense, the cultivation and indulgence of artistic tastes, had all been tried as possible avenues to lasting happiness, and tried in vain. To these must now be added the accumulation by prudent and lawful means, of great wealth. This, too, was discovered to be vanity. It could only be accomplished by years of toil, and brought with it fresh cares; and in the end all that had been gained must be given up to another. Mortifying though the experiments had turned out to be, they had at least been of negative value. Though they had not revealed where happiness was to be found, they had revealed where it was not to be found. The last disappointment, the discovery of the vanity of riches, taught the great truth which might become a clue to lead to the much-desired happiness, that " a man's life consisteth not in the abundance of the things which he possesseth " (Luke xii. 15).—J. W.

Vers. 24—26.—*The condition of pure enjoyment.* Up to this point the thoughts of our author have been gloomy and despairing. Wisdom is better, he declares, than folly, but death sweeps away both the wise and the foolish. The learning of the sage, the fortune accumulated by the successful worker, represent the labours of a lifetime ; but at the end, what are they worth? The results are twofold, partly internal and partly external. The student or worker acquires skill in the use of his faculties, he develops his strength, he becomes, as his life goes on, more proficient in his profession or craft; but death quenches all these attainments. He leaves to those who are perhaps unworthy of them all the external results of his labours, and perhaps in a very little time it will be difficult to find anything to remind one of him. We who have the light of Christian truth may have much to console us and give us strength, even when we are brought face to face with the dark and dreary facts upon which our author dwells. We may think of this life as a preparation for a new and higher existence in the world to come, and believe that every effort we make to use rightly the faculties God has given us will tend to equip us better for service of him in another state of being. But to our author's mind the thought of a future life is not vivid enough to be the source of consolation and strength. What then? Does he find no escape from the gloomy labyrinth of withering doubt, and decide that happiness is a boon for which one may sigh in vain? No; strangely enough, at the very moment when the depression is deepest, light breaks upon him from an unexpected quarter. Simple joys, moderate hopes, contentment with one's lot, thankful acceptance of the gifts of God, may yield a peace and satisfaction unknown to those who are consumed by ambition, who make riches, state, luxury, the object of their desires. The darkness of night will soon close upon our lives, our tenure of our possessions is precarious in the extreme, but some measure of joy is within the reach of us all. In few but suggestive words the Preacher describes—

I. THE NATURE OF A HAPPY LIFE. (Ver. 24.) " There is nothing better for a man than that he should eat and drink, and that he should make his soul enjoy good in his labour." At first one might think the judgment here expressed somewhat poor and gross, and unworthy of the reputation of the wise king to whom it is ascribed, not to say of the Word of God in which we find it. But when we look more closely into it, these impressions disappear. It is not an idle, useless life of self-enjoyment that is here commended to us, but one in which useful labour is seasoned by healthy pleasures. The man eats and drinks, and makes his soul enjoy good *in his labour.* The enjoyment is not such as to waste and exhaust the energies of the soul, otherwise it would be very short-lived. The risk of abusing the counsel in the first part of the sentence is avoided by attending to the safeguard implied in the concluding words. It is not the decision of the sensualist, " Let us eat and drink; for to-morrow we die " (1 Cor. xv. 32), but the admonition of one who perceives that a thankful participation of the good things of life is compatible with the sincerest piety. Eating and drinking mean satisfying the natural appetites, and not ministering to artificial and self-created cravings ; and over-indulgence in so doing is tacitly forbidden. The words suggest to us the simple healthy life and habits of the industrious peasant or workman, who takes pleasure in his daily employment, and finds in the innocent joys which sweeten his lot a happiness which mere wealth cannot buy.

> " The shepherd's homely curds,
> His cold thin drink out of his leather bottle,
> His wonted sleep under a fresh tree's shade,
> All which secure and sweetly he enjoys,
> Is far beyond a prince's delicates,
> His viands sparkling in a golden cup,
> His body couchèd in a curious bed,
> When care, mistrust, and treason wait on him."
> ('Henry VI.,' Part III., act ii. sc. 5.)

II. In the *second* place, our author tells us THE SOURCE OF THIS HAPPINESS—IT IS THE GIFT OF GOD. (Ver. 24*b*.) " This also I saw, that it was from the hand of God. For who can eat or who can have enjoyment apart from him ? " (Revised Version margin). These words are quite sufficient to convince us that a low Epicureanism is far from the writer's thoughts when he speaks of there being nothing better for a man than " to eat and drink, and make his soul enjoy good in his labour." One thing is necessary for the accomplishment of this end, and that is the Divine blessing. Satisfaction in work and in pleasure is a gift bestowed by him upon those who deserve it. " What we get here is the recognition of what we have learnt to call the moral government of God in the distribution of happiness. It is found to depend, not on outward but inward condition, and the chief inward condition is the character that God approves. The Preacher practically confesses that the life of the pleasure-seeker, or the ambitious, or the philosopher, seeking wisdom as an end, was not good before God, and therefore failed to bring contentment " (Plumptre). The source, then, of happiness in life is in obedience to the Divine will. To the gifts of his providence God adds the temper in which to enjoy them ; from his hand both must be sought. Those who seek to be independent of him find that all they may acquire is insufficient to satisfy them ; those who place all their confidence in him are contented with even the hardest lot (Phil. iv. 11—13). " Wisdom, knowledge, and joy " are the portion of the good, whether they be poor or rich in this world's wealth ; but the sinner has only the fruitless labour from which he can derive no satisfaction (ver. 26). And over again the Preacher writes the dreary sentence, " This also is vanity and vexation of spirit," upon the life in which God is not.—J. W.

EXPOSITION.

CHAPTER III.

Vers. 1—22.—Section 4. In confirmation of the truth that man's happiness depends upon the will of God, Koheleth proceeds to show how *Providence arranges even the minutest concerns ; that man can alter nothing, must make the best of things as they are, bear with anomalies, bounding his desires by this present life.*

Vers. 1—8.—The providence of God disposes and arranges every detail of man's life. This proposition is stated first generally, and then worked out in particular by means of antithetical sentences. In Hebrew manuscripts and most printed texts vers. 2—8 are arranged in two parallel columns, so that one " time " always stands under another. A similar arrangement is found in Josh. xii. 9, etc., containing the catalogue of the conquered Canaanite kings; and in Esth. ix. 7, etc., giving the names of Haman's ten sons. In the present passage we have fourteen pairs of contrasts, ranging from external circumstances to the inner affections of man's being.

Ver. 1.—**To every** thing there is **a season, and a time to every purpose under heaven.**

"Season" and "time" are rendered by the LXX. καιρός and χρόνος. The word for "season" (*zeman*), denotes a fixed, definite portion of time; while *eth*, "time," signifies rather the beginning of a period, or is used as a general appellation. The two ideas are sometimes occurrent in the New Testament; *e.g.* Acts i. 7; 1 Thess. v. 1 (comp. also Dan. ii. 21, where the Septuagint has καιροὺς καὶ χρόνους; and Dan. vii. 12, where we find the singular καιροῦ καὶ καιροῦ in Theodotion, and χρόνου καὶ καιροῦ in the Septuagint). So in Wisd. viii. 8, "She [wisdom] foreseeth signs and wonders, and the events of seasons and times (ἐκβάσεις καιρῶν καὶ χρόνων)." *Every thing* refers especially to men's movements and actions, and to what concerns them. *Purpose; chephets*, originally meaning "delight," "pleasure," in the later Hebrew came to signify "business," "thing," "matter." The proposition is—In human affairs Providence arranges the moment when everything shall happen, the duration of its operation, and the time appropriate thereto. The view of the writer takes in the whole circumstances of men's life from its commencement to its close. But the thought is not, as some have opined, that there is naught but uncertainty, fluctuation, and imperfection in human affairs, nor, as Plumptre conceives, "It is wisdom to do the right thing at the right time, that inopportuneness is the bane of life," for many of the circumstances mentioned, *e.g.* birth and death, are entirely beyond men's will and control, and the maxim, Καιρὸν γνῶθι, cannot apply to man in such cases. Koheleth is confirming his assertion, made in the last chapter, that wisdom, wealth, success, happiness, etc., are not in man's hands, that his own efforts can secure none of them—they are distributed at the will of God. He establishes this dictum by entering into details, and showing the ordering of Providence and the supremacy of God in all men's concerns, the most trivial as well as the most important. The Vulgate gives a paraphrase, and not a very exact one, *Omnia tempus habent, et suis spatiis transeunt universa sub cœlo.* Koheleth intimates, without attempting to reconcile, the great *crux* of man's free-will and God's decree.

Ver. 2.—**A time to be born, and a time to die.** Throughout the succeeding catalogue marked contrasts are exhibited in pairs, beginning with the entrance and close of life, the rest of the list being occupied with events and circumstances which intervene between those two extremities. The words rendered, "a time to be born," might more naturally mean "a time to bear;" καιρὸς τοῦ τεκεῖν, Septuagint; as the verb is in the infinitive active, which, in this particular verb,

is not elsewhere found used in the passive sense, though other verbs are so used sometimes, as in Jer. xxv. 34. In the first case the catalogue commences with the beginning of life; in the second, with the season of full maturity : "Those who at one time give life to others, at another have themselves to yield to the law of death" (Wright). The contrast points to the passive rendering. There is no question of untimely birth or suicide; in the common order of events birth and death have each their appointed season, which comes to pass without man's interference, being directed by a higher law. "It is appointed unto men once to die" (Heb. ix. 27). Koheleth's teaching was perverted by sensualists, as we read in Wisd. ii. 2, 3, 5. **A time to plant.** After speaking of human life it is natural to turn to vegetable life, which runs in parallel lines with man's existence. Thus Job, having intimated the shortness of life and the certainty of death, proceeds to speak of the tree, contrasting its revivifying powers with the hopelessness of man's decay (Job xiv. 5, etc.). **And . . . to pluck up** that which is **planted.** This last operation may refer to the transplanting of trees and shrubs, or to the gathering of the fruits of the earth in order to make room for new agricultural works. But having regard to the opposition in all the members of the series, we should rather consider the "plucking up" as equivalent to destroying. If we plant trees, a time comes when we cut them down, and this is their final cause. Some commentators see in this clause an allusion to the settling and uprooting of kingdoms and nations, as Jer. i. 10; xviii. 9, etc.; but this could not have been the idea in Koheleth's mind.

Ver. 3.—**A time to kill, and a time to heal.** The time to kill might refer to war, only that occurs in ver. 8. Some endeavour to limit the notion to severe surgical operations performed with a view of saving life; but the verb *harag* does not admit of the meaning "to wound" or "cut." It most probably refers to the execution of criminals, or to the defence of the oppressed; such emergencies and necessities occur providentially without man's prescience. So sickness is a visitation beyond man's control, while it calls into exercise the art of healing, which is a gift of God (see Ecclus. x. 10; xxxviii. 1, etc.). **A time to break down, and a time to build up.** The removal of decaying or unsuitable buildings is meant, and the substitution of new and improved structures. A recollection of Solomon's own extensive architectural works is here introduced.

Ver. 4.—**A time to weep, and a time to laugh,** grouped naturally with **a time to mourn, and a time to dance.** The funeral and the wedding, the hired mourners and the guests at the marriage-feast, are set against one another. The first clause intimates the spontaneous manifestation of the feelings of the heart; the second, their formal expression in the performances at funerals and weddings and on other solemn occasions. The contrast is found in the Lord's allusion to the sulky children in the market-place, who would not join their companions' play: "We have piped unto you, and ye have not danced; we have mourned unto you, and ye have not lamented" (Matt. xi. 17). Dancing sometimes accompanied religious ceremonies, as when David brought up the ark (2 Sam. vi. 14, 16).

Ver. 5.—**A time to cast away stones, and a time to gather stones together.** There is no question about building or demolishing houses, as that has been already mentioned in ver. 3. Most commentators see an allusion to the practice of marring an enemy's fields by casting stones upon them, as the Israelites did when they invaded Moab (2 Kings iii. 19, 25). But this must have been a very abnormal proceeding, and could scarcely be cited as a usual occurrence. Nor is the notion more happy that there is an allusion to the custom of flinging stones or earth into the grave at a burial—a Christian, but not an ancient Jewish practice; this, too, leaves the contrasted "gathering" unexplained. Equally inappropriate is the opinion that the punishment of stoning is meant, or some game played with pebbles. It seems most simple to see herein intimated the operation of clearing a vineyard of stones, as mentioned in Isa. v. 2; and of collecting materials for making fences, wine-press, tower, etc., and repairing roads. **A time to embrace.** Those who explain the preceding clause of the marring and clearing of fields connect the following one with the other by conceiving that "the loving action of embracing stands beside the hostile, purposely injurious, throwing of stones into a field" (Delitzsch). It is plain that there are times when one may give himself up to the delights of love and friendship, and times when such distractions would be incongruous and unseasonable, as on solemn, penitential occasions (Joel ii. 16; Exod. xix. 15; 1 Cor. vii. 5); but the congruity of the two clauses of the couplet is not obvious, unless the objectionable position of stones and their advantageous employment are compared with the character of illicit (Prov. v. 20) and legitimate love.

Ver. 6.—**A time to get** (*seek*), **and a time to lose.** The verb *abad*, in piel, is used in the sense of "to destroy" (ch. vii. 7), and it is only in late Hebrew that it signifies, as here, "to lose." The reference is doubtless to property, and has no connection with the last clause of the preceding verse, as Delitzsch

would opine. There is a proper and lawful pursuit of wealth, and there is a wise and prudent submission to its inevitable loss. The loss here is occasioned by events over which the owner has no control, differing from that in the next clause, which is voluntary. The wise man knows when to exert his energy in improving his fortune, and when to hold his hand and take failure without useless struggle. Loss, too, is sometimes gain, as when Christ's departure in the flesh was the prelude and the occasion of the sending of the Comforter (John xvi. 7); and there are many things of which we know not the real value till they are beyond our grasp. **A time to keep, and a time to cast away.** Prudence will make fast what it has won, and will endeavour to preserve it unimpaired. But there are occasions when it is wiser to deprive one's self of some things in order to secure more important ends, as when sailors throw a cargo, etc., overboard in order to save their ship (comp. Jonah i. 5; Acts xxvii. 18, 19, 38). And in higher matters, such as almsgiving, this maxim holds good: "There is that scattereth, and yet increaseth. . . . The liberal soul shall be made fat, and he that watereth shall be watered also himself" (Prov. xi. 24, 25). Plumptre refers to Christ's so-called paradox, "Whosoever would (ὃς ἂν θέλῃ) save his life shall lose it, and whosoever shall lose his life for my sake shall find it" (Matt. xvi. 25).

Ver. 7.—**A time to rend, and a time to sew** (καιρὸς τοῦ ῥῆξαι, καὶ καιρὸς τοῦ ῥάψαι). This is usually understood of the rending of garments in token of grief (Gen. xxxvii. 29, 34, etc.), and the repairing of the rent then made when the season of mourning was ended. The Talmudists laid down careful rules concerning the extent of the ritual tear, and how long it was to remain unmended, both being regulated by the nearness of the relationship of the deceased person. In this interpretation there are these two difficulties: first, it makes the clause a virtual repetition of ver. 4; and secondly, it is not known for certain that the closing of the rent was a ceremonial custom in the times of Koheleth. Hence Plumptre inclines to take the expression metaphorically of the division of a kingdom by schism, and the restoration of unity, comparing the Prophet Ahijah's communication to Jeroboam (1 Kings xi. 30, 31). But surely this would be a most unlikely allusion to put into Solomon's mouth; nor can we properly look for such a symbolical representation amid the other realistic examples given in the series. What Koheleth says is this—There are times when it is natural to tear clothes to pieces, whether from grief, or anger, or any other cause, *e.g.* as being old and worthless, or infected; and there are times when it is equally natural to mend them, and to make them serviceable by timely repairs. Connected with the notion of mourning contributed by this clause, though by no means confined to that notion, it is added, **A time to keep silence, and a time to speak.** The silence of deep sorrow may be intimated, as when Job's friends sat by him in sympathizing silence (Job ii. 13), and the psalmist cried, "I was dumb with silence, I held my peace, even from good; and my sorrow was stirred" (Ps. xxxix. 2); and Elisha could not bear to hear his master's departure mentioned (2 Kings ii. 3, 5). There are also occasions when the sorrow of the heart should find utterance, as in David's lament over Saul and Jonathan (2 Sam. i. 17, etc.) and over Abner (2 Sam. iii. 33, etc.). But the gnome is of more general application. The young should hold their peace in the presence of their elders (Job xxxii. 4, etc.); silence is often golden: "Even a fool, when he holdeth his peace, is counted wise: when he shutteth his lips, he is esteemed as prudent" (Prov. xvii. 28). On the other hand, wise counsel is of infinite value, and must not be withheld at the right moment, and "a word in due season, how good is it!" (Prov. xv. 23; xxv. 11). "If thou hast understanding, answer thy neighbour; if not, lay thy hand upon thy mouth" (Ecclus. v. 12; see more, Ecclus. xx. 5, etc.).

Ver. 8.—**A time to love, and a time to hate.** This reminds one of the gloss to which our Lord refers (Matt. v. 43), "Ye have heard that it hath been said, Thou shalt love thy neighbour, and hate thine enemy," the first member being found in the old Law (Lev. xix. 18), the second being a misconception of the spirit which made Israel God's executioner upon the condemned nations. It was the maxim of Bias, quoted by Aristotle, 'Rhet.,' ii. 13, that we should love as if about some day to hate, and hate as if about to love. And Philo imparts a still more selfish tone to the gnome, when he pronounces ('De Carit.,' 21, p. 401, Mang.), "It was well said by them of old, that we ought to deal out friendship without absolutely renouncing enmity, and practise enmity as possibly to turn to friendship." **A time of war, and a time of peace.** In the previous couplets the infinitive mood of the verb has been used; in this last hemistich substantives are introduced, as being more concise and better fitted to emphasize the close of the catalogue. The first clause referred specially to the private feelings which one is constrained to entertain towards individuals. The second clause has to do with national concerns, and touches on the statesmanship which discovers the necessity or the opportuneness of war and peace, and acts accordingly. In this and in all the other examples adduced, the lesson intended is this—that man is not independent; that under all circumstances and relations he is in the hand of a power mightier than himself, which frames time and seasons according to its own good pleasure. God holds the threads of human life; in some mysterious way directs and controls events; success and failure are dependent upon his will. There are certain laws which regulate the issues of actions and events, and man cannot alter these; his free-will can put them in motion, but they become irresistible when in operation. This is not fatalism; it is the mere statement of a fact in experience. Koheleth never denies man's liberty, though he is very earnest in asserting God's sovereignty. The reconciliation of the two is a problem unsolved by him.

Ver. 9.—If thus man, in all his actions and under all circumstances, depends upon time and seasons which are beyond his control, we return to the same desponding question already asked in ch. i. 3. **What profit hath he that worketh in that wherein he laboureth?** The preceding enumeration leads up to this question, to which the answer is "None." Since time and tide wait for no man, since man cannot know for certain his opportunity, he cannot reckon on reaping any advantage from his labour.

Vers. 10—15.—There is a plan and system in all the circumstances of man's life; he feels this instinctively, but he cannot comprehend it. His duty is to make the best of the present, and to recognize the immutability of the law that governs all things.

Ver. 10.—**I have seen the travail which God hath given to the sons of men to be exercised in it;** i.e. to busy themselves therewith (ch. i. 13). This travail, exercise, or business is the work that has to be done under the conditions prescribed of time and season in face of the difficulty of man's free action and God's ordering. We take infinite pains, we entertain ample desires, and strive restlessly to carry them out, but our efforts are controlled by a higher law, and results occur in the way and at the time arranged by Providence. Human labour, though it is appointed by God and is part of man's heritage imposed upon him by the Fall (Gen. iii. 17, etc.), cannot bring contentment or satisfy the spirit's cravings.

Ver. 11.—**He hath made every thing beautiful in his (its) time.** "Everything" (eth hacol) does not refer so much to the original creation which God made very good (Gen. i. 31), as to the travail and business mentioned in ver. 10. All parts of this have, in God's design, a beauty and a harmony, their own season for appearance and development, their work to do in carrying on the majestic march of Providence. **Also he hath set the world in their heart.** "The world;" *eth-haolam*, placed (as *hacol* above) before the verb, with *eth*, to emphasize the relation. There is some uncertainty in the translation of this word. The LXX. has, Σύμπαντα τὸν αἰῶνα; Vulgate, *Mundum tradidit disputationi eorum*. The original meaning is "the hidden," and it is used generally in the Old Testament of the remote past, and sometimes of the future, as Dan. iii. 33, so that the idea conveyed is of unknown duration, whether the glance looks backward or forward, which is equivalent to our word "eternity." It is only in later Hebrew that the word obtained the signification of "age" (αἰών), or "world" in its relation to time. Commentators who have adopted the latter sense here explain the expression as if it meant that man in himself is a microcosm, a little world, or that the love of the world, the love of life, is naturally implanted in him. But taking the term in the signification found throughout the Bible, we are justified in translating it "eternity." The pronoun in "their heart" refers to "the sons of men" in the previous verse. God has put into men's minds a notion of infinity of duration; the beginning and the end of things are alike beyond his grasp; the time to be born and the time to die are equally unknown and uncontrollable. Koheleth is not thinking of that hope of immortality which his words unfold to us with our better knowledge; he is speculating on the innate faculty of looking backward and forward which man possesses, but which is insufficient to solve the problems which present themselves every day. This conception of eternity may be the foundation of great hopes and expectations, but as an explanation of the ways of Providence it fails. **So that no man can find out the work that God maketh from the beginning to the end;** or, *without man being able to penetrate; yet so that he cannot*, etc. Man sees only minute parts of the great whole; he cannot comprehend all at one view, cannot understand the law that regulates the time and season of every circumstance in the history of man and the world. He feels that, as there has been an infinite past, there will be an infinite future, which may solve anomalies and demonstrate the harmonious unity of God's design, and he must be content to wait and hope. Comparison of the past with the present may help to adumbrate the future, but is inadequate to unravel the complicated thread of the world's history (comp. ch. viii. 16,

17, and ix. 1, where a similar thought is expressed).

Ver. 12.—**I know that** there is **no good in them, but for** a **man to rejoice;** rather, *I knew, perceived, that there was no good for them;* i.e. for men. From the facts adduced, Koheleth learned this practical result—that man had nothing in his own power (see on ch. ii. 24) which would conduce to his happiness, but to make the best of life such as he finds it. Vulgate, *Cognovi quod non esset melius nisi lætari*. **To do good in his life;** Τοῦ ποιεῖν ἀγαθόν (Septuagint); *Facere bene* (Vulgate). This has been taken by many in the sense of "doing one's self good, prospering, enjoying one's self," like the Greek εὖ πράττειν, and therefore nearly equivalent to "rejoice" in the former part of the verse. But the expression is best taken here, as when it occurs elsewhere (*e.g.* ch. vii. 20), in a moral sense, and it thus teaches the great truth that virtue is essential to happiness, that to "trust in the Lord . . . to depart from evil, and to do good" (Ps. xxxvi. 3, 27), will bring peace and content (see in the epilogue, ch. xii. 13, 14). There is no Epicureanism in this verse; the enjoyment spoken of is not licentiousness, but a happy appreciation of the innocent pleasures which the love of God offers to those who live in accordance with the laws of their higher nature.

Ver. 13.—**And also that every man should eat and drink . . . it is the gift of God.** This enforces and intensifies the statement in the preceding verse; not only the power to "do good," but even to enjoy what comes in his way (see on ch. ii. 24), man must receive from God. When we pray for our daily bread, we also ask for ability to take, assimilate, and profit by the supports and comforts afforded to us. "It" is better omitted, as "is the gift of God" forms the predicate of the sentence. Ecclus. xi. 17, "The gift of the Lord remaineth with the godly, and his favour bringeth prosperity for ever."

Ver. 14.—**I know that, whatsoever God doeth, it shall be for ever.** A second thing (see ver. 12) that Koheleth *knew*, learned from the truths adduced in vers. 1—9, is that behind man's free action and volition stands the will of God, which orders events with a view to eternity, and that man can alter nothing of this providential arrangement (comp. Isa. xlvi. 10; Ps. xxxiii. 11). **Nothing can be put to it, nor anything taken from it.** We cannot hasten or retard God's designs; we cannot add to or curtail his plans. Septuagint, "It is impossible to add (οὐκ ἔστι προσθεῖναι) to it, and it is impossible to take away from it." Thus Ecclus. xviii. 6, "As for the wondrous works of the Lord, it is impossible to lessen or to add to them (οὐκ ἔστιν ἐλαττῶσαι οὐδὲ προσθεῖναι), neither can the ground of them be found out." **God doeth it, that** men **should fear before him.** There is a moral purpose in this disposal of events. Men feel this uniformity and unchangeableness in the working of Providence, and thence learn to cherish a reverential awe for the righteous government of which they are the subjects. It was this feeling which led ancient etymologists to derive Θεός and *Deus* from δέος, "fear" (comp. Rev. xv. 3, 4). This is also a ground of hope and confidence. Amid the jarring and fluctuating circumstances of men God holds the threads, and alters not his purpose. "I the Lord change not; therefore ye, O sons of Jacob, are not consumed" (Mal. iii. 6). The Vulgate is not very successful: *Non possumus eis quidquam addere, nec auferre, quæ fecit Deus ut timeatur,* "We cannot add anything unto, or take anything away from, those things which God hath made that he may be feared."

Ver. 15.—**That which hath been is now;** so Septuagint; "That which hath been made, the same remaineth" (Vulgate); better, *that which hath been, long ago it is;* i.e. was in existence long before. The thought is much the same as in ch. i. 9, only here it is adduced not to prove the vanity and endless sameness of circumstances, but the orderly and appointed succession of events under the controlling providence of God. **That which is to be hath already been.** The future will be a reproduction of the past. The laws which regulate things change not; the moral government is exercised by him who "is, and was, and is to come" (Rev. i. 8), and therefore in effect history repeats itself; the same causes produce the same phenomena. **God requireth that which is past;** literally, *God seeketh after that which hath been chased away;* Septuagint, "God will seek him who is pursued (τὸν διωκόμενον);" Vulgate, "God reneweth that which is passed (*instaurat quod abiit*)." The meaning is—God brings back to view, recalls again into being, that which was past and had vanished out of sight and mind. The sentence is an explanation of the preceding clauses, and has nothing to do with the inquisition at the day of judgment. Hengstenberg has followed the Septuagint, Syriac, and Targum, in translating, "God seeks the persecuted," and seeing herein an allusion to the punishment of the Egyptians for pursuing the Israelites to the Red Sea, or a general statement that God succours the oppressed. But this idea is quite alien to the intention of the passage, and injures the coherence.

Vers. 16—22.—Acknowledging the provi-dential government of God, which controls events and places man's happiness out of his own power, one is confronted also by the fact that there is much wickedness, much injustice, in the world, which oppose all plans for peaceful enjoyment. Doubtless there shall be a day of retribution for such iniquities; and God allows them now in order to try men and to teach them humility. Meantime man's duty and happiness consist, as before said, in making the best use of the present and improving the opportunities which God gives him.

Ver. 16.—**And moreover I saw under the sun the place of judgment.** Koheleth records his experience of the prevalence of iniquity in high places. *The place of judgment (mishpat);* where justice is administered. The accentuation allows (cf. Gen. i. 1) this to be regarded as the object of the verb. The Revised Version, with Hitzig, Ginsburg, and others, take מָקוֹם as an adverbial expression equivalent to "in the place." The former is the simpler construction. "And moreover," at the commencement of the verse, looks back to ver. 10, "I have seen the travail," etc. That **wickedness** (*resha*) was **there.** On the judicial seat iniquity sat instead of justice. **The place of righteousness** (*tsedek*). "Righteousness" is the peculiar characteristic of the judge himself, as "justice" is of his decisions. That **iniquity** (*resha*) **was there.** The word ought to be translated "wickedness" or "iniquity" in both clauses. The Septuagint takes the abstract for the concrete, and at the end has apparently introduced a clerical error, which has been perpetuated in the Arabic and elsewhere, "And moreover I saw under the sun the place of judgment, there was the ungodly (ἀσεβής); and the place of the righteous, there was the godly (εὐσεβής)." The Complutensian Polyglot reads ἀσεβής in both places. It is impossible to harmonize these statements of oppression and injustice here and elsewhere (*e.g.* ch. iv. 1; v. 8; viii. 9, 10) with Solomon's authorship of the book. It is contrary to fact that such a corrupt state of things existed in his time, and in writing thus he would be uttering a libel against himself. If he was cognizant of such evils in his kingdom, he had nothing to do but to put them down with a high hand. There is nothing to lead to the belief that he is speaking of other countries and other times; he is stating his own personal experience of what goes on around him. It is true that in Solomon's latter days disaffection secretly prevailed, and the people felt his yoke grievous (1 Kings xii. 4); but there is no evidence of the existence of corruption in judicial courts, or of the social and political evils of which he speaks in this book. That he had a prophetical for sight of the disasters that would accompany the reign of his successor, and endeav urs herein to provide consolation for the future sufferers, is a pious opinion without historical basis, and cannot be justly used to support the genuineness of the work.

Ver. 17.—**I said in mine heart, God shall judge the righteous and the wicked.** In view of the injustice that prevails in earthly tribunals, Koheleth takes comfort in the thought that there is retribution in store for every man, when God shall award sentence according to deserts. God is a righteous Judge strong and patient, and his decisions are infallible. Future judgment is here plainly stated, as it is at the final conclusion (ch. xi. 14). They who refuse to credit the writer with belief in this great doctrine resort to the theory of interpolation and alteration in order to account for the language in this and analogous passages. There can be no doubt that the present text has hitherto always been regarded as genuine, and that it does clearly assert future retribution, though not so much as a conclusion firmly established, but rather as a belief which may explain anomalies and afford comfort under trying circumstances. **For there is a time there for every purpose and for every work.** The adverb rendered "there" (םָשׁ, *sham*) is placed emphatically, at the end of the sentence. Thus the Septuagint, "There is a reason for every action, and for every work there (ἐκεῖ)." Many take it to mean "in the other world," and Plumptre cites Eurip., 'Med.,' 1073—

Ἐνδαιμονοῖτον, ἀλλ' ἐκεῖ· τὰ δ' ἐνθάδε
Πατὴρ ἀφείλετ'.

"All good be with you! but it must be *there;*
Here it is stolen from you by your sire."

But it is unexampled to find the elliptical "there," when no place has been mentioned in the context, and when we are precluded from interpreting the dark word by a significant gesture, as Medea may have pointed downwards in her histrionic despair. Where the words, "that day," are used in the New Testament (*e.g.* Luke x. 12; 2 Tim. i. 18, etc.), the context shows plainly to what they refer. Some take the adverb here in the sense of "then." Thus the Vulgate, *Justum et impium judicabit Deus, et tempus omnis rei tunc erit.*" But really no time has been mentioned, unless we conceive the writer to have been guilty of a clumsy tautology, expressing by "then" the same idea as "a time for every purpose," etc. Ewald would understand it of the past; but this is quite arbitrary, and limits the signification of the sentence unnecessarily. It is

best, with many modern commentators, to refer the adverb to God, who has just been spoken of in the preceding clause. A similar use is found in Gen. xlix. 24. With God, *apud Deum*, in his counsels, there is a time of judgment and retribution for every act of man, when anomalies which have obtained on earth shall be rectified, injustice shall be punished, virtue rewarded. There is no need, with some commentators, to read םָשׂ, "he appointed;" the usual reading gives a satisfactory sense.

Ver. 18.—The comfort derived from the thought of the future judgment is clouded by the reflection that man is as powerless as the beast to control his destiny. **Concerning the estate of the sons of men**; rather, *it happens on account of the sons of men.* God allows events to take place, disorders to continue, etc., for the ultimate profit of men, though the idea that follows is humiliating and dispiriting. The LXX. has περὶ λαλιᾶς, "concerning the speech of the sons of men." So the Syriac. The word *dibrah* may indeed bear that meaning, as it is also used for "word" or "matter;" but we cannot conceive that the clause refers solely to words, and the expression in the text signifies merely "for the sake, on account of," as in ch. viii. 2. **That God might manifest them**; rather, *that God might test them; Ut probaret eos Deus* (Vulgate). God allows these things, endures them patiently, and does not at once redress them, for two reasons. The first of these is that they may serve for the probation of men, giving them opportunity of making good or bad use of them. We see the effect of this forbearance on the wicked in ch. viii. 11; it hardens them in impenitence; while it nourishes the faith of the righteous, and helps them to persevere (see Dan. xi. 35 and Rev. xxii. 11). **And that they might see that they themselves are beasts.** The pronoun is repeated emphatically, "that they themselves are [like] beasts, they in themselves." This is the second reason. Thus they learn their own powerlessness, if they regard merely their own animal life; apart from their relation to God and hope of the future, they are no better than the lower creatures. Septuagint. "And to show (τοῦ δεῖξαι) that they are beasts." So the Vulgate and Syriac. The Masoretic reading adopted in the Anglican Version seems best.

Vers. 19—21 are best regarded as a parenthesis explanatory of vers. 16—18, elucidating man's impotence in the presence of the anomalies of life. The conclusion in ver. 22 is connected with vers. 16—18. We must acknowledge that there are disorders in the world which we cannot remedy, and which God allows in order to demonstrate our powerlessness; therefore the wisest course is to make the best of present circumstances.

Ver. 19.—**For that which befalleth the sons of men befalleth beasts;** literally, *chance are the sons of men, and chance are beasts* (see on ch. ii. 14); Septuagint, " Yea, and to them cometh the event (συνάντημα) of the sons of men, and the event of the beast." Koheleth explains in what respect man is on a level with the brute creation. Neither are able to rise superior to the law that controls their natural life. So Solon says to Crœsus (Herod., i. 32), Πᾶν ἐστι ἄνθρωπος συμφορή, " Man is naught but chance; " and Artabanus reminds Xerxes that chances rule men, not men chances (ibid., vii. 49). **Even one thing befalleth them.** A third time is the ominous word repeated, " One chance is to both of them." Free-thinkers perverted this dictum into the materialistic language quoted in the Book of Wisdom (ii. 2): " We are born at haphazard, by chance (αὐτοσχεδίως)," etc. But Koheleth's contention is, not that there is no law or order in what happens to man, but that neither man nor beast can dispose events at their own will and pleasure; they are conditioned by a force superior to them, which dominates their actions, sufferings, and circumstances of life. **As the one dieth, so dieth the other.** In the matter of succumbing to the law of death man has no superiority over other creatures. This is an inference drawn from common observation of exterior facts, and touches not any higher question (comp. ch. ii. 14, 15; ix. 2, 3). Something similar is found in Ps. xlix. 20, " Man that is in honour, and understandeth not, is like the beasts that perish." **Yea, they have all one breath** (*ruach*). This is the word used in ver. 23 for the vital principle, " the breath of life," as it is called in Gen. vi. 17, where the same word is found. In the earlier record (Gen. ii. 7) the term is *nishma*. Life in all animals is regarded as the gift of God. Says the psalmist, " Thou sendest forth thy spirit (*ruach*), they are created" (Ps. civ. 30). This lower principle presents the same phenomena in men and in brutes. **Man hath no pre-eminence above a beast;** *i.e.* in regard to suffering and death. This is not bare materialism, or a gloomy deduction from Greek teaching, but must be explained from the writer's standpoint, which is to emphasize the impotence of man to effect his own happiness. Taking only a limited and phenomenal view of man's circumstances and destiny, he speaks a general truth which all must acknowledge. Septuagint, " And what hath the man more than the beast? Nothing." **For all is**

vanity. The distinction between man and beast is annulled by death; the former's boasted superiority, his power of conceiving and planning, his greatness, skill, strength, cunning, all come under the category of vanity, as they cannot ward off the inevitable blow.

Ver. 20.—**All go unto one place.** All, men and brutes, are buried in the earth (ch. xii. 7). The author is not thinking of Sheol, the abode of departed spirits, but merely regarding earth as the universal tomb of all creatures. Plumptre quotes Lucretius, ' De Rer. Nat.,' v. 260—

" Omniparens eadem rerum commune sepulchrum."

" The mother and the sepulchre of all."

Thus Bailey, ' Festus '—

" The course of nature seems a course of death;
The prize of life's brief race, to cease to run;
The sole substantial thing, death's nothingness."

All are of the dust (Gen. iii. 19; Ps. civ. 29; cxlvi. 4). So Ecclus. xli. 10, " All things that are of earth shall turn to earth again." This is true of the material part of men and brutes alike; the question of the destiny of the immaterial part is touched in the next verse.

Ver. 21.—**Who knoweth the spirit of man that goeth upward, and the spirit of the beast that goeth downward to the earth?** The statement is here too categorically rendered, though, for dogmatical purposes, the Masorites seem to have punctuated the text with a view to such interpretation. But, as Wright and others point out, the analogy of two other passages (ch. ii. 19 and vi. 12), where " who knoweth" occurs, intimates that the phrases which follow are interrogative. So the translation should be, " Who knoweth as regards the spirit (*ruach*) of the sons of men whether it goeth upward, and as regards the spirit (*ruach*) of the beast whether it goeth downward under the earth?" Vulgate, *Quis novit si spiritus*, etc.? Septuagint, Τίς εἶδε πνεῦμα υἱῶν τοῦ ἀνθρώπου εἰ ἀναβαίνει αὐτὸ ἄνω; " Who ever saw the spirit of the sons of man, whether it goeth upward?" The Authorized Version, which gives the Masoretic reading, is supposed to harmonize better with the assertion at the end of the book (ch. xii. 7), that the spirit returns to the God who gave it. But there is no formal denial of the immortality of the soul in the present passage as we render it. The question, indeed, is not touched. The author is confirming his previous assertion that, in one point of view, man is not superior to brute. Now he says, looking at the matter merely externally, and taking not into consideration any higher notion, no one knows the destiny of the living powers, whether God deals differently with the spirit of man and of beast. Phenomenally, the principle of life in both is identical, and its cessation is identical; and what becomes of the spirit in either case neither eye nor mind can discover. The distinction which reason or religion assumes, viz. that man's spirit goes upward and the brute's downward, is incapable of proof, is quite beyond experience. What is meant by "upward" and "downward" may be seen by reference to the gnome in Prov. xv. 24, "To the wise the way of life goeth upward, that he may depart from Sheol beneath." The contrast shows that Sheol is regarded as a place of punishment or annihilation; this is further confirmed by Ps. xlix. 14, 15, "They are appointed as a flock for Sheol: death shall be their shepherd . . . their beauty shall be for Sheol to consume. . . . But God will redeem my soul from the power of Sheol; for he shall receive me." Koheleth neither denies nor affirms in this passage the immortality of the soul; that he believed in it we learn from other expressions; but he is not concerned with parading it here. Commentators quote Lucretius' sceptical thought ('De Rer. Nat.,' i. 113—116)—

"Ignoratur enim quæ sit natura animaï,
  Nata sit, an contra nascentibus insinuetur,
  Et simul intereat nobiscum, morte diremta,
  An tenebras Orci visat vastasque lacunas."

"We know not what the nature of the soul,
  Born in the womb, or at the birth infused,
  Whether it dies with us, or wings its way
  Unto the gloomy pools of Orcus vast."

But Koheleth's inquiry suggests the possibility of a different destiny for the spirits of man and brute, though he does not at this moment make any definite assertion on the subject. Later on he explains the view taken by the believer in Divine revelation (ch. xii. 7).

Ver. 22.—After all, the writer arrives at the conclusion intimated in ver. 12; only here the result is gathered from the acknowledgment of man's impotence (vers. 16—18), as there from the experience of life. **Wherefore I perceive that** there is **nothing better,** etc.; rather, *so,* or *wherefore I saw that there was nothing,* etc. As man is not master of his own lot, cannot order events as he would

like, is powerless to control the forces of nature and the providential arrangements of the world, his duty and his happiness consist in enjoying the present, in making the best of life, and availing himself of the bounties which the mercy of God places before him. Thus he will free himself from anxieties and cares, perform present labours, attend to present duties, content himself with the daily round, and not vex his heart with solicitude for the future. There is no Epicureanism here, no recommendation of sensual enjoyment; the author simply advises men to make a thankful use of the blessings which God provides for them. **For who shall bring him to see what shall be after him?** The Revised Version, by inserting " back "—*Who shall bring him back to see?*—affixes a meaning to the clause which it need not and does not bear. It is, indeed, commonly interpreted to signify that man knows and can know nothing that happens to him after death—whether he will exist or not, whether he will have cognizance of what passes on earth, or be insensible to all that befalls here. But Koheleth has completed that thought already; his argument now turns to the future in this life. Use the present, for you cannot be sure of the future;—this is his exhortation. So he says (ch. vi. 12), "Who can tell a man what shall be after him under the sun?" where the expression, "under the sun," shows that earthly life is meant, not existence after death. Ignorance of the future is a very common topic throughout the book, but it is the terrestrial prospect that is in view. There would be little force in urging the impotence of men's efforts towards their own happiness by the consideration of their ignorance of what may happen when they are no more; but one may reasonably exhort men to cease to torment themselves with hopes and fears, with labours that may be useless and preparations that may never be needed, by the reflection that they cannot foresee the future, and that, for all they know, the pains which they take may be utterly wasted (cf. ch. vii. 14; ix. 3). Thus in this section there is neither scepticism nor Epicureanism. In brief, the sentiment is this—There are injustices and anomalies in the life of men and in the course of this world's events which man cannot control or alter; these may be righted and compensated hereafter. Meantime, man's happiness is to make the best of the present, and cheerfully to enjoy what Providence offers, without anxious care for the future.

HOMILETICS.

Vers. 1—9.—*Times and seasons; or, Heaven's order in man's affairs.* I. THE EVENTS AND PURPOSES OF LIFE. 1. *Great in their number.* The Preacher's catalogue exhausts not, but only exemplifies, the "occupations and interests," occurrences and experiences, that constitute the warp and woof of mortal existence. Between the cradle and the grave, instances present themselves in which more things happen than are here recorded, and more designs are attempted and fulfilled than are here contemplated. There are also cases in which the sum total of experience is included in the two entries, "born," "died;" but the generality of mortals live long enough to suffer and to do many more things beneath the sun. 2. *Manifold in their variety.* In one sense and at one time it may seem as if there were "no new thing under the sun" (ch. i. 9), either in the history of the race or in the experience of the individual; but at another time and in another sense an almost infinite variety appears in both. The monotony of life, of which complaint is often heard (ch. i. 10), exists rather in the mind or heart of the complainant than in the texture of life itself. What more diversified than the events and purposes the Preacher has catalogued? Entering through the gateway of birth upon the mysterious arena of existence, the human being passes through a succession of constantly shifting experiences, till he makes his exit from the scene through the portals of the grave, planting and plucking up, etc.

> "All the world's a stage,
> And all the men and women merely players;
> They have their exits and their entrances;
> And one man in his time plays many parts,
> His acts being seven ages."
>
> ('As You Like It,' act ii. sc. 7.)

3. *Antithetic in their relations.* Human life, like man himself, may almost be characterized as a mass of contradictions. The incidents and interests, purposes and plans, events and enterprises, that compose it, are not only manifold and various, but also, it would seem, diametric in their opposition. Being born is in due course succeeded by dying; planting by plucking up; and killing—it may be in war, or by administration of justice, or through some perfectly defensible cause—if not by actual raising from death, which lies confessedly beyond the power of man (1 Sam. ii. 6; 2 Kings v. 7), at least by healing every malady short of death. Breaking down, whether of material structures (2 Chron. xxiii. 17) or of intellectual systems, whether of national (Jer. i. 10) or religious (Gal. ii. 18) institutions, is after an interval followed by the building up of those very things which were destroyed. Weeping endureth only for a night, while joy cometh in the morning (Ps. xxx. 5). Dancing, on the other hand, gives place to mourning. In short, whatever experience man at any time has, before he terminates his pilgrimage he may almost confidently count on having the opposite; and whatever action he may at any season perform, another season will almost certainly arrive when he will do the reverse. Of every one of the antinomies cited by the Preacher, man's experience on the earth furnishes examples. 4. *Fixed in their times.* Though appearing to come about without any order or arrangement, the events and purposes of mundane existence are by no means left to the guidance, or rather no-guidance, of chance; but rather have their places in the vast world-plan determined, and the times of their appearing fixed. As the hour of each man's entrance into life is decreed, so is that of his departure from the same (Heb. ix. 27; 2 Tim. iv. 6). The date at which he shall step forth upon the active business of life, represented in the Preacher's catalogue by "planting and plucking up," "breaking down and building up," "casting away stones and gathering stones together," "getting and losing;" the period at which he shall marry (ver. 4), with the times at which weddings and funerals (ver. 4) shall occur in his family circle; the moment when he shall be called upon to stand up valiantly for truth and right amongst his contemporaries (Prov. xv. 23), or to preserve a discreet and prudent silence when talk would be folly (Prov. x. 8), or even hurtful to the cause he serves; the times when he shall either suffer his affections to flow forth in an uninterrupted stream towards the good,

or withhold them from unworthy objects; or, if he be a statesman, the occasions when he shall go to war and return from it, are all predetermined by infinite wisdom. 5. *Determined in their durations.* How long each individual life shall continue (Ps. xxxi. 15; Acts xvii. 26), how long each experience shall last, and how long each action shall take to perform, is equally a fixed and ascertained quantity, if not to man's knowledge, certainly to that of the supreme Disposer of events.

II. THE TIMES AND SEASONS OF LIFE. 1. *Appointed by and known only to God.* As in the material and natural world the Creator hath appointed times and seasons, as, *e.g.*, to the heavenly bodies for their rising and setting (Ps. civ. 19), to plants for their growing and decaying (Gen. viii. 22; Numb. xiii. 20; Judg. xv. 1; Jer. l. 16; Mark xi. 13), and to animals for their instinctive actions (Job xxxix. 1, 2; Jer. viii. 7), so in the human and spiritual world has he ordained the same (Acts xvii. 26; Eph. i. 10; Titus i. 3); and these times and seasons, both in the natural and in the spiritual world, hath God reserved to himself (Acts i. 7). 2. *Unavoidable and unalterable by man.* As no man can predict the day of his death (Gen. xxvii. 2; Matt. xxv. 13), any more than know beforehand that of his birth, so neither can he fathom beforehand the incidents that shall happen, or the times when they shall fall out during the course of his life (Prov. xxvii. 1). Nor by any precontriving can he change by so much as a hair's breadth the place into which each incident is fitted, or the moment when it shall happen.

Learn: 1. The changefulness of human life, and the duty of preparing wisely to meet it. 2. The Divine order that pervades human life, and the propriety of accepting it with meekness. 3. The difficulty (from a human point of view) of living well, since no man can be quite certain that for anything he does he has found the right season. 4. The wisdom of seeking for one's self the guidance of him in whose hands are times and seasons (Acts i. 7).

Vers. 11—14.—*All things beautiful; or, God, man, and the world.* I. THE BEAUTIFUL RELATION OF THE WORLD TO GOD. Expressed by four words. 1. *Dependence: no such thing as independence, self-subsistence, self-origination, self-regulation, in mundane affairs.* The universe, out to its circumference and in to its centre, from its mightiest structure down to its smallest detail, is the handiwork of God. Whatever philosophers may say or think upon the subject, it is simple absurdity to teach that the universe made itself, or that the incidents composing the sum of human life and experience have come to pass of themselves. It will be time enough to believe things are their own makers when effects can be discovered that have no causes. Persons of advanced (?) intelligence and culture may regard the Scriptures as behind the age in respect of philosophic insight and scientific attainment; it is to their credit that their writers never talk such unphilosophic and unscientific nonsense as that mundane things are their own creators. Their common sense—if not permissible to say their inspiration —appears to have been strong and clear enough to save them from being befooled by such vagaries as have led astray many modern savants, and to have taught them that the First Cause of all things is God (Gen. i. 1; Exod. xx. 11; Neh. ix. 6; Job xxxviii. 4; Ps. xix. 1; Isa. xl. 28; Acts xiv. 15; xvii. 24; Rom. xi. 36; Eph. iii. 9; Heb. iii. 4; Rev. iv. 11). 2. *Variety: no monotony in mundane affairs.* Obvious as regards both the universe as a whole and its individual parts. The supreme Artificer of the former had no idea of fashioning all things after one model, however excellent, but sought to introduce variety into the works of his hands; and just this is the principle upon which he has proceeded in arranging the programme of man's experiences upon the earth. To this diversity in man's experience the twenty-eight instances of events and purposes given by the Preacher (vers. 2—8) allude; and this same diversity is a mark at once of wisdom and of kindness on the part of the Supreme. As the material globe would be monotonous were it all mountain and no valley, so would human life be uninteresting were it an unchanging round of the same few incidents. But it is not. If there are funerals and deaths, there are as well marriages and births; if nights of weeping, days of laughing; if times of war, periods of peace. 3. *Order: no chance or accident in mundane affairs.* To short-sighted and feeble man, human life is full of accidents or chances; but not so when viewed from the standpoint of God. Not only does no event happen without his permission (Matt. x. 29; Luke xii. 6), but each event occurs at the time and falls into the place appointed for it by infinite wisdom. Nor is this true merely of such events as are wholly and exclusively in his power, like births and deaths (ver. 2), but of such also as to some extent at least are within man's control, as *e.g.* the planting of a field and the plucking up of that which is planted (ver. 2), killing and healing, breaking down and building up (ver. 3), weeping and laughing (ver. 4), etc. Men may flatter themselves that of these latter actions they are the sole originators, have both the choosing of their times and the fixing of their forms; but according to the Preacher, God's supremacy is as little to be disputed in them as in the matter of man's coming into or going out from the world. We express this thought by citing the well-known proverb, "Man proposes, but God disposes," or the familiar words of Shakespeare—

> "There's a divinity that shapes our ends,
> Rough-hew them how we will."
>
> ('Hamlet,' act v. sc. 2.)

4. *Beauty: no defect or deformity in mundane affairs.* This cannot signify that in such events and actions as "killing," "hating," "warring," there is never anything wrong; that God regards them only as good in the making, and generally that sin is a necessary stage in the development of human nature. The Preacher is not pronouncing judgment upon the moral qualities of the actions he enumerates, but merely calling attention to their fitness for the times and seasons to which they have been assigned by God. Going back in thought to the "Very good!" of the Creator when he rested from his labours at the close of the sixth day (Gen. i. 31), the Preacher cannot think of saying less of the work God is still carrying on in evolving the plan and programme of his purpose. "God hath made everything beautiful in its time" (cf. ver. 11): beautiful in itself, so far as it is a work of his; but beautiful not less in its time, even when the work, as not being entirely his, is not beautiful in itself, or in its inward essence. Cf. Shakespeare's—

> "How many things by season seasoned are
> To their right praise and true perfection!"
>
> ('Merchant of Venice,' act v. sc. 1.)

Beautiful in themselves and their times are the seasons of the year, the ages of man, and the changing experiences through which he passes; beautiful, at least in their times, are numerous human actions which God cannot be regarded as approving, but which nevertheless he permits to occur because he sees the hour has struck for their occurring. As it were, the glowing wheels of Divine providence never fail to keep time with the great clock of eternity.

II. THE BEAUTIFUL RELATION OF MAN TO THE WORLD. Also expressed in four words. 1. *Weariness: no perfect rest in the midst of mundane affairs.* Not only is man tossed about continually by the multitudinous vicissitudes of which he is the subject, but he derives almost no satisfaction from the thought that in all these changes there is a beautiful because divinely appointed harmony, and a beneficent because Heaven-ordained purpose. The order pervading the universe is something outside of and beyond him. The fixing of the right times is a work in which he cannot, even in a small degree, co-operate. As a wise man, he may wish to have every action in which he bears a part performed at the set time marked out for it on the clock of eternity; but the very attempt to find out for each action the right time only aggravates the fatigue of his labour, and increases the sense of weariness under which he groans. "What profit hath he that worketh in that wherein he laboureth?" Not, certainly, "no profit," but not enough to give him rest or even free him from weariness. And this, when viewed from a moral and religious standpoint, is beautiful inasmuch as it prevents (or ought to prevent) man from seeking happiness in mundane affairs. 2. *Ignorance: no perfect knowledge of mundane affairs.* "No man can find out the work that God maketh from the beginning to the end." One more proof of the vanity of human life—that no man, however wise and far-seeing, patient and laborious, can discover the plan of God either in the universe as a whole or in his own life; and what renders this a special sorrow is the fact that God hath set "the world [or, 'eternity'] in his heart." If the " world " be accepted as the true rendering (Jerome, Luther, Ewald), then probably the meaning is that, though each individual carries about within his bosom in his own personality an image of the world—is, in fact, a microcosmus in which the macrocosmus or great world is mirrored—nevertheless the problem of the universe eludes his grasp. If, however, the translation " eternity " be adopted (Delitzsch, Wright, Plumptre), then the import of the clause will be that God hath planted in the heart of man "a longing after immortality," given him an idea of the infinite and eternal which lies beyond the veil of outward things, and inspired him with a desire to know that which is above and beyond him, yet he cannot find out the secret of the universe in the sense of discovering its plan. With an infinite behind and before him, he can grasp neither the beginning of the work of God in its purpose or plan, nor the end of it in its issues and results, whether to the individual or to the whole. What his eye looks upon is the middle portion passing before him here and now—in comparison with the whole but an infinitesimal speck—and so he remains with reference to the whole like a person walking in the dark. 3. *Submission: no ground for complaining as to mundane affairs.* Rather in the view presented is much to comfort man. Had the ordering of the universe, or even of his own lot, been left to man, man himself would have been the first to regret it. As Laplace is credited with having said that, if only the Almighty had called him into counsel at the making of the universe, he could have given the Almighty some valuable hints, so are there equally foolish persons who believe they could have drafted for themselves a better life-programme than has been done for them by the supreme Disposer of events. A wise man, however, will always feel grateful that the Almighty has retained the ordering of events in his own hand, and will meekly submit to the same, believing that God's times are the best times, and that his ways are ever " mercy and truth unto such as keep his covenant and his testimonies " (Ps. xxv. 10). 4. *Fear: no justification for impiety or irreverence in mundane affairs.* A proper study of the constitution and course of nature, a due recognition of the order pervading all its parts, with a just consideration both of the perfection and permanence (ver. 14) of the Divine working, ought to inspire men with " fear "—of such sort as both to repress within them irreligion and impiety, and to excite within them humility and awe.

Ver. 15.—*Requiring that which is past.* I. IN THE REALM OF NATURE. God seeks after that which is past or has been driven away, in the sense that he recalls or brings again phenomena that have vanished; as *e.g.* the reappearance of the sun with its light and heat, the various seasons of the year with their respective characteristics, the circling of the winds with other meteorological aspects of the firmament. The thought here is the uniformity of sequence in the physical world (ch. i. 4—7).

II. IN THE SPHERE OF INDIVIDUAL EXPERIENCE. God seeks after that which has been driven away in the sense that he reproduces in the life of one individual experiences that have existed in another, or in himself at a former point in his career. The thought is, that by Heaven's decree a large amount of sameness exists in the phases of thought and feeling through which different individuals pass, or the same individuals at successive stages of their development.

III. IN THE DOMAIN OF HISTORY. God seeks after that which has been driven away, in the sense that, on the broad theatre of action which men name " time," or " the world," he frequently, in the evolutions of his providence, seems to recall the past by reproducing " situations," " incidents," " events," " experiences," similar to, if not identical with, those which occurred before. The thought is that history frequently repeats itself.

IV. IN THE PROGRAMME OF THE UNIVERSE. God will eventually seek after that which has been driven away, by calling up again out of the past for judgment every individual that has lived upon the globe, with every word that has been spoken and every act that has been done, with every secret thought and imagination, whether it has been good or whether it has been bad. The thought is that the distant past and the distant future will one day meet. The place will be before the great white throne; the time will be the last day.

Vers. 16, 18.— *Wickedness in the place of judgment; or, the mystery of providence.*

I. THE PROFOUND PROBLEM. The moral disorder of the universe. " I saw under the sun in the place of judgment that wickedness was there, and in the place of righteousness that wickedness was there " (ver. 16). 1. *The strange spectacle.* What fascinated the Preacher's gaze and perplexed the Preacher's heart was not so much the existence as the triumph of sin—the fact that sin existed where and as it did. Had he always beheld sin in its naked deformity, essential loathsomeness, and abject baseness, receiving the due reward of its misdeeds, trembling as a culprit before the bar of providential judgment, and suffering the punishment its criminality merited, the mystery and perplexity would most likely have been reduced by half. What, however, he did witness was iniquity, not trembling but triumphing, not sorrowing but singing, not suffering the due recompense of her own evil deeds but snatching off the rewards and prizes that belonged to virtue. In short, what he perceived was the complete moral disorder of the world—as it were society turned topsy-turvy ; the wicked up and the righteous down ; bad men exalted and good men despised ; vice arrayed in silks and bedizened with jewels, and virtue only half covered with tattered rags. 2. *Two particular sights.* (1) Iniquity usurping the place of judgment ; thrusting itself into the very council-chambers where right and justice should prevail ; now as a judge who deliberately holds the scales uneven because the one litigant is rich and the other poor, anon as an advocate who employs all his ingenuity to defend a prisoner whom he knows to be guilty, and again as a witness who has accepted a bribe and calmly swears to a lie. (2) Iniquity preoccupying the place of righteousness ; *i.e.* the tribunal, whether secular or ecclesiastical, whose efforts should be all directed to finding out and maintaining the cause of righteousness.

II. THE PERPLEXING MYSTERY. " I said in mine heart " (ver. 17). The Preacher was troubled about it, as David (Ps. xxxvii. 1, 7), Job (xxi. 7), Asaph (Ps. lxxiii. 3), and Jeremiah (xii. 1) had been. To him, as to them, it was an enigma. But why should it have been ? 1. *On one hypothesis it is no enigma.* On the supposition that God, duty, and immortality are non-existent, it is not a mystery at all that vice should prevail and virtue have a poor time of it so long as it remains above ground, for (on the hypothesis) fleeing to a better country beyond the skies is out of the question. The mystery would be that it were otherwise. 2. *On another hypothesis it is an enigma.* What creates the mystery is that these things occur while God is, duty presses, and immortality awaits. Since God is, why does he suffer these things to happen ? Why does he not interpose to put matters right ? If right and wrong are not empty phrases, how comes it that moral distinctions are so constantly submerged ? With " eternity in their hearts," how is it to be explained that men are so regardless of the future ?

III. THE PROPOSED SOLUTION. This lay in three things. 1. *The certainty of a future judgment.* " I said in mine heart, God shall judge the righteous and the wicked; for there is a time for every purpose and for every work " (ver. 17). Convinced that God, duty, and immortality were no fictions but solemn realities, the Preacher saw that these implied the certainty of a judgment in the future world when all the entanglements of this world would be sorted out, its inequalities evened, and its wrongs righted ; and seeing this, he discerned in it a sufficient reason why God should not be in a hurry to cast down vice from its undeserved eminence and exalt virtue to its rightful renown. 2. *The discrimination of human character.* The Preacher saw that God allowed wickedness to triumph and righteousness to suffer, in order that he might thereby " prove them," *i.e.* sift and distinguish them from one another by the free development of their characters. Were God by external restraints to place a check on the ungodly or by outward helps to recompense the pious, it might come to be doubtful who were the sinful and who the virtuous ; but granting free scope to both, each manifests its hidden character by its actions, according to the principle, " Every tree is known by its fruits " (Matt. vii. 16—20). 3. *The revelation of human depravity.* Because a future judgment awaits, it is necessary that the wickedness of the wicked should be revealed. Hence God abstains from interfering prematurely with the world's disorder that men may see to what thorough inherent depravity they have really come ; that, oppressing and destroying one another, they are little better than brute beasts who, without consideration or remorse, prey on each other.

LESSONS. 1. Patience. 2. Confidence. 3. Hopefulness.

Vers. 19—22.—*Are men no better than beasts?* I. BOTH ALIKE EMANATE FROM THE
SOIL. "All are of the dust" (ver. 20). This the first argument in support of the
monstrous proposition that man hath no pre-eminence above a beast. 1. *The measure
of truth it contains.* In so far as it asserts that man, considered as to his material part,
possesses a common origin with the beasts that perish, that both were at first formed
from the ground, and are so allied to the soil that, besides emerging from it, they are
every day supported by it and will eventually return to it, being both resolved into
indistinguishable dust, it accords exactly with the teaching of Scripture (Gen. i. 24;
ii. 7), science, and experience. Compare the language of Arnobius, "Wherein do we
differ from them? Our bones are of the same materials; our origin is not more noble
than theirs" ('Ad Gentes,' ii. 16). 2. *The amount of error it conceals.* It overlooks
the facts that, again according to Scripture (Gen. i. 27; ii. 7; ix. 6), man was created
in the Divine image, which is never said of the lower creatures; was endowed with
intelligence far surpassing that of the creatures (Job xxxii. 8); and so far from being
placed on a level with the lower animals, was expressly constituted their lord (Gen. i.
28). Read in this connection Shakespeare's "What a piece of work is man!" etc.
('Hamlet,' act ii. sc. 2). Moreover, it ignores what is patent on every page of
Scripture as well as testified by every chapter in human experience, viz. that God deals
with man as he does not deal with the beasts, subjecting him as not them to moral
discipline, and accepting of him what is never asked of them, the tribute of freely
rendered service, inviting him as they are never invited to enter into conscious fellowship with himself, punishing him as never them for disobedience, and making of him
an object of love and grace to the extent of devising and completing on his behalf a
scheme of salvation, as is never done or proposed to be done for them. Unless, therefore, Scripture be set aside as worthless, it will be impossible to hold that in respect of
origin and nature man hath no pre-eminence over the beasts.

II. BOTH ALIKE ARE THE SPORT OF CHANCE. "That which befalleth the sons of
men befalleth beasts; even one thing befalleth them;" or, "Chance are the sons of
men, chance is the beast, and one chance is to them both" (ver. 19). 1. *The assertion under limitations may be admitted as correct.* Certainly no ground exists for the
allegation that the course of providence, whether as it relates to man or as it bears
upon the lower animals, is a chance, a peradventure, a haphazard. Yet events, which
in the programme of the Supreme have their fixed places and appointed times, may
seem to man to be fortuitous, as lying altogether beyond his calculation and not within
his expectation; and what the present argument amounts to is that man is as helpless
before these events as the unthinking creatures of the field are—that they deal with
him precisely as with the beasts, sweeping down upon him with resistless force, falling
upon him at unexpected moments, and tossing him about with as much indifference
as they do them. 2. *The assertion, however, must be qualified:* It follows not from
the above concessions that man is as helpless before unforeseen occurrences as the
beasts are. Not only can he to some extent by foresight anticipate their coming, which
the lower creatures cannot do, but, unlike them also, he can protect himself against
them when they have come. To man belongs a power not (consciously at least)
possessed by the animals, of not merely accommodating himself to circumstances—a
capability they to some extent share with him—but of rising above circumstances and
compelling them to bend to him. If to this be added that if time and chance happen
to man as to the beasts he knows it, which they do not, and can extract good from it,
which they cannot, it will once more appear that ground exists for disputing the
degrading proposition that man hath no pre-eminence over the beasts.

III. BOTH ALIKE ARE THE PREY OF DEATH. "As the one dieth, so dieth the other;
yea, they have all one breath" (ver. 19). 1. *Seeming correspondences between the two
in the matter of dying.* (1) In both death means the extinction of physical life and
the dissolution of the material frame. (2) In both the mode of dying is frequently the
same. (3) The same grave receives both when the vital spark has departed. (4) The
only difference between the two is that man commonly gets a coffin and a funeral, a
mausoleum and a monument, whereas the beast gets none of these luxuries. 2. *Obvious
discrepancies between the two in respect of dying.* (1) Man living knows that he must
die (ch. ix. 5), which the beast does not. (2) Man has the choice and power, if he
accepts the provisions of grace, of meeting death without a fear. (3) Even if he does

not, there is something nobler in the spectacle of a man going forth with eyes open to the dread conflict with the king of terrors, than in that of a brute expiring in unconscious stupidity. (4) If one thinks of him dying, as he often does die, like a Christian, it will be seen more absurd than ever to assert that a man hath no pre-eminence over a beast.

IV. BOTH, DYING, PASS BEYOND THE SPHERE OF HUMAN KNOWLEDGE. " Who knoweth the spirit of man, whether it goeth upward? and the spirit of the beast, whether it goeth downward to the earth?" (ver. 21). 1. *Admitted so far as scientific knowledge is concerned.* The agnostics of the Preacher's day, like those of modern times, could not say what became of a man's spirit, if he had one (of which they were not sure), after it had escaped from his body, any more than they could tell where a beast's—and the beast was as likely to have a spirit as the man—went to after its carcase sank into the soil. Whether it was the man's that went upward and the beast's downward, or *vice versâ*, lay outside their ken. Their scientific apparatus did not enable them to report, as the scientific apparatus of the nineteenth century does not enable it to report, upon the post-mundane career of either beast or man; and so they assumed the position from which the agnostics of to-day have not departed, that it is all one with the man and the beast when the grave hides them, and that a man hath no pre-eminence over a beast. 2. *Denied so far as religious knowledge is concerned.* Refusing to hold that the anatomist's scalpel, or chemist's retort, or astronomer's telescope, or analyst's microscope are the ultimate tests of truth, and that nothing is to be credited which cannot be detected by one or other of these instruments, we are not so hopelessly in the dark about man's spirit when it leaves its earthly tabernacle as are agnostics whether ancient or modern. On the high testimony of this Preacher (ch. xii. 7), on the higher witness of Paul (2 Cor. v. 1; Phil. i. 23), and on the highest evidence attainable on the subject (2 Tim. i. 10), we know that when the spirit of a child of God forsakes the body it does not disperse into thin air, but passes up into the Father's hand (Luke xxiii. 46), and that when a good man disappears from earth he forthwith appears in heaven (Luke xxiii. 43; Phil. i. 23), amid the spirits of the just made perfect (Heb. xii. 23); so that another time we decline to endorse the sentiment that man hath no pre-eminence over a beast.

V. BOTH ALIKE, PASSING FROM THE EARTH, NEVER MORE RETURN. " Who shall bring him *back* to see that which shall be after him?" (ver. 29). Accepting this as the correct rendering of the words (for other interpretations consult the Exposition): 1. *It may be granted* that no human power can recall man from the grave any more than it can reanimate the beast; that the realm beyond the tomb, so far as the senses are concerned, is "an undiscovered country, from whose bourne no traveller returns." 2. *It is contended* that nevertheless there is a power which can and ultimately will despoil the grave of its human victims, and that man will eventually come back to dwell, if not upon the old soil and beneath the old sky, at least beneath a new heavens and upon a new earth, wherein dwelleth righteousness.

LESSONS. 1. The dignity of man. 2. The solemnity of life. 3. The certainty of death.

HOMILIES BY VARIOUS AUTHORS.

Vers. 1—8.—*The manifold interests and occupations of life.* There is nothing so interesting to man as human life. The material creation engages the attention and absorbs the inquiring activities of the student of physical science; but unless it is regarded as the expression of the Divine ideas, the vehicle of thought and purpose, its interest is limited and cold. But what men are and think and do is a matter of concern to every observant and reflecting mind. The ordinary observer contemplates human life with curiosity; the politician, with interested motives; the historian, hoping to find the key to the actions of nations and kings and statesmen; the poet, with the aim of finding material and inspiration for his verse; and the religious thinker, that he may trace the operation of God's providence, of Divine wisdom and love. He who looks below the surface will not fail to find, in the events and incidents of human existence, the tokens of the appointments and dispositions of an all-wise

Ruler of the world. The manifold interests of our life are not regulated by chance; for "to everything there is a season, and a time to every purpose under the heaven."

I. LIFE'S PERIODS (ITS BEGINNING AND CLOSE) ARE APPOINTED BY GOD. The sacredness of birth and death are brought before us, as we are assured that "there is a time to be born, and a time to die." The believer in God cannot doubt that the Divine Omniscience observes, as the Divine Omnipotence virtually effects, the introduction into this world, and the removal from it, of every human being. Men are born, to show that God will use his own instruments for carrying on the manifold work of the world; they die, to show that he is limited by no human agencies. They are born just when they are wanted, and they die just when it is well that their places should be taken by their successors. "Man is immortal till his work is done."

II. LIFE'S OCCUPATIONS ARE DIVINELY ORDERED. The reader of this passage is forcibly reminded of the substantial identity of man's life in the different ages of the world. Thousands of years have passed since these words were penned, yet to how large an extent does this description apply to human existence in our own day! Organic activities, industrial avocations, social services, are common to every age of man's history. If men withdraw themselves from practical work, and from the duties of the family and the state, without sufficient justification, they are violating the ordinances of the Creator. He has given to every man a place to fill, a work to do, a service of helpfulness to render to his fellow-creatures.

III. THE EMOTIONS PROPER TO HUMAN LIFE ARE OF DIVINE APPOINTMENT. These are natural to man. The mere feelings of pleasure and pain, the mere impulses of desire and aversion, man shares with brutes. But those emotions which are man's glory and man's shame are both special to him, and have a great share in giving character to his moral life. Some, like envy, are altogether bad; some, like hatred, are bad or good according as they are directed; some, like love, are always good. The Preacher of Jerusalem refers to joy and sorrow, when he speaks of "a time to laugh, and a time to weep;" to love and hate, for both of which he declares there is occasion in our human existence. There has been no change in these human experiences with the lapse of time; they are permanent factors in our life. Used aright, they become means of moral development, and aid in forming a noble and pious character.

IV. THE OPERATION OF DIVINE PROVIDENCE IS APPARENT IN THE VARIED FORTUNES OF HUMANITY. This passage tells of accumulation and consequent prosperity, of loss and consequent adversity. The mutability of human affairs, the disparities of the human lot, were as remarkable and as perplexing in the days of the Hebrew sage as in our own. And they were regarded by him, as by rational and religious observers in our own time, as instances of the working of physical and social laws imposed by the Author of nature himself. In the exercise of divinely entrusted powers, men gather together possessions and disperse them abroad. The rich and the poor exist side by side; and the wealthy are every day impoverished, whilst the indigent are raised to opulence. These are the lights and shades upon the landscape of life, the shifting scenes in life's unfolding drama. Variety and change are evidently parts of the Divine intention, and are never absent from the world of our humanity.

V. THE MORAL AND SPIRITUAL ISSUES OF HUMAN LIFE BEAR MARKS OF DIVINE WISDOM AND ORDER. It cannot be the case that all the phases and processes of our human existence are to be apprehended simply in themselves, as if they contained their own meaning, and had no ulterior significance. Life is not a kaleidoscope, but a picture; not the promiscuous sounds heard when the instrumentalists are "tuning up," but an oratorio; not a chronicle, but a history. There is a unity and an aim in life; but this is not merely artistic, it is moral. We do not work and rest, enjoy and suffer, hope and fear, with no purpose to be achieved by the experiences through which we pass. He who has appointed "a season, and a time for every purpose under the heaven," designs that we should, by toil and endurance, by fellowship and solitude, by gain and loss, make progress in the course of moral and spiritual discipline, should grow in the favour and in the likeness of God himself.—T.

Vers. 9—13.—*The mystery and the meaning of life.* The author of Ecclesiastes was too wise to take what we call a one-sided view of human life. No doubt there are times and moods in which this human existence seems to us to be all made up of either toil or endurance, delight or disappointment. But in the hour of sober reflection we are constrained to admit that the pattern of the web of life is composed of many and diverse colours.   Our faculties and capacities are many, our experiences are varied, for the appeals made to us by our environment change from day to day, from hour to hour. "One man in his time plays many parts."

I. In life there is mystery to solve. The works and the ways of God are too great for our feeble, finite nature to comprehend. We may learn much, and yet may leave much unlearned and probably unlearnable, at all events in the conditions of this present state of being.   1. There are speculative difficulties regarding the order and constitution of things, which the thoughtful man cannot avoid inquiring into, which yet often baffle and sometimes distress him. "Man cannot find out the work that God hath done from the beginning even to the end." 2. There are practical difficulties which every man has to encounter in the conduct of life, fraught as it is with disappointment and sorrow. "What profit hath he that worketh in that wherein he laboureth?"

II. In life there is beauty to admire. The mind that is not absorbed in providing for material wants can scarcely fail to be open to the adaptations and the manifold charms of nature. The language of creation is as harmonious music, which is soothing or inspiring to the ear of the soul. What a revelation is here of the very nature and benevolent purposes of the Almighty Maker! "He hath made everything beautiful in its time." And beauty needs the æsthetic faculty in order to its appreciation and enjoyment. The development of this faculty in advanced states of civilization is familiar to every student of human nature. Standards of beauty vary; but the true standard is that which is offered by the works of God, who "hath made everything beautiful in its time." There is a beauty special to every season of the year, to every hour of the day, to every state of the atmosphere; there is a beauty in every several kind of landscape, a beauty of the sea, a beauty of the heavens; there is a beauty of childhood, another beauty of youth, of healthful manhood and radiant womanhood, and even a certain beauty peculiar to age. The pious observer of the works of God, who rids himself of conventional and traditional prejudices, will not fail to recognize the justice of this remarkable assertion of the Hebrew sage.

III. In life there is work to do. Labour and travail are very frequently mentioned in this book, whose author was evidently deeply impressed by the corresponding facts—first, that God is the almighty Worker in the universe; and, secondly, that man is made by the Creator like unto himself, in that he is called upon by his nature and his circumstances to effort and to toil. Forms of labour vary, and the progress of applied science in our own time seems to relieve the toiler of some of the severer, more exhausting kinds of bodily effort. But it must ever remain true that the human frame was not intended for indolence; that work is a condition of welfare, a means of moral discipline and development. It is a factor that cannot be left out of human life; the Christian is bound, like his Master, to finish the work which the Father has given him to do.

IV. In life there is good to participate. There is no asceticism in the teaching of this Book of Ecclesiastes. The writer was one who had no doubt that man was constituted to enjoy. He speaks of eating and drinking as not merely necessary in order to maintain life, but as affording gratification. He dwells appreciatingly upon the happiness of married life. He even commends mirth and festivity. In all these he shows himself superior to the pettiness which carps at the pleasures connected with this earthly existence, and which tries to pass for sanctity. Of course, there are lawful and unlawful gratifications; there is a measure of indulgence which ought not to be exceeded. But if Divine intention is traceable in the constitution and condition of man, he was made to partake with gratitude of the bounties of God's providence.

V. All the provisions which Divine wisdom attaches to human life are to be accepted with gratitude and used with faithfulness, and with a constant sense of responsibility. In receiving and enjoying every gift, the devout mind will exclaim, "It is the gift of God." In taking advantage of every opportunity, the Christian will bear in mind that wisdom and goodness arrange human life so that it shall afford repeated occasion for fidelity and diligence. In his daily work he will make it his aim to "serve the Lord Christ."

APPLICATION. 1. There is much in the provisions and conditions of our earthly life which baffles our endeavours to understand it; and when perplexed by mystery, we are summoned to submit with all humility and patience to the limitations of our intellect, and to rest assured that God's wisdom will, in the end, be made apparent to all. 2. There is a practical life to be lived, even when speculative difficulties are insurmountable; and it is in the conscientious fulfilment of daily duty, and the moderate use of ordinary enjoyments, that as Christians we may adorn the doctrine of God our Saviour.—T.

Ver. 14.—*The purposes of Providence.* Different minds, observing and considering the same facts, are often very differently affected by them. The measure of previous experience and culture, the natural disposition, the tone and temper with which men address themselves to what is before them,—all affect the conclusion at which they arrive. The conviction produced in the mind of the Preacher of Jerusalem is certainly deserving of attention; he saw the hand of God in nature and in life, where some see only chance or fate. To see God's hand, to admire his wisdom, to appreciate his love, in our human life,—this is an evidence of sincere and intelligent piety.
I. GOD'S WORK IS PERFECT AND UNALTERABLE. "Nothing can be put to it, nor anything taken from it." This cannot be said to be the general conviction; on the contrary, men are always finding fault with the constitution of things. If they had been consulted in the creation of the universe, and in the management of human affairs, all would have been far better than it is! Now, all depends upon the end in view. The scientific man would make an optical instrument which should serve as both microscope and telescope—a far more marvellous construction than the eye. The pleasure-seeker would eliminate pain and sorrow from human life, and would make it one prolonged rapture of enjoyment. But the Creator had no intention of making an instrument which should supersede human inventions; his aim was the production of a working, everyday, useful organ of vision. The Lord of all never aimed at making life one long series of gratification; he designed life to be a moral discipline, in which suffering, weakness, and distress fulfil their own service of ministering to man's highest welfare. For the purposes intended, God's work needs no apology and admits of no improvement.
II. GOD'S WORK IS ETERNAL. All men's works are both unstable and transitory. Fresh ends are ever being approved and sought by fresh means. The laws of nature know no change; the principles of moral government are the same from age to age. When we learn to distrust our own fickleness, and to weary of human uncertainty and mutability, then we fall back upon the unchanging counsels of him who is from everlasting to everlasting.
III. GOD'S WORK HAS A PURPOSE WITH REFERENCE TO MAN. What God has done in this world he has done for the benefit of his spiritual family. Everything that is may be regarded as the vehicle of communication between the creating and the created mind. The intention of God is "that men should fear before him," *i.e.* venerate and glorify him. Our human probation and education as moral and accountable beings is his aim. Hence the obligation on our part to observe, inquire, and consider, to reverence, serve, and obey, and thus consciously and voluntarily secure the ends for which the Creator designed and fashioned us.—T.

Vers. 16, 17.—*Man's unrighteousness contrasted with God's righteousness.* Every observant, judicial, and sensitive mind shares this experience. Human society, civil relations, cannot be contemplated without much of disapproval, disappointment, and distress. And who, when so affected by the spectacle which this world presents, can do other than raise his thoughts to that Being, to those relationships that are characterized by a moral excellence which corresponds to our highest ideal, our purest aspirations?
I. THE PREVALENCE OF WICKEDNESS UPON EARTH AND AMONG MEN. The observation of the wise man was naturally directed to the state of society in his own times and in his own and of the neighbouring countries. Local and temporal peculiarities do not, however, destroy the applicability of the principle to human life generally. Wickedness was and is discernible wherever man is found. Unconscious nature obeys physical laws,

brute nature obeys automatic and instinctive impulse. But man is a member of a rational and spiritual system, whose principles he often violates in the pursuit of lower ends. In the earliest ages "the wickedness of man was great in the earth, and every imagination of the thoughts of his heart was only evil continually." A remedial system has checked and to some extent counteracted these evil tendencies; yet to how large an extent is the same reflection just!

II. WICKEDNESS, IN THE FORM OF INJUSTICE, PREVAILS EVEN WHERE JUSTICE SHOULD BE IMPARTIALLY ADMINISTERED. It is well known that in every age complaints have been made of the venality of Eastern magistrates. In the Old Testament references are frequent to the "gifts," the bribes, by which suitors sought to obtain decisions in their favour. Corruption here is worse than elsewhere, for it is discouraging to uprightness, and lowers the tone of public morals. We may be grateful that, in our own land and in our own day, such corruption is unknown—that our judges are above even temptation to bribery. But the fact has to be faced that injustice, whether from motives of malice or from motives of avarice, has existed widely in human communities.

III. THE UNIVERSAL JUDGMENT OF A RIGHTEOUS GOD. The atheist has no refuge from such observations and reflections as those recorded in ver. 16. But the godly man turns from earth to heaven, and rests in the conviction that there is a Divine and righteous Judge, to whose tribunal all men must come, and by whose just decisions every destiny must be decided. 1. All characters, the righteous and the wicked alike, will be judged by the Lord of all. Has the unjust escaped the penalty due from a human tribunal? He shall not escape the righteous judgment of God. Has the innocent been unjustly sentenced by an earthly and perhaps corrupt judge? There is for him a court of appeal, and his righteousness shall shine as the noonday. 2. All kinds of works shall meet with retribution; not only the acts of private life, but also acts of a judicial and governmental kind. The unjust judge shall meet with his recompense, and the wronged and persecuted shall not be unavenged.—T.

Vers. 18—21.—*The common destiny of death.* The double nature of man has been recognized by every student of human nature. The sensationalist and materialist lays stress upon the physical side of our humanity, and endeavours to show that the intellect and the moral sentiments are the outgrowth of the bodily life, the nervous structure and its susceptibilities and its powers of movement. But such efforts fail to convince alike the unsophisticated and the philosophic. It is generally admitted that it would be more reasonable to resolve the physical into the psychical than the psychical into the physical. The author of Ecclesiastes was alive to the animal side of man's nature; and if some only of his expressions were considered, he might be claimed as a supporter of the baser philosophy. But he himself supplies the counteractive. The attentive reader of the book is convinced that the author traced the human spirit to its Divine original, and looked forward to its immortality.

I. THE COMMUNITY OF MEN WITH BEASTS IN THE ANIMAL NATURE AND LIFE. If we look upon one side of our humanity, it appears that we are to be reckoned among the brutes that perish. The similarity is obvious in: 1. The corporeal, fleshly constitution with which man and brute are alike endowed. 2. The brevity of the earthly life appointed for both without distinction. 3. The resolution of the body into dust.

II. THE SUPERIORITY OF MEN OVER BEASTS IN THE POSSESSION OF A SPIRITUAL AND IMPERISHABLE NATURE AND LIFE. It is difficult for us to treat this subject without bringing to bear upon it the knowledge which we have derived from the fuller and more glorious revelation of the new covenant. "Christ has abolished death, and has brought life and immortality to light by the gospel." We cannot possibly think of such themes without taking to their consideration the convictions and the hopes which we have derived from the incarnate Son of God. Nor can we forget the sublime speculations of philosophers of both ancient and modern times. 1. In his spiritual nature man is akin to God. Physical life the Creator imparted to the animal organisms with which the world was peopled. But a life of quite another order was conferred upon man, who participates in the Divine reason, who is able to think the thoughts of God himself, and who has intuitions of moral goodness of which the brute creation is for ever incapable. Instead of man's mind being a function of organized matter, as a base sensationalism and empiricism is wont to affirm, the truth is that it is only as an expression and vehicle of thought, of reason, that matter has a dependent existence.   2. In his consequent immortality man is distinguished from the inferior animals.   The life possessed by these latter is a life of sensation and of movement; the organism is resolved into its constituents, and there is no reason to believe that the sensation and movement are perpetuated.   But "the spirit of man goeth upward;" it has used its instrument, the body, and the time comes—appointed by God's inscrutable providence—when the connection, local and temporary, which the spirit has maintained with earth, is sundered.   In what other scenes and pursuits the conscious being is continued, we cannot tell.   But there is not the slightest reason for conceiving the spiritual life to be dependent upon the organism which it uses as its instrument.   The spiritual life is the life of God; and the life of God is perishable.

> "The sun is but a spark of fire,
>   A transient meteor in the sky;
> The soul, immortal as its Sire,
>   Can never die."
>
>   T.

Ver. 22.—*The earthly portion.*   When a man is, perhaps suddenly, awakened to a sense of the transitoriness of life and the vanity of human pursuits, what more natural than that, under the influence of novel conceptions and convictions, he should rush from a career of self-indulgence into the opposite extreme?   Life is brief: why concern one's self with its affairs?   Sense-experiences are changeable and perishable: why not neglect and despise them?   Earth will soon vanish: why endeavour to accommodate ourselves to its conditions?   But subsequent reflection convinces us that such practical inferences are unjust.   Because this earth and this life are not everything, it does not follow that they are nothing.   Because they cannot satisfy us, it does not follow that we should not use them.

I. IT IS POSSIBLE TO LIMIT OUR VIEW OF THIS EARTHLY LIFE UNTIL IT LOSES ITS INTEREST FOR US.   1. Man's works, to the observant and reflecting mind, are perishable and poor.   2. Man's joys are often both superficial and transitory.   3. The future of human existence and progress upon earth is utterly uncertain, and, if it could be foreseen, would probably occasion bitter disappointment.

II. IT IS UNWISE AND UNSATISFACTORY SO TO LIMIT OUR VIEW OF LIFE.   There is true wisdom in the wise man's declaration, "There is nothing better than that a man should rejoice in his works; for that is his portion."   The epicurean is wrong who makes pleasure his one aim.   The cynic is wrong who despises pleasure as something beneath the dignity of his nature.   Neither work nor enjoyment is the whole of life; for life is not to be understood save in relation to spiritual and disciplinary purposes. Man has for a season a bodily nature; let him use that nature with discretion, and it may prove organic to his moral welfare.   Man is for a season stationed upon earth; let him fulfil earth's duties, and taste earth's delights.   Earthly experience may be a stage towards heavenly service and bliss.—T.

Vers. 1—10.— *Opportunity; opportuneness; ordination.*   This view of life embraces—

I. OPPORTUNITY, OR THE WISDOM OF WAITING.   Everything comes in its turn; if we weep to-day, we shall laugh to-morrow; if we have to be silent for the present, we shall have the opportunity of speech further on; if we must strive now, the time of peace will return.   Human life is neither unshadowed brightness nor unbroken gloom. "Shadow and shine is life . . . flower and thorn."   Let no man be seriously discouraged, much less hopelessly disheartened: what he is now suffering from will not always remain; it will pass and give place to that which is better.   Let us only patiently wait our time, and our turn will come.   "Weeping may endure for a night, but joy cometh in the morning"—at any rate, and at the furthest, in the morning of eternity.   Only let us wait in patience and in prayerful hope, doing all that we can do in the paths of duty and of service, and the hour of opportunity will arrive.

> '. . . with succeeding turns God tempers all,
> That man may hope to rise, yet fear to fall."

II. OPPORTUNENESS. The words of the text may suggest to us, though the thought may not have been in the writer's mind, that some things are good or otherwise according to their timeliness. There is a time to speak in the way of rebuking, or of jesting, or of contending, and, when well-timed, such words may be right and wise in a very high degree; but, if ill-timed, they would be wrong and foolish, and much to be condemned. The same thought is applicable to the demonstration of friendliness, or of any strong emotion (vers. 5, 7); to the exercise of severity or of leniency (ver. 3); to the manifestation of sorrow or of joy (ver. 4); to the action of economy or of generosity (ver. 6). Hard-and-fast rules will not cover the infinite particulars of human life. Whether we shall act or be passive, whether we shall speak or be silent, what shall be our demeanour and what the tone we shall take,—this must depend upon particular circumstances and a number of new combinations; and every man must judge for himself, and must remember that there is great virtue in opportuneness.

III. ORDINATION. There is a season, an "appointed time for every undertaking" (Cox). "What profit hath he that worketh," when all this "travail" with which "the sons of men" are exercised results in such fixed and inevitable changes? That is the spirit of the moralist here. We reply: 1. That it is indeed true that much is already appointed for us. We have no power, or but little, over the seasons and the elements of nature, and not very much (individually) over the institutions and customs of the land in which we live; we are compelled to conform our behaviour to forces which are superior to our own. 2. But there is a very large remainder of freedom. Within the lines that are laid down by the ordination of Heaven or the "powers that be" on the earth, there is ample scope for free, wise, life-giving choice of action. We are free to choose our own conduct, to form our own character, to determine the complexion and aspect of our life in the sight of God, to decide upon our destiny.—C.

Ver. 11.—"*This unintelligible world.*" How shall we solve all those great problems which continually confront us, which baffle and bewilder us, which sometimes drive us to the very verge of distraction or even of unbelief? The solution is partly found in—

I. A WIDE VIEW OF THE WORTH OF PRESENT THINGS. If we look long and far, we shall see that, though many things have an ugly aspect at first sight, God "has made everything beautiful in its time." The light and warmth of summer are good to see and feel; but is not the cold of winter invigorating? and what is more beautiful to the sight than the untrodden snow? The returning life of spring is welcome to all hearts; but are not the brilliant hues of autumn fascinating to every eye? Youth is full of ardour, and manhood of strength; but declining years possess much richness of gathered wisdom, and there is a dignity, a calm, a reverence, in age which is all its own. There is a joy in battle as well as a pleasantness in peace. Wealth has its treasures; but poverty has little to lose, and therefore little cause for anxiety and trouble. Luxury brings many comforts, but hardness gives health and strength. Each climate upon the earth, every condition in life, the various dispositions and temperaments of the human soul,—these have their own particular advantage and compensation. Look on the other side, and you will see something that will please, if it does not satisfy.

II. THE HELP WE GAIN FROM THE GREAT ELEMENT OF FUTURITY. "Also he hath set eternity" (marginal reading, Revised Version) "in their heart." We are made to look far beyond the boundary of the visible and the present. The idea of "the eternal" may help us in two ways. 1. That we are created for the unseen and the eternal accounts for the fact that nothing which is earthly and sensible will satisfy our souls. Nothing of that order *ought* to do so; and it would put the seal upon our degradation if it *did* so. Our unsatisfiable spirit is the signature of our manhood and the prophecy of our immortality. 2. The inclusion of the future in our reasoning makes all the difference to our thought. Admit only the passing time, this brief and uncertain life, and much that happens is inexplicable and distressing indeed; but include the future, add "eternity" to the account, and the "crooked is made straight," the perplexity is gone. But, even with this aid, there is—

III. THE MYSTERY WHICH REMAINS, AND WILL REMAIN. "No man can find out," etc. We do well to remember that what we see is only a very small part indeed of the whole—only a page of the great volume, only a scene in the great drama, only a field of the large landscape—and we may well be silenced, if not convinced. But even that does not cover everything. We need to remember that we are human, and not Divine; that we, who are God's very little children, cannot hope to understand all that is in the mind of our heavenly Father—cannot expect to fathom his holy purpose, to read his unfathomable thoughts. We see enough of Divine wisdom, holiness, and love to believe that, when our understanding is enlarged and our vision cleared, we shall find that " all the paths of the Lord were mercy and truth "—even those which most troubled and bewildered us when we dwelt upon the earth.—C.

Vers. 12, 13, 22 (with ch. ii. 24).—*The conclusion of folly or the faith of the wise?* In what catalogue shall we place these words of the text? On whose lips are they to be found? Are they—

I. THE REFUGE OF THE SCEPTIC? They may be such. The epicure who has lost his faith in God says, " Let us eat and drink; for to-morrow we die." There is no sacredness in the present, and no solid hope for the future. What is the use of aiming at a high ideal? Why waste breath and strength on duty, on aspiration, on piety? Why attempt to rise to the pursuit of the eternal and the Divine? Better lose ourselves in that which is at hand, in that which we can grasp as a present certainty. The best thing, the only certain good, is to eat and drink and to labour; is to minister to our senses, and to work upon the material which is visible to our eye and responsive to our touch. So speaks the sceptic; this is his miserable conclusion; thus he owns himself defeated and (we may say) dishonoured. For what is human life worth when the element of sacredness is expunged, when piety and hope are left out of it? It is no wonder that the ages of unbelief have been the times when men have had no regard for other people's dues, and very little for their own. Or shall we rather find here—

II. AN ARTICLE OF A WISE MAN'S FAITH? It is not certain what was the mood in which the Preacher wrote; but let us prefer to think that behind his words, actuating and inspiring him, was a true spirit of faith in God and in Divine providence; let us take him to mean—what we know to be true—that, in spite of all evidence to the contrary, a wise and loyal-hearted man will hold that there is much that is worth pursuing and possessing in the simple pleasures, in the daily duties, and in the ordinary services which are open to us all. 1. Daily God invites us to eat and drink, to partake of the bounties of his hand; let us appreciate his benefits with moderation and gratitude. 2. Daily he bids us go forth to " our work and to our labour until the evening;" let us enter upon it and carry it out in the spirit of conscientiousness and fidelity toward both God and man (Col. iii. 23). 3. Daily God gives us the means of getting good to ourselves and doing good to others; let us eagerly embrace our opportunity, let us gladly avail ourselves of our privilege; so doing we shall make our life peaceful, happy, worthy.

In the light that shines into our hearts from the truth of Christ we judge: 1. That these lesser things—pleasure, activity, acquisition—are well in their way and in their measure. " Bodily exercise profiteth a little." But: 2. That human life has possibilities and obligations which immeasurably transcend these things; such, that to put these into the front rank and to fill our life with them is a fatal error. Made subordinate to that which is higher, they take their place and they render their service—a place and a service not to be despised; but made primary and supreme, they are usurpers that do untold injury, and that must be relentlessly dethroned.—C.

Vers. 14, 15.—*Divine constancy and human piety.* With the outer world of nature and with our human nature and character before us, these words may somewhat surprise us; it is necessary to take a preliminary view of—

I. HUMAN ACTION UPON THE DIVINE. 1. There is a sense in which man has *modified* the Divine action according to the Divine purpose. God has given us the material, and he says to us, " Work with it and upon it; mould, fashion, transform, develop it as you will; make all possible use of it for bodily comfort, for mental enlargement, for social enjoyment, for spiritual growth." Man has made large use of this his opportunity, and, with the advance of knowledge and of science, he will make much more in the centuries to come. He cannot indeed " put to " or " take from " the substance with which God supplies him, but he can do much to change its form and to determine the service it shall render. 2. There is a sense in which man has *temporarily thwarted* the Divine idea. For is not all sin, and are not all the dire consequences of sin, a sad and serious departure from the purpose of the Holy One? Surely infidelity, blasphemy, vice, cruelty, crime; surely poverty, misery, starvation, death;— all this is not what the heavenly Father meant for his human children when he breathed into man's nostrils the breath of life. But the leading idea of the text is—

II. THE PERMANENCY OF THE DIVINE THOUGHT. This truth includes: 1. *The fixedness of the Divine purpose.* "The counsel of the Lord standeth for ever, the thoughts of his heart to all generations" (Ps. xxxiii. 11). We believe that from the beginning God intended to work out the righteousness and the blessedness of the human race; and whatever has come between him and the realization of his gracious end will be cleared away. Man will one day be all that the Eternal One designed that he should become. 2. *The constancy of the Divine Law.* The same great moral laws, and the same physical laws also, which governed the action and the destiny of men in primeval times still prevail, and will always abide. Sin has meant suffering and sorrow, righteousness has worked out well-being and joy; diligence has been followed by fruitfulness, and idleness by destitution; generosity has been recompensed with love, and selfishness with leanness of soul, etc. As it was at the beginning, so will it be with the action of all Divine laws, even to the end. 3. *The permanency of the Divine attitude.* (1) What God always felt toward sin he feels to-day; it is the thing which he hates. In Jesus Christ, as fully and as emphatically as in the Law, his holy intolerance of sin is revealed, his Divine determination to conquer and to destroy it. (2) What God always felt toward the sinner he feels to-day—a Divine grief and an infinite compassion; a readiness to forgive and to restore the penitent.

III. THE DIVINE DESIGN. "God doeth it, that men should fear before him." God's one unchanging desire is that his children should live a reverential, holy life before him. All the manifestations of his character that he gives us are intended to lead up to and issue in this. And surely the Divine constancy is calculated to promote this as nothing else would. It is God's desire and his design concerning us, because he knows (1) that it is the only right relationship for us to sustain; and (2) that it is the one condition of peace, purity, blessedness, life.—C.

Vers. 18—21.—*Before and after Christ.* These words have a strange sound in our ears; they evidently do not belong to New Testament times. They bring before us—

I. MAN'S UNENLIGHTENED CONCEPTION OF HIMSELF. It is evidently possible that, under certain conditions, men may judge themselves to be of no nobler nature than that of "the beasts that perish." It may be (1) bodily suffering or weakness; or (2) untoward and disappointing circumstances; or (3) bewilderment of mind after vain endeavours to solve great spiritual problems; or (4) the distracted and unnatural state of the society in which we are placed (see Cox's 'Quest of the Chief Good'); but, owing to some one of many possible causes, men may be driven to take the lowest view of human nature; so much so that they may lose all respect for themselves—may shut the future life entirely out of view, and live in the narrow circle of the present; may confine their ambition and aspiration to bodily enjoyment and the excitements of present occupation; may practically own themselves to be defeated, and go blindly on, 'hoping nothing, believing nothing, and fearing nothing." Such a melancholy conclusion (1) does us sad dishonour; (2) has a demoralizing influence on character and life; (3) yields a wretched harvest of despair and self-destruction. In most happy contrast with this is—

II. THE VIEW OF OUR NATURE WHICH CHRIST HAS GIVEN US. He asks us to think how "much a man is better than a sheep," and reminds us that we are "of more value than many sparrows." He bids us realize that one human soul is worth more than "the whole world," and that there is nothing so costly that it will represent its value. He reveals to us the supreme and most blessed fact that each human spirit is the object of Divine solicitude, and may find a home in the Father's heart of love at once, and in his nearer presence soon. He assures us that there is a glorious future before every man that becomes the subject of his kingdom, and serves faithfully to the end. Under his teaching, instead of seeing that "they themselves are beasts," his disciples find themselves "children of their Father who is in heaven," "kings and priests unto God," "heirs of eternal life." Coming after Christ, and learning of him, we see that we are capable of a noble heritage now, and move toward a still nobler estate a little further on.—C.

Vers. 1—8.—*Opportuneness.* Our author makes a fresh start. He drops the auto-biographical style of the first two chapters, and casts his thoughts into the form of aphorisms, based not merely upon the reminiscences of his own life, but upon the experi-ence of all men. He gives a long list of the events, actions, emotions, and feelings which go to make up human life, and asserts of them that they are governed by fixed laws above our knowledge, out of our control. The time of our entrance into the world, the condition of life in which we are placed, are determined for us by a higher will than our own, and the same sovereign power fixes the moment of our departure from life; and in like manner all that is done, enjoyed, and suffered between birth and death is governed by forces which we cannot bend or mould, or even fully understand. That there is a fixed order in the events of life is, to a certain extent, an instinctive belief which we all hold. The thought of an untimely birth or of an untimely death shocks us as something con-trary to our sense of that which is fit and becoming, and those crimes by which either is caused are generally regarded as specially repulsive. Yet there is an appointed season for the other incidents of life, though less clearly manifest to us. Our wisdom lies, not in mere acquiescence in the events of life, but in knowing our duty for the time. The circumstances in which we are placed are so fluctuating, and the conditions in the midst of which we find ourselves are so varying, that a large space is left for us to exercise our discretion, to discern that which is opportune, and to do the right thing at the right time. The first class of events alluded to, the time of birth and the time of death, is that of those which are involuntary; they are events with which there can be no interference without the guilt of gross and exceptional wickedness. The actions and emotions that follow are voluntary, they are within our power, though the circumstances that call them forth at a precise time are not. The relations of life which are determined for us by a higher power give us the opportunity for playing our part, and we either succeed or fail according as we take advantage of the time or neglect it. The catalogue given of the events, actions, and emotions which make up life seems to be drawn up with-out any logical order; the various items are apparently taken capriciously as examples of those things that occupy men's time and thoughts, and at first sight the teaching of our author does not seem to be of a distinctively spiritual character. To a superficial reader it might appear as if we had not in it much more than the commonplace prudence to be found in the maxims and proverbs current in every country: "Take time by the forelock;" "He that will not when he may, when he would he shall have nay;" "Time and tide wait for no man," etc. But we are taught by Christ himself that knowing how to act opportunely is a large part of that wisdom which is needed for our salvation. He himself came to earth in the "fulness of time" (Gal. iv. 4), when the Jewish people and the nations of the world were prepared by Divine discipline for his teaching and work (Acts xvii. 30, 31; Luke ii. 30, 31). The purpose of the mission of John the Baptist, calcu-lated as it was to lead men to godly sorrow for sin, was in harmony with the austerity of his life and the sternness of his exhortations. It was a time to mourn (Matt. xi. 18). The purpose of Christ's own mission was to reconcile the world to God and to manifest the Father to men, so that joy was becoming in his disciples (Mark ii. 18—20). He taught that there was a time to lose, when all possessions that would alienate the heart from him should be parted with (Mark x. 21, 23); and that there would be a time of gain, when in heaven the accumulated treasures would become an abiding possession (Matt. vi. 19, 20). "That which the Preacher insists on is the thought that the circumstances and events of life form part of a Divine order, are not things that come at random, and that wisdom, and therefore such a measure of happiness as is attainable, lies in adapting ourselves to the order, and accepting the guidance of events in great things and small, while shame and confusion come from resisting it." But such teaching is applicable, as we have seen, to the conduct of our spiritual as well as of our secular concerns. The fact that there are great changes through which we must pass in order to be duly pre-pared for the heavenly state, that we may have to forfeit the temporal to secure the eternal, that the new life has new duties for the discernment and fulfilment of which all our powers and faculties need to be called into full exercise—should make us earnestly desire to be filled with this wisdom that prompts to opportune action. "If any of you lack wisdom," says St. James, "let him ask of God, that giveth to all men liberally, and upbraideth not; and it shall be given him" (i. 5).—J. W.

Vers. 9—11.—*Desiderium æternitatis.* The thought of there being a fixed order in the events of life, of laws governing the world which man cannot fully understand or control, brings with it no comfort to the mind of this Jewish philosopher. It rather, in his view, increases the difficulty of playing one's part successfully. Who can be sure that he has hit upon the right course to follow, the opportune time at which to act? Do not "the fixed phenomena" and "iron laws of life" render human effort fruitless and disappointing? Another conclusion is drawn from the same facts by a higher Teacher. We cannot by taking thought alter the conditions of our lives, and should, therefore, Christ has taught us, place our trust in our heavenly Father, who governs all things, and whose love for the creatures he has made is seen in his feeding the birds and clothing with beauty the flowers of the field (Matt. vi. 25—34). The anxiety which the thought of human weakness in the presence of the immutable laws of nature excites is charmed away by the consolatory teaching of Jesus. But no solution is given of the difficulties that occasioned it. These will always exist as they spring from the limitations of our nature. We are finite creatures, and God is infinite. We endure but for a few years; he is from everlasting to everlasting. Our apprehension of these facts, of infinitude and eternity, prevents our being satisfied with that which is finite and temporal. "God has set eternity" (*vide* Revised Version margin) "in our hearts." Though we are limited by time, we are related to eternity. "That which is transient yields us no support; it carries us on like a rushing stream, and constrains us to save ourselves by laying hold on eternity" (Delitzsch). We cannot rest satisfied with fragmentary knowledge, but strive to pass on from it to the great worlds of truth yet undiscovered and unknown; we would see the whole of God's work from beginning to end (ver. 1), and find ourselves precluded from accomplishing our desire. From Solomon's point of view, in which the possibility or certainty of a future life is not taken into account, this *desiderium æternitatis* is only another of the illusions by which the soul of man is vexed. But we should contradict our better knowledge, and ungratefully neglect the Divine aids to faith which have been given us in the fuller revelation of the New Testament, if we were to cherish the same opinion. Dissatisfaction with the finite and the temporal is not a morbid feeling in those who believe that they have an immortal nature, and that they are yet to come into "an inheritance incorruptible, and undefiled, and that fadeth not away" (1 Pet. i. 4).—J. W.

Vers. 12, 13.—*Another condition of pure happiness.* In these words we have a repetition of the conclusion already announced (ch. ii. 24) as to the method by which some measure of happiness can be secured by man, but there is a very important addition made to the former declaration. Our author is referring to temporal things, and tells the secret by which the happiness they may procure for us is to be won. It consists of two particulars: (1) a cheerful enjoyment of the gifts of God, and (2) a benevolent use of them. This latter is the addition to which I have referred. It is a distinct advance upon the previous utterance, as it introduces the idea of an unselfish use of the gifts which God has bestowed upon us—an employment of them for the benefit of others less fortunately circumstanced than ourselves. "Over and above the life of honest labour and simple joys which had been recognized as good before, the seeker has learnt that 'doing good' is in some sense the best way of getting good" (Plumptre). It may be that beneficence is only a part of what is meant by "doing good," but in the connection in which the phrase is here employed it must be a large part, because it evidently suggests something more as desirable than a selfish enjoyment of the good things of life. This twofold duty of accepting with gratitude the gifts of God and of applying them to good uses was prescribed by the Law of Moses (Deut. xxvi. 1—14); and, to a truly pious mind, the one part of the duty will suggest the other. The thought that God in his bounty has enriched us, who are unworthy of the least of all his mercies, will lead us to be compassionate to those who are in want, and we shall find in relieving their necessities the purest and most exquisite of all joys. We shall in this way discover for ourselves the truth of that saying of our Lord's, "It is more blessed to give than to receive" (Acts xx. 35). While those who selfishly keep all they have for themselves find that, however their goods increase, their satisfaction in them cannot be increased—nay, rather that it rapidly diminishes. Hence it is that the apostle counsels the rich "to do good, to be rich in good works, to be ready to distribute, willing to communicate" (1 Tim. vi. 17—19). The general teaching of the Scriptures, therefore, is in harmony with the results of our own experience, and leads to the same conclusion, that "doing good" is a condition of pure happiness.—J. W.

Vers. 14—17.—An argument in support of the statement that *a present use and enjoyment of the gifts of God is advisable*, is found in the fact of the unchangeable character of the Divine purposes and government. He who has given may take away, and none can stay his hand. While, therefore, we are in possession of benefits he has bestowed on us, we should get the good of them, seeing that we know not how long we shall have them. Exception has been taken to this teaching. "The lesson to cheerfulness under such bidding seems a hard one. Men have recited it over the wine-cup in old times and new, in East and West. But the human heart, with such shadows gathering in the background, has recognized its hollowness, and again and again has put back the anodyne from its lips" (Bradley). But though the thought of the Divine unchangeableness may be regarded by some as a stimulus to a reckless enjoyment of the present, it is calculated to have a wholesome influence upon our views of life, and upon our conduct. Acquiescence in one's lot, and reverential fear of God, leading to an avoidance of sin, are naturally suggested by it. The conviction that the will of God is righteous will prevent acquiescence in it becoming that apathetic resignation which characterizes the spirit of those who believe that over all the events of life an iron destiny rules, against which men strive in vain.

I. THE CHARACTER OF THE DIVINE GOVERNMENT. (Ver. 14.) It is eternal and unalterable. In the phenomena of the natural world, we see it manifested in laws which man cannot control or change; in the providential government of human affairs, the same rule of a higher Power over all the events of life is discernible; and in the revelations of the Divine will, recorded in the Scriptures, we see steady progress to an end foreseen and foretold from the beginning. What God does stands fast; no created power can nullify or change it (Ps. xxiii. 11; Isa. xlvi. 9, 10; Dan. iv. 35).

II. THE EFFECT WHICH THIS UNCHANGEABLENESS SHOULD PRODUCE. (Ver. 14*b*.) "That men should fear before him." It should fill our heart with reverence. This is, indeed, the purpose for which God has given this revelation of himself, and no other view of the Divine character is calculated to produce the same effect. The thought of God's infinite *power* would not impress us in like manner if at the same time we believed that his will was variable, that it could be propitiated and changed. But the conviction that his will is righteous and immutable should lead us to "sanctify him in our hearts, and make him our Fear and our Dread" (Isa. viii. 13), and give us hope and confidence in the midst of the vicissitudes of life (Mal. iii. 6). In the earlier part of his work (ch. i. 9, 10) the Preacher had dwelt upon the uniformity of sequence in nature, as if he were impressed with a sense of monotony, as he watched the course of events happening and recurring in the same order. And now, as he looks upon human history, he sees the same regularity in the order of things. "That which hath been is now, and that which is to be hath already been." But the former feeling of weariness and oppression is modified by the thought of God's perfection, and by the "fear" which it excites. He recognizes the fact of a personal will governing the events of history. It is no mechanical process of revolution that causes the repetition time after time of similar events, the same causes producing the same effects; no wheel of destiny alternately raising and depressing the fortunes of men. It is God who recalls, "who seeks again that which is passed away" (ver. 15*b*). "The past is thought of as vanishing, put to flight, receding into the dim distance. It might seem to be passing into the abyss of oblivion; but God recalls it, brings back the same order, or an analogous order of events, and so history repeats itself" (Plumptre). And out of this belief in God's wise providence a healthy spirit should gather strength to bear patiently and cheerfully the difficulties and trials of life. The belief that our life is governed by an unalterable law is calculated, as I have said, to lead to a listless, hopeless state of mind, in which one ceases to strive against the inevitable. But that state of mind is very different from the resignation of those who believe that the government of the world is regular and unchangeable, because unerring wisdom guides him who is the Creator and Preserver of all things. Their faith can sustain them in the greatest trials, when God's ways seem most inscrutable; they can hope against hope, and, in spite of all apparent contradictions, believe that "all things work together for good to them that love God."—J. W.

Vers. 18—22.—*The darkness of the grave.* In these words our author reaches the very lowest depth of misery and despair. His observation of the facts of human life leads him to the humiliating conclusion that it is almost hopeless to assign to man a higher nature and a more noble destiny than those which belong to the beasts that perish. The moral inequalities of the world, the injustice that goes unpunished, the hopes by which men are deluded, the uncertainty of life, the doubtfulness of immortality, seem to justify the assertion "that a man hath no pre-eminence over a beast." The special point of comparison on which he dwells is the common mortality of both. Man and beast are possessed of bodies composed of the same elements, nourished by the same food, liable to the same accidents, and destined to return to the kindred dust from which they sprang. Both are ignorant of the period of life assigned to them; a moment before the stroke of death falls on them they may be unconscious that evil is at hand, and when they realize the fact they are equally powerless to avert it. What there is in common between them is manifest to all, while the evidence to be adduced in favour of the superiority of man is, from its very nature, less convincing. The spiritually minded will attach great weight to arguments against which the natural reason may draw up plausible objections. Let us, then, see the case stated at its very worst, and consider if there are any redeeming circumstances which are calculated to relieve the gloom which a cursory reading of the words calls up.

I. The *first* statement is that MEN, LIKE BEASTS, ARE CREATURES OF ACCIDENT. (Ver. 19*a*.) Not that they are both the results of blind chance; but that, "being conditioned by circumstances over which there can be no control, they are subject, in respect to their whole being, actions, and sufferings, as far as mere human observation can extend, to the law of chance, and are alike destined to undergo the same fate, *i.e.* death" (Wright). A parallel to the thought of this verse is to be found in the very striking words of Solon to Crœsus (Herodotus, i. 32), "Man is altogether a chance;" and in Ps. xlix. 14, 20, "Like sheep they are laid in the grave. . . . Man that is in honour, and understandeth not, is like the beasts that perish."

II. The *second* statement is that AS IS THE DEATH OF THE ONE, SO IS THE DEATH OF THE OTHER (ver. 19*b*), for in both is the breath of life, and this departs from them in like manner. So that any superiority on the part of man over the beast is incredible in the face of this fact, that death annuls distinctions between them. One resting-place receives them all at last—the earth from which they sprang (ver. 20). A belief in the immortality of the soul of man would at once have relieved the gloom, and convinced the Preacher that the humiliating comparison he institutes only reaches to a certain point, and is based upon the external accidents of human life, and that the true dignity and value of human nature remain unaffected by the mortality of the corporeal part of our being. "Put aside the belief in the prolongation of existence after death, that what has been begun here may be completed, and what has gone wrong here may be set right, and man is but a more highly organized animal, the 'cunningest of nature's clocks,' and the high words which men speak as to his greatness are found hollow. They too are 'vanity.' He differs from the brutes around him only, or chiefly, in having, what they have not, the burden of unsatisfied desires, the longing after an eternity which after all is denied him" (Plumptre).

III. The *third* statement is the saddest of all—that of THE UNCERTAINTY OF KNOWLEDGE AS TO WHETHER, AFTER ALL, THERE IS THIS HIGHER ELEMENT IN HUMAN NATURE—"a spirit that at death goeth upward"—or whether the living principles of both man and beast perish when their bodies are laid in the dust (ver. 21). It is quite fruitless to deny that it is a sceptical question that is asked—If the spirit of the beast goeth downward to the earth, who knows that that of man goeth upward? Attempts have been made to obliterate the scepticism of the passage, as may be seen in the Massoretic punctuation followed in the Authorized Version of our English Bible, but departed from in the Revised Version, "Who knoweth the spirit of man that goeth upward," etc.? as though an ascent of the spirit to a higher life were affirmed. The rendering of the four principal versions, and of all the best critics, convinces us that it is indeed a sceptical question as to the immortality of the soul that is here asked. A very similar passage is found in the great poem of Lucretius (i. 113—116)—

> "We know not what the nature of the soul,
> Or born or entering into men at birth,
> Or whether with our frame it perisheth,
> Or treads the gloom and regions vast of death."

It is to be noted, however, about both the question of the Preacher and the words of the heathen poet, that they do not contain a denial of immortality, but a longing after more knowledge resting on sufficient grounds. Sad and depressing as uncertainty on such a point is to a sensitive mind, a denial of immortality would be infinitely worse; it would mean the death of all hope. The very suggestion of a higher life for man, after "this mortal coil has been shuffled off," than for the beast implies that, far from denying the immortality of the soul, the writer seeks for adequate ground on which to hold it. Arguments in favour of the doctrine of immortality were not wanting to the Preacher. He has just spoken of the *desiderium æternitatis* implanted in the heart of man (ver. 11), which, like the instincts of the lower creation, is given by the Creator for our guidance, and not to tantalize and deceive us. The inequalities and evils of the present life render a final judgment in a world beyond the grave a moral necessity (ch. xii. 14). But still these are, after all, but indirect arguments, which have not the weight of positive demonstration. It is only faith that can return any certain reply to his doubting question; its weight, thrown into the balance, inclines it to the hopeful side. And this happy conclusion he reached at last, as he distinctly affirms in ch. xii. 7, "Then shall the dust return to the earth as it was: and the spirit shall return unto God who gave it." That the Preacher should ever have doubted this great truth, and spoken as though no certainty concerning it were within the reach of man, need not surprise us. In the revelation given to the Jewish people, the doctrine of rewards and punishments in a future state was not set forth. The rewards and punishments for obedience to the Law, and for transgressions against it, were all temporal. Almost nothing was communicated touching the existence of the soul after death. In the passage quoted by Christ in the Gospels, for the confutation of the Sadducees, who denied the resurrection, the doctrine of immortality is implied rather than stated (Matt. xxii. 23—32). And in a matter so far beyond the power of the human intellect to search out, the absence of a word of revelation rendered the darkness doubly obscure. It is, however, utterly monstrous for any of us now who believe in Christ to ask the question, "Who knoweth the spirit of man, whether it goeth upward?" The revelation given us by him is full of light on this point. "He hath brought life and immortality to light through the gospel" (2 Tim. i. 10). His own resurrection from the dead, and ascension to heaven is the proof of a life beyond the grave, and a pledge to all who believe in him of a future and an everlasting life. It was not wonderful that the Preacher, in the then stage of religious knowledge, should have spoken as he does here; but nothing could justify us, to whom so much fresh light has been given, in using his words, as though we were in the same condition with him.

IV. The *fourth* and concluding statement is, strangely enough, that since we know not what will come after death, A CHEERFUL ENJOYMENT OF THE PRESENT is the best course one can take. This is the third time he has given this counsel (ch. ii. 24; iii. 12, 13). A calm and happy life, healthy labour, and tranquil enjoyment, are to be valued and taken advantage of to the full. It is an epicureanism of a spiritual cast that he commends, and not the coarse and degraded animalism of those who say, "Let us eat and drink; for to-morrow we die." He recognizes the good gifts of the present as a "portion" given by God, and says—Rejoice in them, though the future be all unknown. The very gloom out of which his words spring give a dignity to them. "We feel that we are in the presence of one who has the germ given him of some courage, equanimity, and calmness, which may grow into other and better things. His spirit is torn by, suffers with, all the pangs that beset the inquiring human heart. He feels for all the woes of humanity; cannot put them by, and fly to the wine-cup and crown himself with garlands. He has hated life, yet he will not lose his courage. 'Be of good cheer,' he says, even in his dark hour; 'work on, and enjoy the fruits of work; it is thy portion. Do not curse God and die'" (Bradley). His words are not, as they might seem at first, frivolous and heartless. It is a calm and peaceful happiness, a life of honest endeavour and of single-hearted enjoyment of innocent pleasures, that he commends; and, after all, it is only by genuine faith in God that such a life is possible—a faith that enables one to rise above all that is dark and mysterious and perplexing in the world about us.—J. W.

EXPOSITION.

CHAPTER IV.

Vers. 1—16.—Section 5. Koheleth proceeds to give further illustrations of *man's inability to be the architect of his own happiness.* There are many things which interrupt or destroy it.

Vers. 1—3.—First of all, he adduces the oppression of man by his fellow-man.

Ver. 1.—**So I returned, and considered all the oppressions that are done under the sun.** This is equivalent to, "again I saw," as ver. 7, with a reference to the wickedness in the place of judgment which he had noticed in ch. iii. 16. *Ashukim*, "oppressions," is found in Job xxxv. 9 and Amos iii. 9, and, being properly a participle passive, denotes oppressed persons or things, and so abstractedly "oppressions." Τὰς συκοφαντίας (Septuagint); *calumnias* (Vulgate). The verb is used of high-handed injustice, of offensive selfishness, of the hindrances to his neighbour's well-being caused by a man's careless disregard of aught but his own interests (comp. 1 Sam. xii. 4; Hos. xii. 8, etc.). **Behold the tears of** such as were oppressed; τῶν συκοφαντουμένων (Septuagint); *innocentium* (Vulgate). He notes now not merely the fact of wrong being done, but its effect on the victim, and intimates his own pity for the sorrow. **And they had no comforter.** A sad refrain, echoed again at the end of the verse with touching pathos. Οὐκ ἔστιν αὐτοῖς παρακαλῶν (Septuagint); they had no earthly friends to visit them in their affliction, and they as yet knew not the soothing of the Holy Ghost, the Comforter (Παράκλητος). There was no one to wipe away their tears (Isa. xxv. 8) or to redress their wrongs. The point is the powerlessness of man in the face of these disorders, his inability to right himself, the incompetence of others to aid him. **On the side of their oppressors** there was **power** (*koach*), in a bad sense, like the Greek βία, equivalent to "violence." Thus the ungodly say, in the Book of Wisdom ii. 11, "Let our strength be the law of justice." Vulgate, *Nec posse resistere eorum*

violentiæ, cunctorum auxilio destitutos. It is difficult to suppose that the state of things revealed by this verse existed in the days of King Solomon, or that so powerful a monarch, and one admired for "judgment and justice" (1 Kings x. 9), would be content with complaining of such disorders instead of checking them. There is no token of remorse for past unprofitableness or anguish of heart at the thought of failure in duty. If we take the words as the utterance of the real Solomon, we do violence to history, and must correct the existing chronicles of his reign. The picture here presented is one of later times, and it may be of other countries. Persian rule, or the tyranny of the Ptolemies, might afford an original from which it might be taken.

Ver. 2.—In view of these patent wrongs Koheleth loses all enjoyment of life. **Wherefore (***and***) I praised the dead which are already dead;** or, *who died long ago,* and thus have escaped the miseries which they would have had to endure. It must, indeed, have been a bitter experience which elicited such an avowal. To die and be forgotten an Oriental would look upon as the most calamitous of destinies. **More than the living which are yet alive.** For these have before them the prospect of a long endurance of oppression and suffering (comp. ch. vii. 1; Job iii. 13, etc.). The Greek gnome says—

Κρεῖσσον τὸ μὴ ζῆν ἐστιν, ἢ ζῆν ἀθλίως.

"Better to die than lead a wretched life."

The Septuagint version is scarcely a rendering of our present text: "Above the living, as many as are living until now."

Ver. 3.—**Yea, better is he than both they, which hath not yet been.** Thus we have Job's passionate appeal (iii. 11), "Why died I not from the womb? why did I not give up the ghost when I came forth," etc.? And in the Greek poets the sentiment of the text is re-echoed. Thus Theognis, 'Parœn.,' 425—

Πάντων μὲν μὴ φῦναι ἐπιχθονίοισιν ἄριστον,
  Μηδ' ἐσιδεῖν αὐγὰς ὀξέος ἠελίου·
Φύντα δ', ὅπως ὤκιστα πύλας 'Αΐδαο περῆσαι,
  Καὶ κεῖσθαι πολλὴν γῆν ἐπαμησάμενον.

" 'Tis best for mortals never to be born,
Nor ever see the swift sun's burning rays;
Next best, when born, to pass the gates of
death
Right speedily, and rest beneath the
earth."

(Comp. Soph., 'Œd. Col.,' 1225—1228.)
Cicero, 'Tusc. Disp.,' i. 48, renders some
lines from a lost play of Euripides to the
same effect—

" Nam nos decebat, cætus celebrantes,
domum
Lugere, ubi esset aliquis in lucem editus,
Humanæ vitæ varia reputantes mala;
At qui labores morte finisset graves,
Hunc omni amicos laude et lætitia ex-
sequi."

Herodotus (v. 4) relates how some of the
Thracians had a custom of bemoaning a
birth and rejoicing at a death. In our own
Burial Service we thank God for delivering
the departed "out of the miseries of this
sinful world." Keble alludes to this barbarian custom in his poem on 'The Third
Sunday after Easter.' Speaking of a
Christian mother's joy at a child's birth, he
says—

" No need for her to weep
Like Thracian wives of yore,
Save when in rapture still and deep
Her thankful heart runs o'er.
They mourned to trust their treasure on
the main,
Sure of the storm, unknowing of their
guide:
Welcome to her the peril and the pain,
For well she knows the home where they
may safely hide."

(See on ch. vii. 1; comp. Gray's ode 'On a
Prospect of Eton College;' and for the
classical notion concerning life and death,
see Plato, 'Laches,' p. 195, D, *sqq.*;
'Gorgias,' p. 512, A.) The Buddhist religion does not recommend suicide as an escape
from the evils of life. It indeed regards man
as master of his own life; but it considers
suicide foolish, as it merely transfers a man's
position, the thread of life having to be
taken up again under less favourable circumstances. See 'A Buddhist Catechism,' by
Subhadra Bhikshu (London: Redway, 1890).
**Who hath not seen the evil work that is
done under the sun.** He repeats the words,
"under the sun," from ver. 1, in order to show
that he is speaking of facts that came under
his own regard—outward phenomena which
any thoughtful observer might notice (so
again ver. 7).

Vers. 4—6.—Secondly, success meets with
envy, and produces no lasting good to the
worker; yet, however unsatisfactory the result, man must continue to labour, as idleness is ruin.

**Ver. 4.—Again, I considered all travail,
and every right work.** The word rendered
"right" is *kishron* (see on ch. ii. 21), and
means rather "dexterity," "success." Koheleth says that he reflected upon the industry
that men exhibit, and the skill and dexterity
with which they ply their incessant toil.
There is no reference to moral rectitude in
the reflection, and the allusion to the ostra-
cism of Aristides for being called "Just" over-
shoots the mark ·(see Wordsworth, *in loc.*).
Septuagint, σύμπασαν ἀνδρίαν τοῦ ποιήματος,
" all manliness of his work." **That for this
a man is envied of his neighbour.** *Kinah*
may mean either "object of envy" or "envious rivalry;" *i.e.* the clause may be translated
as above, or, as in the Revised Version margin,
" it cometh of a man's rivalry with his neighbour." The Septuagint is ambiguous, Ὅτι
αὐτὸ ζῆλος ἀνδρὸς ἀπὸ τοῦ ἑταίρου αὐτοῦ, "That
this is a man's envy from his comrade;" Vulgate, *Industrias animadverti patere invidiæ
proximi*, " Lay open to a neighbour's envy."
In the first case the thought is that unusual
skill and success expose a man to envy and
ill will, which rob labour of all enjoyment.
In the second case the writer says that this
superiority and dexterity arise from a mean
motive, an envious desire to outstrip a neighbour, and, based on such low ground, can lead
to nothing but **vanity and vexation of spirit**,
a striving after wind. The former explanation seems more in accordance with Koheleth's gloomy view. Success itself is no
guarantee of happiness; the malice and ill
feeling which it invariably occasions are
necessarily a source of pain and distress.

Ver. 5.—The connection of this verse with
the preceding is this: activity, diligence,
and skill indeed bring success, but success
is accompanied by sad results. Should we,
then, sink into apathy, relinquish work, let
things slide? Nay, none but the fool (*kesil*),
the insensate, half-brutish man, doth this.
The fool foldeth his hands together. The
attitude expresses laziness and disinclination
for active labour, like that of the sluggard
in Prov. vi. 10. **And eateth his own flesh.**
Ginsburg, Plumptre, and others take these
words to mean "and yet eats his meat," *i.e.*
gets that enjoyment from his sluggishness
which is denied to active diligence. They
refer, in proof of this interpretation, to Exod.
xvi. 8; xxi. 28; Isa. xxii. 13; Ezek. xxxix.
17, in which passages, however, the phrase
is never equivalent to "eating his food."
The expression is really equivalent to
" destroys himself," "brings ruin upon himself." Thus we have in Ps. xxvii. 2, "Evil-
doers came upon me to eat up my flesh;"

and in Micah iii. 3, "Who eat the flesh of my people" (comp. Isa. xlix. 26). The sluggard is guilty of moral suicide; he takes no trouble to provide for his necessities, and suffers extremities in consequence. Some see in this verse and the following an objection and its answer. There is no occasion for this view, and it is not in keeping with the context; but it contains an intimation of the true exposition, which makes ver. 6 a proverbial statement of the sluggard's position. The verbs in the text are participial in form, so that the Vulgate rendering, which supplies a verb, is quite admissible: *Stultus complicat manus suas, et comedit carnes suas, dicens : Melior est*, etc.

Ver. 6.—**Better is a handful with quietness;** literally, *better a hand full of rest*. **Than both the hands full with travail and vexation of spirit;** literally, *than two hands full of travail*, etc. This verse, which has been variously interpreted, is most simply regarded as the fool's defence of his indolence, either expressed in his own words or fortified by a proverbial saying. One open hand full of quietness and rest is preferable to two closed hands full of toil and vain effort. The verse must not be taken as the writer's warning against sloth, which would be out of place here, but as enunciating a maxim against discontent and that restless activity which is never satisfied with moderate returns.

Vers. 7—12.—Thirdly, avarice causes isolation and a sense of insecurity, and brings no satisfaction.

Ver. 7.—**Then I returned.** Another reflection serves to confirm the uselessness of human efforts. The **vanity under the sun** is now avarice, with the evils that accompany it.

Ver. 8.—**There is one alone, and there is not a second;** or, *without a second*—a solitary being, without partner, relation, or friend. Here, he says, is another instance of man's inability to secure his own happiness. Wealth indeed, is supposed to make friends, such as they are; but miserliness and greed separate a man from his fellows, make him suspicious of every one, and drive him to live alone, churlish and unhappy. **Yea, he hath neither child nor brother;** no one to share his wealth, or for whom to save and amass riches. To apply these words to Solomon himself, who had brothers, and one son, if not more, is manifestly inappropriate. They may possibly refer to some circumstance in the writer's own life; but of that we know nothing. **Yet is there no end of all his labour.** In spite of this isolation he plies his weary task, and ceases not to hoard. **Neither is his eye satisfied with riches;** so that he is content with what he has (comp. ch. ii. 10; Prov. xxvii. 20). The insatiable thirst for

gold, the dropsy of the mind, is a commonplace theme in classical writers. Thus Horace, 'Carm.,' iii. 16. 17—

"Crescentem sequitur cura pecuniam,
    Majorumque fames."

And Juvenal, 'Sat.,' xiv. 138—

"Interea pleno quum turget sacculus ore,
    Crescit amor nummi, quantum ipsa pecunia crevit."

Neither, saith he, **For whom do I labour, and bereave my soul of good ?** The original is more dramatic than the Authorized Version or the Vulgate, *Nec recogitat, dicens, Cui laboro*, etc. ? The writer suddenly puts himself in the place of the friendless miser, and exclaims, "And for whom do I labour," etc. ? We see something similar in ver. 15 and ch. ii. 15. Here we cannot find any definite allusion to the writer's own circumstances. The clause is merely a lively personification expressive of strong sympathy with the situation described (comp. ch. ii. 18). *Good* may mean either riches, in which case the denial to the soul refers to the enjoyment which wealth might afford, or happiness and comfort. The Septuagint has ἀγαθωσύνης, "goodness," "kindness"—which gives quite a different and not so suitable an idea. **Sore travail;** a sad business, a woeful employment.

Ver. 9.—Koheleth dwells upon the evils of isolation, and contrasts with them the comfort of companionship. **Two are better than one.** Literally, the clause refers to the two and the one mentioned in the preceding verse (Ἀγαθοὶ οἱ δύο ὑπὲρ τόν ἕνα, Septuagint); but the gnome is true in general. "Two heads are better than one," says our proverb. **Because** (*asher* here conjunctive, not relative) **they have a good reward for their labour.** The joint labours of two produce much more effect than the efforts of a solitary worker. Companionship is helpful and profitable. Ginsburg quotes the rabbinical sayings, "Either friendship or death;" and "A man without friends is like a left hand without the right." Thus the Greek gnome—

Ἀνὴρ γὰρ ἄνδρα, καὶ πόλις σώζει πόλιν.

"Man helps his fellow, city city saves."

Χεὶρ χεῖρα νίπτει δάκτυλός τε δάκτυλον.

"Hand cleanseth hand, and finger cleanseth finger."

(Comp. Prov. xvii. 17; xxvii. 17; Ecclus. vi. 14.) So Christ sent out his apostles two and two (Mark vi. 7).

Ver. 10.—Koheleth illustrates the benefit of association by certain familiar examples. **For if they fall, the one will lift up his fellow.** If one or the other fall, the companion will aid him. The idea is that two travellers are making their way over a rough road—an experience that every one must have had in Palestine. Vulgate, *Si unus ceciderit.* Of course, if both fell at the same time, one could not help the other. Commentators quote Homer, ' Iliad,' x. 220—226, thus rendered by Lord Derby—

"Nestor, that heart is mine ; I dare alone
  Enter the hostile camp, so close at hand ;
Yet were one comrade giv'n me, I should go
  With more of comfort, more of confidence.
Where two combine, one before other sees
  The better course ; and ev'n though one
    alone
The readiest way discover, yet would be
  His judgment slower, his decision less."

Woe to him that is **alone.** The same interjection of sorrow, אִי, occurs in ch. x. 16, but elsewhere only in late Hebrew. The verse may be applied to moral falls as well as to stumbling at natural obstacles. Brother helps brother to resist temptation, while many have failed when tried by isolation who would have manfully withstood if they had had the countenance and support of others.

" Clear before us through the darkness
  Gleams and burns the guiding light;
Brother clasps the hand of brother,
  Stepping fearless through the night."

Ver. 11.—The first example of the advantage of companionship spoke of the aid and support that are thus given ; the present verse tells of the comfort thus brought. **If two lie together, then they have heat.** The winter nights in Palestine are comparatively cold, and when, as in the case of the poorer inhabitants, the outer garment worn by day was used as the only blanket during sleep (Exod. xxii. 26, 27), it was a comfort to have the additional warmth of a friend lying under the same coverlet. Solomon could have had no such experience.

Ver. 12.—The third instance shows the value of the protection afforded by a companion's presence when danger threatens. **If one prevail against him, two shall withstand him ;** better, *if a man overpower the solitary one, the two* (ver. 9) *will withstand him.* The idea of the traveller is continued. If he were attacked by robbers, he would be easily overpowered when alone ; but two comrades might successfully resist the assault. **And a threefold cord is not quickly broken.** This is probably a proverbial saying, like our " Union is strength." Hereby the advantage of association is more strongly enforced. If the companionship of two is profitable, much more is this the case when more combine. The cord of three strands was the strongest made. The number *three* is used as the symbol of completeness and perfection. *Funiculus triplex difficile rum-*

pitur, the Vulgate rendering, has become a trite saying ; and the gnome has been constantly applied in a mystical or spiritual sense, with which, originally and humanly speaking, it has no concern. Herein is seen an adumbration of the doctrine of the Holy Trinity, the Eternal Three in One ; of the three Christian virtues, faith, hope, and charity, which go to make the Christian life ; of the Christian's body, soul, and spirit, which are consecrated as a temple of the Most High.

Vers. 13—16.—High place offers no assurance of security. A king's popularity is never permanent ; he is supplanted by some clever young aspirant for a time, whose influence in turn soon evaporates, and the subject-people reap no benefit from the change.

Ver. 13.—**Better is a poor and wise child than an old and foolish king.** The word translated " child " (*yeled*), is used sometimes of one beyond childhood (see Gen. xxx. 26 ; xxxvii. 30 ; 1 Kings xii. 8), so here it may be rendered " youth." *Misken,* πένης (Septuagint), *pauper* (Vulgate), " poor," is found also at ch. ix. 15, 16, and nowhere else ; but the root, with an analogous signification, occurs at Deut. viii. 9 and Isa. xl. 20. The clause says that a youth who is clever and adroit, though sprung from a sordid origin, is better off than a king who has not learned wisdom with his years, and who, it is afterwards implied, is dethroned by this young man. **Who will no more be admonished ;** better, as in the Revised Version, *who knoweth not how to receive admonition any more.* Age has only fossilized his self-will and obstinacy ; and though he was once open to advice and hearkened to reproof, he now bears no contradiction and takes no counsel. Septuagint, Ὅς οὐκ ἔγνω τοῦ προσέχειν ἔτι, "Who knows not how to take heed any longer ; " which is perhaps similar to the Vulgate, *Qui nescit prævidere in posterum,* " Who knows not how to look forward to the future." The words will bear this translation, and it accords with one view of the author's meaning (see below) ; but that given above is more suitable to the interpretation of the paragraph which approves itself to us. The sentence is of general import, and may be illustrated by a passage from the Book of Wisdom (iv. 8, 9), " Honourable age is not that which standeth in length of time, nor that which is measured by length of years. But wisdom is the grey hair unto men, and an unspotted life is old age." So Cicero, ' De Senect.,' xviii. 62, " Non cani nec rugæ repente auctoritatem arripere possunt, sed honeste acta superior ætas fructus capit auctoritatis extremos." Some have thought that Solomon is here speaking of himself,

avowing his folly and expressing his contrition, in view of his knowledge of Jeroboam's delegation to the kingdom—the crafty
youth of poor estate (1 Kings xi. 26, etc.),
whom the Prophet Ahijah had warned of
approaching greatness. But there is nothing
in the recorded history of Solomon to make
probable such expression of self-abasement,
and our author could never have so completely misrepresented him. Here, too, is
another proof that Ecclesiastes is not written
by Solomon himself.

Ver. 14.—**For out of prison he cometh to
reign; whereas also he that is born in his
kingdom becometh poor.** The ambiguity of
the pronouns has induced different interpretations of this verse. It is plain that
the paragraph is intended to corroborate the
statement of the previous verse, contrasting
the fate of the poor, clever youth with that
of the old, foolish king. The Authorized
Version makes the pronoun in the first
clause refer to the youth, and those in the
second to the king, with the signification
that rich and poor change places—one is
abased as the other is exalted. Vulgate,
*Quod de carcere catenisque interdum quis
egrediatur ad regnum; et alius natus in
regno inopia consummatur.* The Septuagint
is somewhat ambiguous, Ὅτι ἐξ οἴκου τῶν
δεσμίων ἐξελεύσεται τοῦ βασιλεῦσαι, ὅτι καί
γε ἐν βασιλείᾳ αὐτοῦ ἐγενήθη πένης, "For
from the house of prisoners he shall come
forth to reign, because in his kingdom he
[who?] was born [or, 'became'] poor." It
seems, however, most natural to make the
leading pronouns in both clauses refer to
the youth, and thus to render: "For out
of the house of prisoners goeth he forth
to reign, though even in his kingdom
he was born poor." *Beth hasurim* is also
rendered "house of fugitives," and Hitzig
takes the expression as a description of
Egypt, whither Jeroboam fled to escape
the vengeance of Solomon. Others see here
an allusion to Joseph, who was raised from
prison, if not to be king, at least to an
exalted position which might thus be designated. In this case the old and foolish
king who could not look to the future is
Pharaoh, who could not understand the
dream which was sent for his admonition.
Commentators have wearied themselves with
endeavouring to find some other historical
basis for the supposed allusion in the passage. But although many of these suggestions (*e.g.* Saul and David, Joash and
Amaziah, Cyrus and Astyages, Herod and
Alexander) meet a part of the case, none
suit the whole passage (vers. 13—16). It
is possible, indeed, that some particular
allusion is intended to some circumstance or
event with which we are not acquainted.
At the same time, it seems to us that, without
much straining of language, the reference
to Joseph can be made good. If it is objected that it cannot be said that Joseph
was born in the kingdom of Egypt, we may
reply that the words may be taken to refer
to his cruel position in his own country,
when he was despoiled and sold, and may
be said metaphorically to have "become
poor;" or the word *nolad* may be considered
as equivalent to "came," "appeared," and
need not be restricted to the sense of "born."

Ver. 15.—**I considered all the living which
walk under the sun;** or, *I have seen all the*
population. The expression is hyperbolical,
as Eastern monarchs speak of their dominions as if they comprised the whole world
(see Dan. iv. 1; vi. 25). **With the second
child that shall stand up in his stead.**
"With" (עִם) means "in company with,"
"on the side of;" and the clause should be
rendered, as in the Revised Version, *That
they were with the youth, the second, that
stood up in his stead.* The youth who is
called the second is the one spoken of in
the previous verses, who by general acclamation is raised to the highest place in the
realm, while the old monarch is dethroned
or depreciated. He is named *second,* as
being the successor of the other, either in
popular favour or on the throne. It is the
old story of worshipping the rising sun.
The verse may still be applied to Joseph,
who was made second to Pharaoh, and was
virtually supreme in Egypt, standing in the
king's place (Gen. xli. 40—44).

Ver. 16.—**There is no end of all the
people, even of all that have been before
them.** The paragraph plainly is carrying on
the description of the popular enthusiasm
for the new favourite. The Authorized
Version completely obscures this meaning.
It is better to translate, *Numberless were the
people, all, at whose head he stood.* Koheleth
places himself in the position of a spectator,
and marks how numerous are the adherents
who flock around the youthful aspirant.
"Nullus finis omni populo, omnibus, quibus
præfuit" (Gesenius, Rosenmüller, Volck).
Yet his popularity was not lasting and his
influence was not permanent. **They also
that come after shall not rejoice in him.**
In spite of his cleverness, and notwithstanding the favour with which he is now
regarded, those of a later generation shall
flout his pretensions and forget his benefits.
If we still continue the allusion to Joseph,
we may see here in this last clause a
reference to the change that supervened
when another king arose who knew him not
(Exod. i. 8), and who, oblivious of the services of this great benefactor, heavily
oppressed the Israelites. This experience
leads to the same result; it is **all vanity
and vexation of spirit.**

HOMILETICS.

Vers. 1—3.—*Two pessimistic fallacies; or, the glory of being born.* I. THE FIRST FALLACY. That the dead are happier than the living. 1. *Even on the assumption of no hereafter, this is not evident.* The already dead are not praised because they enjoyed better times on earth than the now living have. But (1) if they had better times when living, they have these no more, having ceased to be; while (2) if their times on earth were not superior to those of their successors, they have still only escaped these by subsiding into cold annihilation, and it has yet to be proved that "a living dog" is not "better than a dead lion" (ch. ix. 4). Besides, (3) it is not certain there is no hereafter, which makes them pause and hesitate to jump the life to come. When they discuss with themselves the question—

> "Whether 'tis nobler in the mind to suffer
> The slings and arrows of outrageous fortune,
> Or to take arms against a sea of troubles,
> And by opposing end them?"—

they generally come to Hamlet's conclusion, that it is better to

> "Bear the ills we have,
> Than fly to others that we know not of."

2. *On the assumption that there is a hereafter, it is less certain* that the dead are more to be praised than the living. It depends on who the dead are, and what the kind of existence is into which they have departed. (1) If they have lived unrighteously on earth, it will not be safe, even on grounds of natural reason, to conclude that their condition in the unseen land into which they have vanished is better than that of the living who are yet alive, even should these also be wicked; since for these there are still time and place for repentance, which cannot be affirmed of the ungodly dead. (2) If their lives on earth have been pious—*e.g.* if as Christians they have fallen asleep in Jesus—it need hardly be doubted that their condition is better even than that of the godly living, who are still dwellers in this vale of tears, subject to imperfections, exposed to temptations, and liable to sin.

II. THE SECOND FALLACY. That better than both the living and the dead are the not yet born. 1. *On the assumption that this life is all, it is not universally true* that not to have been born would have been a preferable lot to having been born and being dead. No doubt it is sad that one born into this world is sure, while on his pilgrimage to the tomb, to witness spectacles of oppression such as the Preacher describes; and sadder that many before they die will be the victims of such oppressions; while of all things, perhaps the saddest is that a man may even live to become the perpetrator of such cruelties; yet no one can truly affirm that human life generally contains nothing but oppression on the one side and tears upon the other, or that in any individual's life naught exists but wretchedness and woe, or that in the experiences of most the joys do not nearly counterbalance, if not actually outweigh, the griefs, while in that of not a few the pleasures far exceed the pains. 2. *On the assumption of a hereafter, only one case or class of cases can be pointed to in which it would have been decidedly better not to have been born,* viz. that in which one who has been born, on departing from this world, passes into an undone eternity. Christ instanced one such case (Matt. xxvi. 24); and if there be truth in the representations given by Christ and his apostles of the ultimate doom of those who die in unbelief and sin (Matt. xi. 22; xiii. 41, 42; xxii. 13; xxiv. 51; John v. 29; 2 Thess. i. 9; Rev. xxi. 8), it will not be difficult to see that in their case also the words of the Preacher will be true. 3. *In every other instance, but chiefly in that of the good, who does not see how immeasurably more blessed it is to have been born?* For consider what this means. It means to have been made in the Divine image, endowed with an intellect and a heart capable of holding fellowship with and serving God. And if it also signifies to have been born into a state of sin and misery in consequence of our first parents' fall, it should not be forgotten that it signifies, in addition, to have been born into a sphere and condition of existence in which God's grace has been before one, and is waiting to lift one up, completely and for ever, out of that sin and misery if one will. No one accepting that grace will ever afterwards deem it a misfortune that he was born. Thomas Halyburton, the Scottish theologian (A.D. 1674—1712), did not so regard his introduction to this lower world, with all its vicissitudes and woes. "Oh, blessed be God that I was born!" were his dying words. "I have a father and a mother, and ten brothers and sisters, in heaven, and I shall be the eleventh. Oh, blessed be the day that ever I was born!"

Learn: 1. The existence of sin and suffering no proof that life is an evil thing. 2. The wickedness of undervaluing existence under the sun. 3. The folly of over-praising the dead and underrating the living. 4. A worse thing than seeing "evil work" beneath the sun is doing it.

Vers. 4—8.—*Three sketches from life.* I. THE INDUSTRIOUS WORKER. 1. *The success that attends his toil.* Every enterprise to which he puts his hand prospers, and in this sense is a "right" work. Never an undertaking started by him fails. Whatever he touches turns into gold. He is one of those children of fortune upon whom the sun always shines—a man of large capacity and untiring energy, who keeps plodding on, doing the right thing to pay, and doing it at the right time, and so building up for himself a vast store of wealth. 2. *The drawbacks that wait on his success.* The Preacher does not hint that his work has been wrong; only that success such as his has its drawbacks. (1) It can only be attained by hard work. By Heaven's decree it is the fruit of toil; and sometimes he who finds it must sweat and labour for it, tugging away at the oar of industry like a very galley-slave, depriving his soul of good, and condemning his body to the meanest drudgery. (2) It often springs from unworthy motives in the worker, as *e.g.* from ambition, or a desire to outstrip his competitors in the race for wealth; from covetousness, or a hungry longing for other people's gold; or from avarice, which means a sordid thirst for possession. (3) It commonly leads to envy in beholders, especially in those to whom success has been denied. That it ought not to do so may be conceded; that it will not do so in those who consider that success, like every other thing, comes from God (Ps. lxxv. 6, 7), and that a man can receive nothing except it be given him from above (John iii. 27) is certain; that it does so, nevertheless, is apparent. In every department of life success incites some who witness it to depreciation, censoriousness, and even to backbiting and slander. "Envy spies out blemishes, that she may lower another by defeat," and when she cannot find, seldom wants the wit to invent them. Detraction is the shadow that waits upon the sun of prosperity. (4) It is usually attended by anxiety. The man to whom success is given is often one to whom success can be of small account, being "one that is alone and hath not a second," without wife or child, brother or friend, to whom to leave his wealth, so that as this increases his perplexity augments as to what he shall do with it.

II. THE HABITUAL IDLER. 1. *The folly he exhibits.* Not indisposed to partake of the successful man's wealth, he is yet disinclined to the labour by which alone wealth can be secured. He is one on whom the spirit of indolence has seized. Averse to exertion, like the sluggard, he is slumberous and slothful (Prov. vi. 10; xxiv. 33); and when he does awake, finds that other men's day is half through. If one must not depreciate the value of sleep, which God gives to his beloved (Ps. cxxvii. 2), or pronounce all fools who have evinced a capacity for the same, since according to Thomson ('Castle of Indolence')—

"Great men have ever loved repose,"

one may recognize the folly of expecting to succeed in life while devoting one's day to indolence or slumber. 2. *The wretchedness that springs from his folly.* That the habitual idler should "eat his own flesh"—not have a pleasant time of it, in spite of his indolence, attain to the fruition of his desires without work (Ginsburg, Plumptre), but reduce himself to poverty and starvation, and consume himself with envy and vexation (Delitzsch, Hengstenberg, Wright)—is according to the fitness of things, as well as the teachings of Scripture (Prov. xiii. 4; xxiii. 21; ch. x. 18; 2 Thess. iii. 10). "Idleness is the bane of body and mind, the nurse of naughtiness, the chief author of all misery, one of the seven deadly sins, the cushion upon which the devil chiefly reposes, and a great cause not only of melancholy, but of many other diseases" (Burton).

III. THE SAGACIOUS MORALIZER. 1. *His character defined.* Neither of the two former, he is a happy mean between both. If he toils not like him who always succeeds, he loafs not about like the fool who never works. If he amasses not wealth, he equally escapes poverty. He works in moderation, and is contented with a competence. 2. *His wisdom extolled.* If he attains not to riches, he avoids the sore travail requisite to procure riches, and the vexation of spirit, or "feeding upon wind," which riches bring. If he succeeds in gathering only one fistful of the goods of earth, he has at least the priceless pearl of quietness, including ease of mind as well as comfort of body.

LESSONS. 1. Industry and contentment two Christian virtues (Rom. xii. 11; Eph. iv. 28; 1 Tim. vi. 8; Heb. xiii. 5). 2. Idleness and sloth two destructive sins (Prov. xii. 24; ch. x. 8).

Vers. 9—12.—*Two better than one; or, companionship versus isolation.* I. THE DISADVANTAGES OF ISOLATION. 1. *Its causes.* Either natural or moral, providentially imposed or deliberately chosen. (1) Examples of the former: the individual who has no wife or friend, son or brother, because these have been removed by death (Ps. lxxxviii. 18); the traveller who journeys alone through some uninhabited waste (Job xxxviii. 26; Jer. ii. 6) or voiceless solitude; a stranger who lands on a foreign shore, with whose inhabitants he can hold no converse, because of not understanding their speech, and who lacks the assistance of a friendly interpreter. (2) Instances of the latter: the younger son, who forsakes the parental roof, leaving behind him parents, brothers, and sisters, as well as friends and companions, acquaintances and neighbours, and departs into a far country alone to see life and make a fortune; the elder brother, who, when the old people have died, and the younger branches of the family have removed, remains unmarried, because he chooses to live entirely for himself; the busy merchant, self-contained and prosperous, who stands apart from his employees, and, without either colleague or counsellor, partner or assistant, takes upon his own broad shoulders the whole weight and responsibility of a large "concern;" the student, who loves his books better than his fellows, and, eschewing intercourse with these, broods in solitude over problems too deep for his unaided intellect, that might be solved in a few hours' talk with a friend; the selfish soul, who has heart to give to no thing or person outside of self, and who fears lest his own stock of happiness should be diminished were he in an inadvertent moment to augment that of others. 2. *Its miseries.* Manifold and richly deserved—at least where the isolation springs from causes moral and self-chosen. Amongst the lonely man's woes may be enumerated these: (1) the absence of those advantages and felicities that arise from companionship —a theme treated of in the next main division of this homily; (2) the intellectual and moral deterioration that inevitably ensues on the suppression of the soul's social instincts, and the attempt to educate one's manhood apart from the family, the community, the race, of which it forms a part; (3) the inward wretchedness that by the just decree of Heaven attends the crime (where the isolation spoken of assumes this form) of living entirely for self; and, (4) aside from ideas of crime and guilt, the insatiable greed of self, which makes even larger demands upon one's labour, and deeper inroads upon one's peace, than all the claims of others would were the soul to honour these, and which, like an unpitying taskmaster, impels the soul to unceasing toil, and fills it with unending care (ver. 8; cf. ch. ii. 23).

II. THE BENEFITS OF COMPANIONSHIP. The "good reward" for their labour which two receive in preference to one points to the advantages that flow from union. These are four. 1. *Reciprocal assistance.* The picture sketched by "the great orator" is that of two wayfaring men upon a dark and dangerous road, who are helpful to each other in turn as each stumbles in the path, rendered difficult to tread by gloom overhead or uneven places underfoot. Whereas each one by himself might deem it hazardous to pursue his journey, knowing that if he fell when alone he might be quite unable to rise, and might even lose his life through exposure to the inclemencies of the night or the perils of the place, each accompanied by the other pushes on with quiet confidence, realizing that, should a moment come when he has need of a second to help him up, that second will be beside him in the person of his friend.

> " When two together go, each for the other
> Is first to think what best will help his brother;
> But one who walks alone, tho' wise in mind,
> Of purpose slow and counsel weak we find."
>
> (Homer, ' Iliad,' x. 224—226.)

The application of this principle of mutual helpfulness to almost every department of life, to the home and to the city, to the state and to the Church, to the workshop and to the playground, to the school and to the university, is obvious. 2. *Mutual stimulus.* Illustrated from the case of two travellers, who on a cold night lie under one blanket (Exod. xxiii. 6), and keep each other warm; whereas, should they sleep apart, they would each shiver the whole night through in miserable discomfort. The counterpart of this, again, may be found in every circle of life, but more especially in the home and the Church, in both of which the inmates are enjoined and expected to be helpers and comforters of each other, considering one another to provoke unto love and good works (Heb. x. 24). 3. *Efficient protection.* The writer notes the peril of the pilgrim whom, if alone, a robber may overpower, but whom, if accompanied by a comrade, the highwayman would not venture to attack. So multitudes of dangers assail the individual, against which he cannot protect himself by his own unaided strength, but which the friendly assistance of another may aid him to repel. As illustrations will at once present themselves, cases of sickness, temptations to sin, assaults upon the youthful believer's faith. In ordinary life men know the value of co-operation as a means of defence against invasions of what are deemed their natural rights; might the Christian Church not derive from this a lesson as to how she can best meet and cope with the assaults to which she is subjected by infidelity on the one hand, and immorality on the other? 4. *Increased strength.* As surely as division and isolation mean loss of power, with consequent weakness, so surely do union and co-operation signify augmented might and multiplied efficiency. The Preacher expresses this by saying, " The threefold cord will not quickly be broken." As the thickest rope may be snapped if first untwisted and taken strand by strand, so may the most formidable army be defeated, if only it can be dealt with in detached battalions, and the strongest Church may be laid in ruins if its members can be overthrown one by one. But then the converse of this is likewise true. As every strand twisted into a cable imparts to it additional strength, so every grace added to the Christian character makes it stronger to repel evil, and gives it larger ability for Christian service; while every additional believer incorporated into the body of Christ renders it the more impregnable by sin, and the more capable of furthering the progress of the truth.

LESSONS. 1. The sinfulness of isolation. 2. The duty of union. 3. The value of a good companion.

Vers. 13—16.—*The vicissitudes of royalty; or, the experience of a king.* I. WELCOMED IN YOUTH. The picture sketched that of a political revolution. " An old and foolish king, no longer understanding how to be warned," who has fallen out of touch with the times, and neither himself discerns the governmental changes demanded by the exigencies of the hour, nor is willing to be guided by his state councillors, is deposed in favour of a youthful hero who has caught the popular imagination, perceived the necessities of the situation, learnt how to humour the fickle crowd, contrived to install himself in their affections, and succeeded in promoting himself to be their ruler. 1. *Climbing the ladder.* Originally a poor man's son, he had raised himself to be a leader of his countrymen, perhaps as Jeroboam, the son of Nebat, did in the days of Rehoboam (1 Kings xi. 26—28), interesting himself in the social and political condition of his fellow-subjects, sympathizing with their grievances, probably acting as their spokesman in laying these before the aged sovereign; and, when their demands were unheeded, possibly fanning their discontent, and even helping them to plot insurrection—for which, having been detected, he was cast into prison. Nevertheless, neither his humble birth nor his forcible incarceration had been sufficient to degrade him in the people's eyes. 2. *Standing on the summit.* Accordingly, when the tide of discontent had risen so high that they could no longer tolerate their senile and imbecile monarch, and their courage had waxed so valiant as to enable them success-fully to carry through his deposition, they bethought themselves of the imprisoned hero who had espoused and was then suffering for their cause, and having fetched him forth from confinement, proceeded with him to the then deserted palace, where they placed upon his head the crown, amid shouts of jubilant enthusiasm, crying, "God save the king!" It is doubtless an ideal picture, which in its several details has often been realized; as, *e.g.*, when Joseph was fetched from the round house of Heliopolis, and seated on the second throne of Egypt (Gen. xli. 14, 40); as when David was crowned at Hebron on Saul's death by the men of Judah (2 Sam. ii. 4), and Jeroboam at Shechem by the tribes of Israel (1 Kings xii. 20); as when Athaliah was deposed, and the boy Joash made king in her stead (2 Kings xi. 12). 3. *Surveying his fortune.* So far as the new-made king was concerned, the commencement of his reign was auspicious. It doubtless never occurred to him that the sun of his royal person would ever know decline, or that he would ever experience the fate of his predecessor. It was with him the dawn of rosy-fingered morn; how the day would develop was not foreseen, least of all was it discerned how the night should fall!

II. HONOURED IN MANHOOD. 1. *Extending his renown.* Seated on his throne, he wields the sceptre of irresponsible authority for a long series of years. As the drama of his life unfolds, he grows in the affections of his people. With every revolution of the sun his popularity increases. The affairs of his kingdom prosper. The extent of his dominions widens. All the kingdoms of the earth come to place themselves beneath his rule. Like another Nebuchadnezzar, Cyrus, Xerxes, Alexander, Cæsar, he is a world-governing autocrat. "All the living who walk under the sun" are on the side of the man who had been born poor, and had once languished in a prison; neither is there any end to all the people at whose head he is. 2. *Enjoying his felicity.* One would say, as perhaps in the heyday of his prosperity he said to himself, the cup of his soul's happiness was full. He had obtained all the world could bestow of earthly glory, power the most exalted, influence the most extended, riches the most abundant, fame the most renowned, popularity the most secure! What could he wish else? The sun of his royal highness was shining in meridian splendour, and prostrate nations were adoring him as a god. No one surely would venture to suggest that the orb of his majestical divinity might one day suffer an eclipse. We shall see! Strange things have happened on this much-agitated planet.

III. DESPISED IN AGE. 1. *The shadows gathering.* The brightest earthly glory is liable to fade. One who has reached the topmost pinnacle of fame, and is the object of admiration to millions of his fellows, may yet sink so low that men shall say of him, as Mark Antony said of the fallen Cæsar—

> "Now lies he there,
> And none so poor to do him reverence."

The idol of one age may become an object of execration to the next. As in ancient Egypt another king arose who knew not Joseph, so in the picture of the Preacher grew to manhood another generation which knew not the poor wise youth who had been his country's deliverer. He of whom it had once been said—

> "All tongues speak of him, and the bleared sights
> Are spectacled to see him . . . and such a pother [made about him],
> As if that whatsoever God who leads him
> Were slily crept into his human powers,
> And gave him graceful posture"—
> ('Coriolanus,' act ii. se. 1.)

lived to be an object of derision to his subjects. 2. *The night descending.* In the irony of history, the same (or a similar) fate overtook him as had devoured his predecessor. As the men and women of a past age had counted his predecessor an imbecile and a fool, so were the men and women of the present age disposed to look on him. If they did not depose him, they did not "rejoice in him," as their fathers had done when they hailed him as their country's saviour; they simply suffered him to drop into ignominious contempt, and perhaps well-merited oblivion. Such spectacles of the vanity of kingly state had been witnessed before the Preacher's day, and have been not unknown since. So fared it with the boy-prince Joash (2 Kings xi. 12; 2 Chron. xxiv. 25), and with Richard II., whose subjects cried "All hail!" to him in the day of his popularity, but to whom, when he put off his regal dignity,

> "No man cried, 'God save him!'
> No joyful tongue gave him his welcome home,
> But dust was thrown upon his sacred head."
>
> ('King Richard II.,' act v. sc. 2.)

Learn: 1. The vanity of earthly glory. 2. The fickleness of popular renown. 3. The ingratitude of men.

HOMILIES BY VARIOUS AUTHORS.

Ver. 1.—*The oppressed and the oppressor.* Liberty has ever been the object of human desire and aspiration. Yet how seldom and how partially has this boon been secured during the long period of human history! Especially in the East freedom has been but little known. Despotism has been and is very general, and there have seldom been states of society in which there has been no room for reflections such as those recorded in this verse. I. THE TYRANNY OF THE OPPRESSOR. 1. This implies *power*, which may arise from physical strength, from hereditary authority, from rank and wealth, or from civil and political position and dignity. Power will always exist in human society; drive it out at one door, and it will re-enter by another. It may be checked and restrained; but it is inseparable from our nature and state. 2. It implies the *misuse* of power. It may be good to have a giant's strength, but "tyrannous to use it like a giant." The great and powerful use their strength and influence aright when they protect and care for those who are beneath them. But our experience of human nature leads us to believe that where there is power there is likely to be abuse. Delight in the exercise of power is too generally found to lead to the contempt of the rights of others; hence the prevalence of oppression. II. THE SORROWFUL LOT OF THE OPPRESSED. 1. The sense of oppression creates grief and distress, depicted in the tears of those suffering from wrong. Pain is one thing; wrong is another and a bitterer thing. A man will endure patiently the ills which nature or his own conduct brings upon him, whilst he frets or even rages under the evil wrought by his neighbour's injustice. 2. The absence of consolation adds to the trouble. Twice it is said of the oppressed, "They had no comforter." The oppressors are indisposed, and fellow-sufferers are unable, to succour and relieve them. 3. The consequence is the slow formation of the habit of dejection, which may deepen into despondency. III. THE REFLECTIONS SUGGESTED BY SUCH SPECTACLES. 1. No right-minded person can look upon instances of oppression without discerning the prevalence and lamenting the pernicious effects of sin. To oppress a fellow-man is to do despite to the image of God himself. 2. The mind is often perplexed when it looks, and looks in vain, for the interposition of the just Governor of all, who defers to intervene for the rectification of human wrongs. "How long, O Lord!" is the exclamation of many a pious believer in Divine providence, who looks upon the injustice of the haughty and contemptuous, and upon the woes of the helpless who are smitten and afflicted. 3. Yet there is reason patiently to wait for the great deliverance. He who has effected a glorious salvation on man's behalf, who has "visited and redeemed his people," will in due time humble the selfish tyrant, break the bonds of the captive, and let the oppressed go free.—T.

Vers. 2, 3.—*Pessimism.* It would be a mistake to regard this language as expressing the deliberate and final conviction of the author of Ecclesiastes. It represents a mood of his mind, and indeed of many a mind, oppressed by the sorrows, the wrongs, and the perplexities of human life. Pessimism is at the root a philosophy; but its manifestation is in a habit or tendency of the mind, such as may be recognized in many who are altogether strange to speculative thinking. The pessimism of the East anticipated that of modern Europe. Though there is no reason for connecting the morbid state of mind recorded in this Book of Ecclesiastes with the Buddhism of India, both alike bear witness to the despondency which is naturally produced in the mental habit of not a few who are perplexed and discouraged by the untoward circumstances of human life.

I. THE UNQUESTIONABLE FACTS UPON WHICH PESSIMISM IS BASED. 1. The unsatisfying nature of the pleasures of life. Men set their hearts upon the attainment of enjoyments, wealth, greatness, etc. When they gain what they seek, the satisfaction expected does not follow. The eye is not satisfied with seeing, nor the ear with hearing. Disappointed and unhappy, the votary of pleasure is "soured" with life itself, and asks, " Who will show us any good?" 2. The brevity, uncertainty, and transitoriness of life. Men find that there is no time for the acquirements, the pursuits, the aims, which seem to them essential to their earthly well-being. In many cases life is cut short; but even when it is prolonged, it passes like the swift ships. It excites visions and hopes which in the nature of things cannot be realized. 3. The actual disappointment of plans and the failure of efforts. Men learn the limitations of their powers; they find circumstances too strong for them; all that seemed desirable proves to be beyond their reach.

II. THE HABIT OF MIND IN WHICH PESSIMISM CONSISTS. 1. It comes to be a steady conviction that life is not worth living. Is life a boon at all? Why should it be prolonged, when it is ever proving itself insufficient for human wants, unsatisfying to human aspirations? The young and hopeful may take a different view, but their illusions will speedily be dispelled. There is nothing so unworthy of appreciation and desire as life. 2. The dead are regarded as more fortunate than the living; and, indeed, it is a misfortune to be born, to come into this earthly life at all. " The sooner it's over, the sooner asleep." Consciousness is grief and misery; they only are blest who are at rest in the painless Nirvana of eternity.

III. THE ERRORS INVOLVED IN THE PESSIMISTIC INFERENCE AND CONCLUSION. 1. It is assumed that pleasure is the chief good. A great living philosopher deliberately takes it for granted that the question—Is life worth living? is to be decided by the question—Does life yield a surplus of agreeable feeling? This being so, it is natural that the disappointed and unhappy should drift into pessimism. But, as a matter of fact, the test is one altogether unjust, and can only be justified upon the supposition that man is merely a creature that feels. It is the hedonist who is disappointed that becomes the pessimist. 2. There is a higher end for man than pleasure, viz. spiritual cultivation and progress. It is better to grow in the elements of a noble character than to be filled with all manner of delights. Man was made in the likeness of God, and his discipline on earth is to recover and to perfect that likeness. 3. This higher end may in some cases be attained by the hard process of distress and disappointment. This seems to have been lost sight of in the mood which found expression in the language of these verses. Yet experience and reflection alike concur to assure us that it may be good for us to be afflicted. It not infrequently happens that

" The soul
Gives up a part to take to it the whole."

APPLICATION. As there are times and circumstances in all persons' lives which are naturally conducive to pessimistic habits, it behoves us to be, at such times and in such circumstances, especially upon our guard lest we half consciously fall into habits so destructive of real spiritual well-being and usefulness. The conviction that Infinite Wisdom and Righteousness are at the heart of the universe, and not blind unconscious fate and force, is the one preservative; and to this it is the Christian's privilege to add an affectionate faith in God as the Father of the spirits of all flesh, and the benevolent Author of life and immortal salvation to all who receive his gospel and confide in the mediation of his blessed Son.—T.

Ver. 4.—Envy. There is no vice more vulgar and despicable, none which affords more painful evidence of the depravity of human nature, than envy. It is a vice which

Christianity has done much to discourage and repress; but in unchristian communities its power is mighty and disastrous.

I. THE FACTS FROM WHICH ENVY SPRINGS. 1. Generally, the inequality of the human lot is the occasion of envious feelings, which would not arise were all men possessed of an equal and a satisfying portion of earthly good. 2. Particularly, the disposition, on the part of one who is *not* possessed of some good, some desirable quality or property, to grasp at what *is* possessed by another.

II. THE FEELINGS AND DESIRES IN WHICH ENVY CONSISTS. We do not say that a man is envious who, seeing another strong or healthy, prosperous or powerful, wishes that he enjoyed the same advantages. Emulation is not envy. The envious man desires to take another's possessions from him—desires that the other may be impoverished in order that he may be enriched, or depressed in order that he may be exalted, or rendered miserable in order that he may be happy.

III. THE MISCHIEF TO WHICH ENVY LEADS. 1. It may lead to unjust and malevolent action, in order that it may secure its gratification. 2. It produces unhappiness in the breast of him who cherishes it; it gnaws and corrodes the heart. 3. It is destructive of confidence and cordiality in society.

IV. THE TRUE CORRECTIVE TO ENVY. 1. It should be considered that whatever men acquire and enjoy is attributable to the Divine favour and loving-kindness. 2. And that all men have blessings far beyond their deserts. 3. It becomes us to think less of what we do not or do *possess*, and more of what we *do*. 4. And to cultivate the spirit of Christ—the spirit of self-sacrifice and benevolence.—T.

Ver. 6.—*The handful with quietness.* The lesson here imparted is proverbial. Every language has its own way of conveying and emphasizing this practical truth. Yet it is a belief more readily professed than actually made the basis of human conduct.

I. ABUNDANT MATERIAL WEALTH ATTRACTS ATTENTION AND EXCITES DESIRE.

II. THE DISPOSITION AND HABIT OF MIND WITH WHICH OUR POSSESSIONS ARE ENJOYED IS OF MORE IMPORTANCE THAN THEIR AMOUNT. 1. This appears from a consideration of human nature. "A man's life consisteth not in the abundance of the things which he possesses." 2. And experience of human life enforces this lesson; for every observer of his fellow-men has remarked the unhappiness and pitiable moral state of some wealthy neighbours, and has known cases where narrow means have not hindered real well-being and felicity.

III. IT IS HENCE INFERRED THAT A QUIET MIND WITH POVERTY IS TO BE PREFERRED TO WEALTH WITH VEXATION. So it seemed even to Solomon in all his glory, and similar testimony has been borne by not a few of the great of this world. Nor, on the other hand, is it uncommon to find the healthy, happy, and pious among the poor rejoicing in their lot, and cherishing gratitude to God for the station to which they were born, and for the work to which they are called.

APPLICATION. 1. The comparison made by the wise man in this passage is a rebuke to envy. Who can tell what, if his two hands were filled with earthly good, he might, in consequence of his wealth, be called upon to endure of sorrow and of care? 2. On the other hand, this comparison is an encouragement to contentment. A handful is sufficient; and a quiet heart, grateful to God and at peace with men, can make what others might deem poverty not only endurable but welcome. It is God's blessing which maketh rich; and with it he addeth no sorrow.—T.

Ver. 8.—*The pain of loneliness.* The picture here drawn is one of pathetic interest. It cannot have originated in personal experience, but must have been suggested by incidents in the author's wide and varied observation. A lonely man without a brother to share his sorrows and joys, without a son to succeed to his name and possessions, is represented as toiling on through the years of his life, and as accumulating a fortune, and then as awaking to a sense of his solitary state, and asking himself for whom he thus labours and endures? It is vanity, and a sore travail!

I. THE COMPANIONSHIP OF DOMESTIC AND SOCIAL LIFE IS THE ORDER OF NATURE AND THE APPOINTMENT OF GOD'S PROVIDENCE. There are cases in which men are called upon to deny themselves such companionship, and there are cases in which they have been, by no action of their own, but by the decree of God, deprived of it. But the constitution of the individual's nature and of human society are evidence that the declaration regarding our first father holds good of his posterity—that is, in normal circumstances—" It is not good for the man to be alone."

II. Such companionship supplies a motive and a recompense for toil. A man can work better, more efficiently, perseveringly, and happily, when he works for others than when he works only for himself. Many a man owes his habits of industry and self-denial, his social advancement and his moral maturity, to the necessity of labouring for his family. He may be called upon to maintain aged parents, to provide for the comfort of a sickly wife, to secure the education of his sons, to save a brother from destitution. And such a call may awaken a willing and cheerful response, and may, under God, account for a good work in life.

III. The absence of such companionship may be a sore affliction, and may be the occasion of unwise and blamable dissatisfaction and murmuring. Under the pressure of loneliness, a man may relax his efforts, or he may fall into a discontented, desponding, and cynical frame of mind. He may lose his interest in life and in human affairs generally. He may even become misanthropic and sceptical.

IV. The true corrective of such unhappy tendencies is to be found in the cultivation of spiritual fellowship with Christ, and in a wide circle of sympathy and benevolence. No one need be lonely who can call his Saviour his Friend ; and Christ's friendship is open to every believer. And all Christ's disciples and brethren are of the spiritual kindred of him who trusts and loves the Redeemer. Where kindred " according to the flesh " are wanting, there need be no lack of spiritual relatives and associates. All around the lonely man are those who need succour, kindly aid, education, guardianship, and the heart purifies and refines as it takes in new objects of pity, interest, and Christian affection. And the day shall come when the Divine Saviour and Judge shall say to those who have responded to his appeal, " Inasmuch as ye did it unto one of the least of these my brethren, ye did it unto me."—T.

Vers. 9—12.—*The advantages of fellowship.*   There is a sense in which we have no choice but to be members of society.   We are born into a social life, trained in it, and in it we must live. " None of us liveth unto himself."   But there is a sense in which it rests with us to cultivate fellowship with our kind.   And such voluntary association, we are taught in this passage, is productive of the highest benefits.

I. Fellowship makes labour effective. " Two have a good reward for their labour."   If this was so in the day of the writer of Ecclesiastes, how much more strikingly and obviously is it so to-day !   Division of labour and co-operation in labour are the two great principles which account for the success of industrial enterprise in our own time.   There is scope for such united efforts in the Church of Christ—for unity and brotherly kindness, for mutual help, consideration, and endeavour.

II. Fellowship provides succour in calamity.   When two are together, he who falls may be lifted up, when if alone he might be left to perish.   This is a commonplace truth with reference to travellers in a strange land, with reference to comrades in war, etc.   Our Lord Jesus sent forth his apostles two and two, that one might supply his neighbour's deficiencies ; that the healthy might uphold the sick ; and the brave might cheer the timid.   The history of Christ's Church is a long record of mutual succour and consolation.   To raise the fallen, to cherish the weakly, to relieve the needy, to assist the widow and fatherless,—this is true religion.   Here is the sphere for the manifestation of Christian fellowship.

III. Fellowship is promotive of comfort, well-being, and happiness. " How can one be warm alone ? " asks the Preacher.   Every household, every congregation, every Christian society, is a proof that there is a spirit of mutual dependence wherever the will of the great Father and Saviour of mankind is honoured and obeyed.   The more there is of brotherly love within the Church, the more effective will be the Church's work of benevolence and missionary aggression upon the ignorance and sin of the world.

IV. Fellowship imparts strength, stability, and power of resistance. Two, placing themselves shoulder to shoulder, can withstand an onset before which one alone would fall. " The threefold cord is not quickly broken." It must be remembered that the work of religious men in this world is no child's play ; there are forces of evil to resist, there is a warfare to be maintained.   And in order to succeed, two things are needful: first, dependence upon God; and secondly, brotherhood with our comrades and fellow-soldiers in the holy war.—T.

Vers. 13, 14.—*Folly a worse evil than poverty.* This is no doubt a paradox.   For one man who seeks to become wise, there are a hundred who desire and strive for riches. For one man who desires the friendship of the thoughtful and prudent, there are ten who cultivate the intimacy of the prosperous and luxurious.   Still, men's judgment is fallible and often erroneous; and it is so in this particular.

I. WISDOM ENNOBLES YOUTH AND POVERTY.   Age does not always bring wisdom, which is the gift of God, sometimes—as in the case of Solomon—conferred in early life. True excellence and honour are not attached to age and station. Wisdom, modesty, and trustworthiness may be found in lowly abodes and in youthful years.   Character is the supreme test of what is admirable and good.   A young man may be wise in the conduct of his own life, in the use of his own gifts and opportunities, in the choice of his own friends; he may be wise in his counsel offered to others, in the influence he exerts over others.   And his wisdom may be shown in his contented acquiescence in the poverty of his condition and the obscurity of his station.   He will not forget that the Lord of all, for our sakes, became poor, dwelt in a lowly home, wrought at a manual occupation, enjoyed few advantages of human education or of companionship with the great.

II. FOLLY DEGRADES AGE AND ROYALTY.   In the natural order of things, knowledge and prudence should accompany advancing age. It is "years that bring the philosophic mind."   In the natural order of things, high station should call out the exercise of statesmanship, thoughtful wisdom, mature and weighty counsel.   Where all these are absent, there may be outward greatness, splendour, luxury, empire, but true kingship there is not.   There is no fool so conspicuously and pitiably foolish as the aged monarch who can neither give counsel himself nor accept it from the experienced and trustworthy.   And the case is worse when his folly is apparent in the mismanagement of his own life.   It may be questioned whether Solomon, in his youth, receiving in answer to prayer the gift of wisdom, and using it with serious sobriety, was not more to be admired than when, as a splendid but disappointed voluptuary, he enjoyed the revenues of provinces, dwelt in sumptuous palaces, and received the homage of distant potentates, but yet was corrupted by his own weaknesses into connivance at idolatry, and was unfaithful to the Lord to whose bounty he was indebted for all he possessed.

APPLICATION.   This is a word of encouragement to thoughtful, pure-minded, and religious youth.   The judgment of inspiration commends those who, in the flower of their age, by God's grace rise above the temptations to which they are exposed, and cherish that reverence toward the Lord which is the beginning of wisdom.—T.

Vers. 1—3.—*Pessimism and Christian life.* It is a very significant fact that this pessimistic note (of the text) should be as much heard as it is in this land and in this age;—in this land, where the hard and heavy oppressions of which the writer of Ecclesiastes had to complain are comparatively unknown; in this age, when Christian truth is familiar to the highest and the lowest, is taught in every sanctuary and may be read in every home.   There are to be found (1) not only many who, without the courage of the suicide, wish themselves in their grave; but (2) also many more who believe that human life is worth nothing at all, even less than nothing; who would say with the Preacher, "better than both is he who hath not been;" who would respond to the English poet of this century in his lament—

> " Count o'er the joys thy life has seen,
>   Count o'er thy days from sorrow free;
> But know, whatever 'thou hast been,
>   'Tis *something better not to be.*"

There is an unfailing remedy for this wretched pessimism, and that is found in an *earnest Christian life.* No man who heartily and practically appropriates all that Christian truth offers him, and who lives a sincere and genuine Christian life, *could* cherish such a sentiment or employ such language as this. For the disciple of Jesus Christ who really loves and follows his Divine Master has—

I. COMFORT IN HIS SORROWS. He never has reason to complain that there is "no comforter." Even if human friends and earthly consolations be lacking, there is One who fulfils his word, "I will not leave you comfortless;" "I will come to you;" "I will send you another Comforter, even the Spirit of truth." Whether suffering from oppression, or from loss, or bereavement, or bodily distress, there are the "consolations which are in Jesus Christ;" there is the "God of all comfort" always near.

II. REST IN HIS HEART. That peace of mind, that rest of soul which is of simply incalculable worth (Matt. xi. 28; Rom. v. 1); a sacred, spiritual calm, which the world "cannot take away."

III. RESOURCES WHICH ARE UNFAILING. In the fellowship he has with God, in the elevated enjoyments of devotion, in the intercourse he has with holy and earnest souls like-minded with himself, he has sources of sacred joy, "springs that do not fail."

IV. THE SECRET OF HAPPINESS IN ALL HIS HUMBLEST LABOUR. He does everything, even though he be a servant or even a slave, as "unto Christ the Lord;" and all drudgery is gone; life is filled with interest, and toil is crowned with dignity and nobleness.

V. JOY IN UNSELFISH SERVICE OF HIS KIND.

VI. HOPE IN DEATH.—C.

Vers. 4—6.—*Practical wisdom in the conduct of life.* What shall we pursue—distinction or happiness? Shall we aim to be markedly successful, or to be quietly content? What shall be the goal we set before us?

I. THE FASCINATION OF SUCCESS. A great many men resolve to attain distinction in their sphere. They put forth "labour, skilful labour," inspired by feelings of rivalry; they are animated by the hope of surpassing their fellows, of rising above them in the reputation they achieve, in the style in which they live, in the income they earn, etc. There is very little that is profitable here. 1. It must necessarily be attended with a large amount of failure: where many run, "but one receiveth the prize." 2. The satisfaction of success is short-lived; it soon loses its keen relish, and becomes of small account. 3. It is a satisfaction of a very low order.

II. THE TEMPTATION TO INDOLENCE. Many men are content to go through life moving along a much lower level than their natural capacities, their educational advantages, and their social introductions fit them and entitle them to maintain. They crave quietude; they want to be free from the bustle, the worry, the burden of the strife of life; they prefer to have a very small share of worldly wealth, and to fill a very little space in the regard of their neighbours, if only they can be well left alone. "The sluggard foldeth his hands; yea, he eateth his meat" (Cox). There is a measure of sense in this; much is thereby avoided which it is desirable to shun. But, on the other hand, such a choice is ignoble; it is to decline the opportunity; it is to retreat from the battle; it is to leave the powers of our nature and the opportunities of our life idle and unemployed.

III. THE WISDOM OF THE WISE. This is: 1. *To be contented with our lot;* not to be dissatisfied because there are others above us in the trade or the profession in which we are engaged; not to be envious of those more successful than ourselves; to recognize the goodness of our Divine Father in making us what we are and giving us what we have. 2. *To let our labours be inspired* by high and elevating motives; to work with all our strength, because (1) God loves faithfulness; (2) we cannot respect ourselves nor earn the esteem of the upright if we are indolent or faulty; (3) diligence and devotedness conduct to an honourable success, and enable us to render greater service both to Christ and to mankind.—C.

Vers. 9—12.—*Mutual service.* There is a measure of separateness, and even of loneliness, which is inseparable from human life. There are times and occasions when a man must determine for himself what choice he will make, what course he will pursue. Each human soul must "bear its own burden" in deciding what shall be its final attitude toward revealed truth; what shall be its abiding relation to God; whether it will accept or decline the crown of eternal life. Nevertheless, we thank

God for human companionship; we rejoice greatly that he has so "fashioned our hearts alike," and so interwoven our human lives, that we can be much to one another, and do much for one another, as we go on our way. " Two *are* better than one." The union of hearts and lives means—

I. SHARING SUCCESS. "They have a good reward for their labour." If two men work apart, and succeed in their labour, each has his own separate satisfaction. But if they confide their hopes, and tell their triumphs, and share their joys together, each man has much more "reward for his labour" than if he strove apart. It is one of the blessings of earlier life that its victories are so much enhanced by their being shared with others; it is one of the detractions from later life that *its* successes are confined to so small a sphere.

II. RESTORATION. (Ver. 10.) The falling of the solitary traveller in the unfrequented and dangerous path is a picture of the more serious and often fatal falling of the pilgrim in the path of life. To fall into disgrace, or (what is worse) into sin and evil habitude, and to have no true and loyal friend to stand by and to hold out the uplifting hand, to cover the shame with the mantle of his unspotted reputation, to lead back the erring soul with his strength and rectitude into the way of wisdom, into the kingdom of God—to such a man, in such necessity, the "woe" of the preacher may well be uttered.

III. ANIMATION. (Ver. 11.) "In Syria the nights are often keen and frosty, and the heat of the day makes men more susceptible to the nightly cold. The sleeping-chambers, moreover, have only unglazed lattices, which let in the frosty air. . . . And therefore the natives huddle together for the sake of warmth. To lie alone was to lie shivering in the chill night air." Moreover, it may be said that to sleep in the cold is, in certain temperatures, to be in danger of losing life, while the warmth given by contact with life would preserve vitality. To be "alone" is to live a cold, cheerless, inanimate existence; to be warmed by human friendship, to be animated by contact with living men, is to have a measure, a fulness, of life not otherwise enjoyed.

IV. DEFENCE. (Ver. 12.) "Our two travellers (see above), lying snug and warm on their common mat, buried in slumber, were very likely to be disturbed by thieves who had dug a hole into the barn or crept under the tent. . . . If one was thus aroused, he would call on his comrade for help" (Cox). It is not only the prowling thief against whom a man may defend his companion. By timely warning, by wise suggestion, by sound instruction, by faithful entreaty, by practical sympathy, we may so stand by one another, that we may save from the worst attacks of our most deadly spiritual enemies; thus we may save one another from falling into error, into unbelief, into vice, into shame and sorrow, "into the pit." We conclude, therefore: 1. That we should prize human friendship most highly, as that which furnishes us with the opportunity of highest service (see Isa. xxxii. 2). 2. That we should so choose our companions that we shall have from them the help we need in the trying hour. 3. That we should gain for ourselves the strength and succour of the Divine Friend.—C.

Ver. 12 (latter part).—*A threefold cord.* Many bonds of many kinds bind us in many ways. Of these some are hard and cruel, and these we have to break as best we can; the worst of them may be snapped when we strive with the help that comes from Heaven. But there are others which are neither hard nor cruel, but kind and beneficent, and these we should not shun, but gladly welcome. Such is the threefold cord which binds us to our God and to his service. It is composed of—

I. DUTY. To know, to reverence, to love, to serve God, is our supreme obligation. For we came forth from him; we are indebted to him for all that makes us what we are, owing all our faculties of every kind to his creative power. We have been sustained in being every moment by his Divine visitation; we have been enriched by him with everything we possess, our hearts and our lives owing to his generous kindness all their joys and all their blessings; it is in him that we live and move and have our being; we sum up all obligations, we touch the height and depth of exalted duty, when we say that "he is our God." Moreover, all this natural obligation is enhanced and multiplied manifold by all that he has done for us, *and all that he has endured for us* in the salvation which is in Jesus Christ, his Son.

II. INTEREST. To know, to love, to serve God,—this is our highest and truest interest. 1. It means the possession of his Divine favour; and that surely is much, not to say *everything*, to us. 2. It constitutes our real, because our spiritual, well-being; it causes us thereby and therein to realize the ideal of our humanity; we are at our very best imaginable when we are in fellowship with God and are possessing his likeness. 3. It secures to us a happy life below, filled with hallowed contentment, and charged with sacred joy, while it conducts to a future which will be crowned with immortal glory.

III. AFFECTION. To live in the service of Jesus Christ is to act as our human relationships demand that we should act. It is to give the deepest and purest satisfaction to those from whom we have received the most self-denying love; it is also to lead those for whom we have the strongest affection in the way of wisdom, in the paths of honour, joy, eternal life.—C.

Vers. 13—16.—*Circumstance and character.* This very obscure passage is thus rendered by Cox ('The Quest of the Chief Good'): "Happier is a poor and wise youth than an old and foolish king, who even yet has not learned to be admonished. For a prisoner may go from a prison to a throne, whilst a king may become a beggar in his own kingdom. I see all the living who walk under the sun flocking to the sociable youth who standeth up in his place; there is no end to the multitude of the people over whom he ruleth. Nevertheless, those who live after him will not rejoice in him; for even this is vanity and vexation of spirit." Thus read, we have a very clear meaning, and we are reminded of a very valuable lesson. We may learn—

I. THE VANITY OF TRUSTING IN CIRCUMSTANCE APART FROM CHARACTER. It is well enough to bear a royal name, to have a royal retinue, to move among royal surroundings. Old age may forget its infirmities in the midst of its rank, its honours, its luxuries. But when royalty is dissevered from wisdom, when it has not learned by experience, but has grown downwards rather than upwards, the outlook is poor enough. The foolish king is likely enough to be dethroned, and to "become a beggar in his own kingdom." An exalted position makes a man's follies seem larger than they are; and as they injuriously affect every one, they are likely to lead to universal condemnation and to painful penalty. It is of little use to be enjoying an enviable position if we have not character to maintain it and ability to adorn it. The wheel of fortune will soon take to the bottom the man who is now rejoicing on the top of it.

II. THE NEEDLESSNESS OF DESPAIR IN THE DEPTH OF MISFORTUNE. Whilst the old and foolish king may decline and fall, the wise youth, who has been disregarded, will move on and up to honour and to power, and even the condemned prisoner may mount the throne. The history of men and of nations proves that nothing is impossible in the way of recovery and elevation. Man may "hope to rise" from the bottom, as he should "fear to fall" from the top of the scale. Let those who are honestly and conscientiously striving, though it may be with small recognition or recompense, hope to attain to the honour and the reward which are their due. Let those who have suffered saddest disappointment and defeat remember that men may rise from the very lowest estate even to the highest.

III. THE ONE UNFAILING SOURCE OF SATISFACTION. The old and foolish king may deserve to be dethroned, but he *may* retain his position until he dies; the wise youth *may* fail to reach the honours to which he is entitled; the innocent prisoner may languish in his dungeon even until death opens the door and releases him. There is no certainty in this world, where fortune is so fickle, and circumstance cannot be counted upon even by the most sagacious. But there is one thing on which we may reckon, and in which we may take refuge. To be upright in our heart, to be sound in our character, to be true and faithful in life—this is to *be what is good*; it is to *enjoy that which is best*—the favour of God and our own self-respect; it is to *move toward that which is blessed*—a heavenly future.—C.

Vers. 1—3.—*Oppression of man by his fellows.* Many different phases of human misery are depicted in this book, many different moods of depression recorded; some springing from the disquietude of the writer's mind, others from the disorders he witnessed in the world about him. Sensuous pleasure he had declared (ch. iii. 12, 13,

22) to be the only good for man, but now he finds that even that is not always to be secured. There are evils and miseries that afflict his fellows, against which he cannot shut his eyes. A vulgar sensualist might drown sorrow in the wine-cup, but *he* cannot. "His merriment is spoiled by the thought of the misery of others, and he can find nothing 'under the sun' but violence and oppression. In utter despair, he pronounces the dead happier than the living" (Cheyne). If he does not actually deny the immortality of the soul, and is therefore without the consolation of believing that in a life to come the evils of the present may be reversed and compensated for, he ignores it as something of which we cannot be sure. We may see in this passage the germ of a higher character than is to be formed by the most elaborate self-culture; the spontaneous and deep compassion for the sufferings of others which the writer manifests tells us that a nobler emotion than the desire of personal enjoyment fills his mind. He tells us what he saw in his survey of society, and the feelings which were excited within him by the sight.

I. THE WIDESPREAD MISERY CAUSED BY INJUSTICE AND CRUELTY. (Ver. 1.) His description has been only too frequently verified in one generation after another of the world's history.

> "Man's inhumanity to man
> Makes countless thousands mourn."

The barbarities of savage life, the wars and crusades carried on in the name of religion, the cruelties perpetrated by despotic rulers to secure their thrones, the hardships of the slave, the pariah, and the down-trodden, fill out the picture suggested by the words, "I considered all the oppressions that are done under the sun." They all spring from the abuse of power (ver. 1), which might and should have been used for the protection and comfort of men. The husband and father, the king, the priest, the magistrate, are all invested with rights and authority of a greater or less extent over others, and the abuse of this power leads to hardships and suffering on the part of those subject to them which it is almost impossible to remedy. For many of the evils that may afflict a community a revolution may seem the only way of deliverance; and yet that in the vast majority of cases means, in the first instance, multiplying disorders and inflicting fresh sufferings. Anarchy is a worse evil than bad government, and the fact that this is so, is calculated to make the most ardent patriot hesitate before attempting to set wrong right with a strong hand.

II. THE FEELINGS EXCITED BY A CONTEMPLATION OF HUMAN MISERY. (Vers. 2, 3.) One good point in the character of the speaker we have already noticed, and that is that he cannot banish the thought of the distresses of others by attending to his own ease and self-enjoyment. He is not like the rich man in the parable, who fared sumptuously every day, and took no notice of the hungry, naked beggar covered with sores that lay at his gate (Luke xvi. 19—21). On the contrary, a deep compassion fills his heart at the thought of the oppressed who have no comforter, and the fact that he cannot deliver them or ameliorate their lot does not lead him to consider it unnecessary for him to distress himself about them; it rather tends to deepen the despondency he feels, and to make him think those happy who have done with life, and rest in the place where "the wicked cease from troubling, and the weary be at rest" (Job iii. 17). Yea, better, he thinks, never to have been than to see the evil work that is done under the sun (ver. 3). The distress which the sight of the sufferings of the oppressed produces is unrelieved by any consolatory thought. The writer does not, as I have said, anticipate a future life in which the righteous are happy, and the wicked receive the due reward of their deeds; he does not invoke the Divine interposition on behalf of the oppressed in the present life, or speak of the salutary discipline of sufferings meekly borne. In short, we do not find here any light cast upon the problem of evil in a world governed by a God of infinite power, wisdom, and love, such as is given in other passages of Holy Scripture (Job, *passim*; Ps. lxxiii.; Heb. xii. 5—11). But we may freely admit that the depth and intensity of feeling with which our author speaks of human misery is infinitely preferable to a superficial optimism founded, not upon Christian faith, but upon an imperfect appreciation of moral and spiritual truth, and generally accompanied by a selfish indifference to the welfare of others. A striking parallel to the thought in this passage is to be found in the teaching of Buddhism. The spectacle of miseries of old age, disease, and death, drove the Indian prince, Cakya Mouni, to find in Nirvana (annihilation, or unconscious existence) a solution of the great problem. But both are superseded by the teaching of Christ, who gives us to understand that "not to have been born" is not a blessing which the more spiritually minded might covet, but a state better only than that exceptional misery which is the doom of exceptional guilt (Matt. xxvi. 24).—J. W.

Vers. 4—6.—*Ambition and indolence.* The Preacher turns from the great, and to him insoluble, problems connected with the misery and suffering in which so many of the children of men are sunk. "His mood is still bitter; but it is no longer on the oppressions and cruelty of life that he fixes his eye, but on its littleness, its mutual jealousies, its greed, its strange reverses, its shams and hollowness. He puts on the garb of the satirist, and lashes the pettiness and the follies and the vain hurry of mankind" (Bradley). As it were, he turns from the evils which no foresight or effort could ward off, to those which spring from preventible causes.

I. RESTLESS AMBITION. (Ver. 4.) Revised Version, "Then I saw all labour and every skilful work, that it cometh of a man's rivalry with his neighbour" (margin). The Preacher does not deny that labour and toil may be crowned with some measure of success, but he notices that the inspiring motive is in most cases an envious desire on the part of the worker to surpass his fellows. Hence he asserts that in general no lasting good is secured by the individual worker (Wright). The general community may benefit largely by the results achieved, the progress of civilization may be advanced by the competition of artist with artist, but without a moral gain being attained by those who have put forth all their strength and exerted to the utmost all their skill. They may still feel that their ideal is higher than their achievements; they may see with jealous resentment that their best work is surpassed by others. The poet Hesiod, in his 'Works and Days,' distinguishes between two kinds of rivalry —the one beneficent and provocative of honest enterprise, the other pernicious and provocative of discord. The former is like that alluded to here by the Preacher, and is the parent of healthy competition.

> " Beneficent this better envy burns—
> Thus emulous his wheel the potter turns,
> The smith his anvil beats, the beggar throng
> Industrious ply, the bards contend in song."

But our author, looking at the motive rather than the result of the work, brands as injurious the selfish ambition from which it may have sprung.

II. INDOLENCE. (Ver. 5.) "The fool foldeth his hands together, and eateth his own flesh." While there are some who fret and wear themselves out in endeavours to surpass their neighbours, others rust out in ignoble sloth. The hands of the busy artist are deftly used to shape and fashion the materials in which he works, and to embody the ideas or fancies conceived in his mind; the indolent fold their hands together, and make no attempt either to excel others or to provide a living for themselves. The one may, after all his toil, be doomed to failure and disappointment; the other most certainly dooms himself to want and misery. "He feeds upon his own flesh," and destroys himself. The sinfulness of indolence, and the punishment which it brings down upon itself, are plainly indicated in many parts of Holy Scripture (Prov. vi. 10, 11; xiii. 4; xx. 4; Matt. xxv. 26; 2 Thess. iii. 10). But the special point of the reference to the vice here seems to be the contrast which it affords to that of feverish ambition. The two dispositions depicted are opposed to each other; both are blameworthy. It is foolish to seek to escape the evils of the one by incurring those of the other. A middle way between them is the path of wisdom. This is taught us in ver. 6: "Better is an handful with quietness, than both the hands full with travail and vexation of spirit." The rivalry that consumes the strength, and leads almost inevitably to disappointment and vexation of spirit, is deprecated; so also, by implication, is the inactivity of the indolent. The "quietness" which refreshes the soul, and gives it contentment with a moderate competence, is not idleness, or the rest of sloth. It is rest after labour, which the ambitious will not allow themselves to take. The indolent do not enjoy it, their strength wastes away from want of exercise;

while those of moderate, chastened desires can both be diligent in business and mindful of their higher interests; they can labour assiduously without losing that tranquillity of spirit and peace of mind which are essential to happiness in life.— J. W.

Vers. 7—12.—*Friendship a gain in life.*   A new thought dawns upon our author. In his observation of the different phases of human life, he notes much that is disappointing and unsatisfactory, but he also perceives some alleviations of the evils by which man is harassed and disturbed.   Amidst all his depreciation of the conditions under which we live, he admits positive blessings which it is our wisdom to discern and make the most of.   Amongst these latter he counts friendship.   It is a positive gain, by which the [difficulties of life are diminished and its enjoyments increased. In vers. 8—12 he describes an isolated life wasted in fruitless, selfish toil, and dilates with something like enthusiasm upon the advantages of companionship.   In order, I suppose, to make the contrast between the two states more vivid, he chooses a very pronounced case of solitariness—not that of a man merely isolated from his fellows, say living by himself on a desert island, but that of one utterly separate in spirit, a miser intent only on his own interests.   We may call the passage a description of the evils of a solitary life and the value of friendship.

I. THE EVILS OF A SOLITARY LIFE.   (Vers. 7, 8.)   The picture is drawn with a very few touches, but it is remarkably distinct and vivid.   It represents a "solitary, friendless money-maker—a Shylock without even a Jessica; an Isaac of York with no faithful Rebecca."   He is alone, he has no companion, no relative or friend, he knows not who will succeed him in the possession of his heaped-up treasures; and yet he toils on with unremitting anxiety, from early in the morning till late at night, unwilling to lose a moment from his work as long as he can add anything to his gains.   "There is no end of all his labour."   The assiduity with which he at first applied himself to the task of accumulating riches distinguishes him to the end of life.   At first, perhaps, he had to force himself to cultivate habits of industry and application, but now he cannot tear himself away from business.   His habits rule him, and take away from him both the ability and the inclination to relax his labours and to enjoy the fruit of them. Have we not often seen instances of this folly in our own experience?   Those who have lived a laborious life, and have been successful in their undertakings, toiling on to the very last, afflicted with an insatiable avarice, never satisfied with their riches, and only enjoying the mere consciousness of possessing them?   Have we not noticed how such a man gets to be penurious and fretful and utterly unfeeling?   He gathers in eagerly, and often unscrupulously, and gives out reluctantly and sparingly.   He starves himself in the midst of abundance, grudges the most necessary expenses, and denies himself and those dependent upon him the commonest comforts.   The misery he inflicts upon himself does not open his eyes to the folly of his conduct; he grows gradually callous to discomforts, and finds in the sordid gains which his parsimony secures an abundant compensation for all inconveniences.   And not only does he doom himself to material discomfort and to intellectual impoverishment by setting his desires solely upon riches, but he degrades his moral and spiritual character.   If he must keep all he has to himself, he must often ignore the just claims of others upon him; he must steel his heart against the appeals of the poor and needy, and he must look with scorn and contempt upon all those who are generous and liberal in helping their fellows. And so we find such men gradually growing harsher and more unsympathetic, until it seems at last as if they regarded every one about them with suspicion, as seeking to wrest from their hands their hard-earned gains.   And what is the pleasure of such a life?   How is it such men do not say within themselves, "For whom do I labour, and bereave my soul of good?"   The folly of their conduct springs from two causes. 1. They forget that unremitting, fruitless toil is a curse.   As a means to an end toil is good, as an end in itself it is evil.   It was never contemplated, even when man was innocent, that he should be idle.   He was placed in the garden of Eden to dress and to keep it.   But it is either his fault or his misfortune if he is all his life a slavish drudge.   It may be that he is forced by the necessities of his position to labour incessantly and to the very end, to make a livelihood for himself and for those dependent upon him, but his condition is not an ideal one.   If he could secure a little leisure and relaxation, it would be all the better for him in every sense of the word.

And therefore for the miser to toil like a mere slave, when he might save himself the trouble, is an evidence of how blinded he is by the vice to which he is addicted. 2. A second cause of the miser's folly is his ignoring the fact that riches have only value when made use of. The mere accumulation of them is not enough; they must be employed if they are to be of service. No real, healthy enjoyment of them is to be obtained by merely contemplating them and reckoning them up. Used in that way they only feed an unnatural and morbid appetite.

II. Over against the miseries of a selfish, solitary life, our author sets THE ADVANTAGE OF COMPANIONSHIP. (Vers. 9—12.) Friendship affords considerable mitigation of the evils by which life is beset, and a positive gain is secured by those who cultivate it. Three very homely figures are used to describe these advantages. The thought which connects them all together is that of life as a journey, or pilgrimage, like that which Bunyan describes in his wonderful book. If a man is alone in the journey of life, he is liable to accidents and discomforts and dangers which the presence of a friend would have averted or mitigated. He may fall on the road, and none be by to help him; he may at night lie shivering in the cold, if he has no companion to cherish him with kindly warmth; he may meet with robbers, whom his unaided strength is insufficient to beat off. All these figures illustrate the general principle that in union there is mutual helpfulness, comfort, and strength, verification of which we find in all departments of life—in the family, in the intercourse of friends, and in the Church. The benefits of such fellowships are undeniable. "It affords to the parties mutual counsel and direction, especially in seasons of perplexity and embarrassment; mutual sympathy, consolation, and care in the hour of calamity and distress; mutual encouragement in anxiety and depression; mutual aid by the joint application of bodily or mental energy to difficult and laborious tasks; mutual relief amidst the fluctuations of worldly circumstances, the abundance of the one reciprocally supplying the deficiencies of the other; mutual defence and vindication when the character of either is injuriously attacked and defamed; and mutual reproof and affectionate expostulation when either has, through the power of temptation, fallen into sin. 'Woe to him that is alone when he' so 'falleth, and hath not another to help him up!' —no one to care for his soul, and restore him to the paths of righteousness" (Wardlaw). So far as the application of the principle to the case of ordinary friendship is concerned, the wisdom of our author is instinctively approved of by all. The writings of moralists in all countries and times teem with maxims similar to his. Some have thought that this virtue of friendship is too secular in its character to receive much encouragement in the teaching of Christianity; that it is somewhat overshadowed, if not relegated to comparative insignificance, by the obligations which a highly spiritual religion imposes. The fact that the salvation of his soul is the one great duty of the individual might have been expected to lead to a new development of selfishness, and the fact that devotion to the Saviour is to take precedence of all other forms of affection might have been expected to diminish the intensity of love which is the source of friendship. And not only have such ideas existed in a speculative form, but they have led, in many cases, to actual attempts to realize them. The ancient hermits sought to cultivate the highest form of Christian life by complete isolation from their fellows; they fled from society, dissevered themselves from all the ties of blood and friendship, and shunned all association with their kind as something contaminating. And in our own time, among many to whom the monastical life is specially repulsive, the very same delusion which lay at the root of it is still cherished. They think that love of husband, wife, child, or friend conflicts with love of God and Christ; that if the human love is too intense it becomes a form of sin. And along with this is generally found a cruel and dishonouring conception of the Divine character. God is thought of as jealous of those who take his place in the affections, and the loss of those loved is spoken of as a removal by him of the "idols" who had usurped his rights. That such teaching is a perversion of Christianity is very evident. The New Testament takes all the forms of natural human love as types of the Divine. As the father loves his children, so does God love us. As Christ loved the Church ought a husband to love his wife, ought his followers to love one another. No bounds can be set to affection; S he that dwelleth in love dwelleth in God." The one great check, that our love for another should not be allowed to lead us to do wrong or condone wrong, is not upon the intensity, but upon the perversion of affection, and leads to a purer, holier, and more satisfying exercise of affection. That Christ, whose love was universal, did not discourage friendship is evident from the fact that he chose twelve disciples, and admitted them to a closer intimacy with himself than others enjoyed, and that even among them there was one whom he specially loved. It was seen, too, in the affection which he manifested to the family in Bethany—Martha and Mary and their brother Lazarus. In the time of his agony in Gethsemane he chose three of the disciples to watch with him, seeking for some solace and support in the fact of their presence and sympathy. The truth of Solomon's statement that "two are better than one" was confirmed by Christ's sending out his disciples "two and two together" (Luke x. 1), and by the Divine direction given by the Holy Ghost when Barnabas and Saul were set apart to go together on their first great missionary enterprise (Acts xiii. 2). But over and above these instances of Christ's example in cultivating friendship, and of the advantages of mutual co-operation in Christian work, the great principle remains that true religion cannot come to any strength in an isolated life. We cannot worship God aright if we "forsake the assembling of ourselves together;" we cannot cultivate the virtues of which holiness consists—justice, compassion, forbearance, purity, and love—if we isolate ourselves; for all these virtues imply our conducting ourselves in certain ways in all our relations with others. We lose the opportunity of helping the weak, of cheering the disheartened, and of co-operating with those who are striving to overcome the evils by which the world is burdened, if we withdraw into ourselves and ignore others. So far, then, from the wisdom of Solomon in this matter being, in comparison with the fuller revelation through Christ, of an inferior and almost pagan character, it is of permanent and undiminished value. Our acquaintance with Christian teaching is calculated to lead us to form quite as decided a judgment as Solomon did as to *the evils of a solitary life,* and the *advantages of friendship.*—J. W.

Vers. 13—16.—*Mortifications of royalty.* Yet another set of instances of folly and disappointment occurs to our author's mind; they are drawn from the history of the strange vicissitudes through which many of those who have sat upon thrones have passed. His references are vague and general, and no success has attended the attempts of those who have endeavoured to find historical examples answering exactly to the circumstances he here describes. But the truthfulness of his generalizations can be abundantly illustrated out of the records of history, both sacred and profane. The reason why he adds these instances of failure and misfortune to his list is pretty evident. He would have us understand that no condition of human life is exempt from the common lot; that though kings are raised above their fellows, and are apparently able to control circumstances rather than to be controlled by them, as a matter of fact as surprising examples of mutability are to be found in their history as in that of the humbler ranks of men. He sets before us—

I. The image of "AN OLD AND FOOLISH KING, WHO WILL NO MORE BE ADMONISHED;" who, though "born in his kingdom, becometh poor." He is debauched by long tenure of power, and scorns good advice and warning. "We see him driven from his throne, stripped of his riches, and becoming in his old age a beggar." His want of wisdom undermines the stability of his position. Though he has in the regular course inherited his kingdom, and has an indefeasible right to the crown he wears—though for many years his people have patiently endured his misgovernment—his tenure of office becomes more and more uncertain. A time comes when it is a question whether the nation is to be ruined, or a wiser and more trustworthy ruler put in his place. He is compelled to abdicate, or is forcibly deposed or driven from his kingdom by an invader, whose power he is unable to resist. His noble birth, his legal rights as a sovereign, his grey hairs, the amiability of his private character, do not avail to secure for him the loyal support of a people whom his folly has alienated from him. The same idea of folly vitiating the dignity of old age is found in Wisd. iv. 8, 9, "Honourable age is not that which standeth in length of time, nor that is measured by number of years. But wisdom is the grey hair unto men, and unspotted life is old age." The biographies of Charles I. and James II. of England, and of Napoleon III., furnish examples of kings who learned nothing from experience, and scorned all warnings, and brought upon themselves misery like that hinted at by Solomon. The first of them met his death at the hands of his exasperated subjects, and the other two, after deep humiliations, died in exile.

II. The second instance of strange vicissitude is that of ONE WHO STEPS FROM A DUNGEON TO A THRONE. It is by his wisdom that he raises himself to the place of ruler over the neglected community. From obscurity he attains in a moment to the height of popular favour; thousands flock to do him homage (vers. 15, 16a, "I saw all the living which walk under the sun, that they were with the youth, the second, that stood up in his stead. There was no end of all the people, even of all them over whom he was," Revised Version). The scene depicted of the ignominy into which the worthless old king falls, and the enthusiasm with which the new one is greeted, reminds one of Carlyle's vivid description of the death of Louis XV. and the accession of his grandson. The courtiers wait with impatience for the passing away of the king whose life had been so corrupt and vile; he dies unpitied upon his loathsome sick-bed. "In the remote apartments, dauphin and dauphiness stand road-ready; . . . waiting for some signal to escape the house of pestilence. And, hark! across the Œil-de-Bœuf, what sound is that—sound 'terrible and absolutely like thunder'? It is the rush of the whole court, rushing as in wager, to salute the new sovereigns: 'Hail to your Majesties!'" The body of the dead king is unceremoniously committed to the grave. "Him they crush down and huddle underground; him and his era of sin and tyranny and shame; for behold! a New Era is come; the future all the brighter that the past was base" ('French Revolution,' vol. i. ch. iv.). The same kind of picture has been drawn by Shakespeare, in 'Richard II.,' act v. sc. 2, where he describes the popularity of Bolingbroke, and the contempt into which the king he displaced had sunk. Yet, according to the Preacher, the breeze of popular favour soon dies away, and the hero is soon forgotten. "They also that come after him shall not rejoice in him." The dark cloud of oblivion comes down and envelops in its shade both those who deserve to be remembered, and those who have been unworthy of even the brief popularity they enjoyed in their lifetime. "Who knows," says Sir Thos. Browne, "whether the best of men be known, or whether there be not more remarkable persons forgot than any that stand remembered on the known account of time?" ('Urn-burial').

The fickle and short-lived character of all earthly fame should convince us of the futility of making the desire of the applause of men the ruling motive of our lives; it should lead us to do that which is good because it is good, and not in order "to be seen of men," and because we are responsible to God, in whose book all our deeds are written, whether they be good or whether they be evil. The sense of disappointment at the vanity of human fame should dispose our hearts to find satisfaction in the favour of God, by whom all our good deeds will be remembered and rewarded (Ps. xxxvii. 5, 6; Gal. vi. 9; Matt. xxv. 21).—J. W.

EXPOSITION.

CHAPTER V.

Vers. 1—7.—Section 6. Man's outward and secular life being unable to secure happiness and satisfaction, can these be found in *popular religion?* Religious exercises need the observation of strict rules, which are far from meeting with general attention. Koheleth proceeds to give instruction, in the form of maxims, concerning public worship, prayer, and vows.

Ver. 1.—This verse, in the Hebrew, Greek, and Latin Bibles, forms the conclusion of ch. iv., and is taken independently; but the division in our version is more natural, and the connection of this with the following

verses is obvious. **Keep thy foot when thou goest to the house of God.** Some read "feet" instead of "foot," but the singular and plural numbers are both found in this signification (comp. Ps. cxix. 59, 105; Prov. i. 15; iv. 26, 27). To "keep the foot" is to be careful of the conduct, to remember what you are about, whither you are going. There is no allusion to the sacerdotal rite of washing the feet before entering the holy place (Exod. xxx. 18, 19), nor to the custom of removing the shoes on entering a consecrated building, which was a symbol of reverential awe and obedient service. The expression is simply a term connected with man's ordinary life transferred to his moral and religious life. *The house of God* is the temple. The tabernacle is called "the house of Jehovah" (1 Sam. i. 7; 2 Sam. xii. 20), and this name is commonly applied to the temple; *e.g.* 1 Kings iii. 1; 2 Chron. viii. 16; Ezra iii. 11. But "house of God" is applied also to the temple (2 Chron. v. 14; Ezra v. 8, 15, etc.), so that we need not, with Bullock, suppose that Koheleth avoids the name of the Lord of the covenant as "a natural sign of the writer's humiliation after his fall into idolatry, and an acknowledgment of his unworthiness of the privileges of a son of the covenant." It is probable that the expression here is meant to include synagogues as well as the great temple at Jerusalem, since the following clause seems to imply that exhortation would be heard there, which formed no part of the temple service. The verse has furnished a text on the subject of the reverence due to God's house and service from Chrysostom downwards. **And be more ready to hear, than to give the sacrifice of fools.** Various are the renderings of this clause. Wright, "For to draw near to hear is (better) than the fools offering sacrifices." (So virtually Knobel, Ewald, etc.) Ginsburg, "For it is nearer to obey than to offer the sacrifice of the disobedient;" *i.e.* it is the straighter, truer way to take when you obey God than when you merely perform outward service. The Vulgate takes the infinitive verb as equivalent to the imperative, as the Authorized Version, *Appropinqua ut audias;* but it is best to regard it as pure infinitive, and to translate, "To approach in order to hear is better than to offer the sacrifice of fools." The sentiment is the same as that in 1 Sam. xv. 22, "Hath the Lord as great delight in burnt offerings and sacrifices, as in obeying the voice of the Lord? Behold, to obey is better than sacrifice, and to hearken than the fat of rams." The same thought occurs in Prov. xxi. 3; Ps. l. 7—15; and continually in the prophets; *e.g.* Isa. i. 11; Jer. vii. 21—23; Hos. vi. 6, etc. It is the reaction against the mere ceremonialism which marked the popular religion. Koheleth had seen and deplored this at Jerusalem and elsewhere, and he enunciates the great truth that it is more acceptable to God that one should go to his house to hear the Law read and taught and expounded, than to offer a formal sacrifice, which, as being the offering of a godless man is called in proverbial language "the sacrifice of fools" (Prov. xxi. 27). The verb used here, "give" (*nathan*), is not the usual expression for offering sacrifice, and may possibly refer to the feast which accompanied such sacrifices, and which often degenerated into excess (Delitzsch). That the verb rendered "to hear" does not mean merely "to obey" is plain from its reference to conduct in the house of God. The reading of the Law, and

probably of the prophets, formed a feature of the temple service in Koheleth's day; the expounding of the same in public was confined to the synagogues, which seem to have originated in the time of the exile, though there were doubtless before that time some regular occasions of assembling together (see 2 Kings iv. 23). **For they consider not that they do evil;** *Ὅτι οὐκ εἰσὶν εἰδότες τοῦ ποιῆσαι κακόν* (Septuagint); *Qui nesciunt quid faciunt mali* (Vulgate); "They are without knowledge, so that they do evil" (Delitzsch, Knobel, etc.); "As they (who obey) know not to do evil" (Ginsburg). The words can scarcely mean, "They know not that they do evil;" nor, as Hitzig has, "They know not how to be sorrowful." There is much difficulty in understanding the passage according to the received reading, and Nowack, with others, deems the text corrupt. If we accept what we now find, it is best to translate, "They know not, so that they do evil;" *i.e.* their ignorance predisposes them to err in this matter. The persons meant are the "fools" who offer unacceptable sacrifices. These know not how to worship God heartily and properly, and, thinking to please him with their formal acts of devotion, fall into a grievous sin.

Ver. 2.—Koheleth warns against thoughtless words or hasty professions in prayer, which formed another feature of popular religion. **Be not rash with thy mouth.** The warning is against hasty and thoughtless words in prayer, words that go from the lips with glib facility, but come not from the heart. Thus our Lord bids those who pray not to use vain repetitions (*μὴ βαττολογήσητε*), as the heathen, who think to be heard for their much speaking (Matt. vi. 7). Jesus himself used the same words in his prayer in the garden, and he continually urges the lesson of much and constant prayer—a lesson enforced by apostolic admonitions (see Luke xi. 5, etc.; Phil. iv. 6; 1 Thess. v. 17); but it is quite possible to use the same words, and yet throw the whole heart into them each time that they are repeated. Whether the repetition is vain or not depends upon the spirit of the person who prays. **Let not thine heart be hasty to utter** any **thing before God.** We should weigh well our wishes, arrange them discreetly, ponder whether they are such as we can rightly make subjects of petition, ere we lay them in words before the Lord. "Before God" may mean in the temple, the house of God, where he is specially present, as Solomon himself testified (1 Kings viii. 27, 30, 43). **God is in heaven.** The infinite distance between God and man, illustrated by the contrast of earth and the illimitable heaven, is the ground of the admonition to reverence and thoughtfulness (comp. Ps. cxv. 3, 16; Isa. lv. 8, 9; lxvi. 1). **Therefore let thy words be few**, as becomes one who speaks in the awful presence of God. Ben-Sira seems to have had this passage in mind when he writes (Ecclus. vii. 14), " Prate not in a multitude of elders, and repeat not (μὴ δευτερώσῃς) the word in prayer." We may remember the conduct of the priests of Baal (1 Kings xviii. 26). Ginsburg and Wright quote the Talmudic precept ('Berachoth,' 68. *a*), " Let the words of a man always be few in the presence of God, according as it is written," and then follows the passage in our text.

Ver. 3.—The first clause illustrates the second, the mark of comparison being simply the copula, mere juxtaposition being deemed sufficient to denote the similitude, as in ch. vii. 1; Prov. xvii. 3; xxvii. 21. **For a dream cometh through** (*in consequence of*) **the multitude of business.** The verse is meant to confirm the injunction against vain babbling in prayer. Cares and anxieties in business or other matters occasion disturbed sleep, murder the dreamless repose of the healthy labourer, and produce all kinds of sick fancies and imaginations. Septuagint, " A dream cometh in abundance of trial (πειρασμοῦ);" Vulgate, *Multas curas sequuntur somnia.* **And a fool's voice** is known **by multitude of words.** The verb should be supplied from the first clause, and not a new one introduced, as in the Authorized Version, " And the voice of a fool (cometh) in consequence of many words." As surely as excess of business produces fevered dreams, so excess of words, especially in addresses to God, produces a fool's voice, *i.e.* foolish speech. St. Gregory points out the many ways in which the mind is affected by images from dreams. "Sometimes," he says, " dreams are engendered of fulness or emptiness of the belly, sometimes of illusion, sometimes of illusion and thought combined, sometimes of revelation, while sometimes they are engendered of imagination, thought, and revelation together " ('Moral.,' viii. 42).

Ver. 4.—Koheleth passes on to give a warning concerning the making of vows, which formed a great feature in Hebrew religion, and was the occasion of much irreverence and profanity. **When thou vowest a vow unto God, defer not to pay it.** There is here plainly a reminiscence of Deut. xxiii. 21—23. Vows are not regarded as absolute duties which every one was obliged to undertake. They are of a voluntary nature, but when made are to be strictly performed. They might consist of a promise to dedicate certain things or persons to God (see Gen. xxviii. 20; Judg. xi. 30), or to abstain from doing certain things, as in the case of the Nazarites. The rabbinical injunction quoted

by our Lord in the sermon on the mount (Matt. v. 33), "Thou shalt not forswear thyself, but shalt perform unto the Lord thine oaths," was probably levelled against profane swearing, or invoking God's Name lightly, but it may include the duty of performing vows made to or in the Name of God. Our Lord does not condemn the practice of *corban*, while noticing with rebuke a perversion of the custom (Mark vii. 11). **For he hath no pleasure in fools.** The non-fulfilment of a vow would prove a man to be impious, in proverbial language " a fool," and as such God must regard him with displeasure. The clause in the Hebrew is somewhat ambiguous, being literally, *There is no pleasure* (*chephets*) *in fools;* i.e. no one, neither God nor man, would take pleasure in fools who make promises and never perform them. Or it may be, *There is no fixed will in fools;* i.e. they waver and are undecided in purpose. But this rendering of *chephets* appears to be very doubtful. Septuagint, Ὅτι οὐκ ἔστι θέλημα ἐν ἄφροσι, which reproduces the vagueness of the Hebrew; Vulgate, *Displicet enim ei* (*Deo*) *infidelis et stulta promissio.* The meaning is well represented in the Authorized Version, and we must complete the sense by supplying in thought " on the part of God." **Pay that which thou hast vowed.** Ben-Sira re-echoes the injunction (Ecclus. xviii. 22, 23), " Let nothing hinder thee to pay thy vow (εὐχήν) in due time, and defer not until death to be justified [*i.e.* to fulfil the vow]. Before making a vow (εὔξασθαι) prepare thyself; and be not as one that tempteth the Lord." The verse is cited in the Talmud; and Dukes gives a parallel, "Before thou vowest anything, consider the object of thy vow" ('Rabb. Blumenl.,' p. 70). So in Prov. xx. 25 we have, according to some translations, " It is a snare to a man rashly to say, It is holy, and after vows to make inquiry." Septuagint, "Pay thou therefore whatsoever thou shalt have vowed (ὅσα ἐὰν εὔξῃ)."

Ver. 5.—**Better is it that thou shouldest not vow.** There is no harm in not vowing (Deut. xxiii. 22); but a vow once made becomes of the nature of an oath, and its non-performance is a sin and sacrilege, and incurs the punishment of false swearing. We gather from the Talmud that frivolous excuses for the evasion of vows were very common, and called for stern repression. One sees this in our Lord's references (Matt. v. 33—37; xxiii. 16—22). St. Paul severely reprehends those women who break their vow of widowhood, "having condemnation, because they have rejected their first faith " (1 Tim. v. 12).

Ver. 6.—**Suffer not thy mouth to cause thy flesh to sin.** " Thy flesh " is equivalent to "thyself," the whole personality, the idea of the flesh, as a distinct part of the man, sinning, being alien from Old Testament ontology. The injunction means—Do not, by uttering rash or inconsiderate vows, which you afterwards evade or cannot fulfil, bring sin upon yourself, or, as others render, bring punishment upon yourself. Septuagint, "Suffer not thy mouth to cause thy flesh to sin (τοῦ ἐξαμαρτῆσαι τὴν σάρκα σου);" Vulgate, *Ut peccare facias carnem tuam.* Another interpretation, but not so suitable, is this— Do not let thy mouth (*i.e.* thy appetite) lead thee to break the vow of abstinence, and indulge in meat or drink from which (as, *e.g.*, a Nazarite) thou wast bound to abstain. **Neither say thou before the angel, that it was an error.** If we take "angel" (*malak*) in the usual sense (and there seems no very forcible reason why we should not), it must mean the angel of God in whose special charge you are placed, or the angel who was supposed to preside over the altar of worship, or that messenger of God whose duty it is to watch man's doings and to act as the minister of punishment (2 Sam. xxiv. 16). The workings of God's providence are often attributed to angels; and sometimes the names of God and angel are interchanged (see Gen. xvi. 9, 13; xviii. 2, 3, etc.; Exod. iii. 2, 4; xxiii. 20, etc.). Thus the Septuagint here renders, "Say not before the face of God (πρὸ προσώπου τοῦ Θεοῦ)." If this interpretation be allowed, we have an argument for the literal explanation of the much-disputed passage in 1 Cor. xi. 10, διὰ τοὺς ἀγγέλους. Thus, too, in ' The Testaments of the XII. Patriarchs,' we have, "The Lord is witness, and his angels are witnesses, concerning the word of your mouth" (' Levi,' 19). But most commentators consider that the word here means "messenger" of Jehovah, in the sense of priest, the announcer of the Divine Law, as in the unique passage Mal. ii. 7. Traces of a similar use of ἄγγελος may be found in the New Testament (Rev. i. 20; ii. 1, etc.). According to the first interpretation, the man comes before God with his excuse; according to the second, he comes to the priest, and confesses that he was thoughtless and overhasty in making his vow, and desires to be released from it, or, at any rate, by some means to evade its fulfilment. His excuse may possibly look to the cases mentioned in Numb. xv. 22, etc., and he may wish to urge that the vow was made in ignorance (Septuagint, Ὅτι ἄγνοιά ἐστι, "It is an ignorance"), and that therefore he was not responsible for its incomplete execution. We do not know that a priest or any officer of the temple had authority to release from the obligation of a vow, so that the excuse made "before" him would seem to be

objectless, while the evasion of a solemn promise made in the Name of God might well be said to be done in the presence of the observing and recording angel. The Vulgate rendering, *Non est providentia,* makes the man account for his neglect by assuming that God takes no heed of such things; he deems the long-suffering of God to be indifference and disregard (comp. ch. viii. 11; ix. 3). The original does not bear this interpretation. **Wherefore should God be angry at thy voice**—the words in which thy evasion and dishonesty are expressed— **and destroy the work of thine hands?** *i.e.* punish thee by calamity, want of success, sickness, etc., God's moral government being vindicated by earthly visitations.

Ver. 7.—**For in the multitude of dreams and many words** there are also **divers vanities.** The Hebrew is literally, *For in multitude of dreams, and vanities, and many words;* i.e., as Wright puts it, "In the multitude of dreams are also vanities, and (in) many words (as well)." Koheleth sums up the sense of the preceding paragraph, vers. 1—6. The popular religion, which made much of dreams and verbosity and vows, is vanity, and has in it nothing substantial or comforting. The superstitious man who puts his faith in dreams is unpractical and unreal; the garrulous man who is rash in his vows, and in prayer thinks to be heard for his much speaking, displeases God and never secures his object. Ginsburg and Bullock render, " For it is (it happens) through the multitude of idle thoughts and vanities and much talking," the reference being either to the foolish speaking of ver. 2 or to the wrath of God in ver. 6. The Septuagint rendering is elliptical, Ὅτι ἐν πλήθει ἐνυπνίων καὶ ματαιοτήτων καὶ λόγων πολλῶν, ὅτι σὺ τὸν Θεὸν φοβοῦ. To complete this, some supply, "Many vows are made or excused;" others, "There is evil." Vulgate, *Ubi multa sunt somnia, plurimæ sunt vanitates, et sermones innumeri.*' The Authorized Version gives the sense of the passage. **But fear thou God.** In contrast with these spurious forms of religion, which the Jews were inclined to adopt, the writer recalls men to the fear of the one true God, to whom all vows should be performed, and who should be worshipped from the heart.

Vers. 8—17.—Section 7. *Perils to which one is exposed in a despotic state, and the unprofitableness of riches.*

Vers. 8, 9.—In political life there is little that is satisfactory; yet one must not surrender one's belief in a superintending Providence.

Ver. 8.—**If thou seest the oppression of the poor.** From errors in the service of God, it is natural to turn to faults in the administration of the king (Prov. xxiv. 21). Koheleth has already alluded to these anomalies in ch. iii. 16 and iv. 1. **Violent perverting**; literally, *robbery;* so that **judgment** is never rightly given, **and justice** is withheld from applicants. **In a province** (*medinah*, ch. ii. 8); the district in which the person addressed dwells. It may, perhaps, be implied that this is remote from the central authority, and therefore more liable to be injuriously dealt with by unscrupulous rulers. **Marvel not at the matter** (*chephets*, ch. iii. 1). Be not surprised or dismayed (Job xxvi. 11) at such evil doings, as though they were unheard of, or inexperienced, or disregarded. There is here nothing of the Greek maxim, reproduced by Horace in his " Nil admirari " ('Epist.,' i. 6. 1). It is like St. John's " Marvel not, my brethren, if the world hate you " (1 John iii. 13); or St. Peter's "Think it not strange concerning the fiery trial among' you" (1 Pet. iv. 12). The stupid and unintelligent observation of such disorders might lead to arraignment of Providence and distrust in the moral government of God. Against such mistakes the writer guards. **For he that is higher than the highest regardeth.** Both the words are in the singular number. Septuagint, Ὑψηλὸς ἐπάνω ὑψηλοῦ φυλάξαι. One thinks of the Persian satraps, who acted much as the Turkish pashas in later times, the petty rulers oppressing the people, and being themselves treated in the same fashion by their superiors. The whole is a system of wrong-doing, where the weaker always suffers, and the only comfort is that the oppressor himself is subject to higher supervision. The verb (*shamar*) translated " regardeth " means to observe in a hostile sense, to watch for occasions of reprisal, as 1 Sam. xix. 11; and the idea intended is that in the province there were endless plottings and counterplottings, mutual denunciations and recriminations; that such things were only to be expected, and were no sufficient cause for infidelity or despair. " The higher one " is the monarch, the despotic king who holds the supreme power over all these maladministrators and perverters of justice. **And there be higher than they.** " Higher " is here plural (*gebohim*), the plural of majesty, as it is called (comp. ch. xii. 1), like *Elohim*, the word for " God," the assonance being probably here suggestive. Over the highest of earthly rulers there are other powers, angels, principalities, up to God himself, who governs the course of this world, and to whom we may leave the final adjustment. Who are meant seems purposely to be left undetermined; but the thought of the righteous Judge of all is intimated in accordance with the view of ch. iii. 17. This

is a far more satisfactory explanation of the passage than that which regards as the highest of all " the court favourites, king's friends, eunuchs, chamberlains," etc. In this view Koheleth is merely asserting the general system of injustice and oppression, and neither accounting for it nor offering any comfort under the circumstances. But his object throughout is to show man's inability to secure his own happiness, and the need of submission to Divine providence. To demonstrate the anomalies in the events of the world, the circumstances of men's lives would be only one part of his task, which would not be completed without turning attention to the remedy against hasty and unfair conclusions. This remedy is the thought of the supreme Disposer of events, who holds all the strings in his hand, and will in the end bring good out of evil.

Ver. 9.—It has been much debated whether this verse should be connected with the preceding or the following paragraph. The Vulgate takes it with the preceding verse, *Et insuper universæ terræ rex imperat servienti;* so the Septuagint; and this seems most natural, avarice, wealth, and its evils in private life being treated of in vers. 10 and many following. **Moreover the profit of the earth is for all : the king** himself **is served by the field.** The writer seems to be contrasting the misery of Oriental despotism, above spoken of, with the happiness of a country whose king was content to enrich himself, not by war, rapine, and oppression, but by the peaceful pursuits of agriculture, by cherishing the natural productions of his country, and encouraging his people in developing its resources. Such was Uzziah, who " loved husbandry " (2 Chron. xxvi. 10); and in Solomon's own time the arts of peace greatly flourished. There is much difficulty in interpreting the verse. The Vulgate rendering, " And moreover the King of the whole earth rules over his servant," probably means that God governs the king. But the present Hebrew text does not support this translation. The Septuagint has, Καὶ περίσσεια γῆς ἐπὶ παντί ἐστι, βασιλεὺς τοῦ ἀγροῦ εἰργασμένου, which makes more difficulties. " Also the abundance of the earth is for every one, or upon every thing; the king (is dependent on) the cultivated land, or, there is a king to the land when cultivated," *i.e.* the throne itself depends on the due cultivation of the country. Or, removing the comma, " The profit of the land in everything is a king of the cultivated field." The Hebrew may safely be rendered, " But the profit of a land in all things is a king devoted to the field," *i.e.* who loves and fosters agriculture. It is difficult to suppose that Solomon himself wrote this sentence, however we may interpret it. According to the Authorized Version, the idea is that the profit of the soil extends to every rank of life; even the king, who seems superior to all, is dependent upon the industry of the people, and the favourable produce of the land. He could not be unjust and oppressive without injuring his revenues in the end. Ben-Sira sings the praises of agriculture: "Hate not laborious work, neither husbandry, which the Most High hath ordained" (Ecclus. vii. 15). Agriculture held a very prominent position in the Mosaic commonwealth. The enactments concerning the firstfruits, the sabbatical year, landmarks, the non-alienation of inheritances, etc., tended to give peculiar importance to cultivation of the soil. Cicero's praise of agriculture is often quoted. Thus ('De Senect.,' xv. *sqq.*; 'De Off.,' i. 42): "Omnium rerum, ex quibus aliquid acquiritur, nihil est agricultura melius, nihil uberius, nihil dulcius, nihil homine libero dignius."

Vers. 10—17.—The thought of the acts of injustice and oppression noticed above, all of which spring from the craving for money, leads the bard to dwell upon the evils that accompany this pursuit and possession of wealth, which is thus seen to give no real satisfaction. Avarice has already been noticed (ch. iv. 7—12); the covetous man now reprobated is one who desires wealth only for the enjoyment he can get from it, or the display which it enables him to make, not, like the miser, who gloats over its mere possession. Various instances are given in which riches are unprofitable and vain.

Ver. 10.—**He that loveth silver shall not be satisfied with silver.** "Silver," the generic name for money, as Greek ἀργύριον and French *argent.* The insatiableness of the passion for money is a common theme of poets, moralists, and satirists, and is found in the proverbs of all nations. Thus Horace ('Ep.,' i. 2. 56): "Semper avarus eget;" to which St Jerome alludes ('Epist.,' 53), "Antiquum dictum est, Avaro tam deest, quod habet, quam quod non habet." Comp. Juvenal, 'Sat.,' xiv. 139—

"Interea pleno quum turget sacculus ore,
Crescit amor nummi, quantum ipsa pecunia crevit."

"For as thy strutting bags with money rise,
The love of gain is of an equal size."
(Dryden.)

There is much more of similar import in Horace. See 'Carm.,' ii. 2. 13, *sqq.*; iii. 16. 17, 28; 'Ep.,' ii. 2, 147; and Ovid, 'Fast.,' i. 211—

"Creverunt et opes et opum furiosa cupido,
Et, quum possideant plura, plura volunt."

"As wealth increases grows the frenzied thirst
For wealth; the more they have, the more they want."

Nor he that loveth abundance with increase. The Authorized Version scarcely presents the sense of the passage, which is not tautological, but rather that given by the Vulgate, *Et qui amat divitias fructum non capiet ex eis,* "He who loveth abundance of wealth hath no fruit therefrom;" he derives no real profit or enjoyment from the luxury which it enables him to procure; rather it brings added trouble. And so the old conclusion is again reached, **this is also vanity.** Hitzig takes the sentence as interrogative, "Who hath pleasure in abundance which brings nothing in?" But such questions are hardly in the style of Koheleth, and the notion of capital without interest is not a thought which would have been then understood. The Septuagint, however, reads the clause interrogatively, Καὶ τίς ἠγάπησεν ἐν πλήθει αὐτῶν (αὐτοῦ, al.) γέννημα; "And who has loved [or, has been content with] gain in its fulness?" But מִי is not necessarily interrogative, but here indefinite, equivalent to "whosoever."

Ver. 11.—Koheleth proceeds to notice some of the inconveniences which accompany wealth, which go far to prove that God is over all. **When goods increase, they are increased that eat them.** The more riches a man possesses, the greater are the claims upon him. He increases his household, retainers, and dependents, and is really none the better off for all his wealth. So Job in his prosperous days is said to have had "a very great household" (Job i. 3), and the servants and labourers employed by Solomon must have taxed to the utmost even his abnormal resources (1 Kings v. 13, etc.). Commentators from Pineda downwards have quoted the remarkable parallel in Xenoph., 'Cyropæd.,' viii. 3, wherein the wealthy Persian Pheraulas, who had risen from poverty to high estate, disabuses a young Sacian friend of the idea that his riches made him happier or afforded supreme content. "Do you not know," said he, "that I neither eat, nor drink, nor sleep with any more pleasure now than I did when I was poor? By having this abundance I gain merely this, that I have to guard more, to distribute more among others, and to have the trouble of taking care of more. For now numerous domestics demand of me food, drink, clothes; some want the doctor; one comes and brings me sheep that have been torn by wolves, or oxen killed by falling down a precipice, or tells of a murrain that has affected the cattle; so that I seem to myself to have more afflictions in my abundance than I had when I was poor. . . . It is obligatory on him who possesses much to expend much both on the gods and on friends and on strangers; and whosoever is greatly pleased with the possession of riches will, you may be assured, be greatly annoyed at the expenditure of them." **What good is there to the owners thereof, saving the beholding of them with their eyes?** What it is that the owners behold is doubtful. Ginsburg considers that the increased number of devourers is meant; but surely this sight could hardly be called *kishron*, " success," " profit." So it is better to take the sight to be the amassed wealth. The contemplation of this is the only enjoyment that the possessor realizes. So the Vulgate, *Et quid prodest possessori, nisi quod cernit divitias oculis suis?* Septuagint, Καὶ τί ἀνδρεία τῷ παρ' αὐτῆς; ὅτι ἀρχὴ τοῦ ὁρᾶν ὀφθαλμοῖς αὐτοῦ, " And in what does the excellence of the owner consist? except the power of seeing it with his eyes." À Lapide quotes Horace's portrait of the miser ('Sat.,' i. 1. 66, *sqq.*)—

" Populus me sibilat; ut mihi plaudo
Ipse domi, simul ac, nummos contemplor in arca . . .
　　. . . congestis undique saccis
Indormis inhians et tanquam parcere sacris
Cogeris aut pictis tanquam gaudere tabellis."

" He, when the people hissed, would turn about,
　And drily thus accost the rabble-rout:
' Hiss on; I heed you not, ye saucy wags,
While self-applauses greet me o'er my bags.' . . .
O'er countless heaps in nicest order stored,
You pore agape, and gaze upon the hoard,
As relics to be laid with reverence by,
Or pictures only meant to please the eye."
　　　　　　　　　　　　　(Howes.)

Ver. 12.—Another inconvenience of great wealth—it robs a man of his sleep. **The sleep of a labouring man is sweet, whether he eat little or much.** The labourer is the husbandman, the tiller of the ground (Gen. iv. 2). The Septuagint, with a different pointing, renders δούλου, " slave," which is less appropriate, the fact being generally true of free or bond man. Whether his fare be plentiful or scanty, the honest labourer earns and enjoys his night's rest. **But the abundance of the rich will not suffer him to sleep.** The allusion is not to the overloading of the stomach, which might occasion sleeplessness in the case of the poor equally with the rich man, but to the cares and anxieties which wealth brings. " Not a soft couch, nor a bedstead overlaid with silver, nor the quietness that exists throughout the house,

nor any other circumstance of this nature, are so generally wont to make sleep sweet and pleasant, as that of labouring, and growing weary, and lying down with a disposition to sleep, and very greatly needing it. . . . . Not so the rich. On the contrary, whilst lying on their beds, they are frequently without sleep through the whole night; and, though they devise many schemes, they do not obtain such pleasure " (St. Chrysostom, ' Hom. on Stat.,' 22). The contrast between the grateful sleep of the tired worker and the disturbed rest of the avaricious and moneyed and luxurious has formed a fruitful theme for poets. Thus Horace, ' Carm.,' iii. 1. 21—

　　　" Somnus agrestium
Lenis virorum non humiles domos
　Fastidit umbrosamque ripam,
　　Non Zephyris agitata Tempe."

" Yet sleep turns never from the lowly shed
　Of humbler-minded men, nor from the eaves
　In Tempe's graceful vale is banished,
　Where only Zephyrs stir the murmuring leaves."

　　　　　　　　　　　(Stanley.)

And the reverse, ' Sat.,' i. 1. 76, *sqq.*—

" An vigilare metu exanimem, noctesque diesque
　Formidare malos fures, incendia, servos,
　Ne te compilent fugientes, hoc juvat?"

" But what are your indulgencies? All day,
　All night, to watch and shudder with dismay,
　Lest ruffians fire your house, or slaves by stealth
　Rifle your coffers, and abstract your wealth?
　If this be affluence—this her boasted fruit,
　Of all such joys may I live destitute."
　　　　　　　　　　　　　(Howes.)

Comp. Juvenal, ' Sat.,' x. 12, *sqq.*; xiv. 304. Shakespeare, ' Henry IV.,' Pt. II., act iii. sc. 1—

" Why rather, sleep, liest thou in smoky cribs,
　Upon uneasy pallets stretching thee,
　And hush'd with buzzing night-flies to thy slumber,
　Than in the perfumed chambers of the great,
　Under the canopies of costly state,
　And lulled with sounds of sweetest melody?"

Vers. 13—17.—Another view of the evils attendant upon riches is here presented: the owner may lose them at a stroke, and leave nothing for his children. This thought is presented in different lights.

Ver. 13.—**There is also a sore evil which**

I have seen under the sun (so ver. 16). The fact that follows is, of course, not universally true, but occasionally seen, and is a very bitter evil. The Septuagint calls it ἀρρωστία; the Vulgate, *infirmitas*. Riches kept for the owners thereof to their hurt; rather, *preserved by the possessor*, hoarded and guarded, only to bring their lord added grief when by some reverse of fortune he loses them, as explained in what follows.

Ver. 14.—Those riches perish by evil travail; thing or circumstance. There is no need to confine the cause of the loss to unsuccessful business, as many commentators do. The rich man does not seem to be a tradesman or speculator; he loses his property, like Job, by visitations for which he is in no way answerable—by storm or tempest, by robbers, by fire, by exactions, or by lawsuits. And he begetteth a son, and there is nothing in his hand. The verb rendered "begetteth" is in the past tense, and used as it were, hypothetically, equivalent to "hath he begotten a son," supposing he has a son. His misery is doubled by the reflection that he has lost all hope of securing a fortune for his children, or founding a family, or passing on an inheritance to posterity. It is doubtful to whom the pronoun "his" refers. Many consider that the father is meant, and the clause says that when he has begotten a son, he finds he has nothing to give him. But the suffix seems most naturally to refer to the son, who is thus left a pauper. Vulgate, *Generavit filium qui in summa egestate erit*. Having a thing in the hand means having power over it, or possessing it.

Ver. 15.—The case of the rich man who has lost his property is here generalized. What is true of him is, in a measure, true of every one, so far as he can carry nothing away with him when he dies (Ps. xlix. 17). As he came forth of his mother's womb, naked shall he return to go as he came. There is a plain reference to Job i. 21, "Naked came I out of my mother's womb, and naked shall I return thither." The *mother* is the earth, human beings being regarded as her offspring. So the psalmist says, "My frame was curiously wrought in the lowest parts of the earth" (Ps. cxxxix. 15). And Ben-Sira, "Great trouble is created for every man, and a heavy yoke is upon the sons of Adam, from the day that they go out of their mother's womb till the day that they return to the mother of all things." 1 Tim. vi. 7, "We brought nothing into the world, neither can we carry anything out." Thus Propertius, 'Eleg.,' iii. 5. 13—

"Haud ullas portabis opes Acherontis ad undas,
  Nudus ab inferna, stulte, vehere rate."

"No wealth thou'lt take to Acheron's dark shore,
  Naked, th' infernal bark will bear thee o'er."

Shall take nothing of his labour; rather, *for his labour*, the preposition being בְּ of price. He gets nothing by his long toil in amassing wealth. Which he may carry away in his hand, as his own possession. The ruined Dives points a moral for all men.

Ver. 16.—This also is a sore evil. The thought of ver. 15 is emphatically repeated. In all points as he came; *i.e.* naked, helpless. And what profit hath he that laboureth for the wind? The answer is emphatically "nothing." We have had similar questions in ch. i. 3; ii. 22; iii. 9. To labour for the wind is to toil with no result, like the "feeding on wind," "pursuing of vanity," which is the key-note of the book. The wind is the type of all that is empty, delusive, unsubstantial. In Prov. xi. 29 we have the phrase, "to inherit the wind." Job calls futile arguments "words of wind" (Job xvi. 3; xv. 2). Thus the Greek proverb, Ἀνέμους θηρᾶν ἐν δικτύοις, "to try to catch the wind:" and the Latin, "Ventos pascere," and "Ventos colere" (see Erasmus, 'Adag.,' *s.v.* "Inanis opera"). Septuagint, Καὶ τίς ἡ περίσσεια αὐτοῦ ᾗ μοχθεῖ εἰς ἄνεμον; "And what is his gain for which he labours for the wind?"

Ver. 17.—The misery that accompanies the rich man's whole life is summed up here, where one has to think chiefly of his distress after his loss of fortune. All his days also he eateth in darkness; *i.e.* he passes his life in gloom and cheerlessness. כָּל־יָמָיו, "all his days," is the accusative of time, not the object of the verb. To eat in darkness is not a common metaphor for spending a gloomy life, but it is a very natural one, and has analogies in this book (*e.g.* ch. ii. 24; iii. 13, etc.), and in such phrases as to "sit in darkness" (Micah vii. 8), and to "walk in darkness" (Isa. l. 10). The Septuagint, reading differently, translates, Καὶ γε πᾶσαι αἱ ἡμέραι αὐτοῦ ἐν σκότει καὶ ἐν πένθει, "Yea, and all his days are in darkness and in mourning." But the other versions reject this alteration, and few modern commentators adopt it. And he hath much sorrow and wrath with his sickness; literally, *and much vexation, and sickness, and wrath*; Revised Version, *he is sore vexed, and hath sickness and wrath*. Delitzsch takes the last words as an exclamation, "And oh for his sorrow and hatred!" The man experiences all kinds of vexation when his plans fail or involve him in trouble and privation; or he is morbid and diseased in mind and body; or he is angry and envious when others succeed better than himself. The sentiment is expressed by St. Paul (1 Tim. vi. 9), "They that desire (βουλόμενοι) to be rich fall into a temptation and a snare, and many foolish and hurtful lusts, such as drown men (βυθίζουσι τοὺς ἀνθρώπους) in destruction and perdition." "For," he proceeds, "the love of money is a root of all kinds of evil, which some reaching after have been led astray from the faith, and have pierced themselves through (ἑαυτοὺς περιέπειραν) with many sorrows." The Septuagint continues its version, "And in much passion (θυμῷ) and in infirmity and wrath." The anger may be directed against himself, as he thinks of his folly in taking all this trouble for nothing.

Vers. 18—20.—Section 8.. The inconveniences of wealth lead the writer back to his old conclusion, that *man should make the best of life, and enjoy all the good that God gives with moderation and contentment.*

Ver. 18.—Behold that which I have seen: it is good and comely, etc. The accentuation is against this rendering, which, however, has the support of the Syriac and the Targum. The Septuagint gives, Ἰδοὺ, εἶδον ἐγὼ ἀγαθὸν, ὅ ἐστι καλόν, "Behold, I have seen a good which is comely;" and it is best to translate, with Delitzsch and others, "Behold, what I have seen as good, what as beautiful, is this." My conclusion holds good. They who seek for traces of Greek influence in Koheleth find Epicureanism in the sentiment, and the familiar combination, καλὸν κἀγαθὸν, in the language. Both ideas are baseless. (For supposed Epicureanism, see on ch. ii. 24 and iii. 12.) And the juxtaposition of καλὸς and ἀγαθὸς is only a fortuitous rendering of the Hebrew, upon which no argument for Grecism can be founded. To eat and to drink, etc.; *i.e.* to use the common blessings which God bestows with thankfulness and contentment. As St. Paul says, "Having food and covering, we shall be therewith content" (1 Tim. vi. 8). Which God giveth him. This is the point so often insisted upon. These temporal blessings are God's gifts, and are not to be considered as the natural and assured result of man's own exertions. Man, indeed, must labour, but God giveth the increase. For it is his portion (ch. iii. 22). This calm enjoyment is allotted to man by God, and nothing more must be expected. Ben-Sira gives similar advice, "Defraud not thyself of a good day, and let not the share in a right pleasure pass by thee. . . . Give, and take, and beguile thy soul; for there is no seeking of dainties in Hades" (Ecclus. xiv. 14. etc.).

Ver. 19.—Every man also. The sentence is anacoluthic, like ch. iii. 13, and may best be rendered, *Also for every man to whom . . . this is a gift of God.* Ginsburg connects the verse closely with the preceding one, supplying, "I have also seen that a man," etc. Whichever way we take the sentence, it comes to the same thing, implying man's absolute dependence upon God's bounty. To whom God hath given riches and wealth. Before he can enjoy his possessions a man must first receive them from God's hands. The two terms here used are not quite synonymous. While the former word, *osher*, is used for wealth of any kind whatever, the latter, *nekasim*, means properly "wealth in cattle," like the Latin *pecunia*, and thence used generally for riches (*volek*). Hath given him power to eat thereof. Abundance is useless without the power to enjoy it. This is the gift of God, a great and special bounty from a loving and gracious God. Thus Horace, 'Epist.,' i. 4. 7—

"Di tibi divitias dederunt artemque fruendi."

"The gods have given you wealth, and (what is more)
Have given you wisdom to enjoy your store."

(Howes.)

Ver. 20.—For he shall not much remember the days of his life. The man who has learned the lesson of calm enjoyment does not much concern himself with the shortness, uncertainty, or possible trouble of life. He carries out the counsel of Christ, "Be not anxious for the morrow, for the morrow will be anxious for itself. Sufficient unto the day is the evil thereof" (Matt. vi. 34). Ginsburg gives an entirely opposite rendering to the clause, "He should remember that the days of his life are not many;" *i.e.* the thought of the shortness of life should urge us to enjoy it while it lasts. But the Authorized Version is supported by the Septuagint and Vulgate and most modern commentators, and seems most appropriate to the context. The marginal rendering, "*Though* he give *not much*, yet he remembereth," etc., which Ginsburg calls a literary curiosity, must have been derived from the version of Junius, which gives, "Quod si non multum (*supple*, est illud quod dederit Deus, *ex versu præc.*)," etc. Because God answereth him in the joy of his heart. The man passes a calm and contented life, because God shows that he is pleased with him by the tranquil joy shed over his heart. The verb מַעֲנֶה (the hiph. participle of עָנָה) is variously rendered. The Septuagint gives, Ὁ Θεὸς περισπᾷ αὐτὸν ἐν εὐφροσύνῃ καρδίας αὐτοῦ, "God distracts him in the mirth of his heart;" Vulgate, *Eo quod Deus occupet deliciis cor ejus*; Ginsburg, "God causeth him to work for the enjoyment of his heart," *i.e.* God assigns him work that he may thence derive enjoyment; Köster, "God makes him sing in the joy of his heart;" Delitzsch, Wright, and Plumptre, "God answers (corresponds with) the joy of his heart," which the latter explains to mean "is felt to approve it as harmonizing, in its calm evenness, with his own blessedness, the tranquillity of the wise man mirroring the tranquillity of God." But this modified Epicureanism is alien from the teaching of Koheleth. Rather the idea is that God answers him with, imparts to him, joy of heart, makes him sensible of his favourable regard by this inward feeling of satisfaction and content.

HOMILETICS.

Vers. 1—7.—*Vanities in worship.* I. IRREVERENCE. Specially exhibited in entering upon Divine service. Discommended and rebuked as: 1. *Inconsistent with the sanctity of the place of worship*—the house of God. Wherever men convene to offer homage to the Divine Being, in a magnificent cathedral or in a humble upper room, upon hillsides and moors, or in dens and caves of the earth, there is a dwelling-place of Jehovah no less than in the temple (Solomonic or post-exilic) or in the synagogue, of both which the Preacher probably thought. What lends sanctity to the spot in which worshippers assemble is not its material surroundings, artificial or natural (architectural elegance or cosmical beauty); it is not even the convening there of the worshippers themselves, however exalted their rank or sacred the character of the acts in which they engage. It is the unseen and spiritual, but real and supernatural, presence of God in the midst of his assembled saints (Exod. xx. 24; Ps. xlvi. 4—7; Matt. xviii. 20; xxviii. 20); and the simple consideration of this fact, much more the realization of that nearness of God to which it points, should awaken in the breast of every one proceeding towards and crossing the threshold of a Christian sanctuary the feeling of awe which inspired Jacob on the heights of Bethel (Gen. xxviii. 17), Ethan the Ezrahite (Ps. lxxxix. 7), and Isaiah in the temple (vi. 1). The thought of God's immediate neighbourhood and of all that it implies, his observance of both the persons of his worshippers (Gen. xvi. 16), and the secrets of their hearts (Ps. cxxxix. 1), should put a hush on every spirit (Hab. ii. 20; Zech. ii. 13), and dispose each one to "keep his foot," metaphorically, to "put off his shoe," as Moses did at the bush (Exod. iii. 5), and Joshua in presence of the Captain of Jehovah's host (Josh. v. 15). 2. *Opposed to the true character of Divine worship.* When congregations assemble in the house of God to do homage to him whose presence fills the house, this end cannot be attained by offering the sacrifice of fools, *i.e.* by rendering such service as proceeds from unbelieving, disobedient, and hypocritical hearts (Prov. xxi. 27), but only by assuming the attitude of one willing to hear (1 Sam. iii. 10; Ps. lxxxv. 8) and to obey not man but God (Ps. xl. 8). If unaccompanied by a disposition to do God's will, mere external performances are of no value whatever, however imposing their magnificence or costly their production. What God desires in his servants is not the outward offering of sacrifices or celebration of ceremonies, but the inward devotion of the spirit (1 Sam. xv. 22; Ps. li. 16, 17; Jer. vii. 21—23; Hos. vi. 6). The highest form of worship is not speaking of or giving to God, but hearing and receiving from God. 3. *Proceeding from ignorance* both of the sanctity of the place and of the spirituality of its worship. However the final clause may be rendered (see Exposition), its sense is that irreverence springs from ignorance—from failing properly to understand the character either of that God they pretend to worship, or of that worship they affect to render. Ignorance of God, of his nature as spiritual, of his character as holy, of his presence as near, of his knowledge as all-observant, of his majesty as awe-inspiring, of his power as irresistible, is the prime root of all wrong worship, as Christ said of the Samaritans (John iv. 22), and as Paul told the Athenians (Acts xvii. 23). II. FORMALITY. Manifested when engaged in Divine service and more particularly in prayer. Two phases of this evil commented on. 1. *Rashness in prayer.* (Ver. 2.) Hasty utterance of whatever comes uppermost, as if any jangle of words might suffice for devotion—a manner of prayer totally inconsistent with the thought that one is standing in the Divine presence. If a petitioner would hardly venture to lay his requests before an earthly sovereign, how much less should a suppliant draw near to Heaven's throne without calm forethought and deliberation? Moreover, it is inconsistent with the real nature of prayer, which is a making known to God of the soul's needs with thankful acknowledgment of the Divine mercies; and how can one either state his own wants or record God's mercies who has never taken time to investigate the one or count up the other? 2. *Prolixity in prayer.* Much speaking, endless and unmeaning repetitions— a characteristic of Pharisaic devotions adverted to by Christ (Matt. vi. 7), and difficult to harmonize either with a due regard to the majesty of God or with the possession of that inward calm which is a necessary condition of all true prayer. As a dreamer's eloquence, usually turgid and magniloquent, proceeds from an unquiet state of the brain, which during day has been unduly excited by a rush of business or by the worries of waking hours, so the multitude of words emitted by a " fool's " voice is occasioned by the inward disquiet of a mind and heart that have not attained to rest in God. At the same time, " the admonition, ' let thy words be few,' is not meant to set limits to the fire of devotion, being directed, not against the inwardly devout, but against the superficially religious, who fancy that in the multitude of their words they have an equivalent for the devotion they lack " (Hengstenberg).

III. INSINCERITY. Displayed after leaving Divine service, more especially in the non-fulfilment of vows voluntarily taken while engaged in worship. Against this wickedness the preacher inveighs. 1. *Because such conduct cannot be other than displeasing to God.* " When thou vowest a vow, defer not to pay it; for he hath no pleasure in fools: pay that which thou hast vowed." As the Almighty himself is " the same yesterday, and to-day, and for ever," " without variableness or shadow of turning," and " changeth not," so he desires in all his worshippers the reflection at least of this perfection, and cannot regard with favour one who plays fast and loose with his promises to men, and far less with his vows to God. 2. *Because such conduct is in no sense unavoidable.* A worshipper is under no obligation to vow anything to Jehovah. Whatever is done in this direction must proceed from the clearest free-will. Hence, to escape the sin of breaking one's vows, one is at liberty not to vow (Deut. xxiii. 21—23). Hence also should one cautiously guard against the utterance of rash and sinful vows like those of Jephthah (Judg. xi. 30) and of Saul (1 Sam. xiv. 24), lest through fulfilling (no less than through breaking) them one should incur sin. Similarly, " we must not vow that which through the frailty of the flesh we have reason to fear we shall not be able to perform, as those that vow a single life and yet know not how to keep their vow " (Matthew Henry). The same remark applies to taking vows of total abstinence from meats and drinks. 3. *Because such conduct cannot escape the just judgment of God.* The rashly uttered vow, afterwards left unfulfilled, sets the speaker of it in the place of a sinner, upon whom as guilty God will inflict punishment. Thus through his mouth, his " flesh," or his body, *i.e.* his whole personality, of which the flesh or body is the outer covering, is caused to suffer. Being just and holy, God can by no means clear the guilty (Exod. xxxiv. 7), although he can justify the ungodly (Rom. iv. 5). Hence the vow-breaker cannot hope to elude the due reward of his infidelity. 4. *Because such conduct is practically indefensible.* To say before the angel or presiding minister in the temple or synagogue in whose hearing the vow had been registered that the registration of it had been an error, was, in the judgment of the Preacher, no excuse, but rather an aggravation of the original offence, and a sure means of drawing down upon the offender the anger of God, and of causing God to effectually thwart and utterly destroy the designs his pretended worshipper had, first in making his vows and afterwards in breaking them; and so, when one retreats from protestations and promises made to God, it is no justification of his conduct in the eyes of others who may have listened to or become aware of his votive engagements, to aver that he had made them in error. Nor is it sufficient to excuse one in God's sight to say that one was mistaken in having promised to do so-and-so. Hence, if one vows before God with regard to matters left in his option, it is his duty to fulfil these vows, even should it be to his hurt. But in all respects it is wiser and better not to vow except in such things as are already enjoined upon one by God; and should it be said that no possible need can arise for taking upon one's self by voluntary obligation what already lies upon one by Divine prescription, this will not be denied. Yet one may vow to do what God has commanded in the sense of resolving to do it—always in dependence on promised grace; and with regard to this no better counsel can be offered than that given by Harvey—

> " Call to thy God for grace to keep
>   Thy vows ; and if thou break them, weep.
> Weep for thy broken vows, and vow again :
> Vows made with tears cannot be still in vain."

LESSONS. 1. The condescension of God in accepting human worship. 2. The dignity of man that he can render such worship as God can accept. 3. The spirituality of all sincere worship of God. 4. The displeasure of God against all worship that is merely external.

Vers. 8, 9.—*The picture of an ideal state.* I. THE SOIL WELL CULTIVATED. As the land of a country is its principal source of wealth, where this is left untilled only destitution to the people upon it can ensue. Access to the broad acres of earth, to extract therefrom by means of labour the treasures therein deposited, constitutes an indispensable prerequisite to the material prosperity of any province or empire. Hence the Preacher depicts, or enables us to depict, a state or condition of things in which this is realized—the common people spread abroad upon the soil and engaged in its cultivation ; the upper classes or feudal lords deriving their support from the same soil in the shape of rents, and even the king receiving from it in the form of taxes his imperial revenues.

II. THE LAW EQUALLY ADMINISTERED. The opposite of this is the picture sketched by the Preacher, who probably transferred to his pages a spectacle often witnessed in Palestine during the years of Persian domination—" the oppression of the poor, and violent perverting of judgment and justice in a province ; " the labouring classes despoiled of their scanty savings, and even denied their fair share in the fruits of their own industry, ground down and oppressed by the tyranny and avarice of their social and political superiors, the satraps and other officers who ruled them, and these again preyed on by fiercer harpies above them, and so on, up through each ascending rank of dignitaries, till the last and highest was reached. Reverse the state of matters thus described, and imagine all classes in the community dwelling together in harmony, and conspiring to advance each other's comfort and happiness—the toiling millions cheerfully, honestly, and diligently cultivating the soil, and manufacturing its products into higher forms of wealth and beauty, the upper classes jealously guarding the rights and furthering the welfare of these industrious artisans, and each regarding the other with confidence and esteem—the poet's dream of Utopia, in which " all men's good" should be "each man's rule," would then be realized.

III. THE SOVEREIGN BENEFICENTLY ENTERPRISING. Not in pushing forward his own personal aggrandizement, which in ancient Oriental countries was often done at the expense of his subjects, as by Pharaoh of Egypt (Exod. i. 11) and Solomon of Israel and Judah (1 Kings xii. 4), but by devoting his energies to further the material (and intellectual) advancement of his people. " But the profit of a land every way is a king that maketh himself servant to the field," or " is a king over the cultivated field " (Revised Version margin), or is a king devoted to agriculture (Rosenmüller, Delitzsch, Wright), like Uzziah of Judah, who "loved husbandry " (2 Chron. xxvi. 10). It is only amplifying this thought to represent the ideal state as one in which the king or emperor consecrates his life and powers to the honourable and laborious task of promoting the material prosperity and temporal happiness of his subjects by removing the yoke from agriculture, fostering trade and commerce, encouraging manufactures and inventions, aiding science and art, diffusing education, and stimulating his people upward in every possible way towards the ideal of all free peoples, viz. self-government.

IV. THE DEITY APPROVING. Here again the Preacher's picture must be changed. What he beheld was wholesale oppression and robbery practised by the upper and powerful classes against the under and powerless classes, or in modern phrase, " the masses," and God over both looking on in calm silence (Ps. l. 21), but by no means imperturbed indifference (Zeph. i. 12), accurately noting all the wickedness going on beneath the sun (Ps. xxxiii. ,13—15), and quietly waiting his own time to call it to account (ch. iii. 15, 17 ; xi. 9 ; xii. 14). What must be substituted is a state of matters in which over the well-organized, industrious, peaceful, co-operating community the almighty Disposer of events, the King of nations and King of kings, presides, beaming on them with his gracious smile (Numb. vi. 24—26) and establishing the work of their hands upon them (Ps. xc. 17).

Learn: 1. The duty of the state to seek the welfare of all. 2. The duty of each to promote the welfare of the state.

Vers. 8—17.—*A sermon on the vanity of riches.* I. FREQUENTLY ACQUIRED BY WRONG. As, for instance, by oppression and robbery (ver. 8). That honest labour sometimes leads to affluence cannot be denied (Prov. x. 4); more often, however, it is the ungodly who increase in riches (Ps. lxxiii. 12), and that, too, by means of their ungodliness (Prov. i. 19; xxii. 16; xxviii. 20; Hab. ii. 6, 9; 1 Tim. vi. 9, 10). Hence the question arises whether, if riches cannot be obtained without plunging into all sorts of wickedness, they are worth seeking to obtain at all; whether, if to secure them a man must not only practise dishonesty, theft, oppression, and perhaps worse, but convert his soul into a harbour of divers pernicious lusts, such as avarice, covetousness, and envy, it is really a good bargain to secure them at such a cost. Christ's question, "What shall it profit a man," etc.? (Matt. xvi. 26) has a bearing on this. (On the evils that have come with the great accumulation of wealth, see 'Socialism New and Old,' p. XXXVIII.: International Scientific Series.)

II. ALWAYS INCAPABLE OF YIELDING SATISFACTION. "He that loveth silver shall not be satisfied with silver; nor he that loveth abundance with increase" (ver. 10). In addition to the well-known fact that material wealth has no power to impart solid satisfaction to the better instincts of the soul (Luke xii. 15)—a fact eloquently commented on by Burns ('Epistle to Davie')—

> "It's no in titles nor in rank,
> It's no in wealth like Lon'on Bank,
> To purchase peace and rest," etc.

—the appetite for wealth grows by what it feeds on. The rich are ever craving for more. "The avaricious man is always wanting," said Horace ('Epist.,' i. 2. 26); while Ovid ('Fasti,' i. 211, 212) wrote of rich men, "Both their wealth and a furious lust of wealth increase, and when they possess the most they seek for more." Hence, to use another rendering, "He whose love cleaveth to abundance hath nothing of it" (Delitzsch). "He who hangs his heart on the continual tumult, noise, pomp, of more numerous and greater possessions if possible, to all real profit—*i.e.* all pleasant, peaceful enjoyment—is lost" (ibid.).

III. OFTEN MULTIPLY THEIR OWNER'S CARES. 1. *Numerous dependents.* Unless he is a miser, "who shuts up his money in chests and only feeds himself in looking at it with closed doors" (Delitzsch), the rich man, like Job (i. 3) and Solomon (1 Kings iv. 2, etc.), will maintain a large and expensive household, which will eat up his substance, so that, notwithstanding all his wealth, he shall have little more for his portion in the same than the satisfaction of seeing it pass through his hands (ver. 11). As Pheraulas the Persian observed to a Sacian youth, who congratulated him on being rich, "Do you think, Sacian, that I live with more pleasure the more I possess? Do you not know that I neither eat nor drink nor sleep with a particle more pleasure now than when I was poor? But by having this abundance I gain merely this, that I have to guard more, to distribute more to others, and to have the trouble of taking care of more; for a great many domestics now demand of me their food, their drink, and their clothes. . . . Whosoever, therefore, is greatly pleased with the possession of riches will, be assured, feel annoyed at the expenditure of them" (Xenophon, 'Cyropædia,' viii. 3. 39—44). 2. *Increased anxieties.* The rich man, through the abundance of his riches, is worried with cares, which pursue him into the night, and will not suffer him to sleep (ver. 12), for thinking of how he shall protect his wealth against the midnight prowler, of how he shall increase it by successful trade and profitable investment, of how he shall employ it so as to extract from it the largest quantity of enjoyment; whereas the labouring man, whether he eats little or much, drops into refreshing slumber the moment he lays his head upon his pillow, untroubled by anxious thoughts as to how he shall dispose of his wealth, which consists chiefly in the fewness of his wants. So sang Horace long ago of "gentle sleep," which "scorns not the humble abodes of ploughmen" ('Odes,' iii. 1. 21—23), and Virgil of the tillers of the soil, who

" want not slumber sweet beneath the trees " (' Georg.,' ii. 469); so wrote Shakespeare of the " honey-heavy dew of slumber " (' Julius Cæsar,' act ii. sc. 1), describing it as

> "Sore labour's bath,
> Balm of hurt minds, great nature's second course,
> Chief nourisher in life's feast;"
>
> (' Macbeth,' act ii. se. 2.)

representing it as lying rather

> " In smoky cribs
> Than in the perfumed chambers of the great ; "
>
> (' Henry IV.,' Part II., act iii. sc. 1.)

and depicting the shepherd's " wonted sleep under a fresh tree's shade " as " far beyond a prince's delicates " (' Henry VI.,' act ii. sc. 5).

IV. NOT SELDOM DISAPPOINT THE HOPES THEY HAVE RAISED. 1. *The hope of never-failing happiness.* The rich man hopes that in future years his wealth will be to him a source of comfort (Luke xii. 19). As the years go by he discovers they have only been kept to his hurt (ver. 13)—if not physically or mentally, at least morally and spiritually (1 Tim. vi. 10, 17); and the fact is often so, whether he discovers it or not. 2. *The hope of never knowing want.* The rich man expects that, having safely locked them up in a prudent speculation, he will keep them at least during his lifetime; but alas! the speculation turns out " an evil adventure," and his much-prized riches perish (ver. 14). 3. *The hope of perpetuating his name.* Once more the rich man pleases himself with the prospect of founding a family by leaving his son the fortune he has heaped up by toil, thrift, and profitable speculation. By the time he comes to die he has nothing in his hand to bequeath, and so is forced to bid farewell to his hopes and leave his son a pauper.

V. MUST EVENTUALLY BE LEFT BY ALL. 1. *Absolutely.* However rich a man may grow in his lifetime, of all he has amassed he must divest himself at the grave's mouth, as Claudio in the prison is reminded by the duke—

> " If thou art rich, thou art poor ;
> For, like an ass whose back with ingots bows,
> Thou bear'st thy riches but a journey,
> And death unloads thee."
>
> (' Measure for Measure,' act iii. sc. 1.)

" As he came forth of his mother's womb, naked shall he return to go as he came, and shall take nothing of his labour, which he may carry away in his hand " (ver. 15; cf. Job i. 21); for as " we brought nothing into this world," so it is " certain we can carry nothing out " (1 Tim. vi. 7). 2. *Without compensation.* " What profit," then, the Preacher asks, has the rich man who has laboured all his days to amass wealth? The answer is, " Nothing ! he has simply laboured for the wind." Nor is this the worst. To have had a pleasant time of it before being obliged to part with his wealth would have been a compensation, however slight, to the rich man; but for the most part even this is denied him. In order to amass his riches he has commonly been found to play the part of a miser, " eating in the dark to save candle-light, or working all day and waiting till nightfall before he sits down to a meal " (Plumptre); or, if the words " eating in darkness " be taken metaphorically, while gathering gold he has passed his existence in gloom and sadness, having no light in his heart (Hengstenberg), he has fallen into sore vexation at the failure of many of his plans, become morbidly disposed, " diseased in mind and body," and even waxed wrathful at God, himself, and all the world.

LESSONS. 1. The duty of moderating one's pursuit of earthly riches. 2. The wisdom of laying up for one's self treasures in heaven. 3. The happiness enjoyed by the poor.

Vers. 18—20.—*The picture of a " good and comely " life.* I. THE LABOUR OF THE HANDS REWARDED. The toiler spends not his strength for nought and in vain (Isa. xlix. 4), but with the sweat of his brow earns for himself bread to eat, water to drink, and raiment to put on (Gen. xxviii. 20). Work and food the two first requisites of a good and comely life.

II. THE GOOD THINGS OF LIFE ENJOYED. Not only has the toiler the pleasant satisfaction of being able to earn through his personal exertions something, yea, enough, to eat and drink and to clothe himself withal, but over and above he can eat and drink and wear that which he has earned, and generally rejoice in that which his hands have won. Health and cheerfulness the next two requisites of a good and comely life.

III. THE ILLS OF EXISTENCE FORGOTTEN. If not entirely exempt from ills, since there is no man born of woman who is not heir to trouble (Job v. 7; xiv. 1), yet these affect him so slightly and leave so small impression on his soul, that the even tenor of his life flows on, and he hardly remembers the days as they pass. Equanimity and hopefulness a third pair of requisites for a good and comely life.

IV. THE GOODNESS OF HEAVEN RECOGNIZED. A "good and comely" life differs from mere animal existence in this, that it acknowledges all it receives and enjoys as a portion marked out for it by the sovereign appointment, and bestowed upon it by the gracious bounty of God (Jas. i. 17). Gratitude and religion a fourth pair of requisites for a good and comely life.

V. THE APPROBATION OF GOD EXPERIENCED. The joy of such a life, being more than mere sensuous gratification, and springing up within the deep recesses of the soul, being in fact pure heart-joy, is not displeasing to God, but, on the contrary, is by him observed, answered, and confirmed. Peace and joy the last and highest pair of requisites for a good and comely life.

Learn: 1. The propriety of striving after an ideal life. 2. The necessity of aiming at improved surroundings of existence. 3. The impossibility of reaching Utopia either for the state or the individual without religion.

HOMILIES BY VARIOUS AUTHORS.

Ver. 1.—*The temple and the worshippers.* It is evident that the services of the pious Israelites were by no means merely sacrificial and ceremonial. There is a reflective and intellectual character attributed to the approach of the Hebrew worshippers to their God. The practical admonitions of this passage have reference, not to a formal, but to an intelligent and thoughtful worship.

I. THE HOUSE OF GOD. By this is to be understood no doubt a place, a building, probably the temple at Jerusalem. But clearly it follows from this language that in the view of the writer of Ecclesiastes the idea of the locality, the edifice, is almost lost sight of in the idea of the spiritual presence of Jehovah, and in the society and fellowship of sincere and devout worshippers. God, it was well understood, dwelleth not in temples made with hands, but abideth in his people's hearts.

II. THE SACRIFICE OF FOLLY. In every large gathering of professed worshippers there is reason to fear there are those with whom worship is nothing but a form, a custom. The sacrifice of such is outward only; their postures, their words, may be unexceptionable, but the heart is absent from the service. Inattention, want of true interest, unspirituality, take the place of those penitential acknowledgments—that heavenward aspiration—which are acceptable to him who searcheth the hearts and trieth the reins of the children of men. The sacrifice of such formal and irreverent worshippers is justly designated a sacrifice of fools. They consider not their own nature, their own needs; they consider not the attributes of him whom they profess to approach with the language of adoration, of gratitude, of petition. They are, therefore, not only irreligious; they are foolish, and they seem to say to every sensible observer that they are fools.

III. THE WORSHIP OF THE WISE. In contrast with the careless and undevout we have here depicted the spirit and the demeanour of true worshippers. They are characterized by: 1. *Self-restraint.* The modest repression of all that savours of self-assertion seems to be intended by the admonition, "Keep thy foot," which is as much as to say, "Take heed to thy steps, observe with care thy way, wander not from the path of sincerity, beware of indifference and of obtrusiveness." 2. *Reverence.* Such as becomes the creature in approaching the Creator in whose hand his breath is, and whose are all his ways;

such as becomes the sinner in addressing a holy God, whose Law has been broken, whose favour has to be implored. 3. *A spirit of attentive and submissive hearing.* " Speak, Lord ; for thy servant heareth," is language becoming to the lowly and reverent worshipper ; he shall be made acquainted with God's Law, and he shall rejoice in God's promises.—T.

Ver. 2.—*Reverence, reticence, and brevity in devotion.* What a contrast is there between this sound and sober counsel, and the precepts and customs prevalent among the heathen ! These latter have corrupted the very practice of devotion ; whilst those who acknowledge the authority of the Scriptures condemn themselves if their worship is superficial, pretentious, formal, and insincere.
I. THE RULES OF DEVOTION. 1. *Avoid profane rashness and precipitancy.* When rashness and haste are forbidden, it is not intended to condemn ejaculatory or extempore prayer. There are occasions when such prayer is the natural and appropriate expression of the deep feelings of the heart ; when one cannot pause to weigh one's words, when one cannot fall back upon liturgy or litany, however scriptural and rich. What is censured is ill-considered prayer, which is not properly prayer at all, but the outpouring of ill temper and petulance. Such utterances may be profane, and are certainly unsuitable, unbecoming. 2. *Avoid verbiage.* When praise and prayer take shape in many words, there is danger of using " vain repetitions," against which our Lord Christ has so urgently warned his disciples. Long and diffuse devotions are probably addressed rather to men than to God. They are unnecessary and unprofitable, for God does not need them ; they are irreverential, for they betoken a mind more occupied about self than about the Supreme. But this precept does not preclude urgency and even repetition when such are dictated by profound feeling and by special circumstances.
II. THE REASON OF THESE RULES. 1. *The nature, the character of God himself.* " He is in heaven." By heaven we are to understand the eternal sphere apart from and above time, earth, and sense. We are not to rank God with earthly potentates, but are to bear in mind his distinctness and superiority. As our Creator, he knows both our emotions and our wants ; as our Lord and Judge, he knows our sins and frailties ; as our Saviour, he knows our penitence and faith. Such considerations may well preclude familiarity, rashness, verbosity, irreverence. To think rightly of God, to feel aright with regard to him, is to be preserved from such faults and errors as are here mentioned with censure. 2. *The position of men.* Being upon earth, men partake in the feebleness and finiteness of the created. They are *suppliants;* and as such they should ever approach the throne of grace with reverence and humiliation. They are *sinners;* and should imitate the spirit of him who, when he came up into the temple to pray, cried, " God be merciful to me a sinner ! " This was a short prayer ; but he who offered it was accepted and justified.—T.

Vers. 4, 5.—*The law of the vow.* There are those who would disapprove of the violation of a promise given to a fellow-man, who think lightly of evading a promise solemnly volunteered to the Creator. It may be said that a fellow-man might suffer from such neglect or dereliction, but that God can suffer no loss or harm if a vow be not fulfilled. Such an extenuation or excuse for violating vows arises from the too common notion that the moral character of an action depends upon the consequences that follow it, and not upon the principles that direct it. A man's conduct may be wrong even if no one is injured by it ; for he may violate both his own nature and the moral law itself.
I. THE NATURE OF THE VOW. When some signal favour has been experienced, some forbearance exercised on a man's behalf, he desires to evince his gratitude, to do something which in ordinary circumstances he would probably not have done, and he makes a vow unto God, sacredly promising to offer some gift, to perform some service. Or even more commonly, the vow is made in hope of some benefit desired, and its fulfilment is conditional upon a petition being favourably answered, a desire being gratified.
II. THE VOLUNTARINESS OF THE VOW. It is presumed that no constraint is exercised, that the promise made to Heaven is the free and spontaneous expression of religious

feeling. The language of Peter to Ananias expresses this aspect of the proceeding: "Whiles it remained, did it not remain thine own? and after it was sold, was it not in thy power?"

III. THE OBLIGATION OF THE VOW. It is questionable whether vows are in all cases expedient. A vow to act sinfully is certainly not binding. And there are some vows which it is unwise in some circumstances, if not in all circumstances, to make; this is the case especially with vows which seem to make too great a demand upon human nature, which are indeed against nature; e.g. vows of celibacy, and of obedience to fellow-creatures as fallible as are those who bind themselves to obey. But if a vow be made knowingly and voluntarily, and if its fulfilment be not wrong, then the text assures us it is obligatory, and should be paid.

IV. THE FOLLY OF DEFERRING TO PAY THE VOW. There are disagreeable duties, which weak persons admit to be duties, and intend to discharge, but the discharge of which they postpone. Such duties do not become easier or more agreeable because deferred. Generally speaking, when conscience tells us that a certain thing ought to be done, the sooner we do it the better. So with the vow. " Defer not to pay it; for God hath no pleasure in fools."

V. THE SIN OF NEGLECTING AND REPUDIATING THE VOW. The vow is an evidence, it may be presumed, that there existed at the time, in the mind of him who made it, strong feelings and earnest purposes. Now, for one who has passed through such experiences so far to forget or abjure them as to act as if the vow had never been made, is a proof of religious declension and of inconsistency. How common is such " back-sliding"! It is said, "Better is it that thou shouldest not vow, than that thou shouldest vow and not pay." He who vows not contracts no special obligation, whilst he who vows and withholds payment repudiates a solemn obligation which he has undertaken. A warning is thus given to which it is important for those especially to give heed who are liable to religious excitement and enthusiasm. If such characters yield as readily to evil influences as to good, their impressions may be a curse rather than a blessing, or at least may be the occasion of moral deterioration. None can feel and resolve and pray, and then afterwards act in opposition to their purest feelings, their highest resolves, their fervent prayers, without suffering serious harm, without weakening their moral power, without incurring the just displeasure of the righteous Governor and Lord of all.—T.

Ver. 8.—*The oppressor's accountability.* We are not taught in this verse to disregard the wrongs of our fellow-creatures, to shut our eyes to deeds of iniquity, to close our ears against the cry of the suffering, to steel our heart against the anguish of the oppressed. But we are cautioned against drawing hasty and ill-considered conclusions from the prevalence of injustice; we are encouraged to cherish faith in the overruling and retributive providence of God.

I. THE FACT OF OPPRESSION. Such cases as are here referred to exist in every state; but in the East they have always existed in great numbers. Despotic governments are more favourable to oppression than those states where free institutions are established and where popular rights are respected. Reference is made: 1. To the maltreatment of the poor, who are powerless to defend themselves, and who have no helper. 2. To the withholding and perversion of justice.

II. THE DISTRESS AND PERPLEXITY NATURALLY OCCASIONED BY THE EXISTENCE OF OPPRESSION. 1. To the sufferers themselves; who are in some cases deprived of liberty, in some cases robbed of their property, in other cases injured in their person. 2. The spectators of such wrongs are aroused to sympathy, pity, and indignation. No rightly constituted mind can witness injustice without resentment. Even those who themselves exercise rights and enjoy privileges lose much of the pleasure and advantage of their own position by reason of the wrongs which their neighbours endure at the hand of power and cruelty. 3. Society is in danger of corruption when the laws are over-ridden by selfishness, avarice, and lust; when righteousness is scoffed at, and when men's best instincts and convictions are outraged.

III. THE REDRESS FOR WRONG IN THE UNIVERSAL GOVERNMENT OF GOD. 1. Oppression is not unnoticed. Whether the oppressor hopes to escape, or fears to be called to account, it is for the spectator of his evil deeds to remember that " One higher than the high regardeth." 2. Oppression is not unrecorded. The iniquities of the unjust judge, of the arbitrary sovereign, of the villainous workman who violently hinders his fellow-workman from earning an honest livelihood,—all are written in the book of God. Even when deeds of oppression are wrought in the sacred name of religion by the persecutor and the inquisitor, such deeds are remembered, and will in due time be brought to light. 3. Oppression will not be unavenged. Either now in this world, or hereafter in the state of retribution, the oppressor, like every other sinner, shall be brought to the bar of Divine justice. God shall bring every man into judgment. As a man soweth, so shall he also reap. The wicked shall not go unpunished.—T.

Ver. 9.—*The earth and man.* Whatever obscurity may attach to the interpretation of this verse, in any case it represents the dependence of the inhabitants of earth upon the produce of the soil.

I. THE FACT OF THE BOUNTEOUSNESS OF THE FRUITFUL EARTH. 1. Man's body is fashioned out of its dust. Whatever may have been the process by which the animal nature of man was prepared as the lodging and the vehicle of the immortal spirit, there is no question as to the fact that the human body is a part of nature, that it is composed of elements of a nature similar to those existing around, that it is subject to physical law. All this seems implied in the statement that the human frame was formed of the dust of the ground. 2. Man's body is supported by its produce. Directly or indirectly, man's corporeal nature is nourished by the material substances which exist in various forms upon the surface of the earth. The vegetable and animal creation minister to man's needs and growth. 3. Man's body is resolved into its substance. "Dust thou art, and unto dust shalt thou return." The earth provides man with his food, his raiment, his dwelling, and his grave.

II. THE UNIVERSALITY OF THE BOUNTEOUSNESS OF THE EARTH. 1. The least is not overlooked, the poorest is cared for, fed, and sheltered. 2. The greatest is not independent. All men share the same nature, and sit at the same table: "The king himself is served by the field."

LESSONS. 1. We have to learn our dependence upon what is lower than ourselves. Whilst we are in this earth, whilst we share this corporeal nature, the material ministers to bodily needs, and must not be disdained or despised. 2. We should rise to an apprehension of our real dependence upon Divine providence. "The earth is the Lord's, and the fulness thereof." It is ordered by God's wisdom that the earth should be the instrument of good to all his creatures, even to the highest. And the enlightened and thoughtful will not fail to ascend from the instrument to him that fashioned it, from the abode to him that built it, from the means of well-being to him who appointed and provided them all, and who intended the earth and all that is in it to teach his intelligent creatures something of his glorious character and gracious purposes.—T.

Vers. 10—17.—*The unsatisfying nature of riches.* To love wealth for its own sake is ridiculous. To desire it for the sake of the advantages it may secure is natural, and (within limits) is not blamable. To set the heart upon it for such purposes, to long for it above higher good, to be absorbed in its quest, is sinful. The wise man points out the insufficiency of material possessions to satisfy the nature of man. The reflections here recorded are the result of wide observation and of personal experience.

I. RICHES CANNOT AFFORD SATISFACTION TO THOSE WHO SET THEIR AFFECTION UPON THEM. A man who uses his property for lawful ends, and regards it in the true light as a provision made by God's wisdom and bounty for his wants, need know nothing of the experience recorded in ver. 10. But he who *loves*—i.e. desires with ardent desire, and as the chief good of life—silver and abundance, shall not be satisfied with wealth when it is attained. It is not in the nature of earthly good to quench the deep desires of man's immortal spirit.

II. RICHES ARE CONSUMED BY THOSE WHO ARE DEPENDENT UPON THEM. A large family, a circle of dependents, needy relatives, are the cause of the disappearance even of large revenues. This is no trouble to a man who judges justly; but to a foolish man whose one desire is to accumulate, it is a distress to witness the necessary expenditure involved in family and social claims.

III. RICHES ARE A SOURCE OF ANXIETY TO THE POSSESSOR. The labouring man, who earns and eats his daily bread, and depends for to-morrow's supply upon to-morrow's toil, sleeps sweetly; whilst the capitalist and investor are wakeful by reason of many anxieties. A ship richly freighted may be wrecked, and the cargo lost; a company in which large sums have been invested may fail; a mine of precious metal upon which money has been spent, and from which much is hoped, may cease to be productive. An estate may no longer be profitable; thieves may break through and steal jewels and bullion. As surely as a man owns more than is needed for the supply of his daily wants, so surely is he liable to solicitude and care.

IV. RICHES MAY EVEN PROVE INJURIOUS TO THEIR OWNER. In some states of society the possession of wealth is likely to bring down upon the rich the envy and cupidity of a despotic ruler, who ill treats the wealthy in order to secure his riches for himself. And in all states of society there is danger lest wealth should be the occasion of moral injury, by enkindling evil passions, envy on the part of the poor, and in return hatred and suspicion on the part of the wealthy; or by leading to flattery, which in turn produces vanity and contemptuousness.

V. RICHES ARE OF NO AVAIL BEYOND THIS LIFE. They thus add, in the case of the avaricious, another sting to death; for clutch and grasp them as he may, they must be left behind. A man spends his whole life, and exhausts all his energies, in gathering together a "fortune;" no sooner has he succeeded than he is summoned to return naked to the earth, carrying nothing in his hand, poor as he came into the scene of his toils, his success, his disappointments. The king of terrors cannot be bribed. A mine of wealth cannot buy a day of life.

VI. RICHES MAY BE WASTED BY THE RICH MAN'S HEIRS. This was a misfortune of which the writer of Ecclesiastes seems to have been well aware from his prolonged observation of human life. One may gather; but who shall scatter? He to whom wealth is everything has no security that his property shall not, after his death, come into the hands of those who shall squander it in dissipation, or waste it in reckless speculations. This also is vanity.

APPLICATION. These things being so, the moral is obvious. The poor man may rest contented with his lot, for he knows not whether increase of possessions would bring him increase of happiness. The prosperous man may well give heed to the admonition, "If riches increase, set not your heart upon them."—T.

Vers. 18—20.—*The good things appointed for man by God.* Some detect in these verses the ring of Epicurean morals. But the difference is vast between desiring and rejoicing in the things of this world as mere means of pleasure, and accepting them with gratitude and using them with moderation and prudence, as the gifts of a Father's bounty and the expression of a Father's love.

I. THE GOOD THINGS OF THIS WORLD COME FROM GOD. It is God's earth which provides our sustenance; it is God's creative wisdom that provides our companionships; it is God who gives us power to acquire, to use, and to enjoy his gifts. All is from God.

II. THE ENJOYMENT OF THINGS IN THEMSELVES GOOD IS INTENDED, AND APPOINTED BY DIVINE WISDOM AND GOODNESS. They were not given to tempt or to curse man, but to gladden his heart and to enrich his life. Benevolence is the impulse of the Divine nature. God is "good to all, and his tender mercies are over all his works."

III. THE ENJOYMENT OF THESE GOOD THINGS MAY BE RENDERED THE OCCASION OF FELLOWSHIP WITH GOD AND THANKSGIVING TO GOD. Thus even the common things of earth may be glorified and made beautiful by their devotion to the highest of all purposes. Through them the Giver of all may be praised, and the heart of the grateful recipient may be raised to fellowship with "the Father of the spirits of all flesh."

IV. THE ABUSE OF GOD'S GOOD GIFTS IS OWING TO HUMAN ERROR AND SIN. They are so often abused that it is not to be wondered at that men come to think them evil in themselves. But in such cases, the blame lies not with the Giver, but with the recipient, who turns the very honey into gall.—T.

Vers. 1, 2.—*Acceptable service.* Although the precise meaning of the Preacher is open to some doubt, we shall not go wrong in letting these words speak to us of—

I. THE FUTILITY OF FORMAL WORSHIP. Reference is made to (1) the offering of sacrifice (ver. 1), and (2) the repetition of devotional phrases. We may find a Christian parallel in the reception of sacraments, and in the "prayers" and psalmody of the Church. We know that the purest spirituality may breathe in these, and may be nourished by these, but we know also (1) that they may fail to express any real and pure devotion; (2) that in this case they also fail in winning the favour of God; and (3) that they leave the soul rather the worse than the better, for in such futile worship there is a dangerous delusiveness which is apt to lead to a false and even fatal sense of security.

II. ACCEPTABLE SERVICE. This is threefold. 1. *Reverence*. This is strongly implied, especially in the second verse. Let the worshipper realize that he is in "the house of God," none other and no less than that (see Gen. xxviii. 17). Let him realize that "God is in heaven," etc.; that he is bowing before the Infinite One himself; that he is addressing him who, in his Divine nature and in his unapproachable rank, is immeasurably removed above himself; that he is speaking to One who sees the actions of every life, and knows the secrets of all hearts, and who needs not, therefore, to be informed of what we do or what we feel. Let language be spared, let sacred thought and solemn feeling flow; let a sense of human littleness and of the Divine majesty silence all insincerity, and fill the soul with reverential awe. 2. *Docility*. "Be more ready ['draw nigh,' Revised Version] *to hear*," etc. There is much virtue in docility. Our Lord strongly commended the child-spirit as the condition of entrance into the kingdom; and was not this principally because the spirit of childhood is that of docility—eagerness to know, readiness to receive? We should draw nigh to God in his house, not that we may hear our favourite dogmas once more exalted or enforced, but that we may hear the mind and know the will of Christ better than we have done before; that we may "be filled with the knowledge of his will;" that it may become increasingly true that "we have the mind of Christ." To desire to part with our errors, our ignorance, our prejudices, our half-views, our misconceptions, and to have a closer vision of our Lord and of his Divine truth,—this is acceptable worship. 3. *Obedience*. "Keep thy foot;" "go to the house of God 'with a straight foot,' a foot trained to walk in the path of holy obedience." Go to the house of God as one that "has clean hands and a pure heart;" as one that "lifts up holy hands" unto God. To go up to "offer sacrifice," or "make long prayers," with the determination in the heart to continue a life of impurity, or intemperance, or dishonesty, or injustice, or harshness toward the weak and the dependent,—this is to mock our Maker; it is to grieve the Father of spirits, the Lord of holiness and love. But, on the other hand, to go up to his sanctuary with a pure desire and real resolve to turn from our evil way, and to strive, against all outward hostility and all inward impulses,'to walk in our integrity,—this is acceptable with God. "To obey is better than sacrifice;" and it is the spirit of obedience rather than the overt act of correctness for which the righteous Lord is looking.—C.

Vers. 4—6.—*Vowing and paying*. We may regard the subject of vows in two aspects.

I. THEIR CHARACTER. They may be of: 1. *An entirely obligatory character*. We may solemnly promise to God that which we may not withhold without sin. But this may be shortly summed up in one word—*ourselves*. We owe to him ourselves, all that we are and have, our powers and our possessions. And the first thing that becomes us all is to present ourselves before God in a most solemn act of surrender, in which we deliberately resolve and undertake to yield to him our heart and life thenceforth and for ever. In this great crisis of our spiritual history we make the one supreme vow with which all others are incomparable. It should be made in the exercise of all the powers of our nature; not under any kind of compulsion, but as freely as fully, as intelligently as heartily. It is one that is, of course, to be renewed, and this both *regularly*, and also on *all special occasions*. It is a vow to be confirmed every time we bow in the sanctuary, and every time we gather at the table of the Lord. 2. *Optional*. And of these vows which may be described as optional, there are (1) those that are *conditional*; as when a man promises that if God give him wealth he will devote a large proportion of it to his direct service (see Gen. xxviii. 22); or that if God restore his health he will consecrate all his time and all his possessions to the proclamation of his truth. (2) Those that are *unconditional*; as when (*a*) a man determines that thenceforth he will give a certain fixed proportion of his income to the cause of Christ; or (*b*) when he pledges himself to abstain from some particular indulgence which is hurtful to himself or is a temptation to others.

II. THE SPIRIT IN WHICH THEY SHOULD BE MADE AND FULFILLED. 1. *With devout deliberation.* It is a serious mistake for a man to undertake that which he fails to carry out. (1) It is offensive to God (ver. 4). (2) It is injurious to the man himself; he is in a distinctly worse spiritual position after failure than he would have been if he had not entered into an engagement (ver. 5). We should not promise anything in ignorance of ourselves, and then lose our self-respect by a humiliating withdrawal. 2. In a spirit of *prompt and cheerful obedience.* What we vow to do we should do (1) without delay, "deferring not." There is always danger in delay. To-morrow we shall be further in time from the hour of solemn resolution, and its force will be lessened by the distance. Also (2) cheerfully; for we may be sure that God loveth a cheerful promise-keeper—one that does what he undertook to do, although it proves to be of greater dimensions or to be attended with severer effort than he at first imagined it would. 3. *With patient persistency;* not allowing anything to come between himself and his honourable fulfilment. (1) Are we fully redeeming our vows of Christian consecration in the daily life that we are living? (2) Are we paying the vows we made in some dark hour of need (see Ps. lxvi. 13, 14)?—C.

Vers. 8—16.—*Comfort in confusion.* In the time and the country to which the text belongs there was a very large amount of injustice, rapacity, insecurity. Men could not count on enjoying the fruits of their labour; they were in serious danger of being wronged, or even "done to death;" there were not the constitutional guards and fences with which we are familiar now and here. The political and social conditions of the age and of the land added much to the seriousness of the great problems of the moralist. But though he was perplexed, he was not without light and comfort. There was that—

I. AFFORDED BY REASON AND EXPERIENCE. What if it were true that oppression was often to be witnessed, and, with oppression, the suffering of the weak, yet it was to be remembered that : 1. There was *often an appeal* to a higher authority, and the unrighteous sentence was reversed (ver. 8). 2. There was always reason to hope that *injustice and tyranny would be short-lived* (ver. 9). The king was served by the field; he was by no means independent of those who lived by manual labour; he was as much their subject in fact and truth as they were his in form and in law; he could not afford to live in their disregard and disapproval. 3. Successful oppression was far from being satisfactory to those who practised it. (1) No avaricious man was ever satisfied with the money he made; he was always coveting more; the thirst for gold lived on, and grew by what it gained (ver. 10). (2) The wealthy man found that he could not enjoy more than a fraction of what he acquired; he was compelled to see others partaking of that which his own toil had earned (ver. 11). The successful man was worried and burdened with his own wealth; the fear of losing balanced, if it did not more than counterbalance, the enjoyment of acquisition (ver. 12). (4) No rich man could be sure of the disposition of his hardly won and carefully stored treasure; his son might scatter it in sin and folly (vers. 13, 14). (5) No man can take a solitary fraction of his goods beyond the boundary of life (vers. 15, 16). 4. *Obscurity is not without its own advantage.* (1) It sleeps the sweet sleep of security; it has nothing to lose; it holds out no bait to the despoiler (ver. 12). (2) It enjoys the fruit of its labour, untroubled by the ambitions, unwearied with the excessive toils, unworried by the frequent vexations of those who aim at higher posts and move in larger spheres.

II. AFFORDED BY REVELATION. The godly man, and more especially he to whom Jesus Christ has spoken, contents himself—so far as it is right and well to be contented in the midst of confusion and perversion—with the peace-bringing considerations: 1. That Infinite Wisdom is overruling, and will direct all things to a right issue. 2. That it is not our circumstances, but our character, that should chiefly concern us. To *be* pure, true, loyal, helpful, Christ-like, is immeasurably more than to *have* and to hold any quantity of treasure, any place or rank whatsoever. 3. That we who travel to a heavenly home, who look forward to a "crown of life," can afford to wait for our heritage.—C.

Vers. 15, 16.—*The difference at death.* Even when we have been long looking for the departure of one whose powers as well as his days are spent, his death, when it does come, makes a great difference to us. Between life at its lowest and death there is a great and felt interval. How much more must this be the case to the departed himself! What a difference to him between this life and that to which he goes! Perhaps less than we imagine, yet doubtless very great. The text suggests to us—

I. WHAT WE MUST LEAVE BEHIND US AT DEATH. 1. *Our worldly goods.* This is an obvious fact, which painfully impressed the Preacher (text), and which comforted the psalmist (Ps. xlix. 16, 17). It is a fact that should make the wise less careful to acquire and to save. 2. *Our reputation.* The reputation for wisdom or folly, for integrity or dishonesty, for kindness or severity, which our life has been building up, death cannot destroy, through whatever experiences we may then pass. We must be content to leave that behind to be associated with our name in the memories of men, for their benediction or for their reproach. 3. *The influence* for good or evil we have exerted on human souls. These we cannot remove, nor can we stay to deepen or to counteract them; they are our most important legacies.

II. WHAT WE MAY LEAVE BEHIND US. 1. *A wise disposition of our property.* A sagacious statesman once said that he never quite made up his mind about his neighbour's character until he had seen his will. What disposition we make of that we leave behind is a very serious act of our life; there are very few single acts so serious. (1) It is usually a good thing for a man to dispose of a large proportion of all that he has earned during his life when he is here to superintend it. (2) It is criminally careless to cause additional sorrow at death by negligence in the matter of disposition of means. (3) The kindest thing we can do for our relatives is not to provide absolutely for their wants, but to facilitate their own self-support. 2. *Wise counsels* to those who will heed them. There are usually those who will pay great regard to the wishes of the dying, apart from any "legal instructions." We may leave with those we love such recommendations as shall save them from grave mistakes, and guide them to good and happy courses. 3. *A valued testimony* to the power and preciousness of the gospel of Jesus Christ.

III. WHAT WE MAY TAKE WITH US. 1. *Our faith in Jesus Christ;* that settled attitude of the soul toward him which is one of trustfulness and love, which determines our place in the kingdom of God (John iii. 15, 16, 18, 36). 2. *Our Christian life*—its record in the heavenly chronicles; that Christian service which, in its faithfulness or its imperfection, will gain for us the larger or the smaller measure of our Lord's approval (Luke xix. 16—19). 3. *Qualification,* gained by steadfastness, patience, zeal, for the sphere which "the righteous Judge" will award us and will have ready for us.—C.

Ver. 1.—*Vanity in religion:* 1. *Thoughtlessness.* From secular life the Preacher turns to religious. He has sought in many quarters for peace and satisfaction, but has found none. Royal palaces, huts where poor men lie, cells of philosophers, banqueting-halls, are all alike, if not all equally, infested by vanities which poison pleasure and add to the burden of care. But surely in the house of God, where men seek to disengage their thoughts from things that are seen and temporal, and to fix them upon things that are unseen and eternal, where they endeavour to establish and maintain communion with their Creator, one may count upon finding a haven of refuge for the soul from vanity and care. But here, too, he perceives that, by thoughtlessness, formalism, and insincerity, the purpose for which worship was instituted, and the blessings it may secure, are in danger of being defeated and nullified. But a change is manifest in the tone in which he reproves these faults. He lays down the whip of the satirist, he suppresses the fierce indignation which the sight of these new follies might have excited within him, and with sober earnestness exhorts his hearers to forsake the faults which separate between them and God, and hinder the ascent of their prayers to him and the descent of his blessings upon them. His feelings of reverence, and his conviction that in obedience to God and in communion with him peace and satisfaction may be found, forbid his saying of genuine religion that it is "vanity and vexation of spirit." So far as the spirit of his exhortation is concerned, it is applicable to all forms of worship, but we find some difficulty in ascertaining the kind of scene which was in his mind's eye when he spoke of "the house of God." If we are convinced that it is Solomon speaking in his own person, we know that he must refer to the stately building which he erected for the service of God in Jerusalem; and we understand from his words that he is not depreciating the offering of sacrifices, but is giving the admonition so often on the lips of the prophets, that the external act without accompanying devotion and love of righteousness, is in vain (1 Sam. xv. 22; Ps. l. 8, 9; Prov. xxi. 3; Isa. i. 11—17; Jer. vii. 22, 23; Mark xii. 33). But if we have here the utterance of a later writer, may there not be a reference to the synagogue service, in which the reading of the Word of God and exposition of its meaning were the principal religious exercises employed? May not the writer be understood as affirming "that a diligent listening to the teaching imparted in the synagogue is of more real value than the 'sacrifices' offered up in the temple by 'fools'"? The answer we give is determined by the opinion we form as to the date of the book. But even if we are unable to decide this point, the exhortation before us will lose none of its significance and weight. The underlying truth is the same, whether the primary reference be to the gorgeous ritual of the temple, or to the simple, unadorned services of the synagogue, which in later times furnished the pattern for Christian worship. The first fault against which the Preacher would have his hearers be on their guard is that of *thoughtlessness*—entering the house of God inconsiderately (ver. 1). The form in which the admonition is expressed is probably intended to remind his readers of the Divine command to Moses in the desert when he drew near to the bush that burned with fire: "Put off thy shoes from off thy feet, for the place whereon thou standest is holy ground" (Exod. iii. 5; cf. also Josh. v. 15).

I. Our first duty in entering the house of God is, therefore, TO BE REVERENT BOTH IN MANNER AND IN SPIRIT. The outward expression of this feeling, whatever form, according to the custom of our time, or country, or Church, it may take, is to be an indication of the frame of mind in which we enter upon the service of God. It is true that there may be a reverent manner without devoutness of spirit, but it is equally true that there cannot be devoutness of spirit without reverence of manner. The true frame of mind is that which springs from a due sense of the solemnity attaching to the house of God, and of the purpose for which we assemble in it. It is not superstition, but genuine religious sentiment, that would lead us to be mindful of the fact that it is no common ground which is enclosed by the sacred walls; that it is here that we meet with him whom "the heaven of heavens cannot contain." Though we are at all times in his presence, his house is the place in which we entreat him to manifest himself to his congregated people. Yet, though we know that the place and the purpose of our frequenting it are of the most holy and solemn nature, it is only by a strong effort that we can maintain the frame of mind we should be in when we wait upon God in his house. It is only by resolutely determining so to do that we can control our wandering thoughts, suppress frivolous and sinful imaginations, and divest ourselves of the secular cares and anxieties which occupy only too much of our attention in the world outside the sanctuary.

II. Our second great duty is THAT OF OBEDIENCE TO THE DIVINE LAW; "for to draw near to hearken is better than to give the sacrifice of fools, for they know not that they do evil" (Revised Version). Not only should there be reverence of manner and spirit in the presence of God, but a desire to know what he requires from us, and a disposition to render it. Love of holiness, and endeavours to exemplify it, are essential to all true service of God. By hearkening is evidently meant an attitude of mind which leads directly to obedience to the words spoken, to repentance and amendment when faults are reproved, and to a love and practice of the virtues commended. In the Epistle of James (i. 19—25) we have an inspired commentary upon this precept in the Book of Ecclesiastes. The Christian teacher enforces the same lesson, and depicts the contrast between the "forgetful hearer" and the "doer of the Word." The one is like a man looking for a moment into a mirror, and going on his way, and speedily forgetting what he looked like; the other is like a man who uses the revelation the mirror gives him of himself, to correct what in him is faulty. The latter returns again and again to examine himself in the faithful glass, for the purpose of removing those stains which it may show are upon him. This reverence of manner and spirit and this love of righteousness alone give value to worship; omission of them through thoughtlessness is a *positive* offence against God.—J. W.

Vers. 2, 3.—*Vanity in religion:* 2. *Rash prayers.* From an admonition as to the spirit in which we should enter the house of God, our author proceeds to counsel us as to the religious exercises we engage in there. Our utterances in prayer are to be calm and deliberate. A multitude of wishes may fill our hearts, and, unless we take care, find expression in a volume of ill-considered words. But we are to remember that only some of our wishes can be lawfully turned into prayers, and that an appropriate expression of the requests we feel we can offer, is due from us. The counsel here given is twofold: (1) it relates to our words, which often outrun our thoughts, and (2) to our hearts or minds, which are often the homes of vain imaginations and desires. Over both we must exercise control if we are to offer acceptable prayers. One great safeguard against offending in this matter is *brevity* in our addresses to heaven's King. In a multitude of words even the wisest are in danger of giving indications of folly. Definite petitions, duly weighed, and expressed in simple, earnest language, become us who stand at such a distance from the throne of God. Our Lord reiterates the admonition in the sermon on the mount (Matt. vi. 7, 8): "When ye pray, use not vain repetitions, as the heathen do: for they think that they shall be heard for their much speaking. Be not ye therefore like unto them: for your Father knoweth what things ye have need of, before ye ask him." And in the parable of the Pharisee and the publican (Luke xviii. 9—14) he contrasts the voluble utterance of the self-righteous and complacent worshipper with the brief, sincere confession and supplication of the true penitent. The greatest of all safeguards against the evil here condemned consists in our having before our minds a true idea of what prayer is. It is our offering petitions to God as creatures who are dependent upon his goodness, as children whom he loves. If we take as our example that offered by our Saviour in the garden of Gethsemane (Matt. xxvi. 39), we learn that the aim of prayer is not to determine the will of God. Some one thing we may ask for, but we leave it to God to grant or to deny, and seek above all that our will may be changed into his will (see Robertson of Brighton, vol. iv. serm. 3, "Prayer").—J. W.

Vers. 4—7.—*Vanity in religion:* 3. *Broken vows.* A vow is a promise to dedicate something to God, on certain conditions, such as his granting deliverance from death or danger, success in one's undertakings, or the like, and is one of the most ancient and widespread of religious customs. The earliest we read of is that of Jacob at Bethel (Gen. xxviii. 18—22; xxxi. 13). The Mosaic Law regulated the practice, and the passage before us is an almost exact reproduction of the section in Deuteronomy (xxiii. 21—23) in which general directions are given about the discharge of such obligations. The vow consisted in the dedication of persons or possessions to sacred uses. The worshipper's self, or child, or slave, or property, might be devoted to God. Vows were entirely voluntary, but, once made, were regarded as compulsory, and evasion of performance of them was held to be highly irreligious (Numb. xxx. 2; Deut. xxiii. 21—23; ch. v. 4). The kind of sin referred to here is that of making a vow inconsiderately, and drawing back when the time of performance comes. No obligation to vow rested upon any man (Deut. xxiii. 22), but when the vow had once been made, no one could without dishonour refuse to fulfil it. Of course, it was to be taken for granted that the vow was such as could be fulfilled without violating any law or ordinance of God. And, accordingly, provision was made in the Mosaic Law for the cancelling of any such obligation undertaken inadvertently, and found on maturer consideration to be immoral. It could be set aside, and the offence of having made it be atoned for as a sin of ignorance (Lev. v. 4—6). But when no such obstacle stood in the way of performance, nothing but a prompt and cheerful fulfilment of the vow could be accepted as satisfactory. A twofold fault is described in the passage before us: (1) an unseemly delay in fulfilling the vow (ver. 4) leading, perhaps, to an omission to fulfil it at all; and (2) a deliberate evasion of it, the insincere worshipper going to the angel (priest), and saying that the vow had been made in ignorance, and should not therefore be kept literally (ver. 6). And in correspondence with the respective degrees of guilt incurred by such conduct, the Divine indignation takes a less or more intense form : ver. 4, "He hath no pleasure in fools;" ver. 6, "Wherefore should God be angry at thy voice, and destroy the work of thine hands?" The idea of the former of the two statements of the Divine displeasure is far from being trivial or from being a tame anticipation of the latter. "The Lord first ceases to delight in a man, and then, after long forbearance, gives him over to destruction" (Wright). The one great source of these three forms of evil which so often vitiate religious life—*thoughtlessness, rash prayers*, and *broken vows*—is irreverence, and against it the Preacher lifts up his voice (ver. 7): "For in the multitude of dreams and many words there are also divers vanities: but fear thou God." Just as occasional dreams may be coherent, so few well-considered utterances may be characterized by wisdom. But a crowd of dreams, and hasty, babbling speech, are sure to contain confused images and offensive folly. The fear of God, therefore, if it habitually influence the mind, will preserve a man from being "rash with his mouth;" it will hinder his making inconsiderate vows, and afterwards seeking excuses for not fulfilling them.—J. W.

Ver. 8.—*A misgoverned state.* From the follies only too prevalent in the religious world, the Preacher turns to the disorders of the political; and although he admonishes his readers in a later section of the book (ch. viii. 2) to be mindful of the duties to which they are pledged by their oath of allegiance, it is very evident that he felt keenly the misery and oppression caused by misgovernment. For these evils he could suggest no cure; a hopeless submission to the inevitable is his only counsel. Like Hamlet, his heart is wrung by the thought of evils against which it was almost useless to strive—

> "The oppressor's wrong, the proud man's contumely
>   . . . the law's delay,
> The insolence of office, and the spurns
> That patient merit of the unworthy takes."

The subordinate magistrates tyrannized over the people, those who were higher in office watched their opportunity for oppressing them. From the lowest up to the very highest rank of officials the same system of violence and jealous espionage prevailed. Those that were in the royal household and had the ear of the king, his most intimate counsellors, who were in a sense higher than any of the satraps or governors he employed, were able to urge him to use his power for the destruction of any whose ill-gotten riches made him an object of envy (comp. ch. x. 4, 7, 16, etc.). The whole system of government was rotten to the core, the same distrust and jealousy pervaded every part of it. "Marvel not," says the Preacher, "at oppression and injustice in the lower departments of official life, for those who are the superiors of the tyrannical judge or governor, and should be a check on him, are as bad as he." Such seems to be the sense of the words. At first sight, indeed, the impression left on one's mind is that the Preacher counsels his readers not to be perplexed or unduly dismayed at the wrong they are forced to witness, on the ground that over and above the highest of earthly tyrants is the power of God, and that it will in due time be manifested in the punishment of the evil-doer. As though he had said, God who is "higher than the highest regardeth," beholds the wrong-doing; and when he comes to judgment, the proudest will have to submit to his power (comp. ch. iii. 17). But this interpretation, though very ancient, is not in harmony with the general character of the utterance. The thought of God's power and justice is indeed calculated to give some consolation to the oppressed, but not to explain why they are oppressed. The latter part of the verse is assigned as a reason for not marvelling at the prevalence of evil. If, therefore, reference be made to the power of God, by which the evil might be restrained or abolished, the marvel of its prevalence would only be increased. We are, therefore, to understand his words as meaning, "Do not be surprised at the corruption and baseness of the lower officials, in so much as the same corruption prevails among those in far higher positions." He is not here seeking to cheer up the sufferer by bidding him look higher; he is describing the evil state of affairs everywhere existing in the empire in his own day (Wright). There is nothing very heroic or inspiring in the counsel. It is simply an admonition, based on prudence, to escape personal danger by stolidly submitting to evils which one's own power can do nothing to abolish or alleviate. To those who under an Oriental despotism had become hopeless and dispirited, the words might seem worthy of a wise counsellor; but surely there is a servile ring about them which ill harmonizes with the love of freedom and intolerance of tyranny which are native to a European mind. There is but one relieving circumstance in connection with them, and that is that submission to oppression is not commanded in them or asserted to be a duty; and therefore those in whose hearts the love of country and of justice burns brightly, and who find that a pure and devoted patriotism moves them to make many sacrifices for the good of their fellows, violate no canon of Scripture when they rise superior to the prudential considerations dwelt upon here. Granted that submission to the inevitable is the price at which material safety and happiness may be bought, it is still a question at many times whether the patriot should not hazard material safety and happiness in the attempt to win for his country and for himself a higher boon.—J. W.

Ver. 9.—*A well-ordered state.* In contrast with the evils produced by an administration in which all the officials, from the lowest to the highest, seek to enrich themselves, our author now sets the picture of a well-governed community, in which the efficient cultivation of the land is a matter of the first consideration, and all classes of the population, up to the king himself, share in the consequent prosperity. (The verse has been differently rendered, but the translation of both our Revised and Authorized Versions is probably the best reproduction of the original words.) From the kings who wasted the resources of the lands over which they ruled in carrying on bloody wars, and in the indulgence of their capricious tastes, he turns to those who, like Uzziah, encouraged agriculture, and under whose beneficent rule Judah enjoyed the blessings of peace and prosperity (2 Chron. xxvi. 10). "The profit of the earth is for all." All are dependent upon the labours of the husbandman for the supply of the necessaries of life. By the judicious cultivation of the soil wealth is accumulated, by which comforts and luxuries are to be procured, so that even "the king himself is served by the field." The king, indeed, is more dependent upon the husbandman than the husbandman upon the king; without his labours there would be no bread for the royal palace, and no luxuries could make up for the absence of this necessary of life. We have, surely, in this consideration a strong proof of the dignity and value of the humblest labour, and in the fact of the mutual dependence of all classes upon each other an argument for the necessity of mutual forbearance and co-operation. A very striking illustration of the teaching here given is afforded in an incident which took place at Heidelberg in the reign of Frederic I. (1152—1190). "This prince invited to a banquet all the factious barons whom he had vanquished at Seckingen, and who had previously ravaged and laid waste great part of the palatinate. Among them were the Bishop of Mentz and the Margrave of Baden. The repast was plentiful and luxurious, but there was no bread. The warrior-guests looked round with surprise and inquiry. 'Do you ask for bread?' said Frederic, sternly; 'you who have wasted the fruits of the earth, and destroyed those whose industry cultivates it? There is no bread. Eat, and be satisfied; and learn henceforth mercy to those who put the bread into your mouths'" (quoted in 'Sketches of Germany,' by Mrs. Jameson).—J. W.

Vers. 10—20.—*The drawbacks upon wealth.* The series of aphorisms which begins in ver. 10 is not unconnected with what precedes it. It is for wealth generally that the unjust judge and oppressive ruler barters his peace of mind, sells his very soul. As the means for procuring sensual gratification, for surrounding one's self with ostentatious luxury, and for carrying out ambitious schemes, riches have great fascination. The Preacher, however, records at length the drawbacks connected with them, which are calculated to diminish the envy with which the poor very often regard those who possess them. Probably the bulk of mankind would say that they are willing to put up with the drawbacks if only they could possess the riches. But surely those who read the Word of God reverently and with a docile spirit are disposed to profit by the wise counsels and warning it contains. The gross and presumptuous frame of mind, which would lead any to laugh at the drawbacks upon wealth as imaginary, when compared with the happiness they think it must secure, deserves severe censure. Both rich and poor may draw appropriate lessons from the Preacher's words: the rich may learn humility; the poor, contentment.

I. INSATIABLENESS OF AVARICE. (Ver. 10.) Those who begin to amass money cultivate an appetite which can never be satisfied, which only grows in fierceness as it is supplied with food. Those who love silver will never count themselves rich enough; they will always hunger for more, and the amount that would once have seemed abundance to them will be spurned as paltry, as their ideas and desires are enlarged. Dissatisfaction with what they have, and greed to acquire more, poison their pleasure in all that they have accumulated. Happy are those who have learned to be content with little, whose wants are few and moderate, who, having food and raiment, desire no more—they are really rich.

II. Another thought calculated to diminish envy of the rich is that, AS WEALTH INCREASES, THOSE THAT CONSUME IT INCREASE ALSO. (Ver. 11.) Along with the more abundant possessions, there is generally a larger retinue of servants and dependants. So that, with more to provide for, the wealthy man may be poorer than he was in earlier days when his means were smaller. Fresh demands are made upon him; the outward display he is forced to make becomes a daily increasing burden; he has to labour for the supply of others rather than for himself. A striking passage in Xenophon—quoted by Plumptre—expresses the same thought. "Do you think that I live with more pleasure the more I possess? . . . By having this abundance I gain merely this, that I have to guard more, to distribute more to others, and to have the trouble of taking care of more; for a great many domestics now demand of me their food, their drink, and their clothes. . . . Whosoever, therefore, is greatly pleased with the possession of riches will, be assured, feel much annoyed at the expenditure of them" ('Cyrop.,' viii. 3). The only compensation that the rich man may have is that of being able to look on his treasures and say, "These are mine." Is it, after all, a sufficient reward for his toils and cares?

III. Another boon which the poor may always enjoy, but which the rich may often sigh for in vain, is SWEET SLEEP. (Ver. 12.) The labourer enjoys refreshing sleep, whether his food be abundant or not; the toils of the day ensure sound slumber at night. While the very abundance of the rich will not suffer him to sleep; all kinds of cares, projects, and anxieties rise within his mind, and will not suffer him to be at rest. The dread of losing his riches may make him wakeful, feverish excitement may result from his luxurious mode of living, and rob him of the power to compose himself to slumber, and, like the ambitious king, he may envy the ship-boy rocked and lulled by the tossing of "the rude, imperious surge" (Shakespeare, 'Henry IV.,' Part II., act iii. sc. 1).

IV. RICHES MAY INJURE ITS POSSESSOR. (Ver. 13.) It may mark him out as a suitable victim for spoliation by a lawless tyrant or a revolutionary mob. Or it may furnish him with the means of indulging vicious appetites, and increase greatly the risks and temptations that make it difficult to live a sober, righteous, and godly life, and ruin him body and soul. As says the apostle, "They that desire to be rich fall into a temptation and a snare, and many foolish and hurtful lusts, such as drown men in destruction and perdition" (1 Tim. vi. 9, 10).

V. Another evil attendant on wealth is THE DANGER OF SUDDEN AND IRRETRIEVABLE LOSS. (Ver. 14.) "Not only do riches fail to give any satisfying joy, but the man who reckoned on founding a family, and leaving his heaped-up treasures to his son, gains nothing but anxieties and cares, he may lose his wealth by some unfortunate chance, and leave his son a pauper." The case of Job would seem to be in the writer's mind as an example of this sudden downfall from prosperity and wealth. In any case, death robs the rich man of all his possessions; in the twinkling of an eye he is stripped of his wealth, as a traveller who has fallen in with a troop of banditti, and is forced to depart from life as poor in goods as when he entered it (vers. 15, 16).

VI. Lastly, come THE INFIRMITY AND PEEVISHNESS WHICH ARE OFTEN THE COMPANIONS OF WEALTH. (Ver. 17.) Riches cannot cure disease, or ward off the day of death, or compensate for the sorrows and disappointments of life, and may only tend to aggravate them; a deeper dissatisfaction with self, and with the providential government of the world, a more intense feeling of misanthropy and embitterment are likely to be the portion of the godless rich than of those who have had all through life to labour for their bread, and have never risen much above the position in which they first found themselves.

As a practical conclusion, the Preacher reiterates for the fourth time his old advice (vers. 18—20): "If you have little, be content with it. If you have much, enjoy it without excess, and without seeking more. God gives life and earthly blessings, and the power to enjoy them." And in words that are less clear than we could wish, he seems to intimate that in this pious disposition of mind and heart will be found the secret of a serene and happy life, which no changes or disappointments will be able wholly to overcast. "For he shall not much remember the days of his life; because God answereth him in the joy of his heart"—words which seem to imply, "The man who has learned the secret of enjoyment is not anxious about the days of his life; does not brood even over its transitoriness, but takes each day tranquilly as it comes, as God's gift to him; and God himself corresponds to his joy, is felt to approve it, as harmonizing, in its calm evenness, with his own blessedness. The tranquillity of the wise man mirrors the tranquillity of God" (Plumptre).—J. W.

EXPOSITION.

CHAPTER VI.

Vers. 1—6.—Section 9. Koheleth proceeds to illustrate the fact which he stated at the end of the last chapter, viz. that the possession and enjoyment of wealth are alike the free gift of God. We may see men possessed of all the gifts of fortune, yet denied the faculty of enjoying them. Hence we again conclude that *wealth cannot secure happiness.*

Ver. 1.—**There is an evil which I have seen under the sun.** The writer presents his personal experience, that which has fallen under his own observation (comp. ch. v. 13; x. 5). **And it is common among men.** *Rab,* translated "common," like πολὺς in Greek, is used of number and of degree; hence there is some doubt about its meaning here. The Septuagint has πολλή, the Vulgate *frequens.* Taking into account the fact that the circumstance stated is not one of general experience, we must receive the adjective in its tropical signification, and render, *And it is great* [lies heavily] *upon men.* Comp. ch. viii. 6, where the same word is used, and the preposition עַל is rather "upon" than "among" (Isa. xxiv. 20).

Ver. 2.—**A man to whom God hath given riches, wealth, and honour.** This is the evil to which reference is made. Two of the words here given, "riches" and "honour," are those used by God in blessing Solomon in the vision at Gibeon (1 Kings iii. 13); but all three are employed in the parallel passage (2 Chron. i. 11). **So that he wanteth nothing for his soul of all that he desireth.** "His soul" is the man himself, his personality, as Ps. xlix. 19. So in the parable (Luke xii. 19) the rich fool says to his soul, "Soul, thou hast much goods laid up for many years." In the supposed case the man is able to procure for himself everything which he wants; has no occasion to deny himself the gratification of any rising desire. All this comes from God's bounty; but something more is wanted to bring happiness. **Yet God giveth him not power to eat thereof.** "To eat" is used in a metaphorical sense for "to enjoy," take advantage of, make due use of (see on ch. ii. 24). The ability to enjoy all these good things is wanting, either from discontent, or moroseness, or sickness, or as a punishment for secret sin. **But a stranger eateth it.** The "stranger" (*nokri*) is not the legal heir, but an alien to the possessor's blood, neither relation nor even necessarily a friend. For a childless Oriental to adopt an heir is a common custom at the present day. The wish to continue a family, to leave a name and inheritance to children's children, was very strong among the Hebrews—all the stronger as the life beyond the grave was dimly apprehended. Abraham expressed this feeling when he sadly cried, "I go childless, and he that shall be possessor of my house is Dammesek Eliezer" (Gen. xv. 2). The evils are two—that this great fortune brings no happiness to its possessor, and that it passes to one who is nothing to him. **An evil disease;** ἀῤῥωστία πονηρά, Septuagint, an evil as bad as the diseases spoken of in Deut. xxviii. 27, 28.

Ver. 3.—**If a man beget an hundred children.** Another case is supposed, differing from the preceding one, where the rich man dies childless. Septuagint, Ἐὰν γεννήσῃ ἀνὴρ ἑκατόν. "Sons," or "children," must be supplied (comp. 1 Sam. ii. 5; Jer. xv. 9). To have a large family was regarded as a great blessing. The "hundred" is a round number, though we read of some fathers who had nearly this number of children; thus Ahab had seventy sons (2 Kings x. 1), Rehoboam eighty-eight children (2 Chron. xi. 21). Plumptre follows some commentators in seeing here an allusion to Artaxerxes Mnemon, who is said to have had a hundred and fifteen children, and died of grief at the age of ninety-four at the suicide of one son and the murder of another. Wordsworth opines that Solomon, in the previous verse, was thinking of Jeroboam, who, it was revealed unto him, should, stranger as he was, seize and enjoy his inheritance. But these historical references are the merest guesswork, and rest upon no substantial basis. Plainly the author's statement is general, and there is no need to ransack history to find its parallel. **And live many years, so that the days of his years be many;** *Et vixerit multos annos, et plures dies ætatis habuerit* (Vulgate). These versions seem to be simply tautological. The second clause is climacteric, as Ginsburg renders, " Yea, numerous as may be the days of his years." The whole extent of years is summed up in days. So Ps. xc. 10, " The days of our years are three score years and ten," etc. Long life, again, was deemed a special blessing, as we see in the commandment with promise (Exod. xx. 12). **And** (*yet if*) **his soul be not filled with good;** *i.e.* he does not satisfy himself with the enjoyment of all the good things which he possesses. Septuagint, Καὶ ψυχὴ αὐτοῦ οὐ πλησθήσεται ἀπὸ τῆς ἀγαθωσύνης, " And his soul shall not be satisfied with his good." **And also that he have no burial.** This is the climax of the evil that befalls him. Some critics, not entering into Koheleth's view of the severity of this calamity, translate, " and even if the grave did not wait for him," *i.e.* " if he were never to die," if he were immortal. But there is no parallel to show that the clause can have this meaning; and we know, without having recourse to Greek precedents, that the want of burial was reckoned a grievous loss and dishonour. Hence comes the common allusion to dead carcases being left to be devoured by beasts and birds, instead of meeting with honourable burial in the ancestral graves (1 Kings xiii. 22; Isa. xiv. 18—20). Thus David says to his giant foe, " I will give the carcases of the host of the Philistines this day unto the fowls of the air, and to the wild beasts of the earth " (1 Sam. xvii. 46); and about Jehoiakim it was denounced that he should not be lamented when he died: " He shall be buried with the burial of an ass, drawn and cast forth beyond the gates of Jerusalem " (Jer. xxii. 18, 19).

The lot of the rich man in question is proclaimed with ever-increasing misery. He cannot enjoy his possessions; he has none to whom to leave them; his memory perishes; he has no honoured burial. **I say, that an untimely birth is better than he** (comp. ch. iv. 3). The abortion or still-born child is preferable to one whose destiny is so miserable (see Job iii. 16; Ps. lviii. 8). It is preferable because, although it has missed all the pleasures of life, it has at least escaped all suffering. The next two verses illustrate this position.

Ver. 4.—**For he cometh in with vanity;** rather, *for it came into nothingness.* The reference is to the fœtus, or still-born child, not to the rich man, as is implied by the Authorized Version. This, when it appeared, had no independent life or being, was a mere nothing. **And departeth in darkness;** *and goeth into the darkness.* It is taken away and put out of sight. **And his** (*its*) **name shall be covered with darkness.** It is a nameless thing, unrecorded, unremembered.

Ver. 5.—It has seen nothing of the world, known nothing of life, its joys and its sufferings, and is speedily forgotten. To " see the sun " is a metaphor for to " live," as ch. vii. 11; xi. 7; Job iii. 16, and implies activity and work, the contrary of rest. **This hath more rest than the other;** literally, *there is rest to this more than to that.* The rest that belongs to the abortion is better than that which belongs to the rich man. Others take the clause to say simply, " It is better with this than the other." So the Revised Version margin and Delitzsch, the idea of " rest " being thus generalized, and taken to signify a preferable choice. Septuagint, Καὶ οὐκ ἔγνω ἀναπαύσεις τούτῳ ὑπὲρ τοῦτον, "And hath not known rest for this more than that "—which reproduces the difficulty of the Hebrew; Vulgate, *Neque cognovit distantiam boni et mali,* which is a paraphrase unsupported by the present accentuation of the text. Rest, in the conception of an Oriental, is the most desirable of all things; compared with the busy, careworn life of the rich man, whose very moments of leisure and sleep are troubled and disturbed, the dreamless nothingness of the still-born child is happiness. This may be a rhetorical exaggeration, but we have its parallel in Job's lamentable cry in ch. iii. when he " cursed his day."

Ver. 6.—**Yea, though he live a thousand years twice** told, **yet hath he seen no good.** What has been said would still be true even if the man lived two thousand years. The second clause is not the apodosis (as the Authorized Version makes it), but the continuation of the protasis: if he lived the longest life, "and saw not good;" the conclusion is given in the form of a question.

The "good" is the enjoyment of life spoken of in ver. 3 (see on ch. ii. 1). The specified time seems to refer to the age of the patriarchs, none of whom, from Adam to Noah, reached half the limit assigned. **Do not all go to one place?** viz. to Sheol, the grave (ch. iii. 20). If a long life were spent in calm enjoyment, it might be preferable to a short one; but when it is passed amid care and annoyance and discontent, it is no better than that which begins and ends in nothingness. The grave receives both, and there is nothing to choose between them, at least in this point of view. Of life as in itself a blessing, a discipline, a school, Koheleth says nothing here; he puts himself in the place of the discontented rich man, and appraises life with his eyes. On the common destiny that awaits peer and peasant, rich and poor, happy and sorrow-laden, we can all remember utterances old and new. Thus Horace, 'Carm.,' ii. 3. 20—

"Divesne prisco natus ab Inacho,
Nil interest, an pauper et infima
De gente sub divo moreris,
Victima nil miserantis Orci.

"Omnes eodem cogimur."

Ovid, 'Met.,' x. 33—

"Omnia debentur vobis, paullumque morati
Serius aut citius sedem properamus ad
unam.
Tendimus huc omnes, hæc est domus
ultima."

"Fate is the lord of all things; soon or late
To one abode we speed, thither we all
Pursue our way, this is our final home."

Vers. 7—9.—Section 10. *Desire is insatiable;* men are always striving after enjoyment, but they never gain their wish completely— which fortifies the old conclusion that man's happiness is not in his own power.

Ver. 7.—**All the labour of man is for his mouth;** *i.e.* for self-preservation and enjoyment, eating and drinking being taken as a type of the proper use of earthly blessings (comp. ch. ii. 24; iii. 13, etc.; Ps. cxxviii. 2). The sentiment is general, and does not refer specially to the particular person described above, though it carries on the idea of the unsatisfactory result of wealth. Luther translates strangely and erroneously, "To every man is work allotted according to his measure." Such an idea is entirely foreign to the context. **And yet the appetite is not filled.** The word rendered "appetite" is *nephesh,* "soul," and Zöckler contends that "'mouth' and 'soul' stand in contrast to each other as representatives of the purely sensual and therefore transitory enjoyment (comp. Job xii. 11; Prov. xvi. 26) as compared with

the deeper, more spiritual, and therefore more lasting kind of joy." But no such contrast is intended; the writer would never have uttered such a truism as that deep, spiritual joy is not to be obtained by sensual pleasure; and, as Delitzsch points out, in some passages (*e.g.* Prov. xvi. 26; Isa. v. 14; xxix. 8) "mouth" in one sentence corresponds to "soul" in another. The soul is considered as the seat of the appetitive faculty—emotions, desires, etc. This is never satisfied (ch. i. 8) with what it has, but is always craving for more. So Horace affirms that a man rightly obtains the appellation of king, "avidum domando spiritum," by subduing his spirit's cravings (' Carm.,' ii. 2. 9).

Ver. 8.—**For what hath the wise more than the fool?** *i.e.* What advantage hath the wise man over the fool? This verse confirms the previous one by an interrogative argument. The same labour for support, the same unsatisfied desires, belong to all, wise or foolish; in this respect intellectual gifts have no superiority. (For a similar interrogation implying an emphatic denial, see ch. i. 3.) **What hath the poor, that knoweth to walk before the living?** The Septuagint gives the verse thus: Ὅτι τίς περίσσεια (A, C, ℵ²) τῷ σοφῷ ὑπὲρ τὸν ἄφρονα; διότι ὁ πένης οἶδε πορευθῆναι κατέναντι τῆς ζωῆς, "For what advantage hath the wise man over the fool? since the poor man knows how to walk before life?" Vulgate, *Quid habet amplius sapiens a stulto? et quid pauper, nisi ut pergat illuc, ubi est vita?* "And what hath the poor man except that he go thither where is life?" Both these versions regard הַחַיִּים as used in the sense of "life," and that the life beyond the grave; but this idea is foreign to the context; and the expression must be rendered, as in the Authorized Version, "the living." The interpretation of the clause has much exercised critics. Plumptre adheres to that of Bernstein and others, "What advantage hath the poor over him who knows how to walk before the living?" (*i.e.* the man of high birth or station, who lives in public, with the eyes of men upon him). The poor has his cares and unsatisfied desires as much as the man of culture and position. Poverty offers no protection against such assaults. But the expression, *to know how to walk before the living,* means to understand and to follow the correct path of life; to know how to behave properly and uprightly in the intercourse with one's fellow-men; to have what the French call *savoir vivre.* (So Volck.) The question must be completed thus: "What advantage has the discreet and properly conducted poor man over the fool?" None, at least in this respect. The poor man, even though he be well versed in the rule of life, has insatiable desires which he has to check or conceal, and so is no better off than the fool, who equally is unable to gratify them. The two extremities of the social scale are taken —the rich wise man, and the prudent poor man—and both are shown to fail in enjoying life ; and what is true of these must be also true of all that come between these two limits, " the appetite is not filled " (ver. 7).

Ver. 9.—**Better is the sight of the eyes than the wandering of the desire** (*nephesh*, "the soul," ver. 7). This is a further confirmation of the misery and unrest that accompany immoderate desires. " The sight of the eyes " means the enjoyment of the present, that which lies before one, in contrast to the restless craving for what is distant, uncertain, and out of reach. The lesson taught is to make the best of existing circumstances, to enjoy the present, to control the roaming of fancy, and to narrow the vast field of appetency. We have a striking expression in Wisd. iv. 12, ῥεμβασμὸς ἐπιθυμίας, by which is denoted the giddiness, the reeling intoxication, caused by unrestrained passion. The Roman satirist lashed the sin of unscrupulous greed—

" Sed quæ reverentia legum,
Quis metus aut pudor est unquam properantis avari ? "
(Juven., ' Sat.,' xiv. 177.)

" Nor law, nor checks of conscience will he hear,
When in hot scent of gain and full career."
(Dryden.)

Zöckler quotes Horace, ' Epist.,' i. 18. 96, *sqq.*—

" Inter cuncta leges et percontabere doctos,
Qua ratione queas traducere leniter ævum ;
Num te semper inops agitet vexetque cupido,
Num pavor et rerum mediocriter utilium spes."

" To sum up all—Consult and con the wise
In what the art of true contentment lies :
How fear and hope, that rack the human will,
Are but vain dreams of things nor good nor ill."
(Howes.)

Marc. Aurel., 'Meditat.,' iv. 26, " Has any advantage happened to you ? It is the bounty of fate. It was all preordained you by the universal cause. Upon the whole, life is but short, therefore be just and prudent, and make your most of it ; and when you divert yourself, be always on your guard " (J. Collier). Well is it added that this insatiability of the soul, which never leads to contentment, is **vanity and vexation of spirit**, a feeding on wind, empty, unsatis-

fying. Commentators refer in illustration to the fable of the dog and the shadow, and the proverb, " A bird in the hand is worth two in the bush."

Vers. 10—12.—Section 11. *All things are foreknown and foreordained by God; it is useless to murmur against or to discuss this great fact;* and as the future is beyond our knowledge and control, it is wise to make the best of the present.

Ver. 10.—**That which hath been is named already**; better, *whatsoever hath been, long ago hath its name been given.* The word rendered "already," *kebar* (ch. i. 10 ; ii. 12 ; iii. 15 ; iv. 2), " long ago," though used elsewhere in this book of events in human history, may appropriately be applied to the Divine decrees which predetermine the circumstances of man's life. This is its significance in the present passage, which asserts that everything which happens has been known and fixed beforehand, and therefore that man cannot shape his own life. No attempt is here made to reconcile this doctrine with man's free-will and consequent responsibility. The idea has already been presented in ch. iii. 1, etc. It comes forth in Isa. xlv. 9, " Shall the clay say to him that fashioneth it, What makest thou ? or thy work, He hath no hands ? " (comp. Rom. ix. 20) ; Acts xv. 18 (according to the Textus Receptus), " Known unto God are all his works from the beginning of the world." The same idea is brought out more fully in the following clauses. Septuagint, " If anything ever was, already hath its name been called," which gives the correct sense of the passage. The Vulgate is not so happy, *Qui futurus est, jam vocatum est nomen ejus,* being rather opposed to the grammar. **And it is known that it is man.** What is meant by the Authorized Version is doubtful. If the first clause had been translated, as in the margin of the Revised Version, " Whatsoever he be, his name was given him long ago," the conclusion would come naturally, " and it is known that he is man " (*Adam*), and we should see an allusion to man's name and to the ground (*adamah*) from which he was taken (Gen. ii. 7), as if his very name betokened his weakness. But the present version is very obscure. Cox gives, " It is very certain that even the greatest is but a man, and cannot contend with him," etc. But the Hebrew will not admit this rendering. The clause really amplifies the previous statement of man's predetermined destiny, and it should be rendered, " And it is known what a man shall be." Every individual comes under God's prescient superintendence. Septuagint, Ἐγνώσθη ὅ ἐστιν ἄνθρωπος, "It is known what man is;" Vulgate, *Et scitur quod homo sit.* But it is not the nature of man that is in question, but his conditioned state. **Neither may he contend with him that is mightier than he.** The *mightier* One is God, in accordance with the passages quoted above from Isaiah, Acts, and Romans. Some consider that death is intended, and that the author is referring to the shortness of man's life. They say that the word *taqqiph*, "mighty" (which occurs only in Ezra and Daniel), is never used of God. But is it used of death? And is it not used of God in Dan. iv. 3 (iii. 33, Hebrew), where Nebuchadnezzar says, "How mighty are his wonders!"? To bring death into consideration is to introduce a new thought having no connection with the context, which is not speaking of the termination of man's life, but of its course, the circumstances of which are arranged by a higher Power. Septuagint, Καὶ οὐ δυνήσεται κριθῆναι μετὰ τοῦ ἰσχυροτέρου ὑπὲρ αὐτόν. With this we may compare 1 Cor. x. 22, "Do we provoke the Lord to jealousy? are we stronger than he? (μὴ ἰσχυρότεροι αὐτοῦ ἐσμέν;)."

Ver. 11.—**Seeing there be many things that increase vanity.** The noun rendered "things" (*dabar*) may equally mean "words;" and it is a question which signification is most appropriate here. The Septuagint has λόγοι πολλοί, "many words." So the Vulgate, *verba sunt plurima.* If we take the rendering of the Authorized Version, we must understand the passage to mean that the distractions of business, the cares of life, the constant disappointments, make men feel the hollowness and unsatisfactory nature of labour and wealth and earthly goods, and their absolute dependence upon Providence. But in view of the previous context, and especially of ver. 10, which speaks of contending (*din*) with God, it is most suitable to translate *debarim* "words," and to understand them of the expressions of impatience, doubt, and unbelief to which men give utterance when arraigning the acts or endeavouring to explain the decrees of God. Such profitless words only increase the perplexity in which men are involved. It is very possible that reference is here made to the discussions on the chief good, free-will, predestination, and the like subjects, which, as we know from Josephus, had begun to be mooted in Jewish schools, as they had long been rife in those of Greece. In these disputes Pharisees and Sadducees took opposite sides. The former maintained that some things, but not all, were the subject of fate (τῆς εἱμαρμένης), and that certain things were in our own power to do or not to do; that is, while they attribute all that happens to fate, or God's

decree, they hold that man has the power of assent, supposing that God tempers all in such sort, that by his ordinance and man's will all things are performed, good or evil. The Sadducees eliminated fate altogether from human actions, and asserted that men are in all things governed, not by any external force, but by their own will alone; that their success and happiness depended upon themselves, and that ill fortune was the consequence of their own folly or stupidity. A third school, the Essenes, held that fate was supreme, and that nothing could happen to mankind beyond or in contravention of its decree ('Joseph. Ant.,' xiii. 5. 9; xviii. 1. 3, 4; 'Bell. Jud.,' ii. 8. 14). Such speculative discussions may have been in Koheleth's mind when he wrote this sentence. Whatever may be the difficulties of the position, we Christians know and feel that in matters of religion and morality we are absolutely free, have an unfettered choice, and that from this fact arises our responsibility. **What is man the better?** What profit has man from such speculations or words of scepticism?

Ver. 12.—This verse in the Greek and Latin versions, as in some copies of the Hebrew, is divorced from its natural place, as the conclusion of the paragraph, vers. 10, 11, and is arranged as the commencement of ch. vii. Plainly, the Divine prescience of vers. 10, 11 is closely connected with the question of man's ultimate good and his ignorance of the future, enunciated in this verse. **For who knoweth what is good for man in** this life? Such discussions are profitless, for man knows not what is his real good—whether pleasure, apathy, or virtue, as philosophers would put it. To decide such questions he must be able to foresee results, which is denied him. The interrogative "Who knows?" is equivalent to an emphatic negative, as ch. iii. 21, and is a common rhetorical form which surely need not be attributed to Pyrrhonism (Plumptre). **All the days of his vain life which he spendeth as a shadow.** These words amplify and explain the term "in life" of the preceding clause. They may be rendered literally, *During the number of the days of the life* (ch. v. 18) *of his vanity, and he passeth them as a shadow.* A life of vanity is one that yields no good result, full of empty aims, unsatisfied wishes, unfulfilled purposes. It is the man who is here compared to the shadow, not his life. So Job xiv. 2, "He fleeth as a shadow, and continueth not." He soon passes away, and leaves no trace behind him. The thought is common. "Ye [Revised Version] are a vapour," says St. James (iv. 14), "that appeareth for a little time, and then vanisheth away." Plumptre well quotes Soph., 'Ajax,' 125—

'Ορῶ γὰρ ἡμᾶς οὐδὲν ὄντας ἄλλο πλὴν
Εἴδωλ', ὅσοιπερ ζῶμεν, ἢ κούφην σκιάν.

" In this I see that we, all we that live,
  Are but vain shadows, unsubstantial
  dreams."

To which we may add Pind., 'Pyth.,' viii.
95—

'Επάμεροι· τί δέ τις; τί δ' οὔ τις; σκιᾶς ὄναρ
Ἄνθρωπος.

" Ye creatures of a day !
  What is the great man, what the poor ?
  Naught but a shadowy dream."

The comparison of man's life to a shadow
or vapour is equally general (comp. ch. viii.
13; 1 Chron. xxix. 15; Ps. cii. 11; cxliv. 4;
Wisd. ii. 5; Jas. iv. 14). The verb used for
" spendeth " is *asah*, "to do or make," which
recalls the Greek phrase, χρόνον ποιεῖν (Acts
xv. 33, etc.; Demosth., 'De Fals. Leg.,' p. 392,
17), and the Latin, *dies facere* (Cic., 'Ad
Attic.,' v. 20. 1); but we need not trace

Greek influence in the employment of the
expression here. **For who can tell a man
what shall be after him under the sun?**
This does not refer to the life beyond the
grave, but to the future in the present world,
as the words, " under the sun," imply (comp.
ch. iii. 22; vii. 14). To know what is best
for him, to arrange his present life according
to his own wishes and plans, to be able to
depend upon his own counsel for all the
actions and designs which he undertakes,
man should know what is to be after him,
what result his labours will have, who and
what kind of heir will inherit his property,
whether he will leave children to carry on
his name, and other facts of the like nature;
but as this is all hidden from him, his duty
and his happiness is to acquiesce in the
Divine government, to enjoy with moderation
the goods of life, and to be content with the
modified satisfaction which is accorded to
him by Divine beneficence.

HOMILETICS.

Vers. 1—6.—*Sore evils beneath the sun ; or, the misfortunes of a rich man.* I. A
RICH MAN WITHOUT THE CAPACITY OF ENJOYMENT. 1. *A frequent occurrence.* The
picture that of one who has attained to great wealth, power, and honour, who has
been conscious of large ambitions and has realized them, who has been filled with
insatiable desires and possessed the means of gratifying them, and yet has been unable
to extract from all his possessions, pleasures, and pursuits any grain of real and solid
happiness. 2. *A sorrowful experience.* The Preacher characterizes it as an evil which
lies heavy upon men. Upon the individual himself, whose hopes are disappointed and
plans frustrated, whose riches, wealth, and honours thus become mocking decorations
rather than real ornaments, and whose pleasures and gratifications turn into apples of
Sodom rather than prove, as he expected they would do, grapes of Eshcol. 3. *An
instructive lesson.* The valuable truth that the soul's happiness is not, and cannot be,
found in any creatures, however excellent, but only in God (Ps. xxxvii. 4), is thus
forcibly pressed home upon the hearts and consciences of rich men themselves, and of
such as observe the experiences through which they pass.

II. A RICH MAN WITHOUT AN HEIR TO HIS WEALTH. A great diminution to the rich
man's happiness, who, in having no son or child, lacks: 1. *That which is dearer to the
heart of man than wealth, power, or fame.* Unless the instincts of human nature have
been utterly perverted by avarice, covetousness, and ambition, the hearts of rich no
less than of poor men cling to their offspring, and, rather than lose these by death,
would willingly surrender all their wealth (2 Sam. xviii. 33). 2. *That without which
wealth and honour lose the greater part of their attractions.* Abraham felt it a
considerable detraction from the sweetness of Jehovah's promise that he had no heir,
and that all his possessions would ultimately pass into the hands of his steward,
Eliezer of Damascus (Gen. xv. 1—3). 3. *That which gives to wealth-gathering and
power-seeking their best justification.* It is not certain that anything will justify these
when inordinate; if anything will excuse a man for heaping up wealth in an honest
and legitimate way, and for endeavouring to acquire power and influence amongst his
fellows, it is the fact of his doing so with a view to promote the happiness of those
God has made dependent on him, and bound to him by the ties of natural affection.

III. A RICH MAN WITHOUT A TOMB FOR HIS CORPSE. (For a different rendering of
this clause, "And moreover he have no burial," see the Exposition.) 1. *The case
supposed.* That of a rich man surrounded by many (an hundred) children, who lives

long, but has no true enjoyment of his good fortune, and when he dies is denied the glory of a funeral such as Dives doubtless had (Luke xvi. 22), and the shelter of a grave such as was not withheld even from Lazarus. How he should come at last to have no burial, though not explained, may be supposed to happen either through the meanness of his relatives or their hatred of him, or through his perishing in such a way (*e.g.* in war, at sea, through accident, by violence) as to render burial by his children impossible. Commentators cite as an illustration of the case supposed the murder by Bagoas of Artaxerxes Ochus (B.C. 362—339), whose body was thrown to the cats. Another may be that of Jehoiakim, of whom it was predicted (Jer. xxii. 19), "He shall be buried with the burial of an ass, drawn and cast forth beyond the gates of Jerusalem." 2. *The judgment pronounced.* That such a case is not to be compared in respect of felicity with that of "an untimely birth," which "cometh in vanity, and departeth in darkness, and the name thereof is covered with darkness;" *i.e.* which enters on a lifeless existence when born, and "is carried away in all quietness, without noise or ceremony," having received no name, and becoming forgotten as if it had never been (Delitzsch). The grounds on which the Preacher rests his judgment are three: (1) that an untimely birth never sees the sun, and so escapes all sight of and contact with the sufferings and miseries of earth; (2) that it never wakes to the exercise of intelligence, and so is never conscious of either the wickedness or the woe that is surging around it; and (3) that it rests better in the grave to which it goes than does the corpse of the joyless rich man. 3. *The correction needed.* This pessimistic view of life may be thus admirably qualified. The allegation here made "contains a thought to which it is not easy to reconcile one's self. For supposing that life were not in itself, as over against non-existence, a good, there is yet scarcely any life that is absolutely joyless; and a man who has become the father of a hundred children has, as it appears, sought the enjoyment of life principally in sexual love, and then also has found it richly. But also, if we consider his life less as relating to sense, his children, though not all, yet partly, will have been a joy to him; and has a family life so lengthened and rich in blessings only thorns, and no roses at all? And, moreover, how can anything be said of the rest of an untimely birth, which has been without motion and without life, as of a rest excelling the termination of the life of him who has lived long, since rest without a subjective reflection, a rest not felt, certainly does not fall under the point of view of more or less good or evil? The saying of the author on no side bears the probe of exact thinking" (Delitzsch).

IV. A RICH MAN WITHOUT A BETTER LOT THAN HIS NEIGHBOURS. "Do not all go to one place?" In the grave rich and poor differ not. The dusts of the patrician and of the plebeian, freely intermingled, no human chemistry can distinguish. A tremendous humiliation, no doubt, to human pride, that Solomon and the harlot's child, Cæsar and his slave, Dives and Lazarus, must ultimately lie together in the same narrow house—that rich and poor, wise and unwise, powerful and powerless, honoured and abject, kings and subjects, princes and peasants, masters and servants, must ultimately sleep side by side on the same couch; but so it is. And this, also, in the eyes of worldlings, but not of good men, is a vanity, and a sore evil beneath the sun.

LESSONS. 1. Riches are not the chief good. 2. Temporal evils may be sources of spiritual good.

Vers. 7—9.—*The insatiableness of desire.* I. IT CONSUMES THE LABOUR OF ALL. "All the labour of man is for his mouth, and yet the appetite is not filled" (ver. 7). The appetite, as an imperious master, urges on the soul to labour with all its powers and energies to furnish food for its delectation; and yet the utmost man can provide is insufficient to fill its capacious maw. However varied man's works may be, they have all this end in common, to appease the hunger of the sensuous nature; and all alike fail in reaching it. The appetite grows by what it feeds on, and hence never cries, "Enough!"

II. IT AFFECTS THE CHARACTERS OF ALL. "What advantage hath the wise more than the fool? or what [advantage] hath the poor man, who knows to walk before the living, over the fool?" (ver. 8). 1. *Intellectual gifts do not argue the absence of desire.* The philosopher, no less than the peasant, is under its dominion. The former may attempt to control, and may even to some extent succeed in controlling, his bodily appetites; but the appetite is there, impelling him to labour equally with the fool. 2. *Material poverty does not guarantee the absence of desire.* The poor man who knows how to walk before the living, *i.e.* who understands the art of living, is no more exempt from its sway than is the rich man, though a fool. The poor man may have learned how to put restraints upon himself, because of inability to gratify his desire, but the appetite is as much felt by him as by his rich neighbour.

III. IT DISAPPOINTS THE HOPES OF ALL. "Better is the sight of the eyes than the wandering of the desire" (ver. 9). Just because desire is never satisfied, it wanders on in pursuit of other objects which are often visionary, and almost always illusory; as a consequence, like the dog which snapped at his shadow and lost the meat he carried in his mouth, desire frequently misses such enjoyments as are within its reach through striving after those that are beyond its power.

LESSONS. 1. The danger of self-indulgence. 2. The difficulty of keeping the lower nature in subjection. 3. The propriety of preferring present and possible to future and perhaps impossible enjoyments.

Vers. 10—12.—*Four aspects of human life.* I. MAN AS A CREATURE OF DESTINY. "Whatsoever hath been, the name thereof was given long ago, and it is known that it is man" (ver. 10); or, "Whatsoever he be, his name was given him long ago, and it is known that he is man" (Revised Version margin); or, "That which hath been, its name hath long ago been named; and it is determined what a man shall be" (Delitzsch, Wright). These different readings suggest three thoughts. 1. *That man's appearance upon the earth had been long ago foreseen.* The sentiment holds good of man collectively or individually, *i.e.* of the race, or of the unit in the race. Neither did "man" originally spring into being by a happy accident, without the direct or indirect cognizance of God, nor does the "individual" so arrive upon the scene of time; but both the hour and the manner of man's arrival upon the globe, and of each individual's birth, were prearranged from eternity by him who "made the earth, and created man upon it" (Isa. xlv. 12), and who "giveth to all life and breath and all things" (Acts xvii. 25). 2. *That man's character as a creature had been long ago foreknown.* In this respect, indeed, he had in no way differed from other creatures. Known unto God had been all his works from the beginning of the world (Acts xv. 18). Human character is not in any instance an accidental product of blind forces, but is determined by fixed laws, moral and spiritual, which have been prearranged and instituted by the supreme moral Governor. Hence, within limits, it is possible for man to predict what himself or another shall become. "He that doeth righteousness" not only "is righteous" in the sense of already possessing the fundamental and essential principle of righteousness, viz. faith in, love of, and submission to God, but his righteousness shall eventually become within him the all-pervading and permanent quality of his being; and similarly "he that doeth unrighteousness" not only is potentially, but shall become permanently, unrighteous. Moral character in all men tends to fixity, whether of good or evil. Hence the greater possibility, amounting to certainty, that the Divine Mind, whose creation the laws are under which these results are wrought out, can, *ab initio*, foresee the issue to which, in every separate instance, they lead. 3. *That man's destiny as an individual had been long ago determined.* The doctrine of Divine predestination, however hard to harmonize with that of human freedom, is clearly revealed in Scripture (Exod. ix. 16; 2 Chron. vi. 6; Ps. cxxxv. 4; Isa. xliv. 1—7; Jer. i. 5; Matt. xi. 25, 26; John vi. 37; Rom. viii. 29; ix. 11), and is supported by the plain testimony of experience, which shows that

> "There's a divinity that shapes our ends,
> Rough-hew them how we will."
>
> ('Hamlet.')

Or, in the words of Cæsar, that nothing

> "Can be avoided
> Whose end is purposed by the mighty gods."
>
> ('Julius Cæsar.')

II. MAN AS THE POSSESSOR OF FREE-WILL. "Neither may [or, 'can'] he contend with him that is mightier than he" (ver. 10); in which are contained the following thoughts: 1. *That mighty as man is* (in virtue of his free-will), *there is a mightier than he.* That mightier is not death (Plumptre), but God (Delitzsch), who also is a Being possessed of free-will, which must still less be interfered with by man's choices and intentions, than man's free-will must be impaired by God's purposes and plans. This thought frequently forgotten, that if man, in virtue of his free-will, must be able to carry out his volitions, much more must God be able to carry out the free decisions of his infinite mind. In this concession the whole doctrine of predestination, or election, is involved. 2. *That if in any instance man's purposes and God's come into collision, those of man must give way.* One has only to put the question, whether it is of greater moment that God's purposes with regard to the universe and the individual should be carried out, or that man's with regard to himself should, to perceive the absurdity of limiting the Divine sovereignty in order to avoid the appearance of restricting human freedom, rather than seeming to impair human freedom in order to preserve intact the absolute and entire supremacy of God. 3. *That God's determinations, when accomplished, will not be impeachable by man.* The veil of mystery now shrouding the Divine procedure will in the end be in great measure, perhaps wholly, uplifted, and man himself constrained to acknowledge that the supreme Ruler hath done all things well (Mark vii. 37).

III. MAN AS A VICTIM OF IGNORANCE. "Seeing there be many things [or, 'words'] that increase vanity, what is man the better? For who knoweth," etc.? and "who can tell?" (vers. 11, 12). 1. *The fact of his ignorance.* Elsewhere in Scripture explicitly asserted (Deut. xxxii. 28; Ps. xiv. 4; Prov. xix. 3; John i. 5; Eph. iv. 18), and abundantly confirmed by experience. 2. *The extent of his ignorance.* Restricting attention to the Preacher's words, two subjects may be noted concerning which man— apart, *i.e.*, from God and religion—is comparatively unenlightened: (1) the supreme good (Ps. iv. 6), which he places now in pleasure, now in possessions, now in philosophy, now in power, never in God; and (2) the future, which is to him so much a sealed book that he cannot tell what a day may bring forth (Prov. xxvii. 1), and far less "what shall be after him under the sun." 3. *The strangeness of his ignorance.* Considering that man is a being possessed of high natural endowments, and is often much and earnestly engaged in searching after knowledge. That with all his lofty capacity, and devotion to intellectual pursuits, he should, if left to himself, be unable to tell either what is good for man in this life (all his discussions upon this subject having been little else than words, words, words), or how the course of events shall shape itself when he has passed from this earthly scene, is a surprising phenomenon which calls for examination. 4. *The explanation of his ignorance* lies in two things: (1) in the natural limitation of his faculties, which are finite, and not infinite; and (2) in the moral depravation of his faculties, which are now those not of an unfallen, but of a fallen, being.

IV. MAN AS A DENIZEN OF EARTH. 1. *His continuance is not permanent.* He and his generation shall pass on, that those coming after may enter in and take possession (ch. i. 4). 2. *His days are not many.* His life he spendeth like a shadow, which has no substance, and abides not in one stay. "Man that is born of a woman is of few days," etc. (Job xiv. 1, 2). 3. *His life is not good.* Apart from God and religion it is "vain," *i.e.* empty of real happiness, and destitute of solid worth.

LESSONS. 1. The sovereignty of God. 2. The weakness of man. 3. The duty of submission to the Supreme. 4. The inability of earthly things to make man better. 5. The chief good for man on earth is God.

Ver. 12.—"*Who can tell?*" *a sermon on human ignorance.* I. THINGS THAT LIE BEYOND THE SCOPE OF HUMAN KNOWLEDGE. 1. *The nature of the Deity.* "Canst thou by searching find out God," etc.? (Job xi. 7). To define God as Spirit (John iv. 24), to characterize him as Love (1 John iv. 8, 16) or as Light (1 John i. 5), to ascribe to him attributes of omnipotence, omnipresence, omniscience, etc., is not so much to explain his essence as to declare it to be something that lies beyond the bounds of our finite understanding (Ps. cxxxix. 6). 2. *The mystery of the Incarnation.* "Great is the mystery of godliness: God was manifest in the flesh" (1 Tim. iii. 16). To show that Jesus Christ must have been "Emmanuel, God with us" (Matt. i. 23), may not surpass the powers of man; to give an adequate exhibition of the way in which in

Christ the human and Divine natures were and are united does. The best proof of this lies in the number of the theories of the Incarnation. 3. *The contents of the atonement.* That Christ, as a matter of fact, bore the sins of men so as to expiate their guilt and destroy their power, one can tell from the general tenor of Scripture declarations on the subject (Matt. xxvi. 28; Rom. iii. 24; 2 Cor. v. 21; 1 Tim. ii. 6; 1 Pet. ii. 24; 1 John ii. 2); but what it was in Christ's "obedience unto death" that constituted the propitiation is one of those "secret things" that belong to God. 4. *The movements of the Spirit.* "Thou canst not tell whence it [the wind] cometh, or whither it goeth; so is every one that is born of the Spirit" (John iii. 8). That the Holy Spirit is the Author of regeneration and of inspiration is perfectly patent to the understanding of the Christian. The theory that shall adequately explain how the Spirit renews or inspires the soul has not yet been elaborated. 5. *The events of the future.* "Who can tell a man what shall be after him under the sun?" or even what shall be on the morrow (Prov. xxvii. 1)?

II. THINGS THAT LIE WITHIN THE SCOPE OF HUMAN KNOWLEDGE. 1. *The character of God.* The Ninevites could not tell whether Jehovah would be gracious to them (Jonah iii. 9); we can tell from the revelation of Scripture, and especially from the teaching of Christ, that God is Love, and willeth not the death of any. 2. *The Divinity of Christ.* Human reason is perfectly competent to decide upon the question whether Jesus of Nazareth belonged to the category of common men, or whether he was a new order of man broken in upon the ordinary line of the race. The evidence for such a decision has been provided, and any one who seriously wishes can arrive at a just conclusion. 3. *The work of the Saviour.* This also has been fully discovered in the Scripture. Christ came to reveal the Father (John xiv. 9), to atone for sin (Matt. xx. 28), to exemplify holiness (1 Pet. ii. 21), and to establish the kingdom of heaven upon earth (Rev. i. 6). 4. *The fruits of the Spirit.* If a man cannot always judge whether the Spirit is in his own or another's heart, he should be at no loss to tell whether the Spirit's fruits, which are love, joy, peace, etc. (Gal. v. 22), are discernible in his or his neighbour's life. 5. *The goals of the future.* If the separate incidents that shall hereafter occur in any individual's life be concealed from view, the two termini, towards one or other of which every individual is moving—heaven or hell —have been clearly revealed.

HOMILIES BY VARIOUS AUTHORS.

Vers. 1, 2.—*The unsatisfactoriness and transitoriness of earthly good.* Men are prone to be guided, in the conclusions they form regarding human life, by their own personal experience, and by the observations they make in their own immediate circle of acquaintance. So judging, they are prone to be one-sided in their estimate, and to take a view either too gloomy or too roseate. The author of Ecclesiastes was a man who had very large and varied opportunities of studying mankind, and who was in the habit of forming impartial conclusions. This accounts for what may perhaps seem to some readers opposed and inconsistent representations of the nature of man's life on earth. In fact, a more definite and decisive representation would have been less correct and fair.

I. MEN LOOKING UPON THEIR FELLOW-MEN ARE PRONE TO GIVE TOO LARGE A MEASURE OF ATTENTION TO THEIR OUTWARD CIRCUMSTANCES. The first question that occurs to many minds, upon forming a new acquaintance, is—What has he? *i.e.* what property? or—What is he? *i.e.* what is his rank in society? A man to whom God has given riches, wealth, and honour, who lacks nothing for his soul of all that he desireth, is counted fortunate. He is held in esteem; his friendship and favour are cultivated.

II. REFLECTING OBSERVERS BEAR IN MIND THAT THERE ARE OTHER ELEMENTS IN HUMAN WELFARE. For instance, it cannot be questioned that health of body and a sound and vigorous mind are of far more importance than wealth. And there may be family trouble, which mars the happiness of the most prosperous. The wise man had observed cases in which there was no power to enjoy the gifts of Providence; and other cases in which there were no children to succeed to the possession of accumulated wealth, so that it came into the hands of strangers. Bodily affliction and domestic disappointment may cast a shadow over the lot which seems the fairest and most desirable. "This is vanity, and it is an evil disease."

III. THESE IMPERFECTIONS IN THE HUMAN LOT OFTEN GIVE RISE TO MELANCHOLY REFLECTIONS AND DISTRESSING DOUBTS. Those who not only remark what happens around them, but reflect upon what they witness, draw inferences which have a certain semblance of validity. If we judge only by the facts which come under our cognizance, we may be led to conclusions inconsistent with true religion   Men come to doubt the rule of a benevolent Governor of the universe, simply because they cannot reconcile certain facts with such convictions as Christianity encourages. Scepticism and pessimism often follow upon bitter experiences and upon frequent contact with the calamities of this mundane state.

IV. WISDOM SUGGESTS A REMEDY FOR SUCH DIFFICULTIES AND DOUBTS. 1. It should be remembered that what any individual observes is but an infinitesimal part of the varied and protracted drama of human life and history. 2. It should not be lost sight of that there are moral and spiritual purposes in our earthly existence. It is a discipline, a proving, an education. Its end is not—as men too often suppose that it should be—enjoyment and pleasure; but character—conformity to the Divine character, and submission to the Divine will. The highest benevolence aims at the highest ends, and to secure these it seems in many cases necessary that lower ends should be sacrificed. If temporal prosperity be marred by what seems misfortune, this may be in order that spiritual prosperity may be promoted. It may not be well for the individual that he should be encouraged to seek perfect satisfaction in the things of this world. It may not be well for society that great and powerful families should be built up, to gratify human pride and ambition. God's ways are not as our ways, but they are wiser and better than ours.—T.

Vers. 3—6.—*The gloom of disappointment.* The case supposed in these verses is far more painful than that dealt with in the preceding passage. It is now presumed that a man not only lives to an advanced age—"a thousand years twice told"—but that he begets "a hundred children." Yet he is unsatisfied with the experience of life, and dies without being regretted and honourably buried. And in such a case it is affirmed that the issue of life is vanity, and that it would have been better for such a one not to have been born. It must be borne in mind, when considering this melancholy conclusion, that it is based entirely upon what is earthly, visible, and sensible.

I. HERE IS AN EXAGGERATION OF THE IMPORTANCE OF OUTWARD PROSPERITY AND OF WORLDLY PLEASURE. The standard of the world may be a real one, but it is far from being the highest. Wealth, long life, important family connections, are good things; but they are not the best. Much of human unhappiness arises from first over-estimating external advantages, and then, as a natural consequence, when these are lost, attaching undue importance to the privation. If men did not exaggerate the value of earthly good, they would not be so bitterly disappointed, so grievously depressed, upon losing it.

II. HERE IS AN UNWARRANTABLE EXPECTATION OF SATISFACTION WITH WHAT EARTH CAN GIVE. Of the person imagined it is assumed "that his soul be not filled with good." The fact is that men seek satisfaction where it is not to be found, and in so doing prove their own folly and short-sightedness. God has given to man a nature which is not to be satisfied with the enjoyments of sense, with the provision made for bodily appetite, with the splendour, luxury, and renown, upon which men are so prone to set the desires of their hearts. If what this world can give be accepted with gratitude, whilst no more is expected from it than reason and Scripture justify us in asking, then disappointment will not ensue. But the divinely fashioned and immortal spirit of man cannot rest in what is simply intended to still the cravings of the body, and to render life tranquil and enjoyable.

III. HERE IS MOROSE DISSATISFACTION RESULTING FROM FAILURE TO SOLVE AN INSOLUBLE PROBLEM. Apply the hedonistic test, and then it may be disputed whether the sum of pain and disappointment is not in excess of the sum of pleasure and satisfaction; if it is, then the "untimely birth" is better than the prosperous voluptuary who fails to fill his soul with good, who feels the utter failure of the endeavour upon which he has staked his all. But the test is a wrong one, however hard it may be to

convince men that this is so. The question—Is life worth living? does not depend upon
the question—Does life yield a surplus of agreeable feeling?   Life may be filled with
delights, and the lot of the prosperous may excite envy.   Yet it may be nothing but
vanity, and a striving after wind.   On the other hand, a man may be doomed to
adversity; poverty and neglect and contempt may be his portion; whilst he may fulfil
the purpose of his being—may form a character and may live a life which shall be
acceptable and approved above.—T.

Vers. 7—9.—*Satisfaction better than desire.* It has sometimes been represented
that the quest of good is better than its attainment. The truth and justice of this
representation lies in the unquestionable fact that it would not be for our good to
possess without effort, without perseverance, without self-denial.   Yet the end is
superior to the means, however excellently adapted those means may be to the
discipline of the character, to the calling out of the best moral qualities.

I. MAN'S NATURE IS CHARACTERIZED BY STRIVING, DESIRE, APPETITE, ASPIRATION.
Man's is a yearning, impulsive, acquisitive constitution. His natural instincts urge
him to courses of action which secure the continuance of his own being and of that of
the race.   His restless, eager desires account for the activity and energy which distinguish his movements. His intellectual impulses urge him to the pursuit of knowledge,
to scientific and literary achievemeut. His moral aspirations are the explanation of
heroism in the individual, and of true progress in social life.

II. OF HUMAN DESIRES, NONE CAN EVER BE FULLY SATISFIED, MANY CANNOT BE
SATISFIED AT ALL. The testimony of those who have gone before us is uniform upon
this point.

> " We look before and after,
>   We pine for what is not;
>   Our sincerest laughter
>   With some pain is fraught :
> Our sweetest songs are those that tell of saddest thought."

Thus it becomes proverbial that man is made to desire rather than to enjoy. Of our
aspirations some can never be gratified on earth. The lower animals have desires for
which satisfaction is provided; but whilst their life is thus thoroughly adapted to their
constitution, this cannot be said of man, who has capacities which cannot be filled,
aspirations which cannot be satisfied, faculties for which no sufficient scope is attainable here on earth.   His, as the poet tells us, is

> " The desire of the moth for the star,
>   Of the night for the morrow;
>   The longing for something afar
>   From the sphere of our sorrow."

III. EVEN WISDOM DOES BUT ENLARGE THE RANGE OF MAN'S INSATIABLE DESIRES.
It is not only upon the lower grade of life that we observe a discordance between what
is sought and what is attained. For the philosopher, as for the uncultured child of
nature, there is an ideal as well as an actual. Prudence may enjoin the limitation and
repression of our requirements. But thought ever looks out from the windows of the
high towers, and gazes upon the distant stars.

> " Who that has gazed upon them shining
>   Can turn to earth without repining,
>   Nor wish for wings to flee away,
>   And mix with their eternal day ?"

IV. THESE CONSIDERATIONS TEND TO INCREASE THE UNHAPPINESS OF THE WORLDLY,
WHILST THEY OPEN UP TO THE SPIRITUAL AND PIOUS MIND A GLORIOUS AND IMMORTAL
PROSPECT. They to whom the bodily life and the material universe are everything,
or even anything regarded by themselves, may well give way to dissatisfaction and
despondency when they learn by experience "the vanity of human wishes." On the
other hand, such reflections may well prompt the spiritual to gratitude, for they cannot
believe the universe to have been fashioned in vain; they cannot but see in the illusions

of earth suggestions of the heavenly realities. The storms of life are not to be hated if they toss the navigator of earth's sea into the haven of God's breast. The wandering of the desire may end in the sight of the eyes, when the pure in heart shall see God. "In his presence is fulness of joy, and at his right hand are pleasures for evermore."—T.

Ver. 10.—*Contending against power.* The limitation which is characteristic of the human life and lot is observable, not only in man's inability to attain the happiness he conceives and desires, but also in his inability to execute the purposes he forms. Conscious of powers which are yet undeveloped, inspired by an ambition that knows no bounds, he puts forth effort in many directions, at first with strong confidence and high hope. Experience alone convinces him of the truth expressed by the wise man in the assertion, " Neither can he contend with him that is mightier than he."

I. THE WAY OF RESISTANCE. The will may be strong, and naturally prone to self-assertion, to energetic volition, and to contention with any resisting force. 1. God is, as the providential Ruler of the world, the Lord and Controller of all circumstances, mightier than man. Men fret against the conditions and limitations of their lot ; they would fain possess greater strength and health, a longer life, enjoyments more varied and unmixed, etc. They resent the imposition of laws in the determination of which they had no voice. They are even disposed to believe that the world has been ordered, not by a benevolent Intelligence, but by a hard and cruel fate. 2. God is, as the moral Administrator and Judge, mightier than man. In their selfishness and prejudice, men may and do question the sway of reason in the universe; they assign all things to chance ; they deny any laws superior to such as are physical and political ; they deem man the measure of all things ; they ridicule responsibility. All this they may do ; but it is of no avail. God is mightier than they. They may violate his laws, but they cannot escape from their action; they may spurn his authority, but that authority is all the same maintained and exercised. The time comes when the insurgent and the rebel are constrained to admit that they are powerless, and that the Almighty is, and that he works and rules, and effects his righteous purposes.

II. THE WAY OF SUBMISSION. It is the province of religion to point out to men that there is a Power in the universe which is above all, and to summon men to yield to this Power a cheerful subjection. 1. Submission is a just requirement on the part of God, and an honourable attitude on the part of man. He is no tyrant, capricious and unjust, who claims our loyalty and service; but the Being who is himself infinitely righteous. To do him homage is to bow, not before irresistible power merely, but before moral perfection. Resistance here is slavery; subjection is freedom. 2. Submission is the one only condition of efficient work and solid happiness. Whilst we resist God, we can do nothing satisfactory and good ; when we accept his will and receive our commands from him, we become fellow-workers with God. Just as the secret of the mechanician's success is in obeying the laws of nature, *i.e.* the laws of God in the physical realm, so the secret of the success of the thinker and the philanthropist lies in the apprehension and acknowledgment of Divine law in the intellectual and moral kingdoms. Man may do great things when he labours under God and with God. And in such a course of life there is true peace as well as true success. "If God be for us, who can be against us ?"—T.

Vers. 11, 12.—*What is man's good ?* The author of this book constantly reverts to this inquiry, from which tendency we cannot fail to see how deep an impression the inquiry made upon his mind. In this he is not peculiar ; the theme is one that grows not old with the lapse of centuries.

I. A NATURAL QUESTION, AND ONE BOTH LEGITIMATE AND NECESSARY. "There be many that say, Who will show us any good ? " Sometimes the inquiry arises upon the suggestion of daily occupation; sometimes as the result of prolonged philosophical reflection. The good of man is certainly not obvious, or there would not be so many and varying replies to the question presented. A lower nature, not being self-conscious, could not consider such a question as the *summum bonum ;* being what he is, a rational and moral creation, man cannot avoid it.

II. A QUESTION TO WHICH NO SATISFACTORY REPLY CAN BE GIVEN UPON THE BASIS

OF EXPERIENCE. 1. The occupations and enjoyments of the present are proved to be productive of vanity. "Many things increase vanity." Man "spendeth his vain life as a shadow." The several objects of human pursuit agree only in their failure to afford the satisfaction that is desired and sought. Yet the path which one has abandoned another follows, only to be misled like those who have gone before, only to be put further than ever from the destination desired. The objects which excite human ambition or cupidity remain the same from age to age; and they have no more power to give satisfaction than in former periods of human history. 2. The future is felt to be clouded by uncertainty. "Who can tell a man what shall be after him under the sun?" This element of uncertainty occasioned perplexity and distress in former times, as now. What shall be a man's reputation after his decease? Who shall inherit his estates? and what use shall be made of possessions accumulated with toil and difficulty? These and similar inquiries, made but not satisfactorily answered, disheartened even the energetic and the prosperous, and took the interest and joy out of their daily life. The present is unsatisfactory, and the future uncertain; where, then, shall we look for the true, the real good?

III. A QUESTION WHICH IS SOLVED ONLY BY FAITH. As long as we confine our attention to what can be apprehended by the senses, we cannot determine what is the real good in life. For that, in the case of rational and immortal natures, lies outside of the province in which supreme good must be sought. Good for man is not bodily or temporal good; it is something which appeals to his higher nature. The enjoyment of God's favour and the fulfilment of God's service—this is the good of man. This renders men independent of the prosperity upon which multitudes set their hearts. "Lord, lift thou up the light of thy countenance upon us:" such is the desire and prayer of those who are emancipated from the bondage to time and sense, who see all things in the light of Heaven, and whose thoughts and affections are not called away from the Giver of life and happiness by the gifts of his bounty, by the shadow of the substance that endures for ever. "Thy loving-kindness is better than life."—T.

Vers. 1—6.—*The insufficiency of circumstance.* The Preacher recurs to the same strain as that in which he spoke before (see ch. ii. 1—11). We have to face the same thoughts again.

I. AN IMAGINARY ENRICHMENT. Let a man have, by supposition: 1. All the money that he can spend. 2. All the honour that waits on wealth. 3. All the luxuries that wealth can buy of every kind, material and mental (ver. 2). 4. Let him have an unusual measure of domestic enrichment and affection; let him be the recipient of all possible filial affection and obedience (ver. 3). 5. Let his life be indefinitely prolonged (ver. 6), so that it extends over many ordinary human lives. Give to a man not only what God does give to many, but give him that which, as things are, is not granted to the most favoured of our race; and what then? What is—

II. THE PROBABLE RESULT. It will very likely end in simple and utter dissatisfaction. "God giveth him not the power to eat thereof;" "His soul is not filled with good;" he gets so little enjoyment out of all that he has at command, that "an untimely birth is better than he;" he feels that it would have been positively better for him if he had never been born. Subtract the evil from the good in his life, and you have nothing left but "a negative quantity." This is quite in accord with human experience. As much of profound discontent is found within the walls of the palace as under the cottage roof. The suicide is quite as likely to be found to be a "well-dressed man," belonging to "good society," as to be a man clad in rags and penniless.

III. ITS EXPLANATION. The explanation of it is found in the fact that God has made us for himself, that he has "set eternity in our hearts" (ch. iii. 11), and that we are not capable of being satisfied with the sensible and the transient. Only the love and service of God can fill the heart that is made for the eternal and the Divine (see homily on ch. i. 7, 8).

IV. ITS CHRISTIAN CORRECTION. There need never live a man who has known Jesus Christ of whom so sad a statement as this has to be made. For a Christian life: 1. Even when spent in poverty and obscurity, is filled with a holy contentment; it includes high and sacred joys; it is relieved by very precious consolations. 2. Contains and transmits a valuable influence on others. 3. Constitutes an excellency which God approves, and the angels of God admire.   4. Moves on to a glorious future.   It does *not* end in the grave.—C.

Ver. 10.—*Heroism; infatuation; wisdom.*   Translating the latter part of this passage thus, "And it is very certain that even the greatest is but man, and cannot contend with him who is mightier than he" (Cox), we have our attention directed to three things.

I. REAL HEROISM.   This is found in opposing ourselves to the strong on behalf of the weak, even though the odds against us are very great, and apparently overwhelming. Wonderful triumphs have been achieved, even though the agents have "been but men," when they have courageously and devoutly addressed themselves to the work before them.   They have triumphed over (1) powerful "interests;" (2) imperious passions; (3) deep-rooted prejudices; (4) mighty numbers, in the cause of (*a*) their country, (*b*) truth, (*c*) Jesus Christ.

II. PITIFUL INFATUATION.   This is seen in those who are foolish enough to measure their poor strength (or their weakness) with the power of God, with "him who is mightier than they."   And this they do when they: 1. Act as if he did not regard them; when they say, "How doth God know? and is there knowledge in the Most High?" (Ps. lxxiii. 11).   2. Imagine they can outwit him; when they think they will sin and be forgiven; will corrupt their lives and waste their powers, and yet find entrance at the last hour into his kingdom.   But "God is not mocked; whatsoever a man sows, *that does* he reap."   Sin always carries its penalty at one time and in some form, if not in another.   3. Live in simple defiance of his rule; go on in conscious wrong-doing, in the vague and senseless hope that somehow they will "escape the judgment of God."

III. TRUE WISDOM.   This is realized in: 1. Submitting to his will; in acknowledging his supreme claims, as Father and Saviour of our spirit, upon our worship and trust, our love, our service, and in yielding ourselves unreservedly to him.   2. Enlisting his Divine strength on our side.   For if we are reconciled to him, and become his true and trusted children—"his disciples indeed"—then is God on our side; there is no need to speak of "contending" with him that is mightier than we; there is no further contest or variance.   Surely "God is with us," bestowing upon us his fatherly favour, admitting us to his intimate friendship, accepting us as his fellow-labourers (1 Cor. iii. 9), over-ruling all adverse (or apparently adverse) forces and making them work our true and lasting good (Rom. viii. 28), guarding us from every evil thing, leading us on to a peaceful end and out to a glorious future.—C.

Vers. 1—6.—*Life without enjoyment valueless.*   The problem which occupies the Preacher (vers. 1, 2) is virtually the same as that in ch. iv. 7, 8.   It is not that which is discussed in the Book of Job, and the thirty-seventh and seventy-third psalms, viz. why the wicked often prosper, and the righteous often suffer adversity.   It is that of men blessed with riches, with children, and with long life, and debarred all enjoyment of these blessings.   In the Law of Moses these had been the rewards promised for obedience to God (Deut. xxviii. 1—14), but the Preacher sees that something more is needed for happiness than the mere possession of them.   There is another "gift of God" needed in order that one may enjoy the good of any one of them.

I. The first picture (vers. 1, 2) is that of A RICH MAN, able to gratify every desire, but incapable of making his wealth yield him any pleasure or satisfaction.   He may be a miser, afraid to make use of his riches; he may be in ill health, and find that his wealth cannot procure for him any alleviation of his pains; his domestic circumstances may be so unhappy as to cast a cloud over his prosperity.   From various causes, such as these, the evil upon which our author remarks is common enough in human society —great wealth failing to procure for its possessor any enjoyment he can relish, and perhaps passing at last, on his death, into the hands of a stranger, for want of an heir to whom he might have had some satisfaction in leaving it.

II. A second case of a different kind is suggested in vers. 3—6.   The rich man is NOT CHILDLESS, but has a numerous family, and lives out all his days; but he, too, often has no happiness in his life, and perhaps even fails to find honourable burial when he dies.   His fate is worse than that of the stillborn child that has never tasted of life. "The abortion has the advantage in not having known anything; for it is better to know nothing at all than to know nothing but trouble. It is laid in the grave without having tasted the miseries of human life; in the grave, where, amid the silence and solitude of death, the cares and disappointments, the disquietudes and mortifications and distresses of this world are neither felt nor dreamed of" (Wardlaw). However gloomy these reflections of our author's may seem at first sight, when we examine them a little more closely we find that they are not so sombre in their character as many of the utterances of pessimistic philosophy. He does not contrast being with not-being, and declare that the latter is preferable, but he declares a joyless life to be inferior to that which has been "cut off from the womb." His teaching that the value of existence is to be measured by the amount of good that has been enjoyed in it, is so far from being the utterance of a despairing pessimism that most sober-minded persons would accept it as reasonable and true. Specimens of utterances which, to a superficial reader, might appear to be closely akin to his, but which really are the expression of a very much darker mood than his, might easily be given. Thus we have in Theognis (425—428)—

> "Best lot for man is never to be born,
> Nor ever see the bright rays of the morn:
> Next best, when born, to haste with quickest tread
> Where Hades' gates are open for the dead,
> And rest with much earth gathered for our bed."

And in Sophocles ('Œd. Col.,' 1225)—

> "Never to be at all
> Excels all fame;
> Quickly, next best, to pass
> From whence we came."

And according to the teaching of Schopenhauer, the non-existence of the world is to be preferred to its existence. The world is cursed with four great evils—birth, disease, old age, and death. "Existence is only a punishment," and the feeling of misery which often accompanies it is "repentance" for the great crime of having come into the world by yielding to the "will to live" (Wright, 'Ecclesiastes,' p. 158). Such despairing utterances, when found in the writings of those who have not known God, move us to compassion, but we can scarcely avoid the feeling of indignation when we find them on the lips of those who have known God, but have not "retained him in their knowledge." And we must beware of concluding, after a hasty and superficial reading of the Book of Ecclesiastes, that its author, even in his darkest mood, sank to the depth of atheism and despair which they reveal.—J. W.

Vers. 7—9.—*The insatiability of desire.* In these words the Preacher lays stress upon the little advantage which one man has over another in regard to the attainment of happiness and satisfaction in life. All are tormented by desires and longings which can never be adequately satisfied. His reference is principally, if not entirely, to the cravings of natural appetites to which all are subject, and which cannot by any gratification or exercise of will be wholly silenced. The instinct of self-preservation, the necessity of sustaining the body with food, inspire labour, and yet no amount of labour is sufficient to put an end, once and for all, to the gnawings of desire. The sensuous element in man's nature is insatiable, and the appetites of which it consists grow in strength as they are indulged. Though the pressure of appetite differs in different cases, none are free from it. The wise as well as the foolish, the man of simple tastes and chastened temper, as well as he who gives free rein to all his impulses, feel it. Gifts of intellect, acquirements in culture, make no difference in this matter. Some little obscurity seems at first to hang over ver. 8*b*, but a little examination of the words disperses it. The whole verse runs (Revised Version), "For what advantage hath the wise man more than the fool? or what [advantage] hath the poor man [more than the fool], that knoweth to walk before the living?" "To know to walk before the living" is, as is now generally acknowledged, to understand the right rule of life, to possess the *savoir vivre*, to be experienced in the right art of living

(Delitzsch). The question accordingly is—What advantage has the wise over the fool? and what the poor, who, although poor, knows how to maintain his social position? The matter treated of is the insatiable nature of sensual desire. The wise seeks to control his desire; he who is spoken of as poor knows how to conceal it, for he lays restraints upon himself, that he may make a good appearance and maintain his reputation. But desire is present in both, and they have in this nothing above the fool, who follows the bent of his desire, and lives for the passing hour. In other words, "The idea of the passage seems to be, the desire of man is insatiable, he is never really satisfied; the wise man, however, seeks to keep his desires within bounds, and to keep them to himself, but the fool utters all his mind (Prov. xxix. 11). Even the poor man, who knows how to conduct himself in life, and understands the right art of living, though he keeps his secret to himself, feels within himself the stirrings of that longing which is destined never to be satisfied on earth" (Wright). The reference here to the poor man may possibly be made because the Preacher has already praised the lot of the labouring man (ch. v. 12) in comparison with that of the rich, whose abundance will not suffer him to sleep. If so, he virtually says here, half-humorously, "Don't imagine that poverty is the secret of contentment and happiness. Poverty covers cares and anxieties as well as riches. Both rich and poor are pretty much on the same level." A very simple and practical conclusion is drawn from the fact of the insatiability of desire, and that is the advisability of enjoying the present good that is within our reach (ver. 9). That which the eyes see and recognize as good and beautiful should not be forfeited because the thoughts are wandering after something which may be for ever unattainable by us. So far the teaching is not above that of the fable of the dog who lost the piece of flesh he had in his mouth, because he snapped at the reflection of it he saw on the surface of the water. And if this be thought but a poor, cold scrap of morality to offer to men for their guidance in life, the answer may be given that multitudes spend their life in fruitless endeavours after what is far above their reach, and bereave their souls of present good, from an insatiable greed which this fable rebukes. Constituted as we are, placed as we are amid many temptations, we need not despise any small scraps of moral teaching which may be even in threadbare fables, and homely, familiar proverbs. To say that the words, "Better is the sight of the eyes than the wandering of the desire," is about equivalent to the proverb, "A bird in the hand is worth two in the bush," may seem irreverent to some, who would fain read into the text more than it contains. But instead of imagining that the Word of God is degraded by the comparison, let them recognize the good sense and prudent advice which lie in the proverb which corresponds so closely to the sense of the Preacher's words.—J. W.

Vers. 10—12.—*Inexorable destiny.* Before considering these words of the Preacher, we need to obtain a clear and precise idea of the statements he makes. A considerable measure of obscurity hangs over the passage, and renders it all the more difficult to catch the writer's meaning. This is apparent from the alternative renderings of several clauses in it which we have in the margin of the Revised Version. The general idea of the passage seems to be—*Man's powerlessness and short-sightedness with respect to destiny.* "Whatsoever hath been, the name thereof was given long ago, and it is known that it is man: neither can he contend with him that is mightier than he" (ver. 10). The difficult phrase is that thus translated—"it is known that it is man." But if we take the Hebrew phrase, as several eminent critics (Delitzsch, Wright) do, to be equal to *scitur id quod homo sit*—"it is known that which a man is"—an intelligible and appropriate meaning of the passage is obtained. It seems to point to the fact that man has been placed in certain unalterable conditions by the will of God, and to urge the advisability of submitting to the inevitable. Both as to time and place, the conditions have been fixed from of old, and no human effort can change them. The same thought occurs in St. Paul's address to the Athenians: "He made of one every nation of men for to dwell on all the face of the earth, having determined their appointed seasons, and the bounds of their habitation" (Acts xvii. 26, Revised Version). It is to be found also in Isaiah's saying, "Woe unto him that striveth with his Maker! a potsherd among the potsherds of the earth! Shall the clay say to him that fashioneth it, What makest thou? or thy work, He hath no hands?" And this passage in Ecclesiastes seems to have been in the mind of the Apostle Paul quite as certainly as that just quoted from Isaiah, when he wrote the famous paragraph in the Epistle to the Romans on the potter and the clay (ix. 20, *et seq.*). That God has predetermined the conditions of our lives, and that it is useless to strive against his power, seems, therefore, the teaching of ver. 10. The obscurity in ver. 11 is caused by the translation, both in our Authorized Version and Revised Version, of the Hebrew דברים as "things" instead of "words." In the Revised Version "words" is given in the margin, but assuredly should be in the text, as in the ancient versions (LXX., Vulgate, Syriac): "Seeing there be many words that increase vanity, what is man the better?" (ver. 11). Most probably the reference is to discussions concerning man's freedom and God's decrees, that were coming into vogue among the Jews. The nascent school of the Pharisees maintained fatalistic views concerning human conduct, that of the Sadducees denied the existence of fate (Josephus, 'Ant.,' xiii. 5. 9; xviii. 1. 3, 4; 'Bell. Jud.,' ii. 8. 14). The uselessness of all such discussions is also asserted later in ch. xii. 12, and is pathetically reiterated in the famous passage of Milton's 'Paradise Lost,' in which some of the fallen angels are described as discussing

> "Fixed fate, free-will, foreknowledge absolute;
> Vain wisdom all, and false philosophy."

The twelfth verse is clear enough. After all discussion as to the true course of life, who can give a decided answer? Life is a shadow; the future is unknown to us. "For who knoweth what is good for man in this life, all the days of his vain life, which he spendeth as a shadow? for who can tell a man what shall be after him under the sun?" No one can read the words without being struck with the dark, despairing Pyrrhonism of their tone. "A cloud of irrepressible, inexpressible melancholy hangs around the writer, a leaden weight is on the spring of his spirit." And it is only when we consider that the spiritual education of the world by God has been gradual, that we can tolerate the words as expressing the thoughts of a mind not yet privileged to see truth in its fulness. If we believe that the light of truth is, like the light of the sun, increasing from the first faint rays that begin to dispel the darkness of midnight to the splendour of noonday, we shall not be surprised at the words of the Preacher. They *would be* highly inappropriate in one to whom the revelation of God in Christ had been given; as used by him, they would necessarily imply a gross unbelief, which would excite our indignation rather than our sympathy. Christianity puts the facts which the Preacher regarded as so sombre in a fresh light, and strips them of all their terror. Let us take them in order.

I. THAT WHICH HE CALLED FATE WE CALL PROVIDENCE. "Since fate bears sway, and everything must be as it is, why dost thou strive against it?" said the Stoic, Marcus Aurelius (xii. 13), and his words seem exactly similar to those before us. The idea of a fixed order in human life, a Divine will governing all things, does not necessarily fill us with the same gloomy thoughts, or summon us to a proud and scornful resignation to that which we cannot change or modify. In the teaching of Christ we have the fact of a preordination of things by God frequently alluded to, in such sentences as "Mine hour is not yet come;" "The hairs of your head are all numbered;" "Many be called, but few chosen;" "No man can come to me except the Father draw him;" "For the elect's sake whom he hath chosen God hath shortened the days." This is not a dark, inexorable fate governing all things, but the wise and gracious will of a Father, in which his children may trust with confidence and joy. The thought, I say, of all things being predetermined by the Divine will is prominent in the teaching of Christ, but it is set in such a light as to be a source of inspiration and strength. It prompts such comfortable assurances as, "Fear not, little flock; it is your Father's good pleasure to give you the kingdom."

II. THE PREACHER WAS HUMILIATED AT THE THOUGHT OF HUMAN WEAKNESS. "Neither may he contend with one that is mightier than he." But we know more clearly than he did of the Divine compassion for the poor and feeble and helpless—a compassion that prompted God to send forth his Son for our redemption. We know that the Son of God took on him our nature, submitted to the toils, trials, privations, and temptations of a mortal lot, and overcame the worst foes by whom we are assailed —sin and death. If, as some think, "the mightier" one here referred to is death, we believe that Christ took away his power, and that in his triumphant resurrection we have the pledge of everlasting life. And the one great lesson taught by the Church's history is that God has chosen the weak things of the world to confound the strong.

III. ANOTHER CAUSE OF GRIEF WAS THE FLEETING CHARACTER OF LIFE. "Vain life which man spendeth as a shadow." But this does not afflict us, who know that the grave is not the end of all things, but the door of a better life. The present existence acquires new value and solemnity when we consider it as the prelude to eternity, the time and place given us in which to prepare ourselves for the world to come. We have his words, "I am the Resurrection and the Life: . . . whosoever liveth and believeth in me shall never die." The sorrows and trials of the present dwindle into insignificance as compared with the reward we anticipate as in store for us if we are faithful to God. "Our light affliction, which is but for a moment, worketh for us a far more exceeding and eternal weight of glory; while we look not at the things which are seen, but at the things which are not seen: for the things which are seen are temporal; but the things which are not seen are eternal" (2 Cor. iv. 17, 18).

IV. A FINAL CAUSE OF GRIEF WAS THAT THE FUTURE WAS DARK AND UNKNOWN. "Who can tell a man what shall be after him under the sun?" This is still true in many departments of life. The mightiest potentate cannot tell how long the dynasty he has founded, or of which he may be the brightest ornament, will last. The conqueror may be distressed by the thought that the power, to obtain which he has squandered myriads of lives and countless treasures, may soon fade away, and in a short time after his death vanish "like the baseless fabric of a vision." The poet does not know that even the most brilliant of his works will be kept alive in the memories of men, and treasured among the things they will not willingly let die, within a generation or two after he has passed away. The successful merchant, who has built up a colossal fortune by the labours of a lifetime, cannot guard against its being dissipated in a very short time by those to whom he leaves it. But the Christian is in no such uncertainty. The cause of his Master he knows will prosper and grow to far vaster proportions in the time to come. The good work he has done will aid in the advancement of the kingdom of God, and no blight of failure will fall upon his efforts; the plans of God in which during his earthly life he co-operated will not be frustrated, and his own personal happiness is for ever secured. All the various causes of despondency by which the Preacher's mind was harassed and perplexed vanish before the brighter revelation of God's will given us in the mission and work of Christ. And it is only because we keep in mind that the truth vouchsafed to us was withheld from him, that we can read his words without being depressed by the burden by which his spirit was borne down and saddened. It would only be by our deliberately sinning against the light we enjoy that we could ever adopt his words as expressing our views of life.—J. W.

EXPOSITION.

CHAPTER VII.

Ver. 1—ch. xii. 8.—Division II. DEDUC-TIONS FROM THE ABOVE-MENTIONED EXPERI-ENCES IN THE WAY OF WARNINGS AND RULES OF LIFE.

Vers. 1—7.—Section 1. Though no man knows for certain what is best, yet there are *some practical rules for the conduct of life which wisdom gives.* Some of these Koheleth sets forward in the proverbial form, recommending a serious, earnest life in preference to one of gaiety and frivolity.

Ver. 1.—**A good name is better than**

precious ointment. The paronomasia here is to be remarked, *tob shem mishemen tob.* There is a similar assonance in Cant. i. 3, which the German translator reproduces by the sentence, "Besser gut Gerücht als Wohl-geruch," or, "gute Gerüche," and which may perhaps be rendered in English, "Better is good favour than good flavour." It is a proverbial saying, running literally, *Better is a name than good oil.* Shem, "name," is sometimes used unqualified to signify a cele-brated name, good name, reputation (comp. Gen. xi. 4; Prov. xxii. 1). Septuagint, Ἀγαθὸν ὄνομα ὑπὲρ ἔλαιον ἀγαθόν. Vulgate, *Melius est nomen bonum quam unguenta pretiosa.* Odorous unguents were very precious in the mind of an Oriental, and formed one of the luxuries lavished at feasts and costly entertainments, or social visits (see ch. ix. 8; Ruth iii. 3; Ps. xlv. 8; Amos vi. 6; Wisd. ii. 7; Luke vii. 37, 46). It was a man's most cherished ambition to leave a good reputation, and to hand down an honourable remembrance to distant posterity, and this all the more as the hope of the life beyond the grave was dim and vague (see on ch. ii. 16, and comp. ch. ix. 5). The complaint of the sensualists in Wisd. ii. 4 is embittered by the thought, " Our name shall be forgotten in time, and no man shall have our works in remembrance." We employ a metaphor like that in the clause when we speak of a man's reputation having a good or ill odour; and the Hebrews said of ill fame that it stank in the nostrils (Gen. xxxiv. 30; Exod. v. 21; see, on the opposite side, Ecclus. xxiv. 15; 2 Cor. ii. 15). **And the day of death than the day of one's birth.** The thought in this clause is closely connected with the preceding. If a man's life is such that he leaves a good name behind him, then the day of his departure is better than that of his birth, because in the latter he had nothing before him but labour, and trouble, and fear, and uncertainty; and in the former all these anxieties are past, the storms are successfully battled with, the haven is won (see on ch. iv. 3). According to Solon's well-known maxim, no one can be called happy till he has crowned a prosperous life by a peaceful death (Herod., i. 32; Soph., 'Trachin.,' 1.—3; 'Œd. Tyr.,' 1528, *sqq.*); as the Greek gnome runs—

Μήπω μέγαν εἴπῃς πρὶν τελευτήσαντ' ἴδῃς.

" Call no man great till thou hast seen him dead."

So Ben-Sira, " Judge none blessed (μὴ μα-κάριζε μηδένα) before his death; for a man shall be known in his children " (Ecclus. xi. 28).

Ver. 2.—It is **better to go to the house of mourning, than to go to the house of feasting.** The thought in the last verse leads to the recollection of the circumstances which accompany the two events therein mentioned —birth and death, feasting and joy, in the first case; sorrow and mourning in the second. In recommending the sober, earnest life, Koheleth teaches that wiser, more enduring lessons are to be learned where grief reigns than in the empty and momentary excitement of mirth and joyousness. The house in question is mourning for a death; and what a long and harrowing business this was is well known (see Deut. xxiv. 8; Ecclus. xxii. 10; Jer. xxii. 18; Matt. ix. 23, etc.). Visits of condolence and periodical pilgrimages to graves of departed relatives were considered duties (John xi. 19, 31), and conduced to the growth in the mind of sympathy,

seriousness, and the need of preparation for death. The opposite side, the house of carousal, where all that is serious is put away, leading to such scenes as Isaiah denounces (v. 11), offers no wise teaching, and produces only selfishness, heartlessness, thoughtlessness. What is said here is no contradiction to what was said in ch. ii. 24, that there was nothing better for a man than that he should eat and drink and enjoy himself. For Koheleth was not speaking of unrestrained sensualism—the surrender of the mind to the pleasures of the body—but of the moderate enjoyment of the good things of life conditioned by the fear of God and love of one's neighbour. This statement is quite compatible with the view that sees a higher purpose and training in the sympathy with sorrow than in participation in reckless frivolity. **For that is the end of all men** viz. that they will some day be mourned, that their house will be turned into a house of mourning. Vulgate, *In illa* (*domo*) *enim finis cunctorum admonetur hominum,* which is not the sense of the Hebrew. **The living will lay** it **to his heart.** He who has witnessed this scene will consider it seriously (ch. ix. 1), and draw from it profitable conclusions concerning the brevity of life and the proper use to make thereof. We recall the words of Christ, " Blessed are they that mourn : for they shall be comforted; " and " Woe unto you that laugh now ! for ye shall mourn and weep " (Matt. v. 4; Luke vi. 25). Schultens gives an Arab proverb which says, " Hearest thou lamentation for the dead, hasten to the spot; art thou called to a banquet, cross not the threshold." The Septuagint thus translates the last clause, Καὶ ὁ ζῶν δώσει ἀγαθὸν εἰς καρδίαν αὐτοῦ, " The living will put good into his heart; " the Vulgate paraphrases fairly, *Et vivens cogitat quid futurum sit,* " The living thinks what is to come." " So teach us to number our days," prays the psalmist, " that we may apply our hearts unto wisdom " (Ps. xc. 12).

Ver. 3.—**Sorrow is better than laughter.** This is a further expansion of the previous maxim. ‪כַּעַס‬ (*kaas*), as contrasted with ‪שְׂחוֹק‬, is rightly rendered " sorrow," " melancholy," or, as Ginsburg contends, " thoughtful sadness." The Septuagint has θυμός, the Vulgate *ira;* but anger is not the feeling produced by a visit to the house of mourning. Such a scene produces saddening reflection, which is in itself a moral training, and is more wholesome and elevating than thoughtless mirth. **For by the sadness of the countenance the heart is made better.** The feeling which shows itself by the look of sadness (comp. Gen. xl. 7; Neh. ii. 2) has a purifying effect on the heart, gives a moral tone to the character. Professor Tayler Lewis renders the clause, " For in the sadness of the face the heart becometh fair;" *i.e.* sorrow beautifies the soul, producing, as it were, comeliness, spiritual beauty, and, in the end, serener happiness. The Vulgate translates the passage thus: *Melior est ira risu; quia per tristitiam vultus corrigitur animus deliquentis*, "Better is anger than laughter, because through sadness of countenance the mind of the offender is corrected." The anger is that either of God or of good men which reproves sin; the laughter is that of sinners who thus show their connivance at or approval of evil. There can be no doubt that this is not the sense of the passage. For the general sentiment concerning the moral influence of grief and suffering, we may compare the Greek sayings, Τὰ παθήματα μαθήματα, and Τί μαθών; τί παθών; which are almost equivalent in meaning (comp. Æschyl., 'Agam.,' 170; Herod., i. 207). The Latins would say, "Quæ nocent, docent," and we, "Pain is gain."

Ver. 4.—**The heart of the wise is in the house of mourning.** This is the natural conclusion from what was said in vers. 2, 3. The man who recognizes the serious side of life, and knows where to learn lessons of high moral meaning, will be found conversant with scenes of sorrow and suffering, and reflecting upon them. **But the heart of fools is in the house of mirth.** The fool, who thinks of nothing but present enjoyment, and how to make life pass pleasantly, turns away from mournful scenes, and goes only there where he may drown care and be thoughtless and merry.

Ver. 5.—**It is better to hear the rebuke of the wise.** *Gearah*, "rebuke," is the word used in Proverbs for the grave admonition which heals and strengthens while it wounds (see Prov. xiii. 1; xvii. 10). The silent lessons which a man learns from the contemplation of others' sorrow are rightly supplemented by the salutary correction of the wise man's tongue. **Than for a man to hear the song of fools.** *Shir*, "song," is a general term used of sacred or profane song; the connection here with the second clause of ver. 4, etc., leads one to think of the boisterous, reckless, often immodest, singing heard in the house of revelry, such as Amos (vi. 5) calls "idle songs to the sound of the viol." Koheleth might have heard these in his own country, without drawing his experience from the licence of Greek practice or the impurity of Greek lyrics. The Vulgate renders the clause, *Quam stultorum adulatione decipi*, "Than to be deceived by the flattery of fools." This is a paraphrase; the correctness is negatived by the explanation given in the following verse.

Ver. 6.—**For as the crackling of thorns under a pot.** There is a play of words in the Hebrew, "The crackling of *sirim* under

a *sir*," which Wright expresses by translating, "Like the noise of the nettles under the kettles." In the East, and where wood is scarce, thorns, hay, and stubble are used for fuel (Ps. lviii. 9; cxx. 4; Matt. vi. 30). Such materials are quickly kindled, blaze up for a time with much noise, and soon die away (Ps. cxviii. 12). **So is the laughter of the fool.** The point of comparison is the loud crackling and the short duration of the fire with small results. So the fool's mirth is boisterous and noisy, but comes to a speedy end, and is spent to no good purpose. So in Job (xx. 5) we have, "The triumphing of the wicked is short, and the joy of the godless but for a moment." All this profitless mirth is again nothing but **vanity.**

Ver. 7.—The verse begins with *ki*, which usually introduces a reason for what has preceded; but the difficulty in finding the connection has led to various explanations and evasions. The Authorized Version boldly separates the verse from what has gone before, and makes a new paragraph beginning with "surely:" **Surely oppression maketh a wise** man **mad.** Delitzsch supposes that something has been lost between vers. 6 and 7, and he supplies the gap by a clause borrowed from Prov. xvi. 8, "Better is a little with righteousness than great revenues without right;" and then the sentence proceeds naturally, "For oppression," etc. But this is scarcely satisfactory, as it is mere conjecture wholly unsupported by external evidence. The Vulgate leaves *ki* untranslated; the Septuagint has ὅτι. Looking at the various paragraphs, all beginning with *tob*, rendered "better," viz. vers. 1, 2, 3, 5, 8, we must regard the present verse as connected with what precedes, a new subject being introduced at ver. 8. Putting ver. 6 in a parenthesis as merely presenting an illustration of the talk of fools, we may see in ver. 7 a confirmation of the first part of ver. 5. The rebuke of the wise is useful even in the case of rulers who are tempted to excess and injustice. The "oppression" in the text is the exercise of irresponsible power, that which a man inflicts, not what he suffers; this makes him "mad," even though he be in other respects and under other circumstances wise; he ceases to be directed by reason and principle, and needs the correction of faithful rebuke. The Septuagint and Vulgate, rendering respectively συκοφαντία and *calumnia*, imply that the evil which distracts the wise man is false accusation. **And a gift destroyeth the heart.** The admission of bribery is likewise an evil that calls for wise rebuke. So Prov. xv. 27, "He that is greedy of gain troubleth his own house; but he that hateth gifts shall live." The phrase, "destroys the heart," means corrupts the understanding, deprives a man of wisdom, makes him no better than a fool (comp. Hos. iv. 11, where the same effect is attributed to whoredom and drunkenness). The Septuagint has, ἀπόλλυσι τὴν καρδίαν εὐγενείας αὐτοῦ, "destroys the heart of his nobility;" the Vulgate, *perdet robur cordis illius*, "will destroy the strength of his heart." The interpretation given above seems to be the most reasonable way of dealing with the existing text; but Nowack and Volck adopt Delitzsch's emendation.

Vers. 8—14.—Section 2. Here follow some *recommendations to patience and resignation under the ordering of God's providence.* Such conduct is shown to be true wisdom.

Ver. 8.—**Better is the end of a thing than the beginning thereof.** This is not a repetition of the assertion in ver. 1 concerning the day of death and the day of birth, but states a truth in a certain sense generally true. The end is better because we then can form a right judgment about a matter; we see what was its purpose; we know whether it has been advantageous and prosperous or not. Christ's maxim, often repeated (see Matt. x. 22; xxiv. 13; Rom. ii. 7; Heb. iii. 6, etc.), is, "He that shall endure unto the end shall be saved." No one living can be said to be so absolutely safe as that he can look to the great day without trembling. Death puts the seal to the good life, and obviates the danger of falling away. Of course, if a thing is in itself evil, the gnome is not true (comp. Prov. v. 3, 4; xvi. 25, etc.); but applied to things indifferent at the outset, it is as correct as generalizations can be. The lesson of patience is here taught. A man should not be precipitate in his judgments, but wait for the issue. From the ambiguity in the expression *dabar* (see on ch. vi. 11), many render it "word" in this passage. Thus the Vulgate, *Melior est finis orationis, quam principium;* and the Septuagint, Ἀγαθὴ ἐσχάτη λόγων ὑπὲρ ἀρχὴν αὐτοῦ, where φωνή, or some such word, must be supplied. If this interpretation be preferred, we must either take the maxim as stating generally that few words are better than many, and that the sooner one concludes a speech, so much the better for speaker and hearer; or we must consider that the word intended is a well-merited rebuke, which, however severe and at first disliked, proves in the end wholesome and profitable. And **the patient in spirit is better than the proud in spirit.** "Patient" is literally "long of spirit," as the phrase, "short of spirit," is used in Prov. xiv. 29 and Job xxi. 4 to denote one who loses his temper and is impatient. To wait calmly for the result of an action, not to be hasty in arraigning Providence, is the part of a patient man; while the proud,

inflated, conceited man, who thinks all must be arranged according to his notions, is never resigned or content, but rebels against the ordained course of events. "In your patience ye shall win your souls," said Christ (Luke xxi. 19); and a Scotch proverb declares wisely, "He that weel bides, weel betides."

Ver. 9.—**Be not hasty in thy spirit to be angry.** A further warning against the arrogance which murmurs at Providence and revolts against the checks of the Divine arrangement. The injunction in ch. v. 2 might be taken in this sense. It is not a general admonition against unrighteous anger, but is levelled at the haughty indignation which a proud man feels when things do not go as he wishes, and he deems that he could have managed matters more satisfactorily. **For anger resteth in the bosom of fools.** Such unreasonable displeasure is the mark of a foolish or sceptical mind, and if it rests (Prov. xiv. 33), is fostered and cherished there, may develop into misanthropy and atheism. If we adopt the rendering "word" in ver. 8, we may see in this injunction a warning against being quick to take offence at a rebuke, as it is only the fool who will not look to the object of the censure and see that it ought to be patiently submitted to. On the subject of anger St. Gregory writes, "As often as we restrain the turbulent motions of the mind under the virtue of mildness, we are essaying to return to the likeness of our Creator. For when the peace of mind is lashed with anger, torn and rent, as it were, it is thrown into confusion, so that it is not in harmony with itself, and loses the force of the inward likeness. By anger wisdom is parted with, so that we are left wholly in ignorance what to do; as it is written, 'Anger resteth in the bosom of a fool,' in this way, that it withdraws the light of understanding, while by agitating it troubles the mind" ('Moral.,' v. 78).

Ver. 10.—The same impatience leads a man to disparage the present in comparison with a past age. **What is the cause that the former days were better than these?** He does not know from any adequate information that preceding times were in any respect superior to present, but in his moody discontent he looks on what is around him with a jaundiced eye, and sees the past through a rose-tinted atmosphere, as an age of heroism, faith, and righteousness. Horace finds such a character in the morose old man, whom he describes in 'De Arte Poet.,' 173—

"Difficilis, querulus, laudator temporis acti
 Se puero, castigator censorque minorum."

"Morose and querulous, praising former days

When he was boy, now ever blaming
youth."

And ' Epist.,' ii. 1. 22—

". . . et nisi quæ terris semota suisque
Temporibus defuncta videt, fastidit et odit."

" All that is not most distant and removed
   From his own time and place, he loathes
   and scorns."

**For thou dost not inquire wisely concerning
this.** In asking such a question you show
that you have not reflected wisely on the
matter. Every age has its light and dark
side; the past was not wholly light, the
present is not wholly dark. And it may
well be questioned whether much of the
glamour shed over antiquity is not false and
unreal. The days of " Good Queen Bess "
were anything but halcyon; the "merrie
England" of old time was full of disorder,
distress, discomfort. In yearning again for
the flesh-pots of Egypt, the Israelites forgot
the bondage and misery which were the
accompaniments of those sensual pleasures.
Ver. 11.—Such hasty judgment is incompatible with true wisdom and sagacity.
Wisdom is good with an inheritance;
Septuagint, Ἀγαθὴ σοφία μετὰ κληρονομίας.
Vulgate, *Utilior est sapientia cum divitiis.*
The sentence thus rendered seems to mean
that wealth lends a prestige to wisdom,
that the man is happy who possesses both.
The inheritance spoken of is an hereditary
one; the man who is " rich with ancestral
wealth " is enabled to employ his wisdom
to good purpose, his position adding weight
to his words and actions, and relieving him
from the low pursuit of money-making. To
this effect Wright quotes Menander—

Μακάριος ὅστις οὐσίαν καὶ νοῦν ἔχει·
Χρῆται γὰρ οὗτος εἰς ἃ δεῖ ταύτῃ καλῶς.

" Blest is the man who wealth and wisdom
   hath,
For he can use his riches as he ought."

(Comp. Prov. xiv. 24.) Many commentators,
thinking such a sentiment alien from the
context, render the particle עם not " with,"
but " as: " Wisdom is [as] good as an inheritance " (see on ch. ii. 16). This is putting
wisdom on rather a low platform, and one
would have expected to read some such
aphorism as " Wisdom is better than rubies "
(Prov. viii. 11), if Koheleth had intended to
make any such comparison. It appears then
most expedient to take *im* in the sense of
" moreover," " as well as," " and " (comp.
1 Sam. xvii. 42, " ruddy, and (*im*) of a fair
countenance "). " Wisdom is good, and an
inheritance is good; " both are good, but the
advantages of the former, as ver. 12 intimates,
far outweigh those of the latter. **And by it
there is profit to them that see the sun;**

rather, *and an advantage for those that see
the sun.* However useful wealth may be,
wisdom is that which is really beneficial
to all who live and rejoice in the light of
day. In Homer the phrase, ὁρᾶν φάος ἠελίοιο,
" to see the light of the sun " (' Iliad,'
xviii. 61), signifies merely " to live; "
Plumptre considers it to be used here and
in ch. xix. 7 in order to convey the thought
that, after all, life has its bright side. Cox
would take it to mean to live much in the
sun, *i.e.* to lead an active life—which is an
imported modern notion.

Ver. 12.—**For wisdom is a defence, and
money is a defence;** literally, *in the shade is
wisdom, in the shade is money;* Septuagint,
Ὅτι ἐν σκιᾷ αὐτῆς ἡ σοφία ὡς σκιὰ ἀργυρίου,
" For in its shadow wisdom is as the shadow
of money." Symmachus has, Σκέπει σοφία
ὡς σκέπει τὸ ἀργύριον, " Wisdom shelters
as money shelters." The Vulgate explains
the obscure text by paraphrasing, *Sicut enim
protegit sapientia, sic protegit pecunia.*
Shadow, in Oriental phrase, is equivalent to
protection (see Numb. xiv. 9; Ps. xvii. 8;
Lam. iv. 20). Wisdom as well as money
is a shield and defence to men. As it is said
in one passage (Prov. xiii. 8) that riches
are the ransom of a man's life, so in another
(ch. ix. 15) we are told how wisdom
delivered a city from destruction. The
literal translation given above implies that
he who has wisdom and he who has money
rest under a safe protection, are secure
from material evil. In this respect they
are alike, and have analogous claims to
man's regard. **But the excellency**—profit, or
advantage—**of knowledge is, that wisdom
giveth life to them that have it.** " Knowledge " (*daath*) and " wisdom " (*chokmah*)
are practically here identical, the terms
being varied for the sake of poetic parallelism. The Revised Version, following
Delitzsch and others, renders, *Wisdom
preserveth the life of him that hath it;* i.e.
secures him from passions and excesses
which tend to shorten life. This seems to
be scarcely an adequate ground for the
noteworthy advantage which wisdom is said
to possess. The Septuagint gives, Καὶ περίσσεια γνώσεως τῆς σοφίας ζωοποιήσει τόν
παρ' αὐτῆς, " And the excellence of the knowledge of wisdom will quicken him that hath
it." Something more than the mere animal
life is signified, a climax to the " defence "
mentioned in the preceding clause—the
higher, spiritual life which man has from
God. Wisdom in the highest sense, that is,
practical piety and religion, is " a tree of
life to them that lay hold of her, and happy
is every one that retaineth her " (Prov. iii.
18), where it is implied that wisdom restores
to man the gift which he lost at the Fall
(comp. also Prov. viii. 35). The Septuagint

expression ζωοποιήσει recalls the words of
Christ, "As the Father raiseth the dead
and quickeneth (ζωοποιεῖ) them, even so the
Son also quickeneth whom he will; " "It is
the Spirit that quickeneth (τὸ ζωοποιοῦν)"
(John v. 21; vi. 63). Koheleth attributes
that power to wisdom which the more
definite teaching of Christianity assigns to
the influence of the Holy Spirit. Some
would explain, "fortifies or vivifies the
heart," *i.e.* imparts new life and strength
to meet every fortune. The Vulgate
rendering is far astray from the text, and
does not accurately convey the sense of
the passage, running thus: *Hoc autem plus
habet eruditio et sapientia: quod vitam
tribuunt possessori suo,* "But this more
have learning and wisdom, that they give
life to the possessor of them."

Ver. 13.—**Consider the work of God.**
Here is another reason against murmuring
and hasty judgment. True wisdom is
shown by submission to the inevitable. In
all that happens one ought to recognize
God's work and God's ordering, and man's
impotence. **For who can make that straight,
which he hath made crooked?** The things
which God hath made crooked are the
anomalies, the crosses, the difficulties, which
meet us in life. Some would include bodily
deformities, which seems to be a piece of
unnecessary literalism. Thus the Septuagint, Τίς δυνήσεται κοσμῆσαι ὃν ἂν ὁ Θεὸς
διαστρέψῃ αὐτόν; "Who will be able to
straighten him whom God has distorted?"
and the Vulgate, *Nemo possit corrigere quem
ille despexerit,* "No one can amend him
whom he hath despised." The thought
goes back to what was said in ch. i. 15,
"That which is crooked cannot be made
straight;" and in ch. vi. 10, man "cannot
contend with him that is mightier than he."
"As for the wondrous works of the Lord,"
says Ben-Sira, "there may be nothing taken
from them, neither may anything be put
unto them, neither can the ground of them
be found out" (Ecclus. xviii. 6). We cannot
arrange events according to our wishes or
expectations; therefore not only is placid
acquiescence a necessary duty, but the wise
man will endeavour to accommodate himself to existing circumstances.

Ver. 14.—**In the day of prosperity be joyful;** literally, *in the day of good be in good*
i.e. when things go well with you, be cheerful (ch. ix. 7; Esth. viii. 17); accept the
situation and enjoy it. The advice is the
same as that which runs through the book,
viz. to make the best of the present. So
Ben-Sira says, "Defraud not thyself of the
good day, and let not a share in a good
desire pass thee by" (Ecclus. xiv. 14).
Septuagint, Ἐν ἡμέρᾳ ἀγαθωσύνης ζῆθι ἐν
αγαθῷ, "In a day of good live in (an

atmosphere of) good;" Vulgate, *In die bona
fruere bonis,* "In a good day enjoy your good
things." **But in the day of adversity consider;**
in the evil day look well. The writer could
not conclude this clause so as to make it
parallel with the other, or he would have
had to say, "In the ill day take it ill,"
which would be far from his meaning; so
he introduces a thought which may help to
make one resigned to adversity. The reflection follows. Septuagint, Καὶ ἴδε ἐν
ἡμέρᾳ κακίας· ἴδε, κ.τ.λ.; Vulgate, *Et malam
diem præcave,* "Beware of the evil day."
But, doubtless, the object of the verb is the
following clause. **God also hath set the one
over against the other;** or, *God hath made
the one corresponding to the other;* i.e. he
hath made the day of evil as well as the
day of good. The light and shade in man's
life are equally under God's ordering and
permission. "What?" cries Job (ii. 10),
"shall we receive good at the hand of
God, and shall we not receive evil?" Corn.
à Lapide quotes a saying of Plutarch to this
effect: the harp gives forth sounds acute
and grave, and both combine to form the
melody; so in man's life the mingling of prosperity and adversity yields a well-adjusted
harmony. God strikes all the strings of our
life's harp, and we ought, not only patiently,
but cheerfully, to listen to the chords produced by this Divine Performer. **To the end
that man should find nothing after him.**
This clause gives Koheleth's view of God's
object in the admixture of good and evil;
but the reason has been variously interpreted, the explanation depending on the
sense assigned to the term "after him"
(אַחֲרָיו). The Septuagint gives ὀπίσω αὐτοῦ,
which is vague; the Vulgate, *contra eum,*
meaning that man may have no occasion to
complain against God. Cheyne ('Job and
Solomon') considers that Koheleth here
implies that death closes the scene, and
that there is then nothing more to fear,
rendering the clause, "On the ground that
man is to experience nothing at all hereafter."
They who believe that the writer held the
doctrine of a future life cannot acquiesce in
this view. The interpretation of Delitzsch
is this—God lets man pass through the
whole discipline of good and evil, that when
he dies there may be nothing which he has
not experienced. Hitzig and Nowack explain the text to mean that, as God designs
that man after his death shall have done
with all things, he sends upon him evil
as well as good, that he may not have to
punish him hereafter—a doctrine opposed
to the teaching of a future judgment.
Wright deems the idea to be that man
may be kept in ignorance of what shall
happen to him beyond the grave, that the
present life may afford no clue to the future.

One does not see why this should be a comfort, nor how it is compatible with God's known counsel of making the condition of the future life dependent upon the conduct of this. Other explanations being more or less unsatisfactory, many modern commentators see in the passage an assertion that God intermingles good and evil in men's lives according to laws with which they are unacquainted, in order that they may not disquiet themselves by forecasting the future, whether in this life or after their death, but may be wholly dependent upon God, casting all their care upon him, knowing that he careth for them (1 Pet. v. 7). We may safely adopt this explanation (comp. ch. iii. 22; vi. 12). The paragraph then contains the same teaching as Horace's oft-quoted ode—

"Prudens futuri temporis exitum," etc.
(' Carm.,' iii. 29. 29.)

Theognis, 1075—

Πρήγματος ἀπρήκτου χαλεπώτατόν ἐστι
  τελευτὴν
Γνῶναι, ὅπως μέλλει τοῦτο Θεὸς τελέσαι·
Ὀρφνη γὰρ τέταται· πρὸ δὲ τοῦ μέλλοντος
  ἔσεσθαι
Οὐ ξυνετὰ θνητοῖς πείρατ' ἀμηχανίης.

"The issue of an action incomplete,
'Tis hard to forecast how God may dispose
  it;
For it is veiled in darkest night, and man
In present hour can never comprehend
His helpless efforts."

Plumptre quotes the lines in Cleanthes's hymn to Zeus, vers. 18—21 (' Poet. Gnom.,' p. 114)—

'Αλλὰ σὺ καὶ τὰ περισσά, κ.τ.λ.

"Thou alone knowest how to change the odd
To even, and to make the crooked straight;
And things discordant find accord in thee.
Thus in one whole thou blendest ill with good,
So that one law works on for evermore."

Ben-Sira has evidently borrowed the idea in Ecclus. xxxiii. (xxxvi.) 13—15 from our passage; after speaking of man being like clay under the potter's hand, he proceeds, "Good is set over against evil, and life over against death; so is the godly against the sinner, and the sinner against the godly. So look upon all the works of the Most High: there are two and two, one against the other."

Vers. 15—22.—Section 3. *Warnings against excesses, and praise of the golden mean,* which is practical wisdom and the art of living happily.

Vers. 15.—**All things have I seen in the days of my vanity.** Koheleth gives his own experience of an anomalous condition which often obtains in human affairs. "All," being here defined by the article, must refer to the cases which he has mentioned or proceeds to mention. "The days of vanity" mean merely "fleeting, vain days" (comp. ch. vi. 12). The expression denotes the writer's view of the emptiness and transitoriness of life (ch. i. 2), and it may also have special reference to his own vain efforts to solve the problems of existence. **There is a just** (*righteous*) **man that perisheth in his righteousness.** Here is a difficulty about the dispensation of good and evil, which has always perplexed the thoughtful. It finds expression in Ps. lxxiii., though the singer propounds a solution (ver. 17) which Koheleth misses. The meaning of the preposition (ב) before "righteousness" is disputed. Delitzsch, Wright, and others take it as equivalent to "in spite of," as in Deut. i. 32, where "in this thing" means "notwithstanding," "for all this thing." Righteousness has the promise of long life and prosperity; it is an anomaly that it should meet with disaster and early death. We cannot argue from this that the author did not believe in temporal rewards and punishments; he states merely certain of his own experiences, which may be abnormal and capable of explanation. For his special purpose this was sufficient. Others take the preposition to mean "through," "in consequence of." Good men have always been persecuted for righteousness' sake (Matt. v. 10, 11; John xvii. 14; 2 Tim. iii. 12), and so far the interpretation is quite admissible, and is perhaps supported by ver. 16, which makes a certain sort of righteousness the cause of disaster. But looking to the second clause of the present verse, where we can hardly suppose that the wicked man is said to attain to long life in consequence of his wickedness, we are safe in adopting the rendering, "in spite of." **There is a wicked man that prolongeth** his life in (*in spite of*) **his wickedness.** The verb *arak*, "to make long," "to prolong," is used both with and without the accusative "days" (see ch. viii. 12, 13; Deut. v. 33; Prov. xxviii. 2). Septuagint, Ἐστὶν ἀσεβὴς μένων ἐν κακίᾳ αὐτοῦ, "There is an ungodly man remaining in his wickedness," which does not convey the sense of the original. According to the moral government of God experienced by the Hebrews in their history, the sinner was to suffer calamity and to be cut off prematurely. This is the contention of Job's friends, against which he argues so warmly. The writer of the Book of Wisdom has learned to look for the correction of such anomalies in another life.

He sees that length of days is not always a blessing, and that retribution awaits the evil beyond the grave (Wisd. i. 9; iii. 4, 10; iv. 8, 19, etc.). Abel perished in early youth; Cain had his days prolonged. This apparent inversion of moral order leads to another reflection concerning the danger of exaggerations.

Ver. 16.—**Be not righteous over much.** The exhortation has been variously interpreted to warn against too scrupulous observance of ritual and ceremonial religion, or the mistaken piety which neglects all mundane affairs, or the Pharisaical spirit which is bitter in condemning others who fall short of one's own standard. Cox will have it that the advice signifies that a prudent man will not be very righteous, since he will gain nothing by it, nor very wicked, as he will certainly shorten his life by such conduct. But really Koheleth is condemning the tendency to immoderate asceticism which had begun to show itself in his day — a rigorous, prejudiced, indiscreet manner of life and conduct which made piety offensive, and afforded no real aid to the cause of religion. This arrogant system virtually dictated the laws by which Providence should be governed, and found fault with divinely ordered circumstances if they did not coincide with its professors' preconceived opinions. Such religionism might well be called being "righteous over much." **Neither make thyself over wise**; Septuagint, Μηδὲ σοφίζου περισσά; Vulgate, *Neque plus sapias quam necesse est*; better, *show not thyself too wise*; i.e. do not indulge in speculations about God's dealings, estimating them according to your own predilections, questioning the wisdom of his moral government. Against such perverse speculation St. Paul argues (Rom. ix. 19, etc.), "Thou wilt say unto me, Why doth he still find fault? For who withstandeth his will? Nay but, O man, who art thou that repliest against God? Shall the thing formed say to him that formed it, Why didst thou make me thus?" A good principle carried to excess may bring evil results. *Summum jus, summa injuria.* The maxim, Μηδὲν ἀγάν, *Ne quid nimis,* "Moderation in all things," is taught here; and Aristotle's theory of virtue being the mean between the two extremes of excess and defect is adumbrated ('Ethic. Nicom.,' ii. 6. 15, 16); though we do not see that the writer is "reproducing current Greek thought" (Plumptre), or that independent reflection and observation could not have landed him at the implied conclusion without plagiarism. **Why shouldest thou destroy thyself?** Septuagint, Μή ποτὲ ἐκπλαγῇς, "Lest perchance thou be confounded;" Vulgate, *Ne obstupescas,* "Lest thou be stupefied." This is the primary

meaning of the special form of the verb here used (hithp. of שָׁמֵם), and Plumptre supposes that the author intends thereby to express the spiritual pride which accompanies fancied excellence in knowledge and conduct, and by which the possessor is puffed up (1 Tim. iii. 6). But plainly it is not a mental, internal effect that is contemplated, but something that affects comfort, position, or life, like the corresponding clause in the following verse. Hitzig and Ginsburg explain the word, "Make thyself forsaken," "Isolate thyself," which can scarcely be the meaning. The Authorized Version is correct. A man who professes to be wiser than others, and, indeed, wiser than Providence, incurs the envy and animosity of his fellow-men, and will certainly be punished by God for his arrogance and presumption.

Ver. 17.—**Be not over much wicked, neither be thou foolish.** These two injunctions are parallel and correlative to those in ver. 16 concerning over-righteousness and over-wisdom. But the present verse cannot be meant, as at first sight it seems to do, to sanction a certain amount of wickedness provided it does not exceed due measure. To surmount this difficulty some have endeavoured to modify the term "wicked" (*rasha*), taking it to mean "engaged in worldly matters," or "not subject to rule," "lax," or again "restless," as some translate the word in Job iii. 17. But the word seems not to be used in any such senses, and bears uniformly the uncompromising signification assigned to it, "to be wicked, unrighteous, guilty." The difficulty is not overcome by Plumptre's suggestion of the introduction of a little "playful irony learned from Greek teachers," as if Koheleth meant, "I have warned you, my friends, against over-righteousness, but do not jump at the conclusion that licence is allowable. That was very far from my meaning." The connection of thought is this: in the previous verse Koheleth had denounced the Pharisaical spirit which virtually condemned the Divine ordering of circumstances, because vice was not at once and visibly punished, and virtue at once rewarded; and now he proceeds to warn against the deliberate and abominable wickedness which infers from God's long-suffering his absolute neglect and non-interference in mortal matters, and on this view plunges audaciously into vice and immorality, saying to itself, "God hath forgotten: he hideth his face; he will never see it" (Ps. x. 11). Such conduct may well be called "foolish;" it is that of "the fool who says in his heart, There is no God" (Ps. xiv. 1). The actual wording of the injunction sounds to us somewhat strange; but its form is determined by the requirements of parallelism, and the aphorism must not be pressed beyond its general intention, "Be not righteous nor wise to excess; be not wicked nor foolish to excess." Septuagint, "Be not very wicked, and be not stubborn (σκληρός)." **Why shouldest thou die before thy time?** literally, *not in thy time;* prematurely, tempting God to punish thee by retributive judgment, or shortening thy days by vicious excesses. (For the former, see Job xxii. 16; Ps. lv. 23; Prov. x. 27; and comp. 1 Sam. ii. 31, 33; and for the latter, Prov. v. 23; vii. 23—27; x. 21.) The Syriac contains a clause not given in any other version, "that thou mayest not be hated." As is often the case, both in this book and in Proverbs, a general statement in one place is reduced by a contrariant or modified opinion in another. Thus the prolongation of the life of the wicked, noticed in ver. 15, is here shown to be abnormal, impiety in the usual course of events having a tendency to shorten life. In this way hasty generalization is corrected, and the Divine arrangement is vindicated.

Ver. 18.—**It is good that thou shouldest take hold of this; yea, also from this withdraw not thine hand.** The pronouns refer to the two warnings in vers. 16 and 17 against over-righteousness and over-wickedness. Koheleth does not advise a man to make trial of opposite lines of conduct, to taste the fruit of the tree of knowledge of good and evil, that from a wide experience he may, like a man of the world, pursue a safe course; this would be poor morality, and unmeet for the stage at which his argument has arrived. Rather he advises him to lay to heart the cautions above given, and learn from them to avoid all extremes. As Horace says ('Epist.,' i. 18. 9)—

"Virtus est medium vitiorum et utrinque reductum."

"Folly, as usual, in extremes is seen,
　While virtue nicely hits the happy mean."
　　　　　　　　　　　　　　　　(Howes.)

The Vulgate has interpolated a word, and taken the pronoun as masculine, to the sacrifice of the sense and connection: *Bonum est te sustentare justum, sed et ab illo ne subtrahas manum tuam,* "It is good that thou shouldst support the just man, nay, from him withdraw not thy hand." **For he that feareth God shall come forth of them all;** shall escape both extremes together with their evil results. The fear of God will keep a man from all excesses. The intransitive verb *yatsa,* "to go forth," is here used with an accusative (comp. Gen. xliv. 4, which, however, is not quite analogous), as in Latin *ingredi urbem* (Livy, i. 29). Vulgate, *Qui timet Deum nihil negligit.* So Hitzig and Ginsburg, "Goes, makes his way with both," knows how to avail himself of piety and

wickedness, which, as we have seen, is not the meaning. St. Gregory, indeed, who uses the Latin Version, notes that to fear God is never to pass over any good thing that ought to be done ('Moral.,' i. 3); but he is not professing to comment on the whole passage. Wright, after Delitzsch, takes the term "come out of" as equivalent to "fulfil," so that the meaning would be, "He who fears God performs all the duties mentioned above, and avoids extremes," as Matt. xxiii. 23, "These ought ye to have done, and not to have left the other undone." But this is confessedly a Talmudic use of the verb; and the Authorized Version may be safely adopted. The Septuagint gives, "For to them that fear God all things shall come forth well."

Ver. 19.—**Wisdom strengtheneth the wise.** The moderation enjoined is the only true wisdom, which, indeed, is the most powerful incentive and support. "Wisdom proves itself stronger" (as the verb is put intransitively) "to the wise man." Septuagint, βοηθήσει, "will help;" Vulgate, *confortavit,* "hath strengthened." The spiritual and moral force of the wisdom grounded upon the fear of God is here signified, and is all the more insisted upon to counteract any erroneous impression conveyed by the caution against over-wisdom in ver. 16 (see note on ver. 17, at the end). **More than ten mighty men which are in the city.** The number *ten* indicates completeness, containing in itself the whole arithmetical system, and used representatively for an indefinite multitude. Thus Job (xix. 3) complains that his friends have reproached him ten times, and Elkanah asks his murmuring wife, "Am I not better to thee than ten sons?" (1 Sam. i. 8). Delitzsch thinks that some definite political arrangement is referred to, *e.g.* the dynasties placed by Persian kings over conquered countries; and Tyler notes that in the Mishna a city is defined to be a place containing ten men of leisure; and we know that ten men were required for the establishment of a synagogue in any locality. The same idea was present in the Anglo-Saxon arrangement of *tything* and *hundred.* The number, however, is probably used indefinitely here as *seven* in the parallel passage of Ecclesiasticus (xxxvii. 14), "A man's mind is sometime wont to tell him more than seven watchmen that sit above in a high tower." The sentence may be compared with Prov. x. 15; xxi. 22; xxiv. 5. The word rendered "mighty men" (*shallitim*) is not necessarily a military designation; it is translated "ruler" in ch. x. 5, and "governor" in Gen. xlii. 6. The Septuagint here has Ἐξουσιάζοντας τοὺς ὄντας ἐν τῇ πόλει; the Vulgate, *principes civitatis.* The persons intended are not primarily men of valour in war, like David's heroes, but rulers of sagacity, prudent statesmen, whose moral force is far greater and more efficacious than any merely physical excellence (comp. ch. ix. 16).

Ver. 20.—The wisdom above signified is, indeed, absolutely necessary, if one would escape the consequences of that frailty of nature which leads to transgression. Wisdom shows the sinner a way out of the evil course in which he is walking, and puts him back in that fear of God which is his only safety. **For** there is **not a just man upon earth.** The verse confirms ver. 19. Even the just man sinneth, and therefore needs wisdom. **That doeth good, and sinneth not.** This reminds us of the words in Solomon's prayer (1 Kings viii. 46; Prov. xx. 9). So St. James (iii. 2) says, " In many things we all offend ; " and St. John, " If we say that we have no sin, we deceive ourselves, and the truth is not in us" (1 John i. 8). A Greek gnome runs—

'Αμαρτάνει τι καὶ σοφοῦ σοφώτερος.

" Erreth at times the very wisest man."

Ver. 21.—**Also take no heed unto all words that are spoken ;** literally, *give not thy heart,* as ch. i. 13, etc. Here is another matter in which wisdom will lead to right conduct. You will not pay serious attention to evil reports either about yourself or others, nor regulate your views and actions according to such distortions of the truth. To be always hankering to know what people say of us is to set up a false standard, which will assuredly lead us astray ; and, at the same time, we shall expose ourselves to the keenest mortification when we find, as we probably shall find, that they do not take us at our own valuation, but have thoroughly marked our weaknesses, and are ready enough to censure them. We have an instance of patience under unmerited reproof in the case of David when cursed by Shimei (2 Sam. xvi. 11), as he, or one like minded, says (Ps. xxxviii. 13), "I, as a deaf man, hear not; and I am as a dumb man that openeth not his mouth. Yea, I am as a man that heareth not, and in whose mouth are no reproofs." Corn. à Lapide comments in words to which no translation would do justice, " Verba enim non sunt verbera ; aerem feriunt non hominem, nisi qui iis attendit mordetur, sauciatur." **Lest thou hear thy servant curse thee.** The servant is introduced as an example of a gossip or calumniator, because he, if any one, would be acquainted with his master's faults, and be most likely to disseminate his knowledge, and blame from such a quarter would be most intolerable. Commentators appositely quote Bacon's remarks on this passage in

his 'Advancement of Learning,' viii. 2, where he notes the prudence of Pompey, who burned all the papers of Sertorius unread, containing, as they did, information which would fatally have compromised many leading men in Rome.

Ver. 22.—**Oftentimes also thine own heart knoweth that thou thyself likewise hast cursed others.** The appeal to a man's own conscience follows. The fact that we often speak ill of others should make us less open to take offence at what is said of ourselves, and prepared to expect unfavourable comments. The Lord has said, " Judge not, that ye be not judged ; for with what judgment ye judge, ye shall be judged ; and with what measure ye mete, it shall be measured unto you " (Matt. vii. 1, 2). This is a universal law. " Who is he," asks Ben-Sira, " that hath not offended with his tongue ? " (Ecclus. xix. 16). Septuagint, "Ὅτι πλειστάκις πονηρεύσεταί σε, καὶ καθόδους πολλὰς κακώσει καρδίαν σου, ὅτι ὡς καίγε σὺ κατηράσω ἑτέρους, " For many times he [thy servant] shall act ill to thee, and in many ways shall afflict thine heart, for even thou also hast cursed others." This seems to be a combination of two renderings of the passage. " It is the praise of perfect greatness to meet hostile treatment, without bravely and within mercifully. . . . Some things are more quickly dismissed from our hearts if we know our own misdemeanours against our neighbours. For whilst we reflect what we have been towards others, we are the less concerned that others should have proved such persons towards ourselves, because the injustice of another avenges in us what our conscience justly accuses in itself " (St. Gregory, 'Moral.,' xxii. 26).

Vers. 23—29.—Section 4. Further insight into essential wisdom was not obtainable ; but Koheleth learned some other practical lessons, viz. *that wickedness was folly and madness ; that woman was the most evil thing in the world ; that man had perverted his nature, which was made originally good.*

Ver. 23.—**All this have I proved by wisdom ;** *i.e.* wisdom was the means by which he arrived at the practical conclusions given above (vers. 1—22). Would wisdom solve deeper questions ? And if so, could he ever hope to attain it ? **I said, I will be wise.** This was his strong resolve. He desired to grow in wisdom, to use it in order to unfold mysteries and explain anomalies. Hitherto he had been content to watch the course of men's lives, and find by experience what was good and what was evil for them ; now he craves for an insight into the secret laws that regulate those external circumstances: he wants a philosophy or theosophy. His desire is expressed by his imitator in the Book of Wisdom (ix.), "O God of my fathers, . . . give me Wisdom, that sitteth by thy throne.... O send her out of thy holy heavens, and from the·throne of thy glory, that being present she may labour with me." **But it was far from me.** It remained in the far distance, out of reach. Job's experience (xxviii.) was his. Practical rules of life he might gain, and had mastered, but essential, absolute wisdom was beyond mortal grasp. Man's knowledge and capacity are limited.

Ver. 24.—**That which is far off, and exceeding deep, who can find it out?** The broken, interjectional style of the original in this passage, as Professor Taylor Lewis terms it, is better brought out by translating, "Far off is that which is, and deep, deep: who can find it out?" Professor Lewis renders, "Far off! the past, what is it? Deep—a deep—oh, who can find?" and explains "the past" to mean, not merely the earthly past historically unknown, but the great past before the creation of the universe, the kingdom of all eternities with its ages of ages, its worlds of worlds, its mighty evolutions, its infinite variety. We prefer to retain the rendering, "that which is," and to refer the expression to the phenomenal world. It is not the essence of wisdom that is spoken of, but the facts of man's life and the circumstances in which he finds himself, the course of the world, the phenomena of nature, etc. These things —their causes, connection, interdependence —we cannot explain satisfactorily (comp. ch. iii. 11; viii. 17). In the Book of Wisdom (vii. 17—21) Solomon is supposed to have arrived at this abstruse knowledge, "for," he says, "God hath given me certain knowledge of the things that are (τῶν ὄντων γνῶσιν ἀψευδῆ)," and he proceeds to enumerate the various departments which this "universitas literarum" has opened to him. The Septuagint (and virtually the Vulgate) connects this verse with the preceding, thus: "I said, I will be wise, and it (αὕτη) was far from me, far beyond what was (μακρὰν ὑπὲρ ὃ ἦν), and deep depth: who shall find it out?" (For the epithet "deep" applied to what is recondite or what is beyond human comprehension, comp. **Prov. xx. 5**; Job xi. 8.)

Ver. 25.—**I applied mine heart to know;** more literally, *I turned myself, and my heart was* [set] *to know.* We have the expression, "turned myself," referring to a new investigation in ch. ii. 20 and elsewhere; but the distinguishing the heart or soul from the man himself is not common in Scripture (see on ch. xi. 9), though the soul is sometimes apostrophized, as in Luke xii. 19 (comp. Ps. ciii. 1; cxlvi. 1). The writer

here implies that he gave up himself with all earnestness to the investigation. Unsatisfactory as his quest had been hitherto, he did not relinquish the pursuit, but rather turned it in another direction, where he could hope to meet with useful results. The Septuagint has, "I and my heart travelled round (ἐκύκλωσα) to know;" the Vulgate, *Lustravi universa animo meo ut scirem.* **And to search, and to seek out wisdom.** The accumulation of synonymous verbs is meant to emphasize the author's devotion to his self-imposed task and his return from profitless theoretical investigation to practical inquiry. **And the reason** of things. *Cheshbon* (ver. 27; ch. ix. 10) is rather "account," "reckoning," than "reason"—the summing-up of all the facts and circumstances rather than the elucidation of their causes. Vulgate, *rationem;* Septuagint, ψῆφον. The next clause ought to be rendered, *And to know wickedness as* (or, *to be*) *folly, and foolishness as* (*to be*) *madness.* His investigation led him to this conclusion, that all infringement of God's laws is a misjudging aberration—a wilful desertion of the requirements of right reason—and that mental and moral obtuseness is a physical malady which may be called madness (comp. ch. i. 17; ii. 12; x. 13).

Ver. 26.—One practical result of his quest Koheleth cannot avoid mentioning, though it comes with a suddenness which is somewhat startling. **And I find more bitter than death the woman.** Tracing men's folly and madness to their source, he finds that they arise generally from the seductions of the female sex. Beginning with Adam, woman has continued to work mischief in the world. "Of the woman came the beginning of sin," says Siracides, "and through her we all die" (Ecclus. xxv. 24); it was owing to her that the punishment of death was inflicted on the human race. If Solomon himself were speaking, he had indeed a bitter experience of the sin and misery into which women lead their victims (see 1 Kings xi. 1, 4, 11). It may be thought that Koheleth refers here especially to "the strange woman" of Prov. ii. 16, etc.; v. 3, etc.; but in ver. 28 he speaks of the whole sex without qualification; so that we must conclude that he had a very low opinion of them. It is no ideal personage whom he is introducing; it is not a personification of vice or folly; but woman in her totality, such as he knew her to be in Oriental courts and homes, denied her proper position, degraded, uneducated, all natural affections crushed or undeveloped, the plaything of her lord, to be flung aside at any moment. It is not surprising that Koheleth's impression of the female sex should be unfavourable. He is not singular in such an opinion. One might fill a large page with proverbs and gnomes uttered in disparagement of woman by men of all ages and countries. Men, having the making of such apothegms, have used their licence unmercifully; if the maligned sex had equal liberty, the tables might have been reversed. But, really, in this as in other cases the mean is the safest;. and practically those who have given the darkest picture of women have not been slow to recognize the brighter side. If, for instance, the Book of Proverbs paints the adulteress and the harlot in the sombrest, most appalling colours, the same book affords us such a sketch of the virtuous matron as is unequalled for vigour, truth, and high appreciation. And if, as in our present chapter, Koheleth shows a bitter feeling against the evil side of woman's nature, he knows how to value the comfort of married life (ch. iv. 8), and to look upon a good wife as one who makes a man's home happy (ch. ix. 9). Since the incarnation of our blessed Lord Jesus Christ, "the Seed of the woman," we have learned to regard woman in her true light, and to assign her that position to which she is entitled, giving honour unto her as the weaker vessel, and, at the same time, heir with us of the glorious hope and destiny of our renewed nature (1 Pet. iii. 7). **Whose heart is snares and nets;** more accurately, *who is snares, and nets in her heart;* Septuagint, "The woman who is a snare, and her heart nets;" Vulgate, *Quæ laqueus venatorum est, et sagena cor ejus.* The imagery is obvious (comp. Prov. v. 4, 22; vii. 22; xxii. 14; Hab. i. 15); the thoughts of the evil woman's heart are nets, occupied in meditating how she may entrap and retain victims; and her outward look and words are snares that captivate the foolish. Μὴ ὑπάντα γυναικὶ ἑταιριζομένη, says the Son of Sirach, "Lest thou fall into her snares" (Ecclus. ix. 3). Plautus, 'Asin.,' i. 3. 67—

"Auceps sum ego;
Esca est meretrix; lectus illex est; amatores aves."

"The fowler I;
My bait the courtesan; her bed the lure;
The birds the lovers."

So ancient critics, stronger in morals than in etymology, derive Venus from *venari*, "to hunt," and *mulier* from *mollire*, "to soften," or *malleus*, "a hammer," because the devil uses women to mould and fashion men to his will. And **her hands as bands,** *Asurim,* "bands" or "fetters," is found in Judg. xv. 14, where it is used of the chains with which the men of Judah bound Samson; it refers here to the wicked woman's voluptuous embraces. **Whoso pleaseth God** (more literally, *he who is good before God*) **shall escape from her.** He whom God regards as

good (ch. ii. 26, where see note) shall have grace to avoid these seductions. **But the sinner shall be taken by her;** בָּהּ, "in her," in the snare which is herself. In some manuscripts of Ecclesiasticus (xxvi. 23) are these words: "A wicked woman is given as a portion to a wicked man; but a godly woman is given to him that feareth the Lord."

Ver. 27.—**Behold, this have I found.** The result of his search, thus forcibly introduced, follows in ver. 28. He has carefully examined the character and conduct of both sexes, and he is constrained to make the unsatisfactory remark which he there puts forth. **Saith the preacher.** *Koheleth* is here treated as a feminine noun, being joined with the feminine form of the verb, though elsewhere it is grammatically regarded as masculine (see on ch. i. 1). Many have thought that, after speaking so disparagingly of woman, it would be singularly inappropriate to introduce the official preacher as a female; they have therefore adopted a slight alteration in the text, viz. אָמַר הַקֹּהֶלֶת instead of אָמְרָה קֹהֶלֶת, which is simply the transference of *he* from the end of one word to the beginning of the next, thus adding the article, as in ch. xii. 8, and making the term accord with the Syriac and Arabic, and the Septuagint, εἶπεν ὁ Ἐκκλησιαστής. The writer here introduces his own designation in order to call special attention to what is coming. **Counting one by one.** The phrase is elliptical, and signifies, adding one thing to another, or weighing one thing after another, putting together various facts or marks. **To find out the account;** to arrive at the reckoning, the desired result.

Ver. 28.—**Which yet my soul seeketh, but I find not;** or, *which my soul hath still sought, but I have not found.* The conclusion at which he did arrive was something utterly different from what he had hoped to achieve. The soul and the ego are separately regarded (comp. ver. 25); the whole intellectual faculties were absorbed in the search, and the composite individual gives his consequent experience. **One man** (*Adam*) **among a thousand have I found.** He found only one man among a thousand that reached his standard of excellence—the ideal that he had formed for himself, who could be rightly called by the noble name of *man.* The phrase, "one of a thousand," occurs in Job ix. 3; xxxiii. 23; Ecclus. vi. 6 (εἷς ἀπὸ χιλίων, as in the Septuagint here). *Adam,* the generic term, is used here instead of *ish,* the individual, to emphasize the antithetical *ishah,* "woman," in the following clause, or to lead the thought to the original perfection of man's nature. So in Greek ἄνθρωπος is sometimes used for ἀνήρ, though generally the distinction between the two is sufficiently marked, as we find in Herodotus, vii. 210, Ὅτι πολλοὶ μὲν ἄνθρωποι εἶεν, ὀλίγοι δὲ ἄνδρες. But a woman among all those have I not found; *i.e.* not one woman in a thousand who was what a woman ought to be. Says the Son of Sirach, "All wickedness is but little to the wickedness of a woman; let the portion of a sinner fall upon her" (Ecclus. xxv. 19). So the Greek gnome—

Θάλασσα, καὶ πῦρ, καὶ γυνὴ, κακὰ τρία.

"Three evils are there—sea, fire, and woman."

Solomon had a thousand wives and concubines, and his experience might well have been that mentioned in this passage.

Ver. 29.—Lo, this only (or, *only see! this*) have I found. Universal corruption was that which met his wide investigations, but of one thing he was sure, which he proceeds to specify—he has learned to trace the degradation to its source, not in God's agency, but in man's perverse will. That God hath made man upright. Koheleth believes that man's original constitution was *yashar*, "straight," "right," "morally good," and possessed of ability to choose and follow what was just and right (Gen. i. 26, etc.). Thus in the Book of Wisdom (ii. 23) we read, "God created man to be immortal, and made him an image of his own nature (ἰδιότητος). Nevertheless, through envy of the devil, came death into the world, and they that are his portion tempt it." But they (*men*) have sought out many inventions (*chishshebonoth*); 2 Chron. xxvi. 15, where the term implies works of invention, and is translated "engines," *i.e.* devices, ways of going astray and deviating from original righteousness. Man has thus abased his free-will, and employed the inventive faculty with which he was endowed in excogitating evil (Gen. vi. 5). How this state of things came about, how

the originally good man became thus wicked, the writer does not tell. He knows from revelation that God made him upright; he knows from experience that he is now evil; and he leaves the matter there. Plumptre quotes, as illustrating our text, a passage from the 'Antigone' of Sophocles, vers. 332, 365, 366, which he renders—

" Many the things that strange and wondrous are,
None stranger and more wonderful than man. . . .
And lo, with all this skill,
Wise and inventive still,
Beyond hope's dream,
He now to good inclines,
And now to ill."

We may add Æschylus, 'Choeph.,' vers. 585, etc.—

Πολλὰ μέν γᾶ τρέφει
δεινὰ δειμάτων ἄχη . . .
ἀλλ' ὑπέρτολμον ἀν-
δρὸς φρόνημα τίς λέγοι;

" Many fearful plagues
Earth nourishes . . .
But man's audacious spirit
Who can tell?"

Horace, 'Carm.,' i. 3. 25—

" Audax omnia perpeti
Gens humana ruit per vetitum nefas."

" The race of man, bold all things to endure,
Hurries undaunted to forbidden crime."

Vulgate, *Et ipse se infinitis miscuerit quæstionibus*, "And he entangled himself in multitudinous questions." This refers to unhallowed curiosity and speculation; but, as we have seen, the passage is concerned with man's moral declension, declaring how his "devices" lead him away from "uprightness."

HOMILETICS.

Ver. 1.—*A good name better than precious ointment.* I. MORE DIFFICULT OF ACQUISITION. Money will buy the "good nard," but the cost of a "good name" is beyond rubies. This which cannot be gotten for gold, neither shall silver be weighed for the price thereof, can be secured only by laborious personal exercise in goodness, always smiled on by Heaven's favour and assisted by Heaven's grace. It is the flower, fruit, and fragrance of a soul long practised in well-living and good-doing. If, therefore, things are valuable in proportion to the cost of obtaining them, the above proverbial utterance bears the stamp of truth.

II. MORE HONOURABLE IN POSSESSION. It is: 1. *An article of greater value in itself.* Precious ointment is, after all, only a production of the earth; whereas a good name is a spiritual aroma proceeding from the soul. 2. *An index of truer wealth.* Precious ointment at the best is material riches; a good name proclaims one possessed of riches which are spiritual. 3. *A mark of higher dignity.* Costly unguent a sign of social rank among the children of men ; a good name attests that one has qualities of soul, of mind, heart, and disposition, proclaiming him a son of God and a peer of heaven.

III. MORE SATISFYING IN ENJOYMENT. Perfumed oil may yield a pleasant fragrance which gratifies the sense of smell and revives the body's vigour; the spiritual aroma of a good name not only diffuses happiness amongst those who come to hear of it, but imparts a sweet joy, holy and refreshing, to him who bears it.

IV. MORE DIFFUSIVE IN INFLUENCE. The odour of precious ointment extends to those in its immediate vicinity; the savour of a good name goes far and wide, often pervades the community in which the owner of it lives; sometimes, as in the instance of Mary of Bethany (Mark xiv. 9), spreads itself abroad through the whole world.

V. MORE ENDURING IN CONTINUANCE. The fragrance of the unguent ultimately ceases. Becoming feebler the longer it is exposed to the air and the wider it diffuses itself, it ultimately dies away. The savour of a good name never perishes (Ps. cxii. 6). It passes on from age to age, being handed down by affectionate tradition to succeeding, frequently to latest, generations. Witness the names of Noah, the preacher of righteousness; Abraham, the father of the faithful; Moses, the law-giver of Israel; David, the sweet singer of the Hebrew Church; John, the beloved disciple; Peter, the man of rock; Paul, the Apostle of the Gentiles; with names like those of Polycarp, Cyprian, Origen, Athanasius, Augustine, Chrysostom, Luther, Calvin, Knox, etc.

VI. MORE BLESSED IN ITS ISSUE. Precious ointment can only secure for one entrance into earthly circles of rank and fashion ; a good name will procure for him who bears it admission into the society of Heaven's peerage.

LESSONS. 1. Seek this good name. 2. Cherish it above all earthly distinctions. 3. Guard it from getting tarnished. 4. Walk worthy of it.

Ver. 1.—*The day of death and the day of birth.* I. The latter begins a life at the longest brief (Ps. xc. 10); the former a life which shall never end (Luke xx. 36).

II. The latter ushers into a field of toil (Ps. civ. 23); the former into a home of rest (Rev. xiv. 13).

III. The latter admits into a scene of suffering (Job v. 7; xiv. 1); the former into a realm of felicity (Rev. vii. 16).

IV. The latter introduces a life of sin (Gen. viii. 21; Job xiv. 4; Ps. li. 5; lviii. 3; Rom. v. 12); the former an existence of holiness (Jude 24; Rev. xxi. 27).

V. The latter opens a state of condemnation (Rom. v. 18); the former a state of glory (2 Cor. iv. 17).

LESSONS. 1. The secret of living well—keeping an eye on the day of one's death (Deut. xxxii. 29; Ps. xc. 12). 2. The secret of dying happily—living in the fear of God (Acts xiii. 36; Phil. i. 21).

Vers. 2—6.—*The house of mourning and the house of feasting.* I. THE HOUSE OF MOURNING A DIVINE INSTITUTION; THE HOUSE OF FEASTING AN ERECTION OF MAN. 1. *The house of mourning a Divine institution.* Though not true that "man was made to mourn" (Burns) in the sense that the Creator originally intended human experience on the earth to be one prolonged wail of sorrow, it is nevertheless certain that days of mourning, equally with days of death—and, indeed, just because of these—come to all by Heaven's decree. As no one of woman born can elude bereavement in some shape or form, so must every one in turn make acquaintance with the house of mourning. Hence mourning for departed relatives (Gen. xxiii. 2; xxvii. 41; l. 4; Numb. xx. 29; Deut. xxxiv. 8; 2 Sam. xi. 27) has not only been a universal custom among mankind, but has commended itself to men's judgments as in perfect accordance with the divinely implanted instincts of human nature. To mourn for the dead in becoming manner is something more than to array one's self in "customary suits of solemn black," to affect the "windy suspiration of forced breath," with "the fruitful river in the eye," or to put on "the dejected 'haviour of the visage, together with all forms, modes, shapes of grief," which are at best only the outward "trappings and suits of woe" (Shakespeare, 'Hamlet,' act i. sc. 2); it is more even than to utter selfish lamentations over one's own loss in being deprived of the society of the departed, sighing like the psalmist, "Lover and friend hast thou put far from me, and mine acquaintance into darkness" (Ps. lxxxviii. 18); it is to bewail their abstraction from the light of heaven and the love of friends, saying, "Alas, my brother!" (1 Kings xiii. 30; the grief of Constance for her son: cf. 'King John,' act iii. sc. 4), though sorrow on this account is greatly tempered by the consolations of the gospel in respect of Christians (2 Thess. iv. 13); it is to express the heart's affection for those who have been removed from its embrace, like Rachel weeping for her children, and refusing to be comforted because they were not (Matt. ii. 18); it is even to pay a tribute of gratitude to God for the temporary loan of the precious gift he has withdrawn, as Job did when he lamented his dead sons and daughters (i. 21)—to record appreciation of its worth, and seek, if not its immediate return, its safe keeping till a future day, when they who have been severed here shall be reunited in immortal love.   Hence it is easy to perceive how the house of mourning may be fitly spoken of as a house of Divine appointment.   2. *The house of feasting a purely human institution.*   Not that feasting and dancing, considered in themselves, are sinful, or that there are not times and seasons when both may be indulged in without sin.   Many such occasions may be found in actual life, as *e.g.* in connection with birthdays (Gen. xl. 20), marriages (Gen. xxix. 22; John ii. 1), and funerals (Deut. xxvi. 14; Job xlii. 11; Jer. xvi. 7; Ezek. xxiv. 17; Hos. ix. 4), with family rejoicings of other sorts and for other reasons.   But the "house of feasting," contrasted with the abode of sorrow, is the tent of carousal, in which wine and wassail, song and dance, mirth and revelry, prevail without moderation, and with no other end in view than the gratification of sinful appetite.   Such-like gatherings, having no sanction from Heaven, may be spoken of as instituted by man rather than as appointed by God.

II. THE HOUSE OF MOURNING FREQUENTED BY THE WISE; THE HOUSE OF FEASTING ATTENDED BY FOOLS.   1. *The heart of the wise in the house of mourning.*   The wise are the good, serious, devout, religious, as distinguished from the wicked, frivolous, profane, and irreligious.   The hearts of the wise are in the house of mourning, "even when their bodies are absent;" "they are constantly or very frequently meditating upon sad and serious things" (Poole); "they are much conversant with mournful subjects" (Henry); and as often as occasion offers and duty calls, they repair to the scene of sorrow and chamber of bereavement to sympathize with and comfort its inmates, as Job's friends did with him (Job ii. 11), and Mary's with her (John xi. 19), recognizing it to be their duty to "weep with them that weep," as well as to "rejoice with them that do rejoice" (Rom. xii. 15); and even on their own accounts to learn the wisdom which such a scene is fitted to impart.   2. *The heart of fools in the house of mirth.*   To this they are attracted on the principle that "like draws to like"—the same principle that constrains the wise to repair to the house of mourning, and by the gratification there found for their folly, in the laughter which there provokes their mirth, and the revelry which there slakes their longing for self-indulgence.

III. THE HOUSE OF MOURNING A SCHOOL OF WISDOM; THE HOUSE OF FEASTING A SCHOOL OF FOLLY.   1. *The lessons taught by the house of mourning.*   (1) The certainty of death for the wise man himself and for all others.   What he sees in the chamber of bereavement is "the end of all men," the end to which all the bravery and glory of all men must eventually come (2 Sam. xiv. 14; Ps. lxxxix. 48; Isa. xl. 7; Heb. ix. 27), the final scene also in his own swiftly fleeting life (Ps. xxxix. 4); and so while he lives he lays it to heart, considers his end, numbers his days, and applies his soul unto wisdom (Deut. xxxii. 29; Ps. xc. 12).   (2) The vanity of all earthly things, and especially of pleasure and frivolity.   The "song of fools," whether the bacchanalian carol, the obscene ballad, the comic ditty, or the amorous sonnet, grates with harshness and pain upon his ear, while the laughter it evokes is like the crackling of thorns under a pot, or of nettles under kettles, noisy, short-lived, evanescent, and profitless, leaving nothing behind but ashes (Isa. xliv. 20), a bad taste in the mouth, a pain in the ear, a taint upon the conscience, a wound in the heart.   (3) The duty and sweetness of sympathy—duty for him and sweetness for the bereaved.   Weeping with them that weep (Rom. xii. 15), he learns how to bear another's burdens (Gal. vi. 2), appreciates the inward satisfaction which flows from the exercise of sympathy (Prov. xi. 17), sees the sustaining strength it yields to the weak and disconsolate (Prov. xvii. 17), and thus has his own soul confirmed and enlarged in goodness.   "Sorrow," says Delitzsch, "penetrates the heart, draws the thought upward, purifies, transforms;" and thus, as the Preacher observes, "by the sorrow of the countenance the heart is made better."   (4) The value of serious talk.   The discourse that prevails in the house of mourning is fitted to improve the serious listener. Should it sometimes lay rebukes upon one's spirit, these are felt to be better from a moral and spiritual point of view than the low and grovelling, frequently prurient and obscene, songs that in the Preacher's day were heard, as in our day they are not unknown, in a pothouse. 2. *The proficiency acquired in the house of feasting.* By no means in wisdom, either human or Divine. One will hardly assert that a person will become shrewder in business or brighter in intelligence by indulging in chambering and wantonness; it is certain he will not grow either holier or more spiritually minded. Whatever apologies may be offered for frequenting carousals—innocent feasting requires none—this cannot be urged, that it tends to make one purer in heart or devouter in spirit, incites one to holy living, or prepares one for happy dying. Rather, the instruction received in such haunts of dissipation is for the most part instruction in vice, or at the best in frivolity— a poor accomplishment for a man with a soul.

Vers. 7—10.—*Counsels for evil times.* I. THE WRONG WAY OF BEHAVIOUR UNDER OPPRESSION. 1. *Allowing it to unsettle one's judgment.* "Surely oppression," or extortion, "maketh a wise man mad," or foolish; *i.e.* driveth him to foolish actions through indignation and vexation, through the misery he endures, the hardship he suffers, the sense of injustice he feels, the rising doubts of which he is conscious. A soul thus driven to the wall and set at bay through the woes inflicted by imperious and pitiless tyranny, is prone to be unsettled in its judgments, fierce and even reckless in its actions. Of course, no amount of oppression or extortion should have this effect on any; but it sometimes has. 2. *Attempting to remove it by bribery.* "And a gift destroyeth the understanding." Equally of him that gives and him that receives a bribe is the saying true, that it perverts the judgment, disturbs the soul's perceptions of right and wrong, and leaves a blot upon the conscience. To seek the removal of oppression by currying favour with the oppressor through presentation of gifts, is to seek a right thing in a wrong way, and is to that extent to be condemned. 3. *Indulging in anger on account of it.* "Be not hasty in thy spirit to be angry." Whether this anger be directed against the oppressor or against the oppression, or against God's providence, who has suffered both to come together and co-operate against the wise man, to give way to it is to part with one's wisdom, since "anger resteth in the bosom of fools," if it is not also (in the last case it is) to sin against God. It is always difficult to be angry and sin not (Ps. iv. 4, margin; Eph. iv. 26); hence Christians are exhorted not to be soon angry (Titus i. 7), indeed, to put off (Col. iii. 8) and put away (Eph. iv. 31) anger, as one of the works of the flesh (Gal. v. 20). 4. *Giving way to despair because of it.* Saying in one's heart that "the former days were better than these," and that all things are going to the bad. The Preacher pretty plainly hints that such a sentiment is an error, and yet it is one widely entertained by the ignorant and prone to be adopted by the unfortunate.

II. THE RIGHT WAY OF BEHAVING UNDER OPPRESSION. 1. *Permitting the evil to avenge itself on its perpetrator.* This it will do, if the propositions be correct that oppression practised even by a wise man will make him mad, and that a bribe accepted by a good man will corrupt his heart and destroy his understanding. "The oppressive exercise of power is so demoralizing that even the wise man, skilled in statecraft, loses his wisdom. There comes upon him, as the history of crime so often shows, something like a mania of tyrannous cruelty. And the same effect follows on the practice of corruption" (Plumptre). 2. *Reflecting that the evil will not continue for ever.* It will run its course, have its day, and come to an end as other evil things have done before it; and " better will its end be than its beginning." In the course of history this has often been observed, that seasons of oppression and periods of persecution have not been suffered to continue for ever, and have often been terminated (by some sudden turn in providence, by the death of the oppressor, or by a change of purpose in the persecutor) sooner than the victims expected. 3. *Exercising patience while the evil day continues.* "Better is the patient in spirit than the proud in spirit," better in respect of moral character and religious profiting. Philosophy and religion both teach that the way to rise superior to injustice and oppression, to extract the largest amount of profiting from it, and to bring it most speedily to an end, is to meekly endure it. Patience disarms the oppressor of his strongest weapon, and imparts to his victim double advantage over his foe. Without patience tribulation cannot work out the soul's good (Rom. v. 3; Jas. i. 4). 4. *Cherishing a hopeful spirit in the darkest times.* Not despairing of the future either for one's self or for the world, but believing that all things work together for good to them that love God, and that through evil times as well as good times the world is slowly but surely moving on towards a better day.

LESSONS. 1. Never oppress. 2. Cultivate meekness. 3. Be hopeful.

Ver. 8.—*The end better than the beginning.* I. THE IMPORT OF THE PROVERB STATED. Not always true that the end of a thing is better than the beginning. Whether it is so depends largely on what the thing is, upon the character of its beginning and the nature of its end. 1. *Cases in which the maxim will not apply.* (1) Evil projects which reach their consummation; as *e.g.* the temptation of Eve by Satan (Gen. iii. 1, etc.), the wrath of Cain against Abel (Gen. iv. 8), the design of David against Uriah and Bathsheba (2 Sam. xi. 2—24), the murder of Naboth by Jezebel (1 Kings xxi. 14), the seduction of a youth by the strange woman (Prov. iv. 3, 4). (2) Undertakings which, though good, nevertheless fail to succeed; as *e.g.* the journey of Jacob and his sons to Egypt, which commenced in gladness and ended in bondage and oppression (Gen. xlvi. 5, 6; Exod. i. 13); the voyage of the corn-ship of Alexandria which carried Paul, and which, though it left the Fair Havens with a soft south wind, was not long after caught by a tempestuous Euroclydon and wrecked on the island of Malta (Acts xxvii. 13, 14). (3) Works and lives which appear promising at the outset, but terminate in disappointment and disaster; as *e.g.* the kingship of Saul (1 Sam. x. 24; xxxi. 6), the apostleship of Judas (Matt. x. 4; xxvi. 14—16), the adventure of the prodigal (Luke xv. 11—16), the ministry of Demas (2 Tim. iv. 10). 2. *Cases in which the maxim will apply.* (1) Evil projects when they are defeated; as *e.g.* that of Satan to ruin man, which was counter-worked by Christ's mission to effect man's salvation (Heb. ii. 14, 15); or that of the same adversary to overthrow Job's faith and allegiance, which was overcome by Job's constancy and trust (Job xlii. 12); that of Haman to exterminate the Jews, which the skilfulness of Mordecai and Esther (Esth. viii. 7, 8) thwarted; and that of the Jews to assassinate Paul, which the tact of his sister's son (Acts xxiii. 16—31) enabled him to escape; that of the Spanish Armada to overthrow the Protestantism of England, and that of St. Bartholomew's Day to crush the Huguenots in France. (2) Good undertakings when successfully completed; as *e.g.* the building of Noah's ark to save himself and family from the Flood (Gen. vi. 22); and of Solomon's temple for the worship of Jehovah (1 Kings vi. 37, 38); the emancipation of Israel from Egypt under the leadership of Moses (Exod. xii. 51; xiv. 31); and afterwards from Babylon under that of Zerubbabel (Ezra i. 11); the work of human redemption which Christ completed on the cross (John xix. 30), and the life of a good man who dies in the faith (2 Tim. iv. 6—8).

II. THE TRUTH OF THE PROVERB JUSTIFIED. Of things to which the maxim will apply. 1. *The beginnings are attended with anxieties and fears as to ultimate success; while from all such the endings are delivered.* As no man can foretell what a day may bring forth, or provide against all possible contingencies, no one can calculate with absolute certainty that any scheme of his contriving will attain to success. Man proposes, but God disposes. When, however, success has been attained there is manifestly no further ground or room for apprehension. 2. *The beginnings have periods of labour before them; while the endings have all such periods behind them.* Not that labour is a bad thing, but that labour accomplished is better to contemplate than labour not yet attempted. In the former case failure is impossible; in the latter case it is still possible. In the latter, energy, thought, care, have still to be expended; in the former these are no more demanded. Instead of toil, there is repose; instead of peril, safety; instead of anxiety, peace. 3. *The beginnings are times of preparation, of effort, and of laying out, while the endings are seasons of fulfilment, of reward, and of gathering in.* Examples will be found in the reaping of a harvest in autumn as contrasted with its sowing in spring, the completion of a house as distinguished from its foundation-laying, the collection of profits from a fortunate speculation or investment in business, the gaining of distinction in learning after a long course of diligent study, the attainment of the " exceeding, even an eternal, weight of glory " at the close of a life of faith.

LESSONS. 1. A stimulus to diligence.   2. An argument for patience.   3. A caution against rashness.

Ver. 10.—" *The good old times*"—*a popular delusion*. I. THE DELUSION STATED. "That the former days were better than these." The proposition may be understood as applying : 1. *To individual experience,* in which case it will signify that the former days of the speaker's life were better than those in which he then was. Or : 2. *To mundane history*, in which case the sense will be that the earlier periods of the world's history were better than the later, or that the times which preceded the speaker's day were better than those in which he was living.
II. THE DELUSION EXEMPLIFIED. 1. *From sacred history*. (1) As to individual experience. Job was neither the first nor the last who cried, "Oh that I were as in months past!" (Job xxix. 2). Probably Jacob was in a similar mood of mind when he heard of Simeon's detention in Egypt, and of Judah's proposal to take Benjamin (Gen. xlii. 36; xliii. 14). The old men who wept at the foundation of the second temple certainly believed that the days when as yet the first temple stood were incomparably more resplendent than those in which they then lived (Ezra iii. 12). (2) As to world-epochs. To many of the Sethites, no doubt, in the antediluvian era, "the days of old," when man lived in innocence in Eden, were regarded as better than those in which their lot had fallen when all flesh had corrupted its way (Gen. vi. 12). To not a few in the days of the judges and of the kings it seemed as if "the years of ancient times," and "of the right hand of the Most High," when he brought forth the bondmen of Pharaoh from Egypt, were the glorious days of Israel as a nation (Ps. lxxvii. 5, 10). To the exiles who had returned from Babylon, the golden age of their country was behind them in the days of David and Solomon, not before them in the era of Persian domination. 2. *From profane history*. "Illustrations crowd upon one's memory. Greeks looking back to the age of those who fought at Marathon; Romans under the empire recalling the vanished greatness of the republic; Frenchmen mourning over the *ancien régime;* or Englishmen over the good old days of the Tudors, are all examples of this unwisdom" (Plumptre). Old men regretting the vanished days of their boyhood, or once rich but now poor men lamenting the disappearance of wealth which was theirs, or fallen great men sighing for the times when they were called "My lord!" are individual instances of this same delusion.
III. THE DELUSION EXPLAINED. Two things account for this widespread delusion as to the relative values of the past and present. 1. *An instinctive idealization of the past.* (1) The good things of the past, which one has either never known at all or counted only moderately good when he did know them, he now esteems as supremely excellent, on the principle that "distance lends enchantment to the view." (2) The bad things of the past, which he complained of when he endured them, he has now through lapse of time largely forgotten; while if the bad things of the past were such as he never himself experienced but has only heard or read of, these are not likely to press him down so heavily as the lesser present evils under which he groans. 2. *An equally instinctive depreciation of the present.* (1) Its good things are never so sweet as some other good things which we have not, or which other people had. As the possession of pleasure is seldom so intoxicating as its pursuit, so is that which one has never so valuable as that which one once had or may yet have. (2) Its evil things being present always appear worse, *i.e.* heavier, than they really are. They are felt more acutely and oppress more severely than either the ills of other people one has never felt, or one's own ills in the past which have been forgotten.
IV. THE DELUSION DISPROVED. The false judgment rests upon two foundations. 1. *A mistaken standard.* If "better" only means in the case of the individual "more free from anxiety, pain, or difficulty," or in the case of communities or nations "more free from wars, troubles, revolutions, or social disturbances, the proposition complained of may be easily established; but if "better" signify more advantageous in the highest sense, *i.e.* more helpful to and beneficial for moral and spiritual good it will frequently be found that the proposition is false, and that for individuals, for instance, times of present trouble and seasons of present affliction may be better than past times of quiet and seasons of prosperity, and for communities and nations periods of social upheaval and foreign war better than antecedent days of stagnation

and civil death.   2. *An incomplete comparison.* It is commonly forgotten that each age has a dark as well as bright side, and that in estimating the worth of two different periods in the experience of an individual or the history of a nation, it will not do to contrast the dark side of the present with the bright side of the past, but the dark and bright sides of both must be brought into view.

LESSONS.   1. The duty of man in evil times, submission rather than complaining. 2. The wisdom of trying to make the best of the present instead of dreaming about the past.   3. The certainty that the most careful calculations concerning the relative values of past and present are tainted with error.

Vers. 11, 12.—*Wisdom and wealth.* I. THE GREAT POWER OF WEALTH. 1. *What it cannot do.* (1) Purchase salvation for the soul (Ps. xlix. 6, 7).   (2) Impart happiness to the mind (Luke xii. 15).   (3) Secure health for the body (2 Kings v. 1; Luke xvi. 22). 2. *What it can do.* (1) Defend the body against want and disease, at least partially.   (2) Protect the mind against ignorance and error, also again to a limited extent.   (3) Shield the heart, once more in a measure, from such anxieties as spring from material causes.

II. THE GREATER POWER OF WISDOM. 1. *It can do things that wealth can.* Nay, without it wealth can effect little.   (1) It can often do much without wealth to avert want and disease from the body.   (2) It can effectually dispel from the mind the clouds of ignorance and error.   (3) It can help to keep anxiety altogether from the heart, to sustain the heart in bearing it when it does come, and to direct the heart how most speedily and effectually to get rid of it. 2. *It can do things that wealth cannot.* It—in its highest form, the fear of the Lord (ch. xii. 13; Ps. cxi. 10; Job xxviii. 28), the wisdom of God (1 Cor. ii. 7), the wisdom which is from above (Jas. iii. 17), the wisdom which consists in believing on Christ, loving God, living in the Spirit, walking in love, and following holiness—can " preserve the life of him that hath it : " (1) the soul's life, by imparting to it the gift of God, which is eternal life; (2) the mind's life, by flooding it with the light of truth; and (3) the body's life, by communicating to it here on earth length of days (the first rule of health being to fear God and keep his commandments), and by restoring it at the resurrection to a condition of immortality.

LESSONS.   1. The superiority of wisdom.   2. The duty of preferring it to wealth.

Vers. 13, 14.—*Crooked things and straight.* I. COMPOSE THE TEXTURE OF HUMAN LIFE. 1. *Crooked things.* Such experiences, events, and dispensations as run counter or lie cross to the inclinations, as *e.g.* afflictions, disappointments, and trials of all sorts.   Few lives, if any, are exempt from crosses; few estates are so good as to have no drawbacks.   Examples: Abraham (Gen. xv. 2, 3), Naaman (2 Kings v. 1), Haman (Esth. v. 13), Paul (2 Cor. xii. 7). 2. *Straight things.* Such experiences as harmonize with the soul's wishes, as *e.g.* seasons of prosperity, dispensations of good, and enjoyments of every kind; and, as nobody's lot on earth is entirely straight, so on the other hand no one's lot is wholly crooked—" there are always some straight and even parts in it." " Indeed, when men's passions, having got up, have cast a mist over their minds, they are ready to say all is wrong with them and nothing right; yet is that never true in this world, since (always) *it is of the Lord's mercies that we are not consumed* (Lam. iii. 22) " (Boston).

II. PROCEED FROM THE HAND OF GOD. Neither come by accident or from second causes, but from him " of whom, to whom, and through whom are all things" (Rom. xi. 36; 2 Cor. v. 18; Heb. ii. 10). 1. *True of straight things.* " Every good gift and every perfect is from above " (Jas. i. 17).   Saint and sinner alike depend on the providential bounty of God (Ps. cxxxvi. 25), who appointeth to all men the bounds of their habitation (Acts xvii. 26) and measureth out their lots (Isa. xxxiv. 17; Jer. xiii. 25).   So elementary is this truth that it needs no demonstration; yet is it so familiar as to be frequently forgotten. 2. *No less correct of crooked things.* These also are from God (2 Kings vi. 33; Amos iii. 6; Micah i. 12).   It is he who lays affliction on the loins of men (Ps. lxvi. 11), distributes sorrows in his anger (Job xxi. 17), shows great and sore troubles (Ps. lxxi. 20), lifts up and casts down (Ps. cii. 10), wounds and heals, kills and makes alive (Deut. xxxii. 39).   The Preacher recognizes God's hand in introducing crooked things into men's lots; in this all should follow his example.

III. DEMAND DIVERSE TREATMENT FROM THE INDIVIDUAL. 1. *Straight things call for cheerfulness.* "In the day of prosperity be joyful," "be in good spirits," be thankfully happy and happily thankful. (1) Gratitude, an element in that treatment God's goodness calls for (Ps. ciii. 1, 2). Every creature of God is good if it be received with thanksgiving (1 Tim. iv. 4). (2) Use, another ingredient in a proper return for God's gifts. These are not to be despised and shunned, but valued and enjoyed. Asceticism, or voluntary abstinence from meats and drinks, as if these were sinful, harmonizes not with the spirit of either the Old (ch. ix. 7) or the New Testament (Col. ii. 20—23) religion. If permissible under the latter as a means of spiritual discipline (1 Cor. ix. 27), or as an expedient for preventing sin in others (Rom. xiv. 21), it should not be forgotten that God "giveth us all things richly *to enjoy*" (1 Tim. vi. 17). 2. *Crooked things demand consideration.* "In the day of adversity consider:" (1) Whence adversity comes, viz. from God (Lam. iii. 32; Job ii. 10). Hence should it be accepted with submission (1 Sam. iii. 18; Job ii. 10; Ps. xxxix. 9). (2) How adversity comes. Not as a strange thing, *i.e.* allotted in an exceptional way to the individual (1 Pet. iv. 12), but rather as an experience common among men (1 Cor. x. 13; 1 Pet. v. 9). Not as an isolated thing, unmixed with good or untempered with mercy (Ps. ci. 1). Not as a constant thing, as if life were a perpetual calamity (Job xxii. 18). Not as an arbitrary thing, as if the sovereign Disposer of events acted without reason in sending troubles upon men (Lam. iii. 33; Heb. xii. 10). Certainly not as a malignant thing, as if the Almighty took pleasure in the sufferings and miseries of his creatures (Lam. iii. 33; Heb. xii. 10). (3) Why adversity comes; because of man's sinfulness, though not always in each instance connected with some particular offence. (4) Wherefore adversity comes; to fulfil the Divine purpose concerning man, which is not one, but manifold (Job xxxiii. 29).

IV. COMBINE TO SERVE A LOFTY PURPOSE. "God hath even made the one side by side with the other, to the end that man should not find out anything that shall be after him." The Almighty's design variously explained. 1. *Unlikely interpretations.* (1) That God, willing man to be rid of all things at death instead of punishing him hereafter, puts evil into his existence here, and allows it to alternate with good (Hitzig). This does not harmonize with the Preacher's doctrine of a future judgment (ch. ix. 9; xii. 14), and is ruled out of court by the general scope of the New Testament. (2) That man might find nothing which he, dying, might take with him into the unseen world (Ewald). But this end is secured by death (ch. v. 15), and if more were needed would have been more effectually attained by making man's lot on earth all adversity and no prosperity, rather than a commingling of the two; while if the proposed interpretation explains the presence of evil alongside of good, it leaves unaccounted for the existence of good alongside of evil in man's lot. (3) That man might pass through the whole school of life, so that on departing from this scene nothing might remain outstanding (in arrears) which he had not experienced (Delitzsch). This seems equivalent to saying that God commingles joy and sorrow in man's experience that man might have a taste of both—which sounds like a truism— or that his discipline might be complete by being subjected to both, so that nothing more should be possible to or required by him in a future state to render him responsible—which, though true, indicates a clearness and fulness of theological conception manifestly beyond the Preacher. (4) That no one coming after God by way of review should be able to find anything of blame to cast on his procedure (Mercator, Poole, Fausset); which, though undeniable, is not warranted by a just translation of the Hebrew. 2. *Likely interpretations.* (1) That the alternation of prosperous and adverse dispensations was designed to prevent man from finding out the course of future events; in other words, that man should never be able certainly to predict his own future, or even what should be on the morrow (Zöckler, Hengstenberg), and therefore should be disposed to trust in God and calmly wait the development of events; with which teaching may be compared Christ's about taking no thought for the morrow (Matt. vi. 34), and that of Horace ('Odes,' iii. 29. 29—38).

> " God in his wisdom hides from sight,
> Veiled in impenetrable night,
> The future chance and change;

> And smiles when mortals' anxious fears,
> Forecasting ills of coming years,
> Beyond their limit range."
>
> (Plumptre, *in loco*.)

The continuity of human experience is not so unbroken that mortal sagacity, at its highest, can forecast the incidents of even the nearest day. (2) That no man should be able to tell precisely what might come to pass on earth after he had left it (Plumptre), a thought already expressed (ch. vi. 12), of which the practical outcome is the same as that just stated, viz. that as the Divine Being desired to keep the times and seasons in his own hand, he mingled crooked things and straight in man's experience, that man should not be able to guess with certainty at what was coming, and might accordingly be impelled to lead a life of sobriety and watchfulness (Prov. iv. 23, 25, 26; Matt. xxv. 13; Luke xii. 15, 35—40). (3) That man might not be able by all his cogitations on the present scene to find out the lot either of himself or of mankind generally in a future state (Wright); and unquestionably this is true that without the gospel the whole subject of a future state for man would be, if not an insoluble enigma, at least a darkly veiled mystery. A consideration of man's experiences on earth would so little guide to accurate knowledge of what his experiences beyond the grave should be, that to thoughtful minds they might rather seem to have been constructed for the very purpose of baffling curiosity on that alluring theme.

Learn : 1. That crooked things may sometimes be better than straight. 2. That men should not always ask the crooked things in their lot to be straightened. 3. That straight things alone might often prove hurtful.

Vers. 15—18.—*Nothing in excess; or, a caution against extremes.* I. IN INTERPRETING THE WAYS OF PROVIDENCE. 1. *As to the perishing of a just man in his righteousness.* Because, though it may sometimes happen that a just or good man loses his life in his righteousness, it does not follow (1) that all just or good men must necessarily lose their lives—which, considering the natural infirmity of the human heart, would certainly prove a check to the progress of righteousness. Or (2) that though good men perish *in* their righteousness, they also perish *because* of their righteousness—which would be asserting that God loved iniquity and hated righteousness, the exact reverse of the truth (Deut. xxxii. 4; Job xxxiv. 10; Ps. xi. 7). Or (3) that therefore being just is not a wise, or doing righteousness a good, thing—which would be constituting temporal success or material prosperity the standard of moral right, and adversity the test of moral wrong. Or (4) that just men should not persevere in their righteousness, even though they should perish temporally, since he that loseth his life for righteousness' sake shall find it unto life eternal (Matt. xvi. 25). Or (5) that the just man may not sometimes be to blame for his own perishing by proceeding to excess in the performance of things in themselves righteous (see below). 2. *As to the prolonging of a wicked man's life in* (or in spite of) *his evil doing.* From this it must not be inferred either (1) that under the moral government of God wickedness has a greater tendency to prolong life than virtue, because the opposite of this is the case (Ps. xxxiv. 12—14; lv. 23). Or (2) that wickedness is not therefore an evil because it occasionally, or even frequently, appears to be rewarded with long life; because no amount or degree of prosperity can ever render sin the same as holiness, or make it less the abominable thing which God hates. Or (3) that wicked men have the best of life because they do not perish prematurely, but rather often live long and become old and mighty in power (Job xxi. 7); because through their wickedness they are separated even here from him who is the Source of all true felicity (Isa. lix. 2). Or (4) that wicked men will not one day be recompensed for their wickedness, although God may permit them through a long life to sin with impunity; because it is written that "destruction shall be to the workers of iniquity" (Prov. x. 29). In either of these directions it is possible for one, by not observing the limits of just judgment, to go astray in interpreting the ways of God.

II. IN REGULATING THE CONDUCT OF LIFE. 1. *In respect of righteousness.* "Be not righteous overmuch; neither make thyself overwise" (ver. 16). (1) The Preacher cannot be supposed to teach that one may be too holy or too ardent in pursuit of righteousness. That seems inadmissible in the case of one whose standpoint was that of the Old Testament—that religion signified the worship of a holy God (Lev. xix. 2), and righteousness a keeping of that holy God's commandments. Hence if this righteousness could always receive from man a pure expression, it would be simply inconceivable that it should ever be too much in the estimation of Heaven—though it might be too much for the safety of the individual performing or expressing it, and through exciting the world's hostility might lead to his destruction. But man's expression of righteousness is never absolutely perfect, but always tainted with defect, and often one-sided, if not insincere and formal. Hence (2) the Preacher may have meant it was possible to push to excess the doing of purely external righteousness simply as an *opus operatum*, and, in doing so under the impression that such was the way to happiness and salvation, to exercise wisdom beyond measure; because no amount of such righteousness and wisdom could (in his estimation) conduct a soul to peace and felicity; but rather the more a soul pushed these to excess, the more inwardly torpid, lifeless, benumbed, and disordered would it become, till eventually it should land the soul in spiritual, if not the body also in temporal, ruin. 2. *In respect of wickedness.* "Be not overmuch wicked, neither be thou foolish" (ver. 17). Here, again, it cannot be supposed the Preacher teaches the permissibility of a moderate indulgence in sin, but merely that if excessive righteousness is no sign of superior wisdom or perfect guarantee of attaining to felicity, but rather an evidence of mistaken judgment and a precursor of inward moral and spiritual deterioration, much more is excessive wickedness a proof of absolute and unredeemed folly, and a sure as well as short road to ruin (1 Tim. vi. 9 ; 2 Pet. ii. 12).

LESSONS. 1. Fear God instead of murmuring at his dark providences. 2. Serve God with intelligent reason and prudence instead of rushing into extravagances either on one side or on another. 3. Perish in righteousness rather than prosper in wickedness.

Vers. 19—22.—*The dangers and defences of a city.* I. A CITY'S DANGERS. 1. *Either external or internal.* Either attacking it from without or assailing it from within. 2. *Either personal or impersonal.* Arising from individuals, as *e.g.* from embattled hosts marching against the city, or from designing traitors proving unfaithful to the city ; or proceeding from material causes, as *e.g.* from such physical conditions and surroundings as endanger the city's safety or the health of its inhabitants. 3. *Either temporal or spiritual.* Such as threaten its prosperity in trade and commerce, or such as menace its civil order, social well-being, and political stability. 4. *Either few or many.* Either one or two of the above-named perils happening at one time, or all of them together confronting the city.

II. A CITY'S DEFENCES. 1. *The prowess of its soldiers.* The ten mighty men or rulers may be regarded as chiefs or generals (*sallith* being probably equivalent to the Assyrian *sâlat*, which signifies a stadtholder or commander; Schrader, 'Die Keilinschriften und das Alte Testament,' p. 588), or viewed as civil governors like the Roman decemvirs (see Adam's 'Roman Antiquities,' p. 130), or perhaps taken simply as persons of wealth and influence, like the ten men of leisure whom the Mishna ('Megillah,' i. 3) declares to have been necessary to constitute a great city with a synagogue. Either way, they may represent the first or outer line of defence to which a city usually resorts in times of danger, viz. that of physical force, expressed for the most part in armies and garrisons. The Preacher says not that such wall of defence is worthless, but merely that there are defences better and more efficient than it. And though battalions and bullets, regiments and fleets, constitute not the highest instruments of safety to which a city or a nation can trust, yet they have their uses in averting, as well as their dangers in inviting, war (Luke xi. 21). 2. *The wisdom of its rulers.* These the wise men are now supposed to be; and the meaning is that a city's safety depends more upon the mental sagacity of those who guide its affairs than upon the extent and depth of its material resources; that "wise statesmen," for instance, "may do more" for it "than able generals" (Plumptre), and skilful inventors than herculean labourers (cf. ch. ix. 16, 18); and if more upon the mental sagacity of its governors, much more upon their moral earnestness. The wisdom to which the Preacher alludes is unquestionably that which fears God, keeps his commandments, and gives life to all that have it.   Hence even more indispensable for a city's safety is it that her dignitaries should be good than that they should be great.   3. *The piety of its people.*   This a legitimate deduction from the statement that "*there is* not a just man upon the earth, that doeth good, and sinneth not" (ver. 20).   In introducing this sentiment, suggested probably by the utterance of Solomon (2 Kings viii. 46), the Preacher may have wished to call up the thought that once upon a time ten righteous men, could they only have been found (which they were not), would have saved a city (Gen. xviii. 32), and to point to the fact that no such expectation as that of saving a city by means of its righteous men need be cherished now as a reason for resorting to the next best defence—that of moral wisdom instead of brute force.   Yet the truth remains that righteousness, holiness, piety, could it only be attained, would be a far more endurable and impregnable wall of protection to a people than either mighty armies or wise statesmen.

LESSONS.   1. Righteousness or wisdom the highest civil good.   2. The permanence of a state determined by the number of its good men.   3. The power of moral goodness in both individuals and empires.   4. The universal corruption of mankind.

Vers. 23—29.—*A great quest, and its sorrowful result.* I. THE GREAT QUEST. 1. *The person of the seeker.*   The Preacher (see on ch. i. 1).   The frequency with which he draws attention to himself shows that he regarded himself as one possessed of ample and perhaps well-known qualifications for the search upon which he had engaged.   2. *The object of his search.*   To be wise—to know and to search out and to seek wisdom and the reason of things; and in particular to know the wickedness of folly, and that foolishness is madness.   In other words, he desired to reach that wisdom in its fulness which would enable him to solve the problem of the universe.   3. *The spirit in which he entered on his quest.*   (1) Calm resolution.   He said to himself, " I will be wise."   (2) Genuine humility.   He understood that wisdom in its ideal vast-ness and elevation was beyond his reach.   (3) Earnest application.   He applied his heart, or turned himself and his heart, to the business he had undertaken.   (4) Patient perseverance.   His soul kept on seeking, laying one thing to another to find out the account.   These qualities should distinguish all seekers after wisdom.

II. THE SORROWFUL FINDING.   1. *Concerning the strange woman.*   Not "heathenish folly" (Hengstenberg), but the flesh-and-blood harlot of Proverbs (ii. 16—19; v. 3—13).   With respect to her the Preacher calls attention—speaking, no doubt, from personal experience, and recording the results of his own observation—to: (1) Her seductive arts.   "Her heart is snares and nets," luring with her false beauty, bewitch-ing voice, and voluptuous person, numerous unthinking and inexperienced persons, chiefly young men devoid of understanding (Prov. vii. 7), into her embrace.   (2) Her deceptive gifts.   While promising her lovers liberty, she only leads them into slavery— "Her hands are as bands; " and while flattering them with promises of hidden sweets, what she gives them is an experience "more bitter than death," *i.e.* an inward wretchedness more intolerable to the soul than even darkness and the grave.   "Her house is the way to hell, going down to the chambers of death" (Prov. vii. 27).   (3) Her powerless charms—in some cases.   Fascinating to the natural heart, and especially to sensual dispositions, her attractions have no influence upon pure minds and religious souls.   "Whoso pleaseth God shall escape from her;" either never be captivated by her spells, or be recovered from them before it is too late.   (4) Her miserable victims.   Those she leads off as prey are "sinners," in whose hearts sin rules as a dominating principle; who are carnally minded, and delight to make provision for the flesh, to fulfil the lusts thereof (Rom. viii. 1; xiii. 14); lovers of pleasure more than lovers of God (2 Tim. iii. 4); foolish and disobedient souls, who serve divers lusts and pleasures (Titus iii. 3).   2. *Concerning womankind.*   (1) The Preacher's finding was incorrect if designed as a universal negative, in the sense that, while in a thousand men taken at random one might be found good, in a thousand women similarly taken not one could be found entitled to be so characterized.   The best refutation of such woman-hating utterances is to point to " the numerous examples of noble women mentioned in Old Testament Writ, and of the devoted heroines of New Testament days, "whose names stand forth conspicuously, side by side with those of men, in the muster-roll of the 'noble army of martyrs'" (Wright).   (2) The

Preacher's finding may have been correct if accepted only as the record of his own individual experience. In this case, either his lot must have fallen in very evil times in respect of moral corruption, rivalling the days that were before the Flood (Gen. vi. 11; vii. 1), or he himself must have mixed with extremely questionable characters and limited his investigations to the lowest strata of society. It is doubtful if in any age, at least since the Flood, the condition of mankind has been so deplorably degenerate as the Preacher's language implies. (3) The Preacher's finding may be endorsed if it only means (as is probably the case) that woman less frequently attains to her ideal than man does to his—which, however, need not argue deeper depravity in woman than in man, but may point either to the loftier character of woman's ideal than of man's, or to the greater difficulties that stand in the way of woman realizing her ideal than hinder man from reaching his. 3. *Concerning the human race.* (1) Their original condition had been one of uprightness. This one of two conclusions to which the Preacher had been conducted, viz. that whatever of evil was now perceptible in man's nature had not proceeded from the hand of God. (2) Their present condition was one of "inventive refined degeneracy" (Delitzsch). A second result to which the Preacher had been led. Man had lapsed from his primitive condition of moral simplicity and had become an ingenious inventor; not always of things indifferent, but frequently of things immoral in themselves, and leading to immorality and sin as their results.

Lessons. 1. The value of wisdom as a human pursuit. 2. The worth of experience as a teacher. 3. The danger of sensuality. 4. The excellence of piety as a protection against impurity. 5. The inestimable worth of a good woman. 6. The rarity of noble men. 7. The certainty that man is not what God made him.

HOMILIES BY VARIOUS AUTHORS.

Ver. 1.—*Reputation.* The connection between the two clauses of this verse is not at first sight apparent. But it may well be intended to draw attention to the fact that it is in the case of the man who has justly gained a good name that the day of death is. better than that of birth.

I. There is a sense in which reputation among men is worthless, and in which solicitude for reputation is folly. If the reality of fact points one way, and the world's opinion points in an opposite direction, that opinion is valueless. It is better to *be* good than to *seem* and to be deemed good; and it is worse to be bad than unjustly to be reputed bad. Many influences affect the estimation in which a man is held among his fellows. Through the world's injustice and prejudice, a good man may be evil spoken of. On the other hand, a bad man may be reputed better than he is, when he humours the world's caprices, and falls in with the world's tastes and fashions. He who aims at conforming to the popular standard, at winning the world's applause, will scarcely make a straight course through life.

II. Yet there is a righteous reputation which ought not to be despised. Such good qualities and habits as justice, integrity, and truthfulness, as bravery, sympathy, and liberality, must needs, in the course of a lifetime, make some favourable impression upon neighbours, and perhaps upon the public; and in many cases a man distinguished by such virtues will have the credit of being what he is. A good name, when deserved, and when obtained by no mean artifices, is a thing to be desired, though not in the highest degree. It may console amidst trials and difficulties, it is gratifying to friends, and it may serve to rouse the young to emulation. A man who is in good repute possesses and exercises in virtue of that very fact an extended influence for good.

III. It is only when life is completed that a reputation is fully and finally made up. "Call no man happy before his death" is an ancient adage, not without its justification. There are those who have only become famous in advanced life, and there are those who have enjoyed a temporary celebrity which they have long outlived, and who have died in unnoticed obscurity. It is after a man's career has come to an end that his character and his work are fairly estimated; the career is considered as a whole, and then the judgment is formed accordingly.

IV. The approval of the Divine Judge and Awarder is of supreme consequence. A good name amongst one's fellow-creatures, as fallible as one's self, is of small account. Who does not admire the noble assertion of the Apostle Paul, " It is a small thing for me to be judged by man's judgment"? They who are calumniated for their fidelity to truth, who are persecuted for righteousness' sake, who are execrated by the unbelieving and the worldly whose vices and sins they have opposed, shall be recognized and rewarded by him whose judgment is just, and who suffers none of his faithful servants to be for ever unappreciated. But they may wait for appreciation until "the day of death." The clouds of misrepresentation and of malice shall then be rolled away, and they shall shine like stars in the firmament. "Then shall every man have praise of God."—T.

Vers. 2—4.—*A Divine paradox.* To many readers these statements appear startling and incredible. The young are scarcely likely to receive them with favour, and to the pleasure-seeking and the frivolous they are naturally repugnant. Yet they are the embodiment of true wisdom; and are in harmony with the experience of the thoughtful and benevolent.

I. FEASTING, LAUGHTER, AND MIRTH ARE TOO GENERALLY REGARDED BY THE FOOLISH AS THE BEST PORTION AND THE ONLY JOY OF HUMAN LIFE. 1. It is not denied that there is a side of human nature to which merriment and festivity are congenial, or that there are occasions when they may be lawfully, innocently, and suitably indulged in. 2. But these experiences are not to be regarded by reasonable and immortal beings as the choicest and most desirable experiences of life. 3. If they are unduly prized and sought, they will certainly bring disappointment, and involve regret and distress of mind. 4. Constant indulgence of the kind described will tend to the deterioration of the character, and to unfitness for the serious and weighty business of human existence.

II. INTERCOURSE WITH THE SORROWFUL AND THE BEREAVED YIELDS MORE TRUE PROFIT THAN SELFISH AND FRIVOLOUS INDULGENCE. 1. Such familiarity with the house of mourning reminds of the common lot of men, which is also our own. In a career of amusement and dissipation there is much which is altogether artificial. The gay and dissolute endeavour, and often for a time with success, to lose sight of some of the greatest and most solemn realities of this earthly existence. Pain, weakness, and sorrow come, sooner or later, to every member of the human race, and it is inexcusable folly to ignore that with which every reflective mind must be familiar. 2. The house of mourning is peculiarly fitted to furnish themes of most profitable meditation. The uncertainty of prosperity, the brevity of life, the rapid approach of death, the urgency of sacred duties, the responsibility of enjoying advantages and opportunities only to be used aright during health and activity,—such are some of the lessons which are too often unheeded by the frivolous. Yet not to have learned these lessons is to have lived in vain. 3. The house of mourning is fitted to bring home to the mind the preciousness of true religion. Whilst Christianity is concerned with all the scenes and circumstances of our existence, and is able to hallow our joys as to relieve our sorrows, it is evident that, inasmuch as it deals with us as immortal beings, it has a special service to render to those who realize that this earthly life is but a portion of our existence, and that it is a discipline and preparation for the life to come. Many have been indebted, under God, to impressions received in times of bereavement for the impulse which has animated them to seek a heavenly portion and inheritance. 4. Familiarity with scenes of sorrow, and with the sources of consolation which religion opens up to the afflicted, tends to promote serenity and purity of disposition. The restlessness and superficiality which are distinctive of the worldly and pleasure-seeking may, through the influences here described, be exchanged for the calm confidence, the acquiescence in the Divine will, the cheerful hope, which are the precious possession of the true children of God, who know whom they have believed, and are persuaded that he is able to keep that which they have committed to him against that day.—T.

Ver. 7.—*The mischief of oppression and bribery.* There is some uncertainty as to the interpretation of this verse: the reference may be to the effect of injustice upon him who inflicts it; it may be to its effect upon him who suffers it. It is usual to regard the observation as descriptive of the result of oppression and bribery in the feelings of irritation and despondency they produce upon the minds of those who are wronged, and upon society generally.

I. JUSTICE IS THE ONLY SOLID FOUNDATION FOR SOCIETY. There is moral law, upon which alone civil law can be wisely and securely based. When those who are in power are guided in their administration of political affairs by a reverent regard for righteousness, tranquillity, and contentment, order and harmony may be expected to prevail.

II. OPPRESSION, EXTORTION, AND VENALITY ON THE PART OF RULERS ARE INCOMPATIBLE WITH JUSTICE AND WITH THE PUBLIC GOOD. Unjust rulers sometimes use the power which they have acquired, or with which they have been entrusted, for selfish ends, and in the pursuit of such ends are unscrupulous as to the means they employ. Such wrong-doing is peculiar to no form of civil government. It is to some extent checked by the prevalence of liberty and of publicity, and yet more by an elevated standard of morality, and by the influence of pure religion. But in the East corruption and bribery have been too general on the part of those in power.

III. THE SPECIAL RESULT OF CORRUPTION AND OPPRESSION IS THE FURTHERANCE AND PREVALENCE OF FOLLY AND UNREASON. To the writer of Ecclesiastes, who regarded wisdom as "the principal thing," it was natural to discern in mischievous principles of government the cause of general unwisdom and foolishness. 1. The governor himself, although he may be credited with craft and cunning, is morally injured and degraded, sinks to a lower level, loses self-respect, and forfeits the esteem of his subjects. 2. The governed are goaded to madness by the impossibility of obtaining their rights, by the curtailment of their liberties, and by the loss of their property. Hence arise murmurings, discontent, and resentment, which may, and often do, lead to conspiracy, insurrection, and revolution.

IV. THE DUTY OF ALL UPRIGHT MEN TO SET THEIR FACES AGAINST SUCH EVIL PRACTICES. A good man must not ask—Can I profit by the prevalence of injustice? Will my party or my friends be strengthened by it? He must, on the contrary, turn away from the question of consequences; he must witness against venality and oppression; he must use all lawful means to expose and to put an end to such practices. And this he is bound to do from the highest motives. Government is of Divine authority, and is to be upon Divine principles. Of God we know that "righteousness and judgment are the habitation of his throne." They are unworthy to rule who employ their power for base and selfish ends.—T.

Ver. 8.—*The end better than the beginning.* There are many persons, especially among the young and ardent, who adopt and act upon a principle diametrically opposed to this. Every beginning has for them the charm of novelty; when this charm fades, the work, the enterprise, the relationship, have no longer any interest, and they turn away with disgust from the end as from something "weary, stale, flat, and unprofitable." But the language of this verse embodies the conviction of the wise and reflecting observer of human affairs.

I. THE REASON OF THIS PRINCIPLE. The beginning is undertaken with a view to the end, and apart from that it would not be. The end is the completion and justification of the beginning. The time-order of events is the expression of their rational order; thus we speak of means and end. Aristotle commences his great work on 'Ethics' by showing that the end is naturally superior to the means, and that the highest end must be that which is not a means to anything beyond itself.

II. THE APPLICATION OF THIS PRINCIPLE. 1. To human works. It is well that the foundation of a house should be laid, but it is better that the top-stone should be placed with rejoicing. So with seed-time and harvest; with a journey and its destination; with a road and its completion, etc. 2. To human life. The beginning may, in the view of men, be neutral; but, in the view of the religious man, the birth of a child is an occasion for gratitude. Yet, if that progress be made which corresponds with the Divine ideal of humanity, if character be matured, and a good life-work be wrought,— then the day of death, the end, is better than the day of birth, in which this earthly existence commenced. 3. To the Christian calling. The history of the individual Christian is a progressive history; knowledge, virtue, piety, usefulness, are all developed by degrees, and are brought to perfection by the discipline and culture of the Holy Spirit. The end must therefore be better than the beginning, as the fruit excels the blossoms of the spring. 4. To the Church of Christ. As recorded in the Book of the Acts of the Apostles, the beginning of the Church was beautiful, marked by power and promise. But the kingdom of God, the dispensation of the Spirit, has a purpose—high, holy, and glorious. When ignorance, error, and superstition, vice, crime, and sin, are vanquished by the Divine energy accompanying the Church of the living God—when the end cometh, and the kingdom shall be delivered unto the Father—it will be seen that the end is better than the beginning, that the Church was not born in vain, was not launched in vain upon the stormy waters of time. III. The lessons of this principle. 1. When at the beginning of a good work, look on to the end, that hope may animate and inspire endeavour. 2. During the course of a good work look behind and before; for it is not possible to judge aright without taking a comprehensive and consistent view of things. We may trace the hand of God, and find reason alike for thanksgiving and for trust. 3. Seek that a Divine unity may characterize your work on earth and your life itself. If the end crown not the beginning, then it were better that the beginning had never been made.—T.

Vers. 8, 9.—*The folly of pride, hastiness, and anger.* The Scriptures are more pronounced and decisive with regard to these dispositions than for the most part are heathen moralists. Yet the student of human character and life is at no loss to adduce facts in abundance to justify the condemnation of habits which philosophy and religion alike condemn.

I. These dispositions and habits have their source in the constitution of human nature.

II. Circumstances in human life occasion their exercise and growth.

III. To yield to such passions and to allow them to rule the life is the part of folly.

IV. The spirit and conduct of the Divine Saviour exemplify the beauty of humility, patience, and meekness.

V. The subjugation of passion and the imitation of Christ contribute to the welfare of the individual and of society.

VI. There are means by the constant and prayerful use of which evil habits may be conquered, and self-control may be attained.—T.

Ver. 10.—*Laudator temporis acti.* It appears from this passage that a tendency of mind with which we are familiar—a tendency to paint the past in glowing colours—is of ancient date, and indeed it is probably a consequence of human nature itself.

I The questionable assertion. We often hear it affirmed, as the author of this book had heard it affirmed, that the former days were better than these. There are politicians in whose opinion the country was formerly more happy and prosperous than now; farmers who fancy that crops were larger, and merchants who believe that trade was more profitable, in former days; students who prefer ancient literature to modern; Christian men who place the age of faith and piety in some bygone period of history. It has ever been so, and is likely to be so in the future. Others who will come after us will regard our age as we regard the ages that have passed away.

II. The ground upon which the questionable assertion is made. 1. Dissatisfaction with the present. It is in times of pain, loss, adversity, disappointment, that men are most given to extol the past, and to forget its disadvantages as well as the privileges and immunities of the present. 2. The illusiveness of the imagination. The aged are not only conscious of their feebleness and their pains; they recall the days of their youth, and paint the scenes and experiences of bygone times in colours supplied by a fond, deceptive fancy. The imaginative represent to themselves a state of the world, a condition of society, a phase of the Church, which never had real existence. By feigning all prosperity and happiness to have belonged to a past age, they remove their fancies from the range of contradiction. All things to their vision become lustrous and fair with " the light that never was on land or sea."

III. The unwisdom of inquiring for an explanation of a belief which is probably unfounded. Experience teaches us that, before asking for the *cause*, it is well to assure ourselves of the *fact*. *Why* a thing is presumes *that* the thing is. Now, in the case before us, the fact is so questionable, and certainty with regard to it is so difficult, if not unattainable, that it would be a waste of time to enter upon the inquiry here supposed.

APPLICATION.   Vain regrets as to the past are as unprofitable as are complaints as to the present.´   What concerns us is the right use of circumstances appointed for us by a wise Providence.   Whether or not the former times were better than these, the times upon which we have fallen are good enough for us to use to our own moral and spiritual improvement, and at the same time they are bad enough to call for all our consecrated powers to do what in us lies—little as that may be—to mend them.—T.

Vers. 13—15.—*The perplexities of life.*   The Book of Ecclesiastes raises questions which it very inadequately answers, and problems which it scarcely attempts to solve. Some of the difficulties observable in this world, in human society, and in individual experience appear to be insoluble by reason, though to some extent they may be overcome by faith.   And certainly the fuller revelation which we enjoy as Christians is capable of assisting us in our endeavour not to be overborne by the forces of doubt and perplexity of which every thoughtful man is in some measure conscious.

I. A SPECULATIVE DIFFICULTY: THE COEXISTENCE OF CROOKED THINGS WITH STRAIGHT.   The philosophical student encounters this difficulty in a more definite form than ordinary thinkers, and is best acquainted with the apparent anomalies of existence. It may suffice to refer to the coexistence of sense and spirit, nature and reason, law and freedom, good and evil, death and immortality.

II. A PRACTICAL DIFFICULTY: THE JUXTAPOSITION AND INTERCHANGE OF PROSPERITY AND ADVERSITY.   " God hath even made the one side by side with the other." The inequality of the human lot has, from the time of Job, been the occasion of much questioning, dissatisfaction, and scepticism.   Opinions differ as to the effect upon this inequality of the advance of civilization.   Riches and poverty, splendour and squalor, refinement and brutishness, exist side by side.   And the observation of every one has remarked the startling transitions in the condition and fortunes alike of the wealthy and the poor; these are exalted, and those depressed.   At first sight all this seems inconsistent with the sway of a just and benignant Providence.

III. A MORAL DIFFICULTY: THE EVIDENT ABSENCE OF A JUST AND PERFECT RETRIBUTION IN THIS LIFE.   The righteous perish, and the wicked live on in their evil-doing, unchecked and unpunished.   There are those who would acquiesce in inequality of condition, were such inequality proportioned to disparities of moral character, but who are dismayed by the spectacle of prosperous crime and triumphant vice, side by side with integrity and benevolence doomed to want and suffering.

IV. THE DUTY OF CONSIDERATION AND PATIENCE IN THE PRESENCE OF SUCH PERPLEXING ANOMALIES.   The first and most obvious attitude of the wise man, when encountering difficulties such as those described in this passage, is to avoid hasty conclusions and immature, unconsidered, and partial judgments.   It is plain that we are confronted with what we cannot comprehend.   Our observation is limited; our penetration is at fault; our reason is baffled.   We are not, therefore, to shut our eyes to the facts of life, or to deny what our intelligence forces upon us.   But we must think, and we must wait.

V. THE PURPOSE OF SUCH DIFFICULTIES, AS FAR AS WE ARE CONCERNED, IS TO TEST AND TO ELICIT FAITH IN GOD.   There is sufficient reason for every thoughtful man to believe in the wisdom and righteousness of the eternal Ruler.   And the Christian has special grounds for his assurance that all things are ordained by his Father and Redeemer, and that the Judge of all the earth will do right.—T.

Vers. 16, 17.—*Moderation.*   This language must be interpreted in accordance with the rules of rhetoric; it is intended to convey a certain impression, to produce a certain effect; and this it does.   The Preacher aims at inculcating moderation, at cautioning the reader against what a modern poet has termed " the falsehood of extremes."   In interpreting this very effective language we must not analyze it as a scientific statement, but receive the impression which it was designed to convey.

I. HUMAN NATURE IS PRONE TO EXTREMES.   In how many instances may it be observed that a person is no sooner convinced that a certain object is desirable, a certain course is to be approved, than he will hear and think of nothing else! Is liberty good? Then away with all restraints! Is self-denial good? Then away with all pleasures! Is the Bible the best of books? Then let no other volume be opened! Is our own country to be preferred to all beside? Then let no credit be allowed to foreigners for anything they may do!

II. THIS TENDENCY TO EXTREMES IS OWING TO THE DOMINANCE OF FEELING. Calm reason would check such a tendency; but the voice of reason is silenced by passion or prejudice. Impulsive natures are hurried into unreasoning and extravagant opinions and habits of conduct. The momentum of a powerful emotion is very great; it may urge men onwards to an extent unexpected and dangerous. Whilst under the guidance of sober reason, feeling may be the motive power to virtue and usefulness; but when uncontrolled it may hurry into folly and disaster.

III. YIELDING TO THIS TENDENCY OCCASIONS THE LOSS OF SELF-RESPECT AND OF SOCIAL INFLUENCE. The man of extremes must, in his cooler moments of reflection, admit to himself that he has acted the part of an irrational being. And he certainly gains among his acquaintances the reputation of a fanatic; and even when he has sound and sober counsel to give, little heed is taken of his judgment.

IV. MODERATION IS USUALLY THE WISEST AND JUSTEST PRINCIPLE OF HUMAN CONDUCT. A great moralist taught the ancient Greeks that the ethical virtues lie between extremes, and adduced many very striking instances of his law. Bravery lies between foolhardiness and cowardice; liberality between profusion and niggardliness, etc. That a very insufficient theory of morals was provided by this doctrine of "the mean" would universally be admitted. Yet no account of virtue can be satisfactory which does not point out the importance of guarding against those extremes of conduct into which men are liable to be hurried by the gusts of passion that sweep over their nature. Who has not learned by experience that broad, unqualified assertions are usually false, and that violent, one-sided courses of action are in most cases harmful and regrettable? There is wisdom in the old adage which boys learn in their Latin grammar, *In medio tutissimus ibis.*—T.

Vers. 20, 29.—*Perfection is not on earth.* It would be a mistake to attribute these statements to anything peculiar in the experience and circumstances of the author of this book. The most attentive and candid observers of human nature will attest the truth of these very decided judgments. Christians are sometimes accused of exaggerating human sinfulness, in order to prepare for the reception of the special doctrines of Christianity; but they are not so accused by observers whose opportunities have been wide and varied, and who have the sagacity to interpret human conduct.

I. THE NATURE OF SIN. It is deflection from a Divine standard, departure from the Divine way, abuse of Divine provision, renunciation of Divine purpose.

II. THE UNIVERSALITY OF SIN. This is both the teaching of Scripture and the lesson of all experience in every land and in every age.

III. THE EXCEPTION TO SIN. The Divine Man, Jesus Christ, alone among the sons of men, was faultless and perfect.

IV. THE SPIRITUAL LESSONS TAUGHT BY THE PREVALENCE OF SIN. 1. The duty of humility, contrition, and repentance. 2. The value of the redemption and salvation which in the gospel Divine wisdom and compassion have provided as the one universal remedy for the one universal evil that afflicts mankind.—T.

Vers. 25—28.—*Bad women a curse to society.* It is generally considered that in this language we have the conclusion reached by Solomon, and that his polygamy was largely the explanation of the very unfavourable opinion which he formed of the other sex. A monarch who takes to himself hundreds of wives and concubines is scarcely likely to see much of the best side of woman's nature and life. And if marriage is divinely intended to draw out the unselfish, affectionate, and devoted qualities of feminine nature, such a purpose could not be more effectually frustrated than by an arrangement which assigns to a so-called wife an infinitesimal portion of a husband's time, attention, interest, and love. For this reason it is not fair to take the sweeping statement of this passage as expressing a universal and unquestionable truth. What is said of the bitterness of the wicked woman, and of the mischief she does in society, remains for ever true; but there are states of society in which good women are as numerous as are good men, and in which their influence is equally beneficial.

I. THE INJURIOUSNESS OF BAD WOMEN EXEMPLIFIES THE PRINCIPLE THAT THE ABUSE AND CORRUPTION OF GOOD THINGS IS OFTEN THE CAUSE OF THE WORST OF ILLS.

II. THE WICKEDNESS OF BAD WOMEN DISPLAYS ITSELF IN THEIR HABIT OF ENSNARING THE FOOLISH; FOR THEY WILL NOT AND CANNOT SIN ALONE.

III. THE PRESENCE OF BAD WOMEN IN SOCIETY IS THE GREAT TEMPTATION TO WHICH MEN ARE LIABLE, AND THE GREAT TEST BY WHICH THEY ARE TRIED.

IV. THE BITTERNESS OF BAD WOMEN MAY BY CONTRAST SUGGEST THE EXCELLENCE OF THE VIRTUOUS AND THE PIOUS, AND MAY PROMPT TO A GRATEFUL RECOGNITION OF THE INDEBTEDNESS OF SOCIETY TO HOLY AND KINDLY FEMININE INFLUENCES.—T.

Ver. 1.—*Reputation.* There is much both of exalted enjoyment and of valuable influence in a man's reputation. It is said of the great explorer and philanthropist, David Livingstone, that he used to live in a village in Africa until his "good name" for benevolence had been established and had gone on before him: following his reputation, he was perfectly safe. A good reputation is—

I. THE AROMA WHICH OUR LIFE SHEDS AROUND US. We are always judging one another; every act of every kind is appraised, though often quite unconsciously, and we stand better or worse in the estimation of our neighbours for all we do and are. Our professions, our principles, our deeds, our words, even our manners and methods,— all these leave impressions on the mind concerning ourselves. What men think of us is the sum-total of these impressions, 'and constitutes our "name," our reputation. The character of a good man is constantly creating an atmosphere about him in which he will be able to walk freely and happily. It is indeed true that some good men seriously injure their reputation by some follies, or even foibles, which might easily be corrected and which ought to be avoided; but, as a rule, the life of the pure and holy, of the just and kind, is surrounded by a radiance of good estimation, as advantageous to himself as it is valuable to his neighbours.

II. THE BEST LEGACY WE LEAVE BEHIND US. At "the day of one's birth" there is rejoicing, because "a man is born into the world." And what may he not become? what may he not achieve? what may he not enjoy? But that *is* a question indeed. That infant may *become* a reprobate, an outcast; he may *do* incalculable, deplorable mischief in the world; he may grow up to *suffer* the worst things in body or in mind. None but the Omniscient can tell that. But when a good man dies, having lived an honourable and useful life, and having built up a noble and steadfast character, he has won his victory, he has gained his crown; and he leaves behind him memories, pure and sweet, that will live in many hearts and hallow them, that will shine on many lives and brighten them. At birth there is a possibility of good, at death there is a certainty of blessedness and blessing.

1. Reputation is not the very best thing of all. *Character* stands first. It is of *vital* consequence that we be right in the sight of God, and tried by Divine wisdom. The first and best thing is not to *seem* but *to be* right and wise. But then: 2. Reputation is of very great value. (1) It is worth much to ourselves; for it is an elevated and ennobling joy to be glad in the well-earned esteem of the wise. (2) It is of great value to our kindred and our friends. How dear to us is the good name of our parents, of our children, of our intimate friends! (3) It is a source of much influence for good with our neighbours. How much weightier are the words of the man who has been growing in honour all his days, than are those of either the inexperienced and unknown man, or the man whose reputation has been tarnished!—C.

Vers. 2—6.—*The evil, the unprofitable, and the blessed thing.* I. THE POSITIVELY EVIL THING. "The laughter of fools," or "the song of fools," may be pleasant enough at the moment, but it is evil; for (1) it proceeds from folly, and (2) it tends to folly. Of the many things which are here implicitly condemned, there may be mentioned: 1. The irreverent or the impure jest or song. 2. The immoderate feast—particularly indulgence in the tempting cup. 3. The society of the ungodly, sought in the way of friendship and enjoyment, as distinguished from the way of duty or of benevolence. 4. The voice of flattery.

II. THE COMPARATIVELY UNPROFITABLE THING. Two things are mentioned in Scripture as being lawful, but as being of comparatively slight value—bodily indulgence and bodily exercise (see 1 Cor. vi. 13; 1 Tim. iv. 8). "The house of feasting" (ver. 2) is a right place to be found in, as is also the gymnasium, or the recreation-ground, or the place of entertainment. But it is very easy to think of some place that is worthier. As those that desire to attain to heavenly wisdom, to a Christ-like character, to the approval of God, let us see that we only indulge in the comparatively unprofitable *within the limits that become us.* To go beyond the bound of moderation is to err, and even to sin. Fun may grow into folly, pleasure pass into dissipation, the training of the body become an extravagant athleticism, in the midst of which the culture of the spirit is neglected, and the service of Christ forsaken. It behoves us to "keep under" that which is secondary, to forbid it the first place or the front rank, whether in our esteem or in our practice.

III. THE DISGUISED BLESSING. It is not difficult to reach the heart of these paradoxes (vers. 2—5). There is pain of heart in visiting the house where death has come to the door, as there is in receiving the rebuke of a true friend; but what are the issues of it? What is to be gained thereby? What hidden blessing does it not contain? How true it is that it is

"Better to have a quiet grief
Than a tumultuous joy"!

that the hollow laughter of folly is a very poor and sorry thing indeed compared with the wisdom-laden sorrow, when all things are weighed in the balances. To have a chastened spirit, to have the heart which has been taught of God great spiritual realities, to have had an enlarging and elevating vision of the things which are unseen and eternal, to have been impressed with the transiency of earthly good and with the excellency of "the consolations which are in Christ Jesus," to be lifted up, if but one degree, toward the spirit and character of the self-sacrificing Lord we serve, to have had some fellowship with the sufferings of Christ,—surely this is incomparably preferable to the most delicious feast or the most hilarious laughter. To go down to the home that is darkened by bereavement or saddened by some crushing disappointment, and to pour upon the troubled hearts there the oil of true and genuine sympathy, to bring such spirits up from the depths of utter hopelessness or overwhelming grief into the light of Divine truth and heavenly promise,—thus "to do good and to communicate" is not only to offer acceptable sacrifice unto God, but it is also to be truly enriched in our own soul.—C.

Ver. 8.—*Patience and pride.* Patience is to be distinguished from a dull indiscriminateness and from insensibility, to which one treatment is much the same as another; it is the calm endurance, the quiet, hopeful waiting on the part of the intelligent and sensitive spirit. Pride is to be distinguished from self-respect; it is an overweening estimate indulged by a man respecting himself—of his power, or of his position, or of his character. Thus understood, these two qualities stand in striking contrast to one another.

I. PATIENCE IS A DIVINELY COMMENDED AND PRIDE A FORBIDDEN THING. *Patience* (Luke xxi. 19; 2 Thess. i. 4; Heb. x. 36; 2 Pet. i. 6; Jas. v. 7, 8, 11; Rev. ii. 2). *Pride* (Ps. ci. 5; cxix. 21; cxxxviii. 6; Prov. vi. 17; Isa. ii. 12; Mark vii. 22; Rom. xii. 3; Jas. iv. 6).

II. PATIENCE IS THE SEAT OF SAFETY, PRIDE THE PLACE OF PERIL. The man that is willing to wait in patience for the good which God will grant him, accepting what he gives him with quiet contentment, is likely to walk in wisdom, and to abide in the fear and favour of the Lord; but the man who over-estimates his strength is standing in a very "slippery place"—he is almost sure to fall. No words of the wise man are more frequently fulfilled than those concerning pride and a haughty spirit (Prov. xvi. 18). The proud heart is the mark for many adversaries.

III. PATIENCE IS A BECOMING GRACE, PRIDE AN UGLY EVIL. Few things are more spiritually beautiful than patience. When under long-continued bodily pain or weakness, or under grievous ill-treatment, or through long years of deferred hope and disappointment, the chastened spirit lives on in cheerful resignation, the Christian workman toils on in unwavering faith, there is a spectacle which we can well believe that the angels of God look upon with delight. Certainly it is the object of our admiring regard. On the other hand, pride is an offensive thing in the eyes of man, as we know it is in the sight of God (Prov. viii. 13). Whether a man shows himself elated about his personal appearance, or his riches, or his learning, or his strength (of any kind), we begin by being amused and end by being annoyed and repelled; we turn away as from an ugly picture or from an offensive odour.

IV. PATIENCE CONDUCTS INTO, PRIDE EXCLUDES FROM, THE KINGDOM OF GOD. 1. Patient inquiry will bring a man into the sunshine of full discipleship to Jesus Christ, but pride will keep him away, and leave him to be lighted by the poor sparks of his own wisdom. 2. Patient steadfastness in the faith will conduct to the gates of the celestial city. 3. Patient continuance in well-doing will end in the commendation of Christ and in his bountiful reward.—C.

Ver. 10.—*Foolish comparison and complaint.* This querulous comparison, preferring former days to present ones, is unwise, inasmuch as it is—

I. BASED UPON IGNORANCE. We know but little of the actual conditions of things in past times. Chroniclers usually tell little more than what was upon the surface. We probably exaggerate and overlook to a very large extent. The good that is gone from us was probably attended with evils of which we have no idea; while the evils that remain we magnify because we experience them in our own person and suffer from them.

II. MARKED BY FORGETFULNESS. Often, though not always so. Often the change for the worse is not in a man's surroundings, but in himself. Leaving his youth and his prime behind him, he has left his vigour, his buoyancy, his power of mastery and of enjoyment. The "times" are well enough, but he himself is failing, and he sees everything through eyes that are dim with years.

III. INDICATIVE OF A SPIRIT OF DISCONTENT. It is the querulous spirit that thinks ill of his companions and his circumstances. He would come to the same conclusion if these were much better than they are. A sense of our own unworthiness and a consciousness of God's patience with us and goodness toward us, filling our souls with humility and gratitude, would dissipate these clouds and put another song into our mouth.

IV. WANTING IN MANLY RESOLUTENESS. If we are possessed of a right spirit, instead of sitting down and lamenting the inferiority of present things we shall gird ourselves to do what has to be done, to improve that which is capable of reform, to abolish that which should disappear, to plant that which should be thriving.

V. LACKING IN TRUSTFULNESS AND HOPEFULNESS. What if things are not all they should be with us; what if we ourselves are going down the hill and shall soon be at the bottom;—is there not a God above us? and is there not a future before us? Let us look up and let us look on. Above us is a Power that can regenerate and transform; before us is a period, an age, nay, an eternity, wherein all lost joys and honours will be "swallowed up of life."—C.

Vers. 13, 14.—*The irremediable.* Before we apply the main principle of the text, we may gather two lessons by the way.

I. THE WISDOM OF APPROPRIATING—of appropriating to ourselves and enjoying what God gives us without hesitation. In the day of our prosperity let us be joyful. We need not be draping our path with gloomy thoughts; we need not send the skeleton round at the feast; we should, indeed, partake *moderately* of everything, and in everything give thanks, showing *gratitude* to the Divine Giver; and we should also have the open heart which does not fail to show *liberality* to those in need. If our success be hallowed by these three virtues, it will be well with us.

II. THE RIGHTNESS OF RECTIFYING—of making straight all the crooked things which can be straightened. We are not to give up great moral problems as insoluble until we are absolutely convinced that they are beyond our reach. Poverty, ignorance, intemperance, irreligion,—these are very "crooked" things; but God did not make them what they are. Man has done that. His sin is the great and sad perverting force in the world, bending all things out of their course and turning them in wrong directions. And though they may seem to be too rigid and fixed to be amenable to our treatment, yet, hoping in God and seeking his aid, we must address ourselves courageously and intelligently to these crooked things until they are made straight. There is nothing that so strongly appeals to, and that will so richly reward, our aspiration, our ingenuity, our energy, our patience.

III. THE DUTY OF SUBMITTING. There are some things in regard to which we have to acknowledge that the evil thing is a "work of God," something he has "made crooked." This is to be accepted as the ordering of his holy will, as something that is balanced and overbalanced by the good things which are on the other side. It may be slenderness of means, lowliness of position, feebleness of intelligence, exclusion from society in which we should like to mingle, incapacity to visit scenes we long to look upon, the inaccessibility of a sphere for which we think ourselves peculiarly fitted, the advance of fatal disease, the reduction of resources or the decline of power, the breaking up of the old home and the scattering of near relatives, the loosening of old ties with the formation of new ones, etc. Such things as these are to be calmly and contentedly accepted. 1. To strive against the inevitable or irremediable is (1) to strive against God and be guilty; (2) to court failure and be miserable; (3) to waste energy that might be happily and fruitfully spent in other ways. 2. To submit to the will of God, after considering his work, is (1) to please him; (2) to have the heart filled with pure and elevating contentment; (3) to be free to do a good if not a great work " while it is day."—C.

Vers. 15—22.—*The lower and the higher standard.* The Preacher is not now in his noblest mood; he offers us a morality to which he himself at other times rises superior, and which cannot be pronounced worthy by those who have heard the great Teacher and learnt of him. We will look at—
I. THE LOWER STANDARD HERE HELD UP. 1. *His view of sin.* And here we find three things with which we are dissatisfied. (1) Sin is not represented to us as *in itself* an intolerable thing (ver. 17). We are allowed to think of it as something that would be allowable if indulged within certain limits; and if it did no serious injury to our life or to our health. But we know that, apart from its fatal consequences, all wickedness is "an abominable thing which God hates," an essentially evil thing. (2) The invariable penalty of sin is overlooked. We are not reminded that wickedness *always* makes us suffer, in spirit if not in health, in soul if not in circumstance. (3) We are likened to one another rather than with the Holy One (vers. 20—22). The strain is this: we need not be much troubled by the presence of some sin in our hearts and lives; all men are guilty, and we are only like our fellows; if there be those who are reproaching us, we are censuring them in return; we are standing on the same level, though it may be a common condemnation. 2. *His view of righteousness.* The Preacher sees two unsatisfactory features in righteousness. (1) It does not always prolong life and secure success (ver. 15). (2) It leads the best men into a painful loneliness. " Why shouldest thou *be desolate*? " (ver. 16, marginal reading); *i.e.* why be so honest and so pure and so true that thou canst not associate with the unscrupulous, whose standard is lower than thine own? Be content with that measure of righteousness which comes up to the common standard. Such is the Preacher's counsel in this mood of his. But we who have learnt of a Greater and Wiser than he, of him who was not only the wisest of men but " the Wisdom of God," cannot be satisfied with this; we aspire to something loftier and worthier; we must rise to—
II. THE HIGHER STANDARD. Taught of Jesus Christ, we: 1. *Have a truer view of sin.* We regard it as a thing which is only and utterly evil, offensive to God, constantly and profoundly injurious to ourselves, to be hated and shunned in every sphere, to be cleansed from heart and life. 2. *Have a truer conception of righteousness.* We look upon it as (1) that which is in itself precious beyond all price; (2) that which allies us to God in nature and character; (3) that which is to be cherished and pursued at all costs whatever; (4) that which makes our present life beautiful and noble, and leads on to far greater excellence and far deeper joy hereafter.—C.

Vers. 23—28.—*Degradation and elevation.* The words of the Preacher painfully remind us of the familiar story of Diogenes and his lantern. Whether we are to ascribe this pitiful conclusion respecting woman to his own infirmity or to the actual condition of Oriental society, we do not know. But there was, no doubt, so much of realism about the picture that we may learn a very practical lesson therefrom. It is twofold.

I. THE AWFUL POSSIBILITIES OF DEGRADATION. That woman, created by God to be a helpmeet for man, and so admirably fitted, as she is at her best, to comfort his heart and to enrich and bless his life—that woman should be spoken of in such terms as these, is sad and strange indeed. It would be unaccountable but for one thing. The explanation is that man, in his physical strength and in his spiritual weakness, has systematically *degraded* woman; has made a mere tool and instrument of her whom he should have treated as his trusted companion and truest friend. And if you once degrade any being (or any animal) from his or her true and right position, you send that being down an incline, you open the gates to a long and sad descent. You take away self-respect, and in so doing you undermine the foundation of all virtue, of all moral worth. Dishonour any one, man or woman, lad or child, in his (her) own eyes, and you inflict a deadly injury. A very vile woman is probably worse than a very bad man, more inherently foul and more lamentably mischievous; it is the miserable consequence of man's folly in wishing to displace her from the position God meant her to hold, and in making her take a far lower position than she has the faculty to fill. To degrade is to ruin, and to ruin utterly.

II. THE NOBLE POSSIBILITIES OF ELEVATION. How excellent is the impossibility of seriously writing such a sentence as that contained in the twenty-eighth verse, in this age and in this land of ours! Now and here it certainly is not more difficult to find a woman worthy of our admiration than to find such a man. In the Churches of Jesus Christ, in the homes of our country, are women, young and old and in the prime of their powers, whose character is sound to the centre, whose spirit is gracious, whose lives are lovely, whose influence is wholly beneficent, who are the sweetness and strength of the present generation, as they are the hope and promise of the next. And this elevation of woman all comes of treating her as that which God meant her to be—giving to her her rightful position, inviting and enabling her to fill her sphere, to cultivate her powers, to do her work, to take her heritage. 1. It is easy as it is foolish and sinful to degrade; assume the absence of what God has given and deny the opportunity which should be offered, and the work is speedily done. 2. It is quite possible as it is most blessed to elevate; treat men and women, wherever found and at whatever stage in worth or unworthiness they may be taken, as those God meant to be his children, and they will rise to the dignity and partake the inheritance of "the sons and daughters of the living God."—C.

Ver. 1.—*The charm of goodness.* When our author wrote these words he had, for a time at any rate, passed into a purer atmosphere; some gleams of light, if not the full dawn of day, had begun to shine upon him. Up to this he has been analyzing the evil conditions of human life, and has depicted all the moods of depression and sorrow and indignation they excited in him. Now he tells us of some things which he had found good, and which had cheered and strengthened him in his long agony. They were not, indeed, efficient to remove all his distress or to outweigh all the evils he had encountered in his protracted examination of the phenomena of human life; but to a certain extent they had great value and power. The first of these compensations of human misery is the beauty and attractiveness and lasting worth of a good character. The name won by one of honourable and unblemished character, who has striven against vice and followed after virtue, who has been pure and unselfish and zealous in the service of God and man, "is better than precious ointment." It is not unwarrantable thus to expand the sentence; for though the epithet " good " is not in the original, but supplied by our translators (Revised Version), it is undoubtedly understood, and also it is taken for granted that the renown so highly praised is fully deserved by its possessor. " Dear," he says, " to the human senses "—speaking, remember, to an Eastern world—" is the odour of costly unguents, of sweet frankincense and fragrant spikenard; but dearer still, more precious still, an honoured name, whose odour attracts the love, and penetrates and fills for a while the whole heart and memory of our friends " (Bradley). There is in the original a play upon words (*shem*, a name; *shemen*, ointment) which harmonizes with the brightness of the thought, and gives a touch of gaiety to the sentence so strangely concluded with the reflection that for the owner of the good name the day of his death is better than the day of his birth.   An exquisite illustration of the justness of our author's admiration for a good name is to be found in that incident in the Gospels of the deed of devotion to Christ, on the part of the woman who poured upon his head the precious ointment.   Her name, Mary of Bethany (John xii. 3), is now known throughout the whole world, and is associated with the ideas of pure affection and generous self-sacrifice.   The second part of the verse, which at first sounds so out of harmony with what precedes it, is yet closely connected with it.   The good name is thought of as not finally secured until death has removed the possibility of failure and shame.   So many begin well and attain high fame in their earlier life which is sadly belied by their conduct and fate in the close.   The words recall those of Solon to Crœsus, if indeed they are not a reminiscence of them, "Call no man happy until he has closed his life happily" (Herod., i. 32); and are to the same effect as those in ver. 8, "Better is the end of a thing than the beginning thereof."   It is not to be denied that there is, however, more in the words than a prudential warning against prematurely counting upon having secured the "good name" which is better than ointment.   They betray an almost heathenish distaste for life, which is utterly out of harmony with the revelation both of the Old Testament and of the New; and are more appropriate in the mouth of one of that Thracian tribe mentioned by Herodotus, who actually celebrated their birthdays as days of sadness, and the day of death as a day of rejoicing, than of one who had any faith in God.   The only parallel to them in Scripture is what is said of Judas by our Lord, "It had been good for that man if he had not been born" (Matt. xxvi. 24).   Ingenuity may devise explanations of the sentiment which bring it into harmony with religious sentiments.   Thus it may be said, at death the box of precious ointment is broken and its odours spread abroad; prejudices that assailed the man of noble character during his lifetime are mitigated, envy and jealousy and detraction are subdued, and his title to fair fame acknowledged on all hands.   It may be said life is a state of probation, death the beginning of a higher and happier existence. Life is a struggle, a contest, a voyage, a pilgrimage; and when victory has been won, the goal reached, the reward of labour is attained.   We may borrow the words and infuse a brighter significance into them; but no trace of any such inspiring, cheering thoughts are in the page before us.   "The angel of death is there; no angel of resurrection sits within the sepulchre."—J. W.

Vers. 2—6.—*Compensations of misery.*   Although in the Book of Ecclesiastes there is much that seems to be contradictory of our ordinary judgments of life, much that is at first apparently calculated to prevent our taking an interest in its business and pleasures—which are all asserted to be vanity and vexation of spirit—there are yet to be found in it sober and well-grounded exhortations, which we can only neglect at our peril.   Out of his large experience the writer brings some lessons of great value.   It is sometimes the case, indeed, that he speaks in such a way that we feel it is reasonable in us to discount his judgment pretty heavily.   When he speaks as a sated voluptuary, as one who had tried every kind of sensuous pleasure, who had gratified to the utmost every desire, who had enjoyed all the luxuries which his great wealth could procure, and found all his efforts to secure happiness vain—I say, when he speaks in this way, and asks us to believe that none of these things are worth the pains, we are not inclined to believe him implicitly.   We are inclined rather to resent being lectured in such a way by such a man.   The satiety, the weariness, the *ennui*, which result from over-indulgence, do not qualify a man for setting up as a moral and spiritual guide; they rather disqualify him for exercising such an office.   In answer to the austere and sweeping condemnation which he is inclined to pass upon the sources from which we think may be drawn a reasonable amount of pleasure, we may say, "Oh yes! it is all very well for you to speak in that way.   You have worn out your strength and blunted your taste by over-indulgence; and it comes with a bad grace from you to recommend an abstemious and severe mood of life which you have never tried yourself.   The exhortations which befit the lips of a John the Baptist, nurtured from early life in the desert, lose their power when spoken by a jaded epicure."   The answer would be perfectly just.   And if Solomon's reflections were all of the type described, we should be justified in placing less value upon them than he did. It is true that more than once he speaks with a bitterness and disgust of all the occupations and pleasures of life, which we cannot, *with our experience*, fairly endorse. But, as a rule, his moralizing is not of the ascetic type. He recommends, on the whole, a cheerful and grateful enjoyment of all the innocent pleasures of life, with a constant remembrance that the judgment draws ever nearer and nearer. While he has no hesitation in declaring that no earthly employments or pleasures can completely satisfy the soul and give it a resting-place, he does not, like the ancient hermits, approve of dressing in sackcloth, of feeding on bread and water only, and of retiring altogether from the society of our fellows. His teaching, indeed, contains a great deal more of true Christianity than has often been found in the writings and sermons of professedly Christian moralists and preachers. All the more weight, therefore, is to be attached to his words from this very fact, that he does not pose as an ascetic. We could not listen to him if he did; and accordingly we must be all the more careful not to lessen the value and weight of the words he speaks to which we should attend, by depreciating him as an authority. It is only of some of his judgments that we can say they are such as a healthy mind could scarcely endorse. This, in the passage before us, is certainly not one of them. It certainly runs counter to our ordinary sentiments and practices, like many of the sayings of Christ, but is not on that account to be hastily rejected; we are not justified either in seeking to diminish its weight or explain it away. It is not, indeed, a matter of surprise that the thoughts and feelings of beings under the influence of sinful habits, which enslave both mind and heart, should require to undergo a change before their teaching coincides with the mind of the Holy Spirit. In this section of the book we have teaching very much in the spirit of the New Testament. Compare with the second verse the sentences spoken by Christ: "Woe unto you that are full! for ye shall hunger; woe unto you that laugh now! for ye shall mourn and weep" (Luke vi. 25). And notice that the visits paid to the afflicted to console them, from which the Preacher declares he had gained moral and spiritual benefits, are recommended to us by the apostle as Christian duties (Jas. i. 27). From even the saddest experiences, therefore, a thoughtful mind will derive some gain; some compensations there are to the deepest miseries. The house of mourning is that in which there is sorrow on account of death. According to Jewish customs, the expression of grief for the dead was very much more demonstrative and elaborate than with us. The time of mourning was for seven days (Ecclus. xxii. 10), sometimes in special cases for thirty days (Numb. xx. 29; Deut. xxiv. 8). The presence of sympathizing friends (John xi. 19), of hired mourners and minstrels (Matt. ix. 23; Mark v. 38), the solemn meals of the bread and wine of affliction (Jer. xvi. 7; Hos. ix. 4), made the scene very impressive. Over against the picture he suggests of lamentation and woe, he sets that of a house of feasting, filled with joyous guests, and he asserts that it is better to go to the former than to the latter. He contradicts the more natural and obvious inclination which we all have to joy rather than to sorrow. But a moment's consideration will convince us that he is in the right, whether we choose the better part or not. Joy at the best is harmless—it relieves an overstrain on the mind or spirit; but when it has passed away it leaves no positive gain behind. Sorrow rightly borne is able to draw the thoughts upward, to purify and transform the soul. Its office is like that attributed to tragedy by Aristotle: "to cleanse the mind from evil passions by pity and terror—pity at the sight of another's misfortune, and terror at the resemblance between the sufferer and ourselves" ('Poetics'). Contradictory of ordinary feelings and opinions though this teaching of Solomon's is, there are three ways in which a visit to the house of mourning is better than to the house of feasting.

I. IT AFFORDS AN OPPORTUNITY FOR SHOWING SYMPATHY WITH THE AFFLICTED. Among our best-spent hours are those in which we have sought to lighten and share the burden of the bereaved and distressed. We may not have been able to open sources of consolation which otherwise would have remained hidden and sealed; but the mere expression of our commiseration may be helpful and soothing. Sometimes we may be able to suggest consolatory thoughts, to impart serviceable advice, or to give needful relief. But in all cases we feel that we have received more than we have given—that in seeking to comfort the sorrowful we come into closer communion with that Saviour who came from heaven to earth to bear the burden of sin and suffering, who was a welcome Guest on occasions of innocent festivity (John ii. 2; Luke vii. 36), but whose presence was still more eagerly desired in the homes of the afflicted (John xi. 3; Mark v. 23).

II. IT ENABLES US TO FORM TRUER ESTIMATES OF LIFE. It gives us a more trustworthy standard of judging the relative importance of those things that engage our attention and employ our faculties. It checks unworthy ambitions, flattering hopes, and sinful desires. We learn to realize that only some of the aims we have cherished have been worthy of us, only some of the pursuits in which we have been engaged are calculated to yield us lasting satisfaction when we come in the light of eternity to review the past of our lives. The sight of blighted hopes admonishes us not to run undue risk of disappointment by neglecting to take into account the transitory and changeful conditions in which we live. The spectacle of great sorrows patiently borne rebukes the fretfulness and impatience which we often manifest under the minor discomforts and troubles which we may be called to endure.

III. IT REMINDS US OF THE POSSIBLE NEARNESS OF OUR OWN END. (Ver. 2.) "It is better to go to the house of mourning, than to go to the house of feasting: *for that is the end of all men; and the living will lay it to his heart.*" Though the brevity of life is a fact with which we are all acquainted from the very first moment when we are able to see and know what is going on about us, it is a fact which it is very difficult for us to realize in our own case. "We think all are mortal but ourselves." No feelings of astonishment are excited in us by the sight of the aged and weakly sinking down into the grave, but we can scarcely believe that we are to follow them. The very aged still lay their plans as though death were far off; the dying can hardly be convinced till perhaps the very last moment that their great change is at hand. But a visit to the house of mourning gives us hard, palpable evidence, which must, though but for an instant, convince us that mortality is a universal law; that in a short time our end will come. The effect of such a thought need not be depressing; it need not poison all our enjoyments and paralyze all our efforts. It should lead us to resolve (1) to make good use of every moment, since life is so brief; and (2) to live as they should do who know that they have to give account of themselves to God. A practical benefit is thus to be drawn from even the saddest experiences, for by them "the heart is made better" (ver. 3). The foolish will seek out something which he calls enjoyment, in order to deliver his mind from gloomy thoughts; but the short-lived distraction of attention which he secures is not to be compared with the calm wisdom which piety can extract even from sorrow (ver. 4). Painful though some of the lessons taught us may be, they wound but to impart a permanent cure; while the mirth which drowns reflection soon passes away, and is succeeded by a deeper gloom (vers. 5, 6). One circumstance renders the teaching of this passage all the more impressible, and that is the absence from it of the ascetic spirit. This perhaps is, you will think, a paradoxical statement, when the whole tone of the utterance is of a sombre, not to say gloomy, character. But you will notice that the author does not lay a ban upon all pleasure; he does not denounce all innocent enjoyments as wicked. He does not say it is sinful to go to the house of feasting, to indulge in laughter, to sing secular songs. There have been and are those who make these sweeping statements. But he says that a wise, serious-minded man will not find these things satisfying all his desires; that he will, on the contrary, often find it greatly for his advantage to familiarize himself with very different scenes and employments. In other words, there are two sides to life—the temporal and the eternal. The soul, like the head of Janus, looks both on the present, with all its varied and transitory events, and on the future, in which there are so many new and solemn experiences in store for us. The epicurean, the worldling, looks to the present alone; the ascetic looks to the future alone. The wise have true appreciation of them both; know what conduct duty prescribes as appropriate in regard to them both. The examples of Christ and his apostles show us that we may partake both in the business and innocent pleasures of life without being untrue to our higher calling. He, though "holy, harmless, undefiled, and separate from sinners," wrought with his own hands, and thus sanctified all honest labour; he graced a marriage-feast with his presence, and supplied by a miracle the means of convivial cheerfulness. The sights and sounds of city and country life, the mirth of happy homes, the splendour of palaces, the pageantry of courts, the sports of children, were not frowned upon by him as in themselves unworthy of attracting the attention of immortal natures; they were employed by him to illustrate eternal truths. And all through the writings and exhortations of his apostles the same spirit is manifest; the same counsel is virtually given to use the present world without abusing it—to receive with thankfulness every good creature of God. And at the same time, no one can deny that great stress is laid by them also upon the things that are spiritual and eternal; greater even than on the others. For we are in greater risk of forgetting the eternal than of neglecting the temporal. Far too often is it true in the poet's words—

> "The world is too much with us; late and soon,
> Getting and spending, we lay waste our powers."

Therefore it is all the more necessary for startling admonitions like these of Solomon's to be given, which recall us with a jerk to attend to things that concern our higher welfare. The fact that there are dangers against which we must guard, dangers springing not merely from our own sinful perversity, but from the conditions of our lives, the danger especially of being too much taken up with the present, is calculated to arouse us to serious thought and effort. Very much easier would it have been for us if a code of rules for external conduct had been given us, so that at any time we might have made sure about being on the right way; but very much poorer and more barren would the life thus developed have been. We are called, as in this passage before us, to weigh matters carefully; to make our choice of worthy employments; to decide for ourselves when to enjoy that which is earthly and temporal, and when to sacrifice it 'for the sake of that which is spiritual and eternal. And we may be sure that that goodness which springs from an habitually wise choice is infinitely preferable to the narrow, rigid formalism which results from conformity with a Puritanic rule. It is not a sour, kill-joy spirit that should drive us to prefer the house of mourning to the house of feasting; but the sober, intelligent conviction that at times we may find there help to order our lives aright, and have an opportunity of lightening by our sympathy the heavy burden of sorrow which God may see fit to lay upon our brethren.—J. W.

Vers. 7—10.—*Patience under provocation.* In these words our author seems to commend the virtues of patience and contentment in trying circumstances, by pointing out that certain evils against which we may chafe bring their own punishment, and so in a measure work their own cure, that others spring from or are largely aggravated by faults in our own temperament, and that others exist to a very great extent in our own imagination rather than in actual fact. And accordingly the sequence of thought in the chapter is perfectly clear. We have here, too, some "compensations of misery," as in vers. 2—6. The enumeration of the various kinds of evil that provoke our dissatisfaction supplies us with a convenient division of the passage.

I. Evils that bring their own punishment and work their own cure. "Surely oppression maketh a wise man mad; and a gift destroyeth the heart. Better is the end of a thing than the beginning thereof" (vers. 7, 8*a*). It is the oppressor and not the oppressed who is driven mad. The unjust use of power demoralizes its possessor, deprives him of his wisdom, and drives him into actions of the grossest folly. The receiver of bribes, *i.e.* the judge who allows gifts to warp his judgments, loses the power of moral discernment, and becomes utterly disqualified for discharging his sacred functions. And this view of the meaning of the words makes them an echo of those passages in the Law of Moses which prescribe the duties of magistrates and rulers. "Thou shalt not wrest judgment; thou shalt not respect persons, neither shalt thou take a gift: for a gift doth blind the eyes of the wise, and pervert the words of the righteous" (Deut. xvi. 19; cf. Exod. xxiii. 8). The firm conviction which any extended experience of life is sure to confirm abundantly, that such moral perverseness as is implied in the exercise of tyranny, in extortion and bribery, brings with it its own punishment, is calculated to inspire patience under the endurance of even very gross wrongs. The tyrant may excite an indignation and detestation that will lead to his own destruction; the clamour against an unjust judge may become so great as to necessitate his removal from office, even if the government that employs him be ordinarily very indifferent to moral considerations. In any case, "the man who can quietly endure oppression is sure to come off best in the end" (cf. Matt. v. 38—41).

II. EVILS THAT SPRING LARGELY FROM OUR OWN TEMPERAMENT. "The patient in spirit is better than the proud in spirit. Be not hasty in thy spirit to be angry: for anger resteth in the bosom of fools" (vers. 8b, 9). That the disposition here reprobated is a very general and fruitful source of misery cannot be doubted. The proud spirit that refuses to submit to wrongs, either real or fancied, that is on the outlook for offence, that strives to redress on the instant the injury received, is rarely long without cause of irritation. If unprovoked by real and serious evils, it will find abundant material for disquietude in the minor crosses and irritations of daily life. While the patient spirit, that schools itself to submission, and yet waits in hope that in the providence of God the cause of pain and provocation will be removed, enjoys peace even in very trying circumstances. It is not that our author commends insensibility of feeling, and deprecates the sensitiveness of a generous nature, which is swift to resent cruelty and injustice. It is rather the ill-advised and morbid state of mind in which there is an unhealthy sensitiveness to affronts and a fruitless chafing against them that he reproves. That anger is in some circumstances a lawful passion no reasonable person can deny; but the Preacher points out two forms of it that are in themselves evil. The first is when anger is "hasty," not calm and deliberate, as the lawful expression of moral indignation, but the outcome of wounded self-love; and the second when it is detained too long, when it "rests" in the bosom. As a momentary, instinctive feeling excited by the sight of wickedness, it is lawful; but when it has a home in the heart it changes its character, and becomes malignant hatred or settled scornfulness. "Be ye angry, and sin not," says St. Paul; "let not the sun go down upon your wrath" (Eph. iv. 26, 27). "Wherefore, my beloved brethren," says St. James, "let every man be swift to hear, slow to speak, slow to wrath: for the wrath of man worketh not the righteousness of God" (i. 19, 20).

III. EVILS THAT ARE LARGELY IMAGINARY. "Say not thou, What is the cause that the former days were better than these? for thou dost not inquire wisely concerning this" (ver. 10). Discontentment with the present time and conditions is reproved in these words. It is often a weakness of age, as Horace has described it—

" Difficilis, querulus, laudator temporis acti
Se puero, censor castigatorque minorum."
('Ars Poet.,' 173, 174.)

But it is not by any means confined to the old. There are many who cast longing glances back upon the past, and think with admiration of the age of heroes or of the age of faith, in comparison with which the present is ignoble and worthless. It would be a somewhat harmless folly if it did not lead, as it generally does, to apathetic discontent with the present and despondency concerning the future. "Every age has its peculiar difficulties, and a man inclined to take a dark view of things will always be able to compare unfavourably the present with the past. But a readiness to make comparisons of that kind is no sign of real wisdom. There is light as well as darkness in every age. The young men that shouted for joy at the rebuilding of the temple acted more wisely than the old men who wept with a loud voice" (Ezra iii. 12, 13). And the question may still be asked—Were the old times really better than the present? Is it not a delusion to imagine they were? Are not we the heirs of the ages, to whom the experience of the past and all its attainments in knowledge and all its bright examples of virtue have descended as an endowment and an inspiration? The disposition, therefore, that makes the best of things as they are, instead of grumbling that they are not better, that bears patiently even with very great annoyances, and that is characterized by self-control, is sure to escape a great deal of the misery which falls to the lot of a passionate, irritable, and discontented man (cf. Ps. xxxvii.).—J. W.

Vers. 11, 12.—*Wisdom and riches.* The precise meaning of ver. 11 is rather difficult to catch. The Hebrew words can be translated either as, "Wisdom is good with an inheritance" (Authorized Version), or, "Wisdom is good as an inheritance" (Revised Version); and it is instructive to notice that the earlier English version has in the margin the translation which the Revisers have put in the text, and that the Revisers have put in the margin the earlier rendering, as possibly correct. Both companies of translators are equally in doubt in the matter. It is a case, therefore, in which one must use one's individual judgment, and decide as to which rendering is to be preferred from the general sense of the whole passage. Our author, then, is speaking of two things which are profitable in life—" for them that see the sun " (ver. 11)—wisdom and riches; and as he gives the preference to the former in ver. 12—" the excellency of knowledge is that wisdom preserveth the life of him that hath it "—we are inclined to think that that is his view all through. And, therefore, though in themselves the translations given of the first clause in the passage are about equally balanced, this consideration is in our opinion weighty enough to turn the scale in favour of that in the Revised Version. Two things, therefore, there are which in different ways provide means of security against some of the ills of life, which afford some " compensation for the misery " of our condition—wisdom and riches. By wisdom a man may to some extent forecast the future, anticipate the coming storm, and take measures for shielding himself against some or all of the evils it brings in its train. Like the unjust steward who acted " wisely," he can win friends who will receive him in the hour of need. By riches, too, he can stave off many of the hardships which the poor man is compelled to endure ; he can secure many benefits which will alleviate the sufferings he cannot avert. But of the two wisdom is the more excellent; " it giveth life " (or " bestoweth life," Revised Version) " to them that have it." " It can quicken a life within; it can give salt and savour to that which wealth may only deaden and make insipid " (Bradley). And surely by " wisdom " here we are not to understand mere prudence, but rather that Heaven-born faculty, that control of man's spirit by a higher power, which leads him to make the fear of God the guide of his conduct. And in order to understand wherein it consists, and what are the benefits it secures, we may identify the quality here praised with " that wisdom that cometh from above," which all through the Word of God is described as the source of all excellence, the fountain of all happiness (Prov. iii. 13—18 ; iv. 13 ; viii. 32—36 ; John vi. 63 ; xvii. 3 ; 2 Cor. iii. 6). —J. W.

Vers. 13, 14.—*Resignation to Providence.* Already in the tenth verse the Preacher has counselled his readers not to chafe against the conditions in which they find themselves. " Say not thou, What is the cause that the former days were better than these ? " It is part of the true wisdom which he has praised " to consider the work of God," to accept the outward events of life, and believe that, whether they be pleasant or the contrary, they are determined by a will or power which we cannot control or change. It is wise to submit. The crooked we cannot make straight (ch. i. 15) ; the cross which is laid upon us we cannot shake off, and had best bear without repining (cf. Job viii. 3 ; xxxiv. 12 ; Ps. cxlvi. 9). A mingled draught is in the cup of life— prosperity and adversity, the sweet and the bitter. Remember that it is commended to your lips by a higher hand, which it is folly to resist; accept the portion which may be assigned to you. In the time of prosperity be in good spirits (ver. 14), let not forebodings of future evil damp the present enjoyment ; in the time of adversity consider that it is God who has appointed the evil day as well as the good. The thought is the same as that in the Book of Job, " What ? shall we receive good at the hands of God, and shall we not receive evil ? " (ii. 10). The reason why both good and evil are appointed us is given by the Preacher, though his words are somewhat obscure : " God also hath even made the one side by side with the other, to the end that man should not find out anything that shall be after him " (ver. 14b, Revised Version). The obscurity is in the thought rather than in the phrases used. The commonest explanation of the words is that they simply assert that to know the future is forbidden us. But the phrase, " after him," is always used to mean that which follows upon the present world (ch. iii. 22 ; vi. 12 ; Job xxi. 21). Hitzig explains the words as implying, " that because God wills it that man shall be rid of all things after his death, he puts evil into the period of his life, and lets it alternate with good, instead of visiting him therewith after his death." This explanation would make the passage equivalent to, *Idcirco ut non inveniat homo post se quidquam, scil. quod non expertus est.* But probably the best explanation of these words is that given by Delitzsch, who accepts this of Hitzig's with some modification : " What is meant is much rather this, that God causes man to experience good and evil, that he may pass through the whole school of life, and when he departs hence that nothing may be outstanding which he has not experienced." This interpretation of the various events of life, joyous and sombre, as forming a complete disciplinary course, through which it is an advantage for us to pass, is the most worthy of the explanations of the words that they have received. And if we accept it as truly representing the author's thoughts, we may say that our author's researches were not so fruitless as he himself seems sometimes to assert. This recognition of a Divine purpose running through all the events of life is calculated to sanctify our enjoyment of the blessings we receive, and to comfort and sustain us in the day of sorrow and adversity.—J. W.

Vers. 15—18.—*Righteousness and wickedness.* This section is one of the most difficult in the whole Book of Ecclesiastes, though there are no various readings in it to perplex us, and no difficulty in translating it. Neither the Authorized Version nor the Revised Version has alternative renderings of any part of it in the margin. The difficulty lies in the uncertainty in which we are as to the writer's standpoint in making out what form of religious life or what phase of thought or conduct he refers to when he says, "Be not righteous overmuch." It is equally humiliating to attempt to explain his words away—to read into them a higher meaning than they evidently bear, or to confess regretfully that we have here a cynical and low-toned depreciation of that which is in itself holy and good. Both courses have been followed by commentators, and both do dishonour to the sacred text.

I. In the first place, the Preacher states in plain terms THE GREAT AND PERPLEXING PROBLEM WHICH SO OFTEN TROUBLED THE HEBREW MIND—that of the adversity of the righteous and the prosperity of the wicked. In his experience of life, in the days of his vanity, in the course of his troubled pilgrimage, he had seen this sight: "There is a just man that perisheth in his righteousness"—in spite of his righteousness; "and there is a wicked man that prolongeth his life in his wickedness"—in spite of his wickedness (ver. 15). It is the same problem of which varying solutions are attempted in the Book of Job and in the thirty-seventh and seventy-third psalms. The old theory, that the good find their reward and the wicked their punishment in this life, was not borne out by his experience. He had seen it violated so often that he could not hold it as even an approximate statement of the facts of the case. What, then, is his inference from his own experience? Does he say, "Cleave to righteousness in spite of the misfortunes which often attend it?" or, "Believe that somehow and somewhere the apparent inequalities of the present will ultimately be redressed, and both righteousness and wickedness will meet with the rewards and punishments they merit"? No; whether he might acquiesce in one or other of these inferences or not, we cannot tell. Other thoughts are in his mind. A third inference he draws, which would not naturally have occurred to us, but which is as legitimate as ours.

II. FROM HIS EXPERIENCE HE DEDUCES THE LESSON: "Be not righteous overmuch; neither make thyself overwise: why shouldest thou destroy thyself? Be not overmuch wicked, neither be thou foolish: why shouldest thou die before thy time?" Neither the righteous nor the wicked being able to count upon reward for goodness or punishment for evil in this life as certain, both are exposed to certain risks—the one is tempted to adopt an exaggerated and feverish form of religious life, the other to enter on a course of unbridled wickedness. That there is a tendency to exaggeration in matters of religion is abundantly proved by the history of asceticism, which has made its appearance in every religion, true or spurious. The ascetic is the man who is "righteous overmuch." He denies himself all pleasures through the fear of sin; he separates himself, not merely from vicious indulgences, but from occupations and amusements which he admits are innocent enough and lawful enough for those who have not the end in view he has set before himself. He is not content with the good works commanded by the Law of God; he must have his works of supererogation. The Pharisee in the parable (Luke xviii. 9—14) is a typical person of this class. He claimed merit for going beyond the requirements of the Law. Moses appointed but one fast-day in the year, the great Day of Atonement; *he* boasted that he fasted twice in the week. The Law commanded only to tithe the fruits of the field and increase of the cattle; but he no doubt tithed mint and cummin, *all* that came into his possession, down to the veriest trifles. And the aim is in all cases the same—the accumulation of a store of merit which will compel a reward if God is not to show himself unjust; an attempt to force from his hand a benediction which others cannot claim who have not adopted the same course. The folly and impiety of such conduct must be apparent to any well-balanced mind. The blessing of Heaven is not to be extorted by any attempt we may make; it may, so far at any rate as outward appearances go, be bestowed capriciously : "The just man may perish in his righteousness, the wicked man may prolong his life in his wickedness." On the other hand, the fact that punishment for sin is not inevitably and invariably visited immediately upon the evil-doer is undoubtedly the source of danger to those who are inclined to vice. The fact that justice is slow and lame tempts the sinner to an unbridled course of evil; it removes one great restraint upon his conduct. He trusts to the lightness of his heels to escape from punishment until he runs into the arms of death. Some have been as shocked at the counsel, "Be not overmuch wicked," as at that "Be not righteous overmuch," as though the writer allowed that a certain moderate degree of wickedness were permissible. They should, if they are logical, be equally horrified at the admonition of St. James, " Wherefore lay apart all filthiness and *superfluity of naughtiness*" (i. 21). It is in both cases a prohibition of a headlong pursuit of sin, without regard to the fearful consequences it entails. The Preacher has in view the consequences in the present life of being "righteous overmuch." The result in both instances is pretty much the same. To the one he says, " Why shouldest thou destroy thyself?"—to the other, " Why shouldest thou die before thy time ?" Both classes lose the pleasure of living, the bright, innocent joys which spring from a grateful acceptance and temperate use of the blessings which God bestows upon men. The ascetic who makes it his aim to torture himself to the very limit of human endurance, and the debauchee who gives himself up to self-indulgence without restraint, each receive, though in different ways, the penalty due for violating the conditions of life in which God has set us. Another warning is given in the same passage against intellectual errors. "Neither make thyself overwise ; neither be thou foolish." Wisdom, too, has limits within which it should be confined. There is a region of the unknowable into which it is presumptuous for it to attempt to intrude. " Fools rush in where angels fear to tread."

III. The Preacher, in conclusion, points out that A MIDDLE COURSE IS THAT OF DUTY AND OF SAFETY. There are dangers on the right hand and on the left, of over-rigorous austerity and of undue laxity. But the God-fearing are able to walk in the narrow path, and emerge at last unscathed from all the temptations with which life is surrounded. " It is good that thou shouldest take hold of this; yea, also from that withdraw not thine hand, for he that feareth God shall come forth of them all." The words " this " and " that " refer to the two different precepts he has given. " Lay thine hand it is good to do so," he says, " on the one precept, ' Be not righteous overmuch ; ' but do not lose sight of the other, ' Be not overmuch wicked.' It is he that feareth God that shall steer his way between both."

Without, therefore, distorting the words of the Preacher to give them a more spiritual meaning or higher tone than they actually possess, we find in them teaching which is worthy of him and of the Word of God. It is remarkable indeed, how, even in his most desponding moods, the fear of God bulks largely in his thoughts as incumbent on men, and as opening up the path of duty, however much else remains dark and unknown. " In his coldest, grayest hour this sense of the fear of God still smoulders, as it were, within his soul ; not, indeed, the quickening love of God, but something that inspires reverence; something that saves him from utter shipwreck amidst the crossing and eddying currents of the sunless sea of hopeless pessimism " (Bradley).—J. W.

Vers. 19—22.— *Wisdom a protection.* The connection between these words and those that precede them seems somewhat loose. But the Preacher has just been speaking of " the fear of God," and some one of those passages of Scripture, which assert that in it is true wisdom (Prov. i. 7; Ps. cxi. 10; Job xxviii. 28), may have been in his mind. He now speaks of the protection and strength which wisdom gives, and of the sort of conduct becoming those who possess it (ver. 19). " Wisdom strengtheneth the wise man more than ten mighty men which are in the city." Why *ten* mighty men are spoken of is a question difficult to answer. It may be that "ten" is meant to suggest "a full number " (cf. Gen. xxxi. 7; Job xix. 3), or perhaps we have here an allusion to some political or other arrangements of the time now unknown to us. But the evident meaning of the verse is that the wisdom that fears God is better than material force, that in it there is a ground of confidence better than weapons of war (cf. Prov. xxiv. 5a, "A wise man is strong"). In the words that follow we have man's fallibility strongly insisted on in words quoted from the prayer of Solomon at the dedication of the temple (1 Kings viii. 46), "For there is not a just man upon earth that doeth good and sinneth not," and the inference seems to be that "the wisest at times commit mistakes, but their wisdom enables them to get the better of their mistakes, and protects them against the evil consequences which happen in such cases to the unwise." This thought leads on to the teaching of vers. 21, 22. The wise man who remembers his own mistakes and offences will judge leniently of others, and not punish them as offenders for their occasional hasty words. Indifference to idle praise or idle blame becomes the possessor of true wisdom. For him, to use St. Paul's words, "It is a very small thing to be judged of man's judgment" (1 Cor. iv. 3). An idle curiosity to know what others think of us or say of us is the source of constant mortification. We expect praise, and forget that others are as frivolous and hasty in their criticism of us as we have been in our criticism of them. The servant who waits on us, and from whom we expect special reverence, would probably, if we could hear him without his knowledge, say much about us that would surprise and mortify us. Let us therefore not be too eager to hear our character analyzed and discussed.

> "Where ignorance is bliss,
> 'Tis folly to be wise."

Some excuse may be found for the motto of the old Scottish family which expresses this indifference to the opinion of others in the most pointed form : "They say. What say they? Let them say."—J. W.

Vers. 23—29.—*Woman*. The limitations of human knowledge are nowhere more plainly indicated than in the opening verse of the present section. The Preacher points out that after his utmost endeavours to obtain wisdom with the view of solving the perplexing questions connected with mankind, their actions and their relation to God, he found all such knowledge to be far beyond mortal ken (Wright). "For that which is," that which exists, the world of things in its essence and with its causes, "is far off," far removed from the sight of man, "and it is deep, deep ; who can discover it?" (vers. 23, 24). Essential wisdom appeared to him as to Job (xxviii.), quite out of reach. But all his efforts after it had not been in vain. In the course of his researches he had discovered some truth of great value. Though the problems of the universe proved to be insoluble, some lessons had been learned of practical value in the conduct of life. Some rules for present guidance he had discovered, though much remained hidden from him. So is it in every age. The sagest philosophers, the profoundest thinkers, are baffled in their endeavours to explain the mysteries of life, but are able to lay down rules for present conduct which approve themselves to the consciences of all. And happy is it for us that it should be so; that while clouds hang over many regions into which the intellect of man would fain penetrate, the way of duty is plain for all. One great truth he learned, that wickedness was folly, that foolishness was madness, that men who lived in the pursuit of folly were beside themselves and were mad (ver. 25). This thought is very closely akin to the teaching of the Stoics, that the wickedness of men is a kind of mental aberration, and that knowledge is but another name for righteousness. One great source of wickedness he introduces in ver. 26—the fatal fascination of so many by scheming and voluptuous women. The picture he draws is like those in Prov. ii. and vii., and, but for the more sweeping condemnation in the verses that follow, might be thought to express reprobation of a certain degraded class rather than a cynical estimate of the whole of womankind. One man, he says, he had found among a thousand, one only what a man ought to be; but not one woman among the same number who corresponded to the ideal of womanhood, who reminded him of the innocence and goodness of Eve as God created her (ver. 29). The race, both men and women, had been created upright, but had become almost utterly corrupt by the devices they had invented by which to gratify their inclinations toward evil. What are we to make of his words? Is the case really as bad as he represents it? The answer to the question is not far to seek. The Preacher is recording his own experience, and if we take his words as a truthful report, we can only say that he was specially unfortunate in his experience. There is no doubt that in some countries and in some ages of the world, corruption is very widespread and deep, and in the land and time in which our author lived matters may have been as bad as he represents them. But the experience of a single life does not afford sufficient ground for broad generalizations concerning human nature. The words may be an expression of that terrible feeling of satiety and loathing which is the curse following upon gross sensuality such as that of the historical Solomon, with his three hundred wives and seven hundred concubines. No sensible person would take the moralizings of the satiated debauchee without very considerable deductions. Those of a chaste, temperate, God-fearing man are much more likely to hit the truth. We may grant that search had been made, and not one woman among the thousand whose dispositions and characters had been passed in review approved herself worthy of praise as like what a true woman should be, and still doubt whether the thousand were fair representatives of their sex. Did he search in the right quarter? or were the women the population of his seraglio? If they were, we cannot wonder that, in an institution which is itself an outrage upon human nature, all its inhabitants were found corrupt. For a very different estimate of the female character as exemplified in some of its representatives, we have only to read the praises of the Shulamite in the Song of Songs, and of the virtuous women described in Prov. v. 18, 19; xxxi. 10—31. And Scripture itself is rich in the histories of good women. There are those of patriarchal times whose tender grace gives such an idyllic charm to so many incidents of that early age. The names of Sarah, Rebekah, and Rachel call up ideas of purity, innocence, piety, and steadfast love, as a rich inheritance they have left to the race. Miriam, Hannah, Ruth, and Esther, too, suggest a world of goodness and holiness which was quite unknown to the experience of the writer of these dark and sombre words in Ecclesiastes. Then in the New Testament we have the luminous figures of the Virgin-mother, the Prophetess Anna, the devout women who ministered to Christ and stood by his cross, and were early in the morning at his sepulchre, and were the first to believe in him as their risen Lord. There are those in the long list recorded in the Epistles of St. Paul, who were zealous fellow-labourers with him in all good works, who, by their deeds of hospitality, their kindly ministrations to the poor and sick and bereaved, reproved the wickedness of the world in which they lived, and gave promise of the rich harvest of goodness which would spring from the holy teaching and example of the Redeemer. And in no Christian country have abundant examples been wanting of the pure and devoted love by which mothers and wives and sisters have enriched and blessed the lives of those connected with them, and redeemed their sex from the stigma cast upon it by gross-minded and corrupt men. No persecutions have ever wasted any section of the Christian Church without finding among women as true and steadfast witnesses for the cause of Christ as among men.

> " A noble army—men and boys,
>   The matron and the maid,
> Around the Saviour's throne rejoice,
>   In robes of light array'd.
> They climb'd the steep ascent of heaven
>   Through peril, toil, and pain;
> O God, to us may grace be given
>   To follow in their train!"

J. W.

EXPOSITION.

CHAPTER VIII.

Vers. 1—9.—Section 5. There is no use in repining or rebelling; *true wisdom counsels obedience to the powers that be, and submission to the dispensations of Providence.* However oppressive a tyrant may prove sure retribution awaits him.

Ver. 1.—**Who** is as the wise man? *i.e.* Who is like, equal to, the wise man? The somewhat sudden question occurs naturally after the results of the search for wisdom mentioned at the end of the last chapter. The thought is not, as in Hos. xiv. 9 and Jer. ix. 12, "Who is wise?" but—No one can be compared with a wise man; he has no compeer. **And who** [like him] **knoweth the interpretation of a thing?** Who, so well as the wise man, understands the proper relation of circumstances, sees into human affairs and God's dispensations in the case of nations and individuals? Such a one takes the right view of life. The word *pesher,* "interpretation," occurs (*peshar*) continually in Daniel, and nowhere else. and is Chaldaic. The Vulgate, which connects these two clauses with ch. vii., renders, *Quis cognovit solutionem verbi?* So the Septuagint. The "word" or "saying" may be the question proposed above concerning the happy life, or the proverb that immediately follows. But *dabar* is better rendered "thing," as ch. i. 8; vii. 8. **A man's wisdom maketh his face to shine;** Septuagint, φωτιεῖ, "will enlighten, illuminate." The serene light within makes itself visible in the outward expression; the man is contented and cheerful, and shows this in his look and bearing. This is an additional praise of wisdom. Thus Ecclus. xiii. 25, 26, "The heart of man changeth his countenance, whether it be for good or evil. A cheerful countenance is a token of a heart that is in prosperity." Cicero, 'De Orat.,' iii. 57, "Omnes enim motus animi suum quemdam a natura habet vultum et sonum et gestum; corpusque totum hominis et ejus omnis vultus omnesque voces, ut nervi in fidibus, ita sonant, ut motu animi quoque sunt pulsæ." **And the boldness of his face shall be changed.** The word translated "boldness" is ʼỳ, which means properly "strength," and is best taken of the coarseness and impudence engendered by ignorance and want of culture. Wisdom, when it fills the heart, changes the countenance to an open genial look, which wins confidence and love. Delitzsch refers to the well-worn lines of Ovid, 'Epist.,' ii. 9. 47—

"Adde, quod ingenuas didicisse fideliter artes
Emollit mores, nec sinit esse feros."

The Septuagint, "And a man shameless in countenance will be hated," shows an alteration in the text, and does not agree with the context. Vulgate, *Et potentissimus faciem illius commutabit,* "And the Almighty will change his face," where again the text is not accurately followed.

Ver. 2.—**I counsel thee to keep the king's commandment.** The pronoun *I* stands in the Hebrew without a verb (the Vulgate, *Ego os regis observo,* is not warranted by the grammar of the clause), and some take it as the answer to the question in ver. 1, "Who is like the wise man?" I, who am now teaching you. But it is better to regard the pronoun as emphasizing the following rule, supplying some verb (which may possibly have dropped out of the text), as, "Say, advise—I, for my part, whatever others may do or advise, I counsel thee;" the injunction being given in the imperative mood. The Septuagint and Syriac omit the pronoun altogether. The warning implies that the writer was living under kingly, and indeed despotic, government, and it was the part of a wise man to exhibit cheerful obedience. Ben-Sira observes that wise men teach us how to serve great men (Ecclus. viii 8). Such conduct is not only prudent, but really a religious duty, even as the prophets counsel submission to Assyrian and Chaldean rulers (see Jer. xxvii. 12; xxix. 7; Ezek. xvii. 15). The liege lord, being God's vicegerent, must be reverenced and obeyed. St. Paul, though he does not quote Ecclesiastes, may have had this passage in mind when he wrote (Rom. xiii. 1), "Let every soul be subject unto the higher powers. For there is no power but of God: the powers that be are ordained of God," etc.; and (ver. 5), "Ye must needs be subject, not only for wrath, but also for conscience' sake." The "king" in the text is understood by some to mean God, but the following clause renders this improbable, and it is wisdom in its political aspect that is here regarded. **And that in regard of the oath of God.** The *vav* is explicative; "in regard of," or "because of," as ch. iii. 18. "The oath of God" is the oath of allegiance to the king, taken in the name of God, under his invocation (comp. Exod. xxii. 11; 1 Kings ii. 43). So we read (2 Kings xi. 17) of a covenant between king and people, and people and king, in the time of Jehoiada; Nebuchadnezzar made Zedekiah swear by God to be his vassal (2 Chron. xxxvi. 13); and Josephus ('Ant.,' xii. 1; xi. 8. 3) relates that Ptolemy Soter, son of Lagus (following herein the example of Darius), exacted an oath from the Jews in Egypt to be true to him and his successors. We know that both Babylonian and Persian monarchs exacted an oath of fealty from conquered nations, making them swear by the gods whom they worshipped, the selection of deities being left to them.

Ver. 3.—Further advice concerning political behaviour. **Be not hasty to go out of his** (the king's) **sight.** Do not, from some hasty impulse, or induced by harsh treatment, cast off your allegiance to your liege lord. We have the phrase, "go away," in the sense of quitting of service or desertion of a duty, in Gen. iv. 16; Hos. xi. 2. So St. Peter urges servants to be subject unto their masters, "not only to the good and gentle, but also to the froward" (1 Pet. ii. 18). Solomon might have given this advice to the Israelites who were ready to follow Jeroboam's lead; though they could have remained loyal to Rehoboam only fro... high religious motives. But it is better to bear even a heavy yoke than to rebel. The Septuagint has, " Be not hasty; thou shalt go from his presence "—which seems to mean, " Be not impatient, and all will be well." But the authorized rendering is correct (comp. ch. x. 4). We may quote Mendelssohn's comment cited by Chance on Job xxxiv. 16, " This is a great rule in politics, that the people must have no power to pronounce judgment upon the conduct of a king, whether it be good or bad; for the king judges the people, and not the reverse; and if it were not for this rule, the country would never be quiet, and without rebels against the king and his law." **Stand not in an evil thing**; Vulgate, _Neque permaneas in opere malo_, " Persist not in an evil affair." But the verb here implies rather the engaging in a matter than continuing an undertaking already begun. The " affair " is conspiracy, insurrection; and Koheleth warns against entering upon and taking part in any such attempt. This seems to be the correct explanation of the clause; but it is, perhaps intentionally, ambiguous, and is capable of other interpretations. Thus Ginsburg, "Do not stand up (in a passion) because of an evil word." Others, "Obey not a sinful command," or " Hesitate not at an evil thing," _i.e._ if the king orders it. Wordsworth, referring to Ps. i. 1. renders, " Stand not in the way of sinners," which seems to be unsuitable to the context. The Septuagint gives, "Stand not in an evil word " (λόγῳ, perhaps " matter "). The reason for the injunction follows. **For he doeth whatsoever pleaseth him.** The irresponsible power of a despotic monarch is here signified, though the terms are applicable (as some, indeed, take them as alone appertaining) to God himself (but see Prov. xx. 2). The Septuagint combines with this clause the commencement of the following verse, " For he will do whatsover he pleases, even as a king using authority _(ἐξουσιάζων)._" Some manuscripts add λαλεῖ, " he speaks."

Ver. 4.—**Where the word of a king is, there is power.** A further confirmation of the last thought. More accurately, " Inasmuch as the word of a king is powerful" _(shilton,_ ver. 8). This last word is used in Daniel (iii. 2) for " a lord," or " ruler." The king does as he thinks fit because his mandate is all-powerful, and must be obeyed. **And who may say unto him, What doest thou?** The same expression is found applied to God (Job ix. 12; Isa. xlv. 9; Wisd. xii. 12). The absolute authority of a despot is

spoken of in the same terms as the irresistible power of Almighty God.

Εἰκὼν δὲ βασιλεύς ἐστιν ἔμψυχος Θεοῦ.

" God's living image is an earthly king."

Ver. 5.—**Whoso keepeth the commandment shall feel no evil thing.** This is an encouragement to obedience to royal authority (comp. Prov. xxiv. 21, 22; Rom. xiii. 3). The context plainly shows that it is not God's commandment that is spoken of (though, of course, the maxim would be very true in this case), but the king's. Nor is it necessarily a servile and unreasoning obedience that is enjoined. Koheleth is dealing with generals. Such cases as that of Daniel and the three children, where obedience would have been sinful, are not here taken into consideration. "Shall feel," literally, " shall know," _i.e._ experience no physical evil. Quiet submission to the powers that be guarantees a peaceful and happy life. Ginsburg and others translate, " knoweth not an evil word," _i.e._ is saved from abuse and reproach, which seems somewhat meagre, though the Septuagint gives, Οὐ γνώσεται ῥῆμα πονηρόν. The Vulgate is better, _Non experietur quidquam mali._ **And a wise man's heart discerneth** (_knoweth_) **both time and judgment.** The verb is the same in both clauses, and ought to have been so translated. The " heart " includes the moral as well as the intellectual faculties; and the maxim says that the wise man bears oppression and remains unexcited even in evil days, because he is convinced that there is a time of judgment coming when all will be righted (ch. xii. 14). The certainty of retributive justice is so strong in his mind that he does not resort to rebellion in order to rectify matters, but possesses his soul in patience, leaving the correction of abuses in God's hands. Septuagint, "The wise man's heart knoweth the time of judgment," making a hendiadys of the two terms. The Vulgate has _tempus et responsionem,_ " time and answer."

Ver. 6.—**Because.** This and the three following clauses all begin with _ki,_ " since," " for," and the conjunction ought to have been similarly rendered in all the places. Thus here, _For_ **to every purpose there is time and judgment.** Here commences a chain of argument to prove the wisdom of keeping quiet under oppression or evil rulers. Everything has its appointed time of duration, and in due course will be brought to judgment (see ch. iii. 1, 17; xii. 14). **Therefore** (_for_) **the misery of man is great upon him.** This is a further reason, but its exact signification is disputed. Literally, _the evil of the man is heavy upon him_ (comp. ch. vi. 1). This may mean, as in the Authorized Version, that the affliction which subjects suffer at the hand of a tyrant becomes insupportable, and calls for and receives God's interposition. Or "the evil" may be the wickedness of the despot, which presses heavily upon him, and under retributive justice will ere long bring him to the ground, and so the oppression will come to an end. This seems to be the most natural interpretation of the passage. The Septuagint, reading differently, has, "For the knowledge of a man is great upon him." Though what this means it is difficult to say.

Ver. 7.—**For he knoweth not that which shall be.** The subject may be man in general, or more probably the evil tyrant. The clause contains a third reason for patience. The despot cannot foresee the future, and goes on blindly filling up the measure of his iniquity, being unable to take any precautions against his inevitable fate (Prov. xxiv. 22). *Quem Deus vult perdere prius dementat.* **For who can tell him when it shall be?** rather, *how it shall be.* The fourth portion of the argument. The infatuated man knows not the time when the blow will fall, nor, as here, the manner in which the retribution will come, the form which it will take. Septuagint, "For how it shall be, who will tell him?" The Vulgate paraphrases inaccurately, *Quia ignorat præterita, et futura nullo scire potest nuntio,* "Because he knoweth not the past, and the future he can ascertain by no messenger."

Ver. 8.—This verse gives the conclusion of the line of argument which confirms the last clause of ver. 5. **There is no man that hath power over the spirit to retain the spirit.** If we take "spirit" in the sense of "the breath of life," explaining the clause to mean that the mightiest despot has no power to retain life when his call comes, we have the same thought repeated virtually in the next clause. It is therefore better to take *ruach* in the sense of "wind" (Gen. viii. 1). No one can control the course of the wind or know its way (comp. ch. xi. 5, where the same ambiguity exists; Prov. xxx. 4). Koheleth gives here four impossibilities which point to the conclusion already given. The first is man's inability to check the viewless wind or to know whence it comes or whither it goes (John iii. 8). Equally impotent is the tyrant to influence the drift of events that is bearing him on to his end. God's judgments are often likened to a wind (see Isa. xli. 16; Wisd. iv. 4; v. 23). **Neither hath he power in the day of death;** rather, *over the day of death.* The second impossibility concerns the averting the hour of death. Whether it comes by sickness, or accident, or design, the despot must succumb; he can neither foresee nor ward it off (1 Sam. xxvi. 10, "The Lord shall smite him; or his day shall come to die; or he shall go down into

battle, and perish;" Ecclus. xiv. 12, "Remember that death will not be long in coming, and that the covenant of the grave is not showed unto thee"). **And there is no discharge in that war.** The word rendered "discharge" (*mishlachath*) is found elsewhere only in Ps. lxxviii. 49, where it is translated "sending," "mission," or "band." The Septuagint here has ἀποστολή; the Vulgate *Nec sinitur quiescere ingruente bello.* The Authorized Version is doubtless correct, though there is no need to insert the pronoun "that." The severity of the law of military service is considered analogously with the inexorable law of death. The Hebrew enactment (Deut. xx. 5—8) allowed exemption in certain cases; but the Persian rule was inflexibly rigid, permitting no furlough or evasion during an expedition. Thus we read that when Œobazus, the father of three sons, petitioned Darius to leave him one at home, the tyrant replied that he would leave him all three, and had them put to death. Again, Pythius, a Lydian, asking Xerxes to exempt his eldest son from accompanying the army to Greece, was reviled by the monarch in unmeasured terms, and was punished for his presumption by seeing his son slain before his eyes, the body divided into two pieces, and placed on either side of the road by which the army passed, that all might be warned of the fate awaiting any attempt to evade military service (Herod., iv. 84; vii. 38). The passage in the text has a bearing on the authorship and date of our book, if, as seems most probable, the reference is to the cruel discipline of Persia. This is the third impossibility; the fourth follows. **Neither shall wickedness deliver those that are given to it;** its lord and master. Septuagint, τὸν παρ' αὐτῆς, "its votary." Ginsburg translates *resha* "cunning;" but this seems foreign to the sentiment, which is concerned with the despot's impiety, injustice, and general wickedness, not with the means by which he endeavours to escape the reward of his deeds. The fact is, no evil despot, however reckless and imperious, can go long unpunished. He may say in his heart, "There is no God," or, "God hideth his face, and sees him not," but certain retribution awaits him, and may not be avoided. Says the gnome—

Ἄγει τὸ θεῖον τοὺς κακοὺς πρὸς τὴν δίκην.

"Heaven drives the evil always unto judgment."

Ver. 9.—**All this have I seen** (ch. v. 18; vii. 23); *i.e.* all that has been mentioned in the preceding eight verses, especially the conviction of retributive justice. He gained this experience by giving his mind to the consideration of men's actions. There is **a** time wherein one man ruleth over another to his own hurt. This version is certainly incorrect. A new sentence is not commenced here, but the clause is closely connected with what precedes ; and " his own hurt " should be " his [equivocally] hurt." Thus Wright and Volck : " All this have I seen, even by applying my heart to all the work that is done under the sun, at a time when man ruleth over man to his hurt." Most modern commentators consider that the hurt is that of the oppressed subject ; but it is possible that the sense is intentionally ambiguous, and the injury may be that which the despot inflicts, and that which he has to suffer. Both these have been signified above. There is no valid reason for making, as Cox does, this last clause commence ver. 10, and rendering, " But there is a time when a man ruleth over men to their hurt."

Vers. 10—15.—Section 6. Koheleth is troubled by apparent anomalies in God's moral government. He notes *the prosperity of the godless and the misery of the righteous*, God's abstention and the seeming impunity of sinners make men incredulous of Providence ; but God is just in reward and punishment, as the end will prove. Meantime, returning to his old maxim, he advises men patiently to acquiesce in things as they are, and to make the best of life.

Ver. 10.—**And so** (וּבְכֵן) ; then, in like manner, under the same circumstances (Esth. iv. 16). The writer notes some apparent exceptions to the law of retribution of which he has just been speaking, the double particle at the beginning of the verse implying the connection with the preceding statement. **I saw the wicked buried.** " The wicked " are especially the despots (ver. 9). These are carried to their graves with every outward honour and respect, like the rich man in the parable, who "died, and was buried " (Luke xvi. 22). Such men, if they had received their due reward, far from having a pompous and magnificent funeral (which would befit only a good and honoured life), would have been buried with the burial of an ass (comp. Isa. xiv. 19 ; Jer. xxii. 19). So far the Authorized Version is undeniably correct. What follows is as certainly inaccurate as it is unintelligible. **Who had come and gone from the place of the holy;** literally, *and they came, and from the place of the holy they went.* The first verb seems to mean, " they came to their rest," they died a natural death. The words, in themselves ambiguous, are explained by the connection in which they stand (comp. Isa. lvii. 2). Wright renders, " they came into being," and explains it with the

following clause, " they went away from the holy place," as one generation coming and another going, in constant succession. But if, as we suppose, the paragraph applies to the despot, such an interpretation is unsuitable. Cox's idea, that oppressive despots " come again " in the persons of their wicked children, is wholly unsupported by the text. The verse admits and has received a dozen explanations differing more or less from one another. A good deal depends upon the manner in which the succeeding clause is translated, **And they were forgotten in the city where they had so done.** As the particle rendered " so " (*ken*) may also mean " well," " rightly," we get the rendering, " even such as acted justly," and thus introduce a contrast between the fate of the wicked man who is honoured with a sumptuous funeral, and that of the righteous whose name is cast out as pollution and soon forgotten. So Cheyne (' Job and Solomon ') gives, " And in accordance with this I have seen ungodly men honoured, and that too in the holy place (the temple, Isa. xviii. 7), but those who had acted rightly had to depart, and were forgotten in the city." Against this interpretation, which has been adopted by many, it may reasonably be urged that in the same verse *ken* would hardly be used in two different senses, and that there is nothing in the text to indicate a change of subject. It seems to me that the whole verse applies to the wicked man. He dies in peace, he leaves the holy place ; the evil that he has done is forgotten in the very city where he had so done, *i.e.* done wickedly. " The place of the holy " is Jerusalem (Isa. xlviii. 2 ; Matt. xxvii. 53) or the temple (Matt. xxiv. 15). He is removed by death from that spot, the very name of which ought to have cried shame on his crimes and impiety. The expression seems to picture a great procession of priests and Levites accompanying the corpse of the deceased tyrant to the place of burial, while the final clause implies that no long lamentation was made over him, no monument erected to his memory (see the opposite of this in the treatment of Josiah, 2 Chron. xxxv. 24, 25). They who consider " the righteous " to be the subject of the last clauses see in the words, " from the holy place they departed," an intimation that these were excommunicated from the synagogue or temple, or banished from the promised land, on account of their opinions. I would translate the passage thus : *In like manner have I seen the wicked buried, and they came to their rest, and they went from the holy place, and were forgotten in the city where they had so* (wickedly) *acted.* The versions have followed various readings. Thus the Septuagint : " And then I saw the impious brought unto graves, and from the holy place; and they departed and were praised in the city, because they had so done;" Vulgate, "I have seen the impious buried, who also, while they still lived, were in the holy place, and were praised in the city as if men of just doings." Commenting on this version, St. Gregory writes, "The very tranquillity of the peace of the Church conceals many under the Christian name who are beset with the plague of their own wickedness. But if a light breath of persecution strikes them, it sweeps them away at once as chaff from the threshing-floor. But some persons wish to bear the mark of Christian calling, because, since the name of Christ has been exalted on high, nearly all persons now look to appear faithful, and from seeing others called thus, they are ashamed not to seem faithful themselves; but they neglect to be that which they boast of being called. For they assume the reality of inward excellence, to adorn their outward appearance; and they who stand before the heavenly Judge, naked from the unbelief of their heart, are clothed, in the sight of men, with a holy profession, at least in words" ('Moral.,' xxv. 26). This is also vanity. The old refrain recurs to the writer as he thinks on the prosperity of the wicked, and the conclusions which infidels draw therefrom. Here is another example of the vanity that prevails in all earthly circumstances.

Ver. 11.—The verse states one of the results of God's forbearance in punishing the evil. **Because sentence against an evil work is not executed speedily.** The verse begins with *asher*, "because," as in ch. iv. 3; vi. 12, which connects the sentence with the allegation of vanity just preceding, as well as with what follows. *Pithgam*, "sentence," "edict," is a foreign word of Persian origin, found in Esth. i. 20 and in Chaldee portions of Ezra (iv. 17) and Daniel (iv. 14, etc.). God seems to us to delay in punishing the guilty because we behold only one little portion of the course of his providence; could we take a more comprehensive view, anomalies would disappear, and we should see the end of these men (Ps. lxxiii. 17). But a contracted, sceptical view leads to two evils—first, a weakening of faith in God's moral government; and second, a miserable fatalism which denies man's responsibility and saps his energy. Of the former of these results Koheleth here treats. **Therefore the heart of the sons of men.** The heart is named as the seat of thought and the prime mover of action (comp. ch. ix. 3; Esth. vii. 5; Matt. xv. 18, 19). **Is fully set in them to do evil;** literally, *is full in them;* i.e. their heart becomes filled with thoughts which are directed to evil, or full of courage, hence "emboldened" (Revised Version margin) to do evil. Vulgate,

absque timore ullo filii hominum perpetrant mala; Septuagint, "Because there is no contradiction (ἀντίρρησις) made on the part of (ἀπὸ) those who do evil speedily, therefore the heart of the sons of men is fully persuaded (ἐπληροφορήθη) in them to do evil." The long-suffering of God, instead of leading such men to repentance, hardens them in their infidelity (Ps. lxxiii. 11). Primarily, the reference is still to tyrannical despots, who, in their seeming impunity, are emboldened to pursue their evil course. But the statement is true generally. As Cicero says, "Quis ignorat maximam illecebram esse peccandi impunitatis spem?" ('Pro Milone,' xvi.).

Ver. 12.—**Though a sinner do evil a hundred times.** The sentence begins again, as ver. 11, with *asher*, followed by a participle; and the conjunction ought to be rendered "because," the statement made in the former verse being resumed and strengthened. The Vulgate has *attamen*, which our version follows. The Septuagint goes astray, translating, ὃς ἥμαρτεν, "He that has sinned has done evil from that time." The sinner is here supposed to have transgressed continually without check or punishment. The expression, "a hundred times," is used indefinitely, as Prov. xvii. 10; Isa. lxv. 20. **And his days be prolonged;** better, *prolongeth his days for it;* i.e. in the practice of evil, with a kind of contentment and satisfaction, the pronoun *lo* being the ethic dative. Contrary to the usual course of temporal retribution, the sinner often lives to old age. The Vulgate has, *Et per patientiam sustentatur,* which signifies that he is kept in life by God's long-suffering. Ginsburg gives, "and is perpetuated," *i.e.* in his progeny—which is a possible, but not a probable, rendering. **Yet surely I know;** rather, *though I for my part know.* He has seen sinners prosper; this experience has been forced upon him; yet he holds an inward conviction that God's moral government will vindicate itself at some time and in some signal manner. **It shall be well with them that fear God, which fear before him.** This is not really tautological; it is compared to St. Paul's expression (1 Tim. v. 3), "widows that are widows indeed" (ὄντως), implying that they are, in fact and life, what they profess to be. Delitzsch and Plumptre suggest that in Koheleth's time "God-fearers" had become the name of a religious class, as the *Chasidim,* or "Assideans," in 1 Macc. ii. 42; vii. 13, etc. Certainly a trace of this so-named party is seen in Ps. cxviii. 4; Mal. iii. 16. *When* this adjustment of anomalies shall take place, whether in this life or in another, the writer says not here. In spite of all contrary appearances, he holds firm to his faith that it will be well with the righteous in the long run. The comfort and peace of a conscience at rest, and the inward feeling that his life was ordered after God's will, would compensate a good man for much outward trouble; and if to this was added the assured hope of another life, it might indeed be said that it was well with him. The Septuagint has, "that they may fear before him," which implies that the mercy and loving-kindness of God, manifested in his care of the righteous, lead to piety and true religion. Cheyne ('Job and Solomon'), combining this verse with the next, produces a sense which is certainly not in the present Hebrew text, "For I know that it ever happens that a sinner does evil for a long time, and yet lives long, whilst he who fears before God is short-lived as a shadow."

Ver. 13.—**But it shall not be well with the wicked.** If experience seemed often to militate against this assertion, Koheleth's faith prevailed against apparent contradictions. **Neither shall he prolong his days, which are as a shadow.** Above we read of a wicked man enjoying a long, untroubled life; here the contrary is stated. Such contradictions are seen every day. There are inscrutable reasons for the delay of judgment; but on the whole moral government is vindicated, and even the long life of a sinner is no blessing. The author of the Book of Wisdom writes (iv. 8), "Honourable age is not that which standeth in length of time, nor that which is measured by number of years;" and Isaiah (lxv. 20), "The sinner being an hundred years old shall be accursed." Man's life is compared to a shadow because it passes away with the setting sun (see on ch. vi. 12). The Vulgate, in order to obviate the apparent discrepancy between this and the preceding verses, renders the verb in a precatory form: *Non sit bonum impio*, etc., " Let it not be well with the wicked, and let his days not be prolonged; but let them pass away as a shadow who fear not the Lord." This is quite unnecessary; and the words, "as a shadow," according to the accents, belong to what precedes, as in the Authorized Version. Hitzig and others have adopted the Vulgate division, and render, "Like a shadow is he who fears not God." But there is no sufficient reason for disregarding the existing accentuation. Septuagint, " He shall not prolong his days in a shadow (ἐν σκιᾷ)." **Because he feareth not before God.** This is the reason, looking to temporal retribution, why the wicked shall not live out half their days (ch. vii. 17; Prov. x. 27; Ps. lv. 23). Koheleth cleaves to the doctrine received from old time, although facts seem often to contradict it.

Ver. 14.—**There is a vanity which is done**

upon the earth. The vanity is named in what follows, viz. the seeming injustice in the distribution of good and evil. **There be just men, unto whom it happeneth according to the work of the wicked** (comp. ver. 10; ch. iii. 16). The melancholy fact is noted that the righteous often experience that fate with which the wicked are threatened, which their conduct might be expected to bring upon them. The verb translated "happeneth" (*naga*), with *el*, "to come to," "strike against," is thus used only in later Hebrew, *e.g.* Esth. ix. 26. **According to the work of the righteous.** The wicked meet with that outward prosperity and success which were thought to be the special reward of those who served God. The Vulgate is explanatory, "There are just men whom evils befall, as if they did the works of the wicked; and there are wicked men who are as free from care as if they had the deeds of the just." Commenting on Job xxxiv. 10, 11, St. Gregory writes, "It is by no means always the case in this life that God renders to each man according to his work and according to his own ways. For both many who commit unlawful and wicked deeds he prevents of his free grace, and converts to works of holiness; and some who are devoted to good deeds he reproves by means of the scourge, and so afflicts those who please him, as though they were displeasing to him. ... God doubtless so ordains it of his inestimable mercy, that both scourges should torture the just, lest their doings should elate them, and that the unjust should pass this life at least without punishment, because by their evil doings they are hastening onwards to those torments which are without end. For that the just are sometimes scourged in no way according to their deserts is shown by this history of Job. Elihu, therefore, would speak more truly if he had said that there is not unmercifulness and iniquity in God, even when he seems not to render to men according to their ways. For even that which we do not understand is brought forth from the righteous balance of secret judgment" ('Moral.,' xxiv. 44). Koheleth ends by repeating his melancholy refrain, **I said that this also** (*indeed*) **is vanity.** This conclusion, however, does not lead to despair or infidelity.

Ver. 15.—**Then** (*and*) **I commended mirth.** In face of the anomalies which meet us in our view of life, Koheleth recommends the calm enjoyment of such blessings and comforts as we possess, in exact accordance with what has already been said (ch. ii. 24; iii. 12, 22; v. 18), though the road by which he arrives at the conclusion is not identical in both cases. In the earlier chapters the injunction is based on man's inability to be the master of his own fate; in the present passage the inscrutable nature of the law that directs God's moral government leads to the advice to make the best of circumstances. In neither instance need we trace veiled Epicureanism. The result obtained is reached by acute observation supplemented by faith in God. **Under the sun.** The phrase occurs twice in this verse and again in ver. 17, and implies that the view taken was limited to man's earthly existence. **To eat, and to drink,** etc. This is not a commendation of a greedy, voluptuous life, but an injunction thankfully to enjoy the good provided by God without disquieting one's self with the mysteries of Providence. So it was said of Israel in its palmy days (1 Kings iv. 20), "Judah and Israel were many, as the sand which is by the sea in multitude, eating and drinking, and making merry." **For that shall abide with him of his labour;** rather, *and that this should accompany him in his labour.* The Greek Version regards the verb as indicative, not subjunctive, nor, as others, as jussive: "This shall attend (συμπροσέσται) him in his work." But it seems better to consider Koheleth as saying that the happiest thing for a man is to make the best of what he has, and to take with him in all his work a cheerful and contented heart.

Ver. 16 — ch. ix. 10. — Section 7 (the division in the theme caused by the introduction of a new chapter is misleading). *Man's wisdom is incapable of explaining the course of God's providential government; death awaits all without any exception, whatever be their condition or actions.* These two considerations conduce to the old conclusion, that man had best enjoy life, only being careful to use it energetically and well.

Vers. 16, 17. — No mortal wisdom, combined with the closest observation and thought, can fathom the mysteries of God's moral government.

Ver. 16. — **When I applied mine heart** (ch. i. 13). The answering member of the sentence is in ver. 17, the last clause of the present verse being parenthetical. **To know wisdom.** This was his first study (see on ch. i. 16). He endeavoured to acquire wisdom which might enable him to investigate God's doings. His second study was **to see the business that is done upon the earth;** *i.e.* not only to learn what men do in their several stations and callings, but likewise to understand what all this means, what it tends to, its object and result. (For "business," *inyan,* see on ch. i. 13.) The Vulgate here renders it *distentionem,* "distraction," which is like the Septuagint περισπασμόν. **For also there is that neither day nor night seeth sleep with**

his eyes. This is a parenthetical clause expressing either the restless, unrelieved labour that goes on in the world, or the sleepless meditation of one who tries to solve the problem of the order and disorder in men's lives. In the latter case, Koheleth may be giving his own experience. To " see sleep " is to enjoy sleep. The phrase is not found elsewhere in the Old Testament, but commentators quote parallels from classical sources. Thus Terence, ' Heautontim.,' iii. 1. 82—

"Somnum hercle ego hac nocte oculis non vidi meis."

" No sleep mine eyes have seen this livelong night."

Cicero, 'Ad Famil.,' viii. 30, "Fuit mirifica vigilantia, qui toto suo consulatu somnum non vidit." Of course, the expression is hyperbolical. The same idea is found without metaphor in such passages as Ps. cxxxii. 4; Prov. vi. 4. Ver. 17.—**Then I beheld all the work of God.** This is the apodosis to the first clause of ver. 16. "God's work" is the same as **the work that is done under the sun,** and means men's actions and the providential ordering thereof. This **a man,** with his finite understanding, **cannot find out,** cannot thoroughly comprehend or explain (comp. ch. iii. 11; vii. 23, 24). **Because though a man labour to seek** it out. The Septuagint has, "Οσα ἀν μοχθήσῃ, " Whatsoever things a man shall labour to seek;" Vulgate, *Quanto plus laboraverit ad quærendum, tanto minus inveniat.* The interpreters waver between " how much so ever," and " wherefore a man labours." The latter seems to be best. **Though a wise** man **think to know** it, **yet shall he not be able to find it.** It is the part of wisdom to determine to know all that can be known; but the resolution is baffled here (comp. ch. vii. 23). The two verses, with their repetitions and tautologous expressions, seem to denote perturbation of mind in the author and his sense of the gravity of his assertions. He is overwhelmed with the thought of the inscrutability of God's judgments, while he is forced to face the facts. An exquisite commentary on this passage is found in Hooker, ' Eccl. Pol.,' i. 2. § 2, quoted by Plumptre; and in Bishop Butler's sermon ' On the Ignorance of Man,' where we read, "From it [the knowledge of our ignorance] we may learn with what temper of mind a man ought to inquire into the subject of religion, namely, with what expectation of finding difficulties, and with a disposition to take up and rest satisfied with any evidence whatever which is real. A man should beforehand expect things mysterious, and such as he will not be able thoroughly to comprehend or go to the bottom of. . . . Our ignorance is the proper answer to many things which are called objections against religion, particularly to those which arise from the appearance of evil and irregularity in the constitution of nature and the government of the world. . . . Since the constitution of nature and the methods and designs of Providence in the government of the world are above our comprehension, we should acquiesce in and rest satisfied with our ignorance, turn our thoughts from that which is above and beyond us, and apply ourselves to that which is level to our capacities, and which is our real business and concern. . . . Lastly, let us adore that infinite wisdom and power and goodness which is above our comprehension (Ecclus. i. 6).

The conclusion is that in all lowliness of mind we set lightly by ourselves; that we form our temper to an implicit submission to the Divine Majesty, beget within ourselves an absolute resignation to all the methods of his providence in his dealings with the children of men; that in the deepest humility of our souls we prostrate ourselves before him, and join in that celestial song, 'Great and marvellous are thy works, Lord God Almighty; just and true are thy ways, thou King of saints. Who shall not fear thee, O Lord, and glorify thy Name?' (Rev. xv. 3, 4)" (comp. Rom. xi. 33).

HOMILETICS.

Ver. 1.—*A wise man's superiority—in what does it consist?* I. IN PENETRATION OF INTELLECT. He knoweth not merely things, but the interpretation thereof. Among the Chaldeans the interpretation of dreams was a special branch of wisdom professed by magicians and astrologers (Dan. ii. 4—13). A wise man—using the term in its widest sense—has clearer insight than ordinary mortals into the essences of things. To him pertains the faculty of searching into and discovering the causes of events (cf. "Naturam cognoscere rerum," Lucretius, iii. 1072). In particular he has insight into: 1. *The secrets of nature.* He is qualified to understand and explain phenomena which to ordinary minds are mysterious and inscrutable. 2. *The events of history.* He is able frequently to trace the under-currents moving society, and bringing about occurrences which to common minds are inexplicable. 3. *The wonders of revelation.* He can discover in sacred Scripture truths veiled to unenlightened eyes. 4. *The mysteries of grace.* Possessed of an unction from the Holy One, he can understand all things (1 John ii. 20, 27).

II. IN ELEVATION OF CHARACTER. "A man's wisdom maketh his face to shine." "It scarcely needs a proof that the countenance or front of the head is regarded in Scripture as the mirror of Divine influences upon the man—of all affections, and of the entire life of soul and spirit." "In the physiognomy is reflected the moral condition of the man" (Delitzsch's 'Bib. Psych.,' p. 301; Clark). "Many a poet, and seer, and martyr, and reformer, and woman of the finest fibre has at times had a face that has looked like porcelain with a light behind it" (Joseph Cook, 'Boston Noonday Lectures,' 2nd series, p. 148). The wise man's face shines because of three things: 1. *The light of truth in his understanding.* The wise man is essentially a child of light. A luminous intellect makes a radiant countenance. 2. *The light of purity in his heart.* There are faces which glow and beam with a soft silver sheen, as if they had shed off all that was gross and material, animal and brutish, and were spiritualized into a fine ethereal essence; because they reflect upon their surface the pure, sweet, chaste, and holy emotions that stir the clear depths of their bosoms within. 3. *The light of life in his conscience.* In the wise man the moral faculty is not dead, torpid, dull, and besotted; but alive, bright, sensitive, and vigorous; and what Cook calls the solar look in a face "arises from the activity of the higher nature when conscience is supreme" ('Boston Noonday Lectures,' 2nd series, p. 149).

III. IN REFINEMENT OF MANNERS. "The hardness," or strength, "of a wise man's face is changed." "The coarse ferocity of ignorance" is in him "transformed by culture" (Plumptre). What Ovid says of human learning—it

"Makes manners gentle, rescues men from strife"—

is true of heavenly wisdom, which is "first pure, then peaceable, gentle, and easy to be entreated," etc. (Jas. iii. 17). "Wisdom gives to a man bright eyes, a gentle countenance, a noble expression; it refines and dignifies his external appearance and his demeanour; the hitherto rude external, and the rude regardless, selfish, and bold deportment, are changed into their contraries" (Delitzsch). The change may be: 1. *Gradual,* as all moral transformations are slow, "from stage to stage," "first the blade and then the ear, and after that the full corn in the ear;" but it must be: 2. *Actual*, otherwise there is no reason to suppose the individual has become possessed of wisdom ; and it will eventually be: 3. *Visible* to all, so that all beholding him shall recognize in him the gentleness of one who has studied in wisdom's school. Christ, in whom are hid all the treasures of wisdom and knowledge (Col. ii. 3), was the highest impersonation the world ever witnessed of true gentleness and refinement.

Vers. 2—6.—"*Honour the king.*" I. THE SUBJECT'S DUTY TOWARDS THE KING. 1. *To keep the king's command.* Unless conscience interposes with a clear and distinct veto, as in the cases of Moses' parents (Heb. xi. 23), Daniel and his companions in Babylon (ch. i. 8; iii. 16—18; vi. 10), and the apostles before the Sanhedrin (Acts iv. 19, 20), it is the duty of all to render obedience to the civil power, kingly or magisterial, even though the doing of this should entail suffering and hardship (Rom. xiii. 1—7; Titus iii. 1; 1 Pet. ii. 13—15). 2. *To abide in the king's service.* The subject should not be hasty " to go out of the king's presence," in the sense of either renouncing allegiance to the king's throne, or deserting the post of duty he has received from the king. The obligation to preserve one's loyalty, however, is not absolute. Times may come when insurrection is a duty, as in the revolution which overthrew Athaliah (2 Chron. xxiii. 15; 2 Kings xi. 16). Nor can it be maintained that statesmen should never desert their sovereigns. When these embark on projects the consciences of their ministers cannot approve, it is incumbent on these ministers to leave them. Only nations should not resort to revolutionary practices without due consideration, and statesmen should not resign their portfolios in a fit of haste. 3. *To preserve the king's favour.* This the subject will usually do, if he " persist not in an evil thing," *i.e.* if he take no part in conspiracies against the king's power or person ; as he certainly will lose the king's favour by acting otherwise.

II. THE GROUNDS ON WHICH THE SUBJECT'S DUTY RESTS. 1. *The sanctions of religion.* These as much bind the subject as if the subject had individually sworn an oath in God's presence. The relationship existing between king and people being of Divine appointment, the subject is practically bound as by a solemn covenant in God's sight to render obedience and loyalty to his sovereign (cf. 2 Chron. xxiii. 16; xxxvi. 13). Nor does religion exempt the subject from such obligation even when the king is unworthy and his rule oppressive (Jer. xxix. 7; Matt. xxii. 21). 2. *The power of the king.* This also a reason why the subject should not raise the standard of rebellion without just cause, or offer unreasonable resistance to the carrying out of royal commands, that the king, as representative of the supreme power of the state, is usually able to enforce obedience and loyalty at least of an external kind. " The king doeth whatsoever pleaseth him," etc. (vers. 3, 4). The language applies to Oriental despots more than to constitutional monarchs. 3. *The safety of the subject.* Under arbitrary rule such as the Preacher alluded to, the way of submission was the way of safety. It might not, indeed, promise much good to the individual quietly to submit to a power he could not resist; but at least it would largely protect him against evil. Ideal rulers should be a fountain of blessing to their loyal as well as a force of repression to their disloyal subjects (Rom. xiii. 3). 4. *The dictates of wisdom.* The subject who might feel impelled to rebellion and disobedience perceives that, as " to every purpose there is a time and judgment " (*i.e.* a boundary beyond which it cannot pass, and a judicial decision upon its character which it cannot evade), since otherwise man's misery beneath the whips and scorns of time would become intolerable, so the oppression under which he groans will one day exhaust itself, come to an end, and be called up for judgment at the bar of the Supreme, if not in time and on earth, at least at the world's close, and in the unseen ; and, perceiving this, the wise subject deems it better to keep the king's commandment, and maintain allegiance to the king's throne, than to enter on the dubious paths of insurrection and revolt.

Learn: 1. The superior honour due from man to him who is the King of kings. 2. The loftier grounds on which the Christian soul's allegiance to God and Jesus Christ is claimed. 3. The blessedness of those who are faithful subjects of the heavenly King. 4. The folly of attempting to elude God's presence, and the danger of persisting in an evil thing. 5. The high argument for patience supplied by the certain prospect of a future judgment.

Vers. 7—9.—*The sorrowful tale of man's misery upon the earth.*   I. No KNOWLEDGE OF THE FUTURE.   Neither himself can foresee, nor can any one inform him, either what shall be or how it shall be.   Man's acquaintance with the future amounts at best to a "perhaps."

II. No EXEMPTION FROM DEATH.   This great truth stated in a threefold form. 1. *No man can retain his spirit,* or hold it back, when the hour strikes for it to be breathed forth, any more than he can hold back the winds of heaven when the moment has arrived for them to blow.   2. *No man has power over the day of his death,* to defer it, to remove it to a dim and distant future, or to hasten it to bring it near, any more than he has power over the day of his birth.   His times both of coming into and of going out from the world are in God's hand.   3. *No man can procure a discharge from the war with the king of terrors,* either for himself or another, any more than a conscript could escape the battle when drawn for service by an Oriental despot.   All without exception must go forth to the final conflict (Heb. ix. 27).

III. No ESCAPE FROM RETRIBUTION.   The wicked may hope that in some way or other it may be possible for them to evade the due reward of their transgressions; but such hope is taken from them by the fact that God will one day bring every secret thing into judgment, whether it has been good, or whether it has been evil (ch. xii. 14).

IV. No IMMUNITY FROM OPPRESSION.   Though it cannot be affirmed that all are oppressed—else where were the oppressors?—yet it cannot be guaranteed beforehand that any one will not be oppressed, since "there is a time wherein one man hath power over another to his hurt" (ver. 9).

LESSONS.   1. Leave the future with God, and live in the present.   2. Prepare for that day which will come on all like a thief in the night.   3. So live that the recompense of the future will be that which belongs to righteousness.   4. Avoid being an oppressor, and rather be oppressed.

Ver. 10.—*Before, at, and after death; or, the wicked and the good—a contrast.* I. BEFORE DEATH.   In the character of their lives.   Each lives and acts in accordance with his character of soul.   1. *The wicked acts wickedly.*   Spends his days (1) without religion, having no fear of God before his eyes (Ps. xxxvi. 1; Rom. iii. 18); (2) without morality, taking pleasure in disobedience to God's Law (Eph. ii. 2; v. 6); (3) and without hope (Eph. ii. 12), having no happy outlook beyond the grave.   2. *The righteous acts rightly.*   (1) Worshipping in the temple of the holy; (2) learning in the school of the holy; (3) walking in the ways of the holy; and (4) cherishing the hopes of the holy.   These different characteristics belong to the wicked and the righteous in all ranks and classes of society.

II. AT DEATH.   In the style of their funerals.   Both come to the grave, the house appointed for all the living (Job xxx. 23), like Dives and Lazarus (Luke xvi. 22); perhaps after having lived respectively as these did—the wicked clothing themselves in fine linen and faring sumptuously every day; the good lying in rags and sores at the rich man's gate, and feeding on the crumbs from the rich man's table.   But from this point their paths and experiences diverge.   1. *The wicked have a burial.*   They are borne to the place of sepulture with pomp and pageantry, and in presence of assembled crowds are committed to the dust.   Wealth and honour wait upon them to their last resting-places, and do the utmost to provide quiet and peaceful couches for their lifeless corpses.   Oftentimes, if not always, is this the fortune of the ungodly who have defied the Almighty, despised religion, insulted morality, and yet increased in riches and grown great in power.   2. *The good simply go away.*   They vanish from the scene of their sufferings and labours, no one knows when or how.   Whether they have a funeral no one cares.   Certainly their departure is not marked by long trains of mourners going about the streets.   Their obsequies, conducted by angels, are not observed by the passing crowds of busy men on earth.   This also is a frequent lot of good men at death, though it must not be assumed that good men are never carried to their graves amid lamentations and tears (2 Chron. xxiv. 16; Acts viii. 2).

III. AFTER DEATH.   In the treatment of their memories.   Both pass into the unseen, and have no more knowledge of what transpires on this side the veil.   But their lots upon the other side are frequently as different from each other as before.   1. *The wicked are remembered.*   Forgotten, it may be, and forsaken by God, but not by men who admired their splendour, and perhaps envied or feared their greatness when living. 2. *The good are forgotten.* Remembered indeed by God, but not by men, who suffer their names to pass into oblivion ; as saith the poet—

> " The evil that men do lives after them;
> The good is oft interrèd with their bones."
>
> ('Julius Cæsar,' act iii. sc. 2.)

LESSONS. 1. Study to live well by acting well. 2. Seek a lodging for thy soul when it must leave thy body. 3. Commit the care of thy memory to God and good men. 4. Envy neither the present nor the future lot of the wicked.

Vers. 11—13.—*Solemn thoughts for serious moments.* I. A GREAT DISTINCTION IN THE CHARACTERS OF MEN. Between the righteous and the wicked (Mal. iii. 18), the sinner and the saint, the man that fears God and the soul that fears him not. This distinction eclipses all others. Other distinctions affect the externals, this the essentials of man's being. The fear of God the root of all goodness in the soul (Ps. cxi. 10).

II. A GREAT FACT IN THE DIVINE ADMINISTRATION. That sentence is already pronounced (Ezek. xviii. 4), and will eventually be executed (unless intercepted by grace) on every evil work (Ps. xi. 6; xxxiv. 21; Rom. i. 18; v. 12; vi. 21, 23; Jas. i. 15). A sermon on the certainty of future judgment. The principle of the Divine government is one of moral retribution. To each man according as his work shall be—evil to the evil, good to the good.

III. A GREAT DISPLAY OF DIVINE CLEMENCY. Though pronounced, yet is sentence not executed against every evil work. Sometimes in God's providence retribution follows swiftly upon the heels of crime. For the most part, however, the infliction of the sentence is deferred—to give the sinner space to repent, to reveal to him the greatness of his guilt, and to melt him by a personal experience of undeserved kindness. " Account the long-suffering of our God salvation " (2 Pet. iii. 15).

IV. A GREAT INSTANCE OF HUMAN IMPIETY. " Because sentence against an evil work is not executed speedily, therefore the heart of the sons of men is fully set in them to do evil." The abuse of clemency a sadder sign of depravity than the violation of commandment ; to trample on God's mercy a greater wickedness than to break his Law.

V. A GREAT DIVERGENCE IN INDIVIDUAL EXPERIENCE. Between that of the long-lived and deeply-dyed sinner who defies the Divine Law and despises the Divine mercy, and that of the good man and humble who fears God and walks in his commandments and ordinances. The former, in spite of all his shameless audacity and boundless impiety, attains not to real happiness—" it shall not be well with the wicked," either here or hereafter (Isa. iii. 11). The former, notwithstanding his depressed condition, and perhaps brief life, is possessed of the secret of inward felicity—" it shall be well with them that fear God," both in this world and the next (Isa. iii. 10; 1 Tim. iv. 8).

Vers. 14, 15.—*A misunderstood providence and a mistaken judgment.* I. THE MISUNDERSTOOD PROVIDENCE. 1. *The providence is undeniable.* " There be righteous men, unto whom it happeneth according to the work of the wicked ; " and " there be wicked men, to whom it happeneth according to the work of the righteous." Of the former, Joseph, David, Job, Asaph, and Jeremiah were examples; as also the apostles and early Christians, the martyrs and confessors of the New Testament Church. Of the latter, Noah's sons, who, though not themselves righteous, were saved in the ark; Pharaoh's butler, who, though guilty of having conspired against the king's life, was nevertheless spared; Haman, who for a time at least flourished, though he was essentially a bad man—besides others—may be cited as examples. 2. *The providence is inevitable.* The constitution of the world being what it is, and the human family interlaced and interdependent as it is, it is impossible but that calamities should sometimes fall upon the righteous, and blessings descend upon the heads of the wicked, and that occasionally even wicked men should be deliberately treated as if they were righteous, and righteous men rewarded as if they were wicked. Good men often suffer the consequences of other people's evil deeds, and *vice versâ* bad men reap the benefits of other people's good works. 3. *The providence is mysterious.* That such things should occur in a world presided over by an all-wise and all-powerful as well as holy and just God, who loves righteousness and hates iniquity, is undoubtedly "hard to be understood," and for the full solution of the enigma it is more than likely the clearer light of the future must be awaited. 4. *The providence is symbolic.* At least it has its counterpart in the spiritual world—in the experience of Christ the Righteous One, who was numbered with transgressors (Mark xv. 28), and made sin for us, though he knew no sin (2 Cor. v. 21); and in that of believers, who, though personally sinful and unrighteous, are yet accepted as righteous in God's sight, and treated as such on account of the righteousness of Christ (Rom. iii. 25, 26; 1 Cor. i. 30; 2 Cor. v. 21; Eph. i. 6). May this not in part explain the occurrence of such phenomena in actual life? Nevertheless, it often happens that: 5. *The providence is misunderstood.* Men because of it rush to conclusions that cannot be sustained—as *e.g.* that there is no such thing as a providential government of the world, that the Supreme Being is indifferent to moral distinctions, that there is no profit in piety, and that no disadvantage follows on the practice of wickedness, and the like.

II. THE MISTAKEN JUDGMENT. 1. *The judgment is wrong.* It may not be wrong to affirm that a man, more especially if good and wise, should eat, drink, and be merry (ch. ix. 7), though such as do so are not always either good or wise (Luke xii. 19); but it certainly is not right to say that a man has nothing better to do under the sun than to eat, drink, and be merry. He who thinks so must have a low conception of both the nature and the destiny of man. 2. *The reason is doubtful.* That mirth will abide with a man in his labour all the days of his life. One fears this cannot be sustained as in perfect accord with experience. Inward happiness or joy in God may abide with a soul through every varying phase of external circumstances; it is not clear that so outward a thing as mirth, hilarity, satisfaction in creature-comforts, will abide with any to the close of life.

Learn: 1. To trust God even in the darkest and most mysterious providences. 2. To rejoice in God rather than in any of his creatures.

Vers. 16, 17.—"*The business that is done upon the earth.*" I. IN ITS RELATION TO GOD. It is his work. 1. *As to its plan.* "He doeth according to his will in the army of heaven, and among the inhabitants of the earth" (Dan. iv. 35). "He worketh all things after the counsel of his will" (Eph. i. 11). 2. *As to its execution.* Not directly, but indirectly—it being in him that men live and move and have their being (Acts xvii. 28). Not so that he is the Author of sin, or that in any way the freedom and efficiency of second causes are taken away; but so that while man freely acts and carries out his purposes, God also as freely acts in and through man and carries out his. 3. *As to its characteristics.* It is unsearchable and past finding out. As God's thoughts are deep, his works are vast and his ways inscrutable (Ps. lxxvii. 19; Rom. xi. 33).

II. IN ITS RELATION TO MAN. It is man's work also, he being the immediate agent engaged in its performance; and as such it is: 1. *Incessant.* It goes on day and night—work, work, work. 2. *Laborious.* So much so that multitudes are able to see sleep with their eyes neither day nor night. 3. *Disappointing.* Man labours on, and not only often makes little of his toil, but never comes to a clear perception of what the garment is he and others are weaving upon the loom of time.

LESSONS. 1. The duty of each man performing his appointed task with fidelity, leaving the ultimate issue in the hands of God. 2. The wisdom of recognizing that the business done upon the earth is after all only a means toward an end. 3. The greater propriety of labouring for that meat which endureth unto everlasting life. 4. The limited extent of man's knowledge as to God's plan in the government of the world.

HOMILIES BY VARIOUS AUTHORS.

Ver. 1.—*The tokens of wisdom.* This book, and those which have affinity with it, both canonical and apocryphal, are in nothing more remarkable than in the stress they lay upon wisdom. This is the quality of the spirit which in its highest manifestation is godliness and piety, which in its ordinary manifestations distinguishes the ruler from the subject, the sage from the fool. The reader of Ecclesiastes cannot fail to admire the independence of the author of common human standards of well-being, such as wealth, prosperity, and pleasure; wisdom is with him "the principal thing." The signs of true wisdom are graphically portrayed in this verse.

I. WISDOM IMPARTS INSIGHT. Ordinary men are not even, as a rule, observant; but there are men who are observant of what strikes the senses, of the phenomena of nature, of external life, but who go no further. Now, it is characteristic of the wise that they are not satisfied to know what lies upon the surface. The first stage of wisdom is science; the scientific man notes resemblances and differences, antecedents and sequences; he arranges phenomena into classes and species and genera upon the one principle, and into physical causes and effects upon the other. He recognizes similarities and uniformities in nature, and terms these arrangements laws. The second stage of wisdom is philosophy, whose province it is not only to proceed to higher generalizations, but to discover in all the processes of nature and in all the activities of mind the presence and operation of reason. The third stage of wisdom is theology, or religion, i.e. the discernment of the ubiquitous presence in the universe of the Eternal Spirit, from whom all individual minds proceed, and whose language, by which he holds communion with those minds, is nature. The scientist, the philosopher, the theologian, are all men who possess wisdom, who are dissatisfied with superficial knowledge, who "know the interpretation of a thing." Their wisdom is limited indeed if they disparage one another's work and service, for the world has need of them all. And there is no occasion why, in a measure, one man should not partake all three characters.

II. WISDOM IMPARTS BRIGHTNESS. The stupid and brutal betray themselves by an expression of stolidity. The cunning and crafty often display their characteristic quality by a keen, designing, "underhand," and sinister glance. But the wise are bright; clearness of perception, width of judgment, decisiveness of purpose, seem written upon the brow, seem to gleam from the steady eye of the wise man. The entrance of a wise man into the council-chamber is like the rising of the sun upon a landscape,—when the mists are cleared away and the dark places are illumined.

III. WISDOM IMPARTS STRENGTH, BOLDNESS, CONFIDENCE. The wise man is prepared for difficulties and dangers, and because he is prepared he is not alarmed. He measures circumstances, and sees how they may be bent to his will, how their threats may be turned into favour. He measures his fellow-men, discerns the strength of the strong, the depth of the thoughtful, the trustworthiness of the firm, the incompetency of the pretender, and the worthlessness of the shifty. He measures himself, and neither exaggerates or underestimates his abilities and his resources. Hence the boldness, the hardness of his face, when he turns to survey his task, to encounter his adversary, to endure his test. His heart is not dismayed, for his trust is ever in his God and Saviour.—T.

Vers. 2—5.—The ruler and the subject. It is possible that some persons, living under a form of government very different from that presumed in the admonitions of this passage—under a limited monarchy or a republic instead of under an absolute monarchy of a special theocratic kind—may fancy that these verses have no special significance for them, no applicability to the practical conduct of their actual life. But reflection may show us that this is not so, that there are valuable principles of interest and import for the civil life of all men.

I. CIVIL AUTHORITY IS IN ITSELF OF DIVINE ORIGIN, AND POSSESSES DIVINE SANCTIONS. The king, the king's word, commandment, and pleasure, are all significant of order in society, of that great reality and power in human affairs—the state. "Order is Heaven's first law." Right does not, indeed, grow out of civil authority, but it is its Divine basis. That kingship has often become tyranny, and democracy mob-rule, that every form of government may be abused, is known to every student of history, to every reader of the newspapers. But law in itself is good, and its maintenance is the only security for public liberty. One of the first duties of a religious teacher is to impress upon the people the sacredness of civil authority, to inculcate reverence for law, to encourage to good citizenship. He is not called upon to flatter the great and powerful, to repress discussion, to enjoin servility. But that freedom which is the condition of the true development of national life, and which can only be preserved by reverence for rightful authority, for constitutional government, should be dear to every Christian, and should be held in honour by every Christian teacher and preacher. "The powers that be are ordained of God."

II. WISE PATRIOTISM LEADS TO CHEERFUL OBEDIENCE AND SUBMISSION TO AUTHORITY. Law for the most part is designed to repress crime, to maintain peace and tranquillity, to afford protection to the honest, industrious, and law-abiding. Therefore to commit wrong of any kind, whether theft, or slander, or violence, is both evil in itself and is transgression of the law. A man who simply contents himself with breaking no civil law may indeed be a villain, for civil law is not all; there is a Divine Law which the civil ruler is not bound to enforce. But the bad citizen cannot be a good Christian; to break the laws of the state is not likely to lead to obedience to the commandments of the King of kings. It is, indeed, not to be expected that a man should approve of every command of the king, of every law which is enforced in his country. But if every man were to refuse to obey every statute of which he disapproved, how could government be carried on? The wonderful word of Christ is decisive, "Render unto Cæsar the things that are Cæsar's." Where no Divine ordinance is violated by conforming to civil law, the duty of the subject, the citizen, is plain; he should obey. He is, of course, at liberty under a constitutional government to use means of an honourable kind to secure a change of law. It is a grand word of the Preacher, "Whoso keepeth the commandment shall know no evil thing."

III. LOYALTY TO EARTHLY, HUMAN AUTHORITY IS SUGGESTIVE OF LOYALTY TO GOD. When submission is enjoined, it is supported by a religious motive—"and that in regard of the oath of God." It is evident that the authority of a parent or a ruler, the subjection of a child or a citizen, are intended to symbolize the even higher facts of the spiritual kingdom—the empire of the "King, eternal, immortal, and invisible," and the loyalty of those who by the new birth have entered "the kingdom of heaven."—T.

Ver. 11.—*A hasty and foolish inference.* In the case of some this conclusion may be reached deliberately, but in that of others the process may be unconscious, or at all events without attentive consideration and reasoned purpose.

I. THE DATA. There is delay in retribution. When we perceive immediate punishment follow upon flagrant sin, we are surprised and startled. We often remark that the course of the wrong-doer who avoids collision with the civil government is a course of uninterrupted prosperity. We see families advanced to honour and wealth who are lacking in moral character. We read of nations persevering for years, and even for centuries, in paths of injustice, rapacity, and violence, and yet growing in power and acquiring renown. And we cannot doubt that many evil deeds wrought in secret remain unpunished. The facts must be admitted. But they are explicable, and may be reconciled with a firm belief in the righteous retribution, the perfect moral government, of God. Stress is to be laid upon the word "speedily." It must be remembered that with God "one day is as a thousand years, and a thousand years are as one day."

"Though the mills of God grind slowly, yet they grind exceeding small;
Though with patience he stands waiting, he exactly judgeth all."

Judgment deferred is not judgment abandoned. From the time of Job the facts here referred to have been a perplexity to the observer of human society.

II. THE ERRONEOUS INFERENCE. "The heart of the sons of men is fully set in them [is emboldened] to do evil." The supposition is that sin may be committed with impunity, and the conclusion is that those sins which yield pleasure should be committed, since they will entail upon the sinner no evil consequences. Of course, an upright, conscientious, and godly man does not reason thus. He does what is right from a conviction of the nobility and beauty of goodness, and from a desire to act in conformity with the will of God, and to enjoy the approval of God; he abstains from evil because his conscience condemns it, because it is contrary to the universal order, because it is a grief to his Saviour's heart. But the self-seeking, pleasure-loving, base mind looks only to the consequences of actions, and does what affords pleasure, and evades painful duty. It is such a man who is referred to in this passage, whose heart is emboldened to sin by the foolish persuasion that no penalty will follow.

III. The practical lessons. 1. The sinner should reflect upon the facts of the Divine government, and upon the express statements of the revealed Word of God. He may thence learn the certainty of retribution. "The wicked shall not go unpunished;" "The way of transgressors is hard;" "The wages of sin is death." The sentence may not be executed speedily; but it is passed, and it will in God's time be carried out. 2. The godly man should rest assured that, however he may be perplexed by the mysteries of Divine providence, however he may be unable to reconcile what he sees in society with his religious convictions, nevertheless the Lord reigneth, and it shall be well with those who fear, obey, and love him. And he may well think less of the consequences of conduct, and more of those principles by which conduct is governed, of those motives by which action is inspired. Loyalty and gratitude, devotion and sympathetic admiration, may well lead to such a life as shall be its own reward. However it may fare with a man in this life, he chooses the good part who hates that which is evil and loves that which is good, whose convictions are just, and whose life is in harmony with his convictions. For such a man all things work together for good.—T.

Vers. 12—14.— *The certainty of retribution.* Again and again the writer of this remarkable book reverts to the same mysterious and perplexing facts of human society. As soon as men began to observe carefully and to think seriously, they were distressed by the inequality of the human lot, and by the apparent absence of a just arrangement of human affairs. If a family is wisely and righteously ordered, the obedient children are rewarded; whilst the selfish, wilful, rebellious children are chastised. In a well-administered government the law-abiding citizens are regarded and treated with favour, whilst the strong arm of the law is brought down heavily upon the idle and the criminal. Now, if God be the Father and the King of humanity, how is it that the affairs of the world are not so administered that the good are recompensed, and the wicked duly, swiftly, and effectively punished? Can there be a just Ruler who is also omniscient to observe and almighty to carry out his purposes of righteous government? Such are the thoughts which have passed through the minds of reflecting men in every age, and which passed through the mind of the writer of this Book of Ecclesiastes, and which are expressed in this passage. I. The perplexing facts of observation. These are recorded in the fourteenth verse, and are described as "a vanity which is done upon the earth." 1. The just suffer the inflictions which seem appropriate to the wicked. 2. The wicked reap the prosperity which might be expected to recompense the righteous. These are facts of human life which belong to no age, to no state of society more than to another. Taken by themselves, they do not satisfy the intellect, the conscience, of the inquirer. II. The assured conviction of faith. The Preacher, regarding the admitted facts with the eye of faith, comes to a conclusion which is not supported by mere reasoning upon observed facts. For him, and indeed for every truly religious man, there is a test of character which determines the destiny of spiritual beings; the discrimination is made between those who fear God and those who fear him not. Time and earth may not witness the award; but it is the award of the Almighty Judge and Lord. 1. It shall not be well with the wicked, even though he may be permitted to continue and to repeat his offences. 2. On the other hand, it shall be well with them that fear God. Such convictions are implanted by God himself; the righteous Lord has implanted them in the mind of his righteous people, and nothing can shake them, deep-seated as they are in the moral nature, which is the most abiding work of the Creator-Spirit. III. The attitude of godly wisdom. Those who, in the face of the facts described, nevertheless cherish the convictions approved, may reasonably apply such convictions to the practical control of the moral life. 1. Patience should be cultivated in the presence of perplexing and often distressing anomalies. We must wait in order that we may see the end, which is not yet. 2. Quiet confidence is ever the strength of God's people. They do not lean upon circumstances; they lean upon God, who never changes, and who will not fail those who place their trust in him. 3. Expectation of deliverance and acceptance. God may tarry; but he will surely appear, and will vindicate and save his own. Our salvation is nearer than when we first believed. Much has happened to test our faith, our endurance; but when the trial has been sufficiently prolonged and severe to answer the purpose of our all-wise Father, it will be brought to an end. "Unto the upright light ariseth out of darkness;" "The Lord is mindful of his own."—T.

Ver. 16.—*Man's busy life.* The Preacher was observant, not only of the phenomena and processes of nature, but also of the incidents and transactions of human life. In fact, man was his chief interest and his chief study. He observed the diligence of the laborious; the incessant activity of the scheming, the restless, the acquisitive. How he would have been affected by the spectacle of modern commercial life—say in London or Paris, New York or Vienna—we can only imagine; but as things were then, he was impressed by the marvellous activity and untiring energy which were displayed by his fellow-men in the various avocations of life.

I. MAN'S OWN NATURE AND CONSTITUTION IS ACTIVE. It would be an absurd misrepresentation of man's being to consider him as capable only of feeling and of knowledge. Intellectual and emotional he is; but, possessed of will, he is enterprising, inquiring, and active. Nature does indeed act upon him; but he reacts upon nature, subdues it to his purposes, and impresses upon it his thoughts.

II. MAN'S CIRCUMSTANCES ARE SUCH AS TO CALL FORTH HIS ACTIVITY. Human nature is endowed with wants, which prove, as a matter of fact, to be the means to his most valuable possessions and his chief enjoyments. His bodily necessities urge him to toil; and their supply and satisfaction, in many cases, absorb almost all disposable energy. His intellectual aspirations constrain to much endeavour; curiosity and inquiry prompt to efforts considerable in themselves, and lasting all through life. The family and social relations are the motive to many labours. Could one enter a market, an exchange, a port, and could one not merely witness the movements of body and of features which strike every eye, but penetrate the motives and purposes, the hopes and fears, which dwell in secret in the breasts of the busy throng, something might be discerned which would furnish a key to the busy activity of life.

III. BUSINESS ACTIVITY IS ACCOMPANIED WITH MANY PERILS. The labourer, the craftsman, the merchant, the lawyer, all have their various employments and interests, which are in danger of becoming engrossing. Perhaps the main temptation of the very busy is towards worldliness. The active and toiling are prone to lose sight of everything which does not contribute to their prosperity, and especially of the higher relations of their being and their immortal prospects. Young men entering upon professional and commercial life need especially to be warned against worldliness, to be reminded that it is possible to gain the whole world, and yet to lose the soul, the higher and worthier life. A man may become covetous, or at least avaricious; he may lose his sensibilities to what is noblest, purest, and best; he may adopt a lower standard of value, may move upon a lower plane of life.

IV. YET THE LIFE OF CONSTANT ACTIVITY IS DESIGNED BY DIVINE WISDOM TO BE THE MEANS OF SPIRITUAL PROFIT. Like all the appointments of providence, this is disciplinary. Business is not only a temptation, it may be an occasion of progress, a means to moral improvement. A busy man may learn to consecrate his powers to his Creator's service and glory; in the discharge of active duties he may grow in wisdom, in patience, even in self-denial. He may do with his might that which his hand findeth to do, he may redeem the time, he may prepare for the account to be rendered at last of the deeds done in the body.—T.

Ver. 17.—*The impenetrable, inscrutable mystery.* Plain people often think that a wise man is a man who knows, if not all things, yet all things to which he has directed his attention. It does not enter into their mind that wisdom lies largely in the consciousness of the limitation of the human powers. A great thinker has justly and beautifully said that the larger the circle of knowledge, the larger the external circumference which reveals itself to the apprehension. The writer of Ecclesiastes was a wise man, but he confesses himself to have been baffled in his endeavour to find out and master all the work of man, and much more the work of God. In this confession he was not singular. The man who knows a little may be vain of his knowledge; but the man who knows much knows full well how much there is which to him is unknown, and how much more is by him unknowable.

I. THE FACT THAT THE THOUGHTFUL MAN IS BAFFLED IN HIS ENDEAVOUR TO COM-PREHEND GOD'S WAYS, AND TO COMPREHEND HUMAN LIFE AND DESTINY.

II. THIS IS JUST WHAT IS TO BE EXPECTED FROM A CONSIDERATION OF (1) man's finite nature, and (2) God's infinite wisdom.

III. THE PROFITABLENESS OF THIS ARRANGEMENT. 1. It tends to raise our thought of God to a juster elevation. 2. It calls forth (1) humility, (2) submission, and (3) faith. 3. It makes the future infinitely interesting and attractive. What we know not here we shall know hereafter. Now we know as in a mirror, dimly; then, face to face.

> " Here it is given only to survey
> Dawnings of bliss and glimmerings of day:
> Heaven's fuller affluence mocks our dazzled sight—
> Too swift its radiance and too clear its light."

T.

Ver. 8.—*Death—our power and our powerlessness.* The Preacher brings before us the familiar fact of—

I. OUR POWERLESSNESS IN THE PRESENCE OF DEATH. There are evils from which large resources, or high rank, or exceptional abilities may secure us ; but in these death is not included. No man may escape it. Some men have lived so long that " death has seemed to have forgotten them; " but their hour has come at last. Death is a campaign in which there is " no furlough " given. Therefore: 1. Let every man be in readiness for it ; let us live " as those who to-day indeed are on the earth, but who to-morrow may be in heaven." Let not death surprise us with some urgent duty undone, the neglect of which will leave our nearest relatives or dearest friends in difficulty or distress. 2. Let us all measure the limit of our life; and let us feel that since so much is to be done by us if we can, for narrower and for wider circles, and since there is but a brief period in which to do it, let us address ourselves seriously, energetically, patiently, devoutly, to the work which the Divine Husbandman has given us to do. But the statement of the Preacher, reminding us of this familiar truth, may suggest to us, by contrast—

II. OUR PROVINCE AND OUR POWER IN THE PROSPECT OF DEATH. Although it is utterly hopeless that we can avert the stroke of the " last enemy," we may do much in regard to it. 1. We can often defer its coming by the wise regulation of our life ; we cannot " retain our spirit " when our hour is come, but we may put that hour much further on by prudence and virtue. Folly will ante-date, but wisdom will post-date it. We cannot, indeed, measure Divine favour by the number of our years—there is a Christian reading of the heathen adage, " Whom the gods love die young "—but it is very often true that " with long life " God will " satisfy " the man who " sets his love upon him " (Ps. xci. 14—16). 2. We can gain a spiritual victory over it ; we can

> " . . . so live, that we may dread
> The grave as little as our bed."

We may so abide in Jesus Christ, and so live in the light of his holy truth, that the idea of death, instead of being a terror or even a dark shadow at its close, will be positively welcome to our spirit. 3. We may find a friend in it when it comes; the friend whose kind hand opens for us the door of immortality, and ushers into the life which is free and full and endless.—C.

Vers. 9, 10.—*Sin in power.* Amid the obscurities and uncertainties in which the precise meaning of this verse is lost, we may allow it to speak to us of the truth that when sin is in power it is in all respects an unsatisfactory thing. It is—

I. INJURIOUS TO THE PEOPLE. " A man ruleth over men to their hurt " (Cox). The evils of misrule are obvious, for they have been only too often illustrated ; they are these : the infliction of grave injustice ; the encouragement of iniquity and discouragement of righteousness ; disturbance and unsettlement, and consequent reduction in various spheres of useful industry ; decline of activity, morality, worship.

II. HURTFUL TO THE HOLDER HIMSELF. " One man hath power over another to his *own* hurt " (Revised Version marginal reading). It is certainly and most profoundly true, whether here stated or not, that the holding of power by a bad man is hurtful to himself. It elevates him in his own eyes when he needs to be humbled therein; it gives him the opportunity of indulgence, and indulgence is certain to feed an evil inclination, or to foster an unholy habit; it makes injurious flattery the probable, and a beneficial remonstrance the unlikely, thing in his experience.

III. OF BRIEF DURATION. If we only wait awhile we shall " see the wicked buried." It is probable enough that sin in power will be guilty of serious excesses, and will therefore bring down upon itself those human resentments or those Divine judgments which end in death. But, apart from this, an evil course must end at death. God has put a limit to our human lives which, though it sometimes takes from the field a brave and powerful champion, on the other hand relieves society of the impure and the unjust. Sin in power is bound fast by the tether which it is quite unable to snap (see Ps. xxxvii. 35, 36).

IV. CONTRACTING GUILT. They "had come and gone from the place of the holy." They had either (1) been professing to administer justice, and had done injustice; or (2) attended the place of privilege, and had despised their opportunity. Either way, they had been " laying up for themselves wrath against the day of wrath."

V. GOING DOWN INTO OBLIVION. The sense *may* be that this happens too often to the righteous; but it is certainly appropriate to the wicked. And is it not more applicable to them? For no man tries to remember them. No one proposes to erect monuments or institute memorials of them. There is a tacit understanding, if nothing more, that their name shall be dropped, that their memory shall perish. The only kind thing that can be done concerning them is to leave their name unspoken.

1. Be content with the exercise of a holy and benignant influence. It is well to be powerful if God wills it. But most men have to live without it, and a human life may be destitute of it, and yet be truly happy, and be of real service to a great many souls.
2. Resolve to leave a holy influence and a fragrant memory behind. We may have to content ourselves with a very simple memorial stone, but if we leave kindly memories and good influences in many hearts, so that in our case " the memory of the just is blessed," we shall not have lived in vain.—C.

Vers. 11—13.—*The perversion of God's patience.* No obscurity hangs over this passage; the evil to which the Preacher refers is clear enough and common enough, while his condemnation of it is distinct and decisive.

I. A PALPABLE FACT IN THE GOVERNMENT OF GOD. The fact is that God often lets sin go unpunished, or, as we should rather say, partly unpunished. The tyrant is not dethroned; the fraudulent dealer is not convicted and sentenced; the murderer is not apprehended; the drunkard and the debauchee are not driven from the society which they disgrace; the hypocrite is not exposed and expelled; the men who fill their purses or satisfy their cravings at the expense of the property or even the character of their neighbours are sometimes allowed to remain in positions of comfort and of honour. And it may be that even their health and their spirits appear untouched by their sins, and even by their vices.

II. ITS MISINTERPRETATION BY MANY. What does it mean that God allows this to happen? The guilty are not slow to convince themselves that it means *safety to them-selves*. It is, they think, that God does not concern himself with the small particulars of human life, and will not therefore visit them with his penalties; or it is that God is too " good," too kind, to punish his children for following the bent of their own nature; or it is that the world is not under the government of any righteous Ruler at all, but only subject to certain laws of which they may prudently make use for their ultimate immunity. It is that they may safely go on in their evil course without fear of consequences.

III. THEIR COMPLETE MISTAKE. They argue that because *we* always make penalty follow crime as soon as we can, and because our non-infliction of it argues our intention to condone it altogether, it is the same with God, and that his forbearance to punish is proof that he does not intend to do so. Thus they think that " God is altogether such a one as ourselves." But they are wrong; he " *will* reprove us and set [our sins] in order before our eyes " (see Ps. l. 21). We always make penalty pursue wrong-doing without any interval, because (1) we are afraid the criminal will escape us, or (2) we fear that we ourselves may be taken from the scene. But God is not hurried by such considerations as these. The guilty can never get beyond his reach, and he is ever present. Time does not enter into the account of him who is " from everlasting to everlasting." God's long forbearance is, therefore, no proof of Divine indifference or of the absence of a ruling hand from the affairs of men.

IV. Its TRUE SIGNIFICANCE. What the Divine long-suffering really means is that God is patient with us in the hope that we shall repent and live (see Ezek. xxxiii. 11; Rom. ii. 4; 1 Tim. ii. 4; and especially 2 Pet. iii. 9). The truth is that (1) while men *do often seem to escape* the retribution that is due to them, and while they do in fact enjoy a large measure of Divine forbearance; (2) sin is always suffering, and is on its way to doom. (*a*) If outward and visible evils are not attending it, inward and spiritual evils are. (*b*) Sin always *tends toward* misery and shame, and is working it out, as the event will show. Even if it should escape the hundredth time, there *is* a number that will prove fatal. (3) The righteous man has a distinct and immeasurable advantage. It is " well with them that fear God." (*a*) Piety and virtue have the promise of the life that now is. Sobriety, chastity, uprightness, diligence, prudence, courtesy, kindness,—these are all making for health and for prosperity, and for the best friendship which earth can offer. (*b*) They lead up to the gates of the heavenly city.—C.

Ver. 1.—" *Sweetness and light.*" The wisdom which is here spoken of as conferring upon its possessor an incomparable superiority is not mere wealth of intellectual knowledge, or a wide and accurate acquaintance with any department of science or philosophy. It is rather a moral condition, a state of heart and mind with an outward life consonant with it, a temperament and disposition attained by long and careful endeavour. In our modern use of the word, wisdom is equivalent to knowledge, and generally indicates mental endowments and equipment which may or may not enable its possessor to act sensibly in the ordinary affairs of life. We are familiar enough with the phenomena of men of science who in practical matters are as helpless as children, who betray a gross and astounding ignorance of things which lie outside the department of knowledge which they have cultivated, or who make it manifest to all that their knowledge has not had a refining influence upon them, and delivered them from the evil of being biassed by the disturbing influence of prejudices and passions. Such wisdom which we admire and respect, in spite of its unpractical character, is not of the same order with that which the Preacher eulogizes. The wisdom which is so often spoken of in the Hebrew Scriptures, especially in the Proverbs, in this Book of Ecclesiastes, and in Job, is a Divine faculty by which a man is enabled to live a well-ordered life. Its source is in God, but it is not confined to the one nation which he chose, or synonymous with the exceptional revelations made to it. Thus the wisdom of Solomon is declared to have been higher in degree than that attained by any in the neighbouring peoples, but not different in kind (1 Kings iv. 29—31). Then, too, its range is very wide. Nothing is too high, nothing is too low, for wisdom "fitly " to " order." Law and government (Prov. viii. 15, 16), and even the precepts of husbandry (Isa. xxviii. 23—29), are equally her productions with those moral observations which constitute in the main the three books of Scripture to which I have referred. She is the source of skill of every kind, the mistress of the arts, the guardian of the vast and inexhaustible stores garnered by experience, from which men may equip themselves for meeting every emergency of life. The wise man is God-fearing, free from superstition and fanaticism, prudent, shrewd, a good counsellor, a safe guide (*vide* Cheyne, ' Job and Solomon,' pp. 117, *et seq.*). The enthusiastic manner in which the influence of wisdom upon a character is described reminds us of the somewhat similar sentiment expressed by Ovid—

" Adde quod ingenuas didicisse fideliter artes,
　　Emollit mores nec sinit esse feros."
　　　　　　　　　　　　　　　('Epp. ex Ponto,' ii. 9, 47.)

" A man's wisdom maketh his face to shine, and the boldness of his face shall be changed." The words depict very vividly and beautifully the almost transfiguring effect of serene wisdom upon the countenance—how it lights up the face, and gives to even homely features an exquisite charm. The coarse, sullen, vacant stare of ignorance is transformed by the "sweetness and light" with which the soul is suffused. There is a reference probably to the literal shining of Moses' countenance when he came down from the mount on which he had seen God face to face (Exod. xxxiv. 29). We must all of us have known cases in which true piety and wisdom, such as is learned from Christ, have had this refining and transforming influence; persons of little ordinary education or culture, to whom religion has given really new intellectual power, and whose tranquillity and peace of spirit has given an air of heavenly serenity to their whole bearing and manner. And, indeed, in every case a holy disposition of mind has a refining effect upon those who cherish it. The face is an index to the character, and if the emotions that are expressed upon it are pure and worthy, they cannot fail in time to transform it in some measure—to tone down what may have been its natural harshness, and to banish from it all traces of coarse and sensual passions. An example of religion giving intellectual power, or rather of drawing out the faculties which but for it would have remained unexercised, we may see in the life of John Bunyan. The genius which is so marvellously displayed in his works, and which gives him a high place in the literature of his country, would never have shown itself but for the wonderful change in his life, when, from being a profane, careless, godless fellow, he became a true-hearted servant of Christ.

The abruptness with which this chapter opens may, it has been supposed, have been intended to call the attention of the reader to the hidden significance of the words that are about to be spoken, as our Lord often emphasized his utterances by the saying, "He that hath ears to hear, let him hear." Something there is in what he is about to add to be read between the lines. And the probable explanation of the suggestive question, and the allusion to a wise man's understanding "the interpretation of a thing," is in the fact that the writer veils a protest against despotism in the garb of the maxims of servility (Plumptre).—J. W.

Vers. 2—5.—*Allegiance of subjects.* It is scarcely to be denied that the wisdom which the Preacher exhorts his readers to exemplify in their relations as subjects with their kings, has something very like a servile tone about it. "There is not a trace of the enthusiastic loyalty of a Hebrew to a native sovereign, 'whose power loveth righteousness, who judgeth God's people with righteousness; in whose days the righteous flourish, and abundance of peace so long as the moon endureth' (Ps. lxxii. 7). Nor do we find the freeman's boldness, with which an Elijah could confront an apostate or a tyrant king. That fire is spent! The counsels here, as where he recurs to the same subject in the last five verses of ch. x., are those of submission, forbearance, self-control, prudence in dealing with a power irresistible, overbearing, often oppressive, yet which carries within itself the seeds of decay. Such advice may well have been needed by a generation of Jews, proud, intractable, detesting foreign rule, and groaning under the tyranny of an alien monarch " (Bradley). Loyal obedience to a duly constituted authority is declared to be (1) *a matter of conscience* (ver. 2); (2) *a prudent course* (vers. 3, 4, 5a); because by it we escape the punishment incurred by rebellion, and enjoy some tranquillity even under the worst rule. And as a consolation to those who are indignant at a tyrannous use of power, the reminder is given (5b) that punishment for evil deeds will be meted out in due time by a higher hand than ours.

I. OBEDIENCE A MATTER OF CONSCIENCE. (Ver. 2.) "I counsel thee to keep the king's commandment, and that *in regard of the oath of God.*" Though the words " counsel thee " are not in the Hebrew text, no better have been suggested to fill up the gap. But the emphasis which is laid upon the *I* by the omission of the verb may be interpreted to mean that the writer is giving a personal opinion, and not speaking authoritatively on a matter concerning which different men might form very diverse judgments. And we may compare with it St. Paul's manner of speaking, " But to the rest say *I*, not the Lord " (1 Cor. vii. 12, Revised Version), as contrasted with " I command, yet not *I*, but the Lord " (1 Cor. vii. 10). If we interpret the words in this way, a considerable measure of what I have called the servility of their tone is taken away. The writer is giving us prudential counsels, but of course the question still remains open whether there are not in certain emergencies higher considerations than those of prudence. He tells how tranquillity may be preserved even under the rule of a tyrant; but it is for us to decide whether higher blessings than that of tranquillity are not to be striven for. The great cautiousness with which he speaks is not unreasonable when we remember how ready men are to make use of passages of Scripture to justify even questionable conduct, and how many errors have sprung from an ignorant and self-willed misinterpretation of isolated texts. The advice, then, given is " to keep the king's commandment " out of regard to the oath of allegiance taken to him or imposed by him. No hasty or ill-advised breach of such an oath is justifiable. It would seem that this passage was in St. Paul's mind, though he does not directly quote from it, when he says, " Wherefore ye must needs be subject, not only for wrath, but *also for conscience' sake* " (Rom. xiii. 5). As is well known, both the words of the Preacher, and the teaching of St. Paul in the thirteenth chapter of Romans, have been taken as laying down the rule of passive obedience for all subjects in all circumstances. However cruel the despot, the duty of subjects to obey him implicitly, and to make no attempt to deprive him of his power, has been held by many to be clearly laid down by the Word of God. And great stress has been laid upon the fact that the ruler of the civilized world, when St. Paul wrote the Epistle to the Romans, was Nero, one of the most infamous and cruel tyrants who ever wore the purple. In our own country during the seventeenth century, when the question of the prerogative of the sovereign and the rights and duties of subjects engaged the attention of all, these portions of Scripture were often interpreted to teach that the king's will was by right, and by the authority of God's Word, above all charters and statutes and acts of parliament, and that no misuse of his power could justify rebellion against him. But those who took up this ground forgot or ignored the fact that kings have duties towards their subjects, that coronation oaths bind them to keep the laws; and that St. Paul, in the very same place in which he commands subjects to obey, describes the kind of rule which has an absolute claim upon their allegiance. " For rulers are not a terror to good works, but to evil. . . . Do that which is good, and thou shalt have praise of the same : for he is the minister of God to thee for good . . . a revenger to execute wrath upon him that doeth evil." It must surely be evident to all whose minds have not been blinded by a grotesque and monstrous theory, that a ruler who is a terror to good works, who rewards vice and punishes virtue, and uses the sword of justice to enforce his own selfish and cruel purposes, cannot claim from subjects the obedience which the apostle commands them to render to one of the very opposite character. But though passive obedience to tyrannical government cannot be commended on any higher ground than that of prudence, there can be no doubt that in ordinary circumstances the faithfulness of subjects to their rulers is a religious duty. And so we find in many passages of Scripture blame attached to those who thought that rebellion against the authority even of heathen kings, to whom the chosen people might be in subjection, was justifiable (Isa. xxviii. 15 ; xxx. 1 ; Ezek. xvii. 15 ; Jer. xxvii. 12 ; cf. Matt. xxii. 21).

II. A PRUDENT COURSE. (Vers. 3, 4, 5a.) In these verses the Preacher " seeks to dissuade his readers from casting off their allegiance to the king, or taking part with the enemies of the monarch under any hasty impulse whatever." " Do not lightly forsake the post of duty, join in no conspiracy against the king's throne or life," the words might be paraphrased. His power is absolute; he is above courts of law, and therefore any action against him must be attended with great risk. Of course, as I have said, the course recommended is a prudential one, and there are circumstances in which many will think that the oppressiveness of a tyrannical government has reached a pitch justifying rebellion against it. But those who seek tranquillity will bear a great deal, and not be eager to enter on any such undertaking. In ordinary circumstances, those who obey the king's commandment will experience no evil thing (5a), cases being left out of view in which the king requires obedience to decrees contrary to the Divine laws (Dan. iii., vi.); while the risk of failure in attempts to overthrow his power, and the anarchy and crime that generally attend insurrection against constituted authority, are calculated to make the wise man pause before he resolves to become a rebel. The advice given by the Preacher is so carefully stated, and based on such reasonable grounds, that perhaps one should not term it servile. And this impression is strengthened by a consideration of what is implied rather than expressed in the latter part of ver. 5. There is hope of a beneficial change even for those who submit in silence to the worst evils of despotism. It is to be found in the conviction of there being a power higher than that of earthly sovereigns, which will in its own time mete out punishment to all transgressors. The wise man's heart "discerneth both time and judgment;" he will wait patiently for the "time and season of judgment which God hath put in his own power" (Lam. iii. 26; ch. iii. 1, 11, 17). Evil-doing cannot escape punishment; however exalted in station the offender may be, the time will come round when his deeds will be weighed in an unerring balance, and receive the chastisement they deserve. His high-handed disregard of equity and mercy may prevail up to a certain point, but retribution will come when the measure of his iniquity has been filled up. And the knowledge that this is so will help to console and strengthen the wise in the dark and evil day.—J. W.

Vers. 6—8.—*The doom of tyrants.* In words which are purposely dark the writer speaks of the fall of unrighteous tyrants. It is with bated breath that he whispers to those who are writhing helplessly under the oppressive rule of cruel despots, that the evil under which they suffer works its own cure in time, and that those who have their own way at present will sooner or later have to succumb to a power greater than their own. It is with considerable difficulty that the drift of the passage is to be made out, but with this clue in our hands it becomes intelligible. In the sixth and seventh verses there are four statements, each introduced by the same conjunction, כִּי, "for," or "because," and by retaining it in each case, instead of varying it as is done in our English versions, the sequence of thought becomes clearer. The sense of the verses is as follows : " The heart of the wise man will know the time and judgment, and will keep quiet; for (1) there is a time and a judgment appointed by God in which the wicked ruler will be duly punished (cf. ch. iii. 17); (2) the wickedness of man is heavy upon him, and will entail its own punishment,—the misery caused by a tyrant is a weight which will bring him down at last; (3) no man knows the future, or that which will take place, and therefore no despot is able absolutely to guard himself against the stroke of vengeance; for (4) who can tell him how the vengeance will be brought about? He may look in this direction and in that for the longed-for information, but in vain (cf. Isa. xlvii. 13, etc.). One thing, however, is certain, that whilst the wicked "are drowned in their carousing, they shall be consumed like stubble fully dry" (Nah. i. 10). The inexorable nature of the doom which will fall upon the cruel despot is described in highly vivid language. There are four things which are impossible for him to do. 1. "There is no man that hath power over the spirit to retain the spirit." Life can be shortened or cut off at any moment, but can by no art be prolonged beyond the fixed term. The despot cannot by his power escape the doom of death, any more than can the meanest of his subjects. Or understanding by רוּחַ not " the *spirit* of man," but " the wind," to which Divine judgments are often likened (Isa. xli. 16; lvii. 13; Jer. iv. 11—13; xxii. 22), it is as fruitless to try to keep back the Divine judgments as to prevent the wind from bursting forth. 2. There is no one who has power over the day of death, or is able to avert the arrival of that "king of terrors" (Job xviii. 14); the pestilence walketh forth in darkness, and the sickness wasteth at noonday (Ps. xci. 6). 3. There was no discharge granted from the ranks in the time of war under the vigorous law of Persia, and the Divine law of requital cuts off with equal certainty all hope of escape from the guilty transgressor ; and lastly : 4. Wickedness will not deliver its master. When the hour of Divine vengeance strikes, the sinner shall receive the meet reward of his actions. "The wages of sin is death" (Rom. vi. 23) (Wright). By no lavish bribes, by no use of power, by no arts or endeavours, can the evil-doer, however high his rank may be, avert the day of judgment, which may precede, but which, if it does not precede, will certainly coincide with the day of death. And in that time, when he will have to stand before the tribunal of the King of kings, none of his deeds of cruelty and oppression will be passed over. Such is the teaching half concealed beneath the words of the Preacher ; but not so veiled as to be hidden from the discernment of a reader made sensitive by the righteous indignation which oppression excites in a healthy mind. His words pass from an apparent servility of tone into a generous anger, and there is a triumphant ring in his voice as he speaks of the immutability of the law or of the will, upon which the moral government of the world is based. But though horror of injustice and hardness of heart is manifest in his words, they are not instinct with any less worthy feeling. He does not justify revenge, or hint at the advisability of subjects taking the law into their own hands when their patience has been long tried. But he raises the matter to a higher level, and makes faith in God the source of consolation; and in his very words of counsel to subjects adduces considerations which are calculated to weigh with their rulers, and make those of them who are still amenable to reason, pause in a course of oppression and cruelty.—J. W.

Vers. 9, 10.—*Unequal lots.* The enunciation in the preceding verses of a firm conviction in the moral government of the world by God might have been expected to have silenced for ever doubts excited by the inequalities and irregularities so often apparent in human society. The possession of a master-key might have been expected to deliver the wanderer from the mazes of the labyrinth. But so great is the power of the actual, so varying is the strength of faith, that at times belief in a God of infinite wisdom and power and love seems a fallacious theory, contradicted and disproved by the facts of everyday life. And so our author, after bidding his readers to wait patiently for the manifestation of God's justice against evil-doers, gives utterance to the perplexity and distress occasioned by his long delay. He thinks of the successful oppressor, prosperous in life and honoured in burial, and contrasts with him the righteous driven into exile, and dying in obscurity and forgotten by all his fellows. Such seems to be the meaning of these verses, according to the translation given in the Revised Version, "All this have I seen, and applied my heart unto every work under the sun : *there is* a time wherein one man hath power over another to his hurt. And withal I saw the wicked buried, and they came *to the grave ;* and they that had done right went away from the holy place, and were forgotten in the city : this also is vanity." It is just the state of matters described in the first part of the parable of the rich man and Lazarus—the one enjoying in this life good things, the other evil—and because the Preacher is not able to draw aside the veil that divides the temporal from the eternal, he cannot be sure that the inequality of the lots of the wicked and the righteous is ever remedied. He describes (1) *the prosperity of the wicked ;* and (2) *the adversity of the righteous.*

I. THE PROSPERITY OF THE WICKED. It is still the despot whom he has in his mind's eye. He sees him ruling over others to their hurt, and at last receiving honourable burial, and finding rest in the grave. No insurrection of oppressed and pillaged subjects cuts short his tyrannous rule; he is undisturbed by enemies from without ; he escapes the dagger of the assassin, and dies peacefully in his bed. And even then, when the fear he inspired in his lifetime is relaxed, no outbreak of popular indignation interferes with the stately ceremonial with which he is laid in the tomb. "There is not wanting the long procession of the funeral solemnities through the streets of Jerusalem, the crowd of hired mourners, the spices and ointment very precious, wrapping the body ; nor yet the costly sepulchre, with its adulatory inscription." He might have been the greatest benefactor his subjects had known, the holiest of his generation, so completely has he received the portion of those who have lived prosperous and honoured lives (cf. 2 Chron. xvi. 14 ; xxvi. 23 ; xxviii. 27). The punishment merited by an evil life has not fallen upon him; the Divine Judge has delayed his coming until it is too late, as far as this life is concerned, for justice to be done, and therefore the faith of those who wait patiently upon God is subjected to a severe strain.

II. THE ADVERSITY OF THE RIGHTEOUS. While the wicked flourish in undisturbed peace, the righteous have often to endure hardships. The decree of banishment goes out against them; with slow and lingering steps they are compelled against their will to depart from the place which they love. They must go forth, and only too soon are they forgotten in the city, *i.e.* the holy city ; a younger generation knows nothing more of them, and not even a gravestone brings them back to the memory of their people. This also is vanity, like the many others already registered—this, viz., that the wicked while living, and also in their death, possess the sacred soil; while, on the contrary, the upright are constrained to depart from it and are soon forgotten (Delitzsch). It seems a stain upon the Divine righteousness that this should be so ; that so long an interval should elapse between the commission of the offence and the dawning of the day of retribution, and that in so many cases it would appear as if retribution never came. This is calculated to try our faith, and happy are we if the trial strengthens our faith. But one thing must not be left out of account—the Preacher dwells upon it in a subsequent verse—and that is that external circumstances of prosperity or adversity are not of supreme importance; that righteousness even with misfortunes is infinitely preferable to wickedness, whatever measure of external prosperity it may enjoy. Whether happiness or misery in this life be their outward lot, in the end "it shall be well with them that fear God" (ver. 12).—J. W.

Vers. 11—13.—*Retribution certain.* The prosperity of the wicked is not only an evil in itself, but it leads the way to a more deliberate and unrestrained course of sin. The fact that the Divine sentence that condemns evil is not executed speedily, leads many to think that they can sin with impunity. They do not see that the slowness with which the messenger of vengeance often travels gives opportunity for repentance and amendment before the stroke of punishment falls. Men think they are secure, and give themselves fearlessly to the practice of evil. Yet the Preacher could not give up his conviction that punishment of evil was but delayed and not averted. Though he *saw* the sinner do evil a hundred times and prolong his days, he *knew* that the righteousness of God, which in the present world seems so often obscured and thwarted, would in the end assert itself (ver. 12). Though the sinner enjoyed prosperity, it was a deceitful calm before the storm; but the righteous who truly feared God had a peace of spirit which no outward misfortunes or persecutions could disturb. "Appearances, the Preacher saw clearly enough, were against him, yet his faith was strong even under all such difficulties, and through it he was victorious" (Wright) (cf. 1 John v. 24). The prosperity of the wicked is, after all, only apparent. It has no sure foundation; can anticipate no long duration. His days may be many in number, but they soon pass away "as a shadow;" and when the last comes, every wish for prolonged life will be in vain. He may be at the very height of enjoyment when the hour strikes for his enforced departure from the world in which he has abused the long-suffering of God; and no prayers or entreaties or struggles will avail to prolong his days. The shadow on the dial cannot be forced to retrace its course, or to journey more slowly. "His breath goeth forth, he returneth to his dust; in that very day his thoughts perish."—J. W.

Vers. 14, 15.—*One way out of perplexity.* The Preacher has just attained for a moment to higher ground, from which he may get a wider view of life with all its changes and anomalies (vers. 12, 13). His hope revives, his faith comes back. " For a moment he has pierced through the ring which has confined him to the interests of common life, and risen also above his own dark misgivings; and there has flashed across his soul for a moment the certainty that there is a power in the world that 'makes for righteousness,' a Divine and supreme law behind all the puzzles and anomalies of life, which will solve them all. He lays his hand on this, but he cannot grasp it" (Bradley). The inequalities in human lots, the just suffering as though they had been wicked, the wicked prospering as though they had been righteous, afflict his heart once more (ver. 13). His recurrence so often to this perplexing phenomenon is almost painful; it reveals a distress so deep that no arguments can diminish it, no exercise of faith can charm it away. Nothing but fresh light upon the mysteries of life and death can give relief, and this is denied him. He is one of those of whom the Saviour spoke (Luke x. 24) who desired to see and hear the things seen and heard by those who were privileged to receive a revelation of God in Christ, but whose longings were doomed never to be satisfied on earth. In the mean time to what conclusion did the Preacher come? To that which he has already expressed four times over (ch. ii. 24; iii. 12, 22; v. 18)—that it is better to enjoy the good things of life than to pine after an impossible ideal; to eat the fruit of one's toil in spite of all that is calculated to sadden and perplex (ver. 14). Yet we must be fair to him. He does not recommend riot and excess, or a life of mere epicurean enjoyment. There is work to be done in life before enjoyment is won; there is a God from whom the blessings come as a gift, and the remembrance of this fact will prevent mere brutish self-indulgence. The fear of God gives a dignity to his counsel which is wanting in the somewhat similar words of heathen poets, in which we have epicureanism pure and simple—in the songs of Anacreon and Horace and Omar Khayyam. It would indeed be a mistake to imagine that the advice he gives, however often it is repeated, is the best that can be given, or even the best that he has to give. It prescribes but a temporary relief from sorrow and care and perplexity. And even when he makes the most of the satisfaction gained by " eating and drinking and being merry," we remember his own words, that " it is better to go to the house of mourning than to the house of feasting " (ch. vii. 2).—J. W.

Vers. 16, 17.—*Vanity of philosophizing.* The endeavour had been in vain to discover the principle according to which it happens that the just sometimes receive the reward of the wicked, and the wicked that of the righteous (ch. viii. 14). Equal failure attends the endeavour to understand the purpose and end of the toil and labour in which men are ceaselessly engaged. That all that was done was " a work of God," the carrying out of a Divine law, the accomplishment of a Divine plan, he did not doubt (ver. 17); but he was unable to see the connection of the individual parts with the whole—the order and symmetry of events in their course he could not recognize. Two things he had sought to attain : (1) to know wisdom, to understand the essence and causes and objects of things ; and (2) to bring this wisdom to bear upon the facts of life, to find in it a clue for the interpretation of that which was perplexing and abnormal. But success in his endeavour was denied him. The toils and cares which fill up laborious days, and drive away sleep from the eyes of the weary, seemed to him to be in many cases utterly fruitless ; to be imposed upon men for no end ; to have no connection with any higher plan or purpose by which one might suppose the world to be governed. What, then, is his conclusion ? It is that the finite cannot comprehend the infinite ; that no effort is adequate for the task ; that the highest human wisdom is but as folly when it is bent upon forcing a solution of this great problem (ver. 17). " Then I beheld all the work of God, that man cannot find out the work that is done under the sun : because however much a man labour to seek it out, yet he shall not find it ; yea, moreover, though a wise man think to know it, yet he shall not be able to find it." The agnosticism of the writer does not tend to atheism. He does not deny—on the contrary, he affirms—his faith in a great Divine plan to which all the labours of men are related, though what it is and how it is being fulfilled he does not know. The tone in which he records his failure is not without a strain of bitterness ; but one would wish to believe that its prevailing note is that of reverent submission to the Almighty, whose ways he could not comprehend, and that the writer's thoughts would find adequate expression in the devout ejaculation of the apostle, " Oh the depth of the riches both of the wisdom and knowledge of God ! how unsearchable are his judgments, and his ways past finding out ! " (Rom. xi. 33). The pregnant words of Hooker describe the attitude appropriate for creatures in presence of their Creator : " Dangerous it were for the feeble brain of man to wade far into the doings of the Most High ; whom although to know be life, and joy to make mention of his Name ; yet our soundest knowledge is to know that we know him not as indeed he is, neither can know him, and our safest eloquence concerning him is our silence, when we confess without confession that his glory is inexplicable, his greatness above our capacity and reach. He is above, and we upon the earth ; therefore it behoveth our words to be wary and few " ('Eccl. Pol.,' i. 2, 3).—J. W.

EXPOSITION.

CHAPTER IX.

Vers. 1—6.—One fate happens to all, and the dead are cut off from all the feelings and interests of life in the upper world.

Ver. 1.—This continues the subject treated above, confirming the conclusion arrived at in ch. viii. 17, viz. that God's government of the world is unfathomable. **For all this**

I considered in my heart even to declare all this ; literally, *for all this laid I in my heart, and all this I have been about* (equivalent to *I sought*) *to clear up.* The reference is both to what has been said and to what is coming. The *ki,* " for " (which the Vulgate omits), at the beginning gives the reason for the truth of what is advanced ; the writer has omitted no means of arriving at a con-

clusion. One great result of his consideration he proceeds to state. The Septuagint
connects this clause closely with the last
verse of the preceding chapter, "For I applied
all this to my heart, and my heart saw all
this." **The righteous, and the wise, and their
works, are in the hand of God** (Ps. xxxi. 15;
Prov. xxi. 1); *i.e.* in his power, under his direction. Man is not independent. Even the good
and wise, who might be supposed to afford
the plainest evidence of the favourable side
of God's moral government, are subject to the
same unsearchable law. The very incomprehensibility of this principle proves that it
comes from God, and men may well be content to submit themselves to it, knowing that
he is as just as he is almighty. **No man
knoweth either love or hatred.** God's favour
or displeasure are meant. Vulgate, *Et tamen
nescit homo, utrum amore an odio dignus sit.*
We cannot judge from the events that befall
a man what is the view which God takes of
his character. We must not, like Job's
friends, decide that a man is a great sinner
because calamity falls upon him, nor again
suppose that outward prosperity is a proof
of a life righteous and well-pleasing to God.
Outward circumstances are no criterion of
inward disposition or of final judgment.
From the troubles or the comforts which we
ourselves experience or witness in others we
have no right to argue God's favour or displeasure. He disposes matters as seems best
to him, and we must not expect to see every
one in this world treated according to what
we should deem his deserts (comp. Prov. i.
32 with Heb. xii. 6). Delitzsch and others
think that the expressions "love" and
"hatred" are too general to admit of being
interpreted as above, and they determine the
sense to be that no one can tell beforehand
who will be the objects of his love or hate,
or how entirely his feelings may change in
regard of persons with whom he is brought
in contact. The circumstances which give
rise to these sentiments are entirely
beyond his control and foresight. This is
true enough, but it does not seem to me to
be intended. The author is concerned, not
with inward sentiments, but with prosperity
and adversity considered popularly as indications of God's view of things. It would
be but a meagre assertion to state that you
cannot know whether you are to love or hate,
because God ordains all such contingencies;
whereas to warn against hasty and infidel
judgments on the ground of our ignorance
of God's mysterious ways, is sound and
weighty advice, and in due harmony with
what follows in the next verses. The interpretation, "No man knows whether he shall
meet with the love or hatred of his fellows,"
has commended itself to some critics, but
is as inadmissible as the one just mentioned.

By all that is before them. The Hebrew is
simply, "all [lies] before them." All that
shall happen, all that shall shape their
destiny in the future, is obscure and unknown, and beyond their control. Septuagint,
Τὰ πάντα πρὸ προσώπου αὐτῶν. The Vulgate
mixes this clause with the following verse,
But all things are kept uncertain for the future.
St. Gregory, "As thou knowest not who are
converted from sin to goodness, nor who turn
back from goodness to sin; so also thou dost
not understand what is doing towards thyself as thy merits deserve. And as thou
dost not at all comprehend another's end, so
art thou also unable to foresee thine own.
For thou knowest now what progress thou
hast made thyself, but what I [God] still
think of thee in secret thou knowest not.
Thou now thinkest on thy deeds of righteousness; but thou knowest not how strictly they
are weighed by me. Woe even to the praiseworthy life of men if it be judged without
mercy, because when strictly examined it is
overwhelmed in the presence of the Judge
by the very conduct with which it imagines
that it pleases him" ('Moral.,' xxix. 34,
Oxford transl.).

Ver. 2.—**All** things come **alike to all**; literally, *all things [are] like that which [happens]
to all persons.* There is no difference in the
treatment of persons; all people of every
kind meet with circumstances of every kind.
Speaking generally, there is no discrimination, apparently, in the distribution of good
and evil. Sun and shade, calm and storm,
fruitful and unfruitful seasons, joy and
sorrow, are dispensed by inscrutable laws.
The Septuagint, reading differently, has,
"Vanity is in all;" the Syriac unites two
readings, "All before him is vanity, all as to
all" (Ginsburg). There is **one event to the
righteous, and to the wicked.** All men have
the same lot, whether it be death or any
other contingency, without regard to their
moral condition. The classes into which men
are divided must be noted. "Righteous"
and "wicked" refer to men in their conduct
to others. **The good.** The Septuagint,
Vulgate, and Syriac add, "to the evil,"
which is said again almost immediately.
To the clean, and to the unclean. "The
good" and "clean" are those who are not
only ceremonially pure, but, as the epithet
"good" shows, are morally undefiled. **To
him that sacrificeth**; *i.e.* the man who attends
to the externals of religion, offers the obligatory sacrifices, and brings his free-will
offerings. **The good . . . the sinner;** in the
widest senses. **He that sweareth, as he that
feareth an oath.** He who takes an oath
lightly, carelessly, or falsely (comp. Zech.
v. 3), is contrasted with him who regards it
as a holy thing, or shrinks in awe from
invoking God's Name in such a case This

last idea is regarded as a late Essenic development (see Josephus, 'Bell. Jud.,' ii. 8. 6); though something like it is found in the sermon on the mount, "I say unto you, Swear not at all," etc. (Matt. v. 34—37). Dean Plumptre, however, throws doubt on the above interpretation, owing to the fact that in all the other groups the good side is placed first; and he suggests that "he who sweareth" may be one who does his duty in this particular religiously and well (comp. Deut. vi. 13; Isa. lxv. 16), and "he who fears the oath" is a man whose conscience makes him shrink from the oath of compurgation (Exod. xxii. 10, 11; Numb. v. 19—22), or who is too cowardly to give his testimony in due form. The Vulgate has, *Ut perjurus, ita et ille qui verum dejerat;* and it seems unnecessary to present an entirely new view of the passage in slavish expectation of a concinnity which the author cannot be proved to have ever aimed at. The five contrasted pairs are the righteous and the wicked, the clean and the unclean, the sacrificer and the non-sacrificer, the good and the sinner, the profane swearer and the man who reverences an oath. The last clause is rendered by the Septuagint, "So is he who sweareth (ὁ ὀμνύων) even as he who fears the oath," which is as ambiguous as the original. A cautious Greek gnome says—

Ὅρκον δὲ φεῦγε, κἂν δικαίως ὀμνύῃς.

"Avoid an oath, though justly you might swear."

Ver. 3.—**This is an evil among all** things **that are done under the sun.** The "evil" is explained in the following words, which speak of the common fate. The Vulgate (followed by Ginsburg and others) takes the first words as equivalent to a superlative: *Hoc est pessimum inter omnia,* "This is the greatest evil of all that is done under the sun." But the article would have been used in this case; nor would this accurately express Koheleth's sentiments. He looks upon death only as one of the evils appertaining to men's career on earth—one of the phases of that identity of treatment so certain and so inexplicable, which leads to disastrous results (ch. viii. 11). **That there is one event unto all.** The "one event," as the end of the verse shows, is death. We have here the old strain repeated which is found in ch. ii. 14—16; iii. 19; v. 15; vi. 12; "Omnes eodem cogimur" (Horace, 'Carm.,' ii. 3. 25). **Yea, also the heart of the sons of men is full of evil.** In consequence of this indiscriminating destiny men sin recklessly, are encouraged in their wickedness. **Madness is in their heart while they live.** The "madness" is conduct opposed to the dictates of wisdom and reason, as ch. i. 17; ii. 2, 12. All their life long men follow their own lusts

and passions, and care little for God's will and law, or their own best interests. This is well called "want of reason" (περιφέρεια, Septuagint). **And after that they go to the dead.** The verb is omitted in the Hebrew, being implied by the preposition אֶל, "to;" the omission is very forcible. Delitzsch, Wright, and others render, "after him," *i.e.* after man's life is ended, which seems rather to say, "after they die, they die." The idea, however, appears to be, both good and evil go to the same place, pass away into nothingness, are known no more in this world. Here at present Koheleth leaves the question of the future life, having already intimated his belief in ch. iii. and viii. 11, etc.

Ver. 4.—**For to him that is joined to all the living there is hope.** As long as a man lives (is one of living beings) he has some hope, whatever it be. This feeling is inextinguishable even unto the end.

Ἄελπτον οὐδέν· πάντα δ' ἐλπίζειν χρεών.

"Hope springs eternal in the human breast."

Thus Bailey sings, in 'Festus'—

"All
Have hopes, however wretched they may be,
Or blessed. It is hope which lifts the lark so high,
Hope of a lighter air and bluer sky;
And the poor hack which drops down on the flints,
Upon whose eye the dust is settling, he
Hopes, but to die. No being exists, of hope,
Of love, void."

This clause gives a reason for the folly of men, mentioned in ver. 3. Whatever be their lot, or their way of life, they see no reason to make any change by reformation or active exertion. They go on hoping, and do nothing. Something may turn up; amid the inexplicable confusion of the ordering of events some happy contingency may arrive. The above is the reading according to the Keri. Thus the Septuagint: Ὅτι τίς ὃς κοινωνεῖ; "For who is he that has fellowship with all the living?" Symmachus has, "For who is he that will always continue to live?" while the Vulgate gives, *Nemo est qui semper vivat.* The Khetib points differently, offering the reading, "For who is excepted?" *i.e.* from the common lot, the interrogation being closely connected with the preceding verse, or "Who can choose?" *i.e.* whether he will die or not. The sentence then proceeds, "To all the living there is hope." But the rendering of the Authorized Version has good authority, and affords the better sense. **For a living dog is better than a dead lion.** The dog in Palestine was not made a pet and companion, as it is among us, but was regarded as a loathsome and despicable object comp. 1 Sam. xvii.

43; 2 Sam. iii. 8); while the lion was considered as the noblest of beasts, the type of power and greatness (comp. Prov. xxx. 30; Isa. xxxi. 4). So the proverbial saying in the text means that the vilest and meanest creature possessed of life is better than the highest and mightiest which has succumbed to death. There is an apparent contradiction between this sentence and such passages as claim a preference for death over life, e.g. ch. iv. 2; vii. 1; but in the latter the writer is viewing life with all its sorrows and bitter experiences, here he regards it as affording the possibility of enjoyment. In the one case he holds death as desirable, because it delivers from further sorrow and puts an end to misery; in the other, he deprecates death as cutting off from pleasure and hope. He may also have in mind that now is the time to do the work which we have to perform: "The night cometh when no man can work;" Ecclus. xvii. 28, "Thanksgiving perisheth from the dead, as from one that is not; the living and sound shall praise the Lord" (comp. Isa. xxxviii. 18, 19).

Ver. 5.—**For the living know that they shall die.** This is added in confirmation of the statement in ver. 4. The living have at least the consciousness that they will soon have to die, and this leads them to work while it is day, to employ their faculties worthily, to make use of opportunities, to enjoy and profit by the present. They have a certain fixed event to which they must look forward; and they have not to stand idle, lamenting their fate, but their duty and their happiness is to accept the inevitable and make the best of it. **But the dead know not anything.** They are cut off from the active, bustling world; their work is done; they have nothing to expect, nothing to labour for. What passes upon earth affects them not; the knowledge of it reaches them no longer. Aristotle's idea was that the dead did know something, in a hazy and indistinct way, of what went on in the upper world, and were in some slight degree influenced thereby, but not to such a degree as to change happiness into misery, or vice versâ ('Eth. Nicom.,' i. 10 and 11). **Neither have they any more a reward;** i.e. no fruit for labour done. There is no question here about future retribution in another world. The gloomy view of the writer at this moment precludes all idea of such an adjustment of anomalies after death. **For the memory of them is forgotten.** They have not even the poor reward of being remembered by loving posterity, which in the mind of an Oriental was an eminent blessing, to be much desired. There is a paronomasia in zeker, "memory," and sakar, "reward," which, as Plumptre suggests,

may be approximately represented in English by the words "record" and "reward."

Ver. 6.—**Also their love, and their hatred, and their envy, is now** (long ago) **perished.** All the feelings which are exhibited and developed in the life of the upper world are annihilated (comp. ver. 10). Three are selected as the most potent passions, such as by their strength and activity might ideally be supposed to survive even the stroke of death. But all are now at an end. **Neither have they any more a portion for ever in any thing that is done under the sun.** Between the dead and the living an impassable gulf exists. The view of death here given, intensely gloomy and hopeless as it appears to be, is in conformity with other passages of the Old Testament (see Job xiv. 10—14; Ps. vi. 5; xxx. 9; Isa. xxxviii. 10—19; Ecclus. xvii. 27, 28; Bar. iii. 16—19), and that imperfect dispensation. Koheleth and his contemporaries were of those "who through fear of death were all their lifetime subject to bondage" (Heb. ii. 15); it was Christ who brightened the dark valley, showing the blessedness of those who die in the Lord, bringing life and immortality to light through the gospel (2 Tim. i. 10). Some expositors have felt the pessimistic utterances of this passage so deeply that they have endeavoured to account for them by introducing an atheistic objector, or an intended opposition between flesh and spirit. But there is not a trace of any two such voices, and the suggestion is quite unnecessary. The writer, while believing in the continued existence of the soul, knows little and has little that is cheering to say about its condition; and what he does say is not inconsistent with a judgment to come, though he has not yet arrived at the enunciation of this great solution. The Vulgate renders the last clause, Nec habent partem in hoc sæculo et in opere quod sub sole geritur. But "for ever" is the correct rendering of לְעוֹלָם, and Ginsburg concludes that Jerome's translation can be traced to the Hagadistic interpretation of the verse which restricts its scope to the wicked. The author of the Book of Wisdom, writing later, takes a much more hopeful view of death and the departed (see ch. i. 15; ii. 22—24; iii. 1; vi. 18; viii. 17; xv. 3, etc.).

Vers. 7—12.—These verses give the application of the facts just mentioned. The inscrutability of the moral government of the world, the uncertainty of life, the condition of the dead, lead to the conclusion again that one should use one's life to the best advantage; and Koheleth repeats his caution concerning the issues and duration of life.

Ver. 7.—**Go thy way, eat thy bread with joy.** This is not an injunction to lead a selfish life of Epicurean pleasure; but taking the limited view to which he here confines himself, the Preacher inculcates the practical wisdom of looking at the bright side of things; he says in effect (though he takes care afterwards to correct a wrong impression which might be given), " Let us eat and drink; for to-morrow we die" (1 Cor. xv. 32). We have had the same counsel in ch. ii. 24; iii. 12, 13, 22; v. 18; viii. 15. **Drink thy wine with a merry heart.** Wine was not an accompaniment of meals usually; it was reserved for feasts and solemn occasions. Bread and wine are here regarded as the necessary means of support and comfort (comp. ch. x. 19; Gen. xiv. 18; 1 Sam. xvi. 20, etc.). The moderate use of wine is nowhere forbidden; there is no law in the Old Testament against the use of intoxicating drinks; the employment of such fluids as cordials, exhilarating, strengthening and comforting, is often referred to (comp. Judg. ix. 13; Ps. civ. 15; Prov. xxxi. 6, 7; Ecclus. xxxi. 27, 28). Thus Koheleth's advice, taken even literally, is not contrary to the spirit of his religion. **For God now** (*long ago*) **accepteth thy works.** The " works " are not moral or religious doings, in reward of which God gives temporal blessings, which is plainly opposed to Koheleth's chief contention in all this passage. The *works* are the eating and drinking just mentioned. By the constitution of man's nature, and by the ordering of Providence, such capacity of enjoyment is allowable, and there need be no scruple in using it. Such things are God's good gifts, and to be received with reverence and thanksgiving; and he who thus employs them is well-pleasing unto the Lord (ch. ii. 24; viii. 15).

Ver. 8.—**Let thy garments be always white.** The Preacher brings into prominence certain particulars of enjoyment, more noticeable than mere eating and drinking. White garments in the East (as among ourselves) were symbols of joy and purity. Thus the singers in Solomon's temple were arrayed in white linen (2 Chron. v. 12). Mordecai was thus honoured by King Ahasuerus (Esth. viii. 15), the angels are seen similarly decked (Mark xvi. 5), and the glorified saints are clothed in white (Rev. iii. 4, 5, 18). So in the pseudepigraphal books the same imagery is retained. Those that " have fulfilled the Law of the Lord have received glorious garments, and are clothed in white" (2 Esdr. ii. 39, 40). Among the Romans the same symbolism obtained. Horace ('Sat.,' ii. 2. 60)—

" Ille repotia, natales aliosve dierum
Festos albatus celebret."

" Though he in whitened toga celebrate
His wedding, birthday, or high festival."

Let thy head lack no ointment. Oil and perfumes were used on festive occasions not only among Eastern nations, but by Greeks and Romans (see on ch. vii. 1). Thus Telemachus is anointed with fragrant oil by the fair Polykaste (Homer, 'Od.,' iii. 466). Sappho complains to Phaon (Ovid, ' Heroid.,' xv. 76)—

" Non Arabo noster rore capillus olet."

" No myrrh of Araby bedews my hair."

Such allusions in Horace are frequent and commonly cited (see 'Carm.,' i. 5. 2; ii. 7. 7, 8; ii. 11. 15, etc.). Thus the double injunction in this verse counsels one to be always happy and cheerful. Gregory Thaumaturgus (cited by Plumptre) represents the passage as the error of " men of vanity;" and other commentators have deemed that it conveyed not the Preacher's own sentiments, but those of an atheist whom he cites. There is, as we have already seen, no need to resort to such an explanation. Doubtless the advice may readily be perverted to evil, and made to sanction sensuality and licentiousness, as we see to have been done in Wisd. ii. 6—9; but Koheleth only urges the moderate use of earthly goods as consecrated by God's gift.

Ver. 9.—**Live joyfully with the wife whom thou lovest**; literally, *see life with a wife whom thou lovest.* The article is omitted, as the maxim is to be taken generally. In correction of the outspoken condemnation of women in ch. vii. 26, Koheleth here recognizes the happiness of a home where is found a helpmate beloved and worthy of love (comp. Prov. v. 18, 19; xvii. 22, on which our passage seems to be founded; and Ecclus. xxvi. 13—18). (For the expression, "see life," *vide* note on ch. ii. 1.) St. Jerome's comment is misleading, " Quæcumque tibi placuerit feminarum ejus gaude complexu." Some critics translate *ishshah* here "woman." Thus Cox: " Enjoy thyself with any woman whom thou lovest; " but the best commentators agree that the married state is meant in the text, not mere sensual enjoyment. **All the days of the life of thy vanity;** *i.e.* throughout the time of thy quickly passing life. This is repeated after the next clause (though there omitted by the Septuagint and Syriac), in order to emphasize the transitoriness of the present and the consequent wisdom of enjoying it while it lasts. So Horace bids man " carpe diem " (' Carm.,' i. 11. 8), " enjoy each atom of the day;'" and Martial sings (' Epigr.,' vii. 47. 11)—

" Vive velut rapto fugitivaque gaudia carpe."

"Live thou thy life as stolen, and enjoy
    Thy quickly fading pleasures."

Which he (*God*) **hath given thee under the
sun.** The relative may refer to either the
"wife" or "the days of life." The Septuagint
and Vulgate take it as belonging to the latter,
and this seems most suitable (comp. ch. v.
17). **That is thy portion in this life, and in
thy labour,** etc. Such moderate enjoyment
is the recompense allowed by God for the
toil which accompanies a properly spent life.

Ver. 10.—**Whatsoever thy hand findeth to
do, do it with thy might.** In accordance
with what has been already said, and to
combat the idea that, as man cannot control
his fate, he should take no pains to work his
work, but fold his hands in resigned inaction, Koheleth urges him not to despair,
but to do his part manfully as long as life
is given, and with all the energies of his
soul carry out the purpose of his being.
The Septuagint gives, "All things whatsoever thy hand shall find to do, do it as
thy power is (ὡς ἡ δύναμίς σου);" Vulgate,
*Quodcumque facere potest manus tua, in-
stanter operare.* The expression at the
commencement may be illustrated by Lev.
xii. 8; xxv. 28; Judg. ix. 33, where it implies ability to carry out some intention,
and in some passages is thus rendered, "is
able," etc. (comp. Prov. iii. 27). It is therefore erroneous to render it in this place,
"Whatever by chance cometh to hand;" or
"Let might be right." Rather it is a call
to work as the prelude and accompaniment
of enjoyment, anticipating St. Paul's maxim
(2 Thess. iii. 10), "If any would not work,
neither should he eat." Ginsburg's interpretation is dishonouring to the Preacher
and foreign to his real sentiments, "Have
recourse to every source of voluptuous
gratification, while thou art in thy strength."
The true meaning of the verse is confirmed
by such references as John ix. 4, "I must
work the works of him that sent me, while
it is day: the night cometh, when no man
can work;" 2 Cor. vi. 2, "Now is the
accepted time; now is the day of salvation;"
Gal. vi. 10, "As we have opportunity, let us
do good unto all men." **For there is no work,
nor device, nor knowledge, nor wisdom, in
the grave.** The departed have no more work
which they can do, no plans or calculations
to make; their knowledge is strictly limited,
their wisdom is ended. It needs body and
soul to carry on the labours and activities of
this world; when these are severed, and can
no longer act together, there is a complete
alteration in the man's relations and capacities. "The grave," *sheol* (which is found
nowhere else in Ecclesiastes), is the place to
which go the souls of the dead—a shadowy
region. **Whither thou goest;** to which all are
bound. It is plain that the writer believes

in the continued existence of the soul, as he
differentiates its life in *sheol* from its life on
earth, the energies and operations which are
carried on in the one case being curtailed or
eclipsed in the other. Of any repentance,
or purification, or progress, in the unseen
world, Koheleth knows and says nothing.
He would seem to regard existence there as
a sleep or a state of insensibility; at any
rate, such is the natural view of the present
passage.

Vers. 11, 12.—Section 8. *It is impossible
to calculate upon the issues and duration of
life.*

Ver. 11.—He reverts to the sentiment of
ver. 1, that we cannot calculate on the
issues of life. Work as we may and must
and ought, the results are uncertain and
beyond our control. This he shows by his
own personal experience. **I returned, and
saw under the sun.** The expression here
does not indicate a new departure, but
merely a repetition and confirmation of a
previous thought—the dependence and con-
ditionality of man. It implies, too, a correction of a possible misunderstanding of
the injunction to labour, as if one's own
efforts were sure to secure success. **The race
is not to the swift.** One is reminded of the
fable of the hare and tortoise; but Koheleth's meaning is different. In the instances
given he intimates that, though a man is
well equipped for his work and uses all
possible exertions, he may incur failure. So
one may be a fleet runner, and yet, owing
to some untoward accident or disturbing
circumstance, not come in first. Thus
Ahimaaz brought to David tidings of Absalom's defeat before Cushi, who had had the
start of him (2 Sam. xviii. 27, 31). There
is no occasion to invent an allusion to the
foot-race in the formal Greek games. **The
battle to the strong.** Victory does not
always accrue to mighty men, heroes. As
David, himself an instance of the truth of
the maxim, says (1 Sam. xvii. 47), "The
Lord saveth not with sword and spear; for
the battle is the Lord's" (comp. 2 Chron.
xx. 15; Ps. xxxiii. 16). **Neither yet bread
to the wise.** Wisdom will not ensure competency. To do this requires other endowments. Many a man of cultivated intellect
and of high mental power is left to starve.
Riches to men of understanding. Aristophanes accounts for the unequal distribution
of wealth thus ('Plutus,' 88), the god himself
speaking—

"I threatened, when a boy,
On none but just and wise and orderly
My favours to bestow; so Zeus in jealousy
Hath made me blind, that I may none of
    these
Distinguish."

Nor yet favour to men of skill. "Skill" here does not mean dexterity in handicrafts or arts, but knowledge generally; and the gnome says that reputation and influence do not necessarily accompany the possession of knowledge and learning; knowledge is not a certain or indispensable means to favour. Says the Greek gnomist—

Τύχης τὰ θνητῶν πράγματ', οὐκ εὐβουλίας.

"Not prudence rules, but fortune, men's affairs."

But time and chance happeneth to them all. We have had the word *eth*, "time," all through ch. iii. and elsewhere; but פֶּגַע, rendered "chance," is uncommon, being found only in 1 Kings v. 4 (18, Hebrew). Everything has its proper season appointed by God, and man is powerless to control these arrangements. Our English word "chance" conveys an erroneous impression. What is meant is rather "incident," such as a calamity, disappointment, unforeseen occurrence. All human purposes are liable to be changed or controlled by circumstances beyond man's power, and incapable of explanation. A hand higher than man's disposes events, and success is conditioned by superior laws which work unexpected results.

Ver. 12.—**Man also knoweth not his time;** Vulgate, *Nescit homo finem suum*, understanding "his time" to mean his death-hour; but it may include any misfortune or accident. The particle *gam*, "also," or "even," belongs to "his time." Not only are results out of man's control (ver. 11), but his life is in higher hands, and he is never sure of a day. **As the fishes that are taken in an evil net,** etc. The suddenness and unforeseen nature of calamities that befall men are here expressed by two forcible similes (comp. Prov. vii. 23; Ezek. xii. 13; xxxii. 3). Thus Homer ('Iliad,' v. 487)—

"Beware lest ye, as in the meshes caught
Of some wide-sweeping net, become the prey
And booty of your foes."

(Derby.)

So are the sons of men snared in an evil time. Men are suddenly overtaken by calamity, which they are totally unable to foresee or provide against. Our Lord says (Luke xxi. 35) that the last day shall come as a snare on all that dwell in the earth (comp. Ezek. vii. 7, 12).

Vers. 13—16.—Section 9. That *wisdom, even when it does good service, is not always rewarded*, is shown by an example.

Ver. 13.—**This wisdom have I seen also under the sun;** better, as the Septuagint, *This also I saw to be wisdom under the sun.*

The experience which follows he recognized as an instance of worldly wisdom. To what special event he alludes is quite unknown. Probably the circumstance was familiar to his contemporaries. It is not to be considered as an allegory, though of course it is capable of spiritual application. The event in Bible history most like it is the preservation of Abel-Beth-maachah by the counsel of the wise woman (whose name is forgotten) narrated in 2 Sam. xx. 15—22. **And it seemed great unto me;** Septuagint, Καὶ μεγάλη ἐστι πρὸς μέ, "And it is great before me." To my mind it appeared an important example (comp. Esth. x. 3). Some critics who contend for the Solomonic authorship of our book, see here an allegorical reference to the foreseen revolt of Jeroboam, whose insurrection had been opposed by certain wise statesmen, but had been carried out in opposition to their counsel. Wordsworth considers that the apologue may be illustrated by the history of Jerusalem, when great powers were arrayed against it in the time of Isaiah, and the prophet by his prayers and exhortations delivered it (2 Kings xix. 2, 6, 20), but was wholly disregarded afterwards, nay, was put to death by the son of the king whom he saved. But all this is *nihil ad rem*. As Plautus says, "Hæc quidem deliramenta loquitur."

Ver. 14.—**There was a little city.** The substantive verb *is*, as commonly, omitted. Commentators have amused themselves with endeavouring to identify the city here mentioned. Thus some see herein Athens, saved by the counsel of Themistocles, who was afterwards driven from Athens and died in misery (Justin., ii. 12); or Dora, near Mount Carmel, besieged unsuccessfully by Antiochus the Great, B.C. 218, though we know nothing of the circumstances (Polyb., v. 66); but see note on ver. 13. The Septuagint takes the whole paragraph hypothetically, "Suppose there was a little city," etc. Wright well compares the historical allusions to events fresh in the minds of his hearers made by our Lord in his parable of the pounds (Luke xix. 12, 14, 15, 27). So we may regard the present section as a parable founded on some historical fact well known at the time when the book was written. **A great king.** The term points to some Persian or Assyrian potentate; or it may mean merely a powerful general (see 1 Kings xi. 24; Job xxix. 25). **Built great bulwarks against it.** The Septuagint has χάρακας μεγάλους, "great palisades;" the Vulgate, *Extruxitque munitiones per gyrum.* What are meant are embankments or mounds raised high enough to overtop the walls of the town, and to command the positions of the besieged. For the same purpose wooden towers were also used (see Deut. xx. 20;

2 Sam. xx. 15; 2 Kings xix. 32; Jer. lii. 4). The Vulgate rounds off the account in the text by adding, *et perfecta est obsidio*, "and the beleaguering was completed."

Ver. 15.—**Now there was found in it a poor wise man.** The verb, regarded as impersonal, may be thus taken. Or we may continue the subject of the preceding verse and consider the king as spoken of: "He came across, met with unexpectedly, a poor man who was wise." So the Septuagint. The word for "poor" in this passage is *misken*, for which see note on ch. iv. 13. **He by his wisdom delivered the city.** When the besieged city had neither soldiers nor arms to defend itself against its mighty enemies, the man of poor estate, hitherto unknown or little regarded, came forward, and by wise counsel relieved his countrymen from their perilous situation. How this was done we are left to conjecture. It may have been by some timely concessions or negotiations; or by the surrender of a chief offender as at Abel-Beth-maachah; or by the assassination of a general, as at Bethulia (Jud. xiii. 8); or by the clever application of mechanical arts, as at Syracuse, under the direction of Archimedes (Livy, xxiv. 34; Plutarch, 'Marcell.,' xv.—xviii.). **Yet no man remembered that same poor man.** As soon as the exigence which brought him forward was past, the poor man fell back into his insignificance, and was thought of no more; he gained no personal advantage by his wisdom; his ungrateful countrymen forgot his very existence. Thus Joseph was treated by the chief butler (Gen. xl. 23). Classical readers will think of Coriolanus, Scipio Africanus, Themistocles, Miltiades, who for their services to the state were rewarded with calumny, false accusation, obloquy, and banishment. The author of the Book of Wisdom gives a different and ideal experience. "I," he says, "for the sake of wisdom shall have estimation among the multitude, and honour with the elders, though I be young. . . . By the means of her I shall obtain immortality, and leave behind me an everlasting memorial" (Wisd. viii. 10—13).

Ver. 16.—**Then said I, Wisdom is better than strength.** The latter part of the verse is not a correction of the former, but the whole comes under the observation introduced by "I said." The story just related leads to this assertion, which reproduces the gnome of ch. vii. 19, wherein it is asserted that wisdom effects more than mere physical strength. There is an interpolation in the Old Latin Version of Wisd. vi. 1 which seems to have been compiled from this passage and Prov. xvi. 13, "Melior est sapientia quam vires, et vir prudens quam fortis." **Nevertheless the poor man's wisdom is de-**

spised, etc. In the instance above mentioned the poor man's wisdom was not despised, and his words were heard and attended to; but this was an abnormal case, occasioned by the extremity of the peril. Koheleth states the result which usually attends wisdom emanating from a disesteemed source. The experience of Ben-Sira pointed to the same issue (see Ecclus. xiii. 22, 23). Horace, 'Epist.,' i. 1. 57—

> "Est animus tibi, sunt mores et lingua
>   fidesque,
>   Sed quadringentis sex septem millia de-
>   sunt;
>   Plebs eris."

> "In wit, worth, honour, one in vain abounds;
>   If of the knight's estate he lack ten
>   pounds,
>   He's low, quite low!"

(Howes.)

"Is not this the carpenter's Son?" asked the people who were offended at Christ (Mark vi. 2, 3).

Vers. 17, 18.—Section 10. Here follow *some proverbial sayings concerning wisdom and its opposite*, which draw the moral from the story in the text.

Ver. 17.—**The words of wise men are heard in quiet more than the cry of him that ruleth among fools.** This verse would be better translated, *Words of the wise in quiet are heard better than the shout of a chief among fools.* The Vulgate takes the tranquillity to appertain to the hearers, thus: *Verba sapientium audiuntur in silentio;* but, as Delitzsch points out, the contrast between "quiet" and "cry" shows that it is the man, and not his auditors, who is quiet. The sentence says that a wise man's words, uttered calmly, deliberately, without pompous declamation or adventitious aids, are of more value than the blustering vociferation of an arch-fool, who seeks to force acceptance for his folly by loudness and swagger (comp. Isa. xxx. 15; and see Isa. xlii. 2 and Matt. xii. 19, passages which speak of the peacefulness, reticence, and unobtrusiveness of true wisdom, as seen in the Son of God). The verse introduces a kind of exception to the general rejection of wisdom mentioned above. Though the multitude turn a deaf ear to a wise man's counsel, yet this tells in the long run, and there are always some teachable persons who sit at his feet and learn from him. "He that ruleth among fools" is not one that governs a silly people, but one who is a prince of fools, who takes the highest place among such.

Ver. 18.—**Wisdom is better than weapons of war.** Such is the moral which Koheleth desires to draw from the little narrative given above (see vers. 14—16; and ch. vii.

19). Wisdom can do what no material force can effect, and often produces results which all the implements of war could not command. **But one sinner destroyeth much good.** The happy consequences which the wise man's counsel might accomplish, or has already accomplished, may be overthrown or rendered useless by the villany or perversity of a bad man. The Vulgate, reading differently, has, *Qui in uno peccaverit, multa bona perdet.* But this seems to be out of keeping with the context. Adam's sin infected the whole race of man; Achan's transgression caused Israel's defeat (Josh. vii. 11, 12); Rehoboam's folly occasioned the great schism (1 Kings xii. 16). The wide-reaching effects of one little error are illustrated by the proverbial saying which every one knows, and which runs in Latin thus: "Clavus unus perdit equi soleam, solea equum, equus equitem, eques castra, castra rempublicam."

HOMILETICS.

Vers. 1—6.—*All things alike to all.* I. ALL MEN EQUALLY IN THE HANDS OF GOD. 1. *Their persons.* The righteous and the wise (ver. 1), but not less certainly the unrighteous and the foolish. God's breath sustains all; God's providence watches over all; God's power encircles all; God's mercy encompasses all. 2. *Their works.* Their actions, whether good or bad, in the sense explained in the last homily, "are conditioned by God, the Governor of the world and the Former of history" (Delitzsch). 3. *Their experiences.* "All lies before them;" *i.e.* all possible experiences lie before men; which shall happen to them being reserved by God in his own power.

II. ALL MEN EQUALLY IGNORANT OF THE FUTURE. "No man knoweth either love or hatred," or "whether it be love or hatred, no man knoweth;" which may signify either that no man can tell whether "providences of a happy nature proceeding from the love of God, or of an unhappy nature proceeding from the hatred of God," are to befall him (J. D. Michaelis, Knobel, Hengstenberg, Plumptre); or that no man can predict whether he will love or hate (Hitzig, Ewald, Delitzsch). In either case the meaning is that no man can certainly predict what a day may bring forth. In so far as the future is in God's hand, man can only learn what it contains by waiting the evolution of events; in so far as it is moulded by man's free determinations, no man can predict what these will be until the moment arrives for their formation.

III. ALL MEN EQUALLY SUBJECT TO DEATH. "All things come alike to all: there is one event" (ver. 2). 1. *To the righteous and to the wicked;* i.e. to the inwardly and morally good and to the inwardly and morally evil. 2. *To the clean and to the unclean;* i.e. to the ceremonially pure and to the ceremonially defiled. 3. *To him that sacrificeth and to him that sacrificeth not;* i.e. to him who observes the outward forms of religion and to him who observes them not. 4. *To him that sweareth and to him that feareth an oath;* i.e. to the openly sinful and to the outwardly reverent and devout. "All alike go to the dead" (ver. 3).

IV. ALL MEN EQUALLY DEFILED BY SIN. "The heart of the sons of men is full of evil, and madness is in their heart while they live" (ver. 3). From which may be learnt: 1. *That sin is a kind of madness.* This will not be doubted by those who consider that sin is the rebellion of a creature against the Creator, and that sinners generally hope both to escape punishment on account of their sin, and to attain felicity through their sin. 2. *That the seat of this madness is in the soul.* It may affect the whole personality of the man, but the perennial fountain whence it springs is the heart, in its alienation from God. "The carnal mind is enmity against God" (Rom. viii. 7). 3. *That the heart is not merely tainted with this madness, but is full of it.* In other words, it is, in its natural condition, wholly under the power of sin. The total corruption of human nature, besides being taught in Scripture (Gen. vi. 5; viii. 21; Job xv. 14; Ps. xiv. 2, 3; ch. vii. 20; Isa. liii. 6; Matt. xv. 19; Rom. iii. 23; Eph. ii. 1—3), is abundantly confirmed by experience. 4. *That, apart from Divine grace, this madness continues unchanged throughout life.* There is nothing in human nature itself or in its surroundings that has power to subdue and far less to eradicate this madness. A new birth alone can rescue the soul from its dominion (John iii. 3).

V. ALL MEN EQUALLY THE SUBJECTS OF HOPE. 1. *Hope a universal possession.* "To him that is joined to all the living there is hope" (ver. 4); *i.e.* while man lives he hopes. *Dum spirat, sperat* (Latin proverb). "Hope springs eternal in the human breast " (Pope). Even the most abject are never, or only seldom, abandoned by this passion. On the contrary, " the miserable hath no other medicine, but only hope " (Shakespeare). When hope expires, life dies. 2. *Hope a potent inspiration.* In ordinary life " we are kept alive by hope " (Rom. viii. 24). The pleasing expectation of future good enables the heart to endure present ills, and nerves the resolution to attempt further efforts. Though sometimes, when ill-grounded, " kings it makes gods, and meaner creatures kings " (Shakespeare), yet when soundly based it

> " Like a cordial, innocent though strong,
> Man's heart at once inspirits and serenes."
>
> (Young.)

Especially is this the case with that good hope through grace (2 Thess. ii. 16) which pertains to the Christian (Rom. v. 5 ; 2 Cor. iii. 12 ; Phil. i. 20 ; 1 Pet. i. 13).

VI. ALL MEN EQUALLY POSSESSED OF INTELLIGENCE. Not of equal intelligence, but equally intelligent. In particular : 1. *All know themselves to be mortal.* " The living know that they shall die " (ver. 5). They may frequently ignore this fact, and deliberately shut their eyes upon it, but of the fact itself they are not ignorant. 2. *In this knowledge they are superior to the dead,* who " know not anything, neither have they any more a reward, for the memory of them is forgotten ; " who in fact, having dropped out of life, have for ever ceased to take an interest in anything that is done under the sun.

Learn : 1. The essential equality of all men. 2. The inherent dignity of life. 3. The value of the present.

Ver. 4.—" *A living dog better than a dead lion.*" I. ANIMATED BEING BETTER THAN INANIMATE. Life a higher product than matter ; and a lion without life is only matter. Life added to matter in its meanest forms imparts to it a dignity, worth, and use not possessed by matter in its most magnificent shapes where life is absent. The higher life, the nobler being.

II. COMPLETED BEING BETTER THAN INCOMPLETE. A living dog is a complete organism ; a dead lion an organism defective. The living dog possesses all that is necessary to realize the idea of " dog ; " the dead lion wants the more important element, life, and retains only the less important, matter. In the living dog are seen the " spirit " and " form " combined ; in the dead lion only the " form " without the " spirit." If presently man is complete naturally, he is incomplete spiritually. Hereafter redeemed and renewed, man will be " perfect and entire, wanting nothing."

III. ACTIVE BEING BETTER THAN INACTIVE. The living dog, if not a person, is yet more than a thing. Along with life and an organism, it has powers and functions it can exercise ; senses through which it can perceive, a measure of intelligence through which it can understand, at least rudimentary affections it can both feel and express, instincts and impulses by and under which it can act. On the other hand, the dead lion has none of these, however once it may have owned them all. It is now passive, still, inert, powerless—an emblem of the soul dead in sin, as a living dog is of the same soul energized by religion.

IV. SERVICEABLE BEING BETTER THAN UNSERVICEABLE. A living dog of some use, a dead lion of none. The gigantic powers of the forest king are by death reduced to a nullity, and can effect nothing ; the feeble capacities of the yelping cur, just because it is alive, can be turned to profitable account. So magnificent powers of body and intellect without spiritual life are comparatively valueless, while smaller abilities, if inspired by grace, may accomplish important designs.

LESSONS. 1. Be thankful for life. 2. Seek that moral and spiritual completeness which is the highest glory of life. 3. Endeavour to turn the powers of life to the best account. 4. Serve him from whom life comes.

Vers. 7—10.—*The picture of an ideal life.* I. A LIFE OF PERENNIAL JOY. The joy should be fourfold. 1. *Material enjoyment.* " Go thy way, eat thy bread with joy, and drink thy wine with a merry heart " (ver. 7). The permission herein granted to make a pleasurable use of the good things of this world, of its meats and its drinks, has not been revoked by Christianity. Not only did the Son of man by his example (Matt.

xi. 19; Luke vii. 34; John ii. 1—11) show that religion did not require men to be ascetics or monks, Rechabites or Nazarites, but the apostolic writers have made it clear that Christianity is not meats or drinks (Rom. xiv. 17; 1 Tim. iv. 3; Heb. ix. 10), and that while no one has a right to over-indulge himself in either, thereby becoming gluttonous and a wine-bibber, on the other hand no one is warranted in the name of Christianity to impose on believers such ordinances as—" Touch not, taste not, handle not" (Col. ii. 21). 2. *Domestic happiness.* "Live joyfully with the wife whom thou lovest all the days of the life of thy vanity" (ver. 9). Marriage is not only honourable and innocent (Heb. xiii. 4) as being a Divine institution (Matt. xix. 4—6), but is one of the purest sources of felicity open to man on earth, provided it be contracted in the fear of God, and cemented with mutual love. As woman was made for man (1 Cor. xi. 9), to be his helpmeet (Gen. ii. 20), *i.e.* his counterpart and complement, companion and counsellor, equal and friend; so he that findeth a wife findeth a good thing, and obtaineth favour of the Lord (Prov. xviii. 22)—findeth one in whose love he may indulge himself, in whose sympathy he may refresh himself, in whose grace he may sun himself without fear of sin. The notion that a higher phase of the religious life is attained by celibates than by married persons is against both reason and revelation, and is contradicted by the fruits which in practical experience it usually bears. Neither the Preacher nor the great Teacher grants permission to men to live joyfully with unmarried females or with other people's wives, but only with their own partners; and neither Old Testament nor New favours the idea that men should take as wives any women but those they love, or should treat otherwise than with affection those they marry (Eph. v. 28). 3. *Religious felicity.* Arising from two things. (1) The cultivation of personal purity. "Let thy garments be always white." Though "white garments" were most probably intended by the Preacher to be a symbol of joy and gladness, they may be used as an emblem of purity, since they are so explained in the Talmud and Midrash. (2) The realization of Divine favour. "God now accepteth thy works," or "God hath already accepted thy works." Here again the Preacher's intention was no doubt to say that such enjoyment as he recommended was not discommended, but rather distinctly approved of by God; that God did not reject, but from long ago had accepted, such works as eating and drinking, etc., and had shown his mind concerning them by furnishing in abundance the materials for them. Yet with greater emphasis the Preacher's words will apply to the works of the Christian believer, who with all his activities is accepted in the Beloved (Eph. i. 6), and entitled to derive therefrom an argument, not for sinful indulgence, but for the cultivation of a joyous and holy life.

II. A LIFE OF UNWEARIED ACTIVITY. The work of a good man ought to be: 1. *Deliberately chosen.* Voluntarily undertaken, not reluctantly endured; the work of one whose hands have been stretched out in search of occupation. "Whatsoever thy hand *findeth* to do." 2. *Widely extended.* A good man's labours should not be too restricted either as to number, character, or sphere. "This one thing I do" (Phil. iii. 13) does not signify that never more than one business at a time should engage a good man's attention. The ideal good man should put his hand to every sort of good work that Providence may place in his way (Gal. vi. 9, 10)—at least so far as time and ability allow. 3. *Energetically performed.* Whatsoever the hands of a good man find to do, he should do with his might. Earnestness an indispensable condition of acceptable service. Fitful and intermittent, half-hearted and indifferent, labour especially in good work, to be condemned (1 Cor. xv. 58). 4. *Religiously inspired.* A good man should have sufficient reasons for his constant activity. The argument to which the Preacher alludes, though not the highest, but the lowest, is nevertheless powerful, viz. that this life is the only working season a man has. "There is no work, nor device, nor knowledge, nor wisdom, in the grave, whither thou goest" (ver. 10). The inhabitants of the under-world are for ever done with the activities of earth. The good man no more than the wicked can pursue his schemes when he has vanished from this mundane scene. Hence the urgency of working while it is called to-day (John ix. 4). Though the Christian has loftier and clearer conceptions of the after-life of the good than Old Testament saints had, the Preacher's argument is not possessed of less, but rather of more, force as an incitement to Christian work, seeing that the "now" of the present life is the only accepted time, and the only day of salvation (2 Cor. vi. 2).

Learn: 1. The twofold aspect of every true life—as one of receiving and giving, of enjoying and working. 2. The essential connection between these two departments of life—the joy being a necessary condition as well as natural result of all true work, and the work being a necessary expression and invaluable sustainer of the joy. 3. The true way of redeeming life—to consecrate its days and years to serving the Lord with gladness, or to rejoicing in God and doing his will.

Ver. 10.—*Words to a worker.* I. THE WORKER DESCRIBED: MAN. 1. *Furnished with capacities for work.* With bodily organs and mental endowments, with speech and reason. 2. *Located in a sphere of work.* The world a vast workshop, in which every creature is busily employed—not only the irrational animals, but even things without life. 3. *Appointed to the destiny of work.* As while sinless in Eden man was set to dress the garden and to keep it, and after the Fall beyond its precincts he was commanded to till the ground and to earn his bread through the sweat of his brow, so is he still charged to be a worker, a Christian apostle even saying that "if a man will not work neither shall he eat" (2 Thess. iii. 10). 4. *Impelled by a desire of work.* Under the compulsion of his own nature and of the constitution of the world, man is constrained to go forth in search of work, of labour for his hands, of exercise for his mind, and generally of employment for his manhood.

II. THE WORKER COUNSELLED. 1. *To do the duty that lies nearest.* This the obvious import of the words, "Whatsoever thy hand findeth to do, do it." To men in earnest about finding their life-work, the duties that lie nearest will commonly be the most urgent; and *vice versâ*, the duties that are most urgent will usually be found to lie nearest. Among these will stand out conspicuously (1) the preservation of the body, (2) the cultivation of the mind, (3) the salvation of the soul; while others will assume their places in the order of succession according to their importance. 2. *To do every duty with energy.* "Whatsoever thy hand findeth to do, do it with thy might." Half-hearted labour, besides wasting time, spoils the work and demoralizes the worker. It is due to God, whose servant man is, to the importance of the work in which he is engaged, and to himself as one whose highest interests are involved in all he does, that man should labour with enthusiasm, diligence, and might. 3. *To do each duty from an impulse of individual responsibility.* "Whatsoever *thy* hand findeth to do, that do *thou!* " As no man can tell what his neighbour's duty is in every instance, so can no man in any case devolve his duty on another. "To every man his work! " is God's great labour law. If other workers are unfaithful, be not thou unfaithful. 4. *To do all duties under a sense of the value of time.* Remembering that this life is man's only opportunity of working, that it is swiftly passing, that death is near, and that there is neither wisdom, knowledge, nor device in the grave whither man goes.

Vers. 11, 12.—*Time and chance for all.* I. AN UNDENIABLE PROPOSITION—that the issues of life are incalculable. This truth set forth in five illustrations. 1. *The race not to the swift.* Sometimes, perhaps often, it is, yet not always or necessarily, so that men can calculate the issue of any contest. Just as swiftness of foot is no guarantee that a runner shall be first at the goal, so in other undertakings the possession of superior ability is no proof that one shall attain pre-eminence above his fellows. 2. *The battle not to the strong.* By many experiences Israel had been taught that "the battle is the Lord's (1 Sam. xvii. 47), and that there is "no king saved by the multitude of a host" (Ps. xxxiii. 16). Neither Pharaoh (Exod. xiv. 27), nor Zerah the Ethiopian (2 Chron. xiv. 12), nor the Moabites and Ammonites who came against Jehoshaphat (2 Chron. xx. 27), nor Sennacherib (2 Kings xix. 35), were the better for their innumerable armies; and though Napoleon was wont to say that God was always on the side of the strongest battalions, instances can be cited in sufficient numbers to show that it is God who giveth the victory to kings (Ps. cxliv. 10), and that he does not always espouse the side of those who can summon the most warriors into the field. 3. *Bread not to the wise.* Here again the sense is that while capacity and diligence are usually rewarded, yet the exceptions to the rule are so numerous as to prove that it cannot certainly be predicted that a man of sagacity will always be able to secure for himself the means of subsistence. 4. *Riches not to men of understanding.* At least not always. Men of talent, and even of industry, sometimes fail in amassing riches, and when they do succeed, cannot always keep the riches they have amassed.

Nothing commoner than to find poor wise men (ver. 15) and rich fools (Luke xii. 20) Though as a rule the hand of the diligent maketh rich (Prov. x. 4), men of splendid abilities often spend their strength for nought. Riches are no sign of wisdom. 5. *Favour not to men of skill.* Even genius cannot always command the approbation and appreciation it deserves. The world's inventors and discoverers have seldom been rewarded according to their merits. The world has for the most part coolly accepted the productions of their genius, and remanded themselves to oblivion. The fate of the poor wise man after mentioned (ver. 15) has often been experienced.

II. An incontrovertible argument—that death, though certain as to fact, is uncertain as to incidence. 1. *The momentous truth stated.* "Man knoweth not his time," *i.e.* of his death, which ever falls upon him suddenly, as a thief in the night. Even when death's approach is anticipated, there is no reason to suppose its actual occurrence is not always unexpected. 2. *The simple illustration given.* "As the fishes that are taken in an evil net, and as the birds that are caught in the snare, even so are the sons of men snared in an evil time," viz. that of death, "when it falleth suddenly upon them." 3. *The easy argument applied.* This being so, it is obvious that no one can surely reckon upon the issues that seem naturally to belong to his several qualities or abilities, to his swiftness, or strength, or wisdom, or understanding, or skill. Death may at any moment interpose—as, for instance, before the race is finished and the goal reached, before the battle is concluded, before the wise plan has been matured or carried out; and then, of course, man's expectations are defeated.

Lessons. 1. Diligence: let every man do his best. 2. Humility: beware of over-confidence. 3. Prudence: neglect not the possibility of failure. 4. Submission: accept with meekness the allotments of Providence.

Vers. 13—18.—*The parable of the little city.* I. The parable. 1. *The picture delineated.* A little city threatened by a powerful assailant, deserted through fear by the main body of its inhabitants, and occupied by a small garrison of men capable of bearing arms, among them a poor wise man. Advancing against it a mighty monarch, who besieges and storms it with armies and engines, but is ultimately compelled to raise the siege by the skill of the aforesaid wise poor man. 2. *The historical foundation.* Probably (1) the deliverance of Abel-Beth-maachah through the wisdom of a wise woman (2 Sam. xx. 15—22) (Wright); or (2) some event not recorded in history, but well known to the public for whom the Preacher wrote (Graetz); rather than (3) an incident which may have occurred in the siege of Dora by Antiochus the Great, in B.C. 218 (Hitzig), since Josephus ('Ant.,' xiii. 7. 2), who describes this siege, relates nothing corresponding to the Preacher's statements, and certainly does not mention its deliverance by any wise man, either rich or poor. 3. *Some suggestive parallels.* Incidents resembling that to which the Preacher here alludes may have happened often; as *e.g.* the deliverance of Athens by the counsel of Themistocles (Smith's 'History of Greece,' xix. § 5; Thucydides, i. 74), and of Syracuse by the skill of Archimedes, who for a time at least delayed the capture of the city by the wonderful machines with which he opposed the enemy's attacks (Livy, xxiv. 34), according to some doubtful accounts, setting fire to their ships by means of mirrors. 4. *Spiritual applications.* (1) "The poor man with his delivering wisdom is an image of Israel" (Hengstenberg); on which hypothesis the little city will be the suffering Hebrew nation, and the great king their Persian oppressors. (2) "The beleaguered city is the life of the individual; the great king who lays siege to it is death and the judgment of the Lord" (Wangemann). (3) "The little city is the Church of God; the great king Satan, the prince of hell and darkness; the poor wise man, the Lord Jesus Christ" (Fausset).

II. The lessons of the parable. 1. *That wisdom and poverty are frequently allied.* Not always, Solomon being witness (1 Kings iii. 12, 13); but mostly, God seldom bestowing all his gifts upon one individual, but distributing them according to his good pleasure—to one wealth and to another wisdom, dividing to each severally as he will (1 Cor. xii. 11). Nor is it difficult to discern in this marks of special wisdom and goodness. (1) Wisdom in not always conjoining with riches high mental endowments; partly in case of leading to undue exaltation on the part of the recipients, and partly to convince such recipients of the worthlessness of wealth apart from knowledge secular, and much more religious, and to show observers how hard it is to guide wealth without wisdom, especially the highest. (2) Goodness towards the poor, whose scanty share of this world's goods he not unfrequently compensates with great intellectual capacity, and even with celestial wisdom. Nothing more remarkable than the number of the world's thinkers, philosophers, poets, painters, writers, astronomers, chemists, inventors, and discoverers that have sprung from the poor; while in religion it is everywhere apparent that God hath not chosen the mighty and the noble and the wealthy as such, but rather the poor of this world, rich in faith, to be heirs of the kingdom (1 Cor. i. 26, 27; Jas. ii. 5). 2. *That wisdom is superior to force.* "Wisdom is better than strength," and "wisdom is better than weapons of war." (1) True of merely human wisdom. Illustrations almost numberless might be furnished of the superiority of wisdom to force, in the way both of overcoming force and of effecting what force is unable to accomplish. Had the Preacher lived to-day, he might have penned a brilliant commentary on his own text in both of these respects. The history of modern civilization but another name for the record of man's victories over brute strength and material force through the power of mind; and the all-important moral of its story, that vast as are nature's powers, huge, gigantic, and irresistible as are the forces slumbering everywhere within its bosom, the human intellect can control and combine these, and compel them to subserve its purposes and schemes. (2) True of wisdom spiritual and Divine. Not only is this not destructible by force, else it would have long since been banished from the world, but it can stand up, as through past centuries it has done, against the fiercest assaults, fixed and immovable, smiling defiance on every assailant, feeling inwardly confident that no weapon formed against her shall prosper (Isa. liv. 17), and that even the gates of hell shall not prevail against her (Matt. xvi. 18); yea, anticipating confidently the advent of a time when she should trample this grim adversary of brute force beneath her feet, and even chase it from the field (Isa. xi. 9; lx. 18). And more, she can do what mere force and weapons of war are powerless to accomplish—change hearts of unbelief and sin into hearts of faith and holiness, rein in, hold down, and even crush out impure lusts and fierce passions, tame and sway human wills, and convert children of the devil into sons of God (Job xxviii. 28; Jas. iii. 17). 3. *That wisdom mostly speaks into unwilling ears.* "Nevertheless the poor man's wisdom is despised." Partly because of the world's want of appreciation of the intrinsic excellence of wisdom, the world usually possessing a keener relish and finer instinct for folly; and partly, perhaps chiefly, because of the wise man's poverty. At all events, it has usually been the world's way to treat its wise men with disdain. The picture of wisdom crying aloud in the street into unheeding ears (Prov. i. 20—25) has often been reproduced, as *e.g.* in the persons of Jehovah's prophets (Lev. xxvi. 43; 2 Chron. xxxvi. 16; Isa. liii. 1; Matt. xxi. 34—36) and of Christ (John v. 40). To this day the world's treatment of Christ is not dissimilar, his words of wisdom being by men for the most part despised, and in particular the special wisdom he displayed in effecting their deliverance from sin and Satan by himself submitting to shame and death, and extending to them the offer of a full and free forgiveness, being frequently regarded with scorn and contempt. 4. *That wisdom is more influential than folly.* "The words of the wise," spoken "in quiet, are more than the cry of him that ruleth among fools," or that is the ringleader among fools, their very prince and chief. This assertion may seem to conflict with that of the preceding verse, but in reality it does not. The noisy demagogue who by sheer vociferation stirs the unthinking populace may appear to be more influential than the quietly speaking man of wisdom, but in the long run it is the latter that prevails. After all, it is ideas that move the world, in science, in philosophy, in religion, and these have their birth in meditative souls rather than in fiery spirits, and diffuse themselves, not amid the tempests of passion, but through the medium of calm and earnest speech. Remarkably was this exemplified in Christ—read in connection Col. ii. 3; John vii. 37; Isa. xlii. 3; and to this day the most powerful force operating in and on society is not that of eloquence, or of intellect, or of learning, all confessedly influential, but of goodness, which works silently and often out of sight like leaven. 5. *That wisdom is commonly repaid with ingratitude.* "No man remembered that same poor man." The Preacher says it with a touch of sadness, as if after all it was a strange and almost a new thing beneath the sun—which it is not. Whether the wise woman who saved the city Abel was remembered by her citizens is not recorded; but history reports that Themistocles, who delivered Athens from the Persians, was afterwards ostracized by his countrymen. Alas! ingratitude has never been an uncommon sin among men. Pharaoh's butler has had many a successor (Gen. xl. 23). The world has never been guilty of overlauding its benefactors or over-loading them with gratitude. Rather the poet accurately likens Time to a sturdy beggar with a wallet on his back—

> " Wherein he doth put alms for oblivion,
> A great-sized monster of ingratitudes."

And goes on to add—

> " Those scraps are good deeds past, which are devoured
> As fast as they are made, forgot as soon
> As done," etc.
> ('Troilus and Cressida,' act iii. sc. 3.)

Nor is it merely the world of which such ingratitude can be predicted, but the Church also has been too often guilty of forgetting him to whom she owes her deliverance. How many of his words, for instance, are not heard by those who profess to have been redeemed and saved by him—words of counsel for the path of duty, words of comfort for the day of trial, words of caution for the hour of danger!. And yet the remembrance of these would be the highest tribute of gratitude they could offer their Divine Redeemer.

HOMILIES BY VARIOUS AUTHORS.

Vers. 1—3.—*The antidote to despondency.* It was said by a famous man of the world, "Life is a comedy to those who think, a tragedy to those who feel." The epigram is more sparkling than true; reflecting men in every age have been oppressed by the solemnity of life's facts, and the insolubility of life's problems. Some men are roused to inquiry and are beset by perplexities when trouble and adversity befall them-selves; and others experience doubts and distress at the contemplation of the broad and obvious facts of human life as it unfolds before their observation. Few men who both think and feel have escaped the probation of doubt; most have striven, and many have striven in vain, to vindicate eternal Providence, and justify the ways of God to men.

I. THE FACT THAT IN THIS EARTHLY STATE THERE IS AN ABSENCE OF COMPLETE RETRIBUTION. "All things come alike to all;" "There is one event unto all." The righteous, the good, and the wise do not seem to meet with more prosperity and greater happiness than the wicked and the foolish. The man who offers due religious observance, and who reveres his oath, is subject to misfortune and calamity equally with the negligent, the impious, the false swearer. No thunderbolt of vengeance smites the sinner, no miraculous protection is round about the upright and obedient. Nay, the righteous is sometimes cut off in the prime of his manhood; the sinner's days are sometimes lengthened, and he dies in a delusive peace.

II. THE DIFFICULTY, DOUBT, AND PERPLEXITY OCCASIONED BY THE OBSERVATION OF THIS FACT. The writer of Ecclesiastes laid to heart and explored the mysteries of Providence; and in this he was not peculiar. Every observant and thoughtful person is sometimes compelled to ask himself whether or not there is a meaning in the events of life, and, if there be a meaning, what it is. Can our reason reconcile these events, as a whole, with belief in the existence, in the government, of a God at once almighty and benevolent? Are there considerations which can pacify the perturbed breast? Beneath the laws of nature is there a Divine heart? or is man alone sensitive to the inequalities of human fate, to the moral contradictions which seem to thrust themselves upon the attention?

III. THE TRUE SOLUTION OF THESE DOUBTS TO BE FOUND IN THE CONVICTION THAT ALL ARE IN THE HAND OF GOD. It is to be observed that faith in God can do what the human understanding cannot effect. Men and their affairs are not in the hand of chance or in the hand of fate, but in the hand of God. And by God is meant not merely the supreme Power of the universe, but the personal Power which is characterized by the attributes Holy Scripture assigns to the Eternal. Wisdom, righteousness, and benevolence belong to God. And by benevolence we are not to understand an intention to secure the enjoyment of men, to ward off from them every pain, all weakness, want, and woe. The purpose of the Divine mind is far higher than this—even the promotion of men's spiritual well-being, the discipline of human character, and especially the perfecting of obedience and submission. Sorrow and disappointment *may* be, and in the case of the pious *will* be, the means of bringing men into harmony with the will and character of God himself.—T.

Vers. 4—6.—*Life and death.* No thoughtful reader can take these remarks upon the living and the dead as complete and satisfactory in themselves. The writer of this book, as we know from other passages, never intended them so to be taken. They are singularly partial; yet when they are seen to be so, they are also singularly just. Just one aspect of life and of mortality is here presented, and it is an aspect which a wise and reflecting reader will see to be of great importance. Life is a fragment, it is an opportunity, it is a probation. Death is an end, that is, an end of this brief existence, and of what especially belongs to it. If we thought of life and death only under these aspects, we should err; but we should err if we neglected to take these aspects into consideration.

I. THE LOSSES OF THE DEAD. 1. They part with opportunities of *knowledge* which they enjoyed on earth. 2. They part with *passions* which they experienced whilst in the bodily life. 3. They part with *possessions* which they acquired in this world. 4. They are soon *forgotten*; for those who remember them themselves depart, and a faint memory or utter forgetfulness must follow. Death is a great change, and they who undergo it leave much behind, even though they may gain immeasurably more than they lose.

II. THE PREROGATIVES OF THE LIVING. 1. They have knowledge. This is doubtless very limited, but it is very precious. Compared with the knowledge which awaits the Christian in the future state, that which is within our reach now and here is as what is seen dimly in a mirror. Yet how can men be too grateful for the faculty in virtue of which they can acquaint themselves with truth of the highest importance and value? Knowledge of self, and knowledge of the great Author of our being and salvation, is within our reach. We know the limitation of our period of earthly education and probation; we know the means by which that period may be made the occasion of our spiritual good. 2. With all the living there is hope. Time is before them with its golden opportunities; eternity, time's harvest, is before them with all its priceless recompense. Even if the past has been neglected or abused, there is the possibility that the future may be turned to good account. For the dead we know that this earthly life has nothing in store. But who can limit the possibilities which stretch before the living, the progress which may be made, the blessing that may be won?

APPLICATION. It is well to begin with the view of life and death which is presented in this passage; but it would not be well to pause here. It is true that there is loss in death; but the Christian does not forget the assertion of the apostle that " to die is gain." And whilst there are privileges and prerogatives special to this earthly life, still it is to the disciple of Christ only the introduction and preparation for a life which is life indeed—life glorious, imperishable, and Divine.—T.

Vers. 7—9.—*The joy of human life.* Optimists and pessimists are both wrong, for they both proceed upon the radically false principle that life is to be valued according to the preponderance of pleasure over pain; the optimist asserting and the pessimist denying such preponderance. It is a base theory of life which represents it as to be prized as an opportunity of enjoyment. And the hedonism which is common to optimist and to pessimist is the delusive basis upon which their visionary fabrics are reared. Pleasure is neither the proper standard nor the proper motive of right conduct. Yet, as the text points out, enjoyment is a real factor in human life, not to be depreciated and despised, though not to be exaggerated and overvalued.

I. ENJOYMENT IS A DIVINELY APPOINTED ELEMENT IN OUR HUMAN EXISTENCE. Man's bodily and mental constitution, taken in connection with the circumstances of the human lot, are a sufficient proof of this. We drink by turns the sweet and the bitter cup; and the one is as real as the other, although individuals partake of the two in different proportions.

II. MANY PROVISIONS ARE MADE FOR HUMAN ENJOYMENT. Several are alluded to in this passage, more especially (1) the satisfaction of natural appetite; (2) the pleasures of society and festivity, (3) the happiness of the married state, when the Divine idea concerning it is realized. These are doubtless mentioned as specimens of the whole.

III. THE RELATION OF ENJOYMENT TO LABOUR. The Preacher clearly saw that those who toil are those who enjoy. It is by work that most men must win the means of bodily and physical enjoyment; and the very labour becomes a means of blessing, and sweetens the daily meals. Nay, "the labour we delight in physics pain." The primeval curse was by God's mercy transformed into a blessing.

IV. THE PARTIAL AND DISAPPOINTING VIEW OF HUMAN LIFE WHICH CONSIDERS ONLY ITS ENJOYMENTS. 1. Pain, suffering, and distress are as real as happiness, and must come, sooner or later, to all whose life is prolonged. 2. Neither pleasure nor pain is of value apart from the moral discipline both may aid in promoting, apart from the moral progress, the moral aim, towards which both may lead. 3. It is, therefore, the part of the wise to use the good things of this life as not abusing them; to be ready to part with them at the call of Heaven, and to turn them to golden profit, so that occasion may never arise to remember them with regret and remorse.—T.

Ver. 10.—*Diligence.* The prospect of death may add a certain zest to life's enjoyments, but we are reminded in this passage that it is just and wise to allow it to influence the performance of life's practical duties.

I. RELIGION HAS REGARD TO MAN'S PRACTICAL NATURE. The hand is the instrument of work, and is accordingly used as the symbol of our active nature. What we *do* is of supreme importance, both by reason of its cause and origin in our character, and by reason of its effect upon ourselves and upon the world. Religion involves contemplation and emotion, and expresses itself in prayer and praise; but without action all is in vain.

II. RELIGION FURNISHES THE LAW TO MAN'S PRACTICAL NATURE. We are expected to put up the prayer, "What wilt thou have me to do?" In response to this prayer, precept and admonition are given; and so the "hand findeth" its work. 1. True religion prescribes the *quality* of our work—that actions should be just and wise, kind and compassionate. 2. And the *measure* of our work. "With thy might" is the Divine law. This is opposed to languor, indolence, depression, weariness. He who considers the diligence and assiduity with which the powers of evil are ever working in human society will understand the importance of this urgent admonition.

III. RELIGION SUPPLIES THE MOTIVES TO DILIGENCE IN THE EMPLOYMENT OF THE PRACTICAL NATURE. 1. There is the very general motive suggested in the context, that what is to be done for the world's good must be done during this present brief and fleeting life. There is doubtless service of such a nature that, if it be not done here and now, can never be rendered at all. 2. Christianity presents a motive of pre-eminent power in the example of the Lord Jesus Christ, who came to work the work of him who sent him, who went about doing good, who found it his food to do his Father's will, whose aim it was to finish the work given him to do. 3. Christianity enforces this motive by one deeper still; the Christian is inspired with the desire to live unto the Lord who lived and died for him. Grateful love, enkindled by the Divine sacrifice, expresses itself by consecrated zeal.

APPLICATION. Let the hand first be stretched out that it may grasp the hand of the Saviour, God; and then let it be employed in the service of him who proves himself first the Deliverer, and then the Lord and Helper of all those who seek him.—T.

Vers. 10, 11.—*The powerlessness of man.* The reflections contained in these verses are not peculiar to the religious. No observer of human life can fail to observe how constantly all human calculations are falsified and all human hopes disappointed. And the language of the Preacher has naturally become proverbial, and is upon the lips even of those for whom it has no spiritual significance or suggestion. Yet it is the devout and pious mind which turns such reflections to profitable uses.

I. HUMAN EXPECTATION. It is natural to look for the success and prosperity of those who are highly endowed, and who have employed and developed their native gifts. Life is a race, and we expect the swift to obtain the prize; it is a battle, and we look for victory to the strong. We think of wealth and prosperity as the guerdon due to skill and prudence; we can hardly do otherwise. When the seed is sown, we anticipate the harvest. There are qualities adapted to secure success, and observation shows us that our expectations are justified in very many cases, though not in all. When we behold a young man begin life with every advantage of health, ability, fortune, and social recommendations, we forecast for such a one a career of advancement and a position of distinction and eminence. Yet how often does such an expectation prove vain!

II. HUMAN DISAPPOINTMENT. Human endeavour is crossed and human hope is crushed. The swift runner drops upon the course, and the bold warrior is smitten upon the battle-field. As the fishes are caught in the net, and the birds in the snare, so are the young, the ardent, the gifted, and the brave cut short in the career of buoyant effort and brilliant hope. All our projects may prove futile, and all our predictions may be falsified. The ways of Providence are inscrutable to our vision. We are helpless in the hands of God, whose thoughts are not as our thoughts. " Man also knoweth not his time." Attention is called to the suddenness with which our aims may be frustrated, our anticipations clouded, and our efforts defeated. And the observation of every experienced mind confirms the warning of the text. It is often when the sun is brightest that the cloud sweeps across its disc, when the sea is calmest that the storm arises in which the barque is foundered.

III. THE RELIGIOUS LESSONS TAUGHT BY THESE OVERTURNINGS OF HUMAN ANTICIPATIONS. 1. They rebuke human pride and self-confidence. It is natural for the young, the vigorous, the prosperous, to glory in their gifts, and to indulge bright hopes of the future, based upon their consciousness of power. Yet we have this lesson which the strong and fortunate will do well to lay to heart, " Let not the strong man glory in his strength," etc. 2. They check worldliness of spirit. We are all prone to attach importance to what is seen and temporal, and to allow our heart's affections to entwine around what is fair and bright, winsome and hopeful. God would teach us the supreme importance of those qualities which are imparted by his own blessed Spirit, and which endure unto everlasting life. 3. They lead the soul to seek a higher and more enduring satisfaction than earthly prosperity can impart. When riches take to themselves wings and fly away, this may enhance the value of the true, the unsearchable riches. When a fair, bright youth is plucked like a rosebud from the stem, and beauty withers, this may lead our thoughts and our hearts' desires away from this transitory scene to that region into which sorrow and death can never enter, and where God wipes away every tear.—T.

Vers. 13—18.—*The praise of wisdom.* It has been remarked that, whilst the leading idea of religion in the earliest stage of Israel's history was the Law, this idea took at a later period the form of *wisdom.* It is not well to discriminate too carefully between that wisdom which is shown in great works and that which is synonymous with piety. All light is from God, and there is no holier prayer than that in his light we may see light. It is a commonplace remark that men may be clever and yet not good; but every reflecting mind discovers in a character so described a lack of harmony. The philosopher, the sage, the leader in learning or science, should, beyond all men, be religious. " An undevout astronomer is mad." No more melancholy and pitiable spectacle is to be seen on earth than the able man whose self-confidence and vanity have led him into atheism. In considering the case of the truly wise man, it is well to regard him as displaying wisdom not only upon the lower but upon the higher plane.

I. WISDOM MAY BE ASSOCIATED WITH LOWLY STATION. Solomon was an example of an illustrious and splendid king who was famed for wisdom. But the instance of the text is striking; poverty and obscurity are not necessarily inconsistent with unusual insight, ability, and skill.

II. WISDOM MAY ACCOMPLISH GREAT WORKS WITH SMALL MEANS. A mighty king with a numerous and formidable army besieges a small city. How shall the besieged offer resistance to the foe? The inhabitants are few, feeble, ill-armed, half-starved;

and their case seems hopeless. But a citizen hitherto unknown, with no apparent resources, arises to lead the dispirited and helpless defenders. Whether by some marvellous device, or by the magnetic power of his presence and spirit, he accomplishes a task which seemed impossible—vanquishes the besiegers and raises the siege. Such things have been, and they are a rebuke to our worldly calculations, and an inspiration to courage and to faith.

III. WISDOM MAY NEVERTHELESS IN PUBLIC BE OVERLOOKED AND DESPISED. "No man remembered that same poor man." How often does it happen that the real originator, the prime mover, gains no credit for the enterprise which he conceived, and for whose success he prepared the way; whilst praise is given to some person of social or political eminence who joined the movement when its success was assured! It is "the way of the world."

IV. YET WISDOM, UNHONOURED IN PUBLIC, MAY BE ACKNOWLEDGED IN SECRET AND IN QUIETNESS. Those who look below the surface and are not dazzled by external splendour, those who listen, not merely to the earthquake, the thunder, and the tempest, but to the "still, small voice," discover the truly wise, and, in their heart of hearts, render to them sincere honour. Much more he who seeth in secret recognizes the services of his lowly, unnoticed servants who use their gifts for his glory, and work in obscurity to promote his kingdom, by whose toil and prayer cities are sanctified and saved.

V. THUS WISDOM IS SEEN TO BE THE BEST OF ALL POSSESSIONS AND QUALITIES. There is greatness which consists in outward splendour, and this may awe the vulgar, may dazzle the imagination of the unthinking. But in the sight of God and of just men, true greatness is that of the spirit; and the truly wise shine with a lustre which poverty and obscurity cannot hide, and which the lapse of ages cannot dim.—T.

Ver. 4.—*Life is everything.* In a world like ours, where appearance goes so far and counts for so much, there is much in *form.* There is much in *machinery,* in organization; when this is perfected, power is powerful indeed. There is much in original *capacity*—in that invisible, immeasurable germ out of which may grow great things in the future. But it is hardly too much to say that everything is in *life.* Where that is absent, nothing of any kind will avail; where that is present, all things are possible. It is better to have life even in the humblest form than to have the most perfect apparatus or the most exquisite form without it. A living dog, with its power of motion and enjoyment, is better than a dead lion, for which there is nothing but unconsciousness and corruption. Of the many illustrations of this principle, we may take the following:—

I. AN EARNEST STUDENT IS BETTER THAN A DEAD WEIGHT OF LEARNING. A man whose mind is nothing more than a storehouse of learning, who does not communicate anything to his fellows, who does not act upon them, who is no source of wisdom or of worth, is of very little account indeed; he has not what he has (see Matt. xxv. 29). But the earnest student, though he be but a youth or even a child, who is bent on acquiring in order that he may impart, in whom are the living springs of an honourable aspiration, is a great treasure, from whom society may look for many things.

II. AN AWAKENED CONSCIENCE IS BETTER THAN UNCONSECRATED GENIUS. Unconsecrated power may be enlisted on the side of peace and virtue. But it is a mere accident if it be so. It is quite as likely that it will be devoted to strife, and will espouse the cause of moral wrong; the history of our race has had too many painful proofs of this likelihood. But where there is an awakened conscience, and, consequently, a devotion to duty, there is ensured the faithful service of God, and an endeavour, more or less successful, to do good to the world.

III. ONE LIVING SOUL IS BETTER THAN A STAGNANT CHURCH. A Christian Church may be formed after the apostolic model, and its constitution may be irreproachably scriptural, but it may fall into spiritual apathy, and care for nothing but its own edification. A single human soul, with an ear sensitive to "the still sad music of humanity," with a heart to feel the weight of "the burden of the Lord," with courage to attempt great things for Christ and for men, with the faith that "removes mountains," may be of far more value to the world than such an apathetic and inactive Church. Similarly, we may say that—

IV. ONE LIVING CHURCH IS BETTER THAN A LARGE COMMUNITY THAT HAS LOST ITS SPIRITUAL ENERGY.—C.

Ver. 10.—*The day of opportunity.* There is great force in the Preacher's words, demanding present diligence and energy in view of future silence and inaction. It may be well to consider—

I. THE TRUTH LEFT UNSTATED. There is no work in the grave; but what is there beyond it? We who have sat at the feet of Jesus Christ know well that the hour is coming in which all who are in their graves shall hear his voice, etc. (John v. 28, 29). The rest which remaineth for the people of God is not the rest of unconsciousness or repose, but of untiring *activity ;* of *knowledge* that will be far removed from the dim visions of the present (see 1 Cor. xiii. 12); of *wisdom* far surpassing the sagacity to which we now attain. In that heavenly country we hope to address ourselves to nobler tasks, to work with enlarged and liberated faculties, to accomplish far greater things, to be "ministers of his that do his pleasure" in ways and spheres that are far beyond us now. But what we have first to face, and have all to face, is—

II. AN ON-COMING EXPERIENCE. "The grave, whither thou goest." Our life is, as we say, a journey from the cradle to the grave. Death is a goal which: 1. Is absolutely inevitable. We may elude many evils, but that we must all encounter. 2. We may reach soon and suddenly. It may be the very next turn of the road which will bring us to it. No man can tell what mortal blow may not be struck on the morrow, what fatal disease may not discover itself before the year is out. 3. Will certainly appear before we are expecting it. So swiftly does our life pass—so far as our consciousness is concerned—with all its pressure of business and all its growing and gathering excitements, and so pertinacious is our belief that, however it may be with others, we ourselves have some life left in us still, and some work to do yet, that when death comes to us it will surprise us. What, then, is—

III. THE CONCLUSION OF THE WISE? It is this: To do heartily and well all that lies within our power. The Master himself felt this (John ix. 4). He knew that there was glorious "work" for him in the long future, even as there had been for his Father in the long past (John v. 17). But he knew also that between the hour of that utterance and the hour of his death on the cross there was that work to be done *which could only be done then and there.* So he girded himself to do all that had to be done, and to bear all that had to be borne, in that short and solemn interval. We should feel and act likewise. We look for a very blessed and noble sphere of heavenly activity ; but between this present and that future there is work to be done which is now within our compass, but will soon be without it. There is: 1. Good work to be done in the direction of self-culture, of gaining dominion over self, in casting out evil from our own soul and our own life. 2. Good service to be rendered to our kindred, to our friends, to our neighbours, whom we can touch and bless now but who will soon pass beyond our reach. 3. A good contribution, real and valuable, if not prominent, towards the establishment of the kingdom of Jesus Christ upon the earth. All, therefore, that our "hand findeth to do" because our heart is willing to do it, let us do with our might, lest we leave undone that which no future time and no other sphere will give us the opportunity to attempt.—C.

Vers. 11, 12.—*Prosperity—the rule and the exception.* We shall find our way to the true lessons of this passage if we consider—

I. THE RULE UNDER GOD'S RIGHTEOUS GOVERNMENT. The Preacher either did not intend his words to be taken as expressing the general rule prevailing everywhere, or else he wrote these words in one of those depressed and doubtful moods which are frequently reflected in his treatise. Certainly the rule, under the wise and righteous government of God, is that the man who labours hard and patiently to win his goal succeeds in gaining it. It is right that he should. It is right that the race should be to the swift, for swiftness is the result of patient practice and of temperate behaviour. It is right that the battle should be to the strong, for strength is the consequence of discipline and virtue. It is right that bread and riches and the favour of the strong should fall to wisdom and to skill. And so, in truth, they do   Where the natural order of things is not positively subverted by the folly and the guilt of men, it is the case that human industry, resting on human virtue as its base, conducts to competence, to honour, to success. It does, indeed, happen that the crown is placed on the brow of roguery and violence; yet is it not the less true that wisdom and integrity constitute the well-worn and open road to present and temporal well-being.

II. THE OBVIOUS AND SERIOUS EXCEPTION. No doubt it is frequently found that "the race is *not* to the swift," etc. No doubt piety, purity, and fidelity are often left behind, and do not win the battle in the world's campaign. This is due to one of two very different and, indeed, opposite causes. It may be due to: 1. Man's interfering wrong. The human oppressor comes down upon the industrious and the frugal citizen, and sweeps off the fruit of his toil and patience. The scheming intriguer steps in, and carries off the prize which is due to the laborious and persevering worker. The seducer lays his nets and ensnares his victim. There is, indeed, a lamentable frequency in human history with which the good and true, the wise and faithful, fall short of the honourable end they seek. 2. God's intervening wisdom. It may often happen that God sees that human strength or wisdom has outlived its modesty, its beauty, and its worth, and that it needs to be checked and broken. So he sends defeat where victory has been assured, poverty where wealth has been confidently reckoned upon, discomfiture and rejection where men have been holding out their hand for favour and reward. What, then, are—

III. THE PRACTICAL CONCLUSIONS? 1. *Do not count too confidently on outward good.* Work for it faithfully, hope for it with a well-moderated expectation, but do not set your heart upon it as an indispensable blessing. Be prepared to do without it. Have those inner, deeper, diviner resources which will fill the heart with grace and the life with an admirable contentment, even if the goal is not gained and the prize is not secured. Be supplied with those treasures which the thief cannot steal, and which will leave the soul rich though the bank be broken and the purse be emptied. 2. *Guard carefully against the worst evils.* Be so fortified with Divine truth and sacred principles within, and secure so much of God's favour and protection from above, that no snares of sin will be able to mislead and to betray—that the feet will never be found entangled in the nets of the enemy. 3. *Anticipate the Divine discipline.* Live in such *conscious* and in such *acknowledged* dependence upon God for every stroke that is struck, for all strength and wisdom that are gained, for all bounties and all honours that are reaped, that there will be no need for the intervening hand of heaven to break your schemes or to remove your treasures.—C.

Vers. 13—18.—*Wisdom and strength.* The picture which is here drawn is both picture and parable; it portrays a constantly recurring scene in human history. It speaks to us of—

I. THE RANGE OF WISDOM. Wisdom is a word that covers many things; its import varies much. It includes: 1. Knowledge; familiarity with the objects and the laws of nature, and with the ways and the history of mankind. 2. Keenness of intellect; that quickness of perception and subtlety of understanding which sees through the devices of other men, and keeps a watchful eye upon all that is passing, always ready to take advantage of another's mistake. 3. Sagacity; that nobler quality which forecasts the future; which weighs well many considerations of various kinds; which baffles the designs of the wicked; which defeats the machinations and the measures of the strong (vers. 14, 15); which is worth far more than much enginery (ver. 18); which builds up great institutions; which goes forth on hazardous and yet admirable enterprises. 4. Wisdom itself; that which is more properly considered and called such, viz. the discernment of the *true end*, with the adoption of the *best means* of attaining it; and this applied not merely to the particulars of human life, but to human life itself; the determination to seek that good thing, as our true heritage, which is in harmony with the will of God, and to seek it in the divinely appointed way. To us who live in this Christian era, and to whom Jesus Christ is himself "the Wisdom of God," this is found in seeking and finding, in trusting and following, in loving and serving *him*.

II. ITS FAILURE TO BE APPRECIATED. "No man remembered that same poor man." Wisdom in each one of its particular spheres is valuable; in the larger and higher spheres it is of very great account, being far more effective than any quantity of mere material force or of worldly wealth ; in the highest sphere of all it is simply invaluable. But it is liable to be disregarded, especially if it be found in the person of poverty and obscurity. 1. It is often forgotten, and thus overlooked (text). 2. It is either rejected or visited with contumely in the person of its author. " Is not this the carpenter's Son ? " it is asked. " And they were offended in him," it is added. Many a man, with much learning in his head, much shrewdness in his speech, much weight in his counsel, much wisdom in his soul, walks, unrecognized and unhonoured, along some very lowly path of life.

III. ITS REWARD. 1. It is often heeded when mere noise and station are disregarded. " The words of the wise are listened to with more pleasure than the loud behests of a foolish ruler (ver. 17) " (Cox). And it is a satisfaction to the wise that they do often prevail in their quietness and their obscurity when the clamorous and the consequential are dismissed as they deserve to be. 2. The time will come when they who speak the truth will gain the ear of the world; there are generations to come, and we may leave our reputation to them, as many of the wisest and worthiest of our race have done. 3. To be useful is a better reward than to be applauded or to be enriched; how much better to have " delivered the city " than to have been honoured by it ! 4. Our record is on high.—C.

Ver. 18.—*The destructiveness of one evil life.* How much of destruction may flow from one single life may be seen if we look at the subject—

I. NEGATIVELY. We may judge of the magnitude of the evil by considering : 1. How one evil life may hinder the work of God; *e.g.* Achan, Sanballat, Herod, Nero. Who shall say how much of Christian influence has been arrested by one grossly inconsistent member of a Church, or by one arch-persecutor of the gospel of Christ? 2. How much a man may fail to do by refusing to spend his powers in the service of God. To a man with large means, great resources, brilliant capacities, almost anything is open in the direction of holy usefulness, of widespread and far-descending influence. All this is lost, and in a sense destroyed, by a selfish and guilty withholdment of it all from the service of God and man.

II. POSITIVELY. We may estimate the serious and lamentable mischief of an evil life if we think that a godless man may be injuring his neighbours : 1. By weakening or undermining their faith ; causing them to lose their hold on Divine truth, and thus sinking into the miseries of doubt or into the darkness and despair of utter unbelief. 2. By undoing the integrity of the upright ; leading them into the fatal morass of an immoral life. 3. By cooling, or even killing, the consecration of the zealous ; causing them to slacken their speed or even to leave the field of noble service. One man, by his own evil example, by his words of folly and falsity, by his deeds of wrong, may enfeeble many minds, may despoil many hearts, may misguide many souls, may blight and darken many lives.—C.

Vers. 1—6.—*Inexorable destiny.* The teaching in this section of the book is very similar to that in ch. vi. 10—12. The Preacher lays stress upon the powerlessness and short-sightedness of man with regard to the future. A higher power controls all the events of human life, and fixes the conditions in which each individual is to live— conditions which powerfully affect his character and destiny. Such a thought has been to many a source of consolation and strength. " My times," said the psalmist, " are in thy hand " (Ps. xxxi. 15). " Your heavenly Father knoweth that ye have need of all these things," said Jesus (Matt. vi. 32), when he counselled his disciples against undue anxiety for the future. But no such comfort is drawn by the Preacher from the consideration that " the righteous, and the wise, and their works, are in the hand of God " (ver. 1). It suggests to him rather an iron destiny, a cage against the bars of which the soul may beat its wings in vain, than a gracious Providence. The loss of freedom implied in it afflicts him—the thought that not even the feelings and emotions of the heart are under man's control. They are excited by persons and things with whom or with which he is brought in contact. A slight change of circumstances would make his love hatred, and his hatred love; and these circumstances he cannot change or modify. Events of all kinds are before us, and God arranges what is to happen to us. " Whether it be love or hatred, man knoweth it not; all is before them" (ver. 1*b*, Revised Version). "The river of life, along which his course lies, is wrapped in mist. Man's destiny is wholly dark, and is out of his own control. But it is not man's ignorance that cuts him to the heart; it is that the injustice of earthly tribunals seems to have its counterpart in a higher region. No goodness, no righteousness, will avail against the persistent injustice of the laws by which the world seems ruled. What a half-blasphemous indictment, what passionate recalcitration against the God whose fear is in his mouth, is embodied in the cold and calm despair of the words which follow in the next verse (ver. 2)!" (Bradley). He names five classes of persons, embracing all the various types of righteousness and wickedness, and affirms that one event comes to them all, that no discrimination on the part of the Divine Ruler between them appears in their earthly lot. The first group is perhaps that of those whose conduct towards their neighbours is righteous or wicked; the second that of those who are pure or impure in heart; the third that of the religious and the irreligious; the fourth perhaps that of those whose characters are in all these relations good or evil; the fifth that of the profane swearer and the man who reverences the solemn oath (Isa. lxv. 16). "There is no mark at all of a moral government in this world. The providence of God is as indiscriminating as the falling tree, or the hungry tiger, or the desolating famine. If the fittest survive for a time, that fitness has nothing in common with goodness or righteousness." And one of the evil consequences of this state of matters is, as already referred to in ch. viii. 11, that those evilly disposed are subject to less restraint than they would be if Divine Providence in all cases meted out reward and punishment immediately to the righteous and the wicked. "Yea, also the heart of the sons of men is full of evil, and madness is in their heart while they live, and after that they go to the dead" (ver. 3). The gloomy thoughts concerning death and the world beyond it which filled his mind, made the "one event" that comes to all seem all the more unjust. For some, doubtless, it is a deliverance from misery, but to others it is an escape from merited punishment. Even life with all its inequalities and wrongs is better than death, and yet the righteous are swept away from the earth indiscriminately with the wicked.

> " Streams will not turn aside
> The just man not t' entomb,
> Nor lightnings go aside
> To give his virtues room:
> Nor is that wind less rough which blows a good man's barge."

That a strong faith in Divine Providence in spite of all outward appearances, and a firm grasp of the truth of immortality, were denied to the Preacher, need not surprise us, when we remember that the confidence we have in God's fatherly love, and in the eternal happiness of those who are faithful to him, is derived from the teaching of Christ, and his triumphant resurrection from the dead. The Preacher had not the consolations which the gospel affords us. To him the world beyond the grave was dreary and uncertain. He was one of those "who through fear of death were all their lifetime subject to bondage" (Heb. ii. 15). The meanest form of life was superior to the condition of even the noblest who had passed within the grim portals of the grave. The living dog, loathed and despised, feeding on the refuse of the streets, was better than the dead lion (ver. 4). Hope survives while life remains, even though it may be illusive; but with death all possible amelioration of one's lot is cut off. The bitterness of the thought is displayed in the touch of sarcasm which marks his words. "For the living know that they shall die: but the dead know not anything, neither have they any more a reward; for the memory of them is forgotten" (ver. 5). The very consciousness of the coming doom gives a distinction to the living which is denied to the dead. The very memory of those who have passed away soon perishes. Others take their place, and carry on the business of the world. A new generation springs up, with interests and concerns and passions with which the dead have nothing to do. The strongest passions of love, hatred, and envy are quenched by the cold hand of death (ver. 6), and those who may in life have been bosom friends, or mortal enemies, or jealous rivals, lie side by side in the grave, in silence and oblivion. Nothing that is done in the earth concerns them any more (cf. Isa. xxxviii. 9—20). The view here given us of the state of the dead is gloomy in the extreme. The darkness is more intense and palpable than that with which the same subject is invested in the Book of Job, and even in some of the psalms. But we must remember that though the world beyond the grave is represented by him as dim and shadowy, he affirms at the same time that "God will bring every secret thing into judgment" in "his own time and season." "Consequently, the dead, even though regarded by him as existing in a semi-conscious state in Hades, are supposed to be still in existence, and destined at some future period to be awakened out of this dreary slumber, and rewarded according to the merit or demerit of their actions on earth. He does not, it is true, speak of this awakening out of sleep, still less does he allude to the resurrection of the body. His book is mainly occupied with the search after man's highest good on earth, and it is only incidentally that he refers at all to the state of the dead" (Wright). The doctrine of a future judgment, in which every man will appear and receive the reward or punishment due to him, is repeatedly dwelt upon by our author; and this of itself implies a conscious existence after death in the case of all. So far, however, as this life is concerned, the grave puts a period to all activity, extinguishes all the passions which animate the children of men. They pass into another state of existence, and have no further concern with that which is done here on earth.—J. W.

Vers. 7—10.—*Enjoyment of the present.* No one who is at all familiar with the Preacher's thoughts can be surprised with the advice here given, following so closely as it does upon the gloomy reflections on death to which he has just given expression. He for the sixth time urges upon his hearers or readers the practical wisdom of enjoying the present, of cheerfully accepting the boons which God puts within our reach, and the mere thought that he is the Giver, will of itself rebuke all vicious indulgence. He permits enjoyment; nay, it is by his appointment that the means for it exist. "Go thy way, eat thy bread with joy, and drink thy wine with a merry heart; for God now accepteth thy works" (ver. 7). That is, God approves of these works—a cheerful, thankful enjoyment of food and drink. The white garment symbolical of a glad heart, the perfume sprinkled upon the head, are not to be slighted as frivolous or as inappropriate for those who are so soon to pass from life unto death (ver. 8). Asceticism, self-imposed scruples, half-hearted participations in the good things that lawfully fall to us, mean loss of the present, and are not in themselves a preparation for the future. The ascetic may have his heart set upon the very pleasures he denies himself, may value them more highly, than he who takes them as they come, and exhausts them of all the satisfaction they contain. The happiness, too, which marriage yields is commended by him. He speaks elsewhere of the wretchedness and shame into which sensuality leads, and of the hateful types of womanhood with which it brings the sensualist into contact (ch. ii. 8; vii. 26); but here he alludes to the calm peacefulness of a happy home, which, though it cannot remove the sense of the vanity and transitoriness of life, at least makes it endurable (Plumptre). A happy life, a useful life, a life filled by a wholesome activity, may be lived by all or by most, and the fact that the end is near, the grave in which there is neither "work, nor device, nor wisdom," should be a stimulus to such activity (ver. 10). Honest, earnest labour, together with whatever enjoyments God's providence brings within our reach, and not an indifference to all sublunary concerns because of their transitoriness, is asserted to be our bounden duty. Had he recommended mere sensuous indulgence, we should turn from him contemptuously. Had he recommended an ascetic severity, we might have felt that only some could follow his advice. But as it is, his ideal is within the reach of us all, and is worthy of us all. And those who speak censoriously of the conclusion he reaches and expresses in these words, would find it a very hard task to frame a higher ideal of life. Zealous performance of practical duties, a reasonable and whole-hearted enjoyment of all innocent pleasures, and mindfulness of judgment to come, are commended to us by the Preacher, and only a stupid fanatic could object to the counsel he gives.—J. W.

Vers. 11, 12.—*Time and chance.* In the preceding passage our author has exhorted the timid and slothful to bestir themselves and put forth all their powers, since death is ever at hand, and when it comes a period will be put to all endeavours; the wisdom that guides, the hand that executes, will be silent and still in the grave. He now exhorts the wise and strong not to be too confident about success in life, to be prepared for possible failure and disappointment. So full and varied is his experience of life that he has useful counsels for all classes of men. Some need the spur and others the curb. Some would from timidity hang back and lose the chances of usefulness which life gives; others are so self-confident and sanguine that they need to be warned of the dangers and difficulties which their wisdom and skill may not succeed in overcoming. Plans may be skilfully constructed and every effort made to carry them into effect, but some unforeseen cause may defeat them, some circumstance which could not have been provided against, may bring about failure. The Preacher records the observations he had made of instances of failure to secure success in life, and gives an explanation of how it is that the strenuous efforts of men are so often baffled.

I. The PHENOMENA OBSERVED. (Ver. 11.) Five instances of failure are enumerated: the swift defeated in the race, the strong in battle, the wise unable to make a livelihood, the prudent remaining in poverty, the gifted in obscurity. In none of the cases is the fault to be traced to the want of faculties or abilities of the kind needed to secure the end in view, or to a half-hearted use of them. The runner endowed with swiftness might reasonably be expected to be first in at the goal, the strong to be victorious in fight, the wise and prudent to be successful in acquiring and amassing riches, the clever to attain to reputation and influence. It is taken for granted, too, that there is no omission of effort; for if there were, the cause of failure would easily be discovered. But the phenomena being noted as extraordinary and perplexing, we are to understand that in none of the cases observed is there anything of the kind. And it is implied that while those who fulfil all the conditions of success sometimes fail, those who do not sometimes succeed. The phenomena referred to are familiar to us all. We have known many who have begun life with the fairest promise, and who have apparently, without any fault of their own, failed to make their mark. The impression they have made upon us has convinced us that they have ability enough to win the prizes in life; but somehow or other they fail, and remain in obscurity. And, at the same time, others whose abilities are in our opinion of a commonplace order come to the front, and succeed in gaining and keeping a foremost place.

II. THE EXPLANATION OF THE MATTER. (Ver. 11b.) "Time and chance happeneth to them all." There need to be favourable circumstances as well as the possession and use of the requisite faculties, if success is to be won. The time must be propitious, and give opportunities for the exercise of gifts and abilities. "There are favourable and unfavourable times in which men's lot may be cast; and such times, too, may occur alternately in the experience of the same individual. A man of very inferior talent, should he fall on a favourable time, may succeed with comparative ease; whereas, in a time that is not propitious, abilities of the first order cannot preserve their possessor from failure and disappointment. And even the same period may be advantageous to one description of business, and miserably the reverse to another; and it may thus be productive of prosperity to men who prosecute the former, and of loss and ruin to those engaged in the latter; although the superiority in knowledge, capacity, and prudence may be all, and even to a great degree, on the losing side" (Wardlaw). At first sight it might seem as if the explanation given of the reason why the race is not always to the swift, or the battle to the strong, were based on a denial of the Divine providence, and unworthy of a place in the Word of God. But this opinion is considerably modified, if not contradicted, if we find a reference, as we may fairly do, in the word "time" to the statements in ch. iii., that there are "times and seasons," for all things are appointed by God himself. And so far from the conclusion here announced by our author being a solitary utterance, out of harmony with the general teaching of Scripture, we may find many parallels to it; e.g. "The Lord saveth not with sword and spear: for the battle is the Lord's, and he will give you into our hands" (1 Sam. xvii. 47). "Some trust in chariots, and some in horses: but we will remember the Name of the Lord our God" (Ps. xx. 7). "There is no king saved by the multitude of an host: a mighty man is not delivered by much strength" (Ps. xxxiii. 16). Probably the unfavourable impression of which I have spoken arises from the ideas suggested by the word "chance" in our English Version, which does not convey exactly the meaning of the Hebrew pega'. It is a word only found twice in Scripture, here and in 1 Kings v. 4, and means a stroke. The general idea is that of adversity or disappointment inflicted by a higher power, and not merely that of something accidental or fortuitous interfering with human plans. "Chance," therefore, must here refer to the great variety of circumstances over which we have no control, but by which our schemes and endeavours are affected, which may take away success from the deserving, and in all cases render it extremely difficult to calculate beforehand the probabilities of success in an undertaking. The final result, whatever we may do, is conditioned by God. Though our author does not here use these terms, yet we cannot doubt that they express his meaning. He does not say that life is a lottery, in which the swift and the slow, the strong and the weak, the wise and the simple, the industrious and the lazy, have equal chances of drawing prizes. He knew, as we all know, that success is won in most cases by those who are best qualified in ability and character for securing it; that the race is generally to the swift, and the battle to the strong. It is the exception to the rule that excites his astonishment, and leads him to the conclusion that mere human skill and power are not sufficient of themselves to carry the day. Failure and disappointment may at any moment and in any case overtake man, and these from causes which no wisdom could have foreseen or exertion have averted. Such a consideration is calculated to humble human pride, and create in the heart feelings of reverent submission to the great Disposer of events. "So then it is not of him that willeth, nor of him that runneth, but of God that showeth mercy" (Rom. ix. 16). This thought of the limitation of man in his efforts, in spite of all his gifts and abilities, is expressed again with still greater emphasis in ver. 12. The time when life must close is a secret hidden from each of us, and we may be arrested in the mid-course of our endeavours just when our labours are about to be crowned with success. It may come upon us so unexpectedly as to take us as fishes are taken in a net or birds in a snare. This may be the event that snatches the prize from the runner, the victory from the strong (2 Chron. xviii. 33, 34). The arrow shot at random may strike down the brave soldier who has successfully borne the brunt of battle, and lay his pride in the dust. To those whose whole interests are centred in the business and pleasures of the world, the sudden summons of death comes in an evil time (Luke xii. 19, 20); but those who are wise are not taken by surprise—"they understand and consider their latter end."—J. W.

Vers. 13—16.—*An apologue.* The truth of the aphorism, that "the battle is not to the strong . . . nor yet favour to men of skill" (ver. 11), is illustrated by the Preacher in a striking little story or apologue, taken doubtless from the history of some campaign familiar to his readers. It represents in a vivid manner the power of wisdom, and also the ungrateful treatment which the possessor of it frequently receives from those who have found him a deliverer in time of danger. A little city, with few in it to defend it, is besieged by a great king. The place is surrounded by his army, and round about it great mounds are erected from which missiles are hurled into it. All hope seems to be gone; no material forces which the besieged can muster for their defence are at all adequate to repel the assailants. When suddenly some poor man, whose name was perhaps known to few in the city, delivers it by his wisdom. The great king and his army are compelled to retire baffled from before the walls of the city, which probably when they first beheld them moved them to scornful laughter by their apparent insignificance and weakness. The picture is not overdrawn; history affords many parallel instances. The defence of Syracuse against the Romans by Archimedes the mathematician (Livy, xxiv. 34), of Londonderry against James II. by Walker, and in later times of Antwerp by Carnot (Alison, 'Europe,' lxxxvii.), show how inferior material is to moral force. This is the bright side of the picture. "Wisdom is better than strength" (ver. 16); "wisdom is better than weapons of war" (ver. 18). The dark side is that it is often rewarded by the basest ingratitude. It was the wisdom of a poor man that delivered the city in which he dwelt; but when the danger was past he sank again into obscurity. No one thought of him as he deserved to be thought of. The public attention was caught by some new figure, and the saviour of the city remained as poor and unnoticed as he had been before the great crisis in which his wisdom had been of such great service. Had he been high-born and rich, his great services would have been acknowledged in some notable manner; but the meanness of his surroundings obscured his merit in the eyes of the thoughtless multitude. It was this vulgar failing which prompted some to despise wisdom itself incarnate in Jesus of Nazareth, and to ask scornfully, "Is not this the carpenter?" (Mark vi. 2, 3). Wisdom is unassuming, calm, and deliberate (cf. Isa. xlii. 2 ; Matt. xii. 19), yet full of strength and resources, and the pity is that it should so often lose its reward, and the public attention be caught by the blustering cry of fools (ver. 17). It is, indeed, often a better defence than weapons of war; and therefore it is sad that it should sometimes be nullified by folly, that one perverse blunderer should sometimes be able through care-lessness or passion to destroy all the defences that wisdom has carefully erected.—J. W.

EXPOSITION.

CHAPTER X.

Vers. 1—3.—Section 11. *A little folly mars the effect of wisdom*, and is sure to make itself conspicuous.

Ver. 1.—**Dead flies cause the ointment of the apothecary to send forth a stinking savour.** This is a metaphorical confirmation of the truth enunciated at the end of the last chapter, "One sinner destroyeth much good." It is like the apostle's warning to his converts, "A little leaven leaveneth the whole lump" (1 Cor. v. 6). The Hebrew expression is literally, "flies of death," which may mean either "dead flies," as in our version and the Vulgate (*muscæ morientes*), or "deadly, poisonous flies," as in the Septuagint (μυῖαι θανατοῦσαι). The latter rendering seems preferable, if we regard the use of similar compound phrases, *e.g.* "instruments of death" (Ps. vii. 14 [13]); "snares of death" (Ps. xviii. 5); and in New Testament Greek, ἡ πληγὴ τοῦ θανάτου, "the death-stroke" (Rev. xiii. 3, 12). The flies meant are such as are poisonous in their bite, or carry infection with them. Such insects corrupt anything which they touch—food, ointment, whether they perish where they alight or not. They, as the Hebrew says, *make to stink, make to ferment, the oil of the perfumer*. The singular verb is here used with the plural subject to express the unity of the individuals, "flies" forming one complete idea. The Septuagint rendering omits one of the verbs : Σαπριοῦσι σκευασίαν ἐλαίου ἡδύσματος, "Corrupt a preparation of sweet ointment." The point, of course, is the comparative insignificance of the cause which spoils a costly substance compounded with care and skill. Thus little faults mar great characters and reputations. "A good name is better than precious ointment" (ch. vii. 1), but a good name is ruined by follies, and then it stinks in men's nostrils. The term, "ointment of the apothecary," is used by Moses (Exod. xxx. 25, etc.) in describing the holy chrism which was reserved for special occasions. So doth **a little folly him that is in reputation for wisdom and honour.** The meaning of the Authorized Version is tolerably correct, but the actual rendering will hardly stand, and one wants some verb to govern "him that," etc. The other versions vary. Septuagint, "A little wisdom is more precious (τίμιον) than great glory of folly;" Vulgate, "More precious are wisdom and glory than small and short-lived folly;" Jerome, "Precious above wisdom and glory is a little folly." This last interpretation proceeds upon the idea that such "folly" is at any rate free from pride, and has few glaring faults. "Dulce est desipere in loco," says Horace ('Carm.,' iv. 12. 28). But the original is best translated thus: "More weighty than wisdom, than honour, is a little folly." It is a painful fact that a little folly, one foolish act, one silly peculiarity of manner or disposition, will suffice to impair the real value of a man's wisdom and the estimation in which he was held. The little element of foolishness, like the little insect in the ointment, obscures the real excellence of the man, and deprives him of the honour that is really his due. And in religion we know that one fault unchecked, one secret sin cherished, poisons the whole character, makes a man lose the grace of God. (For the same effect from another cause, see Ezek. iii. 20 ; xxxiii. 13.) Jerome sees in the "dead flies" wicked thoughts put into the Christian's mind by Beelzebub, "the lord of flies."

Vers. 2, 3.—A tetrastich contrasting wisdom and folly.

Ver. 2.—**A wise man's heart is at his right hand; but a fool's heart at his left.** There is here no reference to the classical use of right and left, as ominous of success and disaster, which is never found in the Old Testament. The right hand is the place of honour, the left of inferiority, as a matter of fact, not of superstition and luck. The symbolism is intimated in Christ's account of the judgment (Matt. xxv. 31, etc.). But in the present passage we should best paraphrase—The wise man's heart, his understanding and sentiments, lead him to what is right and proper and straightforward; the fool's heart leads him astray, in the wrong direction. The former is active and skilful, the latter is slow and awkward. One, we may say, has no left hand, the other has no right. To be at the right hand is to be ready to help and guard.

" The Lord is at thy right hand," to protect thee, says the psalmist (Ps. cx. 5). The wise man's mind shows him how to escape dangers and direct his course safely; the fool's mind helps him not to any good purpose, causes him to err and miss his best object.

Ver. 3.—**Yea, also, when he that is a fool walketh by the way.** As soon as ever he sets his foot outside the house, and mixes with other men, he exhibits his folly. If he remained at home he might keep his real ineptitude concealed; but such persons as he are unconscious of their inanity, and take no pains to hide it; they go where, they act as, their foolish heart prompts them. There is no metaphor here, nor any reference to the fool being put in the right path and perversely turning away. It is simply, as the Septuagint renders, Καί γε ἐν ὁδῷ ὅταν ἄφρων πορεύηται. **His wisdom** (Hebrew, *heart*) **faileth** him. Ginsburg and others render, " He lacketh his mind," want of heart being continually taken in the Book of Proverbs as equivalent to deficiency of understanding (Prov. vi. 32; vii. 7, etc.). But Delitzsch and Wright consider the order of the words and the suffix to be against this view, and they translate as the Authorized Version, *i.e.* his understanding is at fault. **And he saith to every one** that **he is a fool.** The sentence is ambiguous, and capable of two interpretations. The Vulgate has, *Cum ipse insipiens sit, omnes stultos æstimat.* Jerome quotes Symmachus as rendering, " He suspects all men that they are fools." According to this view, the fool in his conceit thinks that every one he meets is a fool, says this in his mind, like the sluggard in Prov. xxvi. 16, " Who is wiser in his own conceit than ten men that can render a reason." Another explanation, more closely in accordance with the foregoing clauses, takes the pronoun in " he is a fool " to refer to the man himself, *se esse stultum* (comp. Ps. ix. 21 [20], " Let the nations know themselves to be but men "). As soon as he goes abroad, his words and actions display his real character; he betrays himself; he says virtually to all with whom he has to do, " I am a fool " (comp. Prov. xiii. 16; xviii. 2). It is hard to say to which interpretation the Septuagint inclines, giving, Καὶ ἃ λογιεῖται πάντα ἀφροσύνη ἐστίν, " And all that he will think is folly."

Vers. 4—7.—Section 12. *Illustration of the conduct of wisdom under capricious rulers,* or when fools are exalted to high stations.

Ver. 4.—**If the spirit of the ruler rise up against thee.** "Spirit" (*ruach*) is here equivalent to "anger," as Judg. viii. 3; Prov. xxix. 11. The idea seems to be that a statesman or councillor gives wise advice to

a monarch, which the latter takes in bad part, and shows strong resentment against the person who offered it. Now, when a man knows himself to be in the right, and yet finds his counsel rejected, perhaps with scorn and reproach added, he is naturally prone to feel sore, and to show by some overt act his sense of the ill treatment which he has received. But what says wisdom? **Leave not thy place** (*makom*); i.e. position, post, office. Do not hastily resign the situation at court to which you have been appointed. Some, not so suitably, take the expression, "leave thy place," figuratively, as equivalent to "give way to anger, renounce the temper which becomes you, lose your self-possession." But Wright, from the analogous use of *matstsale* and *maamad* in Isa. xxii. 19, confirms the interpretation which we have adopted. Compare the advice in ch. viii. 3, where, however, the idea is rather of open rebellion than of a resentment which shows itself by withdrawal. Origen (' De Princip.,' iii. 2) explained " the spirit of the ruler" to be the evil spirit; and Gregory, commenting on this passage, writes (' Moral.,' iii. 43), " As though he had said in plain words, ' If thou perceivest the spirit of the tempter to prevail against thee in aught, quit not the lowliness of penitence; ' and that it was the abasement of penitence that he called ' our place,' he shows by the words that follow, ' for healing [Vulgate] pacifieth great offences.' For what else is the humility of mourning, save the remedy of sin ?" (Oxford transl.). **For yielding pacifieth great offences.** *Marpe,* "yielding," is rendered " healing " by the versions. Thus ἴαμα (Septuagint); *curatio* (Vulgate). But this translation is not so suitable as that of Symmachus, σωφροσύνη, "moderation." The word is used in the sense of "gentleness," "meekness," in Prov. xiv. 30; xv. 4; and the gnome expresses the truth that a calm, conciliating spirit, not prone to take offence, but patient under trying circumstances, obviates great sins. The sins are those of the subject. This quiet resignation saves him from conspiracy, rebellion, treason, etc., into which his untempered resentment might hurry him. We may compare Prov. xv. 1 and xxv. 15; and Horace, 'Carm.,' iii. 3, " Justum et tenacem propositi virum," etc.

" The man whose soul is firm and strong,
        Bows not to any tyrant's frown,
    And on the rabble's clamorous throng
        In proud disdain looks coldly down."
                                        (Stanley.)

They who regard the "offences" as those of the ruler explain them to mean oppression and injustice; but it seems plain from the run of the sentence that the minister, not the monarch, is primarily in the mind of the writer, though, of course, it is quite true that the submission of the former might save the ruler from the commission of some wrong.

Ver. 5.—Koheleth gives his personal experience of apparent confusion in the ordering of state affairs. **There is an evil which I have seen under the sun.** Power gets into the hands of an unwise man, and then errors are committed and injustice reigns. **As an error which proceedeth from the ruler.** The כ here is *caph veritatis*, which denotes not comparison, but resemblance, the idealization of the individual, the harmony of the particular with the general idea. The evil which he noticed appeared to be (he does not affirm that it is) a mistake caused by the ruler; it so presented itself to his mind. The caution observed in the statement may be owing partly to the tacit feeling that such blots occasioned difficulties in the view taken of the moral government of the world. He does not intend to refer to God under the appellation "Ruler." The Septuagint renders, Ὡς ἀκούσιον ἐξῆλθεν, "As if it came involuntarily;" Vulgate, to much the same effect, *Quasi per errorem egrediens.* The idea here is either that the evil is one not produced by any intentional action of the ruler, but resulting from human imperfection, or that what appears to be a mistake is not so really. But these interpretations are unsuitable. Those who adhere to the Solomonic authorship of our book see here a prophetic intimation of the evil of Jeroboam's rule, which evil proceeded from the sins of Solomon himself and his son Rehoboam. (So Wordsworth, Motais, etc.)

Ver. 6.—**Folly is set in great dignity, and the rich sit in low place.** This is an instance of the error intimated in the preceding verse. A tyrannical ruler exalts incompetent persons, unworthy favourites, to "great heights" (ἐν ὕψεσι μεγάλοις, Septuagint), as it is literally—puts them into eminent positions. "Folly" is abstract for concrete, "fools." *And the rich sit in low place.* "The rich" (*ashirim*) are not simply those who have wealth, however obtained, but men of noble birth; ἀρχαιόπλουτοι, as Plumptre appositely notes, persons of ancestral wealth, who from natural position might be looked upon as rulers of men. Such men would seek eminent stations, not from base motives of gain, but from an honourable ambition, and yet they are often slighted by unworthy princes and kept in low estate (comp. 1 Sam. ii. 7, 8; Prov. xix. 10; Ecclus. xi. 5, 6). The experience mentioned in this and the following verses could scarcely have been Solomon's, though it has been always common enough in the East, where the most startling changes have been made, the lowest

persons have been suddenly raised to eminence, mistresses and favourites loaded with dignities, and oppression of the rich has been systematically pursued.

Ver. 7.—**I have seen servants upon horses.** A further description of the effect of the tyrant's perversion of equity. Such an allusion could not have been made in Solomon's reign, when the importation of horses was quite a new thing (1 Kings x. 28). Later, to ride upon horses was a distinction of the nobility (Jer. xvii. 25). Thus Amaziah's corpse was brought on horses to be buried in the city of David (2 Chron. xxv. 28): Mordecai was honoured by being taken round the city on the king's own steed (Esth. vi. 8, etc.). **Princes walking as servants upon the earth.** "Princes" (*sarim*); i.e. masters, lords. Some take the expressions here as figurative, equivalent to "those who are worthy to be princes," and "those who are fit only to be slaves;" but the literal is the true interpretation. Commentators quote what Justin (xli. 3) says of the Parthians, "Hoc denique discrimen inter servos liberosque, quod servi pedibus, liberi non nisi equis incedunt." Ginsburg notes that early travellers in the East record the fact that Europeans were not allowed by the Turks to ride upon horses, but were compelled either to use asses or walk on foot. In some places the privilege of riding upon horseback was permitted to the consuls of the great powers—an honour denied to all strangers of lower degree. Among the Greeks and Romans the possession of a horse with its war-trappings implied a certain amount of wealth and distinction. St. Gregory, treating of this passage ('Moral.,' xxxi. 43), says, "By the name *horse* is understood temporal dignity, as Solomon witnesses. . . . For every one who sins is the servant of si̇n, and servants are upon horses, when sinners are elated with the dignities of the present life. But princes walk as servants, when no honour exalts many who are full of the dignity of virtues, but when the greatest misfortune here presses them down, as though unworthy."

Vers. 8—11.—Section 13. *Various proverbs expressing the benefit of prudence and caution, and the danger of folly.* The connection with what has preceded is not closely marked, but is probably to be found in the bearing of the maxims on the conduct of the wise man who has incurred the resentment of a ruler, and might be inclined to disaffection and revolt. They are intentionally obscure and capable of a double sense—a necessary precaution if the writer lived under Persian despots.

Ver. 8.—**He that diggeth a pit shall fall into it.** This proverb occurs in Prov. xxvi. 27, and, as expressive of the retribution that awaits evil-doers, finds parallels in Ps. vii. 15, 16; ix. 15; x. 2; Ecclus. xxvii. 25, 26. The " pit " (*gummats*, ἅπαξ λεγόμενον) is such a one as was made to capture wild animals, and the maker of it is supposed to approach it incautiously, and to fall into it. But the scope of our passage is rather to speak of what may possibly occur than to insist on the Nemesis that inevitably overtakes transgressors. Its object is to inspire caution in the prosecution of dangerous undertakings, whether the enterprise be the overthrow of a tyrant, or any other action of importance, or whether, as some suppose, the arraignment of the providential ordering of events is intended, in which case there would be the danger of blasphemy and impatience. **And whoso breaketh a hedge, a serpent shall bite him.** The futures throughout vers. 8 and 9 are not intended to express certainty, as if the results mentioned were inevitable, but rather possibility, and might be rendered, with Delitzsch, "may fall," "may bite," etc. The "hedge" is rather a wall (Prov. xxiv. 31), in the crevices of which poisonous snakes have made their abode, which are disturbed by its demolition (comp. Amos v. 19). *Nachash*, here used, is the generic name of any serpent. The majority of the snakes found in Palestine are harmless; but there are some which are very deadly, especially the cobra and those which belong to the viper family. There is no allusion here to the illegal removal of landmarks, a proceeding which might be supposed to provoke retribution; the hedge or wall is one which the demolisher is justified in removing, only in doing so he must look out for certain contingencies, and guard against them. Metaphorically, the pulling down a wall may refer to the removal of evil institutions in a state, which involves the reformer in many difficulties and perils.

Ver. 9.—**Whoso removeth stones shall be hurt therewith.** It is natural to consider this clause as suggested by the breaking of a wall in the preceding verse; but as this would occasion a jejune repetition, it is better to take it of the work of the quarryman, as in 1 Kings v. 17, where the same verb is used. The dangers to which such labourers are exposed are well known. Here, again, but unsuccessfully, some have seen a reference to the removal of landmarks, comparing 2 Kings iv. 4, where the word is translated "set aside." As before said, the paragraph does not speak of retribution, but advises caution, enforcing the lesson by certain homely allusions to the accidents that may occur in customary occupations. **He that cleaveth wood shall be endangered thereby.**

Cutting up logs of wood, a man may hurt himself with axe or saw, or be injured by splinters, etc. If we take the idea to be the felling of trees, there is the danger of being crushed in their fall, or, according to the tenor of Deut. xix. 5, of being killed inadvertently by a neighbour's axe. Vulgate, *Qui scindit ligna vulnerabitur ab eis*, which is more definite than the general term "endangered;" but the Septuagint has, Κινδυνεύσει ἐν αὐτοῖς, as in the Authorized Version. Plumptre sees here, again, an intimation of the danger of attacking time-honoured institutions, even when decaying and corrupt.

Ver. 10.—**If the iron be blunt, and he do not whet the edge.** The illustration at the end of the last verse is continued. The "iron" is the axe used in cutting wood; if this be blunted by the work to which it is put, and he, the labourer, has not sharpened the edge (Hebrew, *the face*, as in Ezek. xxi. 1), what is the consequence? How is he to carry on his work? **Then must he put to more strength.** He must put more force in his blows, he must make up for the want of edge by added power and weight. This is the simplest explanation of the passage, which contains many linguistic difficulties. These may be seen discussed at length in the commentaries of Delitzsch, Wright, Nowack, etc. The translation of Ginsburg is not commendable, "If the axe be blunt, and he (the tyrant's opponent) do not sharpen it beforehand (*phanim*, taken as an adverb of time), he (the tyrant) shall only increase the army." The Septuagint is obscure, 'Εὰν ἐκπέσῃ τὸ σιδήριον, καὶ αὐτὸς πρόσωπον ἐτάραξε· καὶ δυνάμεις δυναμώσει, "If the axe should fall, then he troubles his face, and he shall strengthen his forces (? double his strength);" Vulgate, *Si retusum fuerit ferrum, et hoc non ut prius, sed hebetatum fuerit, multo labore exacuetur*, "If the iron shall be blunted, and it be not as before, but have become dull, it shall be sharpened with much labour." **But wisdom is profitable to direct;** rather, *the advantage of setting right is* (on the side of) *wisdom.* Wisdom teaches how to conduct matters to a successful termination; for instance, it prompts the worker to sharpen his tool instead of trying to accomplish his task by an exertion of mere brute strength. The gnome applies to all the instances which have been mentioned above. Wisdom alone enables a man to meet and overcome the dangers and difficulties which beset his social, common, and political life. If we apply the whole sentence to the case of disaffection with the government or open rebellion, the caution given would signify —See that your means are adequate to the end, that your resources are sufficient to conduct your enterprise to success. Septuagint Vatican, Καὶ περίσσεια τῷ ἀνδρὶ οὐ σοφία, "And the advantage to man is not wisdom." But manuscripts A and C read, Καὶ περίσσεια τοῦ ἀνδρίου σοφία: Vulgate, *Post industriam sequetur sapientia*, "After industry shall follow wisdom."

Ver. 11.—The last proverb of this little series shows the necessity of seizing the right opportunity. **Surely the serpent will bite without enchantment.** The Authorized Version is not quite correct. The particle אם, with which the verse begins, is here conditional, and the rendering should be, *If the serpent bite*, etc.; the apodosis comes in the next clause. The idea is taken up from ver. 8. If one handles a serpent without due precaution or without knowing the secret of charming it, one will suffer for it. The taming and charming of poisonous snakes is still, as heretofore, practised in Egypt and the East. What the secret of this power is has not been accurately determined; whether it belongs especially to persons of a certain idiosyncrasy, whether it is connected with certain words or intonations of the voice or musical sounds, we do not know. Of the existence of the power from remote antiquity there can be no question. Allusions to it in Scripture are common enough (see Exod. vii. 11; Ps. lviii. 5; Jer. viii. 17; Ecclus. xii. 13). If a serpent before it is charmed is dangerous, what then? The Authorized Version affords no sensible apodosis: **And a babbler is no better.** The words rendered "babbler" (*baal hallashon*) are literally "master of the tongue," and by them is meant the ἐπαοιδός, "the serpent-charmer." The clause should run, *Then there is no use in the charmer.* If the man is bitten before he has time to use his charm, it is no profit to him that he has the secret, it is too late to employ it when the mischief is done. This is to shut the stable door after the steed is stolen. The maxim enforces the warning against being too late; the greatest skill is useless unless applied at the right moment. The Septuagint translates virtually as above, "If a serpent bites when not charmed (ἐν οὐ ψιθυρισμῷ), then there is no advantage to the charmer (τῷ ἐπάδοντι)." The Vulgate departs from the context, rendering, *Si mordeat serpens in silentio* (i.e. probably "uncharmed"), *nihil eo minus habet qui occulte detrahit*, "He is nothing better who slanders secretly," which St. Jerome thus explains: the serpent and the slanderer are alike, for as the serpent stealthily infuses its poison, so the secret slanderer pours his venom into another's breast.

Vers. 12—15.—Section 14. The mention of "the master of the tongue" in ver. 11 leads the author to introduce some maxims concerned with *the contrast between the words and acts of the wise, and the worthless prating and useless labours of the fool.*

Ver. 12.—**The words of a wise man's mouth** are **gracious;** literally, *are grace* (χάρις, Septuagint); *i.e.* they not only are pleasing in form and manner, but they conciliate favour, produce approbation and good will, convince and, what is more, persuade. So of our blessed Lord it was said, "All bare him witness, and wondered at the gracious words (τοῖς λόγοις τῆς χάριτος) which proceeded out of his mouth" (Luke iv. 22; comp. Ps. xlv. 2). In distinction from the unready man, who, like the snake-charmer in the preceding verse, suffers by reason of his untimely silence, the wise man uses his speech opportunely and to good purpose. (A different result is given in ch. ix. 11.) **But the lips of a fool will swallow up himself.** This is a stronger expression than "ruin" or "destroy." Speaking without due forethought, he compromises himself, says what he has shamefully to withdraw, and brings punishment on his own head (comp. Prov. x. 8, 21; xviii. 7).

Ῥῆμα παρὰ καιρὸν ῥιφθὲν ἀνατρέπει βίον.

"Untimely speech has ruined many a life."

Ver. 13.—**The beginning of the words of his mouth is foolishness.** A confirmation of the last clause of the preceding verse. The fool speaks according to his nature. "As saith the proverb of the ancients, Out of the wicked cometh forth wickedness" (1 Sam. xxiv. 13; comp. Prov. xv. 2; Isa. xxxii. 6). As soon as he opens his mouth he utters folly, unwisdom, silliness. But he does not stop there. **The end of his talk is mischievous madness.** By the time he has finished, he has committed himself to statements that are worse than silly, that are presumptuous, frenzied, indicative of mental and moral depravity. Intemperate language about the secrets of God's providence and the moral government of the world may be intended. Some think that the writer is still alluding to dangerous talk concerning a tyrannical ruler, seditious proposals, secret conspiracies, etc. The text itself does not confirm such notion with any certainty.

Ver. 14.—**A fool also is full of words.** The word for "fool" here is *sakal*, which implies a dense, confused thinker. Above the word was *kesil*, which denotes rather the self-confidence of the dull and stupid man. *Moreover the fool multiplieth words.* He not only speaks foolishly, but he says too much (comp. ch. v. 2). It is not mere loquacity that is here predicated of the fool, though that is one of his characteristics, but, as the rest of the verse shows, the prating of things about which he knows nothing. He talks as though he knew everything and there were no limitation to human cognition. **A man cannot tell what shall be.** And yet, or although, no man can really predict the future. The fool speaks confidently of such things, and thereby proves his imbecility. Instead of "what shall be," the Septuagint has, Τί τὸ γενόμενον καὶ τί τὸ ἐσόμενον, "What has been and what shall be;" the Vulgate, *Quid ante se fuerit*, "What has been before him." This reading was introduced probably to obviate a seeming tautology in the following clause, **And what shall be after him, who can tell?** But this clause has a different signification from the former, and presents a closer definition. The future intended may be the result of the fool's inconsiderate language, which may have fatal and lasting consequences; or it may refer to the visitation of his sins upon his children, in accordance with the denunciation of Deut. v. 9; xxix. 20—22; or it may include the life beyond the grave. The uncertainty of the future is a constant theme; see ch. iii. 22; vi. 11, 12; vii. 14; viii. 17; and compare Christ's parable of the rich fool (Luke xii. 16—20), and St. James's warning in his Epistle (iv. 13—16).

Ver. 15.—**The labour of the foolish wearieth every one of them, because he knoweth not how to go to the city.** A transition from plural to singular is here made, *The work of fools wearieth him that knoweth not*, etc. "Fools' work" signifies, perhaps, the vain speculations about Providence which Koheleth constantly condemns; or at any rate, all vain and objectless toil and trouble. Not to know the way to the city is probably a proverbial saying expressive of gross ignorance concerning the most obvious matters. How should one, who fails in the knowledge open to all experience, be able to investigate and give an opinion about abstruse questions (comp. Isa. xxxv. 8)? For the last clause other interpretations have been proposed, such as, the fool knows not how to transact public business (which is introducing a modern idea); the oppressed peasant knows not the way to the town where he might obtain redress; he is so foolish that he does not understand where he may find patrons whom he may bribe to plead his cause; he is an Essene, who avoids cities; he cannot make his way to the new Jerusalem, the city of God. But these artificial explanations are to be rejected, while the simple interpretation given above is plainly consistent with the context. The lesson is not to meddle with things too high, especially when you are ignorant of the commonest matters. A little wisdom would prevent endless and useless trouble.

Vers. 16—20.—Section 15. Koheleth re-

turns to the theme mentioned in vers. 4—7. and speaks of *folly in one who holds the position of king, and the need of wisdom and prudence in the subjects of an unworthy ruler.*

Ver. 16.—**Woe to thee, O land, when thy king is a child!** "Child" is *naar*, which term included any age up to manhood. Some interpret the word here, as παῖς in Greek, in the sense of "slave," contrasting it with "the son of nobles" in the following verse. But it can hardly signify more than servitor, attendant; and in ver. 7 the antithesis to "prince" is *ebed*, not *naar*. The child in the present case is a youthful, inexperienced ruler, who does not realize his responsibilities, and is the tool of evil advisers. What particular instance, if any, Koheleth had in view it is impossible to say. Of course, many expositors see a reference to Rehoboam, whom, at forty years of age, his own son Abijah calls *naar* (2 Chron. xiii. 7), and who was certainly childish in his conduct (1 Kings xii. 1—14). Hitzig connects the passage with the reign of Ptolemy Epiphanes, who was but five years old at the death of his father, B.C. 205, the reins of government being assumed by Agathocles and his sister Agathoclea, who occasioned serious disasters to the land. To support this opinion, the date of our book has to be considerably reduced (see Introduction). It is best to take the gnome as a general expression, like that in Isa. iii. 12, "As for my people, children are their oppressors, and women rule over them." **Thy princes eat in the morning.** Eating here implies feasting and banqueting, beginning the day with sensual enjoyment instead of such honest work as attending to state matters, administering justice, etc., as becomes good rulers. None but profligates would thus spend the early morning. "These are not drunken, as ye suppose; seeing it is but the third hour of the day," says St. Peter, repudiating the charge of intoxication (Acts ii. 15). "Woe unto them," cries Isaiah (v. 11), "that rise up early in the morning, that they may follow strong drink!" Even the heathen censured such debauchery. Cicero thus abuses Antonius: "At quam multos dies in ea villa turpissime es perbacchatus. Ab hora tertia bibebatur, ludebatur, vomebatur" ('Philipp.,' ii. 41). Curtius (v. 7. 2) reprehends "de die convivia inire." The Greeks had a proverb to denote abnormal sensuality, Ἀφ' ἡμέρας πίνειν.

Ver. 17.—**Blessed art thou, O land, when thy king is the son of nobles!** *cujus rex nobilis est* (Vulgate), υἱὸς ἐλευθέρων, "son of free men" (Septuagint). Some would regard "son of nobles" as a periphrasis expressive of character, equivalent to the

Latin *generosus*, as "son of strength," equivalent to "strong man;" "son of wickedness," equivalent to "wicked man;" but the phrase may well be taken literally. Koheleth (ver. 7) has expressed his disgust at the exaltation of unworthy slaves to high positions; he here intimates his adherence to the idea that those who descend from noble ancestors, and have been educated in the higher ranks of society, are more likely to prove a blessing to their land than upstarts who have been placed by caprice or favouritism in situations of trust and eminence. Of course, it is not universally true that men of high birth make good rulers; but proverbs of general tenor must not be pressed in particulars, and the author must be understood to affirm that the fact of having distinguished ancestors is an incentive to right action, stirs a worthy emulation in a man, gives him a motive which is wanting in the low-born parvenu. The feeling, *noblesse oblige*, has preserved many from baseness (comp. John viii. 39). **Thy princes eat in due season;** not like those mentioned in ver. 16, but *in tempore*, πρὸς καιρόν, at the right time, the "season" which appertains to all mundane things (ch. iii. 1—8). **For strength, and not for drunkenness.** The preposition ב here is taken as expressing the object—they eat to gain strength, not to indulge sensuality; but it is more in accordance with usage to translate "in, or with, manly strength," *i.e.* as man's strength demands, and not degenerating into a carouse. If it is thought incongruous, as Ginsburg deems, to say, "princes *eat* for drunkenness," we may take drunkenness as denoting excess of any kind The word in the form here used occurs nowhere else. The Septuagint, regarding rather the consequences of intoxication than the actual word in the text, renders, Καὶ οὐκ αἰσχυνθήσονται, "And they shall not be ashamed." Thus, too, St. Jerome, *Et non in confusione*. St. Augustine ('De Civit.,' xvii. 20) deduces from this passage that there are two kingdoms—that of Christ and that of the devil, and he explains the allegory at some length, going into details which are of homiletic utility. Another interpretation is given by St. Jerome, quoted at length by Corn. à Lapide, in his copious commentary.

Ver. 18.—By much slothfulness the building decayeth. The subject is still the state. Under the image of a house which falls into ruin for lack of needful repairs, is signified the decay that surely overtakes a kingdom whose rulers are given up to indolence and debauchery, and neglect to attend to the affairs which require prompt care (comp. Amos ix. 11). Such were they whom Amos (vi. 6) denounced, "That drink wine in bowls, and anoint themselves with the chief

ointments; but they are not grieved for the affliction of Joseph." "Much slothfulness" is expressed in the original by a dual form, which gives an intensive signification. Ewald and Ginsburg take it as referring to the "two idle hands;" but the intensification of the dual is not unprecedented (see Delitzsch, *in loc.*). The rest of this clause is more accurately rendered, *the rafters sink*, i.e. the timber framework, whether of roof or wall, gives way. This may possibly not be noticed at once, but it makes itself known unmistakably ere long. **And through idleness of the hands the house droppeth through;** rather, *the house leaketh*, the roof lets in the rain. Septuagint, Ἐν ἀργίᾳ χειρῶν στάξει ἡ οἰκία, "Through laziness of hands the house will drip." The very imperfect construction of the flat roofs of Eastern houses demanded continual attention. Such common and annoying occurrences as a leaky roof are mentioned in the Book of Proverbs (see xix. 13; xxvii. 15). Plautus, 'Mostell.,' i. 2. 28—

"Ventat imber, lavit parietes; perpluunt
Tigna; putrefacit aër operam fabri."

"The rain comes down, and washes all the walls,
The roof is leaky, and the weather rough
Loosens the architect's most skilful work."

Ver. 19.—**A feast is made for laughter, and wine maketh merry.** Here is a cause of the decay spoken of above. The rulers spend in revelry and debauchery the time and energy which they ought to give to affairs of state. More literally, *for merriment they make bread, and wine [that] cheereth life;* i.e. they use God's good gifts of bread and wine as means of intemperance and thoughtless pleasure. So a psalmist speaks of wine as making glad the heart of man (Ps. civ. 15); and Ben-Sira says, "Wine is as good as life to a man, if it be drunk moderately: what life is there to a man that is without wine? for it was created to make men glad. Wine measurably drunk and in season bringeth gladness of the heart, and cheerfulness of the mind" (Ecclus. xxxi. [xxxiv.] 27, 28). **But money answereth all things;** *i.e.* grants all that such persons want. It requires money to provide rich food and costly wines; this they possess, and they are thus able to indulge their appetites to the utmost. It concerns them not how such resources are obtained—won by extortion from a starving people, exacted in exorbitant taxation, pillaged by unscrupulous instruments; they want gold to expend on their lusts, and they get it somehow, and with it all that in their view makes life worth living. Commentators cite Horace, 'Ep.,' i. 6. 36, "Scilicet uxorem," etc.

" For why—a portioned wife, fair fame, and
　　friends,
Beauty and birth on sovereign Wealth
　　attends.
Blest is her votary throned his bags
　　among!
Persuasion's self sits perched upon his
　　tongue;
Love beams in every feature of his face,
And every gesture beams celestial grace."
　　　　　　　　　　　　　　　　(Howes.)

Corn. à Lapide appositely quotes—

". . . quidquid nummis præsentibus opta,
Et veniet; clausum possidet arca Jovem."

" If thou hast gold, then wish for anything,
And it will surely come; the money-box
Hath in it a most potent deity."

Pineda, followed by Motais, suggests that
this verse may be taken in a good sense.
He would make ver. 18 correspond to ver.
16, characterizing the government of de-
bauchees, and ver. 19 correspond to ver. 17,
representing the rule of temperate princes
where all is peace and prosperity. But
there is nothing grammatical to indicate
this arrangement; and the explanation
given above is doubtless correct. The
Septuagint Version is not faithful to our
present text, though it is followed virtually
by the Syriac: Εἰς γέλωτα ποιοῦσιν ἄρτον, καὶ
οἶνον καὶ ἔλαιον τοῦ εὐφρανθῆναι ζῶντας, καὶ
τοῦ ἀργυρίου ταπεινώσει ἐπακούσεται τὰ πάντα,
" For gladness they make bread and wine
and oil, that the living may rejoice, and to
money all things will humble themselves,
will obey " (doubly translating the word).

Ver. 20.—**Curse not the king, no not in
thy thought.** Under the above-mentioned
circumstances, a man might be tempted to
abuse and curse these ill-conditioned rulers.
Koheleth warns against this error; it is
dangerous to give way to it (comp. Exod.
xxii. 28). In ch. viii. 2 the motive for submission to the king is placed on religious
grounds; in the present passage the ground
is prudence, regard for personal safety,
which might be compromised by plain
speaking, especially when one has to do
with such depraved and unscrupulous
persons. We may compare David's generous
conduct to his cruel persecutor Saul, whom
he spared because he was the Lord's
anointed (1 Sam. xxiv. 6, 10; xxvi. 9, etc.;
2 Sam. i. 14). *Madda*, " thought," " consciousness," is rare, and is supposed to
belong to late Hebrew (see 2 Chron. i. 10,
11, 12; Dan. i. 4, 17). The Septuagint
translates it συνείδησις: Vulgate, *cogitatio*.
To encourage such thoughts in the mind is
to run the risk of openly expressing them at

some unguarded moment; for " out of the
abundance of the heart the mouth speaketh."
Curse not the rich in thy bedchamber. In
ability to injure, the rich stand in the same
category as the king. You are not safe ἐν
ταμιείοις κοιτώνων σου, " in your very bedchamber," where, if anywhere, you would
fancy yourself free from espionage. But
" walls have ears," says the proverb (comp.
Hab. ii. 11; Luke xix. 40); and the King of
Syria is warned, " Elisha, the prophet that
is in Israel, telleth the King of Israel the
words thou speakest in thy bedchamber"
(2 Kings vi. 12). " That which ye have
spoken in the ear in closets (ἐν τοῖς ταμιείοις)
shall be proclaimed upon the housetops"
(Luke xii. 3). **For a bird of the air shall
carry the voice.** A proverbial saying,
common to all languages, and not to be referred especially to the story of the cranes
of Ibycus (see Erasmus, ' Adag.,' *s.v.* " Ultio
malefacti ") or to the employment of carrier
pigeons. We say of secret information, " a
little bird told me." Plumptre quotes
Aristophanes, ' Aves,' 575—

Οὐδείς οἶδεν τὸν θησαυρὸν τὸν ἐμὸν πλὴν εἴ τις
　　　ἄρ' ὄρνις.

" No one knows of my treasure, save, it may
　　be, a bird."

On which the Scholiast notes, " There is a
proverb extant, ' No one observes me but the
passing bird'" (comp. Erasmus, 'Adag.,' *s.v.*
" Occulta "). In Koheleth's day informers
evidently plied their trade industriously,
and here meet, not only with notice, but
ironically with reprobation. On the general
sentiment of the verse, we may quote
Juvenal, ' Sat.,' ix. 102, " O Corydon,
Corydon," thus versified in Ginsburg's commentary—

" And dost thou seriously believe, fond swain,
The actions of the great unknown remain ?
Poor Corydon ! even beasts would silence
　　break,
And stocks and stones, if servants did not,
　　speak.
Bolt every door, stop every cranny tight,
Close every window, put out every light;
Let not a whisper reach the listening ear,
No noise, no motion; let no soul be near;
Yet all that passed at the cock's second
　　crow,
The neighbouring vintner shall, ere day-
　　break, know."

That which hath wings (compare Latin *ales*);
the possessor (*baal*) of a pair of wings, a
periphrasis for " a bird," as in Prov. i. 17.
We had " master of the tongue," ver. 11;
so in Dan. viii. 6, 20, " having horns," is
" master (*baal*) of horns."

HOMILETICS.

Vers. 1—7, 12—15.—*The dispraise of folly.* I. FOLLY MARS THE FINEST REPUTATION. As one sinner destroyeth much good (ch. ix. 18), and flies of death, or poisonous flies, cause the ointment of the perfumer to send forth a stinking savour, so doth a little folly outweigh wisdom and honour. 1. *It mars their beauty.* As the poisonous flies so affect the perfumer's ointment that it begins to ferment and lose its fragrance, a little folly mixed up with a great deal of wisdom and honour impairs these in such a fashion and to such an extent, that they cease to attract the good opinion of beholders, and the person possessed of them is rather known as a fool than esteemed as a wise man. 2. *It destroys their value.* As the dealer in ointments cannot sell his corrupted pigment, so neither can the man whose wisdom and honour are tainted with folly any longer wield that power for good he might otherwise have done. The influence exerted by his wisdom and honour is directly counteracted and frequently overbalanced by the influence of his folly.

II. FOLLY CONSTITUTES AN UNSAFE GUIDE. "The wise man's heart is at his right hand; but a fool's heart at his left." This has been thought to mean: 1. *The fool's heart is in the wrong place,* in contrast to the wise man's, which is always in the right place (Hengstenberg). This sentiment is true. The fool's heart is not directed towards those objects upon which its affections ought to be set, while the wise man's is. This enough to make folly an unsafe conductor. 2. *The fool's heart never acts at the right time,* while the wise man's does (Ginsburg), because the wise man's heart is always at his right hand, his acting hand, his working hand; while the fool's is always at the left hand, the wrong hand, the hand with which a person usually finds it difficult to act. This a second reason why no man should accept folly as a leader. It can never seize the opportunity, never strike while the iron is hot, never do anything at the proper moment or in an efficient manner. 3. *The fool's heart is always unlucky in its auguries,* whereas the wise man's heart is always lucky (Plumptre). If this were the correct interpretation—which we think it is not—it would state what would not be surprising, were it true, that the fool's forecasts were usually falsified, and would present another argument for not committing one's self to the directorship of folly. 4. *The fool's heart always leads in the wrong direction,* as distinguished from the right direction in which the wise man's heart ever goes. This, undoubtedly, is true. The fool is a person wholly destitute of that wisdom which is profitable to direct (ver. 10), and without which no man can walk safely (Prov. iii. 23). A final consideration against enrolling beneath the banner of folly.

III. FOLLY INVARIABLY BETRAYS ITS OWN STUPIDITY. "Yea also, when the fool walketh by the way, his understanding faileth him, and he saith to every one *that* he is a fool." As it is certain that no man can conceal his true character for ever, or even for long, so likewise is it certain that a zany, a buffoon, a fool, will discover his sooner than most people. He will proclaim himself to be a fool: 1. *By his irrational behaviour.* His understanding will fail him at critical times and on important subjects. He will reveal his ignorance, want of sense, lack of principle, emptiness of grace. 2. *In the most public manner.* As he walks by the way. As not being in the least degree ashamed of his folly, perhaps hardly conscious he is making such an exhibition of himself. 3. *To the most unlimited extent.* He will make himself known, not to his friends in private, but to his neighbours in the street, and not to one or two merely of these, but to every one he meets.

IV. FOLLY FREQUENTLY ASCRIBES ITS OWN CHARACTER TO OTHERS. The fool saith of every one he meets, "He is a fool," *i.e.* the individual whom he meets is (Vulgate, Luther, Plumptre). Though this translation is doubtful, it supplies a true thought; that as insane people often count all but themselves insane, so fools—intellectual, moral, and religious—not infrequently regard themselves as the only truly wise persons, and look upon the rest of mankind as fools.

V. FOLLY IS OFTEN GUILTY OF GREAT RASHNESS. "If the spirit of the ruler rise up against thee, leave not thy place; for yielding allayeth great offences" (ver. 4). The folly here alluded to consists in three things. 1. *In flaming up into indignation at an unmerited accusation.* Charges of such sort were to be expected by one who served an

Oriental despot, and are not uncommon in ordinary life in the experience of subordinates who serve choleric masters. "The spurns that patient merit of the unworthy takes" are no doubt hard to bear; but it is not a sign of wisdom to fume against them, and fret one's self into anger. 2. *In hastily retiring from the post of duty.* As a statesman might resign his seals of office on being reprimanded by his sovereign, or a workman lay down his tools on being challenged by his master, or a domestic servant throw up her situation on being found fault with by her mistress. 3. *In failing to see the better way of meekness and submission.* The advantages of gently and patiently bearing false accusations or unjust ebullitions of temper against one are obvious. Such yielding (1) usually has the effect of softening the anger and checking the railing of the accuser (Prov. xv. 1); (2) puts an end to further offences on the part of the irate superior, whether ruler or master, who, were his rage to be increased by resistance, might proceed to greater manifestations of his temper; and (3) prevents the offended himself from rushing into more serious transgressions, as he might do were he to give way in turn to his angry passions.

VI. FOLLY SOMETIMES ATTAINS TO UNDESERVED HONOUR. "There is an evil which I have seen under the sun . . . folly set in great dignity, and the rich in low place . . . servants upon horses, and princes walking as servants upon the earth" (vers. 5—7). 1. *The commonness of this phenomenon.* "The eunuch Bagoas long all-powerful at the Persian court" (Delitzsch), Louis XI. exalting the base-born to places of honour, and Edward II., James I. of England or Henry III. of France, lavishing dignities on their minions, may be cited as examples. Nothing more frequent in everyday life than to see persons of small capacity and little worth promoted over the heads of their superiors in talent and goodness. 2. *The cause of this phenomenon.* In one sense the wisdom of God, the chief Ruler of men and things (Hengstenberg), but in another sense, and that the one here intended, the arbitrary power of men "dressed in a little brief authority." 3. *The evil of this phenomenon.* It discourages merit, and inflates folly with pride; rewards incapacity, and despises real ability; places influence in wrong hands, and weakens the power of good men to benefit their age.

VII. FOLLY SELDOM KNOWS WHEN TO HOLD ITS TONGUE. "The lips of a fool will swallow up himself," etc. (vers. 12—14). 1. *The wise man's words are few, the fool's endless.* The former is "swift to hear, but slow to speak" (Jas. i. 19); the latter hears nothing, learns less, and chatters incessantly. The former is known by his silence (Prov. xvii. 28; xxix. 11); the latter, by the multitude of his words (ver. 3). 2. *The wise man's words are gracious, the fool's ruinous.* The lips of the wise are a tree of life (Prov. xi. 30; xv. 4), and disperse knowledge amongst their fellows (Prov. xv. 7), whilst they preserve themselves (Prov. xiv. 3); but a fool's mouth is his own destruction (Prov. xvii. 7), and the complete beggarment of all that listen to him (Prov. xiv. 23; xvii. 7). 3. *The wise man's words improve as they proceed, the fool's deteriorate as they flow.* The former carry with them the ripe fruits of thought and experience, growing richer and weightier as they move slowly on; the latter progress from bad to worse, beginning with foolishness and ending with mischievous madness.

VIII. FOLLY IS FREQUENTLY UNABLE TO DO THE SIMPLEST THINGS. "The labour of fools wearieth every one of them, for he knoweth not how to go to the city" (ver. 15). 1. *The fool's ignorance is dense.* So simple a matter as finding his way along a country road to the city is beyond his comprehension. Plumptre cites in illustration the proverbs, "None but a fool is lost on a straight road," and "The 'why' is plain as way to parish church." 2. *The fool's presumption is immense.* He who cannot do so small a matter as find his way to the city proposes to "enlighten the world and make it happy" through his words or his works. So people who know nothing about a subject often imagine themselves qualified to teach it to others, and persons of no capacity put themselves forward to attempt undertakings of greatest difficulty. 3. *The fool's labour is vast.* Having neither knowledge nor ability, he labours with "great travail" to expound what he does not understand, and perform what he has neither brains nor hands to execute.

LESSONS. 1. Forsake the foolish and live (Prov. ix. 6). 2. Get wisdom; get understanding (Prov. iv. 5).

Vers. 8—11.—*Gnomic wisdom; or, a string of double-edged proverbs.* I. DIGGING

PITS AND FALLING INTO THEM. " He that diggeth a pit shall [or, ' may '] fall into it " (ver. 8). An old proverb, borrowed from Solomon (Prov. xxvi. 27), who in turn may have learnt it from David (Ps. vii. 15; ix. 15; lvii. 6), it may point to one or other of two thoughts. 1. *The necessity of exercising caution in all works of danger.* One who hollows out a trench or pit for the purpose of snaring wild animals—a perfectly legitimate design—may, either by standing too near the edge and causing the treacherous earth to give way, or by stumbling on it in the dark at an unexpected moment, fall in, in which case he will suffer not for having done wrong, but merely for having failed to act with circumspection and prudence (Prov. xiv. 15; xxii. 3; xxvii. 12). 2. *The possibility of evil-doers overreaching themselves.* In this case the pit is supposed to be dug for a wicked purpose, as *e.g.* to ensnare another to his ruin. In this sense the proverb has found expression in almost all literatures. Shakespeare speaks of the engineer being " hoist with his own petard." Haman was hanged upon the gallows he had built for Mordecai (Esth. vii. 10). " Plots and conspiracies are often as fatal to the conspirators as to the intended victims " (Plumptre).

II. BROKEN HEDGES AND BITING SERPENTS. " Whoso breaketh through a fence, a serpent shall bite him " (ver. 8). The hedge, or rather fence, or stone wall, was a customary haunt of serpents; so that one engaged in breaking down such a structure had need to beware of being bitten by the reptiles infesting it. Hence a variety of lessons according as the words are viewed. 1. *An admonition to workers.* To go cautiously about their employments, if these are dangerous, as a person would who had to pull down or break through an old wall in which serpents were lodged. Many accidents occur, inflicting damage on the workers, for want of a little foresight. 2. *A warning to transgressors.* That Nemesis may overtake them in the very act of their evil-doing. If they break through a neighbour's fence to steal his fruit, or pull down his wall so as to injure his property, they need not be surprised if they are caught in the act. Wickedness has a habit of avenging itself, sometimes with great rapidity and with terrible severity, on those who perpetrate it. This is true of all breaking down of those fences or laws with which God has girt man. Every violation of law —physical, intellectual, moral, social, religious—is visited with its own particular biting serpent of penalty. 3. *A caution to reformers.* If they will set themselves to pull down the old walls of decayed and worthless institutions, or to break through the fences of time-honoured customs, they must prepare themselves for being bitten by the serpents in the crannies—for encountering the opposition, criticism, hate, and often persecution of those who have vested interests in the abuses proposed to be rectified or swept away. Reformers should count the cost before beginning their work of reformation.

III. HEWING OR REMOVING STONES AND HURTING ONE'S SELF. " Whoso heweth out [or, ' moveth '] stones shall be hurt therewith " (ver. 9). Again of double import, teaching : 1. *The duty of guarding one's self against the perils that may attend a perfectly legitimate occupation.* Viewed in this light, the stone-moving may simply mean the pulling down of a wall, which, if it be carelessly performed, may fall and inflict a hurt upon the worker; and the stone-hewing may refer to the work of quarrying, which may be attended with great risk from the flying about of chips. 2. *The inevitable recompense of all wrong-doing.* If the stone-moving alludes to the removing of a neighbour's landmark, then the proverb stands as a reminder of the curse pronounced against that ancient sin (Deut. xix. 14; xxvii. 17). The use of landmarks, at least as then employed, has ceased; but the distinction between " mine" and " thine "remains ; and every invasion of another's rights is a wickedness which in course of providence will receive its just recompense of reward (Exod. xx. 15).

IV. CLEAVING LOGS AND CUTTING FINGERS. " He that cleaveth wood is endangered thereby " (ver. 9). The three thoughts already mentioned are again repeated. 1. *The need of caution.* Wood-splitting being a dangerous occupation. 2. *The certainty of retribution.* The cutting down of trees, especially fruit trees, being regarded as an act of wrongful oppression, and as such forbidden by the Law, even in a siege (Deut. xx. 19, 20), the hurt that might come to one in wood-cutting (Deut. xix. 5) may be viewed as suggestive of the penalty of disobedience. 3. *The peril of reform.* The cutting down of trees is, in this instance, taken as symbolic of the hewing down of decayed institutions.

V. BLUNT TOOLS AND HEAVY BLOWS. "If the iron be blunt, and one do not whet the edge, then must he put to more strength: but wisdom is profitable to direct" (ver. 10). The lessons are two. 1. *Every work has its own appropriate tools.* Wood-cutting requires axes, and not merely blunt pieces of iron; pit-digging demands spades; stone-hewing chisels. Each occupation has its own implement. This the dictate of common sense. 2. *Every tool should be kept in a fit condition for its work.* This the teaching of wisdom. A woodman with a blunt axe must strike oftener and heavier than he would need to do were his axe sharp. So the man who enters on any task without the requisite sharpness of intelligence and sagacity will find his work proportionately hindered.

VI. BITING SERPENTS AND TARDY CHARMERS. "If the serpent bite before it is charmed, then is there no advantage in the charmer;" or, "Surely the serpent will bite without, or where there is no, enchantment" (ver. 11); which again offers two thoughts. 1. *That the serpent of temptation will do its deadly work unless timeously repressed.* This may be done by resisting its first approaches, if they cannot be eluded altogether (Jas. iv. 7), by crushing down the rising inclination within one to yield, by diligently considering the sinfulness of that to which one is solicited (Gen. xxxix. 9), by calling in the help of God against the adversary (Eph. vi. 10—18). 2. *That if once the serpent of temptation has done its deadly work there is no use whatever of resorting to such means of repression.* Such means are then too late. To employ them then is much the same thing as to shut the stable door when the steed has been stolen.

Vers. 8—11.—*Good thoughts for bad times; or, words from the wise.* I. THE NECESSITY OF CAUTION. Especially in difficult and dangerous works. He who digs a pit must be on his guard against falling into it; he who pulls down a stone wall must look out for serpents; he who hews stones or removes them must be careful not to hurt himself in the process; he who cleaves or splits timber must see that he is not endangered thereby. "The prudent man looketh well to his going."

II. THE RECOMPENSE OF WRONG-DOING. 1. *Springing out of the wrong act.* As when one, having dug a pit to ensnare another, falls into it himself. 2. *Suddenly smiting the transgressor.* As when a serpent bites him who pulls down a wall. 3. *Swiftly following on the heels of crime.* As when one who, hewing stones, injures himself with the chips, or, removing a neighbour's landmark, is punished for his offence. 4. *Certainly overtaking the evil-doer.* As when one cutting wood strikes himself with the axe.

III. THE PERIL OF REFORM. The propriety of counting the cost before entering on the arduous career of a reformer. Illustrated by the two proverbs about breaking through fences and cutting down trees. Men are not to be deterred from attempting reforms because of difficulties and dangers; only they should not be surprised when these are experienced.

IV. THE SELECTION OF INSTRUMENTS. Many enterprises fail because the proper instruments have not been selected; or, if selected, have not been managed with wisdom. The man who intends to cut down a tree must first have an axe and then keep it sharp.

V. THE CHOICE OF TIMES. Many good undertakings fail because not begun at the right time. Many dangers might be avoided were precautions against them not adopted too late. To every work there is a time. Strike while the iron is hot. Beware of being too late.

Vers. 16—20.—*The picture of a happy land.* I. A NOBLE KING. 1. *Of royal blood.* "Happy art thou, O land, when thy king is the son of nobles"—like Horace's "Macenas atavis edite regibus," descended from a long line of crowned heads. If countries are to have kings, then decidedly the scion of kingly (more especially if also honourable and good) ancestors is better than the upstart who was yesterday a gentleman of the pavement, but is to-day the occupant of a throne (ch. iv. 14). 2. *Of mature manhood.* "Woe to thee, O land, when thy king is a child." The experiment of boy-kings has seldom proved successful. Witness the case of Joash (2 Chron. xxiv. 1), who made a tolerable sovereign only so long as Jehoiada lived. When the king is a minor there is too much scope for ambition on the part of the regent and of the nobles, who would like to be regents or even kings. 3. *Of princely intellect.* The man who is to rule others should be every inch a king, not in bodily appearance only, but in mental capacity as well. No greater calamity can befall a country than to have its throne filled by a fool or an intellectual baby. In this sense, to be ruled by a "child" is surely the last indignity that can be offered to reasoning and reasonable men. 4. *Of large experience.* Unlike a child, or a boy, or a youth, whose knowledge of men and things must at the best be limited, the ideal sovereign should be one whose accumulated stores of wisdom, gathered in many ways and from many lands, may be used for promoting the welfare of his people.

II. A TEMPERATE ARISTOCRACY. 1. *Dissipation, shameful in all, is specially so in princes. Noblesse oblige.* The higher one's rank, the more incumbent on one is virtue. Hence for princes to eat in the morning, or to be addicted to gluttony and other bodily gratifications, to be so intent upon them as not merely to sit up late indulging them, but to rise up early for the purpose of renewing them, is to degrade their dignity, and trail their honour in the mire, besides shaming virtue and outraging decency. 2. *Moderation, dutiful in all, is specially promotive of health.* Those who live to eat and drink seldom live so long as they might, but by indulgence, setting up disease in their bodies, often shorten their days and die before their time. Those who eat and drink to live, and therefore eat in due season and in due measure, which is what is meant by temperance, take the best means of maintaining themselves in health and strength.

III. A VIRTUOUS PEOPLE. 1. *Industrious.* "By slothfulness the roof sinketh in; and through idleness of the hands the house leaketh" (ver. 18). What is true of a material edifice is also true of the body politic. As the timbers or rafters of a private dwelling will decay unless watched over and from time to time repaired by its inmate, so the fabric of the state will go to ruin unless it be surveyed by vigilant eyes and upheld by untiring hands. 2. *Joyous.* Not only is there nothing sinful in feasting and wine-drinking when these are kept in virtuous moderation, but the absence of gladness from the face of any people is a bad omen. Gloom on the countenance and wretchedness in the heart mean that social disorder and perhaps revolution are at hand. Everything that contributes to the happiness and contentment of a people is a distinct contribution to the stability of a state. 3. *Moneyed.* A people without money or money's worth is a people on the verge of starvation; and no state can stand long whose population consists of paupers. Money there must be, or its equivalent in material goods, and this not concentrated in a few hands, but distributed as widely as possible. The main problem of statesmen should be to secure a population, not only industrious and happy, but well paid, and therefore well fed, well clothed, and well housed. 4. *Loyal.* A people given to treasonable practices cannot be either prosperous or happy. Hence the Preacher dissuades all good subjects from cursing the king even in their thoughts. The impossibility of escaping detection under the all-pervading espionage of an Oriental despotism rendered it unsafe in the times of the Preacher; but, even in times when the liberty of the subject is respected, it is not always prudent to be hatching conspiracies against the crown, however secret these may be; and certainly it is not conducive to the welfare of a people that such should be common in the land. 5. *Law-abiding.* As little given to curse the rich as to plot against the king. Not communistic, socialistic, or revolutionary in the bad sense of these expressions; since a people may be all of these in a good sense without losing its character for virtue.

HOMILIES BY VARIOUS AUTHORS.

Vers. 1, 3.—*Folly self-betrayed.* To the writer of this book it seemed that the great antithesis of human life, of human society, was pointed out by the distinction between wisdom and folly. As by wisdom he meant not merely speculative knowledge or profound statecraft, but, much rather, reflective habits, deliberate judgment, and decisive action, in the practical affairs of life; so by folly he intended exactly the opposite of such character and mental habits. A certain contemptuous and weary abhorrence of the foolish breathes through his language. His remarks are full of sagacity and justice.

I. FOLLY MAY FOR A TIME BE CONCEALED. A grave countenance, a staid demeanour, a reticent habit, may convey the impression of wisdom which does not exist. Men are disposed to take a favourable view of those occupying high station, and even of those possessing great estates. The casual acquaintances of men who are slow and serious in speech, or are exalted in rank, often credit them with wisdom, when there has been no proof of its existence.

II. FOLLY WILL CERTAINLY, SOONER OR LATER, BE REVEALED BY CIRCUMSTANCES. A little folly is the ill savour that vitiates the perfume. The understanding of the fool faileth him while he walketh by the way. The test is sure to be applied which will prove whether the coin is genuine or counterfeit. The hollow reputation must collapse. A critical time comes when counsel has to be given, when action has to be taken, and at such a time the folly of the pompous and pretentious fool is made manifest to all. Sounding phraseology may impose upon men for a season; but there are occasions when something more than words is needed, and such occasions reveal the emptiness and vanity of the foolish. Pedantry is not learning, profession is not religion, pretence is not reality; neither can the show be, for any length of time, taken for the substance.

III. FOLLY, THUS EXPOSED, DESTROYS A MAN'S REPUTATION AND INFLUENCE. The revulsion is sudden and complete, and may even go to unreasonable lengths. It is presumed that, because the highest expectations have been disappointed, not even the slightest respect or confidence is justifiable. A little folly outweighs wisdom and honour.

APPLICATION. The chief lesson of this passage is the value of sincerity, thoroughness, and genuineness of character. It is not every man who has the knowledge, the natural insight, the large experience of life, which go to make up wisdom. But no man need pretend to be what he is not; no man need proclaim himself a sage or a mentor; no man need claim for himself the deferential regard and homage of others. He who will order his way by such light as he can gain by reflection, by the study of the Scriptures, and by prayer, will not go far astray. Sincerity and modesty may not gain a temporary reputation for profundity of wisdom; but they will not expose their possessor to the humiliation and shame of him who, professing himself to be wise, becomes manifest to all men as a fool.—T.

Ver. 4.—*A pacifying spirit.* The circumstances which suggested this admonition were special; we seem to be introduced to the court of a powerful and arbitrary Oriental sovereign. The caprice and injustice of the monarch arouses the indignation of the courtier, who is ready to rise in resentment and anger. But the counsel is given, "Leave not thy place." Resentment fans the flame of wrath; submission assuages it. "Yielding allayeth great offences." Now, the circumstances apply only to a few, but the principle which they suggest is of wide and general application. A submissive and pacificatory spirit promotes harmony.

I. MEN MUST EXPECT TO ENCOUNTER ANGER AND ARROGANCE FROM THEIR FELLOW-MEN. Those who occupy positions of authority expect deference from their inferiors. Birth, rank, station, are apt to foster an arbitrary habit in their possessors. And whilst there are many and beautiful exceptions to this rule, especially owing to the influence of Christ's example and spirit, it is not to be questioned that arrogance is the special fault of the officially great.

II. ANGER AND ARROGANCE NATURALLY AROUSE RESENTMENT. We are so constituted that, apart from the controlling and restraining influence of reason and religious principles, we return blow for blow. Anger enkindles anger, as flint and steel enkindle fire. Hence words are spoken which may never be forgotten, and may ever be regretted; estrangements take place which may lead to bitter feuds; blows may follow, or duels, or war.

III. THE WISDOM AND THE DUTY OF SELF-CONTROL. The common proverb is, " It takes two to make a quarrel." Because offence is given, offence need not be taken; because injury and insult are inflicted, it does not of necessity follow that they should be avenged. Several motives concur to restrain resentment. 1. Self-respect. The man who loses temper and self-command, upon subsequent reflection, feels himself so much less a man; he despises himself. 2. Prudence. This is the motive specially relied upon in this passage. In dealing with "the ruler," whose spirit rises up against him, the courtier is reminded of the ruler's power, and is admonished not to provoke him to the exercise of that power, for in that case disfavour may lead to disgrace and degradation. 3. Religious principle. This is the motive which, in the case of the Christian, is most powerful. The example of the patient and meek Redeemer, who reviled not again, and who besought mercy for his murderers, is never absent from the mind of those who trust and love him. His love constrains, his precept controls, his example impels. And thus forbearance and forgiveness characterize Christ's disciples, in those circumstances in which otherwise resentment and revenge might animate the heart.

IV. THE PACIFYING POWER OF PATIENT SUBMISSION. "Yielding pacifieth [allayeth] great offences." It is not required that the injured party should approve the action of his injurer; or affirmed that no opportunity may occur of just and dignified rebuke. But silence, quietness of spirit, and control of natural impulse, will in many cases produce a good result. He who bears wrong patiently is the stronger and better for the discipline; and his demeanour may melt the wrong-doer to contrition, and will at all events lead him to reflection. Thus the threatened conflict may be avoided; a lesson may be administered to the hasty and arrogant, and the best interests of society may be promoted. Thus the Word of God is honoured, and witness is given to the power which Christ possesses to subdue and govern the unruly nature of man.—T.

Vers. 5—7.—*Social paradoxes.* The evil which the writer of Ecclesiastes here condemns is one of which the history of every nation affords many examples. Princes' favourites have too often been chosen from amongst the worthless herd who seek their own elevation and advantage by ministering to the vices of the young, profligate, and powerful. How many a reign has been marred by this mischief! How many a king has been misled, to his own and his country's harm, by the folly of choosing companions and counsellors not for wisdom, sincerity, and patriotism, but because those chosen are of congenial tastes and habits, or are flatterers and parasites!

I. THE ELEVATION OF FOOLISH FAVOURITES TO POWER IS INJURIOUS TO THOSE SO PROMOTED. Men who might have been respectable and useful in a lowly station are corrupted and morally debased by their elevation to posts of undeserved dignity and emolument. Their heads are turned by the giddy height to which they are raised.

II. THE ELEVATION OF FOOLISH FAVOURITES TO POWER IS INJURIOUS TO THE PRINCES WHOM THEY PROFESS TO SERVE. What kings and rulers need is to be told the truth. It is important that they should know the actual state and needs of the nation. And it is important that any weakness or wrong bias, natural or acquired, should be corrected. But the fools who are set in high places make it their one great rule of conduct never to utter unpalatable truth. They assume the faultlessness of their master; they paint the condition of his subjects in glowing colours, and give the ruler all the credit for national prosperity. Their insincerity and flattery are morally injurious to the prince, who by the companionship of the wise might have been morally benefited.

III. THE ELEVATION OF FOOLISH FAVOURITES TO POWER IS INJURIOUS TO THE COMMUNITY. The example of injustice thus presented is discouraging to the upright and depressing to the reflecting. The throne becomes unpopular, and the people generally are demoralized. The evil is no doubt greater in despotic than in constitutional states, for these latter afford fewer opportunities for rapacity and oppression. Yet nothing more injuriously affects the community generally than the spectacle of a court which prefers folly to wisdom, fashion to experience, vice to virtue, frivolity to piety.—T.

Vers. 8, 9.—*The rebound of evil.* Under these picturesque and impressive figures of speech, the Preacher appears to set forth the important moral lesson, that they who work harm and wrong to their fellow-men shall not themselves escape with impunity.

I. THE SIGNS AND THE SIN OF MALICE. The case is one of intentional, deliberate malevolence, working itself out in acts of mischief and wrong. Such a spirit so expressing itself may be characterized (1) as a perversion of natural sentiment; (2) as a wrong to our social nature, and a violation of the conditions of our social life; and (3) as in flagrant contradiction to the commands of God, and the precepts of our gracious and compassionate Saviour.

II. THE RETRIBUTION OF MALICE. The proverbial language of the text is paralleled by somewhat similar apophthegms in various languages, as, for example, in the Oriental proverb, "Curses, like chickens, come home to roost." 1. Such retribution is often wrought by the ordinary operation of natural laws. The story of the pirate-rover who was wrecked upon the crags of Aberbrothock, from which he himself had cut off the warning bell, is an instance familiar to our minds from childhood. 2. Retribution is sometimes effected by the action of the laws enforced in all civilized communities. The *lex talionis*, "an eye for an eye, a tooth for a tooth," may be taken as an example of a principle the applications of which are discernible in all the various states of society existing among men. 3. Those who escape the penalties of nature and the indignation of their fellow-men cannot escape the righteous judgment of God; they shall not go unpunished.—T.

Ver. 10.—*Force and wisdom.* The homely adage in the first part of this verse prepares for the broad general statement by which it is followed.

I. IN MECHANICAL UNDERTAKINGS THE SUPERIORITY OF SKILL TO BRUTE FORCE IS MOST APPARENT. This is obvious in the superiority of the workmanship of the civilized and cultured to that of the barbarian.

II. WISDOM HAS A VAST ADVANTAGE IN THE ORDINARY AFFAIRS OF HUMAN LIFE. The old fairy stories usually represented the muscular giant as a simpleton easily out-witted by the youth or the dwarf; the lesson being that mere strength avails but little for those ends which men most seek and prize. It is wisdom which is profitable to direct—a truth which applies not merely to mechanics, but to the various arts which men cultivate. What vocation is there in which thought, investigation, the adaptation of means to ends, a calm deliberate judgment, are not serviceable? It is the wise who reap the harvest of life, who sway the realm of humanity.

III. WISDOM IS PRE-EMINENTLY OF SERVICE IN ALL TRUE RELIGIOUS LIFE AND ENTERPRISE. It is true that human wisdom is depreciated in some passages of Holy Writ. But careful attention will show that it is only the lower type of wisdom which inspiration disparages. They who have only "the wisdom of this world," who are "wise in their own conceit," are indeed condemned. But, on the other hand, they are approved who receive the wisdom of God in Christ, and who are wise unto salvation. It is the enlightening influence of God's Holy Spirit that leads to an appreciation of the gospel itself, and that directs those whose endeavour and aim it is to bring their fellow-men into the enjoyment of those blessings which that gospel secures.—T.

Vers. 11—15.—*The obtrusiveness and the condemnation of folly.* Although some of the language employed in this passage is unquestionably obscure, the general tenor of it is clear enough. The contrast which is drawn between wisdom and folly is what we meet with, under other forms, in other portions of the book, and the exposure and censure of the thoughts and the ways of the fool are fitted to warn the young against forsaking the rough but safe paths of true wisdom.

I. FOLLY IS SHOWN IN THE UNNECESSARY MULTIPLICATION OF WORDS. Fools speak when there is no occasion, when they have nothing to say, or when they have already said all that was needful.

II. FOLLY REVEALS ITSELF, THOUGH WITHOUT PROVOCATION. It cannot be concealed; it is obtrusive and glaring. The fool is his own enemy: "his lips will swallow up himself."

III. FOLLY IS DISPLAYED IN DOGMATIC UTTERANCES UPON MATTERS WHICH ARE BEYOND HUMAN KNOWLEDGE. There are many subjects upon which modesty and reticence are required by wisdom. Especially is this the case with regard to the future. But it is presumed in this passage that the fool will not restrain himself from pronouncing upon what is beyond human knowledge or human prescience.

IV. FOLLY IS WEARISOME TO THOSE WHO WITNESS THE WORKS AND WHO LISTEN TO THE WORDS BY WHICH IT REVEALS ITSELF.

V. FOLLY IS MANIFESTED IN INCOMPETENCY FOR THE MANAGEMENT OF PUBLIC AFFAIRS. The fool "knoweth not how to go to the city," *i.e.* how to transact public business, and to give advice regarding civic action.

VI. FOLLY IS SURE TO ISSUE IN MISCHIEF AND DISASTER. It is sometimes represented that fools can do no harm ; that real mischief is wrought by malice, by criminal designs and actions. But a careful inquiry into the facts would show that very much of the evil that afflicts society is brought to pass by mere folly. The Hebrews and the Greeks were agreed in representing wisdom as a cardinal virtue. It is men's duty to cultivate wisdom. If they neglect to do so, it matters not that they have no criminal intentions; the absence of wisdom must needs lead to conduct which will involve themselves and others in much suffering, and even in terrible calamities.—T.

Vers. 16, 17.—*Statesmanship.* It is sometimes assumed that moral qualities are unimportant in relation to political affairs. If a king be brave in his warlike expeditions, splendid in his court, and affable in his demeanour; if a statesman be sagacious in counsel and determined in action, it is too generally assumed that nothing further is wanting to secure national greatness and prosperity. The writer of Ecclesiastes looked far deeper, and saw the necessity of a self-denying and laborious character in order to true kingly and statesmanlike service.

I. INCOMPETENCE AND SELF-INDULGENCE IN THOSE WHO OCCUPY HIGH PLACES ARE A CURSE TO A NATION. Men who are flung into power by the wave of royal favouritism, or by popular caprice and applause, are apt to use their exalted station as a means to personal enjoyment and to the gratification of vanity. Statesmen who pass their time in luxury and social ostentation will certainly neglect the public interests. They account their power and rank as their possession, and not as a sacred trust. Their example tends to debase the national morals, and to lower the standard of public life. They surround themselves with flatterers, and they neglect their proper duty, until they awake to find their country plunged into calamity or threatened with enslavement.

II. SELF-DENIAL, EXPERIENCE, AND DILIGENCE ARE QUALITIES WHICH ENSURE TRUE STATESMANSHIP. In despotic governments it is obvious that the national prosperity depends very largely upon the patriotism and justice, the assiduity and unwearied devotion to duty, of those in high station. The conditions of national life under a constitutional government are different. Yet there is no political community in which unselfishness, temperance, and diligent application to the public service are not valuable qualities on the part of those who deliberate and decide upon great public questions, and of those who administer a nation's affairs.

APPLICATION. In modern states, where the representative principle so largely obtains, great power is placed in the hands of the citizens and subjects. With them accordingly rests much of the responsibility for the righteous government and the true prosperity of the nation. It behoves Christian men to beware of being misled by party spirit, and so of overlooking the grave moral faults of those who solicit their confidence. It is in the power of the people to raise to positions of eminence and authority men whose aim is not personal aggrandizement and enjoyment, but the public good. If this power be wisely and firmly exercised, vice and crime will be repressed, order and liberty will be maintained, and the nation will maintain a high position and exercise a noble influence among the nations of the earth. Then the spectator will be inspired to utter the exclamation, " Happy art thou, O land ! "—T.

Ver. 18.—*The curse of sloth.* Religious teachers are sometimes unwilling to touch upon common faults, such as are noticeable by every observer as prevailing too generally in the everyday life of their fellow-men. The Scriptures give no countenance to such negligence, but, on the contrary, deal faithfully with those errors and evil habits which are alien from the Christian character, and which are injurious to human society. Slothfulness was peculiarly hateful to the writer of this book, who inculcated diligence as a religious duty, and exhibited in homely but effective ways the results of its prevalence.

I. TEMPTATIONS TO SLOTH ARE MANY. Work must be done, some will admit; but it may be left to others, or it may be put off to a more convenient season. Work need not be done, others will declare; much may be left undone which some people think of importance, but which is not really so. Upon the plea of ill health, or mental inability, or preoccupation, multitudes, in this world where there is so much to be done, sink into slothful, indolent habits and a useless life.

II. THE FOLLY OF SLOTH IS EASILY MADE EVIDENT. 1. The slothful man is his own enemy. Had he exerted himself and exercised his powers, he would have grown an abler and a better man. Who does not know persons with undeniable gifts who have "wrapped their talent in a napkin," and who have morally deteriorated, until they have become worthless members of society? 2. The slothful man wrongs society. Every man is born into this world to do a work for the general good. To live in idleness and comfort upon the produce of others' toil is to inflict a positive injury. Others have to labour in order that the idle may be fed. Work is left undone for which the indolent possess, it may be, some peculiar gift. For the life of the slothful the world is none the better.

III. THE SIN OF SLOTH IS CONDEMNED BY THE WORD OF GOD. The Book of Proverbs contains some very striking reflections and statements upon this point. And for the Christian it is enough to consider the example of the Lord Jesus, who with all his consecrated energy devoted himself to his Father's will and work. How alien from the Master's spirit is the habit of the indolent! We cannot lose sight of the fact that, in the last judgment, the "wicked and slothful servant" must hear words of condemnation.

IV. PRESERVATIVES FROM SLOTH MAY BE FOUND IN THE PROVISIONS OF GOD'S GRACE. 1. Prayer prompts to watchfulness and toil. 2. Attention to the counsels and admonitions of God's Word cannot fail to be serviceable in delivering us from temptations to slothfulness. 3. Meditation upon the example of our Saviour and Lord will stimulate to diligence and zeal. They who by the indwelling of his Spirit are one with him will share his devotion to the Father's will, his consecration to the welfare of mankind.—T.

Ver. 1.—*The dead fly in the ointment.* "So doth a little folly outweigh wisdom and honour" (Revised Version). It is a fact well worth a wise man's thought, that the presence of even a very little evil is found to be enough to counterbalance or undo much that is good. We find this in circumstance, in action, in character. Our every-day life supplies many illustrations.

I. THE CIRCUMSTANCES OF A MAN. Not without reason does the moralist speak of the "one crumpled leaf" spoiling the worth of the "bed of roses." Ahab still makes himself miserable because he cannot have Naboth's vineyard in addition to all his property. It is not only true that "*some* murmur when their sky is clear" if one "small speck of dark appear" in their heavens; it is true that *very many* do. If we are depending on our surroundings for our satisfaction, we shall give one more illustration of "the dead fly in the ointment."

II. HUMAN ADVOCACY. A man may present an important case to his audience; he may have made diligent and ample preparation; he may deliver his address with much logical force, with much felicity of style, with much animation of spirit; and yet he may fail to convince, and he may lose his cause through one mistake. He may make use of one offensive expression, or he may produce one palpably weak argument, on which his opponents fasten; then all the good gained by his persuasiveness is lost by the harm done by his simple indiscretion. Much wisdom is outweighed by a little folly.

III. HUMAN CHARACTER, AND THE INFLUENCE IT EXERTS. We are always acting upon our kindred and our neighbours by our character, and by the conduct of which it is the source. And, as a rule, the good and wise man is thus helping to make others good and wise; but there may be the "dead fly in the ointment" here. Truthfulness, righteousness, purity, kindness,—these qualities are calculated to tell powerfully upon those who daily witness them; but if there be in the midst of these an admixture of severity, or of exaggeration, or of parsimoniousness, or of sarcasm, much if not most of the good influence may be lost; the virtues and the graces are forgotten, while the one blemish is remembered. The same thing, in much the same way, applies to—

IV. HUMAN REPUTATION. A man may be building up a most honourable reputation through many years of toilful and virtuous life; he may succeed in winning the regard of his fellow-citizens, and then by one serious indiscretion—pecuniary, social, domestic, political, ecclesiastical—he may have to step down from his high position. It may not be a crime or a sin, but a serious mistake, an act in which he was very ill advised, a proceeding in which his judgment was sadly at fault—but it is enough; it upsets the fabric which had been laboriously constructed, and but little honour will be accorded to him.

1. In our judgment of others we should distinguish between the superficial and the essential, between the exceptional and the common. 2. We should refuse to allow the one insignificant evil to disturb the harmony of our spirit, to spoil the brightness and excellency of our life. 3. We are bound to be devoutly careful lest we permit our influence over others to be materially weakened by a blemish in our character or an indiscretion in our conduct.—C.

Ver. 8 (former part).—*Sin suicidal.* "He that sinneth against me wrongeth his own soul" (Prov. viii. 36); he that seeks to do injury to others brings trouble upon himself; with the measure and after the manner with which he deals will he himself be dealt with. Evil intents, as also good ones, recoil upon their author—in the one case in penalty, and in the other in blessing. As we observe, we see that—

I. EVIL BEGETS EVIL AFTER ITS OWN KIND. 1. *Violence begets violence.* "They that take the sword perish with the sword;" not, of course, with absolute and unfailing regularity, but generally; so commonly that the professional warrior and, still more, the uncontrollably passionate man may expect to come to a violent end. But, apart from fatal consequences, it is a constantly recurring fact that men give back blow for blow, litigation for litigation, hard measure for hard measure. 2. *Cunning begets cunning.* The crafty man is the likeliest of all to be caught with guile. Men have a peculiar pleasure and take especial pride in outwitting the neighbour who is trying to take advantage of them. So that he who is always laying traps for his fellows is in greatest danger of being himself entrapped. 3. *Contempt begets aversion.* There are those who from the pedestal of (often imaginary) superiority look down upon their companions with supercilious disregard; their attitude is one of haughtiness, their language and conduct that of condescension. These proud ones suffer as they deserve; they pay an appropriate penalty; their neighbours resent their assumption; they pass them by with aversion; they speak of them with condemnation; they leave them to loneliness and friendlessness. 4. *Slander begets reproach.* Men that are unscrupulously complaining of others, hastily or ill-naturedly ascribing to them mistakes or misdeeds, are the men whose own shortcoming is quickly detected and unsparingly condemned (see Matt. vii. 1, 2). Thus sin (or folly) smites itself; it thinks to injure others, but it finds in the end that the stone which it threw up into the air comes down upon its own head. On the other hand, we see—

II. GOOD BEGETS GOOD AFTER ITS KIND. 1. The man *of* peace is permitted to dwell *in* peace. 2. Frankness, sincerity, are met with reciprocated open-mindedness and honesty. 3. Honour rendered to worth and to our common manhood creates respect, and calls forth the best that is in men. 4. Generosity in judgment receives in return a kind and brotherly estimate of its own actions and character. While he that digs a pit for others falls into it himself, he that raises a ladder for others' elevation himself rises upon its rungs.—C.

Ver. 8 (latter part).—*The broken hedge.* There are many fences which we have constructed, or which the Lord of our life has erected, and we discover that if we break them we shall find ourselves attacked and bitten by the serpent which is within or upon the other side.

I. THE HEDGE OF SOCIAL REQUIREMENTS. There are certain understood enactments of society which must be regarded by us. They may have no claim to be moral laws; they may not have any place in the statutes of the land; still they are obligatory upon us. If we are so self-willed or self-sufficient, if we are so ignorant or so careless, as to violate these, we must pay the appropriate penalty of general disregard. Even though we be free from all vice and all crime, we shall be numbered among transgressors of the unwritten law of society, and our position will be lowered, our influence will be lessened, our reputation will be reduced, our usefulness will be impaired.

II. THE HEDGE OF HUMAN LAW. Human law requires of us that we shall pay the debts we owe, that we shall make our contribution to the protection of the society of which we are members, that we shall respect the rights of our neighbours. Breaking this hedge, we pay the penalty which the law inflicts; this "serpent" may be only a small fine, or it may be loss of liberty or even life.

III. The hedge of Divine limitation. God has set a limit to our faculties, and thus to our enjoyment, our activity, our achievement; and if we heedlessly or ambitiously pass this limit, we are bitten and we suffer. If we break the hedge of: 1. *Physical appropriation,* or exercise, we suffer in bodily sickness, in nervous prostration, in premature decline. 2. *Mental activity.* If we think, study, strive, labour on at our desk, beyond the limit of our powers, we pay the penalty in irritability, in softening of the brain, in insanity. 3. *Spiritual faculty.* If we attempt to enter regions that are beyond our God-given powers, we end either in a scepticism which robs us of our highest heritage, or in a mysticism which fascinates and misleads us.

IV. The hedge of conscience. Conscience commands us, with imperative voice, to keep well within the line of purity, of sobriety, of truthfulness, of reverence. If we go beyond that line, we suffer. We suffer: 1. The condemnation of God. 2. The disapproval of the wise and good. 3. The reproach of our own soul. 4. The loss of self-respect and the consequent enfeeblement of our character; and of all losses this is, perhaps, the worst, for it is one of a series of downward steps at the foot of which is death.

1. *Be right at heart* with God; you will then have within you a force of spiritual rectitude which will keep you in the path of wisdom and virtue. 2. Be *vigilant;* ever watching character and conduct, so that you are not betrayed unawares into error and transgression. 3. Be *docile;* always ready to receive the counsel and heed the warning of true and faithful friends. 4. *Seek* daily the guidance and guardianship of God.—C.

Vers. 9 (latter part), 10.—*Good workmanship—ourselves and our tools.* This much-debated passage may suggest to us some lessons which may not have been in the mind of the Preacher, but which are appropriate to our time and our circumstances. The question of how much work a man can do is one that depends on two things—on his own strength and skill, and on the quality of the tools he is using. A weak and untried man with poor tools will not do half as much as a strong experienced man with good ones in his hand.

I. The field of work. This is very broad; it includes not only: 1. All manual labour, to which the passage more immediately applies; but: 2. All business transactions, all household activities, all matters of government in which men are often "the tools" with which work is done. And it includes that to which our attention may be especially directed: 3. All Christian work. This is a great field of its own, with a vast amount of work demanding to be done. Here is work (1) of vast magnitude; (2) of great delicacy; (3) of extreme difficulty, for it means nothing less than that change of condition which results from a change of heart and life. In view of this particular field we regard—

II. The conditions of good workmanship. And these are: 1. *Good tools.* Of these tools are: (1) Divine truth; and to be really good for the great purpose we have at heart we need to hold and to utter this truth in (a) its integrity, not presenting or exaggerating one or two aspects only, but offering it in its fulness and symmetry; (b) its purity, uncorrupted by the imaginations and accretions of our own mind; (c) its adaptation to the special spiritual needs of those to whom we minister. (2) An elastic organization; not such as will not admit of suiting the necessities of men as they arise, but one that is flexible, and that will lend itself to the ever-varying conditions, spiritual and temporal, in which men are found, and in which they have to be helped and healed. 2. *Good workmen.* Those that have: (1) *Wisdom* "profitable to direct," that have tools, skill, discretion, a sound judgment, a comprehensive view. (2) *Strength;* those who can use bad tools if good ones are not at hand, who can work on with sustained energy, who can "bear the burden and heat of the day," who can stand criticism and censoriousness, who will not be daunted by apparent failure or by occasional desertion, who can wait "with long patience" for the day of harvest.

1. Seek to be supplied with the most perfect tools in Christian work; for not only will good tools do much more work than poor ones, but bad tools will result in mischief

to the workman. "He that cleaveth . . . is endangered." Half-truths, or truth unbalanced by its complement, or a badly constructed organization, may do real and serious harm to those who preach the one or work through the other. 2. Put your whole strength—physical, mental, spiritual—into the work of the Lord. With the very best tools we can wield, we shall wish we had done more than we shall have accomplished, when our last blow has been struck for the Master and for mankind.—C.

Vers. 17, 18.—*Ruin—its forms and its sources.* A material "ruin" may be a very picturesque and even pleasant sight, when that which has answered its end loses its form and does well to disappear. But otherwise a ruin is a pitiable spectacle.

I. THREE FORMS OF RUIN. 1. *Health.* When a man should be in his prime, with all his physical and mental forces at their best; when he should be able to work effectively and continuously, and should be the stay of his home and a strength to his Church and to his friends; and when, instead of this, he is worn, feeble, incapable, obviously declining, and clearly drawing towards the end,—we have a melancholy ruin. 2. *Circumstance.* The once wealthy merchant, or the once powerful family, or the once strong and influential state, is brought down to poverty, helplessness, and general disregard; this also is a pitiful sight. But the worst of all is that which relates to: 3. *Character.* When a man once upright, pure, godly, respecting himself and living in the enjoyment of general esteem, is brought down to moral ruin and becomes a human wreck, then we see the saddest sight beneath the sun. What was once the fairest and noblest thing in the world—a sound, strong, beautiful human character—has lost all its excellency and become foul and ugly. How does this happen? Here are—

II. TWO SOURCES OF RUIN. 1. *Self-indulgence.* To "eat for strength and not for revelry" (drunkenness) is the right and the becoming thing; "to eat (feast) in the morning," when the precious hours should be given to duty,—this is a shameful and a fatal thing. Self-indulgence, which constantly tends to become greater and grosser, leads down fast to feebleness, to poverty, to demoralization, to shame, to death. 2. *Idleness,* or carelessness. (1) The man who does not think it worth his while to study the laws of health, and to take pains to keep them, need not wonder if he becomes weak and sickly, if his life is threatened. (2) The man who pursues his pleasure when he should be doing his work will certainly find his business "decaying," his credit failing, his prospects of success "dropping through." So also the housewife, the student, the minister, the secretary, the statesman. (3) The man who treats his own spirit as something of secondary importance, who does not read that he may be enlightened, who does not worship that he may be edified, who does not pray that he may be guarded and sustained, who does not seek the companionship of the good and fellowship with Christ, who leaves his spiritual nature at the mercy of all the adverse forces that are circling round him and acting on him, may expect that his soul will be impaired, that his character will decay, that the most precious "house" which man can build will fall, and great and sad will be the fall of it (Matt. vii. 27).—C.

Ver. 1.—*Dead flies.* Among the Jews oil rendered fragrant by being mixed with precious drugs was used for many different purposes. With it priests and kings were anointed when they entered upon their offices; guests at the tables of the rich were treated to it as a luxury. It was used medicinally for outward application to the bodies of the sick, and with it corpses and the clothes in which they were wrapped were besprinkled before burial. Very great care was needed in the preparation of the material used for such special purposes. Elaborately confected as the ointment was, it was easily spoiled and rendered worthless. It was, accordingly, necessary not only to take great pains in making it, but also in preserving it from contamination when made. If the vase or bottle in which it was put were accidentally or carelessly left open, its contents might soon be destroyed. A dead fly would soon corrupt the ointment, and turn it into a pestilent odour. So, says the Preacher, a noble and attractive character may be corrupted and destroyed by a little folly—an insignificant-looking fault or weakness may outweigh great gifts and attainments. It is not a case of the unthinking multitude taking advantage of a foible, or inconsistency, or little slip, to depreciate the

character of one raised far above them in wisdom and honour, in order to bring it down
to their level; of envy leading to an unjust and ungrateful sentence being pronounced
upon an almost faultless character.   But the warning is that deterioration may really
set in, the precious ointment be actually changed into a disgusting odour, the wisdom
and honour be outweighed by the little folly ("outweigh," Revised Version).   The
same teaching is given in the New Testament.   In 1 Corinthians St. Paul warns his
readers that their toleration of a heinous sin in one of their members was poisoning
the whole spiritual life of the Church (ch. v.).   The fervour of their religious emotions,
the hatred of sin and love of holiness which had led them to separate themselves from
heathen society, the aspirations and endeavours after purity and righteousness which
naturally follow upon an intelligent and earnest acceptance of Christian truth, were
all being undermined by their omission of the duty that lay upon them, that of
isolating the gross offender, and of expelling him from their community if he gave no
signs of penitence and amendment.   They might themselves be orthodox in belief and
unblamable in conduct, but this sin would soon, if unchecked, lower the whole tone of
the community, and nullify all the good that had been attained to.   "Know ye not,"
he said, "that a little leaven leaveneth the whole lump?"   It was impossible to allow
the fault to remain and to keep the evil influence it exerted within bounds; it would
spread like infection, and be persistent until it had corrupted the whole community.
And what is true of a society is true of an individual.   The fault which shows itself in
a character is not like a stain or flaw in a marble statue, which is confined to one spot,
and is no worse after the lapse of years, but like a sore in a living body, which weakens
and may destroy the whole organism.   One cause why the evil influence spreads is
that we are not on our guard against it, and it may grow to almost ungovernable
strength before we are really convinced that there is any danger.   We can recognize at
once great errors and heinous vices, and the alarm and disgust they excite, prepare us to
resist them; but little follies and weaknesses often fill us with an amused contempt for
them, which blinds us to their great power for evil.   The dead body of the fly in the
vase of ointment is so insignificant a source of corruption, that it surprises us to discover
that the fermentation it has produced has tainted the whole mass.   Weight for weight,
there is an enormous disproportion between the precious fluid and the wretched little
object which has corrupted it; yet there is no ignoring of the fact that the mischief
has been done.   In like manner does a little folly outweigh wisdom and honour; an
uncorrected fault spreads its influence throughout a whole character and life.   How
often has the lesson been brought home to us, both in our reading of histories and
biographies and in our own experience, of the widespread mischief done by a small
foible or weakness!—

> "The little rift within the lute
> That by-and-by will make the music mute."

So numerous are the sources from which danger arises, that a long list might be made
of the little sins by which the characters of many good men and women are often
marred—indolence, selfishness, love of ease, procrastination, indecision, rudeness,
irritability, over-sensitiveness to praise or blame, vanity, boastfulness, talkativeness,
love of gossip, undue laxity, undue severity, want of self-control over appetites and
passions, obstinacy, parsimony.   Such are some of the follies which outweigh wisdom
and honour—which stamp the character of a man as unworthy of that respect which
his gifts and graces would otherwise have secured for him.   Numerous though these
follies are, they may be reduced to two great classes—*faults of weakness* and *faults of
strength*.

I. FAULTS OF WEAKNESS.   This class is that of those which are largely negative, and
consist principally in omission to give a definite and worthy direction to the nature;
e.g. want of self-control, love of ease, indolence, procrastination, indecision, selfishness,
heartlessness.   That these are faults which create widespread mischief, and excite a
general contempt for the characters of those in whom they appear, will scarcely be
denied by any, and illustrations of them are only too abundant.   Want of self-control
over appetites and passions led David into the foulest crimes, which, though sincerely
and passionately repented of, were most terribly avenged, and have for ever left a stain
upon his name.   Love of ease is the only fault which is implied in the description of

the rich man in the parable (Luke xvi. 19), a desire to be comfortable and avoid all that was disagreeable, but it led him to such callous indifference to the miseries of his fellows as disqualified him for happiness in the world to come. A similar fault stained the character of that young ruler who came running to Christ and asked, "Good Master, what shall I do to inherit eternal life?" From his youth up he had obeyed the commandments, and his ingenuous, sweet character and disposition attracted the love of the Saviour. But his love of the world made him unwilling to practise the self-denial needed to make him perfect. He went away sorrowful, for he had great possessions (Mark x. 17—22). His cowardice that led him to make "the great refusal" was the dead fly that corrupted the precious ointment. A very striking illustration of the deterioration of a character through the sin of weakness and indecision is to be found in the life of Eli. He was a man possessed of many beautiful qualities of mind and spirit—gentle, unselfish, devoid of envy or jealousy, devout and humble; but was "a wavering, feeble, powerless man, with excellent intentions but an utter want of will." His parental indulgence led him to exercise no restraint over his children, and the consequence was that when they grew up their conduct was grossly scandalous and depraved. His authority and power as a ruler were not used to check the evils which in his heart he loathed, and so his folly outweighed all the wisdom and honour he possessed. His good qualities have not preserved his memory from contempt. For contempt is the feeling instinctively excited in those who witness moral weakness and indecision. This is the sting of the rebuke addressed to the Church of Laodicea, "I know thy works, that thou art neither cold nor hot: I would thou wert cold or hot. So then because thou art lukewarm, and neither cold nor hot, I will spue thee out of my mouth" (Rev. iii. 15, 16). In Dante's description of the lower world special infamy is attached to this class of offenders—that of those who have never really lived, who have never awakened to take any part either in good or evil, to care for anything but themselves. They are unfit for heaven, and hell scorns to receive them. "This miserable mode the dreary souls of those sustain who lived without blame and without praise. They were mixed with that caitiff choir of angels, who were not rebellious nor were faithful to God, but were for themselves. Heaven chased them forth to keep his beauty from impair; and the deep hell receives them not, for the wicked would have some glory over them. They are unknown to fame. Mercy and judgment disdain them. Let us not speak of them, but look and pass."

II. FAULTS OF STRENGTH. This class includes those faults which are of a positive character, and consist largely in an abuse of qualities which might have been virtues. For these are not open vices by which characters otherwise good are depraved, but insignificant, unsuspected sources of danger. The very strength of character by which men and women are distinguished may lead, by over-emphasis, into very offensive deterioration. Thus firmness may degenerate into obstinacy, frugality into parsimony, liberality into extravagance, light-heartedness into frivolity, candour into rudeness, and so on. And these are faults which disgust and repel, and cause us to overlook even very great merits in a character; and not only so, but, if unchecked, gradually nullify those merits. We may find in the character of Christ all the virtues which go to make up holiness so admirably balanced that no one is over-prominent, and, therefore, no one pushed to that excess which so often mars human excellence. Over against the sterner and more masculine qualities of mind and spirit we find those that are gracious and tender, and both within such limits as render his a faultless and perfect example of goodness. His tender compassion for the sinful did not lead him to condone their faults or to lower the standard of holiness for their sake. His righteous indignation against sin did not show itself in impatience, censoriousness, or irritability, as he met it from day to day. "His tender tone was the keen edge of his reproofs, and his unquestionable love infused solemnity into every warning."

Two practical lessons may be drawn from our text. The *first* is that all human excellence is exposed to risk. It is not sufficient to have attained to a certain measure of righteousness; there needs also to be care against declining from it. The ointment carefully distilled must be guarded against corruption. And the *second* is that the danger often springs from insignificant and unsuspected quarters. The dead fly, carried by some stray breeze into the unguarded vial, is the centre of a fermentation which in a very short time will destroy the value of all its contents.—J. W.

Vers. 2—15.—From the second verse of this chapter to the fifteenth we have a series of proverbs loosely strung together, but all bearing upon *the wholesome influence of wisdom and the baneful effects of folly* in the varying circumstances of daily life. It would be waste of ingenuity to try to show any logical connection between the proverbs that are thus crowded together in a small space. And we must content ourselves with a few elucidatory remarks upon them in the order in which they come.

I. A DOUBLE PROVERB ON THE DIFFERENCE BETWEEN WISDOM AND FOLLY. (Vers. 2, 3.) "The wise man's heart is at his right hand; but a fool's at his left;" better, "inclines towards his right, towards his left." The heart of the wise man leads him in the proper direction, that of the fool leads him astray. It would be absurd to speak of their hearts as differently situated. The ♭ is that of direction; and that which is at the right hand means the duty and work which belong to us, that at the left what concerns us less. The wise man recognizes the path of duty, the fool wanders aimlessly away from it. Others give a slightly different turn to the thought. "The one with his heart, *i.e.* his mind, ready, at his right side, as he walks along the track that images human life, ready to sustain and guide him; the other, the fool with his wits at the left side, not available when needed to lean upon" (Bradley). The fool proclaims his folly to all (ver. 3); every step he takes reveals his deficiency, but, so far from being ashamed of himself, he displays his absurdity as though it were something to be proud of.

II. WISDOM A PROTECTION IN TRYING CIRCUMSTANCES. (Vers. 4—7.) The first picture (ver. 4) is that of the court of a despotic king, where an official has either deservedly or undeservedly incurred the anger of the sovereign ("spirit" equivalent to "anger," as in Judg. viii. 3; Prov. xxix. 11). The natural feeling of indignation or resentment would prompt such a one to throw up the office entrusted to him, and by so doing probably draw down on himself a still greater storm of anger. The wise courtier will yield to the blast and not answer wrath with wrath, and either pacify the anger he has deservedly incurred, or, if he be innocent, by his patience under injury, avoid giving real cause for offence. We must remember that it is of an Eastern court our author is speaking, in which the Divine right of kings, and the duty of passive obedience on the part of subjects, are doctrines which it would be thought impious to deny. Similar advice is given in Prov. xv. 1. It is not to be supposed, however, that the Preacher regarded all existing governments as commanding respect, and taught only servile maxims. In vers. 5—7 he speaks of grievous inequalities in the state; faults of rulers, the frequent exaltation of the base and the depression of the worthy. His words are studiously cautious, but yet they describe the evil in sufficiently clear terms. It may often be prudent to bow to the wrath of rulers, but rulers are not always in the right. One class of evils he had seen arising from "something like an error" (so cautious is he of speaking evil of dignities), which proceedeth from the ruler—the selection of unworthy men for high positions in the state. "Folly is set in great dignity, and the rich sit in low place." By the rich he means the nobles—those endowed with ample inheritances received from a line of ancestors who have had the leisure, and opportunities and means for training themselves for serving the state, and from whom a wise king would naturally choose counsellors and magistrates. But in Oriental courts, where "the eunuch and the barber held the reins of power," men of no reputation or character had a chance of promotion. And even in Western courts and more modern times the same kind of evils has been only too common, as the history of the reigns of Edward II. and James I. of England, and of Louis XI. and Henry III. of France, abundantly proves. The reason for making favourites of low-born and unprincipled adventurers is not far to seek; they have ever been ready tools for accomplishing the designs of unscrupulous princes, for doing services from which men who valued their station and reputation in society would shrink. "Regibus multi," says Grotius, "suspecti qui excellunt sive sapientia sive nobilitate aut opibus." Even the Preacher's self-control is insufficient to suppress the indignation and contempt which any generous mind must feel at such a state of matters, and he concentrates his scorn in the stinging sentence, "I have seen servants upon horses, and princes walking as servants upon the earth" (ver. 7). Among the Persians only those of noble birth were permitted to ride on horseback. Thus one of the circumstances of the special honour bestowed on Mordecai was his riding on horseback through the streets of the city (Esth. v. 8, 9). But this distinction the Preacher had seen set aside; his eyes had been offended by the spectacle of princes walking on foot like common people, and slaves mounted on horses and clothed with authority (Prov. xix. 10).

III. WISDOM SHOWN IN PROVIDING AGAINST POSSIBLE DANGERS. (Vers. 8, 9.) We need spend no time in the fruitless endeavour to connect vers. 8—11 with those that have gone before. The writer seems to consider wisdom in another of its aspects. He has just spoken of it as prompting one who is under its influence to be patient and resigned in the presence of irradicable evils; he now speaks of it as giving foresight and caution in the accomplishment of difficult and perhaps even dangerous tasks. He mentions four undertakings in which there may be danger to life or limb. He that digs a pit may accidentally fall into it; he that removes a crumbling wall may be bitten by a serpent that has sheltered itself in one of its crannies; the quarryman may be crushed by one of the stones he has dislodged; and the woodcutter may maim himself with his own axe. Whether underneath this imagery he refers to the risks attending all attempts to disturb the existing order of things and to overthrow the powers that be, one cannot say. "The sum of these four classes is certainly not merely that he who undertakes a dangerous matter exposes himself to danger; the author means to say in this series of proverbs which treat of the distinction between wisdom and folly, that the wise man is everywhere conscious of his danger, and guards against it. . . . Wisdom has just this value in providing against the manifold dangers and difficulties which every undertaking brings with it" (Delitzsch).

IV. THE WISDOM OF ADAPTING MEANS TO ENDS. (Ver. 10.) Such, we think, is the general meaning of the words, which are perhaps more difficult to interpret than any others in the whole Book of Ecclesiastes. "If the iron be blunt," if it will not readily lend itself to the work of felling a tree, more strength must be put forth, the stroke must be heavier to penetrate the wood. If there be little sagacity and preparation before entering on an enterprise, greater force will be needed to carry it out. The foresight which leads to sharpening the axe will make the labour in which it is used much easier. "But wisdom is profitable to direct" (ver. 10*b*); it suggests means serviceable for the end in view. It will save a useless expenditure of time and strength.

V. THE FOLLY OF TAKING PRECAUTIONS AFTER THE EVIL HAS BEEN DONE. (Ver. 11.) "If the serpent bite before it be charmed, then is there no advantage in the charmer" (Revised Version). The picture is that of a serpent biting before the charmer has had time to make use of his skill in charming; and the point of the aphorism is that no skill or wisdom is of any avail if made use of too late. "It is too late to lock the stable door when the steed is stolen" (Wright).

VI. WISDOM AND FOLLY IN HUMAN SPEECH. The winning character of the wise man's words, the mischievous and tedious prating of fools (vers. 12—15). The tongue has just been spoken of (ver. 11) as the instrument used by the charmer for taming serpents, and there follows in these verses a reference to wisdom and folly displayed in the words of the wise man and of the fool. "The words of the wise man are gracious" (cf. Luke iv. 22), they win favour for him; both the subject-matter and the manner of his speech gain for him the good will of those that hear him. The words of the fool are self-destructive; they ruin any chance he had of influencing those who were prepared to be persuaded by him, whom he meets for the first time, and who were therefore not biassed against him by previous knowledge of his fatuity. He goes from bad to worse (ver. 13). "The words point with a profound insight into human nature to the progress from bad to worse in one who has the gift of speech without discretion. He begins with what is simply folly, unwise but harmless, but *vires acquirit eundo,* he is borne along on the swelling floods of his own declamatory fluency, and ends in what is 'mischievous madness'" (Plumptre). Especially is this the case when his talk is on subjects as to which even the wisest are forced to confess their ignorance (ver. 14). He speaks voluminously, as though he knew all things past and to come, as though all the mysteries of life and death were an open book to him. And he wearies out every one who hears him or has to do with him. His crass ignorance in all matters of common life forbids any trust being placed in his speculations and vaticinations as to things that are more recondite. The well-known beaten road that leads to the city (ver. 15) he does not know. What kind of a guide would he be in less-frequented paths?

In these various ways, therefore, the contrast is drawn between wisdom which leads men in the right way, which directs their course through the difficulties and dangers that often beset them, and enables them to make the best use of their resources, and that folly which, if it is the ruling element in a character, no art or skill can conceal, which so often renders those in whom it appears both mischievous and offensive to all who have anything to do with them.—J. W.

Vers. 16—20.—*Duties of rulers and subjects.* Some of the evils of life arise from errors and follies which may be corrected by diligence and prudence, and among them are the caprices of unworthy princes, the vices of courtiers, and the disloyalty of subjects. Both kings and those over whom they rule have duties towards each other, the violation of which bring many mischiefs; both need to have before their minds the ideal of righteousness belonging to their respective stations.

I. The evils of misgovernment. The land is miserable whose king is a child in years or in heedlessness, whose princes begin the days with revels instead of attending to the management of affairs of state and the administration of justice. The incapacity of the prince leads to the appointment of unworthy ministers, and prevents a proper check being put upon their profligacy and neglect. The result is soon seen in the disorders of the state. " Through the slothfulness of rulers," he goes on to hint, " the fabric of thy state decays; the neglected roof lets the water through. And meantime there is high revelry within the palace walls; and gold and silver supply all their needs " (vers. 18, 19). Illustrations of such an unhappy state of matters recur only too readily to the student of history. " We may see it exemplified in the condition, shall we say, of some native state within our Indian frontier? or some Eastern empire tottering to its fall nearer home? or a European monarchy at the close of the last century, with luxury and state in the palace, and a hungry people outside its door, and the shadow of the guillotine, and head-crowned pikes and September massacres in the background?" (Bradley).

II. The blessings of a well-ordered government. That land is happy, governed by a king of undisputed title (ver. 17), who sets an example of integrity, and not by some upstart adventurer. He derives his title from his noble descent, but he may establish his power on a firmer foundation if the excellences of his ancestors are reproduced in him; he will secure a large measure of prosperity for his people if he choose for his officers men of simple tastes, who think more of discharging their duties than of self-indulgence.

III. The duty of loyalty on the part of subjects. (Ver. 20.) Even if the sovereign is personally unworthy of respect, the office he holds should be honoured; he is still the servant of God, even if he is grossly neglectful of his duties. There is a worse evil than misgovernment, and that is anarchy. " Curse not the king "—he may not deserve it; there may be reasons of state to explain what seems to be capricious or unjust in his conduct; yield him reverence for conscience' sake, because it is right to do so. And even if he be in the wrong, it is prudent to abstain from words of blame, since he has the power to punish those that speak against him, and may hear in unexpected ways what has been said about him in secrecy. Such counsels are of a kindred character with those which the apostles have given (Rom. xiii. 1—7; 1 Pet. ii. 13—17). At first it might seem as if they commended the cultivation of a slavish spirit on the part of subjects towards their rulers, and it is well known that many have deduced from them the preposterous doctrine of " passive obedience." But it must be kept in mind that while these portions of Scripture prescribe the duties of subjects, they prescribe also the duties of kings; and that it is no slavish doctrine to hold that those who rule in equity have an absolute right to the devotion and loyalty of their subjects. When they depart from equity their claim to implicit obedience is proportionately diminished. The prudential maxim of ver. 20 warns men to count the cost before they assail the power of even a bad king—to beware of provoking his wrath by heedless conduct—but does not command passive obedience to him. Misgovernment may reach such a pitch as to make it a duty for subjects to brave the wrath of kings, and to attempt to put a check upon their folly. We have not here a mean-spirited and time-serving piece of advice, suitable only for those who languish under the tyranny of Eastern despots, but a warning against rashness which is not inapplicable to the most public-spirited citizen of the freest state. The examples of Isaiah under Ahaz, of Jeremiah under Zedekiah, and of St. Paul under Nero, show that it is possible to have a love of righteousness and hatred of iniquity, and yet not be wanting in respect to a bad king.—J. W.

EXPOSITION.

CHAPTER XI.

Approaching the end of his treatise, Koheleth, in view of apparent anomalies in God's moral government, and the difficulties that meet man in his social and political relations, proceeds to give his remedies for this state of things. These remedies are (1) beneficence and active life (vers. 1—6); (2) joyful light-heartedness (vers. 7—9); (3) piety (ver. 10—ch. xii. 7).

Vers. 1—6.—Section 16. Leaving alone unanswerable questions, man's duty and happiness are found in activity, especially in doing all the good in his power, for he knows not how soon he himself may stand in need of help. This is *the first remedy for the perplexities of life*. The wise man will not charge himself with results.

Ver. 1.—**Cast thy bread upon the waters.** The old interpretation of this passage, which found in it a reference to the practice in Egypt of sowing seed during the inundation of the Nile, is not admissible. The verb *shalach* is not used in the sense of sowing or scattering seed; it means "to cast or send forth." Two chief explanations have been given. (1) As to sow on the water is equivalent to taking thankless toil (compare the Greek proverb, Σπείρειν ἐπὶ πόντῳ), the gnome may be an injunction to do good without hope of return, like the evangelical precept (Matt. v. 44—46; Luke vi. 32—35). (2) It is a commercial maxim, urging men to make ventures in trade, that they may receive a good return for their expenditure. In this case the casting seed upon the waters is a metaphorical expression for sending merchandise across the sea to distant lands. This view is supposed to be confirmed by the statement concerning the good woman in Prov. xxxi. 14, "She is like the merchants' ships; she bringeth her bread from far;" and the words of Ps. cvii. 23, "They that go down to the sea in ships, that do business in great waters." But one sees no reason why Koheleth should suddenly turn to commerce and the trade of a maritime city. Such considerations have no reference to the context, nor to the general design of the book. Nothing leads to them, nothing comes of them. On the other hand, if we take the verse as urging active beneficence as the safest and best proceeding under men's present circumstances, we have a maxim in due accordance with the spirit of the rest of the work, and one which conduces

to the conclusion reached at the end. So we adopt the first of the two explanations mentioned above. The bread in the East is made in the form of thin cakes, which would float for a time if thrown into a stream; and if it be objected that no one would be guilty of such an irrational action as flinging bread into the water, it may be answered that this is just the point aimed at. Do your kindnesses, exert yourself, in the most unlikely quarters, not thinking of gratitude or return, but only of duty. And yet surely a recompense will ¡be made in some form or other. **Thou shalt find it after many days.** This is not to be the motive of our acts, but it will in the course of time be the result; and this thought may be an encouragement. In the Chaldee Version of parts of Ecclesiasticus there is extant a maxim identical with our verse, "Strew thy bread on the water and on the land, and thou shalt find it at the end of days" (Dukes, 'Rabb. Blumenl.,' p. 73). Parallels have been found in many quarters. Thus the Turk says, "Do good, throw it into the water; if the fish does not know it, God does." Herzfeld quotes Goethe—

" Was willst du untersuchen,
　Wohin die Milde fliesst !
Ins Wasser wirf deine Kuchen ;
　Wer weiss wer sie geniesst ? "

" Wouldst thou too narrowly inquire
　Whither thy kindness goes !
Thy cake upon the water cast ;
　Whom it may feed who knows ? "

Voltaire paraphrases the passage in his 'Précis de l'Ecclésiaste '—

" Répandez vos bienfaits avec magnificence,
　Même aux moins vertueux ne les refusez pas.
Ne vous informez pas de leur reconnoissance ;
Il est grand, il est beau de faire des ingrats."

Ver. 2.—**Give a portion to seven, and also to eight.** This further explains, without any metaphor, the injunction of beneficence in ver. 1. Give portions of thy "bread" to any number of those who need. Delitzsch and others who interpret the passage of maritime enterprise would see in it a recommendation (like the proceeding of Jacob, Gen. xxxii. 16, etc.) not to risk all at once, to divide one's ventures into various ships. But the expression in the text is merely a mode of enjoining unlimited benevolence. The numbers are purposely indefinite. Instances of this form of speech are common enough (see Prov. vi 16; xxx. 7—9, etc.; Amos i. 3.

etc.; Micah v. 5; Ecclus. xxiii. 16; xxvi. 5, 28).
Wordsworth notes that the word for "portion" (*chelek*) is that used specially for the
portion of the Levites (Numb. xviii. 20); and
in accordance with his view of the date of the
book, finds here an injunction not to confine
one's offerings to the Levites of Judah, but
to extend them to the refugees who come
from Israel. **For thou knowest not what
evil shall be upon the earth.** A time may
come when you yourself may need help; the
power of giving may no longer be yours;
therefore make friends now who may be
your comfort in distress. So the Lord urges,
"Make to yourselves friends by means of the
mammon of unrighteousness" (Luke xvi. 9).
It seems a low motive on which to base
charitable actions; but men act on such
secondary motives every day, and the moralist cannot ignore them. In the Book of
Proverbs secondary and worldly motives are
largely urged as useful in the conduct of
life (see the Introduction to Proverbs, pp.
viii., ix.). St. Paul reminds us that we
some day may need a brother's help (Gal.
vi. 1). The Fathers have spiritualized
the passage, so as to make it of Christian
application, far away indeed from Koheleth's thought. Thus St. Gregory: "By
the number *seven* is understood the whole
of this temporal condition . . . this is
shown more plainly when the number *eight*
is mentioned after it. For when another
number besides follows after seven, it is set
forth by this very addition, that this temporal
state is brought to an end and closed by
eternity. . . . For by the number *seven*
Solomon expressed the present time, which
is passed by periods of seven days. But by
the number *eight* he designated eternal life,
which the Lord made known to us by his
resurrection. For he rose in truth on the
Lord's day, which, as following the seventh
day, *i.e.* the sabbath, is found to be the
eighth from the creation. But it is well
said, 'Give portions,' etc. As if it were
plainly said, 'So dispense temporal goods,
as not to forget to desire those that are
eternal. For thou oughtest to provide for
the future by well-doing, who knowest not
what tribulation succeeds from the future
judgment'" ('Moral.,' xxxv. 17, Oxford
transl.).

Ver. 3.—**If the clouds be full of rain, they
empty** themselves **upon the earth.** This
verse is closely connected with the preceding paragraph. The misfortune there
intimated may fall at any moment; this is
as certain as the laws of nature, unforeseen,
uncontrollable. When the clouds are over-
charged with moisture, they deliver their
burden upon the earth, according to laws
which man cannot alter; these are of irresistible necessity, and must be expected and

endured. **And if the tree fall toward the
south,** etc.; or, it may be, *in the south*; i.e.
let it fall where it will; the particular
position is of no importance. When the
tempest overthrows it, it lies where it has
fallen. When the evil day comes, we must
bend to the blow, we are powerless to avert
it; the future can be neither calculated nor
controlled. The next verse tells how the
wise man acts under such circumstances.
Christian commentators have argued from
this clause concerning the unchangeable
state of the departed—that there is no repentance in the grave; that what death
leaves them judgment shall find them. Of
course, no such thought was in Koheleth's
mind; nor do we think that the inspiring
Spirit intended such meaning to be wrung
from the passage. Indeed, it may be said
that, as it stands, the clause does not bear
this interpretation. The fallen or felled tree
is not at once fit for the master's use; it has
to be exposed to atmospheric influences.
seasoned, tried. It is not left in the place
where it lay, nor in the condition in which
it was; so that, if we reason from this
analogy, we must conceive that there is
some ripening, purifying process in the intermediate state. St. Gregory speaks thus:
"For when, at the moment of the falling of
the human being, either the Holy Spirit or
the evil spirit receives the soul departed
from the chambers of the flesh, he will keep
it with him for ever without change, so that
neither, once exalted, shall it be precipitated
into woe, nor, once plunged into eternal woes,
any further arise to take the means of
escape" ('Moral.,' viii. 30).

Ver. 4.—**He that observeth the wind shall
not sow.** The fact of the uncertainty and
immutability of the future ought not to
make us supine or to crush out all diligence
and activity. He who wants to anticipate
results, to foresee and provide against all
contingencies, to be his own providence, is
like a farmer who is always looking to wind
and weather, and misses the time for sowing
in this needless caution. The quarter from
which the wind blows regulates the downfall
of rain (comp. Prov. xxv. 23). In Palestine
the west and north-west winds usually
brought rain. **He that regardeth the clouds
shall not reap.** For the purpose of softening
the ground to receive the seed, rain was
advantageous; but storms in harvest, of
course, were pernicious (see 1 Sam. xii. 17,
etc.; Prov. xxvi. 1); and he who was anxiously fearing every indication of such
weather, and altering his plans at every
phase of the sky, might easily put off reaping his fields till either the crops were
spoiled or the rainy season had set in. A
familiar proverb says, "A watched pot never
boils." Some risks must always be run if

we are to do our work in the world; we cannot make a certainty of anything; probability in the guide of life. We cannot secure ourselves from failure; we can but do our best, and uncertainty of result must not paralyze exertion. "It is not of him that willeth, nor of him that runneth, but of God that hath mercy" (Rom. ix. 16). St. Gregory deduces a lesson from this verse: "He calls the unclean spirit *wind*, but men who are subjected to him *clouds;* whom he impels backwards and forwards, hither and thither, as often as his temptations alternate in their hearts from the blasts of suggestions. He therefore who observes the wind does not sow, since he who dreads coming temptations does not direct his heart to doing good. And he who regards the clouds does not reap, since he who trembles from the dread of human fickleness deprives himself of the recompense of an eternal reward" ('Moral.,' xxvii. 14).

Ver. 5.—**As thou knowest not what is the way of the spirit.** In this verse are presented one or two examples of man's ignorance of natural facts and processes as analogous to the mysteries of God's moral government. The word translated "spirit" (*ruach*) may mean also "wind," and is so taken here by many commentators (see ch. i. 6; viii. 8; and comp. John iii. 8). In this view there would be two instances given, viz. the wind and the embryo. Certainly, the mention of the wind seems to come naturally after what has preceded; and man's ignorance of its way, and powerlessness to control it, are emblematic of his attitude towards Divine providence. The versions, however, seem to support the rendering of the Authorized Version. Thus the Septuagint (which connects the clause with ver. 4), ἐν οἷς ("among whom," *i.e.* those who watch the weather), "There is none that knoweth what is the way of the spirit (τοῦ πνεύματος);" Vulgate, *Quomodo ignoras quæ sit via spiritus.* If we take this view, we have only one idea in the verse, and that is the infusion of the breath of life in the embryo, and its growth in its mother's womb. Nor **how the bones do grow in the womb of her that is with child.** Our version, by its insertions, has made two facts out of the statement in the Hebrew, which is literally, *how the bones* (are) *in the womb of a pregnant woman.* Septuagint, "As (ὡς) bones are in the womb," etc.; Vulgate, *Et qua ratione compingantur ossa in ventre prægnantis,* "And in what way the bones are framed in the womb of the pregnant." The formation and quickening of the fœtus were always regarded as mysterious and inscrutable (comp. Job x. 8, 9; Ps. cxxxix. 15; Wisd. vii. 1, etc.). Wright compares M. Aurelius, x. 26, "The first principles of life are extremely slender and

mysterious; and yet nature works them up into a strange increase of bulk, diversity, and proportion." Controversies concerning the origin of the soul have been rife from early times, some holding what is called Traducianism, *i.e.* that soul and body are both derived by propagation from earthly parents; others supporting Creationism, *i.e.* that the soul, created specially by God, is infused into the child before birth. St. Augustine confesses ('Op. Imperf.,' iv. 104) that he is unable to determine the truth of either opinion. And, indeed, this is one of those secret things which Holy Scripture has not decided for us, and about which no authoritative sentence has been given. The term "bones" is used for the whole conformation of the body (comp. Prov. xv. 30; xvi. 24); *meleah,* "pregnant," means literally, "full," and is used like the Latin *plena* here and nowhere else in the Old Testament, though common in later Hebrew. Thus Ovid, 'Metam.,' x. 469—

"Plena patris thalamis excedit, et impia diro
    Semina fert utero."

And 'Fast.,' iv. 633—

"Nunc gravidum pecus est; gravidæ sunt semine terræ.
    Telluri plenæ victima plena datur."

Even so thou knowest not the works of God who maketh all. Equally mysterious in its general scope and in its details is the working of God's providence. And as everything lies in God's hands, it must needs be secret and beyond human ken. This is why to "the works of God" (ch. vii. 13) is added, "who maketh all." The God of nature is Lord of the future (comp. Amos iii. 6; Ecclus. xviii. 6); man must not disquiet himself about this.

Ver. 6.—**In the morning sow thy seed.** Do not let your ignorance of the future and the inscrutability of God's dealings lead you to indolence and apathy; do your appointed work; be active and diligent in your calling. The labour of the farmer is taken as a type of business generally, and was especially appropriate to the class of persons whom Koheleth is instructing. The injunction occurs naturally after ver. 4. **And in the evening withhold not thine hand.** Labour on untiredly from morn till evening. It is not an advice to rest during midday, as that was too hot a time to work (Stuart), but a call to spend the entire day in active employment, the two extremities being mentioned in order to include the whole. Work undertaken in a right spirit is a blessing, not a curse, shuts out many temptations, encourages many virtues. Some see here a special reference to the maxim at the beginning of the chapter, as though the author meant, "Exercise thy charity at all times, early and late," the metaphor being similar to that in 2 Cor. ix. 6, "He which soweth sparingly," etc. Others find a figure of the ages of man in the "morning and evening," thus, "From earliest youth practise piety and purity, and continue such conduct to its close." This leads naturally to the subject of the following section; but it may be doubted whether this thought was in the author's mind. It seems best to take the paragraph merely as commending activity, whether in business or in benevolence, without anxious regard to results which are in higher hands. "Withhold not thy hand," *i.e.* from sowing; Μὴ ἀφέτω ἡ χείρ σου (Septuagint). **For thou knowest not whether shall prosper,** which of the two sowings, **either this or that,** the morning or evening sowing. It is a chance, and a man must risk something; if one fails, the other may succeed. **Or whether they both** shall be **alike good.** The uncertainty rouses to exertion; labour may at any rate secure half the crop, or even give a double produce, if both sowings succeed. So in religion and morality, the good seed sown early and late may bear fruit early or late, or may have blessed results all along. The Vulgate is less correct, *Et si utrumque simul, melius erit,* "And if both together, it will be better."

Vers. 7—9.—Section 17. *The second remedy for the perplexities of the present life is cheerfulness*—the spirit that enjoys the present, with a chastened regard to the future.

Ver. 7.—**Truly the light is sweet.** The verse begins with the copula *vav*, "and," which here notes merely transition, as ch. iii. 16; xii. 9. Do not be perplexed, or despondent, or paralyzed in your work, by the difficulties that meet you. Confront them with a cheerful mien, and enjoy life while it lasts. "The light" may be taken literally, or as equivalent to life. The very light, with all that it unfolds, all that it beautifies, all that it quickens, is a pleasure; life is worth living, and affords high and merited enjoyment to the faithful worker. The commentators quote parallels. Thus Euripides, 'Iph. in Aul.,' 1219—

Μή μ' ἀπολέσῃς ἄωρον· ἡδύ γὰρ τὸ φῶς
Λεύσσειν, τὰ δ' ὑπὸ γῆν μή μ' ἰδεῖν ἀναγκάσῃς.

"O slay me not untimely; for to see
The light is sweet; and force me not to view
The secrets of the nether world."

Plumptre cites Theognis—

Κείσομαι ὥστε λίθος
Ἄφθογγος, λείψω δ' ἐρατὸν φάος ἠελίοιο.

"Then shall I lie, as voiceless as a stone,
And see no more the loved light of the sun."

A pleasant thing it is **for the eyes to behold the sun.** To behold the sun is to enjoy life; for light, which is life, is derived from the sun. Virgil speaks of "cœli spirabile lumen" ('Æn.,' iii. 600). Thus Homer, 'Od.,' xx. 207—

Εἴ που ἔτι ζώει καὶ ὁρᾷ φάος ἠελίοιο·
Εἰ δ' ἤδη τέθνηκε καὶ εἰν 'Αΐδαο δόμοισιν.

"If still he live and see the sun's fair light,
Or dead, be dwelling in the realms of Hades."

Ver. 8.—**But if a man live many years, and rejoice in them all.** The conjunction *ki* at the commencement of the verse is causal rather than adversative, and should be rendered "for." The insertion of "and" before "rejoice" mars the sentence. The apodosis begins with "rejoice," and the translation is, *For if a man live many years, he ought to rejoice in them all.* Koheleth has said (ver. 7) that life is sweet and precious; now he adds that it is therefore man's duty to enjoy it; God has ordained that he should do so, whether his days on earth be many or few. **Yet let him remember the days of darkness.** The apodosis is continued, and the clause should run, *And remember,* etc. "The days of darkness" do not mean times of calamity as contrasted with the light of prosperity, as though the writer were bidding one to be mindful of the prospect of disastrous change in the midst of happiness; nor, again, the period of old age distinguished from the glowing light of youth (Virgil, 'Æneid,' i. 590, 591). The days of darkness signify the life in Hades, far from the light of the sun, gloomy, uncheered. The thought of this state should not make us hopeless and reckless, like the sensualists whose creed is to "eat and drink, for to-morrow we die" (1 Cor. xv. 32; Wisd. ii. 1, etc.), but rouse us to make the best of life, to be contented and cheerful, doing our daily duties with the consciousness that this is our day of labour and joy, and that "the night cometh when no man can work" (John ix. 4). Wisely says Ben-Sira, "Whatsoever thou takest in hand, remember the end, and thou shalt never do amiss" (Ecclus. vii. 36). We are reminded of the Egyptian custom, mentioned by Herodotus (ii. 78), of carrying a figure of a corpse among the guests at a banquet, not in order to damp pleasure, but to give a zest to the enjoyment of the present and to keep it under proper control. "Look on this!" it was cried; "drink, and enjoy thyself; for when thou diest thou shalt be such." The Roman poet has many a passage like this, though, of course, of lower tendency. Thus Horace, 'Carm.,' ii. 3—

"Preserve, O my Dellius, whatever thy fortunes,
A mind undisturbed, 'midst life's changes and ills;
Not cast down by its sorrows, nor too much elated
If sudden good fortune thy cup over-fills," etc.
(Stanley.)

(See also 'Carm.,' i. 4.) **For they shall be many**; rather, *that they shall be many*. This is one of the things to remember. The time in Sheol will be long. How to be passed—when, if ever, to end—he says not; he looks forward to a dreary protracted period, when joy shall be unattainable, and therefore he bids men to use the present, which is all they can claim. **All that cometh is vanity.** All that comes after this life is ended, the great future, is nothingness; shadow, not substance; a state from which is absent all that made life, and over which we have no control. Koheleth had passed the sentence of vanity on all the pursuits of the living man; now he gives the same verdict upon the unknown condition of the departed soul (comp. ch. ix. 5). Till the gospel had brought life and immortality to light, the view of the future was dark and gloomy. So we read in Job (x. 21, 22), "I go whence I shall not return, even to the land of darkness and of the shadow of death; a land of thick darkness, as darkness itself; a land of the shadow of death, without any order, and where the light is as darkness." The Vulgate gives quite a different turn to the clause, rendering, *Meminisse debet tenebrosi temporis, et dierum multorum; qui cum venerint, vanitatis arguentur præterita*, "He ought to remember . . . the many days; and when these have come, things passed shall be charged with vanity"—which implies, in accordance with an hagadic interpretation of the passage, that the sinner shall suffer for his transgressions, and shall then learn to acknowledge his folly in the past. It is unnecessary to say that the present text is at variance with this rendering.

Ver. 9.—**Rejoice, O young man, in thy youth.** Koheleth continues to inculcate the duty of rational enjoyment. "In youth" is during youth; not in the exercise of, or by reason of, thy fresh, unimpaired powers. The author urges his hearers to begin betimes to enjoy the blessings with which God surrounds them. Youth is the season of innocent, unalloyed pleasure; then, if ever,

casting aside all tormenting anxiety concerning an unknown future, one may, as it is called, enjoy life. **Let thy heart cheer thee in the days of thy youth.** Let the lightness of thy heart show itself in thy bearing and manner, even as it is said in Proverbs (xv. 13), "A merry heart maketh a cheerful countenance." **Walk in the ways of thine heart** (comp. Isa. lvii. 17). Where the impulses and thoughts of thy heart lead thee. The wording looks as if the personal identity, the "I," and the thought were distinct. We have a similar severance in ch. vii. 25, only there the personality directs the thought, not the thought the "I." **And in the sight of thine eyes.** Follow after that on which thy eyes fix their regard (ch. ii. 10); for, as Job says (xxxi. 7), "The heart walketh after the eyes." The Septuagint, in deference to the supposed requirements of strict morality, has (at least according to the text of some manuscripts) modified the received reading, translating the passage thus: Καὶ περιπάτει ἐν ὁδοῖς καρδίας σου ἄμωμος καὶ μὴ ἐν ὁράσει ὀφθαλμῶν σου, "And walk in the ways of thine heart blameless, and not in the sight of thine eyes." But μὴ is omitted by A, C, S². Others besides the Seventy have felt doubts about the bearing of the passage, as though it recommended either unbridled licence in youth, or at any rate an unhallowed epicureanism. To counteract the supposed evil teaching, some have credited Koheleth with stern irony. He is not recommending pleasure, say they, but warning against it. "Go on your way," he cries, "do as you list, sow your wild oats, live dissolutely, but remember that retribution will some day overtake you." But the counsel is seriously intended, and is quite consistent with many other passages which teach the duty of enjoying life as man's lot and part (see ch. ii. 24; iii. 12, 13, 22; v. 18; viii. 15, etc.). The seeming opposition between the recommendation here and in Numb. xv. 39 is easily reconciled. The injunction in the Pentateuch, which was connected with a ceremonial observance, ran thus: "Remember all the commandments of the Lord, and do them; and that ye go not about after your own heart, and your own eyes, after which ye used to go a-whoring." Here unlawful pleasures, contrary to the commandments, are forbidden; Ecclesiastes urges the pursuit of innocent pleasures, such as will stand scrutiny. Hoelemann, quoted by Wright, observes that this verse is the origin of a famous student-song of Germany, a stanza or two of which we may cite—

"Gaudeamus igitur, juvenes dum sumus;
Post exactam juventutem, post molestam senectutem,
Nos habebit humus. . . .

" Vita nostra brevis est, brevi finietur,
    Venit mors velociter, rapit nos atrociter,
        Nemini parcetur."

It is not epicureanism, even in a modified form, that is here encouraged. For moderate and lawful pleasure Koheleth has always uttered his sanction, but the pleasure is to be such as God allows. This is to be accepted with all gratitude in the present, as the future is wholly beyond our ken and our control; it is all that is placed in our power, and it is enough to make life more than endurable. And then to temper unmixed joy, to prove that he is not recommending mere sensuality, to correct any wrong impression which the previous utterances may have conveyed, the writer adds another thought, a sombre reflection which shows the religious conclusion to which he is working up. **But know thou, that for all these** things **God will bring thee into judgment** (*mishpat*). It has been doubted what is meant by "judgment," whether present or future, men's or God's. It has been taken to mean—God will make thy excesses prove scourges, by bringing on thee sickness, poverty, a miserable old age; or these distresses come as the natural consequences of youthful sins; or obloquy shall follow thee, and thou shalt meet with deserved censure from thy fellow-men. But every one must feel that the solemn ending of this paragraph points to something more grave and important than any such results as those mentioned above, something that is concerned with that indefinable future which is ever looming in the dim horizon. Nothing satisfies the expected conclusion but a reference to the eternal judgment in the world beyond the grave. Shadowy and incomplete as was Koheleth's view of this great assize, his sense of God's justice in the face of the anomalies of human life was so strong that he can unhesitatingly appeal to the conviction of a coming inquisition, as a motive for the guidance of action and conduct. That in other passages he constantly apprehends earthly retribution, as the Pentateuch taught, and as his countrymen had learned to expect (see ch. ii. 26; iii. 17; vii. 17, 18), is no argument that he is not here rising to a higher view. Rather, the fact that the doctrine of temporal reward and punishment is found by experience to fail in many cases (comp. ch. viii. 14) has forced him to state his conclusion that this life is not the end of everything, and that there is another existence in which actions shall be tried, justice done, retribution awarded. The statement is brief, for he knew nothing more than the fact, and could add nothing to it. His conception of the soul's condition in Sheol (see ch. ix. 5, 6, 10) seems to point to some other state or period for this final judg-

ment; but whether a resurrection is to precede this awful trial is left in uncertainty here, as elsewhere in the Old Testament. Cheyne and some other critics consider this last clause to be an interpolation, because it appears to militate against previous utterances; but this argument is unreasonable, as the paragraph comes in quite naturally as the needed conclusion, and without it the section would halt and be incomplete. A similar allusion is contained in the epilogue (ch. xii. 14). A corrector, who desired to remove all seeming contradictions and discrepancies from the work, would not have been satisfied with inserting this gloss, but would have displayed his remedial measures in other places. Of this proceeding, however, no traces are discernible by an unprejudiced eye.

Ver. 10—ch. xii. 7.—Section 18. *The third remedy is piety*, and this ought to be practised from one's earliest days; life should be so guided as not to offend the laws of the Creator and Judge, and virtue should not be postponed till the failure of faculties makes pleasure unattainable, and death closes the scene. The last days of the old man are beautifully described under certain images, metaphors, and analogies.

Ver. 10.—**Therefore remove sorrow from thy heart.** The writer reiterates his advice concerning cheerfulness, and then proceeds to inculcate early piety. *Kaas*, rendered "sorrow," has been variously understood. The Septuagint has θυμόν, the Vulgate *iram*; so the margin of the ' Authorized Version gives " anger," and that of the Revised Version " vexation," or " provocation." Wordsworth adopts this last meaning (referring to 1 Kings xv. 30; xxi. 22; 2 Kings xxiii. 26, etc., where, however, the signification is modified by the connection in which the word stands), and paraphrases, " Take heed lest you provoke God by the thoughts of your heart." Jerome affirms that in the term " anger" all perturbations of the mind are included—which seems rather forced. The word is better rendered, low spirits, moroseness, discontent. These feelings are to be put away from the mind by a deliberate act. **Put away evil from thy flesh.** Many commentators consider that the evil here named is physical, not moral, the author enjoining his young disciple to take proper care of his body, not to weaken it on the one hand by asceticism, nor on the other by indulgence in youthful lusts. In this case the two clauses would urge the removal of what respectively affects the mind and body, the inner and outer man. But the ancient versions are unanimous in regarding the " evil" spoken of as moral. Thus the Septuagint gives πονηρίαν, "wickedness;" the Vulgate, *malitiam.* Similarly the Syriac and Targum. And according to our interpretation of the passage, such is the meaning here. It is a call to early piety and virtue, like that of St. Paul (2 Cor. vii. 1), "Having these promises, let us cleanse ourselves from all filthiness of the flesh and spirit, perfecting holiness in the fear of God." Do not, says Koheleth, defile thy body by carnal sins (1 Cor. vi. 18), which bring decay and sickness, and arouse the wrath of God against thee. **For childhood and youth are vanity.** This time of youth soon passes away; the capacity for enjoyment is soon circumscribed; therefore use thy opportunities aright, remembering the end. The word for "youth" (*shacharuth*) occurs nowhere else in the Old Testament, and is probably connected with *shachon,* "black," used of hair in Lev. xiii. 31. Hence it means the time of black hair, in contradistinction to the time when the hair has become grey. The explanation which refers it to the time of dawn (Ps. cx. 3) seems to be erroneous, as it would then be identical with "childhood." The Septuagint renders it ἄνοια, "folly;" the Vulgate, *voluptas,* "pleasure;" the Syriac, "and not knowledge;" but the word cannot be rightly thus translated. The two terms are childhood and manhood, the period during which the capacity for pleasure is fresh and strong. Its vanity is soon brought home; it is evanescent; it brings punishment. Thus Bailey, 'Festus'—

"I cast mine eyes around, and feel
There is a blessing wanting;
Too soon our hearts the truth reveal,
That joy is disenchanting."

And again—

"When amid the world's delights,
How warm soe'er we feel a moment among them—
We find ourselves, when the hot blast hath blown,
Prostrate, and weak, and wretched."

HOMILETICS.

Vers. 1—6.—*Bread upon the waters; or, rules and reasons for practising beneficence.*
I. RULES. Beneficence should be practised: 1. *Without doubt as to its result.* One's charity should be performed in a spirit of fearless confidence, even though the recipients of it should appear altogether unworthy, and our procedure as hopeless and thankless an operation as "casting one's bread upon the waters" (ver. 1), or "sowing the sea" (Theognis). 2. *Without limit as to its distribution.* "Give a portion to seven, yea even unto eight" (ver. 2); that is, "Give to him that asketh, and from him that would borrow of thee turn not thou away" (Matt. v. 42). Social economics may, but the sermon on the mount does not, condemn indiscriminate or promiscuous giving. One's bread should be cast upon the waters in the sense that it should be bestowed upon the multitudes, or carried far and wide rather than restricted to a narrow circle. 3. *Without anxiety as to its seasonableness.* As "he that observeth the wind will not sow, and he that regardeth the clouds shall not reap" (ver. 4), so he who is always apprehensive lest his deeds of kindness should be ill-timed is not likely to practise much beneficence. The farmer who should spend his days in watching the weather to select just the right moment to plough and sow, or reap and garner, would never get the one operation or the other performed; and little charity would be witnessed were men never to give until they were quite sure they had hit upon the right time to give, and never to do an act of kindness until they were certain the proper objects to receive it had been found. 4. *Without intermission as to its time.* "In the morning sow thy seed, and in the evening withhold not thine hand" (ver. 6). Who would practise beneficence as it should be practised must be as constantly employed therein as the husbandman is in his agricultural operations. Philanthropy is a sacred art, which can only be acquired by pains and patience. Intermittent goodness, charity performed by fits and starts, occasional benevolence, never comes to much, and never does much for either the giver or receiver. Charity to be efficient must be a perennial fountain and a running stream (1 Cor. xiii. 8). The charitable man must be always giving, like God, who maketh his sun to rise on the evil and the good, etc. (Matt. v. 45), and who giveth unto all liberally (Jas. i. 5).
II. REASONS. Beneficence should be practised for the following reasons: 1. *It is certain in the end to be recompensed.* (Ver. 1.) The kindly disposed individual, who fearlessly casts his bread upon the waters by doing good to the unkind and the unthankful (Matt. v. 45; Luke vi. 35), may have a long time to wait for a return

from his venture in practical philanthropy; but eventually that return will come, here on earth, in the inward satisfaction that springs from doing good, perhaps in the gratitude (or, it may be, the temporal and spiritual elevation) of those who experience his kindness, hereafter in the welcome and the glory Christ has promised to such as are mindful of his needy brethren on earth (Matt. xxv. 40). 2. *No one can predict how soon himself may become an object of charity.* As surely as the clouds when full of rain will empty themselves upon the earth, and a tree will lie exactly in the place where it falls (ver. 3), so surely will seasons of calamity, when they come, descend on rich and poor alike; yea, perhaps strike the wealthy, the great, and the good with strokes which the indigent, the obscure, and the wicked may escape. Hence the bare consideration of this fact, that bad times may come—not only depriving one of the ability to practise beneficence, but rendering one a fit subject for the same (the latter of these being most likely the Preacher's thought)—should induce one to be charitable while he may and can. This may seem a low, selfish, and unworthy ground on which to recommend the practice of philanthropy; but does its meaning not substantially amount to this, that men should give to others because, were bad times to strip them of their wealth, and plunge them into poverty, they would wish others to give to them? And how much is this below the standard of the golden rule (Matt. vii. 12)? 3. *No amount of forethought will discover a better time for practising beneficence than the present.* As no one knows the way of the wind (John iii. 8), or the secrets of embryology (Ps. cxxxix. 15)—in both of which departments of nature, notwithstanding the discoveries of modern science, much ignorance prevails—so can no one predict what kind of future will emerge from the womb of the present (Prov. xxvii. 1; Zeph. ii. 2), or what shall be the course of providence on the morrow. Hence to defer exercising charity till one has fathomed the unfathomable is more than merely to waste one's time; it is to miss a certain opportunity for one that may never arrive. As to-day only is ours, we should never cast it away for a doubtful to-morrow, but

> " Act in the living present,
> Heart within and God o'erhead."
>   (Longfellow.)

4. *The issues of beneficence, in the recipients thereof, are uncertain.* That an act of charity, or deed of kindness, whensoever done, will prosper without fail in the experience of the doer thereof, has been declared (ver. 1); that it will turn out equally well in the experience of him to whom it is done is not so inevitable. Yet from this problematical character of all human philanthropy as to results should be drawn an argument, not for doing nothing, but for doing more. An atrabiliar soul will conclude that, because he is not sure whether his charity may not injure rather than benefit the recipient, he should hold his hand; a hopeful and happy Christian will feel impelled to more assiduous benevolence by reflecting that he can never tell when his kindly deeds will bear fruit in the temporal, perhaps also spiritual, salvation of the poor and needy. "The seed sown in the morning of life may bear its harvest at once, or not till the evening of age. The man may reap at one and the same time the fruits of his earlier and later sowing, and may find that both are alike good" (Plumptre).

LESSONS. 1. "As therefore ye have opportunity, do good unto all men" (Gal. vi. 10). 2. Weary not in well-doing (Gal. vi. 9). 3. Take no thought for to-morrow (Matt. vi. 34). 4. Cultivate a hopeful view of life (Prov. x. 28).

Vers. 1—6.—*Conditions of success in business.* I. THE MEASURES TO BE ADOPTED. 1. *Enterprises not free from hazard.* "Cast thy bread upon the waters," meaning, "launch out upon the sea of business speculation." The man who would succeed must be prepared to venture somewhat. A judicious quantity of courage seems indispensable to getting on. The timid merchant is as little likely to prosper as the shrinking lover. 2. *Prudence in dividing risks.* "Divide the portion into seven, yea, eight parts," which again signifies that one should never put all his eggs into one basket, commit all his goods to one caravan, place all his cargo in one ship, invest all his capital in one undertaking, or generally venture all on one card. 3. *Confidence in going forward.* The agriculturist who is always watching the weather—"observing the wind and regarding the clouds" (ver. 4)—will make but a poor farmer; and he who is constantly taking fright at the fluctuations of the market will prove only an indifferent merchant. In business, as in love and war, the man who hesitates is lost. 4. *Diligence and constancy in labour.* The person who aims at success in business must be a hard and incessant, not a fitful and intermittent, worker. If a farmer, he must sow betimes in the morning, and pause not until hindered by the shades of night. If a merchant, he must trade both early and late. If an artisan, he must toil week in and week out. It is " the hand of the diligent " that " maketh rich " (Prov. x. 4).

II. THE MOTIVES TO BE CHERISHED. 1. *The expectation of a future reward.* " Thou shalt find it [thy bread] after many days." Such enterprises, though attended with risk, will not all fail, but will generally prove successful—not immediately, perhaps, but after an interval of waiting, as the ships of a foreign merchant require months, or even years, before they return with the desired profits. 2. *The anticipation of impending calamity.* As no man can foresee the future, the prudent merchant lays his account with one or more of his ventures coming to grief. Hence, in the customary phrase, he " divides the risk," and does not hazard all in one expedition. 3. *The consciousness of inability to forecast the future.* Just because of this—illustrated in vers. 3 and 5—the man who aspires to prosper in his undertakings dismisses all over-anxious care, and instead of waiting for opportunities and markets, makes them. 4. *The hope of ultimately succeeding.* Though he may often fail, he expects he will not always fail; hence he redoubles his energy and diligence. " In the morning he sows his seed, and in the evening withholds not his hand," believing that in the end his labours will be crowned with success.

Learn : 1. That business is not incompatible with piety. 2. That piety need be no hindrance to business. 3. That each may be helpful to the other. 4. That both should be, and are, a source of blessing to the world.

Vers. 7, 8.—*Carpe diem : memento mori ; or, here and hereafter contrasted.* I. HERE, A SCENE OF LIGHT ; HEREAFTER, A PLACE OF DARKNESS. Under the Old Testament the abode of departed spirits was usually conceived of as a realm from which the light of day was excluded, or only dimly admitted (Job x. 21, 22).

II. HERE, A GARDEN OF DELIGHT ; HEREAFTER, A WILDERNESS OF VANITY. Life beneath the sun, even to the most miserable, has pleasures which are wanting to the bodiless inhabitants of the underworld (ch. ix. 10).

III. HERE, A PERIOD OF FEW DAYS ; HEREAFTER, A TERM OF MANY. At the longest, man's duration upon earth is short (Job xiv. 1 ; Ps. xxxix. 5) ; in comparison, his continuance in the narrow house, or in the unseen world, will be long.

LESSONS. 1. Enjoy life heartily, as a good gift of God. 2. Use life wisely, in preparation for the world to come.

Vers. 9, 10.—*Advice to a young man or woman.* I. A GRAND PERMISSION—to enjoy life. " Rejoice, O young man, in thy youth," etc. 1. *Not a sanction to self-indulgence.* The Preacher does not teach that a young man (or, indeed, any man) is at liberty to " make provision for the flesh to fulfil the lusts thereof " (Rom. xiii. 14) ; to have asserted or suggested that a youth was permitted by religion to follow his inclinations wherever they might lead, to plunge into sensuality, to sow his wild oats (as the phrase is), would have been to contradict the Law of God as given by Moses (Numb. xv. 39). 2. *Not a protest (ironical) against asceticism.* The Preacher does not say that God will judge men if they despise his gifts and refuse to enjoy them. Doubtless, in so far as asceticism springs from a contemptuous disregard of God's providential mercies, it is sinful ; but this is hardly the case the Preacher has in view. 3. *But a warrant for reasonable pleasure.* The young man or maiden is informed that he or she may enjoy the morning of life to the utmost of his or her bent, " walking in the ways of his or her heart, and in the sight of his or her eyes," provided always such pleasures as are sinful are eschewed. Moreover, the Preacher's language appears to hint that such enjoyment as is here allowed is both appropriate to the season, the days of youth, and demanded by the nature of youth, being the legitimate gratification of the heart and eyes.

II. A SOLEMN WARNING—the certainty of judgment. " But know thou that for all these things," etc. The judgment of which the Preacher speaks is: 1. *Future.* The great assize will be held, not on earth, but in the unseen world; not in time, but in eternity. That the Preacher had no clear perception of either the time, place, or nature of this judgment, is probably correct, but that he alluded to a dread tribunal in the great hereafter seems a legitimate conclusion from the circumstance that he elsewhere (ch. viii. 14) adverts to the fact that in this life men are not always requited either for their righteousness or for their wickedness. What was comparatively dark to the Preacher is to us clearly illumined, viz. that after death is the judgment (Heb. ix. 27). 2. *Divine.* The Judge will not be man, but God (ch. iii. 17; Ps. lxii. 12; Isa. xxx. 18). This fully discovered in the New Testament, which states that God shall judge men by Jesus Christ (Acts xvii. 31; Rom. ii. 16; 2 Tim. iv. 1). 3. *Individual.* The judgment will be passed, not upon mankind in the mass, or upon men in groups, but upon men as individuals (2 Cor. v. 10). 4. *Certain.* As the Preacher himself was not dubious, so would he have the young to know that the future judgment will be a momentous reality (Heb. xii. 23; 2 Pet. ii. 9).

III. AN URGENT DUTY—to banish sorrow and evil. 1. *To remove sorrow from the heart.* Either (1) the sorrow of vexation, in which case the counsel is to avoid cherishing a peevish, morose, or discontented spirit, such as arises from looking at the dark side of things, and to cultivate a cheerful disposition—a state of mind which accepts whatever lot falls to it in providence (Phil. iv. 11). Or (2) that which causes sorrow to the heart, viz. sin; in which case, again, the exhortation is to abstain from all ungodliness, the real root of heart-bitterness (Deut. xxix. 18; Prov. i. 31; Gal. vi. 8), and to follow holiness, which alone contains the secret of happiness (Ps. cvi. 3; Isa. xlviii. 18). 2. *To put away evil from the flesh.* Doubtless (1) physical evil, pain, suffering, affliction, whether occasioned by the self-inflicted tortures of asceticism or by the accidentally incurred strokes of disease—a clear injunction to promote the body's comfort and health. But also (2) everything that may induce suffering or evil in the flesh; hence once more sin which, apart altogether from those wickednesses which are against the body (1 Cor. vi. 18), has a tendency to engender disease and accelerate death.

IV. A SERIOUS REASON—the vanity of boyhood and manhood. 1. *Both are transient.* Youth and the prime of life will not last, but will pass away. Hence they should be kept as joyous and pure as possible. Only one thing more unfortunate for the after-development of the soul than a sunless youth, namely, a sinful youth. If the opening years of man's pilgrimage on the earth should be radiant with happiness, much more should they be glorified with holiness. 2. *Both are inexperienced.* Hence their fervid impulses should be moderated and restrained by the solemn considerations that spring from the brevity of life and the certainty of a future judgment.

Learn: 1. That youth should be happy and serious. 2. That man's existence has a future and a present. 3. That privilege and responsibility ever go together.

HOMILIES BY VARIOUS AUTHORS.

Vers. 1, 2.—*Works of charity.* There can be little doubt that these admonitions apply to the deeds of compassion and beneficence which are the proper fruits of true religion. Especially in some conditions of society almsgiving is expedient and beneficial. In times of famine, in cases of affliction and sudden calamity, it is a duty to supply the need of the poor and hungry. At the same time, the indiscriminate bestowal of what is called charity unquestionably does more harm than good, especially in a state of society in which few need suffer want who are diligent, frugal, temperate, and self-denying. But there are many other ways in which benevolence may express itself beside almsgiving. The Christian is called upon to care both for the bodies and for the souls of his fellow-men—to give the bread of knowledge as well as the bread that perisheth, and to provide a spiritual portion for the enrichment and consolation of the destitute.

I. THE NATURAL EMOTION OF BENEVOLENCE IS RECOGNIZED AND HALLOWED BY TRUE RELIGION. It may be maintained with confidence that sympathy is as natural to man as selfishness, although the love of self is too often allowed by our sinful nature to overcome the love of others. But when Christ takes possession, by his Spirit, of a man's inner nature, then the benevolence which may have been dormant is aroused, and new direction is given to it, and new power to persevere and to succeed in the attainment of its object.

II. RELIGION PROMPTS TO A PRACTICAL EXPRESSION OF BENEVOLENT FEELING. Too often sympathy is a sentimental luxury, leading to no effort, no self-denial. The poet justly denounces those who,

> "Nursed in mealy-mouthed philanthropies,
> Divorce the feeling from her mate—the deed."

But the spirit of the Saviour urges to Christ-like endeavour, and sustains the worker for men's bodily, social, and spiritual good. The bread must be cast, the portion must be given.

III. BENEVOLENCE MEETS IN ITS EXERCISE WITH MANY DISCOURAGEMENTS. The bread is cast upon the waters. This implies that in many cases we must expect to lose sight of the results of our work; that we must be prepared for disappointment; that, at all events, we must fulfil our service for God and man in faith, and rather from conviction and principle than from any hope of apparent and immediate success.

IV. A PROMISE IS GIVEN WHICH IS INTENDED TO URGE TO PERSEVERANCE. What is, as it were, committed to the deep shall be found after the lapse of days. The waters do not destroy, they fertilize and fructify, the seed. Thus "they who sow in tears shall reap in joy." In how many ways this promise is fulfilled the history of the Christian Church, and even the experience of every individual worker for God, abundantly show. In places and at times altogether unexpected and unlikely, there come to light evidences that the work has been cared for, watched over, and prospered by God himself. He does not suffer the efforts of his faithful servants to come to nought. The good they aim at, and much which never occurred to them to anticipate, is effected in God's time by the marvellous operation of his providence and his Spirit. "Be steadfast, immovable, always abounding in the work of the Lord, forasmuch as ye know that your labour is not in vain in the Lord."—T.

Ver. 1.—*Encouragement to Christian toilers.* The lesson of this verse, if the figure be dropped, may be expressed thus: Act upon principles and not upon likelihoods.

I. A SIMILITUDE. The good we give to men when we preach and teach Divine truth, when we exercise Christian influence, is seed—fruit-bearing seed. It is a blessed, but a sacred and serious, occupation to sow the seed of spiritual life.

II. A DIRECTION. Christian sowers! cast your bread even upon the waters. 1. Even upon an unkindly soil. 2. Even in an unpromising season. 3. Liberally, though at the cost of self-sacrifice. 4. Constantly, even though it seems that the sowing has been long carried on in vain. 5. Bravely and hopefully, although the calculating, short-sighted world deride your efforts.

III. A PROMISE. After lapse of days you shall find the bread you have dispersed. 1. What is cast abroad is not destroyed. 2. Neither is it lost sight of. 3. It shall, perhaps after many days, be found again. It *may* be in time; it *shall* be in eternity. Then "he that soweth and he that reapeth shall rejoice together."—T.

Vers. 4, 6.—*Fulfil duty and disregard consequences.* These statements and admonitions respect both natural and spiritual toil. The husbandman who labours in the fields, and the pastor and the missionary who seek a harvest of souls, alike need such counsel. The natural and the supernatural alike are under the control and government of God; and they who would labour to good purpose in God's universe must have regard to Divine principles, and must confide in Divine faithfulness and goodness.

I. THE DUTY OF DILIGENCE. Good results do not come by chance; and although the blessing and the glory are alike God's, he honours men by permitting them to be his fellow-workers. There is no reason to expect reaping unless sowing has preceded; "What a man soweth that shall he also reap." Toil—thoughtful, patient, persevering toil—such is the condition of every harvest worth the ingathering.

II. DISSUASIVES FROM DILIGENCE. If the husbandman occupy himself in studying the weather, and in imagining and anticipating adverse seasons, the operations of agriculture will come to a standstill.   There are possibilities and contingencies before every one of us, the consideration and exaggeration of which may well paralyze the powers, hinder effective labour, and cloud the prospect of the future, so as to prevent a proper use of present opportunities.   This is a temptation which besets some temperaments more than others, from which, however, few are altogether free.   If the Christian labourer fixes his attention upon the difficulties of his task, upon the obduracy or ignorance of the natures with which he has to deal, upon the slenderness of his resources, upon the failures of many of his companions and colleagues, leaving out of sight all counteracting influences, the likelihood is that his powers will be crippled, that his work will stand still, and that his whole life will be clouded by disappointment. The field looks barren, the weeds grow apace, the enemy is sowing tares, the showers of blessing are withheld: what, then, is the use of sowing the gospel seed ?   Such are the reflections and the questionings which take possession of many minds, to their discouragement and enfeeblement and distress.

III.   INDUCEMENTS TO DILIGENCE.   It is not questioned that the work is arduous, that the difficulties are real, that the foes are many and powerful, that circumstances may be adverse, that the prospect (to the eye of mere human reason) may be sombre. But even granting all this, the Christian labourer has ample grounds for earnest and persevering effort.   Of these, two come before us as we read these verses.   1. Our own ignorance of results.   We have not to do with the consequences, and we certainly cannot foresee them.   Certain it is that amazing blessings have sometimes rested upon toil in most unpromising conditions, in places and among people that have almost stricken the heart of the observer with despair.   "Thou knowest not whether shall prosper, this or that;" "With God nothing is impossible."   2. The express command of our Divine Lord.   Results we cannot foresee.   But direct commands we can understand and obey.   "In the morning sow thy seed, and in the evening withhold not thine hand."   Such is the voice, the behest, of him who has a right to order our actions—to control and inspire our life.   Whilst we have this commission to execute, we are not at liberty to waste our time and cripple our activities by moodily questioning what is likely to follow from our efforts.   Surely the Christian may have faith to leave this in the hand of God !—T.

Vers. 7, 8.—*Light and darkness.*   The alternation of day and night is not only contributive to human convenience, it is symbolical of human experience.

I. THERE IS APPOINTED FOR MEN THE LIGHT OF YOUTH, HEALTH, AND PROSPERITY. He who rises betimes, and, turning to the east, watches for the sunrise, and then beholds the glorious orb of day rise from the plain or from the sea, and flood hill and valley, corn-field and pasture, with the radiant splendour of the morning, can enter into the language of the preacher, "Truly the light is sweet, and a pleasant thing it is for the eyes to behold the sun."   And if then he looks into the face of a companion, a noble and generous youth, unstained by sin, undimmed by care, untouched by disease, he can well understand what is meant by the morning of life, the lustre of youth, and can thank God that such a period, and such strength, joy, and hope, have been appointed as a part of human experience.   In youth and bounding health and high spirits, how fresh and winsome is the present !   how alluring the future!   Who would wish to cast a shadow upon the brightness which God himself has created ?

II. THERE IS APPOINTED FOR MEN THE DARKNESS OF AGE, INFIRMITY, ADVERSITY, AND DEATH.   The same individual whom we have regarded in the prime of his powers and the beauty of his joy will, if his life be prolonged, pass through quite other experiences.   Clouds will gather about his head, the storm will smite him, the dark midnight will shroud him.   There is no discharge in that war—no exemption from the common lot.   He may lose his health, his powers of body or of mind, his property, his friends.   He must walk through the valley of death-shade.   In some form or other trouble and sorrow must be his portion.

III. THE DUTY AND THE WISDOM OF REMEMBERING THE APPROACH OF THE TIME OF DARKNESS.   It may be objected that it will be time enough to think of the afflictions of life when they are actually present, and that it is a pity to cloud the sunny present by gloomy forebodings.   Those who know the young and prosperous are, however, well aware that their natural tendency is altogether to ignore the likelihood of a great change in circumstances and experience. And to remember the providential appointment that our life cannot be eternal sunshine is, in many respects, a most desirable and profitable exercise. Thus shall we learn to place a due value, and no more than a due value, upon the pleasures, the diversions, the congenial pursuits of youth and prosperity. And, what is still better, thus may we be led to seek a deeper and surer foundation for our life—to acquire spiritual treasures, of which we cannot be deprived by lapse of time or change of circumstances. And thus shall we, by God's mercy, find that the darkness through which we needs must walk is but for a season, and that through it the people of God shall pass into the blessed sunshine of eternal day.—T.

Vers. 9, 10.—*In joy remember judgment!* There is certainly no asceticism in the teaching of this book. On the other hand, there is no commendation of worldliness and voluptuousness. Human nature is prone to extremes; and even religious teachers are not always successful in avoiding them. But we seem in this passage to listen to teaching which at once recognizes the claims of human nature and of the earthly life, and yet solemnly maintains the subordination of all our pleasures and occupations to the service of our Master, and to our preparation for the great account.

I. THE DIVINE PROVISION OF LIFE'S JOYS. If this language be not the language of irony—and it seems better to take it as sober serious truth,—then we are taught that the delights of this earthly existence, however they are capable of abuse, are in themselves not evil, but proofs of the Creator's benevolence, to be accepted with devout thanksgiving. In dealing with the young it is especially important to avoid warring with their innocent pleasures. These may sometimes seem to us trivial and unprofitable; but a juster view of human nature will convince us that they are wisely appointed to fulfil a certain place and office in human life.

II. THE DIVINE APPOINTMENT OF FUTURE JUDGMENT. Conscience suggests that we are responsible beings, and that retribution is a reality. What conscience suggests revelation certifies. The Bible lays the greatest stress upon individual accountability. We are taught in the text that we are not only responsible for the work we do in life, but for the pleasures we pursue. Certainly it is of the greatest advantage that men should recollect in the days of happiness the assurances of Scripture, that God shall ere long bring them into judgment. Such recollection will check any inclination to unlawful enjoyments, and will prevent undue absorption in enjoyments which are in themselves lawful, but to which a disproportionate value may be attached. There is a sense in which, as we are here reminded, "youth and the prime of life are vanity." They will prove to be so to those who imagine that they will last, to those who pride themselves in them and boast of them, to those who use them only as the opportunity of personal pleasure, to those who forget their Creator, neglect his Law, and despise his Gospel.

III. THE POSSIBILITY OF ACCEPTING GOD'S GIFTS AND OF USING THEM UNDER A SENSE OF RESPONSIBILITY, AND WITH A VIEW TO THE GREAT ACCOUNT. If every blessing in this life be taken as coming directly from the great Giver's hand, as a token of his favour, and as the result of the mediation of his blessed Son, then may the very enjoyments of this life become to Christians the occasion of present grace and the earnest of fulness of joy.—T.

Vers. 1—4, 6.—*Incentives to Christian work.* These are not the words of some very young man who has much fervour and little experience; they are those of one who has known the disappointment and disenchantment of life. They come, therefore, with the greater force to us. We gather from them—

I. THAT IT IS WELL WORTH WHILE TO SPEND OUR WHOLE STRENGTH IN LOVING SERVICE. "Cast thy bread upon the waters"—scatter the precious bread-corn, drop it into the flood; that is not the act of a fool, but of a wise man. "Give a portion to seven;" ay, go further than even that in your liberality—spend your whole strength in that which is good and beneficent, lavish your resources, let there be a generous overflow rather than a cool calculation in your service; and this whether you are acting as a citizen, as a neighbour, or as a member of the Church of Christ.

II. THAT, IF WE ARE WISE, WE SHALL LET OUR VERY IGNORANCE STIMULATE US TO EXERTION. Is it worth while to sow when we cannot be sure that we shall ever reap? since we do not know what evil may come in a week or a day, had we not better turn the seed of the sower into bread for the eater? No; let our ignorance concerning the future be rather an incentive to activity. Say not, "I do not know what changes may come upon the earth; how little my labours may prove to be profitable; who will appreciate my devotion, and who will be unresponsive and ungrateful; therefore I shall suspend my exertions." Say rather, "I cannot tell what is coming; how soon I may be rewarded; how short may be the term of my life and of my opportunity here; I must therefore lose no time and waste no strength; I must do whole-heartedly all that is in my power. Because I cannot tell which of my words will fall like water on the rock, and which like seed upon the fertile soil, whether the morning or the evening labours will be rewarded, therefore I will do my best; perhaps this present effort I am now making may be the very one which has in it the seed of a glorious harvest." Thus our very ignorance may stimulate us to holy and fruitful action.

III. THAT WE SHOULD NOT ALLOW OURSELVES TO BE DISTURBED BY THE UNSYMPATHETIC FORCES ROUND US. If the clouds are full of rain, they will empty themselves on the earth without any regard to our necessity for fine weather; the tree will fall this way or that, according to the wind, whomsoever or whatsoever it will crush by its weight. The forces of nature are quite unsympathetic. Feebleness may incapacitate or death may take away our most efficient fellow-labourer; the changes that affect our human lives may reduce our means or remove our agents, or even close our agencies; but we must not be daunted, nor must we stay our hand on this account. The full *mind*, like the full cloud, must pour itself forth, and may do so in words and ways we do not like; the man, like the tree, must take the line toward which he strongly inclines, and this may be one that traverses our tastes and wishes. Never mind! We are not to let our good work for Christ be arrested by such incidental difficulty as that. We are to "quit us like men, and be strong," and we are to triumph over such hindrances as these.

IV. THAT WE ARE NOT TO BE IN ANY HURRY FOR THE HARVEST. The seed we cast "shall be found after many days." The husbandman hath "long patience," waiting for the fruits of the earth. The history of the noblest men is one long sermon on the blessedness of patience. It says to the Christian pilgrim and workman, "Work and wait; work diligently, intelligently, devoutly, then wait prayerfully and hopefully. Be not surprised, much less distracted, because the harvest is still far in the future; in due season you will reap, if you faint not."—C.

Ver. 4.—*The true workman.* The idea of the text is that something must be endured, and something must be dared, if we mean to achieve anything of any account. If a man wants to sow, he must not mind being assailed by the wind while he is at work; or if he wants to reap, he must not stay indoors because it threatens to rain. We must be ready to endure, we must be prepared to run risks, if we have any thought of taking rank among the successful workers of our time. God does not give his bounties to those who will only walk the road when it is perfectly smooth and sheltered; nor does he permit us to win triumphs if our heart misgives us at the sight of difficulty or danger. Success is for those, and those only, who can brave wind and rain in the open field of labour, in the wide spheres of usefulness.

I. THE FACT, AS OUR EXPERIENCE TESTIFIES. Everything that is done which is really worth doing is wrought with trouble, with some measure of difficulty and of risk, with the possibility or likelihood of failure, with struggle and some degree of disappointment—*e.g.* the little child in learning to walk and to talk; the boy in mastering his lesson or even his game, or in finding and taking his place in the schoolroom and the playground; the student in acquiring his knowledge, and in facing and passing his examination; the tradesman and merchant in making their purchases and investing their money; the author in writing and printing his book; the statesman in planning and submitting his measure, etc. In all these, and in all such cases, we have to contend with adverse "winds" that blow upon us; we have to "put our foot down" firmly on the ground; we have to run the risk of unpleasant "rains," of falling and of failure. It is the constant condition of human endeavour.

II. THE BENEFICENT RESULT. This is not to be regretted; on the contrary, we may be thankful for it. It develops human character; it calls forth and strengthens all that is best within us. 1. It nourishes *fortitude*—a commendable capacity to endure; a readiness to accept, unmoved and untroubled at heart, whatever may befall us. 2. It creates and sustains *courage*—a deliberate determination to face the evil that may possibly await us. 3. It contributes to true *manliness*—the power to do and to endure anything and everything as God may will, as man may want. We pity those whose field of work, whose path of life, is unvisited by adverse winds and unpleasant rains. If they do grow up into strong and brave souls, it will be in spite of the absence of those circumstances which are most helpful in the formation of character. We have no condolence for those who have to face the strong wind and the rain; we congratulate them that they are placed where the noblest characters are shaped.

III. Its lesson for the Christian worker. Too often the workman in the Master's vineyard is inclined to lay down his weapon when the clouds gather in the heavens. But to act thus is not worthy of him. Not thus did he who "bore such contradiction of sinners against himself." Not thus have the worthiest of his disciples done—they who have done the most, and have left behind them the most fragrant memories. Not thus will they have acted who receive the gladdening commendation of their Lord "in the day of his appearing." Not thus shall we finish the work our Father has given us to do. Let the strong winds of even an unkindly criticism blow, let the dark cloud of possible failure show itself in the horizon, we will not be daunted; we will go forth to sow the good seed of the kingdom, to reap its precious harvest.—C.

Vers. 7, 8.—*The shadow of the tomb.* Let a man rejoice, says the Preacher, in his long bright days of prosperity; but let him remember that the time is drawing on when he will sleep his long sleep beneath the ground; and many as his days have been when the light of the sun was sweet to his eyes, very many more will be the days of darkness which will follow. It is open to us all to indulge in some—

I. Sentimental sadness, in view of this long future. We may stroll in the churchyard, and as we read the names and ages of men who lived for thirty or forty years, but who have been in their graves for, it may be, two hundred years, we may think how small was the measure of the light on which they looked compared with that of the darkness in which they have been sleeping. And as we yield to these thoughts we feel the vanity of human affairs. Thus the shadow of the tomb falls upon and darkens the brightness of our life. It seems to us a poor thing for a man to come out of the infinite darkness behind; to walk in the sunshine for a few swiftly passing, soon-departed decades, and then go out into the immeasurable darkness on the other side. There is, however—

II. A correcting thought. Why should the excellency of human life be spoiled to us by the reflection that it is limited, bound by a line which is not far off us? If it be so that there is nothing but darkness beyond, if it be true that what we see comprises all that is to be seen, then let us, for that very reason, make the most of all that we hold. If the worth of our existence is confined to the present, let us compress into the present time all the action and all the enjoyment which it will hold. Shall we not say—

> "I will drink
> Life to the lees. . . . Life piled on life
> Were all too little, and of one to me
> Little remains : but every hour is saved
> From that eternal silence"?

III. The Christian aspect of the subject. We know that this life will soon be over, *may* reach its terminus any day, and *must* come to its conclusion before many years have gone. What shall we be concerned about in this? 1. Not the hour or act of dying. Common human fortitude will carry us through that experience, as it has done in countless millions of cases already; much more will Christian faith and hope. 2. Not the silence and darkness of the grave. What does it signify to us that our mortal body will lie long in the grave, when we are hoping to be "clothed upon with our house which is from heaven"? 3. The long future of heavenly life. Not the many days of darkness, but the long, the everlasting day of glory is before us who believe in Christ, and who hope to dwell with him for ever. For that endless day of blessedness the life we are now living is not only the preliminary but the preparation. Therefore let every day, every hour, be sacred; be so spent in faith, in love, in holy labour, in ennobling joy, that the future will be but the continuance of the present— the continuance, but also the enlargement, the glorification. Thus shall there not fall upon the life that now is the shadow of the tomb; there shall shine upon it some beams from the glory that is beyond.—C.

Vers. 9, 10.—*Human joy and Divine judgment.* That these words are not to be taken ironically is probable, if not certain, when we consider how frequently the Preacher had given substantially the same counsel before (see ch. ii. 24; iii. 12, 22; v. 18; viii. 15; ix. 9). Moreover, we obtain an excellent meaning by taking them in their natural sense. We may indeed ask for—

I. The necessity for such counsel. It may be said—What need is there for offering such an exhortation? Young manhood is certain to take all the indulgence which is good for it, without any man's bidding; the danger is not on the side of defect, but of excess. That certainly is so generally. But there is the *religious devotee*, who thinks he is pleasing God by abstaining from all bodily comforts, and enduring all physical sufferings. There is also the *ascetic moralist*, who thinks that he is conforming to the highest standard of ethics when he practises a rigorous abstinence, and goes through life denying himself the delights to which outward nature and inward instincts invite him. There is also the *man of prudent policy*, who thinks that in a state of society such as that in which the Preacher lived and wrote, where there is no security for life or property, it is better not to enter into new relationships or to embark in great enterprises; let life be cut down to its smallest limits. Hence the necessity for such a cheery invitation as that in the text. But we must mark—

II. The extent to which it goes. Clearly the words must not be taken in their widest possible sense. That would be not liberty, but licence; that would not encourage enjoyment, but sanction vice. The Preacher would have the young man, who is full of strength, energy, hope, affection, have the full heritage which the Father of spirits and Author of this world intended and provided for him. Let him give play to all the sound impulses of his nature; let him taste the exquisite enjoyment of a pure affection and of happy friendship; let him be an eager and earnest competitor in the contest of strength, of skill, of the studio, of the mart, of the council, of the senate; let him throw his full energies into the activities, recreations, ambitions, aspirations, of his time; let him play his part as his heart inclines and as his capacities enable him. But let him not cross the line which divides virtue from vice, wisdom from folly, conscientiousness from unscrupulousness. For there has to be taken into account—

III. One powerfully restraining thought. God will bring him into judgment. And God's judgment is threefold. 1. He judges us every moment, deciding whether our thought, our feeling, our action, is right or wrong; and he is thus continually approving or disapproving, and is constantly pleased or displeased. Surely this is not a Divine judgment to be disregarded. 2. He causes an evil habit to be visited, sooner or later, with the penalty which appropriately follows it—sickness, feebleness, poverty, mental incapacity, human condemnation, ruin, death, as the case may be. 3. He reserves the day of trial and of account for the hour when life is over.—C.

Ver. 10.—*The vanity and glory of youth.* (See homily on ch. xii. 1.)—C.

Vers. 1—6.—*Provision for the future.* Fruitless though many of the quests had been on which the Preacher had set out, lost though he had often been in the mazes of barren and withering speculation, something he did succeed in gaining, which he now places on record among the concluding sentences of his book. Though truth in its fulness is out of man's reach, the path of duty is plain; essential wisdom may never be discovered, but some practical lessons for the guidance of life, which after all are what most we need, are to be won from the search. Perhaps to many minds these may seem commonplace. It may be thought that after all the bustle of the enterprise, after all the zeal and energy expended in carrying it through, the gain is small. Surely some new thing of greater value might have been brought out of the far-off region of philosophy and specu- lation than the counsels given here to be beneficent and active, since a time may come when we shall need the help of others, and the harvest may far exceed all our expectations. But from the very nature of the case such murmurings are unreasonable. No new thing can be brought to light in the moral world. Conscience proclaims the same duties age after age; and all that is left to him who would advance the cause of righteousness is to give clearer utterance to the voice of God in the heart, to show the imperative claims of duty, and in some instances to suggest new and weighty motives for obedience to them. None need, therefore, scorn the simple terms in which the Preacher sums up the practical lessons he would have us lay to heart. There is nothing novel or wonderful in what he says, but probably those epithets would be fairly applicable to the change that would be produced in our lives if we obeyed his counsels. There is a close connection between verse and verse in this section (vers. 1—6), but a formal division of it into logical parts is impracticable. The Hebrew or Oriental mind had a different mode of ratiocination from ours. We may, however, note the stages in the current of thought.

I. In vers. 1, 2a THE PRACTICE OF BENEVOLENCE TOWARD OTHERS is commended to us—a benevolence that is generous and profuse. "Cast thy bread," he says, "upon the waters." "Do not be afraid of showing kindness, even where thou seest no prospect of result or return; let the flat cake of bread, the type of food to the hungry, aid to the needy, float down the stream of life. Thou wilt find one day that thou hast hit the mark, won some grateful heart" (Bradley). His words remind us of the counsel in the Gospels "to do good, hoping for nothing again, even to the unthankful and the evil" (Matt. v. 44—46; Luke vi. 32—35).

> " Répandez vos bienfaits avec magnificence,
>   Même aux moins vertueux ne les refusez pas."
>   (Voltaire, 'Précis de l'Ecclesiaste.')

Let many experience your beneficence, says the Preacher; confine it not within narrow limits. He speaks of seven or eight, according to the Hebrew manner of indicating an indefinite but large number (Micah v. 5). His specification is not to be taken literally, any more than our Lord's "seventy times seven" as indicating the literal number of times we are to forgive (Matt. xviii. 22).

II. A MOTIVE TO BENEFICENCE is laid down in ver. 2b. "For thou knowest not what evil shall be upon the earth." In the time of prosperity remember that a day of calamity and suffering may come, when the succour of the friends you have made may be of great service. Bad as men are, there are numerous instances of a grateful love recompensing benefits received long ago, which perhaps even the benefactor has long forgotten. "Peradventure for the good man some would even dare to die." No one can tell what vicissitudes of fortune are in store for him; and therefore it is prudent to make some provision in the present against a day of adversity. The same teaching is found in the parable of the unjust steward (Luke xvi. 1—9). Those who spend some of their wealth in doing deeds of kindness and mercy (Luke xiv. 12—14) are described as laying up treasure in bags that wax not old, as providing for themselves friends who will, when this life is over, welcome them into everlasting habitations. To some this may seem but a sordid motive to benevolence; it may seem to turn that virtue into a kind of refined selfishness. But, after all, there is nothing unworthy in the motive. "Self-love is implanted in man's nature, and men who themselves affect to despise such a motive are often themselves, with all their professed loftiness of aim, actuated by no higher objects than those of pleasure, fame, or advancement" (Wright).

III. OUR IGNORANCE OF THE FUTURE FORBIDS OUR KNOWING WHAT EVIL WILL COME UPON THE EARTH. (Ver. 2b.) The world is governed by uniform laws; both good and evil are subject to them. As it is an invariable law of nature that at a certain point the clouds that are filled with rain begin to discharge their load upon the earth, and no human power can seal them up, and as it is an invincible law that the forest tree must fall before the blast, when the force with which it resists the fury of the wind is insufficient to save it from overthrow, so the future is shaped by laws which man cannot control, and it is a mark of prudence to be prepared for any contingencies. The tempest which deluges the earth with rain, and levels the monarchs of the forest with the ground, can neither be foreseen nor averted by man; neither can the future, whether it be charged with prosperity or adversity. The interpretation of ver. 3 as teaching that the fate of man is for ever fixed at death is utterly indefensible; there is nothing whatever in the text to indicate that the writer had any such thought in his mind. And one may say, in passing, that the teaching in question can have very little foundation, when it is principally, if not altogether, founded upon a misinterpretation of this passage. Why the advocates of the doctrine, which in itself is repulsive to our ideas of reasonableness and justice, should make so much of an obscure metaphor in the Book of Ecclesiastes, and shut their eyes to the historical statement in 1 Pet. iii. 18—20, which is decisive upon the point in question, is difficult to understand. No outcry about the obscurity of the latter passage can annul the plain statement of fact in it, viz. that Christ after his death went and preached the gospel to the spirits of those who were overtaken by the flood in the days of Noah. Uncertainty as to the future should not, however, lead to present inactivity (ver. 5). We are not to allow "taking thought for the morrow" (Matt. vi. 25) to hinder our doing good to-day; that would be as absurd as the conduct of the farmer if he were to put off from day to day the sowing or reaping of his fields because of wind or rain, until the time for sowing or for reaping had passed away. Some risk we must run in our undertakings; and if some opportunities come to us without any seeking or effort on our part, we can make others for ourselves by the exercise of our good sense, energy, or tact. "The conditions of success cannot be reckoned on beforehand; the future belongs to God, the all-conditioning" (Delitzsch). This is the idea contained in ver. 5. Two examples are given of processes of nature which are familiar to us all, but the ways and working of which are hidden from our knowledge; they are the course of the wind (not the "spirit," as in the Authorized Version), which "bloweth where it listeth" (John iii. 8), and the formation of the babe "in the womb of her who is with child." These secrets being in nature, it is not wonderful that the methods of the Divine government cannot be searched out by human wisdom or ingenuity, that the ways of God should be inscrutable and past finding out. "Even so thou knowest not the works of God who maketh all."

IV. THE CALL TO BENEFICENT ACTIVITY IS REPEATED. (Ver. 6.) "Since the future rests in the power of One who arranges all things, but who does not act arbitrarily, and since a finite being cannot unravel the secrets of the Infinite, man should act faithfully and fulfil energetically his appointed task" (Wright). The teaching is the same as in ch. ix. 10, "Whatsoever thy hand findeth to do, do it with thy might;" "In the morning sow thy seed, and in the evening withhold not thine hand: for thou knowest not whether shall prosper, either this or that, or whether they both shall be alike good" (ver. 6). "In the morning of life be active; slumber not through its decline. Use well the gifts of youth; use, too, the special gifts of age. Thou knowest not which shall bear good fruit; it may be both." As men sow, they reap; the greater their exertions, the wider the area they cultivate, the richer usually is their harvest. The whole precept, says Plumptre, "is a call to activity in good, not unlike that of him who said, 'I must work the works of him that sent me, while it is called to-day: the night cometh, when no man can work' (John ix. 4); who taught men to labour in the vineyard, even though they were not called to begin their work till the eleventh hour, when it was toward evening, and the day far spent (Matt. xx. 1—16)."—J. W.

Vers. 7, 8.—*Enjoyment of the present.* The cloud of pessimism rises from the Preacher's mind as he thinks of the happiness which a well-ordered life may after all yield. God has placed some pleasures within our reach, and if we do not by our wilfulness defeat his purpose, we may enjoy much innocent peace and happiness. And this assertion, coming so closely as it does upon the admonition to be diligent in carrying out the business that we have to do, implies that it is the well-earned reward of the worker, and not the ease and luxury of the idle sensualist, that wins the word of approval. "This joy of life, based upon fidelity to one's vocation, and sanctified by the fear of God, is the truest and highest enjoyment here below" (Delitzsch). Only those have a right to enjoy life who are zealous in the discharge of the duties that belong to their lot. The order of thought is the same as in Rom. xii. 11, 12, "In diligence not slothful . . . rejoicing in hope." The Revised Version (in ver. 8) brings out the full meaning more clearly than the Authorized Version: "Truly the light is sweet, and a pleasant thing it is for the eyes to behold the sun. Yea, if a man live many years, let him rejoice in them all; but let him remember the days of darkness, for they shall be many.   All that cometh is vanity."   The light here praised is the light of life; the existence passed in the world on which the sun shines, as contrasted with the darkness of the grave, the unseen world, which to the mind of the Preacher, unillumined by the full revelation in Christ, seemed a region of shadows, dreary and insubstantial. To our thoughts such a view of the world beyond the grave, if world it could be called, in which all was dark and without any order (Job x. 21, 22), would seem calculated to rob the present of all delights.   But evidently our author did not regard it as necessarily doing so.   Neither did those ancient Egyptians, who had the representation of a corpse in its cerements at their banquets.   To grosser minds among them the sight probably suggested the thought, "Let us eat and drink; for to-morrow we die."   But doubtless to graver minds it suggested something nobler—that pleasure, chastened and restrained by wise foresight, is pure and more lasting than any other.   So, too, the enjoyment of life commended by the Preacher is not found by him incompatible with a contemplation of death.   He does not say, "Let the young and thoughtless have out their time of frivolity and short-lived mirth; the sad thoughts by which the closing years of life are naturally darkened will only come to them too soon."   He rather would have men to rejoice in all the years of their life, though they be many.   "Days of evil may come; clouds may, during long hours of sorrow, obscure the glory of the sun; but even if a man live many days, he should endeavour to rejoice in them all: and all the more so, if a long night of darkness awaits him at the close of his earthly career" (Wright).   By the days of darkness, which are many, he evidently means the condition after death; for he distinctly differentiates them from the days of life, in all of which there should be joy, in spite of passing trials and distresses.   For all men days of darkness are in store; let all, therefore, make the most of the present, and by a wise guidance of their conduct, by a beneficent activity, let them acquire the right and the ability to enjoy the innocent joys with which God has been pleased to bless and enrich our lives, seeing that "all that cometh" after life is vanity.   It is true that to us the world beyond the grave appears in a different light.   We believe in the everlasting felicity of the righteous in the "many mansions" which remain for those who have during this life been faithful to God, and have qualified themselves for higher service and more perfect enjoyment of him in the world to come.   But this belief need not, should not, lead us to despise the bounties we have in this world from the hand of God.   A devout and grateful acceptance and use of all the blessings he has bestowed upon us, a joy in living and seeing the light of the sun, should be much easier to us if we are conscious of reconciliation to God, and regard death as the entrance to a higher life.—J. W.

Ver. 9—ch. xii. 7.—*Youth and age.*   The greater part of the Book of Ecclesiastes is of a sombre character.   It records the experiences of one who sought on all sides and with passionate eagerness for that which would satisfy the higher wants of his nature —the hunger and thirst of the soul—but who sought in vain.   Ordinary coarse, sensual pleasures soon lost their charm for him; for he deliberately tried—a dangerous experiment—to see if in self-indulgence any real satisfaction could be found.   From this failure he turned to a more promising quarter.   He sought in "culture," the pursuit of beauty and magnificence in art, the pathway to the highest good, on the discovery of which his soul was set.   He used his great wealth to procure all that could minister to a refined taste.   He built palaces, planted vineyards and gardens and orchards; he filled his palaces with all that was beautiful and costly, and cultivated every pleasure which is within the reach of man.   "Whatsoever mine eyes desired," he says, "I kept not from them, I withheld not my heart from any joy. . . . Then I looked on all the works that my hands had wrought, and on all the labour that I had laboured to do: and, behold, all was vanity and vexation of spirit, and there was no profit under the sun." From this he turned to the joys and employments of an intellectual life—acquired knowledge and wisdom, studied the works of nature, analyzed human character in all its phases, and applied himself to the solution of all those great problems connected with the moral government of the world and the destiny of the soul of man.   Here he was baffled.   The discoveries he made were, he found, useless for curing any of the evils of life, and at every point he met with mysteries which he could not solve, and his sense of failure and defeat convinced him that though "wisdom excelleth folly, as far as light excelleth darkness," it does not satisfy the soul. "What, then, is the result of his inquiries, of his pain and labour in searching after the highest good? Do his withering speculations leave anything untouched which may reasonably be the object of our pursuit, and which may afford us the satisfaction for which he sought in vain in so many quarters? Does he decide that life is, after all, worth living, or is his conclusion that it is not? In the closing sections of his book some answer is given to these questions; something positive comes as a pleasing relief from all the negations with which he had shut up one after another of the paths by which men had sought and still seek to attain to lasting happiness. Two conclusions might have been drawn from the experience through which he had passed. "Since the employments and enjoyments of life are insufficient to give satisfaction to the soul's craving, why engage in them, why not turn away from them in contempt, and fix the thoughts solely on a life to come?" an ascetic might ask. "Since life is so transitory, pleasure so fleeting, why not seize upon every pleasure, and banish every care as far as possible?" an Epicurean might ask. "Let us eat and drink; for to-morrow we die." Neither of these courses finds any favour in the mature judgment of Solomon, or of the writer who draws his teaching from the experience of the Jewish king. "Rejoice," he says, rebuking the ascetic; "know thou that for all these things God will bring thee into judgment," he adds, for the confusion of the Epicurean. He speaks with the authority of one who had fully considered the problems of life, and with the solemnity of one whose earthly career was hastening to its close; and he addresses himself to the young, as more likely to profit by his experience than those over whom habits of life and thought have more power. But of course all, both young and old, men and women, can learn from him if they will, according to the gospel precept, "become as little children," and listen with reverence and simplicity. The counsel which the Preacher has to give is bold and startling. "Rejoice, O young man, in thy youth; and let thy heart cheer thee in the days of thy youth, and walk in the ways of thine heart, and in the sight of thine eyes: but know thou, that for all these things God will bring thee into judgment." What does he mean? Are his words ironical, or spoken in sober earnest? A very long time ago they caused some perplexity to translators and commentators. In the earliest translation of this book into another language, that into Greek, this passage was considerably modified and toned down. The translator put in the word "blameless" after "walk," and the word "not" into the next part of the sentence. "Walk *blameless* in the ways of thine heart, and *not* after the sight of thine eyes." But any such tampering with the text was not only profane, but also senseless, for it simply destroyed the whole meaning of the passage. But granting that we have in our English a fair reproduction of the original, can there be any mistake about the interpretation of it? Is it possible that it may mean, "Rejoice if you will, follow your desires, have your fling, go forth on the voyage of life, 'youth at the prow, and pleasure at the helm,' but know that the end of it all are the penal flames"? Some have thought that that is the meaning of the words. But a little consideration of them, and comparison of them with other passages in the book, will show us that it cannot be. Our author on several occasions, after showing us the vanity of earthly pursuits, falls back on the fact that there are many alleviations of our lot in life, which it is true wisdom to make use of—many flowers of pleasure on the side of the hard road which one may innocently pluck. Thus he says (ch. ii. 24), "There is nothing better for a man, than that he should eat and drink, and that he should make his soul enjoy good in his labour. This also I saw that it was from the hand of God." And again (ch. ix. 7), "Go thy way, eat thy bread with joy, and drink thy wine with a merry heart; for God now accepteth thy works. Let thy garments be always white; and let thy head lack no ointment. Live joyfully with the wife whom thou lovest all the days of thy vanity . . . for that is thy portion in this life." And the same lesson he repeats there, but in a tone of deeper solemnity, balancing and steadying the inclination to pleasure, which in few of us needs to be stimulated, with the thought that for every one of our actions we shall have to give an account at the judgment-seat of God. Surely this thought is a sufficient corrective to the abuse of the teaching which a perverse mind might make, and a proof that the enjoyments spoken of are such as do not degrade the soul. A gloomy asceticism which would unlawfully diminish human happiness is forbidden; a thankful acceptance of all the blessings God gives us, and a constant remembrance of our responsibility to him, is commended to us. With all the repugnance of a healthy mind, our author recoils from that narrow and self-righteous fanaticism which has done so much to deepen the gloom of life, and to turn religion into an oppressive yoke. He does not, however, go to the other extreme; but while he bids the young to enjoy the morning of life, he at the same time admonishes them in all things to have the fear of God before their eyes. Youth and manhood are vanity; their joys are fleeting, and will soon be past. Must we, therefore, neglect them, and indulge in equally vain and fleeting regrets? No; but rather put away all morose repining, and spare ourselves all unnecessary pain, and cultivate a cheerful contentedness with our lot. If the morning will soon be past, let us enjoy its light while it lasts, mindful of him who is the Giver of every good and perfect gift. The thought of him will not dull any innocent happiness, for he has made us capable of joy, and given us occasions of experiencing it. That no fears need be felt about the application of this teaching to actual life is abundantly proved by the words that follow, in the solemn and stately passage with which the twelfth chapter opens. The idea all through is that piety should be bound up with the whole life—with the buoyancy and gaiety of youth, as well as with the decaying hopes and failing strength of age. That religion is not merely a consolation to which we may betake when all other things fail, but all through the food by which the soul is nourished. The fact is put very strongly. If in youth God is not remembered, it will be difficult in age, when the faculties begin to lose their vigour, to think of him for the first time, and consecrate one's self to him. The mere accumulation of the weaknesses, both physical and mental, which attend the close of life will absorb the attention and crowd out other thoughts. "Remember now thy Creator in the days of thy youth, while the evil days come not, nor the years draw nigh, when thou shalt say, I have no pleasure in them." And then he goes on to draw a picture, full of pathos and solemnity, of the gradual dissolution of human life with the advance of age, of the decay and death into which the strongest fall, even if they endure for many years. One cannot make out all the successive images with equal clearness, but the evident purpose of the whole passage is clear enough. In the evil days the light of the sun, moon, and stars is darkened, and the sky is time after time overcast with returning clouds. The light of youth has fled, and with it the self-confidence and strength by which the life was sustained. Like some household in Egypt when the plague of darkness came down upon it and put an end to all tasks and pleasures, and filled every heart with a paralyzing terror, so is the state of man "perplexed with fear of change." "The keepers of the house tremble, the strong men bow themselves, the terrified servants cease their labour, none look out of the windows, the street doors are shut, the sound of human bustle and activity dies away, the shrill cry of the storm-bird is heard without, and all the daughters of music are hushed and silent." And then, in language still more enigmatical, other of the humiliating characteristics of old age are set forth—its timidity and irresolution, the blanched hair, the failing appetite. These signs accumulate rapidly; for man goes to his long, his eternal home, and the procession of mourners is already moving along the street. "Remember," he says, "thy Creator ere the day of death; ere the silver cord be loosened which lets fall and shivers the golden bowl that feeds with oil the flame of life; ere the pitcher be shattered by the spring, and the fountain of life can no longer be replenished; ere the wheel set up with care to draw up from the depths of earth the cool waters give way and fall itself into the well. Therefore remember thy God, and prepare while here to meet him, before that the dust shall return upon the earth dust as it was; for the spirit shall then return to God who gave it." "It was a gift from him, that spirit. To him it will return. More he says not. Its absorption, the re-entering of the human unit into the eternal and unknown Spirit, would be a thought, it would seem, alien to a Hebrew. But we must not press his words too far. As just now he spoke of a judgment, but gave us no picture of the sheep on the right hand and the goats on the left, so here he has no more to say, no clear and dogmatic assertion of a conscious and separate future life. '*Into thy hands I commend my spirit,*' said the trustful psalmist. 'Father, into thy hands I commend my spirit,' said he who bowed his head upon the cross, who tasted death for our sakes. Our Preacher leaves the spirit with its God—that is all, and that is much. 'God will call us to judgment,' he has said, and now he adds, 'The body moulders, the spirit passes back to the God who gave it'" (Bradley). Many are the reasons which might be adduced to give weight to the admonition, " Remember now thy Creator in the days of thy youth.   The uncertainty of life, *e.g.*, renders it unwise in any who begin to realize their responsibilities, and to act for themselves, to postpone self-consecration to God.   If not done now, when the affections are fresh, when habits are beginning to form, there is risk of its not being done at all.   Certainly it is more difficult to make a change, and to enter upon the higher life when the heart is taken up with a love of other things, when the attention and interest are absorbed in other cares.   Then, too, love of our Creator and service of him are due from us in the best of our days, in the time of our strength and energy, and not merely when we are weary and worn out with following our own devices, and are anxious merely to escape utter ruin and overthrow.   True it is that the repentant prodigal is welcomed when he returns to his Father's house; the worker beginning even at the eleventh hour receives his wages as though he had been the whole day in the vineyard. But their sense of gratitude, wonder, and awe at the love which has overlooked their faults and shortcomings is the source of a joy far inferior to that of those who have never wandered, who have served faithfully with all the strength and all the day, upon whom the sunshine of God's favour has ever rested.   Another and final reason why it is wise to remember our Creator in the days of youth is that this is the secret of a happy life.   The happiness which is disturbed by remembrance of God is not worth the name.   That alone gives satisfaction—the satisfaction after which the Preacher sought so long and in so many quarters—which springs from communion with God.   It alone is intense, it alone is lasting.   Arising as it does from the relations of the spirit of man with him who created it, it is raised above all the accidents of time and change. The sooner, therefore, that we begin this life of holy communion and service, the longer period of happiness shall we know, the surer will be our ground of confidence for the future, when the day comes for leaving the world.   " Over against the melancholy circumstances of decay and decline, as the end of life draws on, will be set the bright memories of the past, the consciousness of present help, and the hope of a joyous immortality.   "Vanity of vanities; all is vanity ! " was the sentence of one whose wisdom sprang only from his experience of an earthly life, and upon whose mind the burden lay of human sorrows and cares.   But "a greater than Solomon," One whose wisdom is Divine, whose power to remove every burden is daily seen, has an infinitely more hopeful message for us. " Let not your heart be troubled : ye believe in God, believe also in me.   In my Father's house are many mansions : if it were not so, I would have told you.   I go to prepare a place for you. . . . I will come again, and receive you unto myself; that where I am, there ye may be also."—J. W.

EXPOSITION.

CHAPTER XII.

Ver. 1.—The division into chapters is unfortunate here, as this verse is closely connected with ver. 10 of the preceding chapter.   **Remember now thy Creator in the days of thy youth.**   Set God always before thine eyes from thy earliest days; think who made thee, and what thou wast made for, not for self-pleasing only, not to gratify thy passions which now are strong, but that thou mightest use thy powers and energy in accordance with the laws of thy being as a creature of God's hands, responsible to him for the use of the faculties and capacities with which he has endowed thee.   The word for " Creator " is the participle of the verb *bara*, which is that used in Gen. i. 1, etc., describing God's work.   It is plural in form, like *Elohim*, the plural being that of majesty or excellence (comp. Job xxxv. 10; Isa liv. 5).   It is used here as an appellation of God, because the young have to bethink themselves that all they are and all they have come from God.   Such plurals are supposed by some to be divinely intended to adumbrate the doctrine of the Holy Trinity—a dark saying containing a mystery which future revelation should explain.   " He that made thee " is a common phrase in Ecclesiasticus (see iv. 6; vii. 30; xxxix. 5).   It is to be noted that Grätz reads " cistern " or "fountain " in place of " Creator," and explains this term to mean " wife," as in Prov. v. 15—18. But the alteration has nothing to support it, and is most unnecessary, though Cheyne seems inclined to adopt it ('Job and Solomon,' *in loc.*). **While the evil days come not;** *i.e.* before they come.   " Days of evil;" αἱ ἡμέραι τῆς κακίας (Septuagint) (Matt. vi. 34); *tempus afflictionis* (Vulgate).   The phrase refers to the grievances and inconveniences of old age, which are further and graphically described in the following verses, though whether the expressions therein used regard literal anatomical facts, or are allegorical representations of the gradual decay of the faculties, has been greatly disputed. Probably both opinions contain a partial truth, as will be noted in our Exposition. Ginsburg considers that the allusion is not to the ills that in the course of time all flesh is heir to, but rather to that premature decay and suffering occasioned by the unrestrained gratification of sensual passions, such as Cicero intimates ('De Senect.,' ix. 29), "Libidinosa et intemperans adulescentia effetum corpus tradit senectuti." There is nothing specially in the text to support this view, and it is most reasonable to see here generally a figurative description of decay, whatever may be the cause. **I have no pleasure in them.** Ere the time comes when a man shall say, "I have no pleasure in life." Thus the aged Barzillai asks, "Can I discern between good and evil? Can thy servant taste what I eat or what I drink? Can I hear any more the voice of singing-men and singing-women?" (2 Sam. xix. 35).

Ver. 2.—From this verse onwards there is great diversity of interpretation. While some think that the approach of death is represented under the image of a storm, others deem that what is here intended is first the debility of old age, and then, at ver. 6, death itself, which two stages are described under various metaphors and figures. **While the sun, or the light, or the moon, or the stars, be not darkened.** Under these figures the evil days spoken of above, the advent and infirmities of old age, are represented. It would be endless and unprofitable to recount the explanations of the terms used in the following verses. Every commentator, ancient and modern, has exerted his ingenuity to force the poet's language into the shape which he has imagined for it. But, as we said above, there are at least two distinct lines of interpretation which have found favour with the great majority of expositors. One of these regards the imagery as applicable to the effects of a heavy storm upon a house and its inmates, explaining every detail under this notion; the other regards the terms used as referring to the man himself, adumbrating the gradual decay of old age, the various members and powers that are affected being represented under tropes and images. Both interpretations are beset with difficulties, and are only with some straining and accommodation forced into a consistent harmony. But the latter seems to us to present fewer perplexities than the other, and we have adopted it here. At the same time, we think it expedient to give the other view, together with our own, as there is much to

be said in its favour, and many great writers have declared themselves on its side. Wright supposes (and makes a good case for his theory) that Koheleth is referring especially to the closing days of winter, which in Palestine are very fatal to old people. The seven last days, indeed, are noted even now as the most sickly and dangerous of all the year. The approach of this period casts a dark shadow upon all the inhabitants of the house. The theory is partly borne out by the text, but, like the other solutions, does not wholly correspond to the wording. In the present verse the approach of old age, the winter of life, is likened to the rainy season in Palestine, when the sun is obscured by clouds, and the light of heaven darkened by the withdrawal of that luminary, and neither moon nor stars appear. And **the clouds return after the rain;** i.e. one storm succeeds another (Job xxxvii. 6). The imagery is intended to represent the abiding and increasing inconveniences of old age. Not like the spring-time of life and season, when sunshine and storm are interchanged, winter and old age have no vicissitudes, one dreary character invests them both. The darkening of the light is a common metaphor for sorrow and sadness (see Job xxx. 26; xxxiii. 28, 30; Ezek. xxxii. 7, 8; Amos viii. 9). The symbolism of the details in this verse has been thus elucidated: The diurnal lights appertain to the soul, the nocturnal to the body; the sun is the Divine light which illumines the soul, the moon and the stars are the body and the senses which receive their radiance from the soul's effulgence. These are all affected by the invasion of old age. Some consider that this verse depicts the changes which pass over the higher and more spiritual part of man's nature, while the succeeding imagery refers to the breaking-up of the corporeal frame. We should say rather that ver. 2 conveys a general impression, and that this is then elaborated into particulars. According to the interpretation mentioned above, a gathering tempest is here depicted, the details of which are worked out in the following verses.

Ver. 3.—The gradual decay which creeps over the body, the habitation of the spirit, is depicted under the figure of a house and its parts (comp. Job iv. 19; 2 Cor. v. 1; 2 Pet. i. 13, 14). **In the day when the keepers of the house shall tremble;** i.e. this is the case when, etc. The hands and arms are appropriately called the keepers of the house, for with them (as Volck quotes from Galen) man ὁπλίζει καὶ φρουρεῖ τὸ σῶμα παντοίως ("arms and guards his body in various ways"). The shaking and palsy of old men's limbs are thus graphically described. This would be one of the first symptoms discerned by an observer. Taking the alternative interpretation, we should see in these "keepers" the menservants who keep watch before the house. These menials are appalled by the approach of the tempest, and quake. **And the strong men shall bow themselves.** The " men of power " are the legs, or the bones generally, which in the young are " as pillars of marble" (Cant. v. 15), but in the old become feeble, slack, and bent. Delitzsch quotes 3 Macc. iv. 5, where we read of a multitude of old men being driven mercilessly, "stooping from age, and dragging their feet heavily along." In this clause it is this stooping and bending of the body that is noticed, when men are no longer upright in stature, "swifter than eagles," " stronger than lions " (2 Sam. i. 23; 1 Chron. xii. 8), fit for war and active employment. It is therefore less appropriate to see in the " keepers" the legs, and in the "strong men" the arms. Otherwise, the latter are the masters, the wealthy and noble, in contradistinction to the menials before mentioned : both lords and servants are equally terrified at the approach of the tempest, or, as Wright would say, at the touch of the sickly season (see on ver. 2). **And the grinders cease because they are few.** The word for " grinders " is feminine (αἱ ἀλήθουσαι, "the grinding-women," Septuagint), doubtless because grinding was especially women's business (Matt. xxiv. 41). By them are meant the teeth, as we speak of *molars*, though, of course, the term here applies to all the teeth; so the Greeks used the term μύλαι for the *dentes molares*. These, becoming few in number and no longer continuous, cannot perform their office. Otherwise, the grinding-women leave their work or pause in their labours at the approach of the storm, though one does not quite see why they should be fewer than usual, unless the sickly season has prostrated most of their companions, or that many are too frightened to ply their task. Having, therefore, harder work than usual, they stop at times to recruit themselves. But the analogy rather breaks down here; one would be inclined to suppose that their decreased numbers would make them apply themselves more assiduously to their necessary occupation. As the "keepers" in the former part of the verse were slaves, so these-grinders are slaves, such occupation being the lowest form of service (see Exod. xi. 5; Judg. xvi. 21; Job xxxi. 10). **Those that look out of the windows be darkened.** These are the eyes that look forth from the cavities in which they are sunk; they are regarded as the windows of the bodily structure, the eyelashes or eyelids possibly being deemed the lattice of the same. Plumptre cites Cicero, 'De Nat. Deor.,' ii. 140 : " Sensus interpretes ac nuntii rerum, in capite, tam-

quam in arce, mirifice ad usus necessarios et facti et collocati sunt. Nam oculi, tamquam speculatores, altissimum locum obtinent ; ex quo plurima conspicientes, fungantur suo munere." The dimness in the eye and the failing in the powers of sight are well expressed by the terms of the text. It is noted of Moses, as something altogether abnormal, that at a hundred and twenty years of age " his eye was not dim, nor his natural force abated " (Deut. xxxiv. 7). Taking the alternative interpretation, we must regard those that look out of the windows as the ladies of the house, who have no menial work to do, and employ their time in gazing idly from the lattices (comp. Judg. v. 28; 2 Sam. vi. 16; Prov. vii. 6). These "are darkened," they are terror-stricken, their faces gather blackness (Joel ii. 6), or they retire into corners in terror of the storm. These women are parallel to " the strong men" mentioned above; so that the weather affects all of every class—menservants and maidservants, lords and ladies.

Ver. 4.—**The doors shall be shut in the streets.** Hitherto the symbolism has been comparatively easy to interpret. With this verse inextricable difficulties seem to arise. Of course, in one view it is natural that in the bitter weather, or on the appearance of a tempest, the doors towards the street should be closed, and none should leave the house. But what are meant by the doors in the metaphorical house, the body of the aged man? Jewish expositors understood them to be the pores, or excretive apertures of the body, which lose their activity in old age—which seems an unseemly allusion. Plumptre will have them to be the organs which carry on the processes of sensation and nutrition from the beginning to the end; but it seems a forced metaphor to call these "double-doors." More natural is it to see in the word, with its dual form, the mouth closed by the two lips. So a psalmist speaks of the mouth, the door of the lips (Ps. cxli. 3; comp. Micah vii. 5). As it is only the external door of a house that could be employed in this metaphor, the addition, " in [or, 'towards'] the streets," is accounted for. **When the sound of the grinding is low.** The sound of the grinding or the mill is weak and low when the teeth have ceased to masticate, and, instead of the crunching and grinding of food, nothing is heard but a munching and sucking. The falling in of the mouth over the toothless gums is represented as the closing of doors. To take the words in their literal sense is to make the author repeat himself, reiterating what he is supposed to have said before in speaking of the grinding-women—all labour is lessened or stopped. The sound of grinding betokened cheerfulness and prosperity; its cessation would be an ominous sign (see Jer. xxv. 10; Rev. xviii. 22). Another interpretation considers this clause to express the imperfect vocal utterance of the old man; but it is hardly likely that the author would call speech "the voice of the grinding," or of the mill, as a metaphor for "mouth." **And he shall rise up at the voice of the bird.** This is a very difficult sentence, and has been very variously explained. It is usually taken to mean that the old man sleeps lightly and awakes (for "rises up" may mean no more than that) at the chirrup of a bird. The objection to this interpretation is that it destroys the figurative character of the description, introducing suddenly the personal subject. Of course, it has another signification in the picture of the terror-stricken household; and many interpreters who thus explain the allegory translate the clause differently. Thus Ginsburg renders, "The swallow rises to shriek," referring to the habits of that bird in stormy weather. But there are grammatical objections to this translation, as there are against another suggestion, "The bird (of ill omen) raises its voice." We need not do more than refer to the mystical elucidation which detects here a reference to the resurrection, the voice of the bird being the archangel's trumpet which calls the dead from their graves. Retaining the allegory, we must translate the clause, "He [or, 'it,' *i.e.* the voice] rises to the bird's voice;" the old man's voice becomes a "childish treble," like the piping of a little bird. The relaxation of the muscles of the larynx and other vocal organs occasions a great difference in the pitch or power of tone (compare what Hezekiah says, Isa. xxxviii. 14, "Like a crane or a swallow so did I chatter," though there it is the low murmur of sorrow and complaint that is meant). **And all the daughters of music shall be brought low.** "The daughters of song" are the organs of speech, which are now humbled and fail, so that the man cannot sing a note. Some think that the ears are meant, as St. Jerome writes, *Et obsurdescent omnes filix carminis,* which may have some such notion. Others arrive at a similar signification from manipulation of the verb, thus eliciting the sense—The sounds of singing-women or song-birds are dulled and lowered, are only heard as a faint, unmeaning murmur. This exposition rather contradicts what had preceded, viz. that the old man is awoke by the chirrup of a sparrow; for his ears must be very sensitive to be thus easily affected; unless, indeed, the "voice of the bird" is merely a note of time, equivalent to early cock-crowing. We must not omit Wright's explanation, though it does not commend itself to our mind. He

makes a new stanza begin here: "When one rises at the voice of the bird," and sees here a description of the approach of spring, as if the poet said, "When the young and lusty are enjoying the return of genial weather, and the concert of birds with which no musician can compete, the aged, sick in their chambers, are beset with fears and are sinking fast." We fail altogether to read this meaning in our text, wherein we recognize only a symbolical representation of the old man's vocal powers. It is obvious to cite Juvenal's minute and painful description of old age in 'Sat.,' x. 200, etc., and Shakespeare's lines in 'As You Like It' (act ii. sc. 7), where the reference to the voice is very striking—

"His big, manly voice,
Turning again toward childish treble, pipes
And whistles in his sound."

Cox paraphrases, "The song-birds drop silently into their nests," alarmed at the tempest.

Ver. 5.—**Also** when **they shall be afraid of** that which is **high.** There is no "when" in the original, which runs, "Also, or yea, they fear on high." "They" are old men, or, like the French *on*, "people" indefinitely; and the clause says that they find difficulty in mounting an ascent, as the Vulgate renders, *Excelsa quoque timebant.* Shortness of breath, asthmatic tendencies, failure of muscular power, make such an exertion arduous and burdensome, just as in the previous verse a similar cause rendered singing impossible. The description is now arriving at the last stage, and allegorizing the closing scene. The steep ascent is the *via dolorosa,* the painful process of dying, from which the natural man shrinks; for as the gnome says—

Τοῦ ζῆν γὰρ οὐδεὶς ὡς ὁ γηράσκων ἐρᾷ.

"None dotes on life more than the aged man."

The old man is going on the appointed road, **and fears** shall be **in the way;** or, *all sorts of fears* (plural of intensity) *are in the path;* as in his infirm condition he can walk nowhere without danger of meeting with some accident, so analogously, as he contemplates his end and the road he has to travel, "fearfulness and trembling come upon him, and horror overwhelms him" (Ps. lv. 5). Plumptre sees in these clauses a further adumbration of the inconveniences of old age, how that the decrepit man makes mountains of mole-hills, is full of imaginary terrors, always forecasting sad events, and so on; but this does not carry on the picture to the end which the poet has now in view, and seems tame and commonplace. The supporters of the storm-theory explain the passage as denoting the fears of the people at what is coming from on high—the gathering tempest, these fears extending to those on the highway,—which is feeble. **And the almond tree shall flourish;** or, *is in blossom.* The old man is thus figured from the observed aspect of this tree. It blossoms in winter upon a leafless stem, and its flowers, at first of a pale pink colour, turn to a snowy whiteness as they fall from the branches. The tree thus becomes a fit type of the arid, torpid-looking old man with his white hair. So Wright quotes Virgil, ' Æneid,' v. 416—

" Temporibus geminis canebat sparsa senectus ; "

though there the idea is rather of mingled black and grey hair than of a head of snowy whiteness. Canon Tristram ('Nat. Hist. of the Bible,' p. 332), referring to the usual version of this clause, adds, " But the better interpretation seems to be, that as the almond blossom ushers in the spring, so do the signs referred to in the context indicate the *hastening* (*shaked*, 'almond,' meaning also 'hasten') of old age and death." Plumptre adopts the notion that the name of the tree is derived from a stem meaning " to watch," and that thus it may be called *the early-waking tree* (see Jer. i. 11), the enigmatic phrase describing the wakefulness that often attends old age. But this seems a refinement by no means justified by the use of the word. Others find in the verb the signification " to disdain, loathe," and explain that the old man has lost his taste for almond nuts, which seems to be an unnecessary observation after the previous allusions to his toothless condition, the cracking and eating of such things requiring the grinders to be in perfect order. The versions are unanimous in translating the clause as the Authorized Version. Thus the Septuagint, ἀνθήσῃ τὸ ἀμύγδαλον : Vulgate, *fiorebit amygdalus.* (So Venet. and the Syriac.) Wright takes this clause and the next to indicate the opening of spring, when nature reawakens from its winter sleep, and the dying man can no longer respond to the call or enjoy the happy season. The expositors who adhere to the notion of the storm would translate, " the almond shall be rejected," alluding to fear taking away appetite ; but the rendering is faulty. **And the grasshopper shall be a burden.** *Chagab*, rendered " grasshopper" here and Lev. xi. 22; Numb. xiii. 33, etc., is rightly translated " locust" in 2 Chron. vii. 13. It is one of the smaller species of the insect, as is implied by its use in Isa. xl. 22, where from the height of heaven the inhabitants of earth are regarded as *chagabim.* The clause is usually explained to mean that the very lightest burden is troublesome to old age, or that the hopping and chirping of

these insects annoy the querulous senior. But who does not see the incongruity of expressing the disinclination for labour and exertion by the figure of finding a grasshopper too heavy to carry? Who would think of carrying a grasshopper? Plumptre, who discovers Greek allusions in the most unlikely places, sees here an intimation of the writer's acquaintance with the Athenians' custom of wearing a golden grasshopper on their heads as a token that they were *autochthones*, " sprung from the soil." Few will be disposed to concur with this opinion. Ginsburg and others consider that Koheleth is regarding the locust as an article of food, which it was and still is in the East (Lev. xi. 21, 22; Matt. iii. 4). In some places it is esteemed a great delicacy, and is cooked and prepared in a variety of ways. So here the writer is supposed to mean that dainties shall tempt in vain; even the much-esteemed locust shall be loathed. But we cannot imagine this article of food, which indeed was neither general nor at all seasons procurable, being singled out as an appetizing esculent. The solution of the enigma must be sought elsewhere. The Septuagint gives, καὶ παχυνθῇ ἡ ἀκρίς : the Vulgate, *impinguabitur locusta,* " the locust grows fat." Founded on this rendering is the opinion which considers that under this figure is depicted the corpulence or dropsical swelling that sometimes accompanies advanced life. But this morbid and abnormal condition could not be introduced into a typical description of the usual accompaniments of age, even if the verb could be rightly translated as the Greek and Latin versions give it, which is more than doubtful. Delitzsch, after some Jewish interpreters, considers that under the term " locust" is meant the *coxa,* the loins or hips, or *caput femoris,* which is thus named " because it includes in itself the mechanism which the two-membered foot for springing, placed at an acute angle, presents in the locust." The poet is thought to allude to the loss of elasticity in the hips and the inability to bear any weight. We cannot agree to the propriety of this artificial explanation, which seems to have been invented to account for the expressions in the text, rather than to be founded on fact. But though we reject this elucidation of the figure, we think Delitzsch and some others are right in taking the verb in the sense of " to move heavily," " to crawl along." " The locust crawls," *i.e.* the old man drags his limbs heavily and painfully along, like the locust just hatched in early spring, and as yet not furnished with wings, which makes its way clumsily and slowly. The analogy derives another feature from the fact, well attested, that the appearance of the locust was synchronous with the days considered most fatal to old people, namely, the seven at the end of January and the beginning of February. So we now have the figure of the old man with his snow-white hair, panting and gasping, creeping painfully to his grave. One more *trait* is added. **And desire shall fail.** The word rendered "desire" (אֲבִיּוֹנָה) is found nowhere else in the Old Testament, and its meaning is disputed. The Authorized Version has adopted the rendering of some of the Jewish commentators (and that of Venet., ἡ ὄρεξις), but, according to Delitzsch, the feminine form of the noun precludes the notion of an abstract quality, and the etymology on which it rests is doubtful. Nor would it be likely that, having employed symbolism hitherto throughout his description, the writer would suddenly drop metaphor and speak in unfigurative language. We are, therefore, driven to rely for its meaning on the old versions, which would convey the traditional idea. The Septuagint gives, ἡ κάππαρις, and so the Vulgate, *capparis*, by which is designated the caper tree or berry, probably the same as the hyssop, which is found throughout the East, and was extensively used as a provocative of appetite, a stimulant and restorative. Accordingly, the writer is thought here to be intimating that even stimulants, such as the caper, affect the old man no longer, cannot give zest to or make him enjoy his food. Here, again, the figurative is dropped, and a literal, unvarnished fact is stated, which mars the perfection of the picture. But the verb here used (*parar*) is capable of another signification, and is often found in the unmetaphorical sense of "breaking" or "bursting;" so the clause will run, "and the caper berry bursts." Septuagint, καὶ διασκεδασθῇ ἡ κάππαρις: Vulgate, *dissipabitur capparis.* The fruit of this plant, when overripe, bursts open and falls off—a fit image of the dissolution of the aged frame, now ripe for the tomb, and showing evident tokens of decay. By this interpretation the symbolism is maintained, which perhaps is further illustrated by the fact that the fruit hangs down and droops from the end of long stalks, as the man bows his head and stoops his back to meet the coming death. **Because** (*ki*) **man goeth to his long home.** This and the following clause are parenthetical, ver. 6 resuming the allegory. It is as though Koheleth said—Such is the way, such are the symptoms, when decay and death are approaching; all these things happen, all these signs meet the eye, at such a period. "His long home;" εἰς οἶκον αἰῶνος αὐτοῦ (Septuagint), "to the house of his eternity," "his everlasting habitation," *i.e.* the grave, or Hades. There is a similar expression in Tobit iii. 6, εἰς τὸν αἰώνιον τόπον, which in the Hebrew editions of that book is given as, "Gather me to my fathers, to the

house appointed for all living," with which Canon Churton (*in loc.*) compares Job x. 21; xxx. 23. So Ps. xlix. 11 (according to many versions), "Their graves are their houses for ever." The σκηναὶ αἰώνιοι of Luke xvi. 9 are a periphrasis for life in heaven. Diodorus Siculus notes that the Egyptians used the terms ἀίδιοι οἶκοι and ἡ αἰώνιος οἴκησις of Hades (i. 51; i. 93). The expression, "domus eterna," appears at Rome on tombs, as Plumptre observes, both in Christian and non-Christian inscriptions; and the Assyrians name the world or state beyond the grave "the house of eternity" ('Records of the Past,' i. 143). From the expression in the text nothing can be deduced concerning Koheleth's eschatological views. He is speaking here merely phenomenally. Men live their little span upon the earth, and then go to what in comparison of this is an eternity. Much of the difficulty about αἰώνιος, etc., would be obviated if critics would remember that the meaning of such words is conditioned by the context, that *e.g.* "everlasting" applied to a mountain and to God cannot be understood in the same sense. **And the mourners go about the streets.** This can hardly mean that the usual funeral rites have begun; for the death is not conceived as having already taken place; this is reserved for ver. 7. Nor can it, therefore, refer to the relations and friends who are sorrowing for the departed. The persons spoken of must be the mourners who are hired to play and sing at funerals (see 2 Sam. iii. 31; Jer. ix. 17; xxxiv. 5; Matt. ix. 23). These were getting ready to ply their trade, expecting hourly the old man's death. So the Romans had their *præficæ*, and persons "qui conducti plorant in funere" (Horace, 'Ars Poet.,' 431).

Ver. 6.—**Or ever;** *i.e.* before, ere (*ad asher lo*). The words recall us to vers. 1 and 2, bidding the youth make the best use of his time ere old age cuts him off. In the present paragraph the final dissolution is described under two figures. **The silver cord be loosed, or the golden bowl be broken.** This is evidently one figure, which would be made plainer by reading "and" instead of "or," the idea being that the lamp is shattered by the snapping of the cord that suspended it from the roof. But there are some difficulties in the closer explanation of the allegory. The "bowl" (*gullah*) is the reservoir of oil in a lamp (see Zech. iv. 3, 4), which supplies nourishment to the flame; when this is broken or damaged so as to be useless, the light, of course, is extinguished. The Septuagint calls it τὸ ἀνθέμιον τοῦ χρυσίου: the Vulgate, *vitta aurea,* "the golden fillet," or "flower ornament" on a column, which quite sinks the notion of a light being quenched. The "cord" is that by which the lamp is hung in a tent or a room. But of what in man are these symbols? Many fanciful interpretations have been given. The "silver cord" is the spine, the nerves generally, the tongue; the "golden bowl" is the head, the membrane of the brain, the stomach. But these anatomical details are not to be adopted; they have little to recommend them, and are incongruous with the rest of the parable. The general break-up of life is here delineated, not the progress of destruction in certain organs or parts of the human frame. The cord is what we should call the thread of life, on which hangs the body lit by the animating soul; when the connection between these is severed, the latter perishes, like a fallen lamp lying crushed on the ground. In this our view the cord is the living power which keeps the corporeal substance from falling to ruin; the bowl is the body itself thus upheld. The mention of gold and silver is introduced to denote the preciousness of man's life and nature. But the analogy must not be pressed in all possible details. It is like the parables, where, if defined and examined too closely, incongruities appear. We should be inclined to make more of the lamp and the light and the oil, which are barely inferred in the passage, and endeavour to explain what these images import. Koheleth is satisfied with the general figure which adumbrates the dissolution of the material fabric by the withdrawal of the principle of life. What is the immediate cause of this dissolution, injury, paralysis, etc., is not handled; only the rupture is noticed and its fatal result. Another image to the same effect, though pointing to a different process, is added **Or the pitcher be broken at the fountain, or** (*and*) **the wheel broken at** (*in*) **the cistern.** The picture here is a deep well or cistern with an apparatus for drawing water; this apparatus consists of a wheel or windlass with a rope upon it, to which is attached a bucket; the wheel fails, falls into the well, the bucket is dashed to pieces, and no water can be drawn. It is best to regard the two clauses as intended to convey one idea, as the two at the beginning of the verse were found to do. Some commentators, not so suitably, distinguish between the two, making the former clause say that the pitcher is broken on its road to or from the spring, and the latter that the draw-wheel gives way. The imagery points to one notion which would be weakened by being divided into two. The motion of the bucket, the winding up and down, by which water is drawn from the well, is an emblem of the movements of the heart, the organs of respiration, etc. When these cease to act, life is extinct. The fraction of the cord and the

demolition of the bowl denoted the separation of soul and body; the breaking of the pitcher and the destruction of the wheel signify the overthrow of the bodily organs by which vital motion is diffused and maintained, and the man lives. The expressions in the text remind one of the term, "earthen vessel," applied by St. Paul (2 Cor. iv. 7) to the human body; and "the fountain of life," "the water of life," so often mentioned in Holy Scripture as typical of the grace of God and the blessedness of life with him (see Ps. xxxvi. 9; Prov. xiii. 14; John iv. 10, 14; Rev. xxi. 6).

Ver. 7.—**Then shall the dust return to the earth as it was;** rather, *and the dust return*, etc.—the sentence begun above being still carried on to the end of the verse. Here we are told what becomes of the complex man at death, and are thus led to the explanation of the allegorical language used throughout. Without metaphor now it is stated that the material body, when life is extinct, returns to|that matter out of which it was originally made (Gen. ii. 7; iii. 19; comp. Job xxxiv. 15; Ps. civ. 29). So Siracides calls man "dust and ashes," and asserts that all things that are of the earth turn to the earth again (Ecclus. x. 9; xl. 11). Soph., 'Electra,' 1158—

$$\text{'Aντὶ φιλτάτης}$$
$$\text{Mορφῆς σποδόν τε καὶ σκιὰν ἀνωφελῆ.}$$

"Instead of thy dear form,
Mere dust and idle shadow."

Corn. à Lapide quotes a remarkable parallel given by Plutarch ('Apol. ad Apollon.,' 110) from Epicharmus, "Life is compounded and broken up, and again goes whence it came; earth indeed to earth, and the spirit to upper regions." **And the spirit shall return unto God who gave it;** or, *for the spirit*—the clause being no longer subjunctive, but speaking indicatively of fact. In the first clause the preposition "to" is עַל, in the second אֶל, as if to mark the distinction between the downward and the upward way. The writer now rises superior to the doubts expressed in ch. iii. 21 (where see note), "Who knoweth the spirit of man, whether it goeth upward," etc.? It is not that he contradicts himself in the two passages, as some suppose, and have hence regarded ver. 7 as an interpolation; but that after all discussion, after expressing the course of his perplexities, and the various phases of his thought, he comes to the conclusion that there is a future for the individual soul, and that it shall be brought into immediate connection with a personal God. There is here no thought of its being absorbed in the *anima mundi*, in accordance with the heathen view, which, if it believed dimly in an immortality, denied the personality of the soul (see Eurip., 'Suppl.,' 529 —534; Lucret., ii. 998, *sqq.*; iii. 455, *sqq.*). Nor have we any opinion given concerning the adverse doctrines of creationism and traducianism, though the terms used are most consistent with the former.   God breathed into man's nostrils the breath of life; when this departs, he who gave receives it; God "gathereth in" man's breath (Ps. civ. 29).   The clause, taken in this restricted sense, would say nothing about the soul, the personal "I;" it would merely indicate the destination of the vital breath; and many critics are content to see nothing more in the words.   But surely this would be a feeble conclusion of the author's wanderings; rather the sentence signifies that death, releasing the spirit, or soul, from the earthly tabernacle, places it in the more immediate presence of God, there, as the Targum paraphrases the passage, returning to stand in judgment before its Creator.

Ver. 8.—It has been much questioned whether this verse is the conclusion of the treatise or the commencement of the epilogue.   For the latter conclusion it is contended that it is only natural that the beginning of the final summing-up should start with the same words as the opening of the book (ch. i. 2); and that thus the conjunction "and," with which ver. 9 begins, is readily explained.   But the treatise is more artistically completed by regarding this solemn utterance as the conclusion of the whole, ending with the same burden with which it began—the nothingness of earthly things.   Koheleth has laboured to show this, he has pursued the thought from beginning to end, through all circumstances and conditions, and he can only re-echo his melancholy refrain.   **Vanity of vanities, saith the Preacher.**   He does not follow the destiny of the immortal spirit; it is not his purpose to do so; his theme is the fragility of mortal things, their unsatisfying nature, the impossibility of their securing man's happiness : so his voyage lands him at the point whence he set forth, though he has learned and taught faith in the interval. If all is vanity, there is behind and above all a God of inflexible justice, who must do right, and to whom we may safely trust our cares and perplexities. *Koheleth*, "Preacher," here has the article, *the Koheleth*, as if some special reference was made to the meaning of the name—he who has been debating, or haranguing, or gathering together, utters finally his careful verdict.   This is the sentence of the ideal Solomon, who has given his experiences in the preceding pages.

Vers. 9—14.—THE EPILOGUE.   This contains some observations commendatory of the author, explaining his standpoint and the object of the book, the great conclusion to which it leads.

Vers. 9—11.—Koheleth as teacher of wisdom.

Ver. 9.—**And moreover;** וְיֹתֵר; καὶ περισσόν (Septuagint); rather, with the following שׁ, *besides that.* **The Preacher was wise.** If we render "because the Preacher was wise," we are making an unnecessary statement, as the whole book has demonstrated this fact, which goes without saying.   What the writer here asserts is that Koheleth did not merely possess wisdom, but had made good use of it for the instruction of others. The author throws aside his disguise, and speaks of his object in composing the book, with a glance at the historical Solomon whom he had personated.   That he uses the third person in relation to himself is nothing uncommon in historical memoirs, etc.   Thus Daniel writes; and St. John, Thucydides, Xenophon, Cæsar, mask their personality by dropping their identity with the author (comp. also ch. i. 2; vii. 27).   The attestation that follows is compared with that at the end of St. John's Gospel (xxi. 24), and is plainly intended to confirm the authority of the writer, and to enforce on the hearer the conviction that, though Solomon himself did not compose the work, it has every claim to receive attention, and possesses intrinsic value.   **He still taught the people knowledge.**   As well as being esteemed one of the company of sages, he further (*od*) took pains to instruct his contemporaries (τὸν ἄνθρωπον, Septuagint), to apply his wisdom to educational purposes.   **Yea, he gave good heed;** literally, *he weighed* (like our word "ponder"); only thus used in this passage. It denotes the careful examination of every fact and argument before it was presented to the public.   **Sought out, and set in order many proverbs.**   There is no copula in the original; the weighing and the investigation issued in the composition of "proverbs," which term includes not only the wit and wisdom of past ages in the form of pithy sayings and apophthegms, but also parables, truths in metaphorical guise, riddles, instructions, allegories, etc., all those forms which are found in the canonical Book of Proverbs.   The same word (*mishle*) is used here as in the title of that book.   Koheleth, however, is not necessarily referring to that work (or to 1 Kings iv. 29, etc.), or implying that he himself wrote it; he is only putting forth his claim to attention by showing his patient assiduity in the pursuit of wisdom, and how that he adopted a particular method of teaching.   For the idea contained in the verb *taqan*, "to place or make straight" (ch. i. 15 vii. 13), applied to literary composition, Delitzsch compares the German word for " author" (*Schriftsteller*). The notion of the *mashal* being similitude, comparison, the writer's pondering and searching were needed to discover hidden analogies, and, by means of the known and familiar, to lead up to the more obscure and abstruse. The Septuagint has a curious and somewhat unintelligible rendering, Καὶ οὖς ἐξιχνιάσεται κόσμιον παραβολῶν, "And the ear will trace out the order of parables," which Schleusner translates, "elegantes parabolas."

Ver. 10.—**The Preacher sought to find out acceptable words**; literally, *words of delight*; λόγους θελήματος (Septuagint); *verba utilia* (Vulgate); so Aquila, λόγους χρείας. The word *chephets*, "pleasure," occurs in ch. v. 4; xii. 1. Thus we have "stones of pleasure" (Isa. liv. 12). He added the grace of refined diction to the solid sense of his utterances. Plumptre reminds us of the "gracious words" (λόγοις τῆς χάριτος, Luke iv. 22) which proceeded from the mouth of him who, being the Incarnate Wisdom of God, was indeed greater than Solomon. On the necessity of a work being attractive as well as conforming to literary rules, Horace long ago wrote ('Ars Poet.,' 99)—

" Non satis est pulchra esse poëmata ; dulcia sunto,
Et quocunque volent animum auditoris agunto."

" 'Tis not enough that poems faultless be,
And fair; let them be tender too, and draw
The hearer by the cord of sympathy."

St. Augustine is copious on this subject in his treatise, ' De Doctr. Christ. ;' thus (iv. 26): " Proinde illa tria, ut intelligant qui audiunt, ut delectentur, ut obediant, etiam in hoc genere agendum est, ubi tenet delectatio principatum. . . . Sed quis movetur, si nescit quod dicitur ? Aut quis tenetur ut audiat, si non delectatur ?" **And that which was written was upright,** even **words of truth.** The Authorized Version, with its interpolations, does not accurately convey the sense of the original. The sentence is to be regarded as containing phrases in apposition to the "acceptable words" of the first clause; thus: "Koheleth sought to discover words of pleasure, and a writing in sincerity, words of truth." The Septuagint has, καὶ γεγραμμένον εὐθύτητος, "a writing of uprightness;" Vulgate, *et conscripsit sermones rectissimos*. The meaning is that what he wrote had two characteristics—it was sincere, that which he really thought and believed, and it was true objectively. If any reader was disposed to cavil, and to depreciate the worth

of the treatise because it was not the genuine work of the celebrated Solomon, the writer claims attention to his production on the ground of its intrinsic qualities, as inspired by the same wisdom which animated his great predecessor.

Ver. 11.—**The words of the wise** are **as goads.** The connection of this verse with the preceding is maintained by the fact that the "acceptable words," etc., are words of the wise, emanate from the same persons. Herewith he proceeds to characterize them, with especial reference to his own work. The goad was a rod with an iron spike, or sharpened at the end, used in driving oxen (see Judg. iii. 31; 1 Sam. xiii. 21; Ecclus. xxxviii. 25; Acts ix. 5). Words of wisdom are called goads because they rouse to exertion, promote reflection and action, restrain from error, impel to right; if they hurt and sting, the pain which they inflict is healthful, for good and not for evil. **And as nails fastened by the masters of assemblies.** The proposition "by" is an interpolation, and the sentence should run : *And like nails fastened* [are] *the*, etc.—*masmeroth*, "nails," as in Isa. xli. 7. There is much difficulty in explaining the next words, בַּעֲלֵי אֲסֻפּוֹת (*baale asuppoth*). We have had similar expressions applied to possessors in ch. x. 11, "lord of the tongue," and " lord of wings " (ch. x. 20); and analogy might lead us to apply the phrase here to persons, and not things; but in Isa. xli. 15 we find a threshing-instrument termed "lord of teeth ;" and in 2 Sam. v. 20 a town is called Baal-Perazim, " Lord of breaches ;" so we must be guided by other considerations in our exposition. The Septuagint, taking the whole sentence together, and regarding *baale* as a preposition, renders, " As nails firmly planted, (οἱ παρὰ τῶν συνθεμάτων ἐδόθησαν ἐκ ποιμένος ἑνός) which from the collections were given from one shepherd." Schleusner takes οἱ παρὰ τῶν συνθεμάτων to mean, "Ii quibus munus datum erat collectionem faciendi," *i.e.* the author, of collections. The Vulgate has, *Verba . . . quæ per magistrorum consilium data sunt a pastore uno.* The "masters of assemblies" can only be the chiefs of some learned conclaves, like the great synagogue supposed to exist in the time of Ezra and later. The clause would then assert that these pundits are like fastened nails, which seems rather unmeaning. One might say that their uttered sentiments became fixed in the mind as nails firmly driven in, but one could not properly say this of the men themselves. A late editor, Gietmann, suggests that "lords of collection" may mean "brave men, heroes, gathered in line of battle," serried ranks, just as in Prov. xxii. 20 the term *shalishim*, chariot-fighters, chieftains, is applied to choice proverbs. Thus he would say that the words of the wise are as goads because they stimulate the intellect, as nails because they readily find entrance, and like men in battle array when they are reduced to writing and marshalled in a book. This is certainly ingenious, but somewhat too artificial to be regarded as the genuine intention of the writer. It seems best to take the word translated "assemblies" as denoting collections, not of people, but of proverbs; and the compound phrase would thus mean proverbs of an excellent character, the best of their sort gathered together in writing. Such words are well compared to nails; they are no longer floating loosely about, they are fixed in the memory, they secure other knowledge, and, though they are separate utterances, they have a certain unity and purpose. Nails are often used proverbially as emblems of what is fixed and unalterable. Thus Æschyl., 'Suppl.,' 944—

Τῶν δ' ἐφήλωται τορῶς
Γόμφος διαμπὰξ, ὡς μένειν ἀραρότως.

"Through them a nail is firmly fixed, that they
May rest immovable."

Cicero, 'Verr.,' ii. 5. 21, "Ut hoc beneficium, quemadmodum dicitur, trabali clavo figeret;" *i.e.* to make it sure and steadfast (comp. Horace, 'Carm.,' i. 35. 17, *et seq.*). Which are **given from one shepherd.** All these words of the wise, collections, etc., proceed from one source, or are set forth by one authority. Who is] this shepherd? Some say that he is the *archisynagogus*, the president of the assemblies of wise men, to whose authority all these public utterances are subjected. But we do not know that such supervision existed or was exercised at the time when Koheleth wrote; and, as we saw above, there is probably no reference to any such assemblies in the passage. The "one shepherd" is doubtless Jehovah, who is called the Shepherd of Israel, who feeds his people like a flock, etc. (see Gen. xlviii. 15; xlix. 24; Ps. xxiii. 1; lxxx. 1, etc.). The appellation is here used as concinnous with the thought of the ox-goad, intimating that God watches and leads his people like a tender shepherd and a skilful farmer. This is an important claim to inspiration. All these varied utterances, whatever form they take, whether his own or his predecessor's, are outcomes of wisdom, and proceed from him who is only wise, Almighty God. It is no disparagement of this work to imply that it is not the production of the true Solomon; Koheleth is ready to avow himself the writer, and yet claims a hearing as being equally moved by heavenly influence. It is like St. Paul's

assertion (1 Cor. vii. 40), "I think that I also have the Spirit of God."

Vers. 12—14.—The author warns against profitless study, and gives the final conclusion to which the whole discussion leads.

Ver. 12.—**And further, by these, my son, be admonished;** rather, *and what is more than these, be warned.* Besides all that has been said, take this additional and important caution, viz. what follows. The clause, however, has been differently interpreted, as if it said, "Do not attempt to go beyond the words of the sages mentioned above;" or, "Be content with my counsels; they will suffice for your instruction." This seems to be the meaning of the Authorized Version. The personal address, "my son," so usual in the Book of Proverbs, is used by Koheleth in this place alone. It does not necessarily imply relationship (as if the pseudo-Solomon was appealing to Rehoboam), but rather the condition of pupil and learner, sitting at the feet of his teacher and friend. **Of making many books** there is **no end.** This could not be said in the time of the historical Solomon, even if we reckon his own voluminous works (1 Kings iv. 32, 33); for we know of no other writers of that date, and it is tolerably certain that none existed in Palestine. But we need not suppose that Koheleth is referring to extraneous heathen productions, of which, in our view, there is no evidence that he possessed any special knowledge. Doubtless many thinkers in his time had treated of the problems discussed in his volume in a far different manner from that herein employed, and it seemed good to utter a warning against the unprofitable reading of such productions. Juvenal speaks of the insatiable passion for writing in his day ('Sat.,' vii. 51)—

"Tenet insanabile multos
Scribendi cacoethes et ægro in corde senescit;"

which Dryden renders—

"The charms of poetry our souls bewitch;
The curse of writing is an endless itch."

As in taking food it is not the quantity which a man eats, but what he digests and assimilates, that nourishes him, so in reading, the rule, *Non multa, sed multum,* must be observed; the gorging the literary appetite on food wholesome or not impedes the healthy mental process, and produces no intellectual growth or strength. The obvious lesson drawn by spiritual writers is that Christians should make God's Word their chief study, "turning away from the profane babblings and oppositions of the knowledge which is falsely so called" (1 Tim. vi. 20). For as St. Augustine says

('De Doctr. Christ.'), "Whereas in Holy Scripture you will find everything which has been profitably said elsewhere, to a far greater extent you will therein find what has been nowhere else enunciated, but which has been taught solely by the marvellous sublimity and the equally marvellous humility of the Word of God." **Much study is a weariness of the flesh.** The two clauses in the latter part of the verse are co-ordinate. Thus the Septuagint, Τοῦ ποιῆσαι βιβλία πολλὰ οὐκ ἔστι περασμὸς, καὶ μελέτη πολλὴ κόπωσις ("weariness") σαρκός. The word for "study" (lahag) is not found elsewhere in the Old Testament, nor in the Talmud, but the above meaning is sustained by its connection with an Arabic word signifying "to be eager for." The Vulgate (like the Septuagint) renders it meditatio. You may weary your brain, exhaust your strength, by protracted study or meditation on many books, but you will not necessarily thereby gain any insight into the problems of the universe or guidance for daily life. Marcus Aurelius dissuades from much reading: "Would you examine your whole composition?" he says; "pray, then let your library alone; what need you puzzle your thoughts and over-grasp yourself?" Again, "As for books, never be over-eager about them; such a fondness for reading will be apt to perplex your mind, and make you die unpleased" ('Medit.,' ii. 2, 3, Collier). So Ben-Sira affirms, "The finding out of parables is a wearisome labour of the mind" (Ecclus. xiii. 26).

Ver. 13.—The teaching of the whole book is now gathered up in two weighty sentences. **Let us hear the conclusion of the whole matter.** The Revised Version gives, *This is the end of the matter; all hath been heard.* The Septuagint has, Τέλος λόγου, τὸ πᾶν ἄκουε, "The end of the matter, the sum, hear thou;" Vulgate, *Finem loquendi pariter omnes audiamus.* Another rendering is suggested, "The conclusion of the matter is this, that [God] taketh knowledge of all things;" literally, "everything is heard." Perhaps the passage is best translated, *The end of the matter, when all is heard, is this.* The first word of this verse, *soph,* "end," is printed in the Hebrew text in large characters, in order to draw attention to the importance of what is coming. And its significance is rightly estimated. These two verses guard against

very possible misconception, and give the author's real and mature conclusion. When this is received, all that need be said has been uttered. **Fear God (ha-Elohim), and keep his commandments.** This injunction is the practical result of the whole discussion. Amid the difficulties of the moral government of the world, amid the complications of society, varying and opposing interests and claims, one duty remained plain and unchanging—the duty of piety and obedience. **For this is the whole duty of man.** The Hebrew is literally, "This is every man," which is explained to mean, "This is every man's duty." Septuagint, Ὅτι τοῦτο πᾶς ὁ ἄνθρωπος : Vulgate, *Hoc est enim omnis homo.* For this man was made and placed in the world; this is his real object, the chief good which he has to seek, and which alone will secure contentment and happiness. The obligation is put in the most general terms as applicable to the whole human family ; for God is not the God of the Jews only, but of Gentiles also (Rom. iii. 29).

Ver. 14.—The great duty just named is here grounded upon the solemn truth of a future judgment. **For God shall bring every work into judgment.** It will then be seen whether this obligation has been attended to or not. The judgment has already been mentioned (ch. xi. 9); it is here more emphatically set forth as a certain fact and a strong motive power. The old theory of earthly retribution had been shown to break down under the experience of practical life; the anomalies which perplexed men's minds could only be solved and remedied by a future judgment under the eye of the omniscient and unerring God. **With every secret thing.** The Syriac adds, "and manifest thing." The Septuagint renders, "with everything that has been overlooked"—a very terrible, but true, thought. The doctrine that the most secret things shall be revealed in the *dies iræ* is often brought forward in the New Testament, which makes plain the personal nature of this final investigation, which the earlier Scriptures invest with a more general character (see Rom. ii. 16; xiv. 12; 1 Cor. iv. 5). So this wonderful book closes with the enunciation of a truth found nowhere else so clearly defined in the Old Testament, and thus opens the way to the clearer light shed upon the awful future by the revelation of the gospel.

HOMILETICS.

Ver. 1.—"*Remember thy Creator.*" I. REMEMBER: WHOM? "Thy Creator." The language implies: 1. *That man has a Creator.* It would certainly be strange if he had not, seeing that all things else have. And that Creator is not himself, since he is at best a dependent creature (Gen. iii. 19); or an inferior divinity, since there is none such (2 Sam. vii. 22; Isa. xliv. 6); but (1) *God*, the one living and true God (1 Thess. i. 9), the Almighty Maker of the universe (Gen. i. 1; Exod. xx. 11; Ps. cxxiv. 8; Isa. xl. 28; Jer. x. 16), and therefore of man (Gen. i. 26; Deut. iv. 32; Ps. c. 3; Acts xvii. 25, 26, 28); and (2) *Jesus Christ*, the Image of the invisible God (2 Cor. iv. 4; Col. i. 15), and the unbeginning Word of God (John i. 1), by whom all things were made (John i. 3), whether they be things in heaven or on earth, visible or invisible (Col. i. 16), and therefore from whom man derives his being. 2. *That man originally knows God.* That even in his fallen condition he is not entirely destitute of a knowledge of God—not, perhaps, a knowledge clear and full, but still real and true —appears to be the teaching of Scripture (Rom. i. 21, 28) as well as of experience, no man ever requiring to argue himself into a belief in God's existence, though many try to reason themselves out of it. 3. *That man may forget God.* Moses was afraid lest Israel should be guilty of so doing (Deut. vi. 12), in which case they would be no better than the heathen peoples around them (Ps. ix. 17). Practically this is the world's sin to-day (1 John iv. 8), and the sin against which Christians have to guard (Heb. iii. 12). It is specially the sin against which young persons should be warned, that of allowing the thought of God to slip out of their minds.

II. REMEMBER: HOW? 1. *By thinking of his Person.* A characteristic of the wicked is that God is not in all their thoughts (Ps. x. 4); whereas a good man remembers God upon his bed, and meditates upon him in the night watches (Ps. lx. 3). 2. *By reflecting on his character.* The Creator being neither an abstract conception nor an inanimate force, but a living and personal Intelligence, he is also possessed of attributes, the sum of which compose his character or name; and one who would properly remember him must frequently permit his thoughts to dwell on these (Ps. xx. 7), as David (Ps. lx. 3) and Asaph (Ps. lxxvii. 3) did—on his holiness, his loving-kindness, his faithfulness, his truth, his wisdom, his justice, all of which have been revealed in Jesus Christ, and so made much more easily the subjects of study. 3. *By acknowledging his goodness.* God's bounties in providence and mercies in grace must be equally recalled and thankfully retained before the mind, as David aptly said to himself (Ps. ciii. 1, 2) and protested before God (Ps. xlii. 6). One who simply accepts God's daily benefits as the lower animals do, for consumption but not for consideration, is guilty of forgetting God; who knows about, but never pauses to thank God for his unspeakable grace in Christ, comes far short of what is meant by remembering his Creator. 4. *By meditating in his Word.* Those who lovingly remember God will not forget that he has written to them in the Scriptures words of grace and truth, and will, like the good man of the Hebrew Psalter (i. 2), meditate therein day and night. Where God's Law, with its wise and holy precepts, is counted as a strange thing (Hos. viii. 12), no further proof is needed that God himself is forgotten. The surest evidence that "no man remembered the poor wise man" was found in this, that his wisdom was despised, and his words were not heard (ch. ix. 16). 5. *By keeping his commandments.* As Joseph's recollection of Jehovah helped him to resist temptation and avoid sin (Gen. xxxix. 9), so a sincere and loving remembrance of God will show itself in doing those things that are pleasing in his sight. When Christ asked his disciples to remember him, he meant them to do so, not simply by thinking of and speaking about him, or even by celebrating in his honour a memorial feast (Luke xxii. 19), but also by doing whatsoever he had commanded them (John xv. 14).

III. REMEMBER: WHEN? "In the days of thy youth." 1. *Not then only.* The remembrance of God is a duty which extends along the whole course of life. No age can be exempted from it, as none is unsuitable for it. The notion that religion, while proper enough for childhood or youth, is neither demanded by nor becoming in manhood, is a delusion. The heart-worship and life-service of God and Jesus Christ are incumbent upon, needed by, and honourable to, old as well as young. 2. *But then firstly.* The reasons will be furnished below; meantime it may be noticed that Scripture writers may be said to be unanimous in recommending early piety; in teaching that youth, above all other periods, is the season for seeking God. Moses (Deut. xxxi. 13), David (Ps. xxxiv. 11), Solomon (Prov. iii. 1, 2), and Jesus (Matt. vi. 33) combine to set forth the advantage as well as duty of giving one's early years to God and religion.

IV. REMEMBER: WHY? 1. *Why remember one's Creator?* (1) Because he is infinitely worthy of being remembered. (2) Because he is entitled to be remembered on the simple ground of being Creator. (3) Because without this remembrance of him both happiness is impossible here and salvation hereafter. (4) Because the human heart is prone to forget him, and remember only either his creatures or his comforts. 2. *Why remember him in the way above specified?* (1) Because any remembrance short of that is incomplete, insincere, formal, external, and therefore essentially worthless. (2) Because the above is the sort of remembrance that is demanded by Scripture. (3) Because only such remembrance is worthy of being presented to God. 3. *Why remember him in youth?* (1) Because youth, as the first portion of a man's life, is due to God. (2) Because youth, as the formative period of life, is the most important time for acquiring religious habits (Prov. xxii. 6). (3) Because youth, as the happiest season in life, is the time in which God can most easily be remembered. Then " the evil days " of business and worry, of temptation and sin, of affliction and sorrow, of disease and decay, have not come ; and the soul, besides being comparatively disengaged, is also in a mood for yielding to devout and holy impressions. (4) Because if God is not remembered in youth he is apt to be forgotten in age.

Learn: 1. The real essence of religion—fellowship with God. 2. The dignity of man—that he is capable of such fellowship. 3. The responsibility of youth—for shaping all one's after-life. 4. The evanescence of earthly joys—all doomed to be eclipsed by the darkness of evil days.

Vers. 2—8.—*The last scene of all; or, "man goeth to his long home."* I. THE APPROACH OF DEATH. 1. *The decay of man's higher faculties.* " Or ever the sun, and the light, and the moon, and the stars be darkened, and the clouds return after the rain " (ver. 2). Accepting the guidance of the best interpreters (Delitzsch, Plumptre —for other interpretations consult the Exposition), we may see: (1) In the sun an emblem of man's spirit, elsewhere compared to the lamp of Jehovah (Prov. xx. 27), and described by Christ as " the light that is in thee " (Matt. vi. 23), and in its light a symbol of the spirit's activity of apprehension—thought, memory, imagination, etc. (2) In the moon a figure for the animal soul, " by means of which the spirit becomes the principle of the life of the body (Gen. ii. 7)," and which as the weaker vessel (it, according to Hebrew ideas, being regarded as female, while the spirit is male) is comforted by the spirit (Ps. xlii. 6). (3) In the stars an allegorical representation of the five senses, by which the soul has cognizance of the outer world, and the light of which is dim and feeble in comparison with that of the soul and spirit, or of the reason and intelligence of man. (4) In the clouds that return after the rain, a materialized picture of those calamities and misfortunes, sicknesses and sorrows, " which disturb the power of thought, obscure the consciousness, and darken the mind," and which, though leaving man for a while, return again after a season " without permitting him long to experience health " (Delitzsch). 2. *The failure of man's bodily powers.* Picturing man's corporeal frame as a house, the Preacher depicts its ruinous condition as old age approaches. (1) The keepers of the house tremble. The aged person's arms, " which bring to the house (of the body) whatever is suitable for it, and keep away from it whatever threatens to do it injury," now, touched with infirmity, shake, " so that they are able neither to grasp securely, to hold fast and use, nor actively to keep back and forcibly avert evil " (Delitzsch). (2) The strong men bow themselves. The legs, in young men like marble pillars (Cant. x. 15), are in aged persons loose, feeble, and inclined to stoop. (3) The grinders, or the grinding-women, cease. That these are the molars, or teeth, which perform the work of mastication, is apparent; so is the reason why they are not now at work, viz. because in aged persons they are few. (4) Those that look out of the windows are darkened. The eyes, called by Cicero " the windows of the mind " (' Tusc.,' i. 20), become dim, and as a consequence the soul's eyes, which look through the body's eyes, lose their power of perception. (5) The doors are shut in the street. These are probably the lips, which in old age are usually closed and drawn, because the teeth have disappeared. (6) The sound of the grinding is low. The noise made by an old man in mastication is that of a low munching, he being unable any more to crack, crunch, or break his food. (7) One rises up at the sound of a bird. So timid and nervous, and so light a sleeper, is the old man, that if even a bird chirps he awakes, and, being put off his rest, is obliged to rise. (8) The daughters of music are brought low. Not so much the old man's powers of singing are diminished, his once strong and manly treble having become so feeble and low as to be scarcely audible (Isa. xxxviii. 14), as the old man, like Barzillai (2 Sam. xix. 35), has now no longer an ear for the voice of singing-men and singing-women, so that to him as a consequence "the daughters of song" must lower their voices, *i.e.* must retire so as no longer to disturb him, now so feeble as to be "terrified by the twittering of a little bird." (9) That which is high causes fear (ver. 5). To the old man "even a little hillock appears like a high mountain; and if he has to go a journey he meets something that terrifies him" (Targum, 'Midrash'). Decrepit old men "do not venture out, for to them a damp road appears like a very morass, a gravelly path as full of neck-breaking hillocks, an undulating path as fearfully steep and precipitous, that which is not shaded as oppressively hot and exhausting" (Delitzsch). (10) The almond tree blossoms. An emblem of the winter of age, with its silvery white hair. (11) The grasshopper is a burden, or the grasshopper drags itself along. Either so small a thing as the chirping of a grasshopper annoys the old man (Zöckler)—the obvious sense of the former clause; or the middle of the body, which in an old man resembles a grasshopper, drags itself along with difficulty (Delitzsch). (12) The caper-berry fails. The appetite, which this particular condiment is supposed to stimulate, ceases; the stomach can no more by means of it be roused from its dormant and phlegmatic condition. So low and feeble is he that "no quinine or phosphorus can help him now" (Plumptre).

II. The dissolution of the soul and body. 1. *The loosening of the silver cord, and the breaking of the golden bowl.* (1) The figure. A golden bowl or lamp suspended from the roof of a house or tent by a silver cord, through the sudden snapping of which it, the golden bowl or lamp, is precipitated to the ground, thus extinguishing its light. (2) The interpretation. If the silver cord be "the soul directing and bearing the body as living," the lamp or the golden bowl will be "the body animated by the soul and dependent on it" (Delitzsch); or, if the golden bowl be "life as manifested through the body," then the silver cord will be "that on which the continuance of life depends" (Plumptre); or, again, if the silver cord be the spinal marrow, then the golden bowl will be the brain to which the spinal marrow stands related as silver to gold (Fausset). 2. *The breaking of the pitcher at the fountain, and of the wheel at the cistern.* (1) The image. That of a pitcher, which is used for letting down by a rope or chain into a well or fountain, becoming shivered at the fountain's side through the sudden breaking down of the wheel during the process of drawing water. (2) The significance. The action of the lungs and the heart, the one of which, like a pitcher or bucket, draws in the air-current which sustains life, and the other of which pumps up the blood into the lungs; or the wheel and the pitcher may be the breathing apparatus, and the pitcher at the fountain the heart which raises the blood (Delitzsch).

III. The destination of the severed parts. 1. *Of the body.* "The dust returns to the earth as it was" (ver. 7). As the body came forth from the soil, so to the soil it reverts (Gen. iii. 19). 2. *Of the soul.* "The spirit returns unto God who gave it." Whatever may have been the Preacher's opinion at an earlier period (ch. iii. 21), he was now decided as to three things: (1) that man had, or was, a spirit, as distinguished from a body; (2) that this spirit, as to origin, proceeded from God (Gen. ii. 7; Job xxxii. 8); and (3) that on separating from the body it did not cease to be, but ascended to him from whom it came—not to be reabsorbed into the Divine essence, as if it had originally emanated therefrom, but to preserve in God's presence an independent existence, as the Targum translates, "The spirit will return to stand in judgment before God who gave it to thee."

IV. The last tribute of affection. "The mourners go about the streets" (ver. 5). 1. *Sorrowing for the departed.* Probably the Preacher describes either the professional mourners who go about the streets, in anticipation of the dying man's departure, ready to offer their services the moment he expires (Delitzsch), or the actual procession of such mourners following the dead man's funeral to its place of sepulture (Plumptre). Still, it is permissible to think of the deceased's relatives, who, like Abraham mourning for Sarah (Gen. xxiii. 2), and Martha and Mary for Lazarus

(John xi. 31), give expression to their sadness by going about the streets in the garb of sorrow. 2. *Exciting the sympathy of the living.* This is one reason why private griefs are paraded in public. The heart in times of weakness, such as those occasioned by bereavement, instinctively craves the compassion of others, to whom, accordingly, it appeals by the visible cerements of woe.

Learn: 1. The mercy of God as seen in the gradual approach of death. 2. The wisdom of improving the seasons of youth and manhood. 3. The solemn mystery of death. 4. The duty of preparing for a life beyond the grave. 5. The lawfulness of Christian mourning.

Vers. 9, 10.—*A model preacher.* I. A WISE MAN. 1. *Possessed of secular knowledge.* Gathered as precious spoil from all departments of human learning and experience. As much of this sort of wisdom as possible; the more of it the better. All knowledge can be rendered subservient to the preacher's art, and may be utilized by him for the instruction of his hearers. 2. *Endowed with heavenly wisdom.* If that, much more this, is indispensable to an ideal preacher. The wisdom that cometh from above as much superior to that which springeth from below as heaven is higher than earth, and eternity longer than time. A preacher without the former wisdom may be rude; without the latter he must be ineffective.

II. A DILIGENT STUDENT. Like Koheleth, he must ponder, seek out, and set in order the truth he desires to communicate to others; like Timothy, he must give attendance to reading (1 Tim. iv. 13). In particular, he should be a student: 1. *Of the sacred Scriptures.* These divinely inspired writings, being the principal source of heavenly wisdom accessible to man (2 Tim. iii. 16), should be the preacher's *vade mecum,* or constant companion. 2. *Of human nature.* Having to deal directly with this, in the way of bringing to bear upon it the teachings of Scripture, he ought to acquaint himself accurately with it, by a close and patient study of it in himself and others. Much of a preacher's efficiency is derived from his knowledge of the audience to which he speaks. 3. *Of the material creation.* Like Job (xxxvii. 14), David (Ps. viii. 3; cxliii. 5), and Koheleth (ch. vii. 13), he should consider the works of God. Besides having much to tell him of God's glory (Ps. viii. 1; Rom. i. 20), the physical universe can impart to him valuable counsel of a moral kind concerning man and his duties (Job xii. 7; Prov. vi. 6; Matt. v. 26).

III. A SKILFUL TEACHER. As Koheleth taught the people knowledge, as Ezra caused the people to understand the reading (Neh. viii. 8), as Christ according to his Word taught such as listened to him (Mark x. 1), as the apostles taught the things of the Lord to their hearers (Acts iv. 2; xi. 26; xviii. 25), so must a model preacher be an instructor (1 Tim. iii. 2; iv. 11; vi. 2; 2 Tim. ii. 2). To be this successfully, in addition to the wisdom and study above described, he will need four kinds of words. 1. *Words of truth.* These must constitute the burden of his discourse, whether oral or written. What he publishes to others must be objectively true, and no mere guess-work or speculation. Such a word of truth was the Law of God in the Hebrew Scriptures (Ps. cxix. 43), and is the gospel or the doctrine of Christ in the New Testament (Eph. i. 13; Col. i. 5; 2 Tim. ii. 15; Jas. i. 18). 2. *Words of uprightness.* Whether he writes or speaks, he must do so sincerely, with perfect integrity of heart, "not handling the Word of God deceitfully" (2 Cor. iv. 2), but teaching out of honest personal conviction, saying, " We believe, therefore do we speak " (2 Cor. iv. 13). 3. *Words of delight.* Selected and intended, not to gratify the hearer's corrupt inclinations and perverted tastes, or minister to that love of novelty and sensation which is the peculiar characteristic of itching ears (2 Tim. iv. 3), but to set forth the truth in such a way as to win for it entrance into the hearer's heart and mind. For this purpose the preacher's words should be such as to interest and sway the listener, arresting his attention, exciting his imagination, instructing his understanding, moving his affections, quickening his conscience, and impelling his will. Dulness, darkness, dryness, deadness, are inexcusable faults in a preacher.

Vers. 11, 12.—*Reading, writing, speaking.* I. "READING MAKES A FULL MAN." 1. *Pushed to excess,* it becomes hurtful to the body. "Much study is a weariness to the flesh," and as a consequence, reflexively, injurious to the mind. 2. *Pursued in moderation*, it first enlightens the understanding, next quickens the whole spiritual nature, and finally tends to stimulate the health of the body. "A man's wisdom maketh his face to shine" (ch. viii. 1).

II. "WRITING MAKES A CORRECT MAN." If professional authorship in the Preacher's day was a nuisance, much more is it so in ours. Yet in book-writing lie advantages as well as disadvantages. If, on the one hand, the multiplication of books often signifies nothing more than an accumulation of literary rubbish, and a terrible infliction to those who must read them, on the other hand it secures the preservation and distribution of much valuable knowledge; while if the knowledge is not valuable, the formal deposition of it in a book, which may be quietly consigned to a library, secures that it shall not roam at large, to the disquieting of peace-loving minds. But, apart from the multiplication of volumes, the habit of setting down one's thoughts in writing is attended by distinct advantages. It promotes: 1. *Clearness of thought.* One who intends to write, more especially for the information of his fellows, must know what he purposes to say. The effort of putting one's ideas on paper imparts to them a definiteness of outline they might not otherwise possess. 2. *Order in arrangement.* No writer will, voluntarily, fling his thoughts together into a confused heap, but will strive to render them as lucid and luminous as possible. If for no other reason than this, the practice of preparing for public speech by means of writing is to be commended. 3. *Brevity in expression.* If brevity is the soul of wit, and loquacity the garment of dulness, then the sure way of attaining to the former, and avoiding the latter, is to write.

III. "SPEAKING MAKES A READY MAN." "The words of the wise are as goads, and as nails." Though designed to apply to the wise man's "written words," the clause may be accepted as correct also with reference to his "spoken words." Like the former, the latter are as goads and nails. 1. *They stimulate.* The words of a practised speaker, always supposing him to be a wise man, incite the minds and quicken the hearts of his hearer. The true preacher should be progressive, not only in his own discovery of truth, but in conducting his hearers into fresh fields of instruction, leading them out into "regions beyond," causing them to "forget the things that are behind, and reach forward unto those things that are before," persuading them to "leave the first principles of Christ, and to go on unto perfection." 2. *They abide.* They lodge themselves in the understanding and affections so firmly that they cannot be removed. Facility in arousing and fixing conviction can only be attained by diligent and wise cultivation of the art of speech.

Vers. 13, 14.—"*The conclusion of the whole matter;*" or, "*the whole duty of man.*" I. THE ESSENCE OF IT. 1. *The fear of God.* Not servile or guilty, but (1) reverential, such as the Divine greatness and glory are fitted to inspire (Deut. xxviii. 58; Ps. lxxxix. 7; Matt. x. 28; Heb. xii. 28); (2) filial, such as a child might cherish towards a parent (Ps. xxxiv. 11; Heb. xii. 9). 2. *The service of God.* Not that merely of external worship (Deut. vi. 11; Ps. xcvi. 9; Heb. x. 25), but that of inward devotion (John iv. 24), which expresses itself in the homage of the heart and life, or in the keeping of God's commandments—in particular of the three named by the Preacher, charity, industry, hilarity (Cox).

II. THE REASON OF IT. The certainty of judgment. 1. *By God.* He is the Judge of all the earth (Gen. xviii. 25); the Judge of all (Heb. xii. 23), who will yet judge the world in righteousness (Acts xvii. 31). 2. *In the future.* Not merely here upon the earth, but also hereafter in the world to come (Dan. vii. 10; Matt. xi. 22; xvi. 27; 1 Cor. iv. 5; 2 Tim. iv. 1). 3. *Of works.* Not of nations or communities, but of individuals (Mark viii. 38; Rom. ii. 5, 6); not of open actions merely, but of secret things as well (Luke xii. 2; Rom. ii. 16; 1 Cor. iii. 13; iv. 5); not of good deeds only, but also of evil (2 Cor. v. 10; 2 Pet. ii. 9).

HOMILIES BY VARIOUS AUTHORS.

Ver. 1.—*Youthful religion.* The Preacher spoke from a heart taught by long experience. Himself advanced in years, having enjoyed and suffered much, having long observed the growth of human character under diverse principles and influences, he was able to offer to the young counsel based upon extensive knowledge and deliberate reflection.

I. THE DESCRIPTION HERE GIVEN OF THE RELIGIOUS LIFE. Amplifying this terse and impressive language, we may hear the wise man addressing the youthful, and saying, "Remember that thou hast a Creator; that thy Creator ever remembers thee; that he not only deserves, but desires, thy remembrance; that his character should be remembered with reverence, his bounty with gratitude, his Law with obedience and submission, his love with faith and gladness, his promises with prayerfulness and with hope."

II. THE PERIOD HERE RECOMMENDED FOR THE RELIGIOUS LIFE. Religion is indeed adapted to the whole of our existence; and what applies to every age of life, applies with especial force to childhood and youth. 1. Youth has peculiar susceptibilities of feeling, and religion appeals to them. 2. Youth has especially opportunities of acquiring knowledge and undergoing discipline, and religion helps us to use them. 3. Youth has abounding energy, and religion assists us to employ this energy aright. 4. Youth is a time of great and varied temptations, and religion will enable us to overcome them. 5. Youth is introductory to manhood and to age; religion helps us so to live when young that we may be the better fitted for the subsequent stages of life's journey. 6. Youth may be all of life appointed for us; in that case, religion can hallow those few years which constitute the earthly training and probation.

III. THE SPECIAL REASONS FOR ATTENDING TO THIS ADMONITION. 1. It is a tendency of human nature to be so absorbed in what is present to the senses as to overlook unseen and eternal realities. 2. Our own age is peculiarly tempted to forget God, by reason of the prevalence of atheism, agnosticism, and positivism. 3. Youth is especially in danger of forgetting the Divine Creator, because the opening intelligence is naturally interested in the world of outward things, which presents so much to excite attention and to engage inquiry.

IV. THE ADDITIONAL FORCE WHICH CHRISTIANITY IMPARTS TO THIS ADMONITION. The figure of our blessed Lord himself appears to the imagination, and we seem to hear his winning but authoritative voice pleading with the young, and employing the very language of the text. He who said, "Suffer the little children to come unto me," he who, beholding the young inquirer, loved him, draws near to every youthful nature, and commands and beseeches that reverent attention, that willing faith, that affectionate attachment, which shall lead to a life of piety, and to an immortality of blessedness.—T.

Vers. 2—7.—*Old age and death.* By a natural transition, a striking antithesis, youth suggests to the mind of the Preacher the condition and the solemn lessons of old age. How appropriately does a treatise, dealing so fully with the occupations, the illusions, the trials, and the moral significance of human life, draw to a close by referring expressly to the earlier and the later periods by which that life is bounded!

I. THE BODILY SYMPTOMS OF AGE. These are, indeed, familiar to every observer, and are described with a picturesqueness and poetical beauty which must appeal to every reader of this passage. It is enough to remark that the decay of bodily power, and the gradual enfeeblement of the several senses, are among the usual accompaniments of advancing years.

II. THE MENTAL SYMPTOMS OF AGE. Reference is naturally made especially to the effect of bodily enfeeblement and infirmity upon the human emotions. 1. The emotions of desire and aspiration are dulled. 2. The emotions of apprehension, self-distrust, and fear increase.

III. THE NATURAL TERMINATION OF OLD AGE. There is no doubt that there are old persons of a sanguine temperament who seem unable to realize the fact that they are approaching the end of their earthly course. Yet it does not admit of doubt that the several indications of senility described in these verses are reminders of the end, are premonitions of the dissolution of the body, and of the entering upon a new and altogether different state of being.

IV. THE OPPORTUNITIES AND SERVICES OF AGE. 1. There is scope for the exercise of patience under growing infirmities. 2. There is a call to the acquisition and display of that wisdom which the experience of long years is particularly fitted to cultivate. 3. The aged are especially bound to offer to the young an example of cheerful obedience, and to encourage them to a life of piety and usefulness.

V. THE CONSOLATIONS OF AGE. Cicero, in a well-known treatise of great beauty, has set forth the peculiar advantages and pleasures which belong to the latest stage of human life. The Christian is at liberty to comfort himself by meditating upon such natural blessings as "accompany old age," but he has far fuller and richer sources of consolation open to him. 1. There is the happy retrospect of a life filled with instances of God's compassion, forbearance, and loving-kindness. 2. And there is the bright anticipation of eternal blessedness. This is his peculiar prerogative. As the outer man perisheth, the inner man is renewed day by day. The earthly tent is gradually but surely taken down, and this process suggests that he should look forward with calm confidence and hope to his speedy occupation of the "house not made with hands, eternal in the heavens."—T.

Vers. 9—11.—*The religious thinker and teacher.* The author of this book was himself a profound thinker and an earnest teacher, and it is evident that his great aim was to use his gifts of observation, meditation, and discourse for the enlightenment and the spiritual profit of all whom his words might reach. Taught in the quiet of his heart by the Spirit of the Eternal, he laboured, by the presentation of truth and the inculcation of piety, to promote the religious life among his fellow-men. His aim as he himself conceived it, his methods as practised by him in his literary productions, are deserving of the attentive consideration and the diligent imitation of those who are called upon to use thought and speech for the spiritual good of their fellow-creatures. Words are the utterance of the convictions and the desires of the inner nature, and when spoken deliberately and in public they involve a peculiar responsibility.

I. THE WORDS OF THE RELIGIOUS TEACHER SHOULD BE THE EXPRESSION OF WISDOM. They should not be thrown off carelessly, but should be the fruit of deep study and meditation. For the most part, they should embody either original thought, or thought which the teacher should have assimilated and made part of his own nature, and tested in his own individual experience. They should be the utterance of knowledge rather than of opinion; and they should be set forth in the order which comes from reflection, and not in an incoherent, desultory, and unconnected form.

II. THE WORDS OF THE RELIGIOUS TEACHER SHOULD BE WORDS OF UPRIGHTNESS. In order to this they must be the utterance of sincere conviction; they must harmonize with moral intuitions; they must be such as consequently appeal to the same conscience in the hearer or reader, which approves them in the speaker or writer. Crafty arguments, specious and sophistical appeals, sentimental absurdities, do not fulfil these conditions, and for them there is no place in the Christian preacher's discourses, in the volumes of the Christian author.

III. THE WORDS OF THE RELIGIOUS TEACHER SHOULD BE WORDS OF PERSUASIVENESS. The author of Ecclesiastes commends "proverbs" and "words of delight." Harshness, coldness, contemptuousness, severity, are unbecoming to the expositor of a religion of compassion and love. A winning manner, a sympathizing spirit, language and illustrations adapted to the intelligence, the habits, the circumstances of auditors, go far to open up a way to their hearts. No doubt there is a side of danger to this requirement; the pleasing word may be the substitute for the truth instead of its vehicle, and the preacher may simply be as one that playeth upon a very pleasant instrument. But the example of our Lord Jesus, "the great Teacher," abundantly shows how winning, gracious, condescending, and touching language is divinely adapted to reach the hearts of men.

IV. THE WORDS OF THE RELIGIOUS TEACHER SHOULD BE CONVINCING AND EFFECTIVE. The goads that pierce, the nails that penetrate and bind, are images of the language of him who beateth not the air. Let the aim be kept steadily before the eye, and the mark will not be missed. Let the blow be delivered strongly and decisively, and the work will be well done. The understanding has to be convinced, the conscience awakened, the heart touched, the evil passions stilled, the endeavour and determination aroused; and the Word is, by the accompanying energy of the Spirit of God, able to effect all this. "Who is sufficient for these things?"

V. The words of the religious teacher may be the means of religious, spiritual, imperishable blessing. If his word be the Word of God, who commissions and strengthens every faithful herald and ambassador, then he may comfort himself with the promise, "My Word shall not return unto me void; it shall accomplish that which I please, and it shall prosper in the thing whereto I sent it."—T.

Ver. 12.—*The scholar's sorrow.* In these closing paragraphs of his treatise the writer reveals his own feelings, and draws upon his own experience. It is interesting to observe how largely study was pursued and literature cultivated at the remote period when this book was written; and it is obvious to remark how far more strikingly these reflections apply to an age like our own, and to a state of society such as that in which we live. The diffusion of education tends to the multiplication of books and to the increase of the learned professions; whilst growing civilization fosters the habit of introspection, and consequently of that melancholy whose earlier and simpler symptoms are observable in the language of this touching passage.

I. Study and literature are a necessity of educated human nature. As soon as men begin to reflect, they begin to embody their reflections in a literary form, whether of poetry or of prose. A native impulse to verbal expression of thought and feeling, or the desire of sympathy and applause, or the calculating regard for maintenance, leads to the devotion of ever-growing bodies of men to the literary life. Literature is an unmistakable "note" of human culture.

II. Study and literature are, broadly speaking, promotive of the general good. The few toil that the many may profit. Knowledge, thought, art, right feeling, liberty, and peace, are all indebted to the great thinkers and authors whose names are held in honour among men. Doubtless there are those who misuse their gifts, who by their writings pander to vice, incite to crime, and encourage irreligion. But the bulk of literature, proceeding from the better class of minds, is rather contributive to the furtherance of goodness and of the best interests of men. Books are among the greatest of human blessings.

III. Study and literature have been consecrated to the service of religion. We have but to refer to the Hebrew Scriptures themselves in proof of this. There is nothing more marvellous in history than the production of the Books of Moses, the Psalms, and the prophetic writings, at the epochs from which they date. Lawgivers, seers, psalmists, and sages live yet in their peerless writings; some of them inimitable in literary form, all of them instinct with moral power. The New Testament furnishes a yet more marvellous illustration of the place which literature holds in the religious life of humanity. Men have sneered at the supposition that a book revelation could be possible; but their sneers are answered by the facts. Whatever view we take of inspiration, we are constrained to allow for human gifts of authorship. To make up the sacred volume there are "many books," and every one of them is the fruit of "much study."

IV. Study and literature are cultivated at the expense of the exhaustion and sorrow of the producer and student. 1. There is weariness of the flesh arising from the close connection between body and mind. The brain, being the central physical organ of language, is, in a sense, the instrument of thought; and, consequently, brain-weariness, nerve-exhaustion, are familiar symptoms among the ardent students to whom we are all indebted for the discovery, the formulation, and the communication of truth and knowledge. 2. But there is a mental sorrow and distress which deeper thinkers cannot always escape, and by which some among them are oppressed. The vast range of what in itself *can* be known is such as to strike the mind with dismay. Science, history, philosophy, etc., have made progress so marvellous, that no single finite mind can embrace, in the course of a life of study, however assiduous, more than a minute department, so as to know all of it that may be known; and a highly educated man is content "to know something of everything, and every-thing of something." 3. Then beyond the realm accessible to human inquiry lies the vaster realm of what *cannot* be known—what is altogether outside our ken. 4. It must be borne in mind, further, that, whilst man's intellect is limited, his spiritual yearnings are insatiable; no bounds can be set to his aspirations; his nature is akin to that of God himself. Thus it is that sorrow often shades the scholar's brow, and that to the weariness of the flesh there is added the sadness of the spirit, that finds, in the memorable language of Pascal, the larger the circle of the known, the vaster is the circumference of the unknown that stretches beyond.—T.

Vers. 13, 14.—*Religion, righteousness, and retribution.* After all the questionings and discussions, the doubts and perplexities, the counsels and precepts, of this treatise, the author winds up by restating the first, the most elementary, and the most important, principles of true religion. There are, he felt, in this world many things which we cannot fathom, many things which we cannot reconcile with our convictions and hopes; but there are some things concerning which we have no doubts, and these are the things which most nearly concern us personally and practically. Thoughtful men may weary and distress themselves with pondering the great problems of existence; but, after all, they, in common with the plainest and most illiterate, must come back to the essentials of the religious life.

I. THE GREAT SPRING AND CENTRE OF RELIGION. This is the fear of God, reverence for the Divine character and attributes, the habit of mind which views everything in relation to him who is eternally holy, wise, just, and good. This Book of Ecclesiastes is, upon this point, at one with the whole of the Bible and with all deeply based religion. We cannot begin with man; we must find an all-sufficient foundation for the religious life in God himself, his nature, and his Law.

II. THE GREAT EXPRESSION OF RELIGION. This is obedience to the Divine commandments. Our convictions and emotions find their scope when directed towards a holy and merciful God; our will must bend to the moral authority of the eternal Lord. Feelings and professions are in vain unless they are supported by corresponding actions. It is true that mere external compliance is valueless; acts must be the manifestation of spiritual loyalty and love. But, on the other hand, sentiment that evaporates in words, that does not issue in deeds, is disregarded in the court of heaven. Where God is honoured, and his will is cheerfully performed, there the whole duty of the Christian man is fulfilled. It is the work of the mediation of the Divine Saviour, of the operations of the Divine Spirit, to bring about such a religious and moral life.

III. THE GREAT TEST OF RELIGION. For this we are bidden to look forward to the future. Many things, which are significant as to the religious state of a man, are now hidden. They must be brought to light; secret deeds, alike of holiness and of iniquity, must be made manifest before the throne of judgment. Here, in this world, where men judge by appearances, the wicked sometimes get credit for goodness which does not really belong to them, and the good are often maligned and misunderstood. But, in the general judgment hereafter, the secrets of all hearts shall be revealed, and men shall be judged, not according to what they seem to be, but according to what they actually are. With this solemn warning the Preacher closes his book. And there is no person, in whatsoever state of life, to whom this warning does not apply. Well will it be for us if this earthly life be passed under the perpetual influence of this expectation; if the prospect of the future judgment inspire us to watchfulness, to diligence, and to prayer.—T.

Ver. 1 (with ch. xi. 10, latter part).—*The vanity and glory of youth.* I. THE VANITY OF YOUTH. There is an aspect in which it is true that "childhood and youth are vanity." 1. Its thoughts are very simple; they are upon the surface, and there is no depth of truth or wisdom in them. 2. Its judgments are very mixed with error; it has to unlearn a great deal of what it learns; the young will have to find, later on, that the men of whom and the things of which they have made up their minds are different from what they think now; their after-days will bring with them much disillusion, if not serious disappointment. Much that they see is magnified to their view, and the colours, as they see them to-day, will look otherwise to-morrow. 3. Itself is constantly disappearing. Few things are more constantly disturbing, if not distressing, us than the rapid passage of childhood and youth. Sometimes the young life is taken away altogether—the flower is nipped in the bud. But where life is spared, the peculiar beauty of childhood or of youth—its simplicity, its trustfulness, its docility, its eagerness, its ardour of affection, its unreserved delight—this is perpetually passing and "fading into the light of common day." Yet is there—and it is the truer and deeper thought—

II. THE GLORY OF YOUTH. Whatever may be said of youth in the way of qualification, there is one thing that may be said for it which greatly exalts it—*it may be wise with a profound and heavenly wisdom,* for it may be spent in the fear and in the love of God (see Prov. i. 7; Job xxviii. 28). To "remember its Creator," and to order its life according to that remembrance, is the height and the depth of human wisdom. Knowledge, learning, cunning, brilliancy, genius itself, is not so desirable nor so admirable a thing as is this holy and heavenly wisdom. To know God (Jer. ix. 24), to reverence him in the innermost soul, to love him with all the heart (Mark xii. 33), to be obedient to his commandments, to be patiently and cheerfully submissive to his will, to be honouring and serving him continually, to be attaining to his own likeness in spirit and character,—surely this is the glory of the highest created intelligence of the noblest rank in heaven, and surely this is the glory of our human nature in all *its* ranks. It is the glory of our manhood, and it is the glory of youth. Far more than any order of strength (Prov. xx. 29), or than any kind of beauty (2 Sam. xiv. 25), or than any measure of acquisition, does the abiding and practical remembrance of its Creator and Saviour glorify our youth. That makes it pure, worthy, admirable, inherently excellent, full of hope and promise. We may add, for it belongs to the text as well as to the subject—

III. THE WISDOM OF YOUTH. "While the evil days come not," etc. Let the young live before God while they are young; for: 1. It is a poor and sorry thing to offer to God, to a Divine Redeemer, the dregs of our days. To him who gave himself for us it becomes us to give, not our wasted and worn-out, but our best, our freest and freshest, our purest and strongest self. 2. To leave the consecration of ourselves to Christ to the time when faculty has faded, when the power of discernment and appreciation has declined, when sensitiveness has been dulled with long disuse, when the heavenly voices fall with less charm and interest on the ear of the soul,—this is a most perilous thing. To hearken and to heed, to recognize and to obey, in the days of youth is the one wise thing.—C.

Vers. 5—7.—*Death, its meaning and its moral.* Whatever be the true interpretation of the three preceding verses, there is no doubt at all as to the Preacher's meaning in the text; he has death in his view, and he suggests to us—

I. ITS CERTAINTY. Childhood *must* pass into youth, and youth into prime, and prime into old age—into the days which are bereaved of pleasure (ver. 1); and old age *must* end in death. Of all the *tableaux* which human life presents to us, the last one is that of "the mourners going about the streets." Other evils may be shunned by sedulous care and unusual sagacity, but death is the evil which no man may avoid.

II. ITS MEANING. What does death mean when it comes? 1. It means a *shock* to those that are left behind. The mourners in the street express in their way the sadness which is afflicting the hearts of those who weep within the walls. Here and there a death occurs which disturbs no peace and troubles no heart. But almost always it comes with a shock and an inward inexpressible pain to those who are bereaved. Even in old age the hearts of near kindred and dear friends are troubled with a keen and real distress. 2. It means *separation.* Man "goes to his long home." They who are left go to their darkened home, and he who is taken goes to his long home, to dwell apart and alone, to revisit no more the familiar places, and look no more into the faces of his friends. They and he henceforth must dwell apart; the grave is always a very long distance from the old home. 3. It means *loss.* The loss of the *beautiful* or the *useful,* or of both together. "Our life may have been like a golden lamp suspended by silver chains, fit for the palace of a king, and may have shed a welcome and a cheerful light on every side; but even the durable costly chain will be snapt at last, and the beautiful 'bowl be broken.' Our life may have been like 'the bucket' dropped by village maidens into the village fountain, or like the 'wheel' by which water is drawn from the village well,—it may have conveyed a vital refreshment to many lips; but the day must come when the bucket will be shattered on the marble edge of the fountain, and the timeworn wheel drop into the well" (Cox). The most beautiful life vanishes from our sight; the most useful life is taken away. 4. It means *dissolution.* "The dust shall return to the earth as it was." Our body, however fair and strong it may be, however trained, clothed, adorned, admired, must return to "dust and ashes," must be resolved into the elements from which it was constructed. 5. It means *departure*. "The spirit shall return unto God who gave it." This is by far the most solemn view of death. At death we "return to God" (see Ps. xc. 3). Not, indeed, that we are ever far from him (see Acts xvii. 27; Ps. cxxxix. 3—5). We stand and live in his very near presence. Yet does there come an hour—the hour of death—when we shall consciously stand before our Divine Judge, and when we shall learn from him "our high estate" or our lasting doom (2 Cor. v. 10). Death means departure *from* the sphere of the visible and tangible *into* the close and conscious presence of the eternal God.

III. Its moral. The one great lesson which stands out from this eloquent description is this: *Be the servant of God always;* take care to know him and to serve him at the end, by learning of him at the beginning, and serving him throughout your life. Remember your Creater in youth, and he will acknowledge you when old age is lost in death, and death has introduced you to the judgment-scene. Happy is that human soul that has drawn into itself Divine truth with its earliest intelligence, and that has ordered its life by the Divine will from first to last; for then shall the end of earth be full of peace and hope, and the beginning of eternity be full of joy and of glory.—C.

Vers. 9—12.—*The function of the teacher.* 1. The wise man, because he is wise (ver. 9), *teaches*. There is no better, no other thing that he can do, both for his own sake and for the sake of his fellow-men. To know and not to speak is a sin and a cruelty, when men are "perishing for lack of knowledge." To know and to speak is an elevated joy and a sacred duty; we cannot but speak the things we have learned of God, the truth as it is in Jesus. 2. The wise man also takes what measures he can *to perpetuate* the truth he knows; he wants to preserve it, to hand it down to another time; he therefore "writes down the words with truth and uprightness" (ver. 10); or, if he cannot do this, he labours to put his thought into those parabolic or proverbial forms which will not only be preserved in the memory of those to whom he utters them, but can be readily repeated, and will become embedded in the traditions and, ultimately, into the literature of his country (ver. 9). 3. The wise man *restrains* his literary ardour within due bounds (ver. 12). Otherwise he not only causes a drug in the market, but seriously injures his own health. He knows it is better to do a little and do that thoroughly, than to do much and do it hastily and imperfectly. But what is the teacher's function, his sacred duty, as related to the people of his charge or his acquaintance?

I. To search diligently for the truth. It is for him "to ponder and seek out," or to "compose with care and thought" (Cox's transl.). Divine truth, in its various aspects and applications, is manifold and profound; it demands our most patient study, our most reverent inquiry; we should gain help from all possible sources, more particularly should we seek it from the Spirit and from the Word of God.

II. To interest and to console. The Preacher sought to find out "acceptable" or "comfortable" words—"words of delight" (literally). This is not the main duty of the teacher, but it is one to which he should seriously address himself. 1. A teacher may be speaking in the highest strain, and may be uttering the deepest wisdom, but if his words are unintelligible and, therefore, unacceptable, he will make no way and do no good. We must speak in the language of those whom we address. Our thoughts may be far higher than theirs, but our language must be on their level—at any rate, on the level of their understanding. 2. The teacher will do wisely to spend much time and strength in *consoling;* for in this world of trouble and sorrow no words are more often or more urgently needed than "comfortable words."

III. To retain. "The words of the 'masters of assemblies' are like stakes (nails) which the shepherds drive into the ground when they pitch their tents;" *i.e.* they are *instruments of fastening* or of securing; they act as things which keep the cords in their place, and keep the roof over the head of the traveller. It is one function of the Christian teacher—and a most valuable one—so to speak that men shall retain their hold on the great verities of the faith, on the true and real Fatherhood of God, on the atonement of Jesus Christ, on the openness of the kingdom of heaven to every seeking soul, on the blessedness of self-forgetful love, on the offer of eternal life to all who believe, etc.

IV. To INSPIRE. At other times the Preacher's words are "as goads" that urge the cattle to other fields. To comfort and to secure is much, but it is not all that they who speak for Christ have to do. They have to illumine and to enlarge men's views, to shed fresh light on the sacred page, to invite those that hear them to accompany them to fields of thought hitherto untrodden, to induce them to think and study for themselves, to unveil the beauties and glories of the wisdom " that remains to be revealed," to inspire them with a yearning desire and with a full purpose of heart to enter upon works of helpfulness and usefulness; he has to " provoke them to love and to good works."—C.

Vers. 13, 14.—*Divine requirement and human response.* What is the conclusion of this inquiry? what result may be gained from these inconsistencies of thought and variations of feeling? Deeper down than anything else is the fact that there are—

I. TWO GREAT DIVINE REQUIREMENTS. God demands of us: 1. *Reverence.* We are to " fear God." *That* is certain. But let us not mistake this " fear " for a very different thing with which it may be confounded. It is *not* a servile dread, such as that which is entertained by ignorant devotees of their deities. Only too often worship rises no higher than that; it is an abject dread of the malignant spiritual power. This is both a falsity and an injury. It is founded on a complete misconception of the Divine, and it reacts most hurtfully upon the mind of the worshipper, demoralizing and degrading. What God asks of us is a well-grounded, holy reverence; the honour which weakness pays to power, which he who receives everything pays to him who gives everything, which intelligence pays to wisdom, which a moral and spiritual nature pays to rectitude, to goodness, to love, to absolute and unspotted worth. 2. *Obedience.* We must " keep his commandments; " *i.e.* not only (1) abstain from those particular transgressions which he has forbidden, and (2) practise those virtues which he has positively enjoined; but also (3) carefully study his holy will in regard to all things, and strive earnestly and patiently to do it. This will embrace, not only all outward actions observable by man, but all the inward thoughts of the mind, and all the hidden feelings and purposes of the soul. It includes the bringing of everything of every kind for which we are personally responsible " into obedience to the will of Christ." It requires of us rectitude in every relation that we sustain to others, as well as in all that we owe to ourselves. The text suggests—

II. THE TWO GREAT REASONS FOR OUR RESPONSE. One is that such reverent obedience is: 1. *Our supreme obligation.* " This is the whole duty of man," or, rather, " This it behoveth all men to do." This is what all men are in sacred duty bound to do. There is no other obligation which is not slight and small in comparison with this. The child owes much to his father, the pupil to his teacher, the beneficiary to his benefactor, the one who has been rescued to his deliverer; but not one of these obligations, nor all added together, expresses anything that approaches the indebtedness under which we rest to God. To him from whom we came, and " in whom we live and move and have our being," who is the one ultimate Source of all our blessings and of all our powers, who has poured out upon us an immeasurable wealth of pure and patient love; to the gracious Father of our spirit; to the gracious Lord of our life; to the holy and the benignant One,—to him it does indeed *become* all men to render a reverent obedience. The other reason why we should respond is found in: 2. *Our supreme wisdom.* " For God will bring," etc. God is now bringing all that we are and do under his own Divine judgment, and is now approving or disapproving. He is also so governing the world that our thoughts and actions are practically judged, and either rewarded or punished, before we pass the border-line of death. But while this is true, and while there is much more of truth in it than is often supposed, yet much is left to the future in this great matter of judgment. There are " secret things " to be exposed; there are undiscovered crimes to be made known; there are iniquities that have escaped even the eye of the perpetrators, who " knew not what they did," to be revealed. There is a great account to be settled. And because it is true that " we must all appear before the judgment-seat of Christ, that every one of us may receive the things done in his body," because " God will judge the secrets of all hearts," because sin in every shape moves toward exposure and penalty, while righteousness in all its forms travels toward its recognition and reward, therefore let tne spirit be reverent in presence of its Maker, let the life be filled with purity and worth, with integrity and goodness, let man be the dutiful child of his Father who is in heaven.—C.

Vers. 8—12.—*The epilogue.* The sentence, "Vanity of vanities; all is vanity!" with which the Book of Ecclesiastes opened, is found here at its close. And doubtless to many ·it will seem disappointing that it should follow so hard upon the expression of belief in immortality. Surely we might say that the nobler view of life reached by the Preacher should have precluded his return to the pessimistic opinions and feelings which we can scarcely avoid associating with the words, "Vanity of vanities; all is vanity!" But on second thoughts the words are not contradictory of the hope for the future which ver. 7 expresses. The fact that Christians can use the words as descriptive of the worthlessness of things that are seen and temporal, as compared with those that are unseen and eternal, forbids our concluding that they are necessarily the utterance of a despairing pessimism. A great deal depends upon the tone in which the words are uttered; and the pious tone of the writer's mind, as revealed in the concluding passages of his book, would incline us to believe that the sentence, "all is vanity," is equivalent to that in the Gospel, "What shall it profit a man, if he gain the whole world, and lose his own soul?" No one can deny that the ' De Imitatione Christi' is a noble expression of certain aspects of Christian teaching with regard to life. And yet in the very first chapter of it we have these words of Solomon's quoted and expanded. "Vanity of vanities, and all is vanity beside loving God and serving him alone. . . . It is vanity, therefore, to seek after riches which must perish, and to trust in them. It is vanity also to lay one's self out for honours, and to raise one's self to a high station. It is vanity to follow the desires of the flesh, and to covet that for which we must afterwards be grievously punished. It is vanity to wish for long life, and to take little care of leading a good life. It is vanity to mind only this present life, and not to look forward to those things which are to come. It is vanity to love that which passes with all speed, and not to hasten thither where everlasting joy abides." In the opinion of many eminent critics the eighth verse contains the concluding words of the Preacher, and those which follow are an epilogue, consisting of a " commendatory attestation " (vers. 9—12), and a summary of the teaching of the book (vers. 13, 14), which justifies its place in the sacred canon. On the whole, this seems to be the most reasonable explanation of the passage. It seems more likely that the glowing eulogy upon the author was written by some one else than that it came from his own pen; and a somewhat analogous postscript is found in another book of Holy Scripture, the Gospel of St. John (xxi. 24). Those who collected the Jewish Scriptures into one, and drew the line between canonical and non-canonical literature, may have considered it advisable to append this paragraph as a testimony in favour of a book which contained so much that was perplexing, and to give a summary (in vers. 13, 14) of what seemed to them its general teaching. The Preacher, they say, was gifted with wisdom over and above his fellows, and taught the people knowledge; and for this pondered and investigated and set in order many proverbs or parables (ver. 9). Like the scribe, "who had been made a disciple to the kingdom of heaven," "he brought forth out of his treasure things new and old " (Matt. xiii. 52). Knowledge of the wisdom of the past, ability to recognize in it what was most valuable, and to cast it into new forms and zeal in the discharge of his sacred office, were all found in him. He sought to attract men to wisdom by displaying it in its gracious aspect (cf. Luke iv. 22), and to influence them by the sincerity of his purpose, and by the actual truth he brought to light (ver. 10). "He aimed to speak at once *words that would please* and *words which were true*—words which would be at once *goads* to the intellect, and yet *stakes* that would uphold and stay the soul of man, both coming alike from one shepherd " (ver. 11, Bradley). Some of his sayings were calculated to stimulate men into fresh fields of thought and new paths of duty, others to confirm them in the possession of truths of eternal value and significance. Like the apostle, he was anxious that his readers should no longer be like " children tossed to and fro, and carried about with every wind of doctrine, by the sleight of men, in craftiness, after the wiles of error " (Eph. iv. 14); but should "prove all things, and hold fast that which is good " (1 Thess.

v. 21). How much better to study in the school of such a teacher than to weary and perplex one's self with " science falsely so called; " than to be versed in multitudinous literature, which dissipates mental energy, and in which the soul can find no sure resting-place (ver. 12)! All who set themselves, or who have been called, to be teachers of men, may find in the example of the Preacher guidance as to the motives and aims which will alone give them success in their work.—J. W.

Vers. 13, 14.—*The last word.* In the passage with which the Book of Ecclesiastes concludes, the clue is found which leads the speaker out of the labyrinth of scepticism in which for a time he had gone astray. He at last emerges from the dark forest in which he had long wandered, and finds himself under the stars of heaven, and sees in the eastern sky the promise of the coming day. It is true that from time to time in his earlier meditations he had retained, even if it were with but a faltering grasp, the truth which he now announces confidently and triumphantly. "It had mitigated his pessimism and hallowed his eudæmonism" (ch. vii. 18 ; viii. 12 ; xi. 9). And it must be taken as cancelling much of what he had said about the vanity of human life. Over against his sombre thoughts about one fate awaiting both the righteous and the wicked, the wise and the foolish (ch. ix. 2), and the levelling power of death, that makes no distinction between man and the brute (ch. iii. 18—22), and shakes one's faith in the dignity and worth of our nature, is set his final verdict. God does distinguish, not only between men and the brutes, but between good men and bad. The efforts we make to obey him, or the indifference towards the claims of righteousness we may have manifested, are not fruitless; they result in the formation of a character that merits and will receive his favour, or of one that will draw down his displeasure. The nearness of God to the individual soul is the great truth upon which our author rests at last, and in his statement of it we have a positive advance upon previous revelations, and an anticipation of the fuller light of the New Testament teaching. God, he would have us believe, does not deal with men as nations or classes, but as individuals. He treats them, whatever may have been their surroundings or national connections, as personally accountable for the disposition and character they have cultivated. His judgment of them lies in the future, and all, without distinction of persons, will be subject to it. In these points, therefore, the writer of the Book of Ecclesiastes transcends the teaching of the Old Testament, and approximates to that of Christ and the apostles. The present life, with all its inequalities, the adversity which often besets the righteous, and the prosperity which the wicked often enjoy, is not the whole of existence, but there is a world to come in which the righteous will openly receive the Divine favour, and the wicked the due reward of their deeds. The blessings which were promised to the nation that was faithful to the Divine Law will be enjoyed by each individual who has had the fear of God before his eyes. Judgment will go by character, and not by outward name or profession (Matt. vii. 21—23 ; Rev. xx. 12). We have, therefore, here a great exhortation founded on truths which cannot be shaken, and calculated to guide each one who obeys it to that goal of happiness which all desire to reach. " Fear God, and keep his commandments." Both the inward disposition and the outward conduct are covered by the exhortation.

I. In the first place, then, THE PRINCIPLE BY WHICH WE SHOULD BE GOVERNED IS THE " FEAR OF GOD." This is the root from which the goodly leaves and choice fruit of a religious life will spring. If the word " fear " had been used in this passage only, and we had not been at liberty to understand it in any other than its ordinary sense, one would be forced to admit that such a low motive could not be the mainspring of a vigorous and healthy religious life. But all through the Scriptures the phrase, " fear of God," is used as synonymous with a genuine, heartfelt service of him, and as rather indicating a careful observance of the obligations we as creatures owe to him, than a mere dread of his anger at disobedience. It is not to be denied that fear, in the ordinary sense of the word, is reasonably a motive by which sin may be restrained, but it is no stimulus to that kind of service which we owe to God. " I thank God, and with joy I mention it," says Sir Thomas Browne, "I was never afraid of hell, nor ever grew pale at the description of that place. I have so fixed my contemplations on heaven, that I have almost forgot the idea of hell; and am afraid rather to lose the joys of one than endure the misery of the other. To be deprived of them is a perfect hell, and needs methinks no addition to complete our afflictions. That terrible term hath never detained me from sin, nor do I owe any good action to the name thereof. I fear God, yet am not afraid of him; his mercies make me ashamed of my sins, before his judgments afraid thereof. These are the forced and secondary methods of his wisdom, which he useth but as the last remedy, and upon provocation—a course rather to deter the wicked than incite the virtuous to his worship. I can hardly think there was ever any scared into heaven: they go the fairest way to heaven that would serve God without a hell. Other mercenaries, that crouch unto him in fear of hell, though they term themselves the servants, are indeed but the slaves, of the Almighty" ('Rel. Med.,' i. 52). Plainly, therefore, when the fear of God is made equivalent to true religion, it must include many other feelings than that dread which sinners experience at the thought of the laws they have broken, and which may consist with hatred of God and of righteousness. It must be a summary of all the emotions which belong to a religious life—reverence at the thought of God's infinite majesty, holiness, and justice, gratitude for his loving-kindness and tender mercy, confidence in his wisdom, power, and faithfulness, submission to his will, and delight in communion with him. If fear is to be taken as a prominent emotion in such a life, we are not to understand by it the terror of a slave, who would willingly, if he could, break away from his owner, but the loving reverence of a child, who is anxious to avoid everything that would grieve his father's heart. The one kind of fear is the mark of an imperfect obedience (1 John iv. 18); the other is the proof of a disposition which calls forth God's favour and blessing (Ps. ciii. 13).

II. In the second place, THE CONDUCT WE SHOULD MANIFEST IS DESCRIBED: "KEEP HIS COMMANDMENTS." This is the outward manifestation of the disposition of the heart, and supplies a test by which the genuineness of a religious profession may be tried. These two elements are needed to constitute holiness—a God-fearing spirit and a blameless life. If either be wanting the nature is out of balance, and very grave defects will soon appear, by which all of positive good that has been attained will be either overshadowed or nullified. If there be not devotion of the heart to God, no zeal and fidelity in discharging the ordinary duties of life will make up for the loss. The reverence due to him as our Creator—gratitude for his benefits, penitent confession of sins and shortcomings, and faith in his mercy—cannot be wilfully omitted by us without a depravation of our whole character. And, on the other side, an acknowledgment of him that does not lead us to "keep his commandments" is equally fatal (Matt. vii. 21—23; Luke xiii. 25—27).

The Preacher appends two weighty considerations to induce us to attend to his exhortation to "fear God, and keep his commandments." The *first* is that this is the *source of true happiness*. So would we interpret his words, "For this is the whole of man." The word "duty" is suggested by our translators to complete the sense, but it is not comprehensive enough. "To fear God and keep his commandments is not only the whole duty, but the whole honour and interest and happiness of man" (Wardlaw). The quest with which the book has been largely concerned is that for happiness, for the *summum bonum*, in which alone the soul can find satisfaction, and here it comes to an end. The discovery is made of that which has been so long and so painfully sought after. In a pious and holy life and conversation rest is found; all else is but vanity and vexation of spirit. The *second* motive to obedience is the *certainty of a future judgment* (ver. 14). "For God shall bring every work into judgment, with every secret thing, whether it be good, or whether it be evil." Nothing will be omitted or forgotten. The Judge will be One who is absolutely just and wise, who will be free from all partiality; and his sentence will be final. If, therefore, we have no such regard for our own happiness in the present life as would move us to secure it by love and service of God, we may still find a check upon self-will and self-indulgence in the thought that we shall have to give an account of our thoughts, words, and deeds to One from whose sentence there is no appeal.—J. W.

HOMILETICAL INDEX

TO

ECCLESIASTES; OR, THE PREACHER

SONG OF SOLOMON

EXPOSITION BY

R. A. REDFORD

HOMILETICS BY

B. C. CAFFIN

HOMILIES BY VARIOUS AUTHORS

J. R. THOMSON   S. CONWAY

J. D. DAVIES

THE SONG OF SOLOMON

INTRODUCTION

THERE is no book of Scripture on which more commentaries have been written and more diversities of opinion expressed than this short poem of eight chapters. That it was held in great veneration by ancient Jewish authorities; that it was received as part of the canon of the Old Testament, not only by the Jews but by all the early Christian writers, with very few and insignificant exceptions; that it is acknowledged by those who are entirely disagreed as to its interpretation to possess features of extraordinary literary excellence, and to be not unworthy, as a composition, of the wise king whose name it bears,—are reasons amply sufficient to justify the largest amount of attention which can be given to it, and to condemn the neglect to which it has been consigned by a great proportion of the Christian Church in modern times. There are difficulties which still beset the interpreter of its meaning; but they are not insuperable. The ingenuity of theorists must be put aside; the fanatical prejudices of allegorists must be disregarded; the solid facts of the case must be kept in view, such as the undoubted canonicity of the book and the almost universal feeling of both the Jewish and Christian Churches that there is valuable spiritual truth conveyed in it. Under such conditions it is not impossible to find an intermediate ground on which to stand, on the one side recognizing the distinctly human characteristics of the work, on the other tracing in it the marks of inspiration, so that it shall be retained as a genuine portion of the Word of God. We propose in this Introduction to lay before the reader the results which have been carefully gathered by the ablest modern commentators on the questions of *authorship and date, form and method, meaning and purpose.*

§ 1. AUTHORSHIP AND DATE.

The title is not decisive, " The Song of Songs, which is Solomon's." It may be later in date than the book itself, and added by another hand;

but the fact that Solomon is not described by any royal title is in favour of the antiquity of the words, and the opinion of critics is almost unanimous that they may be contemporaneous with the book itself. The meaning undoubtedly is, "The song which Solomon composed," not "The song which celebrates Solomon's love." When we examine the internal evidence, however, we are left in little doubt that the work is at least of the Solomonic period, and is more likely to have been the production of one whose literary qualities were equal to it than of an author who, while capable of such a masterpiece, still remains unknown. The opinions of the critics vary, as they always do when variation is possible. Some have ventured to place it in the period after the close of the canon; but they have not attempted to solve the enigma, how such a work of genius could come from a people who had by that time lost so much of their original qualities. To attribute it to the Alexandrian school would be entirely against both the spirit of it and its linguistic features. The tendency of recent criticism is to go back to the early view and connect the work with the age of Solomon. Davidson is inclined to this, and Ewald decides that it must have emanated from the northern kingdom, and been published soon after the death of Solomon. He withholds his assent to the Solomonic authorship chiefly on the ground of his adherence to the peculiar theory of interpretation which supposes it to describe an unsuccessful attempt on the part of the king to secure the person of a young shepherdess, faithful to her shepherd-lover. There are many references in the book which indicate the time of its composition, and which could scarcely be introduced as they are by a writer at a later period. The scene is laid partly in the beautiful northern country and partly in the neighbourhood of Jerusalem, and in both cases there is a peaceful prosperity and abundance which corresponds to the age of the great king. The knowledge of national objects of all kinds and of the whole land of Israel befits the royal pen (see 1 Kings iv. 23; v. 13). The reference in ch. i. 9 to "the steed in Pharaoh's chariots" is eminently suitable in Solomon's lips, as also the description of the palanquin as made of the "wood of Lebanon" (ch. iii. 9). The familiarity with a great variety of lovely objects and scenes, the reference to the splendour of the royal household, and the poetic beauty of the language throughout, make it probable that it was the recollection of the early life of the monarch employed by him at a subsequent time to embody Divine truth. The following are some of the objects introduced: names of plants and of animals in thirty-one instances; works of art in ten instances; spices and perfumes, wine of Lebanon, pools of Hebron, forests of Carmel, tents of Kedar, mountains of Gilead, the beauty of Tirzah and Jerusalem, the royal crown, the royal bed of state, the royal body-guard, the royal espousals and the connection of the queen-mother with them. While such allusions do not absolutely prove that King Solomon himself was the author, they confirm the likelihood that it dates from his age, and show that it breathed much of his spirit, which was both intensely Jewish and cosmopolitan, dignified and human, profound and poetic.

Again, there is a considerable resemblance between the language of Solomon's Song and that of the Book of Proverbs—especially the first nine chapters and those from ch. xxii. to xxiv. (cf. Prov. v. 15 with Cant. iv. 15, vii. 17 with iv. 14, v. 3 with iv. 11, vi. 30, 31 with viii. 6, 7, xxiii. 31 with vii. 10). This is no proof that Solomon himself wrote Canticles, but is evidence that the two books approach one another in date. The substance of the book accords with the facts of Solomon's history. It is true that the number of queens mentioned, three score, and four score concubines, and virgins without number, seem to differ from the amount given in 1 Kings xi. 3, but that may be explained by the fact that the reference of Canticles is to the early period of Solomon's splendour, when his life was less voluptuous and degenerate. The tone of the book is not that of a corrupt court, but rather of the simple purity of a country maiden blooming in the presence of royal magnificence, transforming for the time being the atmosphere of worldly pleasure into which she is introduced, rebuking the fallen monarch, and setting forth by way of contrast the superior glory of virtue.

The argument for a later date derived from the language itself is of very little force. It is assumed that Aramaic forms certainly betoken the decay of the Hebrew language. But this is by no means the case. In compositions of a highly poetical and lyrical character such forms are found throughout the Old Testament, as in the Song of Deborah (Judg. v. 7), in Job, and in Amos. They were more frequently used, no doubt, in the northern parts of Palestine than in the southern, and would be an evidence of the provincial cast of the book rather than its late origin. This is particularly the case with abbreviated forms such as the שֶׁ for אֲשֶׁר, which we do not find in books of later date such as Jeremiah and Lamentations. Other Aramaisms are שַׁלְּמָה in ch. i. 7; נָטַר for נָצַר (ch. i. 6; viii. 11, 12); בְּרוֹת for בְּרוֹשׁ (ch. i. 17); סְתָו, "winter" (ch. ii. 11), and others; but all these forms are confessedly poetical. There are also some few foreign words, such as *pardes* (ch. iv. 13), *appiryon* (ch. iii. 9), but they are such as do not again appear, and such as we may well suppose to be within the knowledge of such a writer as Solomon. It may be observed of the language generally, that it is much more like the Hebrew of the Augustan age of the language than of times when its native vigour was in decay, and it was rapidly becoming a dead language. There is no work subsequent to the Captivity to be compared with it in literary power, nor can we suppose that all reference to the changes in the national life could have been lacking had it come from a writer of the later times. It is utterly destitute of all philosophical thought, which would certainly have crept into it had it been composed during the Greek period. On the whole, we can scarcely doubt that it is an early work, and the critical authorities who would dispute that conclusion are of no great weight. Umbreit would ascribe it to the time of the exile. Eichhorn, Bertholdt, and Rosen-müller would date it still later, in the Persian age. Grätz, Hartmann, and some few others would assign it to the Greek period. But against such names we must place the much higher authority of Ewald, Döpke, Häver-nick, Bleek, Hengstenberg, Zöckler, Delitzsch, and Davidson, who all agree that it comes from the period of Solomon, though they do not all admit the royal authorship. Had it been of late origin, we could scarcely understand the extreme reverence with which it was regarded in the Jewish Church. "No man in Israel," said Rabbi Akiba in the 'Mishna,' "ever doubted the canonicity of the Song of Songs, for the course of ages cannot vie with the day on which the Song of Songs was given to Israel; all the Kethuvim [*i.e.* the writings of the Hagiographa] are indeed a holy thing, but the Song of Songs is a holy of holies" ('Jadaim,' iii. 5). It seems probable, from the language both of Hosea and Isaiah, and the familiarity of the Jewish people with the fundamental idea of the book, the intimate relation of the truths of religion with the emotions of the human soul, that it was well known from at least as early a period as the eighth century before Christ. There is no direct allusion to it in the New Testament; but the language of the Psalms, especially such as Ps. xlv. and lxxii., corresponds with it; and the cast of the Apostle Paul's thoughts is often in harmony with it; while the appeals of our Saviour himself to the hearts of the people to recognize their loving relation to God and repent of their unfaithfulness, render it at least possible that the tenderness and persuasive beauty of Canticles was not ignored in the religious teaching of his day. He who was, in his own words, the *heavenly Bridegroom*, and who spoke, both by his own life and by those of his apostles, of his bride and her desire towards him, and the joy and glory of his nuptials, can scarcely be said to have left this book unnoticed, although he never quoted from it or mentioned it by name. It stands by itself in the Old Testament, as the Apocalypse stands by itself in the New; but only those who have given it a hasty and superficial reading will long doubt that it contains within itself the mind of the Spirit.

§ 2. The Literary Form and Method of the Poem.

Critics have been almost as much divided on the literary questions arising out of this remarkable book as theological writers have been on the interpretation of its meaning. Some have regarded it as a collection of love-songs, as Herder the great German poet and philosopher, whose interesting and able work on the subject is entitled, 'Love Songs, the most Ancient and Beautiful from the East' (published in 1778). The old name given to the book, 'Canticles,' lends some weight to that view. The fact that no persons are introduced by name, and that the connection between the different parts of the poem is difficult to trace, seems to suggest an anthology of songs rather than a composition with unity of method and purpose. There have been modifications of this extreme view among the critics which have grown out of the more careful study of the poem. Goethe, *e.g.*, while he once held that it was a mere collection of separate songs, afterwards in the 'Kunst und Alterthum' admitted that there was dramatic unity to be recognized in it. The chief representative of Herder's view in later times is Mündt; but there are few writers of any distinction who would deny that at least one mind is traceable in the ordering and placing of the songs. Bleek, *e.g.*, admits one editor who has put together a variety of erotic compositions referring to different persons and composed at different periods. And some Jewish critics have supposed that while the bulk of the poem refers to Solomon, other songs of a later date have been interpolated. The chief authorities for the unity of the composition are Ewald, Umbreit, Delitzsch, and Zöckler. The following considerations must be acknowledged by every candid reader to be amply sufficient to support the view that the poem is not a mere collection of fragments or isolated songs, but has a definite aim, and is the product, at least in arrangement, of some one superintending mind. The *name of Solomon*, and of "the *king*," who is plainly Solomon, is prominent in the poem through-out. The different parts seem to be strung together by the introduction of a *chorus* somewhat after the manner of a Greek play; and the lover and his beloved interchange the language of affection in a kind of *dialogue*. The references to *the family of the bride* are consistent throughout. The mother is introduced, never the father, but only the brothers, as though the father were deceased, which would point to a particular history (see ch. i. 6; iii. 4; and viii. 2). Again, the occurrence again and again of the same or similar words as a *refrain*, and the repetition of similar *illustrations* and *figures*, suggest one mind at work. The bride speaks in much the same language several times. In ch. ii. 16 and vi. 3 she says, "My beloved is mine, and I am his." In ch. ii. 5 and v. 8, "I am sick with love," and over and over again she uses the expression, "he whom my soul loves." She is addressed by the chorus in a similar manner throughout. Delitzsch very rightly says, "He who has any perception whatever of the unity of a work of art in human discourse will receive an impression of external unity from the Song of Solomon which excludes all right to sunder anything from it as of a heterogeneous character or belonging to different periods, and which compels to the conclusion of an internal unity that may still remain an enigma to the Scripture exposition of the present, but must nevertheless exist."

But while unity of authorship, composition, and purpose may be substantiated, it is still a difficult question to decide *what is the literary form and method of the poem*. It is a mere abuse of literary language to call it a *drama*. There is, properly speaking, no dramatic action and progress in it. Ewald has gone so far as to maintain that it was designed for representation, and Böttcher and Renan that it actually was exhibited as a play. But all that can be said in favour of such a view is that there

are *dramatic features* in the poem, such as the dialogue between the lover
and the beloved, the introduction of the chorus, and the scenic character
of some of the descriptions.   But, on the other hand, there is no evidence
that any such representations took place among the Jews at any time,
and the generally idyllic character of the whole makes it extremely
improbable that it was intended to be a drama.   We can no more call the
Song of Solomon a drama than we can give such a title to the Book of Job.
Nor can we say, on the other hand, that it is a mere *epithalamium*, or
idyllic song prepared for some nuptial occasion and adapted to a musical
intention.   The literary problems arising out of the mixed character of
the composition seem to be solved in the higher question of its aim and
purpose.   It is the adaptation of human affection and sentiment to
religious uses.   We need not therefore wait for a satisfactory theory of
its literary style, but rather be content to arrange its contents as they
dispose themselves by the natural divisions of the subject-matter.   It
has been observed by Dr. Henry Green, of Princeton (in a note to his
translation of Zöckler's 'Commentary'), " The scenes portrayed and the
displays of mutual fondness indulged seem to be grouped rather than
linked.   They stand forth in their distinctness as exquisitely beautiful,
and reflecting as much light on each other and on the subject which they
illustrate and adorn as though they had been gathered up into the artificial
unity of a consecutive narration or a dramatic plot.   And this looser
method of arrangement or aggregation, with its abrupt translation and
sudden changes of scene, is no less graceful and impressive, while it is
more in harmony with the Oriental mind and style of composition
generally than the vigorous, external, and formal concatenation which
the more logical but less proud Indo-European is prone to demand."   All
that seems necessary to do as a help to the literary appreciation of the
poem is to indicate the general principle and method of its arrangement,
which may be expressed thus : Love is first set forth simply in its ecstatic
fervour of emotion in the *mutual delight* of the lover and the beloved.   It
is then celebrated as *nuptial love* in the rejoicing of the bridegroom and
the bride.   And in the second half of the poem, ch. v. 1 to the end, love
is set forth as *tried*, for a time in danger of being lost, ultimately recovered
and expanding into *the fulness of joy*.   There are thus three parts in the
poem.   Part I. extends from the beginning to the fifth verse of the third
chapter, and may be described as *The rapture of first love*.   Part II. extends
from ch. iii. 6 to v. 1, and may be called *Nuptial rejoicing*.   Part III.
extends from ch. v. 2 to viii. 14, and may be named *Separation and reunion*.
But while these main divisions are traceable in the composition, there
are subdivisions which enable us to arrange the whole into a series of
lyrical pieces, and to discern in the language some distinction of speakers
and some variety of scene and action which give a wonderful life and
unity to the poem.

   The opening words prepare us for the general scope of the whole work, which is to set forth the theme of *true love*, and thus to lead our thoughts to the highest ideal of love. "Let him kiss me with the kisses of his mouth: for thy love is better than wine." We are prepared for *the rapture of first love*, which is poured out in the first part in exquisite dialogue and monologue.

(1) Shulamith, the beloved, is waiting for the arrival of her lover, and, surrounded by the chorus of ladies, pours out her rapture and longing, which is responded to by her admiring companions (ch. i. 1—8).

(2) The royal lover appears, and the rapturous joy of mutual delight is poured out in the banqueting-house (ch. i. 9 to ii. 7), closing with the refrain of serene contentment addressed by the beloved woman to the fair companions of her chamber: "I adjure you, O daughters of Jerusalem, by the roes and by the hinds of the field, that ye stir not up, nor awaken love until it please."

(3) In the bright, pure atmosphere of this new-found rapture the beloved woman sings the episodes of her love, tells how the loved one wooed her, how the first love mingled with the loveliness of the opening spring and summer and the delights of a pastoral life, how the heart longed for him until he was found, and when it found him would not let him go, concluding with the same refrain of satisfied yearning as in ch. ii. 7. This third subdivision of Part I. occupies from ch. ii. 8 to iii. 5, and contains some of the loveliest poetry in the whole composition.

Part II. *Nuptial rejoicing* (ch. iii. 6 to v. 1). Here we have first a description of the nuptial festival, and then the bride and bridegroom rejoicing in one another.

(1) *The litter of Solomon* is seen surrounded with his body-guard advancing towards Jerusalem. The daughters of Jerusalem go forth to meet him. He is crowned with the splendid crown made by his mother for the day of his espousal. It is but a glimpse of the festival, but it suggests the whole (ch. iii. 6—11).

(2) The greater part of the beautiful song which follows (ch. iv. 1—15) is *the address of the bridegroom to the bride;* but *the bride responds* with a brief rhapsody of delight, in which she surrenders herself entirely to her husband (ch. iv. 16): "Awake, O north wind; and come, thou south; blow upon my garden, that the spices thereof may flow out. Let my beloved come into his garden, and eat his precious fruits;" to which the bridegroom responds with the words of delight and satisfaction (ch. v. 1).

This concludes the first half of the poem. We then pass into another region. The cloud passes over the face of the sun. The brightness of the bridal bliss is obscured for a while. The bride tells of her forgetfulness and the recovery of her peace. This we may call *Separation and reunion*—Part III. (ch. v. 2 to viii. 14). The subdivisions of this concluding portion may be distinguished as follows :—

(1) Under the figure of a dream the bride describes the *temporary separation* of her heart from the bridegroom; her misery; her longing and

searching for the beloved object; and her appeal to her fair companions to help her (ch. v. 2—8).

(2) The *sympathizing companions* of the bride draw out the fulness of her love by their questions, asking "why she so loves him," and whither he is gone from her (ch. v. 9 to vi. 3).

(3) *The royal bridegroom* returns to his bride and rejoices once more in her (ch. vi. 4—9).

(4) The companions of the bride, recognizing the effect of the renewed bliss in the appearance of the bride, burst out into *a song of praise of her beauty* (ch. vi. 10).

(5) The bride responds with a declaration of her *ecstatic delight* (ch. vi. 11, 12).

(6) The companions of the bride pour out their praises as they behold the bride in her *dance of ecstasy* (ch. vi. 13 to vii. 5).

(7) *The royal bridegroom*, approaching the bride, delights in her attractions (ch. vii. 6—9).

(8) The bride, full of satisfaction in the love of her husband, invites him to return with her to *the scenes of her maiden life*, and there his love would beautify all that was familiar to her. In the thought of such bliss she again adjures her companions to acknowledge the perfection of her peace (ch. vii. 10 to viii. 4).

(9) *Bride and bridegroom* are together in the restful joy of a simple country life, exchanging sweet remembrances and confidences (ch. viii. 5—7).

(10) In the peace of the old home others are thought of, and the bliss of the bride overflows upon her *kindred*, to which the royal bridegroom responds and the bride rejoices (ch. viii. 8—12).

(11) *The royal bridegroom*, delighting in his bride, bids her sing (ch. viii. 13).

(12) The poem ends with the sweet melody of *the bride's voice*, inviting the bridegroom to hasten to her side, in one of her familiar love-songs: "Make haste, my beloved, and be thou like to a roe or to a young hart upon the mountains of spices." Thus the voice of the bride, which opens the poem, lingers on the ear in its close, and suggests to us that the whole is as if from *her* standpoint *the aspiration of an ideal love*, breathing itself out in desire after the beloved objects,—that *the king may delight himself in her beauty*.

§ 3. THEORIES OF INTERPRETATION.

No one can accept the Song of Solomon as a book of Scripture, the canonical authority of which is undoubted, without forming some theory of interpretation which shall justify the position of such a book amongst the sacred writings. It will be evident that our fundamental principles in respect to the nature and authority of inspired books will modify the views we hold on any particular portion of Scripture. If the sacred writings are no more than a collection of Jewish literature, in which there would naturally be great variety, and not necessarily in every instance a lofty spiritual aim, then we can regard the Song of Solomon as Herder did, as a collection of beautiful Eastern songs, and there is no need to seek in them either unity of purpose or special significance. But it is more difficult to reconcile such a view with the facts than to find a tenable theory of interpretation. It is simply incredible that such a book, if merely of literary or moral worth, should be introduced into the collection of Jewish Scriptures, to be an inexplicable exception to the whole volume. All other books have some distinct and easily recognizable connection with the religious character and peculiar national position of the Jewish people. Not one is where it is because it is a piece of *literature*. Why should the Song of Solomon be an exception? Moreover, the simple fact that Jews themselves have always sought for an interpretation of the book shows that they were not satisfied with the mere literary value of it. We must either eliminate it altogether from the Bible, or we must find some method for its profitable use. Those who have renounced all attempts to explain it have either been impatient with the difficulties, or out of humour with the expositors. No doubt a very large amount of folly has been published by those who have endeavoured to support a theory by ingenious manipulation of the language. We are apt to be revolted by such extravagance, and treat the whole subject with indifference. But there is no more beautiful book in the Old Testament than the Song of Solomon. We cannot be right in leaving it unstudied and unused. We *must* deal with it as a part of Holy Scripture. As far as possible, therefore, we must put it in intelligible relation to the Word of God, as a progressive revelation of Divine truth. We must understand what is the idea of the book, and how that idea is set forth in the form in which the poem is composed. We proceed, therefore, to give an account of the different theories which have been held as to the interpretation of the book, and so to justify that which we accept in the subsequent Exposition.

The theories of interpretation may be classed under three heads. **1.** Those which assume that the work is an *allegory*, that the facts contained in it are merely employed for the purpose of framework, the language being mystical and figurative. 2. Those which are founded upon a *naturalistic* basis, taking the literary features of the work as the first in importance, and regarding it as some form of *love-poem* or collection of *erotic songs*. 3. Between these two extremes stands the *typical* view, which, without discarding the historical and literary basis, not to be disputed on the very face of the work, endeavours to justify its position in the Word of God by analogy with other portions of Scripture, in which natural and national facts and interests are imbued with spiritual significance. In each of these points of view there is truth, as there is variety of interpretation. We shall be best prepared to understand the results of the most able modern criticism by placing these different theories clearly side by side.

1. *The allegorical theory.* This is much the most ancient method of interpretation. It sprang, no doubt, from the rabbinical school among the Jews, in which the verbal inspiration of Scripture was tenaciously held, while, at the same time, all kinds of fanciful interpretations were foisted into the divinely authorized words. If the veil of the language has to be preserved intact, then the only resource of the dogmatist or the speculator is to bring forth from behind the veil that which suits his purpose. It is of no consequence to prove that there were any real persons, such as Solomon and Shulamith, whose love for one another is celebrated in this book. It might be so or it might not be so ; these things are an allegory. The deepest truths are set forth in the dress of these words of human affection. Some have found in them *God and his Church* throughout all time. Others the *historical and political relations* of the Jewish people. Others have sought in them profound *philosophical mysteries* and *cabalistic secrets.* There is one point, and one alone, in which all these allegorical interpreters agree, and that is, that nothing is to be made of the book taken literally, that there is no consistency and order in it if we attempt to regard it historically; therefore we have nothing in it but words, which may be applied in any manner which is spiritually or otherwise profitable. Such a view condemns itself, for it deprives us of any ground of confidence in seeking the true interpretation. That surely must be the mind of the Spirit which best accords with the facts of the case. If there is not a foundation of historical truth underlying all the Scripture, then it is a mere unsubstantial cloud which may be blown away by the changes in the atmosphere of human opinion. It is against the analogy of Scripture. It opens the way to extravagance and folly, by removing all bounds and inviting the licence of mere individual speculation. It repels the common sense of the ordinary reader of Scripture, and simply shuts the book which it misinterprets, so that many refuse to look into it at all. " This mode of expounding each separate particular, not with a view to its place in the description in which it stands, but as a distinct reference to the spiritual object typified by it, necessarily leads both to a serious distortion of the lessons to be conveyed, and to a marring and mangling of the symmetry and beauty of the objects depicted." Postponing any further discussion of this principle, we proceed to give a summary of the history of the allegorical interpretation.

There is no evidence that the Song of Solomon was allegorically interpreted among the ancient Jews previous to the Christian era. Had it been a well-known, traditional view, it would certainly have appeared in some of the writings of the Apocrypha, or in the works of Philo. But there is no clear trace of it in either. The allusion which is found in the Fourth Book of Esdras (v. 24, 26), in which the terms "lily" and "dove" are employed of the Church, must be referred to a Christian origin, and dates probably about the end of the first century A.D. There is no decided evidence of the allegorical theory until the eighth century, when there appeared a Targum on the book itself, with Ruth, Lamentations, Esther, and Ecclesiastes. The allegory is taken to be a figurative representation of the history of the Israelites from the time of the exodus to their final restoration and salvation. The Targum is marked, like most similar productions, by great extravagance and absurd anachronisms. After an interval of several centuries, distinguished rabbis published commentaries which contained references to older interpreters who had followed the Targum in the allegorical view. Such were Rabbi Solomon ben Isaac (or Rashi), who died 1105; David Kimchi (1190—1250); Ibn Ezra (died 1167); Moses Maimonides (died 1204); Moses ben Tibbon; Immanuel ben Salome, and others. Some of these rabbinical writers have used the book to support their peculiar philosophical views and their rabbinical interpretations of Scripture; but most of the Jewish writers have regarded the allegory as veiled history and prophecy.

It was very different, however, with the Christian commentators. Not only did they almost without exception treat the book as an allegory, but they strained the interpretation beyond all limits of common sense and Scripture analogy, so that their example has remained a warning, which has produced a healthy reaction in the Church, and has led to the more reasonable view which is now adopted by all the best critics. The rise of the allegorical method can be traced chiefly to the Alexandrian school, and to its great representative Origen. It was the fruit of philosophy in union with Christianity. Origen wrote two homilies on the Song of Solomon, which were translated by Jerome, and a commentary, part of which still remains in the Latin of Rufinus. The idea of the book, according to Origen, is the longing of the soul after God, and the sanctifying and elevating influence of Divine love; but he varies in his explanation of the allegory, now taking it of the individual and then of the Church. His example was followed by later Christian writers, as by Eusebius, Athanasius, Epiphanius, Cyril, Macarius, Gregory of Nyssa, Basil, Gregory Nazianzen, Theodoret, Augustine, and Chrysostom. There were slight differences among these early Fathers in their application of the method, but they all adopted it. Ambrose went so far as to suggest in his sermon on the perpetual virginity of Saint Mary, that there are allusions to Mary in such expressions as the "locked garden" and the "sealed fountain" (ch. iv. 12); and Gregory the Great regarded the crown wherewith Solomon's mother crowned him as a mystical emblem of the humanity which the Saviour derived from Mary. There were some of the Fathers, however, as Theodore of Mopsuestia, who advocated the literal and historical method of interpretation, and he was challenged by some of his critics for his sensual view of the book.

When we come to the Middle Ages we meet with larger and fuller commentaries, in which the allegorical method is wrought out with great ingenuity. The highest name, perhaps, is that of the mystic Bernard of

Clairvaux (died 1153), who wrote eighty-six sermons on the first two chapters, followed by his scholar, Gilbert von Hoyland, who wrote fifty-eight discourses on another portion. Bernard's discourses are mystical. The soul is seeking her heavenly Bridegroom, and introduced by him into progressive states of privilege—the garden, the banqueting-hall, the sleeping-chamber. The kiss of Christ is explained of the Incarnation. He was followed by Richard de St. Victor, and by the great theologian Thomas Aquinas, Bonaventura, Gershon, and Isidore Hispalensis. The whole mystery of the soul's intercourse with the Saviour is, according to them, represented in the language of the Song. The book was, of course, greedily laid hold of by the Middle Age mystics, as it has been by the mystico-evangelical school of modern times, and amidst a dense cloud of fanciful extravagance there are here and there to be found in their commentaries gleams of highly spiritual discernment and profound thought. The Spanish mystics went to great lengths of absurdity; the " cheeks " of the bride were outward Christianity and good works; her "golden chains" were faith; the "silver points" of the golden ornaments were holiness in the walk and conversation; "spikenard" was redeemed humanity; "the breath of myrrh" was the Passion of our Saviour; "the thorns about the rose" were temptations by tribulations, crimes, and heretics; "the chariot of Amminadab" represented the power of the devil, and so forth.

When we come to the time of the Reformers, when biblical study received an entirely new impulse and direction, we find the allegorical method, while not altogether discarded, somewhat modified by the historical and critical spirit which was growing in the Church. Martin Luther was to a large extent under the influence of mystical writers in the early part of his theological course, but he did not follow them in their allegorical tendencies. He saw the danger, which they had promoted, to the healthy use of Scripture, and the mist they threw around its simple, practical meaning. In his 'Brevis Enarratio in Cantica Canticorum' he takes the book as written for an historical purpose—to glorify the age and kingly power of Solomon, and so to exalt the theocracy at its highest splendour. It is to help the people to thank God for the blessings of peace and prosperity. God is the Bridegroom, and his people are the bride. Luther was followed in his view by other Reformers. Nicolas de Lyra, in his 'Portilla,' regards it as a representation of the history of Israel from Moses to Christ, and in the later chapters, of the Christian Church from Christ to the time of the Emperor Constantine. Starke (in his 'Synopsis,' pt. iv.) sees in it a prophecy in which is represented the coming of Messiah in the flesh, the outpouring of the Holy Spirit, the gathering of the New Testament Church from Jews and Gentiles, and the special trials and providential leadings of the people of God in every age. Bishop Perez of Valentia, in 1507, published a commentary, in which an elaborate system of chronological interpretation is set forth. There are ten canticles setting forth ten periods—the patriarchs, the tabernacle, the voice of God from the tabernacle, the ark in the wilderness, Moses on Pisgah, the death of Moses, entrance into Canaan, conquest and partition of Canaan, conflicts under the Judges, prosperity and peace under Solomon. To these ten *Old Testament facts* correspond ten *New Testament fulfilments*—the Incarnation, teaching of Christ, his life and miracles, his ascent to Jerusalem, his death on the cross, the ingathering of Jewish converts, the mission to the Gentiles, the conflicts of the martyr Church, prosperity and peace under Constantine. Cocceius (1673), in his 'Cogitationes,' finds in it the prediction of the events of his own time; and Cornelius à Lapide treats it, in a high Roman Catholic manner, as significant of the glory of the Virgin, while he takes it as a kind of *prophetic drama*, setting forth the history of the Church.

When we come to more modern times and to the great " Introductions " to the study of the Bible, written by the most learned critics, we see the influence of a closer attention to the structure and language of the book in the gradual decay of the allegorical method, and the attempt to unite the facts which underlie the words with a distinct spiritual significance. In the beginning of this century, the great Roman Catholic theologian and critic Leon. Hug (1813) made a novel attempt to maintain the allegorical view. The bride represented the ten tribes, the bridegroom King Hezekiah, the brother of the bride a party in the house of Judah opposing the reunion of the rent kingdom. He was followed by Kaiser in 1825. Rosenmüller sought to put fresh life into the worn-out theory by analogies brought from Hindoo and Persian poetry; as Puffendorf (1776) introduced in his paraphrase mystical allusions to the grave and the hope of the resurrection, the " virgins " being " pure and chaste souls shut up in the dark grave," and waiting for the light of the Saviour's resurrection. Until we come to the time of Keil and Hengstenberg, we have no really sensible defence of the theory put forth, and it is scarcely necessary to make the remark that *their* defence is a virtual surrender, for their use of the *allegorical* method is so moderate that it barely exceeds the *ideal* and *typical* view, and is substantially the same as that of Delitzsch and Zöckler. Keil ('Introduction to the Old Testament,' vol. i. p. 503, Eng. transl.) says, " The book depicts in dramatico-lyrical, responsive songs, under the allegory of the bridal love of Solomon and Shulamith, the loving communion between the Lord and his Church, according to its ideal nature as it results from the choice of Israel to be the Church of the Lord. According to this, every disturbance of that fellowship springing out of Israel's infidelity leads to an ever firmer establishment of the covenant of love, by means of Israel's return to the true covenant God, and this God's unchangeable love. Yet we are not to trace in the poem the historical course of the covenant relation, as if a veil of allegory had been thrown over the principal critical events in the theocratic history." Hahn, *e.g.*, finds allegorically represented " that the kingdom of Israel is called in the service of God finally to overcome heathendom with the weapons of love and righteousness, and to lead it back to the peaceful rest of loving fellowship with Israel, and so with God again." Hengstenberg, in his 'Prolegomena to the Song of Solomon,' and in his Exposition (1853), argues for the allegorical view from the use of similar erotic language in the Psalms and prophets, as well as in the general tone of the Old Testament. The beloved of the heavenly Solomon is the daughter of Zion; the whole, therefore, must be explained of Messiah and his Church. But he proceeds to attempt an application of this view to the details of the language, in which he shows that it can only be accepted in a modified form—*the hair of the bride like a flock of goats* represents the mass of nations converted to Christianity; *the navel of Shulamith* denotes the cup from which the Church refreshes those that thirst for salvation with a noble and refreshing draught; *the sixty and eighty wives of Solomon*, the admission of the original Gentile nations into the Church, 140 being 7 multiplied by 2 and by 10—the "signature of the covenant," the kingdom of Christ being prefigured by the diverse nations introduced into Solomon's harem! Such follies tend to blind the reader to the substantial truth of the theory, which is that, under the figure of the pure and beautiful love of Solomon for Shulamith, is imaged the love of God in Christ for humanity, both in the individual and in the Church.

The only other names which require mention in connection with the allegorical theory are those of Thrupp, Wordsworth, and Stowe. Joseph Francis Thrupp published a revised translation with introduction and commentary (Cambridge, 1862). The millenarian view dominates his work throughout. It is a prophecy of the coming of Christ. Wordsworth (Christopher), in his 'Commentary on the Bible,' published 1868, also regards the poem as a prophetic allegory, suggested by Solomon's marriage with Pharaoh's daughter, and describing "the gathering" of the world into mystical union with Christ, and its consecration into a Church espoused to him as the bride. Calvin E. Stowe defends the allegorical view in the *Biblical Repository* (April, 1847), giving a partial translation. The fault of all these writers, able and learned as they are, is that they push their theory too far, and that they are led away by it into a misuse of Scripture to support that which does not fairly rest upon it. This is the danger which must always attend upon the allegorical method. The ingenuity of the interpreter is tempted to supply, out of his own creed, what is lacking in the scheme of the allegory. He has liberty to suggest what analogies he discovers. The highly figurative language of such a poem as the Song of Solomon is easily accommodated to the demands of any system of thought to which the wish is father. But while the allegorical method, *as a formal treatment*, may be erroneous, it recognizes the spiritual meaning and value of the book. The canonical position of such a work requires to be justified. The allegorist attempts to do so. He is certainly right in demanding that a distinct religious purpose shall be the *vital centre* of any system of interpretation put forth. As Isaac Taylor has remarked, in his 'Spirit of Hebrew Poetry,' "The book has given animation, and depth, and intensity, and warrant, too, to the devout meditations of thousands of the most devout and of the purest minds. Those who have no consciousness of this kind, and whose feelings and notions are all 'of the earth, earthy,' will not fail to find in this instance that which suits them, for purposes, sometimes of mockery, sometimes of luxury, sometimes of disbelief. Quite unconscious of these possessions, and happily ignorant of them, and unable to suppose them possible, there have been multitudes of earthly spirits to whom this, the most beautiful of pastorals, has been, not indeed a beautiful pastoral, but the choicest of those words of truth which are 'sweeter than honey to the taste,' and ' rather to be chosen than thousands of gold and silver.' "

2. We must now proceed to describe the theories of interpretation which have been based upon a *naturalistic principle*. These may be styled *the erotic*, as they all regard the work as *a collection of erotic songs*, put together simply on the ground of their literary worth and poetic arrangement, religiously used by being idealized, just as the language of secular poetry may be sometimes mingled with sacred, though the original intention of the words had no such application. There are several varieties in the form of this erotic theory. The songs have been regarded by some as separate *idylls of love*, collected together and formed into a poem only by a predominating reference to Solomon, and by the one pervading spirit of pure love. But others have attempted to trace a *dramatic unity and progress* in the whole, and have elaborated a *history* on which to found the drama, while those who have renounced all such attempts to find a drama in Hebrew poetry have yet clung to the idea of an *epithalamium*, composed on the occasion of Solomon's marriage, either with the Egyptian princess or some Israelitish bride, and have endeavoured to justify their view by the literary form of the poem. It is not necessary entirely to reject *the naturalistic basis* in order to find a reason for the position of Solomon's Song in the Bible. There is an element of truth in all the erotic theories. They help us to remember that *human love* is capable of being mingled with *Divine ideas*. That which is so often impure, and which sinks the life of man below that of the beasts that perish, may yet be sanctified, lifted above the evil of a fallen nature, and so may be taken, ideally, as the fitting vehicle by which to convey the Spirit of God to the spirit of man.

The earliest writer whose treatment of the book was based upon the secular view of it was Theodore of Mopsuestia (died A.D. 429). He dealt with all Scripture much in the same way, in the spirit of a rigid literalism, in which he followed the school of Antioch. Like others of the same class, he found only *human love* in the language, and his ' Commentary ' was publicly condemned on that account in the Fifth Œcumenical Council (A.D. 553). The Church's anathema crushed this commentary out of existence. The *Middle Ages* were dominated by the allegorical spirit, and no other view was put forth for hundreds of years. Until the free spirit of the Reformation introduced a new criticism, the secular view of Solomon's Song did not reappear. In the time of Calvin, Geneva was startled by the *brochure* of Sebastian Castellio (1544), who represented Shulamith as a concubine, and denounced the book as unworthy of a place in Scripture—to the great displeasure of Calvin himself, who is said to have compelled Castellio to withdraw from Geneva. The next name in the bibliography is that of Hugo Grotius, who published his 'Annotations' on the Old Testament in 1664. In his view the work is a *nuptial song*, with allegorical and typical meanings, which he admits are to be found in it, though he does not himself seek them. R. Simon, J. Clericus, Simon Episcopius, are other instances of the same treatment of the book in the latter part of the seventeenth and the beginning of the eighteenth centuries. The rise of *rationalism* was the revival of the theory. Semler and Michaelis led the way, in the middle of the last century, disparaging the book altogether.

It was only as the literary spirit of German criticism began to deal more fairly with the whole of Scripture, as the remains of a great people, that the poetic merits of Solomon's Song began to be recognized, and an attempt was made to understand its position in the canon. Lessing, who was the greatest critical mind of Europe at that time, saw that there was great idyllic beauty in these 'Eclogues of King Solomon,' as he called them, and compared them with those of Theocritus and Virgil; but the most distinguished name is that of Herder, whose celebrated work on 'The Spirit of Hebrew Poetry' did much to revive the interest of the literary world in the Bible. Herder wrote a separate work on Solomon's Song, treating it as a collection of songs of love, and as intended to describe *ideal human love*, for the purpose of setting forth the example of purity and innocence when it was most needed in the ancient world. His criticism is in many respects valuable and highly æsthetic. He draws attention to the exquisite poetry of the songs, and to their surpassing worth as an ideal of human sentiment. But delightful reading as Herder's work undoubtedly is, it is yet but little help to the biblical student, as there is no attempt to follow out the religious intimations of the language, or to find in it any parabolical intention. The rationalistic critics have, most of them, regarded the songs as *fragmentary* and isolated, and thus have deprived themselves of their true position as commentators; for if there be no *unity* in the book, it is hard to find any basis on which to rest the explanation of its meaning as a whole. To suppose a sacred work written simply in praise of human feeling, or even to cherish the ideal of human relationship, is to resist the analogy of Scripture. It may be doubted if even the Proverbs of Solomon should be regarded from so wide and general a point of view as that.

There is no need to trouble the reader with an account of the many books which have appeared in Germany, treating not only Solomon's Song, but every other book in the Bible, in the most flimsy, superficial spirit, as though no deeper meaning need ever be sought in them than that which satisfies the logical understanding of a narrow-minded, pedantic professor. Eichhorn, Jahn, De Wette, Augusti, Kleuker, Döderlein, Velthusen, Gaab, Justi,

Dödke, Magnus, Rebenstein, Lossner,—all such critics have proceeded on the principle of finding a literary explanation of the form, not a spiritual exposition of the matter. Their highest aim is critical, and they have their reward—they shake together a heap of dry bones, and their own dead hearts hear no living voice of response. But there is a little advance upon the barren, dreary emptiness of this rationalistic criticism in what is called the dramatic theory of interpretation, which has received a considerable accession of interest during the present century by the development of a new historical hypothesis by which it is attempted to explain the dramatic unity and progress of the composition. Jacobi, in 1771, led the way, in a work in which he professed to defend the Song of Solomon from the reproaches brought against it, supposing Solomon to have fallen in love with a young married woman, who, with the husband, is brought to Jerusalem. The husband is induced to divorce his wife for Solomon's sake, and she is alarmed at the king's approach, and cries out for her husband's help. The whole is a worthless attempt to work out a baseless hypothesis, which is entirely out of harmony with the pure spirit of the whole book. Other German critics, such as Hezel, Von Ammon, Stäudlin, and Umbreit, have followed Jacobi in endeavouring to unfold the dramatic unity of the poem, but none have gone further than the great historian Ewald, who has translated it with an introduction and critical remarks (1826); see also his work on 'The Poets of the Old Testament' (1866). His view, as set forth in the latter work, is that it was actually prepared for representation. This opinion is supported by the hypothesis that there is an actual love-history at the basis of the poem; a young shepherd, of the north of Palestine, being the real lover of Shulamith, from whom Solomon desires to alienate her affection; and that the main idea of the book is the successful resistance of Shulamith to the allurements of the royal lover and her faithfulness to her first love, to whom she is restored by the king in acknowledgment of her virtue and as an act of homage to faithful affection. This theory has been adopted by many critics in later times, as by Hitzig, Vaihinger, Renan, Reville, and Ginsburg; but it is not only exceedingly improbable in itself, but out of harmony with the place of the work in the canon of Scripture. Even if we could suppose Solomon capable of writing such a history of his own delinquencies, we could still less understand how such a " confession " should be incorporated in the sacred volume. There may be expressions in the mouth of the bride which seem at first sight to favour such a theory, but the position of Solomon throughout is quite inconsistent with the idea of illicit solicitation, or indeed with any other relation to Shulamith than that of chaste and legal marriage. The only forcible argument in favour of this view, which is generally called " *the shepherd* " *theory*, is the use of language in reference to the bridegroom which supposes him a shepherd; but this is explained by the fact which lies on the surface of the poem, that the bride is one brought up in country life, and who in the purity and simplicity of her heart addresses even Solomon himself as her shepherd. The conclusion of the poem bears this out, for Solomon is so captivated by the beauty of her character that he follows her to her native region and rural home where he is surrounded by her relations, to whom he vouchsafes his royal favour. It must not be overlooked, that by this highly artistic method not only is the contrast between the royal splendour and the pastoral simplicity heightened, but ample scope is given for the introduction of spiritual analogies, which must be granted to be the main purpose of the book and the justification of its place in the canon. The theory is seen in all its improbability in the form which is given it by Renan, who represents the shepherd following his beloved one to the foot of the tower of the seraglio where she is confined, being admitted secretly by her, and then exclaiming, in the presence of the chorus, in a state of rapturous delight, " I am come into my garden, my sister, my spouse," etc. (ch. v. 1), carrying her home when she is at last released from the king's harem, asleep in his arms, and laying her under an apple tree when she awakes to call upon her lover to set her as a seal upon his arm, etc. The shepherd-hypothesis is also defective in another respect, and that is, that it fails to give a clear explanation of the two dreams which Shulamith narrates, which certainly must both refer to the same object of love, and would seem to imply that there was some defect of love on her part. The spiritual interpretation is perfectly simple and plain; the bride representing the soul of man, and therefore its inferiority to that with which it would be united. But if we suppose Shulamith shut up in a harem, the representation is most forced and unnatural, for she certainly could not have either wandered by night in the city of Jerusalem, nor dreamed of such an adventure. The whole hypothesis is rendered unnecessary by the arrangement which disposes the language among three classes of speakers only—the bride, the chorus of ladies, and the king. Thus the shepherd-lover is identified with the royal bridegroom, and the basis is still left secure on which a spiritual interpre-tation of the whole can be based. Notwithstanding the very ingenious attempts made by Ginsburg and Reville to defend the theory, it must be given up, with all the erotic explanations, as untenable and lowering to the character of the poem. We can only justify this decisive statement of opinion by setting forth, in opposition to what we oppose, a more excellent way, which we now proceed to do, giving an account, at the same time, of the various shapes which have been given to the *typical view*, which we adopt.

3. *The typical view.* It should be frankly admitted by those who reject both the allegorical and the erotic interpretation of the Song of Solomon that no theory can be sound which does not recognize what forms the principal distinctive element in each of these views. We cannot overlook the fact that the book is a religious book, and is placed as such in the canon ; therefore in some sense and to some extent it must be allegorical, that is, there must be a deeper meaning in it than that which appears on the surface, and that meaning must be in harmony with the rest of

Scripture. So with regard to the various erotic and naturalistic explanations, it cannot be denied that there is an historical basis on which the whole rests, so that as poetry there is an ideal human element running through it which gives it both vitality and form. It is the attempt to carry it out to an extreme which has vitiated the theory in each case. The main principle can be preserved without acceptance of the details. It is true, as Zöckler has observed, that it was "the greatly preponderating inclination of the Fathers in the Middle Ages, which soon obtained exclusive sway, to plunge immediately and at once into the spiritual sense, which stifled at its birth every attempt to assert at the same time an historical sense, and branded it with the same anathema as the profane-erotic interpretation of Theodore of Mopsuestia." But the spirit of the Reformation broke the spell of the allegorists. The desire to know the mind of the Spirit led to a truer searching of the Scriptures. Even in the Roman Catholic Church there were signs of that freedom, especially among the mystics, one of whom, the Spanish mystic Louis de Leon, in the latter part of the sixteenth century, wrote a translation and explanation of the Canticles, in classical Spanish, in which, recognizing the historical basis of the book, he lifted the veil from the spiritual beauties which he said were hidden behind the figures. Others followed in the same track, as Mercerus (Le Mercier), 1573, in his 'Commentary,' and Bossuet in his work on the 'Books of Solomon' (Paris, 1693), and Calmet in his 'Commentary;' but the two great English names in connection with a revival of the study of the book on a more intelligent foundation are John Lightfoot (1684) and Bishop Lowth (1753). The latter, especially in his 'Prelections in Hebrew Poetry,' somewhat after the style of Herder, led the way in this country to a profounder attention to the literary form and critical examination of the Bible. Lowth's view is substantially that which has been adopted by the majority of evangelical writers since his time, that the book is not to be regarded as a "continual metaphor" nor as a "parable properly so called," but rather as a "mystical allegory in which a higher sense is superinduced upon an historical verity." He is certainly wrong, however, in his view that the bride referred to is Pharaoh's daughter. Harmer, the author of the 'Observations on Passages of Scripture,' followed Lowth, in 1778, with a commentary and new explanation of Solomon's Song; but it is merely of a literary kind, no attempt being made to explain the spiritual application of the language, and it is of no great value. Dr. Mason Good, the learned physician, translated the Song with very interesting notes, regarding it as a collection of idylls in praise of Solomon's queen. Charles Taylor has added valuable notes to Calmet's 'Dictionary,' and Pye Smith advocated the merely literary value of the book and its unspiritual character. Hoffmann explained it of Pharaoh's daughter, and Zöckler went back too far towards the allegorical theory. The two great German commentators, Keil and Delitzsch, substantially agree in their view, which, while admitting the allegorical *intent* of the book, refuses to see hidden meanings in every detail of the historical basis. One would find, more distinctly than the other, reference to the Church of Christ, both in Israel and in the new dispensation, but both agree that the love of Solomon for his bride is idealized, and so used spiritually. Keil sums up his view thus : " It depicts in dramatized lyrical expression, by songs, under the allegory of the bridal love of Solomon and Shulamith, the loving communion between the Lord and his Church, according to its ideal nature as it results from the choice of Israel to be the Church of the Lord. According to this, every disturbance of that fellowship, springing out of Israel's infidelity, leads to an even firmer establishment of the covenant of love, by means of Israel's return to the true covenant God, and thus God's unchangeable love. Yet we are not to trace in the poem the historical course of the covenant relation, as if a veil of allegory had been thrown over the principal events in the theocratic history " ('Introd. to Old Testament,' vol. i. p. 504). The Rev. T. L. Kingsbury, M.A., in the ' Speaker's Commentary,' has accepted the suggestion which seems the most natural—that the history which is involved in the Song is genuine, and that it refers to "some shepherd-maiden of Northern Palestine, by whose beauty and nobility of soul the great king has been captivated ; that as the work of one endued by inspiration with that wisdom which ' overseeth all things' (Wisd. viii. 23), and so contemplates them from the highest point of view, it is in its essential character an ideal representation of human love in the relation of marriage ; that which is universal and common in its operation to all mankind being here set forth in one grand typical instance." " No allegorical method of exposition," he rightly observes, " which declines attempting to elucidate an independent literal sense, on the plea that such endeavour would involve the interpretation in a succession of improprieties and contradictions," should be accepted. It is both untrue and dishonouring to a sacred and canonical book. The fundamental idea he would take to be " the awful all-constraining, the at once levelling and elevating powers of the mightiest and most universal of human affections; and the two axes on which the main action of the poem revolves are the twofold invitation, the king's invitation to the bride on bringing her to Jerusalem, the bride's to the king in recalling him to Shunem." While we willingly coincide in the general truth of these remarks, we incline to the view which Keil has expressed so moderately, that the main purpose of the book is not to glorify a human sentiment or relationship, which seems out of place in a Hebrew book, but rather, using the ideal human feeling and relationship to lead the soul of man into the thought of its fellowship with God, the condescending privilege which is included in that fellowship, the exaltation of man which it brings with it, and the mutual character of religion, both in the individual and in the Church, as based upon the mystical union of God and his creature and their interchange of communications. We must not be deterred from a moderate and chastened employment of type in the interpretation of Scripture by the abuse which has been only too frequently made of it. No doubt, if we look above the historical, or natural, or literary aspects of the book, it is easy to find in it the meanings which we may be tempted to put there; but the same thing may be said of the Lord's parables and of all Scripture. The historical, literary, and spiritual aspects blend in one, and that interpretation which is given to the language is most likely to be after the mind of the Spirit, which follows his own method and harmonizes with that which he inspired the man of God to set before us, and his Church to hand down to us with the seal of its approbation upon it. The commentary must always justify, or otherwise, its own main principle; and if as a whole it satisfies the language, it cannot be very far astray.

It has been objected by some that we ought not to employ Solomon as in any sense a type of God or of Christ, because he was a sensual man; but such a principle would simply exclude all types, for they must be inferior in worth to that which they typify. The patriarchs were far from perfect men in their moral features, but they were plainly employed in Scripture typically as well as historically. David himself, the leading typical character and norm of the Old Testament, was guilty of great sins. Moreover, while Solomon appears in the poem itself as a sensual Eastern monarch, there is no reference to the sensuality of his life. Nor need we doubt that, sensualist as he became, and degraded as he was in the latter part of his life, he would in the earlier portion of his manhood be capable of the sincere attachment portrayed in the songs. At the same time, it may be allowed that the facts are idealized. Fundamentally they are historical. For a religious purpose they are lifted up into the region of poetry. To a considerable extent the same may be said of the Book of Job, which builds a splendid poem on a basis of facts.

There remains, then, only, in conclusion, to justify this typical interpretation by showing that it is in analogy with other parts of Scripture. It will not be denied by any one, however much opposed to allegory or type, that the metaphor of marriage is common through the Old Testament in connection with the exhortation to covenant faithfulness. This is so familiar in the prophetical writings that it is quite unnecessary to adduce instances. The fifth, fiftieth, and sixty-second chapters of Isaiah and the first few chapters of Hosea, with the opening words of Malachi, will suffice to remind the reader that it was an illustration which all the sacred writers made use of. It should again be remembered that we have in the forty-fifth psalm an instance of what the title describes as a "Song of Loves," or *Epithalamium*, which no one doubts was composed on the occasion of Solomon's marriage, or on some similar occasion in Israel. It is only a very extreme rejection of typical interpretation which would refuse to such a psalm any higher application than that which appears upon the surface, especially with such language in it as ver. 6, "Thy throne, O God, is for ever and ever: the sceptre of thy kingdom is a right sceptre." Admitting that such terms might be at first employed only as

royal adulation and homage, it can scarcely be doubted that their place in
the Word of God is due to the fact that the Israelitish king was regarded
as the type of him who was called by the believing " Israelite indeed, in
whom was no guile," " the Son of God, the King of Israel " (John i. 49).
The reference to Messiah was certainly believed by the Jews themselves,
as we see from the introduction of it into the Chaldee paraphrase and
others of the Jewish writings, and as such it is cited in Hebrews (i. 8, 9).
No satisfactory explanation of the psalm can be made out on any other
view.   If we deny a Messianic reference in such a case, while the New
Testament confirms it, our position must be that of dealing with the whole
of the Old Testament only as a fragmentary Jewish literature, without
proper unity and without inspired authority.   In that case we are thrown
back upon far greater difficulties than any which the older view meets, for
we cannot explain the history and character of the Jewish people as a
whole, and we must be prepared to answer the full force of the Apostle
Paul's emphatic statement, that " to them were committed the oracles of
God " (Rom. iii. 2).   Such bold rationalism is now completely out of date,
and we must be at the pains to study the language of the Old Testament
with a reverent acknowledgment of the purpose of God in unfolding the
secrets of his mind and will.   Hengstenberg bases his argument for the
allegorical interpretation of Solomon's Song on the fact that Solomon
himself is the author, and that we cannot otherwise account for the title
and place given to the work.   Had it been a mere collection of love-songs,
it would be a dishonour to the Word of God to call it by such a name and
place it side by side with the sublime inspired songs of Moses, Miriam,
Deborah, Hannah, and David.   There is certainly considerable force in
that view.   And the close correspondence between the " Song of Loves,"
the forty-fifth psalm, and the " Song of Songs " seems to confirm the
typical character of both.   We find, for instance, such language as this,
apparently adopted as a religious phraseology, " fairest among the children
of men " (Ps. xlv. 3), " chiefest among ten thousand " (Cant. v. 10).   " The
king," as the highest object of praise; " lilies," as the emblems of virgin
purity and loveliness; *loveliness of the lip*, as representing excellence of
discourse; *heroic might, majesty, and glory* in the king; the idea which
pervades both, of conjugal fidelity, with other minor resemblances, lend
considerable weight to the suggestion that the forty-fifth psalm was a kind
of adaptation of the Canticles for performance by the sons of Korah in
the temple.   Hengstenberg mentions many instances in the prophetical
Scriptures in which he traces allusion to the language or metaphors of the
Song of Solomon, but they are not sufficiently clear to be relied upon as
evidence.   And the same may be said of the instances which he adduces
from the New Testament, which he thinks is " pervaded with references
all of them based on the supposition that the book is to be interpreted
spiritually."   Our Lord refers to " Solomon in all his glory; " can we safely
affirm that he alludes to the description in Canticles?   Hengstenberg

points to the metaphor in ch. ii. 1, "I am a rose of Sharon, a lily of the valley," but unfortunately he has put those words into the lips of Solomon instead of the bride, which defeats his reference. Most of the other instances are equally unsatisfactory. At the same time, it must be admitted that the use of metaphors formed from the marriage relation and from the language of human affection, in application to the highest intercourse of the soul with the objects of faith, is common both in our Lord's discourses and in the writings of the apostles. It is especially prominent in the Apocalypse. The Church is the bride, the Lamb's wife. Would such metaphors be employed by the Apostle John unless he had found them already in the Old Testament? Would the Apostle Paul have spoken as he does of the mystical meaning of marriage as setting forth the union between Christ and his Church, unless the Scriptures had familiarized the people of God with the symbol?

We entirely sympathize with that revulsion of feeling with which healthy minds turn away from the extravagant fancifulness and arbitrariness of the allegorical school of commentators. But we refuse to follow those who, in their avoidance of one extreme, fly to the other. The book cannot be a mere literary product. We must find for it some true place in the sacred volume. "Shall we then," asks Mr. Kingsbury, in the 'Speaker's Commentary,' "regard it as a mere fancy, which for so many ages past has been wont to find in the pictures and melodies of the Song of Songs types and echoes of the actings and emotions of the highest love, of love Divine, in its relations to humanity; which, if dimly discerned through their aid by the synagogue, have been amply revealed in the gospel to the Church? Shall we not still claim to trace, in the noble and gentle history thus presented, foreshadowings of the infinite condescensions of incarnate love?—that love which, first stooping in human form to visit us in our low estate in order to seek out and win its object (Ps. cxxxvi. 23), and then raising along with itself a sanctified humanity to the heavenly places (Eph. ii. 6), is finally awaiting there an invitation from the mystic bride to return to earth once more and seal the union for eternity (Rev. xxii. 17)? With such a conception of the character and purpose of the poem, we may at any rate sympathize with the glowing language of St. Bernard concerning it. This Song excels all other songs of the Old Testament. They being, for the most part, songs of deliverance from captivity, Solomon for such had no occasion. In the height of glory, singular in wisdom, abounding in riches, secure in peace, he here by Divine inspiration sings the praises of Christ and his Church, the grace of holy love, the mysteries of the eternal marriage, yet all the while like Moses putting a veil before his face, because at that time there were few or none that could gaze upon such glories" (vol. iv. p. 674). It is unworthy of any devout interpreter of such a book to despise and disparage the spiritual element in it. What so many of God's people have recognized must be substantially the mind of the Spirit. No doubt, as Delitzsch has observed, "no other book of Scripture has been so much abused by an unscientific spiritualizing and an over-scientific unspiritual treatment." But the errors of commentators are generally gropings towards the light. The truth is more likely to be found in the mean between the two extremes. The allegorist gives the reins to his fancy and ends in absurdities; the literalist shuts himself up in his naturalism and forfeits the blessing of the Spirit. We trust that the following Exposition will show that there is a better way.

THE SONG OF SOLOMON

---◆---

EXPOSITION.

CHAPTER I.

Ver. 1.—The song of songs, which is Solomon's. This is certainly the title of the book which follows, although in our present Hebrew Bible it is the first verse of the book, preceded by the shorter form, 'The Song of Songs.' The Septuagint has simply the title Ἆσμα, so that our English title in the Authorized Version, 'The Song of Solomon,' has no ancient authority. It is well altered in the Revised Version to 'The Song of Songs.' The word "song" (שִׁיר) does not necessarily convey the meaning, composed to be sung to music. If the performance of the words were chiefly in view, the word would have been מִזְמוֹר, *carmen*, "lyric poem," "hymn," or "ode." The Greek Ἆσμα ᾀσμάτων, and the Latin of the Vulgate, *Canticum canticorum*, accord with the Hebrew in representing the work as taking a high place either in the esteem of the Church or, on account of the subject, in the esteem of the writer. Luther expresses the same idea in the title he attaches to it, 'Das Hohelied,' that is, the chief or finest of songs. The reference may be to the excellence of the literary form, but probably that which suggested the title was the supreme beauty of the love which prompted the songs. The title may be regarded as applied to the whole book, or to the first portion of it giving the name to the whole. If it be a collection of separate songs strung together, as some think, by mere resemblance in style and subject, then the words, "which is Solomon's" (אֲשֶׁר לִשְׁלֹמֹה) apply to the first song alone. But the unity which is clearly to be traced through the book to the end makes it probable that the title is meant to ascribe the work to the authorship of Solomon. This is the opinion of the majority of critics. It must have

come either from the wise king himself, or from some one of his contemporaries or immediate successors. The preposition is the *lamedh auctoris*. If the meaning were "referring to," another preposition (עַל) would have been employed. It has been remarked by Delitzsch that the absence of any description of Solomon as "King of Israel" or "son of David," as in Proverbs and Ecclesiastes, confirms the view that Solomon himself was the sole author. Some have argued against the authenticity of the title on the ground that the longer form of the relative, אֲשֶׁר, is used in it, whereas in the book itself the shorter form, שְׁ, is found, but no dependence can be placed on that argument regarded by itself, for the same writer employs both forms, as *e.g.* Jeremiah, who uses the longer form in his prophecies and the shorter in Lamentations. The shorter form is, in fact, the older, being Old Canaanitish or Phœnician, שַׁא, which is a lengthened form of שְׁ, and afterwards became אֲשֶׁר. One writer, however (Fleischer), holds that the relative pronoun has a substantive origin, and compares it with the Arabic *ithe* and the Assyrian *asar*, meaning "track" or "place," like the German *welcher*, which comes from *wo*. But whether this be so or not, it is certainly unsafe to date any book by the form found in it of the relative pronoun. We know that in poetry the abbreviated form is common. It was probably a North Palestine provincialism, as we see in the Book of Kings. It became common in prose writings after the Captivity because of the degradation of Hebrew, but it was not unknown before that time either in prose or poetry. With regard to the exact description of the poetic form of the Song of Songs, the difference among critics is considerable, but the question is scarcely worth discussing. There undoubtedly is unity of conception in the songs which are brought together, but it cannot be of importance to prove that there is dramatic unity strictly speaking; there is no dramatic procedure, nor can we suppose that there is any ultimate aim at dramatic representation. But the Exposition which follows will suffice to show that there are facts of history in the background of the poem; if the suggestions of the language and scenery be followed, the facts are very beautiful and even romantic— the love of the great king for one of his own subjects, a lovely northern maiden, whose simplicity and purity of character are a great attraction and lend much force to the religious sentiment of the song. In 1 Kings v. 12 we read that "the Lord gave Solomon wisdom, as he promised him." That divinely inspired wisdom enabled him, notwithstanding his own personal errors, to idealize and sanctify the lovely episode of his life which lies at the foundation of his poem. And the Church of God in every age has appreciated, more or less widely, the inspiration, both of matter and of form, which breathed in it. We are told that Solomon composed one thousand and five songs (1 Kings iv. 32); whether this is a part of that collection or not we cannot certainly say, but that it is a mere *fasciculus*, or collection of separate songs, strung together by their general erotic character, is what we cannot believe. No doubt, as Dr. Mason Good has observed, the Arabian poets were accustomed to arrange their poems in what they compared to a string of pearls, but we can scarcely carry such a fact into the Bible, and deal with sacred books as mere literary remains. There must be a deep religious meaning in such language, and it is in accordance with Eastern usage that amatory songs should be so employed. What the meaning is we must persistently ask, and however much has been wrongly said in the past, while we believe in the Divine authority of the Old Testament we must not renounce the endeavour to find the Song of Songs worthy of its title and its place.

Ver. 2—ch. ii. 7.—Part I. MUTUAL LOVE. Song of Shulamith in the royal chambers. Chorus of ladies, daughters of Jerusalem.

Ver. 2.—**Let him kiss me with the kisses of his mouth: for thy love is better than wine.** Whether we take these words as put in the lips of the bride herself, or of the chorus as identifying themselves with her, is of little consequence. It is certain that the idea intended to be expressed is that of delight in the approach of the royal bridegroom. The future is used optatively, "Let me be taken up into the closest fellowship and embrace." All attempts to dispense with the amatory phraseology are vain. The "kisses" must

be interpreted in a figurative sense, or the sacred character of the whole book must be removed. The words may be rendered, *with one of his kisses;* i.e. the sweetness of his lips is such that one kiss would be rapture. Some have thought that allusion is intended to the custom among idolaters referred to in Job xxxi. 27, "My mouth hath kissed my hand;" but the meaning is simply that of affection. The great majority of Christian commentators have regarded the words as expressive of desire towards God. Origen said, the Church of the old dispensation longing after higher revelations, as through the Incarnation, "How long shall he send me kisses by Moses and the prophets? I desire the touch of his own lips." It is dangerous to attempt specific applications of a metaphor. The general truth of it is all that need be admitted. If the relation between God and his people is one that can be set forth under the image of human affection, then there is no impropriety in the language of Solomon's Song. "To kiss a kiss" (נָשַׁק נְשִׁיקָה) is the ordinary Hebraic form (cf. "to counsel a counsel"). *Thy love is better than wine.* The plural is used, "loves," as in the word "life" (חַיִּים)—the abstract for the concrete, perhaps in order to indicate the manifestation of love in many caresses. The change from the third person to the second is common in poetry. The comparison with wine may be taken either as denoting sweetness or exhilarating effects. The intoxicating power of wine is but rarely referred to in Scripture, as the ordinary wine was distinguished from strong drink. Some, as Hitzig and Böttcher, would read יַשְׁקֵנִי, changing the pointing, and translating, "Let him give me to drink;" but there is no necessity for a reading so forced and vulgar. The Septuagint, altering the vowels of the word "love," turn it into "breasts," and must therefore have supposed it addressed to the bride. The word is connected with the Arabic, and runs through the languages, *dodh* (cf. Dada, Dido, David). Perhaps the reference to wine, as subsequently to the ointments, may be explained by the fact that the song is supposed to be sung while wine is presented in the chamber, and while the perfumes are poured out in preparation for the entrance of the royal bridegroom. We can scarcely doubt that the opening words are intended to be the utterance of loving desire on the part of the bride in the presence of the daughters of Jerusalem. Some have suggested that vers. 1—8 are from a kind of responsive dialogue, but the view of the older interpreters and of Ewald, Hengstenberg, Weissbach, and others of the moderns, seems more correct, that all the first seven verses are in the mouth of Shulamith, and then ver. 8 comes in naturally as a chorus in reply to the song of the bride. The use of the plural, " We will run after thee," etc., is easily explicable. The bride is surrounded by her admiring companions and attendants. They are congratulating her on the king's love. She speaks as from the midst of the company of ladies.

Ver. 3.—**Thine ointments have a goodly fragrance; thy name is as ointment poured forth; therefore do the virgins love thee.** There is some slight difference among critics as to the rendering of this verse, but it does not affect the meaning. Lovely and delightful thou art. As thy perfumes are so precious, so is thy name; the more it is spread, the more delight is found in it. The idea is that the person is the sweetest, and that his communications are elevating and inspiring. The " virgins " may be taken generally, " Those who are full of the sensibility of youth appreciate thy attractions." The word *almah* is much disputed about, but the meaning is simply that of " young woman," whether virgin or married. " Thou art the delight of all the young." Mason Good renders the verse—

" Rich thy perfumes; but richer far than they
    The countless charms that round thy person play;
Thy name alone, more fragrant than the rose,
Glads every maid, where'er its fragrance flows."

Ver. 4.—**Draw me, we will run after thee: the king hath brought me into his chambers: we will be glad and rejoice in thee, we will make mention of thy love more than of wine: rightly do they love thee.** This is best taken as all spoken by the bride. It is the language of the purest affection and adoring admiration. " I drew them," God says (Hos. xi. 4), " with cords of a man, with bands of love." " The Lord appeared of old unto me," says Jeremiah (xxxi. 3), " saying, Yea, I have loved thee with an everlasting love : therefore with loving-kindness have I drawn thee." In the same sense the Greek word ἑλκύειν is used by our Lord himself of the Father *drawing* to the Son, and of the Son, uplifted on the cross, " drawing " all men unto him (cf. John vi. 44; xii. 32). If the spiritual meaning of the whole poem is admitted, such language is quite natural. The king's chambers are the king's own rooms in the palace, *i.e.* his sleeping-rooms and sitting-rooms—the *penetralia regis*. We may take the preterite as equivalent to the present; *i.e.* " The king is bringing me into closest fellowship with himself, not merely as a member of his household, but as his chosen bride." The concluding words have caused much discussion. The meaning, however, is

the same whether we say, " The upright love thee," or " Thou art rightly loved." The intention is to set forth the object of love as perfect. The plural, מֵישָׁרִים, is used to signify the abstract of the word, thought, or act; *i.e.* " righteous," for " rightly " (cf. Ps. lviii. 2 ; lxxv. 3); but the best critics think it could not be the abstract for the concrete plural, as in the Vulgate, *Recti diligunt te.* The same use of the word is seen in ch. vii. 9, " The best wine that goeth down *smoothly* for my beloved " (cf. Prov. xxiii. 31). Before going further in the song, it is well to observe how chaste, pure, and delicate is the language of love; and yet, as Delitzsch has pointed out, there is a mystical, cloudy brightness. We seem to be in the region of the ideal. It is not a mere love-song, though it may have been the commemoration of an actual past. The Eastern form of the words may be less suited to our taste than it would be to those who first embraced Christianity, and to the nineteenth century than to the first; but the loving rapture of the Church in fellowship with the Saviour is certainly seeking a more vivid expression in song, and there are many of the most simple-minded and devoted Christians whose joy in Christ pours itself out freely in strains not much less fervid and almost as sensuous as anything to be found in Solomon's Song. Some are beginning to remonstrate against this freedom of devotional language, but the instinct of the Church seems to justify it as the demand of the heart under the influence of the Word of God itself. Perhaps there is a state of religious feeling coming into the experience of Christians which will remove the veil from such a book as the Song of Songs, and we shall yet find that its language is needful and is not extravagant.

Ver. 5.—**I am black, but comely, O ye daughters of Jerusalem, as the tents of Kedar, as the curtains of Solomon.** The word " black " (שְׁחוֹרָה) does not necessarily mean that the skin is black, but rather sunburnt, dark-brown, as in Lam. iv. 8, where the same word signifies the livid or swarthy appearance of one who has suffered long from famine and wretchedness. There is certainly no reason to take the word as an argument for the bride being Pharaoh's daughter ; but it points to what is confirmed by the rest of the poem—the rustic birth and northern blood of the bride. She has been living in the fields, and is browned with the ruddy health of a country life. The best explanation of the words is that they are drawn out by the fact that the bride is surrounded by her ladies. Some think that they look askance at her, or with indignation at the boldness of her words; but that is quite unnecessary, and would be inconsistent with the dignity of the bride. The country maiden feels the greatness of the honour, that she is chosen of the king, and with simple modesty, in the presence of courtly ladies around her, sets forth her claim. The simile is not uncommon in poetry, as in Theocritus and Virgil. *Comely;* i.e. attractive, agreeable. *Kedar* (whether from the Arabic, meaning "powerful," or from the Hebrew, "black") designates the tribes of the North-Arabian descendants of Ishmael (Gen. xxv. 13; Isa. xxi. 17), Kedareens, referred to by Pliny, and remaining in Arabia until the time of the Mohammedans. The Bedouin still calls his tent his "hair-house;" it is covered with goat's-hair cloth, mostly black or grey. Whether the reference is to the colour of the goat's hair or to the tents being browned or blackened by the heat of the sun, we cannot doubt that the allusion is to the complexion, and the rest of the simile would then be applicable to the lovely shape and features of the maiden, the curtains of Solomon being the curtains of a pavilion, or pleasure-tent, spread out like "a shining butterfly," *i.e.* the beautiful cloth or tapestry which formed the sides of the tent or the tent-coverings, the clothing of the framework, or tent-hangings (see Isa. liv. 2; Exod. xxvi. 36; 2 Sam. vii.; 1 Chron. xvii. 1, etc.). Egyptian hangings were particularly prized. The custom prevailed among Eastern monarchs of sojourning once in the year in some lovely rural district, and at such times their tents would be very magnificent. The LXX. has, ὡς δερρείς Σολομῶν, "as the skins of Solomon;" but this is a mistake. The word is derived from a root "to tremble," *i.e.* "to glitter in the sun." Those who desire to find an allegorical interpretation think there is an evident allusion here to the sojourn of Israel in the wilderness, or the admission of the Gentiles into the covenant; but there is no reason for any such strain upon the meaning. The simile is merely poetical. The soul realizes its own acceptance before God, and ascribes that acceptance to his grace. "The bride, the Lamb's wife," sees the beauty of the Lord reflected in herself, and rejoices in her own attractions for his sake. There is no immodesty in the consciousness of merit so long as that merit is ascribed to him from whom it comes. There is often more pride in the assumption of humility than in the claim to be acknowledged. The same apostle who declared himself less than the least of all saints also maintained that he was not a whit behind the very chiefest apostles.

Ver. 6.—**Look not upon me, because I am swarthy, because the sun hath scorched me. My mother's sons were incensed against me; they made me keeper of the vineyards; but mine own vineyard have I not kept.** The meaning seems to be—Do not let the swarthiness of my complexion lower me in

your eyes. Literally the words are, *Do not see me that I am;* i.e. do not regard me as being, because I am. There is no necessity to suppose any looks of the ladies to have suggested the words. They are the words of modest self-depreciation mingled with joyful sense of acceptance. It is difficult to render the Hebrew exactly. The word translated "swarthy" (*shecharchoreh*) is probably a diminutive from *shechorah,* which itself means "blackish;" so that the meaning is, "that my complexion is dark." The reference to the sun explains the word still further, as pointing, not to a difference of race, but to mere temporary effects of an outdoor life: "The sun has been playing with my complexion;" or, as the LXX. renders it, Παρέβλεψέ με ὁ ἥλιος, "The sun has been gazing at me." So other Greek versions. Some, however, include the idea of burning or scorching, which is the literal meaning of the verb, though in Job iii. 9 and xli. 10 it is used in the sense of looking at or upon. The sun is the eye of the heavens (see 2 Sam. xii. 11), and with delicate feeling it is spoken of here as feminine, the bride playfully alluding, perhaps, to the lady seen in the heavens preceding the ladies of the court in gazing on her beauty. It is difficult to explain with perfect satisfaction the next clause of the verse. Doubtless "mother's sons" is a poetical periphrasis for brothers —*not* "step-brothers," as some have said. Perhaps the mother was a widow, as no father is mentioned. The best explanation is that the bride is simply giving an account of herself, why she is so browned in the sun. The brothers, for some reason, had been incensed against her, possibly on account of her favour in the eyes of the king, but more probably for private, family reasons. They would not have her shutting herself up in the house to take care of her complexion; they would have her in the vineyards. In the word "keeper" (*noterah,* instead of *notzerah*) we have an instance of the northern dialect—a kind of Platt-Hebrew—hardening the pronunciation. *My own vineyard have I not kept* no doubt refers simply and solely to her complexion, not to her virginity or character. She means—I was compelled by my brothers to go into the vineyards in the heat of the sun, and the consequence was, as you see, I have not been able to preserve the delicacy of my skin; I have been careless of my personal beauty. The sun has done its work. The reference helps us to recognize the historical background of the poem, and leads naturally to the use of the pastoral language which runs through the whole. The king is a shepherd, and his bride a shepherdess. Without straining the spiritual interpretation, we may yet discover in this beautiful candour and simplicity of the bride the reflection of the soul's virtues in its joyful realization of Divine favour; but the true method of interpretation requires no minute, detailed adjustment of the language to spiritual facts, but rather seeks the meaning in the total impression of the poem.

Ver. 7.—**Tell me, O thou whom my soul loveth, where thou feedest thy flock, where thou makest it to rest at noon: for why should I be as one that is veiled beside the flock of thy companions?** These words carry on the associations suggested by the previous verse. The bride is longing for the bridegroom; but she cannot think of him yet in any other light than as a companion of her simple country life—he is a shepherd, and she a shepherdess. "Take me into closer fellowship with thyself; let me not remain still only one amongst the many." Perhaps there is intended to be an allusion to the common metaphor—the king as the shepherd and the people as his flock; but the uppermost thought of the bride is separation unto her husband. The soul which longs for the enjoyment of fellowship with God desires to be carried away out of all distractions, out of all restraints, lifted above reserve and above doubt into the closest and most loving union. The idea of the veil may be either the veil of mourning or the veil of modesty and reserve. Probably the latter is the true reference. The LXX. has, ὡς περιβαλλομένη. There is some difference of opinion among critics. Ewald thinks it refers to strangeness—"like one unknown," and therefore veiled; Gesenius says, "one fainting;" others connect the word with the root "to *roam*," "to *wander*" (see Isa. xxii. 17), which is confirmed by Symmachus, the Vulgate, the Syriac, the Chaldee, Jerome, Venetian, and Luther. The simplest explanation is that the bride compares herself, in her absence from her lord, among the ladies of the court, to a veiled woman travelling beside the flocks of the shepherds, seeking her friend, but not yet brought to him.

Ver. 8.—(*Chorus of ladies.*) **If thou know not, O thou fairest among women, go thy way forth by the footsteps of the flock, and feed thy kids beside the shepherds' tents.** That another voice is here introduced there can be no doubt; and as it is not like the voice of the bridegroom himself, which is heard in the next verse, we must suppose it to be the chorus of attendant ladies. Delitzsch suggests very plausibly that they are pleasantly chiding the simplicity of the country maiden, and telling her that, if she cannot understand her position, she had better return to her country life. In that case, "if thou know not" would mean—If thou canst not rise up to thy privilege; the

knowledge referred to being general knowledge or wisdom. The delicate irony is well expressed, as in the reference to the kids—"feed thy kids," like a child as thou art. But there may be no intentional irony in the words; rather a playful and sympathetic response to the beautiful simplicity of the bride—If thou art waiting to be brought to thy beloved, if thou art seeking thy shepherd, thou most lovely woman, then go quietly on thy way, like a shepherdess tending the kids beside the shepherds' tents; follow the peaceful footsteps of the flock, and in due time the beloved one will appear. This is better than to suppose the ladies presuming to indulge in irony when they must know that Shulamith is the king's favourite. Besides, the first scene of the poem, which is a kind of introduction, thus ends appropriately with an invitation to peaceful waiting for love. We are prepared for the entrance of the beloved one. The spiritual meaning is simple and clear—Those that would be lifted up into the highest enjoyments of religion must not be impatient and doubt that the Lord will reveal himself, but go quietly and patiently on with the work of life, "in the footsteps of the flock," in fellowship with humble souls, and in the paths of peace, in the green pastures and beside the still waters, ready to do anything assigned them, and the time of rejoicing and rapture will come.

Ver. 9.—(*Entrance of the bridegroom.*) **I have compared thee, O my love, to a steed in Pharaoh's chariots.** There can be no reasonable doubt that these words are put into the mouth of the king. The "steed" is in the feminine (סוּסָה); some would point the word with the plural vowels, that is, "to my horses," or a "body of horses." There is no necessity for that. The reference to a particular very lovely mare is more apt and pointed. In 1 Kings x. 26 we read in the LXX. Version of τεσσάρες χιλιάδες θήλειαι ἵπποι, which Solomon had for his chariots—fourteen hundred war-chariots and twelve thousand horsemen. The Pharaoh-chariots were those which the king had imported from Egypt (1 Kings x. 28, 29; 2 Chron. ix. 28). It may be that the reference is to the splendid decoration of the trappings. Delitzsch very rightly sees in such a figure a confirmation of the view that Solomon himself was the author. The horses from Egypt were famed at that time as those of Arabia became afterwards. The names both of horses and chariots in the Egyptian language were borrowed from the Semitic, as they were probably first imported into Egypt by the Hyksos, or shepherd-kings. Other examples of the same comparison are found in poetry, as in Horace, Anacreon, and Theocritus. In the last ('Idyl.,' xviii.

30, 31) occur the following lines, rendered into English verse :—

" As towers the cypress 'mid the garden's bloom,
As in the chariot proud Thessalian steed,
Thus graceful, rose-complexioned Helen moves."

The idea is that of stately beauty and graceful movements. The old commentators see the Divine love of espousals (Jer. ii. 2), as in the wilderness of the Exodus, and afterwards in the wilderness of the world. The Bible is full of the expression of Divine tenderness and regard for man.

Vers. 10, 11.—**Thy cheeks are comely with plaits of hair, thy neck with strings of jewels. We will make thee plaits of gold with studs of silver.** This language may be suggested by the comparison first employed —the trappings of the horse. " The headframe of the horse's bridle and the poitral were then certainly, just as now, adorned with silken tassels, fringes, and other ornaments of silver. *Torim*, 'round ornaments,' which hang down in front on both sides of the head-band or are also inwoven in the braids of hair in the forehead." The strings of jewels were necklaces—three rows of pearls. The ornamentation is, however, quite in accordance with female dress. The king makes the promise of gold and silver decoration as an expression of his personal delight in his bride and acceptance of her. Gold and silver were closely connected; hence silver was called, in the Old Egyptian language, " white gold." The idea seems to be that of silver points sprinkled over golden knobs. Compare the description in ' Faust' of Margaret's delight in the casket she finds in her room. The LXX. and Vulgate have mistaken the word *torim* for a similar word for " doves," taking the simile to be the beautiful colours of the dove's neck. The bride does not seem to reply immediately to the king; but we may suppose that the king takes his bride by the hand, and leads her into the banqueting-chamber. But the next three verses, which are certainly in the lips of the bride, may be taken as her expression of delight in her husband, either while he feasts in the banquet or when it is over. The banquet is a familiar emblem of the delight of mutual love. Hence the feasts of love in the primitive Church were regarded, not only as seasons of fellowship between Christians, but times of rejoicing, when the soul entered into the full appreciation of the Saviour's presence.

Vers. 12—14.—**While the king sat** (or, *sits*) **at his table, my spikenard sent** (*sends*) **forth its fragrance. My beloved is unto me as a bundle of myrrh, that lieth betwixt my breasts. My beloved is unto me as a cluster of henna flowers in the vineyards of Engedi.** The preterite is best taken poetically for the present. The words are evidently a response to those of the king. As such they refer to present feeling and not to a past state. The bride expresses her delight in the king. The table is used generally. The Hebrew word is from a root " to sit round." The habit of reclining at table was introduced much later, during the Persian, Greek, and Roman period. The spikenard was a powerful perfume, probably of Indian origin, as the Indian word *naladâ*, meaning "that which yields fragrance," shows. The Persian is *nârd*, the Old Arabic *nârdû*. It was made from an Indian plant, the *Valeriana*, called *Nardostachys 'Gatâmânsi*, growing in Northern and Eastern India. The hairy part of the stem immediately above the root yields the perfume. That it was " very precious " we see from the account of Mary's offering, which was worth more than three hundred denarii, *i.e.* £8 10s. (Mark xiv. 5; John xii. 2). Horace promised Virgil a whole cask, *i.e.* nine gallons, of the best wine in exchange for a small onyx-box full of the perfume. The metaphor represents the intense longing of love. *Myrrh* was an exotic introduced into Palestine from Arabia, Abyssinia, and India. Like frankincense, it is one of the amyridæ. The *Balsamodendron myrrha* is the tree itself with its leaves and flowers. From the tree came a resin or gum (*Gummi myrrhæ*), which either dropped from the leaves or was artificially obtained by incisions in the bark. The natural product was the more valuable. It was much prized as a perfume, and employed for many purposes. The Hebrew women were accustomed to carry little bags or bottles of myrrh suspended from their necks and hanging down between their breasts under the dress, diffusing an attractive fragrance round them. The word *tseror* is, properly, " a little bag," *sacculus*, " that which one ties up," rather than a " bundle." The meaning, of course, is rhetorical—He is at my heart and delightful to all my thoughts as the fragrance to my senses. The henna flowers, or cypress, in the vineyards of Engedi, is a very beautiful figure. *Copher*, the cypress cluster, —in Greek, κύπρος: in Arabic, *al-henna* (*Lawsonia*)—grows in Palestine and Egypt, as we are told by Pliny ('Nat. Hist.,' xii. 24). It is a tall shrub reaching to eight or ten feet, exceedingly beautiful in appearance, and giving forth a delightful odour. It is named from a root " to be white or yellow-white." The Moslem women stain their hands and feet with it to give them a yellow tint. Engedi was a lovely district on the west of the Dead Sea—Hazezon Tamar, now *Ain Tidy*, where Solomon made terraces on the hillsides and covered them with gardens and vineyards. The allusion confirms the date of the writing as contemporary with Solomon, as the gardens would then be in their perfection. The figure is, perhaps, intended to be an advance in rhetorical force upon that which preceded —the fragrance diffused and almost overpowering, as of a blossoming tree.

Ver. 15.—Behold, thou art fair, my love; behold, thou art fair; thine eyes are as doves; literally, *thine eyes are doves*. The king receives the worship of his bride and delights in her. She is very sweet and fair to him. The dove is a natural symbol of love; hence it was attached by the classical nations to the garden of love, together with the myrtle, rose, and apple, all of which we find introduced in this Hebrew poem. Hence the Arabic name for a dove, *Jemima*, as we see in the Book of Job, was the name of a woman (cf. Columbina). The language of the king is that of ecstasy; hence the interjection and repetition. The enraptured monarch gazes into the eyes of his beloved bride, and sees there only purity, constancy, and affection. In ch. vii. 4 the eyes are compared to fish-ponds, no doubt for their clear, liquid depth and serenity. Some have thought that the allusion is to the very lovely eyes of the doves; but there is no need of the limitation.

Ver. 16—ch. ii. 1.—Behold, thou art fair, my beloved, yea, pleasant; also our couch is green. The beams of our house are cedars, and our rafters are firs. I am a rose of Sharon, a lily of the valley. We take these three verses together as being, in all probability, the address of the bride to her royal husband. This was the view taken by the Masoretic editors and preserved in our present pointing of the Hebrew, as we see in the masculine form of the first word, הִנְּךָ, which replies to the feminine form in ver. 15, הִנָּךְ. The seventeenth verse is apparently abrupt. Why should the bride pass so suddenly from the general address of affection, "Thou art fair, thou art pleasant," to a particular description of a rural scene? The explanation suggested by some of the critics is not far-fetched, that Solomon whispers to her that she shall go back with him to her country life if she pleases, or she reminds him of his promise made at some other time. Undoubtedly the point of Shulamith's response lies in ch. ii. 1, "I am not at ease in this palatial splendour; I am by nature a rose of Sharon, a lily of the valley. Take me to the green couch, and let me lie under the cedars and the firs." The couch is the divan (cf. Amos vi. 4), from a root "to

cover over" (like "canopy" in Greek, κωνω-πεῖον, so called from its protecting the person under it from the κώνωπες, or "gnats"). It is not that the nuptial bed is particularly intended, or even the bridal bower, but the home itself as a bowery resting-place. "Our home is a sweet country home; take me, there, beloved one." The word "green" is very suggestive in the Hebrew. It is said to "combine in itself the ideas of softness and juicy freshness, perhaps of bending and elasticity, of looseness and thus of overhanging ramification, like weeping willow. *Beams*, from a root "to meet," "to lay crosswise," "to hold together." But the meaning depends upon the idea of the whole description. Some would render "fretted ceilings," or "galleries;" but Dr. Ginsburg gives it, "our bower is of cedar arches," which excludes the idea of a formal structure made of cedar beams. The same meaning is conveyed in the last clause, "our rafters are firs." The word rendered "rafters" (רְחִיטִם) literally signifies "a place upon which one runs" (like שׁוּק, a "street "), *i.e.* a charming or pleasant spot. The *beroth* is the cypress tree, an Aramaic word, or one used in the north of Palestine. The meaning is, "our pleasant retreat is cypresses"—is beautiful and fragrant with the cypress tree. Delitzsch, however, and others would take it differently as describing the panels or hollows of a wainscoted ceiling, like φατναί, *lacunæ, lacunaria*, and the LXX., φατνώματα: Symmachus, φατνωσεῖς: Jerome, *laquearii* (cf. Isa. lx. 13). But the concluding words would then be unfitting. The bride is not describing a splendid palace, but a country home. "I am a tender maiden," she says, "who has been brought up in retirement; take me to a forest palace and to the green, fragrant surroundings, where the meadow-flower, the valley-lily will be happy." We are so accustomed to the rendering of ch. ii. 1, which our Revised Version has adopted from the Authorized, that it would be wrong to destroy the effect which it borrows from long familiarity unless it were absolutely necessary. The word *chavatseleth*, however, has been differently translated; it is literally any wild flower—rose, saffron crocus (*Colchicum autumnale*), tulip, narcissus, lily. The crocus is, perhaps, nearest to the meaning, as the name is probably derived from a root "to form bulbs" or bulbous knolls. It occurs only once again, in Isa. xxxv. 1, where it is rendered "rose" in the Authorized Version; LXX., ἄνθος: Vulgate, *flos*. Some derive it from the root *chavaz*, "to be bright," with ל as termination. *Sharon* may be here a general denomination of the open field or plain, from יָשָׁר, "to be straight, plain." There was a district called Sharon on the coast from Joppa to Cæsarea. There was another Sharon beyond the Jordan (see 1 Chron. v. 16). According to Eusebius and Jerome, there was yet another, between Tabor and Tiberias, and this, as being in the north, may be referred to. Aquila renders "a rosebud of Sharon." The lily (*shoshannah*) is only found as here in the feminine form in the Apocrypha. The red and white lily were both known. Some would derive the word from the numeral (*shésh*) "six," because the liliaceæ are six-leaved, while the rosaceæ are five-leaved; but it is pro-

bably akin to *shésh*, "byssus," *shayish*, "white marbles" (cf. Hos. xiv. 5, "He shall bloom as a lily"). Our Lord's reference to "the lilies of the field" reminds us that they were in Palestine both very beautiful and very abundant. Zöckler thinks it is not the strongly scented white lily (*Lilium candidum*) to which reference is made, but the red lily (*Lilium rubens*); but either will convey the same idea of a flower of the field which is meant. "My beauty is the beauty of nature—artless and pure."

HOMILETICS.

Vers. 1—4.—*The prologue.* I. THE INSCRIPTION. 1. *The title.* We are told (1 Kings iv. 32) that the songs of Solomon were a thousand and five. This is the chief of all, the Song of Songs. It stands alone in the Old Testament. It is a pastoral drama of singular loveliness. It shows a delight in the beauties of nature such as we might look for in him who "spake of trees, from the cedar tree that is in Lebanon even unto the hyssop that springeth out of the wall; of beasts also, and of fowl, and of creeping things." It exhibits a touching picture of early affection gradually ripening into the blessed love of wedlock—that love which, when pure and unselfish, tends more than anything that is of this world to elevate and refine the soul. And it has a higher meaning. Holy men of widely different times have seen in it the spiritual converse of the Church, or of the individual soul, with the heavenly Bridegroom. A famous Jewish rabbi, after saying that all the books of the Hagiographa are holy, describes the Song of Songs as a holy of holies; and a great Father of the Church says that in this book the perfected, who have the world beneath their feet, are joined to the embraces of the heavenly Bridegroom. Thus it combines all the elements which give a charm to poetry—beauty of form and elevation of thought; a delicate appreciation of the attractions of external nature; a deep sense of the sweetness and power of the most universal, the most dominant, of human affections; and an uplook to higher things, an uplook from that love which is of God—for such surely is the love of husband and wife (see Eph. v. 25—28)—to God who is love. Thus the title is abundantly justified. There are great difficulties here and there; but yet much of the Song of Songs has ever sounded to believing souls like far-off echoes of the new song which only the redeemed from the earth could learn (Rev. xiv. 3). There are few passages of Holy Scripture sweeter to the Christian heart than those thrice-repeated words, "My Beloved is mine, and I am his." 2. *The authorship.* "Which is Solomon's." The Hebrew preposition may be translated "of" or "for." In the titles of Ps. lxxii. and cxxvii. it is rendered in our Authorized Version "for Solomon," "of Solomon" standing in the margin. Ps. cxxvii., like the rest of the "songs of degrees," is almost certainly post-Exilic; and in Ps. lxxii. the LXX. translators are probably right in regarding Solomon as the subject, not the author, of the psalm. If the Song of Songs was written by Solomon himself, we have in it a most awful warning of the fickleness, the sinfulness, of the human heart. Solomon, who knew so well what is the sweetness of pure and holy love, was led astray by that sensual passion which usurps the name of love. Solomon, who was called Jedidiah, "the darling of the Lord," whom "the Lord loved" (2 Sam. xii. 24), who himself "loved the Lord" (1 Kings iii. 3)—that same Solomon "loved many strange women" (1 Kings xi. 1), and "when he was old, his wives turned away his heart after other gods." "Let him that thinketh he standeth take heed lest he fall;" "Ye that love the Lord, see that ye hate the thing that is evil." The soul that would live in the love of Christ must hate, and reject with horror and loathing, the very smallest beginnings of that sin of impurity which separates a man from God utterly and with a fearful rapidity. If, on the other hand, it was written by some prophet or poet of Northern Palestine in Solomon's time, we have an explanation of those peculiar words which some scholars regard as Aramaic, others as dialectic peculiarities of the Lebanon country; and we have a warning not to trust too much in human leaders. We must not put our trust in man, but only in God. When men, once honoured and esteemed, fall into sin, we cannot but be distressed; but we must not allow our faith to waver. God is the truth; he continueth faithful; we must trust in him. The internal evidence of the song itself points to a time anterior to the separation of the northern and southern kingdoms; this is not the place to discuss the arguments for a later origin. 3. *The meaning.* The song seems to rest on an historical basis; its many details, its geographical notices, its many references to circumstances of Solomon's time, to its peace and prosperity (such a period of peace and prosperity as perhaps never occurred again during the chequered history of Israel), to its commerce, its magnificence, point to a groundwork of actual fact. It relates the love of the great king for some innocent country maiden—a love that was returned, that for a time at least brought happiness to both, and seemed to refine and elevate the characters of both, as a pure love which leads to a blessed marriage ever does. But holy men of old were led by the Spirit to incorporate this beautiful narrative into the canon of Holy Scripture. That fact invests the song with another and a higher meaning. Jewish rabbis regarded it as a parable of the relations between God and Israel. Many of the Christian Fathers have seen in it the love that is between Christ and his Church; the longings of the Christian soul for the presence of the heavenly Bridegroom; the vicissitudes of the spiritual life; the blessed union of the bride, the Lamb's wife, with the Lord of her redemption at the last. There are great difficulties in the spiritual interpretation of some passages; but when we consider the position of the song in the sacred book; when we remember that "every Scripture inspired of God is also profitable for teaching, for reproof, for correction, for instruction which is in righteousness;" when we remember the great value which many of God's saints have set upon this book, the great spiritual benefit which they have derived from it, we feel that it must be right to regard it as a parable of Divine love, to see under this earthly story a deep and holy heavenly meaning.

II. THE FIRST SONG. 1. *The bride's longing for the beloved.* The three verses (2—4) are often regarded as the song of a chorus of virgins, the companions of the bride; perhaps the mingling of the singular and plural pronouns seems rather to suggest that we have in this first song the voice of the bride herself blended with the strains of her virgin-friends. The bride yearns for the embrace of love. In the pure love of Christian man and maid, the maiden long desired gives at last the full treasure of her love in answer to that love which had with earnest devotion sought for her affection. Ancient writers see in these words the longing of the Jewish Church for a closer union with God, for the fulfilment of the promise given through the prophet (Hos. ii. 16), " In that day, saith the Lord, thou shalt call me Ishi ['my Husband'], and shalt call me no more Baali ['my Lord']." The Christian Church, the Christian soul, longs for the enjoyment of the Saviour's love. We notice the abrupt beginning, "Let him kiss me." The bride is speaking of one well known, greatly loved. There is no need of exact description; the pronoun is enough; there is only One whose image is ever present to that loving heart. When the Christian, taught by the Holy Ghost, is learning, slowly and imperfectly (as, alas! it must be here), to fulfil the first of all the commandments, he will yearn above all things for that manifestation of himself which the Lord promises to them that love him (John xiv. 21, 23). The traitor's kiss, treacherous as it was, shows that such a token of affection was usual in the intercourse between our Lord and his apostles. His love is unchanging, everlasting; still the Christian soul may say, " The Son of God loved me, and gave himself for me;" still the soul longs for the sense of that blessed love; " the love of Jesus, what it is, none but his loved ones know." The woman that was a sinner kissed the Saviour's feet. The kiss of peace was in apostolic times the token of the love which Christians had one towards another. The kiss of pure and holy love is a parable of the blessed love which is betwixt Christ and his Church. That love is better than wine. Now the bride speaks to the Lord. " Thy love," she says; she feels that he is coming in answer to the call of love. Earthly joys are poor indeed when compared with that joy which is in the Lord. St. Paul contrasts them in the Epistle to the Ephesians (v. 18, 19). Excess in wine brings degradation, misery. The Christian soul needs not this spurious excitement; it has a source of joy higher beyond all comparison. It is filled with the Spirit, and the fruit of the Spirit is joy—joy which manifests itself in psalms and hymns and spiritual songs. 2. *The response of the chorus.* The attendant virgins assent. The love of the Bridegroom is better than wine, better than the fragrance of the sweetest of perfumes, sweeter than ointment poured forth which sheds its scent around. The odour of the precious ointment which Mary poured upon the Saviour's head filled the house; the sweet odour of the name of Jesus fills the whole Church; it sheds its penetrating influence everywhere throughout the Church; "therefore," the chorus sings, "do the virgins love thee." The plural number seems to remind us that the love of Christ is personal, individual. The bride, the Lamb's wife, is, indeed, the whole company of the elect. But the Lord's love is not only general; it does not bless only the Church as a whole, an aggregate; he loves all and each; the whole Church and each separate Christian soul; therefore each separate Christian soul, all who take their lamps and go forth to meet the Bridegroom, rejoice in the Bridegroom's love, and desire above all things to return it. "We love him, because he first loved us." 3. *The blended voices of the chorus and the bride.* (1) The request: "Draw me, we will run after thee." The bride is listening for the bridegroom's call; she is ready to answer. Her virgin-companions join in assenting chorus; they will accompany her. The Christian soul longs for the fulfilment of the Divine Word, "I drew them with cords of a man, with bands of love" (Hos. xi. 4); it pleads that gracious promise, "I, if I be lifted up from the earth, will draw all men unto me."

> "Break up the heavens, O Lord! and far,
> Thro' all yon starlight keen,
> Draw me, thy bride, a glittering star,
> In raiment white and clean."

It seems too much to ask; none feel their unworthiness, their guilt, so keenly as those whom the Lord is calling nearer to himself. But faith hears his voice and believes in his power. If only he will draw us, we shall run after him. Love is the magnet of love. When God deigns to shine into his people's hearts to give the light of the knowledge of the glory of God in the face of Jesus Christ, when the blessed word, "We have seen the Lord," is realized in the heart, then the soul runneth in ever-deepening desire to respond to that condescending love. None can come to Christ, we know, "except the Father who hath sent me draw him" (John vi. 44); therefore that prayer, "Draw me, we will run after thee," is often in the Christian's heart, often pleaded by the Christian's lips. We are weak and helpless; but when he draws us with that holy invitation, "Come unto me," we must arise, we must run after him. To look back is ruin. "Remember Lot's wife." And his call giveth strength to follow, to run after him. So St. Augustine says in well-known words ('Conf.,' ix. 1), "How sweet did it at once become to me to want the sweetnesses of those toys; and what I feared to be parted from, was now a joy to part with! For thou didst cast them forth from me, thou true and highest Sweetness. Thou castedst them forth, and for them enteredst in thyself, sweeter than all pleasures, though not to flesh and blood; brighter than all light, but more hidden than all depths; higher than all honour, but not to the high in their own conceits." (2) The answer. The prayer is heard; we hear the voice of the bride: "The King hath brought me into his chambers." Christ loved the Church, and gave himself for her, that he might present her to himself a glorious Church. The chorus answers, "We will be glad and rejoice in thee." Individual believers make up the great Church of Christ. Once we were afar off; now we are brought near; we are "fellow-citizens with the saints, and of the household of God." In proportion as we realize our Christian privileges of access unto God we learn to rejoice in the Lord. The fruit of the Spirit is joy; that joy passes all earthly pleasures. Believers will remember the tokens of the Saviour's love, dwelling on them in holy thought; they will leave no place in their hearts for sensual delights; they will love the Lord in uprightness, in sincerity, and truth.

Vers. 5—8.—*Dialogue between the bride and the chorus.* I. THE BRIDE'S SENSE OF UNWORTHINESS. 1. "*I am black.*" The country maiden loved by the great king feels her own imperfections: she artlessly describes her misgivings to the daughters of Jerusalem, who constitute the chorus; she has been accustomed to rustic occupations; she has been ill-treated; the sun has embrowned her cheeks till she is black as the tents of Kedar, the tents of goat's hair in which the wandering Arabs lived. The Christian soul knows its guilt. Worship begins ever with confession; when we draw near to Christ, we are most sensible of the plague of our own hearts. Christians will find help and comfort in communion with the like-minded; they will tell them their spiritual troubles; but such holy communion can be held only with the like-minded, with the daughters of Jerusalem. Christians sometimes have home troubles; they seem unable to keep their own vineyard, to attend to their own spiritual needs, because other work is forced upon them, because their time is taken up in matters which seem not to belong to their peace; they must be patient and meek, and wait for the Bridegroom's call. 2. *" But comely."* In her artless simplicity she mentions her own beauty: she is fair as the curtains of Solomon. The king, we may suppose, had a stately pavilion in the Lebanon country, near the dwelling of the bride. The Christian recognizes with humble and adoring thankfulness the working of the Spirit of God within his soul. " By the grace of God I am what I am: and his grace which was bestowed on me was not in vain; but I laboured more abundantly than they all: yet not I, but the grace of God which was with me." If God is drawing us nearer to himself we must know it. True unaffected humility recognizes his working in our unworthy hearts, and longs to be found in Christ, "not having mine own righteousness, which is of the Law, but that which is through the faith of Christ, the righteousness which is of God by faith." The bride compares herself to the curtains of Solomon; the Christian owes whatever he may possess of the beauty of holiness to his communion with the King of saints.

II. THE BRIDE'S LONGING FOR THE BRIDEGROOM'S PRESENCE. 1. *Her seeking love.* He is not with her now, but her soul goeth forth to him; she apostrophizes her absent lord, and pours forth her yearning in the presence of her companions. (1) The address: " Thou whom my soul loveth." It is an expression of intense affection, repeated several times in the song (ch. iii. 1, 2, 3, 4). The love of Christ is the life-spring of the Christian heart. That love, when real and true, makes the Christian seek always, every day and every hour, the blessed presence of the Saviour. That love is the soul's love. It is not a thing of words and phrases, not a matter of outward form and observance; it is treasured deep in the heart; it is the mainspring of life and action; it comes to Christ with the question, " Lord, what wilt thou have me to do?" and that in the ordinary concerns of life, in the trifles, the little joys and sorrows of everyday life, as well as in the emergencies that come now and then, the dangers and distresses which cross our path from time to time. That true, deep love is exceedingly precious; it is the perfect love that casteth out fear; it can answer like St. Peter, " Lord, thou knowest all things; thou knowest that I love thee." It is of all graces the holiest and the best; it is the first of the fruits of the Spirit; it is granted to the believer in answer to fervent persevering prayer. May we whose hearts have long been so cold and dead seek it, and gain it to be our own through the forgiving mercy of our God! (2) She asks where he feeds his flock. The King of Israel is represented as a shepherd like his father David. The bride thinks more of his love than of his magnificence; she would have loved him with the same entire devotion had he been in her own lowly position. Perhaps it was a relief to her to regard him sometimes not as a king, but as a shepherd; perhaps the great king had been pleased to assume such a character for a time to give pleasure to his beloved one. The bride seems sometimes to hint that this description is figurative (ch. ii. 16; vi. 2, 3); she speaks of the son of David in language like that which David himself had used of Almighty God (Ps. xxiii. 1, 2). The Lord Jesus Christ is the good Shepherd; he laid down his life for the sheep; he knoweth his own, and his own know him. He is King of kings and Lord of lords; but it is a relief to the soul, dazzled by the awful glory of the Godhead, to remember that he laid his glory by that he might save us; and to think of him as made like unto us in all things, sin only excepted, and therefore touched with the feeling of our infirmities, and able to succour them that are tempted. She asks where he feeds his flock. It is like the aspiration of Job, " Oh that I knew where I might find him! that I might come even to his seat!" The Christian soul yearns for the good Shepherd, to draw ever nearer to him, to share his love and mercy. He maketh his sheep to lie down in green pastures; he leadeth them beside the waters of rest. He feeds them; for he is the Bread of life—the Bread that came down from heaven to give life unto the world. Their prayer is, " Lord, evermore give us this bread." They feed on him in the daily life of faith, and in the blessed sacrament. His presence in the heart is the food, the life of the soul. "He that cometh unto me," he saith, "shall never hunger, and he that believeth on me shall never thirst." And he maketh his flock to rest at noon. In the hot sultry noon of life, amid troubles and anxieties and cares, he giveth rest. The weary and the heavy-laden accept his gracious invitation; they find rest—rest for their souls. There is no other rest for this restless, anxious soul of ours, but only that rest which he giveth—rest in the Lord. He can give rest in the midst of trouble, rest even in the busy noon of life; such rest as Daniel found in his many cares, when he kneeled upon his knees and made his supplications three times a day; such rest as St. Paul found when he had learned to count all things as loss for the excellency of the knowledge of Christ Jesus his Lord. 2. *Her fears.* Compare Gesenius, *s.v.*, "Lest I be as one who faints by the flocks of thy companions; lest I should wander in search of thee from flock to flock, languid even to fainting through the noontide heat." The bride seeks the king himself. His companions may be kind and good, but they are not the beloved. The soul seeks the good Shepherd. Other shepherds may be doing what they can to feed the flock of God (see 1 Pet. v. 2—4), but they can only bring the flock to the chief Shepherd. He is the Desire of all nations; he only is the Saviour; without him we can do nothing. It is not safe to wander from flock to flock, to heap up to ourselves teachers (2 Tim. iv. 3). We must seek Christ himself, for the true sheep are his; they hear his voice and follow him. They that are his shall never perish; no man is able to pluck them out of his Father's hand. But they must not listen to other voices which are not his; they must watch with earnest attention for the voice of the good Shepherd, and attend to every intimation of his will; they must ask him with loving entreaty—"O thou whom my soul loveth"—by what way, in what path, he is to be found; they must not weary themselves in wandering from teacher to teacher, seeking always, like the Athenians, to hear some new things; they must walk in the old paths, where is the good way; and they will find rest, for they will find, not Solomon, whose name means "peace," but the Prince of Peace himself, who giveth peace, the peace of God, to all who seek his face with faithful and true hearts.

III. THE COUNSEL OF THE DAUGHTERS OF JERUSALEM. 1. *The address.* "O thou fairest among women." The bride is addressed by the chorus in the same words in two other places (ch. v. 9; vi. 1). She had described herself as "black, but comely." The daughters of Jerusalem see in her the fairest among women. Jerusalem was the holy city, the dwelling-place of the great King. Her daughters are the saints, the children of the kingdom. The true Christian knows his own sinfulness, though he feels with thankfulness the work of grace within his heart; other Christians recognize in him the beauty of holiness. There must be no jealousies among the people of God; they must not dispute among themselves, as even apostles once did, who should be the greatest in the kingdom of heaven; they must gladly acknowledge the workings of the grace of God in other Christian souls; they will do so the more generously, the nearer they themselves are to the Lord. 2. *The direction.* "If thou know not," they say; as if to intimate that one so highly favoured must surely know the way herself. They can but guide her to the old way where all the saints have walked; she must follow the tracks of the sheep, the footsteps of the flock. They have followed the good Shepherd; she must do the like. "Be ye followers of me," said St. Paul, "even as I also am of Christ." It is good to read the lives of the saints, to study the graces of holy men. Holy Scripture bids us to follow their faith, considering the end of their conversation. But the bride is also told to feed her kids beside the shepherds' tents. We shall most surely find the Lord in faithful work for him. If he is to us what he was to the bride, "O thou whom my soul loveth;" if we can say in truth, "Lord, thou knowest all things; thou knowest that I love thee," we shall surely hear his voice speaking in our hearts, "Feed my lambs;" "Feed my sheep." Those who, like St. Paul, labour most abundantly for Christ (if only that labour is wrought in faith and love) are sure, like St. Paul, themselves to win Christ and to be found in him. "He that watereth shall be watered also himself;" "They that turn many to righteousness shall shine as the stars for ever and ever." Christ is most surely found by those faithful servants who do their best to bring others to the Lord.

Vers. 9—17.—*The communion of the bridegroom and the bride.* I. THE APPROACH

OF THE BRIDEGROOM. 1. *His address.* He compares the bride to a beautiful mare of his own in the chariots of Pharaoh. The words come fitly from the lips of the speaker. He was the first king of Israel who took delight in horses and chariots, and he imported them from Egypt. The words are thought to have suggested a similar comparison in Theocritus ('Idyll,' xviii. 30); they indicate the stateliness of the bride's beauty; they remind us of Ps. cxlvii. 10, 11, " He delighteth not in the strength of a horse. . . . The Lord taketh pleasure in them that fear him, in those that hope in his mercy." Men like Solomon take delight in horses; the Lord in the graces of his people. The king calls the bride " my love," or " my friend; " the word is derived from a verb which in its secondary sense means to take delight in the companionship of those whom we love. We are reminded of the Lord's gracious words, " Henceforth I call you not servants; for the servant knoweth not what his lord doeth: but I have called you friends; for all things that I have heard of my Father I have made known unto you " (John xv. 15). The king proceeds to commend the graces of the bride; he promises costly gifts. She was wearing the simple ornaments of a country maiden (the words "jewels " and "gold " are not in the original of ver. 10). " We will make thee," he says (that is, his servants will make at his order), " borders of gold with studs of silver." Whatever graces the Church possesses come from the gift of the heavenly Bridegroom; it is he who will " present her to himself a glorious Church, not having spot, or wrinkle, or any such thing; " but holy and without blemish (Eph. v. 27). It is only God who can " keep us from falling, and present us at the last faultless before the presence of his glory with exceeding joy " (Jude 24). The fine linen, clean and white, the wedding-garment of the bride, is the Bridegroom's gift (Rev. xix. 8). 2. *The bride's delight in the bridegroom.* The king is come; he sitteth at his table in the midst of the circle of his friends. We are reminded that the presence of his father David was once required to complete such a circle. " We will not sit around " (the literal translation of Samuel's words) " till he come hither " (1 Sam. xvi. 11). The bride (like Mary afterwards) anoints him with " ointment of spikenard very costly; " the house is filled with the odour of the ointment. While the heavenly Bridegroom is present in the blessed sacrament, or in the circle of true worshippers, whenever two or three are gathered together in his Name, the sweet odour of prayer and adoration giveth forth its fragrance. Such worship, worship in spirit and in truth, is always acceptable. " My Father," he saith in his condescending love, " seeketh such to worship him." It is his presence which draws forth that holy worship. While he is with us, in the circle of worshippers, the heart goeth forth unto him. " Lord, it is good to be here; " " Thy Name is as ointment poured forth." It is sweet to the believer; it refreshes his soul in sorrow, and in the hour of death; therefore do thy people love thee. The King's presence is very sacred; those whom he deigns to visit must respond with their heart's love, with the sweet odours of true spiritual worship. 3. *What the bridegroom is to her.* The odour of her spikenard is pleasant to him; he is to her as a bag of myrrh, or a cluster of henna flowers. So, in Ps. xlv. 8, the royal Bridegroom's garments smell of myrrh, aloes, and cassia. The bag of myrrh was kept in the bosom for its sweetness and its medicinal properties; the henna flowers which grew abundantly among the vines of Engedi were highly esteemed for their fragrance. The Saviour's presence in the heart sheds a fragrance through the soul. " He that hath the Son hath life; " a principle of life which preserves the soul from the corruption of sin, which heals its diseases, which prepares it for the hour of death. The Saviour's body lay for a while in the mixture of myrrh and aloes which Nicodemus brought; that holy body needed not the earthly unguent. The Christian needs the preservative virtue which the Saviour giveth. No flowers of earth, no earthly fragrance or beauty, can compare for one moment with the blessedness which his presence bringeth.

II. THE CONVERSE OF THE BRIDEGROOM AND THE BRIDE. 1. *The voice of the beloved.* He commends the beauty of the bride; her eyes, as they look on him, are like doves, gentle, innocent, loving. So, in Ps. xlv., the king greatly desires the beauty of the bride. She " is all glorious within: her clothing is of wrought gold." The Lord would have the Church, his bride, to be " a glorious Church, not having spot, or wrinkle, or any such thing; " but holy and without blemish. Alas! in the visible Church the evil are ever mingled with the good, and there is none that sinneth not. But just in proportion as the Christian walks in the light (in the light of his presence who is the

Light of the world), the blood of Jesus Christ is cleansing him from all sin, and he becomes in his poor measure a light, shining with the reflected light of the Saviour's holiness. Christ is made unto his people wisdom, and righteousness, and sanctification, and redemption; whatever beauty of character they possess comes only from communion with him. "Beholding as in a glass the glory of the Lord, they are changed into the same image from glory to glory." They must be harmless as doves, gentle, humble, innocent. The Lord in his condescending love accepts their imperfect service. "I know thy works, and thy love, and faith, and ministry, and patience; and that thy last works are more than the first." 2. *The answer of the bride.* Perhaps they have now gone forth into the air; they are sitting together, as the words seem to imply, on a green couch, on some grassy slope in the Lebanon country, under the interlacing boughs of cedars and fir trees. The bride enjoys the fair prospect around her; she delights still more in the presence and love of the bridegroom. She calls him "my beloved;" the Hebrew word is another form of the name of the king's father, David, which means "beloved." He is very fair in her eyes; yea, pleasant. The Lord is fairer than the children of men; to the Christian there is no vision of earthly beauty which will bear one moment's comparison with the tender loveliness of the Saviour's character, the exalted beauty of his self-sacrificing love. The Christian soul delights in the fair beauty of the Lord; it is to him the one thing to be desired above all others. "One thing have I desired of the Lord, that I will seek after; that I may dwell in the house of the Lord all the days of my life, to behold the beauty of the Lord" (Ps. xxvii. 4). So Isaiah, who alone of the prophets uses the bride's word of endearment, "my Beloved" (Isa. v. 1), has the blessed promise, "Thine eyes shall see the King in his beauty" (Isa. xxxiii 17). The king is pleasant also; not only fair to look upon, but possessed of every charm, of all spiritual grace. We have the same word applied to God in Ps. xxvii. 4 and xc. 17. May God "shine into our hearts, to reveal to us the light of the knowledge of the glory of God in the face of Jesus Christ"!

HOMILIES BY VARIOUS AUTHORS.

Ver. 1.—"*The Song of Songs, which is Solomon's.*" What does this mean?

I. As to the title? "The Song of Songs." It affirms that this song is the most excellent of all songs, the incomparably beautiful song, a song beside which, as one writer says, "all others hide their heads."

II. As to the name affixed to it? *Not that Solomon was the author.* For the very title would convict him of egregious vanity. A writer would hardly thus speak of his own productions. But it would be quite lawful that another should so speak; hence the poem might be Solomon's and the title be added on by another writer. But even then we question his authorship of this song. For: 1. *If we take the literal interpretation of it,* as well-nigh all modern competent Bible scholars do, in greater or less degree (cf. Ginsburg, Ewald, Maurer, Stanley, 'Speaker's Commentary,' Hartwell Horne's 'Introduction,' etc.),—then, since it represents Solomon as foiled and frustrated in his endeavours to persuade the maiden Shulamith, whose constancy and fidelity the poem celebrates, to become his bride, it is hardly likely that he would depict himself in such an unlovely light, or in such undignified guise as that in which, in this song, he certainly appears. Or, if we take the most ancient and most common interpretation of the song, *the spiritual and allegorical,* which affirms that the bride—though there is no bride in the song at all, but only one who is betrothed—represents the Church; and that Solomon, whom this interpretation identifies with "the beloved," is a type of our Lord Jesus Christ; and that the poem is intended to set forth the mutual love of Christ and his Church;—then we say that Solomon is in no sense a fit type of the Lord Jesus Christ, for he was not a man after God's own heart, but very far from it. Moreover, he was not the man to write a spiritual poem of such exalted character. They were "*holy* men of old" whom the Spirit inspired. But, certainly, Solomon can lay no claim to *that* character. Then: 3. David and Solomon are both *spoken of in such manner as would hardly be likely if Solomon were the writer.* (Cf. ch. iii. 9, 11; viii. 11, 12.) It is the manner of one speaking of them, telling facts concerning them; but it is not as they would speak themselves.   4. And even if the words, "which is Solomon's," be held to mean that he was the author, *such ascription need have no more value* than the titles of many of the psalms, which are allowed to be of no authority.   5. But we read the words as *" concerning Solomon."* True, the poem literally understood has nothing to say in his favour; for what was there to say ?   But if he be a type at all, and we think he is, it is of that greedy, selfish, soul-corrupting world, which would draw away the faithful from the pure love of God, and seek to replace that pure love by its own.   Shulamith loved and was beloved.   Solomon tried by all manner of enticements to draw her from that love.   But he utterly fails.   So that the poem is a parable of the faithful soul and its constancy to its true Lord.   By means of a beautiful earthly story, the yet more beautiful fidelity of the soul truly affianced to God is set forth—a fidelity tried so as by fire, and therefore more precious than all gold (cf. 1 Pet. i. 6, 7), which might be taken as a text for the interpretation of very much in this book.   It was written, probably, near the age of Solomon, but we think subsequently; and by some Israelite belonging to the northern tribes; and from the absence of all praise of Solomon, and the conduct it ascribes to him, the writer was probably hostile to him, perhaps one of those who in Rehoboam's day raised the cry of "To your tents, O Israel!" and broke away from the kingdom of Judah altogether.   The poem is sensuous, but not sensual, unless it be where Solomon is to be understood as speaking, when such speech would be in character.   It is Oriental, of course, and not to be interpreted by those far different canons of taste which prevail in our more Northern and Western lands.   And it is not a mere story of a maiden's constancy.   Were it so, however beautiful (and for remarks on its beauty cf. Isaac Taylor's ' Spirit of the Hebrew Poetry '), still it would not, we think, have found a place amongst the sacred writings.   We hold it to be an allegory or parable of *the soul's true love to God,* and, so read, it is like the rest of Holy Scripture, " profitable for doctrine, for reproof," etc.   He who has no love of God in his heart, or even little, will never understand it, and had better leave it alone.   But to the pure, devout, and Christ-loving heart the vision of him who is for them the "altogether lovely" is seen everywhere in it, and delighted in wherever seen.   That vision may *we* see!—S. C.

Vers. 2—4.—*Desire after God.* Translated into language more congenial to our ordinary Christian thought, these verses may be taken as a parabolic setting forth of the blessed truth contained in the well-known words of the psalm, " My soul thirsteth for God, for the living God; when shall I come and appear before God ?"   It surely would be speaking blasphemy, and an abasement of the Bible, if we were to look on the sensuous words with which these verses begin as meaning nothing more than they say in their ordinary plain and literal meaning.   We, therefore, feel bound to lift them up from such low level, and to look upon them as telling—no doubt in a vivid, Oriental way—of the soul's desire after God, the holy thirst of which the verse from the psalm is the expression.   And we observe—

I. That the conscious possession of the love of God is the soul's deep need and desire.   Men try all manner of other delights, but they turn out mere apples of Sodom.   He who wrote the Book of Ecclesiastes had left untried no single source of earthly joy.   All were within his power, and he did his best to get their best out of them.   And no doubt he succeeded.   But what then ?   Was he satisfied ? did they content him ?   " Vanity of vanities; all is vanity !"—that is his verdict upon them all.   And his experience is that of myriads more, all which goes to prove that the love of God alone can satisfy.   " Nostrum cor inquietum est donec requiescat in te."   This saying of St. Augustine's is the sober truth, which finds such impassioned expression in our text.   And the soul's desire for that love is the fruit of that love.   " I, if I be lifted up, will draw all men unto me," said our Lord ; and it is because of his gracious drawings, the mighty lure with which he attracts our wills, that we are possessed by this desire.

II. The Divine love is the exhilaration of the soul.   "Thy love is better than wine."   " Be not drunk with wine, but be filled with the Spirit," says St. Paul ; and he thereby teaches us, as does the text, that there is a likeness between the two—wine and the Spirit of God.   And the resemblance lies here—in the stir and joy of heart which wine for a while causes ; and this, though in no mere physical sense, is the blessed effect of the Spirit of God. For his office it is to shed abroad the love of God in our hearts, and that causes joy indeed.

III. AND IT IS FRAGRANT WHEREVER IT DWELLS. It is likened to " perfume poured forth," and it fills " all the house."

IV. THE PURE IN HEART LOVE IT. "Therefore do the virgins love thee." The desire for the Divine love is not universal—far from it. But " the pure in heart " " see God," and hence their desire.—S. C.

Ver. 3.—*Christ's Name.* " His Name is as ointment poured forth." We apply the text to him. It cannot be shown that such application is wrong. Perfumes largely used in the East—in acts of worship ; in entertainments, as marks of favour to honoured guests (cf. Ps. xxiii.; John xii.). The Name of Christ is here likened to such precious perfume, the sweet odour of which fills the whole house, as did that which Mary poured on the Lord. The " Name " stands for all that Christ is to us. The comparison is appropriate if we consider concerning such perfumes—

I. THEIR COSTLINESS. They were on this account exceeding precious, large sums of money being demanded for them (John xii. 3). But does not this tell of the " *precious* blood of Christ," and how " God *so* loved the world "? Think of the cost of the " unspeakable Gift" of Christ : 1. *To the Father.* Was the heart of God unmoved by the sorrows of the Son? Is not the touching story of Abraham's offering up of Isaac, and of his anguish at having to surrender his son, his only son Isaac, " whom thou lovest," brought before our minds when we read how " God so loved the world, that he gave *his* only begotten Son "? Does it not tell of the anguish of the Divine mind in that sacrifice? A God that cannot know sorrow or joy, that is not " touched with the feeling of our infirmities," is not the God of the Bible, " our *Father* which art in heaven." Therefore what of uttermost sorrow must he not have known when he beheld the " beloved Son, in whom he was well pleased," expire in agony on the cross? 2. *To Christ himself.* Was he not " the Man of sorrows, and acquainted with grief"? " Come, see if ever there was sorrow like unto my sorrow "—to whom do these words apply as to him? Cf. Ps. xxii., that psalm which was in the mind and on the lips of our Lord as he hung upon the cross. The parable of the pearl of great price and of the treasure hid in the field may have other meanings than those commonly given to them. May they not tell of our salvation, and how our blessed Lord was set upon obtaining this, and therefore, though " he was rich, yet for our sakes he became poor," that he might obtain this, to him, most precious pearl, this treasure of untold worth. 3. *To the Holy Spirit.* For he it is who takes of the things of Christ and shows them unto us ; who seeks men, and woos and wins them for Christ. The whole of the Passion of our Lord is patterned forth and perpetuated in the grievings and outrages, in the Gethsemane-like " groanings which cannot be uttered " (Rom. viii.), which tell of what he suffers to save men. 4. And if we think of the Gift itself, *the very Son of God*—no creature, no man, no angel or archangel, but he who was one with the Father—*that* sacrifice was the cost of our redemption. All comparison fails, no matter what of worth and value in earthly things are thought of ; they can but faintly image the worth and preciousness of Christ.

II. THEIR COMBINED EXCELLENCE. The choicest perfumes were composed of many ingredients. Cf. the sacred anointing oil (Exod. xxx. 31—38). And so Christ is "made unto us," not one thing only, but many—" wisdom, righteousness, sanctification, and redemption" (1 Cor. i. 30). Whether we think of the combined excellences that are in his own nature and character, or of those which he bestows upon us—so many, so manifold, so precious all of them—the comparison is true.

III. How GRATEFUL THEY ARE TO THOSE ON WHOM THEY ARE POURED. To this day Orientals delight in such perfumes. They deem them to be as healthful as they are pleasant ; and still they are given to honoured guests, as Simon should have given them but did not, but as the Magdalen and Mary of Bethany also did to our Lord. "Thou anointest my head with oil," tells in the twenty-third psalm of the exuberance of joy that the believer has in his Lord. " How sweet the Name of Jesus sounds ! " so still his people love to sing. And what they sing is true.

IV. THEIR DIFFUSIVE FRAGRANCE. " Poured forth," released from the vessel which contained it, and in consequence spreading its sweet odours all around. Again the comparison is just. Has not human life become sweeter in innumerable places because there the Name of Christ has been poured forth? Heaven is heaven because there his "Name is above every name."

V. THAT THEY MAKE FRAGRANT AS WELL AS ARE SO IN THEMSELVES. By this may we know whether we are Christ's. If character, temper, spirit, life, be of ill odour, how can we have known Christ's Name?—S. C.

Vers. 4—8.—*The Christian soul, its trials and triumphs.* The maiden who speaks has been separated unwillingly from her beloved, after whom she incessantly mourns; she is kept in the king's chambers, the apartments of the women in his palace at Jerusalem. They ridicule her swarthy look, and she tells how her half-brothers had been unkind to her, and had made her work in the drudgery of the vineyards, beneath the scorching sun. Those about her wonder and scoff at her persistent affection. The story may be taken as telling of the Christian soul, its trials and triumphs.

I. ITS TRIALS. The Christian soul may be: 1. *Unwillingly deprived of* conscious enjoyment of her Lord's presence. How often in the psalms do we find the complaint of the Lord being "far from me," of the failure to realize his presence and his love! And how often the same thing occurs now! Our sun is hidden behind a cloud, and the soul grieves over her absent Lord. 2. *Despised.* This is another though a less trial. The child of God is a poor kind of creature in the world's esteem, and it is not slow to let the believer know and feel its contempt. And with many this is a terrible thing. Not a few who would lead a forlorn hope and do any deed of daring that required only physical courage, will shrink and quail beneath the world's scorn. 3. *Persecuted and ill-used* also, as she was who is spoken of here. So, too, is it and has been with the Christian soul. And often a man's foes are they of his own household. Our Lord told us it would be so, and so they have found it; but have found also, as here, that he knows how to sustain his servants in this trial. 4. *Mockery* likewise has to be reckoned with. For though ver. 8 tells a truth which has very real and blessed meaning in regard to the soul's way to God, yet it seems to us to have been spoken mockingly, bidding her to whom it was spoken track the footprints of the sheep if she wanted to know where her beloved was, if she would persist in being so foolish. Such is the force of the words rendered, "If thou know not." They are contemptuous, and contain a sneer. But "cruel mockings" have been the lot of Christ's people in all ages, and when we have to bear them we are not to be surprised "as if some strange thing had happened" unto us. But these verses tell not of trials alone, but of—

II. ITS TRIUMPHS. For: 1. *Her soul still clave unto her beloved.* (Ver. 4.) And so, notwithstanding the Christian soul may be by one cause or another held in captivity and "walk in darkness," yet it will all the more cry out after him whom it loveth, and remember his love more than any of the joys of earth. Thus the very design of her adversary is baffled, for her heart beats true to Christ still. 2. *She is certain that Christ delights in her.* Those about her may despise her because she is "black," because she seems contemptible in their sight. But she knows that the Lord looks upon her with different eyes, that in his sight she is "comely." Others may think what they will, but his estimate is everything to her, and that is as she would have it be. 3. *She desires and obtains yet more of happy communion with him.* (Vers. 7, 8.) Often is it with the faithful soul that as the frown of Christ's foes and her own deepen, the light of Christ's countenance shines on her more steadily, brightly, and fully than ever. He drew her (ver. 4) by her need of his grace, and she ran after him, seeking that grace and finding it. 4. *She knows that her present lot of hardship and trial is not her true portion.* "Why should I be as one that is veiled?" (margin), that is, one despised and despicable. She knows that such portion is not hers. 5. *She cannot be moved.* She is conqueror. So will it ever be.—S. C.

Vers. 4—7.—*The soul's joy in the love of God.* "The king hath brought me into his chambers," etc. If we may take this book as only an allegory, we find suggested in these verses this subject of the soul's joy.

I. SUCH JOY IS BECAUSE OF THE KING'S CHAMBERS. He has opened for her the unsearchable riches of his grace, "filled with all pleasant and precious riches" (cf. Prov. xxiv. 4).

II. IS VERY GREAT. She will be glad and rejoice. She will "remember" his "love more than wine." That is, the soul's joy is more than any earthly means of delight and exhilaration can afford.

III. IS SHARED IN BY ALL THE SAINTS OF GOD. "The upright love thee." "No good thing will he withhold from them that walk uprightly." Our joy is heightened by the fact that those whom we most esteem count it their joy also.

IV. HER OWN UNWORTHINESS DOES NOT SHUT HER OUT FROM IT. "I am black."

> "Since therefore I can hardly bear
>   What in myself I see,
> How vile, how black, I must appear,
>   Most holy God, to thee!
>
> "But oh! my Saviour stands between,
>   In garments dyed in blood;
> 'Tis he instead of me is seen
>   When I approach to God."

The remembrance of her own unworthiness serves as a foil to set off the comeliness with which inwardly he has endowed her. "The king's daughter is all glorious within" (cf. Ezek. xvi. 14). And as she thinks of her unworthiness she tells how it came to be so with her—by the cruelty of others and her own neglect. They made her serve in such way that she became "black." How often our foes are they of our own household! But she, too, was neglectful. "My own vineyard have I not kept." Nevertheless, the king loved her.

V. HENCE SHE WILL BE SATISFIED WITH NOTHING LESS THAN HIMSELF. "Tell me where thou feedest?" etc. (ver. 7). She appeals to him to bring her where he is. She desires to know the rest he can give. His "companions" will not compensate for him (cf. "Whom have I in heaven but thee?" etc.; cf. Ps. xlii. 9; Ezek. xxxiv.; Ps. xxv. 4, 5; xvi. 2, 3).—S. C.

Ver. 6 (part).—*The pastor's peril.* "They made me . . . I have not kept." If we were to understand these words literally, then what is told of might be without either blame or loss. For if, as seems to have been the case, the speaker's neglect of her own vineyard was forced upon her in order that she might keep the vineyards of others, then no fault attached to her. She could not help herself; she was made to work for others. She might grieve, as it is plain she did, to see her own fair vineyard neglected, and, in consequence, overgrown with weeds, and all prospect of fruit gone; but no blame belonged to her, though there might be loss. And it is quite comprehensible that there might be neither blame nor loss, although her own vineyard was neglected. For it might be far more profitable to cultivate the vineyards of others than one's own; and if so, why should there be blame, and how could there be loss? But when we come to the spiritual suggestions of our text, when we look upon it as telling of those whose office and duty it is to cultivate *the vineyard of the soul,* then the conduct told of here can never be without blame and loss both; blame to the vineyard-keeper who kept not his own whilst keeping others, and loss both to him and them. For—

I. MEN'S SOULS ARE GOD'S VINEYARDS. They were created to bring forth fruit for his glory, and for the strengthening, cheering, and every way helping of the souls of their fellows. For this purpose, also, were they redeemed, and for this end are they supplied with manifold Divine gifts—the influences of the Holy Spirit, the aid which the Church, the Scriptures, and the ministers of Christ are appointed to render. Now, such—

II. PASTORS ARE THE KEEPERS OF THESE VINEYARDS. They are to watch over them continually. They are to cultivate them with all diligent care. They are to aim ever to render help to those committed to their care in the formation of that character, and in the exercise of those graces which God regards and rejoices in as fruit. They are to remember always that the vineyards are for fruit, and that whatever else they may yield, if they yield not this, their work has failed. Now, this verse suggests that—

III. THERE IS A GREAT PERIL WHICH BESETS THESE KEEPERS OF THE VINEYARDS. It is this, that whilst keeping the vineyards of others, their own they should not keep. Now, that this is a very real peril is evident from: 1. *Their own confessions.* The words of our text are a confession, and a sorrowful one. And they have been adopted by such vineyard-keepers again and again. Before God, on their knees, they have owned how marred and faulty their work has been, owing to the ill-prepared condition of their own souls. Pastors, teachers, and all who toil for Christ, in striving to tell of him to their fellow-men, and to persuade them to come to him, have mourned—oh, how often!—that their lips have outrun their hearts; that they have uttered words to which their hearts often gave but faint response. They have declared truths which, alas! they have failed to realize. They have spoken of the love of Christ, and had but little consciousness of it within them. As we read the biographies of such men, or as, in the confidence of friendship, they confess how it has been with them, or as we think over our own experiences, who is there of us that may not make the confession of the text our own? It is the perpetual struggle of the right-minded servant of God to maintain the balance between the spoken words and the inward thought; and the struggle is never easy, but often the reverse. These facts show how real the peril is. 2. And *it is evidently possible to be guilty of that which is here said.* For words and work are both external to us, and they can be assumed and adopted even when there is but little or even no spiritual reality behind them. A man can drill himself into saying or doing almost anything. He can become official, perfunctory, and a mere actor in the way of expressing sentiments in which his soul has no share. This is a dreadful possibility, from which may God graciously deliver us all! And our Lord, and the Scriptures generally, declare and denounce such conduct. God says to the wicked in the fiftieth psalm, "What hast thou to do to declare my statutes?" It is certain, therefore, that wicked men can do this and have done it. Our Lord utters his awful warning to those who say "Lord, Lord," prophesy in his name, and in his name do many wonderful works, to whom at the last he will say, "I never knew *you.*" Yes, God's Word is very plain as to the possibility of this sin and its fearful results. 3. *And it is without excuse.* There is no need for it. No amount of busy activity in keeping the vineyards of others need hinder our duly keeping our own. On the contrary, diligent care here will help us mightily when we strive to do good to others and to keep their vineyards. For when we remember that it is the spirit which breathes through what we say or do, rather than the words and deeds themselves, which more than aught besides influences our fellow-men, it is evident that the right cultivation of our own spiritual life is of unspeakable importance. As one has said, "A holy minister is a mighty instrument in God's hand for the conversion and sanctification of souls." Therefore whatever of time and energy we give to the keeping of our own vineyard is the very best preparation and aid in keeping the vineyards of others. Moreover: 4. *Not to give this is fatal to our work.* There is nothing men detect so soon or despise so much as unreality, want of sincerity. The words may be true and well ordered, and lit up with fine imagination and beautiful illustration; be very interesting to hear, and command rapt attention; but if they be lacking in the indispensable quality of sincerity, they will be nothing but words after all, and will have no real effect. Religion must be a reality to ourselves, or we shall never persuade others to become religious men. "Si vis me flêre dolendum est." And not to be thus real ourselves is: 5. *Most perilous for our own souls.* Being so busy in keeping others' vineyards, caring for the interests of others' souls, what can we lack? Must it not be well with us? And people praise and flatter us, and count us to be all we should be: what wonder, then, that we should be deceived? And all the while the holy truths we tell of, like the heated iron that the blacksmith handles, affect us less and less; we scarcely feel them though we talk so fluently about them. And we have already referred to Scripture which make plain the mind of God on this matter. "The sacrifice of the wicked is an abomination unto the Lord." Such is the perpetual language of the Word of God. May he help us to remember it, and that always!

IV. But it is a peril into which they need not fall. For Christ, who called us to keep and cultivate the vineyards, our own and others', which he has entrusted to our charge, will help us therein if continually we look to him. Without him, indeed, we can do nothing; but with him what cannot we do? Therefore, see to it that our souls are committed to him, that day by day we do our all unto him. Only let us abide in him, and then all our outer service will be the natural product of our inner life; not mere fruit fastened on, but fruit grown, produced naturally by our life. And so shall we find that the inner and the outer act and react one upon the other for the mutual good of each. So, whilst we keep the vineyards of others, our own vineyard will also be kept.—S. C.

Ver. 6 (part).—*Not faithless, yet not faithful.* "They made me the keeper of the vineyards . . . kept." Text a sorrowful confession, but it is not the most sorrowful of all. *That* will come from those who cannot say even as much as is said here. For there was, we may readily suppose, the keeping of the vineyards of others, though the speaker's own was not kept. But the confession suggests sin of a deeper dye, a condition of things more sad than this. Let us speak of it first, and consider—

I. THOSE WHO KEEP NEITHER—the vineyards of others nor their own. We take (see previous homily) the vineyard to represent the soul of man. Now, we are all of us, and some especially, appointed to keep the vineyards of others—to watch and tend the spiritual interests of those entrusted to our care; such as our children, our class, our congregation. And all of us, not merely some, are appointed to keep our own vineyard, to care for our own souls. Now, our text speaks of those who did fulfil one part of this duty—they kept the vineyards of others, though they did not keep their own. But partial failure is less terrible than entire failure. And it is of this we speak; of those who keep neither the souls of others nor their own, who neglect both alike. Deplorable is it for those for whom they were appointed to care. What chance have such neglected ones? The mightiest influence that can possibly bear upon them—I speak especially of our children—the influence of parental love and care to train their souls for God, is kept back. What wonder that in such neglected vineyards "ill weeds grow apace"? But yet more deplorable will it be for those thus guilty to such neglect. What will they say when at the last great day it is asked of them what they have done with the vineyards they were appointed to keep? And of course such persons, as a rule, keep not their own vineyards. The same indifference to spiritual things which made them neglect the vineyards of others makes them neglect their own. They have no hunger after God, no thirst for the living water which Christ alone can give. They care not for any of these things. And so the rank undergrowth which the world, the flesh, and sin propagate, spreads over all their spiritual being, and over that of those whom they were appointed to keep. Godless parents have godless children; they have not sought that it should be otherwise. And the teacher who knows not Christ for himself will never persuade his class to yield themselves to Christ. And the unholy minister—ah! what will *his* congregation be? Oh, dreadful will it be for those who have kept neither the vineyards of those others that have been entrusted to them, nor their own. But our text tells especially of—

II. THOSE WHO HAVE KEPT BUT ONE. They have kept the vineyards of others, but not their own. Or it might have been, for it often is, the other way—They might *have kept their own, but not others'.* Let us speak of these first. There are many of them. They think only about their own poor wretched souls, and how they can make them secure. For this they keep up certain religious habits and do many things. But it is all self-contained; it is mere selfishness, for it all centres in the man's own soul. This is the sin of the Church to-day. Its members are so busy keeping each their own vineyards that they care but very little indeed for those of others. But such selfishness brings with it its own proper punishment, as it ought to and cannot but do. "The liberal man deviseth liberal things, and by liberal things he shall stand." But the churlish common Christianity of our day fails to devise liberal things, and therefore does *not* stand. For is it standing high in men's esteem? Is its odour fragrant; its name, like his of whom we read in ver. 3, as "perfume poured forth"? And does it stand strongly, firmly on its faith? Is not that faith faltering in many places? and do not many fall away, and that daily? If we would have our own vineyard yield large luscious fruit to our Lord, care for the vineyards of others as well as our own. 2. But the text tells chiefly of *those who kept others and not their own.* Of this we have spoken already in the former homily. Therefore we come to speak of that most desirable and blessed condition which is found in—

III. THOSE WHO KEEP BOTH—the vineyards of others and their own. Yes, the one we should do, but the other we should not leave undone. Certainly begin with your own. It may be an awful peril to begin with others. But having committed your own soul into Christ's blessed keeping, and found him your very Lord and Saviour, now go straight away and try and persuade others to do just what you have done. Then you shall find fulfilled for you that parable of reward which all nature is full of. See that running brook. How merrily it prattles over the pebbles that form its bed, as it speeds away to render up its little tribute to the larger river, which will bear it on to the great and wide sea at last! The miry pond hard by the brook sneers at it, and says, "You haven't got so much water that you can afford to let it all run away in that wasteful fashion; you should take care of what you have got as I do." But the brook took no heed, and went on singing merrily just as before. And the hot summer came round at last, when, lo! the pond was dried up almost to its last puddle; but the brook went on as before, bright and clear and merry, sparkling and dancing along its appointed way. And we all know the reason why. The brook gave up its strength to the river, and that to the sea; but the sea gave back in vapour all that she had received, and so the fountains from which the brook flowed forth were filled again, and the brook was glad and not sorry that she had given her strength to others, for now her waters had not failed like those of the pond, but were renewed to her day by day. And so, when the water of life flows into our souls, if we let it flow out again to bless the souls of others, be sure that he who first gave us of this grace will give us yet more grace, and we shall find that there is that which scattereth and yet increaseth. The life of the merry healthful child spends itself in the vigorous activity of which it never seems to tire; but that active exercise replenishes the child's life, and it makes increase in strength daily. So, then, as to the vineyards of your own soul and those of others, resolve and pray that you may not be found amongst those who keep neither. Pray, too, that you be not so unhappy as to be a keeper of but one, and especially if that one be not your own. But let this last condition of which we have been telling be yours. Keep your own vineyard *and* your brother's too.—S. C.

Ver. 8.—*How to find God.* The daughters of Jerusalem—the inmates of Solomon's harem—who scornfully addressed these words to the faithful girl who was mourning after her beloved, never meant to utter a great spiritual truth when they thus spoke; any more than Caiaphas did when he said, "It is expedient that one man die for the people." The doctrine of the atonement is in that Caiaphas-speech; and so, sacred suggestions for souls that seek their Lord are found in these words of Jerusalem's daughters. The parallel passage, or comment on this verse, is Heb. xi. 12, "Be ye followers of them who through faith," etc. Now, it is suggested by this verse that if we would find God—

I. WE MUST GO FORTH. (Cf. Heb. xiii. 13, "Let us go forth unto him," etc.) We cannot stay (1) in the world; or (2) in any known sin; or (3) amid the common religionism of the day.

II. OUR WAY MUST BE THE WAY OF THE LORD'S TRUE PEOPLE. We must go by "the footsteps of the flock." As to who the flock are, cf. John x. They are the true sheep of Christ; those whom he calls "my sheep." They consist not of those who are indifferent, still less strangers, and, least of all, hostile to him; but of those who have followed him, and do follow him "whithersoever he goeth." It is good, oftentimes, when we are in doubt as to what we should do, to ask ourselves what some sincere follower of Christ whom we have known would have done in like circumstances. Such people leave footprints, and they are clearly discernible, and if we track them we shall come where they are.

III. WE MUST FEED OUR SOULS UPON THE WORDS OF THE LORD'S SHEPHERDS. (Cf. Heb. xiii. 7, "Remember those who have the rule over you, who have spoken unto you the Word of God," etc.) Such words are spoken in the Scriptures, and from many a Christian pulpit, and they who seek the Lord have ever found strength and help in the preaching of the Lord's true pastors. It is easy to joke and jibe at the pulpit, and to say it is time that it were put away amidst old lumber; but let the pulpit be filled by a real Christ-given pastor, the words that are uttered from it shall still feed the flock of God. But especially let us feed upon the Word of him who is "the good Shepherd." We shall never find him whom we seek unless we obey these counsels.

IV. THOSE WHO WOULD THUS FIND HIM ARE VERY DEAR TO HIM. The speaker had addressed him as "thou whom my soul loveth," and now he addresses her as the "fairest among women." She had said of herself, "I am black," but he says to her, "Thou fairest," etc. All this suggests what so many Scriptures teach as to the children of God being "beautiful" in his sight, and as to his rejoicing over them.—S. C.

Ver. 9—ch. ii. 7.—*Love assailed, but steadfast.* According to the interpretation we have taken of this poem, Solomon is here introduced as endeavouring to win the maiden's consent to become his wife by flatteries and promises of rich gifts of jewels and adornments; but he altogether fails. The above-named subject is therefore suggested. Note, therefore—

I. LOVE ASSAILED. 1. *By flatteries.* Solomon compares her to whom he is speaking to the "horses of Pharaoh's chariot." This comparison is not so coarse as it sounds. It was not unusual amongst the ancients to compare beautiful women to splendid horses (cf. Exposition). The ideas intended are those of grace in form and movement, courage, generosity, rare beauty. Then (ver. 15) he tells her that her eyes are like "doves' eyes." Then (ch. ii. 2) he disparages all other women in comparison with her. They are as thorns, whilst she is amongst them as the lily. All this is just such flattery as Solomon may be well conceived as employing. And it suggests how the soul affianced in God is often assailed. The world seeks to flatter it, that so it may be the more readily bent to evil. What is the self-satisfaction, the pride, the serene content with itself, in which many souls are weak, but just the effects of the world's flatteries? Satan suggests them to the soul, and his servants repeat them continually, and his victims believe them. Flattery, what harm has it not wrought? So seductive, so powerful, so ruinous always when listened to. If we believe what the world, the flesh, and the devil whisper to us about ourselves and our own excellences, such as they are, we shall never think we need the grace of God, or, if for a while we have thought so, we shall soon give up such thoughts altogether. 2. *By promises that the world makes of its pomps, adornments, and wealth.* So Solomon here tries to win her to whom he speaks. "Rows of jewels," for head-dress, strings of pearls for her neck, gold chains studded with silver (vers. 10, 11). Such gewgaws and finery would he give her. Homer tells ('Odyssey,' lib. xv.) how attractive and tempting such things are—

> "A man of theirs, subtle and shrewd, produced
> A splendid collar, gold with amber strung.
> With deep delight my mother and her maids
> Gazed on it."

And thus Solomon appealed to the natural love of adornment in a young maiden all unused to such rich presents. How many a woman's heart has been won by them! how the love of them has made many a home miserable by the extravagance to which they have been the temptation! how many a fair character has been blasted and lives ruined by their deceitful glitter! And are not such facts parables of one of the chief temptations of the soul, whereby it is sought to seduce it from God? Jewels and pearls and gold, how they flash and sparkle! how they dazzle and delight poor human nature! Types are they of more terrible things still—the pomps and vanities of this wicked world, for the sake of which all too many men are only too ready to sell their souls. How Moses was tempted by them! How brilliant was the career offered him! he, the cast-out child of a slave, to be adopted into the house and family, the possessions and honours, of the imperial dynasty, the Pharaohs of Egypt! How our Lord was tempted in like manner! "All these things"—all the kingdoms of the world and the glory of them—"will I give thee if," etc.

II. LOVE STEADFAST. Solomon did not prevail with her whom he tried to win. All his flatteries and fineries failed. Not one word such as the royal tempter would fain have heard did she address to him, though many to her absent beloved. As showing her steadfastness, note here: 1. *How at once her heart turns to him she loved.* (Ver. 12.) The king has left her alone, has gone to his banquet. At once the sweet memories of her beloved fill her soul as with the fragrance of myrrh (ver. 13). "While the king is in his circle, my spikenard sendeth forth," etc. Her heart is always perfumed with these memories, and is bright therewith as well as fragrant, as with fair flowers and myrrh. 2. See, too, how *she transfers all praise from herself to him.* The king had told her she was fair (ver. 15). Her thoughts fly away to him whom she loves, and she gives the praise to him (ver. 16). 3. And her love *consecrates all the scenes* where she has been with him. The soft green turf (ver. 16), on which they had cast themselves down beneath the cedars and fir trees, whose branches over them were as the beams and rafters of a house. 4. And makes her *think all lowlily of herself but very loftily of him.* She is—so she says—but as a common field-flower (cf. ch. ii. 1), just nothing at all. But he, her beloved, was as the citron tree, fragrant, stately, fruitful, affording refreshing shade (ver. 3). Travellers tell of the beauty of this tree. And amid the leafy arcades of the vine, and beneath its o'erarching branches, she had loved to linger with him (ver. 4); for with him, because of his dear love for her, she was safe as if under the protection of an army, following the banners of a mighty chief. 5. *And these are ever the effects of a steadfast love.* "Not I, but the grace of God which was in me:" so does Paul transfer praise from himself to God. Places where fellowship with Christ have been enjoyed are consecrated by that fact. And love is lowly. "Less than the least of all saints:" so speaks Paul of himself. But of Christ, what does he not say of *him?* What is not Christ to him, and all such? Fruit, and shade, and safeguard sure.

III. THE SECRET OF ALL THIS. The heart possessed by the love of Christ. There is no other antidote that will serve as does this against the flatteries and the bribes of the world. Nothing else will make us so deaf to its appeals, so blind to all its blandishments.

> "Lord, let thy fear within us dwell,
> Thy love our footsteps guide;
> That love shall all vain love expel,
> That fear all fear beside."

S. C.

Vers. 9—11, 15.—*Characteristics of those whom Christ loves.* We need not mind who said what is written in these verses; or why it was said, according to their literal interpretation. But we may consider what is said, for it is true of all people who are "of the Lord beloved."

I. THEY ARE HIS BELOVED. This more than justice; for that would have regarded them as they were in themselves—the reverse of well-pleasing to him. It is more than mercy; for that, though it may have spared the wrong-doer, would not have received him into affection. It is grace abounding. And Christ does thus regard his people. "Henceforth I call you not servants, but friends." What rich store of consolation to all cast-down souls there is in this!

II. THEY ARE AS "A COMPANY OF HORSES IN PHARAOH'S CHARIOT." (Cf. Zech. x. 3, "The Lord hath visited his flock, and hath made them as his goodly horse in the day of battle.") And such comparison is frequent both in the Scriptures and in the ordinary literature of that age. In this song the ideas intended are their alacrity and vigour, swiftness, strength, grace, courage, etc. The image suggests: 1. *The alacrity and vigour of the believer's service.* (Cf. Ps. cxix., "I will run in the way of thy commandments when thou shalt enlarge my heart.") And what so enlarges the heart, so causes it to swell with delightful emotion, as the consciousness that the Lord's love rests upon us. 2. *Their courage.* (Cf. Job's description of the battle-horse—how he "paweth in the valley," and "rejoiceth in his strength," "mocketh at fear, and is not affrighted;" "suffereth the quiver to rattle against him, the glittering spear and the shield.") And how often the dauntless courage, of which the horse is a symbol, has been found in God's servants (cf. Daniel; the three Hebrew youths; Paul; and many more)! Think of the martyrs who

> "Mocked the cross and flame.
> They met the tyrant's brandished steel,
> The lion's gory mane."

And in less marked and tragic, but in equally real way, has this courage been shown —is shown—in our own day. Illustrate: Arthur kneeling in prayer before the whole room at Rugby (see 'Tom Brown's School-days'). And such courage is yet needed, and, thank God, is yet found. 3. *The exquisite symmetry of form* for which the choicest Arabian steeds were famous tells of that *moral symmetry* and harmoniousness of character which will one day, and should now, distinguish his Church and people. It is the same idea as in St. Paul's image of the symmetry of the perfected Church. Hence he tells of its " breadth, and length, and depth, and height," which " all saints " are to " comprehend," because they shall share in and exhibit it. 4. *His people's unity* is also suggested by the comparison with "a company" of horses. The Church is militant here upon earth, and therefore the idea of a war-chariot is appropriate. But the company of steeds who draw it, are they not so esteemed because of their ordered obedience? Not struggling hither and thither as each wills, nor each struggling to get its own way and so pulling in different directions. Alas! it is a sarcasm to liken the Church of our day to "a company of horses in Pharaoh's chariot." Would to God it were not, and that what is may not much longer be!

III. THEY ARE BEAUTIFUL WITH ADORNMENTS. (Ver. 10; cf. Prov. i. 8, 9, "My son hear, . . . For they shall be an ornament of grace unto thy head, and chains about thy neck.") What, therefore, these adornments are is evident. They are the graces wrought by the Spirit; what St. Paul calls, " the fruits of the Spirit "—love, joy, peace, etc. These are the golden links of the chain, added one by one, each connected with and dependent on its fellow. Frequently is the adornment of the soul set forth in Scripture under the imagery of the adornment of the body. We read of " the ornament of a meek and quiet spirit," etc. And thus Christ will array his Church and each individual believing soul.

IV. THEY SHALL RECEIVE "GRACE FOR GRACE;" that is, grace upon grace—grace in addition to grace already given (cf. ver. 11, " We will make thee," etc.). And this is so. We are bidden "grow in grace;" and the soul does thus advance, does receive more and more of those beautiful adornments which are the Spirit's workmanship, those good works for which we were created in Christ Jesus.

V. THE LOVELINESS OF THE HOLY SPIRIT IS SEEN IN THEM. This the suggestion of ver. 15, "Thine eyes are doves'." We read of the "evil" eye (Matt. xx. 15); of "eyes full of adultery" (2 Pet. ii. 14); and of the "high look and proud heart" (Ps. ci. 5). But what a contrast to all these have we here! Eyes of gentleness, of purity, of heavenly-mindedness; eyes through which the Holy Spirit—whose chosen emblem is the dove—looks and is seen. What a description! Would that all we who profess and call ourselves Christians corresponded to it far more than we do!—S. C.

Ver. 12.—*Holy Communion.* The form of expression in this verse has suggested thoughts on this theme to so many devout students of this book that, whilst not admitting their interpretation as correct, we may nevertheless avail ourselves of such suggestions in order to set forth some precious and important truths concerning it—the soul's communion with Christ. And we note—

I. THE ORDINANCES OF THE GOSPEL ARE CHRIST'S TABLE. (Cf. Rev. iii. 20, "If any man will open the door, I will come in to him, and sup with him, and he with me.") In such communion we have the "feast of fat things full of marrow" of which the prophet speaks (cf. also our Lord's words, "Come, for all things are ready; my oxen," etc.). Now, such communion is had : 1. *In prayer.* Not mere saying prayers, but in true prayer. 2. *In the worship of the Church.* How often have we found this to be so! On the sabbath, and in the sanctuary, how often we have there found that

"The cares which infest our day
Have folded their tents, like the Arabs,
And as silently steal away!"

3. *The table of the Lord* is especially the King's table. Hence to our service there the name of "holy communion" has been pre-eminently given. All these are opportunities of such communion, and were designed so to be. But—

II. THEIR VALIDITY AND VALUE DEPEND ON THE KING'S PRESENCE. "*While* the King sitteth," etc. How poor and wretched are our prayers if there be no realization of the presence of Christ! And the worship of the Church, what an empty form! And at the table of the Lord not to "discern the Lord's body," that is to make the service worse than useless; it is to incur his judgment and condemnation. Let us never come to this or to any season of communion without invoking his presence.

III. AND ARE MANIFESTED BY THEIR EFFECTS. "While . . . my spikenard sendeth forth," etc. "It is in seasons of communion with the Lord that the graces of the Spirit are called forth in most lively exercise." A holy fragrance, a "sweet smell," well-pleasing and acceptable, is yielded at such seasons by the heart of the Lord's servants. And: 1. *To the Lord himself.* Our prayers rise up before him "as incense, and the lifting up of our hands as the evening sacrifice." He is well pleased. He told Nathanael, "When thou wast under the fig tree I saw thee;" there, where he had poured forth his fervent prayer. And in our assemblies for worship, where that worship is real, the Lord loveth such "gates of Zion." Of such worshippers it is written, "The Lord hearkened and heard, and a book of remembrance was written before him." And of them he says, "They shall be mine in that day when I make up my jewels." And at his table, if we do indeed commune with him, the faith and hope and love, the contrition and humility and self-surrender, all which the soul then and there offers to him, these are fragrant indeed, sweet and precious as were the anointings of his sacred body by the penitent Magdalen and by Mary of Bethany. 2. *And many others* are conscious of, and share in that fragrance. Our fellow-guests. What a source of true blessing and manifold help to any Church is the presence of those who live in constant communion with their Lord! What a hallowed influence such exert! what real good they do! Like their Lord's, in their measure and degree, the name of such is "as ointment poured forth." And all those with whom such persons have to do—their children, servants, neighbours, associates, and the world generally—will, as it was with the apostles, "take knowledge of them that they have been with Jesus." 3. *And they themselves are blessed.* For is it not good to have all that is pure and holy and Christ-like in us quickened, confirmed, strengthened, as is the case through communion with our Lord? Moses' face shone after he had been in the presence of the Lord. The spiritual help which comes to the real worshipper is so great, and has always been so recognized, that for the sake of having opportunity for such communion Christ's people have risked everything. If they would only have kept their religion to themselves no one would have said anything; but they would not. They would come together for worship and for communion; and hence, all over the world, they have been led "as sheep to the slaughter," and for Christ's sake they "have been slain all the day long." What proof and evidence this is of the real blessedness of communion with Christ! May he help us to add each one our testimony to this same sure truth!—S. C.

Vers. 13, 14.—*What Christ is to his people.* He is here said to be as—
I. "A BUNDLE OF MYRRH." See Exposition for explanation of ancient customs alluded to by this "bundle," or small box, or other such receptacle for perfumes. Its religious teachings are such as arise from the fact that: 1. *Myrrh was used in the "anointing oil"* with which Aaron and the priests were anointed. It was "the oil of gladness" with which Christ was anointed above his fellows (cf. Ps. cxxiii. 2). The teaching, therefore, is that Christ is the Joy of his people. Cf. "Then will I go unto the altar of God, unto God my exceeding Joy" (Ps. xliii. 4). Then: 2. *Myrrh was largely used for incense.* Cf. in the Revelation the vision of the angel to whom "was given much incense." It represented the acceptableness of the prayers of God's saints. And it is Christ's Name that gives worth and validity to our poor prayers. We join them on to his all-availing intercession, and we find ourselves "accepted in the Beloved." 3. *Myrrh was used for embalming,* so as to prevent corruption and decay. And this is just what Christ is to us. He prevents the moral corruption which would destroy our souls having power over them. It would fasten upon them as it does on those in whom Christ is not; but he arrests its power, and preserves our souls in life. And he will, he does, stay the corruption of the grave. That does, indeed, fasten on the poor cast-off garment of the soul; but on the soul itself Christ suffers corruption to have no power, for he clothes it with the spiritual body, so that "mortality is swallowed up of life," and "this corruptible puts on incorruption." But note: 4. In order to be all this to us, *he must ever abide in our hearts.* (Cf. "He shall lie always on my bosom.") So

speaks the maiden who is the type of the believing, Christ-loving soul. Can we each, then, say of Christ, "He is 'my Beloved'"? If so, we may go on and say, "He is unto me as myrrh."

II. "A CLUSTER OF CAMPHIRE." (Ver. 14.) Such flowers were used for the decoration of rooms and for personal adornment. It is not easy to fix what precise flower is meant. We are told its habitat, but not its special characteristics, amongst the many flowers amid which it is found. But its name is very significant. It is the same word that elsewhere is rendered "propitiation," or "atonement." The Jewish rabbis took it as a type of the Messiah. Hence they rendered this verse thus: "My beloved is unto me the man who propitiates all things." And is not this a most true and beautiful rendering? For is not this just what our blessed Lord does for us? Is not his cross the antitype of that tree which Moses had shown to him, and which, when he had cast it into the bitter waters of Marah, made those waters sweet? The cross of Christ is the sweetener of life's bitter waters. Well, therefore, might the flower which bore the name of "the propitiation" be taken as telling of him. Is it not he who, by his grace, propitiates the worries and cares of life, so that they no longer irk and fret my will; and the perplexities and mysteries I everywhere meet with, so that they no longer bewilder and beat down my faith; and the temptations which would defile my soul, so that they no more work me such harm; and the sin for which I might have been condemned, so that it is silent for ever against me; and the grave and its corruption, so that they will not hold me therein? True, his gracious work is done on me; but it is as if the mouths of the lions themselves were stopped, so powerless to do me harm are they if Christ be to me my Propitiation. Oh, most sweet and blessed flower! May it ever beautify my home, my life, my heart!—S. C.

Vers. 16, 17, and ch. ii. 4.—*The house of the Lord.* Before the soul delightedly tells of the house of her Lord, she speaks—

I. OF THE LORD OF THE HOUSE. She declares not only that he is fair, but pleasant also. How many of his people fail here! Some are fair, but not pleasant. Some are pleasant, but not fair. Alas! some are neither. But of him supremely can it be said that he is fair and pleasant. Not only fair in outward seeming, but pleasant in his spirit, temper, and demeanour.

II. OF HIS HOUSE. The soul says "our" in speaking of his abode. And so closely are we united with him, that his people may, though out of reverence they seldom do, speak of that which is his as theirs also. The picture drawn in these verses (16, 17) is one of rural delight—the soft and verdant turf, the o'erarching and umbrageous trees, the noble cedar, the stately fir, beneath which those spoken of have cast themselves down. The ideas suggested are those of happy rest. Ps. xxiii., "Thou makest me to lie down in green pastures," etc., tells substantially of the same spiritual rest. And the house of the Lord is the place of such blessed rest of heart and soul and mind. Because of this, we find those many impassioned expressions in the Psalms as to the psalmist's delight in the house of the Lord; how he had rather be a doorkeeper there than hold any place of worldly honour or pleasure, however exalted (Ps. lxxxiv.). The agitations and cares of the mind hush themselves to rest there. The psalmist tells in one place how the mystery of the Divine rule over men—wicked men often prospering and good men cast down—how this distressed, dismayed, and all but destroyed his faith in God, "until," he says, "I went into the sanctuary; then I understood." Yes, the house of the Lord should be, and often is to his people, what this beautiful picture of rest on the green grass, beneath the cool, refreshing shade of fragrant and stately trees, presents to us—a place of pure delight, rest, and refreshment of heart.

III. ITS PROVISIONS. It is a "banqueting-house." It is so when the Lord brings us there and is with us there (cf. on ver. 12).

IV. ITS DEFENCE. "His banner over me is love." That is, the soul's protection and guard, so sure and strong as that of a banner-led host, is the Lord's love. Is it not so? What guards us there and everywhere but his love? What is the defence of the home but the father's love? What the safeguard of the wife but her husband's love? Love is always a mighty protector, a sure defence, a strong bulwark. "How doth the hen protect her brood," but by her love? And love ever guards the beloved ones. And so with our souls, the Lord's love is their defence.—S. C.

Vers. 1—4.—*The Bridegroom and the bride.* Love's native language is poetry. When strong and happy feeling dominates the soul, it soon bursts into a song. As young life in a fruit tree breaks out into leaf and blossom, so the spiritual force of love unfolds in metaphor and music. Among the lyrics composed by King David, those which celebrate the Messiah-Prince have the richest glory of fervour, blossom most into Oriental imagery; and inasmuch as Solomon inherited somewhat the poetic genius of his father, it was natural that he should pour out in mystic song the heart-throb of a nation's hopes. The deep and inseparable union between Christ and his saints is by no one set forth so clearly as by Jesus the Christ; hence love is strong and tender, because love's Object is noble, winsome, kingly, Divine.

I. THE BRIDEGROOM'S CHARMS. 1. *The love of Christ is incomparably precious.* "Thy love is better than wine." All true love is precious—a sacred thing, a mighty force. The love of Jesus is absolutely perfect, without any admixture of alloy. Love is the mightiest force in the universe, a magnet whose attractive power reaches from the throne of God to the very gates of hell. And love is as precious as it is potent. It makes a desert into a paradise; changes base metal into gold; transforms foul rebels into loving sons. It is a banquet for the heart; a perpetual feast; a fountain of purest joy. What the rarest wine is for a fainting body, *that* the love of Jesus is to a burdened soul. 2. *The love of Christ is diffusive.* It is as "unguent poured forth." The love of God's Son existed long before it was manifested. That love is seen in all the arrangements of creation. That love is unfolded in all the methods of daily providence. "By him all things consist." That love is shed abroad in the believer's heart "by the Holy Ghost." As the flowers in our gardens pour out their essential life in their sweet fragrance, so the love of Christ is Christ's life poured out for us. All the love which angels cherish is Christ's love diffused. He is the "Firstborn of the creation of God." All the parental love that has ever glowed on the altar of human hearts is the love of Christ diffused. All practical benevolence for the well-being of mankind is the outflow of Immanuel's love. The love that constrains me to compassionate deeds and to intercessory prayers is the love of Christ diffused. Discovering the heavenly savour inspires our hearts with joy. Heaven is knit with silken cords to earth. 3. *The love of Christ is condescending and gracious.* "The King hath brought me into his chambers." Had we been told that God admitted into his presence-chamber the unsinning angels, we should not have been so profoundly moved. They are meet for his service. But to admit the base and degenerate sons of men into his intimate friendship, *this* reflects a singular glory upon his kindness; this is a miracle of love. By such familiar intercourse he trains us in kingly conduct, communicates to us Divine wisdom, moulds us into his own image. Beyond this deed of grace not even God can go. As there was no depth of humiliation to which he was not willing to stoop for sinners, so there is no height of excellence from which he would exclude us. Such love no human thought can measure. It is higher than heaven: how shall we scale it? It is deeper than hell: how shall we fathom it?

II. THE BRIDE'S RESPONSE. 1. *Her love originates in the high renown of his love.* "*Thy Name* is as ointment poured forth." So long as this strong force of love was confined within the heart of Christ, no human soul could suspect its existence. On what ground could any dweller on earth conjecture or imagine that he was the object of Immanuel's love? That love must be unfolded, declared, made clearly known. And this is what Jesus has done. Not content with warm protestations of his affection, he has stooped to perform impressive deeds of kindness—yea, prodigies of compassion. All the romantic stories of heroic love Jesus has immeasurably surpassed. His renown is sung in all the courts of the heavenly palace. He has made for himself a "Name above every name," human or angelic. This high reputation warrants our approach, our admiration, our trust, our responsive love. "We love him, because he has first loved us." 2. *Our love craves a closer fellowship with his Person.* "Draw me!" We have made such discoveries of excellence in our Immanuel that we long for larger acquaintance. To us he is a vast mine of spiritual wealth, and the deeper we go the rarer jewels do we find. His charms seem infinite, and no fear troubles us that we shall exhaust them. We are troubled that our own love is so inadequate, so unworthy; hence we desire a closer approach, that his spiritual beauty may quicken our languid affection. Feeling the magnetic power of his love, we too may be magnetized. We cannot command, by a mere volition or a mere resolve, that our love shall flow out. So the only way to intensify our love is by coming into fuller contact with his. Only life can generate life, and only the love of Christ can stir into activity the principle of true love in us. Therefore we pray, "Draw us into nearer fellowship, into more vital union!" 3. *Our love desires a prompt obedience.* "We will run after thee." We love to walk in his footsteps, and when we discover where his haunts lie, we run to seek him there. So sincere is our love, that we long to do his will promptly and heartily. We wish to hear every whisper of his commands. We deprecate that anything on our part should chase the smiles from his face. We long that his thoughts may be *our* thoughts, his dispositions *our* dispositions, his purposes *our* purposes; so that between Christ and us there may be perfect concord. As said Ruth to Naomi, so say we, "Whither thou goest, I will go; and where thou dwellest, I will dwell." We can do without food, we can do without friends, we can do without health, but we cannot do without Christ. Wrote Samuel Rutherford to a friend, "If hell-fire stood between you and Christ, you would press through in order to reach him." All service is delight when the feet are winged by love. 4. *Love brings us into the best society.* "The upright love thee." The love that draws the best men near to Christ likewise draws them near each other. As the spokes of a wheel get near to the hub they get into closer proximity to each other. The more love we give out the more substantial good we get. The friendship of the pious is a precious treasure; their wisdom enlightens, their piety stimulates, their love enkindles, ours. In their society we are elevated and gladdened. The story of their experience inspires us for new endeavour; their triumphs awaken our most sacred ambitions. With Moses, we learn meekness; with Elijah, we learn how to pray; with Job, we learn endurance; with Martin Luther, we learn courage. The society of saints throws into the shade the society of sages or of kings. 5. *Love treasures up the recollection of past favours.* "We will remember thy love more than wine." What Jesus Christ has done for us in the past he will do again. Since his love is infinite, he has not exhausted his love-tokens in the past; he has more costly things yet to give, richer dainties yet to place on his banquet-table. Still, there are times when we cannot realize a present Saviour, when the conscious possession of his love is suspended, and at such times it is a cordial to our spirits to bring out the memorials and tokens of past affection. Our memory is a vast chamber, hung round with ten thousand mementoes of Immanuel's love. Thus, in a dark hour of depression, King David sang, "Yet will I remember thee from the land of Jordan, and of the hill Mizar." In winter's dark days we will feast upon the fruits of well-remembered summer. 6. *Love creates the purest joy.* "We will be glad and rejoice in thee." Joy arises when a felt want is satisfied; but so long as we are sensible of needs and cravings for which no supply is at hand we are miserable. A thirsty man upon a scorching desert, leagues removed from any well, is a stranger to gladness. The misery of lost spirits, doubtless, arises from passionate cravings for which there is no supply. On the other hand, when we can feel that Christ is ours—ours in bonds which nothing can sever—we feel that every want is met, every ambition is realized, every aspiration fulfilled. "Then shall I be satisfied, when I awake, in thy likeness." Therefore, although outward surroundings may tend to depress, we can always find in the fulness of Christ sources of hope and joy. "With him is the fountain of life."—D.

Vers. 5, 6.—*Low estimate of self.* A genuine Christian will take a modest estimate of himself. "He has learnt not to think more highly of himself than he ought to think." Many Christians undervalue themselves; and though this practice is not so obnoxious in the eyes of others as over-valuation, yet this also is a fault. It is better to pass no judgment on ourselves; it is seldom called for; it is often a folly. I. EXTERNAL BLEMISH. "I am black." 1. *This blemish (if it be one) is very superficial; it is only skin-deep.* A strong comparison is employed to convey more vividly the impression—"black as the tents of Kedar." These were manufactured from camel's hair, and, from long exposure to sun and dew, were in colour a dingy black. So when a Christian views himself as he appears externally to others, he sees, perhaps, his ignorance, his poverty, his imperfections, his obscurity, the contempt with which he is regarded by others. If the heavenly Friend should view him only in his outward appearance, he is devoid of attraction, destitute of ordinary beauty. 2. *This blemish arises from the hard treatment of others.* "My mother's children were angry with me; they made me keeper of the vineyards." Compulsion was used. The speaker had been coerced into employment which was menial and exhausting. It demanded long exposure to scorching sun and to chilling dews. The effect was to mar the beauty of the countenance. Yet the eye of love would detect beneath the surface a richer beauty—the beauty of patient obedience and unmurmuring submission. Men of the world may oppress and persecute; they cannot injure character. Earthly kings and magistrates may scourge and imprison the bride of Christ; they may despoil her of much external comeliness; but in the eye of reason—in the eye of God—she is more comely than before. Only the dross is consumed; real excellence of soul comes clearer into view. 3. *Or this may be a real blemish through self-neglect.* "My own vineyard have I not kept." Possibly, in the endurance of such hardships, it might have been possible to escape the blemish. Suitable precautions were not taken. Under stress of cruel compulsion, there had been a feeling of self-abandonment—a weak yielding to despair. It is hard to maintain a heavenly temper under daily provocations; yet it can be done. It is hard to cultivate the Christian graces amid scenes of suffering and mockery; yet it ought to be done. The King Omnipotent has said, "My grace is sufficient for thee." We shall render the most faithful and useful service to others when we maintain in vigour our own piety. The healthful face of a holy character must under no circumstances be neglected.

II. INTERNAL BEAUTY. Though black (*i.e.* sun-browned), she was yet "comely"— yea, beauteous "as the curtains of Solomon." Likely enough, there is in this poetic drama a conversation, the parts of which are not distinctly marked. Likely enough, the daughters of Jerusalem here interject the remarks, "comely;" "as the curtains of Solomon." 1. *The judgment of others respecting us is often more equitable than self-judgment.* Some persons, confessedly, have a sad habit of overrating their virtues; but others are diffident and over-modest—they are given to self-depreciation. Through a jealousy for truth, or through a fear of self-delusion, they underrate their real goodness. As we can judge the merit of a painting or a statue a little distance removed, so a judicious onlooker can often more accurately judge us than we can judge ourselves. It is better for our comfort and for our usefulness neither to under-rate nor to overrate ourselves. Very precious is the inward spirit of truth. 2. *Internal beauty is preferable to external.* It is not so apparent to the eye of man, but it is more prized by God, by angels, and by the best class of men. It is superior in itself, because it belongs to the soul. It is more influential for good. It brings more joy to the possessor. It is permanent, and outlasts all changes of time and pain and death. The genuine Christian may be poor in earthly wealth, but he is endowed with the treasures of heaven. He may wear coarse and homespun apparel, yet his soul is clothed in a robe of perfect righteousness. His face may be marred with suffering and ploughed with the effects of arduous toil, yet is he comely with holiness and beautified by the hand of the great Artificer. 3. *Internal beauty is obtained through self-sacrificing service.* The bride was really comely, though she had been compelled to work, like a slave, in the vineyards; yea, she was comely in character, as the result of this toil. Very true is it that no persecution can injure us; it brings, sooner or later, real advantage. The noblest characters have been fashioned and burnished in the furnace of suffering. Even of the Son of God we are told that "he learned obedience by the things which he suffered." The statue is not perfected until it has felt ten thousand strokes of the chisel. The diamond does not sparkle at its best until it has been well cut on the wheel of the lapidary. The pearl of great price is the fruit of pain. The verdict of experience records, "It was good for me that I was afflicted." Suffering is God's lancet, whereby he produces health. A vital lesson is here taught. Without personal piety there can be no permanent usefulness. A man's character is the mightiest instrument for recovering and elevating others. If we long to see the vineyards of others fair and fruitful, our own vineyard must be a pattern of good culture. Our first duty is respecting ourselves. If we are full of light, we can lead others along the path to heaven. Personal holiness is the great desideratum.—D.

Vers. 7—9.—*Seeking and finding.* The Christian pilgrim has to pass through a variety of fortunes in his passage to the celestial city. His fluctuations of joy and sorrow, hope and fear, resemble an April day. Sunshine alternates with storm. *Now* he is on the mountain-top; *now* in the valley of humiliation. *Now* he looks into his Master's face, and sees a smile of heavenly love; *now* that gracious face is hid, like the sun during eclipse.

I. WE HAVE A SENSE OF DESERTION. This is a matter of personal feeling, not an external reality. God does not undergo any change, nor does he ever forsake his friends. But it sometimes happens that we cease to realize our vital interest in Jesus; we lose for a season the enjoyment of his favours. The sun is as near the earth—yea, nearer—in December as in June; yet, because our northern hemisphere is turned away from the sun, flowers do not bloom, nor do fruits ripen, on our side the globe. So we may unintentionally have drifted away from Christ; our hearts may have flagged in devotion or in zeal; the bloom of our love may have vanished; some cloud of earthliness may have intervened, some mist of doubt may have risen up, and we no longer see the radiant face of our Beloved. In proportion to our appreciation of our heart's best Friend will be the sorrow we shall endure. No earthly good will compensate for the loss. No other joy can take its place. It seems as if the natural sun were veiled; as if earth were clad in mourning; as if all music had ceased, because Jesus is not a Guest in the soul.

II. HERE, NOTWITHSTANDING, THERE IS AN UNDER-CURRENT OF HOPE. We find yet, within the soul, strong love to Jesus, although we no longer realize his love to us. This is solid comfort; for it is evident that our love is real, and not simply a desire for self-advantage. It is not a refined form of selfishness, inasmuch as our love to him abides, although it brings no enjoyment. And we still perceive and appreciate his office. We still regard him as the great Shepherd of the sheep. As such he will not allow a single lamb to stray. It is the part of a good shepherd to care for each member of the flock, and to restore the wanderer. Though *we* no longer bask in the sunshine of his favour, we are sure that others do, and we love him for his compassion to them. Further, we are sure that he is not far away. He is busy with his flock, feeding them, caring for their needs; so we will seek him out. We will not sullenly wait until he shall come to us; we will search for him, for we are sure that he will approve our search. If we heartily desire him, this is hopeful.

III. WE HAVE ALSO AN EAGER INQUIRY. "Tell me where thou feedest, where thou makest thy flock to rest at noon." So fully conscious is the soul of its loss and injury, that it longs to end this sad experience. Its main difficulty is what to do, what step to take. No hindrance in the way of finding Jesus shall be allowed to remain. If we have been guilty of any misdeed or neglect, we will confess it honestly. One question only perplexes us—Where shall we find our Well-beloved? We want information, guidance, light. Yet this same Jesus is our All in all. He is our Light. He will reveal himself. In due time he will give us light. So we speak to him directly, and we employ a very discreet argument: "For why should I be as one that turneth aside by the flocks of thy companions?" In other words, "Why should I seek for satisfaction elsewhere but in thee?" If I seek, I shall find only disappointment. These fancied joys will be as apples of Sodom, as the grapes of Gomorrah. I must have *some* object on whom to expend my love. Let it be no other object, no inferior object, than thyself. Only show me *thy* chosen haunt, and I will find thee out. Distance shall be annihilated. Mountains shall be levelled.

IV. A GRACIOUS RESPONSE. "Go thy way forth by the footsteps of the flock, and feed thy kids beside the shepherds' tents." Prayer for light is especially acceptable to God. In him is no darkness, and nothing is further from him than to keep us in darkness. Most of all does he delight in the prayer which yearns after him. It has been his business all through the past eternity to reveal himself, and to come into nearer union with the human soul; hence our prayer is only the echo of his own wish, our desire is *his* desire, and response is ready. How tender is his rebuke of our ignorance! "If thou know not." It is as if he said, "Yet surely you ought to know. You have found the way to me aforetime. It is the same way still, for I change not." Or, "If thou canst not find the way to me directly, then act as my friends act. Learn from the successes of others. I have instructed others how to find me. They have found me, and now they are patterns and helpers for all seekers. Observe the 'footsteps of the flock.'" If we are earnest in our search after Christ, we shall use all and every means likely to ensure our success. Very often it is not more light we want, but a humble and diligent readiness to use the light we have. Unfaithfulness to our light is a common failing. The instruments employed to convey the electric current must be scrupulously clean, and every law must be delicately observed, or the mystic force refuses to act. Our spiritual sensibilities are far more delicate, and a neglect, which may seem minute or insignificant, will defeat our purpose, and rob us of our joy. They who desire intimate fellowship with Jesus must be companions of the friends of Jesus, and must learn lessons in the humblest school. The footprints of other pilgrims we must carefully note and faithfully follow. Jesus is no respecter of persons. Others have found him: why should not we? They have not exhausted his love; they have merely tasted a sip of the infinite ocean. I may, if I will, drink more deeply than any mortal yet has done.—D.

Vers. 12—17.—*Reciprocal esteem.* Love, manifested and known, will always beget love. As every plant has in its womb seed of its own kind, so, too, love has within itself generative power. If any human heart does not love our Immanuel, it is because that heart is ignorant of him, its eyesight is blurred, its vision is obscured. No sooner is Jesus known as a true and substantial Friend, than love in some form springs up. In the form of gratitude it first appears; then in the form of admiration; then in delight; then in intimacy; then in passionate devotement. Jesus known is Jesus loved.

I. OBSERVE THE CHRISTIAN'S LOVE FOR JESUS CHRIST. 1. *The soul esteems him as its Sovereign King.* As love is the mightiest force in the human breast, love's object is at once promoted to the supreme place. No elevation is too great for our Beloved. It would be a restraint upon our love—yea, a pain—if we did not give to Jesus the highest throne. We perceive that he has all the qualities of a king, and that it is for our own advantage that he should rule within. And when we make the experiment we find such rest, such security, such triumphs, that we would fain exalt him to a higher place. To be the servant—ay, the slave—of such a King is honour infinite, joy ineffable. 2. *The renewed soul desires to have the closest friendship with Jesus.* Where the heavenly King comes, he always spreads a feast for the soul. Out of his fulness he freely bestows. As a fountain spontaneously sends up its limpid waters, so doth Christ our Lord. To be in his presence, to listen to his ripe wisdom, to realize all the advantage of his friendship, this is a spiritual feast. The wisdom he has, he gives. His everlasting righteousness he shares with us. His heavenly peace he conveys to us. His own love is shed abroad in our hearts. All the wealth of his kingdom he conveys to his chosen. We are "heirs of God, joint-heirs with Jesus Christ." The friendship of Immanuel is a perpetual feast. They who daily eat at the same table enjoy the closest intimacy with each other. 3. *The presence of Jesus Christ draws out our hidden graces.* "My perfume sends forth its sweetest odours." Just as the summer sun draws out the essence of our garden flowers, so the energy of the Saviour's love stirs into activity the hidden forces of our souls. In every man is a principle of imitation. If we see a splendid deed of generosity, we are impelled to copy it. When the heart is free from sinful bias, it aspires to imitate every excellence it beholds. So, when the glories of Christ's nature are unfolded, like graces begin to unfold in us. Repentance, gratitude, humility, faith, patience, devoted love, are drawn out in the sunny atmosphere of Jesus' presence. Fragrant flowers and spicy herbs, which had lain long hidden in the frozen soil, spring up and send out a rare perfume. When Jesus dwelt in the house, Mary was constrained to break the alabaster box, and to set free the delicious odour; and when Jesus dwells in our hearts, every restraint gives way, and the essence of our graces yields a sweet perfume. 4. *We esteem the love of Jesus for its constancy.* The bundle of myrrh abides with us "all night." Our beloved Friend is not easily offended. "He hates putting away." In darkness as well as at noon, in times of pain and calamity as in days of prosperity, his love remains unchanged. If for a season we should neglect him, and be absorbed in other pursuits, he does not abandon us. He may visit our folly with chastisement, and to the soul there may be temporary night, yet the remembrance of his love will be a sweet and reviving cordial. It will have a healing efficacy. We shall be touched with a sense of shame; and as myrrh soothes and quiets pain, so will the fragrant breath of our Immanuel heal us. 5. *The friendship of Jesus satisfies every want.* "My Beloved is unto me as a cluster of camphire in the vineyards of Engedi." The cluster of camphire flowers had a renown both for beauty and for fragrance. So the excellence of Jesus has a fascination for every sense of the renewed man. Every organ is a channel through which Christ's life flows. We *look* unto Jesus, and we are charmed with the beauty of his character. We *listen*, and his words of promise kindle in us a holy rapture. His deeds and sacrifices for us have a sweet-smelling savour. His intercession for us is like the temple incense. "We taste that the Lord is gracious." He is to us heavenly manna—"the Bread of life." The coming of Christ is like autumn abundance. "He is all our salvation and all our desire;" "My God shall supply all your need, according to his riches in glory by Christ Jesus;" "He that cometh to me shall never hunger; he that believeth on me shall never thirst." Nothing so enchants and satisfies the soul like Jesus. Amongst the verdant and generous vineyards of Engedi, the cluster of camphire was distinguished for fragrance and for usefulness; so among the charms of nature, among the genial society of human friends, Jesus stands out prominently the most precious and the most prized of all. There is nothing on earth we can compare with him. He is without a rival.

II. OBSERVE THE REGARD WHICH JESUS CHRIST HAS FOR HIS FRIENDS. 1. *He fully esteems all the good there is in them.* "Behold, thou art fair, my love." The eye of friendship will discover many virtues in a man which the eye of malice can never find. It is not love that is blind; it is malice that is blind. Love has eyesight keener than an eagle, keener than an archangel. The eye of Jesus sees in us excellences which he himself has created; and though as yet these are only in tiny germ, yet, with the magnifying power of love, Jesus beholds them as they shall be, full-orbed and beautiful. There is no future to him. What *to us* is in the future is with him present. He looks with tenderness upon the tiny blade of pious love, and lo! already 'tis a cedar of Lebanon, among whose branches the feathered minstrels sing. If only a heavenly ambition begins to stir within the breast, he hastens to foster it. Says he, "It is well that it was in thine heart." 2. *He repeats the commendation in order to confirm it.* "Thou art fair; thou art fair, my love." The conscience of the Christian, filled with light from heaven, is painfully sensible of its faults, and asks in astonishment, "Lord, didst thou call me fair?" Then, to banish doubt and to pierce to the heart unbelief, Jesus repeats his approval, "Behold, thou art fair, my love." "Though it may be that our hearts condemn us, God is greater than our hearts, and knoweth all things." Full clearly he sees the young germ of new-born love, and this he will make to grow until it shall fill the soul with beauty. Hence he already says, "Thou art fair, my love." Under the magic wand of love, the nature that had sunk into a beast becomes incarnate beauty. Love creates. Love transfigures. 3. *Love makes like unto itself.* Because Christ our Lord is beautiful, we shall be beautiful. Because Christ is pleasant, we shall be pleasant. Every quality of mind and heart that Jesus possesses he will communicate unto us. "He emptied himself" that he might fill us. It is a special pleasure to discover a new excellence in our Immanuel, inasmuch as that excellence shall be ours. "We shall be like him when we see him as he is." 4. *Jesus identifies himself completely with his ransomed ones.* The couch, or resting-place, in the palace garden is said to be "ours." "*Our* bed is green." It is a verdant oasis in this world's desert. Or, if the palace is described, it is *our* house. To all the possessions of the Bridegroom the bride is encouraged to lay claim. It is always the result of the marriage-tie that the interests and fortunes of the two are identical. One is the complement of the other. Neither is complete alone. There could be no shepherd unless there were sheep. There can be no bridegroom without a bride. There can be no king without subjects. Nor can there be a Saviour unless there are also the saved. The glory of Jesus Christ is seen nowhere but in his ransomed Church. Therefore Jesus completely and generously identifies himself with us. All his possessions are to be our possessions. All his noble qualities are to be our noble qualities. His purity is to be our purity. His throne is to be our throne likewise. It is his everlasting purpose that we shall be "joint-heirs." "They shall have *my joy* fulfilled in themselves."—D.

Ver. 1.—*Holy lyrics.* There are many songs in Old Testament Scripture—the song of deliverance from the Red Sea (Exod. xv.); the song of the well (Numb. xxi. 17, 18); the song of Moses (Deut. xxxii.); the song of Deborah (Judg. v.); the song (pre-eminently such) of David, in Ps. xviii.; and the song of Isaiah (v.). But this of Solomon is described as the Song of Songs, *i.e.* of all the most excellent, as it is the richest in imagery, the intensest in feeling, the most complete in poetic form. Although there is something dramatic in the structure of this poem, inasmuch as several speakers are introduced, uttering varying moods of feeling, still the poem is mainly lyrical, inasmuch as its spirit is prevailingly sentiment. Song expresses—

I. FEELING GENERALLY; AND FEELING OCCUPIES A PRE-EMINENT PLACE IN RELIGIOUS LIFE. True religion has its root in knowledge and belief; a God not known cannot be truly worshipped, a religion not understood cannot be acceptably practised. Yet religion is not merely an exercise, a possession, of the intellect. Our strongest convictions are naturally accompanied by our deepest emotions. The measure of feeling will, indeed, vary with individual temperament, but a religion with no sentiment is mechanical and unlovely. Now, it is in accordance with human nature that feeling should break forth into song. Cheerfulness finds utterance as in the carol of the lark, and melancholy as in the plaintive warble of the nightingale. The Bible without the Canticles would not correspond with the whole constitution of man.

> "The Church delights to raise
> Psalms and hymns and songs of praise."

The words of inspiration, exact or paraphrased and adapted, have ever given shape and form and utterance to the profoundest emotions of God's worshippers.

II. LOVE, WHICH IS THE CHARACTERISTIC ELEMENT OF THE RELIGIOUS LIFE. Human love is the copy, always faint and imperfect, yet not illusive, of love Divine. The love of the Hebrew king and his mountain bride figures forth, as does all true wedded affection—the love which exists between the Eternal and his intelligent creatures, between the Church and the adorable Bridegroom who deigns to address her as his spouse. The language of the Canticles has often seemed to cold natures extravagant, and so unreal. "Love's language is a foreign language to those who do not love." We have the foundation of the Song of Songs laid in the forty-fifth psalm—the "song of love." Christianity is admitted to have introduced into religion an element of deeper personal feeling than was known before. The love of Christ is declared to "pass knowledge;" and love which passes knowledge, which cannot express itself in propositions, must pour itself forth in song. The nuptials of the soul, of the Church, with Christ, demand a poetic epithalamium. How thoroughly in place, so regarded, seems the "Song of Songs"!

III. JOY, WHICH SPRINGS FROM LOVE FELT AND RETURNED. The history of love is not always one of uninterrupted prosperity and gladness. "Our sweetest songs are those which tell of saddest thought." And even in the Canticles we have varying moods; shadows lie upon the land for a season as clouds obscure the face of heaven. Yet the main current of feeling throughout this book is a current of gladness; the music is of the nature of a carol of spontaneous sweetness, a chorale of triumphant delight. The king and the bride alternately give utterance to their joyful emotions, for heart finds heart. So with the relations with the redeeming Lord and those whom he has saved. God rejoices over that which was lost but is found; and man rejoices in the great salvation. It is thus that the lyrics, though sacred, are glad, breathing a "joy unspeakable and full of glory."—T.

Ver. 2.—*Love better than wine.* The desire of the soul awakened to the higher life is a desire which earth cannot satisfy; it is a desire for God, for the manifestations of Divine favour, the proofs of Divine affection. As one has said, "The Christian is not satisfied, like Mary, to kiss the Master's feet; he would kiss the Master's face." The enjoyment of God's kindness enkindles a desire for more knowledge of God, a closer intercourse with God. This is the result of a sense—an imperfect but genuine sense—of the incomparable preciousness of Divine friendship and favour. "Thy love is better than wine."

I. GOD'S GIFTS ARE GOOD. He is good unto all. Every good gift and every perfect boon must be traced to his bounty. Wine is used here poetically as one of the evidences of Divine provision for man's needs. Wine maketh glad the heart of man, oil maketh his face to shine, bread strengtheneth his heart. Heaven bestows in abundance gifts which men often accept with ingratitude or misuse to their own detriment.

II. GOD'S LOVE IS BETTER. Material possessions, temporal enjoyments, the pleasures of sense, are contrasted with what enriches, purifies, and rejoices the spirit. To the spiritual man the favour of Heaven yields more true joy than he experiences in the time when corn and wine increase. 1. This follows from the very nature of man, who is a being made originally in the Divine image, endowed with an immortal nature. Such a being cannot find satisfaction in any lower source of happiness. 2. It follows especially from the fact of man's sin and salvation. As a dependent being, man is a recipient of Divine bounty; but, as a being who has departed from God, and has been restored by forgiving mercy to favour and fellowship, he is especially in need of constant revelations of Divine love. And as Christians we gratefully recognize that, in bestowing upon us his own Son, God has given unto us that love which is better than wine. 3. In partaking of Divine love we are in no danger of excess. It had been better for many a professing Christian had God's providence withheld the gifts which have by the abuse of worldliness been prized above the Giver himself. Not wine only, but the wealth and luxuries of life generally, have too often been the occasion of forgetting and departing from God. But Divine love is a draught of which none can drink in excess. 4. The love of God is a lasting blessing, a perennial joy. The gifts of Divine bounty perish, for they are of the earth. The love of God is imperishable as God himself.—T.

Ver. 3.—*The fragrant name.* The sense of smell furnishes much of the imagery of this poetical book. Perfumes not only gratify the smell, they awaken the emotions, and have a remarkable power of reviving, by association, bygone scenes and far-distant friends and companions, in whose society the fragrant wild flowers or blooms of the garden have been enjoyed. Perfumed unguents were in the East employed for anointing the body, for health and comfort. Their use was associated with hospitable reception and entertainment. The Name of our Saviour is as the unguents poured upon his form, diffusing sweet fragrance abroad.

I. THE NAME OF CHRIST IS FRAGRANT TO THE SPIRITUAL SENSE OF HIS PEOPLE. In fact, the Christ is "the Anointed," who, by his appointment and devotion, is marked out as the beloved Son of God, and the honoured Saviour of the world. The perfume of Divine grace, treasured up from eternity, was poured forth in abundance upon the Word when he "became flesh, and dwelt among us."

II. THE NAME OF CHRIST HAS A COSTLY, PRECIOUS FRAGRANCE. It is well known that large sums of money were lavished on the scented unguents stored in vessels, bottles, and vases of alabaster and other expensive materials. The perfumes used were brought in many cases from distant lands; they were distilled from rare and beautiful flowers; they were purchased by the wealthy and used by the luxurious.

III. THE NAME OF CHRIST POSSESSES A DELIGHTFUL AND REFRESHING FRAGRANCE. As the mere mention of the king's name was welcome to the bride and to her companions, so is the Name of our Saviour, when pronounced in the hearing of his friends, the occasion of delight. The Name of Jesus is music to the ear, and is as "ointment poured forth." It dispels the lassitude, the discouragement, the despondency, which are sometimes apt to steal into the soul of the disciple during the Master's bodily and temporary absence. It is a "Name above every name." "Ointment and perfume rejoice the heart."

IV. THE NAME OF JESUS DIFFUSES A FAR-REACHING FRAGRANCE. The penetrating power of odours is well known. Poets tell of the "spicy breezes" that "blow soft o'er Ceylon's isle;" how "filled with balm the gale sighs on, though the flowers are sunk in death." Thus the precious Name of Christ sheds its sweetness far and wide, bringing life, hope, and salvation to those in remotest lands. The Plant of Renown which was bruised upon the soil of Palestine has given forth perfume of blessing which has reached the uttermost ends of the earth, reviving those ready to perish with its refreshing and reinvigorating power.

V. THE NAME OF CHRIST DIFFUSES A LASTING AND PERMANENT FRAGRANCE. It is known that some perfumes, such as musk, will continue to pour forth their sweetness day after day and year after year, diffusing effluvia unceasingly, and yet suffering no perceptible loss of bulk, no diminution of power to give forth their special odour. Similarly is it with the power of Christ to bless mankind. Generation after generation has found healing, life, and blessing in the gospel; yet is its freshness undimmed and its power undiminished. And to-day more are rejoicing in the ever-fragrant Name than at any former time. Nor shall that Name ever lose its sweetness or its power.—T.

Ver. 4.—*Divine attraction.* There is evidence of attraction throughout the physical universe. The earth draws all things upon it towards its centre; it draws the moon and keeps it revolving round itself. The sun draws the planets, which in their regular orbits unconsciously yield to the influence which he unconsciously exerts. We cannot study any bodies, however distant and however vast, without perceiving the power of attraction. And this power is as manifest in the molecule as in the mass; there is attraction in the smallest as in the greatest of material bodies. As the planets by gravitation are held in their courses by the sun, so are souls led to feel the attraction of our Saviour-God. But whilst material things obey unwittingly, it is for spiritual natures consciously and voluntarily to yield to the spiritual attraction of him who is the Centre, the Law, the Life of all.

I. THE SPIRITUAL DRAWING OF THE KING OF LOVE. 1. The language reveals a dread of being far from God. The soul cries, "Quicken me! lest I remain in death; turn me! lest I continue in error; draw me! lest I live at a distance from thee." 2. The language reveals a recognition of authority. The cry is to the King. Many are the attractions of the world. *Trahit sua quemque voluptas.* Yet these attractions should always be suspected, should sometimes be resisted. But when God draws, his is the drawing of royalty and of right. 3. The language reveals the power of love. "I drew them with cords of a man, with bands of love." "I will draw all men unto myself." Such are the declarations of infinite grace. Those whose souls they reach and touch cannot but seek to be laid hold of by the silken chains, and led and kept near their Lord.

> "O Christ, who hast prepared a place
> For us beside thy throne of grace,
> Draw us, we pray, with cords of love
> From exile to our home above."

II. THE OBEDIENT FOLLOWING OF THOSE WHO FEEL THE DIVINE ATTRACTION. 1. The drawing of the King proves its own effectiveness. "With loving-kindness *have I* drawn thee." The charm is felt, the summons is obeyed, the presence and society which bring spiritual blessing are sought. 2. There is eagerness and haste in the response.

> "He drew me, and I followed on,
> Glad to confess the voice Divine."

Running denotes interest and zeal. The willing following becomes a diligent and strenuous race. The soul finds in Christ a Divine Friend and Lover and Spouse, and in his society satisfaction that never cloys, and joy that never fails.

APPLICATION. Here we have the history of the Divine life in man, related in a few words. In providence, in revelation, in the incarnate Word, in the power of the spiritual dispensation,—in all this God is drawing us. And every movement of the spirit, every impulse towards holiness, every true endeavour after obedience, may be regarded as the practical yielding to the Divine attraction. God's work on earth is just "drawing" us; our religious life is just "running" after him.—T.

Ver. 4.—*The joyful celebration of Divine love.* The king is represented as conducting his friends and guests into his splendid palace, admitting them to the apartments reserved for his most intimate and favoured courtiers, and thus revealing to them his condescension and affection. Such treatment awakens their joy, and calls forth the celebration of his love. The whole scene is symbolical of the privileges and the sacred delights of those who share in the "shining of God's countenance."

I. Divine love is worthy of being celebrated. 1. It is undeserved love, and therefore love of pure compassion. 2. It is condescending love, on the part of the King of heaven towards poor, ignorant, and sinful man. 3. It is too often ill-requited love. 4. Yet it is bountiful and beneficent love. 5. It is sacrificing love—love to display which costs God much. 6. It is forbearing, patient, constant love.

II. There are many ways in which redeemed men may celebrate the Divine love revealed to them. 1. Its pre-eminence may be maintained. There may be other prerogatives and privileges which we may be tempted to make our boast and cause of rejoicing, but we must ever keep before our minds the supreme excellence of the love of God; "more than wine," and more than blessings far more desirable and precious than this. 2. Its most glorious proof may be commemorated. First and foremost among the meanings of the eucharistic meal celebrated in the Church of the Redeemer is its beauty and justice as a memorial of that love "whose height, whose depth unfathomed, no man knows." 3. Its natural power to awaken joy and praise should be practically confessed. To "be glad and rejoice" in God is only just and becoming; and Christians should not so steadfastly contemplate their own unworthiness as to lose sight of the infinite worthiness of him to whom they owe their salvation. 4. Love may be celebrated in the exercise of willing obedience. There is on our part no response to God's kindness so acceptable as consecrated service. "The love of Christ constraineth us;" this is the practical principle of the new life. There is a world of meaning in the language of the text, "In uprightness do they love thee."—T.

Ver. 6.—*The keeper of the vineyards.* Men have put into their charge responsibilities concerning others, and these they may to some extent worthily observe. They may promote the interest of their family, the comfort of their household and dependants. They may even give time and money to advance schemes of benevolence and religion. But the question suggested by the language of the text is this—What are they the better for regarding the welfare of others if they neglect their own? if, being guardians of vineyards, they must acknowledge in all sincerity that their own vineyard they have not kept?

I. Our religion is likely to consist, to a very large extent, in a sense of our proper responsibility for the welfare of our fellow-men. 1. The very position of Britain among the nations of the world favours this view. Our range of influence is immense, our power is vast, our work of colonizing and of governing is heavy and serious. How can we serve our generation according to the will of God? 2. Add to this, the efforts which are called for on behalf of the ignorant and irreligious millions around us, and which seem to demand all the attention and zealous energies of the Church of Christ. 3. Hence a conception of the Christian life as one of constant activity and progressive usefulness.

II. This very sense of responsibility for the welfare of our fellow-men may occasion the neglect of personal devoutness and spirituality. To explain the action of this principle it may be remarked: 1. When we care for others, we naturally take it for granted that all is well with ourselves. In any work and enterprise, if we are engaged in teaching and in leading others, it is natural that we should overlook the importance of examining our own qualifications. 2. The opinion of others acts as an auxiliary in bringing about this state of feeling. Not only do we take it for granted that all is well with ourselves; others do the same, and their attitude encourages us in our good opinion of ourselves. 3. Time and thought may be so taken up in the service in which we are engaged, that attention is drawn away from our own condition, our own obligation to ourselves. A man may awaken to the fact of his own foolish and sinful neglect of his own spiritual state, and may cry aloud, in anguish and remorse, "They made me keeper of the vineyards, and *mine own* vineyard have I not kept!"

III. Yet there is no necessary connection between usefulness to others and neglect of one's own spiritual safety and growth. One duty does not conflict with another. It is in the cultivation of our own hearts that we gain strength and wisdom to be of benefit and service to others. Works of Christian benevolence are to be undertaken, not under the influence of superficial excitement, not under the contagion of enthusiastic example, but from sober conviction, and with a clear understanding of the law that only those who themselves have received can to any purpose give to others.

APPLICATION. Let those whose position is described in the text bestir themselves at once, apply with diligence to their proper work, restore the hedges, dig about the vine-roots, take the "foxes that spoil the grapes," and climb the watch-tower, that they may discern the approach and resist the incursions of their foes. Then shall they be privileged to present, even from their own vineyard, some fruit which shall be acceptable to the Divine Master and Lord, to whom all must at last give in their great account.—T.

Vers. 7, 8.—*The shepherd's care.* As the beloved maiden or bride seeks her shepherd-lover who is yet the king, she makes use of language which gives an insight into pastoral duty and care, and which serves to suggest the relations borne by the flock to the good Shepherd who gave his life for the sheep.

I. THE GOOD SHEPHERD FEEDS THE FLOCK.

II. THE GOOD SHEPHERD PROVIDES NOONDAY REST FOR THE FLOCK.

III. THE GOOD SHEPHERD PROTECTS THE FLOCK, KEEPING HIS SHEEP NEAR THE WELL-GUARDED TENTS.

IV. THE GOOD SHEPHERD GUIDES HIS SHEEP, LEADING THE FOOTSTEPS OF THE FLOCK ACCORDING TO HIS OWN KNOWLEDGE AND WISDOM.

V. THE GOOD SHEPHERD CARES FOR THE KIDS—THE YOUNG OF THE FLOCK.—T.

Vers. 9—15.—*Love and admiration.* It requires imagination and a knowledge of Oriental habits of thinking fully to appreciate the language of this passage, which otherwise to our colder and less fanciful natures may appear extravagant. But expressions which may be open to the charge of extravagance as applied to ordinary human affection, may well come short of the truth if interpreted as indicating the emotions which distinguish those spiritual relations of absorbed delight subsisting between Christ and his spouse, the Church. Beneath the rich metaphors of the poet we discern certain principles which are of deepest moment and beauty.

I. CHRIST'S INTEREST IN HIS PEOPLE IS INTEREST IN HIS OWN WORKMANSHIP, IN HIS OWN PURCHASE AND POSSESSION. The descriptions of the charms of the beloved, couched in the figurative language of Eastern poetry, can only be applied in any sense to the Church of the Lord Christ upon the distinct understanding that whatever excellences she may possess she owes to the Divine care and munificence of the heavenly Spouse. She owes her existence to his power, her safety to his faithful watching, her gifts and excellences to the provision of his love and care, her position to his compassion. Nothing has she which she did not receive from him; nothing of which she can be vain, of which she can boast. For all, her lowly acknowledgments of gratitude are for ever due to her Almighty Lord.

II. CHRIST'S PERFECTIONS DESERVE AND DEMAND THE ADORING AND AFFECTIONATE ADMIRATION OF HIS CHURCH. 1. She admires him for what he is in himself. In him is all that is excellent and valuable, sweet and lovable. His beauty is spiritual, incomparable, delightful, unfading, and unwearying. 2. She adores him for his treatment of herself and his regard for her. The Church knows, from her Lord's own revelation, that he holds her dear, precious, fragrant; that, having laid down his life for her redemption, he never can or will forget her, or cease to cherish towards her the affection of his Divine and loving heart. 3. Hence she commemorates his love in the Eucharist, honours him by her obedience, and by her witness and her praise commends him to the world.—T.

EXPOSITION.

CHAPTER II.

Ver. 2.—**As a lily among thorns, so is my love among the daughters.** The king responds, taking up the lovely simile and giving it a very apt and charming turn, "My love is beyond comparison the chief and all around her are not worthy of notice beside her." The meaning is not thorns on the tree itself. The word would be different in that case. Rather it is thorn-plants or bushes (*choach*); see 2 Kings xiv. 9. *The daughters;* i.e. the young damsels. The word "son" or "daughter" was commonly so used in Hebrew, the idea being that of simplicity, innocence, and gentleness.

Ver. 3.—**As the apple tree among the trees of the wood, so is my beloved among the sons. I sat down under his shadow with great delight, and his fruit** was **sweet to my taste.** That these are the words of the bride there can be no doubt. The apple tree is noted for the fragrance of its blossom and the sweetness of its fruit; hence the name *tappuach*, from the root *naphach*, "to breathe sweetly." The trees of the wood or forest are specially referred to, because they are generally wild, and their fruit sour and rough, and many have no fruit or flower. The Chaldee renders, "citron;" Rosenmüller and others, "quince." The word is rare (see Prov. xxv. 11; Joel i. 12). It is sometimes the tree itself, at other times the fruit. It occurs in proper names, as (Josh. xii. 17), "The King of Tappuah," etc., and that shows that it was very early known in Palestine. It occurs frequently in the Talmud. The word is masculine, while "lily" is feminine. "I sat with delight" is expressed in true Hebrew phrase, "I delighted and sat," the intensity of feeling being expressed by the piel of the verb. By the shadow is intended both protection and refreshment; by the fruit, enjoyment. Perhaps we may go further, and say there is here a symbolical representation of the spiritual life, as both that of trust and participation. The greatness and goodness of the tree of life protects and covers the sinner, while the inner nature and Divine virtue of the Saviour comes forth in delicious fruits, in his character, words, ministry, and spiritual gifts. If there is any truth in the typical view, it must be found in such passages as this, where the metaphor is so simple and apt, and has been incorporated with all religious language as the vehicle of faith and love. Hymnology abounds in such ideas and analogies.

Ver. 4.—**He brought me to the banqueting-house, and his banner over me** was **love;** literally, *to the house of the wine.* Not, as some, "the house of the vines"—that is, the vineyard. The Hebrew word *yayin* corresponds with the Æthiopic *wain*, and has run through the Indo-European languages. The meaning is—To the place where he royally entertains his friends. Hence the reference which immediately follows to the protection with which the king overshadows his beloved. He covers me there with his fear-inspiring, awful banner, love, which, because of its being love, is terrible to all enemies. The word which is used for "banner" (דֶּגֶל) is from a root "to cover," that which covers the shaft or standard; the *pannus*, "the cloth," which is fastened to a shaft (cf. pennon). Her natural fear and bashfulness is overcome by the loving presence of the king, which covers her weakness like a banner. Some versions render it as an imperative. There can be no doubt of the meaning that the banner is the military banner, as the word is always so used (see Ps. xx. 6; Numb. i. 52; ii. 2). Perhaps there is a reference to the grandeur and military strength in which the young bride felt delight as she looked up at her young husband in his youthful beauty and manly vigour. The typical significance is very easily discovered. It would be straining it too much to see any allusion to the ritual of the Christian sacraments; but whether we think of the individual soul or of the people of God regarded collectively, such delight in the rich provisions of Divine love, and in the tender guardianship of the Saviour over those whom he has called to himself, belong to the simplest facts of believing experience.

Ver. 5.—**Stay me with raisins, comfort me with apples: for I am sick of love.** Again the intensive form of the verb is chosen. She is almost sinking; she cries out for comfort. The food for which she longs is the grape-cakes — the grapes sufficiently dried to be pressed together as cakes, which is very refreshing and reviving; not raisins as we know them, but with more of the juice of the grape in them. So date-cakes are now offered to travellers in the East. "Refresh me; for I am in a state of deep agitation because of the intensity of my love." Ginsburg thinks the cakes are baked by the fire, the word being derived from a root "to burn." The translation, "flagons of wine," in the Authorized Version, follows the rabbinical exposition, but it is quite unsupported by the critics. Love-sickness is common in Eastern countries, more so than with us in the colder hemisphere. Perhaps the appeal of the bride is meant to be general, not immediately directed to the king, as if a kind of exclamation, and it may be connected with the previous idea of the banner. The country maiden is dazzled with the splendour and majesty of the king. She gives up, as it were, in willing resignation of herself, the rivalry with one so great and glorious in the expression of love and praise; she sinks back with delight and ecstasy, calling upon any around to support her, and Solomon himself answers the appeal, and puts his loving arm around her and holds up her head, and gives her the sweetest and tenderest embraces, which renew her strength. We know that in the spiritual life there are such experiences. The intensity of religious feeling is closely connected with physical exhaustion, and when the soul cries for help and longs for comfort, the presence of the Saviour is revealed ; the weakness is changed into strength. The apostolic seer in the Apocalypse describes himself as overcome with the glory of the Saviour's appearance, and being brought back to himself by his voice (Rev. i. 17).

Ver. 6.—**His left hand is under my head, and his right hand doth embrace me.** We may render the verb either as indicative or imperative. The hand gently smooths with loving caresses. The historical sense is more in accordance with the context, as the next verse is an appeal to the attendant ladies. Behold my happiness, how my Beloved comforts me !

Ver. 7.—**I adjure you, O daughters of Jerusalem, by the roes, and by the hinds of the field, that ye stir not up, nor awaken love, until it please.** The fact that these words occur again in ch. iii. 5 and viii. 4 shows that they are a kind of chorus or refrain. It is also evident that they are in the lips of Shulamith the bride. Some have suggested that they are uttered by some one else, e.g. the queen - mother subsequently referred to, Solomon himself, the heavenly Bridegroom, the shepherd - lover from whom Shulamith had been taken. But all these suggestions are unnecessary and unsupported. The natural and simple view is that the same voice is speaking as in ver. 6. But what is the meaning of this adjuration ? Is it merely, " I throw myself on the sympathy you have already expressed " ? Ewald well remarks, " In common life people swore by things which belonged to the subject of conversation or were especially dear to the speaker. As, therefore, the warrior swears by his sword ; as Mohammed by the soul, of which he is just about to speak (see Koran, ch. xci. 7) ; so here Shulamith by the lovely gazelles, since she is speaking of love." The Israelites were permitted to adjure by that which is not God, but they would only solemnly swear by God himself. Delitzsch thinks this is the only example of direct adjuration in Scripture without the name of God. The meaning has probably been sought too far away. The bride is perfectly happy, but she is conscious that such exquisite happiness may be disturbed, the dream of her delight broken through. She compares herself to a roe or a gazelle, the most timorous and shy of creatures (see Prov. v. 19). The Septuagint has a peculiar rendering, which points to a different reading of the original, ἐν δυνάμεσι καὶ ἰσχύσεσι τοῦ ἀγροῦ, " by the power and virtues of the field." Per-

haps the meaning is the same—By the purity and blessedness of a simple country life, I adjure you not to interfere with the course of true love. It is much debated whether the meaning is, " Do not excite or stir up love," or, " Do not disturb love in its peaceful delight." It certainly must be maintained that by " love " is meant " the lover." The reference is to the passion of love itself. A similar expression is used of the feeling of jealousy (Isa. xlii. 13). The verb עוּר (piel) is added to strengthen the idea, and is always used in the sense " to excite or awaken," as Prov. x. 12 of strife ; Ps. lxxx. 3 of strength or power. We must not for a moment think of any artificial excitement of love as referred to. The idea is—See what a blessed thing is pure and natural affection : let not love be forced or unnatural. But there are those who dispute this interpretation. They think that the main idea of the whole poem is not the spontaneity of love, but a commendation of pure and chaste conjugal affection, as opposed to the dissoluteness and sensuality fostered by polygamy. They would therefore take the abstract " love " for the concrete " loved one," as in ch. vii. 6 The bride would not have the beloved one aroused by the intrusion of others ; or the word " love " may be taken to mean " the dream of love." Whichever explanation is chosen, the sense is substantially the same—Let me rejoice in my blessedness. The bride is seen at the close of this first part of the poem in the arms of the bridegroom. She is lost in him, and his happiness is hers. She calls upon the daughters of Jerusalem to rejoice with her. This is, in fact, the key-note of the song. The two main thoughts in the poem are the purity of love and the power of love. The reference to the roes and gazelles of the field is not so much to their shyness and timidity as to their purity, as distinguished from the creatures more close to cities ; hence the appeal to the daughters of Jerusalem, who, as being ladies of the metropolis, might not sympathize as they should with the country maiden. The rest of the poem is a remembrance of the part which illustrates and confirms the sentiment of the refrain—Let the pure love seek its own perfection ; let its own pleasure be realized. So, spiritually, let grace complete what grace begins. " Blessed are all those who trust in him."

Ver. 8—ch. iii. 5.—Part II. SONG OF SHULAMITH IN THE EMBRACE OF SOLOMON. Recollections of the wooing-time in the north.

Ver. 8.—**The voice of my beloved ! behold, he cometh, leaping upon the mountains, skipping upon the hills.** There can be little doubt as to the meaning of this song. The bride is going back in thought to the scenes of her home-life, and the sweet days of first love. "The house stands alone among the rocks and deep in the mountain range; around are the vineyards which the family have planted, and the hill-pastures on which they feed their flocks. She longingly looks out for her distant lover." The expression, "The voice of my beloved!" must not be taken to mean that she hears the sound of his feet or voice, but simply as an interjection, like "hark!" (see Gen. iv. 10, where the voice of the blood crying merely means, "Hark how thy brother's blood cries!" that is, "Believe that it does so cry"). So here, "I seem to hear the voice of my beloved; hark, he is coming!" It is a great delight to the soul to go back in thought over the memories of its first experience of the Saviour's presence. The Church is edified by the records of grace in the histories of Divine dealings.

Ver. 9.—**My beloved is like a roe or a young hart; behold, he standeth behind our wall, he looketh in at the windows, he showeth himself through the lattice.** The *tsĕvi* is the gazelle, Arabic *ghazāl*. Our word is derived through the Spanish or Moorish *gazela*. The young hart, or chamois, is probably so called from the covering of young hair (cf. 2 Sam. ii. 18; Prov. vi. 5; Heb. iii. 19). Shulamith represents herself as within the house, waiting for her friend. Her beloved is standing behind the wall, outside before the house; he is playfully looking through the windows, now through one and now through another, seeking her with peering eyes of love. Both the words employed convey the meaning of searching and moving quickly. The *windows;* literally, *the openings;* i.e. a window broken through a wall, or the meaning may be a lattice window, a pierced wooden structure. The word is not the common word for a window, which is *shĕvākā* (now *shabbáka*), from a root meaning "to twist," "to make a lattice." Spiritually, we may see an allusion to the glimpses of truth and tastes of the goodness of religion, which precede the real fellowship of the soul with God.

Ver. 10.—**My beloved spake, and said unto me, Rise up, my love, my fair one, and come away.** The word "spake" conveys the meaning in answer to a person appearing, but not necessarily in answer to a voice heard. We most suppose that Shulamith recognized her beloved, and made some sign that she was near, or looked forth from the window. As the soul responds, it is more and more invited; the voice of the Bridegroom is heard calling the object of his love by name, "I have called thee by thy name; thou art mine "(Isa. xliii. 1).

Vers. 11—13.—**For, lo, the winter is past,**

the rain is over *and* **gone; the flowers appear on the earth; the time of the singing** *of birds* **is come, and the voice of the turtle is heard in our land; the fig tree ripeneth her green figs, and the vines are in blossom, they give forth their fragrance. Arise, my love, my fair one, and come away.** Winter; *i.e.* the cloudy stormy time (*sĕthauv*). The Jews in Jerusalem to this day call rain *shataâ*. The rain; *i.e.* the showers. The flowers, or the flowery time, corresponding with the singing-time. Several versions, as the LXX. and other Greek, Jerome in the Latin, and the Targum and Venetian, render, "the time of pruning," taking the *zāmir* from a root *zamar*, "to prune the vine." It is, however, regarded by most critics as an onomatopoetic word meaning "song," "music," like *zimrah*, "singing." The reference to the voice of the turtle-dove, the cooing note which is so sweet and attractive among the woods, shows that the time of spring is intended. Ginsburg says wherever *zāmir* occurs, either in the singular or plural, it means "singing" (cf. 2 Sam. xxiii. 1; Isa. xxiv. 16). The form of the word conveys the idea of the time of the action, as we see in the words for "harvest" (*asiph*) and "ploughing-time" (*chārish*). The fig tree and the vine were both employed as symbols of prosperity and peace, as the fig and grape were so much used as food (see 1 Kings v. 5; 2 Kings xviii. 31). The little fruits of the fig tree begin, when the spring commences, to change colour from green to red (cf. Mark xi. 13, where the Passover-time is referred to). The word "to ripen " is literally, " to grow red or sweet." The blossoming vines give forth a very delicate and attractive fragrance. The description is acknowledged by all to be very beautiful. The invitation is to fellowship in the midst of the pure loveliness of nature, when all was adapted to meet and sustain the feelings of awakened love. The emotions of the soul are blended easily with the sensations derived from the outward world. When we carefully avoid extravagance, and put the soul first and not second, then the delights of the senses may help the heart to realize the deepest experience of Divine communion. But the bridegroom first solicits the bride. We reverse the true spiritual order when we place too much dependence on the influence of external objects or sensuous pleasures. Art may assist religion to its expression, but it must never be made so prominent that the artistic pleasure swallows up the religious emotion. Love of nature is not love of Christ. Love of music is not love of Christ. Yet the soul that seeks him may rejoice in art and music, because they blend their attractions with its devotion, and help it to be a joy and a passion.

Ver. 14.—**O my dove, that art in the clefts of the rock, in the covert of the steep places, let me see thy countenance, let me hear thy voice; for sweet is thy voice, and thy countenance is comely.** The wood-pigeon builds in clefts of rocks and in steep rocky places (see Jer. xlviii. 28; and cf. Ps. lxxiv. 19; lvi. 1; Hos. vii. 11). The bridegroom is still addressing his beloved one, who has not yet come forth from the house in the rocks, though she has shown herself at the window. The language is highly poetical, and may be compared with similar words in Homer and Virgil (cf. 'Iliad,' xxi. 493; 'Æneid,' v. 213, etc.). The Lord loveth the sight of his people. He delighteth in their songs and in their prayers. He is in the midst of their assemblies. Secret religion is not the highest religion. The highest emotions of the soul do not decrease in their power as they are expressed. They become more and more a ruling principle of life. There are many who need this encouragement to come forth out of secrecy, out of solitude, out of their own private home and individual thoughts, and realize the blessing of fellowship with the Lord and with his people.

Ver. 15.—**Take us the foxes, the little foxes, that spoil the vineyards; for our vineyards are in blossom.** There is some difficulty in deciding to which of the persons this speech is to be attributed. It is most naturally, however, assigned to the bride, and this is the view of the majority of critics. Hence she refers to the vineyards as "our vineyards," which the bridegroom could scarcely say. On the other hand, it must be acknowledged that the words are abrupt regarded as a response to the beautiful appeal of the lover. The following are the remarks of Delitzsch on the subject: "This is a vine-dresser's ditty, in accord with Shulamith's experience as the keeper of a vineyard, which, in a figure, aims at her love-relation. The vineyards, beautiful with fragrant blossoms, point to her covenant of love, and the foxes, the little foxes, which might destroy those united vineyards, point to all the great and little enemies and adverse circumstances which threaten to gnaw and destroy love in the blossom ere it has reached the ripeness of full enjoyment." Some think that Shulamith is giving the reason why she cannot immediately join her beloved, referring to the duties enjoined upon her by her brethren. But there is an awkwardness in this explanation. The simplest and most straightforward is that which connects the words immediately with the invitation of the lover to come forth into the lovely vineyards. Is it not an allusion to the playful pleasure which the young people would find among the vineyards in chasing the little foxes? and may not the lover take

up some well-known country ditty, and sing it outside the window as a playful repetition of the invitation to appear? The words do seem to be arranged in somewhat of a lyrical form—

"Catch us the foxes,
  Foxes the little ones,
    Wasting our vineyards,
When our vineyards are blossoming."

The foxes (*shuâlim*), or little jackals, were very numerous in Palestine (see Judg. xv. 4; Lam. v. 18; Ps. lxiii. 11; Neh. iv. 3; 1 Sam. xiii. 17). The little jackals were seldom more than fifteen inches high. There would be nothing unsuitable in the address to a maiden to help to catch such small animals. The idea of the song is—Let us all join in taking them. Some think that Shulamith is inviting the king to call his attendants to the work. But when two lovers thus approach one another, it is not likely that others would be thought of. However the words be viewed, the typical meaning can scarcely be missed. The idea of clearing the vineyards of depredators well suits the general import of the poem. Let the blossoming love of the soul be without injury and restraint. Let the rising faith and affection be carefully guarded. Both individuals and communities do well to think of the little foxes that spoil the vines.

Ver. 16.—**My beloved is mine, and I am his; he feedeth (his flock) among the lilies.** These are the words of the bride. The latter clause is repeated in ch. vi. 2, with the addition, "in the gardens," and it is evident that Solomon is lovingly regarded as a shepherd, because Shulamith delights to think of him as fully sympathizing with her simple country life. She idealizes. The words may be taken as either the response given 'at the time by the maiden to the invitation of her lover to come forth into the vineyards, or as the breathing of love as she lies in the arms of Solomon. Lilies are the emblem of purity, lofty elevation above that which is common. Moreover, the lily-stalk is the symbol of the life of regeneration among the mystical mediævalists. Mary the Virgin, the *Rosa mystica*, in ancient paintings is represented with a lily in her hand at the Annunciation. The people of God were called by the Jewish priests "a people of lilies." So Mary was the lily of lilies in the lily community; the *sanctissima* in the *communio sanctorum*. There may be an allusion to the lily-forms around Solomon in his palace—the daughters of Jerusalem; in that case the words must be taken as spoken, not in remembrance of the first love, but in present joy in Solomon's embrace. Some would render the words as simply praise of Solomon himself, "who, wherever he abides, spreads radiancy and loveliness about him," or "in whose footsteps roses and lilies ever bloom." At least, they are expressive of entire self-surrender and delight. She herself is a lily, and the beloved one feeds upon her beauty, purity, and perfection.

Ver. 17.—**Until the day be cool, and the shadows flee away, turn, my beloved, and be thou like a roe or a young hart upon the mountains of Bether.** This is generally supposed to be the voice of the maiden addressing her suitor, and bidding him return in the evening, when the day cools, and when the lengthening shadows fall into night. Some have seen in such words a clear indication of a clandestine interview, and would find in them a confirmation of their hypothesis that the poem is founded on a romantic story of Solomon's attempt to draw a shepherdess from her shepherd. But there is no necessity to disturb the flow of the bride's loving recollections by such a fancy. She is recalling the visit of her lover. How, at first, she declined his invitation to go forth with him to the vineyards, but with professions of love appealed to him to return to the mountains, and in the evening come once more and rejoice in her love. But the words may be rendered, " during the whole day, and until the evening comes, turn thyself to me," which is the view taken by some critics. The language may be general; that is, " Turn, and I will follow." " The mountains of Bether" are the rugged mountains; *Bether*, from a root " to divide," "to cut," *i.e.* divided by ravines; or the word may be the abstract for the

concrete—" the mountains of separation," *i.e.* the mountains which separate. LXX., ὄρη τῶν κοιλωμάτων," decussated mountains." The Syriac and Theodotion take the word as for *bĕshâmim*, i.e. offerings of incense (θυμιαματῶν). There is no such geographical name known, though there is Bithron, east of Jordan, near Mahanaim (2 Sam. ii. 29). The Chaldee, Ibn-Ezra, Rashi, and many others render it "separation" (cf. Luther's *scheideberge*). Bochart says, " Montes scissionis ita dicti propter ῥωχμοῦς et χασματὰ." The meaning has been thus set forth: " The request of Shulamith that he should return to the mountains breathes self-denying humility, patient modesty, inward joy in the joy of her beloved. She will not claim him for herself till he have accomplished his work. But when he associates with her in the evening, as with the Emmaus disciples, she will rejoice if he becomes her guide through the new-born world of spring. Perhaps we may say the Parousia of the Lord is here referred to in the evening of the world" (cf. Luke xxiv.). On the whole, it seems most in harmony with the context to take the words as preparing us for what follows—the account of the maiden's distress when she woke up and found not her beloved. We must not expect to be able to explain the language as though it were a clear historical composition, relating facts and incidents. The real line of thought is the underlying connection of spiritual meaning. There is a separation of the lovers. The soul wakes up to feel that its object of delight is gone. Then it complains.

HOMILETICS.

Vers. 1—7.—*Converse of the bridegroom and the bride continued.* I. THE VOICE OF THE BRIDE. 1. *The rose of Sharon.* They were sitting, it seems, in a forest glade at the foot of some lofty cedar, sheltered by its embowering branches; beneath was their grassy seat, bright with many flowers. The bride feels that she is as one of those fair flowers in the bridegroom's eyes. " I am the rose of Sharon," she says, in her artless acceptance of the bridegroom's loving approval. We cannot identify the flower called here and in Isa. xxxv. 1, the rose. Our rose, we are told, was brought from Persia long after the time of Solomon; it is first mentioned in the Apocrypha (Ecclus. xxiv. 14; xxxix. 13; l. 8). The rose of the canonical Scriptures may be, as many have thought, the narcissus, which is very common in the Plain of Sharon, and is still the favourite flower of the inhabitants. The word " Sharon " may mean simply "a plain;" but, as it has the article, it probably stands here for the famous Plain of Sharon, so celebrated in ancient times for its fertility and beauty. The bride is like a lowly flower of the field, not majestic like those lofty cedars, but yet lovely in the bridegroom's sight. The Christian is humble of heart; he is helpless and short-lived as a flower. " All flesh is as grass, and all the glory of man as the flower of grass." But because Christ hath loved him and died for him, he knows that he is dear to his Saviour. 2. *The lily of the valleys.* Here, too, there is an uncertainty. The word rendered " lily " (*shushan*, the name of the famous Persian city, the " Shushan the palace " of the Book of Esther) is used of many bright-coloured flowers. We infer from ch. v. 13 that this lily was red; hence some writers identify it with the scarlet anemone, which is very abundant all over Palestine. Solomon's bride compares herself to the lily; but even Solomon himself, the Lord said, "in all his glory was not arrayed as one of these." The Lord bids us "consider the lilies." When we look up to the heaven, to the vast distances, the enormous magnitude of the heavenly bodies, in their ordered movements, we think, as the psalmist thought, "Lord, what is man, that thou art mindful of him?" But when we consider the lilies, we see that he who framed the universe in its vastness regards things small and humble. The delicate pencilling, the gorgeous colouring of the flowers of the field, the complicated structure of many of them, the arrangements, for instance, for fertilization, show a wisdom, an exact accommodation of means to ends, as astonishing as the celestial mechanism; a great and loving care, too, for us men, in providing us not only with the necessaries of life, but also with objects of rare and exquisite loveliness, to give us pure and innocent pleasures, to teach us lessons of truthfulness. He who thus clothes the grass of the field, which to-day is, and to-morrow is cast into the oven, will surely clothe us, though, alas! we are of little faith. The bride is as one of these flowers, frail as they are; she trusts in the bridegroom's care. The Christian must learn to cast all his anxiety upon God. He careth for us.

II. THE REPLY OF THE BRIDEGROOM. The king takes up the words of the bride. She is to him as a lily; other maidens, when compared with her, are but as thorns in the bridegroom's eyes. Alas! there are tares in the Lord's field, barren fig trees in his garden. They are as thorns; his chosen are as lilies. The thorns set forth by contrast the beauty of the lily; the deformity of sin brings into sharper contrast the beauty of holiness. But whatever beauty the Christian soul possesses comes only from the Bridegroom's gift; he gives it. In his infinite love he condescends to be pleased with that which is truly his, not ours; we hope to be "found in him, not having our own righteousness, which is of the Law, but that which is through the faith of Christ, the righteousness which is of God by faith" (Phil. iii. 9).

III. THE GRATITUDE OF THE BRIDE. 1. *The excellence of the bridegroom.* He had compared the bride to a lily among thorns; she compares him to an apple tree among the trees of the wood. As the apple tree with its sweet fruit and its fragrant smell excels the barren trees of the wood, so the bridegroom excels all other men in the eyes of the bride. It is uncertain what the *tappuach*, called in our version "apple tree," really is; it has been identified by different writers with the quince, the citron, or the orange. It is enough for our purpose to know that it excels the trees of the wood, that its foliage gives a pleasant shade, that its fruit is sweet and fragrant and possesses certain restorative properties. The fact that it is five times mentioned in the Book of Joshua (xii. 17; xv. 34, 53; xvi. 8; xvii. 7) in connection with the name of various towns or fountains, Beth Tappuach or En Tappuach, shows that in the old times it must have been widely cultivated and greatly valued. It excels other trees; so does the beloved excel all other men in the estimate of the bride. Christ is very dear to the Christian soul. He is the Treasure hid in the field, the Pearl of great price; those who have found him and known him by a real spiritual knowledge count other objects of human desire as nothing worth in comparison with him. "What things were gain to me," says St. Paul, "those I counted loss for Christ;" and again, "I do count them but dung, that I may win Christ, and be found in him." 2. *The bride's delight in him.* The tappuach offered a pleasant shade; the bride delighted in it; she sat down beneath its bower of foliage; its fruit was sweet to her taste. We think of the holy women who stood by the cross of Jesus (John xix. 25). The shadow under which the Church finds rest must be the shadow of the cross. The Lord Jesus Christ is to the believer "a refuge from the storm, a shadow from the heat;" "the shadow of a great rock in a weary land" (Isa. xxv. 4; xxxii. 2). He bids the weary and heavy laden to come to him that they may find rest—rest for their souls. There is no other true and abiding rest for these restless, dissatisfied souls of ours, but only the rest which he giveth—rest in the Lord. But it was the agony and bloody sweat, the bitter cross and passion, which made the Lord Jesus what he is to the believer; it is the exceeding great love of our Master and only Saviour manifested forth in that sacred suffering; it is the blessed atonement for the sins of the world wrought once for all through the virtue of the precious blood;—it is this which makes the Saviour's cross a place of rest and refreshment for the weary soul, which causes the Christian to take delight in the shadow of the cross rather than in any form of earthly joy; hence the words of St. Paul, "God forbid that I should glory, save in the cross of our Lord Jesus Christ, by whom the world is crucified unto me, and I unto the world" (Gal. vi. 14). As St. Paul gloried in the cross, so the bride delighted in the shadow of the beloved. "In his shadow I delighted, and I sat down," is the literal rendering of the Hebrew words. It is delight in the Saviour's love which draws the penitent to the cross; as the Lord said, "I, if I be lifted up from the earth, will draw all men unto me." The Lord's love draws the penitent soul burdened with the sense of sin; the cross is to such a soul like the shadow of a great rock in a weary land; there only is a sure refuge from the heat and turmoil of the world, from the cares and the manifold temptations of this life. Therefore the Christian sits down beneath it, taking the cross for his portion, meditating much on the Saviour's cross, seeking to live ever nearer and nearer to it, within the inner depths of its awful shadow, and finding there a deep and holy peace which the world can neither give nor take away. Under the shadow of the cross we learn ourselves to take up the cross, and to follow after Christ; there we learn that in patient self-denials practised in the faith of Christ there is a spiritual delight, a joy severe indeed, but far more abiding, far more precious, than any joy this world can give. There we learn what St. Paul means when he says, "We glory in tribulations also" (Rom. v. 3); what St. James means when he says, "My brethren, count it all joy when ye fall into divers temptations." For "his fruit is sweet to the taste." The soul that sits under the shadow of the cross of Christ feeds upon Christ, in spiritual communion with him, and in the blessed sacrament which he ordained, and finds in that holy food a Divine sweetness, which wholly passes every form of earthly delight. But it is only they who sit under the shadow, who live very near to Christ in daily bearing of the cross, in patient continuance in well-doing, who can realize that blessed sweetness; they "by reason of use have their senses exercised to discern both good and evil" (Heb. v. 14); they know that Christ is the Bread of life, that his flesh is meat indeed, and his blood drink indeed; their earnest, persevering prayer is, "Lord, evermore give us this bread." 3. *Her remembrance of his love.* "He brought me to the banqueting-house," she says; literally, "to the house of wine." The bride passes from metaphor to facts. The bridegroom is no longer a fair and fruitful tree; he is once more the King of Israel who sought and loved the lowly maiden; she recounts her past experience of his love. He had brought her, humble as she was, into his palace, into the banqueting-house. The literal translation brings to our thoughts the Lord's words, "I say unto you, I will not drink henceforth of this fruit of the vine, until that day when I drink it new with you in my Father's kingdom" (Matt. xxvi. 29). It is he who must bring his people into his banqueting-house; it is his presence manifested to faith which makes the holy communion what it is to the believer. He gives us then the wine that maketh glad the heart of man, when he saith, "Drink ye all of it: for this is my blood of the new testament, which is shed for many for the remission of sins." We are not worthy so much as to gather up the crumbs under his table; but when he brings us thither, when we come led by the Spirit, drawn by the constraining love of Christ, then we know that it is his banqueting-house, the house to which he calls his guests, where he seats them at his own board. "With desire have I desired to eat this Passover with you before I suffer." There he bids us drink: "Drink ye all of it;" we all need that cup, for it is the cup of the new covenant. When we take it in faith and love, the new covenant, the covenant of grace, is confirmed to us afresh; for he gives us the blood that was shed for the remission of sins, the blood that cleanseth from all sin those who walk in the light. But we must ask him to bring us; without him we can do nothing. If we approach without him, without his grace and guidance, without faith in him, we shall bring no blessing away with us, but only the judgment of those who discern not the Lord's body (1 Cor. xi. 29). The banqueting-house of the King of Israel was signalized by the royal banner, the standard which had often led to the battle the warriors of Israel. That standard was the centre round which the king's followers were wont to flock, to guard him in the hour of peril, to honour him with their attendance in the time of peace. But what drew the bride thither was the love of the bridegroom; that was the banner which was beautiful in her eyes, which was over her. The banner of the cross goeth onwards before the followers of the Lord; it is the centre round which they press, which is ever drawing them nearer and nearer. The banner which draws

Christians to the blessed sacrament is the love of Christ.   The banner tells of battle and of victory.   We are told that after the conflict between Israel and Amalek in Rephidim, when the victory was won through the sustained persevering prayer of Moses, " Moses built an altar, and called the name of it Jehovah-nissi : for he said, Because the Lord hath sworn that the Lord will have war with Amalek from generation to generation" (Exod. xvii. 15, 16).   Moses said, " Jehovah is my Banner; " the bride says, " His banner over me is love."   The Hebrew words, indeed, are different, but the thought is similar. Jehovah will have war against the enemies of his people.   " When the enemy shall come in like a flood, the Spirit of the Lord shall lift up a standard against him" (Isa. lix. 19).   The Lord is his people's banner, their rallying-point, the centre round which they range themselves in the hour of danger, when trials and temptations thicken, and the fiery darts of the wicked one are most frequent and most deadly.   The banner is the Lord himself—his presence, his love.   But as the standards round which our troops have fought are cherished and honoured, and reverently preserved in our cathedrals ; so the royal banner which had led the soldiers of the cross to victory floats over the banqueting-house of the King.   It is the token of his presence.   He is there with his faithful ones ; he receives them to his board ; his banner is love.   His love, which was their strength in the day of conflict, is the joy of their souls in the blessed hour of holy communion with their Lord.   But the words run, " His banner over *me* was love;" "The Lord is *my* Banner."   We seem to see here a foreshadowing of those very precious words of Holy Scripture, "The Son of God loved *me*, and gave himself for *me*."   The love of the Lord Jesus Christ is a personal, an individual love.   "The Lord knoweth them that are his;" he knows them one and all.   His banner is over each of them as he brings them into his banqueting-house, as he draws them ever nearer to himself; and that banner is love.   That unutterable love is their defence in times of danger, their joy and delight in seasons of spiritual enjoyment.   Their earnest effort is so to lift up their hearts unto the Lord that they "may be able to comprehend with all saints what is the breadth, and length, and depth, and height; and to know the love of Christ, which passeth knowledge."   The banqueting-house to which he brings the faithful here is the ante-room of the true presence-chamber of the King. "Here we see through a glass, darkly; but then face to face : here we know in part ; but then shall we know even as also we are known."   That banqueting-house is the house not made with hands, eternal in the heavens.   There also his banner, which is love, will be over his elected saints.   But it will no longer lead them to the battle, to hard and difficult struggles; it will tell of victory and glory, and of the unveiled presence of the King.   Heart of man cannot tell what is the joy of those who in that banqueting-house sit down at the marriage supper of the Lamb.   Then the bride shall be arrayed in fine linen, clean and white, the fine linen which is the righteousness of saints (Rev. xix. 8). Then each true soldier of the cross, who with that banner floating over him has fought the good fight of faith, shall see that banner in all its glorious beauty, and sit beneath it very near the King ; for it is written, "To him that overcometh will I grant to sit with me in my throne, even as I also overcame, and am set down with my Father in his throne."   4. *The bride's longing.*   She is sick of love.   The joy of the bridegroom's love is too great and overwhelming; she is fainting in delight too sweet for her powers. She asks for restoratives, "cakes of raisins" (as the word seems to mean, not "flagons") and other fruits which were supposed to possess strengthening or reviving powers. When the Christian comes into the very presence of the King, he is oppressed with the deep sense of his own unworthiness, his own cold unloving heart, and the King's awful holiness and adorable, incomprehensible love; he needs the support of the fruit of the Spirit ; he needs to be strengthened with all might by the Spirit in the inner man.   When God reveals his great love to us, it makes us feel all the more the depth of our ingratitude, the coldness, the hardness, of this stony heart of ours.

> " O Love Divine, how sweet thou art !
>   When shall I find my willing heart
>   All taken up by thee ?
>   I thirst, I faint, I die to prove
>   The greatness of redeeming love,
>   The love of Christ to me."

The bride longs for yet tenderer tokens of affection. Perhaps the words of ver. 6 would be better rendered as a wish or prayer, as in ch. viii. 3, where they occur again: "Oh that his left hand were under my head, and his right hand should embrace me!" The Christian longs to be drawn ever closer into the Lord's embrace; he longs to lie in spirit, as the beloved apostle once actually lay, "on the breast of Jesus." Especially he hopes and prays to be supported in those tender, those protecting arms, when he must pass through the dark valley of the shadow of death; then it will be sweet to feel that "the eternal God is thy Refuge, and underneath are the everlasting arms" (Deut. xxxiii. 27). "Blessed are the dead that die in the Lord," in his presence, in his embrace. But if we would have the holy comfort of that dear embrace in our dying hour, we must try to live "in the Lord" now, to walk with him all our days, to cling to him with the embrace of faith. The Hebrew verb "embrace" is that from which the name of the Prophet Habakkuk, the prophet of faith, is derived. He longed for the Lord's coming; he ever watched to see what the Lord would say to him; he had learned to rejoice in the Lord in the midst of great distress; he taught us the holy lesson which St. Paul so earnestly presses upon us, "The just shall live by his faith." Such holy souls, being justified by faith, shall have peace with God through Jesus Christ our Lord. 5. *The bride's charge to the chorus.* There is an error in the old version of this thrice-repeated charge (ch. ii. 7; iii. 5; viii. 4). The bride is not cautioning the chorus not to awake her love, the bridegroom; she is adjuring (the literal translation) them not to awaken love, that is, the emotion, the affection, of love till it please, till it rise spontaneously in the heart. Hence the adjuration by the gazelles and the hinds of the field. They are gentle, timid creatures. Such is love true and pure; it is retiring; it shrinks away from observation; it is a sacred thing, between the lover and the beloved. The bride longs for the bridegroom's love, but the daughters of Jerusalem must not try to excite it; it is more delicate, more maidenly, to wait till love pleases to stir itself, till it springs up spontaneously in the heart of the beloved. The relations of the soul with Christ are very sacred; they may be mentioned only to the like-minded, and even that with a certain awe and reserve. And there are communings of the heart with the heavenly Bridegroom which may be divulged to none, not even to the nearest and dearest. And we must wait in patience for the Bridegroom. If for a time we cannot see him, or discern the tokens of his love, we must wait for his good time. "The vision is yet for an appointed time," wrote the prophet of faith; "at the end . . . it will surely come, it will not tarry" (Hab. ii. 3). God's people must not be impatient; they must trust; they must believe that "he who hath begun a good work in them will perform it until the day of Jesus Christ" (Phil. i. 6); that he will at last "fulfil all the good pleasure of his goodness, and the work of faith with power" (2 Thess. i. 11).

Vers. 8—17.—*The visit of the beloved.* I. THE BRIDE'S NARRATIVE. 1. *The description of his first coming.* The bride seems to be relating to the chorus the circumstances of her first meeting with the bridegroom. The King of Israel sought her in her humble home among the mountains of Lebanon; there he wooed and won her to be his bride. So the heavenly Bridegroom, the true Solomon who built the spiritual temple of living stones, came from his glory-throne to seek his bride, the Church; so he cometh now to seek and to save that which was lost. The bride hears the voice of the beloved; "*my* beloved," she says. In that little pronoun lies a great meaning. If we can only say in sincerity "*my* Saviour," "*my* Lord and *my* God," "*my* King," "*my* Beloved," then we can realize more or less the language of this holy Song of Songs, and see the spiritual meaning which underlies its touching parable of love; then we shall often look back with wondering gratitude and tender joy to the days of our first conversion, when we first heard the Saviour's voice calling us to himself; when we first felt that "he loved *me*, and gave himself for *me*;" when we first tried to give him that poor love of ours, which in his blessed condescension he sought in return for his own exceeding great love. The beloved is seen bounding over the mountains; he is like a gazelle or a young hart, fair to look upon and graceful, fleet of foot; he stands by the clay-built wall of the humble cottage; he looks in at the windows. So the Lord came to this poor earth of ours to seek the Church, his bride; he despised not the stable or the manger. So now he seeketh his chosen often in the lowliest homes; he looks for them shining (such is one possible interpretation of the word) through the lattice, bringing brightness into the poorest abode; the true Light "lighteth every man" (John i. 9). 2. *The call.* Those first words of love are treasured up in the memory of the bride; she remembers every tone of the bridegroom's voice, the place, the time, all the surroundings. The Hebrew word is that which the Lord used when he called the little daughter of Jairus from the sleep of death: "Talitha, cumi." So now he calls his chosen one by one: "Rise up." They that have ears to hear listen to the gracious voice, and, like Matthew the publican, rise and follow Christ. The soul must sleep no longer when that call is heard; it is high time to awake out of sleep, for now is our salvation near at hand. When he bids us rise, we must be up and doing; we must ask, "Lord, what wouldest thou have me to do?" we must follow whither he is leading, and give him the love which in his love he desireth. His call is sweet, exceedingly full of gracious love: "My love, my fair one." "My love," perhaps better, "my friend" (see ch. i. 9). The Lord would have his Church "a glorious Church, not having spot, or wrinkle, or any such thing." The Church, alas! is not without spot; it is stained with many sins; it numbers many evil men within its fold. But the Lord said of the twelve, the first germ of the Church, "Ye are the light of the world," "Ye are the salt of the earth," though there was a Judas among them; and so now his great love for the Church makes the Church with all her faults fair in the Bridegroom's eyes. Whatever beauty of holiness she possesses comes only from his beauty, who in his love has chosen her, and brought her near to himself, making her shine with the reflection of his light, who is the true Light. But the call comes, not only to the Church in the aggregate, but in God's good time to each elect soul. The Lord knows his own; he calls them by their name. "Jesus said unto her, Mary." And they who answer, "Rabboni, my Master," are fair in the Bridegroom's sight. Each awakened soul, as it rises and comes to Christ, and sees something of his heavenly beauty, and of its own deformity and unworthiness, is filled with thankful wonder. There are, alas! so many stains of sin, and yet he says, "My fair one;" so much weakness and unbelief and selfishness, and yet, "My fair one;" so much ingratitude and hardness of heart, and yet, "My fair one." It is the Saviour's great love which makes our sinful souls fair in his sight. If there is any answering love in our hearts; if we rise when he bids us and come to him; if we can say in any sincerity, though, alas! it must be with trembling and a deep sense of sin, "Lord, thou knowest all things; thou knowest that I love thee;"—then the soul that gives its love to Christ, though feebly and imperfectly, is fair in the sight of the Bridegroom. For it is our love that he seeketh. Love covereth a multitude of sins: "Her sins, which are many, are forgiven; for she loved much." The soul that hears the Bridegroom's call must rise and come away; it must give the whole heart to Christ, and come away from other masters, saying, "Rabboni, my Master," and giving itself wholly to the one Master's love; it must come away daily from every little thing which tends to impede its communion with the Lord, or to deaden its sense of his love and presence; it must part with lower ambitions, lower desires, if it is to win the pearl of great price, the hidden treasure. So we are told in Ps. xlv., which is so like the Song of Songs, "Hearken, O daughter, and consider: incline thine ear; forget also thine own people, and thy father's house; so shall the King have pleasure in thy beauty." The soul comes; for the Lord's call is very sacred, and touches the heart with thrilling power. The soul comes; for the joys to which he invites us are beyond all comparison more blessed and holy than all besides. The winter is past when the Lord's voice is heard—the winter of coldness and indifference and unbelief; the spring of hope and holy joy begins; the heart singeth unto the Lord, making in itself a melody which is the foretaste of the new song which only the redeemed of the Lord can learn; the voice of the holy Dove is heard in the heart, which then becomes "our land"—the kingdom of God.

> "And his that gentle voice we hear,
>   Soft as the breath of even,
> That checks each fault, that calms each fear,
>   And speaks of heaven."

When the Holy Spirit dwelleth in the heart, the fig tree is no longer barren, the Lord's vineyard no longer bringeth forth wild grapes; there is promise of the fruits of the Spirit in ever fuller abundance. Again the Bridegroom calls in the earnestness of his blessed love, " Arise, my love, my fair one, and come away." It may be that in that second call we may discern an anticipation of the midnight cry, " Behold, the Bridegroom cometh; go ye forth to meet him." Then he will call his chosen into that blessed Paradise, the true garden of the Lord, into which he led one forgiving soul on the day of his own most precious death. Then the winter will be past indeed; the eternal spring will begin to shine; angel-voices will welcome the redeemed into that blessed rest which remaineth for the people of God. They that are ready shall enter in; and they will be ready who have listened to the first call of the heavenly Bridegroom, who have arisen in answer to his bidding and come to him, giving him their heart's best affections, and forsaking for his dear love's sake earthly desires and earthly ambitions.

II. THE BRIDEGROOM AND THE BRIDE. 1. *The voice of the bridegroom.* He has climbed the steep rock by the ladder-like path, he has found the secluded cottage; he calls the bride his dove; he desires to see her and to hear her voice. The King of Israel climbed the rocks of Lebanon in search of the maiden whom he loved. The heavenly Bridegroom climbed the steep ascent of the awful cross that he might draw to himself the love of the Church, his bride (John xii. 32). The bridegroom had already compared the eyes of the bride to doves (ch. i. 15); now he says, " O my dove." It tells us how dear the Christian soul is to the Lord; it tells us what that soul ought to be—" harmless as doves." The rock-dove lives in clefts of the rocks. The soul which the Lord in his holy love condescends to call his dove, must dwell in the clefts of that true Rock which is Christ. The Rock of ages was cleft for us; the Christian soul must hide itself therein; there only are we safe. The dove is in the secret place, which can be reached only by climbing up the precipitous path. There is a steep ascent to be climbed before we can be hidden in the clefts of the Rock, before we can live that hidden life which is hid with Christ in God, before we can be safe, hidden in the wounded side of our dear Lord. That ascent is the path of self-denial, leading ever upward, ever closer to him who trod the way of the cross for our salvation. That life is hidden. " In the secret of his tabernacle shall he hide me; he shall set me up upon a rock " (Ps. xxvii. 5). The saint-like character is like the dove, retiring, shrinking from observation; some of God's holiest saints live silent, humble lives, in lowly circumstances, unseen of men. But our Father which seeth in secret knows their prayers, their charity, their self-denials; he will reward them openly. The heavenly Bridegroom deigns to see a sweetness and a beauty in a lowly Christian life; such a life is comely in his eyes, for it hath the beauty of holiness—a beauty derived only from communion with him who is the eternal Beauty. The voice of hymn and psalm ascending from that lowly dwelling is sweet in the Saviour's ear. The loftiest melodies of choir and organ, if love and faith and reverence are absent, cannot reach to heaven; but the heart that is practising the new song in thankfulness and adoration maketh a melody which causeth joy in the presence of the angels of God. 2. *The song of the bride.* " Take us the foxes, the little foxes." Some scholars regard this as a fragment of a vintage-song. The bride sings it in order to intimate to the bridegroom, as she does more plainly in ver. 17, that the care of the vineyards (see ch. i. 6) must prevent her from joining him till the shadows lengthen in the evening. The foxes waste the vineyards, and the vines are in blossom; therefore the little foxes must be caught. The little sins as they sometimes seem to us, the small neglects, the prayer carelessly said, the worldly thought, the idle word,—these things spoil the vineyard of the Lord, which is the Christian soul; they check its blossoming, and so prevent the fruit from being formed. The believer must watch, for these things are enemies of his soul; they may seem to be like little foxes, small and of no strength, but they mar the beauty of the Christian character, and tend to check the promise of the fruit of the Spirit. Therefore they must be caught and destroyed by diligent watchfulness, by earnest persevering prayer. The little foxes do not, indeed, root up and devour the vineyard like the wild beasts of Ps. lxxx., but they check its fruitfulness. And the small transgressions, if they do no worse, at least prevent the Christian from attaining that saintliness to which we are called. The little foxes hide and skulk about; the small sins are apt to escape detection. Therefore there is need of constant watchfulness and of very careful and diligent self-examination. For we are " called to be saints " (1 Cor. i. 2; Rom. i. 7); we are bidden to follow after holiness, to aim at perfection, to walk in the light. The little hindrances must be overcome, the little shadows must be driven away. 3. *The happy union of love.* "My beloved is mine, and I am his: he feedeth his flock among the lilies." The favoured maiden, it may be, could not at the moment join her royal lover; but her heart was wholly his, and she knew that his love was fixed upon her. She describes him as a shepherd, but her words are figurative; he feedeth his flock, not in common pastures, but among the lilies of his garden, the garden of spices mentioned again in ch. vi. 2. She delights in dwelling on the union of their hearts; three times she repeats the happy words (ver. 16; ch. vi. 3; vii. 10). The Church is the Lord's. He loved her, and gave himself for her, and presenteth her to himself as his bride (Eph. v. 25, 27); and he is hers, her Bridegroom, her King, her Lord. The Christian soul is the Lord's. "Whether we live or whether we die, we are the Lord's" (Rom. xiv. 8). He gave himself to each one of us individually when he called us to be his own; we give ourselves to him at the moment of our first spiritual awakening; we renew the gift continually in the hour of prayer, in the holy communion: "We offer and present unto thee, O Lord, ourselves, our souls and bodies, to be a reasonable, holy, and lively sacrifice unto thee." "My Beloved is mine, and I am his"—to know that with the knowledge of personal experience is the highest of spiritual blessings. He gives himself first to us, and by that gift he enables us, cold and selfish as we are, to give ourselves to him. None can tell the blessedness of that inner spiritual union with the Lord save those happy souls to whom it is given; and they to whom he has manifested himself must very jealously keep their souls from any unfaithful leaning to other masters, that they may be wholly his, that no unfaithfulness may mar the pure clear truth of their heart's love for him who loved them even unto death, and deigns now to irradiate their hearts with his most sacred presence. He is their Lord, and he is their good Shepherd; he knoweth his own, and his own know him. Once he gave his life for the sheep; now he feeds them, and leads them on their way, till they come to the lilies of Paradise, the garden of the Lord. 4. *The adieus of the bride.* She has expressed her confidence in her lover's affection and her own devotion to him; but now, apparently, she repeats the intimation of ver. 15 in plainer words: her duties in the vineyard will occupy her time till the evening. She wishes her lover to continue his hunting excursion on the mountains of Bether, or, it may be, "of separation"—the mountains which for the time separate the lovers. She invites him to return when the day is cool, when the day breathes; that is, when the breeze comes in the evening, and the shadows lengthen and flee away (see Jer. vi. 4). The Christian must not neglect the ordinary commonplace duties of life; he must not allow himself, like the Thessalonians, to be so distracted with spiritual excitement as to be unable to attend to the pursuits of his calling. The bride tends the vineyards which have been committed to her charge; the Christian must do with his might whatever his hand findeth to do. He must not neglect his duties even for the sake of giving all his time to religious exercises. *Laborare est orare.* If, whatever he does, he does all to the glory of God, Christ is his, and he is Christ's, as fully in the midst of daily work as in the hour of prayer. Daniel, who kneeled upon his knees, and prayed and gave thanks three times a day, was faithful in all things to the king his master; no error or fault could be found in the administration of his arduous office. The bride will welcome her lover back in the cool of the evening, when she has finished her work; the Christian will take delight in his evening prayers when the tasks of the day have been performed.

HOMILIES BY VARIOUS AUTHORS.

Ver. 1.—*The rose and the lily.* We have suggested here the self-consciousness of the renewed soul as to its true character and condition. It is the maiden who speaks, not her beloved, who in the next verse lovingly responds to what she says of herself. She likens herself—

I. To THE ROSE OF SHARON. That is, to a common field flower, not rare or distinguished, but of the lowliest if also of the loveliest kind. 1. *It is the utterance of humility.* (Cf. Paul's word of himself as "less than the least of all saints.") Lowly thoughts of themselves are ever the characteristics of saints. It is not so strong an expression as the "I am black" of ch. i. 5, but it is of similar order (cf. on ch. i. 5)

2. *But not of false humility.* For though a lowly it is yet a lovely flower. The rose of Sharon was that "excellency of Sharon" which Isaiah couples with "the glory of Lebanon." Here, too, the resemblance between this and the "but comely" of ch. i. 5 is evident. And the saintly soul *is* lovely—in the sight of its Lord, in the sight of the Church, and in the sight of men. Of our Lord it is said that "the grace of God was upon him," and that he grew "in favour with God and man." And this is so with his people, for he makes them beautiful and precious in his sight. She who is here the type of such soul is called "the fairest among women." 3. *And the rose is also fragrant.* True, to it as to others the poet's lines apply—

> "Full many a flower is born to blush unseen,
> And waste its fragrance on the desert air."

But the saintly soul is what it is because it is its nature to be so, whether admired or not (cf. on ch. i. 12). And such souls are: 4. *The glory of the places where they are found.* The Plain of Sharon is remembered in the minds of men for this its "excellency"—the roses that grow there. The world would not say that the glory of a place was its saints. It would point to its popular heroes, and those whom it calls its great men. But by the side of such flowers Solomon in all his glory fades by comparison. How plainly the Divine estimate of men is seen in God's choice of Israel—a small, insignificant people, contemptible in the eyes of the great empires of ancient and modern days! But because in them, as in none other, the saints of the Lord were found, therefore on them and on their land the eyes of the Lord rested night and day. According to our character, according as we are governed by the faith, the fear, and the love of God, are we a blessing and an honour to our land and age. And they: 5. *Delight in the sunshine of his love.* The rose is the child of the sun. Its bright rays must rest upon it or its radiant beauty will not be revealed. And we are to "walk in the light," and to be "children of the light."

II. THE LILY OF THE VALLEYS. This is another emblem of the saintly soul. 1. *Of their character.* Purity, sweetness, power of self-multiplication. What numbers of them there are! Bushnell speaks in his 'Christian Nurture' of "the out-propagating power of the Christian stock," by which he means the power given to Christian faith to reproduce itself beyond the like power possessed by that which is unchristian. And it has been so. How soon was the whole Roman empire converted to Christianity! It is the truth taught in the parable of the mustard seed (Matt. xiii.). And it will be so yet more. "The earth shall be filled with the knowledge of the Lord." 2. *Their home is in the "valleys."* (1) The lowly places. They "mind not high things." They "learn of" him who said, "I am meek and lowly in heart;" and, "When thou art bidden to a feast, take the lowest place." It is in such valleys that some of Christ's fairest flowers are found. Amongst the poor. The afflicted. The persecuted. (2) Where, though exposed to much peril, they are yet preserved. How wonderful has been the preservation of the Church when we think of the perils it has had to encounter! As sheep amongst wolves Christ sent them. But yet the sheep outnumber the wolves, and have long done so. The lilies liable to be plucked by any passer-by, trampled on or devoured by any beast, yet they live on, and each spring sees the valleys covered with them again. 3. *They are found where the living streams abound.* The well-watered valleys are the lilies' natural home. And so with the saintly soul. It lives by that river the streams whereof make its home glad. So, then, here is another portraiture of such a soul. Do we behold *our* face in this glass?—S. C.

Ver. 2.—*The Lord's response to the lily.* "As the lily among thorns."

I. HE DOES SET HIS LILIES AMID SUCH SURROUNDINGS. By the thorns we may understand: 1. *The world of the ungodly.* "Among them that are set on fire, even the sons of men, whose teeth are spears and arrows, and their tongue a sharp sword" (Ps. lvii. 4). "The saint must expect to find himself, while in this world, among uncongenial and hostile spirits." 2. *Trials and temptations.* (Cf. Paul's "thorn in the flesh.") 3. *Hindrances to our growth and peril to our life.* "The thorns sprang up and choked them" (Matt. xiii.). 'Tis a wonder, when we think of it, how any of these lilies live at all. 4. *All others than they who are the Lord's.* The speaker in text compares all other daughters with her, and classes them all with the thorns as compared with her. If whatsoever be not of faith be sin, then, whatsoever it be, it comes under this ill-sounding name of "thorns." Such are the surroundings of the saintly soul.

II. NEVERTHELESS, THEY GROW THERE. As a fact, they do and increase. And the reason is that given to Paul when he "besought the Lord thrice" concerning his thorn : "My grace is sufficient for thee: . . . my strength is made perfect in weakness." There is no other account to be given of the matter. It is all a marvel but for that.

III. AND IT IS IN HIS GRACE AND WISDOM THAT THEY ARE WHERE THEY ARE. How many wise and holy ends are secured by it! 1. *God's grace is magnified in and by them.* It is easy to grow amid favourable surroundings, where much helps and but little hinders. Growth there is not remarkable. To be Christ's servants where such service is general, and even popular, is no hardship. But if amid thorns, amid all that hinders, all that makes it difficult to serve Christ, if there we serve him, then is his grace magnified. 2. *The world is kept from being hell.* From being all thorns, dry, barren, hurtful, fit only for the fire. What would this world be if God's saints were taken out of it? Life would, indeed, then be not worth living. It would be better had men never been born. 3. *The thorns may be led to become lilies.* Of course, this is impossible in the natural world, but, thank God, not in the spiritual. And such transformation often occurs, and that it may, God places his lilies where they are. "As the Father hath sent me, so send I you," he said to his disciples. But the Father sent the Son to save the world. This, therefore, in their measure is the mission of his people, and hence they must be where they are.

IV. BUT IT WILL NOT BE SO ALWAYS. The lilies shall be transplanted that they may bloom for ever in the Paradise of God. And the thorns!—what is fit for such will be done. Therefore if we be of the blessed number whom the lilies of the valleys represent, let us not murmur, but remember what our mission is, and seek to fulfil it. And let each one of us ask—Which am I, lily or thorn?—S. C.

Ver. 3.—"*His shadow.*" St. Bernard takes this as telling of the Passion of Christ, and especially of the time when, as he hung on the cross, there was "darkness over all the land." Now, it does not mean this, but rather, as the whole context of the verse tells, of the cool shelter from the sun's fierce heat and glare which the speaker enjoyed beneath the o'erarching of the boughs of the tree under which she had seated herself. Hence it tells of "the shadow of the Almighty," of which Ps. xci. so fully speaks. Therefore let us take this—

I. ITS TRUE MEANING. "Man is born to trouble;" he needs shelter continually. The sun smites him by day; the fierce heat of life's cares and distresses often make him faint and weary. Now: 1. *There are other shelters which men often choose.* The world offers many. (1) Its riches. Men think, if they can only get these, they will be protected from all harm, both they and theirs. Hence men struggle after them incessantly. (2) Its friends. If we can gather round us a sufficient number of these, and of the right kind, we sit down under that shadow with great delight. (3) Its pleasures also. Men plunge into them as into some leafy covert, where they can hide themselves from the darts of all kinds of pursuing pains. But are not all these what the prophet calls "walls daubed with untempered mortar;" or, as in another place another prophet speaks, "battlements" which are "not the Lord's"? 2. *But what harm they do us!* They are short-lived, and when our sorest need comes these Jonah-gourds have all withered. And at the best they are but imperfect. They can for a while affect our circumstances, but the soul, the true seat of all trouble, they cannot better, but only make worse. For they do us this wrong also—they come between us and man's only true Shelter, "the shadow of the Almighty." They hinder our seeing and our seeking it, and then, sooner or later, do assuredly fail us themselves. Under the image of "cisterns, broken cisterns, which can hold no water," and for the sake of which men in their folly forsake the fountain of living waters, Jeremiah mourns the same infatuation. 3. *But the Lord is alone man's true Defence.* The failure of others, the unvaried protection that this affords, is proof incontestable. This blessed shadow, whilst Israel rested in it, sheltered them from all evil; and it does so still for every one that "dwelleth in the secret place of the Most High"—every one, that is, who abides in the trust of him of whom the secret place told. That secret place was the inner chamber in the tabernacle which was known as the most holy place, and which was emphatically secret, for it was never entered but once a year, and then by the high priest alone. But it told of man's need of God's grace, and of that grace provided for him. To trust, then, in that God was, and is, to dwell "under the shadow of the Almighty." May that happy lot be ours!

II. THE MEANING IT HAS SUGGESTED. The shadow of the cross, the shadow into which our Lord entered during his Passion especially. 1. *It was his shadow.* See the agony in the garden; hear the cry from the cross, "My God, my God, why hast," etc. ? Read Ps. xxii., which tells of those dread hours. We read, once and again, in the Gospels of his being troubled, of his sighing, of his tears. Anticipating his death, he said, "Now is my soul troubled." Yes, what wonder that he feared as he entered that dark shadow! 2. *But we may sit under it* "*with great delight*," and its fruit is sweet to our taste. (1) For that shadow has flown away. The cross is taken down. In its special form the Passion is past. Now, "on his head" is not the crown of thorns, but the "many crowns" of his people's love. With great delight do they think of this. (2) And dark as that shadow was, it was the background on which shone out resplendently the love of the heart of God. Man had never really seen that love but for that shadow. (3) And because of all that has come forth from that shadow. Who can reckon up in order or number the sweet fruits of that tree on which the Saviour hung? Have they not been, are they not, and will they not yet more be, blessed for man? What of redeeming force for all men was not set in motion by that act of redemption? Well, therefore, may even those who look not upon our Lord as we do, nevertheless sing, "In the cross of Christ I glory." 3. *But his shadow may, will, must, be ours.* For we also are to take up our cross and follow after him. We have to "know the fellowship of his sufferings, and to be made conformable to his death."

"All that into God's kingdom come
Must enter by this door."

In some this fellowship with his sufferings has been manifest to all in that which they have been called upon to endure. In others, outwardly, there may not have been much, if anything, to tell of such fellowship. But there is the spiritual cross, as real, as sharp, as heavy, as repellent to our nature, as the outward and visible one. And who may escape that? But: 4. *We may sit under such shadow with great delight.* (1) Men have done so (cf. "I glory in tribulations also"). And St. Paul again, throughout the Epistle to the Philippians, whose key-note is joy. Yet he was in prison and in peril of his life all the while. And his experience has been that of "a great multitude which no man can number, out of," etc. (2) Why is this? Because it has been *his* shadow. The reason of suffering is the measure of its power over us. Does the fond mother, watching night after night by the bed of her fever-stricken, darling child, think much or complain of her sufferings? Does she not glory in them if they can but help her child? And so if our shadow be his shadow, that which he has bidden us bear, then because it is his we shall "sit down under it with," etc. St. Paul sprang towards it, counted all things but loss that he might attain to the excellency of its knowledge; *so* he speaks of it with almost rapture, with certainly no complaint. He was one of those who "sat down under . . . to his taste." Then let it be our sole care to see that the shadows which draw over all lives, and which will darken ours sometimes, be *his* shadow, and then all will be well.—S. C.

Vers. 5—7.—*Faint for love.* Keeping to the spiritual, not the historical, interpretation, these verses suggest what is common to all, but confessed here only by the saintly soul.

I. CHRIST SHARES IT. He said when on the cross, "I thirst," and that told not alone of his physical thirst, but of that sacred, insatiable, and still unsatisfied thirst for the love of human hearts. He could say, "I am faint for love." And yet he yearns for that love, though much he already possesses, and will more and more. The Passion was but as a picture thrown upon a sheet to make clear and conspicuous to all what else they had not seen. So the sufferings of Christ serve to show not what was once, but what eternally is, in the heart of Christ—this yearning for man's love. The Holy Spirit, the unseen and spiritual Christ, is yet on earth amongst men; and yet, as he pleads with them, is grieved and done despite to, as he was in the days of his flesh. His thirst is not yet satisfied; all the loving invitations of the gospel prove this. It is our joy to believe that the day will dawn when, though now, as ever in the past, faint for man's love, he will "see of the travail of his soul, and be satisfied." Be it ours to hasten that day!

II. THE WORLD ALSO, BUT KNOWS NOT WHAT IT NEEDS. The love of Christ is what the world wants, though it wanders wearily off, as it has done from the beginning, after what it foolishly deems will satisfy its need. All the unrest, the agitation, the seething discontent, the wild rush after this scheme and that, which promise its betterment,—all show how great its need, and how yet that need remains unmet. If the Church of Christ on earth were but what its name professes, soon would the weary world see where all its wants would find supply, and turn to him for whose love it is that it faints, and is so wretched and woebegone. It needs that love to be the animating principle of Christian people, in their conversation, conduct, habits, business, and ways; which assuredly it is far enough from being at present, else why is society as it is? why are there "submerged tenths" and "darkest Englands," as we know there are? Is this the outcome of a *Christian* civilization? No; only the natural product of a civilization which is everything but Christian. And yet more, the world needs Christ's love in themselves. For lack of that it is as it is.

III. BUT SPECIALLY THE CHRISTIAN SOUL. And the confession of faintness for his love may be true: 1. *In a sad sense.* If such soul be faint, as many are, incapable of real service, weakly, ineffectual, and impoverished, is not the true and sad cause revealed in this confession? As plants cannot grow without the light and warmth of the sun, so Christian souls cannot prosper that do not come into and "continue in" Christ's love. But the confession as made here is not in a sad sense, but: 2. *In a very blessed one.* It is the very presence of his love in the soul that leads to the longing for deeper enjoyment of it. "My soul breaketh for the longing that it hath after thy commandments at all times;" "My soul longeth, yea, even fainteth, for the courts of the Lord;" and Ps. lxiii. 1, are all similar expressions. Great saints have all of them known this holy longing, this going out of the soul after God in great vehemency of desire; and blessed, blessed indeed, are they. My soul, be thou of their number! And such revelations of the Lord's grace often affect the body as well as the soul, causing faintness and overwhelming emotion (cf. Dan. x. 8—19; Judg. vi. 22; Rev. i. 12—18; 2 Cor. xii. 7, in illustration of this). 3. But in such faintness *the soul craves support.* This is suggested by the request made (ver. 5), "Stay me with cordials, comfort me with citrons." These were the refreshments she had enjoyed when "under his shadow," and when she ate of the "fruit sweet to her taste" (ver. 3). Translated into their spiritual meaning, they tell of those precious truths and teachings which come from and cluster round the cross of Christ. The soul would drink again of such "cup of salvation," and eat of the fruit of such "tree of life." It was the power of those truths, brought home by the Holy Spirit, that heretofore had quickened and sustained the soul, and hence they are desired again. And they seem to have been partaken of (cf. Ps. cxxxviii. 3; Prov. xxxi. 6), and the soul to have been thereby brought again to the rich enjoyment of the Divine love. And: 4. *It finds what it has so earnestly desired.* (Ver. 6.)

> "As in the embraces of my God,
> Or on my Saviour's breast."

This sacred enfolding of the soul in the love of God is the meaning of the verse, or, at least, the designed teaching. Think what must have been the joy of the penitent prodigal when, after his weary journey, he found thrown around him, in loving welcome, the arms of his father, against whom he had so sinned; and on his brow the father's kiss. That rapture of the soul when it is filled with the sense of the Divine love,—these are the embraces of God and the fulfilment of the well-known words, "He fell on his neck, and kissed him." That part of the parable which tells of the prodigal's yearning for home, the weary journey, and then the welcome, may be taken as the gospel commentary on these verses. And the soul shall be enfolded in this Divine love; it shall not be faint for it, and ever continue so. For the next verse tells: 5. How *the soul is anxious not to be disturbed* in its blessed condition until the Lord will. The maiden of the song is represented as addressing a passionate adjuration to her companions, "by the roes and hinds"—that is, by all beautiful, loving, timid, and easily startled things, as these were—that they should not awaken her beloved from his repose until he will. And so the soul that rests in the realization of God's love would linger therein.

"My willing soul would stay
In such a frame as this."

And this side of heaven there is no such joy to be realized as this. Alas! how rare it is, or rather, how rarely we find it, though we might if we would! Still, the soul knows that its life is not to be all enjoyment. Service has to be rendered. The disciples would have liked to stay on the Mount of Transfiguration; they said, "It is good to be here;" but the poor lunatic lad down below needed healing, and therefore neither their Lord nor they might linger where they were. Hence, though the soul would rest always in the joy of his realized love, yet it may, probably will, as with Paul, be sent forth to stern duty and patient toil. Therefore it is added, "until he please."

"O Love Divine, how sweet thou art!
When shall I find my willing heart
All taken up by thee?"

S. C.

Vers. 8—17.—*The soul wooed and won.* In this lovely pastoral the literal meaning is, we think, as stated in introduction to homily on ver. 15. But it may be taken as setting forth how Christ woos and wins the souls he loves. The various stages are shown.

I. THE SOUL HEARS HIS VOICE. "The voice of my Beloved" (ver. 8). It is as said in John x., "My sheep hear my voice." *They hear it* in the loving exhortations of those who would win them for Christ; in his Word; in the silent pleadings of his Spirit; in his providence. And *it is gladly heard.* The tone of this ver. 8 shows that she who hears is pleased to hear. There is the response of her heart; cf. "My sheep hear . . . and follow me;" "Speak, Lord; for thy servant heareth."

II. THEN THE SOUL SEES HIM COMING. "Behold, he cometh leaping upon," etc. Christ says to his Church, "Behold, I come quickly." There, as here, his coming is: 1. *Swiftly.* Conversions to Christ very rarely are sudden, but they often seem so (cf. those of penitent thief, Paul, Philippian gaoler). The conviction that Christ alone can save us, and that he will, is borne in upon our souls all in a moment, as it were; the truth rushes in upon us. 2. *No distance can keep him back.* The soul has been distant enough from him; "over the hills, and far away." How we have kept aloof from him! What space we have put between him and ourselves! Gone, maybe, into some "far country." 3. *Difficulties do not daunt him.* Mountains and hills—he leapeth upon them. What impossibilities have sometimes seemed to stand in the way of a soul's salvation! Take the instances above named. What human probability was there that they should be won for Christ? But he makes nothing of them; they cannot hinder him. "Who art thou, O great mountain? before Zerubbabel," etc. (Zech. iv. 7). 4. *Very near.* "He standeth behind our wall." Just outside (cf. "Behold, I stand at the door, and knock"). Often the soul when sought by the Saviour is conscious of his nearness, and that he is seeking her. Sometimes when we are alone and in serious thought; sometimes in sacred services, when his Word has been preached with power.

III. KNOWS THAT HE IS SEARCHING FOR HER. "He looketh in at the windows" (ver. 9). He will find her if she is to be found, and so his eyes search for her. This, too, the soul often knows. "Thou God seest me" (cf. Ps. cxxxix. 1—12, "O Lord, thou hast searched me," etc.). Our hearts' inmost secrets, unknown to our nearest and dearest earthly friend, are known to him; for all our hearts have windows through which his eyes often keenly glance. Conscience shows us those "eyes of the Lord which are in every place." (For illustration of this loving search, cf. parables in Luke xv.)

IV. IS AFFECTIONATELY ENTREATED BY HIM. He: 1. *Addresses her as his much-*

loved one. "My fair one." Such name of endearment tells the truth as to what our souls are to him. So also "my dove" (ver. 16). We should not call them fair—no, indeed! But love invests all it loves with beauty. What mother does not think her child lovelier than everybody else's? Other people do not see it; she does. And so Christ sees in our souls what we certainly cannot see. 2. *Bids her "rise up and come away."* (Cf. "He arose and came to his father.") How many would be saved willingly if only they could stay where they are—in self-indulgence, in gainful trade, in worldly conformity, in allowed sin! But it may not be. The soul *must* "rise up," etc. We must leave our sins behind us when we come to Christ. 3. *He encourages her* by telling of the pleasure he desires for her. He would have her go forth with him in delightful walk amid the flowers and fragrance, the sunshine and song, of a lovely spring morning. No more exquisite description of such a morning was ever penned. And so the Divine wisdom moves us, saying, "Her ways are ways of pleasantness," etc. And we are taught that the course of the soul should be as a going forth amid the loveliness of such a morning in spring. It is not through a vale of tears, but amid what is here told of. Joy should be a chief element in the soul's life in Christ. 4. *He bids her cast away her fear.* (Cf. as to her fearfulness, on ver. 15.) Young souls are often fearful—of themselves, of the world, of the cross. Christ would dispel such fears. 5. *He asks for response.* He would hear her voice. The voice of the soul in prayer, in praise, in self-surrender,—that is the voice Christ loves to hear.

V. IS FINALLY AND FULLY WON. (Cf. ver. 16.) See how gladly: 1. She *confesses him,* openly avowing that he is the Beloved of her heart, and that she is altogether his (cf. "She fell down before him, and told him all the truth"). Confession is the law of love. 2. *She declares that he dwells in her heart.* Those pure graces, the lilies of his creating, are those amongst which he takes delight. Christ dwells in our hearts through faith. 3. *She desires that whilst her life lasts he may come to her as he has done.* (Ver. 17.) So long as the night of life lasts, and until the eternal dawn breaks, will she welcome his presence and rejoice in his coming.

CONCLUSION. Christ does so woo our souls, especially those who, as the one told of here, are young. May he win them as he won this!—S. C.

Vers. 11, 12.—*Spring.* According to St. Paul, God's natural world was intended to be—might, would, and should have been, but for man's sin—the Bible for the great part of mankind. "Nevertheless," said he to the men of Lycaonia, "God left not himself without witness, in that he did good, and gave us rain from heaven, and fruitful seasons, filling our hearts with food and gladness." And again (Rom. i.), he declares that "the invisible things of God from the creation of the world are clearly seen, being understood by the things that are made, even his eternal power and Godhead." Not the Bible alone, then, but nature also, was intended to reveal God, and men ought, as we are assured, to have seen God in the things that he made. But instead of being a revelation of God, it has been perverted into an impenetrable screen to hide and to conceal him; or, still worse, to distort, misrepresent, and dishonour him. So that, left to nature only, men have sunk lower and lower, as all experience proves. This is true of mankind generally. *But it is not universally true.* Long ere the written Scriptures were given, and in parts of the world where they never came, there have been those who by Divine illumination have learnt much of God through the works of God. Doubtless many of those of whom St. Paul speaks as having by nature done the things of the Law, though they never had the Law, these learnt from the great Bible of nature—that page having been, even as the written page must ever be, opened up to them by the teaching of the Spirit of God. Hence was it that their consciences became so enlightened as to approve or condemn according as they did good or evil. But if it was expected of them who had not, as we have, the written Word, but only nature to teach them, that they should understand God and his ways, how much more will be expected, and justly expected, of us! There are many who rejoice in the natural world as a revelation of God. What a proof we have of this in that glorious Ps. civ.! There the devout writer goes over the whole of God's creation, animate and inanimate; that which has, and that which has not, the gift of reason. And he ends his devout meditation saying, "Bless thou the Lord, O my soul. Praise ye the Lord." Here, then, is a worthy model for us to follow in contemplating the works of God. Let us try to imitate so good an example. Our text is a short but beautiful description of an Eastern spring. In that land of the sun it is true, as it is not always here, that in the spring-time "the winter is past, the rain is over and gone . . . heard in the land." But let us listen to some few out of the many holy and helpful lessons which this season of the year is ready to teach us, if only our hearts be open to receive them. These teachings of the spring, then, what are they? Well, one of them is surely this—

I. "REST IN THE LORD, AND WAIT PATIENTLY FOR HIM." Try to imagine, if you can, what your thoughts would have been during the dark winter-time, supposing you had no idea of spring. It is difficult for us even to conceive that we could ever have not known that winter gives way to spring, and that the seasons follow in their orderly round. But suppose one waking up to consciousness for the first time at the beginning of winter. He would have seen the days getting shorter and shorter, the cold becoming more intense, every leaf stripped from well-nigh all trees, and their unclothed, skeleton-like branches quivering and moaning in the wintry wind. He would see the bare, brown fields stiffen and become rigid under the icy blast and the imprisoning frost; and from time to time the whole land would put on its white shroud of snow as if it were indeed dead. He would see all this and the many other familiar features of winter; and had he never known or heard of spring, would he ever think that such a season would come—that all the present dreariness would give way to brightness, the sad silence to the joyful song of birds, and the gloomy grey tints of winter to the brightness of the foliage, the blossoms, and the flowers of spring? I do not think he would. For this is how many of us feel and speak, notwithstanding perpetual reminders to the contrary, *when winter reigns in the heart.* Hearken to Jacob, "All these things are against me," etc.; Moses, praying God to kill him out of hand because he could not bear the people nor endure his wretchedness; Elijah, too, making the same request; and Job, and many more. Are they not all instances of that mournful tendency in our minds, to think that when like sad wintry times are upon us so they will always be? Surely, then, the teaching of the spring is that we should "rest in the Lord," etc.; for spring declares of him that he is *the gladness-giving God;* that though there be winter, yet it has to give way to the bright and joyful spring. In the natural world the "oil of joy is given for mourning, and the garment of praise for the spirit of heaviness." God does turn Nature's mourning into dancing; he puts off her sackcloth and girds her with gladness. "The winter is over and past," etc. Therefore may we not be well assured that so it will be with the winter of our hearts, the sadness and the silence there, if only we will "rest in the Lord," etc.? Let our prayer, then, be—

"Lord, let thy love,
Fresh from above,
Soft as the south wind blow,
Call forth its bloom.

"Now when thy voice
Makes earth rejoice,
And the hills laugh and sing,
Lord, teach this heart
To bear its part,
And join the praise of spring."

II. THE INFINITE TENDERNESS OF GOD. We go forth into the country, and we note all around us the first springings of that plant-life which when matured is to be of such vast value to us all. But how fragile everything looks! How little it would take to destroy the whole of it! A too-severe storm, an over-rough wind, a frost, any out of a thousand casualties, would destroy all. But yet God takes care of it. He will not suffer the too-violent storms to come, but only gentle showers; not the rough wind, but the milder gales. Thus with infinite tenderness he rears up the young plants.
1. Now, how all this *rebukes the hard thoughts of God* which many have held and taught and maintained, in books as innumerable as dreary. We wonder at the heathen, in view of the loveliness of nature, fashioning their gods so cruel and relentless as they did. But that we, with nature and the gospel, should so conceive of God is sad indeed. We little know the mischief such hard representations do, the alienation and the bitter-

ness towards God which they foster.   It is the source of the Madonna and saint worship of Rome, and of worse things still.   For men become as the gods they worship. 2. *It shows us how to deal wisely with all young life,* especially the beginnings of the Divine life in the soul: how to train our children.   3. *And it bids us trust God.*   Will God be so gracious to birds and blossoms and not tenderly care for us ?   Impossible.

III. " WITH HIM IS PLENTEOUS REDEMPTION."   Spring teaches that our God is the redeeming God.   For spring is the redemption of outward nature, its regeneration and resurrection.   She was dead, but is alive again; was lost, but is found.   Darkness has given place to light, barrenness to fruitfulness, and the " hills rejoice on every side."   The vision of Ezekiel is put before us as oft as the spring comes round.   " Can these dry bones live ?" said he.   " Can all this seeming deadness live ?" say we.   And the spring is our answer.   And we are told further of *our dependence upon God* for such redemption.   Who can bring about the renewed life of spring but God ? and who that yet higher life of the soul ?   And *how visible the life is!*   See all around the proofs of the presence of the spring.   Not less visible are the fruits of the spring-tide of the soul.   And *as the spring is promised, so is the better gift of redemption.*   Each blade, blossom, and bud seems to say to us, "Shall God redeem me, and will he not redeem thee ? "   *And the mystery of the cross* is shown.   For what is spring but life out of and through death ?   Redemption must imply a Redeemer, and the life of spring coming forth out of the death of winter patterns forth how the Christ must needs suffer and be raised again.   And for ourselves it tells of him who said for us, " I am the Resurrection and the Life," and bids us say, " I know that *my* Redeemer liveth."

IV. " PUT YE ON THE NEW MAN."   All Nature does this at spring-tide.   We in our dwellings and in our dress try to imitate her and do the like.   They who can, get new garments; they who cannot, try to make the old look new.   Let us learn the lesson in things higher still.   Is there not much room for it ?   In too many even Christian people the remains of what Paul calls " the old man " are too plentifully visible—in homes, in habits, in speech, in thought, in temper.   How much we need yet to be created anew in Christ Jesus, to " put on the new man " !   And he who maketh " all things new " is ready to help us herein if we will have his help.

V. BE DILIGENT.   Spring is a time of great activity.   The husbandman dare not waste those precious hours if he would rejoice when harvest comes.   So with this life of ours, all which is given us for preparation for the great harvest-time.   Then let the activities of the spring remind us that we, too, must be diligent if we would be found at the last faithful before the Lord.—S. C.

Ver. 15.—" *The little foxes.*"   This verse is part of the description which Shulamith, the betrothed, gives of her beloved.   In the verses preceding she relates (ver. 8, etc.) how he was wont to come to her home after her, bounding and leaping over the hills in his loving haste, like a young hart.   And how, when he had reached the house, he would " look in at the windows," and beg her to come forth to him.   And to entice her he would sing the beautiful song of the spring, " The winter is past, the rain is over and gone; the flowers appear on the earth, and the time of the singing of birds is come." And then, because she was still slow to come forth, she tells how he would call her again, and by the tender name of his timid " dove," that hides itself, because of its fear, in the clefts of the rocks, and amid the inaccessible crags and crevices of lofty cliffs; and then how he would ask her to sing to him her song of the foxes, " Take us the foxes, the little foxes . . . grapes."   Such seems to be the circumstantial setting of this verse ; but, like the whole poem of which it forms part, had it no more meaning than lies on the surface it would not, we believe, have found place amongst the sacred Scriptures, the Bible of the people of God.   If, then, the words suggest to devout minds, as they have done in all the centuries since they were written, truths which belong to the region of the soul, to our relationships with God more than to any relationship of earth, surely we may believe that they were designed so to do; and earthly as the story may be on which such truths are grafted, like the parables of our Lord, it has a heavenly meaning, and is designed to help us on our heavenward way.   Now, of some of these suggested truths let us speak.   One word as to the imagery of this verse.   " Foxes, jackals, little foxes, are very common in Palestine, and are particularly fond of grapes. They often burrow in holes in hedges round the gardens, and, unless strictly watched, would destroy whole vineyards. Their flesh was sometimes eaten in autumn, when they were grown fat with feeding on grapes. Thus Theocritus says—

> " ' I hate the foxes with their bushy tails,
>   Which numerous spoil the grapes of Mecon's vines
>   When fall the evening shades.'

And Aristophanes compares soldiers to foxes, because they consume the grapes of the countries through which they pass " (Burrows). But now as to the spiritual teachings which are contained in these words. We have brought before us here—

I. A SAD POSSIBILITY. Vines that promised well, spoiled. Translated into the language of the Spirit, they speak of blessed beginnings of the Divine life in the soul not realized. *Few things are more beautiful than the beginnings of the Divine life.* The promise and hope they give rise to of matured and rich and Christ-like character fill the devout-minded observer—especially if he himself has prayed and watched and toiled for such beginnings—with a deep and sacred joy. What does he not anticipate from them? What of influence on others, in the Church, the home, the business, the world generally? What of service for Christ and truth and all goodness? Hence when he sees that tenderness of conscience, that prayerfulness, that gentleness and humility, that alacrity in service, that delight in worship, all which mark these beginnings, how can he but be glad? or how can any one who has a Christ-like heart in him? *But few things are more sad than to see all this hopefulness and promise spoiled.* And such things do happen. " Ye did run well; who did hinder you?" so said St. Paul to the foolish Galatians who had so bitterly disappointed him. And how often in our Lord's ministry had he to bear this disappointment! Again and again there would come to him those about whom bright hope might have been cherished—amiable, well-disposed, warm-hearted, intelligent, pure-minded, generous, much esteemed, kindly, lovable, and beloved. Such people were irresistibly drawn to him, and for a while they would follow him; but then after a while we find something offending them, and they go away. Christ drew their portrait in his parable of the sower, where he likens such to the seed sown on the stony ground. Quick to spring up and present the appearance of vigorous life, but as quick to wither away when the sun's scorching heat smote them as it smote all else. And surely, in the spoiled vines told of in our text, we have another of these Bible portraitures of the same, or a similar class. And where there is not the actual destruction and perishing of what is good, *there is yet the spoiling.* The vines are not cut down, they are not hindered from bringing forth *any* fruit; the foe told of " spoils," which is less than to destroy. And how often we have to mourn this " spoiling of the vine"! Neither we nor others come up to that elevation of Christian character which might fairly have been expected. Many people are, in the main, worthy; there is very much that is excellent in them, but their characters are sadly marred. They are ineffectual; they do not tell for any real or large amount of good in any one, anywhere. Their type of life is low; they have the name and the form of godliness, but all too little of the power. They are respectable, decorous, outwardly religious, and live, as we say, consistently with their profession. But if you come to know them, how little of their real life is touched by their religion; what a mere veneer it is on their ordinary existence! How little it does for them in making them really holy or happy, or powerful for good! They began well, but they have sunk and settled down to this. He who looks that these people should bring forth their fruit in due season—plentiful fruit, much fruit, the best fruit—will assuredly be disappointed. " And what hinders them? Now, mark you, it is not said here, as in that mournful psalm, 'The wild boar out of the wood doth root it up, and the wild beasts of the field devour it.' It is not said here, 'It is burnt with fire and cut down, and they shall perish at the rebuke of thy countenance." It is not said here, 'Why hast thou then broken down her hedges, so that all they that go by pluck off her grapes?' No; it is the foxes, the little foxes, that spoil the tender grapes." Therefore let us now look at this—

II. ITS TOO MUCH NEGLECTED CAUSE. It is the little sins, the small faults, the slight self-indulgences, what we count as trifles and think nothing, or almost nothing, of—these are the little foxes which spoil the tender grapes. All sins waste and destroy the soul. Not merely the wage but the work of sin is death. Some there are so notorious that they are as St. Paul says, " open beforehand, going before to judgment."

They are as the wild boar out of the wood and the beasts of the field, told of in the psalm we quoted just now. High-handed, bold, Heaven-defying sins, bringing down on the doers of them, sooner or later, the dread judgments of God. But there are other masters of the soul, spoilers of the grapes of God,—those sins which here are pictured to us as "the little foxes." "*Little*," so we call them, and others call them so too ; and hence, though we be all wrong together in so calling them, we have come to think them little as well as call them so. And *fox-like,* which we often forget, for they skulk and lurk and hide; they have, as our Lord said, "their holes," and there they burrow and bury themselves out of sight. And many of them have other characteristics of the fox—deceit, cruelty, foulness; true vermin of the soul are they. And they all of them often feign death as the fox does. And we think them dead, and lo! they spring to life again, and are as active as ever. Hence we do indeed need to be on our guard against them. But it is the *littleness* of these sins to which our thoughts are chiefly turned by the vivid image of the little foxes. Their littleness, like charity, covers a multitude of them, and so conceals them from our own censure and that of others. And if the great adversary of our souls can persuade us not to mind these little sins, he has almost all he cares for. For then he knows that we shall never be what he most of all hates, that is, great saints. 1. For *such have ever shunned them* with holy care. It has often been pointed out how Daniel might have prayed to God notwithstanding the king's decree, and yet never have incurred the awful peril of the lions' den, if he would only have shut his window when he prayed. But he must needs open it, and so, of course, he was seen. But he would not compromise with what he deemed his duty to God even in so slight degree as this. And the martyrs, too. The Roman judges used perpetually to remind them how trifling was the concession asked for—just sprinkling a grain or two of incense on an altar, that was all. "Now, if men have been able to perceive so much of sin in little transgressions, that they would bear inconceivable tortures rather than commit them, must there not be something dreadful after all in these little sins ? " If we would have fellowship with the great saints of God, the eminent and true disciples of our Lord, we must give no quarter to these so-called trifling sins. They did not, or they would not have been what they were. 2. *And the little foxes grow into great ones.* Has not the indulgence in one glass of intoxicating liquor often led on to the liking for two, and that to the taking of three, and that has been followed by the man's becoming a drunkard and a sot ? " Tremblez, tyrans ; nous grandirons ! " was the shout of the young French lads who, drilled and dressed as soldiers, marched, in the days of the Revolution, through many a town and village in France. They bade the tyrants that oppressed their nation tremble, because they, though but little lads now, would one day be grown up into men. And might not our souls be well made to tremble as they contemplate one of these little sins ? for it, too, will grow up, and then will be no longer little, but great and strong. Scarcely more surely does the boy grow into the man than does a little sin tolerated grow into a great one. It is one of the ways of burglars, in effecting an entrance into a house, to attack a small window not nearly large enough to admit a man. But they bring a boy with them, and him they thrust through, and he then undoes larger windows or doors, and so the men enter too. Yes, my brother, if you are allowing yourself in what you are pleased to call a little sin, it may be but the boy getting in at the window who will let in the greater thieves as soon as he is safely in himself. Let us remember that. 3. *And how these little sins multiply themselves!* Great sins are rare. Tremendous transgressions we are guilty of but now and then—but once in our lifetime, it may be; or God's grace may always keep us "innocent from the great transgression; " we trust it will. But these little ones—they are like the myriad insects in our gardens. How they swarm! The more minute they are the more they multiply, until they devour everything if they be let alone. They never come singly, but in troops. And so is it with these little sins that are like them. A man will think it but a trifle if he utter a profane expression, he counts it a very small matter; but it soon comes to pass that he can hardly open his mouth anywhere or anywhen without some miserable profanity dropping from it. A little temper may come to mean an explosion half a dozen times a day, until it is said of the man that he is always in a temper. That great Zuyder Zee, on which Amsterdam is built, was once a fair fertile land covered with farms, villages, and hamlets; a strong embankment shut it off from the Northern Sea. But that embankment had, no doubt, somehow began to yield in very slight degree, when one stormy winter night the whole gave way, and now the once fruitful land is turned into barrenness, and has been so for centuries past. Oh, take heed of these small beginnings of sin. Yes, they "are like the letting out of water : first there is an ooze, then a drip, then a slender stream, then a vein of water, and then at last a flood, and a rampart is swept before it and the whole land is devoured." God help us, therefore, to be on our guard. And, indeed, if we will think of it, *they are not little.* There may be but a handful of men cross the frontier of a state, but that is as much an act of war as if an army had come. There are people who never cease to ridicule the idea that "death and all our woe" were the result of man's once eating the forbidden fruit. But there the fact is, all the same. It was the violation of the Divine Law, and it did not matter how it was done. And so with all those sins which we are pleased to call little. They are as much outrages on the Law of God as if they were acts so flagrant and enormous that all men should denounce them. Broken law is broken law, no matter whether the breach be great or small. Moreover, these sins which we call little *are often greater than those which we call great.* "If you have a friend and he does you a displeasure for the sake of ten thousand pounds, you say, ' Well, he had a very great temptation. It is true he has committed a great fault, but still he has wronged me to some purpose.' But should your friend vex and grieve your mind for the sake of a farthing, what would you think of that ? ' This is wanton,' you would say. ' This man has done it out of sheer malevolence towards me.'" And must not the same verdict be passed when, for the sake of one of these trifles, as we term them, we grieve the Spirit of God and outrage his holy Law ? And, remember, if you be a Christian, *these sins will ruin your peace with God.* You cannot be happy in him whilst you walk contrary to his will. And if you be not a Christian, these same sins will lessen the likelihood of your ever becoming one. They may be but as small stones, but they will build up a strong and high wall of separation between you and God, which will more and more effectually shut you off from him. Every way they are deplorable things. Therefore consider—

III. THE SURE REMEDY. These "little foxes" must be taken and destroyed. You must search them out by prayerful and diligent self-examination. You must drag them forth into the light of conscience and the judgment of God by full and penitent confession of them ; and by vigorous acts of a will inspired by the Spirit of God you must slay them before him. "These mine enemies which would not that I should rule over them, bring them hither and slay them before me." These are our Lord's words, and he who spoke them will, if you do really desire it, give you grace to obey them. May he help you so to do!—S. C.

Ver. 16.—*He mine; I his.* This verse is the oft-repeated and rapturous utterance of her who is the type of the redeemed soul concerning her beloved. Of course, we regard it as telling of the soul's joy in Christ.

I. HE MINE. Let us ask three questions. 1. *How?* (1) By his free gift of himself. "He loved me, and gave himself for me." (2) By believing appropriation. Faith has this marvellous power. (3) By joyful realization of his love to me. His love has been shed abroad in my heart by the Holy Spirit. "I *know* whom I have believed." How unspeakably blessed such realization is! But it is not universal nor even common. A little child will cry even in its mother's arms. But the arms are there all the same. And so is Christ's love. 2. *What for?* "He is mine to look upon, to lean upon, to dwell with ; mine to bear all my burdens, discharge all my debts; mine to answer all my accusers, mine to conquer all my foes ; mine to deliver me from hell, mine to prepare a place for me in heaven ; mine in absence, mine in presence, mine in life, mine in death, mine in the grave, mine in the judgment, and mine at the marriage of the Lamb" (Moody Stuart). 3. *What then?* (1) All that is his is mine. His righteousness, acceptableness, worthiness; his incarnation, atonement, resurrection, and intercession. (2) I ought to know it if I do not. It is all-important to me if he be mine. (3) I ought not to be so anxious about other things. (4) Let me take care not to lose him. It is possible (cf. ch. v. 6).

II. I HIS. We ask the same three questions. 1. *How?* (1) By creation. "It is he that hath made us" (Ps. c.). (2) By the purchase of his blood. (3) By the conquest of his Spirit. (4) By my own free choice. (5) By open avowal. 2. *What for?* To work and to witness, to suffer and to live, and if needs be to die, for him. To care for those for whom he cares, and to minister as he ministered. 3. *What then?* (1) All that is mine, a sad inheritance indeed, is his. My sin,'my guilt, my sorrow, my shame. And he has taken them on himself and away from me for ever. (2) Others should know it. I may not be a secret disciple. (3) He will be *sure* to take care of me, teach me, perfect me, and bring me to himself. (4) I will be 'his even when I cannot realize that he is mine. (5) I will try to win others to him.—S. C.

Ver. 2.—*Eminent piety seen in contrast.* Some similarities must exist, or the contrast could not be seen. The godly and the ungodly are both men, or we could not put their characters in contrast. Thorns are rooted in the same soil as the lily. They are nourished by the same sun, watered by the same rain, enjoy the same course of the seasons. But the inner life of the lily deals differently with the natural elements than does the inner life of thorns. So the ungodly live in the same land as the godly; they have the same access to God's truth; they dwell amid the same forth-puttings of the Spirit's power; yet, for want of self-appropriation, they are barren of good results. They are as noxious thorns compared with the lily. This eminent goodness of the lily implies—

I. LOWLINESS. In the previous verse, the king's bride had designated herself as a mere "lily of the valley." And now the king responds and says, "It is so; but others are as thorns compared with thee." Humility is the distinctive mark of all the godly. Native pride is crucified on the cross. The Christian longs to have a just estimate of himself. He will not "think of himself more highly than he ought to think." If he discovers any goodness in himself, he attributes it to the active grace of his Benefactor. He is content to take the lowest place in the kingdom. If only he may belong to the chosen race, he is ready to be a "hewer of wood and a drawer of water." Hence he sings—

> " The more thy glories strike my eyes
> The humbler I shall lie."

II. PURENESS. The white colour of the lily is a pure white. It has approved itself universally as the best emblem of innocence. All over the world it is a silent messenger from God. As every plant reaches out toward perfection, so the noblest yearning of the human soul is for purity. I may be learned and rich and renowned, but if I am lacking in purity, I despise myself; my heart refuses joy. I have fallen from my high estate. Other virtues in me are only leaves and blossoms; purity is the proper ripe fruit, which the owner longs to see. Yet, so full of grace is our Immanuel, that *he* sees, not only what is now actually in us, but what is coming—the perfect holiness which is slowly developing. As the whiteness of the lily is produced by its reflecting back again *all* the rays of light that fall upon it, and is whitest under the full blaze of the summer sun, so the Christian gains his purity by reflecting all the love and grace from the Sun of Righteousness.

III. FRAGRANCE. The lily of the valley is noted for its delicious odour. The subtle essence of the flower flows out in a perpetual stream of blessing. Its very life is expended in doing good. It cannot do much; it cannot bear clusters of juicy fruit; but what is possible for it to do, *that* it freely does. Is not this a portrait of a genuine disciple? Does he not count it his meat and his drink to spread blessing on every side? And can he prevent the sweet savour of his Master's grace flowing out day and night? However obscure and insignificant he may be, his piety will diffuse a heavenly fragrance, and men will feel his influence.

> " As some rare essence in a vase of clay
>   Pervades it with a sweetness not its own;
> So when thou dwellest in the human soul,
>   All heaven's own fragrance seems around it thrown."

IV. BEAUTY. The lily charms the eye no less than it pleases the nostril. The eye has a native instinct for beauty, and through the eye the soul is enchanted. "A thing of beauty is a joy for ever." And nothing in human character is half so beautiful as genuine piety. Heroism is beautiful, philanthropy is beautiful, parental love is beautiful; but the quality of godly love transcends them all. It has a sublimity which cannot be described. It has a potent influence which ennobles the whole man. It is immortal in its duration, and has a splendid sphere for growth. Well may we think of it as the amaranthine flower that blossoms in the Paradise of God. " Blessed are the pure in heart."

V. THIS EMINENCE IS REACHED THROUGH DIFFICULTY. This lily has grown up "among the thorns." They robbed it of the nutriment that dwelt in the soil. They hindered the free circulation of the balmy air. They shut out some of the quickening sunshine. Yet, in spite of hindrances, the lily grew and flourished. So it happens with the pious love of the Christian. It has to contend with hostile influences. Formidable opposition bars its growth. We have to resist the chilling influence of an ungodly world. Yet these very difficulties have their uses. Difficulties rouse our latent energy; difficulties put us on our mettle; difficulties give scope to heroic effort. No one of us is seen at our best until we are coping with gigantic opposition. As storms root the oak more firmly, so the opposition of the world blows up the fires of our piety into a white heat of sacred fervour. Thank God for the opposition of the world. Out of antagonism springs the noblest life.—D.

Ver. 3.—*The pre-eminence of Immanuel.* In Eastern lands, far more than in Western, men are dependent on ripe fruit to allay their hunger. A man may walk all day among the oaks of Bashan or among the cedars of Lebanon, and find no food. To discover an apple tree or a citron tree among the trees of the forest would come as a surprise—as a meal direct from Heaven. Equally true is it that men wander from teacher to teacher, from one religious system to another, in quest of saving knowledge, and find it nowhere, until they find Jesus, the Christ. In search of soul-rest and soul-purity, men try practical morality, asceticism, bodily mortification, Church sacraments; but they are doomed to disappointment. For Jesus, the Son of God, is the only Saviour, and, apart from him, the soul is starved, diseased, undone. " As the citron tree among the trees of the wood, so is my Beloved among the sons."

I. THE SUPERLATIVE EXCELLENCE OF JESUS CHRIST. 1. *Here is the idea of rareness.* The event was rare to find a citron tree among forest trees. So Jesus stands alone. As Adam stood alone, the head of a new order of life, the Head of the human race; so Jesus is without a parallel, the covenant Head of the new family. He is "the only begotten Son." By nature and by right, as well as by transcendent goodness, he is unapproachable. In him alone " dwells the fulness of the Godhead bodily." He is the God-Man: " God manifest in the flesh." " Let all the angels of God worship him." 2. *Here is implied delicious fragrance.* The blossom of the citron is not only beautiful to the eye; it is sweet and refreshing to the nostril. And it is a constant perfume. While ripe fruit is found on some branches, fresh blossoms are adorning others. Impressive emblem *this* of the rich fragrance of Immanuel's love. With the sweetness of his disposition nothing can compare. It spreads to-day from the frozen plains of Greenland to the sultry cities of Burmah. From the equator to the poles, the fragrance of the Saviour's love is diffused. It refreshes the fainting; it revives again those " who are ready to perish." Some kinds of apples are named " nonpareils." Jesus is the real " Nonpareil;" he has no equal. 3. *The figure suggests fruitfulness.* This is a theme that will loosen into eloquence every Christian tongue. Every part of Christ's nature is fruitful. The woman, afflicted with old disease in Canaan, found fruitful blessing even in the hem of his garment. He is fruitful as a Teacher, for his words dispel all the perplexities and fears of the human family; he is fruitful as a Healer, for his gracious virtue cures every disease of body and of soul; he is fruitful as our Priest, for his one sacrifice atones for every sin; he is fruitful as Intercessor, for his righteous pleadings always prevail; he is fruitful as a King, for his reign brings order, contentment, righteousness, peace; he is fruitful as a Friend, for all that he has he shares with his saints. For fruitfulness he is the Vine.

II. THE SUPERLATIVE USEFULNESS OF JESUS CHRIST. " I sat down under his shadow with great delight, and his fruit was sweet to my taste." Jesus is not simply excellence in his Person; his virtues are suited to the needs of men. 1. *There is shady rest.* The dwellers in the temperate zone can little appreciate what shade is to dwellers in the tropics. The fierce heat of noon means exhaustion, pain, fever. Rest in cool shade is like life from the dead. And the rest which Jesus gives is more precious yet. It is rest from the gloomy fear of hell; it is rest from the drudgery of sin; it is rest from slavish toil to work out a personal righteousness; it is rest from anxious, worldly care. 2. *This fruitfulness of Christ is life-giving.* All other trees in the wood are impotent to sustain life. This is the tree of health—the tree of life. This is the grand prerogative of our Immanuel: " I am the Resurrection and the Life ; " " I am come that ye may have life, and have it more abundantly; " " I give unto my sheep eternal life, and they shall never perish ; " " Because I live, ye shall live also." And Jesus has always acted up to his word. A myriad human souls in heaven to-day join in the testimony, " Once we were dead ; now, by Christ's grace, we live." " Thanks be unto God for his unspeakable Gift." 3. *Jesus Christ, as the citron tree, imparts joy.* " I sat down under his shadow with great delight." It is an unusual joy, an overflowing blessedness. The joy which Christ gives is real, pure, ennobling, abiding. He gives to men " his own joy." Do men rejoice when pain yields to medicine, and new health flows in ? Do men rejoice in the brightness of spring, or amid the plenty of autumn ? Do men rejoice on their marriage-morn, or when fortune crowns their toil with large success ? In Christ's smile all joys are rolled into one. He who has Christ has a pledge of heaven. This joy is a " joy unspeakable." 4. *Jesus Christ is eminently adapted to our needs.* As the ripe fruit of the citron tree was exquisitely suited to travellers in those hot climes, so Jesus is precisely suited to our necessities. You cannot mention a want of yours which Jesus is not competent to satisfy. He is Light for our darkness, Strength for our weakness, Food for our hunger, Rest for our weariness, Freedom for our bondage, Pardon for our guilt, Purity for our uncleanness, Hope for our despondency. As a well-made key fits a lock, so Jesus fits all my needs. I want no other Saviour. He " is all my salvation, and all my desire." Fitness is God's sign-manual.—D.

Ver. 4.—*Royal generosity.* The testimony of personal experience is specially valuable. We may argue from *à priori* data what generous love must reside in God, in order to harmonize with his perfection ; and such a line of reasoning has its value. Or we may argue from analogy, that since fervent love stirs in the human breast, purer love and mightier glows—an uncreated flame—in the heart of God ; and this form of argument leaves a comforting impression on the mind. But personal testimony has a tender force all its own. If God has dealt generously and graciously to one member of the human family, no more deserving than I am, it is evident that he will deal with equal generosity of love toward me. For he is impervious to change. If it brought him joy and renown to show practical love to fallen men centuries ago, it will contribute to his renown and to his joy of heart now. If it added to his glory to save a lost soul in Palestine, it will add to his glory to save me. One deed of the heavenly King is a sample of all his deeds. *Ex uno, omnia disce.*

I. THE ROYAL GRACE OF CHRIST PROVIDES A BANQUET OF GOOD. It is everywhere a mark of friendship if a king invites a man to a banquet; and, through every part of Scripture, God represents himself as providing for penitent men a " feast of fat things." Resentment and vindictiveness towards his frail creatures are things not to be thought of; they are sentiments familiar in hell, but unknown in heaven. 1. *Here is the idea that hunger is satisfied.* At a banquet the primal want of the body is met. And there is no hunger of the soul so widespread, so deep, as the craving for reconciliation with God —the craving for pardon. What bread is to the bodily appetite, God's mercy is to the convicted soul; it is "the one thing needful." Well, God has provided this gift in no stinted fashion. It does not come to us as a bare measure, just enough to meet the case. It is a banquet; it is supplied in sumptuous abundance. Nor is it pardon alone that the heavenly King supplies. It is a banquet of all kinds of substantial good; luxuries gathered from far and near. Wisdom, mercy, righteousness, sonship, hope, victory, eternal life, are some of the viands spread. The Son of God " has given himself for us." And ever and anon we hear the voice of the King himself, " He that cometh to me shall never hunger; he that believeth on me shall never thirst." 2. *Here is also the idea of renewed friendship.* To eat together is an act of friendship. It is a seal impressed in public that a covenant of friendship exists. To have our several bodies nourished from the same meal, from the same loaf, is a beautiful bond of attachment. It was an aggravation of Iscariot's sin, that " he who had eaten bread with Jesus had lifted up the heel against him." If the king invites us to a banquet, it means that he finds a pleasure in our society; he wishes to draw closer the ties of sacred intimacy. Thus Jesus acts. He wants to come into closer fellowship with us. He calls us, not servants, but friends. He undertakes to be our Surety, our Advocate with the Father. He will keep nothing from us, not even his throne. Other friendships may languish; the friendship of Jesus shall eternally abide. From his love nothing shall separate us. 3. *Here is the idea of exuberant joy.* A banquet is not spread, and lavishly embellished with beauty, simply to allay bodily hunger. It is a royal device for promoting joy. And he, who has given to us a great capacity for joy, intends to fill that capacity to the very brim. If there are occasions on earth when joy flows in upon us like a rising tide, these are only prophetic moments of the ineffable and eternal joy of heaven. Desire gratified —this is joy; effort successful—this is joy; hope realized—this is joy; development complete—this is joy. To be with God, to be like God,—this is noontide gladness; this is the "fulness of joy."

II. THE ROYAL GRACE OF CHRIST USES GENTLE CONSTRAINTS. "He brought me into his banquet-house." A man's worst enemy is usually himself. He cannot persuade himself that such generous love is intended for him. Others may perhaps be invited, but not he. Nor does he see that this unbelief is a fresh act of sin. If I discredit a person's word, I may do him a great injustice. If I doubt the promise of a friend, it is an insult. And if I question the faithfulness of my King, I give him pain. 1. *He sometimes uses the rough messenger of affliction to bring us to his banquet-hall.* Many a pardoned man will say with David, "Before I was afflicted I went astray." Saul's blindness made him sensible of Christ's nearness. The peril of Jonah taught him to say, "Salvation is of the Lord." When Manasseh was in affliction he sought unto Jehovah. In times of earthly prosperity men are often self-sufficient; they have all that heart can wish; they have no sense of soul-hunger. But when argosies are wrecked, or harvests fail, or death sweeps, with black pinions, through the house, then they discover their impotence, and long for the heavenly supply. Often has a pitiless storm driven despairing men to the Refuge on Calvary; often has affliction, in some form, been the messenger employed to bring men to the gospel-feast. 2. *Sometimes Christ uses his gospel-heralds to bring men in.* Our heavenly Friend has seen fit to employ renewed men, though imperfect, to persuade the prodigals to return. He does not so employ the angel-bands. Pardoned men know what are the burdens of sin, and what are the seductions of the tempter. Pardoned men have tender sympathies for their fallen fellows. And pardoned men know by experience the joy of acceptance; the blessedness of God's friendship contrasted with his frown. Cleansed and consecrated men are specially fitted to bring sinners to Christ's banquet. Thus Jesus has brought many. 3. *His own Spirit, the Comforter, is the great Agent in filling the banquet-hall.* Said Jesus, prior to his crucifixion, "He shall testify of me;" "He shall take of mine, and show it unto you." To him belongs the prerogative of enlightening the mind, arousing the torpid conscience, convicting of sin, and quickening into life dead souls. He "strives" with the opposition of a rebellious will. By his Divine anointing, men are empowered to use the arts of heavenly persuasiveness. Jesus, the soul's Bridegroom, has furnished the sumptuous banquet; *now* it is the mission of the Holy Spirit to persuade the perishing to come. Have we not heard his "still small voice" within us, imploring us to accept the generous offers of a Saviour's grace? Have we not put off his pleadings again and again with the promise that we would before long come? And has not our promise been as often violated? Thrice happy is the man who can say, "He has conquered." "He brought me into his banquet-house."

III. THE ROYAL GRACE OF CHRIST VOUCHSAFES NEW TOKENS OF AFFECTION. "The device on his banner is love." The beginning and middle and end of the banquet is love. This is the solution of every problem. Whence originated the feast? In love. Why are the guests rebellious and fallen men? Love! What methods are employed to induce them to come? Love! What end is contemplated in the feast? Love! On every banneret the symbol is love. 1. *This banner implies triumph.* It was the banner which our great Champion carried in the war. If we are at the banquet-table, we have been captivated by Immanuel's love. This love pursued us in our wanderings, convinced us of our folly, bore with us patiently, sweetly induced us to lay down our arms and to submit. We were softened and subdued by love. *Now* "we love him, because he first loved us." 2. *This banner means devotement.* We adopt it as our own. We have sworn to serve our Master under this peaceful banner. At the banquet we enlist ourselves on the side of the righteous King. Constrained by love, we freely devote to him all we have, all we are. We must be trained and disciplined for this noble warfare in the school of love. The love that has conquered us shall, through us, conquer others. Love is the heavenly steel from which we fashion all our weapons. Love moulds and inspires our life. "The banner over us is love." 3. *This banner means security.* If I am the object of Immanuel's love, I am safe; no harm can befall me. The brood under the wing of the parent hen cannot be pierced by foeman's arrow, unless that arrow pierce the parent's wing; so the blow which falls on me must strike my Protector first. Whatever apparent evil fall upon me, it is by the permission of infinite love; therefore is only apparent. It is simply disguised blessing; a sweet kernel in a rough shell. If over me floats the banner of Immanuel's love, I have a charmed life. Every foe, visible and invisible, is disarmed.

> " And so, beside the silent sea,
> I wait the muffled oar;
> Assured no harm can come to me,
> On ocean or on shore."

D.

Vers. 8—13.—*Christ's coming makes a new epoch in our history.* Nature is a mirror in which God is seen, and all the processes of nature are samples of God's works in us. Such analogies we ought to expect, because all the forces in nature are the projections of God's thoughts and purposes. The same God who works so mightily in the material world works with mighty grace in us. If, in the visible creation, he gives life to dead matter, so does he likewise give life to dead souls. The sun which rides in royal majesty across the heavens is a picture of the great Sun of Righteousness, who arises on the soul "with healing in his beams." As the coming of spring makes a new epoch in the material world, so the coming of Immanuel is the opening of a new era to the soul. It is nothing short of a spiritual evolution. We pass out of winter into spring; out of death into life.

I. THIS LANGUAGE IS A PICTURE OF CHRIST'S INCARNATION. "The voice of my Beloved! behold, he cometh leaping upon the mountains," etc. 1. *He overleaps all difficulty.* Principles of eternal righteousness stood in the way of man's redemption. The interests of Divine government stood in the way. The peace and welfare of the heavenly hosts seemed to be obstacles. Man's enmity was a tremendous barrier. But the Son of God was deterred by no obstacle. Although the temporary renunciation of his glory and dignity was required, he did not hold back. Immeasurable condescension was demanded; yet to this he cordially submitted. In view of the splendid result, he triumphed over every hindrance. 2. *His coming was a joyful act.* "Leaping upon the mountains, skipping upon the hills." With the affectionate purpose to save men strong in his breast, he felt a joy in self-humiliation; a delicious pleasure in self-sacrifice. "His delights were already with the sons of men." Lo! said he—"lo! I come to do thy will, O God; yea, thy Law is within my heart." When our globe was fashioned, there was new gladness in heaven; "the sons of God shouted for joy." And when the Son of God appeared on earth as its Redeemer, a multitude of the heavenly host broke upon the midnight silence of Bethlehem with the song, "Glory to God in the highest!" Although to execute his task he was "the Man of sorrows," nevertheless in his heart there glowed the fire of sacred rapture. "For the joy that was set before him, he endured the cross, and despised the shame." As a noble Bridegroom "he rejoices over his bride." In his completed work "he shall be satisfied." 3. *His coming was discerned only by his chosen.* The bulk of men knew nothing about his coming; cared nothing about it. To Herod it was a perplexity and a terror. "He came unto his own, and his own received him not." Yet a few chosen ones "waited for the hope and consolation of Israel." Andrew and Simon Peter and Nathanael had been pondering the old prophecies, and were looking hither and thither for signs of fulfilment. Old Simeon's heart overflowed with gratitude when, embracing the holy Child, he said, "Lord, now lettest thou thy servant depart in peace." Not to the eye of man was he revealed. Outwardly, "there was no beauty in him that men should desire him." To many he was known through his voice of wisdom—through his voice of tender invitation and generous love. "The voice of my Beloved." "Faith cometh by hearing." To the heart Jesus Christ still speaks. The sweet tones of his love win us to obedience. 'Tis not only a voice, but "the voice of my Beloved."

II. THIS LANGUAGE IS A PICTURE OF CHRIST'S COMING AT OUR CONVERSION. In the day of our personal regeneration, Immanuel came into our heart to dwell. Then all the mountains of opposition were levelled, and all the abysses of degradation were filled up. We straightway passed out of darkness into light, out of bondage into liberty, out of banishment into sonship. If it were not a time of harvest, when men gather up the ripe sheaves of plenty, it was a spring-time, when young life appears, and gives fair promise of growth and fruitfulness. So we could sing, "For, lo, the winter is past, the rain is over and gone." 1. A surprising change. If ever a miracle has been wrought on earth, our regeneration is a miracle. It is a new departure in life. We, who once loved sin, now hate the abominable thing. We had "sold ourselves for nought;" now we are redeemed with priceless blood. We were righteously condemned; now we are righteously accepted. We are brought into covenant relationship with God. In that day hell was exchanged for heaven. It was a day of jubilee. Through all the ranks in heaven a thrill of gladness ran. The barrenness and death of winter were gone, and spring, fresh with life and hope, filled the soul. The heavenly Bridegroom had arrived. 2. Varied beauty is here represented. "The flowers appear on the earth." Bright and fragrant flowers are fit emblems of Christian virtues. The early flowers of meekness and penitence send forth a goodly smell, and the spicy beds of obedience produce a rich aroma. Some Christians are like violets, unconscious of their sweetness; some are like snowdrops, lacking character; some are full of sacred enthusiasm, rare roses, like Augustines and Ambroses and Luthers. The brightest and noblest specimens of men are found in the Church. 3. And fruitfulness is also foreseen. "The fig tree putteth forth her green figs." True religion is not mere sentiment; it is practical; it is beneficial to mankind. Whence sprang our hospitals, our asylums, our penitentiaries, our almshouses? They have all sprung from Christ, as the Root. When the Spirit of the Lord anointed Jesus, he preached good tidings to the poor; he announced "liberty to the captive, and the opening of the prison to those who were bound." No life has been so fruitful in good results as the life of Jesus Christ, and every true disciple aspires to be fruitful too. In the first age of Christianity, Paul saw many excellent fruits—"love, joy, peace, long-suffering, meekness," etc. And the catalogue has been growing from that day to this. 4. Gladness is another feature in the coming of the Bridegroom. "The time of the singing of birds is come." If any event on earth can awaken joy, surely this must in a superlative degree. If, on the return of spring, lark and linnet and thrush trill their notes afresh, and fill the woods with music, can we restrain our joy when the spring is within us—a new incoming of heavenly life? This joy is joy of the richest quality. It is the cream of all joy. It is joy akin to that which floods the heart of God. We did not know what joy was until Christ visited the heart. Said Rutherford, "Hold, Lord! it is enough. The vessel cannot contain more." "It is meet that we should make merry and be glad." Let nature share in the gladness! It is the birthday and bridal of the soul in one! 5. This new love is held precious by Christ. "Sweet is thy voice, and thy countenance is lovely." We cannot understand why our attachment and our loyalty should be so highly esteemed by Jesus; yet so it is. He "rests in our love." He "rejoices over us with singing." He calls us "his jewels" —his treasures." He has his "inheritance in the saints." Where the disciples meet, he delights to come. "Whoso offereth praise glorifieth" him. And such complacent joy does he find in his consecrated servants, that he says, "I am glorified in them." In the visions of heaven vouchsafed to St. John, the redeemed of earth occupied a place nearer to the throne than the unfallen angels. They are styled "messengers," "servants;" but consecrated men are designated "brethren."

III. THIS LANGUAGE IS DESCRIPTIVE OF REVIVAL AFTER TEMPORARY DEADNESS. The coming of Christ to the soul is like a restoration to life after fainting, or like new life after sleep. 1. The novelty of spiritual life, arising from contrast, does not abide. The joy that springs from pardon does not remain, just as the freshness of spring does not continue all the year. When the new experience becomes a settled thing, the gladness that could not at first but break into a song subsides into a calmer delight.

At conversion the change was so great, the contrast with the former state so striking, the deliverance so welcome, we could not restrain our joy. But the festivities of marriage do not remain perpetual. The rosy hues of dawn do not continue all the day. So the rapture of the new birth does not remain all through the pilgrimage. 2. *The Christian, too, has seasons of dark desertion.* There are seasons when dark clouds gather round him, and the face of his best friend is hidden. Doubts, like malignant spirits, haunt his mind, and rob him of his peace. Satan entangles him in his enchantments, and lures him into the thickets around Doubting Castle. They "cannot read their titles clear to mansions in the skies." They miss the warm sunshine of Immanuel's face. And they are perplexed. If they are the Lord's, why this painful discipline? Why this loss of conscious favour? And in sad despondency they ask, "Will God cast off for ever? Will he be favourable no more?" 3. *Then the return of the Bridegroom brings new life and joy.* "He restoreth my soul." Possibly there was some fault in us that required chastisement, or some rival to our best Beloved may have appeared in the heart not to be tolerated. Whatever was the cause of this temporary eclipse, certain it is that the reappearance of the sun will be a festive day—a jubilee, a resurrection-morn. While under that dark cloud, there may have been some needed preparation of the soul for higher service, as with the fields of earth under wintry skies. Larger fruitfulness may result. The friendship of Jesus will be more prized. "Absence makes the heart grow fonder." Where silence and sadness just now reigned, mirth and music have stirred the echoes. Despondency has given place to hope. The dark shadows of night have fled before a new dawn; and again we can sing, "For, lo, the winter is past, the rain is over and gone."—D.

Ver. 16.—*Marriage jointure.* Marriage is a mutual identification of personal interests, therefore it fully represents the mystic union between Jesus and the believer. We may not have always the conscious sense of our Friend's nearness to us, still we can always say, "My Beloved is mine." For this is an established fact—a fact revealed—and this fact is ascertained by faith, and treasured in the memory, whether we. experience it at the moment or not. If dark clouds hide the face of our Sun of Righteousness, we know still that he is affording us light and heat and life, and still we say, "My Beloved is mine."

I. THE HEART'S CHOICE. The door has been opened to Christ, and he has been admitted to the innermost shrine. He has become the soul's Husband and King by sacred covenant. 1. *This choice is an effect, not a cause.* "We love him, because he first loved us." Said Jesus to his first disciples, "Ye have not chosen me, but I have chosen you." His light has shined into our minds. His spirit has given sensibility to our conscience. He has made us sensible of our need. He has restrained us from further rebellion. He caused us to walk in the King's highway. "By the grace of God I am what I am." 2. *This choice of Christ is our supremest wisdom.* To have made Jesus our soul's Portion is an act of pure wisdom. It is the only right thing to do. He has a right to the chief place, and it would be sacrilege to give our best love to another. Yet, alas! many do. There are men who make money, or social rank, or fame, or pleasure, the best beloved of their heart. The world is their beloved, or their children occupy the place which should be Christ's. We may sincerely congratulate ourselves if we can say, "Jesus is *my* Portion." 3. *Christ has been chosen because of his excellence.* Who, in heaven or on earth, can be compared for worth with Jesus? A person is always more precious than a thing. A man is "more precious than the gold of Ophir." And among all persons Jesus is superlatively precious. Who can compare with him for wisdom? Who has dominion over nature and over the lower world like the Son of God? Who can impart strength like him? Can any one convey life but Immanuel? Or who has such influence for us in heaven as our gracious Intercessor?

> "Infinite excellence is thine,
> Almighty King of grace."

4. *Christ has been chosen by virtue of his love.* Even if he did not possess so many excellences, we should have chosen him for his love. His condescension is wonderful. His sweet compassion has captivated our souls. As soon as we realized his tender, strong affection for us, we felt that we must have his friendship. As the echo responds

to the speaker's voice, our love responded to his love. Or as the flowers respond to the summer sun, so our hearts gave out the fragrance of their love, under the quickening influence of his grace. For his love is not a vapid sentiment. His love is an everlasting force, ever active, beneficent in ten thousand ways. His practical love persevered with us, touched us in a hundred points, and finally melted our ingratitude. Love has made us subjects, servants, slaves. Such love, when known, is irresistible.

II. THIS CHOICE INCLUDES PROPRIETORSHIP. "My Beloved is *mine.*" As I say, "This coat is mine," or "This land is mine," so I can say, "Christ is mine." No one can dispossess me. It is an inalienable possession. 1. *Mark the nature of this possession.* I do not possess it simply with my hands. It is not something outside me, from which I alone can derive advantage. It is a possession within me. It becomes part and parcel of my being. It enters into my very life. I am a totally different being, by virtue of this possession. Jesus is identified with me, and I with him. He is my Life, my Hope. "Christ liveth in me." We possess him, as the branch possesseth the root. 2. *The extent of the possession.* As the bride becomes by marriage participator of all the lands and estates and honours of the bridegroom, so is it with every believer. The righteousness of Christ is mine. All the excellences of Christ are mine. The wealth of Christ is mine. "I am joint-heir" with him. He has chosen to share with me all that he has. His friends are my friends. His servants are my servants. His world is my world. His throne is my throne. "All things are ours, for we are Christ's." 3. *The utility of this possession.* Does it not bring me great and present advantages ? Does it not make me rich indeed ? "He is mine to bear all my burdens ; mine to discharge all my debts ; mine to answer all my accusers ; mine to conquer all my foes." He is "mine in absence, mine in presence ; mine through life, mine in death ; mine in the judgment ; mine at the marriage-supper of the Lamb." I am secure and honoured and happy, because "Christ is mine."

"With him I'm rich, though stripped of all beside ;
Without him poor, though all the world were mine."

III. THIS CHOICE INCLUDES DEVOTEMENT. "I am his." As Jesus has given himself entirely and unreservedly to me, I have given myself wholly and without reserve to him. It is a real surrender. 1. *The dignity of self-devotement.* The man who devotes his whole self to his king or to his country does not degrade himself thereby. He rises in the scale of being ; he rises in honour. Much more does the devoted servant of Jesus Christ rise to the dignity of true living. Better be prime minister of England than king in Dahomey. And nobler far is it to be a servant in Immanuel's kingdom than to boast of vain independence, and be in reality a vassal of Satan. To serve is noble, royal, Divine. Jesus is a King because he stooped to be a servant, and the only road to kingliness is hearty service. The heraldic motto of our Prince of Wales is, "I serve." Devotement to Jesus Christ is eternal honour. 2. *The extent of self-devotement.* It embraces our whole nature, our entire life. The claim of Christ is complete. There is no organ of our body, no faculty of mind, no moment of time, no particle of our wealth, which does not of right belong to him ; therefore we can keep back nothing. We are "not our own." On the grounds of creation, sustenance, redemption, Jesus has a triple claim. And above all, he has our personal consent. By a sacred covenant, we have freely surrendered all we have to his kingly service. The consecration must be complete. 3. *This devotement brings supreme satisfaction.* There is no joy for the human soul like the joy of entire consecration. This is our proper place, and we cannot find our rest elsewhere. On our death-bed, will the review of our life bring us satisfaction, unless that life has been spent, and wholly spent, in the service of our Redeemer ? Can we dare to appropriate to ourselves all that belongs to Christ, if at the same time we do not give up all to him ? As you cannot put pure water into a vessel that is already full of other things, so you cannot put Christ's treasures into a soul until it is emptied of self. To do my Master's will I must surrender all to him. To become like Christ I must be wholly consecrated to his kingdom. Then shall his joy be my joy. Then shall I discover the truth, and shall sing—

"I'm in the noblest sense my own
When most entirely thine."

D.

Vers. 1, 2.—*Wild-flower beauty*. The scene which suggests this imagery is one abounding in rural delights. In a remote country retreat, the lovers are seated on a couch of verdant turf, decked with lovely flowers. It seems as though nature has prepared for them a pleasant house whose rafters and galleries are formed by the lofty cedars and firs above them. The dialogue is coloured by the suggestions of the rustic spot. To the praises of the lover the bride responds with simplicity and humility : " I am as the wild flower of the vale "—the crocus or the rose. He accepts the comparison. "Yes; as a lily among thorns, so is my love among the daughters." Thus love glorifies and hallows the place of meeting, and transforms it into all that is beautiful. If this world is to the poet a gift of the Eternal Father, a revelation of his character, a means and aid to piety—yea, an earnest of heaven itself—then we may well see in the rose of Sharon, in the lily of the valley, an emblem of true virtue and excellence, especially as apparent in the Church, which is the garden of God's delight. Such spiritual excellence is characterized by—

I. BEAUTY. The mind is fashioned so that it must recognize and admire that which is beautiful, both in the natural and in the spiritual realm. There is a beauty, a charm in goodness more to be admired than the crimson petals of the rose or the lily's snow-white chalice. It is given to the spiritual to apprehend the ideal loveliness of virtue and Christian purity. As the flowers of the field and of the forest tell of the Creator's delight in shapeliest forms and fairest hues, so the graces that adorn the Christian character are witnesses to that Spirit, whose workmanship and design and whose vital creation they surely are.

> " Thus beauty here is like to that above,
> And loveliness leads up to perfect love."

II. PURITY. The wild flowers speak to the poet's mind of stainless goodness; the lily is especially the emblem of maiden pureness. Well may such blossoms, blooming far from the city's defilements, serve to symbolize that moral excellence which is uncontaminated by sin and by a sinful world. Where the holy Christ is himself spiritually present, his presence creates a purity akin to, because derived from, his own.

III. FRAGRANCE. The Song of Songs contains many references to the delicate and delightful odours which abound in the plains and gardens of the East. To the sense of smell there is an ethereal side, an aspect of sentiment; and to this the royal poet delights to appeal. The exquisite aroma which breathes from the scented blossoms tells of their nearness and suggests their beauty. There is a perfume in the pure and unselfish character which diffuses itself near and far, witnessing to the Divine grace and power that ever live and work in the spiritual garden of the Lord. This fragrance betrayeth itself, and cannot be hid.

IV. PRE-EMINENCE HEIGHTENED BY CONTRAST. The lily is pictured as "among the thorns," by whose neighbourhood its fairness and sweetness are enhanced. The thorns are a foil to the flower. The plants which our heavenly Father hath planted in this world are hard by the useless and noxious growths of sin. Who has not seen a pure and gentle member of a coarse, worldly, and selfish circle—a family or a community— showing, all unconsciously, as a lily among thorns, more beautiful and charming for the uncongenial surroundings?

V. ATTRACTIVENESS. The rose and the lily draw to them the innocent child, the maiden gathering flowers with which to decorate the lowly home, the poet whose heart is open to the sacred sweetness of nature's symbols. Where there are spirits susceptible to beauty, the flowers will not be unheeded or unsought. A like attractive-ness is exercised by the pure, the devout, the benevolent, and sympathizing. No wonder that Christ himself has been named the Rose of Sharon. Those who share his spirit and witness to his love are the ornaments of his garden, joining to render it the congenial resort, the chosen home, of all who are sensitive to the appeal of Divine love, and responsive to the summons of Divine holiness and authority.—T.

Ver. 3.—*Shadow and fruit*. Pleasant was it at noon to quit the close tent pitched upon the open plain, and to seek the shelter of the spreading tree; pleasant, beneath this refuge from the scorching heat, to partake of the cool and juicy fruit plucked from its boughs. No wonder that the Church has delighted to find in the apple or citron tree, chief in value among the trees of the grove, an emblem of that "Plant of Renown," the Lord and Saviour himself, who has sheltered multitudes beneath his guardian presence, and supplied multitudes from his abundant sufficiency.

I. CHRIST'S SUPREMACY ASSERTED. As the noble citron in the orchard towers above the lesser trees, so is the Saviour exalted above all human teachers and leaders of men, and even above all inspired seers and prophets. This supremacy (1) results from his very nature; (2) is affirmed upon Divine authority; (3) has proved itself in the history of the Church; and (4) is made evident in the experience of every individual friend and disciple of the Lord.

II. CHRIST'S PROTECTION EXPERIENCED. The bride not only looked up to her royal bridegroom with reverence and with pride; she placed herself beneath his guardian care. He was her husband, in whose palace she abode, and in whose keeping she felt secure. He was to her as the spreading tree which protects from noonday heat. So the spiritual spouse of the Divine Bridegroom rests secure beneath the guardianship of her rightful Lord.

"Oppressed with noontide's scorching heat,
    To yonder cross I flee;
Beneath its shelter take my seat—
    No shade like this for me."

III. CHRIST'S SWEETNESS ENJOYED. The tree that yields the shelter supplies also the fruit, which is "sweet to the taste." And the soul partakes of Christ, feeding upon him by faith. As the fruit enters into the body, is assimilated, and refreshes the system, in like manner our Divine Lord condescends to become the life and nourishment of his people. His sacramental love brings health and nourishment, vigour and revival, satisfaction and joy, to the spiritual nature of such as participate by faith in his sacrifice and in his spirit. Such are happy, for they "taste and see that the Lord is good."—T.

Ver. 4.—*The banquet of love.* Both in the Old Testament and in the New the blessings of the gospel are set forth, by anticipation or in reality, under the image of a feast. The composite nature of man gives point and effectiveness to this metaphorical language. The soul is led by the Saviour into his banqueting-house, where hunger is satisfied, and where the provisions of bounty and of love are partaken and enjoyed.

I. IT IS CHRIST WHO BRINGS THE SOUL TO HIMSELF. He does not wait for the needy and poverty-stricken spirit to find him and to come to him. He came in pity to seek and to save. And as when he was upon earth Jesus sought out many a sinner, many a sufferer, so does he still and ever, in the exercise of his Divine compassion, lay his hand upon needy outcasts, and lead them into his banqueting-house.

II. IT IS CHRIST WHO PROVIDES FOR THE SOUL A BOUNTIFUL ENTERTAINMENT. It is not merely bread for the hungry that the gospel offers; it is, in the language of Scripture, a "feast of fat things." Salvation means something more than deliverance from destitution. God comes to us in Christ, saying, "All things are yours." The beggar may be relieved at the gate; but the guest is welcomed to the banquet-hall, and has his place assigned him at the board of the Divine and blessed Host himself. He whom Christ leads to his own fellowship shall not want any good thing; wisdom, righteousness, sanctification, and redemption, all are assured to him.

III. IT IS CHRIST WHO REVEALS TO THE SOUL THE MYSTERY OF DIVINE LOVE. The banner or standard is the sign of the presence of the king or the commander. Even over the "house of wine" there floated the symbol of the royal bridegroom. Thus for the soul that Christ finds and leads, that Christ supplies from the stores of his spiritual bounty, is there an assurance that the King himself keeps guard over its safety. There is the pledge, not only of the king's faithfulness, but of the bridegroom's love. The soul may feast in security and peace, may enjoy the companionship of Christ's friends; for high over the banqueting-house floats the banner, which is the emblem of a Divine presence, and the earnest of an unchanging, an eternal love.—T.

Vers. 8—10.—*The approach of the beloved.* How poetically does this language picture the rural maiden in her mountain home—the lover climbing the hill like a young hart for strength and swiftness, looking in through the lattice window, calling to his beloved, and inviting her to join him amidst the beauty, the fragrance, and the freshness of the spring! So comes Christ unto the soul.

I. THE VOICE OF THE BELOVED. Jesus speaks in his Word and gospel, and his utterance is (1) Divine; (2) authoritative; (3) gracious; (4) encouraging; and (5) welcome. There is no voice like his; he "spake as never man spake."

II. THE GLANCE AND GAZE OF THE BELOVED. 1. Our Saviour's regard is one of interest. Never is his Church forgotten or neglected by him; never does he withdraw his attention or treat with indifference and neglect those for whom he died. 2. He makes himself acquainted with our state and our wants. 3. He looks with affectionate kindness upon those who are dependent upon his favour and bounty. 4. Christ's gracious regard awakens in the minds of his people a desire to know him more intimately. To see him once is to wish to see him again; to see him now and here is to hope for the nearer and perfect vision hereafter.

III. THE INVITATION OF THE BELOVED. We may notice in the tenth verse: 1. The address—remarkably kind, familiar, and affectionate. 2. The appeal: "Rise up!" Is there slothfulness and inactivity? The summons of the Lord is enough to rouse to earnestness and animation. 3. The entreaty: "Come away!" Thus Christ calls his people to himself, and bids them seek his society, accept that spiritual companionship, desire that affectionate intercourse, which are the prerogative of those whom he loves. Even if to act upon this invitation be to leave all that earth can offer, still there is more than compensation for such loss in the joy and privilege of the peerless friendship of the Son of God.—T.

Vers. 11—13.—*Spring-time.* In this poetical language there is an anticipation of that delight in rural scenery which we are accustomed to regard as distinctive of modern feeling and modern literature. But there is no doubt of the power of ardent love to colour all nature to the eye of him who yields himself to the strong emotion— the power of ardent love to make all this world melodious, fragrant, and fair. Emotion gives keenness to the sense and vigour to the imagination. And he whose mind is open, not only to the power of nature to elicit sentiment, but to its power to suggest spiritual truth, the seasons of the year and the shifting panorama of earth speak of a Divine presence and of a thousand sacred realities.

I. WHAT SPRING-TIME BANISHES. "The winter is past, the rain is over and gone." There is a spiritual winter—the winter of darkness and gloom, of ignorance and error, of sterility and death, of vice and crime and sin. It was beneath the rigour and the depression of this winter that the world lay, in seeming hopelessness, until the Sun of Righteousness arose upon the world with healing in his wings. It is well, whilst in the enjoyment of the blessings of the spiritual dispensation, to look back upon the winter of humanity, from whose dreariness we have been delivered.

II. WHAT SPRING-TIME BRINGS. "The flowers appear on the earth; the time of the singing of birds is come, and the voice of the turtle is heard in our land." There is a blessed spiritual spring, bringing beauty and fragrance as of flowers, and sweetness as of the music of the grove. Life is the distinctive note of the new and spiritual economy; and with spiritual life all good things come to us. The beauties and all the treasures of the spring are emblems of peace and joy, of purity and glad service, of obedience and praise. The Easter of humanity is the season for thanksgiving and triumph, for radiant hope and for inspiring song.

III. WHAT SPRING-TIME HERALDS. "The fig tree ripeneth her green figs; and the vines are in blossom, they give forth their fragrance." The blossoms of the spring tell us of the coming fruit in abundance and lusciousness. Far off as the world's spiritual summer may seem, the mission of the Son of God and the mission of the Comforter assure the faithful mind that there is a harvest yet to come. He who could call life out of death, could banish the winter of humanity, can and will, in his own time, bring his work to perfection. The blossom shall mature into fruit, the green of spring shall mellow into autumn's gold. Fruits of the Spirit shall abound, and the heavenly Vine-dresser and Husbandman shall be satisfied and glorified.—T.

Ver. 15.—"*The little foxes.*" The maiden sings a vintage-song, or repeats the admonition of her brothers, who have left her in charge of the vineyard. It is her duty to protect the precious plants and fruits from the incursions of enemies, even of those which seem the most unworthy of notice. It has been usual to regard these " little foxes " as emblematic of evil powers which perhaps insidiously threaten the welfare of the spiritual vineyard.

I. THE CHURCH OF CHRIST IS THE SPIRITUAL VINEYARD WHICH GOD HAS PLANTED IN THE BARREN SOIL OF THE WORLD. As in the Old Testament Israel is often compared to a vine (Ps. lxxx.) or to a vineyard (Isa. v.), so in the New Testament the spiritual society which the Son of God has founded is exhibited under the same similitude.

II. THE CHURCH OF CHRIST EXISTS FOR THE SAKE OF SPIRITUAL FRUIT. The vineyard may be beautiful to behold; it may be a charming addition to the landscape; its gracefulness and verdure may afford pleasure to the passer-by: yet it exists for the sake of fruit. So with the Church, which is indeed an element of interest in history, an important factor in the state, an admirable illustration of the higher capacities of man's being; but which yet exists for the sake of that holy life, those deeds of justice, mercy, and devotion, which are the true fruits of the Spirit, the very vintage of God.

III. THE CHURCH OF CHRIST IS OFTEN ASSAILED BY MISCHIEVOUS INFLUENCES. Like the enemies of the vineyard, evil powers enter in, and damage the spiritual blossom and threaten to destroy the spiritual vintage. False doctrines, heresies, and schisms, delusions, human ambitions, selfish habits, gross corruptions, sins of worldliness and unspirituality,—such are some of these influences which portend disaster to the work which has been undertaken for God upon earth.

IV. THOUGH APPARENTLY TRIFLING, THESE MISCHIEVOUS INFLUENCES MAY DO GREAT HARM. Like the " little foxes," the power of harmful influences must not be measured by appearances, by magnitude. Deflections from truth or from virtue may appear at first slight and insignificant; but the entrance of evil into Christ's Church is like the letting in of water; what is at first a leak becomes a flood. To change the figure, the disease may in its first approach appear unimportant, yet it may grow until it threatens not only health, but life itself. The vineyard, if left open to the incursions of vermin, will soon give evidence of ravages most serious, if not disastrous. Let no one concerned for the safety and welfare of Christ's Church be indifferent to the insidious commencement of harm. No one can say whereunto the thing may grow.

V. THESE EVIL INFLUENCES SHOULD, THEREFORE, BE VIGOROUSLY ATTACKED AND SPEEDILY EXTIRPATED. "Take us the little foxes;" wage war against even apparently insignificant foes. Not by way of force or of fraud, but by the presentation of truth, by admonition and exhortation, openly, feelingly, and prayerfully. It is a duty which at some time or other, and in some way or other, every Christian is called upon to fulfil. The ministers of Christ's Church are especially bound to be upon their guard against the introduction of false doctrine, and of lax and sinful practice; they are set "for the defence and confirmation of the gospel," and it is their office to withstand every foe that threatens the security and the vitality of the Divine society on earth.—T.

Ver. 16.—*Mutual possession.* One-sided affection is incomplete, unsatisfying, and unhappy; it may be disastrous. Real friendship and true marriage imply mutual love, reciprocal kindnesses. So is it in those personal relations between Christ and the Christian soul, which are the foundations of the spiritual life of mankind. It is only well when the friend of the Saviour can truly say, " My Beloved is mine, and I am his."

I. THE CLAIM MADE BY THE CHRISTIAN TO A SPIRITUAL PROPERTY IN CHRIST. 1. Our Lord and Saviour is ours, to exercise in our favour his mediatorial offices, as our Prophet, Priest, and King. 2. He is ours, to reveal his intimate affection to our heart.

> " The opening heavens around me shine
>   With beams of heavenly bliss,
> While Jesus says that he is mine,
>   And whispers I am his ! "

3. He is ours, to impart a value and a charm to all our other possessions. These, whether material or spiritual, are altogether different from what they would otherwise

be; they are irradiated and dignified by the glory which shines upon them from our Divine Friend. "All things are ours."

II. THE CLAIM MADE BY CHRIST TO A SPIRITUAL PROPERTY IN THE CHRISTIAN. 1. The Saviour regards his people with an especial favour and affection. In a sense, all men are Christ's; he assumed the human nature which is common to us all, and he died for all. But in a peculiar manner they are his who acknowledge his mission, receive his gospel, confide in his mediation, obey his commandments. Towards such his regard is one of complacency and personal affection. 2. The Saviour regards his people as his to care for, to protect, and to save. Having loved his own, he loves them unto the end. There are no circumstances in which he will not remember them, interpose upon their behalf and for their deliverance. 3. The Saviour possesses his people in order to exercise over them a peculiar authority. As the husband is the head of the wife, and as his affection does not destroy his authority, but makes it benign and welcome; so our Divine Lord, who loves his spouse, the Church, which he purchased with his precious blood, directs and governs the object of his tender interest with kindness which is yet authoritative. It is the prerogative and joy of Christ's people to take their Lord's will as the binding law of their individual and social life.

APPLICATION. It is for every Christian to remember that in this relation the Lord Jesus is the superior. "We love him, because he first loved us." This fact should infuse gratitude into our affection, and should urge us to responsive consecration and obedience.—T.

EXPOSITION.

CHAPTER III.

Ver. 1.—**By night on my bed I sought him whom my soul loveth: I sought him, but I found him not.** The bride is probably relating a dream. The time referred to is the close of the day on which she had been visited by her lover. She is retired to rest, and dreams that she searches for the beloved object in the neighbouring city (cf. Job xxxiii. 15). It is another way of telling her love. She is always longing for the beloved one. She had been waiting for him, and he came not, and retired to rest with a heart troubled and anxious because her lover did not appear as she expected at the evening hour. The meaning may be "night after night (לֵילֹה)" (cf. ch. iii. 8), or the plural may be used poetically for the singular. Ginsburg observes that "by night on my bed" is opposed to midday couch (cf. 2 Sam. iv. 5), merely to express what came into her thoughts at night in her dreams or as the result of a dream. It is difficult to avoid the conclusion that the bride intends to represent herself as suffering from self-reproach in having grieved her lover and kept him away from her. In that case the typical meaning would be simple and direct. The soul grieves when it is conscious of estrangement from him whom it loves, and the sense of separation becomes intolerable, impelling to new efforts to deepen the spiritual life.

Ver. 2.—**(I said) I will rise now, and go about the city, in the streets and in the broad ways; I will seek him whom my soul loveth: I sought him, but I found him not.**

Delitzsch renders, "So I will arise, then." The words of the maiden are quite inconsistent with the hypothesis of a shepherd-lover, for in that case she would seek him, not in the streets, but outside the city. Some think the city referred to is Jerusalem, with its markets and streets—the royal city (cf. Prov. vii. 11). If it is a dream, it will be unnecessary to decide to what city the words refer. The idea of the speaker would seem to be either that she was at the time within the walls of the city referred to, or that she was in some dwelling near. But a dream is not always consistent with the real circumstances of the dreamer. Taking it as a reminiscence of first love, it seems better to understand the city as only imaginary, or some neighbouring town in the north.

Ver. 3.—**The watchmen that go about the city found me:** (to whom I said) **Saw ye him whom my soul loveth?** The simplicity of these words is very striking. They confirm the view that the bride is recalling what occurred in her country life. The watchmen make no reply, and do not treat her ill, as in the dream related in ch. v. 7, where they are keepers of the walls, and smite her and wound her. In a small country town she might have been recognized, or known to be really in trouble. But such incidents must not be pressed too much in a poem. The allegorical view finds considerable support in the fact that it is difficult on any hypothesis exactly to explain the language as descriptive of real occurrences. In such instances as Ps. cxxvii. 1 and Isa. lii. 8 the reference to watchmen in the city shows that such a metaphor would be familiarly understood. Whether adopted from Solomon's Song or not, the figure of a city watched and guarded, and the people of God as watching for the glory of Zion, was common in the prophetic writings. The soul seeking for its object and for the restoration of its peace calls in the aid of the faithful guardians of the holy city, the friends alike of the Saviour and of those who desire to be his.

Ver. 4.—**It was but a little that I passed from them, when I found him whom my soul loveth : I held him, and would not let him go, until I had brought him into my mother's house, and into the chamber of her that conceived me.** This verse plainly points to the search referred to in the previous verse being limited to the neighbourhood of Shulamith's home. The lover was not far off, though he had delayed his coming. Possibly it is a real occurrence which is related. In that case we must suppose that the night was not very far advanced. But the hypothesis of a dream is the most natural explanation. The word *cherer*, which is used of the house, denotes the inner part, *penetralia*. The modesty of the last clause is very beautiful. The mother would, of course, at that time be in her sleeping-chamber. There alone would the maiden receive her lover at such a time. The mother would gladly welcome the young man, and thus the love which Shulamith declares is set upon the ground of perfect chastity and homely purity. The object of this little episode introduced by the bride into her song as she lies in the arms of Solomon is to show that, ecstatic and intense as her devotion is, it is not the lawless affection of a concubine, but the love of a noble wife. The religious emotions are always presented to us in Scripture, not as wild fanaticism or superficial excitement, but as pure offering of the heart which blends with the highest relations and interests of human life, and sanctifies home and country with all their ties and obligations. The mother and the child are one in the new atmosphere of bridal joy. No religion is worthy of the name which does not bring its object into the chamber of her who conceived us. We love all that are bound with us in life not the less, but the more, because we love Christ supremely. We revere all that is just and holy in the common world the more, and not the less, because we worship God and serve the Lord. What a rebuke to asceticism, monasticism, and all unsocial religion !

Ver. 5.—**I adjure you, O daughters of Jerusalem, by the roes, and by the hinds of the field, that ye stir not up, nor awaken love, until it please.** This is the refrain which divides the poem. We thus perceive that the whole of the preceding passage has been uttered by the bride in the presence of the ladies. There is no occasion to connect a refrain very closely with the words which go before it. Like the ancient Greek chorus, it may express a general sentiment in harmony with the pervading feeling of the whole composition. In this case it seems to be a general note of praise, celebrating the preciousness of pure, spontaneous affection. There have been several beautiful and celebrated imitations of this first part of Solomon's Song, though they all fall far short of the original. Paul Gerhard has caught its spirit ; Laurentius has copied it in his Advent Hymn. Watts, in bk. i. 66—78 of his 'Divine Songs ; ' 'Lyra Germanica ; ' Schaff's ' Christian Song ; ' and Miss Havergal, in some of her compositions, will furnish examples. Delitzsch quotes an ancient Latin imitation—

" Quando tandem venies, meus amor ?
  Propera de Libano, dulcis amor !
  Clamat, amat, sponsula. Veni, Jesu ;
  Dulcis veni Jesu."

This ends Part II., which sets before us the lovely beginning of this ideal love. We must then suppose that the writer imagines himself in Jerusalem, as though one of the court ladies, at the time that Solomon the king returns from the north, bringing with him his bride-elect. We pass, therefore, from the banqueting-chamber, and recall the scenes which accompanied the arrival of Shulamith at Jerusalem. The remainder of the poem is simply the celebration of married love, the delight of the bridegroom in the bride and of the bride in her husband. The whole book concerns a bride, and not one who is about to be made a bride. Here the dream which is introduced is not the dream of a lover awaiting the beloved one, but the dream of a young wife whose bridegroom tarries. The third part is the nuptial rejoicings ; the fourth part is the reminiscence of love-days or of the early married life ; and the fifth part, which is a conclusion, is a visit of Solomon and his bride to the country home of the latter, pointing to the depth and reality of the influence which this pure maiden had upon his royal nature.

Ver. 6—ch. v. 1.—Part III. NUPTIAL REJOICINGS.

Ver. 6.—**Who is this that cometh up out of the wilderness like pillars of smoke, perfumed with myrrh and frankincense, with all the powders of the merchant?** This may be taken as spoken by a single voice, one of the ladies or inhabitants of Jerusalem, or it may be regarded as the exclamation of the whole population going out to see the splendid sight—a gorgeous procession coming towards the city. "Who is this coming?" (עֹלָה, feminine); that is, "Who is this lady coming?" There could be no difficulty in discerning that it was a bridal procession which is seen. Curiosity always asks, "What bride is this?" "Who is *she?*" not, "Who is he?" A maiden from Galilee is being conducted to Jerusalem; the procession naturally passes through the valley of the Jordan (Ghôr). There is splendour and majesty in the sight. It must be some one coming to the royal palace. The censers of frankincense are being swung to and fro and filling the air with fragrant smoke. Columns of dust and smoke from the burning incense rise up to heaven, and mark the line of progress before and after. "The spices of Arabia" were famous at all times. Hence the names of the perfumes are Arabic, as *murr, levona,* and the travelling spice-merchant, or trader, was Arabic (cf. the Arabic elixir). We can scarcely miss the typical colouring in such a representation—the *wilderness,* typical of bondage and humiliation, sin and misery, out of which the bride is brought; the onward progress towards a glorious destination (see Isa. xl. 3; Hos. i. 16; Ps. lxviii. 8). The Church must pass through the wilderness to her royal home, and the soul must be led out of the wilderness of sin and unbelief into everlasting union with her Lord.

Ver. 7.—**Behold, it is the litter of Solomon; three score mighty men are about it, of the mighty men of Israel.** The litter, or palanquin, is easily recognized. The word is *mittâh,* which is literally "bed," or "litter," but in the ninth verse we have another word, *appiryon,* which is a more stately word, "the royal car." It is the bringing home of the bride which is described. In the forty-fifth psalm the idea seems to be that the bridegroom betook himself to the house of the parents and fetched his bride, or that she was brought to him in festal procession, and he went forth to meet her (see 1 Macc. ix. 39). That was the prevailing custom, as we see in the parable of the ten virgins (Matt. xxv. 1—13). In this case, however, there is a vast difference in rank between the bride and bridegroom, and she is brought to him. The long journey through the wilderness is implied in the mention of the body-guard (cf. Isa. iv. 6; xxv. 4). The intention evidently is to show how dear the bride was to Solomon. His mighty men were chosen to defend her. So the Church is surrounded with armies of guardian attendants. Her Lord is the Lord of hosts. The description reminds us of the exquisite lines in Shake-

speare's 'Antony and Cleopatra,' in which he describes the lovely Egyptian in her barge "like a burnished throne," lying "in her pavilion (cloth of gold, of tissue)," with the smiling cupids on each side, while

"... from the barge,
A strange invisible perfume hits the sense
Of the adjacent wharfs."

(Act ii. sc. 2.)

The word *mittâh,* "a bed, or litter," comes from a root "to stretch out," and is also used of a bier (see 2 Sam. iii. 21). The idea is that of a portable bed, or sitting-cushion, hung round with curtains, after the manner of the Indian palanquin, such as is still found in the Turkish caïques or the Venetian gondolas. It was, of course, royal, belonging to Solomon, not to any nobleman or private person; hence its magnificence. The bearers are not named. The body-guard, consisting of sixty chosen men, forming an escort, were one-tenth part of the whole royal guard, as we see from 1 Sam. xxvii. 2; xxx. 9. Delitzsch suggests that in the mention of the number there may be a reference to the twelve tribes of Israel—60 being a multiple of 12. The term, "mighty men," is explained in the next verse as warriors, that is, men "held fast by the sword" (אֲחֻזֵי חֶרֶב), *i.e.,* according to Hebrew idiom, men practised in the use of the sword; so it is explained by some; but others take it as meaning that they "handle the sword;" hence our Revised Version.

Ver. 8.—**They all handle the sword, and are expert in war : every man hath his sword upon his thigh because of fear in the night.** The guard of warriors round the litter secured the bride from any sudden alarm as she travelled through the wilderness, and so gave her quiet rest. The journey from Shunem to Jerusalem would be about fifty miles in a direct course, and it was therefore necessary to pass at least one, if not two, nights on the way; the course being through a wild and solitary region. The Church of God may be often called to pass through dangers and enemies, but he that loveth her will provide against her destruction—she shall have rest in the love of her Lord. He will surround her with his strength. "My peace I give unto thee"—provided by me, coming from myself, the fruit of my self-sacrificing love.

Vers. 9, 10.—**King Solomon made himself a palanquin of the wood of Lebanon. He made the pillars thereof of silver, the bottom thereof of gold, the seats of it of purple, the midst thereof being paved with love, from the daughters of Jerusalem.** The palanquin is described, that the attention may be kept fixed awhile on the bridal procession, which, of course, forms the kernel of the whole poem, as representing the perfect union of the bride and bridegroom. The Greek versions translate φορεῖον: the Vulgate, *ferculum*. We read in Athenæus (v. 13) that the philosopher and tyrant Athemon showed himself on "a silver-legged φορεῖον with purple coverlet." There probably is some connection between the Hebrew *appiryon* and the Greek *phoreion*, but it is exceedingly doubtful if the Hebrew is merely a lengthened form of the Greek. Delitzsch derives the Hebrew from a root *pâráh*, "to cut or carve" anything of wood. The Greek would seem to be connected with the verb φερω, "to bear," "carry." The resemblance may be a mere coincidence. The rabbinical tradition is that the Hebrew word means "couch, or litter." Hitzig connects it with the Sanscrit *paryâna*, meaning "saddle," "riding-saddle," with which we may compare the Indian *paryang*, "bed." Others find a Chaldee root for the word, פְּרָא, "to run," as *currus* in Latin, or from a root אוֹר, "to shine," *i.e.* "to be adorned." At all events, it would not be safe to argue the late date of the book from such a word as *appiryon*, on account of its resemblance to a Greek word. The "wood of Lebanon" is, of course, the cedar or cypress (1 Kings v. 10, etc.). There may be a covert allusion intended to the decoration of the temple as the place where the honour of the Lord dwelleth, and where he meets his people. The frame of the palanquin was of wood, the ornaments of silver. The references to the high value set upon silver, while gold is spoken of as though it was abundant, are indications of the age in which the poem was composed, which must have been nearly contemporaneous with the Homeric poems, in which gold is spoken of similarly. Recent discoveries of the tomb of Agamemnon, etc., confirm the literary argument. The palanquins of India are also highly decorated. The daughters of Jerusalem, *i.e.* the ladies of the court, in their affection for King Solomon, have procured a costly tapestry, or several such, which they have spread over the purple cushion. Thus it is paved, or covered over, with the tokens of love—while all love is but a preparation for this supreme love. (For the purple coverings of the seat, see Judg. v. 10; Amos iii. 12; Prov. vii. 16.) The preposition מִן in the last clause is rendered differently by some, but there can be no doubt that the meaning is "on the part of," that is, coming from. The typical interpreter certainly finds a firm ground here. Whether we think of the individual believer or of the Church of God, the metaphor is very apt and beautiful—we are borne along towards the perfection of our peace and blessedness in a chariot of love. All that surrounds us speaks to us of the Saviour's love and of his royal magnificence, as he is adored by all the pure and lovely spirits in whose companionship he delights.

Ver. 11.—**Go forth, O ye daughters of Zion, and behold King Solomon, with the crown wherewith his mother hath crowned him in the day of his espousals, and in the day of the gladness of his heart.** This seems to be an appeal to a larger company of those who will rejoice in the bride and her happiness. The daughters of Zion are perhaps intended to represent the people generally as distinguished from the ladies of the court, *i.e.* let all the people rejoice in their king and in his royal bride. The mention of the royal mother seems to point to the beginning of Solomon's reign as the time referred to. The crown, or chaplet, with which the proud mother adorned her son, was the fresh wreath round a young king's head, a wedding coronet, no doubt made of gold and silver. It was not the crown placed on the head of Pharaoh's daughter, which would not be so spoken of. According to the Talmud, the custom remained even to later times. There can be no doubt of Bathsheba's special delight in Solomon (see 1 Kings i. 11; ii. 13). We must not, of course, push too far the typical interpretation of such language, which may be taken as the poetical form rather than the spiritual substance. And yet there may be an allusion, in the joy and pride of Bathsheba in her son's gladness, and the consummation of his nuptial bliss, to the Incarnation and the crowning glory of a Divine humanity, which is at once the essential fact of redemption, and the bright expectation which, on the head of the Saviour, lights up eternity to the faith of his people.

HOMILETICS.

Vers. 1—5.—*The dream of the bride.* I. The absence of the beloved. 1. *The bride's distress.* In the last chapter the bride related to her female friends some of the incidents of her early love; here she seems to be relating a dream of those same well-remembered days. The whole narrative, like that of ch. v. 2—8, has a dream-like character. The circumstances are not such as would be likely to occur in real life; but the longing, the wandering, the search, represent in a vivid truthful way the images of dreams. She was lying asleep on her bed; her thoughts were full of the absent bridegroom. "I sought him," she says, "but I found him not." We notice the dream-like repetition, the dwelling upon phrases. Four times in these five verses we have the fond description of the bridegroom, which occurred for the first time in ch. i. 7, "him whom my soul loveth." Twice we have the utterance of unsatisfied longing, "I sought him, but I found him not." She was sleeping, but (as in ch. v. 2, "I sleep, but my heart waketh") her thoughts were busy and active. Her whole heart was given to her beloved. Those oft-repeated words, "him whom my soul loveth," imply a very deep affection, a great love. The believer remembers God in the watches of the night. The psalmist says, "In the night his song shall be with me, and my prayer unto the God of my life;" and again, "I call to remembrance my song in the night: I commune with mine own heart: and my spirit made diligent search" (Ps. xlii. 8; lxxvii. 6). If our heart is given to the heavenly Bridegroom, we shall think of him as we lie on our beds; our first waking thoughts will be of him. Alas! our love for Christ is not like the bride's love in the Song of Songs. How few of us can in truth speak of the Saviour as "him whom my soul loveth"! The bride dwelt upon those words as the simple truth, the sincere expression of her feelings. We dwell upon them, too; but, alas! with a sense of much coldness and ingratitude, a remembrance of much insincerity and unreality.

> "God only knows the love of God;
> Oh that it now were shed abroad
> In this poor stony heart!
> For love I sigh, for love I pine;
> This only portion, Lord, be mine,
> Be mine this better part."

The Christian dwells on the words, longing for grace to make them his own, the utterance of his inmost heart. Here is the spiritual value of the Song of Songs. We see what a great love is; how it absorbs the heart and fills the soul. Such should be our love to Christ; such should be our "songs in the night" (Job xxxv. 10). The bride sought her beloved in the visions of the night. We seem sometimes in our dreams to be going on long trackless journeys, wandering ever in search of something we know not what. So the bride could not find him whom her soul loved. Such are sometimes the experiences of the Christian soul. So Job once complained, "Oh that I knew where I might find him! that I might come even unto his seat! . . . Behold, I go forward, but he is not there; and backward, but I cannot perceive him" (Job xxiii. 3, 8). The Lord has said, "Seek, and ye shall find;" "Every one that seeketh findeth." But he has also said, "Strive to enter in at the strait gate; for many, I say unto you, shall seek to enter in, and shall not be able." Those who seek shall surely find at last; but the seeking must be diligent seeking, patient, persevering; there must be striving too, struggling to overcome obstacles, wrestling against the spiritual enemies who would bar our way. It is not enough to seek by night on our beds; there must be effort, sustained effort, not mere dreamy aspirations; and that not only by night, not only in the hour of darkness: "in the day of my trouble I sought the Lord" (Ps. lxxvii. 2). We must seek the Lord always; in the hour of health and strength, in the days of our youth; giving him our best, doing all things to his glory. Such seeking will surely find him. 2. *The search.* "I will rise now," she says. The Hebrew tense is cohortative. She is addressing herself, arousing herself. Dreaming as she is, she feels that this is not the way to seek; she must leave her bed, she must rise. Perhaps she remembered the bridegroom's words spoken in the freshness of their first love: "Rise up, my love, my fair one, and come away." She seems to rise; in her dreams she goes about the city in the streets, seeking him whom her soul loved. We must arise and seek the Lord; we must not lie still in careless slumber; we must seek him wherever his providence has set us, whether in the quiet country or in the bustling, crowded city. We may find him in any place, provided it be one where a Christian may safely tread; in any employment, provided it be lawful and innocent; in the city, in the streets, and in the broadways.

> "There are in this loud stunning tide
> Of human care and crime,
> With whom the melodies abide
> Of th' everlasting chime;
> Who carry music in their heart
> Through dusky lane and wrangling mart,
> Plying their daily task with busier feet,
> Because their secret souls a holy strain repeat."

Still the bride found not the beloved; she repeats her first lament like a plaintive refrain : " I sought him, but I found him not." The soul does not always find the Lord at once when it first feels its need of the Saviour. We try one plan after another; we make effort after effort; but for a time all our efforts are vain. We know that he may be found, that others have found him and have felt the blessedness of his love. But the search seems long fruitless. God would have our search to be sincere, thoughtful, earnest. Therefore he tries our faith. He proves us, as once he proved Abraham ; as the Lord Jesus tried the faith of the Syro-Phœnician woman. Again and again she sought his help, but for some time there was no response ; silence at first, then what seemed to be a stern refusal. Still she persevered, she urged her prayer; her case was like that of the bride—she sought him, but she found him not. We must follow her example, remembering the Lord's teaching, that men ought always to pray, and not to faint. We must imitate the bride in her dream, and seek on, though for a long season our search may seem unsuccessful—though we find him not.

II. THE ULTIMATE SUCCESS OF THE BRIDE'S SEARCH. 1. *She meets the watchmen.* The watchmen found her (as again in ch. v. 7). She asks them the question which was so near her heart, " Saw ye him whom my soul loveth ? " They were going about the city ; they might be able to guide her to the object of her search. But they were like the watchman of Ps. cxxvii., waking but in vain for the bride's purpose, unable to help her. It is not always that Christian friends, or the ministers of God's holy Word and sacraments, who "watch for our souls" (Heb. xiii. 17), can help us in our search for Christ. We ask them, we seek their help; it is right to do so; sometimes they can help us. But each soul must find Christ for itself. " Work out *your own* salvation," St. Paul said to the Philippians ; and that, " not as in my presence only, but now much more in my absence " (ii. 12). 2. *She finds the bridegroom.* The watchmen could give her no good tidings ; but she did not faint; she did not return home or throw herself down in despair ; she continued her search alone. She would search on till she found the beloved of her soul. And her search was rewarded at last. " It was but a little that I passed from them, but I found him whom my soul loveth." God is not far from us even in the hour of deepest gloom, when we seem to strain our eyes through the darkness, and can see no light. If we seek him earnestly we shall surely find him at the last; for he, we know, is seeking us. The Lord Jesus Christ came to seek and to save that which was lost. He seeketh the lost sheep until he find it. He giveth his life for the sheep. Then we may be quite sure that he who loved us with such a love, a love stronger than death, will not suffer any penitent soul that seeketh him in faith, in sorrow for the past, in earnest painful longings for forgiveness, to lose its way, to wander on without finding, to inquire everywhere without result, " Saw ye him whom my soul loveth ? " He will surely manifest himself according to his blessed promise, as he did to the two disciples who on the first Easter Day were mourning for their lost Master, and would not be comforted by the words of the women who "had seen a vision of angels, who said that he was alive." He will come in his gracious love, and then our heart will burn within us as he manifests himself, and our eyes shall be opened, and we shall know him ; and that knowledge is eternal life (John xvii. 3). 3. *She brings him to her home.* The long wanderings of the dream were over. She had found him whose love filled her waking thoughts, of whom her dreams were full when she slept. She would not let him go. The anguish of that long, almost despairing search should not be in vain. She held him fast, and brought him to her own home, into its inmost chambers. The soul that once has found Christ clings to him with the strong embrace of faith. He may "make as though he would go further " (Luke xxiv. 28), to try our faith, that we may feel our need of him. But as the two disciples then "constrained him, saying, Abide with us, for it is toward evening, and the day is far spent," so the soul holds him and will not let him go. The soul, weak as Jacob was weak, struggles with the strength that the sense of weakness gives. " I will not let thee go, except thou bless me."

" Yield to me now, for I am weak,
    But confident in self-despair :
Speak to my heart, in blessings speak;
    Be conquered by my instant prayer :
Speak! or thou never hence shalt move,
And tell me if thy name is Love.

> " My prayer hath power with God : the grace
> Unspeakable I now receive ;
> Through faith I see thee face to face—
> I see thee face to face, and live !
> In vain I have not wept and strove :
> Thy nature and thy name is Love."

This noble hymn of Charles Wesley's expresses the feelings of a soul that has found Christ. We must not let him go, not for any perplexities, not for any temptations. St. Paul tells us that no difficulties can draw us back from him if we really give him our heart. " I am persuaded that neither death, nor life, nor angels, nor principalities, nor powers, nor things present, nor things to come, nor height, nor depth, nor any other creature, shall be able to separate us from the love of God, which is in Christ Jesus our Lord " (Rom. viii. 38, 39). Then we must cling very closely to him, not letting go any one desire to serve him better and to love him more. We must stimulate every such desire into activity by actual self-denying effort. We must try with all our heart to realize his presence always, at all times and in all places, in our business, our amusements, our intercourse with friends and relations, as well as in the hour of private prayer or public worship. We must try with conscious effort to please him always ; seeking, indeed, to serve him much, like Martha, but still more to please him perfectly, like Mary. And we must bring him into our home, into the very inmost chambers of our heart, opening them all to him, dedicating them all, every purpose of ours, every hope, every aspiration, to him, beseeching him to accept our imperfect offering, to make our hearts his temple, to fulfil in us his blessed promise, " If any man love me, he will keep my words : and my Father will love him, and we will come unto him, and make our abode [our dwelling, our abiding-place] with him " (John xiv. 23). And now we have again the adjuration of ch. ii. 7. The bride has related her dream to the daughters of Jerusalem. The subject of that dream was love—pure and innocent love ; its sorrows and its joys ; separation and blessed reunion. It is a sacred thing. The daughters of Jerusalem were to listen in silent sympathy ; they were not to praise or to blame ; they were not to endeavour to stimulate or increase the love of bride or bridegroom ; they were to leave it to its free spontaneous growth in the heart. Human love is a holy thing. The love that is between Christ and his Church, the love that is between the Lord of our redemption and every elect soul, is holier yet by far. It is not to be much talked of ; it is to be treasured in the heart ; it is the inmost spring of that life which is hidden with Christ in God. It must not be stirred by irreverent talk or disclosure ; it must rest unseen " till it please "—till the fit time shall come for speaking of its blessedness.

Vers. 6—11.—*The espousals.* I. THE APPROACH OF THE BRIDE. 1. *The question.* " Who is this ? " We have here one of those refrains which form a striking characteristic of the song. The question, " Who is this ? " (the pronoun is feminine, " Who is she ? ") is three times repeated (ver. 6 ; ch. vi. 10 ; viii. 5). It indicates always a fresh appearance of the bride. Here the words seem to be chanted by a chorus of young men, the friends of the bridegroom. They are struck with admiration at the beauty of the bride, and the royal state bestowed upon her by the king. She is coming up to Jerusalem from the distant Lebanon country, here described as the wilderness— which word in the Hebrew Scriptures often means, not a desert, but a thinly populated country, fit for feeding flocks, a pasture-land. She comes like pillars of smoke perfumed with myrrh and frankincense. Perfumes are burned around her in such profusion that pillars of smoke appear to attend her progress. The marriage of the Lamb is come, and his wife hath made herself ready. She is prepared as a bride adorned for her husband. She comes up from this lower world to the city of the living God, the heavenly Jerusalem. The incense of adoration and thanksgiving rises as she moves onward. She is the holy Catholic Church, the great congregation of Christian people dispersed throughout the whole world. But the Church is made up of individual Christian souls. And that the Church may come as a whole to Christ the Bridegroom, each soul must come personally, individually. The soul cometh up out of the wilderness, out of the far country, where the world, the flesh, and the devil rule ; up to

Mount Zion, to the city of God, where is the true temple, where God is worshipped in spirit and in truth, where he manifests himself to them that seek him. And the prayer of the faithful, as they draw ever nearer, is set forth in God's sight as the incense, and the lifting up of their hands as the evening sacrifice. The Lord is pleased, in his infinite condescension, to regard our poor prayers when lifted up in faith as holy incense (Rev. viii. 3, 4), because the great High Priest is praying for us. Our poor prayer joins itself through the power of faith with his prevailing prayer, and therefore rises up before the throne as a pillar of sweetest incense-smoke, acceptable to God through Christ. The thought that God is pleased so to honour the prayers of the faithful, that he condescends to *seek* such worship, worship offered up in spirit and in truth, makes prayer a very sacred thing. The approach of the Christian soul to God is very solemn. The soul cometh out of the wilderness, away from its old haunts; it is ascending up to Mount Zion, to the presence-chamber of the King of heaven; it must come with reverence and godly fear, remembering that God's presence is very awful as well as very blessed; it must come with the perfume of holy thoughts and heavenly aspirations, with the offering of prayer and praise rising up like the smoke of holy incense before the mercy-seat. 2. *The bed of Solomon.* The chorus calls attention to the litter (for such seems here to be the meaning of the word) in which the bride is borne in her progress to the royal city. "It is his litter," they say. They add the royal name itself, "Behold his litter, which is Solomon's," to give emphasis to the honour bestowed upon the bride. The king has sent his own litter to convey his bride to the palace, the palanquin in which he himself was carried. It was King Solomon's; it is the bride's, for the king has given it to her. God has given us all things, St. Paul says (Rom. viii. 32). If only we are Christ's, then all things are ours—the world, life, death, things present, things to come (1 Cor. iii. 21, 22). And the Lord himself says, "The glory which thou gavest me, I have given them" (John xvii. 22). It is his will that his chosen should be with him where he is. He gives them now all that is necessary to convey them thither. "God rode upon a cherub" (Ps. xviii. 10). The Lord will "send his angels . . . and they shall gather together his elect from the four winds, from one end of heaven to the other" (Matt. xxiv. 31). The angels carried the soul of Lazarus into Abraham's bosom. But we may learn here another very solemn lesson. The litter of Solomon bore the bride up to Mount Zion; the cross of the Lord Jesus Christ brings the Christian soul to heaven. The Lord was lifted up upon the cross. Several ancient writers tell us that in Ps. xcvi. 10 the earliest reading was, "The Lord hath reigned from the *wood*." The cross is his throne; it drew, and still draws, all faithful souls to him; it has lifted him up to reign over the hearts of all the best and truest. It behoved him first to suffer, and then to enter into his glory. "He humbled himself even unto the death of the cross; *wherefore* God also hath highly exalted him" (Phil. ii. 9). And he brings his elect to God by the same way which he trod himself. The cross lifts the Christian soul to God.

> "Nearer my God, to thee,
>   Nearer to thee;
> E'en though it be a cross
>   That raiseth me."

The Christian is "crucified with Christ" (Gal. ii. 20). He is lifted up by the cross of atonement, the cross of the Lord Jesus Christ, and then by the cross of spiritual self-sacrifice, the cross borne with Christ, into the very presence of the King. Nothing else can bear him thither. He must pray, "Thy will be done," before he asks, "Give us this day our daily bread." He must learn from the suffering Lord the inner meaning of his own holy prayer. "Not my will, but thine be done." He must remember that the cross is the cross of Christ; that the Lord, who was himself lifted up upon the cross, sends the cross to his followers to lift them also upwards; that, purified and refined by holy self-denials, and by suffering meekly borne, they may at length be with him where he is, and behold his glory, and sit with him in his throne (Rev. iii. 21). 3. *The guard.* The king had sent his own guard to escort the bride to her new home. King David had a guard of thirty mighty men; Solomon, it seems, had double the number. All were expert in war; all bore the sword because of fear in the night. From Ps. x., especially vers. 7—10, we learn that parts of Palestine were in David's time dangerous from bands of brigands. The king had cared for the safety of the bride; the escort was not given her merely for honour. So now the Lord giveth his angels charge over his people to keep (to guard) them in all their ways; so now "the angel of the Lord encampeth round about them that fear him, and delivereth them" (Ps. xci. 11; xxxiv. 7). They "shall not be afraid for the terror by night" (Ps. xci. 5), for "they that be with us are more than they" that be against us (2 Kings vi. 16). The description of the armed guard reminds us that we too have to fight the good fight of faith, that we have to wrestle "against the world-rulers of this darkness, against the spiritual hosts of wickedness" (Eph. vi. 12). We have to take to ourselves the panoply of God, the armour of light; like the mighty men of Israel who guarded the bride, we must take "the sword of the Spirit, which is the Word of God." That sword will save us from the "fear of the night," because it is "through patience and comfort of the Scriptures" that we have hope (Rom. xv. 4). Thus the Holy Scriptures are not only the sword of the Spirit; they furnish us also with hope, the hope of salvation, which is the helmet of the Christian warrior. To gain that sword and that helmet we must study the Word of God in faith; that living faith which (St. Paul tells us) is the shield whereby we may "quench all the fiery darts of the wicked." If we do our part, quitting ourselves like men, fighting manfully under the banner of the cross, we need fear no evil. Our angel-guard, sent forth because of them that shall be heirs of salvation, called in Holy Scripture "their angels," because they have charge over them, as well as God's angels, because he is their God and King, will ever encamp around us and keep us till we appear before God in Zion.

II. THE KING GOES FORTH TO MEET THE BRIDE. 1. *The chariot of the king.* The bride approaches in a litter sent for her by the king. Solomon himself goes forth to receive her in his car of state. He had had it made according to his own plans, with that artistic skill and magnificence which were characteristic of him. It was made of the fragrant and imperishable cedar-wood brought from Lebanon, the country of the bride. Its decorations were of the richest—gold and silver, and the costly Tyrian purple; in the midst was a tesselated pavement, a gift of love from the daughters of Jerusalem. The bride, the Lamb's wife, shall have the glory of God (Rev. xxi. 9, 11). When she is "prepared as a bride adorned for her husband," then, we are told, "the tabernacle of God is with men, and he will dwell with them, and they shall be his people, and God himself shall be with them, and be their God" (Rev. xxi. 3). When Christ, the true Solomon, the Prince of Peace, shall bring his bride, the Church, to the heavenly Jerusalem, the foundation of peace, he will manifest himself to her in his glory. Now he is interceding for us, that then we may be with him where he is, that we may behold his glory. Then, if we are his indeed, we shall see him as he is, and shall be made like unto him (1 John iii. 2). It was a great thing for the poor bride from the Lebanon to be brought into the court of the king whose magnificence filled the Queen of Sheba with wonder and delight. But "eye hath not seen, nor ear heard, neither have entered into the heart of man, the things which God hath prepared for them that love him" (1 Cor. ii. 9). None can tell the blessedness of those happy souls who, having washed their robes and made them white in the blood of the Lamb, "shall see the King in his beauty" (Isa. xxxiii. 17); shall sit with him in his throne amid the glories of the golden city; shall see his face, and his Name shall be in their foreheads. Heart of man cannot conceive the exceeding great joy of that moment of most entrancing bliss, when the heavenly Bridegroom shall bring home the Church, his bride. King Solomon issued out of Jerusalem in royal pomp to meet his betrothed. When the marriage of the Lamb is come, "the Lord himself shall descend from heaven with a shout, with the voice of the archangel, and with the trump of God: and the dead in Christ shall rise first: then we which are alive and remain shall be caught up together with them in the clouds, to meet the Lord in the air: and so shall we ever be with the Lord" (1 Thess. iv. 16, 17). 2. *The glory and great joy of the king.* The chorus calls upon the daughters of Zion to go forth and see the splendour of the royal espousals. King Solomon has brought home his bride; his heart is glad; his mother has crowned him with the royal diadem; he is happy in the love of his bride. The Prophet Isaiah comforts Zion with the blessed promises that "as the bridegroom rejoiceth over the bride, so shall thy God rejoice over thee." "Thou shalt no longer be termed Forsaken; neither shall thy land any more be termed Desolate: but thou shalt be called Hephzi-bah ['my delight is in her'], and thy land Beulah ['married']: for the Lord delighteth in thee, and thy land shall be married " (Isa. lxii. 4, 5). So the Lord " Christ loved the Church, and gave himself for her; that he might sanctify and cleanse her with the washing of water by the Word,' that he might present her to himself a glorious Church, not having spot, or wrinkle,'or any such thing; but that she should be holy and without blemish " (Eph. v. 25—27). It was for the joy set before him that Christ endured the cross (Heb. xii. 2). The Lord bringeth home the lost sheep rejoicing. He saith, " Rejoice *with me*; for I have found my sheep that was lost." " Rejoice with *me!* " And they do rejoice, the Saviour of the world and the holy angels round his throne. The Lord's exceeding great love for our poor dying souls makes the salvation of those souls very precious in his sight. Nothing can show the depth and tenderness of the blessed love with which he yearned for our salvation except the great agony of Gethsemane, the awful anguish of the cross. Therefore the day of the resurrection of the blessed will be a day of joy in heaven. " Let us be glad, and rejoice, and give honour to him: for the marriage of the Lamb is come, and his wife hath made herself ready " (Rev. xix. 7). He is King of kings, and Lord of lords; on his head are many crowns (Rev. xix. 12, 16). His virgin-mother saw him once wearing the crown of thorns; now he wears the crown of boundless sovereignty. He had come down from heaven to seek his bride; now she is with him in his glory. " He shall see of the travail of his soul, and shall be satisfied " (Isa. liii. 11).

HOMILIES BY VARIOUS AUTHORS.

Vers. 1—5.—*Love's dream.* It is a dream that is told of in these verses. It was natural for her who tells it to have dreamt such a dream. Lifting up the story to the higher level of things spiritual, what these verses say suggests—

I. CONCERNING DREAMS GENERALLY. They are often revelations of life and character. Sometimes they are mere folly, the misty vapours exhaled by a gross and over-fed body. But at other times, as here, they have a deeper meaning. They show the manner of a man's life, the bent of his inclinations, the character of his soul. Our dreams never play us false. The motives that govern their acts are the motives that govern ours. A man dreams about the sins he loves too well; about the sorrows that haunt his life; about the joys on which his heart is set. Dreams have played a large part in God's governance of men. They often show us what we should avoid and what we should seek after. Though some are foolish, we cannot afford to despise them as if all were so.

II. CONCERNING THIS DREAM. In both its stages it reveals the fervent love of the dreamer. 1. *It began sorrowfully.* She thought she had lost her beloved (vers. 1, 2). This the deepest of distresses to the renewed soul (cf. Ps. lxxvii. 1—4). If heaven would cease to be heaven, as it would were Christ's presence withdrawn, how much more must this life be all dark and drear if we have him not! And she tells how she sought him. (1) In the city, amid the business and turmoil of men. But it is but little that he is there. They would most probably crucify him if they found him, so deadly is the hate the world hath for him. It is not true that virtue needs only to be seen to be loved. As our Lord was dealt with, so would it be. (2) And in the assemblies, in society. And we cannot be surprised that he was not there. Society! does that word summon up the idea of a community who would cherish Christ's presence? (3) But even the watchmen could not tell her of him. How wrong this! Zion's watchmen, and not know where Christ is to be found! They had found her, and very likely found fault with her, but they could not help her to find him. Such pastors there are, and to them "the hungry sheep look up, and are not fed." We can picture the soul's distress when these failed her. To have gone to the house of God hungering for direction Christwards, and to come back with none at all—that is a sorrow not unknown nor slight. But her dream did not end so. 2. *It ended joyfully.* (1) Her beloved revealed himself to her. She "*found him.*" But what is our finding other than his showing? (cf. the four findings of Christ told of in John i.). How often when we have " passed from " Sundays and services and sermons, and have not found Christ, he is found of us in some other season, place, and circumstances! If he be found of them that seek him not—as he says he is—how much more will he fulfil his word, "They that seek me shall find me"! (2) And she clave to him. "I held him," etc. The soul thus holds her Lord by her prayers, her trust, her communion, her service, her self-surrender. These grasp the Beloved, and will not let him go. (3) And she will be content with nothing less than the full assurance of his love (ver. 4). We should resolve to have a religion that makes the soul happy. The religion that does not do this does but little at all. Cf. the elder son in the parable of the prodigal. He had a religion, but it was all gloom. Let us not be satisfied so. And if we seek, and find, and cleave, and so continue as set forth here, the joy of the Lord shall be ours.

III. CONCERNING THE AWAKING. Ver. 5 shows that she is awake, and conscious of the love of her beloved, and would not be torn therefrom until he pleased (cf. on ch. ii. 7). But, awake, the soul finds that what was sad in her dream was but a dread, but what was joyful is an abiding reality. We cannot lose Christ really, though we may think we do; and the soul that seeks him shall find him.—S. C.

Ver. 3.—*The watchmen.* In this verse very much that it concerns Christ's ministers to give heed to is suggested.

I. THE WATCH THEY HAVE TO KEEP. Christ's ministers are meant (Isa. lii. 8; lxii. 6; Ezek. xxxiii. 7). Their watch is to be over themselves, over their teaching, over the Church of God.

II. THE REASON OF THEIR APPOINTMENT. It is night, when men sleep, when the foe takes advantage; hence the need of watchmen (Isa. xxi. 11, 12).

III. THE DUTY THEY HAVE TO DISCHARGE. "To go about the city." The ways and windings of the human heart. The highways of the Word of God. The streets of the city of God, the Church. They need to be acquainted with all these.

IV. WHAT THEY WILL MEET WITH. Such as they found here. They "found me;" that is, a wearied and sorrowful soul. They find such through their preaching or their pastoral work (1 Cor. xiv. 24, 25). So souls are found. True watchmen are sure to find such.

V. THE QUESTION THEY WILL BE ASKED. (Cf. John xii. 21, "Sir, we would see Jesus.") This the suggestion of what we read here. "Saw ye him whom my soul loveth?" And this is what such souls need; and the more they are directed to him, the more will the watchmen be valued and their word heeded. This is what our congregations want from us, and the question which in reality they put to us.

VI. THE IMPORTANCE OF THEIR ANSWER. Had they told her where he was whom she sought, she would have passed from them with gratitude and joy; as it was, because they could not tell her, she went away in deep distress. Such issues depend upon their word. It is good when they have seen Jesus for themselves. It is better when they can direct seeking souls to him. But it is sad indeed if they have neither seen him nor know how to direct inquirers to him. So was it with these watchmen; so let it not be with us.—S. C.

Vers. 6—11.—"*Solomon in all his glory.*" (For explanation of details in these verses, see Exposition.) We have set before us here such glory as pomp and splendour, strength and power, great riches and sensual pleasure, could give. All that in which Solomon delighted, and for which his name became famous. Now, these things suggest—

I. A GREAT TEMPTATION. They were so: 1. *To Solomon*, for he yielded to it. All that these things could do for him he enjoyed to the full. The tradition of "Solomon and all his glory" came down through the centuries that followed. And the like things are a great temptation to men now. What will they not do for them? They were the last of the temptations with which Satan tempted our Lord. And to the good, the temptation of them lies in the suggestion that was doubtless made to the mind of our Lord—so much good may be done by them; they will so help in establishing the kingdom of God. His mind was, we may well believe, absorbed with the question how the great work he had come to do, the establishment of this kingdom, could be accomplished. And here was the point and force of this temptation. To yield to it would have been as if he had fallen down and worshipped the evil one. Hence he spurned both it and him. And still "in the multitude," not of "words" only, but even more of riches, "there wanteth not sin." Therefore these things are not to become the object of desire in a good man's soul. 2. *They were designed to tempt her of whom this song tells.* Solomon would dazzle her with his splendour and wealth, and so would make her "forget" her "kindred" and her "father's house;" for the king desired her beauty. And in like manner the same temptation is held out still. For the sake of these things what sacrifices are made of loyalty and truth and goodness! She resisted by the might of her affection for her "beloved;" the power of her true love enabled her to overcome. And only the presence in our hearts of a higher love, and, best of all, the highest, even the love of God, will drive out and overcome all lower and evil love.

II. A GREAT LACK. There is nothing in all this glory of pomp and wealth which marks the presence of those Godward riches which alone are real; nothing to satisfy the soul of man or to help it in its life. The soul might starve, as Solomon's did, in spite of all this glory; and, on the other hand, the soul can prosper well though it can call none of this glory its own. We cannot help desiring earthly riches—they are designed in due measure to attract and stimulate us; and they will do us no harm if we are careful, all the while we seek them, to be rich towards God; to possess, as we may, "the unsearchable riches of Christ." But poor and miserable is that soul, though he have all Solomon's glory, if he have not these.

III. A VIVID TYPE. This is what expositors in all ages have mostly seen in the pomp these verses describe. Some have seen a *setting forth of the glory of Christ* on his return to heaven. He comes up out of the wilderness of this dreary world. The incense of praise, fragrant and precious, is given to him. He is borne in stately triumph (cf. Ps. xxiv. 7—10). He is attended by his angel-guards. He has prepared a place for them that love him, and will receive them unto himself. All who love him are to go forth and behold his glory. Thus the triumph of Jesus, the King of Zion, is shown forth. Others have read in these verses *the unseen glory of the redeemed soul.* He comes up out of the wilderness, as Lazarus was carried by angels into Abraham's bosom. The entrance into glory is with joy and praise. Angel-guards surround. The King hath prepared a place, a throne—his own throne—on which the redeemed with their Lord shall sit. Love—Christ's love—has paved all the way. The vision of Christ in his glory which the redeemed shall enjoy. In such ways as this have devout souls found this Scripture full of profit; in this or in other ways may we find it likewise.—S. C.

Vers. 1—4.—*The search for the true King.* When once the Spirit of truth has begun his work in the heart, there is a strong yearning after Jesus. In fulfilling his mission as the Revealer of Christ, the Spirit excites within us intense longings to have the friendship of Jesus. We take this as clear proof that a work of grace has begun in us if we feel that none but Christ can satisfy. Now we can part with all we have to obtain this goodly pearl. As the man who had inadvertently slain a fellow flees with lightning speed toward the city of refuge, feeling that the blood-avenger is at his heels, so the convicted sinner has an eye for only one object—Christ. This persistent search for the Saviour is a token for good. The tree that does not easily languish in summer drought, but grows, blossoms, unfolds its fruit, has most certainly deep roots in the soil; so, if under manifold discouragements we steadily seek after Christ, we may be sure that we are planted in the soil of grace by the Lord's right hand. Three main thoughts are in this text.

I. JESUS SOUGHT. "I sought him whom my soul loveth." 1. *True love to Christ glows brightly even in his absence.* Genuine love is of all things the most unselfish. We love him not so much for the benefit to be obtained; we love him because he is lovable. Having once known him, we cannot restrain our love. To give the shrine of the heart to another would be self-degradation, idolatry. On this account it may be that Jesus keeps away. He sees some growing rivalry within. He sees some need for our self-purging. He wants the soul to realize a deeper need. He wants to make his love more prized. Many worthy reasons has Jesus for hiding himself. 'Tis a temporary winter in order to bring about a more prolific harvest. So, whether we have any assurance of his love or not, we will love him; we will seek after him. 2. *The absence of Jesus makes midnight for the soul.* "By night . . . I sought him." If Jesus has been our Sun of Righteousness, then his departure makes our night. All the things relating to the spiritual world are dark to us if Jesus be absent. We cannot see the face of our Father. We cannot read our titles clear to the heavenly inheritance. There is no growth of holy virtues in us. We cannot run the heavenly race. It is a time of wintry darkness and wintry barrenness if Jesus keeps away. No artificial light can take the place of Immanuel. 3. *There is sound resolution.* The soul has reached a noble resolution. " I will rise now." Some resolutions which we make are worthless. They are made under excited feeling, or from a passing fear, or they are the outcome of a shallow nature, which lightly esteems a pledge. But a resolution made in the strength of God is a firm step taken in advance. It is the first step in a series; for the strength of God is behind it. Genuine resolution never waits. It moves onward at once. No sooner had the prodigal boy resolved to return, than " he arose and came to his father." So here the bride says in the same breath, " I will seek him. . . . I sought him." The future is instantly translated into the present. Good resolution is not a pillow to sleep on; it is a horse which we should instantly mount. 4. *There is active and persistent search.* No journey is too great if we can only find our Beloved. Thousands travel every year over hot sands to Mecca in the hope of getting nearer to Mohammed, and so gaining his empty favour. Sharp privations are gladly endured in order to purchase this worthless merit. Gold-seekers will voyage to the antipodes, and will run a thousand risks to obtain the virgin ore. Then does not highest wisdom impel us to seek the " unsearchable riches of Christ " ? Shall the common adventurers of earth put us to shame ? We must seek everywhere, in all likely places. If in one search we have been disappointed, we must try another. Columbus was not easily daunted when he was on the search for a new continent. Many noble lives have been sacrificed in the effort to find a sea-route over the North Pole. Joseph and Mary did not easily abandon the search for the child Jesus. Pressed down with sorrow, they sought him in one company after another, nor gave up their effort until they found the lad.

> " The subtle chemist can dissect
> And strip the creature naked till he find
> The callow principles within their nest.
> What hath not man sought out and found
> But his dear God ? "

5. *First disappointments will not deter us.* " I sought him, but I found him not." The earnest seeker after Christ is not easily daunted. The first hindrance will not depress him, nor the second, nor the twentieth. Delays in finding Jesus only whet his appetite, and spur him on to fresh search. Failure in finding Christ is in no sense a defeat. It is a gain in knowledge. It is helpful in experience. It is part of the process in the attainment of success. Difficulties make the man. If one road does not lead to righteousness and rest, another road will; for there *is* a road. And Christ is watching us carefully to see if we are faint-hearted. The first experiment to utilize electricity for illuminating a city did not succeed, nor the second; yet mechanicians persevered until they reached the goal. And every awakened sinner is resolved to find Christ, or to die in the attempt. Our own blunders, as a rule, are the cause of delay. 6. *There will be inquiry for Christ from qualified persons.* " The watchmen that go about the city found me : to whom I said, Saw ye him whom my soul loveth?" These watchmen fitly represent the pastors of the Church. They know the haunts and habits of the Prince. They know the proneness of man's heart to err. They know the subtleties of the adversary and the deceitfulness of sin. Therefore a faithful pastor is a good guide for seeking souls. These under-shepherds are ever on the look out for Christ-seekers. We read, " They found me." Then they were searching for such. This is their business. As a man who has navigated a ship a hundred times through an intricate rocky channel makes the best pilot, so they who have themselves found Christ and walk daily with him are best qualified to lead wanderers into his fold. Shrink not from asking counsel. Avail yourself of every help.

II. JESUS FOUND. " I found him whom my soul loveth." 1. *Jesus uses consecrated men to bring his chosen ones into his presence.* Those who know him best are honoured to be chamberlains in his palace, and to introduce guests to his banquet-table. His employment of us in this sacred and noble work is an unspeakable honour. A consecrated man is sure to become a guide to others, whether he fill an office in the Church or not. The pious women who talked with each other of Christ in the cottage porch at Elstow led John Bunyan into the friendship of Christ. As men who have travelled through a *terra incognita* erect guide-posts for those who may follow, so every friend of Christ will find a heavenly pleasure in guiding wayward feet into the right way. Never was Paul the apostle a nobler man than when he put into words the burning desire of his heart, "I could wish that myself were accursed from Christ for my brethren, my kinsmen according to the flesh." 2. *Diligent search is always rewarded.* If, in self-diffidence, we follow the light of Scripture, sooner or later we are sure to succeed. "Then shall we know, if we follow on to know the Lord." Men have searched long for the philosopher's stone and for the secret of perpetual motion—have searched long, and searched in vain. But no sincere lover of Christ yet sought him and failed to find him. Not more surely may you expect a harvest where you have sown good seed than success from seeking Christ. It prevails with the uniform regularity of law. "Then shall we find him when we seek him with all the heart." When there is a seeking sinner and a seeking Saviour, they are sure to meet ere long. Calvary is an old trysting-place. 3. *Genuine love appropriates Christ.* "I held him." We naturally value anything a great deal more if we have taken many pains to acquire it. A jewel is valued for its rarity as well as for its intrinsic beauty. There is but one Christ; hence when we find him we hold him fast. But in what way can we hold him? We hold him by frequent communing with him. We hold him fast when we hourly try to please him. We hold him if our love is strong and fragrant. We hold him if in our heart-garden there are ripe fruits of holiness. We hold him if there is harmony of purpose, will, and life. He loves companionship. 4. *Every attempt of Jesus to depart is energetically resisted.* "I would not let him go." In this way Jesus often tests our love. We have displeased him, and he rises to depart. Then will we confess the evil thing? Will we make some fresh self-sacrifice in order to detain him? He is not easily offended. He hateth putting away. But he loves to see in us a delicate sensitiveness of feeling. He delights to find a tender and childlike affection. It is for our highest good that he should be appreciated. As he did at Emmaus he sometimes deals with us: "he made as though he would have gone further; but they constrained him." And now he gladly yields to our constraints. It brings him delicious joy to feel the embraces of our love. If he can only strengthen and elevate our love, he has conferred on us the very highest good. If love grows, every grace will grow. If love grows, we grow like Christ. And this is love's firm resolve, "I would not let him go."

III. JESUS MADE KNOWN. "Until I had brought him into my mother's house." 1. *We wish our best friend to accompany us everywhere.* The genuine disciple desires to take Jesus with him into every circle and into every occupation. He is not content to have Jesus only on sabbath days and on special occasions. He wants Jesus always at his side—yea, better, always in his heart. He has no friend whom he cannot introduce to Jesus. He has no occupation, no recreation, he wants to keep from the eye of Jesus. Into every chamber of the house Jesus is welcome. He is a fitting Guest for every room, a fit Companion on every journey, a fitting Partner in every enterprise. We do all things in the name of Jesus. 2. *This language suggests benevolent effort for our households.* Love is generous. Having found such spiritual treasure in Jesus, we want every member in our household, viz. children, parents, servants, to share in the "unsearchable riches." "I brought him into my mother's house." Happy the man who can testify *that!* If we are under tremendous obligations to earthly parents, how can we better discharge the debt than by making them partakers of Christ? 3. *This language suggests our usefulness to the Church.* As we give to the imagery of this book a spiritual interpretation, so may we properly regard our mother's house as the Church on earth. This is our true *Alma Mater.* We bring the Bridegroom with us into the Church. We cannot enjoy our piety alone. We inspire the whole Church with a nobler life. Our sacred love to Jesus is a contagion. Others feel the heavenly charm, and they desire to have Jesus too. And from the Church the benefit extends to the whole world. Would that all men knew our Lord!—D.

Vers. 6—11.—*The King coming to his capital.* In Asiatic lands wheeled carriages were rare, and are rare still. This is accounted for by the absence of roads. To construct and maintain roads through a hilly country like Palestine required more engineering skill than the people possessed; and further, there was a general belief that to make good roads would pave the way to military invasion. Hence all over Palestine the pathways from town to town were simply tracks marked out by the feet of men and beasts. Over the level plain of Esdraelon Ahab might ride in a chariot; but if Solomon brought up wheeled chariots from Egypt he had a prior undertaking, viz. to make a road from Beersheba to the capital. Therefore travelling princes rode in a covered palanquin, which served to screen from the hot sun by day, and became a bed at night. Owing to the scorching heat, much of the journey would be taken during the cool hours of night, and hence the need for a strong body-guard. Before the rapt imagination of the sacred poet such a scene passed. The stately procession arrested his attention, and he asks, "Who is this?" What great king is this? Such is the poetic imagery. Now, what is the religious instruction? It is the march of Christ through the ages—a march beginning with the wilderness and terminating with his coronation in the new Jerusalem. Though he has been long hidden, the day is coming when the King of Zion shall be revealed to the eyes of men, and he shall "be admired by all who love his appearing."

I. OBSERVE THE MARCH OF CHRIST TO HIS GLORIOUS THRONE. 1. *His lowly beginning is indicated.* "He cometh out of the wilderness." This is how he appeared to the onlooker. His prior state was hidden from mortal eye. So far as men saw, Jesus began his strange career in the cattle-manger of a stable. The world to him was a wilderness, void of all attractiveness. In this respect he followed the fortunes of ancient Israel, for they too had first the wilderness, then the "land flowing with milk and honey." When Jesus began his mission, human life was a veritable wilderness. The beauty and joy of Eden had departed. On every side raged jealousies, hatreds, strifes. The civilized world was under the iron despotism of Rome. The prophets of God had ceased to speak. Hope of a golden age had almost died out, except in a few believing hearts. The glory of Greece and Tyre had waned. The human race was on the verge of reckless despair. Our earth was reduced to a desert. 2. *Christ's coming was fragrant with heavenly hope.* Even in the loneliest desert there are some living plants, and these ofttimes possess aromatic essences. The shrubs are storehouses of fragrant spice. The sweetest perfumes come from the Arabian desert. Such things abate the mischief of noxious miasma. Rare perfumes refresh the senses, and betoken noble rank. The mightiest King did not despise the sweet odours of myrrh and frankincense. So neither did Jesus Christ treat with contempt the simple virtues and courtesies of the people. He stooped to learn from the lips of Jewish rabbis. He gave his benediction to the wedding-feast. He was pleased with the gratitude of a poor leper. He commended the brotherliness of the despised Samaritan. He accepted the hospitality of peasant women. He praised the generosity of a poor widow. A sweet and refreshing savour pervaded all his words, all his deeds. From his cradle to his grave he was perfumed with frankincense and myrrh. 3. *His coming was a conspicuous thing.* The procession was seen afar off. Possibly the flame of torches during the night-march sent up in front and in rear huge pillars of smoke. Or possibly clouds of dust from that dry soil rose from the feet of the host, and in that clear, transparent air was seen thirty or forty miles away—even from the hills of Zion. Anyhow, the procession is seen from a distance. Curiosity is aroused. Many eyes are turned to the novel spectacle, and the question leaps from lip to lip, "Who is this?" So, too, the progress of Jesus through our world has excited the wonder of successive generations. When he read the Scripture in the rustic synagogue of Nazareth, men asked, "Who is this?" When he fed the five thousand on the mountain-side, or ruled nature with a nod, they asked, "Who is this?" When, on the Day of Pentecost, the whole city was thrilled with astonishment, men asked, "Who is this?" At Corinth, at Ephesus, at Antioch, when multitudes left their idols for the new faith, men asked, "Who is this, whose onward march is so kingly, so triumphant?" And still they ask in the bazaars of India and in the temples of China, "Who is this?" His march is the march of a Conqueror: the King of kings, because he is the Prince of Peace.

II. OBSERVE HIS BODY-GUARD. 1. *This is a token of peril.* But the peril is not that of open war. If a bannered host should oppose his march, he would meet it with his invincible forces. Michael and all the powers of heaven would fight his battle. It is not open war. The foes in the desert are Ishmaelites. They seek for plunder. They make sudden and covert attack in the night. So has it been in the progress of our Immanuel. From the band of his own disciples the traitor came, and came by night. The priests of Jehovah were his worst foes. Professed friends, like Ananias and Sapphira, have stabbed his cause in secret. The persecutors of his gospel have usually laid their plots in the dark. Atheists and hypocrites have been his bitterest foes. The enemies to the cause of heavenly truth still lie in ambush. 2. *Variety of service can be rendered to our gracious King.* There were some who bore on their shoulders his palanquin; some who carried torches; some who perfumed his Person; some who wielded swords in his defence. And various service is needed still. If one cannot be a general on the battle-field, he may be an armour-bearer. He who cannot fight in the ranks can be a sentinel at the gate or a watchman on the tower. The child wanting yet in martial strength may be fleet of foot as a messenger. If too old for field-service, we can be mighty at the throne. 3. *The life-guards are well equipped.* "They all hold swords." And in the service of Immanuel the sword is keen and has a double edge. In the olden time a Damascus blade had great renown; but the sword of truth is forged and furbished in heaven, and has a penetration which is irresistible. If once we get this sword of truth into a man's conscience, it does exploits there. The tongues with which we speak winsomely and graciously of our King is a two-edged weapon. The pen is mightier than the sword, and the tongue of fire is mightier than the pen. The Word of the Lord is invincible. 4. *All service is useful in this King's progress.* It made the march a more imposing spectacle. It silenced the murmurers and the scorners. Does Jesus Christ require human service? He has chosen such plans of warfare as require various agencies of man. He prefers to work through feeble and imperfect men, for thereby he confers blessing on friends and on foes at once. Through exercise our spiritual energies become more robust. Through service our faith and love are tested. The more fervid zeal we bring to our Master's cause, the more honour crowns his head. We serve the King, we serve the human race, we serve ourselves, at one stroke. Loving service is the richest spiritual perfume.

III. NOTE HIS PALANQUIN. It is made of cedar-wood from Lebanon; the bed is gold, the pillars are silver, the curtains are resplendent with imperial purple. 1. *This carriage, or palanquin, may fitly represent for us the covenant of grace.* In this our Immanuel rides triumphantly. In order to set this forth so as to impress the dull senses of humanity, the most precious things of earth are used as metaphors. As cedar is the richest and hardest among timber, as gold and silver are the costliest of metals, as the purple colour was selected for royalty, these material splendours feebly adumbrate the eternal covenant of redemption. Nothing on earth can adequately express it. It is notable for its antiquity; notable for its rarity; notable for its splendour; notable for its usefulness. As the palanquin must be made worthy of a king, the covenant of grace is well worthy of our God. To save is his eternal purpose. 2. *The curtains were the handiwork of virgins.* "Worked by the daughters of Jerusalem." All through the East, women are despised, down-trodden, treated as an inferior race. If in Western lands women are ennobled and honoured, it is wholly due to the grace of our King. So from the very beginning Jesus intimated that the service of women would be acceptable. He was dependent on an earthly mother's care. Once and again, women ministered to him "of their substance." The deed which he predicted should be known throughout the world was the deed of a woman. Women gathered round his cross in sweetest sympathy, while others laughed and jeered. Women performed the last acts of care for his dead body. Women were the first to greet him on the resurrection-morn. "In Christ Jesus there is neither male nor female." 3. *These curtains and carpets are adorned with emblems of love.* Our version says, "paved with love." It should rather be, "inwrought with symbols of love." Just as in our day men use the form of a heart, or the figure of a fire, to denote warm and genuine love, so some device of love was interlaced in the manufacture of these curtains by the deft fingers of devoted women. It is not more true that we rest in Christ's love than the converse, "he rests in our love." "If any man love me, he will keep my commandments: and my Father will love him, and we will come unto him, and will make our abode with him." To the same effect we read, "that Christ may dwell in your hearts." Love has a thousand devices for expressing itself.

IV. MARK THE ADORATION WHICH BEFITS THE KING. "Go forth, ye daughters of Zion, and behold King Solomon." In some respects David was the type of Christ. "He was despised and rejected of men," and yet a mighty king. But, in respect to the magnificence of his kingdom and the peacefulness of his reign, Solomon better prefigures Jesus. 1. *To appreciate Jesus as King we must know him.* "Go forth, then, and behold him." Look into his excellences. Examine his claims to Kingship. Note carefully the unstained purity of his character. Behold his hands, bearing the marks of the nails—marks of love! Behold his feet, firm "as fine brass; as if they glowed in a furnace," and set upon the serpent's head. Behold his heart, still pulsating with everlasting love for the fallen sons of men. Learn well all his kingly qualities; for no true loyalty, no complete consecration, can spring up in us until we know him. 2. *Note especially that he is crowned.* He is appointed to this supreme throne as the world's King by the Eternal Father. "By the right hand of God he is exalted." Yet the symbols of his reign we place upon his head. On his head are already "many crowns." Every ransomed sinner is another ornament in the diadem of our King. Never did king wear such a crown as this. He is crowned already with world-wide renown. Every thorn in that crown, which impious mockers thrust upon his brow, is now transmuted into a ray of peerless glory. To-day kings and princes bow before him, and already his "enemies lick the dust." From a hundred empires the shout ascends, "Blessed is he that cometh in the name of the Lord!" We do not hail and welcome him simply as the Victim of the cross; we bow to him as our soul's true King. 3. *This coronation of Jesus is attended with gladness of heart.* It is not always so. Sometimes the heir to a nation's crown is very unfitted to wear it. He is too young to sustain its cares. He would prefer a life of pleasurable ease. Or the crown itself may be disgraced. The throne is planted with sharpest thorns. The empire is reeking with discontent. That coronation may be no better than a crucifixion. Not so with King Jesus. To be crowned means success for his great redemptive mission. "For the joy that was set before him he endured the cross." As his grief was unexampled, so shall be his joy. The globe shall be his empire. Because his capacity for joy is infinite, his joy shall rise until the capacious heart is full. The joy will be eternal, because the triumph can never be reversed.—D.

Ver. 1.—*The soul's love.* This whole book is a glorification of love; it teaches that human love, if true, is sacred, ennobling, and inspiring; it shows the excellence of human love, that it is worthy of being the emblem of that love which is spiritual and Divine. As St. John has taught us, "He that loveth not knoweth not God: for God is love." The Object of the Christian's love is Christ, in whom the love of God has been revealed and communicated to us.

I. THE GROUNDS OF THE SOUL'S LOVE TO CHRIST. The soul that loves the Redeemer is not prompted by blind, unreasonable impulse; such love as that expressed in the language of the text is rational and justifiable. 1. The soul loves Christ for his own Divine, unapproachable excellence, for what he is in himself. He is worthy above all to be thus loved. With an "intellectual love," as the English Platonist phrased it, does the illumined and living soul love him who is the Effulgence of the Father's glory and the Revelation of the Father's heart. 2. The soul loves Christ in gratitude for Divine compassion, ministry, and sacrifice. The cycle of Christian doctrine concerning the Person and mediation of the Redeemer is an exhibition as much of God's love as of his holiness and his wisdom. What our Saviour has done for us is an appeal to the soul which awakens the response of grateful affection. 3. The soul loves Christ because of the revelations of Divine friendship made to the individual nature. The language of the Canticles is rich in portraying the personal element in the relation between the Lord and humanity as redeemed by him. And every Christian is prompted to affection by those intimate displays of Divine affection which experience records in the recesses of the spiritual nature.

II. THE PROOFS OF THE SOUL'S LOVE TO CHRIST. An emotion such as this cannot take possession of the mind, and dwell in the mind, without becoming a principle, controlling and inspiring the nature, and prompting to manifestations of marked, decisive import. 1. The soul keeps him whom it loveth in perpetual memory. 2. The soul takes an ever-growing delight in his society; places the highest happiness in spiritual fellowship with Christ. 3. The soul proves the sincerity of its love to Christ by treasuring up his precepts, by seeking to live under the inspiring influence of his presence and character, by yielding to him a cheerful, constant, and unquestioning obedience. Whom the soul loveth the hand serveth, the tongue witnesseth unto, the whole life honoureth by obeying and glorifying.—T.

Vers. 2—4.—*The soul's quest rewarded.* The romantic incident here poetically related has usually been regarded as a picture of the experiences through which many a soul is permitted to pass during this state of probation and Divine discipline.

I. THE SOUL'S SEARCH. 1. The appreciation of Christ involved in this quest. Men seek for gold because they value it; they dive for pearls and dig for precious stones. Multitudes are indifferent to the Saviour because they know him not; because their spiritual susceptibilities are not awakened. But those to whom he is chief among ten thousand cannot be satisfied until they possess him and enjoy his fellowship. 2. The quest may be both earnest and prolonged. The desire for highest good is amongst the noblest and purest of all human characteristics. And seeking is good, even though finding be better. A search which is sincere and patient is in a sense its own reward. And there are those whose spiritual experience can only thus be justly described. It is a low view of human nature which looks upon such high quest with contempt; which takes for its motto, *Nil admirari*—" Not to desire or admire." The young and ardent will do well to make the search after God's truth, after God himself, the occupation of their life.

II. THE SOUL'S DISTRESS. 1. Seeking does not always issue in speedy finding. The soul may seek with a mistaken purpose, or in the wrong way, or with a misguided aim, or at the wrong time, *i.e.* too late. 2. The absence of the sought Saviour is the cause of distress and complaint.

> "This is the way I long had sought,
> And mourned because I found it not."

There is no repose for the heart until Christ be found. " Cor nostrum inquietum est, donec requiescat in te," says St. Augustine—" Our heart is restless till it rests in thee." There is something of mystery in the providential arrangement that the lot of man should so often be one of seemingly fruitless search and disappointed endeavour. Yet this is discipline for which many have had reason to give thanks; it has called forth courage, it has braced to patience, it has stimulated aspiration, it has sweetened success.

III. THE SOUL'S DISCOVERY. 1. A delayed discovery. The soul has followed hard after him. The moment of revelation has been again and again deferred. The call has been loud, but has met with no answer but the echo. 2. A promised discovery. The word has gone forth from heaven, " Seek ye the Lord while he may be found." The promise has been proclaimed by Christ himself, " Seek, and ye shall find." He does not say, " Seek ye my face in vain." 3. A gracious discovery. " I found him whom my soul loveth." How condescending the revelation! How joyful the sight, the apprehension, the hope's fulfilment! 4. A discovery which the soul uses for its own lasting satisfaction. As the bride in the poem " held " her spouse, grasped him by the arm in the fulness of her joy, and " brought him into the house," there to enjoy his society, so when the soul finds Christ it finds in him One who satisfies every deep craving of its nature. And to find him is to retain him, not as a wayfaring man who tarrieth for a night, but as an inmate never to be displaced from the heart, a friend to go no more out for ever.—T.

Vers. 6—11.—*The bridal entry.* The pomp of Oriental poetry is nowhere more dazzling and imposing than in this passage, where is depicted the procession of the royal bride, who is escorted with magnificent accompaniments, and welcomed into the metropolis with universal and cordial joy. Expositors have seen in this gorgeous picture a description of the dignity and beauty of the Church, the bride of Christ.

The incense rising in perfumed clouds heralds the approach of the bridal procession. The palanquin which contains the bride is of the cedar of Lebanon; silver pillars support its canopy of gold, and the hangings and drapery are of costly purple. The palanquin itself is the provision of the king's munificence, and the ornaments are the gift of the wealthy ladies of Jerusalem. Accompanying the festive procession is an escort of armed and valiant warriors, not only for security, but for state and dignity. The royal bridegroom meets and joins the *cortége*, having upon his head the crown of festivity and happiness, for it is the day of his gladness of heart. The daughters of Jerusalem go forth from the city to join in the welcome, and to swell the number and add to the dignity and attractiveness of the bridal train. "Which things are an allegory."

I. The Church is summoned to quit the wilderness of the world, and become the bride of Christ.

II. The Church is invested by Divine liberality with all that can contribute to her spiritual glory.

III. The Church in her passage through earth is accompanied with the incense of devotion and of service.

IV. The Church is environed with Divine protection.

V. The Church is the object of Christ's affection and the occasion of his joy.

VI. The Church is regarded by angelic intelligences with the deepest interest and satisfaction.

VII. The Church is assured of an eternal house in the favour and communion of the Divine King.—T.

EXPOSITION.

CHAPTER IV.

Ver. 1.—Behold, thou art fair, my love; behold, thou art fair; thine eyes are as doves behind thy veil; thine hair is as a flock of goats, that lie along the side of Mount Gilead. We commence, at this verse, the loving converse of the bridegroom with the bride, which we must suppose is heard as they travel together in the bridal procession. The words of adoring affection are chiefly spoken by the bridegroom, as is natural in the circumstances, and the reference to the journey, and its consummation in ver. 8, make it certain that the intention is to carry us in thought to the palanquin and the breathings of first love in bridal joy. The poetry is exquisite and truly Eastern, while yet absolutely chaste and pure. The praise of the eyes is common in all erotic poetry. Her eyes gleam, in colour, motion, and lustre, like a pair of doves from behind the veil; showing that the bride is thought of as travelling. The bride was always deeply veiled (see Gen. xxiv. 65), as the Roman bride wore the *velum flamineum*. The LXX. have mistaken the meaning, rendering, ἐκτὸς τῆς σιωπήσεώς σου. The veil might typify silence or reserve, but the word is *tsammâh*, which is from a root "to veil," and is rightly rendered by Symmachus κάλυμμα. The hair was long and dark, and lay down the shoulders uncovered and free, which added much to the graceful attraction

of the bride. In later times it was customary for the hair to be adorned with a wreath of myrtle or roses, or a golden ornament representing Jerusalem. The goats in Syria and the neighbouring countries are mostly black or dark brown, while the sheep are white. Delitzsch says, "A flock of goats encamped upon a mountain (rising up, to one looking from a distance, as in a steep slope and almost perpendicularly), and as if hanging down lengthwise on its sides, presents a lovely view adorning the landscape." It would be especially lovely amid the romantic scenery of Gilead. The verb rendered "lie along" is otherwise taken by the LXX., ἀπεκαλύφησαν, and by the Vulgate *ascenderunt*. The rabbis differ from one another in their renderings. One says, "which look down;" another, "make bare," "quit," or "descend;" another, "are seen." The modern translators vary. Luther says, "shorn;" Houbigant, "hang down;" Kleuken and Ewald, "shows itself;" Gesenius and others, "lie down;" Ginsburg, "rolling down," "running down." Our Revised Version gives, *lie along*, which is a very probable meaning. The reference is to the luxuriance and rich colour of the hair. Gilead would be a recollection of the bride's native place.

Ver. 2.—Thy teeth are like a flock of ewes that are newly shorn, which are come up from the washing; whereof every one hath twins, and none is bereaved among them. The

simile is very apt and beautiful. Thy teeth are perfectly smooth, regular, and white; the upper set corresponding exactly to the lower set, like twin-births in which there is no break (cf. ch. vi. 6). The moisture of the *saliva dentium*, heightening the glance of the teeth, is frequently mentioned in love-songs. The whiteness of wool is often used as a comparison (see Isa. i. 18; Dan. vii. 9; Rev. i. 14; Book of Enoch xlvi. 1). Some think that קְצוּבוֹת should not be rendered "newly shorn," but "periodically shorn" (see Ginsburg)—a poetical epithet for וְחֵלִים. The newly shorn would be washed first. תָּאַם, "to be double," "to be pairs," in the hiph. is "to make double," "to make pairs," "to appear paired." Perhaps the reference is to the sheep being washed in pairs, and going up side by side from the water. This would seem almost more exact than the idea of twin-lambs, because the difference in size between the ewe and the lamb would suggest irregularity. The word שַׁכֻּלָה, "deprived," "bereaved" (Jer. xviii. 21), may point merely to the loneliness of the single sheep going up by itself, suggesting one tooth without its fellow. Ginsburg says, "all of which are paired." Each keeps to its mate as they come up from the pool. This is a decided improvement on the Authorized Version. But the figure is clear with either rendering, and is very striking and suggestive of the pleasant country life to which the bride was accustomed.

Ver. 3.—**Thy lips are like a thread of scarlet, and thy mouth is comely; thy temples are like a piece of a pomegranate behind thy veil.** *Scarlet;* that is, shining, glistening red colour. *Thy mouth* (מִדְבָּרֵךְ). Thy mouth as speaking. So the LXX., Jerome, and Venetian, "thy speech," *eloquium,* conversation. But this is questioned, as it should then be דְּבָרֵךְ. The word *midhbâr* undoubtedly means "the mouth," from *dâvâr,* "to speak," with the מ preformative, as the name of the instrument. It is the preterite for פֶּה, but perhaps as referring specially to speech. *Thy temples;* Latin *tempora,* from the adjective רַק, "weak," meaning the thin piece of skull on each side of the eyes, like the German *schläfe,* from *schlaff,* "slack." The inside of the pomegranate is of a red colour mixed and tempered with the ruby colour. Ginsburg, however, thinks that the cheeks are intended, and that the comparison is with the outside of the pomegranate, in which the vermilion colour is mingled with brown, and resembles the round cheek; but then why say, "*piece* of a pomegranate"? פֶּלַח, from the root "to cut fruit" (see 1 Kings iv. 39), certainly must refer to the cut fruit and the appearance of the inside. The

meaning may be a segment, that is, so as to represent the roundness of the cheek. Possibly the reference may be to blushes on the bride's cheek, or to ornaments which appeared through the veil. We can scarcely expect to make out every particular in an Eastern description.

Ver. 4.—**Thy neck is like the tower of David, builded for an armoury, whereon there hang a thousand bucklers, all the shields of the mighty men.** There is an evident change here in the character of the similitudes. The royal bridegroom does not forget to praise the majesty of his bride. The description now suits a royal queen. She is full of dignity and grace in her bearing. The tower referred to was no doubt that which was sometimes called "The tower of the flock" (Micah iv. 4), that from which David surveyed the flock of his people (cf. Neh. iii. 16, 25)—the government building erected on Mount Zion which served as a court of justice. The word *talpiyoth* is an ἅπαξ λεγόμενον: LXX. θαλπιωθ, as if a proper name. Hengstenberg would render it "built for hanging swords," supposing it composed of two words—*tal,* from a root "to hang," and *piyoth,* "swords." But the word *piyoth* does not mean "swords," but the "double edges" of the swords. Kimchi renders, "an erection of sharp-cornered stones." Gesenius takes it from two roots, "to perish" and "to go," that is, *exitialibus armis,* which is very doubtful. Ewald's explanation seems the best, "built for close troops, so that many hundreds or thousands find room therein," taking it from a root, connected with the Arabic, meaning, "to wrap together." Delitzsch, however, observes that both in Aramaic and Talmudic Hebrew words occur, like this, in the sense of "enclosure," *i.e.* joining together, one working into the other, so that it may be taken as meaning, "in ranks together." This view is supported by Döderlein, Meier, Aquila, Jerome, Vulgate (*propugnacula*), and Venetian (ἐπάλξεις). If this be accepted, it may mean "terraced," *i.e.* built in stories one above another. This would convey the appearance of the tall, straight neck better than any. Surrounded with ornaments, the neck would so appear. There is another suggestion, supported by Ginsburg and taken from Rashi and Rashbun, Jewish writers, that the word is a contraction for a noun meaning "instruction," and means "the model tower"—the tower built for an architect's model. It would be rendered, "built for the builder's model." The meaning "armoury" takes it as composed of two words, *tael,* "a hill," and *piyoth,* "swords." It was decorated with a thousand shields, which was a customary adornment of towers and castles (see Ezek. xxvii. 11). *All the* *shields of heroes.* We can scarcely doubt the reference in such words to the time of Solomon, and therefore to his authorship, as the allusion to heroes, or mighty men of valour, would be customary soon after the time of David.

Ver. 5.—**Thy two breasts are like two fawns that are twins of a roe, which feed among the lilies.** This is a beautiful and yet perfectly delicate figure, describing the lovely equality and perfect shape and sweet freshness of the maiden's bosom. The meadow covered with lilies suggests beauty and fragrance. Thus the loveliness of the bride is set forth in seven comparisons, her perfections being sevenfold. "A twin pair of the young of the gazelle, lying in a bed covered with lilies, representing the fragrant delicacy and elegance of a chaste virgin bosom, veiled by the folds of a dress redolent of sweet odour" (cf. ch. i. 13). The bridegroom, having thus delighted himself in praise of his bride's loveliness, then proceeds to declare his desire for her sweet society, but he is interrupted by the bride.

Ver. 6.—**Until the day be cool, and the shadows flee away, I will get me to the mountain of myrrh, and to the hill of frankincense.** If this be the language of the bride, which most modern interpreters think, the meaning is to check the ardour of her lover, in the modesty of her fresh and maidenly feeling—Let me retire from such praises. They are too ardent for me. It is only a moment's interruption, which is followed by still more loving words from the bridegroom. We must naturally connect the words with ch. ii. 17, where the bride certainly speaks. Louis de Leon thinks that the meaning is general, "shady and fragrant places." Anton (1773) suggests that she is desiring to escape and be free. It cannot be included as a description of the neighbourhood of the royal palace. She might, however, mean merely—Let me walk alone in the lovely gardens of the palace until the shades of night shall hide my blushes. It is unlikely that the words are in the mouth of Solomon; for then it would be impossible to explain their use by Shulamith previously. She is not referring to Lebanon and its neighbourhood, and there can be no idea of looking back to a lover from whom she is torn. The interpretation which connects it with maidenly feeling is certainly the most in harmony with what has preceded. Perhaps the typical meaning is underlying the words—Let me find a place of devout meditation to feed my thoughts on the sweetness of this Divine love into which I have entered.

Ver. 7.—**Thou art all fair, my love; and there is no spot in thee.** The bridegroom speaks. The sweet humility and modesty

of the bride kindles his love afresh. He praised the loveliness of her bodily form, and she by her response showed the exceeding loveliness of her soul. It must not be forgotten that, whether borrowed from this book or not, such language is undoubtedly employed in Scripture of the Church, the bride, the Lamb's wife, who is described as "not having spot, or wrinkle, or any such thing" (Eph. v. 27). It should be noticed that the king immediately addresses his love as "bride," and "sister-bride," to show that there is more than admiration of her person in his thoughts. She is his by assimilation and by eternal union, and he invites her to enter fully into the new life which he has prepared for her, as in Ps. xlv., "forgetting her own people, and her father's house." It is not enough that feeling should be stirred, or even that it should take possession of the soul, if it be only feeling; it is required of us that our inner life of emotion should become practical devotedness, "counting all things but loss" for the sake of him we love.

Ver. 8.—**Come with me from Lebanon, my bride, with me from Lebanon: look from the top of Amana, from the top of Senir and Hermon, from the lions' dens, from the mountains of the leopards.** This seems to be simply the bridegroom rejoicing over the bride, the meaning being, "Give thyself up to me"—thou art mine; look away from the past, and delight thyself in the future. Delitzsch, however, thinks that the bridegroom seeks the bride to go with him up the steep heights of Lebanon, and to descend with him from thence; for while ascending the mountain one has no view before him, but when descending he has the whole panorama of the surrounding region lying at his feet. It is stretching poetical language too far to take it so literally and topically; there is no necessity to think of either the lover or his beloved as actually on the mountains, the idea is simply that of the mountainous region—Turn thy back upon it, look away from it. This is clearly seen from the fact that the names connected with Lebanon—Amana, Senir, Hermon—could have no reference to the bride's being in them, as they represent Anti-Libanus, separated from Lebanon by the Cœle-Syrian valley, stretching from the Banias northwards to the plain of Hamath (see 2 Kings v. 12, where Amana is Abana, overlooking Damascus, now the Basadia). Shenir, or Senir, and Hermon are neighbouring peaks or mountains, or possibly different names for the same (see Deut. iii. 9). In 1 Chron. v. 23 they are mentioned as districts. Hermon is the chief mountain of the range of Anti-Libanus on the north-east border of Palestine (Ps. lxxxix. 12). The wild beasts abounded in that district, especially lions and panthers. They were found in the clefts and defiles of the rocks. Lions, however, have now altogether disappeared. In the name *Amana* some think there is an allusion to truth (*amén*) (see Hos. ii. 22); but that would be too obscure. The general intention of the passage is simple and plain —Leave the rough places, and come to my palace. The words "with me" (אִתִּי) are taken by the LXX. and Vulgate as though written אָתִי, the imperative of אָתָה, "to come," as a word of invitation, δεῦρο. The use of the verb תָּבוֹאִי, "thou shalt come," *i.e.* thou hast come and be content, renders it improbable that such should be the reading, whereas the preposition with the pronoun is quite in place. The spiritual meaning is not far to seek. The life that we live without Christ is at best a life among the wild, untamed impulses of nature, and in the rough and dangerous places of the world. He invites us to go with him to the place which he has prepared for us. And so the Church will leave its crude thoughts and undeveloped life, and seek, in the love of Christ and in the gifts of his Spirit, a truer reflection of his nature and will (see Eph. iv. 14—16). The Apocalypse is based upon the same idea, the advancement of the kingdom of Christ from the place of lions and panthers to the new Jerusalem, with its perfection of beauty and its eternal peace.

Ver. 9.—**Thou hast ravished my heart, my sister, my bride; thou hast ravished my heart with one of thine eyes, with one chain of thy neck.** The bridegroom still continues his address of love, which we must not, of course, press too closely, though it is noticeable that the language becomes somewhat more sober in tone, as though the writer were conscious of the higher application to which it would be put. Some translators take the first clause as though the word "ravished" should be rendered "emboldened." Symmachus, ἐθάρσυνας με. The Hebrew word לְבַבְ, literally, "heartened," may mean, as in Aramaic, "make courageous." Love in the beginning overpowers, *unhearts*, but the general idea must be that of "smitten" or "captured." So the LXX., Venetian, and Jerome, ἐκαρδίωσας με, *vulnerasti cor meum* (cf. Ps. xlv. 6). *My sister, my bride,* is, of course, the same as "my sisterly bride," a step beyond "my betrothed." Gesenius thinks that "one of thine eyes" should be "one look of thine;" but may it not refer to the eye appearing through the veil, as again one chain of the neck may glitter and attract all the more that the whole ornamentation did not appear in view? If but a portion of her beauty so overpowers, what will be the effect of the whole blaze of her perfection? As the Church advances in her likeness to her Lord, she becomes more and more the object of his delight, and as the soul receives more and more grace, so is her fellowship with Christ more and more assured and joyful.

Vers. 10, 11.—**How fair is thy love, my sister, my bride! How much better is thy love than wine! and the smell of thine ointments than all manner of spices! Thy lips, O my bride, drop as the honeycomb; honey and milk are under thy tongue; and the smell of thy garments is like the smell of Lebanon.** The expression of thy love, that is, the endearments, the embraces, are delightful. The allusion to the lips may be a mere amplification of the word "love," but it may also refer to speech, and we think of the nineteenth psalm and the description of the words and testimony of the Lord, "more to be desired than gold, and sweeter than honey and the droppings of the honeycomb" (cf. Gen. xxvii. 27; Hos. iv. 7; Ps. xlv. 9). The words of pure, inward joy flowing forth from the lips may be so described. So the Lord has said, in Isa. lxii. 5, that he rejoiceth over his people as the bridegroom rejoiceth over the bride.

Ver. 12.—**A garden shut up is my sister, my bride; a spring shut up, a fountain sealed.** We must bear in mind that these words are supposed to be spoken on the journey in the marriage procession. The bride is not yet brought to the royal palace. She is still travelling in the royal palanquin. The idea of a paradise or garden is carried from the beginning of Scripture to the end, the symbol of perfect blessedness. The figure of the closed or shut-up garden represents the bridegroom's delight in the sense of absolute and sole possession—for himself and no other. The language is very natural at such a time, when the bride is being taken from her home. We may compare with the figures here employed those in Prov. v. 15—20.

Vers. 13, 14.—**Thy shoots are an orchard of pomegranates, with precious fruits; henna with spikenard plants, spikenard and saffron, calamus and cinnamon, with all trees of frankincense; myrrh and aloes, with all the chief spices.** *Thy shoots;* i.e. that which comes forth from thee, thy plants, or, as Böttcher puts it, "all the phenomena and life-utterances of her personality." All the plants had their meaning in flower language. They are mostly exotics. But it is difficult now to suggest meanings, though they may have been familiar to Jewish readers at the time. The *pardes*, "park, or enclosure," was adorned especially with foreign and fragrant plants of great beauty. It is an Old Persian word, perhaps, as Delitzsch suggests, from *pairi* (περί) and *déz* (Pers. *díz*), "a heap."

Precious fruit; literally, *fructus laudum,* "fruits of renown" or excellence (cf. Syriac *magdo,* "dried fruit"). The *carcom,* or saffron, a kind of crocus (Ind. *safran*), yields the saffron colour from its dried flower-eyes, used both as a cosmetic and as a medicine (cf. Sansc. *kuakuma*). The *calamus,* simply a reed, the sweet reed, a corn indigenous to the East. *Cinnamon (Quinnamon), Laurus cinnamomum,* is indigenous on the east coast of Africa and Ceylon, found later in the Antibes. The inner bark peeled off and rolled together forms the cinnamon bark (see Pliny, bk. 12). There are seven spices mentioned. We need not trouble ourselves to identify them all, as they are mostly Indian, and such as Solomon would fetch from the far East in his celebrated ships. The description is highly poetical, and simply means that all sweetness and attractiveness combine in the fair one. But symbolically we may see an allusion to the spread of the Church over the world, and "all the glory and honour of the nations" being introduced into it. So the graces of the individual soul expand themselves under the influence of Christian truth and fellowship.

Ver. 15.—**Thou art a fountain of gardens, a well of living waters, and flowing streams from Lebanon.** Referring, of course, to the clear, cool streams coming down from the snowy heights. The sweet freshness of the country maiden suggested this. May we not see a symbol of the spiritual life in such language (cf. John vii. 38)? Ethically, at least, the blending of the freshness of a mountain stream with the luxuriance and fragrance of a cultivated garden is very suggestive. To an Eastern monarch, such purity and modesty as Solomon found in his bride must have been a rare excellence which might well be made typical.

Ver. 16.—**Awake, 0 north wind; and come, thou south; blow upon my garden, that the spices thereof may flow out. Let my beloved come into his garden, and eat his precious fruits.** This is the answer of the bride to the lavish praises of her husband. I am all his. She is yet unworthy of the king and of his love until the seasonal changes have developed and unfolded and spread forth her excellences. The north represents cold; the south, heat. Let the various influences from different quarters flow gently over the garden and call forth the fragrance and the fruits (cf. Esth. ii. 12). There is rich suggestion in such words. Whether we think of the individual soul or of the Church of Christ, the true desire of those who delight in the love of the Saviour is that all the gifts and graces which can be bestowed may make them worthy of him who condescends to call his people his delight. Surely it is no mere romantic idyll that is before us. Such significance cannot be a mere coincidence when it is so transparent and so apt.

HOMILETICS.

Vers. 1—6.—*The bridegroom with the bride.* I. HIS PRAISE OF THE BRIDE. 1. *The earthly bridegroom.* The bridegroom rejoices over the bride. She is wholly his. He enumerates her beauties; they are very precious to him; his great love leads him to dwell on every point. The love of the espousals (Jer. ii. 2), the young love of the newly wedded, is a beautiful thing, very tender and touching; it leaves a fragrant memory behind—a memory treasured still after the lapse of many years, when the love of wedlock has become, not less true, not less blessed, but calmer and more mellow; and perhaps even more blessed, when no jealousies, no quarrels, have tended to put asunder those whom God hath joined together, but love has continued to increase with increasing years, with less and less of earthly passion, but more and more of holy tenderness and mutual self-denials for the loved one's sake. Such, alas! was not the love of Solomon. The fair promise, so very bright and beautiful at first, was soon blighted. *Corruptio optimi pessima.* Nothing in this world is more beautiful and blessed than that holy estate of matrimony which was instituted of God in the time of man's innocency, which God has consecrated to such an excellent mystery that in it is signified and represented the spiritual marriage and unity betwixt Christ and his Church. And, on the other hand, nothing is more degrading and ruinous than that sensual passion which is the caricature of wedded love. The early goodness of Solomon, the bright promise of future happiness and usefulness which gilded his youth, excites an interest in him so personal, that it makes us feel a real grief and disappointment when we read that "King Solomon loved many strange women;" that "when Solomon was old, his wives turned away his heart;" that "he went after Ashtoreth, the abomination of the Zidonians;" that he "did evil in the sight of the Lord." And so it came to pass that that bright beginning ended in utter gloom, in the mournful cry of disappointment. " Vanity of vanities, saith the Preacher; all is vanity." He could not find satisfaction in his wisdom when he had begun to fall away from God. He found that " in much wisdom is much grief, and he that increaseth knowledge increaseth sorrow" (Eccles. i. 18). And so the wisest of men betook himself to pleasure. " I said in my heart, Go to now, I will prove thee with mirth;" " I got me servants and maidens, and had servants born in my house;" " I gat me men-singers and women-singers;" " Whatsoever mine eyes desired I kept not from them, I withheld not my heart from any joy" (Eccles. ii. 1, 7, 8, 10). He found, as they that are lovers of pleasure rather than lovers of God always find sooner or later, that all this was " vanity and vexation of spirit," nothing better than "striving after wind." " Therefore," he says, " I hated life; because the work that is wrought under the sun is grievous unto me: for all is vanity and vexation of spirit." And this is King Solomon, who surpassed all the kings of the earth for glory and riches; who was wiser than the wisest of his time; who had won in his youth the love of the pure and innocent Shulamite; who (and this is the saddest thought of all) once loved the Lord: " Solomon loved the Lord, walking in the statutes of David his father" (1 Kings iii. 3). While he continued to love the Lord, he was true, we must believe, to the wife of his youth. One who walks in the light of the love of God cannot love the works of darkness, cannot admit into his heart that taint of impurity which so utterly shuts the soul away from the love of God. We wonder whether Solomon repented as his father David did. We know that God warned him, and chastised him for his sins, but we know also that much will be required from those to whom much has been given, and that to fall from such grace as had been bestowed upon Solomon must be a grievous fall indeed; to disobey God who had given him such abundant blessings showed a depth of ingratitude which utterly startles us, till we learn to know in penitence and self-abasement what Solomon impressed upon others, whether he felt it himself or not, "the plague of our own hearts" (1 Kings viii. 38). The pure love of wedlock is maintained in ever-growing affection when husband and wife both live near to God. " If we walk in the light, as he is in the light, we have fellowship one with another" (1 John i. 7). That fellowship which "is with the Father and with his Son Jesus Christ" (1 John i. 3) involves of necessity the holiest grace of charity in our mutual relations with our brother Christians; especially those whom God hath joined together must and will, if they are living as the children of God, live together in holy love unto their lives' end. We wonder whether the fair Shulamite lived to experience the change in her royal bridegroom; if she did, the loss of his affection must have been a bitter trial indeed. Perhaps God in his mercy took her to himself before that trial came.   2. *The heavenly Bridegroom.* It is the will of the Lord Jesus to present the Church unto himself as a glorious Church, holy and without blemish. The Lord shall rejoice in his works. Through the cleansing power of his most precious blood, through the grace of the Holy Spirit, which he giveth to his chosen, the Church, his bride shall at the last be "all glorious within;" for he is able "to present us faultless before the presence of his glory with exceeding joy" (Jude 24). Then shall there be joy in heaven, when the Lord, who endured for the Church's sake the great agony of the cross, sees the reward of his bitter Passion; when he looks upon the Church, a glorious Church indeed, no longer marred and stained by sin and strife and error, but cleansed and purified "even as he is pure" (1 John iii. 3), made like unto him in the vision of his love and holiness. Then he will rejoice over her as the bridegroom rejoiceth over the bride. " In that day it shall be said to Jerusalem . . . The Lord thy God in the midst of thee is mighty: he will save, he will rejoice over thee with joy; he will rest in his love, he will joy over thee with singing" (Zeph. iii. 16, 17). The heavenly Bridegroom will rejoice over his bride; he will see in her the beauty of holiness; he will rejoice in her graces. She is very dear to him, for she is the reward of that long anguish, the agony and bloody sweat, the bitter cross and Passion. And now she is wholly his; she has left all other masters, and given her whole heart to the Lord who bought her, with the full, pure, holy love which she has learned of him—the infinite love.   3. *The bride must make herself ready.* (Rev. xix. 7.) Without holiness no man can see the Lord. The holiness of the Church consists in the holiness of its members. We must follow after holiness, holiness of heart and life; for without the wedding-garment, the white robe of righteousness, none can be admitted to the marriage-supper of the Lamb. We must, each one of us, make ourselves ready and prepare to meet our God. The Lord rejoices in the holiness of his people. We must learn, not to seek glory from one another, not to set so much store on human praise, but to seek that glory which cometh from the only God (John v. 44). There were some who would not confess the Lord Jesus because " they loved the praise of men more than the praise of God" (John xii. 43). We must look onwards to the praise which the heavenly Bridegroom will bestow on the Church, his bride; then shall the true Israelite, who is a " Jew inwardly," " whose praise is not of men, but of God" (Rom. ii. 29), have praise of God (1 Cor. iv. 5). We must seek that praise with a single heart, walking with God, living to his glory, looking for the blessed hour when we trust to see the heavenly Bridegroom face to face.

> " He lifts me to the golden doors;
>   The flashes come and go;
> All Heaven bursts her starry floors,
>   And strews her lights below,
> And deepens on and up! the gates
>   Roll back, and far within
> For me the heavenly Bridegroom waits,
>   To make me pure of sin.
> The sabbaths of eternity,
>   One sabbath deep and wide,
> A light upon the shining sea—
>   The Bridegroom with his bride!"

II. THE ANSWER OF THE BRIDE. 1. *She must withdraw for a while.* She repeats in her modesty the first clause of her own words in ch. ii. 17. Then, apparently, she asked her lover to leave her till she had fulfilled the routine duties of the day. He was to return when the day should be cool, and the shadows should lengthen in the evening. Now it is she who will leave her Lord for a time. Perhaps she felt herself almost over-burdened by his commendations; the poor country maiden, true and simple as she was, could scarcely understand such praises from the great and magnificent king; they were too much for her; she must retire to collect herself. When the Lord commends the faithful, and glorifies their works of love as done unto himself, they seem oppressed, as it were, for a season by the greatness of his praise. They were only doing their duty; they did it, all of them, more or less imperfectly; they did not regard those poor works of theirs as so exceeding beautiful; they did not think that they had been conferring benefits upon the Lord himself, that they had so greatly pleased him; they were humble, self-distrustful; they seem almost to shrink from the praises of the King. The grace of humility is a very holy thing; it lies at the entrance of the kingdom of heaven; it is the first of the Beatitudes. "Not he that commendeth himself is approved, but he whom the Lord commendeth" (2 Cor. x. 18). 2. *Whither the bride retires.* "I will get me to the mountain of myrrh and to the hill of frankincense." The words may, taken literally, signify some retired place in the palace garden, as many scholars think; but myrrh and frankincense are words of frequent occurrence in Holy Scripture, and are often used with a more or less mystical meaning. The Wise Men from the East brought gold and frankincense and myrrh as offerings to the infant Saviour; wine mingled with myrrh was given him on the cross; his sacred body was laid in a mixture of myrrh and aloes brought by the faithful Nicodemus. The mountain of myrrh seems to suggest the necessity of purification before the soul can dwell always in the presence of the Lord. The maidens from among whom the Queen of Persia was to be chosen had to go through a time of purification, "six months with oil of myrrh" (Esth. ii. 12). It tells us also of the bitter draught, the cup of sorrows, which they who are to be nearest Christ must take. "Are ye able to drink of the cup that I must drink of?" Those who aspire to the highest places in the kingdom of heaven must learn the deepest lessons of humility, the severest lessons of entire submission of will to the holy will of God. They must get them to the mountain of myrrh, to the cross. Our self-denials are small and unworthy; the cross of Christ sets before us a mountain of self-sacrifice, a height that reaches unto the heavens. We must draw nearer and nearer to the cross in daily self-denial and self-abasement, if we are to realize at last the full, deep joy of uninterrupted communion with the Lord. And if myrrh means self-denial, the dying unto sin, frankincense means worship. The sweet odour of the incense going up from the golden altar is a meet emblem of the prayers of the saints (see Rev. viii. 3, 4). We must learn the blessed lesson of worship on earth before we can join the choir of happy worshippers around the glory-throne. We must get ourselves to the hill of frankincense, to the Lord's house, where the incense of prayer and thanksgiving ever ascends, where he himself is in the midst, among those who are gathered together in his name. There we may be trained, if we come in the Spirit as Simeon came when he found the Lord Christ, in that holy worship, worship in spirit and in truth, which is the true preparation for the glad adoring worship of triumphant saints in heaven. Till the evening of life comes, till the shadows lengthen into the night, we must get ourselves to the work which the Lord has given us to do—the work of self-discipline, the work of worship here below, that we may be ready when he cometh to take our part in the never-ceasing worship of heaven, and there to be ever with the Lord.

Vers. 7—16.—*Further conversation.* I. THE WORDS OF THE BRIDEGROOM. 1. *His entire love for the bride.* If the view of ver. 6 indicated above gives the true meaning, the bride has left the bridegroom for a time. In the evening they meet again, and the king again expresses his affection: "Thou art all fair, my love; there is no spot in thee." Such shall the Church be in the eyes of Christ, when he has sanctified and cleansed her with the washing of water by the Word; when she is clothed in the fine linen, clean and white, which is the righteousness of saints; when he "of God is made unto her Wisdom, and Righteousness, and Sanctification, and Redemption" (1 Cor. i. 30). Such shall the saints be in his eyes when they have "washed their robes, and made them white in the blood of the Lamb;" "they are without fault before the throne of God" (Rev. xiv. 5). But it is Christ who has cleansed them. They were stained with many sins, as David was when he cried in the anguish of his deep penitence, "Purge me with hyssop, and I shall be clean: wash me, and I shall be whiter than snow" (Ps. li. 7). We have sinned so long and so greatly, we have so often fallen back into sin after imperfect repentance, that to be "whiter than snow" seems a hope altogether too high for us, out of our reach. But we have the sure Word of God. He is able to "present us faultless before the presence of his glory;" he is able to "cleanse us from all unrighteousness;" "the Lamb of God taketh away the sins of the world." Indeed it is true that "we are all as an unclean thing, and all our righteousnesses are as filthy rags" (Isa. lxiv. 6), but we may have, if we come to Christ in faith, "that righteousness which is through the faith of Christ;" that righteousness which is his, not our own; and yet, if we abide in him, it becomes through his grace our own; for it is given to us, imparted to us, infused into us by the indwelling influences of the Holy Spirit of God. Then we may dare to hope for that spotless righteousness; we may, we must, long for it and strive after it. Not to do so is not humility, but unbelief; not distrust of ourselves, but distrust of God; for we have the sacred word of promise, "Blessed are they that do hunger and thirst after righteousness: for they shall be filled." 2. *His invitation.* The Hebrew words are full of life: "With me from Lebanon, O bride, with me from Lebanon shalt thou come." The bride is henceforth to be with the bridegroom, with him always: she is to forget her own people and her father's house (Ps. xlv. 10, 11). She is to come away from her old haunts—from Amana, Shenir, and Hermon; for even Hermon in all its grandeur is but a "little hill" in comparison with the spiritual glory of Mount Zion, where God is pleased to dwell (see Prayer-book Version of Ps. xlii. 6). She must come from the lions' dens, from "the violence of Lebanon" (Hab. ii. 17), to Jerusalem, the foundation of peace. The Church, the bride of Christ, shall be in the eternal blessedness "for ever with the Lord." She shall come away from her old habitation, the earth which is filled with violence (Gen. vi. 11); away from the raging of the roaring lion, who walketh about, seeking whom he may devour (1 Pet. v. 8), to the heavenly Jerusalem, the city of the living God. And the Christian soul, which looks forward in living hope to the inheritance of the saints in light, must now come with Christ away from other masters, from the lusts of the flesh and the lust of the eye, and the pride of life. "To depart and to be with Christ," St. Paul says (Phil. i. 23), "is far better"—"by much very far better," for such is the full meaning of the emphatic words. Then the soul that hopes to be with Christ in Paradise must be much with Christ now; with him in the daily life of faith, in prayer and praise and frequent communion. He bids us come. "Come unto me," he says, "and I will give you rest." He only can give peace. "Peace I leave with you; my peace I give unto you: not as the world giveth, give I unto you." If we listen to his voice, and come with him away from Lebanon, which, though fair to look upon, with grand and wide-reaching prospects, was yet the haunt of noisome beasts; if we leave the love of the world, with its enticements and its dangers, for the blessed love of Christ, we shall have all that we need for our soul's peace and safety. "Let not your heart be troubled, neither let it be afraid." 3. *His praises of the bride.* He calls her repeatedly, "My sister-bride." His heart is hers; every little thing about her, the very smell of her garments, is dear to him; her love is by much better than wine; her voice is sweet as honey. He dwells now less on graces of person, as in vers. 1—5, than on her looks of affection, the depth and beauty of her love, the music of her voice. These words tell of a great love; but the love of Christ for his Church is beyond the power of language. Solomon left his first love—he loved many strange women; but the love of Christ for his Church is "an everlasting love" (Jer. xxxi. 3), unchangeable, unutterable. "Greater love hath no man than this, that a man lay down his life for his friends;" but "God commendeth his love toward us, in that, while we were yet sinners, Christ died for us" (Rom. v. 8). And because he loved the Church with so great a love, the responsive love of the Church is very dear to him. "He is not ashamed to call us brethren" (Heb. ii. 11). The voice of the Church lifted up to him in prayer and praise, making melody in the heart unto God, is sweet to the Saviour. He praises the graces of the Church, though those graces come all from him; they are his gift. He praises in the Book of the Revelation the Churches of Smyrna and Philadelphia; he sees the beauty of holiness in those afflicted and despised Churches: "I know thy works, and tribulation, and poverty, but thou art rich;" "Be thou faithful unto death, and I will give thee a crown of life;" "They shall know that I have loved thee;" "Him that overcometh will I make a pillar in the temple of my God, and he shall go no more out: and I will write upon him the name of my God, and the name of the city of my God, which is new Jerusalem, which cometh down out of heaven from my God: and I will write upon him my new name" (Rev. ii. 9, 10; iii. 9, 12). 4. *He compares her to a garden enclosed.* She is like a garden shut up, barred against intruders, kept sacred for its master's use; she is like a spring shut up, a fountain sealed as with the royal signet which none but the king can touch. The garden, or paradise, is full of the choicest fruits, flowers, and spice-bearing plants, the produce of many countries, some of them brought in Solomon's time by his navy from Arabia or India. The fountain is a well of living waters, fresh as the gushing mountain-streams of Lebanon. Solomon praises the bride not only for her beauty and her rare endowments, but also for her purity and faithfulness. The "garden enclosed," the "fountain sealed," remind us of our marriage vow: "Wilt thou . . . forsaking all other, keep thee only unto him so long as ye both shall live?" Such should the wedded pair be each to the other; such was not Solomon. We cannot but think and believe that the bride, innocent and artless as she is described, kept herself pure unto the end. The Church, which is the bride of Christ, should be as a garden enclosed, kept sacred for the one Lord. The garden of Eden was a garden enclosed, but Satan marred its sanctity; he, in the words of Milton,

> "At one slight bound high overleaped all bound
> Of hill or highest wall, and sheer within
> Lights on his feet. . . .
> So clomb the first grand thief into God's fold:
> So since into his Church lewd hirelings climb."

The Lord has said, "He that entereth not by the door into the sheepfold, but climbeth up some other way, the same is a thief and a robber." Again he has said, "I am the Door: by me if any man enter in, he shall be saved, and shall go in and out, and shall find pasture." They who are called to minister in the Church of God must ever remember that it is God's Church, that "he hath purchased it with his own blood" (Acts xx. 28); that it should be "a garden enclosed," kept for the Master, tilled and watered for him; that every barren tree should be carefully tended, that it may bring forth fruit before the awful word goeth forth, "Every tree that bringeth not forth good fruit is hewn down, and cast into the fire." The trees in the Lord's garden differ much from one another. There are pomegranates with their pleasant fruit, henna with its fragrant flowers, spikenard with its costly perfume, frankincense for sacred uses; all manner of sweet spices—myrrh and aloes, which tell of the bitter healing cup of sorrow, which point to death and burial. The saints of God differ much from one another. Enoch, Abraham, Moses, Daniel, St. Peter, St. John, St. Paul, have each his own place in the garden of the Lord. All bring forth the fruits of the Spirit, but in different forms and degrees; one we call the apostle of love, another the apostle of faith, a third the apostle of hope; "but all these worketh that one and the selfsame Spirit, dividing to every man severally as he will" (1 Cor. xii. 11). It is the Lord himself who giveth the Spirit. Mary Magdalene, on the first Easter Day, supposed him to be the gardener (John xx. 15); and in a very true sense he is the Gardener of the garden enclosed. And here we may remember that it was in a garden that he suffered that dread agony, when his sweat was as it were great drops of blood falling down to the ground. That blood taketh away the sins of the world; it waters the garden enclosed with its cleansing stream. And again we are told that "in the place where he was crucified there was a garden; and in the garden a new sepulchre, wherein was never man yet laid. There laid they Jesus" (John xix. 41). The Lord suffered in a garden; he has purchased with his own blood the Church to be his own, his garden enclosed. But the Church is also "a spring shut up, a fountain sealed;" shut up in a sense, sealed with the Master's signet, as his own sacred tomb was sealed in the garden of Joseph, but yet (ver. 15) "a fountain of gardens, a well of living waters, and streams from Lebanon." The fountain is sealed, for it is the Lord's; it hath "this seal, The Lord knoweth them that are his. And, Let every one that nameth the Name of Christ depart from iniquity" (2 Tim. ii. 19). But its living waters go forth to fertilize the Lord's garden. The healing waters which the Prophet Ezekiel saw in his vision issued out from under the threshold of the temple; they brought fruitfulness wherever they went "because their waters they issued out of the sanctuary" (Ezek. xlvii. 1, 12). In a true sense the whole world is the Lord's field: "The field is the world" (Matt. xiii. 38); and the Church has the Lord's commandment, "Go ye into all the world, and preach the gospel to every creature" (Mark xvi. 15). The well is the Lord's; it is sealed with his seal; but the living waters of that sacred well must issue forth, that "the wilderness and the solitary place may be glad for them: that the desert may rejoice and blossom as the rose" (Isa. xxxv. 1). And as the Church, the bride of Christ, is for him "a garden enclosed, a fountain sealed," so must every Christian soul be wholly his. "We are Christ's," St. Paul says. "Whether we live or die, we are the Lord's;" and again, "God, whose I am, and whom I serve" (Acts xxvii. 23). Each Christian soul must keep itself as "a garden enclosed" ("barred," or "bolted," is the literal meaning of the Hebrew word). We must strive earnestly to keep out earthly passions, earthly ambitions, and every high thing that exalteth itself against the knowledge of God. We must keep the gate barred against the entrance of the evil one. And we must take heed that the house be not left empty; it must be kept for "a habitation of God through the Spirit" (Eph. ii. 22). We must strive to keep out worldly cares, coming to God in all our troubles, whether great or small, that so the peace of God, which passeth all understanding, may keep (guard, protect) our hearts and thoughts through Christ Jesus. The garden must be barred; the peace of God must rule there (Col. iii. 15); and it must bring forth fruit, the blessed fruit of the Spirit, which is "love, joy, peace, long-suffering, gentleness, goodness, faith, meekness, temperance" (Gal. v. 22). The tree that beareth not fruit must be hewn down at last; it cumbereth the ground; "every branch that beareth not fruit is taken away." How carefully, then, we ought, every one of us, to watch for the fruit of the Spirit in our daily life, to see in diligent self-examination whether we are exhibiting these holy graces in our Christian walk and conversation; and if, alas! we find them not, how earnestly we ought to pray, with fervent, untiring supplication for the help of the Holy Spirit of God to work within us, to assist our prayers, to make intercession for us with groanings that cannot be uttered, to lead us nearer to Christ, that we may evermore abide in him, without whom we can bear no fruit, without whom we can do nothing! The garden needs the living water; the saint of God is a fountain sealed.

The living water is the Lord's; it bears his seal. The Lord himself is, in the truest sense, the "Fountain opened . . . for sin and for uncleanness" (Zech. xiii. 1); with him is "the fountain of life" (Ps. xxxvi. 9). He leadeth his redeemed to living fountains of waters (Rev. vii. 17). But they who have received from him the living water become themselves fountains, as the Lord hath said, "Whosoever drinketh of the water that I shall give him shall never thirst; but the water that I shall give him shall be in him a well of water springing up into everlasting life." And again, "If any man thirst, let him come unto me, and drink. He that believeth on me, as the Scripture hath said, out of his belly shall flow rivers of living water" (John iv. 14; vii. 37, 38). The saint of God is indeed "a fountain sealed," sealed with the Lord's seal, dedicated wholly unto him; "a spring shut up" from all other waters save only the living water which the Lord giveth, not "a fountain which sends forth at the same place sweet water and bitter" (Jas. ii. 11). But he must be "a fountain of gardens" (ver. 15); he that is watered of God must water the thirsty ground (Prov. xi. 25). St. Paul, who had received the gift of the Spirit from the Lord, passed on the living waters to Apollos; Apollos watered the garden of the Lord at Corinth (1 Cor. iii. 6). So must all God's people do. They know in their own hearts more or less of that holy calm and blessedness which the living waters of the indwelling of the Spirit (John vii. 39) bring to the faithful; they must do their best to extend to others the blessings which they have themselves received; they must pray and labour for the spiritual well-being of those nearest to them, within the sphere of their personal influence; they must do their best to help missionary work through the world, resting not till "the earth shall be full of the knowledge of the Lord, as the waters cover the sea" (Isa. xi. 9). But each must keep himself as "a fountain sealed" for the Lord and the work of the Lord, that at the last he may be sealed with the seal of the living God, and stand on the Mount Zion among the mystic hundred and forty and four thousand who have the Lamb's Name and his Father's Name written in their foreheads (Rev. vii. 2, 3; xiv. 1).

II. THE VOICE OF THE BRIDE. She accepts the bridegroom's parable. She is a garden enclosed. She calls upon the winds, north and south, to blow upon the garden, that the fragrance of its spices may flow forth to give pleasure to the bridegroom. The garden is hers; for it is herself, her love. And yet it is the bridegroom's, for she has given herself, her love, to him; she invites him to come into his garden, and eat his pleasant fruits. So the Church, the bride of Christ, longs for the heavenly Bridegroom; so each Christian soul seeks the Saviour's presence. The soul that would give itself wholly to the Lord as a garden barred against all other masters, and enclosed for his use, strives ever to please him more and more; she would have her inward life of prayer and meditation and spiritual communion with him to become more and more pleasing to him, more and more fragrant. Therefore she calls for the north wind as well as the south to blow upon the garden, that the spices thereof may flow out. She is willing to submit to the cold blasts of adversity, as well as to be refreshed with the soft breezes of joy and holy gladness. She knows that God will make all things, joy and sorrow alike, to work together for good to them that love him (Rom. viii. 28). Therefore she prays only that his will may be done in her, whether by chastisements or by spiritual joy and blessing. She would have the garden bring forth more fruit, even though it must be purged with the pruning-knife of affliction. For the garden, though it is herself, her own heart, is yet the Lord's; for she has given it to the heavenly Bridegroom; therefore she yearns for his irradiating presence, praying him to enter into his garden, and eat his pleasant fruits.

HOMILIES BY VARIOUS AUTHORS.

Vers. 1—7.—*What Christ sees in those who love him.* As a mere story, these verses may be taken as a further attempt on the part of King Solomon to win her to whom he speaks for himself. Therefore he extols her beauty. Her eyes like the beautiful eyes of the Syrian dove; her dark glossy hair like that of the goats that browse on the slopes of Mount Gilead; her teeth white as the newly cleansed wool, as even and regular as is the fleece that has been first shorn, and perfect as is the breed of sheep he tells of; her lips ruddy; her mouth so comely; her cheeks rosy red, like the opened pomegranate; her neck graceful, and adorned with precious jewels; and so on. Even her home, because it is her home, is as a hill bearing trees of myrrh and frankincense, and thither would he resort. And he sums up his description by declaring that she is "all fair"—that there is no blemish in her. Now, on such flattery, cf. on ch. i. 9—ii. 7. But had these verses no other meaning than this literal one, we cannot think they would have found place in the Holy Scriptures. Therefore we take them as setting forth, under their rich Oriental colouring, the blessed truth that, in the sight of their Lord, his people are without blemish, "all fair." It is the same truth as was meant by that at present unloved phrase, "imputed righteousness." And that it is unloved is owing to the fact that its meaning has been grossly perverted, and made to stand for ideas dishonouring to God and disastrous to the spiritual life of men. But in reality the phrase means just that which in these verses is allegorically set forth. In interpreting these verses it is not the right or reverent way, though many have followed it, to affix some definite meaning to every detail of the description given, but to take the description as a whole, as attesting the beauty of the redeemed in the sight of their Lord. Therefore, though some have interpreted the dove's eyes as the eyes that are ever towards the Lord in holy desire; and the hair as the unshorn locks of the soul's consecration to Christ; and the teeth, undecayed and perfect, as the faith which feeds on Christ; and the lips as those of one once leprous, but now purified by the precious blood of Christ, and so like a scarlet thread; the blushing temples no longer bold and brazen, but suffused with crimson as the pomegranate, telling of the soul's true repentance; the neck, tall, stately, graceful, strong, telling of the liberty and courage Christ has given the soul; the breasts of the twin graces of faith and love, which Paul says are the believer's breastplate;—all this (cf. Stuart), though interesting and ingenious, appears to us unnecessary and, in some hands, injurious. We therefore take the description generally, and note—

I. The fact that Christ does regard as beautiful the redeemed soul. She is spotless in his sight. He says, "The glory thou gavest me I have given them." Christ is made unto us "Righteousness and Sanctification." He shed his blood that his Church might be "a glorious Church, not having spot," etc. (Eph. v. 27). He will present us "faultless before the presence of his glory" (Jude 24). "Now ye are clean through the word which I have spoken unto you," said our Lord (cf. also 1 Cor. vi. 11). And if he did not so regard his people and count them "precious in his sight" (Isa. xliii.), wherefore should he have done and suffered for them all that he has? Whatever we make sacrifices for we count beautiful. Our love pierces through the outer husk of circumstance and evil habit, and sees the beauty within; and it is for that we will make sacrifice if need be. And so with our most blessed Lord—his eye of love pierced through the often hideous husk of men's vile habits and ways to the soul on which his heart was set, that he might redeem and save it, and make it beautiful, like his own. And when that soul turns to him in trust and penitence, then at once that soul is "all fair" in his sight, and "there is no spot in" it.

II. Why should he not? Men say, "It is wrong to represent God as seeing otherwise than according to the truth of things. Therefore to say of a soul, 'There is no spot in it,' when we know that 'from the sole of the foot to the crown of the head there is no soundness in it' (Isa. i.), this is to introduce unreality and make-believe into the most sacred regions." But look at the mother's joy in her babe. Whence comes that? Is it not largely the loving onlook she takes into the future of that child? She sees, or at least believes she sees, that child grown up in purity, intelligence, goodness, and all that is lovely and lovable. She is a believer, and you cannot move her, in imputed righteousness; for what is she doing but imputing all that righteousness to her babe? See the shipbuilder in his yard. There is a ship in its earliest stages of construction. You can see nothing but chips and dirt and confusion. But he sees that ship in her completion—in all her strength, the beauty of her lines, and all the perfectness which he intends shall belong to her. And he "imputes" to her all that. And so with our Lord. He sees all that the soul shall be when he has perfected the "good work" which he has already begun for and in it. This is why, even now, it is fitting that he should see and say, "There is no spot in thee."

III. And what if he does? There is: 1. *All consolation for the anxious, mis-*

trusting soul. The soul is, as it well may be, often overwhelmed with the sense of its own vileness and sin. It clings to Christ with the grasp of all but despair. What a help to know that Christ's estimate of us is not our own! How often we are able to help a man up by letting him see that we believe in him, notwithstanding he has done wrong! Arnold's word, "Trust a boy, and he will become trustworthy," is most true. The fact we are considering is not only full of consolation, but full of help to us poor sinful men. 2. *Inspiration for the better life.* If Christ thinks me so, I will strive to become so. Is this his ideal for me? I will, in his strength, strive to realize it. 3. *The enkindling and constant rekindling of our love for Christ.*—S. C.

Ver. 6.—*Where Christ is now.* "Until the day break," etc.

I. BY THIS IS MEANT THE PRESENT LIFE. It does not matter whether the words be taken as telling of the time until the day break or until the day close. In the former case, the speaker would mean that all the night long he would be on the mountains of myrrh, etc.; but in the latter, he would mean that until the day were done he would be there. It matters not, for the present life may be likened to either night or day. *If to the night,* then night-time is meant to suggest the darkness in which men live. As to knowledge: "We see through a glass, darkly." As to happiness: "Man is born to trouble." As to the use of life: men choose to walk in darkness. The land sits "in darkness and in the shadow of death," because they who dwell in such land are in that deep spiritual darkness of which the prophet tells. *If to the day,* then as the time for toil, the season for diligent work, the period during which the busy affairs of men are transacted—such is our life so long as it continues. On either interpretation the present life is meant.

II. THE PLACE WHERE DURING THIS LIFE WE MAY FIND CHRIST. On "the mountains of myrrh," etc. By this is meant, not heaven, for we cannot ascend into heaven; and the place told of here is evidently a place accessible. Therefore we take the "mountains of myrrh," etc., to mean *the Church* (cf. Isa. ii. 2). And there are many other Scriptures in which the Church is likened to hills or mountains (Ps. lxviii. 15, 16; lxxxvii. 1—3, etc.). Some have thought that the throne of grace, the place of prayer, is meant—and so it is; but more than that is included. Nothing less than the Church of Christ. And the similitude employed here is just. For *the Church is as a mountain.* 1. *For elevation.* The Church should be above the world. Hence, in the magnificent minsters which adorn this and other lands, the sacred fabric towers in lordly height far above all the dwellings that cluster around it. It symbolizes this very truth. Our Lord said, "Ye are a city set on a hill." 2. *For visibility.* "Which cannot be hid." Goodness ever betrays itself; like him from whom it comes, and of whom it was said, "He could not be hid." Does the visibility consist in anything else but character? Is not the Church the company of all the good? 3. *For its majesty.* It is God's vicegerent here on earth. By it "kings rule, and princes decree justice." Kings were its nursing fathers and queens its nursing mothers (cf. Isa. lx.). 4. *For its immovability.* (Ps. cxxxv. 1.) "The gates of hell shall not prevail against it," said our Lord. And here it is to-day, and it never seemed more likely to continue than it does to-day. 5. *For its fruitfulness.* The mountains and hills told of are not mere rocky heights, stony and barren, but rich and fruitful, their sides covered with noblest trees. "They that be planted in the house of the Lord," etc. 6. *For its delightfulness.* Myrrh and frankincense are the product of its trees, and make the whole place fragrant, precious, full of delight to him who dwells or comes there (cf. "The Lord loveth the gates of Zion more than," etc.). Christ loves to be there, and his people love to meet him there. For it is the place of accepted prayer, of hallowed communion, of adoring worship, of manifold spiritual help. *And there Christ is to be found.* He is there according to his Word, in his unseen but real presence, and in his gracious power. Myriads attest this. Therefore—

III. WE SHOULD SEEK HIM THERE. The verse seems to be a suggestion to this effect. To forsake the assemblies, communion, and fellowship of the Church is to suffer great loss. Some say, "We can pray at home;" and when they *must* be at home no doubt they can, but when they need not be we doubt if many do. And when we think of the treasure-store of help that is gained by them who seek the Lord in his

Church, who get them to the mountain, etc., where he is, we commiserate, even whilst we condemn, those who never get themselves there at all.—S. C.

Ver. 7.—*The immaculate soul.* "Thou art all fair, my love; there is no spot in thee." This word has many parallels; cf. "Ye are clean through the word which I have spoken unto you;" "Ye are washed, justified, sanctified;" "Ye are complete in him;" "There is no condemnation to them which are in Christ Jesus," etc. Now, how can all this be? We reply—

I. THROUGH THE ESTIMATE WHICH LOVE FORMS OF THAT WHICH IT LOVES. (Cf. former homily, on vers. 1—7.)

II. THROUGH THE BLOOD OF CHRIST, WHICH "CLEANSETH US FROM ALL SIN." Christ is our Representative, the second Adam. Our connection with him becomes vitalized when our hearts trust in him. But he, in and by his death—his blood—made perfect confession of our sins, and in that confession absorbed them (cf. McLeod Campbell on the Atonement). Forgiveness, therefore, follows for all in him; and thus we are cleansed.

III. THROUGH THE POWER OF THE HOLY GHOST. He is ever acting on our hearts, to lead them along the various stages that will bring us to perfect purity, to complete sanctification. He works in us that deep sense of sin which leads to a genuine repentance. He reveals Christ to us, which leads to a living trust. He inspires us with love to Christ, which leads to the surrender of our will. He prompts us to and aids us in prayer, which perpetuates and deepens every holy purpose. He keeps us in touch with Christ, which bars the entrance of sin to our souls. He makes all the means of grace full of help to our souls. Thus step by step the blessed work is done.

IV. THROUGH CHRIST'S GRACIOUS ANTICIPATION OF THE COMPLETED WORK. He looks on us, not as we are, but as we shall be, and predates what has yet to, but certainly shall, be realized.

CONCLUSION. What a motive all this supplies to our earnest striving to come up to our blessed Lord's ideal!—S. C.

Ver. 8.—*The beautiful but dangerous world.* For once the literal and allegorical interpretation largely agree. For both represent the places spoken of here as full of peril, and both desire the beloved one to "come away" from them, and promise deliverance if she will come. Let the peril of delivering her be what it may—as dens of lions and leopards—yet will he accomplish it. Allegorically we may read here—

I. CHRIST'S DESCRIPTION OF THE WORLD. It is: 1. *Beautiful to look upon.* Some of the finest scenes, the most glorious landscapes the world can show, are to be seen from the mountain summits named here. The view is entrancing, so travellers say. And the world is to the young soul fair indeed. But: 2. *It is full of peril also.* The dizzy heights, the steep cliffs, the lofty crags of mountainous regions, demand a steady head, well-balanced nerves, a sure foothold. The inexperienced may not venture there. Death and destruction track the footsteps of the traveller on such heights, and if he be not well trained, they have him for their prey. The spiritual analogy is illustrated by only too many sad experiences. To preserve the soul's balance on the heights of the world's prosperity, how difficult for all! how impossible for most! "How hardly shall they that have riches enter into the kingdom of heaven!" "Man, vain man, dressed in a little brief authority," etc. But the special perils named here are *the beasts of prey.* These have their haunts in these mountains (cf. Exposition). In all languages and literatures the designation of evil men by the name of some noxious beast is common (cf. Psalms; also our Lord's word, "Go, tell that fox;" and in the Scriptures *passim*). And the world is full of such creatures—pitiless, cruel, fierce, ravenous, terrible. Smooth and soft and sleek as a leopard, so long as you are able to defy them; but fall down, be at their mercy, and what mercy will you get? "The tender mercies of the wicked are *cruel*;" yes, cruel as lion, leopard, or any beast of prey. Ask the world's victims what mercy they have received. Let the soul once give the world a chance, and the world will drive it hellward with relentless cruelty. There is no mercy there. What a contrast to "the mountains of myrrh" (ver. 6)! "No ravenous beast shall be there;" "They shall not hurt nor destroy in all my holy mountain" (Isa. xxxv. 9).

II. CHRIST'S PROMISE OF HELP. "Come with *me*." His Word is full of such promises and of the records of their fulfilment (cf. histories of Joseph, Moses, Nehemiah, Daniel, etc.). And it is the experience of every Christian soul. Christ does not take us out of the world, but he keeps us from the evil. He keeps us "as the apple of his eye;" hides us "under the shadow" of his wing (cf. Ps. xci.). He knows what he will do, therefore he says, "Come with me."

III. THE CONDITION OF THAT HELP. We must "come with" him. Some wonder that he invites us at all; that, loving the soul as he does, he should leave it any choice as to whether it will or will not come; that he does not deal with us as a father who would compel, not merely invite, his child to come out of the burning house. So some wonder that Christ does not compel the soul, carry it off by force. No doubt, in the literal story of this song, he who spoke was prepared to do this by her whom he appeals to. But Christ says, "Come with me." He solicits, entreats, invites. For there can be no deliverance of the soul unless there be the response of its own will. Even Christ cannot save without that. If, as is the case so sadly often, men "will not come unto" him that they "might have life," they have it not. And that response of the will is from faith in Christ's Word as to our peril and his loving power. Then ponder that Word; pray to know the truth; the Divine Spirit shall teach you, and soon the response Christ desires will be given.—S. C.

Vers. 9—15.—"*Cur Deus homo?*" In these verses the beloved tells her whom he has come to deliver wherefore he would run all this risk and endure so much for her sake. And reading them as an allegory, we may take them as setting forth why and wherefore God became Man; why "he who was rich for our sakes became poor." And amongst these reasons are—

I. HIS INTENSE LOVE FOR US. The speaker tells in ver. 9 how but a small portion of the beauty and of the adornments of her whom he so loved had "ravished" his heart, had filled him with intense desire for her. And translated into the style and teaching of the gospel, this tells of the heavenly joy (Luke xv.) over the repentance—the very beginning, the smallest portion of the beauty, of Divine grace in the soul. "Behold, he prayeth," was said of the persecuting Saul to the Christ-taught Ananias, who immediately rejoices, and is ready to receive as "brother" him who had been but a few hours before as a wolf coming to make havoc of the flock of Christ. A very little thing—the mere beginnings of grace—and yet the Spirit of Christ in Ananias leapt for joy.

II. THE SOUL'S RESPONSE. (Ver. 10.) That which Christ sees in the souls he has redeemed gratifies, refreshes, and delights him. As wine, as perfumes, as all spices. Precious is the soul's response of love to Christ. See how he asks for it. "Lovest thou me?" was thrice said to Peter. It is to him "the greatest thing in the world" (cf. 1 Cor. xiii., "The greatest of these is love"). What argument this is for the love that is in Christ! We reason back from the known likings and preferences of a man to what he is himself. So reasoning, what will not our Lord appear?

III. HER GRACIOUS WORDS. (Ver. 11; cf. parallels, Prov. xvi. 24; Ps. cxix. 103.) It is out of the abundance of the heart the mouth speaketh. And the utterances of loving adoration, of contrite confession, of pleading prayer, of grateful praise—these are well pleasing in his esteem. How true the sabbath evening hymn—

> "And not a prayer, a tear, a sigh,
> Hath failed this day some suit to gain;
> To those in trouble thou wert nigh—
> Not one hath sought thy face in vain."

Yes, as the honeycomb, sweet; as milk and honey, delicious and healthful, so are the fruits of the lips of the redeemed soul to Christ. We, therefore, can give him delight. It must be so. For we know we can "grieve" him; but if we can grieve him, we can also give him joy; and it is thus we do so.

IV. THE FRAGRANCE OF HER LIFE. "The smell of thy garments is," etc. (ver. 11). The garments are the symbol of those outward acts and deeds which, as it were, clothe and characterize the man. We know men by their dress; their garb bespeaks their occupation, tells what their work is. Now, the holy deeds of the redeemed soul are as fragrance, full of a sweet acceptableness to Christ (cf. Matt. xxv., where it is told how the loving acts of his people done to the poor and needy for his sake are, though so trifling in themselves, so wonderfully recompensed). Thus the lives of his people diffuse a fragrance most acceptable to him in whose name they are done.

V. HER FIDELITY. (Ver. 12.) The soul of the believer belongs to Christ. It is his possession—a garden closed, open only to him. All manner of intruders seek to find entrance there, and some of them seem for a while to succeed; but Christ sees that in deed and in truth the soul owns only him as her Lord. You can force the needle of a compass right round, so that it should point the reverse of its right direction; but take your hand off, and back it swings to where, if left to itself, it always would be. And so with the soul of the believer. The violence of the world, the flesh, or the devil, or all combined, often make the soul seem to belong to any one rather than Christ. But he sees how it is, and knows that when that violence is withdrawn the soul will surrender itself again to him, with cries and prayers and tears that it may nevermore belong to any but to him, and him alone.

VI. THE SOUL'S RICH FRUIT. (Ver. 13.) What these are, are told of here under the imagery of the fruits of an Oriental garden; and in Gal. v. 22 as the fruits of the Spirit. Like the fruits this ver. 13 speaks of, they are precious, fragrant, healthful, abundant, delightful, varied, beautiful, and spontaneous. Such are the fruits he desires; and, " supposing him to be the gardener," such as he would surely have in his garden.

VII. THE MINISTRIES OF THE SOUL. (Ver. 15.) The grace of the redeemed soul is not confined to itself; it flows out to others. Allusion seems to be made in this verse to the fountains of Solomon, which were " fountains of gardens." And we are reminded of our Lord's words as to the " well of water " which should be in his people, and which should spring up in them " unto everlasting life." And because our Lord foresaw that through the souls he redeemed so many others should be blessed—each one becoming " a fountain of gardens," a well of living waters for the help and salvation of others— herein is another reason why God became man. It was part of " the joy set before him," for which he " endured the cross, despising the shame." Ruskin tells how in the slime taken from a city lane you have clay, soot, sand, and water. Submit these to the laws of crystallization, and the clay becomes sapphire, the sand becomes opal, with blue green, and golden hues; the soot becomes a lustrous diamond, and the water crystallizes into that thing of beauty, a snow-star. And more than science sees in any city slime Christ sees in the soul, sunken in the mire of sin though it be, which he redeems. Already he sees the flashing of the jewels into which he will transform it, and will place in his diadem for ever: such is part answer to the question, " Cur Deus homo?" —S. C.

Ver. 16.—" *Even so, come, Lord Jesus!* " This is the state of mind produced by the consciousness of Christ's gracious estimate of us. We can scarce believe that it is as he says, but that he counts us such makes us long to be such. Therefore in this verse we may hear the cry of the soul, that he would make us to be what he says we are. " Even so, come," etc. Note—

I. WHAT THIS ASPIRATION OF THE SOUL CONFESSES. 1. *The power of Christ to produce all this.* Hence the appeal, " Awake, O north wind," etc. 2. *That power actually at work.* There are various precious plants of his own planting; his garden is not a wilderness. And there are the heavenly gifts of sun and rain and dew. 3. *But nevertheless the full results of his grace are not forthcoming.* The fragrance so delightful and desirable is not yielded; there are fruits, but not yet ripened, so that they might be pleasant to him who eats them. The soul lives, but does not flourish. It has life, but not abundant life. How common all this is! Hence how ineffectual the lives of many Christians are! 4. *And the causes of this are indicated.* The gloom and mist, the clouds so earth-born and dense, which overhang the garden of the soul and hinder it from yielding its fragrance and fruit as it otherwise would. So the sin-and-sorrow-laden clouds, and those which doubt and unbelief produce—these will mar the soul's life, and make it ineffectual for joy or help.

II. FOR WHAT IT IS WILLING. 1. *For the north wind.* (Cf. Prov. xxv. 23; Job xxxviii. 22.) The north wind, often stern and terrible, and very trying to plant-life. Yet here it is invited to come. The spirit of the well-known lines—

> " Nearer, my God, to thee,
> Nearer to thee ;
> E'en though it be a cross
> That raiseth me "—

is in this invocation to the bitter blast—the north wind. And the Christian soul is willing for whatever of trial and distress God may be pleased to send, so only as it may lead to more full likeness to God. As the inhabitants of the Valais, in Switzerland, love the strong, stern winds which, sweeping wildly down their close gorges and shut-up vales, scatters and drives away the miasma, bred of the stagnant air, which for far too long a time broods over them, unchanged, and hence full of evil, until the welcome wild wind tears down the valley, and then the bad air is driven away, and that which is healthful comes instead; so the soul, conscious that its health and joy are hindered, would welcome that which corresponds to the north wind told of here (cf. Rom. v. 3—5). 2. *The south wind.* (For its effects, cf. Job xxxvii. 7.) The soul knows that without the genial influence of Christ's love realized in her she cannot prosper. Therefore she prays for this also.

> " He sendeth sun, he sendeth shower—
> Alike they're needful for the flower;
> And joys and tears alike are sent
> To give the soul fit nourishment."

III. WHAT IT SUPREMELY DESIRES. "Let my beloved come into his garden," etc. This, translated, means that the soul's supreme solicitude is, as Paul's was, to be accepted of her Lord (cf. 2 Cor. v., "I labour, whether present or absent, to be accepted of him"). The renewed soul seeks to be well pleasing to her Lord; she cares little for any other approval (cf. Paul, "It is a small thing to me to be judged of you, or by man's judgment; he that judgeth me is the Lord"). "To give pleasure to those whom we love, to know that any achievements of ours will gratify them, is a greater pleasure than any derived from the applause of strangers, however numerous or distinguished. The lad laden with prizes at his school is pleased enough with the clapping, and the praise of masters and fellow-pupils; but his real pleasure is to come, when he gets his prizes home and shows them to his loved ones there. To see his mother's eyes glisten with gladness, that is better than all the other praise, were it from all the world beside. And so to be approved of Christ, to please *him*, that, to souls like Paul's, is everything."

IV. THE BLESSING IT OBTAINS. Such supreme solicitude cannot exist without obtaining for the soul that cherishes it some of the choicest favours of God. 1. It will be *an ever-present regulating force* in our souls. It will act as a law to ourselves, prompting, checking, directing, impelling, as needs be. 2. It will win *blessed freedom from the tyranny of the world.* Such soul will fear neither the world's frown—so formidable to well-nigh all—nor court the world's favour, all but universally coveted though it be. The Son will have made him free, and he will be free indeed. 3. It will *make every cross light.* Such cross being *his* cross, borne for him, its sharpness, weight, shame, vanish. 4. *Death is abolished.* It becomes for him " an abundant entrance into the kingdom " of Christ. Freedom, strength, peace—these are some of the blessings which that soul wins whose supreme desire is to be accepted of Christ. —S. C.

Ver. 6.—*Night and morning.* In the experiences of the heavenly life in the soul there are fluctuations of health and joy as great as the fluctuations of the seasons, as great as the change from night to day. Our globe is as near to the sun at dead of night as at noon, but, being turned away from the sun, loses the enjoyment of his beams. So Jesus may be equally near to us in our times of depression, though unbelief hides him from our eyes.

I. THIS LANGUAGE WELL DENOTES THE PURPOSE OF A MAN IN A STATE OF INTEL-LECTUAL DOUBT. The gloom of night has fallen upon him. 1. *Note his difficulties.* Grave doubts haunt his mind whether there be a personal God. The probabilities for and against seem to him fairly equal. In the busy world honest men often suffer. Innocent children sometimes starve. The righteous are crushed to the wall, or are pining in a gaol. Is this consistent with the jurisdiction of a benevolent God? Or if there be a God, the man has serious doubts whether the Bible can be accepted as a revelation to men of God's plans and designs. Evidently the book is marked with imperfections, traceable to man. Or he is perplexed with the theories respecting Christ's atonement. Is it possible for one person to bear the penalty of another's guilt? Or he is in darkness touching man's future state. Will there be a resurrection of the body? Will the identical man have a second life? What will become of the ungodly? How can redemption be a success if the majority of men perish? He is compassed and overborne with these shadows. What shall be his course? 2. *Note his conduct.* "I will take me to the mountains of myrrh," etc. Now, mountains are the emblems of substantial durability. Changes may pass over the plains of earth, but the hills abide. So amid all this flux of doubt some things are certain. It is certain that I ought to be truthful. I must ever follow the truth, and must hate falsehood. It is certain that I ought to be meek, patient, industrious, sober, chaste; a diligent inquirer after the truth, a champion of righteousness. These are our "mountains of myrrh," and on these we will dwell until clearer light dawns upon our path. 3. *Mark his expectation.* Certainly these shadows of night shall in due time vanish; the day of perfect certitude will dawn. Perhaps the mind itself, as an instrument for discerning truth, may grow more perfect. Perhaps some element of probability has been under-rated. Perhaps personal inclination has biassed judgment. Very likely new light from some quarter will break upon us touching the destiny of mankind. We will calmly wait. We will keep our minds open to instruction, open to correction, and light will assuredly come. We find a sweet and healthful fragrance in a life of conscientious service, and we are in the best position to catch the first rays of the morning sun.

II. THIS LANGUAGE DESCRIBES THE PURPOSE OF A MAN WHO ASPIRES TO A HIGHER PLANE OF CHRISTIAN LIFE. He is now among the mists of the valley; he resolves to dwell in the clear bracing air of the breezy hills. 1. *Note his lamentations.* He is in darkness respecting his personal relationship with God. He questions the reality of his faith. His religion is devoid of joy. Now and again some old lust reasserts its power. The old life and the new still struggle for the mastery. He makes no progress in holiness or in self-conquest. He finds no liberty in prayer, no sweet sense of the Brother's friendship. He is impotent. He waits for light and help from above. 'Tis a dark and wintry night. 2. *Observe his purpose.* "I will betake me to the hills of frankincense," etc. There are some things he cannot do for himself. But there are some things he can do. He cannot create light, but he can climb into the place where the light is best seen. He will act as a dependent servant, and carefully do his Master's will. He will deny himself all evil indulgence. He will dwell upon the fragrant mountains of Divine promise. He will be a devout searcher of the Scriptures. He will confess his every sin before God, and cherish a temper of self-humiliation. He will hope for clearer proof of sonship. He will aspire for the full light of God's countenance. What God has done for others, he will surely do for him. 3. *Note his outlook.* "Until the day breaks," etc. Most certainly "we have not yet attained." There is a higher experience to be reached, greater conquests to be gained. It is possible to have closer and more joyous friendship with God. It is possible for the principle of generous love to be fully dominant in the soul. There is fine scope for the development of faith. We want a more entire consecration to our Lord. In a word, we want the heavenly King to reign in us more manifestly. And that spring-morn of consecration and of gladness shall come. The "shadows shall flee away, the day shall break."

III. THIS LANGUAGE WILL EXPRESS THE CHRISTIAN'S HOPE RESPECTING THE TRIUMPH OF CHRIST'S KINGDOM. Now darkness and light commingle in the world like a thick mist in the valley. But presently the light shall conquer. 1. *Observe the present condition of Messiah's cause.* In some empires that cause moves forward, in others it apparently retrogrades. Once flourishing Churches are now dead. The Churches of Antioch and Samaria and Carthage have disappeared. Waves of ritual superstition have swept over some regions where once godly Churches flourished. Forms of faith have disappeared. The seraphic zeal of one age yields to spiritual stupor in the next. We scarcely know whether the kingdom of grace is on the ebb tide or on the flow

The outlook is checkered. 2. *Observe the Church's present duty.* In this case duty is clear. She should resort to the mountain of prayer—to the spicy hills of a new devotement. Sensible of her weakness, she must get into closer union with the eternal Source of strength. The methods which have been successful in the past must be plied in the future. We must be better instructed in the will of God. Perhaps our zeal has been sectarian and selfish in the past, and we want a purer purpose, a simpler aim. We must be ready for greater sacrifices in the Master's cause. To please the Bridegroom must be our supreme motive. 3. *The outlook of faith.* The day shall certainly dawn. Great is the truth; it must prevail. The prophecies of saintly seers shall certainly be fulfilled. The covenant with Christ must be observed. "To him every knee shall bow." The heathen is "given to him for an inheritance." "He shall see of the travail of his soul, and shall be satisfied." We can afford to wait. Jesus "*must* reign." Love is the mightiest force in the universe, and must conquer. In due time the sun of conquest shall rise on man's vision, and the light shall expand into the glories of the perfect day.

IV. This language serves to illustrate the Christian's prospect of heaven. 1. *His present depression.* At present he does not perceive any organic difference between himself and unconverted men. He may have a livelier taste for religious pursuits. He may find more enjoyment in prayer. Yet he cannot discover any radical difference to warrant the sublime expectation that he shall be claimed as a son, and join in the occupations of angels. Daily he feels the power of evil principles within him. Certainly the realities of righteousness and the things of the spiritual world do not absorb his thoughts. He is of the earth, earthy. When and how shall the great change pass over me, to fit me for the society of the redeemed? When will the glorified body be assumed? Will it be developed out of the present organism, or will it be a new creation? What will be my location and my experience immediately after death? Will the eternal state be totally different from anything I have expected? Such things disquiet me? 2. *Present duty.* "I will get me to the hills of frankincense." I will get away from secular pursuits as much as I can, and will get into familiar fellowship with God. Inasmuch as his presence is the centre of all joy and activity in heaven, it is well to have his society and fellowship now. The veil that hides him from me is not on his side, but on mine; it is the veil of unbelief. I will get me to the mount of communion, and in close heart-fellowship with God I shall await with calm composure the tremendous change. I want purity of heart wherewith to see God. 3. *Note the glorious prospect.* "The day shall break, and the shadows shall flee away." All dark thoughts of God and of God's dealings shall by-and-by disappear. All his mysterious ways will be illuminated in the blaze of noon. Whereas now we feel some of our earthly conditions hard to bear, then shall we discover that these were ordered by the ripest wisdom, combined with tenderest love. Every puzzling doctrine shall be made plain. Paradoxes will blend in perfect harmony. Gracious reasons will appear for every disappointment, every sorrow, every conflict, we endured on earth. The mysteries of pain and sin and death will all be solved, and God's great plan for training men will be pronounced the best. So on "the mountains of myrrh and on the hills of frankincense" we will cheerfully abide, in filial fellowship with Jesus, "until the day breaks, and the shadows flee away."—D.

Vers. 10, 11.—*Christ's appraisement of believers.* The interest which God takes in men is marvellous. Why he should have designed to save men from sin's curse, at such personal cost, is a mystery, and must remain so. It is equally a mystery why Jesus should have set such strong love on the fishermen of Galilee. Notwithstanding their glaring misconduct, "he loved them to the end." In like manner Jesus speaks in this passage of his high appreciation of his people's love. The love of Christ to us is a theme on which any Christian may well become eloquent. But to hear that Christ sets high store on our poor love to him, this staggers our thoughts, and almost seals our lips. Nevertheless it is a fact. Full of blemish and imperfection as we are, he counts us his jewels, his choicest possessions. He finds "his inheritance in the saints." With his generous heart he discerns all the goodness there is in us. He sets high value on our love, and in this way encourages us to give him more.

I. Note Christ's high appraisement of a Christian's love. 1. *The very indefiniteness of the language is instructive.* "How fair!" He does not say how precious it is. It is not the language of precise, calculating logic. It is the language of strong feeling. It is the generous ejaculation of the heart—"How fair!" This is spoken after the manner of men. When the intellect is overborne by emotion, we break into an exclamation, and say, almost in a spirit of inquiry, "How lovely! how fair!" As if we would say, "We cannot measure the worth; if any one else can, let him say." 2. *It is the love of tender relationship.* "My sister, my spouse." This mention of earthly relatives is used by way of comparison. What form of love among us is winsome, valued, precious? For sweetness and purity, what love is like a sister's? For strength and generousness, what affection like that of a wife? Jesus combines these both in his thought. Blend the love of sister and wife into one, and even then this poorly represents the love which Jesus discovers in us glowing for himself. He sets more value upon our love than we set upon the love of our most intimate friend. 3. *The language impresses us by a comparison.* "It is better than wine." As at a banquet one's bodily sensations are refreshed and quickened and gladdened with choice wine, so Jesus finds a cordial more refreshing, more inspiring, in his creature's love. To his inmost soul this love of man is a luxury. He has many sources of enjoyment in heaven, but this enjoyment is his choicest. The love of his ransomed is his rarest, sweetest joy. When in his lifetime he sat down to meat at the Pharisee's table, the tears of the penitent harlot were more delicious fare than Simon's choicest wine. It is possible that, though the angels "excel in strength," they may be deficient in love. Anyhow, our shallow, inconstant, imperfect love is precious in the eyes of Immanuel; it is a fountain of joy to his heart.

II. OBSERVE CHRIST'S APPRECIATION OF OUR HOLY INFLUENCE. How much better is "the scent of thy perfumes than all spices"! In the East the dwellings are not so sweet as in our own land. Want of general cleanliness, want of water, want of drainage, will account for this. As a consequence, unguents and perfumes about the person are very common. So in the hallowed savour of our piety there is a delicate fragrance very acceptable to Jesus. Our influence over others is something undefinable, yet very potent. It pertains to every habit of life, to every tone of voice, to every expression of countenance. It lives in a smile or in a tear; and results, begun in the minutest circumstance, stretch far away into the great eternity. Jesus highly esteems this quiet, mystic influence. It is a fragrant atmosphere created by love, and, like the savour of Mary's spikenard, it fills the house. Obdurate men may ridicule our pious words; they cannot ridicule nor resist the influence of a holy life. Our humility, our heavenly-mindedness, our consecrated zeal, diffuse a delicate perfume, like the subtle scent of roses, which every man of refinement appreciates, and in it Jesus finds delight. It is richer and rarer than all the spices of Araby.

III. MARK THE FACT THAT JESUS GREATLY ESTEEMS A CHRISTIAN'S TESTIMONY. "Thy lips drop as the honeycomb." The gift of speech is a noble endowment conferred on us by God. It distinguishes man above the animals. The human voice, either in oratory or in song, has potent enchantment for men. Speech is man's glory. By it he rules a nation. By it he enlightens and inspires the young. By it he moulds the destinies of mankind. Jesus loves to see this endowment consecrated to his cause. He loves to hear our testimony to his goodness. He loves to hear our pious songs. On one occasion Jesus cast out a demon from a man who was dumb, and immediately the dumb man spake. So, when Jesus "sheds abroad his love in our hearts," our lips cannot be silent. The desire to speak of his grace will be like a fire in our bones. A strange impulse stirs within to make all men know of his mighty virtue, and the tongue of the dumb will be unloosed. As the richest, sweetest of all honey is that which drops freely and first from the honeycomb, so the words of our fresh, warm love are very sweet in the ear of Jesus. He intertwines the welfare of his kingdom with human speech, for he has ordained preaching to be his great weapon in the sacred crusade with sin. If we did but remember that Jesus is always a hearer—a generous, appreciative hearer—of all that drops from our lips, should we not take care that he heard only what was true and kind and beautiful? Should we not be eager to "order our conversation aright," and to have our speech like the droppings of the honeycomb?

IV. MARK THAT JESUS APPRECIATES OUR PURPOSES TO PLEASE HIM. When David conceived the thought that he would build a substantial temple to Jehovah, and the plan began to ripen into resolve, God sent his prophet to say *this* to David, "It was well that it was in thine heart." We loudly applaud the man who makes heroic self-sacrifice for the cause of Christ; but very likely there is a purpose burning in the soul of some gentle woman to do battle for Christ more noble still, yet which cannot be realized. Well, that secret purpose is sweet as honey to Christ. His searching eye sees it all—sees every right motive, every heavenly disposition, every upward aspiration; and the sight is a delicious joy. It is the fruit of his incarnation. It is the work of his Spirit. Just as every man finds peculiar delight in his work, be it a building, or a painting, or a mechanical invention; so, and much more, does Jesus find exquisite pleasure in his successful work of making us godlike and Divine. "Honey and milk are under thy tongue." Thy secret thoughts and purposes bring me joy.

V. JESUS CHRIST APPRAISES HIGHLY EVERY DISCIPLE'S SERVICE. "The smell of thy garments is like the smell of Lebanon." The scent of pine trees and of cedar forests is peculiarly pleasant, and in this respect Lebanon surpassed all other forests in Palestine. It is in keeping with the symbolism of the Bible to employ "garments" as an emblem of human actions. We have a similar figure in our own language, for we use the word "habit" to denote one kind of apparel, and also to denote a constant line of action. Acts frequently performed become habits. So the "garments of a Christian are his everyday actions—the things he wears wherever he goes." The lesson here is that Jesus finds pleasure in everything we do, however trivial and insignificant. For there is nothing insignificant. You may read a man's character more clearly in the hourly business of every day than in his conduct on Sundays, or than in some great action of his life. The serving-woman in a shop, or the drudge in the scullery, or the hodman on the scaffolding, can serve Christ as well as the bishop in the pulpit. Jesus loves to see how faithfully we do little things. In his sight there is nothing little. It gave him untold pleasure to see the farthing which a poor widow dropped into his treasury. He counts every hair upon our heads. He notes when a sparrow falls. This is a mark of true greatness that it never overlooks the tiniest things. If from a disposition of love, and with cheerful temper, we sew a garment or drive a nail, we bring new pleasure to our Lord. "Therefore," says the apostle, "whatsoever ye do, whether in word or in deed, do all in the name of the Lord Jesus." Sweetly does old Herbert sing—

> " A servant with this clause
> Makes drudgery Divine;
> Who sweeps a room as for thy laws
> Makes *that* and th' action fine."

D.

Vers. 12—16.—*The King's garden.* The Church of Christ is fitly likened to a garden. It is a piece of territory separated from the rest, enclosed from the beaten road of this world's traffic. The distinguishing mark of a Christian Church is separation; *i.e.* separation from evil, separation as a means of blessing. As in a garden a king finds great delight and solace, so in this sacred garden Jesus Christ has a special joy. He calls it "my garden." We do not hear him say, "My star; my snow-capped mountains; my veins of gold;" but we do hear him say, "My garden; my people; my sister; my spouse." Such language is not merely the language of proprietorship; it is the language of endearment. Every plant and tree in this garden has been planted and pruned by himself. The unfolding of every blossom on the fruit trees he has watched with delight; and when the blossom has matured into fruit, his delight has become an ecstasy. One high ambition fills him, viz. that his garden may bear much fruit.

I. OBSERVE THAT THIS EMBLEM OF A GARDEN SUGGESTS MANY TRUTHS. 1. *There is the fact of separateness.* In this text the writer lays emphasis on this point. Every garden is more or less marked off from other ground, but *this* is specially described as "a garden enclosed." It is made inaccessible to thieves, to cattle, and to wild beasts. Boars out of the wood would soon lay it waste. So is it with the life of God in the believer's soul. He is thereby separated from the ungodly world. The chosen of God are separated by God's eternal decree. Their names are registered in the book of life. They have been separated by redemption. "Christ has redeemed us from the curse of the Law." They are separated by virtue of the new birth. They are separated by their own personal choice. They have gone to Christ "without the camp, bearing his reproach." They are no longer "conformed to the world." As Jesus "is not of the world, neither are they." "My kingdom is not of this world." 2. *There is the idea of secrecy.* This is not altogether the believer's choice; it is inevitable. The new life of the Christian is "hid with Christ in God." As a spring or fountain has its source out of sight—yea, far down in secret caverns of the earth—so the believer has the roots of his new life in Christ. He has experiences now which others do not share, and which he had not aforetime; but these are entirely hidden from the public eye. New fellowship with God; new aims in life; new motives and impulses; new peace and hopes; new springs of joy he has, with which a "stranger cannot intermeddle." As the wind in its vagaries defies all the predictions of man (none can "tell whence it cometh, or whither it goeth), so is every one that is born of the Spirit." "The natural man cannot understand the things of the Spirit; they are foolishness unto him." All life is mysterious; spiritual life is specially so. 3. *There is set forth the fact of security.* As a shepherd guards his flock, so the great Husbandman secures from adversaries his garden. "No wolf shall be there, nor any ravenous beast." The enclosure resists successfully even the "little foxes," who spoil the precious vines. The Christian is secure against the world, the flesh, and the devil; for all the attributes of God envelop him for his protection. He dwells under the shield of the Almighty. The omnipotence of Jehovah is his fortress. God is "a wall of fire round about him." Hence "no weapon that is formed against him can prosper." As a garden enclosed, he enjoys impregnable security. 4. *Here is the idea of sacredness.* The enclosed garden is set apart for the use of the king. It is devoted to one person and to one purpose. So Jesus claims this garden as his own, and what is true of the Church is true of every person composing that Church. The believer is a sacred person, a priest consecrated to holy service. He is God's man, attached to the court of heaven. Jesus said that he had "sanctified (or consecrated) himself, that they also might be sanctified (or consecrated) through the truth." Every part of the Christian is consecrated, viz. his endowments, his learning, his property, his time. For "we are not our own; we are bought with a price." Our business is to serve the kingdom. "For us to live is Christ." We are part of the "sacramental host of God's elect."

II. OBSERVE THAT THIS GARDEN IS FAMOUS FOR FRUITFULNESS. "Thy plants are an orchard of pomegranates, with pleasant fruits," etc. 1. *Abundant fruitfulness is asserted.* It was the earnest longing of Jesus Christ that his disciples "should bear much fruit, and that this fruit should abide." Very soon rich clusters of fruit did appear in his Church. The prayerfulness culminating on the Day of Pentecost; the generous communism of the saints; the courage and zeal of many; the fervid piety of Stephen; the practical sympathy for the poor; the magnanimity of Barnabas; the whole-hearted consecration of Paul;—these were the firstfruits of discipleship. And from that day to this fruit has abounded in the Church. The noble qualities of mind and heart; the splendid virtues; the patience, fortitude, and zeal; the consecrated heroism of believers, have been the admiration and astonishment of the world. "Whatsoever things are lovely, excellent, pure, and of good report," *these* have been conspicuous in the Church. The *élite* of mankind is within the Church. 2. *There is also variety of fruit.* In nature God has made his goodness most manifest in the vast variety of fruits with which our earth teems. Equally in the Church may we find a splendid variety of gifts and graces. The early fruits of humility and repentance and tenderness of conscience soon appear. The spice trees of prayer and sympathy send forth a goodly odour. The trees of righteousness and holiness bear large stores of precious fruit. In each succeeding age new excellences have appeared, new fruits have made this garden famous. Here and there you will find a gnarled and crooked tree that bears little fruit. But this is the exception; a blot upon the garden. You will find even in a royal garden some withered branch, some rank shoot that is unlovely and unfruitful. Still, we do not on that account condemn the whole garden. All temperance reforms, all hospitals and asylums, all plans for the betterment of humanity, all alleviations of misery and woe, have appeared among us as the fruits of Christ's life. The fruit abounds in variety almost endless. 3. *Mark the utility of this fruit.* The fruit was choice; the rarest fruits were there. Some were full of cooling juice, pleasant to the taste in hours of scorching heat. Some had a value as medicines for the cure of disease, and for soothing burning pains. Some yielded rich perfumes (as spikenard), and added to the joy of royal or marriage banquets. Others produced myrrh and frankincense, and were consecrated to Divine worship. Others, again, conferred a delicious flavour to human food. Each and all had a mission of usefulness among mankind. So is it also in the Church of Christ. You cannot put finger on a genuine Christian who is not more or less a blessing to the race. His piety has a delicious savour in the circle in which he lives. His prayers bring blessing upon a thousand bosoms. As God blessed Egypt for Joseph's sake, as God blessed Israel for David's sake, so for the Church's sake he often blesses the world. Every Christian is a light, illuminating the world's darkness. "Ye are the salt of the earth." Since Christ lived, and because he now lives in others, the moral and social aspects of the world are changed. Tyrannies have disappeared. War has lost its barbaric rigour. Industry is productive of substantial good. Agriculture prospers.

III. OBSERVE THE DEPENDENCE OF THIS GARDEN UPON SOURCES OF PROSPERITY OUTSIDE ITSELF. It needs the "fountain;" "the well of living waters;" "the streams from Lebanon." 1. *This may well teach us that the Church needs God in the way of providence.* While yet the Church remains on the earth it needs earthly good. It needs, at least, toleration or sufferance from earthly governments. It needs human teachers, and all the aids of human learning. It needs the use of books and printing. It needs material buildings for public worship. It needs earthly wealth to carry on all the agencies of instruction and of blessing. Likewise the individual disciple receives much from God in the way of providence. We have the priceless ministry of angels. We have the pillar of cloud, and the pillar of fire. We have the stimulating influence of godly companions. We have the benefits of parental teaching and holy example. We have the inspirations that come from the biographies of heroic men. These are wells in the desert; "streams from Lebanon." All that is requisite to make this garden fertile, rich in umbrageous shade, rich in luscious fruits, rich in aromatic spices, has been lavishly supplied. No lack can be found in the thoughtfulness of the husbandman. 2. *Equally the Church needs God in the way of spiritual gifts.* "Awake, O north wind; and come, thou south; blow upon my garden, that the spices thereof may flow out." The Hebrew word for "wind" means also "breath," or "spirit;" hence we have here a striking emblem of the work of the Divine Spirit. To him belongs the sole prerogative to impart life to the trees of the garden. We invoke his presence because he is the Lord and Giver of life. For the largest prosperity of the Church the good Spirit of God is needed in all his offices, in all his fulness of power. A blustering gale from the north scatters noxious blight, but the soft wind from the south will quicken the flow of vital sap, and will nurse the tender blossoms into ruddy fruit. So do we often need that the Spirit of God should come like a northern tornado, and scatter to the ground our false hopes and flimsy errors and earthly ambitions. And we need him also as the Comforter, who shall reveal to us the virtues of our Divine Healer, and shall melt us into sweet obedience by the warmth of Immanuel's love. As the fragrant odours of flowers lie hidden in their tiny cells until the fresh south wind coaxes them forth, so, too, the precious graces of the Christian remain concealed and slumbering within until the Spirit of life and power brings them forth, and diffuses them through the Church. Then do the disciples of Christ become "living epistles, known and read of men." "Awake, O north wind; and come, thou south; blow upon my garden."

> "Come as the wind, the dew, the rain;
>   Come, make this heart thy temple-home;
>   Spirit of grace, come as thou wilt,
>   Our souls adjure thee—only come!"

                                                                                  D.

Ver. 16—ch. v. 1.—*Prayer and its quick response.* "Let my beloved come into his garden, and eat his pleasant fruits." "I am come into my garden." It is a sign of spiritual health when we heartily desire God's best gifts; when our prayer is the prayer of faith; when we ask and have. But it is a sign of higher attainment yet when we have but one desire, viz. the desire to have the Giver with us rather than his gifts. A wife highly prizes the love-tokens she receives from her absent lord, but she values far more highly his personal return. So, if we are wise, we shall more desire to have Christ in our hearts than any gift of light or strength. "Let my Beloved himself come." To have the source of life is better than having the streams. If Christ is with me I shall want nothing.

I. THE CHURCH'S INVITATION TO HER LORD. 1. *She addresses him by an endearing title, " My Beloved."* In dealing with Jesus we need make no reserve of our affection. He will never resent our largest confidence. The mere suggestion borders on the profane. If we know anything, we know whether we love the Saviour. Love to him is the same thing in kind, as love to an earthly friend. We may stand in doubt whether Jesus has love to us personally, although such a doubt is sin. But we need never be in doubt whether love to him glows in our hearts. Many tests are available; and when love, however scanty, is found, Jesus delights to hear himself thus addressed, "My Beloved!" Then is he King within, firm seated on the throne. 2. *She recognizes the garden to be his property.* Yes; and not only is the garden his, but each particular tree, each separate fruit. Every holy principle within us he himself planted. It was planted by his own right hand. It has been trained and pruned by his watchful care. Every blossom has been under his protection. The fruit has been stored with juice from his treasuries. It is a delicious joy if I can feel that every grace in me is the handiwork of Jesus. Am I prayerful? Jesus has been teaching me. Am I meek and self-forgetting? Jesus has been busy in me, and has gently moulded my nature. Much trouble has he taken to bend my proud will. No earthly gardener has such labour to produce fruit in his trees as Jesus has to make us fruitful in holiness and love. And the more abundant our spiritual fruits are, the more readily shall we ascribe all the praise to him. 3. *Here is a strong desire to give our Master pleasure.* "Let him come; let him eat his pleasant fruits." This is spoken after the manner of men. It is a peculiar joy for a man to walk in his own garden, and to eat the ripe fruit he himself has carefully nurtured. A similar joy our Lord tastes. But is any virtue or goodness in us so ripe and sweet that Jesus can find joy in it? What generous condescension does he show in partaking of our meekness, and patience, and faith, and sacred zeal! Just as a father finds peculiar pleasure in listening to the first imperfect lispings of his child, and hears sweet music in the broken words, so Jesus sees in our imperfect graces the promise of future good, the promise of illustrious service, the promise of high attainment. Never did a friend show such generous appreciation of our loyalty. To be fruitful in Christian graces is in itself an ample reward, but to know that every attainment in goodness we make adds to our Saviour's joy is a higher reward still. Who will not brace every nerve to bring new pleasure to Immanuel! We seek our joy in the heavenly paradise; Jesus seeks his joy in us. "I am glorified in them."

II. THE BRIDEGROOM'S PROMPT RESPONSE. "I am come." 1. *Observe how swift is the reply.* No advantage, in this case, will come from silence or delay. The Church has asked the best thing, and she shall at once have it. Here he has acted up to his own promise, "Before they call I will answer." That selfsame desire to have Christ's presence was a desire planted and nourished by himself, therefore he answered the desire before it developed into spoken prayer. Already he had visited that garden, and sowed the seed of noble ambition. Now it has grown to fruitage, and he has come to enjoy it. We have never to wrest this gift from a clenched hand; it is a gift waiting our acceptance. Before the invitation is despatched he is knocking at the door. "I am come." 2. *Mark the harmony of feeling and purpose between Christ and his people.* The Church has learnt a lesson of unselfishness from her Lord. Aforetime she had desired him to come for her profit, or for her pleasure; now she asks him to come for his own gratification. She thought that he would find delight in the graces and excellences which flourish in the Church, and her spiritual instincts were true to fact. This is a delightful discovery. When our thoughts harmonize with Christ's thoughts, when our dispositions are the counterpart of his, when one mind, one will, one aim, dwells in the Saviour and the saint, then is heaven begun on earth. This is joy unspeakable; the foretaste of beatific rest. This is the completion of the sacred covenant. This is his seal impressed on us. 3. *Note the satisfaction which Jesus finds in his saints.* This series of metaphors is suggestive of many meanings. In our holy principles, in our sacred dispositions, in our prayers and our praises, in our words and self-sacrificing deeds, Jesus takes delight. The myrrh and spice may indicate the perfume of our intercession, or the pleasure which he finds in our harmony of praise. Since he has· constructed all musical harmonies, and fashioned the human voice to produce this minstrelsy, surely he is moved to delight when love to him stirs all the powers of song. Every endeavour to please him, every aspiration after holiness, every noble purpose, every act of self-denial, all efforts toward a freer communion with him, —these are fruits of the Spirit, in which Jesus finds delight. Blurred as these are with imperfection, we count them very unworthy, and perhaps too much underrate them. If Jesus appreciates them, and derives satisfaction from them, is not this great encouragement to bring forth more fruit? Many products of nature are here brought into service to illustrate a Christian's spiritual fruitfulness. One has said that wine may represent those labours of ours which result from deep thought, self-denial, and generous consecration, for wine must be pressed from the grape with toil and care. But milk is a natural production, and may represent those little deeds of kindness which flow from a quiet outgushing of daily love. A vigorous fancy will find a hundred suggestions in these similitudes. The essential lesson is *this,* that the Son of God has a large accession of joy from all forms of genuine piety. His people are his vineyard, his inheritance, and in them he finds delight.

III. A GENEROUS PARTICIPATION. "Eat, O friends; drink, yea, drink abundantly, O beloved." The satisfaction which Jesus finds, he forthwith shares with his chosen. If there be a smile on the Bridegroom's face, it will soon communicate itself to the bride. If the Head have gladness, so will all the members in the mystical body. 1. *Jesus uses very tender titles to designate his saints.* He calls them "friends." The old explanation of a friend suits well in this place, viz. one soul dwelling in two bodies. Jesus completely identifies himself with us. Once we were aliens, enemies, rebels, but the old enmity is changed into a sacred and inseparable friendship. Jonathan gave proof of his friendship with David when he stripped himself of raiment and put it upon his friend. But our Immanuel has surpassed all orders of creatures in his practical deeds of kindness. Further, he calls them his "·beloved." He presseth into service every human form of speech. May I take this word as addressed to me? Most certainly I may, for I am not excluded. No saint has attained to this rapturous privilege by any personal merit. "He died for the ungodly." Though the chief of sinners, "he loved me; he gave himself for me." Yes; mystery though it is, it is also plainest· among facts, that into my penitent heart Jesus comes to dwell, and into my ear he whispers this endearing word, "Beloved." 2. *Observe the provisions prepared.* They are of two kinds, viz. food and drink. Very properly may we regard the food as revealed truth. To appreciate the eternal facts of God's redemption, this is solid food. This is the manna which cometh down from heaven. The only food for the hungry soul is truth.

> " Christ said not to his first conventicle,
> ' Go forth and preach imposture to the world,'
> But gave them truth to feed on."

This is heavenly nutriment, and is indispensable. And what else can the drink be, but the mercy of our God, flowing from the fount of his eternal love? All truth and all grace are in Jesus; hence he says to us, "He that cometh to me shall never hunger, and he that believeth on me shall never thirst." 3. *Mark the fulness of the entreaty.* " Drink; yea, drink abundantly." No generous host likes to see his guests making pretence of eating or drinking. It implies that they doubted his welcome, and took care to have a meal before they came. This is dishonouring to the giver of the feast. And Jesus will have none of that. He knows well that the thirst of the soul can be allayed nowhere but from him. He knows well that no one can have a surfeit of his mercy. Of other things we may eat and drink more than is for our good, but of the love of Christ we cannot have too much. The love we partake in shall become in us "a well, springing up unto everlasting life." However much we take, we do not diminish the supply. Trembling at his table, I have sometimes said, "Lord, I am too unworthy to sip a drop of thy mercy. My sin is unusual, crimson, aggravated." But he straightway replies, "For thee it is provided. Drink; yea, drink abundantly, O beloved."—D.

Vers. 1—5.—*The charm of true beauty.* The bride is now in the palace which is to be her residence of state. The veil is removed from her countenance, and as her royal lover and spouse gazes upon her form and features, he is filled with admiration, and breaks forth in a poetical commendation of her loveliness. The language is the warm language of love, and the figures employed are more Oriental than those which would be used amongst ourselves. But all is natural to an Eastern imagination, which revels in eulogium ;that to our colder taste would seem extravagant. The beauty of the figure and the face may be taken as emblematical of that higher beauty which attracts and satisfies the spiritual discernment. The description has been taken as applicable to "the bride, the Lamb's wife," faultless and flawless in the view of him who has purchased his Church unto himself.

I. THE SPIRITUAL BEAUTY WHICH CHRIST DISCERNS IN HIS CHURCH IS HIS OWN CREATION. There is no excellence in man apart from God. The highest excellence to be found in human character and history is the effect of the Divine interposition of grace. God in Christ has created anew, and in his own likeness, those whom he has visited with his favour. The beauty of regenerate character and consecrated life is the beauty which the Holy Spirit has imparted. It is Divine grace which bestows upon the human soul the virtues and graces which make that soul admirable and invest it with a spiritual charm.

"Nought God in us but his own gifts doth crown."

II. THIS SPIRITUAL BEAUTY IS AKIN TO CHRIST'S OWN. The influence is well known which the marriage state exercises in the gradual assimilation to one another in character and habits of those wedded for long years. The resemblance between the Divine Head and his spouse the Church is so striking that none can overlook it. They who accept Christ's doctrine, place themselves beneath his guardianship, cherish his love, cultivate his society, are hereby transformed into his likeness. Who has not seen in faithful and devoted friends of Jesus traits of their Lord's spiritual character, lineaments unmistakably his? The sympathy, beneficence, the purity and tenderness, the patience and self-denial, which are "notes" of the true Church, are evidently Christ's; from the Divine Lord, and from no lower source, have all these virtues been derived.

III. HENCE THIS SPIRITUAL BEAUTY YIELDS SATISFACTION AND DELIGHT TO THE SAVIOUR HIMSELF. If it seems at first an extravagance to suppose that the Lord of all can find joy and complacency in beholding his Church on earth, the explanation must be sought in the principles just stated. Humanity was originally created in the image of God and for the glory of God. The purpose of Eternal Wisdom in creating this human race was that his own attributes might be visibly and manifestly embodied and displayed, according to the measure of the creature, in his own highest handiwork on earth. Nor has this purpose been defeated by sin. The image sin has marred, the grace of God in Christ has restored. And it may be that the work of redemption brings out the moral and spiritual beauty in which God himself delights, with a bloom and charm and perfection which would otherwise have been impossible. Christ sees of the travail of his soul, and is satisfied.

APPLICATION. The Church of Christ may well be encouraged and cheered by the assurance that the Divine Spouse appreciates those spiritual excellences which are due to the operation of his own Spirit. "Behold, thou art fair, my love," is the language of the Bridegroom as he looks upon his beloved. And our Saviour is not insensible to those signs of grace, those revelations of spiritual beauty, which he daily discerns in his own. Those who would please Christ may well be animated by the knowledge that he never looks with indifference upon the proofs of sincere affection, upon the evidences of spiritual assimilation to himself. Well may the Christian adopt the language of St. Augustine, "Take from me, Lord, all that injures me and displeases thee; and give me all that is requisite to please thee; give me words, affections, desires, and works which may draw upon me thine eyes, thy delight, and thy love!"—T.

Ver. 7.—"*Without spot.*" Purity is an element of beauty, and to a mind judging justly is also an element of attractiveness. In the maiden he had brought from her mountain-home on the slopes of Lebanon, the royal bridegroom admired a purity like that of the snow that clothes the summit of Hermon. She was meet to be the spouse of the king, who (speaking not only of the absence of any blemish of form or feature, but of the qualities of the mind and heart) exclaimed, as he looked upon her fairness, " There is no spot in thee ! "

I. THE PURITY OF THE CHURCH IS IN CONTRAST WITH THE SINFULNESS OF THE NATURAL, UNREGENERATE STATE.

II. THE PURITY OF THE CHURCH IS EFFECTED BY THE MEANS OF THE SAVIOUR'S REDEMPTION.

III. THE PURITY OF THE CHURCH IS WROUGHT BY THE CLEANSING POWER OF THE HOLY SPIRIT.

IV. THE PURITY OF THE CHURCH RENDERS HER THE ACCEPTABLE AND SUITABLE SPOUSE OF HER HEAVENLY LORD.

V. THE PURITY OF THE CHURCH IS A WITNESS AND REBUKE TO THE MORAL DEFILEMENT OF A SINFUL WORLD.

VI. THE PURITY OF THE CHURCH ON EARTH IS AN EARNEST AND PREPARATION FOR THE STAINLESSNESS OF THE ETERNAL STATE OF FELICITY—THE NUPTIALS OF HEAVEN.—T.

Vers. 8—11.—*Heart calls to heart.* The richness of imagination for which the Song of Songs is justly renowned is especially remarkable in this passage. All the senses are summoned to deepen the impression. The sight is charmed by visible beauty, by the glances of " eyes darting love," by the necklace lying on the fair white neck. Perfumes and unguents, spices, and cedars of Lebanon, address the sense of smell. The taste is appealed to by the pleasant wine, the honey of exceeding sweetness. And what is the emotion which links itself with beauty, sweetness, and fragrance? It is love, with which all this opulence of poetry seems most harmonious. Beneath all this vesture of splendour are certain principles which may well be brought into clearness of knowledge.

I. ALL LOVE INVOLVES LEAVING. The bride is invited to quit her mountain-home, the scenes of grandeur with which she was familiar, the lonely sources of historic rivers, the romantic home of the lion and the leopard. No power but love could have made her think with acquiescence of such a change as that to which she was now urged. Ever must love come down from its proud heights, from its vaulted splendours, from its ancient scenes. It is so with human love; and how willingly is the call obeyed which bids to forsake the surroundings, the very joys and excitements, of the past! It is so with Divine love; and no soul that recognizes the sweet authority of the Saviour's voice will hesitate to quit the scenes and the society which may previously have afforded pleasure, and like the bride to forget her father's house. It is a sound test, and a fair: " Come with me from Lebanon."

II. ALL LOVE INVOLVES HEART-LOSING. " The heart is where it loves, and not where it lives." The lover here avers, " Thou hast ravished my heart with a look from thine eyes." Common language recognizes the distinction between him who is " heart-whole " and him who has " lost his heart." If nothing is lost, nothing is gained. It is the same in the spiritual life. Christ gives his very heart to his people, and he expects and receives from them their hearts in return. As he has loved us with an everlasting love, no wonder that his appeal is, " Give me thy heart."

III. ALL LOVE INVOLVES PREFERENCE. The language of love is the language of comparison. No similitudes are ample or rich enough to set forth the surpassing charm and attractiveness of the bride. Better than all glories and all gifts, better than all rivals, is the chosen of the heart. Certainly in the religious life this is a noticeable characteristic. The Saviour prefers the soul of man to all that ease and pleasure and worldly dignity can offer. Such is the teaching of his humiliation and obedience on earth. And the soul that knows Christ's love deems him chief among ten thousand and fairer than the sons of men. None can compete, none can compare, with him.

IV. ALL LOVE INVOLVES DELIGHT IN MUTUAL SOCIETY. It does not matter whether life be passed in the cottage on the mountain-side, in the tent on the plain, or in the palace in the metropolis, if only it be passed in that companionship which is congenial, in uninterrupted fellowship with the chosen of the heart. However imperfect in its character is this fellowship, however it be suspended in its enjoyment, the communion of the soul with Christ is subject to no such drawback.

> " They who once his kindness prove,
> Find it everlasting love."

Nothing in Christ can mar the perfection of spiritual intimacy, or can bring that intimacy to a close. The love of Christ is the purest possession, and the one unfailing source of strength and joy.—T.

Vers. 12—15.—*The garden and the fountain.* The bride's beauty, purity, sweetness, and delightfulness are set forth in these verses of the song with all the richness of Oriental imagery. The poet's fancy takes him to the sunny garden of the half-tropical En-gedi, to the breezy heights of Lebanon, whence flow the streams that convert the desert into a paradise. Orchards of pomegranates, gardens redolent with spicy odours, murmuring fountains, all serve to suggest the charms of the peerless one whom the king claims as his own.

I. THE CHURCH IS THE GARDEN OF THE LORD. This similitude occurs constantly both in Scripture and in uninspired Christian writers, and has given a tinge of poetry to many a sacred hymn.

> " Thy vineyards and thine orchards are
> Most beautiful and fair,
> Full furnished with trees and fruits
> Exceeding rich and rare.
> Thy gardens and thy gallant walks
> Continually are green;
> There grow such sweet and pleasant flowers
> As nowhere else are seen."

1. The Church, like the garden, is the scene and home of *life.* The world is the arid wilderness, the stony waste. The Church has been breathed upon by the Eternal Spirit, whose influence has called into existence the living plants that adorn the garden of Christ.   2. The Church, like the garden, is a spectacle of beauty. But in this case the beauty is spiritual.

> " The lily white that bloometh there is purity;
> The fragrant violet is surnamed humility;
> The lovely damask rose is here called patience;
> The rich and cheerful marigold is obedience;
> But one there is that bears a crown the rest above,
> A crown imperial, and this flower is holy love."

3. The Church, like the garden, is fruitful. There are not only the lovely flowers, there are precious fruits. The fruits of the Spirit have been described by the apostle. These are they which afford the deepest satisfaction to the Lord of the vineyard himself.   4. The Church, like the garden, is a secure seclusion and a sole possession. Such a representation sometimes, in our active, bustling, philanthropic age, arouses resentment. Yet it contains a delightful truth. The " garden walled round " is secure from the assaults of the foe and the incursion of the wild beast. The Church is indebted to Divine protection; here is its only security. The wall encloses the domain. The Church is Christ's, and his alone. The garden of the Lord has " a wall without, a well within." It is the sacred and exclusive property of him who planted it for his own glory.

II. THE CHURCH IS THE FOUNTAIN OF THE LORD. The garden seems to suggest the fountain, which in the Eastern climate was necessary to keep the enclosure moist, verdant, and fertile. And the garden well-spring gushing forth and watering the many-coloured and fragrant beds, seems to suggest the mountain-springs far up in the northern heights of Lebanon, beyond the early home of the fair bride herself. Such springs are a suitable figure of the living Church of Christ, which to set forth in all her excellence needs all things fair, bright, and fragrant that earth can offer. The Church of Christ, like the fountain, (1) brings from an unseen source the blessings to be diffused ; (2) yields an abundant and perpetual supply of these spiritual gifts; (3) freely and generously diffuses knowledge and purity life and true refreshment, amongst all around ; (4) produces results of beneficence immediate and remote, for which thanksgiving must ever be rendered to God. (5) It may be noted that, as in the similitude of the garden, so here, there is an assurance of ownership and guardianship. As the well-spring was covered with a great stone, sealed with the owner's signet, so the Church is marked by its Divine Lord as his own. "It hath this seal, The Lord knoweth them that are his ; and, Let every one that nameth the Name of the Lord depart from iniquity."—T.

Ver. 16.—*The response of love.* The impassioned encomium of the bridegroom is not disregarded, is not ineffectual; it not only yields satisfaction and pleasure to her who is the object of unstinted praise; it elicits the response of appreciative gratitude and affectionate welcome. If Christ delights in the Church, the Church also delights in Christ, and yields to him the tribute of loyal obedience.

I. DIVINE INFLUENCES ARE ENTREATED. The breath of the Spirit of God passing graciously and gently and yet mightily over the Christian society alone can call forth all its spiritual fragrance. The silent, unseen, benignant influences are to be sought with fervent, earnest prayer : "Awake, O north wind ; and come, thou south ; blow upon my garden ! "

II. THE EXHALATION OF SPIRITUAL FRAGRANCE IS DESIRED. "That the spices thereof may flow out." Because the Church is Christ's, it has great capacities for good ; yet the actual exhibition of the vital qualities, in proofs of piety, in deeds of holiness, in services of benevolence, is dependent upon the "Lord and Giver of life," whose quickening grace is the greatest privilege of the Christian dispensation. There is an aroma of spiritual excellence in the Church of the Lord Jesus which is beyond comparison the sweetest and divinest quality which human society has ever manifested.

III. THE PRESENCE OF THE LORD HIMSELF IS REQUESTED. "Let my beloved come into his garden." True, he has given his Church the promise, "Lo, I am with you alway." He is among his people to know their works, to accept their service, to inspire their devotion. He ever visits his vineyard; comes, "seeking fruit." The Church speaks of itself as both "my" garden and "his" garden ; and it is both. When the Lord is invited and welcomed, it is to his own chosen and congenial possession.

IV. THE FRUIT THAT IS DUE TO THE LORD IS OFFERED. 1. In what do these precious, pleasant fruits consist ? Praise, devotion, love, obedience. 2. To what are they owing ? To Divine care and protection; to the tilling of the wise and forbearing Master; to the genial influences of the Holy Spirit. Hence they are "his" fruits. The weeds are ours ; the fruits are his. 3. How are they regarded ? Christ delights in them, for they are the results of his purpose and of his sacrifice. Christ "eats" of them ; *i.e.* uses them in his condescension. His people may well say to him, "Of thine own have we given thee." There is no satisfaction possible to Christ's people so great and so pure as that they feel when their Lord accepts their offering and approves their endeavours.—T.

EXPOSITION.

CHAPTER V.

Ver. 1.—**I am come into my garden, my sister, my bride ; I have gathered my myrrh with my spice ; I have eaten my honeycomb with my honey; I have drunk my wine with my milk. Eat, O friends ; drink, yea, drink abundantly, O beloved.** *My myrrh with my balsam* (see 1 Kings x. 10). There were celebrated plantations at Jericho. The Queen of Sheba brought "of spices very great store ; " "There came no more such abundance of

spices as these which the Queen of Sheba gave to King Solomon." Is there a reference to the conversion of the heathen nations in this? The wine and milk are what God offers to his people (see Isa. lv. 1) without money and without price. Οἰογάλα is what Chloe gives to Daphnis (cf. Ps. xix. 6). It would seem as though the writer intended us to follow the bridal procession to its destination in the royal palace. The bridal night intervenes. The joy of the king in his bride is complete. The climax is reached, and the rest of the song is an amplification. The call to the friends is to celebrate the marriage in a banquet on the second day (see Gen. xxix. 28; Judg. xiv. 12; Tobit xi. 18; and cf. Rev. xix. 7 and xix. 9). A parallel might be found in Ps. xxii. 26, where Messiah, at the close of his sufferings, salutes his friends, the poor, and as they eat at his table gives them his royal blessing, " Vivat cor vestrum in æternum ! " The perfect state of the Church is represented in Scripture, both in the Old Testament and in the New, as celebrated with universal joy—all tears wiped away from off all faces, and the loud harpings of innumerable harpers. Can we doubt that this wonderful book has tinged the whole of subsequent inspired Scripture? Can we read the descriptions of triumphant rejoicing in the Apocalypse and not believe that the apostolic seer was familiar with this idealized love-song?

Ver. 2—ch. viii. 4.—Part IV. REMINISCENCES OF LOVE-DAYS. *The bridegroom rejoicing in the bride.*

Ver. 2.—*The bride's reminiscence of a love-dream.* I was asleep, but my heart waked. It is the voice of my beloved that knocketh, saying, Open to me, my sister, my love, my dove, my undefiled : for my head is filled with dew, my locks with the drops of the night. There is a resemblance between this account of what was apparently a dream, and that which is related in ch. iii. 1—4; but the difference is very clear. In the former case the lover is represented as dismissed for a season, and then the relenting heart of the maiden sought after him and found him. In this case he " stands at the door and knocks," coming in the night; and the maiden rises to open, but finds him gone, and so is drawn after him. The second dream is much more vivid and elaborate, and seems to be an imitation and enlargement of the other, being introduced apparently more for the sake of dwelling on the attractions of the beloved one and his preciousness in the eyes of the maiden than in self-reproach. Is it not possible that the poem originally concluded at ch. v. 1 with the marriage, and that the whole of the latter half was an amplification, either by Solomon himself, the author of the first half, or by some one who has entered into the spirit of the song? This would explain the apparent repetition, with the variations. But, at all events, the second part certainly is more from the standpoint of married life than the first. Hence the bride speaks at great length, which she does not in the earlier portion. Delitzsch thinks that this second love-dream is intended to represent what occurred in early married life; but there are two objections to that— *first*, that the place is evidently a country

residence; and *secondly*, that such an occurrence is unsuitable to the conditions of a royal bride. It is much more natural to suppose that the bride is recalling what occurred in her dream when the lover, having been sent away until the evening, as on the former occasion, returned, and in the night knocked at the door. " My heart waked " is the same as " My mind was active." The " heart " in Hebrew is the inner man, both intellect and feeling. " I was asleep, but I was thinking" (cf. Cicero, 'De Divinatione,' i. 30). The lover has come off a long journey over the mountains, and arrives in the night-time. The terms with which he appeals to his beloved are significant, denoting (1) equal rank—*my sister;* (2) free choice—*my love;* (3) purity, simplicity, and loveliness—*my dove;* (4) entire devotion, undoubting trust—*my undefiled.* Tammanthi, " my perfection," as Arabic *tam, teim,* " one devoted to another," as a servant. Similar passages are quoted from heathen love-poetry, as Anacreon, iii. 10; Propertius, i. 16—23; Ovid, 'Amor.,' iii. 19, 21. The simple meaning of the dream is that she is full of love by night and by day. She dreamed that she was back in her old country home, and that her lover visited her like a shepherd; and she tells how she sought him, to show how she loved him. When we are united to the Saviour with the bonds of a pledged affection, we lose the sense of self-reproach in the delight of fellowship, and can even speak of our own slowness and backwardness only to magnify his grace. We delight to acknowledge that it was his knocking that led us to seek after him, although we had to struggle with the dull heart; and it was not until it was moved by his approach, by his moving towards us, that we hastened to find him, and were full of the thought of his desirableness. There are abundant examples of this same interchange of affection in the history of the Church's revivals and restorations.

Ver. 3.—I have put off my coat; how shall I put it on ? I have washed my feet; how shall I defile them ? Evidently the meaning is, " I have retired to rest; do not disturb me." She is lying in bed. The *cuttoneth,* or χιτών, was the linen garment worn next the body—from *cathan,* " linen." The Arabic *kutun* is " cotton ;" hence the French *coton,* " calico, or cotton " shift. Shulamith represents herself as failing in love, not meeting the condescension and affection of her lover as she should. Sloth, reluctance, ease, keep her back. " Woe to them that are at ease in Zion !" The scene is, of course, only ideally true ; it is not meant to be a description of an actual occurrence. Fancy in dreams stirs up the real nature, though it also disturbs it. Shulamith has forsaken her first love. She relates it with sorrow, but not with despondency. She comes to herself again, and her repentance and restoration are the occasion for pouring out the fulness of her affection, which had never really changed, though it has been checked and restrained by self-indulgence. How true a picture both of the individual soul and of the Church in its decline! " Leave me to myself ; let me lie at ease in my luxury and my smooth, conventional ways and self-flattering deceit."

Ver. 4.—**My beloved put in his hand by the hole** of the door, **and my heart was moved for him.** The door-hole is a part of the door pierced through at the upper part of the lock, or door-bolt (מִן־הַחוֹר), that is, by the opening from without to within, or through the opening, as if, *i.e.*, to open the door by pressing back the lock or bolt from within. There was some obstacle. He failed to open it. It had not been left so that he could easily obtain admittance. The metaphor is very apt and beautiful. How much he loved her ! How he tried to come to her ! As applied to the Saviour, what infinite suggestiveness ! He would be with us, and not only knocks at the door, but is impatient to enter ; tries the lock, and too often finds it in vain ; he is repelled, he is resisted, he is coldly excluded. *My heart was moved for him.* מֵעַי, "my inner being" (cf. Isa. lxiii. 15, where the same word is used of God). It is often employed to express sympathy and affection, especially with tender regret. The later authorities, as the older translations, have " to him " (עָלָיו), *i.e.* over him, or on account of him, in the thought of his wounded heart.

Ver. 5.—**I rose up to open to my beloved ; and my hands dropped with myrrh, and my fingers with liquid myrrh, upon the handles of the bolt.** The meaning seems to be that the lover had come to the door perfumed as if for a festival, and the costly ointment which he brought with him has dropped on the handles of the bolts. Similar allusions may be found in Lucretius and other heathen writers. This description is, of course, inapplicable to the shepherd-theory. It would not be a rough country swain that came thus perfumed ; but Solomon is thought of as at once king and lover. It would be stretching the poetry too far to suppose that Shulamith meant the natural sweetness of her lover was the perfume. Neither is there any probability in the explanation that she dipped her hand in perfumed oil before she opened the door. That would destroy all the form and beauty of the dream. It is her lover whose fragrance she celebrates, not her own. Whether he brought perfumes with him, or the innate personal sweetness of his

presence left its fragrance on that which he touched, in either case it is the lover himself who is spoken of. His very hand, wherever it has been, leaves behind it ineffable delight. His presence reveals itself everywhere. Those who go after him know that he is not far off by the traces of his loving approaches to them. The spiritual meaning is too plain to need much exposition.

Ver. 6.—**I opened to my beloved ; but my beloved had withdrawn himself, and was gone. My soul had failed me when he spake : I sought him, but I could not find him ; I called him, but he gave me no answer.** The meaning is this—The voice of my beloved struck my heart ; but in the consciousness that I had estranged myself from him I could not openly meet him, I could not offer him mere empty excuses. Now I am made sensible of my own deficiency. I call after him. I long for his return, but it is in vain (cf. the two disciples going to Emmaus, Luke xxiv., "Did not our heart burn within us," etc.?). Similar allusion to the effect of the voice of the beloved is found in Terence, ' And.,' i. 5. 16, "Oratio hæc," etc. The failing or departing of the soul at the sound of the voice must refer to the lack of response at the time, therefore it was that she sought him and cried out after him. *When he spake;* literally, *in his speaking ;* i.e. when he said, "I will not now come because at first refused ;" cf. Prov. i. 20—33, the solemn warning against the loss of opportunity. It is a coincidence between the two books of Solomon which cannot be disregarded. If there is any spiritual meaning at all in Solomon's Song, it certainly is a book which he who wrote the first chapter of Proverbs is likely to have written.

Ver. 7.—**The watchmen that go about the city found me, they smote me, they wounded me ; the keepers of the walls took away my mantle from me.** The intention is to show into what evil she fell by having to seek her beloved instead of being with him. She is mistaken and misjudged ; she is smitten and wounded with reproaches and false accusations, as though she were a guilty and evil-minded woman. She is subjected to abuse and ill treatment from those who should be her guardians. She had hard work to escape, leaving her robe behind her (cf. Gen. xxxix. 12). The *redhidh*, like *ridhâ* in Arabic, is a plaid-like upper garment thrown over the shoulders—so says Aben Ezra ; but it is derived, no doubt, from the root "to make broad or thin," "to spread out"—perhaps, therefore, " a thin, light upper robe" which was worn over the chiton, a summer overdress, a cloak (LXX., θερίστρον: Jerome, *pallium ;* Luther, *Schleier*). If we take the dream thus described, and which seems to conclude at this point, as related to the surrounding ladies, then we must suppose that it is introduced for the sake of what follows. The bride feels that she does not love her beloved one half enough ; she is so conscious of deficiencies, that she might even have acted as her dream represented. It had entered her soul and made her ill with inward grief and self-reproach. She might so act, she might so treat her husband. So she adjures her companions to tell him how much she loves him. The spiritual application is not difficult to see. When the soul loses its joy in Christ, it becomes the prey of fears and self-accusations, and even of reproaches from Christ's servants and the guardians of his Church. For when our religion ceases to be a spontaneous delight to us, we are apt to carry on even the active work of our life in a manner to be misunderstood by sincere believers around us. Yea, the very efforts we make to recover peace may bring reproach upon us. Any Christian minister who has had to deal with religious despondency will quite understand this dream of the bride's. We may often smite and wound, and even deprive of the garment of reputation and esteem, those who are really seeking for Christ, because we have misunderstood them.

Ver. 8.—**I adjure you, O daughters of Jerusalem, if ye find my beloved, that ye tell him, that I am sick of love.** This appeal to the ladies suggests that the bride is speaking from her place in the royal palace; but it may be taken otherwise, as a poetical transference of time and place, from the place where the dream actually occurred, to Jerusalem. It is difficult, in a poem of such a kind, to explain every turn of language objectively. We cannot, however, be far wrong if we say the bride is rejoicing, in the presence of her attendant ladies, in the love of Solomon. He has just left her, and she takes the opportunity of relating the dream, that she may say how she cannot bear his absence and how she adores him. The ladies enter at once into the pleasant scheme of her fancy, and assume that they are with her in the country place, and ready to help her to find her shepherd-lover, who has turned away from her when she did not at once respond to his call. The daughters of Jerusalem will, of course, symbolically represent those who, by their sympathy and by their similar relation to the object of our love, are ready to help us to rejoice—our fellow-believers.

Ver. 9.—**What is thy beloved more than another beloved, O thou fairest among women? what is thy beloved more than another beloved, that thou dost so adjure us?** This, of course, is poetic artifice in order to give the opportunity to the bride to enter upon a glowing description of the object of

her love. She wishes to say that he is perfect, everything that he can be.

Ver. 10.—**My beloved is white and ruddy, the chiefest among ten thousand.** The mingling of colours in the countenance is a peculiar excellence. The word *tsach*, from the root *tsáchach* (cf. Lam. iv. 7), means a bright, shining clearness; it is not the same as *láván*, which would mean "dead white." So in Greek λαμπρὸς differs from λευκός. The red *adhom*, from the root *dâm*, which means "to condense," is dark red (*rouge puce*), no doubt as betokening health and vigour. The pure, delicate white among the Caucasians denotes high rank, superior training, hereditary nobility, as among ourselves the "aristocratic paleness" (cf. Hom., 'Il.,' iv. 141, "*ivory with purple;*" Virg., 'Æn.,' xii. 65; Ovid, 'Am.,' ii.; ' Eleg.,' v. 39; Hor., Od., i. 13, etc.; Tibull., ' Eleg.,' cxi. 4, etc.). The chiefest, that is, the distinguished one, the chosen (so the Greek versions, Syriac, Jerome, Luther). The LXX. has ἐκλελοχισμένος, *e cohorte selectus*. Another rendering is " bannered," furnished with a banner or pennon (דָּגֵל) hence the word דָּגוּל as a past participle (so the Venetian σεσημαιωμένος). The numeral (*revâvâ*) "*ten thousand*" is simply used to represent an innumerable multitude ; " myriad " is so used among ourselves (cf. Ezek. xvi. 7).

Vers. 11—16.—**His head is as the most fine gold, his locks are bushy, and black as a raven. His eyes are like doves beside the water-brooks; washed with milk and fitly set. His cheeks are as a bed of spices, as banks of sweet herbs; his lips are as lilies, dropping liquid myrrh. His hands are as rings of gold set with beryl; his body is as ivory work overlaid with sapphires. His legs are as pillars of marble set upon sockets of fine gold. His aspect is like Lebanon, excellent as the cedars. His mouth is most sweet: yea, he is altogether lovely. This is my beloved, and this is my friend, O daughters of Jerusalem.** This description, which is complete in itself, is best regarded in its unbroken perfection. We must not expect to find a meaning for each separate part of it. There are ten corporeal excellences enumerated. We naturally recall the descriptions in Daniel and in the Apocalypse, which certainly have reference to this, and manifestly combine the attributes of greatness and beauty in the Son of man. Solomon, no doubt, as the son of Bathsheba, was distinguished by his personal attractions. Some of the details of description are differently rendered by different commentators. Delitzsch regards the description of the hair in ver. 11 as compared to a hill or hilly range— " his locks hill upon hill," *i.e.* " his hair, seen from his neck upwards, forms in undulating lines hill upon hill." The black colour is no doubt mentioned as a contrast with the fair, white complexion. The eyes are not only pure and clear, but with a glancing moistness in them which expresses feeling and devotion. So Plutarch has ὑγρότης τῶν ὀμμάτων to denote a languishing look, and we find the same figure in the ' Gitagovinda' and Hafiz, and in Ossian. So Luther, " Und stehen in der Fälle." The pureness of the white of the eye is represented in the bathing or washing in milk. They are full and large, " fine in their setting," referring no doubt to the steady, strong look of fine eyes. " The cheeks" are compared to towers of plants; that is, there is a soft elevation in them. LXX., ψύουσαι μυρεψικά: Jerome. Sicut areolæ aromatum consitæ a pigmentariis. The Targum says, " Like the rows of a garden of aromatic plants, which produce deep, penetrating essences, even as a (magnificent) garden aromatic plants "—perhaps referring to the " flos juventæ," the hair on the face, the growth of the beard. "The lips" are described as the organs of speech as well as inviting to embrace. They drop words like liquid fragrance. "The hands" may be differently described according as they are viewed. Delitzsch says, " His hands form cylinders, fitted in with stones of Tarshish." Gesenius thinks the comparison is of the closed hand and the stained nails, but that seems farfetched. Surely it is the outstretched hands that are meant. The form of the fingers is seen and admired; they are full, round, fleshy like bars of gold. The word " Tarshish " may mean clay-white, as in the Greek versions; that is, topaz, called Tarshish from Tartessus in Spain, where it is found. The description of the body is of the outward appearance and figure only, though the word itself signifies " inward parts." The comparison with ivorywork refers to the glancing and perfect smoothness and symmetry as of a beautiful ivory statue, the work of the highest artistic excellence. The sapphire covering tempers the white. The beautiful blue veins appear through the skin and give a lovely tint to the body. So in the description of the legs

we have the combination of white and gold, the white marble setting forth greatness and purity, and the gold sublimity and nobleness; intended, no doubt, to suggest that in the royal bridegroom there was personal beauty united with kingly majesty, as in the following description of his general aspect, which, like the splendours of the mountains, was awe-inspiring and yet elevating and delightful (cf. Ps. lxxx. 11 (10); Jer. xxii. 7; Isa. xxxvii. 24). His mouth, or palate, is sweetness itself; that is, when he speaks his words are full of winning love (cf. Prov. xvi. 4; Ps. lv. 16). We may compare with the whole description that given of Absalom, Solomon's brother, in 2 Sam. xiv. 25, 26. It has been truly remarked by Zöckler that "the mention of the legs, and just before of the body, could only be regarded as unbecoming or improper by an overstrained prudishness, because the description which is here given avoids all libidinous details, and is so strictly general as not even to imply that she had ever seen the parts of the body in question in a nude condition. It merely serves to complete the delineation of her lover, which Shulamith sketches by a gradual descent from head to foot, and, moreover, is to be laid to the account of the poet rather than to that of Shulamith, who is in everything else so chaste and delicate in her feelings. Certainly it would be much less delicate regarded as the description of a shepherd-lover who is seeking to obtain possession of the maiden taken from him, than of the royal bridegroom to whom Shulamith is at all events affianced, if not already married. The highest spiritual feelings of loving adoration of the Saviour have welcomed some parts of this description, and adopted them into the language of "spiritual songs." To some minds, no doubt, it is repellent; to those to whom it is not so, the warmth and glow of Eastern language is by no means too realistic for the feelings of delight in the Lord which express themselves in rapturous music.

HOMILETICS.

Ver. 1.—*Response to ch. iv.* 16: *the bridegroom accepts the bride's invitation.* He calls her again by the endearing title, " my sister-bride." He comes, as she bids him, into the garden which was hers and yet his. He takes delight in its produce, in the entertainment which she has prepared for him. He invites his friends to share his enjoyment. He addresses, apparently, the chorus of young men, his companions, who have already appeared in ch. iii. 6—11, calling them " O friends," and " O beloved ones;" unless, indeed, the last clause be translated, as the Hebrew at least permits, " Drink abundantly of love." The heavenly Bridegroom accepts the offering of the Church, his bride. He loved her, and gave himself for her ; therefore her love is very precious to him. He comes into her garden. He calls it his—" my garden "—in gracious acknowledgment of the bride's gift. He uses the same pronoun of all its varied products. They are his, each and all. He gave them to the bride. She offers them back to her Lord. He invites his friends to share his joy. He said once to his friends in his holy parable, "Rejoice with me; for I have found my sheep which was lost;" so now he says, "Eat, O friends; drink, yea, drink abundantly of love." "Blessed are they which are called unto the marriage supper of the Lamb" (Rev. xix. 9). So the Lord listens to the call of the Christian soul that thirsts for him. He answers the cry, "Even so, come, Lord Jesus." He will come with the Father, and make his abode with them that love him (John xiv. 23). He graciously accepts the offerings of love. He welcomes the beauty and sweetness of the fruits of the Spirit in the believing soul. They are his, for it was he who gave the Spirit, who watered the growing fruits with the dew of his grace; his, again, because the heart that gives itself to God gives with the gift of self all its belongings, gladly owning that whatever it has of good comes from his only gift. He acknowledges their imperfect efforts: "I know thy works, thy labour, and thy patience." He saith unto his friends, "Rejoice with me;" and "there is joy in the presence of the angels of God over each sinner that repenteth." Then if our love gives joy to the dear Lord who gave up the glory of heaven for us, and for us endured the long torture of the cross, how very earnestly we Christians ought to try to make our heart indeed a "garden enclosed," wholly dedicated unto him, and separated from all profane uses! If our poor growth in holiness pleases him, how earnestly we ought to pray and strive to grow in grace and in the knowledge of our Lord and Saviour Jesus Christ; how earnestly we ought to try never to grieve his Holy Spirit, but to give him our whole heart, with all its affections and desires, that we may be wholly his—his for ever!

Vers. 2—8.—*The second dream of the bride.* I. THE BRIDEGROOM AT THE DOOR. 1. *The voice of the beloved.* The bridegroom is absent; the bride is alone. There is a temporary separation, something approaching to an estrangement; yet the old love is not lost. The bride is sleeping when she should be awake and watching for the bridegroom's approach. Yet her heart waketh. She has a dreamy consciousness of what is going on around her; she seems to hear in her dream the voice of her beloved. So the Church sometimes sleeps—leaves her first love—lapses into something like spiritual apathy; yet her heart waketh. The Lord never leaves himself without a witness. At the worst times of indifference there has always been some dim consciousness of his presence, some faint love for him who loved the Church and gave himself for her. So the soul sometimes sleeps when it is high time to awake, when the night is far spent and the day is at hand. The heavenly Bridegroom will not let us slumber on without a warning. He knocks at the door of our heart. "Behold," he saith, "I stand at the door, and knock: if any man hear my voice, and open the door, I will come in to him, and will sup with him, and he with me" (Rev. iii. 20). The Church of Laodicea was lying wrapped in a deep sleep: the Lord sought to arouse her. So he knocks at the door of our hearts now by his Word, by his ministers, by his chastisements, by the warnings of his Spirit. If we can in truth call him "*my* Beloved;" if we have really set our love upon him, and given him our heart in answer to his seeking love, we shall hear him. We shall know his voice, recognizing it in judgments and in mercies, in warnings and in consolations. When duty calls us, even if it be, as it will sometimes be, hard and displeasing to flesh and blood, we shall say, "It is the voice of my Beloved." It is the Master's call; he speaks. The heart waketh to listen. Does he come with stern reproof for indifference and coldness of heart? No; his words are full of tenderness. "Open to me, my sister, my love, my dove, my undefiled." It is the Lord's great love for the souls of men that produces those utterances of yearning affection. He still calls the bride "my sister," as he had done before the cloud had come upon her love. He still says "my love, my dove," as he said before; and he has a fresh term of endearment, "my undefiled, my perfect one." We know, alas! that we are not undefiled, we are not perfect. ("Not as though I had already attained, either were already perfect," says even the great apostle, St. Paul.) But what the Lord would have us to be, what he will make us at the last if we abide in him, that he is graciously pleased to call us now. How those holy words of deep tenderness should excite in us repentance for the past, and earnest effort to become by his grace less unworthy of those most gracious and loving titles! He asks us to open, that he may enter in.   He has been wandering in the darkness, and as when he came unto his own there was no room for him in the inn, and as during the days of his earthly ministry he had not where to lay his head, so now he knocks at one heart after another, and heart after heart is closely barred against him.   They will not open, that he may enter in and make his abode with them.   He comes now to the sister bride of old times, asking her as if for his own sake (such is the unutterable depth of his infinite, self-abasing love), "Open unto me, my sister, my love, my dove, my undefiled."   Ah, how can any of those souls of men whom he loved even unto death shut up their hearts against that call of unspeakable affection!   He pleads as for himself, as if needing shelter : " My head is filled with dew, and my locks with the drops of the night."   Alas ! the bride, still half asleep, scarcely heeds the bridegroom's call, does not realize its meaning—

> " For none of the ransom'd ever knew
>   How deep were the waters cross'd ;
> Or how dark was the night that the Lord pass'd through
>   Ere he found his sheep that was lost."

It cost more to redeem our souls than our poor thoughts can comprehend.   When we try to realize the Lord's sufferings, we seem to stand afar off beholding, like the people who came together to that sight of awe, who smote their breasts (Luke xxiii. 48).   The Church pleads those bitter sufferings in her solemn Litany : " By thine agony and bloody sweat, by thy cross and passion, good Lord, deliver us."   "Remember, good Lord Jesus," we say in the ancient hymn, " that it was for me thou didst undertake that long, weary journey ; in that long search for me thou didst sit faint and exhausted ; it was to redeem me that thou didst endure the cross.   Let not that toil and labour be in vain, O Lord."   But here it is the Lord himself who pleads with us in our hardness ; he so longs for our salvation.   He bids us remember what he endured for us.   It is the expression of his intense yearning love.   He would have us comprehend with all saints something of the breadth, and length, and depth, and height of that great love ; to return it in our poor way, to open our heart to him, that he may enter in and take that heart to be his own which he bought with the price of his most precious blood.   2. *The answer.*   The bride does not realize the deep, solemn meaning of the bridegroom's call.   She is half asleep still.   She lies dreaming in her bed.   She makes excuses to herself.   And we, alas ! far too often do the like when the Lord calls us to work, to deny ourselves for his sake.   We slumber on in careless sleep ; we forget what he did for us.   We do not hear his voice ; or, if we hear, we listen dreamily, lying still in spiritual sloth, not thinking that when the Lord calls it is time to bestir ourselves, to be up and doing, to " pass the time of our sojourning here in fear : forasmuch as we know that we were not redeemed with corruptible things, as silver and gold . . . but with the precious blood of Christ " (1 Pet. i. 18).   We must not make vain excuses, like those that were bidden in the parable (Luke xiv. 18), for the time is short.   It is our eternal salvation that is at stake.   It is Christ the Son of God who is calling us ; and he loved us, and gave himself for us (Gal. ii. 20).   Alas ! the bride, whom the bridegroom loved with so great a love, makes poor excuses in her dream.   She will not rise and open till it is too late ; she will not take a little trouble for his sake.   3. *The repentance.*   The beloved put his hand through the hole of the door ; he sought to open it.   The bride's heart was moved at last by his earnest appeals.   " My bowels were moved for him," she says, as she repeats her dream.   She thought of her past love for him, of his great love for her, of the hardships he had gone through in seeking her.   She wonders how she could have forgotten all this even in a dream ; she rose up to open to her beloved.   So the soul that has made many excuses, that has slumbered long, that has spent its time as in a dream, forgetting the solemn realities of life, hears at last through the long-suffering grace of God—listens to the patient call of the heavenly Bridegroom.   Then our heart burns within us when we think that he has indeed been talking with us, opening the Scriptures (Luke xxiv. 32) ; our bowels are moved for him.   We think that it is the Saviour of the world, our Saviour, who is standing without, waiting for us to answer ; that the hand with which he seeks to open the door was once pierced through for us, nailed upon the cross for our souls' sake.   We listen to his voice—

> " O Jesu, thou art pleading
>   In accents meek and low:
> ' I died for you, my children,
>   And will ye treat me so?'
> O Lord, with shame and sorrow
>   We open now the door;
> Dear Saviour, enter, enter,
>   And leave us never more."

The bride opens to her beloved. The bridegroom's hand had been dipped in oil of myrrh. Some of the unguent remained upon the bolt; it dropped upon the fingers of the bride. It was a token of the bridegroom's presence. He had gathered his myrrh (ver. 1) from the "garden enclosed" before this passing shadow had fallen upon their love. It may be, too, that we may see in the myrrh a parable of self-denial. It may be regarded as a loving warning left by the bridegroom to teach the bride a necessary lesson. She must not slumber on; it is time to wake and to work. Working for Christ is sometimes like the wine mingled with myrrh (Mark xv. 23); it has a bitter taste to our pampered palate. But if we take the cup which the Lord gives us to drink, we shall find at last that the smell of it is sweet; even as his yoke, hard at first, becomes easy in the discipline of obedience, and his burden, heavy at first, becomes light when he bears it with us. For self-denials meekly borne for him bring us nearer and nearer to him who bore the supreme self-sacrifice of the cross for us; and in his presence there is a depth of sweetness which takes away the bitterness. 4. *It is too late.* The beloved had withdrawn himself. " My beloved withdrew himself, was gone," she says, in the plaintive wailing of disappointment (there is no conjunction in the original). " My soul went forth," she continues, " as he spake." My soul, my heart, my affections, went forth to him at the sound of his voice. The well-known tones aroused the old love. She had once given her heart to him; and now, though in her dream her love seemed to have been chilled, and she seemed to lie heedless, unwilling to rouse herself to exertion, yet now his words at last reached her heart. Her soul went forth to him in response to his calling. Or the Hebrew words may rather mean, as in the Revised Version, " My soul had failed me when he spake." The same words are used in describing the death of Rachel : " It came to pass, as her soul was in departing " (Gen. xxxv. 18). His words awoke in her soul the fear lest she should lose him by her coldness and selfish neglect. The thought was like death to her. " Love is strong as death " (ch. viii. 6). Her soul went forth; it failed her. For the moment she was helpless—prostrate as in a death-like swoon. Then she aroused herself. It was time to act, to bestir herself. He was gone; she might lose him for ever; and her heart was bound up in him. To lose him was death—worse than death. She sought him, but she could not find him ; she called him in her dream, but he gave her no answer. The dream of the bride is a parable of the Christian life. The soul sometimes sinks into a state of listlessness and apathy. There is no actual transgression, perhaps—no open sin. The evil spirit is not there ; the house is empty (Matt. xii. 43, 44). But the Bridegroom is absent, and love has grown cold. There is no recollection of the absent Lord—no regret, no longing for his return. The soul lives on, as it were, in a dream, not realizing the solemn meaning of life, not thinking of the awful future. But God in his gracious mercy will not let us dream away our lives without a warning. He calls us by his blessed Son : " Behold, I stand at the door, and knock." Sometimes, alas! we will not hear; sometimes we listen dreamily, half-conscious, recognizing in a sense the Bridegroom's voice, but not realizing the solemn, holy meaning of the call; not thinking of his love and of our ingratitude, his promises and our broken vows, what he did for us and what return we have made to him ; not thinking of his grace and our responsibility, his longing for our salvation and our fearful danger. That lethargy, that slumber of indifference, creeps over us all from time to time when we have not been watchful—when we have neglected our prayers and other blessed means of grace. But the dear Lord seeketh that which is lost until he find it. He "is long suffering to usward, not willing that any should perish, but that all should come to repentance" (2 Pet. iii. 9). He comes again and again, calling us, sometimes in the gentle tones of entreating love, sometimes in the sterner language of reproof and chastisement. Sometimes he makes as though he would force his way. He puts his hand in at the hole of the door; he lays the cross upon us; he reminds us of the burden which he bore for us; he teaches us that the cross is the very badge and mark of his chosen—that whosoever doth not take up his cross cannot be his disciple. At last we are stirred in our slumbers. We rise from our sleep. But perhaps we are only half awake, half-hearted. Our will goes back to our old slothful rest. We say, like the sluggard in the Proverbs, "Yet a little sleep, a little slumber, a little folding of the hands to sleep" (Prov. vi. 10). Then the Lord deals with us as a wise physician of the soul. He would have us feel our weakness, our danger. "They that be whole need not a physician, but they that are sick" (Matt. ix. 12). He would have us feel our need of him. He withdraws himself; and when we open to him he is gone. He makes as though he would go further, as he dealt with the two disciples on the way to Emmaus (Luke xxiv. 28). Then our soul goes forth to him. It faints within us; we feel how helpless we are without him; we feel that without him life is not worth living; and we try to constrain him, like those two disciples, saying, in their words, "Abide with us; for it is toward evening, and the day is far spent." We seek him in earnest prayer, sometimes with strong crying and tears. But for a time we cannot find him. We call him, but he gives us no answer. It is in love that he thus deals with us, to arouse us, to make us feel the need of exertion, of active effort. He cannot be found without diligent search. The bride said, in relating her first dream, "By night on my bed I sought him whom my soul loveth" (ch. iii. 1). It is not thus that the soul should seek for Christ, still lying, as it were, upon the bed of spiritual sloth, thinking dreamily of Christ, pleasing itself, perhaps, with the poetry of religion, with the beauty of the Saviour's life, with the comfort which the Scriptures offer. Religion is not a dream; it is not mere poetry, mere love of beauty; it is a life—a life of action and energy—a prolonged effort to imitate Christ, to please Christ, to follow Christ's holy example. The first cry of the really awakened soul is, "Lord, what wilt thou have me to do?" (Acts ix. 6). The soul that answers in earnest to the Saviour's call knows and feels instinctively that God has work for us; that that work must be done even in fear and trembling by his help, who worketh in us both to will and to do. The Lord would have us realize this truth; therefore sometimes he withdraws himself, to make us feel that life is blank without him—to make us cry like Job, "Oh that I were as in months past, as in the days when God preserved me; when his candle shined upon my head, and when by his light I walked through darkness; as I was in the days of my youth, when the secret of God was upon my tabernacle!" (Job xxix. 2—4). The contrast makes us feel that God was certainly with us then, even if we cannot feel his presence now. Therefore we seek him, even though for a time we cannot find him. It was so with Job for a season. "He hideth himself," he said; "I cannot see him." He trusted God even in the midst of darkness. "But he knoweth the way that I take: when he hath tried me, I shall come forth as gold" (Job xxiii. 9, 10). So we must believe in his love even when he seems to hide his face from us and not to listen to our prayers. He seemed long to disregard the supplications of the Syro-phœnician woman, but at last there came the gracious answer, "O woman, great is thy faith: be it unto thee even as thou wilt."

II. The search. 1. *The bride goes forth in her dream.* Again, as in ch. iii. 2, she goes about the city seeking the beloved; again the watchmen found her. They had not been unfriendly in the first dream, though they were not able to guide her in her search. Now they seemed to treat her with cruelty. They smote her, and wounded her, and took her mantle from her. Difficulties will always arise in our search after Christ—sometimes dangers and persecutions: "We must through much tribulation enter into the kingdom of God." We may perhaps also see another lesson here. The bride has more trouble now in her search than she had on the former occasion. She has been more blamable. Then she had been for a time listless and slothful; now her sin had been not only sloth, but selfish disobedience. She refused at first to open to the beloved; she did not heed his call; she did not heed the hardships which he had suffered. So it is in the Christian life. To sin against light is very grievous; repeated sin makes repentance each time more difficult. We must be watchful always, as the Saviour bids us: "Watch ye therefore: for ye know not when the master of the house cometh, at even, or at midnight, or at the cockcrowing, or in the morning: lest coming suddenly he find you sleeping. And what I say unto you I say unto all,

Watch" (Mark xiii. 35—37). We must learn the prayer of the child Samuel, "Speak, Lord; for thy servant heareth." Each time we refuse to listen the old torpor steals more and more over our souls, our slumber becomes deeper, the difficulty of awakening us becomes greater, and repentance more doubtful, more encompassed with dangers, calling for more exertion of will, more determined effort. 2. *The charge.* The bride cannot find her beloved. She seeks the help of the chorus of maidens, the daughters of Jerusalem. She adjures them in her eager anxiety, "If ye find my beloved, what will ye tell him? That I am sick of love." She had used the last words once before (ch. ii. 5), but in a different connection. Then his banner over her was love; then the joy of his love was almost too great for her; she was sick of love. Now it is her longing for the absent bridegroom which produces the heart-sickness which she describes. She fondly thinks that if he only knew her yearning for him he would return; he would forgive all that was past, and bring her again under the banner of his love. So the Christian soul, awakened out of sleep, longs for the Saviour's presence. She feels that she is sick. She needs the great Physician. Without him all is dark; without him there is no spiritual health, no joy, no hope. She seeks him in earnest prayer. She asks for the intercession of Christian friends; she would have them bring her distress and longing before the throne. "My God, my soul is cast down within me;" "My soul thirsteth for God, for the living God;" "Why art thou cast down, O my soul? and why art thou disquieted within me? hope in God: for I shall yet praise him, who is the health of my countenance, and my God."

Vers. 9—16.—*The bride's praise of the bridegroom.* I. THE QUESTION OF THE DAUGHTERS OF JERUSALEM. 1. *The bride.* The bride is dreaming still. The chorus seem in her dream to address her again as they had done in ch. i. 8. She is still to them the fairest among women. They are daughters of Jerusalem, the children of the kingdom; and to them the Church, which is the bride of Christ, must appear exceeding fair. She is not, alas! without spot or blemish now. She recognizes her own faults, her many shortcomings. But the children of the kingdom remember the holiness of the saints departed. They see traces of the beauty of holiness existing always in the Church. Being themselves children of God, they are learning that grace of charity which "believeth all things, hopeth all things, endureth all things; which rejoiceth not in iniquity, but rejoiceth in the truth." And so they regard the beauty of the bride rather than her blemishes; they think more of her yearning love for the Bridegroom than of her past shortcomings. It is a sad mistake, a sin against charity, to refuse to recognize the real goodness of Christian people who have from time to time fallen into various inconsistencies. 2. *The bridegroom.* What is he more than others? "What is thy beloved more than another beloved . . . that thou dost so charge us?" The daughters of Jerusalem know King Solomon well, but in her dream the bride seems to hear them asking the question of the text. She has always loved the bridegroom for himself, not for his crown, his magnificence. She fancies that the maidens of the chorus take the same view of wedded love, and ask what are the distinguishing merits of her beloved. Sometimes, indeed, that question is asked in scorn or in temptation, "What think ye of Christ?" What is he more than other masters? Those other masters have their attractions; they offer more of earthly pleasure, more of present ease. What has Christ to offer? What are his attractions? What are the rewards of his service? "What is thy Beloved more than another beloved?" men say sometimes to the Christian. "What is thy Master to us, that thou dost so adjure us?" But the daughters of Jerusalem, in this second dream of the bride, do not ask the question in scorn or irony. It is asked with a dramatic purpose to give the bride an occasion for dwelling upon the glorious beauty, the many endowments of her beloved. She gladly takes advantage of it.

II. THE BRIDE'S ANSWER. 1. *The bridegroom is the chiefest among ten thousand.* "My beloved," she says, "is white and ruddy." We think of him whose "garment was white as snow," and "his throne like the fiery flame" (Dan. vii. 9). Ancient writers have applied the description to our Lord. He was white in his spotless purity; his sacred body was reddened with the precious blood. These are the first thoughts of the Christian when he meditates upon the Lord's perfections—the perfect beauty of his most holy life, the glory of self-sacrifice which sheds a golden light upon his atoning death. His life exhibited a picture of holiness such as the world had never seen, such as none of its greatest sages had ever imagined. It stands alone in its pure beauty, unique, unapproachable. We know that no human intellect could have imagined such a life; no merely human pen could have described it. It is unlike the accepted moral ideals of the time; it stands apart by itself, immeasurably higher than all beside. But it was his death, he said, that should draw all men unto himself. It was the great love manifested upon the cross that would constrain the best and noblest hearts of all times and countries to live no longer to themselves, but unto him who died for them and rose again (2 Cor. v. 14, 15). Therefore he is our Standard-bearer (as the word rendered "chiefest" seems to mean), our bannered One. He is the Captain of our salvation. He goeth before us, bearing the banner of the cross. The thousands of his disciples follow. And he is the chiefest among ten thousand, marked out and distinguished (as the word may perhaps mean) from all others by his unapproachable holiness, by the infinite power and majesty of his self-sacrificing love. The bride enumerates the various points of excellence which together make up the completeness of the bridegroom's beauty. The Christian loves to meditate upon the various graces which make up the holy beauty of the Saviour's character—his lowliness, his gentleness, his long-suffering kindness, his holy wisdom, his absolute unworldliness, his unselfish devotion to his sacred mission, his meekness, his forbearance, his patience with the many mistakes, the obstinate misunderstandings of his disciples, his endurance, his calm and lofty courage, the majestic bearing which forced even Roman soldiers to exclaim, " Truly this Man was the Son of God." 2. *He is altogether lovely.* The bride sums up her praises of the bridegroom. " His mouth is most sweet: yea, the whole of him is desires " (for this is the literal translation). The Prophet Haggai, using another form of the same Hebrew word, says, " The Desire of all nations shall come " (Hag. ii. 7). Daniel is called three times " a man of desires " (Dan. ix. 23; x. 11, 19). The Lord Jesus Christ is the Desire of all nations. He is the Messiah, the Consolation of Israel, for whose coming so many faithful hearts had yearned. He spake as never man spake. His mouth was all sweetnesses (the literal rendering), both his holy words and his gracious looks. How often we are told significantly that Jesus looked upon his disciples as if that look was (as indeed it must have been) a thing to be remembered all one's life, full of heavenly meaning, full of Divine love! We know what power his words had, what power they have now. The very tones of that most sacred voice must have had an indescribable sweetness. " Jesus said unto her, Mary." That one word was enough. It brought sweet comfort to the penitent, joy unutterable, heart-felt gladness to the mourner. And who can tell the entrancing sweetness of those most blessed words which with all our heart's deepest yearning we long one day to hear, " Come, ye blessed children of my Father "? Therefore we desire his presence now. " The whole of him is desires." Therefore God's people have " a desire to be with Christ " (like St. Paul, Phil. i. 23); for they know that to be with him here, and still more to be with him in the paradise of God, is " far better "—by much very far better, than the greatest of earthly joys. " The whole of him is desires." Every one of those holiest graces which adorn his perfect character should be to us a subject of loving study and adoration, with a longing desire to imitate it and to work it in our poor way into our own hearts by the help of the Holy Spirit. He hath all things who hath Christ. He hath enough, and more than enough, to satisfy all his desires, to fill all the yearnings of his heart. He will count all things else as dross—as very dung—in comparison with the excellency of the knowledge of Christ Jesus his Lord. Then how earnestly we ought to pray that by the grace of God we may be enabled to make those last words of the bride our very own, " This is my Beloved, and this is my Friend, O daughters of Jerusalem." If he is indeed ours, our Beloved, our Friend, our Saviour, then we have all that we can need for our soul's truest blessedness, both for this life and for the life to come.

HOMILIES BY VARIOUS AUTHORS.

Ver. 1.—*Christ's response.* " I am come," etc. Here we have for the second time the name of " sister " prefixed to that of " spouse," and it seems to teach that this song is not to be understood in any mere dry, literal, earthly sense; but is to be regarded in such spiritual way as, in fact, most readers have regarded it. How prompt Christ's answer is! Cf. Isa. lxv. 24, "Before they call I will answer," etc. The soul hears the knock of Christ, opens the door, and at once he comes in (Rev. iii.). Cf. Jacob, "Surely the Lord was in this place, and I knew it not;" Mary Magdalene at the sepulchre: "She knew not that it was Jesus." In this verse we learn—

I. SUCH SOUL IS CHRIST'S GARDEN. For it has been chosen, separated, watered, cultivated, adorned, made fruitful.

II. IT HAS CHRIST'S PRESENCE AND IS HIS DELIGHT. 1. The aspirations of such soul proves *his presence*. They are his footprints, though not perceived to be so. Cf. "Their eyes were holden, that they should not know him" (Luke xxiv.). He is the unperceived Author of its holy desires and purposes. 2. *And he delights in it*. He calls it "my garden" (cf. on ch. iv. 9—15).

III. THE ANGELS ARE SUMMONED TO SHARE IN HIS DELIGHT. "Eat, O my friends." Not that we say this address to his "friends" proves this truth, but suggests it. We know that "there is joy in the presence of the angels of God over," etc. (Luke xv.); and see Revelation, *passim*, where the joy of Christ is ever shared in by all heaven. They know what transpires here, and they rejoice in what is joyful. They are the "great cloud of witnesses" by which we are surrounded and surveyed. And what gladdens Christ must gladden them. They "enter into the joy of their Lord." The good conduct of those whom we behold makes *us* glad. Can it be otherwise with them? What great encouragement, therefore, we have in our Christian life in knowing that we can further the joy of our Lord and of the holy angels! Be it ours so to do.—S. C.

Ver. 2.—*The flesh and spirit.* "I sleep, but my heart waketh." The body sleeping, the heart awake.

I. SOMETIMES, AS HERE, BUT ONE OF THESE IS AWAKE. 1. *Here it was the spirit.* (1) This fact an argument against materialism, which insists that the spirit is altogether dependent upon the body. Hence that death ends all. But, as here, the body may be weighed down with sleep, but the mind is active; the body is dead, but the mind alive. Surely, therefore, the mind is something more than some special arrangement of the molecules of the brain. (2) It is well that, if the spirit be willing, the flesh should be weak. As a general rule it is well, for else, unless the wholesome drag of the body were put on, brain-workers would not live out half their days. (3) But it is at times the occasion of much harm. It was so here. It was so to our Lord through his disciples yielding to the sleep that weighed on them. And the flesh is a tyrant which will, if allowed, enslave the spirit. Hence we need to "keep under the body." For: 2. *Often it is only the flesh that is awake.* This a fearful condition. Cf. St. Jude, "These be sensual, not having the Spirit." Men may, do, sink down into gross animalism. It is horrible as well as disgraceful. It was that which led to the destruction of Sodom, of the Canaanites, etc. It is a dread possibility threatening very many. God keep us therefrom!

II. SOMETIMES NEITHER ARE AWAKE. There are many people of whom one would have much more hope if they were a little better or a little worse than they are. They are such as we have just named. They are generally decent people outwardly; they never offend against the conventionalities; they are to be found in all Churches, more's the pity; for they are but caricatures of the Christian character. They are dull, cold, selfish, hard, and spiritually dead. What is to be done with such? They are the despair of the earnest Christian, who would almost be willing that they should fall— were it possible—into some miserable sin if so only their present self-content could be shattered and they made to wake up.

III. SOMETIMES BOTH ARE AWAKE. This the ideal condition. It is that, and more than that, which is meant by the "Sana mens in corpore sano." For wherever this condition is, the spirit will, as is right, rule the flesh, having it well in hand, causing it like a properly trained dog to come to heel at once at the word of command (Huxley). The body will be the active, faithful servant of the master will, the spirit of the man. And when that spirit is inspired by the Spirit of God, then that is salvation, which means "health." May such health be ours!—S. C.

Vers. 2—8.—*The dream of Gethsemane.* Under the imagery of this dream devout students have seen pictured forth the pathetic facts of the garden in which our Lord was in agony, and his disciples slept (cf. Matt. xxvi. 40—43 and parallels). We have—

I. THE DISTRESSED SAVIOUR. (Ver. 2.) He desired his disciples to watch with him. He needed and desired their sympathy and the solace which their watchful love would have given him. His soul was troubled. He was as he who is told of here, and to whom the cold drenching dews and the damp chills of the dreary night had caused much distress, and who therefore asks the aid of her whom he loved. So did Jesus seek the aid of those he loved. He had right to expect it. He said to Peter, "Simon, sleepest *thou?*"—thou so loved, so privileged, so loud in thy profession of love to me, so faithfully warned, sleepest *thou?* And still the like occurs. The Lord looking for the aid of his avowed disciples, distressed by manifold causes, and that aid not forthcoming, though he has such right to expect it. But he too often finds now what he found then—

II. HIS DISCIPLES ASLEEP. (Ver. 3.) So the spouse here, as the disciples there, and as man now, had composed herself to sleep. The repeated calls of him who by voice and knock sought to arouse her failed. And so did the repeated visits of Jesus to his disciples fail. And he finds the same still. The poor excuses of ver. 3 serve well to set forth the excuses of to-day when he calls on us now to aid and sympathize with him. Who really rouses himself for Christ, and puts forth earnest self-denying endeavour to help his work? No doubt the disciples had their excuses, and Christ then, as now, makes all allowances. But the fact remains the same. Christ wants us, and we are asleep. The sleeper told of in this dream evidently was filled with self-reproach. It can hardly have been otherwise with the disciples, and it is so with us now when in our holier moments the vision of our Lord in all his love for us comes before our hearts. Then we confess, "It is high time to awake out of sleep."

III. THE SORROWFUL AWAKENING. The sleeper told of here awoke (ver. 5) to find her beloved gone. And in Gethsemane the disciples awoke at last. In this song (ver. 5) we are told how he had thrust in his hand by the latch-hole (see Exposition). But he had withdrawn it, as she whom he had appealed to had not awaked; and, finding this, her heart was touched, and she rose to open to him. And doubtless when the disciples saw the gleam of the lanterns and heard their Lord's word, "Arise," and the tramp of the armed multitude who had come to arrest him, then their hearts were touched, and they arose. But it was too late. And like as the sleeper here (ver. 5) did not withhold tokens of her affection—she richly perfumed herself, her hands especially, in token thereof as the Oriental manner was—so, too, the disciples in their way made plain their love for their Lord. They would have fought for him—Peter drew his sword at once—had he let them. But the opportunity for real service was gone. The sleeper of this song tells how her heart smote her when her beloved spoke, and we may well believe that it was so when the disciples heard their Lord's voice. But in both cases it was too late. Who does not know the sorrow that smites the soul when we realize that opportunities of succouring, serving, and making glad the heart of some beloved one have been allowed to pass by us unused, and now cannot be recalled? Oh, if we had only been awake then!

IV. THE UNAVAILING SEARCH. (Ver. 6.) Cf. Peter's tears; the sorrow of the disciples. The reproaches of conscience—they were the watchmen who met and sternly dealt with her who is told of here, and made her ashamed. Such failures in duty are followed by unavailing regrets and prayers. "Oh that I knew where I might find him!" Conscience, the Word of God, faithful pastors,—these are as the watchmen who meet such souls, and scant comfort is or ought to be had from them, but only deserved rebuke and reproach. It is all true. What is told of in this verse must have happened then, does happen now. Our Lord has left us, our joy is gone, we cannot find him, tears and prayers and search seem all in vain.

V. THE HELP OF THE HOLY WOMEN. (Ver. 8 and ch. vi. 1.) It was wise of the sleeper, now awake, to solicit help from the friends of her beloved. And in the Gospel narrative it is plain that the holy women who loved and ministered to our Lord when on earth were a great help to his sorrowing disciples. They were last at the cross and first at the sepulchre; they first brought the glad tidings that he was risen. They represent his true Church. And the sorrowing soul cannot do better than seek the sympathy and prayers of those who love the Lord. Restoration often comes by such means. Here is one of their intercessions : " That it may please thee to strengthen such as do stand, to comfort and help the weak-hearted, to raise up them that fall, and finally to beat down Satan under our feet." Blessed is he who hath intercessions such as that offered for him. But better still not to need them.—S. C.

Ver. 9.—*The supremacy of Christ.* "What is thy beloved more," etc. ? *The world asks this question.* Upon the answer the Church gives depends whether the world remains as it is—alienated from Christ or drawn to him. If the Church makes it evident that Christ is "chiefest among ten thousand " and "altogether lovely," then the blessed era of the world's conversion will be at hand. *The Church asks this question* of those whom she receives into communion. It should be clear that Christ is enthroned in the hearts of those whom she receives. They are not really members of the Church unless it is so. *We should ask ourselves this question,* so that we may see to it that we are giving him the chief place in our hearts, and that in all things he has the pre-eminence. *The question may be answered in various ways.* As for example—

I. BY COMPARISON OF CHRIST WITH THE OBJECTS OF WORSHIP IN OTHER FAITHS. (Cf. Hardwick's ' Christ and other Masters.') There have₁ been and are " gods many and lords many ; " it is well to compare and contrast with them the all-worthiness of him whom we serve. Missionaries to heathen lands do well to make themselves acquainted with the points of contrast and resemblance—" the unconscious prophecies of heathendom "—which they will find in the faiths they seek to supplant by the pure faith of Christ. Often will they find in such study that he is " the Desire of all nations."

II. BY COMPARING THE OBJECTS OF MEN'S PRESENT PURSUITS AND AFFECTION WITH CHRIST, who is the Beloved of the believer's heart. Some set their affections only on earthly things—wealth, power, pleasure, fame, the favour of men. Some on those whom God has given them to love—wife, lover, children, friends. It is well to see how Christ surpasses all these, and deserves the chief place in our hearts : such place, when given to him, will not consign to a lower one than they before filled those objects of our lawful love; but, on the contrary, will uplift and enlarge our love for them, making it better both for them and us. But we prefer to take—

III. THE ANSWER GIVEN IN THIS SONG ITSELF. See vers. 10—16, translating its rich imagery into the plain language of "the truth as it is in Jesus." She who was asked this question replied by giving the description of her beloved which we have in these verses. And, translated, they suggest these reasons for counting Christ chief of all. 1. *He is the perfect Pattern and Sacrifice that my soul needs.* (Ver. 10.) It is a representation of the beauty of perfect physical health : "white and ruddy" (cf. 1 Sam. xvi. 12 ; xvii. 42). Fit type, therefore, of that perfect moral and spiritual health which we behold in Christ, and which constitutes him our all-perfect Pattern. His perfect sacrifice also has been seen in this same description, and it has been compared with that similar description of him in Rev. v. 6, " a Lamb that had been slain." Not alone the whiteness of purity, but " ruddy " as with the stain of his precious sacrificial blood. 2. *He is God in his essential Person.* (Ver. 11.) Gold is, in the sacred symbolism of Scripture, ever associated with that which is of God. The head of fine gold suggests, therefore, that which St. Paul says (1 Cor. xi. 3), " The head of Christ is God." 3. *Yet he consecrated himself for our sakes.* The unshorn hair, " his locks are bushy," was the sign of consecration (cf. the vow of Nazarite). 4. *And is evermore mighty to save.* Youth and strength are signified by the " raven " hair. Whilst others wax old as doth a garment, he is " the same yesterday, and to-day, and for ever " (cf. Ps. cii. 27). 5. *Gentleness, purity, and the love and light of the Holy Spirit beam in his eyes.* (Ver. 12.) Cf. New Testament notices of the look of our Lord—how he looked with compassion, how he " looked upon Peter" (Luke xxii. 61). 6. *To see his face is heaven.* (Ver. 13.) To walk in the light of that countenance, to behold it fair and fragrant as sweet flowers. 7. *And from his lips drop words of love.* Men wondered at the gracious words which he spake. " Never man spake like this Man." " Grace is poured into thy lips " (Ps. xlv. 2 ; Isa. l. 4). 8. *He is invested with the authority of God.* (Ver. 14.) "His hands are rings of gold," etc. The ring was the signet and seal of authority. " He spake as one having authority ; " " I by the finger of God cast out devils ; " " All things are put under him." 9. *Stainless purity and heavenly mindedness marked his life.* (Ver. 14.) The body, or rather the robe that covered it, as bright ivory, tells of the purity and perfectness of his life; the heavenly blue of the " sapphires " is the type of heaven. His conversation was in heaven. He walked with God. 10. *He was firm and steadfast in God.* (Ver. 15.) The legs, as " pillars of marble," tell of his steadfast strength; the " sockets of fine gold," of the Divine basis and foundation of that strength. 11. *Full of majesty and beauty,* as Lebanon and its cedars. Cf. his appearance at the Transfiguration; to the guards at his rising from the dead. 12. *And yet full of grace and benignity.* (Ver. 16.) " His mouth "—his smile—" most sweet." The little children nestled in his arms. The poor fallen women read the benignity of that look. Publicans and sinners crowded round him, irresistibly drawn by his exceeding grace. 13. *No human tongue can tell how fair he is.* " Yea, he is altogether lovely." The words tell of the giving up the task, of ceasing from the hopeless endeavour, to fitly fully set forth her beloved. She could only say, " He is altogether," etc.

CONCLUSION. Such was the answer given when asked, " What is thy beloved more," etc. ? (ver. 9). And such answer is the best. The testimony of the loving heart to what Jesus is to such heart is more convincing than any argument. May such testimony be ours !—S. C.

Ver. 16.—" *Altogether lovely.*" We apply these words to the Lord Jesus Christ, and affirm that they are true of him. May he grant us grace to see that they are so! And we remark—

I. THAT WHETHER WE BELIEVE THEM OR NOT, THEY ARE ASSUREDLY TRUE. *All generations* have confessed them true. The hero of one age is not the hero of another; but Christ is the Beloved of all ages. Abraham saw his " day and was glad." Prophets and psalmists beheld him, and to them all it was a beatific vision. They sang of him as " fairer than the children of men; " they exhausted all imagery of beauty and delight to tell of him. And since he came, apostles, martyrs, and generation after generation of those who have loved and toiled, and often died, for him, have confessed the truth of our text. And to-day myriads of souls are aglow with love to him, and gladly take up the same confession. " The goodly fellowship of the prophets, the glorious company of the apostles, the noble army of martyrs, the holy Church throughout all the world, doth acknowledge " him. And so *will all ranks and classes of men.* The rich and the poor, the lofty and the low, have met together in this confession. And *all ages,* the young and the old. And *all lands,* north, south, east, and west. And all *characters and dispositions.* See how varied the characters of those who gathered round our Lord, and of the saints of the Bible, and of all ages. And seen *in all aspects,* he still receives the same confession. As a child, as a man, as a teacher, as a sufferer, in his death, in his resurrection, in his intercession for us in heaven. With the choicest works of art, with the fairest scenes of nature, with the most glorious buildings that men have reared, all depends on the point of view from which we behold them. Seen from the right standpoint, they are beautiful and glorious; seen from another, they excite no admiration, they may appear the reverse of beautiful. And so with the characters of men. They may be excellent in some things, but the best of men are but men at the best. There are faults and flaws in the fairest human soul. But with our Lord, see him how, when, and whence we may, to the heart that loves him he is still " altogether lovely." The testimony has come from every quarter, from every age; it is full, clear, complete, varied, reiterated, and has been tested and tried and found true always and everywhere. The holiest saints gaze on the perfect loveliness of their Lord as the one model to which they would be conformed, but from which they own they are far removed. His enemies themselves being judges confess that " they find no fault in him." He is as a lamb without blemish and without spot. But, alas! *to many he is not this ;* they see in him no form or comeliness, no beauty that they should desire him. Therefore we say of these words of our text—

II. THAT SINCE THEY ARE TRUE WE OUGHT TO SEE THEM TO BE TRUE. If beautiful music, or works of art, or scenes in nature, do not impress men with their beauty, we pity such persons, we deem them lacking in a great good. And if they have no appreciation of moral beauty, we do not merely pity, but we blame. What, then, must we say of those who fail to see any beauty in him who is " altogether lovely "? But what is it that hinders in any soul that fails to see in Christ what the holiest and best of men always and everywhere have seen in him? Well, *if men will not look* they will not see. And this is one hindrance. The portraiture of Christ is given perfectly in the Gospels, but if men will not look into them, read them, and consider them, what wonder that they fail to see? And to see him as *altogether* lovely, that demands that we *look long and attentively*, that we study the portraiture that is given, and that we seek to be rid of all that would hinder the truth of our seeing. But these persons never do this. Moreover, to see him as he is, we must *stay with him.* You cannot know a fellow-man by a short interview. To know a man you must live with him. And so if we would really know Christ and see him as his saints have seen him, we must live with him, keep in his company, commune with him and be in daily intercourse with him. And we must be *in right relationship to him;* we must serve him, for that is his due. And then as we work for him, his true character will dawn upon us more and more; and we, too, shall come to see him as altogether lovely. Therefore—

III. LET US RESOLVE THAT WE WILL THUS SEE HIM. To encourage us herein let us think of the results and recompenses of such beholding him. We shall come : 1. *To resemble him.* For we shall come to love him, and nothing so assimilates character as love. 2. *To rejoice in him.* Of common earthly things the well-known line says, " A thing of beauty is a joy for ever." But of our Lord to behold *him,* it is the very joy of heaven. For there "they shall see his face." 3. *Rest.* The worries and frets of life will vanish in that beatific vision, like as even an unlovely landscape looks beautiful when the bright sun shines upon it. And so will it be with what is unlovely in life, that in itself irks and distresses us. If we see *his* face, if that vision of perfect loveliness shines before us, all will share more or less in that. 4. *Reap for him,* as never we did before. With our souls full of his love, even the stammering tongue will become eloquent, and our words will tell, and we shall wonder and rejoice to see how our children, our people, our friends and neighbours, listen to us and believe, and turn to him from whom we cannot and would not turn away. And at last we shall be: 5. *Received by him* into his own blessed presence, where we shall own that "the half was not told" us, and even the best of our seeing was but as through a glass, darkly.—S. C.

Ver. 2.—*Languid life.* The experiences of the saints are useful guide-posts on the heavenly road. They help by way of counsel, caution, inspiration, comfort, warning. Some experiences recorded serve as lighthouses, some as beacons. A wise pilgrim will not despise any one of them. If a traveller is about to cross Africa from west to east, he will not fail to ask what were the fortunes and experiences of those who have already made that perilous journey. He will learn from their mistakes and their sufferings what to avoid. He will learn from their successes how far he should tread in their footsteps. The journey is not so difficult now as it was to the first adventurer. A similitude this of the heavenly pilgrimage. Others have passed this way before us. We are indebted to them for the record of their checkered fortunes. They tell us how they climbed the hill Difficulty. They tell us how they were overtaken with the foe unwarily. They tell us how they fought, and by what methods they conquered. They tell us how at times spiritual drowsiness crept over them; how they bemoaned their folly; how they aroused themselves afresh. Then we discover that this infirmity is not peculiar to ourselves. We do not deny ourselves the consolation that we really belong to Christ, though we have been foolish enough to sleep in his service. There is blight upon the tree, and a reduction of fruitfulness; nevertheless, the tree has life in its roots. Blemishes are upon me; still I am in Christ.

I. HERE IS A STATE OF INSENSIBILITY CONFESSED. "I sleep." It is a figure of speech borrowed from the sensations of the body. Our physical nature needs periodic sleep. But many indolent persons sleep when they do not need it; and it is this needless sleep— this ignoble sleep—that is here described. Unlike the body, the soul requires no sleep. 1. *It is a state of inaction.* For the time being sight and hearing are suspended. All bodily sensations are awanting. The sleeper is unconscious of all that is occurring round about him. Sleep is the brother of death. So, if the soul sleeps, it is a transient death. Our best Friend is near, but we cannot see him. If he speaks, we do not hear his voice. We have no enjoyment of his friendship. The sun of God's favour may shine upon our path ; we do not perceive it. We have no conscious communion with Jesus. We find no nourishment in the sacred Word. The ordinances of the sanctuary have lost their charm. We do not grow in grace. We make no progress heavenward. It is inglorious inaction. 2. *It is a blamable condition.* We are servants of God, and to sleep is to waste our Master's time. It is an act of unfaithfulness. The Son of God has entrusted to us the campaign against error and sin ; yet, lo! we sleep on the battle-field. Tens of thousands round about us know nothing of God's salvation ; and yet we sleep. Satan is busy ensnaring men in the pitfalls of vice ; and yet we sleep. The heathen world is waiting to hear Heaven's gospel ; now and again a voice booms across the sea, "Come over and help us!" yet we sleep. Our own crown is imperilled ; yet we sleep. This brief life is slipping from us ; the day of service will soon terminate ; the great assize is close at hand ; yet we sleep. Is it not matter for self-condemnation? 3. *It is a state of peril.* A time of sleep is the time for robbers to do their evil work ; and we imperil the heavenly treasures when we slothfully sleep. Our wily adversary lies in wait for our unguarded moments. If he can breathe upon the Church a spirit of slumber, he has gained a great advantage for himself. To lull Christians into sleep is his most successful stratagem. In one of his parables Jesus tells us that "while men slept, the enemy sowed his tares." Saul, the King of Israel, exposed his life to imminent danger when he slept in the cave. If a man is insensible to the deadly paralysis that is creeping over him, he is not far from death. And if we Christians become insensible to our sin, or insensible to our dependence on Christ, or insensible to God's claims, we are in great danger. What if God should say to us, "They prefer their sleep : let them alone"! Then our sleep would deepen into the collapse of death. 4. *Spiritual sleep entails loss.* How much of spiritual blessing the eleven lost, when they slept in Gethsemane, no tongue can tell. We lose the approval of a good conscience, and that is a serious loss. We lose the approving smile of Christ, and that is a loss far greater. We lose the vigour of our piety. We lose the freshness of enthusiasm. We lose courage. We lose spiritual enjoyment. We lose self-respect. A sense of shame sweeps over the soul. The temperature of our love has gone down. Instead of pressing forward, we have gone backward. It is a loss immeasurable.

II. Here is a very promising sign. "My heart waketh." How true is this record to the facts in ourselves! The heart is the spiritual organ that wakes first. For the heart is the seat of feeling, desire, and affection. The heart must move before the will, and the will before the feet. 1. *This language denotes disquietude.* The man is neither quite asleep nor quite awake. This is an uncomfortable state. It denotes a divided heart. It is not altogether with Christ nor altogether with the world. We cannot endure the thought of leaving Christ, and so forego the hope of heaven. We like some of the experiences of religion. But then we love self in about an equal proportion. We grasp as much pleasure as we can. Hence this vacillation. This is a great loss of Christ's friendship ; a sin to treat Jesus thus. This self-indulgence now will produce a large fruitage of remorse by-and-by. 2. *It is a good sign that this indecision is recognized.* It might have been otherwise. The sin might have been unfelt. Conscience might have been drugged with the opiate of self-confidence. When a Christian perceives his own imperfections, and confesses them, there is manifestly some spiritual life within. His state is not hopeless. God's Spirit has not withdrawn his activities from that man. If he will diligently follow the light which he has, it will lead him to his true home and rest. 3. *This language indicates desire for a better state.* The heart is the seat of desire, and, thank God, the heart is awake. If this desire be not overpowered by stronger desires of an evil sort, all will yet be well. This desire, unhindered, will work like leaven, till it has leavened the whole man. It will disturb the man's peace until it is gratified. This desire is the work of God's good Spirit ; and, if we will only yield to his quickening influence, he will make desire ripen into resolve, and resolve into action. A man's desires are a gauge of the man's character. "As a man thinketh in his heart, so is he." 4. *It is another good sign when a sleepy Christian recognizes Christ's voice.* "It is the voice of my beloved that knocketh." The bride in our text not merely heard a sound, but she was so far awake as to know that it was her lover's voice. It is a fact that we hear the voice of one we know, and of one we love, much sooner than we hear the voice of a stranger. A mother will hear the cry of her babe sooner than she will hear the cry of another child. If we hear our Master's voice, then faith is not asleep. "Faith cometh by hearing." Of all Christ's sheep *this* is a sure mark; they hear Christ's voice. "A stranger will they not follow, for they know not the voice of strangers." We know well that if any one strives to arouse us out of sleep, it will be our best Friend. No one else will take such pains to bless us. Ah! if I hear in my soul a rousing voice, if I am moved to holier aspiration, I instinctively say, "It is the voice of my Beloved that knocketh." Then ought I most gladly to respond, "Speak, Lord; for thy servant heareth."

III. HERE IS A GRACIOUS CALL. This is the reason why the Christian's heart is awake: Jesus calls and knocks. A Christian cannot sleep under such an appeal. 1. *Christ's whole Person engages in this call.* He not only speaks with his voice; he knocks with his hand. He knocks by the preaching of faithful ministers. He knocks by the counsels of a pious friend. He knocks by his afflictive providences. He knocks by his royal bounties. Every fresh gift is a fresh appeal. He knocks by many a startling event that happens about us. He knocks at the door of memory, at the door of feeling, at the door of conscience, at the door of affection. He tries every door, if so be his kindly errand may succeed. He has too much earnest love for us easily to desist. Such love is born, not on earth, but in heaven. 2. *He not only knocks; he speaks.* He appeals to our intelligent nature. He will not use force or compulsion. That were unseemly on the part of love. Jesus will use measures equally potent, but of a winsome, spiritual sort. He speaks to the heart of saints in a "still small voice." There is a latent power in his gentleness. When God spake to despondent Elijah in the desert, he did not speak in earthquake, or in thunder, or in whirlwind, but in a soft human voice. No sound breaks on the ear; the message goes straight to the conscience and to the heart. Have we not, in hours of retirement, often heard the music of his voice, gently chiding us for neglect, or sweetly moving us to closer fellowship? We may resist the appeal, but, alas! we increase our guilt; we cheat our souls of joy. 3. *He addresses us by the most endearing epithets.* "My sister, my love, my dove, my undefiled." Every argument that can move us to a better life he will employ. The whole vocabulary of human speech he will exhaust, to assure us of his interest. He reminds us of our many professions of attachment. He brings to our remembrance our plighted troth. Did we not at one time say that we were his? Have we not pledged ourselves to be faithful over and over again? What an array of perjured vows lie on his book? Can we think of them without self-condemnation? 4. *He appeals to us on the ground of his deeds and endurances.* "My head is filled with dew, and my locks with the drops of the night." It is the pathetic picture of a friend who has been refused customary hospitality, and who has spent the cold night appealing for admission. This is the picture, and the meaning thereof is plain. Jesus Christ has to endure hardship and pain through our self-indulgence and our spiritual stupor. Alas! we shut him out from his own temple. We shut out our best Friend. After all that he has done for us, yea, suffered for us, in proof of his strong affection, shall we treat him with cold neglect, with heartless contempt? Shall he be all ardour, and shall we be frigid as an iceberg? Shall his nature be all love, and shall ours be all selfishness? Then we are not like him. Is not this to "crucify our Lord afresh, and put him to open shame"? Surely here is a test of character. He who can hear these gracious appeals unmoved, hath never felt the stirrings of the new life; he hath no part in the covenant of grace.—D.

Vers. 9—16.—*The personal excellences of Jesus.* A man is always greater than his works, for his best work is only a part of himself. As there is more virtue in the tree than ever comes out in the fruit, so there is some quality in the man that has not come forth in his deed. The same is true in larger measure with respect to God. If there is sublimity in his works, how much more in himself! The redemptive work of Jesus is stupendous, yet his love is more stupendous still. That love of his was not exhausted in the great atoning act; it was only disclosed, and made visible. We admire his incarnation, his benevolent labour, his voluntary suffering, his humiliating death, his strange ascension. We love him in return for his great love to us. Yet his greatest claim to our admiration and our praise is, not his deeds of kindness, but himself. His character is so inlaid with excellences that it demands all the worship of our hearts. "He is altogether lovely." Not simply is his doctrine nourishing, his example inspiring, his self-sacrifice attractive, his compassion winsome, but his very Person is an enchantment and a charm. At the outset of our acquaintance we "shall love him, because he first loved us ; " nor will his compassion ever fail to be a spiritual magnet, which shall win and hold our hearts. Yet we gradually rise to a higher level of appreciation. We prize him for what he is in himself, even more than for what he has been unto us. Our best love goes out to him, because he is so transcendently good; so worthy to be loved. Love of gratitude comes first—an early fruit of the Christian life ; but by-and-by, under the culture of the Divine Husbandman, there shall be the sweeter, richer love of complacent delight.

I. WE HAVE HERE A PERTINENT INQUIRY. "What is thy beloved more than another beloved ? " 1. *This may be the language of intellectual curiosity.* The inquiry about Jesus is more eager and widespread to-day than in any epoch since his birth. During the last twenty-five years more than twenty-five lives of Jesus Christ have appeared in the English language. Some inquiries are of a sceptical sort—are not honest searches after truth. Some inquirers hope to reduce Jesus of Nazareth to the level of a common mortal. In a past age, Lord Lyttelton and Gilbert West essayed to demolish the Divine credentials of Jesus; but they were conquered by the evidence, and became disciples. Many inquirers simply attempt to solve an old and curious question, "Is Jesus more than man ? " They are not seeking any practical issues. Hence they obtain no success. 2. *Or it may be the language of simple surprise.* The kingdom of Christ hath in it many nominal adherents. For earthly advantages come from professing an attachment to Christ. It wins respect from men. It brings good reputation. It aids success in our worldly calling. Therefore many persons avow outwardly an indolent belief in Jesus Christ as Lord who yet can give no reasonable account of their belief. These see with wonder the ardour and zeal of genuine disciples. They smile when they hear the effusive and familiar language of true saints. They deem it religious extravagance. They label Christ's friends as fanatics. "*Our* Christ," say they, "is a Being far removed from us. We offer him our set praises and our set prayers on the sabbath. We hope for his rewards by-and-by. What is your Beloved more than ours ? " 3. *Or it may be the language of nascent desire.* The speaker has seen what a real and present Friend Jesus is to his adopted. To them his friendship is sweeter far than the friendship of a thousand others. His name is music, fragrance, health, life. His help is a real blessing, which gladdens every hour. His favour is a present heaven. They consult him in their distress, and he brings to them prompt sympathy and unerring wisdom. They find in him a restfulness of spirit under every circumstance, a peace of soul no one else can impart. Having Jesus within them, their life is trans-figured. This is a mystery to the bulk of men. So one and another yearn to attain this joyous life, and they ask in a spirit of sincere desire, "What is thy Beloved more than another beloved ? "

II. WE HAVE HERE A PARTICULAR DESCRIPTION OF THE BRIDEGROOM'S PERSON. "My beloved is white and ruddy, the chiefest among ten thousand ; " "He is altogether lovely." 1. *Generally, he is pre-eminent.* "Chiefest among ten thousand." Among all the tribes of men he stands alone, for he is sinless. He is pre-eminent among the angels, for they are only servants of the great King; and, when the Father "brought his Only Begotten into the world, he said, Let all the angels of God worship him." Among the gods of the nations he stands pre-eminent in power and in righteousness. They are dumb vanities, while he is absolute Power, eternal Righteousness, essential Love. In respect of the Godhead, he is eminent for condescension, for tender sympathy, and for self-sacrifice. Among all friends he stands pre-eminent, for "he is a Brother born for adversity." Among all orators he is pre-eminent for eloquence, for "never man spake like this Man." Among philanthropists he takes the highest place, for "he gave himself for us." "For our sakes he became poor." "In all things he has the pre-eminence." 2. *He is altogether lovely as the Son of God.* Such perfect Sonship was never before seen. His reverence for his Father was unique, was beautiful. At the tender age of twelve, his delight was "to be about his Father's business." His spirit of childlike trust was perfect. He is "the Leader and Finisher of faith." During all the years of his busy life he "had not where to lay his head," yet he declared that it was his "meat and his drink to do the will of his Father in heaven." His own explanation of his ceaseless benevolence was this : "I do always the things that please him." As he entered the black cloud of the final tragedy, he interrogates himself thus : "What shall I say? Father, save me from this hour?" But instantly he adds, "Father, glorify thy Name." Filial reverence, filial trust, filial love and submission in him were complete—things till then unknown on earth. "Though he were a Son, yet learned he obedience by the things which he suffered." Upon such sacred Sonship the Father expressed audible and public approbation—expressed it again and again : "This is my beloved Son, in whom I am well pleased." "My Beloved is white and ruddy"—the quality of perfect health. 3. *His personal qualities transcend all comparison.* Every virtue, human and Divine, blossom in his soul. There's not an excellence ever seen in men or in angels that is not found, the perfect type, in Jesus Christ. For nearly nineteen centuries shrewd men have turned their microscopes on the Person of Jesus, if haply they could find the shadow of a spot. The acutest eye has failed, and Jesus stands before the world to-day a paragon of moral perfection. His character is better known and better appreciated to-day than in any previous age. Modern criticism confesses at the bar of the universe, "I find no fault in him." As all the colours of the prism meet and blend in the pure rays of light, so all noble qualities blend in our beloved Friend. As in a royal garden or in the fields of nature there is unspeakable wealth of flowery bloom, all forms and colours composing a very paradise of beauty, so is it in the character of Jesus. Other men were noted for some special excellence—Moses for meekness, Job for patience, Daniel for constancy ; but Jesus has every quality of goodness, and has each quality full-orbed and resplendent. "Whatever things are true, pure, just, lovely, honourable, of good report," they all unite in Jesus. Ransack all the homes of humanity if you will, cull out all the excellences that embellish the seraphim, and you shall not find a single grace that does not adorn our Immanuel. Yea, his soul is the seed-bed of all the goodness that flourishes in heaven or on earth. "He is the Firstborn of every creature." The unfallen, no less than the fallen, adore him as worthy to be worshipped. "He has by inheritance a more excellent name than they." As the stars of heaven pale their ineffectual fires when the sun rises, so in the presence of Jesus Christ even Gabriel veils his face and bends his knee. Human thought fails to reach the height of this great theme, and we can simply repeat the ancient words, "Altogether lovely." 4. *He is incomparable in all the offices he fills.* A splendid theme for contemplation is Jesus in his manifold offices. As a Teacher he has no rival, for he still speaks "as one having authority." "In him are hid all the treasures of wisdom and knowledge;" and, with infinite patience, he unfolds these treasures to us in picture and parable, as we "are able to bear them." Who is so competent to teach us heavenly things as the living Truth? "The words he speaks are spirit and life." "His lips are as lilies, dropping sweet-smelling myrrh." As a Priest, does he not excel all who went before him? Other priests had to offer oblation first for their own sin. Jesus had no personal sin. Other priests "could not continue by reason of death." Jesus has no successor; his priesthood is perpetual. The best of earthly priests could only appear in material temples, gorgeous in marble and in gold though some of them were. Our great High Priest has gone on our behalf into the very presence of God. Our Advocate with the Father cannot fail, because he is "Christ the Righteous." And, as a King, Jesus has no compeer. The sceptre belongs to him by eternal right. He is a King by birth. He is a King by reason of inherent fitness. Every fibre of his nature is kingly. He is a King through conquest. Every foe is, or shall be, vanquished. He is a King by universal acclamation. Angels and men combine to accord to him the highest place—"King of kings, and Lord of lords." As the good Shepherd, he has given his very "life for the sheep." As the Husband of his Church, he is perfect in fidelity; for "having loved the Church, he gave himself for her, and has cleansed her for himself a glorious Church, not having spot, nor wrinkle, nor any such thing." View our Master in any aspect or in any office, and he is full of inexpressible charm. "He is altogether lovely."

III. WE HAVE HERE THE IDEA OF INTIMATE RELATIONSHIP. "This is my beloved, and this is my friend, O daughters of Jerusalem." 1. *This means high appreciation.* The believer in this passage means to say, "I have endeavoured to describe my heavenly Friend, but I have failed. I have mentioned some of the features of his character, yet I scarce think that *these* are the most precious. The theme is above me.

I cannot do it justice.   Mayhap I shall only lower Jesus in the estimation of mankind.
Still, I have said enough to establish his superlative excellence, and to account for my
enthusiastic love."   Ah! who can adequately portray the Person of God's dear Son?
Can Gabriel?   Can Michael?   Can Paul, after centuries of sweet companionship with him
in heaven?   I trow not!   "What think ye of Christ?" is a question, likely enough,
often asked one of another among the dwellers in glory.   By-and-by we "shall see him
as he is."   At present we have only imperfect glimpses of his glorious Person; nevertheless, we know enough to warrant our profound admiration, to awaken our unfaltering
faith, and to excite into activity our most passionate love.   2. *This means appropriation.*
This Being of transcendent excellence I claim as "my Friend."   Many of his august
perfections seem to forbid my bold familiarity.   Sometimes it seems like presumption
to say this.   But then his simple condescension to me, his genuine sympathy, his
unlimited grace, his covenant with the fallen, "without respect of person," his
repeated assurances of love for *me*—yes, for *me*—encourage me to call him mine.   He
has said to me, "Thou art mine;" is not, therefore, the converse also a fact?   Must
he not be mine?   And if at present I am quite unworthy to claim this relationship,
will he not, by his great love, make me worthy?   His love would not find full scope
for its exercise, if it were not for such an unworthy object as I.   Though deserving of
hell, I should cast fresh dishonour on his royal goodness did I not believe his promise,
did I not accept his friendship.   Yes, "he is mine."   3. *This means the public avowal
of Christ.*   "This is my Beloved, and this is my Friend."   It is as if the Christian
meant to say, "I have chosen Jesus to be my Friend, and I call the universe to witness
the fact.   No other being was competent to save me, and I publicly pledge myself
loyally to serve him."   Such avowal is a fine trait in a renewed soul.   To profess
loyalty to Jesus while no love glows for him in the breast—this is an offence to him,
a smoke in his eyes, a spear-thrust in his heart.   Nothing to him is so odious as
hypocrisy.   But when there is sincere love to our Immanuel, though it be accompanied
with self-diffidence and timidity, there ought to be an open avowal of our attachment.
It is but little that we can do to make the Saviour known and loved by others, therefore
that little should be done with gladness of heart and with unwavering fidelity.   Nor
can we ever forget the words of our Well-beloved, "Whosoever shall deny me before
men, him will I also deny before my Father which is in heaven."—D.

Ver. 1.—*Hospitality and festivity.*   This verse is the central stanza of the Song of
Songs.   It brings before us the wedding-feast, the crisis of the dramatic interest of the
poem.   The bride is welcomed to her regal home; friends and courtiers are gathered
together to celebrate the joyful union; and festivity and mirth signalize the realization
of hope and the recompense of constancy.   Under such a similitude inspired writers
and Christian teachers have been wont to set forth the happy union between the Son of
God and the humanity to which, in the person of the Church, he has joined himself in
spiritual and mystical espousals.

I. The presence of the Divine Bridegroom and Host.   "I," says he, "have
come into my garden."   It is the presence, first visibly in the body, and since
invisibly in the Spirit, of the Son of God, which is alike the salvation and the joy
of man.

II. The greeting of the divinely chosen bride.   The language in which this
greeting is conveyed is very striking: "My sister-spouse."   It is the language of
affection, and at the same time of esteem and honour.   It speaks of congeniality of
disposition as well as of union of heart.   Christ loved the Church, as is evident from the
fact of his giving himself for it and to it, and as is no less evident from his perpetual
revelation of his incomparable kindness and forbearance.   "All that I have," says he,
"is thine."

III. The provision of Divine bounty.   How often, in both Old and New Testament Scripture, are the blessings of a spiritual nature which Divine goodness has
provided for mankind set forth under the similitude of a feast!   Satisfaction for deep-
seated needs, gratification of noblest appetite, are thus suggested.   The peculiarity in
this passage is the union of the two ideas of marriage and of feasting—a union which
we find also in our Lord's parabolic discourses.   We are reminded that the Divine
Saviour who calls the Church his own, and who undertakes to make it worthy of him-

self, provides for its life and health, its nourishment and happiness, all that infinite wisdom itself can design and prepare.

IV. THE INVITATION OF DIVINE HOSPITALITY. " Eat, O friends; drink, yea, drink abundantly, O beloved!" Thus does the Lord of the feast ever, in the exercise of his benevolent disposition, address those whose welfare he desires to promote. This invitation on the part of the Lord Christ is (1) sincere and cordial; (2) considerate and kind; (3) liberal and generous.

V. THE FELLOWSHIP OF DIVINE JOY. True happiness is to be found in the spiritual companionship of Christ, and in the intimacy of spiritual communion with him whom the soul loveth. The aspiration of the heart to which Christ draws near in his benignant hospitality has been thus well expressed: "Pour out, Lord, to me, and readily will I drink; then all thirst after earthly things shall be destroyed; and I shall seek to thirst only for the pleasures which are at thy right hand for evermore." The spiritual satisfaction and festivity enjoyed by the Church on earth are the earnest and the pledge of the purer and endless joy to be experienced hereafter by those who shall be called to " the marriage supper of the Lamb."—T.

Ver. 2.—*The heart that waketh.* Thus opens the recital of a dream—a dream which was the confused expression of deep feelings, of affection, of apprehension, of anxiety. The expression is poetical; the body slumbers, yet the mind and its feelings are not altogether asleep. A slumbering heart is inaccessible to the Divine approach, the Divine appeal, the Divine mercy. It is well when the heart waketh, for the wakeful heart is—

I. PROMPT TO HEAR THE VOICE OF HEAVEN. The mother awakes at once when the babe cries; the surgeon wakes at once when the bell rings; the nurse wakes at once when the patient asks for medicine or for food. When the heart is awake, the ear hearkens, the eye is ready to unclose, the sleeper is half alert and prepared to rise. The heart that loves the Saviour is prompt to hear any word of his, whether it be a word of encouragement, a word of admonition, a word of command. "Speak, Lord; for thy servant heareth," denotes the vigilant attitude, the true preparedness of the soul.

II. PROMPT TO RESPOND TO THE LOVE OF CHRIST. The true heart is not wakeful to every call, to every presence, to every appeal. It is mutual love that ensures a heart that waketh. The Christian gives love for love. " We love him, because he first loved us." Hence the very sound of Jesus' name enkindles upon the devout and grateful heart the flame of pure and fervent affection. Nothing that concerns the Lord is indifferent to the Christian; for his heart is awake to every token of the Divine presence, and eager for the spiritual communion which is the privilege of the friends of Jesus.

III. WATCHFUL AGAINST THOUGHTS AND PURPOSES OF EVIL. The deep slumber into which the careless may fall is likely to render them a prey to the assaults of the tempter. Christ found his three nearest friends sleeping in the garden whilst he was enduring his bitter conflict. " Watch and pray," was his admonition, "lest ye enter into temptation." As soldiers during a campaign must take rest in sleep, yet, as it were, with one eye and one ear open, so that they may spring up, and fly to arms, if the foe approach them under cover of the darkness; so must the Christian take even his refreshing rest and recreation as upon the alert, and as ready to resist an approaching enemy. Watchfulness and prayer must guard him against surprise. The heart must be ever wakeful. " Keep thy heart with all diligence."

IV. READY TO ENGAGE IN ALL REQUIRED SERVICE. The service of the hands, of the lips, alone is unacceptable to our Divine Lord, who desires above all things the devotion and loyalty of the heart. This, if the heart slumbers, cannot be given. But a wakeful heart, being ready to receive impressions, is ready also to obey commands, to summon all the powers of the nature to engage in that service which combines dignity with freedom, and submission with joy.—T.

Vers. 2—5.—*Open to the beloved who knocketh.* This dream, so significant of fervent affection, and so full of tender pathos, is emblematic of the relation between the Divine Saviour and Lord and those whom he approaches in his grace and kindness, to whom he proffers the blessings of his presence and his love.

I. THE SUMMONS.　1. Its nature.　There is the *knock* which demands attention, and there is the *speech* which articulately conveys the appeal.　Christ comes to the world, and comes to the heart, with such tokens of Divine authority as demand that heed should be given to his embassage.　The supernatural arrests the attention even of the careless and the unspiritual.　That in Christianity which is of the nature of portent, the " mighty works " which have been exhibited, summon men to yield their reverent attention to a Divine communication.　But the miracle is a " sign."　The display of power is revelation of a wisdom, a love, which are deeper and more sacred than itself.　The knock that arouses is followed by the speech that instructs, guides, comforts, inspires.　Authority is not blind; it accompanies the appeal to the intelligence, to the heart.　2. The danger of neglecting it.　To give no heed to the Divine appeal, to sleep on when God himself is calling,—this is to despise the Highest, to wrong our own soul, to increase our insensibility and to confirm ourselves in spiritual deadness, and to tempt the departure of the heavenly Visitor.　3. The duty of welcoming and responding to it.　This appears both from the dignity of him who knocks, his right to the affection, gratitude, and devotion of the soul ; and from the complete dependence of the soul upon his friendship for its highest welfare.

II. THE RESPONSE.　When Christ " stands at the door and knocks," there is but one thing to do—to open wide to him, the Beloved, the door of the heart.　This is the true response, and it should be : 1. *Glad.*　His absence is mourned, his presence is desired ; his summons, therefore, should be joyfully acknowledged.　The heart may well beat strong with gladness, high with hope, when the voice of Jesus is heard ; for it is " the voice of the Beloved."　2. *Grateful.*　The picture is one of poetic pathos and beauty. The head of the Beloved is filled with dew, his locks with the drops of the night.　How suggestive of what the Saviour has endured for our sake, of his earthly humiliation, of his compassionate sacrifice !　The contemplation of Christ's weakness and weariness, distress and anguish, all endured for us, is enough to awaken the strongest sentiments of gratitude on our part.　To whom are we indebted as we are to him ?　Who has such claims upon our heart's gratitude and devotion ?　What language can justly depict the moral debasement of those who are unaffected by a spectacle so touching as that of the Redeemer, the " Man of sorrows," appealing for admission to the nature he died to save and bless ?　3. *Immediate.*　Delay is here altogether out of place.　The sensitive and responsive nature is forward to exclaim, " Apparitio tua est apertio ! "—" To see thee is to open to thee ! "　The hesitation and apologies described in the dream are introduced to show, by suggestion of contrast, how utterly unsuited they are to the circumstances and the occasion.　4. *Eager and expectant.*　" My heart was moved for him ; I rose to open to my Beloved."　The hope is fulfilled, the prayer is answered, the vision is realized, Christ has come.　With him all Divine blessings approach the soul.　The prospect of his entrance into the spiritual nature is the prospect of a fellowship and intimacy fraught with purest joys and tenderest consolations—a fellowship and intimacy which will never fail to bless, and which no power on earth can avail to darken or to close.—T.

Ver. 6.—*The dream of distress.*　No passage in the Canticles is more pathetic than this.　Whilst the prevalent tone of the Song of Songs is a tone of joyful love, we meet here with the sentiment of anxious sorrow.　We are reminded of the grief of Mary, when, on the resurrection-morn, she exclaimed, " They have taken away my Lord, and I know not where they have laid him."　A true transcript of the moods to which experience is subject !　And not without spiritual lessons which may be turned to true profit.

I. A TRANSIENT ESTRANGEMENT AND BRIEF WITHDRAWAL.　There have been periods in the history of the Church of Christ, resembling the captivity of Israel in the East, when the countenance of the Lord has been hidden from the sight of his people.　The heart, which knoweth its own bitterness, is now and again conscious of a want of happy fellowship with the best and dearest Friend.　But it is not Christ who changes.　When the sun is eclipsed, it does not cease to shine, though its beams may not reach the earth.　And when Christ is hidden, he remains himself " the same yesterday, and to-day, and for ever."　But something has come between the Sun of Righteousness and the soul which derives all its spiritual light from him, and the vision is obscured.

Selfishness, worldliness, unbelief, may hinder the soul from enjoying the Saviour's presence and grace. The fault is not his, but ours.

II. DISTRESSING SYMPTOMS OF SUCH ESTRANGEMENT AND WITHDRAWAL. How simple and how touching is the complaint of the bride! "I sought him, but I could not find him; I called him, but he gave me no answer." Yet it is the nature of Christ to delight in the quest and the cry of those he loves, to reveal himself to such as ever ready to approach and to bless. There may, however, be a reason, and faith cannot question that there is a reason, for the withholding of an immediate response. There may be on the Saviour's part a perception that a stronger confidence, a more evident desire, a truer love, are needed, and are thus only to be called forth. It may be well that for a season the soul should suffer for its sin, that it may be encouraged to deeper penitence and to more fervent prayer.

III. AFFECTIONATE YEARNING THE EARNEST OF SPEEDY RECONCILIATION AND RENEWED HAPPINESS. The parable represents the bride as sad and anxious, as enduring bitter disappointment, as oppressed by the heartless insult and injury of those indifferent to her woes; yet as retaining all her love, and only concerned as soon as may be to find her beloved. A true picture of the devout and affectionate friend of Christ, who is only drawn to him the closer by the sorrowful experiences and repeated trials of life. When the Christian offends his Lord, it is a good sign that he is not really forsaken, it is an earnest of the restoration of fellowship, if he ardently desires reconciliation, and takes measures to recover the favour which for a season he has lost. The beauty of Christ appears the more inimitable and supreme, the fellowship of Christ appears the more precious and desirable. And this being so, the hour is surely near when the face of Christ shall appear in unclouded benignity, when the voice of Christ shall be heard uttering Divine assurances and promises in tones of kindliest friendship.—T.

Ver. 10.—" *Chiefest among ten thousand.*" The figure here employed by the bride to depict the superiority and excellence of her royal husband is very striking. In reply to the inquiry of those who mock and taunt her in the season of her sorrow and her loss, asking what her beloved is more than another, she replies that he is the banner in the vast embattled host, rising conspicuous and commanding above the thousand warriors by whom he is encompassed. Christians are often reproached with their attachment to Christ. Men who are willing to acknowledge him as one of many, to rank him with " other masters," cannot tolerate the claims advanced by his Church on his behalf, and ask what there is in him to entitle him to adoration so supreme, to devotion so exclusive. The answer of Christ's people is one which gathers force with the lapse of time and the enlargement of experience. Christ is "chiefest among ten thousand." He excels all other teachers, leaders, saviours of society, in every respect.

I. IN THE PROFUNDITY OF HIS INSIGHT INTO TRUTH, AND IN THE CLEARNESS WITH WHICH HE REVEALS TRUTH. Among the sages and philosophers who have arisen in ancient and in modern times, and to whom the world is indebted for precious communications, for great thoughts, which it will not willingly let die, there is none who can compete with Christ. His sayings are more original in their substance than those of others, with regard both to the character and service of God and to the duty and hopes of men. In fact, he is " the Truth," proved to be such by the persistence of those utterances which have sunk into the minds of men, enlightening and enriching humanity with its choicest treasures.

II. IN THE EFFECTUAL COMPASSION WITH WHICH HE RECOVERS THE MORALLY LOST. The Lord Jesus is not merely a wise Teacher; he is a mighty Saviour. He knew well that little good is done by communicating truth, unless at the same time the heart can be reached and the character moulded anew. During his earthly ministry he put forth his moral power in many and most memorable instances, and rescued the sinful, the degraded, those abandoned by men, restoring them to integrity, to purity, to newness of moral life. And since his ascension he has been exercising the same power with the same results. His Name, by faith in his Name, has made many whole. His gospel loses none of its efficacy, his Spirit exercises the same energy of grace, as generation succeeds generation. Ten thousand attempt what Christ alone performed.

III. IN THE SPIRITUAL POWER WITH WHICH HE RULES OVER HUMAN SOCIETY. If a comparison be made between Christ and other founders of religious systems and Churches, it will be seen that the superiority rests with him, in the sway wielded over the true nature of men. Compare him, for example, with Gautama, the founder of Buddhism, or with Mohammed. What is the result of such a comparison? There can be no question that, in the matter of spiritual authority, it will be to establish the supremacy of the Son of man. He lays hold, as none other has done, of the affections, the moral susceptibilities and convictions, the inner principles, of men's being, and thus controls and inspires their true life. In this respect ten thousand are inferior to him ; but he stands alone—his banner towers above the host.

IV. IN THE WELL-FOUNDED PROSPECT WHICH HE IMPARTS TO THE WORLD'S FUTURE. Every well-wisher to his race, in looking forward to what shall be after him, must often be assailed with fear and foreboding. There is much to make the outlook gloomy and stormy. And there is no principle which can subdue such natural anxiety, which can inspire confident and sustaining hope with regard to the future of human society, except the principle of Christianity, *i.e.* the personal and spiritual power of the Lord Christ to govern and to guide mankind to glorious issues.—T.

Ver. 16.—"*Altogether lovely.*" In the verses from the tenth to the sixteenth, the bride sets forth in detail the excellences and the attractiveness of her spouse. In similitudes according with Oriental imagination she describes the charm of his person, and accounts for the fascination he exercises. And she sums up the characterization by the assertion that he is "altogether lovely"—"totus est desiderabilis, totus est amor." Augustine, in language dictated by the fervour of his heart, expresses the spiritual truths enshrined in this exclamation : "My soul is a sigh of God; the heart conceives and the mouth forms the sigh. Bear, then, my soul, the likeness of the heart and of the mouth of God. Sigh thou for him who made thee ! "

I. CHRIST IS ALTOGETHER TO BE LOVED AND DESIRED FOR WHAT HE IS IN HIMSELF. In his Person and character Christ is a Being who commands and attracts the love of all who are susceptible to the charms of spiritual excellence. There is beauty beyond that which is physical, beauty of which the charms of feature and of form are the appointed symbols. And for this beauty in most perfect manifestation we must look to Christ. Others have their excellences, but they have also their defects. In him alone every virtue is present and complete, in him alone every blemish is absent. He is at once above all praise and free from all blame. The soul that can recognize and delight in moral excellence finds all scope for such recognition and delight in him who is " fairer than the sons of men."

II. CHRIST IS ALTOGETHER TO BE LOVED AND DESIRED FOR WHAT HE HAS ACTUALLY AND ALREADY DONE FOR HIS FRIENDS. These know that he loved them, and that he loved them even "unto the end," that he "gave his life for his friends;" and this knowledge is ever in their memory, is ever affecting their hearts, is ever influencing the attitude of their whole being towards him. Nothing enkindles love like love. " We love him, because he first loved us."

III. CHRIST IS ALTOGETHER TO BE LOVED AND DESIRED AS THE SAVIOUR OF THE WORLD. He who is possessed with the Spirit of Christ is not selfish in his affections. He feels the spiritual power of his Saviour's self-sacrifice. He loves his Lord, because that Lord has pitied and has died for men. Our love to Christ is not pure, is not perfect, until it springs from a grateful and sympathetic recognition of what he has done who " came into the world to save sinners."—T.

EXPOSITION.

CHAPTER VI.

Ver. 1.—**Whither is thy beloved gone, O thou fairest among women? Whither hath thy beloved turned him, that we may seek him with thee?** The dialogue still continues, possibly because, as Delitzsch sug- gests, the effect of the dream which Shulamith narrates is not passed away in the morning. Under the influence of it she goes forth and meets the daughters of Jerusalem, who offer their assistance. But there is no necessity for this. The poetry merely demands that the idea of the dream should be still kept before the mind of the reader. The scene is still in the palace. The ladies playfully carry on the bride's cue, and help her to pour out her feelings. The bridegroom, they know, is near at hand, and is coming to delight himself in his bride; but the bride has not yet drawn him back completely to her side. This is evident from the fact that there is no distress in the language of the bride. She is not complaining and crying out in agony under a sense of desertion; she is waiting for the return of her beloved, and so she calmly sings of his love and his perfect truthfulness, even though absent from her. He is where his perfect beauty and fragrance might well be.

Vers. 2, 3.—**My beloved is gone down to his garden, to the beds of spices, to feed in the gardens, and to gather lilies. I am my beloved's, and my beloved is mine: he feedeth his flock among the lilies.** In Eccles. ii. 5, 6 Solomon says, "I planted me vineyards; I made me gardens and parks, and I planted trees in them of all kinds of fruit; I made me pools of water, to water therefrom the forest where trees were reared." In Rev. vii. 17 it is said, "The Lamb which is in the midst of the throne shall be their Shepherd, and shall guide them unto fountains of water of life: and God shall wipe away every tear from their eyes." We can scarcely doubt that the meaning is— The bridegroom is not gone far; he is where he is congenially employed; where his pure and lovely nature finds that which is like itself—beauty and fragrance and innocence. It is his resort, and it corresponds with his perfection. Delitzsch thinks "thoughtfulness and depth of feeling are intended" (cf. Ps. xcii. 5). "His thoughts are very deep." But it would seem more fitting, in the lips of the bride, that she should dwell on the aspects of her beloved which correspond with her own feelings. She is one of the lilies. The king is coming into his garden, and I am ready to receive him. The shepherd among his flock. They are all like lilies, pure and beautiful. The bride has nothing but chaste thoughts of her husband, because she knows that he is hers, and she is his. Surely such language is not inaptly applied to spiritual uses. Tennyson's lovely poem, 'St. Agnes' Eve,' has caught the spirit of Shulamith. A few of his lines will illustrate this—

"The shadows of the convent towers
    Slant down the snowy sward,
Still creeping with the creeping hours
    That lead me to my Lord.
Make thou my spirit pure and clear
    As are the frosty skies,
Or this first snowdrop of the year
    That in my bosom lies.

He lifts me to the golden doors;
    The flashes come and go;
All Heaven bursts her starry floors,
    And strews her lights below,
And deepens on and up! the gates
    Roll back, and far within
For me the heavenly Bridegroom waits,
    To make me pure of sin.
The sabbaths of eternity,
    One sabbath deep and wide,
A light upon the shining sea—
    The Bridegroom with his bride."

Vers. 4—7.—**Thou art beautiful, O my love, as Tirzah, comely as Jerusalem, terrible as an army with banners. Turn away thine eyes from me, for they have overcome me. Thy hair is as a flock of goats that lie along the side of Gilead. Thy teeth are like a flock of ewes which are come up from the washing, whereof every one hath twins, and none is bereaved among them. Thy temples are like a piece of a pomegranate behind thy veil.** The king is not far off. The bride knows that he is near. She prepares herself for him with words of love. He is coming among his "rosebud garden of girls." His voice is heard as he approaches. And as he enters the chamber he bursts forth with lavish praises of his bride. Tirzah and Jerusalem, two of the most beautiful cities of the world, are taken as symbols of the surpassing beauty of the bride—doubtless also with an intended reference to the symbology of Scripture, where the people of God are compared throughout to a city. Tirzah was discovered by Robinson in 1852, on a height in the mountain range to the north of Nablûs, under the name *Tullûzah*, high and beautiful, in a region of olive trees. The name itself signifies sweetness, which might be so employed even if there were no actual city so called. Jerusalem is said to have been "the perfection of beauty" (Ps. xlviii. 2; l. 2; Lam. ii. 15). Cities are generally spoken of as females, as also nations. The Church is the city of God. The new Jerusalem is the bride of the Lamb. If the prophets did not take their language from this Song of Solomon, then the phraseology and symbology which we find here must have been familiarly known and used among the people of Israel from the time of Solomon. The beauty of the bride is overwhelming, it is subduing and all-conquering, like a warrior-host with flying banners going forth to victory. Solomon confesses that he is vanquished. This, of course, is the hyperbole of love, but it is full of significance to the spiritual mind. The Church of Christ in the presence and power of the Lord is irresistible. It is not until he appears that the bride is seen in her perfection. She hangs her head and complains while he is absent; but when he comes and reveals himself, delighting in his people, their beauty, which is a reflection of his, will shine forth as the sun for ever and ever. The word which is employed, "terrible," is from the root "to be impetuous," "to press impetuously upon," "to infuse terror," LXX., ἀναπτεροῦν, "to make to start up," referring to the flash of the eyes, the overpowering brightness of the countenance. So the purity and excellence of the Church shall delight the Lord, and no earthly power shall be able to stand before it. Heaven and earth shall meet in the latter days. Wickedness shall fly before righteousness as a defeated host before a victorious army. Is there not something like a practical commentary on these words in the history of all great revivals of religion and eras of reformation? Are there not signs even now that the beauty of the Church is becoming more and more army-like, and bearing down opposition? The remainder of the description is little more than a repetition of what has gone before, with some differences. Mount Gilead is here simply Gilead. The flock of shorn sheep is here the flock of ewes with their young. Perhaps there is intended to be a special significance in the use of the same description. The bride is the same, and therefore the same terms apply to her; but she is more beautiful than ever in the eyes of the bridegroom. Is it not a delicate mode of saying, "Though my absence from thee has made thee complain for a while, thou art still the same to me"? There is scope here for variety of interpretation which there is no need to follow. Some would say the reference is to the state of the Church at different periods—as e.g. to the primitive Church in its simplicity and purity, to the Church of the empire in its splendour and growing dominion. The Jewish expositors apply it to the different stages in the history of Israel, "the congregation" being the bride, as under the first temple and under the second temple. Ibn Ezra, and indeed all expositors, recognize the reason for the repetition as in the sameness of affection. "The beloved repeats the same things here to show that it is still his own true bride to whom he speaks, the sameness in the features proving it." So the Targum. The flock of goats, the flock of ewes, the piece of pomegranate, all suggest the simple purity of country life in which the king found so much satisfaction. He is wrapt up in his northern beauty, and idolizes her. One cannot help thinking of the early Jewish Church coming forth from Galilee, when all spoke of the freshness and genuineness of a simple-hearted piety drawn forth by the preaching of the Son of Mary—the virgin-born Bridegroom whose bride was like the streams and flowers, the birds and flocks, of beautiful Galilee; a society of believing peasants untouched by the conventionalities of Judæa, and ready to respond to the grand mountain-like earnestness and heavenly purity of the new Prophet, the Shepherd of Israel, "who feedeth his flock among the lilies." There is a correspondence in the early Church, before corruption crept in and sophistication obscured the simplicity of faith and life among Christians, to this description of the bride, the Lamb's wife. There must be a return to that primitive ideal before there can be the rapturous joy of the Church which is promised. We are too much turned aside from the Bridegroom to false and worthless attractions which do not delight the Beloved One. When he sees his bride as he first saw her, he will renew his praises and lift her up to himself.

Vers. 8, 9.—**There are three score queens, and four score concubines, and virgins without number. My dove, my undefiled is but one; she is the only one of her mother, she is the choice one of her that bare her. The daughters saw her, and called her blessed; yea, the queens and the concubines, and they praised her.** The account given us of Solomon's harem in 1 Kings xi. 3 represents the number as much larger. Is not that because the time referred to in the poem was early in the reign? The words are an echo of what we read in Prov. xxxi. 28 and Gen. xxx. 13. Perhaps the general meaning is merely to celebrate the surpassing beauty of the new bride. But there certainly is a special stress laid on her purity and innocence. There is no necessity to seek for any exact interpretation of the queens and concubines. They represent female beauty in its variety. The true Church is in closer relation to the Bridegroom than all the rest of the world. Even in the heathen and unconverted world there is a revelation of the Word, or, as the ancient Fathers of the Church said, a Λόγος σπερματικός. He was then as light, though the darkness comprehended him not. The perfection of the true bride of the Lamb will be acknowledged even by those who are not professedly Christian.

Ver. 10.—**Who is she that looketh forth as the morning, fair as the moon, clear as the sun, terrible as an army with banners?** This, of course, is the praise which comes from the lips of the queens and concubines, the ladies of the harem, the daughters of Jerusalem. The word rendered "looketh forth" is literally "bendeth forward," i.e. in order to look out or forth (cf. Ps. xiv. 2), LXX., ἐκκύπτουσα: Venet., παρακυπτοῦσα (cf. Jas. i. 25, "stooping down and looking into the Word as into a well"). The idea seems to be that of a rising luminary, looking forth from the background, breaking through the shades of the garden, like the morning star appearing above the horizon (ὡς ἑωσφόρος, Venetian) (cf. Isa. xiv. 12, where the morning star is called שַׁחַר (֖ ֖)). The moon is generally יָרֵחַ, "yellow," but here לְבָנָה, "white," i.e. pale and sweet, as the lesser light, with true womanly delicacy and fairness; but the rest of the description, which plainly is added for the sake of the symbolical suggestiveness of the figures, removes all idea of mere weakness. *Clear* (or, *bright*) *as the sun.* And the word for "sun" is not, as usual, *shemesh*, but *chammâh*, "heat," the warming light (Ps. xix. 7; see Job xxxi. 26; Isa. xlix. 2). The fierce rays of the Eastern sun are terrible to those who encounter them. The glory of the Church is a glory overwhelming as against all that opposes it. The description is pure hyperbole as applied to a fair bride, referring to the blazing beauty of her face and adornments, but symbolically it has always been felt a precious contribution to religious language. Perhaps no sentence in the Old Testament has been more frequently on the lips of devout men, especially when they have been speaking of the victories of the truth and the glowing prospects of the Saviour's kingdom.

Vers. 11, 12.—I went down into the garden of nuts to see the green plants of the valley, to see whether the vine budded and the pomegranates were in flower. Or ever I was aware, my soul set me among the chariots of my princely people. There cannot be much doubt as to the meaning of these words. Taking them as put into the lips of the bride, and as intended to be a response to the lavish praises of the bridegroom, we may regard them as a modest confession that she had lost her heart immediately that she had seen King Solomon. She went down into her quiet garden life to occupy herself as usual with rustic labours and enjoyments, but the moment that her beloved approached she was carried away—her soul was as in a swift chariot. Delitzsch thinks that the words refer to what occurred after marriage. He supposes that on some occasion the king took his bride with him on an excursion in his chariot to a plain called Etam. He refers to a description of such a place to be found in Josephus, 'Ant.,' viii. 7. 3, but the explanation is far-fetched and improbable. The nut or walnut tree (*Juglans regia*, Linn.) came originally from Persia. The name is very similar in the Persian, Æthiopic, Arabic, and Syriac. One cannot help comparing the lovely simplicity of the bride's description with the tender beauty of Goethe's 'Herman and Dorothea.' The main point is this, that she is not the mere captive of the king, taken, as was too often the case with Eastern

monarchs, by violence into his harem; she was subdued by the power of love. It was love that raised her to the royal chariots of her people. She beholds in King Solomon the concentration and the acme of her people's glory. He is the true Israel; she is the glory of him who is the glory of God.

Ver. 13a.—Return, return, O Shulamite; return, return, that we may look upon thee. Shulem is the same as Shunem (see 1 Kings i. 3; 2 Kings iv. 8; Josh. xix. 18). Shulamite will, therefore, mean "lady of Shulem." It is the first occurrence of the name. It cannot be a pure proper name, says Delitzsch, because the article is attached to it. It is a name of descent. The LXX. has ἡ Σοοναμῖτις, i.e. "she who is from Shunem." Abishag was exceedingly beautiful, and she came from the same district. It is the country in the tribe of Issachar, near to little Hermon, to the south-east of Carmel and south of Nain, south-east of Nazareth, south-west of Tabor. It is found at present under the name *Sawlam*, not far from the great plain of Jiszeal (now *Zer'in*), "which forms a convenient way of communication between Jordan and the sea-coast, but is yet so hidden in the mountain range that the Talmud is silent concerning this Sulem, as it is concerning Nazareth." It is impossible to resist the impression of the fact that this part of Galilee so closely associated with our Lord and his ministry should be the native place of the bride. Delitzsch thinks that the Shulamite is on her way from the garden to the palace. That the words are addressed to her by the admiring ladies can scarcely be disputed; hence the "we" of the address. "The fourfold 'come back' (or, 'turn') entreats her earnestly, yea, with tears, to return thither (that is, to the garden) with them once more, and for this purpose, that they might find delight in looking upon her." But Delitzsch is scarcely right in thinking that the garden of nuts to which the bride referred is the garden of the palace. She is, perhaps, turning to leave the company of ladies, Solomon himself being among them, as though she would escape from their gaze, which is too much for her in her simplicity, and the ladies, seeing her intention to leave them, call her back. Another view is that the word "return" is for "turn round;" that is, "Let us see thee dance, that we may admire the beauty of thy form and movements." This would explain the appropriateness of the bride's reply in the latter half of the verse. Moreover, the fourfold appeal is scarcely suitable if the bride was only slightly indicating her intention to leave. She would surely not leave hastily, seeing that Solomon is present. The request is not that she may remain, but that they may look upon her. It would be quite fitting in the mouth of lady-companions. The whole is doubtless a poetic artifice, as before in the case of the dream, for the purpose of introducing the lovely description of her personal attractions. Plainly she is described as dancing or as if dancing. Delitzsch, however, thinks that the dance is only referred to by the ladies as a comparison; but in that case he certainly leaves unexplained the peculiarity of the description in ch. vii. 1—5, which most naturally is a description of a dancing figure.

Ver. 13b.—**Why will ye look upon the Shulamite as upon the dance of Mahanaim?** The Shulamite, in her perfect modesty and humility, not knowing how beautiful she really is, asks why it is that they wish still to gaze upon her, like those that gaze at the dance of Mahanaim, or why they wish her to dance. But at the same moment, with the complaisance of perfect amiability, begins to move—always a pleasure to a lovely maiden—thus filling them with admiration. Mahanaim came in later times to mean "angels," or the "heavenly host" (see Gen. xxxii. 3), but here it is generally thought to be the name of a dance, perhaps one in which the inhabitants of Mahanaim excelled, or one in which angels or hosts were thought to engage. The old translators, the Syriac, Jerome, and the Venetian, render, "the dances of the camps" (*choros castrarum*, θίασον στρατοπέδων), possibly a war-dance or parade. The word, however, is in the dual. Delitzsch thinks the meaning is a dance as of angels, "only a step beyond the responsive song of the seraphim" (Isa. vi.). Of course, there can be no objection to the association of angels with the bride, but there is no necessity for it. The word would be, no doubt, familiarly known in the age of Solomon. The sacred dances were often referred to in Scripture, and there would be nothing degrading to the dignity of the bride in dancing before the ladies and her own husband. "After throwing aside her upper garment, so that she had only the light clothing of a shepherdess or vine-dresser, Shulamith danced to and fro before the daughters of Jerusalem, and displayed all her attractions before them."

HOMILETICS.

Vers. 1—3.—*Dialogue between the bride and the daughters of Jerusalem.* I. THE QUESTION OF THE MAIDENS. The dream is past. The bridegroom is absent for a time, but the bride is not anxious; she knows where he is, and that he will soon return. Perhaps it was such a short absence which filled her thoughts before, and was the occasion of those narratives which are so dream-like, which recall so vividly reminiscences of dreams such as most men have probably experienced. The chorus again address the bride as "fairest among women." They recognize her beauty and graces. They do not see the bridegroom with her; they ask, "Whither is he gone?" They offer to seek him with her. So we sometimes ask others who have more Christian graces, more love of Christ, than we have, where we may find the Lord. We want to seek Christ with them; we ask for their prayers; we will join our prayers with theirs.

II. THE ANSWER. 1. *The bride knows where her beloved may be found.* She has no doubts now, no anxieties, as she had in her dream. She answers without hesitation, "My beloved is gone down into his garden, to the beds of spices, to feed [his flock] in the gardens, and to gather lilies." She invests her beloved with the ideal character of a shepherd, as she had done before (ch. i. 7). We see that the words are not to be taken literally; he is no shepherd in the ordinary sense. He is said, indeed, to be feeding (his flock), but not in ordinary pastures. He is gone to his garden, a garden of costly spices; and he is gone to gather lilies, apparently for his bride. The bride never dwells on the wealth and magnificence of her royal lover as the chorus do. Such thoughts, perhaps, were to her oppressive rather than attractive; she loves to think of him as a shepherd, as one in her own condition in life. The grandeur of the king was dazzling to the country maiden. So the Christian loves to think of the Lord Jesus as the good Shepherd. We know, indeed, that the kingdoms of this world are his; that he is King of kings and Lord of lords; that he is the Word who in the beginning was with God, and himself was God; that all things were made through him, and without him was not anything made that was made. We know that he will come again in majesty and great glory to judge the quick and the dead. But when our souls are dazzled by the contemplation of his glory; when we shrink, as sinful men must shrink, from the thought of the great white throne and him that sitteth on it, from whose face the earth and the heaven flee away (Rev. xx. 11);—it is a relief then to our weakness to remember that the great King humbled himself to our low estate, that he was made as one of us, that he shared all our human infirmities, sin only excepted; that he who is the Life of the world humbled himself for us unto death, even the death of the cross. And of all the titles by which he has been pleased to make himself known to his people, there is none so full of comfort as that of the Shepherd, the good Shepherd, who calls his sheep by name, who guides them and feeds them, who knows his own and his own know him, who once laid down his life for the sheep. Now he feeds them in his garden, the garden enclosed (ch. iv. 12), which is the Church, among the beds of spices, which are the fruit of the Spirit. There he gathers the lilies one by one, the souls of his redeemed, the souls which he has tended and cared for, and glorified with a beauty of holiness which is a faint reflection of his own heavenly beauty. Solomon in all his glory was not arrayed like one of those precious lilies. He gathers them one by one when they have grown into that spiritual beauty for which he planted them at the first, and carries them into a better garden, the true Eden, the Paradise of God, there to blossom into purer and holier beauty.

2. *She is wholly his.* "I am my beloved's, and my beloved is mine: he that feedeth [his flock] among the lilies." She repeats the happy assurance of ch. ii. 16, only she inverts the order of the clauses, and adds the description. "He is feeding his flock among the lilies: but I am his, and he is mine." There is no jealousy, no doubt now, as there seemed to be when she dreamed of his absence. The shepherd is her shepherd, the lilies are for her, she is his. She thinks first now of her gift to the bridegroom. In ch. ii. 16 she put his gift first. He had given his heart to her in the first happy days of their young love; and that gift had won from her the responsive gift of her affection. She knew now that her heart was wholly his; she delights in owning it. And she was sure of his affection. His heart was wholly hers. "We love him, because he first loved us" (1 John iv. 19). It is the love of Christ manifested in his blessed life and precious death, revealed into the believer's heart by the power of the Holy Spirit,—it is that constraining love which draws forth from our cold and selfish natures that measure of love, real and true, though unworthy and intermittent, with which the Christian man regards the Lord. At first we are more sure of his love than of ours. He loved us, that is certain; the cross is the convincing proof. But we are not sure, alas! that we are returning his love. We have learned from long and sad experience to doubt these selfish hearts of ours; we are afraid that there is no real love in them, but only excited feeling, only transitory emotion. But if by his grace we persevere in the life of prayer and faith, little by little his love given to us, manifested in our souls, draws forth the response of earnest love from us; little by little we begin to hope (oh, how earnestly!) that we may be able at last to say with St. Peter, "Lord, thou knowest all things; thou knowest that I love thee." But to say that, with the knowledge that his eye is on us, that he is reading our heart, involves much awe, much heart-searching, as well as much hope, much peace. We can only pray that "the God of hope may fill us with all joy and peace in believing, that we may abound in hope through the power of the Holy Ghost" (Rom. xv. 13). And if that love, though weak, as, alas! it must be, is yet real, we may make the bride's words our own: "I am my Beloved's; I belong to him. My heart is his; I am giving it to him; and he, blessed be his holy Name, is helping me to give it by first giving himself to me. I am my Beloved's, and my Beloved is mine." Therefore the Christian soul may say, "I hope one day to see him face to face, and to be with him where he feedeth his flock among the lilies of Paradise."

Vers. 4—9.—*The bridegroom's praise of the bride.* I. RENEWED ENUMERATION OF HER GRACES. 1. *General praise of her beauty.* Her beauty is compared to the beauty of Tirzah or Jerusalem. She is beautiful as Tirzah, which word means "grace" or "beauty;" comely as Jerusalem, the habitation or foundation of peace. The bridegroom mentions Tirzah as well as Jerusalem, which seems to imply that the song was written before the division of the kingdom. The bride is beautiful as Tirzah was to the inhabitants of Northern Palestine—a fair city in a fertile country, deriving its name from the attractive graces of the surrounding scenery. She is comely as Jerusalem was to every loyal Israelite. "Beautiful for situation, the joy of the whole earth, is Mount Zion, on the sides of the north, the city of the great King;" "Walk about Zion," the psalmist continues, "and go round about her: tell the towers thereof. Mark well her bulwarks, consider her palaces; that ye may tell it to the generation following" (Ps. xlviii. 2, 12, 13). Zion was to the Israelites "the perfection of beauty" (Ps. l. 2 ; Lam. ii. 15). The exiles in the days of the Captivity sang in plaintive strains, "If I forget thee, O Jerusalem, let my right hand forget her cunning. If I do not remember thee, let my tongue cleave to the roof of my mouth; if I prefer not Jerusalem above my chief joy" (Ps. cxxxvii. 5, 6). The great delight in return-ing from their long captivity was to think, "Our feet shall stand in thy gates, O Jerusalem." "Pray for the peace of Jerusalem," they would say: "they shall prosper that love thee. Peace be within thy walls, and prosperity within thy palaces" (Ps. cxxii. 2, 6, 7). And what Jerusalem was to the Israelites, that the Church is to the heavenly Bridegroom. Her salvation was "the joy set before him," for which "he endured the cross, despising the shame" (Heb. xii. 2). He tells her towers; for "the Lord knoweth them that are his." He knows every living stone of the spiritual temple, the Church, which he hath built upon the Rock of ages. He never forgets her. He intercedes for her, and is preparing a place for her, that hereafter "the nations of them which are saved may walk in the light of her" (Rev. xxi. 24). He prays now for her peace, and giveth her his peace—"the peace of God, which passeth all understanding." She is beautiful with the reflection of his perfect beauty. He will cleanse and purify her, and at the last present her to himself a glorious Church. And if the Church is fair in the Bridegroom's eyes, so in a degree is each converted and sanctified soul; in each such soul he sees something of that beauty of holiness which comes from the indwelling presence of the Holy Spirit of God. For they who love him, and seek to live in that fellowship which is with the Father and with his Son Jesus Christ, must, while they "behold as in a glass the glory of the Lord, be changed into the same image from glory to glory" (2 Cor. iii. 18). And if the dear Lord is pleased with the poor holiness of his people, how earnestly we ought to strive to purge ourselves from all pollution of the flesh and spirit, perfecting holiness in the fear of God! Earthly beauty is but a poor endowment; it soon fades and passes away. The inner beauty of a holy soul abides and increases continually, and is very precious and sacred; for such fair souls, washed and made white in the blood of the Lamb, shall see the King in his beauty, and dwell in the light of the golden city. 2. *She is terrible as an army with banners.* The bride is beautiful not only for her attractive gentleness; she has a queenly dignity that could repel any presumptuous advances. The beauty of the Church is a severe beauty, like the martial beauty of a bannered host. For, indeed, the Church is an army, the army of the living God; the banner of the cross shines in the van, advancing ever forward.

> "The royal banners forward go,
> The cross shines forth in mystic glow."

That bannered host is terrible to the enemy. "Our wrestling is not against flesh and blood, but against the principalities, against the powers, against the world-rulers of this darkness, against the spiritual hosts of wickedness" (Eph. vi. 12).

> "They march unseen,
> That sacred band, in serried ranks arrayed,
> Each cheering on his brother to the fight.
> The Spirit-sword flashes in each right hand;
> The shield of faith protects each steadfast breast;
> The red cross banner glitters in their van,
> As they press ever forwards: breathing all
> The selfsame prayer, the selfsame Presence high
> Abiding in each heart, the selfsame hope,
> The glory-crown in heaven, sustaining all."

Each Christian soul has its place in that vast army; each is a sworn soldier of the cross; each such soul is terrible to the enemy, because Christ is the strength of his people, and they are more than conquerors through him who loved them.

> "Satan trembles when he sees
> The humblest saint upon his knees."

Then we must pray for grace to follow the banner of the cross with loyal heart and steadfast purpose, that our service may be acceptable to the Captain of our salvation, and pleasing in his sight, as a bannered host marshalled and ordered, as each noble warrior well equipped and disciplined, is a sight that gives pleasure and joyful pride to the commander. 3. *The bridegroom repeats the praises of ch. iv.* 1—6. But first he says, "Turn away thine eyes from me, for they have overcome me." He had praised her eyes again and again; they were as doves' (ch. i. 15; iv. 1, 9). Now he says, in the tenderness of a great love, "they have overcome me." We may compare the Lord's gracious wonder at the faith of the centurion (Luke vii. 9). He condescended to "marvel at him, and turned him about, and said unto the people that followed him, I say unto you, I have not found so great faith, no, not in Israel." The bridegroom goes on to praise the various features of the bride's beauty. He had done so already in the love of their first espousals. His affection continues unabated; he repeats the same praises in the same words. The heavenly Bridegroom loves his bride the Church with "an everlasting love" (Jer. xxxi. 3). The terms of affection which are bestowed in the Old Testament upon the ancient Jewish Church are repeated in the New Testament, and applied to the Christian Church, the Israel of God. Thus St. Peter (1 Pet. ii. 9) calls Christians "a chosen generation;" the same title (in the Greek of the Septuagint the words are exactly the same) is given in the Prophet Isaiah (xliii. 20) to the Jewish people. St. Peter calls Christians "a royal priesthood;" in Exod. xix. 6 the Israelites are called "a kingdom of priests" (here again St. Peter has used the exact words of the Septuagint). St. Peter calls Christians "a holy nation;" the same thing is said of the Israelites in Exod. xix. 6. St. Peter describes Christians as "a peculiar people;" his words represent Deut. vii. 6, translated in our old version "a special people," in the new version, "a peculiar people." He applies to the Christian Church the words which the Prophet Hosea had used of the Jews, "Which in time past were not a people, but are now the people of God; which had not obtained mercy, but now have obtained mercy" (1 Pet. ii. 10; Hos. ii. 23). The Lord Jesus loves his Church with a love that changes not. Almost at the beginning of the New Testament stands the holy promise, "Thou shalt call his name Jesus: for he shall save his people from their sins;" and almost at the end we read the blessed words, "Whosoever will, let him take the water of life freely." Each faithful Christian may trust his Saviour's love, for it is written, "I will never leave thee, nor forsake thee;" and again, "He which hath begun a good work in you will perform it until the day of Jesus Christ" (Phil. i. 6).

II. COMPARISON OF THE BRIDE WITH OTHERS. 1. *They are many.* David had had sixteen wives. Solomon had early followed that unhappy example; already he had, it seems, "three score queens, and four score concubines." He had transgressed the commandment of Deut. xvii. 17, where it is said of any future king, "Neither shall he multiply wives unto himself, that his heart turn not away." Solomon, alas! broke the commandment of God, and incurred the awful peril denounced against disobedience. "He had seven hundred wives, princesses, and three hundred concubines: and his wives turned away his heart. For it came to pass, when Solomon was old, that his wives turned away his heart after other gods" (1 Kings xi. 3, 4). Now he was young but even in his youth the evil desire was strong within him. His love for the pure country maiden might have saved him; for a time, perhaps, it did check his sensual passions. But, alas! if it was so, the evil spirit that had been cast out soon returned, and brought with him seven other spirits more wicked than himself, and the last state was worse than the first (Matt. xii. 43—45). 2. *She is one alone.* "One is she, my dove, my undefiled; one is she to her mother; the choice one is she to her that bare her." Such is the literal rendering of the touching words. The bride was an only daughter; she was the joy and darling of her mother. The good daughter makes a good wife. She was the bridegroom's dove, his undefiled one, and she stood alone in his affections; no other came near to her. So good was she and so lovely in character as well as in person, that even those who might have been expected to regard her with envy praised her and called her blessed. The luxurious monarch seems to have a glimpse of the blessedness of purity; he seems almost to feel that "to love one maiden and to cleave to her" is the ideal of human love. Alas! "his goodness was as a morning cloud, and as the early dew it passed away" (Hos. vi. 4)

The evil spirit of sensuality returned. When he was old, his wives turned away his heart; and he did evil in the sight of the Lord, and built high places for the worship of idols in the hill that is before Jerusalem (1 Kings xi. 4, 6, 7). How earnestly we ought to strive to retain in our souls those happy feelings, those aspirations after purity and holiness which God sends from time to time, like angels' visits, into our hearts! They can only be fixed and wrought into our characters by immediate action. In themselves they are transitory, and rapidly pass away. But hold them firm, make them the basis of real effort, the beginning and occasion of the healthy discipline of self-denial,—then God will help us to keep them alive in our souls; the little seed will grow till it becomes a great tree; the little leaven will spread through the whole life with its quickening powers. Very precious are those moments of holy emotion; very solemn, too, for they involve a great responsibility. To let them go is perilous exceedingly, to use them aright brings a priceless blessing.

Vers. 10—13.—*Conversation between the chorus and the bride.* I. ADDRESS OF THE CHORUS. 1. *The question.* "Who is she?" This question occurs three times in the song. In ch. iii. 6 it is asked apparently by a chorus of young men, the friends of the bridegroom; here and in ch. viii. 5 it seems to be put into the mouth of the chorus of maidens, the daughters of Jerusalem. It is an expression of admiration. The maidens meet the bride after an interval, and are startled by her surpassing beauty, at once graceful and majestic. Her happy love has shed a new grace around her; she is clothed in queenly attire; it is a vision of rare loveliness. It is the love of Christ which gives the Church whatever beauty she possesses. Christ's love for her, drawing forth her responsive love for him, gives her whatever graces she may possess. She is his creation. He built his Church upon the rock; all that she is, and all that she has, comes only from his gift. 2. *The description.* She looks forth as the dawn. The bride's sudden appearance is like the early dawn, coming forth in its beauty, tinging sky and clouds with rosy light. She is fair as the moon, clear and pure as the sun (poetical words are used here, as in Isa. xxiv. 23; xxx. 26; the moon is the white, the sun the hot luminary); and the comparison of ver. 4 is repeated; in her queenly majesty she is terrible, awe-inspiring, as a bannered host. Christ is the Bright and Morning Star (Rev. xxii. 16); He is the Sun of Righteousness (Mal. iv. 2); He is the true Light, the Light of the world. The true Light lighteth every man (John i. 9); and they who believe in the Light, and walk as children of light, reflect something of its brightness; so that the Lord, in his condescending love, says of them, "Ye are the light of the world" (Matt. v. 14); and so St. Paul says of his Philippian converts that "ye shine as lights [luminaries] in the world" (Phil. ii. 15). "God is light, and in him is no darkness at all." Christians must strive, by his grace and the illumination of his Spirit, to walk always in the light, as he is in the light, that so they may have fellowship with one another in the light of holy love, and that the blood of Jesus Christ may cleanse them continually from all sin, making their souls white and clear in the transparent truth of that purity in heart which must, by the Saviour's compassionate mercy, belong to them who shall see God (Matt. v. 8).

II. ANSWER OF THE BRIDE. 1. *Her lowliness.* The maidens praise her beauty and stateliness; she reminds them of her former low estate. She seems to be looking back to the hour of her first meeting with the bridegroom. She had no thought, country maiden as she was, of the elevation that awaited her. She was engaged in her ordinary occupations. She had gone down into the garden to tend it and to watch the budding of the fruit trees; there she first saw the king. Whatever graces the Church possesses come from the favour of the heavenly Bridegroom. "Through him we have access by one Spirit unto the Father. Now therefore ye are no more strangers and foreigners, but fellow-citizens with the saints, and of the household of God" (Eph. ii. 18, 19). The Gentiles were strangers and foreigners; they knew not the King; they were not looking for him. As the Lord God called Adam and Eve when they were hiding themselves among the trees of the garden, so the Lord called the Gentiles by the mission of his apostles. In the infancy of the human race it was the protevangel, the promise of the Seed of the woman who shall bruise the serpent's head, that first shed light upon the gloom of sin and misery. And in the fulness of time it was the Lord's gracious mission, "Go ye into all the world, and preach the gospel to every creature," that first called the Gentiles into the city of God. Till he calls us we are like the bride in the song, immersed in worldly pursuits and earthly cares; he brings us into the new Jerusalem and makes us fellow-citizens with the saints. We must remember always that "By the grace of God I am what I am;" that whatever we may have done of good or right, it was "Not I, but the grace of God which was with me" (1 Cor. xv. 10). "By grace are ye saved through faith; and that not of yourselves: it is the gift of God" (Eph. ii. 8). The bride was poor in this world's goods; we Christians must be "poor in spirit." That holy poverty, that sense of our own helplessness and need of the Saviour, is very blessed; it has the first place in the Beatitudes. 2. *Her exaltation.* "I knew not," she says, "my soul made me the chariots of my people, a princely [people]." She uses a military figure, perhaps suggested by the words twice addressed to her in this chapter, "Terrible as an army with banners." In a sense she accepts the metaphor. Elijah and Elisha had been severally called "the chariot of Israel and the horsemen thereof" (2 Kings ii. 12; xiii. 14). So now the bride had been raised to a lofty position, and was awe-inspiring in her majesty, like a bannered host, or the chariots of a princely people. Her soul, she says, had made her this; she means her soul's love for the bridegroom, whom she so often describes as "him whom my soul loveth" (ch. i. 7; iii. 1, 2, 3, 4). The king saw her and loved her. His love won her innocent heart; and that pure, artless love of hers, the love which filled her soul, the seat of the affections, had lifted her up into the very highest place in the affections of the king, so that now in her queenly majesty she was not only fair as the moon, but awe-inspiring as a bannered host, as the war-chariots of a princely people. So it is love that makes one man better than another in the sight of God; not riches, or refinement, or learning, but love. There is, as it were, a hierarchy of love in the universe. Good men love, angels love more, but God is love—the infinite, ever-lasting Love. "He prayeth best who loveth best." He is nearest to God who by his Spirit has learned the great grace of love. "God so loved the world, that he gave his only begotten Son, that whosoever believeth in him should not perish, but have everlasting life" (John iii. 16). The love of Christ draws forth the love of his people. Their love, given in response to his most holy love, lifts them nearer to the King; it makes them take up the cross and follow him as his faithful soldiers, quitting themselves like men in the good fight of faith; it makes them terrible to the powers of evil as a bannered host, as the war-chariots of iron were in the days of the Judges (Judg. i. 19; iv. 3).

III. Short dialogue concluding the conversation. 1. *Request of the chorus.* The bride retires; the maidens of the chorus eagerly call her back; they desire to look again upon her beauty. They call her for the first and only time, "O Shulamite!" What is the meaning of the word? Is it equivalent to Shunamite? Was the bride a native of Shunem in the Plain of Esdraelon, where Elisha afterwards was wont to sojourn (2 Kings iv. 8—12)? And if so, can it be that the historical basis of the song is the love of Solomon for Abishag the fair Shunamite of 1 Kings i. 3? Or, again, is it possible, as some scholars have suggested, that the Hebrew name Shula-mith may have been chosen as a near approach to the feminine form (*Shelomith*) of Solomon (*Shelomoh*), signifying the bride's relationship to the great monarch? But the bride seems to belong to the Lebanon district; and wives were not then accustomed to take their husband's name. Again, Shulamith may possibly have been the original name of the maiden, though it occurs nowhere else as a proper name. It is enough for our purpose that the word suggests the meaning "peaceful;" the Vulgate rendering is *pacifica.* The bride is modest and quiet, she is peaceful; such should Christians be. 2. *Question of the bride.* She repeats the name given to her by the chorus, and asks, "What will ye see in the Shulamite?" The question is asked in modesty. The last clause of the verse, whether taken as part of the question or as the answer of the chorus, is exceedingly difficult. The word translated "company" is the second part of Abel-meholah ("the meadow of the dance"), the home of Elisha (1 Kings xix. 16). The Hebrew for "two armies" may be the name of the town in Gilead, "Mahanaim," so called by Jacob when "the angels of God met him" there (Gen. xxxii. 2). Hence the translation of the Revised Version, "Why will ye look upon the Shulamite as upon the dance of Mahanaim?" as if the chorus was inviting

the bride to dance some stately measure called from the Gileadite town.   Some
commentators who take this view understand the bride's words as a modest refusal ;
others, that she complies with their request.   But the second Hebrew word has the
definite article, which would scarcely be used here if it were the name of the city.
And if the first word must mean "dance," as it elsewhere does, may it not be taken
in connection with the preceding titles of praise, "the bannered host" and "the
chariots of a princely people," as a martial dance, or as the stately and well-ordered
evolutions of two bands of warriors?   This interpretation, which is suggested with
much doubt, may perhaps be regarded as yielding a more suitable explanation than
that of the dance, though this last is the view of many accomplished scholars.   The
chorus looks upon the bride with the interest and delight with which they would
watch the evolutions of two hosts with banners and chariots.   Warlike images occur
several times in the song (ch. i. 9; vi. 4, 10, 12).   To the Christian the words recall
the onward march of the army of the soldiers of the cross with the attendant escort
of angels, the two hosts (Mahanaim) of Gen. xxxii. 2.   For the angels of God still,
as in the times of old, encamp round about them that fear him to deliver them
(Ps. xxxiv. 7).   And still, if our eyes were opened, we should see, as the servant of
Elisha once saw, "chariots and horses of fire round about" the faithful.   "They that
be with us are more than they that be with" the enemy (2 Kings vi. 16, 17).

HOMILIES BY VARIOUS AUTHORS.

Vers. 1—3.—*Earnest inquirers after Christ.*   The conversation still goes on between
her who has lost her beloved and the daughters of Jerusalem.   She has just poured out
her heart to them in the description of him whom her soul so loved, and these verses
give their response.   We learn—

I. THAT THERE IS A SPIRITUAL LOVELINESS IN THE SOUL THAT EARNESTLY SEEKS
CHRIST. (Cf. ver. 1, "O thou fairest among women.") It is not merely that Christ sees·
this loveliness, we know he does; but others see it likewise.   It is not the beloved who
speaks here, but the daughters of Jerusalem. (Cf. 2 Cor. vii. 10, 11, where are set
forth some of those graces of character and conduct which are found in the seeking soul.)
And that humility, tenderness of conscience, zeal, devoutness, holy desire, and gentleness of spirit which accompany such seeking of Christ—how beautiful these things are !
And, like all real beauty, there is no self-consciousness in it, but rather such soul mourns
that it is so little like what Christ would have it be.

II. IT WILL WIN SYMPATHY AND HELP, WHICH ONCE IT DID NOT POSSESS. At the
beginning of this song it is plain that the maiden who speaks did not have the sympathy
but rather the contempt of the daughters of Jerusalem (cf. ch. i. 5, 8).   But now all
that is altered.   They are won to her love.   Great love to Christ will blessedly infect
those about us.   We can hardly live with such without coming under the power of its
sweet and sacred contagion. Cf. Jethro, "We will go with you, for we see that the
Lord hath blessed you." See, at the Crucifixion, how Joseph of Arimathæa, Nicodemus,
the centurion, and others ceased from their cold neutrality or open opposition, and
showed that they felt the power of Christ's love.

III. IT WILL BECOME THE WISE INSTRUCTOR OF OTHERS. This inquiry of ver. 1
had its fulfilment when Christ lay in the tomb.   Those who sought him mourned, but
found him not. Cf. Christ's words concerning his absence, "Ye shall have sorrow, but
your sorrow shall be turned into joy.   Also Mark ii. 20.   And the reply of ver. 2
had part fulfilment at that same period. Cf. "This day thou shalt be with me *in
Paradise*" (Luke xxiii. 43).   Yes, the Beloved had gone down into his garden (ver. 2).
But we may also understand by the garden *his Church* (cf. on ch. iv. 6).   And thus the
soul we are contemplating instructs others.   She tells them : 1. *Where Christ is to
be found.*   In his garden, the place he has chosen, separated, cultivated, beautified,
and whither he loves to resort.   And : 2. *What he delights in there.*   The spices—the
fragrant graces of regenerated souls, the frankincense of their worship and prayers.
The fruits on which he feeds—the holy lives, the manifestation of his people's faith and
love. The lilies—the pure, meek, and lowly souls that spring and grow there. 3. *What
he does there.*   He "feeds" there. "He shall see of the travail of his soul and be *satis-*

fied." As his "meat and drink" when here on earth was " to do the will of" the Father, so now his sustenance is those fruits of the Spirit which abound in his true Church. And he " gathers lilies." " He shall gather the lambs in his arms, and carry them in his bosom " (Isa. xl.). Whenever a pure and holy soul, like those of children and of saints, is transplanted from the earthly garden to the heavenly, that is the gathering of the lilies. " O death, where is thy sting?" Thus doth the soul that loves Christ instruct others.

IV. GAINS THE OBJECT OF ITS SEARCH. (Ver. 3.) "I am my Beloved's . . . mine." It is the declaration of holy rapture in the consciousness of Christ's love. They that seek him *shall* find him. There may be, there are, seasons when we fear we have lost him, but they shall surely be succeeded by such blessed seasons when the soul shall sing in her joy, "My Beloved is mine," etc. (ver. 3).—S. C.

Vers. 4—10 and ch. vii. 1—9.—*The friendship of the world.* Those who take the literal and historic view of this song see here a repetition of Solomon's attempts to bend to his will the maiden whom he sought to win. It is a repetition of ch. iv. 1—5. And in the extravagance of his flattery, his mention of her terribleness, his telling of his many queens and concubines, his huge harem, all of whom he says he will set aside for her—all this is like what he would say. Now, it all might be, as it generally has been, taken allegorically, as we have taken it in ch. iv. 1—5, and as setting forth Christ's estimate of his Church. But here the representations are yet more extravagant and even gross, so that we prefer to take them as telling of that which is evil rather than good ; as the language, not of Christ, but of the world. his foe, in attempting to win from him those who are his. Let it, then, teach us concerning this friendship of the world—

I. FLATTERY IS EVER ONE OF ITS FORMS. It is compelled to adopt this in order to hide away the fatal issue of its friendship. Like as the vampire is said to fan its victim with its wings, soothing and stupefying it so that it may the more surely destroy it, thus the world soothes and sends asleep by its flatteries the soul it would destroy.

II. THIS FLATTERY HAS MARKED CHARACTERISTICS. 1. It is *extravagant.* Cf. what is here said in the verses selected concerning her of whom they speak. How monstrous are the representations as addressed to any maiden! And are not the conceits the world engenders in men's souls of this order? 2. It is *always fearful of losing its prey.* (Ver. 4, "Terrible as an army;" also ver. 10.) These expressions seem to indicate consciousness that the soul was as yet anything but fully won. 3. *Has no originality.* It says the same things over and over again. See about her " hair," her " teeth," her " cheeks " (vers. 5, 6, 7; cf. ch. iv. 1—5). And still every poor fool that the world successfully flatters is plied with the same worn-out arguments, and, alas! yields to them. 4. *Sensuous and sensual.* (Cf. ver. 8 and ch. vii. 1—9.) The baser instincts are the world's happy hunting-grounds. It knows that it can get a response there when there is none elsewhere. 5. *Ruthless and cruel.* (Ver. 9.) The flatterer professes, but let all such professions be doubted vehemently—that he would sacrifice all the rest for her whom he would now win. For her, the "dove," whom he, the hawk, would devour, the three score queens and the four score concubines and the virgins without number (ver. 8) should all be set aside and lose favour. Anything, no matter how unjust, so Solomon may please his sensual phantasy. They who are ruthless in winning will be ruthless when they have won (cf. poor Anne Boleyn). Oh, the all-devouring world! Its "words are smoother than butter," but " the poison of asps is under its lips."

III. TRUE LOVE WILL REJECT IT. Such love is the Ithuriel-like spear which detects at once what it is. So this maiden, type of the redeemed soul, will have none of it (cf. ch. vii. 10). And here is suggested—what, indeed, is the theme of the whole song—the invincible strength of the true love of Christ in the soul. Let us have that, and no flatteries or blandishments of the world, nor its fierce frowns either, shall seduce us from him whose we are and whose we hope ever to be. Such love will be " terrible," must be so, to all who would come against it. Christ's love to us is so infinite that, therefore, nothing less than these many dread words of his about the everlasting fire can serve to tell of his wrath against that and those who would destroy us for whom he died. And if we love him as we should, we shall give no quarter to sin; it will be to us " the abominable thing which I hate," even as to him. Oh, may this love dwell in us richly and for evermore!—S. C.

Ver. 10—ch. vii. 9.—*How souls come into perilous places.* "Or ever I was aware." This section contains—so the literalists say—the account of the speaker's coming to Solomon's palace. (For right rendering of text, see the Revised Version and its margin.) She relates how she met the king's court (ver. 11). She was dwelling at home, and occupied in her customary rural labours, when Solomon, on a pleasure tour (ch. iii. 6, etc.), came into the neighbourhood of her town, Engedi. There the ladies of the court saw her, and were greatly struck with her beauty (ver. 10). Bewildered, she would have fled (vers. 12, 13), but thought the royal chariots were those of the nobles of her country (ver. 12). The ladies of the court beg her to return (ver. 13), and when she asks what they want of her (ver. 13), they request, and she consents, that she will dance before them, as the maidens of her country were wont to do. Thus Solomon sees her, and is enraptured with her, and begins to praise her in his gross way from her feet upwards (ch. vii. 2—9; Müller, *in loc.*) as he had seen her in dancing. And he seems to have brought her to Jerusalem and to his palace there, where she relates all this. Such appears to be the history on which this song is founded. It is likely, natural, and enables us, whilst still regarding it allegorically, to avoid assigning to Christ language and conduct which far more befit such a one as Solomon was. From the narrative as above given we may learn that—

I. No PLACES ARE FREE FROM SPIRITUAL PERIL. This maiden is represented as at home and occupied in her usual and proper employ, when suddenly all happened as is here told. And what places are there in which the world, and Satan, do not seek the soul's harm? At home, in our lawful calling, in the Church, everywhere.

II. THOSE WHOM THE WORLD HAS ENSNARED ARE USED TO ENSNARE OTHERS. The women of Solomon's court are represented as actively engaged in trying to secure this maiden for him. It is a true picture of how worldly souls try to make others as themselves.

III. MISTAKES HAVE OFTEN AS HURTFUL CONSEQUENCES AS SINS.

> " Evil is wrought
> By want of thought
> As well as want of heart."

It was so here. There was mistake as to who the people were; as to the motive of the request made her; in not at once escaping; in yielding to their requests. It does seem very hard that when there is no intention of evil, evil should yet come, and often so terribly (cf. 1 Kings xiii. 11, etc.). But it is that we may learn by our mistakes. We learn by nothing so well, and they are never suffered to have irreparable consequences.

IV. THE PERIL OF PARLEYING WITH SPIRITUAL FOES. Had she who is told of here fled away as she intended, none of her after-trial would have followed. To hold converse with a spiritual enemy is next to giving up the keys of the fortress. See how prompt our Lord was in repelling the suggestions of the tempter.

V. THOUGH WE FALL WE SHALL NOT BE UTTERLY CAST DOWN. The tempter in this history was baffled after all. She whom he tried so much kept her faith and love. The soul that loves Christ may wander and fall, but shall assuredly be brought back. "He restoreth my soul." Faithful love will soon reassert its power.—S. C.

Vers. 1—3.—*Successful quest after the chief good.* The inquirer has taken a step in advance. Awhile he asked, "What is there in Jesus that makes him so attractive?" To this question the loving disciple had responded. He had answered the question fully. He had given a full description of the sinner's Friend. He had testified to the worth and excellence of the heavenly King. And now the inquirer asks further, "Where may I find this gracious Friend? My heart craves the good which this Friend alone can bestow. I fain would have him too. Tell me where I may find him."

I. HERE IS SUGGESTED A DILIGENT SEARCH FOR JESUS. 1. *Spiritual life and joy in one attract others.* Genuine piety acts like a magnetic charm. A well-kept garden, stocked with fragrant flowers, has strong attractions for a thousand men, and the fragrant graces of true piety have a like fascination. If "a thing of beauty is a joy for ever," the life of a true Christian, being of all things the most beautiful, is an abiding joy. There is nothing so capable of manifesting beauty as character. If all Christians were as gracious and loving as they might be, what a benign effect would this have on the ungodly! This is Christ's method for propagating his gospel. "I am glorified in them." By which he meant to say, " All the charm of my character and all the fruit of my redemption shall be seen in the lives of my disciples." This will win the world's attention. 2. *Christian Churches are the objects of the world's respect.* This is not true of every community that styles itself a Church. But every true Church commands the respect and homage of mankind. And as a Church is simply an assemblage of individuals, a genuine Christian has a similar influence over men. The bride of Christ is here addressed as " the fairest among women." Purity and magnanimity of character command universal respect. Prejudiced men may malign and slander consistent Christians; they may envy their high attainments; yet in their heart of hearts they do them homage. They crave a good man's benediction. 3. *Active search is needful if we would find Christ.* It is quite true that Jesus seeks the sinner. He came to " seek the lost." This first desire to have the friendship of the Beloved has been awakened in the heart by the good Spirit of Christ. Nevertheless, there is a part we must perform, or we shall not gain success. We must strive to enter into the kingdom, or the portals will not open. The salvation of the soul is not to be attained by indolent passivity. There must be search, exertion, intense effort. We must break away from old companions. We must forego former indulgences. We must gain knowledge of Christ. We must search the Scriptures. We must be much in prayer. We must watch the stratagems of the tempter. We must seek if we would find. 4. *To find Christ it is best to have an experienced guide.* " That we may seek him with thee." The man who has found Christ, and knows well all the favourite haunts of Christ, is the best guide for others. No qualification in a guide is so good as personal experience. Nothing can take its place. No titles, no diplomas, no amount of intellectual learning, will take the place of experience. The pilot who has navigated a hundred ships through the rocky straits, though he may not be able to read a word in any language, is the best guide to bring us safely into port. It is a foolish act to refuse the practical counsels of faithful Christians. A learned man once accounted for his eminent acquisitions by the fact that he had never hesitated to ask questions respecting the unknown. To find Christ is eternal life, therefore let us use every wise measure in order to gain so great a boon.

II. VALUABLE COUNSEL. "My beloved is gone down into his garden." 1. *Here is confident assurance upon the matter.* On the part of a real Christian there is no doubt where Christ can be found. His knowledge is clear, for it is well-founded. As surely as men know in what part of the heavens the sun will rise or will set, so the friend of Jesus knows where he can be found. So he speaks in no doubtful tones. There is no peradventure. " My Beloved is gone down into his garden." There he had always found the Saviour, when devoutly he had sought him. For " his delights are with the children of men." And his gracious promise to his Church has never been broken, " Where two or three are gathered together in my Name, there am I in the midst of them." 2. *In the society of living and fruitful saints Jesus will be found.* He has gone " to the beds of spices." However imperfect and insipid our graces seem to ourselves, Jesus finds in them a sweet savour. The organ through which Jesus discovers these graces, and enjoys their fragrance and sweetness, is far more highly developed in him than in us. To his sensitive nature there is a fine aroma in our lowliness and patience, in our love and praise, which we had not suspected. Nor do the sweetest songs of angels attract him so much as the first lispings of a penitent's prayer. The nearer we get to Jesus the richer joy do we attain. There is a rare delicacy in the gladness, easier felt than described. So in our fresh passionate love, and in our simple zeal, and in our childlike trust, Jesus finds profoundest satisfaction. In the midst of such virgin souls he delights to dwell. These hold him, and will not let him go. What spice-beds are to every lover of innocent pleasure, the piety of true saints is to Jesus. Near such he may at any time be found. If any man longs to find the Saviour, he will find him in the vicinity of genuine believers. He is gone to the " beds of spices," perchance to some bedside, where deep-rooted love is blossoming and bearing fruit. 3. *Purity of heart wins Christ's presence.* He is gone " to gather lilies." Using Oriental language to convey heavenly truth, he is described as a Shepherd who feeds his flock "among the lilies." In the former chapter we read, " His lips are like lilies." To express his fondness for purity, he portrays his bride as " a lily among thorns." In the use of all such language he utters his strong affection for that which is pure in moral character. If he stoops in his pity to save a polluted sinner, he at the same time makes it clear that he loathes and abhors sin. His companions shall be spiritual virgins. Until a man is new-born he cannot see the kingdom of heaven, much less can he see the King. Purity of life may not yet be reached, but if in the central heart the purpose and firm resolve be for purity, then Jesus will soon be found. "Blessed are the pure in heart: for they shall see God." ·

III. FAITHFUL TESTIMONY. "I am my beloved's, and my beloved is mine." 1. *Religion is essentially a matter of the heart.* This title of endearment, "My Beloved," implies that he has won the affections of the heart. True piety is not simply a matter of conviction. It is not merely a doctrine or a creed. It is not a set of forms and ceremonies. It is an affair of the heart. It moves and holds the whole man. Feeling, desire, choice, strong affection, enter into the warp and woof of true religion. I may be very incompetent to set forth Christ's claims to the homage of mankind. But one thing I know—Jesus is supreme in my heart. None is so worthy of the central shrine as he. I have given myself to him, as the only possible return for his love. 2. *This testimony is the outcome of vigorous faith.* The bride of Christ had used this language before, but now she reverses the order. The order of events is not always the order of our experience. There are times when the Christian loses the assurance that he is loved by Christ. The sunshine of the Master's smile is hidden. Yet even then the language of faith is, "Come what may, I give myself afresh to him. Whether he count me worthy of a place in his regards or not, he is worthy of a place in mine. I am his. Therefore faith says (though I do not realize it now), 'My Beloved is mine.'" 3. *This renewed testimony is required by new circumstance.* The daughters of Jerusalem were inquiring where this Friend of sinners might be found. The bride of Christ undertakes to guide into his presence. Then she wishes to make it plain upon what terms Jesus will reveal himself to seekers. So she means to say, "I gave my whole self to him. I opened to him my heart, and made him Monarch there. Do you likewise, and you shall find the Saviour too." Jesus Christ craves the human heart. "Lovest thou me?" is his inquiry still. Even the city harlot, sick of sin, and opening her heart to Jesus, found in him sympathy and pardon and a new life. "She loved much, therefore her sins are forgiven her."—D.

Vers. 4—10.—*Christ's picture of his Church.* The value of an encomium depends on the qualification of the speaker. If a man is a master of eloquent phrases, and knows but little of the person he eulogizes, his encomium is little worth. If, on the other hand, the speaker is a skilful judge of character, and knows well the person, and speaks from pure motives, his estimate is priceless. Now, the best judge of the quality of a wife is her own husband, for no one else has such opportunities of knowing her virtues. If we regard the language in the text as the language of Christ, then he has all the qualities needful to be an accurate judge. As the Bridegroom, he has intimate acquaintance with his bride; and so righteous is he that he will neither exaggerate nor detract in his delineation. He will gauge with perfect accuracy her merit and her worth. Others may not acquiesce in his judgment. She herself may deem it a flattering portrait. But Jesus is an unerring Judge, and we accept with perfect confidence his description of his Church.

I. THIS LANGUAGE PLAINLY CONVEYS THE IDEA OF SPIRITUAL BEAUTY. "Thou art beautiful, my love, as Tirzah; comely as Jerusalem." Tirzah was a city on the mountains of Samaria, that had a wide renown for beauty. The name meant "a delightful place." God has given to the human soul a faculty that discerns and appreciates what is beautiful. We detect what is beautiful in material nature, viz. symmetry of form and harmony of colour. We discern also what is beautiful in human character and in human conduct. All beauty springs from God, the Fount. He is perfect Beauty, as much as perfect Righteousness. The constituent elements of spiritual beauty are humility, holiness, and love. These, wisely blended, form a comely character. It is always unsafe, because an inducement to pride, to praise the bodily beauty of a maiden within her hearing. But one of the elements in spiritual beauty is lowliness; hence public praise is an advantage rather than a peril. For commendation is a spur to fresh effort, and whatever quickens our exertion in the culture of humility and holiness is a boon to be prized. Nor is this spiritual beauty evanescent. It is a permanent acquisition. It will develop and mature towards perfection, as the ages roll on. The sun will be quenched in darkness, the stars will disappear or else assume new forms; but the ransomed saints will be rising in excellence, and adding to their spiritual adornments, world without end. This high estate of beauty may not as yet be *in esse*, but it is *in posse*. It is not yet an actual possession. But it is in course of development, from the bud to the open flower. It is clearly seen in its perfectness by the prescient eye of our Immanuel.

II. This language betokens the unity of the Church. " My dove, my undefiled, is one." In all God's works we find unity amid diversity. Throughout all material forces we discover system. Part is subordinated to part. Everything is linked to everything else. All forces work together for the well-being of the whole. There is organic unity. The universe shows the presence of one Master-mind. God loves order. Confusion, conflict, anarchy, are an abomination to him. Yet variety is not displeasing to him. Very clearly Jesus has not ordained a system of rigid uniformity in his Church. That would not add to her beauty nor to her usefulness. But the heart of Jesus is set upon unity. In his great prayer to his Father, prior to his crucifixion, he pleaded, " That they all may be one, as thou, Father, art in me, and I in thee." In opinions and beliefs it is next to impossible for the Church to be one. For God has created such diversities of taste and temper in men's minds, that for the time present truth presents itself under many aspects. Likely enough, this will continue until the human mind can more easily grasp the system of truth as a whole. Yet, while opinions and beliefs may vary, Christians can be one in feeling, one in love, one in loyalty to their King, one in aggressive service. This unity of life and love, amid diversities of belief and methods of service, will add to the Church's beauty and the Church's success. All the imagery which God has employed in Scripture to set forth his Church conveys this idea of unity. Is the Church a vine, springing out of Christ the Root? Then the manifold branches and twigs imply a united whole. Is a human body employed as an illustration? Then all the members and organs working in harmony imply unity. So, in our text, the bride is the representative of all saints, in all lands and in all ages. A dominant note of Christ's Church is unity. " There are many members, yet are they one body."

III. The language denotes fame. " The daughters saw her, and blessed her; yea, the queens and the women praised her." High and noble qualities of character are sure to command fame. Fame is a doubtful good. Counterfeit excellence, like tinselled brass, sometimes gains currency, and imposes on credulous people. Successful wickedness will, now and then, obtain a transient fame. Nevertheless, real and permanent honour belongs only to substantial goodness. Sooner or later the true Church will secure high renown. " God is in the midst of her." " The highest himself shall establish her." Her spiritual beauty and her beneficent influence shall win for her immortal praise. Beyond all human institutions, the Church will be found the bond of human society, the bulwark of freedom, the inspirer of intellectual life, the guardian of the nation's welfare. Fame is of secondary importance, yet fame must not be despised. For fame is power. Fame is large opportunity for doing good. Fame, as the result of generous and heroic service, is inevitable. Yet the Church will not keep her fame for herself. She will lay it at the feet of her Lord, to whom all belongs. For the present the Church may inherit the world's scorn rather than the world's fame; but when her hidden light and power shall break forth, " the Gentiles shall come to her light, and kings to the brightness of her rising." Resplendent fame is her sure reversion, " for the mouth of the Lord hath spoken it."

IV. Here is further the idea of hope-creating. " Who is this that looketh forth as the morning?" Morning is the dawn of hope to the benighted and the shipwrecked. Such are the evils that infest human society, that many thoughtful men have become pessimists. " Is life worth living?" many ask. If, after all the struggles and toils and endurances of this life, there is only extinction, or if the future is a dark enigma, then may not suicide be true wisdom? Hope, the backbone of all energy, is destroyed. The great questions are—Is there any desirable future for the human race on the earth? Is there a certain prospect of a better life for righteous souls after death? Now, there is no oracle, outside the Church, that can respond to these queries. The Church is the apostle of hope, the champion of humanity. The Church is a pledge of a better future for mankind. The Church proclaims a universal brotherhood. The Church is the foster-mother of all the useful arts; the foster-mother of progress, learning, social order, and peace. She changes deserts into gardens, and prisons into palaces. Where dark despair awhile reigned, she comes like the light of morning, and opens a new day.

V. HERE IS THE IDEA OF USEFULNESS. "Fair as the moon, clear as the sun." As the luminaries of night and of day perform an office of unspeakable usefulness to mankind, so does the true Church. In some respects the Church most resembles the moon. Her light is borrowed, and hence is enfeebled. She passes oft through manifold phases. The world often obstructs her light. It is only now and then that her light is full-orbed and at its best. This shall not always be. Her light shall be soft and gentle, like the light of the moon; yet for clearness and brilliance she shall be like the sun. Who can measure the potent usefulness of light? How destitute of beauty and of life would our earth be without light! If to-morrow the sun should not rise, what consternation would prevail in every home of man! The wheels of commerce would stand still. Agriculture would be suspended. Food would speedily be exhausted. All artificial light would soon come to an end, and, before many months had sped, all animal and vegetable life would expire. Equally useful, yea, more beneficent still, is the Church in the moral world. Apart from the truth embodied in the Church, what would mankind know of God, or his relationship to men, or his purposes of redemption, or his provision for a higher home? Or what would men know of themselves, their spiritual capacities, their Divine origin, their possible developments, or the resources of Divine help open to them? If you could blot out from existence the Church of Christ, this world would speedily sink into darkness and ruin. Within a single generation of men it would be a chaos, a pandemonium. Usefulness is predicated.

VI. A FURTHER IDEA IS DEVELOPMENT. "Who is this that looketh forth as the morning?" The morning is a promise and a pledge of perfect day. Light and warmth advance by regular stages until noon is reached. It is a picture of certain progress—advancement along an appointed way. Such is the destined life of the Church. At her birth she was feeble. Political arrogance at Jerusalem thought to crush out her life. But she steadily grew, passed safely through the stages of infancy and childhood, until now she appears a full-grown, ruddy maiden. Development is evidently God's order. He places trees at zero, and from the lowest point gives them opportunity to reach the highest. At the present hour the Church's development is an impressive fact. She grows in intelligence, in vigour, in power, in influence, in usefulness, day by day. At no period in her history was the Church of Christ so highly developed as she is to-day. Her progress is assured.

VII. HERE IS ALSO THE IDEA OF CONQUEST AS THE RESULT OF CONFLICT. "Terrible as an army with banners." The metaphor imports a majesty of active power that moves onward with confident step to overthrow its foes. "Terrible as a bannered host." The Church on earth is a Church militant. Many regiments of believers make up one army. This consecrated host of God's elect is commissioned to fight against error, ignorance, superstition, vice, and all immorality. Until the day of complete triumph dawns, she must station her sentinels, discipline her recruits, boldly contend with sin, and lead men captives to the feet of Christ. In proportion to her internal holiness and unity and zeal she will be "terrible" to ungodly men. The main secret of her terribleness is the fact that Jehovah dwells in her midst. As the Canaanites of old feared the host of Israel because the rumour of their power had spread on every side, and the mystic presence of Jehovah was with them, so is it still. The more that evil men discern the tokens of God's presence in the Church, the more they tremble. On the banner of the Church, men see the pattern of the cross. This inspires courage in the army, but terror among opponents. And the old battle-cry of the Crusaders is still the battle-cry of the Church, "By this we conquer!"—D.

Vers. 1—3.—*True love is true knowledge.* Knowledge of phenomena and of physical laws is scientific, and is of the intellect. It is not so with knowledge of persons, which is largely intuitive, and depends upon the qualities of the heart. It is sometimes seen that a character, misunderstood by the learned and clever, is apprehended by a very child. A man who is not loved is not truly known; but as love grows warmer, it may well be that knowledge grows clearer. It is certainly so with our experimental acquaintance with our Saviour and Lord.

I. CHRIST IS NOT REALLY KNOWN BY THOSE WHO STUDY HIM AT A DISTANCE. How is it that the Lord Jesus is so utterly misunderstood by many able and distinguished. men? that some such class him with impostors or with fanatics? that others are evidently at a loss to explain the hold he has over the heart of humanity? How many distressing representations of the Saviour's character, sayings, and ministry are to be met with in the writings of even learned and thoughtful men! The explanation is to be found in a law which governs all our knowledge of persons as distinct from our knowledge of phenomena. These latter we may study from without, as cool spectators. But no great man is to be comprehended if studied in such a spirit; far less any man of remarkable moral character and influence. He who will not *sympathize* with such a person must be content to be ignorant of him; for he is only to be known upon a nearer view, a closer acquaintance, and by means of a profound and tender association with him of feeling and of confidence.

II. CHRIST IS, HOWEVER, KNOWN BY THOSE WHO LOVE HIM, AND ARE UPON TERMS OF INTIMATE FRIENDSHIP WITH HIM. The peasant woman who is, in this Song of Songs, pictured as the beloved of the king, cherished for her husband the warmest affection; he was everything to her—ever in her memory when absent, and ever in her heart. Hence she knew him better than others; and those who wished to know of his character and his movements did well to inquire of her. In this simple fact we discern the operation of an interesting and valuable moral principle. To whom shall we go for an appreciative estimate of the character and the work of Immanuel? We shall go in vain to those among the learned and the critical who care not for Christ save as for an object of speculative, psychological, or historical inquiry. We shall fare better if we appeal to the lowly and the unlearned, if only they are persons who feel their personal indebtedness to Christ, who have "tasted that the Lord is gracious," who have learned by their own personal experience what he can do for those who put their trust in him. It is those who, like Mary, can exclaim, "*My* Master;" who, like Thomas, can address him as "*My* Lord and *my* God;" who, like Peter, can appeal to him, saying, "Lord, thou knowest all things; thou knowest that I love thee;"—it is such that can tell of the mystery of the Saviour's love, and the gracious wisdom of the Saviour's ways.

APPLICATION. These considerations are a rebuke to those who despise the experience and undervalue the testimony of lowly and unlettered disciples of Jesus Christ. And they point out to all who desire intimate knowledge of Christ, that the true method for them to adopt to that end is to yield to him their heart's warmest affection and unreserved, ungrudging confidence. By the way of love we may come to enjoy clear knowledge, and to give effectual witness.—T.

Ver. 4.—*The spiritual beauty of the Church of Christ.* There is such a study as the æsthetics of the soul. Beauty is not wholly material; it has a spiritual side appreciable by the spiritual sense. There is beauty of character as well as of form— "beauty of holiness," in which the holy delight. In the human countenance may now and again be seen, shining through symmetrical features, the loveliness of high emotion and aspiration. And in the spiritual society of the redeemed, even where churches are lowly, services inartistic, the ministry far from brilliant, the discerning mind may nevertheless often recognize glimpses of moral majesty, or comeliness, or attractiveness, speaking of a Divine favour and a Divine inspiration.

I. THE REALITY AND NATURE OF SPIRITUAL BEAUTY. It is not merely imaginary, like that

> "Light that never was on sea or land,
> The consecration and the poet's dream."

Though not physical, it exists, and partakes of the character of moral excellence. It is not discernible by the thoughtless, the insusceptible; it may be passed unnoticed by the haughty and the worldly. Yet it is observed by the enlightened and morally sensitive; such contemplate it with a satisfaction deeper than that of the artist who gazes entranced upon a noble statue or a fascinating picture.

II. THE SOURCE OF SPIRITUAL BEAUTY. The Church does not claim to be in possession of such a quality in its own right, to take credit for it as for something due to its own innate power and goodness. On the contrary, it acknowledges that all moral excellence is due to Divine presence and operation. The beauty which adorns the Lord's spiritual house is the Lord's own workmanship, the expression of the Lord's own wisdom and love. It is derived, and it is reflected—the mirrored image of the purity and benignity which are essentially and for ever his own. It is sustained and developed and perfected by the same grace by which it was originally imparted. The language of the Church's prayer is accordingly, " Let the beauty of the Lord our God be upon us," and the language of the Church's grateful praise, " Not unto us, O Lord, not unto us, but unto thy Name give glory."

III. THE IMPRESSIVENESS AND ATTRACTIVENESS OF SPIRITUAL BEAUTY. There are, indeed, unspiritual natures for whom it has no interest and no charm. But it is dear to Christ, who delights in it as the reflection of his own excellence. The King desires and greatly delights in the beauty of his spiritual spouse, the Church; to him she is beautiful and comely, fair as the moon, and clear as the sun. And all who share the mind of Christ take pleasure in that which delights him. The purity and unity, the Christ-like compassion and self-sacrifice of God's people, have exercised an attractive power over natures spiritual, awakened, and sensitive. By his living Church the Lord has drawn multitudes unto himself. And thus the beauty of the Church, reflecting the beauty of Christ, is the means of winning souls to the fellowship of immortal love.—T.

Ver. 4.—*The terribleness of the Church of Christ.* There is nothing inconsistent in the assertion that the same living society is possessed of beauty and of terribleness. To the susceptible mind there is ever something awful in beauty; it is felt to be Divine. There is a side of beauty which verges upon sublimity. We feel this in gazing upon the headlong cataract, the glorious sea. It sometimes seems to us as though God draws near to our souls when we suddenly behold a noble woman's grace and charm and pure ethereal expression. So there is in Christ's Church a severity as well as a winningness of beauty; we are conscious in some phases of Christian life of an aspect of deep and unspeakable awe. How is this to be explained?

I. THE SPIRITUAL CHURCH IS TERRIBLE AS THE DEPOSITARY OF THE MYSTERIOUS AND SUPERNATURAL GRACE OF GOD. It is the scene of the " real presence" of him who ever fulfils his own assurance, " Lo, I am with you alway, even unto the end of the world."

II. AS POSSESSING IN HOLINESS OF CHARACTER A SUBLIMITY WHICH APPEALS TO THE CHASTENED AND APPRECIATIVE IMAGINATION. Moving with spotless garments amidst the world's defilement and contamination, the true Church presents to the enlightened vision a spectacle of true sublimity, and commands our reverence as that which on earth is most truly sublime.

III. AS REBUKING AND FORBIDDING ALL THAT IS MORALLY EVIL. To penitents the attitude of the Church of Christ is, as was the Master's, benignant and compassionate; but to hardened sinners and to contemptible hypocrites there is a sternness and severity in its demeanour which may well make its presence terrible.

IV. AS POSSESSED OF MILITANT PROWESS AND POWERS. " Terrible as an army with banners." The Church has to confront the hosts of ignorance, of error, and of sin; its attitude and its equipment must, therefore, partake of the nature of a warlike force. As an army, the Church of Christ acknowledges the leadership of the Divine Captain of our salvation; is supplied with weapons, not carnal, but mighty to the pulling down of strongholds; is distinguished by a duly martial spirit, shrinking from no conflict to which it is called, by steady discipline and by just order. Well, then, may it be likened to an embattled host, with banners floating on the breeze, and the voice of the Commander ringing through the ranks. The spectacle is grand and awe-inspiring— an earnest of victory, an omen of empire.—T.

Vers. 11, 12.—*Spiritual promotion.* The Shulamite is now the queen; but she has not forgotten her early home, her youthful training, occupations, and companionship. She takes a pleasure in looking back upon bygone days, and calling to mind the remarkable manner in which, through the king's admiration and favour, she was raised from her lowly condition to the highest position amongst the ladies of the land. The contrast may be used to illustrate the change which takes place in the experience

of the soul which has been visited by the mercy of God in Christ Jesus, and has been
raised from a state of pitiable depression and hopelessness to participation in the
fellowship and the life of the Son of God.

I. THE SOUL'S FIRST STATE OF HUMILIATION.

II. THE INTERVENTION OF THE DIVINE FRIEND UPON THE SOUL'S BEHALF. 1. The
several *steps* of this interposition may be connected with the facts of this simple and
beautiful narrative. Christ visits the soul, bringing himself before the attention of
the object of his merciful regard. He loves the soul, and makes his affection known
by words and by deeds. He appropriates the soul as his own chosen possession. He
thus elevates the soul by bidding it share his own nature and life. 2. The *manner* of
the Saviour's approach in many instances corresponds with the king's revelation of
his love to the Shulamite maiden. It may be sudden and impressive, and yet at the
same time unspeakably welcome and appreciated.

III. THE DIGNITY TO WHICH THE OBJECT OF DIVINE CONSIDERATION IS ELEVATED.
The change of condition experienced by the maiden from Northern Palestine, when
she became the consort of Solomon, may serve to set forth the elevation of the soul
that Christ has, in the friendship of his Divine heart, made partaker of his spiritual
life. Such a condition involves: 1. Fellowship with the King himself. 2. Congenial
society. 3. Dignified occupations. 4. Honour from all associates. 5. Imperishable
glories.

APPLICATION. The soul that rejoices most gratefully in the immunities and honours
of the spiritual life and calling will do well to recollect the state of error, sin, and
hopelessness from which the human race was delivered by the compassion and power
of the Divine Redeemer. The Divine communion to which Christians are admitted
is a privilege which was forfeited by sin, and which has been recovered and restored
through the clemency and loving-kindness of him who is love, and whose love is
nowhere so conspicuous as in the salvation of his people. There are many cases in
which there is danger lest this obligation should be overlooked. It is well that the
polished stone in the temple of God should look back to "the hole of the pit whence it
was digged."—T.

EXPOSITION.

CHAPTER VII.

Ver. 1.—**How beautiful are thy feet in
sandals, O prince's daughter! The joints of
thy thighs are like jewels, the work of the
hands of a cunning workman.** To the ladies
who are looking on the bride appears simply
noble and royal. The word *naudhib* which
is used, translated "prince's daughter,"
means "noble in disposition," and so in
birth and rank, as in 1 Sam. ii. 8; Ps. cxiii.
8; so in ch. vi. 12, "the princely people."
The description, which is perfectly chaste,
is intended to bring before the eye the lithe
and beautiful movements of an elegant
dancer; the bendings of the body, full of
activity and grace, are compared to the
swinging to and fro of jewelled ornaments
made in chains. The cunning workman or
artist is one who is master of that which
abides beautiful. אָמָן, like, אָמַן, "whose truthful work can be trusted." The description
passes from the thighs or loins to the middle
part of the body, because in the mode of
dancing prevailing in the East the breast
and the body are raised, and the outlines of
the form appear through the clothing, which

is of a light texture. We must not expect
to find a symbolical meaning for all the
details of such a description. The general
intention is to set forth the beauty and glory
of the bride. The Church of Christ is most
delightful in his sight when it is most full
of activity and life, and every portion of it
is called forth into manifest excellence.
"*Arise, shine,*" is the invitation addressed
to the whole Church, "shake thyself from
the dust," "put on thy beautiful garments,"
be ready for thy Lord.

Ver. 2.—**Thy navel is like a round goblet,
wherein no mingled wine is wanting: thy
belly is like a heap of wheat set about
with lilies.** It must be remembered that
ladies are speaking of one who is in the
ladies' apartment. There is nothing indeli-
cate in the description, though it is scarcely
Western. The "round goblet," or basin, with
mixed wine, *i.e.* wine with water or snow
mixed with it, is intended to convey the
idea of the shape of the lovely body with
its flesh colour appearing through the semi-
transparent clothing, and moving gracefully
like the diluted wine in the glass goblet.
The navel is referred to simply as the centre

of the body, which it is in infants, and nearly so in adults. · Perhaps Delitzsch is right in thinking that there may be an attempt to describe the navel itself as like the whirling hollow of water in a basin. In the latter part of the verse the shape of the body is undoubtedly intended. " To the present day winnowed and sifted corn is piled up in great heaps of symmetrical, half-spherical form, which are then frequently stuck over with things that move in the wind, for the purpose of protecting them against birds. The appearance of such heaps of wheat," says Wetstein, " which one may see in long parallel rows on the threshing-floors of a village, is very pleasing to a peasant; and the comparison of the song every Arabian will regard as beautiful." According to the Moslem Sunnas, the colour of wheat was that of Adam. The white is a subdued white, denoting both perfect spotlessness and the purity of health. The smooth, round, fair body of the maiden is seen to advantage in the varied movements of the dance.

Ver. 3.—**Thy two breasts are like two fawns** that are **twins of a roe.** So in ch. iv. 5; but there the addition occurs, "which feed among the lilies." This is omitted here, perhaps, only because lilies are just before spoken of. The description is now in the lips of the ladies; before it was uttered by the king himself.

Ver. 4.—**Thy neck is like the tower of ivory; thine eyes are as the pools in Heshbon, by the gate of Bath-rabbim; thy nose is like the tower of Lebanon which looketh toward Damascus.** This is plainly a partial repetition of the king's description. The ivory tower was perhaps a tower well known, covered with ivory tablets, slender in structure, dazzlingly white in appearance, imposing and captivating. No doubt in the lips of the court ladies it is intended that this echo of the royal bridegroom's praises shall be grateful to him. Heshbon is situated some five and a half hours east of the northern points of the Dead Sea, on an extensive, undulating, fruitful, high table-land, with a far-reaching prospect. "The comparison of the eyes to a pool means either their glistening like a water-mirror or their being lovely in appearance, for the Arabian knows no greater pleasure than to look upon clear, gently rippling water:" cf. Ovid, 'De Arte Am.,' ii. 722—

"Adspicies oculos tremulo fulgore micantes,
　Ut sol a liquida sæpe refulget aqua."

The nose formed a straight line down from the forehead, conveying the impression of symmetry, and at the same time a dignity and majesty inspiring with awe like the tower of Lebanon. The reference is perhaps to a particular tower, and in the time of Solomon there were many noted specimens of architectural and artistic splendour. "A tower which looks in the direction of Damascus is to be thought of as standing on one of the eastern spurs of Hermon or on the top of Amana (ch. iv. 8), whence the Amana (Barada) takes its rise, whether as a watch-tower (2 Sam. viii. 6) or only as a look-out from which might be enjoyed the paradisaical prospect."

Ver. 5.—**Thine head upon thee is like Carmel, and the hair of thine head like purple; the king is held captive in the tresses thereof.** Carmel is called the "Nose of the mountain range" (*Arf-el-jebel*). It is a promontory. The meaning, no doubt, is the exquisite fitness of the head upon the neck, which is one of the most lovely traits of personal beauty. Some, however, think that the reference is to colour—Carmel being derived from the Persian, and meaning "crimson." This is rejected by Delitzsch, as the Persian would be *carmile*, not *carmel*. The transition is natural from the position and shape of the head and neck to the hair. The purple shell-fish is found near Carmel (cf. Lucian's πορφύρεος πλόκαμος and Anacreon's πορφυραῖ χαῖται, and similar expressions in Virgil's 'Georgics,' i. 405, and Tibullus, i. 4. 63). The locks of hair are a glistening purple colour, *i.e.* their black is purple as they catch the lights. Hengstenberg, however, thinks that the reference is to the temples, and not to the hair itself; but the use of the term in classical poets is decisive. The lovely head shaking the locks as the body moves gracefully in the dance fills the king with delight and admiration. He is quite captivated, and the ladies, having finished their description of the bride, look at the bridegroom, and behold him quite lost in the fascination—"held captive in the tresses." Delitzsch quotes a similar expression from Goethe, in the 'West Ostliche Divan,' "There are more than fifty hooks in each lock of thy hair." The idea of taking captive is frequent in Hebrew poetry (cf. Prov. vi. 25; Sirach ix. 3, 4). Thus ends the song of the ladies in praise of the bride. We must suppose that the king, who is probably present, then takes up the word, and pours out his heart.

Vers. 6—9.—(*Song of the bridegroom rejoicing over the bride.*) **How fair and how pleasant art thou, O love, for delights! This thy stature is like to a palm tree, and thy breasts to clusters of grapes. I said, I will climb up into the palm tree, I will take hold of the branches thereof: let thy breasts be as clusters of the vine, and the smell of thy breath like apples; and thy mouth like the best wine, that goeth down smoothly for my beloved, gliding through the lips of them that are asleep.** The abstract "love" is plainly here used for the concrete, "O loved one." It is just possible that the meaning may be—How delightful is the enjoyment of love! but the bodily description which follows suggests that the words are addressed directly to Shulamith. We certainly have in 1 Cor. xiii. an apostolic apostrophe to love, which Delitzsch calls the Apostle Paul's spiritual song of songs. But it would be somewhat irrelevant here. The king is deeply moved as he watches the beautiful figure before him, and delights in the thought that so lovely a creature is his own. The rapture which he pours out may be taken either as a recollection of how he was captivated in the past, or the past may be used for the present, as it frequently is in Hebrew. The meaning is the same in both cases. The palm tree may be selected on account of its elegance, but it is commonly employed in Eastern poetry as the emblem of love. The mystical writers use it to denote the Divine manifestation. The comparison of the breasts to clusters of grapes is quite natural, but no doubt reference is intended to the fruit as luscious and refreshing. Both the palm and the vine in the East are remarkable for the abundance and beauty of their fruits. In the case of the palm—"dark brown or golden-yellow clusters, which crown the summit of the stem and impart a wonderful beauty to the tree, especially when seen in the evening twilight." The palm and the vine are both employed in Scripture in close connection with the Church. "The righteous shall flourish as the palm tree;" "The vine brought out of Egypt" (Ps. lxxx.), and the "vineyard of the beloved" (Isa. v.), and the "true vine," to which the Lord Jesus Christ compares himself, remind us that the illustration was perfectly familiar among the Jews; and we can scarcely doubt that the reference in this case would be understood. The Lord delighteth in those "fruits of righteousness" which come forth from the life and love of his people. They are the true adornment of the Church. The people of God are never so beautiful in the eyes of their Saviour as when they are covered with gifts and graces in their active expression in the world. Then it is that he himself fills his Church with his presence. The ninth verse is somewhat difficult to explain. The words are no doubt still in the lips of the king. There is no change of speaker until ver. 10, when Shulamith replies to the king's adoring address. Ginsburg says, "Her voice is not merely compared to wine because it is sweet to everybody, but to such wine as would be sweet to a friend, and on that account is more valuable and pleasant." The Authorized

Version is supported by some critics as the best, "causing the lips of those that are asleep to speak." Delitzsch adheres to this. The LXX. renders it thus: ἱκανουμένος χειλεσί μου καὶ ὀδοῦσιν, "accommodating itself to my lips and teeth." So Symmachus, προστιθέμενος. Jerome, Labiisque et dentibus illius ad ruminandum. Luther strangely renders, "which to my friend goes smoothly down and speaks of the previous year" (pointing יְשֵׁנִים as יְשָׁנִים). Another rendering is, "which comes unawares upon the lips of the sleepers." Some think it refers to the smacking of the lips after wine. "Generous wine is a figure of the love-responses of the beloved, sipped in, as it were, with pleasing satisfaction, which hover around the sleepers in delightful dreams, and fill them with hallucinations." Another reading substitutes "the ancient" for "them that are asleep." The general meaning must be wine that is very good and easily taken, or which one who is a good judge of wine will praise. It is possible that there is some slight corruption in the text. The passage is not to be rendered with absolute certainty. Delitzsch and others think that it is an interruption of the bride's, but they have little support for that view. The bride begins to speak at ver. 10.

Ver. 10.—I am my beloved's, and his desire is towards me. So in ch. vi. 3 and ii. 16. It seems possible that a portion of the bride's speech may have dropped out —"My beloved is mine"—or she may wish to adopt the language of Gen. iii. 16, and represent herself as a true wife, whose husband is wrapt up in her love. By "desire" is intended the impulse of love, תְּשׁוּקָה, from a root שׁוּק, "to move or impel." The thought seems to be this—As my beloved is full of worshipping affection, and I am wholly his, let his love have free course, and let us retire together away from all the distractions and artificiality of the town life to the simplicity and congenial enjoyments of the country, which are so much more to my taste. The more real and fervent the religious emotions of the soul and the spiritual life of the Church, the more natural and simple will be their expression. We do not require any profuse ceremonies, any extravagant decorations, any complicated and costly religious services, in order to draw forth in the Christian Church the highest realization of the Saviour's fellowship. We want the Christianity we profess to take possession of us, body and soul. And so it will be as Christians learn more of Christ.

Vers. 11, 12.—Come, my beloved, let us go forth into the field; let us lodge in the villages. Let us get up early to the vine-yards; let us see whether the vine hath budded and its blossom be open, and the pomegranates be in flower: there will I give thee my love. All true poets will sympathize with the exquisite sentiment of the bride in this passage. The solitude and glory and reality of external nature are dearer to her than the bustle and splendour of the city and of the court. By "the field" is meant the country generally. The village or little town surrounded with vine-yards and gardens was the scene of Shula-mith's early life, and would always be delightful to her. The word is the plural of an unused form. It is found in the form *copher* (1 Sam. vi. 18), meaning "a district of level country." Delitzsch renders, "let us get up early," rather differently—" in the morning we will start "—but the mean-ing is the same. The word *dodhai*, "my love," is "the evidences or expressions of my love" (cf. ch. iv. 16; i. 2). No doubt the bride is speaking in the springtime, the Wonnemond of May, when the pulses beat in sympathy with the rising life of nature.

Ver. 13.—**The mandrakes give forth fra-grance, and at our doors are all manner of precious** fruits, **new and old, which I have laid up for thee, O my beloved.** The *dudhai* after the form *Lulai*, and connected probably with דּוּד, are the "love-flowers,"

the *Mandragora officinalis* (Linn.), whitish-green in colour, with yellow apples about the size of nutmegs; they belong to the order of Solanaceæ, and both fruits and roots were employed as *aphrodisiæ*, to pro-mote love. We are, of course, reminded of Gen. xxx. 14, where the LXX. has, μῆλα μανδραγορῶν, when the son of Leah found mandrakes in vintage-time. They produce their effect by their powerful and pleasant fragrance. They are said to be only rarely found in the neighbourhood of Jerusalem, but they were abundant in Galilee, where Shulamith was brought up. The Arabs called them *abd-el-sal'm*, "servant of love" —*postillon d'amour*. We are not wrong in using that which is perfectly natural and simple for the cherishing and increasing of devout feeling. The three elements which coexist in true spiritual life are thought, feeling, and action. They support one another. A religion which is all impulse and emotion soon wears itself out, and is apt to end in spiritual vacuity and paralysis; but when thought and activity hold up and strengthen and guide feeling, then it is scarcely possible to endanger the soul. The heart should go out to Christ in a simple but fervent worship, especially in praise. There are no Christians who are more ready to devote themselves to good works than those who delight much in hearty and happy spiritual songs.

HOMILETICS.

Vers. 1—5.—*The chorus of maidens praise the beauty of the bride.* I. THE PRELUDE. 1. *The address.* They address her as, "O prince's daughter." She is not a king's daughter, like the bride of Ps. xlv., but she is of honourable extraction. Though she lived in the retired district of Lebanon, and had been brought up there in rustic occupations, her family was one of some distinction. So Joseph, the carpenter of Nazareth, was recognized by the angel Gabriel, and was known among men by the testimony of accepted genealogies as "the son of David." The bride always speaks humbly of herself (as in ch. i. 5, 6), but the daughters of Jerusalem praise her. Such praise was common at nuptial festivals; the literal translation of Ps. lxxviii. 63, " Their maidens were not given in marriage," seems to be, " Their maidens were not praised." The daughters of Jerusalem do not regard the bride with envy; they do not despise her because of her former low estate; they rather bring forward every point that may tend to her praise. We should be like them in this respect. Jealousy is one of the most common of evil tempers; even the Lord's apostles were jealous of one another, and that in the very presence of the Master; again and again they disputed among themselves which should be the greatest (Matt. xviii. 1; Luke xxii. 24). We must covet earnestly the blessed grace of charity—charity which "envieth not, vaunteth not itself, is not puffed up, doth not behave itself unseemly, seeketh not her own, is not easily provoked, thinketh no evil, rejoiceth not in iniquity, but rejoiceth in the truth." We must pray fervently, "From envy, hatred, and malice, and all uncharitableness, good Lord, deliver us." 2. *The bride's approach.* "How beautiful are thy feet with shoes!" The word here rendered "feet" more generally means steps; this has been taken as an argument in favour of "the dance of Mahanaim," mentioned above. It is used also for "feet;" but even if we take it in its more common sense, the words of the chorus may be well understood of the approach of the bride, and perhaps also of the queenly grace of her movements. The opening words remind us of the prophecy of Isaiah, quoted by St. Paul in Rom. x. 15, "How beautiful upon the mountains are the feet of him that bringeth good tidings, that publisheth peace; that bringeth good tidings of good, that publisheth salvation; that saith unto Zion, Thy God reigneth!" (Isa. lii. 7). We have learned to see in the bride of the Song of Songs a figure of the Church, which is the bride of Christ. The mission of the Church is to "make disciples of all nations, baptizing them into the name of the Father, and of the Son, and of the Holy Ghost; teaching them to observe all things whatsoever the Lord commanded" (Matt. xxviii. 19). The heavenly Bridegroom is with the bride while she obeys his precept; for he adds, "Lo, I am with you all the days, even unto the end of the ages." Therefore "the Spirit and the bride say, Come" (Rev. xx. 17). The Church, taught and strengthened by the Holy Spirit, calls men to the knowledge of Christ. Her feet are beautiful as, "shod with the preparation of the gospel of peace" (Eph. vi. 15), she moves ever onward, bringing the light of truth into the regions that were lying in darkness and the shadow of death. Missionary work is a most important part of the duty of the Church; when carried on in faith and love and forgetfulness of self, it is beautiful in the sight of God.

II. PRAISES IN DETAIL. 1. *Of her clothing.* The chorus begins by praising, not simply the feet, but the sandalled feet, of the bride; they admire her sandals. From this we may infer that other terms used here relate rather to the clothing which covered the various parts of the body. It is the royal robes, with their ornaments and embroidery, which are like rows of jewels, or like a round goblet (see the word translated "round" in Isa. iii. 18, where it is rendered, "round tires like the moon"), or like a heap of wheat set about with lilies. Comp. Ps. xlv. 9, 13, 14, "Kings' daughters were among thy honourable women: upon thy right hand did stand the queen in gold of Ophir." "The king's daughter is all glorious within: her clothing is of wrought gold. She shall be brought unto the king in raiment of needlework: the virgins her companions that follow her shall be brought unto thee." So the bride, the Lamb's wife, shall be "arrayed in fine linen, clean and white: for the fine linen is the righteousness of saints" (Rev. xix. 8). "The king's daughter is all glorious within." The Hebrew word, indeed, means "within the palace," in the inner apartment. But we know that the adorning of the Church, when she appears "as a bride adorned for her husband" (Rev. xxi. 2), is "not that outward adorning of plaiting the hair, and of wearing of gold, or of putting on of apparel, but the hidden man of the heart" (1 Pet. iii. 3, 4). She will then be all glorious within, in the spiritual sense of the word, a glorious Church, holy and without blemish; and the Christian soul must even now put on that white linen which is the righteousness of saints, with the ornament of a meek and quiet spirit, which is in the sight of God of great price. Indeed, "our righteousnesses are but as filthy rags" (Isa. lxiv. 6); but Christ "of God is made unto us Wisdom and Righteousness" (1 Cor. i. 30); and St. Paul teaches us that "as many as have been baptized into Christ have put on Christ" (Gal. iii. 27). We must "keep ourselves pure" (1 Tim. v. 22); we must take jealous and anxious heed so to live in the faith of Christ and in the communion of the Holy Ghost as to keep that white robe unspotted from the world (Jas. i. 27). And if we have marred and stained it, as, alas! we too often do, by carelessness and sin, we must come to God in humble penitence and confession, asking him to give us grace to wash our robes and make them white in the blood of the Lamb; for we believe that the blood of Jesus Christ cleanseth from all sin, and that even they who have fallen into grievous sin may, if they turn to God in sorrow and contrition, be made "whiter than snow" (Ps. li. 7). The king's daughter must be all glorious within; she must put on the wedding-garment of righteousness. Let us seek that costly robe to be our own; we may gain it through the grace of Christ if we earnestly desire it, hungering and thirsting after it. 2. *Of herself.* Her neck was white as the ivory which King Solomon imported and used largely for purposes of decoration (1 Kings x. 18, 22); her eyes in their liquid beauty were like the pools at Heshbon; her brow stately as the tower of Lebanon; her head beautiful as the summit of Carmel; her hair like the deepest shade of Tyrian purple—the king (the chorus continues) is held captive in its tresses. The beauty of the bride is a stately, regal beauty; her neck and her brow are compared to towers, her head to the mountain so famous in the history of Elijah. So in the Book of the Revelation, when the angel had said to St. John, " Come hither, I will show thee the bride, the Lamb's wife," " he carried me," the evangelist continues, " away in the Spirit to a great and high mountain, and showed me that great city, the holy Jerusalem, descending out of heaven from God " (Rev. xxi. 9, 10). Here, again, the bride, which is the Church, is compared to a city, a city built upon an exceeding high mountain, according to the Saviour's prophecy, " Upon this rock I will build my Church, and the gates of hell shall not prevail against it " (Matt. xvi. 18). St. John dwells in ardent words upon the heavenly beauty of the bride, which is the city of the living God; he tells us of her stately gates, of her vast dimensions, of her jewelled foundations, of her " streets of pure gold as it were transparent glass." The glories of that heavenly city draw the Christian soul mightily with a constraining power, as King Solomon was held captive in the dark tresses of his bride. The Lord " loveth the gates of Zion " (Ps. lxxxvii. 1); the heavenly Bridegroom loved the Church, and gave himself for it. Christians, taught by him, set their affection on the heavenly city; they love to meditate upon its glories; they count its towers and mark its palaces, the many mansions in our Father's house; confessing that they are pilgrims and strangers here, they seek the continuing city, which is to come. " Blessed are they that do his commandments, that they may have right to the tree of life, and may enter in through the gates into the city " (Rev. xxii. 14).

Vers. 6—13.—*Dialogue between the king and the bride.* I. ENTRANCE OF THE KING. 1. *His praise of love.* Perhaps the last words of the chorus were overheard by the king as he approached the bride. He assents; he is content to be held captive in the tresses of the bride's hair; for love is fair and pleasant above all delightful things. The bridegroom is not here using the word with which he so often addresses the bride (as in ch. i. 9; iv. 1; vi. 4), which is translated, " O my love," or perhaps better, " O my friend." In this place we have the word ordinarily used for the affection of love; and perhaps it is best to take it in that sense here. Among all delightful things there is nothing so beautiful, so fair to contemplate, so full of interest; there is nothing so pleasant, nothing which gives so much comfort and peace and joy as true and faithful love. The king is happy in the bondage of which the chorus had spoken. Indeed, true love is not bondage in any proper sense of the word. It was God himself who said, " It is not good for man to be alone; " God who said, " I will make him an help meet for him." God gave man affections. When he made man after his own image, he set in his heart a reflection of that love which more than any other of his attributes enters into the very being and essence of Almighty God. That love needs objects on which to exert itself; the love of parent, child, or wife is a preparation, a training for the highest form of love, the blessed love of God. Loneliness, as a rule, is not good; it tends to concentrate a man's thoughts upon himself. He finds no outlet for the affections which God has given him: some of them, and those among the best and highest, are in danger of sinking into atrophy; there is great risk of his becoming a prey to selfishness, and the bondage of selfishness is hard and grinding and joyless. Sensual love is not love in the true sense; it is one of the worst and most unfeeling forms of selfishness; it thinks only of selfish pleasure, and recks nothing of the misery and ruin which it brings upon others; it makes a man the slave of evil passions; it tends to wretchedness. The service of God is perfect freedom; so, in a lesser sense, is the service of any pure and holy affection. True wedded love tends to set a man free from the bonds of selfishness; it gives him scope for the exercise of his best affections, and helps him to rise upwards towards that highest love which alone can give abiding happiness. Love, the bridegroom says, is among all delightful things the fairest and the most pleasant. The bride in the next chapter expresses the same belief, " Love is strong as death." " Many waters cannot quench love, neither can the floods drown it: if a man would give all the substance of his house for love, it would utterly be contemned." Wedded love is a parable of the holy love of God. The king in the song is led captive by the love of the bride. The saints of God, like St. Paul, St. James, St. Jude, delight in describing themselves as " the servants of God," " the slaves of God." God so formed our nature for himself that the soul can find an adequate object for its supreme affections only in him. Therefore he bids us love him with all our heart, with all our soul, with all our mind, and with all our strength, because our highest powers can find their proper exercise only thus; and it is in the exercise of the highest powers that the highest happiness is found.   It is the love of God that sheds glory and joy and blessedness through heaven, his dwelling-place, because the blessed angels love him perfectly, and, dwelling in love, do his holy will with a glad, undoubting obedience.   And so in various lower degrees it is the love of God which makes religion what it is to his people, very blessed and holy ; which makes life worth living; which gives them in the midst of their shortcomings glimpses more or less vivid of that holiest joy which is the blessedness of heaven.   Joy in the Lord is one of the fruits of the Spirit; it follows immediately upon the highest grace of love; it issues out of it (Gal. v. 22).   And because it issues out of love, it is enjoined upon us as our duty as well as our highest privilege; for " the first of all the commandments is this, Thou shalt love the Lord thy God ; " and a corollary of that first command- ment is, " Rejoice in the Lord alway ; and again I say, Rejoice " (Phil. iv. 4).   Among earthly delights the pure love of wedlock is, as the king says, the fairest and the most pleasant; and of all highest joys that the human soul can attain unto, the supreme, the transcendent joy, comes from the holy love of God.   2. *His praise of the bride.* He compares her to a palm tree, to a vine.   Both are fair to look upon, both have sacred associations.   The image of the vine recalls to our thoughts the holy allegory in John xv.   The Saviour is the true Vine; his people are the branches.   They must bring forth fruit, for the branch that beareth not fruit is taken away ; and in order to bear fruit they must abide in him, in spiritual union with the Lord, who is the Life. The palm tree also occurs in Scripture imagery : " The righteous shall flourish like the palm tree " (Ps. xcii. 12).   Several characteristics make the palm tree an apt emblem of the faithful servant of God.   There is its tall and graceful appearance, its evergreen foliage, its fruitfulness, and perhaps especially the fact that both fronds and fruit grow at the topmost height of the tree, high above the earth and as near as possible to heaven.   An apt illustration by St. Gregory the Great ('Moral.,' on Job xix. 49) is quoted in Smith's ' Dictionary of the Bible:' " Well is the life of the righteous likened to a palm, in that the palm below is rough to the touch, and in a manner enveloped in dry bark, but above it is adorned with fruit fair even to the eye; below, it is compressed by the enfoldings of its bark ; above, it is spread out in amplitude of beautiful greenness.   For so is the life of the elect, despised below, beautiful above. Down below it is, as it were, enfolded in many barks, in that it is straitened by innumerable afflictions ; but on high it is expanded into a foliage, as it were, of beau- tiful greenness by the amplitude of the rewarding." 3. *The bride continues the bride- groom's words.* " I said, I will go up to the palm tree, I will take hold of the boughs thereof."   These words have been regarded by some commentators as spoken by the bride.   In the next verse certainly the bride interrupts the bridegroom and finishes his sentence.   It may well be that here also she corrects the similitude of the bride- groom, and applies it to him rather than to herself; the words, " I said," seem perhaps to favour this view, and to suggest a different speaker.   The bridegroom is the palm tree rather than the bride ; she modestly and humbly transfers the similitude to him. The palm tree resembles the king in its lofty stateliness and beauty.   And certainly this view best lends itself to spiritual applications.   The palm tree to the Christian represents the cross.   We think of St. Peter's words, " His own self bare our sins in his own body on the tree " (1 Pet. ii. 24).   We remember the old traditional reading of Ps. xcvi. 10, " The Lord hath reigned from the tree."   We recall his own words, " I, if I be lifted up from the earth, will draw all men unto me " (John xii. 32).   The Lord reigned from the tree; above him was the title, " This is Jesus, the King of the Jews."   He is the King of the true Israelites, the Israel of God.   And the cross is the throne of his triumph ; it displays, as nothing else could do, the Divine glory of holiness and entire self-sacrifice and self-forgetting love, which are the kingly orna- ments of the Saviour's lofty dignity.   The Saviour's precious death has made the cross a thing most sacred, most awe-inspiring, most dear to Christian souls, most constraining in the power of its Divine attraction.   It draws around itself all the elect of God, all who have ears to hear and hearts to feel the blessed love of Christ.   All such say in their hearts, " I will go up to the palm tree, I will take hold of the boughs thereof."   The first words, " I said," seem to remind us of many faithless promises, of many broken resolutions. It is easy to say, very hard to persevere in bearing the cross. How often we have promised, at our baptism, at our confirmation, in the Holy Communion, in the hour of private prayer and self-examination—how often we have said, "I will go up"! But the ascent is steep and difficult; the palm tree is high, there are no branches to assist the climber; the fruit is at the very top, high out of our reach; there is need of effort, continued persevering effort—effort sometimes very hard and painful to flesh and blood. But we must lift up our hearts, we must look upward. The Lord was lifted up, and his disciples must follow him; they know the way (John xiv. 4). We must set him ever before us, and think of his agony and bloody sweat, his cross and Passion, when we are tempted to regard the cross as hard and painful, and to relax our efforts in the religious life. We must go up. God's saints have gone before us.

> "They climbed the steep ascent of heaven
> Through peril, toil, and pain."

We must do the like; "we must through much tribulation enter into the kingdom" of God. And if we would persevere in well-doing we must go up to the cross of the Lord Jesus; it is only there, in spiritual communion with the crucified Saviour, in his strength which strengthens all who trust in him, through a living and true faith in him, that the Christian can find strength to bear the burden of the cross. It is a heavy burden to flesh and blood, but the Lord makes it light to all who come to him in obedience to his gracious invitation. For he gives to his chosen power to become the sons of God; he strengthens them with all might by his Spirit in the inner man; he bids them cast their burden upon him (Ps. lv. 22), he bears it with them. But they must go up to the palm tree; they may have many times said they will do so, and perhaps many times have failed. They must go up with sustained effort. The Lord, indeed, draws us, but it is by the attraction of love and the motions of his Spirit, not by forcing our will. We must go up, yielding up our will to him, asking him to give us grace to pray aright that holy prayer, "Not my will, but thine be done." And we must take hold of the boughs thereof, clinging to them with the embrace of loving faith. It is not enough once to go up to the tree; the Lord himself has taught us our need of continual perseverance: "Abide in me, and I in you." We must take hold of him with the earnest prayer of Jacob, "I will not let thee go except thou bless me." And we must learn of him who endured the cross for us to take up the cross ourselves, to crucify the flesh with the affections and lusts, so that, like St. Paul, we may be crucified with Christ, and, dying unto the world, may ever live with him. We may well take to ourselves the words which tradition puts into the mouth of St. Andrew when he first saw the cross on which he was to suffer, "Hail, precious cross, that hast been consecrated by the body of my Lord! I come to thee; receive me into thy arms, take me from among men, and present me to my Master, that he who redeemed me on thee may receive me by thee." The cross goeth before the crown. We must go up to the tree, and that with pains and striving, before we can reach the fronds at the summit. They are the prize of victory. The great multitude that no man could number stood before the throne clothed with white robes, and palms in their hands. That blessed vision may, indeed, be understood as a vision of the true Feast of Tabernacles in heaven; but the palm has ever been regarded as the martyr's prize; we must look upwards to it. "Brethren, I count not myself to have apprehended: but this one thing I do, forgetting those things that are behind, and reaching forth unto those things which are before, I press toward the mark for the prize of the high calling of God in Christ Jesus" (Phil. iii. 13, 14).

4. *The bridegroom continues his praises.* He repeats the comparison of the vine, and adds that the breath of the bride is fragrant as the smell of the choicest fruits, and the tones of her voice sweet as the best wine. Here the bride interrupts the king, adding the words, "that goeth down smoothly for my beloved." We mark the loving controversy; each seeks to put the other first. If the king compares the bride to a palm tree, she stops him with the answer that he is to her the stately tree; she will go up to the palm tree, she will take hold of its boughs. If he compares her voice to the flavour of the sweetest wine, she adds, interrupting him, that that wine is for her beloved, to please and refresh him with its sweetness; her joy is to feel that

she is wholly his, to delight in his love, to try always to please him. It is a sweet picture of the happiness of wedded love, when each seeks to please the other, when each puts the other first. Then Christian marriage is indeed a holy estate, a great help in the religious life, representing to the wedded pair the union that is between Christ and his Church, so that having in their own mutual relations a parable of that holy union, they may be drawn continually nearer to Christ, as they learn continually to love one another with a purer and deeper love, and in their daily self-denials for the loved one's sake find how blessed is self-sacrifice for his sake who loved us and gave himself for us.

II. THE BRIDE'S ANSWER. 1. *The mutual love that binds them together.* She repeats the assertion of ch. ii. 16; vi. 3. As in ch. vi. 3, she puts first her own gift, the gift of her whole heart, to her beloved. She knows now, with a confident and happy knowledge, that her heart is his. Perhaps at first there had been some coyness, some hesitations, some doubts; now there is none. She has given her heart, and she knows it. She dwells on the happy truth; she rejoices in repeating it. Blessed is the Christian soul that can say the like, "I am my Beloved's," "I am Christ's." Blessed above all others are they who can say in sincerity that they have given him their whole heart; that they desire only him, his presence, his love; that their one highest hope is to please him better, to live nearer and nearer to him, and at length to see him face to face. Such, in the ancient times, was the hope of the Psalmist Asaph. "Whom have I in heaven but thee? and there is none upon the earth that I desire beside thee. My flesh and my heart faileth: but God is the Strength of my heart, and my Portion for ever" (Ps. lxxiii. 25, 26). And the bride is sure of the bridegroom's love: "his desire is towards me." She is as sure that his heart is hers as that hers is his. She applies to him the Divine words of Gen. iii. 16. As Eve's desire was to her husband, so now the king's desire was toward his bride. The heavenly Bridegroom loved the Church; his desire is toward his people; their salvation was the joy set before him, for which he endured the cross. He said to his little flock, "With desire I have desired to eat this Passover with you before I suffer" (Luke xxii. 15). His desire is toward his bride, that she may be washed and cleansed, that he may in his own good time present her to himself a glorious Church, holy and without blemish (Eph. v. 25—27). 2. *The bride's invitation.* The king had invited her to his royal city at the time of their espousals. "Come with me from Lebanon, my spouse" (ch. iv. 8). She seems here to be inviting the king to visit in her company her old home, the scene of her labours in the vineyards. "Come, my beloved," she says, "let us go forth into the field." So the heavenly Bridegroom calls to himself the souls whom he so dearly loved: "Come unto me, and I will give you rest;" so the Christian, in answer to the Lord's gracious invitation, responds, "Even so come, Lord Jesus." He bids us come to him, and as we come we pray him to come to us, for without him we can do nothing; we cannot come unless he draws us by himself coming to us (John vi. 44; xii. 32). We pray him, "Let us go forth into the field, let us get up early to the vineyards;" for we need his presence always; we cannot do the work which he has given us to do; we cannot work in his vineyard as he bids us without his help. Therefore we ask him to be with us always, according to his gracious promise, "Lo, I am with you all the days, even to the end" (Matt. xxviii. 20); that we may have grace to get up early to the vineyards, not to stand all the day idle, not to wait to the eleventh hour, but to give the best of our life to God, to remember our Creator in the days of our youth, to do with our might whatsoever our hand findeth to do (Eccles. ix. 10). The word here rendered "get up early" is several times figuratively used for "to be earnest or urgent." God calls us to work, to labour for his Name's sake, but not to leave our first love, like the Church at Ephesus (Rev. ii. 3, 4); to work out our salvation with fear and trembling, but all the time to ask him to come and help us, and to remember that it is he who worketh in us both to will and to do of his good pleasure (Phil. ii. 13); for without that inward work of his within our souls we can do no acceptable work for him. But work we must, for he bids us; and it is in that work, wrought ever in faith and in dependence upon him, that the Christian soul keeps itself in the love of God (Jude 21). So the bride says, "There [in the vineyard] will I give thee my loves." It is in working for God that we prove our love for him. "Lovest thou me?" the Saviour said; then "feed my lambs, feed my sheep." "If ye love me, keep my commandments."

Then he will pray for us, sending the gracious Spirit, the Comforter, to strengthen and to help us; then, he promises, he will come himself. " I will not leave you comfortless: I will come to you " (John xiv. 15—18). Then the blessed Spirit will help us to bring forth the fruit of the Spirit—the fruit which is " love, joy, peace, long-suffering, gentleness, faith, meekness, temperance "—that like the bride in the song we may have " all manner of pleasant fruits, new and old,' and may add, in her words, "which I have laid up for thee, O my Beloved." These fruits are treasures laid up in heaven, and we know that he is able to keep that which we have committed unto him against that day (2 Tim. i. 12).

HOMILIES BY VARIOUS AUTHORS.

Vers. 10—13.—*Christian missions.* " I am my beloved's," etc. The scene is still in " the king's chambers " at Jerusalem. What Solomon has said to her whom he would win is of no avail; her heart is true to her beloved. This emphatic redeclaration of her love for that beloved one is all the response that the king's flatteries have obtained. She speaks as if she were already away from the palace and back at her country home; once more occupied in her usual occupations and enjoying her former happy intercourse with her beloved. But the going forth to her work suggests the idea of going forth in spiritual work, and the language she uses points to the manner in which such work may be successfully done. We may take the section as an allegory concerning Christian missions. It suggests—

I. WHAT PROMPTS THEM. (Ver. 10.) The profound and delightful realization of Christ's love towards and within us. Such work, if done only because we are afraid of the judgment-day, when we all must give account of our stewardship; or from mere sense of duty; still less when the motive is ecclesiastical ambition; or even when pity for the ignorance and general sad condition of the heathen is the motive;—all such promptings have but partial, some very partial, power. The true motive is that which the rapturous expression of ver. 10 reveals—

II. HOW THEY SHOULD BE CARRIED ON. " Come, my Beloved, let us," etc. 1. *The presence of Christ should be invoked.* (Ver. 11.) " Let *us* go forth," etc. Then: 2. *There should be the going forth.* Away from accustomed haunts, away from the place of ordinances and privileges, to where none of these things are enjoyed. 3. *With diligence.* " Let us rise early " (ver. 12). 4. *With watchfulness,* not alone in planting, but for growth and progress.

III. THEIR TRUE NATURE. (Ver. 12.) " There will I give thee, " etc. They are an acceptable offering of our love to Christ and its true manifestation. A love to Christ that is not expansive, that does not go forth to bless others, is no true love, but something very different (1 Cor. xv. 10).

IV. THEY SHALL BE REWARDED WITH DELIGHTFUL SUCCESS. (Ver. 13.) May not the lack of this—though, indeed, it is not entirely absent—be owing to some grave defect in motive or manner?

V. ALL THE GLORY WILL BE RENDERED TO CHRIST. " Which I have laid up *for thee.*" (Ver. 13.) Cf. the account of the first missionary meeting and report (Acts xiv. 27).—S. C.

Ver. 10.—" *I am my beloved's.*" (Cf. on ch. ii. 16).—S. C.

Vers. 11—13.—*Useful service.* Earth is a great picture-gallery, full of illustrations of heavenly things. This material universe is the projection of God's thoughts; the visible expression of his dispositions; the blossoming of his love. The God of nature is the God of religion; hence the same lessons appear in both. As we have seen in the home of a great artist the handiworks of his genius adorning parlours and halls, corridors and bed-chambers—works in all stages of development—so is it in God's world. Pictures of him abound. Every garden is a lesson-book for humanity; every well-kept garden is a portrait of a saint; every fruitful vineyard is an emblem of Christ's Church. Said the Prophet Isaiah to the godly man, " Thou shalt be as a well-watered garden." " My Well-beloved hath a vineyard in a very fruitful hill." The highest fruitfulness is the result of patient culture. Prosperity is threatened by many foes. Human agency must co-operate with Divine power in order "to bring forth fruit unto perfection." Every flower and blossom is an outburst of God's glory. Earth is crammed full of heavenly things.

I. IN ALL HOLY SERVICE THE MOTIVE POWER IS LOVE. "Come, my beloved." Thus Jesus speaks. 1. *God's works spring from love.* We cannot conceive any other reason why the eternal God should have begun to create, unless that happiness and love might be multiplied. Love would not permit him to keep all good within himself. Love impelled him to produce various orders of sentient life. His joy is increased by witnessing the joys of others.

> " Yes, he has gemmed with worlds the abyss,
> Filled them with beauty, life, and bliss,
> Only the wider to dispense
> The gifts of his beneficence.
> Oh yes! creation planned above
>   Was but for mercy's stream a vent,
> The outgushings of eternal love—
>   Ay, this is love's embodiment."

2. *This love in us springs from our assurance of Christ's love.* The love that is fruitful in service realizes the personal friendship of Christ. If I am tormented with doubts touching my acceptance by Christ, I shall have no energy for service. I have only a limited capacity of power, and if I expend this in solving difficult questions, or in calming my own fears, I shall be unfit for service. If the Master is saying to me, "Son, go work to-day in my vineyard," and if I reply, "Lord, I know not if I be a son," I shall not accomplish any good. But when I know that I am "accepted in the Beloved," there is a mainspring of love within that stirs all the energies of my soul. Then my daily prayer will be, "Lord, what wilt thou have me to do?" Then, "the love of Christ constraineth me." "For to me to live is Christ." It would be a painful restraint on my new nature if I did not render him service. Then his "service is perfect freedom." 3. *True love hears Immanuel's voice.* "Come, my beloved." Love moves into healthful activity every organ. It not only gives activity to the feet; it gives sensitiveness to the ear. The voice of Christ is not addressed to the bodily organ; it is addressed to the soul. It is a spiritual communication; a "still small voice." As in the days of his flesh the multitude did not understand the speech that came from heaven—"I have both glorified it, and will glorify it again;" they thought that it thundered, or that an angel spake; so is it still. The Christian hears a voice that no one else can hear. The passing crowd may hear a faint hum, as the wind passes through the telegraphic wires, but the message conveyed through the wire is understood only by the person trained to receive it. So the voice of heavenly authority and the voice of heavenly friendship is heard only by wakeful, tender love. 4. *Love craves to give itself expression.* Love is an expansive power. It is a law of its nature to spread; to go out in practical forms. Like the force of steam, it cannot be held in restraint. The hotter steam becomes, the more it expands. The present motive power in commerce, and in swift locomotion, results from the expansive power of steam. So all human philanthropy and all missionary enterprise are the outcome of fervent love. It would be painful to love if no service were permitted. She is girt and sandalled, waiting to scale rugged mountains, waiting to cross tempestuous seas, waiting to traverse perilous deserts, in order to tell the perishing that Jesus can save. Love never wearies. Service is her delight. There is within an irresistible instinct to do good.

II. IN HOLY SERVICE WE HAVE DIVINE COMPANIONSHIP. "Let us go, . . . let us lodge." 1. *This is a real experience.* To many persons the presence of Christ is a fiction; it may be a part of their creed, nothing more. They read of it as a promise, but they have never realized it. Yet they may. For on the part of a faithful servant of Christ his presence is a real enjoyment. Every inspiration of benevolent desire is from him. He talks with us by the way. We ask for strength, and he gives it. We lack courage, and he supplies it abundantly. He makes our dumb lips eloquent. As truly as we hold intercourse with an earthly friend—yea, more truly—do we have real and joyous intercourse with Jesus. If he spake the promise, "Lo, I am with you alway," certainly he will fulfil it. Why should he not? Is anything too hard for him to accomplish? Some imagine that the real presence of Christ is to be found only in the sacrament of the Supper. This is a delusion. His real presence is ever in the spiritual temple, *i.e.* in the temple of a Christian's heart. Saith he, "I will never leave thee, I will never forsake thee;" so that we may boldly say, "The Lord is my Helper." 2. *This companionship with Jesus is a real honour.* When, in olden time, the King of England went out in person to war, every peer in the realm counted it an honour to go with him. It was dishonourable to stay at home. Every duke and earl would rather dwell amid hardship and danger on the battle-field, if the king were there, than amid the luxuries of their own castle-halls. To be near the person of the king was counted high honour. Yet this honour was as nothing—an empty bubble—compared with companion-ship with Jesus Christ. To be companion with the King of heaven is real honour and real advantage. It is Christ alone who can teach us what honour is. Honour is insepar-able from righteousness, and he is Perfect Righteousness. And Christ is a Worker. He is the good Shepherd, ever going out in search of lost sheep; so, if we wish to have companionship with Jesus, we must be workers too. Service is honourable. It is in service that we shall find Christ nearest us. There is a legend of a pious monk in the Middle Ages, who had a vision of the Saviour. The man was ravished with holy joy. It was a season of hallowed communion with his Lord. At that moment the bell rang, and it was the duty of this monk to distribute food to the poor. There was a struggle in his mind. Should he leave this vision, and break up this sweet fellow-ship? The bell called him to a sacred duty, and he responded and went. At the end of an hour he returned, and lo! the vision was still there. Then the lips of the Master moved, and he said, "Unless thou hadst fulfilled thy call of duty, I had departed." If Jesus is with us, almighty strength is assured. Unerring wisdom is ours; sweetest sympathy cheers us; certain success is in sight. "I will go in the strength of the Lord God."

III. IN HOLY SERVICE THERE WILL BE SELF-DENIAL. "Let us go forth into the field; let us lodge in the villages; let us get up early to the vineyards." Now, this language does not seem natural or customary in the lips of an earthly king. But it is natural and seemly in the lips of the Prince of heaven. For it is his delight to humble himself, and to become the Servant of all. 1. *Discomfort and hardship are foretold.* "Let us go into the field." Jesus is very frank and outspoken. Not on any account will he hide from us the hard conditions of his service. Plainly did he tell his first disciples what toils and persecutions they would have to endure. And the Word still abides, "They that will live godly in Christ Jesus must suffer persecu-tion." Paul was forewarned of the perils that awaited him in every city. But the real friend of Jesus is prepared for self-denial. Apart from self-denial, his service would not be like the service of Jesus. "The disciple is not greater than his Master, nor the servant than his Lord." The Son of God says to us, "Let us go forth into the field." We must leave for a time the fair palaces of our Prince, and lodge in narrow tenements. Yet is there any ground for lamentation? Any roof which covers us, however humble, shall be a palace of delight if only Christ be with us there. The palace does not make the dweller therein a king; but the presence of the King makes the house a palace. Difficulties and self-denials will be quietly borne if we are on Christ's errands. Yea, they will be welcome, if love to Jesus prevail. "They have put me," said Rutherford, "into a prison; but Immanuel came and made it into a banquet-house." Yes, if Jesus come with us into our lowly cottage, forthwith "the doors shall be pearls, and the windows agates," and the fence shall be made of all kinds of precious stones. 2. *We shall be willing to continue in this self-denying work.* "Let us lodge in the villages." We must not grow weary in this well-doing. Many a man will rouse his courage to face some herculean task or to fight in some sharp conflict, who will yet faint under the weariness of a long campaign or fail in patient endurance. The service to which Jesus calls us is lifelong, and the discomfort may be long continued. Still, we will embrace it with joy. "He that endureth to the end, the same shall be saved." The Christian missionary who goes into a foreign field to sow the heavenly seed, must be prepared for long-continued sacrifice. So should every true servant of the King. For self-denial is not long-continued pain. The joy of pleasing Christ, and the blessedness of his company, nullifies the pain and overcomes the discomfort. Soon the self-denial loses its sting. The loss becomes a gain, and every thorn blossoms into a rose. "Out of the eater comes forth meat, and out of the bitter comes forth sweetness." The love of Christ changes everything. It makes our hell into heaven. 3. *There will even be eagerness for this arduous work.* "Let us get up early to the vineyards." To enter upon this hard toil in company with Jesus, we shall be ready to forego comfortable sleep. Soon as morn breaks, soon as the opportunity allows, we shall be ready to leap forth to the task. Our old inclinations are overcome and supplanted with new desires and new endeavours. We are burning with ardour to show Jesus our love. We shall feel ashamed if our zeal does not in some measure resemble the zeal of our Immanuel. He was consumed with holy and intensest ardour to do us good. Said he, "How am I straitened till it be accomplished!" He panted to reach the cross. And now he has commissioned us to take his place and to carry out his work. As his Father had sent him into the world, so has he sent us. His love is to be perpetuated through us. His devotion to humanity must reappear in us. His self-consuming zeal must glow in our breasts. As he could not represent among men the everlasting love of his Father except by incessant toil, humiliating suffering, and a death of public shame, so neither can we adequately represent the saving grace of Christ before men except by enthusiastic zeal and completest consecration. There will be a constant watchfulness for every opportunity of service. To do Christ's work will be our meat and our drink. A principle of sacred earnestness must possess us. As the hallowed fire on the temple-altar was not allowed to expire, so must not the fire of holy zeal ever expire on the altar of our hearts. "We are not our own;" we belong to another; "we are bought with a price;" therefore duty demands that we glorify our Master "with our bodies and with our spirits, which are his."

IV. IN HOLY SERVICE THERE IS GREAT VARIETY OF USEFULNESS. "Let us see if the vine flourish, whether the tender grape appear, and the pomegranates bud forth." 1. *Christ's work is the pattern of ours.* The work of Jesus among men was manifold. He opened blind eyes, unstopped deaf ears, straightened paralyzed limbs, fed the hungry, brought the dead back to life, pardoned men's sins, purified corrupt and vicious lives, led the erring into light. We dwell in the same world in which Christ dwelt. We are encompassed with suffering humanity. We have the same motives for labour. Here there is scope for every capacity. If you cannot preach to great assemblies, you can speak to a wayfarer for Christ. If you cannot vindicate the truth against the assaults of the scoffer, you can feed a hungry child, or console a sorrowing widow, or visit the bedridden, or pray for the outcasts. The youngest disciple may find something to do for Christ's kingdom in this world of sin and suffering. "As ye have opportunity, do good unto all men;" "Freely ye have received, freely give." In nature each drop of falling rain produces a distinct effect, so in the kingdom of Christ a cup of cold water given to a thirsty child obtains its reward. 2. *Concern for the young is here suggested.* "Whether the tender grape appear." Every living Church will have special agencies to gain the young. They have special claims on us. The heart is as yet unoccupied. Character is plastic. Feeling is fresh. There is eager inquiry after the truth. Labour among the young is full of promise. In the young Jesus Christ feels special interest. Every parent should see to it that their children's hearts are opening to Christ. We ought to see conversion to God very early. If faith be the great essential, then very early do children put faith in a parent or in a friend, and such faith they can as readily place in Jesus the Saviour. Parents have special promises from God to encourage their hope. "I will pour my Spirit upon thy seed, and my blessing upon thy offspring." Jesus has special love for the lambs in the flock.

> "The flower, when offered in the bud,
> Is no vain sacrifice."

3. *Pious care for all inquirers is indicated.* "Let us see whether the pomegranates bud forth." It is a hopeful sign of grace when one is inquiring after the light. Already there is a stir in that dead soul. The deep sleep of sin is broken. The man is awaking. Possibly, like some inveterate sluggard, he may turn over on the other side, and fall into deeper sleep than before. Such a thing often happens, both in nature and in grace. *Now* is our opportunity while he is half awake. *Now*

let the alarm-bell of the gospel sound in his ear.   Such methods as true wisdom and love can devise should be vigorously employed.   How precious is the moment! Anon it will have fled.   There is much to be done.   Impression has to be made, instruction given, feeling aroused, conviction wrought, desire excited, resolution taken. Every inquirer after God should be sought out—should be the object of the Christian's concern.

V. IN HOLY SERVICE THERE IS A PRESENT REWARD.   "The mandrakes give a smell, and at our gates are all manner of pleasant fruits, new and old."   1. *The reward is the outcome of natural law.*   As the fruit is already in embryo in the seed, so is reward already in the service, though as yet undeveloped.   As hell is the ripe fruit of sin, so heaven is the ripe fruit of holy service.   The faithful steward of ten talents shall have ten talents more entrusted to him: this is his reward.   The pleasant fruits of the garden shall be the reward of the faithful husbandman.   Such fruits are "old and new."   Others preceding us have sown good seed, done noble work in the vineyard. We enter upon the results, and gather in the fruits.   Old fruit at times is preferable to new.   Apples and nuts mellow with age.   So the ripe wisdom of old saints is a spiritual banquet.   The promises given to Abraham have a good flavour.   The faith that has been of long standing—the faith of Elijah and Paul, *e.g.*—is a very pleasant fruit, while fresh zeal and fresh courage are equally delightful.   "Fruits old and new." 2. *God's provision for us is ample.*   If we go diligently about our Master's work, be sure that he will provide.   He had said, "Let us get up early, and go forth into the vineyards;" and lo! when noon came and hunger looked for a meal, here at the gate was a royal provision.   So Jesus taught his first disciples, that if they attended to his business he would take the responsibility for their wants.   He gave to Peter and his comrades a miraculous draught of fishes; then he said, "Feed my sheep;" "Go into all the world, and preach the gospel;" "My God shall supply all your need, out of his riches in glory by Jesus Christ."   3. *Jesus provides a reward suitable to every taste.* "All manner of pleasant fruits, new and old, which I have laid up for thee."   When our Immanuel spreads for us a banquet, nothing shall be wanting.   Is there a fruit anywhere in God's universe that will meet a want of mine or satisfy a longing?   It shall be given me.   "He will give thee the desires of thy heart;" "In his garden is all manner of pleasant fruit."   4. *Present rewards are the pledge of greater.*   These fruits are found "at our gates."   It is as if our Immanuel had said, "This is only the beginning of good.   There's more to follow."   And this is most assuredly true.   Present possessions are only pledges and earnests of higher and richer good.   The love of Christ in the heart is an entrancing joy, but I shall have a larger experience of it by-and-by.   These attainments of piety and excellence are "treasures of the kingdom," but I shall grow richer yet.   My knowledge of God in Christ is a precious possession, but the "half has not been told me."   Jesus has many things to reveal to me, but I cannot bear them yet.   No! "Eye hath not seen, nor hath ear heard, nor has it entered into the heart of man, what God has prepared for them that love him."

VI. IN HOLY SERVICE WE GAIN FULLEST ASSURANCES OF IMMANUEL'S LOVE.   "There will I give thee my love-presents."   Toward the close of his ministry Jesus said to his disciples, "He that keepeth my commandments, he it is that loveth me; and he that loveth me shall be loved of my Father, and we will come unto him, and will make our abode with him."   This is the love-token, or the love-present, which our Immanuel gives us, viz. his abiding presence in our hearts—the sunshine of his love.   The idler in God's vineyard need never be surprised if he lack the full assurance of his sonship.   It had never been promised him.   To give this love-present to such a one would be a premium upon indolence.   Mark that it is in the field of service that Jesus gives his love-tokens.   It is to earnest and faithful labourers he confers the full assurance of hope.   The consensus of observation testifies that in seasons of apathy and slothfulness we lose the assurance of heaven.   But when we run with alacrity in the path of service, then heaven opens to us, and we read our title clear.   Is it a real joy to us when we look into the face of an earthly friend and realize his tender sympathy? Must it not be a greater joy to look into the face of Jesus and feel that he is our Brother?   Do the minstrels of the woods pour out a fresh tide of song when the genial sun of May shines upon them?   And when we come into the warm sunshine of Immanuel's love, and know that he has made with us an everlasting covenant, shall not our hearts be all aglow with joy? For nothing on earth is more sure than *this*, that if I give my whole self unreservedly to Jesus, he has impelled me to do it, and upon me he confers the wealth of his eternal friendship. "My Beloved is mine, and I am his."—D.

Ver. 6.—*The fairness of love.* The commendations of the bride's beauty, which occur in the early verses of this chapter, lead up to the exclamation—so much in harmony with the whole spirit of the Canticles—concerning the fairness, the pleasantness, the delightsomeness, of true love.

I. THE BEAUTY AND GOOD SERVICE OF LOVE, AS A SENTIMENT IN THE HUMAN HEART AND AS A BOND IN HUMAN SOCIETY. As distinguished from mere carnal passion, that conjugal love which is pictured as subsisting between the king and his spouse is justly in this Song of Songs represented as of the purest and highest excellence. It is true that religion and morality put a restraint upon the natural impulses, and the Bible abounds with warnings against yielding to the temptations which are favoured by human nature and by sinful society. But if the way of virtue be a narrow way, it is not without flowers by its borders, both fair and fragrant. The path of self-government and self-denial is a path which has pleasures of its own. And one aim of this Book of Canticles, one justification for its place in canonical Scripture, appears to be its effective depicting of the pure joys of human affection. Where marriage is the result of personal preference and sincere attachment, and where it is entered upon under the guidance of sober reason and forethought, it may well be expected to yield delights. Toil, anxieties, mutual forbearance and self-sacrifice, the endurance in common of life's cares and sorrows, so far from extinguishing love, may refine and hallow it. And maturity of character and spiritual discipline and strength will prove more than a compensation for the abandonment of the "primrose path" of pleasure, in which the unspiritual find their joys. The family and the home are the scene and the embodiment of wedded love. And they are the very basis of human society, the condition and means of true human progress, the earnest of a higher state of Christian civilization in the future.

II. HUMAN LOVE IS THE EMBLEM OF THE DIVINE LOVE WHICH UNITES THE SOUL AND THE SAVIOUR, AND WHICH IS THE SOURCE OF SPIRITUAL AND HEAVENLY JOYS. The highest purpose of that affinity which binds heart to heart is to elicit emotions, and to lead to relations with which our highest welfare here and hereafter is associated. They who read this Book of Canticles without recognizing the divinely appointed connection in question miss not only a literary charm, but a spiritual truth and law. It is to be feared that in the view of some, human love, such as should exist between husband and wife, appears a profane and common, if not a foolish, thing. But God is not honoured by the disparagement of his own provisions and plans. If he has made love so important a factor in human life, he has done so, we may be sure, with a purpose worthy of himself, his wisdom, and grace. As earthly love is elevated and purified by the Divine discipline of this earthly existence, it comes to symbolize, with ever-growing force, the profound affection which subsists between Christ and his Church. And this significance is recognized in the language of St. Paul and St. John regarding the bride and spouse of the Saviour. With reference to the emotions which are cherished by Christ towards his chosen and beloved people, and by his people towards him to whom they are indebted for all they have and for all they hope for, how appropriate is the exclamation, "How fair and how pleasant art thou, O love, for delights!" Divine love is the source of Divine joy. It is immortal love which is the earnest of "pleasures for evermore."—T.

Ver. 9.—*The sweetness of speech.* The figurative language here employed by the royal lover to eulogize the voice and the utterances of the bride is to our colder and more measured habits of thought Oriental extravagance. Yet it is in harmony with the highly coloured character of the book as a whole. And human speech does often awaken within the heart emotions not easily expressed in cool and justifiable panegyric. The human voice is of all music the sweetest, and speech is sweeter even than song, uttering as it does, not the studied and artificial sentiment of the musical composer, but the spontaneous and natural emotions of the speaker's heart.

I. CHRISTIAN SPEECH IS SWEET AS TESTIFYING TO THE CHARACTER OF THE SPEAKER.
1. Sincerity is the first condition of all acceptable speech; it is above all things desirable that there should be no discordance between the utterance and the heart. The flatterer at court and in general society speaks only to please; and in the case of those who know his aim and his motives, he fails of the very object he has in view. The Church is bound to speak "words of truth and soberness," as remembering the sacredness of the gift of utterance, and the responsibility attaching to its exercise. To a just mind sincere words are welcome, even though they be less honeyed than the words of the time-server and men-pleaser. 2. Love prompts to words which are a delight to hear. Whilst the tones of hatred are harsh, and the utterances of coldness are repugnant, kindness, sympathy, affection, give a sweetness to every utterance. Welcome as the words which come from the heart of the beloved, telling of the depth of unchangeable affection, are those Christian declarations in which the Church gives expression to her love for her Saviour and her pity for the world.

II. CHRISTIAN SPEECH IS SWEET WHEN IT TESTIFIES TO THE LOVE AND FAITHFULNESS OF THE LORD. There is no exercise more congenial to Christ's people, more acceptable to Christ himself, than this. The powers of speech cannot be more holily and honourably employed than in uttering forth the high praises of God, in lauding and magnifying the redeeming love of Christ. The hymn which is lisped by the little child, the anthem which rings through the cathedral aisles, the quiet word of witness in which the friend commends the Saviour to him who is dear to his heart,—these are but some of the forms in which language may show forth the greatness, the goodness, the wisdom, of the Eternal. What theme so worthy of the tongue, " the glory of the frame," as this? The voice of praise and thanksgiving is dear to the heart alike of God and man.

III. CHRISTIAN SPEECH IS SWEET WHEN UTTERING TESTIMONY TO THE GOSPEL OF GOD'S LOVE. Men's hearts have to be reached and to be affected by the tidings of Divine mercy and compassion. It is most condescending and gracious on God's part that he deigns to employ human agency in the service of his own Divine beneficence. If men avail themselves of all the resources of human rhetoric in order to obtain earthly ends—power, wealth, and fame—how much more ready should they be to use all the faculties they possess, all the arts and means they can acquire, to bring before their fellow-men the tidings of heavenly and immortal love! Well may every preacher and every teacher of Divine truth put up the prayer—

" Jesus, confirm my heart's desire,
To work, to think, to *speak* for thee:
Still let me guard the holy fire,
And still stir up thy gift in me ! "

T.

Ver. 10.—*The desire of the beloved.* The assurance of mutual possession and affection occurs in an earlier part of the poem; but its repetition here is not without significance. Love has not lessened as time has passed; it has rather deepened, as experience has revealed, to each of the married lovers, the faithfulness and kindness, the purity and devotion, of the other. Hence the bride adds to this later exclamation, "I am my beloved's," the statement which is the expression of experience, " His desire is toward me." Transferring the language to the relations and sentiments distinctive of the mutual attachment of Christ and his people, we observe here a declaration—

I. OF THE GOOD WILL AND COMPASSIONATE AFFECTION OF CHRIST FOR HIS CHURCH.
1. The Lord takes a deep satisfaction in his people, and regards them with a holy complacency. 2. He desires that they should participate in his character and reflect his image. Spiritual fellowship with him tends to bring about this result, than which nothing can be more to the mind of the Head of the Church. 3. He desires that they may be qualified witnesses to himself, and agents in promoting his cause and glory upon earth. And this, for his own sake indeed, yet also for the Church's sake, and for the sake of the world for whose salvation he lived and died on earth.

II. OF THE RESPONSE OF THE CHURCH, HER SURRENDER OF HERSELF COMPLETELY TO HER SPOUSE AND LORD. This attitude of heart has been beautifully expressed in these words: "I attach myself to God, I give myself to him; and he turns to me immediately; his eyes look upon me with favour; his Spirit is attentive to my good; his great heart bows itself and stoops to my nothingness; he unites his heart to mine; he heaps upon it new graces, to attach it more strongly to him. Devote thyself, O my soul, wholly to thy God." 1. Spiritual receptiveness is the just response to Divine desire. If it is the will and pleasure of the Saviour to take possession of the whole nature and life of his people, it is equally their will and pleasure to abandon all other aims in life, and to devote themselves to this, with the view of becoming his only, his altogether, and his for ever. 2. Spiritual consecration completes this just response. Human nature is not merely passive; it is energetic. Human life is an opportunity, not only for getting, but for giving. The Church must indeed receive from the Divine Head every qualification which can fit for the discharge of duty, for the rendering of service. But it is hers to prove her gratitude and her fidelity to the trust reposed in her, by devoting herself to those high ends with a view to which she has been chosen, loved, and redeemed.—T.

Vers. 11, 12.—*Divine companionship.* Man was made, not for solitude, but for society; not for selfishness, but for love. This principle of human nature and life is taken up by religion, and is employed for man's highest, spiritual, immortal interests. The soul which yields itself to Christ delights in his fellowship, and finds therein its true satisfaction. Like the bride who is represented in this poem as saying to her spouse, "Come, my beloved, let us go forth into the field," etc., the soul craves the society of the Saviour, and longs for his perpetual companionship.

I. THE NATURE OF THIS COMPANIONSHIP. 1. It is companionship to which Christ invites his people. None could address him thus unless first assured of the Lord's interest, friendliness, and love. 2. It is spiritual companionship. The twelve who were with him in his earthly ministry were admitted to close, delightful, and profitable intimacy. They saw his form and heard his voice. Yet, in our case, though we cannot perceive him as they did, the association is equally real; for he is with his people alway. 3. It is companionship in which he is the superior, and we are the dependent. It is true he says, "Abide in me, and I in you;" but he is the Vine, and we the branches.

II. THE OCCASIONS AND MANIFESTATIONS OF THIS COMPANIONSHIP. Observe under this consideration how Christ's friendship appears superior to every merely human association. We may enjoy his society: 1. In our occupations, whatever be their special nature. 2. In our enjoyments, which are all hallowed by his gracious presence and approval. 3. In our sufferings, when we perhaps most need him, and when his sympathy is peculiarly precious, consolatory, and helpful. 4. In our services; for how can we do his work, except beneath his direction and the encouragement of his smile?

III. THE BENEFITS OF THIS COMPANIONSHIP. When Christ is with us, in the varied scenes and experiences of our earthly life: 1. Our gratitude to him will be livelier. 2. Our love to him will be warmer. 3. Our conformity to his will and character will be more complete. 4. Our inseparability from him will be more assured. "Who shall separate us from the love of Christ?"

> "His is love beyond a brother's,
> Faithful, free, and knows no end.

                                                                    T.

Ver. 13.—*Garnered fruits.* When the bride invites the king to revisit the home of her childhood and the scenes of their early acquaintance and attachment, among other alluring representations she assures him that there will be found, laid up for his use by her thoughtful affection, all manner of precious fruits, new and old. A suitable emblem this of the gathered and garnered spiritual fruits which in this earthly life Christ's people are expected to prepare for him at his coming, and which it will be their delight to offer to him as the expression of their grateful love. Properly understood, the main purpose of the Christian life is the growing, gathering, and garnering of precious fruits for the approval and service of the Lord.

I. WHAT THESE FRUITS ARE. 1. They are the fruits of spiritual life and experience.

2. They are the "fruits of the Spirit"—the virtues especially Christian, fruits of right-eousness, those qualities of character which are the peculiar growth of grace. 3. They are fruits of service; not things enjoyed so much as things achieved.

II. WHY ARE THEY LAID UP FOR CHRIST? Because: 1. They are the fruit of his own garden, the growth which testifies to the care and culture of the Divine Husbandman. 2. They are of a nature to yield a peculiar satisfaction and pleasure to him. 3. They are such as he will use for his own purposes, and for the display of his own glory and praise.—T.

EXPOSITION.

CHAPTER VIII.

Vers. 1—3.—**Oh that thou wert as my brother, that sucked the breasts of my mother! When I should find thee without, I would kiss thee; and none would despise me. I would lead thee, and bring thee into my mother's house, who would instruct me; I would cause thee to drink of spiced wine, of the juice of my pomegranate. His left hand should be under my head, and his right hand should embrace me.** The meaning seems to be this—Let our relation to one another be the highest and the purest and the most permanent possible. The sisterly relation is not merely one of affection, but one of blood. The bond between husband and wife may be broken by the caprice and weakness of human feeling, but nothing can destroy the bond of blood. "A friend loveth at all times, and a brother is born for adversity" (Prov. xvii. 17); "There is a friend that sticketh closer than a brother" (Prov. xviii. 24). The brotherly bond re-presents the strength of the blood-relation-ship. When to that is added personal affec-tion, then the tie is perfect. Shulamith means that she would have their love freed from all the uncertainties of human fickle-ness. As symbolically interpreted, there-fore, we take this whole passage to signify that the Church, when it is desiring the closest fellowship with the Saviour, would be lifted above all the temptations of earthly life, which so often lower the standard of Christian feeling and service. The words are specially impressive in the lips of the bride of Solomon. It is a testimony to the inspiration of the whole book that the volup-tuous monarch, whose life fell so far below the ideal of a godly king, should yet, in-directly though still powerfully, condemn and rebuke his own departure from God, setting clearly before us the surpassing excellence of pure love and the sanctity of married life. In the king's address to his bride he called her "sister" and "sister-bride;" she now virtually returns his own sentiment and calls him "brother." She shows that she has risen in her love far above the mere fleshly desires—"the lust of the flesh, the lust of the eyes, and the

pride of life." She would blend her whole existence with that of her Lord. *I would kiss thee; yea, and none would despise me.* Nothing can more exquisitely and delicately express the fulness of affection. It is not merely a return for that which is given; it is free and spontaneous. So should our spiritual feelings be. They should be the natural outpouring of the soul towards the Saviour; not a worked-up, artificial, spas-modic impulse, not a cold, dead formalism, not an unsympathetic service of conscience; but "doing the will of God from the heart." "Love is the fulfilling of the Law;" "Faith worketh by love." The second verse is differently rendered by some. Jerome, Venetian, and Luther take it as referring to the bride's dependence on her husband's superior wisdom—"Thou wouldest instruct me;" which, of course, is a very suitable sentiment as addressed to the wise King Solomon. The Targum expounds it thus: "I would conduct thee, O King Messiah, and bring thee into the house of my sanc-tuary; and thou wouldest teach me to fear God and to walk in his ways." Hitzig and our Revisers take the verb as in the third person feminine, and applied to the mother. "She would teach me as a mother teaches a young bride, from her own early experi-ence." The old view that the bride is the personification of wisdom seems quite re-futed by this speech of Shulamith's. She desires and waits for instruction. Solomon is wisdom. She is the soul of man, or the Church of God, delighting to sit at his feet and learn of him. Whichever rendering we choose, whether the mother or Solomon be regarded as teacher, the meaning is the same. It is, as Delitzsch has observed, a deep revelation of Shulamith's heart. "She knew how much she yet came short of being to the king all that a wife should be. But in Jerusalem the bustle of court life and the burden of his regal duties did not permit him to devote himself to her; in her mother's house, if he were once there, he would in-struct her, and she would requite him with her spiced wine and with the juice of the pomegranates." The "spiced wine," *vinum conditura*, aromatic wine, probably grape wine "mixed with fragrant and pungent essences," as in the East. The juice, or pressed juice, of the pomegranate is a delicious drink. There is no allusion to any love-symbol. The grains of the pomegranates were said by the Arabians to be from Paradise (cf. the ῥοΐτης, or "vinum de punicis quod roidem vocant" in Dioscorides and Pliny). Perhaps this reference to exchange of gifts may be taken as symbolizing the happy state of the Church when she pours out her treasures in response to the spiritual blessings which she is freely receiving. The meaning is something beautiful and precious. And that is the highest state of religious life when the service we render and the gifts we place on the altar are felt to be the grateful sacrifices of our hearts under a sense of Divine love. When the Church of Christ depends for its support on such fellowship between itself and the Saviour there will be no limits to its attainments, no achievements beyond its powers. "All that see" such a state of the Church "shall acknowledge" the glory of it, "that they are the seed which the Lord hath blessed" (see the whole of the sixty-first chapter of Isaiah, which breathes the very spirit of Solomon's Song). The rejoicing bride then gives herself up to the thought of her husband's affection. In that beautiful simplicity and purity of her childhood's life she would realize the bliss of her new relation. Delitzsch describes her state of mind thus: "Resigning herself dreamily to the idea that Solomon is her brother, whom she may freely and openly kiss, and her teacher besides, with whom she may sit in confidential intercourse under her mother's eye, she feels herself as if closely embraced by him, and calls from a distance to the daughters of Jerusalem not to disturb this her happy enjoyment." Perhaps the sense of weakness and dependence is meant to be expressed. The bride is conscious that her lord is everything to her. In that identification which the highest love brings vividly into the soul, there is the joy of exultation. "All things are ours; and we are Christ's, and Christ is God's."

Ver. 4.—**I adjure you, O daughters of Jerusalem, that ye stir not up, nor awaken love, until it please.** This, of course, as the refrain of the song, must be taken as a general sentiment. Love is its own lord. Let it have free course. Let it perfect itself in its own best way. The form of the adjuration is abbreviated in this case. The omission of the words, "By the roes and by the hinds of the field," is not without its significance. Is it not intended to intimate that the *natural* love, to which reference was made by the introduction of the beautiful wild creatures of the field, is now no

more in the thoughts of the bride, because it has been sublimated into the higher sisterly love of which she has been speaking? She is not merely the lovely woman on whom the king dotes because of her personal beauty; she is his companion and dearest friend. He opens his heart to her. He teaches her. He lifts her up to his own level. She participates in his royal dignity and majesty. The ἔρως of her first estate of love is now exalted into the ἀγάπη, which is the grace never to be without its sphere, abiding for ever. We must not press too closely the poetic form of the song. Something must be allowed for the framework in which the main ideas are set before us. It may not be possible to answer the question—Who are intended to be symbolized by the daughters of Jerusalem? There is no necessity to seek further into the meaning of the whole poem than its widest and most general application. But the daughters of Jerusalem are in a lower position, a less favoured relation to the bridegroom, than the bride herself. We may, therefore, without hesitation, accept the view that by the adjuration is intended the appeal of the higher spiritual life against all that is below it; the ideal love calling upon all that is around it and all that is related to it to rise with it to perfection. The individual soul is thus represented claiming the full realization of its spiritual possibilities. The Church of God thus remonstrates against all that hinders her advancement, restrains her life, and interrupts her blessedness. Jerusalem has many daughters. They are not all in perfect sympathy with the bride. When they listen to the adjurations of the most spiritual, the most devoted, the most heavenly and Christ-like of those who are named by the Name of the Lord, they will themselves be lifted up into the bridal joy of "the marriage supper of the Lamb."

Vers. 5—14.—Part V. CONCLUSION. THE BRIDEGROOM AND THE BRIDE IN THE SCENE OF THEIR FIRST LOVE.

Ver. 5a.—**Who is this that cometh up from the wilderness, leaning upon her beloved?** We must compare this question with the corresponding one in ch. iii. 6. In that case the inhabitants of Jerusalem are supposed to be looking forth, and behold the bridal procession approaching the capital. In this case the scene is transferred to the country, to the neighbourhood of the bride's home, where she has desired to be with her lord. The country people, or the group of her relatives, are supposed to be gazing at the pair of lovers, not coming in royal state, but in the sweet simplicity of true affection, the bride leaning with loving confidence on the arm of her husband, as they were seen before in the time of their "first love." The restoration of "first love" is often the prayer of the disciple, feeling how far he falls short of the affection which such a Master should call forth. The first feelings of the heart when it is won to Christ are very delightful.

> "Where is the blessedness I knew
> When first I saw the Lord?
> Where is the soul-refreshing view
> Of Jesus and his Word?"

It is a blessedness when we come up from the wilderness. It is a joy to ourselves and a matter of praise to our fellow-believers when we are manifestly filled with a sense of the Saviour's presence and fellowship. The word *midhbaur*, translated "wilderness," does not, however, necessarily mean a desolate and barren desert, but rather the open country, as the Valley of Jezreel. The LXX. had either a different reading in the Hebrew or has mistaken it. They have rendered the last clause "clothed in white," which perhaps Jerome has followed with his *deliciis affluens*. The word is, however, from the root *rauvaq*, which in the hiph. is "to support one's self." The meaning, therefore, is, "leaning for support." It might, however, be intended to represent the loving confidence of married life, and therefore would be equivalent in meaning to the Greek and Latin renderings, that is, "Who is this? Evidently a young newly married wife with her husband." Perhaps this is the best explanation of the words as preparing for what follows, as the bridegroom begins at once to speak of the first love. Some think that the road in which the loving pair are seen to be walking brings their footsteps near to the apple tree over against Shulamith's house where they had first met. But there is no necessity for that supposition. It is sufficient if we imagine the apple tree to be in sight.

Ver. 5b.—**Under the apple tree I awakened thee; there thy mother was in travail with thee; there was she in travail that brought thee forth.** *I awakened thee;* i.e. I stirred thee up to return the affection which I showed thee (cf. ch. ii. 7). The Masoretic reading prints the verb עוֹרַרְתִּיךָ, as with the masculine suffix, but this renders the meaning exceedingly perplexing. The bride would not speak of awakening Solomon, but it was he who had awakened her. The change is very slight, the ך becoming ך, and is supported by the Old Syriac Version. It must be remembered that the bridegroom immediately addresses the bride, speaking of her mother. The apple tree would certainly be most naturally supposed to be situated somewhere near the house where the bride was born, perhaps overshadowing it or branching

over the windows, or trained upon the trellis surrounding the house. The bridegroom points to it. "See, there it is, the familiar apple tree beside the house where thy dear self wast born. There, yonder, is where thy mother dwelt, and where thou heardest my first words of affection as we sat side by side just outside the house under the shade of the apple tree." The language is exquisitely simple and chaste, and yet so full of the tender affection of the true lover. The spot where the first breathings of love came forth will ever be dear in the remembrance of those whose affection remains faithful and fond. The typical view certainly finds itself supported in these words. Nothing is more delightful and more helpful to the believer than to go over in thought, again and again, and especially when faith grows feeble, when the heart is cold and fickle under the influence of worldly temptations and difficulties of the Christian course, the history of the first beginning of the spiritual life. We recall how dear the Lord was to us then, how wonderful his love seemed to us, how condescending and how merciful. We reproach ourselves that we faint and fail; we cry out for the fulness of grace, and it is given us.

Vers. 6, 7.—**Set me as a seal upon thine heart, as a seal upon thine arm: for love is strong as death; jealousy is cruel as the grave: the flashes thereof are flashes of fire, a very flame of the Lord. Many waters cannot quench love, neither can the floods drown it; if a man would give all the substance of his house for love, he would be utterly contemned.** Is this to be regarded as the reply of the bride to the tender allusion of her husband to their first love; or is it, as some think, only the first words which belong to the bride, while the rest of the two verses are a kind of chorus echoing her loving appeal, and bringing the general action of the poem to a conclusion? It is difficult to decide this, and the meaning is not affected either way. Perhaps, however, it is best to take it as spoken by the bride, who continues her address to the end of the eighth verse. She is full of joy in the return of perfect confidence; she prays that the full tide of affection may never cease to flow, that there be no ebbing of that happy feeling in which she now delights; and then sings the praise of love itself, as though a prelude of praise to a long and eternal peace. The seal is the signet-ring, *chothâm*, from a root "to impress." It was sometimes carried by a string on the breast, and would, therefore, be near the heart (see Gen. xxxviii. 18). It was sometimes worn on the hand (see Jer. xxii. 24; and cf. Gen. xli. 42; Esth. iii. 12). It was not worn on the arm like a bracelet (2 Sam. i. 10). Probably it was not the signet-ring which is referred to in the second clause: "Set me as a seal on thine heart, and as a bracelet on thine arm." The same simile is not infrequent in the prophets. The desire of Shulamith was to escape all possibility of those declensions of which she had spoken before. "Let me never be out of thy thoughts; let me never go back from my fulness of joy in thy love." The true believer understands well such language. He knows that the maintenance of devout affection is not a matter of mere desire and will. The Lord himself must help us with his blessed gifts, the influence of his gracious Spirit to overcome the feebleness and fickleness of a fallen heart. We want to be close to the heart of the Saviour; we want to be constantly in his eye, and so diligently employed in his service, so closely associated with the work of his mighty arm, that we shall be ever receiving from him the signs and evidences of his approval and affection. The purity and perfection of true love are the theme of every sincere believer. The priceless value of such love is described in the Book of Proverbs (vi. 30), in Numb. xxii. 18, and 1 Cor. xiii. 3. It is an unquenchable flame —nothing can resist it. We cannot but recall the rapturous language of one who himself was an example of the highest devotedness to the Saviour, who rejoiced over death and the grave in the consciousness of victory through him from whose love nothing can separate us (Rom. viii. 38; 1 Cor. xv. 54). Certainly the history of the sufferings and trials of the true Church form a most striking commentary upon these words. Floods of persecution have swept over it, but they have not quenched love. The flame has burst forth again and again when it seemed to be extinguished, and it has become a very "flame of the Lord." The bush has been burning, but has not been consumed. By jealousy is intended love in its intensity not bearing a rival. The "flame of the Lord" may be compared with "the voice of the Lord," which is described in Hebrew poetry as connected with the fury of the storm. The flame, therefore, would be lightning and the voice thunder. The whole of this passage, which forms a kind of key-note of the poem, is more like a distinct strain introduced to give climax to the succession of songs than the natural expression of the bride's feelings. It has been always regarded as one of the sublimest apostrophes to love to be found anywhere. The enemies of God and of humanity are represented as falling before it, death and the grave. Its vehemence and force of manifestation are brought vividly before us by the comparison of the flash of lightning. It is remarkable that this exaltation of love should be included in the Old Testament, thus proving that the Mosaic Law, with its formal prescriptions, by no means fulfils the whole purpose of God in his reve-

lation to the world. As the New Testament would not have been complete without the message of the beloved disciple, so this Old Testament must have its song of love. Nor is it only the ideal and the heavenly love which is celebrated, but human affection itself is placed very high, because it is associated with that which is Divine. It is a more precious thing than mere wealth or worldly honour, and he that trifles with it deserves the utmost scorn and contempt of his fellows. It is well to remark how consistently the poetic framework is maintained. There is no attempt to leave the lines of human relations even at this point, where evidently the sentiment rises above them. The love which is apostrophized is not removed from earth in order to be seen apart from all earthly imperfections and impurities. We are invited rather to look through the human to the Divine which embraces it and glorifies it. That is the method of the Divine revelation throughout. "The Word was made flesh, and dwelt among us." We do not need to take Solomon's Song as an allegory. It is a song of human love, but as such it is a symbol of that which is Divine.

Ver. 8.—**We have a little sister, and she hath no breasts: what shall we do for our sister in the day when she shall be spoken for?** The term "little" refers, of course, to her tender age, as in 2 Kings v. 2, the "little maid;" and in Gen. xliv. 20, "a child of his old age, a little one," referring to Benjamin. "She hath no breasts" is equivalent to saying she is not yet mature, of marriageable age (see Ezek. xvi. 7). The question which the bride asks of King Solomon refers to the promise which he is supposed to have made, and which he is virtually pledging himself to fulfil by this visit to the country home of his queen. "What shall be done for the advantage of my little sister? Let us consult together" (cf. Gen. xxvii. 37; 1 Sam. x. 2; Isa. v. 4). "The day when she shall be spoken for" is the day when she shall attract the attention of a suitor. It must necessarily be difficult to find satisfactory interpretations for every detail in such a poem of human love as this. It might be sufficient to see in this reference to the younger sister the general idea of love's expansion. Those who are themselves the objects of it, being full of exquisite happiness, desire to call others into the same joy. This is true both of the individual and of the Church. *What shall be done for others?* That is the question which is awakened in every heart where true love is at work. There is no need to explain the language further. But the allegorists have been very ingenious in attempting to find meanings for every allusion of the poem. Who is the little sister? What is her virginity? What is the day in which she shall be spoken for? Some have said that the little sister represents the firstfruits of the Jews and Gentiles received into the Christian Church immediately after the time of our Lord's ascension, as Beza and others. Some, again, take it to mean the whole body of Jews and Gentiles yet to be converted. Others would see in it those that are weak in faith, the beginners in Christian life. And, again, it has been regarded as pointing to the "daughter of Zion" at the time of the first beginnings of her conversion to the heavenly Solomon, which is the view of Hengstenberg and others. There is no end to such fancies. The broad general meaning is all that we can rest upon. The bride naturally thinks of her sister. It is a lovely incident in a perfectly idyllic poem. The visit to the home is quite in harmony with the fresh, pure, and simple life which reveals itself in all the utterances of the bride, and is honoured by the devoted attention of the splendid monarch. It is a real touch of nature when the young bride, in her family life once more, asks what shall become of her sister. It is an exquisite type of that sisterly solicitude with which all true Christians will care for the souls around them. Delitzsch thinks that the question which is asked by the bride is answered by her brothers, as they were the actual guardians of the little sister (see Gen. xxi. 50, 55; xxxiv. 6—8). But there is no necessity to introduce any new interlocutors at this point. The words are certainly addressed to Solomon. It is quite natural that he should reply to them in a royal style, with the *pluralis majestatis* which suits the corresponding position of the bride as a suppliant for her sister.

Ver. 9.—**If she be a wall, we will build upon her a turret of silver: and if she be a door, we will enclose her with boards of cedar.** The interpretation which Delitzsch suggests of these words is that the "wall" represents firmness of character, and the "door" weakness and insecurity. If she firmly and successfully withstands all immoral approaches, then we will bestow high honour upon her, as a tribute to her maidenly virtue and constancy. The turret or castle of silver would mean rewarding her with increase. Silver is the emblem of holiness, gold of nobility. The meaning may, however, merely be, "We will endow her with plenty." The boards of cedar are supposed to be special protections, as cedar is noted for its hardness and durability. But is not the meaning much simpler and more natural? It would be rather a far-fetched use of the figure of a door that it should suggest seduction, and would be rather unsuitable in the lips of the bridegroom when speaking of the little sister of his own bride. May not

the meaning be no more than this?—She may become one of the most substantial parts of the building, like a wall; in that case all that she can be she shall be; we will put the highest honour upon her. She may be a door, that is, though not so great and substantial as the wall, still in the very front of the building and before the eyes of all. In that case we will beautify her with costly and fragrant adornment. The gate shall be enclosed in cedar-wood. "The wall and the door," says Zöckler, "are mostly understood of the steadfast and faithful keeping of the Word of God and of its zealous proclamation to the Gentiles (1 Cor. xvi. 9, etc.); but some also explain them of the valiant in faith and the weak in faith, or of the learned and simple, or of faithful Christians and such as are recreant and easily accessible to the arts of seduction. And then, according to these various interpretations, the 'silver bulwarks' are now the miracles of the first witnesses of Jesus, now the distinguished teachers of the Church, now pious Christian rulers, now the testimonies of Holy Scripture by which faith is strengthened. And, again, by the 'cedar boards' are sometimes understood the ten commandments or the Law, sometimes Christian teachers, sometimes the examples of the saints, sometimes the salutary discipline of the cross and sufferings for Christ's sake," etc. All such attempts at detailed interpretation fail to give satisfaction. Their effect is to repel many from the study of the book altogether, just as the follies and extravagances of the interpreters of prophecy have greatly hindered the study of the prophetic Scriptures. The *wall* and the *door* need not be taken as opposed to one another, as they are not in our conceptions of a city. They fulfil different functions. The *wall* is for *defence;* the *door* is for *admission.* In the one case we think of *strength*, and in the other case of *beauty.* The application of the symbols is very easy if the general meaning alone is regarded. There is a variety of capacity and function in the Church of Christ. There are differences in the forms of Christianity among different nations. But the Lord will receive and bless all. Some are not fitted to be built upon as strong walls, but they may still be beautiful examples of Christian graces in the eyes of the world, through whom many gladly enter into the truth and into the fellowship of Christ.

Vers. 10—12.—**I am a wall, and my breasts like the towers thereof: then was I in his eyes as one that found peace. Solomon had a vineyard at Baal-hamon; he let out the vineyard unto keepers; every one for the fruit thereof was to bring a thousand pieces of silver. My vineyard, which is mine, is**

before me: thou, O Solomon, shalt have a thousand, and those that keep the fruit thereof two hundred. The meaning seems to be affectionate approval of the method just described. Solomon says, "If the young sister be worthy of love, she shall receive more and more of defence and honour; she shall be all that I can make her." The bride takes up this thought. "So it is with me, and, in the spirit of thankful acknowledgments and praise, I will respond to all the favour of the king. King Solomon has loved me, and now I am rising higher and becoming more and more glorious because of his love." The typical reference can scarcely be missed. The Church, the bride of the Lamb, shines only in the light of him whose favour is life, and whose lovingkindness is better than life. The comparison to a city with the walls and towers, while it would seem a little far-fetched in a love-song, is quite in place if the typical intention was in the mind of the writer. He was thinking of the city of God, "beautiful for situation, the joy of the whole earth." "One that findeth peace" is the same as "one that findeth favour," that is, one who is the object of his affection. There are several references which confirm this, such as Esth. ii. 17; Deut. xxiv. 1; Jer. xxxi. 2; Ps. xli. 10. The word "peace" (*shâlôm*) is in all probability purposely chosen in this case as a kind of play on the name *Solomon*, which appears immediately afterwards. "The king of peace delights in me because I am peace in his eyes." The Church is after the image of the King. His likeness in her makes her beautiful. Men take knowledge of Christians that they have been with Jesus (see 1 Chron. xxii. 9). It is scarcely necessary to point out that this language of the bride is entirely against the shepherd-theory. She could not have talked of finding peace in his eyes if she was torn from her true lover. The bride then goes on to express her devotedness to the king and her desire to bring forth abundance for him. She uses as an example, which perhaps was typical in her time and country, some remarkably fruitful vineyard of the king's. She will, in like manner, realize all his highest wishes. All that she has shall be his. The name Baal-hamon (בַּעַל הָמוֹן) in the LXX. Βεελαμών (cf. Judith viii. 3), designates probably a place near to Sunem, somewhere to the north, on the further side of the Plain of Jezreel. The produce of the vineyard must have been very large, as every keeper was to bring in for himself a thousand shekels of silver. It is not stated how many keepers there were, but the word which is employed is not "servants," but "watchers, or overseers." A vineyard was divided into portions, with a certain definite prescribed number of vines in each portion. In Isa. vii. 23 we read, "And it shall come to pass in that day that every place where there were a thousand vines at a thousand silverlings shall even be for briers and thorns." Now, a thousand silverlings was one shekel, so that if this passage can be taken as throwing light on what the bride says, it would imply that, instead of one shekel for every thousand vines, every keeper brought a thousand shekels. That would seem impossible, so that the parallel can scarcely be strict. Perhaps the largeness of the vineyard is referred to, and each of the keepers would have many thousands of vines under his inspection. The general meaning, however, is not obscure. The vineyard was a celebrated one, and was taken as a typical instance of fertility and abundance. When the bride speaks of her vineyard which is before her, there may be an allusion to her previous manner of life as a rustic maiden employed in the vineyards, and to her own position as a keeper or as one of the family. But this is not intended to be prominently expressed. The whole spirit of the poem justifies the view that she is speaking of her person. She invited Solomon to rejoice in the beauty and fragrance of her garden, to pluck the fruits, to revel in the delights. Everything that is pleasant and lovely is before him (see ch. iv. 12; v. 1). *Before me;* that is, in my power is all this delight, and my desire is to my husband; all that I have is his. Like the far-famed keepers of Baal-hamon, I will give the king a thousand shekels, that is, the utmost that the vineyard can produce, and "those that keep the fruit thereof" shall have two hundred—perhaps meaning a hundred each, that is a tenth, which was the ancient tithe due to the priests. It may be, however, that a double tithe is intended. The king shall be satisfied, and all those who labour for the king shall be more than ever rewarded. If we take such words as typical, they point to a state of things in the history of the kingdom of God when the spiritual and the temporal shall be perfectly adjusted. The keepers of the vineyard have often made sad havoc of the vineyard itself because of their greedy discontent. The fruits which have been yielded by the Church have fallen very far short. The husbandmen have ill treated the Lord's servants. But all the judgments which have been poured out both upon ancient Jews and upon the corrupt Christendom of later times have been directed to one end, to make the vineyard of the Lord more fruitful, to remove the things which are offensive in his sight, to satisfy him whose soul travailed for his people; for herein is the Father glorified in the Son, when those who bear the name of the Beloved "bear much fruit." Then the keepers of the vineyard will themselves rejoice, not that they reap a larger harvest of this world's good, not "for filthy lucre's sake," but because their hearts are one with his whose vineyard they keep, and to see the fruit abound is to fill them with joy. Surely we shall recognize in such language an anticipation of the many allusions which are found both in the prophets and psalms and in the discourses of our Lord himself. "The vineyard of the Lord of thosts is the house of Israel, and the men of Judah his pleasant plant" (Isa. v. 7)

Ver. 13.—**Thou that dwellest in the gardens, the companions hearken for thy voice; cause me to hear it.** There cannot be much doubt that these are the words of the bridegroom. They are addressed to the bride. She is the dweller in the gardens; that is, one who is at home in the gardens, whose beauty blends with the rural loveliness around her. The king wishes his bride to understand that she is only acceptable in his sight, and that all that she asks shall be granted. It is delightful to him to hear her voice, as it is delightful to those who have been accustomed to that voice from her childhood. "Dear country girl, sing to me, and let me revel in the sweetness of thy music. 'Thy companions hearken for it'—thy former associates, the playmates of thy youth. And while they gather round us, and you and I rejoice in one another, let the sound of thy voice mingle with the peaceful beauty of this earthly paradise." There is an exquisite tenderness in this conclusion of the poem. The curtain falls, as it were, upon a scene of mutual confidence and affection, the simplicity of the bride's early home being lifted up into the royal splendour of the king's presence, the companions beholding and praising, while, in the midst of all that sunny bliss and peaceful content, the voice of the bride is heard singing one of the old, familiar strains of love with which she poured out her heart in the days when her beloved came to find her in her home. It is impossible to conceive a more perfect conclusion. It leads up our thoughts to the land of light and song, where "the Lamb which is in the midst of the throne shall be the Shepherd" of those who shall "hunger no more, neither thirst any more; neither shall the sun strike upon them, nor any heat;" "and he shall guide them unto fountains of waters of life: and God shall wipe away every tear from their eyes" (Rev. vii. 16, 17). It is sad to think that Solomon himself fell from such an ideal of human affection, and was unfaithful to such a bride. But there is no need to trouble the clear, transparent beauty of this typical poem by any reference to the incidents of the

writer's own history. He placed it on the altar of God, no doubt, at a time when it represented sincere feelings in his heart, and because he was inspired to see that it would be profitable to the people of God as a mirror in which they could behold the reflection of the highest truth. But though he himself fell away from his high place as a prophet of God, the words which he left behind him were still a precious gift to the Church. It is otherwise with him who is typified by the earthly monarch. He who is the heavenly Bridegroom has himself to lift up the weakness and fickleness of his bride by fellowship with her, until she is above the reach of temptation, and partaker of his own glory. And he does so, as this exquisite poem reminds us, by the power of his love. It is the personal influence of the Lord Jesus Christ which must glorify the Church and restore it to its original simplicity and spirituality. The scene into which we are led in this story of bridal affection typifies a state of the Church when the artificiality of court life shall be abandoned, the magnificence of mere external pomp and ritual shall be left behind, and the bride shall simply delight herself in the Bridegroom among the pure and peaceful surroundings of a country home. The Church will realize the greatness of her power when she is delivered from that which hides her Saviour, when she is simply human and yet entirely spiritual; then the Lord of her life, the second Adam, the perfect Man, who is from heaven and in heaven, but still on earth, changing earth to heaven by his love, will fulfil his promise. "He not merely concludes the marriage covenant with mankind, but likewise preserves, confirms, refines, and conducts it step by step to its ideal consummation, which is at the same time the palingenesia and perfection of humanity."

Ver. 14.—**Make haste, my beloved, and be thou like to a roe or to a young hart upon the mountains of spices.** This is a snatch of the old love-songs which the bride used to sing when love was fresh and young. She sings it now at the request of her bridegroom himself, and in the delighted ears of her companions. She goes forth from among them leaning on her beloved, to rejoice in the beautiful scenery and rural pleasures with him whose presence heightens every joy, the life of her life, the soul of her soul, "all her salvation, all her desire." The bridegroom and the bride are seen disappearing together over the flowery hills; and the music of the Song of Songs dies away in the sweet fragrance of that closing scene; the vision of love has, gazelle-like, leapt from point to point, and vanishes away at last among the mountains of spices. It is well to notice that what were before "mountains of Bether," that is, of "separation," are now "mountains of

Besamin "—balsam mountains. There is no more word of separation. Henceforth the only note is one of peaceful enjoyment. *" My beloved is mine, and I am his."* Our home and haunt is the same. The concluding words, we cannot doubt, are intended to open a perfect future to the eye. Yet the poet, with consummate art, connects that future with the past and the present by the voice of the bride heard singing the love-song with which she first expressed her love, now lifted up into anticipation of the ever-lasting hills of fragrant and joyful life.

HOMILETICS.

Vers. 1—4.— *Wishes of the bride.* 1. *That she had known the bridegroom always.* The bride continues the address of ch. vii. She is still speaking to the king, telling him of her love. He had again and again called her his sister—his sister-bride. She now wishes that he were to her as a brother; that they could have been children of the same mother; that they could have known one another from infancy. So in the close union of love between husband and wife there comes sometimes such a longing, a desire that each could have known the other from the beginning; that instead of the years in which they were strangers, and never heard one another's voice, or touched one another's hand, they had always lived together, and known one another through and through in all the varied experiences of child-life, of girlhood or of boyhood; sometimes there comes a sort of innocent envy of the brothers or sisters who then knew one or other of the wedded pair when they were unknown to one another. The bride wishes that she had always thus known the bridegroom; that she could have loved him always with a sisterly affection; that their mutual endearments might have been, like those of brothers and sisters, without shame, attracting no observation. How often the converted soul longs with an intense longing that it had always from the beginning known and loved the heavenly Bridegroom! How utterly wasted and lost those years now seem which were spent without that knowledge of Christ which is eternal life! How ardently we wish that they could be blotted out of our remembrance, with all their ignorance and all their sins, as we humbly hope that through the atonement of the precious blood they are blotted out from the handwriting " that was against us, that was contrary to us " (Col. ii. 14)! Blessed be God we have his holy promise, " I have blotted out, as a thick cloud, thy transgressions, and, as a cloud, thy sins: return unto me; for I have redeemed thee " (Isa. xliv. 22). We know that in his gracious mercy he so putteth away the sins of them that truly repent that he remembereth them no more (Jer. xxxi. 34; Heb. viii. 12; x. 17). But though we believe in the forgiveness of sins, and thank God heartily for that blessed revelation of his love, yet we cannot but long—and that the more earnestly the nearer we draw to him—that we had always known him with the knowledge of faith and love, that we had always remembered him, that we had kept our heart pure from other loves, and loved him always. There is a difference between the love of the forgiven penitent and the love of saints like Enoch or Samuel, who, as far as human imperfection allows, have always in the main bent and purpose of their lives striven to walk with God. The love of the penitent is more demonstrative, more passionate—if the word may be used, more enthusiastic; the love of men like Samuel is calmer, quieter, fuller, dominating the entire life in all its pursuits and amusements; and just because it is not intermittent, but uniform, it is not so much observed of men. The still waters run deepest; the interpenetration of the heart by the long-continued influences of the Holy Spirit, without any marked and sudden change visible to the eyes of men, produces a very high type of Christian character. Enoch seems to have walked with God all his life. " He was not, for God took him; " " He had this testimony, that he pleased God " (Heb. xi. 5). It is a poor offering to give the dregs of our life to God, when the temptations of youth have lost their power over us; " when the evil days come, and the years draw nigh when thou shalt say, I have no pleasure in them " (Eccles. xii. 1). A life dedicated to God from early childhood must be a thing well pleasing in his sight, as Holy Scripture tells us it was in the case of Enoch. Such a life is very rare, and we may well be full of thankfulness to Almighty God for his gracious promises to the penitent sinner. He "will not despise the broken and the contrite heart." "If the wicked will turn from all his sins that he hath committed, and keep all my statutes, and do that which is lawful and right, he shall surely live, he shall not die. All his transgressions that he hath committed, they shall not be mentioned unto him: in his righteousness that he hath done he shall live." We thank God for these gracious words. If we have been called at the sixth or at the eleventh hour, it is enough to fill us with adoring gratitude; we wonder, as we look back upon the past, that God bore with us so long in our sin and unbelief; we thank him with all our heart for his long-suffering mercy. But when we remember that sin and that unbelief, we cannot but long that we had given to God those lost and wasted years; that we had remembered our Creator in the days of our youth, and not grieved the Holy Spirit of God by so many transgressions, so much coldness and hardness of heart. 2. *That she had brought him into her mother's house.* Those lost years involved the loss of many opportunities of doing good to others. The bride, had she known the bridegroom in early youth, would have brought him, she says, into her mother's house. There (she adds in what seems to be the best reading) "*thou shouldest instruct me.*" How much good we might have done in our families, among our friends, if we had given our earliest years to God, if we had lived then as in his presence, and had carried the consciousness of that presence, with all the feelings of awe and reverence and love which attend it, always with us in our family life, in our dealings with relations and friends; if we had given him of our best, and willingly offered up for his service all that we most prized and valued, how much calmer, holier, happier, our life would have been! For he would have instructed us. He bids us learn of him. He is the great Teacher, the Master. "All thy children," he says, "shall be taught of the Lord: and great shall be the peace of thy children" (Isa. liv. 13). 3. *The bride repeats the aspirations of ch. ii.* 7. If we had listened to that instruction from the time when we were first made his disciples, if we had given him from the beginning that for which he thirsted—our affections, our heart's love—then he would now be wholly ours; "his left hand should be under my head, and his right hand should embrace me." That blessed union with the Saviour, growing ever nearer and closer, is the object of the deepest longings of the Christian soul. We think sometimes that if only we had always loved him and walked with him, our walk now might be very close with God; we might have attained to that calm and serene trustfulness which is the privilege of his saints; we might have found rest for our souls in the embrace of his holy love. But though we have greatly sinned, and have lost much through past neglect and unbelief, yet even now that blessed rest is not beyond our grasp. It was to Mary Magdalene, out of whom the Lord had cast seven devils, that those words were said which seemed at first severe and forbidding, but really involved the promise of a holier union, "Touch me not; for I am not yet ascended unto my Father." She was about to embrace his feet, to cling to the human form of him who had done such great things for her. The Lord implies a promise of a better, spiritual communion. When he had ascended into heaven, when he had sent down the blessed Spirit that he might abide for ever with his Church, then the believing soul might touch him with the touch of faith; might cling to him with a holier, a more blessed embrace; then he would be with us all the days, guiding, strengthening, comforting, his left hand under our head to support us when we seem to be ready to fall, his right hand embracing us to shield us from all evil, to assure us of his love. 4. *The thrice-repeated charge to the daughters of Jerusalem.* The bride's longings for the tokens of the bridegroom's love again arouse her feelings of maidenly reserve: as in ch. ii. 7 and iii. 5, she bids her virgin-friends not to stir up or awaken love until it please to manifest itself. The Christian's aspirations after the abiding presence of God arouse in him feelings of reverential awe. He will remember the Lord's caution, "Touch me not;" he will avoid expressions of love which savour too much of merely human tenderness; he will shrink instinctively from any approach to familiarity; he will remember that the Lord Jesus is the Word of God, the King, the Judge of all; he will be reverent in all his approaches to the Saviour; he will endeavour to instil reverence into those around him by example, by tone, by manner, by word. We must wait on the Lord until he pleases to manifest himself; we must not be impatient; we must learn to say with the psalmist, "Why art thou cast down, O my soul? and why art thou disquieted within me? Hope thou in God: for I shall yet praise him, who is the health of my countenance and my God" (Ps. xlii. 11).

Vers. 5—14.—*Entire union of wedded love.* I. COMMUNION OF THE BRIDEGROOM AND THE BRIDE. 1. *Approach of the bride.* "Who is this?" The question is asked for the third time (see ch. iii. 6; vi. 10). In ch. iii. 6 the chorus of youths asks the question as the bride is borne in royal state to meet the king in the city of his kingdom; it occurs again in ch. vi. 10, when the maidens of the chorus are struck with admiration of her queenlike, majestic beauty. Now, apparently, we have a narrative of a visit to the scenes of the bride's early life, according to her invitation in ch. vii. 11; and the question, "Who is this?" is repeated once more. Here the circumstances are changed; there is no magnificence as in ch. iii.; the bride is alone with the king; she is seen coming up from the wilderness, leaning on her beloved. So the Church, the bride of Christ, cometh up from the wilderness, leaning on the heavenly Bridegroom. So the Church of the Old Testament went up from Babylon when the wilderness was glad for them, when the ransomed of the Lord returned and went up with singing to Zion. So the Church of the New Testament came up from the wilderness of persecution, leaning on the strength of Christ; so the same Church shall come up at the call of the same holy Saviour to the heavenly Zion when that blessed promise is fulfilled, "Upon this rock will I build my Church, and the gates of Hades shall not prevail against it." Hades, the abode of the dead, shall not be able to retain within its grasp the bride of Christ. For he saith, "I will ransom them from the power of the grave [Sheol, or Hades]; I will redeem them from death: O death, where are thy plagues? O grave, where is thy destruction? Repentance shall be hid from mine eyes" (Hos. xiii. 14). And so now each Christian soul cometh up, one after another, out of the wilderness, leaning upon her Beloved. When he calls us and bids us come to him, we feel that the world is indeed a wilderness; that it hath nothing to satisfy our cravings, our needs. And the soul cometh, drawn by the Saviour's love. "I, if I be lifted up from the earth, will draw all men unto me." The soul cometh up; it is a continual ascent. As the Lord was lifted up from the earth, so the soul cometh up, away from the world, nearer to the cross. Christ is calling us upwards. The holiness to which he bids us aspire is very high; it seems above our reach; it can be reached only by persevering effort; by climbing, little by little, ever higher; by making all the little matters of daily life opportunities of self-denial, means of disciplining our human wills into submission to the holy will of God. The effort must be continuous, conscious, real; there must be no looking back to the wilderness; no hankering after the flesh-pots of Egypt; no longing for the other masters, the world, the flesh, and the devil, which we renounced when we gave our heart to Christ. The soul cometh up from the wilderness. It is a solemn thing; a sight which causes joy in heaven, for the angels know the meaning of that ascent; they know the perils of the wilderness, the utter vanity of its seeming pleasures; they know the toil, the difficulty of that ascent; they know the great glory and gladness reserved for those that have achieved it; they know, too, how very precious every Christian soul is in the sight of the Lord, who bought it with his blood. At rest in heaven themselves, they watch with a deep interest the heavenward progress of each true disciple of the Lord. The long procession upwards of the ransomed saints must be a spectacle of varied and intense interest in the presence of the angels of God. And they see what was once seen by the King of Babylon, "Behold, I see four men loose, walking in the midst of the fire, and they have no hurt; and the form of the fourth is like the Son of God" (Dan. iii. 25). The angels see that each soul that cometh up is leaning on her Beloved. The journey is long and wearisome; the ascent is steep and rugged; but the soul that has found Christ, and clung to him with the embrace of faith—the soul that can say, "My Beloved is mine, and I am his," is not left alone in its weakness. There is a strong arm, unseen by the outward eye, but felt and realized by faith; there is a hand stretched forth to help—the hand that once caught the sinking Peter, and lifted him up out of the depths. Each faithful soul leaneth on her Beloved. We need that support always, at every point of the long, wearisome path; at every step of the toilsome, upward climbing. Without Christ we can do nothing; we sink backwards; we become listless and slothful. But while we feel his presence, while by faith we lean upon him, resting our weakness on his strength, then our progress is assured. We need that presence always, in all the little trials of our daily lives, in the greater sorrows and perplexities that emerge from time to time. That presence transfigures our life, turning troubles into blessings; making sorrows so many steps upwards, ever nearer to God. To realize that presence, the Lord Jesus must be "*my* Beloved;" I must give him my whole heart; I must know him with that holy knowledge with which the true sheep know the good Shepherd; and to gain the excellency of that blessed knowledge I must be content, like St. Paul, to count all things else as dross, as very dung, that I may win Christ, and be found in him.

> " I need thy presence every passing hour :
> What but thy grace can foil the tempter's power ?
> Who like thyself my guide and stay can be ?
> Through cloud and sunshine, Lord, abide with me.

> " I fear no foe, with thee at hand to bless ;
> Ills have no weight, and tears no bitterness ;
> Where is death's sting ? where, grave, thy victory ?
> I triumph still, if thou abide with me."

2. *The voice of the bridegroom.* According to the present pointing of the Hebrew, the second clause of ver. 5 is an utterance of the bride. Many of the Fathers and other Christian writers assign it to the bridegroom. This last arrangement seems by far the most natural. The king points out the birthplace of the bride; he recalls to her remembrance an incident of their early attachment—he shows her the tree under which they first met. So man and wife now, when united in a happy marriage, love to visit the early haunts of one another, and especially the places endeared to both by the memory of their first vows and promises. So to the Christian those places must be always full of sacred interest where the heavenly Bridegroom first won the love of his bride, the Church—Bethlehem, Gethsemane, Calvary. So to each Christian those spots are hallowed ground which are connected with events in our own religious life—our baptism, our confirmation, our first communion; or associated with any great and abiding impressions or influences for good which Almighty God has been pleased to grant to us from time to time. 3. *The response of the bride.* The bride is leaning on the bridegroom's arm; perhaps she was reclining her head upon his breast. She would ever remain in that dear embrace, near to him as the seal which was attached to the arm or neck. The seal of the king had great weight and value; it gave his authority to the document which bore it (Dan. vii. 17); it was precious and sacred, and would, of course, be jealously guarded. The king himself would wear it; it would be fastened on his arm, or it would be suspended from his neck and rest upon his heart. There the bride would ever be, encircled with her husband's arms, pressed close to his heart; it is her rightful place, for she is bound to him by the indissoluble ties of holy wedlock. So the Church, the bride of Christ, clings to her Lord. Without him she can do nothing; but, borne up in the everlasting arms, she hath a strength not her own. She would be near to him as a seal. She hath the seal of God, for she is "sealed with that holy Spirit of promise, which is the earnest of our inheritance " (Eph. i. 13, 14). She is God's foundation upon the holy hills (Ps. lxxxvii. 1), built upon the Rock of ages; and "the foundation of God standeth sure, having this seal, The Lord knoweth them that are his. And, Let every one that nameth the name of Christ depart from iniquity " (2 Tim. ii. 19). So each Christian longs to be borne up in the arms of Christ—those arms that were opened wide upon the cross, as if to fold his chosen in the embrace of his love; so each Christian longs to rest, as once St. John rested, upon the Saviour's breast; to be near to him, cherished as a seal that lies in its owner's bosom; so each Christian hopes to bear the impress of that sacred seal stamped more and more deeply into his inner life, that being now sealed with the Holy Spirit of promise, he may one day stand among the blessed, sealed with the seal of the living God upon his forehead (Rev. vii. 3). 4. *Her praise of love.* Why does she desire to be so close to the bridegroom, to be as a seal upon his heart? Because, she says, "love is strong as death." She has given him her love, and that love entirely fills and dominates her soul; she has taken him to be her husband till death; she

loves him with a love like that of Ruth: "The Lord do so to me, and more also, if aught but death part thee and me" (Ruth i. 17). That love, strong as death, the love of those wedded souls who in true affection have plighted their troth, either to other, "till death us do part," is a figure of the holy love that is betwixt Christ and his Church. Indeed, the love of the heavenly Bridegroom was stronger than death; stronger than a death of lingering torture, a death of ignominy and horror. "We love him, because he first loved us." His Church, drawn by the constraining power of his most holy love, has striven to return it. Many of his saints have loved him with a love strong as death; they have proved by the martyr's death the strength of their love. How should we have acted if we had lived in those days of fiery trial? It is a question which we should often and earnestly press upon ourselves, for the Lord has taught us that "he that loveth his life shall lose it, and he that hateth his life in this world shall keep it unto life eternal" (John xii. 25). St. Stephen, and the long line of saints who followed him, the noble army of martyrs, loved not their lives unto the death. How would it be with the many half-hearted, careless Christians who come to church, and call themselves disciples of the crucified Saviour, but have not learned to take up the cross and deny themselves for his sake—how would it be with them if they were suddenly summoned to choose between Christ and death? Which of us would be faithful unto death? Which of us would deny his Lord? It is an awful question—a question full of the deepest interest; for it is only such a love, a love strong as death, which can give us strength to overcome temptation, and to fight the good fight of faith. He who for the love of Christ endures hardness now, who puts aside his own wishes, and does habitually for Christ's sake things which but for the love of Christ he would not have done; he who habitually for Christ's sake leaves undone things which but for the love of Christ he would have gladly done,—he is learning to love Christ with a love strong as death, a love which is giving him strength to kill out of his heart worldly thoughts and earthly ambitions, so that, dying unto the world, he may live unto Christ. We must all pray and strive for that love strong as death; it should be the object of our highest ambition, our most fervent longing. We need it now as much as the saints and martyrs of the Lord needed it in the old times. For if they had to lay down their lives for Christ, we have now to give him our hearts, our lives; and to do that always, in times of anxiety, or sickness, or lassitude, requires a great love; a love strong as death; a love which we can only learn of the Máster who loved us with a love stronger than death, who himself set us the high example of self-sacrificing love, and now helps and teaches us by the gracious influences of the Holy Ghost, the other Comforter, whom he sendeth to abide for ever with his people. Love is strong as death, and jealousy is hard as the grave (Sheol, or Hades). Death is strong; he is the last enemy, the king of terrors. Hades is hard and stern; it is rapacious; it hath never enough; it holds its prisoners firm. But love is strong as death and Hades. Christ, who is Love, hath overcome death, and opened unto us the gate of everlasting life; the gates of Hades shall not prevail against his Church. Neither death nor life can separate from his love those who love him with a true love, a love strong as death; they, too, are more than conquerors through him who loved them. And when love is strong as death, the jealousy (in the good sense of the word), which is one of its developments, is hard, tenacious, as Hades. God is love, the infinite love, and he is a jealous God. "Thou shalt worship no other God: for the Lord, whose name is Jealous, is a jealous God" (Exod. xxxiv. 14). He asks for our whole heart; he is jealous of a divided service; he will not accept a service to be shared with another master. Such a service is stigmatized in Holy Scripture with the stern name of adultery. "Ye adulteresses," says St. James, in language of awful severity, "know ye not that the friendship of the world is enmity with God? . . . Do ye think that the Scripture saith in vain, The Spirit which he hath made to dwell within us, jealously yearneth after us?" or, as the words may also be rendered, "he jealously yearneth for the spirit which he made to dwell within us" (Jas. iv. 4, 5). God once breathed into man's nostrils the breath of life. He gave to man as his distinguishing possession a spirit. "I pray God," says St. Paul to the Thessalonians, "that your whole spirit and soul and body may be preserved blameless unto the coming of our Lord Jesus Christ" (1 Thess. v. 23). That spirit, his special gift, should be wholly his. It is that part of our complex nature which is receptive of the Holy Spirit of God, which, when illumined by his presence, can attain unto such knowledge of God as is now granted to us (" Now we see through a glass, darkly . . . now I know in part," 1 Cor. xiii. 12), and dwell in communion with God. God jealously desires the possession of that spirit. Therefore the Christian's love for God must be a jealous love; he must be very jealous of the intrusion of other loves, other ambitions, into the heart, which should be given wholly to God; he must keep his heart for God with a godly jealousy (see 2 Cor. xi. 2)— jealousy stern as that with which Hades retains its prisoners. And this holy jealousy is ardent, too—ardent as flames of fire; " a very flame of the Lord" (ver. 6, Revised Version). For its ardour comes from him; it is he who gives that ardent zeal—that zeal for the Lord which has urged his holiest servants to do and dare such great things for his love's sake. The great love of the Lord Jesus for our souls calls for something more than the lukewarmness of Laodicea. " Be zealous," it says to us; " be zealous and repent " (Rev. iii. 19). The name of God occurs only in this one place in the song; we read it here in the shortened form (*Jah*) of the adorable name, as if to teach us the sacred lesson of the disciple whom Jesus loved, that " God is love: and he that dwelleth in love dwelleth in God, and God in him " (1 John iv. 16). Holy love comes only from him. " Love is of God, and every one that loveth is born of God, and knoweth God " (1 John iv. 7). Such love cannot be quenched. It is so even with pure human love. " Many waters cannot quench it, neither can the floods drown it." The many waters of trouble, suffering, old age, cannot stifle love; it lives on still. It cannot be bought. " If a man would give all the substance of his house for love, he would utterly be contemned." Love cannot be bought or forced; it is essentially free and spontaneous; it springs up spontaneously in the heart (" when it pleases," ver. 4; also ch. ii. 7; iii. 5), in response to love, at the presence of an object capable of calling it forth. So it is with the holy love of God. God's love for us cannot be quenched. The many waters of our unbelief, ingratitude, and sin have not—blessed be his holy Name— quenched his gracious love. It cannot be bought; we cannot buy it with earthly gifts, with gold or silver, or external good works; it is given freely, graciously, and it abides in those who live in the faith of the Son of God. Our love for God is a faint reflection of his blessed love for us. It is called forth by that holy love. " We love him, because he first loved us." The waters of trouble and sorrow and temptation cannot drown it if it is true and real. These verses are the Old Testament psalm of love (see Ps. xlv., title), corresponding to 1 Cor. xiii. or the First Epistle of St. John, in the New Testament. They have a singular power and beauty; they are treasured in the memories of God's people; they have brought peace and comfort to many a death-bed.

II. INTERCESSIONS OF THE BRIDE. 1. *For her sister.* The bride has a sister not yet of marriageable years. What shall be done for her? If she be a wall, firm and steadfast, she shall be richly dowered; but if she be a door, too easily opened, too accessible, she must be carefully guarded. The bride herself is a wall, strong and steadfast in her virtue; therefore it was that she found peace in the bridegroom's eyes. There may possibly be an allusion here to the name Solomon, which follows in the next verse: the bride found peace in the eyes of the peaceful one. The bride is the Church, the little sister perhaps the Gentiles. Those Gentile Churches that will be steadfast in the faith, like Smyrna or Philadelphia, shall be built upon the foundation of the apostles and prophets, Jesus Christ himself being the chief Corner-stone (Eph. ii. 20). Those that are like Thyatira, Sardis, or Laodicea, still open to those other masters, the world, the flesh, and the devil, must be treated with wholesome severity; they must be carefully guarded and fenced in, and closed against the enemies of the Lord. The bride intercedes for her little sister. She herself has set a good example. Christian people must make intercession for the heathen, that they may be converted; for missionary work, that it may be prospered; and while they pray, they must be very careful to set a good example themselves, that the great work may not be hindered by any fault of theirs, but may go on and prosper till the earth be filled with the knowledge of God as the waters cover the sea. 2. *For her brothers.* She had spoken of their harshness (ch. i. 6). " They made me," she said, " keeper of the vineyards; but mine own vineyard [literally, as here, 'my vineyard, which is mine'] have I not kept." Now she intercedes with the king for them. She would have them to be keepers of her vineyard, and to receive a suitable recompense. She compares King Solomon's vineyard with her own. The king, she says, had one of great extent and value; every one of the keepers was to bring him a thousand shekels. Then she adds, "My vineyard, which is mine, is before me." Her vineyard was small; it lay before her eyes. It now passes into the hand of Solomon; it is his. He must have a thousand shekels from it. She wishes the keepers (her brothers, apparently) to have two hundred. The greater than Solomon, the heavenly Bridegroom, has a vineyard. It is the world (comp. Matt. xiii. 38, "The field is the world"). Solomon's vineyard was at Baal-hamon, which means "the Lord of the multitude." We may perhaps see in the word an allusion to him who is called in Holy Scripture "the prince of this world" (John xiv. 30). The Lord has a vineyard in the world, which Satan strives to rule. And men have still, as in Elijah's time, to choose whom they will serve. "If the Lord be God, follow him: but if Baal, then follow him" (1 Kings xviii. 21). But though Satan is called the prince of this world, and in one place (2 Cor. iv. 4) "the god of this world," he is a usurper; the vineyard is the Lord's. And the Lord has done all that could be done for his vineyard: "he has hedged it round about, and digged a winepress in it, and built a tower, and let it out to husbandmen" (Matt. xxi. 33). The husband-men were to bring him in due time of the fruits of his vineyard. They *were to* do so, but, alas! they did not; they served Baal, many of them, rather than the Lord. The Church's vineyard is before her; it lies within a comparatively narrow space; it does not cover a third of the population of the world. It belongs now to the heavenly Bridegroom, for the Church is his. He loved the Church, and gave himself for her; and that unspeakable gift, that stupendous ransom, has made her and all that she has wholly his. The fruits which that vineyard brings forth must be paid duly to the Lord of the vineyard. Those fruits are souls converted, sanctified, saved. The keepers too, if they are found faithful, have their reward. The souls saved through their means, their warnings, their example, their preaching, their labours, are their best and most precious reward in this world (1 Cor. iii. 14), and in the world to come, "when the chief Shepherd shall appear, they shall receive a crown of glory which fadeth not away" (1 Pet. v. 4). Each Christian soul is the Lord's vineyard; it must be cultivated for him, not for Baal. It may be a vineyard in Baal-hamon, set among a multitude who follow the prince of this world; but it is the Lord's, bought with his most precious blood. It must not bring forth wild grapes, fit only for the world, the flesh, and the devil; it must bring forth good fruit—fruit meet to be rendered to the Lord, to be treasured in his granary; the fruit of the Spirit—love, joy, peace, long-suffering, gentleness, goodness, faith, meekness, temperance. And the soul itself which keepeth the fruit; the soul that treasures up the graces of the good Spirit of God, that listens with reverent attention to his gracious warnings, and follows his guidance; the soul that worketh out its own salvation with fear and trembling through the grace of God, who worketh within both to will and to do,—that soul shall receive of the fruit; for "blessed are they that do hunger and thirst after righteousness: for they shall be filled." Love, trustfulness, obedience rendered to Christ, bring their own great reward in the irradiating presence of the Saviour. "If any man love me, he will keep my word; and my Father will love him, and we will come to him, and make our abode with him."

III. FINAL WORDS OF LOVE. 1. *The voice of the bridegroom.* He addresses the bride as "Thou that dwellest in the gardens," meaning, apparently, the vineyard which she had just mentioned. She has done her best for it. He accepts her past service. Now the king and his companions were listening for her voice; it was sweet to hear. "Cause *me* to hear it," the king says, meaning, it seems, that the voice of the bride was very sweet to him; he loved to hear it; and perhaps also implying that he was ready to grant any request that she might make, as well as that which she had already made. When the Church does her duty, dwelling in the gardens of the Lord, tending his vineyard, then there is joy in heaven, joy in the presence of the angels of God; they hearken to the prayers and praises of the Church. The Lord himself, the heavenly Bridegroom, delights to hear the voice of the bride; her prayers and adorations are as the holy incense, acceptable to him (Rev. viii. 3, 4). The Lord would have all Christian men to pray, and that constantly. His will is that men should pray always, and not faint. He graciously listens to the voice of his people when they speak to themselves in psalms and hymns and spiritual songs, when they make melody in their hearts unto the Lord (Eph. v. 19). And he grants their requests. "If ye ask anything in my Name," he says, "I will do it;" "Ask, and ye shall receive, that your joy may be full;" "Whatsoever ye ask in prayer, believing, ye shall receive." We must claim his blessed promise; we must make him hear our voice while we are "dwelling in the gardens," while we are labouring in the Lord's vineyard. True prayer leads to faithful work; faithful work stimulates prayer, and gives it energy and devotion. He will hear our prayers for ourselves, our intercessions for others, if only they are offered up in faith, in the Name of Jesus Christ our Lord.

2. *The response of the bride.* The king sought to hear the voice of the bride. She in response repeats the last clause of her song in ch. ii. 17; but she makes one important change—the mountains are no longer "mountains of Bether," which means "separation," but "mountains of Besamin" ("spices"). Perhaps there is a reference to "the mountain of myrrh and the hill of frankincense" in the royal gardens (ch. iv. 6). The bride no longer thinks of the possibility of separation. Formerly her beloved was separated from her for a while in his hunting excursions; now he is to be as bright and exultant as of old, but with her in their common haunts. The Church prays, "Thy kingdom come." Her prayer is that God of his gracious goodness would be pleased shortly to accomplish the number of his elect, and to hasten his kingdom. The Christian prays and longs for the coming of the Lord, beseeching him in ever-deepening earnestness to come, first in the kingdom of grace, into his people's hearts, then in the kingdom of glory, when the kingdoms of this world shall become the kingdoms of God and of his Christ, and he shall reign for ever and ever, King of kings, and Lord of lords.

HOMILIES BY VARIOUS AUTHORS.

Vers. 1—4.—"*Oh that men would understand!*" Such seems to be the sentiment of these verses. She who speaks grieves that those about her did not see how natural and right was her love for her beloved. She could almost wish he were her brother instead of her betrothed, for then those who saw her love for him would not, as now they did, despise her for it. She could not have been already a bride, as is so constantly assumed, for in that case her love could not have awakened scorn. But they despised her for clinging to one who, compared with Solomon, was in their esteem despicable. We may take the section as in part parallel to the sentiments in Rom. ix. 1—3; x. 1. She who speaks *could* not wish to be not betrothed, and only as a sister. Some, therefore (Newton), have regarded these verses as an address to the unconverted and unsaved. Others have held that the "brother" means only an infant brother. But we take it that as Paul could wish himself unsaved for Israel's sake, so here, she who speaks could even wish that she did not hold so dear a relationship to the beloved, but only that of a sister, so that those about her, etc. (cf. *supra*). The words in Romans and here are to be regarded as hyperbolical expressions, telling of strong desire for others' good, but not to be regarded *au pied de la lettre*. We note that—

I. MEN WILL ACCEPT THAT WHICH THEY REGARD AS NATURAL. The expression of affection between brother and sister all understand, allow, and approve. And some expressions of religious feeling they will also admit, provided they are marked by what they deem sobriety and conformity to general usage. All beyond that they despise.

II. BUT THE VEHEMENT AFFECTION OF THE SOUL FOR CHRIST THEY DESPISE. Several marks of such affection are suggested here. 1. *Open avowal of love to him.* "The religion of every sensible man," said one, "is that which every sensible man keeps to himself." Therefore such confession as is suggested by ver. 1, "When I should find . . . I would kiss thee," is of course extravagant and to be despised. 2. *Proselytizing in the family.* (Ver. 2.) "I would bring thee into my mother's house." Sincere religion is often deprecated as bringing strife into households, and it is difficult to see how our Lord's word, "I came not to send peace on earth, but a sword," can be escaped under such circumstances. And even if there be not absolute proselytizing, the mere presence of an earnest disciple in a house troubles those therein who have no or but little love for Christ. 3. *The habitual heed to his teaching.* (Ver. 2.) "That thou mightest instruct me" (Revised Version, margin). She would, like Mary, sit at her Lord's feet and listen to him. And even good people like Martha think such conduct not " a good part," and that opportunity for it ought to " be taken away from her." 4. *The giving to him of her best.* This the meaning of " the wine prepared from the pomegranate " (ver. 2). Such a sincerely loving soul will not be content with mere ordinary and routine service, but the best of all she has to give she will offer to him. 5. *But all this wins scorn and dislike.* She who speaks here was evidently " despised " for her devotion to her beloved, and so it is still when the like is seen towards Christ.

III. OUR AIM SHOULD, THEREFORE, BE TO SHOW MEN THAT WHAT THEY DESPISE IS ALTOGETHER REASONABLE AND RIGHT. That men might see this is what is so desired here. But men are as a child playing on a railway line in front of an advancing train. Some kind bystander rushes forward and clutches the child and puts it out of danger before the train is upon it. The child probably only stares displeasedly at him who has roughly interrupted its play ; no spark of gratitude is there. So men now do not see what Christ has done for them and is willing to do, and so their hearts are cold to him. The truth, therefore, that " God so loved the world " must be held up, insisted on, and shown by lives consecrated to him under the sense of that love.—S. C.

Ver. 5.—*The home-coming.* " Who is this that cometh up," etc.? The end of this pastoral song is approaching. The speaker in the former verses has finished her recital with words telling of her yearning love for her beloved, and an adjuration to those listening to her that they should not attempt to alter her mind towards him (vers. 3, 4). They are the same as in ch. ii. 7; iii. 5. And now the scene changes. She has been rescued from or permitted to leave her gilded but none the less hated captivity in Solomon's palace, and with her beloved is returning to her old home. A band of friends exclaim, " Who is this," etc. ? Applying the words spiritually, we may take them of the soul's home-coming. And they tell—

I. WHITHER SUCH SOUL COMES. It is ever an upward coming. For all the characteristics of the soul's true home are far above the soul's natural condition. For here, assuredly, *we have not peace.* " Man is born," not to peace, but " to trouble." Who knows not that? For sin is the great troubler. Therefore, for the soul to have what it so desires, it must come up and away from the wilderness. *Purity,* likewise. How here can we keep ourselves undefiled ? Who amongst men unregenerate and unsaved ever does so ? But as the soul in coming home enters into the peace of God, so also shall it partake of his purity. *Rest.* The trials, crosses, and disappointments of life, its manifold adversities, all ceaselessly proclaim to the soul, " This is not your rest." But " there remaineth a rest for the people of God." And the soul, uprising in faith and love towards God, does even here know much of the truth of Christ's promise, " I will give you rest." And then there is *the course and consummation of all these* in the presence of God eternally in heaven. Here we have pledges and foretastes, but there only are we made perfect.

II. WHENCE. " From the wilderness." How fit that word for the soul's condition here ere it is redeemed by Christ ! Are not the distress of conscience, the sense of guilt, the tyranny and cruelty of sin, the trials of life, and at length the grave,—are not all these wilderness-like things ? But when the soul comes home, it comes away from all these. It is not a coming *to* them, as every soul has to make acquaintance with them when it is born into the world; nor is it a coming *through* them—that is what we are occupied in now whilst we linger here; but it is coming *from* them, leaving them all behind. Oh, blessed home-coming of the soul !

III. HOW. " Leaning upon her beloved." This tells of the *soul's relation to Christ.* He is " her Beloved." Of its *union with him.* As it were linked lovingly together as the soul leans upon him. Of its *dependence upon Christ.* It is a long, rough, lonely, and difficult way that the soul has to traverse. It needs, therefore, that the Lord should be her " arm " every day (Isa. xxxiii. 2). Of its *communion with Christ.* Note the affectionate converse of the next verse. The maiden is represented as coming to a particular tree where once she had awaked him from a noonday slumber, and where, too, he had been born. " In Oriente non raro accidit ut mulieres in aperto pariant " (cf. Gen. xxxv. 16). And they talk of these reminiscences. It was natural, and tells of the familiar intercourse, the happy communion, which the soul enjoys with Christ. Yes, it is thus that we make our way homeward, heavenward. In union, in dependence, in communion, with Christ. Thus we come up from the wilderness leaning on our beloved Lord.—S. C.

Ver 6.—*Love's prayer.* "Set me as a seal," etc. 1. That she may *be precious in Christ's esteem.* As a seal, a signet-ring, of great value. 2. That she may *dwell in his love.* "On thine heart." Also: 3. That she may *enjoy the benefit of his intercession.* There is allusion, apparently, to the jewels engraved as a signet, and which were on the breast of the high priest of Israel (Exod. xxviii. 15—30). 4. That she may *be defended by his might.* "On thine arm." 5. That she may *express and satisfy his will.* As a seal does this for any writing on which it is impressed. Let not our "Amen" be lacking to such a prayer.—S. C.

Vers. 6, 7 —*Love's characteristics.* These verses may be regarded as the theme of the entire song. All its chief incidents are illustrative of the vigour, vehemence, and victory of true love. The literal story tells of the triumph of such love as seen in the maiden and her beloved, and as has often been seen in like human love. But as a parable or allegory, it tells of the love of the soul to Christ, and of his to us.

I. Its STRENGTH. "Strong as death." Death reigns. Who can resist his will? "Pallida mors," etc. (cf. Ps. xc.). *So love is all-powerful.* It is a universal passion. It bears away all men in its might. It is an irrepressible force. This is true of human love. And in *the love of the redeemed soul for Christ* it has proved itself again and again "strong as death." Every one of the noble army of martyrs has faced death and vanquished it. "They loved not their lives unto the death;" "For thy sake we are killed all the day long." And yet more in *Christ's love for us.* Physical death, even the death of the cross, could not daunt him. Spiritual death, even that in which we all were—dead in trespasses and sins—has not been and shall not be too strong for him, though sometimes it seems to be so. His love is surely as strong as that death. "Where sin did abound, grace," etc.

II. Its TENACITY. "Jealousy," or, rather, ardent, intense love—this is what is meant, not the mean passion which is known as jealousy. The same love is spoken of all through. And it is "cruel," or rather firm, tenacious, unyielding, "as the grave," as Sheol. Does hell ever give up its dead? Can we call back any from the grave? Can they who are there come back thence? So love holds fast that which it loves. The story of this song, as many a beautiful human story, proves the tenacity of true love. And the story of the Christian Church, in her love for her Lord, shows the same. What has not been done to compel redeemed souls to give up their love for Christ? And his love for us above all. "My sheep shall never perish, neither shall any pluck them out of my hand" (John x.).

III. Its VEHEMENCE. "The coals thereof are coals of fire," etc. Think of what such fire is and does. How it melts, fuses, and subdues that which comes under its power ! How, as in volcanoes, it struggles for the mastery until it finds vent in victory ! How it burns, consumes, tortures! Apply all this to intense human love—to the soul's love for Christ, and his for us. Are not many sinful souls conscious of Divine love's torturing power? See Peter when his Lord's look of love drove him forth in agony from the scene of his denial. Listen to Christ's word to Saul, "It is hard for thee to kick against the pricks." The baptism of the Holy Spirit is a baptism of fire (cf. Luke xii. 49, 50).

IV. Its UNQUENCHABLENESS. "Many waters," etc. There were such "many waters" which tried, in the beautiful human story of this song, but they could not quench the maiden's love for her beloved. And so has it been again and again in human experience. And think of the waters that sought to quench, and the floods to drown, the love of Christ in saintly souls. And they have failed, and will fail. And think of the like that could not extinguish, though so many more and fiercer far, the love which Christ bore towards *us.* Think of them, and see if Christ's love does not pass knowledge.

V. Its INCORRUPTIBILITY. "If a man would give," etc. It is not for sale; it cannot be bought or bribed. Again, apply this test to the three forms of love we have spoken of —human, Christian, Christ's. And apply all these tests to our own love, and see if it will endure them. If it will, be thankful indeed, and make it evident to all that it is so.

If it will not—and this is the sadder and more probable truth—behold, gaze on, contemplate earnestly, Christ's love to us; and then for us, too, it may come to pass, "whilst I was musing, the fire burned."—S. C.

Vers. 8, 9.—*The little sister.* This verse seems to be an inquiry on the part of those who are heard speaking in ver. 5. They probably knew the story of her who was now returning with her beloved, and their question shows their surprise. Then they listen to her entreaty addressed to him whom she so loved (ver. 6), and to her recital of the characteristics of such love as hers. They now interpose with the question in ver. 8 concerning a younger sister, who is not merely young, but, from the answer given (ver. 9), seems also to have been of uncertain and unsatisfactory character. But the question may be taken as addressed to the beloved by her who has just been speaking. Many think this; that it is she who is telling of her little sister, and asking what shall be done for her. If so, then the question and answer lend themselves as parables of great spiritual truths. It is not likely that these verses have been or will be often preached upon; but should they be, they may, perhaps, be profitably used by spiritualizing them as telling of the concern for others which the redeemed soul cherishes. When the woman of Samaria found Christ, she sought that others should find him too. The Prophet Ezekiel says, "Thy younger sister is Sodom" (xvi. 46). Hence we may take this sister as telling of the whole heathen world, and that world in its worst state. If so, then we may learn—

I. THAT THE HEATHEN, EVEN THE VILEST, ARE, AS WE ARE, CHILDREN OF ONE FATHER. "We have a *sister*." "Christ stands in the relation of an elder Brother to the Gentile as well as to the Jewish Church; therefore these two must be sisters." All men are to say, "Our Father which art in heaven."

II. CHRIST WILL CALL FOR THEM TO BE HIS OWN. There will come a "day when she shall be spoken for." Cf. "Other sheep I have" (John x. 16); "Ask of me, and I shall give thee the heathen for," etc. (Ps. ii. 8).

III. THEY ARE NOT READY FOR HIM. Not ready for that spiritual union with Christ into which his Church shall enter. How certain this is! They are sunk in sin.

IV. THIS IS A MATTER OF MUCH CONCERN TO THOSE WHO ARE CHRIST'S. "What shall be done for her?" This has been the impulse of all true missions, of all endeavours to bring in others to Christ.

V. THEY ASK AND GAIN COUNSEL FROM HIM. Ver. 9 gives his answer to the inquiry, "What shall be done?" "If she be a wall," etc. In the literal story this probably refers to her steadfastness in virtue (cf. ver. 10), and the "door" to an opposite character. We may take the words as telling: 1. *Of preparedness to receive the truth.* There is amongst some people a preparedness for the faith which greatly facilitates its reception. That preparedness is as a wall which shuts out the inroads of the vile vices which too commonly belong to heathenism, and, as a wall, strengthens them in the maintenance of many excellences. Where this is, there Christ will build a glorious Church (cf. Ps. xlviii. 12, 13). 2. *Of ordinary heathenism,* which is as a door, in and out of which come and go all manner and kinds of evils. If it be so, then, as in Rom. ii. 7, then she should be shut in, enclosed with sacred restraints, as with boards of cedar. And the providence of God has in the past and will in the future so work that it will restrain the grosser practices of heathenism. For often is it seen that even where the heart is not yielded to Christ, yet the sacred restraints of religious custom do tend to regulate conduct and hinder it from much evil. See the influence of Sunday on our national life. The counsel suggested, therefore, as to what to do in regard to those as yet not Christ's, is that where there is preparedness, encourage it; and where not, restrain the practice of evil, make sin difficult so far as you can.—S. C.

Vers. 10—12.—"*Gaudeamus igitur.*" The question has been asked and the answer given in reference to the "little sister." It was not clear what should be done, because it was not certain what her disposition might be. In contrast to such uncertainty, she who gave the answer speaks with joyous decision about herself that she is as a wall—not at all as a door—yea, as a strong tower; for though she might be assailed, her love could not be conquered. Her word here is like Paul's, "I have fought a good fight . . . I have kept the faith," etc. (2 Tim. iv. 7). Solomon had sought by every means in his power to bend her will to his, but she had remained faithful to her beloved. She tells of his great estate and of the wealth he obtained from it; but—speaking of her own love—she says she has kept her vineyard, and that it needed no guardian. King Solomon may keep his wealth, and his tenants theirs. She desired neither, but was glad and thankful, her heart was filled with joy, that, tried as she had been, she had yet remained true. Taking all this as a parable, we may learn that—

I. THE CONSCIOUSNESS OF SPIRITUAL VICTORY IS FULL OF JOY. (Cf. ver. 10.) What exultant tone there is in it: like that of the psalms which celebrate victory over enemies! The battle may often have wavered, defeat may have been very near, the struggle very severe; all such considerations invest the victory, when it comes, with great joy. To have kept ourselves unspotted from the world, how blessed this! And our own experience, we trust, has often known this union of joy with victory. The calm of spirit, the sense of the Divine approval, the "Well done!" of conscience, the sunshine in the soul when we have overcome some spiritual foe, all attest what we have said.

II. TOWARDS SUCH VICTORS ENEMIES BECOME FRIENDS. "Then was I as one that found peace." The meaning seems to be that the king, finding all his attempts to win her to be in vain, and struck, it may be, also, with admiration of her constancy, ceased from his solicitations, and let her depart. How often the like of this is witnessed! True, there may be foes who will remain so, though they cease from their temptations. Satan so ceased because he found he could not prevail when he tempted our Lord. But there may be those who cease their persecutions because they have ceased to be our foes. The centurion at the cross confessed, "Surely this was a righteous Man." And they who, returning from "that sight," smote their breasts in sorrow and repentance,—they would gladly have undone the work which that morning they had helped to do. And in the history of the Church, how perpetually was it the case that the constancy and fidelity of her martyrs won over those who before had been her foes; so that the saying went forth, "The blood of the martyrs is the seed of the Church"! And similar fidelity still wins similar triumphs; foes become friends (cf. history of Daniel).

III. THE POSSESSION OF ONE'S OWN SOUL IS BETTER THAN ANY OTHER POSSESSION BESIDE. (Cf. *supra* as to the probable meaning of these verses, which tell of Solomon's vineyard and her own.) She spurned all his wealth, but she prized her own truth and faithfulness. She had striven as Paul had, and succeeded in having a conscience void of offence. And no earthly honour or wealth can be put on a level with such possession, and can never compensate for its loss. Judas lost it, and went out and hanged himself. Hence the Bible says, "Keep thine *heart* with all diligence, for out of it," etc. Not only the kingdom of God, but your own kingdom—that which is your own indeed, and the source of your well-being—is *within you.*—S. C.

Vers. 13, 14.—*The last appeal.* These verses are spoken not by but to the beloved. Literalists say that it is the beloved who speaks, and asks his betrothed to sing to him, and that she complies, and sings to him her song, which we have in ch. ii. 17. But we prefer to understand the whole as her appeal to him. Note, therefore—

I. THE TITLE SHE GIVES HIM. "O thou that dwellest in the gardens" (ver. 13). The gardens are the souls of his loving people. Rightly are they so called, for he chose them for himself, loves to dwell in them, and it is needful for them that he should. (Cf. sermon by C. H. Spurgeon on 'Supposing him to be the Gardener.')

II. THE PLEA SHE PUTS FORWARD THAT SHE MAY HEAR HIS VOICE. "The companions hearken to thy voice." We regard these companions as the angels "that do his commandments, hearkening to the voice of his word" (Ps. ciii. 20). They hear his voice; then why should not the soul that loves him? Doubtless *we deserve it less than they*, but *we need it more than they*. Theirs is not, as ours, the perverse and unruly will; theirs is not, as ours, the daily need to confess sin and to seek its forgiveness, for they are holy as we are not. But then all the more we need to hear his voice causing us to know the way wherein we should walk. And *we love it as much as they.* "Sweeter is thy Word to me than honey," etc.; "The law of thy mouth is better unto me than thousands," etc. (and cf. Ps. cxix.). And *we will strive to obey it even as they*; therefore may each soul plead, "Cause *me* to hear it."

III. HER EAGERNESS FOR HIS COMING. (Ver. 14.) Cf. last verse of the Revelation, "Amen, come quickly. Even so, come, Lord Jesus" (cf. ch. ii. 17). Wherefore this eagerness? Because to the soul aglow with love to him all joy is sorrow without him, and all sorrow joy with him. The kingdom of evil needs to be subdued, the kingdom of God to be set up. Therefore would the soul have it that Christ should come swiftly as the bounding hart or the springing roe. That saintly soul, Samuel Rutherford, thus writes on this verse, "Oh, how long is it to the dawning of the marriage-day? O sweet Jesus, take wide steps! O my Lord, come over the mountains at one stride! 'O my Blessed, flee as a roe or young hart upon the mountains of separation!' O time, run, run, and hasten the marriage-day, for love is tormented with delays!" And what is St. Paul's word but an echo of this? "Our conversation is in heaven, from whence also we look for the Saviour, the Lord Jesus Christ." Thus "looking for and hastening unto the coming of the Lord" may we ever be! —S. C.

Ver. 5.—*The Christian pilgrim.* Life with every man is a journey; a march from the cradle to the grave. To the pious man this journey is religious; it has a moral character. It is not simply the inevitable moving on from year to year; beside this, it is a progress in knowledge, faith, holiness, and usefulness. The grave is not the Christian's goal. His goal is perfection—perfect excellence and perfect joy. Every day's experience is related to the great eternity. Each duty well discharged, each sin conquered, each trouble patiently endured, is a distinct step heavenward. It is not merely a movement onward; it is also a movement upward. The journey of the Hebrews through the wilderness to the earthly Canaan furnishes many instructive analogies with the Christian's passage to the skies. We, who possess the new life within, "seek a country, that is, a heavenly."

I. OBSERVE THE CHRISTIAN'S FORMER STATE. It is described as a "wilderness." 1. *It is a wilderness on account of its barrenness.* So in our unregenerate condition there was in us no fertility and no beauty. There may have been a few barren stalks of common morality; but they yielded no fragrance, they bore no fruit. In this wilderness there was nothing to satisfy the desires and aspirations of the soul. This world has its possessions, its pleasures, its honours, its shows, but none of these please or elevate the soul. We aspire after righteousness, after moral excellence, after the friendship of God; and with respect to these things this world is barren and empty. No man can lie down fully contented in it. It is not suitable for us as a possession; so that most men, burdened with care and infirmity, sigh out, "I would not live alway." "He that loveth silver shall not be satisfied with silver." The vapid joys of this world soon pall upon the appetite. They do not increase the capacity for joy; they diminish it. And many a man who has taken his fill of this world's pleasure concludes life with this dismal verdict on his lips, "Vanity of vanities; all is vanity!" 2. *Moreover, this wilderness is infested with foes.* If in the Arabian desert the Hebrews were exposed to human foes, to wild beasts and fierce serpents, so in this world many foes infest the way. Many and subtle are the snares which the enemy sets for our feet. We are liable to ten thousand annoyances. Evil men tempt us with a view to ruin us. "Satan goeth about as a roaring lion, seeking whom he may devour." We have need for perpetual watchfulness. We have to fight with many adversaries. Clearly "this is not our rest."

II. MARK THE CHRISTIAN'S PRESENT ASCENT. "He cometh up." 'Tis an ascent. 1. *Progress is the only way to perfection.* It is true that God might have brought about perfection by some other way; but, as a fact, he has ordained this way, and this only. All the similitudes employed in Scripture to set forth the Christian life describe it as a thing of progress. The progress may be slow or more rapid; nevertheless, if there is life there is growth. In some believers the processes of enlightenment, conversion, and edification may be more rapid than in others (just as in some climates the processes of budding, blossoming, and ripening in fruit trees are more rapid than in our own land); still, in every instance perfection is attained by distinct stages. The life of every Christian is a progress along the heavenly way. 2. *Discomfort is incident to a pilgrimage.* No one expects to find the same comforts on a journey which he finds at home. On a journey one is content with the bare necessaries of existence.

Would it not be madness to encumber one's self with soft couches and luxurious indulgences while on a journey? Would not such things seriously impede our progress? And is it not the one desire of a pilgrim to advance as rapidly as possible? To reach the end of his pilgrimage at the earliest hour is the uppermost desire of every true pilgrim. Therefore needless burdens are left behind. This is how ordinary pilgrims conduct themselves. And should not every Christian be more eager to advance along the way than to cumber himself with lands, or houses, or worldly honours? He who is bent on heavenly progress is bent also on self-denial. To grow like Christ, that is the Christian's daily business. Every day another step. 3. *The pilgrim often pursues a solitary path.* He is much alone. In the vision of the text only one is seen " coming up from the wilderness." She had left the broad path where many were found. She had left her old friends and companions. More and more the Christian has to walk alone. When first he resolved to follow Jesus he had to abandon former acquaintances; and, as often as he essays to reach a loftier level, he has to part with some comrades. He has learnt the art of personal decision. If others will not ascend with him to the higher planes of holy living, he must go alone. He would rather miss the company of a hundred than lose the company of his Well-beloved. Hence the frequent solitariness of the pilgrim. So far as outward connection with Christ's disciples is concerned, he will not separate himself. He cultivates all possible bonds of unity. He fosters Church life. But with regard to the inner life of his soul, *i.e.* his personal fellowship with Jesus, he is much alone. Yet, when most alone, he has the best society.

III. NOTE THE CHRISTIAN'S HELPFUL COMPANION. "Leaning on her Beloved.' 1. *This leaning implies a sense of Christ's nearness.* We cannot lean upon anything that is not close at hand, yea, in actual touch with us. Though we cannot perceive Jesus with the organ of the body, we have a stronger proof still of his nearness. The experience of the soul is far more real and far more reliable than any sensation of the body. No organ is more easily deceived than the eye. Certainly our Immanuel gains immediate entrance to the heart. This fact is contained in his name, " God with us." So, without the intervention of words or other vehicle, he imparts good cheer and strength straight to the soul. He comes nearer than any human friend can come. He knows all the secret doors by which to pass in. He touches all the secret springs of life and reanimates them. He comes "to give life, to give it more abundantly." 2. *Leaning means the transference of all our weakness to Jesus.* To lean is to find support in another. If I am too weak to walk a distance of fifty miles, and I take a seat in a railway train, I transfer my weakness to that steam-engine, and I take the benefit of its strength. At the outset of our Christian life we laid the whole weight of our sin upon our Substitute. We said, " God be merciful, for the sake of Jesus!" This was the foundation of our hope. As we grow in grace we learn more and more to leave our burdens in the hand of Jesus. We overcome the tempter, not by our own native strength, but through Christ, " who strengtheneth us." " I live," said St. Paul: " yet not I, but Christ liveth in me." This righteousness I have is Christ's righteousness. This love for sinful men is Christ's love " shed abroad in my heart." This wisdom to instruct and guide others is Christ's wisdom. I am " leaning on my Beloved." He takes on him all my weaknesses. He imparts to me his all-sufficient strength. It is a sacred and a vital partnership. Faith is perpetual dependence. 3. *This leaning implies that Jesus is a consenting Party.* He loves to be used, loves to be trusted. Our weakness can never be a strain upon him, for his strength is omnipotence. He cannot fail, for such faithfulness was never seen among men—no, nor among angels. I could not trust to him for my eternal well-being if I did not know that he shared in the Godhead. Clearly he is fully competent to take the whole weight of my salvation. And equally certain is it that he is willing. His love is as great as his power. His patience has often been severely tried, but it has proved abundantly adequate. The sun may cease to shine, the mountains may bow their snowy crests, the sea may vacate its bed; yet his loving-kindness and his faithfulness eternally abide—these cannot fail. It is to him a real delight to help the weak and needy. After fifty or sixty years' experience of his tender grace, he says to us, " You have never half used me yet; you have never trusted me half enough. Hitherto you have asked nothing, comparatively nothing. Ask, and ye shall receive." So that our response ought to be spontaneous, " My soul, wait thou only upon God; for my expectation is from him."

As the ivy clings for support to the oak, or as the limpet clings to the solid rock, so may we in our native weakness cling to the eternal Strength. As our faith grows, so will grow our love; and love, again, will encourage faith. There is a beautiful inter-action. We lean upon Jesus because he is our Well-beloved.—D.

Vers. 6, 7.—*Prayer for full assurance.* The marrow and essence of true religion is love. If there is no love to God, there is no religion. If I am not the object of God's love, I have no solid hope of a blissful immortality. Hence it is our primary and supreme concern to ascertain whether we have a place in God's affection. Has God a care for me? Has he put my name on his book of life? Is he engaged by solemn covenant to be my Friend eternally? I want to know this. If I am left in suspense, it is, of all things, most painful. It robs me of the inspiration and the stimulus of hope. It weakens my endeavour after holiness. It damps my zeal. It checks my cheerfulness, and kills my inward peace. Unless the warm sunshine of Immanuel's love encircle me, I shall not produce the ripe fruits of goodness. Will my love be steadfast? Shall I hold out to the end? Well, all is secure if I know that I share in the love of Christ; for that love is endearing, unchanging, tender, all-victorious, everlasting. If my name is on the heart of my Saviour, then my eternal fortune is certain. No ill can come to me through time or through eternity. Therefore this prayer, "Set me as a seal upon thy heart."

I. NOTE THE SUBSTANCE OF THIS PRAYER. 1. *It is a plea for love.* Unless God had revealed to us the fact that in his heart there glowed a vehement flame of love for sinning men, we could never have surmised it. We might have carefully noted his many arrangements in nature for ministering to our happiness. We might have reasoned in our mind that, since he had given us the capacity to love, the spring and fount of that love must be in his own breast. Yet this would have been at the best conjecture. We could not have built on it any hope of enjoying his personal friend-ship, or of sharing his society eternally. But he has given us a veritable gospel. He has assured us that his highest love centres in men. He has given us plain and practical proofs of the ardour of his love. He has given us the sure pledge that his love is a permanent force in his nature; yea, an attribute of his Godhead. Therefore this love kindles our hope, excites our profoundest desire. God loves me; hence I can become a better man. I can rise out of the mire of sin. I can emerge out of the grave of dark despair. I can become a child of God, a prince in the kingdom of heaven. My heart is deeply moved. I love him who gave himself for me. I want to love him more. But he must soften my nature, and draw out my love. Will he condescend to do it? Will he have pity on undeserving me? I want to have this question solved. Jesus, I pray thee make me thy friend! 2. *It is a petition for the assurance of Christ's love.* The language is very probably borrowed from an impressive scene in the temple. It was a part of the duty of the high priest, when he went into the holy place, and came into immediate contact with God, to wear upon his breast and upon his shoulders the names of the tribes of Israel. These names were graven upon precious stones, and this ceremony indicated the affectionate interest which the high priest felt in the welfare of the people. He lived for them. He made oblation for their sins. He interceded with God on their behalf. Their misfortunes and their falls became his misfortunes and his burdens. He identified himself completely with the people. So his influence with God was used for them. Now, we too have a great High Priest; not a frail, erring man like Aaron and his successors. We have a perfect Mediator, even the Son of God himself. He has passed into the heavens as our Representative. If he will identify himself with me, and undertake my salvation, I am fully content. For so excellent is he that his pleading always does and must prevail. Can I be sure that he feels an interest in me? Yes, it is possible. If I ask for this blessing I shall have it. Hence I pray, "Set me as a seal upon thy heart." 3. *This also is a plea for practical help.* "Set me as a signet upon thine arm." The love of Jesus is not an inactive sentiment. It is sympathetic; it is personally helpful. His love puts into gracious operation all the energies of his being. I want the protection of a mighty arm. I want superior help. My heart has grown very insensible through sin, and I want him to soften it. I want him to eradicate from me the old roots of lust and folly. I want him to break off my fetters of evil habit. I want him to remodel and revitalize my whole nature. No one else can do it. His strength is almightiness. If he will use his Divine power for my good, I shall be emancipated and purified and ennobled. I shall run gladly in his ways. And he is willing to do it. He delights in saving men and in doing good. So I will pray, "O Saviour, let thy great power work in me. Put forth thy strength on my behalf. 'Set me as a signet on thy arm.'"

II. OBSERVE THE ARGUMENT IN THIS PRAYER. "For love is strong as death." The Christian has large hope and has large expectation, because the principle or quality in God concerned about his salvation is love. So he argues with his heavenly Friend in this way: "It is for my eternal good that my name should be engraven on thy heart, for this I know that love is strong; yea, the mightiest thing in the world." 1. *This plea for the assurance of God's love is founded on the power of love.* Commentators have differed whether the writer had in view here Immanuel's love to us, or our love to him. But it is evident that the inspired writer is thinking about love in the abstract. Real love everywhere is strong. The timid bird, that usually flees from man or dog, will, to defend its young, risk its own life and attack its fiercest foe. Love is strong. What peril has not a human mother faced to save her child? Can we measure the strength of love by any known test? Can we express it by any metaphor? I cannot conceive any difficult feat too formidable for love. I think of love as I observe its working among men. I think of it as I experience its strength in me. It is next to omnipotent in man. It will readily confront death and grapple that mysterious foe. Amongst men, it is strong as death; yea, stronger, mightier! What, then, must love be in our Immanuel? Here it exists in perfect form, in uncreated measure, without a flaw or blemish. If love in Christ be the same sort of thing as love in my breast (and it is), then that love will endure anything to save its object. If my name is on Jesus' heart, this is my best-founded security for all good, present and eternal. 2. *The argument proceeds on this ground, that baffled love is poignant pain.* "Jealousy is cruel as the grave." This, again, is spoken of jealousy in the abstract. If I love, and my love is encouraged, and for a time reciprocated, until it burns with ardour; then, if a rival comes between me and my object, what pain, what fierce indignation, follows! Such jealousy springs out of injured love, that the heart-passion is uncontrollable. It over-leaps all barriers of law, all limits of reason. You cannot hold it in check. "It is cruel as the grave;" cruel as hell. Now, if Jesus has set his heart upon me; if he has sacrificed much on my account; if he has attested his affection by the cross and by the grave; then will he allow any rival to supplant him? Would there not be a feeling of intense pain, akin to jealousy, burning in his breast if anything came between him and the object of his love? Hence, for his own sake, he will not cast me off. For his own sake he will not cease to love me, nor cease to win my love in return. We are told that "he hates putting away." Here, then, is a very forceful argument, that for his own peace of mind, for his own honour, he will give me—poor, unworthy me—a larger place in his heart. "Having loved his own, he loves them unto the end." 3. *The argument proceeds on love's unchangeableness.* Literally translated, it is, "The coals thereof are the coals of God." This flame never decreases; it is fed from a store-house of infinity. Changeableness is incident to man, but it has no place with God. We may love a person under a false estimate of that person's excellence. The charms may be plausible and pretentious rather than real. Hence our affections may diminish, undergo complete change. This can never happen with God. He does not love us because we are lovable. He loves us in order to make us lovable and worthy of himself. His love chose us when we were aliens, rebels, depraved, dead in sin. As there was nothing in us to attract him at the first, so nothing in us will drive him away. He will correct, chastise, prune, purify us, but will not allow his love to change. Says he, "I have loved thee with an everlasting love." The flame of love which glows in his breast is a flame that cannot die out, so long as God is God.

III. THE RESPONSE TO THIS PRAYER. We may very properly regard this verse as the bridegroom's response. To the pathetic, yearning appeal of the bride, he promptly replies, "Thy argument is most valid; cogent in the extreme. Yea, verily, many waters cannot quench love, neither can the floods drown it." 1. *Love is all-victorious.* If it be imaged forth as a flame of fire, then in one respect the figure fails. You can extinguish flame with water, if only you can pour on a sufficient quantity; but on this flame of love no amount of coldness or opposition will cool it in the least degree. Let Satan and his legions do their very utmost to lessen the intensity of this heavenly flame, their labour is vain. They only prepare for themselves a bitter disappointment. Or let the floods of human vice and human antagonism rise as they may, they can never rise as high as this heavenly flame. The finite can never o'ermaster the Infinite. The love of God to men is a sacred principle, an integral part of the Divine nature. There is nothing outside God to be compared in potency with what is within him. As the creature can never be a match for the Creator, so no kind of opposition can ever injure or diminish the eternal love of God. Just as nothing on earth nor in hell can diminish God's power or tarnish his righteousness, so also nothing can lessen or dim the fervent flame of his eternal pity. "Many waters cannot quench love;" yea, love turns all human hatred into fresh coals to feed the flame. 2. *Love has a priceless value.* The argument on the part of the Bridegroom seems to be, "Wherefore should my love abate? If it should, there must be some reason for it. What reason can there be? what advantage? what gain?" Even were there some advantage to be gained, this would not weigh in the scale. For love scorns all advantage. Love delights in sacrifice. Only let love discover how it can make some new surrender, in order to bless the fallen and the wretched, and straightway love makes the surrender. Jesus will give up his heaven, his joy, his crown, to-day; give all up without hesitation, if he can thereby lift some poor sinner into a righteous life. On his part nothing shall impede the activities of his ardent love. Will he ever listen to any proposal to allow his love to rest? Never! Will he at any time prefer ease, or rule, or fame, or worship, to the outgoings of practical love? Never! A thousand times, never! Do I feel myself now more unworthy of his love than ever in my past history? Then, my soul, be hopeful! Here is greater scope for Immanuel's love! Spirit of truth, show me more clearly yet my guilt, my ingratitude, my inward corruption! For then shall I see how much I need my Saviour's pity, my Saviour's help. Then I know that he will run to my deliverance. For "Christ died for the ungodly." He loves to save the needy. If I have had much sin forgiven, then shall I love much. "Therefore, Lord, write my name upon thy heart, for in me thy love shall have a glorious triumph!"—D.

Ver. 11.—*Stewardship.* This language is Oriental, yet the lesson is cosmopolitan. In every kingdom there must be a system of economics. For a prosperous condition there must be division of labour. The land must be cultivated. The people must have food. The king's household must be sustained. To this end scope should be given to personal skill and personal enterprise. So a wise king farms out his land to husbandmen, who are under obligation to render back a fair proportion of the produce. This system brings the greatest advantage to both parties. Now, all this has its counterpart in the kingdom of God. Every man is a steward entrusted with God's property. He cannot live for himself. A day of reckoning is appointed, when the account must be produced and examined. Life, with all its possessions and privileges, is a sacred responsibility. Independence of God is impossible.

I. OBSERVE THAT GOD IS THE GREAT PROPRIETOR. "The earth is the Lord's, and the fulness thereof; the world, and they that dwell therein." No part of this vast and illimitable universe is exempt from his lordship. 1. *His claim is founded on creation.* God alone is uncreated. The unfallen hosts of angels, all principalities and powers in heaven, no less than the tiniest insect on earth, are the workmanship of his skilful hands. Creation gives a prescriptive and an indisputable right. What I make I claim as my own, though probably the raw material belonged to another. But God created out of nothing, or rather out of himself; therefore his title is without a flaw. 2. *His claim is founded on preservation.* For preservation is simply a continuous act of creation. He sustains in existence every atom of material, every form of life, every dynamic force, and this through every successive hour. In this way he asserts perpetually his supreme rights of property. Every vineyard is his workmanship. The life of every tree is his gift. The nourishing qualities of the soil; the sunshine, dew, and rain; all influences of the revolving seasons—*all* are his contributions to the maintenance of 'the vineyard. This is simply a sample of God's sustaining activity. My life hangs upon him through every hour. "In him I live and move;" "By him all things consist." 3. *His claim is founded on acknowledgment.* We admit that we are not our own. The enlightened conscience of every man testifies that God is the supreme Owner. We are not masters even of ourselves, nor of our own life. We did not choose in what year, or in what city, or in what family, we would be born. We have no control over our continuance in life. The voice from heaven says, " Return to the dust, ye children of men!" We have no control over the mode or the time of our departure. Nor have we unlimited control over our property. Sudden misfortune may scatter our wealth. " Riches make themselves wings and fly away." We feel that we are accountable to God; for to the bar of our own consciences are we frequently brought, to be prejudged of the use we have made of life, and the decision of this court will simply be ratified in the great assize. We are tenants at will. We have only a life-interest in our earthly possessions. We are stewards, not proprietors.

II. Observe that God has made us keepers, or stewards. "He let out the vineyard unto keepers." The interest of the Proprietor is to be kept in view. We are "keepers" of his property. *His* good, not ours, must be sought. 1. *This steward-ship comprises everything.* My body is not my own; it is a temple of the living God. Every organ of body and of mind is simply entrusted to my care. My tongue is not my own; it is an instrument for praising God. My learning is not my own; it should be laid on God's altar. My will is not my own; it should be made submissive to God's will. Hourly my prayer should be, " Lord, what wilt thou have me to do?" Even the skill for gaining money belongs to another. "Say not in thine heart, My power, and the might of my own hand, have gotten me this wealth. But thou shalt remember the Lord thy God, for it is he that giveth thee power to get wealth." If I live to please myself, I am usurping the place of my Lord, and I incur his displeasure. 2. *We are stewards who know the will of our Master.* He has not left us in ignorance respecting the business of our life, or in what way his property should be employed. The vineyard must be " kept," and must be made fruitful. His Word is full of instruction, which demands our careful study and our faithful observation. In these living oracles he clearly speaks, " Son, go work to-day in my vineyard." " As ye have opportunity, do good unto all men." " Follow me," says Jesus. In other words, he means, " Live as I live. Spend life in doing good." We cannot plead as an excuse for slothfulness that we know not the will of our Master. And if we desire to obtain fuller direction, the Master himself is at hand, and guides every submissive soul. " Ask, and ye shall receive." For the promise still runs, " I will guide thee with mine eye." 3. *We are stewards who have the ability to do our Master's will.* He is no hard Task-master, requiring the tale of bricks without providing raw material. On the contrary, " his yoke is easy." In every circumstance, his friendly voice whispers, " My grace is sufficient for thee." Often do we put up the prayer, " Thy kingdom come, thy will be done." But it behoves us to remember that the means for attaining this great end lie within our reach. Had all servants of God been faithful in their office, what a different world would this be to-day! How large a proportion of our fellow-men would be in the kingdom of God! It does not suffice that we serve Christ with one talent, while we allow other talents to lie idle. We cannot, with our money gifts, buy release from personal service. As no man can transfer to another his mental endowments, or his social influence, or his personal responsibility; so no man can transfer to another man his work. In these vineyards, service by proxy is not allowed. That person whom I presume to employ is already under the same obligation as myself, and cannot there-fore serve as my substitute. Nor can we hope to see any great enlargement in the kingdom of Christ until each separate disciple feels and realizes that the burden of the world's salvation rests upon him. " As each one hath received the gift, let him minister the same, as a good steward of the manifold grace of God."

III. Note that God appoints a reckoning-time. In the annual vintage season, the husbandman was required to make a proper return to the owner. This return might be made either in kind or in some equivalent. 1. *There is a special season for this reckoning-time.* Speaking generally, the reckoning-time will be at the day of judgment. Yet, for all practical purposes, this tenure terminates at death. Then our Lord comes, and convoys his servant home. Then the authoritative voice says, " Give an account of thy stewardship, for thou mayest be no longer steward." Then the faithful servant gives in his account with joy. " He has boldness in the day of judgment." It is the end for which he has toiled and waited. Just as the busy farmer rejoices greatly when his last harvest-sheaves are garnered, because his tòil has reached a successful end; so the disembodied Christian presents himself before his Lord with rapturous joy. For, with the fruits of his toil surrounding him, he confidently says, "Here am I, Lord, and the children thou hast given me. It is only thy talent I have thus multiplied. Not unto me, not unto me, but unto thy Name be all the glory." 2. *Note the system of the reckoning.* In God's kingdom the system must be strictly equitable; on God's part generous. That system is that a fair proportion of the gain belongs to God. He that is entrusted with ten talents is required to bring more gains than the man with only five. In proportion to our faith, fidelity, and zeal will be the measure of our success. Divested of all imagery, the simple fact is that each Christian is required to increase righteousness, loyalty, and love in God's world. I am expected to leave this world better, *i.e.* holier, than I found it. My business in life is to bring men nearer to God. If I can increase in men repentance, faith, piety, mutual benevolence, I have fulfilled my stewardship in some measure. If I have persuaded men to abandon a life of sin and to follow Jesus, I have brought honour to my Master's Name. My life-work as a Christian is to enlarge the spiritual empire of Messiah. As in the fields of nature seed-corn will produce sixty, or eighty, or a hundredfold; so each servant of Jesus Christ should lead sixty, or eighty, or a hundred men out of a state of rebellion into the covenant grace of our Immanuel. Saved ourselves, it should be our main business in life to save others.

> "What is my being but for thee,
>   Its sure support, its noblest end?
> Thy ever-smiling face to see,
>   And serve the cause of such a Friend?"

D.

Vers. 13, 14.—*Sacred fellowship.* The love of Christ to men amazes us by its generosity; it amazes us also by its constancy and its condescension. He, who delighted in human companionship when on earth, delights in it still. In his irrepressible longing to do us good, he encourages us to speak freely, to tell out our desires, and to ask largely. Our requests for his gifts are never too large; they are invariably too small. If he can increase our faith in him and draw forth our love, he has done us greatest good. So, with exquisite tenderness, he says, "Cause me to hear" thy voice.

I. OBSERVE THE CHRISTIAN'S ABODE. "Thou that dwellest in the gardens." 1. *This description of the Christian's dwelling implies quiet retirement.* Formerly he loved bustle and excitement; now he loves a place for quiet meditation and prayer. He finds more pleasure in being among the works of God than among the works of men. As at the beginning God provided for Adam a garden, because most suited for healthfulness both of body and of soul; so the man who has the mind of Christ feels strongly the attractiveness of a garden. He loves to be shut out from the world, and to be shut in with God. He is a learner; and in deep quietude he best learns the mysteries of the kingdom of heaven. 2. *A garden implies privilege.* It is a privileged place. It is not open to all comers. The believer is no longer a rover, wandering up and down the earth in quest of some unpossessed good. He is not, like Cain, an outcast. He does not inhabit a wilderness, like the Edomites. The best situation this earth can furnish is for him. The place where God reveals himself is the place for him. Once it was a wilderness, now it is a garden. Among the lilies the good Shepherd feeds his flock; so there the Christian loves to abide. In the cool of the evening God walks among the trees; so there the Christian will walk also. It is Christ's garden, Christ's workmanship; a place of special privilege. This garden is, of course, the Church. Here the Christian sees what beauty and what fruitfulness adorn others; so he is emulated to be fragrant and fruitful also. 3. *A garden implies useful occupation.* For though God himself is the chief Husbandman, there is something for every Christian to do in the garden. He cannot give life to the plants, yet he can water them; he can shield them from peril; he can prune and train the branches. He is a worker along with God; a partner in service. Such occupation is contributive to his own life and health and joy. An idle Christian is an anomaly. So long as I am in the Church, my influence is felt in moulding the Church. The Church will be either better or worse for my presence. My zeal for fruitfulness will be contagious. My devoutness will lift the Church to a loftier elevation. Or my unspirituality will chill the ardour of the Church's love. I cannot be an idle spectator. I must do good work in the Church or bad. I am called unto usefulness. 4. *A garden implies abundance of good.* Whatever can meet the hunger of the body, or gratify the nostrils, or please the eye, or bring delight to the whole man, is found in a perfect garden. The word suggests abundance. So, in the Church, Jesus Christ spreads a perpetual banquet. He well knows our every requirement, and he anticipates every need. Here is truth for the nourishment of the soul, wisdom for practical guidance, refreshing cordials for hours of weariness, strength for daily duty, deep wells of water for the soul's thirst, grace for every time of need. No earthly garden can fitly picture forth the lavish provision God makes for our souls. Not a blessing is withheld. "All things are ours; for we are Christ's, and Christ is God's." Much as I have already received, there's much more to follow.

II. MARK THE CHRISTIAN'S SPEECH. "The companions hearken to thy voice." 1. *This means that a Christian is social.* If he has withdrawn from the society of worldly men, he is the more drawn into the fellowship of the saints. A Christian cannot be a recluse. This is a mistaken idea of his position and his obligation. Christian love excludes selfishness. His new instinct impels him to help others. He yearns that all men may be saved. God has given him the talent of speech. It is a wondrous gift. He can convey *his* thoughts to others. He can express tender feeling and brotherly sympathy to others. He can reprove faults and encourage virtues by his speech. He can have intimate friendships, which shall be helpful to him and to others. He dare not leave neglected the social side of his nature, or he will be disloyal to his Master. 2. *His speech is attractive.* "The companions *hearken* to thy voice." They did not complain of the harshness or bitterness of his speech. The very reverse: "they hearkened." It was pleasant. There was a heavenly savour about it, that made it winsome. It was like a breath of spring that quickened and refreshed them. The Christian's converse sheds new light into others' minds. It stimulates gently all the better impulses of the soul. It strengthens faith and love and hope. He hears new revelations from God's lips, and communicates the message to his fellows. Each Christian can help and instruct other Christians. Each has his own peculiar experience of the new life, and the interchange of experience is comforting and stimulating. If we speak what "we have known, and tasted, and felt, and handled of the good word of life," if we speak under an impulse of love, our speech will be attractive, and will minister grace to the hearers. "As iron sharpeneth iron," so do wise and gracious words quicken friendship. 3. *This Christian speech was praiseworthy.* Had it not been so, the Divine Master would not have asked to hear it. May we not learn here how ready our Immanuel is to find occasion for commending us? Instead of being in a mood for censoriousness, he is always ready to put the best construction on our doings. If he can find in us a virtue to praise, he will do it. It well behoves us, then, to ask ourselves whether our converse with others is always edifying. Our speech greatly influences men; is that influence always on the right side? In the dark days of Israel's fall, there were a few "who spake often one to another: and the Lord hearkened, and heard, and a book of remembrance was written before him." During his earthly ministry, Jesus often reminded men of the power that resides in human speech, and of the tremendous issues that follow. "By thy words thou shalt be justified, and by thy words thou shalt be condemned."

III. THE CHRISTIAN'S FELLOWSHIP SOUGHT BY CHRIST. "Cause me to hear it." 1. *A rare instance of Christ's meekness.* There is nothing more edifying or more delightful to the Christian than to listen to the voice of Jesus. "Never man spake like this Man." His words are like pearls of wisdom, and for sweetness are like the droppings of the honeycomb. But how comes it to pass that Jesus can find pleasure in listening to our imperfect speech? This is almost a crowning act of condescension. He delights to hear our voices. He asks us *so* to speak that he may hear. He loves to hear us speak as his witnesses among men. He is pleased to hear our testimony concerning himself. His ear is gratified with our songs of adoration and gratitude. Specially he rejoices to hear our voices in prayer. "Hitherto," he says, "you have asked nothing" —comparatively nothing—"in my Name. Ask, and ye shall receive, that your joy may be full." As an earthly father delights to hear the silvery prattle of his little child, and no request from an infant's lips goes unheeded; so our God finds peculiar pleasure in hearing our voice of childlike appeal. Before we finish our petition, the answer is on the way. 2. *This request is an outcome of Christ's relationship to us.* Since he has entered into intimate and affectionate union with us—ay, made with us a marriage covenant—it follows that communion with us is a thing to be desired. If he had not been willing to live with us on familiar and reciprocal terms, he would not have entered into this mystic and organic union. Having made the greater sacrifice, he will not refrain from the lesser. It is not his fault that his intercourse with us is not more frequent, more close, more sensibly enjoyed. He is ever asking us to treat him as our bosom-Friend, and to trust him for every kind of need. It is as if he said to us, " You tell your troubles unto others; why not tell them unto me? Cause *me* to hear thy voice!" Would a loyal wife tell her cares and her griefs to one and to another, while refraining from speaking of them to her husband? Would not this be a scandalous folly? Hence Jesus says to us, " Tell me everything. There is nothing that disturbs your peace which is not a care to me." We are charged to " cast *all* our care upon him." And our simple duty is, " in everything . . . to make known our wants unto God." 3. *This request of Christ will serve as a corrective.* To remember that Jesus wants to hear our voice, will this not often be a check upon our speech? Those hasty or unkind words of ours respecting another, did not Jesus hear them? Or, if we are forming in our minds an ungenerous estimate of a neighbour, does not Jesus whisper to us, " Cause *me* to hear thy voice "? Even thoughts are heard by him. The voice that Jesus hears is not always the voice that others hear. They hear the words which escape the lips. Jesus hears the intention uppermost in the mind. Jesus hears the " still small voice " of our motives. Our every feeling, our every ambition, has a voice, and Jesus says, " Let *me* hear it." It is for our good that he should hear it all. My best Beloved is ever listening. How soft and loving and true should my voice always be! I must " set a watch on the door of my lips, that I sin not with my tongue."

IV. THE CHRISTIAN'S RESPONSE TO HIS LORD'S REQUEST. " Make haste, my Beloved, and be thou like to a roe or to a young hart upon the mountains of spices." 1. *Note the promptness of true obedience.* Jesus had said, " Cause me to hear thy voice." Forthwith the loving soul responds, " Lord, thou shalt hear it. Come, Lord Jesus; come quickly!" No word could be more welcome to Jesus than that. It is as if the spouse had said, " Mayhap my voice may express feelings and inclinations which are very faulty; but do thou, beloved One, come, and thou wilt correct all faultiness. Thy presence will be food and medicine, rest and growth, in one. The 'one thing needful' is thyself. I pass by all the streams of help; I come to the Fountain-head. Thou art the Fount of life. 'All my springs are in thee.'" Love is swift to obey 2. *Yet absence is for a time expedient.* The night is as needful to the plant as the day. Winter is as useful to agriculture as summer. It was expedient for the first apostles that Christ's visible presence should be withdrawn. They learnt to use the wisdom and the courage which he had given them. They gave themselves more to the study of Scripture and to prayer. They showed far more enthusiasm and zeal than when he was among them. We see, as a fact, that great advantage accrued to them from the departure of Jesus. So is it still. We have from him all the help we need. We have his mighty Spirit in our souls. To have the visible presence of Jesus would fill us with a new rapture. But enjoyment is not the main thing now. We want personal holiness and personal consecration; these are attained through faith. 3. *The Christian interprets this command of Christ as a fresh proof of his love.* Did he say, " Cause me to hear thy voice "? then this is a love-token. He would not desire to hear my voice unless he loved me. What delicate reminders of his love does our Immanuel give! How he devises to do us good, and plans to give us pleasure! And the more love grows, the stronger grows the desire to see him as he is. We long to have nearer access to Christ, without a veil between. 4. *Love is impatient of all delay.* We cannot climb to the heavenly heights, or sometimes we would. Hence, if there is to be a meeting between Christ and me, he must come down to me. Where he dwells must be a mountain—a mountain of fragrant spice. As mountains are the eminences of nature, the loftiest parts of this material globe, so they help us to ascend to those empyreal heights, where true purity resides, where the Highest dwells. Love can conquer every hindrance. Love annihilates distance and time. Already Love dwells in the future. To her eye the final consummation is reached; and hence she sings, " Come, Lord Jesus; come quickly ! "—D.

Vers. 1—3.—*The ardour of spiritual love.* There is no measure, no restraint, in this language. If it is possible for human love, when duly placed, to be too fervent and absorbing, this is when that is given to the creature which it behoves us to reserve for the Creator. Passion and poetry combine to express the deepest emotions, the most ardent wishes of the soul.

I. THE OBJECT OF SPIRITUAL LOVE. 1. In loving Christ the soul centres its purest and strongest affections upon One who is in himself infinitely excellent. Earthly love is often the creature of the imagination, conceiving beauty and excellence which do not exist, or which exist in a measure extravagantly exaggerated. There is no possibility of thinking too highly of the Saviour, of admiring him too absorbingly, of loving him too warmly. He is all, and more than all, that our imagination can picture. 2. In loving Christ the soul does but render to him what his services and his sufferings deserve from our hearts. " We love him, because he first loved us." He has done for us what none other could or would have done. " While we were yet sinners, Christ died for us." Is it possible to overstate our obligations—to offer him more than he has a right to expect and to claim from us?

II. THE YEARNING OF SPIRITUAL LOVE. Love would *receive* from the beloved. Two points are suggested by the passionate and glowing language of the text. 1. A desire for intimacy, for closest fellowship, for endearing friendship. 2. A desire for instruction, for lessons such as Christ only can convey to the soul of the disciple. It is well that we should look to our Lord for all things, for the wisdom that guides, the love that cheers, the grace that supports and sustains. The proper attitude of the Christian towards his Lord and Saviour is an attitude of dependence, of supplication, of expectation.

III. THE TRIBUTE OF SPIRITUAL LOVE. Love would *give* to the beloved. And the saved, rejoicing soul would fain offer of its best to Christ. The kisses, the spiced wine, and the pomegranate juice which the bride would offer to her spouse may suggest to us that Christ looks for the affection, the holy service, the consecrated devotion, of those for whom he died. What can we give him? If we cannot bathe his feet with tears or anoint his head with precious and fragrant unguents, we can at all events offer to him the sincere affection of the heart, a constant place in our thoughts, the tribute of our praise, and, to crown all, the service which, being rendered to his people, he will accept as given to himself.—T.

Ver. 5.—" *Leaning upon her beloved.*" As a skilled artist by two or three strokes brings some incident vividly and picturesquely before the eye, so does the poet here by a few words picture before us a scene harmonious with the whole composition, and depict the mutual relation of the two personages of this exquisite dramatic idyll. We see the bride returning to the home of her youth, quitting the familiar pastures, and approaching the dear abode; she is " leaning upon her beloved." If true love is suggestive of true religion, as is not to be doubted, then we may regard this attitude as having its analogue in the Christian's wonted experience as related to his Lord.

I. THE CHURCH'S INNATE WEAKNESS. Men sometimes use extravagant language regarding the Church, as though in itself it were great and powerful. But the juster view to take is that suggested by the posture of the beloved coming up out of the wilderness. All the Church has is derived; she can neither stand nor walk alone; her steps would falter if unsupported, would stray and err if unguided.

II. THE CHURCH'S DIVINE FRIEND AND HELPER. Christ, who has called his Church into fellowship with himself, is alone able and willing to take her under his protection and control. He knows the way in which she is to walk, the enemies she will encounter, the dangers by which she will be assailed. And he has all resources of spiritual strength and wisdom, encouragement and love. Every earthly counsellor and friend has limited powers, which sooner or later will surely fail. There is no measure to Christ's capacity to save and bless.

III. THE CHURCH'S WILLING, GRATEFUL, AND CLINGING DEPENDENCE. They who would fain go alone are not Christ's. So surely as he chooses his own, so surely does he put within them a spirit of subjection and attachment to himself. A cry for leading and for support comes up from the depths of the spiritual nature—a cry to which Christ is never indifferent, to which Christ always responds. He bids her " lean hard " upon him.

IV. THE CHURCH'S HAPPY SECURITY. Having given herself into his keeping, she knows that she is safe; that he will lead her aright, that he will never leave and never forsake her; that if she stumbles, she will not be allowed to fall; that if she is faint and weary, he will uphold her tottering steps; that if she is fearful, his words and his smile will banish her apprehensions and restore her peace.—T.

Vers. 6, 7.—*The power and praise of love.* Literature furnishes no eulogy of the passion which most profoundly stirs the heart of man more splendid than this. Some of the clauses have passed into proverbs, and are often upon the lips. Here is a human scintillation from the Divine fire, glowing with something of the brilliancy of the celestial original. Such language as this has been adopted as their own by those ardent souls with whom piety is a passion, and for whom the love of God consumes all earthly emotion and desire. To analyze such poetry seems almost a profanation. Yet we may trace herein some of the characteristics by which the love of the saints of God has ever been in some measure distinguished. Of that love, especially as enkindled by the sacrifice of the Divine Redeemer, we are reminded that it is—

I. ARDENT. "A very flame of the Lord;" " the flashes thereof like flashes of fire." The story of the Church tells us of many whose affection and devotion to their Lord cannot be justly described in less fervent terms. There have been consecrated apostles, zealous missionaries, seraphic saints, who have been consumed with this sacred passion. And lowly Christians have lived, and yet live, unnoticed by the world, and little recognized even by the Church, in whose breasts this pure fire has burned with fervour so glowing as to verify this glowing language.

II. STRONG AND TENACIOUS. There is a frequent belief that as a keen bright flame soon burns itself out, so it is not to be expected that piety should long retain its utmost fervour. It is presumed that the exalted mood must pass away, that the spiritual passion must give place to the cold ashes of indifference. But this is not so with the love which consciously responds to the love which passeth knowledge. This is persistent, and is " strong as death."

III. UNQUENCHABLE. "Many waters" roll over it in vain, "neither can the floods drown it." Opposition and persecution try their power upon this spiritual passion, only to find that it is more than able to resist them. The oil which is poured upon the fire by the hand that is unseen is mightier than the water which is dashed upon it by the carnal, cold, and unbelieving world. Nay, the worldliness and indifference too often distinctive of professing Christian society, more dangerous than open hostility, is powerless to extinguish the flame which God himself has kindled.

IV. UNPURCHASEABLE. How true is this language even of human love, which, if it be sincere, is surely spontaneous and unbought! If love is to be purchased, it is love and not money which must be paid for it; " the substance of a man's house " is no equivalent for the priceless treasure. Gratitude and service may be bought, but love is beyond the value of jewels and of gold. We are taken into another region than that of market value and of merchandise. It is the love of the Saviour, that love which shone through the lurid darkness of Calvary, which wins the love of human hearts.

> " I give my heart to thee,
>   O Jesus most desired;
> And heart for heart the gift shall be,
>   With grateful ardour fired."

V. IMMORTAL. It is *sealed*, i.e. for an everlasting possession. An ancient writer said, " Christ seals us in the heart, that we may love him; in the forehead, that we may confess him; in the hand, that we may profess him, and that we may practise what we profess." Over this love time and death have no power. It burns brighter when the lamp of life burns low; it breaks forth in perfect lustre when, beyond this murky atmosphere of earth, it reaches the clear air of heaven.—T.

Vers. 11, 12.—*The reward of the faithful.* The vine was cultivated very generally in some parts of Palestine, and afforded the Hebrew poets and prophets many similitudes, especially of the life of the nation and the Church. The incident related in these verses is apart from the main interest and plot of the work, but to whomsoever it refers—and it is conjectured to refer to certain rustic brothers of the bride—it suggests valuable spiritual lessons concerning the moral government of God and the responsibility of men.

I. A TRUST GRACIOUSLY COMMITTED. As Solomon let out his vineyard at Baal-hamon to certain tenants, so the Divine Lord and Ruler of all has appointed for each one of us a certain province of opportunity for improvement and for service. This is more strikingly the case with regard to those who occupy positions of eminence, but in reality such is the position of every intelligent and reasonable creature of God. We are tenants to whom his goodness has assigned a sphere of action in which we may be negligent or diligent, responsive to his behests or indifferent to his claims.

II. A TRUST FAITHFULLY FULFILLED. In the parable the keepers or tenants are represented as having cultivated the vineyards entrusted to them with skill and success, so that they were able to pay the king the rent which was agreed upon or the tribute which he required. In this they are representatives of all those who, having received privileges and enjoyed opportunities, turn them to good account. The scholar who cultivates his mind, enlarges his knowledge, and fits himself to influence aright the opinion and convictions of his less-favoured fellow-men; the man of wealth who employs his riches in a spirit of wise and expansive knowledge; the Christian minister who cultivates the corner of the spiritual vineyard committed to his care; every faithful child of God who diligently and prayerfully endeavours to do the will of the heavenly Husbandman, may be said to be faithful in his discharge of the obligations of his trust.

III. FIDELITY TO THE TRUST AMPLY RECOGNIZED AND REMUNERATED. Whilst the king received his thousand pieces of silver, the cultivators of the vineyard were rewarded with two hundred pieces as the recompense of their toil. And God suffers no faithful labourer to be the loser by his service. True, the recompense may not be material or temporal. Many a diligent servant of God is allowed to live a life of privation and to die in poverty. But there is a rich reward reaped by such a faithful trustee and steward of God's grace. He has the recompense of a good conscience; he may have the affectionate gratitude of some whose best interests he has promoted; and he certainly has the approval of him who can appoint to a higher ministry, who can confer lasting honours and true blessedness.—T.

Ver. 13.—*The longed-for voice.* "The companions hearken for thy voice: cause me to hear it." Such is the closing utterance of the royal spouse, who thus invites the bride to give expression to the feelings that animate her breast. May we not believe that the King of kings, who is yet the Lover and the Friend of his Church, in similar language asks for the free communication of the Church's purest thoughts and best desires? Welcome to the Saviour is the outpouring of his people's hearts. Never can they speak to meet with inattention and disregard from him upon whom their all depends.

I. CHRIST DELIGHTS IN THE VOICE OF HIS PEOPLE'S LOVE. He has not refrained from assurances of his love towards us, and he expects that we shall not repress the utterance of our affection towards him. His kindness evokes our affection, and that affection cannot be speechless; it must needs find a voice, whilst its expression will ever be welcome and grateful to his tender heart.

II. CHRIST DELIGHTS IN THE VOICE OF HIS PEOPLE'S SINCERE SUPPLICATIONS. The relation being such as it is, our addresses to our Lord must be constantly taking the form of prayer. There is no reason why we should withhold our petitions. We are altogether dependent upon him, and in our dependence he takes pleasure, because it affords him the opportunity of constantly displaying his kindness. When we come into his presence as suppliants, we do not come unbidden. "Cause me," says Christ, "to hear thy voice."

III. CHRIST DELIGHTS IN THE VOICE OF HIS PEOPLE'S GRATITUDE AND PRAISE. For such acknowledgments there is incessant occasion. He does not cease to give, nor should we cease to bless the Giver. If supplication is the special exercise of the Church on earth, praise is the undying exercise of the Church in heaven. Gratitude and adoration are as immortal as is love itself.—T.

HOMILETICAL INDEX

TO

THE SONG OF SOLOMON

——◆◆◆——